AVIATION MUSEUMS AND COLLECTIONS OF NORTH AMERICA

Second edition – now includes monuments

Bob Ogden

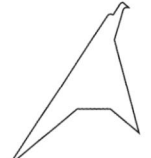 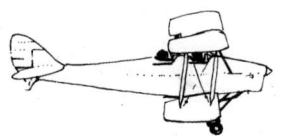

© Bob Ogden & Air-Britain (Historians) Ltd 2011

Published by:
Air-Britain (Historians) Ltd
Website: www.air-britain.co.uk

Membership details:
1 Rose Cottages, 179 Penn Road,
Hazlemere, Bucks HP15 7NE
Email: membership@air-britain.com

Sales Department:
41 Penhurst Road, Leigh,
Tonbridge, Kent TN11 8HL
Email: sales@air-britain.co.uk

Correspondence regarding this publication to:
Bob Ogden, 13 Western Avenue,
Woodley, Berkshire RG5 3BJ
Email: Bob.Ogden@air-britain.co.uk

All rights reserved. No part of the contents of this publication may be reproduced, stored in a retrieval system or transmitted, in any form or by any means, electronic, mechanical, photocopying, recording or otherwise, without the prior written permission of the author and Air-Britain (Historians) Ltd.

ISBN: 978 0 85130 427 4

Printed by Bell and Bain Ltd, Glasgow

Maps and origination by Sue J Bushell

FRONT
Allen Airways award winning Ryan STM-2, painted in its original Dutch East Indies colours, is shown flying over the rugged southern California countryside near its San Diego home. (Allen Airways)

REAR
Top: This de Havilland Moth was delivered to the High Commissioner for Canada in 1928. The aircraft is owned by the Reynolds Museum and has been loaned to the Alberta Aviation Museum for the last few years. (Nigel Hitchman)

Centre: Only a few Kreutzer Tri-motors were built in the 1920s/1930s. The sole survivor is owned by Greg Herrick's Golden Wings Air Museum. The aircraft crashed in mountains in Mexico in 1940 and was recovered and rebuilt in the early 1980s. (Dave Welch)

Bottom: Seen flying near its Boise base is the North American TF-51D Mustang of the Mustang High Flight. (MHF)

CONTENTS

Introduction .... Page 5
Notes .... Page 6

Canada
Map of Canada .... Page 8

Museums and Collections
Alberta .... Page 9
British Columbia .... Page 20
Manitoba .... Page 27
New Brunswick .... Page 33
Newfoundland and Labrador .... Page 35
Northwest Territories .... Page 39
Nova Scotia .... Page 40
Ontario .... Page 43
Prince Edward Island .... Page 64
Québec .... Page 64
Saskatchewan .... Page 70
Yukon .... Page 72
Canada Index .... Page 73

United States of America
Map of United States of America .... Page 80

Museums and Collections
Alabama .... Page 81
Alaska .... Page 93
Arizona .... Page 99
Arkansas .... Page 118
California .... Page 126
Colorado .... Page 190
Connecticut .... Page 198
Delaware .... Page 203
District of Columbia .... Page 207
Florida .... Page 210
Georgia .... Page 239
Hawaii .... Page 254
Idaho .... Page 258

Illinois	Page 266
Indiana	Page 286
Iowa	Page 298
Kansas	Page 307
Kentucky	Page 319
Louisiana	Page 323
Maine	Page 331
Maryland	Page 333
Massachusetts	Page 342
Michigan	Page 346
Minnesota	Page 360
Mississippi	Page 371
Missouri	Page 377
Montana	Page 387
Nebraska	Page 391
Nevada	Page 398
New Hampshire	Page 405
New Jersey	Page 408
New Mexico	Page 417
New York	Page 426
North Carolina	Page 450
North Dakota	Page 461
Ohio	Page 469
Oklahoma	Page 493
Oregon	Page 506
Pennsylvania	Page 518
Rhode Island	Page 533
South Carolina	Page 535
South Dakota	Page 540
Tennessee	Page 543
Texas	Page 550
Utah	Page 599
Vermont	Page 604
Virginia	Page 606
Washington	Page 623
West Virginia	Page 639
Wisconsin	Page 640
Wyoming	Page 654
United States of America Index	Page 657

INTRODUCTION

The second edition of this book has incorporated many of the changes in the recent Mainland Europe volume. These include the revised style of the headings and abbreviations for some manufacturers names to keep the book to a reasonable size. There are many aircraft preserved in towns across the two countries. Some are in shopping malls, others as monuments to local servicemen and a number as attractions at business premises. Also there are colleges and universities with fleets of instructional airframes. I have tried to include all these but I am sure that there are many more. Military aircraft preserved as 'monuments' are fairly well documented but civil ones less so. Some of my local contacts have found aircraft in rather unusual locations so I ask anyone reading the book to send me details of any they find in their area or on their travels. Regarding the colleges, universities and vocational schools I have included what I have been able to find out from research carried out via contacts, websites and promotional videos. There seems to be a reluctance of some institutions to divulge what precisely they have in their workshops. Some of the lists may be a little dated and again I ask readers to provide me with accurate information. In the last three years a number of new museums have opened and a few have sadly closed their doors. New buildings have been constructed at several and others have ambitious plans for improving their facilities. The heightened security at most military bases has made visits by foreigners much more difficult and it is advisable to contact bases well in advance of any planned trips. Despite the recent economic problems the number of private collectors of vintage and classic aircraft seems to be on the increase. I am a member of a number of American organisations and their publications often carry details of these. Again please send me details of any others you may find.

In Canada four major museums have changed their names to reflect their wider roles. In Alberta the Nanton Lancaster Society Air Museum has become the Bomber Command Museum of Canada. Across the country in Ontario the national collection formerly known as Canada Aviation Museum took up the title Canada's Air and Space Museum. At Trenton the Royal Canadian Air Force Memorial Museum is now known as the National Air Force Museum of Canada. Also in the province the Toronto Aerospace Museum has become the Canadian Air and Space Museum. In Calgary the Naval Museum of Alberta closed and the aircraft moved across the city to the new Military Museums. The success of the Canadian Harvard Association has resulted in some members purchasing a fleet of Canadian-built T-33s to set up the Jet Aircraft Museum. At Gatineau Airport Vintage Wings of Canada has added more airworthy warbirds and classic types.

Across the USA there have been developments at most of the major museums. The National Museum of the United States Air Force at Dayton in Ohio has added new galleries and placed more aircraft on show. The National Museum of the Marine Corps near the Quantico base in Virginia has completed further phases of its building programme. Work has also been carried out at the National Museum of Naval Aviation at Pensacola in Florida. The National Air and Space Museum has continued with the development of the Stephen Udvar-Hazy Center near Dulles Airport in Virginia. Aircraft have emerged from the Garber Facility to be put on show and airframes loaned to other institutions have been recalled. Three private museums containing mainly airworthy types from between the wars have opened. At Hood River in Oregon the Western Antique Aeroplane and Automobile Museum has over 70 flying aircraft on show with many more awaiting restoration. Also to be seen is a large collection of cars and motor cycles. In Pennsylvania George Jenkins has set up the Eagles Mere Air Museum at St. Davids. Some rare types can be seen here including some acquired from the estate of the late Dennis Trone of Wisconsin who was killed in the crash of his Dormoy Bathtub in May 2008. An exciting project in Georgia is the Candler Field Museum. Ron Alexander is creating a replica of Atlanta's first airport at the private Peach State Airpark. Some buildings are already constructed and others will follow. Sadly some museums have closed and these include a few which only lasted a short time. Private collections also change as aircraft are sold and acquired.

These are just a few of the significant developments which have taken place since the publication of the first edition. Keeping up with the changes is not always easy and any amendments are always appreciated. Also high resolution photos are welcome. A large number of military aircraft displayed around the country are owned by the service museums and these sometimes move.

ACKNOWLEDGEMENTS

Special thanks are due to Tony Hancock for his meticulous checking of the aircraft lists. He has added a great deal of new information. Through newly-published research we have been able to expand the details of many entries. I would like to thank all who have sent me reports of their travels, helped with aircraft details, loaned me magazines and sent me photographs. Thanks to the staff and volunteer members of museums and colleges who have replied to my requests.

Among the individuals who helped are Nigel Bailey-Underwood, Richard Baker, Dick Barrett, Daniel Berek, Alec Berry, Tony Broadhurst, Chris Chatfield, Glenn Chatfield, Eric Dewhurst, Malcolm Fillmore, Richard Hamblin, Derek Heley, Peter Hellier, Nigel Hitchman, Duncan Kirk, Stewart Lanham, Ruud Leeuw, Tom McGhee, Tony Morris, John Mounce, Mike Ody, Doug Revell, Juha Ritaranta, Lloyd Robinson, Douglas Rough, Kerry Sim, David Skeggs, John Underwood, Dave Welch, John Wickenden.

NOTES

For most museums and collections the following information is stated.

GEOGRAPHY
For each state, province or territory, a two- or three-letter code is allocated. Each museum has been given a number so that the index can be used to trace a particular type of aircraft. The number is also shown on the appropriate map which is normally found after the state, province or territory heading. Maps are drawn to different scales.

ADDRESS
The full postal address is given wherever possible. For some voluntary/private organisations the address stated may be that of the owner or an official of the organisation. The abbreviations ALP (American Legion Post) and VFW (Veteran of Foreign Wars) have been used in the addresses to save space.

TELEPHONE/FAX/E-MAIL
Wherever possible these are given. For some private and voluntary organisations those stated may be that of the owner or an official of the organisation. These details often change so check before making contact. New telephone area codes are regularly introduced as more numbers are allocated. Therefore it is advisable to check these. Many email addresses for museums incorporate the name of an individual. When they leave this is changed.

ADMISSION
The times stated are the most recent available and cannot be guaranteed. Intending visitors should check before travelling. The twenty four hour clock has been used and local times stated. For those not familiar with this system – an a.m. time is as follows 8 a.m. is 0800 – noon is 1200: for a p.m. time add 12 hours i.e. 4 p.m. is 1600. Where 'By prior permission only' is shown the aircraft are on private property or are in restricted areas and normally cannot be seen by the casual caller. Most of the flying collections are based on active airfields and can be seen only with the permission of the airfield operator in addition to that of the owners.

LOCATION
A rough guide to the location of the museum/collection is shown on the map and in the heading. If a museum has aircraft at more than one site a list of these will be given and the number of the location will follow the status symbol.

AIRCRAFT TYPE
Many aircraft have a manufacturer's and service number as well as a name. Where known the full manufacturer's designation is given with the service number in brackets. For a licence-built type which has been given a new designation, the original in the country of design is shown in square brackets.

If the type has been constructed by a number of companies the designing firm is stated.

For homebuilt aircraft and some gliders the designer is named. Shown in brackets after the type name is either its former type if the aircraft has undergone major modifications or the service designations in the order allocated. The symbol (R) denotes a replica which may be an accurate copy built to flying standards. (FSM) denotes a full size model with the correct dimensions.

REGISTRATION/MILITARY SERIAL
The markings normally carried by the aircraft are stated. Many machines are painted in their former markings for display purposes and the serial given may not be a current allocation. False markings are shown in inverted commas i.e. 'A4567'. Some aircraft carry no markings and the current allocation is normally stated.

CONSTRUCTOR'S/ MANUFACTURER'S NUMBERS
This is normally the only true way to identify an aircraft and wherever possible this is stated. Some manufacturers do not allocate c/ns – particularly for military aircraft on the assumption that they will keep the same serial for life. In some cases line numbers or fuselage numbers are given. Although not true c/ns they do provide a means of identification. Some registers quote military serials, part numbers etc. as the c/n.

PREVIOUS IDENTITIES/NOTES
These are given in chronological order starting with the initial allocation. Where the country is unclear this is stated in brackets. Reservations which were not taken up are also shown in brackets. Standard abbreviations have been used for many military serials and the civil country identification markings will be found in registers. Additional information may be given here.

STATUS
The system developed by the Smithsonian Institution is used.

A	Active – capable of flight and in most cases with a current permit.
C	Under restoration or rebuild.
D	Derelict or severely damaged – may be restored eventually.
PV	On public view – normally in the museum premises.
RA	Research accessible – may be seen by serious researchers with prior permission.
S	Stored – may be crated or in a restricted area.
X	Carries false markings.

Combinations of these may be used. If a number is stated after the codes, refer to the location codes for that specific museum.

CANADA

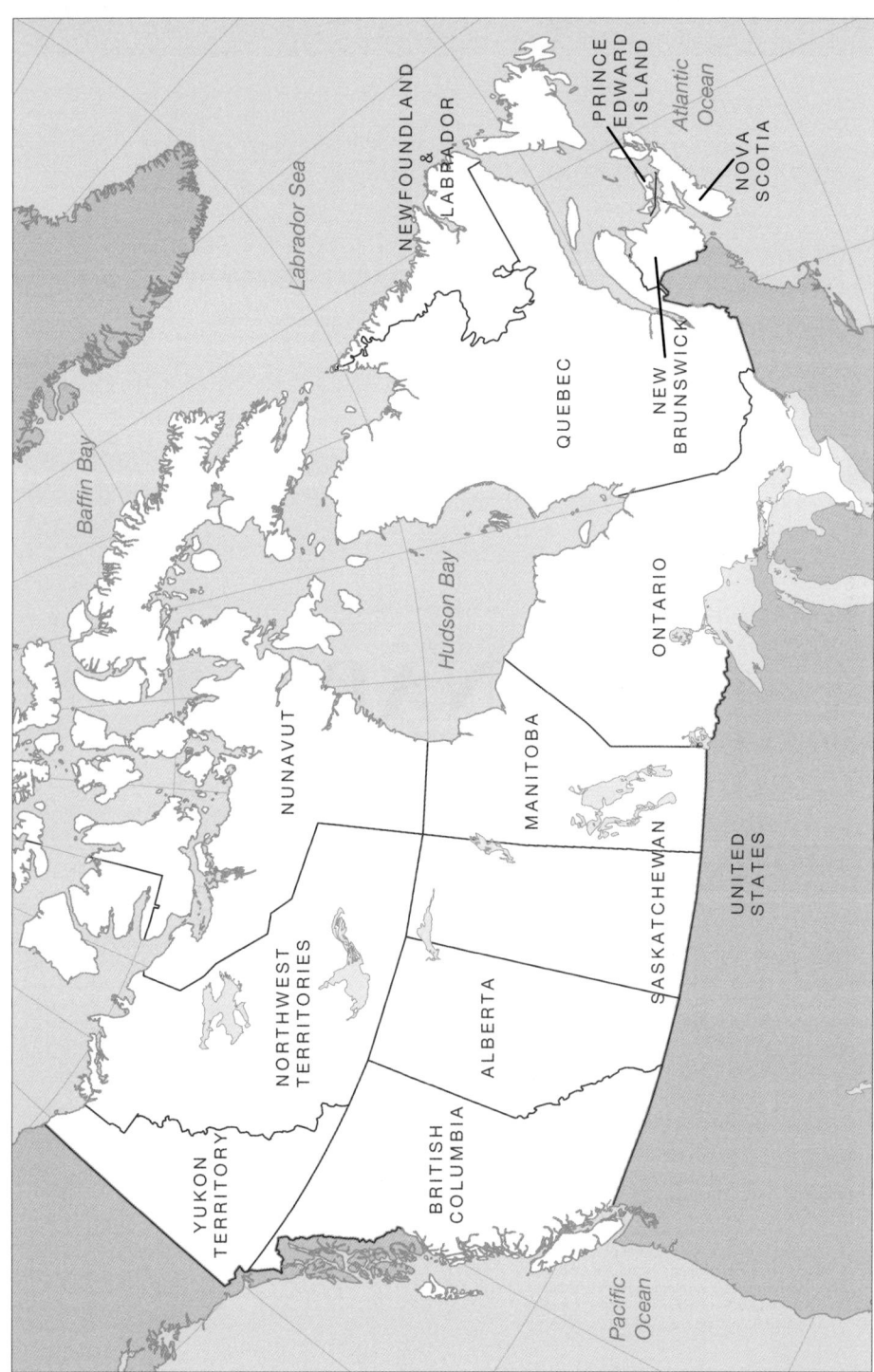

ALBERTA

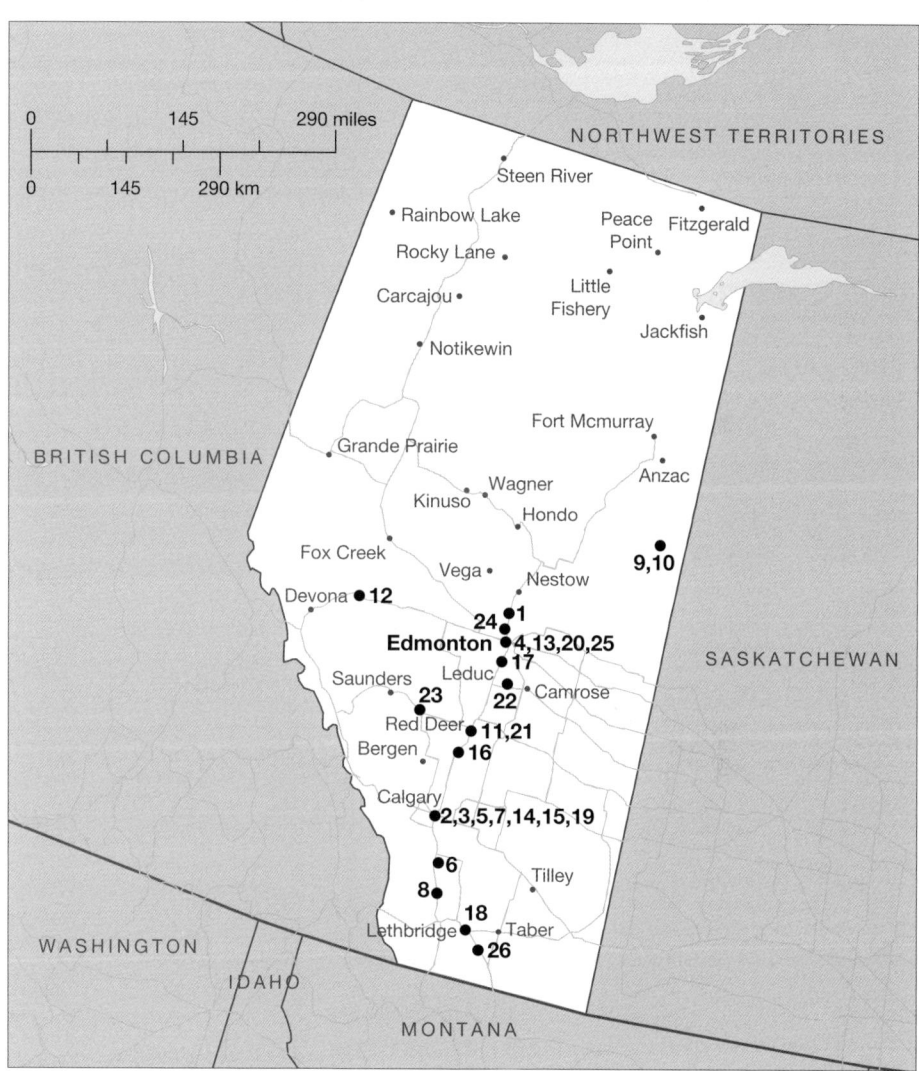

408 SQUADRON MUSEUM (AB1)

Address:	Museum Co-ordinator, Canadian Armed Forces Base Edmonton, Lancaster Park, Alberta T5J 4J5.
Tel:	780-973-8388 **Email:** museum@forfreedom.ca
Admission:	Monday-Friday 1000-1600.
Location:	About 10 km north of the city.

The airfield was home to Air Force units for many years and at the current time helicopters flown by the Army are in residence. 408 Squadron set up a museum at the site and this contains many interesting items. The displays trace the history of the unit with photographs and memorabilia on show.

An outside Air Park and Memorial Garden were established in the 1980s. The aircraft which were on show represented types flown from the field, but have moved to the Alberta Aviation Museum. Only the Kiowa remains at the site.

TYPE	REG/SER	CON. NO.	PI/NOTES	STATUS
☐ Bell 206A Kiowa (COH-58A) (CH-136)	'136408'	44059	71-20924, 136259	PVX

A.V. ROE CANADA HERITAGE MUSEUM (AB2)

Address:	6802 Ogden Road South East, Calgary, Alberta T2C 1B4.
Tel:	403-279-7791 **Email:** info@avromuseum.com
Admission:	First Saturday of each month 0900-1200.
Location:	At Hangar 3 at Springbank Airport.

A.V. Roe acquired Victory Aircraft of Malton, Ontario in 1945. The company had built over 1,000 Avro aircraft during World War II. Its first original design, the C-100 Canuck twin-engined jet fighter, made its maiden flight in January 1950 and 692 were produced. A single C-102 Jetliner flew in 1949. The C-105 Arrow prototype appeared in 1958 but after six aircraft had been completed the project was cancelled.

The museum has been set up to trace the history of the company and its aircraft. The museum closed its display in 2005 in order to concentrate on aircraft building and put its items in store. Members are currently constructing a two-thirds scale replica of the Arrow. Work started in 2005 and the basic fuselage structure is now complete.

TYPE	REG/SER	CON. NO.	PI/NOTES	STATUS
☐ Avro Canada C-105 Arrow (CF-105) (Scale R)				RAC

AERO SPACE MUSEUM OF CALGARY (AB3)

Address:	4629 McCall Way North East, Calgary, Alberta T2E 8A5.
Tel:	403-250-3752 **Fax:** 403-250-8399 **Email:** info@asmac.ab.ca
Admission:	Daily 1000-1700.
Location:	On the south side of the International Airport which is in the north eastern suburbs of the city off Highway 2.

Over the years a number of attempts were made to start an aviation museum in the city. The Air Museum of Canada was set up in the 1960s but did not last long and after a few years donated its assets to the city. The Calgary Centennial Planetarium, which opened in 1967, had a few aircraft on show in its grounds and a display of engines in its building.

In 1974 the Aero Space Museum Association was formed with the aim of maintaining and preserving aircraft and artefacts which existed in the area. In 1983 the association obtained premises at the airport where restoration could be carried out. It now stages an impressive display in one of the early hangars. The story of aviation in the region is portrayed with many models, photographs and personal items on view. One part of the hangar exhibits some superbly restored aircraft with the remaining space used for restoration.

An area outside the building is used to display about a dozen more. Parked here is a Canadian-built Lancaster which was mounted on a plinth at the airport in 1961; a few years ago it was taken down and restored. All of the aircraft from the Planetarium have now been moved to the museum.

Calgary was one of the centres for the British Commonwealth Air Training Plan and examples of types used in the scheme have also been collected. The restoration of an Anson, in the famous yellow colour scheme, has been completed: the type was widely used for training in World War II. Only 11 Barkley-Grow T8P twin engined airliners were constructed in the late 1930s and at least seven were operated in Canada. One can currently be seen in the hangar and another has been loaned to the Alberta Aviation Museum in Edmonton.

TYPE	REG/SER	CON. NO.	PI/NOTES	STATUS
☐ Aerial Experiment Association Silver Dart R)				PV
☐ Auster K AOP.6	C-FOMW	2862	VP 667, 16684, CF-OMW	PV
☐ Auster Q T.7	CF-KYB		16691	PVC
☐ Avro 652A Anson V	'7401'	MDF398	12587 – Composite.	PVX
☐ Avro 683 Lancaster 10(MR) (B.X)	FM136		FM136, (CF-NJQ), 'R5684'	PV
☐ Avro Canada C.100 Canuck 3D (3A) (CF-100)	18126	026	NX26400	PV
☐ Barkley-Grow T8P-1	CF-BQM	8		PV
☐ Bayjo Glider [Hall Cherokee II]	CF-REI	1		PV
☐ Beech D18S	CF-GXC	A-547	N5287C	PV
☐ Beech D18S Expeditor 3NM	C-FQMF	CA-212 (A-862)	2333, CF-QMF	RA
☐ Bell 47G-2	(CF-NHH)	1652		PVX
☐ Bristol 149 Bolingbroke IVT				RAD
☐ Canadian Car & Foundry Harvard 4 [North American NA-186]	C-FRUJ/20273	CCF4-64	20273, CF-RUJ, C-FRUJ	PV
☐ Cessna T-50 Crane 1A (Bobcat – AT-17A)	CF-GEA	2361	42-13677, FJ160, 8811	RAD
☐ Cessna 188 Agwagon 230	C-GXQM	1880007	N5507S	PV
☐ De Havilland DH.98 Mosquito B.35	CF-HMS		RS700	RA
☐ De Havilland DH.100 Vampire F.3	CF-RLK	EEP42387	17069, N6877D	PV
☐ De Havilland DHC.6 Twin Otter	C-FPAT	2	CF-SJB-X, CF-SJB, N856AC, CF-PAT	PV
☐ Douglas DC-3A-456 Skytrain (C-47A)	CF-BZI	13448	42-108960	PV
☐ Fairey Swordfish IV				RAD
☐ Hawker Hurricane XII	5389	42024		RAC
☐ McDonnell M.36BA Voodoo (F-101B) (CF-101B)	101021	499	57-0321,101021, 836B	PV
☐ Mitchell Wing U-2	C-GVUS	476		PV
☐ Müller Stingray Hang Glider				PV
☐ Noorduyn Norseman V	CF-MAM	N29-26	In Atrium of Petro Canada building in the city.	PV
☐ North American NA-151 Sabre (P-86A) (F-86A)	'23175'	151-38433	47-606, N7793C, N57965	PVX
☐ Piasecki PV-18 Retriever (H-25A)	630	59	51-16630	PV
☐ Quickie Aircraft Quickie 2 (Rutan 54)	C-GRNI	009		PV
☐ Sikorsky S-51 Dragonfly	9607	51166		PV
☐ Sikorsky S-55A	CF-JTI	55822	9628, CF-JTI, C-FJTI	PV
☐ Sopwith Triplane (R)	'N6302'	CP101		PVX
☐ Waco 10 (GXE)	CF-AOI	3065	NC7258, N7258 – on loan from Reynolds Alberta Museum, AB.	PV
☐ Waco EQC-6 (ZQC-6)	CF-AZM	4479	NC16520, N16520, CF-AZM, C-FAZM	PV

Alberta

ALBERTA AVIATION MUSEUM (AB4)

Address:	11410 Kingsway Avenue, Edmonton, Alberta T5G 0X4.
Tel:	780-451-1175 **Fax:** 780-451-1607 **Email:** info@albertaaviationmuseum.com
Admission:	Monday-Friday 1000-1800; Saturday-Sunday 1000-1600.
Location:	On the south side of the city airport which is in the northern suburbs.

Formed in 1980, the Alberta Aviation Museum Association started with the restoration of a 1933 Fairchild 71 which had crashed near Yellowknife in 1949, a task completed in 1987. Several other types used in 'bush-flying' have been acquired and some are now on show with others awaiting major rebuilds.

The group then commenced work on a de Havilland Mosquito, one of a batch of 15 bought in England by Spartan Air Services in the 1950s. After being donated to the city of Edmonton the Mosquito was on show at the military base of Namao for five years before being put in store. It was unveiled in September 1995 painted in the colours carried by one flown by Russ Bannock, a former Commanding Officer of 418 Squadron.

In 1991 a dozen organisations combined to set up the Edmonton Aviation Heritage Society and the group obtained the use of one of the former British Commonwealth Air Training Plan hangars at the airport. This wooden building is the only surviving two bay double length hangar from the period. Eventually the museum will house around ten galleries portraying significant events in the development of aviation in Alberta.

A number of private owners have loaned aircraft to the museum and an excellent display can be seen. A rarity is the Cranwell CLA.4 biplane built in the area in the early 1930s. Designed by Nick Comper, two were built at Cranwell for the 1926 Lympne Trials. Plans for the design were bought by Alf Want and with a group of friends the aircraft was constructed at his house. The CLA.4 flew successfully for two years before crashing in 1934 and its remains stored for almost 60 years. The airframe is now almost complete and hopefully this diminutive aircraft will once again take to the skies.

The first Canadair Sabre is a prized exhibit. It was largely assembled from US-built components and made its maiden flight from Dorval on 8th August 1950. The Vickers Viking amphibian first flew as a landplane at Brooklands in late 1919. The design was developed and 31 production examples were constructed. Three were sold to Canada – two for military use and the other was operated by Laurentide Air Services. The replica in the museum was originally displayed at Thorpe Park in England before making the journey across the Atlantic.

An interesting range of types can be seen in one bay of the hangar and many others are under restoration in the second. Boeing 737 airliners have been used by a number of Canadian airlines and an example flown by Air Canada joined the collection a few years ago. Fred Sidlinger of Puyallup in Washington State designed his Hurricane in the early 1970s. The aircraft has the outward appearance of the famous World War II fighter but is only 5/8th size. The airframe is of wooden construction.

TYPE	REG/SER	CON. NO.	PI/NOTES	STATUS
☐ Avro 652A Anson II	'886'			PV
☐ Avro Canada C.100 Canuck 5C (5) (CF-100)	18476	376	18476, 100476	PV
☐ Barkley-Grow T8P-1	CF-BLV	3	On loan from Aero Space Museum of Calgary.	PV
☐ Beech D18S	C-FDSV	A-25	N44617, N745P, N745PD	PV
☐ Beech D18S Expeditor 3NM	C-FRSX	CA-245 (A-895)	2366, CF-RSX	PV
☐ Bell 47G 947D)	CF-GSL	24	NX170B, NC170B, N170B	PVC
☐ Birdman Enterprises MJ-5 Hang Glider				PV
☐ Boeing 737-275	C-GIPW	21712		PVC
☐ Canadair CL-13 Sabre 1 [North American F-86A]	19101	1		PV
☐ Canadair CL-30 Silver Star 3 (CT-133) [Lockheed 580 (T-33AN)]	21506	T33-506	21506, 133506 – parts from c/n T33-535 21535, 133535.	PV
☐ Canadair CL-30 Silver Star 3 (CT-133) [Lockheed 580 (T-33AN)]	21533	T33-533	21533, 133533 – may be c/n T33-122 21722	PV
☐ Canaero Toucan	C-INRO	P.IV		PV
☐ Cranwell CLA.4A				PVC
☐ Curtiss Stinson Special (R)	'901'			PVX
☐ De Havilland DH.60 Moth	G-CYYG	503	On loan from Reynolds Alberta Museum, AB.	PV
☐ De Havilland DH.82C Tiger Moth (PT-24)	C-GDWI/'2114'	DHC.1414	42-1075, FE211, 1211, CF-CTO	PVA
☐ De Havilland DH.90 Dragonfly	CF-BZA	7531	CF-MPB, 7627 – rear fuselage only.	RAD
☐ De Havilland DH.98 Mosquito B.35	'HR147'		VP189, CF-HMQ, (VP-KOM), CF-HMQ	PVX
☐ De Havilland DH.115 Vampire T.35 (T.33)	N11933	4179	A79-657, N11933, (N6528Z)	PV
☐ Douglas DC-3A-456 Skytrain (C-47A) (Dakota III) (CC-129)	C-FROD/12927	13028	42-108918, KG545, 12927, C-GPNW, C-FROD	PV
☐ Douglas DC-6			Front fuselage only.	PV
☐ Eipper MX Quicksilver	C-IBOE	TC021505		PV
☐ Ercoupe 415CD	C-FFYA	4770	NC49759, N49659, CF-FYA	RA
☐ Fairchild 71C	CF-ATZ	17		PV
☐ Fairchild 24W46	CF-EKK	W46-324	NC77624 – privately owned	RAC
☐ Fleet 80 Canuck	'305'	305	CF-MHW, C-FMHW	PVX
☐ Fokker Universal	G-CAHE	408	Front fuselage, tail and other parts.	RA
☐ Kelly D	C-FAPD	02483		PV
☐ McDonnell M.36BA Voodoo (F-101B) (CF-101B)	101060	611	57-0433, 101060, 837B	PV
☐ McDonnell M.36BA Voodoo (F-101B) (TF-101B) (CF-101B)	'17425'	537	57-0359, 101032	PVX
☐ Noorduyn Norseman IV	'CF-HPY'		Composite.	PVX
☐ Noorduyn Norseman IV	CF-EIH	94	494	RAC
☐ North American NA-108 Mitchell (B-25J) (Mitchell III)	5273	108-34066	44-30791	PVC
☐ Quad City Ultralights Challenger				RA
☐ Sheldrake AX-SM Hot Air Balloon	CF-POP	1		PV
☐ Sindlinger HH-1 Hurricane	C-GHHB	LCHH-77		PVA
☐ Stinson SR-9FM Reliant	C-FOAY	5732	CF-OAY	PV
☐ Vickers 60 Viking IV (Scale R)	'G-CAEB'		On loan from BCM, AB.	PV
☐ Waco UIC	CF-AAW	3771		PVA

Above: Members of the Bomber Command Museum of Canada are restoring this Bristol Bolingbroke. (Ruud Leeuw) [AB6]

Left: This replica Curtiss Jenny is on show in the Glenbow Museum. (Nigel Hitchman) [AB14]

This Hawker Sea Fury moved from the Naval Museum of Alberta to the new Military Museums. (Nigel Hitchman) [AB19]

Alberta
ART SMITH AERO CENTRE (AB5)

Address:	1916 McCall Landing North East, Calgary, Alberta T2E 9C2.
Tel:	403-284-7018 **Email:** aerocentre@sait.ca
Admission:	By prior permission only.
Location:	On the south east side of the International Airport which is in the north eastern suburbs of the city off Highway 2.

This new purpose-built facility opened in 2004, prior which the college used a nearby hangar. The organisation is part of the Southern Alberta Institute of Technology. Art Smith was a World War II Lancaster pilot who became a national and local politician as well as a successful businessman. The instructional airframes are used in the many courses offered. The Stolp homebuilt biplane hangs in the foyer of the complex.

TYPE	REG/SER	CON. NO.	PI/NOTES	STATUS
☐ Avro 748 Series 2A/309LFD	8R-GEV	1748	Fuselage section only.	RAD
☐ Beech B90 King Air	C-GTMA	LJ-348	N805K	RA
☐ Bell 206A Jet Ranger	N4802R	225	N4702R, G-AYHN	RA
☐ Bell 206B Jet Ranger	CF-ALE	1074	N83160, CF-ALE, C-FALE	RAD
☐ Bell 206B Jet Ranger	C-GKGO	1416		RA
☐ Boeing 737-2H4	C-GWJU	21117	N26SW	RA
☐ Canadair CL-601-3A Challenger	C-GIOH	5034	C-GLXK	RA
☐ Cessna A185F Skywagon 185	C-GNGD	18503248	(N93802)	RA
☐ Cessna FR172G	SX-AFK	FR172G0155	N7506	RA
☐ Cessna 320E Skyknight	CF-TXL	320E-0093		RA
☐ De Havilland DHC.6-100 Twin Otter	C-GGAW	86	N591MA, VP-BDC, C6-BDC, N2228H	RAD
☐ Grumman G-159 Gulfstream I	C-GKFG	22	N722G, N80G, N8BG – fuselage only.	RA
☐ Grumman G-159 Gulfstream I	C-FHBO	104	N719G, CF-HBO	RA
☐ Mitsubishi MU-2G (MU-2B-30)	C-FTML	525	N150MA, XB-TON, N150MA, YV-O-CDM-1, N360JK	RA
☐ North American NA-76 Harvard II	11643	76-3513	AJ643	RA
☐ Piper PA-31-350 Navajo Chieftain	C-GVAG	317752166	N27411	RA
☐ Robinson R-22 Beta	C-GAAK	2151		RA
☐ Schweizer SGU.1-20	C-FZBS	19	CF-ZBS	RA
☐ Stolp SA.100 Starduster	C-FJOE	SA-1004		RA
☐ Sud SA.319B Alouette III	N91520	2085	2085 (France) – less boom.	RA
☐ Sud-Est SE.3160 Alouette III	C-FCAZ	1358	CF-CAZ	RA

BOMBER COMMAND MUSEUM OF CANADA (AB6)

Address:	PO Box 1051, Nanton, Alberta T0L 1R0.
Tel:	403-646-2270 **Fax:** 403-646-2270 **Email:** nlsCurator@lancastermuseum.ca
Admission:	Mid-April–mid October daily 1000-1600; Mid-October–mid May Saturday-Sunday 1000-1600.
Location:	In the centre of the town.

In 1960 George White, a Nanton resident, heard that three Lancasters were about to be destroyed at the military base at Vulcan and investigated the possibility of acquiring one as a tourist attraction. Howie Armstrong and Fred Garrett joined with George White in the deal and they towed the bomber 25 km across fields to its new home. The aircraft was mounted for display and later donated to the town.

The Nanton Lancaster Society was formed in 1986 and set about the task of raising funds for a display building. In May 1991 the Lancaster was rolled into its new home. The aircraft now carries the code of the one flown by Alberta's only World War II Victoria Cross recipient, Squadron Leader Ian Bazalgette, who was posthumously awarded the decoration in 1944. A display of memorabilia has been set up in the entrance hall to the building and examples of types used in the British Commonwealth Air Training Plan are also being collected.

The Fleet Fawn was delivered to the RCAF in July 1938 and after seven years' service was sold to Ernie Oakman of Stewart Valley in Saskatchewan. The biplane was owned by Harry Whereatt (see Whereatts Warbirds, SK) for a period but went back to Mr. Oakman who donated it to the museum in 1990, along with the Cornell.

Restoration of a number of airframes is underway and more projects are in the planning stages. Mounted outside the museum is a CF-100 which spent over ten years on the gate at the base at Suffield. There are plans to extend the exhibition area and the raising of a Halifax wreck is being investigated. The McHardy Lysander is a scale representation of the famous World War II type and flew for a short time before being put on display at the Alberta Aviation Museum.

In 2010 the name was changed from the Nanton Lancaster Society Air Museum to reflect its wider role.

TYPE	REG/SER	CON. NO.	PI/NOTES	STATUS
☐ Airspeed AS.10 Oxford I			Centre section, cockpit area and other parts.	RAD
☐ Airspeed AS.10 Oxford I			Four centre sections.	RAD
☐ Avro 652A Anson II			More than 20 airframes in store.	RAD
☐ Avro 652A Anson II				RAD
☐ Avro 652A Anson II	7481			PVC
☐ Avro 683 Lancaster 10(MP) (B.X)	FM159			PV
☐ Avro 683 Lancaster B.10 (FSM)	'KB726'		Fuselage only.	PV
☐ Avro Canada C.100 Canuck 3D (3B) (CF-100)	18152	052		PV
☐ Beech D18S	CF-MPI	A-142		PV
☐ Beech D18S Expeditor 3NM	CF-ZOI	CA-213 (A-863)	2334	RAD
☐ Bristol 149 Bolingbroke IVT	9874			RAD
☐ Bristol 149 Bolingbroke IVT	9897			RAD
☐ Bristol 149 Bolingbroke IVT	9994			RAD
☐ Bristol 149 Bolingbroke IVT	9978		Fuselage only.	RAD
☐ Bristol 149 Bolingbroke IVT	9987			PVC

☐ Bristol 149 Bolingbroke IVT		10074			RAD
☐ Bristol 149 Bolingbroke IVT		'R3662'		9989 (?) – front fuselage only.	PVC
☐ Canadair CL-30 Silver Star 3 (CT-133) [Lockheed 580 (T-33AN)]		'21616'	T33-272	21272 – tail from c/n T33-535 21535	PVX
☐ Canadair CL-41A Tutor (CT-114)		114177	1177	26177 – composite.	PV
☐ Canadian Car & Foundry Harvard 4 [North American NA-186]		20419	CCF4-210		PVD
☐ Cessna T-50 Bobcat (C-78) (UC-78)		CF-HGM	3760	42-58269	PVC
☐ Cessna T-50 Crane 1					RAD
☐ Cessna T-50 Crane 1					RAD
☐ Circa Reproductions Nieuport 11				On loan from BCAM, BC.	PV
☐ De Havilland DH.82C Tiger Moth		'4080'	DHC.1534	3873, CF-CKN (?) – Fuselage only	PVCX
☐ Fairchild M-62A-4 Cornell (PT-26A) (Cornell II)		14424		42-71000, FT585	PV
☐ Fleet 7C Fawn II		264	123		PV
☐ McHardy Lysander		'416'	1	C-FOQI	PVX
☐ North American NA-64 Yale		3404	64-2157		PV
☐ North American NA-64 Yale		3462	64-2190	Wings only.	PV
☐ North American NA-64 Yale		3427	64-2230		RAD
☐ Supermarine 349 Spitfire F.V (Scale R)					PV

CALGARY MONUMENT (AB7)

Location:	On permanent view at the Bell Building in the centre of the city.

TYPE	REG/SER	CON. NO.	P/NOTES	STATUS
☐ Bell 206A Kiowa (COH-58A) (CH-136)				PV

CLARESHOLM MONUMENT (AB8)

Location:	On permanent view in the Memorial Park at 43rd Avenue and 4th Street West.

TYPE	REG/SER	CON. NO.	P/NOTES	STATUS
☐ Canadian Car & Foundry Harvard 4 [North American NA-186]			Composite.	PV

COLD LAKE AIR FORCE MUSEUM (AB9)

Address:	PO Box 6550, Station Forces Cold Lake, Alberta T9M 2C6.
Tel:	780-5944-3546 Fax: 780-840-7300 Email:contact@coldlakeairforcemuseum.com
Admission:	By prior permission only.
Location:	About 5 km south west of the town off Highway 28.

Opened in 1954, the base is the largest in the country. Fighter pilot training is carried out at the site and a number of weapons ranges are located nearby. Cold Lake is also home to the military aerospace test and evaluation unit. A small airpark has been set up at the base.

The most interesting aircraft is one of three Dakotas modified in the early 1960s as navigation trainers for the Canadair-built Starfighters then entering service. The other types have all been flown from the field in recent years: the Hornet is the current equipment of the front line squadrons based at the field and examples have joined the collection.

The base is named after Group Captain R.W. McNair and is one of only three military airfields in Canada honouring an individual.

TYPE	REG/SER	CON. NO.	P/NOTES	STATUS
☐ Avro Canada C.100 Canuck 5D (5) (CF-100)	18761	661		PV
☐ Beech C23 Sundowner (CT-134A) (Musketeer II)	134244	M-2332		RA
☐ Canadair CL-30 Silver Star 3 (CT-133) [Lockheed 580 (T-33AN)]	133094	T33-094	21094	PV
☐ Canadair CL-30 Silver Star 3 (CT-133) [Lockheed 580 (T-33AN)]	133181	T33-181	21181	PV
☐ Canadair CL-41A Tutor (CT-114)	114083	1083	26083 – at Joe Heffner Park in the town.	PV
☐ Canadair CL-90 Starfighter (CF-104) [Lockheed 683-04-12]	'104880'		Composite from parts of c/n 683A-1103 12803 and c/n 683A-1116 12816, '12872'	PVX
☐ Canadair CL-90 Starfighter (CF-104) [Lockheed 683-04-12]	'12702'	683A-1004	12704, 104704, 820C – at Joe Heffner Park in the town.	PVX
☐ Canadair CL-219-1A10 Freedom Fighter (CF-116A) (CF-5A) [Northrop N-156A]	116736	1036	Contains parts of c/n 1019 116719 and c/n 2042 116842	PV
☐ Canadair CL-219-1A10 Freedom Fighter (CF-116A) (CF-5A) [Northrop N-156A]	116753	1053		PV
☐ Douglas DC-3A-467 Skytrain (C-47B) (Dakota IV) (CC-129)	12959	15196/26641	43-49380, 979, 'KN979'	PV
☐ McDonnell M.36BA Voodoo (F-101B) (CF-101B)	101056	604	57-0426, 101056, 839B	PV
☐ McDonnell M.267A Hornet (CF-188A)	188702	101/A071		RA
☐ McDonnell M.267B Hornet (CF-188B)	188905	65/B019		PV

COLD LAKE MUSEUM (AB10)

Address:	Cold Lake Information Centre, Cold Lake, Alberta T9M 0A1.
Tel:	780-594-7750 Email: info@coldlake.com
Admission:	Saturday, Sunday 1000-1600.
Location:	On the outskirts of the town.

Alberta

Cold Lake has been the site of an important military airfield for half a century. The municipal museum in the town now has an aviation collection. This is on display at a former radar station. Represented are types used for pilot training as well as combat machines.

Much of the original equipment is still in place and the story of the air defence of the region is portrayed. The displays at the other sites operated by the museum trace the history and development of the local region from the days of the native people up to modern times.

TYPE	REG/SER	CON. NO.	PI/NOTES	STATUS
☐ Avro 652A Anson V				PVD
☐ Beech C23 Sundowner (CT-134A) (Musketeer II)	134241	M-2329		PV
☐ Beech C23-19 Musketeer (CT-134)	134216	M-1340	13416, 134216, 808B	PV
☐ Canadair CL-30 Silver Star 3 (CT-133) [Lockheed 580 (T-33AN)]	133413	T33-413	21413	PV
☐ Canadair CL-30 Silver Star 3 (CT-133) [Lockheed 580 (T-33AN)]	133508	T33-508	21508	PV
☐ Canadair CL-41A Tutor (CT-114)	114114	1114	26114	PV
☐ Canadair CL-219-1A10 Freedom Fighter (CF-116A) (CF-5A) [Northrop N-156A]	116704	1004		PV
☐ Canadair CL-219-1A10 Freedom Fighter (CF-116A) (CF-5A) [Northrop N-156A]	116742	1042	Front fuselage only.	PV
☐ Canadair CL-219-1A10 Freedom Fighter (CF-116A) (CF-5A) [Northrop N-156A]	116761	1061	116761, 116761B, 733B – front fuselage only.	PV
☐ Lockheed 583-04-15 Starfighter (CF-104D)	104666	583A-5336	12666 – front fuselage only.	PV

COTTON COLLECTION (AB11)

Address:	Red Deer, Alberta T4P0J3.
Admission:	By prior permission only.
Location:	At a private house in the town and at a nearby store.

This private collection of jets has been acquired by Ian Cotton. The Sea Harrier was withdrawn from service in 2005 and after storage in two locations in England moved across the Atlantic in 2009. This aircraft is on the front lawn of his house while the other five in store in the region. The Lightning was delivered to the Royal Saudi Air Force in 1969 and returned to England in January 1986. It was on show at the Olympic Flight Museum in Washington State for a period before making the journey north.

One of the Hunters has been identified as a former Singapore Air Force two-seater which initially served in the Netherlands.

TYPE	REG/SER	CON. NO.	PI/NOTES	STATUS
☐ British Aircraft Corporation 167 Strikemaster 80				RA
☐ English Electric P.27 Lightning T.55	N2046J	B1/95024	G-27-70, 55-711 (Saudi), 203 (Saudi), 1315 (Saudi), 234 (Saudi), ZF597	RAC
☐ Hawker P.1099 Hunter F.6				RA
☐ Hawker P.1099 Hunter F.6				RA
☐ Hawker P.1101 Hunter T.75 (T.7)	N91167	HABL 03361	N-303 (Netherlands), G-9-290, 500 (Singapore)	RA
☐ Hawker-Siddeley P.1184 Sea Harrier FA.2 (FRS.1)	ZD615	41H/912054		RA

EDSON MONUMENT (AB12)

Location:	On permanent view in a park in the town off Highway 16.

TYPE	REG/SER	CON. NO.	PI/NOTES	STATUS
☐ Canadair CL-30 Silver Star 3 (CT-133) [Lockheed 580 (T-33AN)]	133097	T33-097	21097	PV

FORT EDMONTON PARK (AB13)

Address:	Whitemud and Fox Drive, Edmonton, Alberta T5A 0A3.
Tel:	780-442-5311 **Fax:** 780-496-8797 **Email:** attractions@edmonton.ca
Admission:	Mid-May-June Monday-Friday 1000-1600; Saturday-Sunday 1000-1800. July-early September daily 1000-1800.
Location:	In the south western suburbs of the city off Highway 2.

This large site has over 75 buildings, many of them original, which trace the development of the area from its early days as a trading station. Regular displays of pioneer life are staged. There are also several working trams and steam trains which run around the large site. Courses are held and workshops at which visitors can learn traditional skills regularly take place.

The Avian replica was built by a team at the Reynolds Museum and was temporarily put on show in the Alberta Aviation Museum at the airport. The Avian biplane was used in some numbers in Canada and several were assembled by the Ottawa Car Manufacturing Company using fuselages supplied by the parent firm in England.

TYPE	REG/SER	CON. NO.	PI/NOTES	STATUS
☐ Avro 594 Avian (R)	'G-CAVB'			PVX

GLENBOW MUSEUM (AB14)

Address:	130 9thAvenue South, Calgary, Alberta T2C 0P3.
Tel:	403-268-4100 **Fax:** 403-265-9769 **Email:** glenbow@glenbow.org
Admission:	Monday–Saturday 0900-1700; Sunday 1200-1700.
Location:	In the centre of the city.

This large museum was founded by Eric Lafferty Harvie and has artefacts tracing the history and culture of Western Canada on show. In 1919 Captain Fred McCall, a World War I pilot, landed his Curtiss Jenny on top of a roundabout at the Calgary Exhibition and Stampede. His engine failed soon after take-off and he stalled the biplane on the carousel. His son Fred built a replica of the Jenny for show in the 'Mavericks of Alberta Gallery'.

TYPE	REG/SER	CON. NO.	PI/NOTES	STATUS
☐ Curtiss 1C Jenny (JN-4D) (R)	'34214'			PVX

HERITAGE PARK HISTORICAL VILLAGE (AB15)

Address:	1900 Heritage Drive South West, Calgary, Alberta T2V 2X3.
Tel:	403-268-8500 Fax: 403-268-8501 Email: info@heritageparrk.ab.ca
Admission:	Gasoline Alley Museum – Daily 0900-1600 closes at 1700 from late May – mid October.
Location:	In the southern part of the city.

The site is one of the largest interactive villages in the country. The visitor can tour historic buildings and sample life from bygone eras. The Gasoline Alley Museum features vintage cars and a reproduction of a 1930s gasoline station. The Tiger Moth hangs above the exhibition and is on long-term loan.

TYPE	REG/SER	CON. NO.	PI/NOTES	STATUS
☐ De Havilland DH.82C Tiger Moth	CF-CJO/3886	DHC.1547	3886 – on loan from ASM, AB.	PV

INNISFAIL MONUMENT (AB16)

Location:	On permanent view at RCL Branch 104 at 5108 49th Avenue in the northern part of the town.

TYPE	REG/SER	CON. NO.	PI/NOTES	STATUS
☐ Lockheed 483-04-08 Starfighter (F-104F)	'104'	283-5070	59-5017, BB+383, 29+17	PVX

LEDUC MONUMENT (AB17)

Location:	On permanent view at the RCL Branch 108 at 5210 50th Avenue in the south western part of the town.

TYPE	REG/SER	CON. NO.	PI/NOTES	STATUS
☐ Canadair CL-30 Silver Star 3 (CT-133) [Lockheed 580 (T-33AN)]	21518	T33-518		PV

LETHBRIDGE MONUMENT (AB18)

Location:	On permanent view at the RCL Branch 44 at 324 Mayor Magrath Drive in the eastern part of the town.

TYPE	REG/SER	CON. NO.	PI/NOTES	STATUS
☐ Canadair CL-30 Silver Star 3 (CT-133) [Lockheed 580 (T-33AN)]	21578	T33-578		PV

MILITARY MUSEUMS (AB19)

Address:	4520 Crowchild Trail South West, Calgary, Alberta T2T 5J4.
Tel:	403-974-2850 Fax: 403-974-2858 Email: moradmin@telusplanet.net
Admission:	Monday–Friday 0900-1700; Saturday–Sunday 0930-1600.
Location:	In the south western suburbs of the city.

The Tecumseh Historical Society was founded in January 1984 with the aim of perpetuating the memory of the thousands from the region who had served in the Royal Canadian Navy. Funds were raised and the exhibition building opened in October 1988.

The museum was dedicated to the memory of Lieutenant Robert Gray, who was the only RCN holder of the Victoria Cross in World War II. He enlisted in the Navy at Tecumseh. On show was an excellent collection of photographs, models of ships, guns, badges, uniforms and artefacts tracing the history of the service.

An extension to the building was ready for the 1997 summer season. Three superbly restored naval fighter aircraft were parked on the exhibition floor. The Seafire was built by Cunliffe-Owen and served with the RCN from 1945 to 1949. In 1954 it was flown to Calgary and used as an instructional airframe at the Southern Alberta Institute of Technology. The Sea Fury arrived at the Institute in 1957 and was passed on to Tecumseh in 1966.

The Naval Museum closed in 2007 and the exhibits transferred to the new site. The new museum aims to trace the military history of the country, with emphasis on the western provinces.

TYPE	REG/SER	CON. NO.	PI/NOTES	STATUS
☐ Canadair CL-219-1A10 Freedom Fighter (CF-116A) (CF-5A) [Northrop N-156A]	116707	1007		PV
☐ Hawker Sea Fury FB.11	WG565	41H/636292		PV
☐ McDonnell M.24 Banshee (F2H-3)	126334	44	Bu126334	PV
☐ Supermarine 377 Seafire F.XV	PR451	CO.9673	PR451, 'PR425'	PV

NORTHERN ALBERTA INSTITUTE OF TECHNOLOGY (AB20)

Address:	11311 120th Street, Edmonton, Alberta T5G 2Y1.
Tel:	780-453-7156 Fax: 780-453-7148 Email: dianest@nait.ca
Admission:	By prior permission only.
Location:	About 1 mile south of the airport in the northern part of the city.

Alberta

The institute was established in the early 1960s and provides technical training in a number of fields. The aviation maintenance school has well equipped workshops with a small fleet of instructional airframes.

TYPE	REG/SER	CON. NO.	PI/NOTES	STATUS
☐ Bell 206 Jet Ranger				RA
☐ Cessna 172				RA
☐ Cessna 337B Super Skymaster	G-GGLZ	3370733	N2433S	RA
☐ Grumman G-89 Tracker (S2F-1) (S-2A) (US-2A)	N422DF	17	Bu133046 – front fuselage only.	RA
☐ Grumman G-89 Tracker (S2F-1) (S-2A) (US-2A)	N429DF	249	Bu133278 – front fuselage only.	RA

RED DEER AIRPORT MONUMENT (AB21)

Location:	On permanent view at the airport which is about 6 km south west of the town.

TYPE	REG/SER	CON. NO.	PI/NOTES	STATUS
☐ Canadian Car & Foundry Harvard 4 [North American NA-186]	20370	CCF4-161		PV

REYNOLDS ALBERTA MUSEUM (AB22)

Address:	Box 6360, Wetaskiwin, Alberta T9A 2G1.
Tel:	780-361-1351 **Fax:** 780-361-1239 **Email:** reynoldsalbertamuseum@gov.ab.ca
Admission:	May 15th–Labor Day 1000-1700; Labor Day–May 14th 0900-1700.
Location:	Adjacent to the airport which is about 1 km west of the town.

The Reynolds family has been connected with aviation for over 90 years. In 1919 Ted Reynolds built a monoplane which first flew on 8th September of that year. Powered by a Ford engine, the aircraft made several short flights over the next three years and is now on show in the museum. In 1925 he constructed the Star, which used a four cylinder water-cooled motor. This aircraft was also preserved and its uncovered fuselage survives.

Ted's son Stan flew with the RCAF during World War II and when he returned to Wetaskiwin in 1945 he set up a car dealership. Over the next few years he amassed a vast number of cars, agricultural machines, military and Indian artefacts and toys as well as a number of aircraft. He founded the Reynolds Museum in 1955 and placed many of these items on show. The family constructed the airport in 1951 and sold it to the town in 1970 with the proviso that the land should be continue to be used as an airfield and that they could have access from the museum.

The Reynolds Aviation Museum was set up with a display hangar and an outside aircraft park. In the 1970s Stan Reynolds started thinking about a large museum to house part of his vast collection. Talks were held with the Provincial Government and in 1981 he donated many items to the province to form the basis of the Reynolds-Alberta Museum. A committee was formed to choose the artefacts which were most significant in the restoration of agriculture, industry and aviation in Alberta and restoration of the potential exhibits began in 1982.

Ground for the main building was broken on 26th July 1988 and the museum was officially opened by the Premier of Alberta, Don Getty, on 12th September 1992. On show in the impressive main building are large numbers of superbly restored cars, motorcycles, commercial vehicles and agricultural implements. All the exhibits are well labelled with their history and technical details highlighted. Outside the building is an exhibition track where vehicles can be demonstrated.

The majority of the aviation exhibits are currently housed in a building close to the active part of the airfield. Long-term plans envisage the construction of a vast new hall where the majority of the 100 aircraft in can be exhibited and the present building will then be used for restoration. The Canada Aviation Hall of Fame was moved to the museum from Edmonton and panels honouring those who have made significant contributions to the development of flying in the country can be seen.

A unique type is the Neys Biplane built near Sexsmith in Alberta in 1932. A rarity is one of the few Miles Whitney Straight monoplanes to survive, as is the 1930 Cessna EC-l monoplane of which only two or three were built. The Canuck 'City of Edmonton' was used by George Gorman to make the first air delivery of newspapers from Edmonton to Wetaskiwin in June 1919. Ted Reynolds acquired the aircraft in 1928 and flew it for a few years. Very few complete Avro Avian biplanes are known to survive. One of the few remaining pointed-wing de Havilland DH.87A Hornet Moth biplanes is a rarity.

In 1946 Northwest Industries built 13 Bellanca Senior Skyrockets at Edmonton. The prototype, which is the last complete survivor from the batch, is on show. The diminutive Kari-Keen Coupe was designed by Swen Swanson and entered production in 1928. Only 25 of the 60 h.p. version were completed along with ten of the higher powered Coupe 90. An earlier type from the same designer is the diminutive Lincoln Sport biplane. The Sznycer-Gottlieb SG VI-D Grey Gull is a helicopter which flew in the late 1940s.

Locally designed homebuilt types are being acquired to show the ingenuity of Alberta aviators. Some airframes are still in the old Reynolds Aviation Museum building on the opposite side of the airfield and in hangars on the active part of the site. Outside a few military aircraft from recent years can also be seen. This superb museum sets excellent standards for both the presentation and restoration of its exhibits.

TYPE	REG/SER	CON. NO.	PI/NOTES	STATUS
☐ Aerial Experiment Association Silver Dart (R)	BAPC.180	4		PV
☐ Aeronca C-3	CF-AQP	A-194	NC12480, N12480	PVA
☐ Aeronca 65LA	CF-WLP	L6249	NC23964, CF-WLP	RA
☐ Aeronca 65TC Grasshopper (O-58B) (L-3B)	CF-XVG	5712	43-1641, N50253	RA
☐ Airspeed AS.10 Oxford II	AS223	3557		RAD
☐ American Eagle A-101 (A-1)	CF-AHY	248	NC6517, N6517, C-FAHY	PV
☐ Arrow Sport F	CF-BGQ	51	NC18508, N18508	PV
☐ Auster K AOP.6	CF-LGM	2580	VP633, 16656	PVA
☐ Avro 616 Avian IVM	CF-CDV	R3/CN/316	137	PV
☐ Avro 652A Anson I				RAD
☐ Avro 652A Anson II	11567			RAD
☐ Avro 652A Anson II				RAD
☐ Avro 652A Anson II				RAD
☐ Avro 652A Anson II				RAD
☐ Avro 652A Anson II				RAD
☐ Avro 652A Anson V	C-FHQZ	MDF289	12477, CF-HQZ	PV
☐ Avro Canada C.100 Canuck 5 (CF-100)	100759	659	18759	PV
☐ Avro Canada C.105 Arrow (CF-105) (FSM)	'25201'			PVX

Alberta

☐ Barkley-Grow T8P-1	CF-BVE	1	NX18388	PV
☐ Beech D17S	CF-DTE	403		RAA
☐ Beech C18S Expeditor 3 (C-45F) (UC-45F)	C-FSIF	6596	43-35850, 1387, CF-SIF	RAA
☐ Beech D18S Expeditor (C-45H)	CF-OME	AF-662	52-10732, N9862Z	RA
☐ Beech C23 Sundowner (CT-134A) (Musketeer II)	134232	M-2319	At the Royal Canadian Legion Post in 50th Street.	PV
☐ Beech C23 Sundowner (CT-134A) (Musketeer II)	134233	M-2320		RA
☐ Beech 35 Bonanza	CF-FYF	D-645		RA
☐ Bell 26D Airacobra (P-39M)	42-4725			RAD
☐ Bell 47J-2	CF-AFK	1805		RA
☐ Bellanca 31-55A Senior Skyrocket	CF-DCH	4		PV
☐ Birdman Atlas XC-215	C-IANB	009		RA
☐ Boeing-Stearman A75 Kaydet (PT-13B)	CF-KQB	75-0255	40-1698	RA
☐ Boeing-Stearman A75N1 Kaydet (N2S-4)	CF-UWK	75-3522	Bu30083, N49366	RA
☐ Boeing-Stearman E75 Kaydet (PT-13D) (N2S-5)	CF-RAF	75-5168	42-17005, Bu61046, N66035, CF-RAF C-FRAF – privately owned.	RAAX
☐ Bristol 149 Bolingbroke IVT	9904			PVD
☐ Bristol 149 Bolingbroke IVT	10120			PV
☐ Bristol 170 Freighter 31M	C-GYQS	13060	G-18-114, NZ5907, ZK-EPD, G-AMLK, ZK-EPD, NZ5907	PV
☐ Canadair CL-2 North Star [Douglas DC-4M-1]	CF-TEP	106	17522 – front fuselage only.	RA
☐ Canadair CL-13 Sabre 3 [North American F-86J]	19200	100	19200, A-613	S
☐ Canadair CL-30 Silver Star 3 (CT-133) [Lockheed 580 (T-33AN)]	21001	T33-001	Composite – At Spar Aerospace.	PV
☐ Canadair CL-30 Silver Star 3 (CT-133) [Lockheed 580 (T-33AN)]	133089	T33-089	21089	RA
☐ Canadair CL-30 Silver Star 3 (CT-133) [Lockheed 580 (T-33AN)]	133351	T33-351	21351	RA
☐ Canadair CL-41A Tutor (CT-114)	114076	1076	26076	PV
☐ Canadair CL-41R Tutor	CF-LTX-X			RAC
☐ Canadair CL-90 Starfighter (CF-104) [Lockheed 683-04-12]	104763	683A-1063	12763	PV
☐ Canadair CL-219-1A17 Freedom Fighter (CF-116D) (CF-5D) [Northrop N-156B]	116815	2015		PV
☐ Cessna EC-1	NC199V	71		PV
☐ Cessna C-37 Airmaster	CF-NEV	355	NC18030, N18030	PV
☐ Cessna T-50 Crane 1				RAD
☐ Cessna T-50 Crane 1				RAD
☐ Cessna T-50 Crane 1				RAD
☐ Cessna T-50 Crane 1A (Bobcat – AT-17A)	8778	2328	42-13644, FJ127, 8778, CF-BTA	PV
☐ Champion 7KC Olympia	CF-OGF	4		RA
☐ Chandelle IV	C-IDPF	O4A 001 185		RAA
☐ Consolidated 21C	NC13289	12	NC13289, N13289	RA
☐ Corben D Baby Ace	CF-RAY	1	In Provincial Building in Edmonton.	PV
☐ Curtiss D Pusher		13	Partial replica.	RAA
☐ Curtiss JN-4 Canuck	'C1347'	AB.24	G-CABX, G-CATE	PVX
☐ Curtiss 50C Robin C-1	CF-ALZ	405	NC51H, N6394T	PVA
☐ De Havilland DH.60M Moth	CF-AGX	DHC.127		PVA
☐ De Havilland DH.82A Tiger Moth	C-GABB	82270	N9151, G-AOYU	PVA
☐ De Havilland DH.82C Tiger Moth	CF-DAL	DHC.644	4314	PVA
☐ De Havilland DH.87A Hornet Moth	CF-AYG	8031	CF-AYG, N8969	PVA
☐ De Havilland DH.89A Dragon Rapide (DH.89)	CF-PTK	6254	G-ACPP	RAC
☐ De Havilland DH.100 Vampire F.3	17071	EEP42389	17071, N6883D	RA
☐ De Havilland DHC.1 Chipmunk 1B-2-S3 (CT-120)	C-FCYO	148-186	(CF-CYO), 186, 18015, (12015), CF-CYO	RAA
☐ Douglas DC-3A-360 Skytrain (C-47)	C-FIAE	4563	41-18471, NC50474, XA-GEQ, N4887V, CF-IAE	PV
☐ Douglas DC-3A-360 Skytrain (C-47)	CF-JWP	9089	42-32863, NC16191, CF-INB, CF-PWF CF-JWP, C-FJWP	RA
☐ Douglas A-26C Invader	C-FCUI	28803	44-35524, N9401Z, CF-CUI	RA
☐ Eagle Delta Rogallo Hang Glider				RA
☐ Edgar Percival EP.9	C-FNWI	30	G-43-2, CF-NWI	PVA
☐ Ercoupe 415G	CF-GLZ	5011		RA
☐ Evans VP-1 Volksplane		9		RA
☐ Great Lakes 2T-1A	NC313Y	200	NC313Y, N313Y	RA
☐ Fairchild 24 C8E	CF-AZT	2825		RA
☐ Fairchild 71	NC24K	686	NC24K, (CF-AAK)	RA
☐ Fairchild M-62A-4 Cornell II	CF-FKB	FA1023	FX192	PVA
☐ Fairey Swordfish II	HS498			RA
☐ Falconar F-11	C-GFST	E6515		RA
☐ Fiberlite Products 104 Viking	CF-REF	FLS2		PV
☐ Fleet 7C Fawn II	220	58	(CF-CHF)	PV
☐ Fleet 16R Finch I	1001	243	1001, A224, CF-AAE, C-FAAE	PVA
☐ Fleet 21C	NC13289	12	NC13289, N13289	RA
☐ Fleet 21M			(Mexico)	RA
☐ Fleet 80 Canuck (Noury N-75)	CF-BYW-X	001	CF-BYW-X, CF-BYW	RAA
☐ Funk B	NC24142	68	NC24142, N24142	RA
☐ Fairchild 22 C7	NC11649	512	NC11649, N11649	PV
☐ Grumman G-40 Avenger (TBM-3)	C-GOEG	2100	Bu69361, N9596C	RAA
☐ Haseloh Gyroplane B	CF-OMO	43118202 (BH-63)		RA
☐ Haseloh Gyroplane J.B.2	C-GUAG	HB2-82		RA
☐ Hawker Hurricane XII	5418	44013		PV

Alberta

TYPE	REG/SER	CON. NO.	PI/NOTES	STATUS
☐ Howard DGA-15P (GH-3)	CF-OJN	1004	Bu45033, NC13943, N13943	RA
☐ Hughes 269A	N8780F	83-0001		RA
☐ Hütter H 17B				RA
☐ Jacobs Jaycopter A				RA
☐ Jacobs Jaycopter B Trainer		2		RA
☐ Jacobs Weihe (DFS 108-68)	N501D	1	At Wetaskiwin School.	RA
☐ Jodel D.9 Bébé	CF-RFK	PMS-1		RAA
☐ Kari-Keen 60 Coupe	CF-ANR	211	NC244K, N244K	RAA
☐ Kinner Sportster K	NC14225	142	NC14225, N14225	RA
☐ Laird LCB-200	CF-APY	196		RA
☐ Lear Learstar (Lockheed 18-10 Lodestar (C-57))	CF-CEC	18-2132	41-23166, NC60200, N60200, N711L	PV
☐ Lincoln Sport				PV
☐ Lockheed 18-10-01 Lodestar	CF-TDB	18-2220		RA
☐ Luscombe 8E Silvaire	CF-JRV	5398	NC2671K	RA
☐ McDonnell M.36BA Voodoo (F-101B) (CF-101B)	101038	546	57-0368, 101038, 838B	RA
☐ Meade C-3 Glider				PV
☐ McNamara Maxim	C-GBND	0001		RA
☐ Meyers MAC-145 (125C)	N34369	212		RA
☐ Miles M.11A Whitney Straight	CF-FGK	509	U-1, G-AFGK, N72511	PVA
☐ Mono Aircraft Monocoupe 90	NC170K	504	NC170K, N170K	PVA
☐ Neys Biplane	CF-ATM	1		PV
☐ Noorduyn Harvard IIB [North American NA-77]	C-FMGO	07-62	3096, CF-MGO	PVA
☐ Noorduyn Norseman IV	CF-SAH	21	679	RA
☐ Noorduyn Norseman VI (C-64A) (UC-64A)	CF-NJK	242	43-5251, NC79909, N79909	RAA
☐ North American NA-64 Yale	3458	64-3024		PV
☐ North American NA-108 Mitchell (B-25J) (Mitchell III)	5237	108-47480	44-86726, 5237, CF-NTP	PVD
☐ Pietenpol B4-A Aircamper	CF-BDH			PV
☐ Piper J-3F-65 Cub	CF-YME	6276	NC35310, N35310	RAA
☐ Piper J-4A Cub Coupe	CF-KIB	4-1255	NC30979, N30979	RA
☐ Piper J-5A Cub Cruiser	CF-HRI	5-897	NC38146, N38146	RA
☐ Pitts S-1C Special	C-GRLJ			RA
☐ Porterfield 35W	NC16401	301	NC16401, N16401	PV
☐ Porterfield LP-65	NC34706	872	NC34706, N34706	RA
☐ Rearwin 7000 Sportster	N14443	401	NC14443	PV
☐ Republic RC-3 Seabee	C-GCEK	149	NC87581, N87581	RA
☐ Reynolds Sport Monoplane		1		PV
☐ Reynolds Star		2		RA
☐ Schneider ESG 31 Grunau Baby IIB (DFS 108-49)	CF-ZBH	1533	(German)	RA
☐ Sikorsky S-58 Seahorse (HUS-1) (UH-34D)	N94495	58730	Bu145731	PV
☐ Sznycer-Gottlieb SG VI-D Grey Gull	CF-FGG	5001-A		RA
☐ Sperry-Verville M-1 Messenger (R)	C-GXYI	HSM-001		RA
☐ Stinson HW.75	CF-BZL	7175	NC22578, CF-BSJ, 3480	RA
☐ Stinson 10A Voyager	CF-BZM	7511	N?????, CF-EZC	RA
☐ Stinson 108-2 Voyager	CF-MPJ	108-2303	NC9303K, CF-COR	RA
☐ Stinson V-77 Reliant (AT-19)	CF-BGM	77-491	43-44204, FB763, Bu30531, N65647	PVA
☐ Stits SA-7D Skycoupe	C-FOWA	400	CF-OWA	RA
☐ Sud-Est SE.3160 Alouette III	CF-CAW	1251	26 (Canada CG)	RA
☐ Taylor J-2 Cub	CF-BEE	1064	NC17564, N17564, C-GNGO	PVA
☐ Taylor-Young BL.65	C-GTJC	1786	NC24449, N24449	RA
☐ Taylorcraft BC-12-65	CF-GUJ	2633	At Wetaskiwin School.	RA
☐ Team Minimax	C-IDCP	TC040316		RA
☐ Travel Air D-4D Speedwing (BE.4000) (B.4000)	CF-JLW	1151	NC9953, N9953	PVA
☐ Vertol V.44A (CH-127)	CF-BSG	602	9592	RA
☐ Waco 10 (GXE)	CF-AQU	1386		RA
☐ Waco NZR Hadrian (CG-4A)				RAD
☐ Waco UPF-7	CF-LEP	5461	NC29964, N29964 – on loan.	RAA
☐ Waco UPF-7 (YPT-14)	CF-LEF	5311	40-025, NC29102, N29102	RAA
☐ Waco YKS-7	CF-KYI	4615	NC17475, N17475 – on loan	PVA
☐ Waco ZQC-6	CF-BDW	4643		RA
☐ Welch OW-8	NC17117	49	CF-PMH, N17117	PVA

ROCKY MOUNTAIN HOUSE MONUMENT (AB23)

Location:	On permanent view at the airport which is about 8 km north of the town.

TYPE	REG/SER	CON. NO.	PI/NOTES	STATUS
☐ Canadair CL-30 Silver Star 3 (CT-133) [Lockheed 580 (T-33AN)]	'21037'	T33-082	21082, 133082 – wings from T33-284 21284 and tail from T33-437 21437 – on loan from Bomber Command Museum of Canada.	PVX

ST. ALBERT MONUMENT (AB24)

Location:	On permanent view at RCL Branch 271 in Tache Street in the centre of the town.

TYPE	REG/SER	CON. NO.	PI/NOTES	STATUS
☐ Canadair CL-30 Silver Star 3 (CT-133) [Lockheed 580 (T-33AN)]	21096	T33-096		PV

VENTURA MEMORIAL FLIGHT ASSOCIATION (AB25)

Address:	11410 Kingsway Avenue, Edmonton Alberta T5J 0X4,
Tel:	780-453-1078 **Fax:** 780-453-1885 **Email:** vmfa@telusplanet.nrt
Admission:	By prior permission only.
Location:	At the Alberta Aviation Museum on the south side of the municipal airport which is in the northern suburbs of the city.

After a period with the US Navy this Ventura was delivered to the Royal Canadian Air Force in 1943 serving for almost eight years. After several years in store the aircraft was bought by Spartan Air Services but after a few months force landed north of Yellowknife in the Yukon and was abandoned. The group was formed in the mid-1980s and on 17th June 1988 recovered the airframe by helicopter and then transported it to Edmonton. Members of the organisation are restoring the Ventura in the hangar of the Alberta Aviation Museum. Several crash sites have been investigated and parts from other aircraft have been moved to Edmonton to aid the rebuild. The aim is to complete it to its original military configuration.

TYPE	REG/SER	CON. NO.	P/NOTES	STATUS
☐ Lockheed 237-27-01 Ventura (PV-1)	CF-ZMR	237-5324	Bu33315, 2195, CF-FAV	RAC

WARNER MONUMENT (AB26)

Location:	On permanent view in the centre of the village.

TYPE	REG/SER	CON. NO.	P/NOTES	STATUS
☐ Canadair CL-30 Silver Star 3 (CT-133) [Lockheed 580 (T-33AN)]	21535	T33-535	21535, N35RV, N133RV	PV

BRITISH COLUMBIA

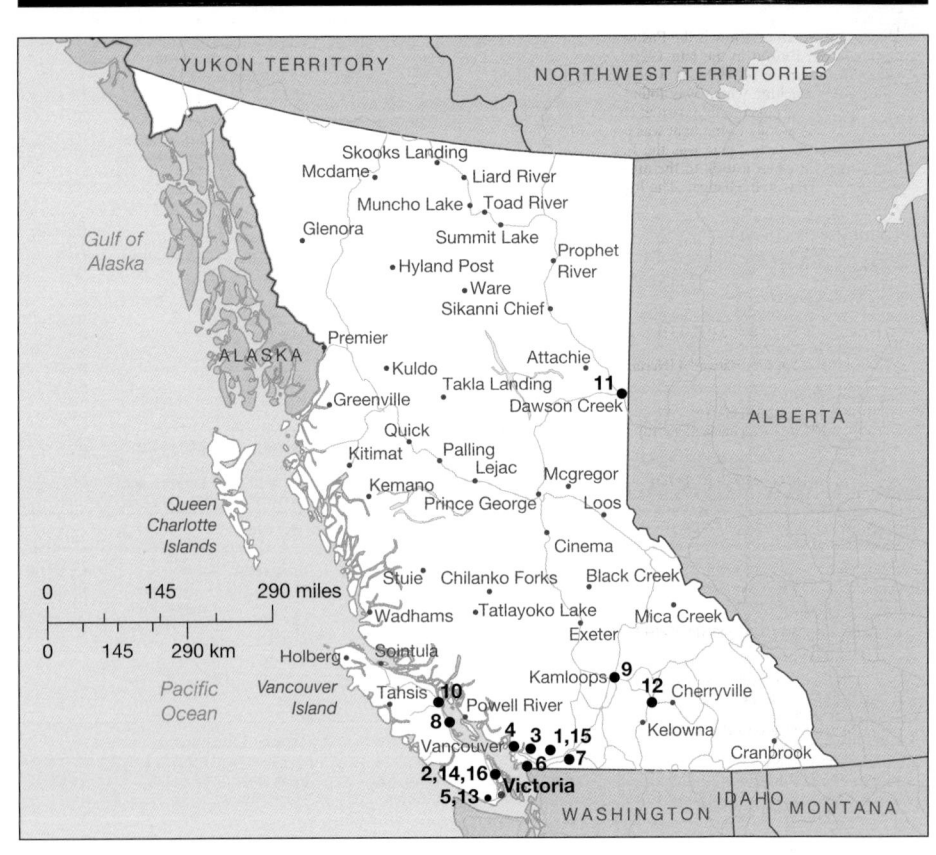

British Columbia
ABBOTSFORD INTERNATIONAL AIRSHOW SOCIETY (BC1)

Address:	PO Box 361 Abbotsford British Columbia V2S 4N9.
Tel:	604-852-8511 Email: info@abbotsfordairshow.com
Admission:	On permanent view.
Location:	About 5 km west of the town off Mount Lehman Road.

Abbotsford Airport regularly stages one of the largest airshows in western Canada and is also home to Conair which operates a large number of water bombers. The Voodoo is parked outside the premises of the society.

TYPE	REG/SER	CON. NO.	PI/NOTES	STATUS
☐ McDonnell M.36BA Voodoo (F-101B) (CF-101B)	101035	541	57-0363, 101035, 873B	PV

BRITISH COLUMBIA AVIATION MUSEUM (BC2)

Address:	1910 Norseman Road, Sidney, British Columbia V8L 5V5.
Tel:	250-655-3300 Fax: 250-655-1611 Email: inquiries@bcam.net
Admission:	Summer daily 1000-1600; Winter daily 1100-1500.
Location:	On the east side Victoria International Airport which is about 15 km north of the city.

The museum was set up in 1980 by the amalgamation of a number of small collections. Initially named the Canadian Military Aircraft Museum, the Department of Defence objected to the title and change was made to Commonwealth Military Aviation Museum. With the broadening of the aims of the collection the current name was adopted. In 1985 a large hangar was constructed and the exhibition expanded considerably. Funds are now being raised to build a new hall. At the rear of the hangar are panels depicting significant events in Canadian aviation. The development of flying in the region is also portrayed. The airfield was originally built as Patricia Bay Airbase during World War II and the story of the field is portrayed.

The rarest aircraft on show is the Eastman Sea Rover. Only 18 were built in Detroit in the late 1920s and five served in Canada. The example on show is a composite made up of Jim Eastman's machine which was found derelict at Fort St. Jean and another discovered in a barn at Duncan in 1988. The restoration of this unique flying boat was completed in August 1995. The Gibson Twin Plane was the first aircraft to fly in British Columbia when it took to the air in September 1910. A replica is on view in the hangar. The Invader was converted to a water bomber and until recently was the only example of this version in a museum.

The Viscount was delivered to Trans Canada Airways (later Air Canada) in March 1957. The airliner was withdrawn in 1980 and used as a ground instructional airframe at two colleges in Vancouver before being transported to the museum by barge in May 2005. The Canadian Government purchased 36 Auster AOP.6s in 1948 and six T.7s three years later. The first Cessna Bird Dogs were acquired in 1954 and these replaced the Austers over the next four years. The museum aircraft flew from bases in Manitoba until withdrawn in November 1954. After nearly three years in store in Alberta it was sold on the civil market and flew in British Columbia until withdrawn in December 1998.

The Pientenpol was built in the late 1970s by Bob McDonnel. The aircraft was completed in 1984 but the builder suffered a heart attack just before he was due to fly it for the first time. He donated it to the museum in 1990 as he did not want anyone else to fly it. The scale Spitfire was built by Bob Noren who died before he could complete it. The Luscombe Silvaire has been rebuilt from components found in South America. BC Airlines, one of the first commercial companies on the West Coast of Canada, operated a Silvaire for pilot training.

TYPE	REG/SER	CON. NO.	PI/NOTES	STATUS
☐ Auster K AOP.6	C-FXNF	2586	VP639, 16662, CF-XNF	PVC
☐ Avro 652A Anson II	FP846			PV
☐ Bell 47D-1 (47B-3)	CF-FZX	71	CF-FZX , C-FFZX – on loan from RBCM, BC.	PV
☐ Bristol 149 Bolingbroke IV	9104	11-880-107	Incorporates parts of 9093 and 10163.	PV
☐ Canadair CL-30 Silver Star 3 (CT-133) [Lockheed 580 (T-33AN)]	133462	T33-462	21462	PV
☐ Canadian Car & Foundry Harvard 4 [North American NA-186]				PVC
☐ Chanute Glider (R)				PV
☐ Circa Reproductions Nieuport 17	C-IRFC	243		PV
☐ De Havilland DHC.1 Chipmunk 22 (T.10)	C-GBRW/WG323	C1/0395	WG323 – privately owned.	PVA
☐ Douglas A-26B Invader	CF-BMS	18506	43-22357, N91348, CF-BMS, C-FBMS	PV
☐ Douglas Super DC-3 (R4D-8) (C-117D)	'CG-JGQ'	43307	Rebuilt from DC-3A-456 (R4D-5) Bu17116, N116DT, C-GJGQ – front fuselage only	PVX
☐ Eastman E-2 Sea Rover	CF-ASY	17	NC472M – with parts from c/n 17 NC471M CF-ASW.	PVC
☐ Fleet 2	CF-AOD	6	On loan from RBCM, BC.	PV
☐ Gibson Twin Plane (R)				PV
☐ Lincoln Sport	CF-AWA			PV
☐ Luscombe 8A Silvaire	'CF-BCR'		Composite.	PVX
☐ Noorduyn Norseman VI (C-64A) (UC-64A)	CF-JDG	538	44-70273, CF-JDG, N538DW- parts from c/n 131 43-5140, NC45380, CF-DRE.	PV
☐ Pacaero Tradewind (Beech D18S Expeditor 3NM)	CF-BCF	CA-176 (A-776)	2303, A625, CF-BCF, C-FBCF	PV
☐ Pietenpol B4-A Aircamper	C-GSNS			PV
☐ Prima 24 Skyseeker 1	C-IFAI	252633		PV
☐ Quickie Aircraft Quickie 1 (Rutan 54)	C-GTDV	1023		PV
☐ Replica Plans S.E.5A	'080279'			PVC
☐ Republic RC-3 Seabee	C-FJLC	710	NC6459K, N6459K, CF-JLC	PV
☐ Sikorsky S-55D (HRS-3)	'961'	55116	Bu129028, N4721 – In false RCN markings.	PVX
☐ Supermarine Spitfire (Scale R)				PV
☐ Vickers 757 Viscount	C-FTHG	224	CF-THG	PVC

BRITISH COLUMBIA FARM MACHINERY AND AGRICULTURAL MUSEUM (BC3)

Address:	9131 King Street, Fort Langley, British Columbia V1M 2R6.
Tel:	604-888-2273 **Email:** bcfm@telus.net
Admission:	April–October daily 1000-1630.
Location:	In the village which is about 5 km north of Langley.

The idea of a museum started in the late 1950s when a vintage plough was presented to the University of British Columbia. The collection finally opened on 19th November 1966. On site is a working sawmill along with a large collection of machinery. The Tiger Moth was the first crop-duster in the area.

TYPE	REG/SER	CON. NO.	PI/NOTES	STATUS
☐ De Havilland DH.82C Tiger Moth	CF-CIE	DHC.986	5811	PV

BRITISH COLUMBIA INSTITUTE OF TECHNOLOGY (BC4)

Address:	3700 Willingdon Avenue, Burnaby, British Columbia V5G 3H2.
Tel:	604-434-5734 **Email:** info@bcit.ca
Admission:	By prior permission only.
Location:	At Vancouver Airport, which is in the western part of the city.

The British Columbia Vocational School was set up in 1960 and changed its name to the current title. Aviation courses have been run for several years. In 2007 a modern Aerospace Technology Campus was opened near the city airport where courses leading to qualifications in aviation maintenance, avionics, airport operations and engines are held. In the hangars are a number of instructional airframes, along with engines and components. The list below is not complete and there are at least four more on site.

TYPE	REG/SER	CON. NO.	PI/NOTES	STATUS
☐ Aero Commander 680V (680T)	C-FAXN	1546-9	N75D, N300HH, N800HH, N800HA, (C-GVCF), N800HA, N9031X, (N800HA), N9031X, C-CJCA, N2549E	RA
☐ Aero 1121 Jet Commander	N710DC	112	N4730E, N91B, N97WG, N4WG, N44WG, N773WB, N372Q	RA
☐ Bell 205 Iroquois (UH-1H)				RA
☐ Bell 206 Jet Ranger				RA
☐ Bell 206 Jet Ranger				RA
☐ Boeing 737-2H4	C-GWJT	21262	N27SW	RA
☐ Cessna 172H	CF-VZQ	56283	(N8083L)	RA
☐ Cessna 172P	CF-QLM	17275669		RA
☐ Cessna 180G	CF-PGY	51370	N4670U	RA
☐ Cessna 310M Blue Canoe (310E) (L-27B) (U-3B)	C-GBDS	310M0005	60-6050, N5331G	RA
☐ Convair 580 (440-77)			Front fuselage only.	RA
☐ Dassault Falcon 20C (CC-117)	C-GWPB	92/421	F-WJMM, 20503 (Canada), 117503 (Canada), C-GWPB, 'N97471'	RA
☐ Piper PA-31-350 Navajo Chieftain	C-GNLM	31-7305053	N74916	RA
☐ Piper PA-60 Aerostar 600A	C-GUTV	0722-8061224	N60765, N8NF	RA
☐ Piper PA-60 Aerostar 602P	C-GRSQ	0896-8161254	N6893S	RA
☐ Quickie Aircraft Quickie 1 (Rutan 54)	C-GOZD	16		RA
☐ Robinson R-22 Beta	C-FAAD	0970		RA
☐ Ted Smith Aerostar 600	C-GBBP	60-0142-062	N17HA	RA
☐ Viking Dragonfly	C-GRLT	090		RA

CANADIAN FORCES BASE ESQUIMALT NAVAL AND MILITARY MUSEUM (BC5)

Address:	Box 17000, Station Forces, Vancouver, British Columbia V9A 7N2.
Tel:	250-363-4312 **Fax:** 250-363-5655 **Email:** info@NavalandMilitaryMuseum.org
Admission:	Monday-Friday 1000-1530.
Location:	About 2 miles west of Victoria on Vancouver Island.

A naval base was established at the site in 1848 and many of the permanent buildings erected at the end of the nineteenth century still survive. The museum focuses on the naval history of the western coast and of the base. There are displays of documents photographs and models. The Tracker is currently in store.

TYPE	REG/SER	CON. NO.	PI/NOTES	STATUS
☐ Grumman G-103 Tracker (CS2F-1) (CP-121)	12148	DHC-47	1548	RA

CANADIAN MUSEUM OF FLIGHT (BC6)

Address:	Hangar 3, 5333 216th Street, Langley, British Columbia V2Y 2N3.
Tel:	604-532-0035 **Fax:** 604-532-0056 **Email:** museum@direct.ca
Admission:	Daily 1000-1700.
Location:	At Langley Airport which is about 2 km north east of the town off Avenue 56.

Started in the early 1970s, the museum battled for many years to find a home. During the 1980s and the early 1990s most of the collection was on view at Surrey but in 1995 the museum was forced to move and has now established an exhibition in a hangar

British Columbia

at Langley Airport. The space for the display is small and about a dozen airframes can be viewed inside the building with a few more outside. The majority of the collection has been placed in store. Nevertheless an interesting display has been set up.

Outside is one of the two known surviving Handley Page Hampden bombers dating from World War II. Crash sites were investigated and the remains of one which had ditched on a training flight were located in Saanich Inlet. After a great deal of effort the airframe was raised in 1986 and work over the last two decades has resulted in an almost complete airframe on show. Components of other Hampdens were also located and used in the rebuild. Recovered from other locations were remains of a Blackburn Shark and a Fairchild 82A. The Shark biplane torpedo bomber made its maiden flight in August 1933 and over 250 were built. Nine Sharks were delivered to Canada from Britain and Boeing Aircraft of Canada at Vancouver constructed 17 under licence. The Fairchild 82 high wing monoplane was produced in Canada. The rugged design proved popular with operators and two dozen were built.

Inside is a rare Nelson Dragonfly powered glider. Developed from the Bowlus Baby Albatross, less than ten were built just after World War II.

The Fleet Finch biplane has seen service in the USA and Mexico as well as in Canada. The airworthy biplane is painted in period RCAF colours and is a popular attraction at local shows. Also in flying condition is 1930 Waco INF. The biplane was converted from the 100 hp Kinner powered RNF by fitting a 125 hp engine. The Mignet HM.290 was built in 1962 by John Sayle of Langley and the aircraft was powered by a 75 hp McCulloch engine. Displays in the hangar are being developed and include one on 'Women in Aviation'.

Parked outside is an early example of the famous Dakota which was first delivered to American Airlines in 1940. Restoration was started by the Friends of the DC-3 and the aircraft has now joined the museum. The collection includes a number of homebuilt designs including an incomplete Jurca Mustang. Fred Struchen of North Vancouver built his helicopter a few years ago. The airframe incorporated a number of motorcycle and car parts. Power was provided by a converted Honda Civic engine. The helicopter only made a few low altitude hover flights.

A great deal of progress has been made since the move and hopefully more space will soon be found to display the many interesting aircraft currently in store.

TYPE	REG/SER	CON. NO.	PI/NOTES	STATUS
☐ Avro 652A Anson II	7139	CF1349		RAD
☐ Avro 652A Anson V	CF-IVK	MDF178	12082, 801	RA
☐ Avro Canada C.100 Canuck 3D (3B) (CF-100)	18138	038	Includes parts of c/n 666 18766 and c/n 691 18791.	PV
☐ Beech D18S Expeditor 3NMT (3N)	CF-CKT	CA-180 (A-780)	2307	PV
☐ Bell 47J-2	CF-IVE	1568	CF-IVE, C-FIVE	RA
☐ Bennett Delta Wing Mariah 170 Hang Glider				RA
☐ Bensen B-8M Gyrocopter	CF-OXO	DF-1		RA
☐ Blackburn Shark III	518	506	Crash remains.	RAD
☐ Bristol 149 Bolingbroke IVT	9896		Front fuselage on show	PV/RA
☐ Canadair CL-30 Silver Star 3 (CT-133) [Lockheed 580 (T-33AN)]	21487	T33-487	At Pitt Meadows Airport.	PV
☐ Canadair CL-41A Tutor (CT-114)	114003	1003	26003	PV
☐ De Havilland DH.60M Moth	CF-APA	1322	G-CYWV	RA
☐ De Havilland DH.60M Moth	CF-AGF	1323	Fuselage only.	RAD
☐ De Havilland DH.82C Tiger Moth	C-GMFT/'4236'	DHC.1178	5875	PV
☐ De Havilland DH.100 Vampire F.3	'17012'	EEP42376	17058, N6860D	PVX
☐ Douglas DC-3-227B (C-49H)	CF-PWH	2198	NC21793, 42-57506, NC21793, CF-HCF	RA
☐ Fairchild 82A	CF-MAI	37	Crash remains.	RAD
☐ Fairchild M-62A-4 Cornell II	C-FFLY	FC.141	10640, CF-FLY	RA
☐ Fairey Battle I	2139		L5306 – major components from several aircraft.	RAD
☐ Fleet 16B Finch II	C-GBJS/4725	542	4725, XB-TUJ, XB-TAX, N16BP, C-GBJS	PVA
☐ Handley Page HP.52 Hampden I	P5436	FAL/CA/80	With parts from AN132 and AN136.	PVC
☐ Hawker Sea Hurricane XIIA	BW862	34		PV
☐ Jurca MJ.7G Mustang	C-FIJB	CCF/R30028	Fuselage section.	RAD
☐ Lockheed 583-04-15 Starfighter (CF-104D)	104645	583A-5315	12645 – wings from two other aircraft.	PV
☐ Mignet HM-290 Pou-du-Ciel	CF-RFH	JDS-1		PV
☐ Müller Arrow Hang Glider				RA
☐ Nelson Dragonfly BB-1	CF-VFA	506	N34922, CF-VFA, CF-IDB – Converted from Bowlus Bumblebee.	PV
☐ Noorduyn Harvard IIB [North American NA-77]	CF-GME	07-144	3275, CF-MGI, N9750M, CF-MGE, C-FGME	PVA
☐ Noorduyn Norseman IVW	CF-PAA	32	2459	RA
☐ Quickie Aircraft Quickie 1 (Rutan 54)		1028	Incomplete.	RA
☐ R.F.D. Dagling	CF-ZAX	1		RA
☐ Replica Plans S.E.5A	CF-QGL	G70 002		PVA
☐ Republic RC-3 Seabee	CF-DYJ	135		RA
☐ Sikorsky S-55D Chickasaw (H-19B) (UH-19B)	'9632'		53-4414 – composite.	PVX
☐ Sopwith F.1 Camel (R)	'B6289'			RAX
☐ Spezio Sport Tuholer	C-GKEL	67		RA
☐ Stampe & Vertongen S.V.4C	F-BDMC	633	633 (Fr.Mil)	RA
☐ Struchen Helicopter				PV
☐ Taylor JT.1 Monoplane				RA
☐ Waco AQC-6 (ZQC-6)	CF-CCW	4646	CF-ZQC	PV
☐ Waco INF (KNF)	CF-CJR	3324	NC605Y, N605Y	PVA
☐ Westland Lysander IIIA	2349	1194	2349, C-GBXL	PV

CHILLAWACK MONUMENT (BC7)

Location:	On permanent view outside the Military Education Centre in the town.

TYPE	REG/SER	CON. NO.	PI/NOTES	STATUS
☐ Grumman G-103 Tracker (CS2F-2) (CP-121)	C-FKVG	DHC-72	1573, 12173	PV

This Canadian-built Harvard 4 is mounted by the entrance to the airport at Red Deer. (Ruud Leeuw) [AB21]

The only aircraft on show at the British Columbia Farm Machinery and Agricultural Museum is this Canadian-built Tiger Moth. (BCFMAM) [BC3]

Among the aircraft on show at the Comox Air Force Museum is this Douglas Dakota III. [BC8]

British Columbia

COMOX AIR FORCE MUSEUM (BC8)

Address:	Box 1000, 19 Wing, Comox, Lazo, British Columbia V0R 2K0.
Tel:	250-339-8162 **Fax:** 250-339-8162 **Email:** info@comoxairforcemuseum.ca
Admission:	June–August daily 1000-1600 September–May Saturday-Sunday 1000-1600.
Location:	About 250 km north west of Victoria east of Highway 19.

Comox began as a Royal Air Force base in 1943 and served as a Transport OTU during the conflict. The site closed in 1946 and re-opened in 1952 as an RCAF station housing maritime units. The museum was established in 1987 in a building just outside the main gate. The excellent displays trace the history of Canadian military aviation from the early days. The development of Comox and the history of the units have flown from the field are portrayed in detail. Uniforms, components, engines, documents and photographs can be seen. Over 1,000 models are also on view. The remains of a Japanese fire balloon launched from Honshu is a prized exhibit. Located a short distance away from the museum is the aircraft park. The Dakota on show represents the early years of the base. The Piasecki helicopter was restored by a group of volunteers.

TYPE	REG/SER	CON. NO.	PI/NOTES	STATUS
☐ Avro Canada C.100 Canuck 5D (5) (CF-100)	18790	690	18790, 100790	PV
☐ Boeing-Vertol 107-II-28 Labrador (CH-113A)	11310	4004	10410	RA
☐ Canadair CL-28-1 Argus 1 (CP-107)	10712	3	20712	PV
☐ Canadair CL-30 Silver Star 3 (CT-133) [Lockheed 580 (T-33AN)]	133102	T33-102	21102	PV
☐ Canadair CL-41A Tutor (CT-114)	114115	1115	26115	PV
☐ Canadair CL-90 Starfighter (CF-104) [Lockheed 683-04-12]	104731	683A-1031	12731	PV
☐ De Havilland DH.100 Vampire F.3	17031		17031, N41J	RA
☐ Douglas DC-3A-456 Skytrain (C-47A) (Dakota III) (CC-129)	12944/FZ671	12256	42-92454, FZ671	PV
☐ Grumman G-103 Tracker (CS2F-2) (CS2F-3) (CP-121)	12188	DHC-87	1588	PV
☐ McDonnell M.36BA Voodoo (F-101B) (CF-101B)	101030	532	57-0354, 101030, 827B	PV
☐ McDonnell M.36BA Voodoo (F-101B) (CF-101B)	101057	607	57-0429, 101057	PV
☐ Piasecki PD-22 Work Horse (H-21B) (CH-21B)	'9641'	B.116	53-4366	PVX
☐ Sopwith F.1 Camel (FSM)				PV

KAMLOOPS MONUMENT (BC9)

Location:	On permanent view at the airport which is about 5 km north west of the town.

TYPE	REG/SER	CON. NO.	PI/NOTES	STATUS
☐ Canadair CL-219-1A10 Freedom Fighter (CF-116A) (CF-5A) [Northrop N-156A]	116740	1040		PV

NORTH ISLAND COLLEGE (BC10)

Address:	1685 South Dogwood Street, Campbell River, British Columbia V9W 8C1.
Tel:	250-923-9793 **Email:** ruedipletscher@nic.bc.ca
Admission:	By prior permission only.
Location:	In the southern part of the town.

The college was established in 1975 and now operates from several sites on Vancouver Island. At the Campbell River Campus a course leading to becoming a qualified Aircraft Structures Technician takes place. Only one airframe, a former RCAF Canadair Silver Star, is currently in use.

TYPE	REG/SER	CON. NO.	PI/NOTES	STATUS
☐ Canadair CL-30 Silver Star 3 (CT-133) [Lockheed 580 (T-33AN]	133543	T33-543	21543	RA

NORTHERN LIGHTS COLLEGE (BC11)

Address:	11401 8th Street, Dawson Creek, British Columbia V1G 4G2.
Tel:	250-784-7503 **Email:** ame@nlc.bc.ca
Admission:	By prior permission only.
Location:	At the airport which is about 2 km south east of the town.

The college operates from seven sites in the northern areas of the province. Courses in a wide range of academic, business and technical subjects are offered. The aviation maintenance department has premises at the airport. In the workshops are a range of engines, components and test rigs along with the aircraft.

TYPE	REG/SER	CON. NO.	PI/NOTES	STATUS
☐ Aero Commander 680V (680T)	C-GSVQ	1544-8	(N1171Z), N357X, N146E	RA
☐ Aérospatiale AS.350D Ecureuil	C-GLNJ	1268		RA
☐ Beech 65-A90 King Air	C-GHVR	LJ-337	N95510, ZS-NOK, N67262, N69J	RA
☐ Bell 205A-1				RA
☐ Bell 206A Jet Ranger				RA
☐ Cessna 150G	C-FCLT	15065150	N3850J, CF-CLT	RA
☐ Cessna 180	C-FING	32229	N4631A	RA
☐ Cessna 310C	C-GWAP	35872	N1772H	RA
☐ Piper PA-23-250 Aztec C	C-FULM	27-3307	N6100Y, CF-ULM	RA
☐ Piper PA-31 Turbo Navajo	C-GSWY	31-595	N6705L, C-GPOP	RA
☐ Robinson R-44 Raven	C-GEMV	0568		RA

OKANAGAN COLLEGE (BC12)

Address:	7000 College Way, Vernon, British Columbia V1B 2N5.
Tel:	250-545-7291 Email: dkeegstra@okanagan.bc.ca
Admission:	By prior permission only.
Location:	At Vernon Airport which is in the south western part of the town.

The college was set up as the British Columbia Vocational school in 1963 and took up its present name in 2005. An aircraft maintenance section is located in a hangar at Vernon Airport. A number of instructional airframes are in use. The list is not complete and more aircraft are inside the hangar.

TYPE	REG/SER	CON. NO.	PI/NOTES	STATUS
☐ Beech 100 King Air				RA
☐ Bell 206B Jet Ranger				RA
☐ Bell 206B Jet Ranger				RA
☐ Cessna 310				RA
☐ De Havilland DHC.1 Chipmunk 1B-2-S3				RA
☐ Mitsubishi MU-2				RA
☐ Rutan 61 Long Ez				RA

ROYAL BRITISH COLUMBIA MUSEUM (BC13)

Address:	675 Belleville Street, Victoria, British Columbia V8W 1A1.
Tel:	250-356-7226 Email: reception@royalbcmuseum.bc.ca
Admission:	Daily 1000-1730, closes at 2000 June–August.
Location:	In the city centre near the Inner Harbour.

Primarily a general history and natural history museum, the collection opened in 1968 as the British Columbia Provincial Museum. Rated as one of the best museums of its type in North America, the imaginative displays trace the development of the culture and social history of the region. The small aeronautical section has components and artefacts on show. The Fleet 2, which was in the main building for many years, has now moved to the British Columbia Aviation Museum along with the Bell helicopter. The biplane was built at Fort Erie in Ontario in 1930 and served in British Columbia for most of its operational life.

SIDNEY MONUMENT (BC14)

Location:	On permanent view at the Army, Navy and Air Force Club on 4th Street in the town.

TYPE	REG/SER	CON. NO.	PI/NOTES	STATUS
☐ Canadair CL-13A Sabre 5 [North American F-86E]	23060	850		PV

UNIVERSITY COLLEGE OF FRASER VALLEY (BC15)

Address:	30645 Firecat Road, Abbotsford, British Columbia V2S 7M8.
Tel:	604-504-7441 Fax: 604-855-7614 Email: aerospace@ufv.ca
Admission:	By prior permission only.
Location:	At the airport which is about 5 miles west of the town.

The college was set up in 1974 and became a university in 2008. An aviation maintenance course takes place in a complex at the airport. The Boeing 737 was donated by a local airline.

Under restoration is the Lockheed Lodestar owned by the Canadian Museum of Flight. Originally delivered to Trans Canada Airlines in 1941, the aircraft was retired in the 1960s and stored for a period at Midway Airport in Chicago. The twin was then on show at the now closed Victory Air Museum at Mundelein, Illinois.

The museum acquired the Lodestar in 1987 and for the past few years it has been displayed at the Delta Air Park south of Vancouver.

TYPE	REG/SER	CON. NO.	PI/NOTES	STATUS
☐ Boeing 737-200				RA
☐ Lockheed 18-10-01 Lodestar	CF-TCY	18-2064		RA
☐ Piaggio P.149D				RA
☐ Sikorsky S-70				RA

WEST COAST MUSEUM OF FLYING (BC16)

Address:	No 19 – 9800 Macdonald Park Road,, Sidney, British Columbia V8L 5W5.
Tel:	250-656-2746 Fax: 250-656-3369
Admission:	Saturday-Sunday 1000-1600.
Location:	On the east side Victoria International Airport which is about 15 km north of the city.

Formed by David Maude, who also set up the British Columbia Aviation Museum, this collection has one aircraft at the moment.

The Kittyhawk was purchased after World War II by David's father George. The aircraft is in original configuration and has been painstakingly restored over the years.

Well over 100 were operated by the Royal Canadian Air Force during World War II. Memorabilia and photographs are also in the hangar. George also acquired at Bolingbroke at the same time and this was later sold to two brothers who put it in store. David bought it in 1980 and it is now in the British Columbia Aviation Museum collection.

TYPE	REG/SER	CON. NO.	PI/NOTES	STATUS
☐ Curtiss A87-A2 Kittyhawk I	C-GHTM	15184	AK803, 1034 (Canada) – wings from c/n 15404 AK933, 1057 (Canada), N94466.	PV

MANITOBA

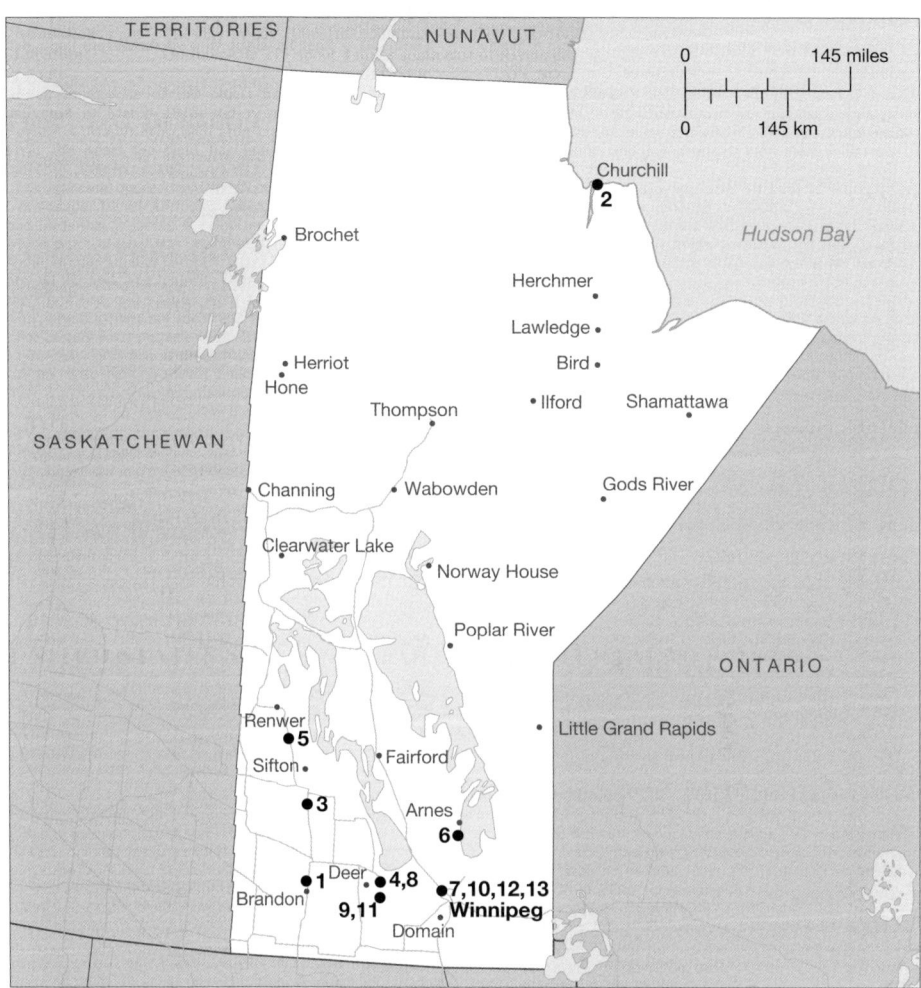

COMMONWEALTH AIR TRAINING PLAN MUSEUM (MB1)

Address:	Box3, Group 520,RR 5, Brandon, Manitoba R7A 5Y5.
Tel:	204-727-2444 **Fax:** 204-725-2334 **Email:** airmuseum@inetlink.ca
Admission:	Daily 1000-1630.
Location:	At McGill Field which is about 1 mile north of the city.

Between 17th December 1939 and the end of World War II the British Commonwealth Air Training Plan trained more than 130,000 aircrew at over 100 bases in Canada. McGill Field, located just north of Brandon, was the home of 12 SFTS.

The idea of a museum started in 1981 with a small private collection of training aircraft assembled by Wes Agnew, who was an instructor during World War II. The display opened on 3rd July 1982 in the old Hangar 1 at McGill Field, now Brandon Municipal Airport.

The exhibition has grown steadily and now has over 5,000 artefacts on show including uniforms, documents, components, log books, maps, badges. The history of the airfield is shown and there are many interesting photographs to be seen.

The hangar contains about a dozen aircraft, most painted in the familiar yellow training scheme. Vehicles and engines can also be seen in this area. Several members of the fleet are maintained in airworthy condition. In order to enhance the display several more aircraft are under restoration, some to flying status.

A short distance away on a local farm is a large outside store containing around 50 derelict airframes recovered from farms in the area. Some of these are capable of being restored.

The wooden hangar was built in 1940 and designed to last ten years. The building now needs major structural work and the museum is raising funds for the rebuild of the hangar and possibly a new exhibition hall. The museum has now been designated a National Historic Site.

TYPE	REG/SER	CON. NO.	PI/NOTES	STATUS
☐ Avro 652A Anson I				PVC
☐ Avro 652A Anson II				RAD
☐ Avro 652A Anson II				RAD
☐ Avro 652A Anson II				RAD
☐ Avro 652A Anson II				RAD
☐ Avro 652A Anson II				RAD
☐ Avro 652A Anson II				RAD
☐ Avro 652A Anson II			Front fuselage only.	RA
☐ Avro 652A Anson II				RAD
☐ Avro 652A Anson V				RAD
☐ Avro 652A Anson V				RAD
☐ Avro 652A Anson V	12125	MDF323 (?)		PVC
☐ Beech D18S Expeditor 3N	C-FBAS	CA-57 (A-657)	1482, CF-BAS	PVC
☐ Beech D18S Expeditor 3TM	1561	CA-161 (A-761)	1561, 5192, CF-ZML	RA
☐ Beech C23-19 Musketeer (CT-134)	134208	M-1332	13408,134208,787C	PV
☐ Boeing-Stearman B75N1 Kaydet (N2S-3)	C-GFMG	75-7972	Bu38351, N63802	PVA
☐ Bristol 149 Bolingbroke IV	9059			PVC
☐ Cessna T-50 Crane 1				RAD
☐ Bristol 149 Bolingbroke IVT				RAD
☐ Bristol 149 Bolingbroke IVT				RAD
☐ Bristol 149 Bolingbroke IVT				RAD
☐ Bristol 149 Bolingbroke IVT	'9944'		At nearby Comfort Inn Hotel.	PVX
☐ Bristol 149 Bolingbroke IVT	10107			PVC
☐ Bristol 149 Bolingbroke IVT	9883			PV
☐ Canadair CL-30 Silver Star 3 (CT-133) [Lockheed 580 (T-33AN)]	21130	T33-130		PV
☐ Cessna T-50 Crane 1				RAD
☐ Cessna T-50 Crane 1				RAD
☐ Cessna T-50 Crane 1				RAD
☐ Cessna T-50 Crane 1				RAD
☐ Cessna T-50 Crane 1				RAD
☐ Cessna T-50 Crane 1				RAD
☐ Cessna T-50 Crane 1				RAD
☐ Cessna T-50 Crane 1	7729	1172		PV
☐ De Havilland DH.82A Tiger Moth	'4188'	85461	DE465, G-ANOS, CF-JNF, C-FJNF	PVAX
☐ Fairchild M-62A-4 Cornell II	C-GATP	1093	FV725	PVA
☐ Fairey Battle I	1317	F4139	P2234 – major components	RAC
☐ Fleet 60K Fort	3562	602	Cockpit only.	RA
☐ Fleet 60K Fort	3613	653		RA
☐ Fleet 60K Fort	3635	675		PV
☐ Frankfort Cinema B (TG-1A)	C-FZCF	B-2-7	(USAAF), CF-ZCF	PV
☐ Hawker Hurricane I (FSM)	'905'			PVCX
☐ Noorduyn Norseman IV				RAC
☐ North American NA-64 Yale	3396	64-2161		RAC
☐ North American NA-66 Harvard II	C-FMGZ	66-2290	AJ540, 2557, CF-MGZ	PVA
☐ Stinson HW.75	C-FDLM	7087	NC22509, CF-BSL, 3478, CF-DLM	PVA
☐ Waco NZR Hadrian (CG-4A)			(USAAF)	PVC

FORT CHURCHILL MONUMENT (MB2)

Location:	On permanent view in the town.

TYPE	REG/SER	CON. NO.	PI/NOTES	STATUS
☐ Curtiss-Wright CW-20B-4 Commando (C-46F)	C-GYHT	22375	44-78552, N3925CN239JL	PVD

FORT DAUPHIN MUSEUM (MB3)

Address:	Box 181, 140 Jackson Street, Dauphin, Manitoba R7N 2V1.
Tel:	204-638-6630 Fax: 204-629-2327 Email: fortdphn@mts.net
Admission:	May–June Monday-Friday 1000-1700; July–August daily 1000-1700.
Location:	In the centre of the town off Highway 20.

The museum resembles an early trading post surrounded by a wooden palisade. Nine original buildings have been moved to the site and these include a blacksmith's shop and a trapper's cabin. There are many interesting period items tracing the history and development of the local area. The fur trade features prominently in the displays.

The museum also serves as a research centre for over 1,000 local archaeological sites.

Major W.G. Barker, who won the Victoria Cross in September 1918, was born in the town. Although wounded, he shot down three Fokker D VIIs before crashing in his Sopwith Snipe. The fuselage of this aircraft is in the Canadian War Museum in Ottawa. On show in this museum is a display of memorabilia, documents and photographs tracing his flying career. There are some original pieces of fabric, including roundels, cut from World War I aircraft.

FORT LA REINE MUSEUM AND PIONEER VILLAGE (MB4)

Address:	PO Box 744, 2652 Saskatchewan Avenue East, Portage la Prairie, Manitoba R1N 3C2.
Tel:	204-857-3259 Fax: 204-857-3259 Email: info@rm.portage-la-prairie.mb.ca
Admission:	May–mid September Monday-Friday 0900-1800; Saturday-Sunday 1000-1800.
Location:	About 5 km east of the town at the junction of Highways 1A and 26.

Manitoba

Pierre Gaultier de la Vérendrye built the original fort in 1738 and the site served as his headquarters for 15 years whilst he explored the region. Several historic buildings and vehicles have been moved to the museum. The official railcar of William van Horn, who built the Canadian Pacific Railway, is a prized exhibit. Nearby is one of the two surviving Superintendent's Cars. Only 22 were built and positioned around the country to ensure the smooth running of the railways. A military museum occupies a hut moved from the local airfield. On show are uniforms, components and memorabilia. The only aircraft is the Beech CT-134A. The example on show served at the nearby airfield in the primary training role for more than two decades.

TYPE	REG/SER	CON. NO.	PI/NOTES	STATUS
☐ Beech C23 Sundowner (CT-134A) (Musketeer II)	134238	M-2326	13238	PV

GARLAND MONUMENT (MB5)

Location:	On permanent view at a house in the town.

TYPE	REG/SER	CON. NO.	PI/NOTES	STATUS
☐ Vickers 757 Viscount	CF-THB	219		PV

GIMLI MONUMENT (MB6)

Location:	On permanent view at the airport which is about 3 km west of the town.

TYPE	REG/SER	CON. NO.	PI/NOTES	STATUS
☐ Canadair CL-30 Silver Star 3 (CT-133) [Lockheed 580 (T-33AN)]	21239	T33-239		PV

MANITOBA MILITARY AVIATION MUSEUM AND AIR PARK (MB7)

Address:	PO Box 17000, CFB Winnipeg, Manitoba R3J 3Y5.
Tel:	204-833-2500 ext 4739 Email: robiwacha@manitobamilitaryaviationmuseum.com
Admission:	Aircraft on permanent display; museum in base open Tuesday-Friday 1300-1700.
Location:	On the south west side of the International Airport which is in the western suburbs of the city.

For a number of years the base had a small airpark just inside the main gate. Three aircraft – a Dakota, one of the Expeditors and a Mitchell – are still located at this site.

A Heritage Park has now been set up close to the Air Command Headquarters. Examples of types used in recent years have been mounted along the road leading to this part of the base. A monument honouring ground crew members has been erected.

A museum tracing the history of military aviation in the province has been set up in one of the buildings on the base. The displays of models, photographs, uniforms, documents and models trace the development of the Air Force in the area.

TYPE	REG/SER	CON. NO.	PI/NOTES	STATUS
☐ Avro Canada C.100 Canuck 5 (CF-100)	100784	684	18784	PV
☐ Beech C23 Sundowner (CT-134A) (Musketeer II)	134228	M-2315		PV
☐ Beech D18S Expeditor 3NM	1577	CA-263 (A-913)		RA
☐ Beech D18S Expeditor 3TM	1528	CA-128	5185	RA
☐ Bell 206A Kiowa (COH-58A) (CH-136)	136248	44048	71-20913	PV
☐ Canadair CL-13B Sabre 6 [North American F-86E]	23605	1395		PV
☐ Canadair CL-30 Silver Star 3 (CT-133) [Lockheed 580 (T-33AN)]	133186	T33-186	21186, 133186, 755B	PV
☐ Canadair CL-41A Tutor (CT-114)	114004	1004	26004, 702B	PV
☐ Canadair CL-90 Starfighter (CF-104) [Lockheed 683-04-12]	104753	683A-1053	12753	PV
☐ Canadair CL-219-1A10 Freedom Fighter (CF-116A) (CF-5A) [Northrop N-156A]	116749	1049	116749, A887	PV
☐ Canadair CL-600 Challenger (CX-144A)	144612	1002	C-GCGS-X	PV
☐ Canadian Car & Foundry Harvard 4 [North American NA-186]	'20301'	CCF4-254	20463, CF-UAE, C-FUAE	PVX
☐ Douglas DC-3A-467 Skytrain (C-47B) (Dakota IV) (CC-129)	12949	14803/26248	43-48987, KJ956, 12949, 746B	RA
☐ Grumman G-103 Tracker (CS2F-2) (CP-121)	1551	DHC-50	1551, 12151, A730, 730B	PV
☐ McDonnell M.36BA Voodoo (F-101B) (CF-101B)	101008	446	57-0268, 101008, 872B	PV
☐ North American NA-108 Mitchell (B-25J) (TB-25J) (Mitchell III)	5203	108-47478	44-86724, 5203, CF-NTU	RA

PORTAGE LA PRAIRIE MONUMENT (MB8)

Location:	On permanent view in Island Park.

TYPE	REG/SER	CON. NO.	PI/NOTES	STATUS
☐ Canadair CL-30 Silver Star 3 (CT-133) [Lockheed 580 (T-33AN)]	21277	T33-277		PV

RED RIVER COLLEGE – PORTAGE LA PRAIRIE (MB9)

Address:	Box 237, Hangar 4, Southport, Manitoba R0H 1N10.
Tel:	204-428-6300 Fax: 204-428-6305 Email: stevensonaviation@rrc.mb.ca
Admission:	By prior permission only.
Location:	At the airport which is south of the town off Highway 240.

The college opened its regional centre at Portage la Prairie in 1985. The aviation maintenance section is located at the airport where a number of instructional airframes and engines are in the hangar.

TYPE	REG/SER	CON. NO.	PI/NOTES	STATUS
☐ Beech C23 Sundowner (CT-134A) (Musketeer II)	134236	M-2324		RA
☐ Beech C23 Sundowner (CT-134A) (Musketeer II)	134245	M-2333		RA
☐ Beech E18S	N651Q	BA-405	Major components.	RA
☐ Bell 204 Iroquois (HU-1B) (UH-1B)	60-3606	252	Probable identity.	RA
☐ Cessna 150G	CF-VGF	15065725	(N2925J)	RA
☐ Mitsubishi MU-2G (MU-2B-30)	N134MA	507		RA
☐ Piper PA-31 Turbo Navajo B	C-FZOW	31-743	N7223L, CF-ZOW	RA

RED RIVER COLLEGE – WINNIPEG (MB10)

Address:	2280 Saskatchewan Avenue, Winnipeg, Manitoba R3J 3Y9.
Tel:	204-945-6001 **Fax:** 245-948-2499 **Email:** stevensonaviation@rrc.mb.ca
Admission:	By prior permission only.
Location:	On the western side of the airport in the western part of the city.

The first vocational college was established in the city in the mid-1930s. The present title was adopted in 1998 and at the current time five sites in the region are in use The aviation maintenance department has several instructional airframes in its workshops at the new facility which opened in January 2002.

TYPE	REG/SER	CON. NO.	PI/NOTES	STATUS
☐ Beech 65-90 King Air	N155S	LJ-14	HB-GCB, I-ERRE, EC-BNN, D-ILTI	RA
☐ Bell 204 Iroquois (UH-1H)	70-16290	12595		RA
☐ Boeing 727-25QC	C-FBWG	19719	N8163G, N127FE	RA
☐ Cessna 150G	C-GPTZ	15066593	N8693J	RA
☐ Cessna 500 Citation I	C-GBNE	500-0378	N3156M	RA
☐ Douglas DC-9-32	C-FTLM	47022	CF-TLM	RA
☐ Mitsubishi MU-2G (MU-2B-30)				RA
☐ Piper PA-31 Turbo Navajo	C-GSIO	31-186	N9139Y, N3ZM, N823PC	ra
☐ Piper PA-34-200T Seneca II	N76PW	34-7670141	N8464C	RA
☐ Robinson R-22HP Beta	N9018P	0023		RA

SOUTHPORT AEROSPACE COLLECTION (MB11)

Address:	PO Box 233, Southport, Manitoba R0M 1N0.
Tel:	204-428-6030 **Fax:** 204-428-6060 **Email:** saci@southport.mb.ca
Admission:	By prior permission only.
Location:	The airfield is south of the town off Highway 240.

Southport Aerospace took over the military base in the mid-1990s and provides pilot training facilities for the services. Four types used for training military pilots are preserved close to the main gate to the site.

TYPE	REG/SER	CON. NO.	PI/NOTES	STATUS
☐ Beech D18S Expeditor 3TM	1560	CA-160 (A-760)		PV
☐ Beech C23-19 Musketeer (CT-134)	134201	M-1325	13401	PV
☐ Canadair CL-41 Tutor	'114000'		CF-LTW-X	PVX
☐ Hiller UH12E	10282	2179		RA

WESTERN CANADA AVIATION MUSEUM (MB12)

Address:	Hangar T-2, 958 Ferry Road, Winnipeg, Manitoba R3H 0Y8.
Tel:	204-786-5503 **Fax:** 204-775-4761 **Email:** info@wcam.mb.ca
Admission:	Monday-Saturday 1000-1600; Sunday 1300-1600.
Location:	At the airport which is in the western suburbs of the city.

Formed in 1972, the Manitoba Aircraft Restoration Group set about investigating crash sites in the province. Restoration work started in 1973 and one of the early projects was the rebuild of the first Canadian helicopter constructed by the Froebe brothers in Homewood, Manitoba. The numbers of enthusiasts grew and the idea of a museum was put forward.

Thus in 1974 the Western Canada Aviation Museum was established. A small display was staged at a club in Winnipeg in 1974 with the aim of gaining publicity. An exhibition was opened in the city in 1979 and development has been maintained over the years. On 7th October 1984 Her Majesty the Queen opened the new museum in a hangar originally used by Trans Canada Airlines in the 1930s and late 1940s.

The museum now has a large storage facility at nearby St. Andrews Airport. One of the first searches carried out was at Cormorant Lake to locate the remains of Vickers Vedette flying boats which had operated in the area. The components of two were found and some of these have been incorporated in the painstaking rebuild which the visitor can see in the Bush Plane Gallery at the rear of the hangar. The design was started in England and completed by Canadian Vickers. In total 61 were built in five versions.

Many pioneering airlines flew in Manitoba in the inter-war period using a variety of aircraft. The museum has recovered a substantial number of airframes and eventually a comprehensive display of types which played significant roles in the development and exploration of the region will be staged. The archive section includes many photographs and taped interviews with pilots from this period.

In 1985 a replica of a single engined Junkers Ju 52 was unveiled. Five examples of the design, which later became famous in its three engined version, were built. The last was delivered to Canadian Airways at Winnipeg in 1931 and flew until 1942. The museum purchased a Spanish-built Junkers Ju 52/3m in Florida in 1982. The aircraft was flown to Manitoba and Bristol Aerospace undertook the conversion.

The Fokker Super Universal on show took to the air again in 1998 after a 17 year rebuild. After a long search the museum located a Fokker Universal at the bottom of Charron Lake and raised the wreck in 2006.

Manitoba

TYPE	REG/SER	CON. NO.	PI/NOTES	STATUS
☐ Auster K AOP.6	CF-KJP	2587	VP640, 16663, CF-KJP	PV
☐ Avro 652A Anson II	FP805	33953		S
☐ Avro Canada Avrocar (R)				PV
☐ Avro Canada C.100 Canuck 5 (CF-100)	18764	664		PV
☐ Beech D18S Expeditor 3NM	1594	CA-280 (A-930)	Front fuselage only.	PV
☐ Beech D18S Expeditor 3NMT (3N)	1477	CA-52 (A-652)	1477	PV
☐ Beech C23 Sundowner (CT-134A)	134235	M-2323		PV
☐ Bell 212 Twin Huey (CUH-1N) (CH-135)				PV
☐ Bellanca 31-55A Senior Skyrocket	CF-DOF	7	Fuselage only.	RAD
☐ Bellanca 66-75 Aircruiser	CF-AWR	719		PV
☐ Bellanca 66-75 Aircruiser	CF-BKV	722	Parts only.	RAD
☐ Bensen B-8 Gyroglider				PV
☐ Bowers Fly Baby 1A	C-FLOP	68.38		RA
☐ Bristol 149 Bolingbroke IVT	9869			RA
☐ Bristol 170 Freighter 31 (31M)	CF-WAE	13219	G-18-195, 9699	PV
☐ Canadair CL-13B Sabre 6 [North American F-86E]	1815	1815	(Luftwaffe) – in Pakistani markings.	PV
☐ Canadair CL-30 Silver Star 3 (CT-133) [Lockheed 580 (T-33AN)]	21075	T33-075		PV
☐ Canadair CL-84 Dynavert (CX-131)	8403	4		PV
☐ Canadian Car & Foundry Harvard 4 [North American NA-186]	CF-MOW	CCF4-???		RA
☐ Cessna C-34 Airmaster	CF-BDI	320	NC15852	RA
☐ Cessna T-50 Crane 1	7673	1116	Fuselage only.	RA
☐ Cessna T-50 Crane 1	7798	1241	Fuselage only.	RA
☐ Cessna 140	C-FGFB	11141	N76709	PV
☐ De Havilland DH.82C Tiger Moth (PT-24)	CF-COU	DHC.1325	42-986, FE122, 1122 (Canada)	PV
☐ De Havilland DH.83C Fox Moth	CF-BNL	FM.4		RA
☐ De Havilland DH.100 Vampire F.3	17020	EEP42312	17020, N6863D	RA
☐ De Havilland DHC.2 Beaver	C-FMAA	1500	CF-MAA	PV
☐ Douglas DC-3A-405 Skytrooper (C-53)	C-FBFV	7340	42-15545, NC49541, CF-BFV	RA
☐ Fairchild 24W40 Forwarder (C-61) (UC-61) (Argus I)	CF-FQA	W40-120	NC41844, 42-94147 or may be c/n 320	PV
☐ Fairchild FC-2	G-CARH	110	NC5740	RAD
☐ Fairchild FC-2	CF-ATG	127	NC6370	RAD
☐ Fairchild FC-2L	G-CYWU	19	G-GYYV, G-CYWU, 625 (Canada), CF-BVR	RA
☐ Fairchild FC-2W2	CF-BXD	513	NC8016 – parts only.	RAD
☐ Fairchild FC-2W2	CF-AKT	516	NC8028	PVC
☐ Fairchild 71	CF-AOU	647	Parts only.	RAD
☐ Fairchild Super 71	CF-AUJ	50	Fuselage and other small parts only.	RA
☐ Fairchild Super 71P	CF-AUT	51	665	RAD
☐ Fairchild Super 71P	666	52	Parts only.	RAD
☐ Fairchild M-62A-4 Cornell II	CF-FXX	1072	FV705	RA
☐ Fleet 60K Fort	3567	607	Fuselage only.	RA
☐ Fleet 60K Fort	3640	680		RA
☐ Fleet 60K Fort	3649	689		RAC
☐ Fairchild F-11-2 Husky (F-11-1)	CF-BQC	1		S
☐ Fairchild F-11-2 Husky (F-11-1)	C-GCYV	2	CF-EIL	PV
☐ Fairchild F-11-2 Husky (F-11-1)	CF-MAN	9		S
☐ Fokker F.XIA (B IVA)	CF-AUV	906	On loan to Aviodrome, Netherlands.	-
☐ Fokker Universal	F-CAJD	430		RA
☐ Fokker Super Universal	G-CASJ	805	Parts only.	RA
☐ Fokker Super Universal	CF-AAM	827	Composite.	PV
☐ Fokker Super Universal	CF-ATJ	AA 853	NC125M – parts only.	RA
☐ Fokker Super Universal	CF-AJC	CV 138		RA
☐ Found 100 Centennial	CF-IOO-X	100		RA
☐ Found 100 Centennial	CF-WFO	102		RA
☐ Froebe Helicopter		1		PV
☐ Froebe Ornithopter				PV
☐ Heath Parasol	CF-ARQ			PV
☐ Junkers F 13 gle	CF-ALX	2050		RAC
☐ Junkers W 34f/fi	CF-AQV	2710		RA
☐ Junkers Ju 52 cao/ce	'CF-ARM'		N99234, C-GARM – converted from CASA 352L c/n 56 T.2B-148.	PVX
☐ Kolb Flyer	C-ITWA	TC202301		PV
☐ Lear Learstar (Lockheed 18-56-23 Lodestar (C-60A))	C-FOZO	18-2209	42-55848, NR66, NC66E, N66E, N815AC, N8157C, CF-OZO, N9987F	RA
☐ Lockheed 10-A Electra	CF-TCC	1116	CF-TCC, N3749, C-FTCC	PV
☐ McDonnell M.36BA Voodoo (F-101B) (CF-101B)	101034	540	57-0362	PV
☐ Noorduyn Norseman IV	CF-CRT	15	CF-BFR, 696	SD
☐ Noorduyn Norseman IV	CF-BTC	29	2456	PV
☐ Noorduyn Norseman VI (C-64A) (UC-64A)	CF-GTM	828	45-41744, NC59775	S
☐ North American NA-64 Yale	3430	64-2223		PV
☐ North American NA-66 Harvard II				RAD
☐ North American NA-66 Harvard II	C-FMWA	66-2249	2516, CF-MWA	RAC
☐ Quickie Aircraft Quickie 2 (Rutan 54)	C-GIKP	004		PV
☐ Republic RC-3 Seabee	CF-FCD	352	NC6164K, N6164K	S
☐ Republic RC-3 Seabee	CF-DKF	740		S

Training aircraft feature prominently at the Commonwealth Air Training Plan Museum. Shown here is a Fleet Fort. (Ruud Leeuw) [MB1]

Pole mounted by Gimli Airport is this Canadair Silver Star. (Ruud Leeuw) [MB6]

This Canadair Challenger is displayed near the military facility at Winnipeg Airport. (John Mounce) [MB7]

Manitoba – New Brunswick

☐ Saunders ST-27 (De Havilland DH.114 Heron 2B)	C-FLOL	006	CF-LOL – original c/n 14054 LN-NPI, LN-SUL, OY-ADV, G-AYLH – with parts of Heron 2B c/n 14093 LN-SUR.	RA
☐ Saunders ST-28	C-GYAP	101	C-GYAP-X	S
☐ Schneider ESG 31 Grunau Baby II (DFS 108-49)	CF-GNJ			PV
☐ Schneider ESG 31 Grunau Baby II (DFS 108-49)	CF-ZEE	012		SD
☐ Schweizer SGU.2-22E	C-FACL	233	N9859E,CF-ACL	PV
☐ Sky Quest Ultralight				RA
☐ Stearman 4EM (4C)	CF-ASF	4010	NV770H – minor components.	RAD
☐ Stinson SR-8B Reliant		9764		RA
☐ Stinson SR-8CM Reliant	CF-AZV	9733		PV
☐ Stinson 108-2 Voyager			Fuselage frame only.	PV
☐ Vickers 757 Viscount	CF-THS	279		PV
☐ Vickers Vedette V	CF-MAG	CV 147	CF-AIS, (CF-MAG), CF-AIS	PV
☐ Vickers Vedette V	G-CASW	CV 91	Parts only.	S
☐ Vultee V-74 Valiant (BT-13A)	CF-HJB	74-5886	41-22027	RA
☐ Waco YKC-S	CF-AYS	4267		SD

WINNIPEG MONUMENT (MB13)

Location:	On permanent view in Woodhaven Park in the St. James suburb of the city.

TYPE	REG/SER	CON. NO.	PI/NOTES	STATUS
☐ Canadair CL-30 Silver Star 3 (CT-133) [Lockheed 580 (T-33AN)]	21232	T33-232		PV

NEW BRUNSWICK

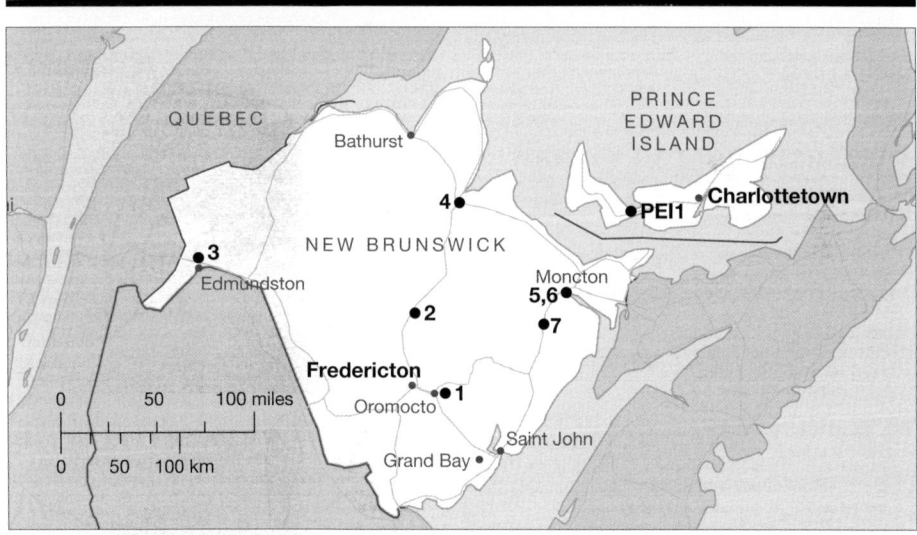

CANADIAN FORCES BASE GAGETOWN MILITARY MUSEUM (NB1)

Address:	PO Box 17000, Oromocto, New Brunswick E2V 4J5.
Tel:	506-422-1304 **Fax:** 506-422-1304 **Email:** museumgagetown@nb.aibn.com
Admission:	June–August Monday-Friday 0800-1600; Saturday-Sunday 1000-1600. September–May Monday-Friday 0800-1600.
Location:	In the south eastern suburbs of the town.

The area is named after General Thomas Gage who was in temporary command of British Forces in North America in the mid-1760s. There has been a camp in the town for many years and the museum has been set up to trace its history and that of Canadians who have served their country.

The displays portray all conflicts in which local men have fought and on show are models, photographs, vehicles, weapons and documents. Helicopter squadrons have flown from the site and the Kiowa is on a pole near the main entrance to the base.

TYPE	REG/SER	CON. NO.	PI/NOTES	STATUS
☐ Avro Canada C.100 Canuck 5 (CF-100)	18773	673		PV
☐ Bell 206A Kiowa (COH-58A) (CH-136)	136216	44016	71-20881	PV
☐ McDonnell M.36BA Voodoo (F-101B) (CF-101B)	101046	562	57-0384, 101046, 817B	PV

CENTRAL NEW BRUNSWICK WOODMEN'S MUSEUM (NB2)

Address:	PO Box 531, Boisetown, New Brunswick E6A 1Z5.
Tel:	506-369-7214 **Fax:** 506-369-9081 **Email:** woodmen@nb.aibn.com
Admission:	Daily 0900-1730.
Location:	About 2 km east of the town off Highway 8.

Forestry work has been an important part of life in the region for many years. The museum consists of many buildings tracing the work of people involved in the industry. Working demonstrations feature prominently and among those on the site there are wheelwrights showing the techniques necessary to construct wooden wheels with steel rims.

The Forester's Hall of Fame has been set up at the site and photographs and texts tell the stories of the people who have made valuable contributions in this field. A steam train runs around the site and a boat-shed houses craft used on the rivers.

The Avenger was delivered to the United States Navy and sold on the civilian market in 1963. It was used on water bombing duties in Idaho and Montana before moving to Québec in 1975. Forest Protection of Fredericton bought the aircraft in 1981 and operated it until a forced landing took place in woods near Miramichi City in 1998. Originally the Avenger was going to the Atlantic Canada Aviation Museum at Halifax Airport in Nova Scotia but they failed to collect it. So a volunteer team recovered the airframe in 2002 and moved it to the museum. The story of aerial fire-fighting is told in the display.

TYPE	REG/SER	CON. NO.	PI/NOTES	STATUS
☐ Grumman G-40 Avenger (TBM-3) (TBM-3E)	C-GLEK	2552	Bu85733, N6824C	PV

LANCASTER KB882 PRESERVATION SOCIETY (NB3)

Address:	c/o St. Jacques Airport, Highway 185, Edmundston, New Brunswick E3V 1T7.
Tel:	506-735-6917 **Fax:** 506-735-7866 **Email:** lancasterkb882@hotmail.com
Admission:	On permanent view.
Location:	About 16 km north west of the town on Highway 185.

During World War II Victory Aircraft of Montreal constructed 430 Lancasters. At the end of the war a number were converted for other roles including air-sea rescue, reconnaissance, navigational training, photo-reconnaissance and as engine test-beds. The Lancaster arrived at the airport for display in July 1964 and has since been parked near the airfield entrance. A group of volunteers has been working on the bomber in recent years to remedy the corrosion that set in. They are now in discussion with the local authority to set up a formal organisation to ensure the preservation of the aircraft.

TYPE	REG/SER	CON. NO.	PI/NOTES	STATUS
☐ Avro 683 Lancaster 10P(AR) (B.X)	KB882			PVC

MIRAMICHI MONUMENT (NB4)

Location:	On permanent view at the airport in the southern part of the town.

TYPE	REG/SER	CON. NO.	PI/NOTES	STATUS
☐ McDonnell M.36BA Voodoo (F-101B) (CF-101B)	101053	596	57-0418	PV

MONCTON MONUMENT (NB5)

Location:	On permanent view in Centennial Park in the south western part of the town.

TYPE	REG/SER	CON. NO.	PI/NOTES	STATUS
☐ Avro Canada C.100 Canuck 5 (CF-100)	18488	388		PV

NEW BRUNSWICK COMMUNITY COLLEGE (NB6)

Address:	1234 Mountain Road, Moncton, New Brunswick E1C 8H9.
Tel:	506-856-2220 **Fax:** 506-856-3288 **Email:** errol.persaud@gnb.ca
Admission:	By prior permission only.
Location:	In the north western part of the town.

Seven sites in the area are in use at the current time. Over 4,000 fulltime and almost 10,000 part-time students take part in a wide range of courses. The aircraft maintenance department has sites at Moncton and Dieppe. Five instructional airframes are known to be in use at the two sites.

TYPE	REG/SER	CON. NO.	PI/NOTES	STATUS
☐ Aero Commander 680V	C-GFAB	1601-43	(N6532V), N5418, N541X, N577VM, N577RH, (N22WG), N577RH	RA
☐ Cessna A185F Skywagon 185	C-GYAZ	18503668	(N8365Q)	RA
☐ Hughes 369HS	C-FFGI	520380S	CF-FGI	RA
☐ Piper PA-11 Cub Special	C-FRTG	11-93	NC4590H, N4590H, CF-RTG	RA
☐ Piper PA-23-160 Apache	C-FPSC	23-1493	N4018P, CF-PSC	RA

PRESERVATION PARK (NB7)

Address:	Steeve's Street, Hillsborough, New Brunswick E0A 1X0.
Admission:	June–August daily 1000-1800.
Location:	On Highway 114 just south of the town which is about 25 km south of Moncton.

New Brunswick – Newfoundland and Labrador

Hillsborough is home to a thriving railway museum and just south of this site is Preservation Park. The Voodoo on show served with 416 Squadron at Chatham, New Brunswick and on 9th August 1984 it made its last flight to CFB Greenwood in Nova Scotia where it served as an instructional airframe. The aircraft was later acquired by the Voodoo Survival Committee and moved to its new home on 28th August 1992.

In addition to the aircraft, the visitor can see a well jack and a pump used to move fresh water around the last steam battleship which operated out of Halifax. The railway museum features many working engines and carriages. The station building houses a large range of artefacts and during the summer season trains run on the Hillsborough to Salem line.

TYPE	REG/SER	CON. NO.	PI/NOTES	STATUS
☐ McDonnell M.36BA Voodoo (F-101B) (CF-101B)	101028	524	57-0346, 101028, 831B	PV

NEWFOUNDLAND AND LABRADOR

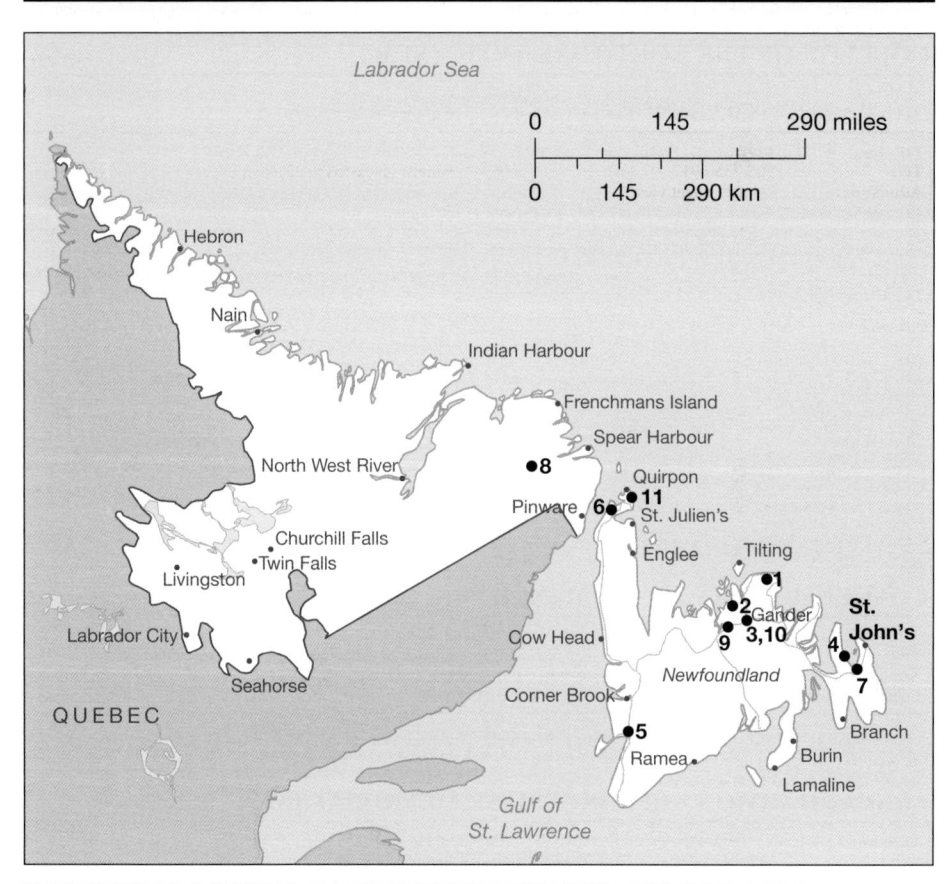

BANTING MEMORIAL PARK INTERPRETATON CENTRE (NF1)

Address:	PO Box 159, Musgrave Harbour, Newfoundland A0G 3J0.
Tel:	709-655-2119 Fax: 709-655-2064 Email: bantinghti@nf.aibn.com
Admission:	Mid June–August Monday-Saturday 1000-1600; Sunday 1000-2000.
Location:	About 40 km north east of Gander off Highway 330.

The Hudson crashed on February 21st 1941 killing Sir Frederick Banting – co-discoverer of insulin. The wreck was later recovered from Three Mile Pond and placed in the park. A replica was unveiled in 2001 and the centre has been built to tell the story of Banting's life and work. On show are photographs and memorabilia.

TYPE	REG/SER	CON. NO.	PI/NOTES	STATUS
☐ Lockheed 414-56-01 Hudson III	T9449	414-2502	Substantial remains.	PVD
☐ Lockheed 414-56-01 Hudson III (FSM)	'T9449'			PVX

BOTWOOD HERITAGE CENTRE (NF2)

Address: PO Box 490, Botwood, Newfoundland A0H 1E0.
Tel: 709-257-2839   **Fax:** 709-257-3330   **Email:** eevans@nf.aibn.ca
Admission: Mid-June-early September daily 1000-2030.
Location: About 30 km north west of Gander.

Botwood served as the terminal for Trans-Atlantic flying boat flights in the 1930s and displays in the centre trace the history of these epic journeys. There are plans to construct a flying boat museum so that more aircraft can be put on show.
The Canadian Vickers-built Catalina has had a varied career. After military service with both the US Navy and Air Force it was stored for a time. From 1949 until 1952 it was flown in Iceland by Flugfelag Islands. The next phase of its career was a decade in Canada on aero-magnetic survey duties. The amphibian returned to airline duties in Ontario for a time before it was converted for water-bombing use in Newfoundland.

TYPE	REG/SER	CON. NO.	PI/NOTES	STATUS
☐ Consolidated 28-5A Catalina (PBV-1A) (OA-10A)	'E1497'	CV 605	Bu68058, 44-34094, NC65715, TF-RVG, CF-DFB, C-FDFB	PVX

COLLEGE OF THE NORTH ATLANTIC (NF3)

Address: 1 Magee Road, Gander, Newfoundland A1V 1W8
Tel: 709-651-4800   **Fax:** 709-651-4854   **Email:** bob.dwyer@cna.nl.ca
Admission: By prior permission only.
Location: In the centre of the town.

The college operates from 18 campuses in the area. A number of vocational schools were established in the early 1960s and were later merged into five community colleges; the current organisation came into being in 1997. The aviation department has premises in Gander where a number of instructional airframes are in use. For many years another Beech 18 was in use and this aircraft can now be seen in the nearby North Atlantic Aviation Museum.

TYPE	REG/SER	CON. NO.	PI/NOTES	STATUS
☐ Aero Commander 680V				RA
☐ Aérospatiale AS.332 Super Puma			Fuselage only.	RA
☐ Beech D18S				RA
☐ Beech A100 King Air	C-FGNL	B-184	CF-GNL	RA
☐ Bell 206B Jet Ranger				RA
☐ Bell 206B Jet Ranger			Fuselage only.	RA
☐ Bell 47G-4				RA
☐ Boeing 737-2E1F	C-GDCC	20681	CF-EPP, C-FEPP, N211PL – dismantled.	RA
☐ Cessna 150F				RA
☐ Cessna 150G				RA
☐ Cessna 172H				RA
☐ De Havilland DHC.8-100			Fuselage only.	RA
☐ Piper PA-18-150 Super Cub				RA
☐ Piper PA-23-250 Aztec				RA
☐ Piper PA-44-180 Seminole			Fuselage only.	RA
☐ Swearingen SA.226TC Metro			Fuselage only.	RA

CONCEPTION BAY MUSEUM (NF4)

Address: Water Street, Harbour Grace, Newfoundland A0A 2MO.
Tel: 709-596-0506   **Fax:** 709-596-5465   **Email:** pfahey@conceptionbaymuseum.nf.ca
Admission: Mid June–early September daily 1000-1700.
Location: About 20 km west of St. John's off Highway 70.

This local history museum is situated in a former 1870 customs building. The development of the community and the industry of the region portrayed in the informative displays. The aviation section contains models, photographs and aviation equipment used on Trans-Atlantic flights.

ERNEST HARMON AIR FORCE BASE MEMORIAL (NF5)

Address: 13 Tennessee Drive, Stephenville, Newfoundland A2N 2Y3.
Tel: 709-643-8440   **Fax:** 709-643-9196   **Email:** tomhutchings@cyjt.com
Admission: On permanent view.
Location: In the southern suburbs of the town.

The airfield was constructed in 1941 for use by United States aircraft crossing the Atlantic. It opened in 1943 and during the time of the Korean war and the increased tension between the USA and the Soviet Union facilities were improved.
Initially known as Stephenville Air Force Base, it was renamed after Captain Ernest Harmon who was killed in a crash in 1933. The base was used by many Strategic Air Command units and for a time a fighter squadron was in residence. The site, which closed as a military airfield in 1966, is now the civil airport for the town and many of the camp buildings have been incorporated into the municipality. Two former barrack blocks are used as halls of residence by the local campus of the College of the North Atlantic. There is a small display in one of the buildings tracing the history of the field with photographs and documents On show is a Convair F-102A, a type which flew from the field which served with three fighter squadrons and the Connecticut Air National Guard before being withdrawn from use and stored.

TYPE	REG/SER	CON. NO.	PI/NOTES	STATUS
☐ Convair 8-10 Delta Dagger (F-102A)	56-1266	8-10-483		PV

This McDonnell CF-101B Voodoo is periodically on show at the North Atlantic Aviation Museum. (Christian Emrich) [NF10]

The Atlantic Canada Aviation Museum has this replica of the AEA Silver Dart mounted above a Canadair Starfighter. Behind is a Bell Jet Ranger. [NS2]

The Shearwater Aviation Museum restored this Fairey Swordfish. The biplane made one flight before going on show. [NS7]

FRENCH SHORE HISTORICAL SOCIETY MEMORIAL (NF6)

Address:	PO Box 29, Conche, Newfoundland A0K 1Y0.
Tel:	709-622-3500 **Fax:** 709-622-3510 **Email:** info@frenchshore.com
Admission:	On permanent view.
Location:	About 30 km south of St. Anthony.

On 30th November 1942 the Boston took off from Gander on a ferry flight to England for use by the Royal Air Force. Several hours later it made a forced landing near Conche as it was running short of fuel. The pilot, Squadron Leader Morrow, and his crew must have become disorientated. The aircraft was cut up into pieces near where it came down. The components serve as a memorial and are looked after by the society which traces the history and traditions of the region. Displays of memorabilia are staged at a number of locations around French Bay and a number of festivals are held in the summer months.

TYPE	REG/SER	CON. NO.	PI/NOTES	STATUS
☐ Douglas Boston IIIA	BZ277		42-33032	PVD

HARBOUR GRACE MEMORIAL (NF7)

Address:	War Memorial Library, PO Box 40, Harbour Grace, Newfoundland A0A 2M0.
Tel:	709-596-3884 **Fax:** 709-596-3884
Admission:	On permanent view.
Location:	About 20 km west of St. John's off Highway 70.

The Dakota was donated to the town by Labrador Airways, based at Goose Bay, in August 1993. It is on show by the side of the main road which runs through Harbour Grace. The aircraft served at a number of military airfields in the southern states before being sold on the civil market in 1945. It arrived in Canada in 1951 for use by Rimouski Airlines.

Quebecair purchased it in 1953 and it later flew with a number of Newfoundland companies before being retired in 1993. The nearby airfield was the starting point for many inter-war Trans-Atlantic flights and a memorial to those epic journeys can also be seen. Among those using the site were Amelia Earhart, in 1932, and Eddie Rickenbacker, four years later.

TYPE	REG/SER	CON. NO.	PI/NOTES	STATUS
☐ Douglas DC-3A-456 Skytrain (C-47A)	CF-QBI	6179	41-38720, , NC86551, CF-GEH, CF-QBI, C-FQBI	PV

LABRADOR MILITARY MUSEUM (NF8)

Address:	Canadian Forces Base Goose Bay, Happy Valley, Labrador, Newfoundland A0P 1S0.
Tel:	709-896-6900 ext 2177 **Email:** smithsc@forces.gc.ca
Admission:	On permanent view.
Location:	About 700 km north west of St. John's.

In 1949 the Royal Air Force set up a detachment at Goose Bay which later handled the ferrying of Canadair-built Sabres to squadrons in Britain and Germany. The unit was expanded in the late 1950s to assist with low-level training for the V-bomber fleet. The Vulcan on show was damaged in November 1981 whilst on a flight to the United Kingdom and was on display at Happy Valley from June 1982. The delta wing bomber was delivered to the Royal Air Force in March 1962 and served with a number of squadrons and the Operational Conversion Unit at RAF Scampton. The aircraft spent a period with the famous 617 'Dambusters' squadron.

The Labrador Heritage Society was formed to look after the Vulcan and has now acquired the T-33 and the Voodoo. Many USAF T-33s passed through the base on their way to operations in Europe. The Voodoo was one of the front line fighters with the Canadian Air Force for many years and the type spent periods in residence at Goose Bay. The aircraft on show arrived in Canada in November 1970 and served at Bagotville in Quebec until withdrawn from use in January 1985. The Voodoo has been on at Goose Bay since 1995.

A museum tracing the military history of the airfield and the region has now been established.

TYPE	REG/SER	CON. NO.	PI/NOTES	STATUS
☐ Avro 698 Vulcan B.2	XL361			PV
☐ Lockheed 580 (T-33A)	53-5413	580-8752		PV
☐ McDonnell M.36BA Voodoo (F-101B) (CF-101B)	101003	292	56-0262	RA

NORRIS ARM HERITAGE MUSEUM (NF9)

Address:	65 Norris Avenue, PO Box 89, Norris Arm, Newfoundland A0G 3M0.
Tel:	709-653-2350 **Fax:** 709-653-2163 **Email:** nahs@nf.aibn.com
Admission:	Mid June–early September Monday-Friday 0900-2000; Saturday-Sunday 1400-1700.
Location:	About 40 km east of Grand Falls.

The collection traces the history and industries of the area and is housed on the upper floor of the Fire Hall. This wooded area has provided employment for many local people. The displays trace the settlement and development of the region over the years. Many pioneer bush fliers operated in the region and there are photographs of these aircraft including a Fox Moth. The stories of these brave pilots are told in detail. Several crashes occurred and a number of lives were lost.

NORTH ATLANTIC AVIATION MUSEUM (NF10)

Address:	PO Box 234, Gander, Newfoundland A1V 1W6.
Tel:	709-256-2923 **Fax:** 709-256-2923 **Email:** naam@nf.aibn.com
Admission:	Late June–August daily 0900-1800. September–late June daily 0900-1600.
Location:	On the Trans Canada Highway in the town.

Newfoundland and Labrador – Northwest Territories

For many years Gander was an important staging post for airliners crossing the North Atlantic. The idea of a museum was put forward in the early 1980s and a modern display building has now been constructed in the town. The story of the development of Gander is portrayed with many photographs and documents. Engines, components and memorabilia can also be seen. The locally-constructed Quickie is on show in this building.

The remaining aircraft are stored during the harsh winter months and placed on display in the museum grounds during the summer. The Canso was formerly used by the Newfoundland Provincial Forestry Department as a water bomber. The Canadian Vickers-built aircraft was delivered to the Royal Canadian Air Force in September 1943 and served for just over two years. It was registered to Canadian Pacific Airlines of Vancouver in late 1945. A move across the country was made in 1957 and service with Trans Labrador Airlines and Eastern Provincial Airlines followed. During World War II many aircraft were ferried to Britain via Gander.

The Hudson in the collection was mounted at the airport several years ago to honour this aspect of the history of the field. It was removed from its pedestal and restored for the museum display. The aircraft has been painted in the markings of one which served with several RAF Squadrons and was lost when it ditched in the sea off Iceland in March 1944.

The Dakota had a long career and flew in the Philippines and Hong Kong before ending its days as a ground instructional airframe with Gander Aviation in the early 1970s. The front and rear fuselage sections and the tail survive after the remainder was scrapped. The rugged Beech 18 has given excellent service to many companies across Canada. The aircraft on show served with the RCAF and was later used at one of their ground schools. It then moved to the College of the North Atlantic in the town where it was used to train students for many years.

TYPE	REG/SER	CON. NO.	PI/NOTES	STATUS
☐ Beech D18S Expeditor 3NM	'CF-VPK'	CA-110 (A-710)	1510, A674 – on loan from the College of the North Atlantic, NF.	PVX
☐ Consolidated 28-5A Canso A	C-FCRP	CV 271	9837, CF-CRP	PV
☐ De Havilland DH.82C Tiger Moth	CF-GPE	DHC.1850	5030, (VO-ABE)	PV
☐ Douglas DC-3A-456 Skytrain (C-47A)	CF-GHX	11780	42-92025, PI-C42, VR-HES, N1514V – front fuselage and tail sections only	PV
☐ Lockheed 414-56-03 Hudson IIIA (A-29)	'T9422'	414-6448	41-23631.BW769, CF-CRJ	PVX
☐ McDonnell M.36BA Voodoo (F-101B) (CF-101B)	101065	622	57-0444, 101065	PV
☐ Quickie Aircraft Quickie 1 (Rutan 54)	C-GZGR	1029		PV

ST. ANTHONY MONUMENT (NF11)

Address:	PO Box 430, St. Anthony, Newfoundland A0K 4SO.
Tel:	709-0454-3864
Admission:	On permanent view.
Location:	In the town.

The Government of Newfoundland and Labrador operated a fleet of Catalinas on water bombing duties for more than 30 years. One has been placed on show in the town to honour the firefighters who flew the amphibian.

TYPE	REG/SER	CON. NO.	PI/NOTES	STATUS
☐ Consolidated 28-6A Catalina (PBY-6A)	C-FIZU	2019	Bu46655, N10014, CF-IZU	PV

NORTHWEST TERRITORIES

PRINCE OF WALES NORTHERN HERITAGE CENTRE (NW1)

Address:	4850 48th. Street, PO Box 1320, Yellowknife, Northwest Territories X1A 2L9.
Tel:	867-873-7551 **Fax:** 867-873-0205 **Email:** joanne_bird@gov.nt.ca
Admission:	June–August daily 1030-1700; September–May Tuesday-Sunday 1030-1730.
Location:	Just north of the town off Highway 3.

Opened in 1979 by the Prince of Wales, the centre serves as the main museum of the Northwest Territories. The displays trace the cultural heritage and history of the development of the region.

Exhibits show the life of the original residents of the area and trace exploration, the fur trade, mining and whaling which took place as settlers arrived.

Bush flying has played an important role in Canada. Just after the end of World War II de Havilland Canada built 53 examples of the Fox Moth. The pre-war biplane was ideally suited to Canadian conditions and was popular with a number of bush airlines. Max Ward, founder of Wardair, bought one in 1946 and flew it from Yellowknife.

In 1977 a local resident started a project to locate and restore a Fox Moth for display. Parts were retrieved from three crash sites and the restoration was undertaken in Alberta. From 1985 to 1987 the aircraft was on show in the Western Canada Aviation Museum in Winnipeg, Manitoba. Money was raised to build an extension to the centre and on 17th October 1987 the gallery was opened in the presence of many dignitaries including Max Ward himself. There are several interesting photographs of bush flying to be seen.

TYPE	REG/SER	CON. NO.	PI/NOTES	STATUS
☐ De Havilland DH.83C Fox Moth	'CF-BNI'		Composite of several aircraft with newly-built components.	PVX

YELLOWKNIFE MONUMENT (NW2)

Location:	On permanent view near the airport.

TYPE	REG/SER	CON. NO.	PI/NOTES	STATUS
☐ Bristol 170 Freighter 31	CF TFX	13137	(G AMRV)	PV

NOVA SCOTIA

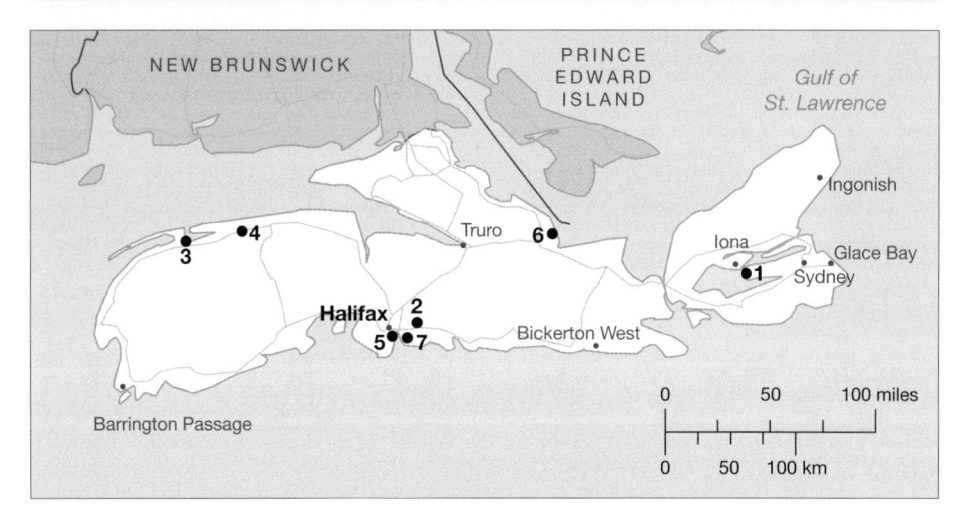

ALEXANDER GRAHAM BELL NATIONAL HISTORIC PARK (NS1)

Address:	PO Box 159, Baddeck, Nova Scotia B0E 1B0.
Tel:	902-955-2069 **Fax:** 902-955-3496 **Email:** information@pc.qc.ca
Admission:	May and late October daily 0900-1700; June–mid October daily 0900-1800.
Location:	Just north east of the town off Highway 105.

Alexander Graham Bell, best known as the inventor of the telephone, set up a vacation home in Baddeck in the 1880s.
 He turned his attention to aviation and initially flew several kites. A group formed the Aerial Experiment Association and hang-gliders and aircraft were produced.
 The displays in the centre trace the work of Bell and there are many photographs, models and documents relating to his aeronautical work.

ATLANTIC CANADA AVIATION MUSEUM (NS2)

Address:	PO Box 44006, Bedford Highway, Bedford, Nova Scotia B4A 3H6.
Tel:	902-873-3773 **Email:** acinfo@atlanticcanadaaviation.com
Admission:	Mid May–mid September daily 0900-1700.
Location:	Close to Halifax International Airport and Exit 6 of Highway 102 about 40 km north east of the city.

In late 1975 a small group of local enthusiasts formed a society with the aim of establishing a museum to trace the rich aeronautical history of the region. Their dreams were realised on 10th May 1986 when a display was staged in a wooden building formerly occupied by the local tourist board. In 1996 a large hangar was added and displays in this building are being developed.
 The oldest known homebuilt aircraft in Nova Scotia is on show in the foyer of the building, part of which is still used by the tourist board. This biplane, believed to be a Lincoln Sport, was started in 1934 by Charles Craig of Truro but never finished. On display in the original building is a replica of the Silver Dart, which made the first powered flight in Canada when it flew at Baddeck, Nova Scotia on 23rd February 1909. This aircraft contrasts vividly with the Lockheed Starfighter parked below the frail biplane.
 The rapid advance in aircraft design which took place in less than 50 years is clearly seen. Also on show in this area is a Bell Jet Ranger used for forestry and fire fighting work.
 The new hangar houses several aircraft under restoration including a Catalina recovered from a crash site. The Aeronca C-3 was one of the last batch of eight imported into Canada in the 1930s.
 The Sabre is painted in the colours of the 'Golden Hawks' aerobatic team. This aircraft was formerly a gate guardian at the now closed base at Chatham.

TYPE	REG/SER	CON. NO.	PI/NOTES	STATUS
☐ Aerial Experiment Association Silver Dart (R)				PV
☐ Aeronca C-3	CF-AQQ	A-159		PVC
☐ Aeronca 11CC Super Chief			Fuselage only.	RA
☐ Aerosport Scamp 1	C-IBEU	S 03042887		PV
☐ Avro Canada C.100 Canuck 5D (5) (CF-100)	18747	647	18747, 100747	PV
☐ Bell 47J-2	'CF-CAF'	1827	CF-PQZ	PVCX
☐ Bell 206B Jet Ranger	C-FDOI	980		PV
☐ British Aerospace 146 Series 200			Front fuselage mock-up.	PV
☐ Canadair CL-13A Sabre 5 [North American F-86E]	23355	1145		PV
☐ Canadair CL-28-1 Argus 1 (CP-107)			Front fuselage only.	PV
☐ Canadair CL-28-2 Argus 2 (CP-107)	10730	21	20730 – rear fuselage only.	PV
☐ Canadair CL-30 Silver Star 3 (CT-133) [Lockheed 580 (T-33AN)]	133174	T33-174	21174	PV

Nova Scotia

Type	Reg/Ser	Con. No.	Pl/Notes	Status
☐ Canadair CL-30 Silver Star 3 (CT-133) [Lockheed 580 (T-33AN)]	133635	T33-635	21635 – front fuselage only.	PV
☐ Canadair CL-90 Starfighter (CF-104) [Lockheed 683-04-12]	104783	683A-1083	12783	PV
☐ Canadair CL-219-1A10 Freedom Fighter (CF-116A) (CF-5A) [Northrop N-156A]	116748	1048		PV
☐ Cessna 305C Bird Dog (L-19E) (O-1E) (CO-119)	119720	24604	56-4037, 16720	RAC
☐ Consolidated 28-5A Catalina (PBY-5A)	CF-HFL	110	Bu05021, NC18444, VP-BAR, VP-JAU	PVD
☐ Craig Biplane				PV
☐ Electroflyer Dove Hang Glider				
☐ Ercoupe 415C	CF-LAK	3234	N2609H	PV
☐ Fieseler Fi 103A-1				RA
☐ Grumman G-40 Avenger (TBM-3) (TBM-3E)	CF-ZYC	3669	Bu53607, N8398H – with parts from c/n 2552 Bu85733, N6824C, C-GLEK and c/n 4194 Bu91289, N7833C, C-GFPN	PV
☐ Grumman G-103 Tracker (CS2F-2) (CS2F-3) (CP-121)	12176	DHC-75	1576, 12176, A744	PV
☐ Lockheed 1329 JetStar 6	C-FDTF	1329-5088	N9244R, CF-DTF	PV
☐ McDonnell M.36BA Voodoo (F-101B) (CF-101B)	101043	558	57-0380	PV
☐ North American NA-81 Harvard II	'2532'	81-4107	3840 – on loan from CASM, ON.	PVX
☐ Piper PA-38-112 Tomahawk				PVC
☐ Pitts S-1C Special	'C-FBIL'			PVX
☐ Rotorway Executive	C-GLYE	RB1992		PV
☐ Scheibe L-Spatz 55	C-GBBI	530	D-7047	PV
☐ Ultralight Flight Mirage	C-IBEO	TC2515		PV

CORNWALLIS MILITARY MUSEUM (NS3)

Address:	726 Broadway, PO Box 31 Clementsport, Nova Scotia B05 1E0.
Tel:	902-638-3118 **Email:** museum.cornwallis@gmail.com
Admission:	Mid June-August daily 1030-1700; September daily 1330-1700. Rest of year by appointment.
Location:	About 10 km east of Digby on Highway 1.

There has been a military presence in the Annapolis Basin area since 1605. Cornwallis was commissioned as a naval base on 1st May 1942 and was responsible for training new entrants to the service. The site became the largest such establishment in the British Commonwealth.

The camp closed in February 1946 but the onset of the 'Cold War' meant it was re-opened in May 1949. When the Canadian forces were unified in 1966 basic training for all recruits was introduced.

Cornwallis closed in the 1995 and a group of people who formerly served at the site worked to establish a museum. This opened its doors in 1997 and large amount of material was on show in two buildings.

The history of the base and the locality are portrayed in detail. The exhibition is steadily being improved and more items are being donated. The T-33 arrived at the site in the early 1970s and the Voodoo in the late 1980s. The aircraft were allocated to the base as Air Force recruits were in training.

TYPE	REG/SER	CON. NO.	Pl/NOTES	STATUS
☐ Canadair CL-30 Silver Star 3 (CT-133) [Lockheed 580 (T-33AN)]	133411	T33-411	21411	PV
☐ McDonnell M.36BA Voodoo (F-101B) (CF-101B)	101006	420	56-0724	PV

GREENWOOD MILITARY AVIATION MUSEUM (NS4)

Address:	PO Box 786, Greenwood, Nova Scotia B0P 1N0.
Tel:	902-765-1494 ext 5955 **Email:** gmam001@hotmail.com
Admission:	June–August daily 0900-1700; September–May Tuesday-Saturday 1000-1600.
Location:	About 3 km south of Kingston off Highway 1.

Royal Air Force Greenwood opened in 1942 as a British Commonwealth Air Training Plan base, providing advanced flying courses to aircrew before overseas posting. Since the end of World War II the field has been home to maritime patrol aircraft.

The museum tracing the history of the base and its units opened in May 1995 and a number of impressive displays have been staged. The history of the base and its units is portrayed with photographs, documents, models and uniforms on view.

The three original aircraft in the collection were parked by the old hangar area. The Lancaster served for ten years from 1945. The Neptune replaced the Lancaster in 1955 and flew until 1958 when the Argus arrived. The Neptune on show, a former US Navy aircraft, was flown into Greenwood on 27th August 1980, has been painted in Canadian colours.

In October 2000 a move was made to a new site outside the base and a new hall was erected. The three large aircraft were towed to the area around the building which was landscaped and includes a memorial garden. More aircraft were acquired including an Anson recovered from a farm. A painstaking rebuild is underway and the project should be finished in the not too distant future. A Bolingbroke has been located in Manitoba and this will soon be moved across the country.

TYPE	REG/SER	CON. NO.	Pl/NOTES	STATUS
☐ Avro 652A Anson II	7135			RAC
☐ Avro 683 Lancaster 10(AR) (B.X)	'FM107'		KB839, 'KB976'	PVX
☐ Boeing-Vertol 107-II-28 Labrador (CH-113A)	11308	4002	10408, 11308, A-697	PV
☐ Bristol 149 Bolingbroke IV				RAD
☐ Canadair CL-28-1 Argus 1 (CP-107)	10717	8	20717	PV
☐ Canadair CL-30 Silver Star 3 (CT-133)	'133434'	T33-345	21345, 133345	PVX
☐ Canadair CL-30 Silver Star 3 (CT-133) [Lockheed 580 (T-33AN)]	133393	T33-393	21393	PV

☐ Canadair CL-601 Challenger (CC-144B)		144613	3035	C-GLXW, C-GCUN – front and rear fuselage only.	RA
☐ Douglas DC-3A-467 Skytrain (C-47B) (Dakota IV)	KN451		16174/32922	44-76590, KN451, 655B	RA
☐ Lockheed 726-45-17 Neptune (P2V-7) (P-2H) (DP-2H)		'24101'	726-7219	Bu147969, '24117'	PVX

NOVA SCOTIA COMMUNITY COLLEGE (NS5)

Address:	357 Pleasant Street, Dartmouth, Nova Scotia B2Y 4N4.
Tel:	902-491-4937 **Fax:** 902-491-4989
Admission:	By prior permission only.
Location:	At

The college was established in 1996 when a number of vocational and post-secondary training institutes merged. At the current time 13 campuses and six community learning centres are located around the province. The Aviation Institute is located on the Dartmouth Campus where at least two instructional airframes are in use.

TYPE	REG/SER	CON. NO.	PI/NOTES	STATUS
☐ Cessna 150G	C-FVDI	15064996	(N3696J), CF-VDI	RA
☐ Piper PA-30 Twin Comanche	C-FUOB	30-323	N7285Y, CF-UOB	RA

PICTOU MONUMENT (NS6)

Location:	On permanent view in the town.

TYPE	REG/SER	CON. NO.	PI/NOTES	STATUS
☐ Canadair CL-30 Silver Star 3 (CT-133) [Lockheed 580 (T-33AN)]	133434	T33-434	21434	PV

SHEARWATER AVIATION MUSEUM (NS7)

Address:	12 Wing Shearwater, PO Box 5000, Station Main, Shearwater, Nova Scotia B0J 3A0.
Tel:	902-720-1083 **Fax:** 902-720-2037 **Email:** info@shearwateraviationmuseum.ns.ca
Admission:	April–May, September–October Tuesday-Friday 1000-1700; Saturday 1200-1600; June–August Tuesday-Friday 1000-1700 Saturday-Sunday 1200-1600.
Location:	About 5 km south east of Dartmouth off Highway 322.

On 18th August 1918 the United States Navy set up a flying boat station at Baker's Point in Dartmouth. This area is part of the current base. In the inter-war period the Canadian military took over the operation of the site and constructed runways and hangars on the opposite side of the road which ran along the shore of the bay.

The Royal Canadian Navy took over RCAF Dartmouth on 1st December 1948 and renamed it HMCS Shearwater. Until 1960 the field also served as the international airport for the area. The airfield was used as a land base for carrier aircraft. At the current time the station is the main maritime helicopter base for the Canadian forces.

The museum was established in 1979 and moved into a magnificent new building in the late 1990s. The displays trace the history of naval aviation in the country with uniforms, photographs, documents and memorabilia on show. A magnificent new exhibition hall has recently been completed and this means that most of the aircraft are now under cover.

Pride of place in the museum is taken by a superbly restored Fairey Swordfish. Recovered from a farm, the biplane flew once before taking its place on the hangar floor. Under restoration on the base is a Fairey Firefly obtained from Ethiopia. Over 60 examples of the type were operated by the Canadian Navy from both carriers and shore bases.

One of the Sikorsky S-55s in the collection is being rebuilt locally by a volunteer team. In 1954 a trio of Piasecki HUP-3s arrived at Shearwater where they were in service for a few years. They were then transferred to Patricia Bay in British Columbia. The first was donated to the British Columbia Institute of Technology as an instructional airframe and in 1982 to the Canadian Museum of Flight. In 2000 the helicopter was purchased by the Classic Rotors Museum in California and a former United States Army machine moved to Langley. This airframe eventually arrived at Shearwater and has now been restored to represent the first Canadian Navy machine.

The remains of one of the Supermarine Stranraer flying boats operated until the end of World War II has been recovered from its crash site and has been put on show.

TYPE	REG/SER	CON. NO.	PI/NOTES	STATUS
☐ Canadair CL-30 Silver Star 3 (CT-133) [Lockheed 580 (T-33AN)]			Front fuselage only.	PV
☐ Canadair CL-30 Silver Star 3 (CT-133) [Lockheed 580 (T-33AN)]	133038	T33-038	21038	PV
☐ Canadair CL-30 Silver Star 3 (CT-133) [Lockheed 580 (T-33AN)]	133618	T33-618	21618	PV
☐ Canadair CL-41A Tutor (CT-114)	114075	1075	26075	PV
☐ Canadair CL-219-1A17 Freedom Fighter (CF-116D) (CF-5D) [Northrop N-156B]	116832	2032		PV
☐ Fairey Swordfish II	HS469	FB3S 126A	HS469, C-GRCN	PV
☐ Fairey Firefly FR.1	PP462	F6173	PP462, (Ethiopia)	PVA
☐ Grumman G-40 Avenger (TBM-3)	85861	2680	Bu85861	PV
☐ Grumman G-89 Tracker (S2F-1) (CS2F-1)	1501	428	Bu136519, 500X, 1500	PV
☐ Grumman G-103 Tracker (S2F-1) (CP-121)	12157	DHC-56	1557, 12157, A706	PV
☐ McDonnell M.24 Banshee (F2H-3)	126402	112	Bu126402	PV
☐ McDonnell M.36BA Voodoo (F-101B) (CF-101B)	101063	620	57-0442, 101063, 832B	RA
☐ North American NA-66 Harvard II	2777	66-2510		PV
☐ Piasecki PD-18 Retriever (H-25A) (HUP-3)	'245'			PV
☐ Sikorsky S-55D (HO4S-3)	55885	55885	55885, A-739, 739B	RAC
☐ Supermarine 304 Stranraer	915	CV 205	915, CF-BYJ	PVD
☐ Supermarine Seafire (Scale R)				PV

ONTARIO

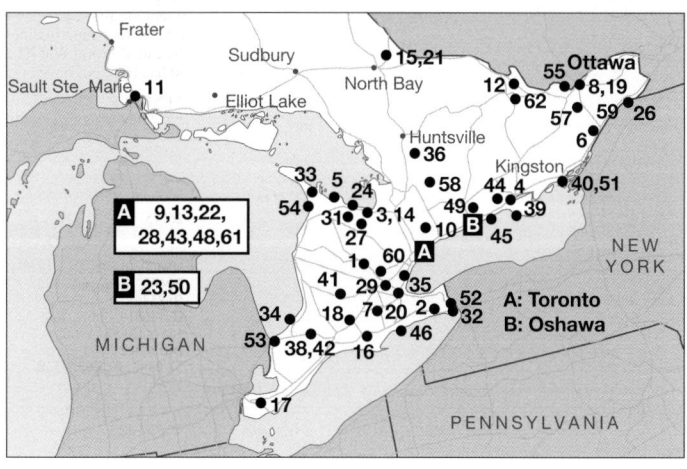

ACTON MONUMENT (ON1)

Location:	On permanent view at RCL Branch 197 in Wright Avenue in the south western part of the town.

TYPE	REG/SER	CON. NO.	PI/NOTES	STATUS
☐ Canadair CL-30 Silver Star 3 (CT-133) [Lockheed 580 (T-33AN)]	21103	T33-103		PV

AEA 2005 (ON2)

Address:	111 Grren Pointe Drive, Welland, Ontario L3C 6Y5.
Tel:	905-734-9005 Email: info@silverdartreplica.com
Admission:	By prior permission only.
Location:	In a private premises in the area.

The group has built a flying replica of Canada's first aircraft the Silver Dart. Construction began in 2005 and on 22nd February 2009 the biplane took to the air in Baddeck, Nova Scotia, the location of the first flight of the original Silver Dart, which took place on 23rd February 1909. The aircraft has since appeared at airshows and museums across the country.

TYPE	REG/SER	CON. NO.	PI/NOTES	STATUS
☐ Aerial Experiment Association Silver Dart (R)	C-IIGY	001		RAA

BASE BORDEN MILITARY MUSEUM (ON3)

Address:	18 Waterloo Road East, Canadian Forces Base Borden, Borden, Ontario L0M 1C0.
Tel:	705-423-3531 Fax: 705-423-3623 Email: marion.jcn@forces.gc.ca
Admission:	Air Force Hangar Saturday-Sunday 1300-1600.
Location:	About 15 km west of Barrie off Highway 90.

Camp Borden opened on 11th July 1916 and the first flying from the site occurred the following March. The Royal Flying Corps arrived in January 1917 and soon established the first airfield in Canada.

The Royal Canadian Air Force was formed at Borden in 1920 and for the next decade all land plane training for the service was carried out at the base. The site is still an important training centre for both Army and Air Force recruits.

A number of museums have been set up each concentrating on a different aspect of the history of the camp. The visitor can see a large collection of armoured vehicles and artillery in Wellington Park and close by is a museum highlighting the role of the Army.

One of the historic hangars on the airfield stages a display tracing the aviation history of Borden. On show here is a Tiger Moth and the Avro 504. The latter was built in 1918 by the Grahame-White Aviation Company at Hendon and served with the Royal Air Force before moving to Canada. The Royal Canadian Air Force flew the trainer until 1928 when six survivors were sold. The Canadian-built Tiger served with the Royal Canadian Air Force before being sold to a civilian owner. The biplane then spent time in the USA before returning home. The aircraft is now painted in period colours. The majority of the aircraft are exhibited nearby.

One of the CF-5s is mounted outside the Officers Mess on the other side of the base.

TYPE	REG/SER	CON. NO.	PI/NOTES	STATUS
☐ Avro 504K	'G-CYCK'		D8971, 'G-CYCK', CF-CYC – on loan from CASM, ON.	PVX
☐ Avro Canada C.100 Canuck 4A (4) (CF-100)	18194	094	18194, A646, 646B	PV
☐ Avro Canada C.100 Canuck 5D (5) (CF-100)	100493	393	18493	PV
☐ Canadair CL-13A Sabre 5 [North American F-86E]	23228	1018	23228, A709	PV
☐ Canadair CL-30 Silver Star 3 (CT-133) [Lockheed 580 (T-33AN)]	21079	T33-079	21079, A668, 668B	PV
☐ Canadair CL-30 Silver Star 3 (CT-133) [Lockheed 580 (T-33AN)]	21100	T33-100	21100, 669C	PV
☐ Canadair CL-30 Silver Star 3 (CT-133) [Lockheed 580 (T-33AN)]	133433	T33-433	21433	PV
☐ Canadair CL-30 Silver Star 3 (CT-133) [Lockheed 580 (T-33AN)]	133540	T33-540	21540	PV
☐ Canadair CL-30 Silver Star 3 (CT-133) [Lockheed 580 (T-33AN)]	133623	T33-623	21623	PV
☐ Canadair CL-41A Tutor (CT-114)	114153	1153	26153, 114153, A753, 753B	PV
☐ Canadair CL-90 Starfighter (CF-104) [Lockheed 683-04-12]	104792	683A-1092	12792, 104792, A794	PV
☐ Canadair CL-219-1A10 Freedom Fighter (CF-116A) (CF-5A) [Northrop N-156A]	116710	1010		PV
☐ Canadair CL-219-1A10 Freedom Fighter (CF-116A) (CF-5A) [Northrop N-156A]	116759	1059	116759, 912B	PV
☐ Canadair CL-219-1A10 Freedom Fighter (CF-116A) (CF-5A) [Northrop N-156A]	116769	1069	116769, 845B, A845, 845B	PV
☐ De Havilland DH.82C Tiger Moth	'4974'	'29552'	(RCAF), CF-EMT, N4446, C-GDPT	PVX
☐ Grumman G-103 Tracker (CS2F-1) (CP-121)	1507	DHC-6	1507, 724B	PVX
☐ McDonnell M.36BA Voodoo (F-101B) (CF-101B)	101011	467	57-0289	PV

BELLEVILLE MONUMENT (ON4)

Location:	On permanent view in the Community Gardens on Highway 62.

TYPE	REG/SER	CON. NO.	PI/NOTES	STATUS
☐ Canadair CL-13A Sabre 5 [North American F-86E]	23053	843		PV

Ontario

BILLY BISHOP HERITAGE MUSEUM (ON5)

Address:	948 Third Avenue West, Owen Sound, Ontario N4K 4P6.
Tel:	519-371-0081 Fax: 519-371-5310 Email: info@billybishop.org
Admission:	June–August Monday-Saturday 1000-1630, Sunday 1200-1630; May, September, October Saturday-Sunday 1300-1630. Rest of year Monday-Friday 1300-1600.
Location:	In the centre of the town.

This house, built between 1882 and 1884, was the home of the Bishop family. William Avery 'Billy' Bishop was born there. During World War I he downed 72 German planes and was awarded the Victoria Cross. After hostilities finished he returned to Canada and for a time ran an air charter business with another 'ace' Billy Barker. He died in 1956 and vast crowds attended his funeral in Toronto. The house opened as a museum in 1987 and the displays trace the history of his life and other Canadians who have served their country. There are rooms dedicated to both World Wars and Canada's aviation history. Many personal items, photographs, models and documents are on show and there is a tribute to von Richthofen.

BROCKVILLE MONUMENTS (ON6)

Location:	At two locations in the town.

TYPE	REG/SER	CON. NO.	PI/NOTES	STATUS
☐ Beech C23-19 Musketeer (CT-134)	134217	M-1341	13417 – at a business about 3 km west of the town.	
☐ Canadair CL-13B Sabre 6 [North American F-86E]	23659	1439	By the Tourist Center.	PV

CAINSVILLE MONUMENT (ON7)

Location:	On permanent view at a business in the town.

TYPE	REG/SER	CON. NO.	PI/NOTES	STATUS
☐ Piper PA-23-250 Aztec				PVX

CANADA'S AVIATION AND SPACE MUSEUM (ON8)

Address:	PO Box 9724, Rockcliffe Airport, Ottawa, Ontario K1G 5A3.
Tel:	613-993-2010 Fax: 613-993-3655 Email: aviation@technomuses.ca
Admission:	May–mid September daily 0900-1700; mid September–April Wednesday-Sunday 1000-1700.
Location:	In the north eastern suburbs of the city

The origins of the collection date back to 1919 when Lieutenant Arthur Doughty, the Dominion archivist, had a number of aircraft and artefacts transported to Canada. Some were put on show at the National Exhibition in Toronto and others at a local airfield. Afterwards they were moved to Camp Borden and in May 1920 some were dispersed around the country.

The German aircraft which remained at Borden were scrapped with the exception of an AEG IV and a Junkers J 1 which went to the Canadian War Museum along with the B.E.2C flown by Lieutenant F. Sowery when he shot down Zeppelin L 32 on 24th September 1916. The two German aircraft are today the last survivors of their type; the Royal Ontario Museum obtained some World War I types but these were scrapped in the 1920s.

The National Research Council, largely through the efforts of John Parkin, began a collection of aeronautical material and opened a museum in 1937. After World War II the RCAF began preserving aircraft but there was little progress until 1959 when the establishment of a National Aviation Museum was announced. A small display containing a replica of the Silver Dart opened in 1959 in the terminal at Ottawa Airport.

In 1964 the RCAF ceased flying at Rockcliffe on the outskirts of Ottawa and three wooden hangars on the south side of the field were allocated to the museum. Over the next few years displays were also staged at the Museum of Science and Technology, at the airport and at the Canadian War Museum. Two of the Rockcliffe hangars were used for exhibition and one for restoration and storage.

In 1983 work started on a new building for the museum. The delta shaped structure with few internal columns provides an excellent setting for the collection. The museum opened in its new home on 17th June 1988. About two-thirds of the building was used for the main exhibition and the remainder for the unrestored airframes. A new storage hall was started in 2001 and on 8th November 2006 the last airframes parked outside moved in. New displays have been set up in the main building.

Over 130 aircraft are now in the collection and these include many unique and historic types. Aircraft from the pioneering days up to the modern era can be seen. Bush flying has played an important part in the development of the country and examples of aircraft used in this work are displayed in typical 'up-country' settings. There is also a fine collection of types from both World Wars. There are many interesting airframes on show including the following. The AEG G IV twin-engined bomber first flew in late 1916 and served on all fronts up to the end of the conflict. It was soon shipped to Canada and led a nomadic life before being restored at Trenton in 1969. The G IV is the only surviving German twin engined bomber of World War I.

A superbly restored Curtiss HS-2L flying boat can be seen. The first bush aircraft in Canada was G-CAAC of Laurentide Air Service; the type served with distinction until the early 1930s. The rebuild commenced in 1975 and parts from three aircraft were used. Completed in 1976, it now carries the markings G-CAAC. Another Curtiss flying boat on show is the Seagull which was used in South America and Canada.

A rare glider is the Harbinger. One was built in England in 1958 and this still survives. Construction of second was started in Toronto in 1949 but after several moves it was not completed until 1975. After 30 flights it was donated to the museum.

The de Havilland Company set up a factory in Canada and its first task was the assembly of DH.60 Moths. Many aircraft were built in World War II and in 1946 its first original design, the Chipmunk, took to the air. The trainer was also built in large numbers in England. This was soon followed by the Beaver and Otter which were sold around the world. The first prototype Beaver and a production Otter can be seen. Other designs from the company are the prototypes of the Twin Otter and DHC.7. Two other Canadian types which failed to achieve production were the Avro Canada Jetliner and Arrow fighter. The front fuselages of these designs, the only major parts remaining, are on show. To interest and inform the visitor the latest technology is being used. Details of all aircraft can be accessed at a number of stations in the main hall. Here the visitor can see their individual operating histories.

Ontario

TYPE	REG/SER	CON. NO.	PI/NOTES	STATUS
☐ Advanced Aviation Buccaneer SX	C-IDWT	9112SX-A A		RA
☐ Aerial Experiment Association Silver Dart (R)		2		PV
☐ Aeronca C-2	'CF-AOR'	A-9	NC525V, N525V	RAX
☐ Allgemeine Electrizitats Gesellschaft G IV	574/18			PV
☐ Apco Aviation Astra 29		300316		RA
☐ Auster K AOP.6	'VF582'	2572	VP629, 16652, CF-KBV	RAX
☐ Avro 504K	'G-CYFG'	2552	H2453, 5918 (US), N8736R, 'A1938' – parts from D8971.	PVX
☐ Avro 616 Avian IVM	CF-CDQ	R3/CN/314	134	RAC
☐ Avro 652A Anson V	12518	MDF329		PV
☐ Avro 683 Lancaster 10(DC) (B.X)	KB848		Front fuselage only.	PV
☐ Avro 683 Lancaster 10(MR) (B.X)			KB944	PVX
☐ Avro Canada C.100 Canuck 5 (CF-100)	18752	652	18752, A793	RA
☐ Avro Canada C.100 Canuck 5D (5) (CF-100)	100757	657	18757	PV
☐ Avro Canada C.102 Jetliner	CF-EJD-X		Front fuselage only.	PV
☐ Avro Canada C.105 Arrow (CF-105)	25206		Front fuselage and other parts.	PV
☐ Bell 47G Sioux (HTL-6) (TH-13M)	1387	1387	Bu142386	PV
☐ Bell 212 Twin Huey (CUH-1N) (CH-135)	135114	32014	(70-15651)	PV
☐ Bellanca CH-300 Pacemaker	CF-ATN	181	NC196N	PV
☐ Bensen B-8 Gyroglider	C-GSXV	BARB.1		PV
☐ Bensen B-8MG Gyrocopter	C-GPJE	P.6174		PV
☐ Blériot XI				RA
☐ Boeing 247D (247)	CF-JRQ	1699	NC13318, CF-BQS, 7638, CF-BVX, NC41809	PV
☐ Boeing-Vertol 107-II-9 Labrador (CH-113)	11301	301	N6680D (?), 10401	PV
☐ Borel-Morane Monoplane				PV
☐ Bowers Fly Baby 1A			Incomplete.	RA
☐ Bristol 14 F.2B Fighter	'D7889'	67626	BAPC.166, G-AANM – composite.	PVX
☐ Bristol 149 Bolingbroke IVT	'9025'		9892	RAX
☐ Bristol 156 Beaufighter TT.10 (TF.X))	RD867			RA
☐ Canadair CL-2 North Star [Douglas DC-4M-1]	17515	122		RAC
☐ Canadair CL-13B Sabre 6 [North American F-86E]	23455	1245		PV
☐ Canadair CL-28-2 Argus 2 (CP-107)	10742	33	20742	RA
☐ Canadair CL-30 Silver Star 3 (CT-133) [Lockheed 580 (T-33AN)]	21574	T33-574		PV
☐ Canadair CL-41A Tutor (CT-114)	114055	1055	26055 – front fuselage only.	PV
☐ Canadair CL-41A Tutor (CT-114)	114108	1108	26108	PV
☐ Canadair CL-84 Dynavert (CX-131)	8402	3		PV
☐ Canadair CL-219-1A10 Freedom Fighter (CF-116A) (CF-5A) [Northrop N-156A]	116763	1063		PV
☐ Canadair CL-604 Challenger (CL-600) (CL-601)	C-GCGT	1003	C-GCGT-X	PV
☐ Canadian Car & Foundry Harvard 4 [North American NA-186]	20387	CCF4-178	20387, CF-GBV	RA
☐ Cessna T-50 Crane 1	8676	2226		RA
☐ Cessna 150H	C-GAZG	15068295	N22457	PV
☐ Consolidated 28-5A Canso A	11087	CV 423		RAX
☐ Consolidated 32 Liberator (B-24L) (B.VIII)	'11130'	5009	44-50154, KN820, HE773 (India)	RAX
☐ Curtiss JN-4 Canuck	'C227'		39158, 111	PVX
☐ Curtiss 8 (HS-2L)	G-CAAC	2901-H-2	A1876 – wings from A1373, NC652 and parts from A1250, C-CAOS.	PV
☐ Curtiss 18 Seagull (MF)				PV
☐ Curtiss A87-A2 Kittyhawk I	1076	18779	AL135 – museum gives c/n as 18780.	PV
☐ Czerwinski-Shenstone Harbinger	C-FZCS	C1	CF-ZCS	RA
☐ De Havilland DH.60X Moth	G-CAUA	630		RA
☐ De Havilland DH.80A Puss Moth	CF-PEI	2187	BuA8877, (DR630), HM534, G-AHLO	PV
☐ De Havilland DH.82C Tiger Moth	4861	DHC.1052		PV
☐ De Havilland DH.82C Tiger Moth	CF-FGL	DHC.724	4394, CF-DTL	RA
☐ De Havilland DH.83C Fox Moth	CF-DJB	FM.28/2	CF-DJB, C-FDJB	PV
☐ De Havilland DH.98 Mosquito B.20	KB336			RA
☐ De Havilland DH.100 Vampire F.1	TG372			RA
☐ De Havilland DH.100 Vampire F.3	17074	EEP42392	Front fuselage only.	PV
☐ De Havilland DH.106 Comet 1XB (1)	5301	06017		RA
☐ De Havilland DHC.1 Chipmunk 1B-2-S5 (CT-120)	12070	208-246	18070, 12070, CF-CIA	RA
☐ De Havilland DHC.2 Beaver			(Pakistan)	RA
☐ De Havilland DHC.2 Beaver	CF-FHB	1	CF-FHB-X, CF-FHB, C-FFHB	PV
☐ De Havilland DHC.3 Otter (CC-123)	9408	370	9408	RA
☐ De Havilland DHC.6 Twin Otter	CF-DHC-X	1	CF-DHC-X, CF-DHC, CF-DHC-X, CF-DHC	PV
☐ De Havilland DHC.7	C-GNBX			RA
☐ Douglas DC-3-454 (C-49J)	C-FTDJ	6261	43-1985, CF-TDJ	PV
☐ Douglas DC-9-32	CF-TLL	47021	CF-TLL, C-FTLL	RA
☐ Evans VP-1 Volksplane	C-GUPY	1938		RA
☐ Fairchild FC-2W2	'G-CART'	128	NC6621	PVX
☐ Fairchild 82A	CF-AXL	61		RA
☐ Fairchild M-62A-4 Cornell II	10738	FC.239		PV
☐ Fairey Swordfish II	'NS122'			PVX
☐ Fairey Battle IT	R7384	F4848		RA
☐ Fairey Firefly FR.1	DK545	F7776		RA

Ontario

☐ Fantasy Sky Promotions Fantasy 7 Hot Air Balloon	C-GEMW	001		RA	
☐ Farman MF-11 Shorthorn			G-AUBC, VH-UBC, N9645Z	PV	
☐ Fleet 2				RAD	
☐ Fleet 16B Finch II	4510	408	4510, CF-SUX, N1327V	PV	
☐ Fleet 50K	CF-BXP	202	799, CF-BJU	RAD	
☐ Fleet 50K	CF-BJW	203	Parts only to assist in rebuild of CF-BXP.	RAD	
☐ Fleet 80 Canuck	CF-EBE	149		RA	
☐ Fokker D VII	10347/18	3659	10347/18, N1178, '2041/18'	RA	
☐ Fokker Universal	NC7029	434	Parts of fuselage and engine.	RAD	
☐ Found FBA-2C	CF-OZV	4	CF-OZV, 'C-GCCF'	RA	
☐ Grumman G-21A Goose (G-39) (JRF-5)	C-FMPG	B77	Bu37824, (CF-BFS), CF-MPG	RA	
☐ Grumman G-103 Tracker (CS2F-2) (CS2F-3) (CP-121)	12187	DHC-86	1587	RA	
☐ Hawker Hind	L7180			RA	
☐ Hawker Hurricane XII	5584	1009/52019	Museum found 522/19308 on aircraft.	PV	
☐ Hawker Sea Fury FB.11	TG119	41H/609977		PV	
☐ Hawker-Siddeley P.1127 Harrier 50 (AV-8A) (AV-8C)	Bu158966	P127	On loan from NMNA, FL.	PV	
☐ Heinkel He 162A-1	120076	120076	120076, AM.59, VH523	RA	
☐ Hispano HA-1112M1L (Messerschmitt Bf 109G)	C.4K-114	183	Museum lists c/n as 164.	RA	
☐ Junkers J 1 (Ju 4)	586/18	252		RA	
☐ Junkers W 34f/fi	CF-ATF	2718		PV	
☐ Lockheed 10-A Electra	CF-TCA	1112	CF-TCA, 1526(Canada), CF-TCA, 1526, CF-BTD NC79237, N79237, N1285, N79237	PV	
☐ Lockheed 12-A Electra Junior	CF-CCT	1219		RA	
☐ Lockheed 183-93-02 Starfighter (F-104A)	12700	183-1058	56-0770	PV	
☐ Lockheed 1329 JetStar 6	C-FDTX	1329-5018	N9287R, (CF-DTX)	RA	
☐ McDonnell M.24 Banshee (F2H-3)	126464	174	Bu126464	PV	
☐ McDonnell M.36BA Voodoo (F-101B) (CF-101B)	101025	518	57-0334	PV	
☐ McDonnell M.267B Hornet (CF-188B)	188901	47/B011		PV	
☐ McDowall Monoplane				PV	
☐ Messerschmitt Bf 109F-4/Z		10132		PV	
☐ Messerschmitt Me 163B-1a Komet	191914	191914	Was thought to be 191916.	PV	
☐ Mikoyan-Gurevich MiG-21MF-75 (MiG-21MF)	4038	96004038	In Czech markings.	RA	
☐ Mitchell Wing B-10				RA	
☐ Moyes Stingray Hang Glider				RA	
☐ Nieuport 12	N1504		N1504, 'A4737'	PV	
☐ Noorduyn Norseman VI (C-64A) (UC-64A)	787	136	43-5145	PV	
☐ North American NA-108 Mitchell (B-25J) (TB-25L) (Mitchell III)	5244	108-47453	44-86699	RA	
☐ North American NA-122 Mustang (P-51D) (Mustang IV)	9298	122-39806	44-73347	RA	
☐ Northrop Delta	673	CV 183	Fuselage only.	RAD	
☐ Piasecki PD-18 Retriever (H-25A)	51-16623	52		PV	
☐ Pitcairn PCA-2	NC2624	8	NR26	RA	
☐ Pitts S-2A Special	C-FAMR	2059	CF-AMR	RA	
☐ Quickie Aircraft Quickie 1 (Rutan 54)	C-GGLC	1001		RA	
☐ Royal Aircraft Factory B.E.2c	5878	1042		PV	
☐ Sheldrake Merritt Spirit of Canada Hot Air Balloon	CF-VOZ	SM101		RA	
☐ Sikorsky VS-316A Hoverfly (R-4B)	43-46565	109		RA	
☐ Sikorsky S-55D (HO4S-3)	55877	55877		PV	
☐ Sopwith 2F.1 Camel	N8156			PV	
☐ Sopwith 7F.1 Snipe	E6938	50131	E6938, N6638	PV	
☐ Sopwith Triplane (R)	'N5492'		CF-CBM	RAX	
☐ SPAD VII	B9913	103		PV	
☐ Spectrum RX550 Beaver	C-IGOW	SB 2331		RA	
☐ Stearman 4EM (4E Special)	'CF-AMB'	4021	NC784H	PVX	
☐ Stinson Junior SR	CF-HAW	8717	NC13464, N13464, CF-HAW, C-FHAW	PV	
☐ Stits SA-3A Playboy	C-FRAD	5501	CF-IGK-X, CF-RAD	RA	
☐ Supermarine 361 Spitfire LF.IXc	NH188	CBAF-IX-2161	NH188, H-109 (Netherlands), H-64 (Netherlands) SM-39 (Belgium), OO-ARC, CF-NUS, 'TE353'	PV	
☐ Taylor E-2 Cub	C-GCGE	289	NC15399, N15399	PV	
☐ Taylorcraft BC-65	CF-BPR	1409		RA	
☐ Travel Air 2000	CF-AFG	720	C6281 (US civil)	RAC	
☐ Ultralight Flying Machines Easy Riser				RA	
☐ Vickers Vedette V	G-CYVP	CV 146	G-CYVP, CF-AIR – front fuselage only.	RA	
☐ Vickers Vedette VA	G-CYWQ	CV 155	C-GYWQ, 814 – fuselage only.	RAD	
☐ Vickers 757 Viscount	CF-THI	270		RA	
☐ Waco 10 (GXE)	C-GAFD	1521		PV	
☐ Waco YKS-7 (VKS-7F)	C-FLWL	6117	NC31676, CF-LWL	RA	
☐ Westland Lysander IIIA	'R9003'	1216	Composite mainly of V9415 but parts of c/n 1286 and c/nY1643.	PVX	
☐ Wills Wings XC-185 Hang Glider				PV	
☐ WSK Lim-2R [MiG-15bis]		1B 003-16		PV	
☐ Yost GB-55 Hot Air Balloon	N53NY			RA	
☐ Zenair CH-300 Tri-Zenith	C-GOVK	300		RA	

47

CANADIAN AIR AND SPACE MUSEUM (ON9)

Address:	65 Carl Hall Road, North York, Ontario M3K 2E1.
Tel:	416-638-6078 Fax: 416-638-5509 Email: casm@casmuseum.org
Admission:	Wednesday 1000-2000; Thursday-Sunday 1000-1600.
Location:	On the north west side of Downsview Airport which is in the northern part of Toronto.

Housed in one of hangars used by the de Havilland company in the 1930s, this museum was set up in the late 1980s. Toronto has been an important centre for the Canadian aviation industry for many years and aircraft are still made at the field. One major project is the restoration of the Lancaster which spent many years mounted in a park by the waterfront in the city. Over 400 examples were built at Malton by Victory Aircraft from 1942 and the last were not withdrawn by the Royal Canadian Air Force until the mid-1960s.

Avro Canada acquired the Victory company in late 1945. The Arrow, which was controversially cancelled in 1959, has evoked many emotions in the intervening years. A full size model of the delta winged fighter was completed in 2006. Other Canadian designs are joining the collection. Found Aircraft was established in 1946 and produced the high wing FBA-1 for bush flying. The design was steadily improved and 27 examples of FBA-2C were completed in the 1960s. Recent military types are now on view.

TYPE	REG/SER	CON. NO.	PI/NOTES	STATUS
☐ Avro 683 Lancaster 10(MR) (B.X)	FM104			PVC
☐ Avro Canada C.105 Arrow (CF-105) (FSM)	'25203'			PVX
☐ Beech C23-19 Musketeer (CT-134)	134220	M-1344	13420,134220, 803B	RA
☐ Bell 206A Kiowa (COH-58A) (CH-136)	136230	44030	71-20895	PV
☐ Canadair CL-30 Silver Star 3 (CT-133) [Lockheed 580 (T-33AN)]	133581	T33-581	21581	PV
☐ Canadair CL-41A Tutor (CT-114)	'114156'	1168	26168, 114168	PVX
☐ Cessna 150D	C-GPXM	15060176	N4176U	PVC
☐ CVT M-100S	C-FRIV	047	CF-RIV	PV
☐ De Havilland DH.82C Tiger Moth	NX820DH/3874	DHC.1535	3874, N820DH	PV
☐ Eipper MX Quicksilver				RA
☐ Fleet 80 Canuck	C-FEAI	127	CF-EAI	PV
☐ Found FBA-1	CF-GMO-X	1		RA
☐ Grumman G-103 Tracker (CS2F-2) (CP-121)	1600	DHC-99	1600, 733B, C-FUDQ	PV
☐ Stinson V-77 Reliant (AT-19)	CF-CAJ	77-166	42-46805, FK979, Bu11490, NC42357	PV
☐ Ultraflight Lazair 1				PV
☐ Ultralight Flying Machines Easy Riser	C-IBYE	WAL.001		PV
☐ University of Toronto Ornithopter	C-GPTR	00001		PV
☐ University of Toronto SHARP UAV				PV
☐ Zenair CH-200 Zenith	C-FEYC	01		PV

CANADIAN AIR SEA LAND MUSEUM (ON10)

Address:	PO Box 518, Markham, Ontario L3P 3RI.
Tel:	905-640-0050 Fax: 905-640-0499 Email: wof@idirect.com
Admission:	By prior permission only.
Location:	At Markham Airport which is about 7 km north of the town on Highway 48.

Alan Rubin started the organisation as International Vintage Aircraft in the mid-1980s. Premises were obtained at Mount Hope Airport but these were demolished after the fire at the nearby Canadian Warplane Heritage. The collection is now based at Markham Airport. Very few Miles Hawk Majors survive and the example in the collection is currently in store. The only Proctor 6, which was operated on floats, is another airframe which has not been seen for many years. A large amount of archive material has been collected and there are long-term plans to construct a museum at Markham or at a nearby location.

TYPE	REG/SER	CON. NO.	PI/NOTES	STATUS
☐ Auster K AOP.6	16679	2857		RA
☐ Avro Canada C.100 Canuck 4 (CF-100)	18506	406	VP662, 16679, CF-KFN	RA
☐ Beech D18S Expeditor 3N	CF-ZYH	CA-100 (A-700)	2302	PV
☐ Beech D18S	CF-RND	A-962	N2912B, N212J	RA
☐ Canadair CL-13A Sabre 5 [North American F-86E]				RAD
☐ Canadair CL-13A Sabre 5 [North American F-86E]	23301	1091		RA
☐ Canadair CL-30 Silver Star 3 (CT-133) [Lockheed 580 (T-33AN)]	133357	T33-357	21357 – tail from c/n T-33-571 21571, 133571.	RA
☐ Canadair CL-30 Silver Star 3 (CT-133) [Lockheed 580 (T-33AN)]	133421	T33-421	21421	RAC
☐ Canadair CL-30 Silver Star 3 (CT-133) [Lockheed 580 (T-33AN)]	133542	T33-542	21542	PV
☐ Canadair CL-30 Silver Star 3 (CT-133) [Lockheed 580 (T-33AN)]	133573	T33-573	21573	PV
☐ Canadair CL-30 Silver Star 3 (CT-133) [Lockheed 580 (T-33AN)]			Fuselage only.	RAD
☐ Canadair CL-219-1A10 Freedom Fighter (CF-116A) (CF-5A) [Northrop N-156A]	116703	1003		RA
☐ Canadair CL-219-1A10 Freedom Fighter (CF-116A) (CF-5A) [Northrop N-156A]	116709	1009		RA
☐ Canadair CL-219-1A10 Freedom Fighter (CF-116A) (CF-5A) [Northrop N-156A]	116712	1012		RA
☐ Canadair CL-219-1A10 Freedom Fighter (CF-116A) (CF-5A) [Northrop N-156A]	116713	1013	116713, 774B, A774	RA
☐ Canadair CL-219-1A10 Freedom Fighter (CF-116A) (CF-5A) [Northrop N-156A]	116714	1014		RA

Ontario

Type	C/N	Serial	PI/Notes	Status
☐ Canadair CL-219-1A10 Freedom Fighter (CF-116A) (CF-5A) [Northrop N-156A]	116717	1017		RA
☐ Canadair CL-219-1A10 Freedom Fighter (CF-116A) (CF-5A) [Northrop N-156A]	116724	1024	116724, 812B	RA
☐ Canadair CL-219-1A10 Freedom Fighter (CF-116A) (CF-5A) [Northrop N-156A]	116726	1026		RA
☐ Canadair CL-219-1A10 Freedom Fighter (CF-116A) (CF-5A) [Northrop N-156A]	116743	1043		RA
☐ Canadair CL-219-1A10 Freedom Fighter (CF-116A) (CF-5A) [Northrop N-156A]	116747	1047		RA
☐ Canadair CL-219-1A10 Freedom Fighter (CF-116A) (CF-5A) [Northrop N-156A]	116750	1050		RA
☐ Canadair CL-219-1A10 Freedom Fighter (CF-116A) (CF-5A) [Northrop N-156A]	116751	1051		RA
☐ Canadair CL-219-1A10 Freedom Fighter (CF-116A) (CF-5A) [Northrop N-156A]	116758	1058		RA
☐ Canadair CL-219-1A17 Freedom Fighter (CF-116D) (CF-5D) [Northrop N-156B]	116810	2010		RA
☐ Canadair CL-219-1A17 Freedom Fighter (CF-116D) (CF-5D) [Northrop N-156B]	116826	2026		RA
☐ Douglas DC-4 Skymaster (C-54E)	C-GFMQ	27265	44-9039, N63309, 44-9039 – front fuselage only.	RA
☐ Fairchild M-62A-4 Cornell II				RAC
☐ Lockheed 583-04-15 Starfighter (CF-104D)	104643	583A-5313	12643, 877C	RA
☐ Lockheed 583-04-15 Starfighter (CF-104D)	104644	583A-5314	12644, 852C	RA
☐ Lockheed 583-04-15 Starfighter (CF-104D)	104658	583A-5328	12658 (Canada), 104658 (Canada) – in Turkish markings.	RA
☐ Lockheed 683-10-19 Starfighter (F-104G)	FX-99	683D-9172	In Belgian markings.	RA
☐ Miles M.2W Hawk Major (M.2H)	C-FAUV	123	G-ACYZ, VH-ACC, CF-AUV	RA
☐ Noorduyn Norseman V				RA
☐ Noorduyn Norseman V				RA
☐ Percival P.47 Proctor 6	CF-EHF	Ae140	X-1	RA

CANADIAN BUSHPLANE HERITAGE CENTRE (ON11)

Address:	50 Pim Street, Sault Ste Marie, Ontario P6A 3G4.
Tel:	705-945-6242 **Fax:** 705-942-8947 **Email:** display@bushplane.com
Admission:	Mid May–mid October daily 0900-1800; Mid October–mid May daily 1000-1600.
Location:	On the waterfront in the town centre.

Established in 1924, the Ontario Provincial Air Service has patrolled the skies of the region for more than 80 years, playing a major role in protecting the forests. The original hangar still stands and is incorporated into the main building which was constructed in 1948 and used until 1991 when the OPAS aircraft moved to Sault Federal Airport.

The complex has been convened into an excellent 'hands-on' museum, which opened in May 1995, tracing the history of bush flying and fire-fighting. In one corner of the large hangar is the historic engine test cell which is in working order. The Pratt and Whitney engine is run regularly.

Displays show a replica of a camp used by fire crews, models and photographs of all types used by OPAS, the history of airlines which started as bush outfits, forest fire equipment, a lightning locator which is still in use and a fire tower. The KR-34 on show was the personal machine of George MacDougall who was Superintendent of Algonquin Park in the 1930s. The biplane was recovered from the shore of Wildcat Lake in 1963 and restored for the 60th anniversary celebrations of the service.

Four Buhl CA-6 Airsedans were built by OPAS at Sault Ste Marie between 1935 and 1937. The remains of two are exhibited in an interesting 'as found' diorama. Nearby is the frame of the prototype Noorduyn Norseman. which was used in the 1941 film 'Captain of the Clouds' starring James Cagney.

TYPE	REG/SER	CON. NO.	PI/NOTES	STATUS
☐ Aerial Experiment Association Silver Dart (R)				PV
☐ Aeronca 7DC Champion (7AC)	CF-IHU	7AC-1934	NC83270, N83270	PVA
☐ Aeronca 11CC Super Chief	C-FNGV	11CC-189	NC4335E, N4335E, CF-NGV	PV
☐ Beech C18S Expeditor 3T (C-45F) (UC-45F)	CF-UWE	8034	44-47626, 1421	PV
☐ Beech D18S Expeditor (C-45H)	CF-MJY	AF-562	52-10632, N3734G	PV
☐ Beech D18S Expeditor 3NM	1506		Front fuselage only.	PV
☐ Bell 47D-1	CF-ODM	665		PV
☐ Buhl CA-6M Airsedan	CF-OAR	2		PVD
☐ Buhl CA-6M Airsedan	CF-OAT	4	Fuselage only.	PVD
☐ Canadair CL-215-II	CF-GVM	1040	F-ZBBT	PV
☐ De Havilland DH.83C Fox Moth	'CF-BNI'	FM.55-1	Parts from c/n FM.28 CF-DJB	PVCX
☐ De Havilland DH.89A Dragon Rapide (DH.89B Dominie I)	C-FAYE	6796	NR697, G-AKGV, F-BFPU, G-AKGV, CF-AYE, (C-GXFJ)	PV
☐ De Havilland DHC.2 Beaver	CF-OBS	2		PVA
☐ De Havilland DHC.2 Turbo-Beaver	CF-PSM-X	1525 (TB1)	CF-PSM-X, CF-PSM, C-FPSM	PV
☐ De Havilland DHC.3 Otter	C-FODU	369	CF-ODU	PVA
☐ Fairchild F-11-2 Husky (F-11-1)	CF-EIR	12		PV
☐ Fokker F.VIIb/3m (R)	'NX4204'			PVX
☐ Fokker Super Universal	CF-AJE	CV 140		PVD
☐ Grumman G-89 Tracker (S2F-1) (S-2A)	Bu133190	161	Bu133190, N423DF	PV
☐ Kreider-Reisner KR-34C Challenger	C-FADH	900	CF-ADH	PV
☐ Noorduyn Norseman I	CF-AYO	1	CF-AYO, CF-HGO	PVD
☐ Noorduyn Norseman IV	CF-BFT	17		PVA
☐ Republic RC-3 Seabee	C-FDKG	822	CF-DKG	PVA
☐ Saunders ST-27 (De Havilland DH.114 Heron 2)	C-GCML	009	Original c/n 14095 G-AOGW	PV
☐ Stinson SR-9FM Reliant	CF-BGN	5702		PV
☐ Taylorcraft 20	CF-FTC	20-012		PV
☐ Thomas Esperanza 4				PV

CANADIAN FORCES BASE PETAWAWA MILITARY MUSEUM (ON12)

Address:	Building 51, PO Box 9999, CFB Petawawa, Petawawa, Ontario K8H 2X3.
Tel:	613-588-6238 **Fax:** 613-588-6446 **Email:** airbornereg@renc.igt.net
Admission:	Monday-Friday 1300-1600; Saturday-Sunday 1100-1600.
Location:	About 140 km north west of Ottawa off Highway 17.

Camp Petawawa was one of the earliest military bases in Canada and on 2nd August 1909 John McCurdy demonstrated the AEA Silver Dart.

The museum incorporates four collections – the Canadian Guards, 427 Squadron, the Royal Canadian Guards and the Canadian Airborne Forces. The camp has been the headquarters of the Airborne Forces Regiment for many years and the display traces the history of the regiment from its early days.

The three aircraft are parked outside along with a large number of military vehicles.

TYPE	REG/SER	CON. NO.	PI/NOTES	STATUS
☐ Bell 206A Kiowa (COH-58A) (CH-136)	136207	44007	71-20872	PV
☐ Cessna 305A Bird Dog (L-19A) (O-1A) (CO-119)	119706	23476	53-8055, 16706, 119706, A745	PV
☐ Douglas DC-3A-456 Skytrain (C-47A) (Dakota III) (CC-129)	KG455	12490	42-92664, KG455, 12924	PV

CANADIAN FORCES COLLEGE MONUMENT (ON13)

Location:	By prior permission only in Yonge Boulevard in northern part of Toronto.

TYPE	REG/SER	CON. NO.	PI/NOTES	STATUS
☐ Lockheed 583-04-15 Starfighter (CF-104D)	104652	583A-5322	12652, 104652, 823C	RA

CANADIAN FORCES SCHOOL OF AEROSPACE TECHNOLOGY AND ENGINEERING (ON14)

Address:	CFB Borden, PO Box 1000, Station Main, Borden, Ontario L0M 1C0.
Tel:	705-424-1200
Admission:	By prior permission only.
Location:	About 15 km west of Barrie off Highway 90.

Flying instruction at Borden decreased in the 1950s and technical training returned from many of the schools set up in World War II.

In the 1960s the Canadian Air Forces Trade School was established by combining seven different organisations. The present name was adopted in 1985. Servicemen are trained in avionics, aircraft structures, airframes and powerplants.

A large number of instructional airframes are in use. Some other aircraft are used for training firefighters but these usually have a limited life and are not listed.

TYPE	REG/SER	CON. NO.	PI/NOTES	STATUS
☐ Beech C23-19 Musketeer (CT-134)	134218	M-1342	13418	RA
☐ Bell 206A Kiowa (COH-58A) (CH-136)	'136228'	44047	136247, 914B, "136288"	PVX
☐ Bell 206A Kiowa (COH-58A)	'136007'		(US Army)	RAX
☐ Canadair CL-41A Tutor (CT-114)	114011	1011	26011, 926B	RA
☐ Canadair CL-41A Tutor (CT-114)	114012	1012	26012	RA
☐ Canadair CL-41A Tutor (CT-114)	114020	1020	26020	RA
☐ Canadair CL-41A Tutor (CT-114)	114023	1023	26023, 936B	RA
☐ Canadair CL-41A Tutor (CT-114)	114026	1026	26026, 899B – rear fuselage and tail only.	RA
☐ Canadair CL-41A Tutor (CT-114)	114030	1030	26030	RA
☐ Canadair CL-41A Tutor (CT-114)	114031	1031	26031 – rear fuselage only.	RA
☐ Canadair CL-41A Tutor (CT-114)	114037	1037	26037	RA
☐ Canadair CL-41A Tutor (CT-114)	114039	1039	26039, 933B	RA
☐ Canadair CL-41A Tutor (CT-114)	114040	1040	26040, 896B – rear fuselage and tail only.	RA
☐ Canadair CL-41A Tutor (CT-114)	114041	1041	26041	RA
☐ Canadair CL-41A Tutor (CT-114)	114043	1043	26043, 889B	RA
☐ Canadair CL-41A Tutor (CT-114)	114046	1046	26046	RA
☐ Canadair CL-41A Tutor (CT-114)	114049	1049	26049	RA
☐ Canadair CL-41A Tutor (CT-114)	114062	1062	26062	RA
☐ Canadair CL-41A Tutor (CT-114)	114066	1066	26066	RA
☐ Canadair CL-41A Tutor (CT-114)	114069	1069	26069, 891B	RA
☐ Canadair CL-41A Tutor (CT-114)	114080	1080	26080, 927B	RA
☐ Canadair CL-41A Tutor (CT-114)	114087	1087	26087, 934B	RA
☐ Canadair CL-41A Tutor (CT-114)	114091	1091	26091, 898B	RA
☐ Canadair CL-41A Tutor (CT-114)	114092	1092	26092, 892B	RA
☐ Canadair CL-41A Tutor (CT-114)	114092	1092	26092	RA
☐ Canadair CL-41A Tutor (CT-114)	114105	1105	26105, 895B – rear fuselage and tail only.	RA
☐ Canadair CL-41A Tutor (CT-114)	114112	1112	26112, 903B	RA
☐ Canadair CL-41A Tutor (CT-114)	114119	1119	26119, A901	RA
☐ Canadair CL-41A Tutor (CT-114)	114124	1124	26124	RA
☐ Canadair CL-41A Tutor (CT-114)	114134	1134	26134, A894	RA
☐ Canadair CL-41A Tutor (CT-114)	114139	1139	26139, 937B	RA
☐ Canadair CL-41A Tutor (CT-114)	114151	1151	26151, 752B – rear fuselage and tail only.	RA
☐ Canadair CL-41A Tutor (CT-114)	114163	1163	26163, 935B	RA
☐ Canadair CL-41A Tutor (CT-114)	114164	1164	26164, 928B	RA
☐ Canadair CL-41A Tutor (CT-114)	114175	1175	26175, 938B	RA

Ontario

☐ Canadair CL-41A Tutor (CT-114)	114178	1178	26178, 939B		RA
☐ Canadair CL-41A Tutor (CT-114)	114181	1181	26181, 897B		RA
☐ Canadair CL-41A Tutor (CT-114)	114189	1189	26189		RA
☐ Canadair CL-219-1A10 Freedom Fighter (CF-116A) (CF-5A) [Northrop N-156A]	116710	1010	116710, 911B		RA
☐ Canadair CL-219-1A10 Freedom Fighter (CF-116A) (CF-5A) [Northrop N-156A]	116768	1068	In Radiation Safety Training Area.		RA
☐ Canadair CL-219-1A17 Freedom Fighter (CF-116D) (CF-5D) [Northrop N-156B]	116835	2035	In Radiation Safety Training Area.		RA
☐ McDonnell M.267A Hornet (CF-188A)	188707	107/A093			RA

CANADIAN FORCES MUSEUM OF AEROSPACE DEFENSE (ON15)

Address:	Canadian Forces Base North Bay, Hornell Heights, Ontario P3A 3YAP.
Tel:	705-494-2011 **Fax:** 705-494-2190 **Email:** berath@forces.gc.ca
Admission:	Sunday 1300-1600.
Location:	About 5 km north east of the town east of Highway 11.

The North American Air Defence Command (NORAD) was formed in May 1958 and North Bay became the site for a data interpretation centre. Fighter Squadrons were based at the field to protect the area against manned bomber attack.

A large complex houses the Regional Operations Control Centre where air defence surveillance and identification are carried out. At the current time there are no operational aircraft based at the field. A museum tracing the history of the base was set up in the late 1990s. The development of defence systems is portrayed in detail.

Two aircraft are currently mounted at the entrance to the site along with radar equipment. In addition a CF-100 and a Bomarc missile can be seen near the lakeshore in the town.

TYPE	REG/SER	CON. NO.	PI/NOTES	STATUS
☐ Avro Canada C.100 Canuck 5D (5) (CF-100)	100500	400	18500	PV
☐ Avro Canada C.100 Canuck 5M (5) (CF-100)	18626	526	In town near the waterfront.	PV
☐ Canadair CL-30 Silver Star 3 (CT-133) [Lockheed 580 (T-33AN)]	133402	T33-402	21402	PV
☐ McDonnell M.36BA Voodoo (F-101B) (CF-101B)	'101067'	598	57-0420, 101054	PVX

CANADIAN HARVARD AIRCRAFT ASSOCIATION (ON16)

Address:	244411 Airport Road, Tillsonburg, Ontario N4G 4H1.
Tel:	519-842-9922 **Fax:** 519-842-3292 **Email:** ray@spitcrazy.comm
Admission:	By prior permission only.
Location:	At Tillsonburg airfield which is about 10 km north of the town on Highway 19.

In 1969 a Woodstock resident acquired a Harvard and based it at the local airfield. Over the next 15 years four more examples of the famous trainer arrived at the airstrip.

The Canadian Harvard Aircraft Association was formed in 1985 and the following year it acquired a hangar at the nearby Tillsonburg Municipal Airport where maintenance and restoration is carried out. Aircraft from the group are regular performers at shows around the country. Other training types have been acquired including one of the more than 1,500 Tiger Moths built by de Havilland's Canadian factory at Downsview.

The fixed undercarriage Yale was originally ordered by France and just over 100 had been delivered when the country fell. The remainder of the batch of 230 was bought by Britain and delivered to the RCAF. One of these is now airworthy.

TYPE	REG/SER	CON. NO.	PI/NOTES	STATUS
☐ Canadian Car & Foundry Harvard 4 [North American NA-186]	C-FWPK	CCF4-33	20242, CF-WPK	RAA
☐ Canadian Car & Foundry Harvard 4 [North American NA-186]	C-FBZT	CCF4-95	20304	RAC
☐ Canadian Car & Foundry Harvard 4 [North American NA-186]	CF-UFZ	CCF4-112	20321	RAA
☐ Canadian Car & Foundry Harvard 4 [North American NA-186]	20407	CCF4-198		RA
☐ Canadian Car & Foundry Harvard 4 [North American NA-186]	C-FRZW	CCF4-213	20422, CF-RZW	RAA
☐ Canadian Car & Foundry Harvard 4 [North American NA-186]	N436WL	CCF4-227	20436, CF-WWI	RAA
☐ De Havilland DH.82C Tiger Moth	C-GCOE	DHC.829	5030, CF-CHT	RAC
☐ Noorduyn Harvard IIB [North American NA-77]	3323	07-190		RAC
☐ Noorduyn Harvard IIB [North American NA-77]	C-FNDB	07-6	3039, CF-NDB	RAA
☐ North American NA-64 Yale				RA
☐ North American NA-64 Yale	C-GLJH	64-2160	3399, C-FAAX	RAA
☐ North American NA-75 Harvard II	C-FMTX	75-3465	3191, CF-MTX, C-FMTX, N3191G	RAA
☐ North American NA-75 Harvard II	C-FMKA	75-3496	3222, CF-MKA	RAA
☐ North American NA-76 Harvard II	C-FHWX	76-3553	AJ583, CF-HWX	RAA
☐ North American NA-81 Harvard II	C-FRWN	81-4097	3830, CF-RWN	RAA
☐ North American NA-88 Texan (AT-6C)			Composite using parts from c/n 121-42490 44-81768 ,N445C	PVX

CANADIAN HISTORICAL AIRCRAFT ASSOCIATION (ON17)

Address:	PO Box 40, Airport Road, Windsor, Ontario N8V 1A2.
Tel:	519-966-9742 **Email:** museum@ch2a.ca
Admission:	By prior permission only.
Location:	In the southern suburbs of the town.

The Lancaster was mounted on a pedestal in the town for many years. The association has been formed to raise funds to construct a building to house this historic bomber. The group has now acquired several other types. Under restoration is a Mosquito which is from the batch imported by Spartan Air Services in the 1950s.

TYPE	REG/SER	CON. NO.	PI/NOTES	STATUS
☐ Avro 683 Lancaster 10P (B.X)	FM212			PV
☐ Boeing-Stearman A75N1 Kaydet (PT-17)	C-FAPG	75-2730	41-25241, N56838, CF-APG	RA
☐ Canadair CL-30 Silver Star 3 (CT-133) [Lockheed 580 (T-33AN)]	133299	T33-299	21299	PV
☐ De Havilland DH.98 Mosquito TT.35 (B.35)	'KB161'		TA661, CF-HMR	RAC
☐ De Havilland DHC.1 Chipmunk 1B-2-S3 (CT-120)	C-FCYR	151-189	(CF-CYR), 189, 18017, CF-CYR, 18017, 12017, CF-CYR	RAA
☐ De Havilland DHC.1 Chipmunk 1B-2-S5 (CT-120)	C-FBNM	192-230	18054, 12054, CF-BNM	RA
☐ Fleet 7B Fawn I	CF-CEQ	68		RAA
☐ Hawker Hurricane I (FSM)	'P3080'			PVX
☐ Piper J-3C-65 Cub	CF-SDR	20050	NC6829H, N6829H, CF-SDR, C-FSDR	PV
☐ Supermarine 359 Spitfire F.VIIIc (FSM)	'JG184'			PVX

CANADIAN MILITARY HERITAGE MUSEUM (ON18)

Address:	347 Greenwich Street, Brantford, Ontario N3R 7X5.
Tel:	519-759-1313 Fax: 519-759-6243 Email: cmhm@execulink.com
Admission:	May–September Tuesday-Saturday 1000-1600; October–November Friday-Sunday 1000-1600.
Location:	In the south eastern part of the town.

The displays at this museum trace the history of the military forces in Canada since 1812. On show are many vehicles, weapons, uniforms, badges, uniforms and items of memorabilia. The four World War I replicas were constructed in the early 1990s by local students for a film which was never made.

TYPE	REG/SER	CON. NO.	PI/NOTES	STATUS
☐ Albatros D Va (R)	'D.5463/17'			PVX
☐ Fokker Dr I (R)				PV
☐ Nieuport 17 (R)				PV
☐ Pfalz D III (R)	'4173/17'			PVX

CANADIAN WAR MUSEUM (ON19)

Address:	1 Vimy Place, Ottawa, Ontario K1A OM8
Tel:	819-776-8600 Fax: 819-776-8623 Email: info@warmuseum.ca
Admission:	May–mid September daily 0900-1700; mid September–April Tuesday-Sunday 0900-1700.
Location:	On Le Breton Flats in the northern part of the city.

The origins of the collection go back to the 1880s but it was not until 1967 that an exhibition opened in the old archive building in Sussex Drive. Plans for a new building were put forward in 2001 and the spectacular structure opened four years later.

The exhibitions trace the story of the battles fought by Canadian forces from the early days up to recent times. There are five main galleries each dealing with a period in the military history of Canada.

On show in the World War I area is the fuselage of the Sopwith Snipe flown by Major W.G. Barker when he won the Victoria Cross over France on October 27th 1918. Wounded in one arm and both legs, Barker shot down three Fokker D VIIs. His Snipe crashed behind the Allied lines and the remains were salvaged.

In Barker's home town, Dauphin in Manitoba, there is a small display of memorabilia at the Fort Dauphin Museum commemorating his deeds. In every one the contribution of Canadians is featured. Dioramas featuring significant events have been constructed and videos can also be viewed. There are photographs, documents, uniforms and weapons to be seen. The collection includes large numbers of military vehicles.

TYPE	REG/SER	CON. NO.	PI/NOTES	STATUS
☐ Bell 204 Iroquois (UH-1B)	63-8504	726		RA
☐ Bell 206A Kiowa (COH-58A) (CH-136)	136274	44074	71-20939	PV
☐ Canadair CL-219-1A10 Freedom Fighter (CF-116A) (CF-5A) [Northrop N-156A]	116702	1002		PV
☐ Fieseler Fi 103A-1/Re4				PV
☐ McDonnell M.36BA Voodoo (F-101B) (CF-101F)	101002	285	56-0260, 101002, 874B	PV
☐ Nieuport 17 (R)	'B1566'		'N2874', CF-DDK – on loan from CASM, ON.	PV
☐ North American NA-66 Harvard II				RA
☐ Sopwith 7F.1 Snipe	E8102		Fuselage only.	PV
☐ Supermarine 329 Spitfire F.IIb	P8332	CBAF-711	P8332, A166, 166B – on loan from CASM, ON.	PV

CANADIAN WARPLANE HERITAGE MUSEUM (ON20)

Address:	9820 Airport Road, Hamilton Airport, Mount Hope, Ontario L0R 1W0.
Tel:	905-679-4183 Fax: 905-679-4186 Email: museum@warplane.com
Admission:	Daily 0900-1700.
Location:	The airport is about 12 km south of Hamilton off Highway 6.

In 1971 four enthusiasts – Dennis Bradley, Alan Ness, Peter Matthews and John Weir – bought a Fairey Firefly in the USA. The quartet formed the Canadian Warplane Heritage the following year and moved the aircraft to Mount Hope Airport at Hamilton. A Chipmunk and a Harvard soon joined the organisation. Over the next few years more aircraft were acquired and in 1975 the group moved into Hangar 4 at the airport.

Ontario

In 1977 Alan Ness was killed when the Firefly crashed into Lake Ontario. The aircraft was eventually replaced with one from Australia which is now flying. Steady progress was made and by 1985 the fleet had grown to around 40 with several in airworthy condition.

For many years a Lancaster had been mounted on a pedestal at Goderich Airport and on 1st July 1977 the bomber was handed over to the group. It was moved to Hamilton under a Chinook helicopter in 1979 and restoration to flying condition commenced.

The museum opened on a full time basis in the early 1980s but disaster struck on February 15th 1993 when fire swept through the wooden Hangar 3 originally built to house aircraft used in the British Commonwealth Air Training Plan. Five aircraft were destroyed: a Hurricane, an Avenger, an Auster AOP.6, a Stinson Voyager and a Spitfire owned by the Confederate Air Force. The Lancaster, which flew again in September 1988, was in the hangar but was separated from the other aircraft by a block wall. This famous bomber is one of two airworthy examples left. A Bolingbroke and a Fleet Finch were also saved. The engineering offices and most of the technical records were lost.

In 1996 a magnificent new delta shaped museum was completed and this now houses the majority of the fleet. A number of rarities are on show including the only airworthy Fleet Fort and the last surviving Fleet 21. The Fort was designed as an intermediate trainer and an order for 200 was placed. The first production model flew in May 1941 but there were several problems after it was introduced into service. The batch was cut to 100 and it was decided to convert them to wireless trainers. A total of 11 biplane 21s was built with 10 being delivered to Mexico. The Finch II made its maiden flight at Fort Erie in March 1940: 404 were delivered to the Royal Canadian Air Force and they served as primary trainers at schools across the country. The majority were withdrawn in 1944 but a few soldiered on until 1947.

Very few Ansons remain in flying condition, as do examples of the Westland Lysander. A Starfighter is spectacularly mounted outside the building and a Vampire arrived from Switzerland. Other jet types will be added as they become available and a Canadair Tutor is a recent arrival. For many years an Auster T.7 was in the collection but this has now been replaced by an AOP.6 which spent a long period in store with a private owner.

Five static aircraft have been loaned by the Canada Aviation Museum to enhance the display. This magnificent museum is one of the major flying collections of warbirds in the world.

TYPE	REG/SER	CON. NO.	PI/NOTES	STATUS
☐ Auster K AOP.6	C-GCID	2859	VP664,16681,CF-KRF	PVA
☐ Avro 652A Anson V	'12417'	BRC1567	12103, PT-AVD, CF-HOT, C-FHOT	PVAX
☐ Avro 683 Lancaster B.I (FSM)	'NG333'		Rear fuselage only.	PVX
☐ Avro 683 Lancaster 10(MR) (B.X)	'KB726'		FM213, C-GVRA	PVAX
☐ Avro Canada C.100 Canuck 5D (5) (CF-100)	100785	685	18785 – on loan from CAM, ON.	PV
☐ Beech D18S	'HB143'	A-156	NC80213, N80213, CF-HHI, TG-JIQ, C-GZCE	PVAX
☐ Bell 206A Kiowa (COH-58A) (CH-136)	136272	44072		PV
☐ Boeing 727-22QC	C-GBWA	19890	N7433U, N112FE	PV
☐ Boeing-Stearman A75N1 Kaydet (PT-17)	'FK107'	75-2180	41-8621, CF-AIU, C-FAIU	PVAX
☐ Boeing-Stearman E75 Kaydet (PT-13D)		75-5315	42-17152, N105H, N72559	PVA
☐ Bristol 149 Bolingbroke IVT	9949			RAD
☐ Bristol 149 Bolingbroke IVT	'9023'		10040, C-GCWO	PVCX
☐ Bristol 149 Bolingbroke IVT	10117			RAD
☐ Canadair CL-13B Sabre 6 [North American F-86E]	23651	1441	On loan from CAM, ON.	PV
☐ Canadair CL-30 Silver Star 3 (CT-133) [Lockheed 580 (T-33AN)]	21275	T33-275	21275, 133275, 768B	PV
☐ Canadair CL-41A Tutor (CT-114)	114038	1038	26038	PV
☐ Canadair CL-90 Starfighter (CF-104) [Lockheed 683-04-12]	'104756'	683A-1090	12790, 104790, 860C, 875C	PVX
☐ Canadair CL-219-1A10 Freedom Fighter (CF-116A) (CF-5A) [Northrop N-156A]	116757	1057	On loan from NAFMC, ON.	PV
☐ Canadian Car & Foundry Harvard 4 [North American NA-186]	C-FUUU	CCF4-4	20213, CF-UUU	PVA
☐ Canadian Car & Foundry Harvard 4 [North American NA-186]	C-FVMG	CCF4-203	20412, CF-VMG	PVA
☐ Cessna T-50 Crane 1	'7862'	1355	7862, CF-FGF	PVA
☐ Consolidated 28-5 Canso	9825	CV 259	Fuselage only.	PV
☐ Consolidated 28-5A Canso A	'9754'	CV 417	11084, CF-PQL, C-FPQL	PVX
☐ De Havilland DH.82C Tiger Moth	C-GCWT	DHC.1724	8922	PVA
☐ De Havilland DH.100 Vampire FB.6		654	J-1145 (Switzerland)	PVX
☐ De Havilland DHC.1 Chipmunk 1B-2-S3	C-FCXP	120-158	CF-CXP	PVA
☐ De Havilland DHC.1 Chipmunk 1B-2-S3 (CT-120)	C-FPOW	173-211	18035, 12035, CF-POW	PVA
☐ De Havilland DHC.1 Chipmunk 1B-2-S5 (CT-120)	C-FBXK	179-217	18041, 12041, CF-BXK	PVA
☐ De Havilland DHC.5 Buffalo	'115461'	85	811 (Sudan)	RAX
☐ Douglas DC-3-201B	'KN458'/'KN563'	2141	NC21729, N21729, C-GDAK	PVAX
☐ Fairchild M-62A-4 Cornell II				RAD
☐ Fairchild M-62A-4 Cornell II	'163'	1070	FV702, CF-CVF – in false Norwegian markings.	PVAX
☐ Fairchild M-62A-4 Cornell II	'10835'	FC.195	10694, C-GCWC	PVAX
☐ Fairchild M-62A-4 Cornell II	CF-FZA	T4-4681	42-65596, 15012, FV111 – wings only.	RA
☐ Fairey Firefly AS.6	'VH142'	F8755	WH632, C-GBDG	PVAX
☐ Fleet 16B Finch II	C-FFUI/'4738'	623	4738, CF-FUI	PVA
☐ Fleet 21K (21M)	C-FDLC	11	CF-DLC-X,	PVA
☐ Fleet 60 Fort	C-FORT	600	3540, CF-BQP	PVA
☐ Fleet 60K Fort	3643	683		PV
☐ Fouga CM.170R Magister	F-FOUG	549	549 (France), NX549M	PV
☐ Grumman G-40 Avenger (TBM-3) (TBM-3E)	F-WQON	3920	Bu53858, N3357G, C-GFPR	PVC
☐ Grumman G-103 Tracker (CS2F-2) (CP-121)	C-FUDH	DHC-76	1577, A732, 732B	PVC
☐ Hawker Hurricane IIB (FSM)	'P3069'			PVX
☐ Hawker Fury FB.10	C-FGAT	41H/623271	324 (Iraq), N58SF, N1324, (C-GGAT), CF-GAT	PVA
☐ Lockheed 583-04-15 Starfighter (CF-104D)	12641	583A-5311	12641, 104641, 876C	PV
☐ McDonnell M.36BA Voodoo (F-101B) (CF-101B)	101045	560	57-0382	PV
☐ Nanchang CJ-6A	N8120L	47-22		PVA

Ontario

☐ North American NA-64 Yale	3400	64-2149	3400 (Canada), N6598Z, N129DB	PVA
☐ North American NA-64 Yale	3411	64-2167		PV
☐ North American NA-64 Yale	'3350'	64-2206	3350, CF-CWZ	PVA
☐ North American NA-108 Mitchell (B-25J)	'HD372'	108-47734	45-8883, NC75755, N75755, (C-GCWA), C-GCWM	PVAX
☐ SCAN 30 (Grumman G-44A Widgeon]	CF-ODR	28	N2812D	PVA
☐ Sikorsky S-51 Dragonfly	9601	5118	On loan from CAM, ON.	PV
☐ Sopwith Pup (R)	'B2167'	C552	CF-RFC – on loan from CAM, ON.	PVX
☐ Supermarine 361 Spitfire LF.XVIe	TE214	CBAF-IX-4424	On loan from CAM, ON.	PV
☐ Westland Lysander IIIA	'2363'	1202	2363, C-GCWL, N1274, C-GCWL	PVAX
☐ Westland Lysander IIIA	C-GCWW	1205	2364	PVA

CANADORE COLLEGE (ON21)

Address:	100 College Drive, North Bay, Ontario P1B 8K9
Tel:	705-474-7600 Fax: 705-474-2384 Email: info@canadorec.on.ca
Admission:	By prior permission only.
Location:	At the airport which is about 5 km north of the town.

Founded as a community college in 1967, Canadore College became an independent organisation five years later. The Aviation Campus opened in September 2002 at Jack Garland Airport.

Courses offered include aircraft structural repairs, aircraft maintenance, avionics maintenance. In addition helicopter and fixed wing pilots licences may be obtained. The workshops contain a fleet of ground instructional airframes and engines.

TYPE	REG/SER	CON. NO.	PI/NOTES	STATUS
☐ Aérospatiale AS.350B Ecureuil	'905'			RAX
☐ Beech A100 King Air	C-GISH	B-152	N25652, N65LC, N65LG, N67LC, (N67LG), N67LC	RA
☐ Beech C23 Sundowner (CT-134A) (Musketeer II)	'702'	M-2313	134226	RAX
☐ Beech C23 Sundowner (CT-134A) (Musketeer II)	'701'	M-2314	134227	RAX
☐ Bell 206A Jet Ranger	C-FOHT'901'	078		RA
☐ Bell 206A Kiowa (COH-58A) (CH-136)	136243/'902'	44043		RA
☐ Bell 47G-2 (47D) (47D-1)	C-FICG/904'	74	NC208B, CF-ICG	RA
☐ Cessna 150	'704'			RAX
☐ Cessna 172	CF-OHP	46098	N4198F	RA
☐ Cessna 177	N3495F/'705'	17700607		RA
☐ Cessna 310Q	C-FSAS	310Q0216		
☐ Cessna 336 Skymaster	'708'			RAX
☐ Mitsubishi MU-2D (MU-2B-10)	C-GWGP/'802'	109	N3573X, N856Q, N1AN	RA
☐ Piper PA-23 Apache	CF-GXP/'803'	23-447		RA
☐ Piper PA-28-140 Cherokee	C-FVLU/'703'	28-22646		RA
☐ Piper PA-31P Pressurised Navajo	C-GLGK	31P-7300117	N7346L, N777JP	RA
☐ Robinson R-22 Alpha	C-GFPY/'903'	0260		RA
☐ Steen Skybolt				RA
☐ Zenair CH-200 Zenith	'707'	269		RAX

CENTENNIAL COLLEGE SCHOOL OF TRANSPORTATION (ON22)

Address:	75 Ashtonbee Road, Scarborough, Ontario M1K 5E9
Tel:	416-289-5000 Email: tbrittain@centennialcollege.ca
Admission:	By prior permission only.
Location:	In the north eastern part of Toronto.

The school offers training on maintaining cars, trucks, coaches, motor cycles and aircraft. In addition a pilot training school is part of the complex. Airframe and avionics courses take place leading to approved qualifications. The fleet of instructional airframes includes an example of the Dash-8 airliner.

TYPE	REG/SER	CON. NO.	PI/NOTES	STATUS
☐ Beech E18S	CF-PER	BA-409		ra
☐ Beech 100 King Air	N777GF	B-241	N777NR, N77GF, N77GS	RA
☐ Bell 47	'CF-CCE'			RAX
☐ Bell 206B Jet Ranger	C-GIWU	174	N209D	RA
☐ Cessna 140		11738	N9999V	RA
☐ Cessna 150G	CF-YSV			RA
☐ Cessna 150G	C-FVXU	15066632	(N2732S), CF-VXU	RA
☐ Cessna 180				RA
☐ Cessna T337C Super Skymaster	CF-WPE	T3370765		RA
☐ De Havilland DHC.8-102	N806LR	093	C-GONH	RA
☐ Piper PA-23 Apache	C-GDNC	23-996	N3078P	RA
☐ Piper PA-23-250 Aztec E	C-GVHL	27-7554153	N54853	RA
☐ Piper PA-44-180 Seminole	C-GWGD	44-7995060	N21856	RA

CLASSIC WINGS (ON23)

Address:	1748 Baseline Road West, Courtice, Ontario L1E 2T1.
Tel:	905-728-7964 Fax: 905-983-5296 Email: hawkfield@sympatico.ca
Admission:	By prior permission only.
Location:	At Oshawa Airport which is just north of the town.

Ontario

This flying school has collected a small fleet of classic types which are regularly operated. Both the Tiger Moth and Piper Cub are Canadian-built examples. A total of J-2s and 150 J-3s were constructed from kits by Cub Aircraft in Hamilton Ontario in 1936/7 and in 1945/7 with a final example emerging in 1952. The Classic Aircraft Corporation of Lansing, Michigan put the F-5, based on the pre-war Waco YMF-5, into production in the mid-1980s and over the next two decades over 100 have been sold. The Canadian Car & Foundry Company built 555 Harvard 4s at its plant in the 1950s. After the taken over of the firm by Avro Canada a few more were completed and sold abroad. The trainer served with the RCAF for many years.

TYPE	REG/SER	CON. NO.	PI/NOTES	STATUS
☐ Beech 95-B55 Baron	C-FMTH	TC-2345		RAA
☐ Canadian Car & Foundry Harvard 4 [North American NA-186]	C-FGUY	CCF4-27	20236, CF-GUY	RAA
☐ Classic Aircraft Waco F-5	C-GKLH	F5-030	N40133	RAA
☐ De Havilland DH.82C Tiger Moth	CF-GTU	DHC.649	4319	RAA
☐ Piper J-3C-65 Cub	CF-FDSD	183C	CF-DSD	RAA
☐ Stinson HW.75	CF-BST	7055	NC21175, CF-BST, 3468	RAA

COLLINGWOOD MONUMENT (ON24)

Location:	On permanent view at RCL Branch 63 in Ontario Street in the eastern part of the town.

TYPE	REG/SER	CON. NO.	PI/NOTES	STATUS
☐ Canadair CL-30 Silver Star 3 (CT-133) [Lockheed 580 (T-33AN)]	21199	T33-199		PV

CONFEDERATION COLLEGE (ON25)

Address:	1450 Nakina Drive, Thunder Bay, Ontario P7C 4W1.
Tel:	807-475-6110 Email: jcelmer@confederationc.on.ca
Admission:	By prior permission only.
Location:	In the southern part of the town.

Founded as a trade school in 1967, the college had as its first president retired Air Vice-Marshal Douglas Bradshaw. Part of his vision was to establish an aviation programme in the area. The college now operates from seven sites in the area.
The Aviation Campus is located at the International Airport. The facility includes workshops and laboratories with the latest equipment.

The fleet of instructional aircraft includes a former Air Canada DC-9. The airliner was in service with the national airline from March 1968 until withdrawn in the early 2000s. The aircraft arrived at Thunder Bay in September 2003.
One of the Kiowas came from the University of Southern Illinois and the college cannot identify it. The other one served with the Canadian Forces.

TYPE	REG/SER	CON. NO.	PI/NOTES	STATUS
☐ Beech 95-B55 Baron	C-FCAL	TC-945	CF-CAL	RA
☐ Bell 206A Kiowa (COH-58A) (CH-136)	136214	44014	71-20879	RA
☐ Bell 206A Kiowa (OH-58A)			(US Army)	RA
☐ Bell 47G-4	CF-RLH	2899	N73293	RA
☐ Cessna 172G	CF-UPQ	17254575	(N4480L)	RA
☐ Cessna 180	CF-DMB	30059	(N2859A)	RA
☐ Cessna 180	CF-HLS	30973	(N3174C), CF-HLS, N9436H	RA
☐ Cessna 180	CF-EBH	31813	N9415C	RA
☐ Cessna 180A	C-FEBG	32894	N9597B, CF-EBG	RA
☐ Cessna 180J	N42256	18052333		RA
☐ Douglas DC-9-32	C-FTLT	47195	CF-TLT	RA

CORNWALL MONUMENTS (ON26)

Location:	On permanent view at two locations in the town.

TYPE	REG/SER	CON. NO.	PI/NOTES	STATUS
☐ Canadair CL-30 Silver Star 3 (CT-133) [Lockheed 580 (T-33AN)]	21347	T33-347	In a park in Water Street	PV
☐ Canadair CL-30 Silver Star 3 (CT-133) [Lockheed 580 (T-33AN)]	133423	T33-423	21423 – at ATC Centre in Montreal Street.	PV

CREEMORE MONUMENT (ON27)

Location:	On permanent view at RCL Branch 397 in Wellington Street West.

TYPE	REG/SER	CON. NO.	PI/NOTES	STATUS
☐ Canadair CL-30 Silver Star 3 (CT-133) [Lockheed 580 (T-33AN)]	21070	T33-070		PV

DEFENCE RESEARCH AND DEVELOPMENT OF CANADA MONUMENT (ON28)

Location:	Near Downsview Airport which is in the northern part of Toronto.

TYPE	REG/SER	CON. NO.	PI/NOTES	STATUS
☐ Canadair CL-219-1A10 Freedom Fighter (CF-116A) (CF-5A) [Northrop N-156A]	116746	1046		RA

DUNDAS MONUMENT (ON29)

| Location: | On permanent view at the RCAFA Club at 128 King Street East in the eastern part of the town. |

TYPE	REG/SER	CON. NO.	PI/NOTES	STATUS
☐ Canadair CL-30 Silver Star 3 (CT-133) [Lockheed 580 (T-33AN)]	21123	T33-123		PV

EAR FALLS DISTRICT MUSEUM (ON30)

Address:	PO Box 309, Ear Falls, Ontario P0V 1T0.
Tel:	807-222-3624 **Fax:** 807-222-2384 **Email:** eftownship@town.earfalls.on.ca
Admission:	Mid May–mid September Monday-Friday 1000-1700.
Location:	Just south of the town on Highway 105 about 100 km north of Vermillion Bay.

This small museum had on show items tracing the history of the area with displays on local transport, the lumber industry, mining and hydroelectric power. Beech 18s have served this remote community for many years and several examples of the type are still in use in the region. The aircraft has been painted in false civil markings.

TYPE	REG/SER	CON. NO.	PI/NOTES	STATUS
☐ Beech D18S Expeditor 3TM	'CF-EAR'	CA-125 (A-725)	1525, 5184, CF-ZQG	PVX

EDENVALE CLASSIC AIRCRAFT FOUNDATION (ON31)

Address:	Hangar F, Edenvale Aerodrome, Stayner, Ontario L0M 1S0.
Tel:	705-818-2223 **Email:** info@classicaircraft.ca
Admission:	Thursdays 1000-1600 or by prior permission.
Location:	At Edenvale Airport which is 15 km west of Barrie on Highway 26.

In the 1990s owners of classic and vintage aircraft in the area decided to establish a museum at Collingwood Airport. The collection has now moved to Edenville Airport. The Canuck is derived from the Noury N-75. Fleet bought the design rights and put the high wing design into production in the immediate post war period. They constructed 198 and another 25 were assembled by Leavens Brothers. Claude Piel built his first aircraft the CP.10 in the 1940s. He went on to design a series of types including the successful Emeraude which was developed into the Diamant.

TYPE	REG/SER	CON. NO.	PI/NOTES	STATUS
☐ Aeronca 7AC Champion	C-FJUJ	7AC-2875	NC84187, N84187, CF-JUJ	RAA
☐ Corben D Baby Ace	C-FABU	PL-1		RAA
☐ De Havilland DH.82A Tiger Moth	C-GSTP	86509	NM201, (French AF), F-BGCP, EI-AUB, N82JS – registered as c/n 86508 NM200.	RAA
☐ Fleet 80 Canuck	C-FDPV	048	CF-DPV	RAA
☐ Piel CP.605 Diamant	C-GUMM	15		RAC
☐ Stinson HW.75	CF-BST	7055	NC21175, CF-BST, 3468	RAA

FORT ERIE MONUMENT (ON32)

| Location: | On permanent view in Sugarbowl Park in Central Avenue in the town. |

TYPE	REG/SER	CON. NO.	PI/NOTES	STATUS
☐ Canadair CL-30 Silver Star 3 (CT-133) [Lockheed 580 (T-33AN)]	133373	T33-373	21373 – tail from c/n T33-512 21512, 133512.	PV

GALLERY OF EARLY CANADIAN FLIGHT (ON33)

Address:	Wiarton-Keppel Airport, Wiarton, Ontario N0H 2T0.
Tel:	519-534-4090 **Fax:** 519-534-3184 **Email:** earlycanflight@sympatico.ca
Admission:	Daily 0830-1830.
Location:	About 2 km east of the town off Highway 26.

The collection at the airport consists of models, photographs, posters and videos tracing the history of pioneer flying in the country. Aviators who have made significant contributions are featured.

GRAND BEND MONUMENT (ON34)

| Location: | On permanent view at a business in the town. |

TYPE	REG/SER	CON. NO.	PI/NOTES	STATUS
☐ Canadair CL-30 Silver Star 3 (CT-133) [Lockheed 580 (T-33AN)]	21591	T33-591	21591, 133591, 869B – tail from c/n T33-303 21303, 133303	PV

GREAT WAR FLYING MUSEUM (THE) (ON35)

Address:	13691 McLaughin Road, PO Box 27, Stn Cheltenham, Caledon, Ontario L7C 3L7.
Tel:	905-838-4936 **Fax:** 905-838-1405 **Email:** info@GreatWarFlyingMuseum.com
Admission:	May–September Sunday 1400-1600 or by arrangement.
Location:	About 10 km north west of Brampton off Highway 10 and 2 km south west of Victoria.

Ontario

The Ontario Historical Aviation Society was formed with the aim of constructing replica aircraft from the World War I period. In the late 1970s a hangar and workshop were built at Brampton Airport.

An adjacent building, resembling an early fighter squadron dispersal hut, serves as a museum with a comprehensive display of memorabilia, photographs, documents etc. tracing the history of the conflict. The first aircraft to arrive was a scale replica of the famous S.E.5A representing one of the types flown by Billy Bishop, Canada's greatest ace.

Construction of a Fokker D VII commenced in the mid-1970s and this biplane took to the air in 1977. A Fokker Dr I triplane followed and this first flew in 1982. A full scale S.E.5A was completed in 1992 and the Nieuport 28C.1 was ready four years later.

Other projects are in the workshops.

TYPE	REG/SER	CON. NO.	PI/NOTES	STATUS
☐ De Havilland DH.2 (R)				RAC
☐ Fokker D VII (R)	C-GWWI	5125/18	Flies as '5324/18'	RACX
☐ Fokker Dr I (R)	C-GFJK	102/17	Flies as '477/17'	PVAX
☐ Fokker Dr I (R)	C-GDRI	AM-1		PVAX
☐ Nieuport 28C.1 (R)	C-FEWL	1918	Flies as '6159'	PVAX
☐ Replica Plans S.E.5A	C-FQGM	G70 003	CF-QGM – flies as 'A8936' was 'B4863'	PVAX
☐ Royal Aircraft Factory S.E.5A (R)	C-GRJC	C1904	Flies as 'C1904'	PVAX
☐ Sopwith 1 ½ Strutter (R)	C-FSOP		Flies as '9739'	PVAX
☐ Sopwith F.1 Camel (R)	C-FCML			RAC

HALIBURTON MONUMENT (ON36)

Location:	On permanent view at RCL Branch 129 on Highland Street in the centre of the town.

TYPE	REG/SER	CON. NO.	PI/NOTES	STATUS
☐ Avro Canada C.100 Canuck 5 (CF-100)	18602	502	18602, A683	PV

IGNACE MEMORIAL (ON37)

Location:	On permanent view in the centre of the town.

TYPE	REG/SER	CON. NO.	PI/NOTES	STATUS
☐ Beech D18S Expeditor 3NM	CF-WUH	CA-222 (A-872)	2343	PV

JET AIRCRAFT MUSEUM (ON38)

Address:	2464 Aviation Lane, Unit 1, London, Ontario N5V3Z9.
Email:	rhewitt@xplornet.com
Admission:	Tuesday 0800-1200, Thursday 1700-2100, Saturday 0900-1300
Location:	At the airport which is in the north eastern part of the town.

The museum was officially set up in September 2009 with the aim of keeping in flying order examples of jets used by the Canadian Forces. The idea stemmed from the success of the Canadian Harvard Aircraft Association. The founder of the Jet Aircraft Museum, Bob Hewitt, had been an active member of the CHAA for many years.

The project was initiated in the autumn of 2007 and negotiations began which led to a home being found at London Ontario International Airport. Six Canadian-built T-33s were purchased from those stored at the base at Mountain View Work started on preparing them for ferry flights. The first pair arrived at London on 15th April 2009 and the last touched down just over six months later. The aim is to acquire other types used by the forces in Canada.

The search is on for a Vampire and the Tutor fleet will be start to be retired in 2012.

TYPE	REG/SER	CON. NO.	PI/NOTES	STATUS
☐ Canadair CL-30 Silver Star 3 (CT-133) [Lockheed 580 (T-33AN)]	C-FUPJ	T33-052	21052, 133052, N53KK	RAA
☐ Canadair CL-30 Silver Star 3 (CT-133) [Lockheed 580 (T-33AN)]	C-FUPK	T33-263	21263, 133263, N263KK	RAA
☐ Canadair CL-30 Silver Star 3 (CT-133) [Lockheed 580 (T-33AN)]	C-FUPM	T33-346	21346, 133346, N346KK	RAA
☐ Canadair CL-30 Silver Star 3 (CT-133) [Lockheed 580 (T-33AN)]	C-FUPN	T33-441	21441, 133441	RAA
☐ Canadair CL-30 Silver Star 3 (CT-133) [Lockheed 580 (T-33AN)]	C-FUPO	T33-500	21500, 133500, N499KK	RAA
☐ Canadair CL-30 Silver Star 3 (CT-133) [Lockheed 580 (T-33AN)]	C-FUPP	T33-573	21573, 133573	RAA

KEITH ALDER MUSEUM (ON39)

Address:	PO Box 792, Picton, Ontario K0K 2T0.
Tel:	613-476-5782
Admission:	By prior permission only.
Location:	About 2 km south of the town.

Keith Alder has set up a museum in a large room at his house. On show are models, components and photographs. The history of Canadian aviation with particular reference to local events is portrayed. The aircraft are parked outside. The Silver Star was used as for instruction and struck off charge in 1989.

TYPE	REG/SER	CON. NO.	PI/NOTES	STATUS
☐ Beech C23-19 Musketeer (CT-134)	134211	M-1335	13411, 134211, A799	PV
☐ Canadair CL-30 Silver Star 3 (CT-133) [Lockheed 580 (T-33AN)]	133238	T33-238	21238, 133238, 863B	PV

The prototype Zenair CH-200 is on show at the Canadian Air and Space Museum. (Richard Hamblin) [ON9]

The Edenvale Classic Aircraft Foundation operates this Fleet Canuck. (Richard Baker) [ON31]

This floatplane Beech 18 is parked by a parade of shops in Ignace. (Ruud Leeuw) [ON37]

Ontario

KINGSTON MONUMENT (ON40)

Location:	On permanent view at Norman Rogers Airport which is in the south western part of the town.

TYPE	REG/SER	CON. NO.	PI/NOTES	STATUS
☐ North American NA-76 Harvard II	AJ693	76-3663		PV

KITCHENER MONUMENTS (ON41)

Location:	On permanent view at two locations in the town.

TYPE	REG/SER	CON. NO.	PI/NOTES	STATUS
☐ Diamond DA-20-A1 Katana	C-FNFA		At the airport which is east of the town.	PV
☐ Supermarine 361 Spitfire LF.IXc (FSM)	'NH357'		At a business in Victoria Street	PVX

LONDON MONUMENTS (ON42)

Location:	On permanent view at three locations in the town.

TYPE	REG/SER	CON. NO.	PI/NOTES	STATUS
☐ Canadair CL-30 Silver Star 3 (CT-133) [Lockheed 580 (T-33AN)]	'133491'	T33-422	21422, 133422 – at the airport.	PVX
☐ Diamond DA-20-A1 Katana			At the Airport Inn.	PV
☐ Diamond DA-20-A1 Katana			At the airport.	PV
☐ Diamond DA-20-A1 Katana			At the Diamond factory.	PV

MALTON MONUMENT (ON43)

Location:	On permanent view off Derry Road in the western part of Toronto.

TYPE	REG/SER	CON. NO.	PI/NOTES	STATUS
☐ Avro Canada C.100 Canuck 5 (CF-100)	18619	519	18619, A682	PV

MEMORIAL MILITARY MUSEUM (ON44)

Address:	226 Albert Street,, Campbellford, Ontario K0L 1L0.
Tel:	705-653-4848
Admission:	Monday-Saturday 1000-1700.
Location:	About 50 km east of Peterborough off Highway 30 and 1 km south of the town.

The late Harold Carlaw ran a business in the town for many years. He started acquiring militaria in the 1950s and gradually built up a sizeable collection; he opened the museum in 1991. The building contains many interesting items including models, uniforms and memorabilia. Two early propellers on show are from a Curtiss Jenny and an Armstrong Whitworth Siskin. There are many engines to be seen including a Ranger which is regularly run. A 60 percent scale model of the ill fated Avro Arrow built for the National Arts Centre production 'The Legend of the Avro Arrow' is a prized possession.

TYPE	REG/SER	CON. NO.	PI/NOTES	STATUS
☐ Avro 652A Anson II			Major components.	PVD
☐ Avro Canada C.100 Canuck 2T (CF-100)	18106	006	18106, A615, 615B	PV
☐ Avro Canada C.105 Arrow (CF-105) (Scale R)				PV
☐ Beech D18S Expeditor 3NM	'6144'		Fuselage only.	PVX
☐ Beech C23-19 Musketeer (CT-134)	134219	M-1343	13419, 134219, A794	PV
☐ Canadair CL-30 Silver Star 3 (CT-133) [Lockheed 580 (T-33AN)]	133303	T33-303	21303, 133303, 865B	PV
☐ Canadair CL-41A Tutor (CT-114)	114063	1063	26063 – front fuselage only.	PV
☐ Canadair CL-41A Tutor (CT-114)	114180	1180	26180	PV
☐ Canadair CL-219-1A10 Freedom Fighter (CF-116A) (CF-5A) [Northrop N-156A]	116730	1030		PV
☐ Cessna T-50 Crane 1A (Bobcat – AT-17A)	8841	2391	42-13707, FJ190	PVC
☐ De Havilland DH.82A Tiger Moth (R)				PVC
☐ Republic RC-3 Seabee	CF-FOY	747		PV
☐ Ultralight Flying Machines Easy Riser				PV
☐ XC-02 Helicopter				PV

NATIONAL AIR FORCE MUSEUM OF CANADA (ON45)

Address:	PO Box 1000, Canadian Forces Base Trenton, Astra, Ontario K0K 3W0.
Tel:	613-965-7223 Fax: 613-965-7352 Email: curator@rcafmuseum.on.ca
Admission:	May–September daily 1000-1700; October–April Wednesday-Sunday 1000-1700
Location:	Just north of the town off Highway 401.

The first Royal Canadian Air Force training airfield was at Borden. In the 1920s a search was made for a new base and Trenton was chosen. Close to Lake Ontario, the site was suitable for both landplane and seaplane operations and was also near to the large cities in the Province.

Trenton became operational in 1931 with the arrival of two squadrons from Borden. During World War II Trenton was a centre for The British Commonwealth Air Training Plan. A small museum was opened on 1st April 1984 to commemorate the sixtieth anniversary of the founding of the RCAF.

Ontario

A decade later to the day the new museum was opened in a former curling club. The superb displays trace the history of the service with models, photographs, uniforms, documents, components and memorabilia. In 1995 the museum obtained a Handley Page Halifax which was shot down over Lake Mjosa in Norway on 13th April 1945. The wreck was raised in September 1995 and transported to Canada. Restoration of this rare bomber soon started and significant progress has been made. Types flown by the Air Force in recent years are on show in an outside area close to the museum building.

TYPE	REG/SER	CON. NO.	PI/NOTES	STATUS
☐ Auster K AOP.6	'VF582'	2598	VP653, 16670, CF-LWK, C-FLWK	PVX
☐ Avro 652A Anson V				RAD
☐ Avro Canada C.100 Canuck 5 (CF-100)	18773	673	18773, A682	PV
☐ Avro Canada C.100 Canuck 5 (CF-100)	18774	674	18774, 100774	PV
☐ Beech C23-19 Musketeer (CT-134)	134213	M-1337	13413, 14213, A800	PV
☐ Bell 205 Iroquois (CUH-1H) (CH-118)	118101	3213		PV
☐ Bell 206A Kiowa (COH-58A) (CH-136)	136204	44004	71-20869	PV
☐ Bell 212 Twin Huey (CUH-1H) (CH-135)	135102	32002	(70-15651)	PV
☐ Boeing-Vertol 107-II-28 Labrador (CH-113A)	11315	4009	10415	PV
☐ Burgess-Dunne Seaplane (FSM)				PV
☐ Canadair CL-13A Sabre 5 [North American F-86E]	23257	1047		PV
☐ Canadair CL-13B Sabre 6 [North American F-86E]	23641	1431	In Community Gardens in town.	PV
☐ Canadair CL-28-2 Argus 2 (CP-107)	10732	23	20732, 10732, 783C	RAC
☐ Canadair CL-30 Silver Star 3 (CT-133) [Lockheed 580 (T-33AN)]	133190	T33-190	21190 – by base gate.	PV
☐ Canadair CL-30 Silver Star 3 (CT-133) [Lockheed 580 (T-33AN)]	133299	T33-299	21299	PV
☐ Canadair CL-30 Silver Star 3 (CT-133) [Lockheed 580 (T-33AN)]	21435	T33-435	21435, 133435	RA
☐ Canadair CL-41A Tutor (CT-114)	114015	1015	26015, CF-OUM-X, 114015, CF-OUM, 114015, A751, 751B	PV
☐ Canadair CL-219-1A10 Freedom Fighter (CF-116A) (CF-5A) [Northrop N-156A]	116721	1021		PV
☐ Canadair CL-219-1A10 Freedom Fighter (CF-116A) (CF-5A) [Northrop N-156A]	116739	1039	At Holiday Inn on Highway 401.	PV
☐ De Havilland DHC.1 Chipmunk T.10	WB550	C1/0002		PV
☐ Douglas DC-3A-456 Skytrain (C-47A) (Dakota III) (CC-129)	12963	12217	42-92419, FZ658, 992, 12963	PV
☐ Grumman G-103 Tracker (CS2F-2) (CP-121)	1545	DHC-44	1545, 12145, A728, 728B, C-FCUS	PV
☐ Handley Page HP.61 Halifax A.VIIA	NA337			PVC
☐ Hawker Hurricane IIB (FSM)	'V7287'			PVX
☐ Hawker P.1099 Hunter F.58	J-4029	41H/697396	In Swiss markings.	PV
☐ Lockheed 414-17-11 Hudson VI (A-28A)	FK466	414-6942	42-47022 – fuselage only.	PV
☐ Lockheed 382-15B Hercules (C-130E)	130314	382-4067	64-17633, 10314	PV
☐ Lockheed 583-04-15 Starfighter (CF-104D)	104646	583A-5316	12646, 104646, 844C	PV
☐ McDonnell M.36BA Voodoo (F-101B) (CF-101B)	101040	551	57-0373, 101040, 816B	PV
☐ McDonnell M.267B Hornet (CF-188B)	188911	97/B029		PV
☐ Mikoyan-Gurevich MiG-21MF	776	96002009	776 (DDR), 23+45	PV
☐ Noorduyn Harvard IIB [North American NA-77 (AT-16)]	3270	07-137		PV

NO.6 ROYAL CANADIAN AIR FORCE DUNNVILLE ASSOCIATION MUSEUM (ON46)

Address:	PO Box 232, Dunville, Ontario N1A 2X5.
Tel:	905-701-7225 Email: jayjay@becon.org
Admission:	June–August daily 1000-1700.
Location:	About 3 km south east of the town off Highway 11.

The airfield opened in November 1940 and until its closure in December 1944 many pilots were trained at the site. The unit was one of 28 schools set up under the British Commonwealth Training Plan. The field lapsed into dereliction and for a time was a turkey farm.

After over half a century without aerial activity a civil airport came into being in July 2000. The association has set up a museum tracing the history of the site with photographs, documents and items of memorabilia. A historical marker tracing the history of the field can be seen.

TYPE	REG/SER	CON. NO.	PI/NOTES	STATUS
☐ Avro 652A Anson I				PVC
☐ Canadian Car & Foundry Harvard 4 [North American NA-186]	'47'		With parts from a Harvard II.	PVX
☐ Canadian Car & Foundry Harvard 4 [North American NA-186]	C-FVIJ	CCF4-173	20382	PVA
☐ De Havilland DH.82C Tiger Moth	C-FDGC	DHC.1020	4830, CF-DGC	PVA
☐ Fleet 16B Finch II	C-GQWE	567	4708	PVA
☐ Grumman G-103 Tracker (CS2F-2) (CP-121)	C-FUCV	DHC-61	1562, 731B	PVC
☐ North American NA-64 Yale	C-FGIR	64-2186	3372	PVA
☐ North American NA-66 Harvard II	2766	66-2499	Outside town library.	PV

NORSEMAN HERITAGE PARK AND MUSEUM (ON47)

Address:	Box 131, Red Lake, Ontario P0V 2M0.
Tel:	807-717-2809
Admission:	Aircraft on permanent view – museum open during town office opening hours.
Location:	About 150 km north of Vermillion Bay on Highway 105.

Ontario

Red Lake has been a centre of bush flying for more than 80 years. The first pilot to fly from the area was Romeo Vachon in 1924. When gold was discovered prospectors flocked to the remote town. Jack Elliott began a service from Sioux Lookout to Red Lake using two Curtiss JN-4s in 1926. The JN-4 could not operate on floats and the service was short lived.

Patricia Airways, using a Curtiss Lark and later a Stinson Detroiter, were soon flying to Red Lake. At the current time several companies operate floatplanes from sites in the town. Six Norseman are based on the lake and every July a Norseman festival is held. In 1991 the town bought an example of the famous bush plane which flew from Red Lake for over 20 years. The aircraft had been in store since 1984 and it was restored to pristine condition.

On July 25th 1992 a park overlooking the lake opened with the Norseman as centrepiece. The setting is spectacular! Informative display boards tell the story of local flying and the development of the Norseman. A small museum is being set up in part of the municipal offices.

The Red Lake Regional Heritage Centre has displays tracing the history and development of the region with many interesting items on view.

TYPE	REG/SER	CON. NO.	PI/NOTES	STATUS
☐ Noorduyn Norseman VI (C-64A) (UC-64A)	CF-DRD	831	45-41747, NC75938	PV

ONTARIO SCIENCE CENTRE (ON48)

Address:	770 Don Mills Road, North York, Ontario M3C 1T3.
Tel:	416-696-1000 Email: webmaster@osc.on.ca
Admission:	Daily 1000-1700
Location:	In the northern suburbs of Toronto.

This superb 'hands-on' exhibition opened in September 1969. The displays cover all aspects of science and technology. New items are added regularly to show the latest developments in many fields.

The only aircraft on show is a Sopwith Pup replica faithfully built using the original drawings. There is a section of the display showing the principles of flight where a number of models can be seen.

TYPE	REG/SER	CON. NO.	PI/NOTES	STATUS
☐ Sopwith Pup (R)	'B1719'			PVX

PETERBOROUGH MONUMENT (ON49)

Location:	On permanent view in Riverside Park in the northern part of the town.

TYPE	REG/SER	CON. NO.	PI/NOTES	STATUS
☐ Canadair CL-13A Sabre 5 [North American F-86E]	'428'	1035	23245	PVX

ROBERT STUART AERONAUTICAL MUSEUM (ON50)

Address:	1000 Stevenson Road North, Oshawa, Ontario L1J 5P5.
Tel:	905-436-6325 Email: museum-chick@rogers.com
Admission:	April–October Saturday-Sunday 1130-1530.
Location:	At Oshawa Airport which is just north of the town.

Robert Stuart began collecting aeronautical material in the 1950s. He opened the collection in 1977 and it is now housed in two original huts used by 20 Elementary Flying Training School in World War II. Robert died in January 2003 and the collection is now maintained by his widow and daughter.

TYPE	REG/SER	CON. NO.	PI/NOTES	STATUS
☐ Canadair CL-13A Sabre 5 [North American F-86E]	23047	837	Nearby outside 420 Wing RCAFA.	PV

ROYAL MILITARY COLLEGE OF CANADA MUSEUM (ON51)

Address:	POBox 17000, Vimy Post Office, Kingston, Ontario K7K 7B4.
Tel:	613-541-6000 ext 6652 Fax: 613-542-3565 Email: mckenzie_r@rmc.ca
Admission:	Mid May-mid September daily 1000-1700.
Location:	Off Highway 2 east of the town.

Founded in 1876, the college trains officers for all branches of the service. From 1789 to 1853 there was a naval dockyard at the site. The museum is housed in a Martello Tower dating from 1846.

The displays trace the history of the college and the early military history of the area. The two aircraft are mounted in the grounds. The Kiowa and CF-116 and located at McNaughton Barracks which is a short distance from the museum.

TYPE	REG/SER	CON. NO.	PI/NOTES	STATUS
☐ Avro Canada C.100 Canuck 5 (CF-100)	'100752'	631	18731.	PVX
☐ Bell 206A Kiowa (COH-58A) (CH-136)	136257	44057	71-20922, 136257, 915C – at nearby barracks.	RA
☐ Canadair CL-13A Sabre 5 [North American F-86E]	23221	1011		PV
☐ Canadair CL-219-1A10 Freedom Fighter (CF-116A) (CF-5A) [Northrop N-156A]	116715	1015	116715, A855 – at nearby barracks.	RA

RUSSELL GROUP AVIATION (ON52)

Address:	12761 Sodom Road, Niagara Falls, Ontario L2E 6S6.
Tel:	905-295-2777 Email: info@russellgroupaviation.com
Admission:	By prior permission only.
Location:	About 6 miles south of the town just north of Highway 116.

This superb collection of airworthy warbirds is housed in a private hangar at Niagara South Airfield. The aircraft appear at shows in the area. The Bf 109 was recovered as a wreck from Russia in 1992. The fighter crashed in 1942 and spent half a century in the tundra. Brought back to England it was restored in an Essex workshop.

The Spitfire was obtained from the Historic Aircraft Collection in England.

TYPE	REG/SER	CON. NO.	PI/NOTES	STATUS
☐ Hawker Hurricane XII	'P2970'	60372	5481 (Canada), G-ORGI, N678DP, C-FDNL	PVAX
☐ Messerschmitt Bf 109E-7 (E-1)	CF-EML	3579	CK+CT, NX81562	PVA
☐ Noorduyn Harvard IIB [North American NA-77 (AT-16] (Sk 16A)	C-GFLR	14-726	42-12479, FE992, Fv16047, LN-MAA, G-BDAM	PVA
☐ Supermarine 361 Spitfire LF.IXc	CF-FLC	CBAF-1875	MK912, B-1, H-119, H-59 (Netherlands), SM-29 (Belgium), G-BRRA	PVA
Supermarine 361 Spitfire LF.IXc (FSM)	'MH415'		BAPC.209, 'MJ751'	PVX

SARNIA MONUMENT (ON53)

Location:	On permanent view in Germain Park in London Road in the centre of the town.

TYPE	REG/SER	CON. NO.	PI/NOTES	STATUS
☐ Canadair CL-13A Sabre 5 [North American F-86E]			23163 – possible identity.	PVX

SAUBLE BEACH MONUMENT (ON54)

Location:	On permanent view in the town.

TYPE	REG/SER	CON. NO.	PI/NOTES	STATUS
☐ Homebuilt Monoplane				PV

SHIRLEY'S BAY MONUMENT (ON55)

Location:	By prior permission only at a military training camp in the town.

TYPE	REG/SER	CON. NO.	PI/NOTES	STATUS
☐ Canadair CL-219-1A17 Freedom Fighter (CF-116D) (CF-5D) [Northrop N-156B]	116834	2034		RA
☐ Canadair CL-30 Silver Star 3 (CT-133) [Lockheed 580 (T-33AN)]	133606	T33-606	21606	RA

SIOUX LOOKOUT MONUMENT (ON56)

Location:	On permanent view outside a bar at 12 First Avenue in the centre of the town.

TYPE	REG/SER	CON. NO.	PI/NOTES	STATUS
☐ Republic RC-3 Seabee	CF-FSG	919	(NC6642K)	PV

SMITHS FALLS MONUMENT (ON57)

Location:	On permanent view in Victoria Park off Highway 15 in the town.

TYPE	REG/SER	CON. NO.	PI/NOTES	STATUS
☐ Canadian Car & Foundry Harvard 4 [North American NA-186]	'443'			PVX

SNOWBIRDS TRIBUTE (ON58)

Address:	Norwood, Ontario K0L 2V0.
Admission:	On permanent view when completed.
Location:	West of the town north of Highway 7.

The Snowbirds aerobatic team was formed at Moose Jaw in 1971 with Canadair Tutors. They delighted audiences around the country with their spectacular displays. The plan is to provide a reminder of the team with the aircraft spectacularly mounted in a typical formation. Display boards will trace the history of the unit.

TYPE	REG/SER	CON. NO.	PI/NOTES	STATUS
☐ Canadair CL-41A Tutor (CT-114)	114024	1024	26024 – with tail from c/n 1070 26070, 114070	PV
☐ Canadair CL-41A Tutor (CT-114)	114070	1070	26070 – with tail from c/n 1067 26067, 114067.	PV
☐ Canadair CL-41A Tutor (CT-114)	114100	1100	26100	PV
☐ Canadair CL-41A Tutor (CT-114)	114101	1101	26101	PV
☐ Canadair CL-41A Tutor (CT-114)	114160	1160	26160 – with tail from c/n 1099 26099, 114099	PV
☐ Canadair CL-41A Tutor (CT-114)	114162	1162	26162 – with tail from c/n 1052 26052, 114052.	PV
☐ Canadair CL-41A Tutor (CT-114)	114167	1167	26167	PV
☐ Canadair CL-41A Tutor (CT-114)	114187	1187	26187 – with tail from c/n 1063 26063, 114063.	PV

Ontario

SWORDS AND PLOUGHSHARES MUSEUM (ON59)

Address:	7500 Reeve Craig North, RR 1, Kars, Ontario K0A 2E0.
Tel:	613-489-3447 Fax: 613-489-1166 Email: swords@calnan.com
Admission:	Mid-May–mid October Sunday 0900-1630 or by appointment.
Location:	At

This privately run museum of militaria has on show a range of vehicles and weapons. Peaceful artefacts are also in the collection. The only aircraft is the former United States military Iroquois.

TYPE	REG/SER	CON. NO.	PI/NOTES	STATUS
☐ Bell 204 Iroquois (UH-1B)	63-8504	726		PV

TIGER BOYS COLLECTION (ON60)

Address:	325 River Road, Kitchener, Ontario N2B 2H2.
Tel:	519-836-6551 Email: tom_bob_tigerboys@hotmail.com
Admission:	By prior permission only.
Location:	At Guelph Air park which is about 8 km north east of the town on Route 7.

The collection was started by Tom Dietrich and the late Frank Evans at this delightful grass airfield which houses many vintage and classic aircraft. The group has two hangars which also serve as workshops. In addition to the aircraft there is a collection of models, airshow posters and photographs.

The Corben Baby Ace is the oldest homebuilt still flying in Canada and first took to the air in the mid-1950s. The Moth was in the initial batch constructed by the Moth Corporation at Lowell in Massachusetts in 1928/9. The Taylor Cub, was the second of its type to be imported into Canada when it was delivered in 1935. In the mid-1950s the Wiltshire School of Flying converted 18 Tiger Moths into four seat cabin versions. Another was modified by Rollason Aircraft at Croydon. Only a few survive and a number have been returned to Tiger Moth standard. The Jackaroo in the collection was initially used by Airspray (Colchester) at Boxted in England in the late 1950s and arrived in Canada in 1971.

The Hurricane is a long-term project and parts are still being sought. One Yale is being rebuilt to static condition and will be displayed outside the hangar. Other projects are underway.

TYPE	REG/SER	CON. NO.	PI/NOTES	STATUS
☐ Aeronca C-3				RA
☐ Aeronca C-3				RA
☐ American Flea Triplane	N5748N			RA
☐ Avro 652A Anson II				RA
☐ Corben C-1 Baby Ace	CF-RAC	4-3856	Register quotes c/n 4-3858.	RAA
☐ Curtiss JN-4 Canuck				RA
☐ De Havilland DH.60G Gipsy Moth	NC373H	1-L		RAC
☐ De Havilland DH.60GM Moth				RA
☐ De Havilland DH.82C Tiger Moth	C-GMTH	DHC.981	5806	RAA
☐ De Havilland DH.82C Tiger Moth	CF-TBS	DHC.1073	4882, CF-DGD	RAA
☐ De Havilland DH.82C Tiger Moth		DHC.1185	5882	RAC
☐ De Havilland DH.82C Tiger Moth	CF-CTN	DHC.1187	5884	RAC
☐ Fairchild M-62A-4 Cornell II				RAC
☐ Fairchild M-62A-4 Cornell II	CF-ILA	FC.110	10609	RAC
☐ Fairchild M-62A-4 Cornell II	CF-ECI	FC.188	10687	RAC
☐ Fleet 16B Finch II	CF-GER	399	4495, A436	RAA
☐ Hawker Hurricane X			5625	RAC
☐ Hickman Biplane				RA
☐ Long Longster III				RA
☐ Marquette Racer				RA
☐ McKinnon Flying Boat				RA
☐ North American NA-64 Yale	3409	64-2158		RA
☐ North American NA-64 Yale	3416	64-2169		RAC
☐ Pietenpol B4-A Aircamper				RA
☐ Sindlinger HH-1 Hurricane	C-GWPN	1015		RAA
☐ Taylor E-2 Cub	CF-ANT	256		RAA
☐ Taylor J-2 Cub				RAC
☐ Taylor-Young A				RA
☐ Thruxton Jackaroo (De Havilland DH.82C Tiger Moth)	C-FPHZ	82168	N6924, G-APHZ, CF-QOT	RAA

VAUGHAN MONUMENT (ON61)

Location:	On permanent view in a shopping mall on Rutherford Road in the western part of the town.

TYPE	REG/SER	CON. NO.	PI/NOTES	STATUS
☐ De Havilland DHC.2 Beaver (L-20A) (U-6A)	C-GVGL	891	54-1736	PV

ZURAKOWSKI PARK AND MUSEUM (ON62)

Address:	Box 1000, 85 Bay Street, Barry's Bay, Ontario K0J 1B0.
Tel:	613-756-2747 Email: bhildebrandt@sympatico.ca
Admission:	In summer months.
Location:	In the town which is at the junction of Highways 60 and 62.

Janusz Zurakowski was born in Poland and joined the Polish Air Force in 1934. He escaped to England in 1940 and served in the Royal Air Force, flying amongst others Spitfires. At the end of the conflict he took up test flying duties and flew several prototypes with the Gloster company. His displays were one of the highlights of Farnborough shows.

He moved to Canada and carried out similar work with Avro Canada. On 25th March 1958 he made the first flight in the CF-105 Arrow prototype. He died in February 2004 in the town which had become his home. A memorial has been erected and funds are being raised to construct a museum honouring his life. His family has his collection of personal items and these will be put on show. The small visitor centre has a few exhibits. There are models of his eight favourite types. These are the Wrona, the R.W.D.8, the P.Z.L. 11c, the Spitfire, the Martin-Baker MB.5, the Meteor F.8, the CF-100 and CF-105 Arrow.

TYPE	REG/SER	CON. NO.	PI/NOTES	STATUS
☐ Avro Canada C.105 Arrow (CF-105) (Scale R)				PV

PRINCE EDWARD ISLAND

HERITAGE AIRCRAFT SOCIETY (PEI1)

Address: 173 Victoria Road, Summerside, Prince Edward Island C1N 2G8.
Tel: 902-436-9145
Admission: On permanent view.
Location: About 8 km north west of the town off Highway 2.

Summerside was an important military airfield for many years housing maritime squadrons – Lancasters, Neptunes and Trackers were among the types flown from the site. It closed in the early 1990s and the three preserved aircraft are now looked after by the society. The Argus was operated from Summerside for more than three decades. The Tracker joined the display in September 1987 to commemorate three decades years of service by the type. The Voodoo was never flown operationally from Summerside. The one on show was allocated to the base for training just before the military moved out.

TYPE	REG/SER	CON. NO.	PI/NOTES	STATUS
☐ Canadair CL-28-2 Argus 2 (CP-107)	10739	30	20739, 10739, 749C	PV
☐ Grumman G-103 Tracker (CS2F-1) (CP-121)	'121131'	DHC-30	1531, 707B	PVX
☐ McDonnell M.36BA Voodoo (F-101B) (CF-101B)	101037	544	57-0366, 101037, 833B	PV

QUÉBEC

Québec

BROME COUNTY HISTORICAL SOCIETY MUSEUM (PQ1)

Address:	Paul Holland Knowlton Memorial Building, 130 Lakeside, Knowlton, Québec J0E 1V0.
Tel:	450-243-6782 **Email:** bchs@endirect.qc.ca
Admission:	mid-May–mid September Monday-Saturday 1000-1630 Sunday 1100-1630.
Location:	The town is about 80 km south east of Montreal on Highway 243.

The society was formed on 18th August 1897 to celebrate the centenary of the first land grant in Brome Township. In 1903 the Old Academy building was taken over for museum use. In 1921 Zelotes Martin funded the construction of an annexe to house a war museum. This building was opened by Sir Robert Borden on 26th August 1921. The old fire hall houses replicas of a general store, a blacksmith's shop, a post office and original farm implements. The centrepiece of the war museum is a Fokker D VII built in 1918 by the Albatros Works at Johannistal near Berlin. The aircraft came to Canada as a war prize and was obtained for the society by a local politician, Senator Foster. The biplane still retains the lozenge fabric applied in the factory and is the most original example of the type surviving. Around the walls are photos relating to the conflict.

TYPE	REG/SER	CON. NO.	PI/NOTES	STATUS
☐ Fokker D VII	6810/18			PV

CANADIAN AVIATION HERITAGE CENTRE (PQ2)

Address:	McGill University, MacDonald Campus, PO Box 64, 21111 Lakeshore, St Anne-de Bellevue, Québec H9X 3V9.
Tel:	514-398-7948 **Email:** info@cahc-ccpa.com
Admission:	By prior permission only.
Location:	In the south western suburbs of Montreal off Highway 20.

The group has its headquarters in the Old Stone Barn on the MacDonald Campus of McGill University. The building was formerly used by the agriculture faculty. The barn has been converted into workshops and several projects are underway.

Fairchild FC-2s served in the area in the inter-war period and the replica will be finished in the markings of one which was based at Grand Mère. The first FC-2s arrived in Canada in the summer of 1927 and were used on passenger services and for exploration in the remote parts of the country. Canadian Vickers based at Montreal built the type under licence. The Blériot replica will represent one which flew at the 1910 meeting in Montreal.

The Canuck based, on the Noury N-75, was developed by the Fleet company in the mid-1940s. Over 200 were eventually built but sales were slow owing to the vast numbers of cheap ex-military aircraft on the market.

The Bolingbroke arrived at the workshops in late 2007. The composite airframe was donated by the Fondation Aérovision Québec. Aircraft 10121 was delivered in 1943 and served as a training aircraft at a Bombing and Gunnery School in Maniitoba. In 1946 it was sold to a local farmer before joining the Canadian Museum of Flight. A collection of artefacts, models, photographs and paintings has been gathered.

TYPE	REG/SER	CON. NO.	PI/NOTES	STATUS
☐ Blériot XI (R)				RAC
☐ Bristol 149 Bolingbroke IVT	'9066'		Composite with main fuselage from 10121	RACX
☐ Fairchild FC-2(R)	'G-CAIH'			RACX
☐ Fleet 80 Canuck	CF-ENH	180		RA
☐ Stinson 10				RA

CANADIAN FORCES BASE MONTREAL MONUMENT (PQ3)

Location:	By prior permission only at St. Jean-sur-Richelieu Garrison in southern part of Montreal

TYPE	REG/SER	CON. NO.	PI/NOTES	STATUS
☐ Avro Canada C.100 Canuck 2T (CF-100)	'100104'	004	18104, A611	RAX
☐ Canadair CL-90 Starfighter (CF-104) [Lockheed 683-04-12]	12784	683A-1084	12784, 104784	RA

CANADIAN FORCES BASE VALCARTIER MONUMENT (PQ4)

Location:	By prior permission only at the site in the northern part of Québec City.

TYPE	REG/SER	CON. NO.	PI/NOTES	STATUS
☐ Bell 206A Kiowa (COH-58A) (CH-136)	136205	44005	71-20870	RA
☐ Canadair CL-13 Sabre 2 [North American F-86E]	'19318'			RAX

CANADIAN MUSEUM OF CIVILIZATION (PQ5)

Address:	100 Rue Laurier, Gatineau, Québec K1A 0M8.
Tel:	819-776-7000 **Fax:** 819-776-8300 **Email:** web@civilization.ca
Admission:	May–mid October Daily 0900-1800; mid October–April Daily 0900-1700.
Location:	About 1 km north east of Ottawa.

The museum focuses on the development of the Canadian people from early times to the modern day. The building also incorporates the Postal Museum and the Children's Museum.

The Bell 47 on show flew in several Canadian Provinces before being retired in 1973. It was then used as an instructional airframe at a college before joining the collection in 2001.

TYPE	REG/SER	CON. NO.	PI/NOTES	STATUS
☐ Bell 47D-1 (B-3)	CF-GWD	64	NC144B, N9391H, (N144B)	PV
☐ Cessna 172				PV

CENTRE D'INTERPRÉTATION DES PIONNIERS D'AVIATION (PQ6)

Address:	640 Rue Notre-Dame Sud, Sainte-Marie, Québec G6E 2W4.
Tel:	418-387-7221　　**Fax:** 418-386-2456　　**Email:** rlapointe@zonartpogz.ca
Admission:	May–mid October Monday-Friday 0900-1700 Saturday-Sunday 1000-1600.
Location:	About 30 km north of Ottawa off Highway 307.

The centre has collected material relating to the early days of flying in the region. On show are photographs, models and documents tracing these days. The pioneers are honoured in the interesting displays.

COLLECTION D'AIR MARCEL (PQ7)

Address:	2035 Dagenais Boulevard West, Suite 200, Laval, Québec H7L 5V1.
Tel:	450-963-4442　　**Email:** info@cf-cpa.ca
Admission:	By prior permission only.
Location:	At St. Hyacinthe Airport which is about 3km south west of the town.

Marcel Deschamps set up collection in 2004 with the aim of collecting, restoring and flying classic aircraft. A major project involves the Lodestar. The aircraft was destined for the Dutch East Indies Air Force in Java but was never delivered because of the Japanese invasion of the country. The Lockheed twin was diverted by the United States Government and delivered to the Army Air Corps who released it to Canadian Pacific Air Lines. It ran out of fuel and force landed near Weeks Lake in Québec whilst being operated by a survey company. Rocks were struck and the resulting fire resulted in damage to the airframe. Teams of volunteers made several journeys to the site to dismantle and recover the airframe.

A replica of a Pietenpol Aircamper has been completed. The 1930s homebuilt high wing monoplane has been a popular design over the years and many have been completed across North America. Two examples of the Kaydet are in the collection. Derived from the Stearman 70, the X75 flew in the late 1930s. The Boeing company acquired Stearman and over 10,000 were delivered to the United States and Allied Air Forces. The Nanchang CJ-6 was designed to replace the CJ-5, a licence-built Yakovlev Yak-18, in Chinese service. The prototype made its maiden flight in August 1958 and over 2,000 were completed. The type was used by a number of Air Forces in Asia and Africa.

TYPE	REG/SER	CON. NO.	PI/NOTES	STATUS
☐ Aeronca 7AC Champion	C-FZXL	7AC-5361	NC1794E, N1794E, CF-ZXL	RAA
☐ Beech B24R Sierra 200	C-GTKA	MC-289	N6506R	RAA
☐ Blériot XI (R)				RAC
☐ Boeing-Stearman A75N1 Kaydet (N2S-3)	CF-DGS	75-7875	Bu38254, N74667	RAA
☐ Boeing-Stearman A75N1 Kaydet ((PT-17)				RAC
☐ Lockheed 18-56A Lodestar (C-60) (18-50-23)	CF-CPA	18-2177	(LT-9-26) (Netherlands), 42-108787	RAC
☐ Nanchang CJ-6A	C-FXMI	1332012	(China), N51800	RAA
☐ Pietenpol B4-A Aircamper				RAA
☐ Piper J-3C-65 Cub	CF-CBU	21032	N2240M	RAA
☐ Temco GC-1B Swift	CF-GDS	2184	N78184	RAA

COLLEGE MILITAIRE ROYALE MONUMENT (PQ8)

Location:	By prior permission only at the site which is just east of the Forces Base in Montreal.

TYPE	REG/SER	CON. NO.	PI/NOTES	STATUS
☐ Avro Canada C.100 Canuck 5 (CF-100)	18746	646		RA

ÉCOLE NATIONALE D'AÉROTECHNIQUE (PQ9)

Address:	5555 De La Savane Place, St. Hubert, Québec, J3Y 8Y8.
Tel:	450-678-3560　　**Email:** dir.generale@college-em.qc.ca
Admission:	By prior permission only.
Location:	About 10 km east of Montreal off Highway 116.

The college, named after Édouard Montpetit, a well known local scientist, was set up in 1967. In the following year it amalgamated with the Dorval Aerotechnical Institute. The campus at St. Hubert was completed in 1972 and all aviation activities moved to the new site.

The complex includes hangars, workshops and sporting facilities. The large fleet of instructional airframes is housed in five hangars. One is used for the construction of homebuilt designs by students and another is allocated for structural repairs.

TYPE	REG/SER	CON. NO.	PI/NOTES	STATUS
☐ Aero Commander 680	C-FPED	408-84	N2003A, N375A, CF-PED	RA
☐ Aero Commander 680	C-FQLR	533-202	N6264D, N13L, CF-QLR	RA
☐ Aero Commander 680E	C-FASL	400-78	N4100S, N4100H, CF-UBM, CF-ASL	RA
☐ Aérospatiale AS.350D Ecureuil	C-GVYL	1062		RA
☐ Aérospatiale AS.350D Ecureuil				RA
☐ Beech C18S Expeditor 3T (C-45B)	CF-ZWY-X	5828	43-35478, HB109, CF-ZWY	RA
☐ Beech 65-90 King Air	C-FUFW	LJ-84	I-SNAT, D-IKOR, N619GS	RA
☐ Bell 47G	'C-XEXA'			RAX
☐ Bell 206B-2 Jet Ranger	C-GUXA	2036	N9961K	RA
☐ Bell 206B-2 Jet Ranger				RA
☐ Bell 206L-1 Long Ranger				RA
☐ Bombardier CRJ200			Major fuselage sections.	RA
☐ Canadair CL-601-3A Challenger	C-GQBQ	5051	C-GLXM, N1903G, N190GG, N300KC, N190SB	RA

Québec

☐ Cessna 150H	C-GACZ	15068585	N22880	RA
☐ Cessna 170B	C-FNNY	25733	N8039A, CF-NNY	RA
☐ Cessna 172I	C-FOSJ	17256637	(N8437L), CF-OSJ	RA
☐ Cessna 172N	C-GQIT	17268584	(N733VN)	RA
☐ Cessna T337B Super Skymaster	C-FVSY	3370703	(N2403S), CF-VSY	RA
☐ Convair 580 (440-77)	C-GDBX	312/103	N8424H, N1000, N1111, N109G, N1092, N73157	RA
☐ Eurocopter EC.120B Colibri	C-GLSP	1061		RA
☐ Gates Learjet 36 (26)	'C-XPWC'	36-001	N26GL, C-GBRW – original c/n 26-001.	RAX
☐ Hughes 269C	C-FFKV	210094	N9663F, CF-FKV	RA
☐ Hughes 269C				RA
☐ Hughes 369HS	'C-XGNY'			RAX
☐ Piper PA-23-250 Aztec	C-GNMA	27-407	XB-KAG, N62525	RA
☐ Piper PA-23-250 Aztec F	C-GPJQ	27-7754021	N9739N	RA
☐ Piper PA-28-140 Cherokee	C-FUYG	28-24367	CF-UYG	RA
☐ Piper PA-31P Pressurised Navajo	C-GAFQ	31P-76	N7323L, N52MC	RA
☐ Piper PA-38-112 Tomahawk	C-FTMK	38-78A0534		RA
☐ Vans RV-6A	C-GENA	22904		RA

FONDATION AÉROVISION QUÉBEC (PQ10)

Address:	5430 Chemin de Chambly,, Saint Hubert, Québec J3Y 3P1.
Tel:	450-678-1720 **Fax:** 450-678-9198 **Email:** maq@aerovision.org
Admission:	Not yet open.
Location:	About 10 km east of Montreal off Highway 116.

Members of the organisation are working to set up a museum at St. Hubert airfield. Negotiations to obtain the use of three buildings soon to be vacated by the military are at an advanced stage.

The province has a rich aeronautical heritage but no general aviation museum within its boundaries. In 1992 the foundation acquired its first aircraft, a Dakota which had seen service with Trans Canada Airlines between 1945 and 1963. This is now stored at St. Hubert, along with a Catalina flown by the Provincial Government for fire-fighting duties.

Military types have joined the collection along with some airframes once used by the National Aerotechnical School at St. Hubert. The list includes some which are owned by members of the foundation as well as others which will join.

Long-term plans envisage the construction of a purpose-built museum which will trace the history of both military and civil aviation in the province.

TYPE	REG/SER	CON. NO.	PI/NOTES	STATUS
☐ Avro Canada C.100 Canuck 5 (CF-100)	100760	660	18760	RA
☐ Bede BD-5B				RA
☐ Bell 47G				RA
☐ Bell 204 Iroquois (UH-1B)	64-14094	1218	Tail boom from c/n 264 60-3618.	RA
☐ Bell 206A Kiowa (COH-58A) (CH-136)	136211	44011	71-20876	RA
☐ Bell 212 Twin Huey (CUH-1N) (CH-135)				RA
☐ Blériot XI (R)				RA
☐ Canadair CL-13 Sabre 2 [North American F-86E]	19118	18	19118, A593	RA
☐ Cessna 305A Bird Dog (L-19A) (O-1A) (CO-119)				RA
☐ Consolidated 28-5A Canso A	C-FPQK	CV 264	9830, CF-PQK	RA
☐ De Havilland DHC.1 Chipmunk 1B-2-S3 (CT-120)	C-FCXI	113-151	(CF-CXI), 18004, 151, CF-CXI, 151, 18004, (12004), CF-CXI	RAA
☐ Douglas DC-3A-456 Skytrain (C-47A) (Dakota III)	C-FDTD	12253	42-92451, FZ668, CF-TER, CF-DTD	RA
☐ Fairchild F-11-2 Husky (F-11-1)	C-FEIM	3	CF-EIM-X, CF-EIM	RAD
☐ Fairchild F-11-2 Husky (F-11-1)	CF-SAQ	8		RA
☐ Gazuit-Valladeau GV-1020				RA
☐ Grumman G-44 Widgeon				RA
☐ Howard 500 [Lockheed 237-27-01 Ventura (PV-1)]				RA
☐ Lockheed 580 Silver Star 1 (T-33A)	14678	580-5310	50-1274, 14678, 599B	RA
☐ Noorduyn Norseman V				RA
☐ Noorduyn Norseman V				RA
☐ Schweizer SGU.2-22				RA
☐ Sopwith Camel F.1 (Scale R)				RA
☐ Supermarine Spitfire (Scale R)				RA
☐ Vickers 757 Viscount	C-FTID	384	CF-TID, C-FTID-X	RA
☐ Wittman W.8 Tailwind				RA

FONDATION DU MÉMORIAL DES MILITAIRES (PQ11)

Address:	34 Rue du Mémorial, Lévis, Québec G6V 8Y1.
Tel:	418-838-4836
Admission:	Not yet open.
Location:	About 5 km south of Québec city off Blvd. Mgr. Ignace-Bourget.

Levis has been an important military site for many years. One of the three forts originally built to protect Québec City is located close to the military memorial. These vast concrete structures replaced earlier wooden ones which had been destroyed in battles.

The Foundation is raising funds for the construction of a museum on Camp Lauzon which was once the headquarters of the Royal Engineers. Archive material and memorabilia have been acquired. There is the potential for an excellent exhibition tracing the complex military history of the area.

The Voodoo is mounted at the entrance to the site and around the main field are several guns and vehicles.

TYPE	REG/SER	CON. NO.	PI/NOTES	STATUS
☐ McDonnell M.36BA Voodoo (F-101B) (CF-101B)	101015	477	57-0299	PV

HUNTINGDON MONUMENT (PQ12)

Location:	On permanent view in the town.

TYPE	REG/SER	CON. NO.	PI/NOTES	STATUS
☐ Lear Learstar (Lockheed 18-56-23 Lodestar (C-60A))	N153T	18-2234	42-32188, IM-21 (Cuba), CU-T45, 215 (Cuba), N75397, N770AC	PV

MIRABEL MONUMENT (PQ13)

Location:	On permanent view at the Bell factory in the town.

TYPE	REG/SER	CON. NO.	PI/NOTES	STATUS
☐ Bell 430	'C-BCHU'			PVX

MONUMENT DE SAINT ESPRIT (PQ14)

Location:	On permanent view in the town.

TYPE	REG/SER	CON. NO.	PI/NOTES	STATUS
☐ Lockheed 18-08A Lodestar	CF-SEQ	18-2246	N9949H, CF-TDD	PV

MUSÉE DE L'AVIATION DE LA BROUSSE (PQ15)

Address:	5460 Avenue Tour du Lac, Lac-à-la-Tortue, Québec G0X 1L0.
Tel:	819-538-6653
Admission:	June–August Tuesday-Sunday 1000-1600.
Location:	On the south side of the lake.

The displays trace the history of bush flying with particular emphasis on operations from the lake. On show are many personal items donated by local pilots.

In 1919 a local businessman persuaded the St. Maurice Forest Protective Association to acquire two Curtiss HS-2L flying boats and this was really the birth of bush flying. Over the years more and more companies were formed using a variety of types.

On show are photographs, models and documents showing the progress of this hazardous work. The parent company operates four floatplanes on passenger and freight charter work from its base on the lake.

TYPE	REG/SER	CON. NO.	PI/NOTES	STATUS
☐ Cessna U206B Super Skywagon	C-FVDG	U2060666	(N4966F), CF-VDG	RAA
☐ Cessna U206G Stationair 6	C-GYXE	U20603801		RAA
☐ De Havilland DHC.2 Beaver (L-20A) (U-6A)	C-GOER	514	52-6128, N99830, Bu150192	RAA
☐ De Havilland DHC.2 Beaver (L-20A) (U-6A)	C-FIDG	718	53-7910, N99872, CF-IDG	RAA

MUSÉE DE LA DÉFENSE AÉRIENNE (PQ16)

Address:	PO Box 567, Alouette, Québec G0V 1A0.
Tel:	418-677-7289 Fax: 418-677-4104 Email: museebagotville@forces.gc.ca
Admission:	Mid-June-September 0900-1700.
Location:	Alongside Highway 170 about 5 km south east of Chicoutimi near the gate of CFB Bagotville.

During World War II the Royal Canadian Air Force selected two sites in the region for the construction of airfields. Bagotville opened in July 1942 and closed in November 1944. Reactivated in July 1951, the field has played an important part in the defence of the country for almost 60 years with fighter units in residence. No 3 Wing currently has its headquarters at the field with two squadrons of CF-188 Hornets.

Plans for the museum were put forward in 1992 and the first exhibition opened five years later in a former chapel. In 2003 the display was redesigned and now presents a comprehensive picture of the history of Bagotville, the aerial defence of Canada and civilian flying in the area. On show are many photographs, models, uniforms and documents.

The outside commemorative park displays types which have served from and visited the airfield. The MiG-23 was presented to the collection by the Czech Republic in recognition of the help given to Czechoslovakia by Canada in World War II. The H-21 on show saved many lives in the mudslide at St. Jean Vianney in May 1971.

TYPE	REG/SER	CON. NO.	PI/NOTES	STATUS
☐ Avro Canada C.100 Canuck 5D (5) (CF-100)	'18437'	372	18472, 100472 – also carries '18741'	PV
☐ Bell 205 Iroquois (CUH-1H) (CH-118)	118106	3218	118106, 917C	RA
☐ Canadair CL-13B Sabre 6 [North American F-86E]	'19454'	1605	BB+275, KE+201, 01+03	PVX
☐ Canadair CL-30 Silver Star 3 (CT-133) [Lockheed 580 (T-33AN)]	133333	T33-333	21333	PV
☐ Canadair CL-41A Tutor (CT-114)	114014	1014	26014	PV
☐ Canadair CL-90 Starfighter (CF-104) [Lockheed 683-04-12]	104774	683A-1074	12774, 104774, A789	RAD
☐ Canadair CL-219-1A10 Freedom Fighter (CF-116A) (CF-5A) [Northrop N-156A]	116733	1033		PVX
☐ De Havilland DH.100 Vampire FB.5	NZ5774		WA411	RA
☐ McDonnell M.36BA Voodoo (F-101B) (CF-101B)	101027	519	57-0341	PV
☐ Mikoyan-Gurevich MiG-23ML	4857	0390324857	In Czech. markings.	PV
☐ Piasecki PD-22 Work Horse (H-21B) (CH-21B)	9642	B.123	54-4373, 9642,CF-JJP, 9642, CF-GQR, (N123HL) – possible identity.	PV

Québec

THETFORD MINES MONUMENT (PQ17)

Location:	On permanent view on Highway 112 in the centre of the town.

TYPE	REG/SER	CON. NO.	PI/NOTES	STATUS
☐ McDonnell M.36BA Voodoo (F-101B) (CF-101B)	101051	???	(USAF) 101051, 815B	PV

VAL D'OR MONUMENT (PQ18)

Location:	On permanent view in 7eme Rue in the centre of the town.

TYPE	REG/SER	CON. NO.	PI/NOTES	STATUS
☐ Canadair CL-30 Silver Star 3 (CT-133) [Lockheed 580 (T-33AN)]	21167	T33-167		PV

VINTAGE WINGS OF CANADA (PQ19)

Address:	1699 Rue Arthur Fecteau, Gatineau, Quebec J8R 2Z9.
Tel:	819-669-9603 Fax: 819-669-9608 Email: cleslie@vintagewings.ca
Admission:	By prior permission only.
Location:	At Gatineau Airport which is about 12 km north east of Ottawa off Highway 50.

The collection is housed in a new hangar at the airfield. The aim is to preserve a fleet of significant types in flying condition. During the summer regular flying days and open houses are held.

Among the highlights of the collection is a pair of Hurricanes. The XII was rebuilt over many years by Harry Wheeratt in Saskatchewan. The now rare IV served with the Royal Air Force and the Yugoslav military before moving to Israel. The airframe was found in a Kibbutz scrapyard near Jaffa in 1983 and brought back to Blackbushe in England. Acquired by the Fighter Collection, the Hurricane was restored at Duxford and Milden and flew again at Earls Colne in July 2003. It is painted in the markings of an aircraft of No 6 Squadron Royal Air Force which flew it in Italy in the tank-busting role.

The Swordfish is one of the batch parked on Ernie Simmonds farm near Tillsonburg in Ontario from 1946 until the auction in 1970. The biplane was acquired by Robert Spence and underwent a restoration lasting two decades before taking to the air again in 1992.

The Lysander, built in Canada, was delivered in 1942 and sold to a private owner in Calgary in 1972. Five years later it was purchased by Harry Whearatt and moved to his farm at Assiniboia in Saskatchewan. Restoration work was carried out and by 2007 the airframe was complete and painted in the yellow and black target tug scheme used by the RCAF. The Lysander was not flown in Saskatchewan and moved to Gatineau in the summer of 2007.

The Castle Bromwich-built Spitfire LF.XVIe has had an interesting history. In the late 1940s it beame the personal aircraft of Air Chief Marshal Sir James Robb and was normally kept at RAF Northolt. In 1954 the Spitfire was purchased by a Worthing garage owner and for a number of years it was displayed in a compound on the forecourt. From 1958 until 1965 it was on show at the Beaulieu Motor Museum. The aircraft moved to Chicago for a period before returning to England. In 1976 it moved to Arizona and from 1983 to 1990 was loaned to the San Diego Aerospace Museum. The fighter moved to the collection in 2001.

Examples of Canadian designs, such as the Beaver and Chipmunk, are also in the collection along with licence built types. Civilian aircraft feature with a Fox Moth, rebuilt in New Zealand, and a Waco ATO in the hangar.

TYPE	REG/SER	CON. NO.	PI/NOTES	STATUS
☐ Beech D17S (UC-43)	CF-GKY	4874	43-10826, N51444, CF-GKY, C-FGKY	RAA
☐ Bellanca 7GCBC Citabria	CF-BSY	387-82	N68548, CF-BSY, C-FBSY	RAA
☐ Canadair CL-13A Sabre 5 [North American F-86E]	C-GSBR	1104	23314 (Canada), CF-BKH, N8687D, '12897'	PVX
☐ Canadian Car & Foundry Harvard 4 [North American NA-186]	CF-ROA	CCF4-242	20451	RAA
☐ Curtiss 87V Warhawk (P-40N) (Warhawk IV)	C-FVWC/'FR350'	28589	42-104827, A29-414, ZK-VWC	RAA
☐ De Havilland DH.82C Tiger Moth	CF-IME	DHC.746	4947, A347, CF-IME, (C-FIME)	RAA
☐ De Havilland DH.82C Tiger Moth	CF-DHQ	DHC.1671	8869	RAA
☐ De Havilland DH.83 Fox Moth	C-FYPM	4033	CF-YPM – original c/n 4033 (G-ACAJ), G-ACDD, OO-ENC, G-ACDD, ZK-AEK, VQ-FAI, ZK-AEK – mainly new aircraft with some parts of original.	RAA
☐ De Havilland DHC.1 Chipmunk 1B-2-S5	CF-RRI	163-201	18025	RAA
☐ De Havilland DHC.2 Beaver	C-GXPM	1588	111 (Kenya), N5595S, 5Y-MMM	RAA
☐ Fairchild M-62A-4 Cornell II	CF-YQR	FC.213	10712 (Canada), (C-FYAY), N226PT	RAC
☐ Fairey Swordfish II	C-GEVS	F/BS35270A	HS554	RAA
☐ Hawker Hurricane IV	CF-TPM/KZ321		KZ321, (Yugoslavia), (Israel), G-HURY	RAA
☐ Hawker Hurricane XII	C-GGAJ	46002	5447	RAA
☐ North American NA-122 Mustang (P-51D) (Mustang IV)	CF-VPM/'KH661'	122-39922	44-73463, 9575 (Canada)- composite with parts from N1335, N6175C, N5478V, N351D	RAAX
☐ Supermarine 361 Spitfire HF.IX	TE294		TE294, 5519 (South Africa) – Less wings.	RAC
☐ Supermarine 361 Spitfire LF.XVIe	C-GVZB	CBAF-IX-4756	SL721, N8R, G-BAUP, N8WK, N721WK	RAA
☐ Supermarine 379 Spitfire F.XIV	RM873	6S.432296	Bu92106, N6897, N106FG	RAC
☐ Vought FG-1D Corsair	C-GVWC/ 'KD658'	3367	NC8531, N8531	RAAX
☐ Waco ATO	CF-BPM	A-65	2365 – composite using parts from four other aircraft.	RAA
☐ Westland Lysander IIIA	C-FVZZ/'416'	1206		RAAX

SASKATCHEWAN

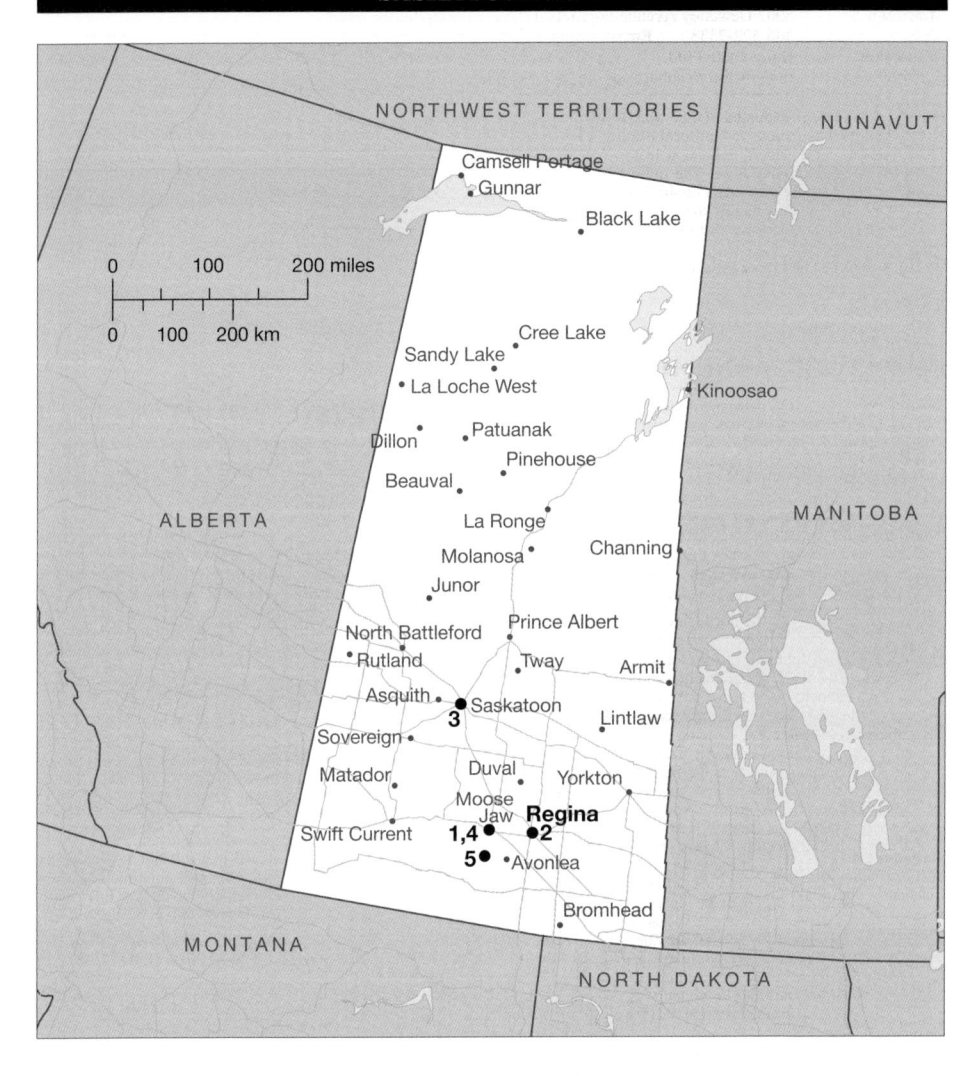

15 WING MILITARY AVIATION MUSEUM (SK1)

Address:	15 Wing, PO Box 5000, Moose Jaw, Saskatchewan S6H 7Z8.
Tel:	306-694-2825 **Fax:** 306-694-2813 **Email:** noel.jr@forces.gc.ca
Admission:	By prior permission only.
Location:	The base is south of the town off Highway 2.

This important training base is home to 'The Snowbirds' aerobatic team. A collection of memorabilia was gathered over the years and a small base museum has been set up. The three preserved aircraft represent types which have flown from the field. The site opened in 1928 and was taken over by the military in 1940.

TYPE	REG/SER	CON. NO.	PI/NOTES	STATUS
☐ Canadair CL-30 Silver Star 3 (CT-133) [Lockheed 580 (T-33AN)]	21297	T33-297		RA
☐ Canadair CL-41A Tutor (CT-114)	114036	1036	26036	RA
☐ Canadian Car & Foundry Harvard 4 [North American NA-186]	20456	CCF4-247		RA

Saskatchewan

ROYAL CANADIAN MOUNTED POLICE HERITAGE CENTRE (SK2)

Address:	5907 Dewdney Avenue, Regina, Saskatchewan S4T 0P4.
Tel:	306-522-7333 Email: info@rcmphc.com
Admission:	Daily 1000-1700.
Location:	In the western suburbs of the town off Highway 6.

The Royal Canadian Mounted Police was formed on 30th August 1873 and its famous red uniform is known throughout the world. The force started collecting historical material in 1933 at its Regina training base. The museum building was opened by Her Majesty the Queen on 4th July 1973 when she visited the town to commemorate the centenary of the force. The history and development of the RCMP is portrayed in detail in a series of imaginative displays. Members of the force have served abroad and there are sections devoted to the Boer and the two World Wars. Aircraft have played an important role in police work in recent years. In 1931/2 the force used a Bellanca of Canadian Airways to search for Albert Johnson (The Mad Trapper) and the following years borrowed RCAF machines to help prevent smuggling and rum running. An Air Division was formed in 1937 with the purchase of four de Havilland Dragonfly biplanes. A large new Heritage Centre with improved displays tracing the history and traditions of the service opened in May 2007.

TYPE	REG/SER	CON. NO.	PI/NOTES	STATUS
☐ Beech D18S	CF-MPH	A-141		PV
☐ De Havilland DHC.3 Otter	CF-MPW	271	Cockpit section only.	RA

SASKATOON MONUMENT (SK3)

Location:	On permanent view at RCAFA branch near the airport in the northern part of the town.

TYPE	REG/SER	CON. NO.	PI/NOTES	STATUS
☐ Canadair CL-30 Silver Star 3 (CT-133) [Lockheed 580 (T-33AN)]	21630	T33-630	May be c/n T33-633 21633.	PV

WESTERN DEVELOPMENT MUSEUM (SK4)

Address:	Box 185, 50 Diefenbaker Drive, Moose Jaw, Saskatchewan S6H 4N8.
Tel:	306-693-5989 Fax: 306-691-0511 Email: moosejaw@wdm.ca
Admission:	Daily 0900-1700. Closed Monday January-March.
Location:	On the north side of the city close to of Highway 2 and the Trans-Canada Highway.

The museum has exhibitions at four locations in the province and many aspects of life in Saskatchewan are portrayed. The Moose Jaw branch, which opened in 1976, houses the transport collection. There are impressive displays of cars, boats and railway equipment.

The British Commonwealth Air Training Plan had many bases in the area and a replica of the front of a typical hangar has been built with examples of aircraft in the famous yellow scheme parked nearby. A dedicated team of volunteers has rebuilt many types for the display. They are currently working on a Cornell having recently taken over six years to restore an Anson which was used at the local military base in 1940. The workshop is located in a replica of the Western Aeroplane Company hangar built at Moose Jaw in 1920.

Two early gliders on show are the Mead constructed by the North Battleford club in 1927/9 and the Zögling. The partially built Zögling was acquired by Norman Eley in 1932 and he stored it for five years before completing and flying it in 1938. In the late 1980s Norman, his two brothers and his son restored the glider and it flew for the last time on 19th April 1991 with Norman at the controls.

A rarity is the Pheasant H-10 which was designed by Orville Hickman in 1927. Memphis, Missouri in 1927. Lee Briggs, who operated a flying school in Memphis, Missouri, built 11 for use by his pupils and later set up the Pheasant company. He was killed in a crash whilst testing the biplane for type approval. Steve Wittman became test pilot for the company and a company reoranisation and take over resulted in a move to Fond du Lac in Wisconsin. Only 41 were completed at both locations before the onset of the depression. Originally bought by Cherry Airways, it is the oldest aircraft in Saskatchewan.

The Gipsy Moth was imported into Canada in 1929 and used by Canadian Pacific Railways. The Norseman on view was one of the first aircraft bought by the Saskatchewan Air Ambulance Service and was bought in 1946. The Cessna 195 was also used on ambulance duties. The Humming Bird replica was built in Calgary, Alberta in 1963 and flew several times. The de Havilland company built the Humming Bird for the 1923 Daily Mail Trials at Lympne in Kent. Powered by troublesome 750 cc Douglas motor cycle engines, the two prototypes failed to win any prizes. A total of 15 were built and the first one survives at the Shuttleworth Collection at Old Warden. The replica on show was built by Stan Greene in Calgary in 1967 and was powered by a 40 hp Continental engine. An addition to the display honours 'The Snowbirds' aerobatic team which is based at the nearby military airfield. The history of Canadian aerobatic teams is told.

TYPE	REG/SER	CON. NO.	PI/NOTES	STATUS
☐ Aeronca K	CF-BIN	K-280		PV
☐ American Aerolights Eagle	C-IATH	TC 012008		PV
☐ Avro 652A Anson I	R9725		Possible identity – composite.	PV
☐ Beech C23 Sundowner (CT-134A) (Musketeer II)	134230	M-2317	On loan from CFB Moose Jaw, SK.	PV
☐ Bensen B-8 Gyroglider				PV
☐ Canadair CL-30 Silver Star 3 (CT-133) [Lockheed 580 (T-33AN)]	'133275'	T33-401	21401	PVX
☐ Canadair CL-41A Tutor (CT-114)	114021	1021	26021, 114021, 779B – on loan from CFB Moose Jaw, SK.	PV
☐ Canadian Car & Foundry Harvard 4 [North American NA-186]	20475	CCF4-266	20475, C-GYYO	PV
☐ Cessna 195	CF-KIY	7628		PV
☐ Cessna T-50 Crane 1	7829	1272	With parts of c/n 1245 7802	PV
☐ De Havilland DH.53 Humming Bird (R)	CF-OVE	DH6063		PV
☐ De Havilland DH.60M Moth	CF-ADI	781		PV

☐ De Havilland DH.82C Tiger Moth	C-GYGU	DHC.1646	3985, CF-BZG	PV
☐ Fairchild M-62A-4 Cornell II				PVC
☐ Funk B-85C	CF-HAR	311	N81181	PVC
☐ Jodel D.9 Bébé	CF-PFB	1		PV
☐ Müller Stingray Hang Glider				PV
☐ Noorduyn Norseman V	CF-SAM	N29-27		PV
☐ Pheasant H-10	G-CASR	121	NC5411	PV
☐ Rogallo Standard Hang Glider				PV
☐ Stamer-Lippisch Z-12 Zögling				PV
☐ Stinson 108-1 Voyager	CF-SFF			PV
☐ Vickers Vedette V			Being rebuilt using some original parts.	PVC
☐ Weber C3 Mead Glider				PV

WHEREATT'S WARBIRDS (SK5)

Address: PO Box 31, Assiniboia, Saskatchewan S0H 0B0.
Tel: 306-642-3147
Admission: By prior permission only.
Location: About 5 km north of the town on the west side of the airport which is 3 km east of Route 2.

Harry Whereatt has been collecting aircraft for many years. Just 100 Fleet Fort trainers were delivered to the RCAF during World War II but the type was not a success and saw only limited use. Several types have left the Assiniboia in recent years and joined other museums and collections in Canada.

TYPE	REG/SER	CON. NO.	PI/NOTES	STATUS
☐ Avro 652A Anson II				RAD
☐ Avro 652A Anson II				RAD
☐ Avro 652A Anson V				RAD
☐ Avro 652A Anson V				RAD
☐ Bristol 149 Bolingbroke IVT	9911			RAD
☐ Canadair CL-30 Silver Star 3 (CT-133) [Lockheed 580 (T-33AN)]	133072	T33-072	21072, 862B	RA
☐ Cessna T-50 Bobcat (C-78) (UC-78)	C-FHAO	3838	42-58437, CF-HAO – fuselage frame only.	RAD
☐ Cessna T-50 Crane 1				RAD
☐ De Havilland DH.60M Moth	CF-CFU	DHC.111	155, CF-CFU, A106	RA
☐ De Havilland DH.82C Tiger Moth	C-FCOF	DHC.1265	5962, CF-COF	RA
☐ Fairchild M-62A-4 Cornell (PT-26B) (Cornell II)	FZ290		43-36340, FZ290, 10843 (Canada)	RAD
☐ Fleet 60K Fort				RA
☐ Fleet 60K Fort	3642	682		RA
☐ North American NA-64 Yale	3414	64-3040		RA
☐ Stinson SR-7A Reliant	CF-AUS	8700		RA
☐ Westland Lysander IIIA	2367	1209	May be 2366.	RA

YUKON

YUKON TRANSPORTATION MUSEUM (YU1)

Address: 30 Electra Crescent, Whitehorse, Yukon Y1A 6E6.
Tel: 867-668-4792 **Fax:** 867-633-5547 **Email:** info@goytm.ca
Admission: Mid May–August daily 1000-1800.
Location: On the Alaska Highway next to the airport which is just south west of the town.

Opened in July 1990, the museum traces the development of all forms of transport in the region. Early native travel, bush planes, river boats, the Alaska Highway and the White Pass and Yukon Railway are all featured.

A replica of the Ryan B-1 'Queen of the Yukon' is on show in the museum. The original was bought by Yukon Airways and Exploration Company in 1927. The B-1 was the first commercial aircraft in the Yukon. The delivery flight left San Diego on 8th July 1927 and the aircraft finally arrived at Whitehorse on 26th October 1927. The Ryan was completely wrecked in a landing at Whitehorse on 5th May 1928. The replica was built for exhibition in the Yukon Pavilion at Expo'86 held at Vancouver.

Mounted on a pylon near the airport and billed as the 'World's Largest Weathervane' is a DC-3. The aircraft was bought by Canadian Pacific Airlines in 1946 and served in the Yukon before being withdrawn in 1970. Now in original CPA colours it took up its present position in 1981.

The museum has recovered the wreck of a Fairchild FC-2W2. The aircraft was used by Northern Airways for many years and then by private owners. Whilst operating on floats it struck a submerged object on take off at Jervis Inlet in British Columbia on 27th June 1963. The high wing monoplane, a type which made a significant contribution to bush flying, is being rebuilt.

Also being restored is another former Northern Airways aircraft. The Waco AQC-6 was damaged by fire at Carcross in the Yukon Territory in October 1949. The wreck languished at the site for many years. The amateur-built Smith DSA-1 flew in the region for several years.

TYPE	REG/SER	CON. NO.	PI/NOTES	STATUS
☐ Douglas DC-3A-456 Skytrain (C-47A)	CF-CPY	4666	41-18541	PV
☐ Fairchild FC-2W2	CF-BXF	523	NC8036	PVC
☐ Ryan B-1 Brougham (R)	'G-CAHR'			PVX
☐ Smith DSA-1 Miniplane	CF-RKN	PH-1		PV
☐ Waco AQC-6 (ZQC-6)	CF-BDZ	5000		RAC

INDEX

All aircraft are listed alphabetically by manufacture or designer (in the case of some gliders and homebuilt aircraft) followed by the type. Each province is denoted by the standard two or three letter code and each museum/collection by a number e.g. ON10 – the tenth museum/collection in alphabetical order in Ontario.

Province codes are as follows:
AB Alberta; **BC** British Columbia; **MB** Manitoba; **NB** New Brunswick; **NF** Newfoundland and Labrador; **NW** Northwest Territories; **NS** Nova Scotia; **ON** Ontario; **PEI** Prince Edward Island; **PQ** Quebec; **SK** Saskatchewan; **YU** Yukon.

Advanced Aviation Buccaneer SX	ON8	Avro Canada C.100 Canuck 5C (5) (CF-100)	AB4
Aerial Experiment Association Silver Dart (R)	AB3, 22, NS2, ON2, 8, 11	Avro Canada C.100 Canuck 5D (4B) (5) (5C) (CF-100)	ON3
Aero Commander 680	PQ9	Avro Canada C.100 Canuck 5D (5) (CF-100)	AB9, BC8, NS2, ON8, 14, 20, PQ16
Aero Commander 680E	PQ9	Avro Canada C.100 Canuck 5M (5) (CF-100)	ON14
Aero Commander 680V	NB6, NF3	Avro Canada C.102 Jetliner	ON8
Aero Commander 680V (680T)	BC4, 11	Avro Canada C.105 Arrow (CF-105)	ON8
Aero 1121 Jet Commander	BC4	Avro Canada C.105 Arrow (CF-105) (FSM)	AB22, ON9
Aeronca C-2	ON8	Avro Canada C.105 Arrow (CF-105) (Scale R)	AB2, ON44, 62
Aeronca C-3	AB22, NS2, ON60	Barkley-Grow T8P-1	AB3, 4, 22
Aeronca K	SK4	Bayjo Glider [Hall Cherokee II]	AB3
Aeronca 65LA	AB22	Bede BD-5B	PQ10
Aeronca 65TC Grasshopper (O-58B) (L-3B)	AB22	Beech D17S	AB22
Aeronca 7AC Champion	ON31, PQ7	Beech D17S (UC-43)	PQ19
Aeronca 7DC Champion (7AC)	ON11	Beech C18S Expeditor 3 (C-45F) (UC-45F)	AB22
Aeronca 11CC Super Chief	NS2, ON11	Beech C18S Expeditor 3T (C-45B)	PQ9
Aérospatiale AS.332 Super Puma	NF3	Beech C18S Expeditor 3T (C-45F) (UC-45F)	ON11
Aérospatiale AS.350B Ecureuil	ON21	Beech D18S	AB3, 4, 6, NF3, ON10, 20, SK2
Aérospatiale AS.350D Ecureuil	BC11, PQ9	Beech D18S Expeditor (C-45H)	AB22, ON11
Aerosport Scamp 1	NS2	Beech D18S Expeditor 3N	MB1, ON10
Airspeed AS.10 Oxford I	AB6	Beech D18S Expeditor 3NM	AB3, 4, 6, MB7, 12, NF10, ON11, 37, 44
Airspeed AS.10 Oxford II	AB22		
Albatros D Va (R)	ON18		
Allgemeine Electrizitats Gesellschaft G IV	ON8		
American Aerolights Eagle	SK4	Beech D18S Expeditor 3NMT (3N)	BC6, MB12
American Eagle A-101 (A-1)	AB22	Beech D18S Expeditor 3TM	MB1, 7, 11, ON30
American Flea Triplane	ON60	Beech E18S	MB9, ON22
Apco Aviation Astra 29	ON8	Beech C23 Sundowner (CT-134A) (Musketeer II)	AB9, 10, 22, MB4, 7, 9, 12, ON21, SK4
Arrow Sport F	AB22		
Auster K AOP.6	AB3, 22, BC2, MB12, ON8, 10, 20, 45	Beech C23-19 Musketeer (CT-134)	AB10, MB1, 11, ON6, 9, 15, 39, 44, 45
Auster Q T.7	AB3		
Avro 504K	ON3, 8	Beech B24R Sierra 200	PQ7
Avro 594 Avian (R)	AB13	Beech 35 Bonanza	AB22
Avro 616 Avian IVM	AB22, ON8	Beech 65-90 King Air	MB10, PQ9
Avro 652A Anson I	AB22, MB1, ON46, SK4	Beech 65-A90 King Air	BC11
		Beech B90 King Air	AB5
Avro 652A Anson II	AB4, 6, 22, BC2, 6, MB1, 12, NS4, ON44, 60, SK5	Beech 95-B55 Baron	ON23, 25
		Beech 100 King Air	BC12, ON22
Avro 652A Anson V	AB3, 10, 22, BC6, MB1, ON8, 20, 45, SK5	Beech A100 King Air	NF3, ON21
		Bell 26D Airacobra (P-39M)	AB22
		Bell 47	ON22
Avro 683 Lancaster 10(AR) (B.X)	NS4	Bell 47D-1	ON11
Avro 683 Lancaster 10(DC) (B.X)	ON8	Bell 47D-1 (B-3)	BC2, PQ5
Avro 683 Lancaster 10(MP) (B.X)	AB6	Bell 47G	PQ9
Avro 683 Lancaster 10(MR) (B.X)	AB3, ON8, 9, 20	Bell 47G 947D)	AB4
Avro 683 Lancaster 10P (B.X)	ON17	Bell 47G Sioux (HTL-6) (TH-13M)	ON8
Avro 683 Lancaster 10P(AR) (B.X)	NB3	Bell 47G-2	AB3
Avro 683 Lancaster B.I (FSM)	ON20	Bell 47G-2 (47D) (47D-1)	ON21
Avro 683 Lancaster B.10 (FSM)	AB6	Bell 47G-4	NF3, ON25
Avro 698 Vulcan B.2	NF8	Bell 47J-2	AB22, BC6, NS2
Avro 748 Series 2A/309LFD	AB5	Bell 204 Iroquois (HU-1B) (UH-1B)	MB9
Avro 748 Series 2B/378	SK3	Bell 204 Iroquois (UH-1B)	ON59, PQ10
Avro Canada Avrocar (R)	MB12	Bell 204 Iroquois (UH-1H)	MB10
Avro Canada C.100 Canuck 2T (CF-100)	ON44, PQ3	Bell 205 Iroquois (CUH-1H) (CH-118)	ON45, PQ16
Avro Canada C.100 Canuck 3D (3A) (CF-100)	AB3	Bell 205 Iroquois (UH-1H)	BC4
Avro Canada C.100 Canuck 3D (3B) (CF-100)	AB6, BC6	Bell 205A-1	BC11
Avro Canada C.100 Canuck 4 (CF-100)	ON10	Bell 206 Jet Ranger	AB20, BC4
Avro Canada C.100 Canuck 4A (4) (CF-100)	ON3	Bell 206A Jet Ranger	AB5, BC11, ON21
Avro Canada C.100 Canuck 5 (CF-100)	AB22, MB7, 12, NB1, 5, ON8, 36, 43, 45, 51, PQ8, 10	Bell 206A Kiowa (COH-58A) (CH-136)	AB7, MB7, NB1, ON9, 12, 15, 19, 20, 21, 25, 45, 51, PQ4, 10

Bell 206A Kiowa (OH-58A)	ON15, 25
Bell 206B Jet Ranger	AB5, BC12, NF3, NS2, ON22
Bell 206B-2 Jet Ranger	PQ9
Bell 206L-1 Long Ranger	PQ9
Bell 212 Twin Huey (CUH-1N) (CH-135)	MB12, ON8, 45, PQ10
Bell 430	PQ13
Bellanca CH-300 Pacemaker	ON8
Bellanca 31-55A Senior Skyrocket	AB22, MB12
Bellanca 66-75 Aircruiser	MB12
Bellanca 7GCBC Citabria	PQ19
Bennett Delta Wing Mariah 170 Hang Glider	BC6
Bensen B-8 Gyroglider	MB12, ON8, SK4
Bensen B-8M Gyrocopter	BC6
Bensen B-8MG Gyrocopter	ON8
Birdman Atlas XC-215	AB22
Birdman Enterprises MJ-5 Hang Glider	AB4
Blackburn Shark III	BC6
Blériot XI	ON8
Blériot XI (R)	PQ2, 7, 10
Boeing 247D (247)	ON8
Boeing 727-22QC	ON20
Boeing 727-25QC	MB10
Boeing 737-200	BC15
Boeing 737-275	AB4
Boeing 737-2E1F	NF3
Boeing 737-2H4	AB5, BC4
Boeing-Stearman A75N1 Kaydet (PT-17)	PQ7
Boeing-Stearman A75 Kaydet (PT-13B)	AB22
Boeing-Stearman A75N1 Kaydet (N2S-3)	PQ7
Boeing-Stearman A75N1 Kaydet (N2S-4)	AB22
Boeing-Stearman A75N1 Kaydet (PT-17)	ON17, 20
Boeing-Stearman B75N1 Kaydet (N2S-3)	MB1
Boeing-Stearman E75 Kaydet (PT-13D)	ON20
Boeing-Stearman E75 Kaydet (PT-13D) (N2S-5)	AB22
Boeing-Vertol 107-II-28 Labrador (CH-113A)	BC8, NS4, ON45
Boeing-Vertol 107-II-9 Labrador (CH-113)	ON8
Bombardier CRJ200	PQ9
Borel-Morane Monoplane	ON8
Bowers Fly Baby 1A	MB12, ON8
Bristol 14 F.2B Fighter	ON8
Bristol 149 Bolingbroke IV	BC2, MB1, NS4
Bristol 149 Bolingbroke IVT	AB3, 6, 22, BC6, MB1, 12, ON8, 20, PQ2, SK5
Bristol 156 Beaufighter TT.10 (TF.X))	ON8
Bristol 170 Freighter 31	NW2
Bristol 170 Freighter 31 (31M)	MB12
Bristol 170 Freighter 31M	AB22
British Aerospace 146 Series 200	NS2
British Aircraft Corporation 167 Strikemaster 80	AB11
Buhl CA-6M Airsedan	ON11
Burgess-Dunne Seaplane (FSM)	ON45
Canadair CL-2 North Star [Douglas DC-4M-1]	AB22, ON8
Canadair CL-13 Sabre 1 [North American F-86A]	AB4
Canadair CL-13 Sabre 2 [North American F-86E]	PQ4, 10
Canadair CL-13 Sabre 3 [North American F-86J]	AB22
Canadair CL-13A Sabre 5 [North American F-86E]	BC14, NS2, ON3, 4, 10, 45, 49, 50, 51, 53, PQ19
Canadair CL-13B Sabre 6 [North American F-86E]	MB7, 12, ON6, 8, 20, 45, PQ16
Canadair CL-28-1 Argus 1 (CP-107)	BC8, NS2, 4
Canadair CL-28-1 Argus 2 (CP-107)	NS2
Canadair CL-28-2 Argus 2 (CP-107)	ON8, 45, PEI1
Canadair CL-30 Silver Star 3 (CT-133) [Lockheed 580 (T-33AN)]	AB4, 6, 9,10, 12, 17, 18, 22, 23, 24, 26, BC2, 6, 8, 10, MB1, 6, 7, 8, 12, 13, NS2, 3, 4, 6, 7, ON1, 3, 8, 9, 10, 14, 17, 20, 24, 26, 27, 29, 32,

Canadair CL-30 Silver Star 3 (CT-133) [Lockheed 580 (T-33AN)] (continued)	34, 38, 39, 42, 44, 45, 55, PQ16, 18, SK1, 3, 4, 5
Canadair CL-41 Tutor	MB11
Canadair CL-41A Tutor (CT-114)	AB6, 9, 10, 22, BC6, 8, MB7, NS7, ON3, 8, 9, 15, 20, 44, 45, 58, PQ16, SK1, 4
Canadair CL-41R Tutor	AB22
Canadair CL-84 Dynavert (CX-131)	MB12, ON8
Canadair CL-90 Starfighter (CF-104) [Lockheed 683-04-12]	AB9, 22, BC8, MB7, NS2, ON3, 20, PQ3, 16
Canadair CL-215-II	ON11
Canadair CL-219-1A10 Freedom Fighter (CF-116A) (CF-5A) [Northrop N-156A]	AB9, 10, 19, BC9, MB7, NS2, ON3, 8, 10, 15, 19, 20, 28, 44, 45, 51, PQ16
Canadair CL-219-1A17 Freedom Fighter (CF-116) (CF-116D) (CF-5D) [Northrop N-156B]	AB22, NS7, ON10, 15, 55
Canadair CL-600 Challenger (CX-144A)	MB7
Canadair CL-601 Challenger (CC-144B)	NS4
Canadair CL-601-3A Challenger	AB5, PQ9
Canadair CL-604 Challenger (CL-600) (CL-601)	ON8
Canadian Car & Foundry Harvard 4 [North American NA-186]	AB3, 6, 8, 21, BC2, MB7, 12, ON8, 16, 20, 23, 46, 57, PQ19, SK1, 4
Canaero Toucan	AB4
Cessna EC-1	AB22
Cessna C-34 Airmaster	MB12
Cessna C-37 Airmaster	AB22
Cessna T-50 Bobcat (C-78) (UC-78)	AB6, SK5
Cessna T-50 Crane 1	AB6, 22, MB1, 12, ON8, 20, SK4, 5
Cessna T-50 Crane 1A (Bobcat - AT-17A)	AB3, 22, ON44
Cessna 140	MB12, ON2
Cessna 150	ON21
Cessna 150D	ON9
Cessna 150F	NF3
Cessna 150G	BC11, MB9, 10, NF3, NS5, ON22
Cessna 150H	ON8, PQ9
Cessna 170B	PQ9
Cessna 172	AB20, ON21, PQ5
Cessna 172G	ON25
Cessna FR172G	AB5
Cessna 172H	BC4, NF3
Cessna 172I	PQ9
Cessna 172N	PQ9
Cessna 172P	BC4
Cessna 177	ON21
Cessna 180	BC11, ON22, 25
Cessna 180A	ON25
Cessna 180G	BC4
Cessna 180J	ON25
Cessna 188 Agwagon 230	AB3
Cessna A185F Skywagon 185	AB5, NB6
Cessna 195	SK4
Cessna U206B Super Skywagon	PQ15
Cessna U206G Stationair 6	PQ15
Cessna 305A Bird Dog (L-19A) (O-1A) (CO-119)	ON12, PQ10
Cessna 305C Bird Dog (L-19E) (O-1E) (CO-119)	NS2
Cessna 310	BC12
Cessna 310C	BC11
Cessna 310M Blue Canoe (310E) (L-27B) (U-3B)	BC4
Cessna 310Q	ON21
Cessna 320E Skyknight	AB5
Cessna 336 Skymaster	ON21
Cessna 337B Super Skymaster	AB20
Cessna T337B Super Skymaster	PQ9
Cessna T337C Super Skymaster	ON22
Cessna 500 Citation I	MB10

Canada Index

Champion 7KC Olympia	AB22	De Havilland DHC.3 Otter	ON11, SK2
Chandelle IV	AB22	De Havilland DHC.3 Otter (CC-123)	ON8
Chanute Glider (R)	BC2	De Havilland DHC.5 Buffalo	ON20
Circa Reproductions Nieuport 11	AB6	De Havilland DHC.6 Twin Otter	AB3, ON8
Circa Reproductions Nieuport 17	BC2	De Havilland DHC.6-100 Twin Otter	AB5
Classic Aircraft Waco F-5	ON23	De Havilland DHC.7	ON8
Consolidated 21C	AB22	De Havilland DHC.8-100	NF3
Consolidated 28-5 Canso	ON20	De Havilland DHC.8-102	ON22
Consolidated 28-5A Canso A	NF4, ON8, 20, PQ10	Diamond DA-20-A1 Katana	ON41, 42
Consolidated 28-5A Catalina (PBV-1A) (OA-10A)	NF2	Douglas A-26B Invader	BC2
		Douglas A-26C Invader	AB22
Consolidated 28-5A Catalina (PBY-5A)	NS2	Douglas Boston IIIA	NF6
Consolidated 28-6A Catalina (PBY-6A)	NF11	Douglas DC-3-201B	ON20
Consolidated 32 Liberator (B-24L) (B.VIII)	ON8	Douglas DC-3-227B (C-49H)	BC6
Convair 8-10 Delta Dagger (F-102A)	NF5	Douglas DC-3-454 (C-49J)	ON8
Convair 580 (440-77)	BC4, PQ9	Douglas DC-3A-360 Skytrain (C-47)	AB22
Corben C-1 Baby Ace	ON60	Douglas DC-3A-405 Skytrooper (C-53)	MB12
Corben D Baby Ace	AB22, ON31	Douglas DC-3A-456 Skytrain (C-47A)	AB3, NF7, 10, YU1
Craig Biplane	NS2	Douglas DC-3A-456 Skytrain (C-47A) (Dakota III)	PQ10
Cranwell CLA.4A	AB4		
Curtiss D Pusher	AB22	Douglas DC-3A-456 Skytrain (C-47A) (Dakota III) (CC-129)	AB4, BC8, ON12, 45
Curtiss JN-4 Canuck	AB22, ON8, 60		
Curtiss 1C Jenny (JN-4D)	AB14	Douglas DC-3A-467 Skytrain (C-47B) (Dakota IV)	NS4
Curtiss 8 (HS-2L)	ON8		
Curtiss 18 Seagull (MF)	ON8	Douglas DC-3A-467 Skytrain (C-47B) (Dakota IV) (CC-129)	AB9, MB7
Curtiss 50C Robin C-1	AB22		
Curtiss 87V Warhawk (P-40N) (Warhawk IV)	PQ19	Douglas Super DC-3 (R4D-8) (C-117D)	BC2
Curtiss A87-A2 Kittyhawk I	BC16, ON8	Douglas DC-4 Skymaster (C-54E)	ON10
Curtiss Stinson Special (R)	AB4	Douglas DC-6	AB4
Curtiss-Wright CW-20B-2 Commando (C-46D)	MB2	Douglas DC-9-32	MB10, ON8, 25
		Eagle Delta Rogallo Hang Glider	AB22
CVT M-100S	ON9	Eastman E-2 Sea Rover	BC2
Czerwinski-Shenstone Harbinger	ON8	Edgar Percival EP.9	AB22
Dassault Falcon 20C (CC-117)	BC4	Eipper MX Quicksilver	AB4, ON9
De Havilland DH.2 (R)	ON35	Electroflyer Dove Hang Glider	NS2
De Havilland DH.53 Humming Bird (R)	SK4	English Electric P.27 Lightning T.55	AB11
De Havilland DH.60 Moth	AB4	Ercoupe 415C	NS2
De Havilland DH.60G Gipsy Moth	ON60	Ercoupe 415CD	AB4
De Havilland DH.60GM Moth	ON60	Ercoupe 415G	AB22
De Havilland DH.60M Moth	AB22, BC6, SK4, 5	Eurocopter EC.120B Colibri	PQ9
De Havilland DH.60X Moth	ON8	Evans VP-1 Volksplane	AB22, ON8
De Havilland DH.80A Puss Moth	ON8	Fairchild FC-2	MB12
De Havilland DH.82A Tiger Moth	AB22, MB1, ON31	Fairchild FC-2 (R)	PQ2
De Havilland DH.82A Tiger Moth (R)	ON44	Fairchild FC-2L	MB12
De Havilland DH.82C Tiger Moth	AB6, 15, 22, BC3, 6, NF10, ON3, 8, 9, 16, 20, 23, 46, 60, PQ19, SK4, 5	Fairchild FC-2W2	MB12, ON8, YU1
		Fairchild 24W46	AB4
		Fairchild 71	AB22, MB12
		Fairchild 71C	AB4
De Havilland DH.82C Tiger Moth (PT-24)	AB4, MB12	Fairchild Super 71P	MB12
De Havilland DH.83 Fox Moth	PQ19	Fairchild 22 C7	AB22
De Havilland DH.83C Fox Moth	MB12, NW1, ON8, 11	Fairchild 24 C8E	AB22
De Havilland DH.87A Hornet Moth	AB22	Fairchild 24W40 Forwarder (C-61) (UC-61) (Argus I)	MB12
De Havilland DH.89A Dragon Rapide (DH.89)	AB22		
		Fairchild 82A	BC6, ON8
De Havilland DH.89A Dragon Rapide (DH.89B Dominie I)	ON11	Fairchild M-62A-4 Cornell (PT-26A) (Cornell II)	AB6
De Havilland DH.90 Dragonfly	AB4	Fairchild M-62A-4 Cornell (PT-26B) (Cornell II)	SK5
De Havilland DH.98 Mosquito B.20	ON8		
De Havilland DH.98 Mosquito B.35	AB3, 4	Fairchild M-62A-4 Cornell II	AB22, BC6, MB1, 12, ON8, 10, 20, 60, PQ19, SK4
De Havilland DH.98 Mosquito TT.35 (B.35)	ON17		
De Havilland DH.100 Vampire F.1	ON8		
De Havilland DH.100 Vampire F.3	AB3, 22, BC6, 8, MB12, ON8	Fairchild F-11-2 Husky (F-11-1)	MB12, ON11, PQ10
		Fairey Swordfish II	AB22, NS7, ON8, PQ19
De Havilland DH.100 Vampire FB.5	PQ16		
De Havilland DH.100 Vampire FB.6	ON20	Fairey Swordfish IV	AB3
De Havilland DH.106 Comet 1XB (1)	ON8	Fairey Battle I	BC6, MB1
De Havilland DH.115 Vampire T.35 (T.33)	AB4	Fairey Battle IT	ON8
De Havilland DHC.1 Chipmunk 1B-2-S3	BC12, ON20	Fairey Firefly FR.1	NS7, ON8
De Havilland DHC.1 Chipmunk 1B-2-S3 (CT-120)	AB22, ON17, PQ10	Fairey Firefly AS.6	ON20
		Falconar F-11	AB22
De Havilland DHC.1 Chipmunk 1B-2-S5	ON20, PQ19	Fantasy Sky Promotions Fantasy 7 Hot Air Balloon	ON8
De Havilland DHC.1 Chipmunk 1B-2-S5 (CT-120)	ON8, 17, 20		
		Farman MF-11 Shorthorn	ON8
De Havilland DHC.1 Chipmunk 22 (T.10)	BC2	Fiberlite Products 104 Viking	AB22
De Havilland DHC.1 Chipmunk T.10	ON45	Fieseler Fi 103A-1	NS2
De Havilland DHC.2 Beaver	MB12, ON8, 11, PQ19	Fieseler Fi 103A-1/Re4	ON19
De Havilland DHC.2 Beaver (L-20A) (U-6A)	ON61, PQ15	Fleet 2	BC2, ON8
De Havilland DHC.2 Turbo-Beaver	ON11	Fleet 7B Fawn I	ON17

Fleet 7C Fawn II	AB6, 22	Hughes 269C	PQ9
Fleet 16B Finch II	BC6, ON8, 20, 46, 60	Hughes 369HS	NB6, PQ9
Fleet 16R Finch I	AB22	Hütter H 17B	AB22
Fleet 21C	AB22	Jacobs Jaycopter A	AB22
Fleet 21K (21M)	ON20	Jacobs Jaycopter B Trainer	AB22
Fleet 21M	AB22	Jacobs Weihe (DFS 108-68)	AB22
Fleet 50K	ON8	Jodel D.9 Bébé	AB22, SK4
Fleet 60 Fort	ON20	Junkers J 1 (Ju 4)	ON8
Fleet 60K Fort	MB1, 12, ON20, SK5	Junkers F 13 gle	MB12
Fleet 80 Canuck	AB4, ON8, 9, 31, PQ2	Junkers W 34f/fi	MB12, ON8
Fleet 80 Canuck (Noury N-75)	AB22	Junkers Ju 52 cao/ce	MB12
Fokker D VII	ON8, PQ1	Jurca MJ.7G Mustang	BC6
Fokker D VII (R)	ON35	Kari-Keen 60 Coupe	AB22
Fokker Dr I (R)	ON18, 35	Kelly D	AB4
Fokker F.VIIb/3m (R)	ON11	Kinner Sportster K	AB22
Fokker F.XIA (B IVA)	MB12	Kolb Flyer	MB12
Fokker Super Universal	MB12, ON11	Kreider-Reisner KR-34C Challenger	ON11
Fokker Universal	AB4, MB12, ON8	Laird LCB-200	AB22
Fouga CM.170R Magister	ON20	Lear Learstar (Lockheed 18-10 Lodestar (C-57))	AB22
Found FBA-1	ON9		
Found FBA-2C	ON8	Lear Learstar (Lockheed 18-56-23 Lodestar (C-60A))	MB12, PQ12
Found 100 Centennial	MB12		
Frankfort Cinema B (TG-1A)	MB1	Lincoln Sport	AB22, BC2
Froebe Helicopter	MB12	Lockheed 10-A Electra	MB12, ON8
Froebe Ornithopter	MB12	Lockheed 12-A Electra Junior	ON8
Funk B	AB22	Lockheed 18-08A Lodestar	PQ14
Funk B-85C	SK4	Lockheed 18-10-01 Lodestar	AB22, BC15
Gates Learjet 36 (26)	PQ9	Lockheed 18-56A Lodestar (C-60) (18-50-23)	PQ7
Gazuit-Valladeau GV-1020	PQ10		
Gibson Twin Plane (R)	BC2	Lockheed 183-93-02 Starfighter (F-104A)	ON8
Goddard Volksplane	AB22	Lockheed 237-27-01 Ventura (PV-1)	AB25
Great Lakes 2T-1A	AB22	Lockheed 382-15B Hercules (CC-130E)	ON45
Grumman G-21A Goose (G-39) (JRF-5)	ON8	Lockheed 414-17-11 Hudson VI (A-28A)	ON8
Grumman G-40 Avenger (TBM-3)	AB22, NS7	Lockheed 414-56-01 Hudson III	NF1
Grumman G-40 Avenger (TBM-3) (TBM-3E)	NB2, NS2, ON20	Lockheed 414-56-01 Hudson III (FSM)	NF1
Grumman G-44 Widgeon	PQ10	Lockheed 414-56-03 Hudson IIIA (A-29)	NF10
Grumman G-89 Tracker (S2F-1) (CS2F-1)	NS7	Lockheed 483-04-08 Starfighter (F-104F)	AB16
Grumman G-89 Tracker (S2F-1) (S-2A)	ON11	Lockheed 580 (T-33A)	NF8
Grumman G-89 Tracker (S2F-1) (S-2A) (US-2A)	AB20	Lockheed 580 Silver Star 1 (T-33A)	PQ10
		Lockheed 583-04-15 Starfighter (CF-104D)	AB10, BC6, ON10, 13, 20, 45
Grumman G-103 Tracker (CS2F-1) (CP-121)	BC5, NS7, ON3, PEI1		
Grumman G-103 Tracker (CS2F-2) (CP-121)	BC7, MB7, ON9, 20, 45, 46	Lockheed 683-10-19 Starfighter (F-104G)	ON10
		Lockheed 726-45-17 Neptune (P2V-7) (P-2H) (DP-2H)	NS4
Grumman G-103 Tracker (CS2F-2) (CS2F-3) (CP-121)	BC8, NS2, ON8		
		Lockheed 1329 JetStar 6	NS2, ON8
Grumman G-159 Gulfstream I	AB5	Long Longster III	ON60
Handley Page HP.52 Hampden I	BC6	Luscombe 8A Silvaire	BC2
Handley Page HP.61 Halifax A.VIIA	ON45	Luscombe 8E Silvaire	AB22
Haseloh Gyroplane B	AB22	Marquette Racer	ON60
Haseloh Gyroplane J.B.2	AB22	McDonnell M.24 Banshee (F2H-3)	AB19, NS7, ON8
Hawker Hind	ON8	McDonnell M.36BA Voodoo (F-101B) (CF-101B)	AB3, 4, 9, 22, BC1, 8, MB7, 12, NB1, 4, 7, NF8, 10, NS2, 3, 7, ON3, 8, 14, 20, 45, PEI1, PQ11, 16, 17
Hawker Hurricane I (FSM)	MB1, ON17		
Hawker Hurricane IIB (FSM)	ON20, 45		
Hawker Hurricane IV	PQ19		
Hawker Hurricane X	ON60		
Hawker Hurricane XII	AB3, 22, ON8, 52, PQ19	McDonnell M.36BA Voodoo (F-101B) (CF-101F)	ON19
Hawker Sea Hurricane XIIA	BC6	McDonnell M.36BA Voodoo (F-101B) (TF-101B) (CF-101B)	AB4
Hawker Fury FB.10	ON20		
Hawker Sea Fury FB.11	AB19, ON8	McDonnell M.267A Hornet (CF-188A)	AB9, ON15
Hawker P.1099 Hunter F.6	AB11	McDonnell M.267B Hornet (CF-188B)	AB9, ON8, 45
Hawker P.1099 Hunter F.58	ON45	McDowall Monoplane	ON8
Hawker P.1101 Hunter T.75 (T.7)	AB11	McHardy Lysander	AB6
Hawker-Siddeley P.1127 Harrier 50 (AV-8A) (AV-8C)	ON8	McKinnon Flying Boat	ON60
		McNamara Maxim	AB22
Hawker-Siddeley P.1184 Sea Harrier FA.2 (FRS.1)	AB11	Meade C-3 Glider	AB22
		Messerschmitt Bf 109E-7 (E-1)	ON52
Heath Parasol	MB12	Messerschmitt Bf 109F-4/Z	ON8
Heinkel He 162A-1	ON8	Messerschmitt Me 163B-1a Komet	ON8
Hickman Biplane	ON60	Meyers MAC-145 (125C)	AB22
Hiller UH12E	MB11	Mignet HM-290 Pou-du-Ciel	BC6
Hispano HA-1112M1L [Messerschmitt Bf 109G]	ON8	Mikoyan-Gurevich MiG-21MF	ON45
		Mikoyan-Gurevich MiG-21MF-75 (MiG-21MF)	ON8
Homebuilt Monoplane	ON54		
Howard DGA-15P (GH-2)	AB22	Mikoyan-Gurevich MiG-23ML	PQ16
Howard 500 [Lockheed 237-27-01 Ventura (PV-1)]	PQ10	Miles M.2W Hawk Major (M.2H)	ON10
		Miles M.11A Whitney Straight	AB22
Hughes 269A	AB22	Mitchell Wing B-10	ON8

Canada Index

Mitchell Wing U-2	AB3
Mitsubishi MU-2	BC12
Mitsubishi MU-2D (MU-2B-10)	ON21
Mitsubishi MU-2G (MU-2B-30)	AB5, MB9, 10
Mono Aircraft Monocoupe 90	AB22
Moyes Stingray Hang Glider	ON8
Müller Arrow Hang Glider	BC6
Müller Stingray Hang Glider	AB3, SK4
Nanchang CJ-6A	ON20, PQ7
Nelson Dragonfly BB-1	BC6
Neys Biplane	AB22
Nieuport 12	ON8
Nieuport 17 (R)	ON18, 19
Nieuport 28C.1 (R)	ON35
Noorduyn Harvard IIB [North American NA-77 (AT-16)] (Sk 16A)	ON52
Noorduyn Harvard IIB [North American NA-77]	AB22, BC6, ON16, 45
Noorduyn Norseman I	ON11
Noorduyn Norseman IV	AB4, 22, MB1, 12, ON11
Noorduyn Norseman IVW	BC6
Noorduyn Norseman V	AB3, ON10, PQ10, SK4
Noorduyn Norseman VI (C-64A) (UC-64A)	AB22, BC2, MB12, ON8, 47
North American NA-64 Yale	AB6, 22, MB1, 12, ON16, 20, 46, 60, SK5
North American NA-66 Harvard II	MB1, 12, NS7, ON46
North American NA-75 Harvard II	ON16
North American NA-76 Harvard II	AB5, ON16, 40
North American NA-81 Harvard II	AB3, NS2, ON16
North American NA-88 Texan (AT-6C)	ON16
North American NA-108 Mitchell (B-25J)	ON20
North American NA-108 Mitchell (B-25J) (Mitchell III)	AB4, 22
North American NA-108 Mitchell (B-25J) (TB-25J) (Mitchell III)	MB7
North American NA-108 Mitchell (B-25J) (TB-25L) (Mitchell III)	ON8
North American NA-122 Mustang (P-51D) (Mustang IV)	ON8, PQ19
North American NA-151 Sabre (P-86A) (F-86A)	AB3
North Tui' Sports	NS2
Northrop Delta	ON8
Pacaero Tradewind (Beech D18S Expeditor 3NM)	BC2
Percival P.47 Proctor 6	ON10
Pfalz D III (R)	ON18
Pheasant H-10	SK4
Piaggio P.149D	BC15
Piasecki PD-18 Retriever (H-25A)	AB3, ON8
Piasecki PD-18 Retriever (H-25A) (HUP-3)	NS7
Piasecki PD-22 Work Horse (H-21B) (CH-21B)	BC8, PQ16
Piel CP.605 Diamant	ON31
Pietenpol B4-A Aircamper	AB22, BC2, ON60, PQ7
Piper J-3C-65 Cub	ON17, 23, PQ7
Piper J-3F-65 Cub	AB22
Piper J-4A Cub Coupe	AB22
Piper J-5A Cub Cruiser	AB22
Piper PA-11 Cub Special	NB6
Piper PA-18-150 Super Cub	NF3
Piper PA-23-Apache	ON21, ON22
Piper PA-23-160 Apache	NB6
Piper PA-23-250 Aztec	NF3, ON7, PQ9
Piper PA-23-250 Aztec C	BC11
Piper PA-23-250 Aztec E	ON22
Piper PA-23-250 Aztec F	PQ9
Piper PA-28-140 Cherokee	ON21, PQ9
Piper PA-30 Twin Comanche	NS5
Piper PA-31-300 Turbo Navajo	BC11, MB10
Piper PA-31-310 Turbo Navajo B	MB9
Piper PA-31-350 Navajo Chieftain	AB5, BC4
Piper PA-31P Pressurised Navajo	ON21, PQ9
Piper PA-34-200T Seneca II	MB10
Piper PA-38-112 Tomahawk	NS2, PQ9
Piper PA-44-180 Seminole	NF3, ON22
Piper PA-60-600 Aerostar	BC4
Pitcairn PCA-2	ON8
Pitts S-1C Special	AB22, NS2
Pitts S-2A Special	ON8
Porterfield 35W	AB22
Porterfield LP-65	AB22
Prima 24 Skyseeker 1	BC2
Quad City Ultralights Challenger	AB4
Quickie Aircraft Quickie 1 (Rutan 54)	BC2, 4, 6, NF10, ON8
Quickie Aircraft Quickie 2 (Rutan 54)	AB3, MB12
R.F.D. Dagling	BC6
Rearwin 7000 Sportster	AB22
Replica Plans S.E.5A	BC2, 6, ON35
Republic RC-3 Seabee	AB22, BC2, 6, MB12, ON11, 44, 56
Reynolds Sport Monoplane	AB22
Reynolds Star	AB22
Robinson R-22 Alpha	ON21
Robinson R-22 Beta	AB5, BC4
Robinson R-22HP Beta	MB10
Robinson R-44 Raven	BC11
Rogallo Standard Hang Glider	SK4
Rotorway Executive	NS2
Royal Aircraft Factory B.E.2c	ON8
Royal Aircraft Factory S.E.5A (R)	ON35
Rutan 61 Long Ez	BC12
Ryan B-1 Brougham (R)	YU1
Saunders ST-27 (De Havilland DH.114 Heron 2)	ON11
Saunders ST-27 (De Havilland DH.114 Heron 2B)	MB12
Saunders ST-28	MB12
SCAN 30 (Grumman G-44A Widgeon]	ON20
Scheibe L-Spatz 55	NS2
Schneider ESG 31 Grunau Baby II (DFS 108-49)	MB12
Schneider ESG 31 Grunau Baby IIB (DFS 108-49)	AB22
Schweizer SGU.1-20	AB5
Schweizer SGU.2-22	PQ10
Schweizer SGU.2-22E	MB12
Sheldrake AX-SM Hot Air Balloon	AB4
Sheldrake Merritt Spirit of Canada Hot Air Balloon	ON8
Sikorsky VS-316A Hoverfly (R-4B)	ON8
Sikorsky S-51 Dragonfly	AB3, ON20
Sikorsky S-55A	AB3
Sikorsky S-55D (HO4S-3)	NS7, ON8
Sikorsky S-55D (HRS-3)	BC2
Sikorsky S-55D Chickasaw (H-19B) (UH-19B)	BC6
Sikorsky S-58 Seahorse (HUS-1) (UH-34D)	AB22
Sikorsky S-70	BC15
Sindlinger HH-1 Hurricane	AB4, ON60
Sky Quest Ultralight	MB12
Smith DSA-1 Miniplane	YU1
Sopwith 1 1/2 Strutter (R)	ON35
Sopwith F.1 Camel (FSM)	BC8
Sopwith F.1 Camel (R)	BC6, ON35
Sopwith F.1 Camel (Scale R)	PQ10
Sopwith 2F.1 Camel	ON8
Sopwith 7F.1 Snipe	ON8, 19
Sopwith Pup (R)	ON20, 48
Sopwith Triplane (R)	AB3, ON8
SPAD VII	ON8
Spectrum RX550 Beaver	ON8
Spencer-Gottlieb SG VI-D Grey Gull	AB22
Sperry-Verville M-1 Messenger (R)	AB22
Spezio Sport Tuholer	BC6
Stamer-Lippisch Z-12 Zögling	SK4
Stampe & Vertongen S.V.4C	BC8
Stearman 4EM (4C)	MB12
Stearman 4EM (4E Special)	ON8
Steen Skybolt	ON21
Stinson Junior SR	ON8
Stinson SR-7A Reliant	SK5

77

Stinson SR-8B Reliant	MB12	Travel Air 2000	ON8
Stinson SR-8CM Reliant	MB12	Travel Air D-4D Speedwing (BE.4000)	AB22
Stinson SR-9FM Reliant	AB4, ON11	(E.4000)	
Stinson V-77 Reliant (AT-19)	AB22, ON9	Ultraflight Lazair 1	ON9
Stinson HW.75	AB22, MB1, ON31	Ultralight Flight Mirage	NS2
Stinson 10	PQ2	Ultralight Flying Machines Easy Riser	ON8, 9, 44
Stinson 108-1 Voyager	SK4	University of Toronto Ornithopter 1	ON9
Stinson 108-2 Voyager	AB22, MB12	University of Toronto SHARP UAV	ON9
Stinson 10A Voyager	AB22	Vans RV-6A	PQ9
Stits SA-3A Playboy	ON8	Vertol V.44A (CH-127)	AB22
Stits SA-7D Skycoupe	AB22	Vickers Vedette V	MB12, ON8, SK4
Stolp SA.100 Starduster	AB5	Vickers Vedette VA	ON8
Struchen Helicopter	BC6	Vickers 60 Viking IV (Scale R)	AB4
Sud SA.319B Alouette III	AB5	Vickers 757 Viscount	BC2, MB5, 12, ON8, PQ10
Sud-Est SE.3160 Alouette III	AB5, 22		
Supermarine 304 Stranraer	NS7	Viking Dragonfly	BC4
Supermarine 329 Spitfire F.IIb	ON19	Vought FG-1D Corsair	PQ19
Supermarine 349 Spitfire F.V (Scale R)	AB6	Vultee V-74 Valiant (BT-13A)	MB12
Supermarine 359 Spitfire F.VIIIc (FSM)	ON17	Waco 10 (GXE)	AB3, 22, ON8
Supermarine 361 Spitfire HF.IX	PQ19	Waco AQC-6 (ZQC-6)	BC6, YU1
Supermarine 361 Spitfire LF.IXc	ON8, 52	Waco ATO	PQ19
Supermarine 361 Spitfire LF.IXc (FSM)	ON41, 45, 52	Waco EQC-6 (ZQC-6)	AB3
Supermarine 361 Spitfire LF.XVIe	ON20, PQ19	Waco INF (KNF)	BC6
Supermarine 377 Seafire F.XV	AB19	Waco NZR Hadrian (CG-4A)	AB22, MB1
Supermarine 379 Spitfire F.XIV	PQ19	Waco UIC	AB4
Supermarine Seafire (Scale R)	NS7	Waco UPF-7	AB22
Supermarine Spitfire (Scale R)	BC2, PQ10	Waco UPF-7 (YPT-14)	AB22
Swearingen SA.226TC Metro	NF3	Waco YKC-S	MB12
Taylor E-2 Cub	ON8, 60	Waco YKS-7	AB22
Taylor J-2 Cub	AB22, ON60	Waco YKS-7 (VKS-7F)	ON8
Taylor JT.1 Monoplane	BC6	Waco ZQC-6	AB22
Taylor-Young A	ON60	Weber C3 Mead Glider	SK4
Taylor-Young BL.65	AB22	Welch OW-8	AB22
Taylorcraft BC-12-65	AB22	Westland Lysander IIIA	BC6, ON8, 20, PQ19, SK5
Taylorcraft BC-65	ON8		
Taylorcraft DCO-65 Grasshopper (L-2M)	NS7	Wills Wings XC-185 Hang Glider	ON8
Taylorcraft 20	ON11	Wittman W.8 Tailwind	PQ10
Team Minimax	AB22	WSK Lim-2R [MiG-15bis]	ON8
Ted Smith Aerostar 600	BC4	XC-02 Helicopter	ON44
Temco GC-1B Swift	PQ7	Yost Hot Air Balloon	ON8
Thomas Esperanza 4	ON11	Zenair CH-200 Zenith	ON9, 21
Thruxton Jackaroo (De Havilland DH.82A Tiger Moth)	ON60	Zenair CH-300 Tri-Zenith	ON8

The Brome County Historical Society Museum has owned this Fokker D VII for over 90 years. [PQ1]

USA

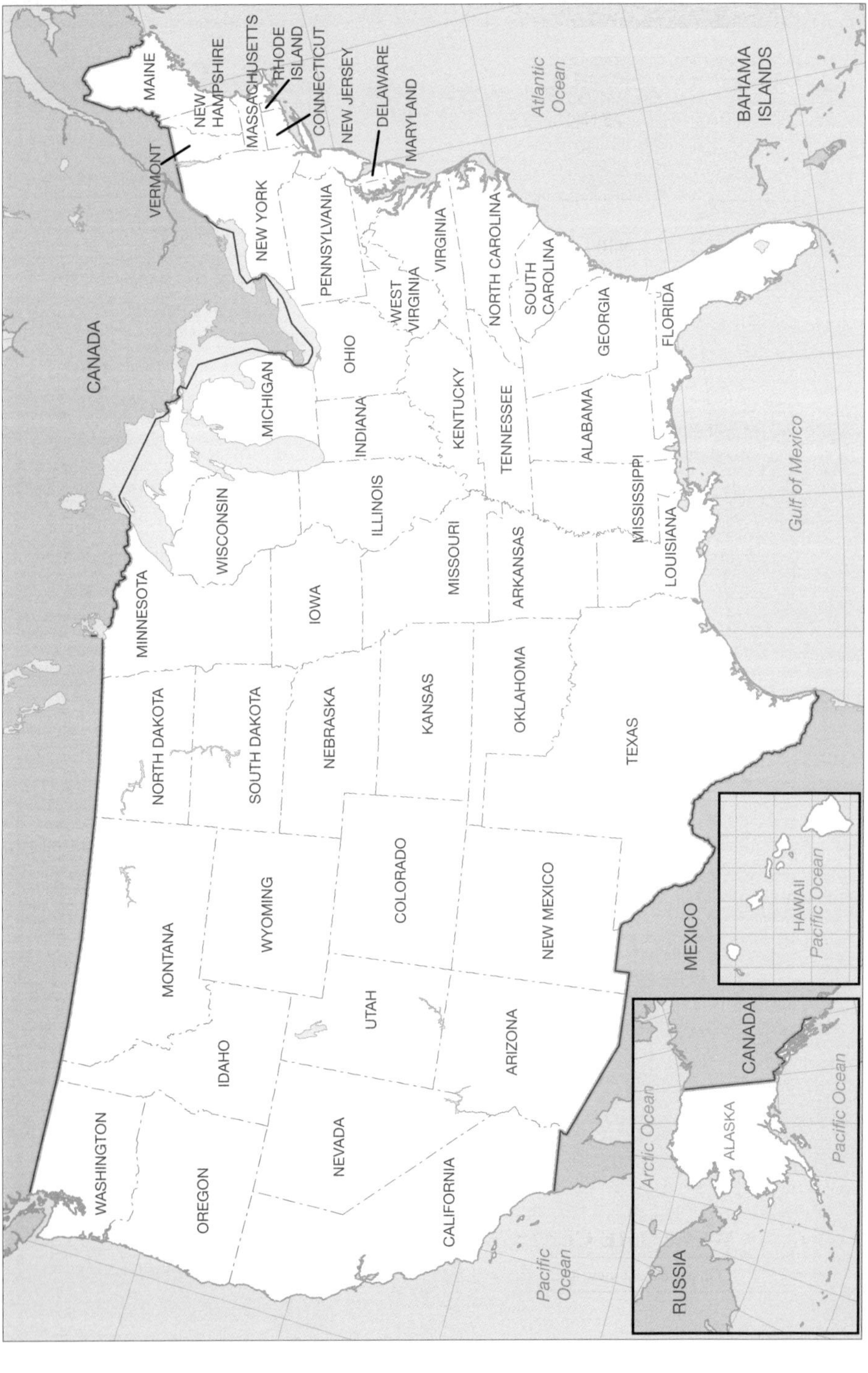
CANADA
MAINE
NEW HAMPSHIRE
VERMONT
MASSACHUSETTS
RHODE ISLAND
CONNECTICUT
NEW YORK
NEW JERSEY
PENNSYLVANIA
DELAWARE
MARYLAND
Atlantic Ocean
BAHAMA ISLANDS
VIRGINIA
WEST VIRGINIA
NORTH CAROLINA
SOUTH CAROLINA
GEORGIA
FLORIDA
OHIO
MICHIGAN
INDIANA
KENTUCKY
TENNESSEE
ALABAMA
MISSISSIPPI
Gulf of Mexico
LOUISIANA
ARKANSAS
MISSOURI
ILLINOIS
WISCONSIN
MINNESOTA
IOWA
NORTH DAKOTA
SOUTH DAKOTA
NEBRASKA
KANSAS
OKLAHOMA
TEXAS
MEXICO
HAWAII
Pacific Ocean
MONTANA
WYOMING
COLORADO
NEW MEXICO
UTAH
ARIZONA
IDAHO
WASHINGTON
OREGON
NEVADA
CALIFORNIA
Pacific Ocean
CANADA
ALASKA
Arctic Ocean
Pacific Ocean
RUSSIA

ALABAMA

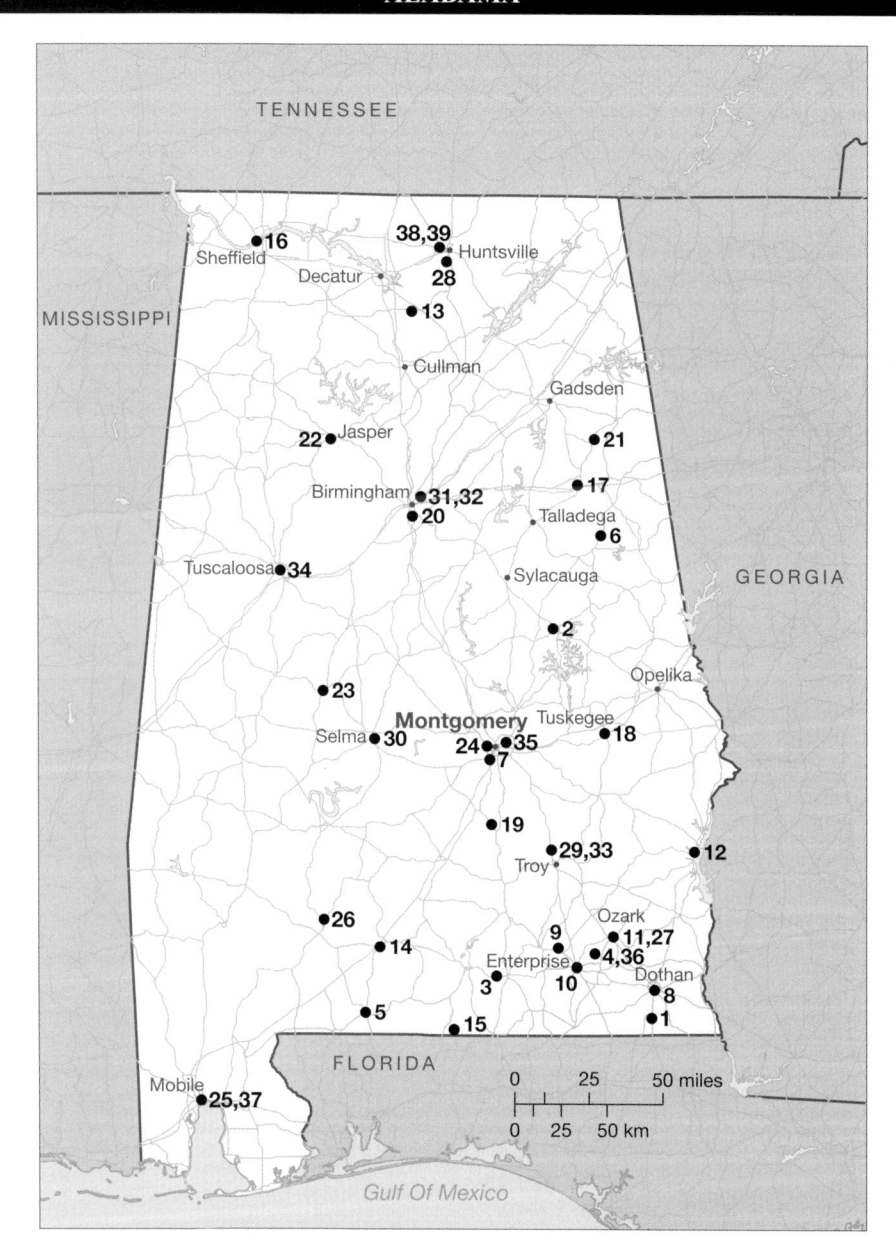

ALABAMA WELCOME CENTER (AL1)

Location:	On permanent view at 15121 Highway 231 in Madrid which is about 15 miles south of Dothan.

TYPE	REG/SER	CON. NO.	PI/NOTES	STATUS
☐ Bell 204 Iroquois (HU-1B) (UH-1B)	62-2018	538		PV

ALEXANDER CITY VETERANS MEMORIAL PARK (AL2)

Location:	On permanent view in the western part of the city off State Route 22.

TYPE	REG/SER	CON. NO.	PI/NOTES	STATUS
☐ Vought A-7D Corsair II	73-1010	D406		PV

ANDALUSIA MONUMENT (AL3)

Location:	On permanent view at Opp airport which is about 3 miles east of the town off Route 84.

TYPE	REG/SER	CON. NO.	PI/NOTES	STATUS
☐ Bell 205 Iroquois (UH-1H)	'13702'	10756	68-16097	PVX

ARMY AVIATION TECHNICAL SCHOOL (AL4)

Address:	1-13th Aviation Regiment, Fort Rucker, Alabama 36362.
Tel:	334-255-1030 Email: ruck.webmaster@conus.army.mil
Admission:	By prior permission only.
Location:	At Yano Hall in the base.

The school has two hangars and workshops on the base. Here technicians are trained using a number of helicopters. There are workshops containing engines, components and test rigs. Some airframes have recently been transferred to the museum and moved to their storage hangars nearby.

TYPE	REG/SER	CON. NO.	PI/NOTES	STATUS
☐ Bell 205 Iroquois (UH-1D) (UH-1H)	64-13644	4351		RA
☐ Bell 205 Iroquois (UH-1D) (UH-1H)	64-13694	4401		RA
☐ Bell 205 Iroquois (UH-1D) (UH-1H)	65-9571	4615		RA
☐ Bell 205 Iroquois (UH-1D) (UH-1H)	65-9668	4712		RA
☐ Bell 205 Iroquois (UH-1D) (UH-1H)	65-12773	5180		RA
☐ Bell 205 Iroquois (UH-1D) (UH-1H)	66-1120	5603		RA
☐ Bell 205 Iroquois (UH-1D) (UH-1H)	68-16402	6096		RA
☐ Bell 206A Kiowa (OH-58A)	69-16373	40594		RA

BREWTON MONUMENT (AL5)

Location:	On permanent view at the airport which is about 3 miles south of the town off Route 41.

TYPE	REG/SER	CON. NO.	PI/NOTES	STATUS
☐ Beech D45 Mentor (T-34C)	Bu160482	GL-39		PV

CLAY COUNTY VETERANS MEMORIAL PARK (AL6)

Location:	On permanent view on Route 9 just north west of Lineville.

TYPE	REG/SER	CON. NO.	PI/NOTES	STATUS
☐ Bell 205 Iroquois (UH-1H)	68-15283	10213	P68-15283, N202BM – probable identity.	PV
☐ North American NA-243 Super Sabre (F-100F)	56-3822	243-98		PV

DANNELLY FIELD AIR NATIONAL GUARD COLLECTION (AL7)

Address:	187 FW, 5187 Selma Highway West, Montgomery Alabama 36108-4829.
Tel:	334-394-7210
Admission:	By prior permission only.
Location:	About 4 miles south west of the city on Route 80.

The unit was allocated to Alabama in October 1947 and initially flew P-51s from Birmingham Airport. The squadron saw active service in Korea and moved to its current base in 1953. For many years it flew in the reconnaissance role using RF-80As and then RF-84F Thunderflashes.

The squadron converted to fighters in the early 1990s with the arrival of the F-4D which served for several years Examples of types used by the group have been preserved around the site. The Iroquois is in the Army base on the other side of the field.

TYPE	REG/SER	CON. NO.	PI/NOTES	STATUS
☐ Bell 205 Iroquois (UH-1H)	68-16378	11037		RA
☐ General Dynamics 401 Fighting Falcon (F-16A)	78-0042	61-38		RA
☐ McDonnell M.98EN Phantom II (F-4D)	66-7745	2381		PV
☐ Republic RF-84F Thunderflash	52-7249			PV

DOTHAN MONUMENTS (AL8)

Location:	On permanent view at two locations in the town.

TYPE	REG/SER	CON. NO.	PI/NOTES	STATUS
☐ Bell 205 Iroquois (UH-1D) (UH-1H)	65-9643	4687	On Highway 84 in the eastern part of the town.	PV
☐ Bell 209 Huey Cobra (AH-1G) (AH-1F)	71-21014	21085	At DAVV Post 87 in the town.	PV

Alabama

ELBA VETERANS MEMORIAL (AL9)

Location:	On permanent view on US 84 in the direction of Enterprise.

TYPE	REG/SER	CON. NO.	PI/NOTES	STATUS
☐ Bell 205 Iroquois (UH-1D) (UH-1V)	66-16877	9071		PV

ENTERPRISE MONUMENT (AL10)

Location:	On permanent view in Johnny Henderson Park which is about 1 mile north of the town on SR 167.

TYPE	REG/SER	CON. NO.	PI/NOTES	STATUS
☐ Bell 205 Iroquois (UH-1D) (UH-1H)	65-9747	4791		PV

ENTERPRISE STATE COMMUNITY COLLEGE – AVIATION CENTER (AL11)

Address:	3405 US Highway 231, Ozark, Alabama 36360
Tel:	334-774-5113 Fax: 334-774-6399
Admission:	By prior permission only.
Location:	At Blackwell Field which is about 3 miles south east of the town.

The college operates at a number of sites in the region. The well equipped Aviation Center at Blackwell Field contains a number of instructional airframes. The Sabre was mounted outside the buildings for many years but is no longer there. The fighter may be stored in the complex.

The Morava, which was once flown by the Cuban Air Force, was in store at the US Army Aviation Museum at nearby Fort Rucker. This and the Short Sherpa were at the Enterprise Campus but reorganisation should mean that they move to Blackwell Field.

TYPE	REG/SER	CON. NO.	PI/NOTES	STATUS
☐ Beech C50 Seminole (L-23D) (U-8D)	'21700'		May be at Enterprise.	RAX
☐ Bell 204 Iroquois (UH-1B)	N87765	616	62-2096	RA
☐ Bell 205 Iroquois (UH-1H)	67-17453	9651	May be at Enterprise.	RA
☐ Cessna 150K	N5790G	15071290		RA
☐ Cessna R172E Mescalero (T-41B)	67-15000	R1720001		RA
☐ Gates Learjet 25	N6NF	25-021	N942GA, N111L, N1JR, N1LL, N40SW, N40SN	PV
☐ Let L-200A Morava	'61-70909'	170709	709 (Cuba), N1040A – may be at Enterprise.	RAX
☐ North American NA-201 Sabre (F-86D) (F-86L)	53-0847	201-291		RA
☐ Short SD.3-30 Sherpa (C-23A)	84-0471	SH.3118	G-14-3118 – may be at Enterprise.	RA
☐ Swearingen SA.26T Merlin IIA	N9032H	T26-007	N2101S, N44BB, C-GGFJ	RA

EUFAULA MONUMENT (AL12)

Location:	On permanent view at VFW 5850 at 5850 Highway 431 South.

TYPE	REG/SER	CON. NO.	PI/NOTES	STATUS
☐ Bell 205 Iroquois (UH-1H) (UH-1V)	68-16349	11008	Possible identity.	PV

EVA MONUMENT (AL13)

Location:	On permanent view at a gas station in the town.

TYPE	REG/SER	CON. NO.	PI/NOTES	STATUS
☐ Beech D18S				PV

EVERGREEN MONUMENT (AL14)

Location:	On permanent view at the airport which is about 3 miles east of the town.

TYPE	REG/SER	CON. NO.	PI/NOTES	STATUS
☐ North American NA-194 Fury (FJ-3) (F-1C)	Bu136032	194-259		PV
☐ North American NA-226 Trojan (T-28C)	Bu140451	226-28		PV

FLORALA MONUMENT (AL15)

Location:	On permanent view in a park near Lake Jackson off Highway 55 in the southern part of the town.

TYPE	REG/SER	CON. NO.	PI/NOTES	STATUS
☐ Lockheed 580 (T-33A)	53-4938	580-8277		PV

FLORENCE VETERAN'S MEMORIAL PARK (AL16)

Location:	On permanent view in James M. Spain Drive in the southern part of the town.

TYPE	REG/SER	CON. NO.	PI/NOTES	STATUS
☐ Bell 209 Huey Cobra (AH-1G) (AH-1F)	67-15803	20467		PV

FORT MCCLELLAN ARMY NATIONAL GUARD COLLECTION (AL17)

Address:	1023 Fort McClellan, Anniston, Alabama 36205
Tel:	256-847-4102
Admission:	By prior permission only.
Location:	About 5 miles north east of the town on Route 21.

The fort closed in 1999 as an Army Base. The site is now home to training units of the Alabama National Guard. Two aircraft are preserved at the site and there is a display tracing the history of the fort in a building.

TYPE	REG/SER	CON. NO.	PI/NOTES	STATUS
☐ Bell 204 Iroquois (UH-1B)	'68935'			RAX
☐ McDonnell M.98EN Phantom II (F-4D)	66-7514	2035		RA

GENERAL DANIEL 'CHAPPIE' JAMES MEMORIAL MUSEUM (AL18)

Address:	Tuskegee University, 1200 West Montgomery Road, Tuskegee, Alabama 36088.
Tel:	334-727-8011 Email: webmaster@tuskegee.edu
Admission:	Aircraft on permanent view. Museum by prior permission only.
Location:	At the airport which is about 3 miles north of the town.
	The Institute is in the centre of the city.

General Daniel James was one of the famous 'Tuskegee Airmen' and rose to become the first black Four Star General. The museum traces the story of his life and many of his personal items are on show.

TYPE	REG/SER	CON. NO.	PI/NOTES	STATUS
☐ Grumman G-105 Cougar (F9F-8T) (TF-9J)	Bu142985		At airport.	PV
☐ McDonnell M.98DJ Phantom II (F-4C)	64-0851	1210		PV

HIGHLAND HOME MONUMENT (AL19)

Location:	On permanent view at the High School at 18434 Montgomery Highway in the town.

TYPE	REG/SER	CON. NO.	PI/NOTES	STATUS
☐ General Dynamics 401 Fighting Falcon (F-16A)	N324DC	61-57	78-0061	PV

HOOVER MONUMENT (AL20)

Location:	By prior permission only at 140 Golden Acorn Drive about 7 miles south of Hoover off Interstate 65.

TYPE	REG/SER	CON. NO.	PI/NOTES	STATUS
☐ Bell 209 Huey Cobra (AH-1G) (AH-1F)	68-17077	20805		PV

JACKSONVILLE MONUMENT (AL21)

Location:	On permanent view at ALP 57 which is south of the town on Highway 21.

TYPE	REG/SER	CON. NO.	PI/NOTES	STATUS
☐ Bell 205 Iroquois (UH-1H)	66-16769	8963		PV

JASPER MONUMENT (AL22)

Location:	On permanent view at VFW 4850 on Highway 78 in the north eastern part of the town.

TYPE	REG/SER	CON. NO.	PI/NOTES	STATUS
☐ McDonnell M.98DF Phantom II (RF-4C)	65-0833	1264		PV

MARION MONUMENT (AL23)

Location:	On permanent view at the Military Institute at 1101 Washington Street in the town.

TYPE	REG/SER	CON. NO.	PI/NOTES	STATUS
☐ Republic F-84F Thunderstreak	51-1688			PV

MAXWELL AIR FORCE BASE COLLECTION (AL24)

Address:	HQ AU/PA, Maxwell Air Force Base, Montgomery, Alabama 36112-5018.
Tel:	334-953-2014 Fax: 334-953-3379
Admission:	Daily 0700-1800.
Location:	On Chennault Circle – the base is in the western suburbs of the city.

Orville Wright chose the site in 1910 as being suitable for the establishment of a flying school. The Army took over in 1918 and the field was later named after Lieutenant William C. Maxwell who was killed in the Philippines in 1920. During World War II pilot training took place at the field.

In 1943 a centre for to familiarise pilots with four engined aircraft pilots was set up using B-24 Liberators and later the B-29 Superfortress. The base houses many units including the Air University, the Air War College and the Historical Research Center.

Alabama

TYPE	REG/SER	CON. NO.	PI/NOTES	STATUS
☐ Boeing 464-201-7 Stratofortress (B-52D)	55-0057	464009		PV
☐ Cessna 305A Bird Dog (L-19A) (O-1A)	N6258	22428	51-12114 (?) – by CAP, HQ.	PV
☐ McDonnell M.36CA Voodoo (RF-101C)	56-0135	395	56-0135, '56-0119'	PV
☐ McDonnell M.98EN Phantom II (F-4D)	65-0660	1674		PV
☐ North American NA-108 Mitchell (B-25J) (TB-25J) (TB-25N)	'253373'	108-33924	44-30649, N9452Z, '44-34974'	PVX
☐ North American NA-161 Sabre (P-86A) (F-86A)	'12760'	161-295	49-1301	PVX
☐ North American NA-223 Super Sabre (F-100D)	55-3678	223-360	55-3678, '63-436'	PV
☐ Northrop N-156T Talon (T-38A)	59-1601	N.5114	59-1601, '3800'	PV
☐ Republic F-105D Thunderchief	61-0176	D-371		PV
☐ Sikorsky S-65A (HH-53C) (MH-53J) (MH-53M)	69-5785	65240		PV

MOBILE MONUMENTS (AL25)

Location:	On permanent view at two locations in the city.

TYPE	REG/SER	CON. NO.	PI/NOTES	STATUS
☐ Boeing 727-22QC	N102FE	19193	N7418U – at a restaurant	RA
☐ Lockheed 580 (T-33A)	53-6123	580-9744	In J. N. Langan Park in the town.	PV

MONROEVILLE VETERANS MEMORIAL PARK (AL26)

Location:	On permanent view in Veteran's Avenue Monroeville which is about 75 miles north east of Mobile.

TYPE	REG/SER	CON. NO.	PI/NOTES	STATUS
☐ Bell 205 Iroquois (UH-1H)	66-17052	9246		PV
☐ Lockheed 580 (T-33A)	52-9436	580-7546		PV

OZARK MONUMENT (AL27)

Location:	On permanent view on Highway 231 in the northern part of the town.

TYPE	REG/SER	CON. NO.	PI/NOTES	STATUS
☐ Bell 205 Iroquois (UH-1H)	65-9770	4814		PV

REDSTONE ARSENAL (AL28)

Address:	Redstone, Alabama 35898-5300.
Tel:	256-876-4261 Email: history@redstone.army.com
Admission:	By prior permission only.
Location:	About 5 miles south west of Huntsville.

The vast Redstone Arsenal was established in 1941 for the production and storage of chemical weapons. In the post-World War II period rocket research and development took place at the site.

Six helicopters are preserved around the camp. Three are outside the Army Aviation Laboratory, one on the airfield, one by the Aviation and Missile Command Headquarters and the other by the Army Aviation Executive Office.

TYPE	REG/SER	CON. NO.	PI/NOTES	STATUS
☐ Bell 204 Iroquois (UH-1C) (UH-1M)	64-14166	1290		RA
☐ Bell 204 Iroquois (UH-1C) (UH-1M)	64-14185	1309		RA
☐ Bell 209 Huey Cobra (AH-1G) (AH-1F)	70-16091	21035		RA
☐ Bell 209 Huey Cobra (AH-1S) (AH-1F)	78-23111	22217		RA
☐ Hughes 77 Apache (AH-64A)	85-25481	PV.302		RA
☐ Vertol V.114 Chinook (CH-47A) (ACH-47A)	64-13149	B.121		RA

SANDERS COLLECTION (AL29)

Address:	PO Box 707, Troy, Alabama 36081-0707.
Tel:	334-392-8017 Fax: 334-566-3257
Admission:	By prior permission only.
Location:	At Troy Airport which is about three miles north of the town off Route 53.

Wiley Sanders operates a trucking company and has owned many warbirds over the years. He has raced a number of fighters at Reno and several of his aircraft have been sold to other collectors in the USA.

The Australian-built Mustang was the first built by Commonwealth Aircraft and made its maiden flight at Fisherman's Bend in May 1946. The aircraft joined the collection in 1981.

The Lodestar spent periods working in Central America before returning to the USA. In the early 1960s it was converted to tricycle undercarriage configuration but has now back in its original state. The Fennec has had a varied career.

TYPE	REG/SER	CON. NO.	PI/NOTES	STATUS
☐ Cessna 305A Bird Dog (L-19A) (O-1A)	N37WM	21690	51-4805, N5185G	RAA
☐ Commonwealth CA-17 Mustang 20 [North American P-51D]	N51WB	1326	A68-1, (VH-EMQ), N7783	RAA
☐ Lockheed 18-56-23 Lodestar (C-60A)	N250JR	18-2232	42-32186, YS-26, XH-TAB, XH-TAL, NC75504, XH-TAL, N75504, N500W, N501W, (N504W), N510RA, N250JG	RAA
☐ North American NA-108 Mitchell (B-25J) (TB-25K)	N5262V	108-47539	44-86705	RAA

| ☐ North American NA-168 Texan (T-6G) | N29939 | 168-138 | 49-3034, C.6-187 (Spain) | RAA |
| ☐ Sud Fennec [North American NA-174 Trojan (T-28A)] | N14112 | 174-395 | 51-7542, 124 (France), N14112, 1242 (Haiti) | RAA |

SELMA MONUMENTS (AL30)

Location:	On permanent view at two locations in the town.

TYPE	REG/SER	CON. NO.	PI/NOTES	STATUS
☐ Lockheed 580 (T-33A)	51-6707	580-6039	At Block Park Stadium on Highway 22 West.	PV
☐ Lockheed 580 (T-33A)	53-5256	580-8595	At Craig Field south of the town.	PV

SMITH AIR NATIONAL GUARD BASE (AL31)

Address:	117th AFW, 5401 East Lake Boulevard, Birmingham, Alabama 35217-5000.
Tel:	205-814-9200
Admission:	By prior permission only.
Location:	In the north eastern suburbs of the city.

The 135th Squadron was allocated to the state in January 1922 and was based at Roberts Field in Birmingham. A variety of observation and training types were used up to 1943. B-25 Mitchells were flown in the Pacific after the USA entered World War II.

The unit returned to Birmingham in November 1946 and, apart from periods of call up during the Korean War and the 1961 Berlin crisis, has always been in residence. The F-4 and RF-84 are in a park near to the gate and should be joined by the Army helicopters in due course.

TYPE	REG/SER	CON. NO.	PI/NOTES	STATUS
☐ Bell 205 Iroquois (UH-1D) (UH-1H)	66-16086	5780		RA
☐ Hughes 369M Cayuse (HO-6) (OH-6A)	67-16243	0628		RA
☐ McDonnell M.98DF Phantom II (RF-4C)	63-7745	496		RA
☐ Republic RF-84F Thunderflash	'11279'		52-7409	RAX
☐ Sikorsky S-64A Tarhe (CH-54B)	69-18479	64087		RA

SOUTHERN MUSEUM OF FLIGHT (AL32)

Address:	4343 73rd Street North, Birmingham, Alabama 35206-3642.
Tel:	205-833-8226 Fax: 205-836-2439 Email: southernmuseumofflight@yahoo.com
Admission:	Tuesday-Saturday 0930-1630.
Location:	In the north eastern suburbs of the city – close to the municipal airport.

The Birmingham Aero Club was formed in 1932 and in 1965 decided to set up an exhibition. The Birmingham Air and Space Museum came into being and a display was staged at Samford University in 1967. A move to larger premises in the airport terminal building took place and the present name was adopted in 1969.

The museum bought its current site in 1977 and over the next six years constructed a purpose-built exhibition hall and workshops. A second hall has been completed and others will be constructed. The displays of photographs, memorabilia and documents trace the history of aviation. in the region.

The Huff-Daland Duster is a rarity. The biplane was one of the first used by a company which became Delta Air Lines. Only two examples survive. The Alexander Eaglerock was built in Colorado in the late 1920s and early 1930s. About 900 were completed before the depression. Several homebuilt types can be seen among them the locally designed and flown Harrison Mini-Mac. John Isaacs designed the Fury as a 7/10ths replica of the famous Hawker fighter. The airframe was based on the Currie Wot. The prototype flew for the first time at Thruxton in England in August 1963. Plans were sold and around 20 have been completed in several countries.

The Beech Starship was an ambitious project which first flew in February 1986. Just over 50 were completed but the type was grounded in 2003. The museum was one of the few to receive an example.

Military aircraft are being added to the collection and a wide range of types can be seen. The early Mitchell force-landed in Lake Murray in North Carolina on 4th April 1943 and remained 150 feet beneath the surface until raised in September 2005. The airframe is now undergoing anti-corrosion treatment and it will be exhibited 'as-raised' in a new hall.

A unique research aircraft is the XV-11A. This was built by Mississippi State University to conduct trials on boundary layer control. The STOL aircraft powered by an Allison T63 turboprop driving a pusher ducted propeller made its maiden flight in December 1965. Modifications later took place and the last took to the air in 1982.

TYPE	REG/SER	CON. NO.	PI/NOTES	STATUS
☐ Aero Commander 680	'USAF'	515-185	N4247D, N800M, N23FC, N131JG	PVX
☐ Aero L-39C Albatros	N82497	430405		PV
☐ Aeronca K	N17799	K-66	NC17799	PV
☐ Aeronca 11AC Chief	NC9180E	11AC-813		PV
☐ Aeronca 15AC Sedan	N1065H	15AC-83	NC1065H	PV
☐ Alexander Eaglerock Long Wing	NC5914	557	On loan	PVA
☐ Beagle B.206 Series 1	N163	B.007	G-ASOF	RA
☐ Beagle B.206 Series 2	N15JP	B.059	G-AVLK	RA
☐ Bede BD-4	N56BT	97		PV
☐ Bede BD-5B	N51CJ	2185		PV
☐ Beech D18S Expeditor (C18S) (SNB-2C) (SNB-3Q) (SNB-5)	N5058	6485	Bu51158	RA
☐ Beech D45 Mentor (T-34B)	N14VY	BG-74	Bu140740	PV
☐ Beech 2000 Starship I	N214JB	NC-14	N5674B	PV
☐ Bell 47G-4A	N1349X	7534		PV
☐ Bell 205 Iroquois (UH-1H)	66-16873	9067		PV
☐ Bell 209 Huey Cobra (AH-1G) (AH-1S)	71-21047	21118		PV

Alabama

	TYPE	REG/SER	CON. NO.	PI/NOTES	STATUS
☐	Bellanca 8KCAB Decathlon	N68501	40-72		PV
☐	Bensen B-8M Gyrocopter	N4470	210		PV
☐	Boeing-Stearman A75N1 Kaydet (PT-17)				RA
☐	Bushby M.II Mustang II	N7XL	M-II-707		PV
☐	Cessna 310	N3051D	35251		PV
☐	Cessna 318B Tweety Bird (318A) (T-37A) (T-37B)	'63-555'	40127	56-3555	PVX
☐	Cessna 337M Super Skymaster (O-2A)	N849AF	337M0214	68-10849	RA
☐	Convair 8-12 Delta Dagger (TF-102A)	56-2352	8-12-84		RA
☐	Convair 8-24 Delta Dart 31 (F-106A)	59-0113	8-31-02	Front fuselage only.	PV
☐	Culver LCA Cadet	N41712	419		PV
☐	Cumulus 2F	N203JS	02	D-5278	PV
☐	Curtiss D Pusher (R)			On loan	PVA
☐	Davis DA-2	N1517C	37		RA
☐	Douglas DC-3A-467 Skytrain (C-47B) (R4D-6) (EC-47J)	N48211	15273/26718	43-49457, Bu50814, 0814 (US Army)	PV
☐	Douglas A-26C Invader	'434517'	29003	44-35724, N7954C	RA
☐	Douglas A-4C Skyhawk (A4D-2N)	Bu148536	12729	Front fuselage only.	PV
☐	Fairchild M-62A Cornell (PT-19A)	'42-83114'		42-2871(?), NC38985 – composite	RACX
☐	Fokker D VII (R)	N904AC	03	F-BNDH, EI-APV	PVA
☐	Forney F.1A	N7574C	5691		PV
☐	General Dynamics F-111A	67-0069	A1-114		PV
☐	Great Lakes 2T-1A-2	N666MT	0748		PV
☐	Grumman G-89 Tracker (S2F-1) (S-2A) (TS-2A)	N91368	469	Bu136560, MM136560	PV
☐	Grumman G-303 Tomcat (F-14A)	Bu162608	530		PV
☐	Harrison Mini Mac	N75GH	3		PV
☐	Heath Super Parasol				RA
☐	Huff-Daland Duster	'NR2953'	62	On loan	PVX
☐	Hughes 369M Cayuse (HO-6) (OH-6A)	67-16087	0472		RA
☐	Isaacs Fury	N1099	1049		PV
☐	Laister-Kauffman LK.10A	N56588	71		PV
☐	Lockheed 383-04-05 Starfighter (F-104C)	56-0929	183-1217		PV
☐	Lockheed 580 (T-33A)	57-0602	580-1251		PV
☐	Lockheed A-12	60-6937	131		RA
☐	McDonnell M.36BA Voodoo (TF-101B) (TF-101F)	57-0302	480	Front fuselage only.	PV
☐	McDonnell M.98AM Phantom II (F-4B) (F-4N)	'64-1049'	1422	Bu152996 –	PVX
☐	Mikoyan-Gurevich MiG-21UM		516999054		PV
☐	Mitchell Wing B-10				PV
☐	Monnett Monerai S	N5587X	0045		PV
☐	Monnett Sonerai II-LT	N64RD	4464		PV
☐	Mooney M-18L Mite	N370A	31		PV
☐	North American NA-82 Mitchell (B-25C)	41-12634	82-5269		RAC
☐	North American NA-168 Texan (T-6G)	N12CC	168-66	49-2962, N9676C	PV
☐	North American NA-190 Sabre (F-86D) (F-86L)	52-4243	190-646	Possible identity.	PV
☐	North American NA-217 Super Sabre (F-100C)	54-1753	217-14		PV
☐	North American NA-226 Trojan (T-28C)	Bu140659	226-236	Bu140659, N75ES –	PV
☐	North American NA-227 Sabre (F-86F)	'12910'	227-268	55-5035 – rear fuselage from c/n 227-247, 55-5014 –	PVX
☐	North American NA-285 Sabreliner (T3J-1) (T-39D)	Bu151338	285-27		PV
☐	North American NA-367 Buckeye (T-2C)	Bu159165	367-16		PV
☐	Northrop N-156T Talon (T-38A)	62-3723	N.5428		PV
☐	Parsons (Marvel) XV-11A	65-13070			PV
☐	Pazmany PL-4A	N43NP	424-18-3854		PV
☐	Piel CP.301 Emeraude	N54144	1048		PV
☐	Piper J-3C-65 Cub	N30451	4840	NC30451	PV
☐	Piper PA-28-140 Cherokee	N3931K	28-23804		PV
☐	Pitts S-1C Special	N14RH	RMH1		PV
☐	Pratt-Read PR-G1 (LNE-1)	N60745	PRG-01-35	(USN) –	PV
☐	Rand Robinson KR-1	N20501	2667		PV
☐	Republic RC-3 Seabee	N6537K	803	NC6537K	PV
☐	Republic F-84F Thunderstreak	51-1487			RA
☐	Republic F-84F Thunderstreak	51-9404			PV
☐	Republic F-105F Thunderchief	63-8365	F-142		PV
☐	Ross Seabird	N667RR	001		PV
☐	Rotec Rally 2B	001			PV
☐	Rotorway Executive	N232TC	3306		PV
☐	Rutan 27 Vari-Viggen	N49VZ	004		PV
☐	Rutan 33 Vari-Eze	N101EZ	1182		PV
☐	Sikorsky S-64A Tarhe (CH-54B)	69-18464	64071	On loan.	RA
☐	Stinson SR-5 Reliant				RAC
☐	Stinson SR-9 Reliant				RAD
☐	Stinson 10A Voyager	N31553	7802	NC31553	PV
☐	Stoddard-Hamilton SH-2 Glasair IIFT	N612WC	4243572040		PV
☐	Stolp SA.100 Starduster	N111JB	JB-01		PV
☐	Taylor J-2 Cub				RA
☐	Vought A-7E Corsair II	Bu159278	E416		PV
☐	Vultee V-79 Valiant (BT-13B)	'762'		42-89762	PV
☐	Wright Flyer (R)				PV
☐	WSK Lim-2 [MiG-15bis]	'2057'	1B 009-17	917 (Poland)' '016'	PVX

TROY MONUMENT (AL33)

Location: On permanent view in Bicentennial Park on Highway 231 in the southern part of the town.

	TYPE	REG/SER	CON. NO.	PI/NOTES	STATUS
☐	Bell 209 Huey Cobra (AH-1G) (AH-1F)	67-15771	20435		PV

TUSCALOOSA MONUMENTS (AL34)

Location:	On permanent view at two locations in the town.

TYPE	REG/SER	CON. NO.	PI/NOTES	STATUS
☐ Bell 205 Iroquois (UH-1H)	66-16907	9101	At the Veterans Park in McFarland Boulevard.	PV
☐ Lockheed 580 (T-33A)	'54109'	580-8448	53-5109 – at the airport.	PV
☐ Vought A-7E Corsair II	Bu159261	E599	At the Veterans Park.	PV

UNITED STATES AIR FORCE ENLISTED HERITAGE HALL (AL35)

Address:	Building 1210, Gunter Air Force Base, Alabama 36114-5000.
Tel:	334-279-1110
Admission:	Monday-Friday 0800-1630
Location:	In the north eastern suburbs of Montgomery on Route 2/21.

The base is administered by Maxwell AFB and houses some departments of the Air University. A small display tracing the traditions of the enlisted airman has been set up. In the building are photographs, documents and uniforms. The C-47 is on show near the exhibition and the BT-15 is by the north gate.

TYPE	REG/SER	CON. NO.	PI/NOTES	STATUS
☐ Boeing 464-201-7 Stratofortress (B-52D)			Rear fuselage only.	PV
☐ Douglas DC-3A-467 Skytrain (C-47B) (R4D-6) (C-47J)	'43-49770'	14943/26388	43-49127, Bu50779, N701, N645, N214GB	PVX
☐ Vultee V-74A Valiant (BT-15)	42-41303	74-8331 (?)	42-41303, N75195 (?) – on base gate.	PV

UNITED STATES ARMY AVIATION MUSEUM (AL36)

Address:	PO Box 620610, Fort Rucker, Alabama 36330-0610.
Tel:	334-255-1069 Email: curator@armyavnmuseum.org
Admission:	Monday-Saturday 0900-1600; Sunday 1200-1600.
Location:	Close to the Daleville entrance to the base off Route 85.

Army aviation in the USA came into being in June 1942 when Piper Cubs were used to direct artillery fire. During the Second World War increasing numbers of light aircraft were used in this and other roles. In the Korean conflict helicopters joined the fixed wing machines.

For the last 40 years the vast site at Fort Rucker has been the home of US Army Aviation. Three airfields and many unprepared sites are used to train crews in all aspects of helicopter and fixed wing operations. Plans for a museum were put forward in 1955 and were accepted officially in 1963. Volunteers started collecting material and in 1966 the first full time staff were appointed.

In 1968 the museum moved into three World War II wooden buildings and around these aircraft parks were set up. The collection expanded rapidly and soon outgrew the space available. Funds were raised and a superb new exhibition hall was completed in 1989. There are plans for further development.

A series of imaginative displays which show the roles of Army aircraft and helicopters in combat conditions are among the highlights in the main hall. The museum has the largest collection of helicopters in the world. The first one to enter service with US forces was the Sikorsky R-4B Hoverfly. The prototype of this design flew in January 1942 and the USAAF took delivery of its first example in 1943. Several were sent to South East Asia and soon the first rescue of a downed pilot by helicopter took place in Burma. The Sikorsky company has been to the fore in the production of rotary winged aircraft and many examples of their products are on show.

Bell was another of the pioneer manufacturers in this field and their Model 30 flew in 1943. This was developed into the 47 which remained in production for more than 30 years and achieved fame in the 'MASH' television series. The Vietnam conflict saw the emergence of the Iroquois in many roles including use as a gunship. The 204 first flew in 1956 and over 11,000 204s, 205s and almost 2,000 of the fearsome 209 Huey Cobra with a redesigned fuselage were built.

Another company to pioneer production of the helicopter was Hiller and several examples of the successful UH12 series are on view along with others produced only in small numbers.

The development of the helicopter as military weapon and in the transport and liaison role is portrayed in the range of types on show and in the associated displays. The Army flew a variety of light fixed wing types during and after World War II and examples of these can be seen.

Several early aircraft and replicas have been acquired to show the work of the US Army Air Service during World War I and in the years after hostilities ended.

TYPE	REG/SER	CON. NO.	PI/NOTES	STATUS
☐ Aero Commander 520 (YL-26) (YU-9A)	52-6219	520-23		PV
☐ Aeronca 65TL Defender	'42-7798'	4760T	NC31309	RAX
☐ Aeronca 7BCM Champion (L-16A)	47-0924	7BCM-299	47-0924, N6408C	PV
☐ American Helicopter XA-8 Jet Jeep (XH-26)	50-1840			RA
☐ Auster B.5 AOP.9	XP277		B5/10/162(?)	RA
☐ Beech C50 Seminole (L-23D) (U-8D)	56-3712	LH-113		RA
☐ Beech C50 Seminole (RL-23D) (RU-8D) (RU-8G)	58-1359	LHC-5 (LH-		PV
☐ Beech 65-A90-1 Ute (RU-21E) (JU-21H)	70-15888	LU-14		RA
☐ Beech 95-B55B Cochise (T-42A)	65-12697	TF-19		RA
☐ Beech A200 Huron (C-12A) (C-12C)	73-22250	BC-1		RA
☐ Beech A200CT Huron (C-12D) (RC-12D)	80-23376	GR-11 (BP-17)		RA
☐ Bell 47D Sioux (H-13B)	48-827	111		RA
☐ Bell 47D Sioux (H-13B) (H-13C)	48-845	129		PV
☐ Bell 47D-1 Sioux (H-13E) (OH-13E)	51-14193	958		RA
☐ Bell 47D-1 Sioux (H-13E) (OH-13E)	51-14218	993		PV
☐ Bell 47G-3B-1 Sioux (TH-13T)	67-17024	3741		RA
☐ Bell 204 (XH-40) (XHU-1)	55-4459	1		RA

Alabama

☐ Bell 204 Iroquois (HU-1A) (UH-1A)	59-1695	154		RA
☐ Bell 204 Iroquois (HU-1B) (UH-1B)	60-3553	199		PV
☐ Bell 204 Iroquois (HU-1B) (UH-1B)	60-3554	200		PV
☐ Bell 204 Iroquois (HU-1B) (UH-1B)	61-0792	372		RA
☐ Bell 204 Iroquois (HU-1B) (UH-1B)	62-1884	404		RA
☐ Bell 204 Iroquois (HU-1B) (UH-1B)	62-2099	619	At Ozark Gate.	PV
☐ Bell 204 Iroquois (UH-1C) (UH-1M)	65-9446	1346		RA
☐ Bell 204 Iroquois (UH-1C) (UH-1M)	65-12740	1467	At Enterprise gate.	PV
☐ Bell 204 Iroquois (UH-1C) (UH-1M)	66-15156	1884		RA
☐ Bell 205 Iroquois (YHU-1D) (YUH-1D) (UH-1D)	60-6030	703		PV
☐ Bell 205 Iroquois (UH-1D) (UH-1H)	63-8781	4073	Near Daleville Gate.	PV
☐ Bell 205 Iroquois (UH-1D) (UH-1H)	65-9567	4611		RA
☐ Bell 205 Iroquois (UH-1D) (UH-1H)	65-9974	5018		PVD
☐ Bell 205 Iroquois (UH-1D) (UH-1H)	66-16197	5891		RA
☐ Bell 205 Iroquois (UH-1H)	66-16325	8519	At Daleville.	PV
☐ Bell 205 Iroquois (UH-1H)	68-16237	10896	At Tank Hill Gate.	RA
☐ Bell 205 Iroquois (UH-1H)	66-16333	8527	Front fuselage only.	PVD
☐ Bell 205 Iroquois (UH-1H)	68-15595	10525		RA
☐ Bell 205 Iroquois (UH-1H)	68-16404	11063		RA
☐ Bell 206 Kiowa (YOH-4A) (YOH-4A)	'62-4201'	001	62-4202	RAX
☐ Bell 206A Kiowa (OH-58A)	'68-1684'	40001	N4768R, 68-16687	PVX
☐ Bell 206A Kiowa (OH-58A)	71-20349	41210		RA
☐ Bell 206A Kiowa (OH-58A)	71-20468	41329		RA
☐ Bell 206A Kiowa (OH-58A)	71-20803	41664		RA
☐ Bell 206A Kiowa (OH-58A)	71-20864	41725	On base.	PV
☐ Bell 206A Kiowa (OH-58A) (OH-58D)	'91-6322'	40543	69-16322	RAX
☐ Bell 207 Sioux Scout	N73927	1		PV
☐ Bell 209 Huey Cobra (AH-1G)	N209J	20001	64-7016	RA
☐ Bell 209 Huey Cobra (AH-1G) (AH-1F)	67-15524	20188	On base.	PV
☐ Bell 209 Huey Cobra (AH-1G) (AH-1Q) (AH-1S)	66-15246	20002		RA
☐ Bell 209 Huey Cobra (AH-1G) (AH-1Q) (AH-1S)	66-15248	20004	66-15248, N736NA	PV
☐ Bell 209 Huey Cobra (AH-1G) (AH-1Q) (AH-1S)	70-16072	21016		RA
☐ Bell 209 Huey Cobra (AH-1G) (AH-1S)	68-17109	20837		RA
☐ Bell 209 Huey Cobra (AH-1G) (AH-1S)	71-15090	21050	71-15090, Z.14-1 (Spain), HA.14-1 (Spain)	PV
☐ Bell 209 Huey Cobra (AH-1S) (AH-1F)	78-23098	22204		PV
☐ Bell 309 King Cobra	'72-2504'	2503	N309J	RAX
☐ Bell 409 (YAH-63A)	73-22247			RA
☐ Blériot XI (R)				PV
☐ Boeing 541 Scout (YL-15)	47-429	20009	47-429, N4210A	RA
☐ Boeing-Sikorsky RAH-66 Comanche	94-0327	66001		RA
☐ Boeing-Sikorsky RAH-66 Comanche	95-0001			RA
☐ Boeing-Stearman B75N1 Kaydet (N2S-3)	'40-7121'	75-7121	Bu07517, N36691	RAX
☐ Boeing-Vertol 237 (YUH-61A)	73-21656		On base.	RA
☐ Boeing-Vertol 347 (Vertol V.114 (CH-47A))	65-7992	B.164		RA
☐ Brantly B.2 (YHO-3)	58-1496	63		RA
☐ Cessna R172E Mescalero (T-41B)	67-15161	R1720162		RA
☐ Cessna 195 (LC-126C) (U-20A)	51-6998	7841		RA
☐ Cessna 305A Bird Dog (L-19A) (O-1A)	50-1327	21001		PV
☐ Cessna 305A Bird Dog (L-19A) (O-1A)	51-4943	21835	51-4943, N4507B	RA
☐ Cessna 305A Bird Dog (L-19A) (O-1A)	51-12349	22675		RA
☐ Cessna 310A Blue Canoe (L-27A) (U-3A)	57-5863	38018		PV
☐ Cessna 318B Tweety Bird (318A) (T-37A) (T-37B)	56-3466	40038	Spent a period as 318D Dragonfly 67-14520.	PV
☐ Cessna CH-1B Seneca (YH-41)	56-4244	45013		RA
☐ Convair 105 (A)	46-159	92		RA
☐ Curtiss 1C Jenny (JN-4D)	'18-2780'	278	N5162	PVX
☐ Curtiss-Wright VZ-7AP Aerial Jeep	58-5508			RA
☐ De Havilland DHC.2 Beaver (YL-20A) (YU-6A)	51-6263	109		PV
☐ De Havilland DHC.3 Otter (U-1A)	57-6135	283		PV
☐ De Havilland DHC.4 Caribou (YAC-1) (YCV-2A) (YC-7A)	57-3080	4	CF-LKU-X	PV
☐ Del Mar DH.1A Whirlymite	002	VA23-204	N3349C	RA
☐ Dornier Do 27B-1	56+67	361	AS+940, GA+390, D-EFIB	RA
☐ Fairchild-Hiller FH-1100 (OH-5A)	62-4208	5	62-4208, N815Z – possible identity.	RA
☐ Firestone 45C (XR-9)	46-001			RA
☐ Fokker E V (FSM)	'143/18'			PVX
☐ Goodyear GA-468 Inflatoplane (XAO-3)	57-6532			RA
☐ Grumman G-134 Mohawk (YAO-1A) (YOV-1A)	57-6539			RA
☐ Grumman G-134 Mohawk (OV-1B)	62-5860	19B		RA
☐ Hawker P.1127 Kestrel (XV-6A)	64-18264		XS690 – on loan from USAFM, OH.	PV
☐ Helio H-391 Courier (YL-24)	52-2540	1	N92859	RA
☐ Hiller UH12A Raven (H-23A)	51-3975	188		PV
☐ Hiller UH12B Raven (H-23B) (OH-23B)	51-16142	296		RA
☐ Hiller UH12E Raven (H-23F) (OH-23F)	62-12508	2284		RA
☐ Hiller 1033 Rotor Cycle (YROE-1)	Bu4004	2		RA
☐ Hiller HJ.1 Hornet (YH-32)	55-4963	6(?)		RA
☐ Hiller HJ.1 Hornet (YH-32)	55-4965	8		RA
☐ Hughes 269A Osage (TH-55A)	'67-18000'		Assembled from parts.	RAX
☐ Hughes 269A Osage (TH-55A)	67-16795	78-0902		PV
☐ Hughes 269A Osage (TH-55A)	67-16966	1073		RA
☐ Hughes 369M Cayuse (HO-6) (OH-6A)	65-12917	340002		RA
☐ Hughes 369M Cayuse (HO-6) (OH-6A)	'65-24213'	340013	65-12928	RAX
☐ Hughes 369M Cayuse (HO-6) (OH-6A)	65-12962	340047		PV
☐ Hughes 369M Cayuse (HO-6) (OH-6A)	68-17340	341300		PV

Alabama

☐ Hughes 77 Apache (YAH-64A)	73-22248	AV.02		RA
☐ Hughes 77 Apache (YAH-64A)	73-22249	AV.03		PV
☐ Interstate S1B1 Cadet (O-63) (L-6)	43-2560	003		RA
☐ Kaman K-600 Huskie (HOK-1) (OH-43D)	'61-38101'		Bu138101, N6062C	RAX
☐ Lockheed 186 (XH-51A)	Bu151262	186-1001		RA
☐ Lockheed 186 (XH-51A)	Bu151263	186-1002		RA
☐ Lockheed 187 Cheyenne (AH-56A)	66-8830	187-1005		RA
☐ Lockheed 187 Cheyenne (AH-56A)	66-8832	187-1007		PV
☐ Lockheed 426-45-15 Neptune (P2V-5) (P2V-5F) (P-2E) (AP-2E)	Bu131485	426-5366		PV
☐ Lockheed CL-475	N6940C	001	On loan from NASM, DC.	RA
☐ Lockheed Q-Star (YO-3A)	69-18000	001		RA
☐ Lockheed/Schweizer SGS.2-32 (X-26B) (QT-2)	67-15345		67-15345, Bu715345, N2471W	RA
☐ McCulloch MC-4C (YH-30)	52-5837	001		RA
☐ McDonnell M.82 (XL-25) (XH-25) (XV-1)	53-4016			RA
☐ Nieuport 28C.1	'17-6531'	6531	N5246, G-BSKS	PVX
☐ North American NA-122 Mustang (P-51D)	44-72990	122-39449	44-72990, 9283 (RCAF), N6322T	RA
☐ North American NA-154 Navion (L-17A)	47-1344	NAV-4-1075 (154-48)		RA
☐ North American NA-200 Trojan (T-28B)	Bu137747	200-110		RA
☐ North American NA-265 Sabreliner (T-39A) (CT-39A)	61-0685	265-88		PV
☐ Piasecki PV-18 Retriever (H-25A)	51-16616	45		PV
☐ Piasecki PD-22 Work Horse (H-21B) (CH-21B)	53-4369	B.119	53-4369, N100RB	RA
☐ Piper J-3C-65 Cub	'40-0003'			PVX
☐ Piper J-3C-65 Cub (L-4B)	43-515	9376	43-515, N14440	RA
☐ Piper J-3C-65 Cub (O-59A) (L-4A)	42-15174	8293		PV
☐ Piper PA-18-95 Super Cub (L-18C)	52-2536	18-2136	52-2536, N555X	RA
☐ Piper PA-18-125 Super Cub (L-21A) (TL-21A) (U-7A)	51-15782	18-947		RA
☐ Rotorway Scorpion 1				RA
☐ Rotorway Scorpion 1	N8565	LWL-H-1		RA
☐ Royal Aircraft Factory B.E.2c (R)	'1780'			PVX
☐ Royal Aircraft Factory S.E.5A (FSM)	'F8010'			PVX
☐ Ryan 143 Vertifan (VZ-11) (XV-5A) (XV-5B)	N705NA		62-4506	RA
☐ Ryan 92 (VZ-3)	56-6941		N705NA (?)	RA
☐ Ryan Navion A (L-17B) (U-18B)	48-1046	NAV-4-1752	48-1046, N555U	PV
☐ Sikorsky VS-316A Hoverfly (R-4B)	43-46592	136		PV
☐ Sikorsky VS-316A Hoverfly (R-4B)	43-46521	65		PV
☐ Sikorsky VS-316B Hoverfly II (R-6A)	43-45473		43-45473, N5282N	PV
☐ Sikorsky S-51	N92805	5107		RA
☐ Sikorsky S-51 Dragonfly (H-5G)	48-0558			PV
☐ Sikorsky S-51 Dragonfly (HO3S-1)	Bu124352	51213		RA
☐ Sikorsky S-51 Dragonfly (R-5A) (R-5D) (H-5D)	43-46645			PV
☐ Sikorsky S-52-2 (YH-18A)	49-2888	52005		RA
☐ Sikorsky S-55B Chickasaw (H-19C) (UH-19C)	51-14272	55225		RA
☐ Sikorsky S-55D Chickasaw (H-19D) (UH-19D)	55-3221			RA
☐ Sikorsky S-55D Chickasaw (H-19D) (UH-19D)	55-5239	551021	On loan to USS *Alabama*, AL.	-
☐ Sikorsky S-56 Mojave (H-37A) (H-37B) (CH-37B)	55-0644	56031		PV
☐ Sikorsky S-58 Choctaw (H-34A) (CH-34A)	53-4526	5888		RA
☐ Sikorsky S-58 Choctaw (H-34A) (VH-34A)	56-4320	58718		RA
☐ Sikorsky S-59 (XH-39)	49-2890		Converted from S-52 (YH-18A)	RA
☐ Sikorsky S-64A Tarhe (CH-54A)	68-18438	64040		PV
☐ Sikorsky S-69 (XH-59A)	73-21942			RA
☐ Sikorsky S-70A Black Hawk (YUH-60A)	73-21651	70002		PV
☐ Sikorsky S-72	N740NA	72-001		RA
☐ Sopwith F.1 Camel (R)	'B6291'			PVX
☐ Stinson V-74 Vigilant (O-49) (L-1)	40-3141			RA
☐ Stinson V-76 Sentinel (L-5)	42-99103	76-1344	42-99103, N6407C	RA
☐ Stinson V-76 Sentinel (L-5G)	45-34985			PV
☐ Taylorcraft DCO-65 Grasshopper (O-57A) (L-2A)	42-35872	O-4333	42-35872, N47652	PV
☐ Taylorcraft DCO-65 Grasshopper (O-57A) (L-2A)	NC47301	L-4567	(USAAF) – on loan	RA
☐ Vertol V.114 Chinook (CH-47A)	60-3451	B.10		PV
☐ Vertol V.43 Shawnee (H-21C) (CH-21C)	56-2040	C.202		PV
☐ Windecker A/C7 Eagle I	N4196G	005		RA
☐ Wright B (R)				PV

UNITED STATES SHIP *ALABAMA* BATTLESHIP COMMISSION (AL37)

Address: PO Box 65, 2703 Battleship Parkway, Mobile, Alabama 36601.
Tel: 251-433-2703/4 **Fax:** 251-433-2777 **Email:** btunnell@ussalabama.com
Admission: October–March daily 0800-1600; April–September daily 0800-1800.
Location: Close to Highways 31,90 and 98 on the west shore of Mobile Bay.

The battleship USS *Alabama* served during World War II in both the North Atlantic and Pacific campaigns. After a period of storage on the West Coast of the USA the authorities decided to scrap the ship. The people of Alabama raised 1,000,000 dollars to save her and she was towed 5,000 miles to Mobile. The battleship was opened to the public in January 1965 and four years later was joined by the submarine USS *Drum*.

A 75-acre park has been set up next to the berth and this serves as a military museum with aircraft and several vehicles on display. The rare Vought Kingfisher is mounted on the ship's catapult. The aircraft ended its military career with the Mexican Air Force which operated it on wheels. The Kingfisher was restored at the now closed Brookley Air Force Base.

The park is dominated by the B-52 which is part of the Vietnam era exhibition. The Northrop F-17 was designed as a

Alabama

lightweight fighter and evaluated by the Air Force against the F-16. Two were built and the example on show was transferred to the Navy to serve as a development prototype for the McDonnell F/A-18A Hornet.
  A few years ago an exhibition hall was constructed and about half the aircraft are now displayed here.

The site was struck by Hurricane Katrina in August 2005 and most of the buildings and several of the aircraft were damaged. Repairs soon started and the complex opened again in February 2006. Restoration of the aircraft is proceeding but it will be some time before all the work is completed. Not all areas can visited at present but an interesting exhibition is still available.

TYPE	REG/SER	CON. NO.	PI/NOTES	STATUS
☐ Bell 205 Iroquois (UH-1H)	69-16730	12307	At nearby Vietnam Memorial Wall.	PVX
☐ Bell 212 Iroquois (UH-1N) (HH-1N)	Bu158551	31422		PV
☐ Boeing 464-201-7 Stratofortress (B-52D)	55-0071	17187		PV
☐ Douglas DC-3A-467 Skytrain (C-47B) (VC-47B)	44-76326	15910/32658	44-76326,'O-76276'	PV
☐ Douglas EA-3B Skywarrioer (A3D-2Q)	Bu146457			PV
☐ Douglas A-4L Skyhawk (A4D-2N) (A-4C)	Bu147787	12551		PV
☐ General Dynamics 401 Fighting Falcon (F-16A)	79-0334	61-119		PV
☐ Grumman G-79 Panther (F9F-5P)	Bu126275			PV
☐ Grumman G-128 Intruder (A-6A) (KA-6D)	Bu151826	I-129		PV
☐ Grumman G-234 Albatross (G-64) (SA-16A) (UF-1G) (UF-2G) (HU-16E)	2129	G-356	52-0129 –	PV
☐ Grumman G-303 Tomcat (F-14A)	Bu161611	470		PV
☐ Kaman K-20 Seasprite (HU2K-1U) (UH-2B) (HH-2C) (SH-2F)	Bu150181	131	Bu150181, N8064F-	PV
☐ Lockheed A-12	60-6938	132		PV
☐ McDonnell M.98DE Phantom II (F-4C)	63-7487	485		PV
☐ McDonnell M.199-1A Eagle (F-15A)	'79-0078'	145/A125	75-0045	PVX
☐ McDonnell M.267 Hornet (F/A-18A)	Bu162417	253/A202		PV
☐ Mikoyan-Gurevich MiG-17	'2087'		87 (Bulgaria) – in false Soviet markings.	PVX
☐ North American NA-108 Mitchell (B-25J) (TB-25J) (TB-25N)	'02344'	108-34279	44-31004, N9463Z	PVX
☐ North American NA-122 Mustang (P-51D)	44-74216	122-40756		PV
☐ North American NA-177 Sabre (F-86D) (F-86L)	51-2993	177-50		PV
☐ Northrop P.600 (YF-17A)	72-1570	C.0002		PV
☐ Piasecki PD-22 Work Horse (H-21B) (CH-21B)	51-15859	B.6		PV
☐ Republic YF-105B Thunderchief	54-0102	B-5		PV
☐ Sikorsky S-55D Chickasaw (H-19D) (UH-19D)	55-5239	551021	On loan from US Army AM, AL.	PV
☐ Sikorsky S-62A Seaguard (HH-52A)	1378	62056		PV
☐ Sikorsky S-70B Sea Hawk (SH-60B)	Bu161562	70373		PV
☐ Vought V-310 Kingfisher (OS2U-3)	'Bu1368'	CV59250	(USN), 03 (Mexico), 'Bu0951'	RACX
☐ Vought RF-8G Crusader (F8U-1P) (RF-8A)	Bu145645			PV

UNITED STATES SPACE AND ROCKET CENTER (AL38)

Address: One Tranquility Base, Huntsville, Alabama 35805-3399.
Tel: 256-837-3400 **Email:** media@spacecamp.com
Admission: Daily 0900-1700 (Closes at 1800 in summer)
Location: West of the town on Route 20.

In 1950 the US Army moved its Missile Command to the Redstone Arsenal Site just outside Huntsville and a number of notable German scientists were employed. Ten years later NASA set up the Marshall Space Flight Center which developed rocket propulsion systems.
  The exhibition opened in March 1970 to show the work of the two research centres. The history of rocketry from the early days of Robert Goddard up to the present time is portrayed in a series of imaginative displays. Werner von Braun, who was responsible for the V-2 rocket, served at Redstone and his work is featured in the exhibition. A number of rockets

and spacecraft are on show along with the equipment needed to fire them.
  In 1908 William Quick made the first powered flight in Alabama. The remains of the aircraft were discovered on the Quick farm in 1964. Members of the local EAA Chapter rebuilt the Monoplane for the display.
  A fairly new venture is the construction nearby of the Aviation Challenge Park where school students experience aspects of the ground training carried out by jet pilots. The majority of the aircraft are on show in this area which is not normally open to the public.

TYPE	REG/SER	CON. NO.	PI/NOTES	STATUS
☐ Bell 204 Iroquois (UH-1B)	64-13954	1078		RA
☐ Bell 205 Iroquois (UH-1H)	70-16441	12746		PV
☐ Bell 209 Huey Cobra (AH-1G)	67-15767	20431		RA
☐ Ford JB-2 [Fieseler Fi 103A-1]				PV
☐ General Dynamics 401 Fighting Falcon (F-16B)	78-0101	62-27		PV
☐ General Dynamics F-111A	63-9775	A1-10		RA
☐ Grumman G-303 Tomcat (F-14A)	Bu160661	280		RA
☐ Hawker-Siddeley Harrier II (YAV-8B)	N704NA		Bu158394 – on loan from NMNA, FL.	RA
☐ Hughes 269A Osage (TH-55A)	67-16703	38-0810		RA
☐ Kaman K-20 Seasprite (SH-2F)	Bu162583	234		RA
☐ Lockheed 185 Orion (P3V-1) (P-3A)			Front fuselage only.	PV
☐ Lockheed A-12	60-6930	127		PV
☐ Martin SV-5P (X-24A) (FSM)				PV
☐ McDonnell M.98DJ Phantom II (F-4C)	64-0838	1187		PV
☐ Northrop N-156T Talon (T-38A)	60-0580	N.5153	60-0580, N580NA	RA
☐ Quick Monoplane				RA
☐ Rutan 33 Vari-Eze	N2VE	842		PV
☐ Vought A-7A Corsair II	Bu153242	A151		RA
☐ WSK Lim-6M (Lim-5P) [MiG-17PF]	511	1D 05-11	In Polish markings.	RA

Amongst the civil aircraft at the Southern Museum of Flight is this Forney F.1A. [AL32]

The crowded hall of the Alaskaland Pioneer Air Museum houses this Fairchild 24J. (Nigel Hitchman) [AK5]

The Kellner KR-1 Seagull can be seen at the Museum of Alaska Transportation and Industry. (Nigel Hitchman) [AK16]

VETERANS MEMORIAL MUSEUM (AL39)

Address: 2060A Airport Road, Huntsville, Alabama 35801.
Tel: 256-883-3737   **Email:** info@memorialmusem.org
Admission: Wednesday-Saturday 1000-1600.
Location: About 5 miles west of the town off Interstate 565.

The museum is run by the Alabama Center of Military History and occupies a building near the local airport. The exhibition traces developments from World War I up to the present day. On show are military vehicles, weapons, uniforms, documents, badges and photographs. Local people who lost their lives in conflict are honoured in the displays. Two Iroquois helicopters were registered to the organisation in 2006.

The Cougar arrived from the now closed M.W. Hamilton Machine Museum in Petal, Mississippi.

TYPE	REG/SER	CON. NO.	PI/NOTES	STATUS
☐ Bell 47G-2 Sioux (H-13H) (OH-13H)				PV
☐ Bell 204 Iroquois (UH-1C) (UH-1M)	66-0623	1605		PV
☐ Bell 205 Iroquois (UH-1D) (UH-1H)	N794CF	4086	63-8794	PV
☐ Bell 205 Iroquois (UH-1D) (UH-1H)	N795CF	5070	65-10026	PV
☐ Bell 206A Kiowa (OH-58A) (OH-58C)	71-20475	41336		PV
☐ Bell 209 Huey Cobra (AH-1G) (AH-1S)	70-15940	20884	70-15940, N794CF	PV
☐ Grumman G-105 Cougar (F9F-8T) (TF-9J)	Bu147418			PV

ALASKA

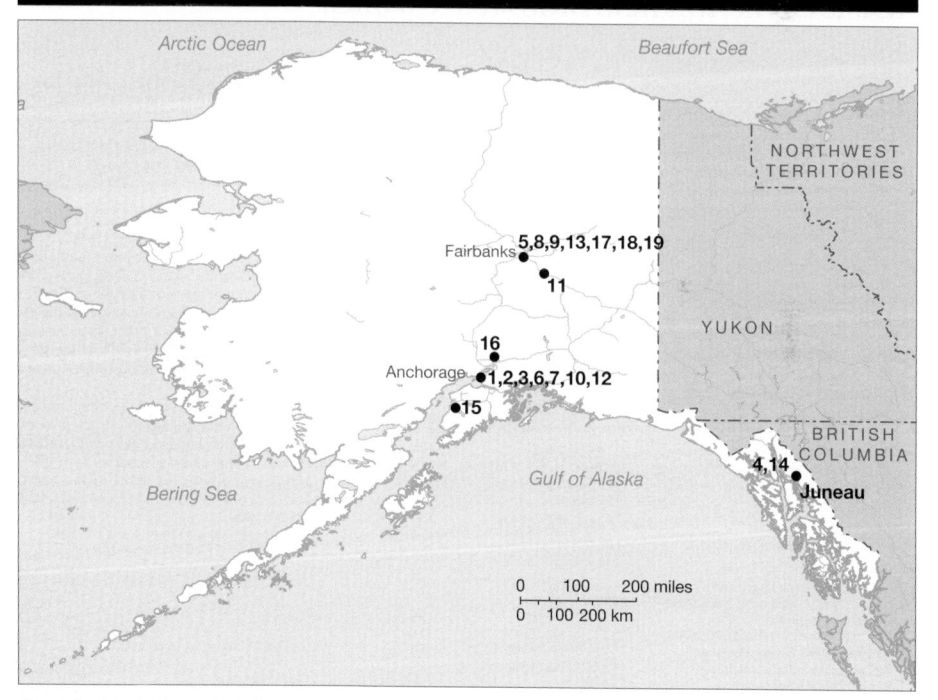

ALASKA AIR NATIONAL GUARD MUSEUM (AK1)

Address: 176th. Wing, Kulis Air National Guard Base, 5005 Raspberry Road, Anchorage, Alaska 99502-1998.
Tel: 907-249-1352
Admission: By prior permission only.
Location: Adjacent to Anchorage International Airport which is in the south western suburbs of the city.

The Alaska Air National Guard was formed in 1952 and for the first three years was located at Elmendorf Air Force Base. The facility on the south side of the international airport is named after Lieutenant Albert Kulis, who was killed on a training flight.

Former Master Sergeant Jim Herrick put forward the idea of a museum and worked for ten years on the project. A collection of memorabilia and photographs is housed in a building on the base. Two aircraft are displayed by the road which passes the site and the remainder, which all served in Alaska, are located just inside the main gate.

The C-47 was operated by the FAA for many years and has now been restored in false military colours. The Shooting Star was the first jet fighter to serve with the unit.

At the time of printing, the base was about to close and the aircraft will be moved to Elmendorf AFB.

TYPE	REG/SER	CON. NO.	PL/NOTES	STATUS
☐ Douglas DC-3A-456 Skytrain (C-47A)	'315497'	19320	42-100857, NC70, N23, N41, (N2273K), N41	RAX
☐ Fairchild 473 Provider (205) (C-123B) (C-123J)	56-4395	20279	56-4395, N4393E	RA
☐ Lockheed 080 Shooting Star (P-80C) (F-80C)	49-1849	080-2676		RA
☐ Lockheed 382-8B Hercules (C-130E)	64-0541	382-4031		RA
☐ Lockheed 580 (T-33A)	'35403'	580-8435	53-5096, (Bu156149)	RAX
☐ North American NA-161 Sabre (P-86A) (F-86A)	'12807'	161-189	49-1195	RAX
☐ North American NA-168 Texan (T-6G)	'34555'	168-119	49-3015	RAX

ALASKA ARMY NATIONAL GUARD COLLECTION (AK2)

Address: 724 Postal Service Loop, Fort Richardson, Anchorage, Alaska 99505-5900.
Tel: 907-384-1110
Admission: By prior permission only.
Location: About 3 miles north of Anchorage.

Helicopter units are in residence at Bryant Army airfield located on this large site. Two types, which have been used in the past, are preserved. The CH-54 was withdrawn from service a short time ago.

TYPE	REG/SER	CON. NO.	PL/NOTES	STATUS
☐ Bell 205 Iroquois (UH-1H)	69-15188	11476		RA
☐ Sikorsky S-64A Tarhe (CH-54B)	70-18488	64096		RA

ALASKA AVIATION HERITAGE MUSEUM (AK3)

Address: 4721 Aircraft Drive, Anchorage, Alaska 99502-1080.
Tel: 907-248-5325   **Fax:** 907-248-6391   **Email:** director@alaskaairmuseum.com
Admission: Mid May–mid September daily 0900-1700; Mid September–mid May Wednesday-Sunday 0900-1700.
Location: On the shore of Lake Hood which is in the south western suburbs of the city.

Formed in 1977, the Alaskan Historical Aviation Society has investigated all aspects of aviation in the state. A vast amount of archive material has been collected and crash sites have been explored. In the late 1980s a plot on the shore of Lake Hood was acquired and this has steadily been developed. A building to house the archives and to stage an excellent display of models, photographs and memorabilia was erected. Workshops and display hangars have been constructed and now most of the aircraft collection is protected from the harsh climate.

Many significant machines which have contributed to Alaskan aviation can be seen. The Stearman C2B arrived in the state in 1928 and the following year was bought by Ben Eielson. The biplane made the first landing on Mount McKinley in 1932. Just over 20 Pilgrim 100As and 100Bs were built and this survivor earned its keep in the state from 1936 until the mid-1980s.

A fairly new acquisition is the Hamilton H-47 which originally came to Alaska in 1937 for use by Wien Alaska Airlines. In recent years the airframe has had several owners in the 'lower 48'. The wreck of a Catalina was brought to the site in 1984 and this has now been joined by a complete example of the amphibian.

A few aircraft are maintained in flying condition including the Goose, the Waco YKC-S and the Stinson SR-9C. There are many wrecks out in the tundra and various groups have laid claim to them over the years. After a long period the museum has been able to recover some including sections of the Liberator. Other crash sites have been investigated and the Curtiss P-40 has been recovered from one and other airframes are sure to follow. The Centrair 101 is a conversion of the three seat L-13 observation aircraft into a six-seat bushplane. A few were produced in California.

This interesting museum is improving its collection and the displays present an informative picture of aviation in the state. Lake Hood houses several hundred active floatplanes and landplanes where the visitor can see modem bush pilots at work A number of interesting types are at the main airport.

TYPE	REG/SER	CON. NO.	PL/NOTES	STATUS
☐ Aeronca 65C Chief	NC22483	C-4339	Parts only – on loan from ASM, AK.	PVD
☐ Bede BD-5				PV
☐ Beech C18S Expeditor (C-45F) (UC-45F)	N1047B	7728	44-47342, N8011H, CF-PSU	PVA
☐ Beech D18S Expeditor (C18S) (SNB-2) (SNB-5)	'265'			PVX
☐ Beech B50 Twin Bonanza	N22W	CH-21		RAA
☐ Bell 205 Iroquois (UH-1D) (UH-1H)	65-12849	5186		PV
☐ Bellanca 31-42 Senior Pacemaker	NC16707	254	On loan from ASM, AK.	PVD
☐ Bellanca CH-300 Pacemaker	NC168N	175		PVD
☐ Bensen B-8M Gyrocopter		EAA004KR		PV
☐ Boeing 727			Front fuselage only.	PV
☐ Boeing 737-290C	N740AS	22578		PV
☐ Centrair 101 (Convair 105 (L-13A))	N3115G		47-0342	RA
☐ Cessna T-50 Bobcat (AT-17B) (UC-78B)				PVD
☐ Cessna T-50 Bobcat (AT-17B) (UC-78B)	NC30023	4629	42-71933	PV
☐ Consolidated 28-5A Canso A	C-FSAT	21986	9757 (Canada), CF-SAT	PV
☐ Consolidated 28-5A Catalina (PBV-1A) (OA-10A)	N57475	CV 465	(Bu67918), 44-33954, N44BY – with parts from c/n 21986 9757 (Canadian), CF-SAT, C-FSAT	PVC
☐ Consolidated LB-30 Liberator	N92MK	55	AL557, G-AGZI, SX-DAA, N9981F, N68735	RAD
☐ Curtiss 1C Jenny (JN-4D)			Front fuselage only – on loan from ASM, AK.	PVD
☐ Curtiss 50C Robin C-1	N76H	446	NC76H	PVA
☐ Curtiss 87-B3 Warhawk (P-40K)	'241'		42-45946, N45826	PVD
☐ De Havilland DHC.2 Beaver				PV
☐ Douglas DWC	23-1229	145	Parts only – on loan from ASM, AK.	PVD
☐ Douglas DC-6A Liftmaster (C-118A)	N43872	446665	53-3294	RA

Alaska

☐ Fairchild FC-2W2	NC7034	136		RAD
☐ Fairchild 24G	NC3212	2933	NC3212, N3212 – in Airport Terminal.	PV
☐ Fairchild 24W40				RAC
☐ Fairchild M-62A-4 Cornell (PT-26) (Cornell I)	FH842	T42-4191	42-14490, FH842, N58749	PV
☐ Fairchild 473 Provider (205) (C-123B) (C-123J)	N4390E	20274	56-4390	PV
☐ Fairchild Pilgrim 100-A	N709Y	6605	NC709Y – on loan	PVA
☐ Grumman G-21A Goose (G-39) (JRF-5)	N789	B102	Bu84807	PV
☐ Grumman G-44A Widgeon (J4F-1)	N13122	1312	Bu32958, N1069M, N69T, N89T, CF-KKF	PVA
☐ Grumman G-44A Widgeon (J4F-2)	N645DH	1329	Bu32975, N66645	PVA
☐ Hamilton H-47	N7791	50		RA
☐ Keystone Loening K84 Commuter	NC374V	313	On loan from ASM, AK.	PVD
☐ Leak Avid Flyer	N621R	621		PV
☐ Lockheed 422-87-23 Lightning (P-38L)			Wing only.	PVD
☐ Luscombe 8E Silvaire	N1347B	5974		PV
☐ McDonnell M.199-1A Eagle (F-15A)	74-0082	054/A043		PV
☐ McDonnell M.199-1A Eagle (F-15A)	74-0084	056/A045		PV
☐ Noorduyn Norseman VI (C-64A) (UC-64A)	N725E	507	43-35433	PV
☐ Piasecki PD-22 Work Horse (H-21B) (CH-21B)	54-4004	B.157	54-4004, 8000132 (France), N6869	PV
☐ Rutan 61 Long Ez	N60AK	1172		PV
☐ Sikorsky S-43	N15062	4302	NC15062 – Front section	RAD
☐ Sikorsky S-51 Dragonfly (H-5G)				RA
☐ Spartan 7W Executive	NC17602	7W-7		RAD
☐ Spencer S-12E Aircar	N10TS	1		PV
☐ Stearman C2B (C2M)	N5415	121	NC5415	PV
☐ Stinson Junior SR	NC13831	8787	NC13831, N13831 – on loan from ASM, AK.	PV
☐ Stinson SM-8A Junior			On loan from ASM, AK.	PVD
☐ Stinson SR-6 Reliant	N15135	9637	NC15135 – on loan from ASM, AK.	PVD
☐ Stinson SR-9C Reliant	NC18419	5350		PVA
☐ Stinson V-74 Vigilant (O-49A) (L-1A) (L-1F)	NL1ZS		41-18915, N704, N704E	PVA
☐ Stinson V-76 Sentinel (L-5G)	N2251	76-3613	(USAAF)	PV
☐ Stinson V-77 Reliant (AT-19)	N79458	77-36	42-46675, FK849, Bu11550	PVA
☐ Stinson V-77 Reliant (AT-19)	N9795H	77-66	42-46705, FK879, Bu?????	PVC
☐ Stinson 108-1 Voyager	N97713	108-713		PVA
☐ Taylorcraft BC-12D	NC43606	7265	NC43606, N43606	PV
☐ Taylorcraft DCO-65 Grasshopper (L-2MK)	N47648	L-5416		PV
☐ Travel Air S-6000B	N8159	6B-967	NC8159	PVC
☐ Volmer Jensen VJ-23				PVC
☐ Waco UIC	N13409	3756	NC13409 – on loan from ASM, AK.	PV
☐ Waco YKC-S	NC14066	3991	NC14066, N14066	PVA

ALASKA STATE MUSEUM (AK4)

Address: 395 Whittier Street, Juneau, Alaska 99801-1718.
Tel: 907-465-2901 **Fax:** 907-465-2976 **Email:** bob.banghart@alaska.gov
Admission: Mid May–mid October Monday-Friday 0900-2100, Saturday-Sunday 1300-1630; mid October–mid May Monday-Friday 0900-1700, Saturday-Sunday 1300-1630
Location: In the port area of the city.

This impressive museum, with its headquarters in Juneau, traces the history and culture of the state. There is a collection of aircraft, which have mainly been recovered from crash sites. For many years the airframes were stored with the Transportation Museum at Palmer and Wasilla. Some restoration work was carried out by volunteers at the two sites. The collection has now moved to the Alaska Aviation Heritage Museum at Anchorage. The DWC crashed in 1924 during its round-the-world flight. The two crew reached safety after a ten-day trek from the wreck to Port Moller.

The Keystone Loening was the personal aircraft of a former State Governor and is one of two known to exist. Restoration of this amphibian should start soon at Anchorage.

There are long-term plans to have some of the airframes on show in Juneau but this will not happen for some time.

ALASKALAND PIONEER AIR MUSEUM (AK5)

Address: PO Box 70437, 2300 Airport Way, Fairbanks, Alaska 99707-0437.
Tel: 907-452-2969 **Fax:** 907-451-0037 **Email:** akttl@imagi.net
Admission: Late May–early September daily 1100-2200
Location: At 2301 Airport Way in the Gold Dome at Alaskaland.

In the mid-1960s several historic buildings were moved to the site which opened as Alaskaland in 1967. On view are railway engines, mining equipment, boats and vehicles.

The aviation museum opened in the late 1980s in the Gold Dome. An interesting collection of aircraft and memorabilia has been acquired tracing the story of aviation in the region with particular emphasis on Fairbanks. There are many models, components, uniforms and documents on view.

In the early 1980s the remains of the Hamilton monoplane in which the famous pioneer Ben Eielson met his death in 1929 were moved from Siberia. The story of his last flight and the recovery of the wreck are shown in an informative display of photographs and press cuttings.

In the late 1920s the Hamilton company produced a series of all metal high wing monoplanes. Their rugged construction proved popular with pilots in Alaska and several of the 25 H-45s and H-47s served in the state.

Three 'bush' aircraft are on view. The Norseman arrived at the museum in the early 1990s and the Fokker Super Universal awaits restoration. Anthony Fokker set up a factory in America in the early 1920s and the Super Universal first flew in 1927. Around 80 were built over the next four years and the type carried out several pioneering flights. The aircraft in the collection was originally delivered to the Goodyear company and later migrated north to Alaska.

A range of homebuilt types can be seen. The parasol wing Bakeng Duce two-seater was designed by former Boeing engineer Jerry Bakeng in the late 1960s. The prototype made its maiden flight in 1970 and plans were soon made available to homebuilders. In 1971 it won the Outstanding New Design Trophy at the EAA Convention at Oshkosh. There is an excellent collection of engines along with models and components.

TYPE	REG/SER	CON. NO.	PI/NOTES	STATUS
☐ Bakeng Duce F.M.1	N75FD	F-01		PV
☐ Beech D18S Expeditor (C-45H)	N701FY	AF-620	52-10690, N9916Z	PV
☐ Bell 205 Iroquois (UH-1D) (UH-1H)	66-0934	5417		PV
☐ Dominator 1	N94LK	1		PV
☐ Eipper MX Quicksilver				PV
☐ Fairchild 24J	N20617	3409	NC20617 – on loan.	PV
☐ Fokker Super Universal	NC9792	840		PVD
☐ Hamilton H-45	NC10002	53		PVD
☐ Mitchell Wing B-10				PV
☐ Noorduyn Norseman VI (C-64A) (UC-64A)	N55555	228	43-5237	PV
☐ Pereira GP.3 Osprey II	N345JD	345		PV
☐ Piper PA-18-150 Super Cub	N2586P	18-4328		PV
☐ Rand Robinson KR-1	N3755F	1024		PV
☐ Raven S-50 Hot Air Balloon				PV
☐ Rotorway Scorpion 133		2925		PV
☐ Rutan 33 Vari-Eze	N37840	1036FK		PV
☐ Ryan ST-3KR Recruit (PT-22)	NC50880	1773	41-15744, NC50880.N50880	PV
☐ Stinson Junior SR	N13482	8734	NC13482	RAC
☐ Stinson V-77 Reliant (AT-19)	NC60924	77-1425	(USAAF), NC60924, N60924	PV
☐ War Aircraft P-47D Thunderbolt				PV

ANCHORAGE COMMUNITY COLLEGE (AK6)

Address:	2811 Merrill Field Road, Anchorage, Alaska 99501.
Tel:	907-204-7000 Email: info@alaska.edu
Admission:	By prior permission only.
Location:	At the airfield which is in the north eastern part of the city.

The college is part of the University of Alaska and trains airframe at engine fitters at its hangars and workshops at Merrill Field. The college also trains commercial pilots and air traffic controllers.

TYPE	REG/SER	CON. NO.	PI/NOTES	STATUS
☐ Bell 205 Iroquois (UH-1H)	N404RH	11162	68-16503	RA
☐ Bell 205 Iroquois (UH-1H)	N404JH	11262	68-16603	RA
☐ Bell 206B Jet Ranger	N793AC	793		RA
☐ Cessna 180A	N4UA	32851		RA
☐ Cessna 310E	N8136Z	31010004		RA
☐ Grumman G-111 Albatross (G-64) (SA-16A) (UF-1L) (LU-16C)	N116AG	G-214	51-7164, Bu142429	RA
☐ Mitsubishi MU-2D (MU-2B-10)	N863Q	117		RA
☐ Piper J-3C-65 Cub	N1561N	23093	NC1561N	RA
☐ Piper PA-38-112 Tomahawk	N9226T	38-78A0284		RA

ANCHORAGE INTERNATIONAL AIRPORT MONUMENT (AK7)

Location:	On permanent view in the terminal – the airport is in the south western part of the city.

TYPE	REG/SER	CON. NO.	PI/NOTES	STATUS
☐ Bell 47B	N105EH			PV

ARCTIC WARBIRDS (AK8)

Address:	PO Box 55596, North Pole, Alaska 99519-0041.
Tel:	907-696-8890 Email: F15Cricket@aol.com
Admission:	By prior permission only.
Location:	At Bradley Sky Ranch which is about 3 miles south east of Fairbanks off Route 2.

This organisation was formed in the 1990s and has three Beech 18s and one T-28 Trojan in its fleet. The Beech 18 served in the state for many years with airlines, companies and private individuals. Two of those in the collection are in a semi-derelict state and are currently used as spares for the airworthy example.

TYPE	REG/SER	CON. NO.	PI/NOTES	STATUS
☐ Beech C18S Expeditor (C-45F) (UC-45F)	N7379C	6373	43-35748	RAD
☐ Beech D18S Expeditor (C-45G)	N9551Z	AF-217	51-11660	RAA
☐ Beech D18S Expeditor (C-45G)	N702FY	AF-326	51-11769, N9330Z	RAD
☐ North American NA-200 Trojan (T-28B)	N887N	200-273	Bu138202	RAC

COLLEGE OF RURAL AND COMMUNITY DEVELOPMENT (AK9)

Address:	Tanana Valley Campus, PO Box 758080, Fairbanks, Alaska 99775.
Tel:	907-455-2921 Email: kwalexander@alaska.edu
Admission:	By prior permission only.
Location:	At the airport which is in the south western part of the city.

Alaska

The college operates from a number of sites around Fairbanks. The aviation department has premises at the airport and two Iroquois helicopters are in use but there may be other airframes in the buildings.

TYPE	REG/SER	CON. NO.	PI/NOTES	STATUS
☐ Bell 205 Iroquois (UH-1H)	68-15769	10699		RA
☐ Bell 205 Iroquois (UH-1H)	68-16513	11162		RA

COMMEMORATIVE AIR FORCE (ALASKA WING) (AK10)

Address:	POBox 190041, Anchorage, Alaska 99519-0041.
Tel:	akwingcaf@alaskawingcaf.org
Admission:	By prior permission only.
Location:	At Merrill Field which is in the northern part of the city.

The wing was formed in 2007 and the Canadian-built Harvard arrived at the airfield on 2nd August of that year. The aircraft is painted in its original Royal Canadian Air Force all-yellow colour scheme.

TYPE	REG/SER	CON. NO.	PI/NOTES	STATUS
☐ Canadian Car & Foundry Harvard 4 [North American NA-186]	N421QB	CCF4-212	20421, CF-UAD	RAA

EIELSON AIR FORCE BASE HERITAGE PARK (AK11)

Address:	354 Wing/PA, 354 Broadway, Eielson Air Force Base, Alaska 99702-3112.
Tel:	907-377-2116 **Email:** 354fw.pa@eielson
Admission:	By prior permission only.
Location:	About 15 miles south east of Fairbanks off Highway 2.

Named after the pioneer aviator Ben Eielson, this base opened in 1944 and houses fighter and strategic units. A heritage park has recently been constructed.

The six aircraft, which all flew from the field, have been placed in a wooded area. The airframe of a KB-29 resides in a nearby lake. The aircraft suffered a collapsed nosewheel when landing at the base on 17th April 1956.

The damaged aircraft was parked on the field for about five years before being pushed into a gravel pit where the cockpit, fin and rudder and one wingtip can be seen.

TYPE	REG/SER	CON. NO.	PI/NOTES	STATUS
☐ Boeing 345 Superfortress (B-29B) (KB-29P)	44-83905			RAD
☐ Boeing 717-148 Stratotanker (KC-135A) (KC-135E)	57-1458	17529		RA
☐ Cessna 337M Super Skymaster (O-2A)	68-11003	337M0279		RA
☐ Fairchild-Republic A-10A Thunderbolt II	75-0289	A10-38		RA
☐ General Dynamics 401 Fighting Falcon (F-16A)	78-0052	61-48		RA
☐ Lockheed 580 (T-33A)	53-6064	580-9667		RA
☐ McDonnell M.98DJ Phantom II (F-4C)	64-0905	1346		RA

ELMENDORF AIR FORCE BASE HERITAGE PARK (AK12)

Address:	3 Wing/PA, 6920 12th Street Suite 120, Elmendorf Air Force Base, Alaska 99506-2530.
Tel:	907-552-4698 **Email:** pateam@elmendorf.af.mil
Admission:	By prior permission only.
Location:	About 3 miles north of Anchorage.

This important base opened in July 1940 and is named after Captain Hugh Elmendorf, who was killed at Wright Field in Ohio in 1933 whilst testing a fighter aircraft.

The Delta Dagger is mounted near one of the gates to the field. The F-4 and T-33 reside in the Paxton Memorial Park which is dedicated to the memory of Colonel Pat Paxton who commanded the 21st Tactical Fighter Wing in the mid-1980s.

Plans have been put forward to enlarge the collection and to possibly construct a museum building to house the memorabilia collected.

TYPE	REG/SER	CON. NO.	PI/NOTES	STATUS
☐ Bell 205 Iroquois (UH-1H) (UH-1V)	67-17208	9406	At Fort Wainwright.	RA
☐ Convair 8-10 Delta Dagger (F-102A)	'56-1274'	8-10-270	56-1053 (?)	RAX
☐ Lockheed 222-68-12 Lightning (P-38G)	42-13400	222-7834	42-13400, N55929	RAC
☐ Lockheed 382-8B Hercules (C-130E)	64-0533	382-4022		RA
☐ Lockheed 580 (T-33A)	53-6021	580-9553		RA
☐ McDonnell M.98DJ Phantom II (F-4C)	'66-0723'	717	63-7628	RAX
☐ McDonnell M.98DE Phantom II (F-4C)	64-0890	1304		RA
☐ McDonnell M.199-1A Eagle (F-15A)	74-0081	053/A042		RA
☐ McDonnell M.199-1A Eagle (F-15A) (FSM)	'43-0139'			RAX
☐ Piasecki PD-22 Work Horse (H-21B) (CH-21B)	'52-8696'	B.119	53-4369, N100RB – identity doubtful.	RAX
☐ Northrop N-68 Scorpion (F-89D)	'53-2453'	N.4539	52-1862	RAX

FAIRBANKS MONUMENT (AK13)

Location:	On permanent view at a business near the airport which is in the south western part of the city.

TYPE	REG/SER	CON. NO.	PI/NOTES	STATUS
☐ Douglas DC-6B	N999SQ	43274	HB-IBA, OY-EAO, N515AO, N515EA – front fuselage only.	

JUNEAU MONUMENT (AK14)

Location:	Will, when restored, be at airport which is about 5 miles north west of the city.

TYPE	REG/SER	CON. NO.	PI/NOTES	STATUS
☐ Douglas DC-3A-456 Skytrain (C-47A)	N8042X	19041	42-100578, N61725	RAC

KENAI MONUMENT (AK15)

Location:	On permanent view at the airport which is in the northern part of the town.

TYPE	REG/SER	CON. NO.	PI/NOTES	STATUS
☐ Lockheed 580 (T-33A)	52-9772	580-8032		PV

MUSEUM OF ALASKA – TRANSPORTATION AND INDUSTRY (AK16)

Address:	3800 Neuser Drive, PO Box 909, Wasilla, Alaska 99687-0646.
Tel:	907-376-1211 Fax: 907-376-3082 Email: mati@mtaonline.net
Admission:	May–September daily 0900-1800; October–April Tuesday-Saturday 0900-1700
Location:	On Neuser/Museum Drive which is off the Parks Highway at Mile 46.7 west of the town near the airport.

This museum was established in 1976 and until 1992 was located at the state showgrounds at Palmer. A move was made to a site near the new Wasilla Airport. Steady development has taken place with the construction of exhibition halls and workshops.

The aircraft collection concentrates on types which have flown in the state. A new aviation exhibition was ready for the 1999 season. An interesting item is a 1942 control tower cab. Originally constructed at Yakatat on the Alaska Gulf, it was moved to other bases and was the first control tower at Anchorage Intentional Airport when it opened in the early 1950s.

The Fairchild 71 was once owned by Bob Reeve who was one of the pioneer airline operators in Alaska. Over 100 of this rugged high wing monoplane were built in the USA and around a further 20 in Canada. The rare Fairchild 42 dates from 1930 and is one of six built.

The Cunningham-Hall PT-6 biplane first appeared in 1929 and only two were sold. One PT-6F, dating from 1938, has recently been restored in Minnesota.

TYPE	REG/SER	CON. NO.	PI/NOTES	STATUS
☐ Beech C18S				PV
☐ Bell 205 Iroquois (UH-1H)	66-17044	9238		PV
☐ Bowers Fly Baby 1A	N5586	64-40		PV
☐ Cessna C-34 Airmaster				RAD
☐ Cessna T-50 Bobcat (C-78) (UC-78)	N44793	5064	43-7544	RAD
☐ Convair 8-10 Delta Dagger (F-102A)	56-1282	8-10-499		PV
☐ Cunningham Hall PT-6	NC692W	2962		PVC
☐ Douglas DC-3A-360 Skytrain (C-47)	N101Z	4574	41-18482, NC5, N99, N101Z, N5	PV
☐ Douglas DC-3A-456 Skytrain (C-47A)	43-15200	19666		PV
☐ Fairchild 42	NC106M	4		PV
☐ Fairchild 71	N119H	657	NC119H	RAD
☐ Fairchild 205 Provider (C-123B)	N98	20219	55-4558, N123, N98, N3144W	PV
☐ Fike F			Incomplete	PV
☐ Ford JB-2 [Fieseler Fi 103A-1]				RA
☐ Kaman K-20 Seasprite (HU2K-1U) (UH-2B) (SH-2F)	Bu150185	135		PV
☐ Kellner KR-1 Seagull	N5552	13FK13		PV
☐ Mitchell Wing B-10				PV
☐ Piasecki PD-22 Work Horse (H-21B) (CH-21B)	53-4362	B.112	53-4362, N109RB	PV
☐ Rotec Panther 2				PV
☐ Sikorsky S-51 Dragonfly (H-5H)	49-2001			PV
☐ Stinson SR-8B Reliant				RAD
☐ Stinson SR-9 Reliant				RAD
☐ Ultralite Products Dragonfly 1 Hang Glider				PV

NORTH POLE MONUMENT (AK17)

Location:	On permanent view at the Vietnam Veterans Motorcycle Club in the town.

TYPE	REG/SER	CON. NO.	PI/NOTES	STATUS
☐ Douglas DC-6	N666SQ	43004	N37515	PV

UNIVERSITY OF ALASKA MUSEUM (AK18)

Address:	PO Box 756960, 907 Yukon Drive, Fairbanks, Alaska 99775-6960.
Tel:	907-974-7505 Email: museum@uaf.edu
Admission:	Aircraft on permanent view at the airport; museum open daily 0900-1700 (opens at 1300 in winter)
Location:	The airport and the university are in the western suburbs of the city.

On show in the main building of this interesting museum are many items tracing the historical and cultural developments which have occurred in the state. Wildlife also features prominently.

The Curtiss Jenny, hanging in the terminal at the International Airport since 1981, was delivered to Fairbanks in February 1923 and flown by Ben Eielson. The original wings were lost and a set from a Swallow was fitted in 1957.

TYPE	REG/SER	CON. NO.	PI/NOTES	STATUS
☐ Curtiss 1C Jenny (JN-4D)	2400			PV

Alaska – Arizona

WEDGEWOOD RESORT (AK19)

Location:	On permanent view in the northern suburbs of Fairbanks.

TYPE	REG/SER	CON. NO.	PI/NOTES	STATUS
☐ Aeronca 7DC Champion (7AC)	N1707E	7AC-5272	NC1707E	PV

ARIZONA

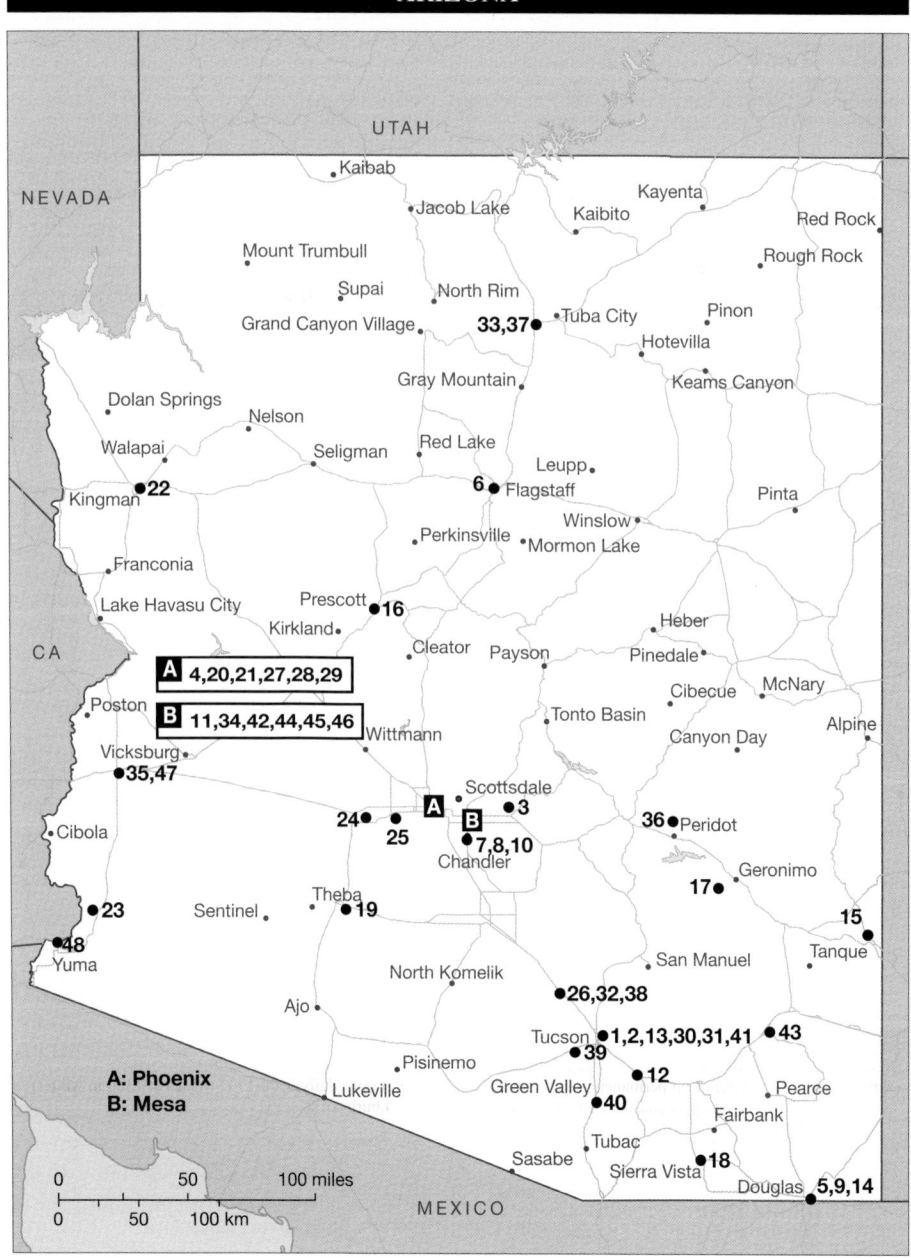

A: Phoenix
B: Mesa

309th AEROSPACE MAINTENANCE AND REGENERATION GROUP
'DISPLAY ROW' (AZ1)

Address:	AMARC/PA, Building 3200, Davis-Monthan Air Force Base, Arizona 85707-5000.
Tel:	520-228-8461 Email: amarc.pa@dm.af.mil
Admission:	By prior permission only – or on tours organised by the Pima Air and Space Museum.
Location:	In the south eastern suburbs of Tucson.

After World War II Davis-Monthan Air Force Base was chosen as the site for storing and preserving aircraft for future use, resale, scrapping or donation to museums. The first types flew in during January 1946 and since then thousands have made the journey to the desert site. Prior to this about 8,000 aircraft had been turned into ingots at Kingman, Arizona and Ontario, California. The Navy moved in from Litchfield Park in 1965 and later in the year the Army began to use the facilities.

During the early 1970s over 6,000 aircraft were present and numbers since then have varied between 3,000 and 5,000. Aircraft have been brought back into service during international crises such as the Berlin Airlift, the Korean and Vietnam Wars and the Desert Shield and Desert Storm operations.

The new name is relatively recent and prior to this a number of titles were in use but many enthusiasts still refer to it as MASDC (The Military Aircraft Storage and Disposition Center) which was in use from October 1964 until 1985.

Regular tours, now operated by the Pima Air and Space Museum, include a drive through the processing site and around some of the vast parking areas. The trip starts at 'Display Row' where an example of almost every type stored can be seen. Some of these aircraft, such as the Canberras, Voodoo and Super Sabre, have been present for many years while others only spend a short time on display.

Two Boeing YC-14As were built in the early 1970s to compete against the McDonnell-Douglas YC-15A in a proposal to replace the C-130 Hercules. The US Coast Guard ordered 41 Dassault Falcons in the late 1970s to replace the Grumman Albatross on coastal patrol duties. The first was delivered in February 1982 and the last in December 1983.

A fairly recent arrival is the Alenia Spartan which is one of a small batch used mainly from bases in Panama. The majority of the airframes have been covered with 'Spraylat', a vinyl preservative to protect them from the hot climate. New types are regularly added.

TYPE	REG/SER	CON. NO.	PI/NOTES	STATUS
☐ Alenia G.222 Spartan (C-27A)	91-0105	4104	I-RAIL, 91-0105, N2286Y	RA
☐ Beech A200C Huron (UC-12B)	Bu161204	BJ-20		RA
☐ Bell 205 Iroquois (HH-1H)	70-2474	17118		RA
☐ Bell 209 Huey Cobra (AH-1G) (AH-1Q) (AH-1S)	71-21000	21071		RA
☐ Bell 209 Sea Cobra (AH-1J)	Bu157785	26029	7H212	RA
☐ Boeing 464-253 Stratofortress (B-52G)	58-0206	464274		RA
☐ Boeing 707-355C (EC-137D)	67-19417	19417	N525EJ, G-AYEX, N525EJ, N707HL	RA
☐ Boeing 717-146 Stratotanker (KC-135A) (EC-135K)	59-1518	18006	59-1518, N96	RA
☐ Boeing 717-166 Stratotanker (KC-135B) (EC-135C)	62-3585	18568		RA
☐ Boeing 727-22	N7004U	18296	NASM, DC aircraft.	RA
☐ Boeing 737-253 (T-43)	71-1403	20685		RA
☐ Boeing 953 (YC-14A)	72-1874		72-1874, N8740B	RA
☐ Cessna 318B Tweety Bird (T-37B)	60-0160	40655		RA
☐ Cessna 337M Super Skymaster (O-2A)	69-7606	337M0404		RA
☐ Convair 340-71 Samaritan (R4Y-1) (C-131F)	Bu141016	299		RA
☐ Convair 8-24 Delta Dart (F-106A)	59-0043	8-24-172		RA
☐ Dassault Falcon 20G (HU-25A)	2115	419	F-WMKJ, N419F	RA
☐ Douglas DC-8-54F (EC-24A)	Bu163050	45881	N8048U	RA
☐ Douglas DC-9-32CF Nightingale (C-9A)	71-0875	47471		RA
☐ Douglas DC-9-32RC Skytrain II (C-9B)	Bu163208	47639	6Y-JIJ, PJ-SND, 6Y-JIJ, PJ-SND, 6Y-JIJ, C-GBWO, EC-DTI, N4549V	RA
☐ Douglas KA-3B Skywarrior (A3D-2) (A-3B) (NA-3B)	Bu142690	11693		RA
☐ Douglas TA-4J Skyhawk (TA-4F)	Bu153486	13552		RA
☐ Douglas TA-4J Skyhawk	Bu158110	14147		RA
☐ Fairchild-Republic A-10A Thunderbolt II	77-0256	A10-181		RA
☐ Fairchild-Republic NGT (T-46A)	85-1596			RA
☐ General Dynamics 401 Fighting Falcon (F-16A)	81-0738	61-419		RA
☐ General Dynamics 401 Fighting Falcon (F-16A)	81-0741	61-422		RA
☐ General Dynamics EF-111A (F-111A)	66-0039	A1-57		RA
☐ General Dynamics F-111E	68-0030	A1-199		RA
☐ General Dynamics F-111G (FB-111A)	68-0244	B1-16		RA
☐ Grumman G-89 Tracker (S2F-1) (S-2A) (S-2F)	Bu136475	384		RA
☐ Grumman G-96 Trader (TF-1) (C-1A)	Bu146038	068	Bu146038, N32709	RA
☐ Grumman G-123 Hawkeye (E-2C)	Bu161783			RA
☐ Grumman G-128 Intruder (A-6E)	Bu164377	I-717		RA
☐ Grumman G-134 Mohawk (OV-1C)	67-18903	104C		RA
☐ Grumman G-159C Academe (TC-4C)	Bu155724	180	N786G	RA
☐ Grumman G-303 Tomcat (F-14A)	Bu161866	502		RA
☐ Grumman G-303 Tomcat (F-14D)	Bu164341	616/D-21		RA
☐ Kaman K-20 Seasprite (HU2K-1U) (UH-2B) (SH-2F)	Bu151314	151		RA
☐ Lockheed 182-1A Hercules (182-44-03) (C-130A) (DC-130A) (C-130A)	57-0497	182-3204	57-0497, Bu570497	RA
☐ Lockheed 185 Orion (P3V-1) (P-3A)	Bu150499	185-5025		RA
☐ Lockheed 185 Orion (P-3C)	Bu159324	185-5614		RA
☐ Lockheed 185 Orion (P-3C)	Bu161131	185-5721		RA
☐ Lockheed 282-3B Hercules (GV-1) (KC-130F)	Bu149800	282-3685		RA
☐ Lockheed 282-6B Hercules (UV-1L) (LC-130F)	Bu148320	282-3565	59-5924	RA
☐ Lockheed 394 Viking (S-3A) (ES-3A)	Bu159404	394A-3040		RA
☐ Lockheed 394 Viking (S-3A) (S-3B)	Bu159732	394A-3061		

Arizona

☐ Lockheed 726-45-17 Neptune (P2V-7) (P2V-7S) (SP-2H)	Bu147963	726-7213	NASM, DC aircraft.	RA
☐ Lockheed 1080-91-08 SeaStar (T2V-1) (T-1A)	Bu142263	1080-1003		RA
☐ Martin 272B Canberra (B-57B) (EB-57B)	52-1506	89		RA
☐ Martin 744 Canberra (272) (B-57B) (RB-57F) (WB-57F)	63-13295	266	53-3918	RA
☐ McDonnell M.36BA Voodoo (F-101B)	57-0436	614		RA
☐ McDonnell M.98DF Phantom II (RF-4C)	68-0551	3342		RA
☐ McDonnell M.98HO Phantom II (F-4E)	68-0337	3381		RA
☐ McDonnell M.98HO Phantom II (F-4E)	68-0531	3730		RA
☐ McDonnell M.199-1A Eagle (F-15A)	76-0116	324/A268		RA
☐ McDonnell YC-15A	72-1876	CX002		RA
☐ North American NA-243 Super Sabre (F-100F) (QF-100F)	56-3880	243-156		RA
☐ North American NA-318 Buckeye (T-2C)	Bu156712	318-27		RA
☐ Northrop N-156T Talon (T-38A)	62-3653	N.5358		RA
☐ Rockwell B-1B Lancer	85-0062	22		RA
☐ Sikorsky S-61B Sea King (SH-3D) (SH-3H)	Bu156483	61429		RA
☐ Sikorsky S-65A Sea Dragon (MH-53E)	Bu163057	65555		RA
☐ Vertol V.107M Sea Knight (CH-46A) (HH-46A) (HH-46D)	Bu151924	2074		RA
☐ Vought RF-8G Crusader (F8U-1P) (RF-8A)	Bu144618			RA
☐ Vought A-7K Corsair II	80-0288	K17		RA

390th MEMORIAL MUSEUM (AZ2)

Address: 6000 East Valencia Road, Tucson, Arizona 85706.
Tel: 602-574-0287
Admission: Daily 1000-1600.
Location: In the grounds of the Pima Air and Space Museum.

This collection is sited in a large building in the grounds of the Pima Air and Space Museum. Activated on 26th January 1943 at Geiger Field, Washington, the 390th Bombardment Group was formed late in the following month. On 6th June the unit moved to Great Falls, Montana for final preparations for the flight to England. The B-17Fs left on 4th July via Iceland and Prestwick in Scotland with the first arriving at their new home at Framlingham on 13th July.

The wing flew over 300 combat missions from its Suffolk base between July 1943 and June 1945 using B-17F and B-17G models of the Fortress. On 10th October 1943 the group destroyed 62 enemy fighters in air to air combat. The only man to fly 100 missions with the 8th Air Force was Master Sergeant Hewitt Dunn, a member of the 390th. The group was deactivated at Sioux Falls, South Dakota in late 1945 and reformed as a Titan missile unit at Davis-Monthan in 1962.

The centrepiece of the display is an immaculately restored B-17G. Around the walls of the building are many photographs, maps, models, uniforms and memorabilia tracing the history of the unit. There is also an exhibition of weapons in the building. The Joseph A. Moller library, named after a former commander of the group, houses a large quantity of archive material. A Titan missile stands outside by the main entrance to the building.

TYPE	REG/SER	CON. NO.	PI/NOTES	STATUS
☐ Boeing 299-O Fortress (B-17G) (PB-1G)	'231892'	8737	44-85828, Bu77254, N9323R – Pima Air and Space Museum aircraft.	PVX

APACHE JUNCTION MONUMENTS (AZ3)

Location: On permanent view at two locations in the town.

TYPE	REG/SER	CON. NO.	PI/NOTES	STATUS
☐ Lockheed 580 (T-33A)	53-6008	580-9540	At ALP 27 in Meridian Road.	PV
☐ Sikorsky S-58 Seahorse (HUS-1) (UH-34D)	Bu147151	581061	Bu147151, N4215Q – at a business at 2646 East Guadelupe Road.	RA
☐ Sikorsky S-58 Seahorse (HUS-1) (UH-34D)	Bu150557	581684	Bu150557, N42171 – at a business at 2646 East Guadelupe Road.	PV

ARIZONA MILITARY MUSEUM (AZ4)

Address: 5636 East McDowall Road, Phoenix, Arizona 85008-3495.
Tel: 602-267-2676   **Email:** david.ervine@azdema.gov
Admission: Tuesday, Thursday 0900-1400; Saturday-Sunday 1300-1600.
Location: In the eastern suburbs of the city – north east of the airport.

Opened in 1981, this museum is housed in the north wing of the 1935 Adobe Arsenal on the Papago Park Military Reservation. The remainder of the building is occupied by the Arizona Military Academy. The displays trace the military history of the state from its early days.

During World War II a German prisoner of war camp was located at the site and there are many relics from this period on show. The museum building was at this time used as workshop. The history of military forces in the state is portrayed in detail with items of memorabilia and uniforms on show.

A pair of prototype fast firing 'chain-guns, donated by McDonnell Douglas Helicopters, based in Mesa, are a prized exhibit. The Iroquois, in the main building, served in Vietnam.

TYPE	REG/SER	CON. NO.	PI/NOTES	STATUS
☐ Bell 204 Iroquois (UH-1C) (UH-1M)	64-14156	1280		PV
☐ Bell 209 Huey Cobra (AH-1G) (AH-1Q) (AH-1S)	68-15264	20598		PV
☐ Vought A-7D Corsair II	74-1741	D416		PV

BORDER AIR MUSEUM (AZ5)

Address:	East 10th Street and Airport Road, Douglas, Arizona 85607
Tel:	520-364-2478 Email: www.drstim@email.com
Admission:	Summer Monday – Friday 1200-1600; Saturday 1100-1500.
Location:	At the airport which is in the eastern part of the town.

The museum was started by the late Richard Westbrook who died before the project was completed. His widow donated the aircraft and building to the town. The prototype Emigh Trojan A-2 made its maiden flight at Douglas on 20th December 1946 and 58 were built before production stopped in 1950. An example of the low wing two-seater has been preserved along with items of memorabilia and photographs.

TYPE	REG/SER	CON. NO.	PI/NOTES	STATUS
☐ Emigh Trojan A-2	NC8301H	4	NC8301H, N8301H	PV

CAMP NAVAJO NATIONAL GUARD BASE (AZ6)

Location:	By prior permission only at the base which is about 10 miles west of Flagstaff off I.40.

TYPE	REG/SER	CON. NO.	PI/NOTES	STATUS
☐ Bell 205 Iroquois (UH-1H)	67-17603	9801		RA

CHANDLER GILBERT COMMUNITY COLLEGE (AZ7)

Address:	2626 East Pecos Road, Chandler, Arizona 85225 – 2499.
Tel:	480-732-7000 Fax: 480-732-7090
Admission:	By prior permission only.
Location:	At Williams Gateway Airport which is in the southern part of Mesa.

The college offers FAA approved courses in pilot training and aviation maintenance. The complex at the former Williams Air Force Base includes workshops and laboratories. Two homebuilts are among the instructional airframes. The Vans RV-3 was built in 1996 and the Evans VP-1 in 1973.

TYPE	REG/SER	CON. NO.	PI/NOTES	STATUS
☐ Beech C35 Bonanza	N5857C	D-2809		RA
☐ Bellanca 17-30A Super Viking	N39848	73-30495		RA
☐ Cessna 172RG	N6335R	172RG0167		RA
☐ Cessna 310	N5288A	35488		RA
☐ Evans VP-1 Volksplane	N73692	1		RA
☐ Gates Learjet 23	N83CE	23-074	5A-DAC, D-IATD, N23TC, N74MW, N23AN, N68WM, N150AG, XA-LAR, XB-GRQ	RA
☐ North American NA-265 Sabreliner (T-39A) (CT-39A)	60-3498	265-26		
☐ Piper PA-23-160 Apache	N6249B	23-1590		RA
☐ Stoddard-Hamilton SH-4 GlaStar	N218GS	5175		RA
☐ Vans RV-3	N41392	10694		RA

CHANDLER MONUMENT (AZ8)

Location:	On permanent view in East Chandler Boulevard in the centre of the town.

TYPE	REG/SER	CON. NO.	PI/NOTES	STATUS
☐ North American NA-173 Sabre (F-86D)	'210115'	173-405	51-6261	PVX

COCHISE COMMUNITY COLLEGE (AZ9)

Address:	4190 West Highway 80, Douglas, Arizona 86507.
Tel:	520-417-4104 Email: greenr@cochise.edu
Admission:	By prior permission only.
Location:	At the college airfield which is about 5 miles west of the town off Highway 80.

The aviation maintenance programme at the college ceased some time ago and the instructional airframes are stored on the airfield. Several of these are in a derelict condition and may be sold or scrapped in the not too distant future. Professional pilot training and courses in avionics still take place.

TYPE	REG/SER	CON. NO.	PI/NOTES	STATUS
☐ Aero Commander 680V	N47HM	1691-70	(N4859E), N4585E	RA
☐ Beech D18S Expediter (C18S) (SNB-1) (SNB-5) (TC-45J) (UC-45J)	N2289	3660	Bu39928	RA
☐ Beech D18S Expediter (C18S) (SNB-1) (SNB-5) (TC-45J) (UC-45J)	N4755	3749	Bu67311	RA
☐ Beech D18S Expediter (C18S) (SNB-1) (SNB-5) (TC-45J) (UC-45J)			Fuselage only.	RA
☐ Beech C50 Seminole (L-23D) (RL-23D) (RU-8D) (RU-8G)	57-6032	RLH-4		RA
☐ Beech C50 Seminole (L-23E) (U-8E) (U-8G)	56-4044	DH-91		RA
☐ Cessna 170B	N2799C	26343		RA
☐ Piper PA-23-250 Aztec (UO-1) (U-11A)	Bu149065	27-347		RA
☐ Piper PA-23-250 Aztec (UO-1) (U-11A)	Bu149068	27-562		RA

Arizona

COLLECTIBLE AIRCRAFT (AZ10)

Address: 4400 West Earhart Drive, Chandler, Arizona 85226-4730.
Admission: By prior permission only.
Location: At the airport which is in the southern part of the town.

This private collection contains a number of interesting types. The Ford Tri-Motor was built in 1929 and was at Pearl Harbor in Hawaii in 1941. The aircraft returned to the mainland in 1946 and three years later was leased to TWA. for its 20th anniversary celebrations. A move to Idaho took place where it was modified as a sprayer. Later it was one of a fleet flown by Johnson Flying Service in Montana to drop smoke jumpers and supplies to fire fighters. Dolph Overton acquired the Ford in 1969 and for a time it was on show at his Wings and Wheels Museum. The aircraft is resplendent in TAT colours.

The Mustang was rebuilt by Trans Florida Aviation at Sarasota in Florida in the 1950s. The Cavalier conversion served in the Dominican Republic until 1984 when it returned to Florida. The fighter moved to Chino in California where it flew again in September 1987.

TYPE	REG/SER	CON. NO.	PI/NOTES	STATUS
☐ Beech D18S	N2913B	A-963		RAA
☐ Bell 47G-4	N474RP	3344		RAA
☐ Cavalier Mustang II (F-51D) (North American NA-122)	N514RP/'472196'	122-41009	44-74469, N7723C, 1919 (Dominican Republic), N7723C	RAAX
☐ Cessna 195B	N2141C	16126	NC2141C	RAA
☐ Ford 4-AT-E	NC9612	4-AT-55	NC9612, N9612	RAA
☐ Mooney M.20K	N98498	25-0534		RAA
☐ Spartan 7W Executive	NC17059	7W-22	NC17059, N17059	RAA

COMMEMORATIVE AIR FORCE (ARIZONA WING) (AZ11)

Address: 2017 North Greenfield Road, PO Box 2969, Mesa, Arizona 85215-2401.
Tel: 480-924-1940   **Fax:** 480-981-1954   **Email:** pio@arizonawingcaf.com
Admission: Daily 1000-1600.
Location: At Falcon Field Airport which is about 3 miles north of the town.

This wing was formed in January 1978 and its first task was the restoration of the B-17G named 'Sentimental Journey'. This aircraft spends each summer on tour and normally visits over 60 cities often accompanied by the Mitchell allocated to the wing. Sadly the group lost a Spanish-built Heinkel He 111 in a fatal crash in 2003.

Ground was broken on 15th April 1987 for the construction of a museum which was completed in 1990. In the entrance hall is a display of memorabilia and photographs of the fleet along with models and flying clothing. The hangar serves as a workshop for the maintenance of the fleet.

Very few examples of the Grumman Guardian attack aircraft survive and almost all these had a brief civil career in the fire-bombing role. Construction of a second hangar is planned so that more aircraft owned by members can be displayed.

TYPE	REG/SER	CON. NO.	PI/NOTES	STATUS
☐ Beech D18S	N145AZ	A-235	CF-GHR, N118R, N20MD	PVA
☐ Boeing 299-O Fortress (B-17G) (RB-17G) (DB-17G) (DB-17P)	N9323Z	32155	44-83514	PVA
☐ Boeing-Stearman A75N1 Kaydet (PT-17) (N2S-4)	N52558	75-4894	(42-16731), Bu55657	PVA
☐ Boeing-Stearman E75 Kaydet (PT-13D)	NC36300	75-5887	42-17724, N36300	PVA
☐ Canadair CL-30 Silver Star 3 (CT-133) [Lockheed 580 (T-33AN)]	N99175	T33-557	21557	PV
☐ Cessna T-50 Bobcat (AT-17B) (UC-78B)	N59188	3084	42-38875 – Wingspan Air aircraft.	PVA
☐ Champion 7EC Traveler	N7436B	7EC-474		PVA
☐ Douglas A-26C Invader	NL202R	28880	44-35601, N202R	PVA
☐ Douglas DC-7C	N90804	45116	G-AOIF – front fuselage only.	PV
☐ English Electric EA.1 Canberra TT.18 (B.2)	N76764	EEP13535	WK142	PV
☐ Fokker D VIII (R)				PVC
☐ Grumman G-82 Guardian (AF-2S)	N9993Z	242	Bu126731	PV
☐ McDonnell M.98AM Phantom II (F-4B) (F-4N)	Bu153016	1496		PV
☐ Mikoyan-Gurevich MiG-15bis	'711'			PVX
☐ Mikoyan-Gurevich MiG-21PF	507	760507	In Hungarian markings.	PV
☐ North American NA-88 Texan (AT-6D) (SNJ-5)	N3246G	88-17873	42-86092, Bu90725	RAA
☐ North American NA-108 Mitchell (B-25J) (TB-25J)	N125AZ	108-35262	43-35972, N9552Z	RAC
☐ North American NA-122 Mustang (P-51D) (Mustang IV)	NL151RJ	122-40944	44-74404, 9276 (Canada), N4132A, N7129E – composite with parts from several unidentified aircraft.	PVA
☐ North American NA-122 Mustang (P-51D) (Mustang IV)	NL151BW	122-41353	44-74813, 9261 (Canada), N6301T, N251KW, N151KW	PVA
☐ Replica Plans S.E.5A	N589D	F8005		PV
☐ Schweizer SGS.2-12 (TG-3A)	'26238'	15	42-52935, N69064	PVX
☐ Sikorsky S-55D Chickasaw (H-19D) (UH-19D)	N6754		54-1686	PV
☐ Titan T-51 Mustang	N5110	M03XXXSOHK0021		PVA
☐ War Aircraft P-47D Thunderbolt	N470J	420473		PV
☐ WSK SBLim-2 (Lim-1) [MiG-15]	N9012	1A 09-012	012	PV

CORONA MONUMENT (AZ12)

Location: On permanent view at ALP 109 at 15921 Houghton Road in the south eastern part of the town.

TYPE	REG/SER	CON. NO.	PI/NOTES	STATUS
☐ McDonnell M.98HO Phantom II (F-4E) (NF-4E)	66-0294	2389		PV

DAVIS-MONTHAN AIR FORCE BASE HERITAGE PARK (AZ13)

Address:	355 Wing Public Affairs, Building 3200, Davis-Monthan Air Force Base, Arizona 85707-5000.
Tel:	520-228-3378 **Fax:** 520-228-4717 **Email:** 355wing.pa@dm.af.mil
Admission:	By prior permission only.
Location:	In the south eastern suburbs of Tucson.

The base, which opened in 1927, is named after two local pilots. Lieutenant Samuel H. Davis was killed in 1921 and Lieutenant Oscar Monthan met his death in 1924. The site was the original civil airport for Tucson.

The Heritage Park is located just inside the main gate. A selection of fairly modern types has been put on show. The Sabre is mounted on a pole near the headquarters of the 358th. Fighter Squadron.

TYPE	REG/SER	CON. NO.	PI/NOTES	STATUS
☐ Boeing 464-201-7 Stratofortress (B-52D)	56-0659	464030		RA
☐ Cessna 305A Bird Dog (L-19A) (O-1A)	51-12670	23125		RA
☐ Fairchild-Republic A-10A Thunderbolt II	79-0116	A10-380	79-0116, '77-0117'	RA
☐ Lockheed 182-1A Hercules (182-44-03) (C-130A) (JC-130A) (RC-130S)	56-0493	182-3101		RA
☐ Lockheed U-2C (U-2A)	56-6716	383		RA
☐ McDonnell M.98AM Phantom II (F4H-1) (F-4B) (F-4N)	'65-0639'	297	Bu150639, '40829'	RAX
☐ McDonnell M.98DJ Phantom II (F-4C)	64-0699	945		RA
☐ North American NA-173 Sabre (F-86D) (F-86L)	51-6071	173-215	51-6071, N3280U, N86RJ	RA
☐ North American NA-243 Super Sabre (F-100F)	56-3727	243-3	56-3727, '56-3951'	RA
☐ North American NA-305 Bronco (OV-10A)	66-13560	305-9		RAX
☐ Republic F-105D Thunderchief	61-0159	D-354	61-0159, '61-355'	RA
☐ Republic F-105G Thunderchief (F-105F)	63-8285	F-62		RA
☐ Sikorsky S-61R (CH-3C) (CH-3E)	'65-5692'	61574	65-12799	RAX
☐ Vought A-7D Corsair II	68-8229	D15		RA

DOUGLAS MONUMENT (AZ14)

Location:	On permanent view in a park on 6th Avenue in the southern eastern part of the town.

TYPE	REG/SER	CON. NO.	PI/NOTES	STATUS
☐ General Dynamics 401 Fighting Falcon (F-16A)	79-0312	61-97		PV

DUNCAN MONUMENT (AZ15)

Location:	On permanent view in a Veterans Park at 115 Williams Street in the southern part of the town.

TYPE	REG/SER	CON. NO.	PI/NOTES	STATUS
☐ North American NA-243 Super Sabre (F-100F)	56-3812	243-88		PV

EMBRY RIDDLE AERONAUTICAL UNIVERSITY VISITOR CENTER (AZ16)

Address:	3200 Willow Creek Road, Prescott, Arizona 86301-3720.
Tel:	520-776-3728 **Email:** pradmit@erau.edu
Admission:	On permanent view.
Location:	In the town which is about 70 miles north of Phoenix off Route 89.

The university has trained many engineers over the years. The former NASA Starfighter is mounted outside the Visitor Center which has a range of exhibits showing the work carried out at the site.

TYPE	REG/SER	CON. NO.	PI/NOTES	STATUS
☐ Lockheed 683-10-19 Starfighter (F-104N)	N811NA	683C-4045	NASA811	PV

FLYING J RANCH AIRPORT MONUMENT (AZ17)

Location:	On permanent view at the airfield which is about 8 miles south west of Pima.

TYPE	REG/SER	CON. NO.	PI/NOTES	STATUS
☐ Fairchild 110 Flying Boxcar (C-119G) (C-119L)	53-8074	177		PV

FORT HUACHUCA MUSEUM (AZ18)

Address:	Fort Huachuca, ATZS-PAM Arizona 85613-6000.
Tel:	520-533-5736 **Email:** finleyj@hua.army.mil
Admission:	Monday-Friday 0900-1600; Saturday-Sunday 1300-1600.
Location:	About 20 miles south of Benson off Highway 90.

This site has been used by the army since the end of the 19th century. The museum is housed in an 1892 structure, one of the few original buildings left on the camp. Displays trace the history of conflicts in the region and include the Civil War, the Mexican Campaign and the battles against Indian tribes; the fort's role in both World War II and the Korean War is also highlighted.

TYPE	REG/SER	CON. NO.	PI/NOTES	STATUS
☐ Beech A200 Huron (C-12D) (RC-12D) (RC-12G)	80-23372	BP-13/FC-3		PV
☐ Grumman G-134 Mohawk (OV-1C)	67-18963	131C		PV

The Arizona Wing of the Commemorative Air Force maintains this Douglas A-26C Invader in flying order. (Nigel Hitchman) [AZ11]

This Republic F-105D Thunderchief is in the Heritage Park at Davis-Monthan Air Force Base. [AZ13]

The Kingman Army Airfield Museum has a number of light aircraft on show including this Bede BD-5. (Nigel Hitchman) [AZ22]

GILA BEND MONUMENTS (AZ19)

Location:	At three locations in the town.

TYPE	REG/SER	CON. NO.	PI/NOTES	STATUS
☐ Bell 205 Iroquois (UH-1H)	68-15760	10690	At a bar on Gila Bridge Road.	PV
☐ McDonnell M.36CA Voodoo (RF-101C)	56-0112	352	At the airport which is about 2 miles north of the town.	PV
☐ McDonnell M.36CA Voodoo (RF-101C)	56-0130	385	At the airport.	PV
☐ Republic F-84F Thunderstreak	52-6503		At the Air Force Station which is south of the town.	RA

GLENDALE MONUMENTS (AZ20)

Location:	On permanent view at two locations in the town.

TYPE	REG/SER	CON. NO.	PI/NOTES	STATUS
☐ North American NA-223 Super Sabre (F-100D)	54-2281	223-161	On permanent view in Harry Bonsall Park on 59th. Street.	PV
☐ Piper PA-18-150 Super Cub			On view during opening hours in Cabela's store at 9380 West Glendale Avenue.	PV

GLOBAL AERONAUTICAL MUSEUM (AZ21)

Address:	2001 South 203rd. Avenue, Phoenix, Arizona 85326-9505.
Admission:	By prior permission only.
Location:	At an airfield in the Phoenix area.

This small private museum operated a Cessna 150 for more than a decade and this was replaced by a 1961 B model. The first Bell helicopter joined the fleet in the early 1990s and two more have now joined the collection. For a number of years a Naval Aircraft Factory N3N-3 biplane was also flown.

TYPE	REG/SER	CON. NO.	PI/NOTES	STATUS
☐ Bell 47G-2	N514SF	30		RAA
☐ Bell 47G-3B-1	N48LL	2823		RAA
☐ Bell 47G-3B-1 Sioux (TH-13T)	N39LL	3694	67-17012, N18831	RAA
☐ Cessna 150B	N7379X	15059479		RAA

KINGMAN ARMY AIRFIELD MUSEUM (AZ22)

Address:	4540 Flightline Drive, Kingman, Arizona 86401.
Tel:	928-757-1892
Admission:	Tuesday-Saturday 1100-1600.
Location:	At the airport which is about 5 miles north east of the town on Route 66.

At the end of World War II large numbers of combat aircraft were stored at the field prior to being scrapped. When the military left the site became the civil airport for the town. At the present time several jet airliners are in store at the site. A group of enthusiasts set up the museum several years ago. A move across the camp to a larger building occurred in the 1990s and for a time some aircraft were on show outside. Photographs, engines, documents and memorabilia can be seen. The varied history of the airfield is portrayed in the display. There are several homebuilt designs in the exhibition hall. Two are replicas of famous World War I types with the Fokker Triplane in a red colour scheme. The original airfield control tower stands near the terminal building. The museum once had two C-45s and two helicopters but these have not been seen for many years.

TYPE	REG/SER	CON. NO.	PI/NOTES	STATUS
☐ Bauer Scale Corsair	N883DL	15		PV
☐ Bede BD-5				PV
☐ Bell 47D-1 (B-3)	N175K	56	NX136B, NC136B, CF-???	PV
☐ Fokker Dr I (R)				PV
☐ Foster Dragonfly III	N86X	655		PV
☐ Neibauer Lancair 235	N235VJ	243		PVA
☐ Nieuport 11 (R)				PVX
☐ Piper PA-20-160 Pacer (PA-22-160 Tripacer)	N8151D	22-5642		PVA

LAGUNA ARMY AIRFIELD MONUMENT (AZ23)

Location:	By prior permission only at the airfield which is in the northern part of the town.

TYPE	REG/SER	CON. NO.	PI/NOTES	STATUS
☐ Bell 205 Iroquois (UH-1H) (JUH-1H)	69-15836	12124		RA
☐ Bell 209 Huey Cobra (AH-1G) (AH-1F)	66-15350	20106		RA

LAURIDSEN AVIATION MUSEUM (AZ24)

Address:	PO Box 570, Carefree, Arizona 85377-5070.
Tel:	480-586-7312 Fax: 480-575-6954 Email: Hans@LauridsenAviationMuseum.com
Admission:	By prior permission only.
Location:	At Buckeye Airport which is in the north eastern part of the town.

Arizona

This private collection of mainly warbirds contains several interesting types. A museum is being set up in a hangar at the field and the aircraft are being to the site. There are plans for more exhibition halls. The Canso is a fairly recent addition to the fleet, having served with the Royal Canadian Air Force from 1944 until 1962 and then spent over four decades as a water bomber in Newfoundland and Labrador. It will be maintained in airworthy condition and taken to shows and other events in the region.

TYPE	REG/SER	CON. NO.	PI/NOTES	STATUS
☐ Beech D18S Expeditor (C-45H)	N6365T	AF-617	52-10687	RAA
☐ Boeing-Stearman A75N1 Kaydet (PT-17)	N56805	75-0828	41-1068	RAA
☐ Boeing-Stearman A75N1 Kaydet (PT-17)	N53131	75-4307	42-16144	RAA
☐ Cessna 305A Bird Dog (L-19A) (O-1A)	N10444	23188	51-12731	RAA
☐ Consolidated 28-5A Canso A	N413PB	CV 343	11047 (Canada), CF-OFI, C-FOFI	RAA
☐ Convair 340-67 Samaritan (VC-131D)	N131CW	205	N8426H, 54-2809, (N6288Y)	RAA
☐ Cub Crafters PA-18-150	N324A	9962CC		RAA
☐ Douglas DC-3A-456 Skytrain (C-47A)	N243DC	9247	42-23385, NC48990, N990, N34116, N66HL, N23AJ	RAA
☐ Douglas A-26B Invader	N126HP	27799	44-34520, N9420Z, C-GHCF, N94207	RAA
☐ Fairchild 110 Flying Boxcar (C-119C)	N15501	10955	22130 (Canada)	RAA
☐ Forney F.1A	N3023G	5716		RAA
☐ Grumman G-40 Avenger (TBM-3) (TBM-3E)	N7001C	2613	Bu85794	RAA
☐ Grumman G-96 Trader (TF-1) (C-1A)	N71456	005	Bu136752	RAA
☐ Grumman G-111 Albatross (G-64) (UF-1) (HU-16C)	N216HU	G-333	Bu131904, N7026X, N904G, N9131	RAA
☐ North American NA-88 Texan (AT-6D) (SNJ-5)	N8151	88-15304	41-34374, Bu43639, N3669F	RAA
☐ North American NA-108 Mitchell (B-25J) (TB-25J)	N3438G	108-47551	44-86797	RAA
☐ North American NA-226 Trojan (T-28C)	N40980	226-141	Bu140564	RAA
☐ Ryan Navion B	N5340K	NAV-4-2240B		RAA
☐ Vought A-7A Corsair II	Bu153241	A150		RA
☐ Waco UIC	NC13434	3786	NC13434, N13434	RAA

LUKE AIR FORCE HERITAGE PARK (AZ25)

Address: 56FW/PA, 4185 West Falcon Drive, Luke Air Force Base, Arizona 85309-1501.
Tel: 623-856-5853 **Email:** 56fw.pa@luke.af.mil
Admission: By prior permission only.
Location: About 20 miles west of Phoenix – about 5 miles north of Interstate 10.

Activated in 1941, this base is named after Lieutenant Frank Luke. He was a World War I observation balloon bursting ace who was the first pilot to receive the Medal of Honor.
The field has been home to fighter units for many years and an attractively landscaped Heritage Park has been set up just inside the main gate.

The Thunderstreak is painted in the colours of the 'Thunderbirds' aerobatic team. The Eagle was the first delivered to the Air Force and arrived at Luke on 14th November 1974.
A collection of memorabilia, documents, photographs, uniforms and trophies is housed in the Wing Headquarters.

TYPE	REG/SER	CON. NO.	PI/NOTES	STATUS
☐ General Dynamics 401 Fighting Falcon (F-16A)	'86-0291'	61-112	79-0327	RAX
☐ General Dynamics 401 Fighting Falcon (F-16A)	81-0687	61-368		RA
☐ Lockheed 383-04-05 Starfighter (F-104C)	'63-13243'	183-1180	56-0892	RAX
☐ Lockheed 580 (T-33A)	'80475'	580-1464	58-0495	RAX
☐ McDonnell M.98HO Phantom II (F-4E)	67-0327	3151	67-0327, '31175'	RA
☐ McDonnell M.199-1B Eagle (TF-15A) (F-15B)	73-0108	021/B003		RA
☐ North American NA-88 Texan (AT-6C)	42-3984	88-11758		RA
☐ North American NA-193 Sabre (F-86F)	52-5323	193-52	52-5323, '52-4530'	RA
☐ North American NA-214 Super Sabre (F-100C)	53-1716	214-8	53-1716, '42009'	RA
☐ Republic F-84F Thunderstreak	'52-6779'		52-6782	RAX

MARANA MONUMENT (AZ26)

Location: On permanent view at VFW 5990 at 15850 West El Tiro Road in the southern part of the town.

TYPE	REG/SER	CON. NO.	PI/NOTES	STATUS
☐ Bell 209 Huey Cobra (AH-1S) (AH-1E)	78-23066	22172		PV

PHOENIX AIR NATIONAL GUARD BASE COLLECTION (AZ27)

Address: 3200 East Old Tower Road, Phoenix, Arizona 85034.
Tel: 602-302-9000
Admission: By prior permission only.
Location: At Phoenix International Airport which is south of the city off Interstate 10/17.

The 197th Squadron was formed at Luke Air Force Base in 1947 with P-51D Mustangs. These were replaced by F-84F Thunderjets and in 1952 a move was made to Phoenix-Sky Harbor and Mustangs were again allocated. F-86As, F-86Ls and F-104As and Bs were used until September 1962 when a transport role was adopted with C-97Gs. A further change to air refuelling took place ten years later and the unit still carries out this work. A small collection of preserved aircraft is located in a park just inside the base gate.

TYPE	REG/SER	CON. NO.	PI/NOTES	STATUS
☐ Lockheed 383-04-05 Starfighter (F-104C)	56-0891		183-1179	RA
☐ Lockheed 580 (T-33A)	'35397'	580-1640	58-0671, NASA936, N936NA	RAX
☐ North American NA-227 Sabre (F-86F)	55-3818	227-3	55-3818, 62-7432 (Japan)	RA
☐ Republic F-84C Thunderjet (P-84C)	47-1486			RA

PHOENIX MONUMENT (AZ28)

Location:	On permanent view at South Mountain High School at 5401 South 7th Street.

TYPE	REG/SER	CON. NO.	PI/NOTES	STATUS
☐ Douglas A-26B Invader	N26GT	6934	41-39221, N9636C, N3035S, N256H	PV

PHOENIX SKY HARBOR AIRPORT DISPLAY (AZ29)

Address:	3400 East Sky Harbor Boulevard, Phoenix, Arizona 85034.
Tel:	602-273-3300 Email: http://phoenix.gov/email/emphx.html
Admission:	On permanent view in Terminal 3.
Location:	South of the city off Interstate 10/17.

The SPAD XIII was put on show in December 2007 and contains about 80% original parts from three aircraft with the remainder newly made. The aircraft was restored by GossHawk Unlimited at Casa Grande and is painted in the markings of one flown by the 27th Squadron of the First Pursuit Group in World War I.

TYPE	REG/SER	CON. NO.	PI/NOTES	STATUS
☐ SPAD XIII	'S15155'		Composite.	PVX

PIMA AIR AND SPACE MUSEUM (AZ30)

Address:	6000 East Valencia Road, Tucson, Arizona 85706.
Tel:	520-574-0462 or 520-791-2929 **Fax:** 520-574-9238 **Email:** jstemm@pimaair.org
Admission:	Daily 0900-1700.
Location:	About 12 miles south east of Tucson, north of Interstate 10.

In the mid-1960s a number of aircraft were put on show near the main gate of Davis-Monthan Air Force Base. These proved to be a popular tourist attraction and the idea of a museum was put forward by the then commander of the Military Aircraft Storage and Disposition Center (now AMARG), Colonel I.R. Perkin. The Tucson Air Museum Foundation was established in 1967 and a 320-acre site owned by the Federal Government was obtained. The area was fenced in and 35 aircraft were delivered from MASDC stocks.

The museum obtained its own aircraft with the first three arriving in 1969/70. A Lockheed F-94A Starfire came from Patagonia, Arizona, a Vultee BT-13A was presented by a local school and a Stinson L-5B was donated by the Arizona Wing of the Civil Air Patrol. The delivery of a former Indian Air Force B-24 Liberator in 1970 brought the name of the museum to the fore. When the collection eventually opened in 1976 around 100 were on show. The site has steadily been developed over the years and the first indoor display building opened in March 1983. This has been subsequently enlarged and a hangar with several World War II types on view was ready in the early 1990s.

The Arizona Aviation Hall of Fame was set up in 1985. Initially known as the Pima County Air Museum, the present title was adopted in 1991. The 390th Memorial Museum is also located in the grounds. There are ambitious plans to construct more exhibition hangars, further workshops and storage facilities and several have been completed. Education features highly and a Visitor Center along with an Aerospace Discovery Building have been completed. An impressive new entrance has been constructed.

The museum has progressed steadily in the last 20 years from just an aircraft park in the desert into a well thought out facility. The aircraft collection now numbers over 250 and most of these are on show. Over the years the outside display has been rearranged so that similar types are now parked near each other. By most aircraft there is a board giving its history and specifications. There are several rarities to be seen. The stainless steel spot welded Budd Conestoga is the sole survivor of the 17 built. The three-engined Northrop Raider is one of two left from the two dozen ordered by the Air Force. During its civilian career it operated in Mexico.

The museum also has the last complete Martin Mariner. Over 1,350 examples of this twin-engined flying boat were constructed between 1939 and 1949. The last one on active duties was retired by the US Coast Guard in 1958. Two well-preserved Mariners are known to exist on the bed of Lake Washington near Seattle and these may be raised in the future. Another unique type is the Curtiss-Wright AT-9A. This aircraft crashed on 30th December 1942 on a flight from Roswell, New Mexico. The wreck was discovered in a remote canyon in 1989 and four years later was lifted out by helicopter before being transported to the museum.

A comprehensive collection of helicopters is displayed by the main entrance. Nearby is one of aircraft used in fire-fighting. These include one of the few surviving Grumman Guardians, a Lockheed Neptune, a Fairchild Flying Boxcar and a Douglas DC-7B. In the centre of the park are lines of fighters and behind several bombers and transports. The B-58 Hustler delta winged bomber set many world speed records in the 1960s. The example on show is the last one built. Only three North American F-107s were built and the first is on view. The type competed against the Republic F-105 Thunderchief for an Air Force order.

Recently restored is the VC-118A that was the last piston powered Presidential aircraft. The interior of this aircraft is now as it was when used by John Kennedy and Lyndon Johnson. Dominating one area of the outside park is the Aero Spacelines Super Guppy. This aircraft was converted from a Boeing Stratocruiser and used by NASA to transport sections of spacecraft from California to Florida.

Inside the halls are light aircraft ranging from a replica of the Wright Flyer up to modem composite homebuilts. The Focke-Wulf Stieglitz served with the Finnish Air Force from 1940-1960. This biplane was then flown on civilian duties before arriving in America. Only two Columbia XJL-1s were built and the type made its maiden flight in 1946. No orders were received and they were placed in store until struck off charge in 1957. Both have survived; the other is in California. Three recent arrivals are the Australian designed Nomad, the Alpha Jet and the Mikoyan-Gurevich MiG-21PF. A number of airframes have now arrived from David Tallichet's Military Aircraft Restoration Corporation in California. These are in a poor state and a restoration programme has started.

TYPE	REG/SER	CON. NO.	PI/NOTES	STATUS
☐ Aero Spacelines 377-SG Super Guppy (Boeing 377-10-26 Stratocruiser)	N940NS	15938	N1038V, N940NA – incorporates parts from c/n 15944 (OY-DFY), G-ALSB, (N103Q), N408Q	PV
☐ Aeronca 65TC Grasshopper (O-58B) (L-3B)	43-27206	13434	43-27206, N46067	RA
☐ Aerosport Quail	N1387J	Q-547-16-9410		PV
☐ Albatros D Va (R)				RA

Arizona

☐ American Eagle A-129	NC520H	538	NC520H, N520H		RA
☐ Avian Falcon II Hot Air Balloon	N4369Z	12			RA
☐ Avro 696 Shackleton AEW.2 (MR.2)	N790WL		WL790		PV
☐ Balloon Works Firefly 7 Hot Air Balloon	N4065D	10008	No gondola		RA
☐ Bede BD-4	N42EE	382			PV
☐ Bede BD-5J	N505MR	2418			PV
☐ Beech C18S Kansan (AT-11)	41-9577	1003	41-9577, N6953C		PV
☐ Beech C18S Navigator (AT-7)	42-2438	4260	42-2438, N68785, N8073H – probably a composite as 42-2438, N8073H has c/n 4118.		PV
☐ Beech D18S Expeditor (C18S) (AT-7C) (SNB-2C) (SNB-3P) (SNB-5) (RC-45J)	'N6000V'	7822	43-50222, Bu29646, N1082		PVX
☐ Beech D18S Expeditor (C18S) (SNB-2) (SNB-2P) (SNB-5P) (RC-45J)	Bu39213	4297			PV
☐ Beech S18D	N55681	177	CF-BKN, YV-AZB		PV
☐ Beech N35 Bonanza	N9493Y	D-6668			PV
☐ Beech C50 Seminole (L-23D) (U-8D)	56-3701	LH-102	On loan from US Army Aviation Museum, AL.		PV
☐ Beech 2000A Starship I	N39TU	NC-23	N8244S, N24VP, (N24UP), N39TW		PV
☐ Bell 26E Airacobra (P-39Q)			Probably either 42-19991 or 42-20339.		RA
☐ Bell 33 Kingcobra (P-63E)	43-11727		43-11727, 400 (Honduras), N9003R		PV
☐ Bell 47D (HTL-2)	Bu122952	39	Bu122952, N1358N -		PV
☐ Bell 47K Sioux (HTL-7) (TH-13N)	Bu145842	2119			PV
☐ Bell 204 Iroquois (UH-1C) (UH-1M)	65-9430	1330			PV
☐ Bell 204 Iroquois (XH-48A) (UH-1F)	63-13141	7001			RA
☐ Bell 205 Iroquois (UH-1D) (UH-1H)	64-13895	4602			PV
☐ Bell 206A Kiowa (OH-58A)	69-16112	40333			PV
☐ Bell 209 Huey Cobra (AH-1G) (AH-1Q) (AH-1S)	70-15985	20929			PV
☐ Bellanca 14-13-2 Crusair Senior	XB-FOU	1551	NC74438, N74438		PV
☐ Boeing 299-O Fortress (B-17E)	41-2446	2257			RAC
☐ Boeing 345 Superfortress (B-29) (TB-29)	44-70016	10848			PV
☐ Boeing 345-9-6 Superfortress (B-50D) (KB-50J)	49-0372	16148			PV
☐ Boeing 367-76-66 Stratofreighter (KC-97C)	53-0151	16933			PV
☐ Boeing 367-76-66 Stratofreighter (KC-97C) (C-97G)	52-2626	16657	52-2626, HB-ILY		PV
☐ Boeing 450-10-9 Stratojet (B-47A)	49-1901	450002	Front fuselage only –		RA
☐ Boeing 450-157-35 Stratojet (B-47E) (EB-47E)	53-2135	44481			PV
☐ Boeing 464-201-0 Stratofortress (B-52A) (NB-52A)	52-0003	16493			PV
☐ Boeing 464-201-7 Stratofortress (B-52D)	55-0067	464019			PV
☐ Boeing 464-253 Stratofortress (B-52G)	58-0183	464251			PV
☐ Boeing 707-153 (VC-137A) (VC-137B)	58-6971	17926			PV
☐ Boeing 717-146 Stratotanker (KC-135A)	N931NA	18615	63-7998		PV
☐ Boeing 717-166 Stratotanker (KC-135B) (EC-135C) (EC-135J)	63-8057	18705			PV
☐ Boeing 953 (YC-14A)	72-1873		72-1873, N8780B		PV
☐ Boeing-Stearman A75N1 Kaydet (PT-17)	N48576	75-2381	41-8822		PV
☐ Bowers Fly Baby 1A	N49992	77-2			PV
☐ Brewster B.340E Bermuda	506				RA
☐ Bristol 149 Bolingbroke IVT	'Z9592'		Composite of at least three derelict airframes including 10076.		PVX
☐ Budd RB-1 Conestoga	XB-DUZ	16	Bu39307, NC33308		RA
☐ Bushby M.II Mustang II	N53RM	581			PV
☐ Canadair CL-13A Sabre 5 [North American F-86E]					RAC
☐ Cassutt IIIM					PV
☐ Cessna T-50 Bobcat (AT-17B) (UC-78B)	42-71830	4526	Front fuselage only.		RAD
☐ Cessna T-50 Bobcat (AT-17D) (UC-78C)		4153	42-72157, N66794 – painted as a JRC-1.		PVX
☐ Cessna 120	NC4191N	13662	NC4191N, N4191N		PV
☐ Cessna 150L Commuter	N18588	15073966			PV
☐ Cessna 310A Blue Canoe (L-27A) (U-3A)	58-2107	38081			RA
☐ Cessna 310C	'182Z'	35909	N1809H, N155G		PV
☐ Cessna 318B Tweety Bird (318A) (T-37A) (T-37B)	57-2267	40200			PV
☐ Cessna 337M Super Skymaster (O-2A)	N37581	337M0190	68-6901		PV
☐ Columbia XJL-1	N54205		Bu31400		PV
☐ Consolidated 28-5A Catalina (PBV-1A) (OA-10A)	'4497'	CV 560	Bu68013, 44-34049, CF-GLX, C-FGLX, N322FA		RAX
☐ Consolidated 28-5A Catalina (PBY-5A)	N10609	1758	Bu48396, 'A24-387' – fuselage only.		RA
☐ Consolidated 28-5A Catalina (PBY-5A)	N68756	1954	Fbu46590 – fuselage only.		RA
☐ Consolidated 32 Liberator (B-24J) (B.VII)	44-44175	1470	44-44175, KH304, HE877 (India), N7866		PV
☐ Convair 4 Hustler (B-58A)	61-2080	116			PV
☐ Convair 8-10 Delta Dagger (F-102A)	56-1393	8-10-610			PV
☐ Convair 8-12 Delta Dagger (TF-102A)	54-1366	8-12-16			PV
☐ Convair 8-24 Delta Dart (F-106A)	59-0003	8-24-132			PV
☐ Convair 36 Peacemaker (B-36J)	52-2827	383	On loan from AHC, TX.		PV
☐ Convair 240-27 (T-29B)	51-7906	318			PV
☐ Convair 340-71 Samaritan (R4Y-1) (C-131F)	Bu141017	300			PV
☐ Convair 340-71 Samaritan (R4Y-1) (C-131F)	Bu141025	308			RA
☐ Culver NR-D Cadet (PQ-14B)	44-21819	N763	44-21819, N1063M		PV

109

☐ Curtiss 85 Owl (O-52)	40-2746	14279		PV
☐ Curtiss 87-B3 Warhawk (P-40K)	42-45984	15785		RA
☐ Curtiss 87V Warhawk (P-40N) (Kittyhawk IV)	42-104961	28723	On loan from MARC, CA.	RA
☐ Curtiss-Wright CW-20B-2 Commando (C-46D)	44-77635	33031		PV
☐ Curtiss-Wright CW-25 Jeep (AT-9A)	42-56882			RAD
☐ Dornier-Breguet Alpha Jet A	40+49	0049		PV
☐ Douglas B-18A Bolo	38-0593	2643	38-0593, N66267	PV
☐ Douglas UC-67 Dragon (B-23)	N61Y	2737	39-0051, NC61Y, N61Y, N34C, N534C, N230SU, N534J, '5340'	PV
☐ Douglas DC-3A-360 Skytrain (C-47)	41-7723	4201		PV
☐ Douglas DC-3A-467 Skytrain (C-47B)	45-1074	17077/34344	Fuselage only.	RA
☐ Douglas Super DC-3 (R4D-8) (C-117D)	Bu50826	43363	Rebuilt from DC-3A-467 Skytrain (C-47B) (R4D-6) c/n 15479/26924 43-49663, Bu50826 –	PV
☐ Douglas DC-4 Skymaster (C-54D)	42-72488	10593		PV
☐ Douglas DC-6A Liftmaster (C-118A) (VC-118A)	53-3240	44611		PV
☐ Douglas DC-7B	N51701	44701		PV
☐ Douglas 1317 Globemaster II (C-124C)	52-1004	43913		PV
☐ Douglas 1430 Cargomaster (C-133B)	59-0527	45578		PV
☐ Douglas DC-9-33RC Skytrain II (C-9B)	Bu164607	47428	EC-BYK, N521MD, Bu164607, N934NA	PV
☐ Douglas A-20G Havoc	43-21627	21274	On loan from MARC, CA.	RAC
☐ Douglas A-24B Dauntless			c/n 17493 42-54654 quoted but museum has found no evidence to substantiate this – on loan from MARC, CA.	PVC
☐ Douglas A-26A Invader (A-26B) (TB-26B) (B-26K)	64-17653	7091	41-39378	PV
☐ Douglas A-26C Invader	44-35272	28651	44-35372, 435372 (France), N8028E – fuselage only.	RA
☐ Douglas A-4C Skyhawk (A4D-2N)	Bu148571	12764	Bu148571, N53996, N401FS –	PV
☐ Douglas TA-4B Skyhawk (A4D-2)	Bu142928	11990		PV
☐ Douglas EA-1F Skyraider (AD-5N) (AD-5Q)	Bu135018	10095		PV
☐ Douglas F-6A Skyray (F4D-1)	Bu134748	10342		PV
☐ Douglas TF-10B Skynight (F3D-2) (F3D-2T)	Bu124629	7499		PV
☐ Douglas WB-66D Destroyer	55-0395	45027		PV
☐ Douglas YEA-3A Skywarrior (YA3D-1)	Bu130361	9262		PV
☐ Ercoupe 415C	N78X	1188	N93865	PV
☐ Evans VP-1 Volksplane	N47188	1		PV
☐ Fairchild M-62A Cornell (PT-19A)	41-14675	T41-613	41-14675, N53963	PV
☐ Fairchild M-62A-4 Cornell II	N1270N	FC.34	10533 (Canada)	PV
☐ Fairchild 78 Packet (C-82A)	44-23006	10050	44-23006, N6997C	PV
☐ Fairchild 110 Flying Boxcar (C-119C)	N13743	10369	49-0157	PV
☐ Fairchild 110 Flying Boxcar (C-119C)	49-0157	10394		PV
☐ Fairchild 205 Provider (C-123B)	4505	20166	55-4505	PV
☐ Fairchild 473 Provider (205) (C-123B) (C-123K)	N3142D	20029	54-0580	PV
☐ Fairchild-Republic A-10A Thunderbolt II	75-0298	A10-47		PV
☐ Fairey Gannet AEW.3	N1350X	F9451	XL482	PV
☐ Fieseler Fi 103A-1		121536		PV
☐ Flaglor Sky Scooter	N6WM	1000		PV
☐ Fleet 2	N605M	181	NC605M	PV
☐ Focke-Wulf Fw 44J Stieglitz	N133JM	2827	D-EYWI, 19 (Norway), SZ-19 (Finland), OH-SZH	PV
☐ Folland Fo.144 Gnat T.1	N694XM	FL-504	XM694	PV
☐ Gates Learjet 23	N88B	23-015		PV
☐ General Dynamics F-111E	68-0033	A1-202		PV
☐ Government Aircraft Factories N.22SL Nomad	N6328	N22S-163	VH-HVZ	PV
☐ Grumman G-36 Wildcat (FM-2)	Bu16161	1360	Bu16161, N4224W	PV
☐ Grumman G-40 Avenger (TBM-3)	Bu69472	2211	Bu69472, N9593C	PV
☐ Grumman G-44A Widgeon (J4F-2)	Bu32976	1330		PV
☐ Grumman G-51 Tigercat (F7F-3)	Bu80410	C.152	Bu80410, N7627C – on loan from NMMC, VA.	PV
☐ Grumman G-79 Panther (F9F-4)	Bu125183			PV
☐ Grumman G-82 Guardian (AF-2S)	'N9995Z'	321	Bu129233, N9994Z	PVX
☐ Grumman G-89 Tracker (S2F-1) (S2F-1S1) (S-2F)	Bu36468	377S		PV
☐ Grumman G-98 Tiger (F11F-1) (F-11A)	Bu141824	141		PV
☐ Grumman G-99 Cougar (F9F-8) (F-9J)	Bu141121	368C		PV
☐ Grumman G-99 Cougar (F9F-8P) (RF-9J)	Bu144426	110		PV
☐ Grumman G-105 Cougar (F9F-8T) (TF-9J)	Bu147397	367		PV
☐ Grumman G-111 Albatross (G-64) (SA-16A) (SA-16B) (HU-16B)	51-0022	G-96		PV
☐ Grumman G-117 Tracer (WF-2) (E-1B)	Bu147227	26		PV
☐ Grumman G-128 Intruder (A-6A) (A-6E)	Bu155713	I-439		PV
☐ Grumman G-134 Mohawk (AO-1C) (OV-1C)	61-2724	67C		PV
☐ Grumman G-159 Gulfstream I	N4NA	151	N741G, NASA4	RA
☐ Grumman G-303 Tomcat (F-14A)	Bu160684	303		PV
☐ Grumman G-1159 Gulfstream II	N948NA	222	N817GA, N5253A	PV
☐ Gyrodyne QH-50C (DSN-2)		DS-1045		PV
☐ Hawker Hurricane IIC	'V6864'		Partial replica.	PVX
☐ Hawker P.1099 Hunter F.58	N159AM	41H/697402	J-4035 (Switzerland) – on loan from Planes of Fame, CA.	PV
☐ Hawker-Siddeley P.1127 Harrier 50 (AV-8A) (AV-8C)	Bu159241	P150		PV
☐ Helton Lark 95	N1512H	9512		RA

Arizona

Arizona

☐ Hiller UH12C	N7725C	J345		RA
☐ Hughes 269A Osage (TH-55A)	67-15418	18-0762		RA
☐ Hughes 369M Cayuse (HO-6) (OH-6A)	67-16381	0766		PV
☐ Hunting-Percival P.84 Jet Provost T.3A (T.3)	XM464	PAC/W/9272		RA
☐ Ilyushin Il-2m3				RAD
☐ Interstate S1B1 Cadet (O-63) (L-6)			(USAAF) – parts only.	RA
☐ Kaman K-20 Seasprite (HU2K-1U) (UH-2B) (SH-2F)	N8062J	105	Bu150155 –	PV
☐ Kaman K-600 Huskie (HOK-1) (OH-43D)	Bu139974			PV
☐ Kaman K-600-3 Huskie (H-43B) (HH-43B) (HH-43F)	62-4531	157	62-4531, N327WN	PV
☐ Lockheed 10-A Electra (UC-36A)	NC14260	1011	NC14260, 42-56638, NC14260, 104 (Honduras), N4963C	PV
☐ Lockheed 15-27-01 Harpoon (PV-2)	N7255C	15-1223	Bu37257 – rear fuselage from c/n 15-1156 '1156' (Brazil), Bu37190, N6856C	RA
☐ Lockheed 18-56-24 Lodestar (R5O-5)	Bu12481	18-2411	Bu12481, NC9200H, ZS-DAX, SA-AAF, N15A	RA
☐ Lockheed 049-46-25 Constellation (049-46-10) (C-69)	N90831	049-1970	42-94549	PV
☐ Lockheed 080 Shooting Star (P-80B) (F-80B)	45-8612	080-1826		PV
☐ Lockheed 182-1A Hercules (182-44-03) (C-130A)	57-0457	182-3164		RA
☐ Lockheed 182-1A Hercules (182-44-03) (C-130A) (C-130D)	57-0493	182-3200		PV
☐ Lockheed 185 Orion (P3V-1) (P-3A) (VP-3A)	Bu150511	185-5037	On loan from NMNA, FL	RA
☐ Lockheed 300 Starlifter (C-141A) (C-141B)	67-0013	300-6264		PV
☐ Lockheed 394 Viking (S-3A) (S-3B)	Bu160604	394A-3184		RA
☐ Lockheed 483-04-06 Starfighter (F-104D)	57-1323	283-5035		PV
☐ Lockheed 580 (T-33A)	53-6145	580-9766		PV
☐ Lockheed 580 (T-33A)				RA
☐ Lockheed 580 (T-33A) (TV-2) (T-33B)	Bu136810	580-7914	53-2704	PV
☐ Lockheed 726-45-14 Neptune (P2V-7) (P-2H) (AP-2H)	Bu135620	726-7052		PV
☐ Lockheed 749A-79-38 Constellation (C-121A) (VC-121A)	48-0614	749A-2606		PV
☐ Lockheed 826-45-14 Neptune (P2V-7) (P-2H)	N14448	826-8013	24113 (Canada) (CF-MQW) – with parts of c/n 726-7207 Bu147957, N7060X.	PV
☐ Lockheed 880-75-13 Starfire (F-97A) (F-94C)	51-5623	880-7686		PV
☐ Lockheed 1049A-55-86 Super Constellation (RC-121D) (EC-121D) (EC-121T)	53-0554	1049A-4369		PV
☐ Lockheed 1080-91-08 SeaStar (T2V-1) (T-1A)	Bu144200	1080-1104		PV
☐ Lockheed 1329 JetStar 6 (VC-140B) (C-140B)	61-2489	1329-5022		PV
☐ Lockheed 1329 JetStar 6 (VC-140B) (C-140B)	62-4197	1329-5041		RA
☐ Lockheed 1329 JetStar 6 (VC-140B) (C-140B)	62-4200	1329-5044		RA
☐ Lockheed Q-Star (YO-3A)	69-18006	007	69-18006, N14425	RA
☐ Lockheed SR-71A Blackbird	61-7951	2002		PV
☐ Martin 162G Mariner (PBM-5A)	N3190G	162	Bu122071 – on loan from NASM, DC.	PV
☐ Martin 179B Marauder (B-26B)	41-31856	3570	Wings from 40-1501 – Rear fuselage from another aircraft – On loan from MARC, CA.	RAC
☐ Martin 272E Canberra (B-57E)	55-4274	376		PV
☐ Martin 4-0-4	N462M	14153	N462M	RA
☐ Martin 744 Canberra (294) (RB-57D) (RB-57F) (WB-57F)	N925NA	012	53-3975, 63-13501	PV
☐ McCulloch J-2	N4309G	019		PV
☐ McCulloch MC-4A (XHUM-1) (HUM-1)	Bu133817	1001	Bu133817, N4072K –	PV
☐ McDonnell M.36BA Voodoo (F-101B)	57-0282	460		PV
☐ McDonnell M.36CA Voodoo (RF-101C)	56-0214	230		PV
☐ McDonnell M.58 Demon (F3H-2) (F-3B)	'Bu143492'	390	Bu145221 –	PVX
☐ McDonnell M.98AM Phantom II (F-4B) (F-4N)	Bu153016	1496	On loan from NMNA, FL but loaned to CAF, AZ.	-
☐ McDonnell M.98AM Phantom II (F4H-1) (F-4B) (YF-4J)	Bu151497	655		PV
☐ McDonnell M.98DJ Phantom II (F-4C)	64-0673	898		PV
☐ McDonnell M.98HO Phantom II (F-4E) (NF-4E)	66-0329	2604		PV
☐ McDonnell M.199-1A Eagle (F-15A)	74-0118	094/A079		PV
☐ Mikoyan-Gurevich MiG-21PF	N21MF	762410	2410 (Poland) – in Soviet markings.	PVX
☐ Mikoyan-Gurevich MiG-23MLD	44	0390323079		RA
☐ Mikoyan-Gurevich MiG-29A	'53'	2960516766	22 (Moldova)	PVX
☐ Mitchell Wing B-10	N4232A	285		RA
☐ Morane-Saulnier MS.500 Criquet [Fieseler Fi 156 Storch]	N42FS	724	724 (France), F-BJQH – on loan from MARC, CA.	RAC
☐ Nakajima Ki-43-IIb Hayabusa		6 (?)	62387, FE-6430, T2-6430 – on loan from NASM, DC.	PV
☐ Naval Aircraft Factory N3N-3	N45084		Bu4497	RA
☐ North American NA-64 Yale	3397	64-2150	3397 (Canada), N4735G	PV
☐ North American NA-108 Mitchell (B-25J) (TB-25J) (TB-25N)	43-27712	108-34725		PV
☐ North American NA-122 Mustang (P-51D)	'44-63272'			RACX
☐ North American NA-147 Tornado (B-45A)	47-0063	147-43463	Front fuselage only –	RA
☐ North American NA-168 Texan (T-6G)	49-2908	168-12	Ex NA-84 (AT-6B) c/n 84-7624 41-17246	PVX

111

Aircraft	Serial	Code	Notes	Status
☐ North American NA-170 Sabre (F-86E)	50-0600	170-22		RA
☐ North American NA-201 Sabre (F-86D) (F-86L)	53-0965	201-409		PV
☐ North American NA-203 Sabre (F-86H)	53-1525	203-297		PV
☐ North American NA-209 Fury (FJ-4B) (AF-1E)	Bu139531	209-151		PV
☐ North American NA-212 (YF-100B) (YF-107A)	55-5118	212-1		PV
☐ North American NA-217 Super Sabre (F-100C)	54-1823	217-84		PV
☐ North American NA-226 Trojan (T-28C)	Bu140481	226-58		PV
☐ North American NA-240 (X-15) (X-15A) (FSM)	'56-6671'			PVX
☐ North American NA-276 Sabreliner (T-39A) (CT-39A)	62-4449	276-2		PV
☐ North American NA-296 Vigilante (NA-269) (A3J-1) (A3J-3P) (RA-5C)	Bu149289	296-67	Original c/n 269-24	PV
☐ North American NA-305 Bronco (OV-10A) (OV-10D)	Bu155499	305-110		PV
☐ North American NA-332 Buckeye (T-2C)	Bu157050	332-21		PV
☐ Northrop N-23 Raider (YC-125A)	XB-GEY	2520	48-0636, N2573B	PV
☐ Northrop N-156B Freedom Fighter (F-5B)	72-0441	N.8092		RA
☐ Northrop N-156T Talon (T-38A)	61-0854	N.5220		PV
☐ Northrop N-160 Scorpion (N-68) (F-89D) (F-89J)	53-2674	N.4805		PV
☐ Pacific Airways 89		KM92514		PV
☐ Panavia PA200 Tornado IDS	43+74	4074		PV
☐ Pentecost E III Hoppicopter	NX31222		On loan from NASM, DC.	PV
☐ Pereira GP.3 Osprey II	N17EH	105A		RA
☐ Piasecki PV-18 Retriever (H-25A) (HUP-3) (UH-25C)	Bu147595	37	51-16608	PV
☐ Piasecki PV-18 Retriever (HUP-2) (UH-25B)	Bu134434	263		PV
☐ Piper J-4A Cub Coupe	NC22783	4-469	NC22783, N22783	PV
☐ Piper PA-23-250 Aztec (UO-1) (U-11A)	Bu149067	27-357		PV
☐ Pitts S-1 Special	N2RB	66		PV
☐ Pitts S-1C Special	N6119	DC1		PV
☐ Quickie Aircraft Quickie 1 (Rutan 54)	N80EB	0297		PV
☐ Republic P-47D Thunderbolt	42-8130			RA
☐ Republic F-84C Thunderjet (P-84C)	47-1433		With parts of F-84B 45-59554.	PV
☐ Republic F-84F Thunderstreak	52-6563			PV
☐ Republic RF-84F Thunderflash	51-1944			PV
☐ Republic F-105D Thunderchief	61-0086	D-281		PV
☐ Republic F-105G Thunderchief (F-105F)	62-4427	F-16		PV
☐ Rutan 61 Long Ez	N82ST	442		PV
☐ Ryan ST-3KR Recruit (PT-22)	41-15736	1765	41-15736, NC54003, N1180C	PV
☐ Scheibe SF-27 Zugvogel IIIB	N111MG	1023		PV
☐ Schempp-Hirth SHK-1	N7732G	13		PV
☐ Schweizer SGS.2-12 (TG-3A)	N69064	15	(USAAF)	PV
☐ Shenyang J-6I [Mikoyan-Gurevich MiG-19SF]	301			PV
☐ Sikorsky S-43	'Bu1061'	4325	NC16394, N326 – on loan from NMMC, VA.	PVX
☐ Sikorsky S-51 Dragonfly (H-5G)	48-0548		48-0548, N9845Z	PV
☐ Sikorsky S-51 Dragonfly (HO3S-1)	232	5108	232, N4925E	PV
☐ Sikorsky S-55D Chickasaw (H-19B) (UH-19B)	52-7537	55640	52-7537, N2256G	PV
☐ Sikorsky S-56 Mojave (H-37A) (H-37B) (CH-37B)	58-1005	56150		PV
☐ Sikorsky S-58 Choctaw (H-34A) (VH-34C)	57-1684	58790		PV
☐ Sikorsky S-61R Pelican (HH-3F)	1476	61638		PV
☐ Sikorsky S-62A Seaguard (HH-52A)	1450	62133		PV
☐ Sikorsky S-64A Tarhe (CH-54A)	68-18437	64039		PV
☐ Sikorsky S-65A (HH-53C) (HH-53H) (MH-53H)	73-1649	65387		PV
☐ Squadron Aviation SPAD XIII	'S42523/1'			PVX
☐ Starr Bumble Bee	N83WS	1		PV
☐ Stinson V-76 Sentinel (L-5B)	44-16907	76-3192	44-16907, N4981V	S
☐ Sud-Est SE.210 Caravelle VI-R	N1001U	86	N1001U, PT-DUW	PV
☐ Swallow A Ultralight				PV
☐ Taylorcraft BC-12D	N43584	7243	NC43584	PV
☐ Taylorcraft DCO-65 Grasshopper (L-2M)	N47583	L-5422	(USAAF)	PV
☐ Taylorcraft ST-100 (TG-6)	N59134	6101	42-58662	PV
☐ Temco D.16 Twin Navion	N5128K	NAV-4-2028B	c/n also given as TTN-29.	PV
☐ Ultralight Flying Machines Easy Riser				RA
☐ Vertol V.43 Shawnee (H-21C) (CH-21C)	56-2159	C.321		PV
☐ Vickers 724 Viscount	N22SN	40	CF-TGI, N22SN, 'VP-ABD'	PV
☐ Vought F4U-4 Corsair	Bu97142	9503	Bu97349 – on loan from NMMC, VA.	PV
☐ Vought DF-8F Crusader (F8U-1) (F-8A)	Bu144427			PV
☐ Vought A-7D Corsair II	70-0973	D119		PV
☐ Vought A-7E Corsair II	Bu160713	E546		PV
☐ Vultee V-74 Valiant (BT-13A)	42-42353	74-9103		PV
☐ Waco NZR Hadrian (CG-4A)	45-14647		Nose section on display – remainder in store.	PV/R
☐ Waco RNF	NC11206	3392		PV
☐ Waco UPF-7	NC30135	5532	NC30135, N30135	PV
☐ Waco ZKS-6	NC16523	4512	NC16523, N16523	PV
☐ War Aircraft P-47D Thunderbolt	N555TN	1	On loan to Phoenix Airport Arts Program, AZ.	-
☐ Wright Flyer (R)				
☐ WSK Lim-2 [MiG-15bis]	'822'	1B 008-22	822 (Poland), N822JM – in false North Korean markings.	PVX
☐ WSK SBLim-2 (Lim-1) [MiG-15] [MiG-15UTI]	038	1A 06-038	038 (Poland), N38BM	PV

Arizona

☐ WSK Lim-5R (Lim-5) [MiG-17F]	'1905'	1C 19-05	1905 (Poland) – In false North Vietnamese markings.	PVX
☐ WSK Lim-6MR (Lim-5P) [MiG-17PF]	'634'	1D 06-34	634 (Poland) – in false Soviet markings.	PVX

PIMA COMMUNITY COLLEGE (AZ31)

Address:	4905 East Broadway Boulevard, Tucson, Arizona 85709-1010
Tel:	520-206-4500 Email: infocenter@pima.edu
Admission:	By prior permission only.
Location:	At the International Airport which is in the southern part of the city on Route 19.

Set up in 1966, the first classes were held in a hangar at Tucson Airport. A campus was soon constructed and now the college has six permanent sites. The Aviation Center is located at the airport. The fleet of instructional airframes includes several withdrawn airliners. This list is not complete and any information would be appreciated.

TYPE	REG/SER	CON. NO.	PI/NOTES	STATUS
☐ Boeing 727-116C	N115FE	19814	CC-CFE, N115FE, C-GBWH	RA
☐ Boeing 727-287A	N914PG	22603	LV-OVN, N914PG, HC-BVT, (N924PG)	RA
☐ De Havilland DHC.8-100	C-GGMP	002		RA
☐ Gates Learjet 45	N453LJ	45-003	N453LJ, (N789H)	RA
☐ Lockheed L-1011-100 Tristar	P4-MED	193L-1064	N10112, C-GIES, N787M	RA
☐ Rand Robinson KR-2	N97WM	7597		RA
☐ Sud-Est SE.210 Caravelle VI-R	N777VV	87	(N1003U), F-WJAM, N1002U, PH-TRY, N777VV, (N240RC)	RA
☐ Vickers 831 Viscount	4X-AVE	403	G-APNE, JY-ADA, G-APNE – fuselage only.	RAD

PINAL AIR PARK MONUMENT (AZ32)

Location:	By prior permission only at the airfield which is about 6 miles north west of Marana.

TYPE	REG/SER	CON. NO.	PI/NOTES	STATUS
☐ McDonnell M.36BA Voodoo (TF-101B) (CF-101F)	57-0332	510	57-0332, 101024 (Canada)	RA

PLANES OF FAME GRAND CANYON (AZ33)

Address:	755 Mustang Way, Valle Williams, Arizona 86046.
Tel:	928-635-1000
Admission:	Daily 0900-1800
Location:	Near the junction of Highways 64 and 180

Now over half a century old Planes of Fame is well established at Chino in California. In the mid-1990s the directors of the museum decided to set up a facility at Grand Canyon Valle Airport. The field was built in 1940 by TWA but closed in the 1960s.
After 30 years of inactivity the airport is now home to this impressive new museum. One hangar and an outside display park are currently in use but there are plans to construct a large building so that the majority of the collection can be protected from the weather. Opened in June 1995, the exhibitions aim to trace the history of aviation.
The World War I period is represented by two replicas, a Bristol Fighter and a Siemens-Schuckert D IV. The story of 'Women in Aviation' and the 'Tuskegee Airmen' is portrayed in the hangar.
The outside park is dominated by a Constellation, which was once the personal transport of General Douglas MacArthur. This aircraft on show at the Army Aviation Museum in Fort Rucker and its future was in doubt until acquired by museum at Chino. After many trials and tribulations it was restored to flying condition and headed slowly west across the country. A team has now restored the interior to MacArthur's executive configuration. The Siebold Collection Ford Tri-Motor is often on show.

TYPE	REG/SER	CON. NO.	PI/NOTES	STATUS
☐ Aero L-29 Delfin	N495D	993219	30 (Soviet)	PV
☐ Boeing-Stearman E75 Kaydet (PT-13D)	NX5279N	75-5926	42-17763, N5279N, '40-2147'	PVX
☐ Bristol 14 F.2B Fighter (R)	1		N29HC	PVX
☐ Cessna 165 Airmaster	N25463	568	NC25463	PV
☐ Cessna 318B Tweety Bird (T-37B)	492		(USAF) – in Peruvian markings.	RA
☐ Cessna 318B Tweety Bird (T-37B)	494		(USAF) – in Peruvian markings.	RA
☐ Convair 105 (L-13A)	N6231C	127	46-0194	RAD
☐ Convair 240-1	N240HH	47	NC8408H, HL-25, JA5092, N8408H	PV
☐ Curtiss 50C Robin C-1	NC74H	47		PVA
☐ De Havilland DH.100 Vampire F.3	17018	EEP2310	17018 (Canada), N6881D	PV
☐ Douglas A-26B Invader	N8026E	28602	44-35323, N8026E, CF-CDD	PVA
☐ Douglas D-4NA Skyraider (AD-4N)	NX409Z	7797	Bu126997, 78 (French), N92053	PVA
☐ Grumman G-32A (UC-107)	N100TF	447	NC1326, 42-97045, NC46110, N7F – piinted as an F3F-2.	PVAX
☐ Grumman G-98 Tiger (F11F-1) (F-11A)	Bu141868	185		PV
☐ Lewann Biplane DD-1	N576A	01		PV
☐ Lockheed 580 (T-33A)	'71-5262'	580-8680	53-5341 – in Japanese markings	PV
☐ Lockheed 749A-79-38 Constellation (C-121A) (VC-121A)	48-0613	749A-2605	48-0613, N422NA	PVA
☐ Macchi M.416 [Fokker S-11]	I-AEMC	1021	MM53223	PVD
☐ Martin 4-0-4	N636X	14135	N40429, N706	PV
☐ Messerschmitt Bf 109G-10/U-4	'13'	611943	'13', FE-122, T2-122, NX700E	PV

☐ Mooney/Cox M-18C-X Mite	N18CX	01		PV
☐ Neibauer Lancair 235	N235B	39		PV
☐ Nieuport 17 (R)	N124PW	621		PV
☐ North American NA-161 Sabre (P-86A) (F-86A)	49-1217	161-211	Front fuselage only.	PV
☐ North American NA-168 Texan (T-6G)	N17498	168-325	49-3221, N7816C, N302V, N990JP	PVA
☐ North American NA-200 Trojan (T-28B)	NX393W	200-381	Bu138310	PVA
☐ North American NA-226 Trojan (T-28C)	N166ER	226-116	Bu140539, N4993Y, N28TN	PVA
☐ Northrop N-160 Scorpion (N-68) (F-89D) (F-89J)	'32601'	N.4530	52-1953	RAX
☐ Republic F-84B Thunderjet (P-84B)	45-59529		Fuselage only.	RA
☐ Republic F-84B Thunderjet (P-84B)	45-59556			PV
☐ Republic F-105B Thunderchief	57-5816	B-53		SD
☐ Rutan 61 Long Ez	N85H	704		PV
☐ Schmidt Commuter	N17RS	101		PV
☐ Siemens-Schuckert D IV (R)	N1094G	S10		PVA
☐ Sorta Baby Lakes	N193TE	001		PV
☐ Standard J-1			Fuselage frame plus engine. 45-34950	PV
☐ Stinson V-76 Sentinel (L-5G)	N6055C			PV
☐ Stinson V-77 Reliant (AT-19)	NC79496	77-131	42-46770, FK944, Bu11469 – Scenic Airlines, NV aircraft	PV
☐ Supermarine 349 Spitfire LF.Vb (FSM)				PVX
☐ Team Minimax 1600	47			PV
☐ Vultee V-74A Valiant (BT-15)	N67629	74A-11513	(USAAF) – mocked up as a Val.	PVA
☐ WSK Lim-2 [MiG-15bis]	1301	1B 13-01	In falseSoviet markings.	PV
☐ Yokosuka D4Y1 Suisei				PVD
☐ Yokosuka MXY-7 Ohka 11	1049			PV

PRESCOTT DC-3 (AZ34)

Address: 5133 East Roadrunner Drive, Mesa, Arizona 85215-2539.
Admission: By prior permission only.
Location: At Falcon Field Airport which is about 3 miles north of the town.

The aircraft, which was registered in 1999, spent three years in Colombia in the late 1940s and early 1950s. It is now painted in a typical World War II colour scheme.

TYPE	REG/SER	CON. NO.	PI/NOTES	STATUS
☐ Douglas DC-3A-456 Skytrain (C-47A)	N53ST	9380	42-23518, NC53426, C-75 (Colombia), C-505 (Colombia), HK-505, N3938C, N66W, N5V, N5144, N514X, N53ST	RAA

QUARTZSITE VETERAN'S MEMORIAL FREEDOM GARDEN (AZ35)

Address: Plymouth Avenue, Quartzsite, Arizona 85346.
Admission: On permanent view.
Location: About ¼ mile west of the Quartzsite Junction of Interstate 10.

On show in this garden are the two Phantoms and memorials honouring local people killed in conflicts. There are plans to add to the display in the future and some military vehicles may appear.

TYPE	REG/SER	CON. NO.	PI/NOTES	STATUS
☐ McDonnell M.98DF Phantom II (RF-4C) (NRF-4C)	65-0941	1763		PV
☐ McDonnell M.98DF Phantom II (RF-4C) (NRF-4C)	66-0384	1809		PV

SAN CARLOS MONUMENT (AZ36)

Location: On permanent view at a school on San Carlos Avenue in the northern part of the town.

TYPE	REG/SER	CON. NO.	PI/NOTES	STATUS
☐ North American NA-173 Sabre (F-86D)	51-5915	173-59		PV

SIEBOLD COLLECTION (AZ37)

Address: Valle Aiport, Arizona 86046.
Admission: By prior permission only.
Location: The airport is near the junction of Highways 64 and 180.

Scenic Airways was formed in 1927 and operated a Ford Trimotor and Stinson Detroiter; its name was changed to Grand Canyon Airways in 1930. Tours over the spectacular Grand Canyon were flown.
 Scenic Airlines was set up in 1967 and this has recently merged with Grand Canyon. The Ford Trimotor was acquired by the owner of Scenic Airlines, John Siebold, in 1977 and since then has made a number of flights around the country.
 The Travel Air 6000 six seater high wing monoplane was designed by Clyde Cessna. The prototype flew in 1928 and was in production for two years. In total over 130 were sold and many operated in the more remote areas of the USA and Canada.
 The Stinson SB-1 Detroiter was the first product of the Detroit based company and first took to the air in January 1926. The design was developed into the SM-2 Junior powered by either a Wright J-5 or J-6 radial. The type proved to be popular and more than 100 were completed over the next few years. The Junior was developed during the 1930s and the SM-8 version appeared in 1929.The high wing four seater was fitted with a 215 hp Lycoming radial and 350 were sold. Other classic types are being acquired.

Arizona

TYPE	REG/SER	CON. NO.	PI/NOTES	STATUS
☐ Curtiss 50 Robin	N74H	47	NC78E	RAA
☐ Fleet 2	N617F	193	NC617M, N617M	RAA
☐ Fokker D VIII (R)				RA
☐ Ford 5-AT-C	N414H	5-AT-74	NC414H, XA-BCX, NC414H, NX414H, NC414H, XA-BKS, LG-AFA	RAA
☐ Payne Knight Twister	N711V	1234		RA
☐ Stinson SM-1B Detroiter	N1517	M267	NC7468, N7468B	RAA
☐ Stinson SM-8A Junior	N483Y	M-4297	NC483Y	RAA
☐ Stinson V-77 Reliant (AT-19)	NC79496	77-131	42-46770, FK944, Bu11469	RA
☐ Travel Air A-6000A	N4942V	1040	CF-AEJ	RAA

SILVERBELL ARMY HELIPORT (AZ38)

Address: Building 4500, Marana, Arizona 85653.
Admission: By prior permission only.
Location: North west of the town which is about 30 miles north west of Tucson.

The site is home to a major training base for Army National Guard Helicopter pilots. Attack units are also based at the site, which was the former Marana Army Airfield but is now used for civil purposes. The three types on show represent those which have been flown from the field in recent years.

TYPE	REG/SER	CON. NO.	PI/NOTES	STATUS
☐ Bell 206A Kiowa (OH-58A)	70-15143	40694		RA
☐ Bell 209 Huey Cobra (AH-1G) (AH-1F)	66-15255	20011		RA
☐ Bell 209 Huey Cobra (AH-1G) (AH-1S)	67-15471	20135		RA

THREE POINTS MONUMENT (AZ39)

Location: On permanent view in the Veterans Memorial Park on Highway 286 just south of the town.

TYPE	REG/SER	CON. NO.	PI/NOTES	STATUS
☐ Bell 209 Huey Cobra (AH-1G) (AH-1F)	68-17104	20832		PV

TITAN MISSILE MUSEUM (AZ40)

Address: PO Box 150, 1580 West Duval Mine Road, Suhuarita, Arizona 85018.
Tel: 520-625-7736   **Fax:** 520-625-9845   **Email:** tmmuseum@qwest.net
Admission: Wednesday-Sunday 0900-1700.
Location: About 25 miles south of Tucson off La Canada Drive, Green Valley.

Operated by the Pima Air and Space Museum, the site is the sole survivor of the 18 which once existed in the area. The 390th Strategic Missile Wing operated the Titan here from 1963 until 1984. Within three years all the complexes had been dismantled except for this one, which was declared a National Historic Landmark on 6th April 1994. The site became operational in July 1963 and was in use until November 1982. Guided tours, lasting an hour, take place every half hour.

The underground Launch Control Center contains most of the communications and monitoring equipment used by the crews which served 24 hour shifts. Visitors walk through a long passage to the silo containing the tenth Titan built. The missile is 110 feet high with a diameter of ten feet. Nearby is a first stage Titan rocket engine. This museum presents a fascinating picture of one aspect of the 'Cold War'. The Iroquois, which was on show for many years, has now returned to the main museum.

TUCSON AIR NATIONAL GUARD BASE COLLECTION (AZ41)

Address: 162FG/PA, 1650 East Perimeter Way, Tucson, Arizona 85706-6052.
Tel: 520-295-6192   **Email:** webmaster@tucsaz.ang.af.mil
Admission: By prior permission only.
Location: At Tucson International Airport which is in the southern suburbs of the city.

The 152nd Squadron took up residence at the field in 1956. This unit was first equipped with F-86A Sabres which were replaced by F-84F Thunderstreaks the following year.
 The F-100A Super Sabre arrived in May 1958 and this type served until the squadron converted to the F-102 in 1966. The F-100C was allocated in 1969 and the F-100D replaced these in 1972. The Vought A-7 Corsair arrived in 1977 and was operated until 1986.
 A park has been constructed just inside the main gate where six immaculately restored aircraft can be seen.

TYPE	REG/SER	CON. NO.	PI/NOTES	STATUS
☐ Convair 8-10 Delta Dagger (F-102A)	56-1134	8-10-351		RA
☐ General Dynamics 401 Fighting Falcon (F-16A)	78-0005	61-11		RA
☐ North American NA-176 Sabre (F-86F) (QF-86F)	51-13278	176-209	Possible identity.	RA
☐ North American NA-235 Super Sabre (F-100D)	56-3055	235-153		RA
☐ Republic F-84F Thunderstreak	52-8973			RA
☐ Vought A-7D Corsair II	75-0394	D444		RA

VALLEY AIRCRAFT RESTORATION SOCIETY (AZ42)

Address: PO Box 30158, Mesa, Arizona 85207.
Tel: 480-981-1258
Admission: By prior permission only.
Location: At Falcon Field Airport which is about 3 miles north of the town.

Over the last few years this group has acquired a number of helicopters in addition to operating a Bonanza.
N.O. Brantly flew his B-l prototype in 1946. The first B-2 followed seven years later and 381 examples of the two seater were built. The five seat 305 first flew in 1965 but suffered from ground resonance problems and only 45 were completed. The Osage was used in large numbers for primary military pilot training.

TYPE	REG/SER	CON. NO.	PI/NOTES	STATUS
☐ American Aviation AA-5A Cheetah	N9592U	AA5A-0092		RAA
☐ Beech A35 Bonanza	N898S	D-1562		RAA
☐ Brantly 305				RA
☐ Brantly 305				RA
☐ Brantly B.2				RA
☐ Hiller UH12C Raven (H-23G) (OH-23G)	64-15190	1699	64-15190, N48167	RA
☐ Hughes 269A Osage (TH-55A)	68-17357			RA
☐ Hughes 369M Cayuse (HO-6) (OH-6A)		1317	68-17357	RAA
☐ Piper PA-28-181 Cherokee Archer II	N4098Q	28-7790471		RAA

WILLCOX MONUMENT (AZ43)

Location:	On permanent view at the Inde Motorsport Ranch which is about 4 miles west of the town.

TYPE	REG/SER	CON. NO.	PI/NOTES	STATUS
☐ North American NA-190 Sabre (F-86D) (F-86L)	52-4239	190-642	52-4239, N5169W	PV

WILLIAMS-GATEWAY MONUMENT (AZ44)

Location:	On permanent view at the airport which is in the southern part of Mesa.

TYPE	REG/SER	CON. NO.	PI/NOTES	STATUS
☐ Northrop N-156T Talon (T-38A)	'82 FTW'	N.5113	59-1600	PVX

WINGS OF FLIGHT FOUNDATION (AZ45)

Address:	5133 East Roadrunner Drive, Mesa, Arizona 85215.
Tel:	480-396-0688 Fax: 480-396-6731 Email: info@WingsOfFlight.org
Admission:	By prior permission only.
Location:	At Falcon Field Airport which is about 3 miles north of the town.

The foundation was established in 2007 by a group of aircraft owners. The aim is to set up a museum of airworthy types and participate in shows around the area. The fleet is housed in hangars at Falcon Field.

TYPE	REG/SER	CON. NO.	PI/NOTES	STATUS
☐ Aeronca KC	NC18866	K-132	NC18866, N18866	RAA
☐ Aeronca 7AC Champion	N82711	7AC-1357	NC82711	RAA
☐ Beech D17S				RAA
☐ Beech E18S				RAC
☐ Douglas DC-3A-456 Skytrain (C-47A)				RAA
☐ Naval Aircraft Factory N3N-3				RAC
☐ North American NA-77 Texan (AT-6A)	N3198G/7673	84-7721	41-17343, NC68386, 7673 (South Africa)	RAA
☐ North American NA-88 Texan (AT-6C)				RAA
☐ North American NA-88 Texan (AT-6D)				RAA
☐ North American NA-124 Mustang (P-51D)	N151X	124-48381	45-11628, N5446V	RAA
☐ North American NA-168 Texan (T-6G)	N3158G	168-256	49-3152	RAA
☐ Waco ZKS-7 (UC-72M)	NC50662	5221	NC20954, 42-94135	RAA

WINGSPAN AIR HERITAGE FOUNDATION / KROPP COLLECTION (AZ46)

Address:	PO Box 21268, Falcon Field, Mesa, Arizona 85277.
Tel:	info@wingspanair.org
Admission:	By prior permission only.
Location:	At the airfield which is about 3 miles north of the town.

The group aims to set up a museum of aircraft, artefacts and vehicles. The majority of the aircraft are in store but a few are active at Falcon Field. A large store of components is also held. The Cessna Bobcat owned by the foundation resides in the hangar of the local wing of the Commemorative Air Force.

TYPE	REG/SER	CON. NO.	PI/NOTES	STATUS
☐ Aero L-29 Delfin				RAA
☐ Bell 47D-1 Sioux (H-13E) (OH-13E)				RA
☐ Cessna 195A				RAA
☐ Douglas DC-3A-456 Skytrain (C-47A)				RA
☐ Lockheed 15-27-01 Harpoon (PV-2)	N7257C	15-1236	Bu37270	RAC
☐ Lockheed 15-27-01 Harpoon (PV-2D)	N7454C	15-1599	Bu37633	RA
☐ Lockheed 580 (T-33A)				RA
☐ Luscombe 8A Silvaire				RA
☐ Piasecki PD-22 Work Horse (H-21B) (CH-21B)				RA
☐ Sikorsky S-55D (HO4S-3) (UH-19F)				RA
☐ Vultee V-74A Valiant (BT-15)				RA
☐ Vultee V-79 Valiant (BT-13B)				RA
☐ Yakovlev Yak-52				RA

On outside display at the Planes of Fame Grand Canyon facility at Valle is this Martin 4-0-4 in Pacific Airlines colours (Nigel Hitchman) [AZ33]

The Arizona Air National Guard has this F-16A preserved at their Tucson base. [AZ41]

This replica of Benny Howard's DGA-6 resides at the Arkansas Air Museum. [AR2]

WOMEN'S AIR SERVICE PILOTS MUSEUM (AZ47)

Address: PO Box 6, Quartzsite, Arizona 85346.
Tel: 928-927-5555 **Fax:** 928-927-4181 **Email:** info@waspmuseum.com
Admission: By prior permission only.
Location: In the western part of the town.

The airfield was used during World War II in the training of women pilots. The museum was set up several years ago by a group of local residents. On show are items of memorabilia, photographs and artefacts tracing the history of the field.

Aircraft have gradually been acquired. The former Belgian Air Force Pembroke is due to move from New Jersey. The Panther was the subject of a dispute and was moved to California for a period.

TYPE	REG/SER	CON. NO.	PI/NOTES	STATUS
☐ Beech C18S Kansan (AT-11)	N68255	1495	41-27650	PV
☐ Beech C50 Seminole (L-23D) (RL-23D) (RU-8D)	58-3086	RLH-87		PV
☐ Grumman G-79 Panther (F9F-5P) (F9F-5KD) (DF-9E)	'Bu123517'		Bu125316	PVX
☐ Percival P.66 Pembroke C.51	N51973	P.66/14	RM-1 (Belgium)	RA
☐ Piasecki PV-18 Retriever (HUP-2) (UH-25B)	Bu133053		Possible identity.	PV

YUMA MARINE CORPS AIR STATION (AZ48)

Address: PO Box 99113, Yuma, Arizona 85369-9113
Tel: 520-341-2275
Admission: By prior permission only.
Location: About 3 miles south of the town off Interstate 8.

This airfield, known as Fly Field, opened in 1928 and during that summer 25 aircraft taking part in a race from New York to Los Angeles stopped at Yuma. When the United States entered World War II a military base was constructed and the field became one of the largest training schools. At the end of the conflict it closed but was reactivated in 1951 and five years later renamed Vincent Air Force Base.

TYPE	REG/SER	CON. NO.	PI/NOTES	STATUS
☐ Douglas A-4L Skyhawk (A4D-2N) (A-4C)	Bu150586	12997	Bu150586, N403FS – on loan from NMMC, VA.	RA
☐ Hawker-Siddeley P.1127 Harrier 50 (AV-8A)	Bu158695	P92	On loan from NMMC, VA.	RA
☐ McDonnell M.98AM Phantom II (F4H-1) (F-4B)	Bu148367	52	On loan from NMMC, VA.	RA
☐ Northrop N-156E Tiger II (F-5E)	74-1570	R.1266	74-1570, Bu741570 –	RA

ARKANSAS

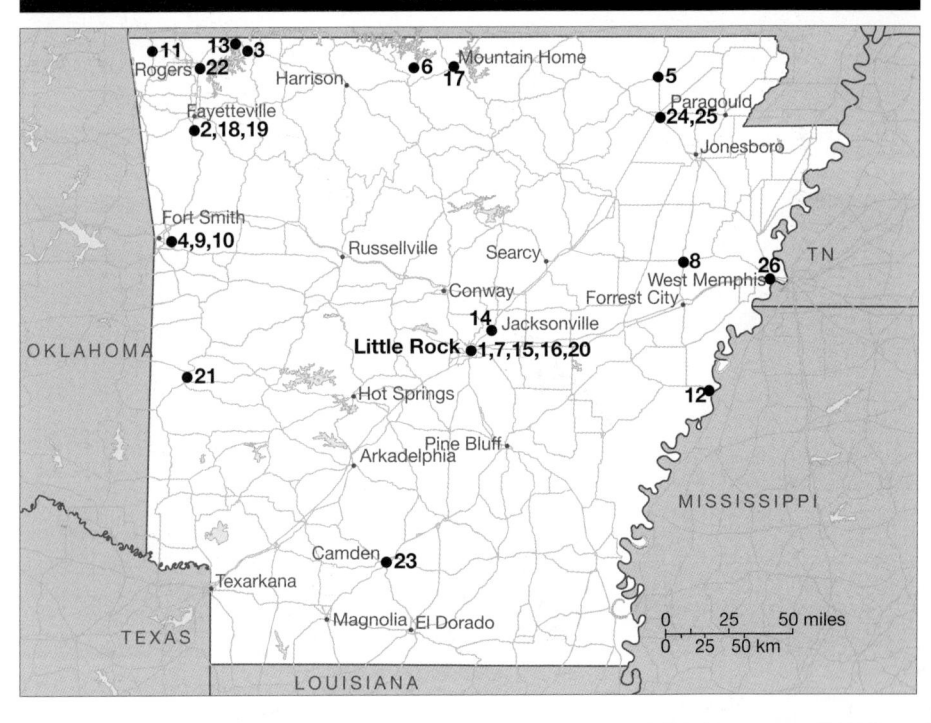

AEROSPACE EDUCATION CENTER (AR1)

Address: 3301 East Roosevelt Road, Little Rock, Arkansas 72206.
Tel: 501-376-4629   **Email:** aerospace@aerospaced.org
Admission: Closed at end of 2010.
Location: Just south of Adams Field which is in the south eastern suburbs of the city.

The Arkansas Aviation Historical Society was formed in 1979 with the aim of recording the history of flying in the state. The Arkansas Aviation Hall of Fame was set up and a collection of aircraft has been acquired. Ground was broken in 1994 for the construction of the museum building which opened in June 1995. The British Caudron-built Sopwith Camel flew in many Hollywood films and has been restored to flying condition. The Arkansas Aircraft was set up at Little Rock in 1926 produced 200 examples of the Command-Aire biplane. Very few of the type have survived. The Forbes Cobra was designed for pylon racing and the type won a number of contests. The complex was closed at the end of 2010.

TYPE	REG/SER	CON. NO.	PI/NOTES	STATUS
☐ Command-Aire 5C3	NC925E	W-88		PV
☐ Curtiss 1C Jenny (JN-4D)	N6898C	34135		PV
☐ Forbes Cobra	N320DW	F-3		PV
☐ Peryra Adventura				PV
☐ Piper J-3C-65 Cub	N42092	14319	NC42092	PV
☐ Sopwith F.1 Camel	'E1537'	3	N6254, 'B7270'	PVX
☐ Stewart JD-HW.1.7Headwind				PV
☐ Travel Air 6000-B	N8112	884	NC8112	PV
☐ Wright Flyer (R)				PV

ARKANSAS AIR MUSEUM (AR2)

Address: 4290 South School Avenue, Fayetteville, Arkansas 72701-8008.
Tel: 479-521-4947   **Email:** arairmuseum@aol.com
Admission: Daily 0930-1630.
Location: At Drake Field which is about 3 miles south of the town on Route 71.

Aviation first came to the area in 1911 and has remained an important part of the life of the community. The museum was established in late 1985 and the City of Fayetteville has restored the original 1940s hangar at Drake Field for the collection.

The aircraft mainly date from the inter-war period. Several have come from the collection of Bob and Jim Younkin, two local men, who have restored many vintage types and have also built replicas of famous racing machines. Benny Howard's DGA-6 'Mister Mulligan' was the only aircraft to win both the Bendix and Thompson Trophy races in the same year. This feat was achieved in 1935. A DGA-11, which was derived from the DGA-6, is on show and only four of this model were produced although others were converted from DGA-8s and DGA-9s. The example on show was restored by Jim Younkin. Younkin's replica of the DGA-6 can also be seen.

The later DGA-15 served in large numbers with the US Navy and over 500 were constructed. A rare low wing Howard DGA-18 trainer was rebuilt in the museum workshops. The aircraft, designed by Gordon Israel, was for the Civil Pilot Training Program. The prototype was constructed in three months and flew in 1941. The 18K version was fitted with a 160 hp Kinner radial engine. The type was based at Fayetteville between late 1941 and March 1943. After primary training on the Piper Cub the cadets moved on to the Howard.

Two other classic pre-war types are the Stinson Junior and the Travel Air D-4000. The S version of the Junior was developed from the SM-8 and first flew in 1931. The Travel air 4000 biplane three seater was manufactured from 1926. The type was almost identical to the earlier 2000 series but was fitted with a variety of radial engines. The D-4000 was powered by a 220 hp Wright.

A few fairly modern types are being acquired to add variety to the display. The Aero Adventure Aventura is an ultralight amphibian design developed in Florida in the 1990s. The type is derived from the Advanced Aeromarine Buccaneer. The company supplies kits of a number of variants of the basic design.

The Revolution Mini 500 helicopter which resembles a scaled down Hughes 500 is powered by a 67 hp Rotax engine. The prototype, built in Excelsior Springs, Missouri flew in the early 1990s. Since then large numbers of kits have been sold around the world. The museum also has an interesting exhibition of aero engines and memorabilia. As many of the aircraft are owned by members of the museum they are sometimes away flying and others from the nearby hangars move into the hall.

TYPE	REG/SER	CON. NO.	PI/NOTES	STATUS
☐ Aero Adventure Aventura				PV
☐ Aeronca 7BCM Champion (L-16A)	N220JK	7BCM-542	47-1171.	PV
☐ Bell 205 Iroquois (UH-1H)	68-15287	10217		PV
☐ Bell 209 Huey Cobra (AH-1G) (AH-1S)	70-16050	20994		PV
☐ Bensen B-8M Gyrocopter	N4840	1		PV
☐ Boeing-Stearman A75N1 Kaydet (PT-17)	N5862	75-2134	41-8575	PVA
☐ Curtiss-Wright CW-1 Junior (R)				PV
☐ Douglas A-4C Skyhawk (A4D-2N)	Bu147733	12497		RA
☐ Ercoupe 415C	N2278H	2903	NC2278H	PV
☐ Gates Learjet 23	N23BY	23-009	N425EJ, N5BL, N13SN, N49CK	PV
☐ Globe GC-1B Swift				PV
☐ Howard DGA-6 (R)	NR273Y	JRY-02		PVA
☐ Howard DGA-11	NC18207	206	NC18207, N18207	PVA
☐ Howard DGA-18K	N39668	668	NC39668	PV
☐ Luscombe 8E Silvaire	N2415K	5142	NC2415K	PVA
☐ Pietenpol B4-A Aircamper				PV
☐ Piper PA-22-160 Tripacer	N86483	22-5777		PV
☐ Revolution Mini-500	N500KZ	325		PV
☐ Royal Aircraft Factory S.E.5A (Scale R)				PV
☐ Stinson Junior S	NC12143	8201		PVA
☐ Taylorcraft BC-12D				PV
☐ Travel Air D-4000	NC6478	798		PV

AVIATION CADET MUSEUM (AR3)

Address:	542 Country Road 2073, Silver Wings Field, Eureka Springs, Arkansas 72632.
Tel:	479-553-5008 Email: av1cadet@arkansas.net
Admission:	By prior permission only at the present time.
Location:	About 30 miles north east of Springfield off Route 62.

An entertainment complex is being built at the field which will honour all who have served in the armed forces of the country. The displays will trace the daily life of an aviation cadet. On show will be memorabilia, photographs, documents and uniforms. Three complete aircraft have arrived and others will follow. The front fuselage of one Thunderchief is mounted on a trailer and tours local events to raise the profile of the museum.

TYPE	REG/SER	CON. NO.	PI/NOTES	STATUS
☐ Convair 240-17 (T-29A)			Front fuselage only.	PV
☐ Lockheed 580 (T-33A)	57-0688	580-1337		PV
☐ North American NA-243 Super Sabre (F-100F)	56-3904	243-180		PV
☐ Northrop N-156E Tiger II (F-5E)	'2401'	R.1186	74-1528	PVX
☐ Republic F-105G Thunderchief (F-105F)	62-4422	F-11	Front fuselage only.	PV
☐ Republic F-105G Thunderchief (F-105F)	63-8306	F-83		PV

BARLING MONUMENT (AR4)

Location:	On permanent view at VVA Post 467 on Fort Smith Boulevard in the town.

TYPE	REG/SER	CON. NO.	PI/NOTES	STATUS
☐ Bell 209 Huey Cobra (AH-1G) (AH-1F)	67-15469	20133		PV

BLACK RIVER TECHNICAL COLLEGE (AR5)

Address:	1410 Highway 304 East, Pocahontas, Arkansas 72455.
Tel:	870-248-4000
Admission:	By prior permission only.
Location:	At Wilson Airport which is in the south-eastern part of the town.

The college, named after the river which flows through the town, was established in 1972 and took up its current name in 1991. The aviation facility is located at the airport. The workshops have a number of piston and turbine engines for use by the students. Two former military aircraft are among the instructional airframes.

TYPE	REG/SER	CON. NO.	PI/NOTES	STATUS
☐ Cessna 150M				RA
☐ Cessna 172K				RA
☐ Cessna 310				RA
☐ Piper PA-23-250 Aztec				RA
☐ Piper PA-28-160 Cherokee				RA
☐ Sikorsky S-62A Seaguard (HH-52A)	1398	62083		RA
☐ Taylorcraft BC-12D				RA
☐ Vought A-7A Corsair II	Bu153150	A59		RA

BULL SHOALS MONUMENT (AR6)

Location:	On permanent view at VFW 1341 at 1206 Central Boulevard in the town.

TYPE	REG/SER	CON. NO.	PI/NOTES	STATUS
☐ Bell 209 Huey Cobra (AH-1G) (AH-1F)	66-15343	20099		PV

CAMP ROBINSON ALL FLAGS HERITAGE PARK (AR7)

Address:	PO Box 1211, Little Rock, Arkansas 72199-9600.
Tel:	501-212-5183
Admission:	On permanent view.
Location:	In the northern suburbs of the city off Route 176.

The 154th Observation Squadron was set up at Little Rock in October 1925 and served in this role until the outbreak of World War II. During the conflict it flew in North Africa and Italy on tactical and weather reconnaissance missions. The unit moved back to Arkansas in 1946 and continued its reconnaissance role until 1986 when it took up the training of transport crews. The 184th Squadron was allocated to the state in 1953 and after periods of active service has been based at Fort Smith. Initially a reconnaissance unit, the group has flown fighters since 1972. The Camp Robinson area is home to a collection of aircraft which have been flown by the state forces. Most personnel do their initial training at the site and the collection reminds them of the heritage of the National Guard. The F-102, which was on show, has been moved to a nearby compound. The site was acquired by the military in 1917 and initially known as Camp Pike. In 1937 it was renamed Camp Robinson. The site was declared as surplus after World War II and in 1950 land was transferred to a number of organisations. The Arkansas National Guard has a museum tracing its history in one of the buildings near the aircraft display. On show are uniforms, vehicles, weapons, photographs, documents and items of memorabilia.

TYPE	REG/SER	CON. NO.	PI/NOTES	STATUS
☐ Bell 204 Iroquois (UH-1C) (UH-1M)	66-15212	1940		PV
☐ Bell 209 Huey Cobra (AH-1G) (AH-1S)	68-15129	20663		RA
☐ Cessna 318B Tweety Bird (318A) (T-37A) (T-37B)	56-3526	40098		RA
☐ Convair 8-10 Delta Dagger (F-102A)	56-1432	8-10-659		RA

Arkansas

☐ McDonnell M.36CA Voodoo (RF-101C)	56-0057	275		PV
☐ McDonnell M.98DE Phantom II (F-4C)	'63463'	443	63-7463	PVX
☐ North American NA-245 Super Sabre (F-100D)	'54434'	245-84	56-3434	PVX
☐ Republic F-84F Thunderstreak	51-1817		51-1817, N94217	PV

CROSS COUNTY VETERANS MEMORIAL AND MUSEUM (AR8)

Address:	204 South Falls Boulevard, Wynne, Arkansas 72396.
Tel:	870-238-7930
Admission:	Tuesday 1400-1600; Thursday 1000-1200.
Location:	Just south of the town centre.

This veterans group was formed in 1999 and the monument to those who lost their lives in conflicts was dedicated on 11th November 2000. Rooms in the nearby Senior Citizen's Center were converted into a museum and a Huey Cobra was mounted outside. The displays contain many personal items, uniforms and photographs. There is a collection of audio and video tapes in which local people tell their war stories.

TYPE	REG/SER	CON. NO.	PI/NOTES	STATUS
☐ Bell 209 Huey Cobra (AH-1G) (AH-1F)	68-17080	20808		PV

FORT SMITH AIR MUSEUM (AR9)

Address:	3 Glen Haven Drive, Fort Smith, Arkansas 72901.
Tel:	479-785-1839
Admission:	Daily 0530-2300.
Location:	At the airport which is in the south eastern suburbs of the town.

The museum was established in August 1999 with the aim of collecting artefacts relating to aviation in Western Arkansas and Eastern Oklahoma.

A display opened in a vacant store in Central Mall in September 2000 but the collection soon moved to Phoenix Mall. From 2002 the display has been located in the new terminal building at the airport. Here over 50 display cases tracing the history of aviation in the region can be seen.

Local aviators are honoured in the exhibition. The Piper Cub is displayed in the Central Mall.

TYPE	REG/SER	CON. NO.	PI/NOTES	STATUS
☐ Piper J-3C-65 Cub	N87710	15418	NC87760	PV

FORT SMITH AIR NATIONAL GUARD BASE (AR10)

Address:	188 FW/PA, Ebbing Air National Guard Base, Fort Smith, Arkansas 72903-5000.
Tel:	501-648-5210
Admission:	By prior permission only.
Location:	In the south eastern suburbs of the city off Interstate 540.

A decision to build an airport was made in 1936 and it opened three years later with two grass strips. The first hangar was built in 1941 and two asphalt runways were laid in 1945. The first services by Braniff Airways began in 1952.

The 184th Squadron was allocated to the Arkansas ANG in October 1953 and took up residence at Fort Smith. The first type used was the Douglas RB-26C Invader which served until the summer of 1956. Lockheed RF-80As followed and these were replaced by Republic RF-84Fs in January 1957. The last reconnaissance type flown was the RF-101C Voodoo which was in service between December 1970 and the summer of 1972. The unit changed to the fighter role with the arrival of F-100D and F-100F Super Sabres. F-4C Phantoms were allocated in the summer of 1979 and these served until April 1989.

TYPE	REG/SER	CON. NO.	PI/NOTES	STATUS
☐ General Dynamics 401 Fighting Falcon (F-16A)	82-0970	61-563		RA
☐ McDonnell M.36CM Voodoo (F-101C) (RF-101H)	56-0011	157		RA
☐ McDonnell M.98DE Phantom II (F-4C)	63-7411	328		RA
☐ North American NA-223 Super Sabre (F-100D)				RA
☐ Republic RF-84F Thunderflash	51-11292			RA

GRAVETTE MONUMENT (AR11)

Location:	On permanent view in Kindley Park in the eastern part of the town on Highway 72.

TYPE	REG/SER	CON. NO.	PI/NOTES	STATUS
☐ Lockheed 580 (T-33A)	53-6073	580-9694		PV

HELENA MONUMENT (AR12)

Location:	On permanent view in a park in Porter Street in the western part of the town.

TYPE	REG/SER	CON. NO.	PI/NOTES	STATUS
☐ Lockheed 580 (T-33A)	51-8965	580-6749		PV

HOLIDAY ISLAND MONUMENT (AR13)

Location:	On permanent view at VFW 77 in the town which is about 5 miles north of Eureka Springs.

TYPE	REG/SER	CON. NO.	PI/NOTES	STATUS
☐ Bell 205 Iroquois (UH-1H)	71-20244	13068	Due soon.	-

JACKSONVILLE MUSEUM OF MILITARY HISTORY (AR14)

Address: 100 Veterans Circle, Jacksonville, Arkansas 72078.
Tel: 501-241-1943
Admission: Unknown.
Location: In the centre of the town just east of Highway 67/167.

The museum is located at the site of the former administration building of the Jacksonville Ordnance Plant. Construction started in 1941 and the first assembly line was ready the following March. By November 1942 just over 1,400 workers were employed.

The factory closed in 1946 and the land was returned to its former owners. In the 1960s the construction of Arkansas Air Force base resulted in some of the land being commandeered again. The museum opened in May 2005 in the former administrative building of the plant. To this has been added further exhibition space. The displays highlight the history of the site and conflicts in which US forces have taken part.

The restored Thunderchief is pylon mounted outside the buildings.

TYPE	REG/SER	CON. NO.	PI/NOTES	STATUS
☐ Republic F-105F Thunderchief	'63261'	F-38	63-8261	PVX

LITTLE ROCK AIR FORCE BASE COLLECTION (AR15)

Address: 19AW/PA, 830 Leadership Drive, Little Rock Air Force Base, Arkansas 72099-4929.
Tel: 501-987-3601
Admission: By prior permission only.
Location: About 12 miles north east of the town off Highway 67/167.

Activated in 1955, the base houses a wing operating C-130 Hercules. The Arkansas Air National Guard is also in residence. The last Titan II missile wing served at Little Rock until it was disbanded in 1987. A building on the camp houses a small display of photographs and memorabilia.

The aircraft preserved around the site represent types flown from the field. The first occupants were Boeing B-47s which were in residence in the early days. The Voodoo flew with Air National Guard units in the 1960s until a role change to a tanker wing operating Boeing KC-135s occurred in 1976. The Thunderflash and Canberra were types flown by the unit when it was based at Adams Field in Little Rock. The C-130A Hercules is displayed by the main gate to the field.

The RF-84F and RF-101C are located outside the Base Operations area. The others are positioned in a heritage park overlooking the airfield. Here there are display boards giving information on the base and the aircraft.

TYPE	REG/SER	CON. NO.	PI/NOTES	STATUS
☐ Bell 204 Iroquois (UH-1C)	66-15195	1923		RA
☐ Bell 205 Iroquois (HH-1H)	70-2460	17104		RA
☐ Boeing 450-157-35 Stratojet (B-47E)	52-0595	450880		RA
☐ Boeing 717-146A Stratotanker (KC-135A) (KC-135E)	56-3630	17379		RA
☐ Fairchild 110 Flying Boxcar (C-119G) (C-119L)	53-8084	187		RA
☐ Fairchild 473 Provider (205) (C-123B) (C-123K)	55-4567	20228		RA
☐ Lockheed 182-1A Hercules (182-44-03) (C-130A)	56-0518	182-3126	56-0518, 60518 (South Vietnam)	RA
☐ Lockheed 382-4B Hercules (C-130E)	61-2362	382-3663		RA
☐ Martin 272C Canberra (B-57C)	53-3841	217	53-3841, '53-521'	RA
☐ McDonnell M.36CA Voodoo (RF-101C)	56-0231	252		RA
☐ Republic RF-84F Thunderflash	'11882'		53-7543	RAX

LITTLE ROCK MONUMENT (AR16)

Location: On permanent view at VFW 9095 at 1121 Gamble Road in the northern part of the city.

TYPE	REG/SER	CON. NO.	PI/NOTES	STATUS
☐ Bell 204 Iroquois (UH-1C) (UH-1M)	66-15107	1835		RA

MOUNTAIN HOME MONUMENT (AR17)

Location: On permanent view at the High School on Bomber Boulevard in the south western part of the town.

TYPE	REG/SER	CON. NO.	PI/NOTES	STATUS
☐ Vought A-7E Corsair II	Bu160614	E538		PV

NORTH WEST ARKANSAS COMMUNITY COLLEGE AVIATION TECHNICAL CENTER (AR18)

Address: 2350 Old Farmington Road, Fayetteville, Arkansas 72701.
Tel: 479-444-3058   **Fax:** 479-444-3017   **Email:** ecannon@nwacc.edu
Admission: By prior permission only.
Location: In the western part of the town.

The college was established in 1899 and has a number of sites in the region. An aviation maintenance course is run in conjunction with another institution. Two instructional airframes have been traced but there are likely to be more in the workshops. The Boeing 727 was donated to the college by FedEx.

TYPE	REG/SER	CON. NO.	PI/NOTES	STATUS
☐ Boeing 727-25QC	N135FE	19853	N8170G	RA
☐ Cessna 152	N25322	15280594		RA

OZARK MILITARY MUSEUM (AR19)

Address:	4360 South School Avenue, Fayetteville, Arkansas 72701.
Tel:	479-587-1941 Email: omm@arkansas.net
Admission:	Sunday-Friday 1100-1630; Saturday 1000-1630.
Location:	At Drake Field which is about 3 miles south of the town on Route 71.

The museum first had its headquarters at Siloam Springs and then proposed to set up a display at Springdale. Initially the collection was called the North West Arkansas World War II Museum but changed its name as more modern items were being acquired.

Now the organisation is at Fayetteville where it occupies a large hangar surrounded by an outside display area. In addition to the aircraft there are several military vehicles and weapons to be seen. Some of the types are maintained in flying condition and regularly visit shows in the area. The inside displays are being developed and will trace the story of Arkansas servicemen who served in all wars.

On show are documents, photographs, models, uniforms and items of memorabilia.

TYPE	REG/SER	CON. NO.	PI/NOTES	STATUS
☐ Aeronca 65TC Grasshopper (O-58B) (L-3B)	N47365	13334		PV
☐ Beech C18S Expeditor (C-45F) (UC-45F) (JRB-4)	N6672	8134	44-77726, Bu44573, N10785	PVA
☐ Beech D18S Expeditor 3NM	N6671	CA-152 (A-752)	1552 (Canada)	PVA
☐ Bell 204 Iroquois (UH-1C) (UH-1M)	66-15050	1778		PV
☐ Bell 205 Iroquois (UH-1D)	65-9640	4684	Possible identity.	PV
☐ Bell 205 Iroquois (UH-1D) (UH-1H)	65-12882	5215		PV
☐ Bell 209 Huey Cobra (AH-1G) (AH-1S)	67-15546	20210		PV
☐ Bell 209 Huey Cobra (AH-1G) (AH-1S)	67-15817	20481		PV
☐ Convair 105 (L-13A)	'47-127'		47-275,N275LG	PVCX
☐ Grumman G-40 Avenger (TBM-3)				RA
☐ Lockheed 580 (T-33A)	56-1673	580-1023		PV
☐ North American NA-88 Texan (SNJ-5)	Bu51968	88-15111	Bu51968, N3263G	PV
☐ North American NA-352 Buckeye (T-28C)	Bu158880	352-5		PV
☐ Piasecki PD-22 Work Horse (H-21B) (CH-21B)	'55-4154'	B.104	53-4354, CF-GMO	PVX
☐ Piper J-3C-65 Cub	N20830	2130	NC20830	PVA
☐ Taylorcraft DCO-65 Grasshopper (L-2B)				PV
☐ Vought A-7B Corsair II	Bu154523	B163		PV

PULASKI TECHNICAL COLLEGE AEROSPACE TECHNOLOGY CENTER (AR20)

Address:	1600 West Maryland Avenue, North Little Rock, Arkansas 72210.
Tel:	501-835-5420 Fax: 501-834-7859 Email: shotle@pulaskitech.edu
Admission:	By prior permission only.
Location:	At North Little Rock Airport in the northern part of the city.

The college was set up in 1945 as the Little Rock Vocational School. The present name was adopted in 1991. The Aerospace complex was built at the airport in 1985 and consists of a large hangar/workshop with associated classrooms and laboratories.

Courses in aviation maintenance, aviation management, and avionics are held. In addition there is a flying training school where commercial pilots licences can be attained.

TYPE	REG/SER	CON. NO.	PI/NOTES	STATUS
☐ Beech D45 Mentor (T-34B)	N4739C	BG-367	Bu144060	RA
☐ Beech C50 Seminole (L-23D) (U-8D)	'N1996A'	LH-168	58-1341, N8041C	RAX
☐ Cessna 150F	N8610S	15061910		RA
☐ Cessna 150F	N3106X	15064506		RA
☐ Cessna 150G	N2402J	15065502		RA
☐ Cessna 150J	N150TG	15069470		RA
☐ Cessna 150M	N66670	15076197		RA
☐ Cessna 152	N5280Q	15285095		RA
☐ Cessna 414	N87TM	4140090		RA
☐ Gates Learjet 24	N995TD	24-149	N294BC, N2945C, N300HH, N300LB, N64HB	RA

RICH MOUNTAIN COMMUNITY COLLEGE (AR21)

Address:	1100 College Avenue, Mena, Arkansas 71953.
Tel:	479-394-7622.
Admission:	By prior permission only.
Location:	In the north eastern part of the town.

The college was founded as a vocational technical school in 1973. A merger with the off campus programmes of Henderson State University took place in 1983 and the present name was adopted. A course in aviation maintenance takes place with a small number of students. The only aircraft used is the Cessna.

TYPE	REG/SER	CON. NO.	PI/NOTES	STATUS
☐ Cessna 172P	N54734	17275043		

ROGERS VIETNAM MEMORIAL (AR22)

Address:	3 Airport Drive, Highway 62 East, Rogers, Arkansas 72756.
Tel:	479-631-1400 (Airport)
Admission:	On permanent view.
Location:	In the north eastern part of the town.

Many local people lost their lives in the Vietnam War. This memorial has been set up at the airport and is slowly being developed. The Voodoo, which was last used as an instructional airframe at Sheppard Air Force Base in Texas, arrived in 1990. The Iroquois joined the display a decade later and is in colours of a 1st Cavalry Division aircraft. The names of local men who lost their lives are highlighted at the site.

TYPE	REG/SER	CON. NO.	PI/NOTES	STATUS
☐ Bell 205 Iroquois (UH-1H)	67-17416	9614		PV
☐ McDonnell M.36BA Voodoo (F-101B)	58-0329	701		PV

SOUTHERN ARKANSAS UNIVERSITY TECH (AR23)

Address: 100 Carr Road, Camden, Arkansas 71701.
Tel: 870-574-4593   **Fax:** 870-574-4520   **Email:** barcher@sautech.edu
Admission: By prior permission only.
Location: At Harrell Field which is about 6 miles north east of the city on Route 79.

The university was created in 1967 on part of the site of the former Schumacher Naval Ammunition Depot which was being developed as an industrial park. The first students in aviation maintenance arrived in 1970. At the present time both degree and certificate courses take place. These take place in the facility at the airport where several instructional airframes are in use. The Boeing 727, donated by FedEx in 2007, provides an opportunity for working on a commercial size airframe. The Aeronca 65LA high wing monoplane appeared in the late 1930s.

TYPE	REG/SER	CON. NO.	PI/NOTES	STATUS
☐ Aeronca 65LA	N26321	L-7850		RA
☐ Beech G18S	N9682R	BA-505	Fuselage only.	RA
☐ Beech G18S	N931GM	BA-568	N579B, N5798 – fuselage only.	RA
☐ Bell 206A Kiowa (OH-58A) (OH-58C)				RA
☐ Bell 206A Kiowa (OH-58A) (OH-58C)	70-15579	41130		RA
☐ Boeing 727-22F	N190FE	19083	N7070U	RA
☐ Cessna 150F	N8232F	15064332		RA
☐ Cessna 150G	N3288J	15065988		RA
☐ Cessna 152	N25301	15280581		RA
☐ Cessna 172F	N5304R	17252826		RA
☐ Cessna 310	N11220	38037		RA
☐ Cessna 310J	N310TP	310J0046	N3046L	RA
☐ Gates Learjet 24A (23)	N105GA	23-116	N461F, N52EN, N77GH, N8FM, N400EP, N40BP, N51B, N105GA, (N12MB), (N1420)	RA
☐ Lockheed 580 (T-33A)	N88769	580-1620	58-0651	RA
☐ Piper PA-23-250 Aztec B	N5118Y	27-2149		RA
☐ Piper PA-25 Pawnee	N6264Z	25-326		RA
☐ Piper PA-42-720 Cheyenne IIIA	N9159Y	42-5501028		RA
☐ Swearingen SA.26T Merlin II	N96RL	T26-116	N216F, N100AW, N80RP, N100AW – fuselage only	RA

WALNUT RIDGE ARMY FLYING SCHOOL MUSEUM (AR24)

Address: 2 Skywatch Drive, Walnut Ridge, Arkansas 72476.
Tel: 870-886-7357
Admission: Saturday-Sunday 1000-1600.
Location: About 4 miles north east of the town off Route 34.

The field opened in 1942 and was home to a basic flight training school until the 1960s. In addition many combat types were serviced and after the end of World War II over 10,000 aircraft were in store awaiting scrapping. The site is now the civil airport for the town.

The museum opened in 1999 in the old industrial park building. The displays trace the history of the field. There are a number of 'nose art' panels taken from the aircraft before they were melted down, photographs of the base and people who served at Walnut Ridge. In addition a large collection of personal items, uniforms, newspapers and letters from abroad can be seen.

The first phases of a new complex opened in 2004 and a much larger exhibition has been staged. In 2002 the museum obtained the collection from the Veterans Museum in Hardy and the vast majority of these items are in store. The Cobra and Expeditor came from this source along with a Link Trainer and several military vehicles.

TYPE	REG/SER	CON. NO.	PI/NOTES	STATUS
☐ Beech D18S Expeditor (C18S) (SNB-1) (SNB-5)				RA
☐ Bell 209 Huey Cobra (AH-1G) (AH-1F)				RA
☐ Vultee V-54D Valiant (BT-13)			Front fuselage only.	PV

WALNUT RIDGE RESTAURANT (AR25)

Location: On permanent view next to the airport which is about 4 miles north east of the town off Route 34.

TYPE	REG/SER	CON. NO.	PI/NOTES	STATUS
☐ Boeing 737-2H4	N86SW	22827	Fuselage only.	PV

WEST MEMPHIS MONUMENT (AR26)

Location: On permanent view at VFW 5225 on South Avalon Street in the southern part of the town.

TYPE	REG/SER	CON. NO.	PI/NOTES	STATUS
☐ McDonnell M.98AM Phantom II (F-4B) (F-4N)	'Bu151463'	977	Bu152263	PVX

The Heritage Park at Little Rock Air Force is home to this Martin B-57C Canberra. [AR5]

Basking in the hot sun of the Mojave Desert area is this General Dynamics F-111A. The fighter is at the Air Force Flight Test Center Museum at Edwards Air Force Base. (Alec Berry). [CA4]

The Blackbird Air Park at Palmdale exhibits an example of the Lockheed U-2 (Alec Berry) [CA21]

CALIFORNIA

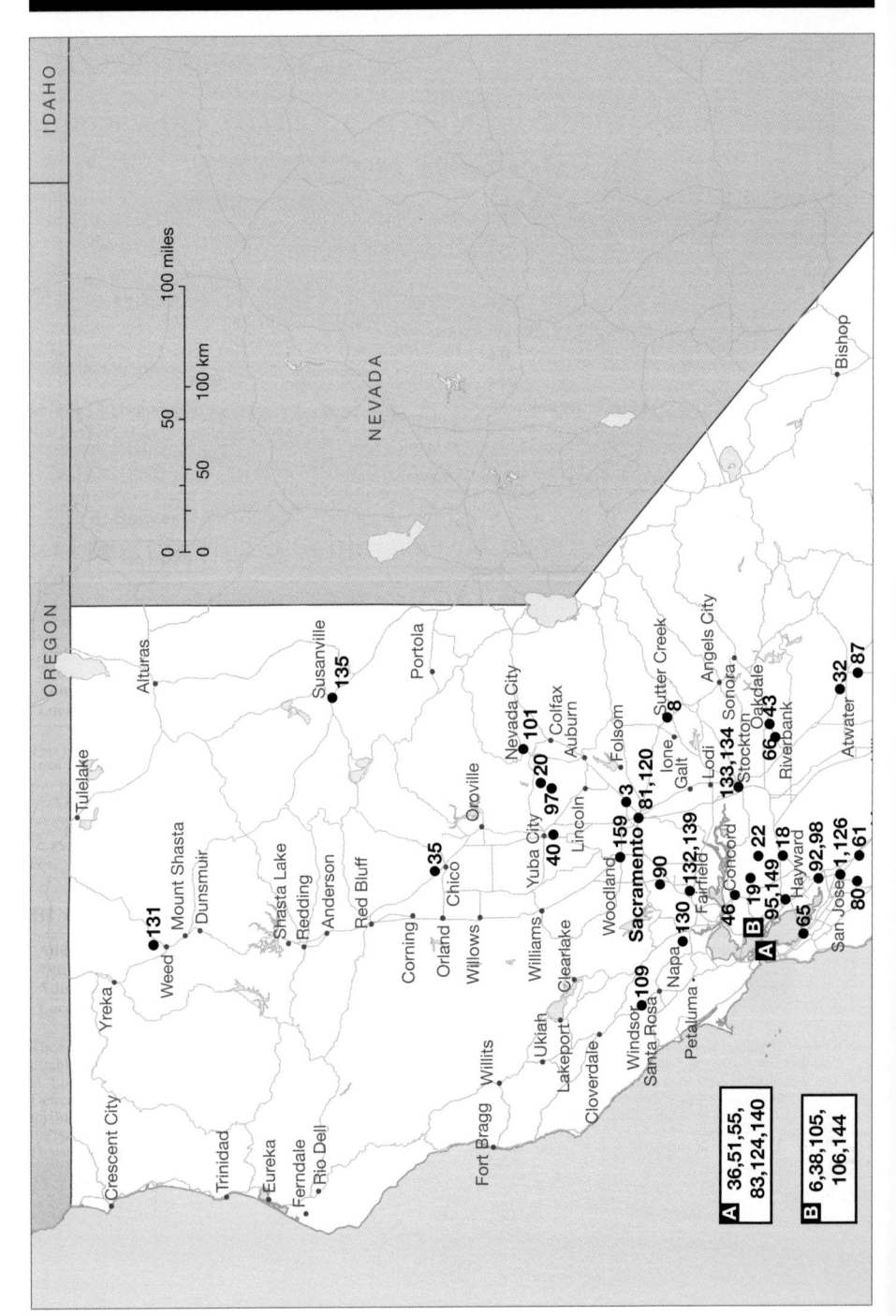

California

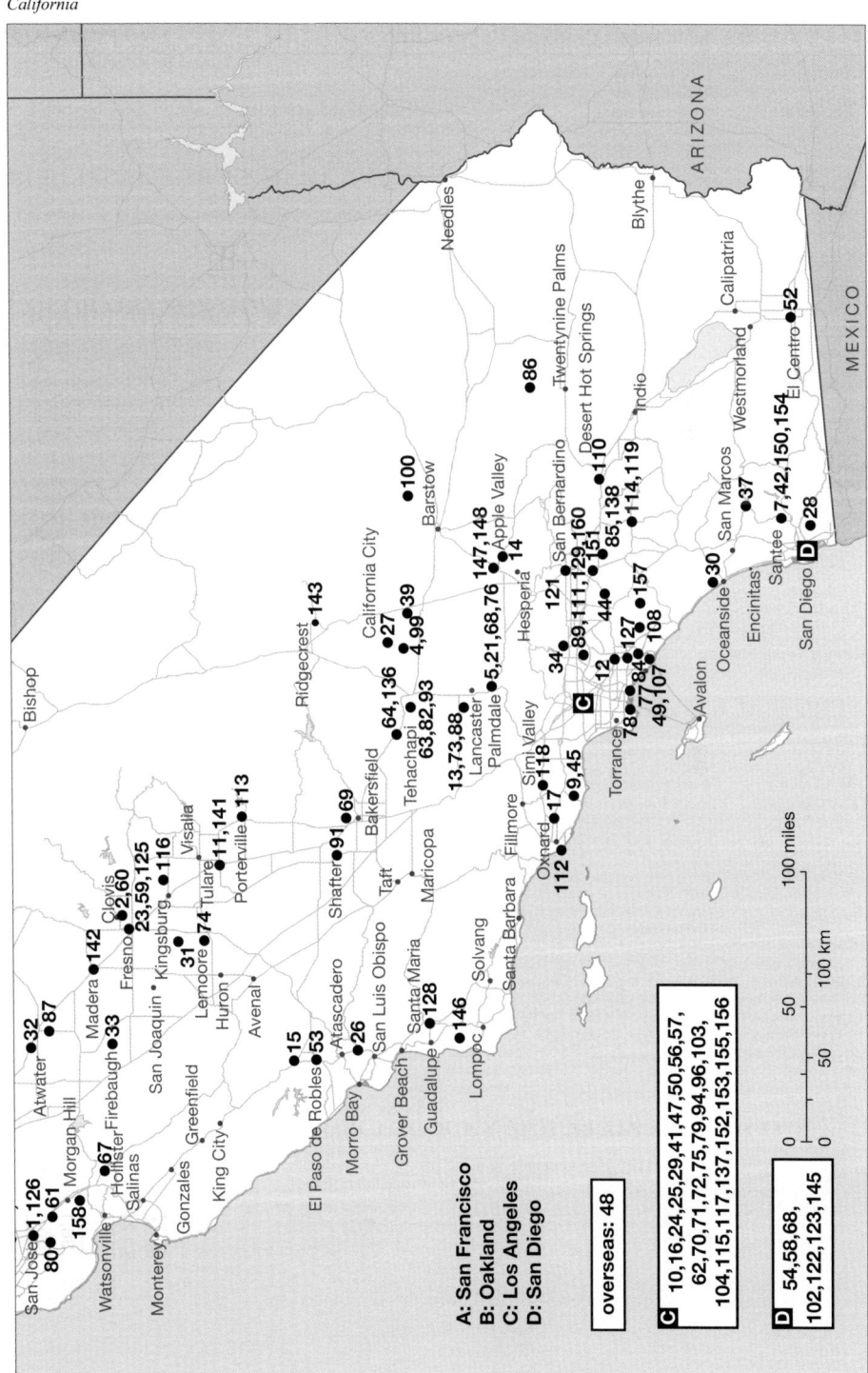

127

- Bishop
- Needles
- Blythe
- Twentynine Palms
- 86
- Desert Hot Springs
- Barstow ●100
- Apple Valley
- Indio
- Westmorland • Calipatria
- 52 El Centro
- San Bernardino
- 85,138 ●110
- 114,119
- 147,148
- 5,21,68,76 ●14
- Hesperia 51
- 121 129,160
- San Marcos
- 37
- 7,42,150,154
- California City
- Ridgecrest ●143
- 27
- 4,99 ●39
- 157
- 30
- Santee ●28
- Bakersfield 64,136
- 44
- 108
- Oceanside
- San Diego D
- Tehachapi 63,82,93
- 89,111, 127
- 34 ●12 C
- Encinitas
- Lancaster 13,73,88
- Palmdale
- 78 84
- Simi Valley
- 49,107 77
- Shafter ●91 ●69
- Taft
- Fillmore
- Avalon
- Porterville ●113
- Maricopa
- Oxnard ●17
- Torrance
- Visalia
- 111,141
- 9,45
- Tulare ●74
- 112 118
- Madera ●142
- Kingsburg ●116
- Fresno 23,59,125
- Clovis ●2,60
- Lemoore ●31
- Firebaugh ●33
- Huron
- San Joaquin
- Atwater ●32
- ●87
- Avenal
- Atascadero
- Santa Maria
- Morgan Hill ●61
- Hollister ●67
- ●158
- Salinas
- Greenfield
- Solvang
- San Jose ●1,126
- ●80
- Watsonville
- Gonzales
- King City
- San Luis Obispo
- El Paso de Robles ●15 ●53
- Morro Bay ●26
- Grover Beach
- Guadalupe ●146
- Lompoc ●128
- Santa Barbara
- Monterey

A: San Francisco
B: Oakland
C: Los Angeles
D: San Diego

overseas: 48

C 10,16,24,25,29,41,47,50,56,57,
62,70,71,72,75,79,94,96,103,
104,115,117,137,152,153,155,156

D 54,58,68,
102,122,123,145

100 miles

100 km

94TH AERO SQUADRON HEADQUARTERS (CA1)

Address: 1160 Coleman Avenue, San Jose, California 95110-1114.
Tel: 408-287-6150.
Admission: Daily 1100-2000.
Location: On the west side of the airport which is in the western suburbs of the town.

This site is one of the chain of speciality restaurants which have an aviation theme. Three full size models have been put on display and inside there are items of memorabilia in the dining areas.

TYPE	REG/SER	CON. NO.	PI/NOTES	STATUS
☐ Fokker Dr I (FSM)				PV
☐ North American NA-122 Mustang (P-51D) (FSM)				PVX
☐ Republic P-47D Thunderbolt (FSM)				PVX

144TH FIGHTER WING COLLECTION (CA2)

Address: 5425 McKinley Avenue, Fresno, California 93727-2199.
Tel: 559-454-5100 **Email:** bryan.williams@cafres.ang.af.mil
Admission: By prior permission only.
Location: At Fresno Air Terminal which is about 5 miles north east of the town centre.

Formed as the 61st Fighter Wing at Alameda in 1948, the unit became the 144th in November 1950. The following year it moved to Hayward and when jets were allocated the squadron transferred to Fresno. In the main building is a display of memorabilia, uniforms, photographs and cups, including the William Tell Trophy won in 1980, tracing the history of the wing. The Mustang was operated from 1949 to 1951 when it was replaced by the Sabre, which served for four years. The F-86L was flown until the delta winged F-102 arrived in 1964. Its successor the F-106 was allocated in 1974 and the Phantom was taken on strength ten years later. This jet served until the arrival of the F-16 in 1989. A small number of T-33s served with the wing for several years. The display of types flown over the last half century is located near the Headquarters Building.

TYPE	REG/SER	CON. NO.	PI/NOTES	STATUS
☐ Convair 8-10 Delta Dagger (F-102A)	53-1804	8-10-14		RA
☐ Convair 8-31 Delta Dart (F-106A)	59-0146	8-31-35		RA
☐ Lockheed 580 (T-33A)	'53-5640'	580-7825	52-9640	RAX
☐ McDonnell M.98EN Phantom II (F-4D)	65-0588	1492		RA
☐ North American NA-122 Mustang (P-51D)	44-73972	122-40512		RA
☐ North American NA-161 Sabre (P-86A) (F-86A)	49-1272	161-266		RA
☐ North American NA-201 Sabre (F-86D) (F-86L)	53-0642	201-86		RA

AEROSPACE MUSEUM OF CALIFORNIA (CA3)

Address: 3200 Freedom Park Drive, McClellan, Sacramento, California 95652.
Tel: 916-643-3192 **Fax:** 916-643-0389 **Email:** info@aerospacemuseumofcalifornia.org
Admission: Monday-Saturday 0900-1700; Sunday 1000-1700.
Location: About 9 miles north east of the city.

The airbase opened in 1939 and was named after Major Hezekiah McClellan, a pioneer of Arctic flying who was killed in 1936. The idea of a museum was put forward in the late 1970s and a foundation established. The exhibition opened on 6th September 1986 as the McClellan Aviation Museum. The base closed in 2001 but the museum survived and soon took up its new name to reflect its wider role.

A small building housed displays tracing the history of the base and of military flying in the Sacramento area. A new exhibition hall opened at the end of 2006. Inside are greatly improved displays and many more artefacts can be seen. The history of the airfield and the region are portrayed. The outside aircraft park has also been landscaped and improved. The museum has a restoration facility nearby. A Memorial Plaza has been constructed to honour local aviators who have lost their lives. This incorporates a garden and plaques. The largest aircraft on show is the Super Constellation, the type was flown from McClellan from 1953 until 1977 on early warning duties over the Pacific Ocean. The F-105 Thunderchief destroyed an Ilyushin Il-28 on a ground attack mission during the Vietnam War. The MiG-21 was the first of its type to be put on show in a US museum when it arrived in May 1989. The A-10 was struck by a surface-to-air missile during Operation Desert Storm. After repairs it was flown to McClellan and later transferred to the museum. The Starfighter served in California with NASA. Two arrivals in 2006 were a pair of former US Navy aircraft which flew into the airfield. These were the Skyhawk and the Tomcat.

More naval and civil types will be acquired to broaden the range of the exhibition.

TYPE	REG/SER	CON. NO.	PI/NOTES	STATUS
☐ Beech D18S Expeditor (C18S) (SNB-2) (SNB-5) (TC-45J) (UC-45J)	'42-51291'	5618	Bu51291, N11248	PVX
☐ Bell 205 Iroquois (UH-1H)	N81114	13850	74-22526	RA
☐ Boeing Stearman E75 Kaydet (PT-13D)	N68830	75-5667	42-17504	PV
☐ Cessna T-50 Bobcat (C-78) (UC-78)	N52390	4834	43-7314	PV
☐ Convair 8-10 Delta Dagger (F-102A)	'55431'	8-10-357	56-1140	PVX
☐ Convair 8-24 Delta Dart (F-106A)	59-0010	8-24-139		PV
☐ Convair 340-67 Samaritan (VC-131C)	54-2822	232	N8455H	PV
☐ Dassault Falcon 10	N55FJ	24	F-WJMJ, N156FJ, N30TH, N518S, N108MR, N5JY	PV
☐ Douglas DC-3A-457 Skytrooper (C-53D)	42-68835	11762	42-68835, NC19924	PV
☐ Douglas DC-4 Skymaster (C-54D) (R5D-3) (C-54Q)	42-72449	10554	42-72449, Bu50874, N27MA	RA
☐ Douglas A-1E Skyraider (AD-5)	Bu132463	9480		PV
☐ Douglas A-4C Skyhawk (A4D-2N)	Bu148503	12696		PV
☐ Fairchild M-62A Cornell (PT-19B)	N46387	T43-5281	42-82706	RAD
☐ Fairchild M-62A-4 Cornell (PT-26)				RA
☐ Fairchild 110 Flying Boxcar (C-119F)	'22124'	10825	22114 (Canada), N15502	PVX

California

☐ Fairchild-Republic A-10A Thunderbolt II	76-0540	A10-87			PV
☐ General Dynamics F-111A			Front fuselage only.		PV
☐ General Dynamics F-111G (FB-111A)	'90159'	B1-01	67-0159		PVX
☐ Grumman G-89 Tracker (S2F-1) (S-2A) (TS-2A)	N412DF	G-222	Bu133251		PV
☐ Grumman G-234 Albatross (G-64) (SA-16A) (UF-1G) (UF-2G) (HU-16E)	7209	G-282	51-7209, 7209, '10047'		PV
☐ Grumman G-303 Tomcat (F-14D)	Bu163897	607/D-12			PV
☐ Lockheed 080 Shooting Star (P-80B) (F-80B)	45-8704	080-1918			PV
☐ Lockheed 283-93-03 Starfighter (F-104B)	57-1303	283-5015	57-1303, N819NA		PV
☐ Lockheed 580 (T-33A)	53-5205	580-8544			PV
☐ Lockheed 1049A-55-137 Super Constellation (1049A-55-86) (WV-2) (EC-121K)	'03-0552'	1049A-4423	Bu141309, '54-0552'		PVX
☐ McDonnell M.36BA Voodoo (F-101B)	57-0427	605			PV
☐ McDonnell M.98DJ Phantom II (F-4C)	64-0706	957			PV
☐ Mikoyan-Gurevich MiG-21F-13	0201	460201	In Czechoslovakian markings.		PV
☐ North American NA-176 Sabre (F-86F)	51-13082	176-13			PV
☐ North American NA-177 Sabre (F-86D) (F-86L)	51-2968	177-25			PV
☐ North American NA-182 Texan (T-6G)	51-15124	182-811			PV
☐ North American NA-200 Trojan (T-28B)	Bu138327	200-398			PV
☐ North American NA-223 Super Sabre (F-100D)	55-3733	223-415	Front fuselage only		PV
☐ North American NA-235 Super Sabre (F-100D)	56-3288	235-386			PV
☐ North American NA-265 Sabreliner (T-39A) (CT-39A)	61-0660	265-63			PV
☐ Pitts S-1S Special	N382SJ	DMR-1			PV
☐ Republic F-84F Thunderstreak	51-1772				PV
☐ Republic F-105D Thunderchief	62-4301	D-500			PV
☐ Sikorsky S-61R (S-61A) (CH-3C) (CH-3E)	65-5690	61541			PV
☐ Taylorcraft DCO-65 Grasshopper (L-2M)	N53792	L-5745	43-26433 (?)		PV
☐ Travel Air B-14B	NC12332	2010	NC12332, N12332		PV
☐ Vertol V.43 Shawnee (H-21C) (CH-21C)	51-15886	C.6	51-15886, N68788, N48082		RA
☐ Vought A-7D Corsair II	70-0998	D144			PV
☐ WSK Lim-5P [MiG-17PF]	'4721'	1D 06-33 (?)	F-1186 (Indonesia),'1186 – in false Chinese markings.		PVX

AIR FORCE FLIGHT TEST CENTER MUSEUM (CA4)

Address: 405 South Rosamond Boulevard, Edwards Air Force Base, California 93524-1850.
Tel: 661-277-8050 **Fax:** 661-277-8051 **Email:** museum@edwards.af.mil
Admission: The museum is technically open Tuesday-Saturday 0900-1700 but this often changes due to the security situation.
Location: East of Rosamond off Route 14.

Muroc Army Airfield opened in 1933 and the site was later renamed after Captain Glen W. Edwards who was killed in June 1948 flying the Northrop YB-49. Flight testing has been carried out at the field since the 1940s. Over 140 types have made their first flights from Edwards. The Air Force Test Center was established in 1951 and since then the base has been the location for nearly all the major test programmes carried out by the service. The site has expanded greatly with the construction of many research facilities. For several years a number of historic aircraft were mounted on pylons around the camp and most of these remain in place.

In the mid-1980s the Flight Test Historical Association was set up with the aim of creating a museum which would trace the history of the site and record developments in testing techniques. Over 60 aircraft and a vast amount of material have been gathered. A small building was modified for a temporary exhibition. On show was a fascinating collection of models, engines, photographs, documents, components and items of memorabilia. A new building opened in July 2000 and this houses a few aircraft with others outside in the Jimmy Doolittle Air Park.

The majority of the collection resides in two storage compounds. One is located near the NASA facility and the other is on the south side of the main airfield. A number of aircraft are still parked on the extensive ranges and these will eventually be moved.

The museum was involved in the setting up of the Blackbird Airpark located at Palmdale where two Lockheed designs built there have been put on show. Only two Piper Enforcers were built in the early 1970s. The design, based on the Mustang, was started by the Cavalier firm and taken over by Piper. The Scaled Composites AT-3 first flew at Mojave in December 1987. Designed by Bert Rutan, the aircraft was a 62% scale prototype of a proposed advanced tactical transport. The Bell Airacomet, the first American jet fighter, was designed in great secrecy. The first example was taken by road to Muroc in September 1942 and assembled in less than three weeks. The XP-59A it made its maiden flight on 1st October. The design was not practical for combat duties and after extensive trials the type was withdrawn in 1946. Some prototypes were taken to the museum at Dayton to be put on show in the Research and Development hangars.

Century Park outside the West Gate opened on 28th July 2007. Displayed here are six fighter types along with one of the two prototypes of the McDonnell YC-15 transport.

TYPE	REG/SER	CON. NO.	PI/NOTES	STATUS
☐ Beech D18S Expeditor (C18S) (SNB-2) (SNB-3) (SNB-5) (TC-45J) (UC-45J)	'408'	5805	Bu67161, N57161, Bu67161, '823'	PVX
☐ Bell 27 Airacomet (P-59B)	44-22633	27-41		PV
☐ Bell 44 (XS-1) (X-1) (FSM)	'46-062'			PVX
☐ Bensen B-8 Gyroglider (X-25B)	68-10771			PV
☐ Boeing 450-67-27 Stratojet (B-47B)	51-2075	450128		RA
☐ Boeing 464-201-3 Stratofortress (RB-52B) (NB-52B)	52-0008	16498	52-0008, NASA008	PV
☐ Boeing 464-201-7 Stratofortress (B-52D)	56-0585	17268		PV
☐ Boeing 717-146 Stratotanker (KC-135A)	56-3591	17340	Front fuselage only.	RA
☐ Boeing 717-157 Stratolifter (C-135A)	60-0377	18152	NASM aircraft.	RA
☐ Boeing 717-158 Stratolifter (C-135B) (C-135C)	61-2669	18345		RA
☐ Cessna 318B Tweety Bird (T-37B)	64-13444	40859	Front fuselage only.	RA
☐ Cessna 318E Dragonfly (A-37B) (NOA-37B)	73-1090	43481		PV
☐ Convair 4 Hustler (YB-58A) (TB-58A)	55-0665	6		RA
☐ Convair 8-12 Delta Dagger (TF-102A)	54-1353	8-12-53		PV

TYPE	REG/SER	CON. NO.	PI/NOTES	STATUS
☐ Convair 8-32 Delta Dart (F-106B)	59-0158	8-32-10		PV
☐ De Havilland DHC.4A Caribou (CV-2B) (C-7B)	63-9765	232		RA
☐ Douglas DC-3A-405 Skytrooper (C-53) (R4D-3)	'41-20093'	4864	41-20094, Bu05074, NC1301	RAX
☐ Douglas TB-26B Invader (A-26B)	N9146H	27444	44-34165	RA
☐ Douglas EF-10B Skynight (F3D-2) (F3D-2Q)	Bu125850	8044		RA
☐ Douglas A-3A Skywarrior (A3D-1)	Bu135434	10327	Bu135434, N816NA	RA
☐ Fairchild 110 Flying Boxcar (C-119B)	48-0352	10334	48-0352, N13746	PV
☐ Fairchild 473 Provider (205) (C-123B) (C-123K)	54-0683	20132	54-0683, N4034L	RA
☐ Fairchild-Republic A-10B Thunderbolt II (A-10A)	73-1664	A10-1		PV
☐ Fairchild-Republic NGT (T-46A)	84-0492			RA
☐ General Dynamics F-111A	63-9766	A1-01		PV
☐ General Dynamics F-111AFTI (F-111A)	63-9778	A1-13		RA
☐ General Dynamics 401 Fighting Falcon (F-16B)	75-0751	62-1		PV
☐ General Dynamics 401 Fighting Falcon (F-16B)	80-0634	62-76		PV
☐ Gloster Meteor NF.11	WD592	5249	WD592, N94709	PV
☐ Lockheed 080 Shooting Star (P-80A) (F-80A) (EF-80A)	44-85123	080-1146		RA
☐ Lockheed 183-93-02 Starfighter (F-104A)	56-0790	183-1078	56-0790, N820NA	PV
☐ Lockheed 183-93-02 Starfighter (F-104A)	56-0801	183-1089		RA
☐ Lockheed 183-93-02 Starfighter (F-104A) (NF-104A)	56-0760	183-1048		PV
☐ Lockheed 300 Starlifter (C-141A) (NC-141A)	61-2779	300-6005		RA
☐ Lockheed 383-04-05 Starfighter (F-104C)	56-0929	183-1217	Maybe due from S. Mus of Ft, AL.	-
☐ Lockheed 580 (T-33A)	58-0669	580-1638		RA
☐ Lockheed 580 (T-33A)	'35540'	580-8152	52-9846	PVX
☐ Lockheed 580 (T-33A)	53-5099	580-8438		PV
☐ Lockheed 580 (T-33A)	53-5123	580-8462		RA
☐ Lockheed 780-76-12 Starfire (TF-80C) (YF-94A)	48-0356	780-5001		RA
☐ Lockheed 1329 JetStar 6 (C-140A)	59-5962	1329-5032		RA
☐ Lockheed SR-71A Blackbird	61-7955	2006		PV
☐ Lockheed YF-22A	N22YF	3997	87-0701	PV
☐ Martin 272B Canberra (B-57B) (RB-57B)	N809NA	166	52-1576	RA
☐ McDonnell M.36BA Voodoo (F-101B)	58-0288	660		PV
☐ McDonnell M.98DE Phantom II (F-4C) (NF-4C)	63-7407	311		PV
☐ McDonnell M.98DF Phantom II (RF-4C)	64-1004	690		RA
☐ McDonnell M.98HO Phantom II (M.98EN) (F-4D) (YF-4EJ)	65-0713	1761		PV
☐ McDonnell M.199-1A Eagle (F-15A)	'835'	009/A008	71-0287	RAX
☐ McDonnell M.199-1B Eagle (TF-15A) (F-15B)	73-0114	041/B009		PV
☐ McDonnell YC-15A	N15YC	CX001'	72-1875	PV
☐ McDonnell-Douglas X-36				PV
☐ North American NA-180 Super Sabre (YF-100A)	52-5755	180-2	52-5755, '10755'	PV
☐ North American NA-191 Sabre (F-86F)	52-5241	191-937		PV
☐ North American NA-192 Super Sabre (F-100A)	53-1688	192-183	53-1688, N100X	RA
☐ North American NA-192 Super Sabre (F-100A)	52-5760	192-5		PV
☐ North American NA-200 Trojan (T-28B)	Bu137702	200-65		PV
☐ North American NA-200 Trojan (T-28B)				RA
☐ North American NA-200 Trojan (T-28B)				RA
☐ North American NA-240 (X-15) (X-15A) (FSM)	'66672'			PVX
☐ North American NA-265 Sabreliner (T-39A) (CT-39A)	60-3505	265-33		PV
☐ North American NA-306 Sabreliner 60 (CT-39G)	Bu159363	306-67	Fuselage only.	RA
☐ Northrop N-26 (XS-4) (X-4)	46-676	3237	46-676, '6677'	RA
☐ Northrop N-156T Talon (T-38A)	61-0810	N.5176		PV
☐ Northrop N-156T Talon (T-38A)	61-0849	N.5515		RA
☐ Northrop N-160 Scorpion (N-68) (F-89D) (F-89J)	52-1883	N.4460		RA
☐ Northrop N-160 Scorpion (N-68) (F-89D) (F-89J)	52-1959	N.4536		RA
☐ Northrop N-160 Scorpion (N-68) (F-89D) (F-89J)	53-2496	N.4627	Rear fuselage only.	RA
☐ Northrop X-21A (Douglas WB-66D Destroyer)	55-0408	45040		RA
☐ Northrop X-21A (Douglas WB-66D Destroyer)	55-0410	45042		RA
☐ Northrop YA-9A	71-1367			RA
☐ Northrop F-20A Tigershark (F-5G) (Mock up)				RA
☐ Piper PA-48 Enforcer	N482PE	48-8301002		RA
☐ Republic F-84F Thunderstreak	51-9350			RA
☐ Republic F-105D Thunderchief	61-0146	D-341		PV
☐ Rockwell B-1A Lancer	74-0159	002	Front fuselage only.	RA
☐ Rockwell B-1B Lancer	85-0067	27	May be c/n 9 84-0049	PV
☐ Rutan 33 Vari-Eze	N309V	354		RA
☐ Scaled Composites 133-4.62	N133SC	001		RA
☐ Sikorsky S-55D Chickasaw (H-19D) (UH-19D)				PV
☐ Sikorsky S-58 Choctaw (H-34A) (VH-34C)	57-1726	58918		PV
☐ Sikorsky S-58 Seabat (HSS-1) (UH-34G)	Bu137856	5812	Bu137856, N9043P	RA
☐ Sikorsky S-61R (CH-3C) (CH-3E) (JCH-3E)	62-12581	61506		PV
☐ Vertol V.43 Shawnee (H-21C) (CH-21C)	52-8623	C.44	52-8623, N8540	RA
☐ Vought YA-7D Corsair II	67-14583	D2		PV
☐ Vought A-7D Corsair II			Front fuselage only.	PV
☐ Vought YA-7F Corsair II (A-7D)	71-0344	D255		RA

AIR FORCE PLANT 42 MONUMENT (CA5)

Location:	By prior permission only at the Air Force HQ at 2503 East Avenue on Palmdale airfield.

TYPE	REG/SER	CON. NO.	PI/NOTES	STATUS
☐ North American NA-187 Sabre (F-86H)	52-2054	187-80		RA

California

ALAMEDA NAVAL AIR MUSEUM (CA6)

Address:	2151 Ferry Point, PO Box 1769, Alameda, California 94501.
Tel:	510-352-4262 Email: info@alamedanavalairmuseum.org
Admission:	Saturday-Sunday 1000-1600.
Location:	In the south western suburbs of Oakland.

Alameda was a major Naval Air Station which opened on 1st November 1940. It was home to both fixed and rotary wing squadrons and a deep-water jetty allowed access to the largest carriers. In addition, the facility carried out major overhauls and modifications on a large number of aircraft types. The base closed in 1997 and part of the vast site is now an industrial park. The airfield was also the Pacific Headquarters of Pan American Airways in the late 1930s, which used flying boats on services to Hawaii and the Far East. There is a section in the display showing the types used and the routes flown. The Navy also left two gate guards on the site but one has now been removed. The museum has opened an exhibition tracing the history of the field. On show are photographs, models, components, engines and documents along with many personal items.

TYPE	REG/SER	CON. NO.	PI/NOTES	STATUS
☐ Douglas A-4C Skyhawk (A4D-2N)	Bu148610	12803	At Encinal High School near site gate –	PV
☐ Vought A-7B Corsair II	'ND-400'			PVX

ALLEN AIRWAYS FLYING MUSEUM (CA7)

Address:	2020/2021 North Marshall Avenue, El Cajon, California 92020.
Tel:	619-596-2020 Email: allenairwy@aol.com
Admission:	By prior permission only.
Location:	At Gillespie Field which is just north of the town which is about 12 miles north east of San Diego.

Bill Allen has acquired a superb collection of memorabilia including over 500 original aviation posters dating from 1876. There are also many helmets, goggles, and photographs. He originally set up a museum at Montgomery Field but a several years ago a move was made to Gillespie.
The exhibition is steadily being developed and many interesting items are on show. Artefacts owned by Charles Lindbergh, A.J. Edwards, Cliff Henderson and Matty Laird can be seen. Over 60 propellers are in the collection along with aircraft models used in films.
In the adjoining hangar several rare aircraft can be seen. The replica of the classic Boeing F4B-1 naval fighter was built in Nevada. The first production F4B-1 flew in May 1929 and only 27 were built and served for a few years. The Stearman C3R has won many trophies including Reserve Grand Champion at Oshkosh in 1984 and Grand Champion at Watsonville in 2006. The standard N2S-3 was the last aircraft owned by the late actor Steve McQueen.
Several years ago a derelict fuselage was found on a Californian farm and this is now thought to be from a Breese Penguin. Two locally produced Ryan aircraft are in the collection. The STM-2 was one of a batch of over 100 for the forces in the Dutch East Indies. Most were destroyed or captured by the Japanese but a few escaped to Australia. This aircraft is now resplendent in its original markings. The Custom Stearman is not owned by Bill but resides in the hangar.

TYPE	REG/SER	CON. NO.	PI/NOTES	STATUS
☐ Boeing 99 (F4B-1) (R)	N8146N			RA
☐ Boeing-Stearman B75N1 Kaydet (N2S-3)	N3188	75-2599	Bu4269, N5146N	RAA
☐ Boeing-Stearman Custom 450 (B75N1 Kaydet (N2S-3))	NC9039H	75-6801	Bu07197	RAA
☐ Breese Penguin			Fuselage only – probable type.	RAD
☐ Ryan STM-2	N466WA	466	S-30 (Dutch East Indies), A50-18, VH-AGR	RAA
☐ Ryan ST-3KR Recruit (PT-22)	N60178	2184	41-20975	RAA
☐ Stearman C3R	NC794H	5036		RAA

AMADOR COUNTY AIRPORT MONUMENT (CA8)

Location:	On permanent view at the field which is about 2 miles south of Sutter Creek.

TYPE	REG/SER	CON. NO.	PI/NOTES	STATUS
☐ North American NA-256 Sabre (F-86F)	57-6416	256-79	57-6416, 02-7959 (Japan) – tail from c/n 238-83, 56-2855	PV

AMERICAN AERONAUTICAL FOUNDATION MUSEUM (CA9)

Address:	1171 Deep Wood Drive, Westlake Village, California 91361.
Tel:	818-887-0550 Email: volunteer@aafgroup.org
Admission:	By prior permission only.
Location:	At Camarillo Airport which is about 40 miles west of Los Angeles off Interstate 101.

Owned by Edward Schnepf, who publishes many aviation magazines, this collection is now all based at Camarillo. The B-25 was delivered to the military in February 1945 the twin engined bomber served at Moody in Georgia and Maxwell in Alabama before being converted as for staff transport duties. Sold on the civil market in 1959 it has since been used as a crop sprayer in Wyoming and in Hollywood films. The collection acquired the Mitchell in 1984. The Convair is a fairly recent addition. Originally delivered to Trans-Australia Airlines in 1948 the airliner served with them for eight years before it was sold to Pakistan International Airlines. After a brief period in Europe it returned to the USA in the summer of 1960. The Prentice, painted in a false Royal Air Force camouflage scheme, is a rarity in the USA.

TYPE	REG/SER	CON. NO.	PI/NOTES	STATUS
☐ Aeronca 15AC Sedan	N1204N	15AC-216		RAA
☐ Beech C50 Twin Bonanza	N113U	CH-69		RAA

☐ Convair 240-5	N396CG	93	VH-TAS, AP-AHS, PH-NLP, PH-EUT, N559R, N559L, N568R	RA
☐ Douglas DC-3A-467 Skytrain (C-47B)	N215CM	15347/26792	43-49531, NC63186, 4X-ADA, 1407/07 (Israel), 4X-ADA, 4X-FNA/007, N215CM, 'C-GFHP'	RAA
☐ Lockheed 580 (T-33A)				RAA
☐ North American NA-108 Mitchell (B-25J) (TB-25J) (VB-25J) (VB-25N)	N30801	108-34076	44-30801, N3699G	RAC
☐ Percival P.40 Prentice T.1	N1041P	5840/7	VS385, G-AOLP	RAA
☐ Piper J-3C-65 Cub	NC70259	17236		RAA

AMERICAN SOCIETY OF MILITARY HISTORY MUSEUM (CA10)

Address: 1918 North Rosemead Boulevard, South El Monte, California 91733.
Tel: 626-442-1776   **Fax:** 626-443-1743   **Email:** tankland@aol.com
Admission: Friday-Sunday 1000-1630.
Location: About 15 miles east of Los Angeles off Route 60.

The society maintains this open air museum which has on display a large number of military vehicles, tanks, weapons and boats. The sole aircraft in the collection is the Iroquois helicopter.

TYPE	REG/SER	CON. NO.	PI/NOTES	STATUS
☐ Bell 204 Iroquois (HU-1C) (UH-1C) (UH-1M)	65-9423	1323		PV

AMERICAN VETERANS MEMORIAL (CA11)

Address: Mefford Field, Tulare, California 93274.
Tel: 559-686-3258   **Email:** tulareveterans@hotmail.com
Admission: On permanent view
Location: Just south of the town off Interstate 99

General Maurice Preston, Commander of the 379th Bombardment Wing based at Kimbolton in England from November 1942 to October 1944, flew the B-17 into Mefford Field in August 1958. The bomber was badly damaged in August 1982 by a truck running off the road which passes the memorial. After restoration it was placed in a compound and plaques honour the local dead of World War II. In 1994 it was joined by an F-4 which is dedicated to Californians who lost their lives in the Vietnam conflict. The aircraft are maintained by local veterans groups who also have a collection of memorabilia in their headquarters in town.

TYPE	REG/SER	CON. NO.	PI/NOTES	STATUS
☐ Boeing 299-O Fortress (B-17G) (DB-17G) (EDB-17G) (DB-17G)	44-85738	8647		PV
☐ McDonnell M.98DJ Phantom II (F-4C)	64-0912	1368		PV

ANAHEIM MONUMENT (CA12)

Location: On permanent view in Boysen Park at 951 South State College Boulevard south of the town centre.

TYPE	REG/SER	CON. NO.	PI/NOTES	STATUS	STATUS
☐ Grumman G-93 Cougar (F9F-6P) (RF-9F)	Bu127484				PV

ANTELOPE VALLEY COMMUNITY COLLEGE (CA13)

Address: 3041 West Avenue K, Lancaster, California 93536-5402.
Tel: 661-722-6300   **Email:** webmaster@avc.edu
Admission: By prior permission only.
Location: In the western part of the town.

This local college has the third of the three Skyrockets built in the late 1940s and early 1950s. The aircraft made its maiden flight from below a Boeing P2B-1S in September 1950. The aircraft was fitted with both jet and rocket engines and made a total of 87 flights before being retired in 1956.

TYPE	REG/SER	CON. NO.	PI/NOTES	STATUS
☐ Aero Commander 560F	N211SR	1042-14	N8467C	RA
☐ Douglas D-558-2 Skyrocket	Bu37975	6569	Bu37975, NACA145	RAA

APPLE VALLEY MONUMENTS (CA14)

Location: At two locations in the town.

TYPE	REG/SER	CON. NO.	PI/NOTES	STATUS
☐ North American NA-203 Sabre (F-86H)	53-1515	203-287	At the airport – north of the town.	PV
☐ Northrop N-156T Talon (T-38A) (AT-38B)	60-0591	N.5164	At Lewis Centre near airport.	RA

ARANGO COLLECTION (CA15)

Address: 501 West Channel Islands Boulevard, Port Hueneme, California 93041-2126.
Admission: By prior permission only.
Location: At a private airfield north of Paso Robles.

California

This private collection of mainly replica aircraft from the World War I period is housed on the owner's ranch near Paso Robles. A few may be seen at the local airport where a number have been built by Antique Aero.
One of the Blériots was built up from original parts at Colerne in England in 1976. This aircraft spent some time on display in the Aviodome in Holland before moving to California. Then owned by Bill Allen, it was on show in the San Diego Aerospace Museum before moving north.
The Pfalz was built in England by Personal Plane Services and the Fokker D VII in France by Rousseau Aviation. Both of these flew in the 'Blue Max' film. A range of classic Sopwith and Fokker types has been acquired and these are painted in period colours.

TYPE	REG/SER	CON. NO.	PI/NOTES	STATUS
☐ Beech C18S Expeditor (C-45F) (Expeditor 3T)	N506PA	7159	44-47216, 1392 (Canada)	RA
☐ Blériot XI	N605WB	1		RAA
☐ Blériot XI		54	BAPC.105	RA
☐ Boeing-Stearman E75 Kaydet (PT-13D) (N2S-5)	N4766V	75-5488	42-17325, Bu61366	RAA
☐ Fokker D VI (R)	N 657JA	1657		RAA
☐ Fokker D VII (R)	N902AC	02	F-BNDG, EI-APU	RAA
☐ Fokker D VII (R)	N29JA	640		RAA
☐ Fokker D VIII (R)	N160E	921		RAA
☐ Fokker Dr I (R)	N37583	F-110217		RAA
☐ Fokker Dr I (R)	N1858S	SCHWERIN-17		RAA
☐ Fokker E III (R)	N5105	105		RAA
☐ Grumman G-40 Avenger (TBM-3) (TBM-3S) (AS.3)	N28SF	2802	Bu85983, 85983 (Canada), N4039A, CF-BEG, C-BFEG	RAA
☐ Nieuport 11 (R)	N161JA	161		RAA
☐ Nieuport 24bis	N1895	W2		RAA
☐ Nieuport 28C.1 (R)	N6190	AA102		RAA
☐ Pfalz D III (R)	N906AC	PPS/PFLZ/1	G-ATIF, EI-ARC	RAA
☐ Royal Aircraft Factory S.E.5A (R)	N911AV	011		RAA
☐ Royal Aircraft Factory S.E.5A (R)	N8936	15		RAA
☐ Sopwith Tabloid (R)	N1213	1213		RAA
☐ Sopwith Triplane (R)	N5483	PPS/REP/9		RAA
☐ Sopwith 1 1/2 Strutter (R)	N5505	AA108		RAA
☐ Sopwith F.1 Camel (R)	N629JA	B6291		RAA
☐ Sopwith F.1 Camel (R)	N8343	DS-200		RAA
☐ Sopwith 7F.1 Snipe (R)	'E8263'			RACX
☐ Sopwith Pup (R)	N6179	008		RAA
☐ SPAD XIII (R)				RAC
☐ Vought FG-1D Corsair	N11Y		Bu67087, (El Salvador)	RAA

ARMED FORCES RESERVE CENTER (CA16)

Address: Los Alamitos Army Airfield, Lexington Drive, Los Angeles, California 90270-5001.
Tel: 562-795-2000
Admission: By prior permission only.
Location: About 25 miles south east of the city centre off Interstate 405.

For many the years the airfield housed front line units of the Air Force. At the current time it is an important reserve base. A display of small items has been set up in the headquarters building.

TYPE	REG/SER	CON. NO.	PI/NOTES	STATUS
☐ Bell 204 Iroquois (UH-1C) (UH-1M)	64-14117	1241		PV
☐ Bell 205 Iroquois (UH-1H)	66-16633	8827		PV
☐ Bell 209 Huey Cobra (AH-1G) (AH-1F)	66-15251	20007		PV

AVIATION MUSEUM OF SANTA PAULA (CA17)

Address: PO Box 908, Santa Paula, California 93061-0908.
Tel: 805-525-1109   Email: amszp@verizon.net
Admission: First Sunday in month 1000-1500.
Location: Just south of the town off Route 126.

The airport opened in the early 1930s but there had been flying in the valley since the mid-1920s. The field has been home to many vintage and classic aircraft. The museum opened in February 2000 and displays have been set up in a number of adjacent hangars.
Long-term plans envisage the construction of a large exhibition hall. The first hangar tells the story of aviation in the region from 1927 to 1930. The aircraft are all privately owned and not all hangars are unlocked on the open days.
The Jungmeister served with the Swiss Air Force before being allocated for aero club use. The DH.60G Moth was originally delivered to Spain and flew with both civilian owners and the military before being retrieved from storage and rebuilt in England.

TYPE	REG/SER	CON. NO.	PI/NOTES	STATUS
☐ Beech G17S	NC80321	B-20	NC80321, N80321	PVA
☐ Boeing-Stearman A75N1 Kaydet (PT-17)	NC66711	75-1675	41-8116, NC66711, N66711	PVA
☐ Boeing-Stearman B75N1 Kaydet (N2S-3)	N65124	75-1260	Bu3483	PVA
☐ Bücker Bü 133D Jungmeister (Bü 133D)	N133JU	1001	HB-HAP, U-51 (Switzerland), HB-MTM, G-AXNI, (N72493), N133WK	PVA
☐ Buhl LA-1 Flying Bull Pup	NC350Y	139	NC350Y, N350Y	PVA
☐ CASA 1.131E [Bücker Bü 131 Jungmann]	N131G		E.3B-391	PVA
☐ CASA 1.131E [Bücker Bü 131 Jungmann]	N1017U	1123 (?)	E.3B-435	PVA
☐ Cessna 195A	N95U	7714		PVA
☐ Cessna 305A Bird Dog (L-19A) (O-1A) (CO-1)	N62364	23484	53-8063, 16714 (Canada), 119813 (Canada), C-FTGJ	PVA
☐ Culver LCA Cadet				PVA

California

☐ De Havilland DH.60G Moth	NX60MZ/ G-AAMZ	1293	MW-134 (Spain), M-CNAN, EC-NAN, 30-52 (Spain), EC-BAU, EC-ABX, G-AAMZ	PVA
☐ De Havilland DH.60X Moth	N1510V	506	G-CAPA	PVA
☐ De Havilland DH.82A Tiger Moth	'G-ADNV'	86572	PG675, G-AMLF, N675LF	PVAX
☐ De Havilland DHC.1 Chipmunk 1B-2-S5 (CT-120)	N77074	212-250	18074, 12074, CF-BXG, C-FBXG	PVA
☐ Dickenson-Howard DGA-21	N273MD	001		PVA
☐ Foss Special	N35C	104	N68732	PVA
☐ Fournier RF-4D	N1700F	4054		PVA
☐ Howard DGA-11	NC57E	88	NC57E, N57E	PVA
☐ Howard DGA-15P	N4638N	1011		PVA
☐ Howard DGA-15P	NC5524N	890	NC5524N, N5524N	PVA
☐ Luscombe 8A Silvaire	N77874	3601	NC77874	PVA
☐ North American NA-88 Texan (AT-6D)	N7096C	88-17699	42-85918	PVA
☐ North American NA-145 Navion	N8667H	NAV-4-667		PVA
☐ Piper J-3C-65 Cub	NC33112	5830	NC33112, N33112	PVA
☐ Ryan STA	NC14987	124	NC16035, N16035	PVA
☐ Ryan ST-3KR Recruit (PT-22)	N47080	1391	41-15362, NC47080	PVA
☐ Ryan ST-3KR Recruit (PT-22)	N78J	1682	41-15653	PVA
☐ Vans RV-6	N406L	936		PVA
☐ Waco ATO	NC11211	3148	NC11211, N11211	PVA
☐ Waco INF	NC864V	3265	NC864V, N864V	PVA
☐ Waco QCF	NC17445	3496	NC11445, N11445	PVA
☐ Waco UPF-7				PVA

BANTA AVIATION CORPORATION (CA18)

Address: 30 Old Rudnick Lane 100, Dover, Delaware 19901.
Admission: By prior permission only.
Location: At Livermore Airport which is about 3 miles west of the town south of Route 580.

Tony Banta has established a collection of flyable warbirds and houses them in his hangar at Livermore. Aircraft in the collection are often seen at shows in the area. A Grumman Bearcat, which served with the French and Vietnamese Air Forces, has just been sold as has another Mustang.

TYPE	REG/SER	CON. NO.	PI/NOTES	STATUS
☐ Curtiss A87-A2 Kittyhawk I	N940AK/'113521'	15411	AK940, 1058 (Canada)	RAAX
☐ North American NA-111 Mustang (P-51K)	NL451TB	111-29286	44-11153, 409 (San Salvador), N34FF, N51WE	RAA
☐ North American NA-182 Texan (T-6G)	N3623K	182-451	51-14764	RAA
☐ Supermarine 361 Spitfire LF.XVIe	N752TB	CBAF-IX-3807	TB252, G-XVIE, N7252B	RAC

BAUMBACH COLLECTION (CA19)

Address: 2369 Hagen Road, Alamo, California 94507-2234.
Admission: By prior permission only.
Location: At an airfield and workshops in the area.

This private collection contains a number of interesting types. The prototype Fleetwings F401 designed by W.A. Sutton and James Reddig emerged from the factory in Pennsylvania in 1936. The amphibian featured a then unique spot-welded stainless steel hull and was powered by a 285hp Jacobs radial engine. Production of the F5 followed but plans to produce 50 were thwarted by the 1938 recession and only five were completed. The American Eagle was designed by Bob McCrum as a replacement for Edward Porterfield's Standard J-1s at his Kansas City flying school.

TYPE	REG/SER	CON. NO.	PI/NOTES	STATUS
☐ American Eagle A-101				RAC
☐ Command-Aire 5C3				RAA
☐ Fleetwings F5 Seabird	N19191	F502	NC19191	RA
☐ Fleetwings F5 Seabird	N19192	F503	NC19192	RA
☐ Piper J-2 Cub	N19518	1718	NC19518	RAA
☐ Waco YKS-7	NC1937	4631	NC17728, NC1937, N1937	RAA

BEALE AIR FORCE BASE COLLECTION (CA20)

Address: 9 SRW/PA, 6000 C Street, Beale Air Force Base, California 95903-1511.
Tel: 530-634-8890   **Email:** 9srw.pao@beale.af.mil
Admission: By prior permission only.
Location: About 13 miles east of Marysville.

This base opened as an Army Camp and was transferred so the Air Force in 1948. Three years later it was named after General Edward F. Beale, who was an Indian Agent in California prior to the Civil War. He unsuccessfully tried to introduce camels into the area for use as pack animals. The large site has proved ideal for classified reconnaissance work. The 9th SRW operated the Lockheed U-2, TR-1 and SR-71 Blackbird; the latest versions of the U-2 are still in service. For many years there was a museum on the base but this closed in the mid-1990s.

TYPE	REG/SER	CON. NO.	PI/NOTES	STATUS
☐ Lockheed SR-71A Blackbird	61-7963	2014		RA
☐ Lockheed U-2C (U-2A)	56-6714	381		RA
☐ Northrop N-156T Talon (T-38A)	60-0570	N.5143		PV
☐ Northrop N-156T Talon (T-38A)	64-13271	N.5700		RA

California

BLACKBIRD AIRPARK (CA21)

Address:	Avenue P, 25th Street East, Palmdale, California 93550.
Admission:	Friday-Sunday 1000-1600.
Location:	On the southern boundary of Air Force Plant 42.

Located close to the gate of Plant 42, this park was dedicated on 27th September 1991. The Air Force Flight Test Center Museum was instrumental in setting up the display. Three aircraft, an A-12, an SR-71 and a U-2 can be seen along with a small indoor exhibition.

The A-12 on show was the first of the type to fly when it took to the air on 25th April 1962 at a secret desert site. The prototype SR-71 made its maiden flight from Plant 42 on 22nd December 1966 and the example here served with the 9th SRW based at Beale. Its final flight took place on 21st July 1987 when it arrived at Palmdale from Mildenhall in England.

The F-117 joined the exhibition in 2008. The stealth fighter was built at Palmdale and was towed to the site from the nearby factory.

TYPE	REG/SER	CON. NO.	PI/NOTES	STATUS
☐ Lockheed A-12	60-6924	121	On loan from AFFTC Museum, CA.	PV
☐ Lockheed F-117A	79-10783	A.4008		PV
☐ Lockheed SR-71A Blackbird	61-7973	2024	On loan from Air Force Plant 42.	PV
☐ Lockheed U-2D (U-2B)	56-6721	388	On loan from AFFTC Museum, CA.	PV

BLACKHAWK MUSEUM (CA22)

Address:	3750 Blackhawk Plaza Circle, Danville, California 94506.
Tel:	925-736-2277 Fax: 925-736-4818 Email: museum@blackhawkmuseum.org
Admission:	Wednesday-Sunday 1000-1700.
Location:	In the centre of the town.

The museum, which has over 90 cars on show, opened its doors for the first time in late 1988. The history and development of the automobile is portrayed in the display. Local history also features. The only aircraft currently on show is a replica of the classic World War I Nieuport 11 fighter.

TYPE	REG/SER	CON. NO.	PI/NOTES	STATUS
☐ Nieuport 11 (R)				RA

BUCHNER COLLECTION (CA23)

Address:	Buchner Aero Specialities, 716 West Kearney Boulevard, Fresno, California 93706.
Tel:	559-233-9547
Admission:	Daily 0900-2100 by prior appointment.
Location:	At Fresno-Chandler airfield which is in the south western suburbs of the city.

Alan Buchner runs an overhaul business at Chandler Field. Over the years he has acquired a collection of vintage aircraft and restored many to airworthy condition. The uncovered fuselage of the Sellmer dating from the 1920s is a rarity. The Waco QDC appeared in 1931 and was the first cabin model produced by the company. In all 36 were built and a few remain active. Alan has won a number of prizes, including Grand Champion at Oshkosh with his QDC. Derived from the Wyandotte Pup, the Porterfield 35-70 first flew in 1934 and 150 were constructed. The Culver Satellite was a post-war development of the Cadet design.

TYPE	REG/SER	CON. NO.	PI/NOTES	STATUS
☐ Cessna 172E	N5790T	17251690		RAA
☐ Culver V Satellite	NC44684	V-75		RAA
☐ Luscombe 8A Silvaire	N71146	2573	NC71146	RAA
☐ Mono Aircraft Monocoupe 90AF				RA
☐ Porterfield 35-70	NC16496	196	NC16496, N16496	RAC
☐ Porterfield 35-70	NC16497	197	NC16497, N16497	RAC
☐ Rearwin 7000 Sportster				RAC
☐ Rearwin 7000 Sportster	NC15857	458	NC15857, N15857	RAA
☐ Ryan ST-3KR Recruit (PT-21)	N7759	1162	41-1962	RA
☐ Ryan ST-3KR Recruit (PT-22)	N48607	1577	41-15548	RA
☐ Ryan ST-3KR Recruit (PT-22)	N48235	1903	41-20694	RA
☐ Ryan ST-3KR Recruit (PT-22)	NC54408	1941	41-20732, N54408	RAA
☐ Ryan ST-3KR Recruit (PT-22)				RA
☐ Sellmer Sportsplane D-1	N512K	1		RA
☐ Waco QDC	NC12438	3579	NC12438, N12438	RAA
☐ Yakovlev Yak-18	N18YA	0532007		RAA

BURBANK AVIATION MUSEUM (CA24)

Address:	PO Box 1215, Burbank, California 91501-1215.
Tel:	818-845-3300
Admission:	Sunday 1200-1600.
Location:	Temporary displays at the Portal of Folded Wings in Valhalla Park at 10621 Victory Boulevard.

The group was founded in 1991 and has collected a large amount of memorabilia relating to the area.

Lockheed had its major factory here for many years and several other companies operated in the area. On Sundays if the weather is fine a small display is staged at the monument to aviators who lost their lives near Burbank.

The search for a permanent home continues as there is the potential for an interesting exhibition.

BURBANK HISTORICAL SOCIETY GORDON HOWARD MUSEUM (CA25)

Address:	1015 West Olive Avenue, Burbank California 91506.
Tel:	818-841-6333 Email: ghowardmuseum@sbcglobal.net
Admission:	Saturday-Sunday 1300-1600 – aircraft on permanent view.
Location:	In the centre of the town.

Lockheed set up a factory in Burbank in the 1930s but in recent years most of the work has been carried out at Palmdale. Displayed outside this local history museum is an example of the famous Starfighter. The displays in the 1887 Victorian House trace the settlement of the area from early times and many interesting items can be seen. There is a section devoted to the local police and another to the fire service. Both contain classic motor vehicles. The work of the film industry is highlighted.

TYPE	REG/SER	CON. NO.	PI/NOTES	STATUS
☐ Lockheed 483-04-06 Starfighter (F-104D)	57-1334	283-5046		PV

CALIFORNIA ARMY NATIONAL GUARD MUSEUM (CA26)

Address:	PO Box 8104, Camp San Luis Opisbo, San Luis Opisbo, California 93403.
Tel:	805-594-6510 Email: webmaster@ca.ngb.army.mil
Admission:	Daily 0800-1630.
Location:	About 4 miles north of the town off Route 1.

Units of the California National Guard have operated a variety of fixed and rotary wing aircraft over the years. A number of types used have been collected and placed in a compound at the camp along with missiles and vehicles. In one of the buildings a collection of photographs, documents, uniforms and memorabilia is on view. These trace the history of National Guard forces in California and highlight the training role of the camp.

TYPE	REG/SER	CON. NO.	PI/NOTES	STATUS
☐ Bell 47D-1 Sioux (H-13E) (OH-13E)	'113738'	379	51-13793	PVX
☐ Cessna 305A Bird Dog (L-19A) (O-1A)	51-7312	22046		PV
☐ De Havilland DHC.2 Beaver (L-20A) (U-6A)	53-2817	614		PV
☐ Hiller UH12C Raven (H-23C) (OH-23C)	56-2259	861		PV
☐ McDonnell M.98DJ Phantom II (F-4C)	64-0827	1165		PV
☐ Sikorsky S-55D Chickasaw (H-19D) (UH-19D)	59-4973	551277	Boom from 56-1547	PV
☐ Sikorsky S-58 Choctaw (H-34A) (CH-34A) (CH-34C)	53-4544	58106		PV

CALIFORNIA CITY MONUMENT (CA27)

Location:	On permanent view at the airport which is about 2 miles north west of the town.

TYPE	REG/SER	CON. NO.	PI/NOTES	STATUS
☐ Convair 240-53 Samaritan (C-131A) (HC-131A)	N54215	53.4	52-5784, 5784 (USCG)	RAA

CALIFORNIA FLIGHT MUSEUM (CA28)

Address:	7049 Curran Road, Brown Field Airport, San Diego, California 92173.
Tel:	619-661-2516 Email: RFinch@san.rr.com
Admission:	Saturday 1000-1700.
Location:	About 10 miles south east of San Diego off Route 905.

Established in the early 1990s, as the San Diego Flight Museum, this collection now occupies two hangars at historic Brown Field located near the Mexican border. The aim is to maintain the majority of the aircraft in flying condition. The former Royal Air Force Gnat and the ex-Hungarian Air Force MiG-21U were restored in the museum buildings. The Fairchild Cornell is a recent addition to the fleet.

TYPE	REG/SER	CON. NO.	PI/NOTES	STATUS
☐ Fairchild M-62A Cornell (PT-19A)	N1110R	T42-3872	42-34206	PVA
☐ Folland Fo.144 Gnat T.1	N316RF	FL-581	XR984, 8571N	PV
☐ Fouga CM.170R Magister	N6222N	334	334	PV
☐ Mikoyan-Gurevich MiG-21U-600	N315RF	664418	4418 (Hungary), N315DM	PV
☐ PZL TS-11 Iskra 200bisC	N902BB	2H 09-02	902 (Poland), N4354S	PVA
☐ Rutan 61 Long Ez	N747SP	713		PVA

CALIFORNIA SCIENCE CENTER (CA29)

Address:	Exposition Park, 700 State Drive, Los Angeles, California 90037.
Tel:	323-724-3623 Email: 4info@csc.mail.org
Admission:	Daily 1000-1700.
Location:	In the city centre in Expostion Park near the Coliseum.

This long established museum was completely refurbished in the early 1980s and a new aerospace section was completed in 1984. In 1998 reconstruction was carried out to improve the exhibition area and a change of name took place. The region has been home to many aviation factories and these have all contributed. Lockheed at Burbank provided the Starfighter which is mounted in a dramatic pose on the outside of the building. Northrop from Hawthorne is represented by a T-38, an HL-l0 lifting body and an F-20 prototype: only three were completed and two of these crashed. Parked outside is a DC-8 once flown by United Air Lines. The Lockheed A-12 is the only two-seat version built and arrived from Palmdale. Early flight is represented by replicas of a Lilienthal and Wright gliders. The Monocoupe will eventually return to the NASM for display there.

California

TYPE	REG/SER	CON. NO.	PI/NOTES	STATUS
☐ Bell 44 (XS-1) (X-1) (FSM)	'6062'			PVX
☐ Bell 47G-5	N4799R	7926		PV
☐ Condor Hang Glider				PV
☐ Douglas DC-8-52	N8066U	45850		PV
☐ Eipper MX Quicksilver				PV
☐ Lilienthal Normal-Segelapparat (R)				PV
☐ Lockheed 483-04-06 Starfighter (F-104D)	57-1333	283-5045		PV
☐ Lockheed A-12	60-6927	124		PV
☐ Mono Aircraft Monocoupe 70	NC6730	133	On loan from NASM, DC.	PV
☐ Northrop N-156T Talon (YT-38) (YT-38A)	58-1196	N.5105		PVX
☐ Northrop F-20A Tigershark (F-5G)	N44671		82-0064	PV
☐ Northrop HL-10				PV
☐ Wright 1902 Glider (R)				PV

CAMP PENDLETON MARINE CORPS BASE MUSEUMS (CA30)

Address: PO Box 555031, History and Museums Office, Marine Corps Base Camp Pendleton, California 92055-5031.
Tel: 760-725-5011 **Fax:** 760-725-5727
Admission: By prior permission only.
Location: Just north of the town off Interstate 5.

This large base is a major training site for the Marine Corps. There are three museums on the camp. By the waterfront is a Mechanised Command Museum housing a range of amphibious vehicles along with a display of photographs, models and vehicle engines.

At another location is the World War II and Korean Museum highlighting the Marines roles in these conflicts. The Ranch House Complex is where the oldest buildings on the base are located. The three helicopters are parked around the camp with the Sea Cobra near the airfield.

TYPE	REG/SER	CON. NO.	PI/NOTES	STATUS
☐ Bell 209 Sea Cobra (AH-1J)	Bu157764	26008		RA
☐ Bell 212 Iroquois (UH-1N)	Bu158260	31601		RA
☐ Vertol V.107M Sea Knight (CH-46D) (CH-46E)	Bu154020	2371		RA

CARUTHERS MONUMENT (CA31)

Location: On permanent view at a garage at 12945 South Elm Avenue about 2 miles east of the town.

TYPE	REG/SER	CON. NO.	PI/NOTES	STATUS
☐ Vultee V-74 Valiant (BT-13A)	N57414	74-2888	41-10571	PV

CASTLE AIR MUSEUM (CA32)

Address: 5050 Santa Fe Drive, Atwater, California 95301-5154.
Tel: 209-723-2178 **Fax:** 209-723-0323 **Email:** cam@vtlnet.com
Admission: June–September daily 0900-1700; October–May daily 1000-1600.
Location: On the west side of the airfield which is about 8 miles north west of Merced.

The base opened in September 1941 and was later named after Brigadier Frederick W. Castle, a noted B-17 pilot who was killed in action on Christmas Eve 1944. For many years the field housed units of Strategic Air Command including the 93rd Bombardment Wing, which trained aircrew for bomber and tanker operations.

The idea of a base museum was put forward several years ago and an area of land near the main gate was acquired along with workshops on the field. An indoor display tracing the history of Castle and its units was set up in a building on this site. The outdoor park was landscaped and in the early 1990s additional land was allocated.

The base closed in the mid-1990s and the foundation set up when the museum opened took over the running of the collection. Castle was a bomber airfield for most of its life and a range of types used by the USAF and its predecessors from World War II to the current time can be seen. Only a few Douglas B-18s and B-23s dating from the late 1930s have survived. The classic four engined B-17 Fortress and B-24 Liberator can be compared with three twins, the B-25 Mitchell, B-26 Marauder and A-26 Invader, all of which were successful in World War II. The first jet bomber to serve with the Air Force was the B-45 Tornado and again only a few have been preserved.

The giant B-36 was for many years on show at Chanute Air Force base in Illinois. When the school closed the aircraft was dismantled and transported across the country by road. The rapid developments in the bomber can be seen with the B-47 and B-52 which were designed in the late l940s and early 1950s.

RAF Vulcans often visited Castle and one is on show. Buildings on the airfield house some of the light aircraft.

TYPE	REG/SER	CON. NO.	PI/NOTES	STATUS
☐ Avro 698 Vulcan B.2	XM605			PV
☐ Avro Canada C.100 Canuck 5 (CF-100)	100504	404	18504	PV
☐ Beech D18S Expeditor (C-45G)	51-11897	AF-454	51-11897, N87681, N608, N87681, '44588'	PV
☐ Beech 45 Mentor (YT-34)	50-0735	G-4	50-0735, N2073A	PV
☐ Bell 47G-2	N2877B	2217		RA
☐ Boeing 299-O Fortress (B-17G) (TB-17G) (EB-17G) (ETB-17G) (TB-17G)	43-38635	9613	43-38635, N3702G	PV
☐ Boeing 345 Superfortress (B-29)	'461535'	10896	44-70064 composite with c/n 11012 44-61535 and a B-29A	PV
☐ Boeing 345-9-6 Superfortress (B-50D) (WB-50D)	49-0351	16127		PV
☐ Boeing 367-76-66 Stratofreighter (KC-97G) (KC-97L)	53-0354	17136		PV
☐ Boeing 450-157-35 Stratojet (B-47E)	52-0166	44020		PV

☐ Boeing 464-201-7 Stratofortress (B-52D)	56-0612	17295		PV
☐ Boeing 717-100A Stratotanker (KC-135A)	55-3139	17255		PV
☐ Boeing-Stearman A75N1 Kaydet (PT-17)	42-16691	75-4854	42-16691, N62929, CF-MSB, VP-HBN, N6028	RA
☐ Cessna T-50 Bobcat (C-78) (UC-78)	43-31838	5776	43-31838, N49445	RA
☐ Cessna 310A Blue Canoe (L-27A) (U-3A)	57-5849	38004		PV
☐ Cessna 337M Super Skymaster (O-2A)	67-21413	337M0119		PV
☐ Consolidated 32 Liberator (B-24M) (PB4Y-1)	44-41916	5852	44-41916, Bu90165, N5141N, N4K, N4907L, CB-76, CP-576	PV
☐ Convair 8-10 Delta Dagger (F-102A)	56-1413	8-10-360		PV
☐ Convair 8-12 Delta Dagger (TF-102A)	56-2364	8-12-96		PV
☐ Convair 8-24 Delta Dart (F-106A)	'72456'	8-24-124	58-0793	PVX
☐ Convair 36 Peacemaker (RB-36H)	51-13730	275	51-13730, '492065'	PV
☐ Convair 105 (L-13A)	47-287	167		RA
☐ Convair 240-11		133	HB-IRT, N1018C, N280P, '5785'	PVX
☐ Curtiss-Wright CW-20B-2 Commando (C-46D)	44-77575	32971	44-77575, 51-1124 (Japan), 71-1135 (Japan), N54510	PV
☐ De Havilland DHC.2 Beaver (L-20A) (U-6A)	54-1707	853	54-1707, N43862	PV
☐ Douglas B-18B Bolo (B-18)	37-029	1890	37-029, NC52056, N52056	PV
☐ Douglas UC-67 Dragon (B-23)	39-047	2733	39-047, NR45361, N45361, N1G, N244AG, N8658E, N409ME, N880L	PV
☐ Douglas DC-3A-456 Skytrain (C-47A)	43-15977	20443	43-15977, NC812, NC112, NC24, N14, N21, N24010, N230GB	PV
☐ Douglas DC-4 Skymaster (C-54E) (R5D-4R) (C-54R)	Bu90407	27363	44-9137, Bu90407, N67038, N51848, N1057R	PV
☐ Douglas A-26B Invader	'44-35648'	7185	41-39472, N86482, N26VC, '24-6093'	PVX
☐ Douglas RA-3B Skywarrior (A3D-2P)	Bu144843	12089	Bu144843, N571HA –	RA
☐ Douglas A-4L Skyhawk (A4D-2N) (A-4C)	Bu149532	12857		RA
☐ Fairchild M-62C Cornell (PT-23A)	42-49354	378HO	42-49354, N52374	RA
☐ Fairchild 110 Flying Boxcar (C-119C)	49-0199	10436	49-0199, N13744	PV
☐ Fairchild 473 Provider (205) (C-123B) (C-123K)	55-4512	20173		PV
☐ General Dynamics FB-111A	69-6507	B1-69		PV
☐ Grumman G-111 Albatross (G-64) (SA-16A) (SA-16B) (HU-16B)	51-7163	G-213	51-7163, N70725	PV
☐ Grumman G-303 Tomcat (F-14D)	Bu164601	629/D-34		PV
☐ Kaman K-600-3 Huskie (H-43B) (HH-43B) (HH-43F)	62-4513	139		PV
☐ Lockheed 080 Shooting Star (P-80B) (F-80B)	45-8490	080-1704		PV
☐ Lockheed 18-08-01 Lodestar	'1373'	18-2035	ZS-ASU, 1373 (SAAF), ZS-ASU, VP-KHW, ZS-DHK, SE-CDR, N6064V, N102V, '12473'	PVX
☐ Lockheed 483-04-06 Starfighter (F-104D)	'57-1312'	283-5042	57-1330, 71318'	PVX
☐ Lockheed 580 (T-33A)	58-0629	580-1598		PV
☐ Lockheed SR-71A Blackbird	61-7960	2011		PV
☐ Martin 272E Canberra (B-57E) (EB-57E)	55-4253	355		PV
☐ McDonnell M.36BA Voodoo (F-101B)	57-0412	590		PV
☐ McDonnell M.98HO Phantom II (F-4E) (NF-4E)	66-0289	2310		PV
☐ McDonnell M.199-1A Eagle (F-15A)	74-0119	095/A080		PV
☐ Mikoyan-Gurevich MiG-17F	N1VC	2507	2507 (China)	PV
☐ North American NA-66 Harvard II	'02684'	66-2684	2951 (Canada), N99839, C-GDJC	PVX
☐ North American NA-108 Mitchell (B-25J) (EB-25) (JB-25J)	44-86891	108-47645	44-86891, N3337G, '02344'	PV
☐ North American NA-147 Tornado (B-45A)	47-0008	147-43408		PV
☐ North American NA-203 Sabre (F-86H)	53-1230	203-2		PV
☐ North American NA-214 Super Sabre (F-100C)	'55-2879'	214-1	53-1709, NASA703, N703NA	PVX
☐ North American NA-265 Sabreliner (T-39A) (CT-39A)	61-0664	265-67		PV
☐ Northrop N-160 Scorpion (N-68) (F-89D) (F-89J)	52-1927	N.4504		PV
☐ Piper J-3C-65 Cub	N3626K	22318	NC3626K	RA
☐ Piper PA-18-95 Super Cub (L-18C)	N6738C	18-2134	52-2534	RA
☐ Piper PA-18-125 Super Cub (L-21A)	51-15713	18-878		PV
☐ Republic F-84F Thunderstreak	51-9433			PV
☐ Republic F-105B Thunderchief	57-5837	B-74	57-5837, '75-887'	PV
☐ Ryan ST-3KR Recruit (PT-22)	41-20850	2058		RAC
☐ Schweizer SGS.2-12 (TG-3A)	42-53129		42-53129, N6449C	RA
☐ Stinson V-76 Sentinel (L-5G)	'42-62091'	76-3419	44-17132 (?), N62091	RAX
☐ Taylorcraft DCO-65 Grasshopper (O-57A) (L-2A)	'42-4759'		(USAAF)	RAX
☐ Vought RF-8G Crusader (F8U-1P) (RF-8A)	Bu145607			RA
☐ Vultee V-74 Valiant (BT-13A)	'6978'		(USAAF)	PVX

CENTRAL CALIFORNIA HISTORICAL MILITARY MUSEUM (CA33)

Address: 11100 Eagle Avenue, Firebaugh, California 93633.
Tel: 209-364-6132   **Email:** barta@telis.org
Admission: March-October Tuesday-Sunday 1000-1700.
Location: About 10 miles north west of the town off Interstate 5.

Eagle Field was constructed in 1942 and became a major training base during World War II. In 1979 Joe Davis bought the site which had several of the original structures still standing. The plan to recreate an operational base of World War II 'somewhere in the Pacific' is slowly being realised. A number of the buildings have been restored and the surviving hangar houses some of the aircraft collection.
An early Lockheed Neptune has been parked here for many years after it moved from a park in Los Angeles. The aircraft is supposed to be moving to the USS Hornet Museum

California

at Alameda but was still present a short time ago. The Spitfire replica is painted in typical Battle of Britain camouflage scheme. In 1985 the first Eagle Field fly-in and dance was held. Many visiting aircraft fly in from neighbouring airfields.

TYPE	REG/SER	CON. NO.	PI/NOTES	STATUS
☐ Bell 204 Iroquois (UH-1C) (UH-1M)	65-9548	1448		PV
☐ Bell 205 Iroquois (UH-1D)	64-13656	4363	Tail boom from c/n 13596 73-22113	PV
☐ Ercoupe 415C			Fuselage only.	PV
☐ Fokker D VII (R)				PV
☐ Fokker D VII (R)				PV
☐ Lockheed 15-27-01 Harpoon (PV-2)	N7414C	15-1428	Bu37462	PVA
☐ Lockheed 326-59-04 Neptune (P2V-3W)	Bu124359	326-1181	May move to USS Hornet.	PV
☐ Lockheed 580 (T-33A)				PV
☐ North American NA-108 Mitchell (B-25J) (TB-25J) (TB-25N)	N8195H	108-34023	44-30748, (N3447G)	RAA
☐ Porterfield CP-65				PVC
☐ Ryan ST-3KR Recruit (PT-21)	N48747	1180	41-1980	RAC
☐ Ryan ST-3KR Recruit (PT-22)				RAC
☐ Supermarine 300 Spitfire F.I (FSM)				PV
☐ Vultee V-74 Valiant (BT-13A)			(USAAF)	RAD

CHAFFEY COLLEGE (CA34)

Address: 5885 Haven Avenue, Rancho Cucamonga, California 91737-3002.
Tel: 909-652-6869   **Email:** russ.baty@chaffey.edu
Admission: By prior permission only.
Location: In the north eastern part of the town.

The college was set up in 1883 by when for the setting up of a private educational establishment. Three sites are now in use and a range of courses are on offer. The aviation maintenance department has two Cessna 150s in use as instructional airframes but there may be others. Also in the workshops are piston and jet engines, and components. Work on instruments, hydraulics and avionics is also undertaken.

TYPE	REG/SER	CON. NO.	PI/NOTES	STATUS
☐ Cessna 150D	N4759U	15060259		RA
☐ Cessna 150J	N3144J	15065844		RA

CHICO AIR MUSEUM (CA35)

Address: 170 Convair Court, Chico, California 95973.
Tel: 530-345-6468   **Email:** chicoairmuseum@digitalpath.net
Admission: Saturday 1000-1600
Location: At the airport which is about 3 miles north of the town

Thaddeus Kearns built and flew an aircraft at Chico in 1913. In the 1940s and 1950s the airfield was a major military base carrying out both primary and multi-engined training along with a gunnery school. In recent years it has been home to Aero Union who were one of the pioneers of aerial fire-fighting. A group of local enthusiasts decided to set up a museum and this became a reality in 2004.

The indoor displays trace the history of the airfield with many photographs, uniforms and items of memorabilia on view. On open days a number of local airworthy machines often fly in to add interest.
The Antonov is painted in the colours of an Aeroflot machine. Grumman Guardians and Lockheed Neptunes have both been widely used as water bombers in California.

TYPE	REG/SER	CON. NO.	PI/NOTES	STATUS
☐ Aero L-29 Delfin	38		In Bulgarian markings.	PV
☐ Antonov An-2R	CCCP-07618	1G 156-58	CCCP-07618, RA-07618	PV
☐ Grumman G-82 Guardian (AF-2S)	N3143G		Bu123088	PVC
☐ Howard Super Ventura (Lockheed 237-27-01 Ventura (PV-1))	N183PL	237-5492	Bu34602, 2226 (Canada), N10476, N100P, N130P, N130PL, N430PL	PV
☐ Lockheed 726-45-17 Neptune (P2V-7) (P2V-7S) (SP-2H)	Bu147968	726-7218	Bu147968, N968L, N716AU, N702AU	PV
☐ Schreder HP-11A	N5992	46VH		PV
☐ Taylor JT.2 Titch				PV
☐ Yakovlev Yak-52	N82623	822310		PV

CITY COLLEGE OF SAN FRANCISCO (CA36)

Address: 50 Phelan Avenue, San Francisco, California 94112.
Tel: 415-239-3000   **Fax:** info@ccsf.edu
Admission: By prior permission only.
Location: Near the International Airport south of the city centre.

The college, established in 1935, now operates from three sites in the city. The aviation department is housed on the campus located on the north side of the international airport. There are a number of instructional airframes in use but there could well be more. Two Hiller UH-12s were present but have not been seen recently.

TYPE	REG/SER	CON. NO.	PI/NOTES	STATUS
☐ Aeronca 65LA	N20902	CA-10020	NC20902	RA
☐ Beech C50 Seminole (L-23D) (U-8D)	57-6038	RLH-10		RA
☐ Cessna 310A Blue Canoe (L-27A) (U-3A)	58-2158	38132	Front fuselage only.	RA
☐ Hughes 269A Osage (TH-55A)				RA

☐ Hughes 269A Osage (TH-55A)	67-16759	58-0866		RA
☐ Lockheed 580 (T-33A)	N73680	580-8336	53-4997	RA
☐ North American NA-265 Sabreliner (T-39A) (CT-39A)	61-0653	265-56		RA

CLASSIC ROTORS MUSEUM (CA37)

Address:	2898 Montecito Road, Hangar G, Ramona, California 92065.
Tel:	760-650-9257 Email: comm@rotors.org
Admission:	Tuesday, Friday and Saturday 1000-1600.
Location:	At Ramona Airport which is about 20 miles north east of San Diego off Route 78.

The main aim of this museum is to rebuild and maintain in flying condition examples of helicopters which have seen service over the last half century.
The first project was the restoration of the Piasecki Work Horse. Over 160 H-21Bs were built and their fuselage shape led them to be known as 'The Flying Banana'. Other twin rotor Piasecki models await their turn in the workshops.
The Montecopter 15 is a three-seat amphibious design produced in Seattle in 1960. The design featured a boat shaped fibreglass fuselage fitted with stub wings and a water rudder.

Only a few McCulloch MC-4s still survive. A small batch of the tandem rotor design was produced and evaluated by both the Army and the Navy but none was ordered. The American Helicopter XA-6 is a small single seater powered by pulse jets and was constructed in the early 1950s. The one man ultralight Goodyear Gizmo first flew in 1954 and was powered by a water colled engine. The museum suffered a setback in the summer of 2009 when is Piasecki HUP-1 was destroyed in a crash which killed its crew. One unidentified type, probably a homebuilt design, can be seen in the exhibition area.

TYPE	REG/SER	CON. NO.	PI/NOTES	STATUS
☐ Adams-Wilson 101 Hobbycopter	N9192Z	02		PV
☐ American Helicopter XA-6	N6232C			PV
☐ Bell 47B-3	LV-AEE	66		PV
☐ Bell 47G-2	N2899B	1999		PVA
☐ Bell 47G-2A	N7576	2666		PVA
☐ Bensen B-8M Gyrocopter	N1820	VWK-1		PVA
☐ Bölkow BO 102B Helitrainer				PV
☐ Brantly 305	CF-UFS	102	CF-UFS, C-FUFS	PV
☐ Doman LZ-5	NX52578	1	N13458	RA
☐ Goodyear GA-400R-3 Gizmo (GA-400R-2J)	N69N	4098	On loan from EAA Museum, WI.	PV
☐ Hiller HJ.1 Hornet (YH-32)	N3955	15		PV
☐ Hiller HJ.1 Hornet (YH-32)	N3781G	2	53-4663	PV
☐ Hiller UH12B Raven (H-23B) (OH-23B)	N7299	729	54-2935, O-1 (Netherlands)	PVA
☐ Kaman K-600 Huskie (HUK-1) (UH-43C)	N3910		Bu146321	PVA
☐ Kaman K-600-1 Huskie (H-43A) (HH-43A)	N2856J		58-1840	PV
☐ Kamov Ka-26	N4106H	7505101	CCCP-19617, RA-19617	PVA
☐ Light Helicopter				PV
☐ McCulloch J-2	N4364G	074		PV
☐ McCulloch MC-4C				PV
☐ Mil Mi-2	OM-LJQ	537326101	OK-LJQ	PV
☐ Montecopter 15	N69P	1		PV
☐ Piasecki PD-18 Retriever (H-25A) (HUP-3)	N7089F	50	51-16621, 16621 (Canada)	PVA
☐ Piasecki PD-22 Work Horse (H-21B) (CH-21B)				RA
☐ Piasecki PD-22 Work Horse (H-21B) (CH-21B)				RA
☐ Piasecki PD-22 Work Horse (H-21B) (CH-21B)	N64606	B.154	54-4001	PVA
☐ Piasecki PV-3 Rescuer (HRP-1)				PV
☐ Piasecki PV-18 Retriever (HUP-2) (UH-25B)	Bu128529			PV
☐ Rotorway Scorpion 133				RA
☐ Sikorsky S-52-2 (YH-18A)				PV
☐ Sikorsky S-55D Chickasaw (H-19D) (UH-19D)	N2256G		57-5962	PV
☐ Sikorsky S-56 Mojave (H-37A) (H-37B) (CH-37B)			On loan.	PV
☐ Sikorsky S-58 Seabat (HSS-1N) (SH-34J)	N87717	581269	Bu148011	PV
☐ Sud SA.341G Gazelle	N505NM	1408		PVA
☐ Sud-Ouest SO.1221S Djinn		62FR112	F-BRGC	PV
☐ Westland Wasp HAS.1	XS562	F.9573		PV
☐ Westland Wasp HAS.1	N612VH	F9734	XV639	RA

COLLEGE OF ALAMEDA (CA38)

Address:	555 Ralph Appezzato Memorial Parkway, Alameda, California 94501
Tel:	510-748-2291 Email: dgunter@peralta.edu
Admission:	By prior permission only.
Location:	Near North Field which is about 5 miles south east of Oakland.

The college offers a variety of courses in aviation related subjects. A fleet of instructional aircraft along with engines and components reside in the workshops. Three European jets are in the collection. A North American CT-39A has recently made the short journey to the Oakland Aviation Museum.

TYPE	REG/SER	CON. NO.	PI/NOTES	STATUS
☐ Bell 47G Sioux (H-13G) (OH-13G)	52-7957	1197		RA
☐ Cessna 150H	N50018	15069013		RA
☐ Cessna 172A	N9896T	47696		RA
☐ Cessna 310B	N43V	35699		RA
☐ Cessna 310H	N62UT	310H0086	N1086Q	RA
☐ Hispano HA.200A Saeta (HA.200R1)	N5485G	20/35	E.14A-27	RA
☐ Hispano HA.200D Saeta	N797DB	20/72	C.10B-66, A10B-66, AE.10B-66, N554GA	RA

California

| ☐ Lockheed 580 (T-33A) | 'NASA715' | 580-8739 | 53-5400, NASA945, N715NA, N94481 | RAX |
| ☐ PZL TS-11 Iskra 100bisB | N2ZB | 1H 05-18 | 0518, 518 | RA |

COLONEL VERNON P. SAXON AEROSPACE MUSEUM (CA39)

Address: 26962 Twenty Mule Team Road, Boron, California 93516.
Tel: 760-762-5810   **Fax:** 760-762-5810   **Email:** director@20muleteammuseum.org
Admission: Daily 1000-1600.
Location: About 30 miles east of Mojave on Route 58.

In the late 1800s Borax was discovered in Death Valley. The nearest railway was 165 miles across the desert and a team of 18 mules and two horses took over two weeks to transport 37 tons of ore to the to station at Mojave. In 1912 a larger deposit was found near Boron and mining began in 1927. Three decades later open cast working started. The idea of a museum was put forward in 1980 and the displays trace the history of the area and the extraction of the ore. The Phantom is on show to highlight the role of Edwards Air Force Base. The Turner Monoplane was designed and built by Eugene Turner. He was a P-47 Thunderbolt pilot in the latter stages of World War II. In civilian life he worked for the Bell company and the FAA.

TYPE	REG/SER	CON. NO.	PI/NOTES	STATUS
☐ Bensen B-8M Gyrocopter				PV
☐ McDonnell M.98EN Phantom II (F-4D) (NF-4D)	66-7716	2337		PV
☐ Turner Monoplane				PV

COMMEMORATIVE AIR FORCE (1st AERO SQUADRON) (CA40)

Address: 1670 Sierra Avenue, Yuba City, California 95993-9411.
Tel: 530-755-3040   **Email:** redwards@optecsolutions.com
Admission: By prior permission only.
Location: At Marysville Airport which is just south of the town.

The Texan was for many years operated by the Golden Gate Squadron at Oakland. The trainer now has moved to this newly formed unit based at Marysville, near Beale Air Force Base. The delivery flight took place in April 2009 and the aircraft has been a regular visitor and performer at shows in the region.

TYPE	REG/SER	CON. NO.	PI/NOTES	STATUS
☐ North American NA-88 Texan (SNJ-5)	N3195G	88-14445	Bu51697	RAA

COMMEMORATIVE AIR FORCE (3rd PURSUIT SQUADRON) (CA41)

Address: 1749 West 13th. Street, Upland, California 91786-2151.
Tel: 951-415-9563   **Email:** cablebob101@aol.com
Admission: By prior permission only.
Location: At Cable Airport which is just west of Upland on Route 66.

The group takes its name from a World War II unit which flew P-40s against Japan from bases in China. Two aircraft are currently allocated – a Polish-built Antonov An-2 and a Harvard which was originally delivered to Canada.

TYPE	REG/SER	CON. NO.	PI/NOTES	STATUS
☐ Antonov An-2R	N43798	1G 210-55	CCCP-43798, N61488, N2AN	RAA
☐ Lockheed Q-Star (YO-3A)	69-18007	008	69-18007, N14426	RAC
☐ North American NA-81 Harvard II	N96281	81-4099	3832 (Canada), CF-NIA	RAA

COMMEMORATIVE AIR FORCE (AIR GROUP ONE MUSEUM) (CA42)

Address: 1905 North Marshall Avenue, Hangar 6, El Cajon, California 92020-1120.
Tel: 619-448-4505   **Fax:** 858-755-5886   **Email:** airgroupone@gmail.com
Admission: By prior permission only.
Location: At Gillespie Field which is just north of the town which is about 12 miles north east of San Diego.

Formed in 1981 as the San Diego Squadron, this unit achieved wing status two years later and took up its current name. The hangar complex contains a museum with photographs and memorabilia on show.

The displays cover many aspects of World War II and trace the history of several campaigns involving US forces.
The early L-5 is painted in Marines colours and the SNJ is being restored in Navy markings.

TYPE	REG/SER	CON. NO.	PI/NOTES	STATUS
☐ Boeing 367-76-66 Stratofreighter (KC-97G) (KC-97L)	53-0200	16982	Front fuselage only.	RA
☐ North American NA-88 Texan (AT-6D) (SNJ-5)	N7300C	88-15754	41-34524, Bu43763	RAA
☐ Stinson V-76 Sentinel (O-62) (L-5)	N59AF	76-137	(USAAF), N65444	RAA

COMMEMORATIVE AIR FORCE (CENTRAL CALIFORNIA VALLEY SQUADRON) (CA43)

Address: 700 Tioga Drive, Modesto, California 95355.
Tel: 209-524-7178   **Email:** dennis-c@sbcglobal.net
Admission: By prior permission only.
Location: At Modesto Airport which is in the south eastern part of the town.

California

This small unit has restored a 1944 Sentinel to original configuration. This liaison aircraft is housed in the squadron hangar at Modesto and is regularly flown at airshows in the region. The Valiant has recently been allocated to the unit and this aircraft is being rebuilt to original configuration.

TYPE	REG/SER	CON. NO.	PI/NOTES	STATUS
☐ Stinson V-76 Sentinel (L-5E)	N5625V		44-17590	RAA
☐ Vultee V-74 Valiant (BT-13A)	N313BT	74-10425	(USAAF)	RAC

COMMEMORATIVE AIR FORCE (INLAND EMPIRE WING) (CA44)

Address:	6936 Flight Road, Riverside, California 92504.
Tel:	909-354-7953 **Email:** bangercaf@sbcglobal.net
Admission:	By prior permission only.
Location:	At Riverside Airport which is about 6 miles south west of the town.

Three aircraft are allocated to this squadron. The USAAF ordered over 800 examples of the Piper J-5 but only a few were completed before the end of the World War II. The Navy ordered 100 for ambulance duties.

The DC-3 was sold on the civil market and the end of World War II and then had a number of corporate and airline owners before joining the CAF in 2001. The aircraft also flew for parachutists and operated joy flights in Nevada.

TYPE	REG/SER	CON. NO.	PI/NOTES	STATUS
☐ Douglas DC-3A-457 Skytrooper (C-53D)	N45366	11757	42-68830, NC45366	RAA
☐ Piper J-5A Cub Cruiser	N35786	5-772	NC35786	RAC
☐ Ryan ST-3KR Recruit (PT-22)	N48742	1298	41-15269	RAA

COMMEMORATIVE AIR FORCE (SOUTHERN CALIFORNIA WING) (CA45)

Address:	455 Aviation Drive, Camarillo, California 93010-9501.
Tel:	805-482-0064 **Fax:** 805-482-0348 **Email:** sdmurphy07@verizon.net
Admission:	Tuesday, Thursday, Saturday 1000-1600.
Location:	The airport is about 40 west of Los Angeles off Interstate 101.

This long established wing was first based at Van Nuys and later moved to Camarillo. The unit has operated the Commando since 1981. The well known World War II nose artist Tony Starcer, whose work adorned more than 130 B-17s including 'Memphis Belle' and 'Shoo Shoo Baby', decorated the C-46 with the famous 'China Doll' motif.

The Bearcat joined the group in the early 1990s and has been painstakingly rebuilt to airworthiness. The B-25 flew in from Texas in 1995 and after a great deal of effort is back in the air. Two large hangers were completed in 2001 – one serves as a museum where items of a memorabilia can be seen and this houses some of the flyable aircraft. The other is used as the workshop where major rebuilds can be carried out.

The Polikarpov I-16 crashed near Leningrad during World War II. In 1994 it and a number of others were transported to Novosibirsk where they were rebuilt for the Alpine Fighter Collection in New Zealand. The fighter flew again at the turn of the century and was shipped to Texas for the CAF airshow at Midland in October 2000. Several private owners also base their aircraft in the complex.

TYPE	REG/SER	CON. NO.	PI/NOTES	STATUS
☐ Beech D45 Mentor (T-34B)	N341MR	BG-65	Bu140731	PVA
☐ Curtiss-Wright CW-20B-4 Commando (C-46F)	N53594	22486	44-78663	PVA
☐ Fairchild 24R46			NC77696, LV-NXI, LV-AFH – with parts from another aircraft.	PVC
☐ Fairchild M-62A Cornell (PT-19)	N641BP	HO.274	42-49250 (?), N64187	PVA
☐ Grumman G-50 Hellcat (F6F-5)	NX1078Z	A-5634	Bu70222	PVA
☐ Grumman G-58 Bearcat (F8F-2)	N7825C	D.1227	Bu122674	PVA
☐ Mitsubishi A6M3 Zero Sen Model 22	N712Z		On loan.	PV
☐ North American NA-88 Texan (SNJ-4)	N6411D	88-10117	Bu10148, NC363, Bu10148 –	PVC
☐ North American NA-88 Texan (AT-6D) (SNJ-5)	N89014	88-16676	42-84895, Bu84865, (Japan)	PVA
☐ North American NA-108 Mitchell (B-25J) (PBJ-1J)	N5865V	108-34263	44-30988, Bu35857	PVC
☐ North American NA-122 Mustang (P-51D) (J 26)	NL44727/'414292'	122-38798	44-73749, Fv26115, 1918 (Dominican Rep), N51EH, N251JC	PV
☐ North American NA-145 Navion	N886MD	NAV-4-486		PVC
☐ North American NA-168 Texan (T-6G)	N116SE	168-406	49-3302, N9609C, N666SS	PVA
☐ Polikarpov I-16 tip 24	N30420	242165	45, ZK-JIP	PVA
☐ Steen Skybolt				PVC
☐ Stinson 108-2 Voyager	N1234			PVA
☐ Supermarine 379 Spitfire FR.XIVe	NX749DP	6S.583887	NH749, T3 (India), G-MXIV – on loan.	PVA
☐ Yakovlev Yak-3		115450123		PV

CONCORD MONUMENT (CA46)

Location:	On permanent view at AMVETS Post 26 at 1333 Willow Pass Road in the south west of the town.

TYPE	REG/SER	CON. NO.	PI/NOTES	STATUS
☐ Bell 205 Iroquois (UH-1H)		10599	67-19493	RAX

CONDOR SQUADRON (CA47)

Address:	7800 Hayvenhurst Avenue, Van Nuys, California 91406.
Tel:	818-997-8472 **Email:** info@condorsquadron.org
Admission:	By prior permission only.
Location:	The airport is in the north western suburbs of Los Angeles off Interstate 405.

California

Former World War II pilot Richard Sykes founded this organisation in 1968. Premises were obtained on the west side of Van Nuys and a large fleet of Texans is maintained in flying condition. A clubroom contains memorabilia and photographs showing the history of the squadron.

The aircraft are mainly painted in US military schemes although a few are in false Luftwaffe colours. The squadron carries out search and rescue work as well as appearing in films and at air shows. Members of the group are usually present at weekends.

TYPE	REG/SER	CON. NO.	PI/NOTES	STATUS
☐ North American NA-75 Harvard II	N16730	75-3473	3199 (Canada), CF-MZI	RAA
☐ North American NA-84 Texan (AT-6B)	N57418	84-7748	41-17370, NC57418	RAA
☐ North American NA-88 Texan (AT-6D)	N8540P		(USAAF), (Portugal) – quoted as ex 42-81646 but this is doubtful.	RAA
☐ North American NA-88 Texan (SNJ-4)	N86WW	88-12291	Bu27255, N9528C	RAA
☐ North American NA-88 Texan (SNJ-4)	N9525C	88-12407	Bu27307	RAA
☐ North American NA-88 Texan (SNJ-5)	N52006	88-15194	Bu52006, N7995C	RAA
☐ North American NA-88 Texan (AT-6D) (SNJ-5)	N7969C	88-16316	42-84535, Bu43974	RAA
☐ North American NA-88 Texan (AT-6D) (SNJ-5)	N3680F	88-16574	42-84793, Bu84843	RAA
☐ North American NA-121 Texan (AT-6D)	N63RB	121-42216	44-81494, 44-81494 (Canada), N7448C	RAA
☐ North American NA-121 Texan (AT-6D) (SNJ-5)	N26BT	121-41634	44-80912, Bu90918, N8158H, N96RM	RAA
☐ North American NA-121 Texan (AT-6D) (SNJ-5)	N3204G	121-41738	44-81016, Bu90920	RAA
☐ North American NA-121 Texan (AT-6F) (SNJ-6)	N3169G	121-42687	44-81965, Bu111974	RAA
☐ North American NA-121 Texan (AT-6F) (SNJ-6)	N2863G	121-43001	44-82279, Bu112168	RAA

CONSTELLATION HISTORICAL SOCIETY (CA48)

Address: 104 East Avenue K-4, Lancaster, California 93535.
Tel: 805-945-2093   **Fax:** 805-945-7055
Admission: By prior permission only.
Location: Aircraft now in Switzerland.

Originally delivered to the Air Force in November 1955, this Constellation was in military use for 17 years before being retired to Davis-Monthan. The aircraft then flew on spraying duties from 1973 until the early 1980s. After a period of storage at Camarillo the 'Connie' was acquired by the society and partially restored.

The aircraft flew to Switzerland in 2004 after lengthy problems with the paperwork necessary to obtain a certificate. The aircraft has since appeared at a number of airshows around Europe over the last three years.

TYPE	REG/SER	CON. NO.	PI/NOTES	STATUS
☐ Lockheed 1049F-55-96 Super Constellation (C-121C)	HB-RSC	1049F-4175	54-0156, N73544 – on loan to Super Constellation Flyers, Switzerland.	–

COSTA MESA MONUMENT (CA49)

Location: On permanent view in a park on Park Avenue in the centre of the town.

TYPE	REG/SER	CON. NO.	PI/NOTES	STATUS
☐ Grumman G-79 Panther (F9F-5)	Bu125180			PV

CRIMSON TECHNICALCOLLEGE (CA50)

Address: 8911 Aviation Boulevard, Los Angeles, California 90301-2904
Tel: 877-852-9706
Admission: By prior permission only.
Location: Just north of the International Airport.

In the late 1930s the California Flyers School of Aeronautics was set up at Mines Field (now Los Angeles International Airport). John K. Northrop founded a school at his nearby factory to train military personnel during World War II. The two merged at the end of the conflict and moved to Inglewood.

The college has since had a number of owners and a variety of names. The present title was adopted in 2008. The workshops contain many engines, components and avionics rigs. A fleet of instructional airframes is in use.

TYPE	REG/SER	CON. NO.	PI/NOTES	STATUS
☐ Aero Commander 560A	N2765B	265		RA
☐ Bell 47D-1 Sioux (HTL-4) (TH-13L)	N5166V	264	Bu128901	RA
☐ Hughes 269A Osage (TH-55A)	N62187	1181017	67-16910	RA
☐ Lockheed 580 (T-33A)	N646	580-6608	51-8824, M-56 (Netherlands)	RA
☐ North American NA-276 Sabreliner (T-39A) (CT-39A)	N1965W	276-9	62-4456	RA
☐ Northrop N-156T Talon (T-38A)				RA
☐ Piper PA-34-200 Seneca				RA

CRISSY FIELD AVIATION MUSEUM (CA51)

Address: Box 210671, San Francisco, California 94121.
Tel: 415-602-8625   **Fax:** 415-977-9344
Admission: Temporary exhibition at Pier 1 Fort Mason.
Location: Just south of the Golden Gate Bridge.

143

California

The group is trying to establish a museum at the historic grass airfield which closed in 1974. The majority of the original buildings, including hangars, survive on the site located inside the former San Francisco Presidio. The Golden Gate Recreation Area was set up and a restoration programme was initiated. The group has constructed a replica DH-4 and this is in store.

TYPE	REG/SER	CON. NO.	PI/NOTES	STATUS
☐ De Havilland DH-4 (R)				RA

EL CENTRO NAVAL AIR FACILITY (CA52)

Address:	335 Kenny Street, El Centro, California 92243-5000.
Tel:	760-339-2519 **Email:** elcnpao@navy.mil
Admission:	By prior permission only.
Location:	About 7 miles west of the town.

The Navy took over the former Marine Corps base in May 1946. Over the years testing and evaluation units of all services had set up facilities at El Centro. The field is regularly used by detachments of training aircraft. Front line and Naval reserve fighter and attack squadrons are often to be seen practising on the nearby bombing range.

Aircraft painted in the colours of the 'Blue Angels' acrobatic team are mounted near the main gate. These are the Skyhawk, Phantom, Tiger and Hornet. The Tomcat was on show at a local museum for many years. The remainder are currently parked on the ramp and will probably be put on display.

TYPE	REG/SER	CON. NO.	PI/NOTES	STATUS
☐ Douglas TA-4J Skyhawk	Bu159798	14497		PV
☐ Grumman G-98 Tiger (F-11F-1) (F-11A)				RA
☐ Grumman G-128 Intruder (A-6E)	Bu159901	I-577		RA
☐ Grumman G-128 Intruder (A-6E)	Bu160996	I-597		RA
☐ Grumman G-303 Tomcat (F-14A)	Bu159620	167		RA
☐ McDonnell M.98DH Phantom II (RF-4B)	'Bu155890'	897	Bu151979	PVX
☐ McDonnell M.267 Hornet (F/A-18A)	Bu162448	297/A242		PV
☐ Vought TA-7C Corsair II (A-7B)	Bu154476	B116		PV

ESTRELLA WARBIRD MUSEUM (CA53)

Address:	4251 Dry Creek Road, Paso Robles, California 93447-9540.
Tel:	805-227-0440 **Fax:** 805-238-9317 **Email:** webmaster@ewarbirds.org
Admission:	Wednesday, Saturday-Sunday 1000-1400.
Location:	At the airport which is about 3 miles east of the town and north of Route 41.

The airfield was constructed in World War II as the Estrella Army Air Force Base and used by P-38 Lightnings. Established in 1994, this museum has made rapid progress in the last few years. Two hangars have been built and in addition a members meeting room has been completed. Several of the aircraft are maintained in flying condition and the museum organises an annual air show. In addition to the aircraft there are military vehicles, weapons, engines, a working Link Trainer and a Titan missile on view. The displays are still being developed and will include the history of the field and local aviation. The Champion is painted to represent an L-16. The collection has grown steadily over the last decade and now includes many recently withdrawn jet types including the Tomcat flew in on 11th December 2004. More aircraft are expected and there are plans to construct hangars with additional space for exhibitions tracing the history of aviation in the area.

TYPE	REG/SER	CON. NO.	PI/NOTES	STATUS
☐ Aero L-29 Delfin	N62187	591234	1234 (Czechoslovakia)	PVA
☐ Aeronca 65TC Grasshopper (O-58B) (L-3B)	'438121'	8212	(USAAF), N47503	PVAX
☐ Aeronca 7AC Champion	N82003	7AC-628		PVA
☐ Bede BD-5J				PV
☐ Beech C18S Kansan (AT-11)	'26997'			PVA
☐ Beech D45 Mentor (T-34B)	N34NL	BG-139	Bu140805, N87642.	PV
☐ Bell 205 Iroquois (UH-1D) (UH-1H)	'61-3859'	5098	65-10054, '61-3859'	PVX
☐ Cessna 318B Tweety Bird (318A) (T-37A) (T-37B)	57-2322	40255		PV
☐ Cessna 337M Super Skymaster (O-2A)	N1041	337M0317	68-11041	PVA
☐ Curtiss 1C Jenny (JN-4D)				PV
☐ De Havilland DH.115 Vampire T.11	'832'		Fuselage pod only.	PVC
☐ Douglas DC-3A-467 Skytrain (C-47B)	N47SJ	14424/25869	43-48608, K-11 (Belgium), 348608 (France), 1416 (Israel), 016/4X-FNN	PV
☐ Douglas A-4A Skyhawk (YA4D-1) (YA-4A)	Bu137826	10523		PV
☐ Douglas TA-4J Skyhawk	Bu158512	14317		PV
☐ Fouga CM.170R Magister	N451FM	451	451, N451FM, N9222T	PV
☐ Grumman G-89 Tracer (S2F-1T) (TS-2A)	'Bu136404'	476	Bu136567, N411DF	PVX
☐ Grumman G-128 Intruder (A-6A) (A-6E)	Bu154171	I-306		PV
☐ Grumman G-303 Tomcat (F-14B)	'Bu159851'	559	Bu162911	PVX
☐ Lockheed 183-93-02 Starfighter (F-104A)	56-0784	183-1072	Fuselage only.	PV
☐ Lockheed 580 (T-33A)	52-9769	580-8029		PV
☐ Lockheed 580 (T-33A)	53-5850	580-9291		PV
☐ Lockheed 583-10-20 Starfighter (TF-104G)	N824NA	583D-5735	61-3064, DA+064, DC+367, 27+33	PV
☐ McDonnell M.98EV Phantom II (F-4J) (F-4S)	Bu155861	3284	Front fuselage only.	PV
☐ McDonnell M.98EV Phantom II (F-4J) (F-4S)	Bu155890	3520	.	PV
☐ North American NA-154 Navion (L-17A)	47-1333	NAV-4-1064 (154-37)		RAC
☐ North American NA-191 Sabre (F-86F) (RF-86F)	'5019'	191-454	52-4758, 52-7401 (Japan) – Rear fuselage from c/n 231-35 55-5082	PVX
☐ North American NA-200 Trojan (T-28B)	N9671N	200-374	Bu138303	PVA
☐ North American NA-305 Bronco (OV-10A)	'155413'	305-23	67-14615, N93LM	PV
☐ Northrop N-311 Tiger II (F-5E)	'741537'/'08'	R.1195	74-1537	PVX

California

☐ Rutan 33 Vari-Eze	N84EZ	2075		PV
☐ Saab 32A Lansen (A 32A)	N4432V	32284	Fv32284	PV
☐ Sikorsky S-62A Seaguard (HH-52A)	1395	62076		PV
☐ Stinson V-76 Sentinel (L-5E)	'417944'	76-3219	44-17932, N4016B, N45CV	PVAX
☐ Stinson V-77 Reliant (AT-19)				PV
☐ Vought F-8K Crusader (F8U-2) (F-8C) (RF-8G)	Bu146931			PV
☐ Vought A-7C Corsair II	Bu156739	E6		PV
☐ Vultee V-74 Valiant (BT-13A)	N56319	74-2167	(USAAF) ,N56319 – painted as an SNV-1	PVX

EVANS ANTIQUE AUTO GARAGE (CA54)

Address: 998 West Mission Bay Drive, San Diego, California 92109.
Tel: 619-539-7600
Admission: By prior permission only.
Location: In the western suburbs of the city.

This private car museum has on show a three quarter scale replica of the de Havilland DH.2
The aircraft was built in California in 1975 and flew for a short time before being donated to the San Diego Aerospace Museum. They have now passed the aircraft on to Bill Evans. There are many interesting cars and motor cycles dating from the early times along with components, engines, photographs and trophies.

TYPE	REG/SER	CON. NO.	PI/NOTES	STATUS
☐ De Havilland DH.2 (Scale R)	N32DH	JM-3		RA

EXPLORATORIUM (THE) (CA55)

Address: 3601 Lyon Street, San Francisco, California 94123.
Tel: 415-563-7337   **Email:** pubinfo@exploratorium.edu
Admission: Tuesday-Sunday 1000-1700.
Location: In the centre of the city.

This general interest museum specialises in the 'hands-on' approach and its displays are designed to educate children in many aspects of science and technology. Modern computer based exhibits can be seen in all areas.

There is a small aeronautical section which contains the hang glider and the ultralight. Many special exhibitions are staged which highlight the latest developments in many different fields.

TYPE	REG/SER	CON. NO.	PI/NOTES	STATUS
☐ Eipper MX Quicksilver				PV
☐ Hang Glider				PV

FLIGHT DECK MUSEUM (CA56)

Address: FAA Western-Pacific Headquarters,15000 Aviation Boulevard, Lawndale, California 90278.
Tel: 310-725-3300
Admission: Not yet open.
Location: In the western part of the town.

This museum is being established in the lobby of the Federal Aviation Administration Western-Pacific Region building. The displays will trace the history of flight and are part of the FAA's education programme. The centrepiece will be a replica Wright Flyer constructed by the Los Angeles Section of the American Institute of Aeronautics and Astronautics. This group built a non-flyable Flyer in 1953 to commemorate the 50th anniversary of the brothers' first flight.

Sadly this aircraft was destroyed in the fire at the San Diego Aerospace Museum in 1977. Work on another was started later that year and this was completed August 1995 The second machine was built as near as possible to original standards and was tested in the wind tunnel at Ames Research Center. The group built another Flyer which was flown to commemorate the centenary of powered flight. This machine is powered by a converted Volkswagen engine.

TYPE	REG/SER	CON. NO.	PI/NOTES	STATUS
☐ Wright Flyer (R)				RA
☐ Wright Flyer (R)				RAA

FLIGHT PATH MUSEUM (CA57)

Address: 6661 West Imperial Highway, PO Box 90234, Los Angeles 90009.
Tel: 310-215-5291
Admission: Tuesday-Saturday 1000-1500.
Location: At the Imperial Terminal at Los Angles International Airport.

Displays at the museum trace the history of aviation in Southern California. A large mural commemorating the centenary of flight and the 75th anniversary of Los Angeles airports can be seen. The history of local aircraft manufacturers and regional airfields are portrayed. Models, photographs, documents and memorabilia are on view with many coming from private collectors and not before seen in public. The DC-3 was delivered to TWA in January 1941 and flew on their services until late 1950. Union Oil of Houston in Texas then used it for more than a decade. The aircraft was at the California Science Center for many years.

TYPE	REG/SER	CON. NO.	PI/NOTES	STATUS
☐ Douglas DC-3-362	N760	3269	NC1944 – on loan from CMSI, CA.	PV
☐ Northrop N-156T Talon (T-38A)	N963NA	N.5116	59-1603	PV

FLYING LEATHERNECK AVIATION MUSEUM (CA58)

Address:	Building T-4203, Anderson Avenue, Box 45316, Marine Corps Air Station Miramar, San Diego, California 92145-0316.
Tel:	877-359-8762 Fax: 858-693-0037
Admission:	Tuesday-Sunday 0900-1530.
Location:	In the northern part of the city off Interstate 15.

El Toro opened in July 1942 and in recent years was the main Marine Corps airfield in the western states. The El Toro Historical Foundation was established in 1989 with the aim of raising funds and providing volunteers to run a museum. Buildings on the base were allocated and an informative exhibition tracing the history of Marine Corps Aviation from World War II to the present day was set up. Three helicopters, which for many years, were on show at nearby Tustin, moved to El Toro in 1998.

El Toro closed as a military base soon after. The museum and aircraft moved to Miramar during 1999 and the new name was adopted. The ground for a new building with an outside airpark was broken in late 2001. This allowed access without entering the base. The area has been landscaped and there are plans to extend the exhibition with more types arriving.

The inside display traces the history of Marine Corps Aviation with many rare items on view. An exhibit devoted to the 'Woman Marine' is the only one in any museum in the United States. A number of aircraft are in store on the base and these will be moved to the museum area in due course.

Several rarities can be seen and these include the Banshee and the Skynight. Very few examples of these types have been preserved. The Skyray was recovered from a school where it had suffered vandalism and has now been rebuilt to original condition. The Marines flew 149 examples of the Fairchild Flying Boxcar. These transports served at bases across the states and airfield in Japan in support of combat operations. After almost a decade of use the last ones were withdrawn in the late 1950s and placed in storage.

Two types not to serve with the Marines are the Czechoslovakian-built MiG-15, which flew with Chinese forces before arriving in the USA and the Bell 214 obtained several years ago from Iraq. Chinese MiG-15s were regularly in combat with Marine aircraft in the Korean War.

TYPE	REG/SER	CON. NO.	PI/NOTES	STATUS
☐ Beech B45 Mentor (T-34B)	Bu140688	BG-22	Bu140688, N2986F	RA
☐ Bell 47G Sioux (H-13G) (OH-13G)	52-7873	1100		RA
☐ Bell 47G-3B Sioux (OH-13S)	'Bu142394'	3206	64-15338	RA
☐ Bell 204 Iroquois (TH-1L)	Bu157824	6419		PV
☐ Bell 209 Sea Cobra (AH-1J)	Bu157784	26028		PV
☐ Bell 212 Iroquois (UH-1N)	Bu159198	31684		PV
☐ Bell 214ST	5722	28166	In Iraqi markings.	PV
☐ Douglas Super DC-3 (R4D-8) (C-117D)	Bu50835	43321	Bu50835, N835TD – rebuilt from DC-3A-467 Skytrain (C-47B) (R4D-6) c/n 15553/26998 43-49737, Bu50835.	PV
☐ Douglas DC-4 Skymaster (C-54A)	'Bu90392'	10314	42-72209, N90432, CF-PWB, N74183 – possible identity.	PVX
☐ Douglas EF-10B Skynight (F3D-2) (F3D-2Q)	Bu124630	7500		PV
☐ Douglas F-6A Skyray (F4D-1)	Bu134875	10469		PV
☐ Douglas A-4B Skyhawk (A4D-2)	Bu142879	11941		RA
☐ Douglas A-4C Skyhawk (A4D-2N)	Bu148492	12685		PV
☐ Douglas A-4F Skyhawk	Bu154204	13661		RA
☐ Douglas TA-4J Skyhawk	Bu158467	14272		RA
☐ Douglas TA-4J Skyhawk	Bu158492	14297		PV
☐ Douglas A-4M Skyhawk	Bu160264	14607		PV
☐ Fairchild 110 Flying Boxcar (R4Q-2)	Bu131708	10893	Bu131708, N7051U.	PV
☐ Grumman G-36 Wildcat (FM-2)	Bu16278	1477		RA
☐ Grumman G-40 Avenger (TBM-3) (TBM-3E)	Bu53726	3788	Bu53726, N7076C.	PV
☐ Grumman G-79 Panther (F9F-2)	Bu123652	K-357		PV
☐ Grumman G-99 Cougar (F9F-8P) (RF-9J)	Bu141722	55		PV
☐ Grumman G-128 Intruder (A-6A) (A-6E)	Bu154170	I-305		PV
☐ Hawker-Siddeley P.1127 Harrier 50 (AV-8A) (AV-8C)	N719NA	P65	(XW647), Bu158387	PV
☐ Kaman K-600 Huskie (HOK-1) (OH-43D)	Bu139990		Bu139990, N5190Q.	PV
☐ Lockheed 080 Shooting Star (P-80C) (F-80C) (TO-1) (TV-1)	Bu33840	080-2073	47-1387, Bu33840, N4425N.	PV
☐ McDonnell M.24 Banshee (F2H-2)	Bu124988	291		PV
☐ McDonnell M.98AM Phantom II (F-4B) (F-4N)	Bu152244	899		RA
☐ McDonnell M.98AM Phantom II (F4H-1) (F-4B)	Bu148373	58		RA
☐ McDonnell M.98DH Phantom II (RF-4B)	Bu151981	1012		PV
☐ McDonnell M.98DH Phantom II (RF-4B)	Bu153110	1590		RA
☐ McDonnell M.98EV Phantom II (F-4J) (F-4S)	Bu157246	3615		RA
☐ McDonnell M.267 Hornet (F/A-18A)	Bu161749	108/A077		PV
☐ McDonnell M.267 Hornet (F/A-18A)	Bu163152	576/A483		PV
☐ Mikoyan-Gurevich MiG-15	81072	81072	81072, N7013L – in Chinese markings.	PV
☐ North American NA-88 Texan (AT-6D) (SNJ-5)	Bu90866	88-18284	42-86503, Bu90866, N3650F, N90766 N100GD.	PV
☐ North American NA-108 Mitchell (B-25J) (TB-25J) (Mitchell III)	44-86727	108-47481	44-86727, 5230 (Canada), N92875 '328217' – in PBJ-1 markings.	PVX
☐ North American NA-194 Fury (FJ-3) (F-1C)	'Bu136022'	194-110	Bu135883.	PVX
☐ North American NA-305 Bronco (OV-10A) (OV-10D)	Bu155494	305-105		PV
☐ Northrop N-311 Tiger II (F-5E)	74-1564	R.1252		PV
☐ Piasecki PV-18 Retriever (HUP-2) (UH-25B)	Bu128596			PV
☐ Sikorsky S-55D (HRS-3) (CH-19E)	Bu130252			PV
☐ Sikorsky S-58 Seahorse (HUS-1) (UH-34D)	Bu150219	581559		PV
☐ Sikorsky S-65A Sea Stallion (CH-53D)	Bu153304	65081		PV
☐ Stinson V-76 Sentinel (O-62) (L-5)	'Bu76121'	76-121	42-14918, N63098 – possible identity.	PVX
☐ Vertol V.107M Sea Knight (CH-46D) (CH-46E)	Bu154803	2410		PV

California

☐ Vought F4U-5N Corsair (F4U-5)	Bu122189		PV
☐ Vought RF-8G Crusader (F8U-1P) (RF-8A)	Bu144617	Bu144617, N110NR.	PV
☐ Vought RF-8G Crusader (F8U-1P) (RF-8A)	Bu146858		RA
☐ Vought F-8J Crusader (F8U-2NE) (F-8E)	Bu150920		PV

FRESNO AVIATION MUSEUM (CA59)

Address:	c/o Chandler Field, Fresno 93706.
Tel:	559-696-4020 **Email:** matt@fresnoairmuseum.com
Admission:	Not yet open.
Location:	The airfield is in the south western suburbs of the city.

A group is working towards building a hangar at Chandler Field to house a display of both civil and military aircraft. The region has a rich aeronautical tradition so there is potential for an interesting exhibition.

A number of aircraft have been promised and several crash sites have been investigated. Progress seems to have slowed down recently but hopefully it will not be too long before these ambitious plans are realised.

FRESNO MONUMENT (CA60)

Location:	On permanent view at the Hammer Field Armory which is north of the International Airport.

TYPE	REG/SER	CON. NO.	PI/NOTES	STATUS
☐ Bell 209 Huey Cobra (AH-1G) (AH-1S)	70-15966	20910		PV

GAVILAN COMMUNITY COLLEGE (CA61)

Address:	5055 Santa Teresa Boulevard, Gilroy, California 95020-9578.
Tel:	408-848-4800 **Email:** tflippen@gavilan.edu
Admission:	By prior permission only.
Location:	At Hollister Airport which is about 3 miles north of the town.

The college has a number of sites in the area. The courses in aviation maintenance technology are carried out in premises at Hollister Airport where a fleet of instructional airframes is in use.

TYPE	REG/SER	CON. NO.	PI/NOTES	STATUS
☐ Aeronca 7AC Champion	N82254	7AC-882	NC82254	RA
☐ Aeronca 7BCM Champion (L-16A)	N4302E	7BCM-310	47-935	RA
☐ Bell 47K (HTL-7)	N81168	2124	Bu145847	RA
☐ Cessna 210A	N9539X	21057839		RA
☐ Champion 7FC Tri-Traveler	N7584E	7FC-272		RA
☐ Hughes 269A Osage (TH-55A)	N62216	0961	67-16854	RA
☐ Piper PA-28-160 Cherokee	N5176W	28-211		RA

GLENDALE COMMUNITY COLLEGE (CA62)

Address:	1500 North Verdugo Road, Glendale, California 91208
Tel:	818-240-1000 **Email:** srubke@glendale.edu
Admission:	By prior permission only.
Location:	Whiteman Air Park is about 1 mile south of San Fernando.

Glendale has a rich aeronautical history and the first airport opened in 1923. Grand Central was in use until 1959 and some of the buildings still exist. For decades the college trained technicians in a number of areas. These programmes have now been terminated. The instructional airframes are at Whiteman Airpark awaiting their fate.

TYPE	REG/SER	CON. NO.	PI/NOTES	STATUS
☐ Cessna 150G	N6660J	15067122		RA
☐ Cessna 172N	N733AM	17268145		RA
☐ Cessna 172N	N738TJ	17270522		RA
☐ Cessna 421B Golden Eagle	N31218	421B0376		RA
☐ Piper PA-32-260 Cherokee Six	N3575W	32-468		RA

HANSEN COLLECTION (CA63)

Address:	PO Box 112, Mojave, California 93502-0112
Tel:	661-824-9729 **Email:** mojojets@antelecom.net
Admission:	By prior permission only.
Location:	At the airport which is just east of the town off Route 58.

Al Hansen and his family have operated warbirds for many years and they have a large hangar on Mojave Airport. Also to be seen are a number of tanks and military vehicles. A display tracing the history of the site has been set up in the hangar. This contains photographs and documents showing the many types which have been flown from the field. The aircraft in the collection are regularly used in film and television work and the hangar area often serves as the backdrop. The types owned vary and several have gone to other collectors in recent years.

TYPE	REG/SER	CON. NO.	PI/NOTES	STATUS
☐ Aero Commander 500A	N313M	1276-99		RAA
☐ Antonov An-2R	N244MJ	1G 172-44	LY-ACP, 12 (Lithuania), LY-APF	RAA
☐ Bell 204 Iroquois (HU-1B) (UH-1B)	N59HP	453	62-1933	RAA

☐ Bell 205 Iroquois (UH-1D) (UH-1H)	N313B	4057	63-8765	RAA
☐ Bell 205 Iroquois (UH-1D) (UH-1H)	N2218N	5057	65-10013	RAA
☐ Bell 205 Iroquois (UH-1D) (UH-1H)	N83CF	5318	66-0835	RAA
☐ Bell 205 Iroquois (UH-1D) (UH-1H)	N19CF	5628	66-1145	RAA
☐ Bell 205 Iroquois (UH-1H)	N312CF	'ACH64'		RAA
☐ Bell 206B Jet Ranger	N59548	1386		RAA
☐ Canadair CL-13B Sabre 6 [North American F-86E]	N38453	1487	23697 (Canada), 378 (South Africa) – flies as '1487'	RAAX
☐ Canadair CL-30 Silver Star 3 (CT-133) [Lockheed 580 (T-33AN)]	N519DL	T33-119	21119, 133119	RAA
☐ Cessna 150M Commuter	N45510	15076954		RAA
☐ Cessna R172E Mescalero (T-41B)	N90252	R1720191	67-15190, 5190 (Thailand)	RAA
☐ Fouga CM.170R Magister	N363F	363	363	RAA
☐ Lake LA-4-200 Buccaneer	N1076L	669		RAA
☐ Lockheed 183-93-02 Starfighter (F-104A)				RAC

HETGE COLLECTION (CA64)

Address: 202510 Woodford-Tehachapi Road, Tehachapi, California 93561.
Admission: By prior permission only.
Location: At an airfield in the area.

This private collection includes a number of classic types including one of the few surviving Buhl Pups. This low wing monoplane first appeared in 1930 and 100 were completed. The J-4E version of the Cub Coupe was fitted with a 75 hp Continental engine and first appeared in 1940. Production commenced the following year.

TYPE	REG/SER	CON. NO.	PI/NOTES	STATUS
☐ Aeronca K	NC17798	K-64	NC17798, N17798	RAA
☐ Buhl LA-1 Flying Bull Pup	NC356Y	145	NC356Y, N356Y	RA
☐ Cessna 175B	N8181T	17556881		RAA
☐ Mono Aircraft Monocoupe 70	NC7820	132	NC6729, N6729	RA
☐ Piper J-4A Cub Coupe	NC32591	4-1284	NC32591, N32591	RAA
☐ Piper J-4E Cub Coupe	NC56599	4-1612		RAA
☐ Taylor J-2 Cub	NC15965	509	NC15965, N15965	RAA

HILLER AVIATION MUSEUM (CA65)

Address: 601 Skyway Road, San Carlos, California 94070-2702.
Tel: 650-654-0200   **Fax:** 650-654-0220   **Email:** museum@hiller.org
Admission: Daily 1000-1700.
Location: At San Carlos Airport which is just north east of the town off Interstate 101.

Stanley Hiller flew his first helicopter, the XH44, in 1944 and his companies subsequently designed and produced a wide range of models over the next 30 years. He collected a number of his machines along with a large archive containing photographs, documents and models. For many years a display was staged in an industrial building in Redwood City.

On 5th June 1998 a new facility was opened at San Carlos Airport covering Hiller's contribution to aviation and the story of flight in northern California. A range of helicopters can be seen including a replica of the XH44. The original, loaned by the National Air and Space Museum, was here for a time but has been recalled. Almost 3,000 examples of the UH12 model were produced for both military and civil use. Many versions of this well used type are in the collection.

The Hornet was the first American helicopter employing the use of tip mounted ramjets to turn the rotor blades. Three variants of this design are on show along with a mock up of the J10 and the prototype 1099. In 1869 Frederick Marriot built and flew the unmanned Avitor Hermes in San Francisco.

In 1883 John Montgomery of the University of Santa Clara flew his Gull glider at San Diego. He carried on developing his ideas over the next three decades. Replicas of three of his designs are on view.

In 1911 Eugene Ely flew a Curtiss Pusher on and off a deck on the USS *Pennsylvania* whilst it was moored in San Francisco Bay. The Gonzales Biplane of 1912 is the sole survivor of three built by two local men. The uncovered airframe fitted with a Kemp I-4 engine has been restored. The aircraft was on show in the museum at Travis Air Force Base for many years. Parts of the mock up of the proposed Boeing supersonic transport is on view.

The displays are being developed but already they present an informative picture of flight in this region which has seen many important developments.

TYPE	REG/SER	CON. NO.	PI/NOTES	STATUS
☐ Aero L-39C Albatros	NX139AF/'68'	533526	(Soviet)	PV
☐ Ames-Dryden AD-1 (Rutan 35)	N805NA	001	On loan from NASA Ames, CA.	PV
☐ Arnold AR-5	N105AR	X-1		PV
☐ Beachey Little Looper (R)	N288QB	001		PV
☐ Bede BD-5B	N644SA	1		PV
☐ Bell Rocket Belt				PV
☐ Boeing 737-222	N9065U	19946	N9065U, CF-NAP – front fuselage only.	PV
☐ Boeing 747-136	G-AWNG	20269	Front fuselage only.	PV
☐ Boeing Condor				PV
☐ Boeing 2707-300 SST (Mock Up)			Fuselage section.	PV
☐ Buhl Autogyro				PV
☐ Cassutt IIIM	N799DM	S101		RA
☐ Cessna 177B Cardinal	N34716	17701954		PV
☐ Christen Eagle II	N2FC	0001		PV
☐ Curtiss 1C Jenny (JN-4D)				PV
☐ Curtiss D Pusher				PV
☐ Curtiss D Pusher (R)				RAC
☐ Curtiss-Thompson A-1			Parts only.	RA
☐ Douglas A-4M Skyhawk			Front fuselage only.	PV

California

☐ Fairchild 22 C7D	NC9481	911	NC9481, N9481	PV
☐ Fairchild 24 C8C	NC15921	2724	NC15921, N15921	PV
☐ Fairchild-Hiller FH-1100	N81005	1		RA
☐ Gonzales Biplane			On loan from Travis AFM, CA.	PV
☐ HD-2M Sportster	N168			PV
☐ Hiller XH44 (R)				PVC
☐ Hiller YHJ.1 Hornet	N8200H	1		RA
☐ Hiller HJ.1 Hornet	N8120H	1	N8170H	PV
☐ Hiller HJ.1 Hornet (YH-32)	55-4967	10		RA
☐ Hiller HJ.1 Hornet (YH-32) (XHOE-1)	Bu138651	4		RA
☐ Hiller 1033 Rotor Cycle (XROE-1)				PV
☐ Hiller 1033 Rotor Cycle (YROE-1)	Bu4002	1		PV
☐ Hiller 1033 Rotor Cycle (YROE-1)	Bu4020	3		RA
☐ Hiller 1033 Rotor Cycle (YROE-1)	Bu4024	7		PV
☐ Hiller 1099	N3776G	1		PV
☐ Hiller Camel (Mock up)				RA
☐ Hiller J10 (R)				PV
☐ Hiller UH4 Commuter	NX68276	1		PV
☐ Hiller UH5B	NX67707	1		PV
☐ Hiller UH12A Model 360	N8118H	118		PV
☐ Hiller UH12A Raven (H-23A)	N55L	284	51-16130	RA
☐ Hiller UH12B Raven (H-23B) (OH-23B)				RA
☐ Hiller UH12B Raven (H-23B) (OH-23B)	54-4031	414		RA
☐ Hiller UH12B Raven (H-23B) (OH-23B)	51-16374	624	51-16374, N47245	PV
☐ Hiller UH12B Raven (H-23B) (OH-23B)	'XB478'	717	54-2926, N90890 – converted to HTE-2 configuration –in false Royal Navy markings.	RAX
☐ Hiller UH12C Raven (H-23C) (OH-23C)	56-2284	898		RA
☐ Hiller UH12D Raven (H-23D) (OH-23D)				RA
☐ Hiller UH12E	N706NA	2265	N9779C	RA
☐ Hiller UH12E Raven (H-23F) (OH-23F)	61-3218	2167	61-3218, N5938	R
☐ Hiller UH12E4 (Mock up)				RA
☐ Hiller UH12E5	N501HA	2534	At Burger King next door.	PV
☐ Hiller UH12L-4				RA
☐ Hiller ULV (HJ.1 Hornet) (YH-32)	53-4664	3		RA
☐ Hiller VXT-8 (R)				PV
☐ Irvin Aero Cycloid (R)				PV
☐ Johnston ONR Flying Platform				PV
☐ Lockheed Q-Star (YO-3A)	69-18001	002		PV
☐ Marriott Avitor Hermes (R)				PV
☐ McCulloch MC-4C				RA
☐ Mono Aircraft Monocoupe 70	NC6740	151	NC6748 N6748	PV
☐ Monte-Copter 12				RA
☐ Montgomery Evergreen (R)				PV
☐ Montgomery Gull (R)				PV
☐ Montgomery Santa Clara (R)				PV
☐ Nelson PG-185B Hummingbird	N68583	83	On loan from NSM, NY.	PV
☐ Pietenpol B4-A Aircamper	N3133	001		PV
☐ Pitts S-1S Special	N18GM	1		PV
☐ Republic RC-3 Seabee	N87482	33	NC87482	PV
☐ Rutan 33 Vari-Eze				PV
☐ Rutan 40 Defiant	N78RA	001		PV
☐ Standard J-1				PV
☐ Stanford Swift				PV
☐ Stearman-Hammond Y-1S	NC15522	307	NC15522, N15522	PVA
☐ Thaden T-1 Argomaut	N3902L	1	X3902	PVD
☐ Thorp TB-3	N30033			PV
☐ Travel Air D-4D Speedwing	N434P	515		PV
☐ Trek Solotrek XFV				RA
☐ Waco 10 (GXE)	NC3807	1197	NC3807, N3807	PV
☐ Watson Hybrid Dirigible Research Vehicle				PV
☐ Wright Flyer (R)				RA
☐ Wright B (R)				RA
☐ Wright EX Vin Fiz (R)				RA

HILLIER AIR MUSEUM (CA66)

Address:	Hangar 7, 700 Tioga Drive, Modesto, California 95354.
Tel:	209-526-8297 Fax: 209-985-9000 Email: tomhillier@msn.com
Admission:	Second Saturday in each month 1000-1600.
Location:	The airfield is about 2 miles east of the town off Route 132.

This private collection concentrates on American aircraft in civilian use in the late 1940s and early 1950s. The Republic Seabee is nearing the end of a long restoration and should soon join the others in the air.

A classic Taylor Cub is currently on show at the College Park Museum in Maryland. Only four aircraft are on show at anytime but arrangements can be made to view the others in nearby hangars.

TYPE	REG/SER	CON. NO.	PI/NOTES	STATUS
☐ Beech D17S (UC-43) (GB-2)	N1196V	6703	44-67726, (Bu23691), FT477, Bu32875	PVA
☐ Beech 35 Bonanza	N3001V	D-400	NC3001V	PVA
☐ Boeing-Stearman A75 Kaydet (PT-13B)	N63378	75-254	40-1697	PVA
☐ Cessna 140	N3065N	13586	NC3065N	PVA
☐ Cessna U206G Stationair 6	N777NY	U20605051		PVA
☐ Globe GC-1B Swift	NC80694	1099	NC80694, N80694	PVA

☐ Piper J-3F-65 Cub	NC26858	4225	NC26858, N26858	PVA
☐ Republic RC-3 Seabee	N6518K	784	NC6518K	PVC
☐ Ryan ST-3KR Recruit (PT-22)	N53190	1477	41-15448	PVA

HUGH'S MUSEUM (CA67)

Address:	PO Box 293, Tres Pinos, California 95075-0293.
Tel:	831-636-9165
Admission:	By prior permission only.
Location:	At Hollister Airport which is about 3 miles north of the town.

This interesting collection is owned by Hugh Bikle and resides in his private hangar at Hollister. A notice on the door states 'Hugh's Museum'. The New Standard D-25 biplane first flew in 1928 and 65 were completed in the next two years. A further ten were produced in the mid-1930s mainly for crop-dusting.

TYPE	REG/SER	CON. NO.	PI/NOTES	STATUS
☐ Boeing-Stearman B75N1 Kaydet (N2S-3)	N5728N	75-2606	Bu4276	RAA
☐ Boeing-Stearman E75 Kaydet (PT-13D)	N4672V	75-5506	42-17343	RAA
☐ Cessna 180	N180HB	31651	N180BN	RAA
☐ New Standard D-25	N149M	156	NC149M	RAA
☐ Schweizer SGS.1-23E	N91893	30		RAA
☐ Travel Air 4000	NC3945	319	NC3945, N3945	RAA

JOE DAVIS HERITAGE AIRPARK AT PALMDALE PLANT 42 (CA68)

Address:	38300 Sierra Highway, Palmdale, California 93550.
Tel:	661-267-5300 **Email:** mlivingstone@cityofpalmdale.org
Admission:	Friday-Sunday 1100-1600.
Location:	On Avenue P between 20th East Street and 25th East Street.

The City of Palmdale has set up this display which honours the contribution Plant 42 has made to the community since it was set up in the late 1940s. The ambitious aim is to exhibit an example of every type which has been tested at the facility. Eventually about 40 aircraft will be on show. Work on the site started in the summer of 1998 and three aircraft were in place by August. The park opened to the public in November 2002 and the official ceremonies took place on 6th August 2004. The site is named after a former Commander of Plant 42 and a Palmdale Councilman.

Restoration work is carried out by a team of volunteers in a workshop donated by the Lockheed Martin Company. The Scaled Composites 143 was designed by Burt Rutan at Mojave and first took to the air in July 1988. The project was initiated by the Beechcraft company and three versions were projected. After the programme was cancelled the aircraft was prserved outside the Mojave factory before making the move to Palmdale. A Visitor Center is planned and the displays here will trace the history of Plant 42, Palmdale Airfield and the companies which operate from the site.

TYPE	REG/SER	CON. NO.	PI/NOTES	STATUS
☐ Boeing 464-260 Stratofortress (B-52F)	57-0038	17432		PV
☐ Canadair CL-13A Sabre 5 [North American F-86E]	N91FS	1021	23231, N231X	PV
☐ Curtiss-Wright CW-20B-2 Commando (C-46D)	44-78019	33415	44-78019, N32229	PV
☐ Douglas YA-4C Skyhawk (A4D-2N) (YA4D-2N)	Bu145067	12313		PV
☐ Lockheed 383-04-05 Starfighter (F-104C)	57-0915	183-1232		PV
☐ Grumman G-303 Tomcat (F-14D)	Bu164350	625/D-30		PV
☐ Lockheed 580 (T-33A)	51-4533	580-5828		PV
☐ Lockheed L-1011-1 TriStar				PV
☐ Lockheed 1329 JetStar 6	N814NA	1329-5003	N9203R, NASA14	PV
☐ McDonnell M.36BA Voodoo (TF-101B) (TF-101F)	58-0324	696		PV
☐ McDonnell M.98EN Phantom II (F-4D)	65-0696	1735	65-0696, N402AV	PV
☐ North American NA-223 Super Sabre (F-100D)	54-2299	223-179		PV
☐ Northrop N-156T Talon (T-38A)	63-8182	N.5529		PV
☐ Northrop N-311 Tiger II (F-5E)	74-1529	R.1187		PV
☐ Republic F-105G Thunderchief (F-105F)	62-4416	F-5		PV
☐ Scaled Composites 143 Triumph	N143SC	001		PV
☐ Vought A-7B Corsair II	Bu154449	B89		PV

KERN COUNTY MUSEUM (CA69)

Address:	3801 Chester Avenue, Bakersfield, California 93301-1345.
Tel:	661-852-5000 **Fax:** 661-322-6415 **Email:** kcmuseum@kern.org
Admission:	Aircraft on permanent view.
Location:	At Meadows Field which is about 4 miles north of the town off Route 99.

The museum which has a number of sites in the county is responsible for the two ex-military aircraft. For many years a Republic XF-84H was mounted at the airport but this was reclaimed by the National Museum of the United States Air Force at Dayton. In return a pair of Northrop T-38 trainers were loaned to Kern County. A replica of the Scaled Composite SpaceShipOne has been built and is suspended in the terminal building. The type made its maiden flight at Mojave in 2004 and appeared at the EAA Convention at Oshkosh the following year. The company has its administrative headquarters in Bakersfield.

The airport opened in 1923 and was in use by the military during World War II. A small display tracing the history of the field has been staged.

TYPE	REG/SER	CON. NO.	PI/NOTES	STATUS
☐ Northrop N-156T Talon (T-38A)	60-0566	N.5139		PV
☐ Northrop N-156T Talon (T-38A)	65-10441	N.5860		PV
☐ Scaled Composites 316 SpaceShipOne (R)	'N328KF'		In Airport terminal	PVX

Several research aircraft including this Vought F-8C Crusader are parked outside NASA's Dryden Flight Research Facility. [CA99]

Right: One of the highlights of the Oakland Aviation Museum is the Short Solent formerly owned by Howard Hughes. (Nigel Hitchman) [CA105]

Below: A team of volunteers at the San Diego Air and Space Museum spent many years restoring this Ford 5-AT-B. (Lloyd Robinson) [CA122]

LA VERNE MONUMENT (CA70)

Location:	On permanent view at Mount San Antonio College in the southern part of the town.

TYPE	REG/SER	CON. NO.	PI/NOTES	STATUS
☐ Bell 205 Iroquois (UH-1D) (UH-1H)	66-16071	5765		PV

LACY COLLECTION (CA71)

Address:	7435 Valjean Avenue, Van Nuys, California 91406.
Tel:	818-989-2000 Fax: 818-904-3450
Admission:	By prior permission only.
Location:	Van Nuys Airport is about 20 miles north west of Los Angeles just west of Interstate 405.

Veteran pilot Clay Lacy has had careers as an airline and fighter pilot and also raced a Mustang at Reno. He runs and aircraft charter business from both Van Nuys and Seattle. The famous purple P-51 has been in his possession for over a quarter of a century. The Republic Seabee amphibian is believed to be stored near Boise in Idaho. Three KC-97s were purchased in the auction of Hawkins and Powers fleet at Greybull in Wyoming and one is being converted into a Stratocruiser with a full airline interior.

TYPE	REG/SER	CON. NO.	PI/NOTES	STATUS
☐ Boeing 367-76-66 Stratofreighter (KC-97G) (KC-97L)	N1365N	16729	52-2698	RA
☐ Boeing 367-76-66 Stratofreighter (KC-97G) (KC-97L)	N29862	16792	52-2761	RA
☐ Boeing 367-76-66 Stratofreighter (KC-97G) (KC-97L)	N972HP	17132	53-0350, N8516Y, N297HP	RA
☐ Douglas DC-3A-467 Skytrain (C-47B)	N814CL	17103/34370	45-1100, NC55414, N5414, (N5410), N541Q, N541GA	RAA
☐ North American NA-88 Texan (AT-6D) (SNJ-5)	N164CL	88-17277	42-85496, Bu85056, N447C	RAA
☐ North American NA-122 Mustang (P-51D)	N64CL	122-40963	44-74423, 9595 (Canada), N6517D, N182XF, N182X	RAA
☐ Republic RC-3 Seabee	N6124K	310	NC6124K	RA
☐ Stinson Junior S	NC10833	8027	NC10833, N10833	RAA

LAKEWOOD KOREAN WAR MEMORIAL (CA72)

Location:	On permanent view in De Valle Park in Lakewood in the south eastern part of the town.

TYPE	REG/SER	CON. NO.	PI/NOTES	STATUS
☐ Douglas F-10B Skynight (F3D-2)	'Bu127039'	8064	Bu125870	PVX

LANCASTER MONUMENTS (CA73)

Location:	On permanent view at two locations in the town.

TYPE	REG/SER	CON. NO.	PI/NOTES	STATUS
☐ McDonnell M.98EN Phantom II (F-4D)	N401AV	1364	64-0952 – on Lancaster Boulevard.PV	
☐ McDonnell M.267 Hornet (F/A-18A)	N842NA	13/A011	Bu161214 – at Municipal Stadium PV on Avenue I.	

LEMOORE NAVAL AIR STATION COLLECTION (CA74)

Address:	730 Enterprise, Room 15, Reeves Field, Lemoore, California 93246-5035.
Tel:	559-998-3393 Email: pao.naslemoore@navy.mil
Admission:	Aircraft are on open part of base.
Location:	About 7 miles west of the town on Route 198.

The field opened in 1961 to serve as a shore base for carrier aircraft of the Pacific Fleet and squadrons flying the F/A-18A Hornet are currently in residence. It is located in a rural area thus easing pressure in the San Francisco Bay area, which at the time had two other active Naval Air Stations. Most aircraft have been painted in false colours to represent ones flown by resident units.

TYPE	REG/SER	CON. NO.	PI/NOTES	STATUS
☐ Douglas A-1H Skyraider (AD-6)	'Bu135300'	10678	Bu137602	PVX
☐ Douglas A-4A Skyhawk (A4D-1)	'Bu150034'	11318	Bu139953 – in the town.	PVX
☐ Douglas A-4B Skyhawk (A4D)	'Bu150033'	11348	Bu142094	PVX
☐ McDonnell M.267 Hornet (F/A-18A)	Bu161366	34/A024		PV
☐ Vought A-7C Corsair II	'Bu160122'	E30	Bu156763	PVX

LEONARD MUSEUM (CA75)

Address:	20114 East Damerel Court, Covina, California 91724.
Admission:	By appointment only.
Location:	At Cable Airport which is just west of Upland on Route 66.

Over the years Lane Leonard collected a vast amount of memorabilia, posters, models, photographs, documents and books. The majority of these are in his hangar at Cable. He died a few years ago and the collection is now maintained by his family. Also in the building are a number of classic cars.

California

TYPE	REG/SER	CON. NO.	PI/NOTES	STATUS
☐ Beech D17S (UC-43)	NC51969	4898	43-10850, N51969	PVA
☐ Cessna 172K	N79924	17258252		PVA
☐ Piper J-3C-65 Cub	N98752	18980	NC98752	PVA
☐ Piper PA-22-150 Tripacer	N2914P	22-3182		RAA
☐ Piper PA-24 Comanche	N7672P	24-2885		RAA
☐ Taylor J-2 Cub	N3WY	935	NC17269, N17269	PVA
☐ Travel Air D-4000	NC9027	828	NC9027, N9027	PVA

LOCKHEED MARTIN SKUNK WORKS DISPLAY (CA76)

Address:	1011 Lockheed Way, Palmdale, California 93599-3740.
Tel:	661-572-4153 **Email:** dianne.m@imco.com
Admission:	By prior permission only.
Location:	About 5 miles east of the town.

The term 'Skunk Works' was first used when the team led by Clarence 'Kelly' Johnson was working on the XP-80. Work on the jet prototype was carried out in temporary quarters. After World War II the Advanced Development Projects section was set up at Burbank. Johnson believed that the aircraft under design should be used for specific military tasks rather than pure research. The F-104, U-2, A-12 and SR-71 and F-117 originated from this skilled team. During the 1960s premises were built at Palmdale and flight testing of the high-speed machines was moved to this new facility. A display of types associated with the 'Skunk Works' can be seen outside the building. The company Shooting Star has been restored to represent the prototype XP-80A which first flew January 1944. The F-117 is a fairly recent addition to the display.

TYPE	REG/SER	CON. NO.	PI/NOTES	STATUS
☐ General Dynamics 401 Fighting Falcon (F-16A)	N816NA	61-569	82-0976	RA
☐ Lockheed 080 Shooting Star (XP-80A)	'44-83021'		Made from P-80C c/n 080-2599 49-0851 and T-33A c/n 580-1297 57-0568.	RAX
☐ Lockheed 683-10-19 Starfighter (F-104N)	N812NA	683C-4053	NASA812 NASA.	RA
☐ Lockheed F-117A	80-0785	A.4010	With parts from the test airframe.	RA

LONG BEACH CITY COLLEGE (CA77)

Address:	1305 East Pacific Coast Highway, Long Beach, California 90808.
Tel:	562-938-3269 **Email:** coshita@lbcc@edu
Admission:	By prior permission only.
Location:	In the northern part of the town.

The college has trained aviation mechanics since 1940. Courses leading to FAA licenses in airframe and engines are held. Three instructional aircraft are known to be in use but there may be more.

TYPE	REG/SER	CON. NO.	PI/NOTES	STATUS
☐ Cessna 152	N66931	15281668		RA
☐ Hughes 269A Osage (TH-55A)	N57953	1018	67-16908	RA
☐ Piper PA-30 Twin Comanche	N7033Y	30-35		RA

LONG BEACH VIETNAM VETERANS MEMORIAL (CA78)

Location:	On permanent view in Houghton Park in the northern part of the town.

TYPE	REG/SER	CON. NO.	PI/NOTES	STATUS
☐ Bell 204 Iroquois (UH-1C) (UH-1M)	66-15028	1756		PV

LOS ANGELES COUNTY MUSEUM OF NATURAL HISTORY (CA79)

Address:	900 Exposition Boulevard, Los Angeles, California 90007.
Tel:	213-744-3466 **Email:** info@nhm.org
Admission:	Daily 1000-1700.
Location:	In the centre of the city in Exposition Park near the Coliseum.

Both aircraft in this collection were on display at the Museum of Flying in Santa Monica. The Douglas DWC was one of four ordered by the Air. Service for a round-the-world flight. They left Seattle on 4th April 1924 and two completed the epic journey on 28th September 1924. The aircraft were fitted with floats for part of the journey. One crashed in Alaska and one sunk whilst it was being towed to a safe harbour in the Faeroe Islands. The trip covered almost 30,000 miles in just over 371 flying hours. One of the survivors was donated to the museum who loaned it to the USAF Museum in Ohio in 1957. This historic biplane returned to California in the early 1990s. At the current time both aircraft are in store; the Nighthawk here and the DWC at the Museum of Flying (CA96) which is planning to open a new facility and the DWC will be back on show.

TYPE	REG/SER	CON. NO.	PI/NOTES	STATUS
☐ Cocke Nighthawk				RA

LOS GATOS MONUMENT (CA80)

Location:	On permanent view in a children's playground in Oak Meadow Park in the town.

TYPE	REG/SER	CON. NO.	PI/NOTES	STATUS
☐ Lockheed 580 (T-33A)	53-5421	580-8760		PV

LOS RIOS COMMUNITY COLLEGE (CA81)

Address:	1919 Spanos Court, Sacramento, California 95825-3905.
Tel:	916-558-2587
Admission:	By prior permission only.
Location:	At the Executive Airport in the southern part of the city.

The college operates a number of sites in the region. The aviation programme is carried out at a facility on the east side of the airport. Four instructional airframes are known to be in use but there may be more.

TYPE	REG/SER	CON. NO.	PI/NOTES	STATUS
☐ Bell 205 Iroquois (UH-1D) (UH-1H)	66-16238	5932		RA
☐ Cessna 150J	N50743	15069523		RA
☐ Cessna 172L	N3965Q	17260065		RA
☐ Cessna 337M Super Skymaster (O-2A)	N464DF	337M0339	68-11063	RA

LOST BIRDS AVIATION HISTORICAL SOCIETY AND MUSEUM (CA82)

Address:	3712 North Rainbow Boulevard, Las Vegas, Nevada 89108.
Tel:	702-646-6524 Email: Info@Lostbirds.com
Admission:	By prior permission only.
Location:	At Mojave Airport which is just east of the town and at a storage site in Nevada.

Scroggins Aviation specialises in the resale and scrapping of large airliners. The museum was set up with the aim of preserving a few interesting types. The first project was to return to flying condition one of the several Convair 880s stored at Mojave. Some work was done but the project seems to have stalled.

TYPE	REG/SER	CON. NO.	PI/NOTES	STATUS
☐ Boeing 367-76-66 Stratofreighter (KC-97G) (KC-97L)	N971HP	17099	53-0317 – front fuselage only.	RA
☐ Boeing 720-023B	N1R	18022	N7536A, N1R, (N81R) – front fuselage only.	RA
☐ Convair 22-1 880	N812AJ	22-00-23	(N817TW), N8483H, N817TW	RAC
☐ Convair 22-1 880	N815AJ	22-00-35	N828TW	RA
☐ Douglas DC-3A (DC-3-201E)	N19968	3252	NC19968, N89C – front fuselage only.	RA
☐ Fairchild F-27A Friendship (F-27)	N753L	48	N2712R, N153L, N753L, C-GEGH, N274PH, (HR-???), N274PH, (YN-CER), N274PH	RAC
☐ Stinson V-77 Reliant (AT-19)	N329AG	77-57	42-46696, FK870, Bu11359	RAC

LOUIS A. TURPEN AVIATION MUSEUM (CA83)

Address:	San Francisco International Airport Terminal, Level Three, Burlingame, California 94128.
Tel:	650-821-9900 Fax: 650-821-9915 Email: curator@flysfo.com
Admission:	Sunday-Friday 1000-1630.
Location:	About 10 miles south of the city on the western shore of San Francisco Bay.

There are a number of museums in the airport buildings and one is devoted to the history of the airport and aviation on the Pacific Coast. A large library and archive collection has been gathered. The Arrow Sport F low wing monoplane first flew in 1934 and although over 100 were sold it had a marginal performance.

TYPE	REG/SER	CON. NO.	PI/NOTES	STATUS
☐ Arrow Sport F	NC18722	85	NC18722, N18722	PV

LYON AVIATION MUSEUM (CA84)

Address:	19300 Ike Jones Road, Santa Ana, California 92707-5229.
Tel:	714-210-4585 Fax: 714-210-4588 Email: info@lyonairmuseum.org
Admission:	Monday-Friday 1000-1500; Saturday 0900-1700.
Location:	At John Wayne Airport which is about 4 miles north of Newport Beach off Interstate 55.

The museum was founded by retired Air Force Major General William Lyon. In addition to the aircraft there are several military vehicles on show along with items of memorabilia.

The B-17G Fortress was once operated by the National Warplane Museum in New York State. The former Israeli C-47B flew in from Europe in 2006. The aim of the museum is to show significant events of the 20th century with particular emphasis on World War II.

The aircraft are displayed in period colours with a range of artefacts around them.

TYPE	REG/SER	CON. NO.	PI/NOTES	STATUS
☐ Boeing 299-O Fortress (B-17G) (CB-17G) (VB-17G)	'297400'	32204	44-83563, N9563Z	PVAX
☐ Cessna 305C Bird Dog (L-19E) (O-1E)				PVAX
☐ Douglas DC-3A-456 Skytrain (C-47A)	NC16005	19394	42-100931, N56U, CF-JUV, (N8153H), N394CA, N1944M	PVA
☐ Douglas DC-3A-467 Skytrain (C-47B)	N791HH	16375/33123	44-76791, 476791 (France), 1434 (Israel), 034/4X-FND	PVA
☐ Douglas A-26B Invader	N34538	27817	44-34538, 434538 (France), N6839D	PVA
☐ North American NA-108 Mitchell (B-25J) (TB-25N)	NL25GL	108-32740	44-29465, N3523G	PVA

California

MARCH FIELD AIR MUSEUM (CA85)

Address:	16222 Interstate 215, Box 6463, March Reserve Base, California 92518-6463.
Tel:	951-902-5949 Fax: 951-697-6605 Email: info@marchfield.org
Admission:	Tuesday-Friday 1000-1600; Saturday-Sunday 1200-1600.
Location:	On Interstate 215 about 4 miles south east of Riverside.

March Field, one of the oldest bases in the USA, was activated in March 1918 and is named after Lieutenant Peyton C. March, who died after crashing earlier that year. Over the years the field has housed many units and is currently a Reserve base.

A museum opened on 19th December 1979 and the then Commander of the 15th Air Force, General James Mullins, had ideas that it should develop into a West Coast Air Force Museum. A display was set up in a building on the base and some of the smaller aircraft were inside with a few more around the hall. The majority of the collection was parked on the flight line and visitors were taken by bus to view these. This situation was not ideal and a foundation was set up to raise money for a purpose-built structure.

In early 1993 a large hangar with associated offices opened off the base near the local main highway. The museum is now a privately run organisation. The indoor display traces the history of March Field, its units and personnel. The early times are told in great detail with several fascinating items on view. There are many models, photographs, components, uniforms, engines and documents on view along with some of the smaller aircraft.

One of the few surviving Bell Airacomets is displayed. Only 66 were built and although unsuitable for combat duties they trained ferry pilots for the next generation of jet fighters. The large outside display contains one of the two Northrop A-9As built to compete in the attack role with the Fairchild-Republic A-10A.

Restoration of the outside aircraft is proceeding and the interior of the B-17 has been brought back to its original state. The aircraft spent many years in Bolivia carrying meat and other freight. The Fleet 7 is painted in its original military colours. Small numbers of the biplane were acquired for training duties in the early 1930s.

TYPE	REG/SER	CON. NO.	PI/NOTES	STATUS
☐ Aero Commander 520 (YL-26) (YU-9A)	52-6218	520-21		PV
☐ Antonov An-2R	'44'	1G 165-50	CCCP-19736, N22AN – in false Soviet markings.	PVX
☐ Beech D18S Expeditor (C18S) (C-45F) (UC-45F) (JRB-4) (SNB-5)	'4588'	8222	44-86963, Bu44588, N9657, '52-10588'	PVX
☐ Bell 26E Airacobra (P-39Q)	42-20000			PV
☐ Bell 27 Airacomet (P-59A)	44-22614	27-22		PV
☐ Bell 204 Iroquois (UH-1F)	63-13143	7003	63-13143, N32281	PV
☐ Bell 209 Huey Cobra (AH-1G) (AH-1F)	69-16416	20848		PV
☐ Bensen B-8M Gyrocopter				PV
☐ Boeing 234 (P-12E) (R)			Due soon.	-
☐ Boeing 299-O Fortress (B-17G) (CB-17G) (VB-17G) (CB-17G) (VB-17G)	44-6393	22616	44-6393, CP-627, CP-891, '230092' – rebuilt with parts of c/n 9300 43-38322, N66568, CP-80, CP-580	PVX
☐ Boeing 345 Superfortress (B-29A) (SB-29)	44-61669	11146	44-61669, N3299P	PV
☐ Boeing 367-76-66 Stratofreighter (KC-97G) (KC-97L)	53-0363	17145		PV
☐ Boeing 450-157-35 Stratojet (B-47E)	53-2275	4501088		RA
☐ Boeing 450-157-35 Stratojet (B-47E) (FSM)			Front fuselage only.	PV
☐ Boeing 464-201-7 Stratofortress (B-52D)	55-0679	464026		PV
☐ Boeing 464-259 Stratofortress (B-52E)	56-0700	464071	Front fuselage only.	RA
☐ Boeing 717-100A Stratotanker (KC-135A)	55-3130	17246		PV
☐ Boeing-Stearman A75N1 Kaydet (PT-17)	N49379	75-4551	42-16388.	PV
☐ Cessna 318B Tweety Bird (318A) (T-37A) (T-37B)	57-2316	40249		PV
☐ Cessna 318E Dragonfly (A-37B)	71-0790	43328	71-0790, (SNVAF)	PV
☐ Cessna 337A Super Skymaster (O-2B)	67-21465	3370261	N6261F	PV
☐ Convair 8-10 Delta Dagger (F-102A)	56-1114	8-10-331		PV
☐ Convair 340-67 Samaritan (VC-131D)	54-2808	204	N8425H	PV
☐ Curtiss 35 Hawk (P-6E) (Scale R)	'32-240'		N90DS	PVX
☐ Curtiss 87V Warhawk (P-40N) (FSM)	'44-7071'			PVX
☐ Douglas DC-3A-456 Skytrain (C-47A) (VC-47A)	43-15579	20045		PV
☐ Douglas DC-4 Skymaster (C-54D) (R5D-3) (C-54Q)	Bu56514	10741	42-72636, Bu56514, N67062	PV
☐ Douglas A-26C Invader	44-35224	28503	44-35224, N9421Z, N6240D	PV
☐ Douglas EA-1E Skyraider (AD-5W)	Bu132789	9385		PV
☐ Douglas TA-4J Skyhawk (TA-4F)	Bu154342	13730		PV
☐ Fairchild M-62A Cornell (PT-19B)	N54270	T43-5598	42-83011	PV
☐ Fairchild 110 Flying Boxcar (C-119F)	N8091	10906	22122 (Canada)	PV
☐ Fairchild 473 Provider (205) (C-123B) (C-123K)	54-0612	20061		PV
☐ Fleet 7 (YPT-6A)	30-385	326	30-385, NS51, NC13933, N13933	PV
☐ Folland Fo.141 Gnat F.1	E1076			PV
☐ General Dynamics FB-111A	68-0245	B1-17		PV
☐ Grumman G-111 Albatross (G-64) (UF-1G) (UF-2G) (HU-16E)	1293	G-370		PV
☐ Grumman G-303 Tomcat (F-14A)	Bu157990	11		PV
☐ Hughes 369M Cayuse (HO-6) (OH-6A)	68-17252	1212		PV
☐ Lockheed 18-56-24 Lodestar (R5O-5)	'833538'	18-2358	Bu12473, N3968B, N1210, N1210L, N505R	PVX
☐ Lockheed 183-93-02 Starfighter (F-104A)	'70925'		Composite.	PVX
☐ Lockheed 300 Starlifter (C-141A) (C-141B)	65-0257	300-6108		PV
☐ Lockheed 580 (T-33A)	58-0513	580-1482		PV
☐ Lockheed SR-71A Blackbird	61-7975	2026		PV
☐ Martin 272B Canberra (B-57B) (EB-57B)	52-1519	102		PV
☐ McDonnell M.36BA Voodoo (F-101B)	59-0418	742		PV
☐ McDonnell M.98DE Phantom II (F-4C)	63-7611	689	On base.	RA
☐ McDonnell M.98DE Phantom II (F-4C)	63-7693	828		PV
☐ McDonnell M.98DF Phantom II (RF-4C)			Front fuselage only.	PV

☐ McDonnell M.98DF Phantom II (RF-4C)	63-7746	509		PV
☐ McDonnell M.98HO Phantom II (F-4E)	68-0382	3465		PV
☐ McDonnell M.199-1A Eagle (F-15A)	76-0008	186/A160		PV
☐ Mikoyan-Gurevich MiG-19S	0409	150409	0409 (Czechoslovakia)	PV
☐ Mikoyan-Gurevich MiG-21FR (MiG-21F-13)	1101	1611101	1101, N1101E – in Czechoslovakian markings.	PV
☐ Mikoyan-Gurevich MiG-23BN	5744	0393215744	In Czechoslovakian markings.	PV
☐ Nieuport 11 (Scale R)	'N437'			PVX
☐ North American NA-88 Texan (SNJ-4)	'Bu51360'		Identity unknown.	PVX
☐ North American NA-108 Mitchell (B-25J) (TB-25J) (TB-25N)	44-31032	108-34307	44-31032, N3174G	PV
☐ North American NA-165 Sabre (F-86D) (F-86L)	50-0560	165-106		RAC
☐ North American NA-203 Sabre (F-86H)	53-1304	203-76		PV
☐ North American NA-217 Super Sabre (F-100C)	54-1786	217-47	54-1786, '53608'	PVX
☐ North American NA-276 Sabreliner (T-39A) (CT-39A)	62-4465	276-18		PV
☐ Northrop N-156T Talon (T-38A)	60-0593	N.5166		PV
☐ Northrop N-160 Scorpion (N-68) (F-89D) (F-89J)	52-1949	N.4526		PV
☐ Northrop YA-9A	71-1368			PV
☐ Piasecki PD-22 Work Horse (H-21B) (CH-21B)	53-4326	B.76	53-4326, N6792	PV
☐ Republic F-84C Thunderjet (P-84C)	47-1595		47-1595, N2884D	PV
☐ Republic F-84F Thunderstreak	51-9432		51-9432, '71595'	PV
☐ Republic F-105B Thunderchief	57-5803	B-40		PV
☐ Republic F-105D Thunderchief	'62-4385'	D-582	62-4383.	PVX
☐ Sauser QC	N90DC	1		PV
☐ Schweizer SGS.2-8	N54301	15		PV
☐ Sikorsky S-61B Sea King (HSS-2) (SH-3A) (SH-3G)	Bu149688			PV
☐ Stinson V-76 Sentinel (O-62) (L-5)	N63085	76-249	42-15046	PV
☐ Vought A-7D Corsair II	69-6188	D18		PV
☐ Vultee V-74 Valiant (BT-13A)	41-1414	74-1524	41-1414, N54865 – mocked up as a Val 'BI-211'	PVX
☐ Vultee V-74 Valiant (BT-13A)	'41-1306'	74-5326	41-21487	PVX
☐ Vultee V-74 Valiant (BT-13A)			Fuselage only.	RAD
☐ WSK Lim-2 [MiG-15bis]	273		In Polish markings.	PV
☐ WSK Lim-5 [MiG-17F]	N170MG	1C 16-05	1605 (Poland)	PV

MARINE CORPS AIR GROUND COMBAT CENTER MUSEUM (CA86)

Address: PO Box 788101, Marine Corps Base, Twentynine Palms, California 92278.
Tel: 760-830-5471
Admission: By prior permission only.
Location: About 10 miles north of the town which is about 60 miles north east of Palm Springs.

Occupying over 900 square miles in the southern Mojave Desert, this base was first used in 1953. A small museum has been established with photographs, uniforms and documents on show.

The history of the site, the units which have served at Twentynine Palms and the tasks carried out are portrayed. The Skyhawk is parked outside along with a number of amphibious vehicles, tanks, artillery and personnel carriers.

TYPE	REG/SER	CON. NO.	PI/NOTES	STATUS
☐ Douglas A-4L Skyhawk (A4D-2N) (A-4C)	Bu145133	12379	.	PV

MERCED MONUMENT (CA87)

Location: On permanent view at the airport which is in the south western part of the town.

TYPE	REG/SER	CON. NO.	PI/NOTES	STATUS
☐ Lockheed 080 Shooting Star (P-80C) (F-80C) (TO-1) (TV-1)	'56467'		Possibly c/n 080-2084 47-1397, Bu33750	PVX

MILESTONES OF FLIGHT MUSEUM (CA88)

Address: PO Box 2585, Lancaster, California 93539.
Tel: 805-942-6555
Admission: Monday-Friday1000-1500; Saturday-Sunday 0800-1200.
Location: At Fox Field which is about 3 miles north west of the town on Avenue F.

This privately run collection was set up in the 1970s by Lee Embree and then called the Antelope Valley Air Museum. The current name was adopted in 1986. A considerable amount of material was collected but display space was limited. In the early 1990s a deal was arranged with Kermit Weeks who acquired a rare Havoc from the museum in return for the construction of a display hangar. The collection is now run in conjunction with a local technical college and students work on the smaller airframes which are in the building.

TYPE	REG/SER	CON. NO.	PI/NOTES	STATUS
☐ Aeronca 7BCM Champion (L-16A)	N4009B	7BCM-380	47-1005 – registered as a 7DC,	PVA
☐ Armstrong Whitworth AW.660 Argosy T.2 (C.1)	N1430Z	6779	XP447	PV
☐ Boeing 367-76-66 Stratofreighter (KC-97G) (C-97G)	53-0272	17054		PV
☐ Briegleb BG-12B	N9767C	12063		PVD
☐ Curtiss D Pusher (R)				PVD
☐ Fairchild 110 Flying Boxcar (C-119B)	N13745	10304	48-0722	PV

California

☐ Globe GC-1A Swift	N90302	316	NC90302	PV
☐ Great Lakes 2T-1A	NC11336	249	NC11336, N11336	PV
☐ Hawker P.1067 Hunter F.51	N72602	41H/680262	G-9-434, 47-403 (Denmark), E-403 (Denmark), – front fuselage only.	PV
☐ Morane-Saulnier MS.505 Criquet (MS.500) [Fieseler Fi 156 Storch]	NX41FS	605	605 (France)	PV
☐ North American NA-64 Yale	N3361	64-2183	3361 (Canada)	PV
☐ North American NA-82 Mitchell (B-25C)	N3968C	82-5886	41-13251, NL75635, 2502 (Dominican)	PVD
☐ Pietenpol B4-A Aircamper	N22EZ	001		PV
☐ Piper PA-22-125 Tripacer	N858A	22-159		PV
☐ Piper PA-38-112 Tomahawk	N6370A	38-78A0396		PV
☐ Polliwagen				PVD
☐ Rotorway Scorpion 1	N37801	021446		PV
☐ Ryan Navion A	N5139K	NAV-4-2039		PV
☐ Sikorsky S-55D Chickasaw (H-19D) (UH-19D)	55-4943	55995	55-4943, N95489	PV
☐ Sikorsky S-58 Seahorse (HUS-1N) (UH-34J)	N85128	580707	Bu143937	PV
☐ Stinson 105				PVD
☐ War Aircraft FW 190	N7334W	102		PV
☐ Wise RW.500				PV

MILITARY AIRCRAFT RESTORATION CORPORATION (CA89)

Address: 2977 Redondo Avenue, Long Beach, California 90806.
Admission: By prior permission only.
Location: Main base is at Chino Airport which is about 7 miles south of Ontario on Route 83.

This collection is part of the business empire of the Tallichet family. A workshop is maintained at Chino but the majority of the aircraft are at other locations in California and elsewhere in the country. Originally called Yesterday's Air Force, a headquarters was set up at Chino. Branches were established in Florida and Kansas and these later became separate entities.
  In the 1970s and 1980s many wrecked World War II aircraft were recovered from islands in the Pacific. Some machines are displayed at Tallichet's chain of Speciality Restaurants across the country. Aircraft are loaned to other groups who carry out restoration but these often move on to other organisations.
  It is almost impossible to obtain an accurate list of the collection as many complex private deals take place and many airframes have not been seen in public for years. Any information on the current state of affairs and the locations of some of the aircraft would be greatly appreciated.

TYPE	REG/SER	CON. NO.	PI/NOTES	STATUS
☐ Beech E18S	N9886A	BA-6	N3600B, PH-LPS, (HB-GBD), CN-MAQ	RAA
☐ Bell 26C Airacobra (P-39N)	42-18811			RAD
☐ Bell 26C Airacobra (P-39N)	42-19034			SD
☐ Bell 26E Airacobra (P-39Q)	42-19991			SD
☐ Bell 26E Airacobra (P-39Q)	42-19995			RAD
☐ Bell 26E Airacobra (P-39Q)	42-20339			SD
☐ Bell 26E Airacobra (P-39Q)	44-2438			SD
☐ Bell 26F Airacobra (P-39N)	42-18403			RAC
☐ Bell 26F Airacobra (P-39N)	42-18408			SD
☐ Bristol 149 Bolingbroke IVT	10073			S
☐ Bristol 152 Beaufort VIII	A9-210			SD
☐ Bristol 152 Beaufort VIII	A9-414			SD
☐ Bristol 152 Beaufort VIII	A9-535			SD
☐ Bristol 152 Beaufort VIII	A9-559			S
☐ Canadair CL-30 Silver Star 3 (CT-133) [Lockheed 580 (T-33AN)]	N84KK	T33-083	21083 (Canada), 133083 (Canada)	RAA
☐ Canadair CL-30 Silver Star 3 (CT-133) [Lockheed 580 (T-33AN)]	N479KK	T33-479	21479 (Canada), 133479 (Canada)	RAA
☐ Canadair CL-30 Silver Star 3 (CT-133) [Lockheed 580 (T-33AN)]	N483KK	T33-483	21483 (Canada), 133483 (Canada)	RAA
☐ Canadair CL-30 Silver Star 3 (CT-133) [Lockheed 580 (T-33AN)]	N560KK	T33-560	21560 (Canada), 133560 (Canada)	RAA
☐ Canadair CL-30 Silver Star 3 (CT-133) [Lockheed 580 (T-33AN)]	N571KK	T33-571	21571(Canada), 133571 (Canada),	RAA
☐ Canadair CL-30 Silver Star 3 (CT-133) [Lockheed 580 (T-33AN)]	N604KK	T33-604	21604 (Canada), 133604 (Canada)	RAA
☐ Cessna 172K	N7342G	17259042		RAA
☐ Consolidated 32 Liberator (B-24D) (B.III)	42-40461	1538	42-40461, BZ734, 599 (Canada) – front fuselage only.	RA
☐ Douglas A-24B Dauntless	42-54593	17432		RA
☐ Douglas A-24B Dauntless	42-54654	17493		RA
☐ Douglas A-26B Invader	N99425		(USAAF), 601 (Nicaragua)	RA
☐ Douglas A-26C Invader	N99422	18815	43-22668, N3691G, 602(Nicaragua)	RA
☐ Douglas A-26C Invader	N4810E	29167	44-35888	RAA
☐ Douglas DC-3A-405 Skytrooper (C-53)	N213MA	7320	42-47378, NC19917, N123BA	PVC
☐ Fairchild 473 Provider (205) (C-123B) (C-123K)	N87DT	20030	54-0581	RAA
☐ Fairchild 473 Provider (205) (C-123B) (C-123K)	N4112A	20110	54-0661	RAA
☐ Fairchild 473 Provider (205) (C-123B) (C-123K)	N94DT	20155	54-0706	RAA
☐ Fairchild M-62A Cornell (PT-19)				RAC
☐ Folland Fo.141 Gnat F.1	E296		In Indian markings	RA
☐ Folland Fo.141 Gnat F.1	E299		In Indian markings	RA
☐ Folland Fo.141 Gnat F.1	IE1214	GT.030	In Indian markings	RA
☐ Hawker Fury FB.10				RA
☐ Hawker Fury FB.10				RA

157

☐ Lockheed 182-1A Hercules (182-44-03) (C-130A)	N223MA	182-3108	56-0500, 60500 (South Vietnam)	RAA
☐ Lockheed 237-27-01 Ventura (PV-1)				RA
☐ Martin 179 Marauder (B-26)	N4299S	1366	40-1501	RA
☐ Nord N.3202	N2253J	30	30	RA
☐ Nord N.3202	N2253W	41	41	RA
☐ Nord N.3202	N2253B	7	7	RA
☐ Nord N.3202	N2255W	84	84	RA
☐ North American NA-108 Mitchell (B-25J) (TB-25J) (TB-25N)	N9455Z	108-33485	44-30210	RAA
☐ North American NA-174 Trojan (T-28A)	N99414	'222'		RAA
☐ North American NA-174 Trojan (T-28A)	N8522Z	174-103	51-3565, 56 (France), CN-AEN, HR-232A	RAA
☐ Potez 842	N9878A	4	CN-MBC, CN-ALL	RA
☐ Stinson V-76 Sentinel (L-5)	N29846	76-709	42-98468, N66913	RAA
☐ Sud Fennec [North American NA-174 Trojan (T-28A)]	N99412	'122'		RAA
☐ Sud Fennec [North American NA-174 Trojan (T-28A)]	N9860A	174-522	51-7669, 2 (France)	RAA

MILLER COLLECTION (CA90)

Address: 6520 Gordon Valley Road, Suisun City, California 94585-9617.
Admission: By prior permission only.
Location: At Nut Tree Airport which is about 3 miles north east of Vacaville of Interstate 505.

This private collection contains two former water bomber Harpoons which operated in several states on the west side of the country. A C-47 has recently moved to the museum at Travis Air Force Base.

TYPE	REG/SER	CON. NO.	PI/NOTES	STATUS
☐ Boeing-Stearman A75 Kaydet (PT-13B)	N52740	75-274	40-1717	RAA
☐ Boeing-Stearman A75N1 Kaydet (N2S-4)	N61248	75-7933	Bu38312	RAA
☐ Boeing-Stearman E75 Kaydet (PT-13D)	N4737V	75-5593	42-17430	RAA
☐ Lockheed 15-27-01 Harpoon (PV-2)	N10PV	15-1182	Bu37216, N7256C	RAA
☐ Lockheed 15-27-01 Harpoon (PV-2)	NL20PV	15-1490	Bu37524, N7262C	RA
☐ Lockheed 18-56-23 Lodestar (C-60A)	N6711	18-2484	42-56011, N67H	RA
☐ North American NA-200 Trojan (T-28B)	N130AS	200-174	Bu138103	RAA
☐ North American NA-200 Trojan (T-28B) (DT-28B)	N93AW	200-390	Bu138319	RAA
☐ Piper J-3C-65 Cub	NC30669	5009	NC30669, N30669	RAA
☐ Stinson V-77 Reliant (AT-19)	NC1141/'FK861'	77-48	42-46687, FK861, Bu11548, NC1141, N1141	RAA
☐ Vultee V-79 Valiant (BT-13B) (SNV-2)	'290026'	79-999	42-90106, (USN), N63282	RAAX

MINTER FIELD AIR MUSEUM (CA91)

Address: 401 Vultee Avenue, Shafter Airport, Route 1, Bakersfield, California 93263-4031.
Tel: 661-393-0291   **Fax:** 661-393-3296   **Email:** mfam@minterfieldairmuseum.com
Admission: Saturday-Sunday 1200-1600.
Location: About 8 miles north west of Bakersfield off Route 99.

Minter Field was an important World War II training base. Many of the original buildings still survive and the museum has set up a display tracing the history of the site.
The airfield opened in 1941 and was dedicated the following year. At one time over 7,000 people were based at Minter. The site is named after local World War I pilot Hugh C. Minter who was killed in a mid-air collision over March Field in July 1936.
The indoor exhibition, which is steadily being improved, contains many photographs, documents, uniforms and models. The aircraft in the collection are slowly being restored to display condition.

TYPE	REG/SER	CON. NO.	PI/NOTES	STATUS
☐ Aeronca 65TC Grasshopper (O-58B) (L-3B)	N48850	3262	(USAAF)	PVD
☐ Atlas-Aermacchi MB.326M Impala I	N153TP	6371/A18	493 (South Africa)	PV
☐ Bell 209 Huey Cobra (AH-1G) (AH-1F)	66-15327	20083		PV
☐ Boeing-Stearman A75N1 Kaydet (PT-17)				PVA
☐ Boeing-Stearman A75N1 Kaydet (PT-17)	N3946	75-1910	41-8351, N60925	PVA
☐ Boeing-Stearman E75 Kaydet (PT-13B)	N46590	75-0297	40-1740	PVA
☐ Cessna T-50 Bobcat (AT-17)	N73580	2060	42-0361	PV
☐ Fokker Dr I (R)				PV
☐ Lockheed 580 (T-33A)	53-6001	580-9533	Front fuselage only.	PV
☐ Lockheed 580 (T-33A) (TV-2) (T-33B)	Bu138995	580-9211	54-2707	PV
☐ Pietenpol B4-A Aircamper				RA
☐ Ryan ST-3KR Recruit (PT-22)	N47708	1731	41-15702	PVA
☐ Sikorsky S-58 Seabat (HSS-1) (UH-34G)	Bu140122	580116		PV
☐ Stinson V-76 Sentinel (L-5G)				RA
☐ Vultee V-54D Valiant (BT-13)	N75789	54-5997	41-22077 (?)	PVC

MOFFETT FIELD MUSEUM (CA92)

Address: PO Box 16, Moffett Field, Moffett Boulevard, California 94035-0016.
Tel: 650-603-9827   **Email:** moffetthistory@mail.org.nasa.gov
Admission: Wednesday-Saturday 1000-1400; First and Third Sunday in month 1200-1400.
Location: About 15 miles north of San Jose off Highway 101.

California

This field opened in 1933 to serve as an airship station and an Army training base. The giant hangars still survive. Hangar One, which is almost 200 feet high, was built in the 1930s to house the USS *Macon*. This structure has been designated as a Naval Historical Monument. In the post-war years the field was home to patrol squadrons until its closure in the mid-1990s. A P-2 Neptune and a P-3 Orion are preserved on the field. These types served with the Navy for many years. A museum has been set up tracing the history of the base and many interesting photographs, models and items of memorabilia can be seen. At the current time NASA Ames operates the site as Moffett Federal Airfield but there are only a few movements each day.

TYPE	REG/SER	CON. NO.	PI/NOTES	STATUS
☐ Lockheed 185 Orion (P3V-1) (P-3A)	Bu150509	185-5035		RA
☐ Lockheed 426-42-13 Neptune (P2V-5) (P2V-5FD) (DP-2E)	Bu128393	426-5239		RA

MOJAVE SPACEPORT LEGACY PARK (CA93)

Address: 1234 Flightline, Mojave, California 93501.
Tel: 661-824-2433 **Email:** wdeaver@mojave.ca.us
Admission: On permanent view.
Location: At the airport which is just east of the town off Route 58.

The park was dedicated on 22nd August 2008 to portray the contributions Eastern Kern County has made to aerospace work. An interactive kiosk has been built to inform the visitor. The 64 feet high Roton was designed for space work and built by Scaled Composites in 1999. Only three flights, reaching a height of 75 feet, were made. A replica of Burt Rutan's Space Ship One can also be seen.

The Coronado, once flown by NASA, and the Phantom are preserved by the airfield gate. Also on show is an early mine cart used in the area.

TYPE	REG/SER	CON. NO.	PI/NOTES	STATUS
☐ Convair 30A-5 Coronado 990	N810NA	30-10-29	N5617, N713NA, N710NA	PV
☐ McDonnell M.98DJ Phantom II (F-4C)	64-0741	1023	64-0741, N403FS – on loan from AFFTM, CA.	PV
☐ Rotary Rocket Company Roton ATV		001		PV
☐ Scaled Composites 316 SpaceShipOne (R)	'N328KF'			PVX

MOUNT SAN ANTONIO COLLEGE AVIATION CENTER (CA94)

Address: 1100 North Grand Avenue, Walnut, California 91789.
Tel: 909-594-5611 **Email:** hlawrence@mtsac.edu
Admission: By prior permission only.
Location: By the entrance to Brackett Field which is just south of La Verne.

The college opened in 1946 to serve the community in the Walnut suburb of Los Angeles. The aviation department trains pilots and air traffic controllers at Brackett Airport. Maintenance training takes at the airfield and the campus. The Sabre was acquired many years ago and may have now departed.

TYPE	REG/SER	CON. NO.	PI/NOTES	STATUS
☐ Beech B24R Sierra 200	N918CD	MC-398		RA
☐ Cessna 150M	N714GM	15079165		RA
☐ Cessna 152	N48968	15281080		RA
☐ Cessna 152	N94364	15285655		RA
☐ North American NA-201 Sabre (F-86D) (F-86L)	N12400	201-598	53-4064	RA
☐ Vans RV-6A	N47PR	001		RA

MUSEUM OF AMERICAN AIRCRAFT (CA95)

Address: 21025 Skywest Boulevard, Hayward, California 94541-4607.
Tel: 510-783-2711
Admission: By prior permission only.
Location: At Hayward Municipal Airport which is about 2 miles east of the town on Hesperia Boulevard.

This private collection of warbirds and classics is owned by Mike Coutches who runs an overhaul and sales business at the airport. One of the Mustangs and the Hellcat spent a long period on display at the now closed Wagons to Wings Museum at Morgan Hill. Only 14 Pinto jets were acquired by the US Navy in 1957 and they had a brief service life before being withdrawn. Mike Coutches bought three. He was unfortunately injured when one crashed in July 1987 but has made a full recovery.

The Bearcat in the collection saw service with the US Navy until in was sold on the civilian market in 1959. Mike Coutches acquired it five years later.

Also in the hangars is an example of the earlier Hellcat. Designed to replace the successful Wildcat the F6F made its maiden flight in June 1942. The first production examples were operational in 1943 aboard the USS *Essex*. When the last one left the factory in 1945 12,275 had been completed. The last ones were withdrawn in Uruguayan service in 1960.

The Republic Seabee amphibian was developed from the C-1 and C-2 which appeared in the last years of World War II. The prototype RC-3 flew late in 1945 and was soon put into production. Just over 1,000 left the factory before the line was closed. Access to this collection is often difficult.

TYPE	REG/SER	CON. NO.	PI/NOTES	STATUS
☐ Beech A45 Mentor (T-34A)	N6122G	1007		RAA
☐ Beech D45 Mentor (T-34B)	N10006	BG-72	Bu140738	RAA
☐ Bellanca 7KCAB Citabria	N53897	559-76		RAA
☐ Cessna 172M	N64262	17265135		RAA
☐ Cessna 182J Skylane	N3069F	18257169		RAA
☐ Cessna 310R	N3458G	310R0842		RAA
☐ Culver LFA Cadet	N34788	LFA-248	NC34788	RAA
☐ Culver LFA Cadet	N41607	LFA-366	NC41607	RAA

☐ Culver LFA Cadet	N41729	LFA-450	NC41729	RAA
☐ Grumman G-50 Hellcat (F6F-5)	N7861C	A-12137	Bu94385	RAC
☐ Grumman G-58 Bearcat (F8F-2)	N818F	D.1053	Bu121679, N4992V	RAA
☐ North American NA-66 Harvard II	N28500	66-2583	2850 (Canada), CF-MIV	RAA
☐ North American NA-122 Mustang (P-51D)	N5074K	122-39540	44-73081	RA
☐ North American NA-124 Mustang (P-51D)	N4223A	124-44720	44-84864, NACA126	RAA
☐ North American NA-126 Mustang (P-51H)	N551H/'464551'	126-37740	44-64314, N1108H	RAAX
☐ North American NA-159 Trojan (T-28A)	N2814G	159-46	49-1534	RAA
☐ Piper J-3C-65 Cub	N24889	3515	NC24889	RAA
☐ Republic RC-3 Seabee	N6232K	435	NC6232K	RAA
☐ Republic RC-3 Seabee	N6317K	540	NC6317K	RAA
☐ Republic RC-3 Seabee	N6485K	739	NC6485K	RA
☐ Ryan ST-3KR Recruit (PT-21)	N2022	1054	41-1933, N53834	RAA
☐ Schweizer SGS.1-26D	N7577	474		RAA
☐ Temco T.51 Pinto (TT-1)	N8K	TE-5	Bu144227, N4091B	RAD
☐ Temco T.51 Pinto (TT-1)	N2695B	TE-14	Bu144236, N7756A	RAC

MUSEUM OF FLYING (CA96)

Address:	2425 Olympic Boulevard, Santa Monica, California 90404.
Tel:	310-752-0555 Email: dryan@museumofflying.com
Admission:	Not yet open.
Location:	About three miles east of the city off Interstate 10.

The Douglas Aircraft Company set its main factory at Santa Monica in 1928. A larger plant was constructed at Long Beach in World War II and eventually all production was transferred to the new site. The factory on the south side of the airfield closed in 1972 and was subsequently demolished. The Donald Douglas Museum and Library was set up on the south side.

A new facilty was built on the north area housing the Museum of Flying. This opened in 1988 and had an interesting collection of aircraft on show. This closed a few years ago and plans for a new museum have been put forward. Funds are being raised and more than half the sum required for the building has been collected.

The opening of the exhibition is not too far away. Aircraft are being acquired and more interesting types have been promised. The museum will incorporate the California Aviation Hall of Fame where local aviators will be honoured.

The mezzanine will feature a replica of the Douglas Aircraft Company Exective Boardroom and a recreation of Donald W. Douglas' original office. The history of the famous company will be portrayed with many photographs, models and documents. The round-the world flight Douglas DWC will once again occupy pride of place in the exhibition. The story of this epic journey will be portrayed in detail with many photographs, maps and memorabilia on view.

The first flight of the DC-3 took place from Santa Monica on 17th December 1935. The museum acquired an example of the famous type a few years ago and this is now mounted at the field. The replicas of the Wright Flyer and the Lockheed Vega featured in the film 'Night at the Museum – Battle of the Smithsonian'. Other movie stars are the BD-5J from the James Bond film 'Octopussy' and The Kaydet which flew in 'Spacecamp'.

TYPE	REG/SER	CON. NO.	PI/NOTES	STATUS
☐ Bede BD-5J				RA
☐ Boeing 727-200			Front fuselage only.	RA
☐ Boeing-Stearman A75N1 Kaydet (PT-17)	N555BF	75-2305	41-8746, N55132	RA
☐ Convair 240			Front fuselage only.	RA
☐ Douglas DC-3A-405 Skytrooper (C-53) (R4D-3)	N242SM	4877	41-20107, Bu05075, (NC36984), NC1075M, N60R, N596AR	PV
☐ Douglas DWC	23-1232	148	On loan from Los Angeles County Museum of Natural History.	RAC
☐ Fokker Dr I (FSM)				RAX
☐ Ercoupe 415C				RAA
☐ Lockheed 5B Vega (R)				RAX
☐ Lockheed 18-56-23 Lodestar (C-60A)				RAA
☐ Lockheed 580 (T-33A)			Front fuselage only.	RA
☐ North American NA-88 Texan (AT-6D) (SNJ-5)				RAA
☐ North American NA-122 Mustang (P-51D)	NL151DP	122-40513	44-73973, 9281 (Canada), N6325T, 407 (El Salvador), (N35DD), N37FF, N51JC, C-GJCJ, N51JC	RAA
☐ Quickie Aircraft Quickie 2 (Rutan 54)				RA
☐ Rutan 27 Vari-Viggen				RA
☐ Waco 10 (GXE)				RA
☐ Wright Flyer (R)				RA
☐ Yakovlev Yak-3				RA

MUSEUM OF FORGOTTEN WARRIORS (CA97)

Address:	5865 A Road, Marysville, California 96901.
Tel:	530-742-3090 Email: cws21779@aol.com
Admission:	Thursday 1900-2100; Saturday 1000-1500.
Location:	About 5 miles east of the town just south of the road to the main gate of Beale Air Force Base.

This small privately run museum has two helicopters in its collection. The indoor displays honour the many military personnel who gave their lives carrying out routine duties during conflicts. There are a number of personal items to be seen. The Hiller Raven served with distinction in Korea and the Iroquois in Vietnam.

TYPE	REG/SER	CON. NO.	PI/NOTES	STATUS
☐ Bell 204 Iroquois (UH-1C)	65-9472	1372		PV
☐ Hiller UH12C Raven (H-23G) (OH-23G)	61-3163	1349	61-3163, N64279	PV

This composite Anson is displayed at the Aerospace Museum of Calgary. (Nigel Hitchman) [AB3]

Above: On show at the Alberta Aviation Museum is this Noorduyn Norseman IV. (Dick Barrett) [AB4]

Right: This Avro Avian can be seen at the Reynolds Alberta Museum. (Nigel Hitchman) [AB22]

C2

The Western Canada Aviation Museum recovered this Vickers Vedette from a site in the bush. The flying boat has been rebuilt and is now on show. (John Mounce) [MB12]

The only surviving twin engined German bomber of World War I is this AEG GIV. The aircraft is displayed at Canada's Air and Space Museum at Rockcliffe. (Dick Barrett) [ON8]

This Republic Seabee can be seen in the Canadian Bushplane Heritage Museum at Sault Ste Marie. (CBHM) [ON11]

This rare Fleet 21 is part of the Canadian Warplane Heritage at Hamilton. (Richard Hamblin) [ON20]

Vintage Wings of Canada operate this Waco ATO. (Nigel Hitchman) [PQ10]

Only a few Pheasant H-10s have survived and this example is at the Western Development Museum in Moose Jaw. (Ruud Leeuw) [SK4R]

On show at the United States Army Museum at Fort Rucker is Piper L-4 in a typical field setting. (John Mounce) [AL36]

This Grumman Albatross formerly operated by the United States Coast Guard is displayed at the USS Alabama Park near Mobile (John Mounce) [AL37]

The Alaska Aviation Heritage Museum on the shores of Lake Hood owns this Grumman Goose. (Nigel Hitchman) [AK3]

Parked outside at the Pima Air and Space Museum is this Sikorsky S-43 painted in false military colours. (Nigel Hitchman) [AZ30]

John Siebold keeps his collection of classic aircraft at Valle Airport. Pictured here is his Curtiss Robin. (Nigel Hitchman) [AZ37]

The Aerospace Museum of California at the former McClellan Air Force Base has a few civil aircraft on show including this Travel Air 14-B. (Alec Berry) [CA3]

The Southern California Wing of the Commemorative Air Force keeps in flying order an example of the Polikarpov I-16. (Alec Berry) [CA45]

On show at the Flying Leatherneck Aviation Museum is this General Motors built Grumman Wildcat. (John Mounce) [CA57]

The impressive Hiller Aviation Museum at San Carlos has this early Monocoupe 70 on show. (Nigel Hitchman) [CA65]

C7

This Vultee BT-13A Valiant has been mocked up to represent a Japanese 'Val' dive bomber. The aircraft is at the March Field Museum. (Alec Berry) [CA85]

Planes of Fame founded by Ed Maloney has many interesting aircraft in their exhibition halls. Shown here is a Douglas SBD-5 Dauntless (Dick Barrett) [CA111]

A number of large transport aircraft can be seen at the Travis Air Force Museum. Shown here is a Douglas C-124C Globemaster II. (Nigel Hitchman) [CA139]

A fairly new arrival at the New England Air Museum is this Waco ZKC-S. (Daniel Berek) (CT9)

Parked outside at the Air Mobility Command Museum at Dover Air Force Base is this former Canadian Fairchild C-119F painted in false USAF colours. (Juha Ritaranta) [DE1]

The Scaled Composite SpaceShipOne is now part of the Milestones of Flight section of the National Air and Space Museum in Washington, DC. (Nigel Hitchman) [DC3]

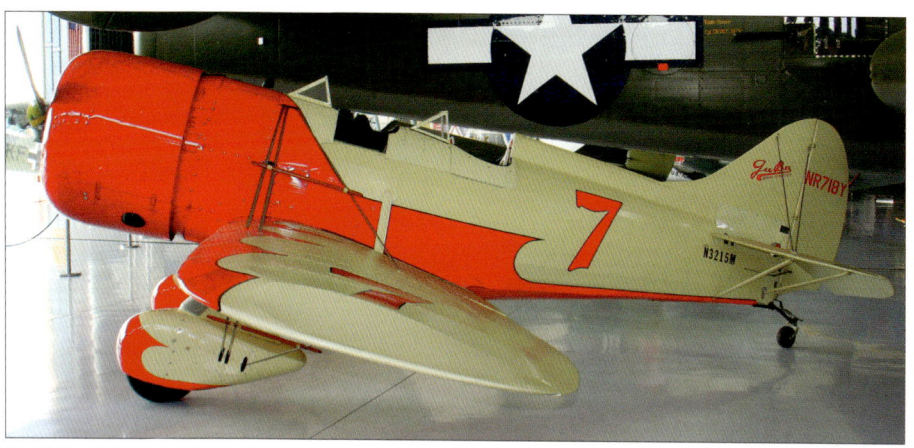

Kermit Weeks' Fantasy of Flight at Polk City is home to three replicas of the Granville brothers racers of the 1930s. Shown here is the Y model. (Juha Ritaranta) [FL22]

Displayed at the Florida Air Museum is this Convair YF2Y-1 Sea Dart. (Chris Chatfield) [FL23]

On show in the crowded hangar of the Kissimmee Air Museum is this Jensen Slipknot midget racer. (Dick Barrett) [FL42]

The crowded halls of the National Museum of Naval Aviation at Pensacola house many interesting aircraft including a Timm N2T-1 Tutor. (Dick Barrett) [FL55]

An exciting project in Georgia is the Candler Field Museum. Amongst its fleet of classic aircraft is this Stearman C3B in 1930s mail colours. (Ron Alexander) [GA17]

A view of part of the large outside exhibition area at the Museum of Aviation at Robins AFB. In the foreground is a Lockheed C-130 with a Lockheed NC-121 to the left. (Eric Dewhurst) [GA45]

On show in the Russell Military Museum is this Hughes OH-6A. (Glenn Chatfield) [IL62]

Only a few Convair B-58 supersonic bombers have been preserved. This example is at the Grissom Air Museum. (Eric Dewhurst) [IN20]

The Airpower Museum is the owner of this Rearwin 7000 Sportster.(Nigel Hitchman) [IA1]

This restored Waco CG-4A Hadrian can be seen at the Don. F. Pratt Memorial Museum at Fort Campbell (Eric Dewhurst) [KY5]

This superbly restored Cessna Bobcat is operated by the Bamboo Bomber Club. (Terry Sullivan) [LA3]

On show at the former England Air Force Base is this Republic F-84F Thunderstreak. (Duncan Kirk) [LA8]

A number of replicas are exhibited at the Owls Head Transportation Museum. Seen here is a Deperdussin Monocoque. (Richard Hamblin) [ME7]

This Taylorcraft BL-65 is on show in the museum at the historic College Park Airport. (Juha Ritaranta) [MD7]

Three aircraft, including this Lockheed C-130A Hercules, are on show in the National Vigilance Park at Fort Meade. (Nigel Hitchman) [MD16]

C14

This Boeing X-32B has been put on show at the Patuxent River Naval Air Museum. (Eric Dewhurst) [MD19]

This Curtiss P-40N was flown for many years at the Air Zoo by Sue Parish. The fighter has now been withdrawn from use and hangs in one of the halls. (Nigel Bailey-Underwood) [MI2]

The Yankee Air Museum owns this Armstrong-Whitworth Argosy. (Nigel Bailey-Underwood) [MI58]

C15

Two Pietenpol aircraft can be seen at the Fillmore County History Center. Shown here is an Aircamper. (Fillmore CHS) [MN15]

This F-101F Voodoo serves as a memorial in Proctor, Minnesota to two local aviators who lost their lives when an example of the type crashed in 1971. (Glenn Chatfield) [MN36]

Only two of the eleven Butler Blackhawks built are known to survive. This one is on show at the Science City in Kansas City. (Science City) [MO35]

This T-33 is parked outside the Valley County Pioneer Museum in Glasgow, Montana. (Glenn Chatfield) [MT15]

The Strategic Air and Space Museum has on display this Lockheed SR-71A. (David Skeggs) [NE23]

The Naval Air Station Wildwood Aviation Museum houses this Air and Space 18A autogyro. (Juha Ritaranta) [NJ21]

California

NATIONAL AERONAUTICS AND SPACE ADMINISTRATION – AMES RESEARCH CENTER MUSEUM (CA98)

Address:	Moffett Field, Mountain View, California 94035.
Tel:	650-604-6274
Admission:	Wednesday-Saturday 1000-1400.
Location:	About 15 miles north of San Jose off Highway 101.

The National Advisory Committee for Aeronautics opened the Ames Research Center in 1939. The complex houses the largest wind tunnel in the world along with a flight operations facility. Over the last 60 years many research programmes have been carried out at the site. A small museum, which highlights the history and the current work of Ames, has been set up in the Visitor Center. Photographs, models, documents, components, instruments and memorabilia can be seen. On weekdays there are tours of the complex. Two aircraft are on show outside the Center. The U-2 was flown in the Earth Resources Survey Programme, the ex-Luftwaffe F-104 Starfighter operated as a chase and test aircraft from the Dryden base. The diminutive AD-1 first flew from the Dryden base in December 1979 and was designed to test the flying characteristics of oblique wings. Much useful information was obtained from this project. The design is one from the fertile brain of Burt Rutan. This aircraft is currently on show in the nearby Hiller Aviation Museum. The Starlifter and Buffalo, which flew on other flight programmes, are parked on Moffett Field and can be seen when visiting the museum there.

TYPE	REG/SER	CON. NO.	PI/NOTES	STATUS
☐ De Havilland DHC.5 Buffalo QSRA (C-8A)	N715NA	2	63-13687	PV
☐ Lockheed 300-50A-01 Starlifter	N714NA	300-6110		PV
☐ Lockheed 583-10-20 Starfighter (TF-104G)	N825NA	583F-5939	KF+239, 2DF+365, (66-13628), 28+09	PV
☐ Lockheed U-2C (U-2A)	N708NA	348	56-6681, NASA708, N801X	PV

NATIONAL AERONAUTICS AND SPACE ADMINISTRATION – DRYDEN FLIGHT RESEARCH FACILITY (CA99)

Address:	PO Box 273, Edwards Air Force Base, California 93523-0273.
Tel:	661-276-3311
Admission:	Monday-Friday 0745-1530 – currently subject to security regulations.
Location:	In the Air Force Base which is east of Rosamond off Route 14.

In 1946 NACA, the forerunner of NASA, established a flight test base at Muroc Army Air Base. The site later became part of the vast Edwards Air Force Base complex. Since then the centre has been used for non-military advanced flight research. On 14th October 1947 Charles Yeager became the first pilot to break the 'sound-barrier' when he flew the Bell XS-1 from Muroc.
On 26th March 1976 the facility was named after Hugh L. Dryden who was NACA's Director of Research in the 1920s. Twice daily tours of the complex used to take place every weekday when visitors could see the aircraft used on current programmes. In the 1950s several 'lifting body' projects were considered and in the next decade some were built and flown in piloted space vehicle trials. The Northrop HL-10 was first flown as a glider in 1966 and was launched from below a B-52. The type made its powered flights two years later. The HL-10 achieved speeds of up to Mach 1.9 and reached an altitude of 90,000 feet.
One of the Crusaders on show was used for super critical wing research and the other in fly-by-wire programmes. Two Grumman X-29s were built for research work and on 13th December 1985 one became the first forward swept wing aircraft to reach Mach 1 in level flight. A replica of the North American X-15 is on show. This rocket powered research aircraft flew into the lower levels of space.

TYPE	REG/SER	CON. NO.	PI/NOTES	STATUS
☐ Bell 44 (XS-1) (X-1) (X-1E)		46-063		PV
☐ Grumman G-712 (X-29A)		82-0049	Rebuilt from Northrop N-156A Freedom Fighter (F-5A) c/n N.7021 65-10573, 573 (Norway)	PV
☐ Lockheed 683-04-10 Starfighter (RF-104G)	N826NA	683D-8213	KG+313, EB+114, 24+64,	PV
☐ Lockheed SR-71A Blackbird	N844NA	2031	61-7980	PV
☐ North American NA-240 (X-15) (X-15A) (FSM)	'66672'			PVX
☐ Northrop HL-10	N804NA			PV
☐ Vought F-8A Crusader (F8U-1)	N810NA		Bu141353	PV
☐ Vought F-8C Crusader (F8U-2)	N802NA		Bu145686	PV

NATIONAL TRAINING CENTER AND 11TH ARMORED CAVALRY REGIMENT MUSEUM (CA100)

Address:	Building 222, Fort Irwin, California 92310.
Tel:	760-380-6607 Fax: 760-380-6609 Email: IRWIN-Museum@conus.army.mil
Admission:	Monday-Friday 1100-1600
Location:	About 35 miles north east of Barstow.

This remote desert fort is used for training purposes. A small museum tracing the history and workings of the site is being set up in a former dining hall. Many vehicles, uniforms, photographs and personal items have been put on show. Displays showing the harsh conditions encountered by soldiers in their training are highlighted. Three of the helicopters are on poles in the Corporal Jerry Wayne Wickam Park He was killed in Vietnam in January 1968 and awarded the Medal of Honor for a single-handed attack on enemy bunkers.

TYPE	REG/SER	CON. NO.	PI/NOTES	STATUS
☐ Bell 204 Iroquois (UH-1C) (UH-1M)		66-0528	1510	PV

☐ Bell 205 Iroquois (UH-1H) (JUH-1H)	69-15312	11600		PV
☐ Bell 205 Iroquois (UH-1H)	70-15839	12449	Possible identity.	PV
☐ Bell 209 Huey Cobra (AH-1G) (AH-1F)	67-15776	20440		PV
☐ Bell 209 Huey Cobra (AH-1G) (AH-1F)				PV
☐ Hiller UH12C Raven (H-23G) (OH-23G)	'54-007'			PVX

NEVADA CITY MONUMENT (CA101)

Location:	On permanent view at Grass Valley Airport which is about 5 miles south of the town.

TYPE	REG/SER	CON. NO.	PI/NOTES	STATUS
☐ Lockheed 183-93-02 Starfighter (F-104A) (NF-104A)	'56-0751'	183-1044	56-0756	PVX

NORTH ISLAND NAVAL AIR STATION FLAG CIRCLE (CA102)

Address:	PO Box 357033, Halsey Field, San Diego, California 92135-7033.
Tel:	619-545-8167 Fax: 619-545-0182 Email: pao@cnrsw.navy.mil
Admission:	By prior permission only.
Location:	In the south western suburbs of the city

The site was first used by naval aircraft in 1912 and over the years has developed into a major airfield along with substantial port facilities capable of handling the largest aircraft carriers. The site was officially commissioned as a Naval Air Station in 1917 and took up its present name in 1955. Eight years later it was given official recognition as the 'Birthplace of Naval Aviation' by the House Armed Services Committee.

Five display aircraft are positioned around the Flag Circle which displays the badges of based units along with flags and guns. A bell from the Japanese carrier 'Junyo' is mounted in the circle. This was presented on behalf of Admiral Chester Nimitz by Rear Admiral W.L. Friedell, Commander of the 11th Naval District, on 24th November 1945.

The world's first seaplane flight was made nearby by Glenn Curtiss on 26th January 1911 and a plaque commemorates this feat. The other preserved types are currently stored around the airfield site. The USS Midway Museum has its workshops and storage area on the field and several aircraft are in residence.

TYPE	REG/SER	CON. NO.	PI/NOTES	STATUS
☐ Douglas A-4C Skyhawk (A4D-2N)	'Bu151134'	12709	Bu148516 –	RAX
☐ Grumman G-123 Greyhound (C-2A)	Bu152795	12		RA
☐ Kaman K-20 Seasprite (HU2K-1) (UH-2A) (SH-2F)	Bu149022	26		RA
☐ Lockheed 394 Viking (S-3A)	Bu159412	394A-3048		RA
☐ McDonnell M.267 Hornet (TF-18A) (F/A-18B)	Bu161714	62/B018		RA
☐ Sikorsky S-61B Sea King (HSS-2) (SH-3A) (SH-3G)	Bu149915			RA
☐ Sikorsky S-70B Sea Hawk (SH-60B)	Bu162983	70470		RA
☐ Vertol V.107M Sea Knight (HRB-1) (CH-46A) (HH-46A) (HH-46D)	Bu150951	2036		RA

NORTHROP GRUMMAN DISPLAY (CA103)

Location:	By prior permission only at the El Segundo factory at 1 Hornet Way.

TYPE	REG/SER	CON. NO.	PI/NOTES	STATUS
☐ Northrop N-156T Talon (T-38A)	N963NA	N.5116	59-1603	PV

NORTH VALLEY OCCUPATIONAL CENTER (CA104)

Address:	11450 Sharp Avenue, Mission Hills, California 91345.
Tel:	818-365-9645
Admission:	By prior permission only.
Location:	At Van Nuys Airport which is in the north western suburbs of Los Angeles off Interstate 405.

The college trains students in aviation and automobile maintenance. FAA courses in airframe and powerplant licenses are held. The fleet of instructional airframes is housed in the hangars at the airfield. The workshops also contain a number of engines, components and test rigs for a number of systems.

TYPE	REG/SER	CON. NO.	PI/NOTES	STATUS
☐ Beech D18S	N9112	A-546	N8652A	RA
☐ Bell 47G-3B-1 Sioux (TH-13T)	N90780	3620	66-8120	RA
☐ Bell 47G-3B-1 Sioux (TH-13T)	67-17103	3810		RA
☐ Bell 206A Kiowa (OH-58A) (OH-58C)	70-15204	40755	Possible identity.	RA
☐ Cessna 150H	N22858	15068567		RA
☐ Cessna 150L	N16102	15073478		RA
☐ Hughes 269A Osage (TH-55A)	N88041	118-1024	67-16917	RA
☐ Lockheed 580 (T-33A)	N17076	580-1400	57-0751, (N18853)	RA
☐ Piper PA-24-250 Comanche	N6863P	24-1969		RA
☐ Sikorsky S-62A Seaguard (HH-52A)	1426	62114		RA

OAKLAND AVIATION MUSEUM (CA105)

Address:	8252 Earhart Road, Boeing Street, PO Box 14264, Oakland, California 94614-2264.
Tel:	510-638-7100 Fax: 510-638-6530 Email: OAMdirector@att.net
Admission:	Wednesday-Sunday 1000-1600.
Location:	Near North Field which is about 5 miles south east of the city.

California

This organisation was formed in 1980 with the aim of preserving the rich aeronautical heritage of the area. On 7th December 986 an exhibition opened in Hangar 5 at the historic North Field. The building was constructed in 1929 and had seen use by Boeing Air Transport, Pacific Air Transport, the Boeing School of Aeronautics, the US Naval Air Reserve and had also served as the passenger terminal.

In late 1988 the museum moved a short distance to the World War II buildings of the Boeing School. North Field is one of the most historic airports in the world. Both civil and military aircraft operate from the site. The museum was first known as the Western Aerospace Museum and took up its present name in 2007. The inside display traces the history of local aviation with many interesting items on view. Engines, components, memorabilia and models are on view.

The collection of aircraft is varied and the outside park is dominated by the Short Solent owned by the Grant brothers. Three examples of the flying boat were acquired by Howard Hughes and spent many years beached at Oakland and Richmond. More types have recently joined the exhibition.

The Yugoslav Aero 3A trainer is the only one of its type in a US museum. Marcel Jurca was born in Romania in 1923 and flew Henschel Hs 129s in World War II. He moved to France after the war and built his first aircraft, a Jodel, in 1949. He then turned his hand to aircraft design and the single seat MJ-2 Tempête flew in 1956. Plans for this were sold and the two seat MJ-5 was ready in 1962. He then turned his attention to producing scale versions of famous World War II fighters. Plans for the North American P-51 Mustang, Focke-Wulf Fw 190, Messerschmitt Bf 109, Supermarine Spitfire and Curtiss P-40 appeared. The MJ-77 is a 2/3rds version of the P-51 and was marketed in North America by Falconar Aircraft in Canada.

The Lockheed 10 was bought in Alaska and flown to Oakland in 1989. This twin has now been restored in its original 1935 colours. The Arrow Sport F dates from the mid 1930s. Just over 100 examples of this low wing monoplane were built. A range of naval aircraft flown from California bases can be seen outside the main building. The exhibition also includes a number of homebuilt designs and ultralights including examples of the BD-5 and Vari-Eze.

TYPE	REG/SER	CON. NO.	PI/NOTES	STATUS
☐ Aerocycle Penguin				PV
☐ Arrow Sport F	NC17093	13	NC17093, N17093	PV
☐ Balloon Works Firefly 7 Hot Air Balloon	N1531P	A7145-S		RA
☐ Bede BD-5B	N325A	3555		PV
☐ Bede BD-5B				PV
☐ Beech M35 Bonanza				PV
☐ Bierman 1600R Eros	N464BB	MK703		PV
☐ Bücker Bü 133 Jungmeister (R)	N713S	11		PV
☐ Curtiss 50C Robin C-1	N389K	550	NC389K	PV
☐ Douglas DC-6B	N444SQ	45320	N579, SU-ANO, 4W-ABF, OY-STT, SE-ENZ, N515TP – front fuselage only.	PV
☐ Douglas KA-3B Skywarrior (A3D-2) (A-3B)	Bu147666	12430		PV
☐ Douglas NTA-4J Skyhawk (TA-4F) (TA-4J)	Bu154332	13720		PV
☐ Douglas A-4M Skyhawk	Bu158195	14232		PV
☐ Funk B	NC9000	B-2	NC9000, N9000	PV
☐ Grumman G-89 Tracker (S2F-1) (S-2A)	Bu136624	533	Front fuselage only.	PV
☐ Grumman G-128 Intruder (A-6A) (KA-6D)	Bu152910	I-214		PV
☐ Grumman G-303 Tomcat (F-14A) (NF-14A)	Bu160666	285		PV
☐ Hawker-Siddeley P.1127 Harrier T.54 (TAV-8A)	'N701NA'	T21	Bu159381	PVX
☐ Ikarus Aero 3A	N9105Y		40169 (Yugoslavia)	PV
☐ Jurca MJ.77 Mustang	N751JR	34P51B-01J.R.M.		PV
☐ Lockheed 10-A Electra	N38BB	1026	NC14937, NC241, NC756, N756, N4846V, N38PB	PV
☐ Lockheed 382-4B Hercules (C-130E)	64-0503	382-3987	Front fuselage only.	PV
☐ Lockheed 382-4B Hercules (C-130E) (WC-130E)	61-2360	382-3559	Front fuselage only.	PV
☐ Mikoyan-Gurevich MiG-15bis			2292 (China), NX90589,'1170'	PV
☐ McDonnell M.267 Hornet (F/A-18A)				PV
☐ Mono Aircraft Monocoupe 110	NC18629	6W00	NC18629, N18629 – On loan from Heritage Aircraft, PA.	PV
☐ North American NA-187 Sabre (F-86H)	52-2090	187-116		PVC
☐ North American NA-265 Sabreliner (T-39A) (CT-39A)	60-3504	265-32		RA
☐ Republic RF-84F Thunderflash	53-7524			RAC
☐ Rutan 33 Vari-Eze	N77NS	592		PV
☐ Rutan 33 Vari-Eze	N45LE	1491		PV
☐ Short S.45 Solent 3 (Seaford 1)	G-AKNP	S.1295	NJ203, G-AKNP, VH-TOB, N9946F, NJ203	PVC
☐ Stoddard-Hamilton SH-2 Glasair	N4473W	385		PV
☐ Ultralight Flying Machines Easy Riser				PV
☐ Vought A-7E Corsair II	'70-945'	E439	Bu159301 –	PVX
☐ Vultee V-74 Valiant (BT-13A)	N59842	74-5057	41-21218	PV
☐ Wright EX Vin Fiz (R)	N1VF	1		PV
☐ Zlin Z-526F Trenér Master	N29RW	1124	N840C	PV

OAKLAND MUSEUM OF CALIFORNIA (CA106)

Address: 1000 Oak Street, Oakland, California 94607.
Tel: 510-238-2200   **Fax:** 510-238-6838   **Email:** webmaster@museumca.org
Admission: Wednesday-Sunday 1000-1700.
Location: In the town which is just east of San Francisco across the bay.

There is a small aeronautical section, containing engines, photographs and models, in this interesting museum. A least 27 examples of the diminutive Irwin Meteroplane were constructed in Sacramento between 1919 and 1931. In addition many kits were supplied to amateur builders and several were completed and flew. The biplane with a span of only 20 feet and a length of 14 feet was powered by a 25 h.p. Irwin engine.

TYPE	REG/SER	CON. NO.	PI/NOTES	STATUS
☐ Irwin F-A-1 Meteroplane	N10685	125	NC10685	PV

ORANGE COAST COLLEGE (CA107)

Address: 2701 Fairview Road, Costa Mesa, California 92626.
Tel: 714-432-0202 **Email:** rfoster@occ.cccd.edu
Admission: By prior permission only.
Location: In the northern part of the town.

The college was set up in 1947 on part of the land formerly occupied by the Santa Ana Army Air Base. A pilot training programme leading to commercial licenses is part of the curriculum. The Airframe and Powerplant Technology course was started in 1970 and there is now a varied fleet of instructional airframes in use.

TYPE	REG/SER	CON. NO.	PI/NOTES	STATUS
☐ Aero Commander 680W	XB-DTD	1788-18	N5021E, N5E, N5EQ, N5EV, XA-DII, N5EV, XA-DII	RA
☐ Beech 200 Super King Air	N15NG	BB-666	N15NA	RA
☐ Beech C50 Seminole (L-23D) (U-8D)	58-3071	RLH-72		RA
☐ Bell 205 Iroquois (UH-1H)	66-16839	9033		RA
☐ Bell 205 Iroquois (UH-1H)	67-17704	9902		RA
☐ Brantly B.2B	N2159U	320		RA
☐ Cessna 150G	N3779J	15065079		RA
☐ Cessna 172N	N4883J	17273690		RA
☐ Cessna 310	N3038D	35238		RA
☐ Douglas DC-9-15			Front fuselage only.	RA
☐ Hughes 269C	N9683F	1010129		RA
☐ Hughes 369HS	N9274F	16-0781S		RA
☐ Nardi FN.333 Riviera	N914NS	0108		RA
☐ North American NA-265 Sabreliner (T-39A) (CT-39A)	'N0647R'	265-50	61-0647	RA
☐ Robinson R-22	N9031Y	0078		RA
☐ Sikorsky S-62A Seaguard (HH-52A)	N4341Q	62069	1388	RA

ORANGE COUNTY GREAT PARK AVIATION AND HERITAGE MUSEUM (CA108)

Address: PO Box 19575, Irvine, California 92623-9575.
Tel: 949-724-6247 **Fax:** 949-724-7407 **Email:** contact@ocgp.org
Admission: Not yet open.
Location: In the northern part of the town off Interstate 5.

The park is being developed on the site of the former El Toro Marine Corps Air Station which closed in 1999. Plans to convert the field into a commercial airport met with local opposition and were eventually dropped.

In 2007 it was decided to develop the site for recreational purposes. The aviation history will not be forgotten and the museum is in the early stages. Three aircraft are currently on the site with more to follow.

TYPE	REG/SER	CON. NO.	PI/NOTES	STATUS
☐ Howard Super Ventura (Lockheed 237-27-01 Ventura (PV-1))	N234P	237-5336	Bu33327, N64004, N234P, (N990PT) – complex see book.	RAA
☐ Naval Aircraft Factory N3N-3	N44879		Bu4425	RA
☐ North American NA-88 Texan (AT-6D) (SNJ-5)	N3685F	88-16183	42-84402, Bu43921	RAA

PACIFIC COAST AIR MUSEUM (CA109)

Address: 2330 Airport Boulevard, Santa Rosa, California 95403-8260.
Tel: 707-575-7900 **Fax:** 707-545-2813 **Email:** canavania@comcast.net
Admission: Tuesday, Thursday 1000-1600; Saturday-Sunday 1000-1600.
Location: At Sonoma County Airport which is about 5 miles north of Santa Rosa.

The idea of a museum was first put forward by owners of warbirds and classic aircraft in the North Bay area. A formal meeting was held in February 1990 with 16 pilots present. Initially the aircraft were housed in private hangars and taken out on special occasions. A setback occurred with the crash of a Lockheed Harpoon and the death of several members. Over the last few years the museum has begun to acquire a number of military jets and the private airworthy machines no longer feature in the display although some may be parked near the museum site for special events.

A small exhibition building has been constructed and photographs, models and memorabilia can be seen. The first aircraft to join the museum was the Douglas Invader which underwent a major restoration after moving to the field.

The F-8K Crusader was found in a poor condition in Larsen Park in San Francisco. Arrivals by air in 2004 included the A-6E Intruder. The fighter is now resplendent in its original Navy colours. Restoration of the Skyhawk has recently been completed and members are working on other airframes.

One of two former Polish Ilyushin Il-14s imported into the USA some years ago is a rare exhibit. This was made airworthy in Reno, Nevada and flown to the museum in August 1994. The Californian Department of Forestry has flown a fleet of Grumman Trackers from bases across the state. An example in their colours is now on view. Construction of the Bede BD-5J diminutive jet was started by a local homebuilder but he never completed the project. Funds are being raised to build a new building on another part of the airfield.

TYPE	REG/SER	CON. NO.	PI/NOTES	STATUS
☐ Bede BD-5J		4174	Unfinished.	PV
☐ Bell 205 Iroquois (UH-1H)	66-16779	8973		PV
☐ Boeing 367-76-66 Stratofreighter (KC-97G)			Front fuselage only.	PVD
☐ Cessna 318B Tweety Bird (318A) (T-37A) (T-37B)	57-2341	40274		PV
☐ Cessna 318B Tweety Bird (318A) (T-37A) (T-37B)	57-2343	40276	Fuselage only.	PV
☐ Convair 8-24 Delta Dart (F-106A)	59-0046	8-24-215		PV
☐ Douglas A-26B Invader	N5589A	7016	41-39303	PV

California

☐ Douglas DC-6A Liftmaster (R6D-1) (C-118A) (R6D-1) (C-118B)	N777SQ	43697	Bu131594, 51-17644, Bu131594, N1383X	RA
☐ Douglas DC-6B	N111AN	44087	HB-IBO, OH-DCB, HB-IBO, SX-DAM, N111AN, CF-QAN – front fuselage only.	PV
☐ Douglas A-4E Skyhawk (A4D-5)	Bu151194	13364		PV
☐ General Dynamics F-111D	68-0162	A6-78	Cockpit section only.	PV
☐ General Dynamics 401 Fighting Falcon (F-16N)	Bu163271	3M-4	85-1372 – on loan from NMNA, FL	PV
☐ Grumman G-89 Tracker (S2F-1) (S-2A) (TS-2A)	N443DF	195	Bu133224	PV
☐ Grumman G-111 Albatross (G-64) (UF-1G) (UF-2G) (HU-16E)	N70262/7245	G-334	7245	PV
☐ Grumman G-128 Intruder (A-6A) (A-6E)	Bu155595	I-321		PV
☐ Grumman G-303 Tomcat (F-14A)	Bu160889	318		PV
☐ Hawker-Siddeley P.1127 Harrier 50 (AV-8A) (AV-8C)	Bu158959	P120		PV
☐ Ilyushin Il-14P	N606RR	4340606	0606 (Polish)	PV
☐ Lockheed 580 (T-33A)	52-9380	580-7565		PV
☐ McDonnell M.98AM Phantom II (F-4B) (F-4N)			Front fuselage only.	PV
☐ McDonnell M.98DJ Phantom II (F-4C)	64-0823	1157		PV
☐ McDonnell M.199-1A Eagle (F-15A)	77-0102	385/A314		PV
☐ North American NA-159 Trojan (T-28A)				PV
☐ North American NA-191 Sabre (F-86F) (RF-86F)	52-4913	191-609	52-4913, 62-7428 (Japan)	PV
☐ North American NA-203 Sabre (F-86H)	53-1328	203-100	Identity doubtful.	PV
☐ Northrop N-156T Talon (T-38A)	62-3659	N.5364		PV
☐ Northrop N-311 Tiger II (F-5E)	72-1387	R.1007		PV
☐ Pitts S-1C Special	N17J	1		PV
☐ Republic F-84F Thunderstreak	52-6475			PV
☐ Republic F-105F Thunderchief	63-8331	F-108		PV
☐ Sikorsky S-58 Choctaw (H-34A) (CH-34A) (CH-34C)	57-1708	58868		PV
☐ Vought RF-8G Crusader (F8U-1P) (RF-8A)	Bu145608		Front fuselage only.	PV
☐ Vought F-8K Crusader (F8U-2) (F-8C)	Bu146995			PV
☐ Vought A-7A Corsair II	Bu153241	A150		RA

PALM SPRINGS AIR MUSEUM (CA110)

Address: 745 North Gene Autry Trail, Palm Springs, California 92262-5464.
Tel: 760-778-6262   **Email:** Sharon@PalmSpringsAirMuseum.org
Admission: Tuesday-Sunday 1000-1700.
Location: On the east side of Palm Springs Regional Airport which is about 2 miles north east of the town.

This modern museum opened in 1996 and is now home to the majority of Bob Pond's collection of warbirds. The complex consists of two well-lit exhibition halls with associated offices and workshops.
Bob Pond, a former Naval pilot, opened a museum in Minnesota in 1984 and then decided to move to California. Also transported to Palm Springs were a number of giant murals depicting World War II scenes. These paintings were restored by the original artist.
The Corsair on view saw combat in the 'soccer war' in El Salvador in 1969. There are a number of famous naval aircraft manufactured by the Grumman company. The Hellcat, Wildcat and Avenger all gave excellent service in World War II. The Bearcat on show was one of two civilian machines built in the late 1940s. The Nomad was designed and built by the Government Aircraft Factories at Fishermens Bend close to Melbourne in Australia. The STOL transport made its maiden flight in July 1971 and 172 were produced. A few were imported into America and the front fuselage of one is on show.
The airworthy aircraft have now been joined by a number of military jets representing the contributions made by the US service in recent years. The first of these to arrive were the F-14 and the F-16. Civil types also feature and an example of the Ercoupe 415 can be seen. The first flew in 1940 but justover 100 had been completed before the onset of World War II. At the end of the conflict the single engine monoplane went back into production and 5,685 were built by a number of companies up to 1970. The displays are being developed with many interesting items on view.

TYPE	REG/SER	CON. NO.	PI/NOTES	STATUS
☐ Bell 33 Kingcobra (P-63A) (RP-63A)	NX163BP		42-68864	PVA
☐ Bell 47G-3B-1 Sioux (TH-13T)	N170HF	3687	67-17005	PV
☐ Bell 206A Kiowa (OH-58A) (OH-58C)	68-16940	40254		PV
☐ Bell 209 Huey Cobra (AH-1G) (AH-1S)	67-15574	20238		PV
☐ Boeing 299-O Fortress (B-17G) (TB-17G) (VB-17G)	N3509G	8687	44-85778	PVA
☐ Boeing-Stearman B75N1 Kaydet (N2S-3)	N81235	75-7990	Bu38369	PVA
☐ Boeing-Stearman B75N1 Kaydet (N2S-3)	N9955H	75-8014	Bu38393	PVA
☐ Boeing-Stearman E75 Kaydet (PT-13D)	N5359N	75-5522	42-17359	PVA
☐ Consolidated 28-5A Catalina (PBY-5A)	N31235	1788	Bu48426	PVA
☐ Curtiss 87V Warhawk (P-40N) (TP-40N)	NX999CD	32824	44-7084, N999CD	PVA
☐ Da Vinci Glider (R)				PV
☐ Douglas DC-3A-467 Skytrain (C-47B) (Dakota IV)	44-76423	16007/32755	44-76423, KN381, K-39 (Belgium), 476423 (France), 4X-FNV/035, 4X-DCE, 4X-FMP/044, N60154	PVA
☐ Douglas SBD-5 Dauntless	Bu36176	4815		RAC
☐ Douglas A-26C Invader	N9425Z	29000	44-35721	PVA
☐ Douglas TA-4J Skyhawk (TA-4F)	Bu154649	13767		PV
☐ Ercoupe 415C	N86965	138	NC86965	PV
☐ General Dynamics 401 Fighting Falcon (F-16N)	Bu163277	3M-10	85-1378 –	PV
☐ Government Aircraft Factory N.24A Nomad	N4817E	N24A-77	VH-IIL – front fuselage only.	PV
☐ Grumman G-36 Wildcat (FM-2)	N47201	3268	Bu55627, N7906C	PVA
☐ Grumman G-58 Goose (JRF-6B) (Goose 1A)	N95950	1161	(BW814), FP511, Bu66331	PV
☐ Grumman G-40 Avenger (TBM-3) (TBM-3E)	'JR456'	3847	Bu53785, N7075C, NL7075C	PVAX
☐ Grumman G-50 Hellcat (F6F-5) (F6F-5N) (F6F-5K)	NX4964X	A-12225	Bu94473, N4964W	PVA

165

☐ Grumman G-51 Tigercat (F7F-3)	NX207F	C.154	Bu80412, N7628C	PVA
☐ Grumman G-58A Bearcat	NL700A	D.1262	N700A, N7700C	PVA
☐ Grumman G-96 Trader (TF-1) (C-1A)	N7171M	078	Bu146048	PV
☐ Grumman G-128 Intruder (A-6A) (A-6E)	Bu154162	I-297		PV
☐ Grumman G-134 Mohawk (AO-1B) (OV-1B)	59-2621	1B		PV
☐ Grumman G-303 Tomcat (F-14A)	Bu160898	327	On loan from NMNA, FL	PV
☐ Let C-11 [Yakovlev Yak-11]	N25YK	25111/25	(Egypt)	RAA
☐ Lockheed 15-27-01 Harpoon (PV-2)	N7273C	15-1177	Bu37211	PV
☐ Lockheed 580 (T-33A) (TV-2) (T-33B)	NX6633D	580-5327	51-4033, Bu126591, N335V	PV
☐ McDonnell M.98EV Phantom II (F-4J) (F-4S) (QF-4S)	Bu153851	2299		PV
☐ McDonnell M.267 Hornet (F/A-18A)	Bu162403	231/A183		PV
☐ Monnett Sonerai II				PV
☐ North American NA-108 Mitchell (B-25J) (TB-25J) (TB-25N)	'42-87293'	108-47501	44-86747, N8163H	PVAX
☐ North American NA-122 Mustang (P-51D)	NX151BP	122-41448	44-74908, 9273(RCAF), N1070Z, N965D	PVA
☐ North American NA-124 Mustang (P-51D)	NL251BP	124-44609	44-84753, N5436V, N51TC, (N51BE)	PVA
☐ North American NA-168 Texan (T-6G) (NA-88) (AT-6C)	N85JR	168-526	42-3890, 49-3402, N9882C-original c/n 88-11594	RAA
☐ North American NA-219 Trojan (T-28B)	NX28BP	219-40	Bu140041, N9995H	RAA
☐ Piper J-3C-65 Cub (J-3L)	N28118	4594	NC28118	RAA
☐ Republic P-47D Thunderbolt	'228473'	399-55744	45-49205, 547 (Peru), 122 (Peru) N47DE, G-BLZW, N47DE, NX47RP	PVA
☐ Ryan STA	NC17343	458	NC17343, N17343	PVA
☐ Sikorsky S-58 Seahorse (HUS-1) (UH-34D)	Bu154895	581805		PV
☐ Supermarine 379 Spitfire FR.XIVc	NX114BP	6S.648206	NH904, SG-108 (Belgium), G-FIRE N8118J	PVA
☐ Vought FG-1D Corsair	NX62290	3890	Bu92629, 215 (El Salvador), N62290 – previously reported as c/n 3790 Bu92529.	PVA

PLANES OF FAME AIR MUSEUM (CA111)

Address: 7000 Merrill Avenue, Suite 17, Chino, California 91710-9084.
Tel: 909-597-3722 **Fax:** 909-597-4755 **Email:** info@planesoffame.org
Admission: Daily 0900-1700.
Location: At Chino Airport which is about 7 miles south of Ontario on Route 83.

The origins of this museum date back to just after World War II when Ed Maloney began collecting aviation memorabilia. He later acquired some engines and larger components. In 1948 the first aircraft, a Mitsubishi Shusui, was purchased. This rocket powered interceptor, based on the Messerschmitt Me 163, had toured the country as an attraction and was residing in a California fairground.

The idea of a museum was born and at the time there were none on the West Coast. Progress was slow and the first exhibition opened at Claremont in 1957. This was not close to an airfield and the number of visitors was small. In 1965 a site at Ontario Airport was obtained and, with almost 50 aircraft in the hangars, business improved. Development at the airport forced a move and in 1969 the collection was transferred to Buena Park which housed the 'Movieland Cars of the Stars' museum. After a short time here the aircraft were taken to Chino Airport.

The museum has grown steadily over the years. There are now five large exhibition hangars, a workshop with a small display gallery attached and a store. In the early 1990s the Fighter Jets Museum was opened in a nearby hangar and in May 1993 the National Air Race Museum was set up in Nevada. The latter project was short lived and the majority of the racers were put in the Fighter Jets Hall. This has closed and a new hangar has been built on the main site to house these aircraft. 1995 saw the opening of a Grand Canyon branch at Valle Airport.

A highlight of the Chino exhibition is the display of World War II Japanese aircraft. The Zero is in flying condition and has made trips back to Japan where it has been seen by vast numbers of people. The Raiden and Shusui were for many years the only complete examples left but wrecks have been found in Japan and rebuilt to display standard. A crashed Mitsubishi 'Betty' bomber has been added to this section. In the early 1950s Ed acquired the remains of one of four Northrop N-9M flying wings built in the 1940s. This aircraft suffered during its many moves. A former Northrop employee saw the airframe and offered to put together a team to rebuild the historic machine. After some initial work at Chino and Hawthorne the project was moved to Signal Hill. In late 1993 the restored N-9 was trucked back to Chino for final assembly and it flew again the following November.

The World War I period is represented by a range of replicas of classic fighters from both sides of the conflict. In recent years replicas of a number of German World War II types have been built to add to the exhibition. A rarity is the only surviving Ryan FR-1 Fireball. The low wing fighter was powered by a Wright piston engine mounted at the front of the fuselage and a a General Electric jet in the rear. The concept was derived from the idea that the early jets were too sluggish for operations from carriers. The prototype few in June 1944 and only 66 were built. The example in the collection was flown by NASA at their Ames facility and was found in a local technical school. The museum holds regular open days when some of the airworthy types are displayed. Planes of Fame is a fitting tribute to the foresight of Ed Maloney who saved many aircraft from the scrapman in the 1940s and 1950s. He still plays a part in the running of this superb collection.

TYPE	REG/SER	CON. NO.	PI/NOTES	STATUS
☐ Aero L-29 Delfin	N495D	993219	30 (Soviet)	PVA
☐ Aichi D3A2-22	N3131G	3179	3179, CF-TZT, 'B11-201'	PVC
☐ Antonov An-2T	'05'	1G 27-22	HA-AND, N90400, NX90400	PVAX
☐ Bachem Ba 349A-1 Natter (BP 20) (FSM)				PV
☐ Beatty-Oram Hang Glider				PV
☐ Beech D18S Expeditor (C18S) (AT-7C) (SNB-2C) (JRB-4) (TC-45J) (UC-45J)	N86470	6321	43-33657, Bu51131	RA
☐ Beech D18S Expeditor (C18S) (JRB-3) (SNB-5) (TC-45J)	N4604		Bu89468	PV

California

☐ Bell 26C Airacobra (P-39N)	42-8784			RAD
☐ Bell 26C Airacobra (P-39N)	'42-19027'		42-4949	PVX
☐ Bell 27 Airacomet (YP-59A)	42-108777	27-3		PV
☐ Bell 44 (XS-1) (X-1) (FSM)	'6062'			PVX
☐ Bell 52 (XS-2) (X-2) (FSM)	'46-0674'			PVX
☐ Bensen B-8 Gyroglider	N4083K	AS-1		PV
☐ Boeing 67 Hawk (FB-5)	'A7126'	810	A7104	PVX
☐ Boeing 234 (P-12E)	NX3360G	1512	32-17, N3360G	PVA
☐ Boeing 266 Pea Shooter (P-26A)	NX3378G	1899	33-123, 0672 (Guatamala), N3378G	PVA
☐ Boeing 299-O Fortress (B-17G) (DB-17G) (DB-17P)	N3713G	32325	44-83684	PV
☐ Boeing 345-2-1 Superfortress (B-29D) (B-50A)	46-0010	15730	Fuselage only	PV
☐ Boeing-Stearman B75 Kaydet (N2S-2)	N61445	75-1335	Bu3558	PVA
☐ Boeing-Stearman E75 Kaydet (PT-13D)	N46CM	75-5122	42-16959, N5006V	RAA
☐ Boeing-Stearman E75 Kaydet (PT-13D)	N5186N	75-5754	42-17591	RAA
☐ Boland Mong Biplane				PV
☐ Bristol 14 F.2B Fighter (R)	'E2624'	2	N34HC	PVX
☐ Brown Miles and Atwood Special (R)	NR225Y	T-6		PV
☐ Bureau of Standards Bat				PV
☐ Callair A-4	N6036C	149		PV
☐ Canadair CL-30 Silver Star 3 (CT-133) [Lockheed 580 (T-33AN)]	N133AT	T33-157	21157, N155X	PVA
☐ Canadair CL-30 Silver Star 3 (CT-133) [Lockheed 580 (T-33AN)]	NX377JP	T33-377	21377, 133377	PVA
☐ Cavalier Mustang II (F-51D) (North American NA-122)	NL20TF		67-14866, 521 (Bolivia), C-GXUR, N20TF	RAA
☐ Cessna 305A Bird Dog (L-19A) (O-1A)	51-12129	22443	51-12129, N5235G, N305TA	PVA
☐ Cessna 305C Bird Dog (L-19E) (O-1E)	N4583V	24729	24729 (France)	PVA
☐ Chanute Glider (R)				PV
☐ Colomban MC-15 Cri-Cri	N128HJ	12-0128		PV
☐ Convair 105 (L-13A)	47-394	274		PV
☐ Convair 440 (340-41)	N138CA	63	(N3445), I-DOGI, OH-LRG, N3756Z – front fuselage only.	PV
☐ Culver LCA Cadet	NC29290	LCA-159		S
☐ Culver NR-D Cadet (PQ-14A) (TD2C-1)	NL15HM	N839	(USAAF), Bu79573, N89573	PVA
☐ Curtiss D Pusher (R)	N1126R	MRP-6-001		PV
☐ Curtiss 42A (R3C-2) (R)	'3'		BAPC.140	PVX
☐ Curtiss 87V Warhawk (P-40N) (Kittyhawk IV)	NL85104	28954	42-105192, 858 (Canada), N1197N	PVA
☐ Curtiss-Wright CW-20B-2 Commando (C-46D)	44-77559	32955		PV
☐ De Havilland DH.100 Vampire FB.6	'WA235'	638	J-1129 (Switzerland), N4024S, NX4024S	PVAX
☐ Deperdussin 1913 (R)	'19'		BAPC.136	PVX
☐ Douglas DC-3A-456 Skytrain (C-47A) (Dakota III)	N47TF	12317	42-92509, KG320, CF-BVF, C-FBVF	RAA
☐ Douglas DC-3A-467 Skytrain (C-47B) (R4D-6) (C-47J)	Bu50802	15213/26658	43-49397 – front fuselage only.	PV
☐ Douglas SBD-5 Dauntless	NX670AM	3883	Bu28536, NZ5062, N670AM	PVA
☐ Douglas D-558-2 Skyrocket	Bu37973	6567	Bu37973, NACA143	PV
☐ Douglas A-4C Skyhawk (A4D-2N)	Bu149547	12872		PV
☐ Douglas A-4E Skyhawk (A4D-5)	Bu151064	13234		PV
☐ Douglas A-4L Skyhawk (A4D-2N) (A-4C)	Bu148316	12626	Bu148316, N157AT	PV
☐ EKW C-3605 (C-3603-1)	NX360BP	263	C-483	RAA
☐ Fairchild M-62A-4 Cornell (PT-26) (Cornell I)	44-19288		44-19288, EW341 – cockpit section only – identity doubtful.	PV
☐ Fieseler Fi 103A-1				RA
☐ Fokker D VII (R)	'5125/18'		BAPC.110	RAX
☐ Fokker Dr I (R)	N5658B			PV
☐ Folland Fo.144 Gnat T.1	NX19GT	FL-540	XP538, 8607M, N19GT	PV
☐ Gloster Meteor F.4	VT260		8813M	PV
☐ Granville Gee Bee R-1 (R)	'NR2100'			PVX
☐ Grumman G-15 Duck (J2F-6)	Bu33594	'A-633504'	Bu33594, N1273N, NL5SF	PVA
☐ Grumman G-36 Wildcat (FM-2)	N29FG	4752	Bu74560, N90523, N16TF	RAA
☐ Grumman G-36 Wildcat (FM-2)	Bu86774	5832		PV
☐ Grumman G-37 (F3F-2)	N20FG		Bu1033	PVA
☐ Grumman G-40 Avenger (TBM-3) (TBM-3E)	NX7835C	4169	Bu91264, KE465	PV
☐ Grumman G-50 Hellcat (F6F-3)	'JV188'	A-3196	Bu41930, N6096C, N103V, N30FG, NX30FG	PVA
☐ Grumman G-51 Tigercat (F7F-3N)	Bu80382	C.124		PV
☐ Grumman G-58 Bearcat (F8F-2)	NX1DF	D.1122	Bu121748, N1029B, N618F, N200N, F-AZRJ, N224RD	RAA
☐ Grumman G-58 Bearcat (F8F-2)	N8TF	D.1190	Bu122637, N1033B, N198F	PVA
☐ Grumman G-79 Panther (F9F-5P)	Bu126277			PV
☐ Grumman G-134 Mohawk (AO-1A) (OV-1A)	N4235Z	2A	59-2604	PVA
☐ Hanriot HD-1	A5624	1398	A5624, N5934	PV
☐ Hawker Sea Hurricane I	NX33TF	CCF/41H/8020	AE977, (G-TWTD)	PVA
☐ Heinkel He 100D-1 (FSM)				PVX
☐ Heinkel He 162A-2	120077	120077	120077, FE-489, T2-489	PV
☐ Hiller UH12E	N702WA	2185	N9756C, XA-TOT, XA-NOI	RA
☐ Hispano HA-1112M1L [Messerschmitt Bf 109G]	NX700E	120	C.4K-???, N700E, N109DW	PV
☐ Horten Ho IVa (DFS 108-251)	N79289	25 (HAC-289)	D-10-1451, LA+AC, VP543, BGA647, N79289, 8-251	PVC
☐ Howard DGA-5 (R)	NR56Y	1		PV
☐ Howard 250 (Lockheed 18-50-23 Lodestar (R5O-3)	N177L	18-2178	Bu30149, N1813M, N67834	PV
☐ Hughes H-1 (R)	'R258Y'			PVX

☐ Keith Rider R-4	NX261Y	6	NR261Y	PV
☐ Keith Rider R-6	NX96Y	8		PV
☐ Laird-Turner LTR-14 Meteor (R)	'NX263Y'			PVAX
☐ Laister-Kauffman LK.10B (TG-4A)	N53612	9	42-43688 (?)	PV
☐ Le Bel Jet				PVD
☐ Le Vier Cosmic Wind	N36C	105		PV
☐ Let C-11 [Yakovlev Yak-11]	'30'	171304	(Egypt)	RAX
☐ Let C-11 [Yakovlev Yak-11]	'11'	171306	(Egypt)	PVX
☐ Lilienthal Normal-Segelapparat (R)				S
☐ Lockheed 18-56-23 Lodestar (C-60A)	'AM711'	18-2622	43-16462, NC44899, NC1000B, N1000B	PVX
☐ Lockheed 080 Shooting Star (P-80A) (F-80A)	44-85488	080-1511		PV
☐ Lockheed 422-81-22 Lightning (P-38J)	NX138AM	422-4318	44-23314, N29Q, N38BP	PVA
☐ Lockheed 422-87-23 Lightning (P-38L) (F-5G)	N74883	422-7965	44-26961, G.C.R-01 (Costa Rica), (Guatemala), 504 (Honduras), N74883, N38DH, N6961.	PVC
☐ Lockheed 422-87-23 Lightning (P-38L) (P-38M)	N9005R	422-8350	44-53095, NL67745, 503 (Honduras), 506 (Honduras)	RAA
☐ Lockheed 580 (T-33A)	53-5156	580-8495		PV
☐ Lockheed 580 (T-33A) (TV-2) (T-33B)	Bu137951	580-8696	53-5357	RA
☐ Lockheed 683-10-19 Starfighter (F-104G)				S
☐ Lockheed 683-10-19 Starfighter (F-104G)	FX-82	683D-9140	In Belgian markings	PV
☐ Luscombe 8A Silvaire	N2050B	6477	NC2050B	PV
☐ Macchi M.39 (FSM)	'5'		BAPC.141	PVX
☐ Martin 210A Mauler (AM-1)	'259'		Bu122403	PVX
☐ Mercury Air Shoestring	N26C			PV
☐ Messerschmitt Bf 108B-2 Taifun		8378	FE-4610, T2-4610	RA
☐ Messerschmitt Bf 109E-1		3523		PV
☐ Messerschmitt Me 163B-1a Komet (FSM)	'191626'			PVX
☐ Mikoyan-Gurevich MiG-15	NX87CN	91051	83277 (China), N87CN	PVA
☐ Mikoyan-Gurevich MiG-15bis	1301			PV
☐ Mikoyan-Gurevich MiG-21R	2149	94R02149	In Czech markings.	PVD
☐ Mitsubishi A6M5 Zero Sen Model 52	NX46770	5357	5357 – flies as 61-120	PVAX
☐ Mitsubishi G4M1				PVD
☐ Mitsubishi J2M3 Raiden	91-101	3014		PV
☐ Mitsubishi J8M1 Shusui	403		FE-300, T2-300	PV
☐ Morane-Saulnier MS.502 Criquet [Fieseler Fi 156 Storch]	'CQ+QS'	381	381 (France), F-BJHP, N57962	PVAX
☐ Naval Aircraft Factory N3N-3			Fuselage frame only.	PV
☐ North American NA-25 (O-47A)	N4725V	25-554	38-284, XB-QEU, XB-KEU	SD
☐ North American NA-25 (O-47A)	38-295	25-565	38-295, N1047P	PV
☐ North American NA-88 Texan (AT-6D)	'FE695'	88-14780	42-44586, 1320 (Brazil), N205SB, N17TF	RAAX
☐ North American NA-88 Texan (AT-6D) (SNJ-5)	N3375G	88-18068	42-86287, Bu90790	PV
☐ North American NA-88 Texan (SNJ-4)	N7407C	88-13345	Bu27729	RAA
☐ North American NA-97 Apache (A-36A)	N251A	97-15949	42-83731, N50452	PV
☐ North American NA-99 Mustang (P-51A)	NX4235Y	99-22354	43-6251, N4235Y	PVA
☐ North American NA-108 Mitchell (B-25J) (TB-25J) (JB-25J) (TB-25J)	NX3675G	108-33698	44-30423	PVA
☐ North American NA-122 Mustang (P-51D)	NL7TF/'463684'	122-40396	44-73856, N5077K, N711UP	RAAX
☐ North American NA-122 Mustang (P-51D)				RAC
☐ North American NA-124 Mustang (P-51D)	''44-13334'	124-44817	44-84961, N7715C, NL7715C	PVAX
☐ North American NA-124 Mustang (P-51D)	NL5441V	124-48335	45-11582	PV
☐ North American NA-145 Navion	N91161	NAV-4-216	NC91161	RAA
☐ North American NA-171 Trojan (T-28A)	N9640C	171-96	50-0290	PV
☐ North American NA-172 Sabre (F-86E)	NX186SE	172-358	51-13067	PV
☐ North American NA-173 Sabre (F-86D)	51-6012	173-156	Cockpit only.	PV
☐ North American NA-191 Sabre (F-86F)	NX186AM	191-708	52-5012, C-127 (Argentina), N30CW, N4TF	RAA
☐ North American NA-194 Fury (FJ-3) (F-1C)	Bu135867	194-94		PV
☐ North American NA-203 Sabre (F-86H)	53-1351	203-123	Composite with c/n 187-100 52-2074.	PV
☐ North American NA-203 Sabre (F-86H)	53-1357	203-129		PV
☐ North American NA-235 Super Sabre (F-100D)	56-3141	235-239		RA
☐ North American NA-253 Buckeye (T2J-1) (T-2A)	Bu147436	253-27		RAD
☐ North American NA-253 Buckeye (T2J-1) (T-2A)	Bu147474	253-65		PV
☐ North American NA-253 Buckeye (T2J-1) (T-2A)	Bu147492	253-83		RAD
☐ Northrop 4A Alpha	'NC999Y'	11	NC986Y	PVDX
☐ Northrop N-9MB	N9MB	0039	N5109R	PVA
☐ Northrop N-160 Scorpion (N-68) (F-89D) (F-89J)	53-2517	N.4648	With components from c/n N.4650 53-2519.	PV
☐ Orlowski HO.1	N426A	1		PV
☐ Pilatus P.2-05	U-142	62	U-113, U-142, G-BONE	PV
☐ Piper J-3C-65 Cub	NC6944H	20183	NC6944H, N6944H	PVA
☐ Piper J-3C-65 Cub (L-4H)	N48679	10732	43-29441	PVA
☐ Pitts S-1S Special				PV
☐ Pratt-Read PR-G1 (LNE-1)			(USN)	RA
☐ PZL TS-11 Iskra 100bisB	N715CM	1H 07-15	0715 (Poland), 715 (Poland)	PV
☐ Quickie Aircraft Quickie 2 (Rutan 54)	N523D	2606		PV
☐ Republic P-47G Thunderbolt	NX3395G		42-25234	PVA
☐ Republic YF-84A Thunderjet (YP-84A)	45-59487			PVA
☐ Republic F-84F Thunderstreak				S
☐ Republic RF-84K Thunderflash (RF-84F) (GRF-84F)	52-7265			PV
☐ Richter Ric Jet 4	N24RJ	001		PV

California

☐ Ryan 28 Fireball (FR-1)	Bu39709			PV
☐ Schopal and Nylander Flying Wing				PV
☐ Seversky 2PA Guardsman (AT-12)	NX55539	483-38	N55539	PVA
☐ Sopwith F.1 Camel (R)	'B1795'			PVX
☐ Summers WH-1 (Hansen Special)	N35TS	1		PV
☐ Supermarine 349 Spitfire LF.Vc	N5TF		JG891, A58-178, ZK-MKV, G-LFVC, N624TB	RAA
☐ Supermarine 361 Spitfire LF.IXc	NX2TF	6S.730116	ML417, G-15-11, HS543 (India), G-BJSG converted to a T.9 for Indian service.	PVA
☐ Supermarine 379 Spitfire F.XIV	NX54SF	6S.663452	SM832, (India), G-WWII, F-AZSJ, G-WWII, N54SF	PVA
☐ Supermarine S.6B (FSM)	'S1595'		BAPC.156	PVX
☐ Tracy Kona Wind				S
☐ Ultralight Flying Machines Easy Riser				PV
☐ Vought F4U-1A Corsair	NX83782		Bu17799 – quoted by FAA as c/n 3884 Bu56198	PV
☐ Vought F4U-4 Corsair	N4TF	9418	Bu97264, N5218V, F-AZVJ, N5118V	PVA
☐ Vought F-8A Crusader (F8U-1)	Bu145336			PV
☐ Vought F-8H Crusader (F8U-2N) (F-8D)				RA
☐ Vultee V-74 Valiant (BT-13A)	'A-II-207'		(USAAF) – mocked up as a Val	PVX
☐ Vultee V-74 Valiant (BT-13A)	'B-II-207'		(USAAF) – mocked up as a Val	PVX
☐ Waco VKS-7				RAD
☐ Williams W.17	N21X	1		PV
☐ Wright Flyer (R)				S
☐ WSK Lim-2 [MiG-15bis]	'14'	1B 006-12	(Poland)	RA
☐ WSK SBLim-2 (Lim-1) [MiG-15}]	NX687	1A 02-005	205 (Poland)	PVA
☐ WSK Lim-5 [MiG-17F]	1020	1C 10-20	1020 (Poland), NX117MG – in Polish markings.	PVX
☐ WSK Lim-5 [MiG-17F]	'1617'	1C 16-17	1617 (Poland) – in false North Vietnamese markings.	PVX
☐ Yakovlev Yak-3U	N130AM	170101	533 (Egypt), G-BTHD – converted from Let C-11	RAC
☐ Yakovlev Yak-18	30	1432030	(China), N7013S, N18YK	PV
☐ Yokosuka MXY-7 Ohka 11	'I-18'			PVX

POINT MUGU NAVAL AIR WEAPONS STATION MISSILE PARK (CA112)

Address: Naval Airfare Weapons Station, 521 9th. Street, Point Mugu, California 93042-5001.
Tel: 805-989-1110
Admission: On permanent view.
Location: Just south of Oxnard off Highway 1.

In 1946 the site was chosen as one or the primary bases for missile evaluation. An airfield was constructed and is now home to the Naval Airfare Weapons Center which operates modern combat types along with earlier aircraft converted for pilotless drone use.

The Missile Park, located on the road which passes the airfield, houses examples of those tested at the base along with the aircraft. The Canadian-built Sabre is mounted outside the headquarters of the nearby Channel Islands Air National Guard Base.

TYPE	REG/SER	CON. NO.	PI/NOTES	STATUS
☐ Canadair CL-13A Sabre 5 [North American F-86E]	'49-1046'	1028	23238 (Canada), N86EB	RAX
☐ Ford JB-2 [Fieseler Fi 103A-1]				PV
☐ Grumman G-123 Hawkeye (E-2C)	Bu161097	A61		RA
☐ Grumman G-303 Tomcat (F-14A)	Bu158623	24		PV
☐ McDonnell M.98EV Phantom II (F-4J) (F-4S)	Bu157259	3666		PV

PORTERVILLE MONUMENTS (CA113)

Location: On permanent view at two locations in the town.

TYPE	REG/SER	CON. NO.	PI/NOTES	STATUS
☐ Bell 205 Iroquois (UH-1H)	'12189'		In a park.	PVX
☐ Douglas A-4C Skyhawk (A4D-2N)	Bu147727	12491	At the airport which is in the south western part of the town.	PV

PROP AND JET AIR MUSEUM (CA114)

Address: 26445 Larkspur Street, Hemet, California 92544-6410
Admission: By prior permission only
Location: At the airport which is about 3 miles south west of the town off Route 74.

The museum has been set up by private owners who base their aircraft at the field. The collection includes a number of interesting types. The Texan and Valiant have been restored to period military markings.

The Fokker Dr I replica is in the familiar all red scheme which has been applied to many homebuilt examples of the type. The Bede BD-5J jet was built in Canada before moving south. The type made its first flight in 1971 and large numbers of kits and plans were sold. The diminutive monoplane could be powered by either a piston or a jet engine. The company soon went bankrupt and only a few hundred were completed.

The collection also includes a classic Cessna 195A which first appeared in the late 1940s and was sold in some numbers.

TYPE	REG/SER	CON. NO.	PI/NOTES	STATUS
☐ Aero L-29 Delfin	N29KJ	491174	52 (Soviet)	RA
☐ Bede BD-5J	N557DM	BS-9	C-GBDA	RA
☐ Beech D18S Expeditor 3N	N62936	CA-38 (A-638)	1463, CF-BCE	RAA
☐ Cessna 195A	N1057D	7669		RA
☐ Cessna 305C Bird Dog (L-19E) (O-1E)	N4845M	24569		RA
☐ Cessna 337M Super Skymaster (O-2A)	N475DF	337M0343	68-11067	RA
☐ Fokker Dr I (R)	N113PC	1		RAA
☐ Mikoyan-Gurevich MiG-21MF			(Czech)	RA
☐ North American NA-159 Trojan (T-28A)	N99394	159-157	49-1645, N2851G, 218 (Nicaragua)	RA
☐ North American NA-168 Texan (T-6G)	N3100G	168-311	49-3207	RA
☐ Northrop N-311 Tiger II (F-5E)	Bu160792	R.1039	73-0858	RA
☐ Piper J-3C-65 Cub (O-59A) (L-4A)	NC58368	8939	42-36815	RA
☐ Ryan ST-3KR Recruit (PT-22)	N56565	1431	41-15402	RAA
☐ Vultee V-74 Valiant (SNV-1)	N59843/'293046'	74-9244	Bu34262	RA
☐ Yakovlev Yak-52	N2327Y	888704		RA

PROUD BIRD RESTAURANT (CA115)

Address: 11022 Aviation Boulevard, Los Angeles, California 90045.
Tel: 310-670-3093 **Email:** gmunit10@srcmail.com
Admission: On permanent view.
Location: Just east of Los Angeles International Airport on Route 1.

This long established restaurant has now set up an aviation display. Inside the building are photographs, models and uniforms. Outside is a large exhibition area. A few genuine aircraft on show. The MiG-15 served in China and is in false Soviet scheme. The Skyhawk is resplendent in the colours of the 'Blue Angels'. Replicas of famous types from both World Wars are now exhibited along with some from the early era of jets.

TYPE	REG/SER	CON. NO.	PI/NOTES	STATUS
☐ Beech C18S Expeditor (C-45F) (UC-45F) (F-2B) (RC-45A)	N81GB	7881	44-47473, N39142	PV
☐ Bell 44 (XS-1) (X-1) (FSM)	'6062'			PVX
☐ Bell 204 Iroquois (UH-1C) (UH-1M)	66-15143	1871		PV
☐ Curtiss H81-A2 Warhawk (P-40C) (Tomahawk IIB) (FSM)				PV
☐ Douglas DST-406 (C-49F)	N715F	4129	NC33643, 42-56636, NC33643, N1R, N71R	PV
☐ Douglas SBD-3 Dauntless (FSM)				PV
☐ Douglas A-4B Skyhawk (A4D-2)	Bu144930	12176		PV
☐ Fokker D VII (FSM)				PVX
☐ Grumman G-36 Wildcat (F4F-4) (FSM)				PV
☐ Grumman G-40 Avenger (TBM-3) (FSM)				PV
☐ Lockheed 080 Shooting Star (P-80C) (F-80C) (FSM)				PV
☐ Lockheed 422-87-23 Lightning (P-38L) (FSM)				PV
☐ Messerschmitt Bf 109E (FSM)				PV
☐ Mikoyan-Gurevich MiG-15bis	'1170'		(China) – in false Soviet markings.	PVX
☐ North American NA-122 Mustang (P-51D) (FSM)	'44-14061'			PVX
☐ North American NA-191 Sabre (F-86F) (FSM)	'24513'			PVX
☐ Republic P-47D Thunderbolt (FSM)				PVX
☐ SPAD XIII (FSM)				PVX
☐ Supermarine 329 Spitfire F.IIa (FSM)	'P8080'			PV
☐ Vought FG-1D Corsair (FSM)				PVX

REEDLEY COLLEGE (CA116)

Address: 995 North Reed Avenue, Reedley, California 93654.
Tel: 559-638-2641 **Email:** rcweb@reedleycollege.edu
Admission: By prior permission only.
Location: In the north western part of the town.

The college has trained aircraft and engine mechanics for over half a century. The Twin Comanche was once used by NASA. The list of instructional airframes is not complete as others can be seen in photos in a brochure.

TYPE	REG/SER	CON. NO.	PI/NOTES	STATUS
☐ Bell 47D (HTL-2)	N1358N	59	Bu122952	RA
☐ Cessna 152	N69214	15282562		RA
☐ Cessna 404 Titan				RA
☐ Hiller UH12B Raven (H-23B) (OH-23B)	N1730	485	51-16292	RA
☐ Piper PA-30 Twin Comanche B	N808NA	30-1498	N8351Y, NASA808	RA

RICHARD NIXON LIBRARY AND BIRTHPLACE (CA117)

Address: 18001 Yorba Linda Boulevard, Yorba Linda, California 92886.
Tel: 714-993-5075 **Fax:** 714-528-0544 **Email:** revjht@msn.com
Admission: Monday-Saturday 1000-1700; Sunday 1100-1700.
Location: About 30 miles east of Los Angeles off Interstate 91.

California

Richard Nixon was born in Yorba Linda and the complex opened in 19th July 1990. The library houses his documents and other items connected with his presidency. The house in which he was born in 1910 has been restored. He was Vice-President from 1953 to 1961 and President from 1969 to 1974. The museum building houses many interesting exhibits from these times. Replicas of rooms in the White House have been constructed. There are exhibits on the American Space Program during his period in office. The only aircraft on show is the Sea King helicopter which was one of those used by the Presidential flight.

TYPE	REG/SER	CON. NO.	PI/NOTES	STATUS
☐ Sikorsky S-61B Sea King (HSS-2Z) (VH-3A)	Bu150617	61123		PV

RONALD REAGAN PRESIDENTIAL LIBRARY (CA118)

Address: 40 Presidential Drive, Simi Valley, California 93065.
Tel: 805-522-8244   **Fax:** 805-577-4074   **Email:** reagan.library@nara.gov
Admission: Daily 1000-1700.
Location: About 30 miles north west of Los Angeles off Route 118.

This complex houses vast numbers of government documents and over 100,000 artefacts tracing the life of the 40th President of the USA. The library is available for research. The VC-137 was used by Ronald Reagan in his eight years in office and also by Presidents Carter, Ford, Nixon, George H Bush, Clinton and George W Bush. In its later years the aircraft served as back-up to the 747 currently in use. The 707 retired in September 2001 and was flown to Simi Valley. The pavilion housing the former 'Air Force One', the Sea King and a Presidential Limousine opened on 24th October 2005. There is a section devoted to his college days. His days as a Hollywood actor are also portrayed with highlights from his films regularly shown.

TYPE	REG/SER	CON. NO.	PI/NOTES	STATUS
☐ Boeing 707-353B (VC-137C)	72-7000	20630	N8459	PV
☐ Grumman G-303 Tomcat (F-14A)	'Bu160403'	514	Bu162592 –	PVX
☐ Sikorsky S-61B Sea King (HSS-2Z) (VH-3A)	Bu150611			PV

RYAN SCHOOL OF AERONAUTICS MUSEUM (CA119)

Address: 4280 Walden Weaver Road, Hemet, California 92545-3823.
Tel: 909-658-2716
Admission: Thursday-Sunday 1000-1500.
Location: On the south side of Hemet-Ryan Airport which is about 3 miles south west of the town.

The Ryan company set up a flying school at Lindbergh Field in San Diego in 1928 which became the Ryan School of Aeronautics in 1931. A new site at Hemet opened in 1940 and over the next four years trained over 6,000 pilots at the airfield. The museum has been set up to commemorate this feat. The base has been used by fire-fighting aircraft for many years and was at one time the busiest in California. Although it is still used for this purpose the main facilities are now at March Reserve Base near Riverside which has longer runways. The two aircraft are by the fire base.

TYPE	REG/SER	CON. NO.	PI/NOTES	STATUS
☐ Bell 205 Iroquois (UH-1H)				PV
☐ Grumman G-89 Tracker (S2F-1) (S-2A)	'70'	654	Bu136745, 4146 (Japan)	PVX

SACRAMENTO MONUMENT (CA120)

Location: On permanent view near Mather Field in the southern part of the city.

TYPE	REG/SER	CON. NO.	PI/NOTES	STATUS
☐ Republic F-105G Thunderchief (F-105F)	63-8278	F-55		PV

SAN BERNARDINO VALLEY COLLEGE (CA121)

Address: 701 South Mount Vernon Avenue, San Bernardino, California 92410.
Tel: 909-384-4441   **Email:** amoore@valleycollege.edu
Admission: By prior permission only.
Location: In the south western part of the city.

Established in 1926, the college operates from two sites. The aviation department offers courses in flight operations, airframe and powerplant maintenance and avionics. The list of airframes is not complete as more are mentioned in a brochure. Engines and components are also present in the workshops.

TYPE	REG/SER	CON. NO.	PI/NOTES	STATUS
☐ Aeronca 7AC Champion	N2559E	7AC-6142		RA
☐ Beech B50 Twin Bonanza	N3568B	CH-28		RA
☐ Bell 205 Iroquois (UH-1H)				RA
☐ Cessna 120	N2699N	12957	NC2699N	RA
☐ Piper PA-28-140 Cherokee	N5907U	28-26894		RA

SAN DIEGO AEROSPACE MUSEUM (CA122)

Address: 2001 Pan American Plaza, Balboa Park, San Diego, California 92101-1636.
Tel: 619-234-8291   **Fax:** 619-233-4526   **Email:** RCVaronfakis@aol.com
Admission: Daily 1000-1630.
Location: In the centre of the city off Interstate 5.
The museum has a facility at Gillespie Field, El Cajon which is open daily.

San Diego has been associated with aviation since the early days. In 1911 Glenn Curtiss made several flights in the area and military bases were soon established. Industry arrived in the region and both Consolidated and Ryan set up factories at the airport in the 1920s.

The city was the obvious site for an aeronautical museum and after an initial period of planning the exhibition opened in February 1963. From 1965 the collection was housed in a temporary building which it shared with the Hall of Science museum. Over the next dozen years an impressive range of aircraft was acquired. A 1909 Chanute glider and a 1911 Montgomery monoplane represented the early era. A Consolidated PT-3 was found in Arkansas and bought by the founder of the firm, Reuben Fleet. In 1969 the biplane was flown to San Diego and a few weeks later the 82-year-old Fleet flew it over his home. Ryan was represented by an original M-l, which was the first monoplane to be put into production in the USA.

In 1977 disaster struck when a vandal started a fire which destroyed most of the aircraft as well as a large library and archive section. Efforts to create a new museum were soon underway and in June 1980 an exhibition opened in a 1935 building in Balboa Park. The circular structure with a centre courtyard was constructed by the Ford Motor Company for the California International Exposition. In the following year it was used as the Palace of Transportation with a 450 foot mural depicting 'The March of Transportation' on the inner wall. This painting was restored before the museum opened.

Another impressive collection has been assembled with many rare aircraft on show. Several of the aircraft are exhibited in period settings. Outside the building are a Convair Sea Dart and a Lockheed Blackbird. In the foyer are replicas of a Curtiss A-l and a Ryan NYP.

The walk round the circular hall traces the development of aviation from the early period up to modern times. The displays are informative with many photographs, documents, models and memorabilia to be seen.

Several of the aircraft lost in 1977 have been replaced by other examples or by accurate replicas. A Consolidated PT-1 has been put on show and a replica Ryan M-1 constructed. The displays are well thought out and there are areas devoted to the Early Days, World War I, Flying the Mail, the Barnstorming Era, General Aviation, Air Racing, World War II and the Korean War.

In the basement is a large workshop where restoration work takes place. For a number of years the Catalina, a Phantom and a MiG-17 have been exhibited in the central courtyard. This area has been covered over and the Ford is placed here.

The museum has two hangars at Gillespie Field, El Cajon where a team of volunteers carries out restoration. A line of military aircraft is parked outside the hangars. Aircraft from the main site are often here for short periods.

TYPE	REG/SER	CON. NO.	PI/NOTES	STATUS
☐ Aeronca C-3	N13094	A-258	NC13094	PV
☐ Albatros D Va (R)	N3767A	AA-106		PV
☐ Bee Aviation Honey Bee	N90859	1	At Gillespie.	PV
☐ Bee Aviation Wee Bee (R)	'NX90840'			PVX
☐ Beech D45 Mentor (T-34B)	Bu140795	BG-129	Bu140795, N795FC – at Gillespie	PV
☐ Beech D45 Mentor (T-34B)	Bu140872	BG-206	Bu140872, N8764T – at Gillespie	PV
☐ Bell 47D-1 Sioux (H-13D) (OH-13D)	51-2461	215 (?)	51-2461, N204W	RAC
☐ Bell 209 Huey Cobra (AH-1S) (AH-1E)	77-22778	22116		PV
☐ Blériot XI (R)	N605WB	1		PV
☐ Boeing 67 Hawk (FB-5)	A7123			PVX
☐ Boeing 235 (F4B-4) (R)	'8426'			PVX
☐ Boeing 266 Pea Shooter (P-26A) (R)				RAC
☐ Boeing-Stearman B75N1 Kaydet (N2S-3)	N1301M	75-6588	Bu05414	PVX
☐ Bowlus Albatross SP-1 (R)	'493'			PVX
☐ Cangie WC.1	N1AE	1	At Gillespie.	PV
☐ Cayley Glider (R)				PV
☐ Chanute Glider (R)				PV
☐ Consolidated 1 Trusty (PT-1)	N1926M		27-150	PV
☐ Consolidated 28-5A Catalina (PBY-5A)	Bu48406	1768	Bu48406, N5590V	PV
☐ Convair 2 Seadart (YF2Y-1) (YF-7A)	Bu135763			PV
☐ Convair 8-10 Delta Dagger (F-102A)	56-1268	8-10-485	At Gillespie.	PV
☐ Curtiss E A-1 (R)				PV
☐ Curtiss Little Looper	N5599N	2		PV
☐ Curtiss 1C Jenny (JN-4D)	N5391	396		PVX
☐ Curtiss 50B Robin B-1	NC9265	329		PV
☐ Da Vinci Ornithopter (R)				PV
☐ Denney Kitfox III	N81LB	792		PV
☐ Deperdussin C				PV
☐ Douglas DC-3A-456 Skytrain (C-47A)	43-15952	20418	Front fuselage only – on loan from NASM, DC.	PV
☐ Douglas SBD-4 Dauntless	Bu06900	1775		PV
☐ Douglas A-26B Invader	N119DR	27592	44-34313, N5457V, C-GHLK – on loan – at Gillespie.	PVA
☐ Douglas A-4B Skyhawk (A4D-2)	Bu142905	11967	Bu142905, N905MD –	PV
☐ Douglas A-4C Skyhawk (A4D-2N)	Bu148517	12710	At Gillespie.	PV
☐ Fleet 2	'C600M'	223	NC648M, N648M	PVX
☐ Fokker Dr I (FSM)	'477/17'			PVX
☐ Fokker E III (FSM)	'246/15'			PVX
☐ Ford 5-AT-B	N9637	5-AT-11	NC9637, NM-22, X-ABCC, AN-AAJ, HI-3, NX1629M, N1629M, XB-KUI, XA-HIL, N1629M, N9637, N76GC	PV
☐ General Atomics RQ-1K Predator				PV
☐ General Dynamics 401 Fighting Falcon (F-16N)	Bu163269	3M-2	85-1370 – at Gillespie.	PV
☐ Gilbert DG-1	N169MB	001	At Gillespie	PV
☐ Gotha Go 229 (Horten Ho IX) (FSM)				PV
☐ Granville Gee Bee R-1 (R)	'NR2100'			PVX
☐ Grumman G-36 Wildcat (F4F-4)	Bu11828	3523		RAC
☐ Grumman G-50 Hellcat (F6F-3)	Bu42874	A-4140		PV
☐ Grumman G-128 Intruder (A-6E)	Bu162195	I-688	At Gillespie.	PV
☐ Grumman G-303 Tomcat (F-14A)	Bu159631	178	At Gillespie.	PV
☐ Hawker-Siddeley P.1127 Harrier 50 (AV-8A)	Bu159239	P148	At Gillespie.	PV
☐ Lilienthal Normal-Segelapparat (R)				PV
☐ Lockheed 5B Vega (FSM)				PV
☐ Lockheed 580 (T-33A)	52-9692	580-7917	Fuselage only – at Gillespie.	PV
☐ Lockheed A-12	60-6933	130		PV

California

☐ McDonnell M.98EV Phantom II (F-4J) (F-4S)	Bu157267	3713		PV
☐ McDonnell M.267 Hornet (F/A-18A)	Bu161963	177/A138	At Gillespie.	PV
☐ Mead Primary Glider (R)				RAC
☐ Mercury Air Shoestring	N16V	101	At Gillespie.	PV
☐ Messerschmitt Bf 109G-4 (FSM)				PV
☐ Mikoyan-Gurevich MiG-15bis	70201	137085	In Chinese markings – at Gillespie.	PV
☐ Mikoyan-Gurevich MiG-17F	'3026'		(Egypt) – in North Vietnamese markings.	PVX
☐ Mikoyan-Gurevich MiG-21PF	64		Front fuselage only – at Gillespie.	PV
☐ Mikoyan-Gurevich MiG-21bis	9099	75049099	In Hungarian markings – at Gillespie.	PV
☐ Mitsubishi A6M7 Zero Sen Model 63	'3-143'	4323	On loan from NASM, DC.	PV
☐ Monnett Sonerai II	N82RX	00045	At Gillespie.	PV
☐ Monnett Sonerai II	N21PC	PM01-0357	At Gillespie.	PV
☐ Monnett Sonex	N116TG	086	At Gillespie.	PV
☐ Montgomery Evergreen	6	6	On loan from NASM, DC.	PV
☐ Nieuport 11 (R)	N1486	102		PV
☐ Nieuport 28C.1 (R)	N28GH	N-1		PVX
☐ North American NA-122 Mustang (P-51D)	'46-17569'	122-40223	44-73683, GN119 (Nicaragua), N12064, NL5551D	PVX
☐ North American NA-227 Sabre (F-86F)	'112958'	227-247	55-5014 –	PVX
☐ Northrop Grumman RQ-8A Fire Scout			At Gillespie.	PV
☐ Pietenpol B4-A Aircamper	N3768Q	PC1-1A	At Gillespie.	PV
☐ Piper J-3C-65 Cub	NC333ED	2844		PV
☐ Pitts S-1S Special	N4HS	10034		PV
☐ Rearwin 8135 Cloudster	N25553	829	NC25553	PV
☐ Rutan 33 Vari-Eze	N24RW	390	At Gillespie.	PV
☐ Robinson R-44 Raven	N544LB	0880		PV
☐ Ryan 69 Vertijet (X-13) (X-13A)	54-1619		On loan from NASM, DC.	PV
☐ Ryan M-1 (R)				PV
☐ Ryan NYP (R)	'NX-211'	AM-1	N211SD – at Gillespie for restoration.	PVX
☐ Ryan B-5 Brougham	'NC731M'	194	NC9236, N9236, NC9236	PVX
☐ Ryan STA	NC17361	166		PV
☐ Ryan ST-3KR Recruit (PT-22)	N47843	1901	41-20692 – at Gillespie.	PV
☐ Ryan ST-3KR Recruit (PT-22)	N60178	2184	41-20975	PV
☐ SPAD VII	'B9916'			PVX
☐ Sopwith Pup (R)				PV
☐ Standard J-1	N2826D	1598		PV
☐ Stinson SM-8A Junior	NC416Y	4251	NC416Y, N416Y – at Gillespie.	PV
☐ Supermarine 361 Spitfire LF.XVIe	SL574	CBAF-IX-4688	SL574, 8391M, 'RV214'	PV
☐ Thomas-Morse S-4C	'A4358'	A51	SC.34544	PVX
☐ Thorp T-18	N48LS	435	At Gillespie.	PV
☐ Vans RV-4	N32KM	476	At Gillespie.	PV
☐ Vought F4U-7 Corsair	'Bu129359'		Bu133704, 704 (France) –	RACX
☐ Vought F-8J Crusader (F8U-2NE) (F-8E)	Bu150297		At Gillespie.	PV
☐ Vought A-7B Corsair II	Bu154554	B194	At Gillespie.	PV
☐ Waco YKS-7	N17713	4625	NC17713, N17713, N48980	PV
☐ Wemple Solitaire	N78DW	12		RA
☐ Wright 1901 Glider (R)				PV
☐ Wright 1902 Glider (R)				PV
☐ Wright Flyer (R)				PV
☐ Wright EX Vin Fiz			Converted from a Wright B.	PV
☐ Zenair CH-200 Zenith			At Gillespie.	PVC

SAN DIEGO MIRAMAR COLLEGE (CA123)

Address: 10440 Black Mountain Road, San Diego, California 92126-2699
Tel: 619-388-7661   **Email:** pchlapec@sdccd.edu
Admission: By prior permission only.
Location: About 15 miles north of the city off Interstate 15.

The college opened in 1969 as a training facility for San Diego's firefighters and law enforcement officers. Flight training is carried out at a local airfield and the workshops contain several instructional airframes.

TYPE	REG/SER	CON. NO.	PI/NOTES	STATUS
☐ Beech B60 Duke	N3LC	P-389		RA
☐ Bell 47G-3B-1 Sioux (TH-13T)	N67186	3543	66-8043	RA
☐ Cessna 150	N6574T	17974		RA
☐ Cessna 150M	N4156G	15078862		RA
☐ Cessna 205	N1813G	2050013		RA
☐ Hiller UH12D Raven (H-23D) (OH-23D)	N4607B	1286	61-3100	RA
☐ Lockheed 580 (T-33A)	53-5850	580-9291	53-5850, N4605B	RA
☐ Piper PA-38-112 Tomahawk	N2491P	38-79A1006		RA

SAN FRANCISCO RESTAURANTS (CA124)

Location: On permanent view at two branches of Lori's Diner.

TYPE	REG/SER	CON. NO.	PI/NOTES	STATUS
☐ Homebuilt Biplane.			At Powell Street.	PV
☐ Smith DSA-1 Miniplane.				PV

The first pre-production McDonnell YF/A-18A is on show at the United States Museum of Naval Armament and Technology. (David Skeggs) [CA143]

A number of aircraft including this Vertol HH-46D Sea Knight, are parked on the flight deck of the USS Midway in San Diego harbour. (Dick Barrett) [CA145]

The largest aircraft on show at the Peterson Air and Space Museum is this Lockheed EC-121T Super Constellation. [CO24]

California

SAN JOAQUIN VALLEY COLLEGE (CA125)

Address:	295 East Sierra Avenue, Fresno, California 93710.
Tel:	866-544-7898
Admission:	By prior permission only.
Location:	At Yosemite Airport. In the north eastern part of the city.

Founded in 1977, the college operates from eight sites around Fresno. The aviation department is located at Yosemite Airport where workshops students are trained in a variety of skills. The Iroquois was flown by a company in Nevada after military service but it still retains its army camouflage scheme.

TYPE	REG/SER	CON. NO.	PI/NOTES	STATUS
☐ Bell 205 Iroquois (UH-1H)	N205JG	9384	67-17686	RA
☐ Cessna 150J	N5521G	15071021		RA
☐ Cessna 172B	N7534X	17248034		RA

SAN JOSE STATE UNIVERSITY DEPARTMENT OF AVIATION (CA126)

Address:	1120 Coleman Avenue, San Jose, California 91605.
Tel:	408-924-3190 Fax: 408-924-3198 Email: avtech@sjsu.edu
Admission:	By prior permission only.
Location:	On the south side of the airport just west of the city.

The university was set up in 1857 as the Minns' Evening Institute in San Francisco, thus making it the oldest public college of higher education on the West Coast of the USA. A move was made to San Jose in 1871 and it still operates from this campus. After a number of name changes it was granted university status in the early 1970s. the aviation department. Students undetake their training on a large fleet of aircraft.

TYPE	REG/SER	CON. NO.	PI/NOTES	STATUS
☐ Aero Commander 100-180	N3734X	5042		RA
☐ Beech 95-B55B Cochise (T-42A)	N19SJ	TF-39	65-12717	RA
☐ Boeing 727-22	N7015U	18307		RA
☐ Cessna 150	N6616T	59016		RA
☐ Cessna 150M	N45386	15076895		RA
☐ Cessna 150M	N7657U	15077783		RA
☐ Cessna 150M	N714HF	15079183		RA
☐ Cessna 310A Blue Canoe (L-27A) (U-3A)	N1SJ	38011	57-5856	RAX
☐ Cessna 310Q	N1535T	310Q0753		RA
☐ Cessna 337M Super Skymaster (O-2A)	N29SJ	337M0318	68-11042	RA
☐ Hughes 269A Osage (TH-55A)	N95881	97-0722	67-15378	RA
☐ North American NA-276 Sabreliner (T-39A) (CT-39A)	'N1SJ'	276-45	62-4492	RAX
☐ Piper PA-23-250 Aztec C	N6480Y	27-3776		RA

SANTA ANA MONUMENT (CA127)

Location:	On permanent view at a Veterans Memorila at 10 Civic Center Plaza in the town.

TYPE	REG/SER	CON. NO.	PI/NOTES	STATUS
☐ Douglas A-4M Skyhawk	Bu160031	14533		PV

SANTA MARIA MUSEUM OF FLIGHT (CA128)

Address:	3015 Airpark Drive, Santa Maria, California 93455.
Tel:	805-922-8758 Fax: 805-922-8958 Email: smmof@msn.com
Admission:	Friday-Sunday 1000-1600
Location:	At the airport which is in the south western suburbs of the town.

The airfield opened in the 1920s and was home to the Hancock Foundation College of Aviation established in 1928. Over the years the field has seen both military and civil use. The Santa Maria Aeronautical and Exhibition Museum was formed in 1984 and initially collected a large number of models and artefacts. A change of name took place and the museum opened in a hangar at the airport in 1990. An informative display of models, components, memorabilia, photographs and uniforms has been set up. A replica 1920s hangar built for a film is being converted to house some of the stored aircraft and there are plans to construct a further hall. The new building will house exhibits from the modern era including space items.

The Stinson Reliant is painted in British military markings. The Royal Navy used 500, supplied under Lend Lease, on communications and navigational training duties. The Fleet 2 has been restored and is now on display. This 1929 biplane is in colours of one used by the Hancock school. The Cessna Airmaster, the modified Great Lakes and the Monocoupe are owned by the husband of a former museum director and are either on show in the museum or parked in his private hangar nearby. A number of homebuilt aircraft, including the unique Parker RP.9, have been added to the collection and some can be seen in the main hall. The new hall will also exhibit classic cars.

TYPE	REG/SER	CON. NO.	PI/NOTES	STATUS
☐ Beech C18S Navigator (AT-7C)	N6776C	5905	43-33474	PV
☐ Bell 204 Iroquois (UH-1C) (UH-1M)	66-0630	1612		PV
☐ Bowers Fly Baby 1A	N9767N	87-491		RA
☐ Cessna C-34 Airmaster	NC15462	301	NC15462, N15462.	RAA
☐ Douglas A-4L Skyhawk (A4D-2N) (A-4C)	Bu147825	12589		PV
☐ Fleet 2	N7629B	157	NC434K, N434K.	PV
☐ Folland Fo.144 Gnat T.1				
☐ Great Lakes 2T-1A (mod)	NC312Y	199	On loan.	RAA

☐ Grumman G-303 Tomcat (F-14A)				PV
☐ Hughes H-1 (R)				PVX
☐ Kaminskas RK-3 Jungster III	N76AQ	1		RA
☐ Lockheed-Boughton Air Rep P-38	N138BB	2001	Possibly this aircraft.	PVX
☐ McDonnell M.98EV Phantom II (F-4J) (F-4S)	Bu153868	2403	On loan from NMNA, FL.	PV
☐ Mikoyan-Gurevich MiG-21PF	N21PF	761811	1811 (POland)	PV
☐ Monnett Moni	N321EW	62		RA
☐ Monnett Sonerai II-LT	N90420	01606LT		PV
☐ Mono Aircraft Monocoupe 90A	NC19434	A-784	NC19434, N19434 – on loan.	RAA
☐ North American NA-231 Sabre (F-86F)	'55014'		Identity unknown.	PVX
☐ North American NA-88 Texan (AT-6D)				PVA
☐ Parker RP.9	N8008H	101		RA
☐ Rand Robinson KR-2	N491SY	1790		PV
☐ Stinson V-76 Sentinel (L-5G)				PVA
☐ Stinson V-77 Reliant (AT-19)	'FK104'	77-104	42-46743, FK917, Bu11542, N9280H	PVX
☐ Volmer Jensen VJ-21				PV
☐ Wright 1902 Glider (R)				RAC

SC VILLAGE PAINTBALL PARK (CA129)

Address:	8900 McCarty Road, Chino, California 91710.
Tel:	949-489-9020 **Email:** info@hollywoodsports.com
Admission:	Friday 1000-1600 1830-2230; Saturday 1830-2230.
Location:	About 3 miles south of Chino Airport.

The sport of paintball is popular in many countries. The 100-acre site at Chino has 25 different terrains from deserts to dense jungles for the participants to play their games. Spread around these areas are buildings and hazards. Four former military Sikorsky S-55s are in use in different areas of the complex.

TYPE	REG/SER	CON. NO.	PI/NOTES	STATUS
☐ Sikorsky S-58 Choctaw (H-34A) (CH-34A) (CH-34C)	N585HS	581745	63-13196	RA
☐ Sikorsky S-58 Seabat (XHSS-1) (YHSS-1) (YSH-34G)	Bu134670	580004		RA
☐ Sikorsky S-58 Seahorse (HUS-1) (UH-34D)	Bu145752	580850		RA
☐ Sikorsky S-58 Seahorse (HUS-1N) (UH-34J)	Bu143865	580451		RA

SCHELLVILLE AIRPORT COLLECTION (CA130)

Address:	23980 Arnold Drive, Sonoma, California 95476.
Tel:	707-938-2444
Admission:	Many hangars open at weekends and there are several 'Open Days' in the year.
Location:	About 8 miles west of Napa off Route 116.

This delightful airfield is home to large numbers of vintage and classic aircraft. At weekends many of the owners open their doors to visitors. Fly-ins occur regularly when many interesting types appear.

The list below includes many of the types that are housed here. The rare Curtiss-Wright CW-19R was recovered from South America in the mid-1990s by Don Carter. The aircraft was restored and is now resplendent in its original Bolivian Air Force colours. The Douglas DST was first delivered to American Airlines in 1935.

Five Luscombe aircraft are at the field. Four are the familiar Silvaires and the other is an 11. The prototype of this four seater first appeared in the late 1940s. The high wing monoplane was built to specifications from the Flying Farmers of America. They required an aircraft that could carry four people and, with the rear seats removed, six milk churns or items of machinery.

The Tiger Moth is one of many that were supplied to French aero clubs in the late 1940s and early 1950s. Under rebuild is the Cirigliano SC-1 biplane dating from the late 1920s. Built in the eastern states it was for a period on show in the Dart Airport Museum in New York State. The aircraft was fitted with a 145 hp Warner engine and at an early stage of its life had its fuselage lengthened.

The Ryan SCW-145 low wing cabin three seater first flew in 1937. Powered by a 150 hp Menasco engine it won acclaim at the National Aircraft Show in Chicago. Only 14 were built and 11 sold as it was too expensive for the private owner. A pair of the classic STA models reside in the hangars. The Grumman F3F biplane fighter first flew in 1935 and 147 were built for use by the Navy. The aircraft at Schelleville is one recovered from a crash site in Hawaii and rebuilt by Herb Tischler's Texas Airplane factory at Fort Worth several years ago.

TYPE	REG/SER	CON. NO.	PI/NOTES	STATUS
☐ Aeronca K	NC18844	K-110	NC18844, N18844	RAA
☐ Aeronca 7AC Champion	N81834	7AC-457	NC81834	RAA
☐ Aeronca 7AC Champion	N1350E	7AC-4911	NC1350E	RAA
☐ American Eagle Eaglet 231	NC479V	1031	NC479V, N479V	RAA
☐ Anderson Phoenix X-1A	N488MA	RB-01-4-88		RAA
☐ Beech B35 Bonanza	N5007C	D-2269		RAA
☐ Bellanca 8KCAB Decathlon	N8753V	201-75		RAA
☐ Blériot XI (R)	N39109	AB3		RAA
☐ Boeing-Stearman A75N1 Kaydet (N2S-4)	N73377	75-3402	Bu29971	RAA
☐ Boeing-Stearman A75N1 Kaydet (PT-17)	N1029P	75-813	41-1053, N38998	RAA
☐ Boeing-Stearman A75N1 Kaydet (PT-17)	N63585	75-2476	41-8917	RAA
☐ Boeing-Stearman B75N1 Kaydet (N2S-3)	N64037	75-6828	Bu07224	RAA
☐ Boeing-Stearman D75N1 Kaydet (PT-27)	N56233	75-3909	42-15720, FJ859	RAA
☐ Boeing-Stearman D75N1 Kaydet (PT-27)	N56749	75-3916	42-15727FJ866	RAA
☐ Bücker Bü 133C Jungmeister	N317D	45	U-98 (Switzerland), HB-MIG, D-EDAD	RAA

California

☐ CASA 1.131E [Bücker Bü 131 Jungmann]	N131JK		E.3B-439	RAA
☐ Cessna 195	N2134C	16119		RAA
☐ Cessna 195B	N775A	7631		RAA
☐ Cessna 195B	N3010B	7893	NC3010B	RAA
☐ Cessna 310	N4844B	35144		RAA
☐ Champion 7EC Traveler	N4738E	7EC-83		RAA
☐ Champion 7ECA Citabria	N86872	1028-74		RAA
☐ Champion 7ECA Citabria	N8564V	1049-74		RAA
☐ Champion 7GCAA	N570MA	496-2005		RAA
☐ Christen Eagle II	N582BB	BLACKWOOD 001		RAA
☐ Cirigliano SC-1 Baby Hawk	N775W	1	NC775W	RAC
☐ Curtiss 1E Jenny (JN-4H)	N3233	8644		RAA
☐ Curtiss 87V Warhawk (P-40N)	N540TP	29068	42-105306	RAA
☐ Curtiss-Wright CW-1 Junior (R)	N4644T	EHS-1		RAA
☐ Curtiss-Wright CW-19R	N19RX	19R-20		RAAX
☐ De Havilland DH.82A Tiger Moth	N838KC	86297	NL838, F-BGEP, N4970	RAA
☐ Douglas DST-217A (C-49E)	N139D	2165	NC21752, 42-43620, NC21752, N110SU,	RAA
☐ Ercoupe 415C	N99133	1756	NC99133	RAA
☐ Ercoupe 415C	N99180	1803	NC99180	RAA
☐ Fairchild 22 C7	N2853	1054	NC2853	RAA
☐ Fairchild 22 C7B	NC13166	1505	NC13166, N13166	RAA
☐ Fairchild 24R46	NC77671	R46-371	NC77671, N77671	RAA
☐ Fairchild 24W46	NC77656	W46-356	NC77656, N77656	RAA
☐ Fleet 1	NC607M	183	NC607M, N607M	RAA
☐ Funk B-75L	NC81115	245	NC81115, N81115	RAA
☐ Globe GC-1B Swift	N80630	1035	NC80630	RAA
☐ Globe GC-1B Swift	N80671	1076	NC80671	RAA
☐ Globe GC-1B Swift	N3307K	1300	NC3307K	RAA
☐ Great Lakes 2T-1A	N844K	91	NC830K	RAA
☐ Grumman G-37 (F3F-2)	N20RW	370	Bu0972	RAC
☐ Hatz CB-1	N2856A	007		RAA
☐ Helio H-295 Super Courier	N6464V	1414		RAA
☐ Kreider-Reisner KR-31 Challenger (C-2)	NC10290	358	NC10290, N10290	RAA
☐ Luscombe 8A Silvaire	N1562K	4289	NC1562K	RAA
☐ Luscombe 8A Silvaire	NC2949K	5676	NC2949K, N2949K	RAA
☐ Luscombe 8A Silvaire	N2041B	6468	NC2041B	RAA
☐ Luscombe 8E Silvaire	NC853K	4580	NC1853K	RAA
☐ Luscombe 11A	N1625B	11-131	NC1625B	RAA
☐ Mono Aircraft Monocoupe 90A	N11795	A-719	NC11795	RAA
☐ Mono Aircraft Monocoupe 90A	N15427	A-727	NC15427	RAA
☐ Nanchang CJ-6A	N6339K	3732012	(China)	RAA
☐ North American NA-88 Texan (SNJ-4)	N7078C	88-11319	Bu26755	RAA
☐ North American NA-121 Texan (AT-6D) (SNJ-5)	N9823C	121-42098	44-81376, Bu91082	RAA
☐ North American NA-122 Mustang (P-51D) (J 26)	N551GP	122-38780	44-72321, Fv26078, 1930 (Dominican Republic)	RAA
☐ Pilatus P.2-05	N6145U	36	A-116 (Switzerland), U-116 (Switzerland), F-AZCD	RAC
☐ Piper J-3C-65 Cub	NC22973	2870	NC22973, N22973	RAA
☐ Piper J-3C-65 Cub	N30202	4684	NC30202	RAA
☐ Piper J-3C-65 Cub	N5869V	9384	NC5869V	RAA
☐ Piper J-3C-65 Cub	N71008	18024	NC71008	RAA
☐ Piper J-5A Cub Cruiser	NC28083	5-99	NC28083, N28083	RAA
☐ Piper PA-16 Clipper	N5875H	16-493		RAA
☐ Piper PA-17 Vagabond	N4865H	17-165		RAA
☐ Piper PA-18-150 Super Cub	N333CP	18-7709189		RAA
☐ Piper PA-18-150 Super Cub	N2592S	18-7909166		RAA
☐ Piper PA-22-108 Colt	N4673Z	22-8208		RAA
☐ Piper PA-22-160 Tripacer	N8959D	22-6122		RAA
☐ Piper PA-24-260 Comanche	N8711P	24-4158		RAA
☐ Pitts S-1S Special	N288BB	8-009		RAA
☐ Porterfield 35-70	NC17490	190	NC17490, N17490	RAA
☐ Porterfield CP-65	NC34726	892	NC34726, N34726	RAA
☐ Porterfield LP-65	NC32362	816	NC32362, N32362	RAA
☐ Republic RC-3 Seabee	N6748K	1036	NC6748K	RAA
☐ Rose Parakeet A4-C	N14882	506		RAA
☐ Ryan SCW-145	NC18900	214	NC18900, N18900	RAA
☐ Ryan STA	NC14984	116	NC14984, N14984	RAA
☐ Ryan STA	NC17357	162	NC17357, N17357	RAA
☐ Schweizer SGU.2-22	N2202	8		RAA
☐ Stinson 108-3 Voyager	NC6982M	108-4982	NC6982M, N6982M	RA
☐ Stinson 10A Voyager	NC36738	8138	NC36738, N36738	RAA
☐ Taylorcraft DCO-65 Grasshopper (L-2M)	N4754K	L-4822	(USAAF)	RAA
☐ Temco GC-1B Swift	N78024	2024		RAA
☐ Vans RV-8	N319H	193		RAA
☐ Waco YKS-6	NC16522	4513	NC16522, N16522	RAA
☐ Waco YKS-6	NC16576	4514	NC16576, N16576	RAA

SISKIYOU FIREFIGHTER MEMORIAL AIR MUSEUM (CA131)

Address: PO Box 128, 1809 Fairlane Road, Yreka, California 96097.
Tel: 530-842-3516
Admission: Not yet open.
Location: At Weed County Airport which is about 4 miles north of Weed off Interstate 5.

The airfield has been an important base for the fleet of aircraft operated by the California Department of Forestry. The Tracker was flown in on 29th July 2005. The aircraft will be placed in a Memorial Garden honouring local fire-fighters. There will also be an exhibition tracing the work of the service.

TYPE	REG/SER	CON. NO.	PI/NOTES	STATUS
☐ Grumman G-89 Tracker (S2F-1) (S-2A)	N404DF	455	Bu136546	PV

SOLANO COMMUNITY COLLEGE (CA132)

Address:	PO Box 246, Suisun Valley Road, Suisun City, California 94585
Tel:	707-864-7000 Email: John.Urrutia@solano.edu
Admission:	By prior permission only.
Location:	In the north eastern part of the city.

Established as Vallejo Community College in 1945, the aviation department offers training in airframe, engine and avionics maintenance. Three instructional aircraft reside in the workshops but there may well be others. Also present are a number of engines and components as well as test rigs.

TYPE	REG/SER	CON. NO.	PI/NOTES	STATUS
☐ Cessna 210	N7488E	57188		RA
☐ Cessna 310C	N222RC	35907	N1807H	RA
☐ Piper PA-24-250 Comanche	N6568P	24-1690		RA

STOCKTON FIELD AVIATION MUSEUM (CA133)

Address:	7432 C.E. Dixon Street, Stockton, California 95206.
Tel:	209-982-0273 Email: museum@twinbeech.com
Admission:	By prior permission only.
Location:	About 3 miles south east of the town.

A civilian airport opened here in the 1930s. The site was taken over by the military and Stockton Field was dedicated in January 1941. An advanced pilot training school using AT-6A Texans moved in. Types also flown included the Boeing-Stearman Kaydet and the Cessna UC-78 Bobcat. Later in the war the Military Air Transport Service used it a centre for delivering supplies. After the hostilities ceased it returned to its former use. A number of restoration companies have been among the tenants in recent years. One of these is Twin Beech which specialises in the type. A number of these classics are always present and pleasure flights are available. A museum is being set up to trace the history of the site. Items of memorabilia have been acquired.

TYPE	REG/SER	CON. NO.	PI/NOTES	STATUS
☐ Boeing 345 Superfortress (B-29)	42-65401		Front fuselage only.	RA
☐ Douglas A-26C Invader			Front fuselage only.	RA
☐ Howard DGA-15P (GH-2)				RA

STOCKTON MONUMENT (CA134)

Location:	On permanent view at ALP 632 on Northrop Street near the airport.

TYPE	REG/SER	CON. NO.	PI/NOTES	STATUS
☐ Bell 209 Huey Cobra (AH-1G) (AH-1S)	70-15987	20931		PV

SUSANVILLE AIRPORT COLLECTION (CA135)

Address:	471-927 Johnstoneville Road, Susanville, California 96130.
Tel:	530-257-2030
Admission:	On permanent view.
Location:	About 5 miles south east of the town.

Three former military aircraft have been put on show at this general aviation airport. The field was active during World War II when it was mainly used by the Civil Air Pilot Training Program. The field is now home to private owners, flying schools and charter firms operating a wide range of types.

TYPE	REG/SER	CON. NO.	PI/NOTES	STATUS
☐ Bell 205 Iroquois (UH-1D) (UH-1H)	66-16374	8568		PV
☐ Bell 209 Huey Cobra (AH-1G) (AH-1F)	67-15684	20348		PV
☐ McDonnell M.98DF Phantom II (RF-4C)	'65-0022'	808	64-1022	PVX

TEHACHAPI MONUMENT (CA136)

Location:	On permanent view at the airport which is just north east of the town.

TYPE	REG/SER	CON. NO.	PI/NOTES	STATUS
☐ Bell 204 Iroquois (UH-1B)	N70105	650	62-4590	PV

TOMORROW'S AERONAUTICAL MUSEUM (CA137)

Address:	961 West Alondra Boulevard, Compton Airport, California.
Tel:	310-618-1155 Email: robin@tamuseum.org
Admission:	Daily 0800-2000.
Location:	In the southern suburbs of Los Angeles just north of Interstate 91.

California   179

Formed in 1997, the organisation was formerly known as the Torrance Aeronautical Museum and acquired premises at Torrance Airport. In 2002 a move was made to larger premises at Compton and a change of name took place.

The main aim of the group is to introduce youngsters from the local area to all aspects of aeronautics by working on aircraft and being flown around the locality.

TYPE	REG/SER	CON. NO.	PI/NOTES	STATUS
☐ Bell 204 Iroquois (HU-1B) (UH-1B)	60-3607	253	60-3607, N3231F, N10605	PV
☐ Bell 205 Iroquois (UH-1D) (UH-1H)	66-0765	5248		PV
☐ Cessna 152	N4644Q	15285046		PVA
☐ Cessna 172N	N734SV	17269085		PVA
☐ Cessna 172RG	N6259V	172RG0600		PVA
☐ Cessna 172S	N6048Z	172S10217		PVA
☐ Cessna 310Q	N315CB	310Q0434		PVA
☐ Cessna 318B Tweety Bird (T-37B)	60-0103	40585		RA
☐ Hughes 369M Cayuse (HO-6) (OH-6A)	67-16091	0476		PV
☐ Northrop N-156T Talon (T-38A)	61-0894	N.5260		PV
☐ Piper PA-23-250 Aztec	N513B	27-416	CF-NED, N1MR	PVA
☐ Piper PA-28-180 Cherokee B	N7506W	28-1418		PVA
☐ Piper PA-38-112 Tomahawk	N23680	38-81A0153		PVA

TONY LE VIER P-38 HANGAR MUSEUM (CA138)

Address: c/o March Field Museum, 16227 Interstate 215, March Reserve Base, California 92518-6463.
Tel: 909-697-6463   **Email:** staff@p38assn.org
Admission: Daily 1000-1600 (Closes at 1700 in Summer).
Location: On Interstate 215 about 4 miles south of Riverside.

This new museum was built in late 1997 in the grounds of the March Field Museum. The late Tony Le Vier joined Lockheed in April 1941 as a ferry pilot. He progressed to P-38 engineering test pilot the following year and became chief of this department in January 1945. He made the first flights of several types including the T-33, F-90, F-94, F-104 and U-2 before retiring in 1974. He was a well-known racing pilot in the late 1930s and in the immediate post-war period. He designed and raced the Cosmic Wind. There is a comprehensive display of photographs and memorabilia on show including some from the P-38 Association. The 475th Fighter Group which flew the P-38 has set up an exhibition in the hangar.

TYPE	REG/SER	CON. NO.	PI/NOTES	STATUS
☐ Lockheed 422-87-23 Lightning (P-38L) (FSM)	'44-27231'			PVX

TRAVIS AIR MUSEUM (CA139)

Address: Building 80, 461 Burgan Boulevard, Travis Air Force Base, California 94535.
Tel: 707-424-5605   **Email:** TravisAirMuseum@travis.af.mil
Admission: Tuesday-Saturday 0900-1600.
Location: Off Interstate 80 at Fairfield which is about 50 miles north east of San Francisco.

Work on the airfield started in 1942 and it was originally intended that medium bombers should be in residence. The Navy used the site for training for a short period. In 1943 Suisun-Fairchild Army Air Base came into being and was used by transports ferrying supplies to the Pacific Theatre. The field was renamed in the 1950s after Brigadier General Robert F. Travis who was killed in a B-29 crash in August 1950. At the current time the site is one of the major Military Airlift Command Bases on the West Coast. The 60th Air Mobility Wing operates its C-5, C-17 and KC-10 aircraft on missions all around the world.

The Travis Air Force Museum opened in 1985. The exhibition is located some distance from the main gate and plans have been put forward to move to a more accessible site but these have not yet come to fruition. The inside displays trace the history of the base and the many units which have been stationed at Travis. There are photographs, documents, uniforms, engines and components on view along with some of the smaller aircraft. The range of transport aircraft in the collection reflects the role of Travis over the last 60 years.

The outside airpark is dominated by the B-52, C-124. and C-133. Only a few Globemasters have survived from the almost 450 operated by the Military Air Transport Service. A C-141 Starlifter is stored on the other side of the airfield and will move to museum when space becomes available. The C-133 Cargomaster was based at Travis between 1958 and 1971. In August 2008 one of the few survivors arrived after a ferry flight from Alaska where it had flown on government contracts. Only 50 examples of the large transport were built between 1956 and 1961.

The Cessna 195 is painted to represent one of the fleet of LC-126s flown on liaison, search and rescue and instrument training duties. The Invader has been rebuilt in B-26K counter-insurgency configuration. The C-54 is parked a short distance from the museum and the F-4 and one of the T-39s are located by the gate to the base hospital.

TYPE	REG/SER	CON. NO.	PI/NOTES	STATUS
☐ Beech C18S Kansan (AT-11)	41-27616	1461	41-27616, N74RT	PV
☐ Beech D18S Expeditor (C-45H)	52-10865	AF-795	52-10865, N87694	PV
☐ Boeing 345 Superfortress (B-29) (SB-29)	42-65281			PV
☐ Boeing 464-201-7 Stratofortress (B-52D)	56-0696	464067		PV
☐ Cessna T-50 Bobcat (C-78) (UC-78)	43-31888	5826	43-31888, N61708	PV
☐ Cessna 195B	'49-7892'	16179	N2194C	PVX
☐ Cessna 310A Blue Canoe (L-27A) (U-3A)	'58-2127'	38005	57-5850, N51731	PVX
☐ Cessna 318B Tweety Bird (318A) (T-37A) (T-37B)	55-2972	40005	Front fuselage only.	PV
☐ Cessna 337M Super Skymaster (O-2A)	68-10848	337M0213		PV
☐ Convair 340-79 Samaritan (C-131D)	54-2806	201		PV
☐ Convair 20-10 Delta Dagger (F-102A)	56-1247	8-10-464		PV
☐ De Havilland DHC.4 Caribou (AC-1) (CV-2A) (C-7A)	60-3767	18		RA
☐ Douglas DC-3A-456 Skytrain (C-47A)	42-92990	12852	42-92990, N16602	PV
☐ Douglas DC-4 Skymaster (C-54B) (R5D-3) (C-54P)	'56505'	10505	42-72560, Bu56505, N67201	PVX
☐ Douglas DC-6A Liftmaster (R6D-1) (C-118A)	51-17651	43705	Bu131602	PV

☐ Douglas 1317 Globemaster II (C-124C)	52-1000	43909		PV
☐ Douglas 1333 Cargomaster (C-133A)	N199AB	45164	56-1999, N199AR, (HI-246)	PV
☐ Douglas A-26C Invader	'43-652'	18799	43-22652, N8018E, C-GHCE	PVX
☐ Fairchild M-62A Cornell (PT-19A)	N46180	T41-1232 (?)	41-20230 – possible identity.	PV
☐ Fairchild 110 Flying Boxcar (C-119F)	22134	10993	22134 (Canada), N15508	PV
☐ Fairchild 473 Provider (205) (C-123B) (C-123K)	55-4507	20168		RA
☐ Grumman G-234 Albatross (G-64) (SA-16A) (UF-1G) (UF-2G) (HU-16E)	7254	G-345	51-7254	RA
☐ Lockheed 18-40-03 Lodestar (C-56)	41-19729	18-2089	(NC33669), NC2333, NX33669, 41-19729, NC2333, N2333, N61M, N2333	PV
☐ Lockheed 183-93-02 Starfighter (F-104A)	56-0752	183-1040		PV
☐ Lockheed 300 Starlifter (C-141A) (C-141B)	63-8088	300-6019		RA
☐ Lockheed 580 (T-33A)	55-3021	580-9518	55-3021, N3497F	PV
☐ Lockheed 1329 JetStar 6 (C-140A)	59-5958	1329-5010		PV
☐ McDonnell M.36BA Voodoo (F-101B)	58-0285	657		PV
☐ McDonnell M.98DE Phantom II (F-4C)	63-7567	611	63-7567, N402FS	PV
☐ Medway Half Pint	G-MNXJ	14/7886		PV
☐ North American NA-174 Trojan (T-28A)	51-3693	174-231	51-3693, N14124 – front fuselage only.	PV
☐ North American NA-192 Super Sabre (F-100A)	52-5770	192-15		RA
☐ North American NA-201 Sabre (F-86D) (F-86L)	53-0704	201-148		PV
☐ North American NA-265 Sabreliner (T-39A) (CT-39A)	60-3483	265-11		RA
☐ North American NA-276 Sabreliner (T-39A) (CT-39A)	62-4452	276-5		PV
☐ Piasecki PD-22 Work Horse (H-21B) (CH-21B)	52-8688	B.50	52-8688, N6795	PV
☐ Piper J-3C-65 Cub (L-4B)	43-0753	9936		PV
☐ Republic F-84F Thunderstreak	52-6359			PV
☐ Republic F-105D Thunderchief	62-4299	D-498		PV
☐ Sikorsky S-58 Choctaw (H-34A) (VH-34C)	57-1705	58865	Identity doubtful.	PV
☐ Stinson V-76 Sentinel (L-5B) (OY-1)	'203917'		(USAAF), Bu03917, N5473V	PVX
☐ Vultee V-74 Valiant (BT-13A)	41-21933	74-5772		PV
☐ Waco NZR Hadrian (CG-4A)			Front fuselage only.	PV

TREASURE ISLAND MUSEUM (CA140)

Address:	Building 1, Treasure Island, California 94130.
Tel:	415-395-5067
Admission:	Variable
Location:	Close to San Francisco International Airport.

The island is man made and was built to be the first airport for the city after use as the site for the city's third World Fair. The Navy took over the area in 1941 and remained in residence until October 1997. The museum is housed in the art deco Building 1 which was planned as the future terminal for the airport.

The site was used as the base for Pan American Airways flying boats for a decade from the late 1930s. The story of the island, the three sea services, the 1939-40 World Fair, the local bridges and lighthouses are portrayed. A display in the lobby is often open.

TULARE RESTAURANT (CA141)

Location:	On permanent view at 240 North L Street in the town in the centre of the town.

TYPE	REG/SER	CON. NO.	PI/NOTES	STATUS
☐ Convair 240-17 (T-29A)	N1184G	223	50-193 – fuselage only.	PV

UNITED STATES AIR POWER MUSEUM (CA142)

Address:	4877 East Norwich Avenue, Fresno, California 93726.
Tel:	559-291-1239 Email: B.Dietzel@aol.com
Admission:	By prior permission only.
Location:	New site near Madera Airport planned or possibly at Fresno.

This organisation was formed in the early part of this century with the aim of restoring to flying condition examples of types which had made significant contribution to the concept of air power. A new complex was planned for Madera Airport but then Fresno was suggested. The project seems to have stalled.

TYPE	REG/SER	CON. NO.	PI/NOTES	STATUS
☐ Folland Fo.141 Gnat F.1				RA
☐ Lockheed 15-27-01 Harpoon (PV-2)	N7251C	15-1516	Bu37750	RA
☐ Saab 32A Lansen (A 32A)	N5468X	32209	Fv32209	RA

UNITED STATES MUSEUM OF NAVAL ARMAMENT AND TECHNOLOGY (CA143)

Address:	PO Box 217, Naval Weapons Center, Ridgecrest, California 93556-0217.
Tel:	760-939-3530 Fax: 760-939-0564 Email: clmfl@ridgenet.net
Admission:	Monday-Saturday 1000-1400 by obtaining a pass in advance.
Location:	In Blandy Avenue on the base which is about 25 miles north west of Barstow.

California

This vast desert base has many ranges within its boundaries. Over the years many surplus airframes have been used as targets and fortunately some of these have been rescued and are now on show at museums across the region. A small display was staged in one of the buildings and on show were examples of weapons used on the ranges. A few aircraft were parked nearby.

A fund raising drive was initiated and a new museum building opened in July 2000. The exhibition has been enlarged with many more interesting items on show. The site has been used for weapons development since its opening in 1943 and the displays trace this heritage. The work was carried out under the strictest security and only now can some of this be revealed. Outside the building are parked aircraft and missiles. This area is still under development and many of the airframes stored close to the airfield and on the ranges will eventually be brought here. The Skyray is the second prototype of the delta wing fighter. The example in the collection set a World Air Speed record in October 1953. The first of a batch of 18 pre-production Douglas Skyhawks is in store on the base and a two seat version is on show.

TYPE	REG/SER	CON. NO.	PI/NOTES	STATUS
☐ Bell 204 Iroquois (HH-1K)	Bu157178	6302		RA
☐ Bell 205 Iroquois (UH-1H)				RA
☐ Boeing 367-76-66 Stratofreighter (KC-97G) (C-97K)	52-2669	16700		RA
☐ Douglas Super DC-3 (R4D-8) (C-117D)	Bu12431	43395	Bu12431, N31310 – converted from DC-3A-456 Skytrain (C-47A) (R4D-5) c/n 9528 42-23666, Bu12431	RA
☐ Douglas XF4D-1 Skyray	Bu124587	7464		PV
☐ Douglas AD-4N Skyraider	Bu125739	7632		PV
☐ Douglas YA-4A Skyhawk (YA4D-1)	Bu137814	10711		RA
☐ Douglas A-4B Skyhawk (AD4-2)	Bu142120	11374		RA
☐ Douglas NTA-4F Skyhawk (TA-4E) (TA-4F)	Bu152102	13490		PV
☐ General Dynamics F-111B	Bu152715	A2-07		RA
☐ Grumman G-98 Tiger (F11F-1F) (F-11B)	Bu138647	44		PV
☐ Grumman G-98 Tiger (F11F-1) (F-11A)	Bu141814	131		RA
☐ Grumman G-105 Cougar (F9F-8T) (TF-9J)	Bu142441			RA
☐ Grumman G-128 Intruder (A-6A) (A-6E)	Bu152936	I-240		PV
☐ Grumman G-128 Intruder (A-6E)	Bu159312	I-550		RA
☐ Hawker-Siddeley P.1127 Harrier 50 (AV-8A)	Bu159249	P158		PV
☐ Hawker-Siddeley P.1127 Harrier 50 (AV-8A) (AV-8C)	Bu158969	P130	XY125	RA
☐ Lockheed 182-1A Hercules (182-44-03) (C-130A) (DC-130A)	57-0461	182-3168		RA
☐ McDonnell M.98AM Phantom II (F4H-1) (F-4B) (YF-4J)	Bu151473	550		RA
☐ McDonnell M.98AM Phantom II (F4H-1) (F-4B) (F-4N)	Bu150423	209		RA
☐ McDonnell M.98DH Phantom II (RF-4B)	Bu157348	3870		PV
☐ McDonnell M.267 Hornet (F/A-18A)	Bu160775	1/A001		PV
☐ McDonnell M.267 Hornet (F/A-18A)	Bu163092	473/A390		RA
☐ North American NA-227 Sabre (F-86F)		227-101	55-3916, 62-7479 (Japan)	PVX
☐ North American NA-316 Vigilante (RA-5C)	Bu156640	316-33		RA
☐ Vought DF-8L Crusader (F8U-1E) (F-8B) (F-8L)	Bu145528			RA
☐ Vought A-7C Corsair II	Bu156797	E64		PV

USS *HORNET* AIR AND SEA MUSEUM (CA144)

Address: 707 West Hornet Avenue, Alameda, California 94501.
Tel: 510-521-8448 **Fax:** 510-521-8327 **Email:** info@uss-hornet.org
Admission: Daily 1000-1700. (1800 in summer)
Location: About 2 miles south west of Oakland.

The original USS *Hornet* was sunk in the battle of the Santa Cruz Islands in October 1942. The famous Doolittle B-25 raid on Japan had been launched from this carrier six months earlier. The new *Hornet* was commissioned in November 1943 and served with distinction in World War II and the Korean and Vietnam wars. The carrier recovered the astronauts on the Apollo 11 and 12 missions before being retired.

After a quarter of a century in store the Hornet was handed over to the museum in 1998 and the ship is now moored at Alameda Point. Many areas are now open and a number of interesting displays can be seen. The history of both ships carrying the name 'Hornet' is told.

Life aboard a carrier in both peace and war is portrayed. The aircraft collection consists of types which have flown from carriers over the last 70 years. The Dauntless and Wildcat both served in World War II. The Dauntless was the main dive bomber flown by the US Navy from 1940 until late 1943. Almost 6,000 were built with the last ones being withdrawn by the Mexican Air Force in 1959. The Wildcat was considered to be one of the outstanding naval fighters of the first years of the conflict. First flown in 1937, 7,885 were built and also served with the US Marines, the Royal Navy and the Canadian military. Combat types and helicopters used in recent years are also on show.

TYPE	REG/SER	CON. NO.	PI/NOTES	STATUS
☐ Douglas SBD-4 Dauntless	Bu10508	2468	Bu10508, NZ5021	RAC
☐ Douglas A-4F Skyhawk				RA
☐ Douglas TA-4J Skyhawk	Bu158137	14174		PV
☐ Grumman G-36 Wildcat (FM-2)	Bu55052			PVD
☐ Grumman G-40 Avenger (TBM-3) (TBM-3R)	Bu69375	2114	Bu69375, N3965A – believed to be a composite.	PV
☐ Grumman G-89 Tracker (S2F-1S) (US-2B)	Bu136691	600	Bu136691, N36AM	PV
☐ Grumman G-98 Tiger (F11F-1) (F-11A)	Bu141821	138	Front fuselage only.	PV
☐ Grumman G-303 Tomcat (F-14A)	Bu162689	535		PV
☐ Kaman K-20 Seasprite (HU2K-1) (UH-2A) (SH-2F)	Bu149021	25	Bu149021, N8059T	PV
☐ Lockheed 394 Viking (S-3A) (S-3B)	Bu160599	394A-3179		PV
☐ McDonnell M.98AM Phantom II (F4H-1) (F-4B)	Bu148423	108	Front fuselage only.	PV

☐ McDonnell M.98EV Phantom II (F-4J) (F-4S)	Bu153879	2461		RA
☐ North American NA-181 Fury (FJ-2)	Bu132057	181-131		PV
☐ North American NA-200 Trojan (T-28B)	Bu138349	200-420	Bu138349, N4614	PV
☐ Piasecki PV-18 Retriever (HUP-1)	Bu124915			PV
☐ Sikorsky S-58 Seahorse (HUS-1) (UH-34D)	Bu150553	581680	Bu150553,N857BA	PV
☐ Sikorsky S-61B Sea King (HSS-2) (SH-3A) (SH-3H)	Bu148999	61073		PV
☐ Vought DF-8F Crusader (F8U-1) (F-8A)	Bu143703			PV
☐ Vought F-8K Crusader (F8U-2) (F-8C)	Bu147034		Front fuselage only.	PV

USS MIDWAY MUSEUM (CA145)

Address:	910 North Harbor Drive, San Diego, California 92101.
Tel:	619-544-9600 Fax: 619-544-9618 Email: dhanson@midway.org
Admission:	Daily 1000-1700.
Location:	At Navy Pier on the Embarcadero waterfront in the centre of the city.

The Midway was launched in March 1945 and served with distinction until April 1992. The ship was involved in the surrender of the Japanese in Tokyo and saw action in many conflicts including the Vietnam War and the 1991 Desert Storm operation. In 1947 a captured German V-2 rocket was launched from the carrier, thus beginning the naval missile programme.

An association was formed to save the ship from being scrapped and their dreams became a reality when the Midway berthed at Davey Pier. A great deal of work was carried out on the interior to make areas of the ship accessible to visitors. More zones are being restored and now large portions of the giant are open. The visitor can see many aspects of carrier life portrayed in the imaginative displays. The history of the carrier is shown in detail.

The collection of aircraft is increasing as more are allocated and a substantial number are now on show both on the flight deck and in the hangar below. The restoration workshops are located in hangars at North Island Naval Air Station where a number of aircraft are also stored.

TYPE	REG/SER	CON. NO.	PI/NOTES	STATUS
☐ Bell 204 Iroquois (HU-1B) (UH-1B)	60-3614	260	60-3614, N70264	PV
☐ Bell 205 Iroquois (UH-1H)	73-22131	13614		RAC
☐ Cessna 305A Bird Dog (L-19A) (O-1A)	51-4882		Possible identity.	RAC
☐ Douglas SBD-1 Dauntless	Bu1612	565		RAC
☐ Douglas SBD-6 Dauntless	Bu54654			PV
☐ Douglas Skyraider AEW.1 (AD-4W)	Bu127922	7937	Bu127922, WT987, G-31-3, SE-EBL, N5469Y	RAC
☐ Douglas EKA-3B Skywarrior (A3D-2) (A-3B)	Bu142251	11577		PV
☐ Douglas A-4F Skyhawk	Bu154977	13793		PV
☐ Grumman G-36 Wildcat (F4F-3)	Bu12290	5950		RAC
☐ Grumman G-40 Avenger (TBM-3) (TBM-3E)	Bu69374	2113	Bu69374, N9650C	RA
☐ Grumman G-40 Avenger (TBM-3) (TBM-3E)	Bu85957	2776	Bu85957, N9547Z	PV
☐ Grumman G-96 Trader (TF-1) (C-1A)	Bu146036	66	Bu146036, N32705 –	PV
☐ Grumman G-79 Panther (F9F-5)	'Bu141136'		Nose cone from F9F-8 Cougar Bu141136	PVX
☐ Grumman G-99 Cougar (F9F-8P) (RF-9J)	Bu141702	35		PV
☐ Grumman G-123 Hawkeye (E-2C)	Bu160701	A49	Front fuselage only.	PV
☐ Grumman G-123 Hawkeye (E-2C)	Bu161227	A67	Tail from c/n A53 Bu160988.	PV
☐ Grumman G-128 Intruder (A-6A) (A-6E)	Bu151782	I-85		PV
☐ Grumman G-303 Tomcat (F-14A)	Bu158978	39		PV
☐ Grumman G-303 Tomcat (F-14A)	Bu150157	107	Front fuselage only.	RA
☐ Kaman K-20 Seasprite (HU2K-1U) (UH-2B) (SH-2F)				
☐ Lockheed 394 Viking (S-3A) (S-3B)	Bu159766	394A-3095		PV
☐ McDonnell M.98AM Phantom II (F-4B) (F-4N) (QF-4N)	Bu153030	1557		PV
☐ McDonnell M.98EV Phantom II (F-4J) (F-4S)	Bu153880	2466		PV
☐ McDonnell M.267 Hornet (F/A-18A)	Bu162901	459/A377		PV
☐ North American NA-121 Texan (AT-6D) (SNJ-5)	Bu91091	121-42107	44-81385	PV
☐ North American NA-316 Vigilante (RA-5C)	Bu156641	316-34		PV
☐ North American NA-318 Buckeye (T-2C)	Bu156697	318-12		PV
☐ Piasecki PV-18 Retriever (HUP-2) (UH-25B)	Bu130059		Bu130059, N88949.	RAC
☐ Sikorsky S-58 Seabat (HSS-1N) (SH-34J)	Bu143939	58709		PV
☐ Sikorsky S-61B Sea King (HSS-2) (SH-3A) (SH-3H)	'Bu161072'		Bu149711	PVX
☐ Sikorsky S-70B Seahawk (SH-60F)	Bu164079	70645		PV
☐ Vertol V.107M Sea Knight (HRB-1) (CH-46A) (HH-46A) (HH-46D)	Bu150954	2040		PV
☐ Vought F4U-4 Corsair	Bu96885	9539	Bu96885, 618 (Honduras) – composite with parts of c/n 9213 Bu97059, 617 (Honduras)	PV
☐ Vought V-366 Cutlass (F7U-3)	Bu128451			RAC
☐ Vought V-366 Cutlass (F7U-3)	Bu129565			RAC
☐ Vought F-8K Crusader (F8U-2) (F-8C)	Bu147030			PV
☐ Vought A-7B Corsair II	Bu154370	B10		PV

VANDENBERG AIR FORCE BASE SPACE AND MISSILE HERITAGE CENTER (CA146)

Address:	747 Nebraska Avenue, Vandenburg AFB, California 93437-6257.
Tel:	805-606-3595 Email: jack.hokanson@vandenburg.af.mil
Admission:	By prior permission only.
Location:	About 10 miles north of Lompoc off Route 1.

California

The site opened as an Army training base in 1941. Orignally named after Major General Philip St. George Cooke, a cavalry officer who served from 1827 to 1873, it took up its current title in 1958. The Air Force took over in 1957 and developed a test centre for space rockets and missiles.

The Center has a exhibition tracing the history of rocket technology and the Cold War. Many examples of rockets tested at the site can be seen along with launching vehicles. In 1972 the field was chosen as the West Coast Space Shuttle site but was never used as such.

TYPE	REG/SER	CON. NO.	PI/NOTES	STATUS
☐ Curtiss 87V Warhawk (P-40N) (FSM)				RA

VICTOR VALLEY COLLEGE (CA147)

Address:	18422 Bear Valley Road, Victorville, California 92395.
Tel:	760-245-4271 Email: greulichb@vvc.edu
Admission:	By prior permission only.
Location:	In the southern part of the town.

The aviation maintenance course at the college has been suspended for the present time. A grant has been made to renovate the facilities up to the standards required by the FAA. The Boeing 727 was donated by FedEx is the only aircraft known to be at the site but there are likely to be others now in temporary storage.

TYPE	REG/SER	CON. NO.	PI/NOTES	STATUS
☐ Boeing 727-22F	N185FE	18871	N7064U	RA

VICTORVILLE MONUMENT (CA148)

Location:	On permanent view at the airport which is in the north western part of the town.

TYPE	REG/SER	CON. NO.	PI/NOTES	STATUS
☐ McDonnell M.98DE Phantom II (F-4C)	63-7519	536		PV

VINTAGE AIR MUSEUM (CA149)

Address:	18011 Incline Road, Hayward, California 94547-4621.
Tel:	510-782-9063
Admission:	Not yet open.
Location:	At Hayward Airport which is about 3 miles west of the town on Hesperian Boulevard.

The late Bud Field acquired a collection of vintage aircraft which are currently based at a number of airfields in the Bay area. Plans to construct a museum hangar at Hayward Airport were put forward but these seem to have stalled. In recent months a number of aircraft have left the collection and the future of the others is unclear. Just 40 Stearman 4s were built in the late 1920s-early 1930s. The 4CM-1 was a single seater designed for mail carrying. The Aristocrat three seat high wing monoplane was built in Buffalo in 1930. About 40 were produced and the sole survivor was restored at Blakesburg in Iowa by Bob Taylor and his sons.

TYPE	REG/SER	CON. NO.	PI/NOTES	STATUS
☐ Aeronca C-3	N16549	A-690	NC16549	RAA
☐ Aeronca C-3	NC17438	A-747	NC17438, N17438	RAA
☐ Boeing-Stearman 75 Kaydet (PT-13)	N75001	75-001	36-002, N53226, N77001	RAA
☐ General Aircraft Corporation Aristocrat 102-A	NC278H	20	NC278H, N278H	RAA
☐ Piper J-5C Cub Cruiser	N65940	5-1461	NC65940	RAA
☐ Piper PA-12 Super Cruiser	N3748M	12-2683	NC3748M	RAA
☐ Stearman 4CM-1	NC489W	4037		RAA
☐ Stinson Junior S	NC10852	8039	NC10852, N10852	RAA

WARBIRDS WEST AIR MUSEUM (CA150)

Address:	1942B Joe Crosson Drive, El Cajon, California 92020.
Tel:	619-449-1504 Email: WarbirdsWest@cox.net
Admission:	Friday-Sunday 1000-1600.
Location:	The airport is just north of the town which is about 12 miles north east of San Diego.

This museum has a hangar at Gillespie Field where four aircraft are based. The Delfin is based at March Reserve Base where there are longer runways. The Navion was designed by the North American company to fulfil the need for a light aircraft after World War II. By mid-1947 over 1,000 had been completed but many were unsold. The type certificate was acquired by the Ryan Aeronautical Corporation who put the type into production and over the years developed the design.

TYPE	REG/SER	CON. NO.	PI/NOTES	STATUS
☐ Aero L-29C Delfin	N443KT	892576	At March Field.	RAA
☐ Beech D18S Expeditor (C-45G)	N181MH	AF-29	51-11472, N602DM, N9576Z	RAA
☐ Beech A45 Mentor (T-34A)	N4WL	G-127	53-3366	RAA
☐ North American NA-145 Navion	N46LJ	NAV-4-312		RAA
☐ North American NA-252 Trojan (T-28C)	NX28CQ	252-17	Bu146254, N910KK, N254PJ	RAA

WATHEN COLLECTION (CA151)

Address:	4130 Mennes Aveune, Riverside, California 92509-6707.
Tel:	951-686-6660
Admission:	By prior permission only.
Location:	At Flabob Airport which is just south of Rubidoux.

Tom Wathen purchased Flabob Airport in May 2001 and it became home for his foundation which promotes education in mathematics, science and technology through aviation. Flabob opened in 1925 as the first civil airport for Riverside and the current field incorporates part of this site. After World War II pioneer homebuilt aircraft designers such as Ray Stits, Ed Marquart and Lou Stolp were in residence. In 1953 Sits asked Paul Poberezny, founder of the EAA, if he could form a local branch and Chapter One came into existence.

Replica aircraft were also built with World War I types emerging from the Appleby workshops and Golden Age racers being constructed by Bill Turner. Tom has acquired a number of these racers. On show at the Planes of Fame Museum at nearby Chino is a copy of the Laird-Turner LTR-14. The original won the Thompson Trophy at Cleveland in 1939 and is now part of the National Air and Space Museum collection. This aircraft was completed in 2000.

The de Havilland Comet was started in the late 1980s and first flew from Flabob in November 1993. The aircraft is painted in the red colours of 'Grosvenor House' which won the 1934 MacRobertson race from Mildenhall in England to Sydney in Australia. Also at Flabob is the Caudron C.460 built by the Aerocraftsmen team with help from graduates of the Wathen Aviation High School. This sleek racer flew in January 2009 and has since been taken to France where it appeared at the Paris Air Show and flown at Oshkosh. The Marquart MA-3 was started at Flabob in the early 1960s and was stored for many years. The biplane was finally completed in 1977.

TYPE	REG/SER	CON. NO.	PI/NOTES	STATUS
☐ Aero Commander 200D	N2980T	354		RAA
☐ Alon A-2	N55HE	A-23		RAA
☐ Caudron C.460 (R)	N6989	100		RAA
☐ De Havilland DH.88 Comet (R)	NX88XD/'G-ACSS'	T-7		RAA
☐ Ercoupe 415D	N3942H	4643		RAA
☐ Marquart MA-3 Maverick	N84F	MA-3-001		RAA
☐ Vans RV-4	N261Y	R-4-261		RAA

WEST COVINA MONUMENT (CA152)

Location:	On permanent view in Palmview Park in the town.

TYPE	REG/SER	CON. NO.	PI/NOTES	STATUS
☐ North American NA-190 Sabre (F-86D)	'6303'	190-187	52-3784 – covered in fibreglass.	PVX

WEST LOS ANGELES COLLEGE (CA153)

Address:	9000 Overland Avenue, Culver City, California 90230.
Tel:	310-287-4200 Email: info@wlac.edu
Admission:	By prior permission only.
Location:	Just north of Los Angeles IAP.

The college came into existence in 1969 and the aviation maintenance programme has been running for many years. Thes courses were started at the Los Angeles Airport College in 1947.

TYPE	REG/SER	CON. NO.	PI/NOTES	STATUS
☐ Bell 47G-3B-1 Sioux (TH-13T)	N9236Z	3534	66-4293	RA
☐ Cessna 150J	N51290	15069900		RA
☐ North American NA-265 Sabreliner (T-39A) (CT-39A)	'0350'	265-35	60-3507	RAX
☐ Cessna 150J	N5548G	15071048		RA
☐ Piper PA-23-250 Aztec B	N5324Y	27-2400		RA

WESTERN GLIDER AND SAILPLANE MUSEUM (CA154)

Address:	1720 Joe Crosson Drive, Hangar A-4, Gillespie Field, El Cajon, California 92020.
Tel:	619-596-2518
Admission:	By prior permission only.
Location:	The airport is just north of the town which is about 12 miles north east of San Diego.

Robert Fronius was the first resident on Gillespie Field when it became a civil airport in 1946. Over the last half century he has collected a number of vintage gliders, several hang gliders and a vast amount of archive material. The majority of the sailplanes are stored dismantled in the roof area of two hangars. Many photographs and flying models can be seen.

The Robinson Glider dating from 1942 was the first to feature a V-tail. Wally Nugent and Irving Culver were members of the Crown City Glider Club at Pasadena in the early 1930s. They designed a number of sailplanes including the Crown City CC-4 which set a world record in the summer of 1939. Culver developed his designs and in 1941 two examples of the Rigid Midget were built. In 1947 one came third in the US National Championships. One is in store at the National Soaring Museum at Harris Hill in New York State. The Williams version is a copy of this design and was built in the mid-1970s.

The Fronius family have constructed a number of gliders and light aircraft and the DF-7 is one of the latter. The PF-1 sailplane dates from the mid-1980s and only one was completed. Waldo Waterman of Santa Monica is best known for his attempts to produce a combined aircraft and car. He also built gliders in the 1930s and a replica of one-off designs is stored in the hangars. The collection also includes a pair of hang gliders. The sport is very popular in California with many clubs operating in the San Diego region.

TYPE	REG/SER	CON. NO.	PI/NOTES	STATUS
☐ Bowlus BA-100 Baby Albatross	N18997	106		RA
☐ Bowlus BA-100 Baby Albatross	N90841	169	Front fuselage only.	RA
☐ Crown City CC-4	N14287	CC4-36	N44W	RA
☐ Fronius DF-7	N39217	2		RA
☐ Icarus I Hang Glider				RA
☐ Laister-Kauffman LK.10A	N53619	48		RA
☐ MacCready Gossamer Penguin				RA
☐ Posnansky-Fronius PF-1	N15PF	1		RA

California

☐ Quickarus Hang Glider			RA
☐ Robinson JR-5	N18984	JR5	RA
☐ Schweizer SGS.2-8	N50796	43	RA
☐ Ultralight Flying Machines Easy Riser			RA
☐ Ultralight Flying Machines Easy Riser			RA
☐ Waterman Gull (R)			RA
☐ Williams Rigid Midget	N215JR	001	RA

WESTERN MUSEUM OF FLIGHT (CA155)

Address: 3315 Airport Drive, Torrance, California 90505.
Tel: 310-326-9544 **Fax:** 310-326-9556 **Email:** WMOFSCHAF@um.att.com
Admission: Wednesday, Friday-Sunday 1000-1500.
Location: Just south of the town on Route 1.

The Southern California Historical Aviation Foundation was set up several years ago by workers at the Northrop factory. This group became well known for the restoration of the N-3PB recovered from Iceland and now exhibited in Norway.

A decision was made to set up a museum and on 1st April 1985 a hangar was obtained on the municipal side of Hawthorne. In 2006 a move was made to Torrance and work on the new display hangar is proceeding. Not all the aircraft made the move and these are currently stored at a number of other airfields in the region. As the new site is developed and more space becomes available they will all be transported to their new home.

The group has a vast amount of memorabilia, models, photographs, components and documents. Only a small proportion can be shown at any time.

The collection includes many interesting types. The Canadian-built Tiger Moth underwent a protracted rebuild and took to the air again in 2004. The former US Navy Texan is being rebuilt as the prototype XAT-6F fined with a Ranger inline engine. The F-5 was obtained from Norway and the recently arrived Sabre is under rebuild.

Two Northrop YF-17s were built in the early 1970s and evaluated against the General Dynamics F-16. One was transferred to the Navy and served as a development prototype for the McDonnell Douglas F-18 Hornet. A pair of YF-23s was ordered to compete with the YF-22.

The JB-1 Bat glider was part of the Northrop flying wing programme which started with the N-1M in 1939 and culminated with the giant B-49 a decade later. The JB-1 was designed as a powered bomb, the project was initiated as a result of German success with the V-1 programme. The prototype was a single seat glider designed to be towed into the air and test flights were made at Muroc Dry Lake in 1944. The JB-1A was the powered version with a jet engine replacing the pilot. A single example of this was also constructed.

The diminutive Ecclestone Airvane is a homebuilt helicopter dating from the 1950s. The Ableiter Green Hornet single seat autogyro was developed in the late 1950s. A small number were completed, mainly by amateur constructors.

John Montgomery was one of the pioneers of flying in California. He constructed his first glider in 1893 and flew it a distance of about 600 feet on its maiden flight at Otay Mesa. The replica in the collection was built by Norman Ward.

The Fellers Sierra was used by the Northrop company as a demonstrator for the AX close support aircraft programme whish was won by the Fairchild-Republic A-10A Thunderbolt II. The Canadian-built Tiger Moth underwent a lengthy rebuild in the old hangar at Hawthorne.

TYPE	REG/SER	CON. NO.	PI/NOTES	STATUS
☐ Ableiter Green Hornet	N2750A	A-1		RA
☐ Bede BD-5B	N2261J	1808		RA
☐ De Havilland DH.82C Tiger Moth	N5994M	DHC.1257	1194 (Canada) (?), CF-CJE, (N822EK)	RA
☐ Douglas A-4A Skyhawk (A4D-1)	Bu142227	11481		RA
☐ Egglestone Airvane				RA
☐ Fellers Sierra Sr.1	N12K	1		RA
☐ Grumman G-303 Tomcat (F-14A)	Bu159830	190		pv
☐ Lockheed 580 (T-33A)	'90505'	580-7305	52-9239 – at airport terminal.	PVX
☐ Montgomery 1893 Glider (R)				RA
☐ North American NA-88 Texan (AT-6D) (XAT-6E)	NX74108	88-16022	42-84241	RAC
☐ North American NA-122 Mustang (P-51D)	NL44727	122-39198	44-72739 – as '414292'	RAA
☐ North American NA-227 Sabre (F-86F)	'52-4401'	227-122	55-3937, 62-7497 (Japan)	PVX
☐ Northrop N-16 Bat (JB-1)				RA
☐ Northrop N-156A Freedom Fighter (F-5A)	207	N.7030	66-9207 – in Norwegian markings.	PV
☐ Northrop N-160 Scorpion (N-68) (F-89D) (F-89J)	52-1870	N.4447	Rear fuselage and tail from c/n N.4445 52-1868	RA
☐ Northrop N-156T Talon (T-38A)	65-10454	N.5873	Fuselage only.	RA
☐ Northrop P.600 (YF-17A)	72-1569	C.0001	.	PV
☐ Northrop F-20A Tigershark (F-5G)		EDF 0889	Test airframe –	RA
☐ Northrop/McDonnell Douglas YF-23A	87-0801	1002	87-0801, N232YF.	PV
☐ Skyfly CA-65	N65CA	2		RA
☐ Stinson 108-1 Voyager	N97913	108-913		RAC
☐ Sunbird Hang Glider				RA
☐ WSK Lim-5 [MiG-17F]	'17'	1C 16-20	1620 (Poland), N317RJ – in false Soviet markings.	RAX

WHITTIER MUSEUM (CA156)

Address: 6755 Newlin Avenue, Whittier, California 90601.
Tel: 562-945-3871 **Fax:** 562-945-9106 **Email:** whittiermuseum@aol.com
Admission: Saturday-Sunday 1300-1600.
Location: In the eastern part of the city about 12 miles from the centre of Los Angeles.

This local history museum displays many aspects of life in the region since settlers moved into the region. The only aircraft on show is one flown by the late Bob Downey in pylon races in the 1970s. He owned the Downey Paper and Paint Store in the town. The Miller Special is mounted in a flying posture. Around the aircraft is a display of memorabilia, flying suits and other items tracing the flying career of Bob Downey. The JM-1 flew from the small airfield set up in the 1920s near the town. The museum has an excellent collection of vintage farm machinery. Many special exhibitions tracing the development of the region are staged.

TYPE	REG/SER	CON. NO.	PI/NOTES	STATUS
☐ Miller Special JM-1	N74J	M-101		PV
☐ Vought A-7B Corsair II	Bu154456	B96	Rear fuselage only.	RA

WINGS AND ROTORS AIR MUSEUM (CA157)

Address:	37350 Sky Canyon Drive, Hangar 7, Murrieta, California 92563.
Tel:	951-662-5653 Email: marketingdirector@wingsandrotors.org
Admission:	By prior permission only Monday-Friday 0630-1500.
Location:	About 4 miles east of the town on Route 79.

This museum was formed a few years ago with the aim of flying former military aircraft. The initial name was the Whittier Air Museum but the current title was soon adopted. The organisation was first based in the grounds of the March Field Museum but then moved to French Valley.

The types will mainly be those used in the Vietnam War. Their first project was a Huey which flew after restoration in 2002 and this was soon followed by the Kiowa. Both helicopters have been painted in typical period colours. At the current time the aircraft are housed in hangars in a secure area of the airport and can only be visited by appointment. Funds are being raised for a move to a larger hangar at the south end of the field. This facility will have public access. The early Phantom was involved in trials work and these led to substantial orders being placed. It last flew in 1964 and the spent 35 years in store at a number of locations. The fighter is undergoing a protracted rebuild to flying condition. A restored Iroquois has recently left the collection and moved to Alabama.

TYPE	REG/SER	CON. NO.	PI/NOTES	STATUS
☐ Bell 204 Iroquois (HU-1B) (UH-1B)	N832M	604	62-2084	RAA
☐ Bell 206A Kiowa (OH-58A)	N317CV	40202	68-16888	RAC
☐ Bell 206A Kiowa (OH-58A) (OH-58C)	N58WR	40809	70-15258, N9113T	RAA
☐ Hughes 269A Osage (TH-55A)	N3083D	0914	67-16807	RAA
☐ Hughes 269A Osage (TH-55A)	N57953	1015	67-16908	RA
☐ McDonnell M.98AM Phantom II (F4H-1F) (F-4A)	Bu145210	11		RAC

WINGS OF HISTORY – CALIFORNIA ANTIQUE AIRCRAFT MUSEUM (CA158)

Address:	PO Box 495, 12777 Murphy Avenue, San Martin, California 95046-0495.
Tel:	408-683-2290 Fax: 408-683-2291 Email: executivedirector@wingsofhistory.org
Admission:	Tuesday, Thursday, Saturday 1000-1500.
Location:	Near South County Airport which is about 20 miles south east of San Jose off Route 101.

Northern California has a rich aeronautical heritage. John Montgomery carried out glider development at Santa Clara from the mid-1880s until the mid-1910s and local resident Harriet Quimby was the first American woman to hold a pilot's licence.

Reid-Hillview Airport at San Jose opened in the late 1930s and aircraft which had been stored at the field during World War II were restored at the end of the conflict. The pilots and rebuilders gathered in the airport café and discussions led to the formation of a group which was named the Northern California Antique Airplane Association.

A fly-in was held at Watsonville in the early 1960s and this now annual event has grown and attracts large numbers of vintage aircraft from all along the West Coast. Proceeds from the event were used to purchase land adjacent to South County Airport. A clubhouse and small workshop were built and in 1989 a group devoted to setting up a museum came into being. Three hangars have now been constructed and an interesting collection of vintage and homebuilt aircraft are now on show with models, components and engines.

The 1928 American Eagle is a former Grand Champion at Watsonville. A rarity is the Alexander Primary Glider of which a large number were reportedly built. Volmer Jensen, who died in 1998, developed a large number of powered microlights and several of these are on show.

A new addition to the collection is the sole surviving Security S-1 B. The type is a simplified version of the Kinner Sportster and about 20 were built in the mid-1930s. A number of aircraft are currently being restored by the team of volunteers.

TYPE	REG/SER	CON. NO.	PI/NOTES	STATUS
☐ Aeronca C-3				PV
☐ Alexander Primary Glider				PV
☐ American Eagle A-101	NC????		Fuselage frame only.	PVD
☐ American Eagle A-101 (A-1)	NC7172	283	NC7172, N7172	PV
☐ Avro 616 Avian IVM	NC806N	104		RAC
☐ Beech 23 Musketeer	N2353J	M-311		PV
☐ Bensen B-8M Gyrocopter	N7801C	1		PV
☐ Bölkow Phoebus C-1	N737XP	838		PV
☐ Bowers Fly Baby 1A	N4722	65-56		PV
☐ Bowlus BA-100 Baby Albatross	N28387	165		PV
☐ Bowlus BS-100 Super Albatross	N21739	100		PV
☐ Bowlus S-1, 000	N317W	26		PV
☐ Breese Penguin (R)				PVA
☐ Culver LFA Cadet	N41719	LFA-436		RAD
☐ Da Vinci Ornithopter (R)				PV
☐ Dobbins Simcopter			Car-helicopter hybrid.	PV
☐ Experimental Aircraft Association P-1 Biplane	N345J	123		PVA
☐ Gross Pioneer II	N54271	3		PV
☐ Kinner Sportster B	NC14201	122	NC14201, N14201	PV
☐ Marketello Stahltaube	N1381N	001		PVA
☐ Nelson Dragonfly BB-1	N4ND	504	On loan from NSM, NY.	PV
☐ Peel Z-1 Glider Boat			On loan from NSM, NY.	PV
☐ Piel CP.305 Emeraude	N106MM	1216		PV
☐ Pietenpol B4-A Aircamper	NX86698	D-1		PV
☐ Quickie Aircraft Quickie 1 (Rutan 54)	N3150Q	397		PVA
☐ Rotorway Scorpion 1	N3225	12139		PV

California

☐ Security S-1-B Airster	NC15536	28		RAC	
☐ SPAD VII (R)				PVC	
☐ Sopwith Pup (R)	N54T	101		PV	
☐ Stinson 10A Voyager	N27740	7690	NC27740	PV	
☐ Stits SA-5A Flut-R-Bug	N37K	101		RA	
☐ Taylor JT.2 Titch				PV	
☐ Vickers 745D Viscount	N220RC	201	N7445, N923RC, N923RA, N500TL N220RC, XA-MOS – front fuselage only.	PV	
☐ Volmer Jensen VJ-21				PV	
☐ Volmer Jensen VJ-22 Sportsman	N5591	55		PV	
☐ Volmer Jensen VJ-23E				PV	
☐ Volmer Jensen VJ-24E				PV	
☐ Volmer Jensen VJ-24W	N55969	1		PV	
☐ Waco 10 (GXE)	NC3931	1201	NC3931, N3931	PV	
☐ Wright Flyer (R)				PV	

WOODLAND MONUMENT (CA159)

Location: On permanent view near the airport which is about 4 miles west of the town off Route 16,

TYPE	REG/SER	CON. NO.	PI/NOTES	STATUS
☐ Cessna 318E Dragonfly (A-37B) (OA-37B)	73-1114	43534		PV

YANKS AIR MUSEUM (CA160)

Address: 7000 Merrill Avenue, PO Box 35, Chino, California 91710-9084.
Tel: 909-597-1734 **Email:** christen@yanksair.com
Admission: Tuesday-Friday 0830-1530; Saturday 0830-1400.
Location: At Chino Airport which is about 7 miles south of Ontario on Route 83.

Charles Nicholls formed the Yankee Air Corps in 1972. Premises at Chino Airport were acquired and former B-17 pilot Stan Hoeffler, who died in 1998, was put in charge of the restoration programme. A large collection of warbirds and classic aircraft has been gathered. Work started in early 2011 on a new complex at Greenfield just off the main highway between Los Angeles and San Francisco.
A new exhibition building to display the restored aircraft was erected next to the Chino workshops in the late 1980s. There are a number of rare aircraft on show. The Curtiss Owl observation monoplane first flew in February 1941 and 203 were built. The YP-47M Thunderbolt is the first of three produced to test the improved Pratt and Whitney Double Wasp C series engine which enhanced the fighters top speed.
More than 20 N3N-3 biplanes were acquired in a derelict condition and a number have now been restored. One of these is displayed on floats. The type was ordered to replace the Consolidated NY-2 and NY-3. The first one flew in August 1935 and 997 were built. The N3N-3 was the last biplane to serve with the US Navy when the final example was retired at the Naval Academy in 1961. In the late 1920s Ray Page of Lincoln Aircraft bought the rights to the New Swallow and

150 slightly modified versions appeared as the LP-3. Clyde Cessna formed his own company in 1927 and its first product was the A series monoplane. Only 78 left the factory before the depression caused the plant to close.
In the early 1990s several aircraft were acquired from Herb Fyfield, who was killed in a forest fire at his home in Connecticut. The Thomas Pigeon flying boat was built in Boston in 1919 and probably never flew. The restored hull is on show. The Kellett autogyro came from the same source and this is now resplendent in its pre-war Army colours.
The Mutual Blackbird biplane was designed by Guiseppe Bellanca and first flew in 1929. The aircraft was damaged in a crash in 1931 and stored in a barn until discovered in 1995. A team at the San Diego Air and Space Museum at Gillespie Field restored the Blackbird in 2008 and soon afterwards it arrived at Chino.
The Schulz ABC glider was built for the 1937 Eaton Design Contest held along with the 8th US National Gliding Championships. The competition was for any new American design which had not been in previous nationals. Only four were completed and one served as a trainer at the military gliding school at Mobile, Alabama in 1942.

TYPE	REG/SER	CON. NO.	PI/NOTES	STATUS
☐ Aeronca C-2	N647W	27	NC647W	PV
☐ American Eagle A-101	N4289	100	NC4289	PVA
☐ Beech D17S (UC-43)	N51746	4890	43-10842, NC51746	PVA
☐ Bell 26F Airacobra (P-39N)	42-8881			RAC
☐ Bell 26F Airacobra (P-39N)	N81575		42-8740	PVA
☐ Bell 33 Kingcobra (P-63A)	N94501		42-69080, NX32750, N32750	PVA
☐ Bell 47D-1 Sioux (H-13E) (OH-13E)	N55230	940	51-14175	PVA
☐ Bellanca 17-31ATC Super Viking	N93669	73-31068		PV
☐ Boeing 464-260 Stratofortress (B-52F)	57-0042	17436	Front fuselage only.	PV
☐ Brunner-Winkle Bird BK	NC731Y	2039-19	NC731Y, N731Y	PV
☐ Canadair CL-13A Sabre 5 [North American F-86E]	'12910'	1100	23310	PVX
☐ Canadair CL-13B Sabre 6 [North American F-86E]	'1472'/'FU-472'	1472	23682 (Canada), 363 (South Africa), N3842H, N86CS, N3842H, (N313M)	PVX
☐ Canadair CL-13B Sabre 6 [North American F-86E]	'1487'/FU-487'	1487	23697 (Canada), 378 (South Africa), N38453	PVX
☐ Cessna AW	NC8782	167	NC8782, N8782	PVA
☐ Cessna T-50 Bobcat (C-78) (UC-78)	N46617	5193	43-7673 – composite.	PV
☐ Cessna 172A	N7791T	47391		PV
☐ Cessna 318B Tweety Bird (318A) (T-37A) (T-37B)	58-1874	40299		RA
☐ Cessna 318B Tweety Bird (318A) (T-37A) (T-37B)	58-1962	40387		PV
☐ Cessna 318B Tweety Bird (T-37B)	59-0289	40451		RA
☐ Cessna 318B Tweety Bird (T-37B)	59-0350	40512		RA

Aircraft	Reg	Serial	Other IDs	Status
☐ Cessna 318B Tweety Bird (T-37B)	64-13426	40841		RA
☐ Command-Aire 3C3	NC136E	532	NC136E, N136E	RA
☐ Consolidated 28-5 Catalina (PBY-5)	N2763A		Bu21232, N5609V, CF-GHU	PVA
☐ Consolidated 40 Privateer (PB4Y-2) (P4Y-2) (P4Y-2G) (Convair 100)	N2872G		Bu66300	PVA
☐ Convair 340-71 Samaritan (R4Y-1) (C-131F)	N9030V	296	Bu141013	PVA
☐ Convair 8-10 Delta Dagger (F-102A)				PV
☐ Convair 8-27 Delta Dart (F-106B)	57-2513	8-27-07		PV
☐ Curtiss 1C Jenny (JN-4D)				PV
☐ Curtiss 1C Jenny (JN-4D)	SC.34091			RAC
☐ Curtiss 1C Jenny (JN-4D)	N1563	D51		RA
☐ Curtiss 1C Jenny (JN-4D) (R)	'A996'	278-50B	N5102, NC996, N996J	PVX
☐ Curtiss 50B Robin B	N3865B	469	NC345K	RA
☐ Curtiss 50C Robin C-1	N374K	538	NC374K	PVA
☐ Curtiss 50H Robin J-1	N679R	679	NC778M, N778M, NC778M	PV
☐ Curtiss 84E Helldiver (SB2C-3)	N4250Y		Bu19075	PV
☐ Curtiss 85 Owl (O-52)	N61241	14302	40-2769	PVA
☐ Curtiss A87-A2 Kittyhawk I	'136483'	15208	AK827, 1038 (RCAF), N1223N, N40245	PVAX
☐ Curtiss-Wright CW-1 Junior	NC11850	1224	NC11850, N11850	PV
☐ Curtiss-Wright CW-20B Commando (C-46A)	N74173	289	43-47218, YV-C-ERB, N5134B, N137R- contains parts from CW-20B-4 (C-46F) c/n 22487 44-78664, N74173	PV
☐ De Havilland DH.60M Moth	NC917M	118	NC917M, N917M	PV
☐ Douglas DC-3A-456 Skytrain (C-47A)	N60480	9530	42-23668, N7252N, 42-23668	PVA
☐ Douglas SBD-4 Dauntless	N4864J	2478	Bu10518	PVA
☐ Douglas AD-4NA Skyraider (AD-4N)	N2692	7724	Bu126924, 19 (France), 126924 (Gabon), N2096P, N924JT	PV
☐ Douglas KA-3B Skywarrior (A3D-2) (A-3B)				PV
☐ Douglas KA-3B Skywarrior (A3D-2) (A-3B)	Bu138965	10826		PV
☐ Douglas A-4A Skyhawk (A4D-1)	Bu139960	11325		RAD
☐ Douglas A-4A Skyhawk (A4D-1)	Bu139969	11334		RAD
☐ Douglas A-4B Skyhawk (A4D-2)	Bu142892	11954		RA
☐ Douglas A-4C Skyhawk (A4D-2N)	N230AT	12961	Bu149636	PV
☐ Douglas A-4E Skyhawk (A4D-5)	Bu151038	13208		PV
☐ Ercoupe 415D	N99229	1852	NC3593H	RA
☐ Ercoupe 415D	N3593H	4218	NC3593H	RA
☐ Fairchild M-62A-4 Cornell (PT-26)				RA
☐ Fieseler Fi 103A-1				PV
☐ Gates Learjet 23	N73CE	23-068	N460F, N902AR, N902AB, N575HW, N9RA, N400PG, N152AG, XA-ARG, XB-GRR	PV
☐ General Dynamics F-111D	68-0092	A6-08		RA
☐ General Dynamics F-111D			Front fuselage only.	RA
☐ Grumman G-21A Goose (JRF-5)	N329	B140	Bu87746, C-151, C-1503, C-1503E, N1503H	PVA
☐ Grumman G-36 Wildcat (FM-2)	N6699K		(USN)	RAC
☐ Grumman G-36 Wildcat (FM-2)	N4629V	5618	Bu86564	PVA
☐ Grumman G-40 Avenger (TBF-1C)	Bu05997	4045		PV
☐ Grumman G-44A Widgeon (J4F-2)	N299CN	1299	Bu32945, N69198, N2PS, C-GWJA	PVA
☐ Grumman G-50 Hellcat (F6F-3)	Bu40467	1733		PVA
☐ Grumman G-50 Hellcat (F6F-5)	N9265A	A-9790	Bu78645	PVA
☐ Grumman G-79 Panther (F9F-2)	Bu123054	K-69		RA
☐ Grumman G-79 Panther (F9F-5)				RA
☐ Grumman G-79 Panther (F9F-5)				RA
☐ Grumman G-98 Tiger (F11F-1) (F-11A)	Bu141735	52		PV
☐ Grumman G-99 Cougar (F9F-8P) (RF-9J)	N9256	8	Bu141675	RA
☐ Grumman G-111 Albatross (G-64) (SA-16A) (SA-16B) (HU-16B)	N7024S	G-258	51-7195	PV
☐ Grumman G-123 Hawkeye (E-2C)	Bu161344	A75		PV
☐ Grumman G-128 Intruder (A-6A) (A-6E)	Bu155644	I-370		PV
☐ Grumman G-128 Intruder (A-6E)	Bu159895	I-571	Front fuselage only.	RA
☐ Grumman G-128 Intruder (A-6E)	Bu160995	I-596		PV
☐ Grumman G-303 Tomcat (F-14A)	Bu158985	46		PV
☐ Grumman G-303 Tomcat (F-14A)	Bu162607	529	Front fuselage only.	RA
☐ Hawker P.1101 Hunter T.7	N576NL	41H/693726	XL576, 8835M	PVD
☐ Hawker-Siddeley P.1127 Harrier GR.3	ZD668	41H/712229	ZD668, C-CBCU	PV
☐ Kellett KD.1 (YG-1B)	37-381	108		PVA
☐ Lincoln Page LP-3	NC3830	156	NC3830, N3830	PVA
☐ Lockheed 12-A Electra Junior (C-40D) (UC-40D)	N93R	1257	38-540, PP-PBV, NC970, N970, N93L	PVA
☐ Lockheed 080 Shooting Star (P-80C) (F-80C)	N729A	080-2467	49-0719	RAC
☐ Lockheed 183-93-02 Starfighter (F-104A)	56-0785	183-1073	Possible identity.	RA
☐ Lockheed 422-87-23 Lightning (P-38L)	N718	422-8187	44-27183, NC62441, N62441, N501MH, N517PA, (N5596V), N517PA	PVA
☐ Lockheed 580 (T-33A)	N48097	580-7086	51-9302	RA
☐ Lockheed 580 (T-33A)	10051	580-1549	58-0580 – in Yugoslav markings.	RA
☐ Lockheed 580 (T-33A)	10054	580-1637	58-0668 – in Yugoslav markings.	RA
☐ Lockheed 1049A-55-86 Super Constellation (RC-121D) (EC-121D) (EC-121T)	N548GF	1049A-4363	53-0548	PVC
☐ Martin 4-0-4				PV

California

☐ McCulloch MC-4A (XHUM-1) (HUM-1)	Bu133818	1002		PV
☐ McDonnell M.98DE Phantom II (F-4C)	'416263'	1055	64-0761	PVX
☐ McDonnell M.98DE Phantom II (F-4C)	64-0915	1378		RA
☐ McDonnell M.98EV Phantom II (F-4J) (F-4S)			Serial quoted as 41623 ?	PV
☐ McDonnell M.267 Hornet (F/A-18A)			Front fuselage only.	RA
☐ Mutual Aircraft Blackbird	X87		X87M	PV
☐ Naval Aircraft Factory N3N-3	N44738		Bu1775	RAD
☐ Naval Aircraft Factory N3N-3	N45117		Bu1780	RAD
☐ Naval Aircraft Factory N3N-3	N45024		Bu1790	RAD
☐ Naval Aircraft Factory N3N-3	N44757		Bu2621	RAD
☐ Naval Aircraft Factory N3N-3	N45283		Bu2623	RAD
☐ Naval Aircraft Factory N3N-3	N45306		Bu1998	RAD
☐ Naval Aircraft Factory N3N-3	N44815		Bu2698	RAD
☐ Naval Aircraft Factory N3N-3	N44713		Bu2704	RAD
☐ Naval Aircraft Factory N3N-3	N45269		Bu2736	RAD
☐ Naval Aircraft Factory N3N-3	N44742		Bu2783	RAD
☐ Naval Aircraft Factory N3N-3	N44744		Bu2785	RAD
☐ Naval Aircraft Factory N3N-3	N45070		Bu2804	PV
☐ Naval Aircraft Factory N3N-3	N45280		Bu2827	PV
☐ Naval Aircraft Factory N3N-3	N45012		Bu2875	RAD
☐ Naval Aircraft Factory N3N-3	N44760		Bu4407	RAC
☐ Naval Aircraft Factory N3N-3	N695M		Bu4480, N?????	PV
☐ Naval Aircraft Factory N3N-3	N44837		Bu4484	RAD
☐ Naval Aircraft Factory N3N-3	N45102		Bu4499	RAD
☐ Naval Aircraft Factory N3N-3				RAD
☐ Naval Aircraft Factory N3N-3				RAD
☐ Naval Aircraft Factory N3N-3				RAD
☐ Naval Aircraft Factory N3N-3				PV
☐ Naval Aircraft Factory N3N-3				PV
☐ Naval Aircraft Factory N3N-3				RAD
☐ Naval Aircraft Factory N3N-3				RAD
☐ Naval Aircraft Factory N3N-3				RAD
☐ North American NA-88 Texan (AT-6D) (SNJ-5)	N43771	88-15762	41-34532, Bu43771, N8099H, N612MD	PVA
☐ North American NA-99 Mustang (P-51A)	N90358	99-22377	43-6274, NX73630, N73630	PVA
☐ North American NA-108 Mitchell (B-25J) (TB-25J)	N6116X	108-47545	44-86791, N8196H, VH-XXV, 'A47-31'	PVA
☐ North American NA-122 Mustang (P-51D)	NL74920	122-41450	44-74910, F-351 (Indonesia), N51SJ	PVA
☐ North American NA-141 Fury (FJ-1)	Bu120349	141-38401		RAC
☐ North American NA-217 Super Sabre (F-100C)	N2011M	217-352	54-2091, 42091 (Turkey)	PVA
☐ Northrop N-156T Talon (T-38A)	61-0908	N.5274		PV
☐ Northrop N-156T Talon (T-38A)	63-8129	N.5476		RA
☐ Northrop N-156T Talon (T-38A)	63-8234	N.5581		RA
☐ Northrop N-156T Talon (T-38A)	64-13179	N.5608		PV
☐ Northrop N-311 Tiger II (F-5E)	5243	V.1143	76-1638 – in Taiwanese markings.	PV
☐ Piasecki PV-18 Retriever (HUP-2) (UH-25B)	Bu130022			RA
☐ Piasecki PV-18 Retriever (H-25A) (HUP-3) (UH-25C)	Bu147610		(USAF)	RA
☐ Republic P-47J Thunderbolt	N3152D	399-55885	45-49346, 4191 (Brazil)	PVA
☐ Republic YP-47M Thunderbolt (P-47J)	N27385/'227385'	93F-12000	42-27385, NX4477N, N4477N, N4477M, N4464N	PVAX
☐ Republic F-84E Thunderjet	49-2155			PV
☐ Republic F-84F Thunderstreak	51-1824		51-1824, N3996	RA
☐ Republic F-105D Thunderchief	59-1759	D-71		RA
☐ Republic F-105D Thunderchief	60-0471	D-159		PV
☐ Republic F-105D Thunderchief	60-0496	D-184	Fuselage only.	RA
☐ Ryan B-1 Brougham	NC6956	141		PVC
☐ Schultz ABC	N25699	G-6		RA
☐ Schweizer SGS.2-12 (TG-3A)	N44787	109	42-53127	RA
☐ Sikorsky VS-316A Hoverfly (R-4B)	43-46534	78		PV
☐ Sikorsky S-58B	N886X	58403		RA
☐ Sikorsky S-61R (CH-3C) (CH-3E)	62-12578	61503		PV
☐ Sikorsky S-62A Seaguard (HH-52A)	1375	62053		PV
☐ Standard J-1				PV
☐ Stearman 4E (4D)	NC11224	4026	NC11724, N11724	PVA
☐ Stearman 6L (6A)	N795H	6004	NC795H	PVA
☐ Stinson V-76 Sentinel (O-62) (L-5)	N723E	76-189	42-14986	PV
☐ Stinson V-76 Sentinel (L-5)	N6438C	76-419	42-98177	PV
☐ Swallow TP	NC8761	161		PV
☐ Thomas-Morse S-4C	N39735		39735	RA
☐ Thomas Pigeon		1		PV
☐ Vought V-310 Kingfisher (OS2U-3)	Bu09643	2731		RAD
☐ Vought F4U-4 Corsair	N47991	9544	Bu97390	PVC
☐ Vought A-7B Corsair II	Bu154475	B115		PV
☐ Vought A-7B Corsair II	Bu154538	B178		RA
☐ Vultee V-79 Valiant (BT-13B)	'79326'	79-326	42-89607, N4425V	PVAX
☐ Waco 10 (GXE)	N7887	1746	NC7665	RA
☐ Waco NZR Hadrian (CG-4A)	42-55896			PVC
☐ Waco NZR Hadrian (CG-4A)	45-13696			RAD
☐ Waco NZR Hadrian (CG-4A)	45-13698			RAD
☐ Waco UEC	NC18613	3684	NC18613, N18613	PVA
☐ Wozniak Double Eagle 1	N2717	1		PV
☐ Wright Flyer (R)				PV
☐ Yokosuka MXY-7 Ohka 11	'I-10'			PVX

COLORADO

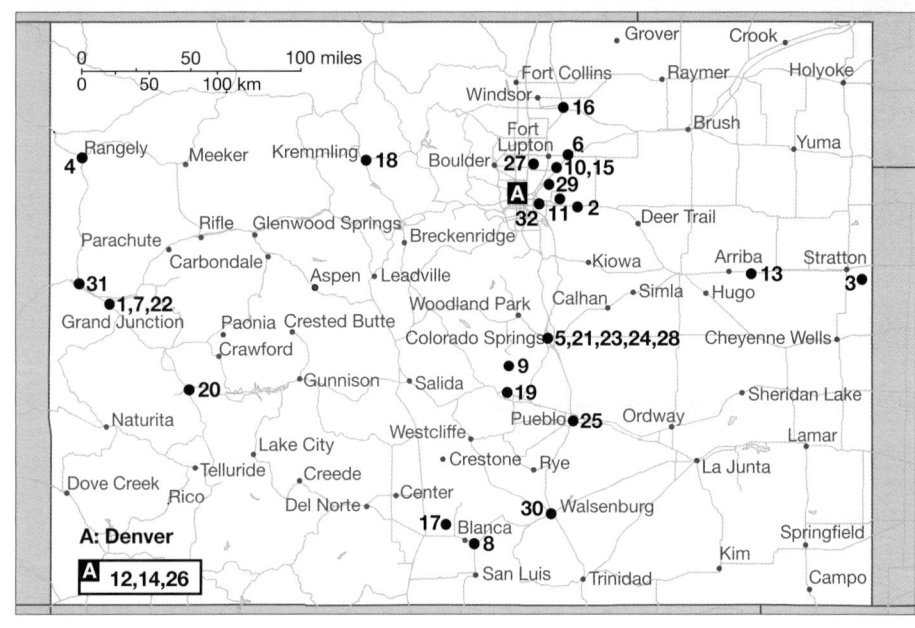

AVIATORS MEMORIAL PARK (CO1)

Address:	2828 Walker Field Drive, Grand Junction, Colorado 81506.
Tel:	970-244-9100 Fax: 970-241-9103
Admission:	On permanent view.
Location:	The airport is about 5 miles north east of the town off Interstate 6.

This park, honouring local aviators, was dedicated in November 1988. A landscaped area with a garden and memorial plaques was built by the approach road to the terminal.

A Grumman Tiger painted in 'Blue Angels' colours was put on show. The aerobatic team used the type from 1957 to 1958.

The fighter entered service with the US Navy in early 1957 and over 200 were built. The last were withdrawn from active units in 1969.

In 1998 a Grumman Intruder was allocated to the display and this is mounted nearby.

TYPE	REG/SER	CON. NO.	PI/NOTES	STATUS
☐ Grumman G-98 Tiger (F11F-1) (F-11A)	Bu141796	113		PV
☐ Grumman G-128 Intruder (A-6A) (A-6E)	Bu154131	I-266		PV

BUCKLEY AIR FORCE BASE COLLECTION (CO2)

Address:	460SW/PA, 510 South Aspen Street, Buckley Air Force Base, Colorado 80011-5000.
Tel:	720-847-9431 Email: 460sw.pa@buckley.af.mil
Admission:	By prior permission only.
Location:	About 12 miles east of Denver on Route 30.

The only flying unit in the Colorado Air National Guard was established in 1923 as the 120th Observation Squadron, based at Lowry with Curtiss JN-4s. The squadron transferred to Denver Municipal Airport in 1938. In 1946 a move was made to Buckley Field where, apart from periods of active service, the unit has remained. Currently the wing flies General Dynamics F-16s.

A Heritage Park is being set up close to the Wing Headquarters. In this building is display of memorabilia, photographs, models and equipment which traces the history of the airfield, the Colorado Air National Guard and its units.

The F-86 is in the colours of the 'Minute Men' which was the official Air National Guard display team in the 1950s. The team consisted of members of the Colorado unit and flew Lockheed T-33s and later F-86E Sabres. The Super Sabre was operated from 1961 until 1974 and the Corsair was in use from 1974 to 1991. A small number of Texans were flown on communications duties in the 1950s. The site is named after Lieutenant Harold Buckley, a Colorado man, who was shot down over France on a strafing mission behind enemy lines on September 17th. 1918. The airfield was transferred back to Air Force control in October 2000 and now houses a space wing.

TYPE	REG/SER	CON. NO.	PI/NOTES	STATUS
☐ Bell 204 Iroquois (UH-1C) (UH-1M)	'4-13484'	1384	65-9484	RA
☐ Bell 204 Iroquois (UH-1C) (UH-1M)	65-9540	1440		RA
☐ Bell 205 Iroquois (UH-1D) (UH-1H)	'O-12994'	4918	65-9874	RAX
☐ Bell 206A Kiowa (OH-58A)	69-16271	40492		RA
☐ Bell 209 Huey Cobra (AH-1S) (AH-1F)	80-23512	22300		RA

Colorado

☐ General Dynamics 401 Fighting Falcon (F-16A)	79-0373	61-158		RA
☐ Hughes 369M Cayuse (HO-6) (OH-6A)	65-12994	0079		RA
☐ North American NA-168 Texan (T-6G)				RA
☐ North American NA-172 Sabre (F-86F)	51-2884	172-167	51-2884, N57966, 51-2884, '112988'	RA
☐ North American NA-192 Super Sabre (F-100A)	'41897'	192-73	53-1578	RAX
☐ North American NA-235 Super Sabre (F-100D)	56-3299	235-397		RA
☐ Vought A-7D Corsair II	70-1001	D147		RA

BURLINGTON MONUMENT (CO3)

Location: On permanent view at VFW 6491 at 884 Rose Avenue in the south eastern part of the town.

TYPE	REG/SER	CON. NO.	PI/NOTES	STATUS
☐ Bell 209 Huey Cobra (AH-1G) (AH-1S)	67-15479	20143		

COLORADO NORTHWESTERN COMMUNITY COLLEGE (CO4)

Address: 500 Kennedy Drive, Rangely, Colorado 81648.
Tel: 970-675-3206   **Email:** lisa.lefevre@cncc.edu
Admission: By prior permission only.
Location: In the south eastern part of the town.

The college also has a flying training school using Cessna 172s. The ground instructional aircraft are at the main campus in the town. Courses for airframe and powerplant licenses are offered to students.

TYPE	REG/SER	CON. NO.	PI/NOTES	STATUS
☐ Beech B95 Travel Air	N9653R	TD-343		ra
☐ Beech C50 Seminole (L-23D) (U-8D)	N26565	LH-155	57-6094	RA
☐ Bell 204 Iroquois (HU-1B) (UH-1B)	62-1971	491		RA
☐ Cessna 170B	N3174A	25818		RA
☐ Cessna 337M Super Skymaster (O-2A)	N6531G	337M0455	69-7657	RA
☐ Cessna T310R	N3517G	310R0860		RA
☐ North American NA-252 Trojan (T-28C)	Bu146265	252-28		RA
☐ North American NA-276 Sabreliner (T-39A) (CT-39A)	N65618	276-42	62-4489	RA
☐ Sikorsky S-62A Seaguard (HH-52A)	1360	62036		RA

COLORADO SPRINGS RESTAURANT (CO5)

Location: On permanent view at Solo's Restaurant at 1665 North Newport Road in the eastern part of the town.

TYPE	REG/SER	CON. NO.	PI/NOTES	STATUS
☐ Boeing 367-76-66 Stratofreighter (KC-97G) (KC-97L)	53-0283	17065		PV

COMMEMORATIVE AIR FORCE (MILE HIGH WING) (CO6)

Address: PO Box 471596, Aurora, Colorado 80047-1596.
Tel: 303-929-0476   **Email:** n727pp@aol.com
Admission: By prior permission only.
Location: At Platte Valley Airport which is about 3 miles north west of Hudson.

The wing was formed in February 1999 and has about 30 members. A Beech Expeditor was maintained in flying condition until lost in a crash in July 2007. Another C-45 has now been allocated which saw active duty with the US Navy from July 1943 until 1965. The aircraft is painted in period colours and is as near as possible in original configuration. The displays in the building concentrate on World War I and World War II with photos, uniforms, models and documents.

TYPE	REG/SER	CON. NO.	PI/NOTES	STATUS
☐ Beech D18S Expeditor (C18S) (SNB-2) (SNB-5) (TC-45J) (UC-45J)	N49205	4784	Bu39265	PVA

COMMEMORATIVE AIR FORCE (ROCKY MOUNTAIN WING) (CO7)

Address: 780 Heritage Way, PO Box 4125, Grand Junction, Colorado 81502-4125.
Tel: 970-256-0693   **Email:** rvtglt@earthlink.net
Admission: By prior permission only.
Location: At Walker Field which is about 5 miles north east of the town off Interstate 6.

The wing was formed in the mid-1980s and over the years has restored the Avenger to World War II configuration. This aircraft was built by General Motors and saw service in with the Royal Canadian Navy before returning to the USA. The aircraft was ferried to Grand Junction from Mesa in Arizona and the rebuild took over four years. The wing has now extended its buildings and an exhibition of World War II memorabilia is on show. The Piper Cub joined the unit in the mid-1990s and is painted in a yellow training scheme. The other two aircraft are owned by members of the wing. The British-built Chipmunk is one of a batch of ten supplied to Burma for use by their Air Force. The aircraft was sold to the USA in the mid-1990s. The trainer is now painted in a silver scheme with yellow bands typical of many used by the Royal Air Force at their flying schools. The Texan is in the original yellow colours it wore when flown by the Navy from Kanahoe Bay in Hawaii in the latter stages of World War II. The wing offers rides in all four aircraft at Grand Junction and at local shows.

191

TYPE	REG/SER	CON. NO.	PI/NOTES	STATUS
☐ De Havilland DHC.1 Chipmunk T.20	N176AB	C1/0678	UB-176	RAA
☐ Grumman G-40 Avenger (TBM-3) (TBM-3E)	N53503	3565	Bu53503, 53503 (Canada), 315 (Canada), N6583D	RAA
☐ North American NA-121 Texan (AT-6F) (SNJ-6)	N5500V	121-42791	44-82069, Bu112023	RAA
☐ Piper J-3C-65 Cub	N6125H	19286	NC6125H	RAA

COSTILLA COUNTY VETERANS MEMORIAL PARK (CO8)

Location:	On permanent view in the eastern part of Fort Garland on Highway 160.

TYPE	REG/SER	CON. NO.	PI/NOTES	STATUS
☐ Lockheed 580 (T-33A) (TV-2) (T-33B)	Bu138064	580-9004	53-5665	PV

CRIPPLE CREEK VETERANS MEMORIAL (CO9)

Location:	On permanent view at the Mount Pisgah Cemetery in the western part of the town.

TYPE	REG/SER	CON. NO.	PI/NOTES	STATUS
☐ Bell 204 Iroquois (UH-1C) (UH-1M)	65-9541	1441		PV

DENVER AEROSPACE SCIENCE MUSEUM (CO10)

Address:	34701 East 56th. Avenue, Watkins, Colorado 80137-7181.
Tel:	303-755-3600
Admission:	By prior permission only.
Location:	At Front Range Airport which is about 20 miles north east of Denver north of Interstate 76.

This organisation was set up in the mid-1980s by John Mulvey. Three helicopters and a Percival Pembroke formed the initial collection but none of these remain. Premises at Centennial Airport were used but in the late 1990s a move was made to Front Range Airport. The Hughes helicopter is mounted on a trailer and is often taken to local events.

TYPE	REG/SER	CON. NO.	PI/NOTES	STATUS
☐ Douglas A-4C Skyhawk (A4D-2N)	Bu145074	12320		RA
☐ Douglas A-4L Skyhawk (A4D-2N) (A-4C)	Bu148600	12793		RA
☐ Evans VP-1 Volksplane				RA
☐ Folland Fo.144 Gnat T.1	N4367L	FL-572	XR955, A2678, XR955	RA
☐ Hughes 269A-1	N8928F	0004		RAA
☐ Rand Robinson KR-1				RA
☐ Smith Termite	N9005Z	1		RA

DENVER INTERNATIONAL AIRPORT DISPLAY (CO11)

Address:	8500 Pena Boulevard, Denver, Colorado 80249-6205.
Tel:	303-342-8477 Email: info@flydenver.com
Admission:	On permanent view.
Location:	About 20 miles east of the city centre.

The airport opened in 1993 replacing Stapleton which had served the city since 1929. Three aircraft can be seen in the terminal buildings. The Jenny was on show for many years at Stapleton. The Eaglerock was produced at Colorado Springs in the 1920s and 1930s. The Learjet was the first aircraft to land at the new airport.

TYPE	REG/SER	CON. NO.	PI/NOTES	STATUS
☐ Alexander Eaglerock A-14	NC205Y	977	NC205Y, N205Y	PV
☐ Curtiss 1C Jenny (JN-4D)	'65'			PVX
☐ Gates Learjet 35	N10BD	35-506	N3819G, N317BG	PV

DENVER SCHOOL (CO12)

Location:	On permanent view at a school at 4140 East Iliff Avenue in the south eastern part of the city.

TYPE	REG/SER	CON. NO.	PI/NOTES	STATUS
☐ Douglas DC-7	N6321C	44285	Fuselage only.	PV

FLAGLER MONUMENT (CO13)

Location:	On permanent view in the town park on Ruffner Avenue in the eastern part of the town.

TYPE	REG/SER	CON. NO.	PI/NOTES	STATUS
☐ Lockheed 580 (T-33A)	57-0587	580-1236		PV

FORNEY MUSEUM OF TRANSPORTATION (CO14)

Address:	4303 Brighton Boulevard, Denver, Colorado 80216.
Tel:	303-297-1113 Email: museum@forneymuseum.com
Admission:	Monday-Saturday 1000-1600.
Location:	In the centre of the city.

Colorado

The Forney company has been involved in many activities in the transport field. In the 1950s it produced 139 Ercoupes at its Fort Collins plant. An example of this type has joined the museum. There is an excellent collection of antique and classic cars to be seen. These include a Rolls Royce once owned by Prince Aly Khan. Motor cycles and bicycles also feature in the exhibition along with horse drawn carriages and carts. The largest steam railway engine in the world the aptly named 'Big Boy' is a prized exhibit. Just 25 of the class were operated by Union Pacific and eight are on show in museums across America. Also to be seen are locomotives made by the Forney company. The Beech 18 was used by the firm as an executive transport.

TYPE	REG/SER	CON. NO.	PI/NOTES	STATUS
☐ Beech C18S Navigator (AT-7)	N312	4137	42-2457	PV
☐ Forney F.1A	N7503C	5611		PV
☐ Quickie Aircraft Quickie 1 (Rutan 54)	N396B	396		RA

FRONT RANGE AIRPORT MONUMENT (CO15)

Location:	On permanent view at the National Guard Armory. which is about 20 miles north east of Denver north of Interstate 76.

TYPE	REG/SER	CON. NO.	PI/NOTES	STATUS
☐ Bell 205 Iroquois (UH-1D) (UH-1H)	66-1087	5570	With boom from c/n 13748 74-22424.	PV

GREELEY/WELD COUNTY AIRPORT MONUMENT (CO16)

Location:	At the airport which is about 3 miles east of the town on Route 34.

TYPE	REG/SER	CON. NO.	PI/NOTES	STATUS
☐ Northrop N-156T Talon (T-38A)	60-0586	N.5159		PV
☐ Vought A-7D Corsair II	69-6242	D72	At ANG base.	PV

HOMELAKE MONUMENT (CO17)

Location:	On permanent view at the Colorado State Veterans Center in the village.

TYPE	REG/SER	CON. NO.	PI/NOTES	STATUS
☐ Vought A-7D Corsair II				PV

KREMMLING MONUMENT (CO18)

Location:	On permanent view at a school on US.40.

TYPE	REG/SER	CON. NO.	PI/NOTES	STATUS
☐ Bell 209 Huey Cobra (AH-1G) (AH-1F)	68-15001	20535		PV

LEO BOSTON VIETNAM MEMORIAL PARK (CO19)

Address:	60298 Highway 50, Fremont County Airport, Penrose, Colorado 81240.
Tel:	719-784-3916 Fax: 719-276-7304
Admission:	On permanent view.
Location:	About 6 miles east of Canon City off Highway 50.

This park is dedicated to the personnel of the 12th Tactical Fighter Wing who flew the F-4C Phantom in the South East Asia during the Vietnam conflict. The memorial opened in 2001 and the names of over 100 members of the unit who lost their lives are on the wall behind the aircraft.

TYPE	REG/SER	CON. NO.	PI/NOTES	STATUS
☐ Bell 205 Iroquois (UH-1D) (UH-1H)	66-16478	8672		PV
☐ Bell 209 Huey Cobra (AH-1G) (AH-1F)	67-15599	20263		PV
☐ McDonnell M.98DE Phantom II (F-4C)	63-7551	585		PV

MONTROSE MONUMENT (CO20)

Location:	On permanent view at the airport which is in the north western suburbs of the town.

TYPE	REG/SER	CON. NO.	PI/NOTES	STATUS
☐ Vought A-7D Corsair II	70-1055	D201		PV

MOUNTAIN POST HISTORICAL CENTER (CO21)

Address:	2160 Barkeley Road, Fort Carson, Colorado Springs, Colorado 80913-2519.
Tel:	719-633-2867 Fax: 719-526-6573
Admission:	Monday-Friday 0900-1630.
Location:	About 3 miles south of the city off Route 83.

The Regiment of Mounted Riflemen fought in the 1847 Mexican War and after this was renamed the 3rd US Cavalry. Since then the unit has been involved in 40 campaigns in nine wars. The museum was set up in 1963 at Fort Meade in Maryland as a trophy room. The collection transferred to Fort Lewis in Washington and Fort Bliss in Texas before moving to Colorado. The indoor displays trace the history of the regiment in detail from the early days. The unit became mechanised in the early 1940s and tanks, armoured cars and personnel carriers from this time up to Desert Storm can be seen. The Iroquois and one of the Cobras are by the airfield, Another Cobra is parked near the main gate and the restored H-34 is outside the museum building.

TYPE	REG/SER	CON. NO.	PI/NOTES	STATUS
☐ Bell 205 Iroquois (UH-1D) (UH-1H)	64-13856	4563		PV
☐ Bell 205 Iroquois (UH-1D) (UH-1H)	65-9899	4943		PV
☐ Bell 206A Kiowa (OH-58A) (OH-58C)	71-20421	41282		PV
☐ Bell 209 Huey Cobra (AH-1G) (AH-1S)	67-15687	20351		PV
☐ Bell 209 Huey Cobra (AH-1G) (AH-1Q) (AH-1S)	68-15067	20601		PV
☐ Bell 209 Huey Cobra (AH-1S) (AH-1F)	79-23247	22292		PV
☐ Sikorsky S-58 Choctaw (H-34A) (VH-34A)	'76141'	58272	54-2874.	RACX

MUSEUM OF THE WEST (CO22)

Address: 462 Ute Avenue, Grand Junction, Colorado 81501.
Tel: 970-242-0971 **Fax:** 970-242-3960
Admission: May–September Monday-Saturday 0900-1700; Sunday 1200-1600. October–April Tuesday-Saturday 1000-1500.
Location: In the centre of the town.

The Museum of Western Colorado is responsible for a number of museums and sites in the area. The displays at the Museum of the West trace the history and development of the area. The visitor can follow the hardships settlers had to endure when they decided to set up homes in the region. There is a small aviation section tracing the history of flying in West Colorado. There are long-term plans to set up a separate museum covering this topic. On show is a Cessna 140.

TYPE	REG/SER	CON. NO.	PI/NOTES	STATUS
☐ Cessna 140				PV

NATIONAL MUSEUM OF WORLD WAR TWO AVIATION (CO23)

Address: 765 Aviation Way, Colorado Springs, Colorado 80916.
Tel: 719-641-0840
Admission: Not yet open.
Location: At the airport which is in the south eastern suburbs of the city.

The museum is being constructed to educate visitors in the contribution American aviation made to the conflict. There will be many interactive displays, artefacts and narrative tapes. The expansion of the aviation industry during this period will be highlighted. Next to the museum is WestPac restorations, noted for their rebuilds of World War II aircraft. Visitors will be able to view the aircraft in the workshops.

PETERSON AIR AND SPACE MUSEUM (CO24)

Address: 150 East Ent Avenue, Peterson Air Force Base, Colorado 80914-1303.
Tel: 719-556-4915 **Fax:** 719-556-8509 **Email:** 21sw.mu@peterson.af.mil
Admission: Tuesday-Saturday 0900-1600.
Location: In the south eastern suburbs of Colorado Springs.

Colorado Springs Municipal Airport opened in 1942 and the site was taken over by the Army Air Corps in May of that year. The base was named after Lieutenant Edward J. Peterson who was killed in a crash at the field on 8th August 1942. During World War II crews were trained here for photographic reconnaissance work. The base now houses the Headquarters of the Air Force Space Command and the North American Aerospace Defense Command. A worldwide network of radar stations and satellites are controlled from Peterson.

The museum was set up in the original civil terminal building in the 1980s and was initially called the Edward J. Peterson Space Command Museum. The history of the base and its units are portrayed in the displays. There is an excellent collection of models, over 1,300 Army Air Corps and Air Force patches, many uniforms, a VELA satellite and a sample of moon rock on show. The two fighters, which flew for many years with the RCAF, in Canadian markings illustrate the co-operation between the USA and Canada in NORAD.

The Curtiss P-40 replica replaced an original example which moved to the museum at Robins in Georgia. Four of the aircraft are mounted on pylons around the base and the others are parked in front of the exhibition building.

TYPE	REG/SER	CON. NO.	PI/NOTES	STATUS
☐ Avro Canada C.100 Canuck 5 (CF-100)	100779	679	18779 – in Canadian markings.	PV
☐ Convair 8-10 Delta Dagger (F-102A)	56-1109	8-10-326		PV
☐ Convair 8-31 Delta Dart (F-106A)	59-0134	8-31-23		PV
☐ Curtiss 87V Warhawk (P-40N) (FSM)	'1356255'		'390'	PVX
☐ Lockheed 383-04-05 Starfighter (F-104C)	'56-0808'	183-1224	56-0936	PVX
☐ Lockheed 580 (T-33A)	57-0575	580-1224		PV
☐ Lockheed 580 (T-33A)	57-0713	580-1362		PV
☐ Lockheed 880-75-13 Starfire (F-97A) (F-94C)	50-1006	880-8051		PV
☐ Lockheed 1049A-55-86 Super Constellation (RC-121D) (EC-121D) (EC-121T)	52-3425	1049A-4343		PV
☐ Martin 272E Canberra (B-57E) (EB-57E)	55-4279	381		PV
☐ McDonnell M.36BA Voodoo (F-101B)	58-0274	646		PV
☐ McDonnell M.36BA Voodoo (F-101B) (CF-101B)	101444	559	57-0381 – in Canadian markings	PV
☐ McDonnell M.98DJ Phantom II (F-4C)	'63-7589'	1118	64-0799	PVX
☐ McDonnell M.199-1A Eagle (F-15A)	76-0024	A176		PV
☐ North American NA-201 Sabre (F-86D) (F-86L)	53-0762	201-216		PV
☐ Northrop N-160 Scorpion (N-68) (F-89D) (F-89J)	52-1941	N.4518		PV
☐ Republic P-47N Thunderbolt	44-89425			PV

Colorado

PUEBLO WEISBROD AIRCRAFT / INTERNATIONAL B-24 MUSEUM (CO25)

Address:	City of Pueblo Memorial Airport, 31001 Magnuson Avenue, Pueblo, Colorado 81001.
Tel:	719-948-9219 **Fax:** 719-948-2437 **Email:** service@pwam.org
Admission:	Monday-Friday 1000-1600; Saturday 1000-1400; Sunday 1300-1600.
Location:	About 3 miles east of the town off Route 50.

In the mid-1970s the then Pueblo City Manager, Fred E. Weisbrod, decided to set up a museum at the city airport which had been an important B-24 training base in World War II. A collection of aircraft moved to the site and they were parked in a compound near the terminal building.

The Pueblo Historical Aircraft Society was set up in the 1980s to restore the airframes and to improve the site. Bill Feder, who formed the PHAS, became involved in constructing a series of display boards to commemorate the 50th anniversary of the B-24. A reunion of crews and factory workers took place at Fort Worth, Texas in 1989 where the 300 foot long panels were on show. These traced the history of the type and of the USAAF Groups which flew the bomber. The reunion committee decided that the panels should have a permanent home in Pueblo. A building close to the Weisbrod Museum was donated by the city to become the International B-24 Museum. The PHAS was reorganised and work started on the aircraft.

The DC-3 is in the high visibility scheme it carried when it served with the Naval Arctic Research Laboratory. The Bell 47 and Piasecki Work Horse were both restored at local schools. A Vought Cutlass has left the exhibition and this is under restoration by the Vought Retirees Group at Fort Worth in Texas. The Starfighter has moved from the USAF Academy in Colorado Springs. Two large hangars have now been completed and now most aircraft are under cover. A recent departure from the display is the first McDonnell Voodoo. The aircraft has now moved to the Evergreen Museum in Oregon.

TYPE	REG/SER	CON. NO.	PI/NOTES	STATUS
☐ Beech D45 Mentor (T-34B)	Bu144018	BG-325	Bu144018, N2086U	PV
☐ Bell 47G-3B-1 Sioux (TH-13T)	N14941	3682	67-15963	PV
☐ Bell 205 Iroquois (UH-1H)	72-21508	13207		PV
☐ Blériot XI (R)				PV
☐ Boeing 345 Superfortress (B-29A)	44-62022	11499		PV
☐ Boeing 450-157-35 Stratojet (B-47E) (NB-47E)	53-2104	44450	53-2104, N1045Y	PV
☐ Boeing-Stearman E75 Kaydet (PT-13D)	42-17780	75-5943		PV
☐ Cessna 318B Tweety Bird (T-37B)	67-22253	41062		PV
☐ Convair 240-53 Samaritan (C-131A) (HC-131A)	N3999P	53.14	52-5794, 5794 (USCG)	PV
☐ Douglas DC-3A-456 Skytrain (C-47A) (R4D-5) (SC-47H)	Bu17217	13227	42-93328, Bu17217, N64605	PV
☐ Douglas A-26C Invader	44-35892	29171	44-35892, 4435892 (France), N4811E	PV
☐ Douglas F-6A Skyray (F4D-1)	Bu134936	10530		PV
☐ Douglas A-4C Skyhawk (A4D-2N)	Bu147702	12466		PV
☐ Fairchild 110 Flying Boxcar (R4Q-2)	Bu131688	10855	Bu131688, N99574	PV
☐ Grumman G-98 Tiger (F11F-1) (F-11A)	Bu141853	170		PV
☐ Grumman G-99 Cougar (F9F-8) (F-9J)	Bu138876			PV
☐ Lockheed 080 Shooting Star (P-80C) (F-80C)	49-1782	080-2699	49-1782, (Ecuador)	PV
☐ Lockheed 137-27-01 Ventura II	AJ311	137-4449	AJ311, (USAAF), 'AF311'	PV
☐ Lockheed 183-93-02 Starfighter (YF-104A) (F-104A)	55-2967	183-1013		PV
☐ Lockheed 426-42-13 Neptune (P2V-5) (P2V-5F) (P2V-5FS) (SP-2E)	Bu128402	426-5248	Bu128402, 'Bu151353'	PV
☐ Lockheed 580 (T-33A) (TV-2) (T-33B)	Bu137939	580-8651	53-5312	PV
☐ North American NA-190 Sabre (F-86D)	52-3653	190-56		PV
☐ North American NA-223 Super Sabre (F-100D)	55-3503	223-185		PV
☐ North American NA-226 Trojan (T-28C)	Bu140064	226-12	Bu140064, N55534	PV
☐ North American NA-283 Vigilante (RA-5C)	Bu151629	283-35		PV
☐ Piasecki PD-22 Work Horse (H-21B) (CH-21B)	53-4347	B.97		PV
☐ Republic F-84C Thunderjet (P-84C)	47-1562			PV
☐ Sikorsky S-58 Seabat (HSS-1N) (SH-34J)	Bu148002	581254		PV
☐ Vought F-8A Crusader (F8U-1)	Bu145349			PV

REDSTONE COLLEGE OF AVIATION TECHNOLOGY (CO26)

Address:	10851 West 120th Avenue, Broomfield, Colorado 80021-3401.
Tel:	303-466-1714
Admission:	By prior permission only.
Location:	At Jefferson County Airport which is in the north western suburbs of Denver on Route 121.

The school was founded in 1965 and is part of the Westwood College empire. Courses in airframes, engines and avionics are offered at the complex at the airport. Four instructional airframes are known to be in use. The Mitsubishi twin was not completed when production ceased in Texas and it moved to the college in 1994.

TYPE	REG/SER	CON. NO.	PI/NOTES	STATUS
☐ Beech C35 Bonanza	N718F	D-2989		RA
☐ Cessna 172N	N2431E	17271280		RA
☐ Gates Learjet 24XR	N7015C	24-235	N51VL	RA
☐ Mitsubishi Marquise (MU-2B-60)		1570SA	(N503MA)	RA

SPIRIT OF FLIGHT CENTER (CO27)

Address:	2650 South Main Street, Building A, Erie, Colorado 80021.
Tel:	303-460-1156 **Fax:** 303-464-7576 **Email:** info@spiritofflight.com
Admission:	Monday-Friday 1000-1400.
Location:	At the airport which is about 2 miles south of the town.

Warbird Recovery has located and brought back to the USA a number of Messerschmitt Bf 109 airframes. These were initially hangared at Broomfield. The company has constructed the new museum building at Erie. Displays of memorabilia have been set up. Several aircraft are now on show and others will be moving from Broomfield.

The Bird Dog which was an instructional airframe at Redstone College is the prototype of the successful observation aircraft and made its maiden flight on 14th December 1949. More than 3,400 were completed over the next few years and the type served with distinction in the Korean and Vietnam conflicts.

TYPE	REG/SER	CON. NO.	PI/NOTES	STATUS
☐ Cessna 305 Bird Dog	N41694	601		PVA
☐ De Havilland DH.112 Venom FB.1	N2X1MJ	737	J-1527 (Switzerland), N9196M	RAA
☐ Fairchild M-62A Cornell (PT-19A)	N19WR	9504AE	43-31512, NC51641, N51641, N164SY, N164S	PVA
☐ Folland Fo.144 Gnat T.1	N572XR	FL-562	XR572	RAA
☐ Gates Learjet 24D	N500SQ	24D-325	N76RV, N416G, N500SW	RA
☐ Hawker Hurricane I	P3311			RAC
☐ Hunting-Percival P.84 Jet Provost T.5	N78SH	EEP/JP/1000	XW336, N8089U	RAA
☐ Lockheed 580 (T-33A)	51-9023	580-6807		RAC
☐ Messerschmitt Bf 109F-4	N441WR	10144	7	RAD
☐ Messerschmitt Bf 109F-4	N541WR	10145		RAD
☐ Messerschmitt Bf 109F-4		10212	Wings and other parts.	RAD
☐ Messerschmitt Bf 109F-4	N109WR	10256		RAD
☐ Messerschmitt Bf 109F-4		10276		RAD
☐ Mikoyan-Gurevich MiG-17A			(Bulgaria)	PVC
☐ North American NA-122 Mustang (P-51D)	N151GP	122-31517	44-63791, 1926 (Dominican Republic))	RAC
☐ North American NA-124 Mustang (P-51D)	N11636	124-48389	45-11636, N5467V	RAA
☐ North American NA-197 Texan (T-6G)	N4269R	197-40	52-8236, (Portugal)	RAA
☐ Shenyang JJ-5	N905DM	551604		RAA

UNITED STATES AIR FORCE ACADEMY COLLECTION (CO28)

Address:	United States Air Force Academy, Colorado Springs, Colorado 80840-5241.
Tel:	719-333-2025 Email: pa.comrel@usafa.af.mil
Admission:	A self-guided tour operates most days between 0900-1800.
Location:	About 5 miles north of the city off Interstate 25.

The academy was built in the late 1950s and occupies a striking setting below the Rampart Range. All Air Force officers undergo a four-year training course.

A collection of aircraft has been acquired and these are displayed at a number of locations around the vast complex.

The aircraft on the parade ground can only be seen from a distance or with an escort. The B-52 served in Vietnam and is one of the few of its type credited with shooting down an enemy fighter. The Schweizer TG-4A and the Northrop T-38A front fuselage are in the Visitor Center.

TYPE	REG/SER	CON. NO.	PI/NOTES	STATUS
☐ Boeing 464-201-7 Stratofortress (B-52D)	55-0083	17199		PV
☐ Cessna 172F Mescalero (T-41A)	N557AF		May be Cessna 150M.	PV
☐ Fairchild-Republic A-10A Thunderbolt II	77-0205	A10-130		PV
☐ General Dynamics 401 Fighting Falcon (F-16A)	75-0748	61-4		PV
☐ Martin SV-5J (X-24A)				PV
☐ McDonnell M.98EN Phantom II (F-4D)	66-7463	1967		PV
☐ McDonnell M.199-1A Eagle (F-15A)	76-0042	224/A194		PV
☐ North American NA-243 Super Sabre (F-100F)	56-3730	243-6		PV
☐ Northrop N-156T Talon (T-38A)	59-1602	N.5115		PV
☐ Northrop N-156T Talon (T-38A)	61-0883	N.5249	Front fuselage only.	PV
☐ Republic F-105D Thunderchief	60-0482	D-170	Composite.	PV
☐ Schweizer SGS.2-33A (TG-4A)	N94TH	566	80-900566	PV

VINTAGE AERO FLYING MUSEUM (CO29)

Address:	7507 County Road 39, Fort Lupton, Colorado 80621-8515.
Tel:	303-502-5347 Email: info@lafayettefoundation.org
Admission:	By prior permission only.
Location:	At Platte Valley Airpark which is north west of Hudson.

The museum is run by the Lafayette Foundation which is dedicated to preserving the memory of World War I. Land was acquired in 2001 and by the following year a hangar and museum building had been constructed. Displays telling the stories of the 'aces' of both world wars can be seen.

On show are many uniforms, photographs and memorabilia from the period. The replica aircraft are regular performers at shows across the country and in 2010 five flew to the EAA convention at Oshkosh in Wisconsin.

TYPE	REG/SER	CON. NO.	PI/NOTES	STATUS
☐ Cessna 140	N89673	8721		PVA
☐ Fokker D VII (R)	N18852	20		RAA
☐ Fokker D VIII (R)	N8105D	2790		RAA
☐ Fokker Dr I (R)	N152RB	20936		RAA
☐ Great Lakes 2T-1A	N435Y	152	NC435Y	PVA
☐ Piper PA-22-160 Tripacer	N86483	22-5777		RAA
☐ Replica Plans S.E.5A	N52RT	078252		RAA
☐ Royal Aircraft Factory S.E.5A (R)	N1917J	F-904		RAA
☐ Sopwith Pup (R)				RAA
☐ SPAD VII (R)				RAC
☐ Taylorcraft BC-12D	N95910	8210		PVA
☐ Vultee V-74 Valiant (BT-13A)	N54679	2990	41-10673	PVA

Colorado

WALSENBURG MONUMENT (CO30)

| Location: | On permanent view at the Colorado State Veterans Nursing Home at 23500 Highway 160. |

TYPE	REG/SER	CON. NO.	PI/NOTES	STATUS
☐ Bell 209 Huey Cobra (AH-1G) (AH-1F)	66-15309	20065		PV

WESTERN SLOPE WAR MEMORIAL PARK (CO31)

| Location: | On permanent view in Fruita near Exit 19 of Interstate 70. |

TYPE	REG/SER	CON. NO.	PI/NOTES	STATUS
☐ Bell 205 Iroquois (UH-1H)	'68-16307'	12634	70-16329	PV

WINGS OVER THE ROCKIES AVIATION AND SPACE MUSEUM (CO32)

Address:	7711 East Academy Boulevard, Denver, Colorado 80230-6929.
Tel:	303-360-5360 Fax: 303-360-5328 Email: curator@wingsmuseum.org
Admission:	Monday-Saturday 1000-1700; Sunday 1200-1700.
Location:	In the eastern suburbs of the town off Sixth Avenue.

Lowry Air Force Base became operational in February 1938 and its primary function was to ease the training load of Chanute AFB in Illinois. The site is named after Lieutenant Francis B. Lowry, a Denver man, who was killed in September 1918. Flying from the airfield ceased in June 1966 and training continued until the base closed on 30th September 1994.

The Lowry Heritage Museum opened on 18th September 1982 in a building used by the Air Force Academy between 1955 and 1958 before it moved to its new premises in Colorado Springs. On 1st November 1994 the Lowry Heritage Museum Foundation obtained a 30-year lease on Hangar 1 and on 1st December 1994, the 100th anniversary of Lowry's birth, the exhibition opened. Rooms around the vast building have been converted for display use. The new name was adopted and in March 1997 the museum was designated the official Air and Space Museum for Colorado.

The science of flight, the history of the base and World Wars I and II are featured. All these displays have been carefully thought out and present an informative view of the topics. President Eisenhower had his Summer White House nearby and one room has been dedicated to him with some of the furniture and fittings from this residence on show. There is also an excellent collection of models.

The aircraft are all displayed in the building with the exception of the B-52. Nearly all the military machines came from the Lowry Heritage Museum or from the training airframes in use.

These include one of the few surviving Douglas B-18s. This aircraft served with the Cuban Air Force in the late 1940s and early 1950s before returning to the USA. In 1958 it was impounded at Miami reportedly involved in gun running to Cuba. The bomber joined the Air Force Museum in 1961 and was on show at Cannon Air Force Base, New Mexico between 1985 and 1988. Civil aircraft are being added to present a comprehensive picture of Colorado aviation.

The restored Alexander Eaglerock was built in Colorado Springs where J. Don Alexander set up an aircraft manufacturing company in 1925. Albert Mooney soon joined the firm and redesigned the unsuccessful Eaglerock biplane. Over the next nine years 900 examples of the three-seater were built. The museum has made excellent progress in a short time.

TYPE	REG/SER	CON. NO.	PI/NOTES	STATUS
☐ Adam Aircraft M309 CarbonAero	N309A	001		PV
☐ Alexander Eaglerock Long Wing	NC2568	122	NC2568, N2568	PV
☐ Ball-Bartoe JW-1 Jetwing	NX27BB	001		PV
☐ Beech C18S Kansan (AT-11)	42-37496	4089	42-37496, N86?10, N209	PVC
☐ Boeing 464-201-3 Stratofortress (RB-52B)	52-0005	16495		PV
☐ Cessna 310A Blue Canoe (L-27A) (U-3A)	57-5894	38049	57-5894, '57-5853', N7502	PVX
☐ Christen Eagle II	N6LA	ANICH 0001		PV
☐ Convair 8-10 Delta Dagger (F-102A)	56-0984	8-10-201		PV
☐ Denney Kitfox I	N32HC	200		PV
☐ Douglas B-18A Bolo	39-025	2673	39-025, N62477, '39-522'	PV
☐ Fisher FP-404	N404RJ	4138		PV
☐ Gates Learjet 24	N241JA	24-131	N659LJ, N232R, N282R, N11FH	PV
☐ General Dynamics FB-111A	68-0287	B1-59		PV
☐ Grumman G-303 Tomcat (F-14A)	Bu159829	189		PV
☐ Hang Glider				PV
☐ Langley Aerodrome 4 (R)				PV
☐ Lockheed 383-04-05 Starfighter (F-104C)	56-0910	183-1198	56-0910, '70910'	PV
☐ Lockheed 580 (T-33A)	56-1710	580-1060		PV
☐ Lunger Beta 1	N12HL	1		PV
☐ Martin 272E Canberra (B-57E) (EB-57E)	55-4293	395		PV
☐ McDonald Primary Glider	N8013	1		PV
☐ McDonnell M.36BA Voodoo (F-101B)	58-0271	643		PV
☐ McDonnell M.98HO Phantom II (F-4E)	66-0287	2280		PV
☐ Miller DK-1	N603DM	003		PV
☐ Monnett Moni Tri-Gear	N39JG	259T		PV
☐ Murray A				PV
☐ Murray T	N7222	1		PV
☐ Nord N.3202	N2254R	62	62 (France)	PV
☐ North American NA-203 Sabre (F-86H)	53-1308	203-80		PV
☐ North American NA-245 Super Sabre (F-100D)	56-3417	245-67		PV
☐ Piper J-3C-65 Cub	N42427	14689		PV
☐ Pitts S-1S Special	N15JB	7-0366		PV
☐ Rand Robinson KR-1	N60BV	BH50		PV
☐ Republic RF-84K Thunderflash (RF-84F) (GRF-84F)	52-7266		52-7266, N4926C	PV
☐ Republic F-105D Thunderchief	60-0508	D-196		PV

☐ Rockwell B-1A Lancer	74-0160	003		PV
☐ Schweizer SGS.1-24	N91888	1	On loan from NSM, NY.	PV
☐ Schweizer SGS.2-33A (TG-4A)	N1192S	202	71-900202 – tail from N1191S c/n 201 71-900201.	PV
☐ Team Minimax 110R				PV
☐ Vought FG-1D Corsair	N194G	3311	Bu92050, N6604C – on loan.	PV
☐ Vought A-7D Corsair II	73-0996	D392		PV
☐ Wizard Hang Glider				PV
☐ Woods Woody Pusher WAS-2	N393EA	225		PV

CONNECTICUT

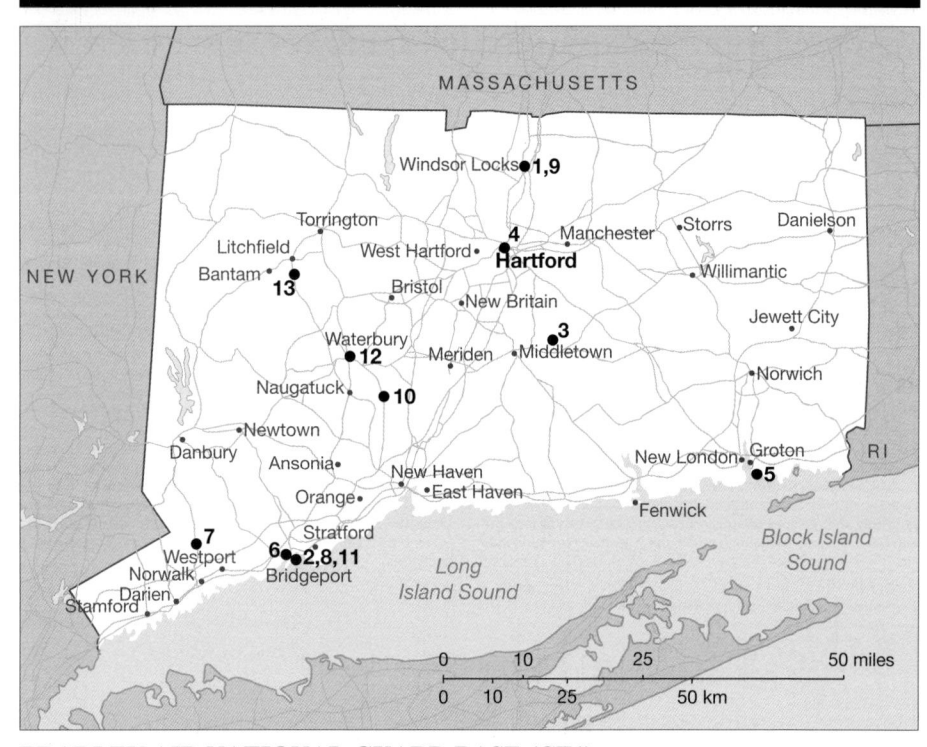

BRADLEY AIR NATIONAL GUARD BASE (CT1)

Address: 103AW/PA, Bradley International Airport, Windsor Locks, Connecticut 06026-5000.
Tel: 860-623-8291   **Email:** 103aw.pa@ctbrad.ang.af.mil
Admission: By prior permission only.
Location: On the north side of the airport which is about 15 miles north of Hartford.

Formed in 1923, the Connecticut Air National Guard was stationed at Brainart Field in Hartford and flew a variety of observation types up to 1941.
After World War II the unit was returned to state control as a fighter squadron and apart from a short period in the 1950s has been based at Bradley. On show by the main gate is an F-100D a type flown by the group from 1971 to 1979.
From 1966 to 1971 the unit flew the Convair F-102A and one has now been put on display along with an A-10A which was used from 1979 to 1993.

TYPE	REG/SER	CON. NO.	PI/NOTES	STATUS
☐ Convair 8-10 Delta Dagger (F-102A)	56-1264	8-10-481		PV
☐ Fairchild-Republic A-10A Thunderbolt II	79-0103	A10-367		PV
☐ North American NA-223 Super Sabre (F-100D)	55-3805	223-487		PV

CONNECTICUT AIR AND SPACE CENTER (CT2)

Address: P550 Main Street, Stratford, Connecticut 06615-7554.
Tel: 203-380-1400   **Fax:** 203-380-9174   **Email:** casc@casc.org
Admission: Not yet open.
Location: In the southern suburbs of the town near the airport.

Connecticut

This museum is being set up in part of a former army camp in Stratford. The area has an important aviation heritage as Sikorsky had a plant in the town until 1943.

The company merged with Vought in 1939 and products from both companies were produced. They subsequently split and Sikorsky built a new plant at Bridgeport. Restoration of the aircraft is taking place and associated items are being collected for the display.

The Corsair spent around four decades on a pole at the airport before recently moving into the workshops.

TYPE	REG/SER	CON. NO.	PI/NOTES	STATUS
☐ Bell 47G-2 Sioux (H-13H) (OH-13H)				RA
☐ Cessna 150L	N7021G	15074606		RA
☐ Cessna 305A Bird Dog (L-19A) (O-1A)			.	RA
☐ Cessna 318B Tweety Bird (318A) (T-37A) (T-37B)	57-2346	40279		RA
☐ Cessna 337M Super Skymaster (O-2A)	Bu721318	337M0024	67-21318	RAC
☐ Christen Eagle II				RA
☐ Lockheed 580 (T-33A) (TV-2) (T-33B)	Bu138084	580-9028	53-5689	RA
☐ Northrop N-156T Talon (T-38A)	61-0900	N.5266		RA
☐ Sikorsky S-52-3 (HO5S-1)	Bu128610	52058	1251 (USCG), Bu128610, N54059	RAC
☐ Sikorsky S-55D Chickasaw (H-19D) (UH-19D)				RA
☐ Sikorsky S-58 Choctaw (H-34A) (CH-34A)				RA
☐ Vought FG-1D Corsair	Bu92460	3721	Bu92460, 201 (El Salvador)	RAC

EAST HAMPTON MONUMENT (CT3)

Location: On permanent view at VFW 5095 in North Maple Street in the north western part of the town.

TYPE	REG/SER	CON. NO.	PI/NOTES	STATUS
☐ Bell 209 Huey Cobra (AH-1G) (AH-1F)	66-15325	20081		PV

EAST HARTFORD MONUMENT (CT4)

Location: On view during opening hours at Cabela's store at 475 East Hartford Boulevard North.

TYPE	REG/SER	CON. NO.	PI/NOTES	STATUS
☐ Aeronca 7AC Champion				PV

GROTON MILITARY MEMORIAL (CT5)

Address: 1109 AVCRAD, 139 Tower Avenue, Groton, Connecticut 06340-5300.
Tel: 860-441-2939 **Fax:** 860-405-2441
Admission: By prior permission only.
Location: At Groton – New London Airport which is in the southern suburbs of Groton on Route 649.

This facility repairs helicopters and other machines for the state forces. Three helicopters have been preserved. The Kiowa is mounted on a trailer and taken around the area as a mobile exhibit.

TYPE	REG/SER	CON. NO.	PI/NOTES	STATUS
☐ Bell 205 Iroquois (UH-1D) (UH-1H)	65-12776	5183		PV
☐ Bell 206A Kiowa (OH-58A)	70-15220	40771		RA
☐ Bell 209 Huey Cobra (AH-1G) (AH-1F)	66-15296	20052		PV

GUSTAVE WHITEHEAD HANGAR (CT6)

Address: Captain's Cove Seaport, Bridgeport, Connecticut 06605
Tel: 203-335-1433 (Seaport Office)
Admission: By prior permission only.
Location: In the south western part of the town.

Gustave Whitehead (formerly Weisskopf) settled in the West End of Bridgeport, in 1900. He conducted numerous experiments with gliders and heavier than aircraft, culminating in a one half mile powered flight over Long Island Sound, on 14th August 1901. This flight, verified by numerous witnesses, took place 28 months before the first flight of the Wright Brothers at Kittyhawk. Whitehead conducted other trials in the area including some near the present site of Captain's Cove Seaport. Unfortunately he kept no photographic records.

Displayed in the hangar is a one-half scale model of the Whitehead 21 aircraft, built by a local model maker.

TYPE	REG/SER	CON. NO.	PI/NOTES	STATUS
☐ Whithead 21 (Scale R)				PV

KNAPP COLLECTION (CT7)

Address: 24 1/2 Richdale Drive, Wilton, Connecticut 06897.
Tel: 203-762-9069
Admission: By prior permission only.
Location: In the town.

This private collection of militaria contains a number of vehicles and weapons with some in running order. The only aircraft is the UH-1M Iroquois. A small number of UH-1Cs were converted for use by the Army in Vietnam. They were fitted with a special Hughes system for night attack duties.

TYPE	REG/SER	CON. NO.	PI/NOTES	STATUS
☐ Bell 204 Iroquois (UH-1C) (UH-1M)				RA

This Boeing B-52D Stratofortress is mounted at one of the gates to the United States Air Force Academy. [CO28]

This Monnett Moni Tri-gear is on show in front of a McDonnell F-4E Phantom in the Wings Over the Rockies Aviation and Space Museum. [CO29]

The Delaware Aviation Museum has recently moved to new premises on Georgetown airport. A number of former Polish Air Force jets, including this Lim-6R, are in the collection. (Juha Ritaranta) [DE5]

Connecticut

NATIONAL HELICOPTER MUSEUM (CT8)

Address:	2480 Main Street, Stratford, Connecticut 06497.
Tel:	203-375-5766 Email: info@nationalhelicoptermuseum.org
Admission:	May–October Wednesday-Sunday 1300-1600. Reduced hours in winter.
Location:	At the Old Train Station which is in the north eastern part of the town close to Interstate 95.

Set up in 1985 the museum has a large collection of photographs and models tracing the development of rotary wing flight in the country. The Sikorsky company has its factories in the area and the town has been to the forefront in helicopter development. The Iroquois cockpit on show contains parts from several machines.

TYPE	REG/SER	CON. NO.	PI/NOTES	STATUS
☐ Bell 204 Iroquois (UH-1B)			Front fuselage only.	PV
☐ Sikorsky S-76			Front fuselage only.	PV

NEW ENGLAND AIR MUSEUM (CT9)

Address:	36 Perimeter Road, Bradley International Airport, Windsor Locks, Connecticut 06096.
Tel:	860-623-3305 Fax: 860-627-2820 Email: staff@neam.org
Admission:	Daily 1000-1700.
Location:	On the north side of the airport off Route 75.

In 1959 the Connecticut Aeronautical Historical Society was established with the aim of preserving the heritage of the region. A decision to set up a museum was soon taken and the Bradley Air Museum opened in May 1968. A large outdoor park housed the aircraft and displays were initially staged inside the larger transport types. In the early 1970s buildings were erected and an indoor exhibition opened.

Plans were put forward for the construction of a large hall but a few seconds of mayhem changed everything. Just before 3p.m. on 3rd October 1979 a tornado ripped through the site, completely destroying more than a dozen aircraft and badly damaging several others. Only a few escaped the attention of the wind.

With great determination the group set about rebuilding the collection. A large display hall was completed in time for the 1981 season and about 40 aircraft were on show. This hall is now known as the Civil Aviation Building. In the early 1990s a second exhibition area was constructed which now houses around 20 military types. In both halls and in the corridors between them a number of imaginative displays featuring photographs, engines and memorabilia have been set up. A hangar housing the B-29 is a new addition.

Outside the buildings around 20 more aircraft are parked. Visitors can see the current restoration projects in the workshop area. A rare aircraft is the last surviving Burnelli design, the CBY-3, which was constructed by the Canadian Car and Foundry firm in the mid-1940s. The museum obtained the twin-engined lifting-fuselage machine in 1973 and plans to restore it in the colours it carried on a 1953 Polar Basin Expedition.

The Sikorsky company has been based in the state for many years and a display tracing the history of the famous firm has been set up. The VS-44 was rebuilt at the Bridgeport factory in the 1990s. A range of the successful helicopters produced by Sikorsky is a highlight of the collection. Another local company, the Kaman Aircraft Corporation, also features prominently.

The Granville Brothers are honoured and a replica of one of their famous racers is on show. The sole surviving Granville Model A sport biplane is a rarity. Only nine examples were constructed in the early 1930s. The first was built at Boston and the others at Springfield. Other famous racers include the Laird Solution which won the 1930 Thompson Trophy at Cleveland and the modified Keith Rider R-3. The R-3 first flew in 1933 and the racer was financed by Edith Clark and Hal Marcoux. The low-wing monoplane crashed on its first flight but was soon repaired and set a record San Francisco to Los Angeles flight. Marcoux took over the aircraft in 1936 and with Jack Bromberg modified it in time to take second place in the 1936 Thompson Trophy.

The present name was adopted in 1984 to reflect the wider role of the museum in tracing the history of aviation in the region.

TYPE	REG/SER	CON. NO.	PI/NOTES	STATUS
☐ Aeronca 50C Chief	NC21070	1018	NC21070, N21070	PV
☐ Bell 47D-1 Sioux (H-13E) (OH-13E)	51-13749	335		RA
☐ Bell 204 Iroquois (UH-1B)	62-12550	708		PV
☐ Bell 209 Huey Cobra (AH-1G) (AH-1Q) (AH-1S)	70-15981	20925		PV
☐ Bensen B-8M Gyrocopter	N3112	JC-1		PV
☐ Blanchard Balloon (FSM)			Basket only.	PV
☐ Blériot XI	N9781	1		PV
☐ Boeing 345 Superfortress (B-29A) (TB-29A)	44-61975	11452		PV
☐ Boeing-Stearman A75N1 Kaydet (PT-17)	41-8786	75-2545	41-8786, N374RA	PV
☐ Brooks Balloon				PV
☐ Burnelli CBY-3 Loadmaster (Cancargo)	N17N	CAM1	CF-BEL	PV
☐ Chalais-Meudon Airship			Nacelle only.	PV
☐ Chanute Glider (R)				PV
☐ Convair 8-10 Delta Dagger (F-102A)	55-3450	8-10-159		RA
☐ Convair 8-10 Delta Dagger (F-102A)	56-1221	8-10-438		RAD
☐ Corben E Junior Ace	N964	164		RA
☐ Curtiss D Pusher		1		PV
☐ De Havilland DHC.2 Beaver (L-20A) (U-6A)	57-2570	1222		PV
☐ De Havilland DHC.4A Caribou (CV-2B) (C-7B)	62-4188	130		PV
☐ Doman LZ-5 (XH-31)	52-5780			PV
☐ Douglas DC-3-454 (C-49J)	N165LG	6314	NC14922, 43-1973, NC44792, N792G	PV
☐ Douglas A-26C Invader	N86481	18584	43-22699	PVC
☐ Douglas A-3B Skywarrior (A3D-2)	Bu142246	11572		PV
☐ Douglas A-4A Skyhawk (A4D-1)	Bu142219	11473		PV
☐ Douglas F-6A Skyray (F4D-1)	Bu134836	10430		PV
☐ Dyndiuk Sport				RA
☐ Fairchild-Republic A-10A Thunderbolt II	79-0173	A10-537		PV

☐ Fokker Dr I (FSM)				PV
☐ Ford JB-2 [Fieseler Fi 103A-1]				PV
☐ Gerath Hang Glider		1		RA
☐ Goodyear K-28 Puritan (ZNPK)	NX21A	C-86	Bu04378 – control car	PV
☐ Granville A Gee Bee Sportster	N901K	8	NC901K	PV
☐ Granville Gee Bee R-1 (R)	'NR2100'			PVX
☐ Great Lakes 2T-1A	N107C	6931K-420		PV
☐ Grumman G-36 Wildcat (FM-2)	Bu74120	4312		RA
☐ Grumman G-40 Avenger (TBM-3)	Bu23602	746	Front fuselage only –	PV
☐ Grumman G-50 Hellcat (F6F-5) (F6F-5K)	Bu79192	A-10337		PV
☐ Grumman G-79 Panther (F9F-2)	Bu125155	K-495		RAC
☐ Grumman G-117 Tracer (WF-2) (E-1B)	Bu147217	16		PV
☐ Grumman G-234 Albatross (G-64) (SA-16A) (UF-1G) (UF-2G) (HU-16E)	7228	G-310	51-7228 –	PV
☐ Grumman G-303 Tomcat (F-14B)	Bu162926	574		PV
☐ Gyrodyne QH-50C (DSN-3)		DS-1320		PV
☐ Gyrodyne XRON-1 (XHOG-1)	4005			S
☐ Heath LNB-4 Parasol	N13296	1		PV
☐ Hiller UH12C Raven (H-23G) (OH-23G)	62-3812	1460		PV
☐ Hughes 369M Cayuse (HO-6) (OH-6A)	67-16127	0512		PV
☐ Kaman K-16B (Grumman G-39 Goose (JRF-5))	Bu04351	1178	Bu04351, N1523V	PV
☐ Kaman K-225	N401A	5		PV
☐ Kaman K-240 Huskie (HTK-1) (TH-43E)	Bu128654	4-2		RA
☐ Kaman K-600 Huskie (HOK-1) (OH-43D)	Bu129801			RA
☐ Kaman K-600-1 Huskie (H-43A) (HH-43A)	58-1837		58-1837, N612	RA
☐ Kaman K-600-3 Huskie (H-43B) (HH-43B)	'60-0289'		Composite built from spares.	PVX
☐ Laird LC-DW-300 Solution	NR10538	192	NC10538	PV
☐ Lazor-Rautenstrauch LR-1A	N11ZZ	11		PV
☐ Lockheed 10-A Electra (XR2O-1)	'NC14262'	1052	Bu0267, NC57573, N57573	PV
☐ Lockheed 383-04-05 Starfighter (F-104C)	56-0901	183-1189		RA
☐ Lockheed 580 (T-33A) (TV-2) (T-33B)	Bu138048	580-8985	53-5646	PV
☐ Lockheed 880-75-13 Starfire (F-97A) (F-94C)	51-13575	880-8359		PV
☐ Marcoux-Bromberg R-3 (Keith Rider R-3)	NX14215	1		PV
☐ Martin 272A Canberra (RB-57A)	52-1488	71		PV
☐ McDonnell M.98EN Phantom II (F-4D)	66-0269	1936		PV
☐ Mead Rhön Ranger		1		PV
☐ Mikoyan-Gurevich MiG-15	N2276H		83277 (China)	PV
☐ Monnett Monerai S	N32WS	22		PV
☐ National Ballooning Ax-8 Hot Air Balloon	N3221B	110		RAA
☐ Navy Gas Training Balloon				RA
☐ Nixon Special				PV
☐ North American NA-98 Mitchell (B-25H)	'34381'	98-22200	43-4999, 2502 (Dominican Republic), N3970C	PVX
☐ North American NA-122 Mustang (P-51D)	N13Y	122-38859	44-72400, NX69406, NX13Y, N502, N913Y	RAC
☐ North American NA-176 Sabre (F-86F)	51-13371	176-302		PV
☐ North American NA-192 Super Sabre (F-100A)	52-5761	192-6		PV
☐ Northrop N-160 Scorpion (N-68) (F-89D) (F-89J)	52-1896	N.4473	Composite.	PV
☐ Piasecki PV-18 Retriever (HUP-2) (UH-25B)	Bu128598			RAD
☐ Piasecki PV-18 Retriever (HUP-2) (UH-25B)	Bu130063			RAD
☐ Piccard AX-5 Hot Air Balloon	N5W	18		RA
☐ Pioneer Flightstar MC	N54209	MC 658		PV
☐ Piper J-3L-50 Cub	NC31091	5374		PV
☐ Pratt-Read PR-G1 (LNE-1)	N5346G		Bu31561 – on loan from NSM, NY.	PV
☐ Quickie Aircraft Quickie 1 (Rutan 54)	N175HM	175		PV
☐ Raven S-40 Hot Air Balloon	N12000	S40-108		RA
☐ Rearwin 8135 Cloudster	N25549	825	NC25549	PV
☐ Republic P-47D Thunderbolt	'45-20344'	399-55997	45-49458, 451 (Peru)	PVX
☐ Republic F-105B Thunderchief	57-5778	B-15		PV
☐ Republic RC-3 Seabee	N6705K	988	NC6705K	PV
☐ Rutan 33 Vari-Eze	N477CM	0003		PV
☐ Ryan ST-3KR Recruit (PT-22)				RA
☐ Sikorsky S-16 (FSM)				PV
☐ Sikorsky S-39-B (S-39-A)	NC803W	904	NC803W, N803W	PV
☐ Sikorsky VS-44A (XJRS-1)	NC41881	4402	NC41881, Bu12391, N41881 -	PV
☐ Sikorsky VS-316A Hoverfly (R-4B)				RA
☐ Sikorsky VS-316A Hoverfly (R-4B)	43-46503	47	NX92820	PV
☐ Sikorsky VS-316B Hoverfly II (R-6A) (Doman mod)	N74146	124	43-45480	PV
☐ Sikorsky S-51 Dragonfly (H-5H)	N5219	5119	(Canada)	PV
☐ Sikorsky S-55D Chickasaw (H-19D) (UH-19D)	56-4257	551138		PV
☐ Sikorsky S-58 Seahorse (HUS-1L) (LH-34D)	Bu145717	58804		RA
☐ Sikorsky S-59	N74150	59004		RA
☐ Sikorsky S-60 Skycrane	N807	60001		PV
☐ Sikorsky S-62A Seaguard (HH-52A)	1428	62116		PV
☐ Sikorsky S-64A Tarhe (CH-54B)	69-18465	64072	Pod from 68-18589.	PV
☐ Stinson SR-5 Reliant	N13838	9203	NC13838	RA
☐ Stinson 10A Voyager	NC34645	8045	NC34645, N34645	PV
☐ Sud-Est SE.210 Caravelle VI-R	N902MW	88	N1003U, OY-SAH	PV
☐ Ultralight 166 Mosquito		166064		PV
☐ Viking B-8 Kittyhawk	N13250	30		PV
☐ Vought XF4U-4 Corsair	Bu80759			PV
☐ Vought A-7D Corsair II	69-6201	D51		PV
☐ Waco YKC-S	NC14614	4236	NC14614, N14614	PV
☐ Zephyr ZAL				RA

PROSPECT MONUMENT (CT10)

Location:	On permanent view at VFW 8075 at 220 Cheshire Road about 2 miles north east of the town.

TYPE	REG/SER	CON. NO.	PI/NOTES	STATUS
☐ Bell 209 Huey Cobra (AH-1G) (AH-1F)	67-15809	20473		PV

STRATFORD SCHOOL FOR AVIATION MAINTENANCE TECHNICIANS (CT11)

Address:	Sikorsky Memorial Airport, 200 Great Meadow Road, Stratford, Connecticut 06615
Tel:	203-381-9250 **Fax:** 203-381-0674 **Email:** sikorsky@ct.gov
Admission:	By prior permission only.
Location:	In the southern part of the town.

This long established school trains technicians in a number of fields. The college has three instructional airframes but work on local private machines is also carried out under supervision of the staff.

TYPE	REG/SER	CON. NO.	PI/NOTES	STATUS
☐ Beech 65-80 Queen Air	N61665	LD-135	N135Q, CR-LLW, 9Q-CRO, G-BDXU, ZS-JWD, G-BDXU, ZS-JWD, N8514N, 85-24373	RA
☐ Bell 205 Iroquois (UH-1D) (UH-1H)	62-12359	4017		RA
☐ Piper PA-28-140 Cherokee		28-22328		RA

WATERBURY MONUMENT (CT12)

Location:	On permanent view in a Veterans Park in the town.

TYPE	REG/SER	CON. NO.	PI/NOTES	STATUS
☐ Bell 209 Huey Cobra (AH-1G) (AH-1F)	70-15896	20930		PV

WINVIAN RESORT (CT13)

Location:	By prior permission only at the complex in Litchfield Hills.

TYPE	REG/SER	CON. NO.	PI/NOTES	STATUS
☐ Sikorsky S-61R Pelican (HH-3F)	1484	61661		RA

DELAWARE

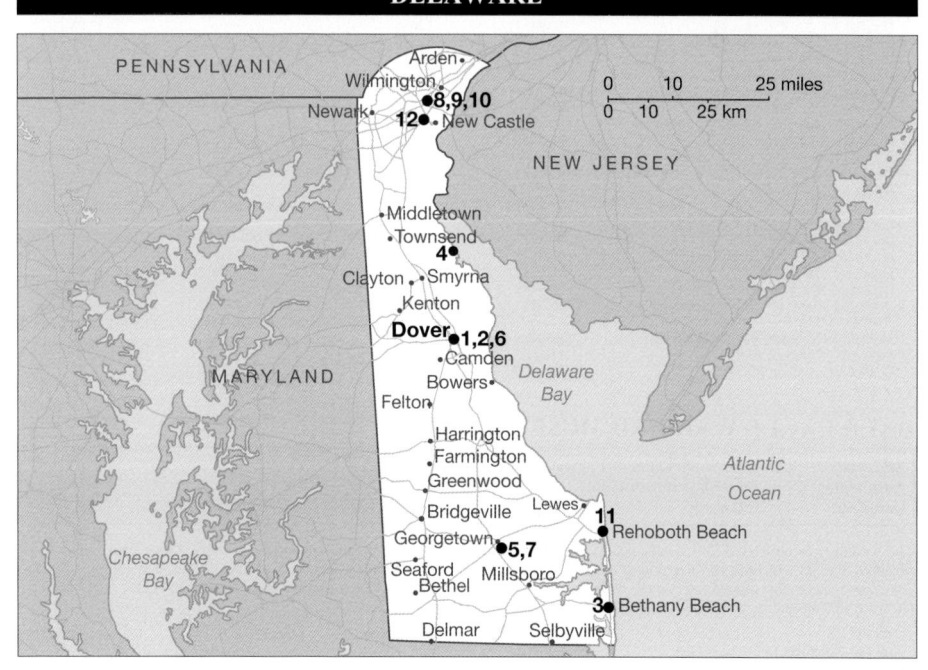

AIR MOBILITY COMMAND MUSEUM (DE1)

Address: 1301 Heritage Road, Dover, Delaware 19902-8001.
Tel: 302-677-5938   **Fax:** 302-677-5940   **Email:** museum@dover.af.mil
Admission: Tuesday-Sunday 0900-1600.
Location: About 3 miles south east of the town on Route 113.

The field has been occupied by the military since 1941 and has housed transport units for over 50 years. In 1978 the famous B-17 Fortress 'Shoo-Shoo Baby' was moved to Dover and rebuilt by volunteers for display at the Air Force Museum at Dayton.

This work led to the idea of starting a base museum which was first housed in three hangars near the north gate. A World War II hangar on the other side of the field was restored for the museum and the display moved in the mid-1990s. This building was once used as the USAAF Rocket Test Center.

The Military Air Transport Service was set up on 1st June 1948. The organisation was soon involved in the Berlin Airlift and aircraft from around the world were moved to Germany. Five US Navy transport squadrons were assigned to MATS. The service was responsible for a number of other tasks including the Air Weather Service, the Air Rescue Service and the Aeromedical Service. Its fleet of transport aircraft became familiar sights at American bases in many countries. A new organisation, the Military Airlift Command, was formed in 1966. In 1992 MAC combined with the Strategic Air Command to set up the Air Mobility Command.

The displays at the museum trace the history of Air Force transport flying. Many of the types used over the last 60 years can be seen. The C-54 Skymaster has been painted in the colours it wore during the Berlin Airlift. Only a few Globemasters have survived and the one in the collection was transported by road from Offutt Air Force Base in Nebraska where it had been on show at the Strategic Air Command Museum. The Cargomaster was the first turbo-prop transport for the USAF and the prototype made its maiden flight in April 1956. Only 50 were completed and the type was withdrawn from service in the early 1970s owing to fatigue problems.

The Fairchild company is represented by the Flying Boxcar and the Provider. A number of informative displays have been set up in rooms around the hangar. Among the subjects covered are the WASP pilots of World War II, the Berlin Airlift and the Fourth Fighter Group Nose Art. A section describes the construction of wood and fabric covered aircraft. The Hall of Heroes honours pilots of the command. The museum has a library and archive section and many tapes of interviews with pilots and crew members have been collected and preserved.

TYPE	REG/SER	CON. NO.	PI/NOTES	STATUS
☐ Beech D18S Expeditor (C-45G)	51-11795	AF-352	51-11795, N7950C – rebuilt from AT-11 Kansan 42-37174.	PV
☐ Bell 205 Iroquois (UH-1H)	'21512'	11763	69-15475	PVX
☐ Boeing 299-O Fortress (B-17G) (MB-17G) (TB-17G) (DB-17G) (DB-17P)	'2107112'	32265	44-83624	PVX
☐ Boeing 367-76-66 Stratofreighter (KC-97G) (KC-97L)	53-0230	17012		RAC
☐ Boeing 717-148 Stratotanker (KC-135A) (KC-135E)	57-1507	17578		RA
☐ Boeing-Stearman A75N1 Kaydet (PT-17)	'41-21741'		Assembled from parts.	PVX
☐ Cessna 310A Blue Canoe (L-27A) (U-3A)	58-2126	38100	58-2126, N5022Z	PV
☐ Convair 340-79 Samaritan (C-131D)	55-0295	223	N8460H	PV
☐ Convair 8-24 Delta Dart (F-106A) (QF-106A)	59-0023	8-24-152		PV
☐ De Havilland DHC.4A Caribou (CV-2B) (C-7B)	63-9760	224		PV
☐ Douglas DC-3A-456 Skytrain (C-47A)	42-92841	12686		PV
☐ Douglas DC-4 Skymaster (C-54E) (C-54M)	44-9030	27560		PV
☐ Douglas 1129A Globemaster II (C-124A)	49-0258	43187		RAC
☐ Douglas 1430 Cargomaster (C-133B)	59-0536	45587		PVC
☐ Douglas DC-9-32CF Nightingale (C-9A)	67-22584	47242		PV
☐ Douglas A-26C Invader	44-35523	28802	44-35523, N3428G	PV
☐ Fairchild 110 Flying Boxcar (C-119F)	'12881'	10870	22118 (Canada), N3559	PVX
☐ Fairchild 473 Provider (205) (C-123B) (C-123K) (UC-123K)	54-0658	20107	54-0658, N97033, (Peru)	PV
☐ Kaman K-600-3 Huskie (H-43B) (HH-43B) (HH-43F)	62-4532	158		PV
☐ Laister-Kauffman LK.10B (TG-4A)	42-53078	135	42-53078, NC58175, N58175	PV
☐ Lockheed 300 Starlifter (C-141A) (C-141B)	64-0626	300-6039		PV
☐ Lockheed 300 Starlifter (C-141A) (NC-141A)	61-2775	300-6001		PV
☐ Lockheed 382C-15D Hercules (C-130E)	69-6580	382C-4356		PV
☐ Lockheed 580 (T-33A)	51-17431	580-7170	At a Legion Post near base.	PV
☐ Lockheed 580 (T-33A)	52-9497	580-7632		PV
☐ Lockheed 1049E-55-115 Super Constellation (1049E-55-93)	'40315'	1049E-4557	CU-P573, N1005C	PVX
☐ McDonnell M.36BA Voodoo (F-101B)	59-0428	752		PV
☐ Vultee V-74 Valiant (BT-13A)	42-1639	74-8673 (?)		PV
☐ Waco NZR Hadrian (CG-4A)	45-15009		Front fuselage on display – remainder in store.	PV

BALD EAGLE WARBIRD MUSEUM (DE2)

Address: 3500 South Dupont Highway, Dover, Delaware 19901.
Admission: By prior permission only.
Location: Unknown.

The Venom was registered to this organisation in the summer of 2006. The jet was built in Switzerland and served with the Air Force there for almost 30 years. The fighter flew to Duxford in England in 1984 and was on show at the Imperial War Museum for about three years. Since then it has had a number of owners in Vermont, Texas and Oregon. Further details of this museum would be appreciated.

TYPE	REG/SER	CON. NO.	PI/NOTES	STATUS
☐ De Havilland DH.112 Venom FB.1	N202DM	826	J-1616 (Switzerland), G-BLIF	RAA

Delaware

BETHANY BEACH MONUMENT (DE3)

Location:	On permanent view at the ANG HQ on Route 1.

TYPE	REG/SER	CON. NO.	PI/NOTES	STATUS
☐ Bell 205 Iroquois (UH-1H)	71-20012	12836	71-20012, N891PM	PV

CHAMBERSVILLE MONUMENT (DE4)

Location:	On permanent view at a house in the town.

TYPE	REG/SER	CON. NO.	PI/NOTES	STATUS
☐ Bell 205 Iroquois (UH-1H)				PV

DELAWARE AVIATION MUSEUM FOUNDATION (DE5)

Address:	21513 Rudder Lane, Georgetown, Delaware 19947-2016.
Tel:	302-854-0244 Fax:
Admission:	Saturday-Sunday 1000-1600.
Location:	At Sussex County Airport which is about 3 miles east of the town.

This museum was set up in 2005 by four owners of vintage aircraft who all had collections of books and memorabilia. The collection was housed in the World War II terminal building at the airport but in 2010 moved across the airfield to a hangar complex.
The author and warbird pilot Jeff Ethell was killed in the crash of a P-38 Lightning near Tillamook in Oregon in June 1997. His widow has loaned his collection of over 3,000 books to the museum., known as the 'Jeffrey L. Ethell Memorial Library'. The aircraft collection contains several interesting types.

The Mitchell was delivered in the spring of 1945 and stored for almost four years. The bomber was converted for training duties and was operational until August 1958. Sold on the civilian market in 1959 it flew as a tanker for a few years. Since then it has had several owners and was repaired by Tom Reilly at Kissimmee after a landing incident in 1988.
The Bobcat, one of few left flying, is painted in its original silver World War II colours. The museum plans to keep the aircraft in flying condition. The MiG-21 is potentially airworthy but needs some work to obtain a certificate.

TYPE	REG/SER	CON. NO.	PI/NOTES	STATUS
☐ Cessna T-50 Bobcat (AT-17B) (UC-78B)	N266C	6582	43-32674	PVA
☐ Champion 7FC Tri-Traveler	N7513E	7FC-233		PVA
☐ Fuji LM-1	N30174	LM-14	21011	PV
☐ Mikoyan-Gurevich MiG-15				PV
☐ Mikoyan-Gurevich MiG-17		131311		PV
☐ Mikoyan-Gurevich MiG-21PFM	7905	94N7905		PV
☐ Mikoyan-Gurevich UTI-MiG-15				PV
☐ Mikoyan-Gurevich UTI-MiG-15	512			PV
☐ Nanchang CJ-6A	N41836	2032108		PVA
☐ North American NA-108 Mitchell (B-25J) (TB-25J) (TB-25N)	N9079Z	108-34009	44-30734, (N9080Z)	PVA
☐ PZL TS-11 Iskra 100bisB	NX7110K	1H 07-11	0711 (Poland), 711 (Poland)	PV
☐ PZL TS-11 Iskra 100bisB	0727	1H 07-27	In Polish markings.	PV
☐ WSK SBLim-2 (Lim-1) [MiG-15]	021	1A 06-021	In Polish markings.	PV
☐ WSK SBLim-2 (Lim-1) [MiG-15]	016	1A 09-016	In Polish markings.	RA
☐ WSK Lim-5 [MiG-17F]	1704	1C 17-04	In Polish markings.	PV
☐ WSK Lim-6R	609	1J 06-09	In Polish markings.	PV

DELAWARE STATE POLICE MUSEUM (DE6)

Address:	PO Box 430, 1425 North DuPont Highway, Dover, Delaware 19903
Tel:	302-739-7700 Email: john.alstadt@state.de.us
Admission:	Monday-Friday 0900-1500; Third Saturday in Month 1100-1500.
Location:	In the north western part of the town off Route 13.

The first Traffic Policeman in Delaware was appointed in 1919 and for a time was the only one in the State. The force was enlarged and the officers were equipped with Harley-Davidson and Indian motor cycles; the first cars were acquired in the mid-1930s. The museum traces the history of police work in Delaware with many interesting photographs and documents to be seen. Also on show are motor cycles and patrol cars along with uniforms, badges and radio equipment. The Kiowa recently moved from the museum at Dover Air Force Base. Helicopters are now an essential part of police work and the unit flies a small number on a variety of duties.

TYPE	REG/SER	CON. NO.	PI/NOTES	STATUS
☐ Bell 206A Kiowa (OH-58A)	'N71SP'	42051	72-21385	PVX

DELAWARE TECHNICAL AND COMMUNITY COLLEGE (DE7)

Address:	24199 Rudder Lane, Georgetown, Delaware 19947.
Tel:	302-855-2307 Fax: 302-855-2311 Email: rhullige@dtcc.edu
Admission:	By prior permission only.
Location:	At Sussex County Airport which is about three miles east of town.

The college offers a range of courses leading to students obtaining licenses in airframes, engines and avionics. Five instructional aircraft are in use along with a number of engines and test rigs. The workshops contain components from a number of aircraft and these are used in teaching repairs and installation of systems.

TYPE	REG/SER	CON. NO.	PI/NOTES	STATUS
☐ Beech 95-A55 Baron	N777RV	TC-345	N9543Y	RA
☐ Cessna 150G	N3455J	15066155		RA
☐ Cessna 150L	N5493Q	15073393		RA
☐ Piper PA-28-140 Cherokee	N3954K	28-23832		RA
☐ Piper PA-28-235 Cherokee	N8610W	28-10126		RA

FRIENDS OF BELLANCA AIRFIELD (DE8)

Address:	PO Box 267, New Castle, Delaware 19720-0267
Tel:	contact@friendsofbellanca.org
Admission:	Not yet open.
Location:	In the western suburbs of the town on Route 273.

In 1928 Guiseppe Bellanca opened an airfield in the town. He designed a number of rugged high wing monoplanes which were produced at the site. The original hangar was destroyed in a fire in 1934 and was replaced the following year by a larger structure. The factory was enlarged and over 3,000 aircraft were produced before manufacture ceased in 1951.

The 1935 building survived even though the old airfield disappeared. The group is restoring the hangar to its original configuration. Several uses have been considered including using part of it as a museum tracing the work of Bellanca. A historic marker was been placed by the roadside in 2002.

MARINE AVIATION MUSEUM (DE9)

Address:	3511 Silverside Road, Suite 105, Wilmington, Delaware 19810-4902.
Tel:	Unknown.
Admission:	Unknown.
Location:	Various.

Four aircraft are registered to this museum which appears to have no permanent exhibition site. A Douglas Skyraider and a Bell Iroquois are on show at the Lone Star Flight Museum at Galveston in Texas.

TYPE	REG/SER	CON. NO.	PI/NOTES	STATUS
☐ Douglas A-26B Invader	N26BP	7072	41-39359, N91281, CF-BMR, C-FBMR	RAA
☐ Folland Fo.144 Gnat T.1	N1CL	FL-585	XR991, 8637M, A2709, G-BOXO	RAA

NEW CASTLE AIR NATIONAL GUARD BASE (DE10)

Address:	166 TAG/PA Greater Wilmington Airport Delaware 19720.
Tel:	302-323-3555 Email: webmaster@denewc.ang.af.mil
Admission:	By prior permission only.
Location:	The airport is about 5 miles south of Wilmington on Route 40.

The unit was set up in September 1946 and in the following February acquired P-47N Thunderbolts. It continued in the fighter role until the spring of 1962 when it became a transport wing. The F-86 on display carries the colours of the one in which Lieutenant-Colonel David McAllister was killed on 4th June 1961. A display of memorabilia is located in the Headquarters Building.

TYPE	REG/SER	CON. NO.	PI/NOTES	STATUS
☐ Bell 205 Iroquois (UH-1H)	73-21809	13497	73-21809, N41909	RA
☐ North American NA-203 Sabre (F-86H)	53-1296	203-68		PV

REHOBETH BEACH MONUMENT (DE11)

Location:	On permanent view at an amusement park in the town.

TYPE	REG/SER	CON. NO.	PI/NOTES	STATUS
☐ Beech C18S Navigator (AT-7)		4253	42-43506, N6401C	PVX

WARBIRDS OF DELAWARE (DE12)

Address:	405 Silverside Road, Wilmington, Delaware 19809-1371.
Tel:	302-746-1211 Email: jgano@nationaleducation.com
Admission:	By prior permission only.
Location:	At Greater Wilmington Airport which is about 3 miles north west of New Castle.

The groups specialises in the operation of former Soviet bloc jets. The aircraft are flown on a variety of tasks including pilot training and contract work. They often appear at air shows in the region.

TYPE	REG/SER	CON. NO.	PI/NOTES	STATUS
☐ Aero L-29R Delfin	N29AD	792405	2405 (Czech)	RAA
☐ Aero L-39C Albatros	N4213A	230105	0105 (Czech)	RAA
☐ Aero L-39MS Albatros	N9016N	040003	0003 (Slovakia)	RAA
☐ Mikoyan-Gurevich MiG-21UM	N1165	01695165	0165 (Czech)	RAA
☐ Mikoyan-Gurevich MiG-21UM	N20739	516931071	3171 (Czech)	RAA
☐ Mikoyan-Gurevich MiG-21US	N63SG	02685141	0241 (Czech0, 0241/F-ZAGR	RA
☐ Mikoyan-Gurevich MiG-23UB	N51734	A1037805	7805 (Czech)	RAA
☐ Mikoyan-Gurevich MiG-23UB	N5106E	A1037827	7827 (Czech)	RAA
☐ Yakovlev Yak-52	N669YK	844206	03	RAA

DISTRICT OF COLUMBIA

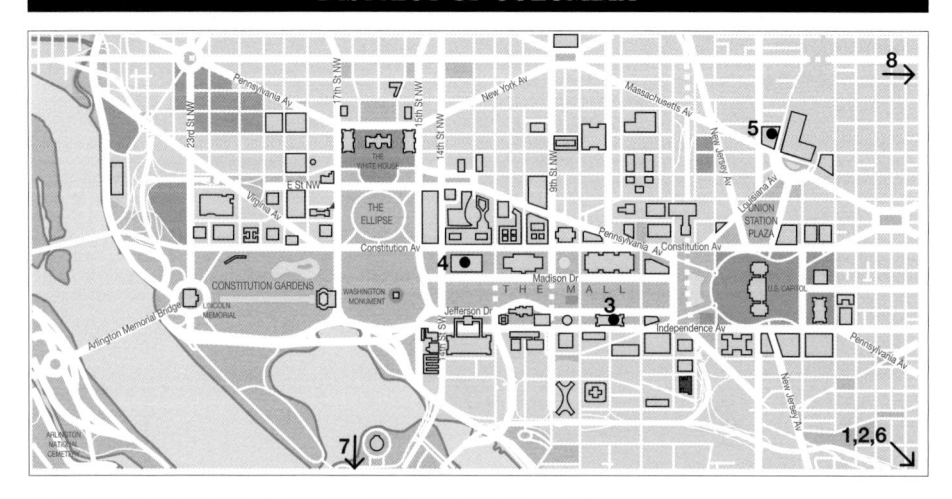

ANACOSTIA NAVAL YARD MONUMENT (DC1)

Location:	On permanent view in the south eastern part of the city.

TYPE	REG/SER	CON. NO.	PI/NOTES	STATUS
☐ North American NA-200 Trojan (T-28B)	Bu137766	200-159		PV

BOLLING AIR FORCE BASE MONUMENT (DC2)

Location:	On permanent view in the south eastern part of the city.

TYPE	REG/SER	CON. NO.	PI/NOTES	STATUS
☐ Republic F-105D Thunderchief	61-0138	D-333		PV

NATIONAL AIR AND SPACE MUSEUM (DC3)

Address: Independence Avenue at 6th. Street, Washington, District of Columbia 20560.
Tel: 202-663-2214 Email: pjakub@si.edu
Admission: Daily 1000-1730.
Location: On Washington Mall in the centre of the city.

The Smithsonian Institution started to collect aeronautical material in 1876 when the then secretary. Samuel Langley acquired a group of Chinese kites. From 1887 to 1903 he designed a number of unmanned flying machines known as 'aerodromes'. In 1920 a temporary World War I structure was acquired and added to the Arts and Industries Building. Space was limited and the vast majority of the aircraft collected remained in store.
The National Air Museum was established by Congress in 1946 and Space was added to the title 20 years later. The dream of a permanent home was realised in 1976 when a superb building was opened on the Washington Mall. Aircraft are on show in 12 major galleries each devoted to a particular theme. Space exhibits occupy several more areas. Hanging above the main entrance is the original Wright Flyer which made the first powered flight on 17th December 1903 when Orville flew for a distance of 100 feet in 12 seconds. Later in the day Wilbur was aloft for 59 seconds covering 852 feet. The aircraft was on show in Boston from 1916 to 1918 when it moved to the Science Museum in England. When Orville resolved his differences with the Smithsonian the Flyer joined the museum in Washington in 1948. Other aircraft in this area include the Ryan NYP flown by Charles Lindbergh on the first solo transatlantic crossing in 1927 and the Bell X-1 in which Charles Yeager broke the 'sound barrier' in October 1947. The X-15A, the first manned aircraft to exceed Mach 6, hangs nearby.
One of the most impressive galleries is devoted to Air Transport where aircraft show the development of passenger and freight flying over 60 years. Two airliners which revolutionised passenger comfort in the 1930s are the Boeing 247 and the Douglas DC-3. The 247 was third in the 1934 MacRobertson race from England to Australia. Among the other significant aircraft on show is one of the Douglas DWCs which made the first round-the-world flight in 1924 and the winner of the 1925 Schneider Trophy, the Curtiss R3C-2 piloted by James Doolittle. The Wright EX 'Vin Fiz' in which C.P. Rogers made the first flight across the US continent in 1911 is also on view. At the end of his epic journey the only original parts remaining were the rudder and two wing struts. Everything had been replaced at least once.
Howard Hughes H-1 record breaking racer was stored in California for many years before he was persuaded to let it go on show. The exhibits change from time to time with aircraft moving to the Steven Udvar-Hazy Center at Dulles Airport in Virginia and others arriving. Several aircraft are still stored at the Paul E. Garber Facility at nearby Silver Hill in Maryland.

TYPE	REG/SER	CON. NO.	PI/NOTES	STATUS
☐ AAI RQ-2A Pioneer	'159'			PV
☐ AAI RQ-7A Shadow	'1076'			PV

☐ AeroVironment MQ-11 Raven	Bu97-0034				PV
☐ Albatros D Va	7161/17				PV
☐ Beech C17L (C-17B)	NC15840	93	NC15840, N15840,		PV
☐ Bell 27 Airacomet (XP-59A)	42-108784	27-17			PV
☐ Bell 44 (XS-1) (X-1)	46-062				PV
☐ Blériot XI		340			PV
☐ Boeing 235 (F4B-4)	Bu9241	1757	Bu9241, NR9329, NX13, NC13		PV
☐ Boeing 247D	NC13369	1953	NC13369, NS11, NC11, N11, NR257Y		PV
☐ Boeing 727-022	N7004U	18296	At AMARC, AZ.		RA
☐ Boeing 747-151	N601US	19778	Front fuselage only.		PV
☐ Boeing X-45A					PV
☐ Breitling Orbiter 3			Gondola only.		PV
☐ Bud Light Spirit of Freedom			Gondola only.		PV
☐ Curtiss 42A (R3C-2)	A6979	26-33			PV
☐ Curtiss 50H Robin J-1	NR526N	723			PV
☐ Curtiss D Pusher	2				PV
☐ De Havilland DH-4	21959	A15101			PV
☐ Douglas DWC	23-1230	146			PV
☐ Douglas DC-3-201	N18124	2000	NC18124		PV
☐ Douglas DC-7	N334AA	45106	Front fuselage only.		PV
☐ Douglas SBD-6 Dauntless	Bu54605	6119			PV
☐ Douglas D-558-2 Skyrocket	NACA144	6568	Bu37974		PV
☐ Douglas A-4C Skyhawk (A4D-2N)	Bu148314	12624			PV
☐ Ecker Flying Boat					PV
☐ Fairchild FC-2	NC6853	139			PV
☐ Fieseler Fi 103A-1					PV
☐ Fokker D VII	4635/18	3533			PV
☐ Fokker F.IV (T-2)	AS64233				PV
☐ Ford 5-AT-B	N9683	5-AT-39	NC9683, XH-TAK, AN-AAP, XA-FUE, XB-WAR, N1142N, XB-YIT, N7791B		PV
☐ Gallaudet Hydro Kite					PV
☐ Goodyear ZPG-3W	Bu144243		Gondola only – at AMARC, AZ.		RA
☐ Grumman G-36 Wildcat (FM-1)	Bu15392	401			PV
☐ Grumman G-712 (X-29A) (R)	'20003'				PVX
☐ Hargrave Ornithopter					PV
☐ Horten Ho IIL	D-10-125	6	D-10-125, FE-7, T2-7 – at DTM, Berlin.		-
☐ Hughes H-1	NR258Y	1			PV
☐ Langley Aerodrome 5					PV
☐ Lilienthal Normal-Segelapparat					PV
☐ Lockheed 140 Shooting Star (XP-80)	44-83020	140-1001			PV
☐ Lockheed 183-93-02 Starfighter (YF-104A) (F-104A)	N818NA	183-1007	55-2961		PV
☐ Lockheed 5B Vega (5)	NR7952	22	NR7952, NC7952		PV
☐ Lockheed 8 Sirius	NR211	140			PV
☐ Lockheed U-2C (U-2A)	56-6680	347			PV
☐ Lockheed-Martin RQ-3A					PV
☐ Macchi MC.202 Folgore	'MM9476'		MM9667, EB300, FE-300, FE-498, T2-498, 'MM7844'		PV
☐ MacCready Gossamer Condor		1			PV
☐ Martin 179B Marauder (B-26B)	41-31773	3487	Front fuselage on show – remainder in store.		PV
☐ McDonnell M.23 Phantom I (FD-1) (FH-1)	Bu111759	11			PV
☐ Messerschmitt Bf 109G-6/R3	'2'	160756	KT+LL, FE-496, T2-496.		PVX
☐ Messerschmitt Me 262A-1a	'7'	500491	500491, FE-111, T2-111- nose from a Me 262A-1a/U3.		PV
☐ Mitsubishi A6M5 Zero Sen Model 52	61-131	4043	(J. Navy), T2-130		PV
☐ North American NA-122 Mustang (P-51D)	44-74939	122-41479			PV
☐ North American NA-240 (X-15) (X-15A)	56-6670	240-1			PV
☐ Northrop 4A Alpha	NC11Y	3			PV
☐ Northrop Gamma	NR12269	2			PV
☐ Northrop M2-F3	N803NA	1			PV
☐ Pfalz D XII	'2486/18'	3504	7517/18		PV
☐ Piper J-2 Cub	NC20137	1937	NC20137, N20137		RA
☐ Pitcairn PA-5 Mailwing	C2895	1	C2895, NC2895		PV
☐ Pitts S-1S Special	N11DR	JDR2			PV
☐ Rockwell HiMAT	NASA807				PV
☐ Royal Aircraft Factory F.E.8 (R)	N17501	300	On loan from Old Rhinebeck, NY.		PV
☐ Ryan NYP	NX211	29			PV
☐ Scaled Composites 316 SpaceShipOne	N328KF	001			PV
☐ SPAD XIII	S7689	7689			PV
☐ Sopwith 7F.1 Snipe	'E8082'	9262C	E8105, N8737R		PVX
☐ Supermarine 359 Spitfire HF.VIIc	EN474	6S.171652	EN474, FE-400		PV
☐ Voisin 8	4640	V.1817			PV
☐ Voyager Aircraft Voyager (Rutan 76)	N269VA	1			PV
☐ Walter Extra EA-260	N618PW	EA260-001			PV
☐ Wittman Buster	NR14855	4	NR12047		PV
☐ Wright 1900 Glider (R)					PV
☐ Wright 1902 Glider (R)					PV
☐ Wright Flyer					PV
☐ Wright Military Flyer					PV
☐ Wright EX Vin Fiz					PV
☐ Wright G		2	Hull only.		RA

District of Columbia

NATIONAL MUSEUM OF AMERICAN HISTORY (DC4)

Address:	Constitution Avenue, Washington, District of Columbia 20560-0605.
Tel:	202-633-3270 Email; info@si.edu
Admission:	Daily 1000-1730.
Location:	In the centre of the city.

This large museum collects all items relation to the history and development of the country. The building closed in the summer of 2005 for a major refurbishment. New galleries were added and others improved. The Iroquois is displayed in the military area where the history of American forces is traced.

TYPE	REG/SER	CON. NO.	PI/NOTES	STATUS
☐ Bell 205 Iroquois (UH-1D) (UH-1H)	65-10091	5135	65-10091, N565TX	RPV

NATIONAL POSTAL MUSEUM (DC5)

Address:	2 Massachusetts Avenue Washington, District of Columbia 20002.
Tel:	202-633-9360 Email: info@si.edu
Admission:	Daily 1000-1730.
Location:	In the city next to the railway station.

This museum is housed in the lower level of the former Washington City Post Office. Exhibits in the magnificent building trace the development of the postal service in the country from the early days of the Colonial Post and the Pony Express up to modern times. Sections include 'Binding the Nation' which is devoted to the early history of the service, Customers and Communities which looks at the expansion of mail deliveries in the 20th century and 'Moving the Mail' which traces the development of transport and technology.

Three aircraft hang in the atrium of the building. In 1911 the Wiseman Cooke biplane made the first sanctioned postal flight from Petaluma to Santa Rosa in California. The distance of 18½ miles took two days to complete. The Stinson Reliant was used in 1939 to test a system for communities which did not have a landing strip. The mail was placed in a container on top of a structure similar to a goal post. A grappling hook was lowered to pick up the container and mail for the village but dropped from the plane. This method was not too successful.

TYPE	REG/SER	CON. NO.	PI/NOTES	STATUS
☐ De Havilland DH-4 (R)	N249B	249	NASM aircraft.	PV
☐ Stinson SR-10F Reliant	NX2311	5910	NC2311 – NASM aircraft.	PV
☐ Wiseman Cooke			NASM aircraft.	PV

NAVY MUSEUM (DC6)

Address:	Building 76, Washington Navy Yard, Washington, District of Columbia 20374-0571.
Tel:	202-433-4882.
Admission:	Monday-Friday 0900-1700; Saturday-Sunday 1000-1700.
Location:	In the south eastern suburbs of the city on the Anacostia River.

Set up in 1799 the yard is the oldest shore establishment of the US Navy. The facility was burned in 1814 to prevent it falling into British hands when they attacked Washington. Only the Commandant's House and the Latrobe Gate survived. The yard was later rebuilt and constructed ships up to the 1850s when it became an ordnance factory remaining in use up to 1961. Technological innovations at the yard included many firsts – a marine railway in 1822, a model ship basin in 1898, a successful shipboard catapult in 1912 and a wind tunnel in 1914.

Since 1962 administration and supplies work have been carried out. The museum, which opened in 1963, is housed in the former Breech Mechanism Shop of the Naval Gun Factory. Exhibits trace the development of the navy over two centuries and include a superb collection of model ships. Uniforms also feature prominently. Outside is a varied display of weapons including some from the Civil War, and moored nearby is the destroyer USS *Barry* which served in the Cuban crisis and the Vietnam War.

TYPE	REG/SER	CON. NO.	PI/NOTES	STATUS
☐ Vought FG-1D Corsair	'Bu17649'	3274	Bu92013, N1978M	PVX
☐ Yokosuka MXY-7-K1 Ohka 11		1084		PV

UNIVERSITY OF THE DISTRICT OF COLUMBIA (DC7)

Address:	4200 Connecticut Avenue North West, Washington, District of Columbia 20008-1122
Tel:	202-274-5000 Email: cc@udc.edu
Admission:	By prior permission only.
Location:	At Reagan National Airport in the southern part of the city.

The university trains airframe and engine mechanics at its hangar at the airport. The Aero Commander was used by the Department of the Interior, the US Army and NASA before becoming an instructional airframe.

TYPE	REG/SER	CON. NO.	PI/NOTES	STATUS
☐ Aero Commander 680W	N514NA	1772-10	N4730E, N615, N611, N611MF, 83-24126	RA
☐ Cessna 182J	N2853F	18256953		RA

WASHINGTON MONUMENT (DC8)

Location:	On permanent view at President Lincoln and Soldiers Home at 4106 North Capitol Street.

TYPE	REG/SER	CON. NO.	PI/NOTES	STATUS
☐ North American NA-203 Sabre (F-86H)	'81833'			PVX

FLORIDA

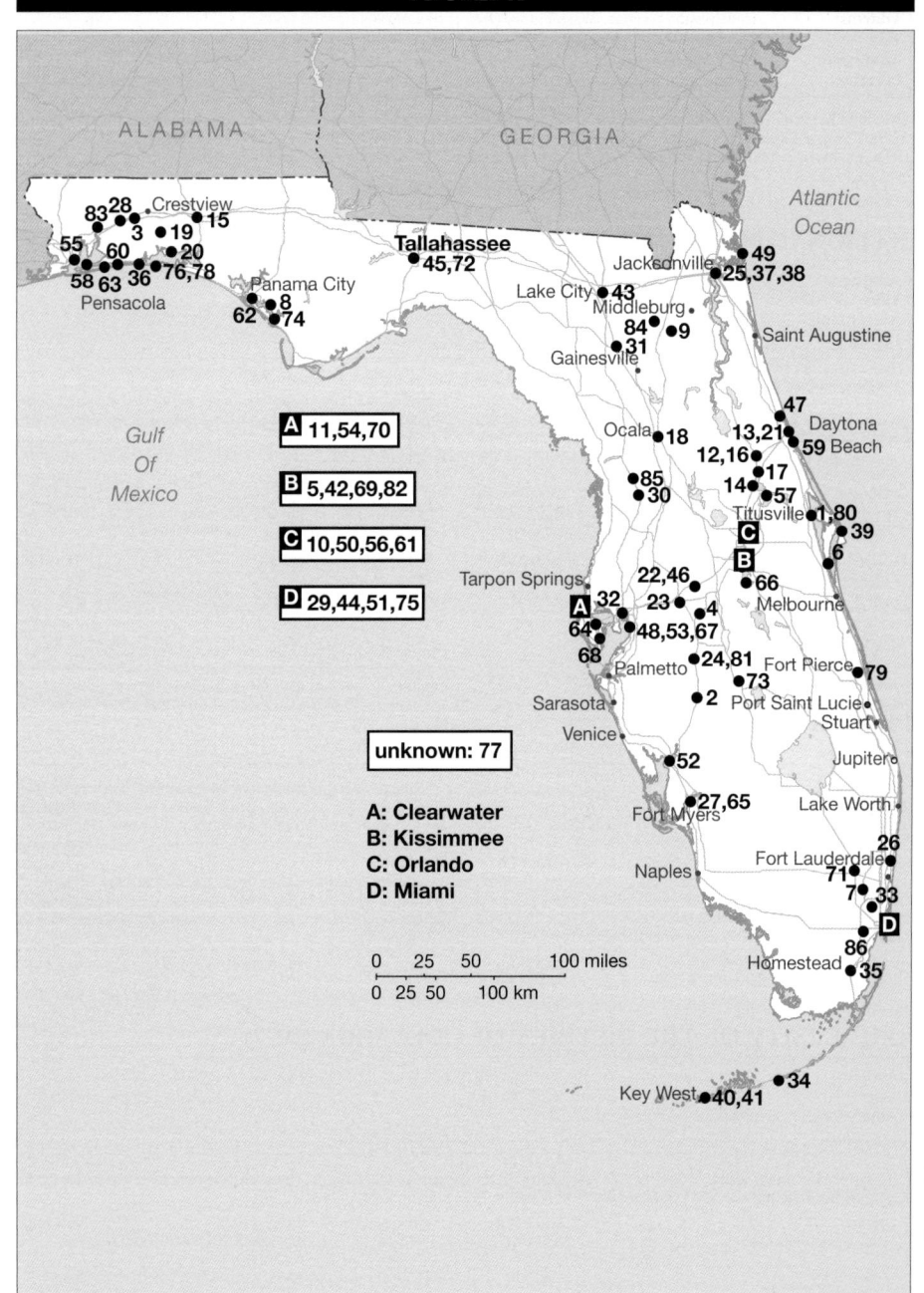

- **A**: 11,54,70
- **B**: 5,42,69,82
- **C**: 10,50,56,61
- **D**: 29,44,51,75

unknown: 77

A: Clearwater
B: Kissimmee
C: Orlando
D: Miami

AIR AMERICA FOUNDATION (FL1)

Address:	1589 South Wickham Road, Melbourne, Florida 32904.
Tel:	321-725-4043 Fax: 321-725-4047 Email: pvasconi@airamericafoundation.org
Admission:	By prior permission only.
Location:	At Titusville Airport which is south of the city close to Highway 1.

The group has been formed to keep alive the memories of 'Air America', the airline which served in Asia from 1946 until America left Vietnam in 1975. Many secretive missions involving US agents were flown around the region. Among the types used was the C-123 and the foundation has an example which is being rebuilt to flying condition. The front fuselage of a Caribou has been obtained.

TYPE	REG/SER	CON. NO.	PI/NOTES	STATUS
☐ De Havilland DHC.4A Caribou (AC-1) (CV-2A) (C-7A)	N6154T	46	61-2389 – front fuselage only.	RA
☐ Fairchild 473 Provider (205) (C-123B) (C-123K)	N38LF	20123	54-0674, N674JK, HR-ALK	RAC

ARCADIA MONUMENT (FL2)

Location:	On permanent view in City Park on Route 70 just west of the town centre.

TYPE	REG/SER	CON. NO.	PI/NOTES	STATUS
☐ Lockheed 580 (T-33A)	52-9696	580-7921		PV

BAKER MONUMENT (FL3)

Location:	On permanent view at a house in Galiver Cutoff in the southern part of the town.

TYPE	REG/SER	CON. NO.	PI/NOTES	STATUS
☐ Mikoyan-Gurevich MiG-23ML	'53'	0390324250	471 (DDR), 20+24	PV

BARTOW MONUMENT (FL4)

Location:	On permanent view at the airfield which is about 3 miles north east of the town on Route 17.

TYPE	REG/SER	CON. NO.	PI/NOTES	STATUS
☐ Cessna 318B Tweety Bird (318A) (T-37A) (T-37B)	56-3346	40118		PV

BLAIR COLLECTION (FL5)

Address:	Hoagland Boulevard, Kissimmee, Florida 32741.
Admission:	By prior permission only.
Location:	On the west side of Kissimmee Airport which is on Highway 192 just west of the town.

This private collection is housed at the Florida airfield. Two Spitfires are currently based in England. A number of aircraft have been sold in recent years. The Warhawk was rebuilt in New Zealand and appeared at shows there.

TYPE	REG/SER	CON. NO.	PI/NOTES	STATUS
☐ Aero L-39TC Albatros	N3467N	432929	(Kyrgyzstan)	RAA
☐ Aviat A-1 Husky	N3XJ	1390		RAA
☐ Beech A45 Mentor (T-34A)	N116RH	G-116	53-3355	RAA
☐ Curtiss 87-B3 Warhawk (P-40K)	NX4436J	21117	42-9733, N4363, (ZK-FRE), ZK-PXL	RAA
☐ De Havilland DH.82A Tiger Moth	N126B	85641	DE712, G-APJL	RAA
☐ North American NA-122 Mustang (P-51D)	'414812'	122-41490	44-74950, N5464V, N511D, N20JS, N7496W, NL51DT	RAAX
☐ Supermarine 361 Spitfire LF.IXe	G-IXCC		PL344, G-IXCC, N644TB – at Duxford in England.	PVA
☐ Supermarine 361 Spitfire LF.IXe (FSM)	'PL344'			PVX
☐ Supermarine 361 Spitfire LF.XVIe	G-OXVI	CBAF-IX-4562	TD248, 7246M– at Duxford in England.	PVA
☐ Supermarine 379 Spitfire FR.XIVc	N201TB	6S.663417	RN201, SG-31 (Belgium), G-BSKP	RAA

BREVARD VETERANS MEMORIAL CENTER MILITARY MUSEUM (FL6)

Address:	400 South Sykes Creek Parkway, Merritt Island, Florida 32952-3547.
Tel:	321-453-1776 Fax: 321-453-1152
Admission:	Monday-Saturday 0830–1630; Sunday 1200-1700.
Location:	In the town which is about 35 miles south of Titusville on Route 3.

The displays at this museum honour all Americans who have served in the military forces. Many artefacts are on show ranging from swords and cannonballs from the early days up to modern electronically controlled weapons. Photographs and documents as well as uniforms and badges can also be seen.

TYPE	REG/SER	CON. NO.	PI/NOTES	STATUS
☐ Bell 205 Iroquois (UH-1H)	71-20139	12963		PV
☐ Bell 209 Huey Cobra (AH-1G) (AH-1F)	68-17023	20751		PV

BROWARD COLLEGE AVIATION INSTITUTE (FL7)

Address:	7200 Pines Boulevard, Pembroke Pines, Florida 33024.
Tel:	954-201-8087 **Fax:** 954-201-8088 **Email:** aviation@broward.edu
Admission:	By prior permission only.
Location:	At the north east side of North Perry Airport off Route 820.

The college offers a variety of courses including flying training. A fleet of single and twin engined types are in use leading up to a commercial pilot rating. Air traffic controllers are also trained at the college. Four airframes are known to be in use in the Aviation Maintenance Technology Department but there are probably more. The Boeing 727 which is parked on the ramp outside the hangar was donated to the school by Federal Express.

TYPE	REG/SER	CON. NO.	PI/NOTES	STATUS
☐ Aero Commander 681	N9058N	6008	N9058N, YV-06CP	RA
☐ Boeing 727-22F	N150FE	19141	N7077U	RA
☐ Cessna 150G	N2803S	15066703		RA
☐ Sikorsky S-62A Seaguard (HH-52A)	1416	62100		PV

CALLAWAY MONUMENTS (FL8)

Location:	On permanent view at two locations in the town.

TYPE	REG/SER	CON. NO.	PI/NOTES	STATUS
☐ McDonnell M.199-1A Eagle (F-15A)	77-0146	436/A358	At Veterans Memorial Park in Cherry Avenue.	PV
☐ McDonnell M.36BA Voodoo (F-101B)	'60417'	595	57-0417 – at a sports complex off Highway 22.	PVX

CAMP BLANDING MUSEUM AND MEMORIAL PARK (FL9)

Address:	Camp Blanding Training School, Route 1, Box 465, Starke, Florida 32091-9703.
Tel:	904-682--3196 **Fax:** 904-682-3276 **Email:** CBMuseum@aol.com
Admission:	Daily 1200-1600.
Location:	About 8 miles east of the town on Route 16.

During World War II nine divisions trained at Camp Blanding. Monuments to these units and to American prisoners of war, winners of the Purple Heart and soldiers who have received the Medal of Honor have been erected in the park. Vehicles used by these regiments are on show. The museum is housed in a renovated World War II barracks and the displays trace the history of the site with particular emphasis on this period.

There are plans for a large purpose-built complex to be constructed. The first aircraft to be put on show was the C-47 painted in typical period colours. A history trail has been set up outside and the features include military vehicles and weapons, a full size replica of a Vietnam Firebase fortification and captured Iraqi tanks. The Vought Corsair has been painted in the colours of one shot down over North Vietnam in December 1972.

TYPE	REG/SER	CON. NO.	PI/NOTES	STATUS
☐ Bell 205 Iroquois (UH-1D) (UH-1H)	66-16056	5750		PV
☐ Bell 205 Iroquois (UH-1H)	68-16114	10773		PV
☐ Bell 206A Kiowa (OH-58A)	72-21455	42120		PV
☐ Convair 8-24 Delta Dart (F-106A)	59-0105	8-24-234		PV
☐ Douglas DC-3A-456 Skytrain (C-47A) (R4D-5) (C-47H)	Bu12436	9619	42-23757, Bu12436	PV
☐ Grumman G-128 Intruder (A-6A) (A-6E)	Bu155661	I-387		PV
☐ Vought A-7E Corsair II	'Bu157503'	E309	Bu157586	PVX

CHURCH STREET STATION (FL10)

Address:	127 West Church Street, Orlando, Florida 32801.
Tel:	407-581-8813 **Email:** info@churchstreetstation.com
Admission:	Daily 1100-0200.
Location:	Just off Interstate 4 in the centre of the city.

A former depot on the South Florida Railroad has been converted into a dining, entertainment and shopping complex. One of the bars has been fitted out as an 1890s ballooning museum with many artefacts on show whilst another large area displays the three replica World War I aircraft painted in period colours. The Fokker Dr I has been identified as once being on show at Thorpe Park in England.

Replicas of a Fokker D VII and a S.E.5A were sold in the same auction in 1987 and these could possibly be that pair.

TYPE	REG/SER	CON. NO.	PI/NOTES	STATUS
☐ Balloon				PV
☐ Fokker D VII (FSM)				PV
☐ Fokker Dr I (FSM)	'102/17'		BAPC.139	PVX
☐ Royal Aircraft Factory S.E.5A (FSM)	'B4853'			PVX

CLEARWATER MONUMENT (FL11)

Location:	On permanent view at the USCG station in the south eastern part of the city.

TYPE	REG/SER	CON. NO.	PI/NOTES	STATUS
☐ Grumman G-111 Albatross (G-64) (SA-16A) (SA-16B) (HU-16B)	7176	G-226	51-7176	PV

Florida

COMMEMORATIVE AIR FORCE (FLORIDA WING) (FL12)

Address:	PO Box 1944, Deland, Florida 32721-1944.
Tel:	386-734-2295 Email: flynavy80@comcast.com
Admission:	Saturday 0900-1600.
Location:	In Hangar F6 at the airport which is just west of the town.

Formed in 2001, the wing has three aircraft allocated to it. The Navions have been restored to flying condition. One has been painted to represent an L-17 with a polished metal airframe with the other in grey colours.

The Avenger was collected from the CAF headquarters at Midland in Texas and moved by road to its new home. Members are slowly restoring the airframe and engine and hope to have it back in the air in another two years.

TYPE	REG/SER	CON. NO.	PI/NOTES	STATUS
☐ Grumman G-40 Avenger (TBM-3) (TBM-3S) (AS.3)	N704QZ	2416	Bu85597, 85597 (Canada), CF-IMK, C-FIMK	RAC
☐ Ryan Navion A	N4321K	NAV-4-1321		RAA
☐ Ryan Navion A	N2995C	NAV-4-1727		RAA

DAYTONA BEACH MONUMENTS (FL13)

Location:	On permanent view at two locations in the town.

TYPE	REG/SER	CON. NO.	PI/NOTES	STATUS
☐ Beech D18S Expeditor (C18S) (SNB-2) (SNB-5) (TC-45J) (UC-45J)	N9651	456	Bu67305 – at Hawaiian Falls Miniature Golf.	PVX
☐ Piper PA-28-140 Cherokee			At Cocos (?) Miniature Golf.	PVX

DE BARY MONUMENT (FL14)

Location:	On permanent view in the Veterans Park in Dirksen Drive in the south eastern part of the town.

TYPE	REG/SER	CON. NO.	PI/NOTES	STATUS
☐ Mcdonnell M.199-1A Eagle (F-15A)	'85-125'	265/A228	76-0076	PVX

DE FUNIAK SPRINGS MONUMENT (FL15)

Location:	On permanent view at the airport which is about 3 miles north west of the town.

TYPE	REG/SER	CON. NO.	PI/NOTES	STATUS
☐ Lockheed 580 (T-33A)	51-8959	580-6743		PV

DELAND NAVAL AIR STATION MUSEUM (FL16)

Address:	910 Biscayne Boulevard, Deland, Florida 32724-2009.
Tel:	386-738-4149 Fax: 386-738-5405 Email: contact@delandnavalairstation.org
Admission:	Tuesday-Saturday 1000-1600.
Location:	At the airport which is just west of the town.

A Naval Air Station opened at Deland in 1942 and was in use until 1946. The site then became the civil airport for the town. The museum was originally set up to trace the history of the field during World War II. In 2010 an annexe was opened to highlight later wars. On show are uniforms, photographs, documents, components and items of memorabilia. The nearby hangar contains the aircraft and also serves as a workshop for restoration of the airframes. About 80 Sikorsky S-52s were used by the Navy and very few have survived. The US Navy used almost 700 versions of the T-33 for training purposes. The Tomcat arrived at the site in 2005 and this fighter represents the recent years of naval aviation.

TYPE	REG/SER	CON. NO.	PI/NOTES	STATUS
☐ Beech D18S Expeditor (C18S) (SNB-2) (SNB-5) (TC-45J) (UC-45J)	N5855	7010	Bu29558, N58559	PV
☐ Bell 47G-2			Cockpit section only.	PV
☐ Grumman G-40 Avenger (TBF-1)	Bu01747	2781	Possible identity.	PV
☐ Grumman G-303 Tomcat (F-14A) (F-14B)	Bu161426	436		PV
☐ Lockheed 580 (T-33A)	51-9098	580-6882	51-9098, N7490C, N233Y	PV
☐ Sikorsky S-52-3 (HO5S-1)	Bu130110	52068	Bu130110, N54065	PV

DELTONA VETERANS MEMORIAL (FL17)

Location:	On permanent view on Evard Drive in the north eastern part of the town.

TYPE	REG/SER	CON. NO.	PI/NOTES	STATUS
☐ Bell 209 Huey Cobra (AH-1G) (AH-1F)	67-15843	20507		PV

DON GARLITS MUSEUMS (FL18)

Address:	13700 Southwest 16th Avenue, Ocala, Florida 34473.
Tel:	352-271-3278 Email: garlits@mfi.net
Admission:	Daily 0900-1700.
Location:	Close to Junction 341 of Interstate 75.

Don Garlits started drag racing in 1950 and has been national champion many times. There are two museums on the site.
One houses classic cars, where many interesting models are on view, and the other drag racers. Most of cars he designed and raced can be seen. Several of these set world records. The Corsair arrived from the former naval base at Cecil Field and is mounted outside the complex.

TYPE	REG/SER	CON. NO.	PI/NOTES	STATUS
☐ Vought A-7A Corsair II	Bu152650	A7		PV

EGLIN AIR FORCE BASE PIERCE FIELD TRAINING SCHOOL (FL19)

Address:	202 West Georgia Avenue, Eglin Air Force Base, Florida 32542.
Tel:	850-882-1110
Admission:	By prior permission only.
Location:	About 3 miles north of Niceville.

The airfield was built in World War II as a satellite for the main base and housed active units for many years. Doolittle's B-25 practised at one of the Eglin fields and it may well have been Pierce. The site was used as a Vietnamese Resettlement Camp in 1975 but it closed some time prior to this.

The field was re-opened and was active until 2000. It is now used as the Base Installation Security Systems Test Site and known as C-3. A number of instructional airframes are in use to assist air force personnel with their work.

TYPE	REG/SER	CON. NO.	PI/NOTES	STATUS
☐ General Dynamics 401 Fighting Falcon (F-16A)	80-0609	61-330		RA
☐ General Dynamics 401 Fighting Falcon (F-16A)	81-0761	61-442		RA
☐ Lockheed 182-1A Hercules (182-44-03) (C-130A) (NC-130A)	55-0022	182-3049		RA
☐ McDonnell M.98EN Phantom II (F-4D)	64-0929	1219		RA
☐ McDonnell M.98EN Phantom II (F-4D)	66-8800	2735		RA

EGLIN MONUMENTS (FL20)

Location:	On permanent view at two locations in the town.

TYPE	REG/SER	CON. NO.	PI/NOTES	STATUS
☐ Bell 205 Iroquois (UH-1H)	69-15171	11459	At the civil terminal at the airfield.	PV
☐ McDonnell M.199-1A Eagle (F-15A)	75-0033	131/A113	On Eglin Boulevard.	PV
☐ McDonnell M.199-1A Eagle (F-15A)	75-0044	144/A124	At the civil terminal at the airfield.	PV

EMBRY RIDDLE AERONAUTICAL UNIVERSITY (FL21)

Address:	600 South Clyde Boulevard, Daytona Beach, Florida 32114-3400.
Tel:	386-226-6000 Email: info@erau.edu
Admission:	By prior permission only.
Location:	At the airport which is in the western part of the town.

The university has a large fleet of aircraft for pilot training. The engineering section uses a former Malaysian Air Force Tebuan as an instructional airframe. The replica Wright Flyer is mounted close to the main entrance to the campus. The 1928 Waco ASO has recently been registered.

TYPE	REG/SER	CON. NO.	PI/NOTES	STATUS
☐ Canadair CL-41G-5 Tebuan	N401AG	2205	FM1134, M22-08	RA
☐ Waco ASO	NC7091	A10	NC7091, N7091	RA
☐ Wright Flyer (R)				PV

FANTASY OF FLIGHT (FL22)

Address:	PO Box 1276, 1400 Broadway Boulevard South East, Polk City, Florida 33868-1276.
Tel:	863-984-3500 Fax: 863-984-9506
Admission:	Daily 0900-1700.
Location:	About 1 mile east of the town just north of Interstate 4.

Kermit Weeks built his first aircraft when he was still at school and in 1978 was runner-up in the World Aerobatic Championships. He started collecting aircraft and in 1985 the Weeks Air Museum opened at Tamiami Airport. In the same year he bought the Tallmantz Collection and other aircraft were later acquired in Idaho.

Several interesting types were on show but disaster struck in August 1992 when the complex was badly damaged by Hurricane Andrew. Some of the aircraft outside were blown across the airfield and those in the hangar suffered when the roof was lifted. The structure was rebuilt and now houses the Wings Over Miami Museum.

In the early 1990s plans were put forward for a new attraction located close to Polk City. Construction started on hangars, workshops, storage buildings, an airfield and a lake to take floatplanes and flying boats. The first phase opened in 1995 and the site has steadily been developed. Kermit has many aircraft and most of those damaged at Tamiami in 1992 are being rebuilt around the USA and in England.

A number of rarities are on show and with many others in store the display will eventually become even more interesting. The exhibition halls contain many innovative 'hands-on' displays. Areas are devoted to the Tuskegee Airmen and the Women Air Force Service Pilots in World War II. A tram takes visitors around the airfield and past the workshops and storage hangars. Types from the early days up to the 1960s can be seen.

One of the stars is the Short Sunderland which was once flown by Charles Blair. The rare Boeing 100 was damaged in the storm and replicas of the military versions of the type are being built. Three of Kermit's own aerobatic designs are in store.

Florida

Some aircraft have been loaned to other museums. Rides are offered in Boeing-Stearman Kaydets and New Standard D-25s owned by the Lock family. Hot Air Balloon trips are also available. Regular demonstrations of some of the airworthy machines take place weather permitting. Flying displays are also held on some weekends.

TYPE	REG/SER	CON. NO.	PI/NOTES	STATUS
Abernathy Streaker	N1LM	1	N344Q	RAD
Aerostar S-60A Hot Air Balloon	N69FF	S60A-3224		RA
Avro 504J	N3182G		B3182	PV
Avro 643 Cadet II	N643AV	1060	A6-25, VH-AEI, VH-PRU	PVA
Avro 683 Lancaster 10(AR) (B.X)	G-BCOH	277	KB976, CF-AMD, CF-TQC – with parts from KB994.	RA
Avro 683 Lancaster B.X			(Canada) – major components	RA
Bachem Ba 349A-1 Natter (BP 20) (FSM)				PV
Barber Valkyrie				PV
Beech D17S (UC-43) (GB-2)	NC67735	6935	(44-76090), Bu23755, N67735, N17VF, N23023, N357MM	PV
Beech D17S (UC-43) (GB-2)	N52962	6880	(44-67772), Bu23694	RAA
Beech C18S Kansan (AT-11)	N92KC	5064	43-10371	RAC
Beech D18S Expeditor (C18S) (SNB-2C) (SNB-3) (SNB-5) (TC-45J) (UC-45J)	Bu29642	7802	Front fuselage only.	PV
Beech 58TC Baron	N7858B	TK-64		RAA
Beech 200 Super King Air	N200PH	BB-1017		RAA
Bell 47G Sioux (HTL-6) (TH-13M)	N147DP	1685	Bu143170	PV
Benoist 14 (R)				RAC
Boeing 100	N873H	1144	C873H, NC873H, NR873H, NX873H	RAC
Boeing 100 (R)				RAC
Boeing 102 (P-12B) (R)				RAC
Boeing 222 (P-12C) (R)				RAC
Boeing 235 (F4B-2) (R)				RAC
Boeing 235 (F4B-2) (R)				RAC
Boeing 299-O Fortress (B-17G) (B-17H) (TB-17H) (SB-17H)	44-83722	32363		RAC
Boeing 299-O Fortress (B-17G) (DB-17G)	N83525	32166	44-83525, N83525, '25053', (N4250)	RAC
Boeing 299-O Fortress (B-17G) (DB-17G) (DB-17P)	'237994'	32183	44-83542, N9324Z	PVX
Boeing 299-O Fortress (B-17G) (VB-17G)	'237994'	31957	44-83316 – fuselage only.	PVX
Boeing 345 Superfortress (B-29)	44-70049	10881	No rear fuselage	RAD
Boeing 345 Superfortress (B-29) (P2B-1S)	N29KW	13681	45-21787, Bu84029, NACA137, N91329	PV
Boeing 345 Superfortress (B-29) (SB-29)	44-84084			RAD
Boeing-Stearman A75N1 Kaydet (PT-17)	NC79466	75-3037	41-25530, N79466	PVA
Bristol 149 Bolingbroke IVT	N4133Z		(Canada)	RA
Bristol 149 Bolingbroke IVT	N4311Z	11-880-202	9983 (Canada)	RA
Bristol 149 Bolingbroke IVT	N4260C	11-880-203	9073 (Canada)	RA
Brown B-2 (R)	N255Y	T-2	On loan.	PVA
Bücker Bü 131B Jungmann	'GD+EG'	82	A-69 (Switzerland), HB-USC, N62200, N317BJ, NX41455	PVX
Bücker Bü 133C Jungmeister	'YR-PAX'	4	U-57 (Switzerland), HB-MIO, G-AYFO, N40BJ	PVX
Cameron A-105 Hot Air Balloon			Capsule only.	PV
CASA 352L [Junkers Ju 52/3m]	'VZ+NK'	155	T.2B-262, G-BFHG, 'D2+600' , 'VK+AZ', 'D-ATABX'	RA
Cierva C.30A (Avro 671)	K4235		K4235, G-AHMJ	PV
Commonwealth CA-13 Boomerang II	A46-165	988		RAC
Commonwealth CA-13 Boomerang II	A46-174	997		RAD
Commonwealth CA-16 Wirraway III	VH-WIR	1101	A20-649	RAA
Consolidated 28-5A Catalina (PBY-5A)	N3936A	1520	Bu33966	PV
Consolidated 28-5A Catalina (PBY-5A)	N96UC	1737	Bu48375, N4937V, ZP-CBA, T-29 (Paraguay, 2002 (Paraguay), N96FP	PVA
Consolidated 32 Liberator (B-24D)	41-11825	321	Front fuselage only.	PV
Consolidated 32 Liberator (B-24J) (B.VII)	'42-50551'	1567	44-44272, KH401, HE771 (India), N94459	PVAX
Convair 440 (340-51)	N114BF	146	XA-KIM, SE-CRM, N29DR, (N29BF), N29DR	PVA
CSS 13 [Polikarpov Po-2]	N50074	0365	(Polish AF), SP-ACN, (SP-FCN), SP-ACP, G-BXYA	PVA
Curtiss D Pusher (R)	N8234E	JP-1		PV
Curtiss D Pusher (R)		PFA/119-1071		RA
Curtiss 1C Jenny (JN-4D) (R)	N2404	5360		PVX
Curtiss 17 Oriole	N61624	181		RA
Curtiss 50B Robin B	N8313	193	NC8313	RA
Curtiss A87-A2 Kittyhawk I	N62435	18815	AL171, 1084 (Canada), '428150'	RAC
Curtiss 87V Warhawk (P-40N) (TP-40N)	NX923	33915	44-47923, N923	PVA
Curtiss-Wright CW-1 Junior	NC10967	1145	NC10967, N10967	PV
Curtiss-Wright CW-22N Falcon (SNC-1)	N888U	3707	(USN), N31686	-
De Havilland DH-4	N358DH	MAILPLANE		RAC
De Havilland DH-4	N434DH	WWI		RAC
De Havilland DH-4B				RAC
De Havilland DH-4BM	'328'			PVX
De Havilland DH.100 Vampire FB.6	N3160Y	649	J-1140 (Switzerland)	RA
Dewoitine D.26	N282DW	10853	282 (Switzerland), HB-RAA, G-BBMI	RAC

☐ Douglas DC-3A-228C	N600RC	2193	NC25653, XA-HAO, NC25653, XB-KEM, N25653, XB-MIL	RA
☐ Douglas DC-3A-467 Skytrain (C-47B)				PV
☐ Douglas SBD-2 Dauntless				PV
☐ Douglas A-20G Havoc	N34920	21844	43-22197, NX34920	RA
☐ Douglas A-24B Dauntless	N51382	17482	42-54643	RA
☐ Douglas A-26B Invader	N39401	7114	41-39401, N3457G	RA
☐ Douglas A-26C Invader	N3248G	28869	44-35590	RA
☐ Douglas B-23 Dragon	'40/17B'	2743	39-057, NR33309, N33309, N400B, N4000B	PVX
☐ EKW C-3605 (C-3603-1)	N31650	275	C-495	RA
☐ Eipper MX Quicksilver				RA
☐ Fairey Swordfish II				RA
☐ Fieseler Fi 103A-1 (FSM)				PV
☐ Fieseler Fi 156C-2 Storch	NX156FS/ 'KF+XL'4642		(Germany), NX464FB	PVX
☐ Focke-Wulf Fw 44J Stieglitz	''TQ+BC'	138	LV-ZAU, NX44FW	PVAX
☐ Fokker D VIII (R)	N94100	941		RAA
☐ Fokker Dr I (R)	N2009V	065		RAC
☐ Fokker Dr I (R)	N5523V	DB1		PV
☐ Ford 4-AT-B	NC7584	4-AT-38	NC7584, N7584	RAC
☐ Ford 5-AT-B	NL9651	5-AT-34	NC9651, NX9651, N9651	PVA
☐ General Aircraft Genairco Cabin	N240G	17	VH-UOH, VQ-FAC, VH-UUI	RA
☐ Gloster Meteor F.4	N229VT		VT229, 7151M, VT229	RAC
☐ Granville Gee Bee R (R)	'NR2101'			PVX
☐ Granville Gee Bee Y (R)	N3215M/ 'NR718Y'	DM002		PVX
☐ Granville Gee Bee Z (R)	NR77V	EK-Z1		PVA
☐ Grumman G-15 Duck (J2F-6)	N1214N		Bu33549	PVA
☐ Grumman G-15 Duck (J2F-6)	N5855S		Bu33614, N55S	RA
☐ Grumman G-36 Wildcat (FM-2)	'Bu86956'	5795	Bu86741, N19K, N222FM	PVX
☐ Grumman G-37 (F3F-2)	NX26KW		Bu1028, N19FG	PVA
☐ Grumman G-40 Avenger (TBM-3) (TBM-3E)	NL9548Z	4503	Bu91598, N9548Z	PVA
☐ Grumman G-50 Hellcat (F6F-3)	N7537U	A-4280	Bu43014	RAC
☐ Grumman G-51 Tigercat (F7F-3)	N7626C	C.146	Bu80404	RA
☐ Grumman G-79 Panther (F9F-2)	N32313	K-125	Bu123420	RAA
☐ Grumman G-89 Tracker (S2F-1) (S-2A)			Front fuselage only.	PV
☐ Grumman G-164A Super Ag-Cat	N8944H	1580		PV
☐ Hawker Hurricane IIB	Z5227		Z5227, (Russia)	RAC
☐ Hawker Hurricane XII				RA
☐ Hawker Hurricane XII		5400		RA
☐ Hawker Tempest V	N7027E		EJ693	RA
☐ Hawker Sea Fury FB.11	G-BWOL	ES.3617	WG599, G-9-66, D-CACY	RAC
☐ Herbert Trautman Road Air	N6892C	1		PV
☐ Hiller HJ.1 Hornet (YH-32)	N125JC	13	55-4970	PV
☐ Ikarus Aero 3A	N9016H	042	40142 (Yugoslavia)	PV
☐ Kawasaki Ki-61-I Hien		379	Fuselage only.	RA
☐ Laird LC-DW-500 Super Solution (R)	'N12048'			PVX
☐ Lavochkin La-11	N2276Y	10142		RA
☐ Leak Avid Flyer				RA
☐ Let C-11 [Yakovlev Yak-11]			(Egypt)	RA
☐ Lockheed 5B Vega (R)	NC105W	72	NC898E, XA-DOK, XB-MAA, N174D, N105D	PV
☐ Lockheed 14-H2 Special Electra	N14126	1500	CF-TCO	RAC
☐ Lockheed 15-27-01 Harpoon (PV-2)	N7483C	15-1168	Bu37202	RA
☐ Lockheed 422-87-23 Lightning (P-38L) (F-5G)	N2897S	422-7765	44-26761, NL5054N, N5054N, CF-GKE, N6190C	PVD
☐ Lockheed 1649A-98-17 Starliner	N974R	1649A-1040	D-ALAN, N45512, D-ALAN, N179AV – on loan.	PVA
☐ Martin 179 Marauder (B-26)	N4297J	1329	40-1464	PVA
☐ Martin 4-0-4	N40415	14119	Fuselage only.	RA
☐ McCulloch J-2	N4342G	052		RAC
☐ Messerschmitt Bf 108B-1 Taifun	N108KW	1914	CC-PWA, CC-PSS	PV
☐ Mikoyan-Gurevich MiG-15				RA
☐ Mitsubishi A6M5 Zero Sen Model 52	'3-108'	4043		PVX
☐ Morane-Saulnier A1	'S1573'			PVX
☐ Morane-Saulnier MS.230	N230MS	1049	1049 (France), F-BGMR, EI-ARG, G-BJCL	PV
☐ Nanchang Y-5 [Antonov An-2]	N4301U	8331		RA
☐ Nardi FN.305D	I-TOMI	007	I-UEBI	RAC
☐ Naval Aircraft Factory N3N-3				PV
☐ Nieuport 17 (R)	'N1653'	LCNC1967	N1290	PV
☐ Nieuport 28C.1 (Scale R)	'6189'			PVX
☐ North American NA-99 Mustang (P-51A)	N51KW	99-22281	43-6178, N8647E	RAC
☐ North American NA-103 Mustang (P-51C)	NX1204	103-26385	42-103831, N1204	PVA
☐ North American NA-108 Mitchell (B-25J) (TB-25N)	N1943J	108-35072	43-28059, N9857C, C-GTIM, N26975	PVA
☐ North American NA-124 Mustang (P-51D)	NL921	124-48260	45-11507, NZ2417, ZK-CCG	PVA
☐ North American NA-168 Texan (T-6G)	N3931Y	168-415	49-3311, C.6-167 (Spain)	PV
☐ Orenco F	N2145	45		PVC
☐ Piper J-3C-65 Cub (L-4J)	N5798N	13623	45-4883, N54783	PVA
☐ Quicksilver Sprint II	N69MX	423		PV
☐ Republic P-47D Thunderbolt				RA
☐ Revolution Mini-500	N51DR	147		PV
☐ Ryan NYP (R)	'NX-211'	DC-001	N211NX	PVX
☐ Santos-Dumont XX Demoiselle (R)	N65269	1		PV
☐ Seversky EP-106 (P-35A)	N106EP	282-11	41-17449, N17MP	PVA

Florida

☐ Shijiazhuang Y-5 [Antonov An-2]	NX4301U	8331		RA
☐ Short S.25 Sunderland MR.V	N814ML	SH.974	ML814, NZ4108, VH-BRF, N158J, G-BJHS, (EI-BYI), G-BJHS, N158J	PVA
☐ Sopwith 1 1/2 Strutter (R)				RAD
☐ Sopwith F.1 Camel (R)	N1920C			PV
☐ Sopwith Pup (R)	'N5452'	5459	N158RC	RACX
☐ SPAD VII	193			RAD
☐ Stampe & Vertongen S.V.4C	NX1606	190	F-BCFI	PVA
☐ Standard E-1	N49128	49128	N3783C	PV
☐ Standard J-1	N2825D	1582		PV
☐ Stephens Super Akro	N1NN	001		PVA
☐ Stinson SM-6000B	NC11170	5023	NC11170, N11170	PV
☐ Stinson V-74 Vigilant (O-49) (L-1)	N63230		40-3102	RAD
☐ Stinson V-74 Vigilant (O-49A) (L-1A)	N1377B		41-19031	RA
☐ Supermarine 361 Spitfire LF.XVIe	NX476TE	CBAF-IX-4610	TE476, 7451M, 8071M, G-XVIB, NX476TE, G-XVIB	PV
☐ Supermarine 379 Spitfire FR.XIVe	G-CCVV	6S.649186	MV262, (India)	RAC
☐ Thomas-Morse S-4C	N1917T	633		PVC
☐ Travel Air B-4000	NC174V	1365	NC174V, N174V	PVA
☐ Tupolev Tu-2S			Front fuselage on show – remainder in store.	PV/RA
☐ Tupolev Tu-2S				RA
☐ Tupolev Tu-2S				RA
☐ Vought F4U-4 Corsair	NX5215V	9440	Bu97286	PV
☐ Vought FG-1D Corsair	N63382	2900	Bu88086, NX63382	RA
☐ Vought A-7B Corsair II	Bu154418	B58	Front fuselage only.	PV
☐ Vultee V-74 Valiant (BT-13A)	41-21821	74-5660		PVC
☐ Vultee V-74 Valiant (BT-15)	'42-16621'	74-11630	42-89261, N56979, N513L – fuselage only – registered as a BT-15.	PVX
☐ Weeks Quicksilver Sprint II	N69MX	423		RA
☐ Weeks S-1W	N69KW	001		RA
☐ Weeks SW-1S Solution	N300KW	001		RA
☐ White D-IX Der Jager	N30KW	003		RA
☐ Wright Flyer (R)				PV
☐ Zlin Z-381 [Bücker Bü 181D Bestmann]	'AM+YA'	461	OK-AVC, OO-AVC, G-AMYA, NX181BU	PVAX

FLORIDA AIR MUSEUM (FL23)

Address:	PO Box 7670, 4175 Medullaq Road, Lakeland, Florida 33807-6795.
Tel:	863-644-0741 **Fax:** 863-648-9264 **Email:** museum@sun-n-fun.org
Admission:	Monday-Friday 0900-1700, Saturday 1000-1600, Sunday 1200-1600.
Location:	On the south side of Lakeland Airport which is south of Interstate 4.

In 1974 the Lakeland Chapter of the EAA held a winter weekend fly-in and this was such a success that it was repeated the following year and extended to one week with the public being admitted. The event is now held annually in April and attracts vast numbers of aircraft and people to the airfield. In the mid-1980s it was decided to set up a museum and aircraft were initially placed on view in one of the hangars. A purpose-built exhibition hall, which opened on 6th April 1992, has now been constructed close to the gate to the EAA. Initially known as the International Sport Aviation Museum, the collection changed its name to reflect its wider role and now houses a collection of mainly homebuilt aircraft.

The aircraft on view show the development of amateur aircraft from the 1930s up to modern designs using composite construction materials. A rarity in the USA is the Auster AOP.9. Many unique types can be seen in the well presented displays. A rarity is the Aeronca L. The company constructed only 65 examples of this low wing design which was powered by a variety of engines. The LB, of which 28 were made, was fitted with an 85 hp Le Blond radial.

TYPE	REG/SER	CON. NO.	PI/NOTES	STATUS
☐ Aeronca C-3	NC13557	A-291	NC13557, N13557	PV
☐ Aeronca LB	N15292	2000	NC15292	PV
☐ American Aerolights Eaglet	N5AQ	005		PV
☐ Anderson Kingfisher	N2EK	84		PV
☐ Anglin Spacewalker 2	N168CM	SW291-F023		PV
☐ Auster B.5 AOP.9	N408XN	B5/10/126	XN408	RAC
☐ Bede BD-4	N8826	128		RA
☐ Bede BD-5B	N51GB	4496		PV
☐ Bell 33 Kingcobra (P-63C)	N91448	33-766	44-4181, NX73744, N73744, N9009 – composite with 43-11117 – on loan from F. of F, FL.	PV
☐ Bensen B-8M Gyrocopter				PV
☐ Boeing-Stearman A75N1 Kaydet (PT-17)	N809RB			PV
☐ Bowers Fly Baby 1A				PV
☐ Briegleb BG-12D	N17EB	220		PV
☐ Brokaw BJ.520 Bullet	N520BJ	1		PV
☐ Cirrus VK-30	N94CM	9105		PV
☐ Colomban MC-10 Cri-Cri	N98DJ	12-0069		PV
☐ Command-Aire Little Rocket (R)	'10403'	2	N345JA	PVX
☐ Convair 2 Seadart (YF2Y-1) (YF-7A)	Bu135765			PV
☐ Culver V Satellite	N3134K	V-270	NC3134K	PV
☐ Denney Kitfox I	N3LB	236		PV
☐ Ercoupe 415D	N99741	2364		PV
☐ Evans VP-1 Volksplane	N24PB	V1522		PV

☐ Fairchild M-62A Cornell (PT-19B)	N46389	T43-5111	42-82724		PV
☐ Fisher FP-303					PV
☐ Ford 1 Flivver (FSM)	'3218'	298			PVX
☐ Grumman G-303 Tomcat (F-14A) (F-14D)	Bu159619	166			PV
☐ Hammond Bill 01	N434SM	01			PV
☐ Hawker Tempest II	N607LA		LA607 – on loan from F of F, FL.		PV
☐ Heath Super Parasol IV	N88EG	41919			PV
☐ Jeffair Barracuda	N118MW	443			PVA
☐ Laird Biplane (R)		02			PV
☐ Lockheed 081-40-01 Salmon (XFV-1)	Bu138657	081-1001			RA
☐ Loving-Wayne WR-1 Love	N100PH	773-88-11	.		PVA
☐ McNeal Ranchaero HR	N4659S	1			PV
☐ Mignet HM-297 Pou-du-Ciel					PV
☐ Mitchell P-38	N435GW	435-6			PV
☐ Monnett Moni	N46431	125			PV
☐ Mooney M-18L Mite	N3159K	3			PV
☐ Palmer Sunshine Clipper	N625C	SH-083-3625	Modified from Stinson 108-3 Voyager c/n 108-3625 N625C		PV
☐ Pereira GP.3 Osprey II	N821H	653			PV
☐ Pietenpol B4-A Aircamper	N3513	100			PV
☐ Pitts P-6 Special	N58P	106			RA
☐ Porterfield CP-65	N37850	997	NC37850		PV
☐ Quickie Aircraft Quickie 1 (Rutan 54)	N303Q	0303			PV
☐ Quickie Aircraft Quickie 200 (Rutan 54)	N150CS	2642			PV
☐ Rand Robinson KR-1	N12NS	NTS 1166			PV
☐ Rans S-9	N218ER	0787012			PV
☐ Rotorway Executive 162F	N77BB	6497			PV
☐ Rutan 27 Vari-Viggen					PV
☐ Rutan 33 Vari-Eze	N4253V	668			PV
☐ Smyth Sidewinder	N727R	212191			PV
☐ Stits SA-11A Playmate	N77JA	126			PV
☐ Stoddard-Hamilton SH-2 Glasair 1-RG	N207SC	207			PVA
☐ Taylor E-2 Cub	NC13177	58	NC13177, N13177		PV
☐ Taylorcraft BL-65	N26653	1995	NC26653		PV
☐ Ultraflight Lazair 1					PV
☐ Viking Dragonfly	N88CU	703			PV
☐ Volmer Jensen VJ-21					PV
☐ Westland Lysander IIIA	'V9312'	1244	Composite – parts from Canadian 2341, 2349 2391, G-BCWL, N3093K, 'V9281', 'V9312' and other airframes – on loan from F of F, FL.		PVX
☐ Woods Woody Pusher	N100FQ	100			PV

FLORIDA MILITARY AVIATION MUSEUM (FL24)

Address:	PO Box 891, Wauchula, Florida 33873.
Tel:	941-773-9700 **Fax:** 941-773-2001
Admission:	Currently closed.
Location:	Some aircraft stored near Fort Meade – others at Wauchula.

The organisation was set up in the late 1970s as a branch of the California-based Yesterday's Air Force. A display was organised at St. Petersburg and the group soon became independent. The change of name was later made to reflect the aims of the museum. The state of Florida has been the location of many military airfields and still houses active bases of all the services. The site close to the airport was lost and the collection was forced to move.

Some of the aircraft are currently stored at Wauchula and others have moved on to other museums. The current position is unclear but little progress seems to have been made.

TYPE	REG/SER	CON. NO.	PI/NOTES	STATUS
☐ Beech C18S Kansan (AT-11)	N241X	1189	41-27344	RA
☐ Bell 205 Iroquois (UH-1D)	64-13614	4321		RA
☐ Cessna R172E Mescalero (T-41B)	67-15006	R1720007	67-15006, N352	RA
☐ Cessna 318E Dragonfly (A-37B)	73-1088	43469		RA
☐ De Havilland DHC.2 Beaver (L-20A) (U-6A)	52-6135	525		RA
☐ Douglas A-4C Skyhawk (A4D-2N)	'Bu148592'	12598	Bu147834	RAX
☐ Douglas DC-3A-405 Skytrooper (C-53)	N90079	7392	42-15875, PJ-ALA, HP-309, HP-729, HI-445	RA
☐ Grumman G-134 Mohawk (AO-1C) (OV-1C)	60-3758	14C	60-3758, N6743	RA
☐ Lockheed 580 (T-33A)	58-0700	580-1669	58-0700, N88232	RA
☐ McDonnell M.58 Demon (F3H-2) (F-3B)			Fuselage only	RAD
☐ McDonnell M.98AM Phantom II (F4H-1F) (F-4A)	Bu145308	9		RA
☐ Sikorsky S-58 Seahorse (HUS-1G) (HH-34F)	1343	581068		RA
☐ Sikorsky S-61R Pelican (HH-3F)	1433	61598		RA

FLORIDA STATE COMMUNITY COLLEGE (FL25)

Address:	13450 Lake Fretwell Street, Jacksonville, Florida 32221.
Tel:	904-317-3800 **Email:** justask@fscj.edu
Admission:	By prior permission only.
Location:	At the former Cecil Field which is about 15 miles southwest of Jacksonville on Route 134.

Florida

The college has facilities at the airport which was the Cecil Field Naval Air Station for many years. Three instructional airframes are in use. The Boeing 727 is one of several donated to educational establishments by Federal Express. The Hornet, which is not owned by the college, is preserved as a memorial to the military era.

TYPE	REG/SER	CON. NO.	PI/NOTES	STATUS
☐ Beech 35 Bonanza	N3818N	D-1045	NC3818N	RA
☐ Boeing 727-25F	N153FE	18286	N8153N, N153FE, C-FBWX	RA
☐ Cessna 150G	N2970J	15065770		RA
☐ McDonnell M.267 Hornet (F/A-18A)	Bu162462	315/A260	Airfield monument –	PV

FORT LAUDERDALE MONUMENT (FL26)

Location:	On permanent view at the Executive Airport which is in the western part of the town.

TYPE	REG/SER	CON. NO.	PI/NOTES	STATUS
☐ North American NA-203 Sabre (F-86H)	53-1255	203-27		PV

FORT MYERS HISTORICAL MUSEUM (FL27)

Address:	2300 Peck Street, Fort Myers, Florida 33901.
Tel:	239-321-7270
Admission:	Tuesday-Saturday 0900-1600.
Location:	In the centre of the old town.

This informative museum is housed in the former Atlantic Coastal Railroad Depot. The displays trace the history and development of south west Florida from the time of the indigenous Calusa Indians. Spanish explorers passed through the region before the area was settled. A 1900s farmhouse and a 1928 Pullman railway car can be seen. There have been a number of military airfields around the town and the Airacobra was recovered from a crash site.

TYPE	REG/SER	CON. NO.	PI/NOTES	STATUS
☐ Bell 26C Airacobra (P-39N)				PVD

GALLIVER MONUMENT (FL28)

Location:	On permanent view at a business in the town.

TYPE	REG/SER	CON. NO.	PI/NOTES	STATUS
☐ Piper PA-28-140 Cherokee				PV

GEORGE T. BAKER AVIATION MAINTENANCE SCHOOL (FL29)

Address:	3275 North West 42 Avenue, Miami, Florida 33142.
Tel:	305-871-3143 Fax: 305-871-5840
Admission:	By prior permission only.
Location:	On the north side of the International Airport which is about 6 miles north west of the city centre.

Aviation classes commenced at Miami High School in 1939 and the school moved into its current premises adjacent to Miami International Airport in 1958.
Over the years a variety of airframes have been used but the climate has caused corrosion problems and several interesting types have been scrapped. The Skyhawk serves as the gate guardian to the school and the MD-82 is a recent donation from American Airlines. This airliner replaced the Boeing 727 which recently fell victim to the weather. More aircraft may be in the workshops.

TYPE	REG/SER	CON. NO.	PI/NOTES	STATUS
☐ Beech D18S Expeditor (C18S) (SNB-1) (SNB-5) (TC-45J) (UC-45J)	N9493	3663	Bu39931	RA
☐ Beech D18S Expeditor (C18S) (SNB-2C) (SNB-3) (SNB-5) (TC-45J) (UC-45J)	N26001	6995	Bu29553	RA
☐ Bell 205 Iroquois (UH-1H)	66-16986	9180		RAX
☐ Cessna 150	'N551'			RAX
☐ Cessna 150A	N7083X	15059183		RA
☐ Cessna 150M	N7589U	15077756		RA
☐ Cessna 172M	N20012	17260929		RA
☐ Cessna 172N	N739KV	17270612		RA
☐ Cessna 172P	N52901	17274632		RA
☐ Cessna 172P	N63425	17275431		RA
☐ Cessna 172P	N63497	17275444		RA
☐ Cessna 421	N3019R	4210056		RA
☐ Douglas A-4B Skyhawk (A4D-2)	Bu142166	11420		RA
☐ McDonnell-Douglas MD-82	N234AA	49181		RA
☐ Piper PA-23 Apache	N1297P	23-336		RA
☐ Piper PA-23 Apache	N2174P	23-780		RA
☐ Piper PA-23-250 Aztec C	N6559Y	27-3855		RA
☐ Rotorway Scorpion 1	N5468M	2560		RA

HERNANDO MONUMENT (FL30)

Location:	On permanent view at VFW 4252 on Route 200 in the northern part of the town.

TYPE	REG/SER	CON. NO.	PI/NOTES	STATUS
☐ Bell 205 Iroquois (UH-1D) (UH-1H)	'8749'	4024	62-12366 – composite.	PVX

The Navy Museum in Washington, DC is home to this Goodyear-built Vought FG-1D Corsair. (Nigel Hitchman) [DC6]

On show at the Hurlburt Field Memorial Airpark is this Curtiss C-46D Commando. (Juha Ritaranta) [FL36]

Preserved just inside the gate of Jacksonville Naval Air Station is this Lockheed P-3A Orion [FL38]

Florida

HIGH SPRINGS MONUMENT (FL31)

Location:	On permanent view at a school on North Main Street in the town.

TYPE	REG/SER	CON. NO.	PI/NOTES	STATUS
☐ Vought A-7A Corsair II	Bu152647	A4		PV

HILLSBOROUGH COUNTY VETERANS MEMORIAL MUSEUM AND PARK (FL32)

Address:	3602 Highway 301, North Tampa, Florida 33617.
Tel:	813-744-5502 Fax: 813-744-5678
Admission:	Saturday-Sunday 1000-1500.
Location:	In the northern part of the city.

Four helicopters have been put on show at this local veteran's museum. Two others are mounted on trailers and often taken to local events to raise the profile of the group. The building houses memorabilia and photographs along with uniforms and badges. Memorials to those who lost their lives in conflicts have been erected.

TYPE	REG/SER	CON. NO.	PI/NOTES	STATUS
☐ Bell 205 Iroquois (UH-1H)	68-15562	10492		PV
☐ Bell 206A Kiowa (OH-58A)	71-20748	41609		PV
☐ Bell 209 Huey Cobra (AH-1G) (AH-1F)	67-15722	20386		PV
☐ Hughes 369M Cayuse (HO-6) (OH-6A)	68-17308	1268	68-17308, N46TP	PV
☐ Hughes 369M Cayuse (HO-6) (OH-6A)	69-16059	1429	69-16059, N56TP	PV
☐ Hughes 369M Cayuse (HO-6) (OH-6A)	69-16062	1432		PV

HISTORIC FLIGHT FOUNDATION (FL33)

Address:	3500 North West 119th Street, Miami, Florida 33167.
Tel:	305-883-2012 Fax: 305-883-2072 Email: info@hffshop.com
Admission:	By prior permission only.
Location:	At Opa-Locka airport which is about 12 miles north west of Miami Beach.

The organisation was formed to keep airworthy an example of the classic DC-7B and to provide flights to airshows for members. N836D was originally delivered to Eastern Airlines in early 1958 and flew on passenger services with them for eight years. After a number of owners it was parked at Holman Field where it remained until ferried to Opa-Locka for restoration. The other aircraft are owned by Florida Air Transport; N381AA is sometimes used on Legendary Airliners flights.

TYPE	REG/SER	CON. NO.	PI/NOTES	STATUS
☐ Beech D18S Expeditor (C-45H)	N9004Z	AF-505	52-10575, N9002Z	RAA
☐ Douglas DC-6A Liftmaster (R6D-1) (C-118B)	N70BF	43720	Bu131617, N70BF, XA-SCZ	RAA
☐ Douglas DC-7B	N836D	45345		RAC
☐ Douglas DC-7BF (DC-7B)	N381AA	44921	N381AA, N750Z, N101LM	RAA

HISTORY FLIGHT (FL34)

Address:	Overseas Highway 101, Marathon, Florida 33050.
Tel:	info@historyflight.com.
Admission:	By prior permission only.
Location:	At the airport which is on the island just off Highway 1.

Four aircraft are operated by the group, whose main aim is to raise funds to try and trace the graves of American servicemen 'Missing in Action'. Flights are offered in the former warbirds and the quartet often appear at shows. The SNJ-6 and N2S-1 are painted in period US Navy colours and the B-25 is in a camouflage scheme.

TYPE	REG/SER	CON. NO.	PI/NOTES	STATUS
☐ Boeing-Stearman A75N1 Kaydet (N2S-1)	N54087	75-1148	Bu3371	RAA
☐ North American NA-88 Texan (AT-6C)				RAA
☐ North American NA-98 Mitchell (B-25H)	N5548N	98-21107	43-4106	RAA
☐ North American NA-121 Texan (AT-6F) ((SNJ-6)	N1044C	121-42857	44-82135, Bu112079	RAA

HOMESTEAD AIR RESERVE STATION MONUMENTS (FL35)

Location:	By prior permission only at the airfield which is about 25 miles south west of Miami off Route 1.

TYPE	REG/SER	CON. NO.	PI/NOTES	STATUS
☐ General Dynamics 401 Fighting Falcon (F-16A)	79-0326	61-111		RA
☐ McDonnell M.98EN Phantom II (F-4D)	66-0267	1934	Composite	RA
☐ McDonnell M.98EN Phantom II (F-4D)	66-0273	1941	In town.	PV

HURLBURT FIELD MEMORIAL AIR PARK (FL36)

Address:	1 SOW/PA, 131 Bartley Street, Suite 326, Hurlburt Field, Florida 32544-5271.
Tel:	850-884-7190 Email: 1sow.pa@hurlburt.af.mil
Admission:	Sunrise-sunset daily subject to security status.
Location:	At the main gate of the field on Highway 98. The field is about 45 miles north east of Pensacola.

Florida

The airfield opened in 1943 and is within the Eglin Air Force Base area. The base is named after Lieutenant Donald W. Hurlburt who was killed in a local crash on 2nd October 1943. The field is the home of all USAF Special Operations and the display features aircraft used on these missions.

The Invader was the first aircraft to join collection. After refurbishment it flew missions over Vietnam from its base in Thailand between 1965 to 1968. Several other machines saw action in South East Asia. The Iroquois is one of 20 converted to the UH-1P model for psychological warfare duties. These helicopters served in Vietnam but their home base was Hurlburt. The Provider is fitted out as a defoliant aircraft although it never flew in this role. The C-47 was flown on a number of special operations tasks but the example on show did not serve in this role, nor did the Skyraider, which has been painted to represent an Air Force aircraft used by an Air Commando Group in Vietnam. The Curtiss Commando is one of 48 operated by the JASDF between 1955 and 1978. Three dozen were supplied under MDAP and the other 12 arrived from the Chinese Nationalist Air Force.

The AC-130 version of the Hercules is one of the small number converted to be used as a gunship for use in the Vietnam conflict. A few Helio Couriers were used on clandestine missions in a number of countries in South East Asia.

TYPE	REG/SER	CON. NO.	PI/NOTES	STATUS
☐ Bell 204 Iroquois (UH-1F) (UH-1P)	64-15493	7043		PV
☐ Cessna 305C Bird Dog (L-19E) (O-1E)	56-4208	23853		PV
☐ Cessna 318E Dragonfly (A-37B) (OA-37B)	70-1293	43308		PV
☐ Cessna 337M Super Skymaster (O-2A)	67-21368	337M0074		PV
☐ Curtiss-Wright CW-20B-2 Commando (C-46D)	44-77424	32820	44-77424, 51-1101 (Japan), N5579Z	PV
☐ Douglas DC-3A-456 Skytrain (C-47A)	'43-510'	19976	43-15510, '49010', '42-510'	PVX
☐ Douglas A-26A Invader (A-26C) (B-26K)	64-17666	28762	44-35483 – (On-Mark B-26K)	PV
☐ Douglas A-1G Skyraider (AD-5N)	'51-598'	8993	Bu132598, 132598 (South Vietnam)	PVX
☐ Fairchild 110 Flying Boxcar (C-119G) (C-119L)	53-3144	11155	53-3144, N8512N, N37484	PV
☐ Fairchild 473 Provider (205) (C-123B) (C-123K)	55-4533	20194		PV
☐ Helio H-395 Super Courier (U-10A)	62-3606	540		PV
☐ Lockheed 182-1A Hercules (182-44-03) (C-130A) (AC-130A)	56-0509	182-3117		PV
☐ North American NA-108 Mitchell (B-25J) (TB-25J)	43-28222	108-35235	43-28222, N5256V	PV
☐ North American NA-159 Trojan (T-28A) (T-28D)	49-1663	159-175		PV
☐ North American NA-305 Bronco (OV-10A)	67-14626	305-34		PV
☐ Sikorsky S-61R (CH-3C) (CH-3E)	65-12784	61559		PV
☐ Sikorsky S-65A (CH-53C) (MH-53J) (MH-53M)	68-10928	65226		PV

JACKSONVILLE AIR NATIONAL GUARD BASE (FL37)

Address: PO Box 18018, Jacksonville International Airport, Florida 32229-0018.
Tel: 904-741-7100   **Email:** publicaffairs@fljack.ang.af.mil
Admission: On permanent view.
Location: The airport is about 10 miles north of the city off Interstate 95.

The 159th Fighter Squadron was allocated to the Florida National Guard in February 1947. Apart from a spell of active duty in the Korean War it has been based at Jacksonville. Five aircraft formerly used by the unit have been preserved outside the main gate to the base.

The T-33 was used in the support role for many years. The F-102A was flown from 1960 to 1964 when they were replaced by the F-106A which was the front line equipment of the unit until 1987. The Eagle was put on show in the late 1990s.

TYPE	REG/SER	CON. NO.	PI/NOTES	STATUS
☐ Convair 8-10 Delta Dagger (F-102A)	'61357'	8-10-783	57-0817	PVX
☐ Convair 8-24 Delta Dart (F-106A)	57-0230	8-24-19		PV
☐ General Dynamics 401 Fighting Falcon (F-16A)	79-0296	61-81		RA
☐ Lockheed 580 (T-33A)	53-5325	580-8664		PV
☐ McDonnell M.199-1A Eagle (F-15A)	76-0080	270/A232		PV

JACKSONVILLE NAVAL AIR STATION COLLECTION (FL38)

Address: 6801 Roosevelt Boulevard,, Jacksonville Naval Air Station, Florida 32122-5000.
Tel: 904-542-7300   **Fax:** 904-542-2413   **Email:** pao@nasjax.navy.mil
Admission: By prior permission only.
Location: About 5 miles south of the city on Route 17.

A military camp was set up in the area in 1909 and for nine months in 1916 a school of aviation using three Curtiss seaplanes was at Black Point. A number of other military units were in the area in the inter-war period. Construction of the airfield started in the late 1930s and the first aircraft moved in during 1940. Since then the site has expanded and now covers a vast area.

The station houses units operating the P-3 Orion and a variety of helicopters. The Naval Air Depot on the site is responsible for the major overhaul of F/A-18s, P-3s and T-2s.

The majority of the collection of preserved aircraft is located in a landscaped area just inside the main gate. The Catalina is one of a batch brought back from Brazil in the early 1980s by David Tallichet.

TYPE	REG/SER	CON. NO.	PI/NOTES	STATUS
☐ Boeing-Stearman A75N1 Kaydet (N2S-4)	'Bu9681'			RAX
☐ Consolidated 28-5A Catalina (PBY-5A)	Bu46582	1946	Bu46582, PT-???, 6520 (Brazil), N4583A	RA
☐ Douglas A-4C Skyhawk (A4D-2N)	Bu147788	12552		RA
☐ Douglas TA-4F Skyhawk				RA
☐ Grumman G-40 Avenger (TBM-3)	Bu91664	4569	Bu91664, N9651C	RA
☐ Grumman G-121 Tracker (S2F-3) (S-2D)	Bu148730	49C	Bu148730, N6750	RA
☐ Grumman G-303 Tomcat (F-14A)	Bu161863	499		RA
☐ Lockheed 185 Orion (P3V-1) (P-3A)	Bu151374	185-5087		RA
☐ Lockheed 394 Viking (YS-3A) (NS-3A)	Bu157993	394A-3002		RA

Florida

☐ Lockheed 426-42-15 Neptune (P2V-5) (P2V-5F) (P-2E)	Bu131410	426-5291	Bu131410, N88487	RA
☐ McDonnell M.267 Hornet (F/A-18A)	Bu161941	147/A112		RA
☐ Sikorsky S-61B Sea King (HSS-2) (SH-3A) (SH-3G)	Bu149695			RA
☐ Sikorsky S-61B Sea King (SH-3D) (SH-3H)	Bu156501	61447		RA
☐ Vought TF-8A Crusader (F8U-1) (F8U-1T)	Bu141351			RA
☐ Vought A-7E Corsair II	Bu160715	E548		RA

KENNEDY SPACE CENTER VISITOR COMPLEX (FL39)

Address: SR 405, Kennedy Space Center, Florida 32899.
Tel: 866-737-5235
Admission: Monday–Friday 0900-1730.
Location: About 5 miles east of Titusville.

The Talon is mounted outside the building where tours of the facility start. Cape Canaveral has been an important location in the space programme for many years. Here launches of rockets, spacecraft and the shuttle have taken place. The visitor will learn about the history of the site, space travel and future developments.

TYPE	REG/SER	CON. NO.	PI/NOTES	STATUS
☐ Northrop N-156T Talon (T-38A)	N969NA	N.5748	65-1029, N511NA	PV

KEY WEST MONUMENTS (FL40)

Location: On permanent view at two locations in the town.

TYPE	REG/SER	CON. NO.	PI/NOTES	STATUS
☐ Antonov An-24RV	CU-T1294	27308105	CCCP-46487, YL-LCF – at airport	PV
☐ Republic RC-3 Seabee			At a business in the town.	PVX

KEY WEST NAVAL AIR STATION COLLECTION (FL41)

Address: PO Box 9001, Stock Island, Florida 33040-9001.
Tel: 305-292-2425   **Fax:** 305-293-4108   **Email:** pao@naskw.navy.mil
Admission: By prior permission only.
Location: About 6 miles east of Key West off Highway 1.

There has been a naval presence at Key West since the mid-1800s. During World War I and the subsequent years flying boats were flown from the site. The base was constructed during World War II to train naval aircrew before they were posted overseas At the current time the site is used for training by transient squadrons.

TYPE	REG/SER	CON. NO.	PI/NOTES	STATUS
☐ Douglas A-4E Skyhawk (A4D-5)	Bu151033	13203		RA
☐ Grumman G-128 Intruder (YA2F-1) (YA-6A) (EA-6A)	Bu148618	I-3		RA
☐ Grumman G-303 Tomcat (F-14B)	Bu162910	558		RA
☐ McDonnell M.98AM Phantom II (F-4B) (F-4N)	Bu153019	1509		PV
☐ North American NA-316 Vigilante (RA-5C)	Bu156612	316-5		PV
☐ Sikorsky S-61B Sea King (SH-3D) (UH-3H)	Bu152710			RA

KISSIMMEE AIR MUSEUM (FL42)

Address: 223 North Hoagland Boulevard, Kissimmee, Florida 34741.
Tel: 407-870-7336   **Email:** info@kissimmeeairmuseum.com
Admission: July–October Monday-Saturday 0900-1700; November–June daily 0900-1700.
Location: At the airport which is on Highway 192 just west of the town.

Warbird Adventures was formed in the late 1990s with the aim of offering flights in a fleet of Texans. The aircraft operated out of the Flying Tigers Warbird Museum. After substantial damage in a 2004 hurricane this facility closed.
  Warbird Adventures then acquired their own premises which has now been enlarged to feature an exhibition hall. In addition to the aircraft listed below other warbirds are often in residence.
  The Taylor Aerocar could also be used on the road. The design dating from the late 1940s was built in small numbers in three versions. The example on show is the last one built and the only one still airworthy.

TYPE	REG/SER	CON. NO.	PI/NOTES	STATUS
☐ Boeing-Stearman B75 Kaydet (N2S-2)	N2JS	75-1349	Bu3572	RAA
☐ Boeing-Stearman E75 Kaydet (PT-13D)	C-GPTD	75-5315	42-17152, N105H, N72759	RAC
☐ Cessna 305A Bird Dog (L-19A)	N4443P	23079	51-12624, 3A-CH (Austria)	PVA
☐ Focke-Wulf Fw 190A-8		173889		RAC
☐ Grumman G-89 Tracker (S2F-1) (S-2A) (US-2B)	N5244B	443	Bu136534	RAA
☐ Grumman G-96 Trader (TF-1) (C-1A)	Bu146029	059	Bu146029, N6192F	PV
☐ Hiller UH12D Raven (H-23D) (OH-23D)	N689HS	1169	59-2689	PVA
☐ Jensen Slipknot	N5381	GDA.002		PVA
☐ Lockheed 683-10-19 Starfighter (F-104G)	'60813'	683D-9094	FX-51 (Belgium)	PVX
☐ Mikoyan-Gurevich MiG-21SMT	52	50019105		PV
☐ North American NA-121 Texan (AT-6F) (SNJ-6)	N452WA	121-42802	44-82080, Bu112034, N3254G N41WD, N2729	PVA
☐ North American NA-121 Texan (AT-6F) (SNJ-6)	N451WA	121-42817	44-82095, Bu112049, N9809C	PVA
☐ North American NA-121 Texan (AT-6F) (SNJ-6)	N455WA	121-43130	44-82408, Bu112227, N9800C	PVA

☐ Ryan ST-3KR Recruit (PT-22)	N55081	1422	41-15393	PVA
☐ Robinson R-44 Raven	N288L	0930		PVA
☐ Taylor Aerocar	N102D	4		PVA
☐ WSK Lim-5 [MiG-17F]	N1705	1C 17-05	1705 (Poland)	PV

LAKE CITY MONUMENT (FL43)

Location:	On permanent view at Cannon Creek Air Park south of the town off I75.

TYPE	REG/SER	CON. NO.	PI/NOTES	STATUS
☐ Vought A-7E Corsair II	Bu158003	E319		PV

LIBERATION AIR FORCE MEMORIAL (FL44)

Address:	PO Box 720328, Miami, Florida 33272.
Tel:	786-200-2816 Fax: 305-675-0375
Admission:	On permanent view.
Location:	At Kendall – Timiami Airport which is south west of Kendall.

The memorial was dedicated on 17th April 2010 to honour the ten Cuban pilots, four CIA volunteer pilots and two technicians who lost their lives in the Bay of Pigs operation. Funds were raised by the Cuban Pilots Association. An obelisk has been erected at the centre of a five pointed star surrounded by a red circle. This is joined by five white and blue bands representing the Cuban flag.

The Invader has been painted in the colours of one flown during the campaign. There are plaques commemorating those who were killed.

TYPE	REG/SER	CON. NO.	PI/NOTES	STATUS
☐ Douglas A-26C Invader	'931'	28719	44-35440, 435440 (France), N6838D, CF-MSB, C-FMSB – in false Cuban markings.	PVX

LIVELY TECHNICAL CENTER AVIATION SCHOOL (FL45)

Address:	3290 Capital Circle South West, Tallahasee, Florida 32310.
Tel:	850-488-2461 Email: hildebrandtw@leonschools.net
Admission:	By prior permission only.
Location:	At the airport which is in the south western part of the city.

The school was set up by Lewis Lively in 1937. The aviation department has facilities at the airport where students can gain their licences. A number of instructional airframes are in use.

TYPE	REG/SER	CON. NO.	PI/NOTES	STATUS
☐ Beech D45 Mentor (T-34B)	N9059R	BG-423	Bu144716	RA
☐ Bell 204 Iroquois (UH-1C) (UH-1M)				RA
☐ Cessna 152	N89177	15282661		RA
☐ Cessna 172	N8188B	29988		RA
☐ Lockheed 580 (T-33A)	58-0470	580-1439	58-0470, N63313	RA

LOCK COLLECTION (FL46)

Address:	6925 Conley Drive, Polk City, Florida 33868-9389
Admission:	By prior permission only – some aircraft at Fantasy of Flight,FL.
Location:	At a number of locations.

The Lock family have a collection of classic biplanes. They now operate from Kermit Weeks Fantasy of Flight. They also have a home in Ohio where some of the aircraft are based in the summer months.

The New Standard D-25 first flew in 1928 and 65 were produced before the depression. A few more appeared in the mid-1930s. The large biplane carried a pilot and four passengers and is ideal for joy riding. A number were converted for crop-dusting duties and the majority of the survivors came from this source.

Arkansas Aircraft was set up at Little Rock in 1926. The following year Albert Voellmecke designed a three seat biplane which soon went into production as the Commandaire 3C3. The 5C3 had a different engine and over 200 were built.

TYPE	REG/SER	CON. NO.	PI/NOTES	STATUS
☐ Aeronca 7AC Champion	N2808E	7AC-6391		RAA
☐ Command-Aire 5C3	NC997E	W-136		RA
☐ Command-Aire 5C3	NC998E	W-137		RA
☐ New Standard D-25	NC9756	105	NC9756, N9756	RAA
☐ New Standard D-25	NC9797	148	NC9797, N9797	RAA
☐ New Standard D-25A	NC9125	205	NC150M, N9125- operates from Fantasy of Flight, FL.	RAA
☐ Stearman 6C	NC786H	6010	NC2143	RA
☐ Travel Air 4000	NC3670	288	NC3670, N3670	RAA
☐ Waco UPF-7	N30102	5499	NC30102	RAA

LUFTWAFFE USA FLYING MUSEUM (FL47)

Address:	770 Airport Road, Ormond Beach, Florida
Tel:	904-806-1214 Fax: 904-823-3418 Email: info@classic-jets.com
Admission:	By prior permission only.
Location:	At the airport and at a base in Germany.

Florida

The group was formed with the aim of returning aircraft of the post World War II Luftwaffe to flying condition. The first project was a Focke-Wulf-built Piaggio P.149 which after restoration was taken back to Germany a few years ago to appear at shows. The two seat Fiat G.91T first flew in 1960 and the type also served with the Italian Air Force. The example being restored was built by the parent company. Dornier constructed 22 under licence between 1971 and 1973 to supplement those already in service in Germany. The original plan was to ship the aircraft to the USA for rebuild to flying condition but it is still at Bielefeld in Germany.

TYPE	REG/SER	CON. NO.	PI/NOTES	STATUS
☐ Fiat G.91T/3 (T/1)	N91GY	91-2-0043	34+39	RAC
☐ Piaggio FWP.149D	N156FW	156	KB+133, GA+406, AC+403, 91+34, D-EMNT	RAA

MacDILL AIR FORCE BASE COLLECTION (FL48)

Address:	6 ABW/PA, 8208 Hangar Road, Suite 5, MacDill Air Force Base, Florida 33621-5202.
Tel:	813-828-2444 **Email:** pao@macdill.af.mil
Admission:	By prior permission only.
Location:	In the southern suburbs of Tampa.

The base was activated in 1941 and is named after Colonel Leslie MacDill, who was killed in a crash near Washington in 1938. The site is the home of a Tactical Training Wing flying the F-16. The F-4 Phantom was formerly flown by the unit and the preserved example was initially by the base headquarters. The collection grew with the arrival of the KB-50 and the F-16. The four engined Boeing bomber, which has been at MacDill since the late 1990s, will eventually move to the Air Mobility Command Museum at Dover Air Force Base in Delaware. The three aircraft are parked near to a gate on the eastern side of the field.

TYPE	REG/SER	CON. NO.	PI/NOTES	STATUS
☐ Boeing 345-9-6 Superfortress (B-50D) (KB-50J)	'48-0114'	16165	49-0389	RAX
☐ General Dynamics 401 Fighting Falcon (F-16A)	81-0721	61-402		RA
☐ McDonnell M.98HO Phantom II (F-4E)	66-0302	2474		RA

MAYPORT NAVAL AIR STATION MONUMENT (FL49)

Location:	By prior permission only at the field which is on the coast north of Atlantic Beach.

TYPE	REG/SER	CON. NO.	PI/NOTES	STATUS
☐ Sikorsky S-70B Sea Hawk (YSH-60B)	Bu161173		Bu161173, ''Bu161172'	RA

McCOY AIR FORCE BASE MEMORIAL (FL50)

Address:	1 Airport Boulevard, Orlando International Airport, Orlando, Florida 32827-4339.
Tel:	407-825-2001
Admission:	On permanent view.
Location:	The airport is about 5 miles south of the city on Highway 528.

Pinecastle Air Force Base opened in 1942 and was closed from 1945 to 1952. The Korean conflict caused the reopening and in 1958 it was renamed after Colonel Michael McCoy who was killed the previous year. In 1962 jet services were moved to McCoy from Orlando Municipal Airport and the base closed. The site was then developed and became the vast Orlando International Airport. The B-52 has been placed in a landscaped park alongside the main entrance road to commemorate military operations from McCoy. Here the visitor can see a small exhibit tracing the military history of the airfield and the development into the airport it is today.

TYPE	REG/SER	CON. NO.	PI/NOTES	STATUS
☐ Boeing 464-201-7 Stratofortress (B-52D)	56-0687	464058		PV

MIAMI INTERNATIONAL AIRPORT DISPLAY (FL51)

Location:	On permanent view in one of the terminal buildings.

TYPE	REG/SER	CON. NO.	PI/NOTES	STATUS
☐ Luton LA.4A Minor	EI-ATP	PAL/1124	G-ASCY, EI-ATP, N924GB	PV

MILITARY HERITAGE AND AVIATION MUSEUM (FL52)

Address:	1200 West Retta Boulevard, Unit 48, Punta Gorda, Florida 33950.
Tel:	941-575-9002 **Email:** info@mhaam.org
Admission:	Monday-Saturday 1000-1800; Sunday 1200-1800.
Location:	In the town which is on Route 41 just south west of Port Charlotte.

This museum traces the military history of the region in its displays which are currently housed in a small building. Funds are being raised to construct a purpose-built complex to house the collection. The aviation collection consists of photographs, models, documents, uniforms and memorabilia.

MUSEUM OF SCIENCES AND INDUSTRY OF TAMPA (FL53)

Address:	4801 Fowler Avenue, Tampa, Florida 33617.
Tel:	813-987-6000 **Email:** info@mosi.org
Admission:	Daily 0900-1800.
Location:	In the northern part of the city centre.

This museum covers many aspects of the sciences in its innovative displays. The large building houses exhibits on three floors. Many of these are designed for children and feature 'hands-on' and computer operated topics.

In the past aircraft, often borrowed from the EAA at Lakeland, have been on temporary display to illustrate a particular theme. In addition to the permanent exhibitions many are staged for a short time to highlight modern innovations.

Currently on show is the Stearman painted in the colours of the now defunct Red Baron Pizza display team.

In one of the display areas are some working flight simulators and models.

TYPE	REG/SER	CON. NO.	PI/NOTES	STATUS
☐ Boeing-Stearman A75N1 Kaydet (PT-17)				PV

NATIONAL AVIATION ACADEMY (FL54)

Address: 6225 Ulmerton Road, Clearwater, Florida 33760.
Tel: 727-531-2080   **Fax:** 727-535-8727   **Email:** admissions@naa.edu
Admission: By prior permission only.
Location: In the city on Route 688.

The Florida branch of this academy opened in 1969 and over the last four decades has trained many mechanics. The school has a number of instructional airframes and engines in its workshops. Students are trained to obtain their FAA licenses in both airframes and powerplants. Courses in avionics also take place.

TYPE	REG/SER	CON. NO.	PI/NOTES	STATUS
☐ Aero Commander 520	N2621B	133		RA
☐ Beech C23 Sundowner 180	N6001V	M-2112		RA
☐ Cessna 310H	N444BR	310H0062		RA
☐ Gates Learjet 24	N100VQ	24-140	N663LJ, N663L, N663LJ, N593KR, N252M, N100VC	RA
☐ Piper PA-28-140 Cherokee	N6377W	28-20440		RA
☐ Piper PA-28-140 Cherokee	N9866W	28-23380		RA

NATIONAL MUSEUM OF NAVAL AVIATION (FL55)

Address: 1750 Radford Boulevard, Pensacola, Florida 32508-5402.
Tel: 850-452-3604   **Fax:** 850-452-3296   **Email:** museuminfo.navalaviation@mchsi.com
Admission: Daily 0900-1700.
Location: On the base which is in the south western suburbs of the city.

The United States Navy acquired its first aircraft, a Curtiss A-1, in 1911. Since then the service has flown a variety of types from both shore and carrier bases and has been involved all the major conflicts in which the nation has participated.

The first plans for a naval aviation museum were put forward in the early 1960s and a building at Pensacola was allocated in 1961. After conversion it opened in December 1962 with a small number of aircraft and items of memorabilia on display. The collection grew rapidly and within five years only about a quarter of the aircraft were on show and the store of uniforms, photographs, documents etc. was increasing at a rapid rate.

In December 1966 the Naval Aviation Museum Association was set up to raise funds for a new building. Ground was broken for the first phase of the complex in November 1972 and when opened on 13th April 1975, over 60,000 square feet of display space was available. The second phase was completed in 1978 almost doubling the area. On 12th October 1990 the third phase, with more than twice the area of the first two stages, was dedicated. Another new hall opened in January 2011.

There are plans for further expansion of the buildings. In addition there is an outside park where larger aircraft are exhibited. At the current time more than 100 aircraft are on show with almost three times that number in store. The museum has obtained some of aircraft by exchanges with private owners, deals which have enabled gaps in the collection to be filled.

In 1911 Glenn Curtiss taught Lieutenant Theodore G. Ellyson to fly and naval aviation in the USA had started. A replica of this aircraft has been constructed. The Curtiss company supplied many aircraft to the Navy in the early years and several products of the firm are on show. The JN series of biplanes, better known as the Jenny, trained vast numbers of military pilots and later flew with many ex-service fliers who tried to earn a living barnstorming around the country.

Curtiss was one of the first producers of flying boats and two examples can be seen. The skill of the woodworkers is evident in the hulls of the pair. The two-seat MF, of which 22 were built by Curtiss at Garden City and another 80 by the Naval Aircraft Factory at Philadelphia, was used for training. The giant NC-4, which dominates part of the exhibition, is also on loan from the NASM. The type was designed as a long-range aircraft which could be delivered by air to France during World War I. The Navy was concerned about loss of aircraft when transported by ship across the Atlantic Ocean. The NC was not ready by the end of the conflict but for publicity the Navy decided to fly three to Europe. The trio left Rockaway, New Jersey on 8th May 1919 and on 31st May one landed at Plymouth in England; the other two had been forced down with engine trouble. The flight, via Newfoundland, the Azores, Ponta Delgada, Lisbon and Ferrol, was the first transatlantic flight. The hull of NC-4 was placed on show in the Smithsonian Institution in Washington, DC to commemorate the 50th anniversary of the flight. The boat was completely rebuilt and loaned to Pensacola in the mid-1970s.

The Grumman company has produced naval aircraft for over 60 years and examples of many of the classic types designed by the Long Island firm are on show. This range from the G-23 that was found derelict in Nicaragua and rebuilt by Grumman to represent an FF-1 which served on the carrier Lexington in the early 1930s, to the modern day Tomcat. The amphibious Duck, the classic Hellcat and Wildcat of World War II, the later Bearcat and Tigercat, jet fighters such as the Panther, Cougar and Tiger and piston-engined twins including the Goose, Widgeon, Albatross, Tracer, Tracker and Trader show the versatility of the famous firm.

The museum has aircraft from many other companies on view including flying boats such as the famous Catalina and the last known survivors of the Consolidated Coronado and the Martin Marlin. There are several significant machines on show including the Douglas Skystreak which set a world speed record in 1947. The increase of the use of helicopters in the last half century is portrayed and many examples are on show.

The indoor displays trace the history of the service and imaginative presentations honour units and individuals as well as famous battles. One part of the new hall has been built to represent the deck of an aircraft carrier. An area is devoted to the US Coast Guard and a number of aircraft are shown in their colours. The museum has recovered several airframes from Lake Michigan and other underwater sites are being

Florida

investigated. Four of the six production Curtiss Sparrowhawks which operated from the airships Akron and Macon have been located off the California coast and it is planned to raise them in the near future.

Several airframes are parked on an apron close to the main exhibition area and these can normally be seen while hangars on the field are used for storage. The indoor exhibitions feature significant developments in US Naval Aviation. The World War I area has the a battered wooden building typical of those used on the Western Front. Nearby is the Curtiss MF on a ramp in front of a tent hangar, replicating the first days of NAS Pensacola. The World War II area highlights many of the bitter battles which took place against the Japanese in the Pacific Ocean. Aircraft carriers played a significant role in these conflicts and aircraft are exhibited in typical conditions. The Korean and Vietnam wars also feature and there is a particularly poignant section dealing with the harsh conditions prisoners endured in the latter conflict.

TYPE	REG/SER	CON. NO.	PI/NOTES	STATUS
☐ Aerostar S-60A Hot Air Balloon				RA
☐ Arado Ar 196A-5	T3+HK	623183	TW+SH	RA
☐ Beech D17S (UC-43) (GB-2)	Bu23688	6700	44-67723 (Bu23688), FT474, Bu32873, NC9459H, N9459H	PV
☐ Beech D18S Expeditor (C18S) (JRB-2) (SNB-5P) (RC-45J)	Bu09771	434	NC1040	PV
☐ Beech D45 Mentor (T-34B)	N85993	BG-92	Bu140758	RA
☐ Beech D45 Mentor (T-34B)	Bu140813	BG-147	Bu140813, N7098U	PV
☐ Beech D45 Mentor (T-34B)	Bu140818	BG-152	Bu140818, N27681	RA
☐ Beech D45 Mentor (T-34B)	Bu140868	BG-202	Bu140868, N7040V, N45283	PV
☐ Beech D45 Mentor (T-34B)	Bu140876	BG-210	Bu140876, N85684	RA
☐ Beech D45 Mentor (T-34B)	Bu140926	BG-260	Bu140926, N8709S	PV
☐ Beech D45 Mentor (T-34B)	Bu140929	BG-263	Bu140929, N7098C	PV
☐ Beech D45 Mentor (T-34B)	N20685	BG-303	Bu143996	RAD
☐ Beech D45 Mentor (T-34B)	Bu144040	BG-347	Bu144040, N159Z	PV
☐ Beech D45 Mentor (T-34B)	Bu144044	BG-351	Bu144044, N4579P	RA
☐ Beech D45 Mentor (T-34B)	N9980Q	BG-377	Bu144070	RA
☐ Bell 47D-1 Sioux (HTL-4) (TH-13L)	Bu128911	280		PV
☐ Bell 47G Sioux (HTL-6) (TH-13M)	Bu142377	1340		RA
☐ Bell 204 Iroquois (HU-1E) (NUH-1E)	Bu151268	6003		PV
☐ Bell 204 Iroquois (HH-1K)	Bu157179	6303	At AMARC, AZ.	RA
☐ Bell 204 Iroquois (HH-1K)	Bu157180	6304	At AMARC, AZ.	RA
☐ Bell 204 Iroquois (HH-1K)	Bu157188	6312		PV
☐ Bell 206A Sea Ranger (TH-57A)	N32536	5024	Bu157378 – at AMARC, AZ.	RA
☐ Bell 206A Sea Ranger (TH-57A)	N32550	5028	Bu157382 – at AMARC, AZ.	RA
☐ Bell 206A Sea Ranger (TH-57A)	N32566	5033	Bu157387 – at AMARC, AZ.	RA
☐ Bell 206A Sea Ranger (TH-57C)	Bu162028	3707		PV
☐ Bell 209 Huey Cobra (AH-1G) (AH-1S)	70-16024	20968		PV
☐ Bell 209 Huey Cobra (AH-1G) (TAH-1F)	66-15341	20097	Front fuselage only.	PV
☐ Bell 209 Sea Cobra (AH-1J)	Bu157773	26017	At AMARC, AZ.	PV
☐ Bell 209 Sea Cobra (AH-1J)			Quoted as c/n 70280.	PV
☐ Blériot XI				RA
☐ Boeing 235 (F4B-4) (FSM)	'Bu9029'			PVX
☐ Boeing 235 (F4B-4) (Scale R)	'Bu9022'			PVX
☐ Boeing 251 (P-12F)	'9029'	1587	32-92, N7037U	PVX
☐ Boeing-Stearman B75N1 Kaydet (N2S-3)	'Bu05369'	75-6543	Bu05409, N75032	PVX
☐ Brewster B.239 Buffalo	'1418'		BW-372 (Finland)	RACX
☐ Brewster B.340 Buccaneer (SB2A-2)			FF860	RAC
☐ Brewster B.340 Buccaneer (SB2A-2)				RAD
☐ Cameron Hot Air Balloon				RA
☐ Cessna T-50 Bobcat (AT-17B) (UC-78B)	'63426'	5515	43-7995, N63426 – as a JRC-1	PVX
☐ Cessna 305A Bird Dog (L-19A) (O-1A)	5L-14981	22300	51-11986 – in Vietnamese markings.	PV
☐ Champion 7EC Traveler	N4331C	7EC-341		RA
☐ Consolidated 28-5A Catalina IB	FP216	805	Fuselage only.	PV
☐ Consolidated 28-5 Catalina (PBY-5)	Bu08317	1241	On loan from NASM, DC.	PV
☐ Consolidated 28-5A Catalina (PBY-5A)	Bu46602	1966	Bu46603, N6071C, CF-FFZ, C-FFFZ, (N4NC), N607CC	PV
☐ Consolidated 29 Coronado (PB2Y-3) (PB2Y-5R)	Bu7099	57	Bu7099, N69003	RAC
☐ Consolidated 40 Privateer (PB4Y-2) (P4Y-2) (P4Y-2G) (Convair 100)	Bu66304		Bu66304, 66304 (USCG), N2870K – composite with parts from Bu59882, N7962C and Bu66313, N3431G	PV
☐ Convair 340-71 Samaritan (R4Y-1) (C-131F)	Bu141003	286	Bu141003, N14100 – at AMARC, AZ.	RA
☐ Convair 340-71 Samaritan (R4Y-1) (C-131F)	Bu141015	298		PV
☐ Curtiss E A-1 (R)				PV
☐ Curtiss 1C Jenny (JN-4D)	A995	490		PV
☐ Curtiss 12 (NC-4)	A2294		On loan from NASM, DC.	PV
☐ Curtiss 18 Seagull (MF)	A5483			PV
☐ Curtiss 34C Hawk (F6C-1) (R)	'A6969'	60	N6969	PVX
☐ Curtiss 43 Seahawk (F7C-1)	A7667			PV
☐ Curtiss 48A Fledgling (N2C-2)	A8529	4		PV
☐ Curtiss 58A Sparrowhawk (F9C-2)	A9058		In Pacific Ocean off Point Sur, CA.	RAD
☐ Curtiss 58A Sparrowhawk (F9C-2)	A9059		In Pacific Ocean off Point Sur, CA.	RAD
☐ Curtiss 58A Sparrowhawk (F9C-2)	A9060		In Pacific Ocean off Point Sur, CA.	RAD
☐ Curtiss 58A Sparrowhawk (F9C-2)	A9061		In Pacific Ocean off Point Sur, CA.	RAD
☐ Curtiss 58A Sparrowhawk (XF9C-2)	9264		9264, 'A9056' – on loan from NASM, DC.	PV
☐ Curtiss 67A Hawk (F11C-2) (BFC-2)	9332			PV
☐ Curtiss 84F Helldiver (SB2C-4)	Bu19866			RAD

☐ Curtiss H81-A2 Warhawk (P-40C) (Tomahawk IIB)	'41-14737'	14737	AK255, (Soviet)	PVX
☐ Curtiss-Wright CW-20B Commando (C-46A)	'Bu39611'	421	43-47350, XT-???, N8364C, N8361C, N1382N, N611Z	PVX
☐ Curtiss-Wright CW-22N Falcon (SNC-1)	Bu05194	4255	Bu05194, N8021J	PV
☐ De Havilland DHC.2 Beaver (L-20A) (U-6A)				RA
☐ De Havilland DHC.3 Otter (UC-1) (U-1B) (NU-1B)	Bu144672	160		PV
☐ Douglas Dolphin 8	N14205	1280	NC14205, N26K	RA
☐ Douglas TBD-1 Devastator			In the ocean to be recovered.	RAD
☐ Douglas TBD-1 Devastator				RAD
☐ Douglas DC-3A-456 Skytrain (C-47A) (R4D-5L) (C-47H)	Bu12418	9358	42-23496	PV
☐ Douglas Super DC-3 (R4D-8) (C-117D)	Bu50821	43322	Rebuilt from DC-3A-467 (C-47B) (R4D-6) c/n 15431/26876 43-49615, Bu50821	PV
☐ Douglas DC-6A Liftmaster (R6D-1) (C-118B)	Bu128424	43207		PV
☐ Douglas DC-6A Liftmaster (R6D-1) (C-118B)	Bu128431	43404	Bu128431, N5176V – front fuselage only.	RA
☐ Douglas DC-9-32RC Skytrain II (C-9B)	Bu163511	47431	(I-DIZI), I-ATIA, N506MD	RA
☐ Douglas SBD-2 Dauntless	Bu2106	632		PV
☐ Douglas SBD-3 Dauntless	Bu06626	1441		RA
☐ Douglas SBD-4 Dauntless	Bu06833	1708		PVD
☐ Douglas SBD-5 Dauntless	Bu36175	4814	Parts only.	RA
☐ Douglas SBD-5 Dauntless	Bu36291	4930		RA
☐ Douglas D-558-1 Skystreak	Bu37970	6564		PV
☐ Douglas F-6A Skyray (F4D-1)	Bu134806	10400		PV
☐ Douglas F-10B Skynight (F3D-2)	Bu124598	7468		RA
☐ Douglas A-26B Invader	'446928'	6928	41-39215, N5292V, N4000M, N200M, N142ER, 'Bu77141'	RAX
☐ Douglas EA-1F Skyraider (AD-5N) (AD-5Q)	Bu132532	8927		PV
☐ Douglas A-1H Skyraider (AD-6)	Bu135300	9944		PV
☐ Douglas A-3A Skywarrior (A3D-1)	Bu135418	10311		RA
☐ Douglas TA-3B Skywarrior (A3D-3T)	N875RS	12111	Bu144865	RA
☐ Douglas XA-4A Skyhawk (XA4D-1)	Bu137813	10710		PV
☐ Douglas A-4C Skyhawk (A4D-2N)	Bu148490	12683	At Santa Rosa Stop on I.10.	PV
☐ Douglas A-4C Skyhawk (A4D-2N)	Bu149505	12830		RA
☐ Douglas A-4C Skyhawk (A4D-2N)	Bu149563	12888	On show in City of Pensacola.	PV
☐ Douglas A-4E Skyhawk (A4D-5)	Bu149656	12981		PV
☐ Douglas A-4E Skyhawk (A4D-5)	Bu150001	13054	At AMARC, AZ.	PV
☐ Douglas A-4E Skyhawk (A4D-5)	'Bu154180'	13129	Bu150076	PVX
☐ Douglas A-4E Skyhawk (A4D-5)	'Bu150122'	13244	Bu151074 – on loan to Atsugi NAS, Japan.	RAX
☐ Douglas A-4F Skyhawk	Bu154176	13633		RA
☐ Douglas A-4F Skyhawk	Bu154217	13674		PV
☐ Douglas A-4F Skyhawk	Bu154983	13799		PV
☐ Douglas A-4F Skyhawk	Bu155033	13849		PV
☐ Douglas TA-4J Skyhawk (TA-4F)	Bu153505	13571		PV
☐ Douglas TA-4J Skyhawk			Front fuselage only.	PV
☐ Douglas TA-4J Skyhawk	Bu158090	14127		RA
☐ Douglas TA-4J Skyhawk	Bu158094	14131		PV
☐ Douglas TA-4J Skyhawk	Bu159795	14494		RA
☐ Douglas A-4L Skyhawk (A4D-2N) (A-4C)	Bu145077	12323		RA
☐ Fleet 2 (N2Y-1)	A8605			PV
☐ Fokker D VII (FSM)				RA
☐ Fokker D VII (FSM)	'1975/18'			PVX
☐ Ford 4-AT-E (4-AT-B)	'A9206'	4-AT-46	NC7861, N7861, 'A9205' – painted as a RR-5.	PVX
☐ Franklin PS-2 Eaglet			N9617	PV
☐ General Dynamics 401 Fighting Falcon (F-16N)	Bu163572	3M-17	86-1690	PV
☐ Goodyear GA-468 Inflatoplane (XAO-3)				RA
☐ Goodyear K-47			Gondola only.	PV
☐ Goodyear Pilgrim	NC19A		Gondola only.	PV
☐ Goodyear ZPG-2 (ZP2N-1)	Bu141561			RA
☐ Grumman G-15 Duck (J2F-6)	Bu33581			PV
☐ Grumman G-23	'Bu9351'		N2803J – mocked up as a G-5 (FF-1)	PVX
☐ Grumman G-36 Wildcat (F4F-3)	Bu3872	754		PV
☐ Grumman G-36 Wildcat (F4F-3)	Bu4039	921		PVD
☐ Grumman G-36 Wildcat (F4F-3A)	Bu3969	851		RA
☐ Grumman G-36 Wildcat (FM-2)	Bu16089	1288		PV
☐ Grumman G-36 Wildcat (FM-2)	Bu86747	5805	Bu86747, N68843	PV
☐ Grumman G-37 (F3F-2)	Bu0976	374 (?)		PV
☐ Grumman G-39 Goose (JRF-3)	V190	1085	V190, N5538N, N12CS	PV
☐ Grumman G-40 Avenger (TBM-3) (TBM-3E)	Bu53593	3655	Bu53593, N6822C, N5567A, N6822C	PV
☐ Grumman G-44 Widgeon (J4F-1)	V212	1260	V212, N743, N2770A, N324BC, N212ST – in USCG markings.	PV
☐ Grumman G-50 Hellcat (F6F-3)	Bu25910			RAD
☐ Grumman G-50 Hellcat (F6F-5)	Bu66237	A-1257		PV
☐ Grumman G-50 Hellcat (F6F-5)	Bu94203	A-11955	Bu94203, N7865C	PV
☐ Grumman G-50 Hellcat (F6F-5) (F6F-5K)	Bu79063	A-10208	On San Nicholas Island.	RA
☐ Grumman G-51 Tigercat (F7F-3)	Bu80373	C.115	Bu80373, N7654C	PV
☐ Grumman G-58 Bearcat (F8F-2) (F8F-2P)	Bu121710	D.1084		PV
☐ Grumman G-79 Panther (F9F-2)	'Bu122563'	K-65	Bu123050	PVX
☐ Grumman G-82 Guardian (AF-2W)	Bu123100	14	Bu123100, N3144G	PV
☐ Grumman G-89 Tracker (S2F-1) (S-2A)			Front fuselage only.	PV

Florida

☐ Grumman G-93 Cougar (F9F-6) (F-9F)	Bu128109			PV
☐ Grumman G-93 Cougar (F9F-6P) (RF-9F)	Bu134451			PV
☐ Grumman G-96 Trader (TF-1) (C-1A)	Bu136748	001	Bu136748, N6194K – at AMARC, AZ.	RA
☐ Grumman G-96 Trader (TF-1) (C-1A)	Bu136754	007		PV
☐ Grumman G-96 Trader (TF-1) (C-1A)	N61932	016	Bu136763 – at AMARC, AZ.	RA
☐ Grumman G-96 Trader (TF-1) (C-1A)	N32619	039	Bu136786 – at AMARC, AZ.	RA
☐ Grumman G-96 Trader (TF-1) (C-1A)	N32628	054	Bu146024 – at AMARC, AZ.	RA
☐ Grumman G-96 Trader (TF-1) (C-1A)	N32636	055	Bu146025 – at AMARC, AZ.	RA
☐ Grumman G-96 Trader (TF-1) (C-1A)	N32637	056	Bu146026 – at AMARC, AZ.	RA
☐ Grumman G-96 Trader (TF-1) (C-1A)	N32654	057	Bu146027 – at AMARC, AZ.	RA
☐ Grumman G-96 Trader (TF-1) (C-1A)	N32658	058	Bu146028 – at AMARC, AZ.	RA
☐ Grumman G-96 Trader (TF-1) (C-1A)	N32689	060	Bu146030 – at AMARC, AZ.	RA
☐ Grumman G-96 Trader (TF-1) (C-1A)	N32695	061	Bu146031 – at AMARC, AZ.	RA
☐ Grumman G-96 Trader (TF-1) (C-1A)	N32709	068	Bu146038 – in AMARC Display Row, AZ.	RA
☐ Grumman G-96 Trader (TF-1) (C-1A)	N32720	071	Bu146041 – at AMARC, AZ.	RA
☐ Grumman G-96 Trader (TF-1) (C-1A)	N5054X	073	Bu146043 – at AMARC, AZ.	RA
☐ Grumman G-96 Trader (TF-1) (C-1A)	N52705	080	Bu146050 – at AMARC, AZ.	RA
☐ Grumman G-96 Trader (TF-1) (C-1A)	N5271B	081	Bu146051 – at AMARC, AZ.	RA
☐ Grumman G-96 Trader (TF-1) (C-1A)	N5271K	085	Bu146055 – at AMARC, AZ.	RA
☐ Grumman G-96 Trader (TF-1) (C-1A)	N32579	087	Bu146057 – at AMARC, AZ.	RA
☐ Grumman G-98 Tiger (F11F-1) (F-11A)			Front fuselage only.	PV
☐ Grumman G-98 Tiger (F11F-1) (F-11A)	Bu141828	145		PV
☐ Grumman G-99 Cougar (F9F-8) (F-9J)	Bu131230	168C		PV
☐ Grumman G-99 Cougar (F9F-8) (F-9J)	'Bu131205'	591C	Bu144365 – at I10 Western Visitor Center, FL.	PVX
☐ Grumman G-117 Tracer (WF-2) (E-1B)	Bu148146	64		PV
☐ Grumman G-121 Tracker (S-2E)	Bu151647	180C		PV
☐ Grumman G-123 Hawkeye (W2F-1) (E-2A) (E-2B)	Bu150540	20	Bu150540, N6166C	RA
☐ Grumman G-128 Intruder (A-6A) (A-6E)	Bu155610	I-336		PV
☐ Grumman G-128 Prowler (EA-6B)	Bu156481	P4		PV
☐ Grumman G-128 Prowler (EA-6B0	Bu158034	P11		RA
☐ Grumman G-159C Academe (TC-4C)	Bu155722	176	N798G	RA
☐ Grumman G-234 Albatross (G-64) (SA-16A) (UF-1G) (UF-2G) (HU-16E)	7236	G-322	51-7236	PV
☐ Grumman G-303 Tomcat (YF-14A)	Bu157984	5		PV
☐ Grumman G-303 Tomcat (F-14A)	Bu159825	185	Front fuselage only.	PV
☐ Grumman G-303 Tomcat (F-14A)	Bu161141	368	On loan to Atsugi NAS, Japan.	RA
☐ Grumman G-303 Tomcat (F-14A)	Bu162710	556		PV
☐ Grumman G-303 Tomcat (F-14A) (F-14D)	Bu161159	386		RA
☐ Gyrodyne XRON-1 (XHOG-1)	4013			PV
☐ Hanriot HD-1	A5625			PV
☐ Hawker-Siddeley P.1127 Harrier 50 (AV-8A)	Bu159244	P153	Front fuselage only.	PV
☐ Hawker-Siddeley P.1127 Harrier 50 (AV-8A)			Front fuselage only.	PV
☐ Hawker-Siddeley P.1127 Harrier 50 (AV-8A)			Front fuselage only.	PV
☐ Hawker-Siddeley P.1127 Harrier 50 (AV-8A) (AV-8C)	Bu158975	P136		PV
☐ Hiller UH12A (HTE-1)	Bu128647	198	51-4017, Bu128647, N3HK	PV
☐ Interstate TDR-1	Bu33529			PV
☐ Kaman K-20 Seasprite (HU2K-1) (UH-2A) (SH-2F)	N8061P	52	Bu149750	RA
☐ Kaman K-20 Seasprite (HU2K-1U) (UH-2B) (SH-2F)	N8064H	149	Bu151312	PV
☐ Kawanishi N1K1 Kyofu				RA
☐ Kawanishi N1K2-J Shiden Kai		5128	(Japan), T2-306	PV
☐ Lockheed 10-A Electra	N19HL	1130	VH-ABV, VH-MMD, N4886V	RA
☐ Lockheed 15-27-01 Harpoon (PV-2)	Bu37230	15-1196	Bu37230, N7459C	RA
☐ Lockheed 026-49-01 Neptune (P2V-1)	Bu89082	26-1003	On loan from NASM, DC.	PV
☐ Lockheed 080 Shooting Star (P-80A) (F-80A)	Bu29689	080-1258	44-85235	PV
☐ Lockheed 185 Orion (P-3A)	Bu152152	185-5122		PV
☐ Lockheed 185 Orion (P3V-1) (P-3A)	Bu151360	185-5073	At AMARC, AZ.	RA
☐ Lockheed 185 Orion [188 Electra] (YP3V-1) (YP-3A) (NP-3A)	Bu148276	185-1003	Built as Electra c/n 188-1003 N1883, N927NA, N428NA	PV
☐ Lockheed 282-3B Hercules (GV-1) (KC-130F)	Bu149798	282-3680		PV
☐ Lockheed 382-4B Hercules (C-130G) (EC-130G) (TC-130G)	Bu151891	382C-3878		PV
☐ Lockheed 394 Viking (S-3A) (S-3B)	Bu159387	394A-3023		PV
☐ Lockheed 580 (T-33A)			Front fuselage only.	PV
☐ Lockheed 580 (T-33A)	58-0480	580-1449	58-0480, N63311	RA
☐ Lockheed 580 (T-33A) (TV-2) (T-33B)	Bu131816	580-6650	51-8866	PV
☐ Lockheed 580 (T-33A) (TV-2) (T-33B)	Bu138983	580-9199	54-2695 – at AMARC, AZ	RA
☐ Lockheed 580 (T-33A) (TV-2) (T-33B)	Bu141516	580-9495	55-2998 – at AMARC,AZ	RA
☐ Lockheed 726-45-14 Neptune (P2V-7) (P2V-7S) (SP-2H)	Bu141234	726-7106		PV
☐ Lockheed 1049A-55-137 Super Constellation (WV-2) (EC-121K)	Bu143221	1049A-4495		PV
☐ Martin 162 Mariner (PBM-5)	Bu59172		In Lake Washington.	RAD
☐ Martin 210A Mauler (AM-1)	Bu122397	13916		PV
☐ Martin 237B Marlin (P5M-2S) (SP-5B)	Bu135533			PV
☐ McDonnell M.23 Phantom I (FD-1) (FH-1)	Bu111793	644	Bu111793, N4282A, N3933N	PV
☐ McDonnell M.24 Banshee (F2H-2P)	Bu126673	402		PV
☐ McDonnell M.24 Banshee (F2H-4) (F-2D)	'Bu126419'	297	Bu127663	PVX
☐ McDonnell M.58 Demon (F3H-2M) (MF-3B)	Bu137078	259		PV
☐ McDonnell M.98AM Phantom II (F-4H) (F-4N)	Bu153915	1796		PV
☐ McDonnell M.98AM Phantom II (F4H-1) (F-4B)	Bu148368	53	Front fuselage only.	PV

☐ McDonnell M.98DH Phantom II (RF-4B)	Bu157349	3892		PV
☐ McDonnell M.98EV Phantom II (F-4J) (F-4S)	Bu155807	3094	On loan to Atsugi NAS, Japan.	RA
☐ McDonnell M.98EV Phantom II (F-4J) (F-4S)	Bu158355	4091	Front fuselage only.	PV
☐ McDonnell M.267 Hornet (F/A-18A)	Bu161948	157/A120		RA
☐ McDonnell M.267 Hornet (F/A-18A)	Bu161955	166/A128		PV
☐ McDonnell M.267 Hornet (F/A-18A)	Bu161959	171/A133		RA
☐ McDonnell M.267 Hornet (F/A-18A)	Bu161960	172/A134		RA
☐ McDonnell M.267 Hornet (F/A-18A)	Bu161975	194/A155	At Officers Club.	RA
☐ McDonnell M.267 Hornet (F/A-18A)	Bu163117	515/A426		RA
☐ McDonnell M.267 Hornet (TF-18A) (F/A-18B)	Bu161746	103/B030		RA
☐ Messerschmitt Me 262B-1A	110639	110639	35, Bu121488	RA
☐ Meyers OTW-160 (OTW-125)	N26482	35	NC26482	RA
☐ Mikoyan-Gurevich MiG-15bis	70007		1317 – in Chinese markings.	PV
☐ Mikoyan-Gurevich MiG-21				PV
☐ Mitsubishi A6M2 Zero Sen Model 21	'EII-140'	5450		PV
☐ Naval Aircraft Factory N3N-3	Bu2693			PV
☐ Naval Aircraft Factory N3N-3	Bu3046		Bu3046, N6399T	PV
☐ Naval Aircraft Factory TS-1 (Curtiss 28)	A6446		On loan from NASM, DC.	PV
☐ New Standard D-29 (NT-1)	A8588	1007	A8588, N155M	PV
☐ Nieuport 28C.1 (R)	5796			PV
☐ North American NA-88 Texan (SNJ-5)	Bu51849	88-14547		RA
☐ North American NA-108 Mitchell (B-25J) (TB-25J) (TB-25N)	'Bu35087'	108-32310	44-29035, N3516G, 4146 (Venezuela), (N61821)	PVX
☐ North American NA-121 Texan (AT-6F) (SNJ-6)	Bu112121	121-42954	44-82232, Bu112121, N2856G, N61JD	RA
☐ North American NA-121 Texan (AT-6F) (SNJ-6)	Bu112165	121-42998	44-82276 – on loan to Atsugi NAS, Japan.	RA
☐ North American NA-181 Fury (FJ-2)	Bu132023	181-97		RA
☐ North American NA-184 Savage (AJ-2)	Bu130418	184-14	Bu130418, N100Z, N68667	PV
☐ North American NA-200 Trojan (T-28B)	Bu138326	200-397		PV
☐ North American NA-200 Trojan (T-28B)			Front fuselage only.	PV
☐ North American NA-209 Fury (FJ-4) (F-1E)	Bu139486	209-106		PV
☐ North American NA-285 Sabreliner (T3J-1) (T-39D)	Bu150985	285-17	Bu150985, N32508 – preserved on base.	RA
☐ North American NA-305 Bronco (OV-10A) (OV-10D)	Bu155472	305-83		RA
☐ North American NA-306 Sabreliner 60 (CT-39G)	Bu160056	306-107	N65798, Bu160056	PV
☐ North American NA-316 Vigilante (RA-5C)	Bu156624	316-17		PV
☐ North American NA-332 Buckeye (T-2C)	Bu157058	332-29		PV
☐ North American NA-340 Buckeye (T-2C)	Bu158320	340-11		RA
☐ North American NA-340 Buckeye (T-2C)	Bu158327	340-18		PV
☐ North American NA-346 Buckeye (T-2C)	Bu158581	346-11		PV
☐ North American NA-346 Buckeye (T-2C)			Front fuselage only.	PV
☐ Northrop N-156T Talon (T-38A)	59-1604	N.5117		RA
☐ Piasecki PV-18 Retriever (H-25A) (HUP-3) (UH-25C)	Bu147607		(USAF), Bu147607, N4953S	PV
☐ Ryan ST-3KR Recruit (PT-22)	N49086	1541	41-15512 – painted as a NR-1.	PV
☐ Schweizer SGS.2-8 (LNS-1)	Bu04385	7		PV
☐ Sikorsky VS-316A Hoverfly (R-4B) (HNS-1)	Bu39047	111	43-46567	PV
☐ Sikorsky S-51 Dragonfly (HO3S-1G)	235	51214	235, N4927E	PV
☐ Sikorsky S-52-3 (HO5S-1)	Bu125519	52012	Bu125519, N8003E	PV
☐ Sikorsky S-55D (HRS-3) (CH-19E)	1258		Bu130151	PV
☐ Sikorsky S-56 Mojave (HR2S-1) (CH-37C)	Bu145864	56099	Bu145864, N7388	RA
☐ Sikorsky S-58 Seahorse (HUS-1) (UH-34D)	Bu150227	581585		PV
☐ Sikorsky S-61B Sea King (HSS-2) (HH-3A)	Bu149682		At AMARC, AZ.	RA
☐ Sikorsky S-61B Sea King (HSS-2) (HH-3A)	Bu149922		At AMARC, AZ.	RA
☐ Sikorsky S-61B Sea King (HSS-2) (HH-3A)	Bu151553		At AMARC, AZ.	RA
☐ Sikorsky S-61B Sea King (HSS-2) (SH-3A) (SH-3H)	Bu152121	61314		PV
☐ Sikorsky S-61B Sea King (HSS-2Z) (VH-3A)	Bu150613	61103		PV
☐ Sikorsky S-61B Sea King (SH-3D) (SH-3H)	'Bu148990'	61430	Bu156484	PVX
☐ Sikorsky S-61B Sea King (SH-3D) (SH-3H)	Bu152704	61367	On loan to Atsugi NAS, Japan.	RA
☐ Sikorsky S-61R Pelican (HH-3F)	1486	61663		PV
☐ Sikorsky S-62A Seaguard (HH-52A)	1355	62024		PV
☐ Sikorsky S-62A Seaguard (HH-52A)	1423	62111	Front fuselage only.	PV
☐ Sikorsky S-65A Sea Stallion (CH-53A)	Bu151687	65004		PV
☐ Sikorsky S-65A Sea Stallion (CH-53A)	Bu153715	65105		PV
☐ Sikorsky S-70B Sea Hawk (SH-60B)	Bu162137	70429		PV
☐ Sopwith F.1 Camel (R)	'A5658'		'C8228'	PVX
☐ Stinson V-76 Sentinel (L-5) (OY-1)	'Bu60645'	76-385	42-98453, Bu60645, N57598	RAX
☐ Thomas-Morse S-4C	A5858	235	A5858, N5858	PV
☐ Timm PT.175K Tutor (N2T-1)	Bu32478	216	Bu32478, N58732	PV
☐ Vertol V.107M Sea Knight (CH-46A) (UH-46D)	Bu151952	2102		RA
☐ Vought O3U Corsair				RAC
☐ Vought V-56 Vindicator (SB2U-2)	Bu1383			PV
☐ Vought V-310 Kingfisher (OS2U-3)	'Bu07534'		Bu5926, A-752 (Uruguay)	PVX
☐ Vought F4U-1 Corsair	Bu02465			RA
☐ Vought FG-1D Corsair	Bu92246	3507	Bu92246, N8050E, N766JD	PV
☐ Vought V-366 Cutlass (F7U-3) (F7U-3M)	Bu129655			PV
☐ Vought DF-8F Crusader (F8U-1) (F-8A)			Front fuselage only.	PV
☐ Vought F-8A Crusader (F8U-1)	Bu145347			PV
☐ Vought F-8H Crusader (F8U-2N) (F-8D)			Front fuselage only.	PV
☐ Vought F-8J Crusader (F8U-2NE) (F-8E)	Bu149139		Front fuselage only – also reported as Bu149134.	PV
☐ Vought A-7A Corsair II			Front fuselage only.	PV
☐ Vought A-7E Corsair II	Bu156804	E71		PV

Florida

☐ Vought A-7E Corsair II	Bu158016	E332	Front fuselage only.	PV
☐ Vought A-7E Corsair II	Bu160714	E547		PV
☐ Vought A-7E Corsair II			Front fuselage only.	PV
☐ Vought A-7E Corsair II			Front fuselage only.	PV
☐ Vultee V-74 Valiant (BT-13A) (SNV-1)	'Bu60828'	74-2365	41-11355, (USN), N57248, N60828	PVX

NATIONAL VIETNAM WAR MUSEUM (FL56)

Address: 3400 North Tanner Road, Orlando, Florida 32826.
Tel: 407-273-2864 **Fax:** 407-273-2864
Admission: Saturday 1000-1700; Sunday 1000-1600.
Location: About 8 miles east of the city centre just north of Route 50.

The group of veterans running this museum was set up in 1982. The display honours the 167 residents of Orange County who lost their lives in the conflict. The indoor displays trace the history of the conflict. On show are uniforms, badges and items of memorabilia along with photographs and documents.

TYPE	REG/SER	CON. NO.	PI/NOTES	STATUS
☐ Bell 205 Iroquois (UH-1D) (UH-1H)	65-12868	5201		RA
☐ Bell 205 Iroquois (UH-1D) (UH-1V)	66-16896	9090		PV
☐ Douglas A-4B Skyhawk (A4D-2)	Bu142741	11803		PV

NAVAL AIR STATION SANFORD MEMORIAL PARK (FL57)

Address: 1200 Red Cleveland Boulevard, Sanford, Florida 32773.
Tel: SAMC@NASSanfordMemorial.com
Admission: On permanent view.
Location: In the south eastern suburbs of the town

The airfield opened in late 1941 and was initially used for twin-engine training using PV-1 Venturas, Hudsons and Expeditors. Later in the war fighter training with Wildcats and Hellcats took place. In 1946 the Navy moved out. The field was reactivated in the 1950s and remained operational until 1968. The site was turned over to the town who have developed it as a major regional airport.

The Ventura, although not a naval model, represents one of the initial types used. This aircraft served in Cuba between 1947 and 1951.

TYPE	REG/SER	CON. NO.	PI/NOTES	STATUS
☐ Lockheed 137-27-02 Ventura IIA (B-34) (RB-34)	N1000X	137-4688	(FD580), 41-38032, 215 (Cuba), N1527V	RAC
☐ North American NA-316 Vigilante (RA-5C)	Bu156632	316-25		PV

NAVAL AIR TECHNICAL TRAINING CENTER (FL58)

Address: 230 Chevalier Field Avenue, Pensacola, Florida 32508-5151.
Tel: 850-452-7446
Admission: By prior permission only.
Location: In the eastern part of the base which is in the south western suburbs of the city.

The original airfield at Pensacola opened in 1922. The site was enlarged in 1935 and named Chevalier Field. With the arrival of jet aircraft the runways were deemed too short and so a new airfield was built three miles to the south.

Chevalier remained open for limited flying but eventually the NATTC was constructed over the south western part of the site. Two museum aircraft are displayed in the atrium of the rebuilt Chevalier Hall– these are the Mentor and the Culver Cadet. Around 1,200 Cadets were transferred from the USAAF to the Navy where they served as target drones. Unfortunately the building was badly damaged by Hurricane Andrew in September 2004. The large hall includes hangars, classrooms and laboratories. Aviation specialists are trained for all US services and some allied nations.

TYPE	REG/SER	CON. NO.	PI/NOTES	STATUS
☐ Beech D45 Mentor (T-34B)	Bu140830	BG-164	Bu140830, N1408N – NMNA aircraft.	RA
☐ Bell 209 Sea Cobra (AH-1J)	Bu157759	26003		RA
☐ Bell 212 Iroquois (UH-1N)	Bu158766	31435		RA
☐ Culver NR-D Cadet (PQ-14A) (TD2C-1)	Bu120082		45-58863 – NMNA aircraft.	RA
☐ Douglas TA-4J Skyhawk	Bu156945	14038	Front fuselage only.	RA
☐ General Dynamics 401 Fighting Falcon (F-16A)	79-0408	61-193		RA
☐ Grumman G-123 Hawkeye (E-2C)	Bu163694	A52		RA
☐ Grumman G-128 Prowler (EA-6B)	Bu158029	P6		RA
☐ Hawker-Siddeley P.1127 Harrier 50 (AV-8A) (AV-8C)	Bu159254	P163		RA
☐ Hawker-Siddeley Harrier II (AV-8B)	Bu161584	16		RA
☐ Hawker-Siddeley Harrier II (AV-8B)	Bu161577	9		RA
☐ Lockheed 394 Viking (S-3A) (S-3B)	Bu159755	394A-3084		RA
☐ McDonnell M.199-1A Eagle (F-15A)	77-0085	365/A297		RA
☐ McDonnell M.267 Hornet (F/A-18A)	Bu161952	162/A124		RA
☐ McDonnell M.267 Hornet (F/A-18A)	Bu161969	186/A147		RA
☐ McDonnell M.267 Hornet (F/A-18A)	Bu162906	467/A384		RA
☐ McDonnell M.267 Hornet (F/A-18A)	Bu161729	81/A057		RA
☐ McDonnell M.267 Hornet (F/A-18F)	Bu165166	1313/F001		RA
☐ Northrop N-156T Talon (T-38A) (AT-38B)	61-0898	N.5264	Front fuselage only.	RA
☐ Sikorsky S-70B Sea Hawk (SH-60B)	Bu162106	70596		RA
☐ Vertol V.107M Sea Knight (CH-46D) (CH-46E)	Bu153397	2239		RA

NEW SMYRNA BEACH MONUMENT (FL59)

Location:	On permanent view at VFW 4250 on Sunset Drive near the airport which is north of the town.

TYPE	REG/SER	CON. NO.	PI/NOTES	STATUS
☐ Bell 209 Huey Cobra (AH-1G) (AH-1F)	71-21028	21099		PV

OKALOOSA MONUMENT (FL60)

Location:	On permanent view at the airport which is south east of the town.

TYPE	REG/SER	CON. NO.	PI/NOTES	STATUS
☐ Bell 205 Iroquois (UH-1H)				PV
☐ Mcdonnell M.199-1A Eagle (F-15A)				PV

ORLANDO MONUMENTS (FL61)

Location:	On view at eleven locations in the city.

TYPE	REG/SER	CON. NO.	PI/NOTES	STATUS
☐ Bell 47G Sioux (H-13G) (OH-13G)	N73550	1168	53-3654 – in Jungle Jim's Restaurant in East Church Street.	PV
☐ Douglas A-4A Skyhawk (A4D-1)	Bu139931	11296	At NAWC in Research Parkway – on loan from NMNA, FL	RA
☐ Grumman G-111 Albatross (G-64) (UF-1) (HU-16C)	N928J	G-401	Bu137928 – at a bar near Universal Studios.	PV
☐ Grumman G-111 Albatross (UF-2S) (HU-16D)	N693S	G-413	Bu141266 – at Universal Studios.	PV
☐ Grumman G-159 Gulfstream I	N234MM	121	N732G – at MGM Theme Park.	PV
☐ Lockheed 18-56-23 Lodestar (C-60A)	N1000G	18-2562	42-56069, NC66110, (C-803), ZS-DAU, SA-AAG, N16A, N1000W, (N88788) – at Disney Hollywood Studios.	PVD
☐ Lockheed 1329 JetStar 6	N488GR	1329-5051	N9217R, N400KC, N44MF, N31S, N310AD, N555BS, N488JS – at Universal Studios.	PV
☐ McDonnell M.267 Hornet (F/A-18A)	Bu161957	169/A131	At Naval Air Support Activity –	RA
☐ Piper J-3C-65 Cub			At the Executive Airport Terminal.	PV
☐ Republic RC-3 Seabee			At a clothing store in the city.	PV
☐ Republic RC-3 Seabee			At a Golf Center in the city.	PV

PANAMA CITY MONUMENTS (FL62)

Location:	On permanent view at two locations in the town.

TYPE	REG/SER	CON. NO.	PI/NOTES	STATUS
☐ Mcdonnell M.36BA Voodoo (F-101B)	'57-0438'	762	59-0438 – at Gulf Coast Community College at 5230 West Highway 98.	PV
☐ McDonnell M.36BA Voodoo (TF-101B) (TF-101F) 59-0478		802	At the Marina in Harrison Avenue.	PV

PENSACOLA MONUMENT (FL63)

Location:	On permanent view in the Veterans Memorial Park on the sea front near 9th. Avenue.

TYPE	REG/SER	CON. NO.	PI/NOTES	STATUS
☐ Bell 209 Sea Cobra (AH-1J)	Bu159226	26066		PV

PINELLAS PARK MONUMENT (FL64)

Location:	On permanent view in Freedom Lake Park on 49th Street North.

TYPE	REG/SER	CON. NO.	PI/NOTES	STATUS
☐ General Dynamics 401 Fighting Falcon (F-16A)	80-0528	61-249		PV

SOUTHWEST FLORIDA DEFENSE ANTIQUITIES MUSEUM (FL65)

Address:	2243 Peck Street, Fort Myers, Florida 33901-3640.
Admission:	By prior permission only.
Location:	At a number of airfields.

Aircraft registered to this museum have been seen at a number of airfields across the country and little is known about the organisation. The red painted MiG-21U was parked at Mojave in California for a time. The former Slovakian MiG-21MF was presented to the RAF Benevolent Fund in 1994 and it appeared at the International Air Tattoo at Fairford. After a couple of abortive sales the fighter arrived in the USA a few years ago. The French Navy ordered 42 examples of the Vought Crusader to serve aboard the carriers *Clemenceau* and *Foch*. The Phantom II was considered but was too large for the ships.

Florida

TYPE	REG/SER	CON. NO.	PI/NOTES	STATUS
☐ Mikoyan-Gurevich MiG-21MF	N7708	967708	7708 (Czechoslovakia), 7708 (Slovakia)	RAA
☐ Mikoyan-Gurevich MiG-21U-600	N121TJ	664718	291 (DDR)	RAA
☐ Slingsby T.67C Firefly	N158GA	2104		RAA
☐ Stoddard-Hamilton SH-2 Glasair III	N340	3008		RAA
☐ Vought F-8P Crusader (F-8E(FN))	N3512Z	1251	Bu151765, 34 (France)	RAA
☐ WSK SBLim-2 (Lim-1) [MiG-15]	N5136T	1A 11-014	114 (Poland)	RAA

ST. CLOUD VETERANS MEMORIAL (FL66)

Location: On permanent view on State Route 192 in the town.

TYPE	REG/SER	CON. NO.	PI/NOTES	STATUS
☐ Bell 209 Huey Cobra (AH-1G) (AH-1F)	68-17052	20780		PV

ST. PETERSBURG MONUMENT (FL67)

Location: On permanent view at Admiral Farragut Academy South in the western part of the city.

TYPE	REG/SER	CON. NO.	PI/NOTES	STATUS
☐ Grumman G-98 Tiger (F11F-1) (F-11A)	Bu138608	6		PV

ST. PETERSBURG MUSEUM OF HISTORY (FL68)

Address: 335 Second Avenue North East, St Petersburg, Florida 33701.
Tel: 727-894-2024   **Fax:** 727-823-7276   **Email:** jessica.ventimiglia@stpetemuseumofhistory.org
Admission: Monday-Saturday 1000-1700; Sunday 1300-1700.
Location: In the eastern part of the city near the Pier.

On 1st January 1914 Tony Jannus flew the world's first scheduled commercial flight in a Benoist flying boat from St. Petersburg to Tampa. On 9th October 1983 a replica of the Benoist, constructed by the Florida Aviation Historical Society, flew from Lake Tarpon with Ed Hoffman at the controls. On the 70th anniversary of the Jannus flight Hoffman flew the original route in the replica.

On 1st January 1992 ground was broken for the museum located only 100 yards from the start of the historic flight. The building opened just over a year later and in addition to the Benoist replica houses the engine from the original aircraft. An excellent local history exhibition is staged in the main hall and here the visitor can see the development of the area.

TYPE	REG/SER	CON. NO.	PI/NOTES	STATUS
☐ Benoist 14 (R)				PV
☐ Ford 1 Flivver (FSM)				PV

STALLION 51 FLYING MUSEUM (FL69)

Address: 3951 Merlin Drive, Kissimmee, Florida 34741-4551.
Tel: 407-846-4000   **Fax:** 407-846-0414   **Email:** mustang@stallion51.com
Admission: By prior permission only.
Location: At the airport which is just west of the town on Route 192.

The company was formed in 1987 and now offers training in two seat Mustangs. The current pair, known as 'Crazy Horse' (NL851D) and 'Crazy Horse 2' (NL351D), have delighted crowds at shows and they are probably the most flown examples of the type at the current time. In addition a number of other examples of the famous fighter are looked after for their owners but these are not always present in the hangar. The Texan is used for initial pilot training.

TYPE	REG/SER	CON. NO.	PI/NOTES	STATUS
☐ North American NA-122 Mustang (P-51D)	N5444V	122-40291	44-73751	RAA
☐ North American NA-122 Mustang (P-51D) (Mustang IV)	N6320T	122-41037	44-74497, 9230 (Canada)	RAA
☐ North American NA-122 Mustang (P-51D) (Mustang IV) (TF-51D)	NL351DT/'413806'	122-41042	44-74502, 9232 (Canada), CF-MWC, N6321T, N70QF, N51VC	RAAX
☐ North American NA-122 Mustang (P-51D) (TF-51D)	NL851D	122-44601	44-84745, N5439V – has fuselage of an El Savador Air Force aircraft.	RAA
☐ North American NA-197 Texan (T-6G)	N5632V	197-22	52-8218 – rebuilt from NA-88 (AT-6D) c/n 121-41996 44-81274.	RAA

STARFIGHTERS (FL70)

Address: 1608 West Jasmine Avenue, Tarpon Springs, Florida 34689-5250.
Tel:
Admission: info@starfighters.net
Admission: By prior permission only.
Location: At Clearwater Airport which is in the south eastern part of the city.

The team flies three Canadian-built Starfighters from its base at Clearwater. The trio all served with the Norwegian Air Force before returning across the Atlantic. Two are single seaters and the third is a two seat training version. In addition to performing at displays the aircraft also fly on NASA programmes.

TYPE	REG/SER	CON. NO.	PI/NOTES	STATUS
☐ Canadair CL-90 Starfighter (CF-104) [Lockheed 683-04-12]	N104RN	683A-1059	12759 (Canada), 104759 (Canada), R-759 (Norway)	RAA
☐ Canadair CL-90 Starfighter (CF-104) [Lockheed 683-04-12]	N104RD	683A-1150	12850 (Canada), 104850 (Canada), R-850 (Norway)	RAA
☐ Lockheed 283-93-03 Starfighter (F-104B)	N65354	283-5008	57-1296, 901 (Jordan)	RA
☐ Lockheed 583-04-15 Starfighter (CF-104D)	N104RB	583A-5302	12632 (Canada), 104632 (Canada), 4632 (Norway), N104NL	RAA

SUNRISE MONUMENT (FL71)

Location:	On permanent view at Sawgrass Mills shopping mall in the town.

TYPE	REG/SER	CON. NO.	PI/NOTES	STATUS
☐ Douglas DC-9-41	N79XS	47779	SE-DDT – front fuselage only.	PV

TALLAHASSEE MONUMENT (FL72)

Location:	On permanent view at VVA 96 at 241 Lake Ella Drive in the northern part of the city.

TYPE	REG/SER	CON. NO.	PI/NOTES	STATUS
☐ Bell 204 Iroquois (TH-1L)	Bu157848	6443	Bu157848, N5530U	PV

TULLIUS COLLECTION (FL73)

Address:	44 Victory Lane, Sebring, Florida 33870-7560.
Admission:	By prior permission only.
Location:	At the airport which is about 5 miles south east of the town off Route 98.

The owner of this private collection is Bob Tullius, a former Jaguar sports car driver. The aircraft have all been restored to a high standard and are housed in an immaculate display hangar. Military trainers feature prominently. Canadair-built 636 examples of the Lockheed T-33, some parts of them being constructed in the USA. These aircraft were powered by the Rolls Royce Nene engine.

A Mustang was donated to the Royal Air Force Museum in England and this is on show in the 'Milestones of Flight' area at Hendon.

TYPE	REG/SER	CON. NO.	PI/NOTES	STATUS
☐ American Eagle A-101	NC3738	82	NC3738, N3738	RA
☐ Beech C90A King Air	N44GP	LJ-1208	(N485JA), N621WP	RAA
☐ Boeing-Stearman E75 Kaydet (PT-13D) (N2S-5)	N44TF	75-8242	42-109209, Bu43148, N1377V	RAA
☐ Canadair CL-30 Silver Star 3 (CT-133) [Lockheed 580 (T-33AN)]	N99195	T33-236	21236, 133236	RAA
☐ Cessna A185F Skywagon 185	N44TU	18503616		RAA
☐ Fairchild M-62A-4 Cornell (PT-26A)	N75LD		42-71130, 14554 (Canada), FT715, N79508	RAA
☐ North American NA-168 Texan (T-6G)	N44FL	168-473	49-3359, E.16-95 (Spain), N5830R	RAA
☐ North American NA-168 Texan (T-6G)	N44CT	168-477	49-3363, E.6-110 (Spain), N5451X, N233TM	RAA
☐ Ryan ST-3KR Recruit (PT-22)	N47620	1857	41-20648	RAA
☐ Vultee V-74 Valiant (BT-13A)	N59572	74-1904	41-9670	RAA
☐ Waco ZPF-6	NC17470	4383	NC17470, N17470	RAA

TYNDALL AIR FORCE BASE COLLECTION (FL74)

Address:	325 TTW/PAO, 445 Suwannee Road, Tyndall Air Force Base Florida 32403-50541.
Tel:	850-283-2953 Email: pao@tyndall.af.mil
Admission:	On permanent view.
Location:	About 13 miles south east of Panama City on Highway 98.

The base is the home of the USAF Air Defense Weapons Center and host to the biennial 'William Tell' fighter weapons contest. The field is named after Lieutenant Frank B Tyndall who flew in World War I and was killed in a Curtiss P-1 in 1930.

The site opened in late 1941 and has been an important fighter base for many years. The four preserved aircraft are located in the domestic area on the opposite side of the road from the airfield. The quartet represent types which have flown from the field in the last half century.

TYPE	REG/SER	CON. NO.	PI/NOTES	STATUS
☐ Convair 8-31 Delta Dart (F-106A)	59-0145	8-31-34		PV
☐ McDonnell M.199-1A Eagle (F-15A)	74-0095	069/A056		PV
☐ McDonnell M.98DE Phantom II (F-4C) (NF-4C)	63-7408	314		PV
☐ North American NA-190 Sabre (F-86D) (F-86L)	'51-5244'	190-858	52-10733	PVX

UNIQUE AIRCRAFT MUSEUM (FL75)

Address:	95 Sunset Drive, Suite 108, Miami, Florida 33155.
Admission:	By prior permission only.
Location:	Presumably in the Miami area.

Florida

The FAA register lists this aircraft with the museum. The Canadian-designed Seawind 2000 amphibian first flew in 1982 powered by a 200 h.p. Lycoming engine. The type was underpowered and the 3000 featured a 300 h.p. powerplant. The design was developed in the USA and over 100 kits have been sold.

TYPE	REG/SER	CON. NO.	PI/NOTES	STATUS
☐ Seawind Seawind 3000	N333ME	006		RA

UNITED STATES AIR FORCE ARMAMENT MUSEUM (FL76)

Address:	100 Museum Drive, Building 3201, Eglin Air Force Base, Florida 32542-5000.
Tel:	850-651-1808 Email: afamf@sprintmail.com
Admission:	Monday-Saturday 0930-1630.
Location:	On Highway 85 about 2 miles south west of Valparaiso just outside the main gate of the base.

Eglin Air Force Base was activated in 1935 as a bombing and gunnery centre. The idea of establishing a museum was first put forward in 1969 and a display opened five years later in a former service club. The exhibition reflected the role of the base and the development of aircraft armament.

The museum closed in the early 1980s and the small number of aircraft were stored on the airfield. A fund-raising drive was started to enable the construction of a purpose-built hall, library, workshops and offices. Work began in 1985 and the complex opened the following year, by which time the aircraft collection had increased as more modern types were allocated.

Four aircraft are on view inside the building along with a number of significant items including, guns, cannons, rockets, bombs and missiles from several countries. These include the MOAB (Mother of all Bombs) which is the largest conventional weapon in the world. Also to be seen is the 'Bunker Buster' which was developed for the 'Desert Storm' operations. The two World War II fighters, the Mustang and the Thunderbolt, can be seen here along with the first Air Force jet to enter squadron service. The Shooting Star is painted in false colours to represent one which served at the field in the late 1940s.

A comprehensive photo display tracing the history of the USAAC, the USAAF and the USAF from the early days up to the present time can be seen. In the theatre is a large mural showing the development of military aircraft. A film showing the history of the base can also be seen. The development of the vast Eglin site is also portrayed.

Outside the building is a park in which most of the aircraft and some of the larger items of armament are displayed. Many of the aircraft have been painted in the markings of those which have taken part in significant missions.

TYPE	REG/SER	CON. NO.	PI/NOTES	STATUS
☐ Bell 204 Iroquois (UH-1C) (UH-1M)	66-15186	1914		PV
☐ Boeing 299-O Fortress (B-17G) (PB-1W)	'46106'	32504	44-83863, Bu77231, N5233V, (N6464D), N5233V	PVX
☐ Boeing 450-171-51 Stratojet (RB-47H)	53-4296	4501320		PV
☐ Boeing 464-253 Stratofortress (B-52G)	58-0185	464253		PV
☐ Cavalier Mustang II (F-51D) (North American NA-109)	44-13571	109-27-202	44-13571, 68-15796, '58-3571'	PV
☐ Cessna 337M Super Skymaster (O-2A)	68-6864	337M0153	68-6864, N37555	PV
☐ Convair 340-70 Samaritan (C-131B)	53-7821	273		RA
☐ Douglas DC-3A-467 Skytrain (C-47B) (R4D-7) (TC-47B) (NC-47K) (NEC-47H)	'43-010'	16070/32818	44-76486, Bu39103, 9103 (US Army), O-39103 (US Army)	PVX
☐ Fairchild-Republic A-10A Thunderbolt II	75-0288	A10-37		PV
☐ Fairchild-Republic A-10A Thunderbolt II			Front fuselage only.	PV
☐ General Dynamics F-111E	68-0058	A1-227		PV
☐ General Dynamics 401 Fighting Falcon (F-16A)	80-0573	61-294		PV
☐ Lockheed 080 Shooting Star (P-80C) (F-80C)	'49-713'	080-2180	49-432	PVX
☐ Lockheed 182-1A Hercules (182-44-03) (C-130A) (AC-130A)	53-3129	182-3001		PV
☐ Lockheed 483-04-06 Starfighter (F-104D)	57-1331	283-5043		PV
☐ Lockheed 580 (T-33A)	53-5947	580-9423		PV
☐ Lockheed SR-71A Blackbird	61-7959	2010		PV
☐ Martin 272B Canberra (B-57B) (EB-57B)	52-1516	99		PV
☐ McDonnell M.36BA Voodoo (F-101B)	56-0250	238		PV
☐ McDonnell M.98DF Phantom II (RF-4C)	67-0452	3003		PV
☐ McDonnell M.98DJ Phantom II (F-4C)	'40813'	1147	64-0817	PVX
☐ McDonnell M.199-1A Eagle (F-15A)	74-0124	100/A085		PV
☐ Mikoyan-Gurevich MiG-21F-13	'85'		In false Soviet markings.	PVX
☐ North American NA-108 Mitchell (B-25J) (JB-25J)	'02344'	108-34129	44-30854	PVX
☐ North American NA-193 Sabre (F-86F)	'12831'	193-242	52-5513, '91122'	PVX
☐ North American NA-217 Super Sabre (F-100C)	'54-954'	217-247	54-1986	PVX
☐ Northrop N-68 Scorpion (F-89D)	53-2610	N.4741	Composite with parts of c/n N.4476 52-1899	PV
☐ Republic P-47N Thunderbolt	44-89320	539-C1527	44-89320, N345GP	PVC
☐ Republic F-84F Thunderstreak	51-9495			PV
☐ Republic F-105D Thunderchief	'58-771'	D-10	58-1155	PVX
☐ Sikorsky S-65A (HH-53C) (MH-53J) (MH-53M)	73-1652	65390		PV

UNITED STATES AIRLINE INDUSTRY MUSEUM FOUNDATION (FL77)

Address:	2 Parkplace Court, Dothan, Alabama 36301.
Tel:	334-702-1010 Email: airlinemuseum@att.net
Admission:	In planning stages.
Location:	To be built at an airfield in Florida.

The group is aiming to establish this museum in Florida and an office has been set up in Alabama. One complete DC-7C has been obtained along with a nose section from another which was scrapped at Chandler Memorial airfield in Arizona. A 1929 American Eagle biplane has been donated to the foundation. Almost 600 of these open cockpit three seaters were built at Kansas City sand several carried out early passenger flights. This aircraft was on show for a period at the Wings of Eagles Discovery Center at Elmira in New York State.

TYPE	REG/SER	CON. NO.	PI/NOTES	STATUS
☐ American Eagle A-101	N523S	393		RA
☐ Convair 240-0	N1022C	147	N894270, N1022C, 4X-AGH, TI-AOC,N2642Z	RA
☐ Douglas DC-7B	N4889C	45353		RA
☐ Douglas DC-7C	N5902	45070	Front fuselage only.	RA

UNITED STATES NAVY EXPLOSIVE ORDNANCE DISPOSAL SCHOOL COLLECTION (FL78)

Address: 304 Mccarthy Road, Suite 117, Eglin Air Force Base, Florida 32542.
Tel: 850-882-8370 **Email:** harold.gilley@eglin.af.mil
Admission: By prior permission only.
Location: Just south of Eglin Air Force Base.

A collection of preserved aircraft is located in the grounds of this naval school. Bomb disposal forces are trained here. The collection consists mainly of recently withdrawn American jets used for training.

TYPE	REG/SER	CON. NO.	PI/NOTES	STATUS
☐ Bell 209 Huey Cobra (AH-1G) (AH-1S)				RA
☐ Fairchild-Republic A-10A Thunderbolt II	75-0262	A10-11		RA
☐ General Dynamics 401 Fighting Falcon (F-16A)	78-0013	61-19		RA
☐ General Dynamics 401 Fighting Falcon (F-16N)	Bu163575	3M-20	86-1693	RA
☐ Grumman G-128 Intruder (A-6A) (KA-6D)	Bu152927	I-231		RA
☐ Grumman G-303 Tomcat (F-14A)				RA
☐ Grumman G-303 Tomcat (F-14A)	Bu160896	325		RA
☐ Hawker-Siddeley P.1127 Harrier 50 (AV-8A)				RA
☐ Hawker-Siddeley P.1127 Harrier 50 (AV-8A)				RA
☐ McDonnell M.199-1A Eagle (F-15A)	76-0036	217/A188		RA
☐ McDonnell M.267 Hornet (F/A-18A)	Bu161702	46/A036		RA
☐ McDonnell M.267 Hornet (F/A-18A)	Bu161979	200/A161		RA
☐ Mikoyan-Gurevich MiG-21				RA
☐ Mikoyan-Gurevich MiG-29UB			(Moldova)	RA

UNITED STATES NAVY UDT AND SEAL MUSEUM (FL79)

Address: 3300 North State Road A1A, North Hutchinson Island, Fort Pierce, Florida 34949-8520.
Tel: 772-595-5845 **Fax:** 72-595-5847
Admission: Tuesday-Saturday 1000-1600; Sunday 1200-1600. 1st January–1st May Monday 1000-1600.
Location: Just east of the town centre.

The first US Navy Frogmen were trained at Fort Pierce in 1943. The museum honours their work and that of the underwater demolition teams. The history of these aspects of special warfare is highlighted in the displays. Their work in all conflicts from World War II up to 'Desert Storm' is portrayed in the displays. Inside the building are weapons, demolition gear, parachutes, uniforms, photographs and memorabilia.

TYPE	REG/SER	CON. NO.	PI/NOTES	STATUS
☐ Bell 204 Iroquois (HU-1B) (UH-1B)	62-1876	396		PV

VALIANT AIR COMMAND WARBIRD MUSEUM (FL80)

Address: 6600 Tico Road, Titusville, Florida 32780-8009.
Tel: 321-268-1941 **Fax:** 321-268-5969 **Email:** vacwarbirds@bellsouth.net
Admission: Daily 1000-1800.
Location: At Titusville Airport which is south of the city close to Highway 1.

The organisation was formed in 1977 by warbird owners who soon set up a base at Titusville. Plans for a museum were put forward in the mid-1980s and a fund raising drive was initiated. The first phase opened in 1992 with an interesting collection of types on view. Over the years the displays have changed significantly with many of the original exhibits moving on.

A rarity in the state is the Yugoslavian designed Utva 66. The first product of the company was the high-wing Utva 56. This was developed into the 60 and eventually the 66. A total of 80 was completed mainly for military use. Later some were sold on the civilian market. The rugged four seater was used in many roles including agricultural and ambulance duties.

The Tiger Moth is one of many supplied to the French Air Force after World War II and then donated to civilian aeroclubs. On 4th January 2006 a ceremony was held to commemorate the rollout of two major restorations. The Nord N.1101 was brought back from France by two members and is now resplendent in a sand Luftwaffe World War II scheme. The other was the Grumman Panther which can be seen in the blue colours which most US naval fighters wore at the time it was in service.

TYPE	REG/SER	CON. NO.	PI/NOTES	STATUS
☐ Bell 205 Iroquois (UH-1D) (UH-1V)	66-16138	5832	66-16138, N985MF	PV
☐ Cessna 337M Super Skymaster (O-2A)	'67-11029'	337M0305	68-11029, N138RM	PVAX
☐ Convair 105 (L-13A)	N164AB	97	46-164	PVD
☐ Convair 8-24 Delta Dart (F-106A)			Front fuselage only.	PV
☐ Dale Fisher Classic				PV
☐ De Havilland DH.82A Tiger Moth	N9TM	86577	PG680, (France), F-BGDS	PV
☐ Douglas DC-3A-456 Skytrain (C-47A)	N3239T	19054	42-100591, 2100591 (Norway), 68-684 (Danish), K-684(Danish)	PVD
☐ Douglas DC-3A-467 Skytrain (C-47A)			Front fuselage only.	PV
☐ Douglas DC-3A-467 Skytrain (C-47A)	N8040L	16975/34236	45-972	RAD
☐ Douglas TA-4J Skyhawk (TA-4F)	'Bu158722'	13513	Bu152867	PVX

Florida

☐ Epps Monoplane (R)	N1907	JP-3		PV
☐ Fischer Mini-Mustang	N81905	001		PV
☐ Grumman G-36 Wildcat (FM-1)	Bu14994	3		PV
☐ Grumman G-40 Avenger (TBM-3) (TBM-3U)	N108Q	4093	Bu91188, N108Z	PVC
☐ Grumman G-79 Panther (F9F-5)	Bu125295			PVC
☐ Grumman G-89 Tracker (S2F-1) (S2F-1S) (S-2F)	N8114T	342	Bu136433	PVA
☐ Grumman G-98 Tiger (F11F-1) (F-11A)	Bu141882	199		PV
☐ Grumman G-128 Intruder (A-6E)	Bu162182	I-675		PV
☐ Grumman G-134 Mohawk (OV-1B)	62-5906	65B	Front fuselage only.	PV
☐ Grumman G-134 Mohawk (OV-1D)	68-16994	5D		PV
☐ Grumman G-134 Mohawk (OV-1D)	68-16998	9D	Composite with parts from OV-1B c/n 93B 64-14265 and OV-1C c/n 138C 68-15934	PV
☐ Grumman G-303 Tomcat (F-14A)	Bu161134	361		PV
☐ Lockheed 580 (T-33A)	57-0569	580-1218	57-0569, N64274 –	PV
☐ McDonnell M.36BA Voodoo (TF-101B) (CF-101F) (TF-101F)	N37647	724	59-0400, 17400 (Canada), 59-0400	PV
☐ McDonnell M.98EV Phantom II (F-4J)	Bu155563	2849		RA
☐ Mikoyan-Gurevich MiG-21U-600	4820	664820	4820 (Slovakia) – in false Soviet colours.	PV
☐ Nieuport 28C.1 (R)				PV
☐ Nord N.1101 Ramier I [Messerschmitt Me 208]	192	192	In false Luftwaffe colours.	PVX
☐ North American NA-108 Mitchell (B-25J) (TB-25J) (Mitchell III)	N62163	108-47451	44-86697, 5239 (Canada), N92876	PV
☐ North American NA-191 Sabre (F-86F)	NX86FR/'31201'	191-655	52-4959, C-109 (Argentina),	PVX
☐ North American NA-305 Bronco (OV-10A) (OV-10D)	N15453	305-20	Bu155409, PNC-3043 (Colombia)	PV
☐ North American NA-318 Buckeye (T-2C)	Bu156702	318-17		PV
☐ Northrop N-311 Tiger II (F-5E)	74-1519	R.1177		PV
☐ Piper J-3C-65 Cub (L-4J)	'43-30426'	12891	44-80595, N1406V	PVAX
☐ Republic F-84F Thunderstreak	52-6600		Front fuselage only.	PV
☐ Republic F-105D Thunderchief	60-0492	D-180		PV
☐ Sikorsky S-55D Chickasaw (H-19B) (UH-19B)	'57-5937'		(USAF), N37788	PVX
☐ Stewart Mustang	N76PH	003		PVC
☐ Utva Fabrica Aviona 66	N404RC		51146 (Yugoslavia), C-GDLZ	PVA
☐ Vought A-7A Corsair II	Bu153135	A44		PV
☐ Vought F-8K Crusader (F8U-2) (F-8C)	Bu146985			PV
☐ Vultee V-74A Valiant (BT-15)	N73402/'241372'	74A-8516	42-41372	PV
☐ WSK Lim-5P [MiG-17PF]	521	1D 05-21	In Polish markings.	PV
☐ WSK SBLim-2 (Lim-1) [MiG-15]	N2400X	1A 06-027	627 (Poland)	PVA

WAUCHULA MONUMENT (FL81)

Location: On permanent view in Palmetto Street in the western part of the town.

TYPE	REG/SER	CON. NO.	PI/NOTES	STATUS
☐ Republic F-84F Thunderstreak	'2007'		52-6379	PVX

WHITE 1 FOUNDATION MUSEUM (FL82)

Address: 822 North Hoagland Boulevard, Kissimmee, Florida 34741.
Tel: 727-365-1713 **Email:** white1foundation@yahoo.com
Admission: Monday-Friday 0900-1700.
Location: At the airport which is just west of the town on Route 192.

Two classic Focke-Wulf 190s are located at the museum. Nearing the end of a major rebuild to flying condition is the F-8 model. This aircraft was allocated to JG5 and served in Finland and Norway. It took part in the defence of the Tirpitz and during the Battle of Fordefjord the pilot Heinz Orlowski was forced to bale out. The aircraft 'White 1' force landed on the side of a mountain and remained there until 1983.

Volunteers from Norwegian aviation societies located the wreck and it was lifted in five parts by helicopter to Flesland Airport near Bergen. In 1988 the fighter moved to the Texas Air Museum in Rio Hondo where it was put on static display. A move to Florida took place in 2001 and the foundation was set up. aircraft. An A-7 model is also now in the hangar.

TYPE	REG/SER	CON. NO.	PI/NOTES	STATUS
☐ Focke-Wulf Fw 190A-7		140668		PV
☐ Focke-Wulf Fw 190F-8	N91FW	931862	KT+YX	PVA

WHITING FIELD NAVAL AIR STATION MUSEUM (FL83)

Address: 7550 Essex Street, Milton, Florida 32570-6155.
Tel: 850-623-7510 **Fax:** 850-623-7601
Admission: By prior permission only.
Location: About 6 miles north of Milton on Route 87.

The station opened in 1943 and consists of two almost identical airfields with a number of outlying small landing sites. Pilot training is carried out on a fleet of about 400 aircraft and helicopters. The base is one of the busiest in the USA.
Captain Kenneth Whiting was one of the pioneers of naval aviation in the USA and he was the Commander of the First Aeronautical Detachment to France in 1917. An area in the headquarters building traces his career with some of his personal effects on show.
The Kaydet and the Texan are suspended in the Atrium Building whilst the other aircraft are positioned around the base. The Tracker has recently been allocated to the base by the Pensacola Museum but may not yet have arrived at Whiting.

TYPE	REG/SER	CON. NO.	PI/NOTES	STATUS
☐ Beech D45 Mentor (T-34B) (YT-34C)	Bu140861	BG-195		RA
☐ Bell 204 Iroquois (TH-1L)	Bu157807	6402		RA
☐ Bell 206A Kiowa (OH-58A) (OH-58C)	71-20572	41433		RA
☐ Bell 206A Sea Ranger (TH-57A)	Bu157362	5008		RA
☐ Boeing-Stearman E75 Kaydet (PT-13D) (N2S-5)	Bu43156	75-8250	42-109217, Bu43156, N66307 –	RA
☐ Grumman G-89 Tracker (S2F-1) (S-2A) (TS-2A)	Bu133255	226		RA
☐ McDonnell M.267 Hornet (F/A-18A)	Bu161961	174/A136		RA
☐ North American NA-121 Texan (AT-6F) (SNJ-6)	Bu112161	121-42994	44-82272, Bu112161, N2862G –	RA
☐ North American NA-200 Trojan (T-28B)	'Bu138701'	200-215	Bu138144 –	RAX
☐ North American NA-200 Trojan (T-28B)	Bu138353	200-424	In nearby town of Milton-	PV
☐ North American NA-332 Buckeye (T-2C)	Bu157057	332-28		RA
☐ Vertol V.107M Sea Knight (CH-46A) (HH-46A) (HH-46D)	Bu152528	2150		RA

WINGS OF DREAMS AVIATION MUSEUM (FL84)

Address: Keystone Heights Airpark, 7100 Airport Road, Starke, Florida 32091.
Tel: 352-256-8037   **Email:** bob@wingsofdreams.org
Admission: By prior permission only.
Location: Just north of the town.

This recently formed museum is planning to build an exhibition hall and warbird restoration centre at the airfield. Funds are being raised to make this a reality. A number of fly-ins have taken place and more are planned. Artefacts are being collected and at the current time one aircraft, a Piper Cub, has been acquired.

TYPE	REG/SER	CON. NO.	PI/NOTES	STATUS
☐ Piper J-3C-65 Cub (L-4J)	N1273V	13998	45-55232	RAA

WINGS OF FREEDOM AVIATION MUSEUM (FL85)

Address: 1784 West New Lenox Lane, Dunnellon, Florida 34434-2261
Tel: 352-464-0797   **Email:** c2mills3@netzero.net
Admission: Not yet open.
Location: About 5 miles east of the town off Route 484.

The group was formed in 2002 and their aim is to set up a museum at the former World War II training airfield. The site is now in civilian use. Artefacts have been acquired and small exhibitions have been staged in the area.

TYPE	REG/SER	CON. NO.	PI/NOTES	STATUS
☐ WSK SBLim-2 (Lim-1) (MiG-15)	105	1A 11-005		PV

WINGS OVER MIAMI MILITARY AND CLASSIC AIRCRAFT MUSEUM (FL86)

Address: 14710 128th. Street, Miami, Florida 33196
Tel: 305-233-5197   **Email:** wingsovermiami@aol.com
Admission: Thursday-Sunday 1000-1700.
Location: At Tamiami Airport which is in the south western suburbs of the city.

The building originally housed the Weeks Air Museum but the structure was severely damaged by Hurricane Andrew in August 1992. The hangar was rebuilt and open for a short time before the Fantasy of Flight at Polk City was ready.

A group of private owners formed Wings Over Miami to display their aircraft. The collection has grown steady and many interesting aircraft are on show. Kermit Weeks has loaned a number of aircraft over the years. One of the highlights is the Brown racer. This small monoplane designed by Dan Holloway made its maiden flight in 1933. The aircraft competed in a number of contests but was damaged when the engine fell out. The B-1 was rebuilt and took part in a few races after World War II. After a long period of storage it emerged and is now resplendent in the exhibition hangar.

TYPE	REG/SER	CON. NO.	PI/NOTES	STATUS
☐ Aero L-39C Albatros	N139LS	330202	(Soviet), N399HB	PVA
☐ Bellanca 8KCAB Decathlon	N86573	132-74		PVA
☐ Brown B-1	NR83Y	3		PV
☐ Consolidated 28-5A Catalina (PBY-5A)	N287	1649	Bu48287, N10017, CF-JMS, VH-UMS, CF-JMS, N16647, C-GGDW, N16647 – on loan from F. of F., FL.	RAA
☐ Douglas DC-3A-456 Skytrain (C-47A)	N705GB	13854	43-30703, NX58099, CF-HBX, TG-SAA	PV
☐ Grumman G-303 Tomcat (F-14D)	Bu164342	617		PV
☐ Hunting-Percival P.84 Jet Provost T.5	NX900LT	EEP/JP/1037	XW415	PV
☐ Nanchang CJ-6A	N92864	1632018		PVA
☐ Nanchang CJ-6A	N92863	2851253		
☐ North American NA-88 Texan (AT-6D)	N42897	88-15992	42-84211, C.6-60 (Spain)	PVA
☐ North American NA-88 Texan (SNJ-5)	N29941	88-15239	Bu52026, N8159H, C.6-130 (Spain), N29941, N144L	PVA
☐ North American NA-121 Texan (AT-6F)	N7460C	121-42606	44-81884	PVC
☐ North American NA-121 Texan (AT-6F) (SNJ-6)	N2118X	121-43178	44-82456, Bu112322	PVA
☐ North American NA-200 Trojan (T-28B)	N107NA/'138191'	200-262	Bu138191, (N54913) – in false US Army markings.	PVAX

Florida – Georgia

☐ Ryan ST-3KR Recruit (PT-22)	N56047	2154	41-20945	PVA
☐ Schweizer SGS.1-26C	N10374	87		PV
☐ Seahawk Industries Condor II				PV
☐ Yakovlev Yak-52	N888YK	9511903		PVA

GEORGIA

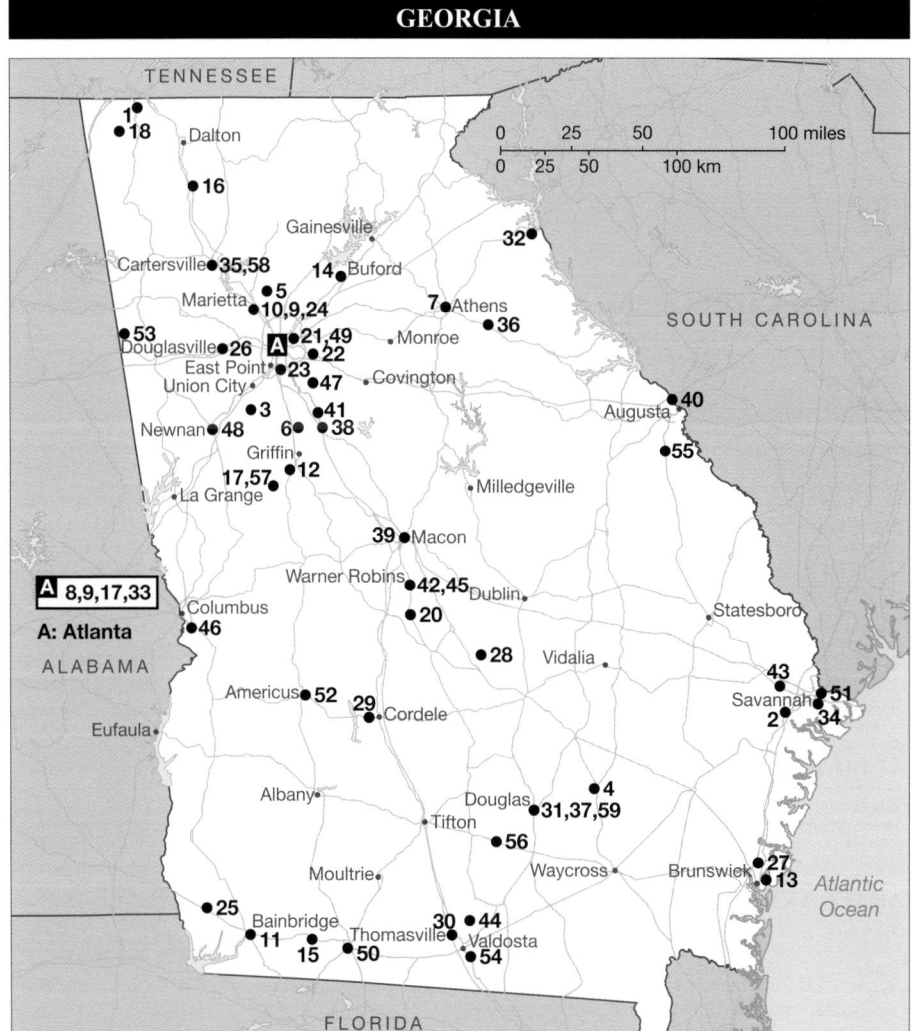

6TH CAVALRY MUSEUM (GA1)

Address: 2 Barnhardt Circle, Fort Oglethorpe, Georgia 30742.
Tel: 706-861-2860   **Email:** info@6thcavalrymuseum.com
Admission: Tuesday-Saturday 0900-1200 1300-1600.
Location: About 5 miles south of Chattanooga, Tennessee off Route 2.

The displays at this museum trace the history of the regiment from the days when it used horses up to the present day role using attack helicopters. The unit was stationed at Fort Oglethorpe from 1919 until 1942. The Huey Cobra has recently been put on show and a Patton tank is also among the exhibits.

TYPE	REG/SER	CON. NO.	PI/NOTES	STATUS
☐ Bell 209 Huey Cobra (AH-1G) (AH-1F)	'73403'			PVX

24TH INFANTRY DIVISION AND FORT STEWART MUSEUM (GA2)

Address:	Building T904, 2022 Frank Cochran Drive, Fort Stewart, Georgia 31314-5028.
Tel:	912-767-7885 **Email:** Walter.Meeks@stewart.army.mil
Admission:	Tuesday-Saturday 1000-1600.
Location:	Just north of Hinesville on Route 118.

Formed in 1941 from the Hawaiian Division, the 24th fought at Pearl Harbor and in other Pacific Islands during World War II. The unit was part of the forces occupying Japan and saw combat in Korea. The Division was inactive between 1970 and 1975 and is now part of the US Rapid Deployment Force. The museum traces the history of the unit and of Fort Stewart. Set up just before World War II, the site served as a training centre for helicopter pilots for the Vietnam War. The display opened in 1976 and has on view a wide range of weapons and memorabilia. The outdoor artillery park features tanks and vehicles used by the division.

TYPE	REG/SER	CON. NO.	PI/NOTES	STATUS
☐ Bell 47D-1 Sioux (H-13E) (OH-13E)	51-13817	403		RA
☐ Bell 47D-1 Sioux (H-13E) (OH-13E)				RA
☐ Bell 204 Iroquois (UH-1C)	65-12741	1468		PV
☐ Bell 204 Iroquois (UH-1C) (UH-1M)	65-9497	1397		PV
☐ Bell 209 Huey Cobra (AH-1G)	'96-00297'		'0811813'	PVX

AIRCRAFT SPRUCE AND SPECIALITY COLLECTION (GA3)

Address:	452 Dividend Drive, Peachtree City, Georgia 30269.
Tel:	770-487-2310 **Fax:** 770-487-2308
Admission:	Monday-Friday 0800-1800; Saturday 0800-1600.
Location:	Just south of the town on Route 74.

The company carries a vast stock of pilot supplies and aircraft parts. Components for a number of homebuilt designs are in stock along with parts for some factory types. Materials for the homebuilder can also be obtained. The company has a display of three aircraft in its premises. The Pitts was built by Dick Rice and first flew in 1963. Two years later it was purchased by Bob Herendeen and flown in the 1966 international aerobatic contest in Moscow. Ralph Mong built the MS-1 in the early 1950s and later decided to make plans available. In 1960 John Young acquired the prototype and lengthened the fuselage.

TYPE	REG/SER	CON. NO.	PI/NOTES	STATUS
☐ Mong MS-1 Sport	N1174	1	N5089N – on loan from EAA, WI.	PV
☐ Pitts SC-1 Special	N66Y	1	On loan from EAA, WI.	PV
☐ Stolp SA.500L Starlet	N2300	500	On loan from EAA, WI.	PV

ALMA MONUMENT (GA4)

Location:	On permanent view in Memorial Park in the northern part of the town.

TYPE	REG/SER	CON. NO.	PI/NOTES	STATUS
☐ Bell 209 Huey Cobra (AH-1G) (AH-1F)	67-15831	20495		PV

ALPHARETTA MONUMENT (GA5)

Location:	On permanent view at ALP 201 at 201 Wills Road in the western part of the town.

TYPE	REG/SER	CON. NO.	PI/NOTES	STATUS
☐ Bell 205 Iroquois (UH-1H)	66-16923	9117		PV

ARMY AVIATION HERITAGE FOUNDATION AND FLYING MUSEUM (GA6)

Address:	506 Speedway Boulevard, Hampton, Georgia 30228-1803.
Tel:	770-897-0444 **Fax:** 770-897-0066 **Email:** President@Armyav.org
Admission:	Monday-Friday 0900-1700.
Location:	At Tara Field which is just north of the town.

This group has been formed to keep in airworthy condition examples of fixed and rotary wing types flown by the US Army. Some of the aircraft are owned by members of the foundation. The Cessna Bird Dog is normally kept on a private strip at nearby Brooks Bridge.

There are workshops at Hampton where some of the fleet are being restored. The museum hopes to increase the number of aircraft as different types become available. Chapters have been set up around the country and more are planned. Some of those listed will move to these groups when they are fully established.

The aircraft regularly appear at shows in the region and are accompanied by a range of military vehicles and display boards highlighting the work of the group.

TYPE	REG/SER	CON. NO.	PI/NOTES	STATUS
☐ Bell 204 Iroquois (TH-1L)	N816HF	6411	Bu157816, N917SF	PVA
☐ Bell 204 Iroquois (UH-1B)	64-13986	1110		PVD
☐ Bell 204 Iroquois (UH-1C) (UH-1M)	64-14182	1306		PV
☐ Bell 205 Iroquois (UH-1D) (UH-1H)	65-9749	4793		PV
☐ Bell 205 Iroquois (UH-1H)	N624HF	8818	66-16724	PVA
☐ Bell 205 Iroquois (UH-1H)	N104HF	10763	68-16104, N104HP	PVA

Georgia

	REG/SER	CON. NO.	PI/NOTES	STATUS
☐ Bell 205 Iroquois (UH-1H)	69-15104	11392		PV
☐ Bell 205 Iroquois (UH-1H)	69-15236	11524		PV
☐ Bell 205 Iroquois (UH-1H)	69-15246	11534		PV
☐ Bell 205 Iroquois (UH-1H)	N354HF	11642	69-15354	PVA
☐ Bell 205 Iroquois (UH-1H)	N221HF	12526	70-16221	PVA
☐ Bell 205 Iroquois (UH-1H)	N426HF	12731	70-16426	PVA
☐ Bell 205 Iroquois (UH-1H)	71-20062	12886		PV
☐ Bell 205 Iroquois (UH-1H)	71-20220	13044		PV
☐ Bell 205 Iroquois (UH-1H)	72-21481	13180		PV
☐ Bell 205 Iroquois (UH-1H)	73-21706	13394		PV
☐ Bell 205 Iroquois (UH-1H)	73-21787	13475		PV
☐ Bell 205 Iroquois (UH-1H)	74-22499	13823		PV
☐ Bell 205 Iroquois (UH-1H) (UH-1V)	69-15229	11517		PV
☐ Bell 205 Iroquois (UH-1H) (UH-1V)	70-16380	12685		PV
☐ Bell 205 Iroquois (UH-1H) (UH-1V)	71-20166	12990		PV
☐ Bell 205 Iroquois (UH-1H) (UH-1V)	74-22312	13631		PV
☐ Bell 205 Iroquois (UH-1H) (UH-1V)	74-22482	13806		PV
☐ Bell 209 Huey Cobra (AH-1G) (AH-1F)	N830HF	20039	66-15283	PVA
☐ Bell 209 Huey Cobra (AH-1G) (AH-1F)	N950LE	20051	66-15295	PVA
☐ Bell 209 Huey Cobra (AH-1G) (AH-1F)	N481HF	20145	67-15481	PVA
☐ Bell 209 Huey Cobra (AH-1G) (AH-1F)	N589HF	20253	67-15589	PVA
☐ Bell 209 Huey Cobra (AH-1G) (AH-1F)	N766HF	20430	67-15766	PVA
☐ Bell 209 Huey Cobra (AH-1G) (AH-1F)	N826HF	20490	67-15826	PVA
☐ Bell 209 Huey Cobra (AH-1G) (AH-1F)	N854HF	20518	67-15854	PVA
☐ Bell 209 Huey Cobra (AH-1G) (AH-1F)	N820HF	20810	68-17082	PVA
☐ Bell 209 Huey Cobra (AH-1G) (AH-1F)	N942HF	20886	70-15942	PVA
☐ Bell 209 Huey Cobra (AH-1G) (AH-1F)	N998HF	21069	71-20998	PVA
☐ Bell 209 Huey Cobra (AH-1G) (AH-1S)	N737HF	20401	67-15737, N209AH	PVA
☐ Bell 209 Huey Cobra (AH-1S) (AH-1F)	N195LE	22240	79-23195	PVA
☐ Bell 209 Huey Cobra (AH-1S) (AH-1F)	N233LE	22278	79-23233	PVA
☐ Bell 209 Huey Cobra (AH-1S) (AH-1F)	N197LE	22345	83-24197	PVA
☐ Cessna 305B Bird Dog (TL-19D) (TO-1D)	N32FL/'72795'	24020	57-2842 – on a private strip at Brooks Bridge.	RAAX
☐ Cessna R172E Mescalero (T-41B)	N78WP	R1720204	67-15203, N96229	RAA
☐ Grumman G-134 Mohawk (AO-1B) (OV-1B) (OV-1D)	N631HF	11B	59-2631, N4376U	PVA
☐ Grumman G-134 Mohawk (OV-1C) (OV-1D)	N605HF	16C	69-17005, N691VY	RAA
☐ Hiller UH12B Raven (H-23B) (OH-23B)	N31621	622	51-16372	PVC
☐ Hughes 269A Osage (TH-55A)	N927AV	1034	67-16927, N82002	PVA
☐ Hughes 369M Cayuse (HO-6) (OH-6A)	N992CH	0346	66-17795	PVA
☐ Hughes 369M Cayuse (HO-6) (OH-6A)	69-15971	1341		RA

ATHENS MONUMENT (GA7)

Location: On permanent view at VFW 2872 at 835 Sunset Drive in the north western part of the town.

TYPE	REG/SER	CON. NO.	PI/NOTES	STATUS
☐ Republic F-84F Thunderstreak	51-1653			PV

ATLANTA HERITAGE ROW (GA8)

Address: 55 Upper Alabama Street, Atlanta, Georgia 30303.
Tel: 404-584-7879
Admission: Tuesday-Saturday 1000-1700; Sunday 1300-1700.
Location: In Underground Atlanta in the city centre.

The exhibition traces the story of the city – there are a several of interactive displays including a replica of a Civil War bomb shelter where the visitor can view episodes from the conflict. The life of Martin Luther King is featured. From the Convair cockpit a simulated approach to Hartsfield International Airport can be experienced.

TYPE	REG/SER	CON. NO.	PI/NOTES	STATUS
☐ Convair 880-22-1	N880AJ	22-00-1	N801TW, N8489H, N871TW – front fuselage only.	PV

ATLANTA TECHNICAL COLLEGE (GA9)

Address: 1560 Metropolitan Parkway Southwest, Atlanta, Georgia 30310-4446.
Tel: 404-225-4400   **Email:** mnwokocha@atlantatech.edu
Admission: By prior permission only.
Location: In the southern part of the city.

The college has a large aviation maintenance facility at its premises. The instructional airframes are mainly parked on the apron outside the buildings. Inside the are workshops containing engines, airframe systems and instrument rigs. The list of aircraft is not complete and an update would be appreciated.

TYPE	REG/SER	CON. NO.	PI/NOTES	STATUS
☐ Aero Commander 680V (680T)	N79BJ	1610-46	(N78D), N79D	RA
☐ Beech D18S Expeditor (C18S) (SNB-2) (SNB-5) (TC-45J) (UC-45J)	N3484	4292	Bu39208	RA
☐ Beech 65-80 Queen Air				RA
☐ Beech D18S Expeditor (C18S) (SNB-2) (SNB-5) (TC-45J) (UC-45J)	N3484	4292	Bu39208	RA
☐ Cessna 150L	N11374	15075364		RA

☐ Cessna 402				RA
☐ Hiller UH12B Raven (H-23B) (OH-23B)	51-16264	456		RA
☐ Sikorsky S-55D (HRS-3) (CH-19E)	N7030		Bu130160	RA

AVIATION WING OF THE MARIETTA MUSEUM OF HISTORY (GA10)

Address:	1 Depot Street, Suite 200, Marietta, Georgia 30060
Tel:	770-794-5710.
Admission:	Aircraft by appointment at the present time.
Location:	Near the airfield which is about 2 miles south of the town on Route 41.

A Government Aircraft Plant was built at Marietta during World War II. In the 1950s the Lockheed company reopened the factory and it has been developed into one of the largest in the world. Many large transport types including the Hercules, Starlifter and Galaxy left the production lines.

The Aviation Museum at Marietta was set up and put forward ambitious plans. These failed to materialise and the venture has been taken over by the Marietta Museum of History. The aircraft, which include some formerly on show at the now closed Atlanta Naval Air Station, are stored on the site while new plans for the exhibition are being discussed.

More aircraft, including types produced at the factory are expected and the collection of associated items is proceeding. The main museum traces the history and development of the local area with many informative displays.

TYPE	REG/SER	CON. NO.	PI/NOTES	STATUS
☐ Bell 205 Iroquois (UH-1H)				PV
☐ Douglas A-4A Skyhawk (A4D-1)	Bu139956	11321		PV
☐ Grumman G-128 Intruder (A-6A) (A-6E)	Bu155648	I-374		PV
☐ Grumman G-303 Tomcat (F-14A)	Bu160909	338		PV
☐ Lockheed 300 Starlifter (C-141A) (C-141B)	66-0186	300-6212		PV
☐ Lockheed 394 Viking (S-3A) (S-3B)	Bu159743	394A-3092		PV
☐ Lockheed 1329 JetStar 6	N428DA	1329-5048	N9215R, N40N, N40NC, N98KR, N98MD, N500WN, N500WZ, N428DA, (N130LW)	PV
☐ Vought A-7E Corsair II	Bu157452	E175		PV

BAINBRIDGE MONUMENT (GA11)

Location:	On permanent view at a business at 1624 Dothan Road in the north western part of the town.

TYPE	REG/SER	CON. NO.	PI/NOTES	STATUS
☐ Bell 205 Iroquois (UH-1D) (UH-1H)	64-13736	4443		PV

BARBERY COLLECTION (GA12)

Address:	1 Lufberry Court, Williamson, Georgia 30292.
Admission:	By prior permission only.
Location:	On an airfield about 5 miles south west of Griffin.

This private collection contains a number of interesting types. The KR-34 biplane was developed from The KR-31 fitted with a variety of radial engines. The Fairchild company acquired Kreider-Reisner in the late 1920s and about 150 KR-34s were completed over the next few years and a small number still survive.

TYPE	REG/SER	CON. NO.	PI/NOTES	STATUS
☐ Bellanca 14-19 Cruisemaster	N536A	2089		RAA
☐ Boeing-Stearman A75N1 Kaydet (PT-17)	N88888	75-4595	42-16432, N61542	RAA
☐ Curtiss 50B Robin B	NC8333	215	NC8333, N8333	RAA
☐ Kreider-Reisner KR-34C Challenger	NC996H	374	NC996H, N996H	RAA
☐ Kreider-Reisner KR-34C Challenger	N221M	390	NC221M, N221M	RAA
☐ Piper J-3C-65 Cub	N42854	15174	NC42854	RAA

BRUNSWICK AIR NATIONAL GUARD MONUMENT (GA13)

Location:	By prior permission only at the airport which about 5 miles north of the town.

TYPE	REG/SER	CON. NO.	PI/NOTES	STATUS
☐ Lockheed 383-04-05 Starfighter (F-104C)	56-0919	183-1207		RA

BUFORD MONUMENT (GA14)

Location:	On permanent view at ALP 127 at 2640 Sawnee Avenue in the north eastern part of the town.

TYPE	REG/SER	CON. NO.	PI/NOTES	STATUS
☐ Bell 205 Iroquois (UH-1H)	67-19519	10125	With boom from c/n 8621 66-16427	PV

CAIRO MONUMENT (GA15)

Location:	On permanent view in Davis Park in the north western part of the town.

TYPE	REG/SER	CON. NO.	PI/NOTES	STATUS
☐ Bell 204 Iroquois (HU-1B) (UH-1B)	60-3572	218	Touring exhibit.	RA
☐ Bell 205 Iroquois (UH-1H)	69-15693	11981		PV

243

This immaculate North American T-6G Texan is part of the Tulius Collection. (Tony Hancock) [FL73]

The USAF Armament Museum at Eglin is home to this Boeing RB-47H Stratojet. (Dick Barrett) [FL76]

The Georgia Veterans Memorial State Park has this Boeing RB-29A Superfortress on show. [GA29]

CALHOUN COLLECTION (GA16)

Address:	Mercer Field, Belwood Road, Calhoun, Georgia 30701.
Admission:	By prior permission only.
Location:	About 4 miles south of the town adjacent to I75.

Lamar Mercer set up the World Aircraft Museum in 1976 at his private airfield. About 15 aircraft were on show. The museum closed some years ago and three of the exhibits remain on the field.

TYPE	REG/SER	CON. NO.	PI/NOTES	STATUS
☐ Convair 240-27 (T-29B)	N1178Q	276	51-5145	RA
☐ Lockheed 580 (T-33A)	52-9574	580-7734		RA
☐ Republic F-84F Thunderstreak	52-6476			RA

CANDLER FIELD MUSEUM (GA17)

Address:	349 Jonathan's Roost Road, Williamson, Georgia 30292.
Tel:	770-467-9490 **Email:** ronalexander@mindspring.com
Admission:	Not yet fully open.
Location:	At Peach State Aerodrome which is about 2 miles west of the town.

In 1909 Asa Griggs Candler, founder of the Coca-Cola company, bought a site just south of Atlanta with the aim of constructing a car race track. The venture lasted for just one season. In 1924 the field was developed as the airport and it was purchased by the city in 1929. Over the years the airfield was developed into the major airport it is today.

This museum is being set up at Peach State Airpark which is being developed as a home for antique and experimental aircraft. Almost 30 lots ranging from one to three acres will be sold and each plot will have its own hangar and access to the airfield. The aim of the museum is to recreate the Candler Field of the 1930s. A replica of the 1930s American Airways Hangar has been completed and others are planned along with a reconstruction of the Art Deco terminal. Doug Davis built the first hangar on Candler Field and set up a flying circus in the early 1920s. Beeler Blevins owned a charter service and flying school as did Davis. Their hangars feature next in the development plan.

The museum has a number of interesting aircraft on show in its hangar. The early DC-3 was delivered to Braniff in 1940 and later served with Trans-Texas. Ron Alexander founder of the museum bought it in 1991. On show are classic types from the interwar period – two Stearman biplanes dating from the 1930s can be seen along with a pair of Curtiss Robins.

TYPE	REG/SER	CON. NO.	PI/NOTES	STATUS
☐ Boeing-Stearman 75 Kaydet (PT-13)	N75009	75-009	36-10, N62546	RAA
☐ Bücker Bü 181B-1 Bestmann (Sk 25)	N94245	25145	Fv25145, D-EHUB	RAA
☐ Curtiss 1C Jenny (JN-4D)	NC1662	6062		RAA
☐ Curtiss 50 Robin	NC7750	24	NC7750, N7750	RAA
☐ Curtiss 50C Robin C-1	N781M	682	NC781M	RAA
☐ Douglas DC-3A-314A	N28AA	2239	NC25666,N N139PB	RAA
☐ Stearman 6L (XPT-912) (6A) (6P)	NC787H	6002	NC787H, N787H	RAA
☐ Stearman C3B	NC8835	241	NC8835, N8835	RAA
☐ Waco YMF-5	N33KD	F5-003		RAA

CHICKAMAUGA MONUMENT (GA18)

Location:	On permanent view in the Veterans Park in the north eastern part of the town.

TYPE	REG/SER	CON. NO.	PI/NOTES	STATUS
☐ Bell 205 Iroquois (UH-1H)	70-16406	12711		PV

COBB COUNTY YOUTH MUSEUM (GA19)

Address:	649 Cheatham Hill Drive, Marietta, Georgia 30061.
Tel:	770-427-2563 **Fax:** 770-427-1060 **Email:** youthmuseum@aol.com
Admission:	Monday-Saturday 0900-1400.
Location:	Off Highway 120 about 3 miles west of Marietta.

Located at the historic Civil War battlefield site of Cheatham Hill the museum has had the Thunderstreak on display for many years. The aircraft has recently been repainted and is in sound condition.

TYPE	REG/SER	CON. NO.	PI/NOTES	STATUS
☐ Republic F-84F Thunderstreak	51-9382			PV

COCHRAN MONUMENT (GA20)

Location:	On permanent view at Bleckley County School in the north eastern part of the town.

TYPE	REG/SER	CON. NO.	PI/NOTES	STATUS
☐ Cessna T310R	N301MG	310R0724	Probable identity.	PV

COMMEMORATIVE AIR FORCE (DIXIE WING) (GA21)

Address:	1200 Echo Court, Peachtree, Georgia 30269-1941.
Tel:	678-364-1110 **Email:** sbdpilot@yahoo.com
Admission:	By prior permission only.
Location:	At Peachtree Airport which is about 8 miles north east of Atlanta on Route 13.

Georgia

The wing was formed in February 1987 and initially was based on a private airfield near Brooks. A move was later made to Peachtree. Members of the group undertook the painstaking restoration the Douglas Dauntless. The unit stripped the airframe right down and manufactured many new parts as the aircraft had been modified for photographic work in Mexico. The four-year task was completed in 1999 and the A-24 took to the air again. Several of the aircraft listed below are owned by members of the wing.

TYPE	REG/SER	CON. NO.	PI/NOTES	STATUS
☐ Aeronca 7BCM Champion (L-16A)	N7620B	7BCM-384	47-1009	PVA
☐ Beech D18S	'KJ508'	A-177	NC1000G, N1000G, XA-POB, N4432B, N70GA	PVAX
☐ Bell 33 Kingcobra (P-63A)	N636GA	33-11	42-68941, NX75488, N75488, N191H	PVC
☐ Canadian Car & Foundry Harvard 4 [North American NA-186]	N7757	CCF4-171	20380 (RCAF) – Mocked up as a Zero	RAAX
☐ Canadian Car & Foundry Harvard 4 [North American NA-186]	'AJ958'	CCF4-206	20415, C-FVCJ, N99CV	RAAX
☐ Douglas A-24B Dauntless	NL82GA	17371	42-54532, NL94513, (Mexican AF), XB-QUC, N54532	RAA
☐ Fairchild M-62A Cornell (PT-19A)	N5215Z	T43-7098	42-53511	RAA
☐ Grumman G-134 Mohawk (OV-1C) (OV-1D) (RV-1D)	N10VD	158C	68-15958	RAA
☐ Nieuport 12 (Scale R)	N12GX	001		RAA
☐ North American NA-88 Texan (SNJ-4)	N103LT	88-12097	Bu27154	RAC
☐ North American NA-88 Texan (SNJ-4)	'BII-310'	88-13171	Bu27675, N7062C – mocked up as a Kate.	RAAX
☐ North American NA-88 Texan (AT-6D) (SNJ-5)	N3771M	88-17109	42-85328, Bu85028, N3273G, N3771M, (N595SH), N3771M	RAA
☐ North American NA-108 Mitchell (B-25J) (TB-25J) (TB-25L)	N3513G	108-37564	44-31489	RAA
☐ North American NA-122 Mustang (P-51D) (Mustang IV)	NL10601	122-40583	44-73843, 9271 (Canada)	RAA
☐ Piaggio FWP.149D	N149WB/'90+32'	046	GA+395, AS+449, AB+449, AB+389, BD+389, 90+32, OO-LWF, TF-LWF, N149WB	RAA
☐ Piaggio FWP.149D	N149DR	070	JA+390, 90+53, D-EEIH, HB-EJX, N149PP	RAA
☐ Soko 522	N210TU	U-210		RAC

CONYERS MONUMENT (GA22)

Location: On permanent view at ALP 77 at 674 American Legion Road in the south eastern part of the town.

TYPE	REG/SER	CON. NO.	PI/NOTES	STATUS
☐ Bell 205 Iroquois (UH-1H)	66-16405	8599		PV

DELTA AIR TRANSPORT HERITAGE MUSEUM (GA23)

Address: 1060 Delta Boulevard, Building B, Department 914, Atlanta, Georgia 30354.
Tel: 404-715-7375   **Email:** museum.delta@delta.com
Admission: By prior permission only.
Location: At the International Airport which is about 10 miles south of the city centre.

Delta Air Service, founded in 1925 by C.E. Woolman, was the first crop-dusting company in the world. The Huff-Daland Duster biplane was the initial type flown by Delta. In 1929 the firm moved into the airline field and opened a route from Atlanta to Birmingham and this was later extended to Dallas. This was short lived and the service was sold to American Airways. Delta applied for routes from Atlanta to Fort Worth and Charleston in 1934 and flew Stinson Trimotors which were replaced by Lockheed Electras in 1936.

The company acquired its first DC-3 in 1940 and the type was in use until 1963. In the mid-1990s the company decided to set up the centre and managed to buy one of its former DC-3s which was originally delivered in December 1940 and used until 1958.

Travel Air 6-Bs and the earlier S-6000B version were used on some services in the early days. The displays trace the history of Delta and many photographs, documents and uniforms are on view.

TYPE	REG/SER	CON. NO.	PI/NOTES	STATUS
☐ Boeing 767-232	N102DA	22214		RA
☐ Douglas DC-3-357	NC28341	3278	NC28341, N29PR	RAA
☐ Lockheed L-1011-1 TriStar	N1011	193A-1001	Fuselage only.	RA
☐ Stinson SR-8D Reliant	NC16181	9755	NC16181, N16181	RAA
☐ Travel Air 6-B	NC8878	6B-2040	NC447W, N447W	RAA

DOBBINS AIR RESERVE BASE COLLECTION (GA24)

Address: 94 AW, 1430 First Street, Dobbins Air Reserve Base, Georgia 30069-5010.
Tel: 678-655-5055   **Email:** 94aw.pav3@dobbins.af.mil
Admission: By prior permission only.
Location: About 2 miles south of Marietta on Highway 41.

The airfield opened in 1943 and the base is named after Captain Charles Dobbins who was killed in action in Sicily during World War II.

The Lockheed company set up a large factory at the field in the 1950s. The 128th Squadron was allocated to the Georgia National Guard in July 1940 and has been a fighter unit since 1946 apart from 1961 to 1973 when it flew transports.

Three aircraft are now preserved at the field. The B-29 is preserved in the Air Force Reserve area, the Mohawk with the ANG and the Hercules is on one of the ramps.

TYPE	REG/SER	CON. NO.	PI/NOTES	STATUS
☐ Boeing 345 Superfortress (B-29) (TB-29)	44-70113	10945		RA
☐ Grumman G-134 Mohawk (AO-1C) (OV-1C)	61-2700	43C		RA
☐ Lockheed 182-1A Hercules (182-44-03) (C-130A) (AC-130A) (C-130A) (JC-130A) (AC-130A)	54-1623	182-3010		RA

DONALSONVILLE MONUMENT (GA25)

Location: On permanent view at ALP 1257 just south of the airport on Highway 39 west of Iron City.

TYPE	REG/SER	CON. NO.	PI/NOTES	STATUS
☐ Bell 209 Huey Cobra (AH-1G) (AH-1F)	70-16001	20945		RA

DOUGLASVILLE MONUMENT (GA26)

Location: On permanent view in Hunter Park at 8830 Gurley Road in the south western part of the town.

TYPE	REG/SER	CON. NO.	PI/NOTES	STATUS
☐ Republic F-105D Thunderchief	'59-1746'	D-359	61-0164	PVX

FEDERAL LAW ENFORCEMENT TRAINING CENTER (GA27)

Address: 1131 Chapel Crossing Road, Glynco, Georgia 31524.
Tel: 912-267-2100
Admission: By prior permission only during working hours.
Location: About 5 miles north of Brunswick.

Glynco Naval Air Station was operational from 1942 until 1974. Two large hangars were built to house patrol airships. The airfield is now operated by the local authority. The Federal Law Enforcement Agency has built an academy on the airship site. A visitor centre shows their work and the history of the airfield.

TYPE	REG/SER	CON. NO.	PI/NOTES	STATUS
☐ Boeing 727-22F	N187FE	19079	N7066U	RA

GEORGIA AVIATION TECHNICAL COLLEGE (GA28)

Address: 71 Airport Road, Eastman, Georgia 31023.
Tel: 478-374-6980   **Email:** drogers@gaaviationtech.edu
Admission: By prior permission only.
Location: About 5 miles east of the town.

The college which was set up many years ago offers courses in a variety of subjects including pilot training. In 2007 a merger with the Middle Georgia Technical College took place. At the current time aviation programmes continue at both sites. Four instructional airframes are known to be in use.

TYPE	REG/SER	CON. NO.	PI/NOTES	STATUS
☐ Cessna 182Q	N821HG	18266354		RA
☐ Cessna 402C	N402HG	402C1016		RA
☐ De Havilland DH.125 Series 400A	N440BC	25218	G-AXTW, N575DU, N575, (N382DA), N711BP	RA
☐ Douglas DC-9-32	N817AT	47323	N1275L, YV-717C, N522MD, N917VV	RA

GEORGIA VETERANS MEMORIAL STATE PARK (GA29)

Address: 2459 Highway 280 West, Cordele, Georgia 31015.
Tel: 912-276-2371
Admission: Museum open daily 0800-1700; park open daily 0700-2200.
Location: About 8 miles west of the town on Route 280.

The museum honours all Georgians who have served in US wars. The indoor displays trace their contribution from the days of the Civil War up to recent conflicts. On show are uniforms, personal items, unit badges, photographs, documents, medals, flags etc. The exhibition gives a comprehensive picture of the state's contribution to national military affairs. A large outside park houses artillery, tanks, vehicles and the aircraft.

TYPE	REG/SER	CON. NO.	PI/NOTES	STATUS
☐ Bell 205 Iroquois (UH-1D)	64-13643	4350		PV
☐ Boeing 345 Superfortress (B-29A) (F-13A) (FB-29A) (RB-29A)	42-93967	7374		PV
☐ Lockheed 580 (T-33A)	51-6699	580-6031		PV
☐ North American NA-244 Fury (FJ-4B) (AF-1E)	Bu143557	244-65		PV
☐ Republic F-84F Thunderstreak	52-6438			PV

GRAND BAY BOMBING RANGE MONUMENT (GA30)

Location: By prior permission only at the site which is about 5 miles south of Moody AFB.

TYPE	REG/SER	CON. NO.	PI/NOTES	STATUS
☐ McDonnell M.98DE Phantom II (F-4C)	64-0675	903		RA

Georgia

GRIFFIN MONUMENT (GA31)

Location:	On permanent view at the airport which is about 3 miles south of the town off Route 19/41.

TYPE	REG/SER	CON. NO.	PI/NOTES	STATUS
☐ Lockheed 580 (T-33A)	53-6096	580-9717		PV

HARTWELL MONUMENT (GA32)

Location:	On permanent view at VFW 8076 at Ack Powell Road about 3 miles north of the town.

TYPE	REG/SER	CON. NO.	PI/NOTES	STATUS
Douglas A-4B Skyhawk (A4D-2)	Bu142105	11359		PV

HERNDON MOBILE WORLD WAR II MUSEUM (GA33)

Address:	125 Heritage Lake Drive, Fayetteville, Georgia 30214-7345.
Tel:	770-719-2365
Admission:	Tours shows.
Location:	Kept in the town.

Retired US Army Chaplain Knox Herndon found the former Pan American DC-3 semi-derelict outside a restaurant at DeKalb Airport. He acquired it in 2002 and mounted the majority of the fuselage on a trailer. He now tours shows across the country. The aircraft is in a period colours with invasion stripes. A display tracing the history of the conflict can be seen in the aircraft. On show are photographs, documents and uniforms.

TYPE	REG/SER	CON. NO.	PI/NOTES	STATUS
☐ Douglas DC-3A-228D		4085	NC28305, XA-GAU, N33639 – front and centre fuselage only.	RA

HUNTER ARMY AIRFIELD COLLECTION (GA34)

Address:	685 Horace Emmet Wilson Boulevard, Hunter Army Airfield, Savannah, Georgia 31409-3517.
Tel:	912-315-3739 **Fax:** 912-315-6424
Admission:	By prior permission only.
Location:	In the south western suburbs of the city off Route 204.

The airfield was constructed for use during World War II and was an Air Force base until the 1970s. The Army then moved in and now flies both fixed and rotary wing aircraft from the field. Local man Frank Hunter was a pioneer of military aviation and rose to the rank of General. He was a fighter ace in World War I and he commanded the 8th Air Force fighter units when they first moved to England in 1942. A room in the operations building traces his career with an excellent display of photographs. The story of the airfield is also portrayed. In an adjoining area, a briefing room of the 352nd Fighter Group based at Bodney in Norfolk during World War II has been recreated. Three of the helicopters are on show outside this building.

TYPE	REG/SER	CON. NO.	PI/NOTES	STATUS
☐ Beech 65-A90-1 Ute (U-21A)	'67-18105'		LM-20	RAX
☐ Bell 204 Iroquois (UH-1C)	'02-00159'		66-18019	RAX
☐ Bell 209 Huey Cobra (AH-1G) (AH-1S)	'00-00609'			RAX
☐ Grumman G-134 Mohawk (OV-1C)	67-18922		123C	RA

L BIRDS FLYING MUSEUM (GA35)

Address:	176 Ridgeview Terrace, Cartersville, Georgia 30210.
Admission:	By prior permission only.
Location:	At the airport which is about 2 miles west of the town.

This collection started in the late 1990s with the aim of flying and maintaining types which have served in the liaison role. A number of types served with distinction in this role during World War II and the museum has acquired examples of some of these.

The Taylorcraft L-2 was developed from the D model designed for the Civilian Pilot Training Program. The Stinson 105 appeared in 1939 and the L-5 is in essence a military derivation of this model. Well over 4,000 Sentinels were completed and served with the US military from 1942 until the late 1950s. The example which was in the collection for many years has recently gone on show in the Museum of Aviation at Robins AFB.

Other collections exist at the airport and the distinction between them is not clear. The L-13A is registered to this collection but the Wings N Wind Museum states that they have an example under restoration. Are there possibly two examples of the type at based at Cartersville?

TYPE	REG/SER	CON. NO.	PI/NOTES	STATUS
☐ Aeronca 65TAC	N39395	C4682TA		RAA
☐ Aeronca 7CCM Champion (L-16B)	N6710C	7CCM-69	48-491 (?)	RAA
☐ Convair 105 (L-13A)	N275LG	155	47-275	RA
☐ Taylorcraft DCO-65 Grasshopper (L-2M)	N43LT	L-5010	(USAAF)	RAA

LEXINGTON MONUMENT (GA36)

Location:	On permanent view at ALP 123 just north of the town on Highway 22.

TYPE	REG/SER	CON. NO.	PI/NOTES	STATUS
☐ Bell 205 Iroquois (UH-1H) (UH-1V)	70-16249	12554	Composite.	PV

LIBERTY FOUNDATION (GA37)

Address:	PO Box 1273, Douglas, Georgia 31534-2770.
Tel:	918-340-0243 Email: smaher@libertyfoundation.org
Admission:	By prior permission only.
Location:	At the airport which is about 3 miles south west of the town off Route 441.

The foundation was set up by Don Brooks a few years ago. He bought a B-17 with an interesting history in 2000. After its military days were over the aircraft was sold for scrap and Pratt and Whitney acquired it for use as an engine test bed. A turboprop engine was mounted in a specially installed cowling in the nose.

When this work was finished it was donated to the Connecticut Aviation Historical Association who run what is now the New England Air Museum. The site was struck by a Tornado in October 1979 and the B-17 suffered major damage. After years in store it was transported to Kissimmee in Florida where Tom Reilly embarked on the rebuild.

The aircraft, now restored to original configuration, is back in flying condition and has visited several shows. A second B-17 owned by Tom is being rebuilt at the airfield

TYPE	REG/SER	CON. NO.	PI/NOTES	STATUS
☐ Boeing 299-O Fortress (299-O) (299-Z) (B-17G)	N390TH/'297849'	8643	44-85734, N5111N, N817BR	RAAX
☐ Boeing 299-O Fortress (B-17G)	44-83790	32431	44-83790	RAC

LOCUST GROVE MONUMENTS (GA38)

Location:	On permanent view at three locations in the town.

TYPE	REG/SER	CON. NO.	PI/NOTES	STATUS
☐ Grumman G-134 Mohawk (OV-1B)	62-5903	62B	At Mallard Landing Strip.	PV
☐ Hughes 369M Cayuse (HO-6) (OH-6A)			In the Package Store.	PVX
☐ Lockheed 580 (T-33A)			North of the town on SR42.	PVX
☐ Piper J-3C-65 Cub	N3411K	22102	In the Package Store.	PV

MACON MONUMENTS (GA39)

Location:	On permanent view at two locations in the city.

TYPE	REG/SER	CON. NO.	PI/NOTES	STATUS
☐ Grumman G-134 Mohawk (OV-1B) (OV-1D)	62-5875	34B	At the Military Institute at 1030 Shurling Drive.	PV
☐ North American NA-190 Sabre (F-86D) (F-86L)	52-3651	190-54	At the ANG base at the airport which is about 8 miles south of the city off Route 129.	PV

MARTINEZ MONUMENT (GA40)

Location:	On permanent view at the Funsville Amusement Park in the town.

TYPE	REG/SER	CON. NO.	PI/NOTES	STATUS
☐ Beech D18S Expeditor (C18S) (SNB-2) (SNB-2P) (SNB-5) (TC-45J) (UC-45J)				PV

MCDONOUGH MONUMENT (GA41)

Location:	On permanent view at a business in the town.

TYPE	REG/SER	CON. NO.	PI/NOTES	STATUS
☐ Lockheed 580 (T-33A)				PVX

MIDDLE GEORGIA TECHNICAL COLLEGE (GA42)

Address:	80 Cohen Walker Drive, Warner Robins, Georgia 31088-2729.
Tel:	478-988-6800 Email: aclark@mgc.edu
Admission:	By prior permission only.
Location:	In the southern part of the town.

The college has workshops where four instructional aircraft are known to reside. A merger with the Georgia Aviation College at Eastman took place in 2007 and there may be movement of the airframes.

TYPE	REG/SER	CON. NO.	PI/NOTES	STATUS
☐ Beech B90 King Air	N425K	LJ-318	N725K	RA
☐ Cessna 150F	N102HA	15064386		RA
☐ Cessna 172M	N12478	17262006		RA
☐ Hunting-Percival P.84 Jet Provost T.5A (T.5)	N8088V	EE/JP/1034	XW412	RA

MIGHTY EIGHTH AIR FORCE HERITAGE MUSEUM (GA43)

Address:	175 Bourne Avenue, PO Box 1992, Pooler, Georgia 31322.
Tel:	912-748-8888 Fax: 912-748-0209 Email: admin@mightyeighth.org
Admission:	Daily 0900-1700.
Location:	In the town near the junction of Interstate 95 and Highway 80.

Georgia

The Eighth Air Force was established on 28th January 1942 at Savannah Army Air Base. Within a short time the force was transferred to England. The plan called for over 3,000 aircraft to be ready for use by April 1943. The B-17 represents the bombers used in this era.

Many new airfields were constructed in Eastern England to house the bombers, fighters and transport types. The last unit returned to the USA in February 1946. The 8th became part of Strategic Air Command when it was set up in 1946.

The B-47 was the backbone of the force for many years. Over 1,300 were built and they served with squadrons both in the USA and abroad.

This impressive museum opened in the late 1990s and traces the history of the units, aircraft and personnel who have served. Modern audio-visual techniques have been employed.

The Messerschmitt Bf 109, which crashed near Murmansk in 1942, was one of several retrieved by Warbird Recovery in Colorado.

TYPE	REG/SER	CON. NO.	PI/NOTES	STATUS
☐ Boeing 299-O Fortress (B-17F)	41-24487	3172	Front fuselage only.	PV
☐ Boeing 299-O Fortress (B-17G)	N66571	32455	44-83814, N66571, CF-HBP – with parts from XA-BEC	RA
☐ Boeing 450-11-10 Stratojet (B-47B) (TB-47B)	50-0062	450077		PV
☐ Boeing-Stearman B75N1 Kaydet (N2S-3)	N555J	75-7811	Bu38190, N68998	PV
☐ Consolidated 32 Liberator (B-24J)	42-51457	2988	Front fuselage only – on loan from IWM, UK.	PV
☐ McDonnell M.98DJ Phantom II (F-4C)	64-0815	1143		PV
☐ Messerschmitt Bf 109E-7	4	5975	Composite with several parts from a G-2.	RAC
☐ Messerschmitt Bf 109G (FSM)	'22'			PVX
☐ Mikoyan-Gurevich MiG-17F	'46'		(Bulgaria) – in false North Vietnam colours.	PVX
☐ Mikoyan-Gurevich MiG-21MF	23+13	967615	490 (DDR) – Front fuselage only.	PV
☐ North American NA-122 Mustang (P-51D) (FSM)	'414061'			PVX

MOODY AIR FORCE BASE HERITAGE PARK (GA44)

Address: 814 Radford Boulevard, Moody Air Force Base, Georgia 31699.
Tel: 229-257-3345   **Email:** 23wg.pa@moody.af.mil
Admission: By prior permission only.
Location: About 10 miles north east of Valdosta on Route 125.

The airfield opened as Valdosta Airfield in September 1941. The site was renamed Moody Army Airfield a few months later. Major George Putnam Moody, a pioneer Air Force pilot, was killed in May 1941 whilst testing a Beech AT-10 at Wichita in Kansas. The 23rd Fighter Group moved into the base in 2006 and brought four preserved aircraft from their former home at Pope AFB in North Carolina. A heritage park will soon be set up.

TYPE	REG/SER	CON. NO.	PI/NOTES	STATUS
☐ Curtiss 87V Warhawk (P-40N)	42-105702	29464		RA
☐ Fairchild-Republic A-10A Thunderbolt II	75-0308	A10-57		RA
☐ General Dynamics 401 Fighting Falcon (F-16A)	79-0352	61-137		RA
☐ Republic F-105D Thunderchief	61-0165	D-360		RA
☐ Vought A-7D Corsair II	72-0230	D352		RA

MUSEUM OF AVIATION (GA45)

Address: 247 and Russell Parkway, Warner Robins, Georgia 31088.
Tel: 478-926-6870/4242   **Email:** ken.emery@robins.af.mil
Admission: Daily 0900-1700.
Location: Just south of Robins Air Force Base on Route 247.

Construction of the Wellston Air Depot started in June 1941 and the base was activated the following March. The site was later named after Brigadier General Augustine Warner Robins, a pioneer of air force logistics, who died in 1940. During World War II a variety of fighter and bomber types were repaired at the field. At the end of the conflict a vast number of B-29 Superfortress bombers were stored at Robins until required. With the onset of the Korean War they were returned to active duty.

As more and more Air Force Depots have closed the Warner Robins Air Logistics Center has assumed greater responsibility and at the current time it undertakes the overhaul of the C-130 Hercules, the C-141 Starlifter and the F-15 Eagle. Airborne avionics and gun systems are also handled by the workshops and many other management programmes are carried out. The airfield is home to several flying units and the Headquarters of the Air Force Reserve is based at Robins.

With this tradition the establishment of a museum was almost a foregone conclusion. The planning for the exhibition started in 1980 and the first phase opened on 9th November 1984. A well thought out display covering a number of topics was set up in a small building. The construction of the base, the work of women in the repair of aircraft in World War II, the history of Strategic Air Command and the roles of modern transport aircraft were all highlighted. Visitors could operate the first bombing and navigation computer used by the Air Force. This vast piece of equipment almost completely occupied one room, thus illustrating the rapid advances in electronics over the last few years.

The aircraft collection, which grew steadily during the 1980s, was parked in a large area behind the building. In 1986 a campaign to raise funds for new exhibition halls, a research centre and a restaurant was initiated. In 1991 a hangar was completed and here a number of aircraft, engines and components etc. are on show. Areas are devoted to helicopters, training aircraft and the development of the aero engine. On 3rd July 1992 after only 12 months construction the 'Phase II' building was dedicated.

The three-storey structure in the form of the insignia of the Air Force houses a fascinating array of exhibits. The rotunda of the building displays the first production F-15 Eagle, a PT-17 Kaydet trainer and a TG-4A glider. On the ground floor the Hump Pilots Association have put on an exhibition. This honours the crews who flew support missions over the Himalayas from bases in India to China in World War II. Also on this level is the P-51D gallery showing a typical airfield scene in Britain in World War II and the Air Rescue Service Hall.

The middle floor houses a superb art gallery, the Georgia Aviation Hall of Fame plus exhibits devoted to the evolution of missiles, electronic counter measures and the development of the propeller. Special sections are devoted to the history of the famous 'Thunderbirds' aerobatic team, the Tuskegee Airmen, aircraft nose art and recipients of the Medal of Honor.

On the top floor is the restaurant which provides an excellent view of the museum grounds and of the activities of the airfield. One non-military aircraft on show is a replica of the Epps Monoplane. Ben Epps was born in 1888 and built his first aircraft in 1907. Five more designs followed and he died in 1937 following injuries received in a crash. All his sons went into aviation and his descendants still run a company bearing his name. He is regarded as the pioneer of aviation in Georgia. A number of machines await their turn in the restoration facility at the rear of the aircraft park.

TYPE	REG/SER	CON. NO.	PI/NOTES	STATUS
☐ Aero Commander 680F	'37948'	1060-58	N37948	PVX
☐ Aeronca 7AC Champion	NC82446	7AC-1079	NC82446, N82446	PV
☐ Beech C18S Kansan (AT-11)	41-27391	1236	41-27391, N6669C	RA
☐ Beech D18S Expeditor (C-45G)	51-11653	AF-210	51-11653, N9306Z	PVX
☐ Bell 47G Sioux (HTL-6) (TH-13M)	Bu142376	1339		PV
☐ Bell 204 Iroquois (UH-1F)	65-7959	7100		PV
☐ Bell 204 Iroquois (UH-1F) (UH-1P)	65-7925	7066		PV
☐ Bell 209 Huey Cobra (AH-1G)	'Bu157795'	20674	68-15140 – at Marine Corps base on the field.	RAX
☐ Bensen B-8M Gyrocopter	N61CN	1977		PV
☐ Boeing 345 Superfortress (B-29A) (TB-29A)	44-61739	11216	Front fuselage only.	RAC
☐ Boeing 345 Superfortress (B-29B) (TB-29B)	44-84053			PV
☐ Boeing 367-76-66 Stratofreighter (KC-97L)	53-0298	17080	53-0298, N2987W – front fuselage from c/n 16635 52-2604, N97GX	PV
☐ Boeing 464-201-7 Stratofortress (B-52D)	55-0085	17201		PV
☐ Boeing 717-157 Stratolifter (C-135A) (EC-135N)	61-0327	18234		RA
☐ Boeing-Stearman A75N1 Kaydet (PT-17)	42-16365	75-4528	42-16365, N9634, CF-DQL	PV
☐ Cessna T-50 Bobcat (AT-17B) (UC-78B)	42-71714	4410		PV
☐ Cessna 152	N634JM			PV
☐ Cessna 305A Bird Dog (L-19A) (O-1A)	'23314'	23314	51-12857, 12857 (France), 51-12857	PVX
☐ Cessna 310M Blue Canoe (310E) (L-27B) (U-3B)	60-6052	310M0007	60-6052, N32086	PV
☐ Cessna 318B Tweety Bird (T-37B)	60-0100	40582		PV
☐ Cessna 318D Dragonfly (318A) (T-37A) (T-37B) (A-37A)	67-14525/'74525'	40043	Converted from 318B Tweety Bird c/n 40043 56-3471	PV
☐ Cessna 337M Super Skymaster (O-2A)	67-21380	337M0086		PV
☐ Chanute Glider (R)				PV
☐ Convair 240-17 (T-29A)	49-1938	205	Front fuselage only.	RA
☐ Convair 8-10 Delta Dagger (F-102A)	56-1151/'56115'	8-10-368		RA
☐ Convair 8-10 Delta Dagger (F-102A)	57-0906	8-10-872		PV
☐ Convair 8-31 Delta Dart (F-106A)	59-0123	8-31-12		RA
☐ Curtiss 1C Jenny (JN-4D) (R)	N217DB	DB-1		PV
☐ Curtiss 87V Warhawk (P-40N) (TP-40N)	42-105927	29689		PV
☐ Curtiss-Wright CW-20B-2 Commando (C-46D)	42-101198	30653	42-101198, N68851, HK-829, CC-CND CC-CDC, HP-977, HH-DGA	PV
☐ De Havilland DHC.2 Beaver (L-20A) (U-6A)	52-6087	454	52-6087, N1477, N30NR	PV
☐ De Havilland DHC.4A Caribou (CV-2B) (C-7B)	63-9756	218		PV
☐ Douglas DC-3A-456 Skytrain (C-47A)	N842MB	19741	43-15275, N842M	RAC
☐ Douglas DC-3A-456 Skytrain (C-47A)			Front fuselage only.	RA
☐ Douglas DC-3A-467 Skytrain (C-47B) (R4D-6) (C-47J)	43-49442	15258/26703	43-49442, Bu50811	PV
☐ Douglas DC-4 Skymaster (C-54G)	45-0579	36032		PV
☐ Douglas 1129A Globemaster II (C-124A) (C-124C)	51-0089	43423		PV
☐ Douglas A-26C Invader	44-35732	29011	Identity doubtful.	PV
☐ Douglas WB-66D Destroyer	55-0392	45024		PV
☐ English Electric P.26 Lightning F.53	ZF593	95298	G-27-62, 53-692 (Saudi Arabia)	PV
☐ Epps Monoplane (R)	N9119	E1		PV
☐ Fairchild M-62A Cornell (PT-19A)	'437220'	T43-7220	42-83633, N54255	PVX
☐ Fairchild 110 Flying Boxcar (C-119C)	51-2566	10524		PV
☐ Fairchild 473 Provider (205) (C-123B) (C-123K) (UC-123K)	54-0633	20082		PV
☐ Fairchild-Republic A-10A Thunderbolt II	75-0305	A10-54		PV
☐ General Dynamics F-111E	68-0055	A1-224		PV
☐ General Dynamics 401 Fighting Falcon (F-16A)	81-0676	61-357		PV
☐ Grumman G-111 Albatross (G-64) (SA-16A) (SA-16B) (HU-16B)	51-7144	G-194		PV
☐ Gyrodyne QH-50C (DSN-3)				RA
☐ Helio H-295 Super Courier (H-395) (U-10B) (U-10D)	'63601'	719	63-13096	PVX
☐ Hiller UH12B Raven (H-23B) (OH-23B)	54-2928	719	51-16372	RAC
☐ Kaman K-600-1 Huskie (H-43A) (HH-43A)	58-1833			PV
☐ Kaman K-600-3 Huskie (H-43B) (HH-43B)	58-1853	13		RA
☐ Laister-Kauffman LK.10B (TG-4A)	42-43740			PV
☐ Lockheed 18-56-23 Lodestar (C-60A)	42-55918	18-2333	42-55918, NC18198, NC66314, N66314, N315, N315F	PV
☐ Lockheed 080 Shooting Star (P-80A) (F-80A)	45-8357	080-1571		PV
☐ Lockheed 182-1A Hercules (182-44-03) (C-130A)	57-0478	182-3185	Fuselage only.	PV
☐ Lockheed 182-1A Hercules (182-44-03) (C-130A) (AC-130A)	55-0014	182-3041		PV
☐ Lockheed 382-8B Hercules (C-130E)	64-0496	382-3980		PV
☐ Lockheed 183-93-02 Starfighter (F-104A)	56-0817	183-1105	56-0817, '70817'	PV
☐ Lockheed 300 Starlifter (C-141A) (C-141B)	65-0248	300-6099		PV
☐ Lockheed 300 Starlifter (C-141A) (C-141B)	66-0180	300-6206		PV
☐ Lockheed 382C-41D Hercules (C-130H) (YMC-130H)	74-1686	382C-4669		PV
☐ Lockheed 580 (T-33A)	52-9225	580-7291	Outside base near Gate 2.	PV
☐ Lockheed 580 (T-33A)	52-9633	580-7818	Rear fuselage and tail section only.	RAD

Georgia

☐ Lockheed 580 (T-33A)	53-5199	580-8538		RAC
☐ Lockheed 726-45-17 Neptune (P2V-7) (P-2H)	'44037'	726-7204	Bu147954	PVX
☐ Lockheed 1049A-55-137 Super Constellation (1049A-55-86) (WV-2) (EC-121K) (NC-121K)	Bu141297	1049A-4421	In false Air Force markings.	PV
☐ Lockheed 1329 JetStar 6 (VC-140B) (C-140B)	61-2488	1329-5017	N9286R	PV
☐ Lockheed SR-71A Blackbird	61-7958	2009		PV
☐ Lockheed U-2C (U-2B)	56-6682	349	56-6682, N709NA	PV
☐ Martin 272A Canberra (RB-57A)	'52-1457'	58	52-1475	PVX
☐ Martin 744 Canberra (272) (B-57B) (RB-57F) (WB-57F)	63-13293	173	52-1583	PV
☐ McDonnell M.36BA Voodoo (TF-101B) (TF-101F)	58-0276	648		PV
☐ McDonnell M.36CA Voodoo (RF-101C)	'60229'	249	56-0229, '5656', 41518' – in false Taiwanese markings.	PVX
☐ McDonnell M.98DE Phantom II (F-4C)	63-7477	469	Front fuselage only.	RA
☐ McDonnell M.98DE Phantom II (F-4C)	63-7465	481		PV
☐ McDonnell M.98DE Phantom II (F-4C)	'68-566'	598	63-7559, '66-7566' – with ANG.	RAX
☐ McDonnell M.98EN Phantom II (F-4D)	66-7554	2091		PV
☐ McDonnell M.199-1A Eagle (F-15A)	73-0085	023/A019		PV
☐ McDonnell M.199-1A Eagle (F-15A)	'77-0099'	042/A033	73-0099 – by base gate.	PVX
☐ McDonnell M.199-1A Eagle (F-15A)	'75-0043'	097/A082	74-0121	RAX
☐ McDonnell M.199-1A Eagle (F-15A)	77-0084	363/A296	Front fuselage only.	PV
☐ McDonnell M.199-1A Eagle (F-15A)				PV
☐ McDonnell M.199-1B Eagle (TF-15A) (F-15B)	76-0132	246/B034		PV
☐ Mikoyan-Gurevich MiG-17F	86	540713	In Bulgarian markings.	PV
☐ North American NA-108 Mitchell (B-25J) (TB-25J)	44-86872	108-47626	44-86872, N2888G, '486874'	PV
☐ North American NA-122 Mustang (P-51D)	'44-13704'		Composite of several aircraft.	PVX
☐ North American NA-168 Texan (T-6G)	49-3217	168-321		PV
☐ North American NA-174 Trojan (T-28A)	51-3612	174-150	Front fuselage only.	PV
☐ North American NA-187 Sabre (F-86A)	52-5751	187-173	Front fuselage only.	RA
☐ North American NA-203 Sabre (F-86A)	53-1511	203-283	53-1511, N5585	PV
☐ North American NA-217 Super Sabre (F-100C)	54-1851	217-112		PV
☐ North American NA-235 Super Sabre (F-100D)	56-2995	235-293		RA
☐ North American NA-276 Sabreliner (T-39A) (CT-39A)	62-4461	276-14		PV
☐ North American NA-305 Bronco (OV-10A)	67-14623	305-31		PV
☐ Northrop N-156T Talon (T-38A)	65-10325	N.5744		PV
☐ Northrop N-160 Scorpion (N-68) (F-89D) (F-89J)	53-2463	N.4594		RA
☐ Piasecki PD-22 Work Horse (H-21B) (CH-21B)	52-8685	B.47		PV
☐ Pitts S-1C Special	N11HC	70-1HC		PV
☐ Republic F-84E Thunderjet	'45-1604'		51-0604	PVX
☐ Republic F-84F Thunderstreak	51-1633		Front fuselage only.	RA
☐ Republic F-84F Thunderstreak	51-9507		With ANG.	PV
☐ Republic F-84F Thunderstreak	52-6701			PV
☐ Republic F-84F Thunderstreak			Front fuselage only.	RA
☐ Republic F-105F Thunderchief	63-8309	F-86	Front fuselage only.	RA
☐ Republic F-105G Thunderchief (F-105F)	62-4438	F-27		PV
☐ Republic F-105G Thunderchief (F-105F)	'24425'	F-122	63-8345 – with ANG.	RAX
☐ Rockwell B-1B Lancer	'86-0098'	6	83-0069	PVX
☐ Ryan ST-3KR Recruit (PT-21)	41-1978	1178	41-1978, N2860D	PV
☐ Sikorsky S-55D Chickasaw (H-19D) (UH-19D)	55-3228			PV
☐ Sikorsky S-58 Seabat (HSS-1N) (SH-34J)	Bu148963	581366		PV
☐ Sikorsky S-61R (CH-3E) (HH-3E)	67-14703	61605		PV
☐ Sikorsky S-61R (CH-3E) (HH-3E)	67-14711	61613	Front fuselage only.	RA
☐ Sikorsky S-61R (CH-3E) (HH-3E)	67-14713	61615	Front fuselage only.	RA
☐ Sikorsky S-65	70-1626	65336		PV
☐ Stinson V-76 Sentinel (L-5)	'44-17421'	76-421	42-98180, N63094	PVX
☐ Vultee V-79 Valiant (BT-13B)	42-90018		(USAAF)	PV
☐ Waco NZR Hadrian (CG-4A)				RAD

NATIONAL INFANTRY MUSEUM (GA46)

Address:	Building 396, Baltzell Avenue, Fort Benning, Georgia 31905-5993.
Tel:	706-545-6762 **Email:** hannerz@benning.army.mil
Admission:	Monday-Friday 1000-1630; Saturday-Sunday 1230-1630.
Location:	About 5 miles south of Columbus off Interstate 185.

The exhibition traces the role of the infantry soldier from the Revolutionary War to the present day. A vast collection of artefacts, documents, photographs, uniforms and weapons can be seen. There are eight major galleries in the building with six devoted to particular periods in America's Military History.

Another is devoted to the history of Fort Benning which shows how raw recruits are trained to be fighting soldiers and how the Fort has impacted on the neighbourhood since it was founded in 1918.

The C-47 has been used to transport soldiers in both peace and wartime and this is parked with the C-119 near the training area for paratroopers. The C-119 on show is one of the batch of 35 supplied to the Royal Canadian Air Force. The first was delivered in September 1952 and they served with squadrons across the country. The final examples were withdrawn in July 1965 and the survivors were mainly sold on the civil market. The one in the collection was flown to Greybull in Wyoming for use by Hawkins and Powers Aviation.

Components of a number of Waco Hadrian gliders have been collected over the years and a long-term project is to exhibit a complete example of the transport glider.

TYPE	REG/SER	CON. NO.	PI/NOTES	STATUS
☐ Bell 205 Iroquois (UH-1H)				RA
☐ De Havilland DHC.2 Beaver (L-20A) (U-6A)				RA
☐ Douglas DC-3A-456 Skytrain (C-47A)	42-93790	13741		PV
☐ Fairchild 110 Flying Boxcar (C-119F)	22116	10860	22116 (Canada), N5217R	PV

Georgia

☐ Sikorsky S-58 Choctaw (H-34A) (CH-34A)	54-2874	58272		RA
☐ Waco NZR Hadrian (CG-4A)			Composite.	RA

NATIONAL MUSEUM OF COMMERCIAL AVIATION (GA47)

Address:	5442 Frontage Road, Suite 102, Forest Park, Georgia 30297.
Tel:	404-675-9266 **Email:** info@nationalaviationmuseum.com
Admission:	Wednesday and Friday 1000-1600.
Location:	About 10 miles south of Atlanta off Interstate 75.

Plans for a large museum, housing mainly airliners, have been put forward. The displays will trace the history of commercial aviation with particular reference to the American contribution.

The nearby Hartsfield Airport at Atlanta was the main base for the now defunct Eastern Airlines and still houses Delta Airlines headquarters.

Replicas of a number of types are proposed along with a number of both piston and jet airliners. A temporary display has been staged with a large amount of airline memorabilia and models on show.

The Martin 4-0-4 first flew in 1947 and just over 100 were produced. The type was in service for many years with a number of companies. The museum has the front fuselage of a former Eastern Airlines aircraft. The ex-Delta 727 is currently stored at Mojave with many withdrawn airliners and will be moved when an exhibition site is found.

TYPE	REG/SER	CON. NO.	PI/NOTES	STATUS
☐ Boeing 727-200			Currently at Mojave, CA.	RA
☐ Martin 4-0-4	N9234C	14143	N452A, N442D, N923RC – front fuselage only.	PV

NEWNAN COWETA MONUMENT (GA48)

Location:	Was on permanent view at the Police hangar on the airfield.

TYPE	REG/SER	CON. NO.	PI/NOTES	STATUS
☐ Bell 205 Iroquois (UH-1D) (UH-1H)	65-10095	5139	Believed to be in store.	RA

PEACHTREE CITY MONUMENT (GA49)

Location:	At Peachtree Airport which is about 8 miles north east of Atlanta on Route 13.

TYPE	REG/SER	CON. NO.	PI/NOTES	STATUS
☐ General Dynamics 401 Fighting Falcon (F-16A)	79-0345	61-130		PV

POWER OF THE PAST MUSEUM (GA50)

Address:	432 Colton Avenue, Thomasville, Georgia 31792.
Tel:	229-226-3010 **Email:** ljdekle@rose.net
Admission:	By prior permission only – someone usually present at weekends.
Location:	At the airfield which is about 7 miles north east of the town on Route 122.

The collection was started by James Dekle and his son John when they acquired a 1918 Anzani engine from a swamp near Macon. Now almost 60 aircraft powerplants are on show in the hangar along with a collection of propellers and aviation memorabilia. The motors include examples of most types which have powered American light aircraft over the last 70 years.

Advertising signs and posters have been acquired and these adorn the walls of the hangar. Two classic biplanes can also be seen. The 1928 Travel Air 2000 was restored over a 4½-year period. The 1931 Waco RNF was found stored in a barn 26 miles from Thomasville. The aircraft took just over a year to be rebuilt to pristine condition. It is named 'City of Roses' after the local area.

TYPE	REG/SER	CON. NO.	PI/NOTES	STATUS
☐ Travel Air 2000	NC4952	450	NC4952, N4952	RAA
☐ Waco RNF	NC11237	3439	NC11237	RAA

SAVANNAH MONUMENTS (GA51)

Location:	On permanent view at two locations in the city.

TYPE	REG/SER	CON. NO.	PI/NOTES	STATUS
☐ Douglas A-4L Skyhawk (A4D-2N) (A-4C)	Bu145122	12368	At Savannah State College in Laroche Avenue in the southern nart of the city.	RA
☐ North American NA-173 Sabre (F-86D) (F-86L)	51-5891	173-35	At the airport which is about 3 miles north west of the city	PV
☐ Republic F-84F Thunderjet	48-0741		At the airport which is about 3 miles north west of the city	PV

SOUTH GEORGIA TECHNICAL COLLEGE (GA52)

Address:	900 South Georgia Technical Parkway, Americus, Georgia 31709
Tel:	229-931-2110 **Fax:** 229-931-5104 **Email:** sbird@southgatech.edu
Admission:	By prior permission only.
Location:	At Souther Field which is about 5 miles north of the town off Route 19.

Georgia

The college was established in 1948 with its main campus in Americus. The airfield was used for military training in both World War I and World War II. The aviation section is housed in the Griffin B. Bell Aerospace Technology Center named after a former US Attorney General. The gate is guarded by the Neptune and a scale model of the F-22 Raptor. The workshops contain engines and some of the latest equipment used in engineering and testing.

TYPE	REG/SER	CON. NO.	PI/NOTES	STATUS
☐ Beech D18S Expeditor (C18S) (AT-7) (SNB-5) (TC-45J) (UC-45J)	N3752	1112	41-21097, NC126, Bu140987	RA
☐ Beech D18S Expeditor (C18S) (SNB-2) (SNB-3) (SNB-5) (TC-45J) (UC-45J)	N3753	5791	Bu67208	RA
☐ Beech B24R Sierra 200	N6500R	MC-232		RA
☐ Beech D45 Mentor (T-34B)	N85995	BG-209	Bu140875	RA
☐ Beech D45 Mentor (T-34B)	N2079A	BG-348	Bu144041, N16116	RA
☐ Bell 204 Iroquois (HU-1B) (UH-1B)	62-1900	420		RA
☐ Bell 204 Iroquois (UH-1B)	N91259	1064	64-13940	RA
☐ Bell 204 Iroquois (UH-1B)	N50023	515	62-1995, 995 (Norway)	RA
☐ Boeing-Stearman E75 Kaydet (PT-13D) (N2S-5)	'C1948'	75-8257	42-109224, Bu43163	RAX
☐ Cessna 182Q	N94709	18266496		RA
☐ Cessna 337M Super Skymaster (O-2A)	68-11149	337M0374	68-11149	RA
☐ Hiller UH12B Raven (H-23B) (OH-23B)	51-16208	388		RA
☐ Hughes 369			Pod only.	RA
☐ Lockheed 726-45-17 Neptune (P2V-7) (P2V-7S) (SP-2H)	Bu147966	726-7216	Bu147966, N4602V	PV

TALLAPOOSA MONUMENT (GA53)

Location:	On permanent view in Helton Howland Park in the eastern part of the town.

TYPE	REG/SER	CON. NO.	PI/NOTES	STATUS
☐ Bell 205 Iroquois (UH-1H) (UH-1V)	66-16992	9186		PV

VALDOSTA MONUMENTS (GA54)

Location:	On permanent view at two locations in the town.

TYPE	REG/SER	CON. NO.	PI/NOTES	STATUS
☐ Lockheed 580 (T-33A)	52-9191	580-7245	At the airport south of the town.	RA
☐ McDonnell M.98DF Phantom II (RF-4C)	66-0467	2615	At the airport south of the town.	RA
☐ North American NA-190 Sabre (F-86D) (F-86L)	52-10057	190-782	In North Ashley Street.	PV

WAYNESBORO MONUMENT (GA55)

Location:	On permanent view in a park near the junction of Routes 24 and 25.

TYPE	REG/SER	CON. NO.	PI/NOTES	STATUS
☐ Lockheed 580 (T-33A)	51-6635	580-5967		PV

WILLACOOCHEE MONUMENT (GA56)

Location:	On permanent view at a business on Route 82.

TYPE	REG/SER	CON. NO.	PI/NOTES	STATUS
☐ Lockheed 580 (T-33A)	51-6612	580-5944		PV

WILLIAMSON MONUMENT (GA57)

Location:	On permanent view on in the centre of the town on Route 362.

TYPE	REG/SER	CON. NO.	PI/NOTES	STATUS
☐ Bell 205 Iroquois (UH-1H)	68-16609	11268		PV

WINGS N WIND MUSEUM (GA58)

Address:	455 Air Acres Road, Woodstock, Georgia 30188.
Tel:	770-928-9042
Admission:	Not yet open.
Location:	At Cartersville Airport which is about 2 miles west of the town and at a local farm.

The museum was established at the turn of the century and currently bases the majority of its aircraft at Cartersville. The Air Acres Museum operated from the field in the 1980s and 1990s and some of the people associated with this are still involved.

The three Beech 18s were transported to the site by road and one is under restoration. Future plans envisage the construction of a display hangar somewhere in the region. There is a connection between this collection and the L-Birds Flying Museum which is also at the airfield.

TYPE	REG/SER	CON. NO.	PI/NOTES	STATUS
☐ Beech D18S Expeditor (C-18S) (SNB-2) (SNB-5P) (RC-45J)	N9254	4122	Bu12354	RAC
☐ Beech D18S Expeditor (C18S) (SNB-2) (SNB-2P) (SNB-5) (TC-45J) (UC-45J)	N2810J	5515	Bu51210	RA

☐ Beech D18S Expeditor (C18S) (SNB-2C) (SNB-3) (SNB-5) (TC-45J) (UC-45J)	N2812J	5722	Bu51317	RA
☐ Boeing-Stearman A75N1 Kaydet (PT-17)				RAC
☐ Cessna 305A Bird Dog (L-19A) (O-1A)	N5234G	22404	51-12090	RAA
☐ Cessna 310D	N310LM/'78467'	39086		RAAX
☐ Convair 105 (L-13A)				RA
☐ Taylorcraft DCO-65 Grasshopper (L-2M)	N49168	L-5980		RAA
☐ Taylorcraft DCO-65 Grasshopper (L-2M)				RA

WORLD WAR TWO FLIGHT TRAINING MUSEUM (GA59)

Address: PO Box 1273, Douglas, Georgia 31534-2770.
Tel: 912-384-7818 **Email:** douglas63rd@accessatc.net
Admission: Friday-Saturday 1100-1600.
Location: At the airport which is about 3 miles south west of the town off Route 441.

Douglas was a major training base in World War II and a display has been set up in one of the buildings. The school was open from 1941 to 1944. The museum was dedicated on 11th October 2006. The three main areas of the display are a recreated barracks, flight training at Douglas and the home front. Aircraft owned by Don Brooks and his friends are in nearby hangars and Tom Reilly's workshop has moved from Florida. These aircraft are listed here as they can normally be seen by visitors to the museum.

TYPE	REG/SER	CON. NO.	PI/NOTES	STATUS
☐ Boeing-Stearman B75N1 Kaydet (N2S-3)	N5503N	75-7768	Bu38147 – registered as an A75N1 (PT-17)	RAA
☐ Curtiss 87-A4 Warhawk (P-40E) (Kittyhawk IA)	N2416X	16701	41-5709, (Soviet AF)	RAC
☐ Douglas DC-3A-456 Skytrain (C-47A) (Dakota III)	N99FS	12425	42-92606, KG395, 12919 (Canada), C-GZCR, (N89BF)	RAA
☐ Lockheed 580 (T-33A)	53-6132	580-9753	At airfield gate.	PV
☐ North American NA-88 Texan (AT-6D) (SNJ-5)	N91073	88-17204	42-85423, Bu85043	PVA
☐ North American NA-108 Mitchell (B-25J) (TB-25J) (Mitchell III)	N62163	108-47451	44-86697, 5239 (Canada), N92876, 0953 (Venezuela)	RAA
☐ North American NA-120 Twin Mustang (XP-82)	44-83887	120-43743	Incomplete	RAD
☐ North American NA-121 Texan (AT-6F)	N4488	121-42770	44-82048	RAA
☐ North American NA-122 Mustang (P-51D)				RAC

HAWAII

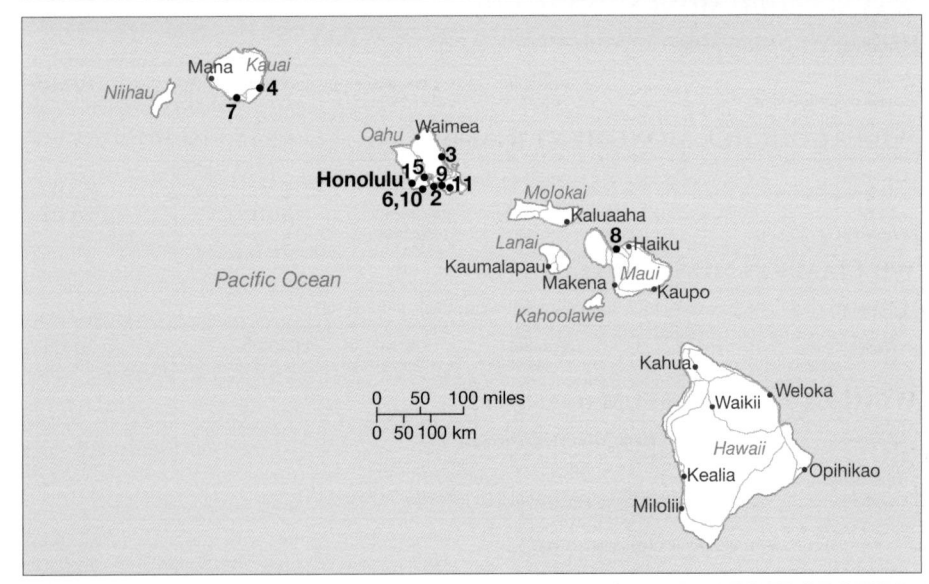

HAWAII MUSEUM OF FLYING/ NAVAL AIR MUSEUM BARBERS POINT (HI1)

Address: PO Box 75253, Kapolei, Hawaii 96707 -0253.
Tel: 808-682-3892   **Fax:** 808-682-4041   **Email:** navairmuseumbp@verizon.net
Admission: Monday-Friday 0800-1630 (By appointment)
Location: About 2 miles south west of Ewa.

Hawaii

Barbers Point airfield was home to squadrons of the Pacific Fleet of the US Navy until it closed in July 1999 after 57 years – the airfield is now used for civil flying. The museum was set up in 1999 and the Orion arrived by air soon afterwards. The displays will trace the story of naval aviation in the area and portray the history of Barbers Point. In addition to the aircraft there is a collection of vehicles.

TYPE	REG/SER	CON. NO.	PI/NOTES	STATUS
☐ Bell 205 Iroquois (UH-1H)	69-15708	11996		PVC
☐ Douglas A-4E Skyhawk (A4D-5)	Bu150023	13076		PV
☐ Douglas A-4E Skyhawk (A4D-5)	Bu151030	13200		PV
☐ Douglas A-4E Skyhawk	Bu152061	13449		PV
☐ Lockheed 185 Orion (P-3A) (UP-3A)	Bu152169	185-5139		PV
☐ McDonnell M.98AM Phantom II (F-4B) (F-4N)	Bu152291	1093		PV
☐ Sikorsky S-61B Sea King (HSS-2A) (SH-3A) (SH-3H)	Bu148043	61021		PV
☐ Sikorsky S-61B Sea King (SH-3D) (UH-3H)	Bu152701	61357		PV
☐ Sikorsky S-65A Sea Stallion (CH-53D)	Bu156964	65211		PV

HICKAM AIR FORCE BASE COLLECTION (HI2)

Address: 15 ABW/PA, 800 Scott Circle, Hickam Air Force Base, Hawaii 96853-5328.
Tel: 808-449-2490   **Fax:** 808-449-3017   **Email:** 15aw.pa@hickam.af.mil
Admission: By prior permission only.
Location: About 6 miles west of Honolulu off Route H1.

Opened in September 1938 on a site adjacent to Pearl Harbor, the base is named after Colonel Horace M. Hickam who was killed in a crash in November 1934. The Japanese raid on 7th December 1941 badly damaged the airfield and most of the buildings. The preserved aircraft represent types which have flown from the field.

TYPE	REG/SER	CON. NO.	PI/NOTES	STATUS
☐ Convair 8-10 Delta Dagger (F-102A)	54-1373	8-10-31		RA
☐ Douglas RB-26C Invader (A-26C)	44-35596	28875	44-35596, N5636V	RA
☐ McDonnell M.98DE Phantom II (F-4C)	63-7540	568		RA
☐ McDonnell M.199-1A Eagle (F-15A)	76-0018	197/A170		RA
☐ North American NA-170 Sabre (F-86E)	50-0653	170-75	50-0653, N5637V	RA

KANEOHE BAY MARINE CORPS AIR STATION COLLECTION (HI3)

Address: Box 63002, Kaneohe Bay, Hawaii 96863-3002.
Tel: 808-257-8839
Admission: By prior permission only.
Location: On the Mokapu Peninsula about 19 miles north east of Honolulu.

The site was chosen as an airfield in 1938 and construction commenced as the threat of war grew closer. Both fixed and rotary wing aircraft are normally in residence.
A history room is located in the Headquarters Building. A display of photographs traces the development of the site and documents, models, uniforms and personal items are also on show. Some of the preserved aircraft moved from Barbers Point when that base closed in 1999.
Five types are located close to the main gate with the others parked around the camp.

TYPE	REG/SER	CON. NO.	PI/NOTES	STATUS
☐ Bell 206A Sea Ranger (TH-57C)				RA
☐ Grumman G-121 Tracker (S2F-3) (S-2D)	Bu147870	10C		RA
☐ Lockheed 185 Orion (P3V-1) (P-3A) (TP-3A)	Bu151392	185-5105		RA
☐ Lockheed 726-45-17 Neptune (P2V-7) (P2V-7S) (SP-2H)	Bu150279	726-7282	Bu150279, (N3767U) –	RA
☐ McDonnell M.98EV Phantom II (F-4J) (F-4S)	'Bu153689'	2515	Bu153889	RAX
☐ Sikorsky S-62A Seaguard (HH-52A)	1356	62025		RA
☐ Sikorsky S-65A Sea Stallion (CH-53D)	Bu157740	65316		RA
☐ Sikorsky S-65A Sea Stallion (RH-53D)	Bu158748	65371		RA
☐ Vought F-8K Crusader (F8U-2) (F-8C)	Bu146973			RA

KAUAI VETERAN'S CENTER (HI4)

Address: 3215 Kapule Highway, Lihue, Kauai, Hawaii 96766.
Tel: kauaiveterans@aol.com
Admission: Aircraft on permanent view – display by prior permission only.
Location: Opposite Lihue Airport which is in the south eastern part of the island.

The local veterans group has set up a display of memorabilia in the building. The former Navy Skyhawk, a type which served in the state, is parked outside the group's headquarters building.

TYPE	REG/SER	CON. NO.	PI/NOTES	STATUS
☐ Douglas A-4E Skyhawk (A4D-5)	Bu151036	13206		PV

PACIFIC AEROSPACE MUSEUM (HI5)

Address: 3000 Rodgers Boulevard, Terminal Box 7, Honolulu International Airport, Hawaii 96819-1897.
Tel: 808-839-0777
Admission: Daily 0900-1800.
Location: In the western suburbs of the city.

A display set up by this museum opened in the terminal building in the late 1980s, tracing the history of aviation in Hawaii since the early days. Modern techniques have been employed to present the information.

There are many photographs, models, engines and components on view. There are a number of 'hands-on' exhibits and videos showing significant events in the aviation history of the islands can be seen.

PACIFIC AVIATION MUSEUM (HI6)

Address:	Hangar 37, Ford Island, 319 Lexington Boulevard, Honolulu, Hawaii 96818.
Tel:	808-441-1016 Fax: 808-441-1019 Email: info@pacificaviationmuseum.org
Admission:	Daily 0900-1700.
Location:	About 8 miles north west of Honolulu off Route H1.

The ambitious plans to set up a museum at Ford Field came to fruition when the display opened on 7th December 2006 in one hangar. This date commemorates the 65th anniversary of the Japanese attack. Three hangars which survived the raid on Pearl Harbor will eventually contain a variety of exhibitions.

Over 300 aircraft were destroyed or damaged and many ships in the Pacific Fleet were sunk. There was a large loss of life as many areas of the base were hit. In addition to these buildings the display will include the control tower. The history of naval aviation on Ford Island and Air Force operations in the Pacific region will be highlighted.

The visitor is transported to the site by shuttle bus and then enters the former seaplane Hangar 37 which survived the 1941 raid. A short film including historic footage is shown. A walk along a corridor with photos is accompanied by sound effects of life before the attack. In this hangar there is a genuine Mitsubishi Zero, displayed as it would have been on the deck of the carrier *Hiryu* at dawn on 7th December 1941. Suspended above is the Aeronca which was actually in the air at the time and saw the first wave of Japanese aircraft attacking.

The P-40 replica in this area is one made for the film 'Tora Tora Tora' The Mitchell honours Doolittle's famous raid on the Japanese mainland. This aircraft was displayed at Hickam Air Force Base for a long period, as were the two Sabres, the Delta Dagger and the Phantom. The B-25 has been modified to represent the B-25B version used on the raid.

The Dauntless is the centrepiece of the Battle of Midway exhibit. The Wildcat is shown in a diorama featuring the bitter fighting which took place around Guadalcanal and highlighting the story of the 'Cactus Air Force'. The Stearman is the aircraft in which President Bush (Senior) made his first solo in 1942.

In June 2010 a new gallery honoring the Korean war was opened. A lifesize diorama depicting 'MiG Alley' has been constructed in Hangar 79. The recently restored Sabre is mounted on a special platform in a takeoff attitude. Suspended overhead in a banked turn is a MiG-15. These classic jet fighters were in combat many times during the conflict.

A collection of types used in the islands after World War II can also be seen in this hangar. All branches of the services have bases on the islands. The Cessna O-2s arrived from the University of Hawaii.

Also on Ford Island are a number of naval exhibits and memorials to sunken ships. The battleship USS *Arizona* was launched in November 1916 and served in the latter stages of World War I. A memorial to the 1,177 men who lost their lives has been erected close to the museum. There are plans to further develop the exhibition over the next few years.

TYPE	REG/SER	CON. NO.	PI/NOTES	STATUS
☐ Aeronca 65TC	NC33768	C-9391T	NC33768, N33768	PV
☐ Beech D18S Expeditor (C18S) (JRB-4) (SNB-5) (TC-45J) (UC-45J)	N44608	8274	Bu44607	RA
☐ Bell 205 Iroquois (UH-1H)	69-15708	11996		PV
☐ Bell 209 Huey Cobra (AH-1G) (AH-1S)	66-15298	20054		PV
☐ Boeing 464-259 Stratofortress (B-52E)	57-0101	464090	Front fuselage only.	PV
☐ Boeing-Stearman B75N1 Kaydet (N2S-3)	N5102N	75-6707	Bu07103	PV
☐ Cessna 337M Super Skymaster (O-2A)	68-10972	337M0248		RA
☐ Cessna 337M Super Skymaster (O-2A)	68-11142	337M0367		RA
☐ Cessna 337M Super Skymaster (O-2A)	68-11145	337M0370		RA
☐ Convair 8-10 Delta Dagger (F-102A)	55-3366	8-10-75		PV
☐ Curtiss A87-A2 Kittyhawk I	'67'	18723	AK979, 1064 (Canada), N5672N, N151U, N9DA, (N151U), N41JR, N41JA, NX40FT	PVX
☐ Curtiss 87-B2 Warhawk (P-40E) (FSM)	'39411'			PVX
☐ Curtiss 87-B2 Warhawk (P-40E) (FSM)	'191 64P'			RAX
☐ Douglas DC-6A Liftmaster (C-118A)	N48AW	44633	53-3262, N44917, N140JR, N87BL, HK-3438X, ETP-10024, XA-TDR	RA
☐ Douglas SBD-2 Dauntless	Bu2173	699		RAC
☐ Douglas SBD-5 Dauntless	Bu36177	4816		PV
☐ Douglas SBD-5 Dauntless (FSM)	'Bu4687'			RAX
☐ Douglas TA-3B Skywarrior (A3D-2T)	Bu144867	12102		PV
☐ Grumman G-36 Wildcat (F4F-3A)	Bu12296	5956	Bu12296, N3210D	PV
☐ Grumman G-50 Hellcat (F6F-5) (F6F-5N)	Bu94352	A-12104		RAD
☐ Grumman G-50 Hellcat (F6F-5) (F6F-5N)	Bu94484	A-12236		RAD
☐ Grumman G-303 Tomcat (F-14D)	Bu163904	614		PV
☐ McDonnell M.98DJ Phantom II (F-4C)	64-0792	1105		PV
☐ McDonnell M.199-1A Eagle (F-15A)	76-0063	249/A215		PV
☐ Mitsubishi A6M2 Zero Sen Model 21				PVD
☐ Mitsubishi A6M2 Zero Sen Model 21	'BII-120'	5358	NX58245, 'EII-142', 'EII-102'	PVX
☐ North American NA-62 Mitchell (B-25B)	'02261'		Composite using parts from TB-25N c/n 108-33352 44-30077, N2849G, c/n 108-33902 44-30627, 4115 (Venezuela), N45HA and one other unidentified aircraft.	PVX
☐ North American NA-88 Texan (AT-6D) (SNJ-5) (SNJ-5B)				RA
☐ North American NA-172 Sabre (F-86E)	51-2841	172-124		RAC
☐ North American NA-190 Sabre (F-86D) (F-86L)	52-4191	190-594	52-4191, N2401H	PV
☐ Sikorsky S-61B Sea King (SH-3D) (UH-3H)	Bu152700	61356		PV
☐ Stinson V-76 Sentinel (L-5E)	'44-16890'	76-4483 (?)	44-18194	RACX
☐ WSK Lim-2 [MiG-15bis]	'1524'	1B 015-24	1524 (Poland) – in false Soviet markings.	RAX

PACIFIC MISSILE RANGE MONUMENT (HI7)

Location:	By prior permission only at the site at Kekaha on the south west coast of Kauai.

TYPE	REG/SER	CON. NO.	PI/NOTES	STATUS
☐ Sikorsky S-61B Sea King (HSS-2) (HH-3A) (UH-3A)	Bu147140	61004		RA
☐ Sikorsky S-61B Sea King (SH-3D) (UH-3H)	Bu154106	61392		RA

PAPER AIRPLANE MUSEUM (HI8)

Address:	70 East Ka'ahumanu Avenue, Kahului, Maui, Hawaii 96732-2176.
Tel:	808-877-8916
Admission:	Monday-Saturday 0900-1700.
Location:	In Maui Mall in the centre of the town.

The displays at this fascinating museum trace the history of aviation in Hawaii from 1910 up to the present day. On show are many historic documents and photographs. Over 2000 model aircraft constructed of paper and metal can be seen. There are also model trains and boats on view. Local musical instruments also feature.

UNITED STATES ARMY MUSEUM OF HAWAII (HI9)

Address:	PO Box 8064, Schofield Barracks, Hawaii 96830.
Tel:	808-955-9552 **Email:** info@hiarmymuseumsoc.org
Admission:	Tuesday-Saturday 0900-1700
Location:	At Fort de Russy in the eastern suburbs of Honolulu near Waikiki Beach.

The military history of the islands along with that of the US Army in the region is portrayed in the displays. The exhibition opened in 1976 in Battery Randolph, a former coastal artillery emplacement at Fort DeRussy. The structure was built in 1911 to house two 14-inch guns that could fire shells around 14 miles and was part of the coastal defence system protecting Honolulu Harbour.

Army aviation arrived in Hawaii in July when 14 men were dispatched from the mainland. Combat types followed four years later. A Huey Cobra is on show at the museum.

TYPE	REG/SER	CON. NO.	PI/NOTES	STATUS
☐ Bell 204 Iroquois (HU-1A) (UH-1A)	59-1659	118		RA
☐ Bell 209 Huey Cobra (AH-1G) (AH-1F)	67-15796	20460		PV

UNIVERSITY OF HAWAII / HONOLULU COMMUNITY COLLEGE (HI10)

Address:	874 Dillingham Boulevard, Honolulu, Hawaii 96817.
Tel:	808-945-9211
Admission:	By prior permission only.
Location:	At Lagoon Drive on the southern side of Honolulu IAP.

The Territorial Trade School was established at Palama in 1920 and was renamed the Honolulu Technical School in 1955. A decade later it became part of the University of Hawaii and took up its present name in 1996. The aviation maintenance section is located in hangars and workshops at the International Airport. A range of instruction airframes is in use including a DC-9 flown in the area by Hawaiian Airlines.

The Emair MA-1B was based on the Boeing-Stearman 75 and designed for agricultural work. The prototype was built in New Zealand in 1969 and production took place at Harlingen in Texas. The MA-1B featured a more powerful engine and 73 examples of all versions had been completed when production ceased in the late 1980s. Emair was part of the Hawaiian Murray company so it is appropriate that one should return to its state of its conception.

TYPE	REG/SER	CON. NO.	PI/NOTES	STATUS
☐ Bell 205 Iroquois (UH-1H)	68-15650	10580		RA
☐ Bell 205 Iroquois (UH-1H)	66-16801	8995		RA
☐ Bell 205 Iroquois (UH-1H)	67-17629	9827		RA
☐ Cessna 172K	N79892	17258227		RA
☐ Cessna 172N	N11446	17270588		RA
☐ Cessna 310F	N699X	39120		RA
☐ Douglas DC-9-51	N699HA	47763	N699HA, (N969HA)	RA
☐ Emroth Emair MA-1B	N88432	044		RA
☐ Hiller UH12C Raven (H-23G) (OH-23G)	N90634	1756	64-15247	RA
☐ Lockheed 580 (T-33A)	51-6533	580-5865		RA
☐ Piper PA-28-140 Cherokee	N3759B	28-22519		RA
☐ Sikorsky S-58 Choctaw (H-34A) (CH-34A)	N73538	58497	55-4490	RA

WHEELER ARMY AIRFIELD COLLECTION (HI11)

Address:	Wahiawa, Hawaii 96854-5000.
Tel:	808-656-1414
Admission:	About 1 mile south of Wahiawa off Route 99.
Location:	By prior permission only.

The airfield opened in February 1922 and is named after Major Sheldon H. Wheeler, the Commanding Officer of Luke Field in Hawaii, who was killed on an exhibition flight in 1921. The Air Force used the base until 1991 when it was turned over to the Army. The Curtiss P-40 replica highlights the role of the field in World War II. At the time of the 1941 Japanese attack most fighter units in the islands were using this type. Army units from Schofield Barracks flew helicopters from the site for many years and a collection of rotary wing types has been put on display since the transfer of the field along with a room containing memorabilia.

TYPE	REG/SER	CON. NO.	PI/NOTES	STATUS
☐ Bell 204 Iroquois (UH-1C) (UH-1M)	66-15127	1855		RA
☐ Bell 206A Kiowa (OH-58A)	70-15358	40909		RA
☐ Bell 209 Huey Cobra (AH-1G) (AH-1S)	'70-15036'	20054	66-15298	RAX
☐ Curtiss 87-B2 Warhawk (P-40E) (FSM)				RAX
☐ Hiller UH12C Raven (H-23G) (OH-23G)	64-15245	1754		RA

IDAHO

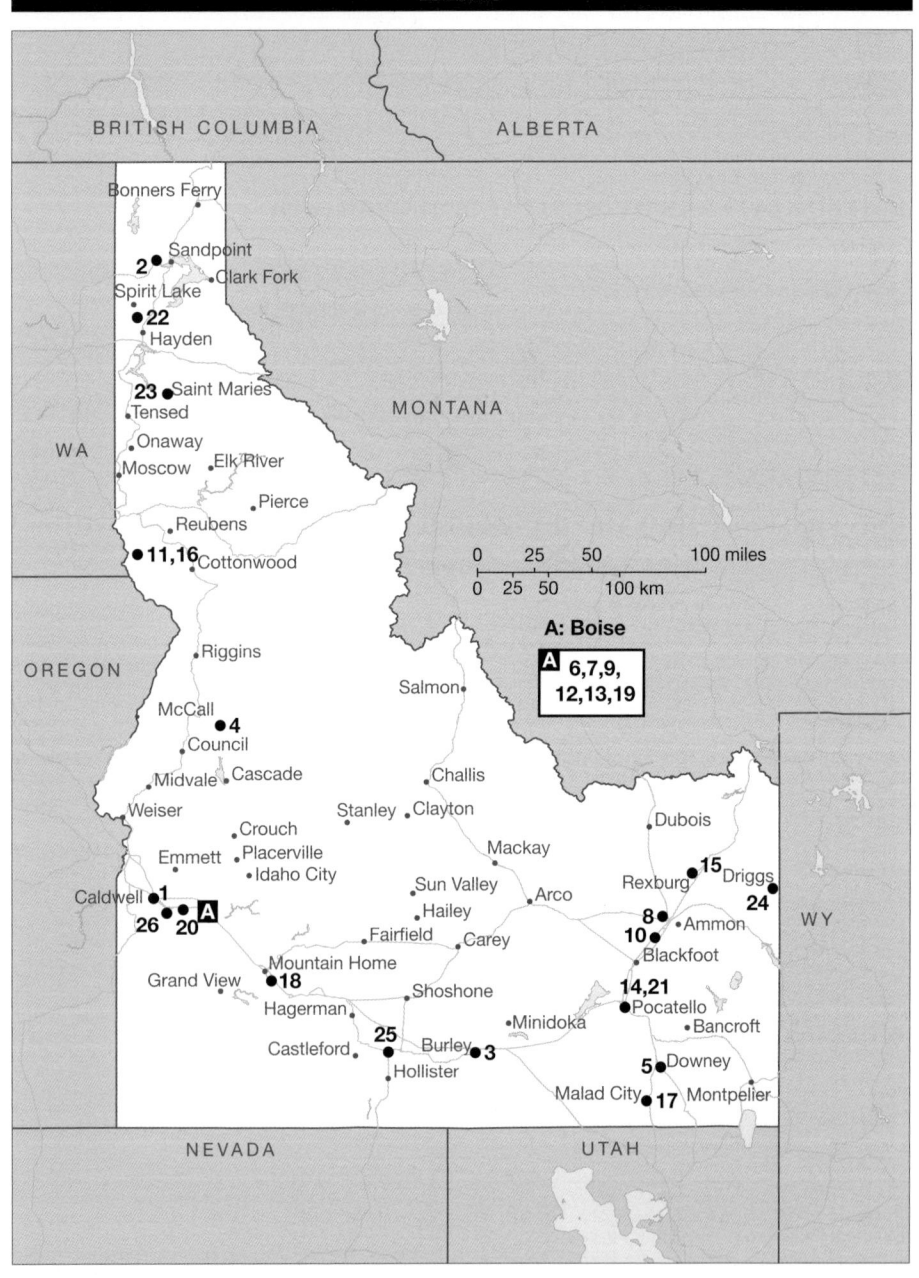

Idaho

AEROPLANES OVER IDAHO MUSEUM (ID1)

Address:	5017 Aviation Way, Caldwell, Idaho 83605.
Tel:	208-455-1708 **Email:** info@aeroplanesoveridaho.com
Admission:	Daily 1000-1600.
Location:	At Caldwell Airport which is in the south eastern suburbs of the town.

This collection opened to the public in 2003 and most of the aircraft are owned by members. The museum also carries out approved maintenance on privately owned types. Education features prominently in the programmes carried out at Caldwell. Displays in the hangar area are being developed.

The founder of the museum Maslen Hollbrook owns a large part of the fleet. He opened the first sky-diving school in California in the 1960s and flew with United Airlines for over three decades. He is also a regular competitor in air races and has been at Reno many times.

There are several interesting aircraft in the collection. Let C-11 was modified for racing from one of the batch of Czechoslavakia-built Yak-11 trainers imported into France by Jean Salis. He acquired over 30 former Egyptian Air Force machines in the 1980s. The aircraft was imported into the USA in 1987 and the initial idea was to convert it into a replica of the Yak-3U. This project was abandoned but the aircraft is still registered as a Yak-3UR.

The Shoestring is a low wing design which was flown in many races by the late Judy Wagner. She set many cross country records in a Beech Bonanza in the early 1970s. Maslen Holbrook has flown the Shoestring at recent Reno races.

Another midget racer is the Lutz Flying Dutchman. This aircraft was involved in a fatal crash in Idaho in the late 1980s. The airframe was rebuilt and it flew again in 1993.

TYPE	REG/SER	CON. NO.	PI/NOTES	STATUS
☐ Aeronca 65TC Grasshopper (O-58B) (L-3B)				PVA
☐ Aeronca 7CCM Champion (L-16B)	N4687E	7CCM-217		PVA
☐ Antonov An-2	N134HS	234025	(Soviet)	PVA
☐ Beech D18S Expeditor (C-45H)	N524C	AF-523	52-10593, N9868Z, N17MM	PVA
☐ Bellanca 14-19-2 Cruisemaster	N9832B	4084		PVA
☐ Cessna 140	N2544N	12800	NC2544N	PVA
☐ Cessna 150H	N50406	15069280		PVA
☐ Cessna 180	N1674C	30374		PVA
☐ Cessna 185 Skywagon	N7801L	'F25023'		PVA
☐ Cessna A188A Agwagon 300	N4401Q	18800801		PVA
☐ Cessna 190	N9320A	7399		PVA
☐ Cessna 195A	N3170G	7590		PVA
☐ Douglas A-4L Skyhawk (A4D-2N) (A-4C)	N156AT	12617	Bu148307	PVA
☐ Gannett Peak Aviation 2PCLM-T LFO-14-1	N95EV	1		PVA
☐ Kreimendahl Shoestring IV	N44JW	WS-711		PVA
☐ Let C-11 [Yakovlev Yak-11]	N134US	DMC003	(Egypt), N134US, (N543SH)	PVA
☐ Lutz Flying Dutchman	N38Z	LFD-13-4		PVA
☐ North American NA-182 Texan (T-6G)	N9701Z	182-536	51-14849, 114849 (France)	PVA
☐ Piper PA-23 Apache	N2214P	23-823		PVA
☐ Piper PA-23 Apache	N2233P	23-842		PVA
☐ Pitts S-1C Special	N8008A	5932		PVA
☐ Snow S-2R	N5511X	1711R		PVA
☐ Snow S-2R	N8523V	2283R		PVA
☐ Stinson V-76 Sentinel (L-5G)	N63370	76-4625	(USAAF)	PVA
☐ Symonds Supercat	N90707	007		PVA
☐ Vollmann Eagle Heli	N135HS	1-23		PVA

BIRD AVIATION MUSEUM AND INVENTION CENTER (ID2)

Address:	1655 Glengary Road, Sagle, Idaho 83860.
Tel:	208-255-4321 **Fax:** 208-255-7630 **Email:** info@birdaviationmuseum.com
Admission:	Monday-Saturday 0800-1600
Location:	About 10 miles west of Sandpoint.

Forest Bird was born in Massachusetts in 1921 and learned to fly in his teens. He joined the army in 1941 and served as a technical training instructor. He also flew most types in service including early jets and helicopters. He was an inventor and designed some of the first mass produced ventilators for heart patients.

In 1967 he developed the Bird Innovator which was a conversion of the PBY Catalina. The aircraft was fitted with two 340 hp Lycoming engines outboard of the normal Pratt and Whitney radials. Only one was completed and it has now been converted back to standard configuration by a later owner. He moved to Idaho many years ago where his company, making breathing equipment, is now based. He received the Presidential Citizens Medal from George Bush in 2007 and in 2009 Barack Obama awarded him the National Medal of Technology and Innovation. Over the years he has collected and restored vintage aircraft, cars and motorcycles.

In 2007 the museum opened in a 16,000 square feet purpose-built facility. The aircraft on show are both modern and classic types. Bird has modified many of the types to incorporate his inventions. The oldest is a 1927 Waco 10 fitted with modern avionics, a type in which he made his first solo at the age of 14. Another classic is the 1937 Beech F17D. This version of the famous Staggerwing was in production between the spring of 1938 and 1941. The biplane is powered by a 275 hp seven cylinder Jacobs radial.

Two Piper Cubs can be seen. Both have been re-engined with 100 hp Continental engines to cope with the high altitude nature of the terrain. N281RD operates on floats and is fitted with a catalytic ignition system. The other was owned by Dr. Bird's father and has been promised to the National Air and Space Museum. The Seabee has been extensively modified with wings of increased span and a higher powered engine. One of the Alon A-2s has been fitted with folding wings and the other has a 150 hp engine and a Lasar ignition system.

Jack Riley has been responsible for modifying and upgrading a number of production types. The Turbine Eagle is a basic Cessna 421C fitted with two Pratt and Whitney PT-6A turboprops. Increased fuel capacity gives the aircraft an endurance of more than six hours and a cruising speed of more than 300 mph. The Schweizer glider was at the Silverwood Theme Park when they had an aircraft exhibition and offered sailplane rides to visitors. The Chipmunk is powered by a 200 hp Lycoming engine and is fitted with a constant speed propeller, an inverted fuel system and a one piece canopy.

This fascinating collection is a fitting tribute to an engineer and inventor and shows the variety and ingenuity of his work in a number of fields. As the majority of the aircraft are airworthy at times some may be away from the museum.

TYPE	REG/SER	CON. NO.	PI/NOTES	STATUS
☐ Alon A-2	N103DB	A-86	N6586Q	PVA
☐ Alon A-2	N21DB	A-232	N5632F	PVA
☐ Beech F17D (UC-43C)	NC291Y	261	NC291Y, 42-97049, NC49704, N49704	PVA
☐ Bell 47G-3B-2	N481RD	6716		PVA
☐ Bell 206B Jet Ranger	N581RD	1497		PVA
☐ Bell 212	N381RD	30850		PVA
☐ Bellanca 8KCAB Decathlon	N276R	713-93		PVA
☐ Boeing-Stearman B75N1 Kaydet (N2S-3)	N2803D	75-6822	Bu07218	PVA
☐ Cessna TU.206G Stationair	N981RD	U20605872		PVA
☐ Cessna T337H Super Skymaster	N181RD	33701881	N1389L	PVA
☐ De Havilland DHC.1 Chipmunk 1B-2-S5	N11PB	177-215	18039 (Canada), CF-RRS	PVA
☐ Grob G.109B	N113DB	6365		PVA
☐ North American NA-75 Harvard II	N901H	75-3439	3165 (Canada), MM?????, N3231H	PVA
☐ Piper J-3C-100 Cub (J-3C-65)	N281RD	16087		
☐ Piper J-3C-100 Cub (J-3C-65)	NC26044	3995	NC26044, N26044	PVA
☐ Piper PA-18-150 Super Cub	N881RD	18-8109047		PVA
☐ Republic RC-3 Seabee	N781RD	511	NC6298K, N6298K	PVD
☐ Riley Turbine Eagle (Cessna 421C)	N81RD	421C0291	N42EW	PVA
☐ Schweizer SGS.2-33A	N1179S	229		PVA
☐ Waco 10 (GXE)	NC4780W	1249	NC4780, N4780	PVA

BURLEY MONUMENT (ID3)

Location:	On permanent view at J.R. Simplot Airport which is about 3 miles east of the town.

TYPE	REG/SER	CON. NO.	PI/NOTES	STATUS
☐ Bell 205 Iroquois (UH-1H)	67-17281	9479		PV
☐ Lockheed 580 (T-33A)	52-9594	580-7754		PV

DC-3 HIGH ADVENTURE CLUB (ID4)

Address:	336 Deinhard Lane, McCall, Idaho 83638
Tel:	208-634-7142 (Airport) Email: dredgeea@micron.net
Admission:	By prior permission only.
Location:	Near the airport which is about 1 mile south of the town.

The group has acquired the DC-3 from the US Forest Service which frequently bases an airworthy example of the type at the field. They aim to restore the aircraft and collect memorabilia relating to the famous transport. A display will be set up in the fuselage. A DC-3 'Wall of Fame' is also planned.

The aircraft was transferred to the US Navy in 1944 and served with them until 1958 when it joined the Army at Fort Huachua in Arizona. After a period in store it moved to McCall in the early 1990s and provided spares for the active fleet.

TYPE	REG/SER	CON. NO.	PI/NOTES	STATUS
☐ Douglas DC-3A-456 Skytrain (C-47A) (R4D-5) (EC-47H)	'O-7220'	13318	42-108947, Bu17220	PV

DOWNEY MONUMENT (ID5)

Location:	On permanent view in the town by Interstate 15.

TYPE	REG/SER	CON. NO.	PI/NOTES	STATUS
Bell 205 Iroquois (UH-1H)				PV

FRUITLAND MONUMENT (ID6)

Location:	On permanent view at the Idaho Motor Pool off Interstate 84.

TYPE	REG/SER	CON. NO.	PI/NOTES	STATUS
☐ Bell 206A Kiowa (OH-58A)	70-15642	41193		PV

GOWEN FIELD AIR NATIONAL GUARD BASE COLLECTION (ID7)

Address:	124th Wing/PA, 3787 West Aeronca Street, Boise, Idaho 83705-8006.
Tel:	208-422-5398 Email: pa.124wg@idbois.ang.af.mil
Admission:	By prior permission only.
Location:	On the south side of the airport which is about 4 miles south of the city off Interstate 84.

The first airfield in Boise opened in 1926 and is now the site of the University. The local authority started purchasing land in the late 1930s and field opened in 1938. In 1941 it was named after local aviator Lt. Paul Gowen, who was killed in Panama in 1938. The first Idaho Air National Guard unit was formed in October 1946 and moved to the airfield the following year. Its commanding officer was Colonel Thomas Lanphier, who was credited with shooting down the Mitsubishi 'Betty' carrying Admiral Yamamoto and his staff. Apart from periods of active service the unit has been based at Boise ever since. Over the years the wing has flown the P-51 Mustang, the F-86A Sabre, the F-94H Starfire, the F-89B Scorpion, the F-86L Sabre, the F-102A Delta Dagger and the RF-4C and F-4G versions of the Phantom. The current equipment is the A-10A Thunderbolt and the C-130E Hercules.

A heritage park is being set up near the Wing Headquarters. The Army National Guard has a helicopter base in the complex and the four Bell types are mounted around the site.

Idaho

TYPE	REG/SER	CON. NO.	PI/NOTES	STATUS
☐ Bell 204 Iroquois (UH-1C) (UH-1M)	65-9426	1326		RA
☐ Bell 204 Iroquois (UH-1C) (UH-1M)	'66-15138'	1957	66-15229.	RAX
☐ Bell 205 Iroquois (UH-1H)	68-15481	10411		RA
☐ Bell 209 Huey Cobra (AH-1G) (AH-1F)	67-15496	20160		RA
☐ Convair 8-10 Delta Dagger (F-102A)	53-1816	8-10-26		RA
☐ Fairchild-Republic A-10A Thunderbolt II	78-0608	A10-228		RA
☐ Lockheed 382-8B Hercules (C-130E)	62-1846	382-3809		RA
☐ Lockheed 580 (T-33A)	55-4351	580-9795	55-4351, N815NA	RA
☐ McDonnell M.98DF Phantom II (RF-4C)	68-0594	3598		RA
☐ McDonnell M.98HO Phantom II (F-4E) (F-4G)	69-7551	3995		RA

HOFF COLLECTION (ID8)

Address: 1940 International Way, Idaho Falls, Idaho 83402-4908.
Tel: 208-524-1202 **Fax:** 208-524-8924 **Email:** aeromark@onewest.net
Admission: By prior permission only.
Location: At the airport which is in the north western suburbs of the city off Interstate 15.

Bob Hoff is a collector and restorer of vintage aircraft. He regularly offers flights in his fleet. The Beech D17S was delivered to a Texas owner in 1939 and two years later was impressed for use by the British Air Commission in Washington, DC. They flew it for another couple of years and after World War II the aircraft has had several owners in a number of states. Hoff carried out a major rebuild in the early 1970s and since then has flown it regularly to meetings around the state.

TYPE	REG/SER	CON. NO.	PI/NOTES	STATUS
☐ Beech D17S	N114H	327	NC21904, EB280, NC21904, NC114H	RAA
☐ Beech D18S	N90552	A-420		RAA
☐ Boeing-Stearman B75N1 Kaydet (N2S-3)	N75808	75-2638	Bu4308	RAA
☐ Cessna 180	N2216C	30516		RAA
☐ Cessna 182Q Skylane II	N4946N	18267471		RAA

IDAHO AVIATION HERITAGE MUSEUM / HALL OF FAME (ID9)

Address: PO Box 6378, Boise, Idaho 83707.
Tel: 208-853-8585 **Email:** millerwilliamc@qwest.net
Admission: In the planning stage.
Location: On the south side of Boise Airport which is about four miles south of the town off Interstate 84.

This museum is raising funds for a purpose-built complex which will be sited on land adjacent to Gowen Field and where the story of aviation in the state will be portrayed. About 30 aircraft have been promised to the museum and three types known are listed. Construction of the facility is yet to start. There will be a Hall of Fame building, two exhibition halls, a restoration facility plus a theatre and library. A collection of artefacts is held by the group and temporary exhibitions have been staged around the area to promote the project. At the present time the Hall of Fame is located at Boise State University and also has displays in eight airport terminals around the state where famous Idaho aviators are honoured with photographs and documents tracing their careers. Hopefully this ambitious project will soon become a reality.

TYPE	REG/SER	CON. NO.	PI/NOTES	STATUS
☐ Curtiss 1C Jenny (JN-4D)				RA
☐ Curtiss 50C Robin C-2				RA
☐ Wright 1902 Glider (R)				RA

IDAHO FALLS MONUMENT (ID10)

Location: On permanent view at the airport which is about 2 miles north west of the city.

TYPE	REG/SER	CON. NO.	PI/NOTES	STATUS
☐ North American NA-201 Sabre (F-86D) (F-86L)	53-1022	201-466		PV

IDAHO FIRST FLIGHT (ID11)

Address: 2309 Ripon Avenue, Lewiston, Idaho 83501-6155.
Admission: By prior permission only.
Location: At Lewiston Airport which is in the southern part of the city.

On 13th October 1910 James Ward took off from the fairgrounds in Lewiston in a Curtiss D and made the first flight in Idaho. The aircraft had been transported by rail by Glenn Curtiss. A number of circuits of the area took place but the plane crashed on the 15th when the engine failed at an altitude of 200 feet and the forward control also failed. The group has built a replica of the aircraft and plan to fly it on the centenary of the event.

TYPE	REG/SER	CON. NO.	PI/NOTES	STATUS
☐ Curtiss D Pusher (R)	N909JJ	WCP-004		RAA

IDAHO MILITARY HISTORY MUSEUM (ID12)

Address: 4040 West Guard Street, Boise, Idaho 83705-5004.
Tel: 208-422-4841 **Email:** gayle.alvarez@idbois.ang.af.mil
Admission: Tuesday-Sunday 1200-1600.
Location: Next to Gowen Field which on the south side of the airport.

The museum has displays tracing the military history of the state. On show are many models, photographs, uniforms and documents. All major conflicts in which Idaho people have served are highlighted.

The history of Gowen Field, which opened in 1936, is portrayed in detail as is that of the Idaho Air National Guard. An engine from a Huey Cobra, components and two flight simulators are on show.

TYPE	REG/SER	CON. NO.	PI/NOTES	STATUS
☐ Fairchild M-62C Cornell (PT-23)	N60994	240HO	42-49216 – possible identity.	RA
☐ McDonnell M.98DF Phantom II (RF-4C)	69-0350	3688		PV

IDAHO STATE HISTORICAL SOCIETY (ID13)

Address:	2205 Old Penitentiary Road, Boise, Idaho 83712
Tel:	208-234-2682 Fax: 208-334-2774 Email: keith.peterson@ishs.idaho.net
Admission:	June–August daily 1000-1700.
Location:	In the eastern part of the city off Warm Springs Road.

The society is responsible for a number of historic sites and exhibitions around the state. In 2002 a new display opened in the Old Penitentiary. The basis was the collection of historic arms and military memorabilia assembled over 60 years by the late J. Curtis Earl. Artefacts from 3500 BC up to modern times were put on show. The MiG-15 flew to Idaho from Arizona and visited many airports to promote the exhibition.

TYPE	REG/SER	CON. NO.	PI/NOTES	STATUS
☐ Mikoyan-Gurevich MiG-15UTI	N2069		2238 (China)	PV

IDAHO STATE UNIVERSITY (ID14)

Address:	921 South 8th Avenue, Pocatello, Idaho 83209.
Tel:	208-232-8485 Email: stewpete@isu.edu
Admission:	By prior permission only.
Location:	At 1455 Flightline, Pocatello Airport which is about 3 miles west of the town off I30.

The Academy of Idaho was established in 1901 and opened a campus in Pocatello. A change of name to the Idaho Technical Institute took place in 1915 and the current title was adopted in 1963. The well-equipped workshops contain a number of engines and test rigs.

The fleet of instructional airframes includes a Fairchild-built F-27. In the mid-1950s Fokker granted Fairchild a licence to build the successful Friendship airliner in the USA. The example at Pocatello spent many years in corporate use before arriving at the university.

The students also undertake work on behalf of local owners and a number of complete rebuilds can be seen in the hangar. New parts are constructed using traditional methods. The owner of the Seabee provided a second fuselage for spares use.

TYPE	REG/SER	CON. NO.	PI/NOTES	STATUS
☐ Beech 58P Baron	N159Z	TJ-178		RA
☐ Beech B100 King Air	N4415L	BE-67	N6035H, N522CF, 90-0060	RA
☐ Beech M35 Bonanza	N762AA	D-6168		RA
☐ Bell 205 Iroquois (UH-1D) (UH-1H)	66-16145	5239		RA
☐ Cessna 140				RAC
☐ Cessna 170				RAC
☐ Cessna 182				RAC
☐ Cessna 210	N7392E	57092		RA
☐ Cessna 310A Blue Canoe (L-27A) (U-3A)	58-2141	38115		RA
☐ Cessna 421	N824LQ	4210135		RA
☐ Fairchild F-27F Friendship	N366SB	97	N20W, N2724R	RA
☐ Piper PA-38-112 Tomahawk	N4265E	38-78A0513		RA
☐ Republic RC-3 Seabee				RAC
☐ Taylorcraft DCO-65 Grasshopper (L-2M)				RA

LEGACY FLIGHT MUSEUM (ID15)

Address:	PO Box 122, 35 Airport Road, Rexburg, Idaho 83440-0122
Tel:	208-351-0004 Email: legacyflightmuseum@hotmail.com
Admission:	June–August Monday-Saturday 0900-1700; September–May Saturday 0900-1700.
Location:	At the airport which is in the western suburbs of the town off Route 33.

Two private owners at the airport have combined to set up the museum. The pride of the fleet is the famous yellow Mustang in which Bob Hoover delighted air show crowds for many years. The Kingcobra has been restored to its original colours and is one of few still airworthy.

Two Skyraiders, one of which served in France and Chad, are in the fleet. The aircraft are all in flying condition and often visit local airshows. An exhibition of memorabilia has been set up in the hangar where photographs and components can be seen.

TYPE	REG/SER	CON. NO.	PI/NOTES	STATUS
☐ Beech D17S (GB-2)	N217SD	3098	Bu12338, NC9595H, CF-FEQ, N1117S, N110WA, N1199S	PVA
☐ Bell 33 Kingcobra (P-63A)	N163FS		42-69021, NX90805, N90805	PVA
☐ Boeing-Stearman B75N1 Kaydet (N2S-3)	N4498N	75-6818	Bu07214	PVA
☐ Cavalier Mustang II (F-51D) (North American NA-122)	N551BJ		67-22579, 519 (Bolivia), C-GXRG, N52BH, N251RM	PVA
☐ Cessna 305C Bird Dog (L-19E) (O-1E)	N305CM	24558	24558 (France)	PVA
☐ Douglas A-1E Skyraider (AD-5)	N39147	9540	Bu12683, 132683 (SNVAF)	PVA
☐ Douglas AD-4NA Skyraider (AD-4N)	NX2088G	7735	Bu126935, 56 (France), 56 (Chad), F-AZFO	PVA
☐ Grumman G-40 Avenger (TBM-3) (TBM-3E)	N7226C	2757	Bu85938	RAA
☐ Howard DGA-15P	N70312	1712	NC70312	PVA

Idaho

☐ Interavia E-3	N9153	0208		PVA
☐ North American NA-78 Texan (AT-6A) (SNJ-3)	N676JD	78-6803	41-16425, Bu01822, N65550, 7676 (South Africa)	PVA
☐ North American NA-88 Texan (AT-6D) (SNJ-5)	N6900C	88-16678	42-84897, Bu84867	PVA
☐ North American NA-122 Mustang (P-51D) (Mustang IV)	N51RH	122-41279	44-74739, 9297 (Canada), N8672E, N151Q	PVA
☐ Taylorcraft DCO-65 Grasshopper (L-2M)				PVA

LEWISTON MONUMENT (ID16)

Location: On permanent view at the airport which is in the southern part of the city.

TYPE	REG/SER	CON. NO.	PI/NOTES	STATUS
☐ Lockheed 580 (T-33A)	51-6717	580-6049		

MALAD CITY MONUMENT (ID17)

Location: On permanent view near the library in the centre of the town.

TYPE	REG/SER	CON. NO.	PI/NOTES	STATUS
☐ Lockheed 580 (T-33A)	53-5007	580-8346		PV

MOUNTAIN HOME AIR FORCE BASE COLLECTION (ID18)

Address: 366 Wing/PA, Mountain Home Air Force Base, Idaho 83648-5000.
Tel: 208-828-6800 **Email:** 366wgpa@mountainhome.af.mil
Admission: By prior permission only.
Location: About 10 miles south west of the town on Route 67.

The field was completed in 1942 and served as a bomber base for three years. The site closed as the end of World War II and for the next 20 years saw only occasional use. In 1972 the F-111 arrived and this was flown until the early 1990s.

A small collection of preserved aircraft is located near the Wing Headquarters. Some have been painted in the markings of examples once based at the field. An F-111 is also mounted in a park in the town.

TYPE	REG/SER	CON. NO.	PI/NOTES	STATUS
☐ General Dynamics F-111A	67-0058	A1-103	In park in town.	PV
☐ General Dynamics EF-111A (F-111A)	66-0049	A1-67		RA
☐ General Dynamics RF-111A (F-111A)	'66-0022'	A1-11	63-9776	RAX
☐ General Dynamics 401 Fighting Falcon (F-16A)	79-0366	61-151		RA
☐ McDonnell M.98DJ Phantom II (F-4C)	'64-0751'	1191	64-0841	RAX
☐ McDonnell M.199-1A Eagle (F-15A)	'86-0177'	189/A162	76-0010	RAX
☐ North American A-217 Super Sabre (F-100C)	'53784'	217-9	54-1748	RAX
☐ Republic F-84F Thunderstreak	'26567'		52-6470	RAX
☐ Rockwell B-1B Lancer	'86-0134'	3	83-0066	RAX

MUSTANG HIGH FLIGHT (ID19)

Address: 10335 West Emerald Street, Boise, Idaho 83704-8241
Tel: 208-323-1022 **Email:** contactus@mustanghighflight.com
Admission: By prior permission only.
Location: At Gowen Field which is about 4 miles south of the city off Interstate 84.

The flagship of the fleet is the two seat Mustang 'Diamond Back'. The aircraft served with the Air Force from 1945 until 1958. Sold on the civilian market, it was flown in a number of races until it crashed in 1979. In the mid-1980s it was rebuilt as a Reno racer and named 'Stiletto'. Skip Holm won the Unlimited Gold Race in 1984.

In 1993 restoration to a standard TF-51 took place and it is now in the colours of a 360th Fighter Group machine. The second P-51 served in Sweden and the Dominican Republic before returning to the USA in 1984. In 2007 a former Luftwaffe Alpha Jet was added to the fleet which appears at many shows on the west coast.

TYPE	REG/SER	CON. NO.	PI/NOTES	STATUS
☐ Dornier-Breguet Alpha Jet A	N120AU	0120	41+20	RAA
☐ North American NA-122 Mustang (P-51D) (J 26)	N7551T	122-38897	44-72438, Fv26131, 1920 (Dominican Republic)	RAA
☐ North American NA-124 Mustang (P-51D) (TF-51D)	N51ZM	124-48224	45-11471, N332, N270MS, N51VW, N51UR	RAA

NAMPA MONUMENT (ID20)

Location: On permanent view in Lakeview Park in the south eastern part of the town.

TYPE	REG/SER	CON. NO.	PI/NOTES	STATUS
☐ Northrop N-35 Scorpion (P-89B) (F-89B)	'9245'	N.2030	49-2457	PVX

POCATELLO MONUMENT (ID21)

Location: On permanent view at the airport which is about 3 miles west of the town off Interstate 86.

TYPE	REG/SER	CON. NO.	PI/NOTES	STATUS
☐ McDonnell M.36BA Voodoo (F-101B)	59-0417	741		PV

The Mighty Eighth Air Force Heritage Museum is home to this McDonnell F-4C Phantom II. [GA43]

This Bell UH-1M Iroquois, in false markings, is preserved at Gowen Field in Boise. [ID7]

On show at the Frasca Air Museum is this Luscombe 8A Silvaire. [IL18]

Idaho

POST FALLS MONUMENT (ID22)

Location:	On permanent view in Cabela's Store at 101 Cabela Way west of the town near the state line.

TYPE	REG/SER	CON. NO.	PI/NOTES	STATUS
☐ Piper J-3C-65 Cub	N23429	3165	NC23429 – possible identity.	PV

ST. MARIES MONUMENT (ID23)

Location:	On permanent view at the airport which is north of the town.

TYPE	REG/SER	CON. NO.	PI/NOTES	STATUS
☐ North American NA-243 Super Sabre (F-100F)	56-3819	243-95		PV

TETON WARBIRD MUSEUM (ID24)

Address:	PO Box 869, 675 Airport Road, Driggs, Idaho 83422.
Tel:	208-354-3200 Fax: 208-354-3100 Email: info@tetonaviation.com
Admission:	During working hours.
Location:	About 2 miles north of the town on Route 33.

This private collection set up by Richard Sugden includes a number of flyable jet warbirds. The Czech designed Albatros, which served in large numbers with air forces throughout the world, has proved very popular in the USA with many imported from former Soviet republics. The North American Buckeye trainer first flew in January 1958 and just over 600 were built. A number were exported to Greece.

TYPE	REG/SER	CON. NO.	PI/NOTES	STATUS
☐ Aero L-39C Albatros	N439RS/'00-0439'	131907		RAA
☐ Aero L-39C Albatros	NX339RS	931338		RAA
☐ Beech D45 Mentor (T-34B)	N934RS	BG-77	Bu140743	RAA
☐ Bell 47G-3B-2	N147RS	2636	CF-NOG, C-FNOG	RAA
☐ Canadair CL-13A Sabre 5 [North American F-86E]	N4688J	999	23209 (Canada)	RAA
☐ Canadair CL-13B Sabre 6 [North American F-86E]	N80FS	1675	KE+104, 01+13	RAA
☐ Douglas TA-4J Skyhawk	N234LT	14178	Bu158141	RAA
☐ Grumman G-111 Albatross (G-64) (UF-1) (HU-16C)	N3HU	G-281	Bu131906, N7026J	RAA
☐ Grumman G-73 Mallard	N730RS	J50	N2980, N1626	RAA
☐ Naval Aircraft Factory N3N-3	N112D		Bu2659, N44774	RAA
☐ North American NA-88 Texan (AT-6D) (SNJ-5)	N85169	88-16992	42-85211, Bu84981	RAA
☐ North American NA-244 Fury (FJ-4B) (AF-1E)	N400FS	244-83	Bu143575, N9255	RAA
☐ North American NA-252 Trojan (T-28C)	N28CV	252-12	Bu146249, N6535K	RAA
☐ North American NA-310 Buckeye (T-2B)	N212TB	310-21	Bu155226, N3174B	RAA
☐ Sportline Aviacija Genesis 2	N262RS	2024		RAA
☐ Sud-Est SE.3130 Alouette II	N70PK	1123	1123 (France), N11233	RAA
☐ Sugden Mini 500	N468RS	468		RAA
☐ Walter Extra EA-300L	N199X	138		RAA
☐ WSK Lim-5 [MiG-17F]	NX717MG	1C 12-10	1210 (Poland), N1210	RAA
☐ WSK SBLim-2 [MiG-15]	N515MG	3508	358 (Poland)	RAA

TWIN FALLS MONUMENT (ID25)

Location:	On permanent view at the airport which is about 4 miles south of the town off Route 3.

TYPE	REG/SER	CON. NO.	PI/NOTES	STATUS
☐ Lockheed 580 (T-33A)	56-1660	580-1010		PV
☐ McDonnell M.98DE Phantom II (F-4C)	64-0828	1167		PV

WARHAWK AIR MUSEUM (ID26)

Address:	201 Municipal Drive, Nampa, Idaho 83687-8582.
Tel:	208-465-6446 Fax: 208-465-6232 Email: suepaul@warhawkairmuseum.org
Admission:	Mid October–March Tuesday-Friday 1000-1600, Saturday 1000-1700; April–mid October Tuesday-Saturday 1000-1700, Sunday 1100-1700.
Location:	At the airport which is in the northern suburbs of the town off Interstate 84.

John Paul has owned and rebuilt several warbirds over the years. In the late 1980s he moved his fleet from California to Idaho via Montana. Two Curtiss fighters and the rare P-51C are the highlights.

Also on show is an excellent collection of World War II memorabilia, engines, clothing, posters, documents, models, flying clothing, uniforms and photographs. The Fokker Dr I was built by Max Fullmer and completed in 1996.

TYPE	REG/SER	CON. NO.	PI/NOTES	STATUS
☐ Bensen B-8M Gyrocopter	N1495	RAC-1		PV
☐ Curtiss A87-A2 Kittyhawk I	NX94466	15404	AK933, 1057 (Canada)	PVA
☐ Curtiss 87V Warhawk (P-40N) (Kittyhawk IV)	NL1195N	30158	42-106396, 880 (Canada), N1195N	PVA
☐ Fokker Dr I (R)	N9224C	2896		PVA
☐ Grumman G-36 Hellcat (FM-2)	N86572	5626	Bu86572, N35MK, N35M	PVA
☐ North American NA-103 Mustang (P-51C)	N4651C	103-26688	43-25057	PVA
☐ North American NA-191 Sabre (F-86F)				PVC
☐ Waco NZR Hadrian (CG-4A)			Fuselage frame only.	PV

ILLINOIS

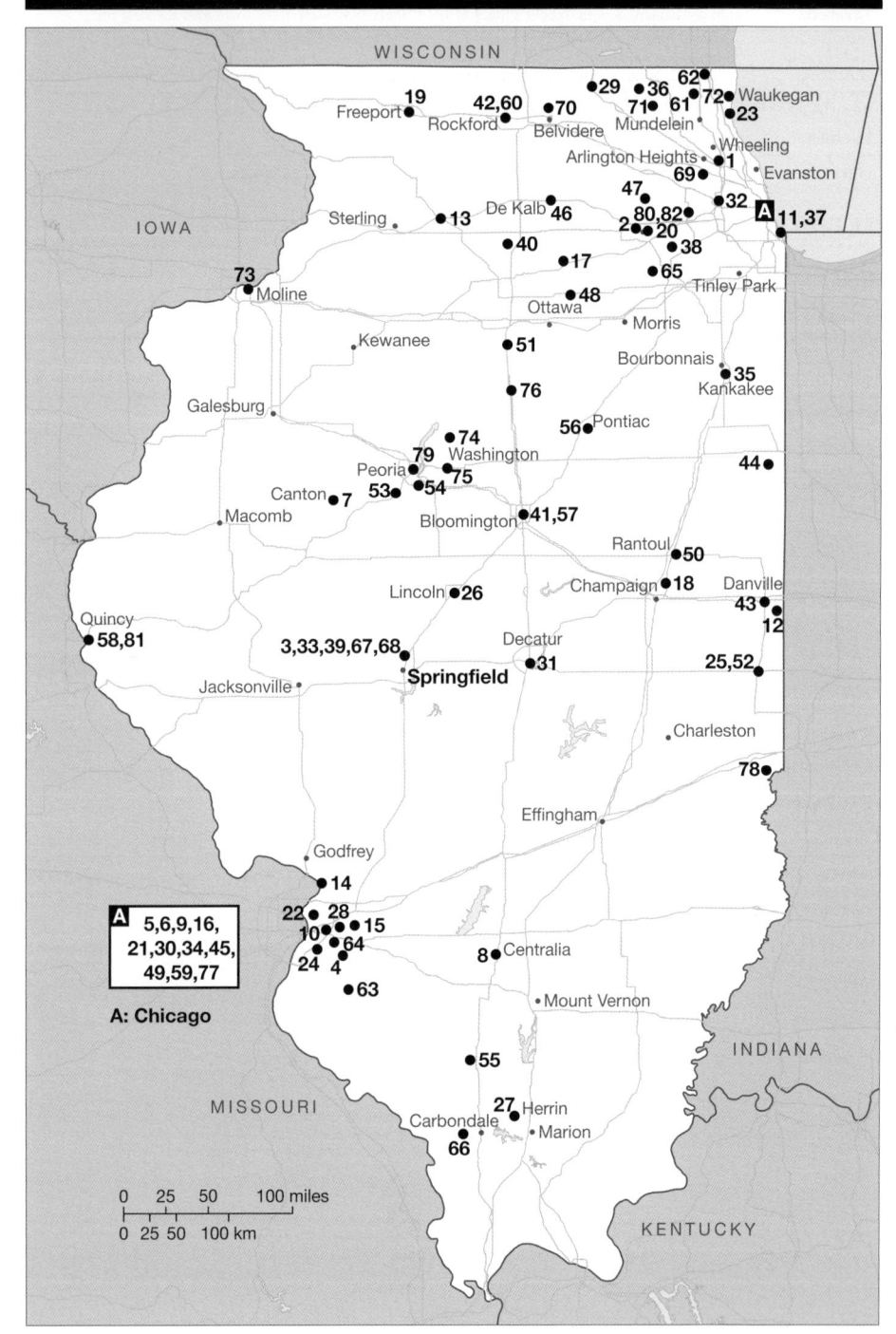

A: 5,6,9,16, 21,30,34,45, 49,59,77

A: Chicago

Illinois

94TH AIR SQUADRON RESTAURANT (IL1)

Address:	1070 South Milwaukee Avenue, Wheeling, Illinois 60090.
Tel:	847-459-3700 **Fax:** 847-215-4592 **Email:** gmunit63@srcmail.com
Admission:	Aircraft on permanent view.
Location:	About 25 miles north west of the centre of Chicago.

Three replica fighters from the World War II era have been put on show at this restaurant. These are painted in typical period markings. Inside are photographs, models and items of memorabilia.

TYPE	REG/SER	CON. NO.	PI/NOTES	STATUS
☐ Lockheed 422-81-14 Lightning (P-38J) (FSM)	'328301'			PVX
☐ North American NA-122 Mustang (P-51D) (FSM)				PV
☐ Republic P-47D Thunderbolt (FSM)				PV

AIR CLASSICS MUSEUM OF AVIATION (IL2)

Address:	43W624 US Route 30, Sugar Grove, Illinois 60554.
Tel:	630-466-0888 **Email:** webmaster@airclassicsmuseum.org
Admission:	Tuesday-Sunday 1000-1500.
Location:	At Aurora Airport which is about 3 miles west of the town.

This museum was set up at Du Page Airport in the mid-1990s and moved to Aurora in 1998. The associated displays have been well thought out and cover many aspects of US military aviation with photographs, models, uniforms and components to be seen.

The F-105 was on show in a park in the town for a period before moving to the museum. The Sabre is one of the batch recovered from the ranges at China Lake in California. The four replicas have recently arrived from a location on the west coast.

TYPE	REG/SER	CON. NO.	PI/NOTES	STATUS
☐ Bell 205 Iroquois (UH-1H)	68-16215	10874		PV
☐ Bell 205 Iroquois (UH-1H)	68-16265	10924		PV
☐ Curtiss H81-A2 Warhawk (P-40C) (Tomahawk IIB) (FSM)				PVX
☐ Douglas TA-4J Skyhawk (TA-4F)	Bu153678	13616		PV
☐ McDonnell M.98AM Phantom II (F4H-1) (F-4B)	Bu148407	92		PV
☐ Messerschmitt Bf 109E (FSM)				PVX
☐ North American NA-122 Mustang (P-51D) (FSM)				PV
☐ North American NA-193 Sabre (F-86F) (RF-86F)	'51-13390'	193-168	52-5439, 62-7416 (Japan) – in Japanese markings – may be c/n 176-321 51-13390 –	PVX
☐ North American NA-265 Sabreliner (T-39A) (CT-39A)	60-3503	265-31		PV
☐ Republic F-105D Thunderchief	61-0099	D-294		PV
☐ Republic P-47D Thunderbolt (FSM)				PVX
☐ Vought A-7E Corsair II	Bu158842	E398		PV

AIR COMBAT MUSEUM (IL3)

Address:	835 South Airport Road, Springfield, Illinois 62707.
Tel:	217-522-2181 **Email:** contact@aircombatmuseum.org
Admission:	Monday-Friday 0900-1600 or by appointment.
Location:	At the airport which is in the north western suburbs of the city off Route 29.

Warbird collector Mike George owns most of the aircraft on show in the museum which opened early in 1994. The exception is the Beech Kansan which was bought by the group and is now airworthy.

The Mustang was acquired in 1990 and is painted in the colours of a 339th Fighter Group aircraft. The Yugoslav designed Soko Galeb jet is a rarity in America and is still in its original camouflage. The Beech T-34 was formerly used by the Indonesian Air Force.

The Fleet 9 biplane dates from 1931 and has recently been restored to flying condition. Only a few examples of this model were built. The identity of the derelict MiG-15 is as yet unknown. The exhibition is slowly being developed and items of memorabilia will be added in the future.

TYPE	REG/SER	CON. NO.	PI/NOTES	STATUS
☐ Aero Commander 500U	N757DD	1652-9	N4521E, N213RC	PV
☐ Beech C18S Kansan (AT-11)	NC64463	4534	42-37538, XH-137, N64463	PVA
☐ Beech A45 Mentor (T-34A)	N634M/B-675	G-761	55-0224, B-675 (Indonesia), N7132M	PVA
☐ Fairchild 24W46	N81378	W46-278	NC81378	PVA
☐ Fleet 9	NC13920	505	NS36, NC13920, N13920	PVA
☐ General Dynamics F-111A			Cockpit only.	PV
☐ Mikoyan-Gurevich MiG-15				PVD
☐ North American NA-122 Mustang (P-51D)	NL951M	122-39746	44-73287, N5445V, N51DF, N5445V, N751JC, NL5445V	PVA
☐ Piccard Balloon				RA
☐ Ryan ST-3KR Recruit (PT-22)	N47306	1358	41-15229	PVA
☐ Ryan ST-3KR Recruit (PT-22)	N522M	2005	41-20796, N60231	PVC
☐ Soko N-60 Galeb G-2A	NX669M		23172 (Yugoslavia), N172PP	PVA
☐ Taylorcraft DCO-65 Grasshopper (L-2B)	N48462	L-5323	(USAAF)	PVA
☐ Taylorcraft DCO-65 Grasshopper (L-2M)	N499M	L-5258	43-25946 (?), N57688	PVA
☐ Vought F4U-5NL Corsair	NX494M		Bu124486, N52??V, 606 (Honduras), N49068, '124453'	PVA
☐ Walter Extra EA-300L	N169M	034		PVA

BELL AERO MUSEUM (IL4)

Address:	206 North 48th. Street, Belleville, Illinois 62223.
Admission:	By prior permission only.
Location:	About 10 miles south east of East St. Louis.

The early Cub is registered to this museum but I would welcome more information. The E-2 first appeared in 1930 and about 350 were produced. The address given is for a residence in the town. The are some private airfields in the Belleville region so if anyone could trace the group it would be appreciated.

TYPE	REG/SER	CON. NO.	PI/NOTES	STATUS
☐ Taylor E-2 Cub	N15632	311	NC15632	PV

BLUE ISLAND MONUMENT (IL5)

Location:	On permanent view in Memorial Park on Highland Avenue in the northern part of the town.

TYPE	REG/SER	CON. NO.	PI/NOTES	STATUS
☐ Vought A-7D Corsair II	71-0347	D258		PV

BROOKFIELD MONUMENT (IL6)

Location:	On permanent view in Ehlert Park in the southern part of the town.

TYPE	REG/SER	CON. NO.	PI/NOTES	STATUS
☐ North American NA-201 Sabre (F-86D) (F-86L)	53-0700	201-144		PV

CANTON MONUMENT (IL7)

Location:	On permanent view at the airport which is about 3 miles west of the town.

TYPE	REG/SER	CON. NO.	PI/NOTES	STATUS
☐ Bell 205 Iroquois (UH-1D) (UH-1H)	65-9819	4863		PV

CENTRALIA MONUMENT (IL8)

Location:	On permanent view in Fairview Park in West Broadway in the town.

TYPE	REG/SER	CON. NO.	PI/NOTES	STATUS
☐ Lockheed 580 (T-33A)	52-9651	580-7536		PV
☐ Republic F-105D Thunderchief	62-4318	D-517		PV

CHICAGO MONUMENT (IL9)

Location:	On permanent view at Midway Airport which is in the south western part of the city.

TYPE	REG/SER	CON. NO.	PI/NOTES	STATUS
☐ Douglas SBD-4 Dauntless	Bu10575	2565		PV

COLLINSVILLE MONUMENT (IL10)

Location:	On permanent view at ALP 365 at 1022 Vandalia Street in the north eastern part of the town.

TYPE	REG/SER	CON. NO.	PI/NOTES	STATUS
☐ Bell 209 Huey Cobra (AH-1S) (AH-1F)	81-23539	22323		PV

COMMEMORATIVE AIR FORCE (GREAT LAKES WING) (IL11)

Address:	630 Winston Drive, Elk Grove Village, Illinois 60007-3340
Tel:	219-977-0324 Email: bobcaf55@aol.com
Admission:	By prior permission only.
Location:	At Lansing Airport which is south of the town.

The group was formed in March 1980 and the following October it became the 21st wing of the CAF. The only aircraft now operated is the C-47 painted in a World War II camouflage scheme.

TYPE	REG/SER	CON. NO.	PI/NOTES	STATUS
☐ Douglas DC-3A-467 Skytrain (TC-47B) (R4D-7) (R4D-6R)	'43-15053'	16597/33345	44-77013, Bu99854, , N7074C, N32, N32A, N227GB	RAAX

DANVILLE MONUMENTS (IL12)

Location:	On permanent view at two locations in the town.

TYPE	REG/SER	CON. NO.	PI/NOTES	STATUS
☐ North American NA-187 Sabre (F-86H)	'24812'	187-9	52-1983 – at Vermillion Airport.	PVX
☐ Vought A-7D Corsair II	68-8223	D9	In Martin Luther King Drive.	PV

Illinois

DIXON VETERANS MEMORIAL PARK (IL13)

Address:	1560 Franklin Grove Road, Dixon, Illinois 61021.
Tel:	815-288-5165 Email: info@vfw540.org
Admission:	On permanent view.
Location:	By the airport which is east of the town on Route 38.

Members of VFW Post 540 have set up this display to honour those who have lost their lives in military service. Three aircraft and a tank are on show along with memorial stones and flags. The Thunderchief has been transported from Jackson in Mississippi and the Huey Cobra is a fairly recent arrival.

TYPE	REG/SER	CON. NO.	PI/NOTES	STATUS
☐ Bell 205 Iroquois (UH-1D) (UH-1H)	66-1039	5522		PV
☐ Bell 209 Huey Cobra (AH-1G) (AH-1F)	67-15475	20139		PV
☐ Republic F-105D Thunderchief	60-0455	D-143		PV

EAST ALTON MONUMENT (IL14)

Location:	On permanent view at St. Louis Regional Airport which is just south of Bethalto.

TYPE	REG/SER	CON. NO.	PI/NOTES	STATUS
☐ McDonnell M.98DE Phantom II (F-4C)	63-7491	491		PV

EDWARDSVILLE MONUMENT (IL15)

Location:	On permanent view in Township Park on Center Grove Road in the centre of the town.

TYPE	REG/SER	CON. NO.	PI/NOTES	STATUS
☐ Vought A-7E Corsair II	Bu159303	E441	On loan from NMNA, FL.	PV

FIRST DIVISION MUSEUM AT CANTIGNY (IL16)

Address:	1S151Winfield Road, Wheaton, Illinois 60189-353.
Tel:	630-260-8185 Email: info@firstdivisionmuseum.org
Admission:	February Friday-Sunday 1000-1600; March–August Tuesday-Sunday 1000-1600;
Location:	In the western part of the town.

The First Infantry Division has seen continuous service since its formation on 24th May 1917. The unit has fought with distinction in all major conflicts. The displays at the museum trace its history with many interesting items on view.

Outside is a park with a range of tanks and military vehicles on show dating from World War I to the present time. The UH-1 has moved from the closed English Field Museum in Texas.

TYPE	REG/SER	CON. NO.	PI/NOTES	STATUS
☐ Bell 204 Iroquois (UH-1C) (UH-1M)	66-15183	1911		PV

FLYING M MUSEUM (IL17)

Address:	PO Box 64, Leland, Illinois 60531-0064.
Admission:	By prior permission only.
Location:	About 25 miles north east of La Salle.

One aircraft is registered to this museum. The DC-3 was delivered to American Airlines in February 1937 and served with them until July 1948. The aircraft then had a number of owners across the country before being acquired by the Confederate Air Force in Texas in early 1982.

The classic transport then moved to the Great Lakes Wing of the CAF in the early 1990s. The local airport, which was used by homebuilt aircraft, is now closed so the location of the fleet is unknown. Again any information would be useful.

TYPE	REG/SER	CON. NO.	PI/NOTES	STATUS
☐ Douglas DC-3-178	N17332	1918	NC17332	RAA

FRASCA AIR MUSEUM (IL18)

Address:	1402 East Airport Road, Urbana, Illinois 61801.
Tel:	217-328-6088 Email: simulators@frasca.com
Admission:	By prior permission only.
Location:	The airfield is about 2 miles north of the town off Route 45.

The Frasca Company is well known for its range of flight simulators. Over the years the founder of the firm, Rudy Frasca, has been acquiring aircraft and housing them at his private airfield. For almost two decades one hangar has been used for the collection and now the adjoining one has been converted for this purpose.

The museum is only open by appointment but there are usually people present at weekends. Items of memorabilia, engines and photographs have been acquired and displays of these are being prepared, An exhibition of simulators dating from the Link Trainer to the present day includes the first one made by the Frasca company.

The warbirds in the collection are regular performers at air shows. Two former Indian Air Force Spitfires were purchased in 1979 and the rebuild of the first was completed at Audley End in England in 1991. The second is currently being restored in the museum workshops. The FW 190 is one of the kits of newly-built aircraft constructed in Germany. The Fiat G.46

trainer has been converted to an example of the G.55 fighter. Examples of classic American types of the 1940s have been joined by several homebuilt aircraft.

The Pitts 12 biplane was produced in Florida in both kit form and as complete aircraft. The biplane is normally powered by a M-12 Russian radial.

Bill Johnson designed the Chris-Tena Mini Coupe in the early 1970s. The aircraft is of similar configuration to the classic Ercoupe but is a single seater. Originally kits could be purchased but at the current time only plans are available. The Pober P-10 was designed by EAA founder Paul Poberezny and is based on the Piper Cub. A number have been constructed. The M-1 Midget Mustang, low wing monoplane, made is debut at the 1948 Cleveland National Air Races. More than 400 have been completed.

The Aeronca C-3, dating from the late 1930s, was rebuilt in the workshops. These distinctive looking high wing monoplanes were built in large numbers and a small batch was also constructed in England. The Chipmunk is one of a batch of 14 used by the Ghanaian Air Force for primary training from 1961 until 1976. Eight survivors were then sold in the USA.

TYPE	REG/SER	CON. NO.	PI/NOTES	STATUS
☐ Aero Commander 690B	N81703	11438		RAA
☐ Aeronca C-3	NC17419	A-730	NC17419, N17419	RAA
☐ Beech V35B Bonanza	N6025T	D-10213		RAA
☐ Beech A45 Mentor (T-34A)	N54RF	G-140	53-3379	RAA
☐ Beech D50 Twin Bonanza	N888BS	DH-14		RAA
☐ Bellanca 14-13 Crusair Senior	N86775	1136	NC86775	RAA
☐ Bellanca 8GCBC Scout	N86756	14-74		RAA
☐ Boeing-Stearman A75N1 Kaydet (PT-17)	N49999	75-1638	41-8079, N59258	RAA
☐ Bushby-Long M-1 Midget Mustang	N451L	177		RAA
☐ Cessna 152	N4648M	15284473		RAA
☐ Cessna 170B	N3572C	26616		RAA
☐ Chris-Tena Mini Coupe	N162JA	JA-1		RA
☐ Curtiss A87-A2 Kittyhawk I	N40PE/'474850'	15376	AK905, 1052 (Canada), CF-OGZ, N11122	RAA
☐ De Havilland DHC.1 Chipmunk 22 (T.10)	N589WK	C1/0613	WK589	RAA
☐ Fairchild 24 C8A	NC957V	2525	NC957V, N957V	RAA
☐ Fairchild M-62C Cornell (PT-23)	N64172	260HO	42-49236	RAA
☐ Fiat G.55 (R)	N46FG	97	I-AEKQ, – built from G.46	RAC
☐ Flug Werk FW 190A-9/N	N190RF	990010		RAA
☐ Goldwing ST				RA
☐ Great Lakes 2T-1A-E (R)	NC3182	6621-G312		RAA
☐ Grumman G-36 Wildcat (FM-2)	N6290C	5804	Bu86746	RAA
☐ Luscombe 8A Silvaire	N71312	2739	NC71312	RAA
☐ Mooney M.20C	N5901Q	3160		RAA
☐ North American NA-88 Texan (SNJ-3)	N7986C	88-14446	Bu51698 – mocked up as a Zero.	RAA
☐ North American NA-121 Texan (AT-6F) (SNJ-6)	N9825C	121-42725	44-82003, Bu111987	RAA
☐ Piper J-3C-65 Cub	N42733	15033	NC42733	RAA
☐ Piper PA-23-250 Aztec F	N20BU	27-7754063	N62828, N20BC	RAA
☐ Piper PA-28-181 Cherokee Archer II	N2070M	28-7890226		RAA
☐ Pitts 12	N805DF	215		RAA
☐ Pober P.10 Cuby	NC23254	2		RAA
☐ Quickie Aircraft Quickie 2 (Rutan 54)	N22TQ	2337		RA
☐ Roloff RLU-1 Breezy	N10TD			RA
☐ Royal Aircraft Factory S.E.5A (R)	N1916J	1		RAA
☐ Schweizer SGS.2-33A	N34298	420		RA
☐ Supermarine 394 Spitfire FR.XVIIIe	HS653	6S.676368	TP276 – in Indian markings.	RAC
☐ Supermarine 394 Spitfire FR.XVIIIe	N280TP	6S.676372	TP280, HS654 (India), G-BTXE	RAA
☐ Temco GC-1B Swift	N2404B	3704		RAA

FREEPORT MONUMENT (IL19)

Location:	On permanent view at Albertus Airport which is about 4 miles south east of the town.

TYPE	REG/SER	CON. NO.	PI/NOTES	STATUS
☐ Northrop N-156T Talon (T-38A)	60-0555	N.5128		PV

GAUNTLET WARBIRDS (IL20)

Address:	43W624 US 30, Sugar Grove, Illinois 60554.
Tel:	630-999-2044 Email: flighttops@gauntletwarbirds.com
Admission:	By prior permission only.
Location:	At Aurora Airport which is about 3 miles west of the town.

The company specialises in aerobatic, warbird and tailwheel training. Two former Soviet Air Force jet trainers are in the fleet. An example of the classic Texan is in use along with the fully aerobatic Extra.

TYPE	REG/SER	CON. NO.	PI/NOTES	STATUS
☐ Aero L-29L Delfin	N919WW/'82'	792383	82 (Soviet)	RAA
☐ Aero L-39C Albatros	N992RT	530509	(Soviet), N239EC, N239BA	RAA
☐ Bellanca 8KCAB Decathlon	N5068G	602-80		RAA
☐ North American NA-88 Texan (AT-6D) (SNJ-5)	N101RF	88-17647	42-85866, Bu90789, N7976C	RAA
☐ Walter Extra EA-300	N7769J	044		RAA

GLENVIEW NAVAL AIR STATION MUSEUM (IL21)

Address:	2040 Lehigh Avenue, Glenview, Illinois 60026.
Tel:	847-657-0000 Email: wam51@comcast.net
Admission:	Saturday 1000-1700; Sunday 1200-1700.
Location:	In the northern suburbs of Chicago.

Illinois

The airfield opened in the 1920s and was built by the Curtiss Wright Flying Service. When constructed, Hangar One was the largest in the country. The Navy was in residence from 1923 to 1995. Hangar One and the Control Tower are on the National Register of Historic Places. The museum opened in 2006 and has on show artefacts tracing the history of the base. The Sikorsky HH-52A moved from the Museum of Science and Industry in Chicago. Future plans include the raising of one of the many World War II aircraft wrecks in Lake Michigan and putting this on display in a new exhibition building along with memorabilia.

TYPE	REG/SER	CON. NO.	PI/NOTES	STATUS
☐ Sikorsky S-62A Seaguard (HH-52A)	1459	62138		PV

GRANITE CITY MONUMENT (IL22)

Location:	On permanent view in Wilson Park on 27th. Street in the north eastern part of the town.

TYPE	REG/SER	CON. NO.	PI/NOTES	STATUS
☐ Republic F-84F Thunderstreak	51-9451			PV

GREAT LAKES NAVAL MUSEUM (IL23)

Address:	Building 158, 2601 Paul Jones Street, Great Lakes, Illinois 60088.
Tel:	847-688-3154 **Email:** therese.gonzalez@navy.mil
Admission:	Friday 1300-1600; Saturday-Sunday 0700-1500.
Location:	About 2 miles south of North Chicago off Route 137.

Training of naval personnel has taken place at the site for almost a century. The Skyhawk is located near the gate to the Recruiting Center. The displays in the building trace the history of the camp.

TYPE	REG/SER	CON. NO.	PI/NOTES	STATUS
☐ Douglas A-4C Skyhawk (A4D-2N)	'Bu149959'	12656	Bu148463	PVX

GREATER ST. LOUIS AIR AND SPACE MUSEUM (IL24)

Address:	2300 Vector Drive, Cahokia, Illinois 62206-1465.
Tel:	618-332-3664 **Email:** info@airandspacemuseum.org
Admission:	Wednesday-Saturday 1000-1600.
Location:	At St. Louis Downtown Airport which is about 1 mile south of East St. Louis.

The organisation was formed in 1982 as the St. Louis Aviation Museum and initially set up a facility at the Spirit of St. Louis Airport. The lease at this site was lost and the group reorganised and moved into a hangar at the Downtown Airport in 2005.

Aviation has been important in the region for many years with both civil and military airfields in use. Displays have been set up tracing this rich heritage with many items on show. The Lockheed JetStar was once owned by Howard Hughes. The Pietenpol has been modified to represent a Curtiss Jenny.

TYPE	REG/SER	CON. NO.	PI/NOTES	STATUS
☐ Bede BD-5B				PV
☐ Hughes 269A Osage (TH-55A)	67-15401	0745		PV
☐ Lockheed 1329 JetStar 8	N511TD	1329-5145	N5509L, N46K, XB-DBJ, XA-JFE	PV
☐ Meyers OTW-125	N34305	50	NC34305	PVA
☐ Osterreichischer Aero Club Standard Austria	N10685	45		RA
☐ Pietenpol / St Croix Jenny Replica				PVX
☐ Taylorcraft DCO-65 Grasshopper (O-57A) (L-2A)	N49904	L-5140	43-25828	RA
☐ Team Minimax				PV

HEARTLAND ANTIQUE AUTO MUSEUM (IL25)

Address:	1208 North Main Street, Paris, Illinois 61944-5709.
Tel:	217-463-1834
Admission:	Daily 0800-1700.
Location:	In the northern part of the town.

The museum has on show a range of cars from the late 1890s up to the 1950s. Also to be seen is a range of motoring memorabilia. Military and aviation sections are planned. Two aircraft are under restoration for the display.

The Lincoln Page LP-3 was developed from the 3-seater New Swallow and about 150 were built in the late 1920s. The Ryan PT-22 was built in large numbers for military primary training in the 1940s.

TYPE	REG/SER	CON. NO.	PI/NOTES	STATUS
☐ Lincoln Page LP-3A				RAC
☐ Ryan ST-3KR Recruit (PT-22)				RAC

HERITAGE IN FLIGHT MUSEUM (IL26)

Address:	1351 Airport Road, Logan County Airport, Lincoln, Illinois 62656.
Tel:	217-732-3333 **Email:** searchlight@midwestcc.net
Admission:	Saturday-Sunday 0800-1700.
Location:	In the eastern suburbs of the town.

The museum was established in 1981 and four years later obtained premises at Logan County Airport. A display was set up in a World War II barrack hut which was originally located at Camp Ellis. The structure was then moved to the airport where it served as the office for 20 years. Artefacts and memorabilia dating from World War I including helmets, uniforms, radios, photographs and documents are on view. The history of the airfield is also portrayed.

A number of military and airport vehicles are also in the collection. The first aircraft obtained was the Beech 18 which was slowly restored to its 1944 configuration. Also displayed nearby on the airfield is a rotating beacon used on the pioneering air route from Chicago to St. Louis.

TYPE	REG/SER	CON. NO.	PI/NOTES	STATUS
☐ Beech C18S Expeditor (C-45F) (UC-45F)	N44569	7044	44-47139	PV
☐ Bell 205 Iroquois (UH-1D) (UH-1H)	65-10030	5074		PV
☐ Bell 47G-3B-1 Sioux (TH-13T)	67-15962	3681		PV
☐ Cessna 152	N757KW	15279810		RAA
☐ Cessna 172E	N3955S	17251155		RAA
☐ Lockheed 580 (T-33A)	51-6680	580-6012		PV
☐ McDonnell M.98AM Phantom II (F4H-1) (F-4B)	Bu148412	97		PV
☐ Vought A-7E Corsair II	Bu158026	E342		PV

HERRIN MONUMENT (IL27)

Location:	On permanent view at VFW 1547 in the town.

TYPE	REG/SER	CON. NO.	PI/NOTES	STATUS
☐ Bell 209 Huey Cobra (AH-1G) (AH-1S)	68-15143	20677		PV

HIGHLAND MONUMENT (IL28)

Location:	On permanent view at VFW 5694 in Poplar Street in the north eastern part of Grantfork.

TYPE	REG/SER	CON. NO.	PI/NOTES	STATUS
☐ Bell 209 Huey Cobra (AH-1G) (AH-1S)	71-20987	21058		PV
☐ Lockheed 580 (T-33A)	53-4914	580-8253		PV

HILL COLLECTION (IL29)

Address:	PO Box 328, 23903 Graf Road, Harvard, Illinois 60033.
Admission:	By prior permission only.
Location:	At Dacy Airport which is just west of the town on Route 173 and at private premises.

This private collection contains three examples of the Brunner Winkle Bird. The A version appeared in 1929 with the B model following two years later; almost 250 were built in the Brooklyn factory before it closed in 1932.

Only a small number have survived. The Cessna Bobcat is one of the few remaining airworthy examples of its type. Two Cubs built by the Taylor company in Pennsylvania are in the fleet.

TYPE	REG/SER	CON. NO.	PI/NOTES	STATUS
☐ Brunner-Winkle Bird A	NC832W	1085	NC832W, N832W	RA
☐ Brunner-Winkle Bird A	NC758Y	1092	NC728Y, N728Y	RA
☐ Brunner-Winkle Bird BK	NC9184	1013	NC9184, N9184	RA
☐ Cessna T-50 Bobcat (C-78) (UC-78)	N30L	3772	42-58281	RAA
☐ Piper PA-22-135 Tripacer	N2149A	22-581		RAA
☐ Piper PA-22-135 Tripacer	N2276A	22-663		RAA
☐ Taylor E-2 Cub	NC13179	60	NC13179, N13179	RA
☐ Taylor J-2 Cub	NC17854	1289	NC17854, N17854	RA

HOFFMAN ESTATES MONUMENT (IL30)

Location:	On view during opening hours in Cabela's store at 5225 Prairie Stone Parkway west of the town.

TYPE	REG/SER	CON. NO.	PI/NOTES	STATUS
☐ Champion 7FC Traveler (7FC Tri-Traveler)	N8573E	7FC-361		PV

HOWIE COLLECTION (IL31)

Address:	555 Greenway Lane, Decatur, Illinois 62521-2532.
Admission:	By prior permission only.
Location:	At a private workshop and airfield in the area.

This collection contains a number of classic open cockpit Waco designs. Two rarities are the Laird and the Pitcairn. Over 120 Mailwings were built in a number of different versions. The Laird, Waco 10 and the Classic Waco are believed to still be airworthy but the condition of the others is unknown.

TYPE	REG/SER	CON. NO.	PI/NOTES	STATUS
☐ Classic Aircraft Waco F-5	N954JD	F5-010		RAA
☐ Laird LC-B-200	NC6906	165	NC6906, N6906	RAA
☐ Mono Aircraft Monocoupe 90A	NC11762	A691	NC11762, N11762	RA
☐ Pitcairn PA-5 Mailwing	NC5808	27	NC5808, N5808	RA
☐ Waco 9	NC2668	306	NC2668, N2668	RA
☐ Waco 10 (GXE)	NC4779	1214	NC4779, N4779	RAA
☐ Waco ASO	NC5020	A-3	NC5020, N5020	RA
☐ Waco ASO	NC5785	A-9	NC5785, N5785	RA
☐ Waco ATO	N5673	A-6	X5673, NC5527X	RA
☐ Waco ATO	N736E	A-104	NC736E,	RA
☐ Waco ATO	NC13917	A-119	NC1391A, N1391A, NC1391A	RA
☐ Waco CSO	NC656N	3136	NC656N, N656N	RA

Illinois

☐ Waco CTO (ATO)	NC7446	A-19	NC7446, N7446	RA
☐ Waco PBF-2	NC13428	3693	NC13428, N13428	RA
☐ Waco QCF	NC13028	3573	NC13028, N13028	RA
☐ Waco RNF	NC686Y	3378	NC686Y, N686Y	RA
☐ Waco ZPF-6	NC16579	4378	NC16579, N16579	RA

ILLINOIS AVIATION MUSEUM (IL32)

Address: 130 South Clow International Parkway, Bolingbrook, Illinois 60490-5508.
Tel: 630-771-1937   **Email:** kent@1demuth.com
Admission: Saturday 1000-1400.
Location: At the airport which is about 2 miles west of the town south of Interstate 55.

The museum currently shares Hangar 1 at the airport with a number of other groups. Plans have been put forward to construct a purpose-built facility nearby. The displays will trace the history of aviation in the state.

The Buckeye was being transported by road from Pensacola Naval Air Station in Florida. A World War I Builders Club is part of the museum organisation and the Fokker E III has been completed. This first flew in October 2008. Funds are being raised for a future project. The two Nieuport biplanes were constructed by local homebuilders.

The two former military jet trainers have been restored by members of the museum.

TYPE	REG/SER	CON. NO.	PI/NOTES	STATUS
☐ Fokker E III (R)	N301AM	001		PVA
☐ Lockheed 580 (T-33A)	58-0632	580-1601		PV
☐ Nieuport 11 (R)				PVA
☐ Nieuport 12 (R)	N317LS	0079		PVA
☐ North American NA-352 Buckeye (T-2C)	Bu158908	352-33		PV
☐ Pazmany PL-1	N85VB	57		PV
☐ Rutan 61 Long Ez				PV

ILLINOIS STATE MILITARY MUSEUM (IL33)

Address: 301 North MacArthur Boulevard, Springfield, Illinois 62702.
Tel: 217-761-3910   **Fax:** 217-761-3709   **Email:** ilmuseum.web@il.ngb.army.mil
Admission: Tuesday-Saturday 1300-1630.
Location: In the north western suburbs of the city.

The site is the headquarters for the Illinois National Guard. The two aircraft, one flown by Army units and the other operated by the 170th Fighter Squadron at nearby Capitol Airport, are on show just inside the fence surrounding the site.

The museum is located in a building on the camp. The displays trace the military history of Illinois from the early days of the settlers up to modern conflicts. Three helicopters are in store.

TYPE	REG/SER	CON. NO.	PI/NOTES	STATUS
☐ Bell 204 Iroquois (HU-1A) (UH-1A)	59-1641	100		PV
☐ Bell 205 Iroquois (UH-1H)				RA
☐ Bell 209 Huey Cobra (AH-1G) (AH-1S)	67-15754	20418		RA
☐ Hughes 269A Osage (TH-55A)				RA
☐ Republic F-84F Thunderstreak	52-7051			PV

ISLAND LAKE MONUMENT (IL34)

Location: On permanent view in Veterans Park on Route 176 in the north western part of the town.

TYPE	REG/SER	CON. NO.	PI/NOTES	STATUS
☐ Bell 209 Huey Cobra (AH-1G) (AH-1F)	67-15736	20400		PV

KANKAKEE MONUMENT (IL35)

Location: On permanent view at ALP 1019 at 739 South Sandbar Road – about 5 miles east of the town

TYPE	REG/SER	CON. NO.	PI/NOTES	STATUS
☐ Bell 205 Iroquois (UH-1H)	67-17539	9737		PV

KELLNER COLLECTION (IL36)

Address: 21010 Anthony Road, Marengo, Illinois 60152-9502.
Admission: By prior permission only.
Location: At private premises in the area.

The star of this private collection is the B-17E. The aircraft was flown during World War II In 1943 it was the second aircraft to be converted as an XC-108A.

In late March 1944 it served in India before being ferried across the North Atlantic to Dow Field in Maine. The Fortress was sold as scrap in 1946 and the pieces were stored on a Maine Farm for almost 30 years before being recovered by brothers Mike and Ken Kellner. The aircraft was in seven large sections and a number of smaller pieces.

Restoration commenced at Galt Airport in 1985 and the project was moved to the farm in Marengo in the mid-1990s where work continues.

TYPE	REG/SER	CON. NO.	PI/NOTES	STATUS
☐ Boeing 299-O Fortress (B-17E) (XC-108A)	41-2595	2406		RAC
☐ Douglas A-26C Invader			44-35696 – identity doubtful.	RA
☐ Grumman G-99 Cougar (F9F-8P) (RF-9J)				RA

LANSING VETERANS MEMORIAL (IL37)

Location:	On permanent view at the airport which is south of the town.

TYPE	REG/SER	CON. NO.	PI/NOTES	STATUS
☐ Bell 204 Iroquois (UH-1C)	66-0731	1713		PV

LEWIS UNIVERSITY (IL38)

Address:	1 University Parkway, Romeoville, Illinois 60446-2200.
Tel:	815-838-0500 Email: webmaster@lewisu.edu
Admission:	By prior permission only.
Location:	At the University Airport which is about 2 miles south of the town.

Founded in 1932 the college now offers a wide range of studies The university has its own airport on campus and is the only one in Illinois to do so. Here flight training, aviation maintenance and air traffic control courses take place. A number of instructional airframes including several homebuilt designs are in the workshops.

TYPE	REG/SER	CON. NO.	PI/NOTES	STATUS
☐ Aero Commander 680F	N6279X	1182-95		RA
☐ Beech D18S Expeditor (C18S) (SNB-2) (SNB-3)	N2808J	5589	Bu51262	RA
☐ Beech E55 Baron	N71GG	TE-835		RA
☐ Bell 205 Iroquois (UH-1H)	72-21615	13314		RA
☐ Boeing 737-222	N9024U	19062		RA
☐ Christen Eagle II	N73JD	DALY-0001		RA
☐ Gates Learjet 24	N68LU	24-163	N701AP, N1AP, N65339, N77AE, (N777JA), N65WM	RA
☐ Hiller UH12C Raven (H-23G) (OH-23G)	N29BK	1398	61-3212	RA
☐ Luscombe 8A Silvaire	N23000	924		RA
☐ North American NA-200 Trojan (T-28B)	N217SF	200-401	Bu138330	RA
☐ Piper PA-23-160 Apache	N4109P	23-1588		RA
☐ Pitts S-1C Special	N56ST	S-1C		RA
☐ Stits SA-3A Playboy	N10159	Q1		RA
☐ Stoddard-Hamilton SH-2 Glasair IIR	N86D	577		RA

LINCOLN LAND COMMUNITY COLLEGE (IL39)

Address:	815 Airport Drive, Springfield, Illinois 62974.
Tel:	217-544-4965 Email:jim.vankleek@llc.edu
Admission:	By prior permission only.
Location:	In the north western suburbs of the city off Route 29.

The college has premises at the airport where a range of technical subjects are taught. Four instructional airframes including an ex-military Iroquois are known to be in use but there may be more.

TYPE	REG/SER	CON. NO.	PI/NOTES	STATUS
☐ Beech C18S Kansan (AT-11)	NC64463	4534	42-37538	RA
☐ Bell 205 Iroquois (UH-1H)	67-17150	9348		RA
☐ Cessna 172	N6448E	46548		RA
☐ Piper PA-22-135 Tripacer	N1601P	22-2416		RA

MARK MONUMENT (IL40)

Location:	On permanent view in the village.

TYPE	REG/SER	CON. NO.	PI/NOTES	STATUS
☐ Bell 209 Huey Cobra (AH-1G) (AH-1F)	67-15474	20138		PV

MCLEAN COUNTY MUSEUM OF HISTORY (IL41)

Address:	200 North Main Street Bloomington Illinois 61701.
Tel:	309-827-0428 Email: marketing@mchistory.org
Admission:	Monday Wednesday-Saturday 1000-1700; Tuesday 1000-2100.
Location:	In the centre of the town.

This excellent local history museum has one aircraft on show. Built in the city in 1933, the diminutive Tilbury Flash racer disappeared from 1935 until the airframe was found in 1947 in store in the Chicago area. Members of the local chapter of the EAA restored it in the early 1970s after it had been given to the museum. The history of the aircraft is highlighted in the display.

TYPE	REG/SER	CON. NO.	PI/NOTES	STATUS
☐ Tilbury Flash	NR12931	SF-1		PV

MIDWAY VILLAGE AND MUSEUM CENTER (IL42)

Address:	6799 Guilford Road, Rockford, Illinois 61107.
Tel:	815-397-9112 Fax: 815-397-9151 Email: danb@midwayvillage.com
Admission:	March–December Monday-Friday 1000-1600; Saturday-Sunday 1200-1600.
Location:	In the eastern suburbs of the city.

Illinois

The village contains many historic buildings which have been moved to the site along with reproductions of others which have been constructed to help portray local life. The Victorian village feature 26 structures along with a number of gardens.

On show is the Stinson 'Greater Rockford'. The monoplane piloted by Bert Hassall left Rockford on a planned flight to Stockholm on 25th July 1928. The aircraft crashed soon after take off but damage was slight and on 16th August the crew started again and made it to Cochrane, Ontario. Two days later they set out for Greenland but ran out of fuel and landed on the ice cap. The pair were rescued but the airframe was not recovered until 1968. The historic machine was flown to Rockford inside a C-46. The superbly restored Stinson is on display along with a photographic record of its flight. The Bell UH-1M has recently arrived.

TYPE	REG/SER	CON. NO.	PI/NOTES	STATUS
☐ Bell 204 Iroquois (UH-1C) (UH-1M)	66-15236	1964		PV
☐ Stinson SM-1 Detroiter	NX5408	M235		PV

MIDWEST AVIATION MUSEUM (IL43)

Address:	Box 325, RR.6, Vermilion County Airport, Danville, Illinois 61832.
Tel:	217-431-2924 Fax: 217-431-8989
Admission:	By prior permission only.
Location:	About 4 miles north east of the town.

This privately run museum is housed in several hangars at Vermilion County Airport. Founded by Butch Schroeder, the collection concentrates on warbirds. The rare F-6D version of the Mustang won the Grand Champion World War II award at the EAA convention at Oshkosh in 1993. The aircraft, which had not flown since 1949, was acquired in 1981. It then underwent a major rebuild in the museum workshops before taking to the air in June 1993.

The Thunderbolt served in Peru from 1952 until the type was withdrawn in the early 1960s. After six years in store at Piura Air Force Base it was sold and returned to Texas by ship. Members of the Confederate Air Force assembled the fighter and it flew again in August 1971. Since then it has had several owners and spent a period on show outside the 56th Fighter Group Restauarant at Farmingdale on Long Island. The aircraft has recently been sold to Oregon.

TYPE	REG/SER	CON. NO.	PI/NOTES	STATUS
☐ Boeing-Stearman E75 Kaydet (PT-13D) (N2S-5)	N52520	75-8347	42-109314, Bu43253, N4918N	RAA
☐ North American NA-124 Mustang (P-51D) (F-6D)	N51BS	124-44642	44-84786	RAA
☐ North American NA-168 Texan (T-6G)	N55897	168-248	49-3144 – ex NA-88 c/n 88-12383	RAA
☐ North American NA-200 Trojan (T-28B)				RAA
☐ Vultee V-74 Valiant (BT-13A)	N56985	74-8557	42-1636	RAA

MILFORD MONUMENT (IL44)

Location:	On permanent view in the town.

TYPE	REG/SER	CON. NO.	PI/NOTES	STATUS
☐ Ford JB-2 [Fieseler Fi 103A-1]				PV

MUSEUM OF SCIENCE AND INDUSTRY (IL45)

Address:	57th Street and Lake Shore Drive, Chicago, Illinois 60637.
Tel:	773-684-1414 ext 2093 Email: msi@msichicago.org
Admission:	Monday-Saturday 0930-1600 Sunday 1100-1600.
Location:	About 4 miles south of the city centre on the shores of Lake Michigan.

The impressive building which houses the museum was constructed in 1893 as the fine arts hall for the Colombian Exposition. The museum opened in 1933 and includes displays on communications, photography, transport, nuclear science, medicine and computing.

The aeronautical collection is spread around the building and a range of engines from a 1910 Wright to modern jets can be seen. There is also a space section with the Apollo 8 command module, a Mercury capsule and several satellites on view. The oldest aircraft in the collection is the Morane-Saulnier H which is believed to have been constructed for the 1914 London-Manchester and London-Paris races.

The Curtiss Jenny was built in large numbers from 1915. Over 6,800 were completed and the biplane was used to train many pilots in World War I and civilians in the years after the end of the conflict. The Boeing 40B is one of four known survivors of the type and was first used by United Air Transport. This can be compared with a modern jet airliner. Visitors can enter the fuselage of the former United Airlines Boeing 727.

The Travel Air R was flown by Frank Hawks who established over 200 records in it in the early 1930s. The Piccard gondola is from the balloon in which he set several altitude records in the 1930s. Hanging over the foyer is an early Spitfire and one of the two complete Junkers Ju 87 Stuka dive bombers surviving.

Also on show in the transport hall are several cars and motor cycles. Craig Breedlove's record breaking jet car 'Spirit of America' is here. A highlight of the museum is the only World War II German submarine on show in the USA. U-505 was attacked by the USS *Chatelain* off the coast of west Africa in June 1944. The ship serves as a memorial to the 55,000 Americans who lost their lives as a result of submarine attacks around the world.

TYPE	REG/SER	CON. NO.	PI/NOTES	STATUS
☐ Boeing 40B-4	NC288	899		PV
☐ Boeing 727-100	N7017U	18309	Fuselage and one wing only.	PV
☐ Curtiss D Pusher (R)	NR10632			PV
☐ Curtiss 1C Jenny (JN-4D)	2421	553		PV
☐ Junkers Ju 87R-2/trop	A5+HL	5954		PV
☐ Morane-Saulnier H				PV
☐ Piccard Balloon			Gondola only.	PV
☐ Supermarine 300 Spitfire F.Ia	P9306			PV
☐ Travel Air R	NR1313	R-2004		PV
☐ Vought A-7A Corsair II	Bu152668	A25		PV

Only a few Boeing 40s have survived and this example has been on show for many years in the Museum of Science and Industry in Chicago. (Nigel Hitchman) [IL45]

This Grumman F4F-3 is a memorial to 'Butch' O'Hare at the Chicago Airport now named after him. (Glenn Chatfield) [IL49]

Parked on the apron at the Octave Chanute Aerospace Museum is this North American CT-39A Sabreliner. [IL50]

NEWHOUSE COLLECTION (IL46)

Address:	45 West 445 Lees Road, Virgil, Illinois 60151-8774.
Admission:	By prior permission only.
Location:	About 8 miles east of De Kalb off Route 38.

This collection, housed on a private airfield near the town, contains a number of interesting types. The two classic Travel Air biplanes date from the mid-1920s and many survived after being used as crop dusters. The Bird A, designed by Michael Gregor, was built in Brooklyn and obtained high ratings in the 1929 Guggenheim safe-plane contest. Over 100 were sold and the biplane was fitted with an OX-5 engine. The improved BK with a 100 hp Kinner appeared in 1931. The CK version biplane had four seats instead of the three in earlier models.

TYPE	REG/SER	CON. NO.	PI/NOTES	STATUS
☐ Aeronca C-3	NC11422	A-156	NC11422, N11422	RAA
☐ Beech E35 Bonanza	N314R	D-3794		RA
☐ Brunner-Winkle Bird CK	NC914V	4004	NC914V, N914V	RAA
☐ Piper J-3C-65 Cub	N7188H	20450	NC7188H	RAA
☐ Travel Air E-4000	N390N	1303	NC382M	RAA
☐ Travel Air E-4000	N390A	1319	NC399N	RAA

NORTHERN ILLINOIS AVIATION MUSEUM (IL47)

Address:	39 West 140, Freeman Avenue, Gilberts, Illinois 60136-9727.
Admission:	By prior permission only.
Location:	Possibly at DuPage airport which is about 1 mile east of St. Charles.

The Dakota, which served with both the Air Force and Navy in the USA, has been acquired from Lamar Mercer's defunct World Aircraft Museum at Calhoun in Georgia. The aircraft was sold on the civil market in 1975 and flown by the State of Florida until moving to Georgia in October 1981. In late 2010 the museum was closed and the aircraft sold.

TYPE	REG/SER	CON. NO.	PI/NOTES	STATUS
☐ Douglas DC-3A-456 Skytrain (C-47A) (R4D-5) (C-47H)	N47060	19066	42-100603, Bu39905, 43-9095	RAA

NORWAY MONUMENT (IL48)

Location:	On permanent view at a business about 2 miles south east of the town on Highway 71.

TYPE	REG/SER	CON. NO.	PI/NOTES	STATUS
☐ Beech D18S Expeditor (C-45H)	N3657G	AF-461	51-11904	PVD

O'HARE MEMORIAL (IL49)

Address:	PO Box 66142, Chicago, Illinois 60666.
Tel:	773-686-3700 Fax: 773-686-3573 Email: aviation@ohare.com
Admission:	When Terminal 2 is open.
Location:	At O'Hare Airport which is in the north western part of the city.

Edward 'Butch' O'Hare was born in 1914 and graduated from the Western Military Academy in 1932. During World War II he became the first US Navy pilot to achieve 'ace' status and to win the Medal of Honor. He was shot down in November 1943 and his aircraft crashed in the Pacific whilst he was leading the first night attack raid from a carrier.

The airport, formerly Chicago International, was named after him in 1949 and the memorial honours his life with photographs and documents.

The Wildcat was recovered almost intact from Lake Michigan and restored by the Air Classics Museum to represent one flown by O'Hare.

TYPE	REG/SER	CON. NO.	PI/NOTES	STATUS
☐ Grumman G-36 Wildcat (F4F-3)	Bu12320	5980	Bu12320, N5254A	PV

OCTAVE CHANUTE AEROSPACE MUSEUM (IL50)

Address:	1011 Pacesetter Drive, Rantoul, Illinois 618663672.
Tel:	217-893-1613 Fax: 217-892-5774 Email: curator@aeromuseum.org
Admission:	Monday-Friday 1000-1700; Saturday 1000-1800; Sunday 1200-1700.
Location:	Just south of Rantoul on Route 45.

The airfield, named after the pioneer aviator Octave Chanute, opened in May 1917. Chanute was born in 1832 in Paris but lived most of his life in America. His main career was as a railroad engineer but he became interested in aviation on a visit to Europe in 1875. When he retired in 1890 he devoted himself to the science of flight and designed a number of gliders, some in partnership with younger aviators who could fly the machines. A replica of one of his designs has been built for the exhibition.

Originally a flying training base, the site became a technical training school in 1921. The last flying mission took place in 1971 but after this aircraft continued to fly in for the base collection and for use by the students. On 26th August 1985 the 'Thunderbirds Air Park' was dedicated and 10 aircraft, many painted in the colours of the aerobatic team, were placed on show. The display also honoured the predecessors of the Thunderbirds. In addition there were many preserved aircraft parked around the base.

The Technical Training Center closed in 1993 and most of the instructional airframes were either scrapped or moved. The site was taken over by the town and part of it is being developed as an airport. A group of enthusiasts, many of whom had helped with the preserved aircraft, decided to set up a museum. Premises were obtained in one of the hangars and a ramp in front of the building was allocated. In a short time several impressive displays were set up in the building. Among those honoured are the pioneer aviators of Illinois and the Commanding Officers of Chanute Air Force Base. The 76-year military history of the field is also portrayed. There is a large display of uniforms and memorabilia. Missile training was carried out at Chanute and the visitor can see an underground ICBM silo.

Several of the preserved aircraft have been put on show in the hangar. The display includes one of the few surviving Convair B-58 bombers The prototype of this delta-winged four-jet-engined bomber made its maiden flight on 11th November 1956. The Hustler was the first operational supersonic bomber and was capable of Mach 2. It entered service in March 1960 and was operational until January 1970, serving at Grissom AFB in Indiana, Carswell AFB in Texas and Little Rock AFB in Arkansas. Only 116 were completed with further versions of the bomber cancelled.

Light aircraft and homebuilt designs have been acquired to enhance the display. The incomplete Tigercat was designed and built by Marcus Foose of Blue Island in Illinois. The diminutive aircraft is powered by a 150 hp Lycoming engine. Lamar Steen designed the Skybolt as a high school engineering project. The tandem seat open cockpit biplane was fitted with a 180 hp Lycoming engine. The first example flew in October 1970. Plans were made available and have been sold in over 30 countries. At least 400 Skybolts, powered by a variety of engines have been completed. An earlier homebuilt biplane design is the Mong Sport. The prototype first flew in Oklahoma in 1953 and several are still flying.

The Wright Flyer replica, built by a volunteer team, commemorates the centenary of powered flight. The displays are being improved but some aircraft have been moved across the country to other USAF collections. These include a giant Consolidated B-36 bomber to Castle in California and a Douglas A-26 Invader to Laughlin in Texas.

TYPE	REG/SER	CON. NO.	PI/NOTES	STATUS
☐ Aeronca 65LB Chief	N34496	L-14881	NC34496	PV
☐ American Aerolights Eagle				PV
☐ Balloon Works Firefly 7-B Hot Air Balloon		F7B-016		PV
☐ Bell 204 Iroquois (HU-1B) (UH-1B)	'60686'	266	61-0686	PVX
☐ Boeing 367-76-66 Stratofreighter (KC-97G) (C-97G)	52-0898	16592		PV
☐ Boeing 450-3-3 Stratojet (XB-47)	46-0066	15973	46-0066, '2278'	PV
☐ Boeing 464-201-7 Stratofortress (B-52D)	55-0095	17211	Front fuselage only.	PV
☐ Cessna 152			Front fuselage only.	PV
☐ Cessna 337M Super Skymaster (O-2A)	'61411'	337M0117	67-21411	PVX
☐ Chanute Glider (R)				PV
☐ Convair 4 Hustler (YB-58A) (YRB-58A)	55-0666	7	55-0666, '12059'	PV
☐ Curtiss 1C Jenny (JN-4D) (R)				PV
☐ Douglas DC-3A-467 Skytrain (C-47B) (VC-47D)	43-49336	15152/26597		PV
☐ Douglas 1333 Cargomaster (C-133A)	56-2009	45246		PV
☐ Douglas A-4A Skyhawk (A4D-1)	Bu139947	11312		PVX
☐ Douglas RB-66B Destroyer	53-0412	44293		PV
☐ Foose Tigercat				PV
☐ General Dynamics F-111A	63-9767	A1-02		PV
☐ Grumman G-111 Albatross (G-64) (SA-16A) (SA-16B) (HU-16B)	'51-5200'	G-267	51-7200	PVX
☐ Lockheed 182-1A Hercules (182-44-03) (C-130A)	55-0037	182-3064		PV
☐ Lockheed 183-93-02 Starfighter (F-104A)	56-0732	183-1020		PV
☐ Lockheed 580 (T-33A)	'59797'	580-8057	52-9797	PVX
☐ Lockheed 1049A-55-137 Super Constellation (1049A-55-86) (WV-2) (EC-121K)	Bu141311	1049A-4435		PV
☐ McDonnell M.36BA Voodoo (F-101B) (NF-101B)	56-0273	330		PV
☐ McDonnell M.98DF Phantom II (RF-110A) (RF-4C)	'20201'	268	62-12201.	PVX
☐ McDonnell M.199-1A Eagle (F-15A)	71-0286	007/A007		PV
☐ Mong Sport	N4253J	1937		PV
☐ North American NA-84 Texan (AT-6B)	'42-805'	84-7750	41-17372, (N96274)	PVX
☐ North American NA-108 Mitchell (B-25J) (TB-25N)	44-30635	108-33910	44-30635, '02344', '2279'	PV
☐ North American NA-126 Mustang (P-51H)	44-64265	126-37691		PV
☐ North American NA-151 Sabre (P-86A) (F-86A)	47-615	151-38442		PV
☐ North American NA-217 Super Sabre (F-100C)	'54785'	217-46	54-1785	PVX
☐ North American NA-276 Sabreliner (T-39A) (CT-39A)	62-4494	276-47		PV
☐ Northrop N-156B Freedom Fighter (F-5B)	63-8441	N.8004		PV
☐ Piper PA-22-135 Tripacer	N8726C	22-1377		PVA
☐ Republic YF-84A Thunderjet (YP-84A)	'488656'		45-59494	PVX
☐ Republic F-84F Thunderstreak	'51531'		51-9531	PVX
☐ Republic F-105B Thunderchief	54-0104	B-7		PV
☐ Republic F-105F Thunderchief	63-8287	F-64		PV
☐ Ryan NYP (FSM)	'NX-211'			RAX
☐ Steen Skybolt	N48BB	0001		PV
☐ Vought A-7D Corsair II	69-6190	D20		PV
☐ Wright Flyer (R)				RAC

OGLESBY MONUMENT (IL51)

Location:	On permanent view in Memorial Park at 500 South Woodland Avenue in the town.

TYPE	REG/SER	CON. NO.	PI/NOTES	STATUS
☐ Bell 205 Iroquois (UH-1H)	71-20066	12890		PV

PARIS MONUMENT (IL52)

Location:	On permanent view at ALP 211 at 1031 Main Road in the northern part of the town.

TYPE	REG/SER	CON. NO.	PI/NOTES	STATUS
☐ Lockheed 580 (T-33A)	'29502'	580-7512	52-9402 – possible identity.	PVX

PEKIN MONUMENTS (IL53)

Location:	On permanent view at two locations in the town.

TYPE	REG/SER	CON. NO.	PI/NOTES	STATUS
☐ Bell 205 Iroquois (UH-1H)			At VFW 1232	PV
☐ McDonnell M.98DJ Phantom II (F-4C)	64-0911	1365	At the airport which is about 8 miles south of Peoria on Route 29.	PV

PEORIA AIR NATIONAL GUARD BASE (IL54)

Address: 182 AW/SCBIM, 2416 South Falcon Road, Peoria, Illinois 61607-1464.
Tel: 309-633-5179   **Fax:** 309-633-5585   **Email:** webmaster@ilpeor.ang.af.mil
Admission: By prior permission only.
Location: About 7 miles south west of the city on Interstate 474.

Units of the Illinois Air National Guard have been based at Peoria since 1941. The squadron flew F-84Fs from 1958 to 1969 and the Cessna O-2 from 1970 to 1980. A new facility was constructed on the opposite side of the field to house the F-16s allocated in 1992. Five preserved aircraft are displayed inside the main gate to the base, representing types flown by units in Illinois. The F-4 is at a nearby American Legion Post.

TYPE	REG/SER	CON. NO.	PI/NOTES	STATUS
☐ Cessna 318E Dragonfly (A-37B) (OA-37B)	'68-428'	43273	69-6428	RAX
☐ Cessna 337M Super Skymaster (O-2A)	68-11160	337M0385		RA
☐ General Dynamics 401 Fighting Falcon (F-16B)	'82-042'			RAX
☐ Lockheed 382-8B Hercules (C-130E)	63-7877	382-3948		RA
☐ McDonnell M.98EN Phantom II (F-4D)	64-0754	1043	At nearby AL Post.	RA
☐ Republic F-84F Thunderstreak	51-9313			PV

PINCKNEYVILLE MONUMENT (IL55)

Location:	On permanent view in the City Park at 104 South Walnut Street in the centre of the town.

TYPE	REG/SER	CON. NO.	PI/NOTES	STATUS
☐ Lockheed 580 (T-33A)	52-9663	580-7848		PV

PONTIAC MONUMENT (IL56)

Location:	On permanent view at ALP 78 on County Road 24 just west of the town.

TYPE	REG/SER	CON. NO.	PI/NOTES	STATUS
☐ Vought A-7D Corsair II	68-8230	D16		PV

PRAIRIE AVIATION MUSEUM (IL57)

Address: 2929 East Empire Street, Bloomington, Illinois 61704-5452.
Tel: 309-663-7632   **Fax:** 309-663-8411   **Email:** frankt@prairieaviationmuseum.org
Admission: Tuesday-Saturday 1100-1600; Sunday 1200-1600.
Location: At Bloomington-Normal Airport which is about 3 miles east of the city off Route 9.

Established in 1983, the museum acquired its first aircraft, a DC-3, the following year. Found in Texas, the transport had not flown for 15 years and after a great deal of work arrived at Bloomington in November 1984. It was repainted in Ozark Airlines' 1950s colours for their 35th anniversary in 1985. The aircraft was sold to Florida in 2009. A building was obtained and an exhibition of memorabilia, photographs, models etc. set up. Subjects featured include the career of Charles Lindbergh and Illinois astronauts.

The majority of the aircraft are parked outside. The Tern is a local homebuilt design dating from the early 1980s. The Tomcat flew into Bloomington in April 2006 and its arrival attracted a large crowd of spectators from the surrounding area.

TYPE	REG/SER	CON. NO.	PI/NOTES	STATUS
☐ Bell 205 Iroquois (UH-1H)	67-17832	10030		PV
☐ Bell 209 Sea Cobra (AH-1J)	Bu157771	26015		PV
☐ Cessna 310B	N900S	35742		PV
☐ Douglas A-4M Skyhawk	Bu160036	14538		PV
☐ Grumman G-303 Tomcat (F-14A) (F-14D)	Bu161163	390		PV
☐ Lockheed 580 (T-33A)	53-5979	580-9461	53-5979, N4698T	RA
☐ Martin 272A Canberra (RB-57A)			Front fuselage only.	RA
☐ McDonnell M.98AM Phantom II (F4H-1) (F-4B) (F-4N)	Bu150444	230		PV
☐ North American NA-217 Super Sabre (F-100C)	'54784'	217-45	54-1784	PVX
☐ Northrop N-156T Talon (T-38A)	60-0549	N.5122		PV
☐ Steckler STS.1 Tern	N37627	STS.1		PV
☐ Vought A-7A Corsair II	Bu152681	A38		PV

QUINCY MONUMENT (IL58)

Location:	On permanent view at the Illinois Veterans Home at 1707 North 12th Street in the town.

TYPE	REG/SER	CON. NO.	PI/NOTES	STATUS
☐ Bell 205 Iroquois (UH-1H)	66-16683	8577		PV

R J DALEY COLLEGE (IL59)

Address:	7500 South Pulaski Road, Chicago, Illinois 60652.
Tel:	773-838-7500
Admission:	By prior permission only.
Location:	In the south western part of the city.

Two instructional airframes were at the college but aviation classes have ceased. The fate of the two known to be there is unclear. The college is named after Richard J. Daley who served as Mayor of the city in the 1970s.

TYPE	REG/SER	CON. NO.	PI/NOTES	STATUS
☐ Grumman G-134 Mohawk (OV-1B)	62-5901	60B		RA
☐ North American NA-265 Sabreliner (T-39A) (CT-39A)	60-3497	265-25		RA

ROCK VALLEY COLLEGE (IL60)

Address:	3301 North Mulford Road, Rockford, Illinois 61114.
Tel:	815-921-3014 Email: ckonkol@ednet.rockvalleycollege.edu
Admission:	By prior permission only.
Location:	At the airport which is about 5 miles south of the town.

Founded in 1964 the college serves the local community in offering a wide range of mainly two year courses. The main campus is in the town and classes are also held at more than 50 sites in the region. The Aviation Maintenance Technology department has a number of instructional airframes in its workshops at the airport.

TYPE	REG/SER	CON. NO.	PI/NOTES	STATUS
☐ Aero Commander 520	N2625B	520-137		RA
☐ Beech D18S Expeditor (C18S) (SNB-2) (SNB-3) (SNB-5) (TC-45J) (UC-45J)	N3024	6049	Bu67234	RA
☐ Beech D18S Expeditor (C18S) (SNB-2C) (SNB-3) (SNB-5) (TC-45J) (UC-45J)	N2813J	5826	Bu51349	RA
☐ Beech C50 Seminole (L-23D) (U-8D)	N51888	LH-116	56-3715 – fuselage only.	RA
☐ Beech C50 Seminole (L-23D) (U-8D)	N3930U	LH-134	57-3098 – fuselage only.	RA
☐ Beech 65-90 King Air	N825K	LJ-91	N2085W	RA
☐ Cessna 150M				RA
☐ Cessna 172F				RA
☐ Hughes 269A Osage (TH-55A)	67-16704	38-0811		RA
☐ North American NA-265 Sabreliner (T-39A) (CT-39A)	61-0641	265-44		RA

ROUND LAKE PARK MONUMENT (IL61)

Location:	On permanent view at ALP 1170 at 111 East Main Street in the village.

TYPE	REG/SER	CON. NO.	PI/NOTES	STATUS
☐ Vought A-7A Corsair II	Bu153220	A129		PV

RUSSELL MILITARY MUSEUM (IL62)

Address:	43363 Old Highway 41, Russell, Illinois 60075.
Tel:	847-395-7020 Fax: 847-395-7025 Email: museum@db3mail.com
Admission:	Wednesday-Sunday 1000-1700.
Location:	Just west of Interstate 41 by Route 165.

This privately run museum occupies a site close to the main Interstate highway. On show are a large number of military vehicles and tanks, some in running order and others requiring complete restoration. These include a British Centurion tank, several motor propelled guns, a armoured launched bridge, several jeeps and the prototype Hummer. Several ships including a Vietnam river patrol boat can be seen. There are weapons and a number of aero engines. The collection was originally located just across the state line in Kenosha, Wisconsin.

A display of memorabilia, documents, photographs and weapons has been set up. The aircraft exhibition includes a number of helicopters and fixed wing aircraft. The giant Sikorsky Tarhe (or Skycrane) can be seen in two variants. One is the fully operational version whilst the other is a ground trainer used for practising many tasks including the suspension of objects below the structure.

The Aero Commander and the TH-55 were obtained from the US Army Transportation Museum in Virginia. The Hercules was used by the Navy at Moffett Field in California and was then transferred to NASA. One of the T-38s was also flown by the organisation.

TYPE	REG/SER	CON. NO.	PI/NOTES	STATUS
☐ Aero Commander 680 (L-26C) (U-9C)	56-4026	344-36	(N68365)	PV
☐ Bell 204 Iroquois (UH-1C) (UH-1M)	65-9534	1434		PV
☐ Bell 205 Iroquois (UH-1D) (UH-1H)	64-13768	4475	64-13768, N43960	PV
☐ Bell 205 Iroquois (UH-1D) (UH-1H)	65-9788	4832		PV
☐ Bell 205 Iroquois (UH-1D) (UH-1H)	65-9931	4975		PV
☐ Bell 205 Iroquois (UH-1D) (UH-1H)	65-10005	5049		PV
☐ Bell 205 Iroquois (UH-1D) (UH-1H)	65-10074	5118		PV
☐ Bell 205 Iroquois (UH-1H)	66-16968	9162		PV
☐ Bell 205 Iroquois (UH-1H)	69-15598	11886	Boom from c/n 13138 71-20314.	PV
☐ Bell 206A Kiowa (OH-58A)	70-15334	40885		RA
☐ Bell 206A Kiowa (OH-58A)	71-20820	41681		PV
☐ Bell 209 Huey Cobra (AH-1G) (AH-1F)	70-15993	20937		PV

Illinois

☐ Cessna 172F Mescalero (T-41A)	N4992R	17256345	67-14992	PV
☐ Cessna 337M Super Skymaster (O-2A)				PV
☐ Grumman G-134 Mohawk (OV-1C)	67-18900	101C		PV
☐ Grumman G-134 Mohawk (OV-1C)	N906KM	107C	67-18906	RAA
☐ Grumman G-134 Mohawk (OV-1D)	68-16992	3D		PV
☐ Gyrodyne QH-50C (DSN-3)				PV
☐ Hiller UH12B Raven (H-23B) (OH-23B)	51-16226	408		RA
☐ Hughes 269A Osage (TH-55A)	67-16879	980586		RA
☐ Hughes 369M Cayuse (HO-6) (OH-6A)	65-12974	0049	65-12974, N570UH	PV
☐ Hughes 369M Cayuse (HO-6) (OH-6A)	67-16017	0402		RA
☐ Lockheed 382C-85D Hercules (EC-130Q)	N427NA	382C-4901	Bu161495	RA
☐ Lockheed 580 (T-33A)				RA
☐ Lockheed 580 (T-33A)	52-9526	580-7661	Tail from c/n 580-7195 52-9141	PV
☐ McDonnell M.199-1B Eagle (TF-15A) (F-15B)	75-0084	0143/B020		PV
☐ McDonnell M.98DE Phantom II (RF-110A) (RF-4C)	'65-0839'		Front fuselage only.	PVX
☐ Mil Mi-24	110			PV
☐ North American NA-305 Bronco (OV-10A) (OV-10D)	N615NA	305-47	Bu155436, PNC-30 (Colombia)	RA
☐ Northrop N-156T Talon (T-38A) (AT-38B)	61-0923	N.5289		PV
☐ Northrop N-156T Talon (T-38A)	61-0941	N.5307		PV
☐ Northrop N-156T Talon (T-38A)	N910NA	N.5771	65-10352	PV
☐ Republic F-84F Thunderstreak	N2250Q		51-9524	PV
☐ Russian Tilt Wing (FSM)				PV
☐ Schweizer SGS.1-26E				PV
☐ Sikorsky S-58 Choctaw (H-34A) (UH-34A)				RA
☐ Sikorsky S-61R (CH-3C) (CH-3E)	65-12789	61564		PV
☐ Sikorsky S-61R Pelican (HH-3F)	N485KM	61662	1485	RA
☐ Sikorsky S-64A Tarhe (CH-54A)	67-18423	64025	Ground trainer version.	PV
☐ Sikorsky S-64A Tarhe (CH-54A)	N446KM	64048	68-18446	RA
☐ Sikorsky S-64A Tarhe (CH-54B)	70-18486	64094		PV
☐ Sikorsky S-65A Sea Stallion (CH-53A)	Bu153292	65069	Bu153292, 67-30044	PV
☐ Vertol V.114 Chinook (CH-47D)	82-23766	M.3017	Front fuselage only – rebuilt from CH-47A c/n B.316 66-19058.	PV
☐ Vertol V.114 Chinook (CH-47D)	85-24365	M.3135	Front fuselage only – rebuilt from CH-47A c/n B.174 65-8002.	PV
☐ Vought EA-7L Corsair II (A-7C) (TA-7C)	Bu156751	E18		PVD

SCHALLER COLLECTION (IL63)

Address: 1414 Baldwin Road, New Athens, Illinois 62264-3002
Admission: By prior permission only.
Location: At an airport in the area.

This private collection contains a number of classic types. The early DC-3, which was delivered to American Airlines in August 1939, is currently parked at Schellville Airport in California. The aircraft, withdrawn in 1987, will eventually be restored and moved across the country. The Mustang has seen service in three countries.

The Piper Cub Special is a development of the famous J-3. The improvements included a fully cowled engine, a more sloping windscreen and fuel tanks in the port wing. The prototype first flew in August 1946 and over 1,500 were sold. Further design work led to the PA-18 Super Cub which was built in vast numbers.

TYPE	REG/SER	CON. NO.	PI/NOTES	STATUS
☐ Beech D17S ((UC-43) (GB-2)	N5074N	6680	(44-76034), Bu32668, NC1826	RA
☐ Bellanca 7GCBC Citabria	N7558F	226-70		RAA
☐ Boeing-Stearman A75N1 Kaydet (PT-17)	N51443	75-4434	42-16271	RAA
☐ Cessna 120	NC1926N	12170	NC1926N, N1926N	RAA
☐ Cessna 180	N9445C	31843		RAA
☐ Douglas DST-217A (C-49E)	N139D	2165	NC21752, 42-43620, NC21752, N110SU – at Schellville, CA.	RA
☐ Meyers OTW-160 (OTW-125)	N34342	87	NC34342	RAA
☐ North American NA-124 Mustang (P-51D)	N9857P	124-44818	44-84962, (South Korea), F-312 (Indonesia)	RAA
☐ Piper PA-11 Cub Special	NC4901M	11-422	NC4901M, N4901M	RAA
☐ Piper PA-22-135 Tripacer	N3479A	22-1749		RAA
☐ Sud Fennec [North American NA-174 Trojan (T-28A)]	N14104	174-158	51-3620, 60 (France), N14104, 1244 (Haiti)	RAA
☐ Taylor J-2 Cub	NC17261	927	NC17261, N17261	RAA
☐ Travel Air 2000	NC6117	615	NC6117, N6117	RAA

SCOTT FIELD HERITAGE AIR PARK (IL64)

Address: 216 East A Street, Belleville, Illinois 62220.
Tel: 618-253-2015 **Fax:** 618-253-2077 **Email:** info@bellevillechamber.org
Admission: On permanent view – others by prior permission only.
Location: About 6 miles east of Belleville off Interstate 64.

Named after Corporal Frank S. Scott, who was the first enlisted man to be killed in an air accident, the base opened in June 1917. Used by airships between 1919 and 1938, the site became a training school during World War II. Transport units moved in during the Korean War and an Airlift Wing is still in residence. The C-45 and the CT-39 are mounted by the hangars.

The Air Park has been constructed outside the base to trace the history of the base and what its units. Ground was broken on 13th June 2008 and the second phase of the project will include a Heritage Center showing the development of military transport aircraft over the last few decades. of the resident wing. A number of types used in recent years by the wing have been moved to the site.

TYPE	REG/SER	CON. NO.	PI/NOTES	STATUS
☐ Beech D18S Expeditor (C-45H)	52-10858	AF-788	52-10858, N7743C	RA
☐ Boeing 717-146 Stratotanker (KC-135A)	63-8010	18627		RA
☐ Boeing 717-146 Stratotanker (KC-135A) (KC-135E)	56-3611	17360		PV
☐ Boeing 717-148 Stratotanker (KC-135A) (KC-135E)	59-1487	17975		RA
☐ Douglas DC-9-32CF Nightingale (C-9A)	71-0877	47495		PV
☐ Lockheed 1329 JetStar 6 (C-140A)	59-5959	1329-5026		PV
☐ Lockheed 300 Starlifter (C-141A) (C-141B)	65-0236	300-6087		PV
☐ Lockheed 300 Starlifter (C-141A) (C-141B) (C-141C)	67-0466	300-6285		RA
☐ Lockheed 382-8B Hercules (C-130E)	62-1862	382-3826		PV
☐ North American NA-265 Sabreliner (T-39A) (CT-39A)	60-3495	265-23		RA

SMITH COLLECTION (IL65)

Address: 23823 West Lockport Street, Plainfield, Illinois 60544-2115.
Admission: By prior permission only.
Location: At an airfield in the area.

This private collection includes three classic Fleet biplanes. The Fleet 1, powered by a 125 hp Warner radial, entered production in 1928 and was soon joined by the Fleet 2 which was fitted with a 100 hp Kinner.

Fleet Aircraft of Canada later acquired the production rights and developed the designs. Over 400 Finch IIs were delivered to the Royal Canadian Air Force between 1939 and 1941 and were used for basic training.

TYPE	REG/SER	CON. NO.	PI/NOTES	STATUS
☐ Aeronca 65C Chief	NC21397	C-2058	NC21397, N21397	RA
☐ Corben C-1 Baby Ace	N10443	1		RA
☐ Fleet 1	NC8626	39	NC8626, N8626	RA
☐ Fleet 2	NC403K	126	NC403K, N403K	RA
☐ Fleet 16B Finch II	N39612	339		RA
☐ Pietenpol B4-A Aircamper	N4991	298365		RA
☐ Piper J-3C-65 Cub	N87937	15555	NC87397	RA
☐ Piper J-3C-65 Cub	N6294H	19473	NC6294H	RA

SOUTHERN ILLINOIS UNIVERSITY (IL66)

Address: 665 North Airport Road, Southern Illinois Airport,, Murphysboro, Illinois 62966.
Tel: 618-536-3371 **Fax:** 618-453-4850 **Email:** wdunkel@siu.edu
Admission: By prior permission only.
Location: About 3 miles north of the town.

The university which was established in 1869 has its main campus in Carbondale. In 1960 it purchased the aircraft and assets of Midwestern Aero Services, a Fixed Base Operator, at Southern Illinois Airport.
Initially the new acquisitions provided services to the university. Academic courses commenced in 1965 in new hangars and workshops constructed at the airport. Over the years the facilities have been improved and courses are now offered in a number of related subjects including Aviation Management. Modern laboratories with computer equipment are in use. In addition to the instructional airframes the university has a fleet used for pilot training.

TYPE	REG/SER	CON. NO.	PI/NOTES	STATUS
☐ Aero Designs Pulsar 912XP	N795P	385		RA
☐ Agusta-Bell 206B1 Jet Ranger	N2414X	9035		RA
☐ Beech 65-80 Seminole (L-23F) (U-8F)	62-3872	LF-70	62-3872, N51UC, N15JD	RA
☐ Bell 47D-1 (HTL-5)	N221S	476	Bu129977	RA
☐ Bell 47G-3B-1	N73991	2897		RA
☐ Bell 47G-3B-1 Sioux (TH-13T)	67-15925	3644		RA
☐ Bell 205 Iroquois (UH-1H)	66-16725	8919		RA
☐ Bell 206A Jet Ranger	N8174J	557		RA
☐ Bell 214J				RA
☐ Bell 222	N222AX	47003		RA
☐ Boeing 737-222	N9009U	19047		RA
☐ Cessna 150	N88DB			RA
☐ Cessna 150L	N18231	15073884		RA
☐ Cessna 310J	N3053L	310J0053		RA
☐ Enstrom F-28A	N509H	327		RA
☐ Lockheed 580 (T-33A)	N49892	580-8162	52-9856	RA
☐ Lockheed 580 (T-33A)	57-0553	580-1202		RA
☐ Piper PA-22-135 Tripacer	N8269C	22-2361		RA
☐ Piper PA-23-250 Aztec D	N13768	27-4418		RA
☐ Sikorsky S-61R Pelican (HH-3F)	1470	61530		RA

SPRINGFIELD AIR NATIONAL GUARD BASE (IL67)

Address: 3101 J. David Jones Parkway, Capital Airport, Springfield, Illinois 62707-5001.
Tel: 217-757-1267 **Email:** webmaster@ilspri.ang.af.mil
Admission: On permanent display.
Location: In the north western part of the city off Route 29.

The 170th Fighter Squadron was allocated to the Illinois Air National Guard in 1948 and based at Springfield. The first equipment was the P-51 Mustang and these were replaced by the F-86 Sabre in 1953. The F-84F served from 1955 to 1972 followed by the F-4 which was flown until the F-16 was allocated in 1989.

Illinois

TYPE	REG/SER	CON. NO.	PI/NOTES	STATUS
☐ Canadair CL-13 Sabre 2 [North American F-86E]	'52-2844'	163	19263 (Canada)	PVX
☐ Mcdonnell M.98EN Phantom II (F-4D)	66-7468	1974		PV
☐ Republic F-84F Thunderstreak	'110822'		51-1822	PVX

SPRINGFIELD MONUMENT (IL68)

Location: On permanent view in the Capital Airport Terminal which is in the north western part of the city.

TYPE	REG/SER	CON. NO.	PI/NOTES	STATUS
☐ Pietenpol B4-A Aircamper				PV

VICTORY AIR MUSEUM (IL69)

Address: 2125 Euclid Street, Arlington Heights, Illinois 60004.
Tel: 815-219-5855
Admission: Not yet open.
Location: At private premises in the area.

Earl Reinert and Paul Polidori established the Victory Air Museum at Mundelein almost 50 years ago. They gathered together an interesting collection of warbirds which included a Brewster Buffalo, an incomplete Vought Cutlass, parts of a Henschel Hs 129, a number of Hispano HA-1112s used in the 'Battle of Britain' film and a Japanese Ohka 11. A number of airframes and components were traded over the years with museum and warbird restorers. The museum closed in the mid-1980s and the collection was dispersed. The recently formed group aims to honour Earl and Paul by setting up a new exhibition in the area. A number of artefacts have been acquired and the search for a permanent home has been started.

TYPE	REG/SER	CON. NO.	PI/NOTES	STATUS
☐ Boeing 727			Front fuselage only.	RA
☐ North American NA-108 Mitchell (B-25J)			Front fuselage only.	RAD

VINTAGE WINGS AND WHEELS MUSEUM / POPLAR GROVE AIRMOTIVE (IL70)

Address: 5151 Orth Road, Hangar 16, Poplar Grove, Illinois 61065-0236.
Tel: 815-547-3115   **Email:** vintagemuseum@gmail.com
Admission: May–October Saturday 1000-1300.
Location: On the north side of the airfield which is about 4 miles north of Belvidere.

This museum opened on 7th June 2003 on a site near Poplar Grove Airport. Historic buildings have been moved and re-erected: a 1930s hangar originally at Waukesha County Airport houses the aircraft exhibits. Two other hangars and a 1920s Sunoco Filling Station can be seen.

A 1920s garage from Green Lake has been fitted out as a dealership and repair shop of the era. A number of aircraft have been placed on show in the building and others owned by members are in hangars on the field. Poplar Grove Airmotive operates several vintage and classic types and tours of their area are often arranged.

The exhibits in the main hangar cover a variety of topics including 'Women in Aviation'. There are several vintage cars and motor cycles on show.

TYPE	REG/SER	CON. NO.	PI/NOTES	STATUS
☐ Aeronca 65CA Super Chief	NC36529	CA-16521	NC36529, N36529	PVC
☐ Beech D18S Expeditor (C-45G)	NC8389H	AF-393	51-11836, N8389H	RAA
☐ Brunner-Winkle Bird BK	N894W	2035-15	NC894W	RAA
☐ Brunner-Winkle Bird BK	NC768Y	2055-35	NC768Y, N768Y	RAA
☐ Cessna 140	N3527V	14796		RAA
☐ Cessna 170	N3839V	18706		RAA
☐ Corben B-1 Baby Ace	NX5502N	1		PV
☐ Corben E Junior Ace	N4954E	1203-8-66		PV
☐ Culver LCA Cadet	NC37843	347	NC37843, N37843	PV
☐ Fleet 7	N788V	369	NC788V	PV
☐ Piper J-3C-65 Cub	N6673H	19877	NC6673H	RAA
☐ Piper PA-23 Apache	N1044P	23-46		RAA
☐ Taylor E-2 Cub	NC42319	303	NC15624, N15624	RAA
☐ Waco ASO	NC31404	3004	NC31404, N31404	RAA
☐ Waco ATO	NC6930	A-14	NC6930, N6930	RAA
☐ Waco SRE (UC-72C)	NC1252W	5153	NC1252, 42-68341, N1252W, NC50857	RAA

VOLO AUTO MUSEUM (IL71)

Address: 27582 Volo Village Road, Volo, Illinois 60073-9613.
Tel: 815-344-6062   **Fax:** 815-385-0703
Admission: Daily 1000-1700.
Location: In the north western part of the town.

The museum is part of a complex which contains Antiques Malls and a sales area for vintage cars. The helicopter was destined for a museum before being stored by the Glenview Historical Society. It is now part of the 'Combat Zone' which opened in 2004. This area exhibits military vehicles and weapons.

TYPE	REG/SER	CON. NO.	PI/NOTES	STATUS
☐ Bell 205 Iroquois (UH-1H)	67-17455	9553		RA

WARBIRD HERITAGE FOUNDATION (IL72)

Address:	3000 Corporate Drive, Waukegan, Illinois 60087.
Tel:	847-244-8701 **Fax:** 847-244-8703 **Email:** INFO@WarbirdHeritageFoundation.org
Admission:	By prior permission only
Location:	At the airport which is in the western suburbs of the town.

This organisation was formed in December 2002 with the aim of acquiring, restoring and maintaining warbirds. The group has made steady progress with the fleet now numbering nine.
  The North American Buckeye served with the Navy in the training role for over 40 years. The first examples were delivered in the late 1950s to Pensacola in Florida. A Skyhawk obtained from the EAA Museum in Oshkosh in 2007 made its maiden flight in June 2010 after a lengthy restoration. The aircraft is in the markings of one flown from the USS *Hornet* be Lt. Cdr Ted Schwarz. He shot down a MiG-17 in May 1967 to record the only air-to-air kill by a Skyhawk in the Vietnam War. The Skyraider represents an Air Force example flown in the attack role in Vietnam and is in a camouflage scheme.
  The Bird Dog was shipped to Japan soon after manufacture in July 1952 and this aircraft also flew in Vietnam. The high wing monoplane was sold on the civil market in 1982.

TYPE	REG/SER	CON. NO.	PI/NOTES	STATUS
☐ Aero L-39C Albatros	NX239PW/'23'	931526	(Kyrgyzstan)	RAA
☐ Boeing-Stearman A75N1 Kaydet (N2S-4)	N52107	75-4924	Bu55687	RAA
☐ Cessna 305A Bird Dog (L-19A) (O-1A)	N677RH/'22677'	22677	51-12351	RAA
☐ Douglas AD-1 Skyraider (BT2D-1)	NX2AD/'52-509'	2085	Bu09257	RAAX
☐ Douglas A-4B Skyhawk (A4D-2)	N49WH /Bu148609'	11366	Bu142112, N41WH, N41CJ	RAAX
☐ North American NA-168 Texan (T-6G)	N584M/'93584'	168-92	49-2988, N7657C, N584DD, N584M	RAA
☐ North American NA-191 Sabre (F-86F)	NX188RL/'24986'	191-682	52-4986, C-125 (Argentina)	RAAX
☐ North American NA-200 Trojan (T-28B)	N73MG	200-431	Bu138360	RAA
☐ North American NA-310 Buckeye (T-2B)	N27WS	310-30	Bu155235	RAA

WARBIRD PRESERVATION FOUNDATION (IL73)

Address:	3455 14th Street, Moline, Illinois 61265-6247.
Admission:	By prior permission only.
Location:	At the airport which is just south of the town.

Two aircraft have been registered to the group. The Albatros is believed to have been used in Krygyzstan. The Texan spent many years with the Spanish Air Force before returning to the USA in 1984.

TYPE	REG/SER	CON. NO.	PI/NOTES	STATUS
☐ Aero L-39C Albatros	N600DM	432935		RAA
☐ North American NA-168 Texan (T-6G)	N57NA	168-431	49-3327, E.16-82 (Spain), N2205G	RAA

WASHBURN MONUMENT (IL74)

Location:	On permanent view at ALP 601 on Highway 89.

TYPE	REG/SER	CON. NO.	PI/NOTES	STATUS
☐ Bell 205 Iroquois (UH-1D) (UH-1H)	66-0761	5244		PV

WASHINGTON VETERANS MEMORIAL (IL75)

Location:	About 8 miles east of Peoria at 815 Lincoln Street on Route 24.

TYPE	REG/SER	CON. NO.	PI/NOTES	STATUS
☐ Bell 209 Huey Cobra (AH-1G) (AH-1F)	70-16045	20989		PV

WENONA MONUMENT (IL76)

Location:	On permanent view at the Wright Brothers Grill by Exit 35 of I19.

TYPE	REG/SER	CON. NO.	PI/NOTES	STATUS
☐ Republic F-84F Thunderstreak	51-9419			PV

WEST CHICAGO MONUMENT (IL77)

Location:	On permanent view at VFW 6791 at 431 North Neltnor Boulevard.

TYPE	REG/SER	CON. NO.	PI/NOTES	STATUS
☐ Republic F-84F Thunderstreak	52-6456			PV

WEST UNION MONUMENT (IL78)

Location:	On permanent view in the Town Park in Walnut Street in the centre of the town.

TYPE	REG/SER	CON. NO.	PI/NOTES	STATUS
☐ Lockheed 580 (T-33A)	52-9604	580-7764	Lacks tail.	PV

Illinois

WHEELS O'TIME MUSEUM (IL79)

Address:	PO Box 9636, 11923 North Knoxville Avenue, Peoria, Illinois 61612-9636.
Tel:	309-243-9020 **Email:** wotmuseum@aol.com
Admission:	May–October Wednesday-Sunday 1200-1700.
Location:	About 8 miles north of Peoria on Route 40.

This interesting museum has many working displays including clocks, model trains, musical instruments and telegraph machines. Rooms depicting life in earlier times have been set up in the main building. There are several cars and commercial vehicles on show along with a steam locomotive and an 1885 fire engine. The only aircraft in the collection is a replica Fokker Triplane painted in the red colours of Baron von Richthofen.

TYPE	REG/SER	CON. NO.	PI/NOTES	STATUS
☐ Fokker Dr I (FSM)				PV

WILLIAMS COLLECTION (IL80)

Address:	9 South 135 Aero Drive, Naperville, Illinois 60540.
Admission:	By prior permission only.
Location:	At a private airfield about 5 miles south west of the town.

Gar Williams has completed many award winning restorations over the years. He owns a number of classic types including a now rare Cessna AW. The aircraft was built as a higher-powered BW in 1928 and at some stage in its life was modified to AW standard. The Bowlus Baby Albatross sailplane first flew in 1937 and over 150 were built. Some were delivered complete by the company and others supplied as kits.

TYPE	REG/SER	CON. NO.	PI/NOTES	STATUS
☐ Bowlus BA-100 Baby Albatross	NC19993	129	NC19993, N19993	RA
☐ Cessna AW (BW)	NC4725	138	NC6442, N6442	RAA
☐ Luscombe 8A Silvaire	N37104	1675	NC37104	RAA
☐ Luscombe 8A Silvaire	N71633	3060		RAA
☐ Luscombe 8A Silvaire	N71955	3382	NC71633	RAA
☐ Pietenpol B4-A Aircamper	N12948	2		RAA
☐ Williams CW-2	N12325	1301		RAA

WORLD AEROSPACE MUSEUM (IL81)

Address:	Baldwin Field, Quincy, Illinois 62301.
Tel:	217-885-3143
Admission:	Monday-Friday 1000-1600 by appointment.
Location:	At the airport which is about 8 miles east of the town.

The aim of the museum is to locate aircraft in the former Soviet Bloc countries and bring them to their premises at Quincy. The majority of the fleet can be seen in the display hangar. Other aircraft have been acquired in the past but these have passed on to other warbird collectors around the country.

TYPE	REG/SER	CON. NO.	PI/NOTES	STATUS
☐ Aero L-39C Albatros	N154XX	730926	(Soviet Union), (Russia)	RAA
☐ Aero L-39C Albatros	N148XX	831104	28 (Soviet Union), 28 (Russia)	RAA
☐ Aero L-39C Albatros	N149XX	831147	(Soviet Union), (Russia)	RAA
☐ Aero L-39C Albatros	N157XX	931401	(Soviet Union), (Ukraine)	RAA
☐ Aero L-39C Albatros	N155XX	931402	(Soviet Union), (Ukraine)	RAA
☐ Aero L-39C Albatros	N156XX	931406	(Soviet Union), (Russia)	RAA
☐ Aero L-39C Albatros	N153XX	931507	(Soviet Union), (Russia)	RAA
☐ Aero L-39C Albatros	NX147XX/0008	931514	(Soviet Union), (Ukraine)	RAA
☐ Aero L-39MS Albatros	N104XX	040002	0002 (Czech), 0002 (Slovakia)	RAA
☐ Aero L-39MS Albatros	N105XX	140005	0005 (Czech)	RAA
☐ Aero L-39MS Albatros	NX106XX/0006	140006	0006 (Czech)	RAA
☐ Mikoyan-Gurevich MiG-21UM	N317DM	516516100	3056 (Poland)	RAA
☐ Mikoyan-Gurevich MiG-29UB	N6394K	2960507662	09 (Kyrgystan)	RAA
☐ Mikoyan-Gurevich MiG-29UB	N6394G	2960520155	32 (Kyrgystan)	RAA

ZILINSKY COLLECTION (IL82)

Address:	9 South Chandelle Drive, Naperville, Illinois 60564-9430.
Admission:	By prior permission only.
Location:	At an airfield in the area.

This private collection contains three versions of the classic Alexander Eaglerock biplane. All are under restoration in the workshops. They differ in the engine installed. The A-4 has a Hispano Suiza, the A-12 a Comet and the A-14 a Wright J-6. The remaining aircraft in the fleet are airworthy.

TYPE	REG/SER	CON. NO.	PI/NOTES	STATUS
☐ Alexander Eaglerock A-4				RAC
☐ Alexander Eaglerock A-12	N308W	957	NC308W	RAC
☐ Alexander Eaglerock A-14				RAC
☐ Cessna 170A	N9971A	19629		RAA
☐ Corben D Baby Ace	N4665T	311		RAA
☐ Piper J-3L-65 Cub	N40827	7531	NC40827	RAA
☐ Royal Aircraft Factory S.E.5A (R)	N8040Z	072040		RAA

INDIANA

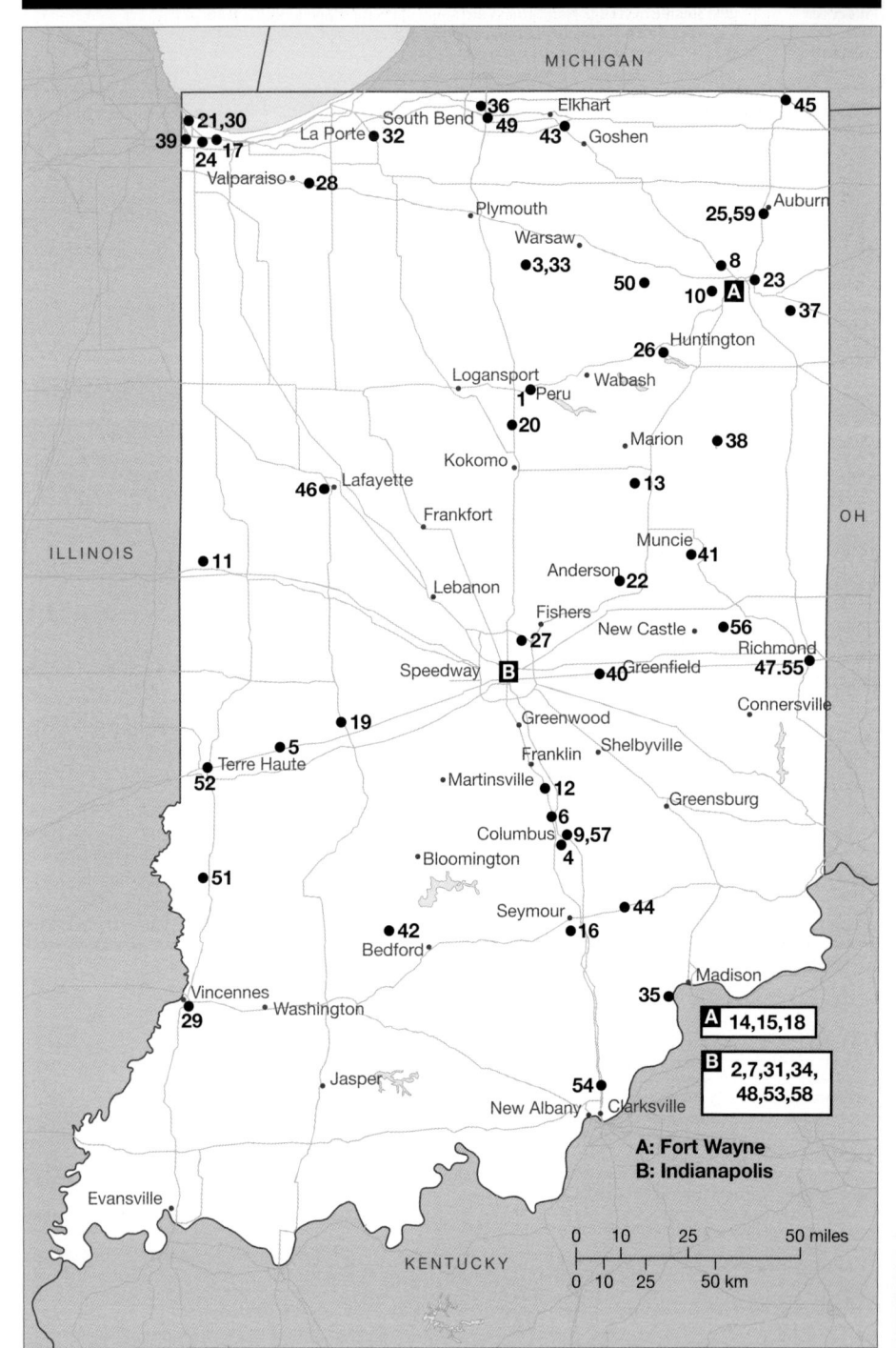

A: Fort Wayne
B: Indianapolis

A: 14, 15, 18
B: 2, 7, 31, 34, 48, 53, 58

Indiana

AMERICAN HUEY 369 (IN1)

Address:	209 South Broadway, Peru, Indiana 46970.
Tel:	765-469-2727 Email: info@americanhuey369.com
Admission:	By prior permission only.
Location:	At the corner of 19 South and 124 East in the town.

The group was formed to keep two examples of the 'Huey' helicopter in airworthy condition in order to educate the public in the role the type played in the Vietnam War. The long-term plan is to set up a museum dedicated to the Iroquois and three more examples of the UH-1 are believed to be in store.

TYPE	REG/SER	CON. NO.	PI/NOTES	STATUS
☐ Bell 205 Iroquois (UH-1D) (UH-1H)	N803UH	4095	63-8803	RAA
☐ Bell 205 Iroquois (UH-1H)	N369UH	12674	70-16369	RAA
☐ Bell 205 Iroquois (UH-1H)				RA
☐ Bell 205 Iroquois (UH-1H)				RA
☐ Bell 205 Iroquois (UH-1H)				RA

AMERICAN MILITARY HERITAGE FOUNDATION (IN2)

Address:	PO Box 29061, 1215 South Franklin Road, Indianapolis, Indiana 46229.
Tel:	317-335-2889 Email: rsuiter700@aol.com
Admission:	Monday-Saturday 0900-1700
Location:	In the Post Air Hangar at the International Airport which is in the south western suburbs of the city.

The group was set up in the early 1990s to maintain the Harpoon in flying condition. The aircraft served as a sprayer in Wyoming when its navy days were over. In 1986 it was sold to the now defunct Historical Aircraft Memorial Foundation in Texas before moving to its current home. Now restored to its original military colours, it regularly visits airshows. The Texan and Valiant are privately owned and reside in the hangar.

TYPE	REG/SER	CON. NO.	PI/NOTES	STATUS
☐ Lockheed 15-27-01 Harpoon (PV-2)	N7265C	15-1362	Bu37396	PVA
☐ North American NA-88 Texan (AT-6D) (SNJ-5) (SNJ-5B)	N600MF	88-16305	42-84524, Bu43763	PVA
☐ Vultee V-74 Valiant (BT-13A)	N413BT	74-6528	41-22450	PVA

ARCHIMEDES ROTORCRAFT AND V/STOL MUSEUM (IN3)

Address:	12296 West 600 South, Mentone, Indiana 46539.
Email:	secretary@pra.org
Admission:	The office is open Thursday-Friday 0900-1600 and they have keys to the museum hangar.
Location:	At the airport which is about 2 miles west of the town.

This collection has been set up by the Popular Rotorcraft Association which has chapters around the country. The aim of the display is to show the development of light helicopters and autogyros. Several examples of Bensen designs are on show including a locally-built B-9 which features co-axial rotor blades. Members of the organisation have designed and built many types and some of these will join the collection. The Helicraft Tip-Jet is a small helicopter designed in Maryland. Two fairly modern Rotorway designs have been acquired.

TYPE	REG/SER	CON. NO.	PI/NOTES	STATUS
☐ Air and Space 18A	N102U	1F		PVD
☐ Air and Space 18A	N6100S	18-6		PV
☐ Bensen B-7 Gyroglider				PV
☐ Bensen B-7M Gyrocopter				PV
☐ Bensen B-8 Gyroglider				PV
☐ Bensen B-8M Gyrocopter				PV
☐ Bensen B-8M Gyrocopter	N63U	1		PV
☐ Bensen B-9 Little Zipster	N976FS	001		PV
☐ Helicraft Tip-Jet				PV
☐ Rotorway Executive	N312SS	3120		PV
☐ Rotorway Scorpion Too				PV

ATTERBURY-BAKALAR AIR MUSEUM (IN4)

Address:	4742 Ray Boll Boulevard, Columbus, Indiana 47203.
Tel:	812-372-4256 Email: lakegc@aol.com
Admission:	Saturday 1000-1600; Sunday 1300-1600.
Location:	At Columbus Airport which is in the northern suburbs of the town.

The field was constructed in 1942 and in 1943 and 1944 training units moved in along with B-25s and B-26s from the early 1950s until its closure in 1970 the field was occupied by transport units. In 1954 its name was changed to Bakalar Air Force Base to honour local World War II pilot Lieutenant John E. Bakalar, killed in France in 1944 when the engine of his P-51 Mustang failed on take off. The airfield was transferred to the local town and is now the municipal airport. The museum was built in 1992 and its exhibits trace the history of the airfield, the aircraft and people who flew from it.

TYPE	REG/SER	CON. NO.	PI/NOTES	STATUS
☐ McDonnell M.98DJ Phantom II (F-4C)	64-0844	1197		PV
☐ Schweizer SGS.2-8 (TG-2)	N47403	53	(USAAF)	RAA
☐ Waco NZR Hadrian (CG-4A)			Front fuselage only.	PV

BRAZIL MONUMENT (IN5)

| Location: | On permanent view outside the Clay County Courthouse in the centre of the town. |

TYPE	REG/SER	CON. NO.	PI/NOTES	STATUS
☐ North American NA-193 Sabre (F-86F)	52-5434	193-163		PV

CAMP ATTERBURY MUSEUM AND MEMORIAL (IN6)

Address:	Edinburgh, Indiana 46124-5000.
Tel:	826-526-1744 Email: JimWest@IndianaMilitary.org
Admission:	January–March Wednesday and Sunday 1300-1600; April–December Wednesday and Sunday 1300-1700, Saturday 1200-1700.
Location:	In the northern suburbs of the town.

The Indiana Army National Guard has placed on display an example of the Iroquois helicopter. This type has given excellent service for many years with units across the state. The history of the base is portrayed in the displays of models, photographs, documents and uniforms. The training of recruits is also portrayed.

TYPE	REG/SER	CON. NO.	PI/NOTES	STATUS
☐ Bell 205 Iroquois (UH-1H)	'66-10584'			PVX
☐ McDonnell M.98EV Phantom II (F-4J) (F-4S)	Bu155900	3576		PV

CHILDREN'S MUSEUM OF INDIANAPOLIS (IN7)

Address:	PO Box 3000, 300 North Meridian Street, Indianapolis, Indiana 46206-3000.
Tel:	317-334-4000 Email: info@childrensmuseum.org
Admission:	Monday-Sunday 1000-1700.Closes at 2000 on Thursday. Closed on Monday September–February.
Location:	At the junction of Thirtieth and North Meridian Streets in the northern part of the city centre.

The museum, opened in 1926, is the largest in the world dedicated specifically to children. The collection moved into the present building in 1976. The five floors house a wide variety of exhibits and 'hands-on' displays.

A 'Flight Where Adventures Take Off' was a temporary attraction in the 1990s. It then toured visiting many sites including Boston, Denver Minneapolis and Philadelphia. The display was designed to introduce young people to the science and myths of flight. The exhibition included a butterfly garden and flight simulators.

In the transport section are several model aircraft and helicopters. The glider and microlight also reside in this area. For some years a Boeing-Stearman Kaydet was loaned to the exhibition but this has returned to its owner.

TYPE	REG/SER	CON. NO.	PI/NOTES	STATUS
☐ Glider				PV
☐ Microlight				PV

CHURUBUSCO MONUMENT (IN8)

| Location: | On permanent view in the Community Park on Route 33 in the northern part of the town. |

TYPE	REG/SER	CON. NO.	PI/NOTES	STATUS
☐ North American NA-203 Sabre (F-86H)	53-1298	203-70		PV

COLUMBUS MONUMENT (IN9)

| Location: | On permanent view at VFW1987 at 215 North National Road in the northern part of the town. |

TYPE	REG/SER	CON. NO.	PI/NOTES	STATUS
☐ Lockheed 580 (T-33A)	54-1547	580-9178	54-1547, E.15-29 (Spain)	PV

COMMEMORATIVE AIR FORCE (INDIANA WING) (IN10)

Address:	14253 Trailwind Court, Carmel, Indiana 46032-7770.
Tel:	317-769-4487 Email: mbacon@indy.rr.com
Admission:	By prior permission only.
Location:	At Terry Airport which is about 5 miles north east of Columbia City.

The Indiana Squadron was formed in 1979 and achieved wing status two years later. The only aircraft now allocated is the Cornell which took to the air again in 1999 after a 13 year restoration.

TYPE	REG/SER	CON. NO.	PI/NOTES	STATUS
☐ Fairchild M-62A-4 Cornell (PT-26A)	N60535	FX-146	42-71412	RAA
☐ Stinson V-76 Sentinel (L-5G)				RAA
☐ Taylorcraft DCO-65 Grasshopper (O-57A) (L-2A)	N53768	L-5135	(USAAF)	RAC
☐ Vultee V-74 Valiant (BT-13A)	N57486	74-5665	41-21826	RAA

COVINGTON MONUMENT (IN11)

| Location: | On permanent view at VFW 2395 in Liberty Street in the south eastern part of the town. |

TYPE	REG/SER	CON. NO.	PI/NOTES	STATUS
☐ Lockheed 580 (T-33A)	52-9326	580-7611		PV

Indiana

EDINBURGH MONUMENT (IN12)

Location:	On permanent view at ALP 233 in High School Drive in the south western part of the town.

TYPE	REG/SER	CON. NO.	PI/NOTES	STATUS
☐ Northrop N-156T Talon (T-38A)	60-0558	N.5131		PV

FAIRMOUNT MONUMENT (IN13)

Location:	On permanent view at ALP 313 on Route 26 in the eastern part of the town.

TYPE	REG/SER	CON. NO.	PI/NOTES	STATUS
☐ Bell 205 Iroquois (UH-1H)	68-16504	11163		PV
☐ McDonnell M.98DE Phantom II (F-4C)	63-7623	709		PV

FORT WAYNE AIR NATIONAL GUARD BASE (IN14)

Address:	122 FW/ACC, 3005 Ferguson Road, Fort Wayne, Indiana 46809-0127
Tel:	260-478-3247 Email: 122FW.WebMaster@inftwa.ang.af.mil
Admission:	By prior permission only.
Location:	The airfield is about 6 miles south west of the city off Route 1.

The 163rd Fighter Squadron was allocated to the Indiana Air National Guard October 1947 and based at Baer Field. The first type to be flown was the P-51D Mustang and and since then fighters have been operated. The four preserved aircraft are located in a park near the gate. The Super Sabre carries false markings.

TYPE	REG/SER	CON. NO.	PI/NOTES	STATUS
☐ General Dynamics 401 Fighting Falcon (F-16C)	84-1264	5C-101		RA
☐ McDonnell M.98HO Phantom II (F-4E)	67-0389	3294		RA
☐ North American NA-235 Super Sabre (F-100D)	'56-3210'			RAX
☐ Republic F-84F Thunderstreak	52-6629		52-6629, N97020	RA

FORT WAYNE MONUMENT (IN15)

Location:	On permanent view at Allen County War Memorial in Parnell Avenue – north of the town centre.

TYPE	REG/SER	CON. NO.	PI/NOTES	STATUS
☐ Republic F-84F Thunderstreak	51-9514			PV

FREEMAN ARMY AIRFIELD MUSEUM (IN16)

Address:	1035 A Avenue, Seymour, Indiana 47274.
Tel:	812-522-2031 Email: sipesj@scsc.k12.in.us
Location:	About 2 miles south of Seymour on Route 11.

The airfield opened on 1st December 1942 and was used for pilot training on Beech AT-10s. The first helicopter training school was established in September 1944. In June 1945 the base was used for the testing and storage of captured enemy aircraft. Over 70 American types later arrived for museum use.

The airfield closed in 1946 after the aircraft were moved across the country and unfortunately some were later scrapped. The museum has been set up to trace the unique history of the field and many digs have taken place to recover components.

GARY-CHIGACO INTERNATIONAL AIRPORT (IN17)

Location:	On permanent view in the terminal of the airport which is in the north western part of the town.

TYPE	REG/SER	CON. NO.	PI/NOTES	STATUS
☐ Chanute Glider (R)				PV

GREATER FORT WAYNE AVIATION MUSEUM (IN18)

Address:	3801 West Ferguson, Fort Wayne, Indiana 46809 -3194.
Tel:	260-747-4146
Admission:	Daily 0600-1900.
Location:	At Baer Field which is which is about 6 miles south west of the city off Route 1.

An excellent display of memorabilia is in the terminal building at Baer Field. Paul Baer was a local man who was killed on military service. The 1911 aircraft built by Art Smith is currently in store. Displays trace the history of flying in the area with sections on the airfield, the aero club and the local Air National Guard unit.

TYPE	REG/SER	CON. NO.	PI/NOTES	STATUS
☐ Smith Aeroplane				RA

GREENCASTLE MONUMENT (IN19)

Location:	On permanent view outside the City Hall.

TYPE	REG/SER	CON. NO.	PI/NOTES	STATUS
☐ Ford JB-2 [Fieseler Fi 103A-1]				

GRISSOM AIR MUSEUM (IN20)

Address:	1000 West Hoosier Boulevard, Peru, Indiana 46970-3723.
Tel:	765-689-8011 **Email:** director@grissomairmuseum.com
Admission:	Tuesday-Sunday 1000-1600 Opens Mondays in summer months. Closed late December–mid February.
Location:	About 7 miles south of Peru on Route 31.

The site opened as a Navy flying training school in January 1943 and closed after World War II. The Air Force took over the facility in 1951 and used it for storage. In 1954 it became Bunker Hill Air Force Base and took up its present title in May 1968 in memory of Colonel Virgil I. Grissom, who was killed in an Apollo Capsule fire at Cape Kennedy in 1967. The first aircraft to arrive at the base for preservation was the B-17 which has now been in residence for over a quarter of a century. The collection grew and was displayed along the road from the main gate to the airfield. The aircraft were moved to a site just outside the gate few years ago and in 1991 a museum building opened. The indoor displays trace the history of the base and the units which have flown from the field. One of the few surviving Convair B-58s is a prized exhibit.

TYPE	REG/SER	CON. NO.	PI/NOTES	STATUS
☐ Bell 204 Iroquois (HH-1K)	Bu157193	6317	Fuselage pod only.	PV
☐ Bell 205 Iroquois (UH-1H)	68-16256	10915		PV
☐ Boeing 299-O Fortress (B-17G) (DB-17G) (DB-17P)	44-83690	32331	44-83690, '231255', '48385'	PV
☐ Boeing 367-76-66 Stratofreighter (KC-97G) (KC-97L)	52-2697	16728		PV
☐ Boeing 450-67-27 Stratojet (B-47B)	51-2315	450368	51-2315, '20271'	PV
☐ Boeing 717-146 Stratotanker (KC-135A) (EC-135L)	61-0269	18176		PV
☐ Cessna 172F Mescalero (T-41A)	65-5100	17251947	N5100F	RA
☐ Cessna 310A Blue Canoe (L-27A) (U-3A)	57-5922	38077		PV
☐ Cessna 318B Tweety Bird (318A) (T-37A) (T-37B)	54-2736	40012		PV
☐ Cessna 337M Super Skymaster (O-2A)	68-6871	337M0160		PV
☐ Convair 4 Hustler (YB-58A) (TB-58A)	55-0663	4		PV
☐ Convair 8-12 Delta Dagger (TF-102A)	56-2317	8-12-49		PV
☐ Douglas DC-3A-467 Skytrain (C-47B) (C-47D)	43-49270	15086/26531		PV
☐ Douglas TA-4J Skyhawk (TA-4F)	Bu153671	13609		PV
☐ Fairchild 110 Flying Boxcar (C-119G)	52-5850	11009		PV
☐ Fairchild-Republic A-10A Thunderbolt II	77-0218	A10-153		PV
☐ Grumman G-96 Trader (TF-1) (C-1A)	Bu136790	043		PV
☐ Grumman G-98 Tiger (F11F-1) (F-11A)	Bu141790	107		PV
☐ Grumman G-303 Tomcat (F-14B)	Bu162912	560		PV
☐ Lockheed 580 (T-33A)	51-6782	580-6114		PV
☐ Lockheed 580 (T-33A)	52-9563	580-7723		PV
☐ McDonnell M.36BA Voodoo (F-101B)	58-0321	693		PV
☐ McDonnell M.98DJ Phantom II (F-4C)	64-0783	1091		PV
☐ McDonnell M.98DJ Phantom II (F-4C)	64-0889	1301	Front fuselage only – on loan from Childrens Museum, IN.	PV
☐ NAMC YS-11-120	P4-KFD	2035	JA8676, OB-R-857, JA8676	PV
☐ North American NA-108 Mitchell (B-25J) (TB-25J) (TB-25N)	44-86843	108-47597	44-86843, N3507G, '486872'	PV
☐ North American NA-214 Super Sabre (F-100C)	53-1712	214-4		PV
☐ North American NA-346 Buckeye (T-2C)	Bu158583	346-9		PV
☐ Northrop N-160 Scorpion (N-68) (F-89D) (F-89J)	52-2154	N.4566	Rear fuselage only.	RA
☐ Northrop N-160 Scorpion (N-68) (F-89D) (F-89J)	53-2601	N.4732	Front fuselage only.	RA
☐ Piasecki PV-18 Retriever (HUP-2) (UH-25B)	Bu129989			RA
☐ Piper J-3C-65 Cub	N98788	19028		RAC
☐ Republic F-84F Thunderstreak	51-9456			RA
☐ Republic F-105D Thunderchief	61-0088	D-283		PV

HAMMOND MONUMENT (IN21)

Location:	On view during opening hours in Cabela's store at 7700 Cabela Drive – south east of the town.

TYPE	REG/SER	CON. NO.	PI/NOTES	STATUS
☐ Aeronca 7AC Champion	N85419	7AC-4159	NC85419	PV

HISTORICAL MILITARY ARMOR MUSEUM (IN22)

Address:	2330 Crystal Street, Anderson, Indiana 46012-1726.
Tel:	765-649-8265 **Fax:** 765-642-0262
Admission:	Tuesday and Thursday 1300-1600.
Location:	In the northern suburbs of the city.

The most complete collection of light tanks in the USA is housed in this museum. They are all in working order and cover the period from World War I to the present day. Other military vehicles are also on show. A range of weapons can also be seen along with examples of bombs and shells. Local interest is provided by a Howe Fire Truck made in the town. A 1947 Cadillac used by President Truman is one of the highlights of the exhibition. The aircraft collection is growing steadily and includes mainly helicopters.

TYPE	REG/SER	CON. NO.	PI/NOTES	STATUS
☐ Bell 204 Iroquois (UH-1C)	65-9547	1447		RA
☐ Bell 205 Iroquois (UH-1H)	N301MD	10960	68-16301	PV
☐ Grumman G-134 Mohawk (OV-1C) (OV-1D)	N939MM	143C	68-15739	PV

Indiana

☐ Hughes 269A Osage (TH-55A)	67-16963	1070	PV
☐ Rotorway Scorpion Too	N53MC	1717MC	RAA

HOAGLAND MONUMENT (IN23)

Location:	On permanent view in the Community Park in the centre of the town.

TYPE	REG/SER	CON. NO.	PI/NOTES	STATUS
☐ Republic F-84F Thunderstreak	51-1763			PV

HOBART MONUMENT (IN24)

Location:	By prior permission only at a house in South Liverpool Road about 3 miles west of the town.

TYPE	REG/SER	CON. NO.	PI/NOTES	STATUS
☐ Lockheed 580 (T-33A)	51-9079	580-6863		RA

HOOSIER AIR MUSEUM (IN25)

Address:	2282 Country Road 62, PO Box 87, Auburn, Indiana 46706.
Tel:	260-927-0443 Email: nileswalton@hotmail.com
Admission:	Mid March–Late December Monday-Saturday 1000-1600; Sunday 1300-1600.
Location:	At the south side of DeKalb County Airport at the junction of County Roads 27 and 62.

Housed in a hangar at the airport, this museum has education high on its priorities. The history of aviation with particular reference to the local area is portrayed in the displays. The visitor can learn about the designers, pilots and engineers who maintained the aircraft.

Over 5,000 Cessna T-50s were built during World War II and used for instruction and communications duties. The Pratt-Read was used to train glider pilots including many who participated in the D-Day landings.

The Fokker D VII replica is under construction in a nearby workshop. The immaculate Bird A is a rarity and carries its original experimental markings.

TYPE	REG/SER	CON. NO.	PI/NOTES	STATUS
☐ Aeronca 7AC Champion				PV
☐ Beech C18S Kansan (AT-11)	N6960C	3306	42-36926	PV
☐ Bell 209 Huey Cobra (AH-1G) (AH-1F)	67-15720	20384		PV
☐ Boeing A75N1 Kaydet (PT-17)				PV
☐ Brunner-Winkle Bird A	X15641	1000	X15641, NC15641, N15641	PV
☐ Cessna T-50 Bobcat (C-78) (UC-78)	N672	5921	43-31983	PV
☐ Fokker D VII (R)				RAC
☐ Howard S-51-D Mustang	N16697	0026		PV
☐ Loving-Wayne WR-3	N553A	3		PV
☐ Nieuport 11 (Scale R)	N42989	00684		PV
☐ Nieuport 24 (Scale R)	N65113	DWM-101		PV
☐ Piper J-3C-65 Cub (J-3C-65)	N98022	18165		PV
☐ Pitts S-1C Special			Incomplete	PV
☐ Pratt-Read PR-G1 (XLNE-1)	Bu31505			PV
☐ Pratt-Read PR-G1 (LNE-1)	N56349		Fuselage only.	PV
☐ Revolution Mini 500	N130GB	130		PV
☐ Smith DSA-2 Miniplane	NX4639S	102		PV
☐ Stinson SR-9C Reliant	NC18408	5315	NC18408, N18408	PV
☐ Stinson V-77 Reliant (AT-19)	N69721	77-152	42-46791, FK965, Bu11479	PV

HUNTINGTON MONUMENTS (IN26)

Location:	On permanent view at two locations in the town.

TYPE	REG/SER	CON. NO.	PI/NOTES	STATUS
☐ Lockheed 483-04-06 Starfighter (F-104D)	57-1322	283-5034	At the airport south of the town.	PV
☐ Lockheed 580 (T-33A)	'51-6754'	580-6077	51-6745 – in Memorial Park in the town.	PVX

INDIANA AIR SEARCH AND RESCUE (IN27)

Address:	20 North Meridian Street, Suite 206, Indianapolis, Indiana 46204.
Tel:	317-636-5007 Email: info@iasar.org
Admission:	By prior permission only.
Location:	At Metro airfield which is about 15 miles north east of the city.

The group was set up to provide air relief and aircraft preservation facilities for the local community. The Bell UH-1H painted in its original army colours is a regular performer at shows in the region. Two DC-3s have been acquired and they are parked at the airport. Restoration of the pair has commenced by members of the organisation.

TYPE	REG/SER	CON. NO.	PI/NOTES	STATUS
☐ Bell 205 Iroquois (UH-1H)	N30111	11222	68-16563	RAA
☐ Douglas DC-3A-456 Skytrain (C-47A) (C-47D) (NC-47B)	N236GB	20743	43-16277, 6277 (US Army)	RA
☐ Douglas DC-3A-467 Skytrain (TC-47B) (R4D-7) (R4D-6R) (TC-47J)	'459838'	16468/33216	44-76884, Bu99838, N7073C, N30, N87814, N20904J, N212GB, N2312GB	RAX

INDIANA AVIATION MUSEUM (IN28)

Address:	4601 Murvihill Road, Valparaiso, Indiana 46383.
Tel:	219-548-3123 Fax: 219-929-1349 Email: info@in-am.org
Admission:	Saturday 1000-1600; Sunday 1300-1600.
Location:	At the airport which is 5 miles east of the town on Route 2.

Most of the aircraft in this museum come from the private collection of James Read. The Corsair which has a complex history flew in the 'Black Sheep' movie. The Mustang was civilianised in the early 1960s but crashed in Missouri soon after. The airframe spent many years in store before being rebuilt.

TYPE	REG/SER	CON. NO.	PI/NOTES	STATUS
☐ Aero L-29 Delfin	N27SR	892829		PVA
☐ Beech D45 Mentor (T-34B)	N234MC	BG-411	Bu144104	PVA
☐ Beech 58 Baron	N7248R	TH-578		PVA
☐ Boeing-Stearman A75N1 Kaydet (PT-17)	N57941	75-1860	41-8301	PVA
☐ Boeing-Stearman A75N1 Kaydet (PT-17)	N54945	75-4458	42-16295	PVA
☐ Cessna 318D Dragonfly (A-37A)	N91RW	40026	67-14510 – converted from 318B 55-4312.	PVA
☐ De Havilland DHC.1 Chipmunk 22 (T.10)	N26JH'18010'	C1/0887	WZ860, G-BDCH, N124VH	PVAX
☐ Lake LA-4-200 Buccaneer	N131ER	940		PVA
☐ North American NA-124 Mustang (P-51D)	NL151W	124-48293	45-11540, N5162V	PVA
☐ North American NA-182 Texan (T-6G)	N92761	182-413	51-14726, 114726 (France)	PVA
☐ North American NA-219 Trojan (T-28B)	N6263T	219-17	Bu140018	PVA
☐ Piper J-3C-65 Cub	N6580H	19773	NC6580H	PVA
☐ Rotorway Executive 90	N4561C	5212		PVA
☐ Taylorcraft DCO-65 Grasshoprrer (L-2M)	N53709	L-5941	43-26629	PVA
☐ Vans RV-4	N91ER	884		PVA
☐ Vought F4U-5N Corsair (F4U-5)	N179PT		Bu123168, (Honduras), N179PT, N179NP – has assumed identity of Bu122179, 604 (Honduras). N4903M	PVA

INDIANA MILITARY MUSEUM (IN29)

Address:	PO Box 977, 2074 Old Bruceville Road, Vincennes, Indiana 47591.
Tel:	812-882-8668 Email: jrosborne@avenuebroadband.com
Admission:	Outside display daily 0800-1600; Buildings daily 1200-1600.
Location:	About 2 miles east of the town.

This has several aeronautical exhibits. Faded airline colours can be seen on the nose of the C-47. The Beech 18, which is an ex Navy example, has been painted in a USAAC colour scheme of the 1941 period.

Inside the building there are displays of uniforms, models documents and photographs. There are many military vehicles and heavy weapons in the collection along with missiles and equipment.

TYPE	REG/SER	CON. NO.	PI/NOTES	STATUS
☐ Beech C18S Expeditor (C-45F) (UC-45F) (JRB-4)				PVX
☐ Bell 205 Iroquois (UH-1D) (UH-1H)	65-9628	4672		PV
☐ Douglas DC-3A-456 Skytrain (C-47A)			Front fuselage only.	PVD
☐ Lockheed 580 (T-33A)	56-1669	580-1019		PV
☐ Lockheed 580 (T-33A) (TV-2) (T-33B)	Bu141547	580-9603	55-3062	PV
☐ Vultee V-74 Valiant (BT-13A)	41-11388	74-2398	41-11388, N59975	PVD

INDIANA WELCOME CENTER (IN30)

Location:	On permanent view at the building at 80/95 and Kennedy South in Hammond.

TYPE	REG/SER	CON. NO.	PI/NOTES	STATUS
☐ Chanute Glider (R)				PV

INDIANAPOLIS MONUMENTS (IN31)

Location:	On permanent view at two locations in the city.

TYPE	REG/SER	CON. NO.	PI/NOTES	STATUS
☐ Cessna 150			At a steakhouse somewhere in the city.	PV
☐ North American NA-170 Sabre (F-86E)	50-0682	170-104	At VFW 7119 at 6500 Lee Road.	PV

LA PORTE COUNTY HISTORICAL SOCIETY MUSEUM (IN32)

Address:	2405 Indiana Avenue, La Porte, Indiana 46350.
Tel:	219-324-6763 Fax: 219-324-9029 Email: info@laportecountyhistory.org
Admission:	Tuesday-Saturday 1000-1630.
Location:	In the south eastern part of the town on Route 4.

The society has a wide range of items on show in the museum and has set up markers at important local sites The development of the area is portrayed in the displays. There are over 10,000 items on show.

Four aircraft can be seen along with a number of vehicles. The development in homebuilt designs can be seen by comparing the 1930s Pietenpol with the 1970s Sonerai. An early example of the Piper Tripacer is on view.

Indiana

TYPE	REG/SER	CON. NO.	PI/NOTES	STATUS
☐ Monnett Sonerai II-S2-MLI	N4ML	18		PV
☐ Pietenpol B4-A Aircamper				PV
☐ Piper PA-22 Tripacer 125	N862A	22-162		PV
☐ Santos-Dumont XX Demoiselle (R)				PV

LAWRENCE D. BELL AVIATION MUSEUM (IN33)

Address: PO Box 411, South Oak Street, Mentone, Indiana 46539.
Tel: 574-353-7318   **Email:** blinda@kconline.com
Admission: June–September Sunday 1300-1700.
Location: In the centre of the town which is about 12 miles south west of Warsaw on Route 19.

Lawrence D. Bell was born in Mentone on 5th April 1894. The family moved to California in 1907 and within a few years he was in the aviation industry and worked for several companies. He formed the Bell Aircraft Corporation in 1935 and many successful designs were produced.

Helicopter development began in 1941 and the company and its successor is still to the forefront. Recently acquired is the collection of Bob Herendeen memorabilia. He was a native of the town and was killed in 1994 in the crash of a Christen Eagle.

TYPE	REG/SER	CON. NO.	PI/NOTES	STATUS
☐ Bell 47G-2 Sioux (H-13H) (OH-13H)				PV
☐ Bell 47H-1	N13172	1348		PV
☐ Bell 47H				PV
☐ Bell 205 Iroquois (UH-1D) (UH-1H)	63-8801	4093		PV

LAWRENCE MONUMENT (IN34)

Location: On permanent view at VFW Post 261 at 10550 Pendleton Pike on Route 36 north east of the town.

TYPE	REG/SER	CON. NO.	PI/NOTES	STATUS
☐ North American NA-170 Sabre (F-86E)	'0682'	170-54	50-0632	PVX

LEE BOTTOM MUSEUM (IN35)

Address: 7296 South River Bottom Road, Hanover, Indiana 47243.
Tel: 812-866-3211   **Email:** info@leebottom.com
Admission: Not yet open.
Location: Next to the Ohio River near the town.

Several antique and classic aircraft reside at the field. Regular fly-ins are held throughout the year. Plans have been put forward to create a museum which will be typical of a 1930s airport. Period hangars will be built along with other facilities. This project is in an early stage and hopefully construction will soon start.

MILITARY HONOR PARK (IN36)

Address: 4300 Veterans Drive, South Bend, Indiana 46628-5509.
Tel: 574-232-4300
Admission: On permanent view.
Location: Off the entrance road to the airport which is about 5 miles north of the town.

The park has been set up to commemorate local people who have fought in the five main services. The T-33 was recovered from Kentland in Indiana. The trainer had spent over 30 years stored in the town and was restored for display. Also on show in the attractive gardens are military vehicles, guns and flags.

TYPE	REG/SER	CON. NO.	PI/NOTES	STATUS
☐ Bell 205 Iroquois (UH-1H) (UH-1V)	68-15529	10459		RA
☐ Lockheed 580 (T-33A)				PV

MONROEVILLE MONUMENT (IN37)

Location: On permanent view in the Community Park in the southern part of the town.

TYPE	REG/SER	CON. NO.	PI/NOTES	STATUS
☐ Republic F-84F Thunderstreak	51-1631			PV

MONTPELIER MONUMENT (IN38)

Location: On permanent view on Route 18 in the western part of the town.

TYPE	REG/SER	CON. NO.	PI/NOTES	STATUS
☐ Republic F-84F Thunderstreak	'52-709'		51-1747	PVX

MUNSTER MONUMENT (IN39)

Location: On permanent view in the Veterans Park in Calumet Avenue in the southern part of the town.

TYPE	REG/SER	CON. NO.	PI/NOTES	STATUS
☐ Bell 205 Iroquois (UH-1H)	67-17288	9486		PV

MUSEUM OF ITALIAN ARMY AVIATION / FROST COLLECTION (IN40)

Address:	784 North Franklin Street, Greenfield, Indiana 46140.
Tel:	317-326-2633
Admission:	By prior permission only.
Location:	About 20 miles east of Indianapolis and 2 miles south of I.70.

Kent Frost obtained a former Italian Army Super Cub in late 1980s and this aroused his interest in the service. Later two more aircraft were acquired and these await restoration. Artefacts have also been collected. The airworthy L-21 was stationed at Urbe Airport near Rome during its Italian service. Several other vintage aircraft owned by Kent's father are based here and at other fields in the area. The two low-wing Aeronca LBs are rarities. Only 65 examples were built in the mid-1930s. Also in the collection are examples of the Aeronca Champion and Chief.

TYPE	REG/SER	CON. NO.	PI/NOTES	STATUS
☐ Aeronca LB	NC16262	2016	NC16262, N16262	RA
☐ Aeronca LB	NC16271	2019	NC16271, N16271	RA
☐ Aeronca 7AC Champion	N82734	7AC-1381	NC82734	RAA
☐ Aeronca 11AC Chief	N9244E	11AC-878	NC9244E	RAA
☐ Aeronca 11AC Chief	N9344E	11AC-982	NC9344E	RAA
☐ Cessna 120	NC72350	9534	NC72350, N72350	RAA
☐ Champion 7GCAA	N199ED	457-2001		RAA
☐ Fleet 2	NC610M	186	NC610M, N610M	RAA
☐ Luscombe 8E Silvaire	N1513B	6140	NC1513B	RAA
☐ Piper PA-18-135 Super Cub (L-21B)	N8056W	18-3376	53-7776, MM53-7776, I-EIHX, EI-147	RAA
☐ Piper PA-18-135 Super Cub (L-21B)	N3021L	18-3554	54-2354, MM54-2354, I-EIXG, EI-168	RAC
☐ Piper PA-18-135 Super Cub (L-21B)	N99323	18-3576	54-2376, MM54-2376, I-EIYH, EI-187	RAC
☐ Stinson V-77 Reliant (AT-19)	N73373	77-77	42-46716, FK890, Bu11352, N73373	RAA
☐ Waco INF	NC11203	3399	NC11203, N11203	RAA
☐ Waco RNF	NC632Y	3343	NC632Y, N632Y	RAA
☐ Waco RNF	NC11245	3405	NC11245, N11245	RAA

NATIONAL MODEL AVIATION MUSEUM (IN41)

Address:	5161 East Memorial Drive, Muncie, Indiana 47302.
Tel:	765-287-1256 Email: michael@modelaircraft.com
Admission:	Monday-Friday 0800-1630; Saturday-Sunday 1000-1600.
Location:	In the south eastern suburbs of the town.

Aeromodelling is a popular hobby throughout the world. The displays trace the history of the sport from simple balsa wood designs to modern radio-controlled types. Also on show are engines, accessories and kits.

NAVAL WEAPONS SUPPORT CENTER MONUMENT (IN42)

Location:	By prior permission only at the base about 4 miles east of Crane.

TYPE	REG/SER	CON. NO.	PI/NOTES	STATUS
☐ Douglas A-4A Skyhawk (A4D-1)	Bu142230	11484		RA

NORTHERN INDIANA AVIATION MUSEUM (IN43)

Address:	Airport Drive, Elkhart, Indiana 46514.
Admission:	By prior permission only.
Location:	About 10 miles south east of the town.

This museum was set up in the mid-1990s at Goshen and has acquired a fleet of airworthy warbirds as well as static examples of more modern types. A move has now been made to larger premises at Elkhart. The Fleet 2 first appeared as the Consolidated Husky Junior in 1928 and the following year the Fleet Aircraft Division was set up to manufacture it. The unique Selcher Sport biplane was once at the Flying Circus Aerodrome in Virginia. The aircraft was completed in the late 1970s and is powered by a Lycoming O-235 engine.

TYPE	REG/SER	CON. NO.	PI/NOTES	STATUS
☐ Beech A45 Mentor (T-34A)	N45RD	G-299	53-4199	RAA
☐ Fleet 2	NC8687	74	NC8687, N8687	RAA
☐ North American NA-88 Texan (AT-6C) (Harvard II)				RAC
☐ North American NA-88 Texan (SNJ-4)				RAC
☐ Selcher Sport	N67JS	JS-1		RAA
☐ Stinson 108-3 Voyager	N108SV	108-4165		RAA
☐ Yakovlev Yak-52	NX8271P	811310	32 (DOSAAF)	RAA

NORTH VERNON MONUMENT (IN44)

Location:	On permanent view at AMVETS Post 7 at 717 Amvets Drive just east of the town

TYPE	REG/SER	CON. NO.	PI/NOTES	STATUS
☐ Vought A-7D Corsair II	68-8226	D52		PV

Indiana

ORLAND MONUMENT (IN45)

Location:	On permanent view at ALP 423 at 6215N SR 327 just north of the town centre.

TYPE	REG/SER	CON. NO.	PI/NOTES	STATUS
☐ Bell 205 Iroquois (UH-1H)	67-17562	9760		PV

PURDUE UNIVERSITY (IN46)

Address:	1401 Aviation Drive, West Lafayette, Indiana 47907-2015
Tel:	765-494-5782 **Fax:** 765-494-2305 **Email:** delongbo@purdue.edu
Admission:	By prior permission only.
Location:	At the airport which is in the south eastern part of the town.

The university, founded in 1869, has a number of sites in the region. Purdue set up its own airport and this is now the home of the aviation department which carries out flight training and research. The workshops contain a number of instructional airframes including one of the four completed Piper Arapaho twin engined monoplanes.

TYPE	REG/SER	CON. NO.	PI/NOTES	STATUS
☐ Beech A23 Musketeer II	N8872M	M615		RA
☐ Boeing 727-22F	N180FE	18867	N7060U, N180FE, C-GBWS	RA
☐ Cessna 152	N757GJ	15279276		RA
☐ Cessna 310R	N3432Y	310R0835		RA
☐ Hughes 269A Osage (TH-55A)	67-18357	17-0669		RA
☐ Piper PA-38-112 Tomahawk	N384PT	38-78A0006		RA
☐ Piper PA-40 Arapaho	N9997P	40-7400003		RA

RICHMOND MONUMENT (IN47)

Location:	On permanent view at the airport which is south west of the town on Route 227.

TYPE	REG/SER	CON. NO.	PI/NOTES	STATUS
☐ Grumman G-128 Intruder (A-6A)	Bu152603	I-151		PV

ROPKEY ARMOR MUSEUM (IN48)

Address:	5649 East 150th North, Crawfordsville, Indiana 47933.
Tel:	317-295-9295 **Email:** tours@ropkeyarmormuseum.com
Admission:	Monday-Friday 0900-1800; weekends by appointment.
Location:	In the south western part of the town.
	Some of the aircraft are at a number of airfields in the Indianapolis area.

Formerly known as the Indiana Museum of Military History, this private museum contains one of the largest collections of military vehicles and equipment in the country. This part of the museum has moved to a new site at Crawfordsville.
The aircraft side is run by Rick Ropkey, son of the founder Fred. One of the Mohawks is maintained in flying condition, as are several other types in the fleet. A fairly recent arrival is the Antonov An-2 which is awaiting restoration.
The Fleet biplane dating from the late 1920s was once used by the famous racing pilot Roscoe Turner. One of the Super Skymasters was flown by the CIA and carries their markings.

TYPE	REG/SER	CON. NO.	PI/NOTES	STATUS
☐ Antonov An-2TP	N9TP	1G 185-01	SP-TWG	PV
☐ Beech D45 Mentor (T-34B)	N662	BG-302	Bu143995	PV
☐ Bell 204 Iroquois (UH-1B)	N2956F	1011	63-12950	PV
☐ Bell 205 Iroquois (UH-1D) (UH-1H)	64-13494	4201	Front fuselage only – possible identity.	PV
☐ Bell 68 (X-14) (X-14A) (X-14B)	N704NA		56-4022, N234NA	RAC
☐ Boeing-Stearman A75N1 Kaydet (PT-17)			Fuselage frame only.	RA
☐ Boeing-Stearman A75N1 Kaydet (PT-17)	NC65851	75-1884	41-8325	RAA
☐ Cessna 337 Super Skymaster	N37536			PV
☐ Cessna 337M Super Skymaster (O-2A)	N5258C	337M0141	67-21435	RAA
☐ De Havilland DH.115 Vampire T.35	N11929	4166	A79-644	RAC
☐ Douglas A-4B Skyhawk (A4D-2)	Bu142834	11896		PV
☐ Fleet 1	N758V	339	NC758V	PV
☐ Government Aircraft Factories Jindivik 203B (IIIB)	A92-653			PV
☐ Grumman G-40 Avenger (TBF-1C)	Bu05954	4010	Bu05954, N5954A	RAC
☐ Grumman G-134 Mohawk (AO-1A) (OV-1A)	N90788	49A	63-13119	RAA
☐ Grumman G-134 Mohawk (AO-1C) (OV-1C)	'N90788'	32C	61-2689	PVX
☐ Grumman G-134 Mohawk (OV-1C) (OV-1D)	66-18884	85C		RA
☐ Homebuilt Monoplane				PVD
☐ North American NA-305 Bronco (OV-10A)				PVD
☐ North American NA-305 Bronco (OV-10A)				PV
☐ Taylorcraft BC-12D	N44170	9970	NC44170	RAA

SOUTH BEND MONUMENT (IN49)

Location:	On permanent view at Jeep Acres at 29430 State Route 2.

TYPE	REG/SER	CON. NO.	PI/NOTES	STATUS
☐ Piasecki PV-17 (HRP-2)				PV

SOUTH WHITLEY MONUMENT (IN50)

Location:	On permanent view in the Community Park in the centre of the town.

TYPE	REG/SER	CON. NO.	PI/NOTES	STATUS
☐ Republic F-84F Thunderstreak	51-1739			PV

SULLIVAN MONUMENT (IN51)

Location:	On permanent view at VFW 2459 in South Section Street in the southern part of the town.

TYPE	REG/SER	CON. NO.	PI/NOTES	STATUS
☐ Bell 205 Iroquois (UH-1H)	66-16665	8859		PV

TERRE HAUTE AIR NATIONAL GUARD BASE (IN52)

Address:	181 IW/PA, 915 South Petercheff Street, Terre Haute, Indiana 47803-5042.
Tel:	812-877-5266
Admission:	By prior permission only.
Location:	About 5 miles east of the city off Route 42.

The 113th Squadron was allocated to the state of Indiana in August 1921. Until 1954 it was based in the Indianapolis area, first at Schoen Field and later at Stout Field. After operating a variety of observation types it became a fighter unit when returned to state control in 1947. The wing moved to Terre Haute in late 1954.

TYPE	REG/SER	CON. NO.	PI/NOTES	STATUS
☐ General Dynamics 401 Fighting Falcon (F-16A)	79-0401	61-186		RA
☐ McDonnell M.98DE Phantom II (F-4C)	63-7565	607		RA
☐ North American NA-235 Super Sabre (F-100D)	56-3320	235-418		RA
☐ Republic F-84F Thunderstreak	52-6617		52-6617, '54-181' – at ALP 104 in town.	PV
☐ Republic F-84F Thunderstreak	'52-7202'		52-7027	RAX

VINCENNES UNIVERSITY (IN53)

Address:	2175 South Hoffman, Indianapolis, Indiana 46241.
Tel:	317-381-6000 Email: dbandy@vinu.edu
Admission:	By prior permission only.
Location:	At Indianapolis IAP in the south western part of the city off the outer ring road.

Founded in 1801, as Jefferson Academy, the university is the oldest public institution of higher education in Indiana. The Aviation Technology Center at the airport is equipped with modern workshops. In additional to the instructional airframes there are a number of engines. The Boeing 737 was acquired from United Airlines.

TYPE	REG/SER	CON. NO.	PI/NOTES	STATUS
☐ Beech 60 Duke				RA
☐ Beech 65-80 Seminole (L-23F) (U-8F)	N62069	LF-64	62-3866	RA
☐ Beech 65-90 King Air	'N90VU'	LJ-3	CF-UAC, C-FUAC,	RAX
☐ Bell 206 Jet Ranger				RA
☐ Boeing 737-222	'N737VU'	19041	N9003U	RAX
☐ Cessna 140	N89848	8897		RA
☐ Cessna 150H	N23400	15068930		RA
☐ Cessna 172	'N72VU'			RAX
☐ Cessna 337 Super Skymaster				RA
☐ Piper PA-23-160 Apache	'N38SVU'			RAX
☐ Piper PA-31 Turbo Navajo				RA
☐ Piper PA-34-200T Seneca II	N32897	34-7570065		RA
☐ Piper PA-44-180 Seminole	N2162K	44-7995198		RA

VINTAGE FIGHTERS (IN54)

Address:	7009 Airport Drive, Sellersburg, Indiana 47172.
Email:	vintagefighters@aol.com
Admission:	By appointment only Monday-Friday 0800-1630.
Location:	At Clark County Airport which is about 15 miles north of Louisville, KY off Interstate 65.

Charles Osborn has been collecting vintage aircraft for a number of years and his warbirds have won awards at several shows. One Mustang (N3751D) flew from 1975 to 1983 with a private owner in Tahiti. The two P-51s have been painted in the colours of famous pilots who flew the type in World War II.

TYPE	REG/SER	CON. NO.	PI/NOTES	STATUS
☐ Commonwealth CA-27 Sabre 1 [North American F-86E]	'6049'	CA27-16	A94-916 – at airport entrance.	PVX
☐ North American NA-88 Texan (SNJ-5)	N3676F	88-14920	Bu51882	RAC
☐ North American NA-122 Mustang (P-51D)	N3751D/413586'	122-39665	44-73206, N7724C, N3751D, F-AZAG	RAAX
☐ North American NA-124 Mustang (P-51D)	N51VF/'472934'	124-48286	45-11553, N5414V, N713DW, N22DC, N51T, N51TZ , N5415V, N38JC, N151GP	RAAX
☐ Vought FG-1D Corsair	N17VF	3997	Bu67070, 201 (El Salvador), N29VF	RAA

Indiana

WAYNE COUNTY HISTORICAL MUSEUM (IN55)

Address:	1150 North A Street, Richmond, Indiana 47374.
Tel:	765-962-5756 **Email:** harlanjd@aol.com
Admission:	Monday-Friday 0900-1600; Saturday-Sunday 1300-1600.
Location:	In the centre of the town.

Located in a former Friends Meeting House the museum displays trace the developments which have taken in the county. The Davis Aviation Company bought the assets of the Vulcan Company and improved the V-3 American Moth design. The Davis V-3 appeared in 1929 and evolved into the D-1 of which almost 40 were built in Richmond. Just 11 D-1Ks and seven D-1Ws were constructed before the factory closed in 1937.

TYPE	REG/SER	CON. NO.	PI/NOTES	STATUS
☐ Davis D-1 (V-3)	NC2851	103		PV

WILBUR WRIGHT BIRTHPLACE MUSEUM (IN56)

Address:	1150 1525 North 750 East, Hagerstown, Indiana 47346.
Tel:	765-332-2495
Admission:	Tuesday-Saturday 1000-1700; Sunday 1300-1700.
Location:	Just north of Milville which is between New Castle and Hagerstown on Highway 38.

Wilbur Wright was born on 16th April 1867 near Milville where his father was a local preacher. The family home burned down in 1884. In 1972 the foundations were revealed and the following year reconstruction started using period techniques. The building has been restored to its original state.

TYPE	REG/SER	CON. NO.	PI/NOTES	STATUS
☐ Republic F-84F Thunderstreak	52-6993			PV
☐ Wright Flyer (R)				PV

WILLIAMS COLLECTION (IN57)

Address:	3811 River Road, Columbus, Indiana 47203-1104.
Admission:	By prior permission only.
Location:	At Columbus Airport which is in the northern suburbs of the town.

This interesting collection has been assembled by Mike Williams who has a business specialising in restoring Tiger Moths. He has a replica of the famous British training biplane. A replica of the Waco STO is being built A version of the Monocoupe 90 was completed in 2000 but this has since been sold.

TYPE	REG/SER	CON. NO.	PI/NOTES	STATUS
☐ Bellanca 14-19-3M Cruisemaster	N68MW	2004/1		RA
☐ Bücker Bü 133C Jungmeister	N26MW	35-7		RAA
☐ De Havilland DH.82A Tiger Moth (R)	N83MW	20618		RA
☐ Pitts S-2S Special	N330HP	1010		RA
☐ Waco STO (R)				RAC
☐ Williams Super 8	N540MW	MW-2		RAA

WOOD COLLECTION (IN58)

Address:	6320 Guildford Avenue, Indianapolis, Indiana 46220.
Admission:	By prior permission only.
Location:	At an airfield in the area.

This private collection of mainly warbirds includes a Grumman Bearcat which after service with the US Navy was delivered to Thailand. From 1965 until 1980 the fighter was displayed outside a building in Bangkok. Jean Salis obtained the aircraft and it was shipped to France. After a short period it moved to Duxford before returning to the USA in 1992. After restoration at Chino in California it took to the air again in February 1999. Tom Wood purchased it from the Yanks Air Museum the previous year. The Sabre, after a period of service in Peru, also was transported to Chino by Dave Zuchel. After a six month rebuild it took to the air in August 1981. The Mustang, which served in Canada from 1951 to 1957, has been owned by Tom Wood since 1969. The aircraft now flies in the colours in carried during service in World War II.

TYPE	REG/SER	CON. NO.	PI/NOTES	STATUS
☐ Beech A36 Bonanza 36	N1089C	E-2989		RAA
☐ Grumman G-58 Bearcat (F8F-1B)	N2209/'122095'	D.779	Bu122095, Kh15-43/93 (Thailand), G-BUCF	RAA
☐ Neibauer Lancair IVP	N132TW	132		RAA
☐ North American NA-88 Texan (AT-6D) (SNJ-5)	N7055C	88-'6756	42-84975, Bu84895, N3189G, 718 (Mexico)	RAA
☐ North American NA-122 Mustang (P-51D) (Mustang IV)	N6306T/'44-74878'	122-41418	44-74878, 9259 (Canada)	RAA
☐ North American NA-191 Sabre (F-86F)	NX86F/'25139'	191-835	52-5139, (Peru), '12849'	RAA

WORLD WAR II VICTORY MUSEUM (IN59)

Address:	PO Box 1, Auburn, Indiana 46706.
Tel:	260-927-9144 **Fax:** 260-927-8043 **Email:** info@dvkfoundation.org
Admission:	Daily 0900-1700.
Location:	At 5634 County Road 11A near Exit 126 of Interstate 69.

The museum is part of the National Military History Center. The complex, which is still being developed, will contain galleries devoted to significant events in the history of the country.

TYPE	REG/SER	CON. NO.	PI/NOTES	STATUS
☐ Stinson V-76 Sentinel (L-5E)				PV
☐ Yakovlev Yak-52				RAA

The World War II Victory Museum opened in early 2003 and since then the exhibition has been enlarged and improved. The only aircraft currently on show is the Stinson Sentinel. Also to be seen are many items of memorabilia.

IOWA

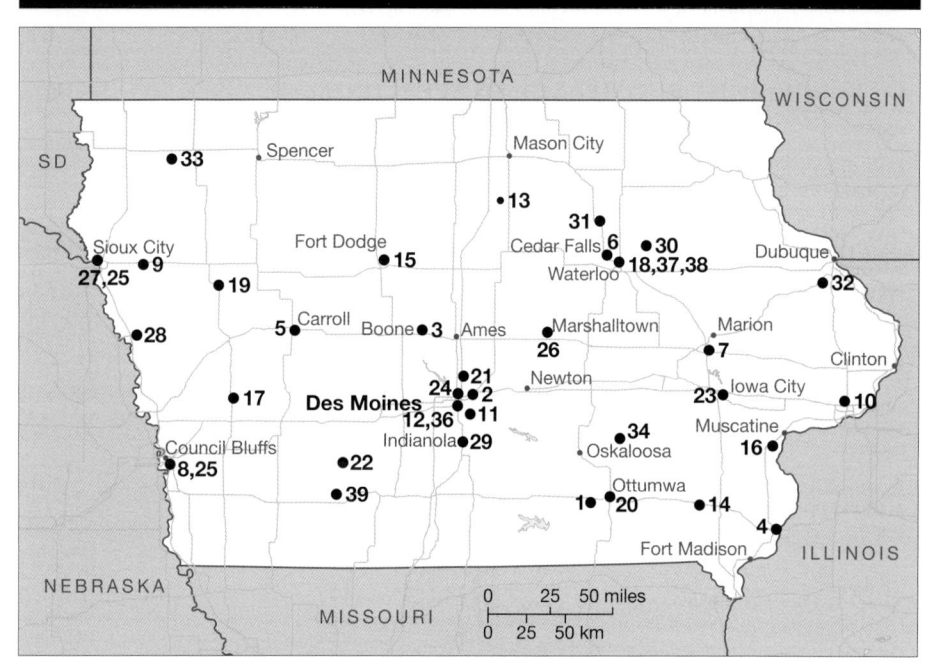

AIRPOWER MUSEUM (IA1)

Address:	Antique Airfield, 22001 Bluegrass Road, Ottumwa, Iowa 52501-8569.
Tel:	641-938-2773 **Fax:** 641-938-2093 **Email:** antiqueairfield@sirisonline.com
Admission:	Monday-Saturday 0900-1700; Sunday 1200-1700.
Location:	About 12 miles west of the town on Route 2.

Founded by Robert L. Taylor in the early 1950s, the Antique Airplane Association set up a museum at Ottumwa Industrial Airport in 1964. Land near to Blakesburg was purchased in the late 1960s and the Antique Airfield opened in 1971.

Almost every year since then the site has been host to the AAA fly in which attracts large numbers of antique and classic aircraft.

The museum moved to the airfield in the early 1970s and has steadily developed over the last four decades. The entrance hail contains an impressive display of models, components and memorabilia. The library has many books autographed by famous pilots from the inter-war period.

Two hangars are used to exhibit the aircraft several of which are maintained in flying condition. A third has airframes awaiting their turn in the rebuilding queue. Funds are being raised for a new restoration building and work on this project has already started.

The museum has managed to obtain several unique types including several homebuilts. The sole Anderson Z was built by a Minnesota farmer in 1925 and the biplane was taxied at the 1994 AAA fly-in, which had OX-5 powered aircraft as its main theme. An excellent collection of Aeronca types from the C-3 to the Chief is one of the highlights of the museum.

Of similar configuration to the Aeronca C-3 is one of three Welch monoplanes known to survive. This aircraft was built up from components stored after the collapse of the company. The Monoprep is and open cockpit version of the earlier Velie powered Monocoupe. About 65 were built and the museum example is one of the few surviving. Although off the beaten track this interesting museum is well worth a visit.

TYPE	REG/SER	CON. NO.	PI/NOTES	STATUS
☐ Aeronca C-3	N14098	A-405	NC14098	RA
☐ Aeronca K	NC18872	K-147	NC18883, N18872	PV
☐ Aeronca 65CA Chief	N29427	CA10220	NC29427	PV
☐ Aeronca 65TC Grasshopper (O-58B) (L-3B)	N50334	12783	(USAAF)	PVC
☐ Aeronca 7AC Champion	N3144E	7AC-6740	NC3144E	PVA
☐ Aeronca 11AC Chief	N9318E	11AC-956	NC9318E	PVA
☐ American Eagle Eaglet B-31	N17007	1111	NC17007	PV

Iowa

☐ Anderson Z	N12041	1	NC12041		PV
☐ Arrow Sport F	N18000	18	NC18000		PV
☐ Backstrom Flying Plank II	N20WB	1			PVA
☐ Bede BD-5B	N3225H	3033	On loan.		PV
☐ Bölkow BO 208A-1 Junior	N208JR	525			RA
☐ Bounsall Prospector	N307K	BSP29NS12			PV
☐ Brewster Fleet B-1 (Fleet 16F)	NC20699	1	NC20699, N20699		PVA
☐ Cessna T-50 Bobcat (AT-17B) (UC-78B)	N64410	6184	43-32246		RA
☐ Culver LCA Cadet (LFA)	NC41725	LFA-443	NC41725, N41725		PV
☐ Culver NR-D Cadet (PQ-14B)	N5526A	N917			PV
☐ Early Bird Jenny					PV
☐ Fleet 7 (2)	NC442K	165	NC442K, N442K		PV
☐ Funk B-85C (B)	N24134	60	NC24134		PVA
☐ Great Lakes 2T-1A	N11339	252	NC11339		PV
☐ Helton Lark 95			Unfinished airframe.		RA
☐ Interstate S-1A Cadet	NC37381	224	NC37381, N37381 – Taylor family aircraft.		RAA
☐ Lark Termite H-1	N1036	10	Taylor family aircraft.		RAA
☐ Lippisch X-114					PV
☐ Luscombe 8A Silvaire					RA
☐ Melfa VCA-1 XP-52					PV
☐ Mono Aircraft Monoprep 218	NC179K	6077	NC119K		PV
☐ Mooney M-18C Mite	N329M	210			PV
☐ Morrisey OM-1-2 Bravo	N37HM	TRGR-1			PVA
☐ Pietenpol B4-A Aircamper	NX4716	AAA-1	Taylor family aircraft.		PV
☐ Pietenpol B4-A Aircamper	N6350	DS1			PV
☐ Pietenpol P-9 Sky Scout (R)	N12942	SL-1			PV
☐ Piper J-3C-65 Cub (L-4H)	N51570	11064	43-29773		PVA
☐ Porterfield CP-40	NC18743	529	NC18743, N18743		PVA
☐ Porterfield CP-50	NC21994	574	NC21994, N21994 – Taylor family aircraft.		PV
☐ Rearwin 190F	N34740	1550	NC34740		PV
☐ Rearwin 7000 Sportster	NC15809	445	NC15809, N15809		PVA
☐ Rearwin 8135 Cloudster	N25555	832	NC25555		PV
☐ Republic RC-3 Seabee	N6019K	189	NC6091K		PV
☐ Ritz Standard A					PVA
☐ Robinson Mere-Merit	NX400KR	A-01	Taylor family aircraft.		PV
☐ Rose Parakeet A-1	NC1367G	101	NC1367G, N1367G		PV
☐ Ryan ST-3KR Recruit (PT-22)	N50664	1254	41-15225		PVA
☐ Ryan STA	NC18902	198	NC18902, N18902		PVA
☐ Smith DSA-1 Miniplane	N44ES	ES-1			PV
☐ Stinson 10A Voyager	N27710	7655	NC27710		PVA
☐ Stinson Junior S	NC12165	8074	NC12165, N12165		PVA
☐ Van Dellen LH-2	N4826E	LH-2			RA
☐ Volmer Jensen VJ-23	N711NK	C-30			PV
☐ Wilkes BMW-1	N17MW	1			PV

ALTOONA MONUMENT (IA2)

Location: On permanent view in a park in the eastern part of the town.

TYPE	REG/SER	CON. NO.	PI/NOTES	STATUS
☐ Vought A-7D Corsair II	71-0334	D245		PV

BOONE ARMY NATIONAL GUARD BASE (IA3)

Location: On permanent view at the airport which is just east of the town.

TYPE	REG/SER	CON. NO.	PI/NOTES	STATUS
☐ Bell 204 Iroquois (UH-1C) (UH-1M)	66-0497	1479		RA
☐ Bell 205 Iroquois (UH-1H) (UH-1V)	67-17250	9448		RA

BURLINGTON MONUMENT (IA4)

Location: On permanent view at the airport which is about 2 miles south of the town of Route 61.

TYPE	REG/SER	CON. NO.	PI/NOTES	STATUS
☐ Lockheed 580 (T-33A)	52-9697	580-7922		PV

CARROLL MONUMENT (IA5)

Location: On permanent view at the airport which is about 4 miles south east of the town.

TYPE	REG/SER	CON. NO.	PI/NOTES	STATUS
☐ Vought A-7D Corsair II	72-0254	D376		PV

CEDAR FALLS MONUMENT (IA6)

Location: On permanent view at AMVETS Post 49 at 1934 Irving Street in the centre of the town.

TYPE	REG/SER	CON. NO.	PI/NOTES	STATUS
☐ Bell 209 Huey Cobra (AH-1G) (AH-1S)	71-21040	21111		PV

CEDAR RAPIDS MONUMENTS (IA7)

Location:	On permanent view at three locations in the town.

TYPE	REG/SER	CON. NO.	PI/NOTES	STATUS
☐ Lockheed 580 (T-33A)	53-5916	580-9392	At Kingston Stadium.	PV
☐ Piper PA-22-150 Tripacer			At Flying Weenies at 103 8th Avenue	PV
☐ Republic F-84F Thunderstreak	51-9444		In Seminole Valley Park – possible identity.	PV

COMMEMORATIVE AIR FORCE (GREAT PLAINS WING) MUSEUM (IA8)

Address:	16803 McCandless Road, Council Bluffs, Iowa 51503-5937.
Tel:	713-322-2435 Email: dales51503@cox.net
Admission:	Wednesday 1800-2100; Saturday 0900-1600; Sunday 0900-1300.
Location:	At Council Bluffs Airport which is about 5 miles south east of the town on old Route 6.

The wing has a hangar at Council Bluffs Airport and there is a display of memorabilia in the rooms at the rear of the building. Also to be seen are engines and components along with uniforms and books.

The P-51 is flown and sponsored by retired General Regis Urschler. The fighter is a popular visitor to many airshows. The two liaison types have been restored to their drab olive World War II colours.

TYPE	REG/SER	CON. NO.	PI/NOTES	STATUS
☐ Aeronca 65TC Grasshopper (O-58B) (L-3B)	N48441	9983	(USAAF)	PVA
☐ North American NA-122 Mustang (P-51D)	N5428V	122-39723	44-73264	PVA
☐ Stinson V-76 Sentinel (L-5B)	N22422		44-17191	PVA

CORRECTIONVILLE MONUMENT (IA9)

Location:	On permanent view in the southern part of the town on Route 31.

TYPE	REG/SER	CON. NO.	PI/NOTES	STATUS
☐ Republic F-84F Thunderstreak	51-1735			PV
☐ Vought A-7D Corsair II	70-0937	D83		PV

DAVENPORT ARMY NATIONAL GUARD BASE (IA10)

Location:	On permanent view at the airport which is about 3 miles north of the town off Route 61.

TYPE	REG/SER	CON. NO.	PI/NOTES	STATUS
☐ Bell 205 Iroquois (UH-1D) (UH-1H)	66-0791	5274		PV

DES MOINES AIR NATIONAL GUARD BASE (IA11)

Address:	132 FW/CC, McKinley Avenue, Des Moines, Iowa 50321.
Tel:	515-256-8210
Admission:	By prior permission only.
Location:	On the north side of the International Airport which is in the southern suburbs of the city.

In July 1940 the 124th Observation Squadron was allocated to the Iowa National Guard and took up residence at Des Moines. Six years later after a period of active service it was reallocated to the state and became a fighter unit. Two types formerly used by the squadron preserved by the main gate. They have been joined by a full size replica of a P-51, a type flown by the unit between 1946 and 1953. The Mustang was replaced by the Lockheed P-80. After periods flying F-84E Thunderjets, F-86L Sabres and F-84F Thunderstreaks the F-100C arrived in 1975. The A-7 was put into service in early 1977 and served until 1993.

TYPE	REG/SER	CON. NO.	PI/NOTES	STATUS
☐ North American NA-122 Mustang (P-51D) (FSM)	'893'			RAX
☐ North American NA-245 Super Sabre (F-100D)	'52783'	245-76	56-3426	RAX
☐ Vought A-7D Corsair II	75-0400	D450		RA

DES MOINES TECHNICAL HIGH SCHOOL (IA12)

Address:	901 Walnut Street, Des Moines, Iowa 50309.
Tel:	515-212-7911
Admission:	By prior permission only.
Location:	At the International Airport which is in the southern suburbs of the city.

The school which has it main campus in the city has a hangar at the airport where the aviation maintenance section resides. Three instructional airframes are known to be in use but there are probably more.

The Sabreliner was transferred to the Wallops Flight Facility in Virginia where it was used as a platform for testing small applications systems. The aircraft was flown to Des Moines in the mid-1990s.

TYPE	REG/SER	CON. NO.	PI/NOTES	STATUS
☐ Cessna 337E Super Skymaster	N8551M	33701251		RA
☐ Grumman G-159 Gulfstream I	N65CE	45	N745G, N7788	RA
☐ North American NA-265 Sabreliner (T-39A) (CT-39A)	N431NA	265-16	60-3488	RA

Iowa

ED DOYLE MUSEUM (IA13)

Address:	824 Glendale Park Drive, Hampton, Iowa 50441-1818.
Tel:	641-456-3464
Admission:	By prior permission only.
Location:	About 3 miles west of the town at Beeds Lake Airport.

This private museum is housed in two hangars at Ed Doyle's airfield which was the old airport for Hampton. In addition to the aircraft there are many artefacts and engines dating from the World War I period. There is also a Merlin engine on view. The Nieuport and Sopwith Pup replicas were built in California by Jim Appleby of Antique Aero who has also supplied machines for many other museums. Construction of a SPAD replica has started and parts are in the hangar. The major components of a Curtiss Pusher are present. Three examples of the classic Fairchild 24 are in the buildings. The 24C8 prototype made its maiden flight in 1932 and over 250 were produced with a variety of engines. The sub type of this aircraft is unknown. The 24G appeared in 1937 and was powered by a Warner Super Scarab radial. Only 100 were completed in the year.

TYPE	REG/SER	CON. NO.	PI/NOTES	STATUS
☐ Blériot XI (R)				RAC
☐ Cessna 310D	N6779T	39079		RAA
☐ Curtiss D Pusher			Major components.	RA
☐ Fairchild 24 C8				RA
☐ Fairchild 24G	N19180	3503	NC19180	RA
☐ Fairchild 24G				RA
☐ Fokker Dr I (R)	N425ED	425		RAA
☐ Nieuport 28C.1 (R)	N6187	AA.104		RAA
☐ SPAD VIII (R)				RAC
☐ Sopwith Pup (R)	N6459	AA.103		RAA

FAIRFIELD MONUMENT (IA14)

Location:	On permanent view at the airport which is north of the town off Route 1.

TYPE	REG/SER	CON. NO.	PI/NOTES	STATUS
☐ Republic F-84F Thunderstreak	'T64-01'		51-1818	PVX

FORT DODGE MONUMENT (IA15)

Location:	On permanent view at the airport which is about 1 mile north of the town off Route 169.

TYPE	REG/SER	CON. NO.	PI/NOTES	STATUS
☐ Republic F-84F Thunderstreak	52-6418			PV

GRANDVIEW ALL VETERANS MEMORIAL (IA16)

Location:	On permanent view in the western part of the town.

TYPE	REG/SER	CON. NO.	PI/NOTES	STATUS
☐ Bell 205 Iroquois (UH-1D) (UH-1H)	66-16304	5998		PV

HARLAN MONUMENT (IA17)

Location:	On permanent view at the airport which is about 5 miles south of the town on Route 59.

TYPE	REG/SER	CON. NO.	PI/NOTES	STATUS
☐ Republic RF-84F Thunderflash	51-1948			PV

HAWKEYE COMMUNITY COLLEGE (IA18)

Address:	1501 East Orange Road, Waterloo, Iowa 50701-9014.
Tel:	319-296-2320
Admission:	By prior permission only.
Location:	In the southern part of the town.

The college was established in 1996 and replaced the Waterloo Area Vocational School. Aviation maintenance training finished in the summer of 2006 and three aircraft are believed to still be present.

TYPE	REG/SER	CON. NO.	PI/NOTES	STATUS
☐ Bell 205 Iroquois (UH-1H)	70-16301	12606		RA
☐ Cessna 310M Blue Canoe (310E) (L-27B) (U-3B)	60-6064	310M0019		RA
☐ North American NA-285 Sabreliner (T3J-1) (T-39D)	Bu151340	285-29		RA

IDA GROVE MONUMENT (IA19)

Location:	On permanent view in Cobb Memorial Park in the centre of the town.

TYPE	REG/SER	CON. NO.	PI/NOTES	STATUS
☐ Bell 209 Huey Cobra (AH-1G) (AH-1S)	71-21041	21112		PV

The Iowa Air National Guard have preserved this North American F-100D Super Sabre at their Des Moines base. (Glenn Chatfield) [IA11]

The only surviving Timm S-2A Aerocraft is displayed at the Iowa Aviation Museum and Hall of Fame. [IA22]

This North American F-86L Sabre can be seen in Iowa City (Glenn Chatfield) [IA23]

INDIAN HILLS COMMUNITY COLLEGE AVIATION CENTER (IA20)

Address:	525 Grandview Avenue, Ottumwa, Iowa 52501.
Tel:	641-683-4255　Email: rbrauhn@indianhills.edu
Admission:	By prior permission only.
Location:	At Ottumwa Industrial Airport which is about 5 miles north of the town on Route 63.

The college has campuses in Ottumwa and Centerville. The Aviation Center at the airport offers pilot training and maintenance courses. The workshops contain a number of instructional airframes.

TYPE	REG/SER	CON. NO.	PI/NOTES	STATUS
☐ Beech D18S Expeditor (C18S) (SNB-2C) (SNB-3) (SNB-5P (RC-45J)	N5245	7817	Bu29645	RA
☐ Bell 204 Iroquois (HU-1B) (UH-1B)	62-4567	627	62-4567, N6810D	RA
☐ Cessna 150K	N5657G	15071157		RA
☐ Cessna 150M	N8353U	15077924		RA
☐ Cessna 310				RA
☐ Cessna 318B Tweety Bird (T-37B)	59-0292	40454		RA
☐ North American NA-276 Sabreliner (T-39A) (CT-39A)	62-4483	276-36		RA
☐ Piper PA-15 Vagabond	N4662H	15-370		RA
☐ Piper PA-22-160 Tripacer	N9821D	22-6708		RA

IOWA AVIATION HERITAGE MUSEUM (IA21)

Address:	3703 Convenience Boulevard, Ankeny, Iowa 50021
Tel:	515-964-2629　Email: MLCallison@aol.com
Admission:	By prior permission only
Location:	About 5 miles north of Des Moines.

Formed in 2000 this museum is being built at the airfield. The collection of aircraft is growing with a number of private owners loaning their aircraft. Memorabilia and other items are being acquired to enhance the display.

TYPE	REG/SER	CON. NO.	PI/NOTES	STATUS
☐ Beech D18S Expeditor (C18S) (SNB-2) (SNB-5) (TC-45J) (UC-45J)	N41005	5563	Bu51236	RAC
☐ Beech D18S Expeditor (C-45H)	N72409	AF-411	51-11854	RAC
☐ Fairchild M-62A Cornell (PT-19A)	N53956	T42-3814	42-34148, NC53956	PVC
☐ Naval Aircraft Factory N3N-3	N45184		Bu2837	RA
☐ Naval Aircraft Factory N3N-3	N45120		Bu4494	PVA
☐ North American NA-88 Texan (AT-6D) (SNJ-5)	N43AF	88-15368	41-34402, Bu43667, N3146G	PVA
☐ Republic F-84F Thunderstreak	51-1655		51-1655, N4930	RA
☐ Temco D.16A Twin Navion	'8587'	TTN-90	N722T	RAAX

IOWA AVIATION MUSEUM AND HALL OF FAME (IA22)

Address:	PO Box 31, 2251 Airport Road, Greenfield, Iowa 50849-0031.
Tel:	515-343-7184　Email: aviation@iowatelecom.net
Admission:	Monday-Friday 1000-1700; Saturday-Sunday 1300-1700.
Location:	About 1 mile north of the town off Route 25.

The late John Schildberg started collecting aircraft in 1964 with the purchase of a Tiger Moth and by 1982 he had acquired a number of interesting machines. For several years the aircraft were maintained by his widow Yvonne and restorer/pilot 'Ace' Cannon.

In the late 1980s it was decided to set up a museum at the airfield and several of the Schildberg aircraft joined the new collection. The exhibition was initially called the Iowa Aviation Preservation Center. One type which did not join the museum was the rare pointed wing de Havilland DH.87A Hornet Moth sold to the Reynolds Museum in Alberta, Canada. A purpose-built hangar with space for associated displays was constructed. The Iowa Aviation Hall of Fame is located at the site and so far over 50 aviators have been honoured.

The Timm 2-SA Aerocraft is the sole survivor of six that were built in 1940. Restored by 'Ace' Cannon it flew again in 1985 and was one of the stars of the AAA fly in at Blakesburg. The low wing design was based on earlier Kinner monoplanes but the military was not interested in ordering the trainer.

The Curtiss Robin dates from 1928 and is the oldest survivor of the more then 760 built at St. Louis. The two primary gliders are also from the late 1920s. The Sioux Coupe is a development of the Kari-Keen Coupe. Only a small number were constructed in Sioux City and just a few survive.

Bernard Pietenpol built the Aircamper in Minnesota in the late 1920s. The parasol monoplane was easy to build and simple to fly. The design is still popular with updated plans available, including the RagWing RW1 Ultra-Piet version.

TYPE	REG/SER	CON. NO.	PI/NOTES	STATUS
☐ Bell 209 Huey Cobra (AH-1G) (AH-1S)	70-16061	21005		PV
☐ Curtiss 50 Robin	N7145	6	NC7145	PVA
☐ De Havilland DH.82C Tiger Moth	N3758U	DHC.1269	5966 (Canada)	PVA
☐ De Havilland DH.82C Tiger Moth	N8966	DHC.1517	8965 (Canada), CF-CVB, CF-FEN	PVA
☐ Hall Cherokee II	N14ET	1		PV
☐ Mead Primary Glider				PV
☐ Northrup Primary Glider				PV
☐ Piper J-3C-65 Cub	NC98733	18963	NC98733, N98733	PVA
☐ Pitts S-1C Special	N20P	101M		PV
☐ RagWing Ultra-Piet				PV
☐ Schweizer SGU.1-20	N2708A	30A		PV
☐ Sioux Coupe 90-B	NC10721	401	NC10721, N10721	PV

☐ Stearman C3R	NC8828	5001	X8828, NC8828, N8828	PV
☐ Taylor J-2 Cub	NC17247	913	NC17247, N17247	PVA
☐ Taylorcraft BC-12D	N95734	8034	NC95734	PVA
☐ Timm (Aetna) 2-SA Aerocraft	N34912	4	NC34912	PVA
☐ Ultralight Flying Machines Easy Riser				PV
☐ Vought A-7D Corsair II	72-0213	D335		PV

IOWA CITY MONUMENT (IA23)

Location:	On permanent view at the airport which is in the south western part of the town.

TYPE	REG/SER	CON. NO.	PI/NOTES	STATUS
☐ North American NA-201 Sabre (F-86D) (F-86L)	53-0750	201-194		PV

IOWA GOLD STAR MUSEUM (IA24)

Address:	7105 North West 70th Avenue, Johnston, Iowa 50131-1824.
Tel:	515-252-4531 Fax: 515-727-3107 Email: GoldStarMuseum@iowa.gov
Admission:	Monday-Saturday 0830-1630.
Location:	About 5 miles north of the town on Route 169 at the airport.

The site at Fort Dodge has been occupied by Iowa military forces for over a century. The museum was established in 1985 to honour their work. The displays trace the history of the state from the early days up to the present time. Iowa citizens have fought in conflicts since the days of the Indian Wars. The development of the units is portrayed in detail. On show are many weapons, uniforms, documents and flags spanning more than two centuries. The history of Fort Dodge over the years is also told in detail.

TYPE	REG/SER	CON. NO.	PI/NOTES	STATUS
☐ Bell 205 Iroquois (UH-1D) (UH-1H)	63-8825	4117		PV
☐ Bell 209 Huey Cobra (AH-1G) (AH-1S)	67-15564	20228		PV
☐ Republic F-84F Thunderstreak	52-6418			PV
☐ Vought A-7D Corsair II	75-0403	D453		PV

IOWA WESTERN COMMUNITY COLLEGE (IA25)

Address:	2700 College Road, Council Bluffs, Iowa 51503
Tel:	712-325-3414 Email: eyoung@iwcc.edu
Admission:	By prior permission only.
Location:	In the eastern part of the town.

The college was established in 1966 and offers a wide range of courses at several sites in the area. Students are trained in airframe and engine maintenance. The workshops contain a number of instructional aircraft.

TYPE	REG/SER	CON. NO.	PI/NOTES	STATUS
☐ Beech 95-B55B Cochise (T-42A)	N9114S	TF-46	65-12724	RA
☐ Bell 206A Kiowa (OH-58A)	N8093U	42087	72-21421	RA
☐ Cessna 182A	N6301B	34201		RA
☐ Hiller UH13C Raven (H-23C) (OH-23C)	55-4080	775		RA
☐ Hughes 269A Osage (TH-55A)	N7058T	108-1009	67-16702	RA
☐ Hughes 269A Osage (TH-55A)	N1040P	16-0438	64-18126	RA
☐ Hughes 269A Osage (TH-55A)	N1040S	56-0534	68-18222	RA
☐ North American NA-265 Sabreliner (T-39A) (CT-39A)	60-3496	265-24		RA
☐ Piper PA-23-250 Aztec C	N5708Y	27-2829		RA
☐ Sikorsky S-55D Chickasaw (H-19D) (UH-19D)	N4669		55-3202	RA

MARSHALLTOWN MONUMENT (IA26)

Location:	On permanent view at ALP 46 in Ingledue Street in the southern part of the town.

TYPE	REG/SER	CON. NO.	PI/NOTES	STATUS
☐ McDonnell M.98DE Phantom II (F-4C)	63-7507	516		PV

MID AMERICA MUSEUM OF AVIATION AND TRANSPORTION (IA27)

Address:	2600 Expedition Court, Sioux City Gateway Airport, Sergeant Bluff, Iowa 51054.
Tel:	712-252-5300 Email: topflite@longlines.com
Admission:	Thursday-Tuesday 0900-1700
Location:	About 7 miles south of Sioux City off Interstate 29.

The Siouxland Aviation Historical Association was formed in November 1991 with the aim of setting up a museum at the airport. The local authority supported the project and land was allocated.

However, progress was slow and a fire in a storage depot in March 2007 destroyed a Thorp T-18 and two hang gliders along with other material. The project became a reality with the opening taking place on 31st July 2010. The displays are still being developed but local aviators feature prominently.

A rarity in the collection is the former Royal Air Force Argosy which is still in military colours although these are fading. The Evangel Aircraft Corporation was set up at Orange City in Iowa to produce a twin engined type suitable for use in rugged conditions. A few Evangel 4500s were built and a new company developed the pusher Angel 44.

The P-40N was involved in a mid-air collision over the Florida Everglades in 1943. The wreck was recovered in 1988 and the local owner has loaned it to the display.

Iowa

TYPE	REG/SER	CON. NO.	PI/NOTES	STATUS
☐ Aero Commander 680			Fuselage only.	PVD
☐ Angel 44			Static test airframe.	PVD
☐ Armstrong Whitworth AW.660 Argosy C.1	N1403Z	6798	XR143, G-BFVT	PVC
☐ Beech 65-80 Queen Air	N68CE	LD-122		PV
☐ Bell 204 Iroquois (UH-1C) (UH-1M)	66-15187	1915		PV
☐ Boeing 727-200			Front fuselage only.	PV
☐ Boeing 727-277F	N246FE	22068	VH-RMP	PV
☐ Curtiss 87V Warhawk (P-40N)	42-24362	32291		PVD
☐ Cvjetkovic CA-61 Mini-Ace	N94283	1		PV
☐ Da Vinci Flying Machine (FSM)				PV
☐ Fairchild 473 Provider (205) (C-123B) (C-123K)	N8190B	20144	54-0695, N8190B, PNP-022 (Peru)	PV
☐ Fokker Dr I (R)				PV
☐ Grumman G-128 Intruder (EA-6A)	Bu156984	I-453		PV
☐ Kotula-Lundy Graflite	N870GF	P-001		PV
☐ Monnett Moni	N153MX	00153		PV
☐ Nieuport 11 (R)	N998S	998		PV
☐ Parker Teenie Too				PV
☐ Rand Robinson KR-2	N1178Z	142		PV
☐ Stolp SA.900 V-Star	N9LS	1		PV
☐ Thorp T-18				PV
☐ Turner T-40	N191T	BB3		PV
☐ Vought A-7K Corsair II	81-0073	K52		PV

MONOMA COUNTY VETERANS MEMORIAL MUSEUM (IA28)

Address: 23 12th Street, PO Box 418, Onawa, Iowa 51040.
Tel: 712-433-3780 **Email:** LestWeForget67@hotmail.com
Admission: May–August Saturday-Sunday 1400-1700.
Location: In the centre of the town.

Three museums are located at the site in the town. The other two are the local Historical Museum and one covering railway history. The veterans display honours local people who have lost their lives in conflicts with many personal items on show. The two aircraft are parked outside along with an M.60 tank and weapons.

TYPE	REG/SER	CON. NO.	PI/NOTES	STATUS
☐ Bell 205 Iroquois (UH-1D) (UH-1H)	64-13601	4308		PV
☐ Vought A-7D Corsair II	70-1008	D154		PV

NATIONAL BALLOON MUSEUM (IA29)

Address: 1601 North Jefferson Way, Indianola, Iowa 50125-0149.
Tel: 515-961-3714 **Email:** balloonmuseum@bfa.net
Admission: May–December Monday-Friday 0900-1600, Saturday 1000-1600, Sunday 1300-1600; February–March Monday-Sunday 1300-1600.
Location: Just north of the town on Route 65/69.

The US National Hot Air Balloon Championships were first held at Indianola in 1970 and now the National Balloon Classic takes place each August. Members of the Balloon Federation of America started collecting memorabilia and artefacts and some of these were on show at the 1975 event. A display was set up at Simpson College in 1979 and this led to plans for a permanent museum.

The building, in the form of two inverted balloons, was completed in 1988. Displays tracing the history of more than two centuries of ballooning have been set up. A large exhibition of photographs, documents, trophies and instruments can be seen.

A number of gondolas and envelopes from both gas and hot air balloons are also on view.

TYPE	REG/SER	CON. NO.	PI/NOTES	STATUS
☐ Adams A.55 Hot Air Balloon	N1063K	107		PV
☐ Avian Hot Air Balloon			Basket only.	PV
☐ Barnes AX-7 Hot Air Balloon				PV
☐ Baum Balloon			Gondola only.	PV
☐ Cameron O-65 Hot Air Balloon	N76GB	220		PV
☐ Cameron Z-105 Hot Air Airship	N5YW	6237		PV
☐ Cutter Hot Air Balloon			Basket only.	PV
☐ Eagle AX-7 Hot Air Balloon	N7001V	ED-81714	Basket and burner only.	PV
☐ Emeott 40 Hot Air Balloon	N4635T	1		PV
☐ Gas Balloon				PV
☐ Gas Balloon				PV
☐ Kersten Merope Hot Air Balloon				PV
☐ National Ballooning Ax-8 Hot Air Balloon				PV
☐ Piccard AX-6 Hot Air Balloon	N88US	688		PV
☐ Piccard AX-6 Hot Air Balloon	N62DP	779	With Thunder envelope.	PV
☐ Piccard AX-7 Hot Air Balloon	N25015	506		PV
☐ Raven CA-50 Hot Air Balloon	N11979	107		PV
☐ Raven Hot Air Balloon			Experimental Double Chair Gondola.	PV
☐ Raven Orbitor Gas Balloon			Basket only.	PV
☐ Raven Rally RX-6 Hot Air Balloon				PV
☐ Raven S-40A Hot Air Balloon			Components.	PV
☐ Raven S-55A Hot Air Balloon	N61AA	S55A-146		PV
☐ Raven S-60 Hot Air Balloon				PV
☐ Raven S-60 Hot Air Balloon	N1200		Basket only.	PV

☐ Semco TC-4 Hot Air Balloon	N2078	SEM 23		PV
☐ Solo System Hot Air Balloon			Basket only.	PV
☐ Thunder AX-7-77A Hot Air Balloon	N68035	065		PV
☐ Universal Systems Hot Air Balloon			Basket and Burner only.	PV

OELWEIN MONUMENT (IA30)

Location:	On permanent view in the City Park in South Frederick Street in the south western part of the town.

TYPE	REG/SER	CON. NO.	PI/NOTES	STATUS
☐ Lockheed 580 (T-33A)	51-4406	580-5701		PV

PARKERSBURG MONUMENT (IA31)

Location:	On permanent view in the City Park in Miners Street in the western part of the town.

TYPE	REG/SER	CON. NO.	PI/NOTES	STATUS
☐ Bell 209 Huey Cobra (AH-1G) (AH-1S)	70-16087	21031		PV

RYAN MONUMENT (IA32)

Location:	On permanent view at VFW 6637 at 909 New Street in the centre of the town.

TYPE	REG/SER	CON. NO.	PI/NOTES	STATUS
☐ Bell 209 Huey Cobra (AH-1G) (AH-1F)	67-15717	20381		PV

SHELDON MONUMENT (IA33)

Location:	On permanent view at the airport which is about 2 miles north east of the town on Route 60.

TYPE	REG/SER	CON. NO.	PI/NOTES	STATUS
☐ Lockheed 580 (T-33A)	52-9614	580-7774		PV

SIGOURNEY MONUMENT (IA34)

Location:	On permanent view in City Legion Park in Spring Street in the southern part of the town.

TYPE	REG/SER	CON. NO.	PI/NOTES	STATUS
☐ Lockheed 580 (T-33A)	58-0579	580-1548		PV

SIOUX CITY AIR NATIONAL GUARD BASE (IA35)

Address:	185 ARW/PA, Sioux City, Iowa 51111.
Tel:	712-223-0809 Email: 185arw.batscan@ang.af.mil
Admission:	By prior permission only.
Location:	The airfield is about 7 miles south of Sioux City off Interstate 29.

The group took up residence at Sioux City in 1946 and since then has operated a range of fighter aircraft with associated types. The collection is preserved in an area near the main gate to the base.

TYPE	REG/SER	CON. NO.	PI/NOTES	STATUS
☐ General Dynamics 401 Fighting Falcon (F-16A)	'85-1547'	61-521	82-0928	RAX
☐ Lockheed 580 (T-33A)	51-9282	580-7066		RA
☐ North American NA-217 Super Sabre (F-100C)	54-2005	217-266		RA
☐ Republic F-84F Thunderstreak				RA
☐ Republic RF-84F Thunderflash	52-7244			RA
☐ Vought A-7D Corsair II	75-0406	D456	Outside ANG HQ.	RA

STATE OF IOWA HISTORICAL BUILDING (IA36)

Address:	East 16th and Grand Avenue, Des Moines, Iowa 50319.
Tel:	515-281-5111 Email: Jerome.Thompson@iowa.gov
Admission:	Tuesday-Saturday 0900-1630; Sunday 1200-1630.
Location:	In the eastern suburbs of the city close to the State Capitol.

The first State Historical Building opened in the early part of the last century and was in use for over 75 years. The present structure opened in 1987 and houses a museum, a library and archives as well as offices. The transport section has, at the present time, only the locally built primary glider on display.

Plans to exhibit some of the other aircraft, which were on show in the old building, are well advanced. The Benoist Biplane dating from 1912 was the first aircraft to be built and flown in the state. Other locally built types are in the collection.

TYPE	REG/SER	CON. NO.	PI/NOTES	STATUS
☐ Benoist Biplane				RA
☐ Blériot XI	N4W	25		RA
☐ Cook and Frazee Primary Training Glider				PV
☐ Curtiss D Pusher				RA
☐ Duede Biplane				RAD
☐ Quickie Aircraft Quickie 2 (Rutan 54)				RA

SULLIVAN BROTHERS IOWA VETERANS MUSEUM (IA37)

Address:	503 South Street, Waterloo, Iowa.
Tel:	319-234-6357 **Email:** cyd.mchone@gmdistricy.org
Admission:	Tuesday-Saturday 0900-1700.
Location:	In the centre of the town.

The museum is one of five operated by the local district. The exhibitions were founded in 1932 by Henry Whittemore Grout, a state legislator and financier, who travelled extensively. The initial display consisted mainly of his personal items. The current building, was completed in 1956 and was open to the public on a regular basis.

A new addition is the Sullivan Brothers Iowa Veterans Museum, completed in 2008, which honours all Iowa residents who have lost their lives in conflicts from the Civil war to the present time. The five Sullivan brothers from Waterloo lost their lives when the USS *Juneau* was sunk at Guadalcanal in November 1942.

TYPE	REG/SER	CON. NO.	PI/NOTES	STATUS
☐ North American NA-122 Mustang (P-51D) (FSM)				PVX

WATERLOO ARMY NATIONAL GUARD BASE (IA38)

Location:	On permanent view at the airport which is about 5 miles north west of the town.

TYPE	REG/SER	CON. NO.	PI/NOTES	STATUS
Bell 204 Iroquois (UH-1C) (UH-1M)	66-15185	1913		RA

WILLE COLLECTION (IA39)

Address:	1139 State Highway 148, Corning, Iowa 50841-7507.
Admission:	By prior permission only.
Location:	At Corning Airport which is about 2 miles north west of the town.

This private collection contains three examples of the Alexander Eaglerock biplane and a Waco 10. Several homebuilt designs are also in the hangar. Dick Johnson won the US National Gliding Championship in May 1963 in a Slingsby Skylark. This success led to a number being imported into the country.

TYPE	REG/SER	CON. NO.	PI/NOTES	STATUS
☐ Alexander Eaglerock 3-POLB	NC81621	531	NC81621, N81621 ?	RAA
☐ Alexander Eaglerock A-1	NC8240	714	NC8240, N8240	RAA
☐ Alexander Eaglerock A-3	NC6341	705	NC6341, N6341	RAA
☐ Bellanca 14-19-3A Cruisemaster	N8890R	4252		RAA
☐ D'Apuzzo D-260	N4030Q	201513B		RAA
☐ Rase R-1	N17R	1		RAA
☐ Slingsby T.50 Skylark 4	N415S	1447		RAA
☐ Waco 10 (GXE)	NC8529	1869	NC8529, N8529	RAA
☐ Wille Excelsior	N3148B	SC-1		RAA
☐ Wille Vancraft	N4109V	009		RAA

KANSAS

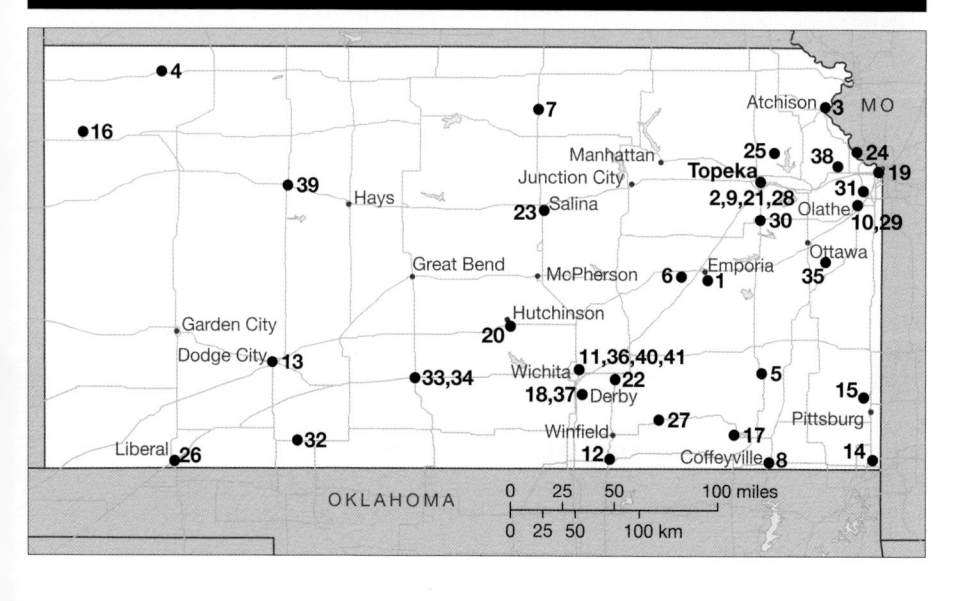

ALL VETERANS MEMORIAL (KS1)

Address:	933 South Commercial Street, Emporia, Kansas 66801.
Tel:	620-342-1803
Admission:	On permanent view.
Location:	Just south of the town on Route 57.

This memorial was dedicated on 26th May 1991 and was the first in the USA to honour the veterans of all wars. The Vietnam tribute was added in March 2001 with the positioning of the Iroquois.

TYPE	REG/SER	CON. NO.	PI/NOTES	STATUS
☐ Bell 205 Iroquois (UH-1H)	68-15652	10582		PV
☐ McDonnell M.98EN Phantom II (F-4D)	65-0585	1483	At nearby airport.	RA

AMERICAN FLIGHT MUSEUM (KS2)

Address:	2945 Wanamaker Drive, Topeka, Kansas 66614.
Tel:	785-266-6462 **Email:** texant6@webtv.net
Admission:	By prior permission only.
Location:	At Forbes Field which is about 4 miles south of the city on Route 75.

The group was formed by former members of the Combat Air Museum which made a decision in the late 1990s to ground its airworthy types.
The Trader was acquired in 1999 and was the only example of the type flying regularly before it crashed in 2002.

The C-47 has been restored to AC-47 'Spooky' gunship configuration. This conversion of the famous transport was first used in Vietnam by the 4th Commando Squadron and about two dozen were modified. All the aircraft are privately owned by members of the group.

TYPE	REG/SER	CON. NO.	PI/NOTES	STATUS
☐ Douglas DC-3A-467 Skytrain (C-47B) (C-47D)	N2805J/'43-770'	20835	43-16369, N2805J, (N9271G)	RAAX
☐ Grumman G-96 Trader (TF-1) (C-1A)	N189G	074	Bu146044, N71459	RAD
☐ Ryan Navion A	N6589D	NAV-4-1702		RAA

ATCHISON COUNTY HISTORICAL SOCIETY MUSEUM / AMELIA EARHART BIRTHPLACE MUSEUM (KS3)

Address:	200 South Tenth Street/ 223 North Terrace Street, Atchison, Kansas 66022.
Tel:	HSM 913-367-6238 B/P 913-367-4217
Admission:	County Museum daily 1300-1600.
	Birthplace Museum Wednesday-Saturday 1000-1600, Sunday 1300-1600.
Location:	In the centre of the town.

The society has set up a local history museum in a restored former railroad depot in the town. On show are items tracing the development of the area.
Amelia Earhart was born in Atchison and a display follows her life in the area and her flying career. She made her first flight in 1920 and soon bought a Kinner Sportster. In this she set an altitude record. More distance flights followed and in 1931 she made the first solo flight across the Pacific Ocean from Honolulu to Oakland in California.
She lost her life in 1937 in a Lockheed Electra during an attempt to fly around the world. Nearby the house in which she was born is preserved.

ATWOOD MEMORIAL (KS4)

Location:	On permanent view at ALP 46 in the town.

TYPE	REG/SER	CON. NO.	PI/NOTES	STATUS
☐ Bell 209 Huey Cobra (AH-1G) (AH-1F)	66-15338	20094		PV

CHANUTE MONUMENT (KS5)

Location:	On permanent view in the Travelers Building in Elm Street in the centre of the town.

TYPE	REG/SER	CON. NO.	PI/NOTES	STATUS
☐ Chanute Glider (R)				

CHASE COUNTY VETERANS MEMORIAL (KS6)

Location:	On permanent view in Swope Park on East Union Street in Cottonwood Falls.

TYPE	REG/SER	CON. NO.	PI/NOTES	STATUS
☐ Bell 205 Iroquois (UH-1D) (UH-1H)	64-13866	4573		PV

CLOUD COUNTY HISTORICAL MUSEUM (KS7)

Address:	635 Broadway, Concordia, Kansas 66901.
Tel:	785-243-2866 **Email:** museum@cloudcounty.ks.org
Admission:	Tuesday-Saturday 1300-1700.
Location:	In the centre of the town.

Kansas

Cloud County Courthouse basement was the first home of the museum which was set up on 30th January 1959. In 1976 the collection moved to the 1908 Carnegie Library building and in January 1990 work started on the Ernest Legasse annexe.
The museum exhibits include radios, railroad items, clothing, furniture, musical instruments, toys and fossils. Among the larger displays are a blacksmith's shop, an early twentieth century kitchen, a broom factory and a peg barn moved from Randall. Also on view are a 1912 windmill, an 1898 Holsman horseless carriage and a 1915 Model T Ford.

The only aircraft in the collection is a 1928 Lincoln Page owned for many years by local aviator Charley Blosser. He purchased his first aircraft in 1923 and in his career owned more than 50 different types. He bought the Lincoln Page in 1928 and during World War II he loaned it to a training school in Wichita. The biplane was damaged during this period and in the mid-1960s Charley and a friend Harold Major rebuilt it.
The biplane was flown a few times a year until donated to the museum.

TYPE	REG/SER	CON. NO.	PI/NOTES	STATUS
☐ Lincoln Page LP-3	NC418V	281	NC418V, N418V	PV

COFFEYVILLE AVIATION HERITAGE MUSEUM (KS8)

Address:	2002 North Buckeye Street, PO Box 774, Coffeyville, Kansas 67337-0774.
Tel:	620-515-1232 Email: bwade@cox.net
Admission:	Saturday 1000-1600; Sunday 1300-1600.
Location:	In Pfister Park which is in the north western part of the town.

The Funk brothers, Joe and Howard, built their first glider in the early 1930s and it flew at the Akron Gliding Club in June 1933 The high-wing design was the first dual control model in the country. In 1934 they completed a high-wing monoplane powered by a Szekely radial. This engine was later replaced by a Ford Model A. A second airframe was then built at the family poultry house where the others had been constructed.
The Akron Aircraft Company was set up and production started using the Funk E engine derived from the Ford B. The firm went into receivership and the brothers moved to

Coffeyville where the design, now powered by a 75 h.p. Lycoming, was manufactured with the first flying in late 1941. When production ceased in 1948 a total of 438 had been built, many with Continental engines.
The museum has been set up to honour the contribution of the brothers to aviation in the country. The collection is housed in a 1933 hangar erected at Big Hill Airport which was operational from 1933 to 1960. The displays inside trace the history of the company and its products. This building is the only surviving structure from the field.

TYPE	REG/SER	CON. NO.	PI/NOTES	STATUS
☐ Brock KB-2	N171TC	TC-6		PV
☐ Funk B-75	NC22678	5	NC22678, N22678	PV
☐ Funk B-75L	NC34768	215	NC34768, N34768	PV
☐ Mitchell Wing U-2				PV
☐ Republic F-84F Thunderstreak	52-6675		52-6675, DD+373, DD+245, DD+345, 26675 (Greece)	PV
☐ Roloff RLU-1 Breezy	N2027	LL-1		PV

COMBAT AIR MUSEUM (KS9)

Address:	Hangars 602-604,J Street, Forbes Field, Topeka, Kansas 66619-1401.
Tel:	785-862-3303 Fax: 785-862-3304 Email: combatairmuseum@aol.com
Admission:	Monday-Saturday 0900-1600; Sunday 1200-1630.
Location:	At Forbes Field which is about 4 miles south of the city on Route 75.

Founded in the mid-1970s, the museum occupies two hangars at Forbes Field. One of the aims is to collect aircraft and artefacts associated with all wars in which US forces have served. The rooms at the rear of one of the hangars are devoted to particular themes. The War Room has items dating from the Spanish-American conflict up to the present day. The Prisoner of War Room highlights the harsh conditions endured by captured servicemen. A World War II Command Post has recreated in another area.
The rarest aircraft in the collection is the North American O-47B. Built in the late 1930s the type was one of the first to serve with the Kansas Air National Guard. Only 74 were built and few survive. The Lockheed Constellation was flown in from Davis-Monthan Air Force base in 1981 and is the largest aircraft in the collection. Examples of classic jet fighters of the last 50 years are being collected and these include a MiG-17

painted in Soviet colours. Not many Douglas Skynights are on show in museums. The jet fighter first flew at El Segundo in California in March 1948. Over 250 were built and most were delivered to the Marine Corps. The type served in Korea and the last examples were withdrawn from service during the Vietnam War.
The prototype Meyers OTW-125 biplane, developed from the Jensen 2, made its maiden flight in November 1936. Civilian Pilot Training Schools operated most of the 102 completed. The production aircraft were powered by either a 145 hp Warner or a 160 hp Kinner radial.
Visitors to the second hangar can see major restoration projects being carried out by the dedicated team of volunteers. Several airframes are in store in this area awaiting rebuild. For many years some aircraft were in flying condition but a change in policy meant they were grounded.

TYPE	REG/SER	CON. NO.	PI/NOTES	STATUS
☐ Baslee Pfalz E-1 (Scale R)				PV
☐ Beech D18S Expeditor (C18S) (SNB-2) (SNB-3) (TC-45J) (UC-45J)	Bu51241	5568	Bu51241, N3716G, N87693	PV
☐ Beech C50 Seminole (RL-23D) (RU-8D)	N4835Z	LHC-4	58-1358 Also reported as c/n LH-185.	PV
☐ Bell 204 Iroquois (UH-1C) (UH-1M)	66-0683	1665	Tail boom from UH-1C c/n 1819 66-15091	PV
☐ Bell 205 Iroquois (UH-1D) (UH-1H)	65-9617	4661		PV
☐ Canadian Car & Foundry Harvard 4 [North American NA-186]	N294CH	CCF4-5.	20294 (RCAF), CF-RUQ, C-FRUQ	PVA
☐ Curtiss 1C Jenny (JN-4D2) (R)	N101JN	R101		PV
☐ Douglas DC-3A-467 Skytrain (TC-47D) (VC-47D)	'476582'	16166/32914	44-76582, N710Z	PV
☐ Douglas A-4A Skyhawk (A4D-1)	Bu142168	11422	Front fuselage only.	PV
☐ Douglas F-10B Skynight (F3D-2)	Bu125807	8001		PV

☐ Douglas TA-4J Skyhawk	Bu158716	14337		PV	
☐ Fairchild 24W46	N81395	W46-295	NC81395	PVA	
☐ Grumman G-79 Panther (F9F-5)	Bu126226			PV	
☐ Grumman G-89 Tracker (S2F-1) (S-2A) (US-2A)	N486GT	395	Bu136486	PV	
☐ Grumman G-98 Tiger (F11F-1) (F-11A)	Bu141811	128		PV	
☐ Grumman G-303 Tomcat (F-14A)	Bu161615	474		PV	
☐ Hiller UH12A Raven (H-23A)	51-16122	276		PV	
☐ Lockheed 580 (T-33A)	52-9632	580-7817		PV	
☐ Lockheed 1049A-55-86 Super Constellation (RC-121D) (EC-121D) (EC-121T)	N4257U	1049A-4336	52-3418	PV	
☐ McDonnell M.36BA Voodoo (F-101B) (JF-101B)	N8234	588	57-0410	PV	
☐ McDonnell M.98EN Phantom II (F-4D)	66-0268	1935		PV	
☐ Messerschmitt Bf 109F (FSM)				PV	
☐ Meyers OTW-125	N15784	1	NC15784	PV	
☐ Mikoyan-Gurevich MiG-21PFM	4315	94A4315	In Czech markings.	PV	
☐ North American NA-51 (O-47B)	N73716	51-1011	39-98, NC73716	PV	
☐ North American NA-203 Sabre (F-86H)	53-1300	203-72		PV	
☐ Republic F-84F Thunderstreak	'0-1159'		51-1659, N65034, 51-1659	PVX	
☐ Republic F-105D Thunderchief	62-4375	D-574		PV	
☐ Shenyang J-8II			Front fuselage only.	PV	
☐ Sikorsky S-64A Tarhe (CH-54A)	67-18424	64026		PV	
☐ Sikorsky S-65A Sea Stallion (CH-53A) (NCH-53A)	Bu152399	65026	Bu152399, NASA543, N39	PV	
☐ Starks Taube (Scale R)	N1914S	001		PV	
☐ Turner Nieuport 27 (Scale R)	N127LT	001		PV	
☐ Vultee V-74 Valiant (BT-13A)	41-11584	74-2594		PV	
☐ WSK Lim-2 [MiG-15bis]	'1016'	1B 010-16	1016 (Poland), N15YY – in false Soviet markings.	PVX	
☐ WSK Lim-6R	'611'	1J 06-11	611 (Poland) – in false Vietnamese markings.	PVX	

COMMEMORATIVE AIR FORCE (HEART OF AMERICA WING) (KS10)

Address:	3 Aero Plaza, New Century, Kansas 66031.
Tel:	913-397-6376 Email: jonmiller2008@gmail.com
Admission:	By prior permission only.
Location:	About 20 miles south of Kansas City off Interstate 69.

The unit was formed as a squadron in 1986 and was initially based at Clinton, Missouri. In 2001 a move was made to a purpose-built hangar at New Century Airport which was once Olathe Naval Air Station. One PT-19 is owned by the wing and the remaining aircraft in the fleet belong to members.

TYPE	REG/SER	CON. NO.	PI/NOTES	STATUS
☐ Aero L-39V Albatros	N139V	630715		RAA
☐ Boeing-Stearman A75 Kaydet (PT-13D)	N234X	75-0260	41-1073	RAA
☐ Fairchild M-62A Cornell (PT-19)	N50303	T43-5905	42-83318	RAA
☐ Fairchild M-62A Cornell (PT-19B)	N50481	6103AE	42-47691 (?)	RAA
☐ North American NA-168 Texan (T-6G)	N6G	168-463	49-3349, E.16-72, N5830Z	RAA
☐ Taylorcraft DCO-65 Grasshopper (L-2M)	N50573	L-4462	(USAAF)	RAA
☐ Taylorcraft DCO-65 Grasshopper (L-2M)	N75891	L-6268	(USAAF)	RAA
☐ Vultee V-74 Valiant (BT-13A)	N2808	74-6488	41-22410	RAA
☐ Vultee V-74 Valiant (BT-13A)	N56665	74-7861	42-1216	RAA
☐ WSK Lim-5 [MiG-17F]	N1717M	1C 17-17	1717 (Poland)	RAA

COMMEMORATIVE AIR FORCE (JAYHAWK WING) (KS11)

Address:	2269 South Kessler Street, Wichita, Kansas 67217-1045.
Tel:	316-943-5510 Email: cafjayhawks@gmail.com
Admission:	By prior permission only.
Location:	At Westport Airport which is off Pawnee Road in the south western suburbs of the city.

Members of the wing restored the Fairchild Cornell which had not flown for many years The Cessna Bobcat also underwent a major rebuild in the workshops. The Ryan PT-22 is privately owned.

TYPE	REG/SER	CON. NO.	PI/NOTES	STATUS
☐ Cessna T-50 Bobcat (AT-17D) (UC-78B)	N44795	6516	43-32578	RAA
☐ Fairchild M-62C Cornell (PT-23)	N64176	256HO	42-49722	RAA
☐ Ryan ST-3KR Recruit (PT-22)				RAA

COWLEY COUNTY COMMUNITY COLLEGE (KS12)

Address:	125 South 2nd Street, Arkansas City, Kansas 67005-2662.
Tel:	620-441-5279 Fax: 620-441-5357 Email: arkcitycte@cowley.edu
Admission:	By prior permission only.
Location:	In the southern part of the town.

The college has seven sites in the south central part of the state and offers a wide range of courses. The aviation maintenance course is known to have two Cessna 152 airframes but there may be more.

TYPE	REG/SER	CON. NO.	PI/NOTES	STATUS
☐ Cessna 152	N25918	15280857		RA
☐ Cessna 152	N93116	15285405		RA

DODGE CITY MONUMENT (KS13)

Location:	On permanent view at the airport which is about 3 miles east of the city

TYPE	REG/SER	CON. NO.	PI/NOTES	STATUS
☐ Douglas A-26C Invader	44-35627	28906		PV

GALENA MINING AND HISTORICAL MUSEUM (KS14)

Address:	319 West 7th Street, Galena, Kansas 66739.
Tel:	620-783-2192
Admission:	Summer months Monday-Saturday 0900-1100 1300-1530; rest of year Monday, Wednesday and Friday 1300-1530
Location:	In the centre of the town.

This interesting museum is housed in the old Missouri-Texas-Kansas railroad depot which was moved to the site. The displays trace the history of the region with particular reference to the Grand Central Mine which was located just east of the town. The Iroquois in mounted nearby outside the city hall.

TYPE	REG/SER	CON. NO.	PI/NOTES	STATUS
☐ Bell 205 Iroquois (UH-1D) (UH-1H)	64-13561	4268		PV

GIRARD VETERANS MEMORIAL (KS15)

Address:	Courthouse Square, Girard, Kansas 66743.
Admission:	On permanent view.
Location:	In the centre of the town.

Dedicated on 15th April 1995, this memorial honours the 777 citizens of Kansas who lost their lives in Vietnam. A replica of the Washington Vietnam Wall has been constructed.

TYPE	REG/SER	CON. NO.	PI/NOTES	STATUS
☐ Bell 205 Iroquois (UH-1D) (UH-1H)	64-13632	4339		PV

HIGH PLAINS MUSEUM (KS16)

Address:	1717 Cherry, PO Box 342, Goodland, Kansas 67735.
Tel:	913-899-4595
Admission:	Monday-Friday 0900-1700 (Closes at 1800 June–September); Saturday 0900-1600: June–August Sunday 1300-1600.
Location:	Just off Interstate 70 in the north western part of the state near the Colorado border.

This excellent local history museum has over 8,000 items on show tracing the struggle of the pioneers to establish settlements in the region. Exhibitions on the depression, the dustbowl and early transport are on view. Many personal items from the early period can be seen along with photographs and documents.

In 1909 two Rock Island machinists William Purvis and Charles Wilson formed the Goodland Aviation Company to raise money in order to complete their helicopter. A flight was attempted early in 1910 but the machine crashed, according to one report, into the local railway water tower sending a spray over the crowd of onlookers. The helicopter never flew again. The inventors left town and returned to work on the railway.

A replica was built in 1976 using as a basis the original patent and the only known photograph of the machine. Two original parts which were rescued from the crashed helicopter are exhibited beside the replica.

TYPE	REG/SER	CON. NO.	PI/NOTES	STATUS
☐ Purvis-Wilson Helicopter (R)				PV

INDEPENDENCE MONUMENT (KS17)

Location:	On permanent view in Riverside Park in Oak Street in the north eastern part of the town.

TYPE	REG/SER	CON. NO.	PI/NOTES	STATUS
☐ North American NA-243 Super Sabre (F-100F)	56-3813	243-89		PV

KANSAS AVIATION MUSEUM (KS18)

Address:	3550 South George Washington Boulevard, Wichita, Kansas 67210-2100.
Tel:	316-683-9242 Fax: 316-683-0573 Email: ksaviation@kansasaviationmuseum.org
Admission:	Monday-Saturday 1000-1700; Sunday 1200-1700.
Location:	In the south eastern suburbs of the city near the ANG entrance to McConnell AFB.

The first airport in Wichita opened in 1925 and soon aircraft builders were setting up factories in the area. Companies such as Beech, Cessna, Mooney, Stearman, Lear and many others have produced aircraft in the city.

In 1928 there were more than 20 manufacturers in the area and plans were put forward for a new airport. In 1930 construction of the administration terminal building started but due to the depression it was not completed until 1934.

During World War II the Army occupied the structure and doubled its size. In the 1950s the Air Force wanted a training base for the B-47 which was being built by the Boeing plant on the field. Eventually they agreed to pay for the construction of new airport for the city and commercial traffic moved out in 1954. The site became known as McConnell Air Force Base. The old terminal building was used by the Kansas Air National Guard for some time but became surplus.

The museum acquired the building and opened its exhibition in 1991. Part of it has been restored to its original state and further work is being carried out. On show here are several early aircraft including Swallow and American Eagle biplanes dating from the time the airport was first opened. These airframes are under restoration at the current time.

A rare aircraft is the Stearman Ariel. Designed by Lloyd Stearman's cousin Glenn, the low-wing monoplane was constructed in Coffeyville, Kansas. Only two or three were completed and parts of another are known to survive. The B-29 which was restored in the nearby Boeing plant has recently been put on show. There are many interesting types in the collection including several one-off homebuilts. The museum plans to raise funds to build an large exhibition hall. When this is complete the aircraft in store around the area and a number of prototypes owned by the local manufacturers will be put on display.

TYPE	REG/SER	CON. NO.	PI/NOTES	STATUS
☐ American Eagle A-129			Fuselage frame.	PV
☐ American Eagle A-129	N536E	397	NC536E	PVC
☐ Bede BD-5B	N26019	3038		PV
☐ Beech B35 Bonanza	N5124C	D-2409		PV
☐ Beech 65-80 Seminole (L-23F) (U-8F)	62-3838	LF-36		PV
☐ Beech 73 Jet Mentor	N134B	F-1		PV
☐ Beech 2000A Starship I	N8283S	NC-41		PV
☐ Boeing 345 Superfortress (B-29) (TB-29)	N69972	10804	44-69972, N6735C, N44697	RA
☐ Boeing 450-17-35 Stratojet (B-47E) (WB-47E)	51-2387	450440		PV
☐ Boeing 464-201-7 Stratofortress (B-52D)	55-0094	17210		PV
☐ Boeing 717-146 Stratotanker (KC-135A) (KC-135E)	56-3658	17407		PV
☐ Boeing 727-173C	N199FE	19509	N695WA, TZ-ADR	PV
☐ Boeing 737-200-2H4	N29SW	21340	(N31SW)	PV
☐ Cessna 177B Cardinal	N1910F	17700002		PV
☐ Cessna 206 Super Skywagon	N5228U	206-0228		RA
☐ Cessna 310F	PP-OTI	310F0103	N5803X, PT-BOJ	PV
☐ Cessna 318B Tweety Bird (318A) (T-37A) (T-37B)	58-1977	40402		RA
☐ Cessna 337A Super Skymaster (O-2B)	67-21469	3370492	N5392S	PV
☐ Detroit Gull	N41775	324		RA
☐ Funk B-85C	N81162	292	NC81162	PV
☐ Gates Learjet 23	N505PF	23-006	N505PF, N578LJ, N23CH, N111JD	RA
☐ Herring Sport Fan	N95SF	DH1001		RA
☐ Jayhawk	N440EM	GP-0001		PV
☐ Laird Swallow				PV
☐ Lockheed 580 (T-33A) (TV-2) (T-33B)	N151	580-5313	51-4019, Bu126583, N151, N1519	PV
☐ Monnett Sonerai II	N719W	719		PV
☐ Mooney M-18C Mite	N492M	245		RA
☐ Oldfield Baby Great Lakes	N4227U	GJ-002		PV
☐ Prescott Pusher	N41PP	001		RA
☐ Rans S-12	N2163X	1289001		RA
☐ Rawdon R-1	N44770	1		RA
☐ Rawdon T-1	N41672	T1-3CS		RA
☐ Republic F-84F Thunderstreak	52-9089			PV
☐ Stearman C3B	NC9067	204	NC9067, N9067	RA
☐ Stearman 4D	NC569Y	4027	NC563Y, N569Y	PV
☐ Stearman 73 (NS-1)	Bu9688	73-0012		PVC
☐ Stearman B Ariel	N32459	1		PV
☐ Swallow OX-5	NC3924	890	Fuselage frame	PV
☐ Swallow OX-5	'C6194'	1008	NC6914	PVCX
☐ Unruh Pretty Prairie Special	N1473V	1		PV
☐ Watkins Skylark SL	N102V	102	NC102V	PV

KANSAS CITY MONUMENT (KS19)

Location:	On view during opening hours in Cabela's store at 10300 Cabela Drive in the western part of the city.

TYPE	REG/SER	CON. NO.	PI/NOTES	STATUS
☐ Piper PA-18-150 Super Cub				PV

KANSAS COSMOSPHERE AND SPACE CENTER (KS20)

Address:	1100 North Plum, Hutchinson, Kansas 67501-1499.
Tel:	316-662-2305
Admission:	Monday-Thursday 0900-1700; Friday-Saturday 0900-1900; Sunday 1200-1700.
Location:	In the centre of the town.

This superb exhibition of space technology features the latest display techniques. A hall contains items from the early days of Robert Goddard's first liquid fuelled rocket up to Neil Armstrong's moon landing. Examples of the Mercury, Gemini and Apollo spacecraft are on view. There is also a planetarium and an Omnimax theatre. The Center runs courses where adults and children experience the training undergone by astronauts. New halls were built some years ago and the exhibition now presents a comprehensive view of space flight.

Two replicas show the development of high speed flight. The Starfighter is due to come here from the long closed Florence museum.

TYPE	REG/SER	CON. NO.	PI/NOTES	STATUS
☐ Bell 44 (XS-1) (X-1) (FSM)				PV
☐ Fieseler Fi 103A-1				PV
☐ Lockheed 283-93-03 Starfighter (F-104B)	57-1301	283-5013		RA
☐ Lockheed SR-71A Blackbird	61-7961	2012		PV
☐ North American NA-240 (X-15) (X-15A) (FSM)				PV
☐ Northrop N-156T Talon (T-38A)	'N948NS'	N.5130	60-0557	PVX

KANSAS MUSEUM OF HISTORY (KS21)

Address:	Kansas State Historical Society, 6425 South West Street, Topeka, Kansas 66615-1099.
Tel:	785-272-8681 Fax: 785-272-8682 Email: reference@kshs.org
Admission:	Tuesday-Saturday 0900-1700; Sunday 1300-1700.
Location:	In the western suburbs of the city at Wanamaker Road and Interstate 70.

The museum opened on its present site in June 1984 and the first permanent galleries were completed the following year. The exhibitions trace the history of the area with a series of imaginative displays.

The first successful aircraft constructed in Kansas was the Longren biplane built in Topeka in 1910. The configuration of the aircraft is similar to the Curtiss Pusher. The Longren was owned by Captain Phil Billard who was killed in World War I and his family later donated the aircraft to the museum.

The Maneval helicopter was completed in 1941 and incorporated a number of innovations. The type suffered from excessive vibration and only made tethered flights. The helicopter was stored by the designer until 1974 when he donated it to the society.

TYPE	REG/SER	CON. NO.	PI/NOTES	STATUS
☐ Longren Pusher		5		PV
☐ Maneval Helicopter				RA

KANSAS MUSEUM OF MILITARY HISTORY (KS22)

Address:	135 South Highway 77, Augusta, Kansas 67010.
Tel:	316-775-1425 Email: info@kmmh.org
Admission:	Saturday-Sunday 1000-1700.
Location:	In the southern part of the town.

Formed in the early 1990s as a detachment of the Combat Air Museum in Topeka, a small display was held in a building in the town in 1991. A move to the current premises, a former oil industry workshop, took place in February 1994.

Since the move a great deal of work has been carried out on the building. Initially known as the Augusta Air Museum the present title was adopted in 2007. A number of light aircraft and homebuilts left the exhibition when it was decided to concentrate solely on military items. The two helicopters arrived from Fort Rucker in Alabama. The collection of military vehicles now numbers around 25 and includes lorries, jeeps and utility vehicles. Over 300 model aircraft are in the collection and there are displays of uniforms, test equipment, communications devices, medical supplies, wartime rations and weapons.

TYPE	REG/SER	CON. NO.	PI/NOTES	STATUS
☐ Bell 205 Iroquois (UH-1D) (UH-1H)	65-9700	4744		PV
☐ Bell 206A Kiowa (OH-58A)	69-16123	40344		PV
☐ Breese Penguin (R)				PV

KANSAS STATE UNIVERSITY (KS23)

Address:	2310 Centennial Road, Salina, Kansas 67401-8196.
Tel:	785-826-2911
Admission:	By prior permission only.
Location:	At the airport which is about 4 miles south of the town off Interstate 135.

The university has a fleet of over 40 aircraft in use for pilot training. The aviation maintenance department is located in a modern complex with classrooms, laboratories and workshops. In addition to the instructional airframes there are several engines and systems test rigs in use. Students also carry out supervised work on the active aircraft. Some of the airframes are stored for future use.

TYPE	REG/SER	CON. NO.	PI/NOTES	STATUS
☐ Bell 206A Kiowa (OH-58A) (OH-58C)	68-16812	40126	68-16812, N670HP	RA
☐ Bell 206A Kiowa (OH-58A) (OH-58C)	N825LS	41828	72-21162	RA
☐ Cessna 150H	N6797S	15067597		RA
☐ Cessna 150H	N7231S	15067931		RA
☐ Cessna 150J	N50570	15069402		RA
☐ Cessna 150L	N10850	15075087		RA
☐ Cessna 421B Golden Eagle	N31KS	421B0662		RA
☐ Hughes 269A Osage (TH-55A)	64-18054	0366		RA
☐ Hughes 269A Osage (TH-55A)	64-18058	0370		RA
☐ Hughes 269A Osage (TH-55A)	64-18217	0529		RA
☐ Hughes 269A Osage (TH-55A)	66-18274	0586		RA
☐ Hughes 269A Osage (TH-55A)	67-16694	0801		RA
☐ Hughes 269A Osage (TH-55A)	67-16825	0932		RA
☐ Hughes 269A Osage (TH-55A)	67-16856	0963		RA
☐ Hughes 269A Osage (TH-55A)	67-16996	1103		RA
☐ Hughes 269A Osage (TH-55A)	N105KT	46-0508	64-?????	RA
☐ Hughes 269A Osage (TH-55A)	N106KT	46-0516	64-?????	RA
☐ Hughes 269A Osage (TH-55A)	N103KT	56-0539	64-18227	RA
☐ Hughes 269A Osage (TH-55A)	N104KT	56-0555	64-?????	RA
☐ Piper PA-28-140 Cherokee C	N5282S	28-26912		RA

LEAVENWORTH MONUMENT (KS24)

Location:	On permanent view at a Mexican Restaurant in the town.

TYPE	REG/SER	CON. NO.	PI/NOTES	STATUS
☐ Piper PA-38-112 Tomahawk				PV

The only Beech Jet Mentor built is awaiting restoration at the Kansas Aviation Museum. (Glenn Chatfield) [KS18]

On show at the Mid-America Air Museum is an example of the Ryan PT-22 Recruit. [KS26]

The unique Krier-Kraft Aero-Master can be seen at the Pioneer-Krier Museum. [KS32]

Kansas

MERIDEN MONUMENT (KS25)

Location:	On permanent view at VFW 10815 on Highway 4 in the northern part of the town.

TYPE	REG/SER	CON. NO.	PI/NOTES	STATUS
☐ Bell 204 Iroquois (UH-1D) (UH-1H)	64-13701	4408		PV

MID-AMERICA AIR MUSEUM (KS26)

Address:	2000 West 2nd Street, PO Box 2585, Liberal, Kansas 67905-2585.
Tel:	620-624-5263 Email: liberalcityam@swko.net
Admission:	Monday-Friday 0800-1700; Saturday 1000-1600; Sunday 1300-1700.
Location:	At the airport which is about 2 miles west of the town.

In 1986 a reunion was held at the former Liberal Army Airfield, the municipal airport for the city. During World War II the field trained Liberator crews and for the gathering David Tallichet flew in his B-24. He suggested that a museum should be established and promised to provide a number of aircraft from his extensive collection.

Plans were made to lease the former Beech factory on the field and the museum moved in during August 1987. By early 1988 five Tallichet machines were on site with only two in display condition. Now only the former Indian Air Force Folland Gnat remains at Liberal.

The Mid-America Air Group was set up by Colonel Tom Thomas in 1983 and he soon acquired over 80 aircraft. A museum was opened at Frederick in Oklahoma in 1985. On 1st June 1985 he flew 65 of his aircraft on the occasion of his 65th birthday. In May 1988 an agreement was made with Tom Thomas to move his collection to Liberal and within six weeks 36 planes had arrived. Over the next few years many more aircraft from the Mid-America Group have joined the museum.

The collection comprises mainly classic American machines produced from the late 1930s as well as a number of homebuilt types including a number of one off types. Several Beech designs are on show from the classic Staggerwing to the innovative Starship.

Cessna types made in the state can also be seen. The museum has also acquired a range of military aircraft from the services and a comprehensive display has been set up.

Exhibitions tracing the history of the airfield during its military days, the Korean and Vietnam wars and the history of NASA have been staged.

A change of name from the Liberal Air Museum took place in the 1990s.

TYPE	REG/SER	CON. NO.	PI/NOTES	STATUS
☐ Aero Commander 520	'52076'	520-76	N4170B, N711YY	PVAX
☐ Aeronca K	N19339	K-208	NC19339	PVA
☐ Aeronca 65C Chief	NC23547	C-5119	NC23547, N23547	PVA
☐ Aeronca 65TC Grasshopper (O-58B) (L-3B)	N48433	9943	43-26587 (?)	PVA
☐ Aeronca 7AC Champion	N2735E	7AC-6316	NC2735E	PVA
☐ Aeronca 7BCM Champion (L-16A)	N66356/'7991'	7BCM-206	(USAAF)	PVAX
☐ Armstrong Aeronaut	N77VA	1		PV
☐ Avro 504K (R)				PVX
☐ Beech F17D	N139KP	257	NC18574, N124D, N500SW	PVA
☐ Beech C18S Navigator (AT-7C)	N65314	7061	43-50128	PVA
☐ Beech B19 Musketeer Sport	N1978W	MB-632		PV
☐ Beech 35 Bonanza	N80441	D-41	NC80441	PVA
☐ Beech D50 Twin Bonanza	N4303R	DH-125		RAA
☐ Beech 2000 Starship I	N1556S	NC-6		PV
☐ Bell 47G-2 Sioux (H-13H) (OH-13H)	55-4619	1648		PV
☐ Bell 205 Iroquois (UH-1D)	66-1204	5687		PV
☐ Bell 209 Huey Cobra (AH-1G) (AH-1S)	71-21038	21109		PV
☐ Bell 209 Huey Cobra (AH-1G) (AH-1S)			Front fuselage only.	PV
☐ Bell 209 Sea Cobra (AH-1T) (AH-1W)	Bu160817	26922		PV
☐ Bellanca 14-13-2 Crusair Senior	N74456	1569	NC74456	PVA
☐ Bellanca 14-19-3 260	N8849R	4203		PVA
☐ Bowers Fly Baby 1A				PV
☐ Bushby M.II Mustang II	N32DC	M.II-343		PVA
☐ Cessna T-50 Bobcat (C-78) (UC-78)	N711UU	3766	42-58275, N68160	PVA
☐ Cessna 120	N72948	10146	NC72948	PVA
☐ Cessna 140	N76483	10915		PVA
☐ Cessna 145 Airmaster	NC19462	414	NC19462, N19462	PV
☐ Cessna 165 Airmaster	NC32450	583	NC32450, N32450	PVA
☐ Cessna 175	N7205M	55505		PVA
☐ Cessna 195A	N9864A	7566		PVA
☐ Cessna 195B	N2196C	16181	NC2196C	PVA
☐ Cessna 318 Tweety Bird (XT-37)	54-0718	40003		PV
☐ Cessna 337A Super Skymaster	'006274'	3370274	N6274F	PVX
☐ Culver V Satellite	N3116K	V-335	NC3116K	PVA
☐ Curtiss-Wright CW-1 Junior	N10973	1151	NC10973	PVA
☐ Douglas A-4L Skyhawk (A4D-2N) (A-4C)	Bu149635	12960		PV
☐ Ercoupe 415C	N2700H	3325		PVA
☐ Ercoupe 415G	N94886	5014		PVA
☐ Experimental Aircraft Association P-9 Pober Pixie	N8509Z	1-S-80		PVA
☐ Fairchild 24 C8F	N16852	3132	NC16852	PVA
☐ Fairchild M-62A Cornell (PT-19A)	N49942	T42-1523	41-20517	PVA
☐ Fairchild M-62A-4 Cornell (PT-26A) (Cornell II)	N91095		42-71241, FT826, 14665 (Canada)	PVA
☐ Fairchild M-62C Cornell (PT-23)	N63739	1223AE	(USAAF)	PVA
☐ Fisher FP-202 Koala II				PVA
☐ Folland Fo.144 Gnat T.1	E1222	GT.038	On loan from MARC, CA. – in Indian markings.	PV
☐ Funk B-75L	N24174	200	NC24174	PVA
☐ Grumman G-40 Avenger (TBM-3)	N6831C	2942	Bu86723	PV

315

☐ Grumman G-89 Tracker (S2F-1) (S-2A)	N5470C	150	Bu133179	PVA
☐ Grumman G-303 Tomcat (F-14A)	Bu160903	332		PV
☐ Hughes 369M Cayuse (HO-6) (OH-6A)	66-7865	0179		PV
☐ Interstate S-1A Cadet	N37214	57	NC37214	PVA
☐ Leak Avid Flyer	N31BL	31		PVA
☐ Lockheed 080 Shooting Star (P-80C) (F-80C)	49-0710	080-2458		PV
☐ Lockheed 383-04-05 Starfighter (F-104C)	56-0933	183-1221		PV
☐ Lockheed 749A-79-43 Constellation (PO-1W) (WV-1)	N1206	749A-2613	Bu124438, N7624C, N120	PV
☐ Luscombe 8A Silvaire	N1172B	5799	NC1172B	PVA
☐ Luscombe T-8F	N1580B	6207	NC1580B	PVA
☐ McCulloch J-2	N4374G	084		PVA
☐ McDonnell M.98EN Phantom II (F-4D)	66-7746	2382		PV
☐ McLeod K & S 102.5 Cavalier	N12RG	1		PVA
☐ Miller S-1 Fly Rod	N22RM	001		PV
☐ Monnett Moni	N124KB	124		PVA
☐ Mooney M-18C Mite	N4140	307		PVA
☐ Nieuport 11 (R)				PV
☐ North American NA-108 Mitchell (B-25J) (TB-25J) (TB-25N)	N9462Z	108-33810	44-30535	PVA
☐ North American NA-145 Navion	N4005K	NAV-4-1005		PVA
☐ North American NA-203 Sabre (F-86H)	53-1501	203-273		PV
☐ North American NA-300 Bronco (YOV-10A)	Bu152880	300-2		PV
☐ Northrop N-156T Talon (T-38A)	60-0583	N.5156		PV
☐ Oldfield Baby Great Lakes	N4628	7010-H-273B		PV
☐ Pereira GP.2 Osprey I (X-28A)	Bu158786			PV
☐ Phoenix 6C Hang Glider				PV
☐ Piasecki PV-18 Retriever (H-25A) (HUP-3) (UH-25C)	Bu147628	57	51-16628	PV
☐ Pietenpol B4-A Aircamper	N2NK	NK-2		PVA
☐ Piper J-3C-65 Cub	NC26815	4196	NC26815, N26815	PVA
☐ Piper J-4F Cub Coupe	NC30426	4-1209	NC30426, N30426	PVA
☐ Piper PA-22-135 Tripacer	N1129C	22-964		PVA
☐ Piper PA-23 Apache	N1015P	23-17		PVA
☐ Piper PA-23-250 Aztec	N4581P	27-90		PVA
☐ Piper PA-24-250 Comanche	N110LF	24-695		PVA
☐ Porterfield CP-65	N32431	861	NC32431	PVA
☐ Quickie Aircraft Quickie 1 (Rutan 54)	N1176L	346		PV
☐ Rand Robinson KR-1	N982GS	1982-1		PVA
☐ Rand Robinson KR-1	N31SB	ONE		PV
☐ Rearwin 175 Skyranger	N32402	1528		PVA
☐ Rearwin 7000 Sportster	NC18768	590	NC18768, N18768	PVA
☐ Republic F-105G Thunderchief (F-105F)	63-8266	F-43		RA
☐ Roloff RLU-1 Breezy	N1380E	4-12-26-ONW		PVA
☐ Rotec Rally 3	N83RE	25071		PVA
☐ Rotorway Scorpion 133				PV
☐ Rutan 33 Vari-Eze	N859	1125		PV
☐ Rutan 33 Vari-Eze	N83BS	168		PVA
☐ Ryan ST-3KR Recruit (PT-22)	N46741	1439	41-15470	PVA
☐ Shober Willie II	N113BT	52925		PVA
☐ Smith DK-1	N601CS	001		PVA
☐ Staib LB-5				PV
☐ Steen Skybolt	N120VL	VL-1		PVA
☐ Stinson 10A Voyager	N34690	7990	NC34690	PVA
☐ Stinson V-76 Sentinel (L-5B)	N66334	76-2942	(USAAF)	PVA
☐ Stinson V-77 Reliant (AT-19)	N9362H''FK814'	77-140	42-46779, FK953, Bu11355	PVAX
☐ Stinson V-77 Reliant (AT-19)	N711NN	77-306	43-44019, FB578, Bu11593, N69377	PV
☐ Sud Fennec [North American NA-189 Trojan (T-28A)]	N8522X	189-41	52-1226, 23 (France), CN-AEC, HR-228A, (228 (Honduras))	PV
☐ Taylorcraft DCO-65 Grasshopper (L-2M)	N49174	L-5962	43-26650	PVA
☐ Temco D.16 Twin Navion	N3797G	TN-13		PVA
☐ Temco GC-1B Swift	N78159	2159		PV
☐ Thorp T-18	N35GW	0Z-3		PVA
☐ Viking Dragonfly	N202RG	1		PVA
☐ Vought F4U-5N Corsair (F4U-5)	Bu124447		Bu124447, 602 (Honduras), N100CV	PV
☐ Vought F-8H Crusader (F8U-2N) (F-8D)	Bu148693			PV
☐ Vought A-7D Corsair II	73-1009	D605		PV
☐ Vultee V-74A Valiant (BT-15)	N67316	74-7652	42-1995	PVA

MOLINE MONUMENT (KS27)

Location:	On permanent view on 3rd Street in the centre of the town.

TYPE	REG/SER	CON. NO.	PI/NOTES	STATUS
☐ Lockheed 580 (T-33A)	52-9258	580-7324		PV

MUSEUM OF THE KANSAS NATIONAL GUARD (KS28)

Address:	6700 South Topeka Boulevard, Topeka, Kansas 66619.
Tel:	785-682-1020 Email: info@kansasguardmuseum.org
Admission:	Tuesday-Saturday 1000-1600.
Location:	At Forbes Field which is about 4 miles south of the city on Route 75.

Kansas

Units of the Kansas Air and Army National Guard have operated fixed wing aircraft and helicopters from Forbes Field for many years.
The decision to set up a museum was made in the mid-1980s and the exhibition opened on 1st February 1997. The history of Kansas forces over the last century and a half is portrayed in detail. There is a mock Civil War encampment to be seen and items on both World Wars feature.
Recent conflicts such as those in Korea, Vietnam and the Gulf can be viewed in the imaginative displays.

TYPE	REG/SER	CON. NO.	PI/NOTES	STATUS
☐ Bell 205 Iroquois (UH-1D) (UH-1H)	64-13569	4276		PV
☐ Bell 205 Iroquois (UH-1D) (UH-1H)	65-10011	5005		PV
☐ Bell 206A Kiowa (OH-58A)	72-21375	42041		PV
☐ Bell 209 Huey Cobra (AH-1G) (AH-1S)	70-16060	21004		PV
☐ Boeing 717-148 Stratotanker (KC-135A) (KC-135E)	57-1429	17500		PV
☐ Hughes 369M Cayuse (HO-6) (OH-6A)	67-16066	0451		PV
☐ Martin 272A Canberra (RB-57A)	52-1480	63		PV
☐ Martin 272B Canberra (B-57B) (EB-57B)	52-1526	109		PV
☐ McDonnell M.98EN Phantom II (F-4D)	65-0801	1880		PV
☐ Sikorsky S-64A Tarhe (CH-54A)	68-18439	64041		PV

NEW CENTURY AIR CENTER DISPLAY (KS29)

Address:	300 Navy Drive, Industrial Airport, Olathe, Kansas 66031-0013.
Tel:	913-715-6000
Admission:	On permanent view.
Location:	About 20 miles south of Kansas City off Interstate 69.

Three aircraft are on show at this former Naval Air Station which now serves as both as an airport and an industrial park. The display was developed in the 1990s and includes two versions of the Corsair II.

TYPE	REG/SER	CON. NO.	PI/NOTES	STATUS
☐ Douglas A-4L Skyhawk (A4D-2N) (A-4C)	'8424'	13009	Bu150598	PVX
☐ Vought TA-7C Corsair II (A-7C)	Bu156782	E49		PV
☐ Vought A-7E Corsair II	'Bu158857'	E350	Bu158657	PVX

OVERBROOK MONUMENT (KS30)

Location:	On permanent view at ALP 239 in Maple Street in the northern part of the town.

TYPE	REG/SER	CON. NO.	PI/NOTES	STATUS
☐ Bell 205 Iroquois (UH-1H)	66-16674	8868		PV

OVERLAND PARK HERITAGE FOUNDATION (KS31)

Address:	7323 West 79th Street, Overland Park, Kansas 66204-2908.
Tel:	913-895-6357
Admission:	By prior permission only.
Location:	About 8 miles south west of Kansas City.

The foundation has been set up to trace the history of the area and to preserve significant sites. William B. Strang founded Overland Park. A replica of an aircraft he designed is being built for future exhibition.

TYPE	REG/SER	CON. NO.	PI/NOTES	STATUS
☐ Strang Flyer (R)				RAC

PIONEER-KRIER MUSEUM (KS32)

Address:	430 West 4th, Box 862, Ashland, Kansas 67831.
Tel:	620-635-2227 Email: pioneer@ucom.net
Admission:	Tuesday-Friday 1000-1200 1300-1700
Location:	On Highway 160 about 35 miles south east of Dodge City.

Opened in May 1968, the museum displays artefacts from the days of the early settlers in the region. Harold Krier was a local man who took part in many aerobatic contests. A number of his mementos and trophies are on show along with three of the aircraft which he flew in competition. He won his first contests in 1953/4. The Krier Kraft, inspired by the Bücker Jungmeister, was constructed by Harold and his brother Larry in 1962.

TYPE	REG/SER	CON. NO.	PI/NOTES	STATUS
☐ Great Lakes Special	N21E	258	On loan	RAA
☐ Krier-Kraft Aero-Master	N5400E	1		PV
☐ Piper J-3C-65 Cub				RA

PRATT COMMUNITY COLLEGE (KS33)

Address:	348 North East Kansas 61, Pratt, Kansas 67124.
Tel:	620-672-9800 Email: daryll@prattcc.edu
Admission:	By prior permission only.
Location:	In the eastern part of the town.

The college operates airframe mechanics and aircraft maintenance technology courses. Only one aircraft is known to be owned by the organisation but there are probably more in the workshops.

TYPE	REG/SER	CON. NO.	PI/NOTES	STATUS
☐ Grumman G-159 Gulfstream I	N47R	69	N769G, N377, N47	RA

PRATT COUNTY HISTORICAL MUSEUM / B-29 ALL VETERANS MEMORIAL (KS34)

Address:	208 South Ninnescah Street, Pratt, Kansas 67124.
Tel:	620-672-7874
Admission:	Monday-Friday 1000-1600 Saturday-Sunday 1300-1600.
Location:	In the town which is about 75 miles west of Wichita.
	The airport is about three miles north of the town on Route 281.

Pratt Army Airfield opened in May 1943 and was built to serve as a training base for the Boeing B-29 Superfortress. A YB-29 flew into the field during the summer and the 40th Bomb Group began forming. The field was closed over the winter of 1945/6 and the last B-29 left on 6th March 1946. The site became the airport and industrial park for the town.

Several buildings from the World War II field survive. A memorial to the B-29 crews has been erected at the airport and two jets have been mounted on poles. The museum in the town has displays tracing the history of the airfield with many interesting items on view.

TYPE	REG/SER	CON. NO.	PI/NOTES	STATUS
☐ Bell 209 Huey Cobra (AH-1G) (AH-1F)	67-15624	20288	At airport.	PV
☐ McDonnell M.98DE Phantom II (F-4C)	63-7702	844	At airport.	PV
☐ Northrop N-156T Talon (T-38A)	61-0814	N.5180	At airport.	PV

RANTOUL MONUMENT (KS35)

Location:	On permanent view at Dodson Aviation at the airport south of the town.

TYPE	REG/SER	CON. NO.	PI/NOTES	STATUS
☐ Lockheed 1329 JetStar 8	'N001DT'	1329-5157	N5521L, N9WP, N29WP, XB-DUH	PVX

RAYTHEON AIRCRAFT CORPORATION DISPLAY (KS36)

Address:	9709 East Central Avenue, Wichita, Kansas 67201-0085.
Tel:	316-681-7811
Admission:	When sales office is open.
Location:	At the factory which is about 5 miles east of the city off Route 55.

The Beech Aircraft Company was formed at Wichita on 1st April 1932. Its first product was the Model 17 which later became known as the 'Staggerwing'. The company is still in residence in the city, albeit under another name, and has on show the third Model 17 which was built in 1934. The aircraft returned to the factory in 1987.

TYPE	REG/SER	CON. NO.	PI/NOTES	STATUS
☐ Beech B17L	N270Y	3	NC270Y	PV

REFLECTIONS OF FREEDOM HISTORICAL AIRPARK (KS37)

Address:	22 ARW/PA, 57837 Coffeyville Street, Suite 240, McConnell Air Force Base, Kansas 67221-3504.
Tel:	316-759-3141 Fax: 316-759-3148 Email: 22.pa@mcconnell.af.mil
Admission:	By prior permission only.
Location:	About 5 miles south east of Wichita.

The Air Force moved into the former Wichita Municipal airport in 1942 and took it over completely in 1954. The base is named after two brothers – Lieutenant Tom McConnell who was killed in a B-17 crash in 1943 and Fred McConnell who died in the crash of a private biplane in 1945. The base houses both Air Force and Air National Guard units. By the Air Force gate are parked a B-47, the EC-135K and the F-105F. Plans to collect all types flown by the Air National Guard unit are nearing fruition. The airpark has been constructed close to the drive which leads to the Kansas Aviation Museum and these aircraft can be seen through the fence. The 120th Fighter Squadron replaced its P-51D Mustangs with the Lockheed P-80C in June 1954. F-86L Sabres arrived in January 1958 and these served until the Spring of 1961 when the unit converted to the F-100C. The Super Sabre was flown for a decade when Republic F-105Ds and F-105Fs became the front line equipment. The F-4D Phantom was flown from late 1979 until 1987 when the Fighting Falcon was put into service.

TYPE	REG/SER	CON. NO.	PI/NOTES	STATUS
☐ Boeing 450-157-35 Stratojet (B-47E)	53-4213	4501237		RA
☐ Boeing 717-100A Stratotanker (KC-135A) (EC-135K)	55-3118	17234		RA
☐ General Dynamics 401 Fighting Falcon (F-16A)	78-0066	61-62		RA
☐ Lockheed 080 Shooting Star (P-80C) (F-80C)	'58612'	080-1976	47-0215, 2058 (Colombia), N10DM	RAX
☐ Lockheed 580 (T-33A)	53-5998	580-9530		RA
☐ McDonnell M.98EN Phantom II (F-4D)	66-0271	1939		RA
☐ North American NA-190 Sabre (F-86D) (F-86L)	52-4256	190-659		RA
☐ North American NA-217 Super Sabre (F-100C)	54-1993	217-254		RA
☐ Republic F-84C Thunderjet (P-84C)	47-1513			RA
☐ Republic F-105D Thunderchief	62-4253	D-452		RA
☐ Republic F-105F Thunderchief	63-8366	F-143		RA
☐ Rockwell B-1B Lancer	83-0068	5		RA

TONGANOXIE MONUMENT (KS38)

Location:	On permanent view at VFW 9721 on Main Street in the centre of the town.

TYPE	REG/SER	CON. NO.	PI/NOTES	STATUS
☐ Bell 205 Iroquois (UH-1H)	67-17267	9465		PV

WAKEENEY MONUMENT (KS39)

Location:	On permanent view at the Kansas Veterans Cemetery at 403 South 13th Street in the town.

TYPE	REG/SER	CON. NO.	PI/NOTES	STATUS
☐ Grumman G-303 Tomcat (F-14A)	Bu160925	354		PV

WICHITA MONUMENTS (KS40)

Location:	On permanent view at three locations in the city.

TYPE	REG/SER	CON. NO.	PI/NOTES	STATUS
☐ Beech D18S Expeditor (C-45G)	N80323	AF-1	51-11444, N7250C – at the Yard Store in Central Avenue.	PV
☐ Beech D18S Expeditor (C-45G)			At Hangar One Steakhouse – front fuselage only.	PV
☐ Gates Learjet 35	N351GL	35-001	N731GA – at Mid-Continent Airport.	PV

WICHITA STATE UNIVERSITY – NATIONAL INSTITUTE FOR AVIATION RESEARCH (KS41)

Address:	1845 Fairmount Street, Wichita, Kansas 67260.
Tel:	316-978-3456 **Email:** jsaunders@niar.wichita.edu
Admission:	By prior permission only.
Location:	In the north eastern part of the city.

The institute carries out research into a number of problems and has well equipped facilities. Most of the complete airframes are used to investigate problems in the structures of 'ageing' aircraft.

TYPE	REG/SER	CON. NO.	PI/NOTES	STATUS
☐ Beech 58P Baron	N135Z	TJ-247		RA
☐ Beech 2000 Starship I	N10TQ	NC-8	N1508S, OY-GEA, N194DB, N10TX	RA
☐ Cessna 402C				RA
☐ General Dynamics 401 Fighting Falcon (F-16A)				RA
☐ Piper PA-31-350 Navajo Chieftain				RA

KENTUCKY

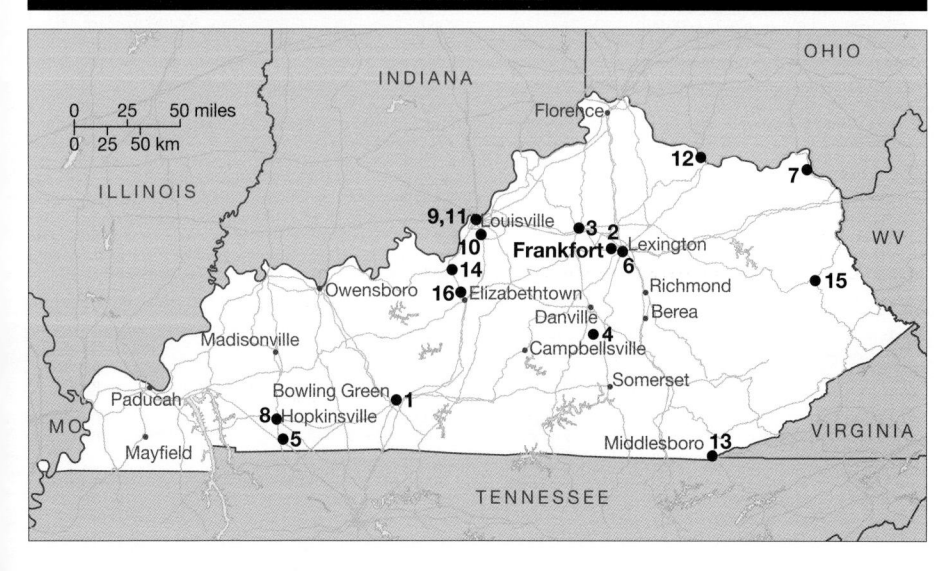

AVIATION HERITAGE PARK (KY1)

Address: PO Box 1256, 1000 Woodhurst Drive, Warren County Airport, Bowling Green, Kentucky 42102-1526.
Tel: 270-779-4186
Admission: On permanent view.
Location: In the south eastern suburbs of the town off Route 884.

The park opened in the autumn of 2006 with just one aircraft on show. During the Vietnam War local man Dan Cherry, who rose to the rank of General, shot down a MiG-21 whilst flying this aircraft. He located the F-4 outside a Veterans Post in Enon, Ohio and negotiated with the museum at Dayton to have it moved. The display will honour other local pilots and the acquisition of more aircraft is planned.

TYPE	REG/SER	CON. NO.	PI/NOTES	STATUS
☐ Grumman G-79 Panther (F9F-5)	Bu125992			PV
☐ McDonnell M.98EN Phantom II (F-4D)	66-7550	2085		PV

AVIATION MUSEUM OF KENTUCKY AND HALL OF FAME (KY2)

Address: PO Box 4118, Blue Grass Airport, Lexington, Kentucky 40544-4118.
Tel: 859-231-1219   **Fax:** 859-381-8739   **Email:** jrm@aviationky.org
Admission: Tuesday–Saturday 1000-1700; Sunday 1300-1700.
Location: The airport is about 5 miles west of the town off Route 60.

This museum has been set up by members of the Kentucky Aviation Historical Society. A hangar at Blue Grass Field was obtained and the displays trace the development of aviation in Kentucky. On show are many photographs, models and documents and the visitor can view some early films. The theory of flight is portrayed with a number of innovative exhibits.

Matthew Sellers built gliders and aircraft in the early years of flight and was the first person to patent a retractable undercarriage. He was born in 1869 and died in 1932. The Quadriplane dates from 1908 and the replica was unveiled, in the presence of his son and granddaughter, at the museum to commemorate the centenary of its first flight.

Five Heath CNA-40 midwings were built by the company in 1933 and many kits were sold. Another rarity is one of the five Crosley Moonbeam biplanes constructed in the late 1920s in Ohio. A Crosley diegned engine was fitted. The Aeronca K was built as a replacement for the C-3 model. The prototype first flew in 1937 and over the next two years almost 500 were constructed.

Jets have been put on show with the Skyhawk in 'Blue Angels' colours and the T-38 in a 'Thunderbirds' scheme. Voodoos, Phantoms, Kiowas and Huey Cobras have been flown from bases in the state and an example of each type is on show. The Tomcat is a fairly recent arrival and flew into the field after being retired from active service. Homebuilt designs over the years and gliders also feature in the exhibition.

The Kentucky Aviation Hall of Fame has been set up in the building and about 50 people have been honoured in recent years.

TYPE	REG/SER	CON. NO.	PI/NOTES	STATUS
☐ Aero Designs Pulsar	N156KB	156		PV
☐ Aeronca K	NC18896	K-165	NC18896, N18896	PV
☐ Arlington Sisu 1-A	N255JB	106	N255JB, N622W – On loan from NSM, NY.	PV
☐ Bell 206A Kiowa (OH-58A)	72-21256	41922		PV
☐ Bell 209 Huey Cobra (AH-1G) (AH-1F)	67-15759	20423		PV
☐ Bensen B-8 Gyroglider			Probable type.	PV
☐ Boeing-Stearman A75N1 Kaydet (PT-17)	N61818	75-4751	42-16588	PV
☐ Crosley Moonbeam	NX147N	4		PV
☐ Douglas A-4L Skyhawk (A4D-2N) (A-4C)	Bu147708	12472		PV
☐ Grumman G-303 Tomcat (F-14A) (F-14B)	Bu161860	496		PV
☐ Heath CNA-40	NR12881	C-51		PV
☐ McDonnell M.36CA Voodoo (RF-101C)	56-0125	375		PV
☐ McDonnell M.98EV Phantom II (F-4J) (F-4S)	Bu153904	2590	Bu138194	PV
☐ North American NA-200 Trojan (T-28B)	NX194RR	200-265		PV
☐ Northrop N-156T Talon (T-38A) (AT-38B)	64-13292	N.5721		PV
☐ Piper J-3C-65 Cub (L-4J)	NC42008	14083	45-55317, NC42008, N42008	PVA
☐ Polliwagen	'N1 AMK'			PV
☐ Pratt-Read PR-G1 (LNE-1)	N60235	PRG-01-73		PV
☐ Schempp-Hirth HS-3 Nimbus 3L	N257JB	107	On loan from EAA Mus, WI.	PV
☐ Sellers Quadriplane (R)	N540KY	80560		PV
☐ Stinson 108-2 Voyager	N928D	108-2928		PV
☐ Vans RV-8	N540KY	80560		PV
☐ Volmer Jensen VJ-22 Sportsman	N68LB	1		PV

BOONE NATIONAL GUARD CENTER (KY3)

Address: TAG Kentucky Air National Guard, Frankfort, Kentucky 40601-6168.
Tel: 502-564-8471
Admission: By prior permission only.
Location: In the north western suburbs of the city off Route 421.

Two aircraft are displayed at the headquarters of the Kentucky National Guard. The only flying unit in the state Air National Guard is based at Standiford Field at Louisville. Reconnaissance Voodoos served with the wing from 1965 to 1976. One was formerly on show. The Kiowa is located in the Army National Guard base.

TYPE	REG/SER	CON. NO.	PI/NOTES	STATUS
☐ Bell 206A Kiowa (OH-58A)	72-21345	42011		RA
☐ Hughes 369M Cayuse (HO-6) (OH-6A)				RA

Kentucky

CRAB ORCHARD MONUMENT (KY4)

Location:	On permanent view at Main Street in the centre of the town.

TYPE	REG/SER	CON. NO.	PI/NOTES	STATUS
☐ Bell 209 Huey Cobra (AH-1G) (AH-1F)	67-15473	20137		PV

DON F. PRATT MEMORIAL MUSEUM (KY5)

Address:	Building 5702, Tennessee Avenue, Fort Campbell, Kentucky 42223-5335.
Tel:	931-431-2617 Email: foundation@fortcampbell.com
Admission:	Monday-Saturday 0930-1630.
Location:	About 10 miles south of Hopkinsville off Route 12 on the Tennessee border.

Brigadier General Don F. Pratt was the first assistant commander of the 101st Airborne Division and was killed during the 1944 Normandy Invasion. The exhibitions trace the history of the unit since its formation in 1942 up to its service in the recent Gulf conflict. Highlighted in the display are several personal items of Don F. Pratt.

The history of Fort Campbell is also portrayed. Inside the building is a fully restored CG-4A glider, the type which carried many soldiers of the division into combat in World War II. The Hughes OH-6 suspended from the ceiling carries a code used by Special Operations units who did not apply the normal military serial. Also on show here are many uniforms, weapons, badges, photographs and documents. There are dioramas showing significant events in the life of the division.

An outside park displays the transport aircraft and equipment used by the unit. One C-47 has been painted in the markings of the aircraft which flew the commander of the 101st, General Maxwell D. Taylor, into Normandy during the invasion. This aircraft was one of several which flew in the 1976 film 'A Bridge Too Far'. False American and British markings were carried during this work. The Lockheed Cheyenne is an attack helicopter from the 1960s. The type experienced development problems and only ten were completed. Several aircraft are preserved around the camp and these are also listed.

TYPE	REG/SER	CON. NO.	PI/NOTES	STATUS
☐ Bell 204 Iroquois (HU-1A) (UH-1A)	58-2091	32	Outside base HQ.	PV
☐ Bell 204 Iroquois (HU-1B) (UH-1B)	62-2010	530		PV
☐ Bell 205 Iroquois (UH-1H)	70-16395	12700		RA
☐ Bell 205 Iroquois (UH-1H)	71-20208	13032		RA
☐ Bell 206A Kiowa (OH-58A) (OH-58C)	68-16747	40061		RA
☐ Bell 209 Huey Cobra (AH-1G) (AH-1S)	68-15088	20622		RA
☐ Bell 209 Huey Cobra (AH-1G) (AH-1S)	70-16090	21034		RA
☐ Douglas DC-3A-456 Skytrain (C-47A)	42-100828	19291	42-100828, 2100828 (Norway), T-AU (Norway), B-WC (Norway), 68-685 (Denmark), K-685 (Denmark), '337185', 'HG618', 'KG912', N3240A	PVX
☐ Douglas DC-3A-456 Skytrain (C-47A)	'43-48910'			PVX
☐ Fairchild 110 Flying Boxcar (C-119F)	N15505	10676	(51-2687), 22101 (Canada)	PVX
☐ Fairchild 110 Flying Boxcar (R4Q-1)	Bu131679	10846		RAX
☐ Fairchild-Republic A-10A Thunderbolt II	78-0687	A10-307		PV
☐ Hughes 369M Cayuse (HO-6) (OH-6A)	'88217'		On base.	PVX
☐ Hughes 369M Cayuse (HO-6) (OH-6A) (AH-6C)	80-TF160			PV
☐ Lockheed 187 Cheyenne (AH-56A)	66-8831	187-1006		PV
☐ Vertol V.114 Chinook (CH-47A)	61-2408	B.12		PV
☐ Waco NZR Hadrian (CG-4A)	'514908'			PVX

FRANKFORT MONUMENT (KY6)

Location:	On permanent view at the airport which is about 3 miles south west of the town off Route 60.

TYPE	REG/SER	CON. NO.	PI/NOTES	STATUS
☐ Bell 206A Kiowa (OH-58A)	72-21345	42011	With ANG.	RA

GREENING COUNTY WAR MEMORIAL (KY7)

Location:	On permanent view in Greenup on Highway 23.

TYPE	REG/SER	CON. NO.	PI/NOTES	STATUS
☐ Bell 205 Iroquois (UH-1H)	68-16594	11253		PV
☐ North American NA-201 Sabre (F-86L) (F-86L)	53-0847	201-291		PV

HOPKINSVILLE MONUMENT (KY8)

Location:	On permanent view in the southern part of the town on Route 41.

TYPE	REG/SER	CON. NO.	PI/NOTES	STATUS
☐ Bell 205 Iroquois (UH-1H) (UH-1V)	67-17589	9787		PV

JEFFERSON COMMUNITY AND TECHNICAL COLLEGE (KY9)

Address:	727 West Chestnut Street, Louisville, Kentucky 40203-2036.
Tel:	502-485-2560 Email: bryan.tutt@kctcs.edu
Admission:	By prior permission only.
Location:	At Bowman Field which is in the eastern part of the city.

The college was established on July 1st 2005 when Jefferson Community College and Jefferson Technical College combined. These institutions had been in existence for many years. Two Hansa aircraft were in use but these have moved on. Two homebuilt projects are now among the instructional airframes.

TYPE	REG/SER	CON. NO.	PI/NOTES	STATUS
☐ Bede BD-5				RA
☐ Cassutt IIIM				RA
☐ Cessna 152	N6353H	15284159		RA
☐ Cessna 172K	N7224G	17258924		RA
☐ Cessna 320C Skyknight	N3062T	320C0062		RA
☐ Ercoupe 415C	N3387H	4012		RA
☐ Piper PA-28-160 Cherokee	N5731W	28-436		RA

JEFFERSTOWN MONUMENT (KY10)

Location:	On permanent view in Veterans Park on Taylorsville Road in the southern part of the town.

TYPE	REG/SER	CON. NO.	PI/NOTES	STATUS
☐ Bell 205 Iroquois (UH-1H)	68-16450	11109		PV

LOUISVILLE AIR NATIONAL GUARD BASE (KY11)

Location:	By prior permission only on the south side of the field which is in the southern suburbs of the city off Interstate 60.

TYPE	REG/SER	CON. NO.	PI/NOTES	STATUS
☐ McDonnell M.36CM Voodoo (F-101C) (RF-101H)	56-0001	136		PV
☐ McDonnell M.98DF Phantom II (RF-4C)	64-1081	1168		PV

MAYSVILLE MONUMENT (KY12)

Location:	On permanent view at Fleming-Mason Airport which is about 10 miles south of the town on Highway 11.

TYPE	REG/SER	CON. NO.	PI/NOTES	STATUS
☐ McDonnell M.98EN Phantom II (F-4D)	66-7500	2015		PV

MIDDLESBORO MONUMENT (KY13)

Location:	On permanent view at Bell County Airport which is in the western part of the town.

TYPE	REG/SER	CON. NO.	PI/NOTES	STATUS
☐ North American NA-203 Sabre (F-86H)	53-1361	203-133		PV

PATTON MUSEUM OF CAVALRY AND ARMOR (KY14)

Address:	PO Box 208, Fayette Avenue, Fort Knox, Kentucky 40121-0208.
Tel:	502-624-3812 **Email:** museum@knox.army.mil
Admission:	Monday-Friday 0900-1630; Saturday-Sunday 1000-1800 (Closes at 1630 October–April)
Location:	Near the Chaffee Avenue entrance off Highway 31/60 about 25 miles south of Louisville.

During World War II several captured armoured vehicles were sent to Fort Knox for testing and evaluation. Many of these came from the area where General George S. Patton's Third Army was operating and they became unofficially known as 'The Patton Collection'. In 1947 it was decided to set up a museum and this opened to the public two years later.

George Patton was born in California in 1885 and joined the army in 1909. He became one of the most colourful commanders of the 20th century and was killed in a car accident in 1945. A gallery is devoted to his life and military career.

The museum moved to its current purpose-built structure in November 1972. New wings were added in 1975, 1982 and 1984. The displays trace the history of Fort Knox and the development of cavalry and armoured equipment over the last 200 years.

TYPE	REG/SER	CON. NO.	PI/NOTES	STATUS
☐ Bell 204 Iroquois (UH-1B)	64-14005	1129		PV

PRESTONBURG MONUMENT (KY15)

Location:	On permanent view at the airport which is about 2 miles east of East point.

TYPE	REG/SER	CON. NO.	PI/NOTES	STATUS
☐ Bell 209 Huey Cobra (AH-1G) (AH-1S)	70-15945	20589		PV

VINE GROVE MONUMENT (KY16)

Location:	On permanent view at VFW 10281 at Briggs Lane in the north western part of the town.

TYPE	REG/SER	CON. NO.	PI/NOTES	STATUS
☐ Bell 209 Huey Cobra (AH-1G) (AH-1F)	67-15495	20159		PV
☐ Republic F-105D Thunderchief	60-0455	D-143		PV

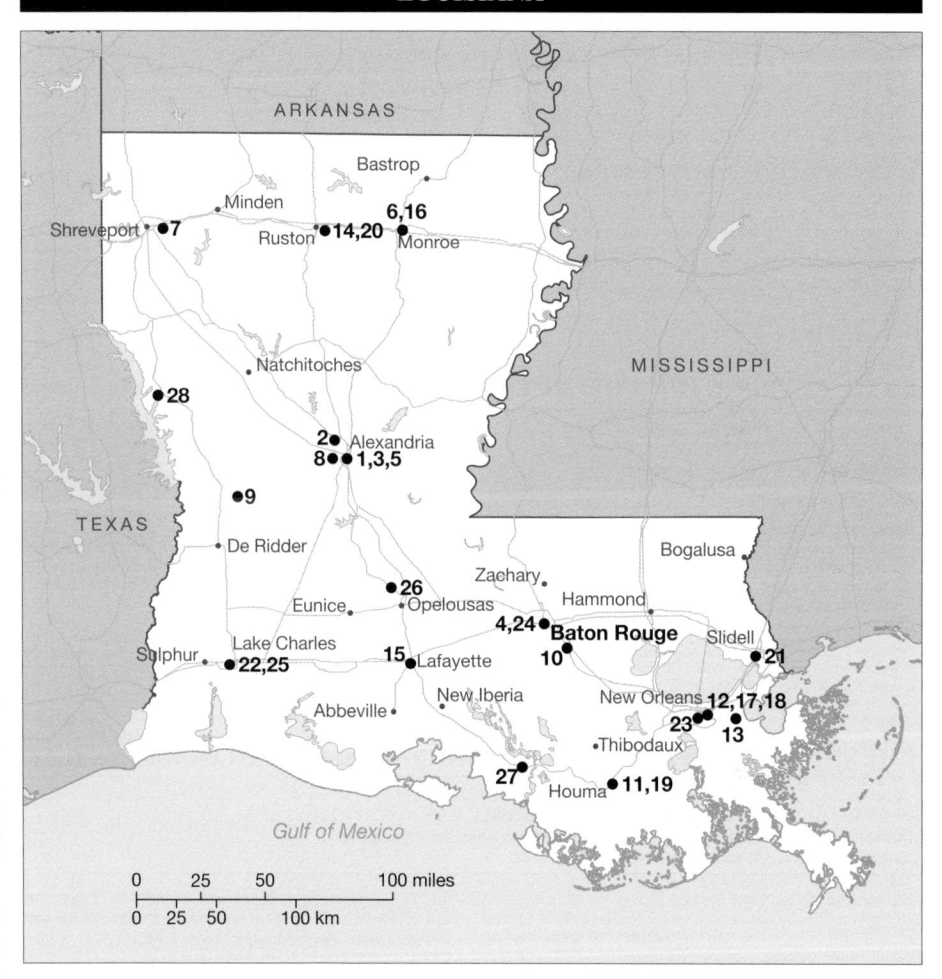

ALEXANDRIA MONUMENT (LA1)

Location:	On permanent view at a company at 2230 South MacArthur Drive in the southern part of the town.

TYPE	REG/SER	CON. NO.	PI/NOTES	STATUS
☐ Lockheed 683-10-19 Starfighter (F-104G)	'60791'	683D-9108	FX-65 (Belgium)	PVX

BALL MONUMENT (LA2)

Location:	On permanent view at the City Hall on Highway 165.

TYPE	REG/SER	CON. NO.	PI/NOTES	STATUS
☐ Bell 205 Iroquois (UH-1H)	67-19526	10132		PV

BAMBOO BOMBER CLUB (LA3)

Address:	454 Linden Street, Shreveport, Louisiana 71104-4424.
Tel:	tmsul@aol.com
Admission:	By prior permission only.
Location:	At an airfield in the area.

The T-50 light transport made its maiden flight on 26th March 1939. In 1940 the US Army Air Corps ordered a small number as multi-engine advanced trainers. The Army Air Force (successor to the USAAC) decided to adopt the type as a light personnel transport. The Royal Canadian Air Force also used the T-50 and named it the Crane. Well over 5,400 had been produced by the end of hostilities.

Many survivors were sold on the civilian market. The club was formed several years ago by Jim Anderson to preserve the history of the famous type and to act as a resource for owners. Terry Sullivan has now taken over the archive. He obtained his aircraft in 1990 and it took to the air again on 21st July 2009 painted in a typical World War II drab olive scheme.

TYPE	REG/SER	CON. NO.	PI/NOTES	STATUS
☐ Cessna T-50 Bobcat (AT-17B) (UC-78B)	N66671/'332426'	6487	43-32549	RAAX

BATON ROUGE MONUMENTS (LA4)

Location:	On permanent view at three locations in the city.

TYPE	REG/SER	CON. NO.	PI/NOTES	STATUS
☐ Lockheed 580 (T-33A)	53-6053	580-9654	At the LSU Tiger Stadium on Nicholson Drive.	PV
☐ McDonnell M.24 Banshee (F2H-2)	Bu128885		In Howell Park in Winborne Avenue.	PV
☐ McDonnell M.98EV Phantom II (F-4J)	'1420'	1683	Bu153088 – at ALP 38 at 151 South Wooddale Boulevard –	PVX

CAMP BEAUREGARD COLLECTION (LA5)

Address:	Pineville, Louisiana 71360.
Tel:	318-641-3358
Admission:	By prior permission only
Location:	In the northern suburbs of Alexandria.

The camp is an important training centre for units of the state forces. The site opened in 1917 and closed in 1919 when the federal government gave the land back to the state. The camp was taken over again in 1940 and returned to Louisiana in 1945. Beauregard closed again in 1947 but was reactivated in 1973. Units of the Louisiana National Guard regularly use its modernised facilities. Two aircraft were put on display in the 1990s. The Iroquois has been flown by the Army National Guard and the Super Sabre arrived from New Orleans JRB in the late 1990s and was followed by the Kiowa. The Eagle is a recent addition to the display.

TYPE	REG/SER	CON. NO.	PI/NOTES	STATUS
☐ Bell 205 Iroquois (UH-1D) (UH-1H)	64-13709	4416		PV
☐ Bell 206A Kiowa (OH-58A)	70-15426	40977		RA
☐ McDonnell M.199-1A Eagle (F-15A)	77-0067	340/A279		RA
☐ North American NA-235 Super Sabre (F-100D)				PVX

CHENNAULT AVIATION AND MILITARY MUSEUM OF LOUISIANA (LA6)

Address:	701 Kansas Lane, Monroe, Louisiana 71213.
Tel:	318-382-5540 Fax: 318-362-5545
Admission:	Monday-Friday 0900-1630; Saturday-Sunday 1000-1700.
Location:	In the town just west of the airport.

The museum is currently located in one of the remaining World War II buildings at Selman Field. The airfield opened in 1942 and at one time was the largest navigator training school in the country. The display opened in 2000 and was originally called the Monroe Aviation Historical Museum. Funds are being raised to construct a purpose-built complex. The displays trace the history of the airfield and local aviators. General Claire Chennault, who was raised in Louisiana, set up the 'Flying Tigers' unit in China in World War II. After the end of the conflict he lived in Monroe. A replica P-40 has been built to honour his work. The story of his life and military career is portrayed in detail. Huff-Daland Dusters was formed in Georgia in 1924 and soon made a move to Monroe. The company changed its name to Delta Air Service in 1928 and over the years expanded into the large airline it is today. The history of these early years is part of the display.

TYPE	REG/SER	CON. NO.	PI/NOTES	STATUS
☐ Beech D18S Expeditor (C18S) (SNB-2C) (SNB-3E) (SNB-5) (TC-45J) (UC-45J)	N15959	6177	Bu23851	PV
☐ Beech D18S Expeditor (C-45G)	N3333G	AF-256	51-11699	RA
☐ Curtiss 87V Warhawk (P-40N) (FSM)				PVX
☐ Douglas DC-3A-269C	N496	2270	NC25622	PVC
☐ Hughes 369M Cayuse (HO-6) (OH-6A)	65-12950	0035		PV

EIGHTH AIR FORCE MUSEUM (LA7)

Address:	88 Shreeveport Road,, Barksdale Air Force Base, Louisiana 71110-2270.
Tel:	318-456-5553 Email: info@8afmuseum.com
Admission:	Daily 0930-1600.
Location:	About 3 miles east of Shreveport off Highway 71.

The Eighth Air Force was formed in January 1942 and became the mainstay of American bombing operations from Britain until the end of the war in Europe. Large numbers of medium and heavy bombers along with escort fighters and transports flew from more than 100 airfields in England during the last years of World War II. The idea of a display at Barksdale was put forward in 1977 and the search to obtain a B-17 Fortress and a B-24 Liberator to put in front of the Headquarters Building was initiated. In April 1978 a B-17 flew in from California and the following December the B-24 arrived, slung under a Skycrane helicopter. The Fortress is the penultimate example built by Douglas at Long Beach in California. It saw service on patrol duties with the Navy before being flown as a civilian water bomber from 1960 to 1977. The Liberator was built by Ford at their Willow Run plant in Michigan. After being withdrawn from service it was allocated to the Spartan School of Aeronautics as an instructional airframe. It now carries the colours of 'Louisiana Belle II' which flew during World War II.

Colonel Kenneth Patterson set about obtaining exhibits portraying the development of strategic bombing for a 1978 contest at Barksdale and the momentum for setting up a proper museum gained pace. A building and a large outside area near the North Gate of the base have been allocated for the display. The range of heavy bombers used in recent years is one of the highlights of the display. The line of Boeing types is impressive with examples of the Superfortress Stratojet and two versions of the Stratofortress to be seen. These show the rapid development of the heavy bomber from the B-17.

The B-29, B-47 and B-52 were the mainstay of the Strategic Air Command force for many years. The B-52 entered service in 1955 and is expected to remain in use for many years to come. Also to be seen are airfield vehicles, missiles and weapons. Inside the exhibitions trace the story of the 8th and its squadrons with models, photographs, documents, uniforms and memorabilia.

An interesting relic is the tail section of a Keystone B-6A. Dating from the early 1930s, this heavy bomber was in front line service from 1931 until 1934 but the last examples soldiered on for a few more years.

TYPE	REG/SER	CON. NO.	PI/NOTES	STATUS
☐ Avro 698 Vulcan B.2	XM606			PV
☐ Beech C18S Kansan (AT-11)	'23267'	3267	42-36887, N3983C	PVX
☐ Beech D18S Expeditor (C18S) (SNB-2) (SNB-5) (TC-45J) (UC-45J)	'447266'	4785	Bu39266, N40081, N3983C	PVX
☐ Boeing 299-O Fortress (B-17G) (PB-1W)	'231340'	32525	44-83884, Bu77244, (N6471D), N5230V, '338289', '333284'	PVX
☐ Boeing 345 Superfortress (B-29) (TB-29)	44-87627	12430		PV
☐ Boeing 367-76-66 Stratofreighter (KC-97G) (KC-97L)	53-0240	17022		PV
☐ Boeing 450-157-35 Stratojet (B-47E)	53-2276	4501089		PV
☐ Boeing 464-201-7 Stratofortress (B-52D)	56-0629	17312		PV
☐ Boeing 464-253 Stratofortress (B-52G)	57-6509	464214		PV
☐ Boeing 717-146 Stratotanker (KC-135A)	56-3595	17344		PV
☐ Consolidated 32 Liberator (B-24J)	'250806'	3636	44-48781	PVX
☐ Consolidated 32 Liberator (B-24J)			Front fuselage only.	PV
☐ Douglas DC-3A-456 Skytrain (C-47A)	43-16130	20596	43-16130, N86453, T.3-33 (Spain) G-BGCF, N3753C	PV
☐ Fairchild-Republic A-10A Thunderbolt II	76-0552	A10-99	On base.	RA
☐ General Dynamics F-111E	'68-0284'	A1-188	68-0019 – cockpit capsule only.	PVX
☐ General Dynamics FB-111A	68-0284	B1-56		RA
☐ Keystone B-6A			Tail section only.	PVD
☐ Lockheed 580 (T-33A)	58-0615	580-1584		RA
☐ Lockheed SR-71A Blackbird	61-7967	2018		PV
☐ McDonnell M.98DE Phantom II (F-4C)	63-7532	556	On base.	PV
☐ Mikoyan-Gurevich MiG-21F	'5060'		185, '80' – in false North Vietnamese markings	PVX
☐ Noorduyn Norseman V	'35314'	N29-5	CF-BEM, N1037Z	PVX
☐ North American NA-122 Mustang (P-51D)	'44-14570'		Composite example.	PVX
☐ Republic F-84F Thunderstreak	51-1386			PV
☐ Vought A-7D Corsair II	71-0339	D250		PV

ENGLAND AIR FORCE BASE HERITAGE PARK (LA8)

Address:	England Drive, England Industrial Air Park, Alexandria, Louisiana 71311-5004.
Tel:	318-449-3504
Admission:	On permanent view.
Location:	About 5 miles west of Alexandria off Route 28.

The base was established in October 1942 and later re-named after Lieutenant Colonel John B. England, a World War II P-51 ace who was killed in the crash of an F-86 in France in 1954. The base closed in 1993 but the Air Force Museum decided to leave five aircraft as a reminder of the history of the field.

TYPE	REG/SER	CON. NO.	PI/NOTES	STATUS
☐ Canadair CL-13A Sabre 5 [North American F-86E]	'24931'	1016	23226 (Canada), N46883	PVX
☐ Fairchild-Republic YA-10A Thunderbolt II	'73-3667'	A10-4	73-1667	PVX
☐ Republic F-84F Thunderstreak	52-7080			PV
☐ Republic F-105G Thunderchief (F-105F)	63-8296	F-73		PV
☐ Vought A-7A Corsair II	'69-6234'	A17	Bu152600	PVX

FORT POLK MILITARY MUSEUM (LA9)

Address:	South Carolina Avenue, PO Box 3916, Fort Polk, Louisiana 71459-0916.
Tel:	337-531-7905.
Admission:	Wednesday-Saturday 1000-1400; Sunday 0900-1600.
Location:	About 7 miles south east of Leesville off Route 171.

The museum was set up in 1972 to trace the history of the site and the 12 divisions which have been stationed at Fort Polk since 1941. In 1974 the display was enlarged to cover in detail the 5th Infantry Division which was reactivated at the fort in the previous September. This division disbanded in November 1992. Helicopters flown from the site have been put on show near the museum and at other locations. The Lockheed Cheyenne programme was cancelled in 1972 after only 10 were completed. One of the few survivors is on show.

TYPE	REG/SER	CON. NO.	PI/NOTES	STATUS
☐ Bell 204 Iroquois (HU-1B) (UH-1B)	61-0727	307		RA
☐ Bell 205 Iroquois (UH-1H)	71-20326	13150		PV

☐ Bell 205 Iroquois (UH-1H)	73-21804	13492		PV
☐ Bell 206A Kiowa (OH-58A) (OH-58C)	69-16143	40364		PV
☐ Bell 206A Kiowa (OH-58A) (OH-58C)	72-21460	42126		RA
☐ Bell 209 Huey Cobra (AH-1G) (AH-1S)	70-15936	20880		PV
☐ Bell 209 Huey Cobra (AH-1S) (AH-1P)	77-22743	24081		PV
☐ Hiller UH12B Raven (H-23B) (OH-23B)	'54-007'			PVX
☐ Lockheed 187 Cheyenne (AH-56A)	66-8827	187-1002		PV
☐ Mil Mi-2			CCCP-88943 (?)	PV

GONZALES MONUMENT (LA10)

Location:	On view during opening hours in Cabela's store at 2200 West Cabela's Parkway in the town.

TYPE	REG/SER	CON. NO.	PI/NOTES	STATUS
☐ Aeronca 7AC Champion				PV

HOUMA MONUMENTS (LA11)

Location:	On permanent view at two locations in the town.

TYPE	REG/SER	CON. NO.	PI/NOTES	STATUS
☐ General Dynamics 401 Fighting Falcon (F-16A)			At the airport which is in the south eastern suburbs of the town.	PV
☐ Lockheed 580 (T-33A)	51-9091	580-6875	At a school at 105 Moffet Road.	PV

JACKSON BARRACKS MILITARY MUSEUM (LA12)

Address:	6400 St. Claude Avenue, Jackson Barracks, New Orleans, Louisiana 70146-0330
Tel:	504-278-8242 Fax: 504-278-8614 Email: jbmuseum@la.ngb.army.mil
Admission:	Monday-Friday 0800-1600.
Location:	In the eastern suburbs of the city.

Jackson Barracks was built between 1833 and 1835 and has seen continuous military use since it opened. At the current time the Headquarters of the Louisiana Army and Air National Guard are located at the site.

The main exhibition is located in the 1837 Powder Magazine, which has also served as a prison for captured German Africa Corps soldiers and as an indoor rifle range. An extension to this area was recently completed. Artefacts and weapons dating from the time of the American Revolution are on show along with many vehicles. Life in the trenches during World War I is shown in a series of realistic tableaux. All major conflicts up to Desert Storm are featured. The history of the Louisiana National Guard is shown from the time of the first militia units established in the 18th century to assist French and Spanish troops in preserving peace in the colony.

The outside airpark was reorganised in 1996. The museum was flooded in the aftermath of Hurricane Katrina and closed for a period. All the aircraft suffered damage as did the inside displays.

Two YF-102s and four YF-102As were built as development aircraft before the delta wing fighter entered production. The Delta Dagger and the Sabre have been painted in false markings to represent ones flown by Louisiana units.

A major restoration programme was set up and now the exhibition is open again although some items are still not on view.

TYPE	REG/SER	CON. NO.	PI/NOTES	STATUS
☐ Beech C18S Kansan (AT-11)	'44951'	951	41-9525, N65423	PVX
☐ Bell 205 Iroquois (UH-1D) (UH-1H)	65-9911	4955		PV
☐ Convair 8-90 Delta Dagger (YF-102A)	'62334'		53-1787	PVX
☐ Douglas A-26C Invader	44-35937	29216	44-35937, 846 (Chile)	PV
☐ Hiller UH12B Raven (H-23B) (OH-23B)	51-16336	572		RA
☐ Lockheed 580 (T-33A)	53-4967	580-8306	53-4967, N47799	PV
☐ McDonnell M.98DE Phantom II (F-4C)	63-7556	593		PV
☐ McDonnell M.98DE Phantom II (F-4C)	63-7657	767	Front fuselage only.	PV
☐ McDonnell M.199-1A Eagle (F-15A)	73-0086	024/A020		PV
☐ North American NA-190 Sabre (F-86D) (F-86L)	'23747'	190-571	52-4168	PVX
☐ North American NA-235 Super Sabre (F-100D)	56-3020	235-118		PV

KENNER NAVAL MUSEUM COMMISSION (LA13)

Address:	2538 Williams Boulevard, Kenner, Louisiana 700662-7675.
Tel:	504-469-8104 Email: iced@kenner.la.us
Admission:	On permanent view off Veterans Boulevard.
Location:	About 4 miles east of New Orleans just east of the airport.

The group is working towards setting up a naval museum in the town and items of memorabilia are being collected. The two aircraft are currently on show in the Veterans Memorial Park in the town. Naval aircraft have flown from New Orleans for many years and the types on show represent ones recently flown.

TYPE	REG/SER	CON. NO.	PI/NOTES	STATUS
☐ Douglas A-4C Skyhawk (A4D-2N)	Bu145082	12328		PV
☐ Grumman G-303 Tomcat (F-14A) (F-14D)	Bu159629	176		RA

LOUISIANA MILITARY MUSEUM (LA14)

Address:	201 Memorial Drive, Ruston, Louisiana 71210.
Tel:	318-251-5099 Email: estevens@sos.louisiana.gov
Admission:	Monday-Friday 1000-1830; Saturday 1000-1700; Sunday 1300-1700.
Location:	On Highway 80 just east of the town.

Louisiana

The displays at this museum trace the military history of the state from early times. There is an excellent collection of uniforms, weapons and documents. Exhibitions are devoted to the early period, World War I, World War II and the conflicts which have taken place since 1945. Outside the building are a number of military vehicles. The Iroquois and Skyhawk represent the Vietnam period in which many Louisiana citizens fought.

TYPE	REG/SER	CON. NO.	PI/NOTES	STATUS
☐ Bell 205 Iroquois (UH-1D) (UH-1H)	65-12873	5206		PV
☐ Douglas A-4C Skyhawk (A4D-2N)	Bu148569	12762		PV
☐ Kaman K-20 Seasprite (UH-2B) (SH-2F)	Bu152201	185	Bu152201, N7096P	RA

LOUISIANA TECHNICAL COLLEGE AVIATION CENTER (LA15)

Address: 205 Shepard Drive, Lafayette, Louisiana 70508.
Tel: 337-262-5186 **Fax:** 337-262-5260 **Email:** cjarrell@ltc.edu
Admission: By prior permission only.
Location: At the airport which is in the south eastern part of the town.

The college has sites across the state. The aviation maintenance section is based in a hangar and workshop area at the airport. One instructional airframe is known to be in use but there may be more.

TYPE	REG/SER	CON. NO.	PI/NOTES	STATUS
☐ North American NA-265 Sabreliner (T-39A) (CT-39A)	61-0635	265-38		RA

MONROE MONUMENT (LA16)

Location: On permanent view at VFW 1809 at 1499 Highway 594 in the south eastern part of the town.

TYPE	REG/SER	CON. NO.	PI/NOTES	STATUS
☐ Bell 205 Iroquois (UH-1D) (UH-1H)	65-10028	5072		PV

NATIONAL WORLD WAR II MUSEUM (LA17)

Address: 345 Magazine Street, New Orleans, Louisiana 70130.
Tel: 504-527-6012 **Email:** info@nationalww2museum.org
Admission: Daily 0900-1700.
Location: In the centre of the city.

This impressive museum opened as the National D-Day Museum on 6th June 2000, the 56th anniversary of the landings, and highlighted all aspects of the operation. The name was changed and the scope of the exhibition widened to deal other battles in World War II. The displays highlight the conditions which led to the outbreak of the conflict and compares the military strengths of the participants. Models of the Normandy beaches have been constructed.

A large electronic map of the Pacific Ocean shows the battles which took place in the many islands and the progress of the Allied forces towards Japan.

TYPE	REG/SER	CON. NO.	PI/NOTES	STATUS
☐ Boeing 299-O Fortress (B-17G)	'293807'	32028	44-83387	RAX
☐ Consolidated 32 Liberator (B-24D)	41-23908		Front fuselage only.	RA
☐ Douglas DC-3A-456 Skytrain (C-47A)	42-93096	12970	42-93096, OH-LCE, DO-12 (Finland), '314013', SE-IOK, (G-BLXV), N58NA, (N211FF), N58NA	PV
☐ Douglas SBD-3 Dauntless	Bu06508	1245		PV
☐ Grumman G-40 Avenger (TBM-3) (FSM)				
☐ Messerschmitt Bf 109G-14			Composite.	PVX
☐ North American NA-108 Mitchell (B-25J) (TB-25J) (TB-25N)	N2854G	108-33087	44-29862	RA
☐ North American NA-122 Mustang (P-51D)				RA
☐ Supermarine 349 Spitfire LF.Vb	BL370			PV

NEW ORLEANS JOINT RESERVE BASE COLLECTION (LA18)

Address: 400 Russell Drive, New Orleans, Louisiana 70143-5012.
Tel: 504-678-3141 **Email:** pao.nrsjrbno@nrs.navy.mil
Admission: By prior permission only.
Location: About 5 miles south east of the city off Route 23.

The station is home to Navy and Marine Reserve squadrons as well as those of the Air Force and Army Reserve. A fighter squadron of the Louisiana Air National Guard is based on the field, as is a US Coast Guard detachment. The F/A-18A in 'Blue Angels' colours is displayed by the main gate. This replaced a Grumman F-11A which is now at Reserve. The preserved aircraft are maintained by volunteer groups from the units on the field. The Hawkeye has recently moved from the now closed Atlanta Naval Air Station at Marietta in Georgia.

TYPE	REG/SER	CON. NO.	PI/NOTES	STATUS
☐ Bell 209 Sea Cobra (AH-1J)	Bu157761	26005		RA
☐ Douglas A-4L Skyhawk (A4D-2N) (A-4C)	Bu147750	12514		RA
☐ Grumman G-123 Hawkeye (E-2C)	Bu161098	A62		RA
☐ Lockheed 185 Orion (P-3B)	Bu153444	185-5240		RA
☐ McDonnell M.199-1A Eagle (F-15A)	73-0100	043/A034		RA
☐ McDonnell M.267 Hornet (F/A-18A)	Bu161726	77/A055		RA
☐ Vought A-7E Corsair II	'Bu151956'	E478	Bu159974	RAX

One of the ten Lockheed AH-56A Cheyennes built can be seen at the Fort Polk Military Museum. [LA9]

On show at the USS Kidd and Veterans Memorial is this replica Curtiss P-40N. [LA24]

This Lockheed SP-2E Neptune is still at the gate of the now closed Brunswick Naval Air Station. (Richard Hamblin) [ME2]

Louisiana

REGIONAL MILITARY MUSEUM (LA19)

Address:	PO Box 10247, 1154 Barrow Street, Houma, Louisiana 70360.
Tel:	985-873-8200 Email: rmmuseum@triparish.net
Admission:	Monday-Friday 0900-1600.
Location:	In the centre of the town.

The museum was set up to honour all personnel who have fought for their country. Houma was the site of an airship base in World War II and there are several photographs from this period. There is an impressive collection of military vehicles, many of which are in running order and often appear at events in the area.

The only aircraft currently in the collection is an Aero Commander. The aircraft, which has been stored at Patterson for many years, was transported by barge to its new home in May 2010. The twin-engined aircraft was once used by President Eisenhower on his shorter trips around the country. The Commander will initially be on display for three years.

TYPE	REG/SER	CON. NO.	PI/NOTES	STATUS
☐ Aero Commander 680 (L-26C) (U-4B)	55-4648	317-12	55-4648, N5380G	PV

RUSTON MONUMENT (LA20)

Location:	On permanent view at Louisiana Technical University west of the town on Highway 80.

TYPE	REG/SER	CON. NO.	PI/NOTES	STATUS
☐ Lockheed 580 (T-33A)	52-9349	580-7434		

SLIDELL MONUMENT (LA21)

Location:	On permanent view at ALP 185 in Kaycee Drive in the north western part of the town.

TYPE	REG/SER	CON. NO.	PI/NOTES	STATUS
☐ Bell 205 Iroquois (UH-1H)	68-16601	11260		PV

SOWELA TECHNICAL COMMUNITY COLLEGE (LA22)

Address:	3280 Senator J. Bennett Johnston Avenue, Lake Charles, Louisiana 70615.
Tel:	337-491-2692 Email: glenn.carter@sowela.edu
Admission:	By prior permission only.
Location:	At Chennault Airport which is about 4 miles east of the town.

The college has premises at the former Chennault Air Force Base which now serves as the local airport. Lake Charles Army Airfield opened in 1941 and was turned over to the city in 1947. The field was reactivated in July 1951 and seven years later was named after the famous pilot.

Strategic Air Command bombers were in residence until the early 1960s and the Air Force finally left in June 1963. The college which runs courses for airframe and engine fitters has a fleet of instructional airframes and associated equipment in workshops at the site.

TYPE	REG/SER	CON. NO.	PI/NOTES	STATUS
☐ Beech 65-A90 King Air	N296A	LJ-208	N29S, N29SA	RA
☐ Bell 204 Iroquois (UH-1B)	N51929	1194	64-14070	RA
☐ Bell 205 Iroquois (UH-1D) (UH-1H)	65-9751	4795		RA
☐ Boeing 727-22F	N188FE	19081	N7068U	RA
☐ Boeing-Stearman A75N1 Kaydet (PT-17)	N49649	75-4678	42-16515	RA
☐ Cessna 150F	N6905F	15063505		RA
☐ Cessna 182D	N9984J	18253084		RA
☐ Hughes 269A Osage (TH-55A)	N9062P	115-0423	64-18111	RA
☐ Piper PA-18-135 Super Cub (L-21B)	N46767	18-3574	53-7774, MM53-7774, EI-145, I-EIWA	RA
☐ Piper PA-23-160 Apache G	N4488P	23-2010		RA

ST. JOHN MILITARY PARK ASSOCIATION (LA23)

Address:	355 Airport Road, Reserve, Louisiana 70084 -6951.
Admission:	On permanent view.
Location:	Just north west of the town off Route 61.

A group known as the American Military Heritage Foundation collected a number of aircraft at the airport. The organisation folded and some types moved on. The association is planning to develop a military airpark.

TYPE	REG/SER	CON. NO.	PI/NOTES	STATUS
☐ Grumman G-98 Tiger (F11F-1) (F-11A)	Bu141875	192	Possible identity.	PV
☐ McDonnell M.98AM Phantom II (F4H-1) (F-4B) (F-4N)	Bu150442	228		PV
☐ Vought A-7B Corsair II	Bu154485	B125		PV

UNITED STATES SHIP *KIDD* AND VETERANS MEMORIAL (LA24)

Address:	305 South River Road, Baton Rouge, Louisiana 70802-6220.
Tel:	225-342-1942 Fax: 225-342-2039 Email: webmaster@usskidd.com
Admission:	Daily 0900-1700.
Location:	In the centre of the city near the Mississippi Bridge.

Docked in the Mississippi River is the destroyer USS *Kidd* which served with distinction in the Pacific in World War II and later in the Korean conflict. The museum building traces the maritime history of the nation with artefacts and an excellent collection of model ships on show. The use of ships on the Mississippi River is also portrayed.

There is a section devoted to General Claire Chennault who was born in the state. He commanded the American Volunteer Group 'Flying Tigers' unit flying P-40s in China during World War II. From December 1941 to July 1942 they destroyed almost 300 Japanese aircraft losing only a dozen of their Warhawks in combat. The Corsair joined the exhibition during the summer of 1994. The A-7 was designed to replace the A-4 Skyhawk in US Navy service as a carrier based attack aircraft. Versions were also adopted by the Air Force and served with many Air National Guard units from the late 1960s until 1991. Over 1,550 were eventually built and the A-7 was also operated by the air forces in Greece, Portugal and the Philippines.

TYPE	REG/SER	CON. NO.	PI/NOTES	STATUS
☐ Curtiss 87V Warhawk (P-40N) (FSM)				PVX
☐ Vought A-7E Corsair II	Bu160724	E557		PV

UNITED STATES SHIP *ORLECK* NAVAL MUSEUM (LA25)

Address:	PO Box 4470, 604 North Enterprise Boulevard, Lake Charles, Louisiana 70606-4470.
Tel:	409-779-1314 Email: volunteer@orleck.org
Admission:	Not yet open.
Location:	At the waterfront in the town.

The destroyer is named after Lieutenant Joseph Orleck who was killed in action when the USS *Nauset* was sunk by German aircraft in the Gulf of Salerno in September 1943. The *Orleck* was launched in May 1945 by his widow. The ship served in Korea and Vietnam and was transferred to the Turkish Navy in 1982.

In August 2000 the destroyer was donated by the Turkish government to the Southeast Texas War Memorial and Heritage Foundation. The ship was berthed at Orange and remained there until badly damaged by Hurricane Rita in September 2005. After repairs she was not allowed to return and spent a period at two temporary berths.

In May 2009 the city of Lake Charles reached an agreement with the Foundation and the *Orleck* moved to her new home on 20th May 2010. On board is an example of the Gyrodyne QH-50 unmanned helicopter.

TYPE	REG/SER	CON. NO.	PI/NOTES	STATUS
☐ Gyrodyne QH-50C (DSN-3)				RA

VILLE PLATTE VETERANS MEMORIAL (LA26)

Location:	On permanent view in Court Street in the western part of the town.

TYPE	REG/SER	CON. NO.	PI/NOTES	STATUS
☐ Bell 205 Iroquois (UH-1D) (UH-1H)	65-9775	4819		PV

WEDELL-WILLIAMS MEMORIAL AVIATION MUSEUM (LA27)

Address:	118 Cotton Road, Patterson, Louisiana 70392.
Tel:	985-399-1268 Fax: 985-399-9910 Email: dkahn@crt.state.la
Admission:	Tuesday-Saturday 1000-1600.
Location:	In the town.

The organisation is the official aviation museum for the state. Jimmy Wedell and Harry Williams set up an air service at Patterson in the early 1930s. They built a series of low wing monoplanes which dominated air racing. Their aircraft won the Bendix Trophy in 1932, 1933 and 1934 and the Thompson Trophy in 1933 and 1934 as well as setting many records.

A hurricane destroyed their premises in 1934 and within two years both had died in crashes. Fate struck again in 1992 when the museum building was badly damaged in Hurricane Andrew and the unique Vincent Starflight was destroyed.

Five replicas of the famous racers have been built for display and in the theatre films of the 1930s meetings can be seen. Hanging in the foyer is one of the two 'Lil' Monster Formula One racers built by Curtis Pitts in the late 1940s/ early 1950s. The aircraft on show was stored in Oklahoma for around 15 years before being rebuilt to fly again in the early 1990s. The Stearman biplane, once used for crop dusting in the area, is exhibited in the Cypress Gallery. Patterson was once the home of the largest cypress sawmill in the world and this area traces the history of the industry.

TYPE	REG/SER	CON. NO.	PI/NOTES	STATUS
☐ Beech D17S	N278WW	264	NC19494, N36E, N90295	PV
☐ Boeing-Stearman A75N1 Kaydet (PT-17)	NC31564			PV
☐ McDonnell M.98AM Phantom II (F-4B) (F-4N)	Bu152986	1373		PV
☐ Mono Aircraft Monocoupe D-145	NC17687	D-128	NC17687, N17687	PV
☐ Piper J-3C-65 Cub			Composite.	PV
☐ Pitts 'Lil' Monster	N1961M			PV
☐ Wedell-Williams 44 (R)	'NR278V'			PVX
☐ Wedell-Williams 44 (R)	'NR536V'			PVX
☐ Wedell-Williams 44 (R)	'NR61Y'			PVX
☐ Wedell-Williams 44 (R)	'NR62Y'			PVX
☐ Wedell-Williams Wee-Will Junior (R)	'NR10377'			PVX

ZWOLLE MONUMENT (LA28)

Location:	On permanent view at DAV Chapter 21 at 120 Lanana Bay Drive about 6 miles south of the town on Highway 191.

TYPE	REG/SER	CON. NO.	PI/NOTES	STATUS
☐ Bell 209 Huey Cobra (AH-1G) (AH-1S)	68-15130	20564		PV

MAINE

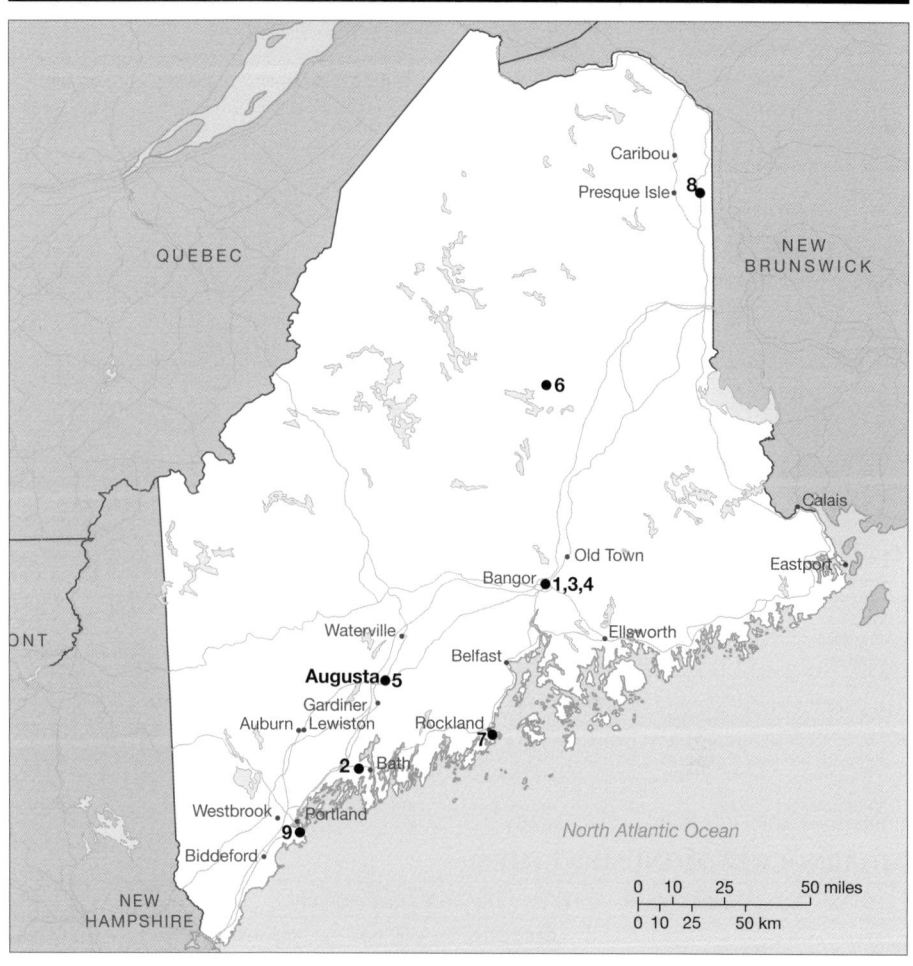

BANGOR AIR NATIONAL GUARD BASE (ME1)

Address:	103 Maineiac Avenue, Suite 505, Bangor, Maine 04401-3099.
Tel:	207-990-7700.
Admission:	By prior permission only.
Location:	At the International Airport which is in the north western suburbs of the city.

Allocated to the state in late 1946, the 132nd Squadron operated fighters from early 1947 until the spring of 1976. Since then it has served in the air-refuelling role. The Voodoo is painted in period Maine ANG colours.

TYPE	REG/SER	CON. NO.	PI/NOTES	STATUS
☐ Bell 205 Iroquois (UH-1D) (UH-1H)	66-0941	5424		RA
☐ McDonnell M.36BA Voodoo (F-101B) (CF-101B)	'70377'	552	57-0374, 101041 (Canada)	RAX
☐ Northrop N-160 Scorpion (N-68) (F-89D) (F-89J)	52-1856	N.4433		RA

BRUNSWICK LANDING BASE (ME2)

Location:	By prior permission only at the airfield which is about 2 miles north east of the town.

TYPE	REG/SER	CON. NO.	PI/NOTES	STATUS
☐ Lockheed 185 Orion (P-3A)	Bu152156	185-5126		RA
☐ Lockheed 426-42-13 Neptune (P2V-5) (P2V-5F) (P2V-5FS) (SP-2E)	Bu128392	426-5238		RA

COLE LAND TRANSPORTATION MUSEUM (ME3)

Address:	405 Perry Road, Bangor, Maine 04401.
Tel:	207-990-3600 Fax: 207-990-2653 Email: mail@colemuseum.org
Admission:	May–mid November daily 0900-1700.
Location:	In the northern part of the city of Route 15.

The displays at the museum trace the history of transport in Maine. On show are vehicles ranging from horse drawn carts up to modern trucks. The collection includes classic cars, farm equipment, snowmobiles, bicycles and military vehicles.

The original Enfield Station on the Maine Central Railroad was moved to the museum in the mid-1980s. Nearby is a locomotive and a number of passenger carriages.

TYPE	REG/SER	CON. NO.	PI/NOTES	STATUS
☐ Bell 205 Iroquois (UH-1D) (UH-1H)	65-9915	4959	65-9915, N4134W	PV

MAINE AIR MUSEUM (ME4)

Address:	PO Box 2641, 98 Maine Avenue, Bangor, Maine 04401.
Tel:	207-941-6757 Email: mam@maineairmuseum.org
Admission:	May–early September Saturday-Sunday 1000-1600.
Location:	At the International Airport which is in the north western suburbs of the city.

For several years the Maine Aviation Historical Society has been collecting artefacts tracing the history of flying in the state. On show in the building, which is a former cold war missile assembly and maintenance facility, are engines and components along with documents, photographs and memorabilia.

TYPE	REG/SER	CON. NO.	PI/NOTES	STATUS
☐ Bell 205 Iroquois (UH-1H)	71-20317	13141	With tail boom from c/n 13349 73-21661, N50823	PV
☐ Luscombe 8A Silvaire	N72025	3452	NC72025	RA
☐ Rotorway Scorpion 1				RA

MAINE MILITARY HISTORICAL SOCIETY MUSEUM (ME5)

Address:	Camp Keyes, 194 Winthrop Street, Augusta, Maine 04333
Tel:	207-626-4338
Admission:	By appointment only.
Location:	In the north western part of the city.

This museum traces the history of Maine citizens who have served their state and country from the early colonial days up to current conflicts, starting with the Revolutionary War and featuring the Mexican, the Spanish American conflict and the two World wars. Conflicts in Korea, Vietnam and the Persian Gulf are also highlighted. Re-constructions of combat conditions have been built. In all area there are uniforms, flags, weapons and many personal items.

The Iroquois served with the Army National Guard for many years.

TYPE	REG/SER	CON. NO.	PI/NOTES	STATUS
☐ Bell 205 Iroquois (UH-1D) (UH-1H)	63-8809	4101		PV

MILLINOCKET MONUMENT (ME6)

Location:	On permanent view at ALP 80 at 970 Central Street in the town.

TYPE	REG/SER	CON. NO.	PI/NOTES	STATUS
☐ Bell 205 Iroquois (UH-1D) (UH-1H)	64-13678	4385		PV

OWLS HEAD TRANSPORTATION MUSEUM (ME7)

Address:	PO Box 277, Owls Head, Maine 04854-0277.
Tel:	207-594-4418/9219 Fax: 207-594-4410 Email: info@ohtm.org
Admission:	April–October daily 1000-1700; November–March Monday-Friday 1000-1600 Saturday-Sunday 1000-1500.
Location:	At Knox County Airport which is 2 miles south of Rockland on Route 73.

Established in 1974 the museum aims to show the development of transport through the ages. Most summer weekends there are special events when some of the aircraft fly, vehicles run and steam engines turn. The collection includes bicycles, cars, motor cycles and traction engines in working order.

The Clark Ornithopter was built in Pennsylvania in about 1900. The current engine, a 5 h.p Waterman air cooled two cylinder, was fitted in 1907. Testing of the design finished in 1910 but it is believed that it never left the ground.

The inter-war period is well represented. The 1930 sailing glider constructed by John Domenjoz is unique. Using a Blériot type fuselage with period wings the aircraft had a mast and sails above the body. The aircraft was towed to an altitude of about 300 feet at Old Orchard Beach but the sails failed to provide power. The Milliken Special was built in Old Town in 1933. It flew three times before turning over on its back when landing. The airframe was placed in store by the family before it joined the museum.

The Fokker C IVA was converted in the 1920s for passenger use. In 1930 it was modified for a flight from Tacoma to Tokyo but crashed soon after take-off and suffered fire damage. The remains languished in a field until recovered by Kenneth Cianchette of Pittsfield, Maine in the early 1970s. He started the rebuild and passed it to the museum in 1992.

The Gazda Helicospeedster helicopter was developed in the mid-1940s and flew for a period. Two examples were completed. The survivor was stored for many years before being restored and the airframe moved to the museum a few years ago.

Maine – Maryland

TYPE	REG/SER	CON. NO.	PI/NOTES	STATUS
☐ Blériot XI (R)	N7899C	3		PV
☐ Boeing-Stearman A75N1 Kaydet (PT-17)	N55361	75-1795	41-8238	PVA
☐ Chanute Glider (R)				PV
☐ Clark Ornithopter				PV
☐ Curtiss D Pusher (R)	N1GJ	M-4		PVA
☐ Curtiss 1C Jenny (JN-4D)	N94JN		34094, N34094, NC2086	PVA
☐ Deperdussin Monocoque (R)	'F-AZAR'	01	N78TJ	PVX
☐ Domenjoz Sailing Glider	N800W	1		PV
☐ Etrich Taube (R)	N11D	D2		PV
☐ Farman HF-3 (R)	N9168X	1		PVA
☐ Fokker Dr I (R)	N425FK	2001		PVA
☐ Fokker C IVA	N439FK	4127	NR439	PVA
☐ Gazda 100 Helicospeeder	NX69154	1		PV
☐ Levasseur Antoinette (R)				RA
☐ Lilienthal Normal-Segelapparat (R)				PV
☐ Mead Rhön Ranger (R)	N306V	1		PV
☐ Milliken M-1 Special	N779V	M1	NC779V	PV
☐ Nieuport 28C.1 (R)	N27226	C-1		PVA
☐ Piper J-3C-85 Cub (J-3C-65)	N6496H	19680	NC6496H	PV
☐ Piper PA-18-150 Super Cub	N703ES	18-7809185		PVA
☐ Royal Aircraft Factory F.E.8 (R)	N928	298		PVA
☐ Royal Aircraft Factory S.E.5A (R)				PV
☐ SPAD XIII (R)	N14574	C-1		PVA
☐ Sopwith Pup (R)	N5139	83213		PVA
☐ Standard J-1	N22581	581		PVA
☐ Waco UBF-2	N13442	3766	NC13442	PVA
☐ Wright Flyer (R)				PVA

PRESQUE ISLE AIR MUSEUM (ME8)

Address:	Northern Maine Regional Airport, 650 Airport Drive, Presque Isle, Maine 04769-2088.
Tel:	207-764-2542 **Email:** piairmuseum@fcmail.com
Admission:	When the terminal is open.
Location:	In the western suburbs of the town.

The airfield was constructed in the 1930s to serve the local community. The site became a military base and during World War II more combat aircraft left for Europe than from any other field in the USA.

The base closed but was reopened in 1950 and was home to fighter squadrons protecting the north east coast until 1959.

For two years a missile wing was in residence. The site was taken over by the region and developed as a civil airport and industrial park.

The museum has been set up to trace the varied history of the site. Displays of photographs, models, documents and memorabilia have been placed in the terminal building.

SCARBOROUGH MONUMENT (ME9)

Location:	On view during opening hours in Cabela's store at 100 Cabela's Boulevard in the town.

TYPE	REG/SER	CON. NO.	PI/NOTES	STATUS
☐ Piper J-3C-65 Cub				PV

MARYLAND

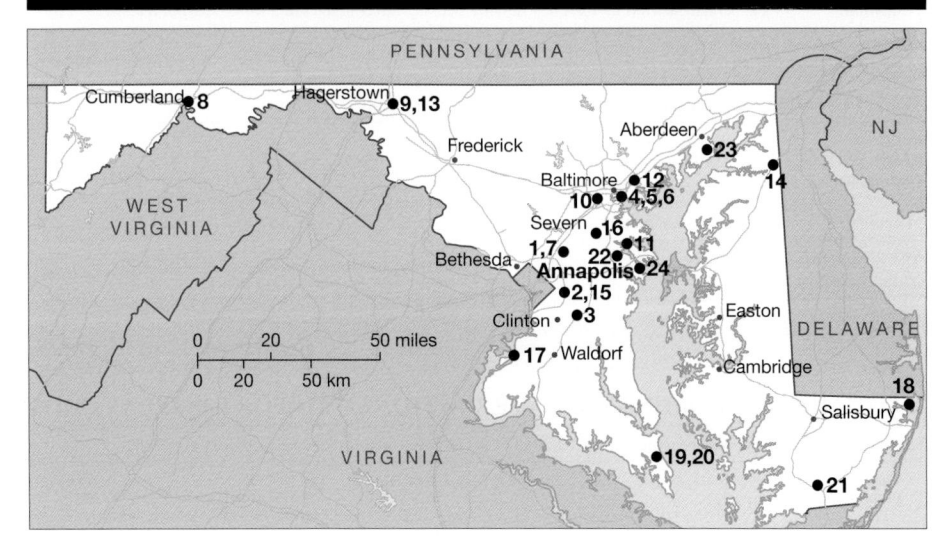

94TH AERO SQUADRON RESTAURANT (MD1)

Address:	5240 Paint Branch Parkway, College Park, Maryland 20740.
Tel:	301-699-9400 **Fax:** 301-779-2305 **Email:** gmunit44@SRCMail.COM
Admission:	Aircraft on permanent view.
Location:	At the eastern end of the airport.

The restaurant was established some years ago and four replicas of World War II fighters were displayed outside the building. In the spring of 2009 the complex was flooded twice in two unrelated events. The business was forced to close and it is hoped that it will be ready for customers in the not too distant future.

TYPE	REG/SER	CON. NO.	PI/NOTES	STATUS
☐ Curtiss 87V Warhawk (P-40N) (FSM)				PVX
☐ North American NA-122 Mustang (P-51D) (FSM)				PVX
☐ Republic P-47D Thunderbolt (FSM)				PVX
☐ Supermarine 361 Spitfire LF.IXc (FSM)				PVX

AIRMEN MEMORIAL MUSEUM (MD2)

Address:	5211 Auth Road, Suitland, Maryland 20746-4339.
Tel:	301-899-8386 **Fax:** 301-899-8136 **Email:** amm@afsahq.org
Admission:	Monday-Friday 0800-1700.
Location:	About 1 mile from Andrews AFB off Route 5 by exit 7B of Interstate 495.

The museum was set up in 1988 by the Air Force Sergeants Association. The main aim is to collect and preserved artefacts, personal papers and photographs relating to all enlisted airmen from 1907 to the present day. There are several fabric portions from World War I aircraft, medals and components to be seen.

ANDREWS JOINT BASE (MD3)

Address:	89AW/PA, Building 1535, Command Room Drive, Andrews Air Force Base, Maryland 20762.
Tel:	301-981-4424 **Email:** 89pa.media@andrews.af.mil
Admission:	By prior permission only.
Location:	About 11 miles south east of Washington DC, off Interstate 95.

Opened as Camp Springs Air Base in September 1942 the field took up its present name in February 1945. Lieutenant General Frank M. Andrews was killed in a B-24 crash in Iceland in May 1943. The base receives many VIP flights for nearby Washington. Units of the Air Force, Air National Guard and Navy are in residence.

TYPE	REG/SER	CON. NO.	PI/NOTES	STATUS
☐ Bell 204 Iroquois (UH-1B)	'12557'	712	62-12554	RAX
☐ Douglas DC-9-32CF Nightingale (C-9A)	71-0876	47475		RA
☐ Grumman G-50 Hellcat (F6F-5)	Bu77722	A-8867		RA
☐ Lockheed 1329 JetStar	'89001'	1329-1002	N329K, N711Z	RAX
☐ McDonnell M.98EN Phantom II (F-4D)	66-7661	2247		RA
☐ Republic F-105D Thunderchief	61-0041	D-236		RA

BALTIMORE MONUMENT (MD4)

Location:	On permanent view at VVA 451 at 6401 Beckley Street in the south eastern part of the city

TYPE	REG/SER	CON. NO.	PI/NOTES	STATUS
☐ Bell 204 Iroquois (UH-1C) (UH-1M)	66-15238	1966		PV

BALTIMORE MUSEUM OF INDUSTRY (MD5)

Address:	1415 Key Highway, Baltimore, Maryland 21230.
Tel:	410-727-4808 **Fax:** 410-727-4869 **Email:** calbert@thebmi.org
Admission:	Mid June–early September Tuesday-Sunday 1200-1700 (opens at 1000 on Saturday); Wednesday 1800-2100; Rest of year Thursday, Friday and Sunday 1200-1700,Sat 1000-1700. Wed 1900-2100
Location:	In the southern suburbs of the city.

This excellent museum is located in a former oyster cannery on the waterfront. Many of the displays are 'hands-on' and visitors can experience trades formerly carried out in the port area.

The Glenn Martin company had a factory in the city for many years and one of their products is on show. The 162A was built in 1938 as a three-eighths scale model of the PBM Mariner to test its flying characteristics.

TYPE	REG/SER	CON. NO.	PI/NOTES	STATUS
☐ Martin 162A	X19168	815	On loan from NASM, DC.	PV

BALTIMORE – WASHINGTON INTERNATIONAL AIRPORT DISPLAY (MD6)

Location:	On permanent view in the terminal of the airport which is in the southern part of the city.

TYPE	REG/SER	CON. NO.	PI/NOTES	STATUS
☐ Boeing 737-293	N462AC	19307	N832PC, N462GB, N462AC, (N648AA) – front fuselage only.	PV

COLLEGE PARK AVIATION MUSEUM (MD7)

Address:	1985 Corporal Frank Scott Drive, College Park, Maryland 20740-2000.
Tel:	301-864-6029 Fax: 301-927-6472 Email: AviationMuseum@pgparks.com
Admission:	Daily 1000-1700.
Location:	About 5 miles north east of Washington, DC off Route 1.

In 1908 the Wright brothers succeeded in persuading the US Government to test one of their aircraft. A field at College Park was chosen for the training of two Army officers as pilots. The site has been in use since then and is the oldest continually operating airport in the world.

Hangars were built for the first Army Aviation School but the unit left after a few years. Civilian operators soon moved in and offered pilot training. A number of aircraft were also constructed at the field. In 1918 the first mail flight in the country left College Park and a hangar and compass rose from this period are still in existence.

In 1977 the airport was entered on the National Register of Historic Places. A small museum was established in the 1990s where history of the airfield was portrayed with photographs, documents and models. Plans for a larger building were been put forward and this opened on 12th September 1998. The Boyd brothers built two aircraft in Baltimore. The A appeared in 1924 and the C2 eight years later. They were both of all metal construction. The A was claimed to be the first design fitted with flaps and the C2 incorporated a variable camber wing. This aircraft is not in a good condition and is store awaiting rebuild.

Emile Berliner began experiments in vertical flight in the early 1900s. He was later assisted by his son Henry. One of his early designs made a tethered flight in 1909. The example on show was demonstrated to the Army at College Park in 1924 and was one of the first successful helicopters in the world. Successful light types from the 1930s and 1940s complete this interesting display.

TYPE	REG/SER	CON. NO.	PI/NOTES	STATUS
☐ Aeronca 11AC Chief				PV
☐ Berliner 5 Helicopter			On loan from NASM, DC.	PV
☐ Blériot XI (R)				PV
☐ Boeing-Stearman A75N1 Kaydet (PT-17)	N8NP	75-2718	41-25229, N57013	PV
☐ Boyd C2				S
☐ Curtiss D Pusher (R)				PV
☐ Curtiss 1C Jenny (JN-4D)			On loan from Fort Sill, OK.	PV
☐ Ercoupe 415C	N99182	1805	NC99182 – front fuselage only.	PV
☐ Ercoupe 415D	NC93942	1265	NC93942, N93942	PV
☐ Mono Aircraft Monocoupe 110	NC12345	6W43	NC12345, N12345	PVA
☐ Taylor J-2 Cub	NC16769	771	NC16769, N16769 – on loan from Hillier AM, CA.	PV
☐ Taylorcraft BL-65	N23624	1349	NC23624	PV
☐ Wright 1902 Glider (R)				PV
☐ Wright B (R)				PV

CUMBERLAND MONUMENT (MD8)

Location:	On permanent view in Constitution Park in the eastern part of the town.

TYPE	REG/SER	CON. NO.	PI/NOTES	STATUS
☐ Lockheed 580 (T-33A)	51-4157	580-5451	51-4157, 14691 (Canada)	PV

DISCOVERY STATION (MD9)

Address:	101 West Washington Street, Hagerstown, Maryland 21740.
Tel:	301-790-0076 Fax: 301-790-0045 Email: info@discoverystation.org
Admission:	Tuesday-Saturday 1000-1700; Sunday 1400-1700.
Location:	In the centre of the town.

This museum with many interactive exhibits is housed in the historic Nicodemus Bank building in the town. The original bank housed the Federal Depository during the Civil War.

The current structure was erected in the early part of the twentieth century. The exhibits cover many aspects of science, transport and technology. The visitor can trace the development of the railways in the area and see local industrial products.

The work of NASA is also highlighted along with agriculture in the region. The Cessna 150 has been prepared for a 'hands-on' exhibit showing how aircraft fly.

At the current time the Hagerstown Aviation Museum have staged a display of memorabilia, photographs and models. The history of aircraft manufacture in the town is told in detail. The museum has most of its aircraft at the local airfield and will eventually have a permanent exhibition there.

TYPE	REG/SER	CON. NO.	PI/NOTES	STATUS
☐ Cessna 150				PV
☐ Truax Papoose	N9DT	001		PV

ELLICOTT CITY MONUMENT (MD10)

Location:	On permanent view at VFW 7472 on VFW Drive in the south western part of the town.

TYPE	REG/SER	CON. NO.	PI/NOTES	STATUS
☐ North American NA-187 Sabre (F-86H)	52-2048	187-74		PV

FORT MEADE MONUMENT (MD11)

Location:	On permanent view at Tipton Airport in the south western part of the town.

TYPE	REG/SER	CON. NO.	PI/NOTES	STATUS
☐ Beech D45 Mentor (T-34B)	N331GK	BG-350	Bu144043	PV

GLENN L MARTIN MARYLAND AVIATION MUSEUM (MD12)

Address:	PO Box 5024, Middle River, Maryland 21220.
Tel:	410-682-6122 Fax: 410-682-8699 Email: contact@marylandaviationmuseum.org
Admission:	Monday-Friday 1000-1400; Saturday 1300-1700.
Location:	At Glenn L. Martin State Airport which is about 10 miles north east of the city on Route 150.

Glenn Martin set up his own aircraft manufacturing company in 1917 and moved to Baltimore in the late 1920s. The firm produced many successful designs and the factory is still in use although aircraft have not been made for a number of years.

Types were produced for both the Air Force, the Navy and the civil market. During World War II the Marauder twin engined bomber served in all theatres of the war. Over 5,200 were completed. The Mariner amphibian also gave excellent service. At the end of the conflict the 2-0-2 twin engined airliner was built. This was developed in to the 4-0-4. Several innovative designs were constructed over the next few years. The company was one of the last to produce flying boats for military use.

The museum was set up in 1990 and an exhibition has been staged in a room at the rear of one of the hangars. The history of the company is shown with displays of models, documents and photographs. A vast archive of company films and photographs is also held. The aircraft in the collection mostly parked on the field and can be seen by appointment. Two Martin-built Canberras are among these. Several types have come from the nearby Aberdeen Proving Grounds. The only known surviving parts of a P6M Sea Master jet flying boat were found in a Navy test facility and the museum now has these in store. A pair of Maulers has arrived for rebuild and other Martin designs are being sought. There are long-term plans to construct a purpose-built museum at the airfield.

TYPE	REG/SER	CON. NO.	PI/NOTES	STATUS
☐ Douglas TA-4J Skyhawk (TA-4F)	Bu153525	13591		PV
☐ Grumman G-105 Cougar (F9F-8T) (TF-9J)	Bu142976	99		RA
☐ Grumman G-111 Albatross (G-64) (SA-16A) (SA-16B) (HU-16B)	'10004'	G-255	51-7193 – at ANG base on field.	RAX
☐ Lockheed 580 (T-33A)	53-5854	580-9295		RA
☐ Martin 210A Mauler (AM-1)	N5586A	13920	Bu22260 – on loan from CAF, TX.	RA
☐ Martin 210A Mauler (AM-1)	Bu122401			RA
☐ Martin 272A Canberra (RB-57A)	52-1446	29		PV
☐ Martin 272A Canberra (RB-57A)	52-1467	50		PV
☐ Martin 275B Seamaster (P6M-2)	Bu145878	P-9	Rear fuselage only.	RA
☐ Martin 4-0-4	N259S	14233	N485A	RA
☐ McDonnell M.36BA Voodoo (F-101B)	58-0303	675		PV
☐ McDonnell M.98DJ Phantom II (F-4C)	64-0919	1390		PV
☐ North American NA-203 Sabre (F-86H)	53-1411	203-183	May be 53-1339 – at ANG base on field.	PV
☐ North American NA-243 Super Sabre (F-100F)	56-3899	243-175		PV
☐ North American NA-243 Super Sabre (F-100F)	56-3905	243-181		PV
☐ Northrop N-156E Tiger II (F-5E)	74-1531	R.1189	74-1531, Bu741531	PV
☐ Republic RF-84F Thunderflash	53-7554			PV
☐ Republic F-105G Thunderchief (F-105F)	63-8274	F-51		PV
☐ Vought A-7D Corsair II	69-6197	D27		PV

HAGERSTOWN AVIATION MUSEUM (MD13)

Address:	14235 Oak Springs Road, Hagerstown, Maryland 21742-1331.
Tel:	301-733-8717 Email: info@hagerstownaviationmuseum.org
Admission:	By prior permission only.
Location:	At 101 West Washington and at the airport which is about 5 miles north of the town off Route 11.

Hagerstown has had a long association with aviation. From 1916 to 1920 Guiseppe Bellanca built his high wing monoplanes in the town. Then in 1921 the Reisner brothers opened an aircraft repair business and Waco dealership. In conjunction with a local shoe manufacture they set up the Kreider-Reisner company which produced a number of biplanes. In 1929 Sherman Fairchild purchased a controlling interest in the Kreider-Reisner firm. A large manufacturing plant was built and this was in operation until 1984.

On 7th July 2005 an exhibition opened on the second floor of the Discovery Station, an interactive museum, in the town. The original Kreider-Reisner shed where doping took place was discovered, dismantled and put in store. The immaculate Challenger biplane was built in the late 1920s. About 200, many powered by the OX-5 engine, were built in the town. The Fairchild 24 was found in a shed in Oxford, Georgia. The high-wing monoplane had spent over 50 years in the small building. Restoration of the airframe has started.

The museum acquired two aircraft in the auction of the Hawkins and Powers fleet at Greybull, Wyoming. The C-82 left Greybull on 12th October 2006 and made its final landing at Hagerstown three days later. This aircraft with a jet mounted on top of the fuselage was a familiar sight in Europe in the 1950s when it was used by TWA to transport engines. The museum is currently negotiating to acquire other Fairchild types so that a comprehensive display can be staged.

TYPE	REG/SER	CON. NO.	PI/NOTES	STATUS
☐ Fairchild 24R9 Forwarder (UC-61C)	NC18653	R9-305	NC18653, 42-70862	RAC
☐ Fairchild M-62A Cornell (PT-19A)	N52164	7343AE	42-65485	RA
☐ Fairchild M-62A Cornell (PT-19A)	N54714	T43-7034	42-83447, NC54714	RA
☐ Fairchild 78 Packet (C-82A)	N8009E	10071	44-23027, N5095V, CC-CRA-0507, N5095V – fuselage only.	RAC
☐ Fairchild 78 Packet (C-82A)	N9701F	10184	45-57814, N2047A, ET-T-12	RAC
☐ Fairchild 110 Flying Boxcar (C-119F)	N8093	10776	22111 (Canada)	RA
☐ Fairchild Black Fly				RA
☐ Grumman G-1159 Gulfstream IISP	N300RD	3	N831GA, N214GP, N311JJ, N555RS, N300GP, N417RD	RA
☐ Kreider-Reisner KR-31 Challenger (C-2)	NC10054	239	NC10054, N10054	RA
☐ North American NA-168 Texan (T-6G)	N9492Z	168-514	49-3390	RA

Maryland

MASSEY AIR MUSEUM (MD14)

Address:	33541 Maryland Line Road, Massey, Maryland 21650.
Tel:	410-928-5270 Email: masseyaero@dmv.com
Admission:	Tuesday-Saturday 1000-1700.
Location:	About 2 miles east of the town on Route 230.

This grass airfield opened in 2001 and the museum was set up the following year. Four local aviators had been planning the project for many years. Hangars were built and displays of engines, components and memorabilia are being set up. In one is an excellent collection of engines from light aircraft. There are many interesting homebuilts in the collection. The Bailey-Moyes Dragonfly ultralight first appeared in 1993 and several have been completed. The Tempest is an ultralight glider. The Pacer has been converted from a Tripacer and now has a standard tailwheel undercarriage. The early DC-3 was delivered to United Airlines in October 1937 and flew on their routes until 1954.

The site is being developed and several more hangars are planned.

TYPE	REG/SER	CON. NO.	PI/NOTES	STATUS
☐ Advanced Aviation Buccaneer II	N959SY	B2B-K021		PVA
☐ Aeronca 7CCM Champion (7BCM)	N6420C	7BCM-499		PVA
☐ Aeronca 7EC Champion	N7489B	7EC-551		PVA
☐ Bailey-Moyes Dragonfly	N103ST	16		PVA
☐ Bailey-Moyes Tempest				PVA
☐ Bell 47G				PV
☐ Boeing-Stearman B75N1 Kaydet (N2S-3)	N747RB	75-6829	Bu07225, N73736	PVA
☐ Cessna 140	N2414N	12663	NC2414N	PVA
☐ Cessna 150H	N22115	15068069		PVA
☐ Cessna 170	N6303D	18015		PVA
☐ CASA 1.131E [Bücker Bü 131 Jungmann]	N211BP		E.3B-172	PVA
☐ Douglas DC-3A-197	N18111	1983	NC18111, N18111, '0795450'	PVA
☐ Eipper MX Quicksilver				PVA
☐ Maxair Super Drifter				PVA
☐ Piper J-3C-65 Cub	N24739	3410	NC24739	PVA
☐ Piper PA-15 Vagabond				PV
☐ Piper PA-20 Pacer (PA-22-150 Tripacer)	N6043D	22-4696		PVA
☐ Piper PA-22-108 Colt	N5832Z	22-9661		PVA
☐ Progressive Aerodyne SeaRey	N96TK	1DK-081		PVA
☐ Schweizer SGU.2-22				PVA
☐ Slipstream Genesis	N1919G	GE02/0001		PV
☐ Slipstream Revelation				PVA
☐ Smith DSA-1 Miniplane	N4092U	021/JK		PVA
☐ Stinson V-77 Reliant (AT-19)	NC64646	77-1492	(USAAF), NC64646, N64646	PVA
☐ Stinson V-77 Reliant (AT-19)	N60890	77-274	43-43987, FB546, Bu?????, NC60890	PVA
☐ Vans RV-7	N715K	71005		PVA
☐ Vought F4U-4 Corsair (FSM)				PVX

NATIONAL AIR AND SPACE MUSEUM – PAUL E. GARBER FACILITY (MD15)

Address:	3904 Old Silver Hill Road, Suitland, Maryland 20746.
Tel:	202-357-1552
Admission:	No longer open.
Location:	About 6 miles south east of Washington DC.

Paul Garber joined the Smithsonian Institution, in 1920 and was responsible for the acquisition of many aircraft in the NASM collection. He suggested to the Institution that they should ask Charles Lindbergh for his 'Spirit of St. Louis'.

After World War II General 'Hap' Arnold was determined that one example of every wartime aircraft from sides should be saved for a national air museum. Hundreds were earmarked for this ambitious project and many were stored in a former aircraft factory at Ridge Park in Chicago. When the Korean War started the plant was needed again and so the aircraft were moved with some lost and many damaged.

Garber found a piece of swampland at Silver Hill and the task of transporting the aircraft to their new home began. A number were scrapped and those which arrived safely were stored in temporary buildings, in crates or left exposed to the elements. In the late 1950s a series of press articles criticised the NASM and the Government for allowing these historic aircraft to rot away in a glorified junkyard.

These struck home and plans for a purpose-built museum in Washington were put forward. More buildings were erected at Silver Hill and a major restoration programme started. After the NASM opened in 1976 its then director, astronaut Mike Collins, issued a directive to clean up Silver Hill.

Within three months all the aircraft bar two were inside and the old crates had gone. It was decided to open the site as a 'no frills' museum and in 1977 the first building was ready. In 1980 the complex was renamed in honour of Paul Garber. Guided tours used to take visitors through a number of the buildings where both restored and unrestored machines could be seen. Sadly, these no longer operate and unless there is a change of policy these machines will not be seen in public.

With the construction of the Udvar-Hazy facility at Dulles Airport in Virginia many aircraft were transported for display. The aircraft listed below are not presently scheduled for exhibition at Dulles so will presumably remain in store for many more years. Restoration of many will not take place until those due to make the move have been completed.

There are many interesting types at this location. Several German and Japanese aircraft which were taken to the USA for testing are in the buildings. Some of these are the last survivors of their type and hopefully they will not be hidden from public view for too long. Two prototype Douglas bombers were moved to the National Museum of the United States Air Force at Dayton in July 2010.

Willard Custer thought up the idea of the channel wing in the late 1930s. He concluded that mounting the engines in a duct in the wing would produce more lift. Four prototypes of the CCW-1 were constructed with the first flying in 1942. Several other versions followed over the next few years.

The Abrams Explorer was designed for aerial survey and the sole example flew in 1938. The Whatsit was Waldo Waterman's first attempt at producing an aircraft that could also serve as a car but it was unstable in flight and he moved on to other projects.

TYPE	REG/SER	CON. NO.	PI/NOTES	STATUS
☐ Abrams Explorer	X19897	15340		RA
☐ Aichi B7A1 Ryusei	T2-N1204	816	FE-1204	RA
☐ Akerman 1-1936 Tailless	X14880	1		RA
☐ Antonov An-2M	N84762	600810	VT-DWH	RA
☐ Applebay Zuni II	N2ZJ	29		RA
☐ Arado Ar 196A-5	'GA+DX'	623167	PO+HG, T3+BH	RAX
☐ Bell Jet Flying Belt				RA
☐ Bellanca 14-13-2 Crusair Senior	N74401	1514	NC74401	RA
☐ Bertelson Aeromobile				RA
☐ Blohm und Voss Bv 155B	T2-505	V-3	(Luftwaffe), FE-505	RA
☐ Boeing 367-76-66 Stratofreighter (KC-97G) (KC-97L)	53-0243	17025	Front fuselage only	RA
☐ Burgess-Curtiss Shoemaker Biplane				RA
☐ Cascade Kasperwing 180B		295		RA
☐ Convair 2 Seadart (YF2Y-1) (YF-7A)	Bu137634			RA
☐ Convair 5 (XFY-1)	Bu138649	1		RA
☐ Convair 240-0	N240K	89	NC94245, N94245	RA
☐ Crowley Hydro Air Vehicle				RA
☐ Culver NR-D Cadet (PQ-14A) (TD2C-1)	Bu120035	E.521846 (?)	45-58816	RA
☐ Custer CCW-1	NX30090	1		RA
☐ Fairchild M-62A Cornell (PT-19A)	43-33842	T43-7427		RA
☐ Franklin PS-2 Eaglet	502M	202		RA
☐ Gotha Go 229 (Horten Ho IX V3)	T2-490	40	(Luftwaffe), FE-490	RA
☐ Granville Gee Bee R (R)	NR2101			RA
☐ Hispano HA.200B Saeta	20063		In Egyptian markings.	RA
☐ Horten Ho IX V3 (See Gotha Go 229)	T2-490	40	(Luftwaffe), FE-490	RA
☐ Icarus I Hang Glider				RA
☐ Kawanishi N1K1 Kyofu	514		514, FE-324 (?), T2-514 (?)	RA
☐ Kyushu J7W1 Shinden			(Japanese Navy), FE-326, T2-326	RA
☐ Langley Aerodrome 6				RA
☐ Lippisch DM 1				RA
☐ Lockheed 10-E Electra (XC-35)	36-353	3501		RA
☐ Lockheed 182-1A Hercules (182-44-03) (C-130A)	56-0512	182-3120	Rear fuselage only.	RA
☐ Martin 272B Canberra (B-57B) (EB-57B)	52-1551	134		RA
☐ Maupin Lanteri Black Diamond				RA
☐ McDonnell M.36CA Voodoo (RF-101C)	56-0119	364	Fuselage only.	RA
☐ McDonnell M.98AM Phantom II (F4H-1F) (F-4A)	Bu145307	8		RA
☐ McDonnell XHJH-1 Whirlaway (XHJD-1)	Bu44318	1		RA
☐ Montgomery Santa Clara			Parts only	RA
☐ Morane-Saulnier MS.500 Criquet [Fieseler Fi 156 Storch]	'80138'	85	85 (Fr.Mil)	RAX
☐ Nakajima B6N2 Tenzan	5350		FE-1200, T2-1200	RA
☐ Nakajima C6N1-S Saiun	4161	4161	4161, FE-4803, T2N-4803	RA
☐ Nakajima J5N1 Tenrai			Rear fuselage wings and other small parts only.	RA
☐ Nakajima Ki-115 Tsurugi		1002	(Japanese Army), FE-156, T2-156	RA
☐ Nakajima Kikka	91ST	7337		RA
☐ NASA DS-1				RA
☐ Nelson PG-185B Hummingbird	N68580	80		RA
☐ New Standard D-25 (1/4 scale)	NX328			RA
☐ Nieuport 12				RA
☐ Noorduyn Norseman IV (YC-64)	42-5046	78		RA
☐ North American NA-141 Fury (FJ-1)	Bu120351	141-38403		RA
☐ North American NA-223 Super Sabre (F-100D)			Front fuselage only.	RA
☐ North American NA-283 Vigilante (RA-5C)	Bu151728	283-43	Front fuselage only.	RA
☐ Northrop M2-F1	N86652	1		RA
☐ Northrop N-2B (XP-56C)	42-38353	326		RA
☐ Northrop N-156T Talon (T-38A)	60-0551	N.5124		RA
☐ Olmstead Amphibian				RA
☐ Piasecki PV-3 Rescuer (XHRP-1)	'Bu01045'		Bu37968	RAX
☐ Pioneer UAV				RA
☐ Pitcairn-Cierva C.8	NC418	R6-4518		RA
☐ Platt-Le Page XR-1	41-001			RA
☐ Princeton Air Scooter				RA
☐ Republic LTV-N-2 [Fieseler Fi 103A-1]				RA
☐ Schneider ESG 29 Grunau 9 (DFS 108-10)				RA
☐ Schneider-Hofmann-Rehberg SG-38 (DFS 108-14)			FE-5004, T2-5004	RA
☐ Schneider-Hofmann-Rehberg SG-38 (DFS 108-14)			FE-5005, T2-5005	RA
☐ Shoemaker Cannonhouse				RA
☐ Sikorsky S-43 (JRS-1)	Bu1063	4346		RA
☐ Saab 29E (29B) (J 29B) (J 29E)	Fv29657	29657		RA
☐ Vertol V.76 (VZ-2)	56-6943			RA
☐ Waco NAZ Primary Glider			Parts only	RA
☐ Waterman Whatsit	X12272	1		RA
☐ Yokosuka MXY-7-K2 Ohka	61			RA
☐ Yokosuka P1Y1-C Ginga		8923	T2-1702	RA
☐ Zimmermann Flying Platform				RA

The Glenn L. Martin Maryland Aviation Museum owns this RB-57A Canberra. [MD12]

Pictured in the hangars of the Massey Air Museum is this Slipstream Genesis. (Dick Barrett) [MD14]

The Boeing B-17G Fortress of the Massachusetts based Collings Foundation spends a large part of the summer months on tour. (CF) [MA4]

NATIONAL VIGILANCE PARK (MD16)

Address:	ANME-OPM, Griffin Avenue, Fort George Meade, Maryland 20755-5094.
Tel:	301-677-6966 **Email:** johnsonr@emh1.ftmeade.army.mil
Admission:	Wednesday-Saturday 1100-1600; Sunday 1300-1600.
Location:	In the southern part of the town off Route 32.

The park was dedicated on 2nd September 1997 to honour the crews who have lost their lives in aerial reconnaissance missions. The Hercules is painted to represent the aircraft shot down over Armenia in September 1958. During the Vietnam War the army lost 68 reconnaissance aircraft and 78 crew. The RU-8 on show flew with the 138th Radio Research Company during the conflict The nearby National Cryptologic Museum has exhibits tracing this aspect of military flying.

TYPE	REG/SER	CON. NO.	PI/NOTES	STATUS
☐ Beech C50 Seminole (RL-23D) (RU-8D)	'92540'	LH-197	59-4991	PVX
☐ Douglas EA-3B Skywarrior (A3D-2Q)	Bu146448	12400		PVX
☐ Lockheed 182-1A Hercules (182-44-03) (C-130A)	'56-0528'	182-3160	57-0453	PVX

NAVAL SURFACE WARFARE CENTER DIVISION MONUMENT (MD17)

Location:	By prior permission only at the base at 101 Strauss Avenue in Indian Head.

TYPE	REG/SER	CON. NO.	PI/NOTES	STATUS
☐ Hawker-Siddeley Harrier II (AV-8B)	Bu161398	3		RA

OCEAN CITY MONUMENT (MD18)

Location:	On permanent view at Lost Treasure Golf at 13903 Coastal Avenue in the town.

TYPE	REG/SER	CON. NO.	PI/NOTES	STATUS
☐ Beech D18S				PVX

PATUXENT RIVER NAVAL AIR MUSEUM (MD19)

Address:	22156 Three Notch Road, Lexington, Maryland 20653.
Tel:	301-863-7148 **Fax:** 301-863-7947 **Email:** director@paxmuseum.com
Admission:	Daily 1000-1700.
Location:	At the junction of Route 235 and Shangri-La Drive in Lexington Park.

The airfield was constructed in 1942 as a test centre to bring together work carried out at a number of locations in the area. A Naval Test Pilots' School was also set up. The base is now home to the Naval Air Warfare Center Aircraft Division, established in 1992 with the role of testing and evaluating all new and modified aircraft and helicopters.

The idea of a museum was first put forward in the early 1970s and a building was allocated. The 1940s structure was initially a social centre and later the enlisted men's club. The inside exhibition traces the work of the base with displays of photographs, models, engines, components and equipment.

The Goodyear Inflatoplane is in this area. Types which have flown from the field have been put on show and include modern combat designs.

Units on the base look after particular machines and they are maintained to a high standard. Funds are being raised to construct a purpose-built complex which will be able to exhibit more artefacts and aircraft.

Two interesting experimental aircraft joined the display in 2006. The Boeing X-32B and the Lockheed-Martin X-35C were both STOL contenders for the Joint Strike Fighter programme.

TYPE	REG/SER	CON. NO.	PI/NOTES	STATUS
☐ Beech D45 Mentor (T-34B)	Bu140921	BG-255	Bu140921, N34PR	PV
☐ Beech PD-373 Texan II	N8284M	PT-2		PV
☐ Bell 204 Iroquois (TH-1L)	Bu157842	6437		PV
☐ Bell 209 Sea Cobra (AH-1J)	Bu159227	26067		PV
☐ Boeing X-32B				PV
☐ Douglas F-6A Skyray (F4D-1)	Bu134764	10358		PV
☐ Douglas NA-4M Skyhawk (A-4F)	Bu155049	13865		RA
☐ Goodyear GA-468 Inflatoplane (XAO-3)			On loan from NASM, DC.	PV
☐ Grumman G-99 Cougar (F9F-8) (F-9J)	Bu144276	497C		PV
☐ Grumman G-121 Tracker (S2F-3) (S-2D)	Bu149240	84C		PV
☐ Grumman G-123 Hawkeye (E-2A) (E-2B)	Bu152476	46		PV
☐ Grumman G-128 Intruder (A-6A) (A-6E) (NA-6E)	Bu156997	I-466		PV
☐ Grumman G-128 Prowler (EA-6B)	Bu158033	P10		PV
☐ Grumman G-303 Tomcat (F-14A) (F-14D)	Bu161623	482		PV
☐ Gyrodyne QH-50D		DS-1679		PV
☐ Kaman K-20 Seasprite (SH-2F)	Bu161642	192		PV
☐ Lockheed 394 Viking (S-3A) (S-3B)	Bu159770	394A-3099		PV
☐ Lockheed-Martin X-35C (X-35A)		PAV-2		PV
☐ McDonnell M.98AM Phantom II (F-4B) (EF-4B)	Bu153070	1770	Front fuselage only.	PV
☐ McDonnell M.98EV Phantom II (F-4J)	Bu153071	1488		PV
☐ McDonnell M.267 Hornet (F/A-18A)	Bu161353	21/A017		PV
☐ McDonnell M.267 Hornet (F/A-18E)	Bu165165	1293/E002		PV
☐ North American NA-285 Sabreliner (T3J-1) (T-39D)	Bu150987	285-19		PV
☐ North American NA-316 Vigilante (RA-5C)	Bu156643	316-36		PV
☐ Northrop X-47A Pegasus (FSM)				PV
☐ Sikorsky S-65A Sea Stallion (CH-53A) (NCH-53A)	Bu151686	65003		PV
☐ Vought A-7A Corsair II	Bu152658	A15		PV

Maryland

PATUXENT RIVER NAVAL AIR STATION COLLECTION (MD20)

Address:	47402 Buse Road, Patuxent River, Maryland 20670-1547.
Tel:	301-342-3510 **Email:** navairpao@navy.mil
Admission:	By prior permission only.
Location:	About 2 miles east of Lexington Park.

Construction of the airfield started in 1942 and the base was commissioned on 1st April 1943. During World War II many pilots test flew aircraft from the field. The Naval Air Test Center was set up in 1945 and the work of this is highlighted along with current units in the nearby museum. The base is also home to a number of operational squadrons. The preserved aircraft are located at outside several different buildings around the large site. They represent those flown from the field in recent years and most have served in considerable numbers with Navy squadrons. In the 1990s the Navy closed test facilities at Trenton, New Jersey and Warminster, Pennsylvania and work carried out at these facilities moved to Patuxent River. Further changes to the tasks carried out at the site have been announced.

TYPE	REG/SER	CON. NO.	PI/NOTES	STATUS
☐ Bell 209 Huey Cobra (AH-1G) (AH-1S)	67-15645	20309		RA
☐ Douglas TA-4J Skyhawk	Bu158106	14143		RA
☐ Grumman G-128 Intruder (A-6E)	Bu159568	I-557		RA
☐ Grumman G-303 Tomcat (F-14A) (F-14D)	Bu162595	517		RA
☐ Grumman G-303 Tomcat (F-14A) (NF-14A)	Bu159455	121		RA
☐ Hughes 369M Cayuse (HO-6) (OH-6A) (TH-6B)	Bu696044	1414	69-16044	RA
☐ Lockheed 185 Orion (P3V-1) (P-3A) (NP-3D)	Bu148883	185-5001		RA
☐ McDonnell M.267 Hornet (F/A-18A) (NF/A-18A)	Bu161367	35/A025		RA
☐ McDonnell M.267 Hornet (F/A-18E)	Bu165164	1285/E001		RA
☐ North American NA-247 Vigilante (A3J-1) (A-5A)	'Bu155697'	247-6	Bu146697 –	RAX
☐ North American NA-340 Buckeye (T-2C)	Bu158328	340-19		RA
☐ Northrop N-156T Talon (T-38A)	62-3625	N.5330	62-3625, 3807 (Taiwan), Bu623625	RA
☐ Sikorsky S-70B Sea Hawk (SH-60B)	Bu162337			RA

POCOMOKE CITY MONUMENT (MD21)

Location:	On permanent view at ALP93 on Worcester Highway north east of the town.

TYPE	REG/SER	CON. NO.	PI/NOTES	STATUS
☐ Lockheed 580 (T-33A)	52-9650	580-7835		PV

QUESTMASTERS MUSEUM (MD22)

Address:	Odenton, Maryland 21113.
Email:	questmasters@hotmail.com
Admission:	By prior permission only.
Location:	At a number of locations in the area.

The museum was set up to preserve all aspects of World War II history. The collection includes vehicles, weapons, uniforms and memorabilia. A number of wrecked aircraft have been acquired and are currently in store. Many crash sites have been investigated and small components from a number of types have been recovered. These include several aircraft downed in Hawaii. Components from B-24s, P-36s, P-47s, P-61s and TBM-3s are held.

TYPE	REG/SER	CON. NO.	PI/NOTES	STATUS
☐ Beech C18S Expeditor (C-45F) (UC-45F)	43-35764		Front fuselage only.	RAD
☐ Douglas DC-3A-456 Skytrain (C-47A)	N89HA	19603	43-15137, NC36699, VP-GAG, 8R-GAG, N9060Y – front fuselage only.	RA
☐ Fairchild M-62A-4 Cornell (PT-26A) (Cornell II)	14528		42-71104, FT689 – fuselage only.	RA
☐ North American NA-88 Texan (AT-6D) (SNJ-5)	Bu84947	88-16868	42-85087 – fuselage and other parts.	RA
☐ Pratt-Read PR-G1 (LNE-1) (TG-32)	43-39557		Bu31556 – front fuselage only.	RAD
☐ Waco NEU (CG-15A)			Partial fuselage frame.	RAD
☐ Waco NZR Hadrian (CG-4A)			Partial fuselage frame.	RAD

UNITED STATES ARMY ORDNANCE MUSEUM (MD23)

Address:	ATSLA-M, Aberdeen Proving Grounds, Maryland 21005-5201.
Tel:	410-278-3602 **Email:** museum@ocs.apg.army.mil
Admission:	Daily 1000-1645.
Location:	Just south of Aberdeen off Route 22.

The site has been used for many years for the testing of weapons. The United States Army Ordnance Museum is located on the base and exhibits a remarkable collection of vehicles and missiles. Inside the museum building displays tracing the work of Aberdeen and the development of weaponry can be seen. On show are many photographs, components and models along with documents.
The Phantom is preserved in front of the Air Force Training School. The type has been flown from the airfield on armaments trials.

TYPE	REG/SER	CON. NO.	PI/NOTES	STATUS
☐ Fieseler Fi 103A-1				PV
☐ Henschel Hs 293A-1				PV
☐ McDonnell M.98EN Phantom II (F-4D)	66-7455	1957		RA

341

UNITED STATES NAVAL ACADEMY MUSEUM (MD24)

Address:	118 Maryland Avenue, Annapolis, Maryland 21402-5034.
Tel:	410-293-2108 Fax: 410-293-5220 Email: jsharmon@usna.edu
Admission:	Monday-Saturday 0900-1700. Sunday 1100-1700.
Location:	In the eastern suburbs of the town which is about 30 miles east of Washington, DC.

Established in 1845, the Naval Academy Lyceum began collecting historic objects, scientific models and works of art for study and discussion. Over the years flags, war trophies and other objects were included. In 1939 the present purpose-built museum opened and an extension was added in 1962.

Highlights of the exhibition include the Rogers Ship Collection with over 150 models of sailing ships from the period 1650 to 1850, the Malcolm Storer Naval Medal Collection, the Beverley Robinson Collection of Naval Prints which depict major battles from the 16th century to 1873 and the US Navy Trophy Flag Collection.

For many years a Naval Aircraft Factory N3N-3 was suspended in the museum building. This was reclaimed by the National Air and Space Museum and can now be seen in the Udvar-Hazy Center.

The museum closed for a period and has now reopened with many new displays including the replica Wright B. The Hornet arrived at the site in the spring of 2009.

TYPE	REG/SER	CON. NO.	PI/NOTES	STATUS
☐ Douglas A-4A Skyhawk (A4D-1)	'2176'	11333	Bu139968 –	PVX
☐ McDonnell M.98AM Phantom II (F4H-1F) (F-4A)	'4783'	47	Bu148275 –	PVX
☐ McDonnell M.267 Hornet (F/A-18A)	Bu161983	205/A165		PV
☐ Wright B-1 (R)				PV

MASSACHUSETTS

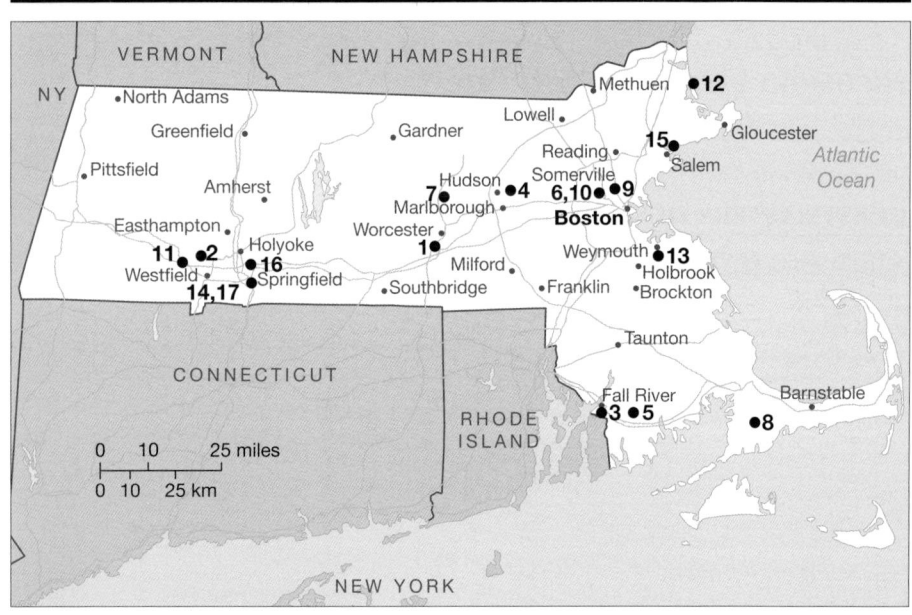

AUBURN MONUMENT (MA1)

Location:	On permanent view at VVA 554 in the eastern part of the town.

TYPE	REG/SER	CON. NO.	PI/NOTES	STATUS
Bell 209 Huey Cobra (AH-1G) (AH-1S)	70-16096	21040		PV

BARNES AIR NATIONAL GUARD BASE (MA2)

Address:	104FW/PA,175 Falcon Drive, Barnes ANG Base, Massachusetts 01085-1482.
Tel:	413-568-9151 Email: pa.104fw@mabarn.ang.mil
Admission:	By prior permission only.
Location:	About 4 miles north of Westfield off Route 10.

In 1947 the 131st. Squadron moved into Barnes Field and since then has flown mainly fighters. The F-100D was operated from 1971 to 1979. A-10s were used from 1979 to 1993 and one was put on display in the late 1990s. This aircraft has been painted to represent one lost in a mid-air collision in 1986.

Massachusetts

TYPE	REG/SER	CON. NO.	P/NOTES	STATUS
☐ Fairchild-Republic A-10A Thunderbolt II	'78-0648'	A10-364	79-0100	RAX
☐ Lockheed 580 (T-33A)	'29681'	580-7959	52-9734	RAX
☐ McDonnell M.199-1A Eagle (F-15A)	77-0104	388/A316		RA
☐ North American NA-203 Sabre (F-86H)	'22042'	203-11	53-1239	RAX
☐ North American NA-235 Super Sabre (F-100D)	'56-3025'	235-106	56-3008	RAX
☐ Republic F-84F Thunderstreak	'19480'		52-6458	RAX

BATTLESHIP COVE (MA3)

Address: 5 Water Street, Fall River, Massachusetts 02721-1540.
Tel: 508-678-1100   **Fax:** 508-674-5597   **Email:** battleship@battleshipcove.org
Admission: June–September daily 0900-1900; October–May daily 0900-1700.
Location: Just north of the bridge on Interstate 195 where it crosses the Taunton River

The USS *Massachusetts* was completed in 1942 at Quincy and served with distinction in 35 major engagements. The *Massachusetts* was the first and last American battleship to fire her large 16-inch guns in World War II. The ship made her final voyage in June 1965 when she docked at Fall River to serve as a memorial to those killed in World War II.

Also on show are the destroyer *Joseph P. Kennedy Junior* and the submarine *Lionfish* along with a patrol boat. Nearby in the complex are the Old Colony Railroad Museum and the Marine Museum, which traces the development of ships from the 1800s to 1930

TYPE	REG/SER	CON. NO.	P/NOTES	STATUS
☐ Bell 204 Iroquois (UH-1C) (UH-1M)	66-0609	1591		PV
☐ Bell 209 Huey Cobra (AH-1G) (AH-1S)	70-16038	20982		PV
☐ Gyrodyne QH-50C (DSN-3)				PV
☐ North American NA-226 Trojan (T-28C)	'Bu137765'	226-31	Bu140454	PVX

COLLINGS FOUNDATION (MA4)

Address: PO Box 248, River Hill Farm, Stow, Massachusetts 01775-1529.
Tel: 978-562-9182   **Fax:** 978-568-8231   **Email:** info@collingsfoundation.org
Admission: By prior permission only.
Location: About 25 miles west of Boston off Route 117.

The two four-engined bombers in the collection have become well known throughout the country as a result of their appearances at shows and on tour. The B-17 was acquired in the mid-1980s and restored to wartime configuration by Tom Reilly in Florida. In 1987 it was damaged at show in Pennsylvania but is now back on the circuit.

The B-24 served with the Royal Air Force and the Indian Air Force before being acquired by the late Douglas Arnold in England. Bob Collings bought the Liberator in 1984 and restoration to static condition commenced at Stow. Soon a decision was taken to rebuild the bomber to flying order. The aircraft was transported to Tom Reilly and it took to the air again in 1989 and has also been restored to its original state.

At Stow the other aircraft are housed in a purpose-built structure along with a number of superbly restored vintage cars. The automobile collection numbers over 100 and they range from 1901 until the 1950s. The early period of aviation is represented by replicas of the two Wright types, the Blériot and the Fokker Dr I.

The World War II types reside for long periods each year at New Smyrna Beach in Florida and the B-17, B-24 and P-51 and take part in the annual 'Wings of Freedom' tour which visits airfields across the country. Spectators are given the opportunity to purchase rides in the classic bombers.

The Korean War is represented by the Invader, Corsair, the AT-6 and the T-33. The A-26 is nearing the end of a long restoration.

Several aircraft in the fleet are usually based at Houston Texas. Operating in period markings they appear as a flight commemorating the Vietnam War. The Saab Viggen has recently been acquired and will initially be stored before restoration commences.

TYPE	REG/SER	CON. NO.	P/NOTES	STATUS
☐ Bell 204 Iroquois (UH-1E)	N911KK	6129	Bu153762	RAA
☐ Blériot XI (R)	N3433	3		RAA
☐ Boeing 299-O Fortress (B-17G) (TB-17G) (SB-17G)	N93012/'231909'	32216	44-83575	RAAX
☐ Boeing-Stearman A75N1 Kaydet (PT-17)	N55171	75-3745	41-25788	RAA
☐ Cessna T-50 Bobcat (C-78) (UC-78)	N6HS	3696	42-58205	RAC
☐ Consolidated 32 Liberator (B-24J) (B.VII) (GR.VI)	N224J	1347	44-44052, KH191, T18 (India)	RAA
☐ Douglas A-26B Invader	NL8036E	28975	44-35696, 435696 (France)	RAC
☐ Douglas TA-4J Skyhawk (TA-4F)	N524CF	13590	Bu153685	RAA
☐ Fieseler Fi 156C-1 Storch	NX156FC	4621		RAA
☐ Fokker Dr I (R)	N14TJ	DR1HB		RAA
☐ Grumman G-40 Avenger (TBM-3) (TBM-3E)	N9590Z	4638	Bu91733	RAC
☐ Grumman G-84 Tracker (S2F-1) (S-2A)	N31957	213	Bu133242	RAA
☐ Lockheed 580 (T-33A)	56-6914	580-1147	56-6914, '51-9128'	RA
☐ Lockheed 580 (T-33A)	N648	580-6285	51-6953, M-52 (Netherlands)	RAA
☐ McDonnell M.98EN Phantom II (F-4D)	NX749CF	1813	65-0749 – flies as '63-7680'	RAAX
☐ Messerschmitt Me 262B-1c	N262AZ	501241		RA
☐ North American NA-97 Apache (A-36A)	N4607V	97-15956	42-83738	PVC
☐ North American 103 Mustang (P-51C)	NL251MX / '2106511'	103-22730	42-103293	RAC
☐ North American NA-108 Mitchell (B-25J) (TB-25J) (TB-25N)	NL3476G /'130669'	108-32207	44-28932, N3476G	RAAX
☐ North American NA-121 Texan (AT-6F)	N4503B	121-42583	44-81861, N124Q	RAA
☐ Saab 37 Viggen (Sk 37) (SK 37J)	Fv37813	37813		RA
☐ Vought F4U-5NL Corsair	N45NL		Bu124692, 607 (Honduras)	RAA
☐ Wright 1902 Glider (R)				RA
☐ Wright EX Vin Fiz (R)	N12A	1-A-5		RA

FREETOWN MONUMENT (MA5)

Location:	On permanent view in the Memorial Park in Chace Road in the town.

TYPE	REG/SER	CON. NO.	PI/NOTES	STATUS
☐ Bell 209 Huey Cobra (AH-1S) (AH-1F)	79-23240	22285		PV

HANSCOM AIR FORCE BASE (MA6)

Location:	By prior permission only at the field which is about 17 miles north west of Boston.

TYPE	REG/SER	CON. NO.	PI/NOTES	STATUS
☐ Curtiss 87V Warhawk (P-40N) (FSM)	'114534'			RAX
☐ McDonnell M.199-1A Eagle (F-15A)	77-0100	383/A312		RA
☐ North American NA-203 Sabre (F-86H)	'53-1328'	203-125	53-1353, '15085'	RAX

LEOMINSTER MONUMENT (MA7)

Location:	On permanent view at a business in the town.

TYPE	REG/SER	CON. NO.	PI/NOTES	STATUS
☐ Republic RC-3 Seabee	N6534K	800	NC6534K	PV

MASSACHUSETTS AIR NATIONAL GUARD MUSEUM (MA8)

Address:	Otis Air National Guard Base, Massachusetts 02542-5001.
Tel:	508-968-4667
Admission:	Saturday 1000-1600; Sunday 1000-1400.
Location:	About 7 miles north east of Falmouth.

The 101st was the fifth National Guard Observation Squadron to be established. From 1921 until 1968, apart from during World War II, the unit was based at Boston.
A move was then made to the former Otis Air Force Base where a museum tracing the history of the site and the Massachusetts ANG units has been set up. Examples of types flown have been acquired and restored. The Albatross is parked in the Coast Guard area.
The future of this station is currently under discussion and it may be closed in the next few years.

TYPE	REG/SER	CON. NO.	PI/NOTES	STATUS
☐ Grumman G-234 Albatross (G-64) (SA-16A) (UF-1G) (UF-2G) (HU-16E)	7250	G-340	51-7250	PV
☐ Lockheed 580 (T-33A)	51-4335	580-5630		PV
☐ Lockheed 580 (T-33A)	53-5960	580-9436		PV
☐ McDonnell M.199-1A Eagle (F-15A)	76-0040	222/A192		PV
☐ North American NA-203 Sabre (F-86H)	53-1235	203-7		PV
☐ North American NA-235 Super Sabre (F-100D)	56-2928	235-26		PV
☐ Republic F-84F Thunderstreak	52-6382			PV

MUSEUM OF SCIENCE (MA9)

Address:	Science Park, Boston Massachusetts 02114-1099.
Tel:	617-723-5000 **Fax:** 617-589-0454 **Email** :information@mos.org
Admission:	Daily 0900-1700 (Closes at 2100 on Friday)
Location:	In the north western part of the city.

The museum has many 'hands-on' exhibits and the displays change at regular intervals. Two man-powered aircraft built by the local Massachusetts Institute of Technology are suspended in the foyer of the main building. The Monarch was a contender for the Kremer Prize in 1984 and the Daedulus flew for 72 miles between two Greek Islands.

TYPE	REG/SER	CON. NO.	PI/NOTES	STATUS
☐ Massachusetts Institute of Technology Daedulus				PV
☐ Massachusetts Institute of Technology Monarch				PV

NATIONAL AVIATION ACADEMY – NEW ENGLAND (MA10)

Address:	150 Hanscom Drive, Bedford, Massachusetts 01730.
Tel:	781-274-8448 **Fax:** 781-274-8490 **Email:** admissions@naa.edu
Admission:	By prior permission only.
Location:	At at the field which is about 17 miles north west of Boston.

The school which is also known as the East Coast Aero Tech was set up in 1932 and later became part of the NAA. The site on the civil side of Hanscom Air Force Base incorporates workshops and laboratories. The varied fleet of instructional aircraft is used to train both airframe and engine fitters.

TYPE	REG/SER	CON. NO.	PI/NOTES	STATUS
☐ Aero Commander 680V	N200TB	1708-83	N4603E, N500HY, (C-GFAC)	RA
☐ Bell 205 Iroquois (UH-1H)	N401AR	12555	70-16250	RA
☐ Cessna 150G	N461SL	15066673	N2377S	RA
☐ Cessna 172G	N1300F	17254795		RA
☐ Cessna 337M Super Skymaster (O-2A)	N4101P	337M0233	68-10768	RA
☐ Hughes 269A Osage (TH-55A)	67-15422	0766		RA

Massachusetts

☐ North American NA-276 Sabreliner (T-39A) (CT-39A)	N15EC	276-22	62-4469	RA
☐ North American NA-276 Sabreliner (T-39A) (CT-39A)	62-4497	276-50		RA
☐ Piper PA-22-150 Caribbean	N3614Z	22-7504		RA
☐ Piper PA-23 Apache	N747EB	23-286		RA
☐ Piper PA-28-140 Cherokee F	N56057	28-7325564		RA
☐ Robinson R-22	N8512K	0417		RA
☐ Stolp SA.300 Starduster Too	N699AA	2144		RA

PIONEER VALLEY MILITARY AND TRANSPORTATION MUSEUM (MA11)

Address: 20 Airport Road, PO Box 1332, Westfield, Massachusetts 01086-1332.
Tel: 413-562-1813   **Email:** info@pvmtm.org
Admission: By prior permission only.
Location: At Barnes Municipal Airport which is about 4 miles north of the town off Route 10.

The group is planning to build a museum on land at the airport. They have already acquired two aircraft and a number of vehicles. The Provost has been advertised for sale and little progress has been made on the site.

TYPE	REG/SER	CON. NO.	PI/NOTES	STATUS
☐ Fairchild M-62C Cornell (PT-23)	N73HA	331HO	42-49307, N60324 –on loan	RAA
☐ Percival P.56 Provost T.1	WV495	P.56/058	WV495, 7697M	RAC

PLUM ISLAND AVIATION MUSEUM (MA12)

Address: Plum Island Airport, Newburyport, Massachusetts 01950.
Tel: 978-463-4222
Admission: When the airfield is open.
Location: About 5 miles east of Newburyport.

The exhibition opened on 1st June 2002 and the first area was devoted to local pioneer W. Starling Burgess who was born in 1878 and died in 1949. In addition to his aviation career he was also a successful racing yacht designer. He established a workshop in Marblehead and aircraft on Plum Island marshes close to the current airfield. In 1915 he was awarded the Collier Trophy for his achievements with the Burgess-Dunne hydroplanes.

SHEA FIELD MEMORIAL GROVE AND NAVAL AVIATION HISTORICAL MUSEUM (MA13)

Address: 495 Shea Memorial Drive, South Weymouth, Massachusetts 02190-5000.
Tel: 781-682-2189   **Email:** inquiries@anapatriotsquadron.com
Admission: By prior permission only.
Location: Just south of the town on Route 18.

Reserve squadrons of both the Navy and Marine Corps flew from the site until it closed in 1997. The airfield was named after Lieutenant Commander John J. Shea. The Skyhawk was flown from the field for many years and the preserved example is still present. There are plans to construct a museum building to house the aircraft.

TYPE	REG/SER	CON. NO.	PI/NOTES	STATUS
☐ Douglas A-4B Skyhawk (A4D-2)	Bu142940	12002		PV

SPRINGFIELD SCIENCE MUSEUM (MA14)

Address: 21 Edwards Street,, Springfield, Massachusetts 01103.
Tel: 413-263-8000   **Email:** info@springfieldmuseums.org
Admission: Tuesday-Saturday 1000-1700; Sunday 1100-1700.
Location: In the city centre.

Four museums surround the quadrangle in the city. Two are devoted to art, one to local history and the fourth is the Science Museum where the story of local aviation history is portrayed. On show is the Zeta designed by Howell W. Miller who was also responsible for the Gee Bee R-1 and R-2 racers. The Zeta was placed in store in 1940 and donated to the museum in 1978. There is a section devoted to the work of the Granville Brothers.

TYPE	REG/SER	CON. NO.	PI/NOTES	STATUS
☐ Miller Zeta	NX1331	1		PV
☐ Ultralight Flight Mirage				PV

VIETNAM MEMORIAL MUSEUM (MA15)

Address: 46 L.P. Henderson Road, Beverly, Massachusetts 01915.
Admission: Helicopter on permanent view.
Location: At Beverly Airport which is about 18 miles north east of Boston off Route 1A.

The Iroquois was mounted at the airport in the to honour the local residents who lost their lives in the conflict. The memorial was dedicated on 21st June 1997. Funds are being raised to construct a building at the airport.

TYPE	REG/SER	CON. NO.	PI/NOTES	STATUS
☐ Bell 204 Iroquois (UH-1C) (UH-1M)	65-9560	1460		PV

WESTOVER AIR RESERVE BASE (MA16)

Location:	By prior permission only at the field which is about 8 miles north of Springfield.

TYPE	REG/SER	CON. NO.	PI/NOTES	STATUS
☐ Hughes 369M Cayuse (HO-6) (OH-6A)	69-16028	1398		RA

WILLIAM C. SULLIVAN VISITOR INFORMATION CENTER (MA17)

Address:	1200 West Columbus Avenue, Springfield, Massachusetts 01105.
Tel:	413-750-2980
Admission:	Daily 0800-1800.
Location:	In the town.

This local tourist centre has put on display a replica of a Granville brothers racer. The type was built in the town. The R-1 was designed for pylon racing and. Jimmy Doolittle won the 1932 Thompson Trophy in the aircraft. There is a small display highlighting their work and aviation achievements.

TYPE	REG/SER	CON. NO.	PI/NOTES	STATUS
☐ Granville Gee Bee R-1 (FSM)	'NR2100'			PVX

MICHIGAN

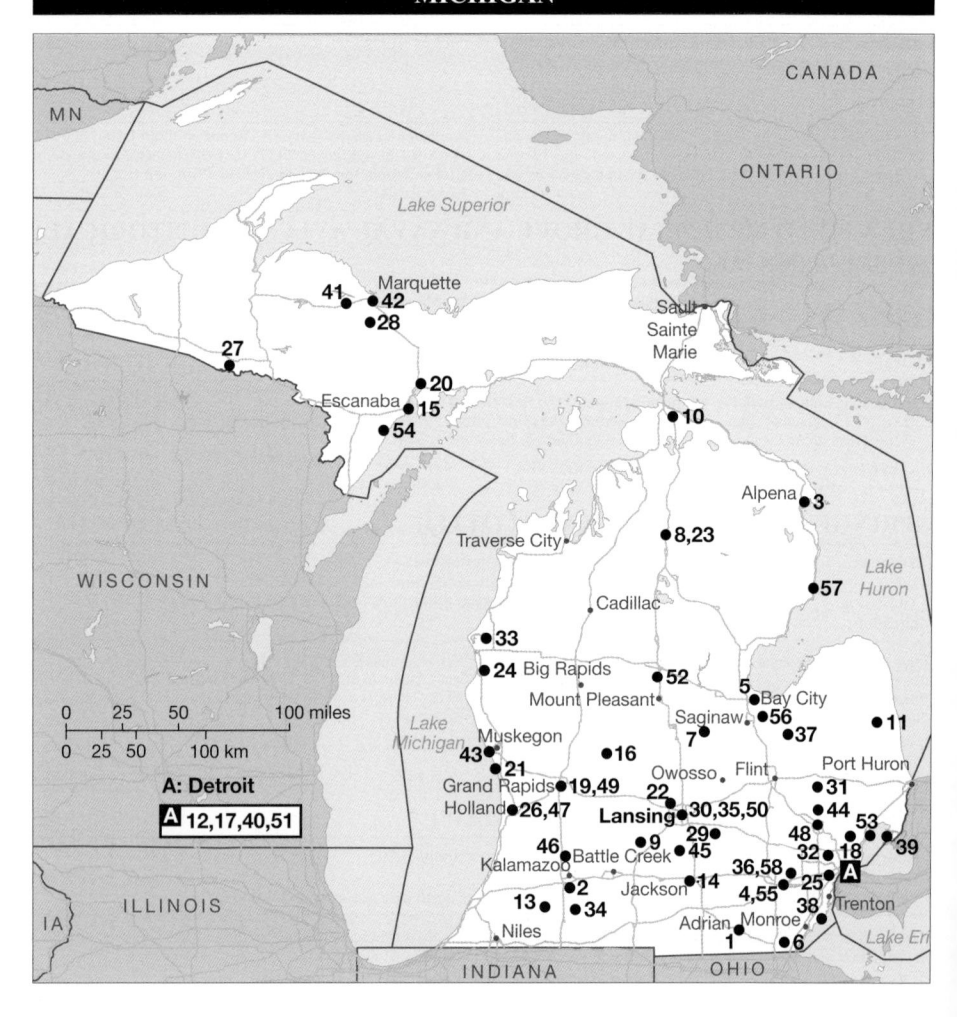

Michigan

ADRIAN MONUMENT (MI1)

| Location: | On permanent view at VFW 1584 at 726 North Main Street in the town. |

TYPE	REG/SER	CON. NO.	PI/NOTES	STATUS
☐ Bell 205 Iroquois (UH-1H)	66-17031	9225		PV

AIR ZOO (MI2)

Address:	6151 Portage Road, Kalamazoo, Michigan 49002-1700.
Tel:	269-382-6555 Fax: 269-382-1813 Email: bellis@airzoo.org
Admission:	Normally Monday-Saturday 0900-1700 Sunday 1200-1700; currently closed for rebuilding.
Location:	At the south east corner of Kalamazoo Municipal Airport which is about 3 miles south of the town.

This excellent museum opened in 1979 and has grown into one of the most impressive displays of warbirds in the country. The original hangar has been extended and improved and another constructed. Nearby is a restoration hangar where several more aircraft can be seen.

The collection of World War II World War II fighters include a P-47 in the markings of Colonel Francis Gabreski's machine, Sue Parish's P-40 painted in desert colours, a P-39 which once raced at Reno and a Hispano HA-1112 in a purple Spanish Air Force scheme. A range of light aircraft have also been acquired and several of these can be seen.

Informative displays have been set up in the main building including the Guadalcanal Memorial Museum which highlights the bitter campaign fought in 1942 when US forces made the first offensive move against the Japanese. A Douglas Dauntless has been restored for this display. This type was one of the first to land on Guadalcanal when the Americans captured the island. For many years there were four classic Grumman fighters in airworthy condition. The Wildcat, Hellcat, Tigercat and Bearcat all won awards including Grand Champion at Oshkosh. Two of these have now been sold to other collections.

Only three Curtiss-Wright XP-55 Ascenders were built along with a lightweight flying mock-up. The design featuring swept wings and an Allison engine driving a pusher propeller first flew from Scott Field in July 1943. The second example survived and spent many years in store at Silver Hill. A team from the museum has painstakingly restored it to original condition.

The museum owns one of the few surviving Ford Tri-Motors. This aircraft was built in 1929 and served with the Ford Motor Company for six years. From 1936 until 1945 it flew in Alaska. The airliner crashed in April 1959 at Moose Creek in Idaho and the airframe remained there for over two decades before it was lifted out by helicopter. The rebuild started soon after and it took to the air again in August 1991.

An excellent collection of engines is in the building and a series of interactive displays have been staged. Jet fighters from the late 1940s also feature prominently in the exhibition. The P-80, F-84 and F-86 all flew in large numbers with the Air Force in from the late 1940s up to the early 1970s.

A range of training aircraft is on show. The Timm N2T Tutor first flew in 1940 and 262 were ordered by the Navy for basic training. Two are preserved in museums and several more are on the US Civil register although few are airworthy. Replicas of a number of types have been acquired. The SPAD VII achieved fame during World War I.

The Travel Air R achieved fame in races in the late 1920s and early 1930s. The prototype of the low wing monoplane was built in great secrecy at Wichita before appearing at the 1929 Cleveland Races. Five were completed and two survive in museums.

The museum is also home to the Michigan Aviation Hall of Fame which was established in 1997 to honour those who had made significant contributions in the state. A number of interactive simulated attractions have been constructed mainly for children.

TYPE	REG/SER	CON. NO.	PI/NOTES	STATUS
☐ Aeronca 65CA Super Chief	N31948	CA-12231	NC31948	PVA
☐ Aeronca 65TC Grasshopper (O-58B) (L-3B)	N47139	9093	43-26772	PVA
☐ Balkema 2/3 Jenny	N2293Y	001		PV
☐ Beech A45 Mentor (T-34A)	N777SU	G-18	52-7637	PV
☐ Beech D45 Mentor (T-34B)	Bu140768	BG-102		S
☐ Beech 95-B55 Baron	N448SP	TC-768		PV
☐ Bell 26E Airacobra (P-39Q) (RP-39Q) (TP-39Q)	'BW146'		44-3908, NX4829N, N4829N, NX40A	PVAX
☐ Bell 209 Sea Cobra (AH-1J)	Bu159211	26051		PV
☐ Boeing 727-25QC	N119FE	19301	N8154G	PV
☐ Boeing-Stearman E75 Kaydet (PT-13D)	N2PP	75-5736	42-17573, N1733B, N244E	PVAX
☐ Cessna 305A Bird Dog (L-19A) (O-1A)	53-8029	23450	53-8029, N2FR –	PV
☐ Christen Eagle II	N960RF	FOXWORTHY0001		PV
☐ Convair 8-10 Delta Dagger (F-102A)	56-1008	8-10-225	Front fuselage only.	PV
☐ Curtiss 87V Warhawk (P-40N)	NL222SU	33359	44-7619, N5038V, N1251N	PVX
☐ Curtiss-Wright CW-24 Ascender (XP-55)	42-78846	P.02	On loan from NASM, DC.	PV
☐ Douglas DC-3A-456 Skytrain (C-47A)	'N90803'	13050	42-93168, NC41398, XB-JIN, XC-BIN, N90830	PVAX
☐ Douglas SBD-3 Dauntless	Bu06624	1439		PV
☐ Douglas A-1D Skyraider (AD-4N) (AD-4NA)	NX92034	7903	Bu127888, 65 (France), NL92034	PVAX
☐ Douglas A-4B Skyhawk (A4D-2)	N21NB	12257	Bu145011 – in false Australian markings – flies as '011'	PVX
☐ Fairchild M-62C Cornell (PT-23)	N52020	291HO	42-49268	PV
☐ Fokker Dr I (R)	N4435C	1		PVX
☐ Ford 5-AT-C	N8419	5-AT-58	NC8419	PVA
☐ Ford JB-2 [Fieseler Fi 103A-1]			Composite.	PV
☐ Francis-Angell A-15 Special	NX84Y	1		PV
☐ Gates Learjet 23	N824LJ	23-083		PV
☐ Grumman G-36 Wildcat (FM-2)	NL1PP	5635	Bu86581, N86581	PVAX
☐ Grumman G-50 Hellcat (F6F-5)	NX4PP	A-10828	Bu79683, N7896C	PVA
☐ Grumman G-73 Mallard	N2954	J14	NC2954	PV
☐ Grumman G-98 Tiger (F11F-1) (F-11A)	Bu141872	189	On loan from MCAGM, VA.	PV
☐ Grumman G-105 Cougar (F9F-8T) (TF-9J)	Bu147283	253		PV
☐ Grumman G-134 Mohawk (OV-1D)	N121AZ	4D	68-16993, 056 (Israel), 4X-JRB	PVA
☐ Grumman G-303 Tomcat (F-14A)	Bu160395	251		PV

☐ Haigh SuperStar	N8HH	12		PV
☐ Heath Parasol				PVC
☐ Hiller UH12A Raven (H-23A)	N4254A	229	51-4007	PV
☐ Hiller UH12B Raven (H-23B) (OH-23B)	51-16225	407		PV
☐ Hispano HA-1112M1L [Messerschmitt Bf 109G]	'C.4K-19'	171	C4K-100, G-AWHJ, N90605, N76GE	PVAX
☐ Howard DGA-15P	'Bu32347'	1713	N67771 – painted as a GH-2	PVX
☐ Karp Pusher 107	N37864	LK475		PV
☐ Laister-Kauffman LK.10B (TG-4A)	N58189	92	(USAAF)	PV
☐ Leak Avid Flyer	N2LF	740		PV
☐ Lockheed 080 Shooting Star (P-80A) (F-80A)	'44-85152'	080-1148	44-85125	PVX
☐ Lockheed 383-04-05 Starfighter (F-104C)	'86800'	183-1186	56-0898	PVX
☐ Lockheed 394 Viking (S-3A) (S-3B)	Bu160123	394A-3105		PV
☐ Lockheed 580 (T-33A) (TV-2) (T-33B)	'31544'	580-9035	53-5696, Bu138090	PVX
☐ Lockheed SR-71B Blackbird	61-7956	2007	61-7956, NASA 831	PV
☐ Long Henderson Longster (R)	N99492	110CB		RA
☐ Martin 272B Canberra (B-57B)	52-1584	174		PV
☐ McDonnell M.98HO Phantom II (F-4E)	74-0658	4809		PV
☐ McDonnell M.267 Hornet (F/A-18A)	Bu161984	207/A167		PV
☐ Mikoyan-Gurevich MiG-21PFM	4107	94A4107	In Polish markings.	RA
☐ Mitchell P-38	'16'			PVX
☐ Montgolfier Balloon (R)	N8985Z	B-07		PV
☐ Murphy Renegade Spirit	N366WS	366		PV
☐ Naval Aircraft Factory N3N-3	Bu2951		Bu2951, N9308Z –	PV
☐ North American NA-98 Mitchell (B-25H) (TB-25H) (RB-25H)	N37L	98-21900	43-4899, N66572, N1582V	PVA
☐ North American NA-121 Texan (AT-6D) (SNJ-5)	N333SU	121-41941	44-81219, Bu91005, N1131U, N7806B N66EG, N141SP	PVAX
☐ North American NA-168 Texan (T-6G)	'112493'	168-653	49-3509, N7057	PVAX
☐ North American NA-191 Sabre (F-86F)	'12852'	191-839	52-5143, N25143	PVX
☐ North American NA-260 Nomad (NA-174 Trojan (T-28A))	N100JE	174-553	51-7700, N8088H	PVA
☐ Pereira GP.2 Osprey I	N2RC	51		PV
☐ Piasecki PV-18 Retriever (H-25A) (HUP-3) (UH-25C)	Bu147600		(US Army) -	PV
☐ Piper J-3C-65 Cub	N4491M	22611	NC4491M	PVA
☐ Piper J-3C-65 Cub (L-4H)	N9245H	12113	44-79817	PV
☐ Republic P-47D Thunderbolt	'226418'	399-55720	45-49181, 539 (Peru), 115 (Peru) N47DC, N159LF, NX444SU	PVAX
☐ Republic F-84F Thunderstreak	'52-6368'		52-6486, N5046, '52-6422'	PVX
☐ Rotorway Executive 90	N4307L	81360		PVA
☐ Ryan ST-3KR Recruit (PT-22)	N5481L	1861	41-20652, N54811	PVA
☐ Schweizer SGS.2-8 (LNS-1)	Bu04383	5		PV
☐ Sikorsky S-65A Sea Stallion (CH-53A)			Front fuselage only.	PV
☐ SPAD VII (R)	N9104A	C-7		PV
☐ Sopwith F.1 Camel (R)	N6313	B-6313		PV
☐ Timm PT.175K Tutor (N2T-1)	Bu32422	360	Bu32622, N66750 –	PV
☐ Travel Air R (R)	'NR1313'			PVX
☐ Vought FG-1D Corsair	NX3PP	3770	Bu92509, N9150Z, N92509, N9PP	PVAX
☐ Vought F-8J Crusader (F8U-2NE) (F-8E)	'Bu150908'	254E	Bu150904	PVX
☐ Vultee V-74 Valiant (BT-13A) (SNV-1)	'11676'	74-3183	41-10866, Bu03022 –	PVX
☐ Waco INF	NC644Y	3382	NC644Y, N644Y – on loan.	PVA
☐ Waco NZR Hadrian (CG-4A)	'42-46574'		45-15965	PVCX
☐ Waco VPF-7	NC74835	4655	NC74835, N74835	PV
☐ War Aircraft F4U Corsair	'812'			PV
☐ Wolf W-II Boredom Fighter	N90553	1		PV
☐ Wright Flyer (R)				PV
☐ WSK Lim-2 [MiG-15bis]	'1621'	1B 016-21	1621 (Poland), N621BM – in false Chinese markings.	PVX
☐ Zenair CH-150	N101LK	736		PV

ALPENA COMBAT READINESS TRAINING CENTER COLLECTION (MI3)

Address:	5884 A Street, Alpena, Michigan 49707-8128.
Tel:	989-356-6284
Admission:	By prior permission only.
Location:	About 5 miles west of the town on Route 321.

Three instructional aircraft are in use at this facility which trains troops in a number of skills to ensure they are ready for fighting duties. Subject to security requirements tours of the site can be arranged locally. The long established airfield formerly housed units of the Michigan Air National Guard and serves as the county airport.

TYPE	REG/SER	CON. NO.	PI/NOTES	STATUS
☐ Bell 205 Iroquois (UH-1H)	68-16088	10747		RA
☐ General Dynamics 401 Fighting Falcon (F-16A)	79-0387	61-172		RA
☐ Lockheed 382-4B Hercules (C-130E)	62-1798	382-3752		RA

ANN ARBOR MONUMENT (MI4)

Location:	On permanent view at VFW 423 at 3230 South Wagner Road in the south western part of the city.

TYPE	REG/SER	CON. NO.	PI/NOTES	STATUS
☐ Bell 205 Iroquois (UH-1H)	68-15275	10205		PV

Michigan

BAY CITY MONUMENT (MI5)

Location:	On permanent view in a park in the western part of the town.

TYPE	REG/SER	CON. NO.	PI/NOTES	STATUS
☐ Bell 205 Iroquois (UH-1H)	70-16358	12663		PV

BLISSFIELD MONUMENT (MI6)

Location:	On permanent view at ALP 325 on Route 223 in the western part of the town.

TYPE	REG/SER	CON. NO.	PI/NOTES	STATUS
☐ Republic F-105G Thunderchief (F-105F)	62-4425	F-14		PV

BRECKENRIDGE MONUMENT (MI7)

Location:	On permanent view at ALP 295 which is in the centre of the town on Route 46.

TYPE	REG/SER	CON. NO.	PI/NOTES	STATUS
☐ Lockheed 580 (T-33A)	51-4067	580-5361		PV

CAMP GRAYLING MILITARY RESERVATION MONUMENT (MI8)

Location:	On permanent view at the gate to the west of Grayling.

TYPE	REG/SER	CON. NO.	PI/NOTES	STATUS
☐ Bell 204 Iroquois (HU-1B) (UH-1B)			Composite.	PVX

CHARLOTTE MONUMENT (MI9)

Location:	On permanent view at ALP 42 at 1000 West Lawrence Highway in the north western part of the town.

TYPE	REG/SER	CON. NO.	PI/NOTES	STATUS
☐ Bell 209 Huey Cobra (AH-1G) (AH-1F)	67-15805	20469		PV

CHEBOYGAN MONUMENT (MI10)

Location:	On permanent view at VVA 274 at 7747 N Black River Road in the town.

TYPE	REG/SER	CON. NO.	PI/NOTES	STATUS
☐ Bell 205 Iroquois (UH-1H)	68-15586	10516		PV

CROSWELL MONUMENT (MI11)

Location:	On permanent view at ALP 255 at West Harrington Road in the north western part of the town.

TYPE	REG/SER	CON. NO.	PI/NOTES	STATUS
☐ Bell 209 Huey Cobra (AH-1G) (AH-1F)	66-15249	20005		PV

DAVIS AEROSPACE TECHNICAL HIGH SCHOOL (MI12)

Address:	10200 Erwin Street, Detroit, Michigan 48234
Tel:	313-866-5401 Fax: 313-866-5408 Email: davisaerospace@yahoo.com
Admission:	By prior permission only.
Location:	Adjacent to Detroit City Airport which is about 2 miles north east of the city centre.

The school was set up in 1941 as an emergency training unit to help fill the needs of the military. In 1943 it became part of the Detroit Public Schools with the name Aero Mechanics Vocational High School.

In 1982 the school was renamed after Benjamin O. Davis Jr, who was commander of the Tuskegee Airmen and rose to the rank of General. Airframe and engine fitters are trained in the well equipped workshops and classrooms.

TYPE	REG/SER	CON. NO.	PI/NOTES	STATUS
☐ Cessna 150J	N51165	15069808		RA
☐ Cessna 150L	N6892G	15072392		RA
☐ Cessna 172M	N20189	17261081		
☐ Cessna 172R	N2083F	17280671		RA
☐ Cessna 190	N4330N	7079		RA
☐ Hiller UH12B	N539DC	539		RA
☐ North American NA-276 Sabreliner (T-39A) (CT-39A)	62-4466	276-19		RA

DECATUR MONUMENT (MI13)

Location:	On permanent view at VFW 6248 at 560 North Phelps Street in the north western part of the town.

TYPE	REG/SER	CON. NO.	PI/NOTES	STATUS
☐ Bell 209 Huey Cobra (AH-1G) (AH-1F)	'15686'	20798	68-17070	PVX

On show at the Massachusetts Air National Guard Museum is this Republic F-84F Thunderstreak. [MA8]

The unique Baumann RB-1 Racer is on show at the Henry Ford Museum. (Nigel Hitchman) [MI25]

This Convair F-106A Delta Dart, painted in false markings, is at the Selfridge Military Air Museum. (Nigel Bailey-Underwood) [MI53]

EAGLE AIRCRAFT MUSEUM (MI14)

Address:	3600 Wildwood Avenue, Jackson, Michigan 49202-1811.
Tel:	517-783-3988 Email: earub@modempool.net
Admission:	Most mornings.
Location:	At Jackson Municipal Airport which is in the western suburbs of the town.

The local chapter (Number 304) of the Experimental Aircraft Association has set up a museum in its hangar. On show are components, models, photographs and memorabilia. The Pazmany was constructed by a member and is mounted outside the building. The group has restored three aircraft for the EAA Museum at Oshkosh.

TYPE	REG/SER	CON. NO.	PI/NOTES	STATUS
☐ Bellanca 14-19-2 Cruisemaster	N7662B	4013		PVA
☐ Lockheed 580 (T-33A)	58-0509	580-1478	58-0509, N57969, N333JX	PV
☐ Pazmany PL-4	N68068	RD-3		PV
☐ Piper PA-22-150 Tripacer	N2748P	22-3055		PVC

ESCANABA MONUMENT (MI15)

Location:	On permanent view at Delta County Airport which is about 3 miles south west of the town.

TYPE	REG/SER	CON. NO.	PI/NOTES	STATUS
☐ Republic F-84F Thunderstreak	'01748'		51-1713	PVX

FIGHTING FALCON MILITARY MUSEUM (MI16)

Address:	515 West Cass Street, Greenville, Michigan 48838.
Tel:	616-754-4838
Admission:	Sunday 1400-1600
Location:	About 20 miles north east of Grand Rapids.

The museum commemorates the many Greenville residents who have fought in conflicts worldwide. The organisation was set up in 2000 and obtained the building the following November. On show are many artefacts, uniforms and weapons. One side of the restored Waco Hadrian glider fuselage has been covered and painted and the other left bare so that the construction can be seen. Plans to construct the other airframe parts have been put forward. There is a large photograph of the Hadrian production line at one end of the exhibition hall. Local companies who contributed to the war effort are featured in the display.

TYPE	REG/SER	CON. NO.	PI/NOTES	STATUS
☐ Waco NZR Hadrian (CG-4A)			Fuselage only.	PV

FRASER MONUMENT (MI17)

Location:	On permanent view at VFW 6691 at 17075 Avenue in the south eastern part of the town.

TYPE	REG/SER	CON. NO.	PI/NOTES	STATUS
☐ Bell 205 Iroquois (UH-1D) (UH-1H)	66-0796	5279		PV

FREEDOM HILL MEMORIAL PARK (MI18)

Address:	15000 Metropolitan, Parkway Sterling Heights, Michigan 48311-0075
Tel:	586-979-7010 Fax: 586-573-2245 Email: FreedomHill@macombcountymi.gov
Admission:	On permanent view.
Location:	On Metro Parkway in the eastern suburbs of the town.

Two aircraft and a number of military vehicles are on show in this municipal park. Just 27 HH-1Ks were built for rescue work and the example on show has been painted to represent a UH-1H flown in Vietnam.

The site is dedicated to all Americans who have served their country in both peace and war. The large area is also home to many recreational facilities including a vast outdoor amphitheatre where concerts are held.

TYPE	REG/SER	CON. NO.	PI/NOTES	STATUS
☐ Bell 204 Iroquois (HH-1K)		6321	Bu157197	PVX
☐ McDonnell M.98EN Phantom II (F-4D)	66-8755	2588		PV

GERALD R. FORD PRESIDENTIAL MUSEUM AND LIBRARY (MI19)

Address:	303 Pearl Street North West, Grand Rapids, Michigan 49504-5353.
Tel:	616-254-0400 Fax: 616-254-0386 Email: ford.museum@nara.gov
Admission:	Daily 0900-1700.
Location:	Just west of the town centre.

Gerald Ford was President from 1974 to 1977 and this museum, tracing aspects of the history of the United States since World War II, opened in September 1981. The period when he ran the country is portrayed in detail with many photographs and documents to be seen. The history of his family is traced in the displays. The library containing many of his personal papers is housed in the Ann Arbor campus of the University of Michigan.

TYPE	REG/SER	CON. NO.	PI/NOTES	STATUS
☐ Bell 205 Iroquois (UH-1H)	67-17153	9351		PV

GLADSTONE MONUMENT (MI20)

Location:	On permanent view in a park in the town.

TYPE	REG/SER	CON. NO.	PI/NOTES	STATUS
☐ Douglas TA-4J Skyhawk	Bu158479	14284		PV

GRAND HAVEN MONUMENT (MI21)

Location:	On permanent view at the airport which is about 2 miles south east of the town.

TYPE	REG/SER	CON. NO.	PI/NOTES	STATUS
☐ North American NA-192 Super Sabre (F-100A)	'22576'	192-7	52-5762	PVX

GRAND LEDGE ARMY NATIONAL GUARD BASE (MI22)

Address:	10600 West Eaton Highway, Grand Ledge, Michigan 48837
Tel:	517-627-9230
Admission:	By prior permission only.
Location:	About 8 miles west of Lansing off Route 100.

This large base houses many flying units of the Michigan Army National Guard. Three helicopters have been put on display. The Hiller Raven was restored in the late 1990s and is stored in the camp. The Huey Cobra, formerly used for ground instruction duties, and the Iroquois have been mounted by the main gate.

TYPE	REG/SER	CON. NO.	PI/NOTES	STATUS
☐ Bell 205 Iroquois (UH-1D) (UH-1V)	66-16041	5735		PV
☐ Bell 209 Huey Cobra (AH-1G) (AH-1S)	67-15822	20486		PV
☐ Hiller UH12B Raven (H-23B) (OH-23B)	51-16255	447		RA

GRAYLING MONUMENT (MI23)

Location:	On permanent view at ALP 106 in the eastern part of the town.

TYPE	REG/SER	CON. NO.	PI/NOTES	STATUS
☐ Lockheed 580 (T-33A)	51-8673	580-6457		PV

HART MONUMENT (MI24)

Location:	On permanent view in the Veterans Park in State Street in the northern part of the town.

TYPE	REG/SER	CON. NO.	PI/NOTES	STATUS
☐ Lockheed 580 (T-33A)	53-5073	580-8412		PV

HENRY FORD MUSEUM AND GREENFIELD VILLAGE (MI25)

Address:	PO Box 1970, 20900 Oakwood Boulevard, Dearborn, Michigan 48124-5029.
Tel:	313-982-6001 Email: info@TheHenryFord.org
Admission:	Daily 0900-1700.
Location:	About 12 miles west of Detroit off Highway 12.

Henry Ford began collecting early American artefacts in the 1920s. His first purchase was the historic Red Horse Tavern located between Boston and Waterford. He planed to set up a museum at the site comprising of an early New England village. He sent out collectors with the brief to acquire one example of every tool, utensil and machine used in America.

He later changed his plans and decided to establish the museum at Dearborn. Work started in 1929 and the complex opened in 1933. Greenfield Village now consists of over 100 buildings many of which have been moved to the site. Included are the Wright brothers' family home and original cycle shop transported from Dayton in 1938. Demonstrations of early crafts can be seen in the period workshops.

Close by is the Henry Ford Museum, a large structure based on the Independence Hall in Philadelphia. The Ford company entered aviation in World War I producing Liberty engines. In 1923 Henry's son Edsel received a request from William Stout for funds to develop an all-metal transport. A factory and airport were built at Dearborn but the two men had a disagreement and Ford bought out Stout. The design was developed to become the famous Tri-Motor of which almost 200 were built. Two Flivver light aircraft were constructed but after the death of a friend in one in the early 1930s Ford closed his aviation factory.

The museum halls cover over 12 acres with displays illustrating all forms of transport and industry. On view are machines which made the first flights over both the North and South Poles. The Arctic aircraft is the Fokker F VII flown by Floyd Bennett on Richard Byrd's expedition which crossed the North Pole on 9th May 1926. Byrd also led the Antarctic expedition and on this the Ford Tri-Motor was flown by Berndt Balcher who made the demanding flight on 28th November 1929.

The Sikorsky VS-300 prototype, which was the first practical helicopter in the USA, made its maiden flight in 1939 and its last in 1943 when Igor Sikorsky landed on the lawn in front of the museum. The Pitcairn PCA-2 carried out over 700 flights for the Detroit News in the early 1930s. This autogyro still carries their colours.

A unique exhibit is the Baumann RB-1. This monoplane featuring a monocoque fuselage, a retractable undercarriage and an enclosed cockpit for the pilot was developed at Dayton just after World War I for the racing contests which were restarting after the end of the hostilities.

Two aircraft, a Curtiss MF Seagull and a Standard J-1 are on long-term loan to the Glenn Curtiss Museum in Hammondsport, New York State. The Junkers W 33 which made the first non-stop east-west crossing of the Atlantic in 1928 is on loan to the city of Bremen and is currently on show at the German airport. The aircraft will not return to America for many years.

Michigan

TYPE	REG/SER	CON. NO.	PI/NOTES	STATUS
☐ Baumann RB-1 Racer				PV
☐ Blériot XI	10211			PV
☐ Boeing 40B-4	NC285	896		PV
☐ Curtiss JN-4 Canuck	8428			PV
☐ Douglas DC-3-201B	N21728	2144	NC21728	PV
☐ Fokker F.VIIa/3m	267	4900	BA-1	PV
☐ Ford 1 Flivver	268			PV
☐ Ford 4-AT-B	NX4542	4-AT-15		PV
☐ Junkers W 33 b	D-1167	2504	On loan to Flughafen Bremen Ausstellung, Germany.	–
☐ Laird Biplane				PV
☐ Lockheed 1 Vega	N965Y	40	NC199E, NR199E	PVX
☐ Pitcairn PCA-2	NC799W	B-6		PV
☐ Ryan NYP (R) (B-1)	'N-X-211'	156	NC7209, N7209	PVX
☐ Sikorsky VS-300	NX28996		NX28996, N28996	PV
☐ Stinson SM-1 Detroiter	NC857	M201	NC4307, NC2931	PV
☐ Wright Flyer (R)				PV

HOLLAND CITY MONUMENT (MI26)

Location: On permanent view at the Park Township Airport which is about 5 miles north east of the town.

TYPE	REG/SER	CON. NO.	PI/NOTES	STATUS
☐ Lockheed 580 (T-33A) (TV-2) (T-33B)	N40186	580-1102	56-1752, Bu143040	PV

IRON MOUNTAIN MONUMENT (MI27)

Location: On permanent view in the town.

TYPE	REG/SER	CON. NO.	PI/NOTES	STATUS
☐ Lockheed 580 (T-33A)	53-5610	580-8949		PV

K.I. SAWYER HERITAGE AIR MUSEUM (MI28)

Address: c/o Elder Agency, 500 South Third Street, Marquette, Michigan 49855.
Tel: 906-249-9389   **Email:** kisham.curator@kishamuseum.org
Admission: On permanent view.
Location: About 20 miles south of Marquette.

The military took over the civilian field in April 1956 and named it after Kenneth I. Sawyer who put forward the original plan for a county airport. Building work started immediately and the first aircraft arrived in 1958. Fighter units were initially stationed at the field but bomber squadrons were then in residence.

The last B-52 left in November 2004 and the base closed the following June. A group has now set up the museum which has a display in the West Branch Community Center in the town.

The museum is negotiating for use of one of the hangars on the airfield so that the smaller aircraft can be protected from the harsh climate.

TYPE	REG/SER	CON. NO.	PI/NOTES	STATUS
☐ Boeing 464-201-7 Stratofortress (B-52D)	55-0062	464014		PV
☐ Cessna 318B Tweety Bird (T-37B)			Due soon.	-
☐ Convair 8-24 Delta Dart (F-106A)	'57-0231'	8-24-11	56-0461	PVX
☐ General Dynamics FB-111A	68-0239	B1-11		PV
☐ Lockheed 580 (T-33A)	51-4263	580-5558		PV
☐ McDonnell M.36BA Voodoo (F-101B)	'58-0308'	663	58-0291	PVX

LANSING COMMUNITY COLLEGE AVIATION TECHNICAL CENTER (MI29)

Address: 3428 West Hangar Drive, Lansing, Michigan 48906-2136.
Tel: 517-267-5942   **Email:** whitehh@lcc.edu
Admission: By prior permission only.
Location: At Capital Airport which is in the northern part of the town.

The college set up the aviation complex at Capital Airport in 1970. Aviation maintenance courses are run along with pilot training. The workshops house engines, components and systems to aid this work. The fleet of ground instructional airframes includes the Fairchild-Hiller FH-227B used locally by Mohawk Airlines.

TYPE	REG/SER	CON. NO.	PI/NOTES	STATUS
☐ Beech E18S	N3131W	BA-436	N10J, N540MC, N549MC	RA
☐ Bell 206A Kiowa (OH-58A) (OH-58C)	69-16275	40496		RA
☐ Cessna 150H	N22543	15068350		RA
☐ Cessna 150H	N22543	15068350		RA
☐ Cessna 172F Mescalero (T-41A)	N5198F	17253175	65-5198	RA
☐ Cessna 172F Mescalero (T-41A)	N5243F	17253328	65-5243	RA
☐ Cessna 172F Mescalero (T-41A)	N5269F	17253392	65-5269	RA
☐ Cessna 172R	N652MA	17280903		RA
☐ Cessna 310	N34TU	35351		RA
☐ Fairchild-Hiller FH-227B (FH-227)	N7806M	515		RA
☐ Hiller UH12C Raven (H-23G) (OH-23G)				RA
☐ Hiller UH12C Raven (H-23G) (OH-23G)	N15NR	1727	64-15218	RA

LANSING VETERANS MEMORIAL (MI30)

Address:	Capital City Airport, Burnham Avenue, Lansing, Illinois 60438.
Admission:	On permanent view.
Location:	In the northern suburbs of the town off Route 96.

This memorial honours Lansing citizens who have lost their lives in War. Plaques bearing their names are located around the site along with flags. The Iroquois is pole mounted in the garden area. The Huey Cobra was on show a few years ago and has been removed for either restoration or scrapping.

TYPE	REG/SER	CON. NO.	PI/NOTES	STATUS
☐ Bell 205 Iroquois (UH-1H)				PV
☐ Bell 209 Huey Cobra (AH-1G) (AH-1S)	71-21002	21073		RA

LAPEER MONUMENT (MI31)

Location:	On permanent view at VFW 4139 at 128 Daley Road in the northern part of the town.

TYPE	REG/SER	CON. NO.	PI/NOTES	STATUS
☐ Bell 205 Iroquois (UH-1D) (UH-1H)	64-13851	4558		PV

LAWRENCE TECHNOLOGICAL UNIVERSITY DISPLAY (MI32)

Address:	Buell Management Building, 2100 West Ten Mile Road, Southfield, Michigan 48075-1058.
Tel:	248-204-4000 Fax: 248-204-3099 Email: info@ltu.edu
Admission:	Monday-Friday 0700-1900; Saturday 0700-1600.
Location:	Southfield is about 15 miles north west of Detroit off Interstate 10.

This unique twin boom pusher aircraft was built as a student exercise in 1947. The airframe incorporated wood, steel tubing, sheet metal, fibreglass, aluminium and fabric to enable students to learn different construction methods. Completed in 1949, the Spirit took part in the Cleveland Races the same year. In 1953 the aircraft was bought by its designer Professor George Martin who flew it until 1957. He then sold it to Mississippi State University where it was used as an instructional airframe. Charles Stevens of Grand Rapids purchased the machine in 1971 but his plans to restore it to flying condition came to nothing and he donated it to Lawrence University in 1984. The aircraft is now on show in the management building.

TYPE	REG/SER	CON. NO.	PI/NOTES	STATUS
☐ Spirit of Lawrence Tech	N138C	1		PV

LUDINGTON MONUMENT (MI33)

Location:	On permanent view at Mason County Airport which is just north east of the town.

TYPE	REG/SER	CON. NO.	PI/NOTES	STATUS
☐ Northrop N-156T Talon (T-38A) (AT-38B)	62-3673	N.5378		PV

MARCELLUS MONUMENT (MI34)

Location:	On permanent view at VFW 4054 at 53550 Michigan 40 about 1 mile south of the town.

TYPE	REG/SER	CON. NO.	PI/NOTES	STATUS
☐ Bell 205 Iroquois (UH-1H)	67-17514	9712		PV

MICHIGAN HISTORICAL MUSEUM (MI35)

Address:	702 Kalamazoo Street,, Lansing, Michigan 48915.
Tel:	517-373-3559
Admission:	Monday-Friday 1000-1700 ;Saturday 1030-1630;Sunday 1300-1700.
Location:	In the centre of the city.

This excellent museum is run by the Michigan Historical Society. Its displays depict many aspects of life in the state from the early times. The museum houses an extensive archive of photographs, flags and documents.

The life of the early settlers is portrayed while the 20th Century area features farming, the Great Depression and World War II in detail. Over 8,600 B-24s were built at Willow Run during World War II and a display of photographs can be seen. The nose of a Liberator has been placed on show.

The society is also responsible for other museums around the state and a number of historic buildings and gardens. They have also erected historic markers at significant locations.

TYPE	REG/SER	CON. NO.	PI/NOTES	STATUS
☐ Consolidated 32 Liberator (B-24L) (B.VII)	44-49112	3967	44-49112, 11120 (Canada) – front fuselage only.	PV

MICHIGAN INSTITUTE OF AVIATION AND TECHNOLOGY (MI36)

Address:	2955 Hagerty Road, Canton, Michigan 48188.
Tel:	734-423-2100 Email: bdevoe@miat.edu
Admission:	By prior permission only.
Location:	Willow Run Airport which is about 5 miles north east of the Belleville.

Michigan

The institute has premises at Willow Run where technicians are trained in both airframe and power plant work. In the past the instructional airframes included a Douglas C-124C Globemaster which made the last flight by the type when it was flown to the McChord Air Museum in Washington State on 5th October 1986. Four instructional airframes are known to be in hangars but there may be others. A number of engines, components and test rigs are in use in the well equipped workshops and laboratories in the complex.

TYPE	REG/SER	CON. NO.	PI/NOTES	STATUS
☐ Beech C50 Seminole (L-23D) (RL-23D) (RU-8D)	N201GB	RLH-32	57-6060	RA
☐ Cessna 152				RA
☐ Cessna 337B Super Skymaster	'67-695'	3370695	N2395S	RAX
☐ North American NA-265 Sabreliner (T-39A) (CT-39A)	61-0681	265-84		RA

MICHIGAN'S OWN MILITARY AND SPACE MUSEUM (MI37)

Address:	1250 Weiss Street, Frankenmuth, Michigan 48734.
Tel:	989-652-8005 Fax: 989-652-3179 Email: michown@ejourney.com
Admission:	March–December Monday-Saturday 1000-1700; Sunday 1100-1700.
Location:	In the centre of the town which is about 10 miles south east of Saginaw.

Michigan military veterans of foreign wars are honoured in the displays at this museum. The collection was started in 1980 when Stan Bozich opened a small display in the basement of a local school. He enlisted the support of the City of Frankenmuth and they obtained a state grant so that land could be purchased. A purpose-built structure was erected and the exhibition opened in 1987. In World War I an army unit nicknamed 'The Polar Bears' served in Northern Russia and their work is highlighted. On show are the uniforms of the state's Medal of Honor servicemen and the suits of Michigan's astronauts. An exhibit traces the story of prisoners of war and another the 'missing in action' personnel from the Vietnam and Gulf conflicts. All wars in which Michigan personnel have served are featured.

The Sabre is mounted outside the building and carries the colours of Michigan's two Korean War aces – Iven Kincheloe (five kills) and Cecil Foster who downed nine enemy aircraft.

TYPE	REG/SER	CON. NO.	PI/NOTES	STATUS
☐ Canadair CL-13B Sabre 6 [North American F-86E]	'12731'/'12738'			PVX

MONROE VIETNAM VETERANS MEMORIAL AND MUSEUM (MI38)

Address:	1095 North Dixie Highway, Heck Park, Monroe, Michigan 48161.
Tel:	734-240-7780 Email: glenn.podhola@dcma.mil
Admission:	Museum Mid May–October Wednesday and Saturday 1200-1600.
Location:	In the centre of the town.

The building contains artefacts tracing the history of the conflict with particular emphasis on the contributions made by local servicemen. On show are uniforms, photographs, weapons and documents. The museum is staffed by veterans of conflict who give guided tours and relate their personal experiences.

The two helicopters are mounted outside in the park which contains a number of memorials to those who perished.

TYPE	REG/SER	CON. NO.	PI/NOTES	STATUS
☐ Bell 204 Iroquois (UH-1C) (UH-1M)	'632'	1614	66-0632 – possible identity.	PVX
☐ Bell 209 Huey Cobra (AH-1G) (AH-1Q) (AH-1S)	68-15074	20608		PV

MOUNT CLEMENS MONUMENT (MI39)

Location:	On permanent view at ALP 4 on Route 97 in the western part of the town.

TYPE	REG/SER	CON. NO.	PI/NOTES	STATUS
☐ McDonnell M.36BA Voodoo (F-101B)	57-0430	608		PV

NATIONAL MUSEUM OF TUSKEGEE AIRMEN (MI40)

Address:	Historic Fort Wayne, 6325 West Jefferson Avenue, Detroit, Michigan 48209-3287.
Tel:	313-843-8849 Fax: 313-843-1540 Email: chehaw@ix.netcom.com
Admission:	April–September Tuesday-Sunday 1000-1500.
Location:	In the south western part of the city centre off Interstate 75 Exit 46.

This informative museum traces the story of the Black Americans who joined the Army Air Corps during World War II. At the time they were not thought of as equals but their contributions to the conflict changed many opinions. Those who were selected as pilots underwent their training at Tuskegee Army Airfield in Alabama. mechanics were sent to Chanute Air Base in Illinois and those chosen to be navigators, bombadiers and gunners were trained at selected bases across the country. Many came from the large cities in the north so the choice of Detroit is appropriate. On show are models, equipment, photographs, uniforms and documents as well as video films. Many local people have donated their personal items to the display. The First Fort Wayne was built by the French in 1701 and the current one – the third – was completed in 1845 and some of the original buildings still survive. Also on the site is an exhibition tracing the history of the fort and its occupants.

NEGAUNEE MONUMENT (MI41)

Location:	On permanent view at VVA 380 on the shore of Teal Lake on US 41.

TYPE	REG/SER	CON. NO.	PI/NOTES	STATUS
☐ Bell 205 Iroquois (UH-1H) (UH-1V)	67-17599	9797		PV

NORTHERN MICHIGAN UNIVERSITY (MI42)

Address:	1401 Presque Isle Avenue, Marquette, Michigan 49855.
Tel:	906-227-2920 Fax: 906-227-2928 Email: knorton@nmu.edu
Admission:	By prior permission only.
Location:	At the airport which is about 20 miles south of the town.

Established in 1899, the university normally has over 8,500 students. A wide range of degree courses are offered. A fleet of instructional aircraft resides in a hangar at the airport. Several other airframes can be seen in a promotional video issued by the department but these cannot be positively identified.

TYPE	REG/SER	CON. NO.	PI/NOTES	STATUS
☐ Bell 205 Iroquois (UH-1D) (UH-1H)	N32741	4665	65-9621	RA
☐ Cessna 152				RA
☐ Cessna 152				RA
☐ Cessna 310				RA
☐ Cessna 402				RA
☐ Piper PA-28-140 Cherokee				RA
☐ Sikorsky S-62A Seaguard (HH-52A)	1409	62094		RA

NORTON SHORES MONUMENT (MI43)

Location:	On permanent view in Hidden Cove Park which is south of the town.

TYPE	REG/SER	CON. NO.	PI/NOTES	STATUS
☐ Bell 205 Iroquois (UH-1D) (UH-1H)	66-0958	5441	Possible identity.	PV

OLD WORLD CANTERBURY VILLAGE (MI44)

Location:	On permanent view in the Toy World section at the site in Lake Orion.

TYPE	REG/SER	CON. NO.	PI/NOTES	STATUS
☐ Royal Aircraft Factory S.E.5A (R)				PV

ONONDAGA WAR MEMORIAL (MI45)

Location:	On permanent view in the centre of the town.

TYPE	REG/SER	CON. NO.	PI/NOTES	STATUS
☐ Bell 209 Huey Cobra (AH-1G) (AH-1S)	70-16056	21000		PV

PLAINWELL MONUMENT (MI46)

Location:	On permanent view at the airport which is about 2 miles north of the town.

TYPE	REG/SER	CON. NO.	PI/NOTES	STATUS
☐ Northrop N-156T Talon (T-38A)	67-14956	T.6097		PV

POLL MUSEUM OF TRANSPORTATION AND MILITARY HISTORY (MI47)

Address:	US Highway 31, Holland, Michigan 49464-1403.
Tel:	616-399-1955
Admission:	May–October Monday-Saturday 1000-1600.
Location:	About 2 miles north of the town.

A number of vehicles and weapons are on show at the museum. These range from a 1921 Pierce Arrow up to fairly modern examples. There are motor cycles and bicycles to be seen along with a large collection of models. The two Iroquois helicopters are the only aircraft currently on display. Military memorabilia is exhibited together with photographs, weapons and components.

TYPE	REG/SER	CON. NO.	PI/NOTES	STATUS
☐ Bell 204 Iroquois (UH-1B)				PV
☐ Bell 204 Iroquois (UH-1C)				PV

PONTIAC MONUMENT (MI48)

Location:	On permanent view at Oakland Airport which is about 8 miles north west of the town.

TYPE	REG/SER	CON. NO.	PI/NOTES	STATUS
☐ Bell 205 Iroquois (UH-1D) (UH-1H)	66-1130	5613		PV

PUBLIC MUSEUM OF GRAND RAPIDS (MI49)

Address:	272 Pearl Street Northwest, Grand Rapids, Michigan 49504-5351.
Tel:	616-456-3977 Fax: 616-456-3873
Admission:	Monday 0900-1700; Tuesday 0900-2000; Wednesday-Saturday 0900-1700; Sunday 1200-1700.
Location:	In the south western suburbs of the town

Michigan

The museum operates a number of sites in the area and the main exhibition is located at the Van Andel Museum Center. Historic buildings in the area have been preserved and some are open regularly.
  Founded in 1854, the collection traces the natural and cultural history of West Michigan. The history of the local indigenous people is portrayed in detail with many personal items on view. There are many innovative displays to be seen and there is a planetarium at the site. One of the highlights is a 1928 carousel which offers rides to all visitors.
  The only aeronautical exhibit is one of the Driggs Skylarks built in the early 1930s at Lansing.

TYPE	REG/SER	CON. NO.	PI/NOTES	STATUS
☐ Driggs Skylark III	NC11301	3016	NC11301, N11301	PV

R.E. OLDS TRANSPORTATION MUSEUM (MI50)

Address: 240 Museum Drive, Lansing, Michigan 48933-1905.
Tel: 517-372-0529   **Email:** autos@reoldsmuseum.org
Admission: Monday-Saturday 1000-1700; May–October Sunday 1200-1700.
Location: In the centre of the city.

Ransom Eli Olds was involved in the manufacture of steam engines in Lansing in the 1890s and later turned his attention to petrol-powered vehicles. The museum highlights his work and covers all forms of transport used in the region. Several types produced by the company are on show including one modified for drag racing and another used by a local congressman. Many historic vehicles are in the collection.
  Ivan Driggs set up a factory at Lansing in 1926 and 15 Darts were built. In 1930 the improved Skylark III appeared but only two dozen were made before the company failed.

TYPE	REG/SER	CON. NO.	PI/NOTES	STATUS
☐ Driggs Skylark III			Fuselage only.	RAD

RIVER ROUGE MONUMENT (MI51)

Location: On permanent view in Jefferson Street just south of the town centre.

TYPE	REG/SER	CON. NO.	PI/NOTES	STATUS
☐ Bell 205 Iroquois (UH-1H)	73-21712	13400		PV

ROSEBUSH MONUMENT (MI52)

Location: On permanent view at ALP 383 in the northern part of the town

TYPE	REG/SER	CON. NO.	PI/NOTES	STATUS
☐ Lockheed 580 (T-33A)	53-6081	580-9702		PV

SELFRIDGE MILITARY AIR MUSEUM (MI53)

Address: 27333 C Street, Building 1011, Selfridge Air National Guard Base, Michigan 48045.
Tel: 586-307-5035   **Fax:** 586-307-6646   **Email:** 127.wg.selfridgeairmuseum@ang.af.mil
Admission: April–October Sunday 1200-1630.
Location: On the northern side of the base which is off Interstate 94 about 25 miles north east of Detroit.

The field was the first real airport in the state and began operations as a training base in July 1917. The site has been in continuous use ever since and is named after Thomas Selfridge who was killed when flying with Orville Wright at Fort Myers, Virginia in September 1908. Selfridge was the first US military officer to pilot an aircraft and also the first fatality in the era of powered flight.
  The site was the home of the First Pursuit Squadron, the oldest combat group in the USA. In the inter-war period a number of races were held and during World War II the field was home to fighter squadrons but training also took place. The first three squadrons of the all-black 332nd Fighter Group were set up at the base. In 1971 the field was transferred to the Michigan Air National Guard and now also houses Reserve and Coast Guard units.
  The museum was set up in the early 1980s by members of the Michigan Air Guard Historical Society. The indoor displays trace the history of Selfridge and its units. Major conflicts are also portrayed in detail. On show are models, uniforms, components, maps photographs and documents.
  The SPAD XIII replica was constructed over a three year period by a group of volunteers. The type was flown by 15 of the 16 squadrons in the American Expeditionary Forces in World War I. The majority of the aircraft are in the outside airpark. The World War II period and the immediate years after are represented by the two Beech twins the Vought FG-1D Corsair and the Douglas Invader. Jet fighters feature prominently in the display ranging from an early F-86A Sabre to the F-16A. Two versions of the ubiquitous Hercules transport can be seen along with a Lockheed Orion.
  The presence of the Coast Guard at Selfridge is shown by the Sikorsky Seaguard in its striking red and white colours. Helicopters which featured in the Vietnam war are also on show with fighters used in the conflict.

TYPE	REG/SER	CON. NO.	PI/NOTES	STATUS
☐ Beech C18S Navigator (AT-7)	'1430'	467	41-1175, NC57776, N57776, '51108'	PVX
☐ Beech C18S Kansan (AT-11)	'9513'	4507	42-37511, NC53209, N33E	PVX
☐ Bell 205 Iroquois (UH-1H)	67-17368	9566		PV
☐ Bell 209 Huey Cobra (AH-1G) (AH-1F)	67-15675	20399		PV
☐ Cessna 310A Blue Canoe (L-27A) (U-3A)	58-2111	38085	58-2111, N9062Y, '58-3111'	PV
☐ Cessna 337M Super Skymaster (O-2A)	67-21340	337M0046		PV
☐ Convair 8-12 Delta Dagger (TF-102A)	54-1351	8-12-1		PV
☐ Convair 8-24 Delta Dart (F-106A)	'59-0082'	8-24-01	56-0451	PVX
☐ Convair 440-79 Samaritan (C-131D)	55-0293	316	N8436H	PV
☐ Douglas A-26C Invader	'435884'	29265	44-35986, N6382T	PVX
☐ Douglas A-4B Skyhawk (A4D-2)	Bu142761	11823		PV

357

☐ Fairchild-Republic A-10A Thunderbolt II	78-0708	A10-328		PV
☐ General Dynamics 401 Fighting Falcon (F-16A)	78-0059	61-55		PV
☐ General Dynamics 401 Fighting Falcon (F-16A)			Front fuselage only.	PV
☐ Grumman G-89 Tracker (S2F-1) (S-2A) (US-2B)	Bu144721	682		PV
☐ Grumman G-303 Tomcat (F-14A)	Bu161620	479		PV
☐ Lockheed 182-2A Hercules (RC-130A) (C-130A)	57-0514	182-3221		PV
☐ Lockheed 185 Orion (P-3B)	Bu152748	185-5188		PV
☐ Lockheed 382-4B Hercules (C-130E)	62-1848	382-3811		PV
☐ Lockheed 580 (T-33A)	53-6099	580-9720		PV
☐ Martin 272A Canberra (RB-57A)	52-1485	68	Contains parts of c/n 39 52-1456	PV
☐ McDonnell M.36CA Voodoo (RF-101C)	56-0048	263		PV
☐ McDonnell M.98DE Phantom II (F-4C)	63-7534	559		PV
☐ McDonnell M.98DJ Phantom II (F-4C)	64-0705	955	Tail section only.	PV
☐ North American NA-161 Sabre (P-86A) (F-86A)	'24387'	161-89	49-1095	PVX
☐ North American NA-235 Super Sabre (F-100D)	56-3025	235-123		PV
☐ North American NA-243 Super Sabre (F-100F)	56-3894	243-170		PV
☐ Republic F-84F Thunderstreak	51-1664			PV
☐ Republic RF-84F Thunderflash	51-1896			PV
☐ Sikorsky S-62A Seaguard (HH-52A)	1466	62145		RA
☐ SPAD XIII (FSM)				PVX
☐ Vought FG-1D Corsair	Bu92085	3346		PV
☐ Vought A-7D Corsair II	72-0461	D583		PV
☐ Vought A-7D Corsair II			Front fuselage only.	PV

THOMAS ST. ONGE VIETNAM VETERANS MUSEUM AND PARK (MI54)

Address:	16462 Linden Street, Hermansville, Michigan 49847.
Email:	choppertweety@hotmail.com
Admission:	June–November Saturday-Sunday 1300-1600.
Location:	In the centre of the town.

The museum opened in 2002 and the displays honour local military personnel who served in the conflict. The idea of the exhibition came from a group of veterans who were friends of Thomas St. Onge, killed during the war. The outside park contains the pole mounted Iroquois and an M-60 tank.

Inside the building there are two exhibition rooms with artefacts, documents, photographs, weapons maps, badges and models. The life and service career of Thomas is told in detail with his medals and the flag which covered his coffin.

TYPE	REG/SER	CON. NO.	PI/NOTES	STATUS
☐ Bell 205 Iroquois (UH-1H)	71-20333	13157		PV

UNIVERSITY OF MICHIGAN (MI55)

Address:	1320 Beal Avenue, Ann Arbor, Michigan 48109-2140.
Tel:	734-704-3310 **Email:** lszuma@umich.edu
Admission:	By prior permission only.
Location:	In the north eastern part of the town.

Edgar Lesher was for many years an assistant professor of engineering at the university. He started construction of the Nomad in 1959 and it flew two years later. It was powered by a 100 hp Continental engine with the propeller at the rear of the fuselage. In the 1960s and 1970s it set many speed records in its class and also flew for a distance of over 1,800 miles in a straight line. The Nomad was donated to the EAA Museum in Oshkosh in Wisconsin in 2000 but has been loaned to the university and is currently displayed in the atrium of the Francis-Xavier Bagnoud Building on the North Campus.

Lesher followed the Nomad with the similarly configured Teal which flew in 1965 and set more world records in the 500kg class in the 1960s and 1970s. In 2002 his children gave the Teal to the EAA Museum where it is currently exhibited.

TYPE	REG/SER	CON. NO.	PI/NOTES	STATUS
☐ Lesher SN-1 Nomad	N1066Z	1	On loan from EAA, WI.	RA

YANKEE AIR FORCE – SAGINAW VALLEY DIVISION (MI56)

Address:	4821 Janes Road, Saginaw, Michigan 48601.
Tel:	517-797-6123
Admission:	By prior permission only.
Location:	At Harry Browne Airport which is about 3 miles east of the town off Route 46.

This division of the YAF flies the Taylorcraft rebuilt in the form of an L-2B. Almost 500 L-2Bs were built in 1943 for observation and liaison duties during World War II and in the years after the conflict. The O-57 was a military version of the pre-war DC series designed for the Civilian Pilot Training Program. Production of the O-57, later L-2, commenced in 1941 and continued for five years. The Army used the type on liaison duties.

TYPE	REG/SER	CON. NO.	PI/NOTES	STATUS
☐ Taylorcraft DCO-65 Grasshopper (O-57A) (L-2A)	N48102	L-4974	(USAAF) – modified as an L-2B.	RAA

YANKEE AIR FORCE – WURTSMITH DIVISION (MI57)

Address:	3961 East Airport Drive, Oscoda, Michigan 48750.
Tel:	989-739-7555 **Fax:** 989-739-1794 **Email:** yafray@yahoo.com
Admission:	Mid-May–mid-October Friday-Sunday 1100-1500.
Location:	About 50 miles north east of Bay City on the shores of Lake Huron.

Michigan

This group has several aircraft in its hangar at the former Wurtsmith Air Force Base which closed in 1993. The airfield opened in the mid-1920s, initially as a gunnery range for aircraft based at Selfridge. During World War II Free French pilots trained at the field.

In 1953 the base was named after Michigan pilot General Paul B. Wurtsmith who was killed when his B-25 crashed in North Carolina in September 1946. Fighter units were in residence from 1951 to 1973. Strategic Air Command squadrons flying the B-52 moved in during 1961 along with supporting KC-135s.

Members of the group are restoring a number of the airframes and the Iroquois will be painted in the colours in wore in Vietnam. A display of memorabilia can be seen in the division's hangar. On show are artefacts collected by members, flying clothing and equipment. There is also a library.

TYPE	REG/SER	CON. NO.	PI/NOTES	STATUS
☐ Bell 205 Iroquois (UH-1D) (UH-1H)	N13YA	5742	66-16048	PV
☐ Cessna 305A Bird Dog (L-19A) (O-1A)	N3302T	22421	51-12107	PVC
☐ Jeffair Barracuda	N29M			PV
☐ Lockheed 580 (T-33A)	52-9843	580-8149	52-9843, N58417 – possible identity.	PV
☐ Lockheed 580 (T-33A)	53-5948	580-9424	53-5948, N62519	PVC
☐ Stinson 10A Voyager	NC32235	7883	NC32235, N32235	PVA
☐ Waco NZR Hadrian (CG-4A)				PVC

YANKEE AIR MUSEUM (MI58)

Address: PO Box 1100, Belleville, Michigan 48112-0590.
Tel: 734-483-4030   **Fax:** 734-483-5076   **Email:** info@yankeeairmuseum.org
Admission: Tuesday-Saturday 1000-1600; Sunday 1200-1600.
Location: On the south west of Willow Run Airport which is about 5 miles north east of the town.

During World War II the Ford plant at Willow Run produced over 8,600 B-24s in 3½ years; at its peak one aircraft rolled out of the factory every 55 minutes. The Yankee Air Force was formed in 1981 with the aim of acquiring a Willow Run B-24 for preservation but this still remains a dream. A 1942 hangar was obtained and aircraft soon joined the museum.

The collection gained publicity when on 26th October 1983 a B-52 was flown in from Dyess Air Force Base in Texas. This was the first B-52 to join a private museum and the giant bomber has recently been repainted. Maintained in flying condition are the C-47 and B-25, both regular attenders at shows. In 1995 they were joined in the air by the B-17 which had been undergoing a lengthy restoration since it joined the museum in 1986. The efforts of the team were rewarded when the bomber won a major award at the 1995 Oshkosh Convention. The aircraft had only flown a few days before the event.

The Stinson V-77 has been restored to airworthiness and joy rides are regularly offered to visitors. The collection contains a number of interesting types including one of three surviving Privateers and one of three Armstrong-Whitworth Argosies preserved in the United States. Riddle Airlines ordered seven examples of the British transport in 1960 for military support duties. When they lost the contract the aircraft were sold to other airlines and were later joined by a few former-RAF examples. The DC-6 on show served with Alitalia and the Italian Air Force before returning to the USA.

In October 2004 the museum hangar was completely destroyed by fire. A number of aircraft, a vast amount of memorabilia and workshop equipment was lost. Types consumed in the fire included the prototype North American Bronco, a former Thunderbirds F-105 Thunderchief, an Aero L-39 Albatros and a Waco CG-4A Hadrian glider which was undergoing a prolonged rebuild. The three active warbirds were saved, but only just, by the heroic efforts of a few members who managed to drag them out of the hangar before the fire reached them.

The museum has relocated to a temporary home whilst a new complex is constructed on the east side of the airport. The Yankee Air Force organised the annual 'Thunder Over Michigan' airshow which attracts large numbers of warbirds from across the country to Willow Run.

TYPE	REG/SER	CON. NO.	PI/NOTES	STATUS
☐ Armstrong Whitworth AW.650 Argosy 100	N896U	6651	G-AOZZ, G-11-1	PV
☐ Beech C18S Kansan (AT-11)	N7340C	5097	43-10404	RAC
☐ Bell 205 Iroquois (UH-1D) (UH-1H)	66-16006	5700		PV
☐ Boeing 299-O Fortress (B-17G) (PB-1G)	N3193G	8738	44-85829, Bu77255	PVA
☐ Boeing 464-201-7 Stratofortress (B-52D)	55-0677	464024		PV
☐ Consolidated 32 Liberator (B-24A) (RB-24A)	40-2369	1 or 527	Front fuselage only.	RA
☐ Consolidated 40 Privateer (PB4Y-2) (P4Y-2) (Convair 100)	N6816D		Bu59905 – parts only.	PV
☐ Consolidated 40 Privateer (PB4Y-2) (P4Y-2G) (Convair 100)	N6813D		Bu59876, 'N6319D'	PV
☐ De Havilland DHC.4 Caribou	'24171'	2	CF-LAN, N6080 – in false USArmy markings.	PVX
☐ Douglas DC-3A-467 Skytrain (TC-47B) (TC-47D)	N8704	16300/33048	44-76716	PVA
☐ Douglas DC-6B	N4913R	44493	I-DIMB, MM61900, I-DIMB	PV
☐ Grumman G-40 Avenger (TBM-3) (TBM-3E)	NL9584Z	2701	Bu85882	PV
☐ Grumman G-128 Intruder (A-6A) (A-6E)			Composite of c/n I-169 Bu152621, c/n I-237 Bu152933, c/n I-450 Bu156981 and c/n I-458 Bu156989.	
☐ Lockheed 580 (T-33A)	58-0492	580-1461	58-0492, N24852	PV
☐ Lockheed 580 (T-33A)	51-8786	580-6570		PV
☐ Martin 272A Canberra (RB-57A)	52-1426	9		PV
☐ McDonnell M.36BA Voodoo (F-101B) (JF-101B) (NF-101B)	56-0235	128		PV
☐ McDonnell M.98DE Phantom II (F-4C)	63-7555	592		PV
☐ North American NA-100 Mitchell (B-25D)	N3774	100-23560	43-3634, KL148, CF-NWV, NX3774	PVA
☐ North American NA-201 Sabre (F-86D) (F-86L)	53-1060	201-504		PV
☐ Republic F-84F Thunderstreak	51-9501		51-9501, N5006	PV
☐ Republic RF-84F Thunderflash	52-7421			PV
☐ Stinson V-77 Reliant (AT-19)	N43YF	77-452	43-44165, FB724, Bu11644, NC95693, N15JH	PVA

MINNESOTA

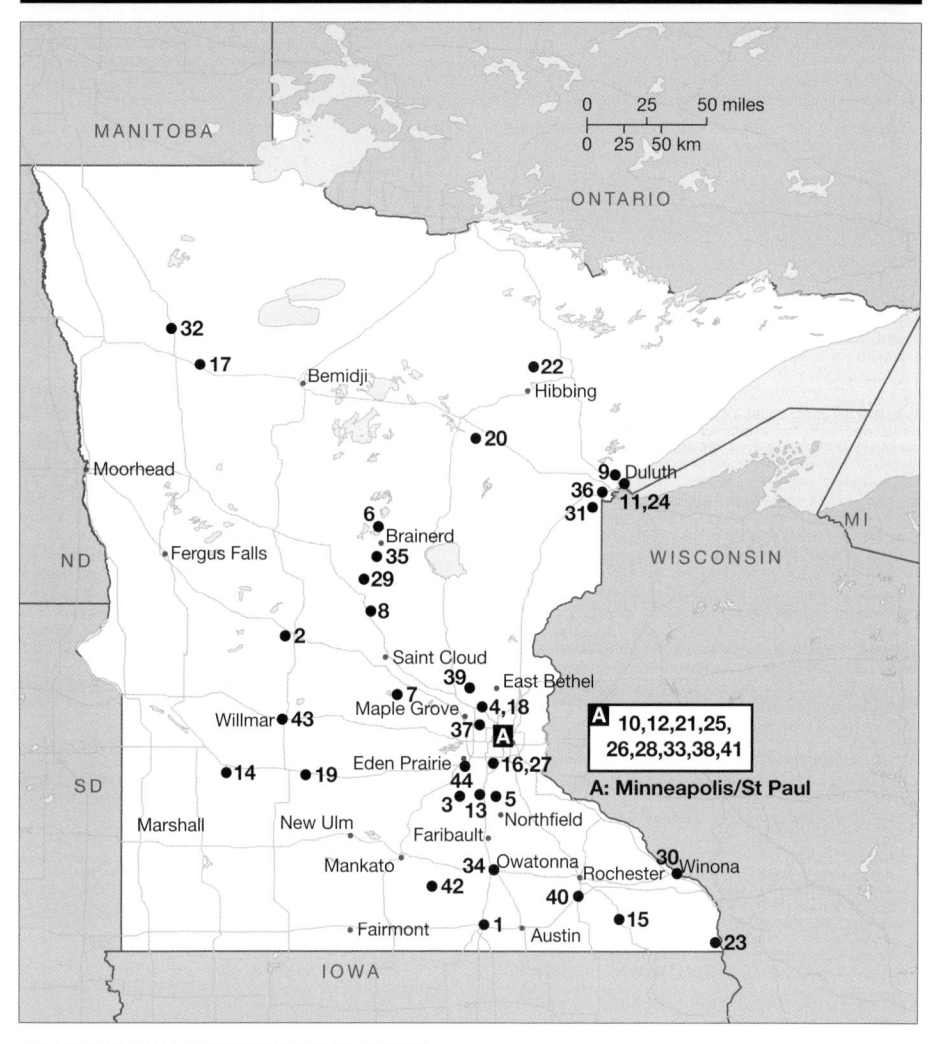

ALBERT LEA MONUMENT (MN1)

Location:	On permanent view at the airport which is about 2 miles north of the town.

TYPE	REG/SER	CON. NO.	PI/NOTES	STATUS
☐ Lockheed 580 (T-33A)	53-5158	580-8497		PV

ALEXANDRIA MONUMENT (MN2)

Location:	On permanent view at the airport which is in the south eastern part of the town.

TYPE	REG/SER	CON. NO.	PI/NOTES	STATUS
☐ Lockheed 580 (T-33A)	52-9171	580-7225		PV

Minnesota

ARLINGTON MONUMENT (MN3)

Location:	On permanent view at ALP 250 at 807 West Chandler Street which is in the north western part of the town.

TYPE	REG/SER	CON. NO.	PI/NOTES	STATUS
Bell 209 Huey Cobra (AH-1G) (AH-1S)	68-17042	20770		PV

AMERICAN WINGS AIR MUSEUM (MN4)

Address:	PO Box 120901, 2141 Rhode Island Avenue, St. Paul, Minnesota 55112-0901.
Tel:	763-786-4146 Email: lburgers@pro-ns.net
Admission:	Tuesday 1500-2000; Saturday 0800-1700.
Location:	At Anoka County Airport which is about 10 miles north of Minneapolis off Route 65.

The museum was set up a few years ago with the aim of concentrating on military trainers, forward air controllers, gunships and photo-reconnaissance aircraft. Hangars and workshops were acquired at Janes Field. A large collection of support material relating to the above roles has been assembled including armament, gunsights, radios, cameras etc.

In 2009 the main exhibition building closed and a smaller display was set up on the other side of the field. Many aircraft are now in store while a permanent solution is sought. The collection includes a number of variants of the Grumman Mohawk. The prototype of this twin-engined turboprop aircraft made its maiden flight in April 1959. The type was designed for a number of roles including attack, battlefield surveillance and observation. In total 380 were produced mainly for the US Army and it was finally withdrawn in the USA in 1996. The OV-1 also flew with the military in Argentina and Israel. Several were sold to civilian owners and museums. The Cessna Bird Dog, developed from the 170, was used for observation duties for many years.

A rarity in the USA is the Fauvel glider. Charles Fauvel flew his first flying wing sailplane in the 1930s and prior to World War II a number of designs appeared including some powered versions. The AV-36 made its maiden flight in 1951 and the longer wingspan AV-361 nine years later. Well over 100 of both versions were made. Two jet fighters are parked outside along with the Sikorsky S-58 helicopter.

TYPE	REG/SER	CON. NO.	PI/NOTES	STATUS
☐ Cessna 305A Bird Dog (L-19A) (O-1A)	N269TH/'22819'	22819	51-12408, N5073Z	PVAX
☐ Cessna 337M Super Skymaster (O-2A)	69-7644	337M0442		RAC
☐ Fauvel AV.361	N9L	361-1		PV
☐ Grumman G-89 Tracker (S2F-1) (S2F-2U) (US-2C)	N8114Z	449	Bu136540	PVA
☐ Grumman G-134 Mohawk (AO-1A) (OV-1A)	N75207	15A	59-2617	RA
☐ Grumman G-134 Mohawk (AO-1A) (OV-1A) (JOV-1A)	60-3734	33A		RA
☐ Grumman G-134 Mohawk (AO-1A) (OV-1A)	N134GA	35A	60-3736	RA
☐ Grumman G-134 Mohawk (OV-1A)	N2036P	58A	63-13128	PV
☐ Grumman G-134 Mohawk (AO-1B) (OV-1B)	59-2629	9B		RA
☐ Grumman G-134 Mohawk (OV-1B) (RV-1D)	62-5891	50B	Front fuselage only.	PV
☐ Grumman G-134 Mohawk (OV-1B) (RV-1D)	N134RV	90B	64-14262	RAA
☐ Grumman G-134 Mohawk (AO-1C) (OV-1C)	60-3748	4C	Front fuselage only.	PV
☐ Grumman G-134 Mohawk (AO-1C) (OV-1C)	61-2718	61C		RA
☐ Grumman G-134 Mohawk (OV-1C)	N134AW	140C	68-15936	PVA
☐ Grumman G-134 Mohawk (OV-1D)	69-17021	32D	69-17021, 055 (Israel), 4X-JRA,	RA
☐ Naval Aircraft Factory N3N-3	N51H		Bu2660, N6394T	RAA
☐ Northrop N-156E Tiger II (F-5E)	74-1539	R.1197		PV
☐ Sikorsky S-58 Seahorse (HUS-1) (UH-34D)	Bu147174	581115		PV
☐ Taylorcraft DCO-65 Grasshopper (L-2M)	N9060K	L-5373	43-26753 (?)	PVA
☐ Vought TA-7C Corsair II (A-7B)	Bu154500	B140		PV

BELLE PLAINE MONUMENT (MN5)

Location:	On permanent view in the Veterans Park off Highway 25 in the town.

TYPE	REG/SER	CON. NO.	PI/NOTES	STATUS
☐ Bell 205 Iroquois (UH-1H)	68-15369	10299		PV

BRAINERD MONUMENT (MN6)

Location:	On permanent view at Crow Wing County Airport whch is about 3 miles north east of the town.

TYPE	REG/SER	CON. NO.	PI/NOTES	STATUS
☐ Grumman G-93 Cougar (F9F-6) (F-9F)				PVX

BUFFALO MONUMENT (MN7)

Location:	On permanent view at the airport which is about 4 miles south east of the town.

TYPE	REG/SER	CON. NO.	PI/NOTES	STATUS
☐ Lockheed 580 (T-33A)	51-9235	580-7019		PV

CHARLES A. LINDBERGH HISTORIC SITE (MN8)

Address:	620 Lindbergh Drive South, Little Falls, Minnesota 56345
Tel:	320-616-5421 Email: lindbergh@mnhs.org
Admission:	May–August Thursday-Saturday 1000-1700 Sunday 1200-1700;
Location:	About 2 miles south of the town.

Charles Lindbergh was born in Detroit on 4th February 1902 but spent most of his childhood in Little Falls. The famous aviator's boyhood home is the centrepiece of the display. The Visitor Center traces the life of Lindbergh from his early years up to his death.

He learnt to fly in Nebraska in 1922 and was soon barnstorming as a wing walker and parachutist across Nebraska, Colorado, Kansas and Wyoming. He did not make his first solo flight until May 1923 at Americus in Georgia when he bought a Curtiss JN-4D. His later flying exploits, including his time as a mail pilot, feature prominently.

A partial fuselage of a Ryan NYP has been constructed to show the cramped conditions he endured on his trans-Atlantic flight. Models of other types he flew are displayed along with documents. A Volkswagen 'Beetle' which he drove across Africa in 1959 is on view.

TYPE	REG/SER	CON. NO.	PI/NOTES	STATUS
☐ Ryan NYP (FSM)			Partial fuselage.	PV

COMMEMORATIVE AIR FORCE (LAKE SUPERIOR SQUADRON 101) (MN9)

Address:	4931 Airport Road,, Hangar 101, Duluth International Airport Hermantown, Minnesota 55811-1515.
Tel:	218-733-0639 Email: corsa@aol.com
Admission:	By prior permission only.
Location:	In the western suburbs of the town off Route 53.

This unit is a detachment of the Minnesota Wing. N7179Y was damaged in a gale and N324FA was grounded with corrosion problems. The wings of the former have been mated with the fuselage of the latter and restoration continues. The other components will be rebuilt in the future.

TYPE	REG/SER	CON. NO.	PI/NOTES	STATUS
☐ Consolidated 28-5ACF Catalina (28-6A) (PBY-6A)	N324FA	2163	Bu64092, N6881C, CF-PIU, C-FPIU	PVC
☐ Consolidated 28-6A Catalina (PBY-6A)	N7179Y	2167	Bu64097, N7082C, F-ZBAW, C-FHNF	PVC

COMMEMORATIVE AIR FORCE (MINNESOTA WING) (MN10)

Address:	310 Airport Road, Hangar 3, Fleming Field, South St. Paul, Minnesota 55075-3551.
Tel:	651-455-6942 Email: info@cafsmw.org
Admission:	Wednesday and Saturday 1000-1600.
Location:	The airfield is about 6 miles south of St. Paul off Route 75.

Housed at Fleming Field the unit maintains six aircraft in airworthy condition. Now flying is one of the few surviving P-51C versions of the famous Mustang. The aircraft moved to the wing in 1985 after spending over a decade in Omaha, Nebraska with another CAF unit. The fighter has been painted in the colours one of the Tuskegee Airmen units. A display of memorabilia has been set up in rooms around the hangar.

TYPE	REG/SER	CON. NO.	PI/NOTES	STATUS
☐ Canadian Car & Foundry Harvard 4 [North American NA-186]	N13595	CCF4-97	20306 (Canada)	PVA
☐ North American NA-103 Mustang (P-51C)	NL61429	103-26199	42-103645, N9288, N215CA	PVA
☐ North American NA-108 Mitchell (B-25J) (TB-25J) (TB-25K)	'327493'	108-33144	44-29869, N3160G, N27493	PVAX
☐ Ryan ST-3KR Recruit (PT-21)	N9753N	1023	41-1902	PVA
☐ Stinson V-76 Sentinel (L-5)	N68591/'268591'		42-98667	PVAX
☐ Vultee V-74 Valiant (BT-13A)	N52411	74-2548	41-11538	PVA

DULUTH MONUMENTS (MN11)

Location:	On permanent view at two locations in the town

TYPE	REG/SER	CON. NO.	PI/NOTES	STATUS
☐ Lockheed 580 (T-33A)	'52-9406'	580-1129	56-1779 – at ALP 71 on Grand Avenue.	PV
☐ McDonnell M.98EN Phantom II (F-4D)	65-0608	1545	At ANG Base at the International Airport which is in the western part of the town.	PV

EAGEN MONUMENT (MN12)

Location:	On permanent view at a motel in the area.

TYPE	REG/SER	CON. NO.	PI/NOTES	STATUS
☐ Luscombe 8A Silvaire				PV

EXPERIMENTAL AIRCRAFT ASSOCIATION CHAPTER 25 MUSEUM (MN13)

Address:	Airlake Airport, 8140 220th Street West, Lakeville, Minnesota 45044.
Tel:	952-831-5142 Email: jfkoser@comcast.net
Admission:	By prior permission only.
Location:	About 20 miles south of Minneapolis off Interstate 38.

Minnesota

Members of this chapter are constructing the Bert Sisler Aviation Education Center at the airport. He was one of the founder members of the group in 1956. He designed and built several aircraft and one of these is in the hangar. He also restored a number of classic types.

The Limbach Gusty was developed from the Tipsy Nipper and first flew in 1967. This aircraft is hanging in the building. The pair of Pietenpols and the Curtiss Wright Junior are owned by members of the chapter and can normally be found at the field.

TYPE	REG/SER	CON. NO.	PI/NOTES	STATUS
☐ Curtiss-Wright CW-1 Junior	N8639E	1055		RA
☐ Limbach Gusty	N55Y	1		RA
☐ Pietenpol B4-A Aircamper	N2RN	RMN01		RAA
☐ Pietenpol B4-A Aircamper	N25RN	RMN02		RAA
☐ Sisler SF-2M	N5901T	1		RA

FAGEN COLLECTION (MN14)

Address:	501 Highway 212 West, Granite Falls, Minnesota 56241-1308.
Admission:	By prior permission only.
Location:	The airport is about 4 miles south of the town off Route 23.

Aircraft from this private collection have won awards at a number of events. The P-40K was Grand Champion at the 2006 EAA Airventure at Oshkosh. One of the Kittyhawks was transported from a crash site in Russia in the late 1980s. After a major rebuild in Georgia using components from other aircraft it took to the air again in July 1998. The now rare Helldiver crashed in 1945 and the wreck was recovered in 1993 by the National Museum of Naval Aviation. The Lightning has had a varied civil career. Sold on the civilian market in the summer of 1946 it took part in a number of races. From 1958 until 1976 it was stored in two locations in California before being acquired by the late David Tallichet. The fighter was eventually rebuilt and flew in 1995. Ron Fagen acquired the aircraft in 2004 and it was again restored to airworthy condition. Two examples of the classic Mustang reside in the hangars. Both aircraft moved to Sweden in the late 1940s and were flown there for around four years before one went to Israel and the other to the Dominican Republic.

TYPE	REG/SER	CON. NO.	PI/NOTES	STATUS
☐ Curtiss 84G Helldiver (SB2C-5)	Bu83393			RAC
☐ Curtiss 87-B3 Warhawk (P-40K)	N401WH	21640	42-10256	RAA
☐ Curtiss A87-A2 Kittyhawk I	N4420K	15134	AK753, (Soviet) – composite.	RAA
☐ Curtiss A87-A2 Kittyhawk I	N7205A	15244	AK863, 1044 (Canada)	RAD
☐ Fairchild M-62A Cornell (PT-19)	N46197	T43-7272	(USAAF), N46197, G-BRUP – identity doubtful.	RAA
☐ Fairchild M-62A-4 Cornell (PT-26) (Cornell I)	N75463/'215429'	T42-4299	42-15429, FH950	RAA
☐ Lockheed 422-87-23 Lightning (P-38L) (F-5G)	N79123	422-8235	44-27231, NX79123	RAA
☐ North American NA-122 Mustang (P-51D) (J 26)	N251L	122-31590	44-63864, Fv26158, 2338 (Israel), 38 (Israel), N251L, N42805	RAA
☐ North American NA-122 Mustang (P-51D) (J 26)	N68JR/'422051'	122-31910	44-72051, Fv26026, 1912 (Dominican Republic)	RAA
☐ Piper J-3C-65 Cub	N88175	15792	NC88175	RAA
☐ Pitts 12	N79EF	004		RAA
☐ Vultee V-74 Valiant (BT-13A)	N54841	74-5225	41-21386	
☐ Walter Extra EA-300L	N51NL	108		RAA
☐ Yakovlev Yak-55M	N572ST	950901		RAA

FILLMORE COUNTY HISTORY CENTER (MN15)

Address:	202 County Road 8, Fountain, Minnesota 55935.
Tel:	507-268-4449 Email: FCHC@mleaf.net
Admission:	Monday-Friday 0900-1600.
Location:	In the town which is about 25 miles south east of Rochester on Route 52.

This local history museum has many original buildings located in its grounds. Early houses, a school and barns have been moved and rebuilt. The rooms have been fitted with period items. A Pietenpol Sky Scout constructed in the region in 1932 has been moved to the site along with its hangar. This has now been joined by an example of the Aircamper. The history of these two homebuilts is highlighted with photographs and documents.

TYPE	REG/SER	CON. NO.	PI/NOTES	STATUS
☐ Pietenpol B4-A Aircamper				PV
☐ Pietenpol P-9 Sky Scout				PV

FORT SNELLING MILITARY MUSEUM (MN16)

Address:	511 Constitution Avenue, Fort Snelling, Minnesota 55111-4027.
Tel:	612-713-3291 Email: FortSnellingMuseum@usarc-emh2.army.mil
Admission:	By appointment Monday-Friday 0600-1630.
Location:	In the south of the city next to the International Airport.

This historic fort was constructed in 1819 and for over 30 years was an outpost in the wilderness. As settlers moved further west the site served as a supply depot for a time and during the civil war became a training centre. New buildings were constructed at the end of the 19th century and the fort remained in use until 1945. In 1960 it was designated as the first National Historic Landmark in Minnesota. Tours of the site take place and a history centre has been built to trace the development over the years.

TYPE	REG/SER	CON. NO.	PI/NOTES	STATUS
☐ Bell 205 Iroquois (UH-1H)				RA
☐ Bell 209 Huey Cobra (AH-1G) (AH-1S)				RA

FOSSTON MONUMENT (MN17)

Location:	On permanent view in the Veterans Memorial Park on Highway 2 in the centre of the town.

TYPE	REG/SER	CON. NO.	PI/NOTES	STATUS
☐ Bell 209 Huey Cobra (AH-1G) (AH-1F)	68-15000	20534		PV

GOLDEN WINGS FLYING MUSEUM (MN18)

Address:	8891 Airport Road C-6, Blaine, Minnesota 55449.
Tel:	763-786-5004 **Email:** goldenwings@minn.net
Admission:	By prior permission only.
Location:	At Anoka County Airport which is about 10 miles north of the Minneapolis off Route 65.

Greg Herrick started this collection in the mid-1990s and has constructed a purpose-built museum at the airport. All types will be restored to flying condition and members of the fleet are regular visitors to shows around the country.

There are many rarities to be seen. The Buhl Air Sedan was built in the late 1920s and is believed to be the last complete survivor of the 70 built. Another large biplane is the all metal Cunningham Hall PT-6. Only two were sold, the freighter version with the collection and the six-seater which is with the Alaska Museum of Transportation.

Just nine Paramount Cabinaires were produced at Lansing in Michigan in 1929/30 and again only one survives. The high-wing three-seater was designed by Walter Carr and was similar to Travel Air types. Six were powered by Warner 110 hp radials. The 165 variant was a four seater fitted with a 175 hp Wright engine.

The Kreutzer K-5 was rescued in the late 1980s from a mountain strip in Mexico where it had crashed in the 1940s. After a protracted rebuilt it joined the collection and is the only known example. The Fleetwings F-401 amphibian featured a spot-welded stainless steel hull and made its maiden flight in 1936. Five production F-5s followed and one is still active in Florida.

The Stinson company constructed a number of three engined transports. A total of 53 high wing SM-6000Bs were built in the early 1930s and used by some of the major airlines in the country such as American and Eastern. The low wing Model A made its first flight in April 1934 and 30 were sold. Both these aircraft are the last survivors of their type. Fairchild became known in the 1930s for a series of successful high wing monoplanes. In 1935 they built the low wing five seater cabin Model 45. The aircraft featured a retractable undercarriage and was designed for the executive market.

Only 21 Alliance Argo biplanes were sold. One other and components of a third exist. Three of the surviving Ford Tri-Motors are owned with two currently airworthy. The Busmaster 2000 was developed from the Ford design and the example in the collection was completed in the 1964. The second first flew in 1985 and was destroyed in a crash in California in 2004.

The Taylor Aerocar is another rarity. Six examples of the roadable aircraft were built. The Avro Avian carries the markings of one sold to Lady Mary Heath in 1927. The aircraft was flown in Africa and eventually arrived in the USA where it was flown by Amelia Earhart. The Avian in the hangar was acquired in 2001 and flown on an Earhart commemorative flight.

TYPE	REG/SER	CON. NO.	PI/NOTES	STATUS
☐ Aeronca C-3	NC15295	A-623	NC15295, N15295	RAA
☐ Alliance Argo	NC2M	108	NC2M, N2M	RAA
☐ Arrow Sport M (F)	NC18764	105	NC18764, N18764	RAC
☐ Aviat A-1 Husky	N9623Z	1188		RAA
☐ Aviat A-1B Husky	N48GH	2049		RAA
☐ Avro 594 Avian II	'G-EBUG'	R3/AV/127	G-AUFZ, VH-UFZ, NC7083	RAAX
☐ Bellanca 31-42 Pacemaker	N16707	254	NC16707	RAC
☐ Boeing-Stearman E75 Kaydet (PT-13D)	N317PT	75-5474	42-17311, N4782V	RAA
☐ Buhl CA-3D/E Airsedan	NC8451	57	NC8451, N8451	RAA
☐ Bushmaster 2000	NC7501V	1	N7501V	RAA
☐ Callair A-2	N2921V	136	NC2921V	RAC
☐ Cessna 182Q Skylane II	N735AZ	18265283		RAA
☐ Cunningham Hall PT-6F	NC444	381	NC444, NPC-44	RAA
☐ Curtiss 51 Fledgling	N250H	B-31	NC250H, N250H	RAC
☐ Fairchild FC-2W2	NC13934	531	NC13934, N13934	RAA
☐ Fairchild 45A	N65F	4003	NC16362	RAC
☐ Fairchild M-62A Cornell (PT-19A)	N55406	T42-1394	41-20388	RAA
☐ Fairchild M-62A-4 Cornell (PT-26) (Cornell I)	N63568	T43-4499	44-19387, EW440	RAA
☐ Fairchild M-62A-4 Cornell II	N79185	FC.180	10679 (Canada)	RAA
☐ Fairchild M-62C Cornell (PT-23A)	N64097	129SL	42-49705	RAA
☐ Fleetwings F401 Seabird	NC16793	1	NC16793, CF-BGZ, N16793	RAA
☐ Ford 4-AT-A	N1077	4-AT-10	NC1077	RAA
☐ Ford 4-AT-B (4-AT-A)	NC9610	4-AT-42	NC7684, N7684	RAC
☐ Ford 4-AT-E	NC8403	4-AT-65		RAD
☐ Frankfort Cinema B (TG-1A)	N54308	B-2-4	(USAAF)	RAC
☐ Interstate S-1A Cadet	NC37280	123	NC37280, N37280	RAA
☐ Keystone Loening K84 Commuter	N63K	305	NC63K	RAC
☐ Kreider-Reisner KR-34C Challenger	N261K	327	NC261K	RAC
☐ Kreutzer K-5 (K-2) (K-3)	NC612A	102	NC612, N612A	RAC
☐ Paramount Cabinaire 165	NC17M	7	NC17M, N17M	RAC
☐ Sikorsky S-39-C (S-39-A)	NC809W	911		RAC
☐ Spartan C-2-160	N11904	J-11	NC11904	RAC
☐ Stearman 6L (6F)	NC788H	6003	NC788H, N788H	RAC
☐ Stearman C3B (C3L)	NC6438	169	X6438, NC6438, N6438	RAC
☐ Stinson A	NC15165	9125	NC15165, N15165	RAA
☐ Stinson SM-1B Detroiter (SM-1DX)	X7654	M262	N7654	RAC
☐ Stinson SM-6000B	NC11153	5021	NC11153, N11153	RAA
☐ Stinson SM-7A Junior	NC216W	M3002	NC216W, N216W	RAC
☐ Taylor Aerocar III	N101D	3		RAA
☐ Travel Air A-6000A	N377A	A6A-2003	NC377M, N377M	RAA
☐ Waco CUC-1	NC15233	4318	NC15233, N15233	RAA
☐ Waco UKC	N13897	3842	NC13897	RAA

HECTOR MONUMENT (MN19)

Location:	On permanent view at the airport which is just south of the town on Route 4.

TYPE	REG/SER	CON. NO.	PI/NOTES	STATUS
☐ Lockheed 580 (T-33A)	52-9842	580-8148		PV

HILL CITY MONUMENT (MN20)

Location:	On permanent view in Don Beerbower Memorial Park in the town.

TYPE	REG/SER	CON. NO.	PI/NOTES	STATUS
☐ Bell 209 Huey Cobra (AH-1G) (AH-1F)	67-15513	20177		PV

HOLLIDAY COLLECTION (MN21)

Address:	PO Box 243, Lake Elmo, Minnesota 55042-0243.
Admission:	By prior permission only.
Location:	At Lake Elmo airfield in the Minneapolis area.

Mark Holliday has acquired an interesting collection. The aircraft also spent some time at Platte Valley Airport in Colorado. 'Pop' Johnson worked for the Globe company for several years. After World War II he set up a firm to produce his own designs. The first was the Rocket of which only a handful were made. The next, the Bullet, was in the planning stage when he ran out of money. The design was taken over by the Aircraft Manufacturing Company who completed six. Three were destroyed in crashes. In 1982 Jim Younkin and

Bud Dake decided to construct an aircraft similar to Benny Howard's famous 'Mr. Mulligan'. Three were built and Mark acquired Bud's aircraft after his death. The high-wing aircraft has a forward fuselage similar to the Howard design but the rear is based on the Monocoupe. The fuselage is constructed of steel tubing with the wooden wings skinned with plywood.
Jim Younkin has also built a number of other replica racers of the inter-war period including one of 'Mr Mulligan'. Several Globe/Temco Swifts are maintained in flying condition.

TYPE	REG/SER	CON. NO.	PI/NOTES	STATUS
☐ Aircraft Manufacturing Company Texas Bullet 205	N78849	103		RAA
☐ Cessna 140	N1940V	14146	NC1940V	RAA
☐ Cessna 140A	N462A	15283		RAA
☐ Cessna 140A	N5613C	15546	NC5613C	RAA
☐ Cessna 150C	N7913Z	15060013		RAA
☐ Cessna U206F Stationair	N2097U	U20602342		RAA
☐ Dake Mullicoupe	NX274Y	JRY 03-2		RAA
☐ Globe GC-1A Swift	N90340	354	NC90340	RAA
☐ Globe GC-1A Swift	N80573	76	NC80573	RAA
☐ Great Lakes 2T-1A	N435Y	152	NC435Y	RAA
☐ Luscombe 8A Silvaire	N276Y	2723		RAA
☐ Luscombe 8F Silvaire	N2045B	6472		RAA
☐ Maule M-4-220C Strata Rocket	N40648	2164C		RAA
☐ Piper PA-20 Pacer 125	N7007K	20-112		RAA
☐ Temco GC-1B Swift	N78069	2069		RAA
☐ Temco GC-1B Swift	N78191	2191		RAA
☐ Temco GC-1B Swift	N78218	2218		RAA
☐ Temco GC-1B Swift	N78225	2225		RAA
☐ Temco GC-1B Swift	N2372B	3672		RAA
☐ Temco GC-1B Swift	N2390B	3690		RAA
☐ Temco GC-1B Swift	N2428B	3728		RAA
☐ Temco GC-1B Swift	N2446B	3746		RAA
☐ Temco GC-1B Swift	N2460B	3760		RAA

IRON RANGE VETERANS MEMORIAL (MN22)

Address:	PO Box 108, Chisholm, Minnesota 55719.
Admission:	On permanent view
Location:	About 1 mile north of the town off Route 73.

This well-maintained memorial honours veterans of all wars. Two aircraft are mounted on poles. The Starfire was at the nearby Minnesota Museum of Mining for many years before moving to its new home in 2003. F-94s were flown by squadrons of the Minnesota Air National Guard in the late 1950s from both Minneapolis-St. Paul and Duluth.

The Iroquois is dedicated to those who served in Vietnam. Also on show are a M-60A tank, flags and weapons. The mining museum contains many impressive displays showing the work carried out over the years. A range of equipment, including a 1907 steam train, can be seen in the informative displays.

TYPE	REG/SER	CON. NO.	PI/NOTES	STATUS
☐ Bell 205 Iroquois (UH-1H)	69-15416	12203		PV
☐ Lockheed 880-75-13 Starfire (F-97A) (F-94C)	'51-13570'	880-8344	51-13560 – incorporates parts of c/n 880-8347 51-13563.	PVX

LA CRESCENT MONUMENT (MN23)

Location:	On permanent view in a park in the northern part of the town.

TYPE	REG/SER	CON. NO.	PI/NOTES	STATUS
☐ Bell 205 Iroquois (UH-1H)	66-17454	9248		PV

LAKE SUPERIOR COLLEGE AIRCRAFT RESCUE AND FIRE FIGHTING TRAINING CENTER (MN24)

Address:	11501 Highway 23, Duluth, Minnesota 55808-2200.
Tel:	218-733-7600
Admission:	By prior permission only.
Location:	In the southern part of the town.

The college offers specialised training for airfield firefighters. Three airframes are known to be in use. A proposal to construct a specialised aviation centre has been put forward and this may involve moving some of the courses from the Minnesota Southeast College campus at Winona.

TYPE	REG/SER	CON. NO.	PI/NOTES	STATUS
☐ Lockheed 580 (T-33A)	N86905	580-7807	52-9622	RA
☐ North American NA-265 Sabreliner (T-39A) (CT-39A)	61-0668	265-71		RA
☐ Sikorsky S-62A Seaguard (HH-52A)	1446	62129		RA

MINNEAPOLIS VIETNAM MEMORIAL (MN25)

Location:	On permanent view at Flying Cloud Airport which is about 12 miles south west of Minneapolis.

TYPE	REG/SER	CON. NO.	PI/NOTES	STATUS
☐ North American NA-203 Sabre (F-86H)	53-1250	203-22		PV

MINNESOTA AEROPLANE COLLECTION (MN26)

Address:	2141 Dudley Avenue, St. Paul Minnesota 55103.
Admission:	By prior permission only.
Location:	At Fleming Field which is in the south eastern suburbs of the city off Route 56.

Founded in the late 1990s this organisation started restoring the Stinson which once served with the Royal Navy in England. Parts of two other examples were acquired to assist with the project. The aircraft was been reregistered some years ago so is presumably either airworthy or nearly so.

TYPE	REG/SER	CON. NO.	PI/NOTES	STATUS
☐ Stinson V-77 Reliant (AT-19)	N715FB	77-443	43-44156, FB715, Bu1570, N66274 – Contains parts from c/n 77-487 43-44200, FB759, Bu30496, N69794 and one other unidentified aircraft.	RAC

MINNESOTA AIR GUARD MUSEUM (MN27)

Address:	670 General Miller Drive, Minneapolis-St. Paul International A/P, Minneapolis 55111-4114.
Tel:	612-713-2523 **Fax:** 612-713-2525 **Email:** msp04332@isd.net
Admission:	Mid April–mid October Saturday-Sunday 1100-1600. (Provisional)
Location:	In the north east corner of the airport by the intersection of Highways 55 and 62.

In 1921 the 109th Aero Squadron became the first federally recognised National Guard aviation unit. Operations started at Holman Field with a leased Curtiss Oriole before Curtiss JN-4s arrived in January 1922. Three hangars were constructed at a former racetrack which is now covered by the international airport. From 1923 until 1940 the 109th Observation Squadron flew a variety of types. The unit was called up to active duty and moved to England in August 1942. The role was changed and Mustangs were operated in the photo-reconnaissance role. Fighters were flown from a number of airfields in the area until 1960. The wing then moved into the airport and has since been flying transport types on missions around the world.

With this rich heritage a museum was needed and approval was granted in June 1982. The collection opened two years later in a group of converted alert hangars. A large amount of material including an archive of cuttings and photographs saved by Captain Ray Miller, one of the early officers of the Minnesota Air National Guard, is on view. There is a large collection of uniforms, unit badges, models and components some of which are on view. Types used by the Minnesota ANG at Minneapolis and Duluth have been acquired and been

have been restored by the museum volunteers over the years. The Curtiss Oriole replica was completed in the late 1990s. This biplane commemorates one of first types flown by the unit and it currently hangs from the roof of one of the hangars used by the active aircraft.

The early Texan is painted in the colours of a BC-1. The type entered service in 1937 and was used for combat training. The North American Mustang was flown from the field in the autumn of 1946 and operated until the arrival of the T-28A a decade later. An ex-Navy T-28B represents this period. From June 1957 until December of the same year the Lockheed F-94 was in service. These were replaced by the Northrop F-89 Scorpion which was used until June 1960 when conversion to the Boeing C-97 was started. The Lockheed Hercules was put into service in the winter of 1970. Restoration of the C-131, flown on aeromedical duties, has started. The museum was closed for a period as its hangars were needed for combat types during Gulf War conflicts. This happened again when a fighter squadron flew in from Duluth whilst the runways there were being resurfaced. The collection is once again open on a regular basis and the displays are being developed.

TYPE	REG/SER	CON. NO.	PI/NOTES	STATUS
☐ Beech D18S Expeditor (C-45H)	52-10884	AF-814	52-10884, N9453Z	PV
☐ Bell 205 Iroquois (UH-1D) (UH-1H)	64-13882	4589		PV
☐ Bell 205 Iroquois (UH-1D) (UH-1H)	65-10077	5121		PV
☐ Boeing 367-76-66 Stratofreighter (KC-97G) (KC-97L)	53-0218	17000	53-0218, N97KC	PV
☐ Cavalier Mustang II (F-51D) (North American NA-122)	'475024'		68-15795	PVX

Minnesota

☐ Convair 440-61 Samaritan (TC-131E)	55-4757	344		PVC
☐ Convair 8-10 Delta Dagger (F-102A)	'56-1476'	8-10-436	56-1219	PVX
☐ Curtiss 17 Oriole (R)	N109NG	320A		RA
☐ Douglas DC-3A-467 Skytrain (C-47B) (R4D-6) (R4D-6R)	N33	15138/26583	43-49322, Bu50793, N7092C, N7072C	PV
☐ General Dynamics 401 Fighting Falcon (F-16A)	81-0807	61-488		PV
☐ Lockheed 182-1A Hercules (182-44-03) (C-130A) (C-130D)	'55-016'	182-3192	57-0485	PVX
☐ Lockheed 580 (T-33A)	55-3025	580-9522	55-3025, N512NA	PV
☐ Lockheed 880-75-13 Starfire (F-97A) (F-94C)	51-13560	880-7811		RA
☐ McDonnell M.36BA Voodoo (F-101B) (CF-101B)	101067	672	58-0300 – in Canadian markings Front fuselage only.	PV
☐ McDonnell M.98AM Phantom II (F4H-1) (F-4B)				PV
☐ McDonnell M.98DE Phantom II (F-4C)	63-7482	476		PV
☐ McDonnell M.98DF Phantom II (RF-4C)	64-1061	1017		PV
☐ North American NA-59 Texan (AT-6)	'798'	59-1948	40-2122, NC63625, N63625 – painted as a BC-1.	PVX
☐ North American NA-200 Trojan (T-28B)	'51-3659'	200-277	Bu138206, (N5493G), Bu138206	PVX
☐ Northrop N-160 Scorpion (N-68) (F-89D) (F-89J)	53-2677	N.4808		PV
☐ Piper J-3C-65 Cub (L-4H)				PVC
☐ Supermarine 349 Spitfire LF.V (Scale R)				PV
☐ WSK SBLim-2M (Lim-2) [MiG-15bis] (MiG-15UTI)	'11'	3506	306 (Poland), N15HQ	PVX

MINNESOTA HISTORICAL SOCIETY (MN28)

Address: 345 West Kellogg Boulevard, St. Paul, Minnesota 55102-1906.
Tel: 651-296-6126   **Email:** reference@mnhs.org
Admission: May–August Monday-Saturday 1000-1700 Sunday 1000-1600; September–October Saturday-Sunday 1000-1600.
Location: In the centre of the city.

The society is responsible for a number of sites and museums across the state. Displays tracing the history of Minnesota can be seen in the main building in St. Paul. Special exhibitions are also staged on a regular basis.

The Curtiss Jenny replica is hanging without fabric in the central rotunda. This aircraft was built by volunteers at the Air National Guard Museum. The Jenny was the first equipment of the local unit.

TYPE	REG/SER	CON. NO.	PI/NOTES	STATUS
☐ Curtiss 1C Jenny (JN-4D) (R)			On loan from Minnesota ANG Museum.	PV

MINNESOTA MILITARY MUSEUM (MN29)

Address: 15000 Highway 115, Camp Ripley, Little Falls, Minnesota 56345-4173
Tel: 320-632-7374   **Fax:** 320-632-7779   **Email:** MNMuseum@yahoo.com
Admission: May–September daily 1000-1700.
Location: About 7 miles north of the town on Route 371.

Collection of items relating to the military history of the state was initiated in 1976 as a Bicentennial project. The museum moved into a 1930 building at Camp Ripley in 1987. Displays tracing the history of the frontier forts including Fort Ripley, which was in use from 1849-1877, can be seen. The Minnesota National Guard was formed in 1856 at St. Paul and the story of all units is told. There is an excellent collection of 19th and 20th century small arms along with military vehicles used in recent years.

The aircraft and helicopters in the collection show some of the types flown in the state and from Fort Ripley over the last half century.

TYPE	REG/SER	CON. NO.	PI/NOTES	STATUS
☐ Bell 47G Sioux (H-13G) (OH-13G)	52-7807	1034		PV
☐ Bell 204 Iroquois (HU-1A) (UH-1A)	57-6097	12	Possible identity.	PV
☐ Bell 205 Iroquois (UH-1H)	69-15122	11410	Possible identity.	PV
☐ Bell 206A Kiowa (OH-58A)	70-15122	40673		PV
☐ Bell 209 Huey Cobra (AH-1G) (AH-1F)				PV
☐ Cessna 305A Bird Dog (L-19A) (O-1A)	50-1328	21002		PV
☐ Hiller UH12C Raven (H-23C) (OH-23C)	56-2285	899		PV

MINNESOTA STATE COLLEGE SOUTH EAST TECHNICAL AIRPORT CAMPUS (MN30)

Address: 110 Galewski Drive, Winona, Minnesota 55987.
Tel: 887-853-8328   **Email:** info@southeasternmn.edu
Admission: By prior permission only.
Location: About 3 miles north west of the town off Route 61.

The college trains airframe and engine fitters at its premises at Max Conrad Field. A number of instructional airframes are in use. Proposals to set up a new centre at Duluth may result in some aircraft moving.

TYPE	REG/SER	CON. NO.	PI/NOTES	STATUS
☐ Beech D18S Expeditor (C18S) (SNB-2C) (SNB-3Q) (SNB-5) (TC-45J)	N3785	6101	Bu23823 – possible identity	RA
☐ Cessna 150H	N6766S	15067566		RA
☐ Ercoupe 415C	N3920H	4621	NC3920H	RA

☐ Hiller UH12C Raven	'N1987AP'			RAX
☐ Luscombe 8A Silvaire	N1361K	4088	NC1361K	RA
☐ Piper PA-22-108 Colt				RA
☐ Piper PA-23-250 Aztec	N4580P	27-89		RA
☐ Sikorsky S-62A Seaguard (HH-52A)	1464	62143	Or 1460/62139	RA

MOOSE LAKE MONUMENT (MN31)

Location:	On permanent view at Carlton County Airport which is about 5 miles south east of the town.

TYPE	REG/SER	CON. NO.	PI/NOTES	STATUS
☐ Bell 209 Huey Cobra (AH-1G) (AH-1F)	67-15608	20272		PV

NORTHLAND COMMUNITY AND TECHNICAL COLLEGE (MN32)

Address:	1101 Highway One East, Thief River Falls, Minnesota 56701.
Tel:	218-683-8800 Fax: 218-683-8801
Admission:	By prior permission only.
Location:	About 2 miles north east of the town.

The college trains students for FAA licences in airframe, power plant and systems. The fleet of instructional airframes is used for these courses. The list is not complete and any information would be welcome.

TYPE	REG/SER	CON. NO.	PI/NOTES	STATUS
☐ Beech 23 Musketeer				RA
☐ Beech 65-80 Seminole (L-23F) (U-8F)	N112AR	LF-20	60-5786	RA
☐ Bell 47G				RA
☐ Bell 47G				RA
☐ Bell 205 Iroquois (UH-1H)	68-16126	10785		RA
☐ Bell 205 Iroquois (UH-1H)				RA
☐ Bell 205 Iroquois (UH-1H)				RA
☐ Boeing 727-14	N460US	18910	N972PS, XA-IUP, N972PS	RA
☐ Boeing 727-200				RA
☐ Cessna 172	N6889A	28989		RA
☐ Cessna 305A Bird Dog (L-19A) (O-1A)				RA
☐ Cessna 337M Super Skymaster (O-2A)				RA
☐ Cessna 402				RA
☐ Douglas A-4C Skyhawk (A4D-2N)	Bu145135	12381		PV
☐ Douglas DC-9-14	N930RC	45729	N946L, OH-LYE	RA
☐ Douglas DC-9-14				RA
☐ Hughes 269A Osage (TH-55A)	67-16752	0859		RA
☐ Hughes 269A Osage (TH-55A)				RA
☐ Mitsubishi MU-2B	N2176D	028	HB-LEC, SE-FGP, LN-DAB, SE-FGP, N53JL, ZP-CCQ, CP-1962	RA
☐ North American NA-265 Sabreliner (T-39A) (CT-39A)	60-3492	265-20		RA
☐ Piper PA-23-250 Aztec C	N6451Y	27-3741		RA
☐ Piper PA-25 Pawnee	N6244Z	25-299		RA
☐ Piper PA-28-151 Cherokee Warrior	N41935	28-7415362		RA
☐ Republic F-84F Thunderstreak				RA

NORTHWEST AIRLINES HISTORY CENTER (MN33)

Address:	8101 34th Avenue South, Bloomington, Minnesota 55425.
Tel:	952-997-8000
Admission:	Monday-Friday 1000-1700.
Location:	Just south of the airport which is in the eastern part of the town.

The company was set up in 1926 as an air-mail carrier flying from Minneapolis/St Paul to Chicago. Volunteers have set up the exhibition to trace the history of the company. On show are uniforms, models of types of aircraft flown by the company from the early days and memorabilia. There is a reconstruction of a vintage office showing equipment used in the pre-war period. Also on show is a large collection of photographs.

OWATONNA MONUMENT (MN34)

Location:	On permanent view near the airport which is about 2 miles north of the town.

TYPE	REG/SER	CON. NO.	PI/NOTES	STATUS
☐ Northrop N-156T Talon (T-38A) (AT-38B)	60-0573	N.5146		PV
☐ Northrop N-156T Talon (T-38A) (AT-38B)	60-0589	N.5162		PV
☐ Northrop N-156T Talon (T-38A) (AT-38B)	61-0828	N.5194		PV

PILLAGER MONUMENT (MN35)

Location:	On permanent view on Highway 210 in the town.

TYPE	REG/SER	CON. NO.	PI/NOTES	STATUS
☐ Bell 204 Iroquois (UH-1B)				PV

Parked in the hangar of the Golden Wings Air Museum is this rare Alliance Argo. (Dave Welch) [MN18]

The Minnesota Air National Guard Museum have painted this North American T-28B in the markings of one flown by the state forces.(MANGM) [MN27]

This Kreider-Reisner KR-21A is often on show in the main hangar of the Historic Aircraft Restoration Museum. [MO15]

PROCTOR MONUMENT (MN36)

Location:	On permanent view on Highway 2 in the town.

TYPE	REG/SER	CON. NO.	PI/NOTES	STATUS
☐ McDonnell M.36BA Voodoo (TF-101B) (TF-101F)	59-0407	731	59-0407, 17407 (Canada) – identity doubtful.	PV

ROGERS MONUMENT (MN37)

Location:	On view during opening hours at Cabela's store at 20200 Rogers Drive in the south eastern part of the town.

TYPE	REG/SER	CON. NO.	PI/NOTES	STATUS
☐ Piper J-3C-65 Cub				PV

SHAKOPEE MONUMENT (MN38)

Location:	On permanent view in the eastern part of the town.

TYPE	REG/SER	CON. NO.	PI/NOTES	STATUS
☐ Bell 209 Huey Cobra (AH-1G) (AH-1F)	70-16032	20976		PV

ST. FRANCIS MONUMENT (MN39)

Location:	On permanent view at ALP 622 at 3073 Bridge Street in the south eastern part of the town.

TYPE	REG/SER	CON. NO.	PI/NOTES	STATUS
☐ Grumman G-134 Mohawk (AO-1A) (OV-1A)	'92622'	15A	59-2617, N75207	PVX

STEWARTVILLE MONUMENT (MN40)

Location:	On permanent view at a business in the town.

TYPE	REG/SER	CON. NO.	PI/NOTES	STATUS
☐ Culver LCA Cadet				PV

THREE RIVER FALLS MONUMENT (MN41)

Location:	On permanent view at VVA 331 in the town.

TYPE	REG/SER	CON. NO.	PI/NOTES	STATUS
☐ Bell 205 Iroquois (UH-1H)				PV

WELLS MONUMENT (MN42)

Location:	On permanent view at the airport which is about 2 miles west of the town on Route 109.

TYPE	REG/SER	CON. NO.	PI/NOTES	STATUS
☐ North American NA-201 Sabre (F-86D) (F-86L)	53-0719	201-163		PV

WILLMAR MONUMENT (MN43)

Location:	On permanent view at the airport which is in the south western part of the town.

TYPE	REG/SER	CON. NO.	PI/NOTES	STATUS
☐ Grumman G-303 Tomcat (F-14A)	Bu160914	343		PV

WINGS OF THE NORTH (MN44)

Address:	9960 Flying Cloud Drive, Suite 204, Eden Prarie, Minnesota 55347-4011.
Tel:	952-746-6100 Email: info@wotn.org
Admission:	By prior permission only.
Location:	At Flying Cloud Airport which is about 12 miles south west of Minneapolis off Route 169/212.

The long-term aim of the group is to construct a museum tracing the history of aviation. Plans have been put forward for a display building and education centre.

They have acquired a share in a Texan and this is displayed regularly at shows in the region. The aircraft was delivered to Luke Field in Texas in January 1942 and was flown from several field in the south of the country until it was put in store at Albuquerque in New Mexico in October 1945. In 1949 the Texan was one of a batch sent to Portugal where it was operated both in Europe and the African colonies until the late 1970s.

The Valiant is under restoration in the workshops. This aircraft was in military service between March 1943 and September 1944 and after a number of owners joined the group in 1992.

TYPE	REG/SER	CON. NO.	PI/NOTES	STATUS
☐ North American NA-78 Texan (AT-6A)	N77TX	78-6698	41-16320, 1620 (Portugal), G-TIDE, N3762J, N42DQ	RAA
☐ Vultee V-74A Valiant (BT-15)	N69987	74A-9536	42-41689	RAC

MISSISSIPPI

ANGLO-AMERICAN LIGHTNING ASSOCIATION (MS1)

Address: Vintage Aeroplane Company, 7110 Road C, Kiln, Mississippi 39556.
Tel: 601-467-7078 **Fax:** 601-467-8484 **Email:** bob@lightningusa.org
Admission: By prior permission only.
Location: At Stennis International Airport which is about 40 miles west of Biloxi north of Interstate 10.

Two Lightnings were shipped to Stennis in late 1997. Rebuilding the T.5, which had served at Coltishall, Wattisham and Boscombe Down soon commenced. The aircraft was rolled out on 23rd September 2001. Volunteers aim to return the classic jet fighter to airworthy status. The second was sold to the Olympic Flight Museum in Washington State.

TYPE	REG/SER	CON. NO.	PI/NOTES	STATUS
☐ English Electric P.27 Lightning T.5	N422XS	B1/95007	XS422	RAC

ARMED FORCES MUSEUM (MS2)

Address: Building 850, Camp Shelby, Mississipi 39407-5500.
Tel: 601-558-2337 **Fax:** 601-558-2377 **Email:** chad.daniels@ms.ngb.army.mil
Admission: Tuesday-Saturday 0900-1630.
Location: About 15 miles south of Hattiesburg off Route 49.

A museum was set up in a building on the site and the displays traced the role of the camp and the history of the units which have been in residence. This exhibition closed in December 2000 and moved to a purpose-built complex in 2001. On show are military vehicles, flags, uniforms etc. and monuments to units trained at the camp.

TYPE	REG/SER	CON. NO.	PI/NOTES	STATUS
☐ Bell 205 Iroquois (UH-1D) (UH-1H)	66-0877	5360		RAC
☐ Bell 205 Iroquois (UH-1H)	68-16608	11267	68-16608, N166UA	PV
☐ Bell 205 Iroquois (UH-1H)	69-15937	12225		PV
☐ Bell 205 Iroquois (UH-1H)				RA
☐ Bell 205 Iroquois (UH-1H)				RA
☐ Bell 209 Huey Cobra (AH-1G) (AH-1Q) (AH-1S)	67-15607	20271		RAC
☐ Douglas DC-3A-467 Skytrain (C-47B)			Fuselage only.	RA
☐ Grumman G-134 Mohawk (OV-1B) (RV-1D)	64-14252	80B		PV
☐ Hughes 369M Cayuse (HO-6) (OH-6A)	66-7804	0118		PV
☐ Sikorsky S-64A Tarhe (CH-54A)	66-18412	64014		PV

COLUMBIA MONUMENT (MS3)

Location: On permanent view at Marion County Airport which is about 5 miles north east of the town.

TYPE	REG/SER	CON. NO.	PI/NOTES	STATUS
☐ Lockheed 580 (T-33A)	'3930'	580-7396	52-9311	PVX

COLUMBUS AIR FORCE BASE (MS4)

Address: 14FTW/PA., 555 Seventh Street Suite 203, Columbus, Mississippi 39710-7068.
Tel: 662-434-7068 **Email:** 14FTW.PA@columbus.af.mil
Admission: On permanent view.
Location: About 10 miles north of the town off Route 45.

Opened in 1941 the base was used for training until it closed five years later. The Air Force took back the field in 1955 and Strategic Air Command units moved in. In 1969 the base reverted to the training role and examples of the types flown in recent years have been preserved. The number on the T-38 is changed every six weeks and is that of the senior class.

The T-37 number '7101' honours the first class to graduate in 1971.

TYPE	REG/SER	CON. NO.	PI/NOTES	STATUS
☐ Cessna 318B Tweety Bird (318A) (T-37A) (T-37B)	'54-2737'	40004	54-2729, '7101'	PVX
☐ Cessna 318B Tweety Bird (318A) (T-37A) (T-37B)	58-1914	40339	Outside base.	PV
☐ Cessna 318B Tweety Bird (318A) (T-37A) (T-37B)	59-0274	40436	Monument in town.	PV
☐ Northrop N-156T Talon (T-38A)	'00-7101'	N.5824	65-10405	PVX

COMMEMORATIVE AIR FORCE (MISSISSIPPI WING) (MS5)

Address: PO Box 3042, Madison, Mississippi 39130.
Tel: 601-853-3542 **Email:** ehollingsworth@cellularsouth.com
Admission: By prior permission only.
Location: At Bruce Campbell Field which is about two miles north east of the town.

The airworthy Stinson 10A is now the only aircraft allocated to the wing. This high wing monoplane is painted in the colours it wore when flown by the New Jersey Wing of the Civil Air Patrol. The remaining aircraft are owned by members and several of these are based at other airfields in the region.

TYPE	REG/SER	CON. NO.	PI/NOTES	STATUS
☐ Cessna 337A Super Skymaster	N5320S	3370420		RAA
☐ Cessna 337M Super Skymaster (O-2A)	N97632	337M0430	69-7632	RAA
☐ North American NA-88 Texan (SNJ-4)	N22KD	88-13072	Bu27616, N7065C	RAA
☐ Stinson 10A Voyager	NC34693	7993	NC34693, N7065C	RAA
☐ Wittman W-18 Tailwind	N52WB	513		RAA

Mississippi

D'IBERVILLE VETERANS MEMORIAL PARK (MS6)

| Location: | On permanent view at the junction of Auto Mall Parkway and Brodie Road in the town. |

TYPE	REG/SER	CON. NO.	PI/NOTES	STATUS
☐ Bell 205 Iroquois (UH-1H)	67-19532	10138		PV

GEORGE R. HALL MEMORIAL PARK (MS7)

Address:	Academy Drive, Hattiesburg, Mississippi 39401.
Tel:	601-544-8661 **Email:** info@hattiesburgairport.com
Admission:	On permanent view.
Location:	At the airport which is about 10 miles north of the city off Route 11.

The T-33 was donated to the city by the Air Force in 1974 and the other two aircraft arrived in August 1985. The trio have been mounted at the regional airport to honour local men who have served in the Air Force.

TYPE	REG/SER	CON. NO.	PI/NOTES	STATUS
☐ Lockheed 580 (T-33A)	'52595'	580-7750	52-9590	PVX
☐ McDonnell M.36CA Voodoo (RF-101C)	56-0217	235		PV
☐ Republic RF-84F Thunderflash	53-7636		53-7636, 37636 (France)	PV

GREENVILLE AIR FORCE BASE MUSEUM (MS8)

Address:	Greenville Airport, Greenville, Mississippi 38701.
Tel:	662-334-3121 **Email:** benelk@techinfo.com
Admission:	Daily 0700-1800.
Location:	About 6 miles east of the town.

Construction of the airfield started in 1942 and the site was used for pilot training. The field was reactivated in 1951 and two years later became Greenville Air Force Base. The flying training school closed in 1960 and five years later the airfield was turned over to the local area and is now the regional airport. The museum is located in the terminal building and photographs, documents and memorabilia trace the military use of the site. The T-33 pole mounted outside the building was acquired in Louisiana and moved to the field. The original Greenville airport, in the south western suburbs of the town, opened in the 1930s and was active until the mid-1960s. This site is now an industrial park but some of the original buildings are still in use.

TYPE	REG/SER	CON. NO.	PI/NOTES	STATUS
☐ Lockheed 580 (T-33A)	51-6601	580-5933		PV

GRENADA MONUMENT (MS9)

| Location: | On permanent view at the High School in Charger Drive in the southern part of the town. |

TYPE	REG/SER	CON. NO.	PI/NOTES	STATUS
☐ Douglas A-4M Skyhawk	Bu160255	14598		PV

GULFPORT-BILOXI NATIONAL GUARD BASE COLLECTION (MS10)

Address:	14035 Airport Road, Gulfport, Mississippi 39503.
Tel:	228-214-6001
Admission:	By prior permission only.
Location:	At the regional airport which is about 2 miles north of Gulfport off Route 49.

Units of the Army National Guard operate helicopters from this base and the two preserved types are parked close to the main gate. The F-4 is at the nearby Combat Readiness Training Center. The Kiowa is used as a touring exhibit. It is mounted on a trailer and can often be seen at local events. Within this site are several buildings remaining from the World War II period including a large hangar.

TYPE	REG/SER	CON. NO.	PI/NOTES	STATUS
☐ Bell 206A Kiowa (OH-58A)	72-21456	42122		RA
☐ Hughes 369M Cayuse (YHO-6) (YOH-6A)	62-12624			RA
☐ McDonnell M.98DE Phantom II (F-4C)	63-7513	526		RA

HAZLEHURST MONUMENT (MS11)

| Location: | On permanent view at VFW 2567 on Highway 28 in the western part of the town. |

TYPE	REG/SER	CON. NO.	PI/NOTES	STATUS
☐ North American NA-201 Sabre (F-86D) (F-86L)	53-1061	201-505		PV

HINDS COMMUNITY COLLEGE (MS12)

Address:	4100 Airport Road, Bolton, Mississippi 39154-1100.
Tel:	601-857-3884 **Email:** mmjackson@hindscc.edu
Admission:	By prior permission only.
Location:	At the airport which is just north of Raymond.

The college was established in 1917 and has five sites in the area. Aviation Maintenance Technology has a facility at the airport where the instructional airframes are located. The college also runs a course for air traffic controllers and some of the aircraft are airworthy and also used for this purpose.

TYPE	REG/SER	CON. NO.	PI/NOTES	STATUS
☐ Beech 58TC Baron	N100HP	TK-116		RA
☐ Beech C 90 King Air	N708DG	LJ-508	N938K, N801MP, N706DG	RA
☐ Beech A200 Huron (C-12A) (C-12C)	76-0170	BD-27		RA
☐ Bell 206A Kiowa (OH-58A) (OH-58C)	68-16940	40254	Possible identity.	RA
☐ Cessna 150L	N18115	15073796		RA
☐ Cessna 172K	N79429	17258078		RA
☐ Cessna 172R	N35367	17281068		RA
☐ Piper PA-28R-200 Cherokee Arrow II	N44SM	28R-7635076		RA

JACKSON AIR NATIONAL GUARD BASE COLLECTION (MS13)

Address: 172nd AW/PA, Allen C. Thompson Field, Jackson, Mississippi 39208-0810.
Tel: 601-405-8311
Admission: By prior permission only.
Location: About 7 miles east of Jackson off Route 80.

The 183rd Squadron was allocated to the Mississippi Air National Guard in July 1953. In September of the same year Douglas RB-26 Invaders moved into Hawkins Field at Jackson. In the spring of 1957 the unit began training on the Republic RF-84F but as the Hawkins facilities were not suitable for jets a change of base was made.

The squadron later became the first in the ANG to serve in the aeromedical evacuation role. Fairchild C-119s were flown until July 1962 when a change to transport duties with Lockheed C-121s was made. In January 1963 a move to the new Jackson Airport took place and since then C-124s, C-130s and C-141s have been used.

TYPE	REG/SER	CON. NO.	PI/NOTES	STATUS
☐ Bell 205 Iroquois (UH-1H)	'6-2036'			RAX
☐ Douglas A-26B Invader	44-34559	27838		RA
☐ Hughes 369M Cayuse (HO-6) (OH-6A)	66-14405	0286		RA

KEESLER AIR FORCE BASE MUSEUM (MS14)

Address: Keesler Technical Training Center, Mississippi 39354-2120.
Tel: 228-377-2783 **Email:** 81trw.pa1@keesler.af.mil
Admission: By prior permission only.
Location: In the western suburbs of Biloxi, north of Highway 90.

Activated in June 1941 the base is named after Lieutenant Samuel R. Keesler who was killed in action on 9th October 1918 near Verdun. During World War II the field was home to large numbers of Tuskegee Airmen who trained as radio operators, airframe and engine mechanics and bombadiers. B-24 Liberator maintenance was the primary function of the school. The primary role of the field has always been training and at the current time work on avionics is carried out.

When Chanute AFB in Illinois closed the weather forecasting courses moved south. A wing operating C-130s on weather reconnaissance and airborne command duties is based at the field. A small display tracing the history of the base has been set up in one of the buildings and the preserved aircraft are located around the site. On show are photographs, documents, uniforms and memorabilia highlighting the work carried out.

The second YF-100A Super Sabre was removed from its position near the gate as it was suffering from corrosion. This aircraft is now at Edwards AFB in California. Over the last few years the base has suffered considerable damage from hurricanes and several areas have been completely rebuilt.

TYPE	REG/SER	CON. NO.	PI/NOTES	STATUS
☐ Ford JB-2 (Fieseler Fi 103A-1)				RA
☐ Lockheed 383-04-05 Starfighter (F-104C)	56-0938	183-1226		RA
☐ Lockheed 580 (T-33A)	58-0567	580-1536		RA
☐ McDonnell M.36CA Voodoo (RF-101C)	56-0068	290	56-0068, '56-3380'	RA
☐ North American NA-174 Trojan (T-28A)	'13747'	174-327	51-3789, '13389'	RAX
☐ Republic F-105D Thunderchief	60-0535	D-223	60-0535,'60-534'	RA

MAGEE MONUMENT (MS15)

Location: On permanent view at VFW 9122 in the northern part of the town.

TYPE	REG/SER	CON. NO.	PI/NOTES	STATUS
☐ Bell 205 Iroquois (UH-1H)	67-17219	9541		PV

MERIDIAN MONUMENT (MS16)

Location: On permanent view at a business north east of the city on Route 39.

TYPE	REG/SER	CON. NO.	PI/NOTES	STATUS
☐ North American NA-253 Buckeye (T2J-1) (T-2A)	Bu147516	253-107		PV

MERIDIAN NAVAL AIR STATION (MS17)

Address: 255 Rosenbaum Avenue, Meridian. Mississippi 39309.
Tel: 601-679-2602 **Email:** public_affair_nasmer_fct@navy.mil
Admission: By prior permission only.
Location: About 15 miles north of the town on Route 39.

Mississippi

Construction of the base started in 1959 and the first units moved in two years later. Since 1971 the base has been the home of Training Wing 1 offering intermediate and advanced courses for strike jet naval pilots. Currently in use are some of the last remaining T-2 Buckeyes and recently introduced T-45 Goshawks. In addition a rescue flight operates helicopters. The preserved aircraft are located around the station.

TYPE	REG/SER	CON. NO.	PI/NOTES	STATUS
☐ Douglas TA-4J Skyhawk	Bu158490	14295		RA
☐ Douglas TA-4J Skyhawk	Bu158526	14331		RA
☐ McDonnell-Douglas T-45A Goshawk (FSM)	'Bu165485'			RAX
☐ North American NA-253 Buckeye (T2J-1) (T-2A)	Bu147522	253-113		RA
☐ North American NA-367 Buckeye (T-2C)	Bu159727	367-48		RA

MISSISSIPPI VIETNAM VETERANS' MEMORIAL (MS18)

Address: PO Box 721, Biloxi, Mississippi 39533-0721.
Tel: 228-392-7190   **Email:** mvvmc@bellsouth.net
Admission: On permanent view
Location: In the eastern part of Ocean Springs on Route 90.

The memorial consists of a wall on which the names of Mississippi people who lost their lives in the war can be seen. The Iroquois is painted in the colours of one which served on medical evacuation duties in South East Asia. In addition there is the top of a mast from a ship and an avenue of unit flags.

TYPE	REG/SER	CON. NO.	PI/NOTES	STATUS
☐ Bell 205 Iroquois (UH-1H)	66-16909	9103		PV

NATIONAL AGRICULTURAL AVIATION MUSEUM (MS19)

Address: 1150 Lakeland Drive. Jackson. Mississippi 39216.
Tel: 601-713-3365   **Fax:** 601-982-4292   **Email:** Charlie@mdac.state.ms.us
Admission: Monday-Saturday 0900-1700
Location: On Route 25 just east of Interstate 55.

The museum is part of the Jim Buck Ross Agriculture and Forestry Museum. The displays reflect Mississippi life from the pioneer days and a typical early town has been put together by moving buildings from around the state. Many interesting structures, several containing working machinery, can be seen. Regular demonstrations of country crafts are held in these buildings. There are several vintage tractors on show.

A modern Heritage Center traces the history of agriculture and forestry in the state. The National Agricultural Aviation Museum occupies part of this building. Crop dusting started in Mississippi in the 1920s and a video traces its history. Many interesting shots of types from the past can be seen. Four aircraft used in this work are currently on show. The Stearman and the Piper Cub were modified for this work whilst the Pawnee and Ag-Cat were specially designed for the task.

The first prototype of the Grumman design is on view. This aircraft made its maiden flight on 22nd May 1957. Production aircraft were built under licence by the Schweizer company at Elmira in New York State as the Grumman factories were busy with military contracts.

TYPE	REG/SER	CON. NO.	PI/NOTES	STATUS
☐ Boeing-Stearman E75 Kaydet (PT-13D)	N3998B	75-5292	42-17129, N5221N	PV
☐ Grumman G-164 Ag-Cat	N74054	X-1		PV
☐ Piper J-3C-65 Cub	N78423	23164	NC78423	PV
☐ Piper PA-25 Pawnee	N6755Z	25-2375		PV

NORTHWEST MISSISSIPPI COMMUNITY COLLEGE (MS20)

Address: 5197 W.E. Ross Parkway, Southaven, Mississippi 38671.
Tel: 662-342-1570   **Email:** ccooper@northwestms.edu
Admission: By prior permission only.
Location: In the southern part of the town off Route 55,

The college has three sites in the area. A course in Aviation Maintenance Technology is offered. Three aircraft are known to be in use. The Seminole was at the Olive Branch campus but is believed to have moved to the new W.E. Ross complex. The Cessna 310 was donated in 2009 and the Magnum is a recent arrival.

TYPE	REG/SER	CON. NO.	PI/NOTES	STATUS
☐ Avid Magnum	N7216A	39M		RA
☐ Beech C50 Seminole (RL-23D) (RU-8D) (U-8G)	58-1363			RA
☐ Cessna 310B	N163HC	35676		RA

PEARL RIVER COMMUNITY COLLEGE (MS21)

Address: 101 Highway 11 North, Poplarville, Mississippi 39470-2216.
Tel: 603-403-1000   **Email:** webmaster@prcc.cc.ms.us
Admission: By prior permission only.
Location: At Stennis International Airport which is about 40 miles west of Biloxi north of Interstate 10.

Pearl River was the first community college to be set up in Mississippi. The aviation department has a facility at Stennis Airport. One Cessna 310 is in use as an instructional airframe but there are believed to be others.

TYPE	REG/SER	CON. NO.	PI/NOTES	STATUS
☐ Cessna 310D	N6866T	39166		RA

PETAL MONUMENT (MS22)

Location:	On permanent view by the City Hall.

TYPE	REG/SER	CON. NO.	PI/NOTES	STATUS
☐ Douglas DC-3A-456 Skytrain (C-47A)	N4003	11672	42-68745, NC49543, N705M, N400S, N400B	PV

PHILADELPHIA MONUMENT (MS23)

Location:	On permanent view in Northside Park just north of the town centre.

TYPE	REG/SER	CON. NO.	PI/NOTES	STATUS
☐ North American NA-253 Buckeye (T2J-1) (T-2A)	Bu147494	253-85		PV

STENNIS SPACE CENTER (MS24)

Address:	Building 1200, National Air and Space Administration, Stennis Space Center, Mississippi 39529.
Tel:	228-688-2370 **Email:** pao@ssc.nasa.gov
Location:	About 40 miles west of Biloxi off Interstate 10.

The site opened in 1961 and amongst its duties is the testing of rocket motors. A visitor centre tracing the work of the centre has been set up. Several interactive exhibits have been built and guided tours take place regularly along with residential space camps. A number of space rockets are on show along with the Lear Jet. This aircraft was flown from the site on a variety of duties. The Corsair is preserved at a naval facility on the site.

TYPE	REG/SER	CON. NO.	PI/NOTES	STATUS
☐ Gates Learjet 25	N566NA	25-064	N266GL	PV
☐ Vought A-7B Corsair II	Bu154474	B114		RA

SUMRALL MONUMENT (MS25)

Location:	On permanent view in the centre of the town.

TYPE	REG/SER	CON. NO.	PI/NOTES	STATUS
☐ Bell 205 Iroquois (UH-1H)	66-16999	9193		PV

TUPELO ARMY NATIONAL GUARD BASE (MS26)

Location:	By prior permission only at the field which is 3 miles west of the town off Route 6.

TYPE	REG/SER	CON. NO.	PI/NOTES	STATUS
☐ Bell 206A Kiowa (OH-58A)	69-16227	40448		RA
☐ Hughes 369M Cayuse (HO-6) (OH-6A)	66-7799	0113		RA

UNION MONUMENT (MS27)

Location:	On permanent view on Route 492 in the eastern part of the town.

TYPE	REG/SER	CON. NO.	PI/NOTES	STATUS
☐ Grumman G-105 Cougar (F9F-8T) (TF-9J)	Bu147395	365	Possible identity.	PV

VETERANS MEMORIAL MUSEUM (MS28)

Address:	920 Hillcrest Drive, Laurel, Mississippi 39440.
Tel:	601-428-4008
Admission:	Tuesday-Saturday 1000-1700.
Location:	In the south western part of the town.

This museum opened in 2005 and has acquired a large collection of artefacts, books, photographs, medals, uniforms, flags, trophies and memorabilia from local veterans. The displays highlight the major conflicts in which United States forces have participated. The work of aviation pioneers features in the exhibition. On show is a replica Santos-Dumont Demoiselle. The aircraft owned by the National Museum of Naval Aviation was displayed at the Intrepid Museum in New York for a period. In 2008 a Pearl Harbor exhibit opened. The centrepiece is a small rusted steel plate from the deckhouse of the USS *Arizona*. The battleship was sunk on the day of the raid on 7th December 1941 and 948 members of the crew lost their lives and their bodies remain in the wreck. Outside the building a tank is displayed along with a range of weapons.

TYPE	REG/SER	CON. NO.	PI/NOTES	STATUS
☐ Santos-Dumont XX Demoiselle (R)				PV

WALNUT MONUMENT (MS29)

Location:	On permanent view in the City Park in the town off Highway 72.

TYPE	REG/SER	CON. NO.	PI/NOTES	STATUS
☐ Bell 205 Iroquois (UH-1H)	72-21639	13338		PV

MISSOURI

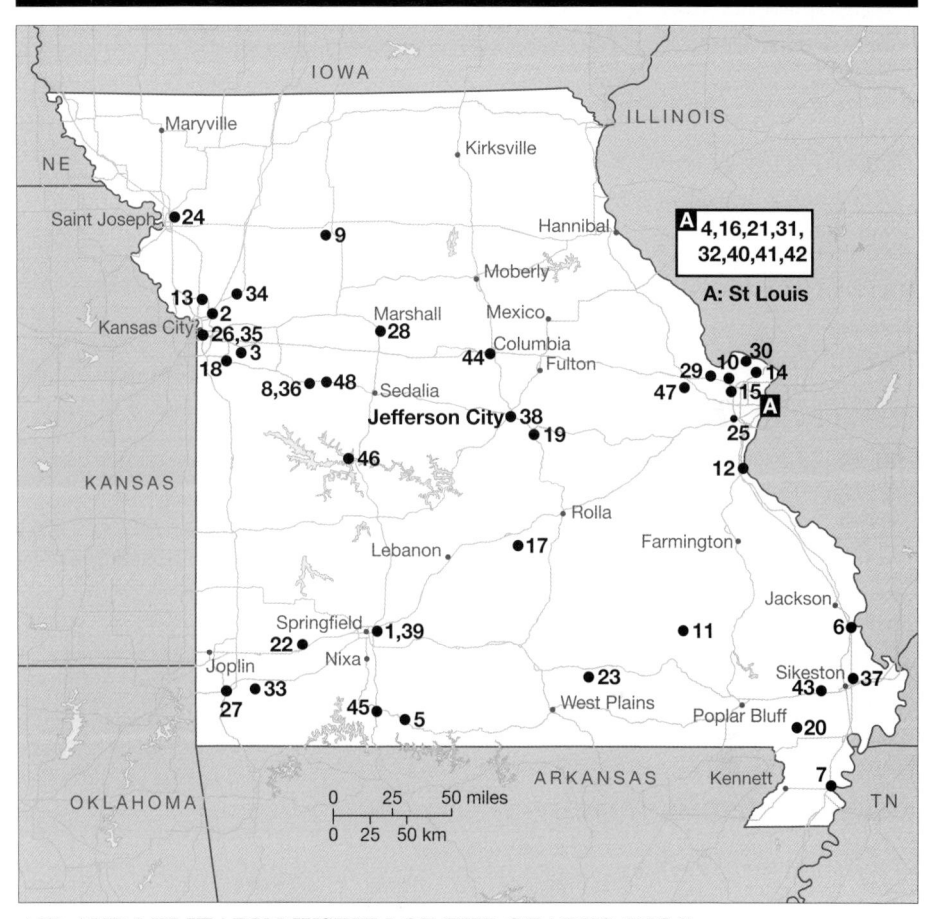

AIR AND MILITARY MUSEUM OF THE OZARKS (MO1)

Address:	2305 East Kearney Street, Springfield, Missouri 65803.
Tel:	417-864-7997 Fax: 417-882-0188 Email: ammo@ammomuseum.org
Admission:	Thursday-Saturday 1200-1600.
Location:	In the eastern suburbs of the town.

This museum is dedicated to all who have served in the armed forces. Military memorabilia has been collected along with items relating to civil aviation in the region. The Huey Cobra was flown into Springfield in 1993 and after being disarmed joined the museum. The Stearman has been registered to the collection since 1992.

TYPE	REG/SER	CON. NO.	PI/NOTES	STATUS
☐ Aeronca 65TC Grasshopper (O-58B) (L-3B)				PV
☐ Bell 209 Huey Cobra (AH-1G) (AH-1S)	70-16086	21030		PV
☐ Boeing-Stearman A75N1 Kaydet (PT-17)	N25191	75-2117	41-8558, N55163	RA
☐ Lockheed 580 (T-33A)	53-6055	580-9658	53-6055, N99095	PV
☐ Schweizer SGS.2-12 (TG-3A)			Fuselage frame only.	PV

AIRLINE HISTORY MUSEUM (MO2)

Address:	201 Lou Holland Drive, Kansas City, Missouri 64116-4234.
Tel:	816-421-3401 Fax: 816-421-3241 Email: info@AirlineHistoryMuseum.com
Admission:	Monday-Saturday 1000-1600; Sunday 1200-1600.
Location:	At Kansas City Airport which is in the northern part of the city.

In July 1986 the group acquired the Super Constellation in Arizona and flew it to Kansas City. The aircraft is now painted to represent one of the fleet operated by TWA which flew the type from the city for more than two decades. In November 1989 it obtained an airworthiness certificate and since then has been a great attraction at air shows throughout the country. In late 1990 a Martin 4-0-4 was bought in Florida and flown to Kansas City for restoration. The former Eastern Airlines aircraft is resplendent in TWA colours and it joined the airshow circuit in July 1993. A second example of the type was acquired and this is stored as a source of spares for the active one.

A DC-3 has been purchased and is currently undergoing a major rebuild. The society has set up an excellent museum of airline memorabilia in part of its building which also houses the huge spares inventory necessary to keep the airliners in flying condition.

TYPE	REG/SER	CON. NO.	PI/NOTES	STATUS
☐ Douglas DC-3-262	NC1945	3294	NC1950, NC1945, NC17334	RAC
☐ Lockheed L-1011-1 Tristar	N700TS	193B-1066	N31019, 3D-NEG, C5-WAL, 9Q-CTS	PV
☐ Lockheed 1049H-03-152 Super Constellation (1049H-03-148)	N6937C	1049H-4830	N5400V	PVA
☐ Martin 4-0-4	N145S	14142	N451A	PVA
☐ Martin 4-0-4	N144S	14150	N459A	RA

BATES CITY MONUMENT (MO3)

Location:	On permanent view at White Industries in the north western part of the city.

TYPE	REG/SER	CON. NO.	PI/NOTES	STATUS
☐ Gates Learjet 23	N20EP	23-008	N825LJ, N1203, N20S, N20BD	PV

BISSELL COLLECTION (MO4)

Address:	3000 Chouteau Avenue, St. Louis, Missouri 63103-2906.
Tel:	314-865-3030
Admission:	By prior permission only.
Location:	In the centre of the city.

The owners of this car business in the city have a number of former military aircraft stored in a compound at their premises. Some have arrived from storage yards around Davis-Monthan AFB in Arizona. Their plans for the aircraft are not known and any further information would be most welcome.

TYPE	REG/SER	CON. NO.	PI/NOTES	STATUS
☐ Lockheed 580 (T-33A) (TV-2) (T-33B)	Bu137790	580-8777	53-5438	RA
☐ North American NA-190 Sabre (F-86D)	52-4138	190-441		RA
☐ Republic F-105D Thunderchief	60-0452	D-140		RA
☐ Republic F-105D Thunderchief	59-1731	D-43		RA
☐ Sikorsky S-58 Choctaw (H-34A) (CH-34A) (CH-34C)	56-4319	58717		RA
☐ Sikorsky S-58 Choctaw (H-34A) (CH-34A) (CH-34C)	56-4339	58771		RA
☐ Sikorsky S-58 Seabat (HSS-1) (UH-34G)	Bu137970	5826		RA

BRANSON MONUMENT (MO5)

Location:	On permanent view at a golf centre in the town.

TYPE	REG/SER	CON. NO.	PI/NOTES	STATUS
☐ Lockheed 15-27-01 Harpoon (PV-2)				PVX
☐ Republic RC-3 Seabee				PV

CAPE GIRARDEAU MONUMENT (MO6)

Location:	On permanent view at the regional airport which is about 5 miles south west of the town.

TYPE	REG/SER	CON. NO.	PI/NOTES	STATUS
☐ Douglas TA-4J Skyhawk (TA-4F)	Bu152861	13507		PV

CARUTHERSVILLE MONUMENTS (MO7)

Location:	On permanent view at two locations in the town.

TYPE	REG/SER	CON. NO.	PI/NOTES	STATUS
☐ Bell 205 Iroquois (UH-1D) (UH-1H)	66-1193	5676	In a park on West 3rd Street	PV
☐ Lockheed 580 (T-33A)	53-5004	580-8343	In England Park on Highway U.	PV

CENTRAL MISSOURI STATE UNIVERSITY (MO8)

Address:	306 Broad Street, Warrensburg, Missouri 64093-5000.
Tel:	660-543-6969 **Email:** rthompson@ucmo.edu
Admission:	By prior permission only.
Location:	In the town and at the airport which is about 5 miles north west of the town.

The University has a large fleet of aircraft used for pilot training. Also in use by the students are a small number of hot air balloons. Four instructional airframes are known to be at the airport and at the campus in town.

Missouri

TYPE	REG/SER	CON. NO.	PI/NOTES	STATUS
☐ Bell 209 Huey Cobra (AH-1G) (AH-1S)	71-21048	21119		RA
☐ Grumman G-159 Gulfstream I	N193PA	125	N738G, N205G, N10NA, N5NA	RA
☐ Hughes 269A Osage (TH-55A)	N3078U		67-16755	RA
☐ North American NA-265 Sabreliner (T-39A) (CT-39A)	'1068'	265-83	61-0680, N32010	RAX

CHILLICOTHE MONUMENT (MO9)

Location:	On permanent view at the airport which is about 5 miles south east of the town

TYPE	REG/SER	CON. NO.	PI/NOTES	STATUS
☐ Republic F-105B Thunderchief	57-5817	B-54		PV

COMMEMORATIVE AIR FORCE (MISSOURI WING) (MO10)

Address:	PO Box 637, St. Charles, Missouri 63302-0637.
Tel:	636-250-4515 Fax: 636-250-4515 Email: pkf4@earthlink.net
Admission:	Tuesday, Thursday, Saturday 1000-1430.
Location:	At Smartt Airport which is about 4 miles north of the town on Route B.

A former Navy World War II hangar at Smartt Field is home to the fleet of warbirds operated by the wing. All the aircraft are airworthy except the T-33 which is preserved on the airfield. The area was flooded in 1993 and the buildings were damaged with almost all the memorabilia lost. A new museum opened in 2005.

TYPE	REG/SER	CON. NO.	PI/NOTES	STATUS
☐ Aeronca 65TAC	N36681	C1121TA	NC36681	PVA
☐ Grumman G-40 Avenger (TBM-3)	N5264V	3415	Bu53353	PVA
☐ Lockheed 580 (T-33A)	53-5933	580-9409		PV
☐ North American NA-108 Mitchell (B-25J) (TB-25J)	N345TH/'1361'	108-37460	44-31385, N3481G,	PVAX
☐ North American NA-121 Texan (AT-6F)	N81854	121-42579	44-81857	PVA

ELLINGTON MONUMENT (MO11)

Location:	On permanent view at VFW 6043 at 485 College Avenue in the northern part of the town.

TYPE	REG/SER	CON. NO.	PI/NOTES	STATUS
☐ Bell 209 Huey Cobra (AH-1G) (AH-1S)	68-15018	20552		PV

FESTUS MONUMENT (MO12)

Location:	On permanent view at ALP 253 at 849 American Legion Drive in the southern part of the town.

TYPE	REG/SER	CON. NO.	PI/NOTES	STATUS
☐ Republic F-84F Thunderstreak	51-9422			PV

FLAGSHIP DETROIT FOUNDATION (MO13)

Address:	POBox 96137, Southlake, Texas 76092.
Email:	Membership@FlagshipDetroit.org
Admission:	By prior permission only.
Location:	At Kansas City IAP which is about 12 miles north west of the city centre off Interstate 29.

The group acquired the early DC-3 in 2004 and it has been restored in its original American Airlines colours. The airliner was the 21st of 84 delivered to American Airlines. Entering service in March 1937 it flew on their routes for just over ten years before being sold in Mexico. The aircraft is normally based in the American Airlines hangars at Kansas City and maintained by a team of volunteers.

TYPE	REG/SER	CON. NO.	PI/NOTES	STATUS
☐ Douglas DC-3-178	NC17334	1920	NC17334, XB-JAD, XB-HED, N4843N, N177H,	RAA

FLORISSANT MONUMENT (MO14)

Location:	On permanent view outside the Civic Center.

TYPE	REG/SER	CON. NO.	PI/NOTES	STATUS
☐ McDonnell M.36BA Voodoo (TF-101B) (TF-101F)	58-0269	641		PV

HISTORIC AIRCRAFT RESTORATION MUSEUM (MO15)

Address:	3127 Creve Coeur Mill Road. Maryland Heights. Missouri 63146.
Tel:	314-434-3368 Fax: 314-878-6453 Email: a.stix@sbcglobal.net
Admission:	Saturday-Sunday 1000-1600 or by appointment.
Location:	At Dauster Field which is about 12 miles north east of St. Louis.

Vintage aircraft have been based at the delightful airfield at Creve Coeur for many years. Some time ago the owners of some of these machines decided to set up a museum and a large hangar was constructed. Around two dozen aircraft are normally on show and these are rotated with others from the private hangars at the field.

The museum suffered a set back in the 1993 floods when the airfield was covered with 22 feet of water. Most of the aircraft were flown out or removed by road before the waters reached their maximum height but some material was lost and the cleaning up operations took many months.

The rarest type in the collection is the Russian Shavrov Sh-2 amphibian which was restored a few years ago. Built in the 1930s, the aircraft was found in the early 1980s in a swamp near Murmansk. It was then taken to a technical college where it was rebuilt using parts from another airframe. The Sh-2 flew again in 1986 and was obtained by the museum after protracted negotiations. The aircraft arrived in St. Louis in January 1993.

Only 38 Star Cavalier high wing monoplanes were constructed between 1928 and 1936 and a handful are now in existence. The Driggs Dart biplane was built in 1927 and is believed to be the sole survivor of the 15 built. The aircraft spent several years in a Texas museum before joining the collection.

Only about five Timm Collegiate parasol wing monoplanes were built in the late 1920s and the example on show is one of three still in existence. The American-built DH-4 was completed in the autumn of 2006 after a major rebuild. This biplane is resplendent in the colours of one used on mail services.

The Monosport was a Warner powered de-luxe version of the Velie engined Monocoupe. Only 16 were sold and several of these were fitted with Kinner motors. The example at the airfield is under restoration in one of the workshops. The Zenith biplane was built in California in the late 1920s and was later used as a crop duster.

TYPE	REG/SER	CON. NO.	PI/NOTES	STATUS
☐ Aeronca K	NC19780	K-265	NC19734, N19780	PVA
☐ Aeronca 7AC Champion	N85057	7AC-3784	NC85057	PVA
☐ Aircraft Dynamics Nuwaco T-10	N813TW	183		RAA
☐ Antonov An-2P	N147AS	1G 132-45	CCCP-70790, RA-70790, 02763 (Lithuania), FLARF-02163	PVA
☐ Antonov An-2TP	N147SP	1G 238-19	SP-FBP	RAA
☐ Beech G17S	N911	B-12	NC80313, NC911	PVA
☐ Beech S35 Bonanza	N5610K	D-7378		RAA
☐ Boeing-Stearman A75 Kaydet (PT-13B)	N53280	75-0261	40-1704	RAA
☐ Boeing-Stearman B75N1 Kaydet (N2S-3)	N5521N	75-7931	Bu38310	PVA
☐ Brunner-Winkle Bird A	NC9115	1007	NC9115, N9115	RAA
☐ Cessna 172	N8841B	36541		RAA
☐ Culver LCA Cadet	N41621	LCA-380	NC41621	PVA
☐ Curtiss 50B Robin B	NC263E	116	NC263E, N263E	PVA
☐ Curtiss JN-4 Canuck	N496C	496		RAA
☐ Curtiss-Wright CW-15C Sedan	N436W	15C-2001	NC436W, N436W	PVA
☐ Curtiss-Wright CW-16E Light Sport	'E-35'	3548	LV-HHM, N71068 – in Argentinean markings.	PVAX
☐ Dart GC	N31692	66	NC31692	PVA
☐ De Havilland DH-4M2A	NX3249H	3		PVA
☐ De Havilland DH.89A Dragon Rapide (DH.89B Dominie I)	N2290B	6588	X7446, VT-ASA	RAA
☐ Driggs Dart II	NC1927	6	NC1927, N1927	PVA
☐ Fairchild 24 C8A	N9384	2514	NC9384	PVA
☐ Fairchild 24R46	N690FA	R46-104		PVA
☐ Fairchild 71	NC9727	603	NC9727, X-ABCI, X-ABEF	RA
☐ Flagg F-13	NX13625	1	NC13625	RAA
☐ Fleet 7	NC637M	212	NC637M, N637MJ	RAA
☐ Granville Gee Bee R-1				RAC
☐ Kreider-Reisner KR-21A	NC962V	1053	NC962V, N962V	PVA
☐ Kreider-Reisner KR-31 Challenger (C-2)	NC3615	119	NC3615, N3615	PVA
☐ Laister-Kauffman LK.10A	N54573	111		RAA
☐ Mono Aircraft Monocoupe 90	NC119V	628		PVA
☐ Mono Aircraft Monocoupe 90A	N2701C	AF-826	NC2701C	RAA
☐ Mono Aircraft Monocoupe 90AF	N38927	A-850	NC38927	RAA
☐ Mono Aircraft Monocoupe 90AF	N52271	A-860	NC52271	RAA
☐ Mono Aircraft Monocoupe 90AL-115	N18185	A-811		RAA
☐ Mono Aircraft Monocoupe 90AL-115	N1161	A-865	N87617	RAA
☐ Mono Aircraft Monocoupe D-145	NC86570	D-122	NS56, NC86570, N86570	RAA
☐ Mono Aircraft Monosport	NC152K	2012	NC152K, N152K	PVC
☐ Mooney M-18C Mite				RA
☐ Mooney M.20A	N8394E	1572		RAA
☐ Naval Aircraft Factory N3N-3	N12063		Bu2996, N?????	PVA
☐ Nicholas-Beazley NB-8G	NC543Y	K-8		PVA
☐ North American NA-88 Texan (SNJ-5)	N543LB	88-15205	Bu52017, N3260G	RAA
☐ Piper J-3L-65 Cub	NC25894	3750	NC25894, N25894	RAA
☐ Piper PA-11 Cub Special	N4615M	11-119		RAA
☐ Piper PA-15 Vagabond	NC4313H	15-97	N4313H	PVA
☐ Piper PA-28-140 Cherokee	N7332J	28-24686		RAA
☐ Porterfield LP-65	NC34706	872	NC34706, N34706	RAA
☐ Rawdon T-1	N5160	T1-6		PVA
☐ Rearwin 7000 Sportster	NC15856	457	NC15856, N15856	PVA
☐ Ryan M-1	N2073	7		RAA
☐ Ryan STA Special (ST-3KR Recruit (PT-22))	N48587	2073	41-20864	PVA
☐ Shavrov Sh-2	CCCP-E1986			PV
☐ Skandinavisk Aero Industri (SAI) KZ III U-2	N76KZ	76	OY-DVO	RAA
☐ Sopwith Pup (R)	N5192	01		PVA
☐ Spartan C-3-225	NC720N	A-14		RAA
☐ Spartan 7W Executive (UC-71)	NC4444	7W-18	NC17631, 42-38267, NC4444, N4444, N3LL	RAA
☐ St. Louis C-2-110 Super Cardinal	NC951B	C-106	NC951K, N951K	RAA
☐ Standard J-1	'187'	T-4595	N62505	PVA
☐ Star Cavalier B	NC14860	138	NC14860, N14860	PVA
☐ Star Cavalier E	NC219E	126	NC219E, N219E	RA

Missouri

☐ Stinson SM-8A Junior		NC245W	M4064		PVA
☐ Stinson SR-5A Reliant		N13853	9227A	NC13853	RAC
☐ Stinson SR-5B Reliant		N13855	9230A	NC13855	RAC
☐ Stinson SR-6 Reliant		NC15112	9603	NC15112, N15112	RAA
☐ Taylor E-2 Cub		NC15676	341	NC15676, N15676	PVA
☐ Taylorcraft DCO-65 Grasshopper (L-2M)		N47727	L-4776	(USAAF)	RAA
☐ Timm Collegiate		NC337	101		PVA
☐ Travel Air 2000		NC5290	490		RAA
☐ Travel Air 3000		NC3947	321	NC3947, N3947	RAC
☐ Travel Air 4000		NC6116	614	NC6116, N6116	PVA
☐ Waco 10 (GXE)		NC6675K	1388	NC6675K, N6675K	PVA
☐ Waco ATO		NC5533	A-7	NC5533, N5533	RAA
☐ Waco ATO		NC1023S	A-69	NC8537	RAA
☐ Waco ATO		N741EA	A-75	NC741E	PVA
☐ Waco ATO		NC906H	A-103	NC906H, N906H	PVA
☐ Waco AVN-8		NC19378	5111	NC19378, N19378	PVA
☐ Waco AVN-8		NC90H	5114	NC19387, NC90	RAA
☐ Waco CSO		NC671N	3140	NC671N, N3767X	RAA
☐ Waco CTO		NC280W	A-3596	NC280W, N280W	PVA
☐ Waco JWM		NX8550	A-86		PVA
☐ Waco JYM		NC991H	D-3	NC991H, N991H	RAA
☐ Waco JYM		NC631N	J-3183	NC631N, N631N	RAA
☐ Waco PBA		NC12445	3598	NC12445, N12445	RAA
☐ Waco QCF		NC20922	3489	NC11273, N11273	RA
☐ Waco QCF		NC11497	3567	NC11488, N11488	RAA
☐ Waco QCF		NC12428	3569	NC12428, N12428	RAA
☐ Waco QCF-2		NC9220J	3491	NC11429, N11429	RAA
☐ Waco SRE (UC-72)		NC20961	5086	NC20961, NC71, 42-38271, N46329	RAA
☐ Waco UBF-2		N1244G	3607	NC12447	RAA
☐ Waco UBF-2		NC2091K	3608	NC12454, N12454	PVA
☐ Waco UBF-2		NC155Y	3618	NC155Y, N155Y	PVA
☐ Waco UBF-2		NC12002	3619	NC12002, N12002	RAA
☐ Waco YKC-S		N3NX	4202	NC14083, N3N	RAA
☐ Waco YKS-7		NC17457	4600	NC17457, N17457	RAA
☐ Waco ZKS-7		NC20902	5214	NC20902, N20902	RAA
☐ Waco ZPF-6		NC9130S	4377	NC15707, N15707	RAA
☐ Yakovlev Yak-52		N107GC	833800		PVA
☐ Yakovlev Yak-52		N203AS	867207	N51114, C-GFDJ	PVA
☐ Zenith Z6A		NX392V	3	NC392V, N392V	RAA

JAMES S. MCDONNELL PROLOGUE ROOM (MO16)

Address: Building 100, Boeing Works, St. Louis Missouri 63166.
Tel: 314-232-6891
Admission: June–August Monday-Friday 1000-1600.
Location: At the International Airport which is about 10 miles north west of the city centre off Interstate 70.

The exhibits in the room trace the history of flight from the 1920s to the present day. James McDonnell worked for a number of aircraft companies before setting up his own firm in 1939. The first design, the XP-67, flew in January 1944 and was not a success. Over the next three decades a range of jet fighters for the navy emerged. In 1967 the McDonnell Douglas Corporation was formed and this is now part of the vast Boeing empire.

JOHN B. MAHAFFEY MUSEUM COMPLEX (MO17)

Address: ATZTPTM-PM, Building 1607, 495 South Dakota Avenue, Fort Leonard Wood, Missouri 65473-5165.
Tel: 573-596-0780   **Fax:** 573-596-0169   **Email:** atztptmm@wood.emh1.army.mil
Admission: Monday-Friday 0800-1600; Saturday 1000-1600.
Location: About 80 miles north east of Springfield off Interstate 44.

This large site is home to four Army museums. The Chemical Corps Museum was established soon after World War I at Englewood Arsenal in Maryland. A move to Fort McClellan in Alabama followed.
The history of chemical and biological warfare is traced. The Military Police Corps Regimental Museum has items on show from the setting up of the force in 1775. The tasks carried out are highlighted. The Army Engineer Museum has a wide range of equipment on show. Fort Leonard Wood Museum covers the history of the site and is housed in World War II barracks. Two aircraft are displayed on the camp.

TYPE	REG/SER	CON. NO.	PI/NOTES	STATUS
☐ Bell 204 Iroquois (UH-1B)	63-8505	727		PV
☐ Fairchild-Republic A-10A Thunderbolt II	76-0519	A10-66		PV

LEES SUMMIT MONUMENTS (MO18)

Location: On permanent view at two locations in the town.

TYPE	REG/SER	CON. NO.	PI/NOTES	STATUS
☐ Bell 205 Iroquois (UH-1D) (UH-1H)	66-0970	5453	At VVA243.	PV
☐ Piper PA-38-112 Tomahawk			At Habaneros Restaurant at 1008 Southeast Blue Parkway.	PVX

LINN STATE TECHNOLOGY COLLEGE (MO19)

Address: 1 Technology Drive, Linn, Missouri 65051.
Tel: 573-897-5181 **Email:** mel.williams@linnstate.edu
Admission: By prior permission only.
Location: At the airport which is about 3 miles south east of the town.

The college has a small aviation department with premises at the airport. A number of instructional airframes have left and four are believed to remain. An annual fly-in is organised by the aviation club.

TYPE	REG/SER	CON. NO.	PI/NOTES	STATUS
☐ Beech 58TC Baron	N152Z	TK-33		RA
☐ Cessna 152	N48895	15281037		RA
☐ Cessna 210	N9538T	57338		RA
☐ Hughes 269A				RA

MALDEN ARMY AIRFIELD PRESERVATION SOCIETY MUSEUM (MO20)

Address: 167 Mitchell Drive, Malden, Missouri 63863.
Tel: 573-276-2279 **Email:** info@maaps.net
Admission: Monday-Friday 0800-1200 1300-1700.
Location: About 3 miles north of the town off Route 25.

The airfield opened in 1942 and for six years was a military pilot training school. From 1951 until 1960 a civilian company carried out a similar task. The site then became the airport for the region.

In September 2002 the museum opened in the airport office building. Displays of photographs, documents, memorabilia and components were put on show. The history of the airfield and the school are portrayed.

MISSOURI HISTORICAL SOCIETY HISTORY MUSEUM (MO21)

Address: Jefferson Memorial Building, 5700 Lindell Boulevard, Forest Park, St. Louis, Missouri 63112-0040.
Tel: 314-454-4599 **Email:** info@mohistory.org
Admission: Daily 1000-1800 (closes at 2000 Tuesday)
Location: Forest Park is in the southern suburbs of the city.
The IAP is about 10 miles north west of the city on Interstate 70.

The society has a collection of aviation memorabilia in its premises in the city. These include several items relating to Charles Lindbergh. The 'Spirit of St. Louis' replica honours his famous solo flight across the North Atlantic. The B-1 was converted by Paul Mantz for use in the film of his flight. It was purchased in 1962 by a group of donors and presented to the society on 7th June 1963. It was at the airport from 1975 until 1998 and then moved to the new display at Forest Park opened in the autumn of 1999.

TYPE	REG/SER	CON. NO.	PI/NOTES	STATUS
☐ Mono Aircraft Monocoupe 110 Special	N606G	5W98	NC10746 – in East Terminal at St. Louis IAP.	PV
☐ Mono Aircraft Monocoupe D-145	NX211		In Main Terminal at St. Louis IAP.	PV
☐ Ryan NYP (R) (B-1)	'N-X-211'	153	NC7206.	PVX

MONETT MONUMENT (MO22)

Location: On permanent view in South Park in the town.

TYPE	REG/SER	CON. NO.	PI/NOTES	STATUS
☐ McDonnell M.98HO Phantom II (F-4E) (NF-4E)	66-0315	2538		PV

MOUNTAIN VIEW MONUMENT (MO23)

Location: On permanent view in a park on East 5th Street in the town.

TYPE	REG/SER	CON. NO.	PI/NOTES	STATUS
☐ Lockheed 580 (T-33A)	58-0545	580-1514		PV

NATIONAL MILITARY HERITAGE MUSEUM (MO24)

Address: 701 Messanie Street, St. Joseph, Missouri 64501.
Tel: 816-233-4321 **Fax:** 816-279-4667 **Email:** info@nationalmilitaryhistorymuseum.com
Admission: Monday-Friday 0900-1700; Saturday 0900-1300.
Location: In the centre of the city.

The museum is housed in the original St Joseph police station. The displays trace the history of American forces from the 1800s to the present day. There are also several military vehicles and weapons to be seen. A replica of the famous Fokker D VII has been built and this is on show with three helicopters.

TYPE	REG/SER	CON. NO.	PI/NOTES	STATUS
☐ Bell 205 Iroquois (HU-1D) (UH-1D) (UH-1H)	62-2113	4008	Identity doubtful.	PV
☐ Bell 205 Iroquois (UH-1H) (UH-1V)	67-17465	9840		PV
☐ Bell 209 Huey Cobra (AH-1G) (AH-1S)	68-15200	20574		PV
☐ Fokker D VII (FSM)				PV

Missouri

NATIONAL MUSEUM OF TRANSPORTATION (MO25)

Address:	2967 Barrett Station Road, St. Louis, Missouri 63122-3398.
Tel:	314-965-6885　**Fax:** 314-965-0242
Admission:	May–mid September Monday-Saturday 0900-1700 Sunday 1100-1700; Mid September–April Tuesday-Saturday 0900-1600 Sunday 1100-1600.
Location:	About 15 miles south west of the city centre on Route 141.

Barrett Station Depot was located on the original Pacific Railroad. The 39 acre site contains a large number of railway engines and rolling stock from many countries. The halls also house horse drawn vehicles, cars and lorries. The C-47 has recently been repainted in a World War II camouflage scheme.

TYPE	REG/SER	CON. NO.	PI/NOTES	STATUS
☐ Bensen B-8M Gyrocopter	N2283W	RWC-1		RA
☐ Douglas DC-3A-456 Skytrain (C-47A)	43-15635	20101	43-15635, (NC58139)	PV
☐ Gyrodyne XRON-1 (XHOG-1)		4001		RA
☐ Lockheed 580 (T-33A)	52-9446	580-7556		PV
☐ Quickie Aircraft Quickie 1 (Rutan 54)	N79TT	0067		RA
☐ Wright Type Glider				RA

NATIONAL WORLD WAR ONE MUSEUM (MO26)

Address:	100 West 26th Street, Kansas City, Missouri 64108.
Tel:	816-784-1918　**Email:** info@theworldwar.org
Admission:	Tuesday-Sunday 1000-1700.
Location:	In the centre of the city.

The museum has its origins in the collections of local people who brought back items from the Great War. Originally known as the Liberty Memorial Museum, the name was changed to reflect its wider role. Entry to the exhibition is via a Western Front poppy field.

The displays trace the history of the conflict in vivid detail in a number of innovative displays. On show are uniforms, weapons, photographs and documents along with panels tracing the story of the conflict. Three full scale replica aircraft are on show.

TYPE	REG/SER	CON. NO.	PI/NOTES	STATUS
☐ De Havilland DH.2 (R)				PV
☐ Fokker D VII (R)	N86500	524		PV
☐ Nieuport 12 (R)				PV

NEOSHO MONUMENT (MO27)

Location:	On permanent view in Morse Park in East Spring Street in the eastern part of the town.

TYPE	REG/SER	CON. NO.	PI/NOTES	STATUS
☐ Bell 205 Iroquois (UH-1H)	68-15533	10463		PV

NICHOLAS BEAZLEY AVIATION MUSEUM (MO28)

Address:	PO Box 740, 1985 South Odell, Marshall, Missouri 65340.
Tel:	660-886-5575　**Fax:** 660-886-2689　**Email:** mccbam@mmuonline.net
Admission:	Saturday 1000-1600; Sunday 1300-1600.
Location:	At the airport which is just south of the town on Route 65.

Russell Nicholas and Howard Beazley established a flying school and aviation supply house in the town in 1921. Six years later they put the Barling designed NB-3 low-wing three-seater into production. More than 100 were built with many being sold in Latin America, most being powered by either 60 h.p. Anzani or 60 h.p. Le Blond engines. In 1931 the high-wing NB-8 appeared and around 60 were completed over the next four years. The design featured folding wings and the power plant was a 80 h.p. Genet radial. The local museum has had a display tracing the history of the company in one of its rooms for a long time. This collection has recently been established and has one of the few remaining NB-3s on show along with an NB-8G.

TYPE	REG/SER	CON. NO.	PI/NOTES	STATUS
☐ Mignet HM-14 Pou-du-Ciel				PV
☐ Nicholas-Beazley NB-3G	NC885H	26	NC885H, N885H	PV
☐ Nicholas-Beazley NB-8G	NC583Y	K-24	NC583Y, N583Y	PV
☐ Taylorcraft ST-100 (TG-6)				PV

O'FALLON MONUMENT (MO29)

Location:	On permanent view at VFW 5077 at 8500 Veterans Memorial Parkway in the town.

TYPE	REG/SER	CON. NO.	PI/NOTES	STATUS
☐ Bell 209 Huey Cobra (AH-1G) (AH-1S)	68-15204	20738		PV

OVERLAND MONUMENT (MO30)

Location:	On permanent view at VFW 3944 at 10815 Midland Boulevard in the town.

TYPE	REG/SER	CON. NO.	PI/NOTES	STATUS
☐ Bell 209 Huey Cobra (AH-1G) (AH-1S)	70-15204	20888		PV

OZARK AIRLINES MUSEUM (MO31)

Address:	638 Bellerive Estate Drive, St. Louis, Missouri 63141-6229.
Tel:	314-576-1747 Email: C47oami@aol.com
Admission:	By prior permission only.
Location:	At the International Airport which is in the north western suburbs of the city.

Ozark Airlines was formed in the late 1940s and began scheduled services with DC-3s on 26th September 1950. Over 25 examples of the type were operated with the last being withdrawn in 1968.

The company has set up a museum at its St. Louis headquarters and a DC-3 which recently arrived from Israel has been bought. The airliner will be restored in period markings and visit shows in the area.

TYPE	REG/SER	CON. NO.	PI/NOTES	STATUS
☐ Douglas DC-3A-360 Skytrain (C-47)	N150D	4463	41-18401, 118401 (France), F-BCBB, 4X-FNE/032, (Uganda), 4X-FNE/032, N155JM, N150D, (N150JD)	RAA

PARKS COLLEGE (MO32)

Address:	3450 Lindell Boulevard, St. Louis, Missouri 63103.
Tel:	314-977-8203 Fax: 314-977-8403 Email: 314-977-8403
Admission:	By prior permission only.
Location:	In the western part of the city centre.

The college was founded by Oliver Parks in 1927 and was the first certified school of aviation in the country. In 1946 it became part of St. Louis University. A pilot training school uses a fleet of modern types. The aviation maintenance section has a number of instructional airframes. In the late 1920s a number of KR-31s were reworked and sold as the Parks P-1. The P-2 soon followed. A P-1 is preserved at the airport facility.

TYPE	REG/SER	CON. NO.	PI/NOTES	STATUS
☐ Canadair RJ-200				RA
☐ Cessna 152	N4965Q	15285066		RA
☐ Cessna 152	N5082Q	15285067		RA
☐ Cessna 152	N5091Q	15285072		RA
☐ Cessna 180B	N5103F	50403		RA
☐ Cessna 310A	N10PC	38058		RA
☐ Parks P-1	NC964K	198-16		RA
☐ Piper PA-23 Apache	N2290P	23-901		RA
☐ Piper PA-28-161 Warrior II	N2905M	28-7916531		RA

PURDY MONUMENT (MO33)

Location:	On permanent view in a park on Highway C in the town.

TYPE	REG/SER	CON. NO.	PI/NOTES	STATUS
☐ Douglas A-4B Skyhawk (A4D-2)	Bu142678	11740		PV

RICHMOND MONUMENT (MO34)

Location:	On permanent view in Maurice G. Roberts City Park off East Lexington Street in the town.

TYPE	REG/SER	CON. NO.	PI/NOTES	STATUS
☐ Lockheed 580 (T-33A)	53-5990	580-9472		PV

SCIENCE CITY (MO35)

Address:	30 West Pershing Road, Kansas City, Missouri 64108.
Tel:	816-460-2020 Email: archive@unionstation.org
Admission:	Monday-Friday 0900-1700; Saturday 1000-1700; Sunday 1200-1700.
Location:	In the city centre.

This museum, with many interactive exhibits, is housed in the old Union Station in the city. The building was completed in 1914 and closed in 1988. The structure was restored and the museum opened in 1999. There is a large exhibition of railway engines and rolling stock. The only aircraft on show is the Butler Blackhawk which was constructed in the city. Just 11 examples of the biplane were built in the late 1920s/early 1930s. The one in the collection, the last constructed, was flown in shows and as a crop duster until 1938 when it was dismantled and put in store. Rediscovered in 1957 the Blackhawk was rebuilt to flying condition. The Butler company, which now makes buildings, acquired it in 1991 and stored it locally whilst a suitable exhibition site was found. Another Blackhawk is registered to an Illinois owner and these are believed to be the only survivors.

TYPE	REG/SER	CON. NO.	PI/NOTES	STATUS
☐ Butler Blackhawk	NX299N	111	NC299N	PV

SHORT COLLECTION (MO36)

Address:	655 South West 51st Road, Warrensburg, Missouri 64093-7544.
Admission:	By prior permission only.
Location:	At an airfield in the area.

Missouri

This private collection contains only classic types. The Monocoupe 90 appeared in the mid-1930s and was a delight to fly. The type, designed by Clayton Folkerts, was derived from a special version of the Velie Monocoupe raced by the company test pilot Vern Roberts. Only about 100 were built.

TYPE	REG/SER	CON. NO.	PI/NOTES	STATUS
☐ Aeronca 7AC Champion	N841MC	7AC-2851	NC84164 (?), N84164 (?)	RAA
☐ Boeing-Stearman A75N1 Kaydet (PT-17)	N52573	75-2136	41-8577	RAA
☐ Mono Aircraft Monocoupe 90A	NC15440	A-739	NC15440, N15440	RAA
☐ Piper J-3C-65 Cub (L-4J)	N33548	13986	45-55220	RAA
☐ Taylor J-2 Cub	NC17837	1272	NC17837, N17837	RAA

SIKESTON VETERANS MEMORIAL PARK (MO37)

Address:	501 Campanella Drive, Sikeston, Missouri 63801
Tel:	573-432-375
Admission:	On permanent view.
Location:	On the south side of the airport which is in the north eastern suburbs of the town.

Local veterans groups have set up this display to honour local people who lost their lives in conflicts. The Phantom, which arrived in the late 1990s, once flew with the 'Blue Angels' aerobatic team.

The fighter now carries the markings of one which served on the carrier USS *Enterprise*. The Bell 47J is a fairly recent arrival and is in a blue colour scheme. Also on show is a M60 tank along with several guns and memorial plaques.

TYPE	REG/SER	CON. NO.	PI/NOTES	STATUS
☐ Bell 47J (HUL-1) (UH-13P)	Bu143143	1611		PV
☐ McDonnell M.98EV Phantom II (F-4J)	Bu153839	2227		PV

SKELTON NATIONAL GUARD BASE (MO38)

Location:	By prior permission only at the base in the northern part of Jefferson City

TYPE	REG/SER	CON. NO.	PI/NOTES	STATUS
☐ McDonnell M.199-1A Eagle (F-15A)	76-0094	289/A246		RA

SPRINGFIELD MONUMENTS (MO39)

Location:	On permanent view at two locations in the city.

TYPE	REG/SER	CON. NO.	PI/NOTES	STATUS
☐ Bell 205 Iroquois (UH-1H)	69-15051	11339	At ALP 639 at 2600 South Scenic.	PV
☐ Bell 209 Huey Cobra (AH-1G) (AH-1S)	71-21016	21087	At ALP 639 at 2600 South Scenic.	PV
☐ Republic F-84F Thunderstreak	51-1639		At Branson Airport north west of the town.	PV
☐ Wright Flyer (R)			At Branson Airport.	PV

ST. LOUIS AIR NATIONAL GUARD BASE (MO40)

Address:	131 FW/PA, 10800 Lambert International Boulevard, Bridgetown, Missouri 63044-2371.
Tel:	314-527-6410
Admission:	On permanent view.
Location:	On the south side of St. Louis IAP off Route 67.

The Missouri National Guard moved its flying units to Lambert Field (now the International Airport) in 1931 and was initially an observation squadron. In 1946 it became a fighter unit with P-51s and apart from a short spell with B-26s in the early 1950s has served in this role ever since.

The F-100 was flown from 1972 to 1979 and the F-4 used from 1979 to 1992. The F-100 is mounted by the main gate where it has been joined by an example of the current equipment, the F-15 Eagle. The F-4 is behind the headquarters building.

TYPE	REG/SER	CON. NO.	PI/NOTES	STATUS
☐ McDonnell M.199-1A Eagle (F-15A)	76-0088	280/A240		PV
☐ McDonnell M.98HO Phantom II (F-4E)	68-0338	3383		PV
☐ McDonnell M.98HO Phantom II (F-4E)	68-0465	3622	At Jefferson Barracks in city.	RA
☐ North American NA-223 Super Sabre (F-100D)	55-3667	223-349		PV

ST. LOUIS CITY MUSEUM (MO41)

Address:	701 North 15th. Street, St. Louis, Missouri 63103.
Tel:	314-231-2489 **Email:** mpr@citymuseum.org
Admission:	Monday-Thursday 0900-1700; Friday 0900-1300; Saturday 1000-1300; Sunday 1100-1700. (Closed Monday and Tuesday in winter.)
Location:	In the city centre.

This museum specialises in sculpture made from recycled materials. The two Sabreliners are part of exhibit called 'Monstrocity' where they are mixed with a fire engine and a series of iron railings.

TYPE	REG/SER	CON. NO.	PI/NOTES	STATUS
☐ Lockheed 1329 JetStar 731	N171JL	1329-5074/22	N9234R, N67B, N267P, N267GF, N168DB, N777SG	PV
☐ North American NA-282 Sabreliner 40	N40BP	282-40	N6395C, N738R, N715MR	PV
☐ North American NA-282 Sabreliner 40	N225LS	282-51	N733R, N108G, N108X, N227LS	PV

ST. LOUIS MONUMENTS (MO42)

Location:	On permanent view at three locations in the city.

TYPE	REG/SER	CON. NO.	PI/NOTES	STATUS
☐ McDonnell M.36BA Voodoo (F-101B)	58-0281	786	At Spirit of St. Louis Airport.	PV
☐ McDonnell M.98AM Phantom II (F4H-1) (F-4B)	Bu148392	77	At a business at 3000 Chateau.	PV
☐ McDonnell M.267 Hornet (F/A-18A)			At Science Center.	PV
☐ North American NA-190 Sabre (F-86D)	52-4138	190-541	At a business at 3000 Chateau.	PV
☐ North American NA-276 Sabreliner (T-39A) (CT-39A)	62-4501	276-54	At O'Fallon Technical School – may still be here.	RA

STARS AND STRIPES MUSEUM (MO43)

Address:	17377 Stars and Stripes Way, PO Box 1861, Bloomfield, Missouri 63825.
Tel:	573-568-2055 Email: stripes@newwavecomm.net
Admission:	Monday, Wednesday-Friday 1000-1600, Saturday 1000-1400; Sunday 1300-1800.
Location:	In the southern part of the town.

The museum was founded by a group dedicated to preserving the history of the United States Armed Forces newspaper 'The Stars and Stripes'. The publication first saw the light of day on 9th November 1861 when it was distributed in the Bloomfield area. A group of Illinois soldiers set up camp in the area and found the local newspaper office deserted. They set about producing a paper telling the story of their expedition against the Confederate forces. The exhibition opened in 1999 and has thousands of artefacts in its collection. An Iroquois has now joined the display.

TYPE	REG/SER	CON. NO.	PI/NOTES	STATUS
☐ Bell 205 Iroquois (UH-1H)	74-22453	13777		PV

STRICKER COLLECTION (MO44)

Address:	2801 Butternut Court, Columbia, Missouri 65201-3538.
Admission:	By prior permission only.
Location:	At the Columbia Regional Airport which is about 10 miles south east of the town.

The star of the collection is the airworthy Seafire which took to the air again on 1st July 2010. The aircraft was transferred to the Royal Canadian Air Force in late 1945 and shipped to HMCS Dartmouth in Nova Scotia.
In April 1950 it was assigned for fire practice but was never set alight. In April 1972 it moved to the Canadian Warplane Heritage which owned it for two decades. The fighter was then in Minnesota for 13 years before being bought by Wes Stricker.
Another example of the type which served in Israel and Burma is in store. The collection also owns three examples of the Grumman Avenger, two of which flew as water bombers in Canada.

TYPE	REG/SER	CON. NO.	PI/NOTES	STATUS
☐ Grumman G-40 Avenger (TBM-3)	N65VC	2534	Bu85175, N1369N, C-GLEF	RAA
☐ Grumman G-40 Avenger (TBM-3) (TBM-3E)	N9429Z	4619	Bu91714	RAA
☐ Grumman G-40 Avenger (TBM-3) (TBM-3E) (AS.3)	N6VC	3201	Bu53159, 53159 (Canada), CF-IMN	RAA
☐ Grumman G-89 Tracker (S2F-1) (US-2B)	N31984	482	Bu136573, N31984, N34S	RAA
☐ Piper J-3C-65 Cub	N35363	6330		RA
☐ Supermarine 386 Seafire F.XV	N462XV	COA.30621	PR503, PR503 (Canada), (C-GCWK), N535R, N503PR	RAA
☐ Supermarine 386 Seafire F.XV	N9413Z	WASE14106	SR462, (Israel), UB414, 'UB415'	RA

VETERANS MEMORIAL MUSEUM (MO45)

Address:	1250 West 76 Country Boulevard, Branson, Missouri 65616.
Tel:	417-336-2300 Fax: 417-336-2301
Admission:	Daily 0800-2100.
Location:	In the western part of the town.

This impressive museum has ten large halls displaying artefacts from many wars. The display opened on November 11th. 2000. On show are vehicles, uniforms, flags, weapons and badges and a giant bronze sculpture depicting a soldier from each of the 50 states. Many personal stories are told in the exhibition.

TYPE	REG/SER	CON. NO.	PI/NOTES	STATUS
☐ North American NA-122 Mustang (P-51D) (FSM)				PVX

WARSAW MONUMENT (MO46)

Location:	On permanent view at ALP 217 on Wildcat Drive about 3 miles south of the town.

TYPE	REG/SER	CON. NO.	PI/NOTES	STATUS
☐ Bell 209 Huey Cobra (AH-1G) (AH-1F)	66-15306	20062		

WENTZVILLE MONUMENT (MO47)

Location:	On permanent view at VFW 5327 on Highway Z about 5 miles south of the town.

TYPE	REG/SER	CON. NO.	PI/NOTES	STATUS
☐ Bell 209 Huey Cobra (AH-1S) (AH-1E)	78-23063	22169		PV

WHITEMAN AIR FORCE BASE (MO48)

Address:	509BW/PA, 509 Spirit Boulevard, Knob Knoster, Missouri 65035-5000.
Tel:	660-687-6123 Fax: 660-687-7948 Email: 509bwpa@whiteman.af.mil
Admission:	By prior permission only.
Location:	About 2 miles south of the town on Route D.

Opened in 1942 as Sedalia Glider Base, the site had seven more names before taking up its present title in 1955. A P-40 flown by Lieutenant George Whiteman was attacked on 7th December 1941 whilst taking off from Wheeler Field in Hawaii during the attack on Pearl Harbor. He was the first USAAF airman to be shot down in World War II. The field was closed between 1946 and 1951.

A bomb wing moved in during October 1952 and stayed for almost 11 years. A Minuteman missile wing took over the base and in the 1990s major work took place to accommodate the Northrop B-2 'stealth bomber'.

Three of the aircraft, the B-29, the B-52 and the KC-97, were moved from Pease Air Force Base in New Hampshire when it closed in 1991.

TYPE	REG/SER	CON. NO.	PI/NOTES	STATUS
☐ Bell 204 Iroquois (UH-1F)	65-7941	7082		RA
☐ Bell 209 Huey Cobra (AH-1S) (AH-1G)	80-23515	22303		RA
☐ Boeing 345 Superfortress (B-29A) (SB-29)	44-61671	11148		PV
☐ Boeing 367-76-66 Stratofreighter (KC-97G) (KC-97L)	53-0327	17109		RA
☐ Boeing 450-67-27 Stratojet (B-47B)	51-2120	450173		RA
☐ Boeing 464-201-7 Stratofortress (B-52D)	56-0683	464054		RA
☐ Fairchild-Republic A-10A Thunderbolt II	76-0530	A10-77		RA
☐ General Dynamics F-111G (FB-111A)	69-6509	B1-71		RA
☐ Northrop N-156T Talon (T-38A)	62-3640	N.5345		RA

MONTANA

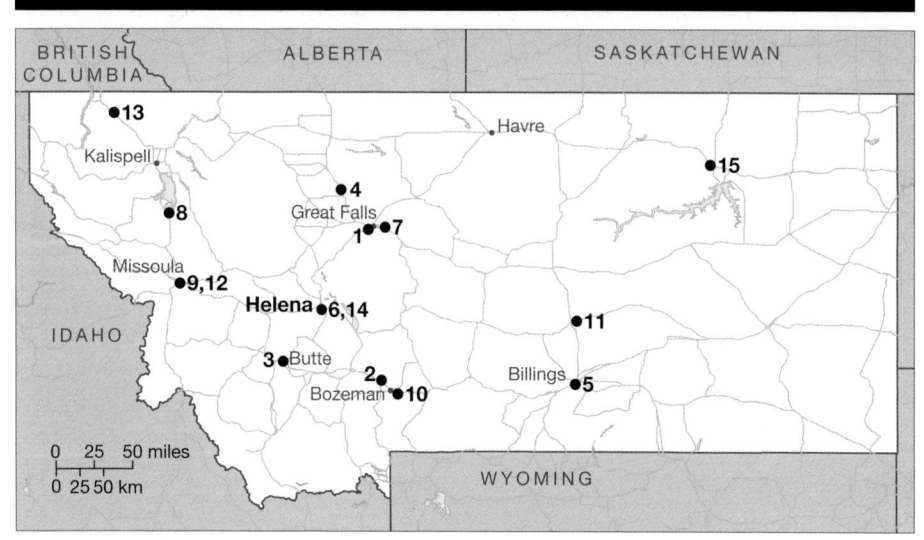

120TH FIGHTER INTERCEPTOR GROUP COLLECTION (MT1)

Address:	2920 Airport Drive, Great Falls, Montana 59404-5570.
Tel:	406-791-0233 Email: goguard@mtgrea.ang.af.mil
Admission:	By prior permission only.
Location:	The airport is west of the town off Interstate 15.

The Montana Air National Guard was formed in June 1947 and flew P-51D Mustangs. In November 1953 it became the first Guard unit to operate the F-86A Sabre which was used until the F-94 Starfire arrived in June 1955.

The F-89 Scorpion was flown from 1956 to 1966, the F-102 from 1966 until 1972 and the F-106 from 1972. The current equipment, the F-16, arrived in 1987. The F-89 was mounted on the roof of the guard post.

TYPE	REG/SER	CON. NO.	PI/NOTES	STATUS
☐ Convair 8-10 Delta Dagger (F-102A)	56-1105	8-10-322	56-1105, '68259' – in the town.	PV
☐ Convair 8-24 Delta Dart (F-106A)	'57-2463'	8-24-198	59-0069, '72492'	RAX
☐ General Dynamics 401 Fighting Falcon (F-16A)	79-0290	61-75		RA
☐ Lockheed 580 (T-33A)	52-9672	580-7857		RA
☐ North American NA-151 Sabre (P-86A) (F-86A)	'2637'	151-38464	47-0637	RAX
☐ Northrop N-160 Scorpion (N-68) (F-89D) (F-89J)	53-2547	N.4678		RA

BIG SKY WARBIRDS (MT2)

Address: PO Box 502, Belgrade, Montana 59714-0502.
Admission: By prior permission only.
Location: At Gallatin Field Airport which is just east of the town off Route 205.

This organisation has acquired a fleet of mainly jet warbirds. The four two seat Super Sabres were flown by the Danish Air Force for many years and were ferried to the USA via England. They flew out of Mojave in California before journeying north. The Canadian built Sabre and T-33 also operated from the same airfield

TYPE	REG/SER	CON. NO.	PI/NOTES	STATUS
☐ Canadair CL-13B Sabre 6 [North American F-86E]	N87FS	1491	23701 (Canada), 382 (South Africa), N3847H	RAA
☐ Canadair CL-30 Silver Star 3 (CT-133) [Lockheed 580 (T-33AN)]	N305FS	T33-159	21159 (Canada), 133159 (Canada), N96186	RAA
☐ North American NA-243 Super Sabre (F-100F)	N417FS	243-118	56-3842, GT-842 (Denmark), N32511	RAA
☐ North American NA-243 Super Sabre (F-100F)	N416FS	243-192	56-3916, GT-916 (Denmark), (N3251X), N3251W	RAA
☐ North American NA-243 Super Sabre (F-100F)	N419FS	243-247	56-3971, GT-971 (Denmark), N3251U	RAA
☐ North American NA-243 Super Sabre (F-100F)	N418FS	243-272	56-3996, GT-996 (Denmark), N3251S	RAA
☐ Vultee V-74 Valiant (BT-13A)	N10458	74-2775	41-10458, N57335, N450BT	RAA

BUTTE MONUMENT (MT3)

Location: On permanent view at Bert Mooney Airport which about 3 miles south of the town.

TYPE	REG/SER	CON. NO.	PI/NOTES	STATUS
☐ North American NA-201 Sabre (F-86D) (F-86L)	53-0997	201-441		PV

DUTTON MONUMENT (MT4)

Location: On permanent view at ALP 64 at the Legion Memorial Field in the eastern part of the town.

TYPE	REG/SER	CON. NO.	PI/NOTES	STATUS
☐ Lockheed 483-04-06 Starfighter (F-104D)	57-1332	283-5044		PV

EXPERIMENTAL AIRCRAFT ASSOCIATION CHAPTER 57 MUSEUM (MT5)

Address: Billings, Montana 59105.
Email: mlelshore@msn.com
Admission: By prior permission only.
Location: At the airfield which is in the northern suburbs of the town.

This thriving group has many projects in its hangar. Etienne Dormoy had flown with the French Air Force in World War I. He then moved to America and in 1924 built the Bathtub for the 1924 Rickenbacker Trophy for light aircraft. The design, powered by a 20 h.p. Henderson motor, won the cross-country competition.

TYPE	REG/SER	CON. NO.	PI/NOTES	STATUS
☐ Chanute Glider (R)				RA
☐ Chanute Triplane (R)				RA
☐ Dormoy Flying Bathtub (R)				RAC
☐ Wright 1900 Glider (R)				RA

HELENA NATIONAL GUARD BASE (MT6)

Address: Helena Regional Airport, Helena, Montana 59601.
Tel: 406-442-1720
Admission: By prior permission only.
Location: The airport is about 3 miles east of the city on Route 12.

The Montana Army National Guard has a helicopter base at the airport. An Iroquois, formerly flown by the unit, is mounted on a pylon near the airfield boundary. Two other helicopters are being prepared for display.

TYPE	REG/SER	CON. NO.	PI/NOTES	STATUS
☐ Bell 204 Iroquois (UH-1C) (UH-1M)	64-14101	1225		PV
☐ Bell 204 Iroquois (UH-1C) (UH-1M)	66-15024	1752		RA
☐ Bell 209 Huey Cobra (AH-1G) (AH-1S)	68-17025	20753		RA

MALMSTROM AIR FORCE BASE MUSEUM AND AIR PARK (MT7)

Address: 341 Missile Wing, 21 77th North Street Suite 144. Malmstrom Air Force Base, Montana 59402-5000.
Tel: 406-731-4050   **Fax:** 406-731-4048   **Email:** 341mwpa@malmstrom.af.mil
Admission: Monday-Friday 1000-1600.
Location: About 3 miles east of Great Falls.

Montana

Great Falls Army Air Base was activated in December 1942 and during the conflict prepared lend-lease aircraft for delivery to the Soviet Union. The airfield is now home to a missile wing, which was the first to be equipped with the Minuteman intercontinental ballistic rocket. The museum, established in 1982, traces the history of the site and its units. The indoor display has many photographs, models, documents, components, uniforms and personal items. The last fixed wing unit to operate from Malmstrom was the 301st Air Refuelling Wing using the KC-97 and the example on show has been painted in their colours.

TYPE	REG/SER	CON. NO.	PI/NOTES	STATUS
☐ Bell 204 Iroquois (UH-1F)	'13157'	7097	65-7956	PVX
☐ Boeing 367-76-66 Stratofreighter (KC-97G) (KC-97L)	'2638'	17142	53-0360	PVX
☐ Lockheed 580 (T-33A)	'61779'	580-1223	57-0574.	PVX
☐ Martin 272B Canberra (B-57B) (EB-57B)	52-1505	88		PV
☐ McDonnell M.36BA Voodoo (TF-101B) (TF-101F)	59-0419	743		PV
☐ North American NA-108 Mitchell (B-25J) (TB-25J) (TB-25N)	44-30493	108-33768	44-30493, N9451Z	PV
☐ Republic F-84F Thunderstreak	'52-6974'		'52-6969', N84JW	PVX

MIRACLE OF AMERICA MUSEUM (MT8)

Address: 36094 Memory Lane, Polson, Montana 59860.
Tel: 406-863-6804 **Email:** info@MiracleofAmericaMuseum.org
Admission: Summer daily 0800-2000; rest of year Monday-Saturday 0800-1700, Sunday 1330-1700-1800
Location: About one mile south of Junction 35 of Highway 93.

The museum was set up in 1981 by Gil and Joanne Mangles. A large collection of objects traces the progress of the country from the early days up to the present time. Over 100,000 items are on show. Several original buildings have been moved to the site to create the pioneer village which depicts life in the area when it was first being settled.

The transport and military section includes many vehicles from horse drawn carts up to modern cars and commercial vehicles. A range of bicycles, motor cycles and boats is also on show. A number of former military aircraft have been displayed to show to the work of the forces.

TYPE	REG/SER	CON. NO.	PI/NOTES	STATUS
☐ Bell 204 Iroquois (UH-1B)	64-13914	1038	64-13914, N87944 – boom from UH-1A 58-3019.	PV
☐ Bell 47G-2 Sioux (H-13H) (OH-13H)				PV
☐ Bell 47G-2 Sioux (H-13H) (OH-13H)	56-2179 (?)	1891 (?)	Could be 47D-1 (H-13E) c/n 889 51-14179 or 47G-3B (OH-13S) c/n 3065 63-9179.	PV
☐ Lockheed 580 (T-33A)	54-1549	580-9180		PV
☐ McDonnell M.98DJ Phantom II (F-4C)	64-0677	907	Front fuselage only.	PV
☐ Piper J-3C-65 Cub			Fuselage frame only.	PVD
☐ Sikorsky S-55D Chickasaw (H-19D) (UH-19D)	54-1417			PVD
☐ Vought A-7D Corsair II	71-0342	D253		PV

MUSEUM OF MOUNTAIN FLYING (MT9)

Address: 713 South 3rd. West Street, Missoula, Montana 39801.
Tel: 406-721-3644 **Fax:** 406-555-5555 **Email:** info@museumofmountainflying.org
Admission: May–October daily 1000-1600.
Location: At the airport which is about 3 miles north west of the town on Route 90.

Established in 1993 this museum highlights the special skills needed to fly in the rugged mountain terrain. Photographs and memorabilia can be seen in the hangar.

The DC-3 was operated by the locally based Johnson Flying service and was used in the fire-fighting role from 1945 until it crashed in 1954. In 1949 it took part in a mission to put out a large fire at Mann Gulch. A dozen of the 15 fire-fighters who jumped lost their lives.

The aircraft was recovered from its crash site and rebuilt. Before returning to Montana it served as a freighter in Arkansas. Johnson's also operated a number of Ford Tri-Motors on this work.

The BJ Sportster is a Piper Cub modified for flying from high altitude airfields.

A number of locally constructed homebuilts can also be seen. The Kaminskas Jungster flew in prototype form in 1966 and several have been built by amateur constructors. The Clark Special is an original design dating from the late 1970s.

The American-built Gipsy Moth spent many years hanging in the terminal building at Helena Airport before joining the exhibition. There is a superb collection of photographs tracing the history of aviation in the mountainous landscape. The story of smoke-jumping work is told in the exhibition with a number of models and documents to be seen.

TYPE	REG/SER	CON. NO.	PI/NOTES	STATUS
☐ Aeronca 65TC Grasshopper (O-58B) (L-3B)				RAC
☐ Aeronca 11AC Chief				PV
☐ Beech C18S Expeditor (C-45F) (UC-45F)	N8037H	8449	(USAAF)	PVA
☐ BJ Sportster (Piper J-3C-65 Cub modified)	N21BJ	001		PVA
☐ Boeing-Stearman A75N1 Kaydet (PT-17)	N500JV	75-440	40-1883	PVA
☐ Clark Special 3	N50RR	3		PVA
☐ De Havilland DH.60GMW Moth	N617R	179	NC617V – on loan from Montana HS.	PV
☐ Douglas DC-3A-456 Skytrain (C-47A)	N24320	20197	43-15731, NC24320	PVA
☐ Fairchild F-27 Friendship	N222DG	31	N1924, C-GJON, N54506	PV
☐ Ford 5-AT-D	NC435H	5-AT-102	Wreck to be recovered from crash site.	RAD
☐ Helmerichs 32	N12752	1		PV
☐ Kaminskas RK-3 Jungster II	N805	100JH		PVA
☐ Rutan 33 Vari-Eze	N5SB	1455		PV
☐ Snow S-2A				RAC

MUSEUM OF THE ROCKIES (MT10)

Address:	Montana State University, 600 West Kagy Boulevard, Bozeman, Montana 59717-2730.
Tel:	406-994-2251 Fax: 406-994-2682 Email: wwwmor@montana.edu
Admission:	June–August daily 0900-2000; September–May Monday-Saturday 0900-1700 Sunday 1230-1700.
Location:	In the southern part of the town.

This superb museum traces the natural and local history of the region. In the geology hall four billion years of the life of the Earth are traced.
There is a reconstruction of the dinosaur nesting colony discovered by the museum's Curator of Palaeontology. On show are many other fossils found in the area. The lives of the local Indians are portrayed in detail.
The transport section contains many vehicles, including some superb motorcycles. The restored 1932 Pietenpol was built locally and flew for several years.

TYPE	REG/SER	CON. NO.	PI/NOTES	STATUS
☐ Pietenpol B4-A Aircamper	NC12752	1		PV

MUSSELSHELL VALLEY HISTORICAL MUSEUM (MT11)

Address:	524 First Street West, Roundup, Montana 59672.
Tel:	406-323-1463 Email: info@mvhm.us
Admission:	May–September daily 1300-1700.
Location:	In the town which is about 50 miles north of Billings on Route 12.

The museum displays trace the history and development of the region. David Comstock was born in the town and in the 1920s he designed and built a glider. He then acquired an Avro 504 and operated this for a time. In 1932 he started the construction of the Aircamper. Over the next three years he made over 250 flights in the aircraft.
When he went to college in 1935 the airframe was placed in store where it remained until his death in 2005. In his will he left money for an exhibition hall for the aircraft.
The wings were lost over this period and new ones were constructed by EAA members at Billings who also restored the fuselage.

TYPE	REG/SER	CON. NO.	PI/NOTES	STATUS
☐ Pietenpol B4-A Aircamper	N12724		NC12724	-

ROCKY MOUNTAIN MUSEUM OF MILITARY HISTORY (MT12)

Address:	PO Box 7263, Fort Missoula, Montana 59807
Tel:	406-549-5346 Email: info@fortmissoula.org
Admission:	June–August Daily 1200-1700; September–May Saturday-Sunday 1200-1700.
Location:	In the suburbs of the town.

The museum is housed in two 1930s buildings at Fort Missoula. The site is still used by the Montana National Guard.
Local collectors were asked to help with the setting up of the exhibition. The military history of the area is portrayed in detail and there are exhibits tracing all major conflicts involving American forces.
Close by is the Fort Missoula Museum where the story of the site, first occupied in 1877, is portrayed.

TYPE	REG/SER	CON. NO.	PI/NOTES	STATUS
☐ Bell 205 Iroquois (UH-1D) (UH-1H)	66-16019	5713		PV

SMITH COLLECTION (MT13)

Address:	Crystal Lake Resort, Fortine, Montana 59918.
Tel:	406-882-4114
Admission:	By prior permission only.
Location:	At a private airfield about 50 miles north west of Kalispell on Route 93.

This interesting collection of warbirds and classics contains several rarities. The oldest design is the Curtiss Jenny. Almost 11,000 were built in the World War I period and a few survive. The Curtiss-Wright Sport Trainer first flew in 1930 and around 40 were constructed before the onset of the depression. The Kittyhawk was buried on a farm in Alberta in 1953 and recovered by John Paul two decades years later. The airframe was sold to Col Pay in Australia who rebuilt in between 1985 and 1989. The fighter was badly damaged in a crash in 1991 and after repair flew again in 1994 before returning to the USA. The Seafire was imported into the country in the early 1970s and a rebuild was started at San Antonio in Texas.

TYPE	REG/SER	CON. NO.	PI/NOTES	STATUS
☐ Beech D17S (GB-2)	NC17643	4827	Bu33028	RAA
☐ Beech A36 Bonanza 36	N9286Q	E-291		RAA
☐ Beech A45 Mentor (T-34A)	N563DP	CCF34-83	53-4114	RAA
☐ Beech 95-B55 Baron	N2042E	TC-2188		RAA
☐ Bell 206B Jet Ranger	N10699	2857		RAA
☐ Boeing-Stearman D75N1 Kaydet (PT-27)	N77AA	75-3780	42-15591, FD989, N59980	RAA
☐ Canadian Car & Foundry Harvard 4 [North American NA-186]	N600LM	CCF4-191	20400, CF-SRJ, C-FSRJ	RAA
☐ Cessna 318E Dragonfly (A-37B)	N437B	43284	69-6439, (Vietnam), VH-IVI	RAA
☐ Curtiss 1C Jenny (JN-4D)	N400JN	400		RAA
☐ Curtiss A87-A2 Kittyhawk I	N440PE	15133	AK752, 1028 (Canada), N96045, VH-KTH	RAA
☐ Curtiss-Wright CW-12W Sport Trainer	NC17463	12W-2017	NC413W, N413W	RAA
☐ De Havilland DH.82A Tiger Moth	N995DH	85855	DE995, (Fr. Mil), F-BKFL	RAA
☐ Fokker Dr I (R)	N72517	H-1		RAA

Montana – Nebraska 391

☐ Goodyear GA-466 Inflatoplane				RA
☐ Great Lakes 2T-1A-2	N3805F	0773		RAA
☐ Lake LA-250 Renegade	N8409B	63		RAA
☐ Lincoln PT-W	N20731	804	NC20731	RAA
☐ Lockheed 580 (T-33A)	N22ES	580-1214	57-0565	RAA
☐ Montanair Scale Mustang	N192M	M1-92		RAA
☐ Montanair Spirit 2180	N882MA	M302-90		RAA
☐ North American NA-122 Mustang (P-51D) (Mustang IV)	N6519D	122-40552	44-74012, 9243 (Canada), N6518D, N6519D, C-GPSI	RAA
☐ Northrop N-156A Freedom Fighter (F-5A)				RAA
☐ Piper J-3L-65 Cub	N32635	5504	NC32635	RAA
☐ Piper PA-42-1000 Cheyenne 400LS	N500LM	42-5527016		RAA
☐ Rutan 61 Long Ez	N88BE	1317		RAA
☐ Supermarine 388 Seafire FR.47	N47SF	6S.73229	VP441	RAA
☐ Valentin Taifun 17E	N66BV	1070		RAA
☐ Vought F4U-5N Corsair (F4U-5P)	N65WF		Bu122184, N3764A, 605 (Honduras), N4901E, N49051, N65HP	RAA

UNIVERSITY OF MONTANA COLLEGE OF TECHNOLOGY (MT14)

Address: 1115 North Roberts Street, Helena, Montana 59601.
Tel: 406-444-6800 **Email:** info@umhelena.edu
Admission: By prior permission only.
Location: The airport is about 3 miles east of the city on Route 12.

The University has an aviation facility at the airport where it trains airframe and engine fitters Two recent departures are a Lockheed Super Constellation and a Northrop Scorpion. The four engined classic has been gone to the Evergreen Aviation Museum in Oregon where it will be restored.

TYPE	REG/SER	CON. NO.	PI/NOTES	STATUS
☐ Bell 47D-1 Sioux (H-13E) (OH-13E)	51-14045	755		RA
☐ Bell 47G-2 Sioux (H-13H) (OH-13H)	58-1497	2261		RA
☐ Bell 205 Iroquois (UH-1H)	70-16265	12570		RA
☐ Bell 205 Iroquois (UH-1H)	66-17078	9272	Boom from c/n 12781 70-16476.	RA
☐ Cessna 150	N6557T	17957		RA
☐ Convair 8-10 Delta Dagger (F-102A)	56-1116	8-10-333	56-1116, N8970	RA
☐ North American NA-265 Sabreliner (T-39A) (CT-39A)	61-0677	265-80	61-0677, (N9166Y)	RA

VALLEY COUNTY PIONEER MUSEUM (MT15)

Address: 816 Highway 2 West, Glasgow, Montana 59230.
Tel: 406-228-8692 **Email:** vcmuseum@nemontel.net
Admission: June–August daily 1000-1800.
Location: Near the town centre on Route 2.

This pioneer museum was built in 1970 by the local historical society. The story of the early settlers is portrayed in detail. One of the major dinosaur finds of the 20th century was made in the county and this is featured in the display. Also on show are farm machinery, tractors and railway equipment. The T-33 was donated to the town in 1968 and is now mounted outside the building.

TYPE	REG/SER	CON. NO.	PI/NOTES	STATUS
☐ Lockheed 580 (T-33A)	52-9564	580-7724		PV

NEBRASKA

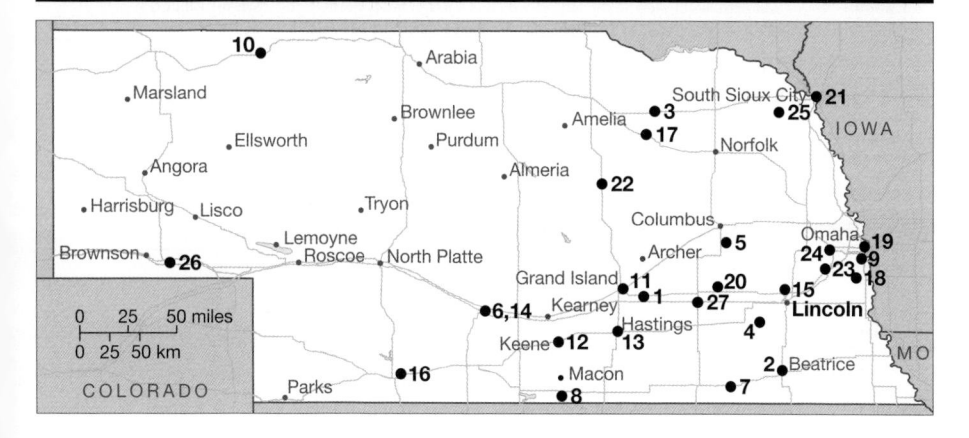

AURORA MONUMENT (NE1)

Location:	On permanent view at the airport which is north of the town on Route 14.

TYPE	REG/SER	CON. NO.	PI/NOTES	STATUS
☐ North American NA-243 Super Sabre (F-100F)	56-3825	243-101		PV

BEATRICE MONUMENT (NE2)

Location:	On permanent view at the airport which is north of the town on Route 77W.

TYPE	REG/SER	CON. NO.	PI/NOTES	STATUS
☐ Lockheed 580 (T-33A)	51-8880	580-6664		PV

CREIGHTON MONUMENT (NE3)

Location:	On permanent view in the centre of the town on Route 59.

TYPE	REG/SER	CON. NO.	PI/NOTES	STATUS
☐ Republic F-84F Thunderstreak	52-6642			PV

CRETE MONUMENT (NE4)

Location:	On permanent view at the airport which is about 2 miles east of the town.

TYPE	REG/SER	CON. NO.	PI/NOTES	STATUS
☐ North American NA-190 Sabre (F-86D)	52-3735	190-138		PV

DAVID CITY MONUMENT (NE5)

Location:	On permanent view at the airport which is about 1 mile south of the town.

TYPE	REG/SER	CON. NO.	PI/NOTES	STATUS
☐ Republic RF-84F Thunderflash	53-7560			PV

DAWSON COUNTY HISTORICAL MUSEUM (NE6)

Address:	805 North Taft, Lexington, Nebraska 68850.
Tel:	308-324-5340 Email: dcmuseum@atcjet.net
Admission:	Monday-Saturday 0900-1700.
Location:	In the north eastern suburbs of the town.

This excellent museum traces the history of the region. The Union Pacific Railroad arrived in Dawson County in 1866 and the oldest depot in the area was moved to the museum site in 1967. Other pioneer buildings can also be seen.

The only aviation exhibit features a local man Ira McCabe. He built successful gliders in Lexington whilst still at school. In 1915 he designed and constructed a powered biplane. On show in the museum is his second biplane which was completed in 1917. After more than half a century in store in Chicago the aircraft with its distinctive wing form returned to its birthplace. Also on show are a number of vintage cars and farm vehicles.

TYPE	REG/SER	CON. NO.	PI/NOTES	STATUS
☐ McCabe Aeroplane				PV

FAIRBURY MONUMENT (NE7)

Location:	On permanent view at the airport which is about 3 miles north of the town off Route 15.

TYPE	REG/SER	CON. NO.	PI/NOTES	STATUS
☐ Lockheed 580 (T-33A)	51-9111	580-6595		PV

FRANKLIN MONUMENT (NE8)

Location:	On permanent view in a park in the northern part of the town.

TYPE	REG/SER	CON. NO.	PI/NOTES	STATUS
☐ Lockheed 580 (T-33A)	52-9205	580-7271		PV

FREEDOM PARK UNITED STATES NAVAL MUSEUM (NE9)

Address:	2497 Freedom Park Road, Omaha, Nebraska 68110.
Tel:	402-345-1959 Fax: 402-345-3418 Email: info@freedomnavymuseum.org
Admission:	April-October daily 1000-1700.
Location:	One mile south of Eppley Airfield on the west bank of the Missouri River.

This voluntarily run museum on the banks of the Missouri River has on show three ships. The USS *Hazard* is an Admirable class minesweeper dating from 1944. The ship served in the Pacific for a short time and was decommissioned in 1946. After years in store *Hazard* was bought by a group of Omaha businessmen in the early 1970s and moved to the museum. The submarine

Nebraska

USS *Marlin* was launched in October 1953 and was designed for training purposes. She served until January 1973 and moved to museum in August 1974. The LSM-45 is an amphibious landing craft. Three aircraft are on the site. The A-4 is mounted on a pylon and the former Air Force A-7 has been repainted in naval colours. The Sikorsky helicopter has recently been retired from service with the US Coast Guard. There are also several guns to be seen.

TYPE	REG/SER	CON. NO.	PI/NOTES	STATUS
☐ Douglas A-4C Skyhawk (A4D-2N)	'Bu149618'		Composite.	PVX
☐ Sikorsky S-62A Seaguard (HH-52A)	1370	62048		PV
☐ Vought A-7D Corsair II		D21	69-6191	PVX

GORDON MONUMENT (NE10)

Location:	On permanent view at ALP 34 at 404 South Elm Street in the southern part of the town.

TYPE	REG/SER	CON. NO.	PI/NOTES	STATUS
☐ Bell 209 Huey Cobra (AH-1G) (AH-1F)	70-15967	20911		PV

GRAND ISLAND MONUMENT (NE11)

Location:	On permanent view at Hall County Veterans Park in the southern part of the town.

TYPE	REG/SER	CON. NO.	PI/NOTES	STATUS
☐ Lockheed 580 (T-33A)	53-5882	580-9358		PV

HAROLD WARP PIONEER VILLAGE (NE12)

Address:	138 East Highway 6, PO Box 68, Minden, Nebraska 68959-0068.
Tel:	308-832-2750 Email: Manager@PioneerVillage.com
Admission:	June–August daily 0800-1800; September–May daily 0900-1630.
Location:	In the centre of the town at the intersection of Routes 10 and 6/34.

Harold Warp was born in Minden and made his fortune presiding over a plastics empire based in Chicago. He died in the early 1990s and a foundation was set up to continue the running of the museum. The village contains around two dozen historic buildings which have been moved to the site. The collection started when Warp purchased the country school he attended as a boy. Many original items are on show in the buildings which include a church, a fire station, a log fort, a pony express station and a number of barns. The displays have been designed to show the harsh conditions encountered by the early settlers.

There is also a large collection of cars, agricultural vehicles, motor cycles, bicycles, railway vehicles, boats and household machines. The cars include the oldest surviving Buick which was built in 1905. A railroad depot contains two steam locomotives and a number of carriages.

Harold Warp gained his pilot's licence in the 1920s and over the years he obtained an interesting collection of aircraft and engines for the museum. The 1910 Hartman Monoplane was the first to fly in Iowa when it took to the air at Burlington Race Course. In use until 1920 it was put into store until Hartman flew it again at Clinton in 1955. Photos of the two events show that there are considerable differences in the monoplane so at some time major modifications were made.

The Cessna AW is now a rarity. The high-wing four-seat monoplane was the first produced by the new company. Clyde Cessna had a disagreement with Walter Beech, who favoured biplanes, and sold his stake in the Travel Air company. The AW was successful in races but only 78 had been sold before the Depression caused Cessna to close the factory in 1930.

The Pitcairn PAA-1 first flew in 1931 and was of similar configuration to his earlier designs. Only 25 were produced and fitted with a Kinner B-5 radial. The Sikorsky Hoverfly was the first American helicopter to be produced in large numbers and this also heralded a new age in flight.

The Bell P-59 was the first American jet fighter but it was not a great success and the Army Air Force cancelled the contract when only 68 had been completed.

TYPE	REG/SER	CON. NO.	PI/NOTES	STATUS
☐ Bell 27 Airacomet (P-59B)	44-22656	27-64	44-22656	PV
☐ Bensen B-6 Gyroglider				PV
☐ Bensen B-7M Gyrocopter	N719DP	1		PV
☐ Cessna AW	NC8141	156	NC8141, N8141	PV
☐ Curtiss D Pusher				PV
☐ Curtiss 1C Jenny (JN-4D)	1350	3044		PV
☐ De Havilland DH.60GM Moth				S
☐ Ercoupe 415C	N37100	67	NC37100 – believed correct.	PV
☐ Hartman Monoplane	N286Y	1		PV
☐ Heath Parasol	N13538	1		PV
☐ Lincoln Page LP-3				S
☐ Piper PA-23 Apache	N1030P	23-32		PV
☐ Pitcairn PAA-1	NC11638	C-55	NC11638, N11638	PV
☐ Sikorsky VS-316A Hoverfly (YR-4B) (HNS-1)	N75378	26	43-28229, Bu39034	PV
☐ Standard J-1				S
☐ Stinson SM-8A Junior	NC903W	M4080	NC903W, N903W	PV
☐ Swallow 3POLB	NC5070	924	NC5070, N5070	PV
☐ Taylor J-2 Cub	N19250	1650	NC19250	PV
☐ Weedhopper JC-24				PV
☐ Wright Flyer (R)				PV

HASTINGS MONUMENT (NE13)

Location:	On permanent view at the airport which is about 2 miles north west of the town.

TYPE	REG/SER	CON. NO.	PI/NOTES	STATUS
☐ McDonnell M.98EN Phantom II (F-4D)	65-0735	1794		PV

The National World War One Museum has on show this replica Nieuport 12. (NWWOM) [MO26]

This Boeing KC-97L Stratofreighter at the Malmstrom Air Force Base Museum is painted in the colours of one which used to operate from the field. [MT7]

The Harold Warp Pioneer Village exhibits the Hartman Monoplane first flown in 1910. [NE12]

HEARTLAND MUSEUM OF MILITARY VEHICLES (NE14)

Address:	600 Heartland Road West, Lexington, Nebraska 68850.
Tel:	308-324-6329 Email: tlauby@hotmail.com
Admission:	Monday-Saturday 1000-1700; Sunday 1300-1700.
Location:	Just north of Interstate 80 by Junction 237.

In 1986 four Lexington residents formed the museum. Over 60 vehicles are now in the collection with the majority in running order. A site was obtained near the Lexington junction to Interstate 80 and the large area has been landscaped. A building to house most of the vehicles has now been erected and the museum opened in June 1994. Future plans include the construction of more halls to accommodate the remainder of the vehicles.

TYPE	REG/SER	CON. NO.	PI/NOTES	STATUS
☐ Bell 204 Iroquois (UH-1C) (UH-1M)	66-0513	1495		PV
☐ Bell 204 Iroquois (UH-1C) (UH-1M)	66-15211	1939		PV
☐ Bell 205 Iroquois (UH-1D) (UH-1H)	66-1168	5651		PV
☐ Bell 205 Iroquois (UH-1H)	68-16329	10988		PV

LINCOLN AIR NATIONAL GUARD BASE (NE15)

Address:	155 ARW/PA, 2420 West Butler Avenue, Lincoln Municipal Airport, Nebraska 68524-1888.
Tel:	402-309-1234 Email: 155arw.pa@ang.af.mil
Admission:	By prior permission only.
Location:	About 3 miles north west of the city off Interstate 80.

The 173rd Squadron was assigned to the Nebraska Air National Guard in 1946 and, equipped with P-51 Mustangs, moved into Lincoln. In April the unit was called up for active duty and did not return home until January 1953. Over the years fighters were flown until 1994, when the unit changed to a tanker squadron with KC-135Rs. Examples of types previously flown have been preserved around the base. The F-86D version of the Sabre was in use between January 1957 and the winter of 1959 when the type was replaced by the RF-84F Thunderflash. The RF-4C arrived in February 1972 and these were operated until the unit converted to tankers. A military base was built on the site of the old civil airport in the early 1940s. This was closed at the end of the conflict. In 1952 it was reactivated as a Strategic Air Command base which housed bombers and missiles until 1966. The two helicopters are preserved in the Army National Guard area.

TYPE	REG/SER	CON. NO.	PI/NOTES	STATUS
☐ Bell 205 Iroquois (UH-1H)	69-15330	11618		RA
☐ Bell 209 Huey Cobra (AH-1S) (AH-1F)	78-23108	22214		RA
☐ Boeing 717-148 Stratotanker (KC-135A) (KC-135E)	57-1495	17566		RA
☐ Lockheed 580 (T-33A)	52-9264	580-7330		RA
☐ McDonnell M.98DF Phantom II (RF-4C)	64-0998	661		RA
☐ North American NA-201 Sabre (F-86D) (F-86L)	'52-3760'	201-275	53-0831	RAX
☐ Republic RF-84F Thunderflash	51-11259			RA

McCOOK AIRBASE HISTORICAL SOCIETY/ HIGH PLAINS MUSEUM (NE16)

Address:	PO Box B-29, McCook, Nebraska 69001-0029.
Tel:	308-345-3081
Admission:	Tuesday-Saturday 1300-1700. (Museum)
Location:	The museum is in the centre of the town.
	The old airbase is about 5 miles north of the town west of Route 83.

The airfield was activated on 1st April 1943 and until its closure on 31st December 1945 was a major training base for bomber crews. Types in use at this time included the B-17 Fortress, B-24 Liberator and B-29 Superfortress.
The site became a civil airport in 1947 but closed in the early 1960s. Five hangars and several other buildings survive but the three runways have almost disappeared. The society was formed to preserve the history of this once important field. An exhibition has been staged in one of the rooms in the High Plains Museum in the town. Memorabilia, models, photographs and documents can be seen. The site also served as a camp for German prisoners of war and there are a number of artefacts from this period in the display.
The Sabre is on show by the passenger terminal at the new airport for the town which was built on eastern side on Route 6.

TYPE	REG/SER	CON. NO.	PI/NOTES	STATUS
☐ North American NA-203 Sabre (F-86H)	53-1503	203-275	At new airport east of the town.	PV

NELIGH MONUMENT (NE17)

Location:	On permanent view on Route 275 just south of the centre of the town.

TYPE	REG/SER	CON. NO.	PI/NOTES	STATUS
☐ Republic RF-84F Thunderflash	51-1929			PV

OFFUTT AIR FORCE BASE (NE18)

Address:	55W/PA, 906 Sac Boulevard, Nebraska 68113-5000.
Tel:	402-294-2663 Email: 55wg.pa@offutt.af.mil
Admission:	By prior permission only.
Location:	About 10 miles south of Omaha off Route 75.

Fort George Cook was established on the site in March 1891 and the first aerial activity occurred in 1918 when an Army balloon unit took up residence. The airfield was built in 1921 and three years later was named after Lieutenant Jarvis Offutt who was the first Omaha resident to be killed in World War I when his S.E.5 crashed in France in August 1918. During World War II a factory operated by the Glenn L. Martin company was built. A concrete runway two miles in length was laid down along with an assembly plant and six large hangars. The plant produced 1,585 Martin B-26 Marauders and 531 Boeing B-29 Superfortresses.

In November 1948 the Headquarters of Strategic Air Command moved to Offutt. The site was chosen as it was believed that a location in the centre of the country was out of range of most bombers and missiles. The Strategic Air Command Museum was located at the airfield until the mid-1990s.

TYPE	REG/SER	CON. NO.	PI/NOTES	STATUS
☐ Boeing 299-O Fortress (B-17F) (RB-17F)	'230230'	8310	42-3374	RAX
☐ Boeing 464-253 Stratofortress (B-52G)	57-6468	464173		PV
☐ Boeing 717-146 Stratotanker (KC-135A) (EC-135A)	61-0287	18194		PV

OMAHA MONUMENTS (NE19)

Location:	On permanent view at two locations in the city.

TYPE	REG/SER	CON. NO.	PI/NOTES	STATUS
☐ Bell 205 Iroquois (UH-1H)	66-16935	9129	At ALP 374 at 4618 South 139th. Street.	PV
☐ Republic F-84F Thunderstreak	52-6385		At VFW 2503 at 8904 Military Road in the north western part of the city.	PV

SEWARD MONUMENT (NE20)

Location:	On permanent view at the airport which is about 2 miles north of the town on Route 15.

TYPE	REG/SER	CON. NO.	PI/NOTES	STATUS
☐ Bell 205 Iroquois (UH-1H)	68-16475	11134		PV

SOUTH SIOUX CITY MONUMENT (NE21)

Location:	On permanent view at the airport which is in the south western part of the town on Route 20.

TYPE	REG/SER	CON. NO.	PI/NOTES	STATUS
☐ Vought A-7D Corsair II	70-0963	D109		PV

SPALDING MONUMENT (NE22)

Location:	On permanent view on Route 91 in the eastern part of the town.

TYPE	REG/SER	CON. NO.	PI/NOTES	STATUS
☐ Northrop N-156T Talon (T-38A)	60-0567	N.5140		PV

STRATEGIC AIR AND SPACE MUSEUM (NE23)

Address:	28210 West Park Highway, Ashland, Nebraska 68003.
Tel:	402-944-3100 **Fax:** 402-944-3160 **Email:** scott@strategicairandspace.com
Admission:	Daily 0900-1700.
Location:	About 35 miles south west of Omaha off I80.

Strategic Air Command moved its Headquarters to Offutt Air Force Base in 1948. The first aircraft for the museum, a giant B-36, arrived in May 1959 but progress was slow and very few exhibits appeared over the next five years. The museum officially opened on Armed Forces Day in 1966.

The State of Nebraska took over the running of the museum in 1971 but control has since passed to a private foundation. A move was made to a new site at Ashland where the first ground was broken on 22nd March 1996, the 50th anniversary of the setting up of the command. This excellent complex opened on 16th May 1998. The aircraft are now protected from the harsh climate and many new displays have been created.

The change of name took place on 15th June 2001 as major space exhibits are now on view. Most of the types operated by SAC since its formation can be seen, ranging from the B-17 Fortress to the supersonic B-1 Lancer.

The Fortress was delivered from the Douglas plant in Long Beach in California in April 1945, too late to see active service. The bomber served in a number of roles including a period as a ground instructional airframe before flying from Patrick Air force Base in Florida to Offutt in May 1959. A range of later Boeing bombers can also be seen. The B-29 was the first bomber type allocated to SAC when it was set up. They were used in the Korean war to drop conventional bombs. Just over 2,000 B-47s were delivered to the Air Force and they were the first swept wing bombers produced in large numbers by any country. The Stratojet was operational as a bomber between 1951 and 1965. Reconnaissance and test bed aircraft flew for another dozen years. In the early days of its existence the command used fighters for escort duties and examples of these are on show along with helicopters, training and transport aircraft used by the force.

One of three Avro Vulcan delta wing bombers presented to US museums by the Royal Air Force is on show. The delta flew into Offutt in June 1982. Dwarfed by all the other aircraft is the diminutive McDonnell XF-85 Goblin, two of which were built; they were designed to be carried as parasite fighters suspended below B-36 bombers. Trials were carried out under a B-29 but the programme was abandoned in 1949.

The B-45 Tornado first flew in March 1947. Just over 100 bomber versions were built along with 33 RB-45Cs. The example on show is one of four survivors and the only reconnaissance version preserved. Also on show are displays tracing the history of the 9th Air Force, the Doolittle Raiders and the Martin Bomber plant at Offutt Air Force Base. Clayton Anderson, a Nebraska astronaut in 2007, is honoured in the exhibition. A range of missiles used in recent years has been assembled and a Vietnam Memorial Wall has been constructed.

Nebraska

TYPE	REG/SER	CON. NO.	PI/NOTES	STATUS
☐ Avro 698 Vulcan B.2	XM573			PV
☐ Boeing 299-O Fortress (B-17G) (DB-17G) (DB-17P)	44-83559	32200	44-83559, '23474'	PVX
☐ Boeing 345 Superfortress (B-29) (TB-29)	44-84076			PV
☐ Boeing 367-76-66 Stratofreighter (KC-97G)	53-0198	16980	With tail from c/n 17092 53-0310	PV
☐ Boeing 450-157-35 Stratojet (B-47E)	52-1412	44096		PV
☐ Boeing 464-201-3 Stratofortress (RB-52B)	52-8711	16839		PV
☐ Boeing 717-166 Stratotanker (KC-135B) (EC-135C)	63-8049	18666		PV
☐ Convair 36 Peacemaker (B-36J)	52-2217	358		PV
☐ Convair 4 Hustler (B-58A)	61-2059	95		PV
☐ Convair 8-10 Delta Dagger (F-102A)	54-1405	8-10-63		PV
☐ Convair 240-17 (T-29A)	50-0190	220		PV
☐ Douglas DC-3A-456 Skytrain (C-47A)	43-48098	13914/25359		PV
☐ Douglas DC-4 Skymaster (C-54D)	42-72724	10829		PV
☐ Douglas VB-26B Invader (A-26B) (TB-26B)	44-34665	27944		PV
☐ Fairchild 110 Flying Boxcar (C-119F) (C-119G)	51-8024	10767		PV
☐ General Dynamics FB-111A	68-0267	B1-39		PV
☐ General Dynamics FB-111A	68-0283	B1-55	Cockpit section only.	PV
☐ Grumman G-111 Albatross (G-64) (SA-16A) (SA-16B) (HU-16B)	51-0006	G-79		PV
☐ Lockheed 580 (T-33A)	58-0548	580-1517		PV
☐ Lockheed SR-71A Blackbird	61-7964	2015		PV
☐ Lockheed U-2C (U-2A)	56-6701	368		PV
☐ Martin 272E Canberra (B-57E)	55-4244	346		PV
☐ McDonnell M.27D Goblin (XF-85)	46-0524	2	46-0524, '8652'	PV
☐ McDonnell M.36BA Voodoo (F-101B)	59-0462	786		PV
☐ McDonnell M.98DF Phantom II (RF-4C)	65-0903	1556		PV
☐ Mikoyan-Gurevich MiG-21F	'4422'	2105	2105 – in North Vietnamese markings.	PVX
☐ North American NA-108 Mitchell (B-25J) (TB-25J)	44-30363	108-33638		PV
☐ North American NA-108 Mitchell (B-25J) (TB-25J) (TB-25N)	44-28738	108-32013	44-28738, N3441G – fuselage only.	PV
☐ North American NA-153 Tornado (RB-45C)	48-0017	153-38493		PV
☐ North American NA-203 Sabre (F-86H)	53-1375	203-147		PV
☐ North American NA-276 Sabreliner (T-39A) (CT-39A)	62-4487	276-40		PV
☐ Piasecki PD-22 Work Horse (H-21B) (CH-21B)	52-8676	B.39		PV
☐ Republic F-84F Thunderstreak	51-1714			PV
☐ Republic F-105D Thunderchief	61-0069	D-264	On a pole by Interstate 80.	PV
☐ Rockwell B-1A Lancer	76-0174	004		PV
☐ Sikorsky S-55D Chickasaw (H-19B) (UH-19B)	53-4426			PV

VALLEY MONUMENT (NE24)

Location: On permanent view in the City Park at 400 West Vass Street in the town.

TYPE	REG/SER	CON. NO.	PI/NOTES	STATUS
☐ Republic RF-84F Thunderflash	52-7251			PV

WAKEFIELD MONUMENT (NE25)

Location: On permanent view at ALP 81 at 211 Main Street in the town.

TYPE	REG/SER	CON. NO.	PI/NOTES	STATUS
☐ Bell 209 Huey Cobra (AH-1G) (AH-1F)	67-15772	20436		PV

WESTERN NEBRASKA COMMUNITY COLLEGE (NE26)

Address: 371 College Drive, Sidney, Nebraska 69162.
Tel: 308-254-7448   **Fax:** 308-254-7444   **Email:** leeverj@wncc.edu
Admission: By prior permission only.
Location: In the south eastern part of the town.

Originally established in 1926 as Scottsbrook Junior College the organisation has undergone a number of name changes over the years. Three sites are now in use with the aviation maintenance department located in the technology area at Sidney. Three airframes are known to be in use although there may well be others. A range of engines is also used in the training programme along with components and test rigs.

TYPE	REG/SER	CON. NO.	PI/NOTES	STATUS
☐ Cessna 172A	N7604T	47204		RA
☐ Cessna P206A Super Skylane	N2690X	P2060190		RA
☐ Cessna 414	N8145Q	4140045		RA

YORK MONUMENT (NE27)

Location: On permanent view at the airport which is just north of the town on Route 81.

TYPE	REG/SER	CON. NO.	PI/NOTES	STATUS
☐ Republic RF-84F Thunderflash	51-1935			PV

NEVADA

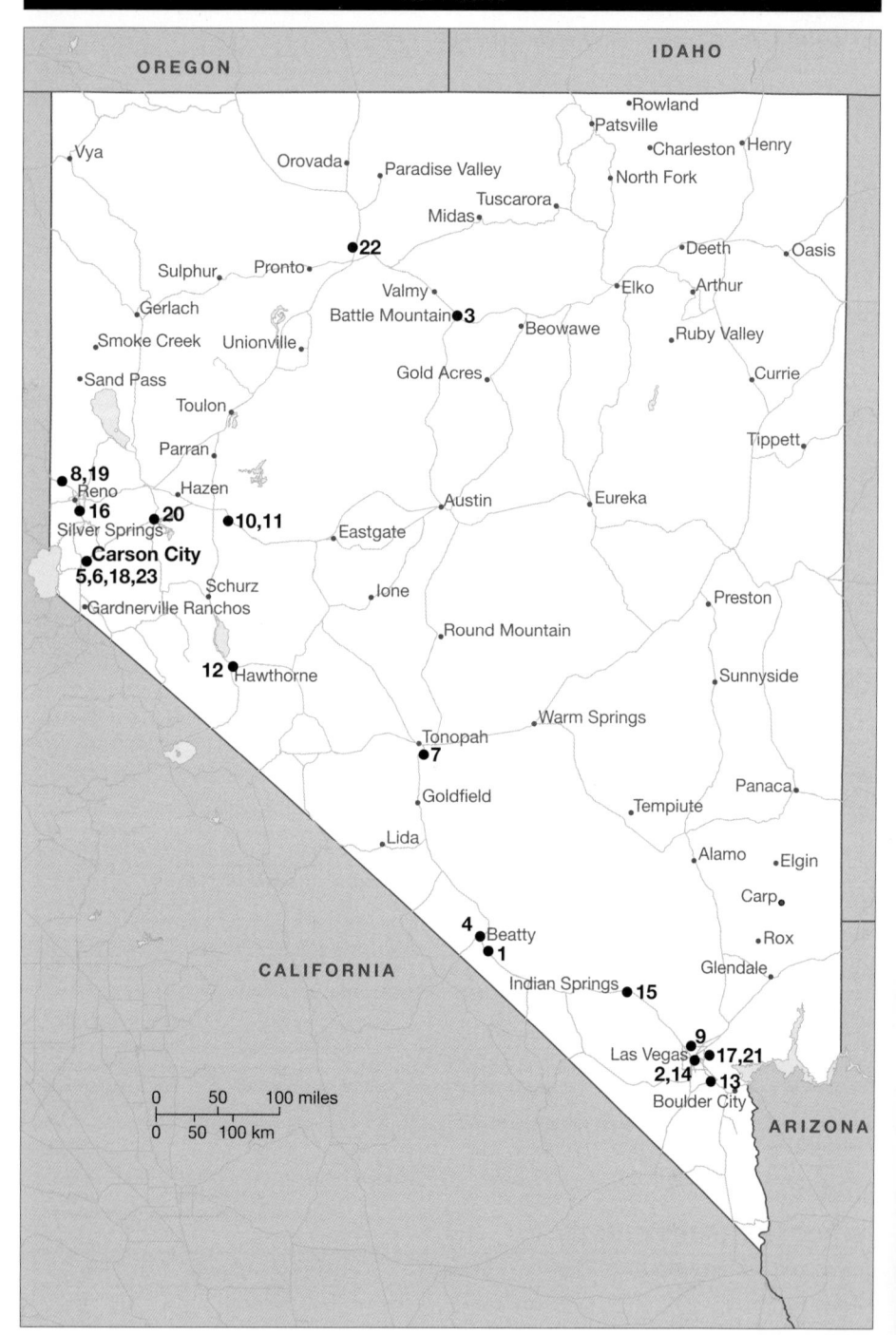

Nevada

AMARGOSA VALLEY MONUMENT (NV1)

| Location: | On permanent view at VFW 6826 in the town. |

TYPE	REG/SER	CON. NO.	PI/NOTES	STATUS
☐ Bell 205 Iroquois (UH-1H)	66-17004	9198		PV

ATOMIC TESTING MUSEUM (NV2)

Address:	755 East Flamingo Road, Las Vegas, Nevada 89119.
Tel:	702-794-5161
Admission:	Monday-Saturday 1000-1700; Sunday 1200-1700
Location:	In the eastern part of the city centre.

The Nevada deserts have been used for testing nuclear weapons for many years. The displays at the museum trace the development of the bombs and show in detail how the work was carried out. Equipment used in monitoring the explosions can be seen along with photographs of the results of the tests. Aircraft have been used to drop weapons and to observe tests.

BATTLE MOUNTAIN AIRPORT COLLECTION (NV3)

Address:	Battle Mountain Airport, Nevada 89820.
Tel:	775-635-2885
Admission:	Museum closed but aircraft on permanent view.
Location:	About 4 miles east of the town.

A museum was set up as the airport in the mid-1990s but only remained open for a short time. Five aircraft were parked at the site but now only two remain along with a virtually empty display building. The F-111A is expected to move soon. The Flying Boxcar was used for fire-fighting duties in the state.

TYPE	REG/SER	CON. NO.	PI/NOTES	STATUS
☐ Fairchild 110 Flying Boxcar (C-119F)	N5216R	10956	22131 (Canada)	PVX
☐ General Dynamics F-111A	66-0012	A1-30		PV

BEATTY MONUMENT (NV4)

| Location: | On permanent view at a business about 1 mile north of the town on Route 95. |

TYPE	REG/SER	CON. NO.	PI/NOTES	STATUS
☐ Beech D18S Expeditor (C-45G)	N6065G	AF-206	51-11649, N6065V	PVD

BUEHN COLLECTION (NV5)

Address:	2600 College Parkway, Carson City, Nevada 89706.
Admission:	By prior permission only.
Location:	At the airport which is about 3 miles north east of the town.

A number of Harvards and Texans are flown by Dennis and Tami Buehn. One is painted in a period US Marines scheme and another in Royal Canadian Navy colours. The collection includes a number of early examples of the famous trainer. The Harvard IIs were delivered to the Royal Canadian Air Force in 1941 and served for almost two decades. The AT-6A was in as an instructional airframe at the Cleveland Technical Institute for many years.

TYPE	REG/SER	CON. NO.	PI/NOTES	STATUS
☐ Aeronca 11CC Chief	N4094E	11CC-4		RAA
☐ Canadian Car & Foundry Harvard 4 [North American NA-186 (T-6J)]	N4290	CCF4-290	51-17108, MM?????	RAA
☐ Cessna 172M	N1990V	17263183		RAA
☐ North American NA-66 Harvard II	N2757	66-2490	2757 (Canada)	RAA
☐ North American NA-66 Harvard II	N2832F	66-2565	2832 (Canada), N9787Z	RA
☐ North American NA-77 Texan (AT-6A)	N648DB	77-4215	41-256, 'CTI-70'	RA
☐ North American NA-88 Texan (SNJ-4)	N694US	88-13627	Bu51360, N6424D	RAA
☐ North American NA-121 Texan (AT-6D) (SNJ-5)	N752V	121-42105	44-81383, Bu91089, N3194G – possible identity.	RA
☐ North American NA-168 Texan (T-6G)	N51KT/'284602'	168-370	49-3266, N9604C	RAAX
☐ North American NA-168 Texan (T-6G)	N3171P/'17320'	SA-058	7708 (South Africa), 0116 (Paraguay)	RAAX
☐ Piper J-3C-65 Cub	N42842	15162	NC42842	RAA

CACTUS AIR FORCE (NV6)

Address:	2230 Mouton Drive, Carson City, Nevada 89702.
Admission:	By prior permission only.
Location:	At the airport which is about 3 miles north east of the town.

Carson City Airport is home to many warbirds and a company specialising in the maintenance of Grumman Albatross amphibians. The name of the group is taken from the one applied to the air force flown in the battle of Guadalcanal in 1942. The Bronco is one of 18 procured by the US Navy for use by the Luftwaffe. The Trojans are from the first batch delivered to the Air Force in the early 1950s.

TYPE	REG/SER	CON. NO.	PI/NOTES	STATUS
☐ Canadair CL-30 Silver Star 3 (CT-133) [Lockheed 580 (T-33AN)]	N613RC	T33-613	21613, 133613	RAA
☐ Canadair CL-30 Silver Star 3 (CT-133) [Lockheed 580 (T-33AN)]	N615RC	T33-615	21615, 133615	RAA
☐ North American NA-159 Trojan (T-28A)	N28NA	159-142	49-1630	RAA
☐ North American NA-159 Trojan (T-28A)	N7245C	159-231	49-1719	RAA
☐ North American NA-338 Bronco (OV-10B)	N338RC	338-10	Bu158301, D-9554, 99+25	RAA

CENTRAL NEVADA MUSEUM (NV7)

Address:	PO Box 326, 1900 Logan Field Road, Tonopah, Nevada 89049.
Tel:	775-482-9676 Fax: 775-482-5423
Admission:	April–September daily 0900-1700; October–March Monday-Saturday 1100-1700.
Location:	In the southern part of the town.

This informative museum traces the history of the region. Pioneer life, mining, geology and plant life feature in the displays. There are many interesting items of machinery to be seen. Tonopah Army Airfield was constructed in the early 1940s and served as a training base for P-39 Airacobra fighters and Consolidated B-24 Liberator bombers.

The history of the airfield is portrayed in detail in the museum with many photographs and items of memorabilia. The airfield closed after the end of hostilities and now serves as the civil airport for the town. Four original hangars in various stages of dereliction survive at the site which is about seven miles east of the town.

COMMEMORATIVE AIR FORCE (HIGH SIERRA SQUADRON) (NV8)

Address:	316 California Avenue, Reno, Nevada 89509-1650.
Email:	cgsqd@sbcglobal.net
Admission:	By prior permission only.
Location:	At Stead Airport which is about 15 miles north west of the city off Route 395.

The unit currently operates an example of the N3N-3 biplane trainer dating from the 1940s. The aircraft, painted in period yellow colours, is a regular participant at events in the area. The Sabre is a recent arrival in the workshops. This classic jet fighter is being painstakingly rebuilt by volunteers.

TYPE	REG/SER	CON. NO.	PI/NOTES	STATUS
☐ Naval Aircraft Factory N3N-3	N4009A		Bu2733	RAA
☐ North American NA-191Sabre (F-86F)	N186SR	191-812	52-5112	RAC

COMMEMORATIVE AIR FORCE (NEVADA WING) (NV9)

Address:	2730 Airport Drive, Suite 101, Las Vegas, Nevada 89032.
Tel:	702-646-1340 Email: airphoto@cox.net
Admission:	By prior permission only.
Location:	At North Las Vegas Air Terminal which is in the north western suburbs of the city on Route 95.

Two aircraft are operated by this wing, which was formed in the early 1990s. The Invader served in the fire-fighting role in the 1970s and joined the Confederate Air Force in 1982. Restoration to military configuration is taking place.

The Stinson Reliant arrived at Las Vegas soon after the unit was established. The high wing monoplane seved in the Far East with the Fleet Air Arm before returning to the USA in the summer of 1946.

TYPE	REG/SER	CON. NO.	PI/NOTES	STATUS
☐ Douglas A-26B Invader	N9682C	6943	41-39230	RAA
☐ Stinson V-77 Reliant (AT-19)	N67227	77-496	43-44209, FB768, Bu11530	RAA

FALLON MONUMENT (NV10)

Location:	On permanent view at a car showroom in town.

TYPE	REG/SER	CON. NO.	PI/NOTES	STATUS
☐ Vought A-7E Corsair II	Bu159467	E456		PV

FALLON NAVAL AIR STATION AIR POWER HERITAGE PARK (NV11)

Address:	4755 Pasture Road, Van Voorhies Field, Fallon, Nevada 89406-5000.
Tel:	775-426-2880 Fax: 775-426-2930 Email: webmaster@fallon.navy.mil
Admission:	By prior permission only.
Location:	About 7 miles south east of the town.

The airfield was built in 1942 as part of the defensive network designed to repel a posssible Japanese invasion across the Pacific. Today it is home to the Naval Strike Warfare Center and the Naval Fighter Weapons School, units that moved in during 1976 from Miramar when the Californian base was transferred to the Marine Corps. The field is named after Lieutenant Commander Van Voorheis, a local man, who won the Medal of Honor in World War II. The regional history museum in the town stages a display tracing his life. A heritage park has been set up at the airfield.

TYPE	REG/SER	CON. NO.	PI/NOTES	STATUS
☐ Bell 204 Iroquois (HU-1B) (UH-1B)	60-3593	239		RA
☐ Bell 212 Iroquois (UH-1N) (HH-1N)	Bu158272	31613		RA

Nevada

☐ Douglas AD-4B Skyraider	Bu132261	8369	Bu132261, N68625	RA
☐ Douglas A-4B Skyhawk (A4D-2)			Front fuselage only.	RA
☐ Douglas A-4B Skyhawk (A4D-2)	Bu142100	11354		RA
☐ Douglas A-4F Skyhawk	Bu155025	13841		RA
☐ General Dynamics 401 Fighting Falcon (F-16N)	Bu163576	3M-21	86-1694	RA
☐ Grumman G-123 Hawkeye (E-2C)	Bu159496	A22		RA
☐ Grumman G-128 Intruder (A-6A) (A-6E)	Bu155627	I-353		RA
☐ Grumman G-303 Tomcat (F-14A)	Bu159626	173		RA
☐ Lockheed 394 Viking (S-3A) (S-3B)	Bu160571	394A-3151		RA
☐ McDonnell M.98AM Phantom II (F4H-1) (F-4B) (F-4N)	Bu151510	700	Bu151510, '63411', '37411', 'Bu155800'	RA
☐ McDonnell M.267 Hornet (F/A-18A)	Bu161708	54/A040		RA
☐ Mikoyan-Gurevich MiG-21bis	3964	75033964	In Hungarian markings.	RA
☐ Mikoyan-Gurevich MiG-21F-13				RA
☐ Mikoyan-Gurevich MiG-23ML	353	0390324640	353 (DDR), 20+23	RA
☐ Mikoyan-Gurevich MiG-29A	15		In Moldovan markings.	RA
☐ North American NA-231 Sabre (F-86F)	'29371'		(USAF), (Japan), '25484'	RAX
☐ North American NA-316 Vigilante (RA-5C)	Bu156638	316-31		RA
☐ Northrop N-156E Tiger II (F-5E)	Bu160796	R.1092	73-0900, (South Vietnam)	RA
☐ Vought DF-8L Crusader (F8U-1E) (F-8B) (F-8L)	Bu145449			RA
☐ Vought A-7B Corsair II	Bu154420	B60		RA
☐ Vought NA-7C Corsair II (A-7C)	Bu156734	E1		RA
☐ WSK Lim-2 [MiG-15bis]	'8170'	1B 016-14	1614 (Poland), N614BM – in false Soviet markings.	RAX
☐ WSK Lim-5 [MiG-17F]	'3020'	1C 13-19	1319 (Poland) – in false North Vietnamese markings.	RAX

HAWTHORNE ORDNANCE MUSEUM (NV12)

Address:	925 East Street, Hawthorne, Nevada 89415.
Tel:	775-945-5400 **Fax:** 775-945-5402 Email: ordnancemuseum@yahoo.com
Admission:	Monday-Friday 1000-1600;Saturday 1000-1400.
Location:	In centre of the town.

In 1930 the US Navy set up an ammunitions depot at Hawthorne. In 1926 an explosion at a facility in New Jersey had destroyed most of the town and killed over 50 people. The Nevada site was chosen because it was in a sparsely populated area. The site was transferred to the Army in 1977 and was named Hawthorne Army Ammunition Plant. Production of weapons ceased in 1994 and it became the Hawthorne Army Depot. The displays at the museum trace the history of the site with an excellent collection of ordnance on show. Photographs and documents can also be seen. Two helicopters are on view. The Piasecki HUP-1 twin rotor helicopter first flew in 1948 and was used by the navy for transport and search and rescue duties. The one on show moved to the exhibition from the USS *Hornet* Museum in California. The Gyrodyne QH-50 is a remote controlled unmanned helicopter delivered to the navy in the 1960s. Operating mainly from destroyers the QH-50s were used for carrying torpedoes and depth charges. Total production of all versions was 377.

TYPE	REG/SER	CON. NO.	PI/NOTES	STATUS
☐ Gyrodyne QH-50D		DS-1914		PV
☐ Piasecki PV-18 Retriever (HUP-1)	Bu128561		Bu128561	PV

HENDERSON RESTAURANT (NV13)

Location:	On permanent view at the Baja Beach Cafe in the Fiesta Casino Complex in the town.

TYPE	REG/SER	CON. NO.	PI/NOTES	STATUS
☐ Beech D18S Expeditor (C18S) (SNB-1) (SNB-4) (SNB-5) (TC-45J) (UC-45J)	N68619	5013	Bu67313	PV

HOWARD W. CANNON AVIATION MUSEUM (NV14)

Address:	5757 Wayne Newton Boulevard, Las Vegas, Nevada 89119.
Tel:	702-455-7968
Admission:	On permanent view in the main and general aviation terminals.
Location:	At McCarran International Airport which is in the southern suburbs of the city.

This collection has been set up in the main terminal at the airport. The exhibition is been renamed in honour of a retired senator. The history of flying in southern Nevada from the first flight in 1920 is portrayed. There are many photographs, documents, models and items of memorabilia on view. The stories of the many airlines which have flown from airfields in the Las Vegas region is portrayed in detail. The first airport in the city was Alamo and the widow of the founder, George Crockett operator of Alamo Airways, donated many personal items to the display. The Cessna took off from the field in 1968 and stayed aloft for over 64 days. The pilots on this record flight, which still stands, were John Cook and Robert Timms. who made low passes along the runway for fuel and supplies. Works of art can also be seen in the buildings.

TYPE	REG/SER	CON. NO.	PI/NOTES	STATUS
☐ Cessna 172	N9172B	36772		PV

INDIAN SPRINGS MONUMENT (NV15)

Location:	On permanent view in the City Park in the centre of the town.

TYPE	REG/SER	CON. NO.	PI/NOTES	STATUS
☐ Republic F-84F Thunderstreak	'1776'			PVX

This Republic RF-84F Thunderflash is one of the gate guards at Lincoln Air Force Base. (David Skeggs) [NE15]

On show in the Fallon Naval Air Station Freedom Park is this Grumman A-6E Intruder. [NV11]

The Howard W. Cannon Aviation Museum at McCarran International Airport displays this record breaking Cessna 172. (Malcolm Fillmore) [NV14]

Nevada 403

MAY AIR NATIONAL GUARD BASE (NV16)

| Location: | On permanent view at Cannon International Airport which is about 5 miles south east of Reno. |

TYPE	REG/SER	CON. NO.	PI/NOTES	STATUS
☐ McDonnell M.36BA Voodoo (F-101B) (CF-101B) (RF-101B)	59-0483	807	59-0483, 17483 (Canada)	PV
☐ McDonnell M.98DF Phantom II (RF-4C)	65-0886	1490		PV

NELLIS AIR FORCE BASE FREEDOM PARK (NV17)

Address:	HQAWC/PA, 4370 Washington Boulevard, Suite 117, Nellis Air Force Base, Nevada 89191-2915.
Tel:	702-652-2750 Email: 99abw.pa@nellis.af.mil
Admission:	By prior permission only.
Location:	About 8 miles north east of Las Vegas on Route 604.

This important base, named after Lieutenant William H. Nellis who was killed in a P-47 crash in Europe in 1944, opened as a gunnery school in July 1941.

Among the units housed at the field are the Tactical Fighter Weapons Center and the 'Thunderbirds' acrobatic team. A display of preserved aircraft has been set up just inside the secondary gate to the field. The types on view represent some of the fighters which have flown from Nellis over the last few years. The Soviet designed types are parked by a training facility and can be seen on base tours.

TYPE	REG/SER	CON. NO.	PI/NOTES	STATUS
☐ Fairchild-Republic A-10A Thunderbolt II	77-0255	A10-180		RA
☐ General Dynamics F-111A	67-0100	A1-145		RA
☐ General Dynamics 401 Fighting Falcon (F-16A)	79-0371	61-156		RA
☐ Lockheed YF-117A	79-10780	A.4005		RA
☐ McDonnell M.98DJ Phantom II (F-4C)	'94806'	1128	64-0806	RAX
☐ Mikoyan-Gurevich MiG-21F-13	'64'		F-2153 (Indonesia)	RAX
☐ Mikoyan-Gurevich MiG-23ML	20+25	0390324254	475 (DDR)	RA
☐ Mikoyan-Gurevich MiG-29	'309'	2960517473	16 (Moldova)- in false DDR markings.	RAX
☐ Mikoyan-Gurevich MiG-29	'30'	2960517464	06 (Moldova) – in false Soviet markings.	RAX
☐ Mil Mi-8T				RA
☐ Mil Mi-14PL				RA
☐ Mil Mi-24D			In Iraqi markings.	RA
☐ North American NA-172 Sabre (F-86E)	51-13010	172-301	51-13010, '27523'	RA
☐ North American NA-223 Super Sabre (F-100D)	'56-3298'	223-277	55-3595.	RAX
☐ Northrop N-156E Tiger II (F-5E)	'73-0865'	R.1229	74-1571	RAX
☐ Republic F-105G Thunderchief (F-105F)	63-8276	F-53		RA
☐ Sukhoi Su-7BM	'547'	7505	7643 (Egypt) – in false Iraqi markings.	RAX
☐ WSK Lim-5 [MiG-17F]	'547'	1C 11-18	(Indonesia) – in false North Korean markings.	RAX

NEVADA MUSEUM OF MILITARY HISTORY (NV18)

Address:	PO Box 186, Wellington, Nevada 89444-0186.
Tel:	hhatfiel@pacbell.net
Admission:	Not yet open.
Location:	To be built at Carson City Airport.

Members of this recently formed museum are raising funds to build an exhibition hall and hangar at Carson City Airport. The Mentor is owned by the museum and the pair of Mitchells by members.

The Douglas Invader has been stored for over 30 years and a complete restoration is planned. The three active aircraft are regular performers at air shows in the region. When the facility is complete more aircraft may be acquired.

TYPE	REG/SER	CON. NO.	PI/NOTES	STATUS
☐ Beech A45 Mentor (T-34A)	N3799G	G-709	55-0152	RAA
☐ Douglas A-26B Invader				RA
☐ North American NA-108 Mitchell (B-25J) (TB-25J) (TB-25N)	N9117Z	108-32474	44-29199	RAA
☐ North American NA-108 Mitchell (B-25J) (TB-25J) (TB-25N)	N201L	108-33881	44-30606, N5249V – painted as PBJ-1 '430606'	RAAX

RENO ARMY NATIONAL GUARD BASE (NV19)

| Location: | By prior permission only at Stead Airport which is about 15 miles north west of the city. |

TYPE	REG/SER	CON. NO.	PI/NOTES	STATUS
☐ Bell 205 Iroquois (UH-1H)	68-16084	10743		RA
☐ Sikorsky S-64A Tarhe (CH-54A)	67-18418	64020		RA

SILVER SPRINGS MONUMENT (NV20)

| Location: | On permanent view at the airport just south west of the town. |

TYPE	REG/SER	CON. NO.	PI/NOTES	STATUS
☐ General Dynamics EF-111A (F-111A)	66-0047	A1-65		PV

THUNDERBIRDS MUSEUM (NV21)

Address:	4445 Tyndall Avenue, Nellis Air Force Base, Nevada 89191.
Tel:	702-652-9902
Admission:	On the Tuesday and Thursday tours of the base which are not operating at the current time.
Location:	About 8 miles north east of Las Vegas off Route 604.

This aerobatic team was originally formed in 1953 as the 3600th Air Demonstration Team at Luke Air Force Base in Arizona. Five F-84G Thunderjets were used and four were normally flown with one in reserve. The name 'Thunderbirds' was chosen the following year. In the spring of 1955 F-84F Thunderstreaks were acquired and these were operated for two years. The F-100C Super Sabre arrived in May 1966 and the team moved to Nellis. For a brief spell in 1964 the F-105B Thunderchief was used but after six shows these were replaced by the F-100D. After 13 years with the Super Sabre they were withdrawn and the F-4E Phantom arrived. In 1974 the team changed to the T-38 Talon and these stayed until 1982 when the current equipment, the F-16, was introduced. The museum traces the history of the team with photographs, models, trophies, uniforms and memorabilia. Films of the team in action are shown. A team aircraft is on show when the museum is open.

TYPE	REG/SER	CON. NO.	PI/NOTES	STATUS
☐ General Dynamics 401 Fighting Falcon (F-16A)			One of the team aircraft.	PV

WINNEMUCCA VETERANS MEMORIAL (NV22)

Address:	Veterans Memorial Highway, Winnemucca, Nevada 89445.
Admission:	On permanent view.
Location:	About 1 mile north of the town on Highway 95.

This memorial to local military dead is situated on a hill overlooking the town. The Sabre, which has been here for many years, honours the people who fought in Korea in the 1950s. The Iroquois is dedicated to those who lost their lives in the Vietnam conflict. Also on show are a tank, memorial plaques, weapons and flags.

TYPE	REG/SER	CON. NO.	PI/NOTES	STATUS
☐ Bell 205 Iroquois (UH-1H)	66-16654	8848		PV
☐ North American NA-201 Sabre (F-86D) (F-86L)	53-0568	201-12		PV

YESTERDAYS FLYERS (NV23)

Address:	Carson City Airport, 3020 Graves Lane No.14, Carson City, Nevada 89701.
Tel:	702-883-1050
Admission:	Saturday-Sunday 0900-1700 or by appointment.
Location:	About 3 miles north east of the town.

Owners of vintage aircraft in the region formed this group in the 1980s. The collection has grown steadily and now has a display hangar and workshop facilities at the airport. An exhibition of photographs and memorabilia has been put on show.

The Stearman 4E was bought from the manufacturers by Keith Scott of Reno in 1929. He sold the biplane in 1942 and after a spell as a crop duster it was restored to original configuration in 1970. On 17th October 1985, then aged 81, he repurchased the 4E which is now owned by his son. This superb biplane has won many awards at shows. The biplane took part in the 2003 National Air Tour. The first event organised in 1925 by the Ford company was intended to show local communities the potential of air travel. The 2003 journey was carried out to relive the epic journeys flown in 1932. About two dozen aircraft from the inter-war period flew the route starting and finishing at Detroit. Almost 30 airfields were visited between 8th and 24th September.

Two replicas of early aircraft have been constructed and these are occasionally flown on calm days. The Pfalz replica was airworthy for many years and the Halberstadt has now been completed. This pair have not flown for some years. A Nieuport 24 was built but this was destroyed in 1993.

The Breese Penguin replica won a prize at the 1998 Watsonville show in California. About 300 examples of this design were built and used for training pilots in the ground handling of aircraft. The airframe was fitted with an engine which would enable it to reach taxying speeds without leaving the ground. The Robin is an early example of this classic design and the type was the first three seat cabin design to be produced in the USA. The Stinson Junior, built in 1930 is powered by a 300 h.p. Pratt and Whitney Wasp Junior radial.

The Franklin PS-2 glider, dating from the 1920s, has arrived from Harris Hill and is undergoing restoration. The Eaglet was very successful and the first four US Soaring Championships were won by pilots flying the type. Most of the aircraft are owned by individuals in the group and are often away from Carson City.

Members of the local chapter of the Experimental Aircraft Association have their premises nearby and a number of vintage types are being rebuilt.

TYPE	REG/SER	CON. NO.	PI/NOTES	STATUS
☐ Blériot XI (R)				RAA
☐ Breese Penguin (R)	'33741'			PVX
☐ Curtiss 50 Robin	N8303	178	NC8303	PVC
☐ Curtiss-Wright CW-1 Junior	NC10943	1121	NC10943, N10943	PVA
☐ Curtiss-Wright CW-1 Junior	NC11888	1258	NC11888, N11888	RAA
☐ Deperdussin Monoplane (R)				PVA
☐ Franklin PS-2 Eaglet	N452Y	113	On loan from National Soaring Museum, NY.	PV
☐ Halberstadt CL II (R)	N5601	000117		PV
☐ Hang Glider				PV
☐ Howard DGA-3 Pete (R)				RAA
☐ Pfalz D III (R)	N4115	1		PV
☐ Santos-Dumont XX Demoiselle (R)	N121RC	SD20		PVA
☐ Stearman 4E Junior Speedmail	NC663K	4005		PVA
☐ Stinson SM-1F Detroiter				RAA
☐ Stinson SM-7B Junior	NC10812	M3013	NC10812, N10812	PV
☐ Vultee V-74 Valiant (BT-13A)	N69041	74-6462	41-22784	PVA

NEW HAMPSHIRE

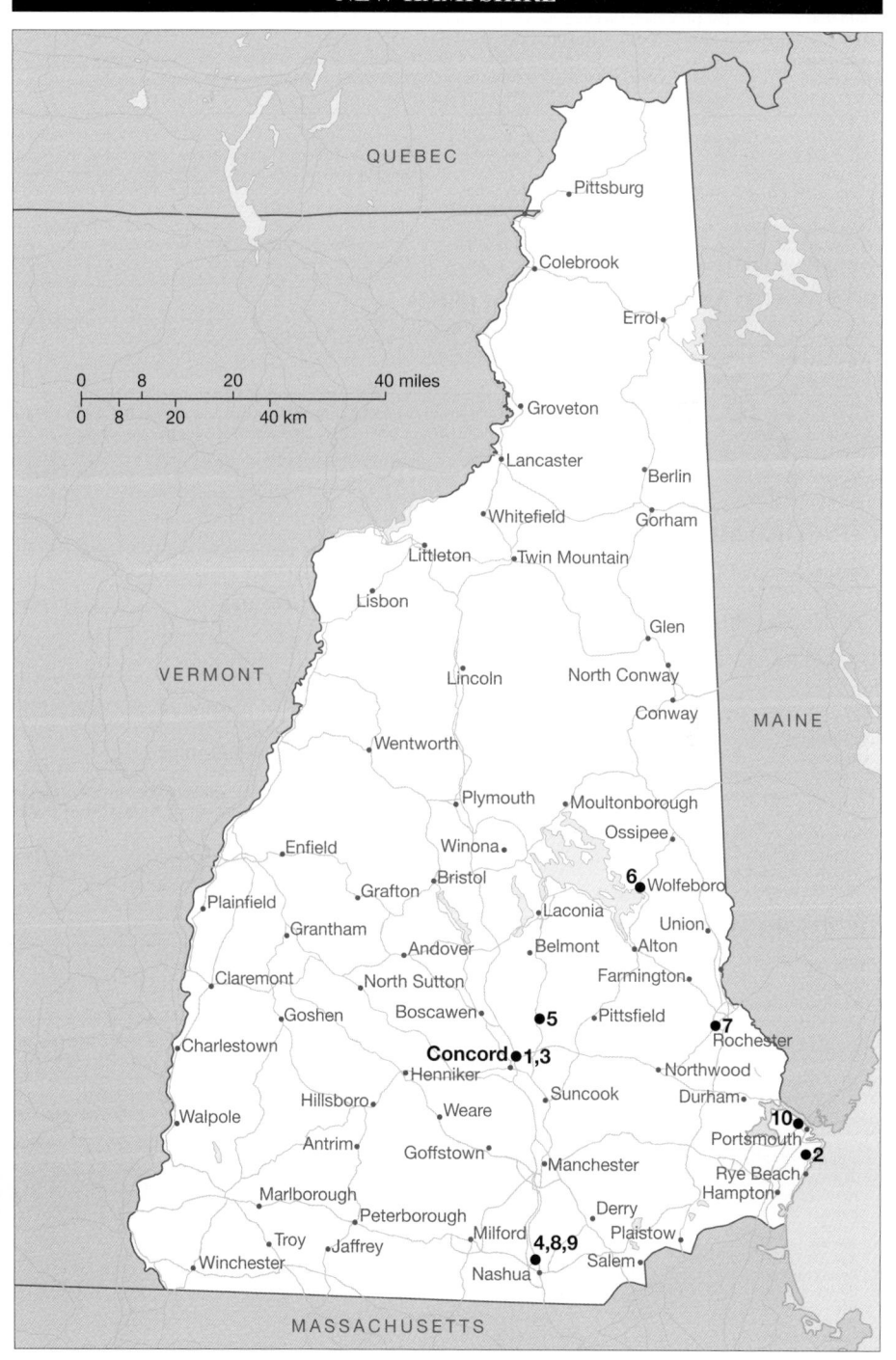

AVIATION MUSEUM OF NEW HAMPSHIRE (NH1)

Address:	PO Box 3653, Concord, New Hampshire 03302-3653.
Tel:	603-669-4820 Email: Avmuseum1@myfairpoint.net
Admission:	Friday-Saturday 1000-1600 ; Sunday 1300-1600.
Location:	At 13 East Perimeter Road at Manchester Airport which is about two miles south of the town off Route 29.

The society was formed in 1995 and has collected many artefacts tracing the history of aviation in the state which has seen many significant events over the years.

The first balloon flight was made at Manchester when Eugene Goddard took to the air astride a horse suspended below the envelope. The first airport in the state was constructed at Concord in 1920. Regular meetings are held and exhibitions have been staged at local shows. Funds were raised to save the now unused 1937 'Art Deco' terminal at Manchester Airport. The society was supported by the airport authorities and two local towns in this project. In June 2004 the building was transported across two runways to a site on the south east side of the field.

The displays trace the history of aviation in the state with many models, photographs and documents on show. New exhibitions are being developed.

BONEYARD AVIATION MUSEUM (NH2)

Address:	PO Box 1062, 271 Harbor Road, Rye, New Hampshire03870-1062.
Admission:	By prior permission only.
Location:	At an airfield in the area.

This former Czechoslovakian jet trainer was registered to the museum in 2002. After its active days were over the Delfin was put on show at Pardubice Air Force Base. It was imported into the USA in 1997. I have been unable to trace any further details of the group which does not appear to have any other aircraft.

TYPE	REG/SER	CON. NO.	PI/NOTES	STATUS
☐ Aero L-29 Delfin	N29SV	892828	2828 (Czechoslovakia)	RAA

CONCORD MONUMENT (NH3)

Location:	By prior permission only at the Army NG base at the airport which is just south east of the town.

TYPE	REG/SER	CON. NO.	PI/NOTES	STATUS
☐ Bell 205 Iroquois (UH-1H)	69-15395	11683		RA

DAKOTA AVIATION MUSEUM (NH4)

Address:	492 Old Ashby Road, Mason, New Hampshire 03048.
Tel:	603-878-1622
Admission:	By prior permission only.
Location:	At Nashua Airport which is in the north western part of the town off Route 101A.

The group bought two examples of the classic transport in the mid-1990s. Both were in flying condition and arrived at Nashua from Canada. One is still flying and the other has been sold and is now with a Texas owner The remaining aircraft was delivered to the USAAF in May 1944 and entered civilian life in March 1946.

TYPE	REG/SER	CON. NO.	PI/NOTES	STATUS
☐ Douglas DC-3A-456 Skytrain (C-47A)	N33623	20215	43-15749, NC20754, N36MK, N364K, C-GYBA, N347AB	RAA

DEXTER COLLECTION (NH5)

Address:	PO Box 7009, Loudon, New Hampshire 0330-7001.
Admission:	By prior permission only.
Location:	At a private airfield in the area.

This collection contains a number of interesting types including several of a range of Aeronca Chiefs. The Aeronca K appeared in 1937 and was powered by a 40 h.p. Aeronca E113 engine. The KCA with a 50 h.p. Continental was developed into the 65C Chief with higher powered motors. Over 1,000 examples of the model 65 appeared before production turned to military models. The basic design was revived after World War II as the 11AC. This was again a success with well over 1,000 being sold from 1947 up to 1951. In 1958 John Grega modernised the 1930s Pietenpol design into a two seater powered by a 50 h.p. Continental motor. Plans were made available and many are now flying around the country.

TYPE	REG/SER	CON. NO.	PI/NOTES	STATUS
☐ Aeronca K	NC18838	K-104	NC18838, N18838	RAA
☐ Aeronca 65C Chief	NC22384	C-3849	NC22384, N22384	RAA
☐ Aeronca 65C Chief	NC24217	C-6839	NC24217, N24217	RA
☐ Aeronca 65CA Super Chief	N33783	CA-13531	NC33783	RA
☐ Aeronca 11AC Chief	N9051E	11AC-682	NC9051E	RAA
☐ Aeronca 11AC Chief	N9284E	11AC-921	NC9284E	RAA
☐ Boeing-Stearman A75L3 Kaydet (B75N1) (N2S-3)	N58969	75-7871	Bu38250	RA
☐ Boeing-Stearman A75N1 Kaydet (N2S-1)	N48190	75-993	Bu3216	RA
☐ Boeing-Stearman A75N1 Kaydet (PT-17)	N52673	75-2840	41-25345	RA
☐ Boeing-Stearman A75N1 Kaydet (PT-17)	N58212	75-762	41-1002	RA
☐ Curtiss 50B Robin B	N3115L	55	NC52E	RA
☐ Curtiss 50C Robin C-2	NC323J	480	NC323K, N9740N	RAA

New Hampshire

☐ Enstrom F-28A	N9220	206		RAA
☐ Enstrom F-28F	N19BZ	727		RAA
☐ Grega GN-1 Aircamper	N2308C	GN-1-632		RAA
☐ Stinson SR-5 Reliant	NC14592	9333A	NC14592, N14592	RA

E. STANLEY WRIGHT MUSEUM OF AMERICAN ENTERPRISE (NH6)

Address:	PO Box 1212, 77 Center Street, Wolfeboro, New Hampshire 03894.
Tel:	603-569-1212 **Fax:** 603-569-6326 **Email:** wrmuseum@aol.com
Admission:	May–October Monday-Saturday 1000-1600; Sunday 1200-1600:
Location:	In the centre of the town.

Stanley Wright was a World War I veteran. His son David began collecting military vehicles and memorabilia in the late 1970s. Over 50 tanks, armoured carriers, jeeps and lorries were acquired. He set up a foundation named after his father and in 1993 obtained a five-acre complex at Wolfeboro. The exhibition opened two years later and the site is still being developed.

Displays in the 'Home Front' hall focus on the contribution of Americans in the USA during World War II. A large building houses the collection of military vehicles. A new attraction being constructed is the 'Time Tunnel'. The first room dedicated to 1945 opened in August 2004 and was followed by the 1939 exhibition. Exhibitions covering other eras are planned.

TYPE	REG/SER	CON. NO.	PI/NOTES	STATUS
☐ Cessna 305A Bird Dog (L-19A) (O-1A)	'11090'	21041	50-1367	PVX
☐ Taylorcraft DCO-65 Grasshopper (L-2M)				PV

JACKSON COLLECTION (NH7)

Address:	156 Rochester Hill Road, Rochester, New Hampshire 03867-3347.
Admission:	By prior permission only.
Location:	At a private airfield about 3 miles west of the town.

This family collection contains a number of interesting types. The Waco S3HD first flew in 1934 and only two were built. The one in the collection has spent all its life in the USA and the other was sold to Cuba for military use in 1936. Only 14 D models with differing engines were built with sales to the air forces of Guatemala, Nicaragua and Venezuela. The Waco P series did not prove to be very popular with only one PLA and five PBFs sold. The UMF was also not produced in large numbers so these three classic biplanes are all of great interest. The Sikorsky S-39 was a smaller version of the S-38 and prototype first flew in 1929. Just 23 were built and only four are known to survive. The development of the famous Cub series can also be seen in this collection.

TYPE	REG/SER	CON. NO.	PI/NOTES	STATUS
☐ Aeronca KC	NC19716	K-228	NC19716, N19716	RAA
☐ Piper J-3C-65 Cub	N7486H	20754	NC7486H	RAA
☐ Piper J-4A Cub Coupe	NC26188	4-865	NC26188, N26188	RAA
☐ Piper PA-18-105 Super Cub Special	N7218K	18-102		RAA
☐ North American NA-154 Navion	N4043K	NAV-4-1043 (154-16)	NC4043K	RAA
☐ Sikorsky S-39-C (S-39-B)	N50V	912	NC50V	RAA
☐ Stinson Junior SR	NC13462	8715	NC13462, N13462	RAA
☐ Taylor J-2 Cub	NC16734	863	NC16997, N16997	RAA
☐ Waco PBF	NC13029	3616	NC13029, N13029	RAA
☐ Waco S3HD	NC14048	3814	NC14048, N14048	RAA
☐ Waco UMF (YMF-3)	NC14031	3944	NC14031, N14031	RAA

NASHUA COMMUNITY COLLEGE (NH8)

Address:	505 Amherst Street, Nashua, New Hampshire 03063.
Tel:	603-882-6923 **Fax:** 603-882-8690 **Email:** dvallaerand@ccsnh.edu
Admission:	By prior permission only.
Location:	In the north western part of the town.

The college offers a course in aviation maintenance technology. The Baron is currently registered to the college and the non-airworthy Apache used to be.

TYPE	REG/SER	CON. NO.	PI/NOTES	STATUS
☐ Beech 58P Baron	N158Z	TJ-180	N185Z	RA
☐ Piper PA-23 Apache	N2137R	23-728		RA

NASHUA MONUMENT (NH9)

Location:	On permanent view at a FAA facility at 35 North Eastern Boulevard in the town.

TYPE	REG/SER	CON. NO.	PI/NOTES	STATUS
☐ Douglas A-4B Skyhawk (A4D-2)	Bu142777	11839		PV

PEASE AIR NATIONAL GUARD BASE (NH10)

Location:	By prior permission only at the field which is about 1 mile west of Portsmouth.

TYPE	REG/SER	CON. NO.	PI/NOTES	STATUS
☐ Boeing 717-148 Stratotanker (KC-135A) (KC-135E)	57-1455	17526		RA

NEW JERSEY

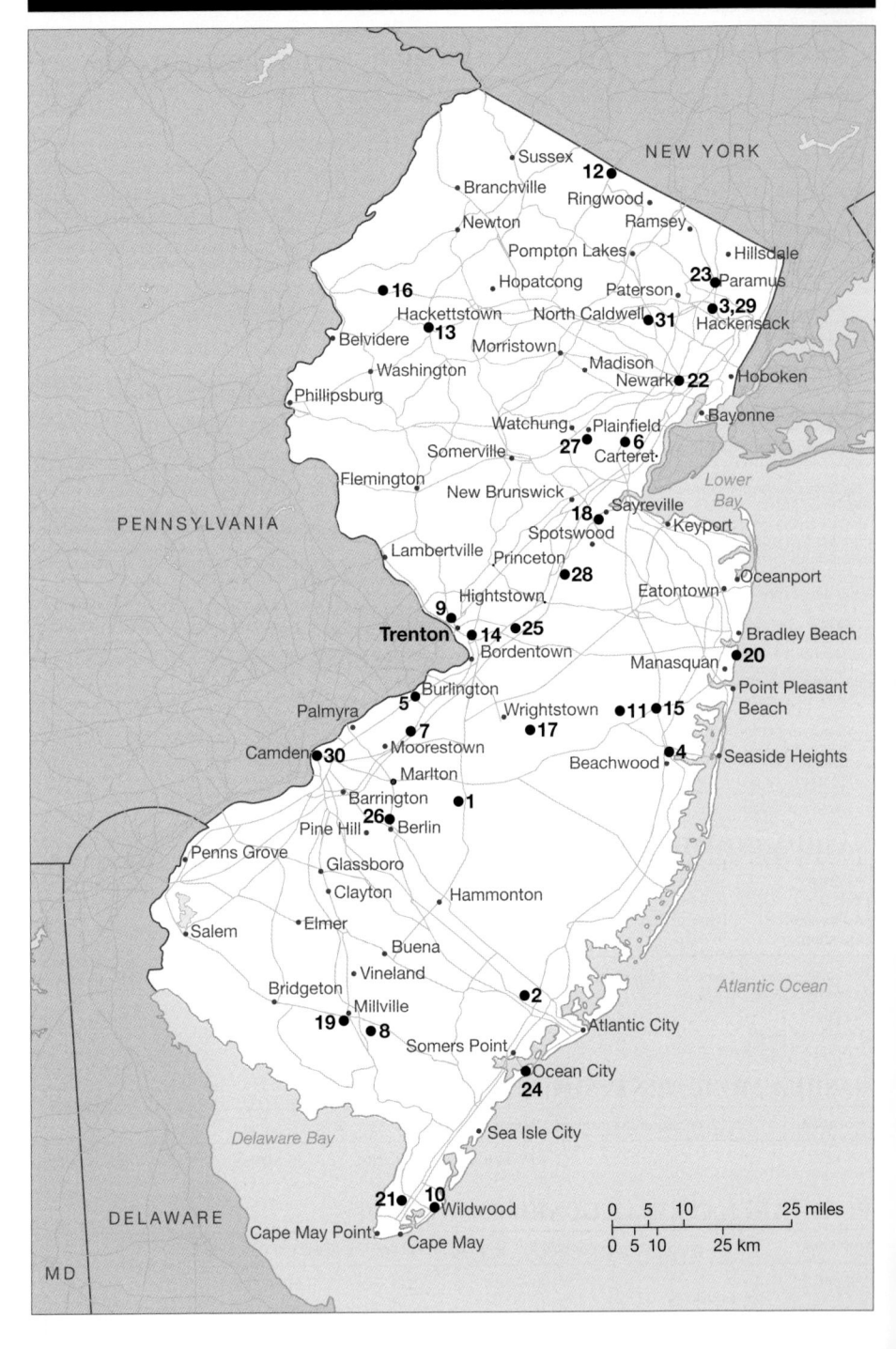

AIR VICTORY MUSEUM (NJ1)

Address:	68 Stacy Haines Road, Lumberton, New Jersey 08055.
Tel:	609-267-4488 Fax: 609-702-1852 Email: info@airvictorymuseum.org
Admission:	Wednesday-Saturday 1000-1600; Sunday 1100-1600.
Location:	At South Jersey Regional Airport which is about 5 miles north east of the town on Route 612.

The museum was set up in late 1993 and its first building was completed three years later. The collection of mainly military aircraft features recently withdrawn types. Also on show are engines, models, components and some vehicles.

One of the aims of the museum is to show the development of combat aircraft. The Starfighter was built by SABCA at Gosselies in Belgium and was initially kept in store as a replacement for aircraft lost. After this it served with 10 Wing at Kleine Brogel. The aircraft was sold to the USA and has now been painted in the colours of a Dutch Air Force machine which was transferred to Turkey. The Sabre has been restored in recent years and is also painted in false colours.

One of the founders of the museum was involved in the programme of building new Messerschmitt Me 262s and a replica example has been put on show. The display rooms house an extensive collection of uniforms and badges. Also on show are components excavated from crash sites, models and photographs. The excellent engine collection contains many significant models. These range from large radials to modern jets. There are long-term plans to construct a larger facility.

TYPE	REG/SER	CON. NO.	PI/NOTES	STATUS
☐ Douglas A-4C Skyhawk (A4D-2N)	Bu145072	12318		RA
☐ Fisher FP-404				PVA
☐ Grumman G-123 Hawkeye (E-2A) (E-2B)	Bu152484	54		PV
☐ Grumman G-303 Tomcat (F-14A)	Bu158998	59		PV
☐ Lockheed 080 Shooting Star (P-80A) (F-80A)	44-85391	080-1414	Front fuselage only.	PV
☐ Lockheed 683-10-19 Starfighter (F-104G)	'D-8090'	683D-9139	FX-81 (Belgium) – in false Dutch markings.	PVX
☐ McDonnell M.98AM Phantom II (F4H-1F) (F-4A)	Bu148273	45		PV
☐ Messerschmitt Me 262B-1 (FSM)				PVX
☐ North American NA-201 Sabre (F-86D) (F-86L)	'52-10110'	201-79	53-0635	PVX
☐ Sikorsky S-65A Sea Stallion (RH-53D)	Bu158690	65363		PV
☐ Vought A-7B Corsair II	Bu154550	B190		PV
☐ Wright Flyer (R)				PV

ATLANTIC CITY AIR NATIONAL GUARD BASE (NJ2)

Address:	400 Langley Avenue, Egg Harbor, New Jersey 08234.
Tel:	609-645-6225 Email: webmaster@njatla.ang.af.mil
Admission:	By prior permission only.
Location:	About 10 miles west of the city off Route 327.

Allocated to the state in 1930, the 119th Squadron flew a variety of types from Newark Airport in the observation role until America entered World War II. The unit was inactivated in 1944 and formed again in May 1946. In 1947 the wing returned to Newark. It moved to McGuire AFB in 1956 and two years later transferred to Atlantic City.

The F-100 was flown from 1965 to 1970 and the F-106 from 1972 to 1988. The F-16 arrived in 1988 and during the 1990s a move was made to the new International Airport. The Super Sabre has now been painted in its correct markings after carrying a false serial for many years.

TYPE	REG/SER	CON. NO.	PI/NOTES	STATUS
☐ Convair 8-27 Delta Dart (F-106B)	57-2523	8-27-17		RA
☐ General Dynamics 401 Fighting Falcon (F-16B)	81-0816	62-85		RA
☐ North American NA-243 Super Sabre (F-100F)	56-3897	243-173	56-3897, '56-3902'	RA

AVIATION HALL OF FAME AND MUSEUM OF NEW JERSEY (NJ3)

Address:	400 Fred Wehran Drive, Teterboro Airport, New Jersey 07608.
Tel:	201-288-6344 Fax: 201-288-5666 Email: njahof@verizon.net
Admission:	Tuesday-Sunday 1000-1600.
Location:	Just south of Route 46 and about 5 miles west of the Hudson River.

In the early part of the century the Witteman brothers constructed almost 100 gliders and in 1907 started to build powered aircraft. They moved their operation from Newark to Teterboro in 1918 and their factory soon became the largest aircraft works in the country.

The Barling NBL-1 triplane bomber was built at the field and shipped to Dayton for trials. In 1924 Anthony Fokker rented the Witteman factory for production of his aircraft in the USA. The Wright engine plant was also located on the airport. In the inter-war period Teterboro was home to the Gates Flying Circus.

In recent years the field has been developed as a major general aviation airport. An exhibition was opened in the early 1980s in the old control tower on the west side of the field. In 1985 a new Hall of Fame and museum was completed on the east side. The Bell 47 is exhibited in a typical 'MASH' scene from the Korean War period with a tented field hospital and landing pad.

The Snyder R-1 was registered in 1962 but is believed to have made only a few flights. Very few examples of 47 Martin 2-0-2 airliners produced have survived for preservation and a former TWA aircraft is displayed outside the building.

TYPE	REG/SER	CON. NO.	PI/NOTES	STATUS
☐ Bell 47D-1 Sioux (H-13E) (OH-13E)	51-14077	777	Probable identity	PV
☐ Bell 209 Huey Cobra (AH-1G) (AH-1S)	69-16437	20869		PV
☐ Bensen B-8 Gyroglider				PV
☐ Convair 880-22-1	N801AJ	22-00-3	N803TW – front fuselage only.	PV
☐ Grumman G-134 Mohawk (AO-1A) (OV-1A)	60-3740	39A		PV
☐ Lockheed 402-2 Bushmaster	N1601L	1009		PV
☐ Martin 2-0-2A	N93204	14074		PV
☐ Mikoyan-Gurevich MiG-21MF	23+03	967603	427 (DDR) – Front fuselage only.	PV

☐ Rotorway Scorpion Too	N96328	8350951	PV
☐ Sikorsky S-62A Seaguard (HH-52A)	1455	62134	PV
☐ Snyder R-1	N905Z	1	PV
☐ Stinson 108-1 Voyager	N8379K	108-1379	PV

BERLIN AIRLIFT HISTORICAL FOUNDATION (NJ4)

Address:	PO Box 782, Farmingdale, New Jersey 07727.
Tel:	732-818-0034 Fax: 732-818-0456 Email: airlift48@aol.com
Admission:	By prior permission only.
Location:	At Miller Airpark, Toms River which is about 6 miles south east of Lakehurst.

The organisation was formed in 1988. The DC-4 has been painted to represent an aircraft of the 48th Troop Carrier Squadron which took part in the Berlin Airlift.
The aircraft honours the crews which flew in the 1948/9 operation to relieve the besieged city. The transport was delivered to the Air Force in the latter stages of World War II and transferred to the Navy in May 1945. It served with a number of Navy and Marine units until being sold in the mid-1970s. For several years it flew in Canada with Millardair. The interior of the aircraft is fitted out as a museum tracing the history of the airlift.

The Stratofreighter was bought in April 1996 and has been restored to airworthy condition. This aircraft was delivered to the Air Force in 1954 and flew with many units in the air-refuelling and transport role until being put in store at Davis-Monthan in 1976. After spending in ten years in the Arizona desert it was sold and converted as a pure freighter. The US Marshalls seized the Stratofreighter and it was leased out to operate on humanitarian flights to South America and to fly fish from Alaska. The aircraft is now painted in the colours of YC-97 '45-59595' which flew regularly into the besieged German city. A second example has been acquired for spares use.

TYPE	REG/SER	CON. NO.	PI/NOTES	STATUS
☐ Boeing 367-76-66 Stratofreighter (KC-97G)	'45-56595'	16749	52-2718, N1175K, N117GA	RAAX
☐ Boeing 367-76-66 Stratofreighter (KC-97G)	53-3816	17149	Major components.	RA
☐ Douglas DC-4 Skymaster (C-54E) (R5D-4R) (C-54R)	N500EJ	27370	44-9144, Bu90414, N48163, N904DS, C-GQIB	RAA

BURLINGTON MONUMENT (NJ5)

Location:	On permanent view in the Veterans Park in the centre of the town.

TYPE	REG/SER	CON. NO.	PI/NOTES	STATUS
☐ Bell 205 Iroquois (UH-1D) (UH-1H)	65-9884	4928		PV
☐ North American NA-187 Sabre (F-86H)	52-5737	187-159		PV

CLARK MONUMENT (NJ6)

Location:	On permanent view at ALP 328 at 78 Westfield Avenue in the eastern part of the town.

TYPE	REG/SER	CON. NO.	PI/NOTES	STATUS
☐ Bell 209 Huey Cobra (AH-1G) (AH-1F)	70-16043	20987		PV

COMMEMORATIVE AIR FORCE (DELAWARE VALLEY WING) (NJ7)

Address:	325 Frankford Avenue, Blackwood, New Jersey 08012-3726.
Tel:	856-228-3172 Email: skiptora@aol.com
Admission:	By prior permission only.
Location:	At Princeton Airport which is just west of Rocky Hill.

The Avengers Squadron was formed in 1991 at Trenton, New Jersey. Its move to North East Philadelphia Airport, and the change of name, took place in 1994 with the arrival of its first aircraft. A total of 250 examples of the high wing Cadet were ordered in 1943 and served in the liaison role.

The wing also operates the Criquet. In 1942 production of the Fieseler Storch commenced at the Morane-Saulnier facory at Puteaux. At the end of hostilities the French company produced more than 700 examples of the type.

TYPE	REG/SER	CON. NO.	PI/NOTES	STATUS
☐ Boeing-Stearman A75N1 Kaydet (PT-17)				RAA
☐ Cessna 150				RAA
☐ Ercoupe 415C				RAA
☐ Interstate S1B1 Cadet (O-63) (L-6)	'432716'	159	43-2716, N46336	RAAX
☐ Morane-Saulnier MS.502 Criquet [Fieseler Fi 156 Storch]	N40FS	361	361 (France)	PVA
☐ North American NA-88 Texan (AT-6D) (SNJ-5)	N3242G	88-15771	41-34527, Bu43766 – mocked up as Kate 'AI-313'	RAAX
☐ Piper J-3C-65 Cub				RAA

DUFFY COLLECTION (NJ8)

Address:	Millville RAP, 104 Leddon Street, Millville, New Jersey 08332.
Admission:	By prior permission only.
Location:	About 2 miles west of the town south of Route 49.

This collection of warbirds includes several classic fighters of the World War II period. The Spitfire was delived to the Royal Netherlands Air Force in 1946 and later spent 15 years pole mounted at Eindhoven Air Base. The aircraft arrived in the USA in 1993 and took to the air again in Texas in February 2004.

New Jersey

TYPE	REG/SER	CON. NO.	PI/NOTES	STATUS
☐ Beech 58 Baron	N930DJ	TH-1946		RAA
☐ Cessna 170B	N3442C	26485		RAA
☐ Grumman G-40 Avenger (TBM-3) (TBM-3E)	N188TD	3584	Bu53522, N7410C, N88HP	RAA
☐ Grumman G-44 Widgeon	N1340V	1228	V203 (USCG)	RAA
☐ North American NA-88 Texan (AT-6D) (SNJ-5)	N6437D	88-17085	42-85304, Bu85004	RAA
☐ North American NA-108 Mitchell (B-25J) (TB-25J) (TB-25N)	N3155G/'430832'	108-34107	44-30832	RAA
☐ North American NA-122 Mustang (P-51D)	N63476	122-31202	44-63476, 252 (Uruguay), N51HT, N2092P	RAA
☐ Piper J-3C-65 Cub (L-4B)	N11190	9692	43-507	RA
☐ Republic P-47D Thunderbolt	N147PF/'226671'	399-55571	(USAAF), N47DD, G-THUN – composite of several aircraft including 45-49192.	RAA
☐ Supermarine 361 Spitfire LF.IXc	N959RT/'MK959'		MK959, H-15 (Netherlands), 'MJ829'	RAA
☐ Vought FG-1D Corsair	N773RD/'92433'	3732	Bu92471	RAAX
☐ Vultee V-74 Valiant (BT-13A)	N40018	74-10547	42-88708	RAA

EWING MONUMENT (NJ9)

Location:	On permanent view in General Betor Veterans Memorial Park in the centre of the town.

TYPE	REG/SER	CON. NO.	PI/NOTES	STATUS
☐ Douglas A-4B Skyhawk (A4D-2)	Bu142848	11910		PV

FORGOTTEN WARRIORS VIETNAM MUSEUM (NJ10)

Address:	529 Forrestal Road, Cape May Airport, Rio Grande, New Jersey 08242.
Tel:	609-374-2987 Email: tcollins@forgottenwarriors.org
Admission:	May–September daily 0900-1700; October–April Saturday-Sunday 1000-1600.
Location:	About 5 miles north of the town off Route 9.

The museum started as a collection of artefacts at the adjacent NAS Wildwood Museum. An exhibition hall has been constructed and the display honours all New Jersey servicemen who took part in the conflict.

TYPE	REG/SER	CON. NO.	PI/NOTES	STATUS
☐ Hughes 269A Osage (TH-55A)	67-15438	0782		PV
☐ Hughes 269A Osage (TH-55A)	67-16699	0806		PV
☐ Hughes 269A Osage (TH-55A)	67-16742	0849		PV
☐ Hughes 269A Osage (TH-55A)	67-16863	88-0945		PV

FORT DIX MUSEUM (NJ11)

Address:	6501 Pennsylvania Avenue, Fort Dix, New Jersey 08640-5010.
Tel:	609-562-0256 Email: webmaster@dix.army.mil
Admission:	Monday-Friday 0800-1600.
Location:	About 6 miles west of Lakehurst on Route 539.

Fort Dix was established in 1918 and soon became a major training centre. The post is named after General John Adams Dix who fought in the 1812 and Civil Wars. This large site still trains many soldiers in a variety of tasks. The museum traces the history of Fort Dix and the people and regiments who have served at the camp.

TYPE	REG/SER	CON. NO.	PI/NOTES	STATUS
☐ Bell 205 Iroquois (UH-1H)	71-30326	13150		PV
☐ Bell 209 Huey Cobra (AH-1G) (AH-1F)	67-15502	20166		PV

GREENWOOD LAKE MONUMENT (NJ12)

Location:	On permanent view at the airport which is about 2 miles east of West Milford.

TYPE	REG/SER	CON. NO.	PI/NOTES	STATUS
☐ Lockheed 049-51-26 Constellation	N9412H	049-2072	F-BAZA	PV

HACKETTSTOWN MONUMENTS (NJ13)

Location:	By prior permission only at a children's area in the town.

TYPE	REG/SER	CON. NO.	PI/NOTES	STATUS
☐ Piper PA-23-160 Apache	C-FNTE	23-1717	N4222P, CF-NTE	RA
☐ Piper PA-28-161 Cherokee Warrior II	N43774	28-7816018		RA

HAMILTON MONUMENT (NJ14)

Location:	On permanent view in the Veterans Park in Yardville Hamilton Square Road.

TYPE	REG/SER	CON. NO.	PI/NOTES	STATUS
☐ Bell 209 Huey Cobra (AH-1S) (AH-1F)	83-24193	22341		PV
☐ McDonnell M.98HO Phantom II (F-4E) (NF-4E)	66-0286	2565		PV

One of the first Lockheed F-117s to be preserved was this example in the Nellis Air Force Base Freedom Park. [NV17]

This Lockheed Bushmaster is parked outside the main building of the Aviation Hall of Fame and Museum of New Jersey. (Dick Barrett) [NJ3]

Millville Army Airfield Museum is home to this Short C-23A Sherpa. (Juha Ritaranta) [NJ19]

New Jersey

LAKEHURST NAVAL AIR ENGINEERING STATION INFORMATION CENTER (NJ15)

Address:	PO Box 328, Highway 547, Lakehurst, New Jersey 08733-0328.
Tel:	732-323-2811 (NAES): 723-244-8861 (Historical Society)
	Fax: 732-244-8897 (Historical Society) Email: thomas.worsdale@navy.mil
Admission:	Wednesday 1000-1300; second and fourth Saturday in month 1000-1300 – by prior permission only.
Location:	About 1 mile north of the town on Route 70.

During World War I munitions for the Russian Imperial Army were tested at the site, then known as Camp Kendrick. In 1921 the Navy took over the station as its main base for airship operations. Six large hangars were constructed and a number still survive. The USS *Shenandoah* was built and flown from the field and later the German *Graf Zeppelin* and *Hindenburg* flew into Lakehurst.

The *Hindenburg* was tragically destroyed mooring in 1937 and a monument has been erected at the spot. Hangar One was designated a national historical monument in 1967.

The Information Center has been set up by the Navy Lakehurst Historical Society and contains a fascinating display of components and memorabilia. The preserved aircraft are parked around the site.

TYPE	REG/SER	CON. NO.	PI/NOTES	STATUS
☐ Douglas A-4B Skyhawk (A4D-2)	Bu142106	11360		RA
☐ Grumman G-98 Tiger (F11F-1) (F-11A)	Bu141851	168		RA
☐ Grumman G-303 Tomcat (F-14A)	Bu160658	277		RA
☐ McDonnell M.98EV Phantom II (F-4J)	Bu153074	1541		RA
☐ Northrop-Grumman RQ-8A Fire Scout	Bu166401			RA
☐ Vought F-8A Crusader (F8U-1)	Bu145397			RA
☐ Vought A-7B Corsair II	Bu154443	B83		RA

LAND OF MAKE BELIEVE (NJ16)

Address:	354 Great Meadows Road, Hope, New Jersey 07844.
Tel:	908-459-9000
Admission:	May–early June Saturday-Sunday 1000-1800; early June–early September 1000-1800
Location:	About 3 miles south of the town.

This large theme and water park has many attractions for the family. A civil war locomotive operates a train ride and there are many fairground items. The front fuselage of a former US Navy R4D is on show.

TYPE	REG/SER	CON. NO.	PI/NOTES	STATUS
☐ Douglas DC-3A-456 Skytrain (C-47A) (R4D-5)			Front fuselage only.	PV

MCGUIRE AIR FORCE BASE COLLECTION (NJ17)

Address:	305 MW/PA, 2901 Falcon Lane, McGuire Air Force Base, New Jersey 08641-5002.
Tel:	609-754-2273 Fax: 609-754-6999 Email: pa.staff@mcguire.af.mil
Admission:	By prior permission only.
Location:	About 18 miles south of Trenton on Route 545.

The airfield opened as Fort Dix Airport in 1941 and took up its present name in 1948. It is named after Major Thomas B. McGuire, the second leading ace of World War II who was killed in action in the Philippines in January 1945. The Lightning on view by the main gate is painted in the colours of McGuire's machine. During World War II the field was used by Douglas B-18s patrolling the New York and Boston shipping lanes. The field closed in 1946 but was reopened two years later. Initially it was home to Strategic Air Command bombers and Air Defense Command fighters. In 1954 the Eastern Division of the Military Air Transport Service moved in from Westover AFB in Massachusetts.

Three transport types have been preserved.

TYPE	REG/SER	CON. NO.	PI/NOTES	STATUS
☐ Boeing 717-148 Stratotanker (KC-135A) (KC-135E)	59-1497	17985		RA
☐ Douglas DC-6A Liftmaster (C-118A) (C-118B) (VC-118A)	'52687'	44626	53-3255, Bu152687, 53-3255, '33300'	RAX
☐ Lockheed 300 Starlifter (C-141A) (C-141B)	66-7947	300-6239		RA
☐ Lockheed 422-87-23 Lightning (P-38L)	'44-27183'	422-8270	44-53015, NX57492, N9957F	RAX
☐ McDonnell M.98HO Phantom II (F-4E)	67-0270	2997		RA
☐ Republic F-84F Thunderstreak	'57-2543'		51-1658	RAX
☐ Republic F-105B Thunderchief	57-5776	B-13		RA

MILLTOWN MONUMENT (NJ18)

Location:	On permanent view at ALP 25 at 4 JFK Drive in the south eastern part of the town.

TYPE	REG/SER	CON. NO.	PI/NOTES	STATUS
☐ Bell 209 Huey Cobra (AH-1G) (AH-1F)	68-17072	20800		PV

MILLVILLE ARMY AIRFIELD MUSEUM (NJ19)

Address:	1 Leddon Street, Millville Municipal Airport, New Jersey 08332.
Tel:	856-327-2247 Email: museum@p47millville.org
Admission:	Tuesday-Sunday 1000-1600.
Location:	About 2 miles west of the town south of Route 49.

Millville was opened in 1941 as the first Defense Airport in the country. During World War II its main function was P-47 gunnery training. The military moved out in 1945 and the field became the civil airport for the town. The museum opened in 1988 and has put on show an informative display tracing the history of the base and the resident units. There are many photographs showing the aircraft in residence during the conflict. The origins of the collection go back to the early 1970s. Michael Stow, an aviation enthusiast found out about some underground bunkers just south of the airfield. He explored these and the surrounding areas and over the next decade found a large number of artefacts. He approached the city authorities in 1983 about obtaining a permanent home at the airfield for his collection. These remain the basis of the exhibition. The Skyhawk arrived at the museum in the mid-1990s. The Short Sherpa is a freighter version of the SD-330 airliner. The C-23A entered service with the USAF in 1985 and flew in both America and Europe. The aircraft on show joined the exhibition over a decade ago. The C-47 front fuselage is used as a travelling exhibit to publicise the museum.

TYPE	REG/SER	CON. NO.	PI/NOTES	STATUS
☐ Douglas A-4F Skyhawk	Bu154200	13657		PV
☐ Douglas DC-3A-467 Skytrain (C-47B) (R4D-6) (C-47J)	Bu50837	15563/27008	43-49747, Bu50837, N7998A, N375AS – front fuselage only	PV
☐ Short SD.3-30 Sherpa (C-23A)	85-25343	SH.3011	G-14-3011, G-BEWT, N331GW	PV

NATIONAL GUARD MILITIA MUSEUM OF NEW JERSEY (NJ20)

Address:	PO Box 277, Sea Girt, New Jersey 08750-0277.
Tel:	732-974-5766
Admission:	Tuesday and Thursday 1000-1500.
Location:	About 5 miles south of Belmar.

This museum was set up to trace the history of the forces of New Jersey from the early days. The area was colonised by the Dutch, Swedish and British and items from this era can be seen. The war of Independence, the Civil War, World War I, World War II and subsequent conflicts feature prominently.

The inside displays cover all aspects of these with many photographs, uniforms, documents and weapons to be seen. The museum has an artillery annexe at Lawrenceville where tanks, vehicles and cannons are displayed.

TYPE	REG/SER	CON. NO.	PI/NOTES	STATUS
☐ Bell 47G Sioux (H-13G) (OH-13G)				RA
☐ Bell 204 Iroquois (UH-1H)				RA
☐ Bell 209 Huey Cobra (AH-1G) (AH-1S)	67-15685	20349		RA
☐ Hughes 369M Cayuse (OH-6A)	67-16172	0557		RA
☐ McDonnell M.98EN Phantom II (F-4D)	66-0259	1923		PV
☐ Republic F-84F Thunderstreak	'52-7066'		51-9430	PVX

NAVAL AIR STATION WILDWOOD AVIATION MUSEUM (NJ21)

Address:	500 Forrestal Road, Cape May Airport, New Jersey 08204.
Tel:	609-886-8787 Fax: 609-886-1942 Email: aviationmuseum@comcast.net
Admission:	April–September daily 0900-1700; October–November daily 0900-1600; December–March Monday-Friday 0900-1600.
Location:	About 5 miles north of Cape May off Route 9.

The foundation has set up a museum in Hangar 1 at the former Naval Air Station. The building is listed on the National Register of Historic Places and has been restored by the group. The station opened 1943 and the displays honour the 38 airmen who lost their lives whilst undergoing training at Wildwood.

An exhibition tracing the history of the site during its military days and its subsequent use as a civil airport can be seen. There are a number of interactive displays in the building. The Skyhawk has been painted in the colours of the 'Blue Angels' aerobatic team which flew the type from 1974 until 1986.

Two famous Grumman naval types are on view. The prototype of the Avenger torpedo bomber made its maiden flight on 7th August 1941. Almost 10,000 were produced by the parent company and General Motors. The last examples were withdrawn from military service in the mid-1960s. The one in the collection ended its days as a water bomber in Canada.

The Tomcat was the last fighter made by Grumman and the type was in service with the US Navy from 1974 until 2006. The prototype Piper Tomahawk is now here after many years on show in the Franklin Institute Science Museum in Philadelphia. The aircraft was built at Vero Beach in Florida in late 1977 and almost 2,500 had been sold when production ceased in 1984. The Air and Space 18A autogyro first flew in 1959 and about 70 were produced. The McCulloch J-2 was originally a Jovair design and 96 were completed in the early 1970s.

TYPE	REG/SER	CON. NO.	PI/NOTES	STATUS
☐ Air and Space 18A	N6169S	18-59		PV
☐ Bell 204 Iroquois (UH-1C) (UH-1M)	65-9462	1362		PV
☐ Bell 204 Iroquois (UH-1C) (UH-1M)	'61182'	1888	66-15160	PVX
☐ Bell 205 Iroquois (UH-1H) (EH-1X)	69-15905	12193		PV
☐ Bell 209 Huey Cobra (AH-1G) (AH-1F)	67-15633	20297		PV
☐ Bell 47G Sioux (H-13G) (OH-13G)	52-7834	1061		PV
☐ Boeing-Stearman A75N1 Kaydet (PT-17)	'40-75382'	75-382	40-1825, N55437, N56Z	PVAX
☐ Boeing-Stearman A75N1 Kaydet (PT-17)	NX33171	75-7562	Bu07958	PVA
☐ Boeing-Stearman B75N1 Kaydet (N2S-3)	N9844H	75-7694	Bu38073	PVA
☐ Boeing-Stearman E75 Kaydet (PT-31D) (N2S-5)	N75668	75-8710	42-109677, Bu43616	PVA
☐ Cessna 321 Bird Dog (OE-2) (O-1C)	'Bu140089'		51-1653, Bu140090	PVX
☐ Douglas A-4A Skyhawk (A4D-1)	Bu142180	11434		PV
☐ Douglas TA-4J Skyhawk	Bu156891	13984	Front fuselage only.	PV
☐ Grumman G-40 Avenger (TBM-3) (TBM-3S) (AS.3)	N145WB	2279	Bu84560, 84560 (Canada), N7032C, C-GFPS	PVC
☐ Grumman G-40 Avenger (TBM-3) (TBM-3S) (AS.3)	CF-MUD	2999	Bu86180, 86180 (Canada)	PVC
☐ Grumman G-303 Tomcat (F-14A) (F-14B)	Bu161422	432		PV
☐ Hiller UH12D Raven (H-23D) (OH-23D)	N22SP	1214	59-2734	PV

New Jersey

	Type	REG/SER	CON. NO.	PI/NOTES	STATUS
☐	Hughes 269A Osage (TH-55A)	67-16835	0942	With parts of c/n 0806 67-16699	PV
☐	Hughes 269A Osage (TH-55A)	67-17002	1109		PV
☐	Hughes 369M Cayuse (HO-6) (OH-6A)	67-16638	1023		PV
☐	Lockheed 580 (T-33A)	10032	580-6816	51-9032, FT-13 (Belgium) – in Yugoslav markings.	PV
☐	Lockheed 580 (T-33A)	10055	580-7032	51-9248, FT-14 (Belgium) – in Yugoslav markings.	PV
☐	McCulloch J-2	N4326G	036		PV
☐	Mikoyan-Gurevich MiG-15	23		1961 (China), N51MG	PVX
☐	North American NA-226 Trojan (T-28C)	Bu140557	226-134		PV
☐	Northrop N-311 Tiger II (F-5E)	74-1572	R.1270		PV
☐	Piper PA-38-112 Tomahawk	N38PA	38-78A0001		PV
☐	Sikorsky S-62A Seaguard (HH-52A)	1462	62141		PV
☐	Vultee V-74 Valiant (BT-13A)	N40018	74-10547	42-88708	PV

NEWARK MONUMENT (NJ22)

Location:	On permanent view at Barringer High School at 90 Parker Street in the northern part of the city.

	TYPE	REG/SER	CON. NO.	PI/NOTES	STATUS
☐	Ercoupe 415C				PV

NEW JERSEY CHILDREN'S MUSEUM (NJ23)

Address:	599 Valley Heath Plaza, Paramus, New Jersey 07652.
Tel:	201-262-5151
Admission:	Tuesday-Sunday 1000-1700.
Location:	In the northern part of the town.

The museum has sections on many topics. All contain innovative exhibits designed to interest and educate children. The space and aviation area has an interactive 'air traffic control tower' and a large model airport. Visitors can sit in the Hughes helicopter and operate the controls. Space flight is featured with photographs ad models of rockets and the shuttle on view. Among other highlights is a 1954 Ahrens Fire Truck in which visitors can simulate a ride to a fire.

	TYPE	REG/SER	CON. NO.	PI/NOTES	STATUS
☐	Hughes 269A				PV

OCEAN CITY MONUMENTS (NJ24)

Location:	On permanent view at two locations in the town.

	TYPE	REG/SER	CON. NO.	PI/NOTES	STATUS
☐	Hughes 369			At the gate of a golf complex.	PV
☐	Smith DSA-1 Miniplane	N116JF	DSA-1	On the roof of a business.	PV

PITCAIRN COLLECTION (NJ25)

Address:	Trenton-Robbinsville Airport, Robbinsville, New Jersey 08691
Tel:	609-259-3309
Admission:	By prior permission only.
Location:	About 1 mile east of Robbinsville.

Harold Pitcairn was born at Bryn Athyn in Pennsylvania in 1897 and he built his first glider in 1913. In 1924, after military pilot training and a career in business he decided to set up an aircraft factory. An airfield was built on the family farm and in 1925 the Pitcairn PA-l biplane was completed. Other models followed and within a few years Pitcairn won an Air Mail contract.

The company produced the PA-5 Mailwing for the work. Between 1927 and 1931 the design was improved and several versions of the Mailwing appeared. In the late 1920s he became interested in the autogyro and on 18th December 1928 he flew the Cierva C.8 at Bryn Athyn. His first autogyro the PCA-1 appeared in 1929 and the decision was taken to build new factory at Willow.

Harold's son, Stephen, has been collecting examples of his father's aircraft for a number of years. He restored the famous PCA-2 'Miss Champion' in the 1980s and flew it to the EAA Convention at Oshkosh in 1986. In 2005 he donated it to the museum at the Wisconsin airfield. The autogyro had taken part in the 1931 Ford National Air Tour. The three other types in the hangar are owned by members of the family.

	TYPE	REG/SER	CON. NO.	PI/NOTES	STATUS
☐	Bellanca 17-30A Super Viking	N2667M	89-301008		RAA
☐	Globe GC-1B Swift	N7BR	1416		RAA
☐	Luscombe 8A Silvaire	NC1294M	4021	NC1294M, N1294M	RAA
☐	Pitcairn PA-5S Sport Mailwing	NC6708	30	NC6708, N6708 – fitted with PA-6 wings and tail surfaces.	RAA
☐	Pitcairn PA-7S Sport Mailwing	NC13158	151	NC13158, N13158	RAA
☐	Pitcairn PA-8 Mailwing	N10751	162	NC10751	RAA

SIX FLAGS THEME PARK (NJ26)

Address:	1 Six Flags, Boulevard, Jackson, New Jersey 08527-5369.
Tel:	732-928-1821
Admission:	April–September daily 0900-1700.
Location:	In the northern part of the town.

This large park has many attractions including a drive through a 30 acre wild life reserve. There are a number of rides for the public and entertainment is provided for people of all ages. The Starfighter, which was parked at Davis-Monthan for a time, is currently in store at the park. This aircraft will be put on show in due course.

TYPE	REG/SER	CON. NO.	PI/NOTES	STATUS
☐ Lockheed 483-04-06 Starfighter (F-104D)	57-1320	283-5032		RA

SOUTH PLAINFIELD MONUMENT (NJ27)

Location:	On permanent view near Spring Lake which is about 1 mile north of the town.

TYPE	REG/SER	CON. NO.	PI/NOTES	STATUS
☐ Bell 209 Huey Cobra (AH-1G) (AH-1F)	69-16442	20874		PV

STONE MUSEUM (NJ28)

Address:	608 Spotswood-Englishtown Road, Monroe, New Jersey 08331.
Tel:	732-521-2232 Fax: 732-521-3338 Email: displayworld@erols.com
Admission:	Monday-Saturday 0800-1600; Sunday 1000-1600.
Location:	In the town which is just east of Interstate 95.

This fascinating collection of minerals from around the world is housed in a number of exhibition rooms. The displays have been arranged to show the rocks in an innovative way. There is also a large adventure area for children on the site. The Huey Cobra was obtained from storage at Fort Drum.

TYPE	REG/SER	CON. NO.	PI/NOTES	STATUS
☐ Bell 209 Huey Cobra (AH-1G) (AH-1F)	68-15116	20650		

TETERBORO SCHOOL OF AERONAUTICS (NJ29)

Address:	80 Moonache Avenue, Teterboro, New Jersey 07608.
Tel:	201-288-6300 Fax: 201-288-5609 Email: admissions@teterboroschool.com
Admission:	By prior permission only.
Location:	Just south of Route 46 and about 5 miles west of the Hudson River.

The school has been in existence for over half a century and has trained many engineers. Courses in airframe and engine maintenance are run. There is a small fleet of instructional airframes.

TYPE	REG/SER	CON. NO.	PI/NOTES	STATUS
☐ Bell 47G-3B-1 Sioux (TH-13T)	N48358	3638	67-15919	RA
☐ Cessna 150J	N60920	15070704		RA
☐ Cessna 150M	N7572U	15077741		RA
☐ Lockheed 402-2 Bushmaster				RA
☐ Piper PA-23-250 Aztec C	N6395Y	27-3683		RA
☐ Piper PA-23-250 Aztec C	N58PG	27-3772	N6477Y	RA

UNITED STATES SHIP *NEW JERSEY* BATTLESHIP MUSEUM (NJ30)

Address:	62 Battleship Place, Camden, New Jersey 08103
Tel:	866-877-6262
Admission:	January–February Friday-Monday 0900-1500; March daily 0900-1500; April–September daily 0900-1700; October–December daily 0900-1500.
Location:	Just north of the Walt Whitman Bridge.

The *New Jersey* was built at the Philadelphia Naval Shipyard and launched on 7th December 1942, being commissioned five months later. The battleship was the second ship to carry the name. The *New Jersey* had a long and distinguished career. During World War II she served mainly in the Pacific and took part in most of the major battles in that region. The ship was decommissioned in 1948 but activated again in 1950 for use in the Korean War. Stored again from 1957 until 1968 she was again put into service for Vietnam. By this time the *New Jersey* was the last active battleship in the world. Withdrawn again in 1991 she was berthed at Bayonne before being sold. In November 1999 a journey to Camden was undertaken and the ship opened in October 2001. Visitors can tour the ship and see displays of naval life in both peacetime and combat conditions.

TYPE	REG/SER	CON. NO.	PI/NOTES	STATUS
☐ Kaman K-20 Seasprite (HU2K-1U) (UH-2B) (SH-2F)	Bu150175	125		PV

YANKEE AIR FORCE – NORTHEAST DIVISION (NJ31)

Address:	PO Box 1729, West Caldwell, New Jersey 07007-1729.
Tel:	201-438-6276
Admission:	By prior permission only.
Location:	At Essex County Airport which is about 25 miles west of New York City off Route 46.

This division was set up in the mid-1980s and currently has the Taylorcraft in flying condition. The Convair L-13 is stored in one of the hangars and an ex-Belgian Pembroke has moved to Arizona.

TYPE	REG/SER	CON. NO.	PI/NOTES	STATUS
☐ Convair 105 (L-13A)	N65893	269	47-389	RAD
☐ Taylorcraft DCO-65 Grasshopper (O-57A) (L-2A)	'43-5049'	L-5041	(USAAF), N9666N	RAAX

C17

This replica Curtiss Jenny was built in Texas for the Pancho Villa State Park and Museum. (PVSP) [NM16]

The Southwest Soaring Museum at Moriarty exhibits this Argentinean registered ABSA Genesis 2. (Derek Heley) [NM20]

On show in the War Eagles Museum is this Hawker Sea Fury painted in Australian Navy colours. (Derek Heley) [NM24]

This Grumman F-11F-1 Tiger in 'Blue Angels' colours can be seen at the Cradle of Aviation Museum. (Nigel Hitchman) [NY14]

This Nesmith Cougar is one of the many homebuilt designs that can be seen at the Dart Airport Aviation Museum. (Dick Barrett) [NY16]

This Mooney M.18LA Mite is on show at the Empire State Aerosciences Museum. (Richard Baker) [NY21]

Above: This Curtiss NC-4 replica is part of the collection at the Glenn H Curtiss Museum. The flying boat was flown from a local lake. (Dick Barrett) [NY24]

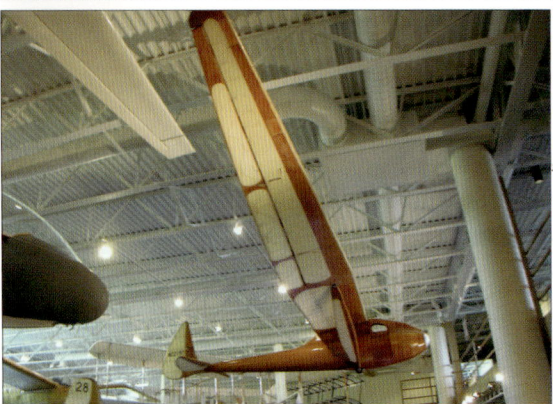

Right: Hanging in the National Soaring Museum is this graceful Bowlus Senior Albatross. (Dick Barrett) [NY50]

This New Standard D-25 is used for joy riding at the Rhinebeck Aerodrome Museum. The biplane was restored in Georgia. (Dick Barrett) [NY63]

The Wings of Eagles Discovery Center has on show this Fairchild PT-19B Cornell (Dick Barrett) [NY82]

The airpark at Pope Air Force Base has this Fairchild C-123K Provider in its grounds. (Eric Dewhurst) [NC30]

This Aeronca C-3 is at the Western North Carolina Air Museum. (Doug Revell) [NC40]

C21

The Dakota Territory Air Museum has on show this active Callair A-3 (DTAM) [ND5]

Three aircraft including this AH-1 Cobra are on show at the Motts Military Museum. (MMM) [OH54]

The National Museum of the United States Air Force houses an impressive collection of research aircraft including this LTV XC-142A (Eric Dewhurst) [OH55]

The 45th Infantry Division Museum in Oklahoma City displays a number of aircraft mounted on poles. Shown here is a Cessna U-3A. (John Mounce) [OK1]

The prototype Aero Commander is awaiting restoration at the Metro Tech Aviation Center in Oklahoma City. (John Mounce) [OK23]

The unique Krist Cloud Cutter is in the main hall of the aviation section of the Oklahoma Science Museum. (John Mounce) [OK28]

C23

On show at the Evergreen Aviation Museum is this Curtiss Fledgling (EAM) [OR7]

Several helicopters including this Vertol CH-21C are parked outside the American Helicopter Museum and Education Center. (Juha Ritaranta) [PA4]

The only known surviving General Aircraft Company Thunderbird W-14 is now part of George Jenkins' Eagles Mere Air Museum. (Nigel Hitchman) [PA17]

This airworthy Brunner-Winkle Bird CK resides at the Golden Age Air Museum. (Nigel Hitchman) [PA23]

Below: The National Museum of Naval Aviation has loaned this Piasecki HUP-2 to the Harold F. Pitcairn Wings of Freedom Museum. (Nigel Hitchman) [PA26]

Left: Only 28 Inland Sport W-500s were built and a handful survive including this one owned by Heritage Aircraft. (Nigel Hitchman) [PA29]

C25

Shown in the hangar of the Mid-Atlantic Air Museum is this Culver LCA Cadet. (Nigel Hitchman) [PA35]

The Oil Region Preservation Museum keep their Franklin A at the local airport. (Dick Barrett) [PA43]

On show at the Piper Aviation Museum is this PA-12 Super Cruiser which is one of a pair that flew around the world in 1947. (Dick Barrett) [PA47]

Displayed outside at the South Dakota Air and Space Museum is this Rockwell B-1B. Behind is a Boeing B-52D. (Glenn Chatfield) [SD7]

The only aircraft at the Lane Motor Museum is this Mignet HM-380 Pou-du-Ciel. (LMM) [TN22]

Many red painted replica Fokker Dr Is can be seen at museums and airfields in the USA. This example is at the Cavanaugh Flight Museum. (John Mounce) [TX16]

C27

Formerly flown by NASA this Boeing KC-135A is preserved at Ellington Air National Guard Base. (Derek Heley) [TX35]

The Temple Monoplane was designed and built in Texas. The aircraft is now on show in the Frontiers of Flight Museum. (Derek Heley) [TX69]

The Historic Aviation Memorial Museum is home to this Douglas TA-4J Skyhawk. (John Mounce) [TX80]

The Texas Air Museum rebuilt a small number of Focke-Wulf Fw 190s recovered from crash sites in Norway. One has remained in the state and is on show at the Stinson Field branch of the museum. (John Mounce) [TX135]

A large number of aircraft have been preserved at Lackland Air Force Base which is home to the USAF History and Traditions Museum. This North American F-82E Twin Mustang is by the main parade ground. (John Mounce) [TX147]

This North American T-2C Buckeye is parked on the flight deck of the USS Lexington. (John Mounce) [TX149]

C29

The Vintage Flying Museum in Texas has recently sold this B-17G Fortress to the Military Aircraft Museum in Virginia. (John Mounce) [TX151]

Cabela's stores across the country have put a number of light aircraft on show. This Aeronca Champion is in the Lehi, Utah branch. (Mike Glasgow) [UT8]

The Air Power Park and Museum is home to this XV-6A Kestrel. (Nigel Hitchman) [VA2]

Jerry Yagen's Military Aviation Museum has on show this Hurricane and Spitfire. (Nigel Hitchman) [VA14]

The Steven-Udvar-Hazy Center of the National Air and Space Museum has on show this Bell 30 helicopter. (Eric Dewhurst) [VA19]

On show at the Virginia Aviation Museum is this replica SPAD VII. (Eric Dewhurst) [VA36]

Paul Allen's impressive Flying Heritage Collection includes this Nakajima Hayabusa. (Nigel Hitchman) [WA14]

The Museum of Flight have restored this Boeing 100 in the colours of a P-12.(Museum of Flight) [WA25]

The Skagit Aero Education Museum's Ryan STA Special is shown visiting a fly-in at Arlington. (Kerry D Sim) [WA37]

Local designer and pilot Steve Wittman is honoured in the EAA Airventure Museum. Shown here is a W.8C Tailwind. (Dick Barrett) [WI17]

The unique Scott-Mathieu-Russell is part of the Kelch Collection. (Nigel Hitchman) [WI27]

The Richard Ira Bong World War II Heritage Center has this P-38L Lightning painted in the colours of his aircraft. (Glenn Chatfield) [WI48]

NEW MEXICO

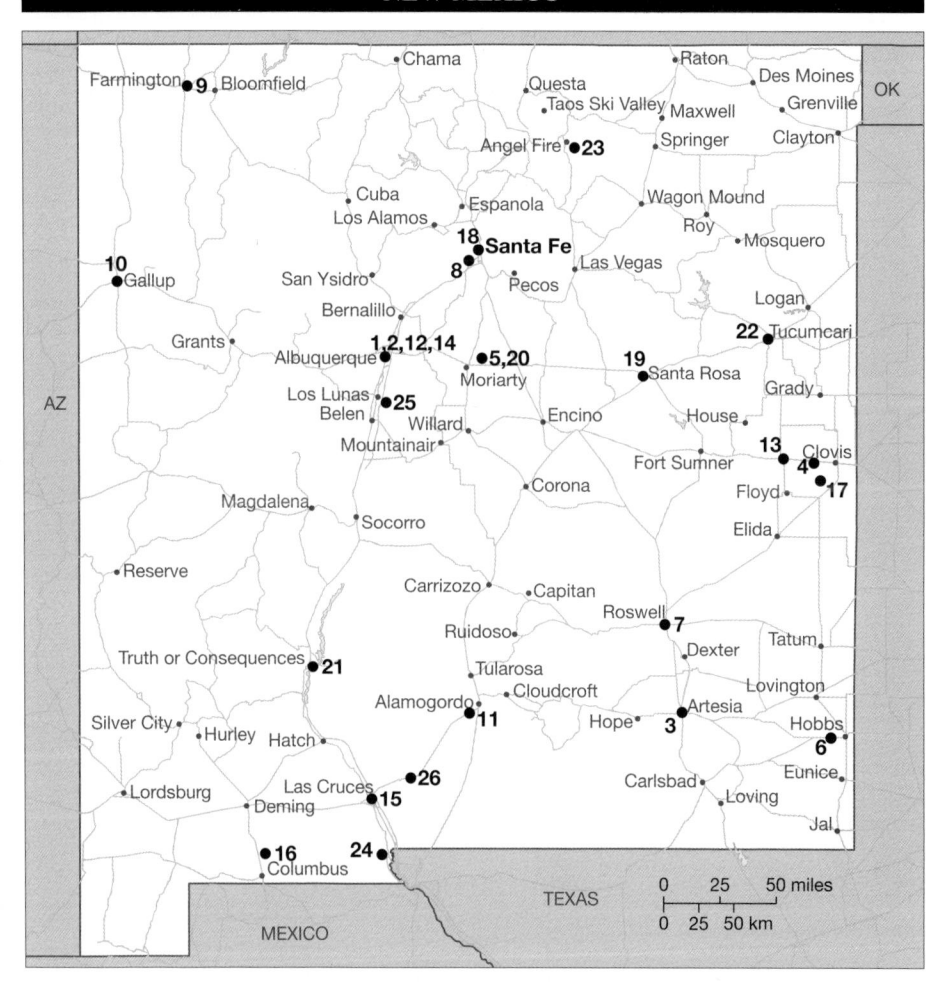

ALBUQUERQUE MUSEUM OF ART, HISTORY AND SCIENCE (NM1)

Address: 2000 Mountain Road North West, PO Box 1293, Albuquerque, New Mexico 87103.
Tel: 505-243-7255   **Email:** albuquerquemuseum@cabq.gov
Admission: Tuesday-Sunday 0900-1700 – the aircraft is on permanent view in the airport terminal.
Location: The museum is in the old town – the airport is in the southern suburbs of the city.

This museum has an excellent display of local history, scientific equipment and works of art at its premises in the city. The centrepiece of the display was a 1911 Curtiss Pusher which is now on show in the terminal building at the city airport. The aircraft is believed to be the sole survivor of those built by the Texas Aeroplane Company. Just before the outbreak of World War I the founder of the company, Dr. Ingram, put it into a crate and stored it in a family warehouse. Over 70 years later it was acquired by John Bowden who reassembled the pusher and ran the engine. A photograph display traces the history of this aircraft.

TYPE	REG/SER	CON. NO.	PI/NOTES	STATUS
☐ Curtiss D Pusher				PV

ANDERSON ABRUZZO INTERNATIONAL BALLOON MUSEUM (NM2)

Address: 9201 Balloon Museum Drive North East, Albuquerque, New Mexico 87113.
Tel: 505-768-6020   **Fax:** 505-768-6021   **Email:** info@balloonmuseum.com
Admission: Tuesday-Sunday 0900-1700.
Location: In the northern part of the city.

The town has hosted a balloon festival every year since 1972. The first one attracted 13 participants and at the 25th commemoration in 1996 a dozen of the original pilots attended. The event now attracts large numbers of balloonists from around the world.

Albuquerque was an obvious site for a museum and the display opened on 1st October 2005. Ben Abruzzo and Maxie Anderson made the first gas balloon crossing of the Atlantic Ocean in 1978. Anderson was killed in a balloon accident in Europe in 1983 and Abruzzo died in a plane crash two years later. (His son Richard, also a noted balloonist, died during the Gordon Bennett Balloon Race in September 2010 when his balloon came down in the Adriatic Sea; also lost was Richard Abruzzo's ballooning partner Carol Rymer Davis.)

The two families felt that a museum should be built and the City of Albuquerque became involved in financing the project. The impressive structure houses a fascinating collection tracing the history of the sport from the days of the first human carrying flight by the Montgolfière hot air balloon in 1783. The Grand Hall houses several balloons which have made significant flights. The Raven 'Double Eagle V' (N4003A) was used by a crew of four which included Ben Abruzzo. This made the first Pacific Ocean crossing from Nagashima in Japan to Covelo in California on 13th November 1981. In May 1980 Kris and Maxie Anderson carried out the first North America transcontinental flight from Fort Baker in California to Sainte Felicitie in Quebec. They used a Raven design named 'Kitty Hawk' (N80KH). This balloon was later rebuilt as the 'Jules Verne'. Maxie Anderson and Don Ida made three world record attempts in this balloon in 1981/2.

In 1980 the Soukup and Thomas International Balloon and Airship Museum opened in Tyndall, South Dakota. The exhibition moved to a purpose-built facility in Mitchell in 1992. The museum closed in 2000 and the large collection of balloon equipment and memorabilia moved to Albuquerque.

In the museum there is a section tracing the history of the airship. The work of Zeppelin is highlighted and the crash of the *Hindenburg* at Lakehurst in New Jersey is portrayed in detail. Furniture, crockery and cutlery from the era of the great passenger carrying airships is on view.

The United States Navy was a major user of airships in the inter-war period and carried on using dirigibles up to the mid-1960s. During World War II over 100 were in use and hangars used to house them still survive at a number of locations.

Airships and balloons have always featured prominently on postage stamps and a large philatelic exhibition has been staged. There are many baskets, burners and items of balloon equipment on view along with many photographs, documents, instruments and models.

TYPE	REG/SER	CON. NO.	PI/NOTES	STATUS
☐ Avian Falcon II Hot Air Balloon	N6AV	15		PV
☐ Balloon Works Firefly 7 Hot Air Balloon	N69130	F7-131		RA
☐ Balloon Works Firefly 7 Hot Air Balloon	N2077F	F7-725	Basket only.	RA
☐ Balloon Works Firefly 8B Hot Air Balloon	N7410M	F8B-071	Less envelope.	RA
☐ Cameron AT-165 Hot Air Balloon	G-BIAZ	400		PV
☐ Cameron R-36 Gas Balloon	G-ROZY	1141		PV
☐ Cameron V-65 Hot Air Balloon	N126CB	324		RA
☐ Foster AA-1 Hot Air Balloon			Less envelope.	RA
☐ Foster AS-2 Hot Air Balloon			Less envelope.	RA
☐ Foster AX-1 Hot Air Balloon			Less envelope.	RA
☐ Foster AX-2 Hot Air Balloon			Less envelope.	RA
☐ Gas Balloon			Basket only.	RA
☐ Gas Balloon			Basket only.	RA
☐ Gas Balloon			Basket only.	RA
☐ Goodyear S-94 Hot Air Balloon	N9074H	P4	N9074H, N31374	PV
☐ Homebuilt Hot Air Balloon			Less envelope.	RA
☐ Hot Air Balloon				RA
☐ Krieg Ax.6 Smoke Balloon	N33PK	4	Less envelope.	RA
☐ Lithuanian Hot Air Balloon				RA
☐ Military Gas Balloon			Basket only.	RA
☐ Military Gas Balloon			Basket only.	RA
☐ Omega 7 Hot Air Balloon	N79330			RA
☐ Padelt Grom 1 Peak Express Hot Air Balloon	N96YD	798		RA
☐ Piccard AX-6 Body Glove Hot Air Balloon	N2CT	105T	Gondola only.	PV
☐ Raven Jules Verne Hot Air Balloon (Kittyhawk)	N80KH	1		PV
☐ Raven NO5ST-15/15T Hot Air Balloon	N4003A	103		PV
☐ Raven R Hot Air Balloon			Gondola only.	RA
☐ Raven R Hot Air Balloon			Less envelope.	RA
☐ Raven RX.6-56 Hot Air Balloon	N6414L	Rx6.108	Less envelope.	RA
☐ Raven S-40A Hot Air Balloon			Gondola only.	RA
☐ Raven S-50 Hot Air Balloon				RA
☐ Raven S-55A Hot Air Balloon	N64AA	S55A-0164	Gondola only.	RA
☐ Raven S-55A Hot Air Balloon	N50DE	S55A-0454		PV
☐ Raven S-55A Hot Air Balloon	N81DS	S55A-0748		PV
☐ Raven S-55A Hot Air Balloon	N2806L	S55A-1096		RA
☐ Raven S-60A Hot Air Balloon	N3097R	S60A-132		RA
☐ Raven S-60A Hot Air Balloon	N5681T	S60A-137	Bottom half of envelope.	RA
☐ Raven S-60A Hot Air Balloon	N4273D	S60A-239		RA
☐ Raven S-100 Hot Air Balloon	N54693	EXP-400		RA
☐ Semco Ax.5 Model T Hot Air Balloon	N36003	SEM-162	Basket, burners and tanks.	PV
☐ Semco Ax.5 Model T 65 K Hot Air Balloon	N24424	SEM-109	Basket, burners and tanks.	
☐ Semco Ax.6 Hot Air Balloon (Ax.5)	N65241	SEM-117		RA
☐ Thunder Hot Air Balloon.			Less envelope.	
☐ Thunder Hot Air Balloon.			Less envelope.	
☐ Yost GB-47 Hot Air Balloon	N9289Z			PV
☐ Yost GBN-41-1000 Gas Balloon	N611SP	125	Less envelope.	RA
☐ Yost GBN-41-1000 Helium Balloon	N61SP	112		RA
☐ Yost GBN-41-1000 Hot Air Balloon	N47SP	119		RA
☐ Yost GBN-41-1000 Helium Balloon	N767SP	126		PV
☐ Yost Helium Balloon			Lees envelope.	RA

ARTESIA MONUMENT (NM3)

Location:	On permanent view in a park in the northern part of the town.

TYPE	REG/SER	CON. NO.	PI/NOTES	STATUS
☐ Republic F-84F Thunderstreak	51-9485			PV

New Mexico

CANNON AIR FORCE BASE MEMORIAL PARK (NM4)

Address:	27th FW/PA, 110 East Sextant, Suite 1150, New Mexico 88103-5216.
Tel:	505-784-4131 Email: 27fwpublicaffairs@cannon.af.mil
Admission:	During daylight hours.
Location:	About 7 miles west of Clovis off Route 60/84.

Portair Field opened in the mid-1920s and later became Clovis Municipal Airport. A military glider detachment arrived in 1942 and was soon followed by a unit training bomber crews and the site became Clovis Army Airfield. The base closed in 1947 but the USAF returned in 1951 with the 140th Fighter Bomber Wing operating Mustangs. The field was renamed in June 1957 after General John K. Cannon who commanded Allied Air Forces in the Mediterranean in World War II and later became Commander of Tactical Air Command.

The Memorial Park was opened on 4th June 1976 to commemorate the bicentennial celebrations. Examples of types which have served at the base have been put on show and many have been painted in the markings of aircraft used by the resident 27th Tactical Fighter Wing which arrived at Cannon in February 1959. The Voodoo is in the colours of she one flown by Major Adrian E. Drew of the 27th when he set a world air speed record of 1207.6 mph over a course at Edwards Air Force Base on 12th December 1957.

TYPE	REG/SER	CON. NO.	PI/NOTES	STATUS
☐ General Dynamics EF-111A (F-111A)	66-0016	A1-34		PV
☐ General Dynamics F-111A	63-9771	A1-06	63-9771, '27-234'	PV
☐ General Dynamics F-111D	68-0140	A6-56	In Clovis town centre	PV
☐ General Dynamics 401 Fighting Falcon (F-16A)	79-0307	61-92		PV
☐ Lockheed 580 (T-33A)	58-0503	580-1472		PV
☐ McDonnell M.36CA Voodoo (RF-101C)	'32426'	178	56-0187	PVX
☐ North American NA-203 Sabre (F-86H)	'31404'	203-23	53-1251	PVX
☐ North American NA-235 Super Sabre (F-100D)	'56-3141'	235-38	56-2940, '56-3141'	PV
☐ Republic F-84F Thunderjet (P-84C)	'11027'		47-1530	PVX
☐ Republic F-84F Thunderstreak	51-1810			PV

COMMEMORATIVE AIR FORCE (LOBO WING) (NM5)

Address:	PO Box 20576, Albuquerque, New Mexico 87154-0576.
Tel:	505-856-1615 Email: smwitschger@cs.com
Admission:	Saturday 0800-1600 or by prior permission.
Location:	At Moriarty Airport which is about 1 mile east of the town.

This unit was formed in September 1984 as part of the New Mexico Wing. The Cornell, built by Fleet in Canada, was assigned to the squadron in January 1986 and was returned to flying condition after a 12-year rebuild.

After a long period at Coronado Airport the wing moved to Double Eagle Airport in the mid-1990s. In 2004 a new hangar was completed at Moriarty Airport and this became their home. A museum is being set up in the building and several interesting items have been acquired. These include a World War II Link Trainer, a Willys Jeep and a Ramp Scooter, which was built up from aircraft parts at Hobbs Army Airfield in the 1940s.

The Kansan arrived in 2002 from a now defunct unit in Michigan and is under rebuild in the hangar. This aircraft served in the training role at Albuquerque in 1941/2. The tail turret of the B-29 will be mounted on a trailer and taken to shows. The remainder of the rear fuselage is displayed in the museum along with items of memorabilia.

TYPE	REG/SER	CON. NO.	PI/NOTES	STATUS
☐ Beech C18S Kansan (AT-11)	N320A	877	41-9451	RAC
☐ Boeing 345 Superfortress (B-29)			Rear fuselage only.	RA
☐ Fairchild M-62A-4 Cornell II	N5519N	FC.18	10520 (Canada), CF-FDF	RAA

COMMEMORATIVE AIR FORCE (NEW MEXICO WING) (NM6)

Address:	5901 Carlsbad Highway, PO Box 2796, Hobbs, New Mexico 88241.
Tel:	505-392-3119 Email: one-n-christ@hotmail.com
Admission:	Daily 0800-sunset.
Location:	At Lea County Airport which is about 8 miles west of the town on Route 62/180.

This wing was the first successful unit to be formed away from the then main base of Harlingen. A hangar was moved from a former World War II B-17 training airfield just north of Hobbs. A display of engines, photographs and memorabilia has been set up in the building.

The rarest aircraft in the fleet is a German-built Messerschmitt Bf 108. After service in the Luftwaffe this aircraft spent some time in England before being sold unconverted to Switzerland in January 1950. The Taifun is now airworthy after a protracted rebuild by members of the unit.

The Beech 18 and North American SNJ-4 are allocated to the wing. The other aircraft are owned by members and are either in the unit hangar or those nearby. There is a museum containing mainly World War II memorabilia, uniforms, badges, photographs and components at the back of the hangar.

TYPE	REG/SER	CON. NO.	PI/NOTES	STATUS
☐ Beech D18S	N79AG	A-806	N8866A	PVA
☐ Boeing-Stearman A75N1 Kaydet (N2S-3)	N63542	75-3684	Bu37937	PV
☐ Boeing-Stearman E75 Kaydet (PT-13D) (N2S-5)	N66306	75-8103	42-109070, Bu38482	PVA
☐ Fairchild M-62A Cornell (PT-19A)	N49232	T43-555	42-34389	PVA
☐ Fairchild M-62A-4 Cornell (PT-26A) (Cornell II)	N59916	T42-65619 (?)	42-65619, FV134, 15035 (Canada)	PV
☐ Messerschmitt Bf 108D-1 Taifun	N2231	3059	D-ERPN, VE+LI, AM87, G-AKZY, HB-DUB, HB-ESK, NX2231	PVC
☐ North American NA-88 Texan (SNJ-4)				PVA
☐ North American NA-168 Texan (T-6G)	N7000S	168-410	49-3306, N5278V	PVA
☐ Stinson V-76 Sentinel (L-5)	N48083		42-98701	PVA

This 1911 Curtiss D Pusher owned by the Albuquerque Museum of Art, History and Science is on show in the terminal at the airport. [NM1]

The Veterans Square Memorial at Holloman Air Force Base is home to this McDonnell F-15A Eagle. [NM11]

The New Mexico Air National Guard have this Lockheed F-80B Shooting Star outside their Kirtland Headquarters. [NM12]

New Mexico

EASTERN NEW MEXICO UNIVERSITY (NM7)

Address:	52 University Boulevard, Roswell, New Mexico 88203.
Tel:	575-624-7000 Email: webmaster@roswell.enmu.edu
Admission:	By prior permission only.
Location:	At the airport whch is about 3 miles south of the town.

The university offers courses in many subjects. The aviation section is located in a complex at the airport. Here are the instructional airframes along with engines and systems rigs. This list is probably not complete.

TYPE	REG/SER	CON. NO.	PI/NOTES	STATUS
☐ Beech C50 Seminole (L-23D) (U-8D)	N49290	RLH-82	58-3081.	RA
☐ Bell 47G-2 Sioux (H-13H) (OH-13H)	57-6205	2134		RA
☐ Bell 47G-2 Sioux (H-13H) (OH-13H)	58-5380	2393		RA
☐ Bell 204 Iroquois (UH-1B)	N96250	733	63-8511	RA
☐ Boeing 727-22F	N191FE	19084	N7071U	RA
☐ Cessna 210E Centurion	N4955U	21058655		RA
☐ Cessna 310A Blue Canoe (L-27A) (U-3A)	57-5907	38062		RA
☐ Cessna 421	N124LB	4210175		RA
☐ Mitsubishi MU-2D (MU-2B-10)	N28DC	106	N3570X, N853Q, N518T, N518TQ	RA
☐ Republic F-105D Thunderchief	61-0110	D-305		RA

FANTASY FIGHTERS (NM8)

Address:	3662 Cerrillos, Suite S-A3, Santa Fe, New Mexico 87501.
Tel:	505-471-4151 Fax: 505-471-6335 Email: info@jetwarbird.com
Admission:	By prior permission only.
Location:	At the airport which is about 5 miles west of the town on Route 284.

This organisation offers pilot training in jet warbirds. The Canadian-built T-33 is painted in the colours of the famous 'Thunderbirds' aerobatic team. The company often holds 'open-days' when the fleet can be viewed.

TYPE	REG/SER	CON. NO.	PI/NOTES	STATUS
☐ Aero L-29 Delfin				RAA
☐ Aero L-39C Albatros	N39VM	131536	38 (Soviet)	RAA
☐ Aero L-39C Albatros	N24189	633721		RAA
☐ Beech A45 Mentor (T-34A)	N334LS	G-813	55-0256	RAA
☐ Canadair CL-30 Silver Star 3 (CT-133) [Lockheed 580 (T-33AN)]	N33HW	T33-375	21375 (Canada), N12430, N33WR	RAA
☐ Fouga CM.170R Magister	N316FM	316	316 (France)	RAA
☐ WSK SBlim-2 (Lim-1) [MiG-15] [MiG-15UTI]	N150MG	1A 07-031	731 (Poland)	RAA

FARMINGTON MONUMENT (NM9)

Location:	On permanent view at the National Guard Armory near the airport which is just north of the town.

TYPE	REG/SER	CON. NO.	PI/NOTES	STATUS
☐ Vought A-7D Corsair II	74-1746	D421		PV

GALLUP MONUMENT (NM10)

Location:	On permanent view at the airport which is about 2 miles south west of the town.

TYPE	REG/SER	CON. NO.	PI/NOTES	STATUS
☐ Northrop N-156T Talon (T-38A)	61-0829	N.5195		PV

HOLLOMAN AIR FORCE VETERAN'S SQUARE MEMORIAL (NM11)

Address:	49 FW/PA, 596 Fourth Street, Building 224 Suite 105, Holloman Air Force Base, New Mexico 88330-5000.
Tel:	575-572-7383 Fax: 575-572-3650 Email: 49fw.pa@holloman.af.mil
Admission:	By prior permission only.
Location:	About 6 miles south west of Alamogordo on Route 70/82.

The base was activated in 1942 and called Alamorgdo Army Airfield. In 1948 it was named after Colonel George V. Holloman, a guided missile pioneer, who was killed in a B-17 crash in Formosa in 1946. The airfield houses many units including a fighter wing and test facilities for the nearby White Sands Missile Ranges. The Veteran's Square was set up in the early 1990s and most of the aircraft which were preserved around the base were brought together. The exceptions are the Iroquois, parked near the Army facility, and the Sabre which is mounted on the far side of the airfield by the 49th Wing Headquarters.

TYPE	REG/SER	CON. NO.	PI/NOTES	STATUS
☐ Bell 204 Iroquois (UH-1B)	63-8515	737	At Army facility.	RA
☐ Convair 8-24 Delta Dart (F-106A) (QF-106A)	56-0454	8-24-04		RA
☐ Lockheed 080 Shooting Star (P-80C) (F-80C)	49-1853	080-2680		RA
☐ Lockheed 383-04-05 Starfighter (F-104C)	56-0886	183-1174		RA
☐ Lockheed F-117A	79-10782	A.4007		RA
☐ Lockheed F-117A	85-0816	A.4046		RA
☐ McDonnell M.98DE Phantom II (F-4E)	'67-435'	564	63-7571	RAX
☐ McDonnell M.199-1A Eagle (F-15A)	76-0037	219/A189		RA

☐ North American NA-172 Sabre (F-86E)	51-13028	172-319	51-13028, '53154'	RA
☐ North American NA-235 Super Sabre (F-100D)	56-3220	235-318		RA
☐ Northrop N-156T Talon (T-38A) (AT-38B)	60-0576	N.5149		PV
☐ Panavia PA200 Tornado IDS	45+11	4211		PV
☐ Republic F-84F Thunderstreak	51-9396		51-9396, '51-5396'	RA
☐ Republic F-105D Thunderchief	61-0145	D-340	61-0145, '61-0141'	RA

KIRTLAND AIR FORCE BASE (NM12)

Address:	2000 Wyoming Boulevard South East, Albuquerque, New Mexico 87117-5000.
Tel:	505-846-5991 Email: 377abw.pa@kirtland.af.mil
Admission:	By prior permission only.
Location:	In the southern suburbs of the city off Gibson Boulevard.

Named after Colonel Roy S. Kirtland who was the Commander of Langley Field in the 1930s, the base shares its runways with Albuquerque Airport. The military set up the site in 1941 and at the present time is home to a variety of units.
Four aircraft are preserved outside the Headquarters of the Air National Guard and the others are located around the vast site. The MiG-21 is one of several obtained by the USAF for test purposes. The Rescue Heritage Hall was on the base for many years. The displays showed how aircraft were used on rescue missions around the world. This has now closed but the aircraft are still around the building.

TYPE	REG/SER	CON. NO.	PI/NOTES	STATUS
☐ Bell 204 Iroquois (UH-1F)	'61240'	7045	64-15495, '57956'	RAX
☐ Bell 47D-1 Sioux (H-13E) (OH-13E)	51-13747	333	51-13747, N82853	RA
☐ Consolidated 28-5A Catalina (PBY-5A)	'433882'	1821	Bu46457, 6510 (Brazil), N4582U, '34077',	RAX
☐ Douglas DC-3A-456 Skytrain (C-47A) (SC-47A)	'43-15732'	19458	42-100995, 100995 (Norway), LN-IAS, PH-SCC, OO-AVG, N3433E – identity doubtful.	RAX
☐ Grumman G-111 Albatross (G-64) (UF-1) (UF-2S) (HU-16B)	1280	G-428	Bu141280, 1280, '10071'	RA
☐ Kaman K-600-3 Huskie (H-43B) (HH-43B)	59-1578	59		RA
☐ Lockheed 080 Shooting Star (P-80B) (F-80B)	45-8501	080-1715		RA
☐ Mikoyan-Gurevich MiG-21F	150		In Soviet markings.	RA
☐ North American NA-122 Mustang (P-51D) (FSM)	'51400'			PVX
☐ North American NA-192 Super Sabre (F-100A)	53-1532	192-27		RA
☐ North American NA-265 Sabreliner (T-39A) (CT-39A)	59-2868	265-1	59-2868, N2259U	RA
☐ Piasecki PD-22 Work Horse (H-21B) (CH-21B)	'8706'	B.53	52-8691, '34876', '34343' – composite with c/n B.68 52-8706.	RAX
☐ Sikorsky S-51 Dragonfly	'5122'	5122	N92808, '8555'	RAX
☐ Sikorsky S-55D (HO4S-3) (UH-19F)	'27540'		Bu138499,'13893'	RAX
☐ Sikorsky S-58 Seabat (HSS-1N) (SH-34J)	Bu148938	581313		RA
☐ Sikorsky S-61R (CH-3C) (HH-3E)	64-14232	61535		RA
☐ Sikorsky S-65A (HH-53B) (MH-53B) (MH-53J)	66-14433	65048		RA
☐ Vought A-7D Corsair II	'72-0245'	D299	72-0177	RAX

MELROSE MONUMENT (NM13)

Location:	On permanent view in Baxter Memorial Park on Highway 64 in the southern part of the town.

TYPE	REG/SER	CON. NO.	PI/NOTES	STATUS
☐ North American NA-192 Super Sabre (F-100A)	53-1533	192-28		PV

NATIONAL MUSEUM OF NUCLEAR SCIENCE AND HISTORY (NM14)

Address:	601 Eubank Boulevard South East,, Albuquerque, New Mexico 87123.
Tel:	505-245-2137 Fax: 505-245-4537 Email: info@atomicmuseum.com
Admission:	Daily 0900-1700.
Location:	In the south eastern suburbs of the city off Wyoming Boulevard.

Housed in a former missile repair building, the collection opened in September 1969 as the Sandia Atomic Museum. Later the name was changed to the National Atomic Museum.
The first atomic bomb was conceived at the Los Alamitos Scientific Laboratory located just north of the town. The development of nuclear weapons is portrayed in detail including replicas of those dropped on Hiroshima and Nagasaki. The peaceful use of atomic reactors is also shown.
The first bombs were dropped on Japan by B-29s and in the mid-1990s an example of this famous type arrived by road from Chanute Air Force Base in Illinois.

TYPE	REG/SER	CON. NO.	PI/NOTES	STATUS
☐ Boeing 345 Superfortress (B-29)	'45-21749'	13642	45-21748	PVX
☐ Boeing 464-201-3 Stratofortress (RB-52B)	52-0013	16503		PV
☐ Republic F-105D Thunderchief	61-0107	D-302		PV
☐ Vought TA-7C Corsair II (A-7B)	Bu154407	B57		PV

NEW MEXICO VETERANS MEMORIAL MUSEUM (NM15)

Address:	PO Box 8939, Las Cruces, New Mexico 88005.
Admission:	Unknown.
Location:	In the centre of the town.

New Mexico

The Super Sabre arrived in the town as a memorial to members of the New Mexico Air National Guard who had lost their lives in Vietnam. Local veterans groups have now constructed a small museum containing memorabilia, uniforms and badges to show the contribution of local servicemen in the conflict.

TYPE	REG/SER	CON. NO.	PI/NOTES	STATUS
☐ North American NA-243 Super Sabre (F-100F)	56-3855	243-131		PV

PANCHO VILLA STATE PARK AND MUSEUM (NM16)

Address: POBox 450, Columbus, New Mexico 88029-0224.
Tel: 505-531-2711   **Fax:** 505-531-2115   **Email:** victore.trujillo@state.nm.us
Admission: Daily 1000-1700.
Location: About 5 miles north of the town.

The museum opened in March 2006 and commemorates the March 1916 raid on Columbus by Villa when 500 of his troops attacked the town. The replica Jenny was constructed by Vintage Aviation Services in Texas. The biplane is in the markings of the one flown by Lieutenant Carleton G. Chapman of the 1st Aero Squadron.

TYPE	REG/SER	CON. NO.	PI/NOTES	STATUS
☐ Curtiss 1C Jenny (JN-3) (R)	'53'			PVX

PORTALES MONUMENT (NM17)

Location: On permanent view in the south western part of the town.

TYPE	REG/SER	CON. NO.	PI/NOTES	STATUS
☐ General Dynamics F-111F	70-2364	E2-03		PV

SANTA FE MONUMENTS (NM18)

Location: On permanent view at two locations in the city.

TYPE	REG/SER	CON. NO.	PI/NOTES	STATUS
☐ General Dynamics 401 Fighting Falcon (F-16A)	79-0404	61-189	At National Guard Headquarters.	PV
☐ General Dynamics F-111F	70-2408	E2-47	At the airport west of the town.	PV

SANTA ROSA MONUMENT (NM19)

Location: On permanent view at the airport which is about 2 miles east of the town on Highway 84.

TYPE	REG/SER	CON. NO.	PI/NOTES	STATUS
☐ Vought A-7D Corsair II	72-0245	D367		PV

SOUTHWEST SOARING MUSEUM (NM20)

Address: PO Box 3626, Moriaty, New Mexico 87035-3636
Tel: 505-832-0755   **Email:** gapplebay@aol.com
Admission: Daily 0900-1600.
Location: About 20 miles east of Albuquerque off Interstate 40.

Formed in 1996, the museum opened in one hangar the following year. A second hall was completed in 1999 and plans envisage the construction of a purpose-built complex close to Interstate 40.

The main aim is to trace the history of gliding in the western states of the country. A 24 foot mural by a local artist can be seen on one wall of the building. This shows the development of man's desire to fly. A collection of almost 100 models of important glider designs is another highlight.

The number of sailplanes on show is increasing. A replica of a Zögling has been built. This type which appeared in 1924 was soon produced in large numbers.

TYPE	REG/SER	CON. NO.	PI/NOTES	STATUS
☐ AB Sportline Aviacija Genesis 2	LY-GEN			PV
☐ Applebay Zia	N202Z	2		PV
☐ Bensen B-8M Gyrocopter	N5317	T.P.2		PV
☐ Bowlus BS-100 Super Albatross	N64JJ	3		PV
☐ Briegleb BG-12B	N1352	1000		PV
☐ Campbell CSG-1	N112CC	112		PV
☐ Cascade Kasperwing 180B				PV
☐ Elliott AP.5 EoN Olympia 2				PV
☐ Fibera KK-1e Utu	N1070	18		PV
☐ Focke-Wulf Weihe 50	YU-4048			PV
☐ Frankfort Cinema B (TG-1A)	NC54138	B-2-26	(USAAF), NC54138, N54138	PV
☐ Frankfort Cinema B (TG-1A)	NC54139	B-2-29	(USAAF), NC54139, N54139	PV
☐ Franklin PS-2 Eaglet	N452Y	113	On loan from NSM, NY.	PV
☐ Glasflügel H303 Mosquito	N235A	79		PV
☐ Glasflügel H401 Kestrel	N59LL	32		PVA
☐ Hall Cherokee II	N1510U	1001		PV
☐ Hall Cherokee RM	N3034	RS-1		PV
☐ Jansson BJ-1B Duster	N11BJ	002		PV
☐ Kensrue MSK-10				PV
☐ Laister LP-46	N46LP	46		PV
☐ Laister-Kauffman LK.10A	NC53613	28	NC53613, N53613	PVA
☐ McEwan M-2-153	N1376	101		PV

☐ Mitchell Wing B-10				PV
☐ Monnett Monerai S	N9020C	219		PV
☐ Moore SS-1	N4072B	SS-1		PV
☐ Nelson PG-185B Hummingbird	N68582	82		PVA
☐ Northrup Primary Glider				PV
☐ Oldershaw O-2	N7799C	1		PV
☐ Oldershaw O-3	N2560B	1		PV
☐ Schleicher ASW-15				PV
☐ Schleicher Ka-3				PV
☐ Schleicher Ka-4 Rhönlerche II	N791D	270		PV
☐ Schleicher Ka-4 Rhönlerche II	N7984	93/58		PVA
☐ Schleicher Ka-6CR Rhönsegler	N424ES	6350		PV
☐ Schleicher Ka-6E Rhönsegler	N99DW	4081		PV
☐ Schreder HP-11A	N251F	45		PV
☐ Schreder HP-18	N897EN	EN-1		PV
☐ Schweizer SGS.2-12 (TG-3A)	CF-ZAY		42-52993	PV
☐ Schweizer SGU.2-22				PV
☐ Schweizer SGS.1-26A	N8661R	194		PV
☐ Schweizer SGS.1-34	N17973	73		PV
☐ Seagull Hang Glider				PV
☐ Slingsby T.21B Sedbergh TX.1	N941WB	608	WB941, BGA.3219	PV
☐ Slingsby T.31B Cadet TX.3	N7012Z	898	XE785	PV
☐ Stamer-Lippisch Z-12 Zögling (R)				PV
☐ Ultralight Flying Machines Easy Riser				PV
☐ UP Hang Glider				PV
☐ Wills Wing Hang Glider				PV

TRUTH OR CONSEQUENCES MONUMENT (NM21)

Location: On permanent view at the airport which is just north of the town.

TYPE	REG/SER	CON. NO.	PI/NOTES	STATUS
☐ Lockheed 580 (T-33A)	51-9022	580-6806		PV

TUCUMCARI HISTORICAL MUSEUM (NM22)

Address: 416 South Adams Street, Tucumcari, New Mexico 88401.
Tel: 575-461-2201
Admission: May–August Monday-Saturday 0800-1700.
Location: In the northern part of the town.

The museum is housed in a 1903 schoolhouse and has displays tracing the history and development of the region on three floors. Outside is Firehouse Number 1 housing a 1926 Chevrolet Fire Truck in working order. The original railroad depot nearby has an early truck on show. Another highlight is an early ranch roundup wagon.

TYPE	REG/SER	CON. NO.	PI/NOTES	STATUS
☐ North American NA-192 Super Sabre (F-100A)	53-1600	192-95		PV

VIETNAM VETERANS NATIONAL MEMORIAL (NM23)

Address: PO Box 608, Angel Fire, New Mexico 87710.
Tel: 505-377-6900   **Fax:** 505-377-3223
Admission: On permanent view.
Location: Just north west of the town on Route 64.

The site is now operated by New Mexico as one of its state parks. It took over the running from a private foundation in 2005. A Visitor Center and Chapel are in the grounds. The history of the Vietnam War and the contributions by local military personnel are portrayed in the exhibition.

TYPE	REG/SER	CON. NO.	PI/NOTES	STATUS
☐ Bell 205 Iroquois (UH-1D) (UH-1H)	64-13670	4377		PV

WAR EAGLES AIR MUSEUM (NM24)

Address: 8012 Airport Road, Santa Teresa, New Mexico 88008-1225.
Tel: 505-589-2000   **Email:** mail@war-eagles-air-museum.com
Admission: Tuesday-Sunday 1000-1600.
Location: At Doña Ana County Airport which is about 15 miles north west of El Paso,TX. and 8 miles off Interstate 10 Exit 8.

Warbird collector John MacGuire established this museum in 1991. A large exhibition building and a nearby workshop were constructed at the airport. The majority of the aircraft are in flying condition. The Curtiss Kittyhawk was restored in Louisiana and was to have been the centrepiece of a museum devoted to the exploits of Chennault's 'Flying Tigers' force in World War II. This aircraft flew in the film 'Tora Tora Tora'.

Two Tupolev Tu-2s were obtained China. One has been restored to static condition and the other has been sold to a private owner. A batch of Polish-built MiG-15s was acquired and several of these are still in the collection.

Five derelict Mustangs were purchased from a number imported from Indonesia. The Lightning was converted for photographic duties during World War II. The aircraft was sold for civilian use in 1946 and was bought by John MacGuire in 1984. This classic is now resplendent in an all black scheme.

A new hall has been added to the main hangar and here the visitor can view around two dozen vintage and classic cars.

New Mexico

TYPE	REG/SER	CON. NO.	PI/NOTES	STATUS
☐ Boeing-Stearman A75N1 Kaydet (PT-17)	N75855	75-4413	42-17250	PVA
☐ Canadair CL-13B Sabre 6 [North American F-86E]	365	1474	23684 (Canada), 365 (South Africa), N106JB	PV
☐ Canadair CL-30 Silver Star 3 (CT-133) [Lockheed 580 (T-33AN)]	N92JB	T33-582	21582 (Canada), N99202	PV
☐ Cessna 140A	N992F	15599		PV
☐ Cessna 318B Tweety Bird (T-37B)	66-7966	40926		PV
☐ Convair 105 (L-13A)	N316LG	196	47-316	PVA
☐ Curtiss A87-A2 Kittyhawk I	N95JB	18796	AL152, 1082 (Canadian), N1207V	PV
☐ De Havilland DH.82A Tiger Moth	N7158N	84569	T6102, G-ANNC, OO-SOM	PVA
☐ Douglas DC-3A-456 Skytrain (C-47A)	N574JB	20145	43-15679, NC59534, N998Z, N101ZG	PVA
☐ Douglas RB-26C Invader (A-26C)	N576JB	28772	44-35493, N2852G	PVA
☐ Globe GC-1B Swift	N80649	1054		PVA
☐ Grumman G-40 Avenger (TBM-3) (TBM-3E)	NL8397H	2198	Bu69459, N8397H	PV
☐ Hawker Fury FB.10	NX57JB	41H/37703	253 (Iraq), N40SF, VH-HFA	PV
☐ Lockheed 422-87-23 Lightning (P-38L) (F-5G)	N577JB	422-8091	44-27087, NX65485, N65485, NX345, N345, N345DN	PVA
☐ Mikoyan-Gurevich MiG-21SPS (MiG-21PFM)	22+24	94A4213	729 (DDR)	PV
☐ Morane-Saulnier MS.502 Criquet [Fieseler Fi 156 Storch]	N28670	728	728 (France)	PVA
☐ North American NA-121 Texan (AT-6F)	N578JB	121-42563	44-81841, N10590	PVA
☐ North American NA-122 Mustang (P-51D)	N96JM	122-41564	44-75024, F-??? (Indonesian) N4261U	PV
☐ North American NA-124 Mustang (P-51D) (TF-51D)	N51TF	124-44514	44-84658, N851D, F-361 (Indonesia)	PVA
☐ North American NA-181 Fury (FJ-2)	Bu132028	181-102		PV
☐ North American NA-200 Trojan (T-28B)	N572JB	200-318	Bu138247, N54911	PV
☐ Northrop N-156T Talon (T-38A) (AT-38B)	64-13267	N.5696		PV
☐ Piper J-3C-65 Cub	N20240	2042	NC20240	PVA
☐ Piper PA-18-125 Super Cub	N1588P	18-3751		PVA
☐ Republic F-84F Thunderstreak	'52-7343'		Composite.	PVX
☐ Stinson V-76 Sentinel (O-62) (L-5)	N40002	76-220	42-15017	PVA
☐ Stinson V-77 Reliant (AT-19)	'FK887'	77-74	44-46713, FK887, Bu11348, NC69996	PVA
☐ Tupolev Tu-2S		1011112		PV
☐ Vought F4U-4 Corsair	NX53JB	8423	Bu81698, N3763A	PV
☐ Vought A-7E Corsair II	Bu157455	E178		PV
☐ Vultee V-79 Valiant (BT-13B) (SNV-2)	N63697	79-1293	42-90296, (USN)	PVA
☐ Waco EGC-8	NC19354	5002	NC19354, N19354	PVA
☐ WSK Lim-2 [MiG-15bis]	N13KM	1B 010-13	1013 (Poland) – in false Soviet markings.	PVX
☐ WSK Lim-2 [MiG-15bis]	N416JM	1B 014-16	1416 (Poland)	RA
☐ WSK Lim-2 [MiG-15bis]	N629BM	1B 016-29	1629 (Poland)	RA
☐ WSK SBLim-2A (Lim-1) [MiG-15] [MiG-15UTI]	'640'	1A 006-40	640 (Poland), N40BM – in false Soviet markings.	PVA

WAR HEROES MEMORIAL (NM25)

Address:	Highway 109, Jarales, New Mexico 87023.
Admission:	On permanent view.
Location:	In the northern part of the town.

This monument honours local men who met their death on the infamous Bataan Death March which took place in the Philippines. Captured America soldiers were forced to march over 100 miles to a prisoner of war camp. Many perished on the way as they were denied food and water. Others were tortured before being executed. The T-33 has been painted in the colours of one flown by the New Mexico Air National Guard.

TYPE	REG/SER	CON. NO.	PI/NOTES	STATUS
☐ Lockheed 580 (T-33A) (TV-2) (T-33B)		580-8652	53-5313, Bu137940	PVX

WHITE SANDS MISSILE RANGE MUSEUM (NM26)

Address:	Headquarters Avenue, White Sands Missile Range, Las Cruces, New Mexico 88002-5047.
Tel:	505-678-8824 Email: darren.court@us.army.mil
Admission:	Monday-Friday 0800-1600; Saturday-Sunday 1000-1500.
Location:	About 15 miles north east of the town south of Route 70.

This range was established on 9th July 1945 as the White Sands Proving Ground and took up its present name in 1958. Over the last half century almost all types of missiles used by the US Military have been developed at the vast site.

The first atomic device in the world was tested at the Trinity Site, about 80 miles north of the headquarters, on 16th July 1945 and the crater is still visible. The park, located just inside the main gate to the complex, has developed over the years and many missiles are on show. The indoor display traces the history of the site with many photographs, documents, components and memorabilia on view.

TYPE	REG/SER	CON. NO.	PI/NOTES	STATUS
☐ Beech 65-A90 King Air (VC-6A)	66-15361	LJ-153		PV
☐ Bell 204 Iroquois (UH-1C) (UH-1M)	66-0416	1598		PV
☐ Gyrodyne QH-50D		DS-1570		PV
☐ McDonnell M.98NQ Phantom II (F-4F)	72-1135	4410	72-1135, 37+25	PV
☐ Republic LTV-N-2 [Fieseler Fi 103A-1]	'1156'			PV

NEW YORK

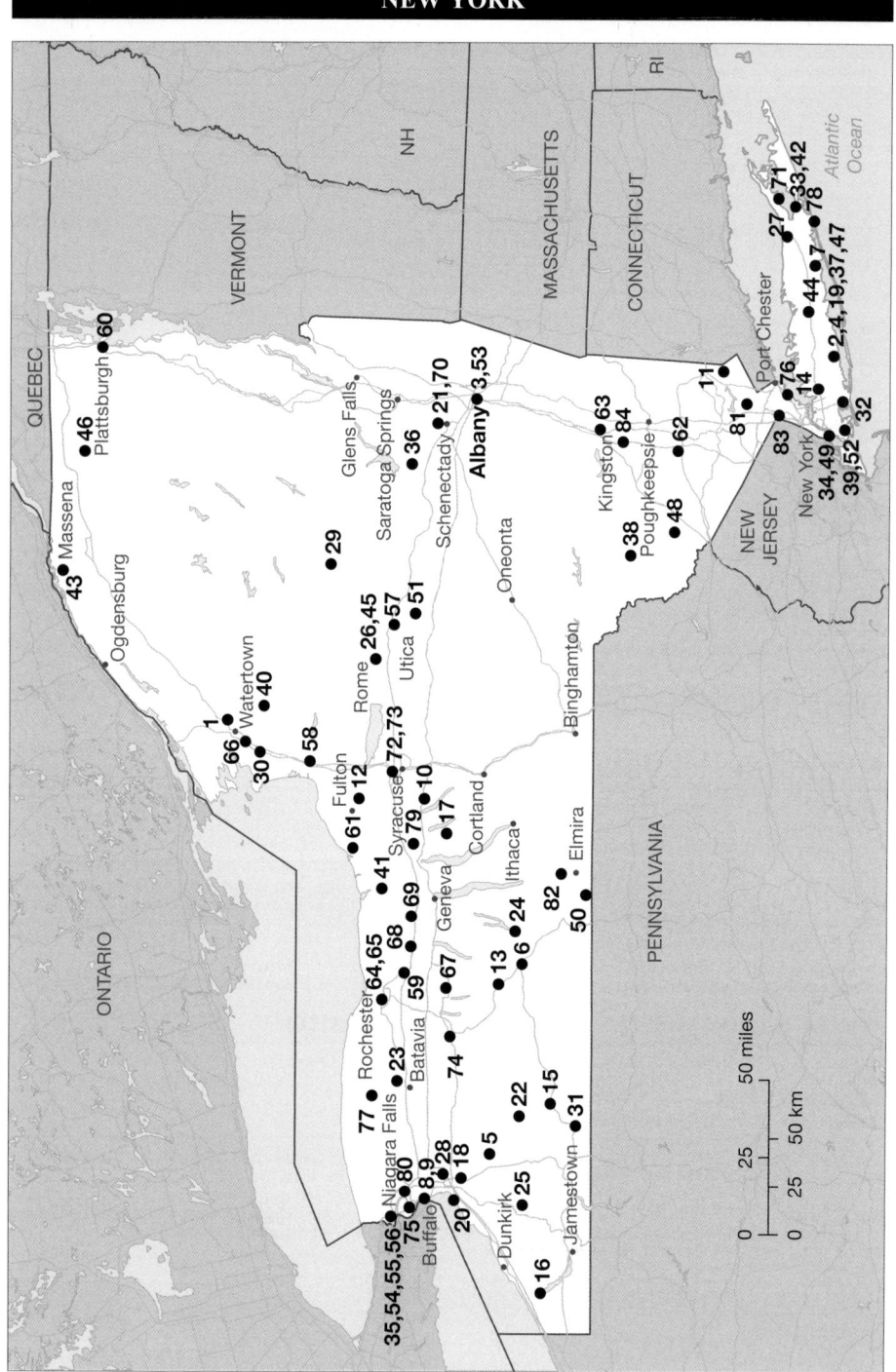

New York

10th MOUNTAIN DIVISION AND FORT DRUM MUSEUM (NY1)

Address:	Building 10502, South Ridge Loop, Fort Drum, New York 13602-5000.
Tel:	315-7724-0355 Fax: 315-774-6309 Email: kent.bolke@us.army.mil
Admission:	Monday-Friday 1000-1700.
Location:	About 5 miles north east of Watertown off Route 11.

A museum has been set up at the site which is home to units of the Army and a large helicopter overhaul company. The displays trace the history of the area and the units which have served there. There are many uniforms, flags and unit badges in the exhibition. A quantity of personal items has been donated by former soldiers. The five helicopters are displayed around the camp along with military vehicles and weapons.

TYPE	REG/SER	CON. NO.	PI/NOTES	STATUS
☐ Bell 205 Iroquois (UH-1H) (UH-1V)	69-15253	11541	On base.	RA
☐ Bell 206A Kiowa (OH-58A) (OH-58C)	70-15098	40649	On base.	RA
☐ Bell 209 Huey Cobra (AH-1G) (AH-1S)	71-20994	21065	On base.	RA
☐ Bell 209 Huey Cobra (AH-1S) (AH-1F)	79-23219	22264	On base.	RA
☐ Bell 209 Huey Cobra (AH-1S) (AH-1P)	76-22702	24055		PV

56th FLYING GROUP RESTAURANT (NY2)

Address:	7160 Republic Airport, East Farmingdale, New York 11735.
Tel:	631-694-8280
Admission:	Replicas on permanent view.
Location:	At Republic Airport which is about 2 miles east of the town on Route 24.

The restaurant building is in the style of a 1917 Allied Headquarters farmhouse in France is located on the site of the old Republic factory where P-47s were produced. Inside are several large models of World War II types. Visitors have an excellent view over the airport and the three replica aircraft are in the grounds.

TYPE	REG/SER	CON. NO.	PI/NOTES	STATUS
☐ Curtiss H81-A2 Warhawk (P-40C) (Tomahawk IIB) (FSM)				PVX
☐ Republic P-47D Thunderbolt (FSM)				PVX
☐ Vought F4U-4 Corsair (FSM)				PVX

ALBANY MONUMENT (NY3)

Location:	On permanent view at the airfield which is about 5 miles north west of the town.

TYPE	REG/SER	CON. NO.	PI/NOTES	STATUS
☐ Bell 209 Huey Cobra (AH-1S) (AH-1F)	78-23120	22226		PV

AMERICAN AIRPOWER MUSEUM (NY4)

Address:	1230 New Highway, Farmingdale, New York 11735.
Tel:	212-843-8010 Email: info@americanairpowermuseum.com
Admission:	Thursday-Sunday 1030-1600.
Location:	At Republic Airport which is about 2 miles east of the town on Route 24.

This impressive collection of warbirds was dedicated on 7th December 1999 in premises at the historic Republic Airport. A display of memorabilia has been set up in the adjacent control tower. The story of American involvement in World War II is portrayed in detail. The service history of the types in the collection is traced. The story of the war in the Pacific can be followed with the details of many of the famous battles shown vividly.

The majority of the aircraft are owned by Jeff Clyman who has had the dream of establishing a museum for many years. The P-47D Thunderbolt, built at Farmingdale, was acquired from the Museum of Flying in California in 2000. Once part of Harrah's Aircraft Museum in Reno, Nevada the P-40 was rebuilt by the well-known racing pilot Bill Destefani at Minter Field in California before joining the Lone Star Flight Museum at Galveston in Texas. After disposal by the Navy in 1958 the Corsair flew with several owners and for a period in the early 1980s was raced by a team based in Wyoming.

The Mitchell is believed to be the oldest survivor of the type and in 1943/4 served as General 'Hap' Arnold's personal transport. A group of retired Grumman employees acquired a Tomcat which is parked a short distance from the museum.

TYPE	REG/SER	CON. NO.	PI/NOTES	STATUS
☐ Aero L-39C Albatros	N4207W	834605	4605 (Czech)	PVA
☐ Aero L-39ZA Albatros	N7511Q	232424	2424 (Czech)	PVA
☐ Beech D18S			Front fuselage only.	PV
☐ Beech D18S			Front fuselage only.	PV
☐ Beech B95 Travel Air				PVA
☐ Cessna 310A Blue Canoe (L-27A) (U-3A)	N195M	TD-373		
☐ Cessna 310L	N222FB	38112	58-2138	PVA
☐ Consolidated 28-6A Catalina (PBY-6A)			Front fuselage only.	PVA
☐ Curtiss 87-A3 Warhawk (P-40M) (Kittyhawk III)	N7057C	2142	Bu64072	PVA
☐ Douglas DC-3A-467 Skytrain (C-47B)	NX1232N	27483	43-5795, 845 (Canada)	PVA
☐ Douglas DC-3A-467 Skytrain (C-47B) (Dakota IV)	N15SJ/'476717'	16301/33049	Front fuselage only.	PV
			44-76717, KN512, K-29 (Belgium), 476717 (France), 1406/4X-FNK/006	PVA
☐ Fairchild-Republic A-10A Thunderbolt II			Front fuselage only.	PV
☐ Fouga CM.170R Magister	N224PS	224	224	PV
☐ General Dynamics F-111A	67-0047	A1-92		PV
☐ Grumman G-40 Avenger (TBM-3)	N9586Z	2705	Bu85882	PVA

☐ Grumman G-303 Tomcat (F-14D)	Bu164603	631	With nearby Grumman Retiree Club.	PV
☐ Lockheed 580 (T-33A)	N43856	580-1097	56-1747	PV
☐ Mikoyan-Gurevich MiG-21UM	23	516915001	01 044 (?) – front fuselage only.	PV
☐ North American NA-62 Mitchell (B-25) (RB-25)	NL2825B	62-2837	40-2168, (XB-GOG), NL75831, N75831, N2825B	PVA
☐ North American NA-88 Texan (SNJ-4)	N9523C	88-12349	Bu27293	PVA
☐ North American NA-88 Texan (AT-6D) (SNJ-5)	N26862	88-17767	42-85978, Bu90819	PVC
☐ North American NA-122 Mustang (P-51D) (FSM)	'44-14151'			PVX
☐ Republic P-47D Thunderbolt	NX1345B	399-55592	44-90447, (Yugoslavia)	PVA
☐ Republic F-84E Thunderjet	49-2348			PV
☐ Republic RF-84F Thunderflash	53-7595	581		PV
☐ Republic F-105D Thunderchief	62-4361	D-560		PV
☐ Rotorway Scorpion 1	N8PA	3289		PV
☐ Stinson 108-2 Voyager	N348C	108-3348		PVA
☐ Vought FG-1D Corsair	NX83JC		Bu67089, N4716C, N4715C, N97GM, N83JC	PVA
☐ Waco UPF-7	N32006	5637	NC32006	PVA

ARCADE MONUMENT (NY5)

Location:	On permanent view at VFW 374 at 550 Main Street in the western part of the town.

TYPE	REG/SER	CON. NO.	PI/NOTES	STATUS
☐ Bell 205 Iroquois (UH-1D) (UH-1V)	66-16155	5849	With boom from UH-1H c/n 13135 71-20311.	PV

BATH MONUMENT (NY6)

Location:	On permanent view at VFW 1420 in Geneva Street in the north eastern part of the town.

TYPE	REG/SER	CON. NO.	PI/NOTES	STATUS
☐ Bell 209 Huey Cobra (AH-1G) (AH-1S)	68-15086	20620		PV

BAYPORT AERODROME SOCIETY (NY7)

Address:	PO Box 728, Bayport, New York 11708
Tel:	516-764-3429 Email: sbain@emediaofny.com
Admission:	By prior permission only.
Location:	In the northern suburbs of the town which is on the southern coast of Long Island.

The airfield opened in 1947 on area of farmland and was taken over by the town of Islip in 1974. Owners of vintage aircraft based at the airfield formed the society in l972. At weekends some of the 16 hangars are opened so that visitors can view the classic machines.

The Brunner-Winkle Bird was designed by Michael Gregor and 100 A models were sold in 1929/30. The improved B and C models appeared in 1931 and almost 130 were built in the Brooklyn factory before the firm folded in 1932.

All the aircraft are privately owned so changes to those on show occur frequently. The active Tiger Moth is one of many exported sold to France from England in the early 1950s. This biplane served with the club at Pau for four years. The Tiger then spent 18 years in store before being sold to the USA.

The Experimental Aircraft Association has promoted private flying for over 50 years and has also produced several designs suitable for the amateur builder. The P-1 Biplane was one of the first designs produced by the organisation. Jim Stewart and three other Allison engineers worked on the plans. The first was constructed by Robert Blacker and students at St. Rita's High School in Chicago.

TYPE	REG/SER	CON. NO.	PI/NOTES	STATUS
☐ Aeronca 7AC Champion	N2470E	44327C9 (?)	NC2470E	RAA
☐ Aeronca 7AC Champion	N2274E	7AC-5848	NC2274E	RAA
☐ Aeronca 7AC Chief	N9013E	11AC-644	NC9013E	RAA
☐ Auster K AOP.6	N3675	2853	VP658, 16675 (Canada), CF-LPA, C-FLPA	RAA
☐ Auster K AOP.6				RA
☐ Auster K AOP.6				RA
☐ Auster K AOP.6				RAC
☐ Blériot XI (R)				RA
☐ Boeing-Stearman B75 Kaydet (N2S-2)	N57811	75-1355	Bu3578	RAA
☐ Boeing-Stearman B75N1 Kaydet (N2S-3)	N5820V	75-7728	Bu38107	RAA
☐ Brunner-Winkle Bird BK	NC767Y	2054-34	NC767Y, N767Y	RAA
☐ Brunner-Winkle Bird BK	N10619	2065-45	NC10619	RAA
☐ Cessna 140	N89918	8963	NC89918	RAA
☐ Cessna 170B	N4446B	26790		RAA
☐ Cessna 190				RAA
☐ Curtiss 50C Robin C-1	N591	428	NR59H	RAA
☐ De Havilland DH.82A Tiger Moth	N82EK	83216	T5483, VH-BCL, VH-PCE, N31191	RAA
☐ De Havilland DH.82A Tiger Moth				RAC
☐ Ercoupe 415C	N99127	1750	NC99127	RAA
☐ Experimental Aircraft Association P-1 Biplane	N907V	2004		RAA
☐ Fairchild 24G	NC336E	2934		RAA
☐ Fairchild 24G				RAC
☐ Fleet 16B Finch II	N343SF	343	(Canada)	RAA
☐ Globe GC-1B Swift	N80977	1170	NC80977	RA
☐ Mono Aircraft Monocoupe 90	N19438	A-788	NC19438	RA
☐ Naval Aircraft Factory N3N-3	N44907		Bu1991	RAA

New York

☐ Pheasant H-10	N5738B	118		RAA
☐ Piper J-2 Cub	N19202	1602	NC19202	RAC
☐ Piper J-3C-65 Cub	N2049M	20819	NC2049M	RAA
☐ Piper J-3C-65 Cub	NC1542N	23074	NC1542N, N1542N	RAA
☐ Piper PA-15 Vagabond	N4159H	15-42	NC4159H	RAA
☐ Piper PA-20 Pacer 125	N7781K	20-607		RAA
☐ Pitts S-2A Special	N188JP	JP8-88		RAA
☐ Polikarpov Po-2				RAC
☐ Republic RC-3 Seabee				RA
☐ Republic RC-3 Seabee				RAA
☐ Royal Aircraft Factory S.E.5A (R)	N84847	074168		RAA
☐ Stinson 108-3 Voyager				RA
☐ Yakovlev Yak-12				RAC

BUFFALO AND ERIE COUNTY HISTORICAL SOCIETY MUSEUM (NY8)

Address: 25 Nottingham Court, Buffalo, New York 14216.
Tel: 716-873-9644   **Email:** collections@bechs.org
Admission: Tuesday-Saturday 1000-1700; Sunday 1200-1700.
Location: In the northern part of the city off Highway 198.

Opened in 1901, the museum displays trace the history of the region. Its aviation collection includes photographs, documents and memorabilia.
One of the two Standard biplanes has been restored to represent a Curtiss Jenny and this hangs in the atrium of the Rich company building in the city. About a dozen H-3s were built in 1916/7. The Bell Aircraft Corporation was formed in 1935 and moved into the former Consolidated plant at Buffalo.
The company's first helicopter, the model 30, designed by Arthur Young flew in December 1942. This design was developed into the successful 47 series which was produced in large numbers.

TYPE	REG/SER	CON. NO.	PI/NOTES	STATUS
☐ Bell 30	NX41869	3A		RA
☐ Standard A-3			Restored to represent a Curtiss Jenny – on show in the Rich Atrium.	PV
☐ Standard H-3				RA

BUFFALO AND ERIE COUNTY NAVAL & SERVICEMEN'S PARK (NY9)

Address: 1 Naval Park Cove, Buffalo, New York 14202.
Tel: 716-847-1773   **Email:** info@buffalonavalpark.org
Admission: April-October daily 1000-1700. November Saturday-Sunday 1000-1600.
Location: In the centre of the city near the junction of Pearl and Scott Streets.

The park opened on 30th June 1979 and now has four ships on view. The cruiser *Little Rock*, the submarine *Croaker*, the destroyer *The Sullivans* and a fast patrol boat. *The Sullivans* is named after the five brothers who were lost when the cruiser *Juneau* was sunk off Guadalcanal in November 1942.
The new museum building houses displays featuring famous conflicts of World War II. The Airacobra on show was recovered from the New Guinea jungle and later restored for display. The Voodoo was based at Niagara Falls with the New York National Guard from 1971 to 1982. The North American Fury flew with the United States Navy for many years. Also on show are a number of military vehicles.
The park underwent a major rebuild in 2006 and a number of new exhibitions have been set up. These include Marine Corps and former Prisoner of War memorabilia, the Polish Armed forces and Vietnam veterans stories.

TYPE	REG/SER	CON. NO.	PI/NOTES	STATUS
☐ Bell 205 Iroquois (UH-1D) (UH-1H)	63-12982	4178		PV
☐ Bell 26E Airacobra (P-39Q)	42-19995	26E-399	If identity correct.	PV
☐ Gyrodyne XRON-1 (XHOG-1)				PV
☐ McDonnell M.36BA Voodoo (TF-101B) (TF-101F)	58-0338	710		PV
☐ North American NA-244 Fury (FJ-4B) (AF-1E)	Bu143610	244-118		PV

CAMPBELL MONUMENT (NY10)

Location: On permanent view at ALP 1279 on Main Street in the town.

TYPE	REG/SER	CON. NO.	PI/NOTES	STATUS
☐ Bell 209 Huey Cobra (AH-1G) (AH-1F)	67-15688	20352		PV

CARMEL MONUMENT (NY11)

Location: On permanent view in Putnam County Memorial Park just north west of the town.

TYPE	REG/SER	CON. NO.	PI/NOTES	STATUS
☐ Bell 209 Huey Cobra (AH-1G) (AH-1F)	66-15318	20074		PV

CENTRAL SQUARE MONUMENT (NY12)

Location: On permanent view at ALP 915 on New York Route 49 in the north western part of the town.

TYPE	REG/SER	CON. NO.	PI/NOTES	STATUS
☐ North American NA-203 Sabre (F-86H)	'53-0915'	203-78	53-1306	PVX

CLARCQ COLLECTION (NY13)

Address:	3878 Jones Road, Cohocton, New York 14826.
Tel:	585-384-5333
Admission:	By prior permission only.
Location:	About 2 miles outh of the town off Route 371.

Richard Clarcq operates DC Helicopters from a site near the town. He also acquires examples of classic models and these are stored at the premises. An initial batch of 11 Bell 47s was produced for test work and the last of these is in the buildings. Interesting types are being sought to enhance the collection.

TYPE	REG/SER	CON. NO.	PI/NOTES	STATUS
☐ Bell 47	N1HQ	11		RA
☐ Bell 47G-2	N9010N	2198		RA
☐ Bell 47G-4	N9010B	3167		RA
☐ Bell 204 Iroquois (UH-1B)				RA
☐ Fairchild-Hiller FH-1100	N5024K	49		RA
☐ Hiller UH12A	N69085	103		RA
☐ Hiller UH12D Raven (H-23D) (OH-23D)	N62MC	1203	59-2723	RA
☐ Hiller UH12D Raven (H-23D) (OH-23D)	N3346F	980	57-3022	RA
☐ Hughes 369HS	N1042N	90-0251S		RAA
☐ Sikorsky S-58				RA

CRADLE OF AVIATION MUSEUM (NY14)

Address:	Charles Lindbergh Boulevard, Garden City, New York 11530.
Tel:	516-572-4111 Fax: 516-572-4065 Email: info@CradleOfAviation.org
Admission:	Tuesday-Saturday 0930-1730.
Location:	About 30 miles east of Manhattan on Long Island.

Long Island has been the scene of many developments in aviation. Glenn Curtiss made the first flight in the region when he flew from Hempstead Plains. Mitchel Field and the adjacent Roosevelt Field featured in many epic flights; Charles Lindbergh took off from the latter on his solo flight to Paris in 1927. The two fields are now part of a vast housing and recreational complex but a line of hangars survives at Mitchel Field.

Nassau County allocated Numbers 3 and 4 for museum use along with associated buildings. The museum was set up in the early 1980s and soon acquired an impressive collection of aircraft. The exhibition closed in June 1995 so that a major rebuilding programme could start. The two display hangars were refurbished along with an adjoining one used by the police. They are now linked by a new structure which contains the main entrance.

This excellent exhibition opened in May 2002. Its aim is to trace the history of the airfields and companies on the island. There are many interesting displays to be seen. These trace the history of aviation on Long Island from the days of the early balloon flights.

Many famous manufacturers such as Fairchild, Grumman, Republic, Seversky and Sperry located their factories on the island. Grumman, until recently based at Bethpage, achieved fame with its naval fighters dating from XFF-1 of 1931 up to the recently withdrawn F-14 Tomcat. A rarity is the low-wing Kitten. This aircraft was designed for the post-World War II civil market. The tailwheel Kitten I took to the air in March 1944 and a tricycle version – the Kitten II – followed two years later. Neither model was put into production as there were many ex-military aircraft available for private owners.

The Seversky company was formed in 1931 and reorganised into the Republic Aviation Corporation in 1939. Classic aircraft from both firms have been acquired.

The Curtiss Jenny owned by the museum was Lindbergh's first aircraft. The Ace was the first type to be produced commercially after World War I for the civil market but only two were completed. First flown in 1919 the aircraft was designed for the Aircraft Engineering Company on Long Island. The sales manager Horace Keane took over the firm and built a few of a modified version. The Ace returned to Long Island from the Owl's Head Transportation Museum in Maine.

Only two Gyrodyne GCA-2s were built. The first flew in 1949 and the example in the collection took to the air seven years later. The design was a five seater helicopter powered by two Continental motors. The company later produced the single seat XRON-1 for the US Navy and the unmannned QH-50 flown from frigates.

TYPE	REG/SER	CON. NO.	PI/NOTES	STATUS
☐ Aircraft Engineering Company Ace	N69097	1		PV
☐ Bellanca Monoplane (R)	N1911G	2		PV
☐ Blériot XI		153		PV
☐ Boeing 707-458	4X-ATA	18070	Front fuselage only.	PV
☐ Breese Penguin	33622			PV
☐ Brewster B.239 Buffalo (F2A-2) (R)				PV
☐ Brunner-Winkle Bird A	NC78K	1067	NC78K, N78K	PV
☐ Cassutt B Special				PV
☐ Cessna 172			Front fuselage only.	PV
☐ Convair 340			Front fuselage only.	PV
☐ Convertawings A Quadrotor	N63N	101		PV
☐ Curtiss 1A Jenny (JN-4A)	1187			PV
☐ Curtiss 1C Jenny (JN-4D)			Fuselage only.	PV
☐ Curtiss 50C Robin C-1				RAC
☐ Douglas DC-3A-467 Skytrain (C-47D)			Front fuselage only.	PV
☐ Fairchild-Republic A-10A Thunderbolt II	76-0535	A10-82		PV
☐ Fairchild-Republic A-10A Thunderbolt II	77-0252	A10-177	Front fuselage only.	PV
☐ Fairchild-Republic NGT (T-46A)				PV
☐ Fleet 2	NC614M	190	NC614M, N614M,	PV
☐ Grumman G-21A Goose (OA-13A)	'NC16913'	1058	NC3021, 42-38214	PVX
☐ Grumman G-36 Wildcat (F4F-3)	Bu12297	5957		PV
☐ Grumman G-37 (F3F-2) (R)	'0968'			PVX
☐ Grumman G-40 Avenger (TBM-3) (TBM-3E)	Bu91586	4491	Bu91586, N9433Z	PV
☐ Grumman G-50 Hellcat (F6F-5) (F6F-5K)	Bu94263	A-12015		PV
☐ Grumman G-63 Kitten I	NX41858	1	NX41808	PV

New York

☐ Grumman G-93 Cougar (F9F-7) (F-9H)	Bu130763			PV
☐ Grumman G-98 Tiger (F11F-1) (F-11A)	Bu141832	149		PV
☐ Grumman G-123 Hawkeye (E-2C)	Bu160012	A34		PV
☐ Grumman G-123 Hawkeye (E-2C)			Front fuselage only.	PV
☐ Grumman G-128 Intruder (A-6E)			Front fuselage only.	PV
☐ Grumman G-128 Intruder (A-6F)	Bu162184	I-677		PV
☐ Gremman G-134 Mohawk (AO-1B) (OV-1B)	'0-12994'	13B	59-2633	PVX
☐ Grumman G-164 Ag-Cat		883		S
☐ Grumman G-303 Tomcat (YF-14A)	Bu157982	3		PV
☐ Grumman G-303 Tomcat (F-14A)	Bu159432	98	Front fuselage only.	PV
☐ Grumman G-303 Tomcat (F-14A)	Bu160899	328	Front fuselage only.	PV
☐ Gyrodyne GCA.2C	N6594K	1002		PV
☐ Gyrodyne QH-50C (DSN-3)		DS-1235		PV
☐ Gyrodyne XRON-1 (XHOG-1)	4014			PVX
☐ Herring-Curtiss 1 (R)				PV
☐ Langley Aerodrome 5 (R)				PV
☐ Lilienthal Normal-Segelapparat (R)				PV
☐ Merlin Hang Glider				PV
☐ Monnett Monerai S	N52SS	75		PV
☐ Paramotor FX-5				PV
☐ Peel Z-1 Glider Boat	N822W	15		PV
☐ Piper PA-28-140 Cherokee			Front fuselage only.	PV
☐ Rearwin 175 Skyranger	N92972	1705		PV
☐ Republic P-47N Thunderbolt	44-89444			PV
☐ Republic F-84B Thunderjet (P-84B)	45-59504			PV
☐ Republic F-84F Thunderstreak	51-9480			PV
☐ Republic F-105B Thunderchief	57-5783	B-20		PV
☐ Republic F-105D Thunderchief			Front fuselage only.	PV
☐ Republic JB-2 [Fieseler Fi 103A-1]	631			PV
☐ Republic RC-3 Seabee	N6461K	712	NC6461K	PV
☐ Rutan 73	N73RA	0001		S
☐ Ryan NYP (R) (B-1)	'N-X-211'	159	NC7212, N7212	PVX
☐ Savoia-Marchetti SM.56	NC349N	12		PV
☐ Sperry Aerial Torpedo (R)				PV
☐ Sperry-Verville M-1 Messenger (R)	'AS.22-328'			PVX
☐ Thomas-Morse S-4C	N1115	552	38934	PV
☐ Waco NZR Hadrian (CG-4A)	45-15574			PV
☐ Wright EX Vin Fiz (R)				PV

CUBA MONUMENT (NY15)

Location:	On permanent view at VFW 2721 at 305 North Shore Road about 2 miles north of the town.

TYPE	REG/SER	CON. NO.	PI/NOTES	STATUS
☐ Bell 205 Iroquois (UH-1H) (UH-1V)	70-15815	12425		PV

DART AIRPORT AVIATION MUSEUM (NY16)

Address: 6167 Plank Road, Mayville, New York 14757.
Tel: 716-753-2160
Admission: April–October Tuesday-Sunday 1000-1700.
Location: About 2 miles east of the town off Route 430.

The airfield has been in existence for over 50 years and for a quarter of a century was owned by the late Bob Dart. His family and friends are continuing with the project.

Around 50 classic aircraft and gliders reside in the hangars. The airfield has many attractions including joy rides in aircraft and gliders, fly-ins and a weekly flea market in summer. A building that was formerly used by an engineering company has been turned into the museum. In addition to the aircraft there are displays of engines, models, photographs, documents and memorabilia.

On show are a number of homebuilt aircraft including a few whose origins are not known. They have been donated to the museum by people who have come across them in their travels around the region.

TYPE	REG/SER	CON. NO.	PI/NOTES	STATUS
☐ Aaaro Aeroncopy C3L-65	N106DC	101		PV
☐ Bell 204 Iroquois (UH-1C) (UH-1M)	64-14179	1303		PV
☐ Bensen B-6 Gyroglider				PV
☐ Bensen B-8M Gyrocopter				PV
☐ Bensen B-8M Gyrocopter				PV
☐ Bowers Fly Baby 1A Biplane				PV
☐ Briegleb BG-7				PV
☐ Champion 7ECA Citabria	N6397N	356		PV
☐ Corben D Junior Ace	N8696R	1		PV
☐ Corben E Junior Ace	N7222D	RGD47		PV
☐ Curtiss-Wright CW-1 Junior				PVD
☐ Dart BAC-2 [Bensen B-8M Gyrocopter]	N8823	1002		PV
☐ Dart CW-3	N12306	1		PV
☐ Dart CW-3	N12324	2		PV
☐ Dart JN-4D	N3929X	X2939		PV
☐ Dart Special	N27128	2005-2		PV
☐ Dart Special	N2067H	3		PV
☐ Dart ULA-1 Skycycle	NC1371K	RDES-001		PV
☐ Elliott GE-2	N25071	GE2		PV
☐ Ercoupe 415C				PV
☐ Ercoupe 415C	NC99643	2566	NC99643, N99643	PV

☐ Ferguson Monoplane				PV
☐ Fleet 16B Finch II				PV
☐ Hatz CB-1	N148GD	148		PV
☐ Heath Super Parasol				PV
☐ Heath Super Parasol	NC4834T	99Z		PV
☐ Henderson Power				PV
☐ Homebuilt Helicopter				PV
☐ Homebuilt Helicopter	N6277H			PV
☐ Homebuilt Monoplane				PVD
☐ Homebuilt Monoplane				PV
☐ Hughes 369M Cayuse (HO-6) (OH-6A)	65-12949	0034		PV
☐ Hughes 369M Cayuse (HO-6) (OH-6A)	67-16208	0593		PV
☐ Laister-Kauffman LK.10A	N52181	108		PV
☐ Long Henderson Longster (R)				PV
☐ Martin Sport Plane	N9647H	1		PV
☐ Maxair Drifter				PV
☐ Mead Rhön Ranger				PV
☐ Mignet HM-14 Pou-du-Ciel				PV
☐ Nesmith Cougar	N1112V	C-1		PV
☐ Nieuport 11 (R)				PV
☐ Piel CP.301C Emeraude			Incomplete.	PV
☐ Piper J-2 Cub				PV
☐ Piper J-3C-65 Cub	N3592N	22839	NC3592N	RAA
☐ Piper J-3C-65 Cub	N40763	7476	NC40763	PV
☐ Piper J-4A Cub Coupe	N25993	4-829	NC25993	PV
☐ Royal Aircraft Factory S.E.5A (R)				PV
☐ Schweizer SGS.2-12 (TG-3A)				PV
☐ Schweizer SGU.2-22	N91851	23		RAA
☐ Slingsby T.56 [Royal Aircraft Factory S.E.5A (R)]	N912AC	1594	G-AVOX, EI-ARM, 'A5435, 'A1313'	PV
☐ Smith DSA-1 Miniplane	N18B	LK-1		PV
☐ Stevens Jet			Incomplete.	PV
☐ Stits SA-6B Flut-R-Bug	N59255	P-2047		PV
☐ Taylorcraft BC-12D	N96588	8888	NC96588	PV
☐ Ultralight Flying Machines Easy Riser				PV
☐ Volmer Jensen VJ-22 Sportsman	N2921	206		PV
☐ Volmer Jensen VJ-23				PV

DERUYTER MONUMENT (NY17)

Location:	On permanent view at ALP 894 in the town.			

TYPE	REG/SER	CON. NO.	PI/NOTES	STATUS
☐ Bell 205 Iroquois (UH-1H)				PV

EAST AURORA MONUMENT (NY18)

Location:	On permanent view at ALP362 on Center Street in the town.			

TYPE	REG/SER	CON. NO.	PI/NOTES	STATUS
☐ Bell 205 Iroquois (UH-1H)	67-17798	9996		PV
☐ Republic F-84F Thunderstreak	51-1748			PV

EAST COAST SKYTYPERS (NY19)

Address:	Atlantic Aviation, Route 109, Farmingdale Airport, New York 11735.
Tel:	888-759-8273 Fax: 631-350-1583
Admission:	By prior permission only.
Location:	At Republic Airport which is about 2 miles east of the town on Route 24.

Skytypers was set up in 1932 when the Pepsi Cola company wanted to promote is product. A fleet of early model Texans is currently in use. The aircraft carry out advertising sorties at many locations along the east coast.

TYPE	REG/SER	CON. NO.	PI/NOTES	STATUS
☐ North American NA-65 Texan (SNJ-2)	N52900	65-1999	Bu2010, NC52900	RAA
☐ North American NA-65 Texan (SNJ-2)	N60734	65-2021	Bu2032, NC60734	RAA
☐ North American NA-65 Texan (SNJ-2)	N62382	65-2028	Bu2039, NX62382	RAA
☐ North American NA-78 Texan (AT-6A) (SNJ-3)	N7648E	78-6987	41-16609, Bu01882, NC64299, XB-XYZ-923, 7648 (South Africa), N733RE	RAA
☐ North American NA-79 Texan (SNJ-2)	N58224	79-3988	Bu2553, NC58224	RAA
☐ North American NA-79 Texan (SNJ-2)	N65370	79-3997	Bu2562, NC65370	RAA

EDEN MONUMENT (NY20)

Location:	On permanent view at ALP 880 at 2912 Legion Drive in the northern part of the town.			

TYPE	REG/SER	CON. NO.	PI/NOTES	STATUS
☐ Bell 209 Huey Cobra (AH-1G) (AH-1F)	67-15506	20170		PV

New York

EMPIRE STATE AEROSCIENCES MUSEUM (NY21)

Address:	250 Rudy Chase Drive, Glenville, New York 12302.
Tel:	518-377-2191 Fax: 518-377-1959 Email: esam@esam.org
Admission:	Friday-Saturday 1000-1600; Sunday 1200-1600. Mid June–August also open Wednesday-Thursday 1000-1600.
Location:	At Schenectady County Airport which is about 2 miles north of Scotia on Route 50.

The museum was formed in 1984 and acquired a ten-acre plot at the airport. Aviation in New York State has played an important part in the life of the people. Many aircraft manufacturing companies had factories in the region and there are still a number of active military bases in the state. Major civil airports and general aviation fields along with private airstrips are also located in New York. The museum aims to highlight these contributions. An indoor display has on show models, photographs and artefacts. The main hangar was formerly used by the General Electric company and served as the main base for their engine test-beds. Two small hangars have been erected and are used for restoration and storage.

The collection includes a number of interesting homebuilt machines. In 1910 the then 19-year-old John von Pomer built a biplane based on the Curtiss D Pusher.

The Strat was designed by Mischa Kantor, a Russian born engineer, who was trained by the Messerschmitt company.

After arriving in the USA he worked for North American and Luscombe. The low-wing four-seater, powered by a 150 h.p. Franklin engine, first flew in 1949.

The Huntington Chum high-wing featured side-by-side seating. It was designed in the early 1930s and restored in the 1980s. The replica of the 1922 De Pischoff Biplane was built in the 1970s by a group of students at Ruburn in New York. A converted Volkswagen engine was fitted.

The Murray JN-2D-1 is a scale replica of the famous Curtiss Jenny biplane. The example on show was in the EAA Airventure Museum at Oshkosh for several years. A number of modern homebuilt types have been added to the display. The Lockheed Electra fuselage was built for use in a film.

The majority of the military types are displayed in the outside aircraft park and include a former Indian Air Force Folland Gnat, two ex Polish Air Force MiG fighters and a range of types flown by all branches of the American military.

TYPE	REG/SER	CON. NO.	PI/NOTES	STATUS
☐ Aeronca 65LB Chief	N33725	L-13001	NC33725	RAC
☐ Bell 204 Iroquois (UH-1C) (UH-1M)	65-9435	1335	Boom from c/n 10553 68-15623	PV
☐ Bell 205 Iroquois (UH-1D) (UH-1H)	64-13513	4220		PV
☐ Brown Star-Lite	N170BH	170		PV
☐ Chanute Glider				PV
☐ Convair 8-10 Delta Dagger (F-102A)	56-1365	8-10-582		PV
☐ De Pischoff Biplane (R)	N183	001		PV
☐ Douglas A-4F Skyhawk	Bu155009	13825		PV
☐ Fairchild-Republic A-10A Thunderbolt II	75-0263	A10-12		PV
☐ Fisher FP-303				PV
☐ Folland Fo.141 Gnat F.1	E315		In Indian markings.	PV
☐ Grumman G-89 Tracker (S2F-1) (S2F-1T) (TS-2A)	Bu133264	235S		PV
☐ Grumman G-128 Intruder (A-6A) (A-6E)	Bu152935	I-239		PV
☐ Grumman G-303 Tomcat (F-14A)	Bu160411	267		PV
☐ Hughes 369M Cayuse (HO-6) (OH-6A)	68-17343	1303		PV
☐ Kantor Strat M-21	NX74106	101		RA
☐ Lockheed 10-E Electra (FSM)	'16020'		Fuselage only.	PVX
☐ Lockheed 382-4B Hercules (EC-130E) (HC-130E)	1414	382-4158	66-4299 – front fuselage only.	PV
☐ McDonnell M.36BA Voodoo (TF-101B) (TF-101F)	59-0413	737		PV
☐ McDonnell M.98EN Phantom II (F-4D)	65-0626	1588		PV
☐ Mikoyan-Gurevich MiG-21PF	2406	762406	In Polish markings.	PV
☐ Monnett Sonerai II	N38HC	00191		PV
☐ Mooney M-18LA Mite	N4089	128		PV
☐ Murray JN-2D-1	N1005Z	101		PV
☐ North American NA-316 Vigilante (RA-5C)	Bu156621	316-14	.	PV
☐ North American NA-318 Buckeye (T-2C)	Bu156730	318-45	.	PV
☐ Northrop N-311 Tiger II (F-5E)	Bu162307	R.1191	74-1533	PV
☐ Peterson J-4 Javelin	N7976S	002		RA
☐ Rand Robinson KR-2	N20463	3234		PV
☐ Rensselaer Polytechnic Institute RP-1	N8482U	001		PV
☐ Republic F-84F Thunderstreak	51-1620			PV
☐ Republic F-105G Thunderchief (F-105F)	62-4444	F-33		PV
☐ Stits SA-7D Skycoupe	N3834	P-328		PV
☐ Stockwell Chum (Huntington Chum)	NX707Y	1	NX741Y	PV
☐ Stoddard-Hamilton SH-4 GlaStar IIR2	'0-159001'	494R	N580GS	PVX
☐ Von Pomer Pusher				PV
☐ Vought A-7E Corsair II	Bu160613	E537		PV
☐ Wallis WA.116/6-1	N135A			PV
☐ WSK Lim-5 [MiG-17F]	605	1C 06-05	In Polish markings.	PV

FRANKLINVILLE MONUMENT (NY22)

Location:	On permanent view at VFW 9487 at 2027 Cemetery Hill Road about 2 miles east of the town.

TYPE	REG/SER	CON. NO.	PI/NOTES	STATUS
☐ Bell 209 Huey Cobra (AH-1S) (AH-1F)	78-23097	22203		PV

GENESEE WARBIRDS (NY23)

Address:	16 West Main Street, Suite 310, Rochester, New York 14614.
Tel:	585-234-5257 Email: info@genesseewarbirds.org
Admission:	By prior permission only.
Location:	At Batavia Airport which is about 3 miles north of the town. On Route 98.

The aim of this collection is to maintain classic jets in flying condition. All the types originate from Europe and trained generations of military pilots. Four former Spanish Air Force Saetas are flying and another is in the workshops. The Lim-2 has recently been transported across the country from Reno in Nevada.

TYPE	REG/SER	CON. NO.	PI/NOTES	STATUS
☐ Aero L-29 Delfin				RAA
☐ British Aircraft Corporation 167 Strikemaster 84	N2146G	EEP/JP/1928	308 (Singapore)	RAA
☐ De Havilland DH.100 Vampire F.3	N6878D	EEP.42390	(VP773(	RA
☐ De Havilland DH.115 Vampire T.55	N172LA		BY385 (India)	RAA
☐ Fouga CM.170-2 Magister (CM.170A)	NX19JV	39	FM-39 (Finland)	RAA
☐ Hispano HA.200A Saeta (HA.200R1)	N607HA	20/12	E.14A-7	RAA
☐ Hispano HA.200A Saeta (HA.200R1)	N631HA	20/26	E.14A-31	RAA
☐ Hispano HA.200A Saeta (HA.200R1)	N922BB	20/30	E.14A-22, N622HA, N9170J, N922SP	RAC
☐ Hispano HA.200B Saeta				RAA
☐ Hispano HA.200B Saeta				RAA
☐ Hispano HA.200D Saeta	N3180T	20/91	E.14B-85, C.10B-85, A.10B-85	RAA
☐ WSK SBLim-2 (Lim-1) [MiG-15]	N7800W	1A 06-011	011	RAC

GLENN H. CURTISS MUSEUM (NY24)

Address: 8419 State Route 54, Hammondsport, New York 14840.
Tel: 607-569-2160   **Fax:** 607-569-2040
Admission: May–October Monday-Saturday 0900-1700; Sunday 1000-1700: November–April Monday-Saturday 1000-1600; Sunday 1000-1600.
Location: About ½ mile south of the town which is at the southern end of Lake Keuka.

Glenn Curtiss was born in Hammondsport in May 1878 and whilst still in his teens he opened a cycle shop in the town. By the turn of the century he had commenced motorcycle manufacture and he gained fame with racing successes. In 1907 he joined Alexander Graham Bell's Aerial Experiment Association and the following year they tested aircraft at Hammondsport. In 1909 Curtiss set up his own firm and soon his aeroplanes won world-wide recognition. He died in 1930 but companies producing aircraft bearing his name were in existence until 1947. The museum was set up in 1960 by local residents who renovated a former school building in the town. The displays traced all aspects of local life with exhibitions of farm machinery, fire engines, cars, cycles, toys and every day items from the turn of the century. Examples of aircraft designed by Curtiss were collected and restored.

The space available for the exhibition was small and in the early 1990s a move was made to a derelict wine store on the edge of town. The building was refurbished and an excellent exhibition is now staged.

The Curtiss aircraft on view start with a replica of the 1908 AEA 'June Bug' and includes a Pusher, a Jenny, an Oriole and a Robin. A replica of an E flying boat was built in the workshops in the late 1990s using the hull of one loaned by the NASM as pattern.

A major project, which was completed in 2007, was the building of the replica NC-4 flying boat. The 72-foot span biplane was transported to a nearby lake where it flew for the first time on 13th September 2008.

Curtiss left Hammondsport to move to Buffalo in 1917 where a vast factory was built. The Warhawk fighter was built in large numbers during World War II and a three-quarters scale replica built in Canada is now on show. The Commando loaned by the National Air and Space Museum is parked outside the building.

The Aerial Service Corporation, later to become Mercury Aircraft, moved into Hammondsport. On show is a 1929 Chic, which was unsold by the company and then donated to the museum. Another product of the company, the 1931 White Racer can also be seen. A few types from other companies are also on show. The Standard J-1 first flew in 1916 and just over 1,600 were produced for use by Army Flying Schools around the country.

TYPE	REG/SER	CON. NO.	PI/NOTES	STATUS
☐ Aerial Experiment Association Glider (R)				PV
☐ Aerial Experiment Association June Bug II (R)	N1908C	MAJB-001		PV
☐ Aerial Experiment Association Silver Dart (R)		3		PV
☐ Baldwin Airship (R)			Gondola only.	PVA
☐ Curtiss A-1 (R)	N511GC	002		PVA
☐ Curtiss D Pusher (R)	NR10362	1	On loan from Curtiss-Wright Corporation.	PV
☐ Curtiss D Pusher (R)	N2120	EC-1		PV
☐ Curtiss E (R)	N1913E	001		PV
☐ Curtiss Albany Flyer (R)		001		PVA
☐ Curtiss 1C Jenny (JN-4D)	5086			PV
☐ Curtiss H-1 (R)				PV
☐ Curtiss 12 (NC-4) (R)	N914GC	1		PVA
☐ Curtiss 17 Oriole	N853	559		PV
☐ Curtiss 25 Seagull (MF)	257		A4411 – on loan from Ford Museum, MI.	PV
☐ Curtiss 50B Robin B	NC924KS	511	NC924K	PV
☐ Curtiss 51 Fledgling				PV
☐ Curtiss 87-A4 Warhawk (P-40E) (Scale R)				PV
☐ Curtiss-Wright CW-1 Junior	N683V	1065	NC683V	PV
☐ Curtiss-Wright CW-1 Junior				PV
☐ Curtiss-Wright CW-20B-4 Commando (C-46F)	N800FA	22595	44-78772, N67996, N614Z, CF-ZQX – on loan from NASM, DC.	PV
☐ Mercury Chic T-2	N53N	82	NC53N	PV
☐ Mercury S-1 White Racer	X13223	52		PV
☐ Putzer/Raab Doppleraab				PV
☐ Royal Aircraft Factory S.E.5A (Scale R)	'N9841'			PVX
☐ Standard J-1	N823H		NC823H, 41236 – on loan from Ford Museum, MI.	PV
☐ Travel Air D-4D Speedwing	NC477C	1379	NC477V, N477V	PV
☐ War Aircraft P-40	'68'	001		PVX

A number of aircraft, including this Kaman HH-43B Huskie, are still parked outside the closed Rescue Heritage Hall at Kirtland Air Force Base. [NM12]

This Bell UH-1C flown on range duties is now preserved at the White Sands Missile Range Museum. [NM26]

On show at the 82nd Airborne Division War Memorial Museum is this Fairchild C-123K Provider. [NC1]

GOWANDA MONUMENT (NY25)

Location:	On permanent view at ALP 409 at 100 Legion Drive just east of the town centre.

TYPE	REG/SER	CON. NO.	PI/NOTES	STATUS
☐ Bell 205 Iroquois (UH-1H)	67-17611	9809		PV

GRIFFISS AIR FORCE BASE MEMORIAL DISPLAY (NY26)

Address:	325 Erie Boulevard West, Rome, New York 13441.
Tel:	315-336-2680 **Email:** post24@borg.com
Admission:	By prior permission only.
Location:	About 1 mile north east of Rome off Route 46.

Opened as Rome Air Depot in 1942, the site took up its present title in January 1948 and was named after Lieutenant Colonel Townsend E. Griffiss who was mistakenly shot down in England in February 1942. The last operational aircraft left the base on 15th November 1994 and at the current time the site is home to the Rome Laboratory.

The B-52 on show arrived at Griffiss on 12th January 1960. It was withdrawn from use in May 1991 and placed on display. Members of a local veterans' post have taken over responsibility for the aircraft and are constructing a memorial around it. A number of military vehicles will be put on view.

TYPE	REG/SER	CON. NO.	PI/NOTES	STATUS
☐ Boeing 464-253 Stratofortress (B-52G)	58-0225	464293		PV

GRUMMAN MEMORIAL PARK AND AEROSPACE MUSEUM (NY27)

Address:	Box 147, Calverton, New York 11983.
Tel:	631-369-9488 **Fax:** 631-369-9489 **Email:** grummanpk@aol.com
Admission:	Daily 0900-1700.
Location:	About 2 miles east of the town on Route 25.

This park has been set up at Calverton Airport which was the site of a new Grumman plant opened in 1952, 40 miles from the main factory at Bethpage.

The display, with a Calverton built Tomcat as centrepiece, was unveiled on 28th October 2000. The F-14 is the last of a long line of Grumman fighters produced for the US Navy. The prototype made its maiden flight in December 1970 and 712 aircraft were completed with a batch going to Iran in the mid-1970s. The type was withdrawn from frontline service in America in September 2006. The Intruder was allocated in late 2006. This twin jet attack aircraft was designed to replace the Douglas Skyraider in Marine and Navy service. The A-6 was in use between 1963 and 1997.

A genuine Grumman guard shack is by the entrance to the car park. A small piece of the runway from Bethpage has been moved to the site. There are long-term plans to construct a museum and visitor centre and obtain more aircraft.

TYPE	REG/SER	CON. NO.	PI/NOTES	STATUS
☐ Grumman G-128 Intruder (A-6E)	Bu164384	I-724	.	PV
☐ Grumman G-303 Tomcat (F-14A)	Bu160902	331	.	PV

HAMBURG MONUMENT (NY28)

Location:	On permanent view at VFW 1419 at 2985 Lakeview Road in the north eastern part of the town.

TYPE	REG/SER	CON. NO.	PI/NOTES	STATUS
☐ Bell 209 Huey Cobra (AH-1G) (AH-1F)	69-16446	20878		PV
☐ Douglas A-4E Skyhawk (A4D-5)	Bu149977	13030		PV

HAMILTON COUNTY SEAPLANE MUSEUM (NY29)

Address:	Piseco Airport, Old Piseco Road, Piseco, New York 12139.
Tel:	518-548-8794 (Airport)
Admission:	Daily 0800-1600.
Location:	About 3 miles north west of the town which is about 40 miles north east of Utica.

The region has many lakes and several of these are regularly used by seaplanes and amphibians. The displays, mainly of photographs, trace the history of this form of flying over the years. A number of interesting aircraft are based at the field.

Also on show are models, documents, and items of memorabilia. Tourist seaplane flights over the picturesque region are offered by a number of companies.

HENDERSON MONUMENT (NY30)

Location:	On permanent view at a Veterans Memorial on Route 3 about 2 miles south of the town.

TYPE	REG/SER	CON. NO.	PI/NOTES	STATUS
☐ Bell 209 Huey Cobra (AH-1G) (AH-1F)	71-21033	21104		PV

HINSDALE MONUMENT (NY31)

Location:	On permanent view at ALP 1434 on Highway 16 south of the town centre.

TYPE	REG/SER	CON. NO.	PI/NOTES	STATUS
☐ McDonnell M.98AM Phantom II (F4H-1) (F-4B)	Bu149457	174		PV

New York

HISTORIC AIRCRAFT RESTORATION PROJECT (NY32)

Address:	Building 69, Floyd Bennett Field, Brooklyn, New York 11234-7097.
Tel:	718-338-5986 Email: harpfb@hotmail.com
Admission:	Tuesday, Thursday, Saturday 0900-1700.
Location:	On Flatbush Avenue off the Belt Parkway.

Floyd Bennett Field, built in the 1930s, was the first municipal airport for the city of New York. The site became a Naval Air Station in 1941 and served in this role until it closed in the 1960s.

The airfield and a number of surrounding sites became part of the Gateway National Recreation Area in 1972. One of the features of the park is the nature reserve which is home to several species of rare plants and a variety of wildlife. A number of walks around this area have been created.

A new museum tracing the aviation history of the airfield is being set up. This project started in 1995 and the society was formed soon afterwards. The historic hangars will be restored in the future. The C-47, which was for some time on show at Stout Field in Indiana, was the first aircraft to arrive. This has now been joined by several others including the Catalina, a type which was frequently seen at the field in the 1940s and 1950s.

The US Coast Guard maintains a station at the site and the HH-3 was restored by members of the service. The Albatross also flew with the Guard from a number of bases. The Goose served for many years with the Department of the Interior in Alaska after its naval service.

TYPE	REG/SER	CON. NO.	PI/NOTES	STATUS
☐ Beech D18S Expeditor (C18S) (C-45F) (UC-45F) (JRB-4) (SNB-5)	Bu90536	6999	44-47109, Bu90536, N9659	PV
☐ Boeing-Stearman E75 Kaydet (PT-13D) (N2S-5)	N1922M	75-8675	42-109642, Bu43581	PV
☐ Consolidated 28-5A Catalina (PBY-5A)	N4582T	1820	Bu46456, 6509 (Brazil)	PVC
☐ Douglas DC-3A-467 Skytrain (C-47B)	44-76457	16041/32789		PV
☐ Douglas A-4B Skyhawk (A4D-2)	Bu142829	11891	Bu142829, 'Bu144992'	PV
☐ Fairchild M-62A-4 Cornell (PT-26B) (Cornell II)	N1321V		43-36278, 10781 (Canada), FZ228	PVC
☐ Grumman G-21A Goose (G-39) (JRF-5)	N644R	B130	Bu87736	PV
☐ Grumman G-121 Tracker (S-2E)	Bu151664	197C	.	PV
☐ Grumman G-234 Albatross (G-64) (SA-16A) (UF-1G) (UF-2G) (HU-16E)	7216	G-292	51-7216	PV
☐ Lockheed 426-45-15 Neptune (P2V-5) (P2V-5F) (P2V-5FS) (SP-2E)	Bu131542	426-5423	.	PV
☐ Sikorsky S-61R Pelican (HH-3F)	1434	61599		PV
☐ Wright Flyer (R)				PV

HMM-361 VETERANS ASSOCIATION (NY33)

Address:	PO Box 429, Cutchogue, New York 11935-0429.
Tel:	631-827-5526 Email: ajweiss@34restoration.org
Admission:	By prior permission only.
Location:	On private property near Jamesport which is about 6 miles east of Riverhead on Route 22.

The unit was formed in California in 1952 and became HMM-361 when Marine Corps helicopter squadrons were redesignated. Service in the Cuban missile crisis and Vietnam followed. The Seahorse was flown in the latter conflict. A group of personnel who once served with HMM-361 have restored the UH-34D to flying condition.

The S-58 was moved from Arizona where it had been in store. Members of the group took four years to complete the task and the helicopter took to the air again in November 2005. Now resplendent in the colours it wore during the conflict the aircraft has been seen at many shows in the area and at veterans reunions.

TYPE	REG/SER	CON. NO.	PI/NOTES	STATUS
☐ Sikorsky S-58 Seahorse (HUS-1) (UH-34D)	N19YN	581699	Bu150570, N4218K	RAA

INTREPID AIR-SEA-SPACE MUSEUM (NY34)

Address:	Intrepid Square, West 46th Street and 12th Avenue, New York 10036-4103.
Tel:	212-245-0072 Fax: 212-957-7044 Email: jzukowsky@intrepidmuseum.org
Admission:	October–March Tuesday-Sunday 1000-1700; April–September Monday-Friday 1000-1700, Saturday-Sunday 1000-1800.
Location:	On the west side of Manhattan at Pier 86.

The *Intrepid* was one of 24 Essex class carriers built. Work started on the ship six days before the Japanese attack on Pearl Harbor and the carrier served with distinction in the Pacific during World War II. In the 1960s she took part in the recovery of the early astronauts and served for three tours in the Vietnam War.

Retired in 1974, the ship was stored before being donated to the Intrepid Museum Foundation in December 1980. The carrier was towed to Bayonne for conversion to a museum and docked at Pier 86 in June 1982. Now it has been joined by the Nantucket lightship, the fleet destroyer *Edson*, the submarine *Growler*, the escort destroyer *Slater* and the research ship *Elizabeth M. Fisher*. A new addition is the helicopter carrier *Guadalcanal* which from 1997 has served as a public heliport and museum ship berthed next to the *Intrepid*. The complex now regards itself as the largest naval museum in the world.

The hangar deck of the *Intrepid* is divided into four halls. These are the Pioneer Hall, the US Navy Hall, the *Intrepid* Hall and the Technologies Hall. In all areas informative displays have been staged and aircraft are on show on this deck.

The majority of the aircraft are parked on the flight deck and include machines from all four services. A few types operated by foreign services have been acquired to enhance the display. The Dassault Etendard first flew in 1956 and was the company's entry in a contest for a NATO competition for a light fighter. The competition was won by the Fiat G.91 and the French Navy ordered 90 in two versions to serve on their carriers. The Israeli Kfir was developed from the Dassault Mirage V. Several versions were built and the type gave excellent service for many years. The US Navy and Marines loaned 25 for training in the late 1980s.

The display closed in late 2006 and the ship was moved away for a major restoration. The exhibition reopened in 2009 with many new displays in the hangar deck. The *Intrepid* is home to one of the two former British Airways Concorde supersonic airliners displayed in the USA.

TYPE	REG/SER	CON. NO.	PI/NOTES	STATUS
☐ Aermacchi MB.339A	'MM54476'	6640/037	MM54461	PVX
☐ Aérospatiale / British Aircraft Corporation Concorde 102	G-BOAD	100-010	G-BOAD, G-N94AD	PV
☐ Beech A45 Mentor (T-34A)	N34Z	G.283	53-4183, N4934E	PV
☐ Bell 204 Iroquois (HU-1A) (UH-1A)	59-1621	80		PV
☐ Bell 209 Huey Cobra (AH-1G) (AH-1S)	70-15956	20900		PV
☐ Bell 209 Sea Cobra (AH-1J)	Bu159218	26058		PV
☐ Dassault Etendard IVM	60	60		PV
☐ Douglas TF-10B Skynight (F3D-2) (F3D-2T)	Bu127074	8132		PV
☐ Douglas A-4B Skyhawk (A4D-2)	Bu142833	11895	.	PV
☐ General Dynamics 401 Fighting Falcon (F-16A)	79-0403	61-188		PV
☐ Grumman G-40 Avenger (TBM-1)	Bu24803			PV
☐ Grumman G-98 Tiger (F11F-1) (F-11A)	Bu141884	201	.	PV
☐ Grumman G-99 Cougar (F9F-8) (F-9J)	Bu141117	364C	.	PV
☐ Grumman G-117 Tracer (WF-2) (E-1B)	Bu147212	11	.	RA
☐ Grumman G-128 Intruder (A-6F) (A-6DSD)	Bu162185	I-678	.	PV
☐ Grumman G-303 Tomcat (YF-14A) (YF-14B) (YF-14D)	Bu157986	7	.	PV
☐ Hawker-Siddeley P.1127 Harrier 50 (AV-8A) (AV-8C)	Bu159232	P141		PV
☐ Israeli Aircraft Industries Kfir C.1 (F-21A)	999734			PV
☐ Lockheed A-12	60-6925	122		PV
☐ McDonnell M.58 Demon (F3H-2N) (F-3C)	Bu133566	78	.	PV
☐ McDonnell M.98AM Phantom II (F4H-1) (F-4B) (F-4N)	Bu150628	286	.	PV
☐ Mikoyan-Gurevich MiG-15	'624'		In false North Korean markings.	PVX
☐ Mikoyan-Gurevich MiG-21PFM	4105	94A4105	In Polish markings.	PV
☐ North American NA-194 Fury (FJ-3) (F-1C)	Bu135868	194-95	.	PV
☐ Piasecki PV-18 Retriever (HUP-2) (UH-25B)	Bu128519		Bu128519, N8SA	PV
☐ Sikorsky S-55D (HO4S-3G)	1308	55729	1308, N16861	PV
☐ Sikorsky S-62A Seaguard (HH-52A)	1429	62117		PV
☐ Supermarine 544 Scimitar F.1	XD220			PV
☐ Vought F-8J Crusader (F8U-2NE) (F-8E)	Bu145550			PV
☐ WSK Lim-5 [MiG-17F]	'0327'		In false North Vietnamese markings.	PVX

IRA G ROSS AEROSPACE MUSEUM (NY35)

Address: HSBC Arena, 1 Seymour H Knox III Plaza, Buffalo, New York 14203.
Tel: 716-858-4340 **Email:** info@wnyaerospace.org
Admission: End May–mid June Saturday-Sunday 1100-1600; mid-June–August Thursday-Sunday 1100-1600.
Location: Near the Convention Center.

This museum opened on 16th May 1998 in premises in a shopping mall. The collection moved to a larger building in November 2002 and has recently transferred the exhibition to a temporary site near the waterfront.

At the current time the majority of the aircraft are in store at the old Bell plant. The Bell Aircraft Corporation had a major factory at the airport which is about a mile from the museum. The company set up a plant at Niagara Falls in 1940 and during World War II many aircraft were produced there and at the nearby Buffalo complex.

Two products of the company are on view. The company was one of the pioneers in helicopter development and the prototype 30 flew on December 1942. The famous 47 was built at the Niagara Falls factory and made its maiden flight on 8th December 1945. Over 5,000 variants were constructed in the USA, England, Italy and Japan. Two versions are on show – the fifth example built and an early B model delivered to Argentina in 1947. Two others are in store. The X-22A V/STOL design with twin ducted propellers dates from 1965

and the two prototypes were the last aircraft to be built at Niagara Falls. The first made its maiden flight in March 1966 and crashed the following August. The second took to the air in August 1967 but the programme was soon cancelled. The surviving X-22A moved to the Cornell Aeronautical Laboratory for further tests and last flew in 1988.

The General Aircraft company took over the former Fokker plant and produced a small number of all metal low wing monoplanes. The unique GA-36 is a prized exhibit. The all-metal low wing monoplane started life as the GA-21 side-by-side two seater. Over the next few years the airframe was modified several times. The final version, the GA-36, was a tandem two-seater.

The Airacobra, one of many supplied to the Soviet Union, was lifted from a Russian lake by a British recovery team and now resides in a workshop where restoration has started. Hopefully the museum will soon obtain a site where it can display its interesting collection.

TYPE	REG/SER	CON. NO.	PI/NOTES	STATUS
☐ Bell 26E Airacobra (P-39Q)	23		44-2911 – in Soviet markings.	RAC
☐ Bell 47	NC3H	5	On loan from Buffalo and Erie CHS, NY.	PV
☐ Bell 47B-3	LV-AEF	67		PV
☐ Bell 47H-1	N996B	1349		RA
☐ Bell 47H-1	N2818B	1370		RA
☐ Bell 205 Iroquois (UH-1D) (UH-1H)	65-9839	4883		RA
☐ Bell 209 Huey Cobra (AH-1G) (AH-1F)	67-15690	20354		RA
☐ Bell D2127 (X-22A)	Bu151521			RA
☐ Cunningham-Hall GA-36	X14324	211	.	RA
☐ Curtiss A Pusher (R)	N4124A	2	On loan from Rhinebeck AM, NY.	PV
☐ Curtiss 1C Jenny (JN-4D)	N3409D	MSC-1		RA
☐ Lockheed 780-76-12 Starfire (F-94A)	49-2500	780-7022		RA
☐ Pietenpol B4-A Aircamper				RA
☐ Pitts S-1C Special				RA
☐ Republic F-84E Thunderjet	49-2285			RA
☐ Schweizer SGS.1-23HM	N94298	70	On loan from NSM, NY.	RA

New York

JOHNSTOWN MONUMENT (NY36)

Location:	On permanent view at Fulton County Airport which is about 3 miles south east of the town.

TYPE	REG/SER	CON. NO.	PI/NOTES	STATUS
☐ Douglas XA-3 Skywarrior (XA3D-1)	Bu125413	7589		PV

L. A. WILSON TECHNICAL CENTER (NY37)

Address:	7200 Republic Airport, Farmingdale, New York 11735.
Tel:	631-261-3600 Email: webmaster@wsboces.org
Admission:	By prior permission only.
Location:	At Republic Airport which is about 2 miles east of the town on Route 24.

The college has operated Aviation Maintenance Technician courses for over 30 years. At least four instructional airframes and a number of engines are known to reside in the workshops. Courses are also run for private pilots so that they can carry out basic maintenance on their aircraft. A ground school for student pilots also takes place with instruction in the principles of flight and meteorology.

TYPE	REG/SER	CON. NO.	PI/NOTES	STATUS
☐ Aero Commander 680V	N87BT	1705-81	N87D	RA
☐ Bell 205 Iroquois (UH-1H)	68-15362	10292		RA
☐ Cessna 310A Blue Canoe (L-27A) (U-3A)	N31612	38153	58-2179 – possible identity.	RA
☐ North American NA-88 Texan (AT-6C)				RA

LEONARD COLLECTION (NY38)

Address:	102 Hall Hill Road, Parksville, New York 12768-5002.
Admission:	By prior permission only.
Location:	About 1 mile north east of the town.

This private collection of militaria contains military vehicles, tanks, artillery and memorabilia. The owner also has a range of weapons, uniforms and badges along with maps, documents and photographs. Two widely used helicopters have arrived at the site and fixed wing aircraft are being sought to enhance the display.

TYPE	REG/SER	CON. NO.	PI/NOTES	STATUS
☐ Bell 205 Iroquois (UH-1D) (UH-1H)	65-12880	5213		RA
☐ Hughes 269A Osage (TH-55A)	68-18???			RA

LONG ISLAND CITY MONUMENT (NY39)

Location:	On permanent view in the Cockpit store at 4818 Northern Boulevard in the city.

TYPE	REG/SER	CON. NO.	PI/NOTES	STATUS
☐ North American NA-88 Texan (AT-6D)				PV

LOWVILLE MONUMENT (NY40)

Location:	On permanent view at Marine Corps League 754 on Route 12 in the western part of the town.

TYPE	REG/SER	CON. NO.	PI/NOTES	STATUS
☐ Bell 209 Huey Cobra (AH-1G) (AH-1F)	68-17074	20802		PV

LYONS MONUMENT (NY41)

Location:	On permanent view at VFW 5092 at 202 Geneva Street about 1 mile south of the town.

TYPE	REG/SER	CON. NO.	PI/NOTES	STATUS
☐ Bell 205 Iroquois (UH-1H)	66-17019	9213		PV

LUCILLE M. WRIGHT AIR MUSEUM (NY42)

Address:	21 East Third Street, Suite 301, Jamestown, New York 14701.
Tel:	716-664-9500
Admission:	By appointment only.
Location:	At Chautauqua County Airport which is about 4 miles north of the town off West Oak Hill Road.

Set up in 1986, the museum is an aviation orientated learning centre designed to assist pupils in their studies. There are two sections at the airport. The 'Overlook' is an elevated area from which airfield operations may be observed. This contains a number of interactive exhibits designed to show the principles of flight. Also on show are models, photographs and documents tracing the history of the airport and local aviation. Nearby is a Quonset hangar housing the early Tripacer which is being rebuilt by students. The aircraft was built in 1951 and was active for over 25 years before being placed in store. The Iroquois is parked by the hangar but all markings have been removed and a report suggested the possible identity of the helicopter.

TYPE	REG/SER	CON. NO.	PI/NOTES	STATUS
☐ Bell 204 Iroquois (UH-1C)	64-14102	1226	Possible identity.	PV
☐ Piper PA-22 Tripacer 125	N887A	22-188		PVC

MASSENA MONUMENTS (NY43)

Location:	On permanent view at two locations in the town.

TYPE	REG/SER	CON. NO.	PI/NOTES	STATUS
☐ Bell 205 Iroquois (UH-1D) (UH-1V)	66-0831	5314	At ALP 79 at 40 East Orvis Street.	PV
☐ Bell 209 Huey Cobra (AH-1G) (AH-1F)	67-15790	20454	At AMVETS 4 at 12 Andrews Street.	PV

MILITARY & VEHICLES & COLLECTIONS ASSOCIATION (NY44)

Address:	228 Dix Hills Road, Dix Hills, New York 11746.
Admission:	Unknown.
Location:	Just north of Junction 51 of Interstate 495 on Long Island.

A UH-1H Iroquois has been reported as being with this organisation. Presumably this is a group of individuals who collect and preserve military vehicles. Any information would be appreciated.

TYPE	REG/SER	CON. NO.	PI/NOTES	STATUS
☐ Bell 205 Iroquois (HU-1D) (UH-1D) (UH-1H)	64-13754	4461		RA

MOHAWK VALLEY COMMUNITY COLLEGE (NY45)

Address:	1101 Floyd Avenue, Rome, New York 13440.
Tel:	315-339-3470 Email: rhaubert@mvcc.edu
Admission:	By prior permission only.
Location:	About 1 mile north east of the town off Route 46.

The aviation maintenance department offers courses leading to certificates in both airframes and powerplants. The workshops occupy a hangar at the former Griffiss Air Force Base and three aircraft are known to be there. Also in the workshops are a number of jet and turboprop engines along with test equipment.

TYPE	REG/SER	CON. NO.	PI/NOTES	STATUS
☐ Boeing 727-25QC	N136FE	19855	N8172G	RA
☐ Cessna 210				RA
☐ Cessna 310				RA

MOIRA MONUMENT (NY46)

Location:	On permanent view at ALP 939 on Route 11 in the eastern part of the town.

TYPE	REG/SER	CON. NO.	PI/NOTES	STATUS
☐ Northrop N-156T Talon (T-38A) (AT-38B)	61-0806	N.5172		PV

MOLLOY COLLEGE (NY47)

Address:	1196 Prospect Avenue, Farmingdale, New York 11735.
Tel:	631-732-1957 Email: dsantiag@wesboces.org
Admission:	By prior permission only.
Location:	At Republic Airport which is about 2 miles east of the town on Route 24.

The academy is part of the Nassau Community College which offers courses in a wide range of subjects. The aviation department has premises at the Republic Airport which was once home to the famous company.

TYPE	REG/SER	CON. NO.	PI/NOTES	STATUS
☐ Beech 1079 (QU-22B)				RA
☐ Bell 205 Iroquois (UH-1D) (UH-1H)	64-13513	4220		RA
☐ Cessna 337A Super Skymaster	N5333S	3370433		RA

MONROE MONUMENT (NY48)

Location:	On permanent view in Airplane Park off Route 17M in the town.

TYPE	REG/SER	CON. NO.	PI/NOTES	STATUS
☐ North American NA-190 Sabre (F-86D) (F-86L)	52-10052	190-777		PV

MUSEUM OF MODERN ART (NY49)

Address:	11 West 53rd. Street, New York City, New York 10019-5491.
Tel:	218-708-9400 Email: info@moma.org
Admission:	Wednesday-Monday 1030-1730 (Closes at 2000 Friday)
Location:	In the centre of the city.

A Bell 47 has been placed on show in one of the galleries at this renowned art museum. The curator has no records of the identity of the helicopter or its origins and any information would be most useful.

TYPE	REG/SER	CON. NO.	PI/NOTES	STATUS
☐ Bell 47D-1				PV

New York

NATIONAL SOARING MUSEUM (NY50)

Address:	51 Soaring Hill Drive, Harris Hill, Elmira, New York 14903-9204.
Tel:	607-734-3128 Fax: 607-732-6745 Email: nsm@soaringmuseum.org
Admission:	Daily 1000-1700.
Location:	About 8 miles west of the town.

Harris Hill was chosen as the site for the first National Gliding Contest in 1930 and has been in continuous use ever since.

In 1969 a small museum opened in a manor house loaned by Chemung County. Artefacts traced the story of gliding with particular reference to the USA. During the 1970s gliders were added but in 1977 a fire at the administrative building at Harris Hill destroyed a large part of the collection including a 1906 Herring-Arnot hang glider.

A fund raising drive was started and in 1980 a superb purpose-built complex was ready. The large exhibition area could display several gliders and alongside were workshops, offices and a storage area.

The collection has now grown so large that further storage buildings are in use and several gliders are not on site. Two machines can be seen in the nearby Arnot Mall shopping area. The museum displays trace the development of gliders with particular reference to the methods of construction. There are components showing the evolution from the use of wood up to modern composite materials.

A superb exhibition of photographs portrays designers, pilots and their sailplanes. The history of gliding at Harris Hill is also told. In 1911 Orville Wright was aloft for nine minutes and 45 seconds in the Wright Glider 5 and a replica of this machine is on show.

Gliders from the early days to modern times can also be seen. These include two inter-war classics from Germany and a pair from Slingsby in England. A highlight is the Evolution of Gliders and Sailplanes Exhibit. Superbly crafted models of over 120 significant types from around the world are displayed in chronological order.

Regular vintage glider meetings are held at the airfield and the museum has loaned several sailplanes to other collections.

TYPE	REG/SER	CON. NO.	PI/NOTES	STATUS
☐ Arlington Sisu 1-A	N6391X	103		RA
☐ Backstrom EPB-1A Flying Plank	N7634B	1		RA
☐ Backstrom EPB-1C Flying Plank	N19C	1		RA
☐ Baker-McMillen Cadet	G10265	113		RA
☐ Berkshire Concept 70	N6BM	6		RA
☐ Bölkow Phoebus C	N1770	865		RA
☐ Bowlus BA-100 Baby Albatross				PV
☐ Bowlus BA-100 Baby Albatross	NX33630	104		RA
☐ Bowlus BA-102-2 Senior Albatross	NC219Y	25		RA
☐ Bowlus BS-100 Super Albatross	N33658	1	NC33658	RA
☐ Briegleb BG-12ABD	N12RK	162		PV
☐ Chanute-Herring Glider				PV
☐ Croff Batwing Hang Glider				RA
☐ Culver Rigid Midget	N90871	1001		
☐ Dawydoff UT-1 Cadet	N30422			
☐ Elmira Dagling				PV
☐ Franklin PS-2 Eaglet				RA
☐ Franklin PS-2 Eaglet	N451Y	112		RAC
☐ Franklin PS-2 Eaglet	NX20646	1234-7		RAC
☐ Franklin PS-2 Eaglet	G12185	129A		PV
☐ Glasflügel BS-1	N6959	8		RA
☐ Glasflügel H301 Libelle	N25KD	59		PV
☐ Glasflügel H301B Libelle	N260E	51		PV
☐ Göppingen Gö 1 Wolf (DFS 108-58)	N31635	CPS-1		PV
☐ Göppingen Gö 3 Minimoa	G16923	56	NC1306	PV
☐ Gross Sky Ghost	G11348			PV
☐ Hall Cherokee IIRM	N1658	CS-1		RA
☐ Hall SAH-1 Ibex	N63P	SAH-8		RA
☐ Herring-Arnot Hang Glider (R)			In Arnot Mall in Horseheads.	PV
☐ Hütter H 17	CF-RCD	WB153624		PV
☐ Laister Nugget JP-15	N3MH	3		PV
☐ Laister-Kauffman LK.10A	N54191	60		PV
☐ Marske Genesis I	N94GC			PV
☐ Miller Tern	N8591	9		RA
☐ Mitchell Nimbus 3L	N7864C	001		RA
☐ Mitchell Wing U-2	N103WT	175		RA
☐ Nelson Dragonfly BB-1	N34921	505		RA
☐ Nelson PG-185B Hummingbird	N68584	84		RA
☐ Nord N.2000 [Jacobs Meise]	N74ZH	10381/51	F-CAIV	RA
☐ Perl PG-130 Penetrator	N8146H	PG 130-1		RA
☐ Politechnika Warszawska PW-5 Smyk	N737BS	1705009		RA
☐ Prue 215				RA
☐ Prue IIA	N86671	1		RA
☐ Rogallo Hang Glider				PV
☐ Ross Johnson RHJ-6 Adastra	N4921C	101		RA
☐ Ross Johnson RJ-6	N34H	R-6		RA
☐ Ross Johnson RJK-5	N79T	1	N3722C	RAC
☐ Scheibe L-Spatz 55	N1346D	777		RA
☐ Schleicher Ka-6E Rhönsegler	N139N	4038		PV
☐ Schreder HP-8	N34Y	1		RAC
☐ Schreder HP-10	N4718G	AC-1		RA
☐ Schreder HP-11A	N4777G	7		PV
☐ Schreder HP-16	N45HP	CS-2		RA
☐ Schreder HP-18	N1YV	18-107		PV
☐ Schweizer SGP.1-1 (R)	N50SZ	1		PV
☐ Schweizer SGU.1-7	NR23026	2		PV
☐ Schweizer SGS.2-8	N10VV	2		RA
☐ Schweizer SGS.2-12 (TG-3A)	N61279	43	(USAAF)	RA

☐ Schweizer SGU.1-19				Fuselage frame.	RA
☐ Schweizer SGU.1-19	CF-ZBE				RA
☐ Schweizer SGU.1-19	NC981	1		Fuselage frame.	PV
☐ Schweizer SGU.1-19	N91806	14			RA
☐ Schweizer SGS.1-23D	N91899	36			PV
☐ Schweizer SGS.1-26	N91889	1		At Arnot Mall, Horseheads.	PV
☐ Schweizer SGS.1-26E	N36122	700			PV
☐ Schweizer SGS.1-29		1			RA
☐ Schweizer SGS.1-34				Front fuselage only.	PV
☐ Schweizer SGS.1-35	N17900	1			PV
☐ Schweizer SGS.2-32	N2767Z	11			RA
☐ Slingsby T.15 Gull	N41829	1			PV
☐ Slingsby T.38 Grasshopper TX.1	XA237	870			RA
☐ Slingsby T.43 Skylark 3B	CF-ZDH	1093			RA
☐ Stamer-Lippisch Z-12 Zögling					PV
☐ Waco NZR Hadrian (CG-4A)				Front fuselage only.	PV
☐ Wright 1902 Glider (R)					PV
☐ Wright 1911 Glider (R)					PV

NEW HARTFORD MONUMENT (NY51)

Location:	On permanent view at ALP 1376 at 8616 Clinton Street in the north western part of the town.

TYPE	REG/SER	CON. NO.	PI/NOTES	STATUS
☐ Bell 209 Huey Cobra (AH-1G) (AH-1F)	68-15110	20644		PV

NEW YORK AVIATION HIGH SCHOOL (NY52)

Address:	4530 36th Street, Long Island City, New York 11101.
Tel:	718-361-2032 Fax: 718-784-8654 Email: mcotumaccio@schools.nyc.gov
Admission:	By prior permission only.
Location:	In the city which is in the north western part of the island.

The school was originally set up as a building trades college in 1925. A number of moves were made before the aviation section moved into a purpose-built facility in 1957. The school now has an annexe, dedicated in 1999, at JFK Airport where the Boeing 727 donated by Federal Express is located.

TYPE	REG/SER	CON. NO.	PI/NOTES	STATUS
☐ Beech 95-B55B Cochise (T-42A)	65-12713	TF-35		RA
☐ Boeing 727-24C	N114FE	19527	N2474, N5474, N1781B, N1355B, CC-CAN	RA
☐ Boeing-Stearman A75N1 Kaydet (PT-17)				RA
☐ Cessna 150H	N59036	15069272		RA
☐ Cessna 150J	N64618	15071054		RA
☐ Cessna 310A Blue Canoe (L-27A) (U-3A)	N3766U	38022	57-5867	RA
☐ Cessna 411	N999RS	411023		RA
☐ Douglas TA-4F Skyhawk	Bu154639	13757		RA
☐ Experimental Aircraft Association P-1 Biplane	N919	AHS105		RA
☐ North American NA-88 Texan (SNJ-5)	N3674F	88-16771	Bu84910	RA
☐ North American NA-88 Texan (SNJ-5)				RA
☐ North American NA-121 Texan (AT-6F)	N10434	121-42548	44-81826	RA
☐ North American NA-168 Texan (T-6G)	N3142G	168-293	49-3189	RA

NEW YORK STATE MUSEUM (NY53)

Address:	Cultural Education Center, 222 Madison Avenue, Albany, New York 12230.
Tel:	518-474-5877 Email: info@mail.nysed.gov
Admission:	Daily 0930-1700.
Location:	In the centre of the city.

The museum has its origins in the State Geological Survey of the 1830s. The first exhibition was set up in the late 1850s and the present building opened in 1976. The displays trace all aspects of life in the state and there is a large library and research centre.

The only powered aircraft on show is one of seven Fleet 8 three-seater biplanes built. The example in the collection was the first aircraft to be purchased by the New York State Conservation Department. Delivered in the summer of 1931,

it was used for fire spotting, aerial photography and transport duties. After a crash of another Model 8 flown by the State Police the Fleet was sold in September 1932. The aircraft served in six other states before returning to New York in 1966. It last flew in 1986 and joined the museum the following year.

The RP-3 is a glider designed by the Troy based college. The 57-foot wingspan sailplane made its maiden flight at Schenectady County Airport in the late 1980s.

TYPE	REG/SER	CON. NO.	PI/NOTES	STATUS
☐ Fleet 8	N49V	803	NS69V	PV
☐ Rensselaer Polytechnic Institute RP-3	N397RP	Dash3		PV

NIAGARA FALLS AIR RESERVE BASE COLLECTION (NY54)

Address:	107AW/PA, 9910 Blewitt Avenue, Niagara Falls, New York 14304-5000
Tel:	716-236-2394
Admission:	By prior permission only.
Location:	About 6 miles east of Niagara Falls on Route 62.

New York

Allocated to the state in December 1948, the 136th Squadron moved into Niagara Falls Naval Air Station. The field was re-designated as an International Airport in 1959 but the unit remained in residence. Fighters were operated until 1994 when the unit took up an air-refuelling role. Reserve units are also stationed on the base.

TYPE	REG/SER	CON. NO.	PI/NOTES	STATUS
☐ Douglas DC-3A-467 Skytrain (C-47B) (R4D-6) (C-47J)	'43-15851'	14773/26218	43-48957, Bu150190, 43-48957 –	RAX
☐ Fairchild 110 Flying Boxcar (C-119F)	'51-2680'	10736	22105 (Canada), N15506, '51-8101'	RAX
☐ McDonnell M.36CA Voodoo (RF-101C)	56-0185	172		RA
☐ McDonnell M.98DJ Phantom II (F-4C)	64-0660	877		RA
☐ North American NA-235 Super Sabre (F-100D)	56-2993	235-91		RA

NIAGARA FALLS MONUMENT (NY55)

Location:	By prior permission only in the foyer of Veridian Flight Research near the IAP.

TYPE	REG/SER	CON. NO.	PI/NOTES	STATUS
☐ Bell 44 (XS-1) (X-1) (FSM)	'6062'			RAX

NIAGARA FRONTIER VINTAGE AIRCRAFT GROUP (NY56)

Address: 2168 Adams Circuit, Ransomville, New York 14131-9713.
Admission: By prior permission only.
Location: At a private airfield near Niagara Falls International Airport.

For many years the group worked on a Lysander for the Canadian Warplane Heritage. This aircraft has now returned to Hamilton. The Fleet 1 was built in Buffalo. This two-seat biplane powered by a 125 h.p. Warner radial entered production in 1928 and the basic design fitted with other engines was built as the 2 and 7. Well over 600 were completed over the next seven years. The Taylorcraft has not flown for several years.

TYPE	REG/SER	CON. NO.	PI/NOTES	STATUS
☐ Fleet 1	NC8600	14	NC8600, N8600	RAA
☐ Taylorcraft BC-12-65	N1510T	2868		RA

ORISKANY VILLAGE MUSEUM (NY57)

Address: 420 Utica Street, PO Box 284, Oriskany, New York 13424-0517.
Tel: 315-736-7529
Admission: Wednesday-Saturday 1000-1730.
Location: In the centre of the village which is about 8 miles north west of Utica.

The museum commemorates the 1777 Battle of Oriskany, the village of Oriskany, the aircraft carrier USS *Oriskany* and a turn of the century amusement park which used to be located in the village. The original display was in a local house. The Navy donated a few more items from the ship which was sunk off the Florida coast in 2006 to serve as an artificial reef. The Skyhawk is located in a park next to the USS *Oriskany* Anchor Memorial where a purpose-built museum was dedicated in 1997. The displays have been improved with many more items on show. including dioramas of the battle. The museum aircraft did not serve aboard the carrier and is in false colours. On one side of its rudder is a blue boomerang and on the other an orange one. These were the markings of the two squadrons which served on the ship in the Vietnam War.

TYPE	REG/SER	CON. NO.	PI/NOTES	STATUS
☐ Douglas YA-4E Skyhawk (YA4D-5)	Bu148613	12806	.	PV

PARISH MONUMENT (NY58)

Location:	On permanent view at ALP on Route 69A in the south western part of the town.

TYPE	REG/SER	CON. NO.	PI/NOTES	STATUS
☐ Bell 209 Huey Cobra (AH-1S) (AH-1E)	78-23047	22153		PV

PERINTON MONUMENT (NY59)

Location:	On permanent view at VFW 8495 at 300 Macedon Center Road in the eastern suburbs of Rochester.

TYPE	REG/SER	CON. NO.	PI/NOTES	STATUS
☐ Bell 205 Iroquois (UH-1H) (UH-1V)	69-15593	11881		PV

PLATTSBURGH MUSEUM CAMPUS (NY60)

Address: Plattsburgh, New York 12903.
Admission: Aircraft on permanent view.
Location: In the southern suburbs of the city off Interstate 87.

Plattsburgh has been a military base since 1814 although prior to this British and French forces took part in campaigns in the area. In 1946 the barracks were transferred to New York State for student housing. The construction of an Air Force Base started in 1954 and the site was ready the following year. During most of its life the field was home to a bomb wing but tanker squadrons were also in residence. There are long-term plans to develop the base campus into a number of museums with one tracing the military history of the region.

TYPE	REG/SER	CON. NO.	PI/NOTES	STATUS
☐ Boeing 450-157-35 Stratojet (B-47E)	53-2385	4501198		PV
☐ General Dynamics FB-111A	68-0286	B1-58		PV

RED CREEK MONUMENT (NY61)

Location:	On permanent view at Paradise Airport in Maroney Road about 2 miles south east of the town.

TYPE	REG/SER	CON. NO.	PI/NOTES	STATUS
☐ Beech D18S Expeditor (C-45G)	N302F	AF-95	51-11538, N9924Z, N175H	PV

RED STAR AVIATION MUSEUM (NY62)

Address:	1188 First Street, Stewart International Airport, New Windsor, New York 12553.
Tel:	845-567-0000 **Email:** Flight@RedStarAviation.org
Admission:	By prior permission only.
Location:	About 5 miles west of Newburgh off Interstate 84.

Red Star Aviation owned and flew a number of European light aircraft. Over the next few years a Fouga Magister arrived and this led to the idea of operating jet fighters and trainers. The company now offers training on warbirds with experienced instructors and also opens its hangar as a museum. It carries out its work at a number of airfields and hires in other aircraft for these tasks. Members of the fleet are often away from Stewart Airport. Some of the aircraft are painted in false Soviet colour schemes.

The Yakovlev company has produced low wing monoplanes for many years. The Yak-50 and Yak-55 were specially designed for aerobatics.

TYPE	REG/SER	CON. NO.	PI/NOTES	STATUS
☐ Aero L-29 Delfin	'47'			RAAX
☐ Aero L-39C Albatros	N9050H	630640		RAA
☐ De Havilland DH.100 Vampire FB.6				RAA
☐ De Havilland DH.115 Vampire T.55	N835HW	973	U-1213 (Switzerland), N935HW	RAA
☐ Fouga CM.170R Magister	N431PS	431	431	RAA
☐ Fouga CM.170R Magister	N925WD	463	463, N531PA	RAA
☐ Grumman G-134 Mohawk (AO-1C) (OV-1C)	N4376D	35C	61-2692	RAA
☐ Hispano HA.200A Saeta (HA.200R1)	N606HA	20/6	E.14-6, E.14A-6	RAA
☐ Mikoyan-Gurevich MiG-21U-600				RAA
☐ North American NA-200 Trojan (T-28B)				RAA
☐ WSK SBLim-2 (Lim-1) [MiG-15] [MiG-15UTI]	'69'	1A 07-009	709 (Poland), N50CS – in false Soviet markings.	RAAX
☐ Yakovlev Yak-50	N3016	842708		RAA
☐ Yakovlev Yak-52	N1139X	844610		RAA
☐ Yakovlev Yak-55M	N955SF	961009		RAA
☐ Zlin Z-526 Trenér Master	N112TM	1053		RAA

RHINEBECK AERODROME MUSEUM (NY63)

Address:	PO Box 229, Rhinebeck, New York 12572-0229.
Tel:	845-752-3200 **Fax:** 845-758-6481
Admission:	Mid May–October daily 1000-1600; Air shows June–October Saturday-Sunday 1430.
Location:	North of Rhinebeck at the intersection of Norton and Stone Church Roads off Route 9.

In 1951 Cole Palen was on a mechanics course at Roosevelt Field on Long Island. He found six aircraft from the former museum at the airfield stored in the corner of a hangar. This historic site, which was the starting point for Charles Lindbergh's flight to Paris, was being turned into a housing and shopping complex.

Cole obtained the six for the princely sum of $1500. The aircraft were an Avro 504K, an Aeromarine 39, a Curtiss Jenny, a Standard J-1, a Sopwith Snipe and a SPAD XIII. The Standard was soon sold for $1500 and the Jenny was traded for a Nieuport 28. Restoration of the SPAD started and it flew again in 1956.

In 1959 a derelict farm at Old Rhinebeck was acquired with the idea of starting a general aviation business and restoring the vintage aircraft in spare time. A runway was hacked out of the trees and soon the plan for a museum with regular air shows was conceived. Other enthusiasts joined the venture and more aircraft were collected. In the early 1960s aircraft were transported by road to shows around the USA and Canada and the name of Old Rhinebeck became well known.

Heavy snow in the severe winter of 1962/3 caused the collapse of a hangar and several aircraft were damaged. The Avro 504 was later sold to the National Aviation Collection of Canada to cover losses incurred in winter shows in Florida in 1964/5.

Replica construction was started at this time with Dick King's Sopwith Pup flying in 1966 and Cole's Fokker Dr I the following year.

This trend has continued with a steady stream emerging from the Rhinebeck and Florida workshops. The active aircraft are housed in hangars on the airfield and across the road is the museum with three small exhibition halls. In 1993 a new large museum building was completed and displays have been set up inside. In the addition to the aircraft there is a superb collection of aero engines ranging from types from the early days of aviation up to the outbreak of World War II.

The regular summer airshows are held from May to October. The themes on Saturday are the pioneers and barnstorming in the inter-war period and on Sunday World War I. Joy riding is carried out in 1928 New Standard D-25s – Cole purchased five examples of the large biplane from a Texas crop dusting outfit in the early 1980s.

There are many rare types in the collection. The original Aeromarine company was founded before World War I and produced a number of original designs. The 39 was a biplane trainer ordered by the US. The design set an endurance record for a two-seater. The sole survivor was accidentally burnt and suffered minor damage. Hopefully this aircraft will be rebuilt in the not too distant future.

W.T. Thomas of Bath in New York State built a number of original types. Twelve Es were constructed in 1912 for 'barnstorming' work. The airframe was found on a farm but the wings were in poor condition as they had been used to protect crops from frost. Cole rebuilt the aircraft in the early 1960s and flew it for a few years before it was retired in 1966.

New York

Early in 1993 Cole suffered a stroke and he then decided to set up the Rhinebeck Aerodrome Museum Foundation. Sadly he died at his winter home in Florida on 8th December 1993.

His foresight has ensured that the tradition of Old Rhinebeck will continue and delight the many visitors to this picturesque site.

TYPE	REG/SER	CON. NO.	PI/NOTES	STATUS
☐ Aeromarine 39B	N347N	55923	NC347N – components only.	RA
☐ Aeromarine-Klemm AKL-26A	N320N	2-59	NC320N	PV
☐ Aeronca C-3	N17447	A-754	NC17447	PVA
☐ Albatros D Va (R)	N12156	17-D-7517		PV
☐ Albree Pigeon Fraser		3		PV
☐ American Eagle A-129	N513H	534	NC513H	PV
☐ Ansaldo A-1 Balilla (R)				PVC
☐ Avro 504K (R)	'E2939'	HAC1	G-ATXL, N4929	RAD
☐ Blériot XI	N99923	3856		PV
☐ Blériot XI	N60094	56		PVA
☐ Breguet Biplane			Components only.	S
☐ Bristol 20 M.1C (R)				PV
☐ Brunner-Winkle Bird CK	N850W	4012	NC850W	PV
☐ Caudron G.3 (R)	N3943P	1914-2		PVA
☐ Chamberlin Monoplane				PVD
☐ Chanute Glider (R)				PV
☐ Curtiss D Pusher (R)	N68014	1976		PVA
☐ Curtiss 1E Jenny (JN-4H)	'A-6226'	3919	38278, N3918, 38278	PVAX
☐ Curtiss 50H Robin J-1	NC534N	737	NC534N, N534N	PVA
☐ Curtiss 51 Fledgling	N271Y	B-52	271H	PVA
☐ Curtiss-Wright CW-1 Junior	NC605EB	1025	NC643V, N605EB	PV
☐ Davis D-1W	N532K	115	NC532K	PVA
☐ De Havilland DH.80A Puss Moth	N770N	2140	G-ABIH, NC770N, N770N, N770M	RAC
☐ De Havilland DH.82A Tiger Moth	'G-ACDB'	86556	PG647, F-BGDH, N3529	PVAX
☐ Deperdussin Monoplane (R)	N8448	11		PV
☐ Dickson Primary (R)	N5666	PHC-1		PV
☐ Fairchild 24 C8F (24H)	N19129	3224	NC19129	RAC
☐ Fleet 16B Finch II	NC666J	350	4498, NC39631	RAC
☐ Fokker D VII (R)	'4649/18'	1918-1989	N70814	PVAX
☐ Fokker Dr I (R)	N3221	322		PV
☐ Fokker Dr I (R)	N220TP	F1-103		PVA
☐ Fokker E III (R)				RA
☐ Great Lakes 2T-1A-2	N707RM	0737		PVA
☐ Great Lakes 2T-1MS	N304Y	191	NC304Y,	RA
☐ Great Lakes 2T-1R	NX306Y	H003	NC306Y, N306Y	PVA
☐ Hanriot Monoplane (R)	N8449	11		PVA
☐ Heath LNA-40 Parasol	N5719	1000		PV
☐ Mono Aircraft Monocoupe 90	N429N	618	NC429N	PV
☐ Mono Aircraft Monocoupe 113	NC8955	322	NC8955, N8955	PV
☐ Morane-Saulnier A1	N1379M	1591/417		PV
☐ Morane-Saulnier N (R)	N5356J	1915-84		PV
☐ Morane-Saulnier MS.130Et2	N7MS	001	F-AJRQ (?)	PV
☐ New Standard D-25	NC176H	138	NC176H, N176H	PV
☐ New Standard D-25	N31K	150	NC31K	PVA
☐ New Standard D-25	N19157	162J	NC19157	PVA
☐ New Standard D-25				RA
☐ Nicholas-Beazley NB-8G	N576Y	K-18	NC576Y	PV
☐ Nieuport 2N (R)	N9147A	1911-78		PV
☐ Nieuport 10/83E	N680CP	680		PV
☐ Nieuport 11 (R)	'N1334'	1915-78	N9163A	PVA
☐ Nieuport 24bis (R)	N5246	1		PVA
☐ Passett Ornithopter (R)				PV
☐ Piccard AX-3M Hot Air Balloon	N7132	23		RAA
☐ Pietenpol B4-A Aircamper	N6262	1		PVA
☐ Pitcairn PA-6 Super Mailwing	N15307	159	NC15307	PVA
☐ Raab-Katzenstein RK 7 Schmetterling				RA
☐ Royal Aircraft Factory F.E.8 (R)	N17501	300		RA
☐ Royal Aircraft Factory S.E.5A (R)				RAC
☐ Ryan NYP (R)	N211XC	30		PVA
☐ Santos-Dumont XX Demoiselle (R)				PV
☐ Santos-Dumont XX Demoiselle (R)	N6551	1		PV
☐ Short S.29 (R)	N4275	2		PV
☐ Siemens-Schuckert D IV (R)	N1918G	1918-70		PV
☐ Sopwith 5F.1 Dolphin (R)	N47166	1533		PVC
☐ Sopwith F.1 Camel (R)	'B6299'	1990	N7157Q, 'F6034'	PVAX
☐ Sopwith Triplane (R)				RAC
☐ SPAD VII (R)	N8096L	1999		PVA
☐ SPAD XII	'2'			RAC
☐ Spartan C-3-165	NC285M	120	NC285M, N285M	PV
☐ Stampe & Vertongen S.V.4B	N51SV	460	460	PVA
☐ Thomas E Pusher	N4720G	2		PV
☐ Thomas-Morse S-4B	4328	153	4328, N74W	PV
☐ Voisin 8 (R)	N38933	1		PV
☐ Waco 9	N2574	359	NC2574	PV
☐ Waco 10 (GXE)	N940	751	NC940	PV
☐ Waco QCF	NC11478	3559	NC11478, N11478	PVA
☐ Wright 1903 Glider (R)				PV
☐ Wright EX Vin Fiz (R)	N1911P		1911-1981	PV
☐ Wright Flyer (R)				PV

ROCHESTER ARMY NATIONAL GUARD BASE (NY64)

Location:	By prior permission only at Greater Rochester Airport which is in the south western part of the city.

TYPE	REG/SER	CON. NO.	PI/NOTES	STATUS
☐ Bell 205 Iroquois (UH-1D) (UH-1H)	63-12990	4186		PV
☐ Bell 209 Huey Cobra (AH-1G) (AH-1F)	67-15829	20493		PV

ROCHESTER INTERNATIONAL AIRPORT DISPLAY (NY65)

Address:	1200 Brooks Avenue, Rochester, New York 14624.
Tel:	585-753-7020 **Fax:** 583-753-7008 **Email:** mcairport@monroecounty.gov
Admission:	On permanent view when the terminals are open.
Location:	In the south western part of the city.

The airport has set up a display tracing the history of the site. Two aircraft can be seen. The Ohm and Stoppelbein Special set a closed circuit international speed record for its class in 1956. A replica of the Taylor Chummy has been constructed. C.G. Taylor and his brother, Gordon, built the high wing monoplane in Rochester in 1926 but the type did not sell. Gordon was killed in another Taylor design in 1928 and C.G. moved to Bradford, Pennsylvania where the successful Cub series was developed and the company became Piper.

TYPE	REG/SER	CON. NO.	PI/NOTES	STATUS
☐ Ohm & Stopplebein Special	N6H	O-1		PV
☐ Taylor Chummy (R)				PV

SACKETS HARBOR MONUMENT (NY66)

Location:	On permanent view at ALP 1757 in the south western part of the town.

TYPE	REG/SER	CON. NO.	PI/NOTES	STATUS
☐ Bell 209 Huey Cobra (AH-1G) (AH-1S)	68-15091	20625		PV

SAMPSON NAVAL MUSEUM (NY67)

Address:	Sampson State Park, Romulus, New York 14541.
Tel:	315-585-6023 **Email:** Krystal.Westfall@oprhp.state.ny.us
Admission:	June–August Friday-Sunday 1000-1600; September–mid October Saturday-Sunday 1000-1600.
Location:	On the east shore of Lake Seneca off Route 96A.

During World War II over 5,000 naval recruits were trained at this base near to Lake Seneca. Much of the area is still under military control but a State Park has been established. A museum has been set up to trace the naval heritage and many interesting items can be seen. The former Sampson Army Airfield was close by and the World War II control tower and other buildings survive.

TYPE	REG/SER	CON. NO.	PI/NOTES	STATUS
☐ Lockheed 580 (T-33A)	51-8604	580-6388		PV
☐ North American NA-346 Buckeye (T-2C)	Bu158596	346-22	.	PV

SHORTSVILLE MONUMENT (NY68)

Location:	On permanent view in a Childrens Park in the town.

TYPE	REG/SER	CON. NO.	PI/NOTES	STATUS
☐ North American NA-203 Sabre (F-86H)	53-1337	203-109		PV

STITTVILLE MONUMENT (NY69)

Location:	On permanent view at VFW 8259 at 8999 Olin Road which is about 1 mile south of the town.

TYPE	REG/SER	CON. NO.	PI/NOTES	STATUS
☐ Bell 209 Huey Cobra (AH-1G) (AH-1F)	67-15528	20192		PV

STRATTON AIR NATIONAL GUARD BASE (NY70)

Location:	By prior permission only at the north east corner of Schenectady County Airport which is about 2 miles north of Scotia on Route 50.

TYPE	REG/SER	CON. NO.	PI/NOTES	STATUS
☐ Lockheed 182-1A Hercules (182-44-03) (C-130A) (C-130D)	57-0490	182-3197		PV

SUFFOLK COUNTY AIR NATIONAL GUARD BASE (NY71)

Location:	At the airfield in eastern Long Island about 3 miles north of Westhampton on Route 31.

TYPE	REG/SER	CON. NO.	PI/NOTES	STATUS
☐ Convair 8-10 Delta Dagger (F-102A)	57-0788	8-10-754		RA
☐ Sikorsky S-61R (HH-3E)	66-13290	61-588		PV

New York

SYRACUSE 'DISCOVER THE AIRPORT' (NY72)

Address:	1000 Colonel Eileen Collins Boulevard, Syracuse 13212.
Tel:	315-454-4330 **Email:** information@syrairport.com
Admission:	When the terminal is open.
Location:	About 5 miles north east of the city off Interstate 81.

The exhibition opened in 1966 and shows the work of the airport. The front fuselage of a Boeing 727 can be entered and there is also a fuselage section from the aircraft. Some of the working areas can be seen on the tours.

TYPE	REG/SER	CON. NO.	PI/NOTES	STATUS
☐ Boeing 727			Front fuselage and another section.	PV

SYRACUSE AIR NATIONAL GUARD BASE (NY73)

Address:	174FW/PA, 6001 East Molloy Road, Syracuse, New York 13211-7099.
Tel:	315-223-2651
Admission:	By prior permission only.
Location:	At Hancock Field which is about 5 miles north east of the city off Interstate 81.

Assigned to the state in late 1947 the l38th. Squadron has mainly served in the fighter role. The unit has been based at Hancock Field since 1947 apart from active duty during the Berlin and Pueblo crises and the Gulf War.

TYPE	REG/SER	CON. NO.	PI/NOTES	STATUS
☐ Cessna 318B Tweety Bird (318A) (T-37A) (T-37B)	56-3493	40065		RA
☐ Fairchild-Republic A-10A Thunderbolt II	76-0523	A10-70		RA
☐ General Dynamics 401 Fighting Falcon (F-16A)	80-0504	61-225		RA
☐ Lockheed 780-76-12 Starfire (F-94B) (YF-94A) (YF-94C)	50-0877	780-7183		RA
☐ North American NA-203 Sabre (F-86H)	53-1519	203-291		RA
☐ Republic F-84B Thunderjet (P-84B)	46-600			RA

THE 1941 HISTORICAL AIRCRAFT GROUP (NY74)

Address:	PO Box 185, 3489 Big Tree Lane, Geneseo, New York 14454.
Tel:	585-243-2100 **Fax:** 585-245-9802 **Email:** office@1941HAG.org
Admission:	By prior permission only.
Location:	The airport is about 1 mile west of the town which is 30 miles south of Rochester.

This group, formed in 1993 by former members of the National Warplane Museum, has a hangar and other buildings at Geneseo.

The two World War II fighters are owned by one of the founders of the organisation. The Spitfire was with an Air Training Corps unit at Tynemouth in England from 1951 to 1963 and then sat outside a public house in Herefordshire for another dozen years before crossing the Atlantic Ocean. This fighter is undergoing a long restoration to flying condition as is the Spanish-built Messerschmitt. The HA.1112 was used at Tablada in taxiing scenes for 'The Battle of Britain' film. This aircraft was at the Victory Air Museum in Illinois from 1970 to 1976.

The group held a successful warbird show at Geneseo in 1995 and this has now become an annual event. Three of David Tallichet's aircraft are being worked on by members of the organisation. The Fortress was in store at Davis-Monthan AFB from 1954 to 1959. The bomber was then sold and converted for water bombing duties. Just over 20 years of service in California followed. David Tallichet purchased it and it was on show at the March Field Museum for a time. The B-17 was one of those flown to Duxford for the 'Memphis Belle' film and it is still in these markings. The Canadian operated Flying Boxcar arrived at Geneseo for the National Warplane Museum but was left behind when this group moved out.

There are several homebuilt aircraft, owned by members of the group, based at the airfield. The Parker Jeanie's Teenie is an all metal low wing single seater. The prototype made its maiden flight in 1969. The design was modified into the Teenie Two and many sets of plans have been sold. Bert Floyd has constructed several types and the BF-6 dates from 1997.

TYPE	REG/SER	CON. NO.	PI/NOTES	STATUS
☐ Aero Commander 100	N4110X	208		PVA
☐ Aeronca 7AC Champion	N3033E	7AC-6619		PVA
☐ Air Command Autogyro				PV
☐ American Eagle Eaglet 231				PV
☐ Antonov An-2R	N26AN	1G 226-56	CCCP-33397, LY-ACM	RAA
☐ Beech D17S (UC-43) (GB-2)	NC582	6704	44-67727, (Bu23692), FT478, Bu32876, N1183V, N582	PV
☐ Beech D18S Expeditor (C-45G)	N45GC	AF-489	52-10539, N450C, N9154R	PV
☐ Boeing 299-O Fortress (B-17G) (CB-17G) (VB-17G)	N3703G	32187	44-83546 – on loan from MARC, CA.	PV
☐ Canadair CL-30 Silver Star 3 (CT-133) [Lockheed 580 (T-33AN)]				PV
☐ Cessna 150M	N45636	15076999		PVA
☐ Cessna 195A	N1033D	7777	Fuselage only.	PV
☐ Culver LCA Cadet	N29271	140	NC29271	RA
☐ Douglas A-20H Havoc	N99385	23243	44-20, N5066N, 50 (Nicaragua) – on loan from MARC, CA.	PVC
☐ Douglas DC-3A-456 Skytrain (C-47A)	N345AB	13803	43-30652, NC65135, CF-RTB	RA
☐ Douglas DC-3A-467 Skytrain (C-47B)	N54402	15635/27080	43-49819, KN214, G-AMJX, 49819 (Morocco), CN-ALJ, N54602, '316250' – on loan from MARC, CA.	PVX
☐ Douglas UC-67 Dragon (B-23)	N62G	2724	39-38, NR56249, NC56249, N56249	PVC

☐ Ercoupe 415C	N2389H	3014		PVA
☐ Ercoupe 415C			Fuselage only.	PV
☐ Ercoupe 415C			Fuselage only.	PV
☐ Fairchild 110 Flying Boxcar (C-119F)	N8092	10678	(51-2689), 22103 (Canada)	PV
☐ Floyd BF-6	N62594	1		PV
☐ Grumman G-50 Hellcat (F6F-5) (FSM)				PVX
☐ Hispano HA-1112M1L [Messerschmitt Bf 109G]	C.4K-121	178	Believed to be in Texas.	RA
☐ Kolb III Classic				PV
☐ Naval Aircraft Factory N3N-3	N45053		Bu1983	PVD
☐ Naval Aircraft Factory N3N-3			Fuselage frame only.	RAD
☐ Neibauer Lancair 235				PV
☐ North American NA-66 Harvard IIA (II)	N9435H	66-2401	2668 (Canada)	PVC
☐ Parker Jeanie's Teenie	N2486	1		PV
☐ Piper PA-30 Twin Comanche	N10JR	30-39	N7036Y, N10JR, (N10UP)	PVA
☐ Ryan Navion B	N5308K	NAV-4-2208B		PVA
☐ Stinson 10A Voyager				PVC
☐ Stinson V-77 Reliant (AT-19)	N70012	77-284	43-43997, FB556, Bu1397 – on loan from MARC, CA.	PVC
☐ Supermarine 361 Spitfire LF.XVIe	TD135	CBAF-IX-4218	TD135, 6798N	RAC
☐ Wag Aero Cuby L-21B-135	N90293	690		PVA

TONAWANDA MONUMENT (NY75)

Location:	On permanent view in a park in Colvin Boulevard in the northern part of the town.

TYPE	REG/SER	CON. NO.	PI/NOTES	STATUS
☐ Grumman G-93 Cougar (F9F-6P) (RF-9F)				PV

VAUGHN COLLEGE OF AERONAUTICS (NY76)

Address:	86-01 23rd Avenue, Flushing, New York 11369.
Tel:	718-429-6600 Email: paul.miranda@vaughn.edu
Admission:	By prior permission only.
Location:	Just south of La Guardia Airport.

The college was set up in New Jersey in 1932 and moved to a site near La Guardia Airport eight years later. The workshops contain a number of instructional airframes along with engines and systems rigs.

TYPE	REG/SER	CON. NO.	PI/NOTES	STATUS
☐ Aero Jet Commander 1121	N910MH	1121-45	N920R, N340DR, N340ER, N121PG	RA
☐ Beech 65-90 King Air	N795K	LJ-95		RA
☐ Beech 95-B55B Cochise (T-42A)	N9177Y	TF-22	65-12700	RA
☐ Beech B95 Travel Air	N2745Y	TD-103		RA
☐ Cessna 150H	N22685	15068448		RA
☐ Cessna 310A Blue Canoe (L-27A) (U-3A)				RA
☐ Piper PA-18-95 Super Cub (L-18C)	N2779K	18-2110	52-2510	RA
☐ Piper PA-23-160 Apache	N3404P	23-1368		RA

VINTAGE AIRCRAFT GROUP (NY77)

Address:	4906 Pine Hill Road, Albion, New York 14411-9241.
Tel:	585-589-7758 Email: vintage26@aol.com
Admission:	By prior permission only.
Location:	At Pine Hill Airport which is about 5 miles south west of Albion.

Formed with the aim of maintaining and operating vintage aircraft, this group has several projects underway. One Cornell is airworthy and the other is undergoing a major rebuild to flying condition. This low-wing monoplane was produced in large numbers for basic training. A vintage fire truck is also in the collection. The T-33 has been on display at the airport for many years and the group now looks after the jet. Two Stinson designs are in the collection. The Sentinel was developed from the pre-war series of high wing monoplanes.

TYPE	REG/SER	CON. NO.	PI/NOTES	STATUS
☐ Fairchild M-62A Cornell (PT-19A)	N53953	T41-1342	41-20296	RAA
☐ Fairchild M-62A Cornell (PT-19A)		T42-3374	42-33708	RAC
☐ Lockheed 580 (T-33A)	51-4353	580-5648		RA
☐ Stinson V-76 Sentinel (L-5G)	N60410			RAA
☐ Stinson V-77 Reliant (AT-19)	N4608N	77-197	42-46836, FL110, Bu11508	RAC

WARBIRDS OVER LONG ISLAND (NY78)

Address:	Brookhaven Calabro Airport, Shirley, New York 11967
Tel:	info@warbirdsoverlongisland.com
Admission:	By prior permission only.
Location:	In the northern part of the town.

Formed by father and son Robert and Christopher Baranaskas, the group maintains a number of World War II types in airworthy condition. Robert, who died in 2009, was the son of a World War II fighter pilot. He flew for American Airlines for many years. The aircraft attend many airshows in the region. The Mustang has a complex history and underwent a major rebuild in Californian where Australian components were used.

New York

TYPE	REG/SER	CON. NO.	PI/NOTES	STATUS
☐ Boeing-Stearman D75N1 Kaydet (PT-27)	N53292	75-3856	44-15767, FJ806	RAA
☐ Cessna 195A	N41X	7775		RAA
☐ Curtiss A87-A2 Kittyhawk I	N740RB/'11456'	15370	AK899, 1051 (Canada), N9837A – quoted as ex 44-7368.	RAA
☐ North American NA-121 Texan (AT-6D) (SNJ-5)	N276RB	121-41944	444-81222, Bu91008, N3202G, N144KM, N9048P, N29GK	RAA
☐ North American NA-121 Texan (AT-6D) (SNJ-5)				RAA
☐ North American NA-122 Mustang (P-51D) (Mustang IV)	N751RB'413903'	122-40993	44-74453, 9597 (Canada), N9150R, C-GJCJ, N151JP, N251HR – rebuilt with parts of a Commonwealth Mustang and adopted identity 44-13903.	RAAX

WATERLOO MONUMENT (NY79)

Location: On permanent view at VFW 6433 at 29 West Elisha Street just north of the town centre.

TYPE	REG/SER	CON. NO.	PI/NOTES	STATUS
☐ Bell 205 Iroquois (UH-1H)	68-16521	11180		PV

WHEATFIELD MONUMENT (NY80)

Location: On permanent view at the Highways Department at 6860 Ward Road in the town.

TYPE	REG/SER	CON. NO.	PI/NOTES	STATUS
☐ Bell 205 Iroquois (UH-1D) (UH-1H)	65-9690	4734		PV

WHITE PLAINS MONUMENT (NY81)

Location: On permanent view at Westchester County Airport which is about 5 miles north east of White Plains.

TYPE	REG/SER	CON. NO.	PI/NOTES	STATUS
☐ Lockheed 580 (T-33A) (TV-2) (T-33B)	55-3053	580-9594	55-3053, Bu141538	PV

WINGS OF EAGLES DISCOVERY CENTER (NY82)

Address: 17 Aviation Drive, Horseheads, New York 14845-1102.
Tel: 607-739-8200   **Fax:** 607-739-8374   **Email:** info@wingsofeagles.com
Admission: November–April Wednesday-Saturday 1000-1600, Sunday 1200-1600: May–October Monday-Saturday 1000-1600, Sunday 1200-1600.
Location: At Elmira Airport which is about 6 miles north of the town, north of Route 17.

Founded in 1982, this museum has grown into one of the major flying collections of warbirds in the country. An annual airshow was one of the highlights of the aviation calendar. Two exhibition halls, a visitor centre containing a display of artefacts and a shop were constructed at Geneseo.

In the late 1990s a move was made to Elmira. The aim of the museum is to cover all aviation aspects of World War II and the Korean and Vietnam conflicts. The story of these conflicts is portrayed with many models, photographs, uniforms and documents on show. Many interesting items are on show here.

A large number of the aircraft have been restored to flying condition. Pride of the fleet was the B-17G Fortress. The bomber was painted in the colours of 'Fuddy Duddy' which suffered a mid-air collision over Germany after 96 missions. This was sold to the American Airpower Museum in early 2002 and moved to California. Transport, liaison and training types are steadily being added. The rare Douglas Destroyer has been loaned by the museum at Pensacola. Only 28 were completed and another 330 were cancelled at the end of World War II.

The static aircraft collection is growing and the two early McDonnell jet fighters are now comparatively rare exhibits. The FH-1 Phantom was the first US jet aircraft designed for carrier operations. The prototype flew in January 1945 and 60 production models were delivered. The Banshee was basically an enlarged version of the FH-1. The design proved to be successful with almost 900 leaving the production lines. The type saw extensive service in the Korean War and the last examples were not withdrawn until the mid-1960s.

The replica of the Heinkel He 162 jet fighter, operated in the last years of World War II, was completed recently. Pleasure flights in the Kaydet, Cornell and Piper Cub are available on most days.

The Schweizer company produced many gliders at its factory on the airport and a number of types owned by the firm can be seen in the hangars along with a Piper Pawnee used for aerial tows.

TYPE	REG/SER	CON. NO.	PI/NOTES	STATUS
☐ Aeronca 65TC Grasshopper (O-58B) (L-3B)	N39351	F4142TA		PVA
☐ Aeronca 65TF Defender	N33769	F9381T		PV
☐ American Eagle A-129	N523S	393		PVA
☐ Bell 205 Iroquois (UH-1D) (UH-1H)	65-9589	4633		PV
☐ Bell 205 Iroquois (UH-1H)	66-16906	9100	Fuselage only.	RA
☐ Bell 205 Iroquois (UH-1H)	69-16723	12300		PV
☐ Bell-Boeing V-22A Osprey			Front fuselage only.	PV
☐ Boeing-Stearman B75N1 Kaydet (N2S-3)	N64604/'07190'	75-6811	Bu07207	PVAX
☐ Cessna 318E Dragonfly (A-37B)	N496WM	43364	71-0826, 826 (Vietnam)	RA
☐ Douglas DC-3A-456 Skytrain (C-47A) (R4D-5)	N293WM	13560	43-30079, Bu39091, NC88765, N91221, (N141A), N91221, CF-AOH, C-FAOH	PVA
☐ Douglas BTD-1 Destroyer	Bu04959	1891	Bu04959, N7035U	PV
☐ Douglas A-26B Invader	N237Y	7229	41-39516	PV
☐ Fairchild M-62A Cornell (PT-19)				PV
☐ Fairchild M-62A Cornell (PT-19A)	N50341	T41-446	41-57	PVA

☐ Fairchild M-62A Cornell (PT-19B)	N49830	5203AE	42-47871		PVA
☐ Fairchild-Republic A-10A Thunderbolt II	75-0293	A10-42			PV
☐ Glasflügel H201B Standard Libelle	N7190	93			PV
☐ Grumman G-40 Avenger (TBM-3)	Bu91752	4657	Possible identity.		PV
☐ Grumman G-93 Cougar (F9F-7) (F-9H)	Bu130802				RA
☐ Grumman G-99 Cougar (F9F-8P) (RF-9J) (TAF-9J)	Bu144402	86			PV
☐ Grumman G-134 Mohawk (OV-1C)	N6744	79C	62-5856		RAC
☐ Grumman G-303 Tomcat (F-14A)	Bu161605	464	.		PV
☐ Heinkel He 162A-1 (R)	'120241'				PVX
☐ Hughes 369M Cayuse (HO-6) (OH-6A)	'16668'	0961	67-16576		PVX
☐ Martin 272A Canberra (RB-57A)	52-1459	42			PV
☐ McDonnell M.23 Phantom I (FD-1) (FH-1)	Bu111768	20	Bu111768, N4283A		PV
☐ McDonnell M.24 Banshee (F2H-2P)	Bu125690	348			PV
☐ McDonnell M.98AM Phantom II (F-4B)	Bu152256	946	.		PV
☐ McDonnell M.199-1A Eagle (F-15A)	'83-0033'	122/A106	75-0026		PVX
☐ Mikoyan-Gurevich MiG-21PFM	4102	94A4102	In Polish markings.		PV
☐ North American NA-78 Texan (AT-6A) (SNJ-3)	N696WM	78-7045	41-16667, Bu01902, 7666 (South Africa)		PVA
☐ Piper J-3C-65 Cub	NC25769	3722	NC25769, N25769		PVA
☐ Piper J-4B Cub Coupe	NC26726	4-867	NC26726, N26726		PVA
☐ Piper PA-25-235 Pawnee D	N235WE	25-7556108	N9795P.		PV
☐ Pratt-Read PR-G1 (LNE-1)	NC4467U		Bu31506		PVA
☐ Schweizer SGS.2-8 (LNS-1)	N53275	6	Bu04384		PV
☐ Schweizer SGS.1-26E	N2740H	680			PV
☐ Schweizer SGS.2-32	N232WE	87			PV
☐ Schweizer SGS.2-33A	N233WE	570	N3621A		PV
☐ Schweizer SGS.2-33A	N3620G	569			PV
☐ Schweizer SGS.1-36	N236WE	44	N3623B		PV
☐ Stinson V-76 Sentinel (L-5)	N69887	76-419	42-98178		RA
☐ Vought FG-1D Corsair			Composite.		PVC
☐ Vought A-7D Corsair II	69-6200	D30			RA
☐ Westland-Sikorsky WS-55 Whirlwind HAR.10 (HAR.1)	XJ763	WA.109	XJ763, G-BKHA		PV
☐ WSK Lim-5P [MiG-17PF]	NX620PF	1D 06-20	0620 (Poland)		PV
☐ Yokosuks MXY-7 Ohka 11 (R)					PV

WINGS OVER WESTCHESTER AVIATION MUSEUM (NY83)

Address:	1 Blauvelt Place, Scarsdale, New York 10583-2709.
Tel:	914-723-0957
Admission:	Unknown.
Location:	At a private location

The Mackie is the only aircraft registered to the organisation. Built in the late 1990s nothing further is known about the design or the museum. Further information would be most welcome.

TYPE	REG/SER	CON. NO.	PI/NOTES	STATUS
☐ Mackie 1	N50007	0068		RAA

WOODRIDGE MONUMENT (NY84)

Location:	On permanent view in William Krieger Memorial Park in the south eastern part of the town.

TYPE	REG/SER	CON. NO.	PI/NOTES	STATUS
☐ Grumman G-105 Cougar (F9F-8T) (TF-9J)	Bu142442			PV

NORTH CAROLINA

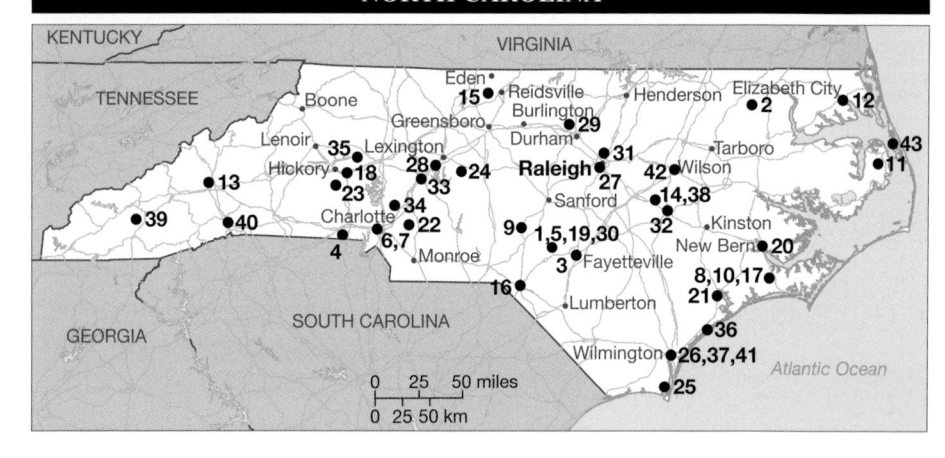

North Carolina

82nd AIRBORNE DIVISION WAR MEMORIAL MUSEUM (NC1)

Address:	Building C-6841, Ardennes Street, Fort Bragg, North Carolina 28310.
Tel:	910-344-5307 **Email:** aarsenj@bragg.army.mil
Admission:	Tuesday-Saturday 1000-1630.
Location:	About 10 miles north west of Fayetteville on Ardennes Street.

The 82nd began life as an infantry division in World War I and took up its present role during World War II. The unit served in France soon after its formation and since then has seen duty in Vietnam, the Caribbean and the Middle East.

The museum was set up in 1945 and the displays trace the history of the division. Artefacts from the early days of the unit are on show and a complete picture of the personnel who have served and of the campaigns fought is portrayed. The initial home of the exhibition was in a wooden hut which caught fire in the 1950s. A new building opened in 1957 and this has since been enlarged several times. The outside park contains vehicles and artillery used by the 82nd and types of aircraft which have carried paratroopers of the unit.

The front fuselage of the CG-15 glider is in the main building. Over 400 were delivered in the latter stages of World War II. The Caribou is one of the batch of five evaluated by the Army before the type was ordered some years later. Two of the helicopters are parked by regimental buildings on the camp.

TYPE	REG/SER	CON. NO.	PI/NOTES	STATUS
☐ Bell 204 Iroquois (HU-1A) (UH-1A)	59-1711	170		PV
☐ Bell 204 Iroquois (UH-1C) (UH-1M)	65-9559	1459	Outside HQ Building.	PV
☐ Bell 209 Huey Cobra (AH-1S) (AH-1E)	77-22784	22122	Outside 82nd. HQ.	PV
☐ Curtiss-Wright CW-20B-4 Commando (C-46F)	44-78573	22396	44-78573, N1685M	PV
☐ De Havilland DHC.4 Caribou (YAC-1) (YCV-2A) (YC-7A)	57-3083	8		PV
☐ Douglas DC-3A-467 Skytrain (C-47B) (VC-47D)	43-48932	14748/26193	43-48932, N2568	PV
☐ Fairchild 110 Flying Boxcar (C-119G) (C-119L)	53-8087	190		PV
☐ Fairchild 473 Provider (205) (C-123B) (C-123K)	54-0609	20058		PV
☐ Lockheed 382-8B Hercules (C-130E)	64-0525	382-4009		PV
☐ Waco NEU (CG-15A)	45-5276		Front fuselage only.	PV

AHOSKIE MONUMENT (NC2)

Location:	On permanent view at Tri-County Airport which is about 9 miles west of the town.

TYPE	REG/SER	CON. NO.	PI/NOTES	STATUS
☐ Lockheed 580 (T-33A)	51-4505	580-5800		PV

AIRBORNE AND SPECIAL OPERATIONS MUSEUM (NC3)

Address:	100 Bragg Boulevard, Fayetteville, North Carolina 28301.
Tel:	910-643-2766 **Fax:** 910-643-2793 **Email:** info@asomf.org
Admission:	Tuesday-Saturday 1000-1700; Sunday 1100-1600.
Location:	In the centre of the town at the corner with Hay Street.

This impressive museum opened in the late 1990s. The six acre site includes a large exhibition hall, theatre and a memorial garden. The histories of Airborne and Special operations are shown in vivid detail. There are walk-through dioramas and audio visual presentations. The training of paratroopers in 1940 is portrayed along with operations in World War II. The visitor can wander through a video enhanced Normandy village and sit on crates in an Army briefing hut in the Philippines. The work of the forces in Korea, Vietnam and Desert Storm is also shown. The C-47 is mounted in a flying position with paratroops leaving through the side door. Almost 14,000 examples of the Hadrian were built by manufacturers around the counttry.

TYPE	REG/SER	CON. NO.	PI/NOTES	STATUS
☐ Bell 205 Iroquois (UH-1H)	72-21524	13223		PV
☐ Douglas DC-3A-456 Skytrain (C-47A)	'315623'	12975	42-93101	PVX
☐ Hughes 369M Cayuse (HO-6) (OH-6A) (MH-6C)	68-17191	1151		PV
☐ Waco NZR Hadrian (CG-4A)	45-15073			PV

BESSEMER CITY MONUMENT (NC4)

Location:	On permanent view at ALP 243 in Long Creek Road in the town.

TYPE	REG/SER	CON. NO.	PI/NOTES	STATUS
☐ Lockheed 880-75-13 Starfire (F-97A) (F-94C)	51-5576	880-7639		PV

CAMP MACKALL MONUMENT (NC5)

Location:	On permanent view at the site which is about 3 miles west of Fort Bragg.

TYPE	REG/SER	CON. NO.	PI/NOTES	STATUS
☐ Bell 205 Iroquois (UH-1H)				PV

CAROLINAS AVIATION MUSEUM (NC6)

Address:	4672 First Flight Drive, Charlotte North Carolina 28208-5770.
Tel:	704-359-8442 **Fax:** 704-359-0057 **Email:** info@carolinasaviation.com
Admission:	Tuesday-Saturday 1000-1600; Sunday 1300-1700.
Location:	About 4 miles west of the city off Route 521.

In 1991 Floyd and Lois Wilson heard that two historic hangars at Charlotte Airport were to be demolished. They called a meeting which led to the formation of the Carolinas Historic Aviation Commission.

One aim was to set up a museum tracing the rich aeronautical traditions of the state. The first aircraft, a T-28, arrived in September 1992 and was stored in one of the hangars. In January 1993 the museum acquired the former Southern Airways hangar built in 1936. Work soon started to make it fit for an exhibition hall.

A number of the aircraft are maintained in flying condition including the DC-3 in Piedmont colours. The Salem-based airline used the type on its regional services from its formation in 1948 until 1963. The three seat Bellanca is labelled 'The World's Smallest Airliner'. In the 1940s it flew with State Airlines.

Under restoration is the Douglas Skystreak. Three examples of this jet research aircraft were built with the first flying in April 1947. The second crashed in 1948 and the third made the last flight in the programme in June 1953. The example in the workshops spent many years in store at the Marine Corps Museum at Quantico in Virginia and had deteriorated before arriving at Charlotte. This aircraft was flown by the late Scott Crossfield.

A replica of the Wright Glider which made many flights in the state in the first decade of the 20th century has been constructed to honour the brothers' contribution to aviation.

Jet fighters of the post World War II period are well represented along with helicopters used in the Vietnam conflict. Locally constructed homebuilt types as well as classic light aircraft are being added in order to present a varied display. The Fogle V-333 is an experimental tilt rotor design which never flew.

A large collection of artefacts is being assembled to present a comprehensive record of aviation in the area.

TYPE	REG/SER	CON. NO.	PI/NOTES	STATUS
☐ Beech D45 Mentor (T-34B)	Bu140931	BG-265		PV
☐ Bell 205 Iroquois (UH-1D) (UH-1H)	64-13731	4438		RA
☐ Bell 206A Kiowa (OH-58A)	71-20516	41377		RA
☐ Bell 209 Sea Cobra (AH-1J)	Bu159216	26056		PV
☐ Bellanca 14-9L Crusair	N1KQ	1037	In the airport terminal	PV
☐ Boeing 367-76-66 Stratofreighter (KC-97G)	53-0335	17117	Front fuselage only.	PV
☐ Boeing-Stearman A75N1 Kaydet (PT-17)	N48272	75-4086	42-15923 – as stated by this museum. However NMMC say ex 41-8706 which is c/n 75-2265 and N61986	PV
☐ Bushby-Long M-1 Midget Mustang	N373	100001		PV
☐ Cessna 305A Bird Dog (L-19A) (O-1A)	'20777'	21210	50-1536, N5257G, N777VN	RAX
☐ Convair 8-90 Delta Dagger (YF-102A)	53-1788			PV
☐ Douglas DC-3A-360 Skytrain (C-47)	N44V	4545	41-38596, NC15585, N1916, N555CR, C-GQHK, N46BF	PVA
☐ Douglas DC-3A-467 Skytrain (C-47B) (Dakota IV)	'349926'	15742/27187	43-49926, KN258, 12907 (Canada), A754 (Canada), N92BF, N12907	RA
☐ Douglas A-26C Invader	NL81797	29031	44-35752, N8627E, CF-KBZ, C-FKBZ	RA
☐ Douglas D-558-1 Skystreak	Bu37972	6566	NACA142	RAC
☐ Douglas A-4A Skyhawk (A4D-1)	Bu142226	11480		PV
☐ Ercoupe 415C	N3180H	3805		PV
☐ Fogle Skycat V-333				PV
☐ Grumman G-134 Mohawk (OV-1B) (OV-1D)	N1171Y	33B	62-5874	PVA
☐ Grumman G-134 Mohawk (OV-1B) (OV-1D)	N1209P	49B	62-5890	RAA
☐ Grumman G-303 Tomcat (F-14A) (F-14D)	Bu161166	393		PV
☐ Gyrodyne QH-50C (DSN-3)		DS-1355		PV
☐ Hawker-Siddeley Harrier II (AV-8B)	Bu161397	2		RA
☐ Kaman K-600 Huskie (HOK-1) (OH-43D)	Bu139982		Bu139982, N5185Q	PV
☐ Lockheed 080 Shooting Star (P-80C) (F-80C) (TO-1) (TV-1)	Bu33866	080-2100	48-0377	RA
☐ Lockheed 080 Shooting Star (P-80C) (F-80C) (TO-1) (TV-1)			Fuselage only.	RA
☐ Lockheed 580 (T-33A) (TV-2) (T-33B)	Bu131762	580-6433	51-8649	RA
☐ Lockheed 580 (T-33A) (TV-2) (T-33B)	Bu131870	580-6859	51-9075	RA
☐ McDonnell M.36BA Voodoo (F-101B) (F-101F)	56-0243	190		PV
☐ McDonnell M.98EV Phantom II (F-4J) (F-4S)	Bu155872	3384	.	PV
☐ McDonnell M.98EV Phantom II (F-4J) (F-4S)	Bu158353	4078	Front fuselage only.	PV
☐ North American NA-121 Texan (AT-6D) (SNJ-5)	Bu90906	121-41622	44-80900	RAC
☐ North American NA-168 Texan (T-6G)	N5296V	168-161	49-3057	RA
☐ North American NA-190 Sabre (F-86D) (F-86L)	52-4139	190-542		RA
☐ North American NA-200 Trojan (T-28B)	'37285'	200-356	Bu138285	RAX
☐ North American NA-235 Super Sabre (F-100D)	56-2992	235-90		RA
☐ North American NA-266 Buckeye (T2J-1) (T-2A)	Bu148239	266-90		RA
☐ Piper J-3C-65 Cub				RA
☐ Republic P-47D Thunderbolt	42-22331		Crash remains.	RAD
☐ Republic F-84G Thunderjet	'01191'		52-3253	PVX
☐ Sikorsky S-51 Dragonfly (HO3S-1)	'5136'	51-36	N92868 – possible identity.	PVX
☐ Sikorsky S-58 Choctaw (H-34A) (CH-34A) (CH-34C)	53-4496	5854		RA
☐ Sikorsky S-61R (CH-3C) (CH-3E)	65-12797	61572		RA
☐ Vertol V.107M Sea Knight (CH-46D) (CH-46E)	Bu153389	2287	With rear fuselage of c/n 2225 Bu153735	PV
☐ Vought A-7E Corsair II	Bu159971	E475		PV
☐ Waco NEU (CG-15A)				PV
☐ Wright 1902 Glider (R)			In the airport terminal.	PV

CHARLOTTE AIR NATIONAL GUARD BASE (NC7)

Location: By prior permission only at the airfield which is about 4 miles west of the city off Route 521.

TYPE	REG/SER	CON. NO.	PI/NOTES	STATUS
☐ Lockheed 382-4B Hercules (C-130E)	61-2367	382-3712		RA
☐ North American NA-190 Sabre (F-86L)	52-4142	190-545		RA

North Carolina

CHERRY POINT MARINE CORPS AIR STATION COLLECTION (NC8)

Address:	PO Box 8003, Building 198, Cherry Point, North Carolina 28533-0003.
Tel:	252-466-4241 **Email:** mary.bhill1@usmc.mil
Admission:	By prior permission only.
Location:	Just east of the town on Route 70.

The airfield opened in 1942 and has been a Marine Corps base ever since. In the 1990s there were plans for a major aviation museum at this important airfield. About 20 aircraft were allocation by the Marine Corps Museum and many were moved to the airfield. This came to nothing and a few are still stored on the base.

TYPE	REG/SER	CON. NO.	PI/NOTES	STATUS
☐ Grumman G-128 Intruder (YA2F-1) (YA-6A) (EA-6A)	Bu147865	2		RA
☐ Hawker-Siddeley Harrier II	Bu162969	90		PV
☐ McDonnell M.98DH Phantom II (RF-4B)	Bu157346	3749	.	RA
☐ McDonnell M.98EV Phantom II (F-4J)	Bu153073	1522		RA
☐ Vertol V.107M Sea Knight (CH-46A) (HH-46A) (HH-46D)	Bu151912	2060	.	RA

COMMEMORATIVE AIR FORCE (CAROLINAS WING) (NC9)

Address:	PO Box4984, Pinehurst, North Carolina 28374-4984.
Tel:	336-855-1958 **Email:** rworthin@bellsouth.net
Admission:	By prior permission only.
Location:	At Moore County Airport which is about 5 miles south of Carthage on Route 22.

Formed in 1983, the wing has restored a Stinson Reliant to flying condition. The aircraft served with the Royal Navy from 1944 to 1945 and is in these colours. A batch of 500 examples of the high-wing type were ordered and delivered to Great Britain. They were produced at Wayne, Michigan under Air Force control. The type was used on a number of duties including navigational training. At the end of the conflict about 350 were repatriated.

TYPE	REG/SER	CON. NO.	PI/NOTES	STATUS
☐ Stinson V-77 Reliant (AT-19)	N60634/FB605	77-333	43-44046, FB605, Bu11608, 'FK810'	RAA

CRAVEN COMMUNITY COLLEGE (NC10)

Address:	305 Cunningham Boulevard, Havelock, North Carolina 28532.
Tel:	252-447-5727 **Email:** ashburnl@cravencc.edu
Admission:	By prior permission only.
Location:	Just south of the airfield.

The college was established in 1965 as an industrial education centre. Several years later a school was added and the current title adopted. The site at Havelock is home to the aviation maintenance department where there are workshops and classrooms. The fleet of instructional airframes includes both civil and military types.

TYPE	REG/SER	CON. NO.	PI/NOTES	STATUS
☐ American Aviation AA-1A Trainer	N9371L	AA1A-0071		RA
☐ Beech 95-A55 Baron	N8599M	TC-451		RA
☐ Bell 209 Huey Cobra (AH-1G) (AH-1F)	66-15252	20008		RA
☐ Cessna 150F	N6502F	15063102		RA
☐ Cessna 150G	N3354J	15066054		RA
☐ Cessna 150H	N66642	15067464		RA
☐ Cessna 150M	N66458	15076062		RA
☐ Cessna 152	N67860	15282064		RA
☐ Cessna 152	N69048	15282460		RA
☐ Cessna 172N	N737UA	17269675		RA
☐ Gates Learjet 24	N16HC	24-126	N653LJ, N352WR, N332FP, (N345SF)	RA
☐ Hughes 269A	N8844F	43-0206		RA
☐ Piper PA-28-140 Cherokee F	N55655	28-7325452		RA
☐ Piper PA-38-112 Tomahawk	N25163	38-80A0037		RA
☐ Sikorsky S-70B Sea Hawk (SH-60B)				RA
☐ Sikorsky S-70B Sea Hawk (SH-60F)	Bu164104	701590		RA
☐ Vertol V.107M Sea Knight (HRB-1) (CH-46A) (UH-46A) (HH-46D)	Bu150963	2049		RA

DARE COUNTY REGIONAL AIRPORT MUSEUM (NC11)

Address:	PO Box 429, 410 Airport Road, Manteo, North Carolina 27954.
Tel:	252-473-2600 **Fax:** 252-473-1196 **Email:** museum@darenc.com
Admission:	Daily 0800-1900.
Location:	Just south of the town.

In the 1930s there was a nearby private airstrip but it was not until the early 1940s that the county set up a committee to construct a municipal airport. The attack on Pearl Harbor changed the plans and on 3rd March 1943 Naval Air Station Manteo was commissioned. A number of squadrons carried out training at the site before they moved to serve on carriers or at airfields in the Pacific Theatre. The field was closed on 15th December 1945 and two years later Dare County took over the site. The museum has been set up in the terminal building and has on show models and memorabilia tracing the history of the airfield. Kill Devil Hills is not far away and the earliest design is the Wright Flyer. Several Navy types are hanging from the beams and there are also a few civil models. An excellent display of photographs spanning several decades can also be seen.

ELIZABETH CITY COAST GUARD AIR STATION COLLECTION (NC12)

Address:	Consolidated Road, Elizabeth City, North Carolina 27909.
Tel:	252-335-5634
Admission:	By prior permission only
Location:	At the airfield which is about 3 miles south east of the town off Route 34.

The station was commissioned on 15th August 1940 with ten aircraft on strength. When America entered World War II the field was taken over by the US Navy for search and rescue, antisubmarine patrols and training duties.

Three types which have been used by the service have been preserved. The Grumman Albatross amphibian entered service in 1954 and over 70 were flown before the final example was withdrawn in August 1976 and flown to the museum at Pensacola. The Coast Guard flew the Dassault Falcon on patrol, pollution control and drug interdiction duties. Also on the site is a training school where student mechanics work on airframes and engines.

TYPE	REG/SER	CON. NO.	PI/NOTES	STATUS
☐ Aérospatiale AS.366G Dauphin (HH-65A)	'6500'		In Aviation Training Center.	RAX
☐ Aérospatiale AS.366G Dauphin (HH-65A)	'6509'		In Aviation Training Center.	RAX
☐ Dassault Falcon 20G (HU-25B)	2136	460	F-WJML, N467F	RA
☐ Grumman G-234 Albatross (G-64) (SA-16A) (UF-1G) (UF-2G) (HU-16E)	7247	G-336	51-7247, N227S	RA
☐ Sikorsky S-62A Seaguard (HH-52A)	1384	62065		RA
☐ Sikorsky S-70B Sea Hawk (SH-60B)	'6096'		In Aviation Training Center.	RAX

ENKA MONUMENT (NC13)

Location:	On permanent view outside the Middle School in Sand Hill Road in the south eastern part of the town.

TYPE	REG/SER	CON. NO.	PI/NOTES	STATUS
☐ Republic RF-84F Thunderflash	53-7570			PV

GOLDSBORO MONUMENT (NC14)

Location:	On permanent view in a park in East Chestnut Street just south of the town centre.

TYPE	REG/SER	CON. NO.	PI/NOTES	STATUS
☐ North American NA-203 Sabre (F-86H)	53-1370	203-142		PV

GUILFORD TECHNICAL COMMUNITY COLLEGE (NC15)

Address:	260 North Regional Road, Piedmont Triad International Airport, Greensboro, North Carolina 27409.
Tel:	336-665-9425 **Email:** khonstetter@gtcc.edu
Admission:	By prior permission only.
Location:	About 3 miles west of the town off Route 70.

The college has workshops and classrooms at the T.H. Davis Aviation School at the airport. A number of instructional airframes are in use along with engines and testing equipment. The Corben Baby A, parasol-wing single-seater, it first appeared in 1929. Plans were made available and the college aircraft was built in the 1980s.

TYPE	REG/SER	CON. NO.	PI/NOTES	STATUS
☐ Aero Commander 680				RA
☐ Beech 23 Musketeer	N2325J	M-276		RA
☐ Beech A45 Mentor (T-34A)				RA
☐ Beech B90 King Air	N7BF	LJ-350	N579DU, (N5798), N579DU	RA
☐ Boeing 727-22F	N148FE	19086	N7073U	RA
☐ Cessna 310				RA
☐ Corben C-1 Baby Ace	N8154	NH-1		RA
☐ North American NA-276 Sabreliner (T-39A) (CT-39A)	'66866'	276-20	62-4467	RAX
☐ Piper PA-23-250 Aztec D	N6795Y	27-4133		RA
☐ Piper PA-28-140 Cherokee	N4244J	28-22599		RA

HAMLET MONUMENT (NC16)

Location:	On permanent view at a site on Route 177 in the south western part of the town.

TYPE	REG/SER	CON. NO.	PI/NOTES	STATUS
☐ Bell 204 Iroquois (UH-1B)				

HAVELOCK TOURIST AND EVENT CENTER (NC17)

Address:	202 Tourist Center Drive, Havelock, North Carolina 28532.
Tel:	252-444-4348 **Email:** ktownsend@havelock.nc.us
Admission:	Monday-Saturday 0900-1700.
Location:	In the centre of the town.

North Carolina

The City of Havelock has maintained close ties with the nearby Cherry Point Marine Corps base for over 60 years. A display tracing this link has been set up in the centre. The history of Marine Corps aviation is portrayed in an exhibition of models, photographs and uniforms.
A range of ejector seats can also be seen. The squadrons which have served at Cherry Point are featured. A special display, which changes regularly, features a particular unit. In the inter-war period the Boeing company produced a range of successful biplane fighters which served with both Army and Navy units.
The F4B-3 was similar to the Army P-12E. A total of 21 was ordered and all were delivered in December 1931 and January 1932. Several were transferred to the Marine Corps.

TYPE	REG/SER	CON. NO.	PI/NOTES	STATUS
☐ AAI RQ-2B Pioneer	Bu300307	1506	.	PV
☐ Boeing 235 (F4B-3) (R)	'Bu8891'	1506	N8891 – constructed from Boeing-Stearman 75 parts.	PVX
☐ Douglas A-4M Skyhawk	Bu160024	14526	.	PV
☐ Grumman G-128 Intruder (A-6E)	Bu164378	I-718	By Hampton Inn.	PV
☐ Grumman G-93 Cougar (F9F-6P) (RF-9F)	Bu127487	287	.	PV
☐ Hawker-Siddeley P.1127 Harrier 50 (AV-8A)	Bu158976	P137	.	PV
☐ McDonnell M.98DH Phantom II (RF-4B)	Bu157342	3689	.	PV
☐ Vertol V.107M Sea Knight (HRB-1) (CH-46A) (HH-46A) (HH-46D)	Bu150941	2024	.	RA

HICKORY AVIATION MUSEUM (NC18)

Address: PO Box 3152, Hickory, North Carolina 28603.
Tel: 828-322323-1963 **Email:** jeffw@commscope.com
Admission: Saturday 1000-1700; Sunday 1300-1700.
Location: At Hickory Airport which is about 2 miles north west of the town off Route 321.

The Sabre Society of North Carolina came into being in the early 1990s when it acquired a semi-derelict North American Fury fighter. Over the next decade more jet fighters arrived at the field and restoration work was carried out. The dream of a museum became a reality in the spring of 2007 when a display opened in the former flight service station in the airport terminal. The history of flying in the region is portrayed in the exhibition with many photographs, documents, models and documents on show. Engines and weapons can also be seen.

TYPE	REG/SER	CON. NO.	PI/NOTES	STATUS
☐ Bell 205 Iroquois (UH-1H)				PV
☐ De Havilland DH.115 Vampire T.11	'WD187'	15283	XD538, 7951M, (N675LF), N70877	PVX
☐ Douglas A-4L Skyhawk (A4D-2N) (A-4C)	Bu148538	12731	.	PV
☐ Douglas A-4L Skyhawk (A4D-2N) (A-4C)			Front fuselage only.	PV
☐ Fokker F.27 Friendship 500	N705FE	10367	PH-FMO, F-BPNB, G-BNZE, G-FEDX	PV
☐ Grumman G-303 Tomcat (F-14D)	Bu163902	612	.	PV
☐ Hispano HA.200D Saeta	N4551W	20/60	E.14B-54, C.10B-54, A.10B-54	PV
☐ Lockheed 580 (T-33A)	52-9529	580-7664	.	PV
☐ McDonnell M.98AM Phantom II (F4H-1) (F-4B)	Bu148400	85	.	PV
☐ North American NA-215 Fury (FJ-3M) (MF-1C)	Bu145125	215-99	Bu141393, N92321	PV
☐ North American NA-244 Fury (FJ-4B) (AF-1E)	Bu143596	244-104	Possible identity.	RA
☐ Northrop N-311 Tiger II (F-5E)	74-1540	R.1198	74-1540, Bu741540	PV
☐ Republic F-105B Thunderchief	54-0107	B-9	.	PV
☐ Republic LTV-N-2 [Fieseler Fi 103A-1]				RA
☐ Vought A-7A Corsair II	Bu154345	A184	.	PV

JOHN F. KENNEDY SPECIAL WARFARE MUSEUM (NC19)

Address: Building D.2502, Ardennes and Marion Streets, Fort Bragg, North Carolina 28307-5200.
Tel: 910-432-1533 **Email:** merrittr@soc.mil
Admission: Tuesday-Sunday 1130-1600.
Location: About 10 miles north west of Fayetteville.

The displays trace the history of unconventional warfare over the last two and a half centuries. The 18th century Rangers, the Alamo Scouts and the Airborne Rangers of Korea are all highlighted in the exhibition. The development of psychological warfare is chronicled in detail. A Courier will be put on show.

TYPE	REG/SER	CON. NO.	PI/NOTES	STATUS
☐ Helio H-395 Super Courier (U-10B)				RAC

NEW BERN MONUMENTS (NC20)

Location: On permanent view at two locations in the town.

TYPE	REG/SER	CON. NO.	PI/NOTES	STATUS
☐ Grumman G-98 Tiger (F11F-1) (F-11A)	Bu141802	119	On Route 17.	PV
☐ Hawker-Siddeley P.1127 Harrier 50 (AV-8A)	Bu158963	P124	At the airport south of the town.	PV

NEW RIVER MARINE CORPS AIR STATION (NC21)

Address: PSC Box 2110, New River, Jacksonville North Carolina 28545-1001.
Tel: 919-451-6197/8 **Email:** mcasnrjpao@usmc.mil
Admission: By prior permission only.
Location: About 3 miles south of the town to the east of Route 17.

455

The airfield is located close to the vast Camp Lejeune training area and houses several helicopter squadrons. Three types which have seen service at the base have been preserved just inside the main gate. The Osprey is located on the base and will join the display in due course.

TYPE	REG/SER	CON. NO.	PI/NOTES	STATUS
☐ Bell-Boeing YV-22A Osprey	Bu163911	D0001		RAC
☐ Sikorsky S-58 Seahorse (HUS-1Z) (VH-34D)	Bu147191	581142		PV
☐ Sikorsky S-65A Sea Stallion (CH-53A)	'Bu153698'	65025	Bu152398 –	PVX
☐ Vertol V.107M Sea Knight (CH-46D) (CH-46E)	Bu153402	2300		PV

NEW SALEM MONUMENT (NC22)

Location:	On permanent view at ALP 440 at 7321 Highway 218 West.

TYPE	REG/SER	CON. NO.	PI/NOTES	STATUS
☐ Bell 209 Huey Cobra (AH-1G) (AH-1F)	67-15587	20251		PV

NEWTON MONUMENT (NC23)

Location:	On permanent view at VFW 5305 on Highway 10 in the north western part of the town.

TYPE	REG/SER	CON. NO.	PI/NOTES	STATUS
☐ Bell 205 Iroquois (UH-1D) (UH-1H)	64-13729	4436		PV

NORTH CAROLINA AVIATION MUSEUM (NC24)

Address:	2222-G Pilots View Road, Asheboro, North Carolina 27205-9667.
Tel:	336-625-0170 Fax: 336-629-2984 Email: ncam@triad.twcbc.com
Admission:	April–October Monday-Saturday 1000-1700, Sunday 1300-1700; November Tuesday-Saturday 1000-1700, Sunday 1300-1700; December–March Wednesday-Saturday 1000-1700, Sunday 1300-1700.
Location:	At the airport which is about 5 miles south west of the town on Route 49.

This flying museum has in its collection military aircraft from World War II to the Vietnam conflict. In the hangar is one of the largest collections of military uniforms and memorabilia in the South Eastern States. Newspapers covering the period have been mounted on the walls of the hangar and big band music can be heard. There are several military vehicles to be seen. The aircraft are regular attenders at air shows throughout the region and the museum hosts an annual event in the first weekend in June. A rarity is the Savoia-Marchetti SM.56. The prototype of this single engined biplane flying boat first flew in Italy in 1924. The SM.56A was an amphibian version and the American Aeronautical Corporation built more than 40 under licence.

TYPE	REG/SER	CON. NO.	PI/NOTES	STATUS
☐ Aerosport Quail	N99HS	7		PV
☐ Beech A45 Mentor (T-34A)	N3648G	G-774	55-217	PVA
☐ Beech D18S Expeditor (C-45H)	N213DE	AF-392	51-11835, N6307D, N7313N	PVA
☐ Beech D18S Expeditor (C-45H)	'602271'	AF-586	52-10656, N9550Z – rebuilt from C18S Kansan (AT-11) c/n 1270 41-27425	PVAX
☐ Boeing-Stearman A75N1 Kaydet (PT-17)	N49926	75-808	41-1048	PVA
☐ Cessna 305A Bird Dog (L-19A) (O-1A)	N5472V	21410	50-1680	PVA
☐ Cessna R172E Mescalero (T-41B)	N899SP	R1720101	67-15700	PVA
☐ Fairchild 22 C7F	N14339	916	NC14339	PVA
☐ Pilatus P.3-05	N842JM	480-29	A-842	PVA
☐ Piper J-3C-65 Cub	NC78689	17793	NC78689, N78689	PVA
☐ Piper J-3C-65 Cub	NC1776	6600		PVA
☐ Savoia-Marchetti SM.56A	NC194M	7		PVA
☐ Vans RV-8	N123SG	74-2990	81425	PV

NORTH CAROLINA MILITARY HISTORY MUSEUM (NC25)

Address:	Fort Fisher, Kure Beach, North Carolina 28412.
Admission:	April–October Friday-Sunday 1200-1600; November–March Friday-Saturday 1200-1600.
Location:	Just south of the town.

The exhibition has been set up by the North Carolina Military History Society. The displays trace the development of forces in the state. On show are many artefacts, models, uniforms, photographs and documents. The Iroquois helicopter is parked outside along with a number of military vehicles.

TYPE	REG/SER	CON. NO.	PI/NOTES	STATUS
☐ Bell 205 Iroquois (UH-1H)	68-16289	10548		PV

NORTH CAROLINA MUSEUM OF AVIATION (NC26)

Address:	1903 Hall Drive, Wilmington, North Carolina 28405.
Tel:	910-254-9989
Admission:	When the terminal is open.
Location:	In the north eastern suburbs of the town.

The group has collected a large amount of material tracing the history of aviation in the region. Displays of memorabilia have been set up in the new terminal building at Wilmington Airport.

North Carolina

Parked outside at the Carolinas Aviation Museum is this Grumman OV-1D Mohawk. (Derek Heley) [NC6]

The Hickory Aviation Museum has this Vought A-7A Corsair II on show. [NC18]

Mounted on the USS North Carolina *is this Vought OS2U-2 Kingfisher. (Derek Heley) [NC37]*

NORTH CAROLINA MUSEUM OF HISTORY (NC27)

Address:	5 East Edenton Street, Raleigh, North Carolina 27601-1011.
Tel:	919-807-7900 **Fax:** 919-733-**8655** **Email:** john.campbell@ncdcr.gov
Admission:	Monday-Saturday 0900-1700; Sunday 1200-1700.
Location:	In the eastern part of the city centre.

Founded in 1902 the museum traces the history of the state since early times. The Bensen company is based in the state and has produced many autogyro designs over the last 50 years. The Wright brothers carried out experiments at Kill Devil Hill so a replica of the Flyer is appropriate.

TYPE	REG/SER	CON. NO.	PI/NOTES	STATUS
☐ Bensen B-8M Gyrocopter				PV
☐ Rogalo Standard Hang Glider				PV
☐ Wright Flyer (R)				PV

NORTH CAROLINA TRANSPORTATION MUSEUM (NC28)

Address:	411 South Salisbury Street, Spencer, North Carolina 28159.
Tel:	704-636-2889 **Fax:** 704-639-1881 **Email:** nctrans@nctrans.org
Admission:	May–October Monday-Saturday 0900-1700, Sunday 1300-1700; November–April Tuesday-Saturday 1000-1600, Sunday 1300-1600.
Location:	In the town which is about 40 miles north east of Charlotte off Interstate 85.

The site was the location of the Southern Railway's repair shops and it is now being developed into a state transport museum. Construction of the facility started in 1896 and the workshops finally closed in 1970. The museum opened in 1983. Over a dozen buildings are on the 100 acre site and these are gradually being converted for display purposes.

Four aircraft are on show along with a small collection of aviation memorabilia. Molt Taylor designed an amphibian soon after World War II. This was not built as he turned his attention to the roadable Aerocar. The Coot is a low wing two seat amphibious aircraft fitted with a pusher engine. The wings and horizontal tail surfaces can be folded so that the aircraft can easily be towed on a trailer. The prototype flew in 1969 and at least 70 have been completed by amateur constructors.

The Wright Flyer was built to commemorate the centenary of powered flight. A steam locomotive pulling several restored coaches now takes visitors around the site at weekends. A large number of vehicles are displayed in the halls.

TYPE	REG/SER	CON. NO.	PI/NOTES	STATUS
☐ Douglas DC-3A-405 Skytrooper (C-53)	N56V	4900	41-20130, NC18600	PV
☐ Rearwin 185 Skyranger	N92910	1641		PV
☐ Taylor Coot A	N79BM	WM-1		PV
☐ Wright Flyer (R)				PV

NORTH CAROLINA VIETNAM HELICOPTER PILOTS ASSOCIATION (NC29)

Address:	2822 Franklin Road, Hillsborough, North Carolina 27278.
Admission:	By prior permission only.
Location:	At a number of locations in the area.

The group was formed in 1989 by pilots who flew helicopters in the conflict. Their aim was to acquire types used in combat and display them around the region. The airframes were restored and mounted on trailers so that they could be easily transported. Visits are made to local schools, air shows, festivals and parades.

TYPE	REG/SER	CON. NO.	PI/NOTES	STATUS
☐ Bell 204 Iroquois (UH-1C) (UH-1M)				RA
☐ Bell 205 Iroquois (UH-1D) (UH-1H)	64-13767	4474		RA
☐ Bell 205 Iroquois (UH-1H)	68-15217	10147		RA
☐ Bell 209 Huey Cobra (AH-1G) (AH-1S)	68-15095	20629		RA
☐ Hughes 369M Cayuse (HO-6) (OH-6A)	65-12925	0010		RA
☐ Hughes 369M Cayuse (HO-6) (OH-6A)	65-12958	0043		RA

POPE AIR FORCE BASE COLLECTION (NC30)

Address:	43AW/PA, Pope Air Force Base, North Carolina 28308-5000.
Tel:	910-424-3183
Admission:	By prior permission only.
Location:	About 12 miles north west of Fayetteville off Route 24.

The airfield, which is situated next to Fort Bragg, now the home of the airborne forces of the US Army, opened in 1919. The site is named after Lieutenant Harley H. Pope who was killed in 1917 when his Curtiss Jenny ran out of fuel near Fayetteville.

The based transport aircraft provide support for the Army units. An air park is now being constructed near the main gate and currently four transport types are on show. A number of preserved aircraft moved to Moody AFB in when a fighter unit was transferred to the Georgia airfield.

TYPE	REG/SER	CON. NO.	PI/NOTES	STATUS
☐ Douglas DC-3A-467 Skytrain (TC-47B) (R4D-6) (R4D-6R) (R4D-6S) (SC-47J) (TC-47J)	'293496'	16046/32794	44-76462, Bu39098, N7478C, N35, '118427'	RAX
☐ Fairchild 110 Flying Boxcar (C-119G)	'33182'	10446	50-0128	RAX
☐ Fairchild 473 Provider (205) (C-123B) (C-123K)	'372'	20118	54-0669	RAX
☐ Lockheed 382C-15D Hercules (C-130E)	70-1269	382C-4423		RA

North Carolina

RALEIGH-DURHAM AIR NATIONAL GUARD BASE (NC31)

| Location: | At the International Airport which is about 6 miles south east of Durham on Route 70. |

TYPE	REG/SER	CON. NO.	PI/NOTES	STATUS
☐ Bell 204 Iroquois (UH-1C) (UH-1M)	66-15000	1728		RA

SEYMOUR JOHNSON AIR FORCE BASE (NC32)

Address:	4FW/PA 1510 Wright Brothers Avenue, Goldsboro, North Carolina 27351-2418.
Tel:	919-722-1110.
Admission:	By prior permission only.
Location:	In the south eastern suburbs of the town.

Opened in June 1942, the base is named after a local pilot Lieutenant Seymour A. Johnson who was killed in a crash in 1941. The site was inactive from 1946 until the 4th Fighter Interceptor Group took up residence in 1956. It still operates from the base and was the first operational unit to fly the F-15E, which arrived in the late 1980s. The Canadian-built Sabre has been restored to represent one flown from the base. The Mustang has arrived from Dover AFB in Delaware and at one time was due to go on display at Bolling.

TYPE	REG/SER	CON. NO.	PI/NOTES	STATUS
☐ Canadair CL-13B Sabre 6 [North American F-86E]	'112972'			RAX
☐ McDonnell M.98DJ Phantom II (F-4C)	64-0770	1069		RA
☐ McDonnell M.98HO Phantom II (F-4E)	74-0649	4800	Also reported as 74-1649	RA
☐ McDonnell M.199-1B Eagle (TF-15A) (F-15B)	77-0161	394/B052		RA
☐ North American NA-122 Mustang (P-51D)	'415569'	122-31339	44-63613, 270 (Uruguay) – possibly c/n 122-31341 44-63615.	RAC
☐ North American NA-192 Super Sabre (F-100A)	'41814'	192-68	53-1573	RAX
☐ Republic F-105D Thunderchief	61-0056	D-251		RA

SALISBURY MONUMENT (NC33)

| Location: | On permanent view at VFW 3006 at 1200 Brenner Avenue in the north western part of the town. |

TYPE	REG/SER	CON. NO.	PI/NOTES	STATUS
☐ Bell 205 Iroquois (UH-1D) (UH-1H)	66-16236	5930		PV

STANLEY MONUMENT (NC34)

| Location: | By prior permission only at a private house in the town. |

TYPE	REG/SER	CON. NO.	PI/NOTES	STATUS
☐ Lockheed 1049A-55-137 Super Constellation (1049A-55-86) (WV-2) (EC-121K) (NC-121K)	Bu141292	1049A-4416	Front and centre fuselage only.	RA

STATESVILLE MONUMENT (NC35)

| Location: | On permanent view at ALP 65 at 2446 Salisbury Highway. About 3 miles east of the town centre. |

TYPE	REG/SER	CON. NO.	PI/NOTES	STATUS
☐ Bell 209 Huey Cobra (AH-1G) (AH-1F)	68-17040	20768		PV

TOPSAIL ISLAND MUSEUM (NC36)

Address:	720 Channel Boulevard, Topsail Beach, North Carolina 28445.
Tel:	910-328-2488 Email: info@topsailhistoricalsociety.org
Admission:	April–mid October Monday, Tuesday, Thursday-Saturday 1400-1600. Winter by appointment only.
Location:	About 25 miles north east of Wilmington.

During the 1940s the area was used for the testing of missiles. The display, in the local Assembly Building, includes photographs, models and actual rockets. One, now on show, was washed ashore a few years ago. The history of the region from early times is also portrayed. A number of local Indian artefacts can be seen.

UNITED STATES SHIP *NORTH CAROLINA* BATTLESHIP MEMORIAL (NC37)

Address:	1 Battleship Road, Wilmington, North Carolina 28402-0480.
Tel:	910-251-5797 Fax: 910-251-5807 Email: ncbb55@battleshipnc.com
Admission:	Daily 0800-2000 (closes at sunset September–May)
Location:	East side of the bridge over the Cape Fear River in the centre of the town.

Commissioned in 1941, the USS *North Carolina* served with distinction in every major Pacific campaign. The ship was placed in store at Bayonne in 1947 and was due to be scrapped in 1960 but when the people of the state heard the news they rapidly raised the sum required to purchase her. The warship opened as a museum in 1962 and the visitor can undertake a self-guided tour through many parts of the vast structure. Mounted on the fantail of the ship is one of the few surviving Vought Kingfishers. The aircraft was flying from Washington State to Alaska when it crashed in a remote area of Calvert Island in British Columbia – only the engine, instruments, radio and armament were salvaged at this time. The wreck was rediscovered in 1963. The airframe was moved to Wilmington in 1969 and then sent to Dallas to be restored by workers at the Vought plant. The prototype of the catapult-launched floatplane first flew in 1938 and served on battleships and cruisers during World War II. The type was in service with the US Navy, the US Marines, the US Coast Guard, the Royal Navy and the Soviet Navy. The Australian Navy flew a few from shore bases. A landplane version also served in small numbers. Over 1,500 were built and the last examples were withdrawn from use by the Cuban Navy, which flew four, in 1959.

TYPE	REG/SER	CON. NO.	PI/NOTES	STATUS
☐ Vought V-310 Kingfisher (OS2U-2)	Bu3073			PV

WAYNE COMMUNITY COLLEGE (NC38)

Address:	3000 Wayne Memorial Drive, Goldsboro, North Carolina 27534.
Tel:	919-735-5151
Admission:	By prior permission only.
Location:	At the airport which is about 5 miles north of the town.

The college was set up in 1957 as the Goldsboro Industrial Education Center and took up its current name in 1967. The aviation department has a facility at the airport. In the hangar are a number of instructional airframes and engines. The Tebuan was flown by the Royal Malaysian Air Force.

TYPE	REG/SER	CON. NO.	PI/NOTES	STATUS
☐ Aero Commander 560A (L-26B) (U-4A)	N14WC	269	N2769B, 55-4646	RA
☐ Beech D18S	N80231	A-211		RAD
☐ Canadair CL-41G-5 Tebuan	M22-07	2203	FM1132	RA
☐ Cessna 150L	N11437	15075420		RA
☐ Piper PA-25 Pawnee				RA
☐ Piper PA-28-180 Cherokee				RA

WAYNESVILLE MONUMENT (NC39)

Location:	On permanent view at VFW 5202 at 325 Miller Street in the north eastern part of the town.

TYPE	REG/SER	CON. NO.	PI/NOTES	STATUS
☐ Bell 205 Iroquois (UH-1H)	67-17145	9543		PV

WESTERN NORTH CAROLINA AIR MUSEUM (NC40)

Address:	PO Box 2343,1340 Gilbert Street, Hendersonville, North Carolina 28793-2343.
Tel:	878-698-2482 Email: info2009@WNCAirMuseum.com
Admission:	April–October Saturday 1000-1800, Sunday and Wednesday 1200-1800; November–March Wednesday, Saturday-Sunday 1200-1700.
Location:	At Hendersonville Airport which is about 1 mile east of the town.

The museum was founded by three local aviators who owned a number of vintage aircraft. In May 1992 a temporary home was obtained in a hangar at Hendersonville Airport.
Construction of a purpose-built museum at the field soon started and the official opening took place on 22nd May 1993. Displays tracing the history of aviation in the region are being set up and a collection of engines and flight manuals can also be seen. Members of the museum own a number of vintage and classic aircraft and there are plans to double the size of the hangar in the near future. A replica of the ornithopter designed in 1510 by Leonardo da Vinci has been built and this is taken to many local events where it has proved a popular attraction. The remainder of the aircraft are all in flying condition or are in the process of being restored to airworthiness.
The display building is currently so full that a number of the aircraft have been suspended from the ceiling. The majority of the airworthy types are in an adjacent hangar and are sometimes away from the field. The collection includes a range of homebuilt designs spanning the years. The Parker JP.001, powered by a 100hp Continental engine, first flew in 1976. The Gilbert Robert DGA-1A was built in 1988 and was for a time on show in the museum at Lakeland in Florida.

TYPE	REG/SER	CON. NO.	PI/NOTES	STATUS
☐ Aeronca 7AC Champion	N85582	7AC-4235		PVA
☐ Aeronca C-3	NC11293	A-125		PV
☐ Bellanca 7KCAB Citabria	N53843	550-73		PVA
☐ Bensen B-2 Gyroglider				PV
☐ Cessna 170B	N3533C	26756		PV
☐ Corben E Junior Ace	N28LW	LWM2		PVA
☐ Curtiss 50C Robin 4C-1A	N563N	712		PVA
☐ Da Vinci Ornithopter (R)				PV
☐ Ercoupe 415C	N36494	4274	NC36494	PVA
☐ Fairchild 24R46	N81236	R46-137	NC81236	PVA
☐ Gilbert Robert DGA-1A	N37835	1		PVA
☐ Heath LNB-4 Parasol	N47529	121033		PVA
☐ Nieuport 11 (R)	N8217U	DWE001		PV
☐ Oldfield Baby Great Lakes Special	N11311	2		PV
☐ Parker JP.001 American Special	N113JP	001		PV
☐ Piper J-3C-65 Cub	N92133	1675c		PVA
☐ Piper J-5 Cub Cruiser	NC38499	5-982	NC38499, N38499	PVA
☐ Piper PA-22-108 Colt	N5360Z	22-8688		PVA
☐ Royal Aircraft Factory S.E.5E (R)	N4327S	DWE 002		PVA
☐ Stampe & Vertongen S.V.4C				PV
☐ Taylor E-2 Cub	N12664	36	NC12664	PV
☐ Taylor J-2 Cub	NC16315	548	NC16315, N16315	PVA
☐ Wittman W.8 Tailwind	N14470	558		PVA

WILMINGTON MONUMENTS (NC41)

Location:	On permanent view at two locations in the town.

TYPE	REG/SER	CON. NO.	PI/NOTES	STATUS
☐ Grumman G-98 Tiger (F11F-1) (F-11A)	Bu138619	17	At a business at 5915 Carolina Beach Road in the south eastern part of the city.	PV
☐ Lockheed 580 (T-33A)	52-9766	580-8026	At VFW 2572 at 2772 Carolina Beach Road in the south eastern part of the city.	PV

WILSON MONUMENT (NC42)

Location:	By prior permission only at the Industrial Air Center in the north western part of the town.

TYPE	REG/SER	CON. NO.	PI/NOTES	STATUS
☐ Bell 204 Iroquois (UH-1F)	N485DF	7088	65-7947	RA

WRIGHT BROTHERS NATIONAL MEMORIAL (NC43)

Address: 1401 National Park Drive, Box 675, Manteo, North Carolina 27954.
Tel: 252-473-2111 **Fax:** 252-473-2595 **Email:** wrbr_information@nps.gov
Admission: Daily 0900-1700.
Location: At Kill Devil Hills on Route 158.

A 60 foot high granite monument was erected in 1960 at Kill Devil Hill to commemorate the Wright brothers' pioneering flights. In the early years of the century the pair carried out over 1,000 glider flights before Orville achieved the first controlled powered flight on 17th December 1903. The original Wright Flyer can be seen just inside the main entrance of the National Air and Space Museum in Washington, DC.
 A visitor centre has been constructed close to the site of their first powered flight and this houses replicas of the brothers' 1902 glider and of the 1903 Flyer and associated displays. The pair built their first glider in 1900 and flew it mostly as a kite. However Wilbur did make a short ten-second glide late in the year. The 1901 Glider was a larger version and their research culminated with the 1902 version which was flown over 400 times. The addition of an engine resulted in the successful flights.
 The paths of the first four flights on the historic day are denoted by markers and there is also a portion of the original wooden guide rail. In 1963 replicas of their living quarters and their hangar/workshop were constructed. A second Flyer was donated in 2004.

TYPE	REG/SER	CON. NO.	PI/NOTES	STATUS
☐ Wright 1902 Glider (R)				PV
☐ Wright Flyer (R)				PV
☐ Wright Flyer (R)				PV

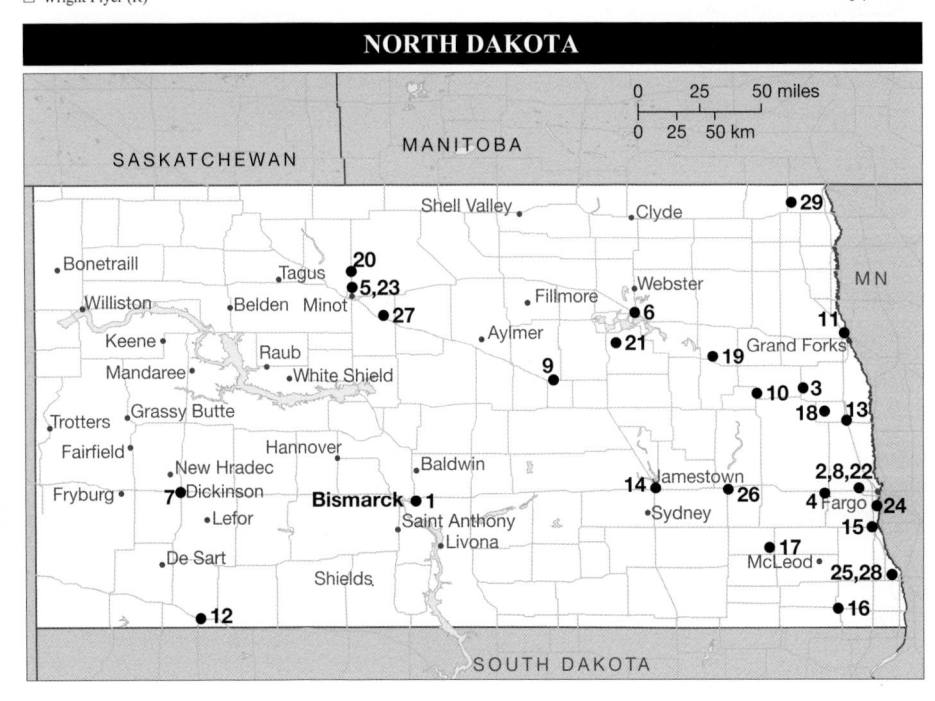

NORTH DAKOTA

BISMARCK MONUMENT (ND1)

Location:	On permanent view at the airport in the south eastern part of the town.

TYPE	REG/SER	CON. NO.	PI/NOTES	STATUS
☐ Bell 205 Iroquois (UH-1H) (UH-1V)	70-16440	12745	Tail boom from c/n 10196 68-15266	PV

BONANZAVILLE EAGLES AIRCRAFT MUSEUM (ND2)

Address:	1351 West Main Street, West Fargo, North Dakota 58078-0719.
Tel:	701-282-2822 Email: info@bonanzaville.com
Admission:	May–mid November daily 0900-2000; mid–November-April Monday-Friday 0930-1630.
Location:	About 3 miles west of Fargo on Route 10.

Bonanzaville is operated by the Cass County Historical Society and first opened in the early 1970s. The Red River and Northern Plains Museum houses one of the largest American Indian collections in the Midwest. Many historic buildings have been moved to the site and replica structures have been constructed to present a vivid picture of life in the region from the time of the first settlers. There are also displays of farm machinery, a railway depot with an 1883 locomotive, a car museum and horse drawn vehicles. In 1980 a large hangar was constructed to house the aircraft collection.

This museum is dedicated to Charlie Klessig who was born in the state in 1911 and died in 1985. He learnt to fly in 1928 and had a varied career in aviation until he returned to the area in 1963. In his retirement he restored and flew many vintage aircraft and some of these can be seen in the museum.

A rarity is the McKinnie 165. The aircraft was built over a five-year period from 1948 and was completed at Fargo Airport. After 20 hours of flying the prototype was stored for two decades. Charlie restored the plane, flew it once, and delivered it to the museum. A second incomplete airframe was stored on Charlie's farm in the 1980s and its fate is unknown.

The C-47 was used by the Governor of North Dakota in the 1960s. The F-4 has been painted in the colours of the North Dakota Air National Guard Centennial Phantom.

The Swallow Airplane Manufacturing Company was formed in 1923 in Wichita, Kansas to take over the Laird company. The New Swallow biplane, which differed slightly from the Laird Swallow, flew in 1924. The design was steadily improved and in total around 300 of all versions were sold. The higher powered Wright J-5 engine was fitted to a number used commercially.

The Boeing historian and aircraft designer Peter Bowers flew the prototype of his low wing single seater Fly Babv in 1962. The aircraft structure was of wood with fabric covering. A variety of engines could be fitted. The aircraft could be built in the average car garage. The design won the EAA's 1962 competition. To date over 500 have been completed including a few biplane versions. Also on show is an earlier homebuilt design, the Pietenpol Aircamper, which has been popular for many years.

TYPE	REG/SER	CON. NO.	PI/NOTES	STATUS
☐ Beech D18S Expeditor (C18S) (C-45F) (SNB-5) (TC-45J) (UC-45J)	Bu89484		(USAAF), Bu89484, N40093 – on loan from ND ANG.	PV
☐ Bell 205 Iroquois (UH-1D) (UH-1H)	64-13879	4586		PV
☐ Bowers Fly Baby 1A	N47243	1		PV
☐ Bowers Fly Baby 1A			Incomplete.	PV
☐ Briegleb BG-12A	N7198	198		PV
☐ Curtiss D Pusher				PV
☐ Douglas DC-3A-456 Skytrain (C-47A) (VC-47A)	42-93800	13752	On loan from ND ANG, ND.	PV
☐ Hawker P.1067 Hunter F.51	E-407	41H/680266	47-407 (Denmark), G-9-435 – in Danish markings.	PVC
☐ McDonnell M.98DJ Phantom II (F-4C)	'40949'	885	64-0665	PVX
☐ McKinnie 165	N9MX	125001		PV
☐ Pietenpol B4-A Aircamper	N12072	B-2		PV
☐ Piper J-3F-65 Cub	N25132	6288	NC25132	PV
☐ Pitts S-1 Special	N2CK	540H		PV
☐ Pratt-Read PR-G1 (LNE-1)	N56660	PRG-01-63		PV
☐ Stits SA-3B Playboy	N7609U	1-67		PV
☐ Swallow J-5	N3753K	963	NC6065	PV
☐ Vultee V-74 Valiant (BT-13A)	N54886	74-1879	41-9725	PV
☐ Weedhopper JC-24		W80335		PV

CARL BEN EIELSON MUSEUM (ND3)

Address:	405 8th Street, POBox278, Hatton, North Dakota 58240.
Tel:	701-543-3828 Email: eielsonmuseum@gra.midco.netm
Admission:	May–September Sunday 1300-1630.
Location:	In the centre of the town.

Exhibits relating to the history of the region are on show in the museum. Carl Ben Eielson was born in Hatton and there are displays tracing his life and his Polar flights with many of his personal effects on view. He arrived in Alaska in 1922 and was the first 'bush' pilot in the territory using a Curtiss JN-4 which he based at Fairbanks. In 1928 he and Hubert Wilkins became the first to cross the North Pole by air when they flew from Point Barrow to Spitsbergen in a Lockheed Vega. The pair also made many pioneering flights in Antarctica before Eielson returned to Alaska and was killed in the crash of a Hamilton H-45 in Siberia in 1929 (the remains of this aircraft are on show in the Alaskaland Pioneer Air Museum in Fairbanks).

For their 1926 expedition to the Arctic Eielson and Wilkins used a single engined Fokker F VIIa and a three engined F VII/3m. The fuselage of the F VIIa was presented to the State Historical Society many years ago. The aircraft has now been loaned to Hatton and a new building has been constructed to house it. The T-33 has been in the town for over four decades.

TYPE	REG/SER	CON. NO.	PI/NOTES	STATUS
☐ Fokker F.VIIa		4909	Fuselage only – on loan from ND State Historical Society	PVC
☐ Lockheed 580 (T-33A)	51-6721	580-6053		PV

North Dakota

CASSELTON MONUMENT (ND4)

Location:	On permanent view at the airport which is about 2 miles south of the town.

TYPE	REG/SER	CON. NO.	PI/NOTES	STATUS
☐ Mcdonnell M.98DE Phantom II (F-4C)	63-7417	349		PV

DAKOTA TERRITORY AIR MUSEUM (ND5)

Address:	100 34th. Avenue North East, PO Box 195, Minot North Dakota 58703-0195.
Tel:	701-852-8500 Email: airmuseum@minot.com
Admission:	Saturday 1000-1700: Sunday 1300-1800.
Location:	At Minot Airport which is about 2 miles north of the town on Route 83.

Founded in the early 1990s, the museum has now constructed a building on the north side of Minot Airport. The entrance hall area is being fitted out with displays and there are many interesting items on show. The displays are being developed to trace the history of flying in the region. Many photographs, models and items of memorabilia can be seen.

Two DC-3s are appropriately in the collection. One saw service with several US Government agencies, including the FAA, before ending its active life with the Forestry Service. The oldest aircraft on show is the Waco 10 of which over 1,100 were built between 1927 and 1929. Dating from the early 1930s is an example of the Monocoupe 110 which has been restored to pristine condition.

The diminutive Arrow Sport biplane, first flown in 1926, was derived from the Lincoln Sport by its designer Swen Swanson. Initially fitted with a 35 hp Anzani engine it was underpowered and few were sold. The installation of the 55 hp Le Blond radial changed its fortune and eventually just under 100 were completed. The low wing Arrow Sport F, designed by Louis Imm and C.F. Biesemeir was built to test a Ford V8 car engine conversion. The prototype flew in 1934 and 105 were built in 1936/7. The performance was marginal but the F was cheap to fly.

The other pre-war machines are the Taylor Cub and the now fairly rare Stinson SR-5A Reliant. The Stinson R appeared in 1932 and was developed into the first Reliant the SR. About 100, including a few specials, were sold over the next couple of years. The SR-5 first flew in 1934 and was the first aircraft in its class to be fitted with flaps. About 150 were sold including a small number for the Navy and Coast Guard. The Reliant was steadily improved during the 1930s. The final Reliant model was the V-77, derived from the SR-10, navigational trainer many of which were leased to the Royal Navy.

A number of homebuilt aircraft an on show including an uncompleted BD-5. The Pietsch SD-TWO is a modified version of Stolp Starduster Too biplane. Lou Stolp flew his single seat Starduster in 1964 and this was soon followed by the two seater design. William Evans designed the low wing VP-1 with the amateur constructor in mind. The structure was kept simple and the aircraft was fitted with a converted Volkswagen car engine. Many have been built in countries around the world.

TYPE	REG/SER	CON. NO.	PI/NOTES	STATUS
☐ Arrow Sport A2-60	N530A	304		PVC
☐ Arrow Sport F				PVC
☐ Bede BD-5B			Incomplete.	S
☐ Beech D18S Expeditor 3NM	NC3647	CA-262 (A-912)	1576 (Canada), 5194 (Canada)	PVA
☐ Callair A-3	N2901V	117		PVA
☐ Cessna 195A	N714E	7271		PVA
☐ Curtiss A87-A2 Kittyhawk Ia	N7205A		(Canada) – identity doubtful.	PVC
☐ Douglas DC-3A-456 Skytrain (C-47A)	N102Z	20560	43-16094, NC182, N100, N76, N76AB	PV
☐ Douglas DC-3A-467 Skytrain (C-47B) (R4D-6) (R4D-6E) (R4D-6S)	43-49707	15523/26968	43-49707, Bu50829, N7676C, N53, N73, N73AH, N237GB – fuselage only.	PVD
☐ Ercoupe 415C	N99208	1831	NC99208	PVC
☐ Ercoupe 415C	N2594H	3219	NC2594H	PVA
☐ Evans VP-1 Volksplane	N22VP	PS289		PVA
☐ Fairchild 24 C8C	NC14799	2671	NC14799, N14799	PVA
☐ Lockheed 580 (T-33A)	57-0616	580-1265		PV
☐ Luscombe 8A Silvaire	N71219	2646	NC71219	PVA
☐ Mono Aircraft Monocoupe 110	NC114V	6W23	NC114V, N114V – on loan from Pietsch Coll, ND.	PVA
☐ North American NA-88 Texan (AT-6D) (Harvard IIIA)	N9272A	88-15693	41-34062, EZ189, 7615 (South Africa)	PVA
☐ North American NA-171 Trojan (T-28A)	N28JD	171-106	50-0300, N3292G, N213PC	PVA
☐ Pietenpol B4-A Aircamper	N5592	100		PVA
☐ Pietsch SD-TWO	N30110	P-10	On loan from Pietsch Coll, ND.	PVA
☐ Piper J-3C Cub (Scale R)				PV
☐ Piper J-3C-65 Cub	NC3632K	22324	NC3632K, N3632K	PVA
☐ Roloff RLU-1 Breezy	N2383	265-74-1		PVA
☐ Rotec Rally 2B				PV
☐ Rotorway Executive	N145LC	1320		PVA
☐ Rutan 33 Vari-Eze	N203DB	2032		PVA
☐ Stinson SR-5A Reliant	N13872	9251A	NC13872	PVA
☐ Taylor J-2 Cub	NC14419	1607	NC14119, N14119 – on loan from Pietsch Coll, ND.	PVA
☐ Taylorcraft BC-12D	N39215	6469		PVA
☐ Unknown Glider				PVD
☐ Vought A-7D Corsair II	68-8222	D8		PV
☐ Waco 10 (GXE)	NC5132	1498	NC5132, N5132	PVA
☐ Waco QCF-2	NC11490	3572	NC11487, N11487, NC11100, N11490 – on loan from Pietsch Coll, ND.	PVA
☐ Waco UPF-7	N50176	5590	NC50176	PVA
☐ Wolf W-II Boredom Fighter	N45RB	157		PVA
☐ Wright Flyer (R)				PV

DEVILS LAKE MONUMENT (ND6)

Location:	On permanent view at the airport which is in the western part of the town.

TYPE	REG/SER	CON. NO.	PI/NOTES	STATUS
☐ McDonnell M.36BA Voodoo (TF-101B) (TF-101F)	58-0311	683		PV

DICKINSON MONUMENT (ND7)

Location:	On permanent view in a park in 9th. Street West in the town.

TYPE	REG/SER	CON. NO.	PI/NOTES	STATUS
☐ Lockheed 580 (T-33A)	'30748'	580-8417	53-5078	PVX

FARGO AIR MUSEUM (ND8)

Address:	1609 19th. Avenue North, Fargo, North Dakota 58109-8190.
Tel:	701-293-8043 Fax: 701-293-8103 Email: fran@fargoairmuseum.org
Admission:	Tuesday-Saturday 0900-1700; Sunday 1200-1600.
Location:	At Hector Airport which is in the north western suburbs of the city on Route 81.

A number of warbird owners have set up this museum at Fargo Airport. The collection opened in July 2001 and around the building are displays of memorabilia.

The rarest aircraft in the fleet is the F2G-1 Corsair. Developed by Goodyear for low altitude work, eight were converted from the licence-built FG-1 models and five new F2G-1s were constructed along with ten F2G-2s. The example in the collection is currently the only airworthy one among the three known to exist. It is painted in its 1949 Cleveland Air Race winning colours.

Canadian collector Bob Diemert recovered three Zeros and a Val from Bougainville in the Solomon Islands in 1968 and the airframes were transported to his farm in Manitoba. In 1990 the Blayd Corporation in the nearby town of Carman started building a new aircraft using the Diemert parts as pattern. A few original components were used. The aircraft was trucked to Wahpeton in the spring of 1999 for completion. The fighter flew in July 2004 and is fitted with a Pratt and Whitney radial engine.

Aircraft often come on short term periods from the Tri-State Warbirds Collection. The early military C-47 is resplendent in a yellow colour scheme and is used in educational programmes. Members of the fleet are regular performers at shows in the region.

TYPE	REG/SER	CON. NO.	PI/NOTES	STATUS
☐ Bell 205 Iroquois (UH-1H)		67-17406	9604	Fuselage only.	PV
☐ Boeing-Stearman E75 Kaydet (PT-13D) (N2S-5)	N5057N	75-8143	42-109110, Bu38522	PVA
☐ Canadian Car & Foundry Harvard 4 [North American NA-186]	N7431	CCF4-222	20431, CF-UZW, NX7431	PVA
☐ Cessna 305A Bird Dog (L-19A) (O-1A)	N5258K	22736	51-16702	RAA
☐ Douglas DC-3A-360 Skytrain (C-47)	N1XP	4733	41-38630, NC843, N843K, CF-DOT, C-FDOT	PVA
☐ Fairchild M-62A Cornell (PT-19A)	N51437	6563AE	42-48007	PVA
☐ Fisher FP-404				PVC
☐ Interstate S1B1 Cadet (O-63) (L-6)	N52413	206	(USAAF) – on loan from Tri-State Warbirds, ND.	PVA
☐ McDonnell M.98EN Phantom II (F-4D)	'67478'	2300	66-7693	PVX
☐ Merlin Aircraft Merlin GT				RAC
☐ Mitsubishi A6M2 Zero Sen Model 21	'AI-I-129'	1498	N8280K – new built aircraft with a few original components.	PVAX
☐ North American NA-122 Mustang (P-51D)	N63476	122-31202	44-63476, 252 (Uruguay), N51HT, N2092P	PVA
☐ PZL TS-11 Iskra 100bisA	N66EN	1H 03-14	0314 (Poland), 314 (Poland)	PVA
☐ Pitts S-1 Special	N19JP	397H		PVA
☐ Standard J-1	N9477	2434		PV
☐ Stinson V-76 Sentinel (O-62) (L-5)	'298593'	76-269	42-15066, N58648, N46JB	PVAX
☐ Stinson V-77 Reliant (AT-19)				RAC
☐ Sud Fennec [North American NA-174 Trojan (T-28A)]	N9103F	174-459	51-7606, 136 (France), 136/3-A-309 (Argentina)	PVA
☐ Taylorcraft DCO-65 Grasshopper (L-2M)	N46955	L-5397	43-26085	PVA
☐ Vans RV-8	N222BC	80457		PVA
☐ Vought F4U-4 Corsair	N72378	9542	Bu97388, 610 (Honduras) – on loan from Tri-State Warbirds, ND.	PVA
☐ Vought F2G-1 Corsair	N5588N	6166	Bu88457	PVA
☐ Vultee V-54D Valiant (BT-13)				PVC
☐ War Aircraft FW 190	N317DG	153		PV

FESSENDEN MONUMENT (ND9)

Location:	On permanent view on Route 15 in the centre of the town.

TYPE	REG/SER	CON. NO.	PI/NOTES	STATUS
☐ North American NA-235 Super Sabre (F-100D)	56-3208	235-306		PV

FINLEY MONUMENT (ND10)

Location:	On permanent view on Route 32/200 in the centre of the town.

TYPE	REG/SER	CON. NO.	PI/NOTES	STATUS
☐ Lockheed 580 (T-33A)	53-6007	580-9539		PV

465

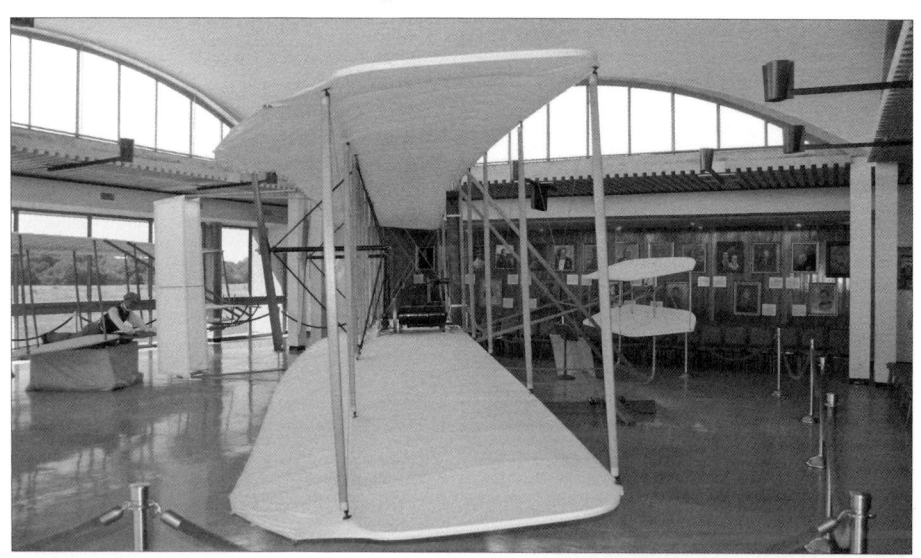

The Wright Brothers National Memorial houses this replica Wright Flyer. (Derek Heley) [NC43]

The only completed McKinnie 165 can be seen at the Bonanzaville Eagles Aircraft Museum. [ND2]

This Douglas A-26C Invader is part of the collection of the Grand Forks Air Base Museum. [ND11]

GRAND FORKS AIR FORCE BASE MUSEUM (ND11)

Address:	319AW/PA, Grand Forks Air Force Base, North Dakota 58205-5000.
Tel:	701-747-5023 Email: pa@grandforks.af.mil
Admission:	Tuesday-Thursday 0930-1600.
Location:	About 16 miles west of the town on Highway 2.

The base was opened in 1957 as one of the new facilities designed to protect the northern part of the country. The site was chosen in 1954 and citizens of Grand Forks purchased the land.
Originally used in the defence role to combat potential attacks by Soviet aircraft, F-101s were the first type to fly from Grand Forks. In 1962 the 30th Bombardment Squadron arrived from Homestead Air Force Base in Florida with B-52Gs. Theses heavy bombers were in residence for many years. The field is now home to the 319th Air Refueling Wing flying Boeing KC-135R Stratotankers.

The museum opened in 1982 and exhibitions tracing the history of the base and its units have been set up. On show are photographs, documents, models, components, uniforms and items of memorabilia tracing the history of the airfield and its units. The line of preserved aircraft is parked outside the main gate.
There are also a few missiles. Examples of three types which have been regularly based at Grand Forks can be seen.
Helicopters have been based at the field in support and rescue roles and two are on view.

TYPE	REG/SER	CON. NO.	PI/NOTES	STATUS
☐ Bell 204 Iroquois (UH-1F)	65-7946	7087		PV
☐ Boeing 464-253 Stratofortress (B-52G)	59-2577	464340		PV
☐ Boeing 717-146 Stratotanker (KC-135A)	63-8005	18622		PV
☐ Douglas A-26C Invader	'434220'		(USAAF), N36B, N36BB, N94445	PVX
☐ McDonnell M.36BA Voodoo (F-101B)	58-0315	687		PV
☐ North American NA-108 Mitchell (B-25J) (TB-25N)	'327899'	108-34609	43-27596, N9865C – quoted by FAA as ex 44-28834.	PVX
☐ Sikorsky S-55D Chickasaw (H-19D) (UH-19D)	'41428'		57-5959, '27561'	PVX

HETTINGER MONUMENT (ND12)

Location:	On permanent view at the airport which is in the north western part of the town.

TYPE	REG/SER	CON. NO.	PI/NOTES	STATUS
☐ North American NA-203 Sabre (F-86H)	53-1372	203-144		PV

HILLSBORO MONUMENT (ND13)

Location:	On permanent view at the National Guard Armory on Highway 81 South.

TYPE	REG/SER	CON. NO.	PI/NOTES	STATUS
☐ Lockheed 580 (T-33A)	'35326'	580-1350	57-0701	PVX

JAMESTOWN MONUMENT (ND14)

Location:	On permanent view at the airport which is in the north eastern part of the town.

TYPE	REG/SER	CON. NO.	PI/NOTES	STATUS
☐ North American NA-203 Sabre (F-86H)	53-1253	203-25		PV

KINDRED MONUMENT (ND15)

Location:	On permanent view at the airport which is just east of the town.

TYPE	REG/SER	CON. NO.	PI/NOTES	STATUS
☐ Lockheed 580 (T-33A)	58-0619	580-1588		PV

LIDGERWOOD MONUMENT (ND16)

Location:	On permanent view in a park in the northern part of the town.

TYPE	REG/SER	CON. NO.	PI/NOTES	STATUS
☐ Bell 209 Huey Cobra (AH-1G) (AH-1F)	67-15769	20433		PV

LISBON MONUMENT (ND17)

Location:	By prior permission only at a Veterans Home in Rose Street in the south eastern part of the town.

TYPE	REG/SER	CON. NO.	PI/NOTES	STATUS
☐ Bell 205 Iroquois (UH-1H)				RA

MAYVILLE MONUMENT (ND18)

Location:	On permanent view on Route 200 near the Motel 8 in the centre of the town.

TYPE	REG/SER	CON. NO.	PI/NOTES	STATUS
☐ Republic F-84F Thunderstreak	51-1462			PV

MCVILLE MONUMENT (ND19)

Location:	On permanent view on Route 15 in the eastern part of the town.

TYPE	REG/SER	CON. NO.	PI/NOTES	STATUS
☐ Bell 205 Iroquois (UH-1H)	73-21687	13375		PV

MINOT AIR FORCE BASE MUSEUM (ND20)

Address:	201 Summer Drive, Suite 105, Minot Air Force Base, North Dakota 58705-2000.
Tel:	701-723-6212
Admission:	By prior permission only.
Location:	About 13 miles north of the city on Route 83.

The base opened in 1957 and the first aircraft, Boeing KC-135A Stratotankers, arrived in September 1959. Fighters followed with the arrival of the 5th Fighter Interceptor Squadron from Suffolk County Airport in New York State, flying delta-wing fighters until 1979. In July 1961 bomber units flying the B-52H Stratofortress took up residence and this long serving bomber is still flown by the 5th Bomb Wing. A display of memorabilia has been set up in a building and the history of the site is portrayed with a range of photographs. The five preserved aircraft are displayed around the site along with a number of missiles.

TYPE	REG/SER	CON. NO.	PI/NOTES	STATUS
☐ Bell 204 Iroquois (UH-1F)	66-1215	7111		RA
☐ Convair 8-10 Delta Dagger (F-102A)	56-1505	8-10-722		RA
☐ Convair 8-24 Delta Dart (F-106A)	56-0460	8-24-10		RA
☐ Lockheed 580 (T-33A)	58-0466	580-1435		RA
☐ Northrop N-156T Talon (T-38A) (AT-38B)	61-0888	N.5254		RA

NEW ROCKFORD MONUMENT (ND21)

Location:	On permanent view on Route 281 in the town.

TYPE	REG/SER	CON. NO.	PI/NOTES	STATUS
☐ Bell 205 Iroquois (UH-1H)	67-17500	9698		PV

NORTH DAKOTA AIR NATIONAL GUARD COLLECTION (ND22)

Address:	119 FG/PA, Box 5536, State University Station, Fargo, North Dakota 58105-5536.
Tel:	701-237-6030 Email: pa@ndfargo.ang.af.mil
Admission:	On permanent view.
Location:	At Hector Field which is in the north western suburbs of the city on Route 81.

The 178th Squadron was allocated to the North Dakota Air National Guard and moved into Hector field in January 1947 where it has remained except for periods of active duty. P-51s were the initial equipment and they served until 1954. The Lockheed F-94 then arrived and was flown for four years until the Northrop F-89 was allocated. Subsequently the Convair F-102, the McDonnell F-101, and the McDonnell F-4 were successively used before the unit converted to the General Dynamics F-16 Fighting Falcon in 1990.

TYPE	REG/SER	CON. NO.	PI/NOTES	STATUS
☐ Convair 8-10 Delta Dagger (F-102A)	'53432'	8-10-719	56-1502	PVX
☐ General Dynamics 401 Fighting Falcon (F-16A)	'82-1012'	61-326	80-0605.	PVX
☐ Lockheed 580 (T-33A)	58-0619	580-1268		RA
☐ Lockheed 880-75-13 Starfire (F-97A) (F-94C)	51-5605	880-7668		PV
☐ McDonnell M.36BA Voodoo (F-101B)	58-0341	713		PV
☐ McDonnell M.98EN Phantom II (F-4D)	64-0972	1443		PV
☐ McDonnell M.199-1A Eagle (F-15A)	74-0112	086/A073		PV
☐ North American NA-122 Mustang (P-51D)	44-74407	122-40947		PV
☐ Northrop N-160 Scorpion (N-68) (F-89D) (F-89J)	'32604'	N.4596	53-2465	PVX

PIETSCH COLLECTION (ND23)

Address:	2216 North Broadway, Minot, North Dakota 58703-1011.
Admission:	By prior permission only.
Location:	At Minot Airport and a number of private airfields in the area.

Pietsch Aviation is one of the Fixed Base Operators at Minot. Aircraft restoration and overhaul is carried out and flying training and crop dusting work performed.
Members of the family have acquired an interesting collection of aircraft and a few of these can be seen in the Dakota Territory Air Museum on the other side of the field. Two original homebuilt designs have been constructed and a Taylorcraft has been extensively modified. Three Luscombe Phantoms have recently been acquired and hopefully at least one will be seen in the air in the not too distant future. Three examples of the graceful Waco biplanes are in the collection.
Agricultural flying has taken place in North Dakota for many years and among the types used in this work is the Callair A-9.

TYPE	REG/SER	CON. NO.	PI/NOTES	STATUS
☐ Aeronca 7CCM Champion (L-16B)	N4600E	7CCM-171		RAA
☐ Beech D17S (UC-43)	N985SW	4870	43-10822, NC260, NC1027M, N7778B, CF-GWL	RAA
☐ Callair A-9B	N2851F	1367		RAA
☐ Callair A-9B	N7769V	1526		RAA
☐ Cessna 150L Commuter	N10394	15074790		RAA

☐ Cessna 195 (LC-126B) (U-20B)	N6747C	7603	50-1253	RAA
☐ Interstate S-1A Cadet	NC37361	204	NC37361, N37361	RAA
☐ Interstate S-1A Cadet	NC37428	273	NC37428, N37428	RAA
☐ Let L-13 Blanik	N9NV	175220		RAA
☐ Luscombe 1 Phantom	NC1286	106	NC1286, N1286	RA
☐ Luscombe 1 Phantom	NC1249	120	NC1249, N1249	RA
☐ Luscombe 1 Phantom	NC272Y	131		RA
☐ Mono Aircraft Monocoupe 110 Special	NC101H	6W60	NC101H, N101H	RAA
☐ Mooney M.20C	N1366W	2647		RAA
☐ Mooney M.20E	N79335	545		RAA
☐ Mooney M.20F	N3484N	680067		RAA
☐ Mooney M.22	N66179	680005		RAA
☐ North American NA-88 Texan (AT-6D) (Harvard III)	N9272K	88-15693	41-34062, EZ189, 7615 (South Africa)	RAA
☐ Pietsch-Warren IT	N214GP	Z1A-0016		RAA
☐ Pietsch-Warren Taylorcraft GJ	N180WP	XT-1		RAA
☐ Piper PA-11 Cub Special	N4967M	11-453	NC4967M	RAA
☐ Pitts S-2A Special	N43JC	2019		RA
☐ Waco ASO	N9129C	A-129	NC797E, N797E	RAA
☐ Waco ATO	NC915H	A-125	NC915H, N915H	RA
☐ Waco BSO (DSO)	NC861M	3006	NC605N, N605N	RAA

TRI STATE WARBIRD COLLECTION (ND24)

Address:	PO Box 843, Wahpeton, North Dakota 58074.
Tel:	701-642-5777
Admission:	By prior permission only.
Location:	At Harry Stein Airport which is just south of the town off Route 127.

Gerry Beck operates a crop dusting service from the airfield at Wahpeton. His hangars also contain a fascinating collection of warbirds.

The Avenger was purchased in 1990 and had spent several years in the USA and Canada as a fire-fighting machine. The aircraft was lacking bomb doors and as these could not be obtained a new set was built. The company has since supplied sets to over a dozen owners. Tri-State Aviation also makes parts for P-51s and is now capable of building the fighter from scratch.

The incomplete Mignet HM-290 was obtained from a local homebuilder and will be finished in due course.

TYPE	REG/SER	CON. NO.	PI/NOTES	STATUS
☐ Bellanca 7GCBC Citabria	N88416	782-75		RAA
☐ Boeing-Stearman B75N1 Kaydet (N2S-3)	N74683	75-1252	Bu2475	PVC
☐ Grumman G-40 Avenger (TBM-3) (TBM-3E)	NL293E	3891	Bu53829, N9591C, CF-AYG, N293E	PVA
☐ Howard DGA-15P	N981GB	981	CF-OGI	PV
☐ Mignet HM-290 Pou-du-Ciel				PVC
☐ North American NA-121 Texan (AT-6D) (SNJ-5)	N8005V	121-42062	44-81340, Bu91066	RAA
☐ North American NA-124 Mustang (P-51D)	N305PM	124-48232	45-11479, A68-810, 29 (Bolivia), 501 (Bolivia) – identity doubtful.	RAC
☐ Piper J-3C-65 Cub (L-4J)	N6037V	13660	45-4920	PVA
☐ Raven Rally RX-6 Hot Air Balloon	N5557N	RX6-346		RAA
☐ Vans RV-4	N780GW	780		RAA
☐ Vought F4U-4 Corsair	N72084	9474	Bu97320, N52??V, 616 (Honduras)	PVC
☐ Waco 10 (GXE)	NC5132	1498	NC5132, N5132	RAA

VALLEY CITY MONUMENT (ND25)

Location:	On permanent view in the Veterans Memorial Park in Main Street East.

TYPE	REG/SER	CON. NO.	PI/NOTES	STATUS
☐ Lockheed 383-04-05 Starfighter (F-104C)	56-0926	183-1214		PV

VELVA MONUMENT (ND26)

Location:	On permanent view at a campsite on 1st Avenue West.

TYPE	REG/SER	CON. NO.	PI/NOTES	STATUS
☐ Lockheed 580 (T-33A)	51-9100	5880-6884		PV

WAHPETON MONUMENT (ND27)

Location:	On permanent view at Harry Stein Airport which is just south of the town off Route 127.

TYPE	REG/SER	CON. NO.	PI/NOTES	STATUS
☐ Vought A-7D Corsair II	69-6208	D58		PV

WALHALLA MONUMENT (ND28)

Location:	On permanent view at the airport which is about 1 mile north of the town.

TYPE	REG/SER	CON. NO.	PI/NOTES	STATUS
☐ North American NA-203 Sabre (F-86H)	53-1392	203-164		PV

OHIO

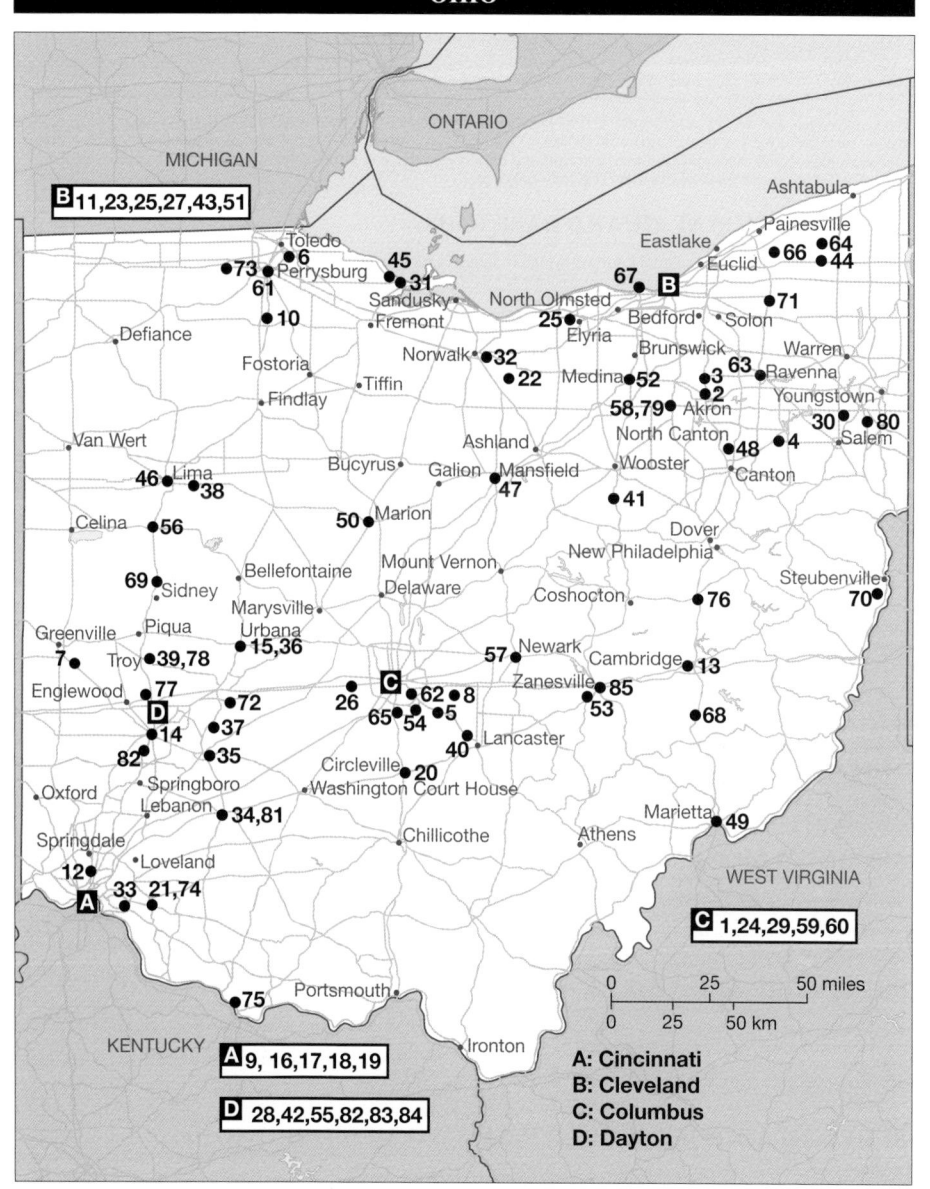

A: Cincinnati
B: Cleveland
C: Columbus
D: Dayton

94TH AERO SQUADRON RESTAURANT (OH1)

| Location: | On permanent view at the site at 5030 Sawyer Road to the east of Port Columbus Airport. |

| TYPE | REG/SER | CON. NO. | PI/NOTES | STATUS |
| ☐ North American NA-122 Mustang (P-51D) (FSM) | | | | PVX |

AKRON AIRSHIP HISTORICAL CENTER (OH2)

Address:	Lighter Than Air Society, 526 South Main Street, Akron, Ohio 44311.
Tel:	330-535-5827 **Email:** Sugges@BlimpInfo.com
Admission:	Not yet open.
Location:	In the centre of the city.

The Lighter Than Air Society was formed in 1952 by workers making airships at the Goodyear factory in the city. A large number of photographs and artefacts have been collected over the last half century and small displays are regularly staged at events in the area. The aim is to raise funds for a museum tracing the history of airship development with particular reference to those constructed in Akron by Goodyear.

AKRON NATIONAL GUARD BASE (OH3)

Location:	At Akron-Canton Airport which is about 5 miles north of Canton.

TYPE	REG/SER	CON. NO.	PI/NOTES	STATUS
☐ Bell 209 Huey Cobra (AH-1G) (AH-1S)	67-15800	20464		RA

ALLIANCE MONUMENT (OH4)

Location:	On permanent view at a high school at 400 Glamorgan Street in the southern part of the town.

TYPE	REG/SER	CON. NO.	PI/NOTES	STATUS
☐ Vought A-7A Corsair II	Bu153142	A51	On loan from NMNA, FL	PV

AMERICAN WAR MUSEUM (OH5)

Address:	4316 Winchester Southern Road, Canal Winchester, Ohio 43110-8938.
Admission:	Unknown.
Location:	About 12 miles south east of Columbus off Route 33.

The Iroquois was registered to this museum in 1997. Efforts to obtain further information have not been successful and it is not known if the organisation is still in existence. The museum is still listed on a number of tourist web sites but no details of any exhibits or opening times are stated.

TYPE	REG/SER	CON. NO.	PI/NOTES	STATUS
☐ Bell 205 Iroquois (UH-1H)	N48951	10191	68-15261	RA

AMHERST MONUMENT (OH6)

Location:	On permanent view at the Lorain County Veterans Memorial on North Lake Street in the town.

TYPE	REG/SER	CON. NO.	PI/NOTES	STATUS
☐ Bell 205 Iroquois (UH-1H)				PV

ARCANUM MONUMENT (OH7)

Location:	On permanent view at VFW 4161 at 311 South Albright Street in the south eastern part of the town.

TYPE	REG/SER	CON. NO.	PI/NOTES	STATUS
☐ Bell 205 Iroquois (UH-1D) (UH-1H)	65-9888	4932		PV

BALTIMORE MONUMENT (OH8)

Location:	On permanent view at VFW 3761 on Route 256 in the western part of the town.

TYPE	REG/SER	CON. NO.	PI/NOTES	STATUS
☐ Lockheed 426-42-15 Neptune (P2V-5) (P2V-5F) (P-2E)	Bu131522	426-5403		PV

BLUE ASH AIRPORT WORLD WAR TWO MEMORIAL (OH9)

Address:	4393 Glendale Milford Road, Cincinnati, Ohio 45242.
Tel:	513-984-3881 **Email:** bob_ready@hotmail.com
Admission:	Not yet open.
Location:	In the north eastern suburbs of Cincinnati.

Only six B-17Es are known to exist and the example under restoration at Blue Ash Airport will form the centrepiece of a memorial at the airfield. The bomber, named 'My Girl Sal', crashed on the Greenland ice cap on 27th June 1942 on a flight to England. The wreck was discovered in 1964 by a USAF reconnaissance flight but it was not recovered until 1985. The bomber will be displayed on its belly. The Corsair is mounted on a pole at the ANG facility about ½ mile from the airport.

TYPE	REG/SER	CON. NO.	PI/NOTES	STATUS
☐ Boeing 299-O Fortress (B-17E)	41-9023	2504		RAC
☐ Vought A-7D Corsair II	71-0360	D271	At ANGS Gate.	PV

BOWLING GREEN MONUMENT (OH10)

| Location: | On permanent view at Wood County Airport in the north eastern part of the town. |

TYPE	REG/SER	CON. NO.	PI/NOTES	STATUS
☐ Lockheed 580 (T-33A)	53-4932	580-8271		PV

BROOKLYN MONUMENT (OH11)

| Location: | On permanent view by the Municipal Center in Memphis Avenue in the town. |

TYPE	REG/SER	CON. NO.	PI/NOTES	STATUS
☐ Lockheed 580 (T-33A)	51-9263	580-7047		PV

BUTLER COUNTY WARBIRDS MUSEUM (OH12)

Address:	PO Box18771, Fairfield, Ohio 45018-0771.
Tel:	513-702-3602 Email: tim@ephisservices.com
Admission:	By prior permission only
Location:	At Butler County Airport which is about 3 miles south east of Hamilton.

The museum was set up with the aim of collecting and maintaining historic aircraft in airworthy condition. The PT-19 was rolled out a gathering in June 2007 and is resplendent in a typical World War II silver colour scheme. The Stearman is in yellow US Navy markings and both aircraft regularly attend events in the area. Artefacts are being acquired with the eventual aim of setting up a permanent display.

TYPE	REG/SER	CON. NO.	PI/NOTES	STATUS
☐ American Aviation AA-5A Cheetah	N1000S	AA5-0107		RAA
☐ Boeing-Stearman A75 Kaydet (PT-13A)	N55252	75-107	38-459	RAA
☐ Fairchild M-62A-3 (Fairchild M-62A Cornell (PT-19A))	N51090	T43-5048	42-34382	RAA

CAMBRIDGE MONUMENT (OH13)

| Location: | On permanent view at the airport which is about 5 miles south of the town. |

TYPE	REG/SER	CON. NO.	PI/NOTES	STATUS
☐ Lockheed 580 (T-33A)	'91-9766'			PVX

CARILLON HISTORICAL PARK (OH14)

Address:	1000 Carillon Boulevard, Dayton, Ohio 45409.
Tel:	937-293-2841 Fax: 937-293-5798
Admission:	April–October Tuesday-Saturday 1000-1700; Sunday 1200-1700.
Location:	In the southern suburbs of the city close to the Great Miami River.

The museum is located in a former swamp and was the idea of local businessman Colonel William A. Deeds. His aim was to preserve buildings and inventions which were significant to the region.

Historic buildings were moved to the site including the Newsome Tavern (Dayton's oldest building), a schoolhouse, a mill and a blacksmith's shop along with several railway engines and cars. The Wright Brothers were residents of the city and an accurate replica of their cycle shop has been built (the original is at Greenfield Village in Michigan).

In the Wright Hall is the Flyer 3 which according to Orville was the aircraft in which they really learned to fly.

TYPE	REG/SER	CON. NO.	PI/NOTES	STATUS
☐ Wright Flyer 3		3		PV

CHAMPAIGN AVIATION MUSEUM (OH15)

Address:	Grimes Field 174, 1636 North Main Street, Urbana, Ohio 43078.
Tel:	937-484-6947
Admission:	Monday-Friday 1000-1600.
Location:	At the airport which is in the northern part of the town.

The museum occupies premises at Grimes Field and its members are restoring a B-17 Fortress. The airframe is being rebuild from the remains of two aircraft: N6694C was used by the Curtiss-Wright company as a research machine with a fifth engine fitted in the nose– the airframe was later rebuilt to standard configuration and the B-17 flew on firefighting duties until it crashed in 1980. Major components were recovered and incorporated in the rebuild of another. 44-83722 was used for atomic tests in Nevada and the hulk moved around over the years until it arrived at the museum in 2007. The Invader is another former water bomber. The aircraft served in this role with Conair and Airspray in Canada from the mid-1970s until 2008. The 1932 Pitcairn PA-18 autogyro restored to flying condition by Jack and Kate Tiffany and Jim Hammond over a ten year period is often displayed at the museum. Only 19 examples of the type were built and two are known to survive. Two replicas of early designs have been put on show to illustrate how designs have progressed over the last century.

TYPE	REG/SER	CON. NO.	PI/NOTES	STATUS
☐ Boeing 299Z Fortress (299-O) (B-17G) (EB-17G) (JB-17G)	N3154S	32363	44-83722 – composite with c/n 8722 44-85813, N6694C	PVC
☐ Douglas A-26C Invader	N381EC/C-GHLX	29227	44-35948, NL67764, N67764, N1244, N910H, N161H, C-GHLX	PVA

Ohio

☐ Douglas DC-3A-456 Skytrain (C-47A)	N105CA	14275/25720	43-48459, N47071, N85FA	PVA
☐ Nieuport 27 (R)	NX27XZ	1000603		PVA
☐ North American NA-88 Texan (AT-6C) (Harvard IIA)	N7176	88-10154	41-33371, EX398, 7176 (South Africa)	PVA
☐ North American NA-108 Mitchell (B-25J) (TB-25J) (TB-25N)	N744CG	108-32141	44-28866, N5277V, CF-OND, N225AJ	PVA
☐ Pitcairn PA-18	NC1267B	G-65	N12678 – on loan from Hammond Collection.	PVA
☐ Santos-Dumont XX Demoiselle (R)	PU-FNB	005		PV
☐ Wright B (R)				PV

CINCINNATI AVIATION HERITAGE SOCIETY AND MUSEUM (OH16)

Address:	262 Wilmer Avenue, Cincinnatti, Ohio 45226
Tel:	513-407-3104
Admission:	Monday and Friday 1000-1400.
Location:	In the South Terminal at Lunken Airport which is in the eastern suburbs of the city off Route 52.

The society has collected a vast amount of archive material and has now opened a display at the historic Lunken Airport. The Aeronautical Corporation of America was established at the field in 1928. The company soon changed its name to Aeronca. Their first product was the C-2 which was developed into the successful C-3 of which almost 500 were built. One hangs in the terminal.

TYPE	REG/SER	CON. NO.	PI/NOTES	STATUS
☐ Aeronca C-3	N16553	A-695	NC16553	PV

CINCINNATI MONUMENT (OH17)

Location:	Was on permanent view at Lunken Airport which is in the eastern suburbs of the city off Route 52 – aircraft moved to Georgia.

TYPE	REG/SER	CON. NO.	PI/NOTES	STATUS
☐ North American NA-203 Sabre (F-86H)	53-1528	203-300		PV

CINCINNATI STATE TECHNICAL AND COMMUNITY COLLEGE (OH18)

Address:	3520 Central Parkway, Cincinnati, Ohio 45223.
Tel:	513-569-4976 **Email:** jeffrey.wright@cincinnatistate.edu
Admission:	By prior permission only.
Location:	At Cincinnati West Airport at 10030 West Road, Harrison.

The college was established in 1969. The aviation facility consists of a hangar and laboratories. The fleet of instructional aircraft includes a number of homebuilt designs including an example of the Hipp's Reliant. The design is based on the J-3 Kitten which is a ¾ scale version of the Piper Cub. The Reliant is powered by a Rotax engine.

Richard van Grunsven founded Vans Aircraft in 1973. Over the years he has developed a series of successful designs and supplied kits to homebuilders. Well over 6,500 Vans aircraft are now flying in many countries. The RV-4 is a low wing tandem two seater which can be fitted with engines up to 180 hp.

TYPE	REG/SER	CON. NO.	PI/NOTES	STATUS
☐ Aero Commander 680V	N4682E	1630-56		RA
☐ Aeronca 11AC Chief	N9413E	11AC-1050	NC9413E	RA
☐ Bell 47G				RA
☐ Bell 47G				RA
☐ Bowers Fly Baby 1A	N441H	J1130H		RA
☐ Cessna 150D	N4422U	15060422		RA
☐ Cessna 320C Skyknight	N3166T	320C0001		RA
☐ Flightstar FS-II SL				RA
☐ Hipp's Reliant				RA
☐ Vans RV-4				RA

CINCINNATI WARBIRDS (OH19)

Address:	262 Wilmer Avenue, Cincinnatti, Ohio 45266. (Airport)
Email:	towerjim@aol.com
Admission:	By prior permission only.
Location:	At Lunken Airport which is in the eastern suburbs of the city off Route 52.

This organisation is part of the EAA warbirds movement and has a hangar at the historic airfield. The aircraft are all owned by members and appear at local shows. The Ercoupe is painted in the colours of VX147 which was evaluated by the Royal Air Force in the 1940s. The early Harvard served in New Zealand.

TYPE	REG/SER	CON. NO.	PI/NOTES	STATUS
☐ Beech A45 Mentor (T-34A)	N421NM/ '550720'	G-720	55-0163	RAAX
☐ Ercoupe 415C	N99933/'VX147'	2556		RAAX
☐ North American NA-66 Harvard II	N8994	66-2814	NZ948	RAA
☐ North American NA-200 Trojan (T-28B)	NX194RR	200-265	Bu138194	RAA
☐ North American NA-226 Trojan (T-28C)	NX462NA	226-147	Bu140570	RAA
☐ PZL TS-11 Iskra 100bisB	N315JB	1H 07-04	0704 (Poland), 704 (Poland), N94DW	RAA

Ohio

CIRCLEVILLE MONUMENT (OH20)

Location:	On permanent view at AMVETS 2256 in Tarlton Road in the southern part of the town.

TYPE	REG/SER	CON. NO.	PI/NOTES	STATUS
☐ Republic F-105D Thunderchief	59-1771	D-83		PV

CLEARWATER AIR AND AUTO MUSEUM (OH21)

Address:	2845 Highway 50, Batavia, Ohio 45103-9518.
Admission:	Unknown.
Location:	About 20 miles east of Cincinnati off Route 32.

Two Polish types are among the aircraft owned by this museum which is believed to have a collection of vintage and classic cars. Further information on the organisation would be most welcome.

TYPE	REG/SER	CON. NO.	PI/NOTES	STATUS
☐ Cessna 150J	N60138	15070099		RAA
☐ PZL TS-11 Iskra 100bisB	N818CM	1H 08-18	0818 (Poland), 818 (Poland)	RA
☐ Taylorcraft BC-65	N27671	2313		RAA
☐ WSK Lim-5 [MiG-17F]	N2503U	1C 16-03	1603 (Poland)	RA

CLEAVER COLLECTION (OH22)

Address:	State Route 18, Clarksfield, Ohio 44826.
Admission:	By prior permission only.
Location:	In the area of the town.

Leon Cleaver has gathered a collection of derelict airframes at his property. Many of the aircraft have been recovered from crash sites and others from airfields where they were rotting away. He also has a shed full of components and engines. A North American Yale recently left the collection for static restoration.

TYPE	REG/SER	CON. NO.	PI/NOTES	STATUS
☐ Aero Commander 520 (YL-26) (YU-9A)	52-6217	520-17		RAD
☐ Beech D18S Expeditor (TC-45G)	51-11555	AF-112	51-11555, (N6851D)	RAD
☐ Beech D18S Expeditor (C-45H)	N322X	AF-857	52-10927	RAD
☐ Bell 205 Iroquois (UH-1D) (UH-1H)	63-8828	4120	Crash remains.	RAD
☐ Curtiss-Wright CW-20B Commando (C-46A)	N9905F	30316	42-96654 – front fuselage only.	RAD
☐ Fairchild M-62A Cornell (PT-19)			Major components.	RAD
☐ Fairchild M-62A Cornell (PT-19)			Major components.	RAD
☐ Fairchild M-62A Cornell (PT-19)	NC47985		42-33484 – fuselage only.	RAD
☐ Fairchild M-62C Cornell (PT-23)			Major components.	RAD
☐ Grumman G-93 Cougar (F9F-6P) (RF-9F)	Bu128298			RAD
☐ Grumman G-99 Cougar (F9F-8) (F-9J)	Bu144388			RAD
☐ Hiller UH12D Raven (H-23D) (OH-23D)	57-3036	994		RAD
☐ Lockheed 580 (T-33A)	51-6546	580-5878		RAD
☐ Lockheed Schweizer SGS.2-32 (X-26A)	Bu158818	74		RAD
☐ Naval Aircraft Factory N3N-3				RAD
☐ North American NA-88 Texan (SNJ-4)	Bu27842	88-13578	Identity doubtful.	RAD
☐ Northrop N-156T Talon (T-38A)	Bu158197	T.6199	68-8194	RAD
☐ Piasecki PD-22 Work Horse (H-21B) (CH-21B)	53-4365	B.115		RAD
☐ Piasecki PV-18 Retriever (HUP-2) (UH-25B)	Bu128566			RAD
☐ Sikorsky S-55B Chickasaw (H-19C) (UH-19C)	51-14306			RAD
☐ Sikorsky S-55D Chickasaw (H-19D) (UH-19D)	56-4254			RAD
☐ Vultee V-79 Valiant (BT-13B) (SNV-2)				RAD

CLEVELAND MONUMENT (OH23)

Location:	On permanent view at Gillespies Map Room at 1283 West Street in Cleveland.

TYPE	REG/SER	CON. NO.	PI/NOTES	STATUS
☐ Homebuilt Biplane				PV

COLUMBUS STATE COMMUNITY COLLEGE (OH24)

Address:	5355 Alkire Road, Columbus, Ohio 43228.
Tel:	614-287-7100 Email: khill@cscc.edu
Admission:	By prior permission only.
Location:	At Bolton Field which is about 8 miles south west of the city.

The college has a large hangar at the field where the instructional airframes reside. The complex has well equipped workshops and laboratories to aid the students. The Boeing 727 served with United Airlines and FedEx before being donated to the college in 2006. Only 15 T-47As were used by the Navy at Pensacola in Florida.

TYPE	REG/SER	CON. NO.	PI/NOTES	STATUS
☐ Beech 65-90 King Air	N900BP	LJ-61	N764K, N900BP, N3078W	RA
☐ Bell 47G	N8270E	162		RA
☐ Boeing 727-22QC	N107FE	19202	N7427U	RA
☐ Cessna 210E Centurion	N2363F	21058563		RA
☐ Cessna 310Q	N69942	310Q1033		RA

☐ Cessna 552 Citation II (T-47A)	N12566	552-0012	Bu162766	RA
☐ Gates Learjet 25D	N100WN	25D-288	N31WT, N61WT, N40BC, N100WN, (N40BC)	RA
☐ Piper PA-23 Apache	N3179P	23-1116		RA
☐ Piper PA-24 Comanche	N1220Z	24-800	N5726P	RA
☐ Piper PA-28-151 Cherokee Warrior	N41995	28-7415382		RA

COMMEMORATIVE AIR FORCE (CLEVELAND WING) (OH25)

Address:	44050 Russia Road, Elyria, Ohio 44035.
Tel:	440-323-8335 Email: kdonovan@fwdlaw.com
Admission:	By prior permission only.
Location:	At Lorain County Airport which is about 5 miles west of the town.

The wing was formed in 1988 and the Texan was allocated in 1991. The trainer is regularly flown at shows. The group plans to build a hangar to house this and other aircraft owned by members.

TYPE	REG/SER	CON. NO.	PI/NOTES	STATUS
☐ North American NA-88 Texan (SNJ-4)	N224X	88-13041	Bu27585, N7438C	RAA

COMMEMORATIVE AIR FORCE (OHIO VALLEY WING) (OH26)

Address:	2000 Norton Road, Columbus, Ohio 43228.
Tel:	330-426-3199 Email: adjutant@cafohio.org
Admission:	By prior permission only.
Location:	At Bolton Field which is about 8 miles south west of the city.

Only one aircraft is now allocated to the wing. The L-5 is in flying condition and painted in typical World War II colours. A small number of OY-1s were fitted with modified equipment and re-designated OY-2. The unit has a mobile exhibition which is taken to shows at which Sentinel is displayed.

TYPE	REG/SER	CON. NO.	PI/NOTES	STATUS
☐ Stinson V-76 Sentinel (L-5E) (OY-1) (OY-2)	N5138B		(USAAF), Bu04013	RAA

CRAWFORD AUTO-AVIATION MUSEUM (OH27)

Address:	10825 East Boulevard, Cleveland, Ohio 44106-1777.
Tel:	216-721-5722 Email: allan@wrhs.org
Admission:	Monday-Saturday 1000-1700; Sunday 1200-1700.
Location:	In the eastern suburbs of the city off Route 322.

The Western Reserve Historical Society was formed in 1867 and the museum came into being in 1937 as the Thompson Auto Album and Aviation Museum when Frederick Crawford bought a 1910 car. He started collecting in earnest and by 1943 the society had set up an exhibition in temporary premises. A change of name to the Thompson Products Museum took place and it moved to its current site in 1965.

On show are over 100 cars along with bicycles and motorcycles. The collection is considered to be one of the best in the country and contains a range of vehicles from the early days. Many items of memorabilia can also be seen.

Crawford had worked for Thompson Products who sponsored the Thompson Trophy at the National Air Races. This event was a closed circuit race and was first held in 1930. The last race took place in 1949. A number of significant racing aircraft are currently on show. Wedell-Williams racers won the cross-country Bendix Trophy for three years in succession from 1932 to 1934 and the Thompson in 1933 and 1934. Roscoe Turner won the 1934 Thompson in the aircraft on show. The racer was left at Cleveland Airport in 1939 and acquired by the museum in 1946. Art Chester and Benny Howard were well-known racing pilots and examples of their designs are on view. The Goon first appeared in 1938 and the following year achieved success in the Cleveland meeting. The racer reappeared after World War II and flew with several owners before joining the collection in 1991. The Mustang was flown in the 1949 Bendix by Robert Swanson.

Three F2G-1 Corsairs achieved success in the contests in the late 1940s. The example in the collection spent many years in Walter Soplata's yard before being acquired. This Corsair is now being rebuilt and should appear in its racing colours.

TYPE	REG/SER	CON. NO.	PI/NOTES	STATUS
☐ Chester Goon	NX93Y	2		PV
☐ Curtiss E Hydro				PV
☐ Curtiss 17 Oriole	NC1660	189		RA
☐ Granville Gee Bee R-1 (R)				PV
☐ Great Lakes 2T-1	NC9462	264	NC9462, N9462	PV
☐ Howard DGA-3 Pete	N2YX	67		PV
☐ North American NA-111 Mustang (P-51K)	NX79161	111-30249	44-12116	PV
☐ Thomas-Morse S-4C	N5452	633	NC5452	RA
☐ Vought F2G-1 Corsair	NX5577N	6172	Bu88463	RAC
☐ Wedell-Williams 44	NX61Y	109	NX54Y	PV
☐ Wright 1902 Glider (R)				PV

DAYTON INTERNATIONAL AIRPORT DISPLAY (OH28)

Location:	On permanent view in the terminal of the airport which is about 5 miles north of the city.

TYPE	REG/SER	CON. NO.	PI/NOTES	STATUS
☐ Wright 1902 Glider (R)				PV
☐ Wright Flyer (R)				PV

DEFENSE CONSTRUCTION SUPPLY DEPOT MONUMENT (OH29)

Location:	By prior permission only at 3990 East Broad Street in the eastern part of Columbus.

TYPE	REG/SER	CON. NO.	PI/NOTES	STATUS
☐ Bell 205 Iroquois (UH-1H)	69-15939	12227		RA

ELLSWORTH MONUMENT (OH30)

Location:	On permanent view at VFW 9571 at 11937 Ellsworth Road in the town.

TYPE	REG/SER	CON. NO.	PI/NOTES	STATUS
☐ Bell 209 Huey Cobra (AH-1G) (AH-1F)	69-16441	20873		PV

EXPERIMENTAL AIRCRAFT ASSOCIATION TIN GOOSE CHAPTER 1247 (OH31)

Address:	3255 East State Road, Port Clinton, Ohio 43452.
Email:	mail@tingoose.org
Admission:	By prior permission only.
Location:	At Keller Field which is about 2 miles east of the town.

The chapter was set up in 1995 by the late James Parker and the members now own and operate a variety of types. Island Airlines flew Ford Tri-Motors from the field for around 40 years with the last leaving in the mid-1980s. A volunteer team is restoring a 5-AT-B version to flying condition, the airframe of which arrived in 2003. The eventual aim is to set up a museum tracing the history of the type and its operations from Port Clinton.

TYPE	REG/SER	CON. NO.	PI/NOTES	STATUS
☐ Ford 5-AT-B	N9667	5-AT-13	NC9667, AN-AAR	RAC

FIRELANDS MUSEUM OF MILITARY HISTORY (OH32)

Address:	202 Citizens Bank Building, Norwalk, Ohio 44857-1542.
Tel:	419-668-8161 Fax: 419-668-0440 Email: rench@accnorwalk.com
Admission:	By prior permission only.
Location:	At Huron County Airport which is about 3 miles east of the town on Route 20.

Started in the 1990s by Richard Rench, the museum now has over 60 military vehicles with the majority in working order, including a 1942 Harley-Davidson motor cycle and a 60-ton M-60 tank. Two of the Iroquois helicopters, both of which served in Vietnam, are kept in airworthy condition and are used to give rides to members. Also on show are many weapons, badges, flags and uniforms.

TYPE	REG/SER	CON. NO.	PI/NOTES	STATUS
☐ Bell 205 Iroquois (UH-1D) (UH-1H)	64-13873	4580		RA
☐ Bell 205 Iroquois (UH-1D) (UH-1H)	N825HX	5308	66-0825	RA
☐ Bell 205 Iroquois (UH-1D) (UH-1H)	N992H	5475	66-0992	RAA
☐ Bell 209 Huey Cobra (AH-1G) (AH-1S)	70-16080	21024		RA

GLEN ESTE MONUMENT (OH33)

Location:	On permanent view in a Veterans Memorial Park in Clough Pike in about 12 miles east of Cincinnati.

TYPE	REG/SER	CON. NO.	PI/NOTES	STATUS
☐ Bell 205 Iroquois (UH-1D) (UH-1H)	'63-12972'			PVX

GREAT OAKS INSTITUTE OF TECHNOLOGY – LAUREL OAKS CAMPUS (OH34)

Address:	300 Oak Drive, Wilmington, Ohio 45177.
Tel:	937-382-14411 Fax: 937-383-2095
Admission:	By prior permission only.
Location:	At the airport which is in the south eastern part of the town.

The college has four locations in the region. The aviation complex at Wilmington Airport trains students for airframe, avionics and engine licences. Instructional airframes, engines and test rigs are used.

TYPE	REG/SER	CON. NO.	PI/NOTES	STATUS
☐ Beech 65-90 King Air	N9901	LJ-93	N48W, N48A	RA
☐ Bell 47G Sioux (H-13G) (OH-13G)	N68371	1039	52-7912	RA
☐ Bell 47G Sioux (H-13G) (OH-13G)	N68372	1188	52-7948	RA
☐ Bell 206A Kiowa (OH-58A)				RA
☐ Cessna 150F	N8695S	15061995		RA
☐ Gates Learjet 23	N153AG	23-058	N363EJ, N66MP, N7FJ	RA
☐ Hiller UH12B Raven (H-23B) (OH-23B)	N68370	590	51-16352	RA
☐ Piper PA-23-250 Aztec C	N6481Y	27-3777		RA
☐ Schweizer SGM.2-37 (TG-7A)	N31AF	1	81-0886	RA
☐ Schweizer SGM.2-37 (TG-7A)	N27AF	7	82-0041	RA

GREENE COUNTY HISTORICAL MUSEUM (OH35)

Address: 74 West Church Street, Xenia, Ohio 45385-2902.
Tel: 937-372-4406
Admission: Tuesday-Friday 0900-1200; Saturday-Sunday 1300-1500.
Location: In the centre of the town which is about 15 miles south east of Dayton on Route 42.

The Greene County Historical Society was formed in 1925 and is now responsible for a number of historic sites in the area. The museum opened in 1971 in a large building which had served as the county home for the poor for a century from the 1860s.

The exhibitions trace the history of Greene County with many interesting artefacts on show. The Wright B replica was one of a number built as part of the centenary of flight. The aircraft will eventually be put on show in one of the sites administered by the museum.

TYPE	REG/SER	CON. NO.	PI/NOTES	STATUS
☐ Wright B (R)				RA

GRIMES FLYING LAB FOUNDATION (OH36)

Address: 1399 Edinger Road, Urbana, Ohio 43078-8769.
Tel: 877-873-5764
Admission: Saturday 0900-1300.
Location: At the Grimes Field which is in the northern part of the town.

Warren Grimes acquired a Beech 18 in 1963 and he converted it into a lighting demonstration aircraft. He used the aircraft to develop his lighting products until 1986 when it was damaged in a fly-by at Tremont Airport.

The aircraft was purchased by Honeywell in 1999 and it has now been restored to flying condition. The foundation has now acquired two other examples of the type and work is being carried out on these.

TYPE	REG/SER	CON. NO.	PI/NOTES	STATUS
☐ Beech D18S Expeditor (C-45G)	N87689	AF-276	51-11719	RAC
☐ Beech D18S Expeditor (C-45H)	N8640E	AF-510	52-10580	RAA
☐ Beech D18S Expeditor (C-45H)	N87692	AF-619	52-10689	RAC

HAMMOND COLLECTION (OH37)

Address: 3073 US Route 68 North, Yellow Springs, Ohio 45387-9747.
Admission: By prior permission only.
Location: About 15 miles east of Dayton on Route 68.

This private collection contains a number of interesting aircraft. The Standard J-1 biplane was designed by Charles Day and first flew in 1916. Just over 1,600 were built and used for pilot training. After World War I the Lincoln company converted a number into three seaters and these were flown by many of the early 'barnstormers'. The Stinson Junior S was a 1931 development of the SM-8A. The Pitcairn PA-18 autogyro in the collection spends long periods on show at the Champaign Aviation Museum and is listed there.

TYPE	REG/SER	CON. NO.	PI/NOTES	STATUS
☐ Aeronca C-3	NC12407	A-173	NC12407, N12407	RAA
☐ Aeronca C-3	NC13021	A-236	NC13021, N13021	RAA
☐ Aeronca 65TF Defender	N27307	1210T	NC27307	RAA
☐ Aeronca 65TL Defender	NC33782	L9341T	NC33782, N33782	RAA
☐ Cessna 180	N40GP	32174		RAA
☐ Consolidated 2 Trusty (PT-3)	N311PT		28-311	RA
☐ Fairchild M-62A Cornell (PT-19A)	N49795	T41-1222	41-20220	RA
☐ Hatz CB-1	N659JH	90		RAA
☐ Standard J-1	N7063X	1000		RA
☐ Stinson Junior S	NC10886	8058	NC10886, N10886	RA

HARROD MONUMENT (OH38)

Location: On permanent view at the Veterans Memorial Park in the centre of the village.

TYPE	REG/SER	CON. NO.	PI/NOTES	STATUS
☐ Bell 205 Iroquois (UH-1D) (UH-1H)	65-9587	4631		PV

HEINS AND PARTNERS COLLECTION (OH39)

Address: 50 La Belle Street, Dayton, Ohio 45403-2324.
Admission: By prior permission only.
Location: At Waco Field which is about 2 miles south of Troy on Route 25A.

Andy Heins is curator of the Waco Aircraft Museum. In partnership with his wife and friends they have acquired several variants of the classic biplane which are kept in hangars near the museum and are nearly all airworthy. The earliest type is the Waco 10, over 1,150 of which were sold in the late 1920s. The rare 125, of which only 31, were built was similar to the 10 but was fitted with a Siemns-Halske radial engine. Later open cockpit types and a cabin YKC are in this interesting collection.

TYPE	REG/SER	CON. NO.	PI/NOTES	STATUS
☐ Waco 10 (GXE)	NC4777	1211	NC4777, N4777	RAA
☐ Waco 10 (GXE)	NC5955	1308	NC5955A	RAA

Ohio

☐ Waco 125	NC7122	1544	NC7122, N7122	RAA
☐ Waco ATO	NC719E	A-97	NC719E, N719E	RAA
☐ Waco KNF (RNF)	NC113Y	3297	NC113Y, N113Y	RAA
☐ Waco RNF	NC863V	3278	NC863V, N863V	RAA
☐ Waco RNF	NC663Y	3356	NC663Z	RAA
☐ Waco UMF-3	NC14041	3836	NC14041, N14041	RAA
☐ Waco UPF-7	NC29300	5327	NC29300, N29300	RAA
☐ Waco UPF-7	NC29988	5485	NC29988, N29988	RAA
☐ Waco UPF-7	NC32065	5697	NC32065, N32065	RA
☐ Waco UPF-7	NC5528N	5824	NC32192, N32192	RA
☐ Waco UPF-7	NC39717	5850	NC39717, N39717	RA
☐ Waco YKC-S	NC14620	4234	NC14620, N14620	RAA
☐ Waco YMF-5 (YMF-3)	NC14132	3957	NC14132, N14132	RA

HISTORICAL AIRCRAFT SQUADRON (OH40)

Address:	PO Box 156, 3266 Old Columbus Road, Fairfield County Airport, Carroll, Ohio 43112.
Tel:	740-653-4778 **Fax:** 740-653-2387 **Email:** info@historicalaircraftsquadron.com
Admission:	Wednesday, Saturday 0900-1700.
Location:	About 20 miles south east of Columbus off Route 33.

The group was formed in 1994 and their first hangar opened in June 2000. Another one plus a museum building are planned. The aim is to restore and fly warbirds and to collect military vehicles. The Invader, which last flew many years ago, is nearing completion after a major rebuild. Members own a number of other aircraft and these will join the display when the new hangar is built. Two aircraft, including the former Indian Air Force Gnat, are on loan from MARC in California.

TYPE	REG/SER	CON. NO.	PI/NOTES	STATUS
☐ Beech C18S Expeditor (C-45B)	N9045V	5844	43-35482, HB113, CF-SFI, C-FSFI	PVC
☐ Burgess Scale P-51D	N51DZ	1		PVA
☐ Douglas A-26B Invader	N99420	27383	44-34104, N9484Z, 420 (Nicaragua), 604 (Nicaragua) – on loan from MARC, CA.	PVC
☐ Folland Fo.141 Gnat F.1	E276		In Indian markings – on loan from MARC, CA.	RAPV
☐ Hiller UH12B Raven (H-23B) (OH-23B)	N68370	590	51-16352	PV
☐ North American NA-88 Texan (AT-6D)				PVA
☐ Stinson V-76 Sentinel (L-5)	N2561C/'298730'	76-961	42-98720	PVAX
☐ Vultee V-74 Valiant (BT-13A)				RAC
☐ Wright 1902 Glider (R)				PV

HOLMESVILLE MONUMENT (OH41)

Location:	On permanent view at ALP 551 at 9510 State Route 83 in the northern part of the town

TYPE	REG/SER	CON. NO.	PI/NOTES	STATUS
☐ Bell 205 Iroquois (UH-1H)	70-16349	12654		PV

HUFFMAN PRAIRIE FLYING FIELD AND INTERPRETIVE CENTER (OH42)

Address:	2380 Memorial Road, Wright-Patterson Air Force Base, Ohio 45473.
Tel:	937-425-0008 **Fax:** 937-425-0011 **Email:** daav_info@nps.gov
Admission:	Daily 0830-1730.
Location:	About 8 miles north east of Dayton off Highway 4.

The Wright Brothers Interpretative Centre has been built at Huffman Prairie Flying Field, which is now part of Wright Patterson Air Force base. This display, which opened on 17th December 2002, is run by the National Park Service and a replica of the Wright B will eventually be on view.

The brothers used the field to develop their designs and carried out a number of significant flights. Several sites in the area, where the pair worked, have been designated as part of the Dayton Aviation Heritage National Historical Park.

TYPE	REG/SER	CON. NO.	PI/NOTES	STATUS
☐ Wright B (R)				RA

INTERNATIONAL WOMEN'S AIR AND SPACE MUSEUM (OH43)

Address:	Burke Lakefront Airport, 1501 North Marginal Road, Cleveland, Ohio 44114.
Tel:	216-623-1111 **Fax:** 216-623-1113 **Email:** cluhta@iwasm.org
Admission:	When the terminal is open.
Location:	In the north eastern part of the city off Interstate 90.

The collection of items for this museum started in the 1970s and the first museum opened in Centerville, a suburb of Dayton in 1986.

A move was made to Cleveland where an impressive display has been staged. On show are photographs, documents, trophies and memorabilia. Many significant contributions by women are portrayed. These include Katharine sister of the Wright brothers, Amelia Earhart, Jacqueline Cochrane, Jacqueline Auriol and Valentina Tereshkova.

The only aircraft currently on display is the Smith Miniplane.

TYPE	REG/SER	CON. NO.	PI/NOTES	STATUS
☐ Smith DSA-1 Miniplane	N1189			PV

The North Dakota Air National Guard have several aircraft, including this Northrop F-89J Scorpion, on show at their Fargo Base. [ND22]

This replica of the Waco Cootie is on show at the Waco Aircraft Museum. (Andy Heins)

This Douglas EA-1E Skyraider is operated by the Oklahoma Museum of Flying. (Glenn Chatfield) [OK27]

JEFFERSON MONUMENT (OH44)

| Location: | On permanent view at VFW 3334 at 341 South Elm Street in the southern part of the town. |

TYPE	REG/SER	CON. NO.	PI/NOTES	STATUS
☐ Bell 209 Huey Cobra (AH-1G0 (AH-1F)	67-15450	20114		PV

LACARNE MONUMENT (OH45)

| Location: | On permanent view on Route 2 just north of the town. |

TYPE	REG/SER	CON. NO.	PI/NOTES	STATUS
☐ Convair 340-31	N707NA	3	N73103, NASA707, N707NA, N8048X – fuselage only.	PV

LIMA MONUMENT (OH46)

| Location: | On permanent view at a business in the town. |

TYPE	REG/SER	CON. NO.	PI/NOTES	STATUS
☐ Cessna 310	N3660D	35360		PV

MANSFIELD AIR NATIONAL GUARD BASE (OH47)

| Location: | By prior permission only at Mansfield-Lahm Airport which is about 3 miles north of the town off Route 13. |

TYPE	REG/SER	CON. NO.	PI/NOTES	STATUS
☐ North American NA-235 Super Sabre (F-100D)	'56783'	235-120	56-3022, N405FS	RAX
☐ Republic F-84F Thunderstreak	52-7021			PV

MAPS AIR MUSEUM (OH48)

Address:	2260 International Parkway, North Canton, Ohio 44720.
Tel:	330-896-7722 Email: jkohan@neo.rr.com
Admission:	Monday-Tuesday Thursday-Saturday 0900-1600; Wednesday 0900-2100.
Location:	On the west side of Akron-Canton Airport which is about 5 miles north of Canton off Route 241.

The Military Aviation Preservation Society was formed in July 1990 and two years later moved into a building at the airport. Displays have been set up in the rooms at the back of the building and these include models, photographs and memorabilia. One area is devoted to the Tuskegee Airmen and another to the WASP pilots.

Some of the aircraft in the collection have been obtained on long-term lease from the Tallichet family Military Aircraft Restoration Corporation in California. The rare Marauder made a wheels up forced landing near Smiths River in British Columbia in January 1941. The airframe was recovered in 1971 and it spent almost two decades years in store at Chino in California. The B-26 was with two other collections for short periods before moving to the museum.

There were two Dauntless airframes here for a long time but these have moved on. The engines on the Beech 18 are now in running order and the aircraft can be taxied. The early Martin Glider has been recovered from storage at the nearby McKinley Museum and it has now been assembled. The type was built in Canton in 1908 and Martin's wife made the first hop because she was lighter than her husband. Eventually over 100 flights were carried out.

The Goodyear company is based in Akron and has constructed over 300 airships. A gondola from the GZ-22 dating from the late 1980s can be seen in the hangar.

This interesting collection includes types which have flown with all three services in the USA over recent years.

TYPE	REG/SER	CON. NO.	PI/NOTES	STATUS
☐ Beech D18S Expeditor (C18S) (SNB-2) (SNB-5) (TC-45J) (UC-45J)	N200KU	5479	Bu67103 – on loan from MARC, CA	PV
☐ Bell 206A Kiowa (OH-58A)	69-16153	40374		PV
☐ Bell 209 Huey Cobra (AH-1G) (AH-1S)	70-16084	21028		PV
☐ Cessna 318B Tweety Bird (318A) (T-37A) (T-37B)	54-2732	40008		RA
☐ Cessna 337M Super Skymaster (O-2A)	N202AF	337M0227	68-10862	PV
☐ Convair 8-10 Delta Dagger (F-102A)	56-0986	8-10-203		RA
☐ Douglas DC-3A-467 Skytrain (C-47B)	N54599/'50928'	16931/34189	45-928, 05928 (Morocco), CNALE (Morocco), N9853A – on loan from MARC, CA.	PV
☐ Fairchild M-62A Cornell (PT-19A)	N51798	8033AE	43-31365	RAC
☐ Goodyear GZ-22			Gondola only.	PV
☐ Grumman G-89 Tracker (S2F-1) (S-2A) (US-2A)	N4225F	373		RAA
☐ Grumman G-98 Tiger (F11F-1) (F-11A)	Bu141783	100		PV
☐ Grumman G-303 Tomcat (F-14A) (F-14B)	Bu162694	540		PV
☐ Hughes 269A Osage (TH-55A)	64-18059	0371	64-18059, N10471	PV
☐ Martin 179 Marauder (B-26)	N4299K	1324	40-1459 – on loan from MARC, CA	PVC
☐ Martin W.M. Glider				PV
☐ McDonnell M.36BA Voodoo (TF-101B) (TF-101F)	57-0342	520		PV
☐ McDonnell M.98EV Phantom II (F-4J) (F-4S)	Bu155764	2980		PV
☐ North American NA-88 Texan (AT-6D)	N83H	88-14989	42-44675,N75206	PVA
☐ North American NA-201 Sabre (F-86D) (F-86L)	53-0658	201-102		RA
☐ North American NA-235 Super Sabre (F-100D)	56-3081	235-179	.	PV
☐ Republic F-84F Thunderstreak	52-6476			PV
☐ Republic F-105B Thunderchief	57-5820	B-57		PV

☐ Ryan Navion A (L-17B) (U-18B)	N91173	NAV-4-1781	48-1075		PVA
☐ Sopwith Triplane (R)	'N6291'				PVX
☐ Sud Fennec [North American NA-174 Trojan (T-28A)]	51-3565	174-103	51-3565, 56 (France), CN-AEN, HR-232A, N8522Z.		PVC
☐ Taylorcraft DCO-65 Grasshopper (L-2M)	N61720	L-5638	(USAAF)		PVA
☐ Vought FG-1D Corsair	Bu76671		Centre fuselage only.		PV
☐ Vought A-7E Corsair II	Bu159268	E406			PV
☐ WSK Lim-6R [MiG-17F]	'419'	1J 04-19	419 (Poland) – in false Soviet markings.		PVX

MARIETTA MONUMENT (OH49)

Location: On permanent view at VFW 5108 at 319 Pike Street in the eastern part of the town.

TYPE	REG/SER	CON. NO.	PI/NOTES	STATUS
☐ Lockheed 580 (T-33A)	52-9785	580-8045		PV

MARION MONUMENT (OH50)

Location: On permanent view at VFW Post 7201 at 1614 Marion-Marysville Road just south of the town.

TYPE	REG/SER	CON. NO.	PI/NOTES	STATUS
☐ Bell 209 Huey Cobra (AH-1G) (AH-1F)	66-15286	20042		PV

MARJORIE ROSENBAUM PLAZA (OH51)

Address: Burke Lakefront Airport, Cleveland, Ohio 44114.
Tel: 216-781-6411
Admission: On permanent view.
Location: In the north eastern part of the city off Interstate 90.

The airport was home to the famous National Air Races from 1929 to 1949 and a major air show is still held annually at the field. The plaza has been set up by the Cleveland Air Show Foundation to honour the pilots and aircraft who have flown from Lakefront. Two Phantoms, one in Thunderbirds and the other in Blue Angels schemes, are mounted either side of an area of lawn. Memorial plaques to those who died in the races can be seen.

TYPE	REG/SER	CON. NO.	PI/NOTES	STATUS
☐ McDonnell M.98EV Phantom II (F-4J)	Bu153812	2088		PVX
☐ McDonnell M.98HO Phantom II (F-4E)	66-0284	2234		PVX

MEDINA MONUMENT (OH52)

Location: On permanent view at VFW 5137 at 3916 Pearl Road in the northern part of the town.

TYPE	REG/SER	CON. NO.	PI/NOTES	STATUS
☐ Bell 205 Iroquois (UH-1H)	70-16428	12733		PV

MOROZOWSKY COLLECTION (OH53)

Address: 1629 Wheeling Avenue, Zanesville, Ohio 43701-4528.
Tel: 740-453-6889
Admission: By prior permission only.
Location: At John's Landing Airfield which is about 6 miles south west of the town.

This large private collection contains many interesting types. The Laird LC series of biplanes first appeared in 1924 and 45 were built. The LC-Rs featured a more powerful engine and shorter wings. A dozen of this model were completed with differing engines.

The low-wing Buhl Pup suffered because of its unreliable Szekely engine and the Depression but 100 were built before the firm closed in 1932. Only a few have survived and most of these have been fitted with modern engines.

The American Eagle was designed as a cheap low powered aircraft. The prototype first flew in June 1930 with a 25 h.p. Cleone two cylinder motor. A total of 98 was built and these used 30 or 45 h.p. Szekely engines. The Luscombe Phantom is now a rarity. The collection of Waco biplanes contains several models which now only exist in very small numbers.

The majority of the aircraft are not complete and some exist as major restoration projects from a few original components.

TYPE	REG/SER	CON. NO.	PI/NOTES	STATUS
☐ Aeronca C-2	N8082Y	21	NC641W	RA
☐ Aeronca C-2	N8196U	A-93	NC651Y	RA
☐ Aeronca C-3	NC11277	A-107	NC11277, N11277	RA
☐ Aeronca C-3	NC13024	A-238	NC13023, N13023	RA
☐ Aeronca C-3	NC14555	A-507	NC14555, N14555	RA
☐ Aeronca 11BC Chief (11AC)	N86301	11AC-107		RA
☐ American Eagle Eaglet A31-1B	NC805J	1203	NC805J, N805J	RA
☐ Beech C17B	NC17072	130	NC17072, N17072	RA
☐ Bensen B-8M Gyrocopter	N309W	1142		RA
☐ Buhl LA-1 Flying Bull Pup	NC392Y	181	NC392Y, N392Y	RA
☐ Cessna 182	N5673	33673		RA
☐ Curtiss JN-4 Canuck	N7982C	1-G.C.		RA
☐ Curtiss JN-4 Canuck	NC1639	4048		RA
☐ Curtiss JN-4 Canuck	N39193	56618		RA

Ohio

☐ Curtiss-Wright CW-1 Junior	NC11808	1183	NC11808, N11808		RA
☐ Franklin PS-2 Eaglet	NC15195	140	NC15195, N15195		RA
☐ Funk B	NC22681	7	NC22681, N22681		RA
☐ Funk B	NC24118	44	NC24118, N24118		RA
☐ Funk B-75L	N22683	10	NC22683		RA
☐ Great Lakes 2T-1A	NC839K	103	NC839K, N839K		RA
☐ Laird LC-1B-300	NC9170N	186	NC170N, NC9170N, N9170N		RA
☐ Laird LC-B-200	NC8106L	147	NC8106L, N8106L		RA
☐ Laird LC-R-200 (LC-B)	NC746W	187	NC746W, N746W		RA
☐ Laird LC-RW300	NC5793	161	NC5793, N5793		RA
☐ Laird LC-RW300	NC7216	162	NC7216, N7216		RA
☐ Laird LC-RW300	NC14803	194	NC14803, N14803		RA
☐ Laird LC-RW300 (LC-R-200)	NC634	177	X634, NC634, N634		RA
☐ Laird LCR-300	N867M	182	NC56K		RA
☐ Luscombe 1 Phantom	N263M	107	NC1007		RA
☐ Payne Knight Twister	N14130	A2			RA
☐ Piper J-3C-65 Cub (L-4B)	N3922A	10093	43-1232		RA
☐ Proctor-Varner-Austin Clip Wing Dart	N3116	RP1-S			RA
☐ Spartan C-2-45	N992N	I-1	NC992N		RA
☐ Stinson SM-8A Junior	NC963W	M4215	NC963W, N963W		RA
☐ Taylorcraft A	NC18305	36	NC18305, N18305		RA
☐ Waco 9	NC139E	218	NC139, N139		RA
☐ Waco 9	N1066	250	NC2766, N2766		RA
☐ Waco 9	NC997	288	NC997, N997		RA
☐ Waco 10 (GXE)	NC8545	1916	NC8545, N8545		RA
☐ Waco 10 (GXE)	NC758E	2010	NC758E, N758E		RA
☐ Waco ASO	NC662N	C-3204	NC662N, N662N		RA
☐ Waco ASO	N268M	DS3001	NC268M		RA
☐ Waco ATO	NC1933R	822	NC1933, N1933		RA
☐ Waco CJC	NC14039	3893	NC14037, N14037		RA
☐ Waco CPF-1	NC15249	4376	NC15249, N54948		RA
☐ Waco CRG	NC660Y	3350	NC660Y, N660Y		RA
☐ Waco CSO	NC2130	AT-3007	NC265M, N2130		RA
☐ Waco KNF	NC699N	3243	NC699N, N699N		RA
☐ Waco PCF	NC11483	3563	NC11483, N11483		RA
☐ Waco PCF	NC13046	3574	NC12439, N12439		RA
☐ Waco PLA	NC81769	3714	NC13067, N13067		RA
☐ Waco PLA	NC13410	3758	NC13073, N13073		RA
☐ Waco PLA	NC13401	3759	NC13401, N13401		RA
☐ Waco QCF-2	NC11444	3495	NC11444, N11444		RA
☐ Waco QDC	NC11443	3503	NC11443, N11443		RA
☐ Waco RNF	NC677N	3222	NC677N, N677N		RA
☐ Waco UBA	NC12449	3600	NC12449, N12449		RA
☐ Waco UBA	NC13032	3612	NC13032, N13032		RA
☐ Waco ULA	NC13049	3761	NC14300, N14300		RA
☐ Waco UMF-3	NC13894	3835	NC13894, N13894		RA
☐ Waco UPF-7	NC29958	5455	NC29958, N29958		RA
☐ Waco UPF-7	N5078X	5468	NC29971, N29971, NC8573		RA
☐ Waco UPF-7	NC30129	5526	NC30129, N30129		RA
☐ Waco UPF-7	N152E	5530	(NC30133), NC152		RAA
☐ Waco UPF-7	NC30171	5568	NC30171, N30171		RA
☐ Waco UPF-7	N174M	5593	NC174		RAA
☐ Waco UPF-7	NC14085	5836	NC14085, N14085		RA
☐ Waco YMF-3	N286Y	3962	NC86Y		RAA
☐ Waco YMF-5	NC14300	3965	NC14063, N14063		RA
☐ Waco YMF-5	NC14607	4214	NC14607, N14607		RA
☐ Waco YPF-6	NC15711	4374	NC15711, N15711		RA

MOTTS MILITARY MUSEUM (OH54)

Address:	5075 South Hamilton Road, Groveport, Ohio 43125-9336.
Tel:	614-836-1500　　Fax: 614-836-5110　　Email: info@mottsmilitarymuseum.org
Admission:	Tuesday-Saturday 0900-1700; Sunday 1300-1700.
Location:	About 10 miles south east of Columbus.

The museum was started by Groveport resident Warren E. Mott and opened its doors in 1987. Originally housed in the 1870 family home, the collection moved into a purpose-built facility in 1999.

All conflicts in which Americans have fought are portrayed. These range from the 1776 War of Independence up to modern times. In each area there are impressive displays of weapons, uniforms, memorabilia and documents.

Military vehicles spanning several years can be seen. A rarity is a World War II landing craft of which only a few survive. Units of the Ohio Air National Guard flew A-7 Corsairs from Rickenbacker Air Force Base in the 1990s.

TYPE	REG/SER	CON. NO.	PI/NOTES	STATUS
☐ Bell 205 Iroquois (UH-1H)	66-17048	9242		PV
☐ Bell 209 Huey Cobra (AH-1G) (AH-1F)	67-15480	20144		PV
☐ Vought A-7D Corsair II	73-1006	D402		PV

NATIONAL MUSEUM OF THE UNITED STATES AIR FORCE (OH55)

Address:	1100 Spaatz Street, Wright Patterson Air Force Base, Dayton, Ohio 45433-6518.
Tel:	937-255-3286　　Fax: 937-656-4081　　Email: nationalmuseum.usaf@wpafb.af.mil
Admission:	Monday-Friday 0900-1700; Saturday-Sunday 1000-1700.
Location:	About 4 miles north east of the city off Highway 4.

The museum has the largest collection of aircraft in the world since it is responsible for most of the former USAF airframes loaned to museums and bases throughout the USA and other countries. Only aircraft actually at Dayton are listed below.

The origins of an Air Force Museum go back to 1923 when equipment and aircraft were put on show at McCook Field Aeronautical Engineering Center near Dayton. In 1927 the display transferred to Wright Field and was named the Engineering Division Museum but space was limited. The collection, by then known as the Army Aeronautical Museum, moved to a new building in 1936 but this closed in 1940 and some of the material was lost.

On 2nd January 1948 a former engineering shop at Patterson Air Force Base was opened as the Air Force Technical Museum but no complete airframes were on show. Aircraft joined the collection in 1954 and by the early 1960s the outside display park was full. Eugene W. Kettering, a Dayton resident, set up the Air Force Museum Foundation to raise 6,000,000 dollars for a new building. Construction started at Wright Field in April 1970 and the magnificent structure opened in August 1971. Sadly Kettering did not live to see his dream realised as he died in 1969.

The aircraft were towed the seven miles to their new home along public roads. The museum initially consisted of two hangars later joined by an administrative area, shop, research centre and theatre. The displays were arranged in a chronological order tracing the history of military flying with special reference to the American contribution.

In 1909 the Signal Corps purchased a Wright Military Flyer and a full size replica is on view. The World War I area includes the first guided missile ever built, the Dayton designed Kettering Aerial Torpedo. On loan from the Caproni Museum in Italy is a superbly restored Ca 36 bomber. In the inter-war area several unique types are on show. From World War II are aircraft from the USA, Great Britain, Germany and Japan These two areas are now known as the Early Years and Air Power Galleries.

Construction of a vast new building started in 1986 and opened two years later. This hall is the Modern Flight Gallery which holds aircraft from the Korean and Vietnam wars. The Eugene W. Kettering Building, which opened in 2003, is home to types from the Cold War and modern conflicts. An impressive Space and Missile Hall was completed in 2004.

Across the field is the annexe consisting of two large hangars. Approximately 50 aircraft are on show including a collection of aircraft used by American Presidents over the years. Also here are many types specifically designed for research tasks. This area has been renamed the Presidential and Research Development Hangars. As these are on an active part of the site tours are run when the security situation allows.

Close by are the workshops which are housed in three World War II hangars. Here more types are being prepared for display. Put on show in late 2006 after a major rebuild is the former Australian Air Force Beaufighter.

In addition to the aircraft there are many displays tracing the history of the service, its personnel, significant developments in military flying and major aerial conflicts. The complete display presents a detailed history of the American Air Force under its different names.

TYPE	REG/SER	CON. NO.	PI/NOTES	STATUS
☐ Aero Commander 680 (L-26C) (U-4B)	55-4647	315-10	N5379G	PV
☐ Aeronca 65TC Grasshopper (O-58B) (L-3B)	42-36200	2262	42-36200, N48407	PV
☐ Albatros D Va (R)				RA
☐ American Helicopter XA-8 Jet Jeep (XH-26)	50-1841			RA
☐ Applebay Zuni II	N9JK			RA
☐ Avro 504K (R)	'D9029'		G-CYEI	PVX
☐ Avro Canada C.100 Canuck 4D (4) (CF-100)	18241	141		PV
☐ Avro Canada Model 1 Avrocar (VZ-9V)	58-7055	AV-7055	On loan from NASM,DC.	PV
☐ Beech D17S (UC-43) (GB-2)	'39-139'	6913	(44-76068), Bu23733, NC67198, N67198	PVX
☐ Beech C18S Kansan (AT-11)	42-37493	4086	42-37493, N64044, N341X	PVX
☐ Beech D18S Expeditor (C-45H)	52-10893	AF-823	52-10893, '54-823'	PV
☐ Beech 26 (AT-10)	'41-27193'		42-35143	PVX
☐ Beech A45 Mentor (T-34A)	53-3310	G-71	53-3310, N6458C	PV
☐ Beech B90 King Air (VC-6A)	66-7943	LJ-230	N2085W	PV
☐ Beech 1079 (QU-22B)	69-7699	EB-7	69-7699, N90697	PV
☐ Bell 26E Airacobra (P-39Q) (RP-39Q)	'41-7073'		44-3887 – displayed as a P-39D	PVX
(TP-39Q)				
☐ Bell 27 Airacomet (P-59B)	44-22650	27-58		PV
☐ Bell 33 Kingcobra (P-63E)	'269654'		43-11728, 401 (Honduras), NX41964	PVX
☐ Bell 47J-1 Sioux (H-13J) (UH-13J)	57-2728	1575		PV
☐ Bell 58 (X-1B)	48-1385			PV
☐ Bell 60 (X-5)	50-1838			RAC
☐ Bell 200 (XH-33) (XV-3A)	54-148	2		RAC
☐ Bell 204 Iroquois (UH-1F)	65-7922	7063		RA
☐ Bell 204 Iroquois (UH-1F) (UH-1P)	64-15476	7026		PV
☐ Bensen B-8M Gyrocopter (X-25A)	68-10770			PV
☐ Blériot XI			Partial replica	PV
☐ Boeing 234 (P-12E)	31-559	1466		PV
☐ Boeing 266 Pea Shooter (P-26A) (R)	'33-391'			PVX
☐ Boeing 299H Fortress (B-17D) (RB-17D)	40-3097	2125		RA
☐ Boeing 299-O Fortress (B-17F) (TB-17F)	41-24485	3170		RAC
☐ Boeing 299-O Fortress (B-17G)	42-97683	7048	Parts only.	PVD
☐ Boeing 345 Superfortress (B-29)	44-27297			PV
☐ Boeing 345 Superfortress (B-29A)	44-62139	11616	Fuselage only.	PV
☐ Boeing 345-9-6 Superfortress (B-50D) (WB-50D) (JB-50D)	49-0310	16086		PV
☐ Boeing 367-76-66 Stratofreighter (KC-97L) (KC-97L)	52-2630	16661		PV
☐ Boeing 450-157-35 Stratojet (B-47E)			Front fuselage only.	RA
☐ Boeing 450-157-35 Stratojet (B-47E) (JB-47E)	53-2280	4501093		RA
☐ Boeing 450-157-35 Stratojet (B-47E) (EB-47E)	52-0410	450695	Front fuselage only.	RAC
☐ Boeing 450-171-51 Stratojet (RB-47H)	53-4299	4501323		PV
☐ Boeing 464-201-7 Stratofortress (B-52D)	56-0665	464036		PV
☐ Boeing 464-201-7 Stratofortress (B-52D)	56-0682	464053	Front fuselage only.	RA
☐ Boeing 707-353B (VC-137C) (C-137C)	62-6000	18461		PV
☐ Boeing 717-100A Stratotanker (KC-135A) (JKC-135A) (NKC-135A)	55-3123	17239		PV
☐ Boeing 717-157 Stratolifter (C-135A) (EC-135N) (EC-135E)	60-0374	18149		PV

Ohio

☐ Boeing Bird of Prey				PV
☐ Boeing X-32A				RA
☐ Boeing X-40A				PV
☐ Boeing X-45A				PV
☐ Boeing X-46A				PV
☐ Boeing-Stearman E75 Kaydet (PT-13D)	42-17800	75-5963	42-17800, N41766	PV
☐ Bristol 156 Beaufighter IC	A19-43		T5049 – in Australian markings	PV
☐ Caproni Ca.36M (Ca.3 mod)	'CA3 11504'	3808	25811	PVX
☐ Caquot Balloon				PV
☐ Cessna T-50 Bobcat (AT-17B) (UC-78B)	42-71626	4322	42-71626, N43BB, N4403N	PV
☐ Cessna 172F Mescalero (T-41A)	N5251F	17253351	65-5251	PV
☐ Cessna 195 (LC-126A)	49-1949	7328		RA
☐ Cessna 305D Bird Dog (305A) (L-19A) (O-1A) (O-1G)	51-11917	22231		PV
☐ Cessna 310A Blue Canoe (L-27A) (U-3A)	58-2124	38098		PV
☐ Cessna 318B Tweety Bird (318A) (T-37A) (T-37B)	57-2289	40222		PV
☐ Cessna 318D Dragonfly (318C) (T-37C) (YAT-37D) (YA-37A)	62-5951	40719		PV
☐ Cessna 337M Super Skymaster (O-2A)	67-21331	337M0037		PV
☐ Chanute Glider (R)				PV
☐ Consolidated 1 Trusty (PT-1)	26-233			PV
☐ Consolidated 28-5A Catalina (PBY-5A)	'44-33879'	1959	Bu46595, N9501C, PT-AXM, 6551 (Brazil), N4583B – painted as an OA-10A.	PVX
☐ Consolidated 32 Liberator (B-24D)	42-72843	2413		PV
☐ Consolidated 37 (XC-99)	43-52436		43-52436, N5009F	RAC
☐ CASA 2.111B [Heinkel He 111H-16]		152	B.2I-22	RA
☐ CASA 352L [Junkers Ju 52/3m]	T.2B-244	135		PVX
☐ Convair 4 Hustler (B-58A)	59-2458	61		PV
☐ Convair 7-002 (XF-92A)	46-682			PV
☐ Convair 8-10 Delta Dagger (F-102A)	56-1416	8-10-633		PV
☐ Convair 8-24 Delta Dart (F-106A)	58-0787	8-24-118		PV
☐ Convair 36 Peacemaker (B-36J)	52-2220	361		PV
☐ Convair 102 (XP-81) (XF-81)	44-91000			RA
☐ Convair 102 (XP-81) (XF-81)	44-91001			RA
☐ Convair 340-70 Samaritan (C-131B) (EC-131B) (C-131H), (NC-131H)	N793VS	245	53-7793	PV
☐ Convair 440-79 Samaritan (C-131D)	55-0301	329	N8443H	PV
☐ Corben Super Ace				RA
☐ Culver NR-D Cadet (PQ-14B)	44-68462	W1059	44-68462, N5389N	PV
☐ Curtiss D Pusher (R)	'2'			PVX
☐ Curtiss 1C Jenny (JN-4D)	2805			PV
☐ Curtiss 35 Hawk (P-6E)	'32-240'		32-261	PVX
☐ Curtiss 75L Hawk (P-36A)	'38-086'	12415	38-001, N52203, 38-001	PVX
☐ Curtiss 84B Shrike (S84) (A-25A) (SB2C-1A)	Bu76805		42-80449	RAC
☐ Curtiss 85 Owl (O-52)	'11907'	14296	40-2763, '41-2150'	PVX
☐ Curtiss A87-A2 Kittyhawk I	'104'	18731	AK987, 1068 (Canada), N1237N, N5673N	PVX
☐ Curtiss-Wright CW-20B-2 Commando (C-46D)	44-78018	33414		PV
☐ Curtiss-Wright CW-25 Jeep (AT-9)	41-12150	362		PV
☐ Curtiss-Wright 200 (X-19A)	62-12198			PV
☐ Dassault Mystère IVA	57	57		RA
☐ De Havilland DH-4B				PV
☐ De Havilland DH.82A Tiger Moth	N39DH	85674	DE744, G-ANCN, OO-NCN	PV
☐ De Havilland DH.89A Dragon Rapide (DH.89B Dominie I)	'X7454'	6794	NR695, VT-ASQ, N2290F,	PVX
☐ De Havilland DH.98 Mosquito TT.35 (B.35)	'NS519'		RS709, G-ASKA, 'HR113', N9797, G-MOSI	PVX
☐ De Havilland DHC.2 Beaver (L-20A) (U-6A)	51-16501	277	51-16501, N9239	PV
☐ De Havilland DHC.4A Caribou (CV-2B) (C-7B)	62-4193	138		PV
☐ Douglas O-38F	33-324	1177		PV
☐ Douglas O-46A	35-179	1441		RA
☐ Douglas SBD-4 Dauntless	'115786'	2565	Bu10575 – painted as an A-24A.	PVX
☐ Douglas B-18A Bolo	37-469	2469	37-469, NC56847, N56847	PV
☐ Douglas B-23 Dragon	39-37	2723	39-37, NR41821, N41821, N800L, N800N	RA
☐ Douglas RB-66B Destroyer	53-0475	44356		PV
☐ Douglas DC-2-243 (C-39)	38-515	2072	38-515, XA-DUF, XB-YAV, N6097C	RA
☐ Douglas DC-3A-467 Skytrain (C-47B) (C-47D)	'315174'	15323/26768	43-49507	PVX
☐ Douglas DC-4 Skymaster (C-54A) (VC-54C) (C-54A)	'272252'	7470	42-107451	PVX
☐ Douglas DC-6 Liftmaster (VC-118)	46-505	42881		PV
☐ Douglas 1317 Globemaster II (C-124C)	'10135'	43975	52-1066	PVX
☐ Douglas 1333 Cargomaster (C-133A)	56-2008	45245		PV
☐ Douglas A-20G Havoc	'321475'	21847	43-22200, NL63004, N63004, 43-22200 – painted as a P-70.	PVX
☐ Douglas A-26A Invader (A-26B) (B-26K)	64-17676	7309	41-39596, 64-17676, N29939, N268G, C-GXTF, N29939 –	PV
☐ Douglas A-26C Invader	44-35733	29012		PV
☐ Douglas X-3 Stiletto	49-2892			PV
☐ Douglas A-1E Skyraider (AD-5)	52-132649	9506	Bu132649	PV
☐ Douglas A-1H Skyraider (AD-6)	'51-630'			RAX
☐ Douglas XB-42A Mixmaster (XB-42)	43-50224	27224		RA
☐ Douglas YB-43 Jetmaster	44-61509			RA

☐ Ercoupe 415C	N37119	86		RA
☐ Fairchild 24 C8F	NC16817	3118	NC16817, N16817	PVX
☐ Fairchild 24R40A (UC-86) (XUC-86A)	42-68852	R40-422	NC28530, 42-68852, N18652	RA
☐ Fairchild M-62A Cornell (PT-19A)	'41-14666'	T42-3689	42-34023, N1070N	PVX
☐ Fairchild M-62A-4 Cornell II		FC.120	10619 (Canada), N2039A	RAX
☐ Fairchild 78 Packet (C-82A)	'45-57735'	10216	48-581, N4752C	PVX
☐ Fairchild 110 Flying Boxcar (C-119F) (C-119J)	51-8037	10915		PV
☐ Fairchild 473 Provider (205) (C-123B) (UC-123B) (C-123K) (UC-123K)	56-4362	20246	56-4362, (South Vietnam)	PV
☐ Fairchild-Republic A-10A Thunderbolt II	78-0681	A10-301		PV
☐ Fairchild-Republic NGT (T-46A)	84-0493			RA
☐ Fieseler Fi 156C-2 Storch	'5F+YK'	4389	??+??, Fv3808, D-EBOY, N156SV	PVX
☐ Fisher P-75A Eagle	44-44553	5	On loan from NASM, DC.	RAC
☐ Focke-Achgelis Fa 330A-1 Bachstelze	T2-4617		FE-4617	PV
☐ Focke-Achgelis Fa 330A-1 Bachstelze			FE-4618, T2-4618 – on loan to NASM, DC.	-
☐ Focke-Wulf Fw 190D-9	'8'	601088	601088, T2-120 – on loan from NASM, DC.	PV
☐ Fokker D VII (R)	'7625/18'	1918-1961	N10408, '452/18' – original wing from a C II – on loan from Old Rhinebeck, NY.	PVX
☐ Fokker Dr I (R)	N1387B	16		PV
☐ Fokker D XII	286			RA
☐ Ford JB-2 [Fieseler Fi 103A-1]				PV
☐ General Atomics RQ-1A Predator	94-3009	P-009		PV
☐ General Atomics MQ-9 Reaper				PV
☐ General Dynamics F-111A	63-9780	A1-15	Cockpit only.	PV
☐ General Dynamics EF-111A (F-111A)	66-0057	A1-75		PV
☐ General Dynamics F-111A	67-0067	A1-112		PV
☐ General Dynamics F-111F	70-2390	E2-29		PV
☐ General Dynamics 401 Fighting Falcon (F-16A)	81-0663	61-344		PV
☐ General Dynamics 401 Fighting Falcon (F-16A) (NF-16A) (AFTI/F-16)	75-0750	61-6		PV
☐ Grumman G-15 Duck (J2F-6)	'48-563'		Bu33587, N67790	PVX
☐ Grumman G-111 Albatross (G-64) (SA-16A) (SA-16B) (HU-16B)	51-5282	G-163		PV
☐ Grumman G-712 (X-29A)	82-0003		Built from Northrop N-156A Freedom Fighter (F-5A) c/n N.6009 63-8372.	PV
☐ Halberstadt CL IV (C-5)	4205/18		4205/18, D-144, D-E??O – on loan from NASM, DC.	PV
☐ Halberstadt CLS I			Fuselage only	PV
☐ Hawker Hurricane XII	'Z3174'	42025	5390 (Canada)	PVX
☐ Hawker P.1127 Kestrel (XV-6A)	64-18262		XS688	PV
☐ Helio H-295 Super Courier (U-10D)	'66-14374'	1262	66-14360, N42022	PVX
☐ Hispano HA-1112M1L [Messerschmitt Bf 109G]	C.4K-64	133	Displayed as a Bf 109G-5	PVX
☐ Interstate S1B1 Cadet (O-63) (L-6)	43-2680	123	43-2680, N60458	PV
☐ Junkers Ju 88D-1/trop	'105'	430650	F6+AL, HK959, FE-1598, F6+AL – in Romanian colours.	PVX
☐ Kaman K-600-3 Huskie (H-43B) (HH-43B)	60-0263	87		PV
☐ Kawanishi N1K2-J Shiden Kai	62387	5312		PVX
☐ Kellett K-3	NC10767	2	NC10767, N10767	PV
☐ Laister-Kauffman LK.10B (TG-4A)	42-43734			PV
☐ Ling-Temco-Vought XC-142A	NASA522		62-5924	PV
☐ Lockheed 15-27-01 Harpoon (PV-2)	N7086C	15-1410	Bu37444	RA
☐ Lockheed 18-56-23 Lodestar (C-60A)	43-16445	18-2605	43-16445, 316445 (France), F-BAMA, , N94540, XA-SEX, (XB-SEX), N51605,	PV
☐ Lockheed 080 Shooting Star (P-80B) (P-80R)	44-85200	080-1223		PV
☐ Lockheed 080 Shooting Star (P-80C) (F-80C)	49-696	080-2444	49-696, (Uruguay)	PV
☐ Lockheed 090-32-01 (XP-90) (XF-90)	46-688	090-1002		RA
☐ Lockheed 182-1A Hercules (182-44-03) (C-130A) (AC-130A)	54-1626	182-3013		PV
☐ Lockheed 182-1A Hercules (182-44-03) (C-130A) (JC-130A) (C-130A) (AC-130A)	54-1630	182-3017		PV
☐ Lockheed 183-93-02 Starfighter (F-104A)	'56-0879'	183-1042	56-0754, (Jordan)	PVX
☐ Lockheed 300 Starlifter (C-141A) (C-141C)	66-0177	300-6203		PV
☐ Lockheed 383-04-05 Starfighter (F-104C)	56-0914	183-1202		PV
☐ Lockheed 422-87-23 Lightning (P-38L)	'42-67855'	422-8487	44-53232, NX66678, 505 (Honduras)	PVX
☐ Lockheed 580 (T-33A)	53-5974	580-9456		PV
☐ Lockheed 580 (T-33A) (NT-33A)	51-4120	580-5414		PV
☐ Lockheed 780-76-12 Starfire (F-94A)	49-2498	780-7020		PV
☐ Lockheed 880-75-13 Starfire (F-97A) (F-94C)	'50-1054'	880-8025	50-980	PVX
☐ Lockheed 1049A-55-86 Super Constellation (RC-121D) (EC-121D)	53-0555	1049A-4370		PV
☐ Lockheed 1049B-55-97 Super Constellation (1049B-55-75) (R7V-1) (VC-121E)	53-7885	1049B-4151	(Bu131650)	PV
☐ Lockheed 1329 JetStar 6 (VC-140B) (C-140B)	61-2492	1329-5031		PV
☐ Lockheed SR-71A Blackbird	61-7976	2027		PV
☐ Lockheed U-2A	56-6722	389		PV
☐ Lockheed YF-117A	79-10781	A.4006		PV
☐ Lockheed YF-12A	60-6935	1002		PV
☐ Lockheed-Boeing Dark Star				PV
☐ Lockheed-Martin YF-22A Raptor	N22YF	3997	87-0700	PV

Ohio

Ohio

☐ Lockheed-Martin F-22A Raptor	91-4003	4003		PV
☐ Lockheed-Martin X-35				RA
☐ Luscombe 8A Silvaire	N2085K	4812	NC2085K	RA
☐ Macchi MC.200 Saetta	MM8146			PV
☐ Martin MB-2 (R)	'14'		Contains some original parts.	PVX
☐ Martin 139A (YB-10)	33-146 (?)	514 (?)	33-146 (?), (Argentina)	PV
☐ Martin 179G Marauder (B-26G)	'42-95857'	8701	43-34581, 334581 (France)	PVX
☐ Martin 272B Canberra (B-57B) (EB-57B)	52-1499	82		PV
☐ Martin 294 Canberra (RB-57D) (EB-57D)	53-3982	006		PV
☐ Martin SV-5J	'13551'	2	Painted as the X-24A	PVX
☐ Martin SV-5P (X-24A) (X-24A)	66-13551			PV
☐ Martin X-23A (SV-5D)				RA
☐ McDonnell M.27D Goblin (XF-85)	46-523	1		PV
☐ McDonnell M.36BA Voodoo (F-101B)	58-0325	697		PV
☐ McDonnell M.36CA Voodoo (RF-101C)	56-0166	127		PV
☐ McDonnell M.38 (XR-20) (XH-20)	46-689			PV
☐ McDonnell M.98AM Phantom II (F4H-1) (F-4B) (F-4N)	'66-7660'	404	Bu151424 – front fuselage only.	PVX
☐ McDonnell M.98DF Phantom II (RF-4C)	64-1047	947		PV
☐ McDonnell M.98DF Phantom II (YRF-110A) (YRF-4C) (YF-4E)	62-12200	266		RA
☐ McDonnell M.98DJ Phantom II (F-4C)	64-0763	1059		RA
☐ McDonnell M.98DJ Phantom II (F-4C)	64-0829	1169		PV
☐ McDonnell M.98EN Phantom II (F-4D)	66-7626	2195		RA
☐ McDonnell M.98HO Phantom II (F-4E) (F-4G)	69-7263	3947		PV
☐ McDonnell M.199-1A Eagle (F-15A)	72-0119	019/A017		PV
☐ McDonnell M.199-1A Eagle (F-15A)	76-0027	207/A179		PV
☐ McDonnell-Douglas X-36				PV
☐ Messerschmitt Bf 109G-14	'4'	610824	610824 (Bulgaria), 9664 (Yugoslavia), N109MS.	PVX
☐ Messerschmitt Me 163B-1a Komet	191095	191095	191095, AM211	PV
☐ Messerschmitt Me 262A-1a		501232	(Luftwaffe), Bu121442	PV
☐ Mikoyan-Gurevich MiG-15	2057	2015357	In North Korean markings.	PV
☐ Mikoyan-Gurevich MiG-17	'3020'		799 (Egypt) – in false North Korean markings.	PVX
☐ Mikoyan-Gurevich MiG-19S	0138	0915372		PV
☐ Mikoyan-Gurevich MiG-21F-13	'5063'	560301	0301 (Czechoslovakia) – in false North Vietnamese markings.	PVX
☐ Mikoyan-Gurevich MiG-21PF	408	760408	In Hungarian markings.	RA
☐ Mikoyan-Gurevich MiG-21UM	535			RA
☐ Mikoyan-Gurevich MiG-23K				PV
☐ Mikoyan-Gurevich MiG-23MLD	44	0390316216		PV
☐ Mikoyan-Gurevich MiG-25RB	25105		In Iraqi markings.	RAC
☐ Mikoyan-Gurevich MiG-29A	25	2960516761		RA
☐ Mitsubishi A6M2 Zero Sen Model 21	51553			PV
☐ Nieuport 28C.1 (R)	'N6301'	7171-2-19	N8539	PVX
☐ Noorduyn Norseman VI (C-64A) (UC-64A)	'44-70534'	561	44-70296, CF-KVB, NC55860, N57WS	PVX
☐ North American NA-51 (O-47B)	'37-328'	51-1025	39-112, N73722, XB-YUW, N73722	PV
☐ North American NA-64 Yale	'38-224'	64-2168	3417 (Canada) – modified to represent a NA-29 (BT-9C).	PVX
☐ North American NA-88 Texan (AT-6C)	41-32406	88-10543		RA
☐ North American NA-88 Texan (AT-6D)	42-84216	88-15997	42-84216, (Korea)	PV
☐ North American NA-97 Apache (A-36A)	42-83665	97-15883	42-83665, NX39502, N39502, N6458C	PV
☐ North American NA-100 Mitchell (B-25D) (F-10) (RB-25D)	'40-2344'	100-23700	43-3374	PVX
☐ North American NA-122 Mustang (P-51D)	'44-15174'	122-41476	44-74936	PVX
☐ North American NA-123 Twin Mustang (P-82B) (F-82B)	N12102	123-43748	44-65162	RAC
☐ North American NA-123 Twin Mustang (P-82B) (F-82B)	44-65168	123-43754	44-65168, NACA132	PV
☐ North American NA-153 Tornado (B-45C)	48-0010	153-38486		PV
☐ North American NA-154 Navion (L-17A)	'48-928'	NAV-4-1078) (154-51)	47-1347	PVX
☐ North American NA-159 Trojan (T-28A) (JT-28A)	49-1494	159-6		PV
☐ North American NA-161 Sabre (P-86A) (F-86A)	'49-1236'	161-61	49-1067	PVX
☐ North American NA-165 Sabre (F-86D)	'52-3863'	165-23	50-477	PVX
☐ North American NA-191 Sabre (F-86F)	'24978'	191-445	52-4749	PVX
☐ North American NA-191 Sabre (F-86F) (RF-86F)	52-4492	191-188		PV
☐ North American NA-203 Sabre (F-86H)	53-1352	203-124		PV
☐ North American NA-212 (YF-100B) (YF-107A)	55-5119	212-2		PV
☐ North American NA-219 Trojan (T-28B)	'38365'	219-47	Bu140048 – in false South Vietnamese markings.	PVX
☐ North American NA-223 Super Sabre (F-100D)	55-3754	223-436		PV
☐ North American NA-240 (X-15) (X-15A) (X-15A-2)	56-6671	240-2		PV
☐ North American NA-243 Super Sabre (F-100F) (QF-100F)	56-3837	243-113		PV
☐ North American NA-276 Sabreliner (T-39A)	62-4478	276-31		PV
☐ North American NA-278 Valkyrie (XB-70)	62-0001	278-1		PV
☐ North American NA-321 Bronco (OV-10A)	68-3817	321-113		PV
☐ North American X-10				PV
☐ Northrop Gamma 2F (A-17A)	36-207	234		PV

☐ Northrop N-8E Black Widow (N.C)	'42-39468'	N.1399	43-8353	PVX
☐ Northrop N-23 Raider (YC-125B)	'48-622'	2510	48-626, XA-LOU	RACX
☐ Northrop N-26 (XS-4) (X-4)	46-0677	3238		PV
☐ Northrop N-156F Freedom Fighter (YF-5A)	'13332'	N.6003	59-4989	PVX
☐ Northrop N-156T Talon (T-38A) (AT-38B)	63-8172	N.5519		PV
☐ Northrop N-160 Scorpion (N-68) (F-89D) (F-89J)	'53-2509'	N.4488	52-1911	PVX
☐ Northrop B-2 Spirit	'82-1070'		Static test airframe.	PVX
☐ Northrop Tacit Blue				PV
☐ Northrop-Grumman RQ-4A Global Hawk	98-22003			PV
☐ Northrop/McDonnell Douglas YF-23A	87-0800	1001	87-0800, N231YF	RA
☐ Packard C2	SC42133	6		PV
☐ Panavia PA200 Tornado GR.1B (GR.1)	ZA374	3088		PV
☐ Piasecki PD-22 Work Horse (H-21B) (CH-21B)	51-15857	B.4		PV
☐ Piper J-3C-65 Cub (O-59A) (L-4A)	NC42050	8570	42-36446, NC42050, N42050	PV
☐ Piper J-3C-65 Cub (O-59A) (L-4A)	'42-36389'	8914	42-36790, N5777N	PVX
☐ Piper PA-48 Enforcer	N481PE	48-8301001		PV
☐ Pratt-Read PR-G1 (LNE-1)	N69215	PRG-01-11	Bu31523	RA
☐ Raytheon T-6A Texan II [Pilatus PC-9]		PT-3		RA
☐ Republic P-47D Thunderbolt	'42-22668'		42-23278, N5087V, N347D, 42-23278	PVX
☐ Republic P-47D Thunderbolt	'44-32718'	399-55706	45-49167, 540 (Peru), 116 (Peru) N47DB	PVX
☐ Republic F-84E Thunderjet	'51-10454'		50-1143	PVX
☐ Republic YF-84F Thunderstreak (YF-96A)	49-2430			RA
☐ Republic F-84F Thunderstreak	52-6526			RA
☐ Republic RF-84K Thunderflash (RF-84F) (GRF-84F)	52-7459			PV
☐ Republic XF-84H Thunderstreak (XF-106)	51-17059			PV
☐ Republic XF-91 Thunderceptor (XP-91)	46-680			PV
☐ Republic F-105D Thunderchief	60-0504	D-192		PV
☐ Republic F-105G Thunderchief (F-105F)	63-8320	F-97		PV
☐ Rockwell B-1B Lancer	84-0051	11		PV
☐ Royal Aircraft Factory S.E.5E	'22-335'		22-325	PVX
☐ Ryan 69 Vertijet (X-13) (X-13A)	54-1620			RAC
☐ Ryan STA	'40-44'	312	NC18922	PVX
☐ Ryan ST-3KR Recruit (PT-22)	41-15721	1750	41-15721, N51713	PV
☐ Schweizer SGS.2-12 (TG-3A)				RA
☐ Schweizer SGS.2-12 (TG-3A)	42-52988			PV
☐ Schweizer SGS.2-25	N91892	1		RA
☐ Seversky AP-1 (P-35)	'41-17449'	95 (?)	36-404	PVX
☐ Sikorsky VS-316A Hoverfly (R-4B)	43-46506	50		PV
☐ Sikorsky VS-316B Hoverfly II (R-6A)	43-45379			PV
☐ Sikorsky VS-372 Dragonfly (YR-5A) (YH-5A)	43-46620	164		PV
☐ Sikorsky S-55D Chickasaw (H-19B) (UH-19B)	'51-3893'		52-7587	PVX
☐ Sikorsky S-61R (CH-3C) (CH-3E)	63-9676	61508		PV
☐ Sikorsky S-61R (CH-3E) (HH-3E)	67-14709	61611		PV
☐ Sikorsky S-65A (HH-53C) (MH-53J) (MH-53M)	68-10357	65163		PV
☐ SPAD VII	'3730'		'AS94099'	PVX
☐ SPAD XIIIC.1	'1'	1924E	N2030A	PVX
☐ Sopwith F.1 Camel (R)	'F6034'			PVX
☐ Sperry-Verville M-1 Messenger	'AS68533'		On loan from NASM, DC.	PVX
☐ Standard J-1	'AS22692'			PVX
☐ Standard J-1	1141			PV
☐ Stinson V-74 Vigilant (O-49A) (L-1A)	'41-19039'		40-0291	PVX
☐ Stinson V-76 Sentinel (L-5)	'42-98667'	76-466	42-98225, N66225	PVX
☐ Sukhoi Su-22M4	25+33	31203	724 (DDR)	RA
☐ Supermarine 349 Spitfire F.Vc	MA863		MA863, A58-246	PV
☐ Supermarine 365 Spitfire PR.XI	'MB950'	6S.417723	PA908, M342 (India), PA908	PVX
☐ Taylorcraft DCO-65 Grasshopper (L-2M)	'42-26753'			PVX
☐ Thomas-Morse S-4C	SC38944	160		PV
☐ Vought A-7D Corsair II	70-0970	D116		PV
☐ Vultee V-79 Valiant (BT-13B)	42-90629	79-1706	42-90629, NC62605	PV
☐ Waco NZR Hadrian (CG-4A)	45-27948			PV
☐ Wright B Modified				PV
☐ Wright Flyer (R)				PV
☐ Wright Military Flyer (R)				PV
☐ Yokosuka MXY-7-K1 Ohka 11				PV

NEIL ARMSTRONG AIR AND SPACE MUSEUM (OH56)

Address: 500 Apollo Drive, PO Box 1978, Wapakoneta, Ohio 45985-9780.
Tel: 419-738-8811   **Fax:** 419-738-3361   **Email:** rmacwhinney@ohiohistory.org
Admission: April–November Monday-Saturday 0930-1700 Sunday 1200-1700;
Location: Just east of the town at the junction of Interstate 75 and Route 67.

Astronaut Neil Armstrong was born close by in 1930 and spent his early years in the area. The museum opened on 20th July 1972, the third anniversary of his historic moon walk.

The story of his life is portrayed in an interesting display. There are a number of models he built as a boy along with other personal artefacts. The Aeronca Champion in which he learned to fly in 1946 is mounted vertically on a wall. Armstrong obtained his pilot's licence before he could drive and he used to cycle to the airport for lessons. Outside is the Douglas Skylancer he flew at NASA in the early 1960s. Four examples of the type were built and used for research work. Initially flown from Edwards Air Force Base they were later transferred to Moffett Field.

The Gemini 8 capsule in which he and David Scott carried out the first space docking in 1966 can be seen. A sample of moon rock is a prized exhibit.

Ohio

Roy Knabenshue was an early pioneer of airship design. His first appeared in 1905 and in the Toledo 2 he flew around Central Park in New York. He later carried out regular passenger services in California. He also became the manager for the Wright brothers on their tours around the country. The museum makes use of modern audio-visual techniques to trace the story of space flight. One gallery portrays early flight in the state.

TYPE	REG/SER	CON. NO.	PI/NOTES	STATUS
☐ Aeronca 7AC Champion	NC83423	7AC-2090	NC83423, N83423	PV
☐ Douglas F5D-1 Skylancer	NASA802		Bu142350, NASA213	PV
☐ Knabenshue Toledo 2 Airship			Gondola only – on loan from NASM, DC.	PV
☐ Razor Balloon				PV

NEWARK MONUMENTS (OH57)

Location:	On permanent view at two locations in the town.

TYPE	REG/SER	CON. NO.	PI/NOTES	STATUS
☐ Bell 204 Iroquois (UH-1B)	63-8662 (?)	887 (?)	In a compound in 6th. Street.	PV
☐ McDonnell M.98DE Phantom II (F-4C)	64-0683	917	At Licking County Airport which is about 10 miles south east of the town.	PV

NORTHERN OHIO MUSEUM OF AVIATION (OH58)

Address:	320 Deepwood Drive, Wadsworth, Ohio 44281.
Tel:	330-242-0550 Email: gaairracers@aol.com
Admission:	By prior permission only.
Location:	At the airport which is about 2 miles south west of the town.

This private museum owns two of Benny Howard's famous racers. One of the aims is to set up a Museum of Air Racing in Cleveland to commemorate the meetings held between 1929 and 1949. In 1930 the DGA-3 'Pete' was third in the race. Howard decided to built a larger aircraft and two DGA-4s named 'Mike' and 'Ike' were soon ready. The pair have survived and are being restored by Karl Engelskirger and Tom Matowicz.

TYPE	REG/SER	CON. NO.	PI/NOTES	STATUS
☐ Cessna 180K Skywagon 180	N2986K	18053149		RAA
☐ Howard DGA-4	N55YV	68	NR55Y	RA
☐ Howard DGA-4	N56YV	69	NR56Y	RAC
☐ Piper J-3C-65 Cub	N98737	18966		RAA
☐ Piper J-3C-65 Cub (L-4J)	N5930V	13081	44-80785	RAA
☐ Piper PA-12 Super Cruiser	N4364M	12-3302	NC4364M	RAA
☐ Waco UPF-7	NC32032	5663	NC32032, N32032	RAA

OHIO HISTORY OF FLIGHT MUSEUM (OH59)

Address:	2610 West Case Road, Columbus, Ohio 43235.
Tel:	614-777-5488 Email: rbujarski@columbus.rr.com
Admission:	Not Open
Location:	In storage in the area.

The museum was set up in 1983 and originally staged a small exhibition in a hangar at the airport. Funds were raised to construct a purpose-built exhibition hall and this opened in 1991.

One of the founders of the museum was Foster Lane who died in the summer of 1995. His company Lane Aviation is resident at the airport and celebrated its 70th anniversary in 2005. Several aircraft in the collection were owned by him and presented to the museum when it opened.

The museum was forced to close when the airport decided to take over the land for expansion of its facilities. The majority of the collection is in store but two aircraft have been put on show. A group is raising funds for the construction of a new facility at Ohio State University Airport.

Foster Lane bought the Waco 9 in 1927 and repurchased it in 1985. He also owned the Waco 10, the Taylor Cub and the Alliance Argo. The Argo was built in Alliance and first flew in 1928. Only 20 were completed before the factory closed in 1930 and two now survive. Only 40 Simplex Red Arrows were constructed in Defiance and the major components of one are owned by the museum. A complete example is somewhere in Illinois.

TYPE	REG/SER	CON. NO.	PI/NOTES	STATUS
☐ Aeronca C-2	NC10304	A-66	NC10300, N10300	RA
☐ Alliance Argo	N596K	106	NC596K – at the Ohio Historical Center in the city.	PV
☐ American Eagle RF-1 Frigate	N81RF	001		RA
☐ Bensen B-8M Gyrocopter	N7087	1		RA
☐ Blériot XI (Scale R)				RA
☐ Bowers Fly Baby 1A				RA
☐ Culver LCA Cadet	NC20989	100	NC20989, N20989 – on show at Port Columbus IAP.	PV
☐ Curtiss D Pusher				RA
☐ Curtiss-Wright CW-1 Junior	N10939	1118	NC10939	RA
☐ Dart G				RA
☐ Goodyear GA-33 Inflatoplane	N39635			RA
☐ Piccard AX-6 Hot Air Balloon	N72LL	641		RA
☐ Piccard AX-6 Hot Air Balloon	N333AJ	713		RA
☐ Simplex Red Arrow K2C	NC7581	18	Components.	RA
☐ Smith Termite				RA

| ☐ Taylor E-2 Cub | N14757 | 150 | NC14757 | RA |
| ☐ Williams WAF-2C | | | | RA |

OHIO'S CENTER OF SCIENCE AND INDUSTRY (OH60)

Address:	333 West Broad Street, Columbus, Ohio 43215.
Tel:	614-228-2674 Fax: 614-629-3226 Email: knowinsky@mail.cosi.org
Admission:	Monday-Saturday 1000-1700; Sunday 1200-1730.
Location:	In the centre of the city.

Displays at the museum are designed to introduce young people to all aspects of science and engineering. The museum opened in 1964 in the old Memorial Hall building and moved to its present location in 1999.

The only aircraft on show is the microlight produced at Delaware in Ohio. The design is a three-quarter scale replica of the Curtiss Jenny of World War I. Over 30 examples, in either complete or kit form, were sold.

TYPE	REG/SER	CON. NO.	PI/NOTES	STATUS
☐ Cloud Dancer Jenny				PV

OWENS COMMUNITY COLLEGE (OH61)

Address:	30335 Oregon Road, Perrysburg, Ohio 43551.
Tel:	567-661-7000
Admission:	By prior permission only.
Location:	In the south eastern part of Rossford.

The airliner was donated to the college by FedEx who had operated the aircraft for more then 18 years. The Boeing is used at the Center for Emergency Preparedness where disasters are simulated.

TYPE	REG/SER	CON. NO.	PI/NOTES	STATUS
☐ Boeing 727-22F	N186FE	18872	N7065U	RA

PICKERINGTON MONUMENT (OH62)

Location:	On permanent view at ALP 283 in Refugee Road in the north western part of the town.

TYPE	REG/SER	CON. NO.	PI/NOTES	STATUS
☐ Bell 209 Huey Cobra (AH-1G) (AH-1S)	71-21009	21080		PV

RAVENNA ARSENAL (OH63)

Location:	By prior permission only at the site which is about 5 miles east of the town.

TYPE	REG/SER	CON. NO.	PI/NOTES	STATUS
☐ Bell 205 Iroquois (UH-1H)				RA
☐ Bell 209 Huey Cobra (AH-1G) (AH-1F)				RA

REED COLLECTION (OH64)

Address:	5782 Trask Road, Leroy, Ohio 44057.
Tel:	216-298-1314
Admission:	By prior permission only.
Location:	About 2 miles west of Thompson which is south of Interstate 90.

Charles Reed has acquired an interesting collection of aircraft at his private airfield. Three hangars house the flyable aircraft, all of which have been restored to immaculate condition. In the workshop area others are under rebuild.

Two replica World War I fighters can be seen. The Fokker Triplane is painted in the standard red scheme and was completed in 1988. The S.E.5A was registered in 1996 and is painted in Royal Flying Corps colours. The Snow has been mocked up to represent a German monoplane of this period.

The remainder of the collection comprises mainly of classic post-war types and homebuilt machines. An exception is the replica of the Miles and Atwood Racer. The original was built in 1933 by Lawrence Brown and powered by a Menasco engine. The aircraft achieved several prizes at the 1933 Cleveland meeting. However, in 1937 Lee Miles was killed when a bracing wire to the wing snapped and the low wing monoplane dived into the ground during a race.

TYPE	REG/SER	CON. NO.	PI/NOTES	STATUS
☐ Aeronca 7AC Champion	N81760	7AC-381	NC81760	RAA
☐ Aeronca 7AC Champion	NC1255E	7AC-4813	NC1255E, N1255E	RAA
☐ Bowers Fly Baby 1A	N747X	19340		RAA
☐ Brown Miles and Atwood Special (R)	'NR225Y'			RAX
☐ Corben C-1 Baby Ace				RA
☐ Fleet 2	NC764V	332	NC764V, N764V	RAA
☐ Fokker Dr I (R)	N1917W	102		RAA
☐ Interstate S1B1 Cadet (O-63) (L-6)	N3771Z	196	(USAAF)	RAA
☐ Luscombe 8A Silvaire	NC45527	2054	NC45527, N45527	RAA
☐ Meyers OTW-160	N34356	101	NC34356	RAA
☐ New Standard D-31	NC29090	100		RAA
☐ Oldfield Baby Great Lakes WR-1	N6067	M-0171		RAA
☐ Royal Aircraft Factory S.E.5A (R)	N1917S	71023		RAA
☐ Ryan ST-3KR Recruit (PT-22)	N53072	1828	41-20619	RAA
☐ Smith DSA-1 Miniplane	N60CR	EN-7	N500RD, N6067	RAA

Ohio

☐ Snow S-2A N9426R 1056A RAA
☐ Spezio Sport Tuholer RAC

RICKENBACKER AIR NATIONAL GUARD BASE (OH65)

Address:	121ARW/PA, 7370 Minuteman Way, Lockbourne, Ohio 43217-5887.
Tel:	614-492-4223 **Fax:** 614-492-4215 **Email:** publicaffairs@ohcolu.ang.af.mil
Admission:	By prior permission only.
Location:	About 13 miles south of Columbus on Route 317.

The field was activated in 1942 as Lockbourne Army Air Base and was renamed in 1974 after World War I ace Captain Edward V. Rickenbacker who died the previous year. The Air National Guard took over the site in April 1980. The 166th Squadron came under state control in late 1946 at Port Columbus Airport but soon moved to Lockbourne. The unit served in the fighter role for many years. The collection of preserved aircraft has been steadily growing and represents types flown by the wing. Recently several types have left for other collections.

TYPE	REG/SER	CON. NO.	PI/NOTES	STATUS
☐ Bell 209 Huey Cobra (AH-1G) (AH-1S)	70-16104	21048	At Army NG Headquarters.	RA
☐ North American NA-224 Super Sabre (F-100D)	55-2884	224-151		RA
☐ Republic F-84F Thunderstreak	51-1346			RA
☐ Vought A-7D Corsair II	72-0247	D369	At nearby Naval Reserve Facility.	RA
☐ Vought A-7D Corsair II	73-0999	D395		RA

ROCK CREEK MONUMENT (OH66)

Location:	On permanent view at VFW 4953 in the town.

TYPE	REG/SER	CON. NO.	PI/NOTES	STATUS
☐ Bell 209 Huey Cobra (AH-1G) (AH-1F)	66-15264	20020		PV

SHEFFIELD MONUMENT (OH67)

Location:	On permanent view at a private site in the town.

TYPE	REG/SER	CON. NO.	PI/NOTES	STATUS
☐ Convair 240-0	N314H	31	NC94218, N1L, N7779	PV

SHENANDOAH AIRSHIP DISPLAY (OH68)

Address:	50495 State Route 21, Ava, Ohio 43711.
Tel:	740-732-2624
Admission:	By prior permission only.
Location:	About 15 miles south of Cambridge on Route 821.

This private collection, housed in a mobile trailer, commemorates the airship which crashed near the town. On show are memorabilia and photographs tracing the history of the *Shenandoah* which was the first rigid airship built in America. Sites have been excavated and a number of interesting items, including small components, have been found. The first flight of the 680 feet long monster took place in 1922. Two years later she was ripped apart in a gale and fell to the ground. The airship was also the first to use helium for lift. Around the town are a number of informative markers showing where pieces of the giant crashed.

SIDNEY MONUMENTS (OH69)

Location:	On permanent view at three locations in the town.

TYPE	REG/SER	CON. NO.	PI/NOTES	STATUS
☐ Bell 209 Huey Cobra (AH-1G) (AH-1F)	66-15250	20006	At VFW 4239at 2841 Wapakoneta Avenue north of the town	PV
☐ Bell 209 Huey Cobra (AH-1G) (AH-1F)	67-15683	20347	At AMVETS Post 1986 at 1319 North 4th. Avenue.	PV
☐ Lockheed 580 (T-33A)	52-9776	580-8036	At airport south of the town.	PV

SMITHFIELD MONUMENT (OH70)

Location:	On permanent view in Friendship Park in the northern part of the town.

TYPE	REG/SER	CON. NO.	PI/NOTES	STATUS
☐ Cessna 337M Super Skymaster (O-2A)				PV
☐ Northrop N-160 Scorpion (N-68) (F-89D) (F-89J)	53-2646	N.4777		PV

SOPLATA COLLECTION (OH71)

Address:	PO Box 65, Newbury, Ohio 44065.
Tel:	216-564-5256
Admission:	By prior permission only.
Location:	Just to the north of the town which is about 18 miles east of Cleveland on Route 87.

Ohio

The late Walter Soplata was born in Cleveland and learned to fly in 1944. Three years later he acquired a derelict Vultee BT-13 and moved it to Newbury. Over the next few years he travelled miles across the country to move airframes to his home. The B-36 was dismantled and transported in small sections and this alone took over 50 trips. A few aircraft in the collection have been sold and are under restoration with their new owners.

A rarity is the Fleetwings BT-12 trainer. Only 25 examples of this stainless steel low wing monoplane were completed in 1942/3. The Douglas XAD-1 Destroyer first flew in 1944 and 25 were ordered by the Navy for trials. The design was developed into the successful Skyraider. Very few examples of the Vought Cutlass survive. This unconventional jet fighter first flew in from Patuxent River in September 1948.

In the 1990s a museum was set up at a nearby airfield but this venture did not last long. Around five aircraft were moved to this facility. The airframes at Newbury were regularly sprayed with oil to minimise corrosion and this has helped their survival.

An accurate list is difficult to obtain but the one below is based on two visits when Walter was alive.

TYPE	REG/SER	CON. NO.	PI/NOTES	STATUS
☐ Avro Canada C.100 Canuck 5 (CF-100)	18775	675		RAD
☐ Beech C18S Kansan (AT-11C)	N6783C	1177	41-27332	RA
☐ Beech D18S Expeditor (C-45G)	N9966Z	AF-143	51-11586	RAD
☐ Beech D18S Expeditor (C18S) (SNB-2) (SNB-5) (TC-45J) (UC-45J)	Bu51228	5555	Bu51228, N2024 – incomplete	RAD
☐ Beech D18S Expeditor 3TM	N7598	CA-172 (A-772)	1572 (Canada)	RAD
☐ Bell 26C Airacobra (P-39N)			Wings only.	RAD
☐ Bell 33 Kingcobra (P-63A)	42-68895	33-35		RAD
☐ Bell 47G			Cabin only.	RAD
☐ Boeing 367-76-29 Stratofreighter (KC-97F)	51-0253	16320		RAD
☐ Boeing 464-201-3 Stratofortress (B-52B)	53-0394	16873	Front fuselage only.	RA
☐ Cessna T-50 Bobcat (C-78) (UC-78)	NC60145	5173	43-7653	RA
☐ Consolidated 36 Peacemaker (YB-36) (YB-36A) (RB-36E)	42-13571		Incomplete	RAD
☐ Curtiss-Wright CW-20B-2 Commando (C-46D)			Front and rear fuselage only.	RA
☐ Douglas A-26B Invader	N919P	28056	44-34777, N66661, N1242, N910F	RA
☐ Douglas XAD-1 Destroyer II (XBT2D-1)	Bu09103	1931		RAD
☐ Douglas A-1H Skyraider (AD-6)	Bu135273	9917		RA
☐ Douglas 1129A Globemaster II (C-124A)	51-0119	43453	Incomplete	RAD
☐ Douglas DC-7B	N757Z	44924	N390AA	RAD
☐ Fairchild 78 Packet (C-82A)	44-22991	10035	Less wings.	RAD
☐ Fairchild M-62A Cornell (PT-19)			Fuselage only.	RAD
☐ Fleetwings XBT-12	39-719	1		RA
☐ Grumman G-40 Avenger (TBM-3) (TBM-3N)				RAD
☐ Grumman G-40 Avenger (TBM-3) (TBM-3N)				RAD
☐ Grumman G-89 Tracker (S2F-1) (S-2A) (US-2A)			Front fuselage only.	RA
☐ Grumman G-98 Tiger (F11F-1) (F-11A)	Bu141849	166		RA
☐ Handley Page HP.80 Victor K.2 (B.2)	XL191		Front fuselage only.	RAD
☐ Howard DGA-15P				RAD
☐ Lockheed 580 (T-33A)	51-6747	580-6079	51-6747, (Canada) – fuselage only.	RAD
☐ Lockheed 726-45-14 Neptune (P2V-7) (P-2H)	Bu140436	726-7095		RAD
☐ Martin 272A Canberra (RB-57A)				RAD
☐ McDonnell M.24 Banshee (F2H-3)			Incomplete.	RAD
☐ North American NA-121 Texan (AT-6F) (SNJ-6) (SNJ-7)	N4133A	121-43157	44-82435, Bu112303	RAD
☐ North American NA-168 Texan (T-6G)				RAD
☐ North American NA-172 Sabre (F-86E)				RAD
☐ North American NA-200 Trojan (T-28B)				RAD
☐ North American NA-201 Sabre (F-86D) (F-86F)	53-0715	201-159		RA
☐ North American NA-201 Sabre (F-86D) (F-86F)	53-0959	201-403		RA
☐ Republic P-47D Thunderbolt			Fuselage only.	RAD
☐ Republic F-84E Thunderjet				RAD
☐ Republic F-84F Thunderstreak	52-6524			RA
☐ Republic RF-84F Thunderflash	52-7262			RA
☐ Sikorsky S-55D Chickasaw (H-19D) (UH-19D)	54-1412			RA
☐ Sikorsky S-58 Seabat (HSS-1) (UH-34G)	Bu140121	58165		RA
☐ Vought FG-1A Corsair	NX69900		Bu13481 – Front fuselage only.	RAD
☐ Vought FG-1D Corsair	Bu88026	2840		RAD
☐ Vought FG-1D Corsair	Bu82850	7279		RA
☐ Vought V-366 Cutlass (F7U-3)	Bu129685			RA
☐ Vultee V-74 Valiant (BT-13A)				RAD
☐ Vultee V-74A Valiant (BT-15)	N9781H	74A-9189	42-41597	RAD

SPRINGFIELD AIR NATIONAL GUARD BASE COLLECTION (OH72)

Address: 178FW/PA, 706 Regula Avenue, Springfield-Beckley MAP, Ohio 45502-8784.
Tel: 937-327-2321   **Email:** 178ththunderer@ohspri.ang.af.mil
Admission: By prior permission only.
Location: About 5 miles south of the town off Highway 68 on Road 794.

Allocated to the state in November 1947, the 162nd Squadron first flew the P-51D Mustang from Cox Field at Dayton.

In September 1955 it moved to Springfield where it received its first jet fighter, the F-84E Thunderjet. Since then F-84Fs, F-100Ds, F-100Fs and A-7Ds were flown before the current equipment the F-16 arrived, in late 1993.

The F-84F on show served from 1957 to 1970 and was one of the last flown by the squadron. The F-100D was in use from 1970 until 1978 and the type is represented by the F-100A which was towed to Springfield from the USAF Museum at Dayton early one Sunday morning.

TYPE	REG/SER	CON. NO.	PI/NOTES	STATUS
☐ North American NA-192 Super Sabre (F-100A)	'52-559'	192-54	53-1559	RAX
☐ Republic F-84F Thunderstreak	51-1797			RA

☐ Republic F-84G Thunderjet	51-0791		51-0791, N5582A	RA
☐ Vought A-7D Corsair II	72-0178	D300		RA

TOLEDO AIR NATIONAL GUARD BASE (OH73)

Address:	180 TFG, Toledo Express Airport, 2660 South Eber Road, Swanton, Ohio 43558.
Tel:	419-868-4219 Email: 180.webmaster@ohtole.ang.af.mil
Admission:	By prior permission only.
Location:	About 14 miles west of the city on Route Alternative 30.

The 112th Squadron was allocated to Ohio in June 1927 and was based at Hopkins Field in Cleveland flying observation aircraft. Among the types operated were Consolidated PT-1s and a variety of Curtiss and Douglas designs.

After World War II the unit turned to state control and flew Douglas A-26es from Cleveland Military Airport. After a move to Georgia during the Korean conflict the squadron took up residence at Berea with P-51Hs but within a few months had moved to Akron-Canton. In April 1956 the unit transferred to Toledo whew it flew T-28As, T-33As and F-84Es.

In 1959 the squadron moved to Toledo Express Airport and since then has operated F-84Fs, F-100Ds, F-100Fs and A-7Ds before the F-16 arrived in mid-1992.

TYPE	REG/SER	CON. NO.	PI/NOTES	STATUS
☐ North American NA-224 Super Sabre (F-100D)	55-2855	224-122		RA
☐ Republic F-84F Thunderstreak	51-9525			RA
☐ Vought A-7D Corsair II	72-0211	D333		RA

TRI-STATE WARBIRD MUSEUM (OH74)

Address:	4021 Borman Drive, Batavia, Ohio 45163
Tel:	513-735-4500 Fax: 513-735-4533 Email: tristatewarbirdmuseum@fuse.net
Admission:	Wednesday 1600-1900; Saturday 1000-1500.
Location:	The airport is about 2 miles west of the town off Route 32.

The museum was established in 2003 by a group of warbird owners. The first phase of a superb new facility has been constructed at Clermont County Airport. Display rooms tracing the history of all aircraft in the collection have been set up. The fleet will be maintained in airworthy condition and the hangar contains fully equipped workshops.

The Avenger served with the Royal Canadian Navy in the late 1940s. A long career as a water bomber followed. From 1961 until 1977 the TBM was based in British Columbia. Conair of Abbotsford sold her for operations in New Brunswick where the aircraft was damaged in a 1981 crash. The airframe was stored and then sold back to America in 1994. The Corsair had an interesting career when its military days were over. From 1958 until 1973 it was owned by Ed Maloney and was part of his Planes of Fame Museum in California. After being sold to David Tallichet it was one of the aircraft flown in the television series 'Baa Baa Black Sheep'. The story of Marine Corps Squadron VMF-214 and its leader 'Pappy' Boyington was told with some artistic licence in these episodes featuring their World War II adventures in the Pacific. The Corsair was then stored at Chino for several years before moving to Danville, Illinois. Here it was rebuilt to flying condition by Mike Vadeboncoeur for 'Butch' Schroeder's Midwest Aviation Museum.

The museum hopes to acquire more aircraft when the hangar complex is extended.

TYPE	REG/SER	CON. NO.	PI/NOTES	STATUS
☐ Boeing-Stearman B75N1 Kaydet (N2S-3)	N224DF	75-7899	Bu38278, N75947	PVA
☐ Curtiss 87-A4 Warhawk (P-40M) (Kittyhawk III)	N5813	27501	43-5813, NZ3119	PVC
☐ Flug Werk FW 190A-8/N				PVA
☐ Grumman G-40 Avenger (TBM-3) (TBM-3S) (AS.3M)	NL420GP	3482	Bu53420, 53420 (Canada), CF-KCM, C-FKCM	PVA
☐ North American NA-88 Texan (AT-6D)	N7RK	88-16560	42-84779, N7210C – painted as an SNJ-4.	PVAX
☐ North American NA-108 Mitchell (B-25J) (TB-25J) (TB-25N)	N898BW	108-47749	45-8898, N3681G – rebuilt with centre section and other components from c/n 108-32040 44-28765, N9443Z	PVA
☐ North American NA-124 Mustang (P-51D)	N83KD	124-44266	44-84410	PVC
☐ Piper PA-16 Clipper	N5693H	16-304		PVC
☐ Vought FG-1D Corsair	N3466G	3393	Bu92132	PVC

UNION TOWNSHIP MONUMENT (OH75)

Location:	On permanent view in the town.

TYPE	REG/SER	CON. NO.	PI/NOTES	STATUS
☐ Bell 205 Iroquois (UH-1H)				PV

UNITED STATES SHIP *RADFORD* NATIONAL NAVAL MUSEUM (OH76)

Address:	238 West Canal Street, Newcomerstown, Ohio 43832.
Tel:	740-498-4446 Email: vanescott@sbcglobal.net
Admission:	By appointment.
Location:	In the western part of the town.

The destroyer USS *Radford* served in World War II and the Korean conflict. The museum was set up to trace its history and has on show photographs and memorabilia. A Gyrodyne QH-50 unmanned helicopter can be seen.

TYPE	REG/SER	CON. NO.	PI/NOTES	STATUS
☐ Gyrodyne QH-50C (DSN-3)		DS-1199		PV

VANDALIA MONUMENT (OH77)

Location:	On permanent view at VFW 9582 at 4170 Old Springfield Road in the northern part of the town.

TYPE	REG/SER	CON. NO.	PI/NOTES	STATUS
☐ Bell 205 Iroquois (UH-1D) (UH-1H)	65-9696	4740		PV

WACO AIRCRAFT MUSEUM (OH78)

Address:	PO Box 62 A, Troy, Ohio 45373-0062.
Tel:	937-335-9226 Email: info@wacoairmuseum.orgom
Admission:	May–December Saturday-Sunday 1300-1700.
Location:	At Waco Field which is about 2 miles south of the town on Route 25A.

The Weaver Aircraft Corporation was set up in Lorain, Ohio in 1919 and used the Waco trade name. Two of the four founders formed the Advance Aircraft Company in Troy in 1923, kept the Waco name for their products and six years later the firm became the Waco Aircraft Company.

By the late 1920s the company was the largest producer of civil aircraft in the world with its successful 9 and 10 series of biplanes: a total of 236 9s and 1,152 10s left the factory. In the 1930s large numbers of open cockpit and cabin biplanes were constructed. During World War II many examples of the CG-4A transport glider were produced by firms around the country along with smaller numbers of the CG-3, CG-13 and CG-15. The company ceased aircraft manufacture in 1947.

The museum has been set up trace the history of Waco and the aircraft. A small display was set up in the town but in April 2006 this moved to larger premises at Waco Field. Here an 1856 barn has been re-erected to house the main exhibition and a hangar has been built for the aircraft.

The parasol wing Cootie 1 was built in 1920 by George Weaver and Elwood Junkin. Powered by a 28 hp Lawrance engine it crashed on landing after its first flight. The aircraft was rebuilt as the Cootie 2 with a stronger undercarriage and larger tail surfaces. This was more successful and lasted until a 1923 crash.

In 1921 one Waco 4, which was based on the Curtiss Jenny, was built. This aircraft had a wider fuselage and high-lift wings. The replica was started in Toledo by Ray Vaughan, who had worked on the original 4, but ill health caused the project to be abandoned. Members of the society finished the replica which is now flying. The airfield is home to many other Waco biplanes.

TYPE	REG/SER	CON. NO.	PI/NOTES	STATUS
☐ Waco Cootie (R)	N920W	001		PV
☐ Waco 4 (R)	'N920W'	2	N1921V	PVAX
☐ Waco 9	C116	358	NC116, N1160	PV
☐ Waco 10 (GXE)	NC4899	1464	NC4899, N4899	PV
☐ Waco CTO (ATO)	NR13918	A-118	NS25, NC13918	RAA
☐ Waco NAZ Primary Glider				PV
☐ Waco NEU (CG-15A)			Front fuselage only.	RAC
☐ Waco NZR Hadrian (CG-4A)			Front fuselage only.	RAC
☐ Waco UPF-7	NC32114	5746	NC32114, N32114	PV
☐ Wright 1902 Glider (R)				PV

WADSWORTH MONUMENT (OH79)

Location:	On permanent view at the airport in the south western part of the town

TYPE	REG/SER	CON. NO.	PI/NOTES	STATUS
☐ Lockheed 580 (T-33A)	53-5545	580-8884		PV

WASHINGTONVILLE MONUMENT (OH80)

Location:	On permanent view at VFW 5532 at 575 Leetonia Road in the southern part of the town.

TYPE	REG/SER	CON. NO.	PI/NOTES	STATUS
☐ Bell 205 Iroquois (UH-1H)	68-16610	11269		PV

WILMINGTON MONUMENT (OH81)

Location:	On permanent view at the airport which is in the south eastern part of the town.

TYPE	REG/SER	CON. NO.	PI/NOTES	STATUS
☐ McDonnell M.36BA Voodoo (F-101B)	57-0308	486		PV

WRIGHT B MUSEUM (OH82)

Address:	10550 Springboro Pike, Dayton General Airport, Miamisburg, Ohio 45342.
Tel:	937-885-2327 Email: wbflyer@dayton.net
Admission:	Tuesday, Thursday, Saturday 0900-1430.
Location:	About 10 miles south of Dayton on Route 741.

The Wright B was the first mass produced aircraft in the world and dates from 1911. One replica made its maiden flight on 21st July 1982 and since then has made regular appearances at shows.

In 1992 the group opened the hangar built to resemble the original Wright building on Huffman Prairie. The displays inside trace the work of the Wright Brothers in Dayton with a range of photographs on view along with models and engines.

TYPE	REG/SER	CON. NO.	PI/NOTES	STATUS
☐ Wright B (R)	N3786B	001		PVA
☐ Wright B (R)	N2283D	1903-09		PVA

WRIGHT BROTHERS AEROPLANE COMPANY (OH83)

Address:	PO Box 204, West Milton, Ohio 45383.
Email:	orville@wright-brothers.org
Admission:	By prior permission only.
Location:	At a number of locations.

Members of the group have built replicas of Orville and Wilbur's designs. The majority of these have flown – many at Kitty Hawk in North Carolina and Huffman Prairie near Dayton in Ohio.

The aircraft are taken to schools and colleges to educate students in the pioneering days of aviation. There is also an informative touring exhibition about the brothers. A range of plans and publications have also been produced

TYPE	REG/SER	CON. NO.	PI/NOTES	STATUS
☐ Wright 1899 Glider (R)				RA
☐ Wright 1900 Glider (R)				RA
☐ Wright 1901 Glider (R)				RA
☐ Wright 1902 Glider (R)				RA
☐ Wright Flyer (R)	N193WF	001		RAA
☐ Wright Flyer 3 (R)	N196WF	002		RAA
☐ Wright EX Vin Fiz (R)				RA

WRIGHT-PATTERSON AIR FORCE BASE (OH84)

Address:	88ABW/PA, 5215 Thurlow Street, Wright-Patterson Air Force Base, Ohio 45433-5547.
Tel:	937-522-3252 Email: 88abw.pawebmaster@wpafb.af.mil
Admission:	By prior permission only.
Location:	About 8 miles north east of Dayton off Highway 4.

The base was formed in 1948 by the amalgamation of Wilbur Wright Field and Fairfield Aviation Supply Depot which became Patterson Field. The site houses research units as well as operational units and the USAF Museum occupies part of the old Wright Field. The three aircraft are preserved near the main gate.

TYPE	REG/SER	CON. NO.	PI/NOTES	STATUS
☐ General Dynamics 401 Fighting Falcon (F-16A)	79-0399	61-184		RA
☐ McDonnell M.199-1A Eagle (F-15A)	75-0039	138/A119		RA
☐ Mikoyan-Gurevich MiG-29UB	'62'	50903012308	62, 61 (Moldova)	RAX

ZANESVILLE MONUMENTS (OH85)

Location:	On permanent view at two locations in the town.

TYPE	REG/SER	CON. NO.	PI/NOTES	STATUS
☐ Bell 209 Huey Cobra (OH-1G) (OH-1F)	67-15490	20154	At VVA 42 at 534 Shinnick Street.	PV
☐ Republic F-105B Thunderchief	57-5792	B-29	At the airport which is on Route 797 north of the town.	PV

OKLAHOMA

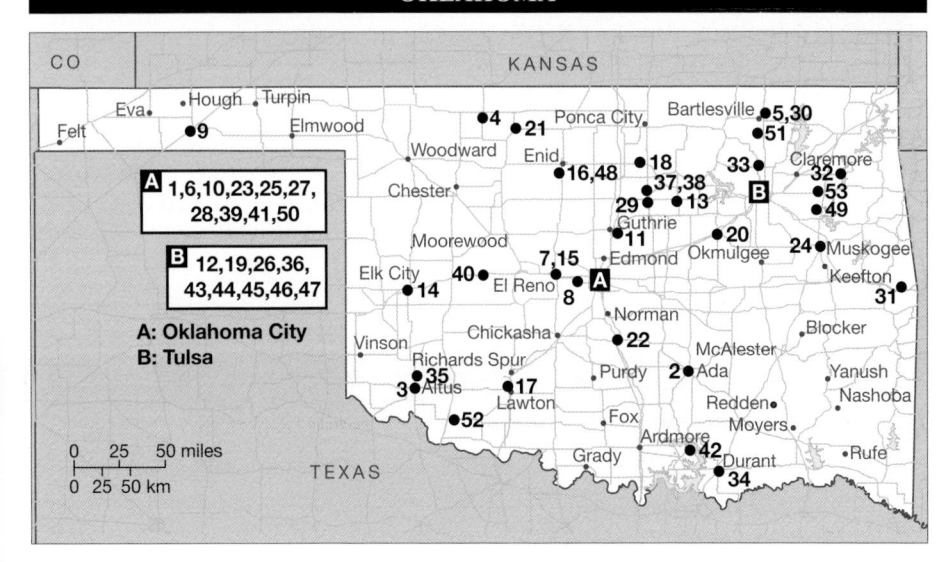

A: Oklahoma City
B: Tulsa

45TH INFANTRY DIVISION MUSEUM (OK1)

Address:	2145 North East 36th Street, Oklahoma City, Oklahoma 73111.
Tel:	405-424-5313 Email: curator@45thdivisionmuseum.com
Admission:	Tuesday-Friday 0900-1700; Saturday 1000-1700; Sunday 1300-1700.
Location:	In the northern suburbs of the city.

The museum is named after the famous Oklahoma 'Thunderbird' Division but its displays trace the complete military history of the state. In addition the contribution of local people to the nation's forces is portrayed. The majority of the collection is housed in the former Lincoln Park Armory and there is also an outside park where the larger items are exhibited. One gallery shows the Jordan B. Reeves Collection of Military Weapons, which is one of the best in the country. The aircraft are types formerly used by local Army and Air National Guard units.

TYPE	REG/SER	CON. NO.	PI/NOTES	STATUS
☐ Bell 47D-1 Sioux (H-13E) (OH-13E)	51-13965	551		PV
☐ Bell 204 Iroquois (UH-1B)	62-4588	648		PV
☐ Bell 206A Kiowa (OH-58A)	'71-15425'	40976	70-15425 – possible identity.	PVX
☐ Cessna 305A Bird Dog (L-19A) (O-1A)	51-4651	21536	51-4651, N26848, N26847P	PV
☐ Cessna 310A Blue Canoe (L-27A) (U-3A)	58-2166	38140	58-2166, N88SM	PV
☐ De Havilland DHC.2 Beaver (L-20A) (U-6A)	56-0367	1062	56-0367, N90880	PV
☐ Hiller UH12C Raven (H-23C) (OH-23C)	55-4124	830		PV
☐ Hughes 369M Cayuse (HO-6) (OH-6A) (MH-6B)	68-17193	1153	68-17193, N5185H	PV
☐ Lockheed 580 (T-33A)	'58555'	580-1474	58-0505	PVX
☐ North American NA-145 Navion	'4953'	NAV-4-953	N7612B	PVX
☐ North American NA-190 Sabre (F-86D)	'24043'	190-157	52-3754	PVX
☐ North American NA-224 Super Sabre (F-100D)			Front fuselage only.	PV
☐ Piper J-3C-65 Cub (L-4B)	43-1074	9935	On loan from NASM, DC.	PV
☐ Vought A-7D Corsair II	'72-0240'	D431	74-1756	PVX

ADA MONUMENT (OK2)

Location:	On permanent view at the airport which is about 2 miles north of the town.

TYPE	REG/SER	CON. NO.	PI/NOTES	STATUS
☐ Beech J35 Bonanza	'EAA1005'			PVX

ALTUS AIR FORCE BASE (OK3)

Address:	97AMW/PA, 305 East Avenue, Oklahoma 73523-5000.
Tel:	580-481-7700 Email: 97amw.pa@altus.af.mil
Admission:	By prior permission only.
Location:	About 3 miles east of the town on Route 62.

Opened in 1942, the base was closed at the end of World War II but activated again in 1953 and is now the main training site for KC-135, C-5 and C-17 crews. Four aircraft are displayed inside the camp; the C-118 which was on display was unfortunately scrapped in 2000. Also on the base is a school to train loaders on the C-17 Globemaster III.

TYPE	REG/SER	CON. NO.	PI/NOTES	STATUS
☐ Beech D18S Expeditor (C18S) (C-45F) (UC-45F) (JRB-4) (SNB-5)	Bu44617	8355	44-87096, Bu44617, N40084	RAX
☐ Bell 206A Kiowa (OH-58A)	70-15441	40992	Instructional airframe.	RA
☐ Bell 206A Kiowa (OH-58A)	71-20571	41432	Instructional airframe.	RA
☐ Bell 209 Huey Cobra (AH-1G) (AH-1S)	70-16017	20961	Instructional airframe.	RA
☐ Bell 209 Huey Cobra (AH-1G) (AH-1S)	71-21004	21075	Instructional airframe.	RA
☐ Boeing 450-157-35 Stratojet (B-47E)	'520413'	450614	51-7071 on Route 62 just east of the town.	PV
☐ Boeing 717-148 Stratotanker (KC-135A)	58-0070/'56-3617'	17815		RA
☐ Douglas DC-3A-467 Skytrain (C-47B)	'11843'	15022/26467	43-49206, 49206 (Morocco), CNALD (Morocco), N54611	RAX
☐ Lockheed 300 Starlifter (C-141A) (C-141B)	65-9400	300-6137		RA

ALVA MUNICIPAL AIRPORT MUSEUM (OK4)

Address:	Route 3, Box 263A, Alva, Oklahoma 73717.
Tel:	580-327-2898 Fax: 580-327-4965 Email: alvaair@sbcglobal.net
Admission:	When the airfield is open.
Location:	About 2 miles south of the town on Route 45.

The display has been set up to trace the history of the field from the 1930s. There are many photographs, models and documents to be seen. The development of the site from a grass field to one capable of taking jets is portrayed. The prisoner of war camp at Alva in World War II is highlighted with memorabilia on view.

BARTLESVILLE MONUMENT (OK5)

Location:	On permanent view at a Veterans Memorial in Washington Boulevard in the north western part of the town.

TYPE	REG/SER	CON. NO.	PI/NOTES	STATUS
☐ Douglas A-4C Skyhawk (A4D-2N)	Bu148485	12678		PV

Oklahoma

CAMP GRUBER ARMY NATIONAL GUARD BASE MONUMENT (OK6)

Location:	On permanent view at the site in the northern part of Braggs.

TYPE	REG/SER	CON. NO.	PI/NOTES	STATUS
☐ Bell 204 Iroquois (UH-1B)				PV

CANADIAN VALLEY TECHNOLOGY CENTER (OK7)

Address:	6505 East Highway 66, El Reno, Oklahoma 73036-9117.
Tel:	405-262-2629
Admission:	By prior permission only.
Location:	In the southern part of the town.

The college has four sites in the area. The aviation facility is based at the El Reno campus. Two instructional airframes are known to be in use but it is likely that there are more in the workshops.

TYPE	REG/SER	CON. NO.	PI/NOTES	STATUS
☐ Cessna 172F Mescalero (T-41A)	N5185F	17253128	65-5185	RA
☐ Piper PA-23 Apache	N2046P	23-629		RA

CIMARRON FIELD / MUSTANG FIELD MUSEUM (OK8)

Address:	15237 Worthington Lane, Edmond, Oklahoma 73013
Tel:	405-659-8988 Email: mhoward3@cox.net
Admission:	By appointment only.
Location:	At Clarence E. Page Airport which is about 2 miles west of Yukon.

This private museum set up by Mark Howard aims to preserve the history of the two World War II training fields. C.E. Page Airport at Yukon is the former Cimarron Field and El Reno Airport was Mustang Field. In the hangar are engines, display cases containing memorabilia and documents tracing the story of the two sites. Both used Cornells and the PT-19A currently under restoration to flying condition served at Cimarron and Mustang. The other PT-19 on static display was recovered from Lake Rice in Wisconsin. There is also a memorial to those who lost their lives during training at the two fields.

TYPE	REG/SER	CON. NO.	PI/NOTES	STATUS
☐ Douglas DC-6A Liftmaster (R6D-1) (C-118A)	N1037F	43688	Bu131585 – front fuselage and other major components.	RA
☐ Fairchild M-62A Cornell (PT-19A)	NC47774	T42-1393	41-20387	RA
☐ Fairchild M-62A Cornell (PT-19A)	N879CF	T42-1967	42-2879, NC51920, N51920	RAC
☐ Fairchild M-62A Cornell (PT-19B)	42-83001	T43-5588	Fuselage only.	RA
☐ Fairchild M-62A-4 Cornell (PT-26A)	N9279H	FV-391	15292 (Canada), 42-65876	RAA

COMMEMORATIVE AIR FORCE (CIMMARON STRIP WING) (OK9)

Address:	PO Box 604, Guymon, Oklahoma 73942-0604.
Tel:	580-338-7700 Email: bdow@ptsi.net
Admission:	By prior permission only.
Location:	The airport is 2 miles west of the town.

The unit operates just one aircraft the Beech 18, which is at the civil airport for the town. The twin is painted in the colours of the C-45 used by General Ira C. Eaker when he commanded the Eighth Air Force in 1943.

TYPE	REG/SER	CON. NO.	PI/NOTES	STATUS
☐ Beech D18S Expeditor (C-45H)	N40074	AF-834	52-10904	RAA

COMMEMORATIVE AIR FORCE (OKLAHOMA WING) (OK10)

Address:	PO Box 42352, 7100 North West 63rd Street, Oklahoma City, Oklahoma 73123-3532.
Tel:	405-205-7452 Email: drandallok@aol.com
Admission:	By prior permission only.
Location:	At Wiley Post Airport which is in the north western suburbs of Oklahoma City.

The wing has completed a painstaking restoration of the Cornell as a PT-19 and painted it in a typical World War II scheme. This features a blue fuselage with yellow wings and tail surfaces.

TYPE	REG/SER	CON. NO.	PI/NOTES	STATUS
☐ Fairchild M-62A Cornell (PT-19A)	N519SH	T43-5954	42-83367, N51589	RAC

COMMEMORATIVE AIR FORCE (SIERRA HOTEL A-26 GROUP) (OK11)

Address:	PO Box 20452, Oklahoma City, Oklahoma 73156-0452.
Tel:	405-249-9852 Email: starwars5@sbcglobal.net
Admission:	By prior permission only.
Location:	At Guthrie Airport which is about 3 miles south of the town.

The Invader first flew with the USAAF and USAF before being one of a batch supplied to France in 1954. The aircraft flew for a short time in Indochina before being returned in being returned in the winter of 1955. After two years in store at Clark AFB in the

Philippines it was bought, along with five others, by a company in Kansas. The Confederate Air Force acquired it from Bob Diemert in Canada in 1984 and for a long period it was based with the now defunct wing in Arkansas. The aircraft is now undergoing a major rebuild in a hangar at at Guthrie but will probably move when it is completed.

TYPE	REG/SER	CON. NO.	PI/NOTES	STATUS
☐ Douglas A-26C Invader	N626SH	28922	44-35643, 435643 (French), N6841D, C-GCES, N8015H, N226RW	RAC

COMMEMORATIVE AIR FORCE (SPIRIT OF TULSA SQUADRON) (OK12)

Address:	PO Box 158, Jenks, Oklahoma 74037-0158
Tel:	918-794-4182 Email: squadron@caftulsa.org
Admission:	By prior permission only.
Location:	At Tulsa Technology Center Riverside Campus, adjacent to Jenks Airport which is in the north western suburbs of the town.

The group, which was formed in 1988, has recently moved into workshops at the Center. Two projects are in progress. The Cornell is being completely rebuilt and progress is being made. This aircraft will be finished in a period colour scheme.
From 2000 to 2006 the group assisted in the maintenance of the CAF. B-24 Liberator 'Diamond Lil'. The bomber spent time in Tulsa each winter between its annual tours of the country. The squadron has plans to construct another hangar to house members' aircraft.
A collection of World War II memorabilia is in store and displays are planned with the eventual aim of setting up a museum. The group has acquired a vintage aircraft tow truck and this is being rebuilt to original condition.

TYPE	REG/SER	CON. NO.	PI/NOTES	STATUS
☐ Aeronca 65TC	N27336	F-1490T	NC27336	RAC
☐ Fairchild M-62A Cornell (PT-19A)	N46876	T42-1957	42-2869	RAC

CUSHING MONUMENT (OK13)

Location:	On permanent view at the airport which is about 2 miles south of the town.

TYPE	REG/SER	CON. NO.	PI/NOTES	STATUS
☐ Bell 205 Iroquois (UH-1H) (UH-1V)	70-16460	12765		PV

ELK CITY MONUMENT (OK14)

Location:	On permanent view at the airport which is north east of the town.

TYPE	REG/SER	CON. NO.	PI/NOTES	STATUS
☐ Lockheed 580 (T-33A)	51-8896	580-6680		PV

EL RENO MONUMENT (OK15)

Location:	On permanent view at VFW 382 at 1515 South Rock Island Avenue in the eastern part of the town.

TYPE	REG/SER	CON. NO.	PI/NOTES	STATUS
☐ Douglas A-26B Invader	44-34746	28025	At VFW 382.	PV

ENID MONUMENT (OK16)

Location:	On permanent view at Woodring Airport which is about 5 miles east of the town.

TYPE	REG/SER	CON. NO.	PI/NOTES	STATUS
☐ Cessna 318B Tweety Bird (318A) (T-37A) (T-37B)	56-3519	40091		PV
☐ McDonnell M.98DE Phantom II (F-4C)	63-7440	401		PV

FORT SILL MUSEUM (OK17)

Address:	437 Quanah Road, Fort Sill, Oklahoma 73503-5100.
Tel:	580-442-5123 Fax: 580-442-8120 Email: spiveyt@doimex.sill.army.mil
Admission:	Tuesday-Sunday 0830-1700.
Location:	About 4 miles north of Lawton off Highway 277/281/62.

General Philip H. Sheridan established the fort on 8th January 1869 during a campaign against the South Plains tribes. Since 1911 it has been the home of the US Army Field Artillery Center and School.
The museum occupies several buildings of the old fort and the displays trace the history of the site, the Indian Wars of the region and the evolution of field artillery. The Indian Chief Geronimo was imprisoned at Fort Sill on several occasions and he is buried close by. There is a display portraying the story of his life and his battles against the American forces. There are many historic items on view and the exhibits show both the early civilian and military life in the region.
The Cannon Walk exhibits a number of rare pieces including 'Atomic Annie', the gun which fired the first atomic artillery round. There is also a missile park with several interesting types on show.
The aircraft, apart from the Piper Cub, are positioned near the hangars at the Fort airfield.

TYPE	REG/SER	CON. NO.	PI/NOTES	STATUS
☐ Bell 204 Iroquois (UH-1B)	63-8510	732		PV
☐ Cessna 305A Bird Dog (L-19A) (O-1A)	51-12303	22617	51-12303, N13025	PV

Oklahoma

☐ Cessna R172E Mescalero (T-41B)	67-15140	R1720141	67-15140, N102RL	PV
☐ Hiller UH12C Raven (H-23G) (OH-23G)	62-3791	1439	Identity doubtful.	PV
☐ Hiller UH12E Raven (H-23F) (OH-23F)	62-12510	2293		RA
☐ Piper J-3C-65 Cub (L-4J)	45-5136	13876		RA

GLENCOE MONUMENT (OK18)

Location:	On permanent view at VFW 1843 about 3 miles south of the town at 9121 East VFW Road.

TYPE	REG/SER	CON. NO.	PI/NOTES	STATUS
☐ Bell 205 Iroquois (UH-1D) (UH-1H)	66-16135	5829		PV

HARRIS COLLECTION (OK19)

Address:	PO Box 470350, Tulsa, Oklahoma 74147.
Tel:	918-622-8400
Admission:	By prior permission only.
Location:	At Richard L. Jones Airport which is in the southern suburbs of the city off 81st. Street.

This collection contains several classic types. They are housed in a private hangar at the airport and are all in an immaculate condition.

The Luscombe Silvaire first flew in December 1937. The all metal high wing monoplane was powered by a 50 h.p. motor. The design was developed and 8A with a 65 h.p. Continental and the 8B fiited with a 65 h.p. Lycoming appeared in 1939. Later in the year Jackie Cochran set several new lightplane records. Eventually over 6,000 were constructed in several versions. The 8F made its maiden flight in January 1948 and was intended to compete with the Cessna 120/140 series. The Monocoupe 90 was designed by Clayton Folkerts and made its maiden flight in January 1930. The improved 90A appeared in 1934 and more than 150 were sold. The 90AL is a version re-engined with a Lycoming flat four engine of higher power to improve performance. The original used a 90 h.p. Lambert radial.

Several modern classic types are in the hangar. The Super Cub was built in large numbers and was in production for many years.

TYPE	REG/SER	CON. NO.	PI/NOTES	STATUS
☐ American Aviation AA-1B Trainer	N5751L	AA1B-0051		RAA
☐ Beagle B.206 Series 2	N26GW	B.070	G-35-24, G-AWRM, (LV-PLE), N54JH	RAA
☐ Cessna 210N Centurion	N5336Y	21064170		RAA
☐ Culver LFA Cadet	N41716	LFA-433	NC41716	RAA
☐ Globe GC-1B Swift	NC90394	389	NC90394, N90394	RAA
☐ Luscombe 8A Silvaire	NC45965	2492	NC45965, N45965	RAA
☐ Luscombe 8A Silvaire	N1220K	3947	NC1220K	RA
☐ Luscombe 8F Silvaire	NC1902B	6329	NC1902B, N1902B	RAA
☐ Luscombe 8F Silvaire	NC1924B	6351	NC1924B, N1924B	RAA
☐ Luscombe 8F Silvaire	NC2126B	6553	NC2126B, N2126B	RAA
☐ Luscombe 8F Silvaire	NC831B	6762	NC831B, N831B	RAA
☐ Mono Aircraft Monocoupe 90AL-115	NC87621	869	NC87621, N87621	RAA
☐ Piper J-3C-65 Cub	NC42773	15084	NC42773, N42773	RAA
☐ Piper PA-18-150 Super Cub	N9670P	18-7509014		RAA

HEARTLAND AIR MUSEUM (OK20)

Address:	24495 South, 385 West Avenue, Bristow, Oklahoma 74010.
Email:	info@heartlandairmuseum.com
Admission:	Unknown.
Location:	At the airport which is about 6 miles south west of the town.

The museum has been formed with the aim of keeping in airworthy condition vintage military aircraft. Military vehicles and memorabilia are also being acquired. The Stinson Sentinel is in the process of a major rebuild.

TYPE	REG/SER	CON. NO.	PI/NOTES	STATUS
☐ Douglas DC-3A-467 Skytrain (C-47B) (R4D-6)	N231GB	14663/26108	43-48847, Bu50749, N3455G, N63, N79, N87819, N2002J	RAA
☐ Grumman G-40 Avenger (TBM-3) (TBM-3E)	N124TB	2062	Bu69323, N7961C, C-GLEJ	RAA
☐ Piper J-3C-65 Cub	N53602	8580	NC53602	RAA
☐ Stinson V-76 Sentinel (L-5E)				RAC
☐ Vultee V-79 Valiant (BT-13B) (SNV-2)		79-253	Bu52291, NC57807	RAC

JET MONUMENT (OK21)

Location:	On permanent view in the eastern part of the town.

TYPE	REG/SER	CON. NO.	PI/NOTES	STATUS
☐ Cessna 318B Tweety Bird (318A) (T-37A) (T-37B)	56-3563	40135		PV

LEXINGTON ARMY NATIONAL GUARD MONUMENT (OK22)

Location:	By prior permission only at General Howell Mudrow Airport which is about 6 miles east of the town on Route 39.

TYPE	REG/SER	CON. NO.	PI/NOTES	STATUS
☐ Hiller UH12A Raven (H-23A)	'01975'			PVX

The collection at the Tinker Air Force Base Heritage Museum includes this Boeing C-135C Stratolifter. [OK44]

This replica Wright 1902 Glider can be seen in the Thomas P. Stafford Air and Space Museum. (TASM) [OK40]

Among the exhibits and the Oregon Air and Space Museum is this Roloff RLU-1 Breezy. [OR13]

Oklahoma

METRO TECH VOCATIONAL TECHNICAL CENTER (OK23)

Address:	5600 South MacArthur, Oklahoma City, Oklahoma 73179.
Tel:	405-424-8324
Admission:	By prior permission only.
Location:	At Will Rogers Airport which is in the south western part of the city.

The aviation campus is located at Will Rogers Airport and offers courses leading to airframe and engine licences. The instructional airframes include two which were once on show at the State Fairgrounds in the city. The Aero Commander is the 1948 prototype of the series of high wing twins which were built in large numbers up to the mid-1980s. After restoration it will again be put on show.

TYPE	REG/SER	CON. NO.	PI/NOTES	STATUS
☐ Aero Commander L.3805	N1946	1		RA
☐ Beech 65-90 King Air	N601TA	LJ-120	N601T	RA
☐ Bell 205 Iroquois (UH-1H) (UH-1V)	69-15758	12046		RA
☐ Boeing 727-81	N3211M	18951	JA8316, HP-620, N500JJ, N55AJ, HP-620, D-AJAA, OO-JAA, D-AJAA, G-BMUE, N55AJ, TC-AJU, G-BMUE,	RA
☐ Cessna 152	N93342	15285471		RA
☐ Cessna 152	N94789	15285787		RA
☐ Cessna 172E	N5382T	17251282		RA
☐ Cessna 172F	N5550R	17253137		RA
☐ Cessna 172G	N3642L	17253811		RA
☐ Cessna 195A	N9397A	7555		RA
☐ Douglas DC-3A-456 Skytrain (C-47A)	'892953'	12683	42-92838, NC65162, N65162	RAC
☐ North American NA-265 Sabreliner (T-39A) (CT-39A)	61-0669	265-72	61-0699	RA
☐ North American NA-276 Sabreliner (T-39A) (CT-39A)	N988MT	276-32	62-4479	RA

MUSKOGEE MONUMENT (OK24)

Location:	On permanent view at the airport which is about 2 miles south of the town

TYPE	REG/SER	CON. NO.	PI/NOTES	STATUS
☐ Lockheed 580 (T-33A)	53-4971	580-8310		PV

MUSTANG MONUMENT (OK25)

Location:	On permanent view in Wild Horse Park in South West 59th Street.

TYPE	REG/SER	CON. NO.	PI/NOTES	STATUS
☐ North American NA-201 Sabre (F-86D) (F-86L)	53-0566	201-10		PV

NATIONAL AVIATION MUSEUM AND FOUNDATION OF OKLAHOMA (OK26)

Address:	2715 North Sheridan Road, Hangar 4, Tulsa International Airport, Oklahoma 74115-2345.
Admission:	By prior permission only.
Location:	In the north eastern suburbs of the city

Former Royal Air Force pilot John Baines has set up the museum which once kept its aircraft with the Aero Group.
A former Swiss Air Force Hunter was sold to the Texas Air Command Museum in 1995.
The Canberra was built by Handley Page in 1953 and converted for use by the Navy as a TT.18 in the early 1970s.

It is still registered to the museum but is no longer airworthy.
The Aero Group maintains a fleet of jets which it operates on military contract work. Types usually flown include Hunters and MiG-21s.
The Canberra has been parked at Melbourne Airport in Florida for many years and shows little signs of moving.

TYPE	REG/SER	CON. NO.	PI/NOTES	STATUS
☐ English Electric EA.1 Canberra TT.18 (B.2)	N77844	HP/HI/161B	WJ574, G27-182, WJ574, (N5291J)	RA

OKLAHOMA MUSEUM OF FLYING (OK27)

Address:	7110 Millionaire Drive, Bethany, Oklahoma 73008-7021.
Admission:	By prior permission only.
Location:	At Wiley Post Airport which is the north western suburbs of Oklahoma City.

The Albatros which has seen military service in the Soviet Union and the Ukraine was registered to the museum in August 2006. A number of sources state that the aircraft owned by the group is hangared at Wiley Post Airport. Further details of this organisation and its future plans would be most welcome.

TYPE	REG/SER	CON. NO.	PI/NOTES	STATUS
☐ Aero L-39C Albatros	N639RH/'1025'	232203	(Soviet Union), (Ukraine), N98796	RAA
☐ Douglas EA-1E Skyraider (AD-5W)	N188RH	10265	Bu135188, NX188BP	PVA
☐ Ercoupe 415D	N87359	532	NC87359	RAA

☐ Fokker E III (R)				PVC
☐ North American NA-122 Mustang (P-51D)	N991R	122-41076	44-74536, N5452V, N991RC	RAA
☐ North American NA-226 Trojan (T-28C)	N2800N	226-57	Bu140480	RAC

OKLAHOMA SCIENCE MUSEUM (OKLAHOMA AIR AND SPACE MUSEUM) (OK28)

Address:	Kirkpatrick Center, 2100 North East 52nd Street, Oklahoma City, Oklahoma 73111.
Tel:	405-602-6664 **Fax:** 405-602-3768 **Email:** communications@sciencemuseum.org
Admission:	Monday-Friday 0900-1700; Saturday 0900-1800; Sunday 1100-1800.
Location:	In the north eastern suburbs of the city

Opened in 1982, the museum displays trace the history of flight from the early days to modern space travel. The contribution of Oklahomans to aviation is well represented in the Hall of Fame. Sections devoted to the Wright Brothers, the Pioneers, World War I, the Barnstorming Era, World War II and the Conquest of Space all contain many interesting items.

A number of rare aircraft are on show including the sole surviving Wiley Post biplane. Derived from the Straughan A, only 13 were built before the company folded soon after the death of Wiley Post. The biplane was powered by a 40 h.p. Straughan engine.

The Star Cavalier was built in the state. Just 38 were constructed between 1928 and 1935 and an example is on show. Awaiting restoration is the sole surviving Coffman Monoplane of which about three were built in the 1930s. Sam Coffman set up his company in Clinton in 1928 but soon moved to Oklahoma City. Several designs were built but all in small numbers. The collection includes many interesting homebuilt types. The Sole Cloud Cutter was built by Chester Krist in northern Texas and was active for some time before being sold to the museum. The low wing Pierce-Sawyer JP-51 is another unique type. Ralph Mong of Tulsa in Oklahoma constructed his first aircraft, the MS.1 Sport, in the early 1950s. He developed the concept and the MS.3 was specifically designed for pylon racing. The Jungster is a basically a scaled down Bücker Jungmeister for homebuilding. This can be compared with the full sized model. The Jungmeister on show was newly-built after World War II. The Duster glider was sold in kit form and over 70 have been completed.

A fairly recent arrival is the Gulfstream Peregrine business aircraft dating from the 1980s. The design was developed from the American Jet Industries Hustler and Peregrine trainer after they took over Grumman. Also on show are a range of engines and several items from the space programme. The DC-3 operated by the FAA was restored to airworthy condition for the 'Centenary of Flight' celebrations in 2003. One day it will retire and join the exhibition. The complex has been extended to include a science museum and the theatre.

TYPE	REG/SER	CON. NO.	PI/NOTES	STATUS
☐ American Eagle A-101	N215N	724	NC215N	PV
☐ Banks Lonestar Spirit Helico	N31022	011		PV
☐ Bede BD-5B	N8065V	673		PV
☐ Bücker Bü 133 Jungmeister (R)	N133JS	12		PV
☐ Cirrus 3 Hang Glider				PV
☐ Coffman Monoplane				RAD
☐ Colomban MC-12 Cri-Cri	N32236	0061		PV
☐ Curtiss D Pusher (R)				PV
☐ Douglas DC-3A-467 Skytrain (TC-47B) (R4D-7) (R4D-6R) (R4D-6V)	N34	16611/33359	44-77027, Bu99856, N7091C – due when retired by FAA.	RAA
☐ DSK Aircraft Corporation BJ.1B Duster	N85968	199		PV
☐ Fokker Dr I (FSM)				PV
☐ General Dynamics FB-111A	68-0263	B1-35	Cockpit only.	PV
☐ Gulfstream 550 Peregrine	N84GP	551	N9881S, N550GA	PV
☐ Hickman Jungmeister DH-1	N28DH	1		PV
☐ Krist Cloud Cutter	N157CK	001		PV
☐ Lockheed 580 (T-33A)	58-0633	580-1602	On loan from Tinker AFB.	PV
☐ Lockheed 683-10-19 Starfighter (F-104G)	D-8331	683D-8331	(KG+431) – in Dutch markings – on loan from Tinker AFB.	PV
☐ Maupin Woodstock 1	N5553V	173		PV
☐ Mitchell Wing B-10	N579C	1		PV
☐ Monarch Hang Glider				PV
☐ Mong Special MS.3	N119F	711		PV
☐ Nieuport 11 (R)	N7082	4		PV
☐ Pierce-Sawyer JP-51	N31420	1		PV
☐ Ryan ST.3KR Recruit (PT-22)	N53173	2149	41-20940	PV
☐ Schweizer SGS.2-12 (TG-3A)				PV
☐ Star Cavalier E ((B)	N7239	101	NC7239 – possible identity.	PVX
☐ Stinson 108-2 Voyager	N435D	108-3435		PV
☐ Travel Air D-4000	R671H	1266	NC671H, N671H – on loan from 99s Museum of Women Pilots.	PV
☐ Wiley Post A	NC13961	12		PV

OKLAHOMA STATE DEPARTMENT FOR VOCATIONAL TRAINING (OK29)

Address:	1500 West 7th Avenue, Stillwater, Oklahoma 74074.
Tel:	405-377-2000 **Email:** steve.marks@okstate.edu
Admission:	By prior permission only.
Location:	At a number of locations around the state.

The department operates a number of vocational schools around the state. Aviation technology courses are held at several of these and instructional airframes are allocated to the colleges.

I have not been able to find out the exact location of the aircraft listed below. The list is probably not complete as others can be seen in the background of photographs in college literature. Any information would be appreciated.

Oklahoma

TYPE	REG/SER	CON. NO.	PI/NOTES	STATUS
☐ Beech 65-A90 King Air	N42CQ	LJ-245	N3000C, N68395, N58W, N42CC, N42CQ, (N221ML)	RA
☐ Beech 95-55 Baron	N9318Y	TC-11		RA
☐ Cessna 172N	N738CN	17269873		RA
☐ Cessna 172N	N4576E	17271630		RA
☐ Cessna 177RG Cardinal RG	N8070G	177RG0070		RA
☐ Cessna 210C	N3690Y	21058190		RA
☐ Cessna 401	N8007M	4010056		RA
☐ Cessna 411	N411JN	4110172		RA
☐ Hughes 269A Osage (TH-55A)	N9064Y	0441	64-18129	RA
☐ Hughes 269A Osage (TH-55A)	N9064Q	0531	64-18219	RA
☐ Mooney M.20E	N1326W	214		RA
☐ Piper PA-28R-200 Cherokee Arrow II	N4310T	28R-7235005		RA

PHILLIPS PETROLEUM COMPANY MUSEUM (OK30)

Address:	410 Keeler Street, Bartlesville, Oklahoma 74004.
Tel:	918-661-8687 Fax: 918-662-2600 Email: jenny.l.brown@conocophillips.com
Admission:	Monday-Saturday 1000-1600.
Location:	In the centre of tht town.

The Phillips company was formed in 1905 when Frank Phillips found his first oil well in the region. Over the last century it has grown into one of the major oil producing firms in the world. In 2002 it combined with the Conoco company.

The museum tracing this history opened on 11th May 2007. On show are many items, photographs and documents showing the development of oil manufacture and distribution.

The only aircraft on show is the 1914 Parker Pusher. Billy Parker constructed about 10 aircraft in Colorado between 1910 and 1916. In 1927 he became the first manager of the Phillips Petroleum Company's aviation department. The aircraft was flown at shows from the 1940s up to the 1960s. For many years it was exhibited at the Oklahoma Air and Space Museum (Oklahoma Science Museum) in Oklahoma City.

TYPE	REG/SER	CON. NO.	PI/NOTES	STATUS
☐ Parker Pusher	N66U	1		PV

ROLAND MONUMENT (OK31)

Location:	On permanent view near the town offices.

TYPE	REG/SER	CON. NO.	PI/NOTES	STATUS
☐ Bell 205 Iroquois (UH-1D) (UH-1H)	65-9937	4981		PV

SALINA MONUMENT (OK32)

Location:	On permanent view on Route 20 in the western part of the town.

TYPE	REG/SER	CON. NO.	PI/NOTES	STATUS
☐ Northrop N-156T Talon (T-38A)	61-0926	N.5292		PV

SKIATOOK MONUMENT (OK33)

Location:	On permanent view at the airport which is in the south western part of the town

TYPE	REG/SER	CON. NO.	PI/NOTES	STATUS
☐ Cessna 318B Tweety Bird (318A) (T-37A) (T-37B)	57-2338	40271		PV
☐ Lockheed 580 (T-33A)	51-9380	580-6564		PV

SOUTH EASTERN OKLAHOMA STATE UNIVERSITY AVIATION SCIENCES INSTITUTE (OK34)

Address:	1405 North 4th Street, Durant, Oklahoma 74701.
Tel:	580-745-2000
Admission:	By prior permission only.
Location:	At Eaker Field which is about 3 miles south of the town.

The university operates a professional pilot training school at Eaker Field with a fleet of Cessna types. In addition courses in many aspects of aviation management are held. These include safety and security along with business administration. A Fairchild-built Friendship is used in this work.

TYPE	REG/SER	CON. NO.	PI/NOTES	STATUS
☐ Fairchild F-27F Friendship (F-27F)	N432NA	35	N1000L, N291WX, N768RL	RA

SOUTHWEST TECHNOLOGY CENTER (OK35)

Address:	711 West Tamarack Road, Altus, Oklahoma 73521-1527.
Tel:	580-482-7705 Email: rsmith@swtc.tech.edu
Admission:	By prior permission only.
Location:	Aircraft at Quartz Mountain Airport which is about 3 miles north of the town.

The aviation department of the college is located in hangar workshops at the airfield. A small fleet of instructional airframes resides here and courses leading to airframe and engine licenses are held.

TYPE	REG/SER	CON. NO.	PI/NOTES	STATUS
☐ Cessna 150				RA
☐ Cessna 172				RA
☐ Cessna 172F Mescalero (T-41A)	N5137F	17252930	65-5137	RA
☐ Lockheed 300 Starlifter (C-141A) (C-141B)	64-0642	300-6055	Fuselage only.	RA
☐ Piper PA-31 Turbo Navajo				RA

SPARTAN SCHOOL OF AERONAUTICS (OK36)

Address:	8820 East Pine Street, Tulsa, Oklahoma 74115-5800.
Tel:	918-836-6886 Email: bfespero@mail.spartan.edu
Admission:	By prior permission only.
Location:	At Tulsa International Airport which is in the north eastern suburbs of the city.

The school was founded in September 1928 by W.G. Skelly who also established the Spartan Aircraft Company. He also formed the firm which built the airfield which is now Tulsa International Airport. Over the years the school has trained over 80,000 pilots and technicians. The list of instructional airframes is not complete.

Undergoing a rebuild is an example of a C-3 biplane produced from the late 1920s. The aircraft was popular and sold in considerable numbers before the onset of the depression. The aircraft spent a period on show at the Tulsa Air and Space Museum before moving across to the school.

TYPE	REG/SER	CON. NO.	PI/NOTES	STATUS
☐ Bell 47J	N6759D	1781		RA
☐ Cessna 150B	N1255Y	15059655		RA
☐ Cessna 150F	N7026F	15063662		RA
☐ Cessna 150L	N16242	15073566		RA
☐ Cessna 150L	N11753	15075613		RA
☐ Cessna 150L	N11903	15075699		RA
☐ Cessna 150M	N2970V	15076337		RA
☐ Cessna 310				RA
☐ Piper PA-23-160 Apache	N3342P	23-1295		RA
☐ Piper PA-38-112 Tomahawk	N2536F	38-79A0483		RA
☐ Spartan C-3-225	NC720N	A-14	NC720N, N720N	RA

STILLWATER AIRPORT MEMORIAL MUSEUM (OK37)

Address:	2020-1 West Airport Road, Stillwater, Oklahoma 74075.
Tel:	405-372-7881 Fax: 405-372-8460
Admission:	Sunday 1300-1700.
Location:	About 5 miles north of the town off Route 177.

Searcy Field started life as a grass strip in the late 1930s but by the end of World War II it was a large Navy base with three hard runways. For the next few years it became the first of a number of storage sites for surplus aircraft. In February 1946 Paul Mantz bought the 475 airframes on the site. Most were scrapped but 11 survived. The museum was established in 1992 and now occupies a large room. The displays trace the history of the field and many small parts from the scrapped aircraft are on show.

STILLWATER MONUMENT (OK38)

Location:	On permanent view at Oklahoma State University at Elm Street in the northern part of the town.

TYPE	REG/SER	CON. NO.	PI/NOTES	STATUS
☐ Republic RF-84F Thunderflash	53-7604			PV

THE 99'S MUSEUM OF WOMEN PILOTS (OK39)

Address:	4300 Amelia Earhart Road, Oklahoma City, Oklahoma 73159-0965
Tel:	405-685-9990 Email: museum@ninety-nines.org
Admission:	Monday-Friday 0900-1600; Saturday 1000-1600.
Location:	At Will Rogers Airport which is in the south western suburbs of the city.

The 99's organisation has been in existence for over 70 years. The museum was opened on 23rd July 1999 on the second floor of the headquarters building at Will Rogers Airport.
A large collection of memorabilia is on show. The stories of many notable women pilots are portrayed in detail with photographs and documents tracing their achievements. The only aircraft currently in the collection is a Travel Air, once flown by Louise Thaden. She was born in 1905 and in the 1920s and 1930s set several records and also won many races. In 1989 it re-enacted the course of the 'Powder Puff Derby' which it had won 60 years earlier. This biplane was obtained from the Allen Airways Museum at Gillespie Field in California. The famous aircraft is currently in the main hall at the Oklahoma Science Museum in the city.

THOMAS P. STAFFORD AIR AND SPACE MUSEUM (OK40)

Address:	300 East Logan Road, Weatherford, Oklahoma 73096.
Tel:	580-772-5871 Fax: 580-772-0498 Email: director@staffordmuseum.com
Admission:	Monday-Saturday 0900-1700; Sunday 1300-1700.
Location:	At the airport which is just east of the town off Interstate 40.

Oklahoma 503

Thomas P. Stafford, born in Weatherford in 1930, was America's 13th man in space. In 1975 he was commander of the Apollo craft which made the first meeting in space with a Soyuz capsule. He graduated from the USA Naval Academy at Annapolis in Maryland in 1952 and then joined the Air Force. After undergoing pilot training at Connally Air Force Base in Texas he became a fighter pilot and for a time flew F-86E Sabres at Hahn in Germany.

A museum honouring him opened in the airport terminal in 1983. On show are models, NASA photographs and memorabilia along with videos of his four space flights. In 2000 a hangar was constructed to house a collection of aircraft and engines which is steadily being enlarged. The Starfighter was once on show outside the now closed California Air National Guard base at Van Nuys Airport.

Several replicas have been added to the display. These highlight significant periods in the history of aviation. The Curtiss Pusher inspired many similar types in the period before World War I. The rapid advance in design can be seen in the Sopwith Pup of a few years later. The Ryan NYP honours Charles Lindbergh's contribution to popularising flying.

The former Czechoslovakian MiG-21R is painted in typical Soviet colours of the Cold war era. This jet was withdrawn in the mid-1990s and stored for a period.

TYPE	REG/SER	CON. NO.	PI/NOTES	STATUS
☐ Blériot XI (R)				PV
☐ Canadair CL-13B Sabre 6 [North American F-86E]	'81075'	1075	23285, CF-BKG, N8686D, N87FS, N92FS – probable identity.	PVX
☐ Canadair CL-30 Silver Star 3 (CT-133) [Lockheed 580 (T-33AN)]	'29846'	T33-555	21555 (Canada), 21555 (France), N301FS	PVX
☐ Curtiss D Pusher				PV
☐ General Dynamics 401 Fighting Falcon (F-16B)	79-0430	62-62		PV
☐ Lockheed 383-04-05 Starfighter (F-104C)	56-0932	183-1220		PV
☐ Mikoyan-Gurevich MiG-21R	'15'	94R02109	2109 (Czechoslovakia) – in false Soviet markings.	PVX
☐ Northrop N-156T Talon (T-38A)	'67-14956'	N.5108	59-1595	PVX
☐ Ryan NYP (R)	N-X-211'			PVX
☐ Sopwith Pup (R)				PV
☐ Wright Flyer (R)				PV
☐ Wright Glider (R)				PV

TINKER AIR FORCE BASE HERITAGE MUSEUM (OK41)

Address: OC-ALC/PA, Tinker Air Force Base, Oklahoma 73145-5900.
Tel: 405-739-2026   **Fax:** 405-739-5441   **Email:** oc-alc.pa@tinker.af.mil
Admission: Daily Dawn-Dusk.
Location: About 8 miles south east of Oklahoma City on Interstate 40.

Opened in 1941 as the Midwest Air Depot the base was later named after General Clarence L. Tinker, the Commander of the Seventh Air Force. He was killed when leading a raid on Wake Island in June 1942.

During and just after World War II the Douglas factory produced over 5,000 A-26s, C-47s and C-54s at the site. During this period repairs were carried out on B-17s, B-24s and B-29s by the depot.

For the last few years a small team has worked hard to try and establish a museum tracing the history of the field. An air park has been set up just inside Gate I and the majority of the aircraft are on show here.

The B-29 has a special association with the base, as in 1944 almost all produced were flown to Tinker for the addition of long range tanks before they were delivered to bases in Asia. Also on show are examples of two other outstanding Boeing bombers. The Lockheed WV-2 is positioned near the AWACS complex on the airfield. The B-1 bomber arrived for display over the winter of 2002/3. The T-38 is parked at the nearby Oklahoma Welcome Center.

TYPE	REG/SER	CON. NO.	PI/NOTES	STATUS
☐ Boeing 345 Superfortress (B-29)	44-27343		Composite	PV
☐ Boeing 450-158-36 Stratojet (RB-47E)	53-4257	4501281		PV
☐ Boeing 464-201-7 Stratofortress (B-52D)	56-0695	464066		PV
☐ Boeing 717-158B Stratolifter (C-135B) (WB-135B) (C-135C)	61-2671	18347		PV
☐ Douglas DC-3A-467 Skytrain (C-47B) (R4D-6) (EC-47J)	'2150761'	14828/26273	43-49012, Bu50761, O-50761 (US Army), N219GB	PVX
☐ Lockheed 382C-32D Hercules (EC-130Q) (TC-130Q)	Bu159348	382C-4601	Outside Navy HQ.	RA
☐ Lockheed 1049A-55-86 Super Constellation (WV-2) (EC-121K)	'O-30552'	1049A-4347	Bu137890	RAX
☐ McDonnell M.98EN Phantom II (F-4D)	66-7518	2040		PV
☐ Northrop N-156T Talon (T-38A) (AT-38B)	61-0817	N.5183	At the OK Welcome Center.	PV
☐ Republic F-105D Thunderchief	62-4360	D-559		PV
☐ Rockwell B-1B Lancer	83-0071	8		PV
☐ Vought A-7D Corsair II	72-0175	D297		PV

TISHOMINGO MONUMENT (OK42)

Location: On permanent view at Murray State College in the southern part of the town.

TYPE	REG/SER	CON. NO.	PI/NOTES	STATUS
☐ Grumman G-98 Tiger (F11F-1) (F-11A)	'Bu141824'	176	Bu141859	PVX

TULSA AIR AND SPACE MUSEUM (OK43)

Address: 3624 North 74th Avenue East, Tulsa, Oklahoma 74115-3708.
Tel: 918-834-9700   **Fax:** 918-834-6723   **Email:** curator@tulsamuseum.com
Admission: Tuesday-Saturday 1000-1700; Sunday 1300-1700.
Location: At Tulsa International Airport which is in the north eastern suburbs of the city.

This museum was set up in the late 1990s and features the latest interactive techniques to educate visitors in the principles of flight and space travel. There are simulators in which the visitor can experience a flight in a modern jet. The space exhibits trace the history of this form of travel and exploration.

The Mid-Continent Aircraft Company was set up at Tulsa in 1926 and their first product was the C-3 biplane. The company was re-organised as the Spartan Aircraft Company in 1928 and the C-3 was improved and offered with a number of engines. About 100 were completed before the depression.

Over 200 similar NP-1 trainers were also delivered to the United States Navy. These served mainly with reserve units. The C-2-60 low wing monoplane made its maiden flight in 1931 and 16 were built. The engine was a 60 h.p. Jacobs three cylinder radial. A number of successful designs, including the all metal Executive, followed and the company made its last aircraft in 1945. In October 1928 the renowned Spartan School of Aeronautics was established to train pilots and mechanics.

The Pitbull autogyro was constructed by Kenneth Cottle of Columbia, Missouri.

TYPE	REG/SER	CON. NO.	PI/NOTES	STATUS
☐ Aeromet Aura	N16AU	002		PV
☐ Bell 47K Sioux (HTL-7) (TH-13N)	N5710	2216	Bu145849	PV
☐ Bilstrom and Jucewick BJ-1 Glider			Frame only.	PV
☐ Deutsch Aerospace / Rockwell Ranger 2000	N204NA	RP-03		PV
☐ Diehl Aeronautical XTC				PV
☐ Douglas DC-3-277	N2237C	2137	NC18141, N38PB, XA-RPE	PV
☐ Fokker Dr I (R)			Incomplete.	PV
☐ Gates Learjet 24D	'N1TL'	24D-323	N61AW, N744JC, N104MC, N453N27AL	PVX
☐ Grumman G-303 Tomcat (F-14A)	Bu161598	457		PV
☐ Hugo Hu-Go Craft VPS	N29H	1		RA
☐ North American Rotorworks Pitbull				PV
☐ Schleicher Ka-6E Rhönsegler				PV
☐ Spartan C-2-60				PV
☐ Spartan C-3-220 (NP-1)	Bu3691	47	Bu3691, N28700	PV
☐ Star Cavalier (R)				PV

TULSA AIR NATIONAL GUARD BASE COLLECTION (OK44)

Address: 138 FW, 4200 North 93rd East Avenue, Tulsa, Oklahoma 74115-5000.
Tel: 918-832-8300 **Email:** webmaster@oktuls.ang.af.mil
Admission: By prior permission only.
Location: At Tulsa International Airport which is in the north eastern suburbs of the city.

The 125th Observation Squadron was constituted at Tulsa in 1940. After active duties in World War II it was returned to state control in 1946. The initial equipment after the conflict was the P-51D Mustang which served from 1947 until 1950.

The squadron operated the F-86D/L from 1957 to 1960 when it changed to the transport role with C-97s. Fighters returned in 1973 with the F-100 which was flown until the arrival of the A-7.

TYPE	REG/SER	CON. NO.	PI/NOTES	STATUS
☐ General Dynamics 401 Fighting Falcon (F-16A)	80-0505	61-226		RA
☐ North American NA-173 Sabre (F-86D) (F-86L)	51-8409	173-542		RA
☐ North American NA-223 Super Sabre (F-100D)	55-3650	223-332		RA
☐ Vought A-7D Corsair II	70-1028	D174		RA

TULSA TECHNOLOGY CENTER (OK45)

Address: 801 East 91 Street, Tulsa, Oklahoma 74132-4008.
Tel: 918-828-4000 **Fax:** 918-828-4009 **Email:** mike.highland@tulsatech.org
Admission: By prior permission only.
Location: At Richard Lloyd Jones Airport which is in the southern part of the city.

The college was established in 1965 and now operates from a number of sites in the area. The aviation department is at the Riverside Campus near Richard Lloyd Jones Airport. The T-33 is mounted outside the building. The workshops contain a fleet of instructional airframes along with engines and components.

TYPE	REG/SER	CON. NO.	PI/NOTES	STATUS
☐ Aero Commander 680W	N17JG	1802-24	N5078E, N17JG, (N102US), HP-898	RA
☐ Boeing 727-214	N218TT	19684	N529PS, F-BPJV	RA
☐ Cessna 150F				RA
☐ Cessna 150F				RA
☐ Cessna 337M Super Skymaster (O-2A)	N470DF	337M0254	68-10978	RA
☐ Convair 440-71 (C-131E) (R4Y-2) (C-131G)	N221TT	482	(57-2552), Bu145963, N42883, (N63280), N42883	RA
☐ Lockheed 580 (T-33A)	53-6011	580-9543		PV
☐ North American NA-282 Sabreliner 40	N61RH	282-27	N6381C, N720R, N129GP, N129GB, N111EA	RA
☐ North American NA-282 Sabreliner 40 (CT-39E)	N825SB	282-92	N2676B, Bu158382	RA
☐ Schweizer SGM.2-37 (TG-7A)	N764AF	12	87-0764	RA
☐ Vought A-7D Corsair II	71-0297	D208		RA

TULSA MONUMENT (OK46)

Location: On permanent view at Tulsa International Airport which is in the north eastern suburbs of the city.

TYPE	REG/SER	CON. NO.	PI/NOTES	STATUS
☐ Parker Pusher	N62E		In the terminal.	PV
☐ Mitsubishi MU-2B				PV

UNITED STATES AVIATION MUSEUM (OK47)

Address:	4141 North Memorial Road, Tulsa, Oklahoma 74115-1400.
Tel:	918-836-5387
Admission:	Monday-Friday 0800-1700.
Location:	At Tulsa International Airport which is in the north eastern suburbs of the city

Two aircraft are registered to the organisation. The early Harvard flew with the Royal Canadian Air Force whilst the Two seat F-5 saw service in the Netherlands. Little information is available on the activities of the museum.

TYPE	REG/SER	CON. NO.	PI/NOTES	STATUS
☐ Canadair CL-226 Freedom Fighter (NF-5B) [Northrop N-156B]	N8910	4003	K-4003 (Netherlands), N3206Y	PVA
☐ North American NA-81 Harvard IIA	N196FC/'02196'	81-4121	BW196, N3176U	PVA

VANCE AIR FORCE BASE COLLECTION (OK48)

Address:	71 FTW/PA, Vance Air Force Base, Oklahoma 73705-5000.
Tel:	580-213-7476 Email: 71ftw.pa@vance.af.mil
Admission:	By prior permission only.
Location:	About 3 miles south west of Enid.

Opened in 1941 as Air Corps Basic Flying School Enid, the site was closed at the end of World War II. Types in use during this period were the BT-13 Valiant, the TB-25 Mitchell and the TB-26 Invader. Re-opened as Enid Air Force Base in 1948, it took its present name in 1949 in honour of local man Colonel Leon R. Vance, killed in 1944. North American T-6 Texans moved in and later the Lockheed T-33 arrived. Subsequently the Cessna T-37 and Northrop T-38 were in service.

TYPE	REG/SER	CON. NO.	PI/NOTES	STATUS
☐ Cessna 172F Mescalero (T-41A)	65-5168	17253060	N5168F	RA
☐ Cessna 318B Tweety Bird (318A) (T-37A) (T-37B)	56-3498	40070		RA
☐ Cessna 318B Tweety Bird (T-37B)	68-8050	41155		RA
☐ Douglas TB-26B Invader (A-26B)	44-34156	27435	44-34156, XB-COM, XC-CAZ, N190M – composite with c/n 18632 43-22523, N4050A.	RA
☐ Lockheed 580 (T-33A)	51-4301	580-5596		RA
☐ North American NA-88 Texan (AT-6D)	42-44660	88-14974		RA
☐ North American NA-159 Trojan (T-28A)	49-1689	159-201		RA
☐ Northrop N-156T Talon (T-38A)	65-10426	N.5845		PV
☐ Republic F-105D Thunderchief	62-4242	D-441		RA
☐ Vultee V-74 Valiant (BT-13A)	41-10683	74-3000		RA

WAGONER MONUMENT (OK49)

Location:	By prior permission only at the Tuskogee Conference Center in the town.

TYPE	REG/SER	CON. NO.	PI/NOTES	STATUS
☐ Beech D18S	N2635	A-169		RA

WILEY POST HERITAGE OF FLIGHT CENTER (OK50)

Address:	7101 Millionaire Drive, Bethany, Oklahoma 73008.
Tel:	405-691-2632 Fax: 405-789-5315 Email: hangarmail@wileyposthangar.org
Admission:	Not yet open.
Location:	At the airport which is the north western suburbs of Oklahoma City.

In the late 1920s the Curtiss-Wright company built an airport at Tulsa. One of the buildings was a large art-deco hangar. Between 1929 and 1934 the famous local pilot Wiley Post kept and maintained his aircraft in the hangar. From 1932 until 1937 it was used by Braniff Airlines.
  During World War II the airfield was home to a training school. The field closed in 1955 and over the years the building became surrounded by commercial and industrial sites. The owner feared the hangar had become a hazard and planned to demolish it.
  A group of local pilots stepped in and persuaded him to take it down carefully and the building was stored. Funds have been raised to re-erect it at the modern Wiley Post Airport. The famous building was dedicated on 4th October 2003.

WOOLAROC MUSEUM (OK51)

Address:	Route 3, PO Box 2100, Bartlesville, Oklahoma 74003.
Tel:	918-336-0307 Fax: 918-336-0084 Email: woolarocmail@woolaroc.org
Admission:	June–August Tuesday-Sunday 1000-1700; September–May Wednesday-Sunday 1000-1700.
Location:	About 12 miles south west of the town on Route 123.

A specially constructed building houses the Travel Air 5000, which won the Dole Race from mainland USA to Hawaii. On 16th August 1927 Frank Goebel set off from Oakland, California and 26 hours and 17 minutes later landed at Wheeler Field. The aircraft was sponsored by oil magnate Frank Phillips and was stored on his family ranch for many years. The aircraft was built as a standard 5000 but Goebel required several modifications for the flight, On show in the main building are works of art, a collection of Colt revolvers and items showing the traditions of the Indians and settlers of the region.

TYPE	REG/SER	CON. NO.	PI/NOTES	STATUS
☐ Travel Air 5000MA	NX869	N0082		PV

WWII AIRBORNE DEMONSTRATION TEAM (OK52)

Address:	3200 Paul Tibbets Avenue, Frederick, Oklahoma 73542-1000.
Tel:	580-335-3344 Fax: 580-335-3344 Email: admin@wwiiadt.org
Admission:	Daily 0800-2000.
Location:	At Frederick Airport which is about 5 miles south east of the town.

The group was formed a decade ago and carries out parachute drops at shows. For several years aircraft were leased, including the C-47 then owned by the Oklahoma Airborne Museum. This aircraft has now joined the group.

The organisation acquired its own aircraft, a pre-war DC-3 first flown by Eastern Airlines, in 2007 and is setting up a 'living' museum in a World War II hangar at Frederick Airport.

TYPE	REG/SER	CON. NO.	PI/NOTES	STATUS
☐ Douglas DC-3-201F	N79MA	4089	NC28381, N168LG	PVA
☐ Douglas DC-3A-456 Skytrain (C-47A) (Dakota III)	N751A/'292277'	12060	42-92277, FL633.TC-YOL, CS-TAI, 1429/4X-FNT/029	PVA

YL-37 VIETNAM VETERANS ASSOCIATION (OK53)

Address:	14157 East 580 Road, Inola, Oklahoma 74036.
Tel:	918-543-8175 Fax: 918-543-3766 Email: yl37@aol.com
Admission:	By prior permission only.
Location:	At Inola/Dobies Heliport which is in the northern part of the town.

The group and its members keep three Sikorsky S-58s in flying condition. This type served in Vietnam with Marine squadron HMM-362 for three years. The fourth airframe is used for spares.

TYPE	REG/SER	CON. NO.	PI/NOTES	STATUS
☐ Sikorsky S-58 Seabat (HSS-1) (SH-34J)	'Bu145782'	58706	Bu143936, N62292	RAAX
☐ Sikorsky S-58 Seahorse (HUS-1) (UH-34D)	145810	581048	Bu145810 – in SVNAF markings.	RAD
☐ Sikorsky S-58 Seahorse (HUS-1) (UH-34D)	N855BA	581356	Bu148783	RAA
☐ Sikorsky S-58 Seahorse (HUS-1) (UH-34D)	'Bu148786'	58996	Bu145794, N7936C	RAAX

OREGON

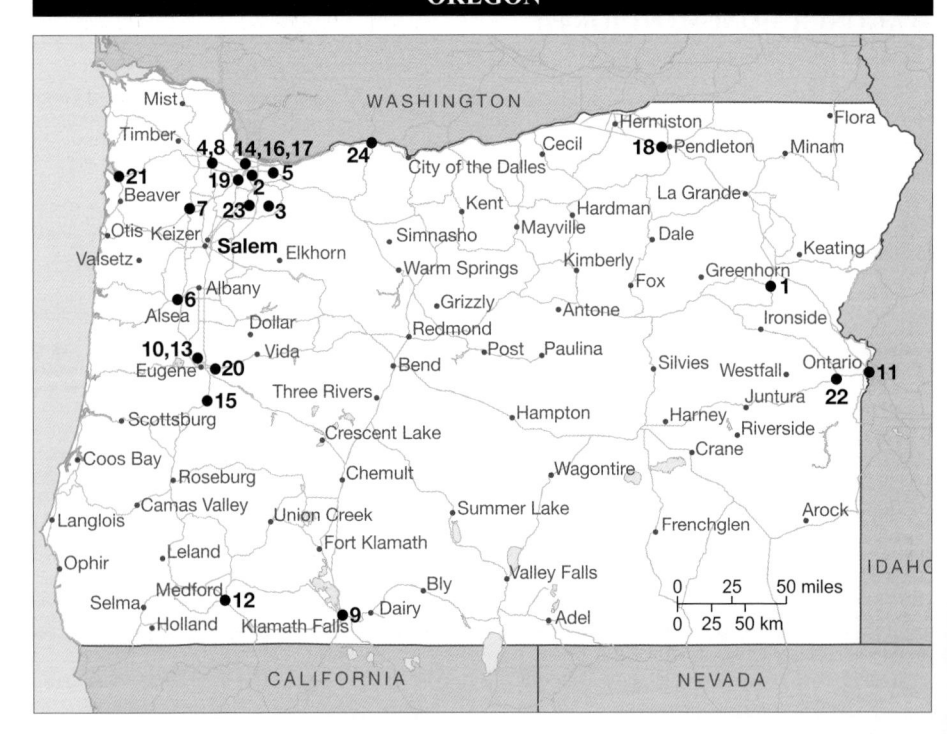

BAKER CITY MONUMENT (OR1)

Location:	On permanent view at the airport which is about 3 miles north of the town.

TYPE	REG/SER	CON. NO.	PI/NOTES	STATUS
☐ Lockheed 580 (T-33A)	51-6653	580-5985		PV

BOMBER FOUNDATION (OR2)

Address:	13515 South East McLoughlin Boulevard, Milwaukie, Oregon 97222.
Tel:	503-654-6491
Admission:	On permanent view.
Location:	On Route 99E in the town which is about 5 miles south of Portland.

This Fortress was built at Burbank and delivered to the Army Air Force in June 1945. In March 1947 it made it last flight from Altus in Oklahoma to Portland when it was bought by Art Lacey and mounted above his petrol station.
In 2003/4 the site was redeveloped as a garden centre but the bomber remained. The group has been formed to restore the bomber which has suffered after 50 years exposure to the harsh climate and to vandalism.
A building is used for the work and the forward fuselage was removed in the first phase of the rebuild. When this is completed other parts will be taken down and moved into the workshop.

TYPE	REG/SER	CON. NO.	PI/NOTES	STATUS
☐ Boeing 299-O Fortress (B-17G)	44-85790	8699		PVC

BORING MONUMENT (OR3)

Location:	On permanent view at a business in the town.

TYPE	REG/SER	CON. NO.	PI/NOTES	STATUS
☐ Bell 204 Iroquois (UH-1B)	62-2067	587	Cabin only.	PV

CLASSIC AIRCRAFT AVIATION MUSEUM (OR4)

Address:	2140 North East 25th Street, Hillsboro, Oregon 97291-0430.
Tel:	503-693-1414 Email: donkel@classicaircraft.org
Admission:	Monday-Friday 0900-1600.
Location:	At the airport which is about 3 miles north east of the town off Route 6.

The first aircraft acquired by the museum was the former Belgian Air Force Starfighter which is being rebuilt in the museum workshops. Other jet fighters have since joined the collection.
Three aircraft have recently been acquired from Airspray at Red Deer in Alberta. These are a former Luftwaffe Sabre and two Douglas Invaders. The Sabre was used by Dornier at Oberpfaffhofen after its military days were over. The fighter was then sold in the USA and was operated from Mojave in California for several years. Airspray bought it in 1998 and it flew on military target towing duties. The company operated almost 20 Invaders on water bombing duties. The type was in use for over 30 years and a 1,000 gallon tank was fitted in the fuselage.
The prototype Jet Provost flew for the first time in 1954 and improved versions were ordered by the Royal Air force for training duties. Almost 600 were built with several exported.
The Hunter is painted in the red scheme of the modified prototype flown by Neville Duke when he set a when he set a World Air Speed Record of 727.63 mph off the Sussex coast on 7th September 1953. Displays of memorabilia are being set up in the buildings.

TYPE	REG/SER	CON. NO.	PI/NOTES	STATUS
☐ Bell 33 Kingcobra (P-63C)	43-11247	33-115		RAC
☐ Canadair CL-13B Sabre 6 [North American F-86E]	N186PJ	1710	JB+240, D-9541, N1039L, N89FS, C-GBUI	PVA
☐ Douglas A-26C Invader	N26FK	28723	44-35444, N7656C, CF-TFB, C-FTFB	PVA
☐ Douglas A-26C Invader	N26PJ	28987	44-35708, 435708 (France), N5530V, C-GXGY	PVA
☐ Douglas DC-3A-456 Skytrain (C-47A) (Dakota III)	N115SA	13310	42-93402, KG587, 12931 (Canada), (C-GXAU), C-GRTM	PVA
☐ Fouga CM.170-2 Magister (CM.170A)	N71FM	38	FM-38 (Finland)	PVA
☐ Hawker P.1067 Hunter F.51	'WB188'	41H/680272	47-418 (Denmark), E-418 (Denmark), G-9-440, G-HUNT, N5097Z, N611JR	RAX
☐ Hunting-Percival P.84 Jet Provost T.3A (T.3)	N27357	PAC/W/6314	XM357	PVA
☐ Lockheed 583-10-20 Starfighter (TF-104G)	N104TF	583F-5926	KF+226, BB+119, 27+96, 5926 (Turkey)	PV
☐ Lockheed 683-10-19 Starfighter (F-104G)	63-12699	683D-6051	63-12699, R-699 (Denmark), 4420 (Taiwan)	RA
☐ Mikoyan-Gurevich MiG-21F-13	N6285L	261109	1109 (Czechoslovakia)	PV
☐ Mikoyan-Gurevich MiG-21UM	N7238T	516913036	3036 (Czech)	PVA
☐ Mikoyan-Gurevich MiG-21UM	N57GS	516999343	9343 (Poland)	PVA
☐ WSK Lim-5 [MiG-17F]	N1426D	1C 14-26	1426 (Poland)	PVA

DAMASCUS MONUMENT (OR5)

Location:	On permanent view at a business in the town.

TYPE	REG/SER	CON. NO.	PI/NOTES	STATUS
☐ Bell 205 Iroquois (UH-1H)				PVX

DC-3 AVIATION MUSEUM (OR6)

Address:	3301 North West Walnut Boulevard, Corvallis, Oregon 97330.
Email:	dc3@dc3museum.org
Admission:	Not yet built.
Location:	In the northern part of the town.

The group is raising funds for a building to house archive material relating to the famous aircraft. There will be taped and video interviews with those who have flown and maintained the type.

EVERGREEN AVIATION AND SPACE MUSEUM (OR7)

Address:	500 North East Captain Michael Smith Road, McMinnville, Oregon 97128-8877.
Tel:	503-434-4180 Fax: 503-434-4058 Email: stewart.bailey@sprucegoose.org
Admission:	Daily 0900-1700 (Closes at 1800 June-September)
Location:	At McMinnville Airport which is about 3 miles south of the town

Delford M. Smith, who formed the Evergreen Group, was born in McMinnville. The company now operates a fleet of helicopters and fixed wing aircraft around the world. A large new complex, which opened on 6th June 2001, has been constructed at the airfield.

The centrepiece of the display is the giant Hughes H-4 'Spruce Goose' which made one brief flight on 2nd November 1947. After years in store in California it was put on display at Long Beach from 1983 until the early 1990s. The flying boat was then dismantled and moved to Oregon, arriving at McMinnville on 22nd February 1993.

Amongst the aircraft on show is the prototype Curtiss Wright Falcon, a Messerschmitt Bf 109 restored in Colorado and the second Hughes 269 helicopter. The Ford Tri-Motor was once part of the Harrah Collection in Nevada before moving to Silverwood in Idaho. Only eight Beech D17As were built in the late 1930s and early 1940s. The example in the collection was the only one of this variant to be impressed. Other Beech designs are an early version of the classic Bonanza and one of the few Starships allocated to museums.

The Fortress has had a varied career. During its service life it was converted for transport duties and later further modified carrying high-ranking officers. The aircraft was sold on the civilian market and was used by the CIA for a time. The B-17 was then modified for fire-fighting work and flew on these duties for over a quarter of a century. Now the Fortress is displayed in its original military configuration. Helicopters also feature prominently.

After World War I the Boeing company built about 350 examples of the de Havilland DH.4. Several of these were fitted with steel tube fuselages. The Vampire, painted in false RAF colours, was originally used in India. This superb exhibition has many interesting types on show and others are being restored for the display.

Mounted outside is an F-15 Eagle. This aircraft is a memorial to Michael King Smith, son of the founder of the company and Rhory Draeger, both members of the Oregon Air National Guard who died from injuries sustained in a car crash in March 1995. Other military jets are joining the exhibition.

TYPE	REG/SER	CON. NO.	PI/NOTES	STATUS
☐ Adams-Wilson 101 Hobbycopter				S
☐ American Aerolights Eagle II				S
☐ Auster K AOP.6	N52874	2845	VF644, (Hong Kong) – on loan.	PV
☐ Bede BD-5B	N110CJ	2392		PV
☐ Beech D17A (UC-43F)	NC50959	305	NC19453, 42-49071	PVA
☐ Beech 35 Bonanza	N3870N	D-1111		PVA
☐ Beech D45 Mentor (T-34B)	Bu140938	BG-272	Bu140938, N9334B –	PV
☐ Beech 2000A Starship I	N74TD	NC-27	N8225Y, N47TF	PV
☐ Bell 47D-1 Sioux (H-13E) (OH-13E)	51-13934	520		PV
☐ Bell 47E (HTL-3)	Bu124564	168		PV
☐ Bell 205 Iroquois (UH-1D) (UH-1H)	64-13502	4209	On loan from Oregon MM, OR.	PV
☐ Bell 206B Jet Ranger	N10729	2876		PV
☐ Bell 209 Huey Cobra (AH-1G) (AH-1F)	69-16434	20866		PV
☐ Bensen B-8M Gyrocopter				PV
☐ Blériot XI (R)				PV
☐ Boeing 299-O Fortress (B-17G) (CB-17G) (VB-17G) (CB-17G) (VB-17G)	N207EV	32426	44-83785, N809Z	PVA
☐ Boeing 747-132C	N481EV	19896	N9896, LV-LRG, N9896, N40108, B-1868, N902PA	PV
☐ Boeing-Stearman E75 Kaydet (PT-13D) (N2S-5)	N450UR	75-5300	42-17137, Bu61178, N9302H	PVA
☐ Cessna 310	N198R	35150	N4850B	RA
☐ Chadwick C122S Helicopter				PV
☐ Christen Eagle II	N4221H	POIER-001		PV
☐ Convair 8-10 Delta Dagger (F-102A)	56-1368	8-10-585	56-1368, '57-0776'	PV
☐ Convair 8-31 Delta Dart (F-106A)	59-0137	8-31-26		PV
☐ Curtiss D Pusher (R)			On loan from Hiller AM, CA.	PV
☐ Curtiss 1A Jenny (JN-4A) (R)				PV
☐ Curtiss 50C Robin C-1	NC9283	337	NC9283, N9283	PV
☐ Curtiss 51 Fledgling	NC868N	B-51	NC868N, N868N	PV
☐ Curtiss 87-B3 Warhawk (P-40K)	N293FR	21133	42-9749, N67253	PVA
☐ Curtiss-Wright CW-15D Sedan	NC12314	15-2214		PVC
☐ Curtiss-Wright CW-A22 Falcon	N500G	A22-1	NX18267	PVA
☐ De Havilland DH-4M	'166'	ET-4	N3258	PVX
☐ De Havilland DH.100 Vampire FB.52	'VZ309'		IB1686 (India), N174LA	PVX
☐ Douglas DC-3A-197	NC16070	1910		PV
☐ Douglas DC-3A-456 Skytrain (C-47A)	'315512'	19978	43-15512, NC62376, 'N56589'	PVX
☐ Douglas DC-9-32	N998R	47030	N3321L – fuselage section only.	PV
☐ Douglas A-26C Invader	N74833	28718	44-35739	PV
☐ Douglas EA-1F Skyraider (AD-5N) (AD-5Q)	Bu132534	8929	Bu152070	PV
☐ Douglas A-4E Skyhawk	'Bu149996'	13458		PVX
☐ Fairchild M-62A Cornell (PT-19B)	42-83239	T43-8239	42-83239, NC49081, N49081	PV
☐ Fisher FP-404				PV

Oregon

☐ Fisher Q-Lite				PV
☐ Fokker Dr I (R)				PV
☐ Ford 5-AT-B	N9645	5-AT-8	NC9645, XH-???, AN-AAS, XA-FUB, XB-NET, N58996	PVA
☐ Ford JB-2 [Fieseler Fi 103A-1]	'325'			PVX
☐ Gates Learjet 23				PV
☐ Granville Gee Bee Sports E (R)	'NR2101'	X-9	N11044	PVX
☐ Grumman G-40 Avenger (TBM-3) (TBM-3E)	N5260V	4631	Bu91726	PVA
☐ Grumman G-50 Hellcat (F6F-3)	Bu41476	A-2742	Bu41476, N41476 – on loan from NMMC, VA.	PV
☐ Grumman G-105 Cougar (F9F-8T) (TF-9J)	Bu146417			RA
☐ Grumman G-134 Mohawk (OV-1C) (OV-1D)	67-18902	103C	On loan from Or. Mil. Mus., OR.	PV
☐ Grumman G-303 Tomcat (F-14D)	Bu164343	618		PV
☐ Handley Raven 2300	N711WH	003-89-5003		PV
☐ Hiller 1033 Rotor Cycle (YROE-1)	Bu4021	5 (S2/7588)	G-46-1 – in Evergreen Offices – on loan from Hiller AM, CA.	RA
☐ Hiller UH12B Raven (H-23B) (OH-23B)	51-16245	437		PV
☐ Hiller UH12E	N5363V	2049		PV
☐ Hiller UH12E	N1H	2100	In Evergreen Offices.	PV
☐ Hughes H-4 Hercules (HK-1)	NX37602		NX37602, N37602	RA
☐ Hughes 269A	N79P	002/380002		PV
☐ Hughes 369D	N11035	0810D		PV
☐ Insitu A-20 Scan Eagle				PV
☐ Israeli Aircraft Industries-Mazlat Mastiff III				PV
☐ Kaman K-20 Seasprite (HU2K-1U) (UH-2B) (SH-2F)	Bu151321	158	Bu151321, N8064Z –	PV
☐ Lockheed 422-87-23 Lightning (P-38L)	N505MH	422-8441	44-53186, NL62350, N62350, N505MH (G-MURU), N505MH, N38EV	PVA
☐ Lockheed 426-45-15 Neptune (P2V-5) (P2V-5S) (SP-2E)	N202EV	426-5383	Bu131502	PV
☐ Lockheed 580 (T-33A)	'30943'	580-9419	53-5943	PVX
☐ Lockheed 683-10-19 Starfighter (F-104C)	FX-84	683D-9142	FX-84 (Belgium), N104PJ	PV
☐ Lockheed 1049A-55-86 Super Constellation (RC-121D) (EC-121D) (EC-121T)	N4257L	1049A-4353	52-3417	RAC
☐ Lockheed SR-71A Blackbird	61-7971	2022	61-7971, N832NA	PV
☐ McDonnell M.36W Voodoo (F-101A)	53-2418	1	53-2418, N9250Z	PV
☐ McDonnell M.98DE Phantom II (F-4C)	63-7647	750	On loan from Oregon MM	PV
☐ McDonnell M.199-1A Eagle (F-15A)	76-0014	193/A166		PV
☐ McDonnell M.199-1A Eagle (F-15A)	73-0089	28/A023		RAC
☐ Messerschmitt Bf 109G-10/U4	N109EV	610937	610937, FE-124, T2-124	PV
☐ Messerschmitt Me 262A-1 (R)		110999		PV
☐ Mikoyan-Gurevich MiG-17	'115'	541393	115 (Czechoslovakia), N75490 – In false Soviet markings.	PVX
☐ Mikoyan-Gurevich MiG-21MF-75	'84'	96007600	7600 (Poland) – in false Soviet markings.	PVX
☐ Mikoyan-Gurevich MiG-29	23	2960505561	41 – possibly c/n2906721930	PV
☐ Mitsubishi A6M3 Zero Sen Model 32		3318		RAC
☐ Naval Aircraft Factory N3N-3	Bu2831			PV
☐ Neibauer Lancair 320	N44BH	313		PV
☐ North American NA-88 Texan (AT-6C)	N33CC	88-13466	42-43973, N7405C	PVA
☐ North American NA-122 Mustang (P-51D)	N51DH	122-31302	44-63576, NX37492, N37492	PVA
☐ North American NA-194 Fury (FJ-3) (F-1C)	Bu136119	194-346	On loan from NMMC, VA.	PV
☐ North American NA-200 Trojan (T-28B)	NX394W	200-405	Bu138334	RAA
☐ North American NA-240 (X-15) (X-15A) (FSM)	'66672'			PVX
☐ North American NA-243 Super Sabre (F-100F)	56-3832	243-108		PV
☐ North American NA-265 Sabreliner (T-39A) (CT-39A)	60-3481	265-9		RA
☐ North American NA-340 Buckeye (T-2C)	Bu158312	340-3		PV
☐ Northrop N-156T Talon (T-38A) (AT-38B)	'N968NA'	N.5571	63-8224	PVX
☐ Northrop N-160 Scorpion (N-68) (F-89D) (F-89J)	53-2534	N.4665		RAC
☐ Northrop N-311 Tiger II (F-5E)	74-1556	R.1216		PV
☐ Northrop-Grumman RQ-4A Global Hawk (FSM)				RAC
☐ Oldfield Baby Great Lakes	N44ET	6907M-187		PVA
☐ Pietenpol B4-A Aircamper				RAC
☐ Piper J-3C-65 Cub (L-4H)	N61827	10750	43-29459	PV
☐ Piper J-3L-65 Cub	NC46471	G-31		PVA
☐ Pitts S-2B Special	N5352E	5105		PVA
☐ Quickie Aircraft Quickie 2 (Rutan 54)	N84GK	2402		PVA
☐ Republic RC-3 Seabee	N6481K	736	NC6481K	PV
☐ Republic F-84F Thunderstreak	'52-6877'		51-9522, N6950N	PVX
☐ Republic F-105G Thunderchief (F-105F)	62-4432	F-21		RA
☐ Ryan ST-3KR Recruit (PT-22)	N53438	2161	41-20952	PV
☐ Schweizer SGS.2-32	N8600R	1	On loan from NSM, NY.	PV
☐ Sikorsky S-51 Dragonfly	N65760	5105		RA
☐ Sikorsky S-51 Dragonfly (HO3S-1G)	233	51209		PV
☐ Sikorsky S-55D Chickasaw (H-19D) (UH-19D)	52-7602	55542		PV
☐ Sikorsky S-56 Mojave (H-37A) (CH-37A) (CH-37B)				RAC
☐ Sikorsky S-58 Seahorse (HUS-1) (UH-34D)	Bu138460	580128	Bu138460, (South Vietnam)	PV
☐ Sikorsky S-61B Sea King (HSS-2) (SH-3A) (SH-3H)	Bu149006	61080		PV
☐ Sopwith F.1 Camel (R)				PV
☐ Stoddard-Hamilton SH-2 Glasair II	N306AT	306		PV
☐ Supermarine 361 Spitfire LF.XVIe	N356TE	CBAF-11470	TE356, G-SXVI, N356EV	PVA
☐ Thorp T-18	N3BF	413		PV
☐ Thunder & Colt Hot Air Balloon			Basket only.	PV

☐ Vertol V.43 Shawnee (H-21C) (CH-21C)	'53-4379'	C.172	55-4218	RACX
☐ Vought FG-1D Corsair	NX67HP	3356	Bu92095, N62344	PVA
☐ Vought A-7D Corsair II	69-6230	D60		RA
☐ Wright Flyer (R)				PV
☐ WSK SBLim-2 [MiG-15bis]	'22'	242271	2271 (Poland), NX271JM	PVX
☐ Yakovlev Yak-50	'CCCP-01'	832604	NX7144F	PVX

HILLSBORO MONUMENT (OR8)

Location: By prior permission only at a private site in the town.

TYPE	REG/SER	CON. NO.	PI/NOTES	STATUS
☐ Boeing 727-284	N727SH	20005	SX-CBC	RA

KINGSLEY FIELD AIR NATIONAL GUARD BASE (OR9)

Address: 211 Arnold Avenue, Suite 11, Klamath Falls, Oregon 97603-2111.
Tel: 541-885-6677 **Email:** webmaster@orklam.ang.af.mil
Admission: By prior permission only
Location: The airfield is about 4 miles south east of the town off Route 39.

The base is named after Lieutenant David Kingsley, a native of the state, who was killed in action in the Pacific during World War II. The three preserved aircraft are mounted in an area close to the Headquarters Building.

TYPE	REG/SER	CON. NO.	PI/NOTES	STATUS
☐ General Dynamics 401 Fighting Falcon (F-16A)	82-0910	61-503		RA
☐ McDonnell M.98DE Phantom II (F-4C)	63-7479	472		RA
☐ McDonnell M.199-1A Eagle (F-15A)	76-0009	188/A161		RA

LANE COMMUNITY COLLEGE (OR10)

Address: 28715 Airport Road, Eugene, Oregon 97402.
Tel: 541-463-5340 **Email:** stegalll@lanecc.edu
Admission: By prior permission only.
Location: In the southern part of the town.

The college was set up in 1964 and offers pilot training on Cessna and Piper types. Aircraft maintenance courses are run and two instructional airframes are known to be in use but there are probably more.

TYPE	REG/SER	CON. NO.	PI/NOTES	STATUS
☐ Cessna 182F	N3488U	18254888		RA
☐ Piper PA-28-140 Cherokee	N6253W	28-20300		RA

MAINE COLLECTION (OR11)

Address: 3196 South West 12th Avenue, Ontario, Oregon 97914-4600
Admission: By prior permission only.
Location: At Ontario airport which is in the south western suburbs of the town off Route 20.

This private collection owned by Merle Maine consists of mainly flyable and static ex-military aircraft.
The Vampire is one of a batch of ex-Australian machines imported into the USA in 1970. The Sea Venom also made a similar journey.

The rarest aircraft in the collection is the Douglas Skylancer of which only four were built. The origin of some of the MiG fighters is not known at the current time.
Several aircraft have suffered at other locations and will need a great deal of work to bring them up to exhibition standard.

TYPE	REG/SER	CON. NO.	PI/NOTES	STATUS
☐ Aero L-39C Albatros	N139MM	931411	(Ukraine)	RAA
☐ Bellanca 17-30A Super Viking	N6710V	30314		RAA
☐ De Havilland DH.112 Sea Venom FAW.53	N7022H	12786	WZ944, N4-944	RAA
☐ De Havilland DH.115 Vampire T.35	N11924	4140	A79-618	RAA
☐ Douglas A-4L Skyhawk (A4D-2N) (A-4C)	N148AT	12557	Bu147793	RAA
☐ Douglas A-4L Skyhawk (A4D-2N) (A-4C)	N130AT	12639	Bu148446, N3E	RAA
☐ Douglas A-4L Skyhawk (A4D-2N) (A-4C)	Bu150581	12992	Bu150581, (N235AT)	RA
☐ Douglas F5D-1 Skylancer	NASA 708	11282	Bu139208, NASA 212	RA
☐ General Dynamics F-111A			Test airframe.	RA
☐ Grumman G-51 Tigercat (F7F-3)	N7195C	C.268	Bu80532	RAC
☐ Grumman G-89 Tracker (S2F-1) (S-2A)	N8110X	307	Bu136398	RAA
☐ Grumman G-89 Tracker (S2F-1) (S-2A)	N8115M	628	Bu136719	RAA
☐ Grumman G-89 Tracker (S2F-2) (S2F-2U) (US-2C)	N8110Q	N23	Bu133351	RAA
☐ Lockheed 183-93-02 Starfighter (F-104A)				RA
☐ Lockheed 580 (T-33A)	N82852	580-1258	57-0609	RAC
☐ Lockheed 580 (T-33A)	52-9803	580-8063		RA
☐ Lockheed 580 (T-33A)	53-6117	580-9738	Fuselage only.	RA
☐ Lockheed 580 (T-33A)			Fuselage only. Coded TR-221	RA
☐ Lockheed 580 (T-33A) (RT-33A)	MM53-5587	580-8926	53-5587	RA
☐ McDonnell M.98EN Phantom II (F-4D)	66-0266	1932		RA
☐ Mikoyan-Gurevich MiG-17				RA
☐ Mikoyan-Gurevich MiG-21FR (MiG-21F-13)	NX1011E	061011	1011 (Czechoslovakia)	RAA
☐ Mikoyan-Gurevich MiG-21PFM		94A6611	6611 (Poland)	RAX
☐ Mikoyan-Gurevich MiG-23MF	147	0390217147	In Polish markings.	RA
☐ North American NA-159 Trojan (T-28A)	N9862C	159-239	49-1727	RAA

Oregon

☐ North American NA-159 Trojan (T-28A)	N2867G	159-65	49-1553	RAA
☐ North American NA-172 Sabre (F-86E)	51-2826	172-109		RA
☐ North American NA-201 Sabre (F-86D)	53-0809	201-253	Possible identity.	RAD
☐ North American NA-201 Sabre (F-86D)	53-0897	201-341	Possible identity.	RAD
☐ Republic F-105D Thunderchief			Front fuselage only.	RA
☐ Vought A-7D Corsair II	70-0964	D110		RA

MEDFORD AIRPORT MUSEUM (OR12)

Address:	4002 Cirrus Drive, Medford, Oregon 97504.
Tel:	541-776-7222 Fax: 541-776-7223 Email: airportadmin@jacksoncounty.org
Admission:	Saturday 0900-1600.
Location:	About 2 miles north of the town off Route 62.

The original Medford Airport which opened in 1922 was the first municipal airfield in the state. Airlines and the US Forest service were among the first users. A move to the current site was made in the late 1920s and air mail aircraft used the facilities.

The KC-97 was a regular visitor on fire-fighting duties as a number of companies have a base at Medford. The aircraft has a display of this work inside the fuselage. The F-16 is mounted near the terminal building and honours the Oregon Air National Guard who operate the fighter.

TYPE	REG/SER	CON. NO.	PI/NOTES	STATUS
☐ Boeing 367-76-66 Stratofreighter (KC-97G) (KC-97L)	N1365D	16589	52-0895	PV
☐ General Dynamics 401 Fighting Falcon (F-16A)	81-0759	61-440		PV

OREGON AIR AND SPACE MUSEUM (OR13)

Address:	90377 Boeing Drive, Eugene, Oregon 97402.
Tel:	503-461-1101.
Admission:	April–October Wednesday-Sunday 1200-1600; November–March Wednesday-Saturday 1200-1600.
Location:	At Eugene Airport which is about 5 miles north west of the city off Route 99.

The museum hangar opened in August 1991 and within the next year a new wing doubling the exhibition space was ready. There are long-term plans to construct a larger facility nearby.
 The history of aviation in the state is portrayed in detail and there is a section devoted to Oregon's Fighter Aces. In 1924 two of the Douglas World Cruisers landed at Eugene on their record-breaking visit and a display honours this. There is a collection of over 600 models, built by one man, tracing developments from the Wright Brothers to the Stealth Fighter. Also on show are engines, components and many items of memorabilia. There is an exhibition of photographs showing the development of flying both in Oregon and the Eugene area.
 A prized exhibit is a 'space ball' retrieved by a local resident. This metallic sphere originates from a Gemini mission. The aircraft display contains a number of homebuilts including a locally designed scale Zero fighter and Molt Taylor's experimental pusher, the Bullet 2100. The prototype Adams-Wilson Hobbycopter flew in 1958 and a number of kits were sold to amateur constructors. Four former military jets have been loaned by other museums across the country.

TYPE	REG/SER	CON. NO.	PI/NOTES	STATUS
☐ Adams-Wilson 101 Hobbycopter				PV
☐ Beech D45 Mentor (T-34B)	Bu144030	BG-337	Bu144030, N349MF	PV
☐ Breeze Bee				PV
☐ Coffee Mitsubishi A6M2-21 (R)	N4217	1		PV
☐ Douglas A-4C Skyhawk (A4D-2N)	Bu148491	12684		PV
☐ Fokker Dr I (R)	N35PH	1981-A		PV
☐ Grumman G-128 Intruder (A-6E)	Bu162206	I-699		PV
☐ Gyrodyne QH-50C (DSN-3)		DS-1289		PV
☐ Homebuilt Aircraft				PV
☐ Icarus I Hang Glider				PV
☐ Long Henderson Longster (R)	N930AL	LL-1	On loan from Oregon AM, OR.	PV
☐ Messerschmitt Bf 109 (Scale R)				PV
☐ Mikoyan-Gurevich MiG-17	NX306DM	0704	(China)	PV
☐ Mitchell Wing B-10				PV
☐ Monnett Monerai S	N8534P	206		PV
☐ Nieuport 17 (R)	N25PH	1985-B		PV
☐ North American NA-191 Sabre (F-86F)	'12892'	191-451	52-4755, (S.Korea) – on loan from Oregon MM	PVX
☐ Roloff RLU-1 Breezy	N2545	5537-HS	N254E	PV
☐ Smith Termite				PV
☐ Striplin Lone Ranger				PV
☐ Taylor-Berry 2100 Bullet				PV
☐ Thorp T-18				PV
☐ War Aircraft F4U Corsair	N86RD	1-1986		PV
☐ Xiamen AD-100T	N168Y	012		PV

OREGON AIR NATIONAL GUARD MEMORIAL PARK (OR14)

Address:	6801 North East Cornfoot Avenue, Portland International Airport, Oregon 97218-2797.
Tel:	503-335-4104 Email: webmaster@orport.ang.af.mil
Admission:	By prior permission only.
Location:	On the south side of the airport which is in the northern suburbs of the city.

The 123rd. Squadron was allocated to the Oregon National Guard in 1941 and became a fighter unit five years later. Apart from periods of active duties it has always been based at Portland. A memorial park is located inside the base with three aircraft formerly used by the unit on show.

TYPE	REG/SER	CON. NO.	PI/NOTES	STATUS
☐ McDonnell M.199-1A Eagle (F-15A)	76-0066	253/A218		RA
☐ McDonnell M.36BA Voodoo (F-101B)	58-0301	673		RA
☐ McDonnell M.98DE Phantom II (F-4C)	63-7679	805		RA

OREGON AVIATION HISTORICAL CENTER (OR15)

Address:	PO Box 553, Cottage Grove, Oregon 97424.
Tel:	541-942-2567
Admission:	May–September Saturday 1000-1600.
Location:	In the town – aircraft are at a number of locations.

Formed in 1987, this museum is still searching for a permanent home. The Long Longster was built from 1931 plans by the aviation construction technology class at Lane Community College in Eugene. The project was started in 1981 and completed four years later and is now loaned to the Oregon ASM.

The Rupert Special is a local homebuilt design from 1934. The parasol-wing monoplane was constructed at Beaverton and was fitted with a Heath engine. This did not generate enough power so a Salmson radial was installed. The majority of the collection, is in store in the Cottage Grove and Eugene areas.

TYPE	REG/SER	CON. NO.	PI/NOTES	STATUS
☐ Great Lakes 2T-1A	NX315Y	202		RA
☐ Long Wimpy				RAC
☐ McManiman Springfield Cadet				RAC
☐ Rupert Special				RA
☐ Stinson SR-5E Reliant	NC14585	9322A	NC14585, N14585	RAC

OREGON MILITARY MUSEUM (OR16)

Address:	PO Box 2516, 10101 Southeast Clackamas Road, Camp Withycombe, Clackamas, Oregon 97015-2516.
Tel:	503-557-5359
Admission:	Friday-Saturday 0900-1700 and by prior permission.
Location:	In the southern suburbs of Portland just east of Highway 205.

The first Militia Company was established in Oregon in 1843 and state units have served in all major conflicts since this date.
The museum was set up in 1974 to preserve this rich heritage. A small exhibition building was erected at the camp and a display or artefacts and memorabilia can be seen along with vehicles and armaments.
Most of the aircraft in the collection are either in store or loaned out to other museums until a new hall is built. The only one on show is the Bird Dog parked near the museum building.

TYPE	REG/SER	CON. NO.	PI/NOTES	STATUS
☐ Bell 205 Iroquois (UH-1D) (UH-1H)	64-13502	4209	At Salem AGB.	RA
☐ Bell 206A Kiowa (OH-58A)	72-21361	42027	At Salem AGB.	RA
☐ Cessna 305A Bird Dog (L-19A) (O-1A)	50-1333	21007	50-1333, N5280G	PV
☐ Hiller UH12B Raven (H-23B) (OH-23B)	N	410	51-16228, N23PC	RA
☐ Hiller UH12B Raven (H-23B) (OH-23B)	54-0868	682		RA

OREGON MUSEUM OF SCIENCE AND INDUSTRY (OR17)

Address:	1945 Southeast Water Avenue, Portland, Oregon 97214-3354.
Tel:	503-797-4586 Email: webmaster@omsi.com
Admission:	Tuesday-Sunday 0930-1730.
Location:	In the city.

The museum covers many aspects of the sciences with many innovative displays. Engineering and local industry feature prominently. The only aircraft on show is the Long Ez hanging in one of the halls.

TYPE	REG/SER	CON. NO.	PI/NOTES	STATUS
☐ Rutan 61 Long Ez	N1382Y	921		PV

PENDLETON AIR MUSEUM (OR18)

Address:	PO Box 639, Pendleton, Oregon 97801.
Tel:	541-231-4384 Email: info@pendletonairmuseum.org
Admission:	By prior permission only.
Location:	About 2 miles west of the town.

The museum has been set up to trace the history of the airfield. During World War II Pendleton Army Airfield was home to the 17th Bombardment Group. This unit became famous as 'The Doolittle Raiders'. A flight of 16 B-25s took off from the USS *Hornet* and carried out a daring raid on Tokyo in April 1942.
A memorial stone has been erected at Pendleton to honour those who lost their lives. Members of the museum working with the Oregon National Guard have restored a Mitchell which is now on show near the military hangars. The Iroquois is also displayed in this area. A collection of memorabilia tracing the development of the airfield, which is now the Eastern Oregon Regional Airport, is being assembled. The National Guard also has artefacts in its camp which show the history of the local units and the helicopters they have operated.

TYPE	REG/SER	CON. NO.	PI/NOTES	STATUS
☐ Bell 205 Iroquois (UH-1H)				RA
☐ North American NA-108 Mitchell (B-25J) (CB-25J) (TB-25J) (TB-25N)	N17666	108-33518	44-30243, N9622C	RA

Oregon

PORTLAND COMMUNITY COLLEGE (OR19)

Address:	17705 Northwest Springville Road, Portland, Oregon 97229.
Tel:	503-614-7238 Email: rfrasco@pcc.edu
Admission:	By prior permission only.
Location:	At the Rock Creek Campus which is about 10 miles west of the city.

The college has a large aviation maintenance department with 16 instructional airframes and more than 40 engines for the use of the students. The workshops also contain a range of test equipment and components.

TYPE	REG/SER	CON. NO.	PI/NOTES	STATUS
☐ Aero Commander 680T	N6540V	1571-26		RA
☐ Beech 65-A80 Queen Air	N3800	LD-155		RA
☐ Beech D18S Expeditor (C18S) (JRB-4) (SNB-5) (TC-45J) (UC-45J)				RA
☐ Bell 47G-2 Sioux (H-13H) (OH-13H)				RA
☐ Bell 205 Iroquois (UH-1H)				RA
☐ Cessna 150				RA
☐ Cessna 150M	N6451K	15077709		RA
☐ Cessna 305A Bird Dog (L-19A) (O-1A)				RA
☐ Cessna 310Q	N7507Q	310Q0007		RA
☐ Cessna T337G Super Skymaster	N54E	P3370156		RA
☐ Hiller UH12C Raven (H-23C) (OH-23C)	N26PC	800	55-4097	RA
☐ Hiller UH12C Raven (H-23C) (OH-23C)	N24PC	880	56-2272	RA
☐ Hughes 369M Cayuse (HO-6) (OH-6A)				RA
☐ Piper PA-28-140 Cherokee				RA
☐ Piper PA-31T Cheyenne				RA
☐ Piper PA-38-112 Tomahawk	N2472D	38-79A0327		RA

RAGWOOD REFACTORY COLLECTION (OR20)

Address:	86094 Panorama Road, Springfield, Oregon 97478.
Tel:	541-746-6572
Admission:	By prior permission only.
Location:	In the northern suburbs of the town.

This private collection is owned by restorer Tim Talen. Work is carried out in the old Springfield Airport hangar which was moved to his home and at a local airfield.

There are many rarities among the fleet, which are nearly all restoration projects. Only five Timm Collegiates were built in the late 1920s and a pair await their turn in the restoration queue. Another rarity is the Rearwin Speedster of which only ten were built in the late 1930s.

The General Skyfarer appeared in 1941 but only about 20 emerged from the factory before America entered World War II. This high wing monoplane was based on the 1939 Puritan and was reputedly spin proof.

Clarence Prest built a small number of the Baby Pursuit parasol wing single-seater in the late 1920s – the fuselage was diamond shaped. The last survivor of the type is in store. In May 1930 one set a then closed circuit speed record of 101 m.p.h.

TYPE	REG/SER	CON. NO.	PI/NOTES	STATUS
☐ Aeronca 50F Chief	NC22137		NC22137, N22137	RA
☐ Aeronca K	NC19759	K-270	NC19754, N19754	RA
☐ Aircraft Builders Corporation Student Prince X	NC263V	101		RA
☐ American Eagle A-101 (A-1)	N844E	375	NC844E	RA
☐ Cessna C-34 Airmaster	N17054	337	NC17054	RA
☐ Corben T.1 Baby Ace	N68647	1		RA
☐ Curtiss 50B Robin B	NC315E	135	NC315E, N315E	RA
☐ Curtiss-Wright CW-1 Junior	NC10938	1117	NC10938, N10938	RA
☐ Curtiss-Wright CW-1 Junior	NC11880	1250	NC11880, N11880	RA
☐ Fairchild 24 C8C	N15346	2689	NC15346	RA
☐ Fairchild 24 C8C	N15347	2690	NC15347	RA
☐ General G-1-80 Skyfarer	NC29025	12		RA
☐ Great Lakes 2T-1	NC820K	134	NC873K, N873K	RA
☐ Heath Parasol				RA
☐ Interstate S-1A Cadet	NC28314	6		RA
☐ Interstate S-1A Cadet	NC37270	14	NC37270, N37270	RA
☐ Interstate S-1A Cadet	NC37270	113		RA
☐ Interstate S-1A Cadet	N37334	177	NC37334, N37334	RAA
☐ Maule M-4C	N9850M	5C		RAA
☐ Porterfield CP-40	N20702	532	NC20702	RA
☐ Prest Baby Pursuit				RA
☐ Rearwin 6000M Speedster	NC19410	306		RA
☐ Rearwin 8135 Cloudster	N25547	824	NC25547	RA
☐ Ryan NYP (R)	'NX-211'			RA
☐ Sioux Coupe 60	N16N	Q217	NC161N, N161N	RA
☐ Stearman C3B	NC6154	140	NC6154, N6154	RA
☐ Stearman C3B	NC6499	195	NC6499, N6499	RA
☐ Stearman C3MB	NC6496	207	NC6496, N6496	RA
☐ Swallow OX-5	NC6711	991		RA
☐ Taylor J-2 Cub	N15971	515	NC15971	RA
☐ Taylorcraft A	N8136N	89	NC8136N	RA
☐ Timm Collegiate	NC887E	102		RA
☐ Timm Collegiate	NC888E	103		RA
☐ Travel Air 2000	NC9857	1113	NC9875	RA
☐ Travel Air 2000	NC167V	1402		RA
☐ Woods Woody Pusher				RA

TILLAMOOK NAVAL AIR STATION MUSEUM (OR21)

Address:	6030 Hangar Road, Tillamook, Oregon 97141.
Tel:	503-842-1130 Fax: 503-842-3054 Email: info@tillamookair.com
Admission:	Daily 0900-1700.
Location:	About 2 miles south of the town off Highway 101.

Naval Air Station Tillamook was commissioned in December 1942 to house airships used for coastal patrol and convoy escort duties. Two large wooden hangars were constructed. Squadron ZP-33 operating eight Goodyear K-class blimps moved in. The station closed in 1948 but the two hangars were left. In 1992 Hangar A was destroyed in a fire and only the support posts remain. Hangar B, which was the first built, has housed the current museum since 1994. This building, which is the largest wooden clear span structure in the world, has a length of 1,072 feet, a width of 296 feet and a height of 192 feet. Prior to 1994 a display tracing the history of airship operations had been staged. This exhibit can still be seen.

The majority of the aircraft on show are owned by Jack Erickson who operates a helicopter and airfreight business at Medford, Oregon. The oldest type on show is a SPAD XIII dating from 1917.

Only 18 Bellanca Airbus monoplanes were built in the early 1930s and these were followed by five improved Aircruisers. This high-wing type with a span of 65 feet is one of the largest single-engined aircraft ever built.

The Grumman Duck is something of a rarity these days. First flown in 1936, well over 600 were flown by the US Navy and Coastguard. The Hayabusa was recently restored to airworthy condition.

Parked outside is one of the Boeing Stratocruisers modified by Aero Spacelines to carry large loads for the space programme. A modern airship reminds the visitor of the first use of the site.

TYPE	REG/SER	CON. NO.	PI/NOTES	STATUS
☐ Aero L-29 Delfin	N7149E	993629	A-2918 (Indonesia), LL-2918 (Indonesia)	PVA
☐ Aero Spacelines 377-MG Mini-Guppy (Boeing 377-10-26 Stratocruiser)	N422AU	15937	NC1037V, N1037V, N422AJ -with parts of c/n 15967 NC31227, G-ANTZ, N106Q, N411Q.	PVA
☐ Bell 26C Airacobra (P-39N)				PVC
☐ Bell 206A Kiowa (OH-58A)			Front fuselage only.	PV
☐ Bell 206A Sea Ranger (TH-57A)	Bu157363	5009		PV
☐ Bellanca 66-75 Aircruiser	N2191K	721	NCP-40, CF-BTW	PVA
☐ Bensen B-8M Gyrocopter				PV
☐ Boeing-Stearman A75N1 Kaydet (PT-17)	N65727	75-4405	42-16242	PVA
☐ Cessna 180F	N2146Z	18051246		PV
☐ Chris-Tena Mini Coupe	N62ME	MC106		PV
☐ Commonwealth CA-17 Mustang 20 [North American P-51D]	N551D	1364	A68-39, VH-BOY – adopted c/n 124-48242 45-11489, N5421V, N551D, N5421V in one rebuild then c/n 109-28459 44-14826, N1740B, 14826 (Haiti), 826 (Haiti), (Dominican) Republic, N551D in a further rebuild.	PVA
☐ Consolidated 28-5A Catalina (PBY-5A)	NX2172N	1886	Bu46522, N5585V, CF-FFA, C-FFFA	PVA
☐ Douglas DC-3A-360 Skytrain (C-47) (R4D-1)	N737H	6062	(43-30631), Bu12396, NC39340, N69011, N7H	RAA
☐ Douglas DC-3A-467 Skytrain (C-47B) (Dakota IV)	N56V	16405/33153	44-76821, KN547, 44-76821, GA+110, AS+590, AB+590, BD+590, 14+06, Fv79008, SE-IKL, N5467Y	PVA
☐ Douglas A-24A Dauntless	NX5254L	2350	42-60817, N9142H, N15749	PV
☐ Douglas TB-26B Invader (A-26B)	NX3222T	28001	44-34722, N3222T, N62289	PVA
☐ Douglas AD-4NA Skyraider (AD-4N)	NX4277P	7712	Bu126912, 41 (France), 126912 (Gabon)	PV
☐ Douglas AD-4W Skyraider (AEW.1)	NX4277N	7850	Bu126867, WV181, SE-EBK, G-BMFB	PVA
☐ Douglas A-3A Skywarrior (A3D-1)			Cockpit section only.	PV
☐ Douglas A-4B Skyhawk (A4D-2)	Bu142922	11984	On loan from NMNA, FL – possible identity	PV
☐ Douglas A-4C Skyhawk (A4D-2N)			Front fuselage only. only.	PV
☐ Ercoupe 415C	N99903	2526	NC99903	PV
☐ Fairchild 24W40 (GK-1)	Bu7703	W40-171	N3779C –	PV
☐ Grumman G-15 Duck (J2F-6)	N3960C		Bu33559, N3960C, N910CM	PVA
☐ Grumman G-36 Wildcat (FM-2)	NX58918	5812	Bu86754	PVA
☐ Grumman G-40 Avenger (TBM-3) (TBM-3E)	NX6447C	3637	Bu53575, N6447C	PVA
☐ Grumman G-303 Tomcat (F-14A)	Bu159848	208		PV
☐ Hispano HA-1112M1L [Messerschmitt Bf 109G]	N90602	193	C.4K-130, G-AWHN	PV
☐ Kaman K-240 Huskie (HTK-1) (TH-43E)	Bu129313	4-22		PV
☐ Lockheed 15-27-01 Harpoon (PV-2D)	N83L	15-1501	Bu37535, N7079C, N83L, (N11559)	PV
☐ Lockheed 422-87-23 Lightning (P-38L) (F-5G)	NX2114L	422-8087	44-27083, NX75551, N75551, N502MH	PVA
☐ Lockheed 726-45-17 Neptune (P2V-7) (P2V-7S) (SP-2H)	N360RR	726-7256	Bu148360	PV
☐ Martin 210A Mauler (AM-1)	N7163M	12155	Bu22275	PV
☐ Mustang Golden Commuter				PV
☐ Nakajima Ki-43 Hayabusa	NX43JE			PVA
☐ Nord N.1101 Noralpha (Ramier I) [Messerschmitt Me 208]	N2758	175	175 (France) –	PV
☐ North American NA-168 Texan (T-6G)	N100XK	168-430	49-3326, E.16-69	PVA
☐ North American NA-200 Trojan (T-28B)	N28DE	200-346	Bu138275, N75AF	PVA

Oregon

☐ North American NA-200 Trojan (T-28B)	N28EV	200-405	Bu138334, N394W	PVA
☐ Quickie Aircraft Quickie 2 (Rutan 54)	N5588L	DL1		PV
☐ Republic P-47D Thunderbolt	NX47DA/'226641'	399-55616	44-90471, 532 (Peru), 114 (Peru)	PVA
☐ Rotorway Scorpion 133				PV
☐ SPAD XIII	S7571			PV
☐ Stinson V-77 Reliant (AT-19)	N9112H	77-311	43-44024, FB583, Bu11321	PVA
☐ Thompson 28	N99TW	01		PV
☐ United States Lighter Than Air Corporation 138-SC (Grace GAC-20)	N25BP	0001	(Avotek 100)	PV
☐ Vanek Gyrocopter C	N1331	VC2860		PV
☐ Vought F4U-7 Corsair	NX1337A		Bu133722, 722 (France)	PVA
☐ Vought F-8J Crusader (F8U-2NE) (F-8E)			Cockpit section only.	PV
☐ Vought A-7E Corsair II			Cockpit section only.	PV
☐ Vought A-7E Corsair II	Bu158819	E375		PV
☐ WSK Lim-6bis (LiM-5M)	'319'	1F 03-19	319 (Poland), N2503N – in false Soviet markings.	PV

VALE MONUMENT (OR22)

Location: On permanent view in Wadleigh Park in the southern part of the town.

TYPE	REG/SER	CON. NO.	PI/NOTES	STATUS
☐ North American NA-201 Sabre (F-86D) (F-86L)	53-0781	201-225		PV

VIETNAM ERA VETERANS MEMORIAL (OR23)

Address: 3834 North East View Court, Gresham, Oregon 97030.
Tel: 503-669-7941 **Email:** john@wamc.com
Admission: On permanent view.
Location: Just south of Canby on Highway 99.

This memorial has been constructed to honour local people who lost their lives in the conflict. A mock Vietnamese 'paddy field' has been put in place showing the conditions the troops would have encountered.

TYPE	REG/SER	CON. NO.	PI/NOTES	STATUS
☐ Bell 205 Iroquois (UH-1H)	70-16351	12656		PV

WESTERN ANTIQUE AEROPLANE AND AUTOMOBILE MUSEUM (OR24)

Address: 1600 Air Museum Road, Hood River, Oregon 97031.
Tel: 541-308-1600   **Fax:** 541-308-1601   **Email:** info@waamuseum.org
Admission: Daily 0900-1700.
Location: About 3 miles south of the town which is about 60 miles east of Portland.

This museum has been set up by two collectors Terry Brandt and John Thurmond. The museum opened for the first time on 7th September 2007. A new large facility has been built for the collection. Terry Brandt has acquired a substantial number of airframes over the years. Currently there are about 70 airworthy aircraft and several more will be restored in the near future.

There are several antique and classic cars with the earliest being a 1914 Model T Ford Depot Hack. Military vehicles from World War II up to the late 1950s will also be on show. The majority of these are in working order and rides will be available. Around 40 aircraft engines are in the display halls. Many propellers, components and instruments will be put on show. The original Longster was built in 1932 by Les Long in Cornelius, Oregon. The replica in the collection was built in 1990 and has now been fitted with the correct power unit a 30 h.p. Henderson motorcycle engine.

The fleet includes the largest known number of airworthy 1930s types powered by three cylinder motors. These have now been joined by the greatest number fitted with the Curtis OX-5 engine. The low-wing Buhl Pup with an all-metal monocoque fuselage first flew in late 1930 and 100 were built before the depression of 1932.

The low wing side-by-side Spartan C-2 dates from 1931 and only 16 were completed. One, powered by a 55 h.p. Jacobs is in flying condition and two more airframes await their turn The Davis D-1K parasol wing was built in Richmond, Indiana. The prototype took to the air in November 1929 and was powered by a Kinner radial. Around 60 of all versions were sold.

TYPE	REG/SER	CON. NO.	PI/NOTES	STATUS
☐ Aeronca C-3	NC12423	A-189	NC12423, N12423	PVA
☐ Aeronca C-3	NC13000	A-215	NC13000, N13000	PVA
☐ Aeronca K	N19718	K-236	NC19718	SD
☐ Aeronca KCA	NC21041	KCA-19	NC21041, N21041	PVA
☐ Aeronca LC	NC17442	2056	NC17442, N17442	PVA
☐ Aeronca 65-TAL Defender	N36874	L-1971TA	NC36874	PVA
☐ Aeronca 65TC Grasshopper (O-58B) (L-3B)	N47751	5242	(USAAF)	PVA
☐ Aeronca 7AC Champion	NC81513	7AC-135	NC81513, N81513	PVA
☐ Alexander Eaglerock 3-POLB	NC3641	365	NC3641, N3641	SD
☐ Alexander Flyabout D-2	N11076	3005	NC11070, NC11070	SD
☐ Alon A-2	N6354V	A-30		PVA
☐ American Eagle A-101 (A-1)	NC7157A	278	NC7157, N7157A	PVA
☐ American Eagle Eaglet B-31	NC595Y	1103	NC595Y, N595Y	PVA
☐ Arrow Sport F	N16483	5	NC16483	SD
☐ Arrow Sport Pursuit	N853H	412	NC853H	PVA
☐ Beech D17S (GB-2)	NC59832	4837	Bu33038, N52832, N900C, N97P	PVA
☐ Beech E18S	NC18BY	BA-275	N227, N2279	PVA
☐ Boeing 40C	N5339	1043	NC5339	PVA

Oregon

☐ Boeing-Stearman A75 Kaydet (PT-13B)	N57444	75-166	40-1609 – painted as an N2S-3.	PVA
☐ Boeing-Stearman A75N1 Kaydet (PT-17)	N2978T	75-0824	41-1064	SD
☐ Boeing-Stearman A75N1 Kaydet (PT-17)	N59231	75-4367	42-16204	PVA
☐ Boeing-Stearman A75N1 Kaydet (PT-17)	N62911	75-4496	42-16333	RA
☐ Brunner-Winkle Bird A	NC945V	1046	NC945V, N945V	PVA
☐ Brunner-Winkle Bird CK (BK)	NC14K	1060	NC14K, N14K – registered as a Bird A	PVA
☐ Buhl LA-1 Flying Bull Pup	NC365Y	154	NC365Y, N365Y	PVA
☐ Cessna T-50 Bobcat (AT-17B) (UC-78B)	N58542	4203	42-71507	PVA
☐ Culver LCA Cadet	NC34785	236	NC34785, N34785	PVA
☐ Curtiss D Pusher (R)	NX5704N	1		PVA
☐ Curtiss D Pusher (R)	N8Y	101		PVC
☐ Curtiss 1C Jenny (JN-4D)	NC1282	1		PVA
☐ Curtiss 1C Jenny (JN-4D)	N5137	5137		SD
☐ Curtiss 50H Robin J-1	NC8332	213	NC8332, N8332	PVA
☐ Curtiss 50H Robin J-1	NC511N	705	NC511N, N511N	PVA
☐ Curtiss-Wright CW-1 Junior	NC671V	1052	NC670V, N670V	PVA
☐ Curtiss-Wright CW-1 Junior	N11890	1263	NC11893, N11893	SD
☐ Curtiss-Wright CW-12W Sport Trainer	NC11715	12W-2040	NC11715, N11715	PVA
☐ Dart G	N20993	G-11	NC20993	PVA
☐ Davis D-1K	NC151Y	510	NC151Y, N151Y	PVA
☐ Emigh Trojan A-2	N8323H	26	NC8323H	PVA
☐ Fairchild 22 C7A	NC2816	1053	NC2816, N2816	PVA
☐ Fairchild 22 C7B	NC12454	1503	NC13107, N3107	PVA
☐ Fairchild 24R40 (UC-86)	NC48411	R40-405	NC25331, 42-78040, N48411	PVA
☐ Fairchild M-62A Cornell (PT-19B)	N56268	T43-5242	42-34576	PVA
☐ Fleet 7 (2)	N682M	230	NC682M	PVA
☐ Franklin Sport 90	NC13271	106	NC13271, N13271	PVA
☐ Heath Super Parasol				RA
☐ Lincoln Page LP-3	NC136W	259	NC136W, N136W	PVA
☐ Long Henderson Longster III (R)	N10115	3		PVA
☐ Luscombe 8A Silvaire	NC77918	3645	NC77918, N77918	PVA
☐ Naval Aircraft Factory N3N-3	N45042		Bu2582	PV
☐ Naval Aircraft Factory N3N-3	N45047		Bu2641	SD
☐ Nicholas-Beazley NB-8	NC436V	K-1	NC436V, N436V	SD
☐ Pietenpol P-9 Sky Scout (R)	N1933A	007		PVA
☐ Piper J-3C-40 Cub	N20258	2058	NC20258	SD
☐ Piper J-3C-65 Cub	NC20255	2055	NC20255, N20255	PVA
☐ Piper J-3C-65 Cub	N21595	2443	NC21595	SD
☐ Piper J-3C-65 Cub	N23325	3076	NC23325	SD
☐ Piper J-3C-65 Cub	N30210	4693	NC30210	PVA
☐ Piper J-3C-65 Cub	N30596	4963	NC30596	PVA
☐ Piper J-3C-65 Cub	N41273	8199	NC41273	SD
☐ Piper J-3C-65 Cub	N6036V	9394	NC6036V	PVA
☐ Piper J-3C-65 Cub	N92394	16856	NC92394	SD
☐ Piper J-3C-65 Cub	N48686	G236		PVA
☐ Piper J-3C-65 Cub (O-59A) (L-4A)	N8370H	8874	42-36750, NC8370H	PVA
☐ Piper J-3C-65 Cub (L-4J)	N1071N	13284	45-4544	PVA
☐ Piper J-3F-50 Cub	N232PB	3011		SD
☐ Piper J-3L-65 Cub	N41121	7772	NC41121	SD
☐ Piper J-3P Cub	NC21561	2474	NC21561, N21561	PVA
☐ Piper J-4A Cub Coupe	N21867	4-410	NC21867	PVA
☐ Piper J-5 Cub Cruiser (HE-1) (AE-1)	N63557	5-1465	Bu30262	PVA
☐ Piper J-5A Cub Cruiser	N3202J	5-1108		RA
☐ Piper PA-18A-150 Super Cub	N14319	18-6359		RA
☐ Piper PA-20-135 Pacer (PA-22-135 Tripacer)	N1418C	22-1175		PVA
☐ Piper TG-8	N88683	G-129	43-3137	RA
☐ Rearwin 185 Skyranger	NC90685	1780	NC90685, N90685	PVA
☐ Rearwin 6000M Speedster	N19415	309	NC19415	PVA
☐ Rearwin 8500 Sportster	N4478B	428	NC15480	SD
☐ Rearwin 9000L Sportster	N18008	549	NC18008	PVA
☐ Ryan ST-3KR Recruit (PT-22)	N57026	1764	41-15735	PVA
☐ Ryan ST-3KR Recruit (PT-22)	N56711	2084	41-20875	SD
☐ Ryan ST-3KR Recruit (PT-22)	N27575	2210	41-21002	SD
☐ Spartan C-2-60	N11016	J-3	NC11016	PVA
☐ Sperry-Verville M-1 Messenger				SD
☐ Stearman 70	N571Y	70-001	X571Y	RAC
☐ Stinson 108-1 Voyager	N8238K	108-1238		PVA
☐ Stinson HW.75	N22539	7105	NC22539	SD
☐ Stinson Junior R	N4472N	8506	NC12152	SD
☐ Stinson V-76 Sentinel (L-5)	N58726	76-510	42-98269	PVA
☐ Taylor E-2 Cub	NC12610	18	NC11647, N11647	PVA
☐ Taylor J-2 Cub	NC16743	580	NC16343, N16343	PVA
☐ Taylorcraft BC-65	NC21239	1029	NC21239, N21239	PVA
☐ Taylorcraft BC-12-65	NC29840	2691	NC29840	PVA
☐ Taylorcraft ST-100 (TG-6)	NX39177	4183	NC39177 – built from a BC-12D.	PVA
☐ Taylorcraft DCO-65 Grasshopper (L-2M)	'43-12498'	L-5615	43-26303, N3072Z	PVAX
☐ Travel Air 2000	N3677	289	NC3671, N3671	RA
☐ Travel Air 3000	N5432	519	NC5430, N5430	RA
☐ Travel Air 4000	N6297	744	NC6297	RA
☐ Waco 10 (GXE)	NC6513	1810	NC6513, N6513	PVA
☐ Waco CSO (10 (GXE))	NC7662	1657	NC7662, N7662	PVA
☐ Waco CTO	NC516M	AT-3605	NC516M, N516M	PVA
☐ Waco DSO	NC605N	3006	NC605N, N605N	PVA
☐ Waco NAZ Primary Glider				RA
☐ Waco RNF	NC143Y	3417	NC11224, N11224, CF-AMD	PVA

Parked outside the giant airship hangar at the Tillamook Naval Air Station Museum is this Aerospacelines Mini-Guppy. [OR21]

The 169th Fighter Wing Memorial Park is home to this North American F-86H Sabre. [SC1]

Parked on the deck of the USS Yorktown at Patriot's Point is this Grumman S-2E Tracker. [SC18]

PENNSYLVANIA

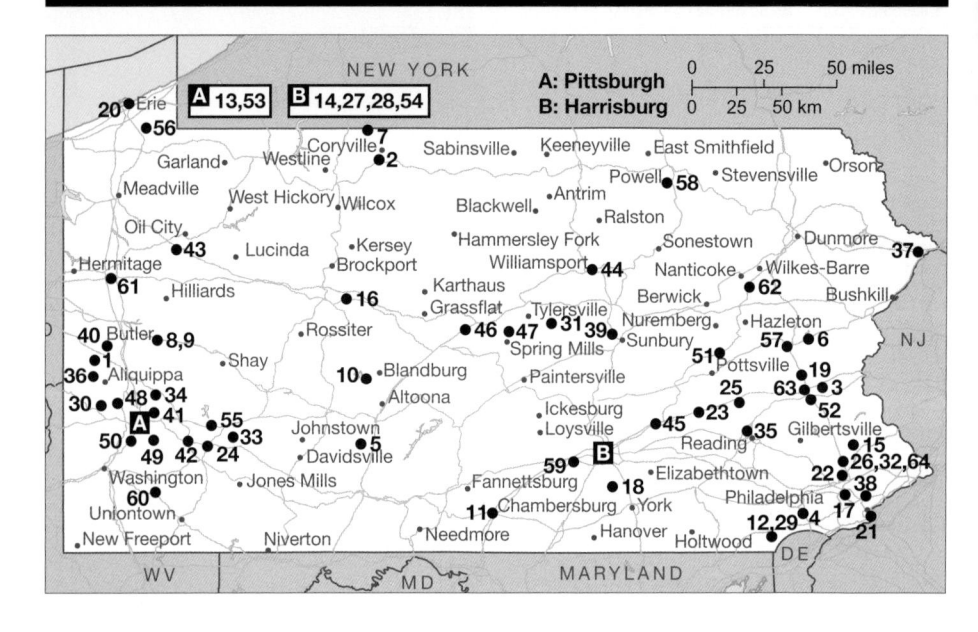

AIR HERITAGE (PA1)

Address:	Beaver County Airport, Beaver Falls, Pennsylvania 15010-1043.
Tel:	724-843-2820 **Fax:** 724-847-4581 **Email:** airheritage@airheritage.org
Admission:	Monday-Saturday 1000-1700; Sunday 1200-1700.
Location:	About 5 miles north west of the town off Route 51.

The group was formed in 1983 and in 1987 helped in the restoration of the Collings Foundation B-17 which had been damaged when it ran off the runway at an airshow at Beaver Falls.

In 1987 the group obtained its first aircraft a former Italian Air Force Super Cub. This was joined by a Fairchild Provider in the mid-1990's. In 1990 an agreement was reached with the Military Aircraft Restoration Corporation of California to rebuild to flying condition some of their aircraft.

A hangar at the airport has been set up as a working museum and visitors can see restoration in progress. The Sabre has been mounted at the airport for over 20 years.

TYPE	REG/SER	CON. NO.	PI/NOTES	STATUS
☐ Beech D45 Mentor (T-34B)	N4738C	BG-366	Bu144059	RAC
☐ Bell 26C Airacobra (P-39N)	42-18814		On loan from MARC, CA.	PVC
☐ Fairchild 24 C8C	NC14749	2655	NC14749, N14749	PVC
☐ Fairchild 473 Provider (205) (C-123B) (C-123K)	N22968	20113	54-0664, 40664 (Thai)	PVA
☐ Grumman G-134 Mohawk (OV-1C) (OV-1D)	N947AH	151C	68-15947	PVA
☐ McDonnell M.199-1A Eagle (F-15A)	76-0012	191/A164		PV
☐ North American NA-200 Trojan (T-28B)	N214SF	200-382	Bu138311, N4781E	PVA
☐ North American NA-203 Sabre (F-86H)	53-1338	203-110		PVC
☐ Piper PA-18-135 Super Cub (L-21B)	N10365	18-3953	54-2553, MM54-2553, I-EIUB	PVA

ALLEGHENY ARMS AND ARMOR MUSEUM (PA2)

Address:	502 ½ Main Street West, Smethport, Pennsylvania 16749.
Tel:	814-887-0947 **Fax:** 814-558-6112 **Email:** hvonzog@pennswoods.net
Admission:	Daily 1000-1800.
Location:	About 2 miles north of Smethport on Route 46.

The display was set up as a memorial to those who have served in all branches of the US services. On show are a large number of military vehicles, tanks and guns, many of which are in working order. There are also several boats in the collection. Displays of photographs, uniforms and memorabilia can also be seen.

TYPE	REG/SER	CON. NO.	PI/NOTES	STATUS
☐ Bell 205 Iroquois (UH-1H) (UH-1V)	N4374T	9612	67-17414	PV
☐ Grumman G-128 Intruder (YA2F-1) (YA-6A) (NA-6A)	Bu147867	4		PV
☐ Sikorsky S-58 Choctaw (H-34A) (CH-34A)	'Bu144275'	58842	57-1698, N94485 –	PVX

Pennsylvania

ALLENTOWN MONUMENT (PA3)

Location:	Being restored for display in the area.			
TYPE	**REG/SER**	**CON. NO.**	**PI/NOTES**	**STATUS**
☐ Bell 204 Iroquois (UH-1C) (UH-1M)	66-15098	1826		RA

AMERICAN HELICOPTER MUSEUM AND EDUCATION CENTER (PA4)

Address: 1220 American Boulevard, West Chester, Pennsylvania 19380-4268.
Tel: 610-436-9600 **Fax:** 610-436-8642 **Email:** info@helicoptermuseum.org
Admission: Wednesday-Saturday 1000-1700; Sunday 1200-1700.
Location: About 25 miles west of Philadelphia on Route 3.

This museum was formed in the 1990s and has already acquired a number of interesting designs. The aim is to trace the development of rotary wing flight in the USA. The exhibition features helicopters and autogyros artefacts, models and several 'hands-on' displays. At the end of August 1995 the museum obtained a long-term lease on the former MBB helicopter service building at Brandywine Airport.

The first really successful helicopter in the USA was the Sikorsky VS-300. This was soon followed by designs from other manufacturers such as Bell, Hiller and Piasecki. Types from all these manufacturers can be seen. The Bell 30 made its maiden flight on 19th December 1942. Two of the three built still survive. The design was developed into the Model 47 which was produced in large numbers for both military and civilian use. The Iroquois and Huey Cobra became well known after their use in Vietnam.

Stanley Hiller flew his first helicopter, the XH44, in 1944 and his most successful design was the UH12. The Piasecki company constructed the PV-2 in 1943. A range of twin rotor designs many with the distinctive 'flying banana' fuselage followed. Kaman developed a number of types using intermeshing rotors.

Edward Glatfelter of Newton Square, Pennsylvania built and flew the XRG-65 in 1959. The helicopter was powered by a 65 h.p. Continental engine. The design incorporated several novel ideas and was used to carry out research into rotor control and drive systems. The single example used a Bell 47 tail rotor, Piasecki HUP main blades and a number of parts from Sikorsky designs. Modern light helicopters can also be seen.

In the inter-war period autogyros were being developed. One of the pioneers in America was Harold Pitcairn and an example of his PCA-1 design is on view. In the early 1950s Igor Bensen developed a series of small gyrogliders and gyrocopters. This concept has been developed by both companies and amateur constructors and several examples of these designs are on view.

The Osprey is the first tilt-rotor aircraft to enter production. The concept had been tested in the 1960s but the idea took time to come to fruition. The V-22 can carry about 20 troops and can take off vertically with the rotors in a horizontal position. Once airborne the engines and rotors at the end of the wings can be turned through a right angle and the Osprey behaves as a conventional aircraft.

TYPE	REG/SER	CON. NO.	PI/NOTES	STATUS
☐ Air Command 447 Commander Sport				PV
☐ Bell 47B	NC5H	3		PV
☐ Bell 47D-1 Sioux (H-13D) (OH-13D)			Composite.	PV
☐ Bell 47H-1	N8010E	1355		PV
☐ Bell 204 Iroquois (TH-1L)	Bu157817	6412		PV
☐ Bell 206A Jet Ranger		4		PV
☐ Bell 209 Huey Cobra (AH-1G) (AH-1F)			Front fuselage only.	PV
☐ Bell 209 Huey Cobra (AH-1G) (AH-1F)	68-15138	20672		PV
☐ Bell-Boeing YV-22A Osprey	Bu163913	D0003		PV
☐ Bensen B-8M Gyrocopter	N1938	C-A-M-423-2525		PV
☐ Bensen B-8M Gyrocopter	N1536	CT-1		PV
☐ Boeing-Vertol BV.360	N360BV	001		PV
☐ Bölkow BO 105C			Pod only.	PV
☐ Brantly B.2B	N2294U	467		PV
☐ Enstrom F-28A	N501EH	5		PV
☐ Glatfelter Galaxie XRG-65 Glaticopter	N6576D	XRG-165-A-1		PV
☐ Gyrodyne QH-50C (DSN-3)		DS-1277		PV
☐ Hiller UH12C Raven (H-23G) (H-23G)	62-3759	1407		RA
☐ Hughes 269A Osage (TH-55A)	67-15412	0756		PV
☐ Hughes 369M Cayuse (HO-6) (OH-6A)	65-12916	0001	Also reported as c/n 4.	PV
☐ Hughes 369M Cayuse (MH-6E)	81-23655			PV
☐ Kaman K-20 Seasprite (HU2K-1) (UH-2A) (HH-2D)	Bu149031	35		RA
☐ Parsons Sport Autogyro	N54WP	128		PV
☐ Piasecki 59K Aerial Jeep (VZ-8P)	58-5510			PV
☐ Piasecki PD-22 Work Horse (H-21B) (CH-21B)	54-4003	B.156	54-4003, 800131 (France)	RAD
☐ Piasecki PV-14 (XHJP-1)			Either Bu37976 or Bu 37787	RA
☐ Piasecki PV-17 (HRP-2)	Bu111831			RA
☐ Piasecki PV-18 Retriever (HUP-2) (UH-25B)	Bu128479			PV
☐ Pitcairn PCA-1A	X95N	A-2	On loan from NASM.	PV
☐ PrincetonGem X-2 Air Scooter				PV
☐ Robinson R-22	N9036S	97		PV
☐ Rotorway Scorpion 133	N9011Z	3279		PV
☐ Rotorway Scorpion Too				PV
☐ Sikorsky S-51 Dragonfly	9603	5130	In Canadian markings.	PV
☐ Sikorsky S-51 Dragonfly (H-5G)	N1052		48-0531	RA
☐ Sikorsky S-52-3 (HO5S-1)	Bu130136	52094		PV
☐ Sikorsky S-61B Sea King (HSS-2) (HH-3A)	Bu151556			PV
☐ Sikorsky S-62A Seaguard (HH-52A)	1383	62054		PV
☐ Sikorsky VS-300 (R)			Front fuselage only.	PV
☐ Sikorsky VS-316B Hoverfly II (R-6A)	N75610		43-45531	RA
☐ Sud-Ouest SO.1221S Djinn	57-6106	1025FR75	F-WIFM	PV
☐ Vertol V.43 Shawnee (H-21C) (CH-21C)				RAD
☐ Vertol V.43 Shawnee (H-21C) (CH-21C)	55-4140	C.94		PV

BEAVERDALE MONUMENT (PA5)

| Location: | On permanent view at ALP 460 at 506 Cedar Street in the centre of the town. |

TYPE	REG/SER	CON. NO.	PI/NOTES	STATUS
☐ Bell 209 Huey Cobra (AH-1G) (AH-1F)	68-15085	20619		PV

BLAKESLEE MONUMENT (PA6)

| Location: | At the Jack Frost Mountain Resort south of the town. |

TYPE	REG/SER	CON. NO.	PI/NOTES	STATUS
☐ Bell 204 Iroquois (HU-1A) (UH-1A)	60-3535	181		PV

BRADFORD MONUMENT (PA7)

| Location: | On permanent view at the airport which is about 12 miles south of the town on Highway 59. |

TYPE	REG/SER	CON. NO.	PI/NOTES	STATUS
☐ Bell 205 Iroquois (UH-1D) (UH-1V)	66-0902	5385		PV

BUTLER COUNTY HISTORICAL SOCIETY (PA8)

Address:	119 West Castle Street, Butler, Pennsylvania 16003.
Tel:	724-283-8116 **Fax:** 724-263-2505 **Email:** bchissoc@zoominternet.net
Admission:	Monday-Friday 0900-1600.
Location:	In the centre of the town.

The society was founded in 1927 when a group of residents met to discuss ways to preserve local history. Now four historic sites are maintained and a large archive has been gathered. The Heritage Center opened in 1995 in a three storey building in the town. Examples of vehicles produced in Butler by the Bantam company can be seen. The development of other local industries is portrayed. The Taylorcraft is currently in store.

TYPE	REG/SER	CON. NO.	PI/NOTES	STATUS
☐ Taylorcraft BL-65	N23853	1489	NC23853	RA

BUTLER MONUMENT (PA9)

| Location: | On permanent view at the airport which is west of the town. |

TYPE	REG/SER	CON. NO.	PI/NOTES	STATUS
☐ Bell 209 Huey Cobra (AH-1G) (AH-1F)	68-15057	20591		PV

CARROLLTOWN MONUMENT (PA10)

| Location: | On permanent view in the American Legion Park on Highway 219 in the northern part of the town. |

TYPE	REG/SER	CON. NO.	PI/NOTES	STATUS
☐ Bell 209 Huey Cobra (AH-1G) (AH-1F)	67-15795	20459		PV

CHAMBERSBURG MONUMENT (PA11)

| Location: | On permanent view in the town. |

TYPE	REG/SER	CON. NO.	PI/NOTES	STATUS
☐ Bell 209 Huey Cobra (AH-1G) (AH-1F)	67-15653	20317		PV

COLONIAL FLYING CORPS MUSEUM (PA12)

Address:	New Garden Aviation Inc, Newark Road, PO Box 481, Toughkenamon, Pennsylvania 19374-0481.
Tel:	610-268-2048 **Email:** everitt@n57.com
Admission:	Now closed; most aircraft sold.
Location:	The airfield is about 1 mile west of the town just off Route 1.

Set up in the early 1970s, the collection is housed in several hangars at the airfield. In addition to the aircraft there are vehicles, engines and photographs. The airfield is owned by members of the Dupont family with flying schools and an overhaul business also in residence.

The Fairchild company was based Hagerstown in Maryland for many years and several products from their factory can be seen. The 24 series of high wing monoplanes achieved fame worldwide and the Cornell was a successful trainer during World War II. Piper was based at Lock Haven in Pennsylvania for over 50 years and a number of their designs are in residence. The field is home to a Tiger Moth and a Chipmunk.

The University of Liverpool Man Powered Aircraft was a redesign of the Hatfield Puffin II with a new fuselage.

The Alarus CH200 is a two seat low wing monoplane designed by Chris Heintz. The type was put into production in Eastman Georgia and a military version is constructed in Jordan and Iraq. The HP-10 glider was designed by R.E. Schreder and flown in the 1961 US National Championships. Steve Dupont later carried out some modifications to the sailplane. The Helisoar company bought the rights to the design but they only completed a few examples before they ceased production. Most of the aircraft listed are privately owned and are often in locked hangars.

Pennsylvania

TYPE	REG/SER	CON. NO.	PI/NOTES	STATUS
☐ Aircraft Manufacturing and Design Alarus CH2000	N8501Q	200066		PV
☐ Bellanca 14-13-3 Crusair Senior	N6506N	1624		RAC
☐ Cessna 140A	N1160D	15723		PVA
☐ Cessna 150L	N1592Q	15072892		PVA
☐ Cessna 170	N3958V	18277		PVA
☐ Cessna 182A	N4825D	34925		PVA
☐ De Havilland DH.82A Tiger Moth	N4808	82700	R4759, G-ANKN, CF-JJI	PVA
☐ De Havilland DHC.1 Chipmunk 22 (T.10)	N48250	C1/0251	WD308, G 150 (Ghana)	PVA
☐ Ercoupe 415CD	N415CD	4523		PVA
☐ Fairchild 24G	N19146	2994	NC19146	RA
☐ Fairchild M-62A Cornell (PT-19A)	N54254	T42-1831	42-2743	PVA
☐ Fairchild M-62A Cornell (PT-19B)	N60112	T43-5457	42-82870	PVA
☐ Grumman G-36 Wildcat (FM-2)	N1352N	5831	Bu86773	RA
☐ Helisoar HP-10	N916Z	007		PV
☐ Mann SB-26	N57SM	002		PVA
☐ Nanchang CJ-6A				PVA
☐ Piper J-3C-65 Cub	N41110	7756	NC41110	PVA
☐ Piper J-3C-65 Cub	N98248	18417	NC98248	PVA
☐ Piper J-3C-65 Cub	N6731H	19942	NC6731H	PVA
☐ Piper J-3C-65 Cub	N6825H	20048	NC6825H	PVA
☐ Piper J-3C-65 Cub	NC6925H	20158	NC6925H, N6925H	PVA
☐ Piper J-3C-65 Cub	NC2211M	21002	NC2211M, N2211M	PVA
☐ Piper J-3L-50 Cub	N26197	7076	NC26197	RAC
☐ Piper PA-15 Vagabond	N4551H	15-325	NC4551H	PVA
☐ Piper PA-18-150 Super Cub	N7769D	18-5948		PVA
☐ Piper PA-20 Pacer 125	N6941K	20-45		PVA
☐ Piper PA-23-160 Apache	N6000P	23-1236		PVA
☐ PZL Koliber 150A	N150AY	04940073		PVA
☐ Scheibe SF-24A Motor Spatz	N4664T	4009		S
☐ Spartan C-3-135	NC61K		Fuselage only.	RA
☐ Stolp SA.300 Starduster Too	N14MM	62		PVA
☐ Taylorcraft BC-12D	N43172	6831	NC43172	PVA
☐ Taylorcraft DCO-65 Grasshopper (L-2B)	N3113S	L-4960	(USAAF)	PVA
☐ Taylorcraft DCO-65 Grasshopper (L-2M)	N50135/'326128'	L-5440	43-26128	PVA
☐ University of Liverpool Man Powered Aircraft				PV
☐ Vultee V-79 Valiant (BT-13B) (SNV-2)	N396	79-266	944-31765), Bu52304, N52210	RAC
☐ Wittman W.10 Tailwind	N228JL	970		PVA

COMMEMORATIVE AIR FORCE (KEYSTONE WING) (PA13)

Address:	Hangar 20, Allegheny County Airport, West Mifflin, Pennsylvania 15122-2673.
Tel:	724-693-8078 **Email:** TomB17G@verizon.net
Admission:	By prior permission only.
Location:	In the southern suburbs of the town off Route 51.

The wing was formed in February 1986 and the L-5G was assigned the following June. The Sentinel was dismantled and restored to its original configuration over a two year period. This aircraft flies in a military colour scheme.

The Stinson Voyager arrived in October 1991 and was completely restored over the next few years. The high-wing monoplane arrived as a basket case in 2002. Members of the wing have been steadily restoring the aircraft in the colour scheme of one operated by the Civil Air Patrol. The rebuild was completed in the summer of 2010 and it will now be flying again after half a century of inactivity.

TYPE	REG/SER	CON. NO.	PI/NOTES	STATUS
☐ Stinson 10A Voyager	N26295	7582	NC26295	RA
☐ Stinson V-76 Sentinel (L-5G) (OY-1)	N2581B		(USAAF), Bu120473	RAA

DEFENSE DISTRIBUTION CENTER EAST (PA14)

Location:	By prior permission only at the site which is on the west side of Capital City Airport just east of Harrisburg.

TYPE	REG/SER	CON. NO.	PI/NOTES	STATUS
☐ Bell 209 Huey Cobra (AH-1G) (AH-1S)				RA
☐ Fairchild-Republic A-10A Thunderbolt II	75-0303	A10-52		RA
☐ North American NA-332 Buckeye (T-2C)	Bu157060	332-31		RA

DOYLESTOWN MONUMENT (PA15)

Location:	Due to go on view in a park in the town.

TYPE	REG/SER	CON. NO.	PI/NOTES	STATUS
☐ Bell 205 Iroquois (UH-1H)				RA

DU BOIS MONUMENT (PA16)

Location:	On permanent view at VFW 813 at 114 Fuller Avenue in the north western part of the town.

TYPE	REG/SER	CON. NO.	PI/NOTES	STATUS
☐ Bell 209 Huey Cobra (AH-1G) (AH-1F)	66-15348	20104		PV

EAGLES MERE AIR MUSEUM (PA17)

Address:	467 Belrose Lane, St. Davids, Pennsylvania 19087-4418.
Tel:	570-946-7663 Email: merrittcapital@earthlink.net
Admission:	July–September Sunday 1000-1700 or by prior permission only.
Location:	At the airport which is about 2 miles east of the town on Route 42.

George Jenkins has assembled an interesting collection of aircraft, aircraft engines, and artefacts from the golden age of flying. The museum is located on a private airfield and the majority of the aircraft are airworthy. A number were acquired when the Trone Collection at Brodhead in Wisconsin was dispersed following Dennis Trone's death in 2008. The oldest type is the Swanson biplane built in the early 1920s and active until at least 1936. The aircraft was initially powered by a 90 hp Curtiss OX-5 engine. In the 1930s it was re-engined with an 80 hp Le Rhone radial. The airframe was stored in a museum near the University of South Dakota and sold in an auction in the mid-1980s. The airframe is awaiting a major rebuild.

The Polson Special was designed in California and one was built in 1922 and another five years later. The Thunderbird Aircraft Company was set up at Glendale in California in the late 1920s. About 40 examples of the W-14 two seat biplane, powered by a variety of engines, were produced. The Bellanca CH-400 Skyrocket is the only surviving genuine example.

The other in the Virginia Aviation museum is a conversion of a CH-300 Pacemaker. Charles Lindbergh wanted to use a Skyrocket on his solo-Atlantic flight but this plan did not materialise. The rugged high-wing monoplane was popular in the harsh conditions encountered in Alaska and Canada.

The Bird CK which is being rebuilt was once owned by Wiley Post. The Aeronca C-3 originally belonged to Bill Piper and is believed to have operated on floats from the Susquehanna River. Travel Air built only 11 examples of the high wing 10-D before the factory closed. The aircraft operated in Illinois and Idaho until 1955. After a period in store it moved to California as a rebuild project but this never took place. The museum acquired it in 2004 and it was taken to Florida. The 10D flew again in July 2006. The two diminutive Lincoln Bird biplanes, designed by Swen Swanson, are now rarities. One is powered by an Anzani three cylinder radial and the other by a Salmson nine cylinder motor. Also in the hangars are aircraft toys, signs, posters and pictures.

TYPE	REG/SER	CON. NO.	PI/NOTES	STATUS
☐ Aeronca PC-3 (C-3)	NC13082	A-246	NC13082, N13082	PVA
☐ Aeronca 7AC Champion	N1813E	7AC-5380	NC1813E	PVA
☐ Alexander Eaglerock A-4	NC6927	578	NC6927, N6927	PVC
☐ Bellanca CH-400 Skyrocket	NC779W	617	NC779W, N779W	PVA
☐ Boeing-Stearman E75 Kaydet (PT-13D) (N2S-5)	N75MW	75-8405	42-109372, Bu43311, XB-SEF	PVA
☐ Brunner-Winkle Bird CK	NC765N	CK4033		PVA
☐ Curtiss 50 Robin	NC76F	45	NC76E, N7890C	PVA
☐ De Havilland DH.82A Tiger Moth	N8232	3963	N6659	PVA
☐ General Aircraft Company Thunderbird W-14	NC5830	2812	NC5830, N5830	PVA
☐ Kinner Sportster B	NC13776	102	NC13776, N13776	PVC
☐ Kreider-Reisner KR-31 Challenger (C-2)	NC7744	219	NC7744, N7744	PVA
☐ Lincoln Sport	NC1047	101	NC1047, N1047	PVA
☐ Lincoln Sport LS-2	N956	1		PVA
☐ Luscombe 8C Silvaire	N28588	1417	NC28588	PVA
☐ Nussbaumer Baumer-Heath	N7123	12		PVA
☐ Piper J-3C-65 Cub (L-4B)	N51502	9790	43-605	PVA
☐ Pitcairn PA-6 Super Mailwing	NC548K	48	NC548K, N548K	PVA
☐ Polson Special	N271	102		PVA
☐ Swanson SF-4	N1035	4	NC3522	PVC
☐ Travel Air 10-D	NC418N	10-2011	NC418N, N418N	PVA
☐ Travel Air 3000	NC49603	458		PVA
☐ Waco 10 (GXE)	NC6974	1554	NC6974, N6974	PVA
☐ Waco CTO	NC657N	3166	NC657N, N657N	PVA

EAST BERLIN MONUMENT (PA18)

Location:	On permanent view at VFW 8896 on Locust Street in the western part of the town.

TYPE	REG/SER	CON. NO.	PI/NOTES	STATUS
☐ Grumman G-303 Tomcat (F-14B)	Bu162916	564		PV

EGYPT MONUMENT (PA19)

Location:	On permanent view at VFW 7293 on Spring Mill Road in the north eastern part of the town.

TYPE	REG/SER	CON. NO.	PI/NOTES	STATUS
☐ Grumman G-303 Tomcat (F-14A)	Bu158617	18		PV

ERIE MONUMENT (PA20)

Location:	On permanent view in a cemetery on Edinboro Road in the southern part of the town.

TYPE	REG/SER	CON. NO.	PI/NOTES	STATUS
☐ Lockheed 880-75-13 Starfire (F-97A) (F-94C)	51-5671	880-7734		PV

FRANKLIN INSTITUTE SCIENCE MUSEUM (PA21)

Address:	222 North 20th Street, Philadelphia, Pennsylvania 19103.
Tel:	215-448-1200 Fax: 215-448-1235 Email: membership@fi.edu
Admission:	Daily 0930-1700.
Location:	In the centre of the city close to the Schuylkill River.

Pennsylvania

Founded in 1824, the Institute is one of the oldest museums in the country. Sections cover the physical sciences, mechanical and nuclear engineering, transport and communications. In all areas there are many innovative 'hands-on' displays.

The aeronautical collection was started many years ago and includes the complete engineering notes, sketches and plans of the Wright Flyer.

These historic documents were presented to the museum by Orville Wright and also on show is the 13th aircraft to be built by the brothers. This biplane last flew in December 1934 to commemorate the 31st anniversary of the first flight.

Outside is the Budd amphibian which is based on the Savoia-Marchetti SM.56. The aircraft was built in the city in 1931 to demonstrate spot welding stainless steel construction. Since 1934 it has been exhibited without fabric to show the durability of the airframe.

The Quickie has been acquired to show a modern innovative design using composite materials. Also on view are a number of models explaining the principles of flight.

TYPE	REG/SER	CON. NO.	PI/NOTES	STATUS
☐ Bölkow BO 105 (FSM)				PV
☐ Budd BB-1	NR749N	1		PV
☐ Lockheed 580 (T-33A)	53-6038	580-9641		PV
☐ Mitchell Nimbus 3L	N7864C	001	On loan from NSM, NY.	PV
☐ Quickie Aircraft Quickie 1 (Rutan 54)	N11794	131		PV
☐ Wright B	NR14333			PV

GLENSIDE MONUMENT (PA22)

Location:	On permanent view in the town.

TYPE	REG/SER	CON. NO.	PI/NOTES	STATUS
☐ Bell 205 Iroquois (UH-1D) (UH-1H)	65-9897	4941		PV

GOLDEN AGE AIR MUSEUM (PA23)

Address:	371 Airport Road, Bethel, Pennsylvania 19507-9692.
Tel:	717-933-9566 Fax: 717-933-9566 Email: info@goldenageair.org
Admission:	May–October Friday-Saturday 1000-1700; Sunday 1100-1700.
Location:	About 1 mile north east of the town.

This museum was established in 1997 by Paul D. Dougherty and his son. A hangar at Grimes Field houses this interesting collection of aircraft mainly from the inter-war period. Two biplanes dating from the end of World War I are the famous Curtiss Jenny and Standard J-1 biplanes. Both types have been restored and the Jenny last flew in the late 1920s.

A replica of the 1924 Dormoy Flying Bathtub can be seen. Featuring a parasol wing with a nacelle clad in sheet metal its 20 h.p. Henderson engine gave it a speed in excess of 70 m.p.h. In September 1924 it won the 140-mile Rickenbacker Trophy at the National Air Races at Dayton. The sole Winstead Special was built by two brothers in Wichita in 1926. The biplane flew with a circus and was put into store in 1937. Acquired from the Airpower Museum in Iowa the Special has been restored to its flying circus condition.

Only 38 Star Cavalier high wing monoplanes were built between 1928 and 1936 and these were in five versions depending upon the engine fitted. The unique Allison Sport Plane was built in 1930 and is awaiting restoration. The collection also includes a number of classic motor vehicles.

TYPE	REG/SER	CON. NO.	PI/NOTES	STATUS
☐ Aeronca C-3	NC17404	A-717	NC17404, N17404	PVA
☐ Allison Sport Plane				PV
☐ Brunner-Winkle Bird CK	NC726N	4037	NC726N, N726N	PVA
☐ Cessna AW	N4180G	196	NC9801, N9801	PV
☐ Cessna 195	N195PD	7460		PVA
☐ Culver LFA Cadet	N34856	LFA-269	NC34856	PVA
☐ Curtiss 1C Jenny (JN-4D)	N2946	8047	N2407	PVA
☐ Curtiss 51 Fledgling			Fuselage frame only.	PV
☐ Curtiss-Wright CW-1 Junior				PV
☐ Dormoy Flying Bathtub (R)				PVC
☐ Ercoupe 415C	N93687	1010	NC93687	PVA
☐ Experimental Aircraft Association P-1 Biplane				PVA
☐ Fokker Dr I (R)	N2009S/'425/17'	1		PVA
☐ Great Lakes 2T-1A	N75M	6914-G-408		PVA
☐ Great Lakes 2T-1L	NX430Y	6824J-384		PVA
☐ Heath Parasol				PV
☐ Mono Aircraft Monocoupe 70	N6731	134	NC6731	PVA
☐ Mono Aircraft Monocoupe 90A	N11750	A-679	NC11750	PV
☐ Pietenpol B4-A Aircamper	NX54N	1		PVA
☐ Roloff RLU-1 Breezy	N2766	GE-1		PVA
☐ Rumpler C V (R)	'C.V 1704/17'	1704	N1915E	PVAX
☐ Schleicher Ka-4 Rhönlerche II	N144KA	1046	D-6316	PVA
☐ Sopwith Pup (R)				RAC
☐ Sperry-Verville M-1 Messenger (R)				PV
☐ Standard J-1				RAC
☐ Star Cavalier B	N451	105	NC450	RA
☐ Star Cavalier E	N350V	121	NC350V	PV
☐ Taylor E-2 Cub	NC13146	54	NC13146, N13146	PVA
☐ Taylor-Young A				RAC
☐ Taylorcraft BC-12D	NC43277	6936	NC43277, N43277	PV
☐ Travel Air 2000 (B)	N1081	206	NC1083	PVA
☐ Waco ASO	NC4453Y	1998	NC4453Y, N4453Y	PVA
☐ White D-XII Der Jager	N49JA	174		PV
☐ White P	N81AC	AW-1		PVA
☐ Winstead Special	N2297	1	NX2297	PVA

GREENSBURG MONUMENT (PA24)

Location:	On permanent view at Lynch Field on Highway 119 in the northern part of the town.

TYPE	REG/SER	CON. NO.	PI/NOTES	STATUS
☐ Bell 205 Iroquois (UH-1D) (UH-1H)	66-1129	5612		PV

HAMBURG MONUMENT (PA25)

Location:	On view during opening hours in Cabela's store at 100 Cabela Drive west of the town.

TYPE	REG/SER	CON. NO.	PI/NOTES	STATUS
☐ Piper PA-18-150 Super Cub				PV

HAROLD F. PITCAIRN WINGS OF FREEDOM MUSEUM (PA26)

Address:	NAS-JRB, Willow Grove, Pennsylvania 19090
Tel:	215-672-2277 Fax: 215-675-4005 Email: dvhaacurator@dvhaa.org
Admission:	April–October Wednesday 1030-1500 1700-2000, Saturday-Sunday 1030-1600; November–March Wednesday 1030-1500.
Location:	About 15 miles north of Philadelphia on Route 611.

In 1942 the Navy took over Pitcairn Field and the following year it became Willow Grove NAS. At the present time the site is home to reserve units of the Air Force, Army, Marine Corps and Navy along with squadrons of the Pennsylvania Army and Air National Guard.

For many years a display of preserved aircraft was sited by the main road alongside the base. Those on show including an Arado Ar 196, a Kawanishi N1K1, a Kawanishi N1K2, a Messerschmitt Me 262B and a Nakajima B6N1 These were exhibited in the open for many years. The historic aircraft, suffering from years of exposure to the elements, were reclaimed by their owners, the National Air and Space Museum and the National Museum of Naval Aviation after plans for an ambitious museum complex came to nothing. One of the five Convair Sea Darts built remained and the spaces were filled by more modern types. The Delaware Valley Historical Aircraft Association was formed with the aim of creating a museum. An exhibition building has now been completed and the Messerschmitt Me 262, which went away for restoration, is now inside. A display tracing the history of the historic airfield is being set up. The Sea Dart delta was fitted with a ski undercarriage enabling it to operate from sheltered waters. The prototype first flew in January 1953 when it inadvertently took off on a fast taxi run in San Diego Bay. The official maiden flight was on 9th April. Only five examples were completed with one disintegrating in flight in November 1954. The project was cancelled and the remaining four aircraft have all survived for preservation.

Another rarity is one of the few surviving Vought Cutlass tailless jet fighters. Two other combat types from this period are the Fury and the Panther which gave excellent service to Navy and Marine squadrons. The Messerschmitt, which went away for restoration, returned and has been reclaimed by the National Museum of Naval Aviation, Pensacola.

TYPE	REG/SER	CON. NO.	PI/NOTES	STATUS
☐ Bell 47G Sioux (H-13G) (OH-13G)	52-7833	1060		PV
☐ Bell 205 Iroquois (UH-1H) (UH-1V)	68-16614	11273		PV
☐ Convair 2 Seadart (YF2Y-1) (YF-7A)	Bu135764			PV
☐ Douglas A-4M Skyhawk	Bu158182	14219		PV
☐ Fokker D VIII (Scale R)				PV
☐ Grumman G-79 Panther (F9F-2)	Bu127120	K-526		PV
☐ Grumman G-96 Trader (TF-1) (C-1A)	Bu146034	064		PV
☐ Grumman G-303 Tomcat (F-14A)	Bu160386	242	On base	PV
☐ Kaman K-20 Seasprite (SH-2F)	Bu162576	227		PV
☐ Lockheed 080 Shooting Star (P-80C) (F-80C) (TO-1) (TV-1)	Bu33824	080-1982	47-0221	PV
☐ North American NA-244 Fury (FJ-4B) (AF-1E)	Bu143568	244-76		PV
☐ Piasecki PV-18 Retriever (HUP-2) (UH-25B)	Bu128517			PV
☐ Sikorsky S-58 Seabat (HSS-1N) (SH-34J)	Bu145694	58997	Bu145694, N46920	PV
☐ Vought F-8A Crusader (F8U-1)	Bu143806			PV
☐ Vought V-366 Cutlass (F7U-3)	Bu129642			PV

HARRISBURG AIR NATIONAL GUARD BASE (PA27)

Location:	At the International Airport which is about 5 miles south east of the city on Route 230.

TYPE	REG/SER	CON. NO.	PI/NOTES	STATUS
☐ North American NA-122 Mustang (P-51D) (FSM)	'44-73240'			PVX

HARRISBURG MONUMENT (PA28)

Location:	On permanent view in the Bass Pro Shop at 3601 Paxton Street in the town.

TYPE	REG/SER	CON. NO.	PI/NOTES	STATUS
☐ Cessna 140				PV

HERITAGE AIRCRAFT (PA29)

Address:	600 Horizon Drive, Chalfont, Pennsylvania 18914-3961.
Tel:	215-643-3617
Admission:	By prior permission only.
Location:	Some aircraft at Toughkenamon Airfield which is about 1 mile west of the town – others in store.

Pennsylvania

This private collection contains many interesting types. The Inland Sport was designed by L.D. Bonebrake and first flew in 1928. Three versions of the parasol monoplane were built. The S-300 was powered by a 65 h.p. Le Blond, the R-400 by a 90 h.p. Warner and the W-500 by a 125 h.p. Warner. Only 28 were manufactured and the Sport had some racing successes.

One Vega was originally delivered to the Shell Aviation Company in 1933. This aircraft was one of seven built as the 5C model with larger vertical tail surfaces and was the penultimate Vega produced by Lockheed. The prototype Kinner Playboy R-l flew in 1934 and later eight examples of the R-5 were made. The Playboy in the collection was the last one built and left the Glendale factory in 1935.

Well over 1,000 Waco 10s were manufactured in the late 1920s. The ASO was an improved version with a Wright J-5 radial. The ATO incorporated the 'taperwing' which became a feature on many Waco designs.

The Curtiss Fledgling trainer was developed for the navy in the late 1920s and about 50 were ordered. A civil version of the biplane with a less powerful engine followed and the Curtiss Flying service operated over 100 in the 1930s.

TYPE	REG/SER	CON. NO.	PI/NOTES	STATUS
☐ Beech D17S (UC-43) (GB-2)	N25K	6881	44-67775, FT511, Bu32901, NC25	RA
☐ Boeing-Stearman D75N1 Kaydet (PT-27)	N58957	75-3850	42-15661, FJ800	RA
☐ Curtiss 51 Fledgling	N656M	B-109	NC656M	RA
☐ Curtiss 51 Fledgling	N470K	B-74	NC470K	RA
☐ Fokker D VI (R)	N29WR	2620		RA
☐ Inland Sport W-500	NC8088	W-505	NC8088, N8088	RA
☐ Kinner Playboy R-5	NC14963	228	NC14963, N14963	RA
☐ Lockheed 1 Vega	N7044	11	N7044	RA
☐ Lockheed 5 Vega	NC7429	18	NC7429, N7429	RA
☐ Lockheed 5C Vega	NC13705	203	NC13705, N13705	RA
☐ Piper J-3C-65 Cub	N70596	17606	NC70596	RA
☐ Piper PA-18-105 Super Cub	N116T	18-2230		RA
☐ Pitcairn PA-6 Super Mailwing	NC214H	39	NC214H, N214H	RA
☐ Pitcairn PA-7S Sport Mailwing	NC54W	144	NC54W, N54W	RA
☐ Pitcairn PA-7S Sport Mailwing	N97WA	149	NC97W	RA
☐ Royal Aircraft Factory S.E.5A (R)	N5348	5348		PV
☐ Sopwith F.1 Camel (R)	N2346	6234		RA
☐ Standard J-1				RA
☐ Travel Air S-6000B	NC411N	6B-2024	NC411N, N411N	RA
☐ Waco 10 (GXE)	NC5273	1470	NC5273, N5273	RA
☐ Waco 10 (GXE)	NC8564	1927	NC8564, N8564	RA
☐ Waco ASO	NC931H	A-143	NC931H, N931H	RA
☐ Waco ASO	NC4902	A-2	NC4902, N4902	RA
☐ Waco ASO	NC604N	A-3107	NC604N, N604N	RA
☐ Waco ASO (DSO)	NC9538	A-37	NC9539, N9539	RA
☐ Waco ATO	NC926H	A-121	NC926H, N926H	RA
☐ Waco ATO	NC949H	A-134	NC949H, N949H	RA
☐ Waco BSO	NC752K	A-153	NC752K, N752K	RA
☐ Waco YKS-6	NC16517	4508	NC16517, N16517	RA
☐ Waco ZGC-7	NC17725	4584	NC17725, N17725	RA
☐ Waco ZQC-6	NC16590	4494	NC16590, N16590	RA

IMPERIAL MONUMENT (PA30)

Location: On permanent view at VFW 7714 on Old Steubenville Pike in the south eastern part of the town.

TYPE	REG/SER	CON. NO.	PI/NOTES	STATUS
☐ North American NA-201 Sabre (F-86D) (F-86L)	53-0665	201-109		PV

JERSEY SHORE MONUMENT (PA31)

Location: On permanent view at ALP 36 at 320 Seminary Road in the north eastern part of the town.

TYPE	REG/SER	CON. NO.	PI/NOTES	STATUS
☐ Bell 205 Iroquois (UH-1D) (UH-1H)	66-16014	5708		PV

JOHNSTOWN ARMED SERVICES MUSEUM (PA32)

Address: PO Box 2381, Warminster, Pennsylvania 18974.
Admission: Not yet open.
Location: About 20 miles north of Philadelphia off Route 263.

The Naval Air Station at Warminster closed in the late 1990s. A group of enthusiasts are working hard to set up a military museum in the area. Archive material along with memorabilia has been acquired. Three helicopters have been acquired and these are stored at Cambria Airport with the National Guard.

TYPE	REG/SER	CON. NO.	PI/NOTES	STATUS
☐ Bell 209 Huey Cobra (AH-1G) (AH-1S)	70-15984	20928		RA
☐ Bell 209 Huey Cobra (AH-1S) (AH-1F)	79-23209	22254		RA
☐ Hughes 369M Cayuse (HO-6) (OH-6A)	66-14379	0520		RA

KLBE AIR MUSEUM (PA33)

Address: Westmoreland County Airport Authority, R.D.1, Box 396, Latrobe, Pennsylvania 15650.
Tel: 412-539-8100
Admission: Sunday 1000-1600
Location: Latrobe is about 25 miles south east of Pittsburgh off Route 30.

On 12th May 1939 a Stinson Reliant made the first mail pick up at Latrobe Airport. Westmoreland County decided that they should look for a Reliant as centrepiece of their proposed museum. An example was found in Montana. The aircraft had crashed in Alaska in 1952 and was recovered and rebuilt in 1980.

The Stinson was flown to Latrobe in 1986 and in 1990 was restored to the colours of the original mailplane by the Pittsburgh Institute of Aeronautics. The dream became a reality when the museum opened on May 29th 2010 in a hangar at the airport. In addition to the aircraft there is a theatre showing aviation films.

TYPE	REG/SER	CON. NO.	PI/NOTES	STATUS
☐ Cessna 150				PV
☐ Great Lakes 2T-1A				PV
☐ Stinson V-77 Reliant (AT-19)	NC29767	77-61	42-46700, FK874, Bu11441, NC29767, N29767	PV
☐ WSK SBlim-2 (Lim-1) (MiG-15)	N302LA/'302'	1A 03-302	3302 (Poland) – in false Soviet markings.	PV

LOWER BURRELL MONUMENT (PA34)

Location:	On permanent view at VFW 92 at 1836 Wildlife Lodge Road to the south of the town.

TYPE	REG/SER	CON. NO.	PI/NOTES	STATUS
☐ Bell 204 Iroquois (UH-1C) (UH-1M)	'092'	1299	64-14175	PVX

MID-ATLANTIC AIR MUSEUM (PA35)

Address:	11 Museum Drive, PO Box 105, Reading Regional Airport, Pennsylvania 19605.
Tel:	610-372-7333 Email: maam@maam.org
Admission:	Daily 0930-1600.
Location:	About 3 miles north west of the town off Route 183.

The museum was formed in 1980 and made its first home at Harrisburg International Airport, the former Olmstead Air Force Base. In 1986 a move was made to Schuylkill Airport where a purpose-built museum was planned. These plans came to nothing and on 28th December 1987 the collection transferred to Reading Regional Airport.

A large hangar is in use along with workshops, a small indoor exhibition and storage buildings. Many of the aircraft are maintained in flying condition including a number of two- and four-engined transports, airliners and warbirds. The museum has won many awards at shows with its fleet.

The Northrop Black Widow force landed 7,000 feet up a mountain in New Guinea in 1945. The aircraft survived in reasonably good condition and returned to the USA in 1985. Restoration to flying condition is underway and when complete it will be the only airworthy example of its type. In the spring of 2006 the P-61 fuselage and inner wings were joined and the aircraft was rolled out on its undercarriage. There is still a long way to go before this major project is finished.

Local industry is represented by the Piper designs and a number of homebuilts. Only a small number of autogyros

from the inter-war period exist and the museum has a Kellett KD-1A on display. Kellett was given a licence by Cierva and Pitcairn to develop the concept and his first design flew in 1935. The first scheduled autogyro service was flown by a KD-1 from the roof of the main post office in Philadelphia to Camden New Jersey.

A rarity is the Custer CCW-5 featuring the channel wing. The prototype CCW-5 was built by Baumann Aircraft in 1952/3 and the first production model was completed by Custer in 1964. The restored Heath Parasol is one of the small number of factory-built examples and the less common CNA-40 Midwing is in store. The unique Troyer VX-1 was completed in 1939. The Spratt 108 was built in Pennsylvania in 1973 by Robert Quaintance and flew for many hours.

In the early part of the 20th century George Spratt developed the idea of a tilting wing to control flight. He and his son built several designs to test this theory. The museum is steadily acquiring aircraft and has many airframes in store awaiting restoration. A wide range of types can now be seen and this should increase in future years as more are brought out of store and restored for the exhibition.

TYPE	REG/SER	CON. NO.	PI/NOTES	STATUS
☐ Aeronca C-3	N16259	A-647	NC16259	S
☐ Aeronca K	N17495	K-13	NC17495	S
☐ Aeronca K	N18834	K-100	NC18834	S
☐ Aeronca K	N19336	K-204	NC19336	S
☐ American Aerolights Double Eagle	N749AA	400164		PV
☐ American Aerolights Eagle				PV
☐ American Eagle Eaglet 231	NC467V	1022	NC467V, N467V	RA
☐ Arrow Sport F	NC16470	2	NC16470, N16470	RA
☐ Auster J/1 Autocrat	N22443	2034	OO-ABH, LX-ABH, LX-ACD, F-BEPC	RAC
☐ Bede BD-5B	N5BE	2931B		RA
☐ Bede BD-5B	N472MA	472		RA
☐ Beech G18S	N404H	BA-590	N404G	PVA
☐ Bensen B-8M Gyrocopter	N338SM			PV
☐ Boeing-Stearman A75N1 Kaydet (PT-17)	N26M	75-1925	41-8366	RA
☐ Briegleb BG-12B-GT	N4105G	GET-004		PV
☐ Brunner-Winkle Bird A-T (A)	N15K	1062	NC15	RA
☐ Bushby-Long M-1 Midget Mustang	N12RR	1		RA
☐ Cessna T-50 Bobcat (C-78) (UC-78)	N41793	5855	43-31917	RA
☐ Cessna 150M Commuter	N714GR	15079169		RA
☐ Cessna 172L Skyhawk	N80522	17256252		RA
☐ Culver LCA Cadet	N34781	237	NC34781	PV
☐ Custer CCW-5	N5855V	1		PV
☐ De Havilland DH.104 Dove 5A	N557JC	04380	N1576V, N1900H	PV
☐ De Havilland DH.104 Dove 6A (2A)	N234D	04387	N1557V, CF-EYL	RAD
☐ Douglas DC-3A-467 Skytrain (C-47D) (R4D-6) (R4D-6S) (SC-47J)	N229GB	15429/26874	43-49613, Bu50819, N9119Z, N60, N68, N68AH	PVA
☐ Elias EC-1 Aircoupe	NX3981	401	X3981	RAC

Pennsylvania

☐ Ercoupe 415G	N3430H	4055		PV
☐ Fairchild 24G	N19139	2987	NC19139	PVA
☐ Fairchild M-62A Cornell (PT-19)	N119EC	T40-308	40-2594	RA
☐ Fairchild M-62A Cornell (PT-19B)	N50024	6143AE	42-47965	RA
☐ Fairchild M-62A Cornell (PT-19B)	N60651	T43-5651	42-83064	RA
☐ Fairchild 110 Flying Boxcar (R4Q-2)	N175ML	10844	Bu131677	PV
☐ Fleet 7	N63V	402	NC63V	RA
☐ Grumman G-40 Avenger (TBM-3)	NL109K	3700	Bu53638, CF-KCL, C-FKCL, N109K	PVA
☐ Heath CNA-40	N12882	C-52	NC12882	S
☐ Heath LNB-4 Parasol	NC15792	1006	NC15792, N15792	PVA
☐ Hild-Marshonet 17 (R)				RA
☐ Kellett KD.1A (KD.1)	NC14742	101	X14742, NC14742, N14742, N109K	PV
☐ Kinner Sportster B-1	N727W	138	NC14235	PV
☐ Lockheed 726-45-17 Neptune (P2V-7) (P2V-7S) (SP-2H)	N45309	726-7180	Bu145915	PV
☐ Martin 4-0-4	N450A	14141	N450A, N149S	PV
☐ Mitchell Wing B-10				RA
☐ Monnett Sonerai II	N86FF	37		PVA
☐ Naval Aircraft Factory N3N-3	N44718		Bu2782	PVA
☐ North American NA-88 Texan (SNJ-4)	N24554	88-12281	Bu27245 – museum states it is ex Bu27753 which is c/n 88-13369 and N6419D.	PVA
☐ North American NA-108 Mitchell (B-25J) (TB-25J) '327638' (TB-25N)		108-33214	44-29939, N9456Z	PVAX
☐ North American NA-176 Sabre (F-86F)	N51RS	176-348	51-13417, C.5-235 (Spain)	RA
☐ Northrop N-8D Black Widow (P-61B)	N550NF	N.964	42-39445	PVC
☐ Piasecki PD-22 Work Horse (H-21A) (CH-21A)			Front fuselage only.	RA
☐ Piasecki PD-22 Work Horse (H-21B) (CH-21B)	N4367M	B.117	53-4367	PVD
☐ Pietenpol B4-A Aircamper	N4979E			PVC
☐ Piper J-3C-65 Cub (NE-1)	N41529	8187	Bu26276	S
☐ Piper PA-18-135 Super Cub (L-21B)	N50084	18-3220	53-7720, MM53-7720, I-EIKC, EI-103	PVA
☐ Piper PA-22 Tripacer 125	N600A	22-3		RA
☐ Piper PA-22-150 Caribbean	N3601Z	22-7489		RA
☐ Piper PA-34-200 Seneca	N5297T	34-7250245		RA
☐ Rand-Robinson KR-2	N303JV	1		PV
☐ Rearwin 185 Skyranger	N93248	1753		RA
☐ Rearwin 8135 Cloudster	N25545	823	NC25545	PV
☐ Reid Flying Submarine		1		S
☐ Republic F-84B Thunderjet (P-84B)	46-666			PV
☐ Republic RC-3 Seabee	N6202K	398	NC6202K	RA
☐ Rutan 33 Vari-Eze	N95E	107		PV
☐ Sikorsky S-58 Seabat (HSS-1N) (SH-34J)	N46922	581069	Bu145712 – tail from c/n 581807 Bu154897.	PV
☐ Sikorsky S-62A Seaguard (HH-52A)	N1394	62075	1394, N6647L	PVA
☐ Spratt 108	N49888	1		PV
☐ Steen Skybolt	N827DH	001		RA
☐ Taylor J-2 Cub	N16330	567	NC16330	S
☐ Taylor JT.1 Monoplane	N4991C	JT1/89		PV
☐ Taylor-Young A	N18339	72	NC18339	S
☐ Troyer VX-1	N18471	1	NC18471	RAC
☐ Vickers 798D Viscount (745D)	N7471	233	(N7471), N6591C, N820BK, N1898T, N98KT, N555SL	PV
☐ Vultee V-74 Valiant (BT-13A)	N60277	74-6519	41-22441	PVA
☐ Wright Flyer (Scale R)				PV

MIDLAND MONUMENT (PA36)

Location:	On permanent view at VFW 8168 on Midland Avenue in the north western part of the town.

TYPE	REG/SER	CON. NO.	PI/NOTES	STATUS
☐ Bell 209 Huey Cobra (AH-1G) (AH-1F)	71-21031	21102		PV

MILFORD MONUMENT (PA37)

Location:	On permanent view at ALP 139 on Route 2001 in the town.

TYPE	REG/SER	CON. NO.	PI/NOTES	STATUS
☐ Bell 205 Iroquois (UH-1H) (UH-1V)	68-15543	10473		PV

NAVAL INVENTORY CONTROL POINT COLLECTION (PA38)

Address:	700 Robbins Street, Philadelphia, Pennsylvania 19111-5096.
Tel:	215-697-2667
Admission:	By prior permission only.
Location:	About 6 miles north east of the city centre.

A collection of aircraft has been assembled at this large naval depot which controls supplies for the service. The six types are parked outside the entrance to the main building of the complex. The Tomcat arrived at the site in 1997 and the others have appeared over the years with the most recent being the Fire Scout.

TYPE	REG/SER	CON. NO.	PI/NOTES	STATUS
☐ Douglas AD-3 Skyraider	Bu122811	6933		RA
☐ Grumman G-128 Intruder (A-6A) (A-6E)	Bu157001	I-470		RA
☐ Grumman G-303 Tomcat (F-14A)	Bu159448	114		RA
☐ Hawker-Siddeley P.1127 Harrier 50 (AV-8A)	Bu159247	P156		RA
☐ McDonnell M.267 Hornet (F/A-18A)	Bu161982	204/A164		RA
☐ Northrop-Grumman RQ-8A Fire Scout	Bu166415			RA

NEW BERLIN MONUMENT (PA39)

Location: On permanent view at ALP 957 at 640 Water Street in the centre of the town.

TYPE	REG/SER	CON. NO.	PI/NOTES	STATUS
☐ Bell 205 Iroquois (UH-1H) (UH-1V)	68-15526	10456		PV

NEW GALILEE MONUMENT (PA40)

Location: On permanent view at VFW 8106 at 100 Monroe Street in the centre of the town.

TYPE	REG/SER	CON. NO.	PI/NOTES	STATUS
Bell 209 Huey Cobra (AH-1G) (AH-1F)	68-17043	20771		PV

NEW KENSINGTON MONUMENT (PA41)

Location: On permanent view in a park on Highway 56 in the eastern part of the town.

TYPE	REG/SER	CON. NO.	PI/NOTES	STATUS
☐ Lockheed 580 (T-33A)	51-8513	580-6297		PV

NORTH IRWIN MONUMENT (PA42)

Location: On permanent view at VFW 781 off Highway 30 in the town.

TYPE	REG/SER	CON. NO.	PI/NOTES	STATUS
☐ Lockheed 580 (T-33A)	49-0955	580-5105		PV

OIL REGION MUSIC PRESERVATION MUSEUM (PA43)

Address: Debence Antique Music World, 1261 Liberty Street, Franklin, Pennsylvania 16323-1329.
Tel: 814-432-8350   **Email:** debencemusicworld@usachoice.net
Admission: May–October Tuesday-Saturday 1000-1700; Sunday 1230-1700.
Location: In the town which is about 50 miles south of Erie.

The Franklin A biplane was conceived in Illinois by Jos Bauer. Finance for the project was provided by W.E. Barrow a Franklin resident. The first prototype of the biplane was flown in Franklin in February 1930. Powered by a 55 h.p. Velie engine, a small number were completed. The biplane resides at the local airfield. The museum which features mainly antique musical instruments. The history of the region is also portrayed.

TYPE	REG/SER	CON. NO.	PI/NOTES	STATUS
☐ Franklin A	NC10147	8	NC10149, N10149	RAA

PENNSYLVANIA COLLEGE OF TECHNOLOGY (PA44)

Address: 1 College Avenue, Williamsport, Pennsylvania 17701
Tel: 570-320-8037   **Email:** aviation@pct.edu
Admission: By prior permission only.
Location: At the airport which is about 7 miles south of the town.

At adult education college was set up in the town in 1914 and this became the Williamsport Technical Institute in 1941. During World War II the college operated 24 hours a day to train personnel for the defence industry.

In 1988 it became part of Pennsylvania State University and adopted its current name. Four sites are now in use including the Kathryn Wentzel Lumley Aviation Center at the airport. The students are trained on a fleet of instructional airframes and in addition there is a licensed facility to carry out work on private aircraft.

Students have carried out restoration work for the American Helicopter Museum.

TYPE	REG/SER	CON. NO.	PI/NOTES	STATUS
☐ Aero Commander 680W	N5RE	1818-32	(N6517V), N5418, , N1NR, N15ES, N3RA, C-GKMV, N3RA	RA
☐ Beech 58P Baron	N155Z	TJ-368		RA
☐ Beech C50 Seminole (L-23D) (U-8D)	N9048C	LH-178	58-1351	RA
☐ Bell 204 Iroquois (UH-1B)	N9434A	889	63-8664	RA
☐ Bölkow BO 105C			Pod only.	PV
☐ Cessna R172E Mescalero (T-41B)	N38932	R1720125	67-15142	RA
☐ Grumman G-128 Intruder (A-6E)	Bu161676	I-653		RA
☐ Hiller UH12B Raven (H-23B) (OH-23B)	54-4024	309		RA
☐ North American NA-276 Sabreliner (T-39A) (CT-39A)	N1PC	276-46	62-4493	RA
☐ Piper PA-36-285 Pawnee Brave	N9957D	36-7560068		RA
☐ Velocity Aircraft Velocity	N70ED	DM-104		RA

PENNSYLVANIA NATIONAL GUARD MILITARY MUSEUM (PA45)

Address:	Building T-8-57, Fort Indiantown Gap, Pennsylvania 17003-5003.
Tel:	717-801-8352 Email: c-coelig@state.pa.us
Admission:	Monday and Friday 1000-1630; Tuesday-Thursday by appointment – aircraft on permanent view.
Location:	About 23 miles north east of Harrisburg off Interstate 81.

The historic site at Fort Indiantown Gap was first used as a military installation in the 17th century when Fort Swatara was built just north of the present base. The Pennsylvania National Guard moved into the fort in the 1930s and a small museum has been set up in one of the buildings. The F-102 is mounted in front of the Headquarters Building. The type was flown by the state ANG at Pittsburgh from 1960 to 1975.

TYPE	REG/SER	CON. NO.	PI/NOTES	STATUS
☐ Bell 205 Iroquois (UH-1H)	70-16469	12774		PV
☐ Bell 209 Huey Cobra (AH-1G) (AH-1F)	70-15969	20913		PV
☐ Convair 8-12 Delta Dagger (TF-102A)	56-2346	8-12-78		PV
☐ Hughes 369M Cayuse (HO-6) (OH-6A)	68-17204	1164		PV
☐ Lockheed 382-8B Hercules (C-130E) (EC-130E)	63-7773	382-3839		PV

PHILIPSBURG MONUMENT (PA46)

Location:	On permanent view at the Mid-State Airport which is about 10 miles east of the town.

TYPE	REG/SER	CON. NO.	PI/NOTES	STATUS
☐ McDonnell M.36BA Voodoo (F-101B)	58-0328	700		PV

PIPER AVIATION MUSEUM (PA47)

Address:	One Piper Way, Lock Haven, Pennsylvania 17745.
Tel:	570-748-8283 Fax: 570-893-8357 Email: info@pipermuseum.com
Admission:	Monday-Friday 0900-1600; Saturday 1000-1600; Sunday 1200-1600.
Location:	At W.T. Piper Memorial Airport, Lock Haven.

In 1930 William T. Piper acquired the assets of the Taylor Aircraft Company which was formed in 1927 under another name. Production of the E-2 Cub started in 1931 and the design was developed over the next few years. Taylor left the firm in 1935 and two years later a move was made to Lock Haven when the name was changed to the Piper Aircraft Corporation. The factory remained in use until 1987 when the firm moved all production to its Vero Beach plant in Florida which had opened in 1957.

The museum was set up in the mid-1980s with the aim of collecting Piper aircraft and artefacts. In the 1990s the former Piper Engineering block was purchased and this was converted for museum use. The displays trace the history of the company and its aircraft with many models, photographs and documents on view. The J-2 Cub on show was the first produced at Lock Haven after the move from Bradford and was donated by William T. Piper Jnr, the son of the founder.

The PA-12 Super Cruiser is one of a pair which made a round-the-world flight in 1947. The epic journey started on 9th August at Teteboro and finished on 10th December. The PT-1 was in the EAA collection at Oshkosh until 2006. This type was the first low wing design by the company and only a single prototype was built. Several aircraft are currently in store and in the workshops is an example of the Tripacer which sold in large numbers. The search for more types from the famous company continues.

TYPE	REG/SER	CON. NO.	PI/NOTES	STATUS
☐ Piper J-2 Cub	NC19555	1755	NC19555, N19555	PV
☐ Piper J-3C-65 Cub	N70676	17696	NC70676	RA
☐ Piper PA-12 Super Cruiser	NX8671M	12-2623	N8671M	PV
☐ Piper PA-22-150 Tripacer	N3840P	22-3530		RAC
☐ Piper PA-23-250 Aztec E	N14230	27-4788		PV
☐ Piper PA-24 Comanche	N5785P	24-864		PVA
☐ Piper PA-29 Papoose	N2900M	29-01		PV
☐ Piper PA-31-300 Turbo Navajo			Fuselage only.	RA
☐ Piper PA-31-350 Navajo Chieftain			Fuselage only	RA
☐ Piper PA-31 353 T-1020	N353PA	31-8558001	N353PX	RAD
☐ Piper PA-31P-350 Mojave	N9198Y	31P-8414002		RAD
☐ Piper PA-31T Cheyenne	N7500L	31T-1		RAD
☐ Piper PA-38-112 Tomahawk	N2467D	38-79A0328		PV
☐ Piper PA-41P (pressurized Aztec)	N9941P	41P-1		PV
☐ Piper PA-42-1000 Cheyenne 400 (R)				PV
☐ Piper PT-1	NX4300	1		PVC

PITTSBURGH AIR NATIONAL GUARD BASE COLLECTION (PA48)

Address:	171 ARW/PA 300 Tanker Road 4200, Pittsburgh International Airport, Coraopolis, Pennsylvania 15108-4200.
Tel:	412-474-7321 Email: webmaster@papitt.ang.af.mil
Admission:	During daylight hours – a pass must be obtained from the gate.
Location:	On the south side of the airport which is about 12 miles north west of the city.

Two units of the Pennsylvania Air National Guard are based at the field. The 146th Squadron arrived in mid-1948 and flew P-47s, P-51s, F-84Fs, F-86Ls, F-102s and A-7s up to the summer of 1991 when it became a tanker unit. The 147th arrived in April 1949 and was a fighter unit until 1961 when it changed to an aeromedical outfit. Tankers arrived in October 1972 and the unit has served in this role ever since. The line of preserved aircraft is located along the road from the main gate to the base and shows types flown by the wing up to its conversion to tankers. For some years a genuine P-51 Mustang was on show but this was replaced by a full scale replica in period markings. A P-47 Thunderbolt replica has now joined the collection.

TYPE	REG/SER	CON. NO.	PI/NOTES	STATUS
☐ Convair 8-10 Delta Dagger (F-102A)	56-1415	8-10-632		RA
☐ North American NA-122 Mustang (P-51D) (FSM)	'44-84900'			RAX
☐ North American NA-201 Sabre (F-86D) (F-86L)	53-0894	201-338		RA
☐ Republic P-47D Thunderbolt (FSM)				PVX
☐ Republic F-84F Thunderstreak	51-1508			RA
☐ Vought A-7D Corsair II	73-1002	D398		RA

PITTSBURG INSTITUTE OF AERONAUTICS (PA49)

Address: 5 Allegheny County Airport, West Mifflin, Pennsylvania 15122.
Tel: 412-346-2122   **Email:** ssabold@pia.edu
Admission: By prior permission only.
Location: At the airport which is about 5 miles west of the town.

The Institute opened in 1929 and offer courses in a variety of subjects. The aviation department trains students for airframe, engine and avionics licences. The fleet of instructional aircraft housed at the airport includes a number of withdrawn homebuilt types. Floyd S Bert, based in Carnegie in Pennsylvania, has constructed a number of original designs and a small number of Pitts Specials. His BF-2, dating from 1959 is still active in Texas. The BF-5 was completed in the mid-2000s. The Bakeng Double Duce is a biplane version of the parasol wing monoplane designed by Jerry Bakeng in the early 1970s.

TYPE	REG/SER	CON. NO.	PI/NOTES	STATUS
☐ Aero Commander 1121B	N1944P	142		RA
☐ Bakeng Double Duce	N2XD	78-1		RA
☐ Beech 35-33 Debonair	N156J	CD-285		RA
☐ Beech C 50 Twin Bonanza	N3743B	CH-169		RA
☐ Beech C50 Seminole (L-23D) (U-8D)	'N2038P'	LH-138	57-6077, N138LH	RAX
☐ Beech C50 Seminole (L-23D) (U-8D)	'N2020P'	RLH-33	57-6061, N3274N	RAX
☐ Beech D50C Twin Bonanza	N1DU	DH-262		RA
☐ Bell 206A Kiowa (OH-58A) (OH-58C)	72-21430	42096		RA
☐ Bell 206A Kiowa (OH-58A) (OH-58C)	73-21884	42150		RA
☐ Cessna 152	N757XW	15280095		RA
☐ Cessna 172C	N7682T	17249073		RA
☐ Cessna 310A	N12144	38118		RA
☐ Cessna 310B	N5400A	35600		RA
☐ Floyd BF-5	N3402B	5		RA
☐ North American NA-282 Sabreliner 40	N399P	282-87	N87, N36P	RA
☐ Revolution Mini-500	N343JB	375		RA

PLEASANT HILLS MONUMENT (PA50)

Location: On permanent view at ALP 712 on Old Clairton Road in the southern part of the town.

TYPE	REG/SER	CON. NO.	PI/NOTES	STATUS
☐ Bell 209 Huey Cobra (AH-1G) (AH-1F)	68-17088	20816		PV

PORT CARBON MONUMENT (PA51)

Location: On permanent view at VVW 29 at 612 Fifth Street in the nothern part of the town.

TYPE	REG/SER	CON. NO.	PI/NOTES	STATUS
☐ Bell 205 Iroquois (UH-1D) (UH-1H)	66-16012	5706		PV

SEA WOLF MUSEUM (PA52)

Address: Queen City Aviation 1730 Vultee Street, Allentown, Pennsylvania 18103.
Tel: 610-797-7430
Admission: Not yet open.
Location: At Queen City Airport which is just south of the town off Interstate 78.

In 1942 the Navy proposed that Vultee, later Convair, should build the Vought designed TBY Sea Wolf. The Mack International Motor Truck Corporation plant at Allentown was taken over and converted for aircraft production.

A batch of 1,100 TBY-2s were ordered in September 1943 and the first was delivered to Philadelphia on 7th November 1944. Eventually only 180 were completed and the plant closed in late 1945.

The museum was set up in August 1994 and plans to trace the history of the factory and the TBY-2. A full size replica incorporating some original parts will be built and placed on show in front of the old delivery hangar which now serves as the garage for the town vehicles. Archive material and photographs along with components have been collected and the site for a suitable display is being investigated by members of the group.

TYPE	REG/SER	CON. NO.	PI/NOTES	STATUS
☐ Consolidated TBY-2 Sea Wolf (R)				RAC

SENATOR JOHN HEINZ HISTORY CENTER (PA53)

Address: 1212 Swallow Street, Pittsburgh, Pennsylvania 15222-4268.
Tel: 412-454-6000   **Email:** rostakeley@hswp.org
Admission: Daily 1000-1700.
Location: Aircraft at Pittsburg IAP which is which is about 12 miles north west of the city.

Pennsylvania

This museum traces the history and development of the region. A large extension was opened in 2004 and many new displays were added. The Historical Society of Western Pennsylvania has an extensive library and archive in the building. Other museums in the town including one focussing on sport are administered by the society. The 1926 Waco 9 was registered to the society in 2001. This biplane has been restored and hangs in the terminal at Pittsburgh International Airport. There are nearby display boards about the museum.

TYPE	REG/SER	CON. NO.	PI/NOTES	STATUS
☐ Waco 9	N2574	359	NC2574	PV

STATE MUSEUM OF PENNSYLVANIA (PA54)

Address:	300 North Street, Harrisburg, Pennsylvania 17120-0024.
Tel:	717-787-4980 Fax: 717-783-4558 Email: hpollman@state.pa.us
Admission:	Tuesday-Saturday 0900-1700; Sunday 1200-1700.
Location:	At the junction of Third and North Streets in the centre of the city.

The museum was founded in 1905 and since 1965 has been housed in the William Penn Memorial Building. The exhibitions trace the history of the state from early times up to the present day. Sections on early history, anthropology, military history, industry and technology, geology, natural sciences and ecology are all presented in an informative manner.

The small aeronautical section has the two aircraft, engines and photographs on show. The Piper factory was at Lock Haven for almost 50 years and the Cub is one of their famous products. The unique Knepper Crusader was built in 1941 at Andreas in Pennsylvania. The high-wing monoplane was powered by a 75 h.p. Lycoming engine. Members of the Knepper family donated the aircraft to the museum in 1990.

TYPE	REG/SER	CON. NO.	PI/NOTES	STATUS
☐ Knepper KA-1 Crusader	NX28856			PV
☐ Piper J-3C-65 Cub	NC98629	18854	NC98629, N98629	PV

STOYSTOWN MONUMENT (PA55)

Location:	On permanent view at ALP 257 in the eastern part of the town.

TYPE	REG/SER	CON. NO.	PI/NOTES	STATUS
☐ Bell 205 Iroquois (UH-1H)	66-16993	9187		PV

THERMAL GLIDERPORT AIR MUSEUM (PA56)

Address:	9001 Hamot Road, Waterford, Pennsylvania 16441.
Tel:	814-866-1131
Admission:	By prior permission only.
Location:	About 8 miles south of Erie between Routes 19 and 99.

This interesting private collection has been built up by the late Lawrence Gehrlein. His sons now run the glider repair business at the airstrip.

The collection is housed in two buildings and includes photographs, models and documents. The Heath Parasol was built in 1938 by G. Palmer Bates and features a floatplane from Lake Chautauqua. An immaculate replica of the 1928 Heath Baby Bullet been constructed and the aircraft was taken to the 1995 Oshkosh Convention.

Five Gehrlein GP-1 gliders were built in the 1960s and three of these are now in the collection with one on show. The Bowlus Baby Albatross dating from the 1930s was produced in both finished and kit form. Another early glider is the Baker-McMillen Cadet. This design dates from the early 1930s and around 30 were completed. In one demonstration three were towed behind an airship. Over 100 kits were sold.

There are a number of balloons in the collection and these are flown regularly.

TYPE	REG/SER	CON. NO.	PI/NOTES	STATUS
☐ Aeronca C-3	NC14646	A-532	NC14646, N14646	PV
☐ Aeronca 65CA Super Chief	NC47385	CA-16781	NC47385, N47385	PVA
☐ Baker-McMillen Cadet	N10500	121		PV
☐ Bamber Glider (R)				PV
☐ Bede BD-5B				RA
☐ Bensen B-8 Gyroglider				PV
☐ Bensen B-8M Gyrocopter				PV
☐ Bobcat Ultralight				PV
☐ Bowlus BA-100 Baby Albatross				PV
☐ Corben D Baby Ace	N111B	B-1		PV
☐ Exline PX-1	N14E	EX-2		PV
☐ Fisher Mk1 912 Floatplane				PV
☐ Gehrlein GP-1	N5471	1		RAA
☐ Gehrlein GP-1	N99Z	2		RAA
☐ Gehrlein GP-1	N3973	7		PV
☐ Gehrlein Precursor				PV
☐ General Balloon Ax-6	N2429Z	429		RA
☐ General Balloon Ax-6	N2473Z	473		RAA
☐ Griswold Slotted Wing				PV
☐ Heath Baby Bullet (R)	NX6784	GH001		RAA
☐ Heath Parasol	N99Z	101		PVC
☐ Jacobs Rhönadler 35 (DFS 108-47)	NX34192			RAC
☐ Laister-Kauffman LK.10A	NC60258	105		PVA
☐ Maxair Hummer	N2775F	0112A		PVA
☐ Nieuport 11 (R)	N124RJ	GP04053		PVA
☐ Parker-Thompson Tiny Mite	N68731	1		RAD
☐ Piccard AX-4 Hot Air Balloon	N53PB	4101		RAA
☐ Piper J-3C-65 Cub (mod)	N7315H	20577		PVA

☐ Pitts S-1D Special	N14E	7-0012		PVA
☐ Rolladen-Schneider LS-1F	N77VL	449		RA
☐ Rolladen-Schneider LS-1F	N585	477		RA
☐ Scheibe L-Spatz 55	N8364	731		RA
☐ Schweizer SGS.1-26A	N8693R	213		RA
☐ Schweizer SGS.1-26B	N9909J	336		RA
☐ Schweizer SGS.1-26B	N9914J	337		RA
☐ Schweizer SGS.1-26D	N1126P	481		RA
☐ Schweizer SGU.1-19	NC91821	42	N91821	PV
☐ Steinhauser S-2				PV
☐ Volmer Jensen VJ-23				PV

TOBYHANNA ARMY DEPOT COLLECTION (PA57)

Address:	11 Hap Arnold Boulevard, Tobyhanna, Pennsylvania 18446.
Tel:	570-615-7000
Admission:	By prior permission only.
Location:	In the town off Route 611.

The site houses a logistics centre specialising in electronic systems. These are designed manufactured and repaired in the advanced laboratories and workshops. The site has been in use by the army since World War I when it served as a tank and ambulance crew training centre. The aircraft are preserved around the site.

TYPE	REG/SER	CON. NO.	PI/NOTES	STATUS
☐ Bell 204 Iroquois (UH-1C) (UH-1M)	66-15193	1921		RA
☐ Bell 205 Iroquois (UH-1H)				RA
☐ Bell 209 Huey Cobra (AH-1G) (AH-1S)				RA
☐ Grumman G-134 Mohawk (OV-1B) (RV-1D)	64-14247	75B		RA
☐ Grumman G-303 Tomcat (F-14A)	Bu161151	378		RA
☐ Hughes 369M Cayuse (HO-6) (OH-6A)	66-17829	0380		RA

TOWANDA MONUMENT (PA58)

Location:	On permanent view at VFW 1568 in Bridge Street in the south western part of the town.

TYPE	REG/SER	CON. NO.	PI/NOTES	STATUS
☐ Bell 205 Iroquois (UH-1H)	70-16432	12737		PV

UNITED STATES ARMY HERITAGE CENTER MUSEUM (PA59)

Address:	950 Soldiers Drive, Carlisle, Pennsylvania 17013-5021.
Tel:	717-258-3419 **Fax:** 717-258-1576 **Email:** carl_ahec-ahm@conus.army.mil
Admission:	Monday-Friday 0900-1645; April–October also open Saturday 1000-600 Sunday 1200-1600.
Location:	In the eastern part of the town.

The aim of the centre is to inform the public on the history of the service and to show its current role. The museum has on show, uniforms, documents, photographs and weapons of the early days. The experiences of individual soldiers will be portrayed as the displays are developed. A touring exhibition is based at the museum. Two helicopters are preserved at the site and more are expected.

TYPE	REG/SER	CON. NO.	PI/NOTES	STATUS
☐ Bell 205 Iroquois (UH-1D) (UH-1H)	66-1071	5554		PV
☐ Bell 209 Huey Cobra (AH-1G) (AH-1S)	67-15663	20227		PV

WEST BROWNSVILLE MONUMENT (PA60)

Location:	On permanent view at ALP 800 at 800 Middle Street in the northern part of the village.

TYPE	REG/SER	CON. NO.	PI/NOTES	STATUS
☐ Bell 205 Iroquois (UH-1H) (UH-1V)	67-17813	10011		PV

WEST PENNSYLVANIA WARBIRD MUSEUM (PA61)

Address:	58 Cribbs Road, Mercer, Pennsylvania 16137.
Tel:	724-794-6747
Admission:	By prior permission only
Location:	About 3 miles south of the town.

The museum is being set up by a group of enthusiasts with the aim of portraying the military aviation heritage of the region. A Sabre and a Phantom have been put on static display. One of the museum members has aircraft based in the area. The Funk B-75L has been reported as stored in a dismantled state.

TYPE	REG/SER	CON. NO.	PI/NOTES	STATUS
☐ Beech D18S	N33G	A-274	N50661	RA
☐ Byfield HTH-1	N110HT	001		RAA
☐ Ercoupe 415C	N93340	663	NC93340	RAA
☐ Funk B-75L	N2088W	203		RAA
☐ McDonnell M.98DE Phantom II (F-4C)				RA
☐ North American NA-193 Sabre (F-86F)	52-5303	193-32		RA

WHITE HAVEN MONUMENT (PA62)

Location:	On permanent view at VFW 6615 at 519 Ash Lane in the village.

TYPE	REG/SER	CON. NO.	PI/NOTES	STATUS
☐ Bell 204 Iroquois (UH-1C) (UH-1M)	66-15102	1830		PV

WHITEHALL MONUMENT (PA63)

Location:	On permanent view at VFW 7293 on Spring Hill Road in the town.

TYPE	REG/SER	CON. NO.	PI/NOTES	STATUS
☐ Grumman G-303 Tomcat (F-14A)	Bu158617	18		PV

WILLOW GROVE JOINT RESERVE BASE COLLECTION (PA64)

Address:	Public Affairs, Willow Grove JRB, Pennsylvania 19090-5030.
Tel:	215-443-6033
Admission:	By prior permission only.
Location:	About 15 miles north of Philadelphia on Route 611.

The airfield was set up by Harold Pitcairn in 1926. The site was purchased by the military in the early days of World War II. The airfield has been used by all branches of the services. After September 2011 the site will probably be turned over to the Pennsylvania Air National Guard.

TYPE	REG/SER	CON. NO.	PI/NOTES	STATUS
☐ Bell 204 Iroquois (HU-1B) (UH-1B)	62-1920	440	By Army gate.	PV
☐ Cessna 318E Dragonfly (A-37B) (OA-37B)	69-6370	43215		RA
☐ Fairchild-Republic A-10A Thunderbolt II	77-0248	A10-173		RA
☐ Lockheed 185 Orion (P-3B)	Bu154574	185-5255		PV
☐ McDonnell M.267 Hornet (F/A-18A)	'Bu162436'	573/A480	Bu163150	RA
☐ Sikorsky S-65A Sea Stallion (RH-53D)	Bu158754	65377		RA

RHODE ISLAND

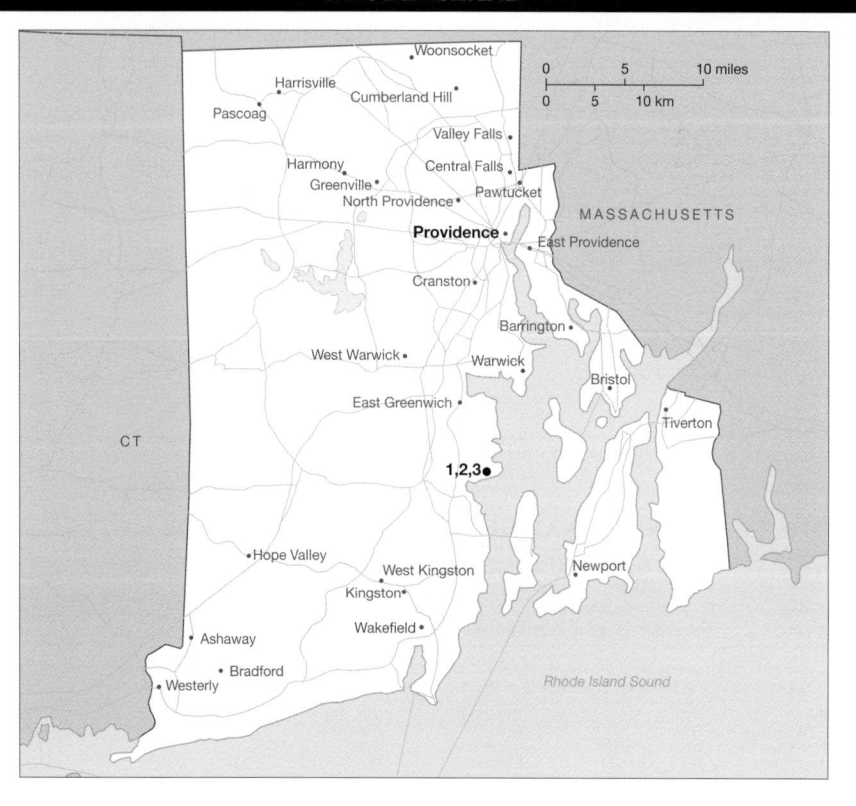

QUONSET AIR MUSEUM (RI1)

Address:	488 Eccleston Avenue, Quonset State Airport, North Kingstown, Rhode Island 02852.
Tel:	401-294-9540 Fax: 401-294-9887 Email: info@theqam.org
Admission:	July–September daily 1000-1600; October–June Saturday-Sunday 1000-1600.
Location:	About 15 miles south of Providence off Route 403.

Quonset Point was once the largest naval air station in the country. Work started on the site in July 1940 and the field was ready the following year. During World War II it was home to many land- and carrier-based squadrons. Training of air crews was one of the main tasks. During its latter years it was one of the primary overhaul and maintenance facilities in the Navy. The base closed in 1974 and is now the municipal airport.

The Rhode Island Aviation Heritage Association was formed in 1989 and opened the museum in 1992. The collection is housed in Hangar 488 which was used as a paintshop for the Naval Air Rework Facility.

Under long-term rebuild is a Grumman Hellcat recovered after spending almost 50 years in the Atlantic Ocean. The fighter will be restored in its original markings. Naval aircraft feature prominently in the display with several examples of the Skyhawk on show. A rare Skynight, which served in Korea and Vietnam, was transported from Arizona. The Avenger was airlifted from its crash site in Maine and is being restored.

The museum is gradually acquiring civil aircraft for display. The American Eagle Eaglet first flew in 1930 and about 90 were built. This parasol wing monoplane was fitted with a variety of engines. Only three examples of the Curtiss XF15C fighter were built. The Grumman C-1A on show was the last aircraft tp fly from the Naval Air Station.

Displays are being set up in the rooms alongside the hangar to trace the history of the base and aviation in Rhode Island.

TYPE	REG/SER	CON. NO.	PI/NOTES	STATUS
☐ Aero Commander 680	N2100M	432-105	N6902S, N200M	RA
☐ American Eagle Eaglet B-31	NC597Y	1104		PV
☐ Bell 204 Iroquois (UH-1C) (UH-1M)	66-15083	1811		PV
☐ Bell 205 Iroquois (UH-1D) (UH-1H)	64-13492	4199		PV
☐ Bell 206A Kiowa (OH-58A)	70-15117	40668		PV
☐ Bell 209 Huey Cobra (AH-1G) (AH-1S)	66-15317	20073		PV
☐ Bensen B-8 Gyroglider	N88774			PV
☐ Curtiss 99 (XF15C-1)	Bu01215			PV
☐ Cessna 140				PVD
☐ Cessna 337B Super Skymaster	N2434S	0734	Fuselage only.	RA
☐ Cessna 337M Super Skymaster (O-2A)	68-10997	337M0273	Fuselage only.	RAD
☐ Douglas EF-10B Skynight (F3D-2) (F3D-2Q)	Bu124620	7490		PV
☐ Douglas A-4C Skyhawk (A4D-2N)	Bu147790	12554		PVC
☐ Douglas A-4F Skyhawk	Bu155027	13843		PV
☐ Douglas A-4M Skyhawk			Front fuselage only.	PV
☐ Douglas A-4M Skyhawk	Bu158148	14185		PV
☐ Grumman G-40 Avenger (TBM-3) (TBM-3E)	Bu53914	3976	Bu53914, N7029C, CF-BQS	PV
☐ Grumman G-50 Hellcat (F6F-5)	Bu70185	A-5597		PVC
☐ Grumman G-96 Trader (TF-1) (C-1A)			Front fuselage only.	PV
☐ Grumman G-96 Trader (TF-1) (C-1A)	Bu136780	033	Front fuselage only.	PV
☐ Grumman G-96 Trader (TF-1) (C-1A)	Bu136792	045		PV
☐ Grumman G-128 Intruder (A-6A) (A-6E)	Bu155629	I-359		PV
☐ Grumman G-134 Mohawk (AO-1C) (OV-1C)	N4376D	35C	61-2692	RAA
☐ Grumman G-303 Tomcat (F-14A)	Bu162591	513		PV
☐ Hughes 369M Cayuse (HO-6) (OH-6A)	67-16570	0955		PV
☐ Lockheed 426-42-15 Neptune (P2V-5) (P2V-5F) (P2V-5FS) (SP-2E)	Bu131403	426-5272	Composite.	PV
☐ Lockheed 426-42-15 Neptune (P2V-5) (P2V-5F) (P2V-5FS) (SP-2E)	Bu131427	426-5308	Rear fuselage from c/n 426-5272 Bu131403.	PV
☐ McDonnell M.24 Banshee (F2H-3)	Bu126292			PVD
☐ McDonnell M.98AM Phantom II (F4H-1F) (F-4A)	Bu148252	24		PV
☐ Meyers Racer				RA
☐ Mikoyan-Gurevich MiG-21F-13				RA
☐ Nord N.1101 Ramier I [Messerschmitt Me 208]	187	187		RA
☐ Pietenpol B4-A Aircamper				PV
☐ Rutan 77-6 Solitaire				PV
☐ Sikorsky S-61B Sea King (HSS-2) (SH-3A) (SH-3H)	Bu149738			PV
☐ Sisler SP.1 Pipit	N154S	111		PV
☐ Stinson 10A Voyager				RA
☐ Stolp SA.300 Starduster Too	N100LF	FAR05		RA
☐ Vought A-7D Corsair II	75-0408	D458		PV
☐ WSK Lim-6bis (LiM-5M)	325	1F 03-25	In Polish markings.	PV
☐ WSK SBLim-2 (Lim-1) [MiG-15]	N669MG	1A 07-009	709 (Poland), N60CS	PVA

RHODE ISLAND NATIONAL GUARD COLLECTION (RI2)

Address:	Quonset State Airport, North Kingstown, Rhode Island 02852.
Tel:	401-275-4193
Admission:	By prior permission only.
Location:	The airport is about 15 miles south of Providence off Route 403.

Units of the state guard are based at the former naval airfield which is now serves as the airport for the region. Three helicopters which have seen service at the field are preserved in the army site.

TYPE	REG/SER	CON. NO.	PI/NOTES	STATUS
☐ Bell 205 Iroquois (UH-1H)	68-15556	10486		RA
☐ Bell 209 Huey Cobra (AH-1G) (AH-1F)	67-15530	20194		RA
☐ Hughes 369M Cayuse (HO-6) (OH-6A)	67-16627	1012		RA

UNITED STATES SHIP *SARATOGA* MUSEUM (RI3)

Address:	PO Box 845, North Kingstown, Rhode Island 02852.
Tel:	401-398-1000 Fax: 401-885-1290 Email: saratogamuseum@aol.com
Admission:	Saratoga not coming here – aircraft parked with Quonset Air Museum.
Location:	About 15 miles south of Providence off Route 403.

The *Saratoga* entered service in 1958 and was involved in the 1962 blockade of Cuba. The following year she became the first to operate the A-6 Intruder and has since served in Southeast Asia, the Mediterranean and the Persian Gulf.

The foundation is setting up a museum which will, in addition to the history of the ship, cover many aspects of maritime and aviation technology. Aircraft are being allocated for the display.

Funds are being raised for the purchase of a ship which hopefully will be berthed next to the old Quonset Air Station. The Foundation has heard that the *Saratoga* will not now be donated for display and is likely to be scrapped. However there is a chance that the carrier USS *John F. Kennedy* may become available. Other organisations had made approaches for this ship so there is still some way to go before a carrier is docked at Quonset.

TYPE	REG/SER	CON. NO.	PI/NOTES	STATUS
☐ Cessna 318B Tweety Bird (318A) (T-37A) (T-37B)	57-2291	40224		PV
☐ Hawker-Siddeley P.1127 Harrier 50 (AV-8A) (AV-8C)	Bu158710	P107		PV
☐ Lockheed 580 (T-33A) (TV-2) (T-33B)	Bu137936	580-8582	53-5243	PV
☐ McDonnell M.98AM Phantom II (F4H-1) (F-4B)	Bu148371	56		PV
☐ Northrop N-156T Talon (T-38A)	63-8197	N.5544		PV

SOUTH CAROLINA

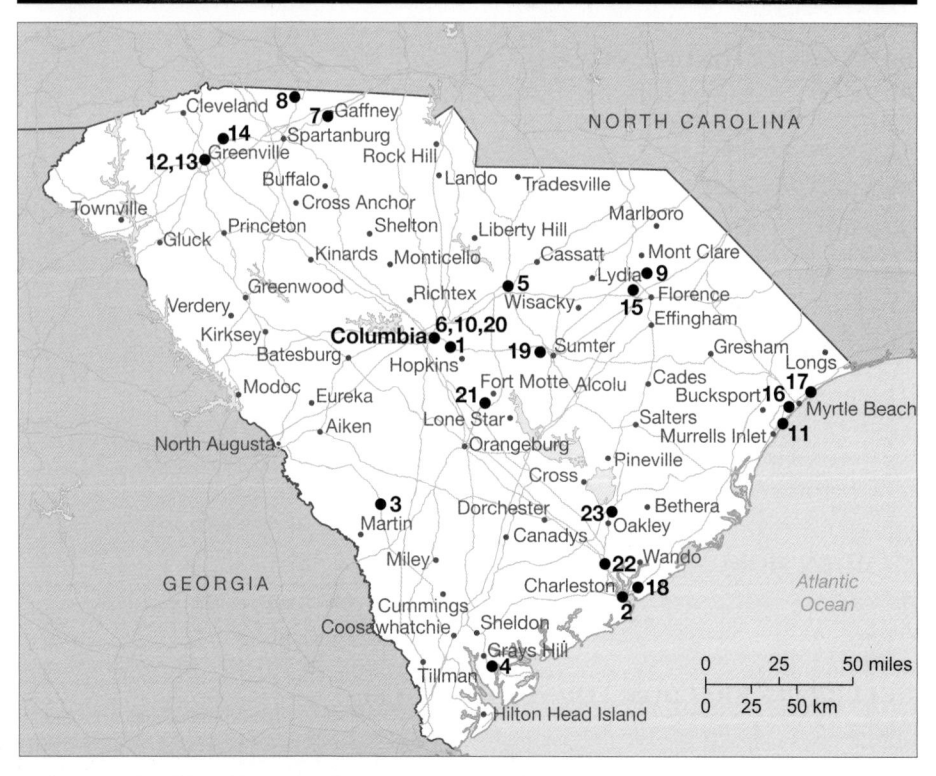

169TH FIGHTER WING MEMORIAL PARK (SC1)

Address:	McEntire Air National Guard Base, Route 1, Eastover, South Carolina 29044-9690.
Tel:	803-776-5121 Email: pa.169fw@scmcen.ang.af.mil
Admission:	By prior permission only.
Location:	About 12 miles east of Columbia on Route 76.

The 157th Squadron was allocated to the South Carolina Air National Guard in May 1946 and has been based at McEntire (formerly Congaree Air Base) ever since, apart from periods of active duty.

The base is named after Brigadier General B. B. McEntire, the commander of the SC ANG, who was killed on 25th May 1961. Piloting an F-104A Starfighter he stayed with the aircraft to avoid it crashing into Harrisburg in Pennsylvania.

TYPE	REG/SER	CON. NO.	PI/NOTES	STATUS
☐ Bell 204 Iroquois (UH-1C) (UH-1M)	66-0643	1625	By Army NG area.	RA
☐ Bell 205 Iroquois (UH-1H)	67-17545	9743	By Army NG area.	RA
☐ Bell 206A Kiowa (OH-58A)			By Army NG area.	RA
☐ Convair 8-10 Delta Dagger (F-102A)	56-0985	8-10-202		RA
☐ General Dynamics 401 Fighting Falcon (F-16A)	75-0746	61-2		RA
☐ Lockheed 383-04-05 Starfighter (F-104C)	'60920'	183-1237	57-0920	RAX
☐ Lockheed 580 (T-33A)	51-6915	580-6247		RAX
☐ North American NA-111 Mustang (P-51K) (FSM)	'473919'			RAX
☐ North American NA-201 Sabre (F-86D) (F-86L)	53-1064	201-508		RA
☐ North American NA-203 Sabre (F-86H)	53-1386	203-158		RA
☐ Vought A-7D Corsair II	'73-1010'	D181	73-1035	RAX

AIR FORCE RESERVE OFFICER TRAINING CENTER (SC2)

Address: The Citadel, 171 Moultrie Street, Charleston, South Carolina 29049.
Tel: 803-953-5000 **Email:** aero@citadel.edu
Admission: By prior permission only.
Location: In the north western part of the city centre.

This long established school with a military background has officer training centres for all three services. There are displays of militaria in a number of buildings. The Phantom is mounted in the Air Force ORTC area.

TYPE	REG/SER	CON. NO.	PI/NOTES	STATUS
☐ Bell 209 Huey Cobra (AH-1S) (AH-1P)	76-22699	24052		RA
☐ McDonnell M.98DJ Phantom II (F-4C)	64-0816	1145		RA

BARNWELL MONUMENT (SC3)

Location: On permanent view at the airport which is off Highway 278 in the northern part of the town.

TYPE	REG/SER	CON. NO.	PI/NOTES	STATUS
☐ Bell 205 Iroquois (UH-1H)	67-17338	9536		RA

BEAUFORT MARINE CORPS AIR STATION (SC4)

Address: POBox 55001, Beaufort, South Carolina 29904-5001.
Tel: 843-228-6123 **Email:** bfrt_jpao@usmc.mil
Admission: On permanent view.
Location: About 2 miles north west of Beaufort on Highway 21.

The airfield is the main F/A-18 Hornet base for the Atlantic Fleet of the Marine Corps. Several types which have flown from the field in the past have been preserved and put on display near the main gate.

TYPE	REG/SER	CON. NO.	PI/NOTES	STATUS
☐ Douglas A-4L Skyhawk (A4D-2N) (A-4C)	Bu147772	12536		RA
☐ McDonnell M.267 Hornet (F/A-18A)	Bu163157	586/A493		PV
☐ McDonnell M.267 Hornet (F/A-18A)	Bu163163	596/A503		RA
☐ McDonnell M.267 Hornet (F/A-18D)	Bu163486	719/D016		RA
☐ McDonnell M.98AM Phantom II (F-4B) (F-4N)	Bu152270	1006		PV
☐ North American NA-215 Fury (FJ-3M) (MF-1C)	'Bu135841'	215-82	Bu141376	PVX
☐ Vertol V.107M Sea Knight (CH-46A) (HH-46A) (HH-46D)	Bu152530	2152		PV
☐ Vought F-8K Crusader (F8U-2) (F-8C)	Bu146963		Bu146963, 'Bu149220'	PV

CAMDEN MONUMENT (SC5)

Location: On permanent view at Woodward Field which is about 5 miles north east of the town off Route 1.

TYPE	REG/SER	CON. NO.	PI/NOTES	STATUS
☐ McDonnell M.98DE Phantom II (F-4C)	63-7422	708		PV

CELEBRATE FREEDOM FOUNDATION (SC6)

Address: 455 Andrews Road, Suite 1, Columbia, South Carolina 29210
Tel: 803-772-2945 **Fax:** 803-731-0341 **Email:** celebratefreedom@earthlink.net
Admission: By prior permission only.
Location: In the south eastern suburbs of the city.

Owens Field opened in 1929 and served as the main airport for the town until 1965. The Curtiss-Wright Flying Service hangar was constructed at the same time.

The group is raising funds to restore the building to its original condition and work has started. The site will serve as an aviation museum and house the South Carolina Aviation Hall of Fame and a collection of artefacts is being assembled for the display. The Mitchell, recovered in 1983 after crashing in Lake Greenwood in June 1944. is currently in store in the building.

The helicopters are used in the foundation's education programme and are taken to functions in the area.

South Carolina

TYPE	REG/SER	CON. NO.	PI/NOTES	STATUS
☐ Bell 209 Huey Cobra (AH-1G) (AH-1F)	N5628Q	20108	66-15352	RA
☐ Bell 209 Huey Cobra (AH-1G) (AH-1F)	N5627D	20184	67-15520	RA
☐ Bell 209 Huey Cobra (AH-1S) (AH-1F)	N56269	22256	79-23211	RA
☐ Bell 209 Huey Cobra (AH-1S) (AH-1F)	N5627C	22305	80-23517	RA
☐ Bell 209 Huey Cobra (AH-1S) (AH-1P)	N56267	22001	76-22567	RA
☐ North American NA-82 Mitchell (B-25C)	41-13285	82-5920	At Owens Field.	RA

CHEROKEE COUNTY VETERANS MUSEUM (SC7)

Address:	VFW Post 3447, PO Box 746, 200 Logan Street, Gaffney, South Carolina 29342.
Tel:	864-489-4704
Admission:	Saturday 0900-1100; Sunday 1400-1600.
Location:	Just south of the town centre off Route 29.

The local veterans' group has set up this museum with artefacts on show from the 1776 War of Independence up to Desert Storm. The history of all conflicts is portrayed in detail with mention of significant battles. On show are many personal items of memorabilia, uniforms, photographs, weapons and documents tracing the military lives of local people.
Two aircraft are displayed. The Iroquois served in vast numbers in Vietnam. Many local Air Force pilots were trained on the T-37 and the one on show is the fifth production example.

TYPE	REG/SER	CON. NO.	PI/NOTES	STATUS
☐ Bell 205 Iroquois (UH-1D) (UH-1H)	66-0764	5247		PV
☐ Cessna 318B Tweety Bird (318A) (T-37A) (T-37B)	54-2733	40009		PV

CHESNEE MONUMENT (SC8)

Location:	On permanent view at ALP 48 south of the town on Highway 221.

TYPE	REG/SER	CON. NO.	PI/NOTES	STATUS
☐ Bell 209 Huey Cobra (AH-1G) (AH-1F)	70-16034	20978		PV

DARLINGTON MONUMENT (SC9)

Location:	On permanent view at the airport which is about 10 miles north east of the town.

TYPE	REG/SER	CON. NO.	PI/NOTES	STATUS
☐ Lockheed 580 (T-33A)	53-6089	580-9710		PV

FORT JACKSON MUSEUM (SC10)

Address:	ATZJ-PTM-M, 2179 Sumpter Street, Fort Jackson, South Carolina 29207-5100.
Tel:	803-751-7419/7355 Email: matteson@jackson.army.mil
Admission:	Monday-Friday 0900-1600.
Location:	In the eastern suburbs of Columbia off Route 12.

The Army set up Camp Jackson in 1917 and the site has been in use ever since. The museum opened in 1972 with only 20 artefacts in its collection. This has now grown to over 3,000 items.
The displays include a reconstructed World War II Army barracks scene and a replica of a village built at the Fort for training personnel before they were sent to Vietnam.
An outside park contains vehicles and artillery from the time of the opening of the installation. The Iroquois on show has recently been returned to the exhibition after a period of restoration.
There are three other interesting displays at the Fort Jackson. These are the Adjutant General Corps Museum, the Chaplains Museum and the Finance Corps Museum.

TYPE	REG/SER	CON. NO.	PI/NOTES	STATUS
☐ Bell 204 Iroquois (UH-1B)	64-13972	1096		PV

GARDEN CITY MONUMENT (SC11)

Location:	On permanent view at a business in the town.

TYPE	REG/SER	CON. NO.	PI/NOTES	STATUS
☐ Republic RC-3 Seabee				PVX

GREENVILLE MONUMENT (SC12)

Location:	On permanent view in Cleveland Park in the town.

TYPE	REG/SER	CON. NO.	PI/NOTES	STATUS
☐ North American NA-187 Sabre (F-86H)	52-1976	187-2		PV

GREENVILLE TECHNICAL COLLEGE (SC13)

Address:	111 Connecticut Court, Greenville, South Carolina 29605-5410.
Tel:	864-422-1762 Email: Carl.Washburn@gvltech.edu
Admission:	By prior permission only.
Location:	At the airport which is about 10 miles south of the town.

537

The college was established in the early 1960s and now operates from six sites in the area. The aviation maintenance courses are held in a facility at the Donaldson Industrial Air Park. The airfield opened as Greenville Army Air Base in 1942. In 1951 the base was named after Captain John Donaldson, a local pilot who was killed in 1930 at an air race in Philadelphia. Among the instructional airframes are two retired business jets.

TYPE	REG/SER	CON. NO.	PI/NOTES	STATUS
☐ Beech C50 Seminole (RL-23D) (RU-8D) (RU-8G)	NL23D	LH-150	57-6089	RA
☐ Bell 205 Iroquois (UH-1D) (UH-1H)	N7420	4786	65-9742	RA
☐ Bell 205 Iroquois (UH-1H)	68-16505	11164	Boom from c/n 5556 66-1073.	RA
☐ Bell 205 Iroquois (UH-1H)	67-17195	9593		RA
☐ Cessna 337M Super Skymaster (O-2A)				RA
☐ Lockheed 1329 JetStar 8	N801	1329-5138	N5502L, N1301P, N333RW, N31DK, N801, (N700MJ)	RA
☐ North American NA-306 Sabreliner 60	N4LG	306-9	N4717N, N47MN, N998R, N958R, N1298, N32UT, N5071L	RA

GREER MONUMENT (SC14)

Location:	On permanent view in a park in the town.

TYPE	REG/SER	CON. NO.	PI/NOTES	STATUS
☐ Bell 209 Huey Cobra (AH-1G) (AH-1F)	67-15768	20432		PV

HARTSVILLE MONUMENT (SC15)

Location:	On permanent view at the airport which is about 3 miles north west of the town.

TYPE	REG/SER	CON. NO.	PI/NOTES	STATUS
☐ Lockheed 580 (T-33A)	58-0504	580-1473		PV

MYRTLE BEACH AIR FORCE BASE HERITAGE PARK (SC16)

Address:	1181 Shine Avenue, Myrtle Beach, South Carolina 29577.
Tel:	803-238-7211
Admission:	On permanent view
Location:	Just south of the town off Route 17.

The town set up a small civil airport in the late 1930s which was soon taken over as a military airfield; it remained in use until 1948 when it reverted to town ownership. An Air Force base was constructed in the mid-1950s for use by Tactical Air Command squadrons and it was operational until 1993. Three aircraft have been left as a reminder of the military presence at the field.

TYPE	REG/SER	CON. NO.	PI/NOTES	STATUS
☐ Fairchild-Republic A-10A Thunderbolt II	79-0097	A10-361		PV
☐ North American NA-235 Super Sabre (F-100D)	56-2967	235-65		PV
☐ Vought A-7D Corsair II	70-1019	D165		PV

NORTH MYRTLE BEACH MONUMENTS (SC17)

Location:	On permanent view at two locations in the town.

TYPE	REG/SER	CON. NO.	PI/NOTES	STATUS
☐ Bell 204 Iroquois (UH-1B)			Probably a composite – at Mayday Golf Course.	PV
☐ Lockheed 15-27-01 Harpoon (PV-2)	N72707	15-1458	Bu37492, N7270C – at Mayday Golf Course.	PVX
☐ Republic RC-3 Seabee			At a crazy golf attraction.	PV

PATRIOTS POINT NAVAL AND MARITIME MUSEUM (SC18)

Address:	PO Box 986, 40 Patriots Point Road, Mount Pleasant, South Carolina 29464.
Tel:	803-884-2727 **Email:** ntompkins@patriotspoint.org
Admission:	Daily 0900-1700.
Location:	On the east side of Charleston Harbour.

In 1973 the Patriot's Point Development Authority was established and it purchased land the following year.
The aircraft carrier the USS *Yorktown* arrived in June 1975 and was opened to the public on 3rd January 1976. The ship was commissioned in April 1943 and served with distinction in many of the Pacific battles of World War II. Later it operated in the Korean War and in December 1968 recovered the crew of Apollo 8 after the first flight around the moon. The three other ships on view are the destroyer USS *Laffey* which took part in the D-Day landings, the submarine USS *Clamagore*, and the Coast Guard cutter *Comanche*. All four vessels are open for inspection.
The aircraft are mainly displayed on the *Yorktown* and the majority have seen carrier use. Some are on the flight deck and others in the hangar. The Mitchell was not designed for ship operation but the type achieved fame after Jimmy Doolittle's spectacular raid on Tokyo. On 18th April 1942 he led a formation of 16 B-25s from the deck of the USS *Hornet* on the 800 mile flight to bomb the Japanese capital.
The Grumman company has been a supplier of aircraft to the Navy for more than 60 years and a number of the products of the Long Island firm are on view. The Dauntless was ditched in Lake Michigan in March 1944 and remained under water until recovered in 1987. The aircraft was rebuilt at Griffin in Georgia and joined the exhibition in 1993. A reconstruction of a Vietnam Naval Support Base has been built on the shore and the Bell helicopters are on view in this area along with a river patrol boat, weapons of the period and a replica combat centre.

South Carolina

TYPE	REG/SER	CON. NO.	PI/NOTES	STATUS
☐ Bell 204 Iroquois (UH-1C) (UH-1M)	66-15005	1733		PV
☐ Bell 205 Iroquois (UH-1D)	'65-10132'	5615	66-1132	PVX
☐ Bell 209 Sea Cobra (AH-1J)	Bu159210	26050		PV
☐ Boeing-Stearman B75N1 Kaydet (N2S-3)	Bu07526	75-7130	On loan from NMNA, FL	PV
☐ Douglas SBD-5 Dauntless	Bu36173	4812		PV
☐ Douglas A-1D Skyraider (AD-4N) (AD-4NA)	Bu127007	7807		PV
☐ Douglas EA-3B Skywarrior (A3D-2Q)				PV
☐ Douglas A-4L Skyhawk (A4D-2N) (A-4C)	Bu149623	12948		PV
☐ Grumman G-36 Wildcat (F4F-3A)	'Bu3872'	838	Bu3956	PVX
☐ Grumman G-40 Avenger (TBM-3) (TBM-3E)	Bu53842	3904	Bu53842, N7025C, N603, N60393	PV
☐ Grumman G-50 Hellcat (F6F-5) (F6F-5K)	Bu79593	A-10538	Was painted as F6F-3 Bu41476	PV
☐ Grumman G-105 Cougar (F9F-8T) (TF-9J)	Bu147385	355		PV
☐ Grumman G-117 Tracer (WF-2) (E-1B)	Bu147225	24		PV
☐ Grumman G-121 Tracker (S-2E)	Bu151657	190C		PV
☐ Grumman G-128 Intruder (A-6A) (A-6E)	Bu152599	I-147		PV
☐ Grumman G-303 Tomcat (F-14A)	Bu159025	86		PV
☐ Gyrodyne QH-50C (DSN-3)		DS-1323		PV
☐ Gyrodyne XRON-1 (XHOG-1)				PV
☐ Lockheed 394 Viking (S-3A) (S-3B)	Bu159731	394A-3060		PV
☐ McDonnell M.98EV Phantom II (F-4J)	Bu153077	1579	Carries 'Bu157282' on port side	PV
☐ McDonnell M.267 Hornet (F/A-18A)	Bu162435	278/A224		PV
☐ North American NA-87 Mitchell (B-25D) (TB-25D)N2XD		87-7549	41-29784, NL5078N, N5078N, N122B, N2DD	PV
☐ Sikorsky S-58 Seahorse (HUS-1) (UH-34D)	Bu147171	581087		PV
☐ Sikorsky S-61B Sea King (HSS-2) (SH-3A) (SH-3G)	Bu149932			PV
☐ Vought FG-1D Corsair	Bu88368	3182		PV
☐ Vought F-8K Crusader (F8U-2) (F-8C)	Bu146939			PV
☐ Vought A-7E Corsair II	Bu159291	E429	Carries 'Bu153176' on port side	PV
☐ Wright Flyer (R)				PV

SHAW AIR FORCE BASE COLLECTION (SC19)

Address: 20 FW/PA, 517 Lance Avenue, Suite 106, Shaw Air Force Base, South Carolina 29152-5041.
Tel: 803-895-2019.
Admission: By prior permission only.
Location: About 10 miles north west of Sumter on Route 76/378.
Poinsett Range is about 4 miles south of Wedgefield off Route 261.

Lieutenant Ervin D. Shaw was one of the first Americans to see action in France in World War I. He was killed in July 1918 when his Bristol Fighter was shot down on a reconnaissance mission. The base was activated in August 1941 and houses a tactical fighter wing.

The field has been in continuous use since it opened. A collection of preserved aircraft has been set up close to the main gate and two others are parked at the nearby Poinsett gunnery range. There is a collection of memorabilia in a room in the base headquarters.

TYPE	REG/SER	CON. NO.	PI/NOTES	STATUS
☐ Cessna 337M Super Skymaster (O-2A)	'98-962'	337M0238	68-10962	RAX
☐ Douglas EB-66C Destroyer (RB-66C)	54-0465	44765		RA
☐ Fairchild-Republic A-10A Thunderbolt II	'81-0964'	A10-58		RA
☐ General Dynamics 401 Fighting Falcon (F-16A)	'93-0324'	61-94	75-0309 – possible identity	RAX
☐ Gyrodyne QH-50C (DSN-3)	'64-0158'			RAX
☐ McDonnell M.36BA Voodoo (F-101B)	58-0273	645	At Poinsett Range.	RA
☐ McDonnell M.36CA Voodoo (RF-101C)	56-0099	333		RA
☐ McDonnell M.98DF Phantom II (RF-4C)	63-7748	532		RA
☐ Republic F-105B Thunderchief	'75817'	B-56	57-5819 – at Poinsett Range.	RAX
☐ Republic P-47D Thunderbolt (FSM)	'226420'			PVX

SOUTH CAROLINA STATE MUSEUM (SC20)

Address: 301 Gervais Street, Columbia, South Carolina 29201-3091.
Tel: 803-898-4948   **Fax:** 803-898-4969   **Email:** webmaster@scmuseum.com
Admission: Tuesday-Saturday 1000-1700; Sunday 1300-1700.
Location: In the centre of the city.

Housed in the large Columbia Mill built in 1893 this museum traces the story of the state in a number of fields. These include art, natural history, cultural history, science and technology. The transportation area includes the aviation section. On show is the 1928 monoplane built by Clemson College Aeroclub. The high-wing design is believed to be the first aircraft in the USA to be built by college students. The engine was unreliable and it crashed on most of its few flights. The history of aviation in the state is portrayed with photographs and documents.

The oldest rubber-band powered model aircraft in the country is a prized exhibit.

TYPE	REG/SER	CON. NO.	PI/NOTES	STATUS
☐ Clemson AM A-100	X-372			PV

ST. MATTHEWS MONUMENT (SC21)

Location: On permanent view at a business in the town.

TYPE	REG/SER	CON. NO.	PI/NOTES	STATUS
☐ Lockheed 580 (T-33A)	58-0539	580-1508	58-0539, N37998	PV

TRANSPORT AIRCRAFT MUSEUM (SC22)

Address:	437 AW/PA, 102 East Hill Road, Suite 223, Charleston Air Force Base, South Carolina 29404-5000.
Tel:	843-963-5608 Email: publicaffairs@charleston.af.mil
Admission:	By prior permission only.
Location:	About 8 miles north west of the city off Interstate 26.

The site was first used in 1931 as the civil airfield for the city. The Army Air Corps established a base in December 1941 and training of B-17 Fortress and B-24 Liberator crews was carried out. From 1946 until 1952 it was again the Charleston Airport. An agreement for joint use of the runways was agreed in the early 1950s. Tactical Air Command squadrons were in residence from 1952 to 1956. For the last half century the field has been home to transport units. Four significant types flown from the site have been preserved.

TYPE	REG/SER	CON. NO.	PI/NOTES	STATUS
☐ Cessna 172F Mescalero (T-41A)	N5223F	17253260	65-5223 – by Aero Club.	RA
☐ Douglas DC-3A-467 Skytrain (C-47B) (VC-47D)	'2100972'	15171/26616	43-49355	RAX
☐ Douglas 1317 Globemaster II (C-124C)	52-1072	43981		RA
☐ Lockheed 300 Starlifter (C-141A) (C-141B)	63-8079	300-6010		RA
☐ Lockheed 1049F-55-96 Super Constellation (C-121C)	'40153'	1049F-4199	54-0180	RAX

TRIDENT TECHNICAL COLLEGE (SC23)

Address:	1001 South Live Oak Drive, Moncks Corner, South Carolina 29461-7224.
Tel:	843-899-8000 Email: d.coombs.73662@ttc.mailcruiser.com
Admission:	By prior permission only.
Location:	In the south western part of the town.

The college came into being in 1973 when two local educational institutions merged. Courses leading to FAA licences are held along with an associate degree in aircraft maintenance technology. The well equipped workshops house engines and test rigs. The list of instructional aircraft is not complete.

TYPE	REG/SER	CON. NO.	PI/NOTES	STATUS
☐ Bell 204 Iroquois				RA
☐ Bell 205 Iroquois (UH-1D) (UH-1H)	63-8831	4123		RA
☐ Cessna 152				RA
☐ Cessna 172N	N2039E	17271128		RA
☐ Cessna 310A	N4568	38138		RA
☐ Cessna 421				RA
☐ Ercoupe 415D				RA
☐ North American NA-265 Sabreliner (T-39A) (CT-39A)	61-0651	265-54		RA
☐ North American NA-276 Sabreliner (T-39A) (CT-39A)	62-4462	276-15		RA
☐ Piper PA-30 Twin Comanche				RA

SOUTH DAKOTA

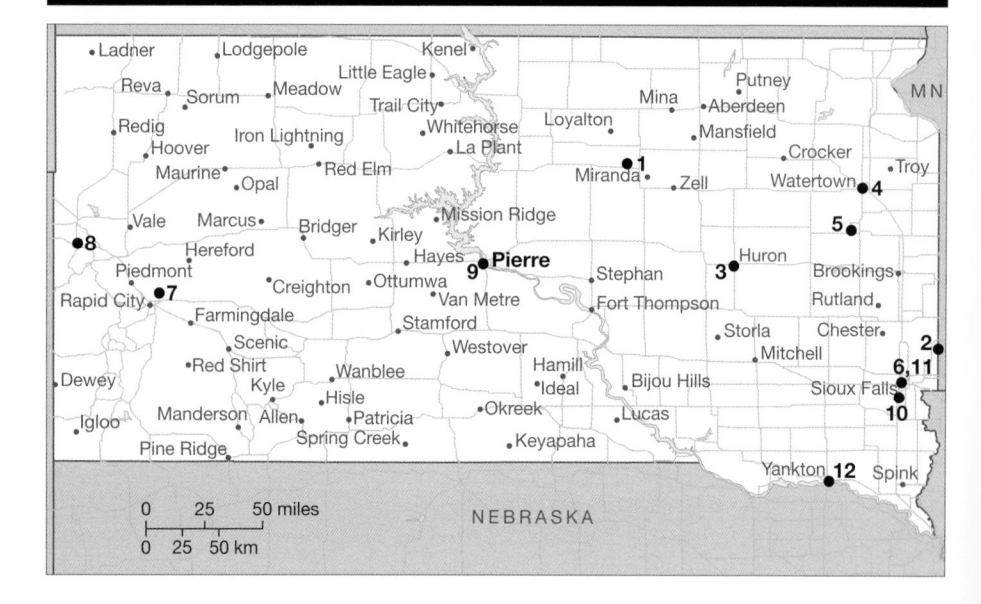

FAULKTON MONUMENT (SD1)

Location:	On permanent view at the airport in the eastern part of the town.

TYPE	REG/SER	CON. NO.	PI/NOTES	STATUS
☐ Vought A-7D Corsair II	69-6239	D69		PV

GARRETSON MONUMENT (SD2)

Location:	By prior permission only at a farm in the area.

TYPE	REG/SER	CON. NO.	PI/NOTES	STATUS
☐ Northrop N-160 Scorpion (N-68) (F-89D) (F-89J)	51-11443	N.2408		RA

HURON MONUMENTS (SD3)

Location:	On permanent view at two locations in the town.

TYPE	REG/SER	CON. NO.	PI/NOTES	STATUS
☐ Lockheed 580 (T-33A)	53-6100	580-9721	At VFW 1776 on Huron Street.	PV
☐ Vought A-7D Corsair II	70-1012	D158	At airport north of the town.	PV

LAKE AREA TECHNICAL INSTITUTE (SD4)

Address:	230 11th Street North East, Watertown, South Dakota 57201
Tel:	605-882-6311
Admission:	By prior permission only.
Location:	At airport which is just south of the town.

The college was established in 1965 and offers a wide range of courses at its campus in the town. The aviation department has premises at the airport. The Cessna 337 and Schweizer motor glider are also used for pilot training.

The fleet of instructional aircraft includes an example of the Falco. The low-wing two-seater was designed by Stelio Frati and the prototype made its maiden flight in 1955. Small numbers were built by three companies in Italy. The high performance coupled with pleasing looks soon attracted amateur constructors. Sequoia Aircraft based in Richmond, Virginia sell kits and plans. The aircraft in the workshops was built by Laurence Wohlers and first flew in the mid-1980s.

The workshops contain several engines both piston and jet.

TYPE	REG/SER	CON. NO.	PI/NOTES	STATUS
☐ Aero Commander 100	N3653X	307		RA
☐ Beech C23 Sundowner 180	N6717K	M-2266		RA
☐ Beech 58P Baron	N165SD	TJ-314		RA
☐ Beech 65-A90-1 Ute (U-21A)	N518NA	LM-80	67-18080	RA
☐ Bell 206A Kiowa (OH-58A)	71-20804	41665		RA
☐ Cessna R172E Mescalero (T-41C)	N7886N	R1720277	68-7886	RA
☐ Cessna 337M Super Skymaster (O-2A)	N337SD	337M0266	68-10990, N465DF	RAA
☐ North American NA-265 Sabreliner (T-39A) (CT-39A)				RA
☐ Schweizer SGM.2-37 (TG-7A)	N762AF	10	87-0762	RAA
☐ Sequoia F.8L Falco	N33LW	1		RA
☐ Vought A-7E Corsair II	Bu157435	E158	Airport monument.	PV

LAKE NORDEN MONUMENT (SD5)

Location:	On permanent view in a park on Park Street in the north western part of the town.

TYPE	REG/SER	CON. NO.	PI/NOTES	STATUS
☐ Lockheed 580 (T-33A)	51-8665	580-6449		PV

SIOUX FALLS AIR NATIONAL GUARD BASE (SD6)

Address:	114 FG/PA, 1201 West Algonquin Street, Sioux Falls, South Dakota 57104-0264.
Tel:	605-988-5700 Email: webmaster@sdsiou.ang.af.mil
Admission:	By prior permission only.
Location:	On the south side of the field which is in the northern suburbs of the city.

The sole flying unit of the South Dakota Air National Guard has been based in its home state since its formation in September 1946. The 175th Squadron initially operated P-51s from Sioux Falls but during its call-up for active service in the Korean War period it only made the short move to Ellsworth Air Force Base on the other side of the state.

The types operated include the F-94, the F-89, the F-102, the F-100, the A-7 and now the F-16.

The air park is by the base gate and in the Wing Headquarters is a display of memorabilia. The Convair delta fighter was first put on show in the mid-1980s and the others have been added over the years.

TYPE	REG/SER	CON. NO.	PI/NOTES	STATUS
☐ Convair 8-10 Delta Dagger (F-102A)	'56-1114'	8-10-11	53-1801	RAX
☐ General Dynamics 401 Fighting Falcon (F-16A)	81-0723	61-404		RA
☐ General Dynamics 401 Fighting Falcon (F-16C)	85-1469	5C-249		RA
☐ Lockheed 580 (T-33A) (TV-2) (T-33B)	Bu137993	580-8848	53-5509	RA
☐ North American NA-235 Super Sabre (F-100D)	56-3178	235-201		RA
☐ Vought A-7D Corsair II	70-0931	D77		RA

SOUTH DAKOTA AIR AND SPACE MUSEUM (SD7)

Address:	Ellsworth Heritage Foundation, PO Box 871, Box Elder, South Dakota 57719-0871.
Tel:	605-385-5189 Fax: 605-385-6295 Email: ronalley@ellsworth.af.mil
Admission:	Mid May–mid September daily 0830-1800; mid September–mid May daily 0830-1630.
Location:	About 11 miles north east of Rapid City off Interstate 90 near Ellsworth Air Force Base.

Formerly known as Rapid City Army Air Base, the site opened as a bomber field in 1942 and has retained this role throughout its existence. The current name was adopted in 1954 to honour General Richard E. Ellsworth who was killed in the crash of a RB-36 in Newfoundland in March 1953. He was commander of the 28th Wing which moved in during 1954 and is still resident.

A small museum opened on the base in 1981 and on show were items tracing the history of the field and its units. The Ellsworth Heritage Foundation set about raising funds for a purpose-built museum located outside the main gate. An excellent building opened in 1989. In 1956 the B-52, parked on a hill, was the first of its type to land at Ellsworth.

TYPE	REG/SER	CON. NO.	PI/NOTES	STATUS
☐ Beech D18S Expeditor (C-45H)	'40796'	AF-796	52-10866, N2797A, N311SA, N4111A	PV
☐ Beech C50 Seminole (L-23D) (U-8D)	56-3708	LH-109		PV
☐ Bell 47G-2 Sioux (H-13H) (OH-13H)	58-1520	2284		PV
☐ Bell 204 Iroquois (UH-1F)	65-7951	7092		PV
☐ Boeing 345 Superfortress (B-29) (TB-29) (B-29M) (KB-29B)	44-87779	12582		PV
☐ Boeing 464-201-7 Stratofortress (B-52D)	56-0657	464028		PV
☐ Boeing 717-146 Stratotanker (KC-135A) (EC-135A)	61-0262	18169		PV
☐ Cessna 310A Blue Canoe (L-27A) (U-3A)	57-5872	38027		PV
☐ Cessna 337M Super Skymaster (O-2A)	67-21422	337M0128		PV
☐ Convair 440-79 Samaritan (C-131D)	55-0292	315	N8435H	PV
☐ Convair 8-10 Delta Dagger (F-102A)	56-1017	8-10-234		RAC
☐ Douglas DC-3A-456 Skytrain (C-47A) (R4D-5)	'42-93149'	13004	42-93127, Bu17193, N6517C, N55, N67, N226GB	PVX
☐ Douglas DC-4 Skymaster (C-54D) (R5D-3) (C-54S)	42-72592	10697	42-72592, Bu56511, N67029	PV
☐ Douglas A-26A Invader (A-26C) (B-26K)	64-17640	29175	44-35896, 64-17640, N267G, N2294B – (On-Mark B-26K)	PV
☐ General Dynamics FB-111A	68-0248	B1-20		RA
☐ Lockheed 580 (T-33A)	57-0590	580-1239		PV
☐ Martin 272B Canberra (B-57B) (EB-57B)	52-1548	131		PV
☐ McDonnell M.36BA Voodoo (F-101B)	59-0426	750		PV
☐ North American NA-108 Mitchell (B-25J) (VB-25J)	'44-39340'	108-24356	43-4030, N3339G, 43-4030	PVX
☐ North American NA-192 Super Sabre (F-100A)	53-1553	192-48		RA
☐ North American NA-203 Sabre (F-86H)	53-1302	203-74		PV
☐ Northrop B-2 Spirit (Scale R)	'89-1001'			PVX
☐ Northrop N-156T Talon (YT-38) (YT-38A)	58-1192	N.5102		PV
☐ Republic F-84F Thunderstreak	52-8886			PV
☐ Republic F-105B Thunderchief	57-5839	B-76		PV
☐ Rockwell B-1B Lancer	83-0067	4		PV
☐ Stinson V-76 Sentinel (L-5G)	45-34996	76-4628	45-34996, N63273	PV
☐ Vought A-7D Corsair II	74-1739	D414		PV
☐ Vultee V-74 Valiant (BT-13A)	41-22204	74-6124	41-22204, N58268	PV

SOUTH DAKOTA AVIATION HALL OF FAME (SD8)

Address:	424 Aviation Place, Spearfish, South Dakota 57783-6350.
Tel:	605-642-0277 Email: bha@mato.com
Admission:	Not yet open.
Location:	At the airport which is about 2 miles east of the town.

Funds are being raised to construct a building to house memorabilia and aircraft. The site will be at Black Hills Airport. Two aircraft are owned by the organisation and others have been promised.

TYPE	REG/SER	CON. NO.	PI/NOTES	STATUS
☐ American Flea Triplane	N6001V			RAC
☐ Stits SA-11A Playmate	N6515	HCB-1		RA

SOUTH DAKOTA NATIONAL GUARD MUSEUM (SD9)

Address:	425 East Dakota Avenue, Pierre, South Dakota 57501-3225.
Tel:	605-224-9991 Email: bobkusser@state.sd.us
Admission:	Monday, Wednesday, Friday 1300-1700.
Location:	In the centre of the city.

The museum was set up in 1982 and traces the history of the forces which have served in the region. Many items date from the South Dakota territorial military units established before the state came into being. On show are weapons, medals, uniforms, photographs, documents etc. On view in the building is a Hughes OH-6 which was flown by the state Army Air Guard and outside is an A-7 operated by the South Dakota Air National Guard at Sioux Falls. The Sioux helicopter was formerly on show at the US Army Transportation Museum in Virginia.

TYPE	REG/SER	CON. NO.	PI/NOTES	STATUS
☐ Bell 47A Sioux (YR-13) (YH-13)	46-0234	7		PV
☐ Hughes 369M Cayuse (HO-6) (OH-6A)	65-13000	0085		PV
☐ Vought A-7D Corsair II	70-0996	D142		PV

TEA MONUMENT (SD10)

Location:	On permanent view at the airport which is about 4 miles north east of the town.

TYPE	REG/SER	CON. NO.	PI/NOTES	STATUS
☐ Vought A-7D Corsair II	70-1050	D-196		PV

VAMPIRE JET MUSEUM (SD11)

Address:	3700 South Westport Avenue, Sioux Falls, South Dakota 57106-6360
Admission:	By prior permission only.
Location:	Possibly at the airport which is in the northern part of the town.

The former Royal Air Force Vampire Trainer was restored to flying condition by a group in Great Britain. The jet has been registered to the museum since the summer of 2007 but little is known about their activities.

TYPE	REG/SER	CON. NO.	PI/NOTES	STATUS
☐ De Havilland DH.115 Vampire T.11	N920DH	15621	XE920, 8196M, G-VMPR, N94019	PVA

YANKTON MONUMENT (SD12)

Location:	On permanent view at the closed airport at 610 East 31st Street.

TYPE	REG/SER	CON. NO.	PI/NOTES	STATUS
☐ Northrop N-156T Talon (T-38A) (AT-38A)	60-0595	N.5168		PV

TENNESSEE

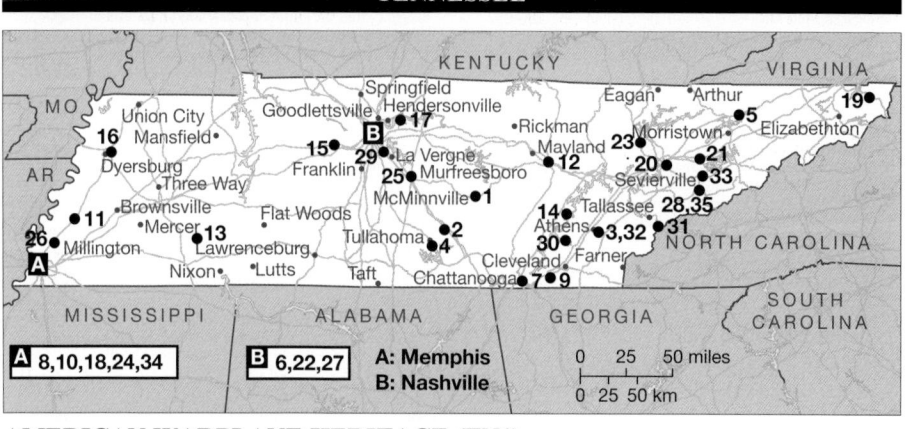

AMERICAN WARPLANE HERITAGE (TN1)

Address:	4187 Nashville Highway, McMinnville, Tennessee 37110-5380
Admission:	By prior permission only.
Location:	At the airport which is about 4 miles west of the town on Route 1

This collection has a number of interesting types in its fleet. Under restoration is a Grumman Tiger which when completed will be the only airworthy example of the classic jet fighter. The F11F prototype made its maiden flight on 30th July 1954 at Grumman's new factory at Calverton on Long Island.

TYPE	REG/SER	CON. NO.	PI/NOTES	STATUS
☐ Beech A45 Mentor (T-34A)	N999SC	G-306	53-4206	RAA
☐ Beech D45 Mentor (T-34B)	N34JW	BG-374	Bu144067, N4947C	RAA
☐ Canadair CL-30 Silver Star 3 (CT-133) [Lockheed 580 (T-33AN)]	N72JR	T33-295	21295 (Canada), N4TM, N33EL	RA
☐ Cessna 305A Bird Dog (L-19A) (O-1A)	N70542	21231	51-4539 (?)	RAA
☐ Grumman G-98 Tiger (F11F-1) (F-11A)	N81682		(USN)	RAC
☐ North American NA-88 Texan (AT-6D)	N7214C	88-17532	42-85751	RAA

ARNOLD AIR FORCE BASE (TN2)

Address:	AEDC/PAO, 100 Kindel Drive, Suite B-213, Arnold AFB, Tennessee 37389-2213.
Tel:	931-454-4204
Admission:	By prior permission only.
Location:	About 5 miles south of Manchester on Route 16.

The complex was opened in January 1950 and houses the Engineering Development Center of the Air Force. The area was formerly Camp Forrest, a training base for the Tennessee National Guard.

TYPE	REG/SER	CON. NO.	PI/NOTES	STATUS
☐ General Dynamics 401 Fighting Falcon (F-16A)	79-0407	61-192		RA
☐ Grumman G-303 Tomcat (F-14D)	Bu163893	603		RA
☐ Mcdonnell M.98DE Phantom II (F-4C)	63-7644	745		PV
☐ Mcdonnell M.199-1A Eagle (F-15A)	77-0068	342/A280		PV
☐ Mcdonnell M.267 Hornet (F/A-18A)	Bu162838	358/A299		RA
☐ Republic F-105D Thunderchief	62-4328	D-527		PV

ATHENS MONUMENT (TN3)

Location:	On permanent view at VFW 5146 on Highway 11 just north of the town.

TYPE	REG/SER	CON. NO.	PI/NOTES	STATUS
☐ Mcdonnell M.98HO Phantom II (F-4E) (NF-4E)	66-0319	2562		{V

BEECHCRAFT HERITAGE MUSEUM (TN4)

Address:	570 Old Shelbyville Highway, PO Box 550, Tullahoma, Tennessee 37388-0550.
Tel:	931-455-1974 **Fax:** 931-455-1994 **Email:** info@beechheritagemuseum.org
Admission:	Tuesday-Saturday 0830-1630
Location:	At Parish Aerodrome which is just south of Tullahoma Municipal Airport west of Route 130.

Walter Beech was born near Pulaski, Tennessee in 1891. In 1925 he was one of the founders of the Travel Air Company which set up its factory in Wichita, Kansas. The firm was sold to Curtiss-Wright in 1929 but during its brief existence it produced a series of types which were thought by many to be the best of their era.
Beech left in 1932 to form his own company which is still in the forefront of the aviation industry. The first product of the Beech Aircraft Company was the biplane Model 17 which soon became known as the Staggerwing because of its unique wing form. The prototype first flew on 4th November 1932 and just over three years later crashed near Nunda in New York State. The remains were recovered by the late Steve Pfister who set about rebuilding the historic machine at his Santa Paula workshops in California. Sadly he died before the aircraft could be completed. The Staggerwing was purchased by the museum in 1991. It was then taken to Arkansas for completion.

The museum was set up in 1973 by members of the Staggerwing Club and its first building a 100-year-old log cabin was moved to the site the following year. Named the Louise Thaden Office and Library after the pilot who set many records in Travel Airs and won the 1936 Bendix Race in a Staggerwing, the cabin houses many trophies and memorabilia relating to her accomplishments.
The Walter H. Beech hangar was opened in 1975 and on show are examples of Travel Airs and every model of the Staggerwing. A second set of buildings to honour the classic Beech 18 series was constructed a few years ago and recently a hangar housing models of the Bonanza series has been completed. A fairly recent arrival is the Starship. The prototype of this advanced twin engined pusher design made its maiden flight in February 1986. Only 53 were completed and the type was grounded in 2003. The history of the company is portrayed in the displays.

TYPE	REG/SER	CON. NO.	PI/NOTES	STATUS
☐ Beech 17R	NC499N	1		PVA
☐ Beech B17L	NC14409	21	NC14409, N14409	PVA
☐ Beech C17L	NC962W	100	NC16441	PV
☐ Beech D17S	N20753	395	NC20753	PVA
☐ Beech E17L (E17B) (UC-43D)	NC19467	231	NC19467, 42-53511, N19467 – rebuilt with fuselage of E17B c/n 209 NC40Y.	PV
☐ Beech F17D (E17B) (UC-43D)	NC17083	138	NC17083, 42-47447, N57839	PVC
☐ Beech F17D (UC-43C)	NC20798	333	NC20798, 42-38238	PVA
☐ Beech G17S	N44G	B-3	NC80304	PV
☐ Beech G17S	N80308	B-7		PVA
☐ Beech D18S	N4477	A-935	N2049D	PVA
☐ Beech D18S Expeditor (C-45H)	N7916A	AF-824	52-10894 – formerly C18S Kansan (AT-11) c/n 3628 42-37199.	PVA
☐ Beech D18S Expeditor (C18S) (UC-45F) (JRB-4) (SNB-5) (TC-45J)	N20003	8142	44-47733, Bu44580 – front fuselage only.	PV
☐ Beech E18S	N712JS	BA-553	N435A, N4351	PVA
☐ Beech S18D	CF-BKO	178	N87AZ	PVA
☐ Beech 35 Bonanza	NC40818	D-18	NC40818, N40818	PV
☐ Beech H35 Bonanza	N5404D	D-4887		PV
☐ Beech V35 Bonanza			Cutaway airframe.	PV
☐ Beech A36 Bonanza 36	N9697R	E-2503		PVA
☐ Beech D45 Mentor (T-34B)	N434RM	BG-322	Bu144015	PVA
☐ Beech D50E Twin Bonanza	N14VU	DH-326		PV
☐ Beech 95-55 Baron	N9695R	TC-1		PV
☐ Beech 2000A Starship I	N8224Q	NC-49	N8224Q, XA-TQF	PV
☐ Cianchette Lionhart	N985CC	003		PV
☐ Fleet Super V (Beech 35 Bonanza)	N3124V	SV-109-D-549		PV
☐ Travel Air 1000	NC241	1	NC241, N241 – on loan from EAA, WI.	PV
☐ Travel Air 4000	N367M	1295	NC367M	PVA
☐ Travel Air R	NR614K	2002		PV
☐ Travel Air R	NR1313	R-2004	Original wings -complete aircraft at Museum of Science and Industry, IL. New aircraft will be built by museum.	PV

BLOOMQUIST COLLECTION (TN5)

Address:	219 Brooks Road, Mooresburg, Tennessee 37811-2105.
Admission:	By prior permission only.
Location:	About 10 miles north of Morristown on Route 11.

This private collection of light aircraft contains many interesting types. The four replica World War I designs are painted in period colours. Under construction is a replica of a Gotha G IV twin engined bomber.

TYPE	REG/SER	CON. NO.	PI/NOTES	STATUS
☐ Bellanca 8GCBC Scout	N8667V	17-75		RAA
☐ Bloomquist Staggerwing	N6086N	85445		RAC
☐ Boeing 99 (F4B-1) (R)	N6086R	85446		RAC
☐ Fokker Dr I (R)	N7049P	085		RAA
☐ Gotha G IV (R)				RAC
☐ Pietenpol P-9 Sky Scout	N81746	001		RAA
☐ Ramsey Bathtub				RAC
☐ Royal Aircraft Factory S.E.5A (R)	N30255	7549		RAA
☐ Rumpler C IV (R)	N1916E	1705	G-AXAM – built from de Havilland DH.82A Tiger Moth c/n 85835 DE975, G-AODU	RAA
☐ Sopwith Pup (R)	N6086K	85444		RAA

BRISTOL HERITAGE COLLECTION (TN6)

Address:	210 Cub Parkway, Nashville, Tennessee 37221-1900.
Tel:	615-383-9091 Email: graybrstl@prodigy.net
Admission:	By prior permission only.
Location:	At Clifton Airport which is about 3 miles east of the town.

This collection has been set up by Bristol born Graham Kilsby. The main aim is to preserve aircraft, engines and cars built at Filton by the Bristol Aeroplane Company. The first aircraft to arrive were the Bolingbroke, Beaufort and Bristol powered Gnat which came from the Military Aircraft Restoration Company at Chino.

TYPE	REG/SER	CON. NO.	PI/NOTES	STATUS
☐ Bristol Boxkite (R)				RAC
☐ Bristol 149 Bolingbroke IVT	10076	49306-28	In Canadian markings.	RAC
☐ Bristol 152 Beaufort VIII	A9-555		Rear fuselage from A9-182.	RA
☐ Fairey Swordfish III				RAD
☐ Folland Fo.141 Gnat F.1				RA
☐ Percival P.66 Pembroke C.51	N510RP	P.66/29	RM-9 (Belgium), N51964, HR-ITA, N702JM,	RAC
☐ Westland Lysander IIIA		1176	On loan from MARC, CA.	PVC

CHATTANOOGA AIR NATIONAL GUARD BASE (TN7)

Location:	On permanent view at the airport which is in the north eastern suburbs of the city off Interstate 153.

TYPE	REG/SER	CON. NO.	PI/NOTES	STATUS
☐ McDonnell M.36BA Voodoo (F-101B)	59-0412	736		PV

CHILDREN'S MUSEUM OF MEMPHIS (TN8)

Address:	25 Central Avenue, Memphis, Tennessee 38104-5926.
Tel:	901-458-2678 Fax: 901-458-4033 Email: children@cmom.com
Admission:	Monday-Saturday 0900-1700; Sunday 1200-1700.
Location:	In the centre of the city.

The 'Going Places' section of this informative and innovative museum has the front fuselage of a Boeing 727 on show along with a flight simulator, an air traffic control tower and a wind tunnel.

TYPE	REG/SER	CON. NO.	PI/NOTES	STATUS
☐ Boeing 727-22	N7025U	18317	N7025U, (N160FE) – front fuselage only.	PV
☐ Hot Air Balloon				PV

COLLEGEDALE MONUMENT (TN9)

Location:	On permanent view in a Veterans Memorial Park off Apison Pike in the northern part of the town.

TYPE	REG/SER	CON. NO.	PI/NOTES	STATUS
☐ Bell 209 Huey Cobra (AH-1G) (AH-1F)	67-15642	20306		PV

COMMEMORATIVE AIR FORCE (MEMPHIS SQUADRON) (TN10)

Address:	1684 Peach Avenue, Memphis, Tennessee 38112-5216.
Tel:	901-522-7764 Email: mwray2@bellsouth.net
Admission:	By prior permission only.
Location:	At General De Witt Spain Airport which is in the north western suburbs of the city.

The squadron was formed in December 2005 and now operates the former Royal Navy Sea Fury The aircraft was restored to flying condition in the mid-1990s and was donated it to the newly formed unit in 2006. The Lockheed T-33 arrived in 2010 from the currently dormant Golden Gate Wing in California.

TYPE	REG/SER	CON. NO.	PI/NOTES	STATUS
☐ Hawker Sea Fury FB.11	N15S	41H/696792	WJ288, G-SALY	RAA
☐ Lockheed 580 (T-33A)	NX9124Z	580-5913	51-6581, Bu128706	RAA

COVINGTON MONUMENT (TN11)

Location:	On permanent view on Highway 51 in the eastern part of the town.

TYPE	REG/SER	CON. NO.	PI/NOTES	STATUS
☐ Douglas A-4L Skyhawk (A4D-2N) (A-4C)	Bu149508	12833		PV

CROSSVILLE MONUMENT (TN12)

Location:	On permanent view at Cumberland County High School at 660 Stanley Street in the centre of the town.

TYPE	REG/SER	CON. NO.	PI/NOTES	STATUS
☐ Douglas A-4C Skyhawk (A4D-2N)	Bu148572	12765		PV
☐ Lockheed 580 (T-33A)	51-6756	580-6088		PV

CRUMP MONUMENT (TN13)

Location:	On permanent view at the City Hall in the centre of the town.

TYPE	REG/SER	CON. NO.	PI/NOTES	STATUS
☐ Bell 209 Huey Cobra (AH-1G) (AH-1F)	70-16053	20997		PV

DAYTON MONUMENT (TN14)

Location:	On permanent view at Mark Anton Airport which is about 4 miles east of the town.

TYPE	REG/SER	CON. NO.	PI/NOTES	STATUS
☐ Lockheed 580 (T-33A)	51-6861	580-6193	51-6861, N62278	PV

DICKSON MONUMENT (TN15)

Location:	On permanent view at VFW 4641 at 215 Marshall Stuart Drive in the south eastern part of the town.

TYPE	REG/SER	CON. NO.	PI/NOTES	STATUS
☐ Bell 205 Iroquois (UH-1D) (UH-1H)	66-0868	5351		PV

DYERSBURG ARMY AIR BASE VETERANS' MUSEUM (TN16)

Address:	100 Veteran's Avenue, Halls, Tennessee 38040.
Tel:	731-836-7400 Email: higdon@ten-nash.ten.k12.tn.us
Admission:	Saturday-Tuesday 1400-1700.
Location:	In the western part of the town.

The airfield opened in 1942 and was used mainly for training B-17 crews. The site closed in 1945 and a few original buildings still survive. A group of local people had gathered together memorabilia and used to display them at local shows. This led to the idea of a museum and the first building opened in 1997 on the site of the ramp of the former base. The exhibition area was doubled in 2004.

TYPE	REG/SER	CON. NO.	PI/NOTES	STATUS
☐ Vought A-7E Corsair II	Bu160869	E585		PV

GALLATIN MONUMENT (TN17)

Location:	On permanent view at Sumner County Airport which is about 3 miles south east of the town.

TYPE	REG/SER	CON. NO.	PI/NOTES	STATUS
☐ McDonnell M.98DE Phantom II (F-4C) (NF-4C)	63-7654	762		PV

GRACELAND (TN18)

Address:	3434 Elvis Presley Boulevard, PO Box 16508, Memphis, Tennessee 38116.
Tel:	901-332-3322 Email: Graceland@Elvis.Com
Admission:	March–May Monday-Saturday 0900-1600, Sunday 1000-1600; June–August Monday-Saturday 0900-1700, Sunday 0900-1600; September–February daily 1000-1600 (Closed Tuesday December–February)
Location:	In the southern suburbs of the city off Route 51.

Elvis Presley lived at Graceland for more than 20 years. The house was opened to the public in 1982 and contains many of his personal effects. At the time of his death he owned two aircraft and these are on show.

TYPE	REG/SER	CON. NO.	PI/NOTES	STATUS
☐ Convair 22-2 880	N880EP	38	N8809E	PV
☐ Lockheed 1329 Jetstar 6	N777EP	1329-5004	N9204R, N13304, N524AC, N777EP, N69HM	PV

JOHNSON CITY MONUMENT (TN19)

Location: On permanent view at Bowser Ridge Model Airfield which is north west of the town.

TYPE	REG/SER	CON. NO.	PI/NOTES	STATUS
☐ Lockheed 580 (T-33A)	53-6009	580-9541		PV

KNOXVILLE AIR NATIONAL GUARD BASE (TN20)

Address: 134 AREFG McGhee-Tyson Airport, Knoxville Tennessee 37901.
Tel: 865-985-3210   Email: webmaster@tnknox.ang.af.mil
Admission: By prior permission only.
Location: On the west side of the airport which is about 10 miles south of the city on Route 129.

The 151st Squadron was formed on December 15th 1957 at McGhee-Tyson Airport. Initially a fighter with F-86D Sabres, it later used F-86Ls, F-104 Starfighters and F-102 Delta Daggers. In 1965 it changed to the air-refuelling role. The Starfighter is mounted by the base gate.

TYPE	REG/SER	CON. NO.	PI/NOTES	STATUS
☐ Lockheed 383-04-05 Starfighter (F-104C)	'56-0880'	183-1178	56-0890	RAX
☐ North American NA-190 Sabre (F-86D)	52-3679	190-82		RA

KODAK MONUMENT (TN21)

Location: On permanent view at a business in the town.

TYPE	REG/SER	CON. NO.	PI/NOTES	STATUS
☐ Sikorsky S-58 Seahorse (HUS-1) (UH-34D)				PV

LANE MOTOR MUSEUM (TN22)

Address: 702 Murfreesboro Pike, Nashville, Tennessee 37210.
Tel: 615-742-7445   Email: info@lanemotormuseum.org
Admission: Thursday-Monday 1000-1700.
Location: In the south eastern suburbs of the city off Interstate 24.

This private museum opened in 2003. The exhibition is located in the former Sunbeam Bakery Factory which was in use from 1951 until 1994. Jeff Lane had collected cars for many years specialising in those made in Europe. Over 150 are normally on show along with over 50 motor cycles. Several prototypes and limited production models can be seen. The aim is to have all the vehicles in running order. A large collection of associated equipment can also be seen.

The only aircraft in the collection is the Flea which was built in the late 1990s.

TYPE	REG/SER	CON. NO.	PI/NOTES	STATUS
☐ Mignet HM-380 Pou-du-Ciel	N380FG	001		PV

LOUISVILLE MONUMENT (TN23)

Location: On permanent view at VFW 5154 at 2561 Hobbs Road just north of the airport.

TYPE	REG/SER	CON. NO.	PI/NOTES	STATUS
☐ Bell 209 Huey Cobra (AH-1G) (AH-1F)	66-15421	20077		PV

MEMPHIS MONUMENT (TN24)

Location: By prior permission only at the FedEx Headquarters at 942 South Shady Grove in the eastern part of the city.

TYPE	REG/SER	CON. NO.	PI/NOTES	STATUS
☐ Dassault Falcon 20C	N9FE	84	F-WJMK, N975F, N530L, N1FE, (N150FE)	RA

MIDDLE TENNESSEE STATE UNIVERSITY (TN25)

Address: 1301 East Main Street, Murfreesboro, Tennessee 37132-0001.
Tel: 615-898-2788   Fax: 615-904-8273   Email: asymonds@mtsu.edu
Admission: By prior permission only.
Location: At the airport which is about 3 miles north of the town.

The Middle Tennessee Normal School was established in Murfreesboro in 1911. University status was achieved in 1965. The aviation department is located at the airport and has a fleet of types used for single and multi engine pilot training.

The former military Beaver is used for instruction and as a flying advertisement for the aerospace programmes.
The Boeing 727 is one of a number donated to colleges by FedEx.

TYPE	REG/SER	CON. NO.	PI/NOTES	STATUS
☐ Bell 206A Kiowa (OH-58A)	70-15276	40827		RA
☐ Boeing 727-25QC	N117FE	19299	N8152G	RA
☐ De Havilland DHC.2 Beaver (L-20A) (U-6A)	N8306	533	52-6140	RAA
☐ North American NA-276 Sabreliner (T-39A) (CT-39A)	N741MT	276-34	62-4481, N33UT	RA

MILLINGTON MONUMENT (TN26)

Location: On permanent view at the airport which is just north east of the town.

TYPE	REG/SER	CON. NO.	PI/NOTES	STATUS
☐ Grumman G-98 Tiger (F11F-1) (F-11A)			On loan from NMNA, FL	PV
☐ North American NA-316 Vigilante (RA-5C)	Bu156608	316-1		PV

NASHVILLE MONUMENTS (TN27)

Location: On permanent view at three locations in the city.

TYPE	REG/SER	CON. NO.	PI/NOTES	STATUS
☐ North American NA-201 Sabre (F-86D) (F-86L)	53-0668	201-112	In Centennial Park in the centre of the city.	PV
☐ Northrop N-156T Talon (T-38A)	62-3643	N.5348	At Tennessee State University on 33rd Avenue North.	PV
☐ Republic RF-84F Thunderflash	53-7529		In the Air National Guard Base at the International Airport.	RA

PIGEON FORGE MONUMENT (TN28)

Location: On permanent view outside Professor Hacker's Lost Treasure Golf Course in the town.

TYPE	REG/SER	CON. NO.	PI/NOTES	STATUS
☐ Beech D18S			N218SD or N9561	PV

SMYRNA MONUMENT (TN29)

Location: On permanent view at the National Guard gate at the airfield which is just north of the town.

TYPE	REG/SER	CON. NO.	PI/NOTES	STATUS
☐ Bell 209 Huey Cobra (AH-1G) (AH-1F)	68-15131	20665		RA

SODDY-DAISY MONUMENT (TN30)

Location: On permanent view in a park in the south western part of the town.

TYPE	REG/SER	CON. NO.	PI/NOTES	STATUS
☐ Bell 205 Iroquois (UH-1D) (UH-1H)	64-13786	4493		PV

SWEETWATER MONUMENT (TN31)

Location: On permanent view at VFW 5156 at 127 Veterans Road about 2 miles south east of the town.

TYPE	REG/SER	CON. NO.	PI/NOTES	STATUS
☐ Bell 209 Huey Cobra (AH-1G) (AH-1F)	68-17085	20813		PV

SWIFT MUSEUM FOUNDATION (TN32)

Address: PO Box 644, Athens, Tennessee 37371-0644.
Tel: 423-745-9547   Fax: 423-745-9869
Email: swiftlypam@aol.com
Admission: Monday-Saturday 0800-1600.
Location: At McMinn County Airport which is about 3 miles south of the town off Route 30.

The airport is the home of the International Swift Association which has acquired the type certificate, jigs and parts holding for the type.
The GC-1 Swift first flew in 1941 and featured a steel tube fabric covered fuselage. The all-metal GC-1A went into production in 1945 with the delay being due to the company producing the Beech AT-10. Manufacture was subcontracted to Temco who in 1947 acquired the assets of Globe aircraft.

They put into production the improved GC-1B model when manufacture ceased in 1951 well over 1000 examples of both models had been sold. The Swift National Convention is held annually at Athens when large numbers of the type fly in to the field.
Temco also built 20 Buckaroo tandem seat trainers and two are in the collection. One was donated to the museum by the Royal Saudi Air Force who used ten examples.

TYPE	REG/SER	CON. NO.	PI/NOTES	STATUS
☐ Aircraft Manufacturing Company Texas Bullet 205	N78851	105		PVA
☐ Globe GC-1A Swift	NC80760	163	NC80760, N80760	PVA
☐ Globe GC-1A Swift	N80500	3	NC80500	RA
☐ Globe GC-1B Super Swift (GC-1B Swift)	N80637	1042	NC80637	PVA
☐ Globe GC-1B Swift	N3788K	1481	NC3788K	PVA
☐ Globe GC-1B Swift	N2379B	3679		RA

Tennessee

| ☐ Temco TE.1B Buckaroo (T-35A) | N68773 | TE-6008 | 53-4470, (Saudi) | PVA |
| ☐ Temco TE.1B Buckaroo (T-35A) | N909B/'1021' | TE-6016 | 53-4466, (Saudi) | PVA |

TENNESSEE MUSEUM OF AVIATION (TN33)

Address:	135 Air Museum Way, PO Box 5587, Sevierville, Tennessee 37862.
Tel:	865-908-0171 **Fax:** 865-908-8421 **Email:** info@tnairmuseum.com
Admission:	Monday-Saturday 1000-1800; Sunday 1300-1700.
Location:	At Gatlinburg Airport which is about 20 miles south east of Knoxville.

The museum opened on 15th December 2001 in a hangar at Gatlinburg Airport. A restoration building is also in use.
The founder of the collection is R. Neal Melton who owns many of the warbirds. The aim is to present a display tracing the history of aviation in the state. The Tennessee Aviation Hall of Fame is located at the museum.

The highlight of the aircraft fleet is the pair of restored Thunderbolts, another example of the fighter resides nearby. Two of these served in Brazil and the other in Yuogoslavia. The exhibits often change as owners sell their aircraft. The Bell 222 replica came from the short lived Halson's Helicopter Museum.

TYPE	REG/SER	CON. NO.	PI/NOTES	STATUS
☐ Beech D18S Expeditor (C18S) (SNB-2) (SNB-2P) (SNB-5P) (RC-45J)	N145J	5560	Bu51233	PV
☐ Bell 222 (FSM)				PV
☐ Canadair CL-13B Sabre 6 [North American F-86E]	N50CJ	1490	23700, 381 (South Africa)	PVA
☐ Canadair CL-30 Silver Star 3 (CT-133) [Lockheed 580 (T-33AN)]	N307FS	T33-566	21566, N99193	PVA
☐ Cessna P172D	N99RT	P17257165	N8565X	PVC
☐ Douglas A-4C Skyhawk (A4D-2N)			Front fuselage only.	PV
☐ Grumman G-111 Albatross (SA-16B) (HU-16B) (HU-16E)	N29853	G-335	51-7246, 7246 (USCG)	PVA
☐ Lockheed 580 (T-33A)	N133CK	580-7138	51-17445, FT-15 (Belgium), N1180C, N410GH	PV
☐ Lockheed 580 (T-33A)	53-6069	580-9690		PV
☐ McDonnell M.267 Hornet (F/A-18A)	'300'		Front fuselage only.	PVX
☐ Mikoyan-Gurevich MiG-21US	4007	07685140	In Polish markings.	PV
☐ North American NA-88 Texan (SNJ-4)	N6423D	88-13519	Bu27823	RAA
☐ North American NA-108 Mitchell (B-25J)			Front fuselage only.	PV
☐ North American NA-122 Mustang (P-51D) (FSM)	'44-13318'			PVX
☐ North American NA-200 Trojan (T-28B)	NX32257	200-200	Bu138129	PVA
☐ North American NA-305 Bronco (OV-10A) (OV-10D)	N12320	305-62	Bu155451, PNC-3045 (Colombia)	PVA
☐ Republic P-47D Thunderbolt	NX647D/'490438'	399-55583	44-90438, 13021 (Yugoslavia)	PVA
☐ Republic P-47D Thunderbolt	NX9246B	399-55605	44-90460, 4175 (Brazil)	PVA
☐ Republic P-47D Thunderbolt	N9246T	399-55669	45-49130, 4181(Brazil)	RAA
☐ Sikorsky S-58 Seabat (HSS-1) (SH-34G) (UH-34G)	Bu140376	58190		PV
☐ Wright 1902 Glider (R)				PV
☐ WSK Lim-5 [MiG-17F]	1706	1C 17-06	1706 (Poland) – in false North Vietnamese markings.	PV
☐ WSK Lim-5R (Lim-5) [MiG-17F]	1728	1C 17-28	In Polish markings.	PV

TENNESSEE TECHNOLOGY CENTER (TN34)

Address:	3435 Tchulahoma Road, Memphis, Tennessee 38118.
Tel:	901-543-6180 **Email:** pat.thompson@ttcmemphis.edu
Admission:	By prior permission only.
Location:	On the eastern side of the International Airport.

The college has sites Covington, Knoxville and Memphis. The aviation complex at the airport offers courses leading to licenses in airframes, engine, and avionics. Five instructional airframes are known to be in use.

TYPE	REG/SER	CON. NO.	PI/NOTES	STATUS
☐ Aero Commander 680W	N951HE	1751-4	N5052E, VH-KRX, N5052E, N951HF	RA
☐ Boeing 727-25F	N510FE	18282	N8131N, HK-2705X, HK-2705, N4556W, N8131N	RA
☐ Mitsubishi MU-2J (MU-2B-35)	N19GU	574	N243MA	RA
☐ North American NA-265 Sabreliner (T-39A) (CT-39A)	59-2869	265-2	59-2869, N4999G	RA
☐ Piper PA-34-200 Seneca	N40759	34-7450075		RA

VETERANS MEMORIAL MUSEUM (TN35)

Address:	110 Showplace Boulevard, Pigeon Forge, Tennessee 37868.
Tel:	865-908-6003 **Email:** info@veteransmemorialpf.com
Admission:	Daily 0900-2000.
Location:	In the centre of the town.

The museum opened a few years ago under the name of National Freedom Museum but the building now carries the above title. The exhibition is run by the local veterans group and honours all Americans who lost their lives in military service. On show are items of memorabilia, photographs, documents, uniforms and weapons.

TYPE	REG/SER	CON. NO.	PI/NOTES	STATUS
☐ North American NA-122 Mustang (P-51D) (FSM)	'450895'		Contains some original parts.	PVX

TEXAS

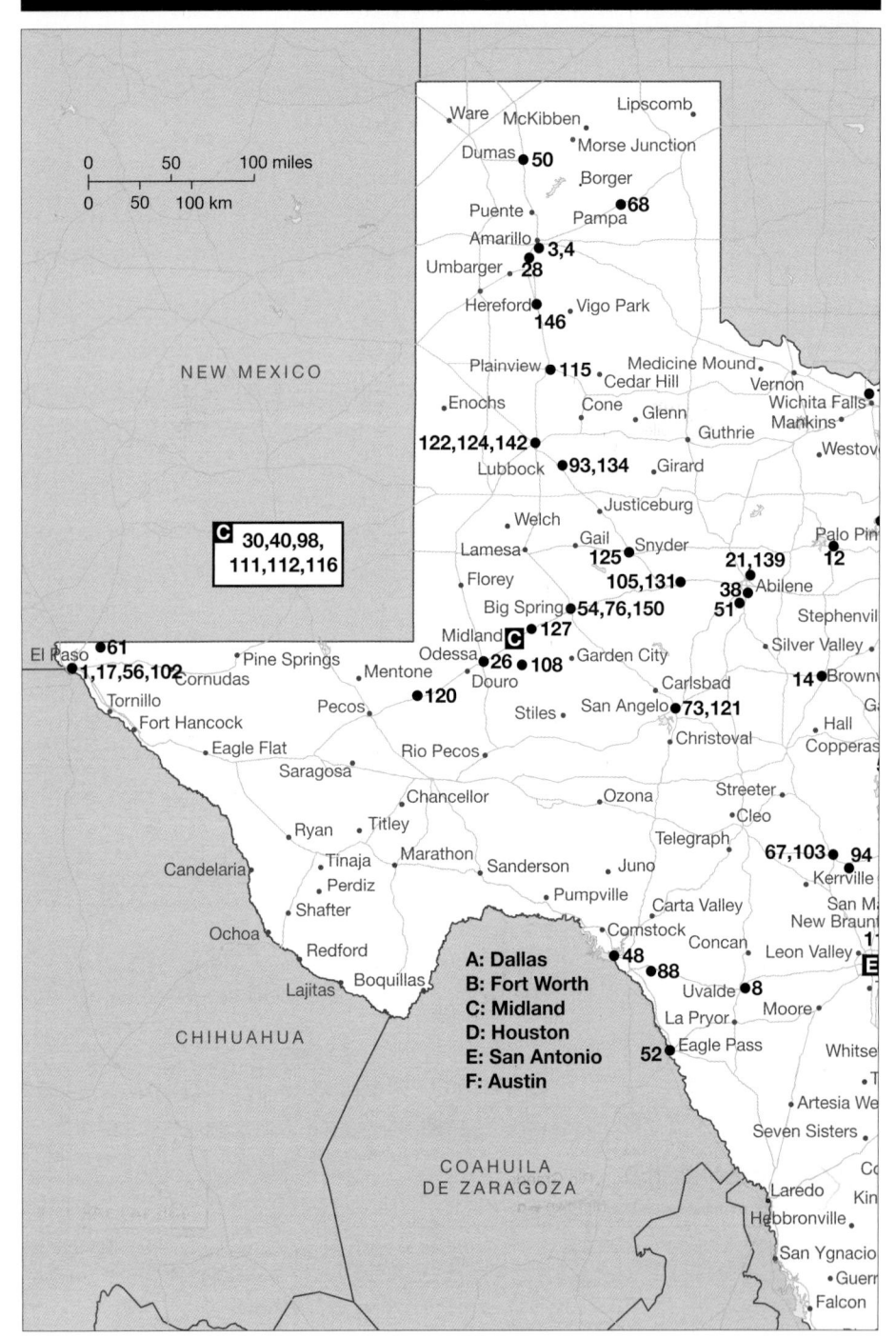

A: Dallas
B: Fort Worth
C: Midland
D: Houston
E: San Antonio
F: Austin

551

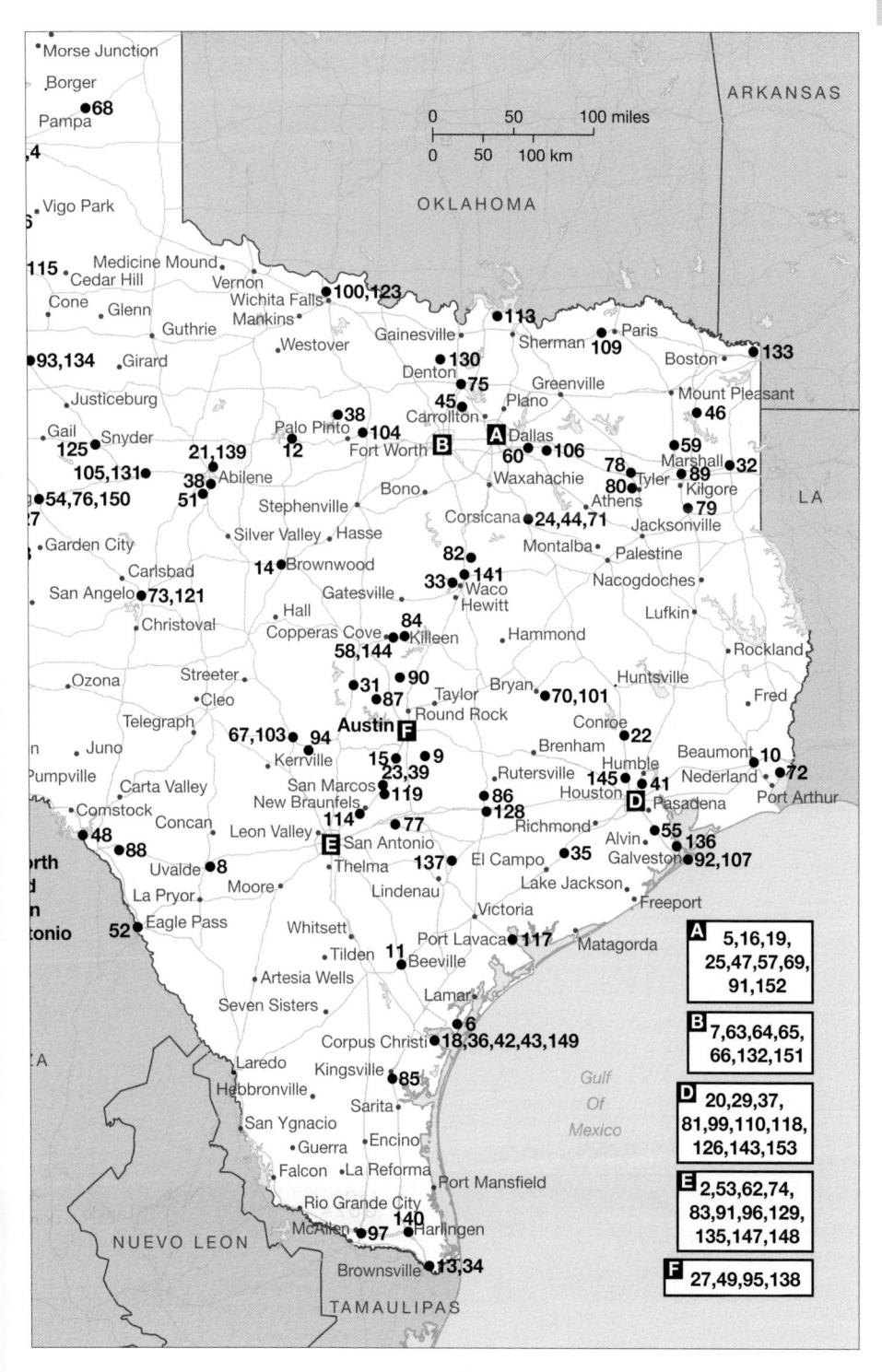

AIR WAR AIR MUSEUM (TX1)

Address:	Box 4850, El Paso, Texas 79914.
Admission:	Unknown
Location:	At an airfield in the area.

The two light aircraft have been registered to this museum since 1985. Neither has a valid certificate of airworthiness for several years. No trace has been found of the collection and it might have been connected to now defunct West Texas Air Museum which was also in the El Paso area. Further information would be welcome.

TYPE	REG/SER	CON. NO.	PI/NOTES	STATUS
☐ Piper PA-22-150 Tripacer	N3362A	22-1662		RAA
☐ Taylorcraft BC-12D	N44075	9875	NC44075	RAA

ALAMO LIAISON GROUP (TX2)

Address:	16518 Ledgestone Road, San Antonio, Texas 78232.
Tel:	210-490-4572
Admission:	By prior permission only.
Location:	At a private airfield about 14 miles south of the city on Loop 1604.

Formed in 1981 with the aim of collecting and flying World War II liaison aircraft, the organisation is based on a private field. By the late 1980s the group had collected at least one example of all types from the L-l to the L-6. Now the L-l has been sold and in the 1990s two of their aircraft collided over San Antonio killing all four people on board. The group initially found it difficult to come to terms with this disaster but more aircraft are now being added. The majority of the machines are painted in their period colours. The three Piper Cubs are all civilian machines but have been acquired to honour the large numbers used in military service. One of the Taylorcrafts was built as a training glider during World War II. A total of 250 was ordered for this role. At the end of the conflict several of the survivors were sold and converted to standard L-2 configuration. In a building at the airstrip is a small collection of memorabilia highlighting the role of liaison types in combat.

TYPE	REG/SER	CON. NO.	PI/NOTES	STATUS
☐ Aeronca 65TC Grasshopper (O-58B) (L-3B)	NC52169	1782	42-36152	RAA
☐ Interstate S1B1 Cadet (O-63) (L-6)	N46951	168	(USAAF)	RAA
☐ Piper J-3C-65 Cub	N87769	15427	NC87769	RAA
☐ Piper J-3C-65 Cub	NC23413	3150	NC23413, N23413	RAA
☐ Piper J-3C-65 Cub	NC142BN	4764	'004644'	RAA
☐ Stinson V-76 Sentinel (L-5C)	N45TX		44-17397	RAA
☐ Taylorcraft DCO-65 Grasshopper (L-2M)	N53771	L-4915	(USAAF)	RAA
☐ Taylorcraft DCO-65 Grasshopper (L-2M)	N87787/'43-26173'	L-5485	43-26173	RAA
☐ Taylorcraft DCO-65 Grasshopper (L-2M)	N57538	L-5922	43-26610	RAA
☐ Taylorcraft DCO-65 Grasshopper (L-2M)	N596BH	L-5963	43-26651	RAA
☐ Taylorcraft DCO-65 Grasshopper (ST-100D) (TG-6) (L-2M)	N61080	L-6238	(USAAF)	RAA

AMARILLO COLLEGE (TX3)

Address:	PO Box 447, Amarillo, Texas 79111.
Tel:	806-371-5000 Email: moseley-dm@actx.edu
Admission:	By prior permission only.
Location:	At the East Campus which is at 2000 East Avenue just east of the International Airport.

The college was originally set up in 1929 and now has four locations in the city and two in the vicinity. The East Campus was originally part of the Texas State Technical College. In 1995 the site was transferred to Amarillo College and now houses a number of departments. Most buildings date from the time when the airfield was Amarillo Air Force Base – the military were at the field from 1942 until 1968. Bomber squadrons were in residence for most of the time and in addition technical training was carried out.

The aviation section is housed in a hangar on the campus where the instructional airframes are located along with some engines.

TYPE	REG/SER	CON. NO.	PI/NOTES	STATUS
☐ Beech 35 Bonanza	N2780V	D-172	NC2780V	RA
☐ Bell 47G-3B Sioux (OH-13S)	N9263Z	2971	63-9085	RA
☐ Cessna 210	N9699T	57499		RA
☐ Cessna 310A Blue Canoe (L-27A) (U-3A)	N6476	38103	58-2129	RA
☐ Piper PA-28-140 Cherokee	N4530R	28-21233		RA
☐ Piper PA-28-140 Cherokee	N8709N	28-25531		RA
☐ Sikorsky S-62A Seaguard (HH-52A)	1397	62082		RA

AMARILLO MONUMENTS (TX4)

Location:	On permanent view at three locations in the city.

TYPE	REG/SER	CON. NO.	PI/NOTES	STATUS
☐ Grumman G-134 Mohawk (OV-1B)	N512NA	39B	62-5880 – at Tradwind Airport, which is in the southern part of the city.	PV
☐ North American NA-223 Super Sabre (F-100D)	56-3046	235-144	At the Texas Panhandle War Memorial at 4111 South Georgia Street.	PV
☐ Republic F-84F Thunderstreak	52-6553		In the city.	PV

AMERICAN AIRLINES C.R. SMITH MUSEUM (TX5)

Address:	4601 Highway 360, Fort Worth, Texas 76261-9617
Tel:	817-967-1560 Email: barbra.lancaster@aa.com
Admission:	Tuesday -Saturday 1000-1800.
Location:	About 2 miles south of Dallas-Fort Worth International Airport.

American Airlines was founded in April 1934 and in the following month C.R. Smith was appointed president. Later in the year he opened discussions with the Douglas company about a new airliner. The design materialised as the Douglas Sleeper Transport (or DST) and its daytime version the DC-3. American ordered eight DSTs and a dozen DC-3s with the first being delivered on 8th June 1936. The museum opened on 3rd July 1993 in a new building at the company training site.

The only complete aircraft displayed is DC-3 'Flagship Knoxville' which was delivered to the airline in March 1940 and used for over eight years. It was parked outside for a period but it now resides in a glass fronted hangar. There are plans to acquire other types which have been used by the company. Inside the museum the history of American Airlines and commercial aviation is told and there are many hands on displays giving an insight into the workings of the industry.

TYPE	REG/SER	CON. NO.	PI/NOTES	STATUS
☐ Douglas DC-3-277B	NC21798	2202	NC21798, N393SW	PV
☐ Fokker 100 (FSM)			Front fuselage only.	PV

ARANSAS PASS MONUMENT (TX6)

Location:	On permanent view at VFW 2932 at 620 West Wheeler Avenue in the town.

TYPE	REG/SER	CON. NO.	PI/NOTES	STATUS
☐ Bell 204 Iroquois (UH-1B)				PV

AVIATION HERITAGE ASSOCIATION (TX7)

Address:	1201 Forum Way South, Fort Worth, Texas 76140.
Tel:	817-551-7179 Email: musdevelop@yahoo.com
Admission:	Not yet built.
Location:	Some aircraft stored in factory at Forth Worth.

In 1959 the last production Convair B-36 was flown into Amon Carter Field for preservation by the Museum of Aviation Group. When the airfield was incorporated into the new Dallas-Fort Worth International Airport the giant bomber moved closer to its birthplace at the now defunct Southwest Aerospace Museum just outside the gates of the General Dynamics (now Boeing) factory.

A local congressman and the Mayor of Forth Worth were determined to keep the B-36 in the area and it was moved into the plant for a much needed restoration. The bomber has now been loaned to the Pima Air and Space Museum in Arizona.

The remaining aircraft are currently in store in the city. Land was allocated at the new Alliance Airport for a museum but this project was abandoned. A new site in the area is being sought and negotiations with the local authorities are currently in progress. Hopefully it will not be too long before a home can be found for this collection.

TYPE	REG/SER	CON. NO.	PI/NOTES	STATUS
☐ Aviation Restoration and Testing ART-38	N90611	001		RA
☐ Lockheed 580 (T-33A)				RA
☐ Lockheed A-10 (FSM)				RA
☐ Vultee V-54D Valiant (BT-13)	'39-64960'			RAX

AVIATION MUSEUM OF TEXAS (TX8)

Address:	PO Box 453, Uvalde, Texas 78802.
Tel:	830-278-2552
Admission:	Monday, Tuesday, Friday 0900-1600; Saturday 0900-1200.
Location:	About 5 miles east of the town which is about 50 miles west of San Antonio.

The museum is housed in Hangar 1 at Garner Field. The base was operational between 1942 and 1945 and was used to train pilots. The types flown were the PT-17 and PT-19. Exhibits on the local region feature prominently in the displays.

An excellent collection of warbirds has been assembled with almost all in flying condition. The Invader served with the French Air Force in Indochina for a short period in 1954 before returning to the USAF. It was civilianised in 1963 and from 1985 to 1993 was flown by the Collings Foundation but crashed on take off at Kankakee in Illinois. The bomber is nearing the end of a major rebuild. The wartime history of the site is represented by the two Kaydets and the Cornell.

The majority of the aircraft are privately owned and are not always on show in the historic hangar. Burt Rutan designed the Vari-Viggen in the 1960s and the prototype flew in April 1972. Large numbers of plans were sold but only about a dozen aircraft were completed and few are now flying. A display of memorabilia tracing the history of the airfield can be seen and on show are photographs, uniforms and documents.

TYPE	REG/SER	CON. NO.	PI/NOTES	STATUS
☐ Bede BD-5B				PVA
☐ Boeing-Stearman A75N1 Kaydet (PT-17)	N75160	75-2224	41-8665	PVA
☐ Boeing-Stearman E75 Kaydet (PT-13D)	N54JH	75-5603	42-17740	PVA
☐ Douglas A-26B Invader	NL8036E	28975	44-35696, 435696 (France) – Collings Foundation, MA aircraft.	PVC
☐ Fairchild M-62A Cornell (PT-19A)	N50480	T43-7022	42-83675	PVA
☐ Fairchild M-62A-4 Cornell (PT-26)			Fuselage frame only.	PV
☐ Piper J-3C-65 Cub (L-4J)	N33576	14053	45-55287	PVA
☐ Rutan 27 Vari-Viggen	N9VV	003		PVA

Amongst the preserved aircraft at Charleston Air Force Base is this Lockheed C-121C Super Constellation. [SC22]

The first Beech 17 is a prized exhibit at the Beechcraft Heritage Museum. [TN4]

The Swift Museum Foundation has this Temco TE.1B Buckaroo in Saudi colours on show.. [TN32]

BASTROP MONUMENT (TX9)

Location:	On permanent view at ALP 533 on Loop 150 in the eastern part of the town.

TYPE	REG/SER	CON. NO.	PI/NOTES	STATUS
☐ Mcdonnell M.98EN Phantom II (F-4D)	66-8768	2620		PV

BEAUMONT MONUMENT (TX10)

Location:	On permanent view in Babe Didrikson Zaharas Park in the northern part of the town.

TYPE	REG/SER	CON. NO.	PI/NOTES	STATUS
☐ Mcdonnell M.36BA Voodoo (F-101B)	59-0430	754		PV

BEEVILLE MONUMENT (TX11)

Location:	On permanent view at the Bee County Court House in the centre of the town.

TYPE	REG/SER	CON. NO.	PI/NOTES	STATUS
☐ Douglas A-4B Skyhawk (A4D-2)	Bu142717	11779		PV

BRECKENRIDGE AVIATION MUSEUM (TX12)

Address:	PO Box 388, Breckenridge, Texas 76024.
Tel:	817-559-3201 **Email:** brkcofc@breckenridgetexas.com
Admission:	Monday-Friday 0800-1700.
Location:	At Stephens County Airport which is about 2 miles south of the town off Route 183.

Warbird owners at Breckenridge set up the museum in the mid-1980s. Howard Pardue owns several of the aircraft. The Bearcat is the oldest surviving example and was one of 23 development machines which followed the two prototypes. From 1952 to 1976 it was stored at Silver Hill by the National Air and Space Museum but was then exchanged with Darryl Greenamyer for his record breaking F8F-2.

TYPE	REG/SER	CON. NO.	PI/NOTES	STATUS
☐ Beech D17S ((UC-43) (GB-2)	N666TX	6897	44-67791, Bu32911, FT527, NC1336V, N1336V	PVA
☐ Fouga CM.170-2 Magister (CM.170A)	N904DM	80	FM-80 (Finland)	PVA
☐ Grumman G-36 Wildcat (FM-2) (FM-2P)	NL5HP	5835	Bu86777, N90541	PVA
☐ Grumman G-58 Bearcat (F8F-1) (F8F-1D)	NL14HP	D.10	Bu90446, N99279	PVA
☐ Hawker Fury FB.10	NX13HP	41H/37536	255 (Iraq), N34SF, NX666HP	PVA
☐ Piper J-3C-65 Cub (O-59A) (L-4A)	N48975	8588	42-36464	PVA

BROWNSVILLE MONUMENT (TX13)

Location:	On permanent view on San Padre Island east of the town.

TYPE	REG/SER	CON. NO.	PI/NOTES	STATUS
☐ Vickers 757 Viscount	CF-TGZ	144	CF-TGZ, (N3832S)	PV

BROWNWOOD MONUMENT (TX14)

Location:	On permanent view at the airport which is just west of the town.

TYPE	REG/SER	CON. NO.	PI/NOTES	STATUS
☐ General Dynamics F-111A	67-0046	A1-91		PV
☐ Mcdonnell M.98HO Phantom II (F-4E)	67-0249	2944		PV

BUDA MONUMENT (TX15)

Location:	On view during opening hours in Cabela's store at 15570 Highway 35 in the eastern part of the town.

TYPE	REG/SER	CON. NO.	PI/NOTES	STATUS
☐ Piper J-3C-65 Cub				PV

CAVANAUGH FLIGHT MUSEUM (TX16)

Address:	4572 Claire Chennault Drive, Addison Airport, Dallas, Texas 75001-5321.
Tel:	972-380-8800 **Fax:** 972-248-0907 **Email:** cavmaint@aol.com
Admission:	Monday-Saturday 0900-1700; Sunday 1100-1700.
Location:	About 10 miles north of the city off Belt Line Road.

Jim Cavanaugh bought his first aircraft, a Piper Cub, in 1980. He and his father soon followed this by building a Pitts Special. Nine years later he acquired the PT-19 and his collection of warbirds had begun. The fleet grew in number and it was decided to set up a museum. The exhibition opened on 15th September 1993 and now four hangars are in use. There is a restoration facility close by. The aim is to maintain the majority of the aircraft in flying condition. A number of static types has been acquired to enhance the exhibition. Three World War I replicas highlight this period of aviation. The Second World War is well represented with a range of bombers, fighters, transports and training types. The Spitfire was found in India by the late Ormond Haydon-Baillie and was rebuilt in Italy before returning to England. It is one of the few surviving Mark VIIIs.

The jets on show are from US manufacturers along with a number of Warsaw Pact machines. A rarity is the airworthy Grumman Panther. Over 1,300 examples of the jet fighter were built and the design was developed into the Cougar which was also constructed in large numbers. Helicopter types used in the Vietnam conflict are also on show. A recent acquisition is the Dassault Falcon. The prototype of this twin-engined jet made its maiden flight in 1963 and the design has been developed into a number of variants which have sold in large numbers. Homebuilt designs are also being acquired.

The museum donated a sum of money to the Commemorative Air Force to be used for re-engining their B-29. As a result this aircraft and the CAF B-24 spend periods at the museum. There is an aviation art gallery at the site where the work of several well-known artists can be seen.

TYPE	REG/SER	CON. NO.	PI/NOTES	STATUS
☐ Aeronca 65TC Grasshopper (O-58B) (L-3B)	N47373	10233	43-26886	PVA
☐ Bell 47G-3B-1 Sioux (TH-13T)	N4077	3473	65-8040, N67261	PVA
☐ Bell 47G-3B-1 Sioux (TH-13T)	N55ER	3803	67-17098	PVA
☐ Bell 204 Iroquois (UH-1B)	62-4567	627		PV
☐ Bell 209 Huey Cobra (AH-1G) (AH-1F)	'Bu159220'	20497	67-15733	PVX
☐ Boeing-Stearman A75 Kaydet (PT-13B)	N1207	75-0207	40-1650	PVA
☐ Boeing-Stearman A75N1 Kaydet (N2S-4)	'Bu05256'	AR-36	N741BJ – rebuild from spares.	PVAX
☐ Canadair CL-13A Sabre 5 [North American F-86E]	NX4689H	1083	23293 – carries '51-2821'	PVAX
☐ Canadian Car & Foundry Harvard 4 [North American NA-186]	NX1811B	CCF4-38	20247 (Canada), CF-UZO –	PVA
☐ CASA 2.111B [Heinkel He 111H-16]	NX99230	155	B.2I-27, N99230	PV
☐ Christen Eagle II	N724RC	002		PVA
☐ Curtiss 87V Warhawk (P-40N)	NL40PN	33109	44-7369, N94500, C-GTGR	PVA
☐ Dassault Falcon 200	N200CU	499	F-WZZJ, N213FJ, N565A, N14CJ	PVA
☐ De Havilland DH.82C Tiger Moth (PT-24)	'R5130'	DHC.1317	42-978, FE114, 1114 (Canada), CF-CSX, NX18840	PVAX
☐ De Havilland DHC.4 Caribou (CV-2A) (C-7A)	N149HF	85	62-4149, N9249Q	PVA
☐ Douglas DC-3A-456 Skytrain (C-47A)	'320401'	20401	43-15935, VH-BHC, G-ALFO, N94529, N300A, N700E, N20DH, N3BA, N890P, N12RB, N33VW, '31595'	PVAX
☐ Douglas A-26C Invader	N7705C	28989	44-35710, N7705C, OO-INV	PVA
☐ Douglas EA-1E Skyraider (AD-5W)	N65164	10299	BU135152	PVA
☐ Fairchild M-62A Cornell (PT-19B)	'305226'	T43-5226	42-34560, N58307	PVAX
☐ Fokker D VII (R)	N1258	1		PVA
☐ Fokker Dr I (R)	N1839	1839		PVA
☐ General Dynamics F-111D	68-0125	A6-41	Cockpit section only.	PV
☐ Grumman G-36 Wildcat (FM-2)	'Bu86960'	6014	Bu86956, N18PK, N18P	PVAX
☐ Grumman G-40 Avenger (TBM-3) (TBM-3E)	NL86280	3099	Bu86280, N7219C	PVA
☐ Grumman G-79 Panther (F9F-2) (F9F-2B)	NX9525A	K-93	Bu123078	PVA
☐ Grumman G-89 Tracker (S2F-1) (S-2A) (US-2B)	N37AM	340	Bu136431	PVA
☐ Grumman G-111 Albatross (G-64) (UF-1) (HU-16C)	N7027Z	G-384	Bu137911, N89LH	PVA
☐ Grumman G-134 Mohawk (AO-1B) (OV-1B)	N134GM	48B	62-5889	PVA
☐ Hawker Sea Fury T.20	NX51SF	ES.3613	VX302, D-CACE, G-BCOV, N613RD	RAC
☐ Hispano HA-1112M1L [Messerschmitt Bf 109G]	NX109GU	235	C.4K-172, N48157, G-BJZZ, G-HUNN	PVA
☐ Lockheed 15-27-01 Harpoon (PV-2D)	N86493	15-1604	Bu84060, N6656D – composite with parts of c/n 15-1468 Bu37502, N7269C and c/n 15-1608 Bu84064, N7415C	PV
☐ Lockheed 183-93-02 Starfighter (F-104A)	56-0780	183-1068	56-0780, 4203 (Taiwan), 908 (Jordan), N66342	PV
☐ Lockheed 1329-25 JetStar II	N814K	1329-5204	N5530L, N19ES, N59AC, N500PR, N167R, N25WZ (N220ES), N202ES	PV
☐ McDonnell M.98DJ Phantom II (F-4C)	64-0777	1080		PV
☐ Mikoyan-Gurevich MiG-21US	N211MG	02685145	4502 (Poland)	PVA
☐ Mikoyan-Gurevich MiG-21US	4504	04685145	4504 (Poland), N1121M , '0524'	PVX
☐ North American NA-88 Texan (AT-6D)	N29947	88-17478	42-85697, AE.6-178 (Spain), C.6-178 (Spain)	PVA
☐ North American NA-88 Texan (AT-6D) (SNJ-5)	N39403	88-15838	41-34588, Bu43794, C.6-153 (Spain)	PVA
☐ North American NA-108 Mitchell (B-25J) (TB-25J) (TB-25N)	N7687C	108-32200	44-28925	PVA
☐ North American NA-122 Mustang (P-51D)	NL51JC	122-38798	44-72339, Fv26115, 1918 (Dominican Republic), N51EH, NL251JC	PVA
☐ North American NA-200 Trojan (T-28B)	NX52424	200-152	Bu137789	PVA
☐ Piper J-3C-65 Cub	NC24935	3536	NC24935, N24935	RAA
☐ Piper J-3C-65 Cub (L-4J)	N9073C	13976	45-55210	PVA
☐ Pitts S-1S Special	N215JC	21546		PVA
☐ PZL TS-11 Iskra 100bisB	NX524SH/'0524'	1H 05-24	0524 Poland), 524 (Poland)	PV
☐ Republic F-84F Thunderstreak	N9450		51-9420	PV
☐ Republic F-84G Thunderjet			Fuselage only.	PV
☐ Republic F-105F Thunderchief	63-8343	F-120		PV
☐ Ryan ST-3KR Recruit (PT-22)	N46217	1363	41-15734	PVA
☐ Sikorsky S-58 Seahorse (HUS-1) (UH-34D)	Bu150213	581545		RPV
☐ Sikorsky S-58 Seahorse (HUS-1N) (UH-34J)	N54526	581055	Bu145709	RA
☐ Sopwith F.1 Camel (R)	N86678	DS 100	B7270	PVA
☐ Stinson V-76 Sentinel (L-5E)	N40020	76-3547	44-17260	PVA

Texas

☐ Supermarine 359 Spitfire LF.VIIIc	NX719MT	6S.479770	MT719, HS??? (India), I-SPIT, G-VIII	PVA
☐ Vought FG-1D Corsair	N451FG	3660	Bu92399, N4717C, N448AG, (N17VW), N448AG, G-CCHM	PVA
☐ Vought A-7D Corsair II				PV
☐ Vultee V-79 Valiant (BT-13B) (SNV-2)	N61483	79-1420	(USAAF), Bu44177	PVA
☐ WSK SBLim-2 [MiG-15bis]	'115	512036	536 (Poland), NX115PW – in false Soviet markings.	PVX
☐ WSK Lim-5 [MiG-17F]	N1917M	1C 05-08	508 (Poland)	RA
☐ WSK Lim-5 [MiG-17F]	'228'	1C 12-28	1228 (Poland), N1817M – in false Soviet markings.	PVX

CENTURY AIRLINES COLLECTION (TX17)

Address: 7335 Boeing Drive, El Paso, Texas 79925.
Tel: 915-779-3097
Admission: By prior permission only.
Location: At the International Airport which is about 3 miles east of the city.

The owner of the collection acquired six F-106s from Tyndall Air Force Base in Florida in the late 1990s. The aircraft had all been used as pilotless target machines. One was subsequently scrapped. Restoration commenced in 2000 but progress has been slow. The aim is to have two in airworthy condition

TYPE	REG/SER	CON. NO.	PI/NOTES	STATUS
☐ Convair 8-24 Delta Dart (F-106A) (QF-106A)	58-0786	8-24-117		RA
☐ Convair 8-24 Delta Dart (F-106A) (QF-106A)	59-0047	8-24-176		RA
☐ Convair 8-27 Delta Dart (F-106B) (QF-106B)	57-2509	8-27-03		RAC
☐ Convair 8-27 Delta Dart (F-106B) (QF-106B)	57-2543	8-27-37		RAC
☐ Convair 8-27 Delta Dart (F-106B) (QF-106B)	57-2545	8-27-39		RA
☐ North American NA-243 Super Sabre (F-100F)	N26AZ	243-120	56-3844	RAA

CHRISTIAN AIR MUSEUM (TX18)

Address: PO Box 260154, Corpus Christi, Texas 78246-0154,
Admission: By prior permission only.
Location: At an airfield in the area.

Four aircraft listed have been registered to the organisation over the last six years. An Aeronca Champion was with the museum for a period but has now been sold to a private owner in the Houston area.

One of the Texans is mocked up as a Japanese 'Kate' and has been reported at airshows in the region. Attempts to find out more information on the group and its activities have so far been unsuccessful.

TYPE	REG/SER	CON. NO.	PI/NOTES	STATUS
☐ Cessna 180	N3383D	32181		RAA
☐ North American NA-88 Texan (AT-6D) (SNJ-5)	N7130C	88-17780	42-85999, Bu90712 – mocked up as a Kate.	RAA
☐ North American NA-121 Texan (AT-6F) (SNJ-6)	N9806C	121-43155	44-82433, Bu112301	RAA

COLD WAR AIR MUSEUM (TX19)

Address: 7750 North MacArthur Boulevard, Suite 120-990, Irving, Texas 75063-7574.
Tel: 972-869-2471   **Fax:** 240-376-1111   **Email:** bruce@shadowsoft.com
Admission: Saturday 1000-1600
Location: At Lancaster Airport, which is about 10 miles south of Dallas off Belt Line Road.

The museum was set up a few years ago to acquire and fly aircraft and helicopters from this period. The first to arrive were the four Mil Mi-2s registered to the museum in late 2006. The quartet had been in store at Krumovo before being sold in the spring of 2003.
Bulgaria has supplied several other members of the collection. One of the fearsome Mil Mi-24s is now airworthy and should prove to be a popular attraction at shows in the region. This type can be compared with the Bell Huey Cobra. The MiG-21UM and the MiG-23 are being restored to flying condition. The Magister was built in Finland and served with the Air Force until the late 1980s when it was one of many sold to the USA.
The Delfin first flew in 1959 and was subsequently selected to be the standard Warsaw Pact jet trainer. Over 3,500 were produced between 1963 and 1974. The type served in more than 20 countries. The Albatros was designed to replace the Delfin and this type was again successful with over 2800 completed.
Not all the aircraft are on show in the main hangar.

TYPE	REG/SER	CON. NO.	PI/NOTES	STATUS
☐ Aero L-29 Delfin	N129TX	194236	86 (Bulgaria)	PV
☐ Aero L-29 Delfin		892779	41 (Bulgaria)	RA
☐ Aero L-29 Delfin	N68SJ	892783	45 (Bulgaria)	RA
☐ Aero L-29 Delfin	N12DN	892814	2814 (Czechoslovakia)	PVA
☐ Aero L-39C Albatros		633647	25 (Ukraine)	PV
☐ Aero L-39ZA Albatros	NX909ZA	633909	909 (Bulgaria)	RA
☐ Aero L-39ZA Albatros	N107ZA	734107	107 (Bulgaria)	RA
☐ Aero L-39ZA Albatros	NX109ZA	734109	109 (Bulgaria)	PVA
☐ Antonov An-2				RAA
☐ Bell 204 Iroquois (HU-1B) (UH-1B)	N333WN	410	62-1890	PV
☐ Bell 209 Huey Cobra (AH-1G) (AH-1S)	70-16088	21032		PV
☐ Ercoupe 415C	N3245H	3870	NC3245H – painted as a PQ-13.	PVA
☐ Fouga CM.170-2 Magister (CM.170A)	N904DM	80	FM-80	PV

☐ Hughes 269A	N8856F	43-0194		PVA
☐ Hughes 269C-1	N6145V	0045		PVA
☐ Mikoyan-Gurevich MiG-21UM	N921UM	516979001	38 (Bulgaria)	PV
☐ Mikoyan-Gurevich MiG-23UB	N923UB	A1037622	022 (Bulgaria)	PV
☐ Mil Mi-2	NX211PZ	515021126	211 (Bulgaria)	PVA
☐ Mil Mi-2	NX212PZ	515249077	212 (Bulgaria)	PV
☐ Mil Mi-2	NX213PZ	515250087	213 (Bulgaria)	PV
☐ Mil Mi-2	NX214PZ	515303087	214 (Bulgaria)	PV
☐ Mil Mi-24D	NX120NX	110155	120 (Bulgaria)	PV
☐ Mil Mi-24D	NX118NX	150153	118 (Bulgaria)	PVA
☐ Nanchang CJ-6A	N36CJ	3532022		RAA
☐ Nanchang CJ-6A	N193LN	3632009		PVA

COMANCHE FIGHTERS (TX20)

Address: 109 North Post Oak Lane Suite 600, Houston, Texas 77024-7753.
Admission: By prior permission only.
Location: At an airfield in the area.

This collection of fighter aircraft has a number of interesting types. The Spitfire crashed in New Guinea in 1944 and the wreck was recovered 30 years later. The aircraft was shipped to New Zealand for a major rebuild. The fighter arrived in England in 1999 and took to the air again at Duxford in November 2006.

The Lightning has had an interesting career serving in Honduras between 1948 and 1960. After it returned to the USA it has had a number of owners including the Lone Star Flight Museum at Galveston. The four Mustangs all saw combat duties in World War II and are painted in typical period markings. Two classic jets complete the collection.

TYPE	REG/SER	CON. NO.	PI/NOTES	STATUS
☐ Canadair CL-13B Sabre 6 [North American F-86E]	N186FS	1461	23671 (Canada), 352 (South Africa), N38301	RAA
☐ Lockheed 422-87-23 Lightning (P-38L)	N38TF	422-8350	44-53095, NL67745, 503 (Honduras), 506 (Honduras), N9005R	RAA
☐ North American NA-103 Mustang (P-51C)	NL487FS	103-26778	43-25147, N51PR, G-PSIC – composite	RAA
☐ North American NA-111 Mustang (P-51K)	N98CF	111-30149	44-12016	RAA
☐ North American NA-111 Mustang (P-51K) (F-6K)	N357FG	111-36135	44-12852, NX66111, N90013, N22B 1900 (Dominican Republic), N21023	RAA
☐ North American NA-122 Mustang (P-51D)	N351MX	122-40931	44-74391, 351 (Guatemala), N38229	RAA
☐ Supermarine 349 Spitfire LF.Vc	N5TF		JG891, A58-178, ZK-MKV, G-LFVC, N624TB	RAA
☐ WSK SBLim-2M (Lim-1) [MiG-15]	N687	1A 02-005	205 (Poland)	RAA

COMMEMORATIVE AIR FORCE (BIG COUNTRY SQUADRON) (TX21)

Address: 4886 Newman Road, Abilene, Texas 79601-6718.
Tel: 325-676-1944   **Email:** nancy@weekshunter.com
Admission: By prior permission only
Location: At Elmdale Airpark which is just east of the city north of Interstate 20.

Situated on a grass airfield close to Abilene the squadron has constructed its own hangar and a museum is being set up. The Cessna is allocated to the wing and the other two aircraft are privately owned.

TYPE	REG/SER	CON. NO.	PI/NOTES	STATUS
☐ Cessna 165 Airmaster	N25462	567	NC25462	RAC
☐ Culver LFA Cadet	N37819	LFA-330		RAA
☐ Vultee V-74 Valiant (BT-13A)	N826BT	74-1638	41-1528	RAA

COMMEMORATIVE AIR FORCE (BIG THICKET WING) (TX22)

Address: Cleveland Municipal Airport, Highway 787, Cleveland, Texas 77328.
Tel: 409-321-1520
Admission: By prior permission only.
Location: At the airport which is about 15 miles east of San Antonio.

The wing now has only the Valiant allocated to it. There was a hangar fire at the airport a decade ago and several members' aircraft were destroyed. The BT-15 was away at the time and escaped. Also on the airfield is a chapter of the Experimental Aircraft Association and a number of vintage types can be seen in their hangar.

TYPE	REG/SER	CON. NO.	PI/NOTES	STATUS
☐ Vultee V-74A Valiant (BT-15)	N66681	74A-1268	41-10147	RAA

COMMEMORATIVE AIR FORCE (CENTRAL TEXAS WING) (TX23)

Address: 1841 Airport Drive, San Marcos, Texas 78666-9664.
Tel: 512-396-1943   **Email:** cafcentex@centurytel.net
Admission: Monday, Wednesday, Friday, Saturday 1000-1600.
Location: About 3 miles north east of the town off Route 21.

Texas

The wing, which has been in existence for about a quarter of a century, was the seventh chartered by the CAF. The unit is housed in a former World War II hangar at San Marcos which is also home to a number of warbirds owned by members. This building constructed in 1943 is the only original one left at the airfield.

The group completed a seven year rebuild of a P-38 but in 1994 it crashed during an airshow at Breckenridge. The wreck was eventually moved to the headquarters at Midland where it is was stored for a period. The P-39 is one of the few left flying.

The Cessna 310 has been painted in the colours of one of the U-3 Blue Canoe aircraft operated by the Air Force. There is a museum of memorabilia in the building. On show are many World War II items including documents, uniforms, components, photographs and models.

One part of the display is dedicated to the 'Doolittle Raiders' and their attack on Tokyo. A prized possession is an armoured seat from the B-25 piloted by Doolittle himself. A number of engines, including an Allison V-12, are on show.

The wing has also set up a excellent library where many books, log books and other archive materials can be seen.

TYPE	REG/SER	CON. NO.	PI/NOTES	STATUS
☐ Beech A45 Mentor (T-34A)	N99L	G-122	53-3361	PVA
☐ Bell 26E Airacobra (P-39Q)	N6968		42-19597	PVA
☐ Bell 33 Kingcobra (P-63E)	N6763		43-11719, NX1719, N1719, N443, N447AG	PVA
☐ Canadian Car & Foundry Harvard 4 [North American NA-186]	N2047	CCF4-83	20292 (Canada) – mocked up as a Kate.	PVA
☐ Canadian Car & Foundry Harvard 4 [North American NA-186]	N7754	CCF4-215	20424, CF-WPN (Canada) – mocked up as a Zero.	PVA
☐ Cessna 310B	N5435A/'58310'	35635		PVAX
☐ Curtiss 87V Warhawk (P-40N) (Kittyhawk IV)	N1226N	29629	42-105867, 867 (Canada)	PVA
☐ Interstate S-1A Cadet	NC37412	255		PVA
☐ Lockheed 580 (T-33A)	N155SF	580-1099	56-1749, N61749	PV
☐ Nanchang CJ-6A	N4184G	1332008		PVA
☐ Nanchang CJ-6A	N53HM	3051201		RAA
☐ North American NA-88 Texan (AT-6C) (Harvard IIA)	N9272C/'93555'	88-12054	41-33583, EX610, 7303 (South Africa),	PVAX
☐ Piper J-3C-65 Cub (L-4B)	N75066	9720	43-0535	RAA

COMMEMORATIVE AIR FORCE (COYOTE SQUADRON) (TX24)

Address:	515 Hidden Oaks Lane, Corsicana, Texas 75109.
Tel:	903-872-7627 Email: steveandchris757@att.net
Admission:	By prior permission only.
Location:	About 5 miles south east of the town off Route 287.

This recently formed wing maintains the Cornell in flying condition. The trainer is currently housed in the Tucker Hardgrave Memorial Hangar. The prototype Cornell first flew in May 1939 and large numbers were ordered for military primary pilot training. Also on the field is the informative Glenn Cumbie Museum.

TYPE	REG/SER	CON. NO.	PI/NOTES	STATUS
☐ Fairchild M-62A Cornell (PT-19A)	N49238	T42-3530	42-33864	RAA

COMMEMORATIVE AIR FORCE (DALLAS-FORT WORTH WING) (TX25)

Address:	DFW Hangar, Ferris Road, Lancaster, Texas 75146.
Tel:	972-227-9119 Email: littlecharkie@aol.com
Admission:	Saturday 0900-1600.
Location:	At Lancaster Airport which is about 10 miles south of Dallas off Belt Line Road

Formed in 1971, the wing constructed a large hangar at Lancaster in the late 1980s. An excellent museum of World War II memorabilia has been set up. There are many interesting items to be seen including some original combat maps. Also on view are period furniture, uniforms, instruments, documents and badges.

Three aircraft are currently allocated and a number of privately owned machines also reside in the building. The R4D is painted in period colours and is regularly flown to airshows. The L-5 and BT-l5 are also in typical World War II markings. The Canadian-built Harvard was in service with the Royal Canadian Air Force from 1952 until 1967. The trainer then spent 31 years in civilian use before moving south to the United States.

A former Bulgarian Mil Mi-24 has moved from the Cold War Air Museum and is now on show by the wing hangar.

TYPE	REG/SER	CON. NO.	PI/NOTES	STATUS
☐ Boeing-Stearman A75N1 Kaydet (PT-17)	N27933	75-630	41-870, N2809D, N22JH	PVA
☐ Canadian Car & Foundry Harvard 4 [North American NA-186]	N244SM	CCF4-35	20244, CF-WPM, C-FWPM – at nearby private strip.	RAA
☐ Douglas DC-3A-467 Skytrain (C-47B) (R4D-6) (SC-47J)	N151ZE	14963/26408	43-49147, Bu50783, N151Z, N151ZL	PVA
☐ Mil Mi-24D	122	730203	In Bulgarian markings.	PV
☐ North American NA-88 Texan (AT-6D) (SNJ-5)	N30JF	88-16411	42-84630, Bu44009, N6639C	PVA
☐ North American NA-168 Texan (T-6G)	N49RR	168-464	49-3255, E.16-120 (Spain), N4993X	PVA
☐ Stinson V-76 Sentinel (O-62) (L-5)	N57789	76-272	(USAAF)	PVA
☐ Vought FG-1D Corsair	N9964Z	3729	Bu92468	PVA
☐ Vultee V-74A Valiant (BT-15)	N69605	74A-1258	41-10137	PVA

COMMEMORATIVE AIR FORCE (DESERT SQUADRON) (TX26)

Address:	411 East Yukon Road, PO Box13112, Odessa, Texas 79763.
Tel:	432-550-6537 Email: ccpt13@sbcglobal.net
Admission:	By prior permission only.
Location:	About 3 miles north of the town on Route 385.

The group has its own hangar at the airport. A display of memorabilia has been set up in the building. On view are many World War II items. This small unit has an N2S-3, painted in original colours, allocated and this regularly attends events in the area. Also airworthy is the Cornell which has recently joined the squadron.
The T-33 is mounted at the field and is in the care of the local American Legion Post.

TYPE	REG/SER	CON. NO.	PI/NOTES	STATUS
☐ Boeing-Stearman B75N1 Kaydet (N2S-3)	N65666	75-7318	Bu07714	RAA
☐ Fairchild M-62A Cornell (PT-19A)	N40265	T41-562	41-14624, NC51822	RAA
☐ Lockheed 580 (T-33A)	52-9233	580-7299		PV
☐ Stinson V-76 Sentinel (L-5C)	N178	76-3571	44-17284, PI-C279, RP-C279	RAA

COMMEMORATIVE AIR FORCE (DEVIL DOG SQUADRON) (TX27)

Address:	209 Corsair Drive, Georgetown, Texas 78268.
Tel:	512-869-1759 Email: info@devildogsquadron.com
Admission:	By prior permission only.
Location:	At the airport which is about 5 miles north of the town.

The unit maintains the Mitchell which has been painted in the colours of a PBJ-1J. The Marine Corps operated nine squadrons of the type during World War II. The bomber was mainly used on low altitude missions and the glass nose was replaced by a solid one. The Devil Dog Squadron highlights the missions carried out by PBJs.

TYPE	REG/SER	CON. NO.	PI/NOTES	STATUS
☐ North American NA-108 Mitchell (B-25J) (TB-25K)	N9643C	108-47512	44-86758	RAAX

COMMEMORATIVE AIR FORCE (DEWLINE SQUADRON) (TX28)

Address:	4105 Tradewind Road, Tradewind Airport, Amarillo, Texas 79118.
Tel:	806-355-8705 Email: coljowell@gmail.com
Admission:	By prior permission only.
Location:	In the south western suburbs of the city.

The squadron has restored to original World War II condition a Stinson L-5 built in 1942. The type flew in the liaison and observation role for many years and almost 4,000 were built.
The unit was originally based at Pampa and it moved to Amarillo several years ago. A number of members' aircraft are housed in the squadron hangar on the west side of the airport. Several of these carry military markings.
Inside the building is a display of World War II memorabilia and artefacts. The display highlights history of the unit and the airport.

TYPE	REG/SER	CON. NO.	PI/NOTES	STATUS
☐ Aeronca 65CA Super Chief	NC31797	CA-11140	NC31797, N31797	RAA
☐ Beech A45 Mentor (T-34A)	N234RJ	G-773	55-0216	RAA
☐ Boeing-Stearman E75 Kaydet (PT-13D) (N2S-5)	N5539N	75-5198	42-17035, Bu61076	RAC
☐ Fairchild M-62A-4 Cornell II	N1132N	FC.27	10521 (Canada)	RAA
☐ Fairchild M-62A-4 Cornell (PT-26) (Cornell II)	N9165H	T43-4459	44-19347, EW400	RAA
☐ North American NA-121 Texan (AT-6F) (SNJ-6)	N2861G	121-42990	44-82268, Bu112167	RAA
☐ Stinson V-76 Sentinel (L-5)	N63777	76-526	(USAAF)	RAA
☐ Vultee V-74 Valiant (BT-13A)	N59840	74-2459	41-11449, NC59840	RAA

COMMEMORATIVE AIR FORCE (GULF COAST WING) (TX29)

Address:	Hangar ER-7, 8411 Nelms Street, Houston, Texas 77061.
Tel:	281-484-0098 Email: wing.leader@gulfcoastwing.org
Admission:	By prior permission only.
Location:	At William P. Hobby Airport which is in the south eastern suburbs of the city off Route 35.

The wing was formed in 1972 and has recently moved into its new headquarters at Hobby Airport. The B-17 'Texas Raiders' was assigned to the unit in the mid-1970s and it is now painted in the World War II colours of a 381st Bomb Group aircraft.
Delivered on 12th July 1945, the Fortress was transferred to the Navy four days later and flown until January 1955. After a career as a survey aircraft the bomber was purchased by the CAF in September 1967. The aircraft was based at nearby Ellington Field before its move to Hobby in late August 2006.
Not all of the fleet is at the new home and they are based at a number of other airfields in the area of Houston. The wing is responsible for the operation of a number of Texans and Valiants converted to represent Japanese aircraft for the film 'Tora Tora Tora'. The wing has provided the Pearl Harbor sequence at the annual CAF airshow at first Harlingen and then Midland for around 30 years.

TYPE	REG/SER	CON. NO.	PI/NOTES	STATUS
☐ Boeing 299-O Fortress (B-17G) (PB-1W)	N7227C	32513	44-83872, Bu77235	RAA
☐ Canadian Car & Foundry Harvard 4 [North American NA-186]	NX15799	CCF4-117	20326 (Canada), – mocked up as Zero 'AI-113'	RAA
☐ Canadian Car & Foundry Harvard 4 [North American NA-186]	N9097	CCF4-158	20367 (Canada), CF-URH – mocked up as Zero 'AI-112'	RAA
☐ Canadian Car & Foundry Harvard 4 [North American NA-186]	N15797	CCF4-199	20408 (Canada) – mocked up as Zero 'AI-114'.	RAA
☐ Canadian Car & Foundry Harvard 4 [North American NA-186]	N4447	CCF4-241	20450 (Canada) – mocked up as Zero 'AI-111'	RAA
☐ North American NA-84 Texan (AT-6B)	N11171	84-7800	41-17422, N62144 – mocked up as Zero 'AI-115'	RAA
☐ North American NA-88 Texan (AT-6D) (SNJ-5)	N3725G	88-16686	42-84905, Bu84875, – mocked up as Kate 'AII-356'	RAA

Texas

☐ North American NA-121 Texan (AT-6F) (SNJ-6)	N9820C	121-43036	44-82314, Bu112178 – Mocked up RAA as Zero 'AI-118'	
☐ Vultee V-74 Valiant (BT-13A)	N67208	74-2307	41-11297 – mocked up as a Val 'BI-257' – formerly 'BII-235'.	RA
☐ Vultee V-74 Valiant (BT-13A)	N56478	74-7356	41-22926 – mocked up as a Val	RAA

COMMEMORATIVE AIR FORCE (HIGH SKY WING) (TX30)

Address: PO Box 61064, Midland, Texas 79711-1064.
Tel: 432-563-5112   **Email:** randy@rwebs.org
Admission: Saturday 1000-1800.
Location: At Midland International Airport which is about 8 miles west of the city.

A hangar close to the headquarters building of the CAF is home to the wing. Some restoration on a Douglas B-23 bomber, which was converted for transport duties during its service life, was carried out but this aircraft has now moved back to the main museum.

Four aircraft are currently assigned to the unit. The Fairchild is painted in the colours of an aircraft used by the US Coast Guard in the late 1930s. The wing has a display of memorabilia in its hangar and this includes a 'Veteran's Wall' where those lost in military service are remembered.

TYPE	REG/SER	CON. NO.	PI/NOTES	STATUS
☐ Fairchild 24R46	N81348/'V-165'	R46-248	NC81348	RAAX
☐ Fairchild M-62A Cornell (PT-19A)	N49797	T42-3273	42-33607	RAA
☐ Fokker Dr I (R)				RA
☐ North American NA-88 Texan (SNJ-4)	N101X/'9450'	88-9450	Bu09935, NC367, Bu09935	RAAX
☐ Stinson HW.75	N23784	7244	NC23784	RAA

COMMEMORATIVE AIR FORCE (HIGHLAND LAKES SQUADRON) MUSEUM (TX31)

Address: PO Box 866, Burnet, Texas 78611-0866.
Tel: 512-756-2266   **Email:** caf@star.net
Admission: Saturday 0900-1700; Sunday 1200-1700.
Location: At the airport which is about 1 mile south west of the town on Route 281.

The museum houses a large collection of World War II items including a Norden bomb sight, a Japanese mortar, a nose turret from a B-24 and many uniforms, radio equipment, photographs and personal memorabilia. The Navion which is painted to represent an L-17. The four former military jets were obtained from Davis-Monthan.

TYPE	REG/SER	CON. NO.	PI/NOTES	STATUS
☐ Cessna 318B Tweety Bird (T-37B)		40545		PV
☐ Douglas DC-3A-467 Skytrain (C-47B) (Dakota IV)	N47HL	15758/27203	43-49942, KN270, 12909 (Canada), C-GCKE, N595AM	PVA
☐ Fairchild M-62A-4 Cornell (PT-26A) (Cornell II)	N6072C	T42-6020 (?)	42-6935, FV450, 15361 (Canada), CF-GDX	PVA
☐ North American NA-88 Texan (SNJ-4)	N7024C	88-13517	Bu27821,	PVA
☐ North American NA-243 Super Sabre (F-100F)	56-3990	243-266		PV
☐ Northrop N-156T Talon (T-38A) (AT-38B)	60-0594	N.5167		PV
☐ Piper J-3C-65 Cub				PVA
☐ Ryan Navion A	N444AC		NAV-4-1463	PVA
☐ Stinson V-76 Sentinel (O-62) (L-5)	N55723	76-193		PVA
☐ Vought A-7D Corsair II	72-0188	D310		PV

COMMEMORATIVE AIR FORCE (LONE STAR WING) (TX32)

Address: 2020 Warren Drive, Marshall Texas 75672-5513.
Tel: 903-923-8335   **Email:** gtent@mcc4u.com
Admission: By prior permission only.
Location: About 3 miles south east of the town off Route 31.

The wing was first formed at Tyler in 1982 and operated a PBY-6 Catalina. Sadly this was destroyed in a fatal crash in 1984. A squadron was established at Longview in 1987 and three years later it became the Lone Star Wing. A museum was set up in the centre of Longview. On show was an impressive display of memorabilia, military vehicles, models, photographs and documents highlighting significant events in World War II. This display closed in 1995 and the items were put into store.

A move to Marshall took place in the late 1990s where the wing has its own hangar. The SG-38 replica is painted in period World War II 'Hitler Youth' colours.

TYPE	REG/SER	CON. NO.	PI/NOTES	STATUS
☐ Aeronca 11AC Chief				RAA
☐ Aeronca 65-TAL Defender	N47309	L-4822TA		RAA
☐ Beech D18S				RA
☐ Beech D18S Expeditor 3NM	N1002N	CA-64 (a-664)	1489 (Canada), N6132, N300NL – possible identity.	RA
☐ Boeing-Stearman A75N1 Kaydet (PT-17)	N7058Q	75-1543	41-7984, N56186	RAA
☐ Fairchild M-62A Cornell (PT-19)	N51173	10564AE	(USAAF)	RAA
☐ Piper J-3C-65 Cub	N91946	16366	NC91946	RAA
☐ Schneider-Hofmann-Rehberg SG-38 (DFS 108-14) (R)				PVX
☐ Taylorcraft DCO-65 Grasshopper (L-2M)	N50569	L-4546	(USAAF)	RAA
☐ War Aircraft P-51 Mustang				RA

COMMEMORATIVE AIR FORCE (RANGER WING) (TX33)

Address:	PO Box 1218, Bruceville, Texas 76630-1218
Tel:	254-754-6478 Email: darlene@ramaircraft.com
Admission:	By prior permission only.
Location:	At Waco Airport which is about 5 miles west of the town.

In 1979 the Ranger Squadron was formed at Waco and in the following year it was allocated the Invader. Over the next two years the bomber was completely restored. The unit has now been granted wing status.

TYPE	REG/SER	CON. NO.	PI/NOTES	STATUS
☐ Douglas A-26B Invader	N240P/'437140'	7140	41-39427, N75Y	RAAX

COMMEMORATIVE AIR FORCE (RIO GRANDE VALLEY WING) MUSEUM (TX34)

Address:	955 South Minnesota Avenue, Brownsville Texas 78521-5731.
Tel:	956-541-8585 Email: tes2ces@yahoo.com
Admission:	Wednesday-Saturday 0930-1530.
Location:	At Brownsville Airport which is about 4 miles north east of the town off Route 2519,

An excellent museum has been set up at Brownsville by the wing. On show are many items tracing the history of aviation in the area, items from World War II and a large collection of photographs, documents and uniforms. There are also models, components and engines to be seen.

The aircraft collection includes a number of unusual types some of which are privately owned. The de Havilland Moth Minor is painted in false Royal Air Force impressment colours. The aircraft was sold new to Switzerland in 1939 and arrived in the USA in the early 1970s.

The German-built Focke-Wulf Stieglitz was used by the Luftwaffe and the Finnish Air Force until sold on the civil market in 1960 and it came on the American register in late 1969.

TYPE	REG/SER	CON. NO.	PI/NOTES	STATUS
☐ Aeronca 65TC Grasshopper (O-58B) (L-3B)				PVA
☐ Beech D18S Expeditor (C-45G)	N75Q	AF-423	51-11866, N5265V	PVA
☐ Boeing-Stearman E75 Kaydet (PT-13D) (N2S-5)	N65877	75-8274	42-109241, Bu43180	PVA
☐ British Aircraft Corporation 167 Strikemaster 80	N799PS	EEP/JP/3688	G-27-232, 1121 (Saudi Arabia), G-CCAI	RAA
☐ Cessna 172N	N75702	17267884		PVA
☐ De Havilland DH.94 Moth Minor	N94DH	94020	HB-OMU, 'AV977'	PVA
☐ Ercoupe 415C	N2214H	2837	NC2214H	PVA
☐ Fairchild M-62A Cornell (PT-19A)	N46693	7033AE	42-65454	PVA
☐ Fairchild M-62A-4 Cornell (PT-26B) (Cornell II)	N4732G		(FZ293), 43-36343, FZ293, 10846 (Canada)	PVA
☐ Fleet 16B Finch II	N16BR	383	(Canada), XB-ZOQ(?)	PVA
☐ Focke-Wulf Fw 44J Stieglitz	'RF+GJ'	2936 (?)	SE+IY, SZ-33 (Finland), OH-SZD, N2497	PVAX
☐ North American NA-145 Navion	N8867H	NAV-4-867		PVA
☐ Piper J-3C-65 Cub	N41161	7782	NC41161	PVA
☐ Ryan ST-3KR Recruit (PT-22)	N22AL	1831	41-20622, N54098	PVA
☐ Stinson V-76 Sentinel (L-5E)	N66535	76-3918	44-17631	PVA
☐ Taylorcraft DCO-65 Grasshopper (L-2M)	N47731	L-4628	(USAAF)	PVA

COMMEMORATIVE AIR FORCE (RIVER BEND SQUADRON) (TX35)

Address:	Wharton Airport, Route 1, Highway 59, Wharton, Texas 77488.
Email:	ronfountain@swmuseum.com
Admission:	By prior permission only.
Location:	About 5 miles south west of the town on Route 59.

The squadron acquired the Yale, formerly with the New Mexico Wing, in the summer of 2005. The former RCAF trainer is undergoing a major restoration to airworthy status. The French Air Force ordered large numbers but these were diverted to Canada when the country fell to the Germans. They were used as primary trainers under the Commonwealth Air Training Plan.

TYPE	REG/SER	CON. NO.	PI/NOTES	STATUS
☐ North American NA-64 Yale	N4574Y	64-2214	3450 (Canada)	RAC

COMMEMORATIVE AIR FORCE (THIRD COAST SQUADRON) (TX36)

Address:	PO Box 8192, Corpus Christi, Texas 78468-8192.
Tel:	361-661-0321 Fax: 361-883-4840 Email: preflys@aol.com
Admission:	By prior permission only.
Location:	At the airport which is about 3 miles west of the city.

The squadron maintains the Interstate Cadet in flying condition. In total 250 examples of the type, powered by a 100 h.p. Continental O-200 engine, were ordered for liaison work. The Canadian-built Cessna T-50 is a recent addition to the fleet. This aircraft has moved from the now defunct Wright Stuff Squadron in Ohio.

TYPE	REG/SER	CON. NO.	PI/NOTES	STATUS
☐ Boeing-Stearman A75N1 Kaydet (N2S-1)	N48182	75-967	Bu3190	RAA
☐ Cessna T-50 Crane 1	N1238N	1632	8139 (Canada)	RAA
☐ Interstate S1B1 Cadet (O-63) (L-6)	N46337	163	43-2720	RAA

COMMEMORATIVE AIR FORCE (WEST HOUSTON SQUADRON) (TX37)

Address:	Hangar B-5, West Houston Airport, 18000 Groeschke Road, Houston, Texas 77084.
Tel:	281-579-2131 Email: info@WestHoustonSqdn.org
Admission:	Saturday 0800-1700.
Location:	The airport is about 20 miles west of the city north of Interstate 10.

The squadron was formed in 1978 and has been based at the airport since its early days. In 1993 a hangar was bought to house the aircraft. A museum of memorabilia opened in September 2003. A collection of engines can be seen here. Five aircraft are assigned to the unit and a number owned by members are also in residence.

TYPE	REG/SER	CON. NO.	PI/NOTES	STATUS
☐ Boeing-Stearman E75 Kaydet (PT-13D)	N11ZW	75-5436	42-17273, N3954B	RAC
☐ Lockheed 18-56-23 Lodestar (C-60A)	N60JT	18-2478	42-56005, NC45330, AN-ADI, N9980F, N60DX	RAC
☐ Mooney M.20E	N6993U	353		RAA
☐ Naval Aircraft Factory N3N-3	N44741		Bu2781	PVA
☐ North American NA-121 Texan (AT-6D) (SNJ-5)	N991VR	121-41842	44-81120, Bu90991, N8203E, N73SL	RAA
☐ Stinson 108-1 Voyager	N97040	108-1040	N97902	PVA
☐ Vultee V-74 Valiant (BT-13A)	NX27003	74-5017	41-21178	PVC

COMMEMORATIVE AIR FORCE (WEST TEXAS WING) MUSEUM (TX38)

Address:	PO Box 861, Graham, Texas 76450.
Tel:	817-549-5560 Email: web@wtwcaf.org
Admission:	By prior permission only.
Location:	In a workshop in the town – and at Abilene Airport.

In the late 1980s the wing was restoring a Martin Mauler but this is now in store at the headquarters at Midland. Kept at Graham is the Curtiss Helldiver, one of the few remaining examples of the World War II scout bomber and the only one currently airworthy.

The hangar, constructed in 1984, houses a museum dedicated to the first leader of the unit, Robert E. Richeson. On show are items of World War II memorabilia, uniforms, weapons and models. An exhibition entitled 'Life on the Home Front' is being set up.

TYPE	REG/SER	CON. NO.	PI/NOTES	STATUS
☐ Beech D18S	N80197	A-171		RAA
☐ Curtiss 84G Helldiver (SB2C-5)	N92879		Bu83589	RAA
☐ North American NA-88 Texan (AT-6C)	N5WS	88-11170	41-32815	RAC

COMMEMORATIVE AIR FORCE (YELLOW ROSE SQUADRON) (TX39)

Address:	1841 Airport Drive, San Marcos, Texas 77666-9664.
Tel:	512-396-1943
Admission:	By prior permission only.
Location:	The airport is about 3 miles north east of the town off Route 21.

The squadron has maintained the B-25 for a number of years. The aircraft was based at Stinson Field in San Antonio before moving to San Marcos. The bomber is a regular performer at air shows. The Mitchell was delivered in 1943 and was operational for only three years serving at a number of bases in the eastern USA. After three years in store it was transferred to Sheppard Air Force Base as an instructional airframe. The aircraft was sold on the civil market in 1959 and was soon converted for crop spraying duties. A number of private owners followed before the Confederate Air Force acquired it in 1979.

TYPE	REG/SER	CON. NO.	PI/NOTES	STATUS
☐ North American NA-108 Mitchell (B-25J) (TB-25N)	N25YR	108-34881	43-27868, N9077Z	RAA

COMMEMORATIVE AIR FORCE AMERICAN AIRPOWER HERITAGE MUSEUM (TX40)

Address:	PO Box 62000, Midland, Texas 79711-2000.
Tel:	432-563-1000 Fax: 432-563-8046 Email: publicrelations@cafhq.org
Admission:	Monday-Saturday 0900-1700; Sunday 1200-1700.
Location:	At Midland International Airport which is about 8 miles west of the city.

Lloyd Nolen and four friends bought a P-51 Mustang in 1957 and based it at Mercedes Airport. Soon after they formed the Confederate Air Force. The following year a Grumman Bearcat was added and the search for other World War II aircraft was started. By 1961 there were nine aircraft in the fleet and the organisation became a non-profit Texas corporation.

The members were amazed to find that large numbers of 1939-1945 combat aircraft being scrapped and that no real attempts were being made to save them. They set themselves the aim of trying to find and maintain in airworthy condition one example of each type flown in combat by US forces during the conflict. Visits were made to the storage depots for the Navy at Litchfield and the Air Force at Davis-Monthan to see what could be salvaged.

In 1965 a museum was opened at Mercedes but the field was too small for the bombers then being acquired and a move was made to Harlingen. At the new site three hangars were in use and more aircraft were acquired. The searches covered the world and in 1969 six P-47 Thunderbolts were purchased in Peru. All were flying by 1974 but most were later sold to avoid unnecessary duplication.

Wings and squadrons were set up across the USA and abroad and many of these units now have their own premises and have set up museums. The annual airshow each October brought thousands of enthusiasts to Harlingen and at the time was the only opportunity for many of the types to be seen in the air.

In 1991 a move was made to Midland where a new facility has been constructed. The American Airpower Heritage Museum has a superb collection of World War II artefacts and memorabilia. The building has several phases of its exhibit now open. The Silent Wings and Airborne Gallery was ready for the October 1994 airshow. The Aviation Nose Art Gallery opened on 5th October 2001. Here a number of panels showing the typical paintings used on American aircraft of the period can be seen. Also on show are military vehicles and weapons along with many uniforms and documents. The story of World War II with particular emphasis on the American contribution is portrayed in detail. There is an extensive library and archive section which includes over 1,700 taped interviews with World War II veterans.

The fleet held by the headquarters is listed here and in addition the units are required to send aircraft to Midland for a three month period so all aircraft owned to the organisation are shown with their normal location.

TYPE	REG/SER	CON. NO.	PI/NOTES	STATUS
☐ Aeronca 65TAC	N36681	C1121TA	NC36681 – [St. Charles, MO]	-
☐ Aeronca 65TAC	N36687	L1441TA	NC36687	PVA
☐ Antonov An-2R	N43798	1G 210-55	CCCP-43978, N61488, N2AN – [Cable, CA]	-
☐ Beech C18S Kansan (AT-11)	N320A	877	41-9451 – [Moriarty, NM]	-
☐ Beech C18S Kansan (AT-11)	N65494	3258	42-36878 (?)	RA
☐ Beech C18S Expeditor (C-45F) (UC-45F) (JRB-4)	N1553V	8698	44-87439, Bu66469	RAA
☐ Beech D18S Expeditor (C18S) (SNB-2) (SNB-5P) (RC-45J)	N4207	4664	Bu67124 – [Heber Valley, UT]	-
☐ Beech D18S Expeditor (C18S) (SNB-2) (SNB-5) TC-45J) (UC-45J)	N49265	4784	Bu39265 – [Platte Valley, CO]	-
☐ Beech D18S	N80197	A-171	[Graham, TX]	-
☐ Beech D18S	'KJ508'	A-177	NC1000G, N100G, XB-POB, N4432B, N70GA – [Atlanta, GA]	-
☐ Beech D18S	N145AZ	A-235	CF-GHR, N118R, N20MD – [Mesa, AZ]	-
☐ Beech D18S	N79AG	A-806	N8866A – [Hobbs, NM.]	-
☐ Beech D18S Expeditor (C-45H)	N40074	AF-834	52-10904 – [Guymon, OK]	-
☐ Bell 26E Airacobra (P-39Q)	N6968		42-19597 – [San Marcos, TX]	-
☐ Bell 33 Kingcobra (P-63A)	N636GA	33-11	42-68941, NX7775488, N75488, N191H – [Atlanta, GA]	-
☐ Bell 33 Kingcobra (P-63F)	N6763		43-11719, NX1719, N1719, N443, N447AG – [San Marcos, TX]	-
☐ Bell 47G	N633EB	26	N172B	PV
☐ Bell 205 Iroquois (UH-1H)	69-15500	11788		PV
☐ Bell 209 Huey Cobra (AH-1G) (AH-1S)	68-15146	20680		PV
☐ Boeing 299-O Fortress (B-17G) (PB-1W)	N7227C	32513	44-83872, Bu77235 – [Houston, TX]	-
☐ Boeing 299-O Fortress (B-17G) (RB-17G) (DB-17G) (DB-17P)	N9323Z	32155	44-83514 – [Mesa, AZ]	-
☐ Boeing 345 Superfortress (B-29A)	N529B	11547	44-62070, N4249	RAA
☐ Boeing-Stearman A75N1 Kaydet (PT-17)	N27933	75-630	41-870, N2809D, N22JH – [Marshall, TX]	-
☐ Boeing-Stearman A75N1 Kaydet (PT-17)	N7058Q	75-1543	41-7984, N56184 – [Marshall, TX]	-
☐ Boeing-Stearman B75N1 Kaydet (N2S-3)	N65666	75-7318	Bu07714 – [Odessa, TX.]	-
☐ Boeing-Stearman E75 Kaydet (PT-13D) (N2S-5)	N1387V	75-8291	42-109258, Bu43197 – [Heber Valley, UT]	-
☐ Canadian Car & Foundry Harvard 4 [North American NA-186]	N2047	CCF4-83	20292 (Canada) – mocked up as a Kate – [San Marcos, TX]	-
☐ Canadian Car & Foundry Harvard 4 [North American NA-186]	N13595	CCF4-97	20306 (Canada) – [St. Paul, MN.]	-
☐ Canadian Car & Foundry Harvard 4 [North American NA-186]	NX15799	CCF4-117	20326 (Canada) – mocked up as Zero 'AI-113' – [Houston, TX]	-
☐ Canadian Car & Foundry Harvard 4 [North American NA-186]	N9097	CCF4-158	20367 (Canada), CF-URH – mocked up as Zero 'AI-112' – [Houston, TX]	-
☐ Canadian Car & Foundry Harvard 4 [North American NA-186]	N15797	CCF4-199	20408 (Canada) – mocked up as Zero 'AI-114' – [Houston, TX]	-
☐ Canadian Car & Foundry Harvard 4 [North American NA-186]	N421QB	CCF4-212	20421 (Canada), C-FUAD – [Anchorage, AK]	-
☐ Canadian Car & Foundry Harvard 4 [North American NA-186]	N4447	CCF4-241	20450 (Canada) – mocked up as Zero 'AI-111' – [Houston, TX]	-
☐ Cessna 165 Airmaster	N25462	567	NC25462 – [Abilene, TX]	-
☐ Cessna T-50 Bobcat (AT-17B) (UC-78B)	N44795	6516	43-32578 – [Wichita, KS]	-
☐ Cessna T-50 Crane 1	N1238N	1632	8139 (Canada) – [Corpus Christi, TX]	-
☐ Cessna 310B	N5435A	35635	[San Marcos, TX]	-
☐ Champion 7EC Traveler	N7436B	7EC-474	[Mesa, AZ]	-
☐ Consolidated 28-5ACF Catalina (28-6A) (PBY-6A)	N324FA	2163	Bu64092, N6681C, CF-PIU, C-FPIU – [Duluth, MN]	-
☐ Consolidated 28-6A Catalina (PBY-6A)	N7179Y	2167	Bu64097, N7082C, F-ZBAW, C-FHNF – [Duluth, MN]	-
☐ Consolidated RLB-30 Liberator (LB-30A)	N24927	18	AM927, NL24927, N1503, XC-CAY, N12905	RAA
☐ Curtiss 84G Helldiver (SB2C-5)	N92879		Bu83589 – [Graham, TX]	-
☐ Curtiss 87V Warhawk (P-40N) (Kittyhawk IV)	N1226N	29629	42-105867, 867 (Canada) – [San Marcos, TX]	-
☐ Curtiss-Wright CW-20B-4 Commando (C-46F)	N53594	22486	44-78663 – [Camarillo, CA.]	-
☐ Curtiss-Wright CW-20B-4 Commando (C-46F)	N78774	22597	44-78774, N74178, N680SE	PVA
☐ De Havilland DH.94 Moth Minor	N94DH/'AV977'	94020	HB-OMU – [Brownsville, TX]	-

Texas

☐ Douglas DC-3A-457 Skytrooper (C-53D)	N45366	11757	42-68830, NC45366 – [Riverside, CA]
☐ Douglas DC-3A-467 Skytrain (C-47B) (Dakota IV)	N47HL	15758/27203	43-49942, KN270, 12909 (Canada), C-GCKE, N595AM – [Burnet, TX]
☐ Douglas DC-3A-467 Skytrain (C-47B) (R4D-6) (SC-47J)	N151ZE	14963/26408	43-49147, Bu50783, N151Z, N151ZL – [Lancaster, TX]
☐ Douglas DC-3A-467 Skytrain (TC-47B) (R4D-7) (R4D-6R)	N227GB	16597/33345	44-77013, Bu99854, N7074C, N32, N32A,'43-15033' – [Lansing, IL]
☐ Douglas DC-4 Skymaster (C-54D)	N4470M	10780	42-72675 – fuselage only. PV
☐ Douglas A-24B Dauntless	NL82GA	17371	42-54582, NL94513, XB-QUC, N54532 [Atlanta, GA]
☐ Douglas A-26B Invader	N9682C	6943	41-39230 – [Las Vegas, NV]
☐ Douglas A-26B Invader	N240P/437140'	7140	41-39427, N75Y – [Waco, TX.]
☐ Douglas A-26C Invader	N626SH	28922	44-35643, 435643 (France), N6841D, C-GCES, N8015H, N226RW – [Guthrie, OK] RAA
☐ Ercoupe 415C	N2354H	2979	PVA
☐ Fairchild 24R46	N81348/'V-165'	R46-248	NC81348 – [Midland, TX]
☐ Fairchild M-62A Cornell (PT-19A)	N40265	T41-562	41-14624, NC51882 – [Odessa, TX]
☐ Fairchild M-62A Cornell (PT-19A)	N46876	T42-1957	42-2869 – [Tulsa, OK]
☐ Fairchild M-62A Cornell (PT-19A)	N49797	T42-3273	42-33607 – [Midland, TX] RAA
☐ Fairchild M-62A Cornell (PT-19A)	N49238	T42-3530	42-33864 – [Corsicana, TX] RAA
☐ Fairchild M-62A Cornell (PT-19A)	N46693	7033AE	42-65454 – [Brownsville, TX] PVA
☐ Fairchild M-62A Cornell (PT-19B)	N50481	6103AE	42-47961 – [New Century, KS]
☐ Fairchild M-62A Cornell (PT-19A)	N46693	7033AE	42-65454 – [Brownsville, TX]
☐ Fairchild M-62A-4 Cornell (PT-26A)	N60535	FX-146	42-71412 – [Indianapolis, IN]
☐ Fairchild M-62A-4 Cornell II	N5519N	FC.18	10520 (Canada), CF-FDF – [Albuquerque, NM]
☐ Fairchild M-62A-4 Cornell (PT-26A) (Cornell II)	N519SH	T43-5954	42-83367, NC51589, N51589 – [Oklahoma City, OK]
☐ Fairchild M-62A-4 Cornell (PT-26A) (Cornell II)	N6072C	T4-6020 (?)	42-65935, FV450, 15361 (Canada), CF-GDX – [Burnet, TX] PVA
☐ Fairchild M-62A-4 Cornell (PT-26B) (Cornell II)	N4732G		(FZ293), 43-36343, FZ293, 10829 (Canada) – [Brownsville, TX] PVA
☐ Fairchild M-62C Cornell (PT-23)	N64176	256HO	42-49232 – [Wichita, KS]
☐ Fairey Swordfish IV	'HS164'		(Canada), N2235R, N2F RAX
☐ Fleet 16B Finch II	N16BR	383	(Canada), XB-ZOQ(?) – [Brownsville, TX]
☐ Focke-Wulf Fw 44J Stieglitz	'RF+GJ'	2936 (?)	SE+IY, SZ-33 (Finland), OH-SZD, N2497 – [Brownsville, TX]
☐ Fokker Dr I (R)			PV
☐ General Dynamics F-111E	68-0027	A1-196	PV
☐ Grumman G-36 Wildcat (FM-2)	NX681S	3226	Bu55585 – [Leesburg, VA]
☐ Grumman G-36 Wildcat (FM-2)	N5833	5877	Bu86819 – [El Cajon, CA]
☐ Grumman G-40 Avenger (TBM-3)	N5264V	3415	Bu53353 – [St. Charles, MO]
☐ Grumman G-40 Avenger (TBM-3) (TBM-3E)	N53429	3565	Bu53503, 53503 (Canada), 315 (Canada), N6583D – [Grand Junction, CO]
☐ Grumman G-40 Avenger (TBM-3) (TBM-3S)	N40402	4331	Bu91426, 91426 (Canada), CF-MUE – [Frederick, MD]
☐ Grumman G-40 Avenger (TBM-3) (TBM-3S) (AS.3)	N704QZ	2416	Bu85597, 85597 (Canada), CF-IMK, C-FIMK – [Deland, FL]
☐ Grumman G-50 Hellcat (F6F-5)	NX1078Z	A-5634	Bu70222 – [Camarillo, CA]
☐ Grumman G-58 Bearcat (F8F-2)	N7825C	D.1227	Bu122674 – [Camarillo, CA]
☐ Grumman G-82 Guardian (AF-2S)	N9993Z	242	Bu126731 – [Mesa, AZ]
☐ Grumman G-303 Tomcat (F-14A)	Bu160403	259	PV
☐ Hawker Sea Fury FB.11	N15S	41H/696792	WJ288, G-SALY – [Memphis, TN]
☐ Hispano HA-1112M1L [Messerschmitt Bf 109G]	N109ME	67	C.4K-31, G-AWHE PV
☐ Interstate S1B1 Cadet (O-63) (L-6)	N46336/'432716'	159	43-2716 – [Princetown, NJ]
☐ Interstate S1B1 Cadet (O-63) (L-6)	N46337	163	43-2720 – [Corpus Christi, TX]
☐ Lockheed 15-27-01 Harpoon (PV-2D)	Bu37537, N6651D	15-1503	Bu37537, N6651D PV
☐ Lockheed 18-56-23 Lodestar (C-60A)	N30N	18-2274	42-55884, YS-22, NC66322, N66322 – [Hampton Roads, VA]
☐ Lockheed 18-56-23 Lodestar (C-60A)	N60JT	18-2478	42-56005, NC45330, AN-ADI, N9980F, N60DX – [West Houston, TX]
☐ Lockheed 580 (T-33A) (TV-2) (T-33B)	NX9124Z	580-5913	51-6581, Bu128706 – [Memphis, TN]
☐ McDonnell M.98HO Phantom II (F-4E)	68-0366	3436	PV
☐ Messerschmitt Bf 108D-1 Taifun	N2231	3059	D-ERPN, VE+LI, AM87, G-AKZY, HB-DUB, HB-ESK, NX2231 – [Hobbs, NM]
☐ Mikoyan-Gurevich MiG-17F	N1VC/'01'	2507	2507 (China) – [Castle, CA]
☐ Mitsubishi A6M3 Zero Sen Model 22	N712Z	3869	N6582L -[Camarillo, CA]
☐ Morane-Saulnier MS.502 Criquet [Fieseler Fi 156 Storch]	N40FS	361	361 (France) – [Princetown, NJ]
☐ Naval Aircraft Factory N3N-3	N44741		Bu2781 – [West Houston, TX]
☐ Naval Aircraft Factory N3N-3	N4009A		Bu2733 – [Reno, NV]
☐ Nieuport 12 (Scale R)	N12GX	001	[Atlanta, GA]
☐ Noorduyn Harvard IIB [North American NA-77]	N9790Z	07-15	3048 (Canada) – [West Houston, TX] PVA

☐ North American NA-64 Yale	N4574Y	64-2214	3450 (Canada) – [Wharton, TX]	-
☐ North American NA-81 Harvard II	N96281	81-4099	3832 (Canada), CF-NIA – (Cable, CA]	-
☐ North American NA-84 Texan (AT-6B)	N11171	84-7800	41-17422, N62144 – mocked up as a Zero – [Houston, TX]	-
☐ North American NA-88 Texan (SNJ-4)	N101X/'9450'	88-9450	Bu09935, NC367, Bu09935 – [Midland, TX]	
☐ North American NA-88 Texan (SNJ-4)	N6411D	88-10117	Bu10148, NC363, Bu10148 -- [Camarillo, CA]	-
☐ North American NA-88 Texan (SNJ-4)	N103LT	88-12097	Bu27154 – [Atlanta, GA]	
☐ North American NA-88 Texan (SNJ-4)	N224X	88-13041	Bu27585, N7438C [Elyria, OH]	
☐ North American NA-88 Texan (SNJ-4)	N7024C	88-13517	Bu27821 – [Burnet, TX]	
☐ North American NA-88 Texan (SNJ-5)	N3195G	88-14445	Bu51697 – [Maryville, CA]	-
☐ North American NA-88 Texan (AT-6D) (SNJ-5)	N7300C	88-15754	41-34524, Bu43763 – [El Cajon, CA]	-
☐ North American NA-88 Texan (AT-6D) (SNJ-5)	N89014	88-16676	42-84895, Bu84865 – [Camarillo, CA]	-
☐ North American NA-88 Texan (AT-6D) (SNJ-5)	N3725G	88-16686	42-84905, Bu84875 – mocked up as a Kate 'AII-356' – [Houston, TX]	-
☐ North American NA-88 Texan (AT-6D) (SNJ-5)	N3246G	88-17873	42-86092, Bu90725 – [Mesa, AZ]	-
☐ North American NA-103 Mustang (P-51C)	NL61429	103-26199	42-103645, N9288, N215CA – [St. Paul, MN]	-
☐ North American NA-108 Mitchell (B-25J) (PBJ-1J)	N5865V	108-34263	44-30988, Bu35857 – [Camarillo, CA]	-
☐ North American NA-108 Mitchell (B-25J) (TB-25J)	N345TH/'1361'	108-37460	44-31385, N3481G – [St. Charles, MO.]	-
☐ North American NA-108 Mitchell (B-25J) (TB-25J) (TB-25K)	N27493/'327493'	108-33154	44-29869, N3160G -[St. Paul, MN]	-
☐ North American NA-108 Mitchell (B-25J) (TB-25J) (TB-25N)	N125AZ	108-35262	43-35972, N9552Z – [Mesa, AZ.]	-
☐ North American NA-108 Mitchell (B-25J) (TB-25K)	N9643C	108-47512	44-86758 – [Georgetown, TX]	-
☐ North American NA-108 Mitchell (B-25J) (TB-25N)	N25YR	108-34881	43-27868, N9077Z – [San Marcos, TX]	-
☐ North American NA-121 Texan (AT-6F) (SNJ-6)	N9820C	121-43036	44-82314, Bu112178 – mocked up as Zero 'AI-118' – [Houston, TX]	-
☐ North American NA-122 Mustang (P-51D)	N5428V	122-39723	44-73264 – [Council Bluffs, IA]	-
☐ North American NA-122 Mustang (P-51D) (Mustang IV)	NL10601	122-40383	44-73843, 9271 (Canada) – [Atlanta, GA]	-
☐ North American NA-159 Trojan (T-28A)	N70743	159-158	49-1646, (Dominica), HI-276	RA
☐ North American NA-191 Sabre (F-86F)	N186SR	191-812	52-5112 – [Reno, NV]	-
☐ North American NA-192 Super Sabre (F-100A)	52-5773	192-18		PV
☐ Piper J-3C-65 Cub	N6125H	19286	[NC6125H – [Grand Forks, CO]	-
☐ Piper J-5A Cub Cruiser	N35786	5-772	NC35786 – [Riverside, CA]	-
☐ Polikarpov I-16 tip 24	N30425	2421645	28, ZK-JIR – [Camarillo, CA]	-
☐ Reno P-5151	N5148Z	140H7198		RA
☐ Republic P-47N Thunderbolt	N47TB		44-89436, (Guatemala), GN71 (Nicaragua), N478C	PVA
☐ Republic F-105D Thunderchief	59-1739	D-51		PV
☐ Ryan Navion A	N444AC	NAV-4-1463	[Burnet, TX]	-
☐ Ryan Navion A	N2995C	NAV-4-1727	[Deland, FL]	-
☐ Ryan ST-3KR Recruit (PT-22)	N48742	1298	41-15629 – [Riverside, CA]	-
☐ Ryan ST-3KR Recruit (PT-22)	N22AL	1831	41-20622, N54098 – [Brownsville TX]	-
☐ Schweizer SGS.2-12 (TG-3A)	N87603	67	42-52925 (?)	PV
☐ Sikorsky S-55D Chickasaw (H-19D) (UH-19D)	N6735		54-1416 – [Mesa, AZ]	-
☐ Stinson HW.75	N23784	7244	NC23784, – [Midland, TX]	
☐ Stinson 10A Voyager	N26295	7582	NC26295 – [West Miffin, PA]	-
☐ Stinson 10A Voyager	N34693	7993	NC34693 – [Madison, MS]	-
☐ Stinson 108-1 Voyager	N97040	108-1040	N97902 – [West Houston, TX]]	-
☐ Stinson V-76 Sentinel (O-62) (L-5)	N9315H		42-15060 – [Hampton Roads, VA]	-
☐ Stinson V-76 Sentinel (O-62) (L-5)	N59AF	76-137	(USAAF], N65444 – [El Cajon, CA]	-
☐ Stinson V-76 Sentinel (O-62) (L-5)	N57789	76-272	42-15069 (?) – [Lancaster, TX]	-
☐ Stinson V-76 Sentinel (L-5)	N68591/'268591'		42-98667 – [St. Paul, MN]	-
☐ Stinson V-76 Sentinel (L-5)	N61100	76-361	(USAAF] – [Chantilly, VA]	-
☐ Stinson V-76 Sentinel (L-5)	N63777	76-526	(USAAF] – [Amarillo, TX]	-
☐ Stinson V-76 Sentinel (L-5)	N121MC/ '299186'	76-1684	(USAAF] – [Hausen-am -Albis -Switzerland]	-
☐ Stinson V-76 Sentinel (L-5) (OY-1)	N1156V/'298758'		42-98752, Bu60507 – [Manassas, VA]	-
☐ Stinson V-76 Sentinel (L-5B) (OY-1)	N2581B		(USAAF], Bu120473 – [[West Miffin, PA]	-
☐ Stinson V-76 Sentinel (L-5E)	N5625V		44-17590 – [Modesto, CA]	-
☐ Stinson V-76 Sentinel (L-5E) (OY-1)	N5138B		(USAAF], Bu04013 – [Columbus, OH]	-
☐ Stinson V-77 Reliant (AT-19)	N60634/FB605	77-333	43-44037, FK887, Bu11608, FK810' – [Carthage, NC]	-
☐ Stinson V-77 Reliant (AT-19)	N67227	77-496	43-44209, FB768, Bu11530 – [Las Vegas, NV]	-
☐ Supermarine 379 Spitfire FR.XIVe	NX749DP	6S.583887	NH749, T3 (India), G-MXIV – [Camarillo, CA]	-
☐ Taylorcraft DCO-65 Grasshopper (O-57A) (L-2A)	N53768	L-5135	(USAAF] – [Blountville,TN]	-

Texas

☐ Vought FG-1D Corsair	N9964Z	3729	Bu92468 – [Lancaster, TX]	-
☐ Vultee V-54D Valiant (BT-13)			[Aurora, CO]	-
☐ Vultee V-74 Valiant (BT-13A)	N67208	74-2307	41-11297 – mocked up as Val	-
			–'BI-257' – [Houston, TX]	
☐ Vultee V-74 Valiant (BT-13A)	N52411	74-2548	41-11538 – [St. Paul, MN]	-
☐ Vultee V-74 Valiant (BT-13A)	NX27003	74-5017	41-21178 – [West Houston, TX]	-
☐ Vultee V-74 Valiant (BT-13A)	N56360	74-5946	41-22026 – [Manassas, VA]	-
☐ Vultee V-74 Valiant (BT-13A)	N56478	74-7356	41-22926 – mocked up as a Val	- -
			[Houston,TX]	
☐ Vultee V-74 Valiant (BT-13A)	N313BT	74-10425	42-43210 (?) – [Modesto, CA]	-
☐ Vultee V-74A Valiant (BT-15)	N69605	74A-1258	41-10137 – [Lancaster, TX]	-
☐ Vultee V-74A Valiant (BT-15)	N66681	74A-1268	41-10147 – [Cleveland, TX]	-
☐ Vultee V-79 Valiant (BT-13B) (SNV-2)	N57807		(USAAF), (USN) – [Jenks, OK]	-
☐ Waco NZR Hadrian (CG-4A)			(USAAF)	PVC
☐ Wolf W-II Boredom Fighter	N90SQ	91		PV

CONROE MONUMENT (TX41)

Location:	On permanent view at VFW 4709 at 1303 West Semands Avenue in the north western part of the town.

TYPE	REG/SER	CON. NO.	PI/NOTES	STATUS
☐ Bell 205 Iroquois (UH-1H)	67-17456	9654		PV

CORPUS CHRISTI MONUMENT (TX42)

Location:	On permanent view on Shoreline Drive at McGee Beach in the town.

TYPE	REG/SER	CON. NO.	PI/NOTES	STATUS
☐ Bell 205 Iroquois (UH-1H)			Composite.	PVX

CORPUS CHRISTI NAVAL AIR STATION COLLECTION (TX43)

Address:	Ocean Drive, Corpus Christi, Texas 78419.
Tel:	361-961-2811 Email: nascc-pao@navy.mil
Admission:	By prior permission only.
Location:	About 10 miles south east of the town off Route 358.

Primary and intermediate training on single engined aircraft and an advanced course for pilots who will fly multi-engined types takes place at the field. There is a depot which overhauls Army and Coast Guard helicopters.

Several of the aircraft which were preserved at the base have moved to the USS *Lexington* moored in Corpus Christi Bay. The five remaining are located around the large site.

TYPE	REG/SER	CON. NO.	PI/NOTES	STATUS
☐ Beech A200C Huron (UC-12B)	Bu161185	BJ-1		RA
☐ Douglas TA-4J Skyhawk	Bu158087	14124		RA
☐ McDonnell M.267 Hornet (F/A-18A)	Bu163093	475/A591		RA
☐ McDonnell-Douglas T-45A Goshawk (FSM)	'Bu176455'			RA
☐ North American NA-219 Trojan (T-28B)	Bu140046	219-45		RA

CORSICANA MONUMENT (TX44)

Location:	On permanent view at Navarro College at 3200 7th Avenue in the south western part of the town.

TYPE	REG/SER	CON. NO.	PI/NOTES	STATUS
☐ McDonnell M.98EN Phantom II (F-4D)	65-0747	1810		PV

COWTOWN AEROCRAFTERS COLLECTION (TX45)

Address:	15719 Bonanza Drive, Justin, Texas 76247-6618.
Tel:	940-648-2280
Admission:	By prior permission only.
Location:	At Propwash Field which is about 2 miles west of the town on County Road 407.

The company carries out restoration of classic World War II liaison and training types at the field which is flying community where a number of light aircraft reside. The workshop contains a number of Stinson Sentinels. Three examples are currently airworthy with another few nearing completion.

TYPE	REG/SER	CON. NO.	PI/NOTES	STATUS
☐ Aeronca 65TC Grasshopper (L-3C)			43-1835	RAA
☐ North American NA-121 Texan (AT-6F)	N4708C	121-42592	44-81870	RAA
☐ Stinson V-76 Sentinel (O-62) (L-5)	N1718M		42-14927	RAC
☐ Stinson V-76 Sentinel (O-62) (L-5)	N56851		42-14880	RAC
☐ Stinson V-76 Sentinel (L-5)			42-98376	RAA
☐ Stinson V-76 Sentinel (L-5)	N67174/'298344'	76-397	42-98156	RAAX
☐ Stinson V-76 Sentinel (L-5)	N142LB	76-935	42-98694, CF-FLV, C-FFLV	RAA
☐ Stinson V-76 Sentinel (L-5)				RAA
☐ Stinson V-76 Sentinel (L-5B)	N3955A		44-17139	RAC
☐ Vultee V-74 Valiant (BT-13A)	N76W	74-1624	41-1514	RAA

The Rio Grande Valley Wing of the Commemorative Air Force keeps this de Havilland Moth Minor in flying order. [TX34]

The Linear Air Park at Dyess Air Force Base contains this de Havilland YC-7A Caribou. [TX51]

The Edward H White II Memorial Museum has this Curtiss JN-4D in its 1918 hangar. [TX53]

Texas

DAINGERFIELD MONUMENT (TX46)

Location:	On permanent view at a business south of the town on Highway 259.

TYPE	REG/SER	CON. NO.	PI/NOTES	STATUS
☐ Bell 205 Iroquois (UH-1H)				PV

DALLAS MONUMENT (TX47)

Location:	On permanent view at a business somewhere in the city.

TYPE	REG/SER	CON. NO.	PI/NOTES	STATUS
☐ Republic RC-3 Seabee				PV

DEL RIO MONUMENT (TX48)

Location:	On permanent view by the Chamber of Commerce on Highway 90 in the town.

TYPE	REG/SER	CON. NO.	PI/NOTES	STATUS
☐ Lockheed 580 (T-33A)	53-6124	580-9745		PV

DEL VALLE MONUMENT (TX49)

Location:	On permanent view at Del Valle High School at 5201 Ross Road south east of the town.

TYPE	REG/SER	CON. NO.	PI/NOTES	STATUS
☐ McDonnell M.98DF Phantom II (RF-4C)	68-0570	3485		PV

DUMAS MONUMENT (TX50)

Location:	On permanent view in a park in the southern part of the town.

TYPE	REG/SER	CON. NO.	PI/NOTES	STATUS
☐ McDonnell M.98DF Phantom II (RF-4C)	'67-224'	2880	67-0444	PVX

DYESS LINEAR AIR PARK (TX51)

Address:	7BW/PA, 7 Lancer Loop, Suite 136, Dyess Air Force Base, Texas 79607-1960.
Tel:	325-696-4300 **Email:** 7bw.pa@dyess.af.mil
Admission:	Daily sun up to sunset with authorisation.
Location:	About 3 miles south west of Abiline off Interstate 20.

Opened as Abilene Army Air Base in December 1942, the field was used for pilot training until it closed in 1945. Allocated to Strategic Air Command in 1953, it was rebuilt for bomber use and the first B-47s moved in during September 1955. B-52s were flown from 1963 and the first operational B-1s in the USAF arrived in June 1985. The base is named after Colonel William B. Dyess who was a Japanese prisoner of war for a year. He escaped and fought with guerrilla forces in Mindanao. He returned to the USA but was killed when his P-38 caught fire over Burbank in December 1943.
Over the years aircraft were allocated to the base for preservation and these were parked along the main road from the gate to the Headquarters building. The first one to arrive was the B-17, which was given to the city for display at the municipal airport. It was moved to Dyess under a Skycrane helicopter in the mid-1970s and the B-47 followed in 1977.
The Texas Museum of Military History was founded in 1981 and plans were put forward for a major complex at Dyess. These have now been shelved. On 12th June 1991 the Linear Air Park was officially dedicated by General Robert D. Beckel, the Commander of the Fifteenth Air Force. The grounds along the road have been landscaped and the aircraft have been arranged in small groups with paved walkways around them.

TYPE	REG/SER	CON. NO.	PI/NOTES	STATUS
☐ Beech D45 Mentor (T-34B)	Bu140810	BG-144	Bu140810, N137Z	PV
☐ Boeing 299-O Fortress (B-17G) (EDB-17G) (DB-17G) (DB-17P)	'238133'	8508	44-85599	PVX
☐ Boeing 367-76-66 Stratofreighter (KC-97G) (KC-97L)	53-0282	17064		PV
☐ Boeing 450-157-35 Stratojet (B-47E) (EB-47E)	'24120'	450697	52-0412	PVX
☐ Boeing 464-201-7 Stratofortress (B-52D)	56-0685	464056		PV
☐ Boeing 717-146 Stratotanker (KC-135A)	56-3639	17388		PV
☐ Cessna 318B Tweety Bird (318A) (T-37A) (T-37B)	54-2734	40010		PV
☐ Cessna 337M Super Skymaster (O-2A)	67-21326	337M0032		PV
☐ Convair 240-27 (T-29C)	52-1175	414		PV
☐ Curtiss 87V Warhawk (P-40N) (FSM)				PVX
☐ De Havilland DHC.4 Caribou (YAC-1) (YCV-2A) (YC-7A)	'58-3082'	7	CF-LKG-X, 57-3082	PVX
☐ Douglas DC-3A-456 Skytrain (C-47A) (R4D-5) (R4D-6)	42-108808	11928	42-108808, Bu17106, N9881C, N51, N71, N916, N223GB	PV
☐ Douglas A-26C Invader	44-35913	29192	44-35913, N3522G, N303W, N303WC	PV
☐ Douglas RB-66B Destroyer	53-0466	44347		PV
☐ Fairchild 473 Provider (205) (C-123B) (C-123K) (UC-123K)	54-0604	20053		PV
☐ General Dynamics F-111A	67-0057	A1-102		RA

☐ Grumman G-111 Albatross (G-64) (SA-16A) (SA-16B) (HU-16B)	51-7251	G-341	51-7251, 7251	PV
☐ Lockheed 080 Shooting Star (P-80C) (F-80C)				RA
☐ Lockheed 182-1A Hercules (182-44-03) (C-130A)	55-0023	182-3050		PV
☐ Lockheed 183-93-02 Starfighter (F-104A)	56-0748	183-1036		PV
☐ Lockheed 382C-15D Hercules (C-130E)	69-6579	382C-4354		PV
☐ Lockheed 580 (T-33A)	51-4300	580-5595		PV
☐ Martin 272B Canberra (B-57B) (EB-57B)	52-1504	87		PV
☐ McDonnell M.36BA Voodoo (TF-101B) (TF-101F)	57-0287	465		PV
☐ McDonnell M.98EN Phantom II (F-4D)	65-0796	1874	At school near to base.	PV
☐ North American NA-121 Texan (AT-6F)	44-81819	121-42541	44-81819, N7446C, (N88RT), N7446C	PV
☐ North American NA-201 Sabre (F-86D) (F-86L)	53-4035	201-569		PV
☐ North American NA-217 Super Sabre (F-100C)	'54-1753'	217-13	54-1752	PVX
☐ North American NA-265 Sabreliner (T-39A) (CT-39A)	61-0634	265-37		PV
☐ Northrop N-138 Scorpion (F-89H)	54-0298	N.4932	54-0298, '57-1752'	PV
☐ Northrop N-156T Talon (T-38A)	60-0592	N.5165		PV
☐ Republic F-84F Thunderstreak	51-9364			PV
☐ Republic RF-84F Thunderflash	51-11293			PV
☐ Republic F-105D Thunderchief	'60-517'	D-50	59-1738	PVX
☐ Rockwell B-1B Lancer	83-0065	2		PV

EAGLE PASS MONUMENT (TX52)

Location: On permanent view at Maverick County Lake Park which is east of the town on Highway 277.

TYPE	REG/SER	CON. NO.	PI/NOTES	STATUS
☐ Bell 205 Iroquois (UH-1H)	68-16536	11195		PV
☐ Lockheed 580 (T-33A)	53-6102	580-9723		PV

EDWARD H. WHITE II MEMORIAL MUSEUM (TX53)

Address: Hangar 9, Brooks Air Force Base, San Antonio, Texas 78235-5397.
Tel: 210-536-2204 **Fax:** 210-536-3224 **Email:** museum@brooks.af.mil
Admission: Monday-Friday 0800-1600.
Location: In the south eastern suburbs of the city off Route 13 (Military Drive).

Hangar 9 was one of 16 built at Brooks Field which opened in February 1918 as a satellite of Kelly Field. The building is the only surviving World War I hangar in the USA. The base is named after Cadet Sidney Brooks who was killed at Kelly Field when his Curtiss JN-4 crashed on landing.

In 1926 the Air Service Medical Research Laboratory moved to Brooks from New York State. The unit transferred to Randolph Field in 1931 but returned to Brooks in 1959. In 1966 it was decided to set up a Museum of Flight Medicine and name it after San Antonio astronaut Edward H. White, who lost his life at Cape Kennedy in January 1967. The hangar was restored in 1969 and houses a JN-4 to reflect the original training role of the field. Also on show are personal effects of Colonel White and many items tracing the development of Aviation Medicine.

The Super Sabre is positioned near the main gate to the base and the Phantom is by the School of Aerospace Medicine Headquarters.

TYPE	REG/SER	CON. NO.	PI/NOTES	STATUS
☐ Curtiss 1C Jenny (JN-4D)	3805			PV
☐ McDonnell M.98DE Phantom II (F-4C)	63-7431	383		PV
☐ North American NA-255 Super Sabre (F-100F)	'63944'	255-28	58-1232	PVX

EDWARDS COLLECTION (TX54)

Address: Box 2341, Big Spring Texas 79721-2431.
Admission: By prior permission only.
Location: About 5 miles south east of the town.

This private collection is not often opened to visitors. Over the years aircraft have been offered for sale yet few seem to leave. The Spanish-built Messerschmitts were acquired after the 'Battle of Britain' film in the late 1960s and have not moved since. There are a number of amphibians in the fleet including several built by Grumman.

An accurate list has not been obtained for some years so any information would be appreciated.

TYPE	REG/SER	CON. NO.	PI/NOTES	STATUS
☐ Beech 95-B55 Baron	N1830B	TC-2410		RAA
☐ Beech H18S	N245M	BA-646		RAA
☐ Consolidated 28-5A Canso A	N222FT	CV 397	11074 (Canada), CF-OWE, C-FOWE, N691RF, C-FOWE, N69RF	RA
☐ Consolidated 28-6A Catalina (PBY-6A)	N4NC	2026	Bu46662, N9588C, N788C, CF-VIG, N1022G, N999AR	RAA
☐ Grumman G-21A Goose (G-39) (JRF-5)	N3282	1110	Bu6440, 0182 (Argentina), 0128 (Paraguay)	RA
☐ Grumman G-21A Goose (G-39) (JRF-5)	N7211	B24	Bu37771, N721, N7211, C-GPIA	RA
☐ Grumman G-21A Goose (G-39) (JRF-5)	N322	B73	Bu37820	RA
☐ Grumman G-21A Goose (G-39) (JRF-6B) (Goose IA)	N68157	1138	(BW791), FP488, Bu66325	RA
☐ Grumman G-40 Avenger (TBM-3) (TBM-3E) (AS.3M)	N33BM	3181	Bu53119, 53119 (Canada)	RA
☐ Grumman G-73 Mallard	N775WA	J21	N2961, CF-MHG	RAA

☐ Grumman G-111 Albatross (SA-16B) (UF-2G) (HU-16E)	N226CG	G-307	51-7226, 7226, N5402G	RAA	
☐ Grumman G-234 Albatross (G-64) (SA-16A) (UF-1G) (UF-2G) (HU-16E)	N1026A	G-357	52-0130, 2130 (USCG)	RA	
☐ Hispano HA-1112M1L [Messerschmitt Bf 109G]	C.4K-30			RA	
☐ Hispano HA-1112M1L [Messerschmitt Bf 109G]	G-AWHF	129	C.4K-61	RA	
☐ Hispano HA-1112M1L [Messerschmitt Bf 109G]	N90604	187	C.4K-99, G-AWHM	RA	
☐ Hispano HA-1112M1L [Messerschmitt Bf 109G]	N90603	190	C.4K-126, G-AWHD	RA	
☐ Hispano HA-1112M1L [Messerschmitt Bf 109G]	C.4K-154	219		RA	
☐ Hispano HA-1112M1L [Messerschmitt Bf 109G]	N4109G	220	C.4K-152, G-AWHR	RA	
☐ Hispano HA-1112M4L [Messerschmitt Bf 109G] (two seater)	N1109G	40/2	C.4K-112, G-AWHC	RA	
☐ North American NA-88 Texan (AT-6D) (SNJ-5)	N15090	88-17311	42-85530, Bu85090, N9050Z	RAA	
☐ North American NA-122 Mustang (P-51D)	N38227	122-40442	44-73902, 315 (Guatemala)	RA	
☐ North American NA-226 Trojan (T-28C)	N8084V	226-187	Bu140610	RAA	
☐ Piaggio P.136L-1	N6354T	199		RAA	
☐ Piaggio P.166AL-1	N166Y	356		RAA	
☐ Piaggio P.166AL-1	N7651E	358		RAA	
☐ Piper PA-18-150 Super Cub	N82486	18-7709156		RAA	
☐ Piper PA-18-150 Super Cub	N4044Z	18-8005		RAA	
☐ Snow S-2R	N8904Q	1574R		RAA	
☐ Supermarine 361 Spitfire LF.IXb	N415MH	CBAF-IX-533	MH415, H-108 (Netherlands), H-65 (Netherlands), B-12 (Belgium), SM-40 (Belgium), OO-ARD, G-AVDJ	RA	

ELLINGTON AIR NATIONAL GUARD BASE (TX55)

Address: 147 FG/DPR, 14657 Schneider Street, Ellington Field, Texas 77034-5586.
Tel: 713-929-2525 **Email:** 147fg.pa@txelli.ang.af.mil
Admission: By prior permission only.
Location: About 17 miles south east of Houston on Route FM 1959.

Named after Lieutenant Eric L. Ellington who was killed in a crash in 1913, the field was formerly an Air Force base. Now it houses units of the Texas Air and Army National Guard, the US Coast Guard, the FAA and NASA as well as civil aircraft. The KC-135A is parked on a mound near to the NASA entrance. The aircraft was withdrawn from service after cracks had been found in the wings. The F-84F is mounted nearby.

TYPE	REG/SER	CON. NO.	PI/NOTES	STATUS
☐ Boeing 717-148 Stratotanker (KC-135A)	N930NA	17769	59-1481, N98, 59-1481, NASA930	RA
☐ Convair 8-10 Delta Dagger (F-102A)	56-1252		8-10-469	RA
☐ General Dynamics 401 Fighting Falcon (F-16A)	82-0930		61-523	RA
☐ Lockheed 580 (T-33A)	52-9223		580-7289	RA
☐ McDonnell M.36BA Voodoo (F-101B)	59-0424		748	RA
☐ McDonnell M.98EN Phantom II (F-4D)	66-0280		1952	RA
☐ Republic F-84F Thunderstreak	52-6455		At ALP post by main gate.	PV

EL PASO MONUMENT (TX56)

Location: By prior permission only at the International Airport which is in the eastern part of the city.

TYPE	REG/SER	CON. NO.	PI/NOTES	STATUS
☐ Northrop N-156T Talon (T-38A)	'N999NA'	N.5746	65-10327, (USN)	RAX

FIGHTER JETS (TX57)

Address: 302 Saint Andrews Drive, Mabank, Texas 75156-7281
Tel: 214-676-0323 **Fax:** 903-451-5910 **Email:** randy@fighterjets.com
Admission: By prior permission only.
Location: At a number of airfields in the Dallas area.

The company specialises in providing jet aircraft to airshows where demonstrations of the versatility of the types can be seen. Two of the aircraft have been painted in false Soviet colours.

TYPE	REG/SER	CON. NO.	PI/NOTES	STATUS
☐ Aero L-29L Delfin	N28NR/'75'	194144	75 (Bulgaria) – in false Soviet markings.	RAAX
☐ Lockheed 580 (T-33A)				RAA
☐ Mikoyan-Gurevich MiG-21MF				RAA
☐ PZL TS-11 Iskra 100bisB	N21HW	1H 06-03	603 (Poland)	RAA
☐ WSK Lim-5 [MiG-17F]	N217SH/'1611'	1C 16-11	1611 (Poland) – in false Soviet markings.	RAAX

FIRST CAVALRY DIVISION MUSEUM (TX58)

Address: AFVA-GE-M, Building 2218, PO Box 5187, Fort Hood, Texas 76545-5101.
Tel: 254-286-5684 **Fax:** 254-287-6427 **Email:** steven.c.draper@usarmy.mil
Admission: Monday-Friday 0900-1600; Saturday-Sunday 1200-1600.
Location: About 25 miles west of Temple off Route 190.

The First Cavalry Division was formed at Fort Bliss in 1921. In keeping with its name it has been first in several operations. The unit was the first to enter Manila when the city was liberated, it led Allied forces into Tokyo, it launched the first amphibious landing during the Korean War and it was the first United Nations unit to enter Pyongyang.

The museum opened on 13th September 1971, the 50th anniversary of the formation of the division. The displays trace the history of the unit from the early days up to its service in the Gulf conflict and Iraq. Early wars fought against the local Indian tribes in the area are also highlighted.

An outside park contains aircraft, military vehicles and large weapons including some captured in action. More are located around the large camp whilst others are the responsibility of the Third Armored Cavalry Division Museum.

TYPE	REG/SER	CON. NO.	PI/NOTES	STATUS
☐ Beech A200CT Huron (C-12D) (RC-12D)	78-23143	GR-8 (BP-4)		PV
☐ Bell 47D-1 Sioux (H-13E) (OH-13E)	51-13993	579		PV
☐ Bell 204 Iroquois (HU-1A) (UH-1A)	59-1625	84		PV
☐ Bell 205 Iroquois (UH-1D)	'O-11556'			PVX
☐ Bell 205 Iroquois (UH-1H)	73-21839	13527		PV
☐ Bell 205 Iroquois (UH-1H) (UH-1V)	67-17586	9784	At Darnell Hospital.	PV
☐ Bell 206A Kiowa (OH-58A) (OH-58C)	69-16369	40590		PV
☐ Bell 206A Kiowa (OH-58A) (OH-58C)	72-21103	41769	At Sturt Building.	PV
☐ Bell 209 Huey Cobra (AH-1G)	67-15865	20529		PV
☐ Bell 209 Huey Cobra (AH-1G)	68-15013	20547	At Sturt Building.	PV
☐ Bell 209 Huey Cobra (AH-1G) (AH-1S)	68-17113	20841		PV
☐ Fairchild-Republic A-10A Thunderbolt II	76-0518	A10-65		PV
☐ Grumman G-134 Mohawk (AO-1C) (OV-1C)	60-3747	3C		PV
☐ Grumman G-134 Mohawk (OV-1D)	69-17007	18D		RA
☐ Hughes 369M Cayuse (HO-6) (OH-6A)	65-12920	0005		PV
☐ Sikorsky S-64A Tarhe (CH-54A)	66-18409	64011		RA

FLIGHT OF THE PHOENIX AVIATION MUSEUM (TX59)

Address: PO Box 610, Gilmer, Texas 75644.
Tel: 903-843-5543 **Fax:** 903-843-5554 **Email:** sawdust@texasforestproducts.com
Admission: Monday-Friday 0900-1600.
Location: At Gilmer-Upsher County Airport which is about 10 miles north west of Longview.

Set up to honour the aviators of east Texas, this museum opened in 1999. The Dean Lumber company constructed a large wooden hangar to house their business aircraft. Steve and Linda Dean have set up the collection in this building.

The Texan is one of 30 remanufactured to T-6G standard by the South African Air Force in the early 1950s. The Tiger Moth spent a period in civilian use in Australia before crossing the Pacific Ocean.

TYPE	REG/SER	CON. NO.	PI/NOTES	STATUS
☐ Aero Commander 520	N11L	520-109	N4198D	PV
☐ Beech D18S	N412K	A-263	N80353, N112K	PVA
☐ CASA 1.131E [Bücker Bü 131 Jungmann]				PVA
☐ Great Lakes 2T-1A-2				PVA
☐ North American NA-168 Texan (T-6G)	N725SD	SA-070	7725 (South Africa)	PVA

FORNEY MONUMENT (TX60)

Location: On permanent view in the eastern part of the town.

TYPE	REG/SER	CON. NO.	PI/NOTES	STATUS
☐ WSK Lim-5 [MiG-17F]	'003'		In false Soviet markings.	PVX

FORT BLISS MUSEUM (TX61)

Address: Building 1735, Marshall Road, Fort Bliss, Texas 79916-3802.
Tel: 915-568-3390 **Fax:** 915-566-9407 **Email:** fanning@bliss.army.mil
Admission: Monday-Saturday 0900-1630.
Location: About 5 miles north east of El Paso off Route 375.

Fort Bliss was home to three museums all of which existed in cramped conditions. Plans to centralise the collections were put forward in the late 1990s and the new exhibition housed in the former Exchange Building opened in 2002. The Air Defense Artillery Association were the prime movers of the project.

There is a display tracing the history and lives of the early residents of the El Paso area. The development of anti-aircraft weapons features prominently. The Museum of the Non-Commissioned Officer and the Army Medical Collection will both have sections in the new enlarged exhibition.

TYPE	REG/SER	CON. NO.	PI/NOTES	STATUS
☐ Beech A200CT Huron (C-12D) (RC-12D)	80-23379	FC-1 (BP-20)		PV
☐ Bell 209 Huey Cobra (AH-1G) (AH-1F)	67-15460	20124		PV
☐ Bell 209 Huey Cobra (AH-1G) (AH-1F)	68-17096	20824		pv
☐ Cessna 318B Tweety Bird (T-37B)	61-2496	40590		PV
☐ Grumman G-134 Mohawk (OV-1C) (OV-1D)	68-15960	164C		PV

FORT SAM HOUSTON MUSEUM (TX62)

Address: MCCS-GTPS-M, 1210 Stanley Road, Fort Sam Houston, Texas 78234-7501.
Tel: 210-221-1886 **Email:** john.manguso@amedd.army.mil
Admission: Wednesday-Saturday 1000-1600.
Location: Off Wilson Road in the Fort which is in the north eastern suburbs of San Antonio

Texas

The museum displays trace, in chronological order, the history of the military presence in the area from the early frontier days. Famous Americans who served here include Theodore Roosevelt and Dwight Eisenhower. Geronimo was imprisoned at the camp and this event features in the exhibition. Visitors can undertake a self-guided tour of the fort and view a number of historic buildings and sites. There are plaques at each location. The sole aircraft owned by the museum is the 'Huey'.

TYPE	REG/SER	CON. NO.	PI/NOTES	STATUS
☐ Bell 204 Iroquois (HU-1B) (UH-1B)	62-2027	547		PV

FORT WORTH JOINT RESERVE BASE (TX63)

Address: 1510 Chenault Drive, Fort Worth, Texas 76127-5000.
Tel: 817-782-5000   **Email:** pao.nasjrbf@nrs.navy.mil
Admission: By prior permission only.
Location: About 7 miles west of Fort Worth off Route 183.

The base was activated in 1942 and was later named after Major Horace S. Carswell who was killed in a B-24 crash off the China coast in October 1944. For many years it was a bomber base. The site now houses Air Force Reserve fighters and transports. The Air National Guard and Naval units from Hensley Field (Dallas Naval Air Station) moved to the field in the late 1990s and when the present name was adopted. The preserved aircraft are displayed around the large site. Some are positioned by the main gate and others are alongside the main road into the camp. The types on display represent those which have flown from the airfield as well as those which are frequent visitors. One of the Skyhawks, the Shooting Star and the Sabre were moved from Hensley Field. A number of modern jets have been loaned by the National Museum of Naval Aviation.

TYPE	REG/SER	CON. NO.	PI/NOTES	STATUS
☐ Bell 205 Iroquois (UH-1D) (UH-1H)	66-0932	5415		RA
☐ Bell 206A Kiowa (OH-58A) (OH-58C)	70-15469	41020		RA
☐ Douglas A-4M Skyhawk	Bu158430	14252		RA
☐ Douglas A-4M Skyhawk	Bu159789	14488		RA
☐ General Dynamics 401 Fighting Falcon (F-16N)	Bu163569	3M-14	86-1687	RA
☐ Grumman G-303 Tomcat (F-14A)	Bu158999	60		RA
☐ Lockheed 080 Shooting Star (P-80C) (F-80C) (TO-1) (TV-1)	'056607'	080-2078	47-1392, Bu33845, '58607'	RAX
☐ McDonnell M.98EN Phantom II (F-4D)	66-8714	2491		RA
☐ McDonnell M.98HO Phantom II (F-4E)	'66-375'	3264	67-0375	RAX
☐ McDonnell M.267 Hornet (F/A-18A)	Bu161712	59/A043		RA
☐ McDonnell M.267 Hornet (F/A-18A)	Bu162440	285/A230		RA
☐ North American NA-201 Sabre (F-86D) (F-86L)	53-1030	201-474		RA
☐ Republic F-105D Thunderchief	61-0100	D-295		RA
☐ Sikorsky S-58 Seahorse (HUS-1) (UH-34D)	Bu148764	581315		RA

FORT WORTH MONUMENT (TX64)

Location: On view during opening hours in Cabela's store at 12901 Cabela Drive in the northern part of the city.

TYPE	REG/SER	CON. NO.	PI/NOTES	STATUS
☐ Piper J-3C-65 Cub				PV

FORT WORTH MUSEUM OF SCIENCE AND HISTORY (TX65)

Address: 1600 Gendy Street, Fort Worth, Texas 76107.
Tel: 817-255-9300   **Fax:** 817-255-9322   **Email:** info@fwmsh.org
Admission: September–February Monday-Wednesday 0900-1700, Thursday-Saturday 0900-2100, Sunday 1200-2100, March–August Monday-Saturday 0900-2100; Sunday 1200-2100.
Location: In the centre of the city.

The collection was set up in 1941 as the Fort Worth Children's Museum and over the years has steadily developed the range of exhibits to appeal to a wider audience. The engineering section has three aeronautical exhibits. Features include a planetarium, an Omni-theatre, and an outdoor dig for fossils.

TYPE	REG/SER	CON. NO.	PI/NOTES	STATUS
☐ Bell 47G				PV
☐ Boeing 727			Front fuselage only.	PV
☐ Boeing-Stearman A75N1 Kaydet (PT-17)				PV

FORT WORTH VETERANS MEMORIAL AIR PARK (TX66)

Address: 3300 Ross Avenue, Forth Worth, Texas 76106.
Tel: 817-575-0535   **Fax:** 817-488-8170   **Email:** jbloomberg@aim.com
Admission: Daily 1000-1700.
Location: At Meacham Field which is in the north western suburbs of the city.

The OV-10 Bronco Association originally set up a museum to preserve the history of the type. The prototype of this twin engined light attack and observation aircraft made its maiden flight in July 1965 and entered service four years later, serving with the Air Force, Marines and the Navy in the USA and in six foreign countries. NASA also operated a small number and the type has also served as a fire fighter. The decision to extend the displays to cover all aspects Forward Air Controllers' work was made. These pilots and crew suffered heavy losses in battle. The collection has expanded to honour veterans from all services. Aircraft from the Vietnam era have been acquired and are several are now on show with others under restoration.

TYPE	REG/SER	CON. NO.	PI/NOTES	STATUS
☐ Bell 206A Kiowa (OH-58A)	71-20606	41467	71-20606, N604MP	PV
☐ Cessna 318B Tweety Bird (318A) (T-37A) (T-37B)	57-2261	40194		PV
☐ Cessna 337M Super Skymaster (O-2A)	67-21418	337M0124		PV
☐ Cessna 337M Super Skymaster (O-2A)	67-21430	337M0136	67-21430, N37542	PV
☐ Convair 8-12 Delta Dagger (TF-102A)	56-2337	8-12-69		PV
☐ Douglas A-4C Skyhawk (A4D-2N)	Bu147715	12479	On loan tfrom NMNA, FL.	PV
☐ Douglas TA-4J Skyhawk	Bu158073	14110		PV
☐ General Dynamics F-111E	68-0009	A1-178		PV
☐ Grumman G-303 Tomcat (F-14A) (F-14D)	Bu159600	147		PV
☐ McDonnell M.98DJ Phantom II (F-4C)	64-0825	1162		PV
☐ McDonnell M.98EV Phantom II (F-4J) (F-4S) (QF-4S)	Bu153821	2135		PV
☐ North American NA-300 Bronco (YOV-10A)	Bu152879	300-1		PV
☐ North American NA-305 Bronco (OV-10A)	N97LM	305-37	Bu155426	PV
☐ North American NA-321 Bronco (OV-10A)	N646	321-151	68-3825	PV
☐ Northrop N-311 Tiger II (F-5E)	74-1558	R.1218		PV
☐ Republic F-105D Thunderchief	60-5385			PV
☐ Vought RF-8G Crusader (F8U-1P) (RF-8A)	Bu146898			PV
☐ Vought A-7B Corsair II	Bu154479	B119		PV

FREDRICKSBURG MONUMENT (TX67)

Location:	On permanent view at the airport which is about 4 miles south west of the town

TYPE	REG/SER	CON. NO.	PI/NOTES	STATUS
☐ North American NA-145 Navion	N91500	NAV-4-295	NC91500	PV

FREEDOM MUSEUM (TX68)

Address:	VFW Post 1657, PO Box 66, 600 North Hobart Street, Pampa, Texas 79065.
Tel:	806-669-6066
Admission:	Tuesday-Saturday 1200-1600.
Location:	About 11 miles east of the town.

The airfield opened in the summer of 1942 and was used for advanced twin engine training using Beech AT-10s. Curtiss AT-9s, Cessna AT-17s and North American B-25s were also in residence. A group of 16 B-25s from this airfield took part in the famous Doolittle raid on Tokyo. The site closed on 30th September 1945 and was abandoned. The museum was set up in 1972 and memorabilia, photographs documents and badges can be seen along with weapons and military vehicles. The Iroquois is mounted on a pole and honours the Vietnam conflict. Funds are being raised to construct a hangar to house the Mitchell which is now painted in the markings of the one flown by Doolittle. The former Coast Guard Pelican is a recent arrival.

TYPE	REG/SER	CON. NO.	PI/NOTES	STATUS
☐ Bell 205 Iroquois (UH-1H)	67-17859	10057		PV
☐ McDonnell M.98HO Phantom II (F-4E)	67-0384	3283		PV
☐ North American NA-100 Mitchell (B-25D) (Mitchell II)	'43-3308'	100-23634	43-3308, KL156, N8011, HP-428, CP-915	PVX
☐ Sikorsky S-61R Pelican (HH-3F)	1471	61633		PV

FRONTIERS OF FLIGHT MUSEUM (TX69)

Address:	6911 Lemmon Avenue, Dallas, Texas 75209-3603.
Tel:	214-350-3600 Fax: 214-351-0101 Email: woodul@flightmuseum.com
Admission:	Monday-Saturday 1000-1700; Sunday 1300-1700.
Location:	In the north western suburbs of the city

George Haddaway, the editor of the American 'Flight' magazine, donated his personal collection of artefacts, documents, books and magazines to the University of Texas at Austin. In 1978 the items were moved to the Dallas campus and Ed Rice, who was appointed curator, brought in other important private collections, including the Admiral Charles Rosendahl lighter-than-air collection of one million items. By the late 1980s the space at the university was too small and it was decided to look for a site to exhibit the artefacts. An area in the Love Field terminal was obtained and a superb exhibition was staged. Funds were raised for the construction of a purpose-built museum and this opened in late 2005. An excellent display has been set up tracing the history of flight. There is an interesting collection of aircraft to be seen with a number of rare types on show.

TYPE	REG/SER	CON. NO.	PI/NOTES	STATUS
☐ Balloon Works Firefly 7 Hot Air Balloon	N40524	10072	Basket only.	PV
☐ Beech E17B (UC-43D)	N57829	198	NC187755, 42-61093	PV
☐ Bell 47G-3B-1 Sioux (TH-13T)	67-17059	3766	67-17059, N595	PV
☐ Bell 204 Iroquois (TH-1L)	N7UW/'38362'	6433	Bu157838, '38632', 'N1JW'	PVX
☐ Boeing 737-200-2H4	N102SW	23108	Front fuselage only.	PV
☐ Bücker Bü 133S Jungmeister	N21KL	222		PV
☐ Christen Eagle II	N999WD	DENTON 1		PV
☐ Dart GC	N4HM	GC-64		PV
☐ De Havilland DH.82A Tiger Moth	VH-PCC/DE664	85605	DE664, VH-PCC, N4MH, N8MH, N4MH, N8WH, N1XW, N82AK – on loan from Flt. of Phoenix, TX.	PV
☐ Ercoupe 415C (XPQ-13)	41-25196	110	NC37143, 41-25196, N37143	RA
☐ Gates Learjet 24D	N281FP	24D-281	SE-DFB, OY-BIZ, N23MJ	PV
☐ Gates Learfan 2100	N21LF	E-003	N327ML, N21LF, (N327ML)	PV
☐ General Dynamics F-111F	70-2412	E2-51	Front fuselage only.	PV

Texas

☐ General Dynamics 401 Fighting Falcon (F-16B)	75-0752	62-2		PV
☐ Glasflügel BS-1	N1710	9		PV
☐ Hallock Road Wing HT.1	N2721C	1		PV
☐ Ling-Temco-Vought L450F (XQM-93A)	N5592S		72-1287 – on loan from AHA, TX.	PV
☐ Lockheed 580 (T-33A)	56-1767	580-1117		PV
☐ MacCready Gossamer Penguin				RA
☐ Meyers Little Toot	N217J	JDM-3		PV
☐ North American NA-182 Texan (T-6G)	N729AM	182-116	51-14429, 114429 (France), N896WW	PV
☐ Northrop N-156T Talon (T-38A)	62-3645	N.5350		PV
☐ Piper PA-18-125 Super Cub	N350CC	18-1172		PV
☐ Piper PA-20 Pacer 125				PV
☐ Pitts S-2B Special	N56FC	5207		PV
☐ Ryan ST-3KR Recruit (PT-22)	N46745	2131	41-20923	RA
☐ Sopwith Pup (R)	N914W	NCH-1		PV
☐ Temple Sportsman	N987N	107R	X852H	PV
☐ Thorp T-18	N2WW	772		PV
☐ Vought RF-8G Crusader (F8U-1P) (RF-8A)	Bu146882			PV
☐ Vought A-7B Corsair II	Bu154502	B142		RA
☐ Wittman W.8 Tailwind	N103BJ	1		PV
☐ Wright Flyer (R)				PV

GEORGE BUSH PRESIDENTIAL LIBRARY AND MUSEUM (TX70)

Address:	1000 George Bush Drive West, College Station, Texas 77845.
Tel:	979-691-4000 Email: library.bush@nara.gov
Admission:	Monday-Saturday 0930-1700; Sunday 1200-1700.
Location:	About 2 miles south east of Bryan off Route 6.

The history of America since 1941 is one of the themes of this museum. On show are many items relating to the life of the former President and his family. George Bush flew with the Navy in World War II and an Avenger is on show. During his term Germany was reunified, the Soviet Union collapsed and the Gulf War occurred.

TYPE	REG/SER	CON. NO.	PI/NOTES	STATUS
☐ Grumman G-40 Avenger (TBM-3)	Bu53229	3291	Bu53229, N7236C	PV

GLENN CUMBIE MUSEUM (TX71)

Address:	9000 Old Navarro Road, Corsicana, Texas 75109.
Tel:	903-654-4847 (Airport)
Admission:	When the airport is open.
Location:	The airport is about 5 miles south east of the town off Route 287.

The airfield opened in 1940 and for four years was used for pilot training. The site then served as a storage depot until the end of hostilities. Since 1946 it has been the airport for the town.

The Corsicana Field Heritage Association has set up a display. This exhibition traces the history of flying from World War I up to the present day. On show are photographs, documents, models and items of memorabilia.

TYPE	REG/SER	CON. NO.	PI/NOTES	STATUS
☐ Fairchild M-62A Cornell (PT-19A)	N193AR	T43-7155	42-83568, N54018	PV

GOLDEN TRIANGLE VETERANS MEMORIAL PARK (TX72)

Address:	VFW Post 4820, Port Neches, Texas 77658.
Tel:	409-962-8070
Admission:	On permanent view.
Location:	At Port Arthur on Route 73 in the Orange direction.

Members of local veterans groups have set up this display. A large memorial building dominates the site. Around this is a landscaped park where a tank and an assault landing craft and the aircraft are displayed.

TYPE	REG/SER	CON. NO.	PI/NOTES	STATUS
☐ Bell 205 Iroquois (UH-1D) (UH-1H)	65-10090	5134		PV
☐ McDonnell M.98EN Phantom II (F-4D)	'924'	2669	66-8788	PVX

GOODFELLOW AIR FORCE BASE (TX73)

Address:	Building 158, 17TRW/PA, Texas 76908-5000.
Tel:	325-654-3876 Email: 17trw.pa@goodfellow.af.mil
Admission:	By prior permission only.
Location:	About 4 miles east of San Angelo off Route 380.

Named after Lieutenant John J. Goodfellow, who was killed in combat in France in 1918, the base was activated in 1940. The field was initially used to train pilots but operational flying ceased in 1975. A technical training school is now in residence. The preserved aircraft are on show around the camp.

TYPE	REG/SER	CON. NO.	PI/NOTES	STATUS
☐ Douglas DC-3A-456 Skytrain (C-47A) (C-117C) (VC-117A)	'43204'	12508	42-108866, N53425, 42-108866	RAX
☐ Kaman K-600-3 Huskie (H-43B) (HH-43B)	58-1841	1		RA

☐ McDonnell M.98DF Phantom II (RF-4C)	69-0367	3853		RA
☐ Mikoyan-Gurevich MiG-23ML	'136'	0390324618	345 (DDR), 20+20 – in false Soviet markings.	RAX
☐ Mikoyan-Gurevich MiG-29	'17'	2960512124	27 (Moldova)	RAX
☐ North American NA-88 Texan (AT-6C)	'14319'			RA
☐ North American NA-108 Mitchell (B-25J) (TB-25J) (TB-25N)	44-28875	108-32150		RA
☐ North American NA-159 Trojan (T-28A)	49-1679	159-191		RA
☐ Vultee V-74 Valiant (BT-13A)	'424130'			RAX

HALLMARK COLLEGE (TX74)

Address: 8901 Wetmore Road, San Antonio, Texas 78216-4229.
Tel: 210-826-1000   **Email:** sross@hallmarkcollege.edu
Admission: By prior permission only.
Location: On the south side of the airport.

The college was established in 1969 and was until recently known as the Hallmark Institute of Aeronautics. The only aircraft owned is the Boeing 727 donated by FedEx. Students also work under supervision in the adjacent Hallmark Jet Center which maintains and services many corporate business jets.

TYPE	REG/SER	CON. NO.	PI/NOTES	STATUS
☐ Boeing 727-22F	N168FE	18865	N7058U	RA

HANGAR 10 FLYING MUSEUM (TX75)

Address: 1945 Matt Wright Lane, Denton, Texas 76207.
Tel: 940-565-1945   **Email:** ary@hangar10.org
Admission: Monday-Saturday 0830-1500.
Location: About 40 miles north west of Dallas.

In the 1980s the Fighting Air Command Museum was located at Denton. With the demise of this organisation plans were put forward to open another exhibition.

The museum is named after the first aviation exhibit in the state which was in Hangar 10 at Brooks Air Force Base in the 1920s. The collection moved into a new facility in 2001 and aims to build two more hangars and obtain additional aircraft representing all periods of aviation.

Most of the fleet are airworthy and regularly participate in airshows in the region.

TYPE	REG/SER	CON. NO.	PI/NOTES	STATUS
☐ Cessna 140	NC2194V	14423	NC2194V, N2194V	PVA
☐ Cessna 195 (LC-126C) (U-20A)	N4929C	7803	51-6960	PVA
☐ Cessna 195B (190)	N725J	7672		PVA
☐ Globe GC-1B Swift	N3801K	1494	NC3801K	PVA
☐ Howard DGA-15P (NH-2)	N1366		Bu32348	PVC
☐ Lancair Legacy 2000	N410RH	L2K-276		PVA
☐ North American NA-145 Navion	N91750	NAV-4-470	NC91750	PVA
☐ Piper J-3C-65 Cub	N7066H	20317	NC7066H	PVA
☐ Pitts S-1S Special	N26SM	483-H		PVA

HANGAR 25 MUSEUM (TX76)

Address: 1911 Apron Drive, PO Box 2925, Big Spring. Texas 79721.
Tel: 432-264-1999   **Fax:** 432-466-0316   **Email:** hangar25@crcom.net
Admission: Tuesday-Friday 0800-1600; Saturday 0900-1500:
Location: About 3 miles south west of the town off Interstate 20.

Big Spring airfield opened in September 1942 and housed a Bombardier School operating AT-11 Kansans and B-18 Bolos. The base closed four years later after almost 6,000 students had been trained and the site became the municipal airport. In October 1951 the Air Force returned and it was home to a training wing. On 18th May 1952 the field was renamed Webb Air Force Base after Lieutenant James Webb, a local man killed in a P-51 crash off the Japanese coast in 1949. Fighter squadrons with F-102s arrived in 1956 and these were replaced by the F-104 in 1963. The base closed on 30th September 1977 and became Big Spring Industrial Airpark. The museum has been set up in Hangar 44 (refurbished with parts from the now demolished Hangar 25) and the displays trace the history of two periods of military residence. The active aircraft are from a private collection and are all resplendent in military markings. The F-100F arrived recently and this has been assembled and restored. An exhibition tracing the history of the airfield and its units has been set up.

TYPE	REG/SER	CON. NO.	PI/NOTES	STATUS
☐ Beech C18S Kansan (AT-11)	N88KD	929	41-9703	PVA
☐ Boeing 464-201-7 Stratofortress (B-52D)	58-0232	464300	Front fuselage only.	PV
☐ Cessna 318D Dragonfly (318A) (T-37A) (T-37B) (A-37A)	55-4305	40019	67-14504 – Cessna 318A 55-4305 converted – with parts of 318D 67-14531 converted from 318A c/n 40050 56-3478.	PV
☐ Fairchild-Republic A-10A Thunderbolt II			Front fuselage only.	PV
☐ Hawker-Siddeley P.1127 Harrier 50 (AV-8B) (AV-8C)	Bu159238	P147		PV
☐ Lockheed 580 (T-33A)	N5848F	580-9923	51-6573, N97477, N7477	PVA
☐ Lockheed 580 (T-33A)	57-0606	580-1255		PV
☐ North American NA-159 Trojan (T-28A)	N6FY	159-56	49-1544	PVA
☐ North American NA-243 Super Sabre (F-100F)	56-3982	243-258		PV
☐ Northrop N-156T Talon (T-38A)	64-13198	N.5627		PV

Texas 577

HARWOOD PAINTBALL (TX77)

| Location: | By prior permission only at Tactical Paintball at 12590 Route 794 in the town. |

TYPE	REG/SER	CON. NO.	PI/NOTES	STATUS
☐ Bell 204 Iroquois (UH-1B)			May be Bell 205.	RA
☐ Bell 204 Iroquois (UH-1B)			May be Bell 205.	RA

HAWKINS MONUMENT (TX78)

| Location: | On permanent view in the Veterans Memorial Park in the northern part of the town. |

TYPE	REG/SER	CON. NO.	PI/NOTES	STATUS
☐ Bell 209 Huey Cobra (AH-1G) (AH-1F)	69-16440	20872		PV

HENDERSON MONUMENT (TX79)

| Location: | On permanent view at Rusk County Airport which is south west of the town. |

TYPE	REG/SER	CON. NO.	PI/NOTES	STATUS
☐ Lockheed 580 (T-33A)	51-6656	580-5988		PV

HISTORIC AVIATION MEMORIAL MUSEUM (TX80)

Address:	2198 Dixie Drive, Tyler Pounds Airport, Tyler, Texas 75704.
Tel:	903-526-1945 Fax: 903-592-1202 Email: cjverver@aol.com
Admission:	Tuesday-Saturday 1000-1700; Sunday 1300-1700.
Location:	About 6 miles west of the town on Route 64.

A foundation was established in 1985 to raise funds for the construction of a museum. The original idea was to house the PBY-6A of the Lone Star Wing of the Confederate Air Force but this was destroyed in a fatal crash and plans were changed. Building work started some years ago and the first phases of the complex are ready. There is an area displaying memorabilia, a set of meeting rooms and a hangar for the aircraft.

In July 2007 the museum moved into the North Terminal Building which was formerly used by airlines; this more than doubled the exhibition space. The collection of military types contains some interesting machines. The Fury was parked near to the water at Sea Wolf Park in Galveston for almost 30 years. The FJ-4 was transported to Tyler and is now resplendent in the colours of Marine Squadron VMF-232 who operated it in Japan in the late 1950s. The Sikorsky helicopter has moved from the Texas Air Museum. The museum now has a Canso on show. This aircraft is a Canadian-Vickers-built example which served in Brazil.

TYPE	REG/SER	CON. NO.	PI/NOTES	STATUS
☐ Aero L-29 Delfin	N29NR/'75'	194144		PVA
☐ Cessna 318B Tweety Bird (T-37B)	62-5952	40720		PV
☐ Consolidated 28-5A Canso A	N4934H	CV-272	9838 (Canada), 6525 (Brazil)	PV
☐ Douglas NA-1E Skyraider (AD-5) (A-1E)	Bu132443	9460		PV
☐ Douglas TA-4J Skyhawk	Bu154291	13679		PV
☐ General Dynamics F-111A	67-0051	A1-96		PV
☐ Grumman G-99 Cougar (F9F-8) (F-9J)	Bu141058		Possible identity.	PV
☐ Lockheed 183-93-02 Starfighter (F-104C)	'56-0763'	183-1114	56-0826	PVX
☐ Lockheed 580 (T-33A)	'80221'	580-1590	58-0621	PVX
☐ McDonnell M.98EN Phantom II (F-4D)	66-8812	2799		PV
☐ North American NA-192 Super Sabre (F-100A)	53-1684	192-179	53-1684, '53537'	PV
☐ North American NA-209 Fury (FJ-4) (F-1E)	Bu139516	209-136		PV
☐ North American NA-332 Buckeye (T-2C)	Bu157034	332-5		PV
☐ PZL TS-11 Iskra 100bisB	N44ZR	1H 05-21	0521 (Poland), 521 (Poland)	PVA
☐ Republic F-105D Thunderchief	60-0500	D-188		PV
☐ Sikorsky S-55B (HO4S-1)	Bu125506			PV

HOUSTON MONUMENT (TX81)

| Location: | On permanent view at ALP 560 in Alba Street in the north western part of the city. |

TYPE	REG/SER	CON. NO.	PI/NOTES	STATUS
☐ McDonnell M.98DE Phantom II (F-4C)	64-0772	1072		PV

HUBBARD MONUMENT (TX82)

| Location: | On permanent view in the town centre. |

TYPE	REG/SER	CON. NO.	PI/NOTES	STATUS
☐ Bell 209 Huey Cobra (AH-1G) (AH-1S)	68-15179	20713		PV

KELLY FIELD ANNEX COLLECTION (TX83)

Address:	San Antonio, Texas 78241.
Tel:	210-925-4883
Admission:	By prior permission only.
Location:	In the western part of the city

The first airfield opened in 1916 when Major Benjamin Foulois chose an area for use by the Army. In June 1917 it was named after Lieutenant George Kelly who was killed in May 1911 when attempting to land an aircraft at Fort Sam Houston.

Kelly Field remained open in the inter-war period and during World War II vast numbers of aircraft were maintained. This work continued during the Korean conflict. The base finally closed in the mid-1990s. The site is now split with the Boeing company occupying the former overhaul site and other organisations in residence around the site. The Texas Air National Guard still fly from the base.

A number of preserved aircraft remain and the Inter-American Air Force Academy has a several instructional airframes. This organisation has trained personnel for Latin American nations since 1943. After its premises at Homestead Air Force Base in Florida were almost destroyed by Hurricane Andrew in 1992 it moved to its current home. The preserved aircraft are at a number of locations around the site.

TYPE	REG/SER	CON. NO.	PI/NOTES	STATUS
☐ Bell 205 Iroquois (HH-1H)	70-2485	17129	Instructional airframe.	RA
☐ Cessna 318E Dragonfly (A-37B) (OA-37B)	68-7967	43114	Instructional airframe.	RA
☐ Convair 4 Hustler (B-58A)	59-2437	40		RA
☐ Convair 8-27 Delta Dart (F-106D)	57-2533	8-27-27		RA
☐ General Dynamics 401 Fighting Falcon (F-16A)	80-0526	61-247	Instructional airframe.	RA
☐ Lockheed 382-8B Hercules (C-130E)	64-0519	382-4003	Instructional airframe.	RA
☐ McDonnell M.98DE Phantom II (F-4C)	63-7515	529		RA
☐ McDonnell M.199-1A Eagle (F-15A)	76-0108	310/A260		RA
☐ North American NA-235 Super Sabre (F-100D)	56-3000	235-98	56-3000, '53000'	RA
☐ Northrop N-311 Tiger II (F-5F)	73-0889	W.1001	Instructional airframe.	RA

KILLEEN MONUMENT (TX84)

Location:	On permanent view in the centre of the town.

TYPE	REG/SER	CON. NO.	PI/NOTES	STATUS
☐ Bell 209 Huey Cobra (AH-1S) (AH-1E)	77-22795	22133		PV

KINGSVILLE NAVAL AIR STATION (TX85)

Address:	802 Dealey Avenue, Suite 103, Kingsville, Texas 78363-5720.
Tel:	361-516-6375 Email: knsv.nask-pao@navy.mil
Admission:	By prior permission only.
Location:	About 3 miles south of the town off Route 77.

The airfield opened in July 1942 and has been active ever since. Intermediate and advanced strike jet pilot training are carried out at the station. In January 1992 it became the first to operate the T-45A Goshawk. This aircraft replaced the North American Buckeye and the Douglas Skyhawk with the resident units.

Examples of types flown have been preserved with several positioned outside the Headquarters building.

TYPE	REG/SER	CON. NO.	PI/NOTES	STATUS
☐ Douglas A-4C Skyhawk (A4D-2N)				RA
☐ Douglas A-4C Skyhawk (A4D-2N)	Bu145113	12359	In town park.	PV
☐ Douglas TA-4J Skyhawk (TA-4F)	Bu154338	13726		RA
☐ Douglas TA-4J Skyhawk	Bu156904	13997	In town.	RA
☐ McDonnell M.267 Hornet (F/A-18A)	Bu161967	183/A144		RA
☐ McDonnell-Douglas T-45A Goshawk (FSM)				PV
☐ North American NA-346 Buckeye (T-2C)	Bu158586			RA

LA GRANGE MONUMENT (TX86)

Location:	On permanent view at Fayette County Airport which is 2 miles west of the town on Highway 71.

TYPE	REG/SER	CON. NO.	PI/NOTES	STATUS
☐ North American NA-243 Super Sabre (F-100F)	56-3929	243-205		PV

LAGO VISTA AIRPOWER MUSEUM (TX87)

Address:	Hangar 9, Rusty Allen Airport, Lago Vista, Texas 78645.
Tel:	512-267-7403
Admission:	Saturday-Sunday 1300-1700.
Location:	About 20 miles north west of Austin off Route 1431.

The indoor displays at the museum feature a large collection of models portraying the development of combat aircraft. In addition there are uniforms, documents, photographs and items of memorabilia on view. The Phantom joined the collection in the mid-1990s and is parked outside.

TYPE	REG/SER	CON. NO.	PI/NOTES	STATUS
☐ Boeing-Stearman E75 Kaydet (PT-13D)	N3992B	75-5992	42-17829	PV
☐ McDonnell M.98DF Phantom II (RF-4C)	64-1000	665		PV
☐ Piper J-3C-65 Cub (O-59) (L-4)	N50784	7563	42-7832	PV

LAUGHLIN AIR FORCE BASE HERITAGE PARK (TX88)

Address:	47 FTW/PA, 598 4th Street, Laughlin Air Force Base, Texas 78843-5202.
Tel:	830-298-5988 Fax: 830-298-5047 Email: 47ftw.pa@laughlin.af.mil
Admission:	Monday-Friday 0830-1630 – by prior permission only from Wing Public Affairs Office.
Location:	About 6 miles east of Del Rio off Highway 90.

Texas

Named after Lieutenant Jack T. Laughlin, the first Del Rio resident to be killed in World War II when his B-17 was shot down over Java, the base opened in 1942 to train bombardiers. The site closed in 1945 and was then modernised in the early 1950s for training on the F-84 and the T-33.

From 1957 to 1963 Strategic Reconnaissance Wings flying the Martin RB-57 and the then secret Lockheed U-2 were in residence. Since April 1962 the field has been used for pilot training.

A Heritage Foundation was set up in August 1983 and this has collected a large number of items. These are mainly in store in the offices in town. Most of the aircraft are by the main gate. The Invader arrived from Chanute AFB in Illinois in the mid-1990s.

TYPE	REG/SER	CON. NO.	PI/NOTES	STATUS
☐ Beech D18S Expeditor (C18S) (SNB-2C) (SNB-5) (TC-45J) (UC-45J)	'5-2274'	5850	Bu23774	PVX
☐ Beech D45 Mentor (T-34B)	'74112'	BG-419	Bu144112, N155ZL	PVX
☐ Cessna 318B Tweety Bird (318A) (T-37A) (T-37B)	54-2739	40015		PV
☐ Douglas A-26C Invader	44-35204	28483	44-35204, '434314'	PV
☐ Lockheed 580 (T-33A)	'51-8595'	580-6413	51-8629	PVX
☐ Lockheed U-2C (U-2A)	56-6707	374		PV
☐ Martin 272B Canberra (B-57B) (EB-57B)	52-1509	92		PV
☐ North American NA-88 Texan (AT-6C)	'801428'			PVX
☐ North American NA-159 Trojan (T-28A)	49-1682	159-194		PV
☐ Northrop N-156T Talon (T-38A)	60-0574	N.5147		PV
☐ Republic F-84F Thunderstreak	52-9060			PV

LE TOURNEAU UNIVERSITY (TX89)

Address:	PO Box 7001, Longview, Texas 75607-7001.
Tel:	800-759-8811 **Email:** admissions*letu.edu
Admission:	By prior permission only.
Location:	In the southern part of the town.

This private university was set up in 1946 as a technical institute on the site of an abandoned World War II hospital. The site has been developed and the last of the original buildings were demolished in 2003.

The Aeronautical Science Department operates a flying training school at the local airfield. Three instructional airframes have been reported as being used in buildings on the main campus.

TYPE	REG/SER	CON. NO.	PI/NOTES	STATUS
☐ Beech 65-A90-1 Ute (U-21A)	N70503	LM-43	66-18042	RA
☐ Luscombe 8E Silvaire				RA
☐ North American NA-265 Sabreliner (T-39A) (CT-39A)	60-3500	265-28		RA

LEANDER MUSEUM (TX90)

Address:	Leander
Tel:	Unknown
Admission:	Unknown
Location:	Unknown

There have been reports of a private museum in the area with the former Czechoslovakian MiG-21 in the collection. I have been in correspondence with the town authorities and they could not help with details.

TYPE	REG/SER	CON. NO.	PI/NOTES	STATUS
☐ Mikoyan-Gurevich MiG-21F-13	1104	161104	In Czech markings.	RA

LEWIS AERONAUTICAL COLLECTION (TX91)

Address:	10101 Reunion Place, Suite 1000, San Antonio, Texas 78216-4157.
Admission:	By prior permission only.
Location:	At The International Airport in the northern part of the town.

This warbird collection contains many interesting machines. On 15th July 1942 two B-17s and six P-38s were flying from the USA to England. Bad weather over Iceland forced them back and they landed on the Greenland ice cap.

In 1981 Pat Epps, Roy Schoffner and Richard Taylor of Atlanta formed the Greenland Expedition Society to find and retrieve the aircraft. After seven trips the machines were located in 1989 three miles from their landing site and over 250 feet below the surface. The following year a group reached one B-17 and found that it had been crushed. The smaller and stronger P-38s were in much better condition. In 1992 members returned to raise one of the Lightnings. A large heated cone was used to melt the ice and once the aircraft had been reached a cavern around it was maintained by use of a hot water cannon. By the 50th anniversary of the landings one of the aircraft had been brought to the surface. The components were transported to Middlesboro in Kentucky. Restoration began in October 1992 and the aircraft took to the air again on 26th October 2002.

Examples of the famous naval aircraft produced by the Grumman company are owned. The Tigercat was the first twin-engined fighter to enter service with the US Navy. First flown in 1944 it was operated for a decade and 364 were built. Four Bearcats are in the fleet. This single-engined fighter, inspired by the Focke Wulf Fw 190, was designed as the successor to the Hellcat. The prototype flew in August 1944 but the type never saw use in World War II. The Bearcat flew with the 'Blue Angels' aerobatic team and saw use in Southeast Asia with the French, Thai and Vietnamese forces. Bearcats have also flown successfully as racers and set speed records.

Two Hawker Sea Furies, one a single seater and the other a two seat trainer, are in the collection. The T.20 served as a target tug in Germany between 1959 and 1972. The aircraft then moved to a collector in Belgium where it was hardly touched for ten years. After a few moves around the USA it flew again in California in 1997. Fitted with a Wright radial it was raced at Reno.

The only other British aircraft is the Spitfire. After RAF and Royal Navy service it was found derelict in Cornwall and shipped to Australia. A rebuild took place in England, Australia and New Zealand before it flew at Ardmore in 2007.

TYPE	REG/SER	CON. NO.	PI/NOTES	STATUS
☐ Bell 26E Airacobra (P-39Q)	G-CEJU	26E-397	42-19993, N139DP, N793QG	RAA
☐ Canadair CL-219-1A17 Freedom Fighter (CF-116D) (CF-5D) [Northrop N-156B]	N805FF	2005	116805 (Canada)	RAA
☐ Commonwealth CA-18 Mustang 22 [North American P-51D]	N50FS/'44-74839'	1512	A68-187, VH-AGJ, VH-FHT, VH-UFO, N919WJ, (N151SU)	RAAX
☐ Douglas A-20J Havoc	N3WF	21356	43-21709, NC67932, N67932, N22M	RA
☐ Grumman G-36 Wildcat (F4F-3)	N12260	5920	Bu12260	RAA
☐ Grumman G-51 Tigercat (F7F-3)	NX700F	C.132	Bu80390, N6129C, N700F, (N700FM)	RAA
☐ Grumman G-51 Tigercat (F7F-3P)	N805MB	C.245	Bu80503, N800RW	RAA
☐ Grumman G-58 Bearcat (F8F-1)	N58204	D.527	Bu95255, 95255 (France), 95255 (SNVAF), N65135, N41089	RAA
☐ Grumman G-58 Bearcat (F8F-2)	NX747NF	D.988	Bu121614, N7957C – in false Thai Air Force colours	RAAX
☐ Grumman G-58 Bearcat (F8F-2)	NX14WB	D.1148	Bu122619, N7958C, N700F	RAA
☐ Grumman G-58 Bearcat (F8F-2)	N777L	D.1170	Bu122629, N1031B	RAA
☐ Hawker Sea Fury FB.11	N232MB	41H/609972	TG114, CF-OYF, N54M, N232J, G-BVOE, N232J	RAA
☐ Hawker Sea Fury T.20S (T.20)	N233MB	41H/620508/ ES.9506	VZ351, D-CEDO, (OO-SFY)	RAA
☐ Lockheed 222-60-15 Lightning (P-38F)	NX17630	222-5757	41-7630, N5757	RAA
☐ North American NA-50	N250NA	050		RAA
☐ North American NA-108 Mitchell (B-25J) (TB-25N)	N125PF	108-33731	44-30456, N3512G, C-GTTS, N43BA – in false Soviet colours.	RAAX
☐ North American NA-122 Mustang (P-51D) (Mustang IV)	N74190	122-40992	44-74452, 9225 (Canada)	RAA
☐ North American NA-168 Texan (T-6G)	N884TA/248884'	168-294	49-3190, N8399H	RAAX
☐ Republic P-47D Thunderbolt	N767WJ	399-53778	44-32817, 15B36 (Venezuela)	RAA
☐ Ryan ST-3KR Recruit (PT-21)	N1616	1062	41-1941, N57030	RAA
☐ Supermarine 349 Spitfire LF.Vb	N628BL	CBAF 1660	BL628, G-BTTN, VH-FVB	RAA
☐ Vought FG-1D Corsair	N29VF	3997	(USN)	RAA

LONE STAR FLIGHT MUSEUM (TX92)

Address:	2002 Terminal Drive, Galveston, Texas 77554-9279.
Tel:	409-740-7722 **Fax:** 409-740-7612 **Email:** flight@lonestarflight.org
Admission:	Daily 0900-1700.
Location:	At Scholes Field which is in the western suburbs of the city.

The museum was set up in 1985 and obtained premises at Hobby Airport in Houston. All of the aircraft then came from the private collection of Robert Waltrip. After a long search for a suitable exhibition site the museum opened in 1990 in a purpose-built facility at Galveston Airport formerly Galveston Army Air Field. Over 30 aircraft were shown and this number has now increased.

The museum came to public attention with the purchase of a B-17 Fortress in England. The aircraft served for many years in France on survey work before being acquired by Warbirds of Great Britain. The bomber flew across the North Atlantic in 1987, 42 years after most of the type made the journey home. The aircraft then underwent a three-year restoration to bring it back to pristine condition.

A range of bombers, fighters and trainers is on view in the two exhibition halls. Most of the aircraft are airworthy but an exception is the Convair B-58 Hustler obtained from the defunct Southwest Aerospace Museum at Fort Worth. The aircraft are restored and maintained to a high standard and regularly appear at airshows. The Hurricane is nearing the end of a protracted rebuild.

The museum is home to the Texas Hall of Fame and most of the aircraft are registered to this organisation. The Hall opened in 1977 and each year there is a ceremony where people who have made outstanding contributions to aviation in the state are inducted. A special exhibition was set up for the centenary of powered flight. The scale Wright Flyer is here along with many photographs and documents tracing the work of the brothers. Replicas of early types have been constructed to enhance the display.

In 1913 the Burgess H was the first tractor monoplane purchased by the US Army who eventually ordered five.

TYPE	REG/SER	CON. NO.	PI/NOTES	STATUS
☐ Aero L-29R Delfin	N82601	792661	(Soviet)	PVA
☐ Aeronca 7DC Champion (7AC)	N84057	7AC-2744	NC84057	PV
☐ Beech H18S	N954	BA-670		PVA
☐ Bell 205 Iroquois (UH-1H) (UH-1V)	N22490	13814	74-22490 – on loan from Marine AM, DE.	PV
☐ Blériot XI (R)				PV
☐ Boeing 299-O Fortress (B-17G)	'238050'	8627	44-85718, F-BEEC, ZS-EEC, F-BEEC, G-FORT, N900RW	PVAX
☐ Boeing-Stearman B75N1 Kaydet (N2S-3)	N84LK	75-7322	Bu07718, N9753H	PVA
☐ Boeing-Stearman E75 Kaydet (PT-13D) (N2S-5)	N75272	75-8115	42-109078, Bu38490	PVA
☐ Burgess H (R)				PV
☐ Cavalier Mustang II (F-51D) (North American NA-122) (Mustang IV)	N4151D	122-39917	44-73458, 9294 (Canada), N6525D, N6347T, N554T, N36FF	PVA
☐ Cayley Glider (R)				PV
☐ Cessna T-50 Bobcat (AT-17B) (UC-78B)	N51469	6644	43-32706	PVA
☐ Cessna 318E Dragonfly (318A) (T-37A) (T-37B) (A-37A)	N134RA	40055	67-14534, (N534RW) – converted from 318A 56-3482	RAC
☐ Consolidated 28-5A Canso A	N68740	407	9742 (Canada), N68740, (N6208N)	PVA
☐ Consolidated 40 Privateer (PB4Y-2) (P4Y-2) (Convair 100)	N3739G		Bu59719	PVC
☐ Convair 4 Hustler (YB-58A) (TB-58A)	55-0668	9		PV
☐ Curtiss A-1 (R)				PV

Texas

☐ De Havilland DH.82A Tiger Moth	N9714	83896	T7467, G-ANIZ	RAA
☐ Douglas DC-3-277B	NC25673	2213	NC25673, N130PB, N30PB, N130PB	RAA
☐ Douglas A-24B Dauntless	N93RW	17521	42-54682, (Mexican AF), XB-ZAH, N74133	RAC
☐ Douglas A-1D Skyraider (AD-4N) (AD-4NA)	NX91945	7682	Bu126882, 85 (France), 126882 (Gabon) – on loan from Marine AM, DE.	PVA
☐ Evans VP-1 Volksplane	N11VP	VP-DH1		PV
☐ Evans VP-1 Volksplane				RA
☐ Grumman G-40 Avenger (TBM-3) (TBM-3U)	N700RW	2068	Bu69329, N73642	PVA
☐ Grumman G-50 Hellcat (F6F-5) (F6F-5N)	N4998V	A-11956	Bu94204	PVA
☐ Grumman G-58 Bearcat (F8F-2)	'Bu94996'	D.1162	Bu121776, N1030B, N68RW	RACX
☐ Grumman G-96 Trader (TF-1) (C-1A)	N81193	082	Bu146052	PVA
☐ Hawker Hurricane IIB	N96RW/'BG974'	'CCF-96'	(Canada), N68RW	PVAX
☐ Lilienthal Normal-Segelapparat (R)				PV
☐ Lockheed 15-27-01 Harpoon (PV-2D)	N6655D	15-1600	Bu37634	PVC
☐ Luscombe 8C Silvaire	N25270/'279550'	1177	NC25270	PVAX
☐ Monnett Moni	N943M	143		RA
☐ Murphy Renegade Spirit	N427EK	533P		PV
☐ Naval Aircraft Factory N3N-3	N3NZ		Bu1974, N44970	PVA
☐ Noorduyn Norseman VI (C-64A) (UC-64A)				RAC
☐ North American NA-88 Texan (AT-6D) (SNJ-5)	N566TX	88-17274	42-85493, Bu85053, N8210E, N777WS	PVA
☐ North American NA-108 Mitchell (B-25J) (TB-25N)	N333RW	108-47488	44-86734, N9090Z, N600DM	PVA
☐ North American NA-235 Super Sabre (F-100D)	'63-154'	235-252	56-3154	PVX
☐ Oldfield Baby Great Lakes	N15RF	7318 B471		PV
☐ Piaggio FWP.149D				RAA
☐ Republic P-47D Thunderbolt	'433240'		44-90368, 22B-36 (Venezuela), NX4747P, '432773'	PVAX
☐ Sino-Swearingen SJ30-2	N30SJ	001		PV
☐ Steen Skybolt	N31CS	1		PV
☐ Stinson V-76 Sentinel (L-5)	'214999'	76-1039	42-98798, N68MH	PVAX
☐ Supermarine 361 Spitfire LF.XVIe	N97RW	CBAF-IX-4551	TE392	PVA
☐ Turner T-40A	N585N	59		PV
☐ Vought F4U-5N Corsair (F4U-5)	N43RW	9873	Bu121823, 0434 (Argentina)	PVA
☐ Wright Flyer (Scale R)				PV

LUBBOCK MONUMENT (TX93)

Location: On permanent view at Lubbock State School in the northern part of the town.

TYPE	REG/SER	CON. NO.	PI/NOTES	STATUS
☐ Lockheed 580 (T-33A)	'9202'			PVX

LYNDON B. JOHNSON NATIONAL HISTORICAL PARK (TX94)

Address: PO Box 329, Johnson City, Texas 78636.
Tel: 830-868-7128   **Fax:** 830-868-7863
Admission: Daily 0845-1700.
Location: About 5 miles east of Stonewall.

The park has two sites. These are the boyhood home of the former President in Johnson City and his ranch near Stonewall where the visitor can take a self guided driving tour. The Texas White House is at the latter. The JetStar has been painted in the colours it wore when he flew in the aircraft between 1963 and 1968.

TYPE	REG/SER	CON. NO.	PI/NOTES	STATUS
☐ Lockheed 1329 JetStar 6 (VC-140B) (C-140B)	61-2490	1329-5024		PV

MANCHACA MONUMENT (TX95)

Location: On permanent view at VFW 3377 at 12921 Lowden Lane in the southern part of the town.

TYPE	REG/SER	CON. NO.	PI/NOTES	STATUS
☐ McDonnell M.98DE Phantom II (F-4C)	64-0791	1104		PV

MARTINDALE ARMY AIRFIELD (TX96)

Location: By prior permission only at the site in the eastern part of San Antonio.

TYPE	REG/SER	CON. NO.	PI/NOTES	STATUS
☐ Bell 205 Iroquois (UH-1H)	70-16478	12783		PV

MCALLEN INTERNATIONAL AIRPORT MUSEUM (TX97)

Address: 2500 Bicentennial, McAllen, Texas 78503.
Tel: 956-682-9101
Admission: On permanent view.
Location: Just south of the city.

Constructed by former RAF member Fred Leech, the replica of the locally built 1912 White Monoplane now hangs in the terminal building. This newly constructed version was flown before being put on display. The local museum is setting up an exhibition entitled 'Wings over the Rio Grande' in a number of cabinets close to the White. The displays trace the history of flying in the area and the development of the airport. On show are models, photographs, documents, flying clothing, maps and many items of memorabilia.

TYPE	REG/SER	CON. NO.	PI/NOTES	STATUS
☐ White Monoplane (R)				PV

MIDLAND COLLEGE (TX98)

Address:	Hangar E, 2405 Windecker Road, Midland, Texas 79711.
Tel:	432-563-8952 Email: tbranon@midland.edu
Admission:	By prior permission only.
Location:	At Midland International Airport which is about 8 miles west of the city.

The college has its main campus in the town. The Aviation Maintenance Department has a facility at the airport where a number of instructional airframes are in known to be in use. Also at the field is a fleet of active aircraft used for training students up to commercial pilot standards.

TYPE	REG/SER	CON. NO.	PI/NOTES	STATUS
☐ Beech F33A Bonanza	N33UB	CE-1496		RA
☐ Bell 205 Iroquois (UH-1H)				RA
☐ Bell 206 Jet Ranger				RA
☐ Cessna 172S	N65536	172S9723		RA
☐ Cessna 172S	N66045	172S9772		RA

MILITARY MUSEUM OF TEXAS (TX99)

Address:	8611 Wallisville Road, Houston 77029.
Tel:	713-673-1234 Email: mail@texasmuseum.org
Admission:	Saturday-Sunday 0800-1800.
Location:	About 7 miles east of the city centre.

The state of Texas has a long military history and the displays at the museum trace this heritage. On show are weapons and military vehicles along with uniforms and memorabilia. Members stage historical re-enactments of significant battles on a number of weekends. The only aircraft on show is the Iroquois.

TYPE	REG/SER	CON. NO.	PI/NOTES	STATUS
☐ Bell 205 Iroquois (UH-1D) (UH-1H)	65-9779	4823		PV

MUSEUM OF NORTH TEXAS HISTORY (TX100)

Address:	720 Indiana Avenue, Wichita Falls, Texas 76301-6512.
Tel:	940-322-7628
Admission:	Museum Tuesday-Friday 1000-1400. Call Field exhibit Saturday 1000-1400.
Location:	Museum in town – aircraft at Kickapoo Airport.

The displays at the museum trace the history of the region. The Heritage Hall features a remarkable collection of cowboy hats. Nat Fleming ran a business in the town for 54 years and when a customer bought a new hat the old one was hung on the wall. Reproductions of store fronts, a replica of an early post office can be seen. The Oil Exhibit presents the story of the exploration for crude in the area. The development of the industry is portrayed in a series of models and photographs.

The Military Collection displays items from the civil war up to modern times. During the latter stages of World War I many pilots were trained at Call Field. At the time it was one of five military airfields in Texas. Closed in 1920 its dirt runways were located in what is now the University Park.

A Curtiss Jenny resides in the hangar and this is flown on special occasions. This aircraft was used as a barnstormer just after the conflict. After a crash in 1920 it spent 50 years dismantled in an Iowa barn. Restoration of biplane was started in Spencer, Iowa and completed in Oklahoma City. The Jenny was in England for a time. Also on show are many photographs from the period along with uniforms and memorabilia.

TYPE	REG/SER	CON. NO.	PI/NOTES	STATUS
☐ Curtiss 1C Jenny (JN-4D)	N2525S	1917	(US Army), N2525, G-ECAB	PVA

MUSEUM OF THE AMERICAN GI (TX101)

Address:	PO Box 9599, 1303 Cherokee Street, College Station, Texas 77840.
Tel:	972-567-7151
Admission:	Monday-Saturday 1000-1800.
Location:	About 1 mile south of the town off Route 6.

This new museum traces the history and life of the American serviceman. On show are many uniforms, badges and documents along with photographs and posters. An impressive collection of military vehicles, tanks, heavy weapons and boats has been obtained. Several of these have been restored to working order. The island of the USS *Iwo Jima*, which was scrapped in 1993, has been moved from the now closed Rio Hondo site of the Texas Air Museum. The Iroquois has arrived from a period of storage at Ellington Air National Guard Base and needs to be restored for display. Regular open days are held an on these re-enactments of famous battles are fought. A genuine World War II Bailey Bridge can be seen in the grounds.

TYPE	REG/SER	CON. NO.	PI/NOTES	STATUS
☐ Bell 204 Iroquois (TH-1F)	66-1225	7301		PVC

NATIONAL BORDER PATROL MUSEUM (TX102)

Address:	4315 Transmountain Road, El Paso, Texas 79924.
Tel:	915-759-6060　　Fax: 915-759-0992　　Email: npbm@borderpatrolmuseum.com
Admission:	Tuesday-Saturday 0900-1700.
Location:	In the northern suburbs of the city just west of Route 54.

The US Immigration Service started patrolling the southern border on horses in the early years of the twentieth century. The Border Patrol was officially set up in 1924 and its duties have varied over the years. During World War II the service first used aircraft and autogyros in its work. At the current time the majority of its agents are employed along the Mexican border trying to stop illegal immigration and drug shipments.

This museum traces the history of the Border Patrol with many fascination exhibits. There are photographs, documents and uniforms from the early days. Vehicles used in their work can be seen and these include motor cycles and cars.

The Super Cub is hanging in the main exhibition hall and the Hughes helicopter is on the museum floor.

TYPE	REG/SER	CON. NO.	PI/NOTES	STATUS
☐ Hughes 369				PV
☐ Piper PA-18-150 Super Cub	N4464Z	18-8811		PV

NATIONAL MUSEUM OF THE PACIFIC WAR (TX103)

Address:	340 East Main Street, PO Box 777, Fredericksburg, Texas 78624.
Tel:	830-997-4379　　Fax: 830-997-8220　　Email: joe.cavanaugh@thc.state.tx.us
Admission:	Daily 0800-1700.
Location:	In the town which is about 70 miles north west of San Antonio off Highway 10.

This excellent museum is housed in the building where Admiral Nimitz was born. The story of the Pacific War is told in great detail and in the Pearl Harbor Room are relics from a number of shot down aircraft. A short distance away is the History Walk of the Pacific War. Here a number of military vehicles are on show. The Aichi D3A1 was the first Japanese type to drop bombs on US soil when Oahu was attacked in December 1941.

The Kawanishi N1K1 floatplane served in small numbers near the end of the conflict.

TYPE	REG/SER	CON. NO.	PI/NOTES	STATUS
☐ Aichi D3A2-22		3357	3105	PVD
☐ Grumman G-36 Wildcat (FM-2)		Bu74161	4353	PV
☐ Grumman G-40 Avenger (TBM-3) (TBM-3E)		Bu53403	3465	PV
☐ Kawanishi N1K1 Kyofu			562	PV
☐ North American NA-108 Mitchell (B-25J) (TB-25J)	44-86880		108-47634	PV

NATIONAL VIETNAM WAR MUSEUM (TX104)

Address:	PO Box 146, 12685 Mineral Wells Highway, Weatherford, Texas 76068.
Tel:	940-664-3918　　Email: info@nationalvnwarmuseum.org
Admission:	Daily dawn-dusk
Location:	About 1 mile east of the Mineral Wells off Route 180.

In 2001 land was purchased for the construction of this museum to trace the history of the war. The first memorial garden is now open and ground should soon be broken for the first phase of the building. The plans show 11 exhibit rooms each tracing a particular aspect of the conflict. Mineral Wells was chosen as the site for the exhibition as the majority of Army helicopter pilots received basic flying training at nearby Fort Wolters. That site, now an industrial park, was in use from 1956 until 1973 when the school moved to Fort Rucker in Alabama. A number of helicopters have been acquired and are in store in the area.

TYPE	REG/SER	CON. NO.	PI/NOTES	STATUS
☐ Bell 47D-1 Sioux (H-13E) (OH-13E)				RA
☐ Bell 205 Iroquois (UH-1D) (UH-1H)	65-10068	5112		PV
☐ Bell 205 Iroquois (UH-1H)	N3757Z	11035	68-16376	RA
☐ Bell 205 Iroquois (UH-1H)	N15707	12317	70-15707	RA
☐ Hiller UH12D Raven (H-23D) (OH-23D)				RA
☐ Hughes 369M Cayuse (HO-6) (OH-6A)	68-17331	1291		RA
☐ North American NA-305 Bronco (OV-10A) (OV-10D)	N10957	305-57	Bu155446	RA
☐ North American NA-305 Bronco (OV-10A) (OV-10D)	N97854	305-81	Bu155470	RA
☐ North American NA-305 Bronco (OV-10A) (OV-10D)	N88970	305-90	Bu155479	PV
☐ North American NA-305 Bronco (OV-10A) (OV-10D)	N373SV	305-94	Bu155483	RA
☐ North American NA-305 Bronco (OV-10A) (OV-10D)	N85967	305-100	Bu155489	PV
☐ North American NA-305 Bronco (OV-10A) (OV-10D)	N97854	305-104	Bu155493	PV
☐ Northrop N-156T Talon (T-38A)	61-0809	N.5175	Airport monument.	PV

NATIONAL WASP WWII MUSEUM (TX105)

Address:	210 Loop 170, PO Box 456, Sweetwater, Texas 79956.
Tel:	325-235-0099　　Email: nancy@avengerfield.org
Admission:	Thursday-Monday 1300-1700.
Location:	About 5 miles west of the town on Route 170.

From February 1943 until December 1944 Sweetwater was the largest female pilot training school in the country. Over 1,700 gained their wings in this period.

The museum, which opened on 28th May 2005, traces the history of the Women Air Force Service Pilots and Avenger Field. The exhibition is housed in Hangar 1 which was built in 1929 for the original Sweetwater Airport. A number of informative displays showing the life of the students during their time at the school have been set up in the hangar. A typical living quarter area with period furniture can be seen.

An archive of taped interviews with surviving WASP pilots has been gathered over the last few years. Uniforms, flying clothing, photographs and documents are exhibited. Funds are being raised for a memorial to the 38 pilots who lost their lives in military service. The Bobcat was moved from Midland to an adjacent hangar where it will be rebuilt.

TYPE	REG/SER	CON. NO.	PI/NOTES	STATUS
☐ Cessna T-50 Bobcat (AT-17B) (UC-78B)	N64513	5598	43-8078	RAC

NO.1 BRITISH FLYING TRAINING SCHOOL MUSEUM (TX106)

Address: 119 Silent Wings Drive, Terrell Municipal Airport, Terrell, Texas 75160.
Tel: 972-524-1714
Admission: Wednesday, Friday and Saturday 1000-1600.
Location: About 2 miles south east of the town off Route 429.

During World War II there were six flying training schools for British pilots and Terrell was the largest of these. When the United States entered the war American students joined the classes. The museum has been set up to trace the story of the school.

On show are many log books, training material, items of memorabilia and uniforms. Among the types used were Boeing-Stearman PT-13D Kaydets and North American AT-6A Texans. Over 2,000 pilots gained their wings at Terrell before the unit closed in 1945.

OCEAN STAR OFFSHORE DRILLING RIG AND MUSEUM (TX107)

Address: Pier 19, Harborside Driave and 20th Street, Galveston, Texas 77550.
Tel: 409-706-7827   **Fax:** 409-766-1424   **Email:** osmuseum@aol.com
Admission: October-April daily 1000-1600; May-September daily 1000-1700.
Location: On the coast in the city.

The workings of a modern rig are portrayed at the museum. Exhibits are on three decks and show how oil and gas are obtained and transported around the world. There are many working models and video presentations to be seen. The environmental implications are explained in detail. Also on the site is the Oil Industry Hall of Fame which honours those who pioneered the work of drilling under the sea. Helicopters have played an important role in taking crew members to offshore platforms and a Bell Jet Ranger is parked on the flight deck. This aircraft is only a shell and has been assembled from parts of several withdrawn machines.

TYPE	REG/SER	CON. NO.	PI/NOTES	STATUS
☐ Bell 206A Jet Ranger			Composite.	PV

ODESSA MONUMENT (TX108)

Location: On permanent view at Ector County Airport which is north of the town on Highway 385.

TYPE	REG/SER	CON. NO.	PI/NOTES	STATUS
☐ Lockheed 580 (T-33A)	52-9233	580-7017		PV

PARIS MONUMENT (TX109)

Location: On permanent view at Tiger Field which is about 5 miles west of the town.

TYPE	REG/SER	CON. NO.	PI/NOTES	STATUS
☐ Martin 4-0-4	N255S	14246	N498A	PV

PASADENA MONUMENT (TX110)

Location: On permanent view at ALP 521 at 2300 Preston Road.

TYPE	REG/SER	CON. NO.	PI/NOTES	STATUS
☐ McDonnell M.98EN Phantom II (F-4D)	65-0777	1849		PV

PERMIAN BASIN PETROLEUM MUSEUM (TX111)

Address: 1500 Interstate 20 West, Midland, Texas 79701-2041.
Tel: 432-683-4403/4   **Email:** info@petroleummuseum.org
Admission: Monday-Saturday 0900-1700; Sunday 1400-1700.
Location: Off Interstate 20 just west of the city.

Exhibits tracing the development of the oil industry in Texas are on show in this excellent museum. The history of the region is also covered.

The Luscombe Silvaire on show was used for 23 years on pipeline patrol duties. There is a gallery devoted to the innovative Chapparal cars which won many races in the 1960s, 1970s and 1980s. Jim Hall and Hall Sharp set up the company and these vehicles were designed and built in a Midland workshop. They achieved notable success at long distance races around the world.

TYPE	REG/SER	CON. NO.	PI/NOTES	STATUS
☐ Luscombe 8F Silvaire	N2645	6282	NC1862B	PV

585

On show at the Fort Worth Veterans Memorial Park is this Northrop F-5E. (John Mounce) [TX66]

This dramatically posed pair of Northrop T-38As can be seen outside the Space Center at Houston. (Derek Heley) [TX126]

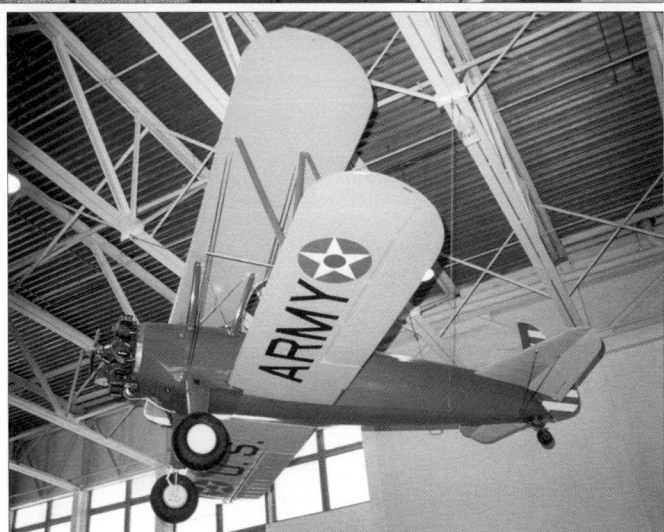

This Boeing-Stearman PT-17 hangs in one of the halls at the Hill Aerospace Museum. [UT5]

PERMIAN BASIN VIETNAM VETERANS MEMORIAL (TX112)

Address:	9000 Wright Drive, PO Box 2178, Midland, Texas 79702.
Tel:	info@veteransmemorial.org
Admission:	On permanent view.
Location:	At the airport which is about 8 miles west of the city off Interstate 20.

This memorial honours local people who were killed in military service. Their names are recorded on plaques. The Iroquois moved to the site in late 2002 and was restored for the display. The type served in large numbers in a variety of roles in the conflict so it is appropriate that one has been put on display.

TYPE	REG/SER	CON. NO.	PI/NOTES	STATUS
☐ Bell 205 Iroquois (UH-1H)	73-21676	13364		PV

PERRIN AIR FORCE BASE MUSEUM (TX113)

Address:	4575 Airport Drive, Denison, Texas 75020.
Tel:	903-786-8741 **Email:** jimfarr@texoma.net
Admission:	Tuesday-Saturday 1000-1600.
Location:	About 4 miles west of the town.

The airfield was constructed soon after the Pearl Harbor attack and became a large flying training school, a role that was continued until its closure in 1946. The site was reactivated in 1948 and housed a variety of training and combat types up to 1971 when the Air Force left. In the late 1950s longer runways were built and jets moved in. Among the types operated was the F-86D Sabre The airfield is now the local county airport. The museum, which opened in 2004, moved into the first phase of a new building the following year. A fascinating display of uniforms, photographs, documents, and memorabilia can be seen.

The T-37 arrived from Sheppard Air Force Base.

TYPE	REG/SER	CON. NO.	PI/NOTES	STATUS
☐ Cessna 318B Tweety Bird (T-37B)	59-0361	40523		PV
☐ North American NA-173 Sabre (F-86D) (F-86L)	51-6144	173-288		PV

PIONEER FLIGHT MUSEUM (TX114)

Address:	190 Pershing Lane, Kingsbury, Texas 78638
Tel:	830-639-4162 **Email:** vahf@gvtc.com
Admission:	Monday-Friday 0900-1600.
Location:	About 10 miles north east of San Antonio off Route 78.

Ground was broken for museum building in 2000. The group has now acquired an original World War I hangar from Dodd Field at Fort Sam Houston and this will be assembled and rebuilt as the main exhibition hall. An appeal has been launched to raise funds for the restoration of this historic building.

Roger Freeman has built a number of replicas over the last few years and some of these will be on show. The Farman biplane now on show at the new Hong Kong Airport was built here. The Blériot is the earliest design attempted. This aircraft has been constructed to the original plans but is powered by a modern engine. There are a number of World War I types completed and others are planned. Many of these projects are being worked on by teams of volunteers. The Alexander Eaglerock was built in Colorado Springs between 1925 and 1934 with over 900 sold. Two other classic biplanes from the 1920s are the KR-31 and the now rare Rearwin Ken-Royce design. Only five of the latter were built and just the one in this collection survives. This biplane is being rebuilt in a nearby workshop and will join the museum when completed.

Two Bristol Fighter projects have been acquired. One is a replica and the other a genuine airframe. The latter was one of a batch of fuselages used as roof trusses in a barn at Weston-on-the-Green in Oxfordshire in England. This one went to Canada before moving south to Texas.

The majority of the Thomas Morse scouts were registered to the Freeman Heritage Collection in the autumn of 2006 and it is believed a number of original components have been acquired for future rebuilds.

TYPE	REG/SER	CON. NO.	PI/NOTES	STATUS
☐ Alexander Eaglerock A-1	NC8225	790	NC8221, N8221	PVA
☐ Blériot XI (R)	N1909E	VA1		PVA
☐ Bristol 14 F.2B Fighter	N2751D		D2751	RAC
☐ Bristol 14 F.2B Fighter (R)	N2743A	A-2743		RAC
☐ Curtiss 1C Jenny (JN-4D)	N3229	3229		RA
☐ Curtiss JN-4 Canuck	N308F	C-308		PVC
☐ Dormoy Flying Bathtub (R)	N14HD	143		PV
☐ Fairchild 22 C7D	NC14302	915	NC14338, N14338	RA
☐ Fokker D VII (R)	N1918H	VA3		PVA
☐ Fokker Dr I (R)	N1917H	VA4		PVA
☐ Kreider-Reisner KR-31 Challenger (C-2)	NC7563	200	NC7563, N7563	PVA
☐ Luscombe 8A Silvaire	NC25144	1068	NC25144, N25144	PVA
☐ Meyers OTW-125	N34310	53	NC34310	PVA
☐ Pietenpol P-9 Sky Scout (R)	N1932G	VA2		PVA
☐ Piper J-3C-65 Cub				RA
☐ Piper J-3C-65 Cub	NC88313	15931	NC88313, N88313	RAC
☐ Piper J-4A Cub Coupe				RA
☐ Rearwin 7000 Sportster	NC15896	477	NC15897, N15897	PV
☐ Rearwin Ken-Royce 2000C	NC592H	103	NC592H, N592H	RAC
☐ Royal Aircraft Factory S.E.5A (R)	N8152	F8157		PVA
☐ Sopwith F.1 Camel (R)	N6337	N6337		PVA
☐ Standard J-1	N598EF	T-4598		RA
☐ Thomas-Morse S-4C	N38663		38663	RA
☐ Thomas-Morse S-4C	N3880P		38802, NC4725	RA
☐ Thomas-Morse S-4C	N3885L		38850	RA

Texas

☐ Thomas-Morse S-4C	N38882		38882, NC3932	RA
☐ Thomas-Morse S-4C (R)				RAC
☐ Thomas-Morse S-4C (R)	N38923	1		PVA
☐ Thomas-Morse S-5	N761VA	761		RA
☐ Wilcox Great Lakes Replica	N318Y	6829-D-367		RA

PLAINVIEW MONUMENT (TX115)

Location: On permanent view at Hale County Airport just south west of the town.

TYPE	REG/SER	CON. NO.	PI/NOTES	STATUS
☐ Lockheed 580 (T-33A)	51-6753	580-6085		PV

PLISKA AIRCRAFT MUSEUM (TX116)

Address: PO Box 60305, Midland International Airport, Midland, Texas 79711.
Tel: 432-560-2000
Admission: At all times.
Location: About 8 miles west of the city off Interstate 20.

John Pliska settled in Midland in 1903 and six years later he opened his own blacksmith's shop. On 19th November 1911 Robert Fowler landed at Midland in his Wright Flyer II whilst attempting to win the prize for the first coast-to-coast flight.

This aroused Pliska's interest and with the help of Gray Coggin he set about building an aircraft. They took photographs and made sketches of the Wright to aid construction. Their aircraft flew distances up to two miles and it was the first aircraft to be built in Texas.

The biplane was stored in his workshop until 1962 when the building was demolished. His children gave the aircraft to the city and the machine was restored and placed in a special building in 1965. Expansion of the airport facilities caused the museum to be in a restricted area.

The aircraft has now been moved to a site in the new terminal building. There is also a display tracing the history of the field from its opening in 1927 and this features its military role in World War II.

TYPE	REG/SER	CON. NO.	PI/NOTES	STATUS
☐ Pliska Biplane				PV

PORT LAVACA MONUMENT (TX117)

Location: On permanent view at VFW 4403 at 16 Conrad Road in the town.

TYPE	REG/SER	CON. NO.	PI/NOTES	STATUS
☐ Bell 209 Huey Cobra (AH-1G) (AH-1F)	67-15700	20364		PV

RAMIN COLLECTION (TX118)

Address: 5902 FM1960 West, Houston, Texas 77069.
Admission: By prior permission only.
Location: At an airfield in the area.

This private collection contains one of the few surviving Luscombe Phantoms. This aircraft made its maiden flight in October 1936 and was sold to a Cuban pilot soon afterwards. The aircraft has had many owners since and in the 1970s spent a period in the old EAA Museum at Hales Corners in Wisconsin.

The Luscombe 11A appeared in the late 1940s and just over 90 were sold. The Eaglet is a 1980s homebuilt design. Over 280 Mooney Mites were built in Wichita, Kansas and Kerrville, Texas between 1947 and 1955. The low-wing single-seater is of mainly wooden construction and the M-18C used a 65 hp Continental.

TYPE	REG/SER	CON. NO.	PI/NOTES	STATUS
☐ Eaglet 1A	N8381	001		RA
☐ Luscombe 1 Phantom	NC1025	112	NC1025, 1025	RAA
☐ Luscombe 8A Silvaire	N4580	1123	NC25218	RA
☐ Luscombe 8A Silvaire	N45939	2466	NC45939	RA
☐ Luscombe 8A Silvaire	N72059	3486	NC72059	RA
☐ Luscombe 8A Silvaire	N1946K	4673	NC1946K	RA
☐ Luscombe 8A Silvaire	N2564K	5291	NC2564K	RA
☐ Luscombe 8A Silvaire	N2867K	5594	NC2867K	RA
☐ Luscombe 8A Silvaire	N2132B	6559	NC2132B	RA
☐ Luscombe 11A	N6895C	11-116	NC1610B, N1610B	RA
☐ Mooney M-18C Mite	N4160	326		RA
☐ Piper J-3L-65 Cub	N21659	2552	NC21659	RA
☐ Stinson 108-1 Voyager	N8761K	108-1761		RA

RANDOLPH AIR FORCE BASE HERITAGE PARK (TX119)

Address: 12 FTW/PA, 1 Washington Court, Randolph Air Force Base, Texas 78150-5001.
Tel: 210-652-4410   **Email:** public.affairs@randolph.af.mil
Admission: By prior permission only.
Location: About 20 miles north east of San Antonio off Route 78.

The site opened as Aviation Field, San Antonio in 1928 but was soon named after Captain William M. Randolph who was killed in the crash of an AT-4 in February 1928. Until the outbreak of World War II its main role was the training of pilots but towards end of the conflict B-29s moved in.

After the declaration of peace the base reverted to its former task. Conversion training on a variety of types occurred during the 1950s and from 1948 a basic flying school has been in residence. A heritage park has been set up within the base.

TYPE	REG/SER	CON. NO.	PI/NOTES	STATUS
☐ Beech C18S Expeditor (SNB-1)	'4460'	4460	Bu39819, N1389M, N450M, '24066'	RAX
☐ Beech D45 Mentor (T-34B)	'6552'	BG-397	Bu144090, '33309'	RAX
☐ Boeing 737-253 (T-43A)	73-1153	20700		RA
☐ Cessna 172F Mescalero (T-41A)	65-5226	17253271	65-5226, N5226F	RA
☐ Cessna 318B Tweety Bird (318A) (T-37A) (T-37B)	'62-730'	40006	54-2730	RAX
☐ Convair 240-27 (T-29C)	53-3489	443		RA
☐ Lockheed 580 (T-33A)	53-6147	580-9768		RA
☐ North American NA-121 Texan (AT-6F)	'84560'	121-42632	44-81910	RAX
☐ North American NA-159 Trojan (T-28A)	'17882'	159-207	49-1695	RAX
☐ Northrop N-156T Talon (T-38A)	61-0838	N.5204	61-0838, '61638'	RA

RATTLESNAKE BOMBER BASE MUSEUM (TX120)

Address:	PO Box 120, Pyote, Texas 79777.
Tel:	432-389-5660
Admission:	Saturday 0900-1800; Sunday 1400-1800.
Location:	About 1 mile south west of the town off Route 1927.

Construction of the airfield started in 1942 and it opened on 5th January 1943. Bomber crews for B-17s and B-29s were trained at the base. At the end of the conflict the vast site was used for storing surplus aircraft and by 1948 just over 2,000 were parked there.

When the Korean War started many of the B-29s were put back into service. Operations were run down and in the late 1950s a radar station was installed but this did not last for long. The site was sold off in 1966. The five large hangars were gradually demolished.

The main gate has now been restored and two plaques trace the history of the field. In the town a museum has been set up to honour those who served at Pyote. Uniforms, documents, photographs and memorabilia are on show.

SAN ANGELO MONUMENTS (TX121)

Location:	On permanent view at two locations in the town.

TYPE	REG/SER	CON. NO.	PI/NOTES	STATUS
☐ Bell 205 Iroquois (UH-1D) (UH-1H)	65-9889	4933	At a Vietnam Memorial at Mathis Field which is about 8 miles south of the town on Route 277.	PV
☐ Lockheed 580 (T-33A)	58-0542	580-1511	58-0542, N10265 – at the JROTC on Highway 67.	PV

SCIENCE SPECTRUM MUSEUM (TX122)

Address:	2579 South Loop 289, PO Box 93178, Lubbock, Texas 79423.
Tel:	806-745-6299 **Fax:** 806-745-1115 **Email:** spectrum@door.net
Admission:	Tuesday-Friday 1000-1700; Saturday 1000-1800; Sunday 1300-1700.
Location:	On Route 289 south of the city.

This modern centre has over 200 interactive exhibits and the Omnimax Theatre which shows films on many aspects of science. There is an area devoted to flight highlighting the work on NASA.

Other exhibitions focus on the wild life of the region and the visitor can see a large aquarium. Another section is devoted to the science of sport where the visitor can try out many machines to test their performance and health.

TYPE	REG/SER	CON. NO.	PI/NOTES	STATUS
☐ Northrop N-156T Talon (T-38A)	61-0902	N.5268		PV

SHEPPARD AIR FORCE BASE HERITAGE CENTER AND TECHNICAL TRAINING CENTER (TX123)

Address:	STTC/PA, Sheppard Air Force Base, Texas 76311-5000.
Tel:	940-676-2732 **Email:** 82trw.pawebteam@sheppard.af.mil
Admission:	By prior permission only.
Location:	About 4 miles north of Wichita Falls on Route 240.

Set up in 1941 as Technical School, Wichita Falls, the base was soon renamed Sheppard Field after Senator Morris E. Sheppard who had recently died. He was a Texan and chairman of the Senate Military Affairs Committee. The site closed in 1945 but was reactivated three years later for basic flying training and aircraft maintenance instruction. A bomb wing used the field between 1959 and 1966. In 1967 the training of German pilots for the Luftwaffe started and other NATO countries have also sent their personnel to the base.

At the current time the 82nd Wing is in residence. This unit operates the Euro-NATO Joint Jet Pilot Training Scheme. Also on the field is the Sheppard Technical Training Center which has a wide range of instructional aircraft. Technicians receive instruction in all aspects of airframe, engine and systems maintenance. The future of the base in its present form is in some doubt as a report in 2005 recommended that many of its tasks should move. The Heritage Center traces the history of the site from the early days.

TYPE	REG/SER	CON. NO.	PI/NOTES	STATUS
☐ Boeing 464-201-7 Stratofortress (B-52D)	56-0589	17272		RA
☐ Boeing 464-253 Stratofortress (B-52G)	58-0200	464268	Without tail – instructional airframe.	RA
☐ Boeing 464-261 Stratofortress (B-52H)	61-0022	464449	Instructional airframe.	RA
☐ Boeing 464-261 Stratofortress (B-52H)	61-0025	464452	Instructional airframe.	RA
☐ Boeing 717-146 Stratotanker (KC-135A) (KC-135E)	56-3607	17356	Instructional airframe.	RA

Texas

☐ Boeing 717-146 Stratotanker (KC-135A) (KC-135E)	56-3623	17372	Instructional airframe.	RA
☐ Boeing 717-146 Stratotanker (KC-135A) (KC-135E)	56-3645	17394	Instructional airframe.	RA
☐ Boeing 717-148 Stratotanker (KC-135A) (KC-135E)	57-1431	17502	Instructional airframe.	RA
☐ Boeing 717-148 Stratotanker (KC-135A) (KC-135E)	57-1485	17556	Instructional airframe.	RA
☐ Boeing 717-148 Stratotanker (KC-135A) (KC-135E)	57-1503	17574	Instructional airframe.	RA
☐ Cessna 318B Tweety Bird (318A) (T-37A) (T-37B)	56-3520	40092		RA
☐ Cessna 318B Tweety Bird (318A) (T-37A) (T-37B)	58-1891	40316	Instructional airframe.	RA
☐ Cessna 318D Dragonfly (318C) (T-37C) (YAT-37D) (YA-37A)	62-5950	40718		RA
☐ Convair 240-17 (T-29A)	49-1934	201		RA
☐ Convair 8-10 Delta Dagger (F-102A)	57-0826	8-10-792		RA
☐ Fairchild-Republic YA-10A Thunderbolt II	73-1665	A10-2	Instructional airframe.	RA
☐ Fairchild-Republic A-10A Thunderbolt II	75-0260	A10-9	Instructional airframe.	RA
☐ Fairchild-Republic A-10A Thunderbolt II	77-0199	A10-124	Instructional airframe.	RA
☐ Fairchild-Republic A-10A Thunderbolt II	79-0225	A10-489	Instructional airframe.	RA
☐ Fairchild-Republic A-10A Thunderbolt II	80-0143	A10-493	Instructional airframe.	RA
☐ Fairchild-Republic A-10A Thunderbolt II	80-0216	A10-566	Instructional airframe.	RA
☐ General Dynamics F-111A	63-9773	A1-08		RA
☐ General Dynamics 401 Fighting Falcon (F-16A)	79-0330	61-115	Instructional airframe.	RA
☐ General Dynamics 401 Fighting Falcon (F-16A)	80-0481	61-202		RA
☐ General Dynamics 401 Fighting Falcon (F-16A)	81-0678	61-359	Instructional airframe.	RA
☐ General Dynamics 401 Fighting Falcon (F-16A)	81-0782	61-463	Instructional airframe.	RA
☐ General Dynamics 401 Fighting Falcon (F-16A)	81-0789	61-470	Instructional airframe.	RA
☐ General Dynamics 401 Fighting Falcon (F-16A)	82-0919	61-512	Instructional airframe.	RA
☐ General Dynamics 401 Fighting Falcon (F-16A)	82-1006	61-599	Instructional airframe.	RA
☐ General Dynamics 401 Fighting Falcon (F-16B)	78-0080	62-6	Instructional airframe.	RA
☐ General Dynamics 401 Fighting Falcon (F-16B)	78-0088	62-14	Instructional airframe.	RA
☐ General Dynamics 401 Fighting Falcon (F-16B)	78-0089	62-15	Instructional airframe.	RA
☐ General Dynamics 401 Fighting Falcon (F-16B)	79-0420	62-52	Instructional airframe.	RA
☐ General Dynamics 401 Fighting Falcon (F-16B)	79-0422	62-54	Instructional airframe.	RA
☐ General Dynamics 401 Fighting Falcon (F-16B)	79-0427	62-59	Instructional airframe.	RA
☐ General Dynamics 401 Fighting Falcon (F-16B)	80-0633	62-75	Instructional airframe.	RA
☐ General Dynamics 401 Fighting Falcon (F-16C)	89-2146	1C-299	Instructional airframe.	RA
☐ General Dynamics 401 Fighting Falcon (F-16C)	83-1124	5C-7	Instructional airframe.	RA
☐ General Dynamics 401 Fighting Falcon (F-16C)	83-1125	5C-8	Instructional airframe.	RA
☐ General Dynamics 401 Fighting Falcon (F-16C)	83-1127	5C-10	Instructional airframe.	RA
☐ General Dynamics 401 Fighting Falcon (F-16C)	83-1143	5C-26	Instructional airframe.	RA
☐ General Dynamics 401 Fighting Falcon (F-16C)	87-0251	5C-512	Instructional airframe.	RA
☐ General Dynamics 401 Fighting Falcon (F-16C)	87-0295	5C-556	Instructional airframe.	RA
☐ General Dynamics 401 Fighting Falcon (F-16C)	87-0305	5C-566	Instructional airframe.	RA
☐ General Dynamics 401 Fighting Falcon (F-16C)	87-0313	5C-574	Instructional airframe.	RA
☐ General Dynamics 401 Fighting Falcon (F-16C)	87-0329	5C-590	Instructional airframe.	RA
☐ General Dynamics 401 Fighting Falcon (F-16D)	86-0039	5C-415	Instructional airframe.	RA
☐ Lockheed 182-1A Hercules (182-44-03) (C-130A)	57-0471	182-3178	Instructional airframe.	RA
☐ Lockheed 182-1A Hercules (182-44-03) (C-130A) (C-130D)	57-0486	182-3193	Instructional airframe.	RA
☐ Lockheed 382-4B Hercules (C-130E)	61-2361	382-3662	Instructional airframe.	RA
☐ Lockheed 382-4B Hercules (C-130E)	61-2371	382-3716	Instructional airframe.	RA
☐ Lockheed 382-4B Hercules (C-130E)	62-1790	382-3737	Instructional airframe.	RA
☐ Lockheed 382-4B Hercules (C-130E)	62-1795	382-3746	Instructional airframe.	RA
☐ Lockheed 382-4B Hercules (C-130E)	62-1807	382-3761	Instructional airframe.	RA
☐ Lockheed 382-4B Hercules (C-130E)	62-1812	382-3774	Instructional airframe.	RA
☐ Lockheed 382-4B Hercules (C-130E)	63-7813	382-3883	Instructional airframe.	RA
☐ Lockheed 382-8B Hercules (C-130E)	63-7768	382-3834	Instructional airframe.	RA
☐ Lockheed 382-4B Hercules (C-130E)	63-7838	382-3908	Instructional airframe.	RA
☐ Lockheed 382-4B Hercules (C-130E)	63-7849	382-3919	Instructional airframe.	RA
☐ Lockheed 382-4B Hercules (C-130E)	63-7779	382-3968	Instructional airframe.	RA
☐ Lockheed 382-8B Hercules (C-130E)	64-0535	382-4024	Instructional airframe.	RA
☐ Lockheed 382-8B Hercules (C-130E)	64-0542	382-4032	Instructional airframe.	RA
☐ Lockheed 382-8B Hercules (C-130E)	64-17680	382-4064	Instructional airframe.	RA
☐ Lockheed 383-04-05 Starfighter (F-104C)	56-0912	183-1200		RA
☐ Lockheed 580 (T-33A) (TV-2) (T-33B)	'91151'	580-6941	51-9157, Bu131878	RAX
☐ Lockheed 580 (T-33A) (TV-2) (T-33B)	'32155'	580-8594	53-5255, Bu156157	RAX
☐ McDonnell M.36CM Voodoo (F-101C)	56-0009	153		RA
☐ McDonnell M.98DE Phantom II (F-4C)	63-7426	371		RA
☐ McDonnell M.199-1A Eagle (F-15A)	72-0115	15/A013	Instructional airframe.	RA
☐ McDonnell M.199-1A Eagle (F-15A)	74-0113	88/A074	Instructional airframe.	RA
☐ McDonnell M.199-1A Eagle (F-15A)	76-0022	201/A174	Instructional airframe.	RA
☐ McDonnell M.199-1A Eagle (F-15A)	76-0054	238/A206	Instructional airframe.	RA
☐ McDonnell M.199-1A Eagle (F-15A)	76-0067	254/A219	Instructional airframe.	RA
☐ McDonnell M.199-1A Eagle (F-15A)	76-0079	268/A231	Instructional airframe.	RA
☐ McDonnell M.199-1A Eagle (F-15A)	76-0083	273/A235	Instructional airframe.	RA
☐ McDonnell M.199-1A Eagle (F-15A)	76-0101	300/A253	Instructional airframe.	RA
☐ McDonnell M.199-1A Eagle (F-15A)	77-0095	377/A307	Instructional airframe.	RA
☐ McDonnell M.199-1A Eagle (F-15A)	77-0125	412/A337	Instructional airframe.	RA
☐ McDonnell M.199-1A Eagle (F-15A)	77-0150	441/A362	Instructional airframe.	RA
☐ McDonnell M.199-1B Eagle (TF-15A) (F-15B)	76-0135	274/B037	Instructional airframe.	RA
☐ McDonnell M.199-1B Eagle (TF-15A) (F-15B)	76-0136	281/B038	Instructional airframe.	RA
☐ McDonnell M.199-1B Eagle (TF-15A) (F-15B)	77-0154	339/B045		RA
☐ McDonnell M.199-1B Eagle (TF-15A) (F-15B)	77-0156	357/B047	Instructional airframe.	RA
☐ McDonnell M.199-1B Eagle (TF-15A) (F-15B)	77-0157	366/B048	Instructional airframe.	RA
☐ McDonnell M.199-1B Eagle (TF-15A) (F-15B)	74-0142	90/B015		RA
☐ McDonnell M.199-1D Eagle (F-15D)	80-0061	727/D033	Instructional airframe.	RA
☐ McDonnell M.199-1E Eagle (F-15E)	96-0203	1339/E213	Instructional airframe.	RA
☐ North American NA-223 Super Sabre (F-100D)	54-2151	223-31		RA
☐ Northrop N-156T Talon (T-38A)	61-0858	N.5224		RA
☐ Northrop N-156T Talon (T-38A)	61-0859	N.5225	Instructional airframe.	RA
☐ Northrop N-156T Talon (T-38A)	61-0895	N.5261	Instructional airframe.	RA
☐ Northrop N-156T Talon (T-38A)	62-3690	N.5395		RA

☐ Northrop N-156T Talon (T-38A)	63-8125	N.5472		RA
☐ Northrop N-156T Talon (T-38A)	64-13281	N.5710		RA
☐ Republic F-105D Thunderchief	61-0175	D-370		RA
☐ Rockwell B-1B Lancer (FSM)			Instructional airframe.	RA
☐ Sikorsky S-65A (HH-53C) (MH-53J) (MH-53M)	73-1648	65386	Instructional airframe.	RA
☐ Sikorsky S-65A Sea Stallion (CH-53A)	'70052'	65138	Bu154867, 67-30052 – instructional airframe.	RAX

SILENT WINGS MUSEUM (TX124)

Address:	6202 North I-27, Lubbock, Texas 79403-9710.
Tel:	806-775-2047 Fax: 806-775-3133 Email: info@silentwingsmuseum.com
Admission:	Tuesday-Saturday 1000-1700; Sunday 1300-1700.
Location:	At the airport which is about 5 miles north of the town off Interstate 27.

The National World War II Glider Pilots Association was formed in 1971. Their first aim was to locate a Waco Hadrian glider and restore it for public display. One was found in Fresno in California which had been parked on top of a tyre shop to advertise the business. The aircraft was bought and restored for their 1979 reunion.

They decided to set up a museum and this opened on 10th November 1979 at Terrell. A vast amount of memorabilia, documents, photographs, uniforms etc. were on show and they traced the story of glider operations in the conflict. Films were shown of the training of glider pilots and of airborne troops in action. The majority of the glider pilots had trained at South Plains Army Airfield, the former Lubbock Municipal Airport.

Funds were raised for a purpose-built museum which opened at the airport in Lubbock on 19th October 2002. The centrepiece of the display is the restored Waco CG-4A and also on show are a number of training gliders.

TYPE	REG/SER	CON. NO.	PI/NOTES	STATUS
☐ Airspeed AS.58 Horsa II (FSM)				RAC
☐ Coffman Glider				PV
☐ Douglas DC-3A-467 Skytrain (C-47B) (R4D-6) (SC-47J)	Bu17278	14379/25824	43-48563, Bu17278, N7634C, N40, N40180	PV
☐ Laister-Kauffman LK.10B (TG-4A)	N58178	129	(USAAF)	PV
☐ Pratt-Read PR-G1 (LNE-1) (TG-32)				PV
☐ Schweizer SGS.2-8 (TG-2)	N47902	52	(USAAF)	PV
☐ Schweizer SGS.2-12 (TG-3A)	N64307		(USAAF)	PV
☐ Waco NZR Hadrian (CG-4A)			Front fuselage only.	PV
☐ Waco NZR Hadrian (CG-4A)	45-15691			PV

SNYDER MONUMENT (TX125)

Location:	On permanent view at the airport which is about 3miles south west of the town.

TYPE	REG/SER	CON. NO.	PI/NOTES	STATUS
☐ McDonnell M.36BA Voodoo (F-101B)	59-0423	747		PV
☐ Republic F-105B Thunderchief	57-5789	B-026		PV

SPACE CENTER HOUSTON (TX126)

Address:	1601 NASA Parkway, Houston Texas 77058.
Tel:	281-244-2100
Admission:	Monday-Friday 1000-1700; Saturday-Sunday 1000-1800.
Location:	About 25 miles south of the city.

The Johnson Space Center has many exhibits tracing the history of space exploration. There are several interactive displays and historic exhibits to be seen. Regular tours of the operational part of the complex are offered.

TYPE	REG/SER	CON. NO.	PI/NOTES	STATUS
☐ Northrop N-156T Talon (T-38A)	N968NA	N.5821	65-10402	PV
☐ Northrop N-156T Talon (T-38A)	'N900NA'	T.6138	68-8133	PVX

STANTON MONUMENT (TX127)

Location:	On permanent view at a business on Route 137 in the town.

TYPE	REG/SER	CON. NO.	PI/NOTES	STATUS
☐ Bell 204 Iroquois (UH-1B)				PV

STANZEL MODEL AIRCRAFT MUSEUM (TX128)

Address:	311 Baumgarten Street, Schulenburg, Texas 78956.
Tel:	979-743-6559 Fax: 979-743-2525 Email: museum@stanzelmuseum.org
Admission:	Monday, Wednesday, Friday and Saturday 1030-1630.
Location:	In the southern part of the town off Route 77.

The museum honours the work of brothers Victor and Joe Stanzel who were pioneers in model aircraft design and manufacture. They first carved wooden models of famous types in the 1920s.

The first control line model, the 'Tiger Shark', appeared in 1939 and was put into production soon after. The original prototype is one of the highlights of the exhibition. Victor developed control line flying over the next few decades.

The museum, which opened in March 1999, has over 30 displays showing the development of their designs over the 70 years they were produced. The company is still in existence supplying kits to shops around the world.

ST. PHILIP'S COLLEGE (TX129)

Address:	800 Quintana Road, San Antonio, Texas 78211.
Tel:	210-486-7294 **Email:** rcoller@alamo.edu
Admission:	By prior permission only.
Location:	Near Kelly Field.

The college was founded in 1898 and is part of the Alamo Community College District. The Southwest Campus located on part of the old Kelly Air Force base is the home to a wide range of technical courses. Four instructional airframes are known to be in use but there are believed to be several others.

TYPE	REG/SER	CON. NO.	PI/NOTES	STATUS
☐ Bell 206A Kiowa (OH-58A)	N99147	41729	72-21063	RA
☐ Bell 47D-1 Sioux (H-13E) (OH-13E)	51-14093	857		RA
☐ Cessna 318B Tweety Bird (T-37B)	67-14750	41007		RA
☐ Piper PA-23-250 Aztec				RA

SUNSET COLLECTION (TX130)

Address:	Sunset, Texas 76270.
Admission:	By prior permission only.
Location:	Just south of the town off US 71/287.

This private collection is located in a yard in the town. One of the T-33s will be restored to display condition using parts from the other two. The Sikorsky helicopter will also be put on show.

TYPE	REG/SER	CON. NO.	PI/NOTES	STATUS
☐ Lockheed 580 (T-33A)	57-0643	580-1292	Fuselage less tail.	RA
☐ Lockheed 580 (T-33A)	58-0497	580-1466		RA
☐ Lockheed 580 (T-33A)	53-5346	580-8685	Fuselage less tail.	RA
☐ Sikorsky S-61R (CH-3C) (CH-3E)	64-14228	61531		RA

SWEETWATER MONUMENT (TX131)

Location:	On permanent view in Newman Park in the northern part of the town.

TYPE	REG/SER	CON. NO.	PI/NOTES	STATUS
☐ Bell 205 Iroquois (UH-1D) (UH-1H)	65-10014	5058		PV
☐ Lockheed 580 (T-33A)	51-4380	580-5675		PV

TARRANT COUNTY COLLEGE (TX132)

Address:	1500 Houston Street, Fort Worth, Texas 76102.
Tel:	817-515-8223 **Email:** james.grant@tccd.edu
Admission:	By prior permission only.
Location:	At Meacham Field in the north western part of the city.

The large college operates from several sites in the Fort Worth area. The Northwest Campus is home to the aviation department. Hangars and workshops house the fleet of instructional airframes. There are also a number of engines, components and test rigs in use along with a wide range of electronic equipment. Courses leading to FAA airframe, powerplant and avionics licences are run at regular intervals.

TYPE	REG/SER	CON. NO.	PI/NOTES	STATUS
☐ Aero Commander 520	N4121B	520-24		RA
☐ Cessna 152	N6448M	15284732		RA
☐ Cessna 310A Blue Canoe (L-27A) (U-3A)	N1384K	38051	57-5896	RA
☐ Cessna 310B	N709SH	35573		RA
☐ Cessna T210G Turbo Centurion	N2981F	T2100277		RA
☐ Hiller UH12C Raven (H-23G) (OH-23G)	N43441	1382	61-3196	RA
☐ Hughes 269A Osage (TH-55A)	N70552		67-16804	RA
☐ Mitsubishi MU-2B	N2GZ	025	N3557X, N2GT	RA
☐ Piper PA-18-135 Super Cub (L-21B)	N87930	18-4038	54-2638	RA
☐ Piper PA-23 Apache	N2296P	23-908		RA
☐ Piper PA-23-160 Apache	N3379P	23-1339		RA
☐ Piper PA-23-250 Aztec C	N3234L	27-3626		RA

TEXARKANA MONUMENT (TX133)

Location:	On permanent view in Spring Lake Park in the northern part of the town.

TYPE	REG/SER	CON. NO.	PI/NOTES	STATUS
☐ Lockheed 580 (T-33A)	51-4025	580-5319		PV

TEXAS AIR MUSEUM – SOUTH PLAINS CHAPTER (TX134)

Address:	PO Box 667, 12102 FM 400, Slaton, Texas 79364-75528.
Tel:	806-828-4664
Admission:	Saturday 0900-1600.
Location:	At the airport which is about 2 miles north of the town.

The Texas Air Museum was formed in 1985 and set up a display at the Texas Dusting Service airfield near Rio Hondo. Several hangars were constructed and an interesting display was staged. The founding director John Houston died in November 2002 and after a period of little activity the display closed in 2005. This chapter was set up in the mid-1990s and a hangar/workshop was erected.

The exhibition has grown steadily over the years and a number of interesting types can be seen. Several aircraft are maintained in flying condition. The Mitsubishi Ki-51 was designed for ground attack and tactical reconnaissance duties. The prototype flew in the summer of 1939 and by the end of the year 11 were being evaluated. Almost 2,400 were produced by the parent firm and the Tachikawa company. The low-wing monoplane was of similar configuration to the Funk F-23 crop sprayer. The first conversion appeared at many displays and proved to be a popular attraction.

This aircraft was sold in California but more have been modified to represent the Japanese type. The Dove was sold to the USA in 1951 for use as an executive transport. The twin was later used by a number of private owners and small airlines. Also on show are many models and military vehicles along with weapons including a rare Japanese artillery gun. A collection of recently with drawn military types is on show and more aircraft are expected.

Two Messerschmitt Bf 109 projects owned by Malcolm Laing are being rebuilt. The F model was acquired in Italy and one wing carries a Spanish identity plate and the was built by Avia in Czechoslovakia. This will be rebuilt to airworthy standard. The G-2 crashed in the Murmansk region of Russia in April 1943 and the pilot was captured and survived the war. The Stinson 10A is a fairly recent arrival and is now undergoing a major rebuild in the workshops. The aircraft has not flown for several years and needs a great deal of work.

TYPE	REG/SER	CON. NO.	PI/NOTES	STATUS
☐ Beech D18S Expeditor (C18S) (SNB-2) (SNB-2P) (SNB-5) (TC-45J) (UC-45J)	N3483	4335	Bu39219	PV
☐ De Havilland DH.104 Dove 2A	N551JC	04306	N4262C, N640H	PV
☐ Funk F-23	N1127Z	4		RA
☐ Funk F-23	N1128Z	5	Converted to Mitsubishi Ki-51 replica.	PVA
☐ Funk F-23	N1129Z	6	Converted to Mitsubishi Ki-51 replica.	RA
☐ Funk F-23B (F-23)	N1131Z	9	Converted to Mitsubishi Ki-51 replica.	PVA
☐ Grumman G-99 Cougar (F9F-8) (F-9J)	Bu131063	1C		PV
☐ Grumman G-134 Mohawk (OV-1A)				PV
☐ Grumman G-303 Tomcat (F-14A)	Bu160391	247		PV
☐ Hughes 77 Apache (AH-64A)				PV
☐ Lockheed 580 (T-33A)	53-5219	580-8558		PV
☐ McDonnell M.36BA Voodoo (F-101B)	59-0429	753		PV
☐ McDonnell M.98EV Phantom II (F-4J) (F-4S)	Bu157293	3907		PV
☐ McDonnell M.267 Hornet (F/A-18A)	Bu162473	331/A275		PV
☐ Messerschmitt Bf 109F-4/trop		8461		PVC
☐ Messerschmitt Bf 109G-2		10394		PVC
☐ North American NA-168 Texan (T-6G)	N5557V	168-257	49-3153	RAA
☐ North American NA-200 Trojan (T-28B)	N365FL	200-436	Bu138365	PVA
☐ North American NA-346 Buckeye (T-2C)	Bu158599	346-25		PV
☐ Republic F-105D Thunderchief	61-0093	D-288		PV
☐ Stinson 10A Voyager				PVC
☐ Stinson V-77 Reliant (AT-19)	N88026	77-411	43-44126, FB683, Bu11431	PV
☐ Taylorcraft BC-12D	N95004	9404	NC95004	PVC
☐ Taylorcraft DCO-65 Grasshopper (L-2M)	N47344	L-5362	43-26050	PVC
☐ Vought A-7B Corsair II	Bu154431	B71		PV

TEXAS AIR MUSEUM – STINSON CHAPTER (TX135)

Address: 1234 99th Street, San Antonio, Texas 78214.
Tel: 210-977-9885   **Fax:** 210-927-4447   **Email:** info@texasairmuseum.org
Admission: Tuesday-Saturday 1000-1700.
Location: At Stinson Field which is in the southern suburbs of the city.

This branch of the museum was formed in the late 1990s and has premises at the historic Stinson Field which is the second oldest airport in the United States. The old 1930s terminal building still stands and now serves as the control tower. The site opened in 1915 and the Stinson family operated a flying school. Katherine Stinson was the fourth licensed pilot in the country and a replica of her Blériot XI can be seen.

The Christofferson company was established in Washington State in 1910 and later moved to California. The firm ceased to exist after the death of Silas Christofferson in 1916. A number of designs were produced and the Mexican Army ordered a few.

Another replica from the early period is the scale Roe Triplane. A.V. Roe built four triplanes in 1910 all differing in design. The Curtiss Pusher was a popular type in the early days of flying in the USA, a number were built by the firm and several pilots built very similar models for their own use.

When the museum was at Rio Hondo it negotiated a deal with the Norwegian Armed Forces Museum in Oslo. The remains of several Focke-Wulf Fw 190s were recovered from crash sites and transported to Texas. The deal was that the museum would carry out rebuilds of the airframes and one would remain in Texas. The aircraft on show has been rebuilt for static display. A display board showing its history along with photographs of the rebuild is positioned nearby.

The Aerobat III crashed at Brownsville Airport in 1997. Ellis Eichmann built his first flying wing, the Aerobat I, in the late 1930s and it made its maiden flight in 1942. The Pietenpol Aircamper was built by Robert Nortcutt in the late 1970s. Displays tracing the history of the airport and local aviation are being developed. Portrayed are the history of the Stinsons and the aircraft produced by the company. San Antonio is considered to be the birthplace of American military aviation and there are photographs showing activity in the area.

TYPE	REG/SER	CON. NO.	PI/NOTES	STATUS
☐ Blériot XI (R)				PV
☐ Christofferson Biplane (R)				PVC
☐ Curtiss D Pusher (R)				PV
☐ Eichmann Aerobat III	NX17638	1003		PVD
☐ Focke-Wulf Fw 190A-8		732070		PV
☐ Funk B-85C	N77712	342	NC77712	PV

Texas

☐ McDonnell M.36BA Voodoo (F-101B)	59-0421	745		PV
☐ McDonnell M.98DE Phantom II (F-4C)	63-7415	342		PV
☐ Northrop N.35 Scorpion (P-89A) (F-89A) (F-89B) (EF-89B)	49-2434	N.2008		PV
☐ Pietenpol B4-A Aircamper	N36RN	RN-1		PVA
☐ Piper J-3C-65 Cub	NC32851	5660	NC32851, N32851	PVA
☐ Republic F-105G Thunderchief (F-105F)	63-8363	F-140		PV
☐ Roe 1910 Triplane (Scale R)	N46756			PV
☐ Sikorsky S-58 Seahorse (HUS-1A) (UH-34E)	Bu145728	58896		PV
☐ Waco 10 (GXE)	NC7970	1801	NC7970, N7970	PVA

TEXAS CITY MONUMENT (TX136)

Location: On permanent view in Bay Street Park in the eastern part of the town.

TYPE	REG/SER	CON. NO.	PI/NOTES	STATUS
☐ Burgess H (R)				PV
☐ North American NA-243 Super Sabre (F-100F)	56-3814	243-90		PV

TEXAS INFORMATION CENTER (TX137)

Location: On permanent view north of Halletsville on Route 77.

TYPE	REG/SER	CON. NO.	PI/NOTES	STATUS
☐ Bell 209 Huey Cobra (AH-1G) (AH-1F)	67-15470	20134		PV

TEXAS MILITARY FORCES MUSEUM (TX138)

Address: 2200 West 35th Street, PO Box 5218, Austin, Texas 78703-1222.
Tel: 512-782-5659 **Email:** museum@tx.ngb.army.mil
Admission: Wednesday-Sunday 1000-1600.
Location: At Camp Mabry in the north western suburbs of the city.

Camp Mabry is named after Brigadier General Woodford H. Mabry who was Adjutant General of Texas in the 1890s. The site is the headquarters of the military forces of the state.

A project to establish a museum was started in 1986. In 1990 Building 6, constructed in 1916, was allocated for display purposes. The exhibition opened on 14th November 1992. The museum is dedicated to Brigadier John C.L. Scribner. He was born in Laredo and after serving in the Army joined the Texas State Guard. After he retired the Adjutant General asked him to set up the museum.

The history of Texas forces and their role in conflicts around the world are told in detail. There are some superb dioramas to be seen including one depicting the final assault on the Alamo. Uniforms, equipment and vehicles feature prominently.

Two Piper liaison aircraft obtained from the US Army Transportation Museum in Virginia have been restored for the indoor display. A line of missiles, tanks, guns and aircraft is located by the fence close to the main road which passes the site. Items captured during World War II are on view.

TYPE	REG/SER	CON. NO.	PI/NOTES	STATUS
☐ Bell 204 Iroquois (UH-1C) (UH-1M)	64-14142	1266		PV
☐ Bell 205 Iroquois (UH-1D) (UH-1H)	66-16189	5883		PV
☐ Bell 206A Kiowa (OH-58A)	71-20486	41347		PV
☐ Bell 209 Huey Cobra (AH-1G) (AH-1S)	68-15153	20687		PV
☐ Hiller UH12B Raven (H-23B) (OH-23B)	51-16386	637	Fitted with boom from c/n 452 51-16260.	RA
☐ Hiller UH12B Raven (H-23B) (OH-23B)	51-16387	638	51-16387, N4784C	PV
☐ McDonnell M.98DJ Phantom II (F-4C)	64-0712	969		PV
☐ North American NA-190 Sabre (F-86D) (F-86L)	52-3770	190-173		PV
☐ Piper J-3C-65 Cub (L-4B)	'36833921'	10134	43-949,N9064C	PVX
☐ Piper PA-18-125 Super Cub (L-21A)	'18573'	18-573	51-15656, N3970A	PVX

TEXAS STATE TECHNICAL COLLEGE – ABILENE (TX139)

Address: 650 East Highway 80, Abiline, Texas 79601.
Tel: 325-672-7091 **Email:** clark.evans@tstc.edu
Admission: By prior permission only.
Location: On the northern side of the airport.

The airfield is home to the TSTC West Texas Air Academy which trains pilots up to commercial standard. A fleet of Piper Warriors, Arrows and Seminoles are in use. There are a number of ground instructional aircraft in the hangars where courses leading to airframe, and engine and avionics licenses take place.

TYPE	REG/SER	CON. NO.	PI/NOTES	STATUS
☐ Bell 205 Iroquois (UH-1H)	66-16652	8846		RA
☐ Cessna 337M Super Skymaster (O-2A)	N455DA	337M0401	69-7603	RA
☐ Hughes 269A Osage (TH-55A)	N76878	980985	67-16878	RA
☐ Mitsubishi MU-2J (MU-2B-35)	N245MA	576		RA

TEXAS STATE TECHNICAL COLLEGE – HARLINGEN (TX140)

Address: 1902 North Loop 499, Harlingen, Texas 78550.
Tel: 956-364-4756 **Email:** tomcross@harlingen.tstc.edu
Admission: By prior permission only.
Location: Near Valley International Airport in the north eastern part of the town.

The college has a fleet of instructional airframes in the Aviation Maintenance Building on the main campus just across the road from the airport. The list is not complete and other types are believed to be in use. The ex-military Hiller helicopter has been present for many years. Several engines are also in the workshops.

TYPE	REG/SER	CON. NO.	PI/NOTES	STATUS
☐ Aero Commander 680V (680T)	N66FV	1676-59	N4345R, N580M	RA
☐ Bell 205 Iroquois (UH-1H) (UH-1V)	68-15743	10673		RA
☐ Hiller UH12D Raven (H-23D) (OH-23D)	N49777	1137	58-5488	RA
☐ Piper PA-23-250 Aztec				RA
☐ Piper PA-28-180 Cherokee				RA

TEXAS STATE TECHNOLOGY COLLEGE – WACO (TX141)

Address: 3801 Campus Drive, Waco, Texas 76705.
Tel: 254-799-3611 **Email:** jan.osburn@tstc.edu
Admission: By prior permission only.
Location: At Connally Field which is about 8 miles north east of the town.

The college operates from the airport and pilot training is carried out at the site. The instructional airframes include several of interest. The Ag-Cat was designed for agricultural work and first flew in 1957. The second prototype of this type which has been produced in substantial numbers is in the workshops. The Helton Lark is based on the Culver Cadet and first flew in the mid-1960s but only a few were built.

TYPE	REG/SER	CON. NO.	PI/NOTES	STATUS
☐ Beech 65-A90 King Air	N457CP	LJ-275	N905K, N985K, N457SR	RA
☐ Bell 205 Iroquois (UH-1H)	66-16823	9017		RA
☐ Cessna 150J	N51142	15069790		RA
☐ Cessna 150J	N60281	15070194		RA
☐ Cessna 150J	N60730	15070531		RA
☐ Cessna 172RG	N9452D	172RG1168		RA
☐ Cessna 172S	N584SP	172S8511		RA
☐ Cessna 310A Blue Canoe (L-27A) (U-3A)	N5754	38021	52-5866	RA
☐ Convair 580 (440) (340-38)	N4811C	101		RA
☐ Grumman G-164 Ag-Cat	N74055	X-2		RA
☐ Helton Lark 95	N1513H	9513		RA
☐ Lockheed 185 Orion (P-3A)			Fuselage only.	RA
☐ Lockheed 185 Orion (P-3A)			Fuselage only.	Ra
☐ Piper PA-23 Apache	N3040P	23-951		RA
☐ Piper PA-24-250 Comanche	N7450P	24-2639		RA
☐ Piper PA-44-180 Seminole	N5321R	4496045		RA

TEXAS TECHNICAL UNIVERSITY VIETNAM CENTER (TX142)

Address: Math Room 4, Texas Technical University, Lubbock, Texas 79409.
Tel: 806-742-3742 **Fax:** 806-742-8664 **Email:** vietnam.center@ttu.edu
Admission: By prior permission only.
Location: In the western part of the city centre.

The university has set up the Center to trace the history of the conflict which cost so many American lives. The moral and economic effects of the war are portrayed. The site houses one of the largest and most comprehensive archives on the war in the world. The helicopters have been obtained to show types flown.

TYPE	REG/SER	CON. NO.	PI/NOTES	STATUS
☐ Bell 205 Iroquois (UH-1D) (UH-1H)	66-1189	5672		RA
☐ Bell 206A Kiowa (OH-58A)	72-21244	41910		RA
☐ Bell 209 Huey Cobra (AH-1G) (AH-1F)	67-15532	20196		RA
☐ Hughes 269A Osage (TH-55A)	64-18407	0596		RA

THE 1940 AIR TERMINAL MUSEUM (TX143)

Address: 8325 Travelair Street, Houston, Texas 77061.
Tel: 713-454-1940 **Email:** coats@1940airterminal.org
Admission: Tuesday-Saturday 1000-1700; Sunday1300-1700.
Location: At William P. Hobby Airport which is in the south eastern suburbs of the city off Route 35.

The first project for the Houston Aeronautical Heritage Society is the restoration of the 1940 art deco terminal which was in use until 1954. The building was empty for a number of years and when work is complete it will house a museum tracing the history of aviation in the region.

The first phase of the exhibition opened in 2004. An early hangar has now been allocated for the display. The Lodestar was donated to the collection by a local owner and this Lockheed twin will be maintained in airworthy condition.

The Sikorsky S-43, which was once flown by Howard Hughes, was due to be donated to the society but the death of the owner has resulted in further negotiations.

Several more aircraft have been promised in the not too distant future.

TYPE	REG/SER	CON. NO.	PI/NOTES	STATUS
☐ Douglas DC-3A-456 Skytrain (C-47A) (Dakota III)	CU-T1192	10028, FL5110028	42-24166, FL510, G-AOYE, 706B, 24166 (France), F-BTDB, CF-POY	PV
☐ Douglas DC-6B	N841TA	44891	CF-CZE, N45502, CC-CEV, CC-PJG – front fuselage only.	PV
☐ Lockheed 18-56-23 Lodestar (C-60A)	N31G	18-2302	42-55897, YS-25, TI-73, C-251, NC4495N, N4495N, N67K	PV

Texas

☐ Potez 25 (R)			Under construction from GrummanRAC G-164 Ag-Cat parts.	
☐ Sikorsky S-43 (OA-11)	N440	4327	NR440, NX440, 42-001, NX440 – hopefully will join collection	–
☐ Sikorsky S-58B	N887	58482		PV

THIRD ARMORED CAVALRY DIVISION MUSEUM (TX144)

Address: Building 418, PO Box 5917, Fort Hood, Texas 76546-0719.
Tel: 254-287-8811 **Fax:** 254-287-3833 **Email:** celia.stratton@hood.army.mil
Admission: Monday-Friday 0900-1600; Saturday-Sunday 1200-1600.
Location: About 25 miles west of Temple off Route 190.

The Fourth Armored Division was established in 1940 and was among the first US units to see combat during World War II. One of its commanders in the conflict was General George S. Patton.
The Fourth Armored Division Museum was set up in 1949 and became officially recognised in 1963. In 1991 the name was changed to the III Corps and Fort Hood Museum to reflect the nature of the displays. It reverted to the original title in the mid-1990s and later in that decade took up its present name.
Outside the building is a park where military vehicles, weapons and three helicopters can be seen. The remaining aircraft are located around the camp.

TYPE	REG/SER	CON. NO.	PI/NOTES	STATUS
☐ Bell 47D-1 Sioux (H-13E) (OH-13E)				PV
☐ Bell 204 Iroquois (HU-1A) (UH-1A)	'58-01632'	91	59-1632 – at Headquarters Building.	PVX
☐ Bell 204 Iroquois (HU-1B) (UH-1B)	61-0693	273		PV
☐ Bell 205 Iroquois (UH-1H)	68-15727	10657	Near airfield.	PV
☐ Bell 209 Huey Cobra (AH-1G) (AH-1Q) (AH-1S)	68-15052	20586	At Headquarters Building.	PV

TOMBALL MONUMENT (TX145)

Location: On permanent view in a park on Alice Road in the south western part of the town.

TYPE	REG/SER	CON. NO.	PI/NOTES	STATUS
☐ Lockheed 580 (T-33A)				PV

TULIA MONUMENT (TX146)

Location: On permanent view at VFW 1798 on South East 2nd Street in the town.

TYPE	REG/SER	CON. NO.	PI/NOTES	STATUS
☐ North American NA-170 Sabre (F-86E)	50-0593	170-15		PV

UNITED STATES AIR FORCE HISTORY AND TRADITIONS MUSEUM (TX147)

Address: 37thTRW/PA, Lackland Air Force Base, Texas 78236-5218.
Tel: 210-925-3055 **Email:** publicaf@lackland.af.mil
Admission: Security clearance required at the current time.
Location: About 8 miles west of San Antonio off Highway 90.

The original Lackland site had no airfield and is used for basic military training, technical training for security police, instructor training and houses an officer school.
The museum opened in 1956 and has on view a number of engines, dioramas showing significant events in aviation warfare and uniforms. The displays have been improved and the renovated museum reopened on 12th August 2010.
A number of interactive exhibits have been added to show the history of the service and the development of Lackland and Kelly. The preserved aircraft are now displayed in several areas. Around the parade ground the World War II types can be seen along with several others including the Lockheed Blackbird.
A Liberator was once on show but this moved to the American Air Museum at Duxford in England and was replaced by a full size replica. A new airpark has been set up in the residential part of the camp. Others are in training areas used by the military police.

TYPE	REG/SER	CON. NO.	PI/NOTES	STATUS
☐ Beech D18S Expeditor (C18S) (SNB-2C) (SNB-5) (TC-45J) (UC-45J)	'42-9637'	7777	Bu29637	PVX
☐ Beech A45 Mentor (T-34A)	55-0206	G-763		PV
☐ Bell 33 Kingcobra (RP-63G) (QF-63G)	45-57295			PV
☐ Bell 204 Iroquois (HU-1B) (UH-1B)	60-3601	247		PV
☐ Bell 205 Iroquois (UH-1D) (UH-1H)	65-9641	4685		PV
☐ Boeing 299-O Fortress (B-17G) (TB-17G)	44-83512	32153		PV
☐ Boeing 345 Superfortress (B-29A)	44-62220/'4614'	11697		PVX
☐ Boeing 464-201-7 Stratofortress (B-52D)	55-0068	17184		PV
☐ Boeing 717-148 Stratotanker (KC-135A) (KC-135E)	57-2589	17725		PV
☐ Cessna 318E Dragonfly (A-37B) (NOA-37B)	67-14790	43015		PV
☐ Cessna 337A Super Skymaster (O-2B)	67-21440	3370518	N5418S	PV
☐ Consolidated 32 Liberator (B-24M) (FSM)	'44-51228'			PVX
☐ Convair 240-27 (T-29B) (VT-29B)	51-5172	303		PV
☐ Curtiss 1C Jenny (JN-4D)			Fuselage only.	PV
☐ Douglas A-26C Invader	44-35918/'434287'	29197	44-35918, N7953C, TI-1040L, TI-1040P, HR-276, 276 (Honduras), 510 (Honduras), N2781G	PVX

☐ Douglas DC-3A-467 Skytrain (C-47B)	'43-201'	14231/25676	43-48415, 348415 (France) 348415 (South Vietnam)	RAX
☐ Douglas DC-3A-467 Skytrain (C-47B) (VC-47D)	44-76671	16255/33003		PV
☐ Douglas DC-6A Liftmaster (R6D-1) (C-118A)	51-17640	43692	Bu131589	PV
☐ Douglas DC-9-32CF Nightingale (C-9A)	71-0878	47536		PV
☐ Douglas WB-66D Destroyer	55-0390	45022		PV
☐ Fairchild 110 Flying Boxcar (C-119C)	51-2567	10525		PV
☐ Fairchild 473 Provider (205) (C-123B) (C-123K)	54-0593	20042		PV
☐ Fairchild 473 Provider (205) (C-123B) (C-123K)	54-0668	20117		PV
☐ Fairchild-Republic A-10A Thunderbolt II	'79-547'	A10-94	76-0547	PVX
☐ Ford JB-2 [Fieseler Fi 103A-1]				PV
☐ General Dynamics 401 Fighting Falcon (F-16A)	78-0062	61-58		RA
☐ General Dynamics 401 Fighting Falcon (F-16A)	78-0069	61-65		RA
☐ General Dynamics 401 Fighting Falcon (F-16A)	79-0332	61-117		PV
☐ General Dynamics 401 Fighting Falcon (F-16A)	79-0334	61-119		RA
☐ General Dynamics 401 Fighting Falcon (F-16A)	79-0360	61-145		PV
☐ General Dynamics 401 Fighting Falcon (F-16A)	80-0511	61-232		RA
☐ General Dynamics 401 Fighting Falcon (F-16B)	78-0107	62-33		PV
☐ General Dynamics FB-111A	68-0275	B1-47	68-0275, '90275'	RA
☐ Lockheed 282-1B Hercules (C-130B)	59-1531	282-3579		PV
☐ Lockheed 422-87-23 Lightning (P-38L) (FSM)	'43-78538'			PVX
☐ Lockheed 483-04-06 Starfighter (F-104S)	57-1319	283-5031		PV
☐ Lockheed 1049F-55-96 Super Constellation (C-121C) (EC-121S)	54-0155	1049F-4174		PV
☐ Lockheed SR-71A Blackbird	61-7979	2030		PV
☐ Martin 272A Canberra (RB-57A)	52-1482	65		PV
☐ McDonnell M.36BA Voodoo (F-101B)	56-0241	176		PV
☐ McDonnell M.36BA Voodoo (TF-101B) (TF-101F)	58-0290	662		PV
☐ McDonnell M.98AM Phantom II (F4H-1) (F-4B)	'49-421'	138	Bu149421, '37680'	PVX
☐ McDonnell M.98DF Phantom II (RF-4C)	'65-895'	482	63-7744, '64-467'	RAX
☐ McDonnell M.199-1A Eagle (YF-15A) (F-15A)	'85-114'	001/A001	71-0280	PVX
☐ North American NA-88 Texan (SNJ-5)	'93477'	88-14226	Bu51584, N1395N, '49-3584'	PVX
☐ North American NA-108 Mitchell (B-25J) (TB-25J) (VB-25J) (TB-25J) (TB-25N)	'35103'	108-33110	44-29835, N3676G, 44-29835	PVX
☐ North American NA-126 Mustang (P-51H)	'44-14151'	126-37802	44-64376	PVX
☐ North American NA-144 Twin Mustang (P-82E) (F-82E)	46-0262	144-38148		PV
☐ North American NA-151 Sabre (P-86A) (F-86A) (EF-86A)	'11295'	151-38432	v	PVX
☐ North American NA-159 Trojan (T-28A)	49-1611	159-123	49-1611, '11916'	PV
☐ North American NA-192 Super Sabre (F-100A)	53-1629	192-124		PV
☐ North American NA-192 Super Sabre (F-100A)	52-5759	192-4		PV
☐ Northrop N-156B Freedom Fighter (F-5B)	'55-668'	C.8123	Static test airframe.	PVX
☐ Northrop N-156T Talon (T-38A)	59-1605	N.5118		PV
☐ Republic P-47N Thunderbolt	'226418'		44-89348	PVX
☐ Republic F-84F Thunderstreak	52-8889			PV
☐ Republic JF-105B Thunderchief	54-0105	JF-1 (B-006)		PV
☐ Republic F-105D Thunderchief	61-0106	D-301		PV
☐ Republic F-105D Thunderchief	61-0108	D-303		PV
☐ Republic F-105D Thunderchief	61-0115	D-310		PV
☐ Republic F-105D Thunderchief	61-0199	D-394		PV
☐ Republic F-105D Thunderchief	62-4228	D-427		PV
☐ Republic F-105D Thunderchief	62-4259	D-458		PV
☐ Republic F-105D Thunderchief	62-4279	D-478		PV
☐ Republic F-105D Thunderchief	62-4346	D-545		PV
☐ Republic F-105D Thunderchief	62-4353	D-552		PV
☐ Republic F-105D Thunderchief	62-4387	D-586		PV
☐ Sikorsky S-65A (HH-53C) (MH-53J) (MH-53M)	73-1648	65380		PV
☐ Vought A-7D Corsair II	71-0337	D248		PV

UNITED STATES ARMY MEDICAL DEPARTMENT MUSEUM (TX148)

Address: MCCS-BRL-MM, Building 1046, 2310 Stanley Road, Fort Sam Houston, Texas 78234-6100.
Tel: 210-221-6358 **Fax:** 210-221-6181 **Email:** ameddmus@aol.com
Admission: Tuesday-Saturday 1000-1600.
Location: In the north eastern suburbs of San Antonio.

The US Army Medical Department was set up in 1775 and over the years its constituent units saved many significant items for posterity. The first display opened in Washington, DC, in 1882. In 1920 the Medical Field Service School at Carlisle Barracks established a small museum to aid their training and this was transferred to Fort Sam Houston in 1946.

The site is named after the first President of the Republic of Texas and the complex opened in 1876. Many historic buildings survive around the fort including the Quadrangle which once housed Geronimo and other captured Apaches.

The museum opened in its present buildings in July 1989.

Further phases of the exhibition have been added in recent years. Artefacts from the Civil War period are on show along with uniforms, photographs etc. The development of medicines and surgical techniques is portrayed with particular emphasis on military applications.

The Bell OH-13 was used in the Korean conflict and the example in the collection was restored to 'MASH' configuration a few years ago.

The Iroquois operated on aeromedical evacuation duties in the Vietnam conflict. One of the seven evaluation Model 205s ordered is parked outside the Headquarters Building.

TYPE	REG/SER	CON. NO.	PI/NOTES	STATUS
☐ Bell 47D-1 Sioux (H-13D) (OH-13D)	51-2456	194		PV
☐ Bell 205 Iroquois (YHU-1D) (YUH-1D) (UH-1D)	'06031'	704	60-6031 – at Aeromedical HQ.	PVX
☐ Bell 205 Iroquois (UH-1D) (UH-1H)	64-13675	4382	64-13675, N361SP	PV
☐ Bell 205 Iroquois (UH-1D) (UH-1H)	'65-9668'	5180	65-12773	PVX

UNITED STATES SHIP *LEXINGTON* MUSEUM ON THE BAY (TX149)

Address:	PO Box 23076, 2914 North Shoreline Drive, PO Box 23076, Corpus Christi, Texas 78403-3076.
Tel:	361-888-4873 **Fax:** 361-883-8361 **Email:** rocco@usslexington.com
Admission:	Daily 0900-1700. (Closes at 1800 May-August)
Location:	In the city harbour.

The aircraft carrier the USS *Lexington* is the fifth ship to bear the name: the first was launched in 1776 and the present holder of the title was commissioned on 17th February 1943. During World War II she served in the Pacific and her aircraft shot down more than 370 enemy machines in aerial combat and destroyed 475 on the ground.

The ship was modernised after the end of the war and rejoined the fleet in 1955 serving off Formosa, Laos and Cuba during the periods of tension in these areas. In 1962 the *Lexington* was a training carrier for shore based squadrons operating out of Pensacola in Florida. On 26th November 1991 she was decommissioned and soon after sailed to Corpus Christi to begin her new career. The carrier served longer than any other in the US Navy. It also set more records than any carrier in the history of naval aviation.

Visitors can now tour large parts of the ship and view the living and working areas where informative displays have been set up The aircraft collection is displayed in the hangar area and on the flight deck. There are several interesting types to be seen.

In 1942 a number of Douglas Dauntless dive-bombers were ditched from a training carrier into Lake Michigan. They remained under the surface until the early 1990s when they were recovered for the National Museum of Naval Aviation in Florida. The example in the hangar moved to Texas soon after. The aircraft is undergoing a restoration to original configuration. One of the Skyhawks is by the entrance on the shore.

TYPE	REG/SER	CON. NO.	PI/NOTES	STATUS
☐ Beech D45 Mentor (T-34B)	Bu140936	BG-270	Bu140936, N7035P –	PV
☐ Bell 209 Huey Cobra (AH-1S) (AH-1E)	77-22758	24096	Possible identity – but marked as '77-22754'	PV
☐ Douglas SBD-3 Dauntless	Bu06694	1509		PVC
☐ Douglas KA-3B Skywarrior (A3D-2) (A-3B)	Bu138944	10805		PV
☐ Douglas A-4B Skyhawk (A4D-2)	Bu142675	11737		PV
☐ Douglas A-4B Skyhawk (A4D-2)	Bu142929	11991		PV
☐ Douglas TA-4J Skyhawk	Bu158722	14343		PV
☐ Douglas DC-9-32RC Skytrain II (C-9B)				RA
☐ Grumman G-40 Avenger (TBM-3) (TBM-3E)	Bu53804	3866	Bu53804, 53804 (Canada), N9710Z –	PV
☐ Grumman G-105 Cougar (F9F-8T) (TF-9J)	Bu147276	246	Bu147276, 'Bu142470'	PV
☐ Grumman G-128 Intruder (A-6E)	Bu158532	I-515		PV
☐ Grumman G-303 Tomcat (F-14A)	Bu160694	313		PV
☐ Howard DGA-15P (GH-3)	Bu44947	918		PV
☐ McDonnell M.24 Banshee (F2H-2)	Bu125052	375		PV
☐ McDonnell M.98AM Phantom II (F4H-1F) (F-4A)	Bu145315	16		PV
☐ McDonnell M.98EV Phantom II (F-4J) (F-4S)	Bu158366	4150	Front fuselage only.	PV
☐ McDonnell M.267 Hornet (F/A-18A)	Bu161942	149/A114		RA
☐ Naval Aircraft Factory N3N-3	Bu2959		Bu2959, N6358T –	PV
☐ North American NA-88 Texan (SNJ-5)	Bu52020	88-15208	Bu52020, N8211E –	PV
☐ North American NA-200 Trojan (T-28B)	Bu138271	200-342		PV
☐ North American NA-352 Buckeye (T-2C)	Bu158898	352-23		PV
☐ Vought FG-1D Corsair (FSM)	'Bu92095'			PVX
☐ Vought A-7B Corsair II	Bu154548	B-188		PV

VIETNAM MEMORIAL PARK (TX150)

Address:	PO Box 2854, Big Spring, Texas 79721-2854.
Email:	info@bigspringvietnammemorial.org
Admission:	On permanent view.
Location:	About 3 miles south west of the town off Interstate 20.

This impressive memorial consists of a wall of remembrance, a pleasant garden and a display of flags. The two acre park was dedicated in May 1991 and a memorial to the residents of Howard County who were either killed or disappeared in the conflict was erected. The three aircraft, representing types flown in the conflict, are parked nearby. Also on show are a tank and a display of unit flags.

TYPE	REG/SER	CON. NO.	PI/NOTES	STATUS
☐ Bell 205 Iroquois (UH-1D) (UH-1H)	'66-1678'	5561	66-1078	PVX
☐ Bell 209 Huey Cobra (AH-1G) (AH-1S)	68-15054	20588		PV
☐ McDonnell M.98HO Phantom II (F-4E)	66-0368	2762		PV

VINTAGE FLYING MUSEUM (TX151)

Address:	505 North West 38th. Street, Hangar 33, Fort Worth, Texas 76106.
Tel:	817-624-1935 **Fax:** 817-485-4454 **Email:** vfm@vintageflyingmuseum.org
Admission:	Friday 1000-1700; Saturday 0900-1700; Sunday 1200-1700.
Location:	At Meacham Field which is in the north western suburbs of the city.

Dr. William Hospers bought a Fortress in October 1979 and it was flown to Fort Worth. Built in late 1944, its military records have been lost but it is believed to have seen combat action. In 1959 it was sold for civilian use and was later used on cargo and crop spraying duties. The bomber has been restored to its original configuration; in late 2010 it was sold to the Military Aviation Museum in Virginia.

A rarity is the American Flea Triplane. Inspired by the Mignet designs, the aircraft was put into production in Forth Worth. The third wing served as ailerons and only a few were sold. The SD-1A was built in the early 1980s by Tim Yanc and was active for several years. Another interesting type is the Ling-Temco-Vought 450F. The low wing monoplane was designed for high altitude surveillance missions.

TYPE	REG/SER	CON. NO.	PI/NOTES	STATUS
☐ Aero Falcon Knight Falcon	N401ES	600502		PV
☐ Aeronca 65TF Defender	N31484	5680T	NC31484	PVA
☐ Aeronca 11AC Chief	N9108E	11AC-741	NC9108E	PVA
☐ American Flea Triplane				PV
☐ Beech D18S Expeditor (C-18S) (JRB-2) (SNB-5)	N3761	1052	Bu4725	PV
☐ Beech D18S	N80152	A-112		PVA
☐ Beech D18S	N197L	A-361	N80497	PV
☐ Boeing-Stearman D75N1 Kaydet (PT-17)	N450HS	75-3876	42-15687, FJ826, N56862	PVA
☐ Canadair CL-30 Silver Star 3 (CT-133) [Lockheed 580 (T-33AN)]	N165KK	T33-565	21165 (Canada), , 133165 (Canada)	PV
☐ Cessna 310A Blue Canoe (L-27A) (U-3A)	N6747	38106	58-2132	PV
☐ Convair 640 (340-32)	N3407	GD.4 (20)		PV
☐ Convair 640 (340-33)	N860FW	10	N727A, N7263, CF-PWU, C-FPWU, N2569D	
☐ Daphne SD-1A	N42524	1	42-100903, NC57278, CF-CUC	PVA
☐ Douglas DC-3A-456 Skytrain (C-47A)	N141JR	19366		PVA
☐ Douglas A-26A Invader (A-26B) (B-26K)	N4988N	27477	44-34198, 64-17679, N269G, C-GXTG	PVA
☐ Ling-Temco-Vought L450F	N2450F	002		PV
☐ Morrisey 2000C	N58789	1A		PVA
☐ North American NA-88 Texan (AT-6D) (Harvard III)	N101NZ	88-15611	41-34050, EZ177, NZ1079, N111PB	PV
☐ North American NA-108 Mitchell (B-25J) (TB-25J) (VB-25J) (VB-25N)	NL1042B'/29710'	108-34098	44-30823	PVAX
☐ North American NA-191 Sabre (F-86F)	N8630	191-385	52-4689, (Venezuela), 658 (Bolivia)	PVA
☐ Piaggio P.136L-1	N40025	216		PV
☐ Ryan ST-3KR Recruit (PT-22)	N48748	1683	41-15654	PVA
☐ Stinson V-76 Sentinel (L-5E)	44-17925	76-3199	44-17925,	PV
☐ Stinson V-77 Reliant (AT-19)	N5490N	77-473	43-44186, FB745, Bu30491	PVA

VOUGHT AIRCRAFT HERITAGE FOUNDATION (TX152)

Address:	PO Box 655907, Dallas, Texas 75265-5907.
Tel:	972-946-4054 Fax: 972-946-3371 Email: heritage@voughtaircraft.com
Admission:	By prior permission only.
Location:	Just east of Grand Prairie south of Route 80.

The Vought company was formed in 1917 and merged with the Northrop Grumman group in 1995. The first factories were in New York State and later plants were set up in Connecticut.

The Vought Retirees Group came into being in 1996 and a volunteer team has workshops in the Dallas factory. Two aircraft – a Crusader and a Corsair – have been completed and are on show in the Frontiers of Flight Museum at Love Field. The A-7 was the last type to be produced at Dallas. Since the late 1970s components for other production lines have been made.

The VE-7 biplane was the first type built by the new company. Only 14 were ordered by the Signal Corps. A replica is under construction and this will also eventually go to the Frontiers of Flight Museum.

The company was well-known for its naval designs and the group now has a F4U Corsair. After a long period of negotiations with the National Air and Space Museum the Vought V-173 moved to Dallas. This experimental design, known as the 'Flying Pancake', made its maiden flight in November 1942 at Bridgeport Airport in Connecticut. The aircraft was a wooden prototype for the XF5U-1 fighter which was cancelled before it flew. At the end of the programme the V-173 was presented to the Smithsonian Institute who stored it for more than half a century.

Another innovative fighter was the Cutlass. This tailless jet first flew in November 1948 and was the first of this configuration in the USA The example in the collection was on show at the Weisbrod Museum in Colorado before being moved by road to the workshops.

The Pirate was the first jet fighter produced by the company and flew in 1946. Only 33 were produced and the example here is being rebuilt for the New England Air Museum. The group also has a large archive of Vought papers and photographs.

TYPE	REG/SER	CON. NO.	PI/NOTES	STATUS
☐ Vought VE-7 (R)				RAC
☐ Vought V-173	Bu02978		On loan from NASM, DC.	RAC
☐ Vought F4U-4 Corsair	Bu97330	9584	Bu97330, N5222V, N912CM	RAC
☐ Vought V-352 Pirate (F6U-1)	Bu122479		On loan from NEAM, CT.	RAC
☐ Vought YF-8C Crusader (F8U-1) (YF8U-2)	Bu140448			RA

WESTWOOD AVIATION INSTITUTE (TX153)

Address:	8800 Telephone Road, Houston, Texas 77061-5114.
Tel:	866-782-1253 Email: amtcoordamh@aviationmaintenance.edu
Admission:	By prior permission only.
Location:	At William P. Hobby Airport which is in the south-eastern suburbs of the city off Route 35.

This long established college has premises at Hobby Airport. The hangars house four instructional airframes along with a number of engines and components. Students are trained to obtain FAA licences.

TYPE	REG/SER	CON. NO.	PI/NOTES	STATUS
☐ Cessna 150C				RA
☐ Cessna 150J				RA
☐ Lockheed 1329 JetStar 2				RA
☐ Piper PA-28-140 Cherokee				RA

UTAH

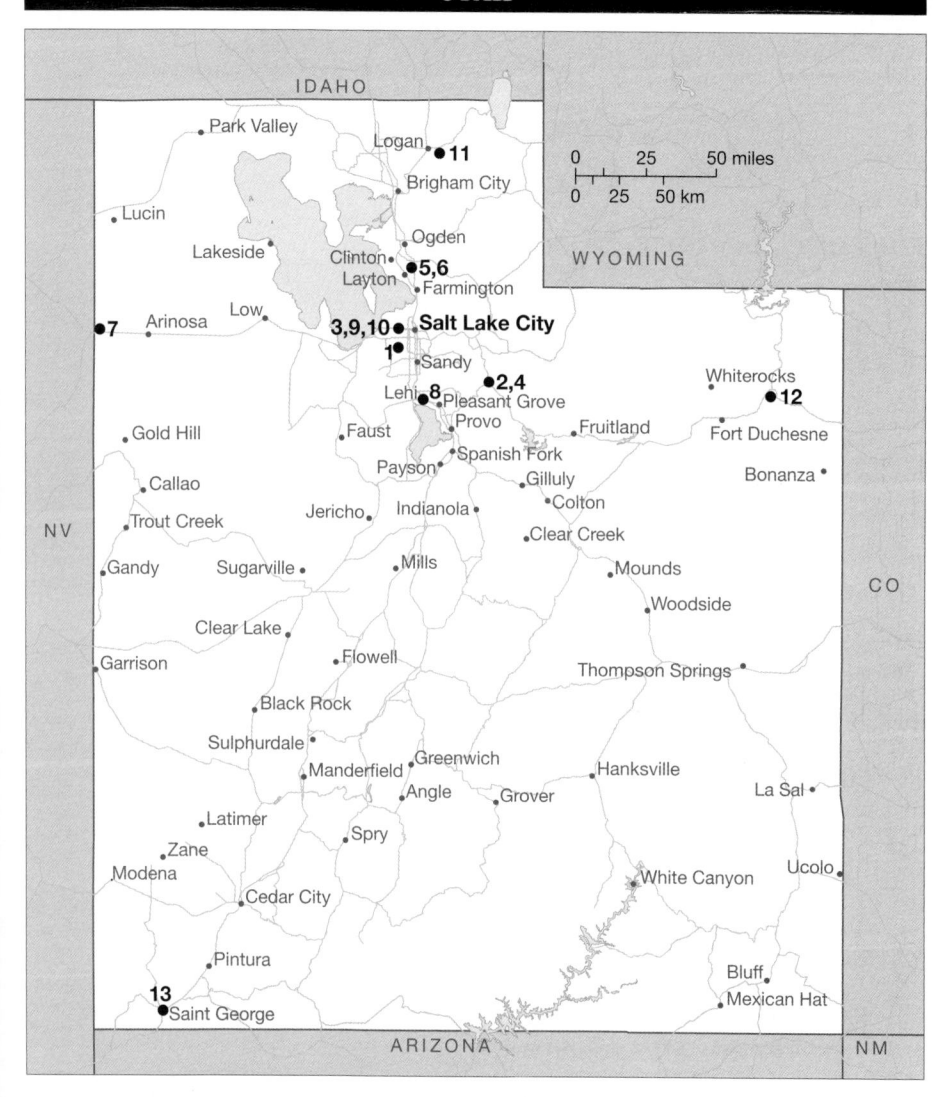

CAMP W. G. WILLIAMS MONUMENT (UT1)

Location:	On permanent view at the site in which is about 3 miles south of Bluffdale.

TYPE	REG/SER	CON. NO.	PI/NOTES	STATUS
☐ Bell 204 Iroquois (UH-1C) (UH-1M)	66-0546	1528		PV

COMMEMORATIVE AIR FORCE (UTAH WING) (UT2)

Address:	PO Box 26333, Salt Lake City, Utah 84126-0333.
Tel:	801-571-4613 Email: richardmeyer3610@msn.com
Admission:	By prior permission only.
Location:	At Heber Valley Airport which is in the south western part of the city off Route 189.

The wing evolved from the Great Basin Squadron which operated the Kaydet for many years. The unit has moved from Salt Lake City and the hangar now houses a number of aircraft owned by members.

TYPE	REG/SER	CON. NO.	PI/NOTES	STATUS
☐ Beech D18S Expeditor (C18S) (SNB-2) (SNB-5P) (RC-45J)	N4207	4664	Bu67124	RAA
☐ Boeing-Stearman E75 Kaydet (PT-13D) (N2S-5)	N1387V	75-8291	42-109258, Bu43197 – flies as N2S-5 '3217'	RAAX
☐ Ercoupe 415D	N99924	2547	NC99924	RAA
☐ Hunting-Percival P.84 Jet Provost T.3A (T.3)	N455XM		XM455, 8960M	RAA
☐ Lockheed 15-27-01 Harpoon (PV-2)	N7670C	15-1438	Bu37472	RAA
☐ Nanchang CJ-6A	N75480	2951265	(China AF)	RAA
☐ North American NA-174 Trojan (T-28A)				RAA
☐ Piper J-3C-65 Cub (L-4J)	N5580	13236	45-4496	RAA
☐ Stinson V-76 Sentinel (L-5)	N4914	76-1120	42-98879	RAA

FORT DOUGLAS MILITARY MUSEUM (UT3)

Address:	32 Potter Street, Fort Douglas, Utah 84113.
Tel:	801-581-1251 **Email:** edickson@fortdouglas.org
Admission:	Tuesday-Saturday 1200-1700
Location:	In the eastern suburbs of Salt Lake City.

The first military establishment in the area was Camp Floyd which was set up in 1858 to ensure that the Mormon Settlers were law abiding. The site closed in 1861 when the troops were moved east to serve in the Civil War. Fort Douglas opened in October 1862 to protect the overland mail route. Over the next few years troops were involved in a number of local conflicts. In World War I it served as a training centre and as a prisoner of war camp.

The Fort was closed in 1991 and large areas of the site were transferred to the University of Utah. The museum was set up in 1976 and has steadily expanded over the last 30 years. The history of the site is portrayed in the exhibition. The helicopters are fairly recent arrivals with the Cobra making the short journey from the National Guard Base at Salt Lake City and the Cayuse from the Hill Aerospace Museum.

TYPE	REG/SER	CON. NO.	PI/NOTES	STATUS
☐ Bell 205 Iroquois (UH-1H)	67-19527	10133		PV
☐ Bell 209 Huey Cobra (AH-1G) (AH-1Q) (AH-1S)	70-16042	20986		PV
☐ Hughes 369M Cayuse (HO-6) (OH-6A)	67-16432	0517		PV

HEBER VALLEY AERO MUSEUM (UT4)

Address:	Russ McDonald Field, 2002 Airport Road, Heber City, Utah 84068.
Tel:	435-657-1826 **Email:** info@hebervalleyaeromuseum.org
Admission:	May–October Tuesday-Sunday 1000-1800.
Location:	In the south western part of the city off Route 189.

This collection has been set up by warbird owners at the field. The former US Navy T-28 trainer was converted for ground attack duties and was operated by the Air Force in Laos until the mid-1970s when it was taken to Australia. The Stearman Kaydet is currently being rebuilt in the museum workshops. The Jet Provost was imported into the USA in 1993 and spent a few years on the East Coast before moving across the country. A small display of photographs and memorabilia has been set up in rooms around the main hangar.

The local unit of the Commemorative Air Force has moved to the field and the two organisations co-operate closely.

TYPE	REG/SER	CON. NO.	PI/NOTES	STATUS
☐ Boeing-Stearman B75N1 Kaydet (N2S-3)	N7995	75-7995	Bu38374	PVC
☐ Hunting-Percival P.84 Jet Provost T.3A (T.3)	N77506	PAC/W/11795	XN506	PVA
☐ North American NA-200 Trojan (T-28B) (AT-28D)	N28YF	200-162	Bu137799, 54-137799 (Laos), 3412 (Laos)	PVA
☐ Piper J-3C-65 Cub	N92003	16396	NC92003	PVA
☐ Pitts S-1S Special				PVA
☐ WSK SBLim-2 [MiG-15bis]	N15UT	522546	546 (Poland), N14687	PVA

HILL AEROSPACE MUSEUM (UT5)

Address:	75ABW/MU, 7961 Wardleigh Road, Hill Air Force Base, Utah 84056-5842.
Tel:	801-777-6868 **Email:** 75abw.mu.webmaster@hill.af.mil
Admission:	Daily 0900-1630.
Location:	About 7 miles south of Ogden off Interstate 15.

This museum opened in 1986 in a small World War II warehouse building on the base along with an outside aircraft park. The collection grew rapidly and by the mid-1980s over two dozen airframes were on show.

The Heritage Foundation put forward plans for a new facility which would include an aircraft hall, rooms for smaller items and offices. This superb building was ready for the 1992 season and in late 1998 work started on a second hall. The outdoor park was landscaped and enlarged and a separate entrance constructed.

Displays in the building trace the history of Hill, its units and military aviation in Utah. There are many models, engines, uniforms, photographs and documents to be seen. The Utah Aviation Hall of Fame was set up in the building and the initial 13 inductees were honoured in 1996. Areas are devoted to the Women Airforce Service Pilots (WASP) highlighting their work in World War II. American Aerospace Pioneers also feature prominently.

In the mid-1930s the Army Air Corps began the search for a major base in Utah and a site near Ogden was chosen. Work started in late 1939 and the base was named Hill Field During World War II the site was used to repair and maintain many types. At the end of the conflict a large number of aircraft were flown to Hill for storage and parts reclamation. In the 1950s

Utah

the Ogden Air Materiel Area began its work in supporting the jet types which were entering service and this task continues to the present day.

The first aircraft to arrive for the museum was a B-17. After a period of service with the Brazilian Air Force it returned to the USA in 1968. Owned by the Air Force Museum, it was loaned to a group in Florida and was on display at St. Petersburg from 1983 until 1986. This bomber has now been restored to its original World War II state. Parked outside is a B-29 Superfortress. Before the outbreak of the Korean War over 150 were stored at Hill.

Around the building is a comprehensive display of missiles used on the local ranges. Inside smaller rockets and bombs can be seen along with associated aircraft equipment, components, engines and vehicles.

The SR-71 Blackbird in the hall is the only two-seat trainer version built. About 70 aircraft are now on show and most of the major types used by the Air Force over the last half century are represented.

Several wrecks have been recovered from Alaska and restored for the display. The Liberator is one of these and now incorporates a Privateer fuselage. The Burgess-Wright F is a license built version of the Wright B and the type was one of the first to serve with the US Army.

The displays have been carefully thought out and trace the history and development of the Air Force.

TYPE	REG/SER	CON. NO.	PI/NOTES	STATUS
☐ Beech D18S Expeditor (C-45H)	52-10862	AF-792	52-10862, N87688	PV
☐ Bell 47G-3B-1 Sioux (TH-13T)	67-17053	3760	67-17053, N62233	PV
☐ Bell 205 Iroquois (HH-1H)	70-2470	17114		PV
☐ Boeing 299-O Fortress (B-17G) (TB-17G)	44-83663	32304	44-83663, 5400 (Brazil), N47788	PV
☐ Boeing 345 Superfortress (B-29A)	44-86408		44-86408	PVX
☐ Boeing 450-157-35 Stratojet (B-47E) (WB-47E)	51-2360	450413		PV
☐ Boeing 464-253 Stratofortress (B-52G)	58-0191	464259		PV
☐ Boeing 717-148 Stratotanker (KC-135A) (KC-135E)	57-1510	17581		RA
☐ Boeing-Stearman A75N1 Kaydet (PT-17)	41-25284	75-2573	41-25284, N264H, N264HC	PVC
☐ Burgess-Wright F				PVX
☐ Cessna 310A Blue Canoe (L-27A) (U-3A)	57-5869	38024		PV
☐ Cessna 318B Tweety Bird (318A) (T-37A) (T-37B)	57-2259	40192		PV
☐ Cessna 318B Tweety Bird (T-37B)	60-0122	40605		PV
☐ Cessna 318B Tweety Bird (T-37B)	64-13418	40833		RA
☐ Cessna 337M Super Skymaster (O-2A)	68-10653	337M0218		PV
☐ Consolidated 32 Liberator (B-24D)	41-23908	393	Using fuselage from PB4Y-2 Bu59932, N9829C.	PV
☐ Convair 8-10 Delta Dagger (F-102A)	57-0833	8-10-799		PV
☐ Convair 8-24 Delta Dart (F-106A)	58-0774	8-24-105		PV
☐ Convair 240-27 (T-29C)	52-1119	358		PV
☐ Convair 340-79 Samaritan (C-131D) (VC-131D)	55-0300	233	N8440H	PV
☐ Curtiss 1C Jenny (JN-4D)	'SC5002'	5002	N5001	PVX
☐ Curtiss 87V Warhawk (P-40N) (R)	'42-105270'		Contains original parts from a number of aircraft.	PVX
☐ De Havilland DHC.4A Caribou (CV-2B) (C-7B)	63-9757	220		PV
☐ Douglas DC-3A-467 Skytrain (C-47B) (VC-47B)	43-49281	15097/26542	43-49281, N55C, N55CE , O-49281 (US Army), N143Z	PV
☐ Douglas DC-4 Skymaster (C-54G)	45-0502	35955	45-0502, N1022A, HH-JMA	PV
☐ Douglas 1317 Globemaster II (C-124C)	53-0050	44345		PV
☐ Douglas RB-26C Invader (A-26C)	44-35617	28896	44-35617,N7660C, N600WB	PV
☐ Douglas A-1E Skyraider (AD-5)	'52-0247'		Composite assembled in Vietnam.	PVX
☐ Fairchild 110 Flying Boxcar (C-119F)	'52-2107'	10738	22107 (Canada), N966S	PVX
☐ Fairchild 473 Provider (205) (C-123B) (C-123K)	54-0610	20059	54-610, N3836A	PV
☐ Fairchild-Republic A-10A Thunderbolt II	73-1666	A10-3		PV
☐ General Dynamics F-111E	68-0020	A1-189		PV
☐ General Dynamics 401 Fighting Falcon (F-16A)	79-0388	61-173		PV
☐ Kaman K-600-3 Huskie (H-43B) (HH-43B)	62-4561	187		PV
☐ Lockheed 080 Shooting Star (P-80A) (F-80A)	'44-84999'		Converted from Lockheed 580 (T-33A) possibly c/n 580-7670 52-9535.	PVX
☐ Lockheed 183-93-02 Starfighter (F-104A)	'60753'			RAC
☐ Lockheed 282-1B Hercules (C-130B) (JC-130B) (C-130B) (NC-130B)	57-0526	282-3502		PV
☐ Lockheed 382-4B Hercules (C-130E)	64-0569	382-4079		RA
☐ Lockheed 422-81-22 Lightning (P-38J)	42-67638	422-2149		PV
☐ Lockheed 580 (T-33A)	51-9271	580-7055	51-9271, (N16697), N1452	PV
☐ Lockheed 1329 JetStar 6 (VC-140B) (C-140B)	62-4201	1329-5045		PV
☐ Lockheed SR-71C Blackbird	61-7981	2000	Composite using rear fuselage of YF-12A c/n 1001 60-6934 and static test front fuselage	PV
☐ Martin 179 Marauder (B-26)	40-1370	1235		RAD
☐ Martin 272A Canberra (RB-57A)	52-1492	75		PV
☐ McDonnell M.36BA Voodoo (F-101B)	57-0252	430		PV
☐ McDonnell M.36Y Voodoo (RF-101A)	54-1503	53	Front fuselage only.	RA
☐ McDonnell M.98DE Phantom II (F-4C)	63-7424	366		PV
☐ McDonnell M.98DF Phantom II (RF-4C)	65-0905	1565		RA
☐ McDonnell M.98DF Phantom II (RF-4C)	66-0469	2632		PV
☐ McDonnell M.98DJ Phantom II (F-4C)	64-0664	884		PV
☐ McDonnell M.98EN Phantom II (F-4D)	66-8711	2483		RA
☐ McDonnell M.98HO Phantom II (F-4E)	68-0304	3318		RA
☐ McDonnell M.98HO Phantom II (F-4E)	68-0476	3642		RA
☐ McDonnell M.199-1A Eagle (F-15A)	77-0090	371/A302		PV
☐ McDonnell M.267 Hornet (F/A-18A)	Bu161725	76/A054		PV
☐ Mikoyan-Gurevich MiG-21F-13	'2118'		585 – in false North Vietnamese markings.	PVX
☐ North American NA-78 Texan (AT-6A)	'039'		Composite.	PVX
☐ North American NA-108 Mitchell (B-25J)			Front fuselage only.	PV
☐ North American NA-108 Mitchell (B-25J) (TB-25J) (TB-25N)	44-86772	108-47526	44-86772, N9333Z, (CX-BAL), N9333Z	PV

☐ North American NA-109 Mustang (P-51D)	44-13371	109-27004	Possible identity.	PV
☐ North American NA-173 Sabre (F-86D) (F-86L)	'19055'	173-199	51-6055	PVX
☐ North American NA-191 Sabre (F-86F)	'12834'	191-674	52-4978	PVX
☐ North American NA-192 Super Sabre (F-100A)	52-5777	192-22	52-5777, N1453	PV
☐ North American NA-200 Trojan (T-28B)	Bu137749	200-112		PV
☐ North American NA-265 Sabreliner (T-39A) (CT-39A)	61-0674	265-77		PV
☐ North American NA-305 Bronco (OV-10A)	67-14675	305-83		PV
☐ Northrop N-138 Scorpion (F-89H)	54-0322	N.4956		PV
☐ Northrop N-156B Freedom Fighter (F-5B)	63-8440	N.8003		RA
☐ Northrop N-156T Talon (T-38A)	61-0824	N.5190		PV
☐ Northrop N-156T Talon (T-38A)	62-3634	N.5339		RA
☐ Northrop N-311 Tiger II (F-5E)	73-1640	R.1095		PV
☐ Piper J-3C-65 Cub	'45-4655'	16028	NC88410, N88410	PVX
☐ Republic P-47D Thunderbolt	44-32798		44-32798, 450 (Peru), N987R	RAC
☐ Republic F-84F Thunderstreak	51-1640			PV
☐ Republic RF-84F Thunderflash	51-17046		51-17046, AZ-P (Norway) – front fuselage only.	PV
☐ Republic F-84G Thunderjet	'23275'		52-3242	PVX
☐ Republic F-105D Thunderchief	'61-743'	D-55	59-1743	PVX
☐ Republic F-105G Thunderchief (F-105F)	62-4440	F-29		PV
☐ Republic JB-2 [Fieseler Fi 103A-1]				PV
☐ Rockwell B-1B Lancer	83-0070	7		PV
☐ Sikorsky S-58 Seabat (HSS-1N) (SH-34J)	'48943'	581327	Bu148943 – in false USAF markings.	PVX
☐ Sikorsky S-61R (CH-3C) (CH-3E)	65-12790	61565		PV
☐ Sikorsky S-65A (HH-53C) (MH-53J) (MH-53M)	68-10369	65175		PV
☐ Vertol V.43 Shawnee (H-21C) (CH-21C)	56-2142	C.304	56-2142 , '54-4002'	PV
☐ Vought YA-7F Corsair II (A-7D)	70-1039	D185		PV
☐ Vultee V-79 Valiant (BT-13B)	42-90406	79-1423 (?)	42-90406, N66743 (?)	PV
☐ Wright Flyer (R)				PV
☐ WSK Lim-5 [MiG-17F]	406	1C 04-06	In Polish markings.	PV

HILL AIR FORCE BASE COLLECTION (UT6)

Address: OOALC/PA, 7285 4th Street, Building 180, Suite 109, Hill Air Force Base, Utah 84056-5824.
Tel: 801-777-5201 **Email:** 75sfawebmaster@hill.af.mil
Admission: By prior permission only.
Location: About 7 miles south of Ogden off Interstate 15.

In the late 1930s the military authorities took over this site and constructed the airfield. The base is named after Major Ployer P. Hill who was killed on 30th October 1935 at Wright Field in Ohio. He was the pilot of the prototype Boeing 299, the forerunner of the B-17 series. Unfortunately the aircraft took off with the controls locked.

This large base houses the Ogden Air Logistics Center which provides support for both missiles and aircraft, particularly the F-16 and A-10. Fighter squadrons are also in residence. One of the Fighting Falcons is positioned by the secondary gate and the other two are positioned by the main entrance to the base.

TYPE	REG/SER	CON. NO.	PI/NOTES	STATUS
☐ General Dynamics 401 Fighting Falcon (F-16A)	79-0402	61-187		RA
☐ General Dynamics 401 Fighting Falcon (F-16A)	78-0065	61-61		RA
☐ Republic F-105D Thunderchief	62-4347	D-546		RA

HISTORIC WENDOVER AIRFIELD MUSEUM (UT7)

Address: 345 South Airport Apron, Wendover, Utah 84083.
Tel: 435-665-2308 **Email:** admin@wendoverairbase.com
Admission: Daily 0800-1800.
Location: Just east of the town off Interstate 80.

Wendover Army Air Base opened in March 1942 and was used for training B-17 and B-24 crews. Bombing ranges were used in the remote areas around the site. Over the next two years 21 Bomb Groups passed through the school before transferring to active duties. For a short time in 1944 P-47 pilots received instruction. September 1944 saw the arrival of the B-29 Superfortress bombers involved in the 'Manhattan Project'. These were equipped to carry the atomic bomb and they carried out many test flights from the field. The remote location was ideal for missile work and the site was used for a period before the unit moved to White Sands in New Mexico. Strategic Air Command used Wendover for training in the late 1940s. The airfield was turned over to the town in the 1970s and it serves as the local airport. Many hangars and buildings remain from the World War II period and a slow programme of restoration is underway. The museum traces the history of the airfield and on show are many dioramas showing period scenes. There are also uniforms, components, documents and photographs to be seen. The visitor can also tour the surviving buildings and the former military ramp.

TYPE	REG/SER	CON. NO.	PI/NOTES	STATUS
☐ North American NA-201 Sabre (F-86D) (F-86L)	53-1045	201-489		RAC

LEHI MONUMENT (UT8)

Location: On view during opening hours in Cabela's store at 2502 Grand Terrace Parkway in the northern part of the town.

TYPE	REG/SER	CON. NO.	PI/NOTES	STATUS
☐ Aeronca 7AC Champion	N81793	7AC-616	NC81793	PV

Utah

SALT LAKE CITY ARMY NATIONAL GUARD BASE (UT9)

Address:	7602 South Airport Road, Salt Lake City Municipal Airport No.2, West Jordan, Utah 84122.
Tel:	801-565-4422
Admission:	On permanent view.
Location:	About 7 miles south west of the city off Route 48.

The Utah Army National Guard operates helicopters from its base on the south west side of the field. Two types flown by the unit have been put on display in front of the base Headquarters Building. The Sabre is mounted outside the State HQ and is in the colours of local Korean War 'Ace' Captain Clifford Jolley.

TYPE	REG/SER	CON. NO.	PI/NOTES	STATUS
☐ Bell 204 Iroquois (UH-1C) (UH-1M)	64-14138	1262		PV
☐ Hughes 369M Cayuse (HO-6) (OH-6A)	67-16241	0626		PV
☐ North American NA-161 Sabre (P-86A) (F-86A)	'49-1273'	161-267 (?)	At Guard HQ in nearby Sandy.	PVX

SALT LAKE COMMUNITY COLLEGE (UT10)

Address:	551 North 2200 West, Salt Lake City, Utah 84107.
Tel:	801-957-4448 **Email:** contactcenter@slcc.edu
Admission:	By prior permission only.
Location:	At the International Airport which is in the northern part of the city.

The college has workshops and a pilot training centre at the airport with other classes held at its Meadowbank Campus. A number of instructional airframes are in use along with engines and components. After Beech withdrew support for the Starship most were withdrawn and one of these airframes is now at the college.

TYPE	REG/SER	CON. NO.	PI/NOTES	STATUS
☐ Alarus CH2000	N8500R	200061		RA
☐ Beech 2000 Starship I	N401AS	NC-19	N8025L	RA
☐ Bell 206A Kiowa (OH-58A) (OH-58C)	68-16793	40107		RA
☐ Bell 206A Kiowa (OH-58A) (OH-58C)	71-20739	41600		RA
☐ Cessna 150G	N2747S	15066647		RA
☐ Cessna 172	N5974A	28574		RA
☐ Cessna 182	N5415B	33415		RA
☐ Cessna 310F	N5841X	3100141		RA
☐ Hunting-Percival P.84 Jet Provost T.3	N77506	PAC/W/11795	NX506	RA
☐ North American NA-276 Sabreliner (T-39A) (CT-39A)	62-4498	276-51		RA
☐ Piper PA-23-250 Aztec (UO-1) (U-11A)	Bu149052	27-268		RA

UTAH STATE UNIVERSITY (UT11)

Address:	0500 Old Main Hill, Logan, Utah 84322-0500.
Tel:	435-797-1351 **Fax:** 435-797-1250 **Email:** prm@usu.edu
Admission:	By prior permission only.
Location:	At the airport which is in the northwester part of the town.

The university operates a pilot training school using Diamond DA.40Fs and DA.42s. Older types formerly used have been transferred to the aviation maintenance programme along with some specifically acquired.

TYPE	REG/SER	CON. NO.	PI/NOTES	STATUS
☐ Beech 58P Baron	N146Z	TJ-426		RA
☐ Cessna 152	N67508	15281877		RA
☐ Cessna 152	N934JH	15283001		RA
☐ Cessna 337M Super Skymaster (O-2A)	N5252C	337M0059	67-21353	RA
☐ Cessna 337M Super Skymaster (O-2A)	N468DE	337M0312	68-11036	RA
☐ North American NA-276 Sabreliner (T-39A) (CT-39A)	62-4464	276-17		RA
☐ Sikorsky S-62A Seaguard (HH-52A)	1377	62055		RA

VERNAL MONUMENT (UT12)

Location:	On permanent view at VFW 5560 on 241 North in the town.

TYPE	REG/SER	CON. NO.	PI/NOTES	STATUS
☐ Bell 209 Huey Cobra (AH-1S) (AH-1F)	78-23110	22216		PV

WESTERN SKY AVIATION WARBIRD MUSEUM (UT13)

Address:	2050 West Canyon View Drive, St. George, Utah 84770-5802.
Tel:	801-391-8376 **Email:** westernwarbirds@gmail.com
Admission:	By prior permission only.
Location:	At the airport which is in the south western part of the town.

The museum currently has three aircraft in its fleet. The MiG-15bis, imported from China, is being restored to flying condition. The other aircraft regularly attend airshows in the region. The former Polish Air Force Lim-5 was imported in late 1997 and was flown in Texas until its move north. The Jet Provost was delivered to the Royal Air Force in late 1961 and flew with a number of training establishments for almost 30 years before spending a short period serving as an instructional airframe at RAF Halton.

… *Utah – Vermont*

TYPE	REG/SER	CON. NO.	PI/NOTES	STATUS
☐ Hunting-Percival P.84 Jet Provost T.3A (T.3)	N4421B	PAC/W/11803	XN548, N9014M	RAA
☐ Mikoyan-Gurevich MiG-15bis			(China)	RAC
☐ WSK Lim-5 [MiG-17F]	N509	1C 15-09	1509 (Poland)	RAA

VERMONT

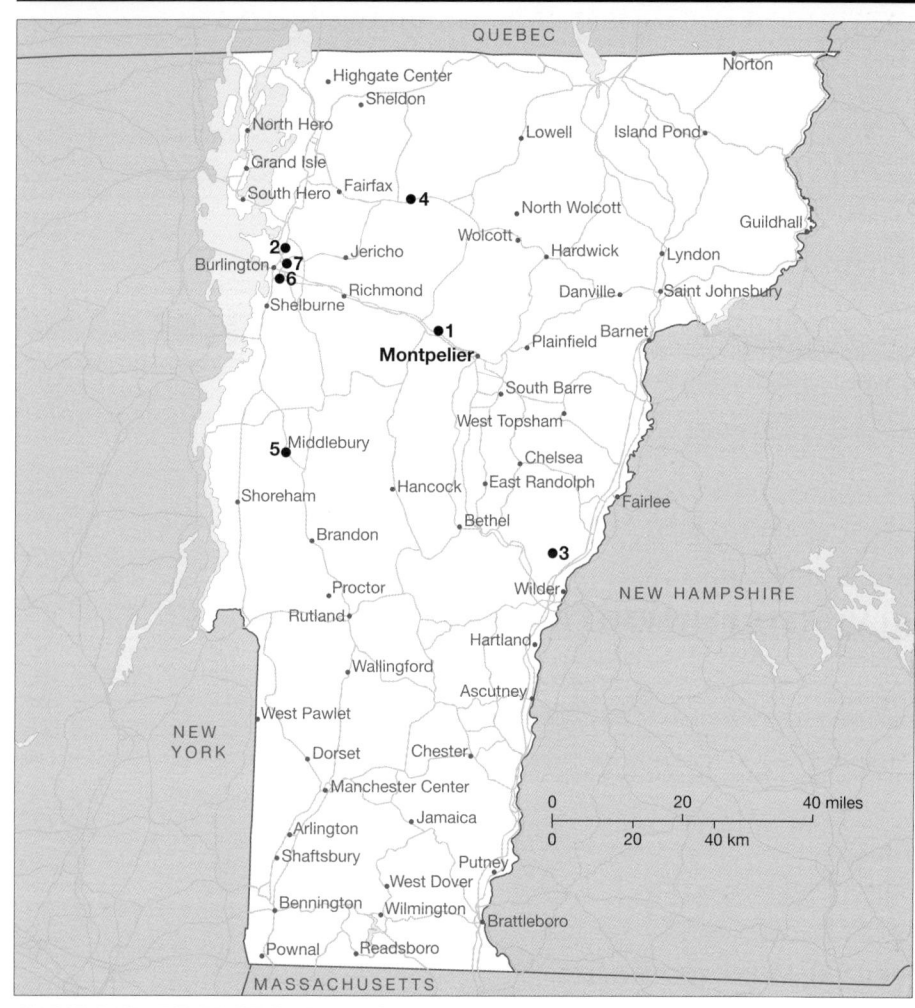

CAMP MEADE VICTORY MUSEUM (VT1)

Address: 961 Route 2, Middlesex, Vermont 05602.
Tel: 802-223-5537   **Email:** campmeade@together.net
Admission: Mid May–mid October Tuesday-Saturday 0900-1600.
Location: About 15 miles north west of Montpelier near exit 9 of I-89.

The camp opened in the 1930s as a Civilian Conservation Corps Camp. Here men put out of work by the Great Depression were given board and lodging and took part in training programmes. The exhibits highlight this period and also cover World War II. Period music can be heard and the hardships endured are portrayed in detail. Items of memorabilia and every day objects feature prominently. A number of military vehicles are on show and three aircraft can be seen. The Kansan was flown in Canada after its military days were over. The cabins on the site are now used as a motel and the canteen serves food reminiscent of the 1930s and 1940s.

TYPE	REG/SER	CON. NO.	PI/NOTES	STATUS
☐ Beech C18S Kansan (AT-11)	CF-JNW	4616	42-37620	PV
☐ North American NA-190 Sabre (F-86D)	52-10068	190-793		PV

COLCHESTER MONUMENT (VT2)

Location:	On permanent view at a business in the town.

TYPE	REG/SER	CON. NO.	PI/NOTES	STATUS
☐ Kamov Ka-26	HA-MPX	7806401		PV

EXPERIMENTAL BALLOON AND AIRSHIP MUSEUM (VT3)

Address:	PO Box 51, Robinson Hill Road, Post Mills Airport, Vermont 05058-0051.
Tel:	802-333-9254 Email: balloons@vermontel.net
Admission:	During working hours.
Location:	About 20 miles north of White River Junction off Route 113.

Brian Boland built his first balloon in 1971. Over the last three decades he has constructed large numbers of balloons and several airships.
  He has made a number of innovations in both design and construction. He developed a lightweight collapsible seat and has used parachute fabric in the construction of envelopes. This has led to balloons which can be easily transported as standard luggage. His first airship design flew in the mid-1970s and several developments have now flown. Brian has also set up the Experimental Balloon and Airship Association to co-ordinate the work of amateur builders.

  In the mid-1990s a large two-storey building was constructed at the airport. The ground floor houses the museum and the upper is used for balloon manufacture and layout. The museum literature states that over 100 balloons are in the exhibition along with components, photographs and documents.
  Brian Boland has said to me that he does not know what exactly is on show and has no list. A visitor has told me not many of the exhibits are labelled. I would appreciate further details. Those listed below are registered to Boland Balloons and some are still regularly flown.

TYPE	REG/SER	CON. NO.	PI/NOTES	STATUS
☐ Boland Albatross Hot Air Balloon	N14BJ	A-1		PV
☐ Boland Ax.1-5 Hot Air Balloon	N31220	5		PV
☐ Boland Ax.8 Hot Air Balloon	N5589B	12		PV
☐ Boland Baggage Hot Air Balloon	N24072	132		PV
☐ Boland Fred Hot Air Balloon	N8295	3		PV
☐ Boland Phoenix Hot Air Balloon	N11895	1		PV
☐ Boland Polywog Air Balloon	N10324	11		PV
☐ Boland Rover Hot Air Balloon	N9029Q	A-2		PV
☐ Boland/Raven RX.6 Hot Air Balloon	N8752L	RX6-139		PVA
☐ Boland/Raven RX.6 Hot Air Balloon	N9511L	RX6-146		PVA
☐ Cameron V-77 Hot Air Balloon	N148CB	341		PVA
☐ Cameron O-105 Hot Air Balloon	N2925L	5050		PVA
☐ Galaxy 7 Hot Air Balloon	N5335M	GLX-1497		PVA

HYDE PARK MONUMENT (VT4)

Location:	On permanent view at VFW 7779 in the western part of the town on Route 15.

TYPE	REG/SER	CON. NO.	PI/NOTES	STATUS
☐ Hughes 369M Cayuse (HO-6) (OH-6A)	68-17197	1157		PV

MIDDLEBURY MONUMENT (VT5)

Location:	On permanent view at ALP 27 at 49 Wilson Road in the south eastern part of the town.

TYPE	REG/SER	CON. NO.	PI/NOTES	STATUS
☐ Douglas TA-4J Skyhawk	Bu158090	14127	On loan from NMNA, FL	PV

VERMONT AIR NATIONAL GUARD HERITAGE PARK (VT6)

Address:	150 NCO Drive, Burlington, Vermont 05402.
Tel:	802-660-5210 Email: webmaster@vtburl.ang.af.mil
Admission:	By prior permission only.
Location:	About 3 miles east of the city off Route 2.

The 158th Squadron was allocated to the Vermont Air National Guard in August 1946. The unit initially flew the P-47D Thunderbolt. In July 1950 the P-51D Mustang arrived and later F-94 Starfires, F-89D Scorpions and F-102 Delta Daggers were flown. In 1974 a change in role occurred with the arrival of the Martin EB-57.

Fighters returned in January 1982 when F-4D Phantoms were allocated. These served until 1986 when they were replaced by the F-16 Fighting Falcon. The squadron has been collecting aircraft for preservation for a number of years.
  A heritage park has been built near the main gate and almost all the aircraft are now located here.

TYPE	REG/SER	CON. NO.	PI/NOTES	STATUS
☐ Beech D18S Expeditor (C-45H)	'01880'	AF-771	52-10841, N9590Z, N128VC, N128V	RAX
☐ Bell 205 Iroquois (UH-1H)	70-16355	12660	At Army NG site.	RA
☐ Convair 340-79 Samaritan (C-131D)	54-2810	207		RA
☐ Convair 8-10 Delta Dagger (F-102A)	55-3462	8-10-171		RA
☐ Convair 8-10 Delta Dagger (F-102A)	57-0858	8-10-824		RAD
☐ Douglas DC-3A-467 Skytrain (C-47D)	N54610	20507	43-16141, 316141 (Morocco), CNALC (Morocco)	RA
☐ General Dynamics 401 Fighting Falcon (F-16A)	79-0357	61-142	Recruiting aid.	RA
☐ General Dynamics 401 Fighting Falcon (F-16A)	78-0425	61-31		RA

☐ General Dynamics 401 Fighting Falcon (F-16C)	83-1165	5C-48		RA
☐ Hughes 369M Cayuse (HO-6) (OH-6A)	68-17206	1166	At Army NG. site.	RA
☐ Lockheed 580 (T-33A)	'29734'	580-1561	58-0592	RAX
☐ Lockheed 780-76-12 Starfire (F-94A)	49-2517	780-7039		RA
☐ Martin 272B Canberra (B-57B) (EB-57B)	52-1500	83		RA
☐ McDonnell M.98EN Phantom II (F-4D)	'65-0793'	1899	66-0240	RAX
☐ Northrop N-160 Scorpion (N-68) (F-89D) (F-89J)	'21883'	N.4625	53-2494	PVX

VERMONT VETERANS MILITIA MUSEUM (VT7)

Address: 789 National Guard Road, Colchester, Vermont 05466-3099.
Tel: 802-338-3360   **Email:** museumadm@gmail.com
Admission: Tuesday-Thursday 1000-1500. (Only open on Tuesday in winter)
Location: In the northern suburbs of Burlington off Interstate 89.

A small museum has been set up in a building on the camp. The displays trace the history of the state forces and special exhibitions are regularly staged. All wars in which the units have served are highlighted.

Three aircraft, flown by Vermont Guard Units, are on show outside the museum along with a collection of military vehicles. An exhibition hall houses the S.E.5 replica and the Sioux along with items of memorabilia.

TYPE	REG/SER	CON. NO.	PI/NOTES	STATUS
☐ Bell 47D-1 Sioux (H-13E) (OH-13E)				PV
☐ Bell 205 Iroquois (UH-1D) (UH-1H)	65-9613	4657		PV
☐ Hughes 369M Cayuse (HO-6) (OH-6A)	66-14390	0271		PV
☐ McDonnell M.98EN Phantom II (F-4D)	65-0712	1760		PV
☐ Royal Aircraft Factory S.E.5A (Scale R)				PVX

VIRGINIA

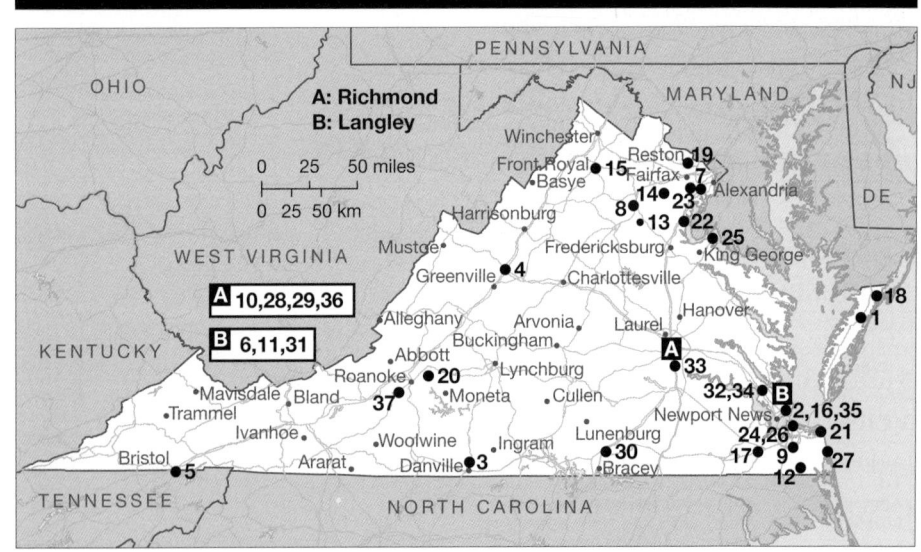

ACCOMACK MONUMENT (VA1)

Location: On permanent view at the airport which is about 4 miles south of the town.

TYPE	REG/SER	CON. NO.	PI/NOTES	STATUS
☐ Douglas A-4F Skyhawk	Bu155036	13852		PV

AIR POWER PARK AND MUSEUM (VA2)

Address: 413 West Mercury Boulevard, Hampton, Virginia 23666.
Tel: 757-727-1163
Admission: Daily 0900-1630.
Location: In the northern suburbs of the city off Route 167.

Virginia

The park was set up in the early 1960s to honour the contribution of Langley Air Force Base and NASA's Langley Research Center to the community. An exhibition building, which also houses a tourist bureau, was later erected. Inside there are displays tracing the history of aviation in the area with a superb range of photographs from the early days of Langley up to the present time. A collection of models is also on show.

The outside park contains the aircraft and several missiles. Nine Kestrels were built to serve as development aircraft between the prototype Hawker P.1127 and the operational Harrier. Six went to the USA at the end of the trials in Britain and the example on show was flown by NASA at Langley.

The history of the United States space programme from the early days up to current Space Shuttle flights is portrayed.

TYPE	REG/SER	CON. NO.	PI/NOTES	STATUS
☐ Hawker P.1127 Kestrel (XV-6A)	NASA520		XS694, 64-18268 – wings from XS692, 64-18266	PV
☐ Lockheed 580 (T-33A)	51-9086	580-6870		PV
☐ Mcdonnell M.36BA Voodoo (F-101C)	56-0246	211		PV
☐ McDonnell M.98DF Phantom II (RF-4C)	69-0372	3906		PV
☐ North American NA-177 Sabre (F-86D) (F-86L)	51-3064	177-121		PV
☐ North American NA-223 Super Sabre (F-100D)	54-2145	223-25		PV
☐ Northrop N-160 Scorpion (N-68) (F-89D) (F-89J)	52-2129	N.4541		PV
☐ Republic F-105D Thunderchief	61-0073	D-268		PV
☐ Republic LTV-N-2 [Fieseler Fi 103A-1]				PV
☐ Vought A-7E Corsair II	'Bu157500'	E229	Bu157506	PVX

AMERICAN ARMORED FOUNDATION TANK MUSEUM (VA3)

Address: 3410 Highway 29B, Danville, Virginia 24540.
Tel: 434-836-5273 **Fax:** 434-836-3532 **Email:** aaftank@gamewood.net
Admission: Monday-Saturday 1000-1700.
Location: About 5 miles north of the town.

This museum, run by the American Armored Foundation, was originally located at Mattituck in New York State. On 24th December 1998 the Sandvik company donated a large building on an 89-acre site to the group. The structure had been empty for many years and it has now been converted for the display. Over 100 tanks are on show along with a similar number of heavy weapons. There is an extensive collection of uniforms and items of memorabilia.

The displays have been enhanced with dioramas which feature large murals as backgrounds and genuine weapons and equipment in typical combat scenes from wars around the world.

TYPE	REG/SER	CON. NO.	PI/NOTES	STATUS
☐ Bell 209 Huey Cobra (AH-1G) (AH-1F)	68-17022	20750		PV

BLUE RIDGE COMMUNITY COLLEGE (VA4)

Address: PO Box 80, 1 College Lane, Weyers Cave, Virginia 24486-0080.
Tel: 540-234-2306 **Email:** dyenf@brcc.edu
Admission: By prior permission only.
Location: At Shenandoah Valley Airport which is about 4 miles south east of the town

The college has a facility at the airport which includes classrooms and workshops. Students are trained in a variety of skills leading to obtaining airframe and power plant certificates.

TYPE	REG/SER	CON. NO.	PI/NOTES	STATUS
☐ Beech 65-A90 King Air	N77SS	LJ-230	N750K, N938A	RA
☐ Cessna 172M	N20515	17261353		RA
☐ Cessna 172M	N9591V	17264393		RA

BRISTOL MONUMENT (VA5)

Location: On permanent view at a Veterans Memorial in Cumberland Street in the eastern part of the town.

TYPE	REG/SER	CON. NO.	PI/NOTES	STATUS
☐ Bell 209 Huey Cobra (AH-1G) (AH-1F)	66-15299	20055		PV

CENTRAL INTELLIGENCE AGENCY MONUMENT (VA6)

Location: On permanent view at the Headquarters in Langley.

TYPE	REG/SER	CON. NO.	PI/NOTES	STATUS
☐ Lockheed A-12	'77835'	128	60-6931	PVX

COLD WAR MUSEUM (VA7)

Address: PO Box 178, 10824 West 1st Street, Fairfax, Virginia 22038.
Tel: 703-273-2381 **Fax:** 703-273-4903 **Email:** museum@coldwar.org
Admission: Not yet open.
Location: At Vint Hill which is near Warrenton about 30 miles south of Washington DC.

On 1st May 1960 Gary Powers was shot down in a U-2 over Sverdlovsk in the Soviet Union. Parts of crashed U-2s are on show in the Central Museum of the Armed Forces in Moscow and the Museum of Military Technology in Ekaterinburg in Russia– both wrecks are claimed to be his aircraft! After his release he returned to the USA and served as a test pilot for the Lockheed company. The museum has been established by his son Gary Jnr. and John Welch. A travelling exhibit tracing the

story of the mission has been set up at this has been on temporary display in a number of museums across the country.
After a number of setbacks a site has now been obtained at Vint Hill. This site is being developed and hopefully will be ready in the not too distant future. The area is a former Army communications base used by the NSA and CIA during the period of the Cold War. The main hall will feature items from the Berlin Airlift, the USS *Pueblo*, the U-2 incident, the Bay of Pigs mission and the Cuban Missile Crisis. The collection includes a number of missiles from this era.

COMMEMORATIVE AIR FORCE (NATIONAL CAPITOL SQUADRON) (VA8)

Address:	12499 Beverly Ford Road, Hangar C2, Brandy Station, Virginia 22714.
Tel:	540-727-0018 Email: Mike.Hogan@landmarkaviation.com
Admission:	By prior permission only.
Location:	At Culpepper Airport which is about 7 miles north east of the town.

This unit has a Stinson Sentinel and Vultee Valiant allocated to it. Both are in flying condition and painted in typical period colours. The remaining aircraft are owned by members and are often attend meetings at the airfield. The Chipmunk has retained its Portuguese Air Force markings.

Art Nalls, former AV-8 pilot, owns the Sea Harrier which he purchased in 2005. The aircraft made its first flight in the USA at St. Mary's County Airport in Maryland in November 2007. Since then it has appeared at several shows in the region.

TYPE	REG/SER	CON. NO.	PI/NOTES	STATUS
☐ Aero L-39C Albatros	N39WF	232218	91 (Soviet), ES-YLC, N39MQ	RAA
☐ De Havilland DHC.1 Chipmunk T.20	N46TR	P.10	1320 (Portugal), N64746	RAA
☐ Grumman G-40 Avenger (TBM-3) (TBM-3E) (AS.3M)	N40402	4331	Bu91426, 91426 (Canada), CF-MUE	RAC
☐ Hawker-Siddeley P.1184 Sea Harrier FA.2 (FRS.1)	N94422	41H/912002	XZ439	RAA
☐ North American NA-88 Texan (AT-6D) (SNJ-5)	N3931R	88-16874	42-85003, Bu84923, (Spain)	RAA
☐ North American NA-121 Texan (AT-6D)	N36	121-42215	44-81493, N7230C, N36JM	RAA
☐ North American NA-168 Texan (T-6G)	N66JB/'49-2821'	168-19	49-2915, N7813C	RAAX
☐ North American NA-182 Texan (T-6G)				RAA
☐ North American NA-200 Trojan (T-28B)	NX228JK	200-31	Bu137668, 37688 (US Army), N228KM	RAA
☐ North American NA-219 Trojan (T-28B)	N281CM	219-34	Bu140035, N281MS	RAA
☐ Piper J-3C-65 Cub	N26457	3999	NC26457	RAA
☐ Stinson V-76 Sentinel (L-5) (OY-1)	N1156V/'298758'		42-98752, Bu60507	RAA
☐ Vultee V-74 Valiant (BT-13A)	N56360	74-5946	(USAAF)	RAA
☐ Yakovlev Yak-3UA	N20669	0470110		RAA

COMMEMORATIVE AIR FORCE (OLD DOMINION SQUADRON) (VA9)

Address:	32454 John Beverly Rose Drive, Franklin Virginia 23851-3923.
Tel:	757-838-3003 Email: johnbarbara@verizon.net
Admission:	By prior permission only.
Location:	At Chesapeake/Hampton Roads Airport which is about 5 miles west of Chesapeake on Route 58.

For many years the wing had a hangar at Richmond International Airport and there were plans for a museum. A move was made to Danville Airport before the current home was found. Funds are being raised to construct a flying museum. The Sentinel and Lodestar are allocated to the wing and the others are owned by members.

TYPE	REG/SER	CON. NO.	PI/NOTES	STATUS
☐ Boeing-Stearman B75N1 Kaydet (N2S-3)				RAA
☐ Lockheed 18-56-23 Lodestar (C-60A)	N30N	18-2274	42-55884, YS-22, NC66322, N66322	RA
☐ Naval Aircraft Factory N3N-3	N66CV		Bu4384, N44957	RAA
☐ North American NA-182 Texan (T-6G)				RAA
☐ North American NA-200 Trojan (T-28B)	N65491	200-316	Bu138245	RAA
☐ Ryan ST-3KR Recruit (PT-22)	N53004	1888	41-20679	RAA
☐ Stinson V-76 Sentinel (O-62) (L-5)	N9315H		42-15060	RAA

DEFENSE SUPPLY CENTER (VA10)

Address:	8000 Jefferson Davis Highway, Richmond, Virginia 23219-5001.
Tel:	804-279-3139 Fax: 804-279-6052
Admission:	By prior permission only.
Location:	On Highway 301 south of the city.

This large complex houses many government offices. Opened in 1942 as the Richmond General Depot it served the Army with Quartermaster supplies. The site was expanded in the early 1960s when it took on the role of supporting all the military services and civilian agencies worldwide. A collection of preserved aircraft has been assembled over the last few years. They represent types which have connections with the work carried out.

TYPE	REG/SER	CON. NO.	PI/NOTES	STATUS
☐ Bell 205 Iroquois (UH-1H)	69-15851	12139		RA
☐ Bell 209 Huey Cobra (AH-1G) (AH-1S)				RA
☐ Fairchild-Republic A-10A Thunderbolt II	75-0273	A10-22		RA
☐ Grumman G-128 Intruder (A-6A) (A-6E)	Bu157024	I-493		RA
☐ Grumman G-303 Tomcat (F-14A)	Bu159853	213		RA
☐ McDonnell M.199-1A Eagle (F-15A)	71-0283	004/A004		RA
☐ McDonnell M.267 Hornet (F/A-18A)	Bu163119	518/A629		RA
☐ Republic F-84F Thunderstreak	52-6643			RA

Virginia

DELMONT MONUMENT (VA11)

Location:	On permanent view in a park in northern suburbs of Richmond

TYPE	REG/SER	CON. NO.	PI/NOTES	STATUS
☐ Lockheed 580 (T-33A)	51-6742	580-6074		PV

FENTRESS NAVAL AUXILLIARY LANDING FIELD MONUMENT (VA12)

Location:	By prior permission only at the airfield which is just east of the town.

TYPE	REG/SER	CON. NO.	PI/NOTES	STATUS
☐ Grumman G-123 Hawkeye (E-2C)	Bu160420	A40	Instructional airframe	RA
☐ McDonnell M.267A Hornet (YF-18A)	Bu160776	2/A002		RA

FLYING CIRCUS AERODROME (VA13)

Address:	5114 Ritchie Road, Bealeton, Virginia 22728.
Tel:	540-439-8661 **Email:** Info@FlyingCircusAirShow.com
Admission:	May–October Saturday-Sunday 1000-1700.
Location:	About 14 miles south east of Warrenton off Route 17.

The organisation started in the early 1970s using a number of World War I replicas bought in England. The site at Bealeton was purchased in 1973 and hangars and buildings typical of the period were erected. Weekend shows were held throughout the summer months. After three years of operations the emphasis changed to include classic American biplanes. The shows relive the barnstorming days with typical inter-war stunts, including wing-walking, aerobatics and parachute drops.

TYPE	REG/SER	CON. NO.	PI/NOTES	STATUS
☐ Aeronca K	NC17774	K-42	NC17774, N17774	RAA
☐ Aeronca 7AC Champion	N4300E	7AC-7173		PVA
☐ Bellanca 14-13-2 Crusair Senior	N74228	1341		RAA
☐ Bellanca 7GCBC Citabria	N1670G	137		RAA
☐ Boeing-Stearman A75N1 Kaydet (PT-17)	N53414	75-773	41-1013	PVA
☐ Boeing-Stearman A75N1 Kaydet (PT-17)	N49986	75-1726	41-8167	PVA
☐ Boeing-Stearman A75N1 Kaydet (PT-17)	N66004	75-2446	41-8887, N6904	PVA
☐ Boeing-Stearman A75N1 Kaydet (PT-17)	N46592	75-2759	41-25270	PVA
☐ Boeing-Stearman A75N1 Kaydet (PT-17)	N1209N	75-4646	42-16483	PVA
☐ Boeing-Stearman A75N1 Kaydet (PT-17)	N68853	75-5418	42-17255	PVA
☐ Boeing-Stearman A75N1 Kaydet (PT-17) (N2S-4)	N4786N	75-3293	41-25855, Bu28018	PVA
☐ Boeing-Stearman B75N1 Kaydet (N2S-3)	N27WE	75-6651	Bu07007, N58255	PVA
☐ Boeing-Stearman B75N1 Kaydet (N2S-3)	N1066M	75-7932	Bu38311	PVA
☐ Boeing-Stearman E75 Kaydet (PT-13D) (N2S-5)	N75665	75-8556	42-109523, Bu43462	RAA
☐ Corben MJA Sport	N4731C	1		PVA
☐ Fleet 7	N9433	81	NC9433	PVA
☐ Piper J-3C-65 Cub	N30551	4925	NC30551	RAA
☐ Piper J-3C-65 Cub	N70593	17604	NC70593	PVA
☐ Piper J-3C-65 Cub	N4693S	18373		PVA
☐ Piper J-3C-65 Cub (L-4J)	N33554	14028	45-55262	PVA
☐ Pitts S-1T Special	N666BD	1018		PVA
☐ Waco UPF-7	N185V	5604	NC185	PV
☐ Waco UPF-7	NC32162	5794	NC32162, N32162	PVA
☐ Waco UPF-7 (PT-14)	N2291	5312	NC2291, 40-26, NC2291	PVA
☐ Walter Extra EA-300	N300XT	023		PVA

FREEDOM MUSEUM (VA14)

Address:	PO Box 568, Manassas, Virginia 20108.
Tel:	703-393-0660 **Email:** FreedomMuseum7@FreedomMuseum.org
Admission:	Monday-Saturday 0900-1700; Sunday 1200-1600.
Location:	At the airport which is about 5 miles west of the town on Route 28.

The museum opened on 4th July 1999 and has on show photographs and artefacts tracing the contribution of the American nation in establishing freedom in many parts of the world. At the current time the exhibition is housed in an unused terminal building at Manassas Regional Airport. There are plans have to expand the display.

FRONT ROYAL MUSEUM (VA15)

Address:	229 Stokes Airport Road, Front Royal, Virginia 22630.
Tel:	540-636-7751 **Email:** airportmanager@warrencountyva.net
Admission:	When the clubhouse is open.
Location:	About three miles west of the town.

The local aeroclub has set up a small display in its building at the airport. The Sabre has been mounted at the field for a number of years. On show inside are local artefacts, photographs, parts from WW II aircraft and uniforms. The MB-2 autogyro was built locally in the mid-1980s and is powered by a Volkswagen engine.

TYPE	REG/SER	CON. NO.	PI/NOTES	STATUS
☐ Boland Hot Air Balloon			Basket only.	PV
☐ Boyce-Maynard MB-2	N5206X	002		PV
☐ North American NA-187 Sabre (F-86H)	52-2044	187-70		PV

HAMPTON UNIVERSITY (VA16)

Address:	Science and Technology Building, Hampton, Virginia 23668.
Tel:	757-727-5418 **Email:** aviation@hamptonu.edu
Admission:	By prior permission only.
Location:	At Newport News Airport which is about 7 mile north of Hampton.

The University offers courses in subjects such as Air Traffic Control, Aviation Computer Science, Aviation Electronics, Aviation Management and Flight Education. Well equipped laboratories are used and a hangar at the airport houses the instructional airframes. The Beech Mentor was flown locally by NASA. The Sabreliner joined the collection in the 1990s. The two Learjets were acquired a few years ago.

TYPE	REG/SER	CON. NO.	PI/NOTES	STATUS
☐ Beech D45 Mentor (T-34C)	N510NA	GL-108		RA
☐ Gates Learjet 24D	N48FN	24D-238	N262GL, N472EJ, N49DM	RA
☐ Gates Learjet 25	N97FN	25-003	N594GA, N11JC, N4PN, N97DM	RA
☐ North American NA-282 Sabreliner 40	N88	282-88		RA
☐ Northrop N-156T Talon (T-38A) (AT-38B)	63-8117	N.5464		RA

MILITARY AIRCRAFT MUSEUM / FIGHTER FACTORY (VA17)

Address:	1341 Princess Anne Road, Virginia Beach, Virginia 23457
Tel:	757-721-7767 **Fax:** 757-539-5331 **Email:** epy1@aol.com
Admission:	Daily 0900-1700.
Location:	At Virginia Beach Airport which is about 3 miles south of the town on Route 615. Restoration at Suffolk County Airport.

This private collection set up by Jerry Yagen contains several interesting types. In 2003 an airport at Virginia Beach was purchased. The grass runway was lengthened and a new hangar complex was built. A museum building has also been erected.

An original Luftwaffe World War II hangar has been acquired from Cottbus and this will eventually house the German aircraft in the fleet. A control tower from the same period was transported from the former Goxhill airfield in England.

The Spitfire was recovered from Israel by Robert Lamplough in 1979. Restoration started in the mid-1980s in England and it took to the air in November 1998. This classic fighter arrived in Virginia in 2000. The Invader was once owned by Robert Pond whose fleet of warbirds now reside at the Palm Springs Air Museum in California.

There are a number of Russian aircraft in the collection. The Polikapov fighters have been rebuilt from wrecks discovered in the former Soviet Union. Two came via the Alpine Fighter Collection in New Zealand.

Many aircraft are being rebuilt in workshops around the world and will move to Virginia when complete. The three Focke-Wulf Fw 190s were all found in Norway and spent some time at the Texas Air Museum workshops in Rio Hondo. A newly-built Flug Werk example has also been acquired. Replicas of World War I types are joining the collection.

The Tupolev ANT-7 prototype first flew in September 1929 and soon entered production in a number of versions. The type was used for military reconnaissance and escort duties. Aeroflot also used the twin engined monoplane on its services. The wreck of one recovered from a crash site is being restored at a workshop near Moscow.

The Dragon Rapide has been rebuilt in New Zealand and flew again in early 2010. This classic biplane now wears the colours of one used by the Prince of Wales in the 1930s. The Hawker Fury replica was built for the late Patrick Lindsay and first flew at Booker in December 1985. The aircraft spent many years in Belgium before joining the collection in the autumn of 2009. No doubt more interesting types will arrive here to enhance the wide range already present.

TYPE	REG/SER	CON. NO.	PI/NOTES	STATUS
☐ Albatros D Va (R)	N17DV	JP1991DV		RAA
☐ Avro 504K (R)	'H5991'			PVX
☐ Avro 504K (R)	N504K	PSA-001		PVX
☐ Beech A45 Mentor (T-34A)	N56NT	G-778	55-0210	PVA
☐ Bell 14 Airacobra (P-400)				RAD
☐ Bell 26E Airacobra (P-39Q)				RAC
☐ Bell 26E Airacobra (P-39Q)				RAC
☐ Bell 33 Kingcobra (P-63A)	'270609/17'		42-70609 – in Soviet markings.	PVX
☐ Bell 33 Kingcobra (P-63E)				RAC
☐ Blériot XI (R)				RA
☐ Boeing 266 Pea Shooter (P-26D) (R)	N26PX	32-06		PVA
☐ Boeing 299-O Fortress (B-17G) (TB-17G) (ETB-17G) (JTB-17G)	NL3701G	7943	44-8543, N3701G	PVC
☐ Boeing-Stearman A75N1 Kaydet (PT-17)	N41EE	75-2743	41-25254, N52507	PVA
☐ Bücker Bü 133C Jungmeister	N38BU	38	U-91, HB-MIW, G-AYSJ, D-EHVP, G-AYSJ	PVA
☐ CASA 352L [Junkers Ju 52/3m]	'1Z+AR'	67	T.2B-176, N99059, N352JU	PVAX
☐ Cessna 172F	N8723U	17252627		RAA
☐ Cessna 337 Super Skymaster	N2399Q	33700172		RAA
☐ Classic Aircraft Waco F-5	N40116	F5-024		PVA
☐ Commonwealth CA-27 Sabre 31 [North American F-86F]	N5686	CA27-22	A94-922	RAC
☐ Consolidated 28-5A Catalina (PBY-5A)	N9521C	1656	Bu48284	PVA
☐ Curtiss 87-A4 Warhawk (P-40E) (Kittyhawk IA)	N1941P/'41-5658'	18539	41-35918, (RAF) (Soviet)	PVAX
☐ De Havilland DH.82A Tiger Moth	N6463/T5525	83244	T5525, VH-BFO, VT-CSZ, CF-EIQ	PVA
☐ De Havilland DH.89A Dragon Rapide (DH.89B Dominie I)	'G-ADDD'	6709	HG724, G-AKPA, EI-AML, F-BLHZ, NX89DH	RAAX
☐ De Havilland DH.98 Mosquito FB.26	KA114			RAC
☐ De Havilland DHC.1 Chipmunk T.10	N559WK	C1/0576	WK759	PVA
☐ Douglas A-20G Havoc				RAC
☐ Douglas A-26B Invader	N26RP/'436874'	6874	41-39161, N1470V, N317V, N317W	RAAX

Virginia

☐ Douglas AD-4 Skyraider	N23827/'123827'	7133	Bu123827, N54162	PVA
☐ Fiat G.59-4B	N5955F	185	MM53778	RA
☐ Fieseler Fi 103A-1				RA
☐ Fleet 1	N63J	229		RAA
☐ Flug Werk FW 190A-8/N	D-FMFW	990002		RAA
☐ Focke-Wulf Fw 190A-8	N4247L	350177		PVC
☐ Focke-Wulf Fw 190A-8	N90FW	732183		RAC
☐ Focke-Wulf Fw 190A-8	N447FW	739447		RA
☐ Focke-Wulf Fw 44J Stieglitz	N183FW	183	LV-YYX, D-EHDH, OO-JKT, G-STIG	RAA
☐ Fokker D VII (R)	N1918F	1		PVA
☐ Fokker D VII (R)	N425VT	0033	D-EAWM, G-BFPL, I-BFPL	PVA
☐ Fokker Dr I (R)	NX900TP	001TP		PVAX
☐ Fokker Dr I (R)	N757FK	1972		PVAX
☐ Fokker Dr I (R)	NX417RB	42118	Carries '103/17'	PVA
☐ Grumman G-36 Wildcat (FM-2)	N315E	2183	Bu47030	PVA
☐ Grumman G-40 Avenger (TBM-3) (TBM-3E)	NL7030C	3516	Bu53454	PVA
☐ Halberstadt CL IV (R)	N6175J	CL-IV		RAA
☐ Hawker Fury (R)	N31FY/'K1930'	WA/6	G-BKBB, OO-XFU, OO-HFU, G-BKBB	PVAX
☐ Hawker Hurricane II				RA
☐ Hawker Hurricane XII	'V6793'	56022	5667 (Canada), N2549, N943HH	PVA
☐ Hawker Sea Fury FB.11	N60SF	41H/656816	WN480, 308 (Iraq)	RAA
☐ Hispano HA-1112M1L [Messerschmitt Bf 109G]	N109FF		C.4K-64 (?), N7800P	RAA
☐ Kawasaki Ki-61-I Hien				RAC
☐ Laister-Kauffman LK.10A	NC51462	126		PV
☐ Lavochkin La-9	N415ML	828		RA
☐ Lockheed 422-87-23 Lightning (P-38L)			Remains of seven airframes.	RAD
☐ Messerschmitt Bf 109E-7		2023		RAA
☐ Messerschmitt Bf 109G			Wings and other parts.	RAD
☐ Messerschmitt Me 262A-1				RAC
☐ Mikoyan-Gurevich MiG-3	'17'	3457	N107FB	RAAX
☐ Morane-Saulnier MS.500 Criquet [Fieseler Fi 156 Storch]	N42FM	751	751 (France), D-EAML	RAA
☐ Naval Aircraft Factory N3N-3	N120BH		Bu2892, N45067	RAA
☐ Nieuport 27 (R)	NX27XZ	100603		PVA
☐ Nord N.1002 Pingouin II [Messerschmitt Bf 108B]	N108ZZ	258	F-BDYT	RAA
☐ Nord N.1101 Noralpha (Ramier I) [Messerschmitt Me 208]	N208K/'14'	162	162 (France)	PVAX
☐ North American NA-65 Texan (SNJ-2)	N55729	65-2000	Bu2011	PVA
☐ North American NA-88 Texan (SNJ-4)	N43NA/'26939'	88-11798	Bu26939, 7647 (South Africa), N50BZ	RAA
☐ North American NA-108 Mitchell (B-25J) (TB-25J)	N3453G	108-47598	44-86844	RAC
☐ North American NA-108 Mitchell (B-25J) (TB-25N)	N7947C	108-33404	44-30129	PVA
☐ North American NA-122 Mustang (P-51D) (Mustang IV)	N51EA/'463684'	122-31223	44-63507, 9554 (Canada), N6345T, (N12073), (N38FF), N13410	PVAX
☐ North American NA-159 Trojan (T-28A) (AT-28D)	NX99160	159-146	49-1634, N9878C, FG-634 (Zaire)	PVA
☐ Pietenpol B4-A Aircamper	NX29GM	1986		RA
☐ Polikarpov I-15bis	N3815R/'7'	3994	RA-02915	PVAX
☐ Polikarpov I-153	N153RP/'16'	6316	16, ZK-JKN	PVA
☐ Polikarpov I-16	21			RA
☐ Polikarpov I-16 tip 24	N1639P/'28'	2421028	28, ZK-JIR	PVAX
☐ Polikarpov Po-2	'01'	0717	N3602	RAAX
☐ Ryan ST-3KR Recruit (PT-22)	N56081	1926	41-20717	RA
☐ Sopwith Pup (Scale R)	N98LM	10201		PVA
☐ Stinson V-76 Sentinel (L-5E)	N57WT/'417588'	76-3786	44-17499	RAAX
☐ Supermarine 361 Spitfire LF.IXe	N730MJ/MJ730	CBAF-7243	MJ730, MM4094, 0606 (Israel), 20-66 (Israel), (G-FEDX), G-BLAS, G-HFIX	PVA
☐ Tupolev ANT-7 (R-6)				RAC
☐ Vought FG-1D Corsair	N46RL	3769	Bu92508, N7225C, N46WB, N46LF, (N70RP), N46LF	RAC
☐ Vought V-310 Kingfisher (OS2U-3)				RAC
☐ Vultee V-72 Vengeance I (A-35A)				RAC
☐ Vultee V-79 Valiant (BT-13B) (SNV-2)	N56867	79-1220	(USAAF), (USN) – mocked up as Val 'BI-211'	PVAX
☐ Wright B (R)				RAA
☐ Yakovlev Yak-3M	N42YK	0470103		RAA
☐ Yakovlev Yak-18	N98LM	1160314		RAA
☐ Yakovlev Yak-55	N90RY	901204		RAC

NATIONAL AERONAUTICS AND SPACE ADMINISTRATION – WALLOPS ISLAND VISITOR CENTER (VA18)

Address:	Building J-7, Wallops Island, Virginia 23337.
Tel:	757-824-2298 Email: April.M.Davis@nasa.gov
Admission:	Thursday-Monday 1000-1600.
Location:	About 8 miles south of the Maryland border off Route 13.

The site was developed in the late 1940s for testing rocket powered missiles. The Pilotless Aircraft Research Division moved in during June 1945. A small exhibition tracing the work of the facility has been staged.

TYPE	REG/SER	CON. NO.	PI/NOTES	STATUS
☐ Beech C23 Sundowner 180	NASA504	M-1608	N6624R, N504NA	PV

NATIONAL AIR AND SPACE MUSEUM – STEVEN F. UDVAR-HAZY CENTER (VA19)

Address:	14930 Air and Space Parkway, Chantilly, Virginia 20151.
Tel:	202-633-1000 Email: jakub.p@nasm.edu
Admission:	Daily 1000-1730.
Location:	About 20 miles west of Washington, DC near Dulles Airport.

Plans for a new facility close to house the ever-growing collection were put forward several years ago. In 1990 the site was chosen to be near Dulles Airport. President Clinton signed the legislation in 1993 and a fund raising drive was initiated. Ground was broken in 2000 and the building opened to the public on 15th December 2003, four days after the formal dedication which commemorated the centenary of the Wright brothers historic flight. The complex has been named after the major donor to the project. Now over 100 aircraft are on show and more will arrive in the near future.

The James S. McDonnell Space Hangar was completed in December 2004. Here the visitor can see the Space Shuttle 'Enterprise' and a large number of rockets, spacecraft and satellites. Funds are being raised for a second phase which when complete will result in many more of the aircraft at Silver Hill making the short journey to the site. Restoration workshops, an archive centre and a storage hangar will eventually be built.

In the 1980s and 1990s some of the larger aircraft in the collection were stored at Dulles and in March 1990 a Lockheed SR-71 Blackbird flew into the airport. The first aircraft to be installed in the main display area, known as the Boeing Aviation Hangar, was the Piper Cub and this was soon followed by many more from the Garber Facility at Silver Hill in nearby Maryland. Just before the opening two significant airliners arrived by air.

The Boeing S-307 Stratoliner flew in after a journey from Seattle and a former Air France Concorde came from Paris. These two types show vividly the advances in transport design over half a century.

Many unique designs and the last survivors of a number of types can be seen in this ever developing display. Among the helicopters are examples of early designs from the Bell and Piasecki companies. The Arado Ar 234 is the only surviving German jet bomber of World War II.

Also on show are engines, components and models and displays tracing the history of flight from the early days. The aircraft are exhibited on three levels and a series of walkways enables the visitor to view them from a number of angles.

NB: The aircraft marked 'RA' will be put on show gradually over the next few years. Also aircraft loaned to other museums will be recalled and exhibited when the current deals have expired.

TYPE	REG/SER	CON. NO.	PI/NOTES	STATUS
☐ Aero Commander 500S	N500RA	3127		PV
☐ Aeronca C-2	X626N	291-2	NC626N	PV
☐ Aérospatiale / British Aircraft Corporation Concorde 101	F-BVFA	100-005	F-BVFA, N94FA	PV
☐ Aichi M6A1 Seiran	47	1600228		PV
☐ American Aerolights Double Eagle		200146		PV
☐ Arado Ar 234B-2	FI+GS	140312	140312, FE-1010, T2-1010	PV
☐ Arlington Sisu 1-A	N1100Z	102		PV
☐ Arrow Sport A2-60	NC9325	341	NC9325, N9325, G-AARO, N280AS	PV
☐ Bachem Ba 349B-1 Natter (BP-20)	T2-1		FE-1	RA
☐ Baldwin Red Devil				PV
☐ Bede BD-5A/B	N234BD	2731-001		PV
☐ Beech D18S	N522B	A-481		PV
☐ Beech 35 Bonanza	N80040	4	NX80040	PV
☐ Beech 65-90 King Air	N275DP	LJ-34	N1920H, N10LE, N1920M, N200SW	PV
☐ Bell 30	NX41867	1A		PV
☐ Bell 26E Airacobra (P-39Q)	44-2433	26E-433	44-2433, NX57591, N57591	RA
☐ Bell 33 Kingcobra (P-63A)	42-70255	33-131		RA
☐ Bell 47B	N116B	36		PV
☐ Bell 47J-1 Sioux (H-13J) (UH-13J)	57-2729	1576		PV
☐ Bell 65 ATV	N1105V	1		RA
☐ Bell 205 Iroquois (UH-1D) (UH-1H)	65-10126	5170		PV
☐ Bell 206L-1 Long Ranger	N3911Z	45658		RA
☐ Bell 301 (XV-15)	N703NA	002		PV
☐ Bellanca CF		C.56	11036, NR11036	PV
☐ Bennett Delta Wing 162 Hang Glider				PV
☐ Bennett Delta Wing Mariah M-9 Hang Glider		91		PV
☐ Bennett Delta Wing Phoenix 6 Hang Glider				PV
☐ Bennett Delta Wing Phoenix 6B Hang Glider				PV
☐ Bennett Delta Wing Phoenix Streak 130 Hang Glider		9		PV
☐ Bennett Delta Wing Phoenix Viper 175 Hang Glider				PV
☐ Benoist-Korn		32		PV
☐ Bensen B-6 Gyroglider		1		PV
☐ Bensen B-8M Gyrocopter	N2588B	194		PV
☐ Boeing 67 Hawk (FB-5)	A7114	820		PV
☐ Boeing 266 Pea Shooter (P-26A)	33-135	1911		PV
☐ Boeing 299-O Fortress (B-17G)	42-32076	7190	42-32076, SE-BAP, OY-DFA, 67-672 (Denmark), F-BGSH	PV
☐ Boeing S-307 Stratoliner	N19903	2003	NC19903, ZS-BWV, 2003 (Haiti), N9703R	PV
☐ Boeing 345 Superfortress (B-29)	44-86292			PV
☐ Boeing 367-80	N70700	17158		PV
☐ Boeing-Stearman E75 Kaydet (PT-13D) (N2S-5)	Bu61064	75-5186	42-17023	PV
☐ Bogardus Little Gee Bee	NX31250			PV
☐ Bowlus BA-100 Baby Albatross	NX18979	BA-100	NX18979, N18979	PV
☐ Bowlus-Dupont 1-S-2100 Falcon	G13763	3		PV

Virginia

☐ Bücker Bü 133C Jungmeister	N15696	42	YR-PAX	PV
☐ Bücker Bü 181B-1 Bestmann		2227	(Luftwaffe), FE-4611, T2-4611	RA
☐ Caudron G.4	2170	C-4263		PV
☐ Cessna 150L Commuter	N11213	15075257		RA
☐ Cessna A152 Aerobat	N7557L	A1520817		PV
☐ Cessna 180	N1538C	30238		PV
☐ Cessna 305A Bird Dog (L-19A) (O-1A)	51-11963	22277	(N4508B)	PV
☐ Cessna 337M Super Skymaster (O-2A)	67-21396	337M0102		RA
☐ Construcciones Aeronáuticas (CASA) 352L [Junkers Ju 52/3m]	'D-ADLH'	146	T2B-255 (Spain), G-BFHD	PVX
☐ Cosmos Phase II	C-IEQU	B21128		PV
☐ Crosley-Mignet Pou-du-Ciel	X15749	1		PV
☐ Curtiss E			Hull only.	PV
☐ Curtiss 1C Jenny (JN-4D)	4983			PV
☐ Curtiss 5 (N-9H)				PV
☐ Curtiss 35 Gulfhawk 1	N982V	1	NR636E	PV
☐ Curtiss 58A Sparrowhawk (XF9C-2)	'A9056'		A9264	PVX
☐ Curtiss 84G Helldiver (SB2C-5)	Bu83479			RA
☐ Curtiss A87-A2 Kittyhawk I	'194'	15346	AK875, 1047 (Canada), NX1048N, N1048N	PVX
☐ Curtiss-Wright CW-1 Junior	N10965	1143	NC10965	RA
☐ Curtiss-Wright X-100	N853	1		RA
☐ Dassault Falcon 20C	N8FE	199	F-WMKH, N4388F	PV
☐ De Havilland DH.98 Mosquito B.35 (TT.35) (B.35)	TH998			RA
☐ De Havilland DHC.1 Chipmunk 1A-1 (mod)	N13Y	23	18001 (RCAF)	PV
☐ Dornier Do 335A-1	VG+PH	240102	FE-1012, Bu121447	PV
☐ Double Eagle II			Gondola only	RA
☐ Douglas M-2	C150	244		PV
☐ Douglas VB-26B Invader (A-26B)	44-34610	27889		RA
☐ Douglas A-1H Skyraider (AD-6)	'Bu132463'	9976	Bu135332, 135332 (South Vietnam), (N32162), N39148	RAX
☐ Eipper-Formance Cumulus 10 Hang Glider				PV
☐ Ercoupe 415	NC15692	1		RA
☐ Farman F.65 Sport	NC72	15		PV
☐ Felixstowe F.5L	3022		Hull only – may be A 3882.	RA
☐ Focke-Achgelis Fa 330A-1 Bachstelze		60133	FE-4618, T2-4618 – on loan from NMUSAF, OH.	PV
☐ Focke-Wulf Fw 190F-8/R1 (A-7)	'7'	931884	931884, FE-117, T2-117 – built as Fw 190A-7 c/n 640069	PV
☐ Focke-Wulf Ta 152H-0	'4'	150010	150010, FE-112, T2-112	RA
☐ Fowler Gage Tractor				PV
☐ Frankfort Cinema B (TG-1A)	N53601	B-2-39		PV
☐ Fulton FA-3 Aerocar	NC74154		NC74154, N74154	RA
☐ Gates Learjet 23	N802L	23-002		PV
☐ Gittens Ikenga 530Z	N5032	DK001		PV
☐ Globe GC-1A Swift	NC80518	21	NC80518, N80518	PV
☐ Goodyear K-47			Gondola only.	RA
☐ Grob G.102 Standard Astir III	N17999	5558S		PV
☐ Grumman G-21A Goose	NC702A	1048	YV-VOD, HC-AAM, HC-SBA, N702A, N14CS	PV
☐ Grumman G-22 Gulfhawk II	NR1050	355		PV
☐ Grumman G-40 Avenger (TBF-1)	Bu24085	4968		RA
☐ Grumman G-50 Hellcat (F6F-3)	Bu41834	A-3100		PV
☐ Grumman G-58 Bearcat (F8F-2)	N1111L	D.1020	Bu121646, N7699C	PV
☐ Grumman G-93 Cougar (XF9F-6)	Bu126670	L-01		RA
☐ Grumman G-128 Intruder (A-6A) (A-6E)	Bu154167	I-302		PV
☐ Grumman G-164 Ag-Cat	N332Y	207		PV
☐ Grumman G-303 Tomcat (F-14A) (F-14D)	Bu159610	157		PV
☐ Halberstadt CL IV	8013/18	135		PV
☐ Hawker Hurricane IIC	LF686			PV
☐ Heinkel He 162A-2	120230	120230	120230, FE-504, T2-504 – tail from 120222.	RA
☐ Heinkel He 219A	GI+KQ	290202	GI+KQ, FE-614, T2-614	PV
☐ Helio No.1	N9390H	1		RA
☐ Herrick HV2A Convertoplane	N13515	1		RA
☐ Hiller XH44	NX30033	1		PV
☐ Hiller 1031 Flying Platform (VZ-1)		2		RA
☐ Hiller 1033 Rotor Cycle (YROE-1)	Bu4022	4 (S2/7589)		PV
☐ Hiller HJ.1 Hornet (XHOE-1)	Bu138652	5		PV
☐ Horten Ho IIIf (DFS 108-250)	T2-5042	32	FE-5042 – fuselage only.	PV
☐ Horten Ho IIIh (DFS 108-250)	LA-AI	31	LA-AI, FE-5039, T2-5039	PV
☐ Horten Ho VI V2 (DFS 108-253)		34	FE-5040, T2-5040	PV
☐ Huff-Daland Duster			.	PV
☐ Ilyushin Il-2m3				PV
☐ Junkers Ju 388L-1	560049	560049	560049, FE-4010, T2-4010	RA
☐ Kaman K-225 Huskie (XHOK-1)	Bu125477			PV
☐ Kawanishi N1K2-J Shiden Kai	'343-35'	5341	(J Navy), FE-305, T2-305	PV
☐ Kawasaki Ki-45 Toryu	4268	4268	4268, FE-701, T2-701	PV
☐ Kellett KD.1 (XO-60)	42-13610	118		PV
☐ Kellett XR-8	43-44714			PV
☐ Kreider-Reisner KR-34C Challenger	N30M	384	NC30M	PV
☐ Laird-Turner LTR-14 Meteor	NX263Y			PV
☐ Langley Aerodrome A				PV
☐ Lockheed 5C Vega (5B)	NR105W	122	NC105W, NR105W, NC195W	PV
☐ Lockheed 182-1A Hercules (182-44-03) (C-130A)	57-0460	182-3167	57-0460, 70460 (South Vietnam)	RA
☐ Lockheed 422-81-22 Lightning (P-38J)	42-67762	422-2273		PV

613

Aircraft	Reg 1	Reg 2	Reg 3	Status
☐ Lockheed 580 (T-33A)	53-5226	580-8565		PV
☐ Lockheed 1049F-55-96 Super Constellation (C-121C)	54-0177	1049F-4196	54-0177, N1104W	PV
☐ Lockheed SR-71A Blackbird	61-7972	2023		PV
☐ Lockheed-Martin X-35B	'301'			PV
☐ Loening OA-1A	26-431			PV
☐ Mahoney Sorceress	N89TT	1		PV
☐ Manta Pterodactyl				PV
☐ Martin J.V. K-III Kitten				PV
☐ McDonnell M.82 (XL-25) (XH-35) (XV-1)	53-4017			RA
☐ McDonnell M.98EV Phantom II (F-4J) (F-4S)	Bu157307	4018		PV
☐ Messerschmitt Me 163B-1a Komet	191301	191301	191300, FE-500, T2-500	PV
☐ Messerschmitt Me 410A-2/U1	F6+WK	10018	DI+NN, F6+WK, FE-499, T2-499	RA
☐ Mikoyan-Gurevich MiG-15bis	70919	70919	4320 (China)	PV
☐ Mikoyan-Gurevich MiG-21F-13	'2163'	21067 (?)	F-2163 (Indonesia)	PV
☐ Mitchell Wing U-2	N582U	PU-646		PV
☐ Mitsubishi G4M3	3041	3041	3041, FE-2205, T2-2205 – front fuselage only.	RA
☐ Monnett Moni	N23HW	154		PV
☐ Mono Aircraft Monocoupe 110 Special	N36Y	7W96	NC36Y	PV
☐ Mooney M-18C Mite	N3199K	201		PV
☐ Nagler-Rolz NR 54		V-2		PV
☐ Nakajima J1N1-S Gekko	7334	7334	7334, FE-700, T2-700	PV
☐ NASA Parasev 1L-B	X9765C	1		PV
☐ NASA Pathfinder Plus				PV
☐ Naval Aircraft Factory N3N-3	Bu3022		Bu3022, N44843	PV
☐ Nelson Dragonfly BB-1	N34923	507		PV
☐ Nieuport 28C.1 (R)	N4123A	1958E		PV
☐ North American NA-25 (O-47A)	37-279	25-222		RA
☐ North American NA-88 Texan (SNJ-4)	Bu51398	88-13780		PV
☐ North American NA-108 Mitchell (B-25J) (TB-25N)	N10564	108-33162	44-29887	RA
☐ North American NA-111 Mustang (P-51C)	NX1202	111-29080	44-10947, NX1202, N1202.	PV
☐ North American NA-151 Sabre (P-86A) (F-86A)	48-0260	151-43629		PV
☐ North American NA-245 Super Sabre (F-100D)	56-3440	245-90		RA
☐ Northrop N-1M	NX28311			PV
☐ Northrop N-8E Black Widow (P-61C)	43-8330	N.1376		PV
☐ Piasecki PV-2	NX37061			PV
☐ Piper J-3C-65 Cub	NC35773	6578	NC35773, N35773	PV
☐ Piper PA-12 Super Cruiser	NX2365M	12-1618		PV
☐ Piper PA-18-135 Super Cub	N1872P	18-4151		PV
☐ Piper PA-23 Apache	N114DA	23-14	N1011P	PV
☐ Pitcairn AC-35	NX70	J-91	X70	PV
☐ Pitts S-1 Special	N22E	2	NX86401	PV
☐ Quickie Aircraft Quickie 1 (Rutan 54)	N169H	169		PV
☐ Raven S-50A Hot Air Balloon	N1960R	S50A-179		PV
☐ Republic P-47D Thunderbolt	44-32691			PV
☐ Republic JB-2 [Fieseler Fi 103A-1]				PV
☐ Republic RC-3 Seabee	N6709K	992	NC6709K	RA
☐ Republic XF-84 Thunderjet (XP-84)	45-59476		Front fuselage only	RA
☐ Republic F-105D Thunderchief	60-0445	D-133		PV
☐ Robinson R-22	N32AD	0002		PV
☐ Robinson R-44 Astro	G-MURY	0201		PV
☐ Rockwell OV-101 Space Shuttle				PV
☐ Rotorway Scorpion Too	N18849	707		PV
☐ Rutan 33 Vari-Eze	N4EZ	002		PV
☐ Ryan ST-3KR Recruit (PT-22A)	N46501	1777	42-57481	PV
☐ Scaled Composites 311	N277SF	001		PV
☐ Schneider ESG 31 Grunau Baby II (DFS 108-49)	LZ+NC	031016	LZ+NC, FE-2600, T2-2600	PV
☐ Schweizer SGU.2-22	N2790Z	212		PV
☐ Sharp J-4 Nemesis	N18JS	36		PV
☐ Sikorsky VS-316A Hoverfly (XR-4)	41-18874	2		PV
☐ Sikorsky VS-372 Dragonfly (XR-5)	43-47954	37		RA
☐ Sikorsky S-52-3 (HO5S-1)	Bu125157	52010		PV
☐ Sikorsky S-55B (HRS-1)	'49-2012'		Bu127799, N4782S	PVX
☐ Sikorsky S-58 Seahorse (HUS-1) (UH-34D)	Bu148768	581319		RA
☐ SPAD XVI	AS9392	959		PV
☐ Sportswings Valkyrie Hang Glider				PV
☐ Standard J-1	N1375	177		RA
☐ Stanley Nomad	NX20645	1		PV
☐ Stearman-Hammond Y-1S	NC15533	319		RA
☐ Stephens Akro	N10LL	3		PV
☐ Stinson V-76 Sentinel (L-5)	42-14798	76-1		PV
☐ Stout Skycar	X10899			PV
☐ Sukhoi Su-26M	N726GM	02-05		PV
☐ Travel Air D-4D Speedwing	N434N	1340	NC434N	PV
☐ Ultraflight Lazair SS EC	N911MP	A838		PV
☐ Verville AT Sportsman	NC457M	8		RA
☐ Vought V-310 Kingfisher (OS2U-3)	Bu5909	2400		PV
☐ Vought F4U-1D Corsair	Bu50375	5622		PV
☐ Vought RF-8G Crusader (F8U-1P) (RF-8A)	Bu146860			PV
☐ Vultee V-74 Valiant (BT-13A)	41-22124	74-6044		RA
☐ Waco 9	N452	389	NC452	RA
☐ Waco UIC	N13062	3715	NC13062	RA
☐ Waterman W-5 Arrowbile	N54P	1		PV
☐ Weedhopper JC-24C		1845		PV

Virginia

☐ Westland Lysander IIIA	'N7791'	1185	2346 (Canada), N7791	PV
☐ Windecker A/C7 Eagle I	N4197G	006		RA
☐ Yakovlev Yak-18	'59'		In North Korean markings.	RA
☐ Yokosuka MXY-7 Ohka 22				PV
☐ Yost GB-55 Hot Air Balloon	N50DE	108		PV

NATIONAL D-DAY MEMORIAL (VA20)

Address: PO Box 77, 3 Overlord Circus, Bedford, Virginia 24523.
Tel: 540-586-3329 **Fax:** 540-586-7200 **Email:** dday@dday.org
Admission: Tuesday-Sunday 1000-1700.
Location: In the western part of the town.

This impressive memorial was dedicated on 6th June 2001 after more than seven years of fund raising. The site occupies almost 90 acres and consists of three main areas.

The Reynold's Garden symbolises the planning stages of the operation and has the shape of the Supreme Headquarters Allied Expeditionary Force combat patch.

The Gary Plaza honours the landing and subsequent fighting during the operation. Here is a pool with typical beach obstructions and a representation of a landing craft.

The Estes Plaza celebrates the victory and includes the Overlord Arch flanked by the flags of the 12 nations which took part in the invasion.

TYPE	REG/SER	CON. NO.	PI/NOTES	STATUS
☐ Aeronca 65TC Grasshopper (O-58B) (L-3B)				PV

NATIONAL HISTORIC AIRCRAFT FOUNDATION (VA21)

Address: 5324 Lake Lawson Road, Virginia Beach, Virginia 23455.
Tel: 757-961-2926
Admission: Not yet open.
Location: At the airport which is about 3 miles south of the town on Route 615.

The foundation was set up in 2004 with the primary aim of informing the public of the role of aviation in the history of the nation. A building will be constructed at Virginia Beach Airport and the display will concentrate on the role Naval Aviation has played in the local community.

TYPE	REG/SER	CON. NO.	PI/NOTES	STATUS
☐ Grumman G-36 Wildcat (F4F-4) (Scale R)				PVX

NATIONAL MUSEUM OF THE MARINE CORPS (VA22)

Address: 18900 Jefferson Davis Highway, Triangle, Virginia 22172.
Tel: 877-635-1775 **Email:** info@usmcmuseum.org
Admission: Daily 0900-1700.
Location: About 55 miles south of Washington DC west of Highway 1.

In 1912 the first Marine Corps pilots started their training at the Naval Academy at Annapolis. The first to obtain his licence was Alfred A. Cunningham who is honoured in the museum. The base at Quantico was set up during World War I and is thus an appropriate site for the museum.

The Marine Corps Aviation Museum opened in one hangar in 1977 and two years later a second was ready. The third was converted for display use in the late 1980s. The museum was a long way inside the camp so a decision was taken to raise funds for a purpose-built complex outside the security gate.

This superb exhibition opened on 10th November 2006 and its displays cover all aspects of marine duties. In all areas there are battle scenes with equipment on show in a typical environment. Use is made of audio-visual effects to create realism. The first phase consists of a large atrium where some aircraft hang and galleries covering specific themes. Several aircraft are exhibited in 'operational scenes' which show how they were used under combat conditions.

Two of the galleries feature the weather conditions encountered by the Marines. One shows the below zero temperatures encountered in Korea and another the sweltering heat and humidity of Vietnam.

Three new halls opened in June 2010 covering events up to the end of World War I. A further stage will see the construction of two more halls. One will cover the years from the end of the Vietnam conflict up to the Gulf Wars and the other will focus on terrorism.

When these areas are complete aircraft will be taken out of store on the base and put on view in appropriate settings. New well equipped workshop and storage areas are planned.

TYPE	REG/SER	CON. NO.	PI/NOTES	STATUS
☐ AAI RQ-2B Pioneer				PV
☐ Bell 47D-1 Sioux (HTL-4) (TH-13L)	Bu128635	218	Bu128635, N10320	RA
☐ Bell 204 Iroquois (UH-1E)	Bu154760	6145		PV
☐ Bell 209 Sea Cobra (AH-1J)	Bu159212	26052		RA
☐ Bell 209 Sea Cobra (AH-1T) (AH-1W)	Bu164591	26290		RAC
☐ Curtiss A-2 (R)	N67263	MC1975		PV
☐ Curtiss 1E Jenny (JN-4HG)	A-4160		Replica (?)	PV
☐ Curtiss 34H Hawk (F6C-4)	A-7114			PV
☐ De Havilland DH-4A (R)	'A3295'			PVX
☐ Douglas SBD-3 Dauntless	Bu06583	1351		RAC
☐ Douglas EF-10B Skyknight (F3D-2) (F3D-2Q)	Bu124618	7488		RA
☐ Douglas OA-4M Skyhawk (TA-4F)	Bu154638	13756	On loan to MCAS Iwakuni, Japan.	RA
☐ Douglas A-4E Skyhawk	Bu152080	13468		PV
☐ Grumman G-36 Wildcat (F4F-4)	Bu12114	3809		PV
☐ Grumman G-40 Avenger (TBM-3) (TBM-3E)	Bu85890	2709	Bu85890, N1952M	PV
☐ Grumman G-79 Panther (F9F-2)	Bu123526	K-228		PV
☐ Gyrodyne XRON-1 (XHOG-1)	4012			RA
☐ Hawker-Siddeley Harrier II (AV-8B)	Bu161396	1		PV

615

☐ Hawker-Siddeley Harrier II (AV-8B)	Bu163194	109	Fuselage only.	PV
☐ Lockheed 237-27-01 Ventura (PV-1)	Bu34807	237-5697	Bu34807, 2247 (Canada), N5779N, N151V	RA
☐ McDonnell M.98AM Phantom II (F4H-1F) (F-4A)	Bu143388	3		RA
☐ North American NA-88 Texan (AT-6D) (SNJ-5)	Bu84962	88-16973	42-85192 – fuselage only.	PV
☐ North American NA-108 Mitchell (B-25J)			Front fuselage only.	PV
☐ Sikorsky S-51 Dragonfly (HO3S-1)	Bu124344	51201	Bu124344, N5182C	PV
☐ Sikorsky S-55B (HRS-1)	'Bu127834'	55066	Bu127828	PVX
☐ Sikorsky S-58 Seahorse (HUS-1Z) (VH-34D)	Bu147161	581077		RAC
☐ Sikorsky S-65A Sea Stallion (CH-53A)	Bu151692	65009		RA
☐ Stinson V-76 Sentinel (L-5E) (OY-1)	Bu120454	76-4471	44-18182	PV
☐ Thomas-Morse S-4B/C	NR66Y	1		PV
☐ Vertol V.107M Sea Knight (CH-46D)	Bu153986	2337	Rear fuselage only.	PV
☐ Vought F4U-4 Corsair	Bu97369	9523	Bu97369, N5214V	PV
☐ Vought FG-1A Corsair	'Bu13486'	2495	Bu13459	PVX
☐ Yokosuka MXY-7 Ohka 11	I-13	1018		PV

NATIONAL MUSEUM OF THE UNITED STATES ARMY (VA23)

Address: 6098 Abbot Road, Fort Belvoir, Virginia 22060.
Tel: 703-805-5001
Admission: By prior permission only.
Location: About 15 miles south of Washington, DC off Route 1.

Two helicopters are currently stored close to the airfield at the camp. On 16th October 2001 the fort was selected as the home for the National Museum of the US Army which is scheduled to open in 2015.

TYPE	REG/SER	CON. NO.	PI/NOTES	STATUS
☐ Bell 205 Iroquois (UH-1H)	69-15594	11882		RA
☐ Bell 205 Iroquois (UH-1H)	70-16493	12798		RA
☐ Bell 209 Huey Cobra (AH-1S)	68-17051	20779		RA
☐ Grumman G-134 Mohawk (OV-1B)	62-5898	57B		RA

NAUTICUS – THE NATIONAL MARITIME CENTER (VA24)

Address: PO Box 3310, 1 Waterside Drive, Norfolk, Virginia 23510.
Tel: 757-664-1000   Fax: 757-623-1287
Admission: June–early September daily 0900-2100; early-September–May Saturday-Sunday 0900-2100.
Location: In the centre of the city.

Opened on 1st June 1994, the structure has been designed to represent the form of a boat hull. Overlooking one of the busiest shipping areas in the world, the displays feature the latest 'Virtual Reality' techniques. The Hampton Roads Naval Museum has moved to the new site.

The only aircraft on show is the Skyhawk painted in 'Blue Angels' colours, which is mounted on the roof of the building. Berthed next to the exhibition is the battleship USS *Wisconsin* which was launched at Philadelphia Naval Yard in 1943.

TYPE	REG/SER	CON. NO.	PI/NOTES	STATUS
☐ Douglas A-4E Skyhawk (A4D-5)	Bu150058	13111		PV

NAVAL SURFACE WARFARE CENTER DAHLGREN (VA25)

Location: By prior permission only at the site which is about 2 miles north east of the town.

TYPE	REG/SER	CON. NO.	PI/NOTES	STATUS
☐ McDonnell M.267 Hornet (F/A-18A)	Bu162458	310/A255		RA

NORFOLK NAVAL AIR STATION – ELY MEMORIAL PARK (VA26)

Address: 9420 Third Avenue, Norfolk, Virginia 23511-2127.
Tel: 757-445-6647   Email: webmaster@nsn.car.navy.mil
Admission: By prior permission only.
Location: In the eastern suburbs of the city off Interstate 564.

The airfield is situated close to the largest naval complex in the western world. About two dozen squadrons are normally based at the field and there is also a large depot which carries out major overhauls of naval aircraft.

The park is named after the pioneer aviator Eugene Ely. On 14th November 1910 he made the first take off from a ship when he flew to land from the USS *Birmingham*. In January of the following year he achieved another first when he landed on a strengthened platform on the USS *Pennsylvania* with an aircraft fitted with a tailhook. He was killed in an aircraft crash at Macon, Georgia later in the year.

TYPE	REG/SER	CON. NO.	PI/NOTES	STATUS
☐ Grumman G-123 Hawkeye (W2F-1) (E-2A) (E-2B)	'Bu165826'	21	Bu150541, 'Bu159492'	PVX
☐ Grumman G-128 Intruder (A-6A) (A-6E)	Bu152923	I-227		PV
☐ Grumman G-303 Tomcat (F-14A)	Bu159445	111		PV
☐ Kaman K-20 Seasprite (HU2K-1) (UH-2A) (SH-2F)	Bu149026	30		PV
☐ McDonnell M.267 Hornet (F/A-18C)	Bu163437	637/C009		PV

Virginia

☐ Sikorsky S-61B Sea King (HSS-2) (SH-3A) (UH-3A) (SH-3H)	Bu148042	61020	Bu148042, 'Bu158362'	PV
☐ Sikorsky S-65A Sea Stallion (RH-53D)	Bu158692	65365	Bu158692,'Bu158687' – on loan from NMNA, FL.	PV
☐ Vertol V.107M Sea Knight (HRB-1) (CH-46A) (HH-46A) (HH-46D)	Bu151953	2103		PV

OCEANA NAVAL AIR STATION AVIATION HISTORICAL PARK (VA27)

Address:	1750 Tomcat Boulevard, Naval Air Station Oceana, Virginia Beach, Virginia 23460-2191.
Tel:	757-433-3131 **Email:** troy.snead@navy.mil
Admission:	By prior permission only.
Location:	About 5 miles south east of the town Highway 44.

The airfield opened in 1940 as an auxiliary field and was gradually improved. In 1952 it became a full Naval Air Station and is now home to the Commander of the Atlantic Tactical Wings. For many years an F-4 Phantom was mounted in front of the Officers Club and in the mid-1980s it was joined by several other aircraft. The collection has been steadily enlarged and includes a rare Douglas Destroyer, the forerunner of the Skyraider. Tours of the base take place subject to security considerations and the park is on the normal itinerary.

TYPE	REG/SER	CON. NO.	PI/NOTES	STATUS
☐ Douglas XAD-1 Destroyer II (XBT2D-1)	Bu09102	1930		RA
☐ Douglas A-4E Skyhawk (A4D-5)	Bu151186	13356	Bu151186, 'Bu155167' – on loan from NMNA, FL.	RA
☐ Douglas F-6A Skyray (F4D-1)	'Bu141414'	10544	Bu134950, 'Bu133633'	RAX
☐ Grumman G-79 Panther (F9F-2)	Bu123612	K-317		RA
☐ Grumman G-98 Tiger (F11F-1) (F-11A)	Bu141864	181		RA
☐ Grumman G-123 Hawkeye (E-2C)				RA
☐ Grumman G-128 Intruder (A2F-1) (A-6A) (KA-6D)	Bu151579	I-61	Bu151579 , 'Bu161662', 'Bu162179'	RA
☐ Grumman G-303 Tomcat (F-14A)	Bu157988	9		RA
☐ Grumman G-303 Tomcat (F-14A)	'350701'	257	Bu160401 – at Air Control Facility.	RAX
☐ Grumman G-303 Tomcat (F-14D)	Bu164604	632	On loan from NMNA, FL	RA
☐ McDonnell M.24 Banshee (F2H-4) (F-2D)	'Bu147369'	327	Bu127693	RAX
☐ McDonnell M.98AM Phantom II (F4H-1F) (F-4A)	'Bu155847'	33	Bu148261	RAX
☐ McDonnell M.267 Hornet (F/A-18A)	Bu162454	304/A249		RA
☐ North American NA-194 Fury (FJ-3) (FJ-3M) (MF-1C)	Bu136008	194-235		RA
☐ Vought F-8E Crusader (F8U-2NE)	'Bu145802'		Bu149150	RAX
☐ Vought A-7E Corsair II	Bu158650	E355		RA

SANDSTON AIR NATIONAL GUARD BASE (VA28)

Address:	192 FW, Byrd International Airport, Sandston, Virginia 23150.
Tel:	804-236-6000 **Email:** webmaster@varich.ang.af.mil
Admission:	On permanent view.
Location:	About 7 miles east of Richmond off Route 60.

Assigned to the state in June 1947, the 149th Squadron took up residence at Byrd Field flying P-47D Thunderbolts. Apart from spells on active duty during the Korean War and the 1961 Berlin crisis the unit has remained at the Sandston base. The three preserved aircraft are on view just outside the gate to the base.

TYPE	REG/SER	CON. NO.	PI/NOTES	STATUS
☐ Republic F-84F Thunderstreak	52-8837			PV
☐ Republic F-105D Thunderchief	61-0050	D-245		PV
☐ Vought A-7D Corsair II	72-0192	D314		PV

SCIENCE MUSEUM OF VIRGINIA (VA29)

Address:	2500 West Broad Street, Richmond, Virginia 23220.
Tel:	804-864-1400 **Fax:** 804-864-1509 **Email:** info@smv.com
Admission:	Monday-Saturday 0930-1700; Sunday 1130-1700.
Location:	In the western part of the city.

This impressive museum is housed in the former Broad Street Station which opened in 1917. Passenger services ceased in 1975 and the building was converted for museum use. All aspects of science are covered and there are many 'hands-on' displays. Also on site are an IMAX theatre and a Planetarium. The aeronautical section has grown steadily over the last few years and in addition to the aircraft there are models and components on show. The Flaglor Sky Scooter first appeared in the late 1960s. The all wooden design won awards at the 1967 EAA Convention. A space section has been set up and this covers all aspects of the topic.

TYPE	REG/SER	CON. NO.	PI/NOTES	STATUS
☐ American Aerolights Eagle				PV
☐ Cirrus 2 Hang Glider				PV
☐ Eipper MX Quicksilver				PV
☐ Flaglor Sky Scooter	N3886	75		PV
☐ MacCready Solar Challenger	N1815C	1	On loan from NASM, DC.	PV
☐ Piper J-3C-65 Cub	N77552	22043	NC77552	PV
☐ Wright 1902 Glider (R)				PV

617

The Aviation Historical Park at Oceana Naval Air Station exhibits this McDonnell F2H-4 Banshee (Eric Dewhurst) [VA27]

This Pietenpol Aircamper hangs in the Super Mall in Auburn. (Super Mall) [WA3]

This OA-10A Catalina is on show at the McChord Air Museum. [WA22]

Virginia

SOUTH HILL MONUMENT (VA30)

Location:	On permanent view at VFW 7166 at 1472 North Mecklenburg Avenue in the north eastern part of the town.

TYPE	REG/SER	CON. NO.	PI/NOTES	STATUS
☐ Bell 205 Iroquois (UH-1D) (UH-1H)	64-13745	4452		PV

TACTICAL AIR COMMAND MEMORIAL PARK (VA31)

Address:	1 FW/PA, 159 Sweeney Boulevard, Langley Air Force Base, Hampton, Virginia 23665-5548.
Tel:	757-764-2018 **Email:** 1fwpa.msstraffic@langley.af.mil
Admission:	By prior permission only.
Location:	The base is about 3 miles north of Hampton off Route 172.

The airfield was activated on 30th December 1916 and is the oldest continuously active air force base in the USA The field is named after the pioneer aviator and scientist Samuel Pierpoint Langley who died in 1906. The Headquarters of Tactical Air Command are located at Langley along with several operational units.

A display of three aircraft mounted on pylons was set up some years ago to commemorate the 30th anniversary of the command. Recently the area has been enlarged and dedicated as a memorial to all who have served with TAC. The B-52 is positioned just inside the main gate and is a short distance from the park.

TYPE	REG/SER	CON. NO.	PI/NOTES	STATUS
☐ Boeing 464-253 Stratofortress (B-52G)	59-2601	464364		PV
☐ General Dynamics 401 Fighting Falcon (F-16A)	78-0001	61-7		PV
☐ McDonnell M.98DJ Phantom II (F-4C)	64-0748	1033		RA
☐ McDonnell M.199-1A Eagle (YF-15A) (F-15A)	71-0281	002/A002		PV
☐ North American NA-187 Sabre (F-86H)	'53-1483'	187-169	52-5747	PVX
☐ Republic F-105D Thunderchief	'61-0217'	D-383	61-0188	PVX

UNITED STATES ARMY LOGISTICS SCHOOL (VA32)

Address:	705 Read Street, Fort Eustis, Virginia 23604.
Tel:	757-878-0400 **Email:** eust.usaals.webdir@conus.army.mil
Admission:	By prior permission only.
Location:	About 11 miles south east of Williamsburg off Interstate 64.

The site has had a long military history. The first settlers arrived in the early 1600s and the area also saw fighting in the Civil War. The land, known as Mulberry Island, was bought by the Army in 1918.

Camp Abraham Eustis was named after a brigadeer general who was the first commanding officer of nearby Fort Monroe. The title Fort Eustis was taken up in 1923 when it became a permanent military installation. The Transportation Corps was established in 1942 and units have been based at the site for many years.

The Logistics School has been teaching aviation maintenance since 1954. A large fleet of instructional airframes is in hangars and workshops around the site. The Transportation School is also on the base but some parts of it are moving to Fort Lee. The Public Affairs Office told me that not many of the helicopters would be transferred but they would not provide an inventory of those present.

Those listed have been reported in recent years but some may have left and others arrived. Most of the Apaches reside in the Apache Maintenance School.

TYPE	REG/SER	CON. NO.	PI/NOTES	STATUS
☐ Bell 204 (YH-40) (YUH-1B)	56-6723	4		RA
☐ Bell 205 Iroquois (UH-1D) (UH-1H)	63-12960	4156		RA
☐ Bell 205 Iroquois (UH-1D) (UH-1H)	66-16087	5781		RA
☐ Bell 205 Iroquois (UH-1H)	67-17177	9375		RA
☐ Bell 205 Iroquois (UH-1H)	68-15446	10376		RA
☐ Bell 205 Iroquois (UH-1H)	68-16178	10837		RS
☐ Bell 205 Iroquois (UH-1H)	70-16318	12623		RA
☐ Bell 206A Kiowa (OH-58A)	68-16721	40035		RA
☐ Bell 206A Kiowa (OH-58D)	90-0347	43214		RA
☐ Bell 206A Kiowa (OH-58D)	90-0350	43217		RA
☐ Bell 206A Kiowa (OH-58D)	90-0354	43221		RA
☐ Bell 206A Kiowa (OH-58D)	90-0355	43222		RA
☐ Bell 206A Kiowa (OH-58D)	90-0362	43229		RA
☐ Bell 206A Kiowa (OH-58D)	90-0367	43234		RA
☐ Bell 206A Kiowa (OH-58D)	90-0375	43242		RA
☐ Bell 206A Kiowa (OH-58D)	91-0536	43249		RA
☐ Bell 209 Huey Cobra (AH-1G) (AH-1F)	68-17028	20756		RA
☐ Bell 209 Huey Cobra (AH-1G) (AH-1F)	68-17065	20793		RA
☐ Bell 209 Huey Cobra (AH-1G) (AH-1F)	70-16018	20962		RA
☐ Bell 209 Huey Cobra (AH-1G) (AH-1F)	79-23244	22589		RA
☐ Bell 209 Huey Cobra (AH-1G) (AH-1S)	68-15127	20661		RA
☐ Hughes 77 Apache (AH-64A)	83-23791	PV.16		RA
☐ Hughes 77 Apache (AH-64A)	83-23792	PV.17		RA
☐ Hughes 77 Apache (AH-64A)	83-23799	PV.24		RA
☐ Hughes 77 Apache (AH-64A)	88-0205	PV.535		RA
☐ Hughes 77 Apache (AH-64A)				RA
☐ Hughes 77 Apache (AH-64A)				RA
☐ Hughes 77 Apache (AH-64A)				RA
☐ Hughes 77 Apache (AH-64A)				RA
☐ Hughes 77 Apache (AH-64A)				RA
☐ Sikorsky S-65A Sea Stallion (CH-53A) (NCH-53A)	63-13693		Bu??????	RA

☐ Sikorsky S-70A Black Hawk (UH-60A)	77-22715	70009		RA
☐ Sikorsky S-70A Black Hawk (UH-60A)	77-22719	70013		RA
☐ Sikorsky S-70A Black Hawk (UH-60A)	77-22721	70015		RA
☐ Sikorsky S-70A Black Hawk (UH-60A)	77-22726	70020		RA
☐ Sikorsky S-70A Black Hawk (UH-60A)	78-22963	70026		RA
☐ Sikorsky S-70A Black Hawk (UH-60A)	78-22964	70027		RA
☐ Sikorsky S-70A Black Hawk (UH-60A)	78-22970	70033		RA
☐ Sikorsky S-70A Black Hawk (UH-60A)	78-22972	70035		RA
☐ Sikorsky S-70A Black Hawk (UH-60A)	78-22981	70044		RA
☐ Sikorsky S-70A Black Hawk (UH-60A)	78-22987	70050		RA
☐ Sikorsky S-70A Black Hawk (UH-60A)	86-24562	701086		RA
☐ Sikorsky S-70A Black Hawk (UH-60A)	79-23336	70153		RA
☐ Sikorsky S-70A Black Hawk (UH-60A)	79-23352	70169		RA
☐ Sikorsky S-70A Black Hawk (UH-60A)	80-23418	70176		RA
☐ Sikorsky S-70A Black Hawk (UH-60A)	80-23466	70224		RA
☐ Sikorsky S-70A Black Hawk (UH-60A)	80-23505	70263		RA
☐ Sikorsky S-70A Black Hawk (UH-60A)	81-23565	70286		RA
☐ Sikorsky S-70A Black Hawk (UH-60A)	82-23663	70356		RA
☐ Sikorsky S-70A Black Hawk (UH-60A)	83-23879	70724		RA
☐ Sikorsky S-70A Black Hawk (UH-60A)	84-23972	70799		RA
☐ Vertol V.114 Chinook (CH-47D)	85-24340	M.3010	Converted from CH-47C c/n B.636 69-17121	RA
☐ Vertol V.114 Chinook (CH-47D)	85-24351	M.3121	Converted from CH-47A c/n B.143 65-7971	RA
☐ Vertol V.114 Chinook (CH-47D)	85-24368	M.3138	Converted from CH-47A c/n B.302 66-19044	RA
☐ Vertol V.114 Chinook (CH-47D)	86-1639	M.3144	Converted from CH-47A c/n B.156 65-7984	RA
☐ Vertol V.114 Chinook (CH-47D)	87-0084	M.3203	Converted from CH-47A c/n B.48 62-2132	RA
☐ Vertol V.114 Chinook (CH-47D)	88-0105	M.3279	Converted from CH-47C c/n B.6587 68-15995	RA
☐ Vertol V.114 Chinook (CH-47D)	90-0194	M.3346	Converted from CH-47C c/n B.713 74-22294	RA

UNITED STATES ARMY TRANSPORTATION CENTER AND SCHOOL (VA33)

Address:	Fort Lee, Petersburg, Virginia 23801.
Tel:	804-765-3000
Admission:	By prior permission only.
Location:	About four miles east of the town.

Camp Lee was established as a state mobilisation centre just after war was declared on Germany in 1917. On 15th July 1917 the site was named after Confederate Civil War commander General Robert E Lee. A new camp was built in 1940/41 and served as a quartermaster training centre. This role has continued to the present day.

Parts of the Transportation School are moving to Fort Lee from Fort Eustis over the next few years. Two aircraft have so far arrived for this purpose and more are expected. Some helicopters may be transferred but this has not been fully decided. The C-17A fuselage arrived in the summer of 2009 and the Hercules the following spring.

TYPE	REG/SER	CON. NO.	PI/NOTES	STATUS
☐ Lockheed 382-4B Hercules (C-130E)	64-0527	382-4013		RA
☐ McDonnell-Douglas C-17A Globemaster III		F3	Static test fuselage only.	RA

UNITED STATES ARMY TRANSPORTATION MUSEUM (VA34)

Address:	300 Washington Boulevard, Besson Hall, , Fort Eustis, Virginia 23604-5260.
Tel:	757-878-1115 Email: tcmuseum@eustis.army.mil
Admission:	Tuesday-Sunday 0900-1630.
Location:	About 11 miles south east of Williamsburg off Interstate 64.

'Nothing Happens Until Something Moves' is the slogan of this museum. Set up in 1960 in an old warehouse on the base, it moved around the site several times before obtaining a permanent home. The money for the main building was raised by donation and it was handed over to the Army in August 1975.

The museum was officially opened on 9th July 1976. The exhibition covers all aspects of army transport over the last two centuries. The displays range from the horse and wagon of 1776 up to modern day vehicles. Excellent dioramas depict scenes from the 1848 Mexican War, the Civil War, the Spanish-American War and all conflicts of the 20th century.

Army aviation in the USA dates from 1942 when liaison aircraft were used in military exercises. In the indoor display are components, engines and models. The visitor can sit in the cockpit of a helicopter and view a slide show of operations in Vietnam.

Two examples of vehicles designed to give the soldier more mobility in the field are on show. The De Lackner Aerocycle was tested in 1956 and had contra-rotating propellers. The Bell Rocket Belt was strapped around the brave 'volunteer' who upon ignition was propelled into the air and hopefully flew over and past any obstacles.

A hall to house the aircraft and helicopter collection was constructed in the late 1980s. The Sikorsky VH-34C used by President Kennedy on his 1962 trip to Bermuda and the lead Bell UH-1B of the trio which made the first rotary-wing flight to the South Pole in February 1963 are notable exhibits. The experimental Doak 16 VTOL machine has ducted propellers at the wing tips which can be rotated through 90 degrees. Only one was built and this was tested at Fort Eustis.

The flying saucer like Avro Canada VZ-9 was not a success and proved to be uncontrollable rising only three feet above the ground. More successful were the two flying jeeps built by the Piasecki company between 1958 and 1962. Designed to carry up to 1,000 pounds over any terrain, they showed promise but were not developed. Several aircraft have left the exhibition and have been transferred to other army museums.

Virginia

TYPE	REG/SER	CON. NO.	PI/NOTES	STATUS
☐ Avro Canada Model 1 Avrocar (VZ-9V)	59-4975		On base.	RA
☐ Beech C50 Seminole (L-23D) (U-8D)	58-3051	RLH-52		PV
☐ Bell 47D-1 Sioux (H-13E) (OH-13E)	51-14010	596		PV
☐ Bell 204 (YH-40) (YUH-1B)	56-6723	4	On base.	PV
☐ Bell 204 Iroquois (HU-1A) (UH-1A)	59-1616	75	Front fuselage only.	PV
☐ Bell 204 Iroquois (HU-1B) (UH-1B)	61-0788	368		PV
☐ Bell 205 Iroquois (UH-1H)	74-22376	13700		PV
☐ Bell Jet Flying Belt				PV
☐ Cessna 305A Bird Dog (L-19A) (O-1A)	51-12745			PV
☐ Curtiss-Wright Gem		2-X		PV
☐ De Havilland DHC.2 Beaver (L-20A) (U-6A)	58-1997	1322		PV
☐ De Havilland DHC.3 Otter (U-1A)	55-3270	116		PV
☐ De Havilland DHC.4 Caribou (YAC-1) (YCV-2A) (YC-7A)	57-3079	5	CF-LKF-X	PV
☐ De Lackner Aerocycle				PV
☐ Doak 16 (VZ-4)	56-6942			PV
☐ Hiller UH12B Raven (H-23B) (OH-23B)	'0111'	328	51-16168	PVX
☐ Hughes 269A Osage (TH-55A)	67-16944	1051		PV
☐ Piasecki 59K Aerial Jeep (VZ-8P)	58-5511			PV
☐ Piasecki PV-18 Retriever (HUP-2) (UH-25B)	Bu130043			PV
☐ Sikorsky S-55D Chickasaw (H-19D) (UH-19D)	'114299'		56-1550	PVX
☐ Sikorsky S-56 Mojave (H-37A) (H-37B) (CH-37B)	57-1651		57-1651, N14462	PV
☐ Sikorsky S-58 Choctaw (H-34A) (VH-34C)	57-1725	58910		PV
☐ Sikorsky S-64A Tarhe (YCH-54A)	64-14203	64005		PV
☐ Vertol V.43 Shawnee (H-21C) (CH-21C)	56-2077	C.239		PV
☐ Vertol V.114 Chinook (YHC-1B) (YCH-47A) (YCH-47B)	59-4986	B.5		RA

VIRGINIA AIR AND SPACE CENTER (VA35)

Address:	600 Settlers Landing Road, Hampton, Virginia 23669-4033.
Tel:	757-727-0900 **Email:** ahoilman@vasc.org
Admission:	June–August Monday-Wednesday 1000-1700, Thursday-Sunday 1000-1900; September–May Daily 1000-1700.
Location:	In the centre of the city close to the Hampton Roads Bridge.

This superb museum opened on 5th April 1992. Space features highly in the exhibits with many items coming from the NASA Langley facility. An Apollo Lunar Excursion Module Simulator which was used to train astronauts is on show along with the hatch from the Gemini 10 spacecraft. A replica of one of the aircraft built by Langley in the first few years of this century can be seen. Aircraft used by NASA have been acquired.

The Convair Delta Dart was operated by the organisation in its research into the effects of lightning on aircraft. The F-106 was deliberately flown into storms and was struck about 700 times between 1980 and 1986. The AA-1A Trainer on show was developed from the AA-1 Yankee. NASA carried out trials with leading edge cuffs and end plates fitted to an AA-1. Over 400 examples of both versions were delivered to customers.

The Thunderstreak and the Starfighter were formerly on show at the Air Power Park. The Northrop HL-10 was one of five designs for a heavyweight lifting body tested at the Dryden Flight Research Center in California between 1966 and 1975. A total of 37 flights of the HL-10 took place and it set a fastest speed of 1,228 mph on one of these and an altitude of 90,030 feet on another.

The Pitts and Vari-Eze were specially constructed for the exhibition to show examples of homebuilt designs. The Kitfox designed by Dan Denney made its first flight in November 1984 and over 4,500 kits of the high-wing folding wing monoplane have been delivered.

The exhibition was enlarged a few years ago with the opening of the 'Adventures in Flight' gallery which contains many interactive exhibits. There are several flight simulators which the visitor can use. Audio-visual displays have been set up and the DC-9 airliner can be walked through.

The main theme of this area is the development of aviation over the last century and this is portrayed with a range of models, photographs, documents and historic videos.

TYPE	REG/SER	CON. NO.	PI/NOTES	STATUS
☐ American Aviation AA-1A Trainer	N501NA	AA1-001		PV
☐ Bell 204 Iroquois (UH-1C) (UH-1M)	66-0648	1630		PV
☐ Bell 26E Airacobra (P-39Q)	42-20007			PV
☐ Boeing-Stearman B75N Kaydet (N2S-3)	Bu07481	75-7085	Bu07481, N95440 –	PV
☐ Consolidated 32 Liberator (B-24D) (B.III)	42-40557	1634	44-40557, BZ755, 600 (Canada) – front fuselage only – probable identity.	PVD
☐ Convair 8-27 Delta Dart (F-106B)	N816NA	8-27-10	57-2516, N616NA	PV
☐ Denney Kitfox IV Speedster	N177CA	1777		PV
☐ Douglas DC-9-32	N903VJ	47261	N1266L, N903VJ, N803AT	PV
☐ General Dynamics 401 Fighting Falcon (YF-16A)	72-1567	60-1		PV
☐ General Dynamics 401 Fighting Falcon (F-16A)			Front fuselage only.	PV
☐ Grumman G-128 Intruder (A-6A) (A-6E)	Bu152941	I-245	Front fuselage only.	PV
☐ Hawker P.1127 Kestrel (XV-6A)	NASA521		XS689, 64-18263 – on loan from NASM, DC.	PV
☐ Lockheed 383-04-05 Starfighter (F-104C)	57-0916	183-1233		PV
☐ McDonnell M.98HO Phantom II (F-4E)	67-0392	3301	67-0392, '67-0393'	PV
☐ McDonnell M.267 Hornet (F/A-18A)	NASA840	6/A006	Bu160780, NASA840, N840SN	PV
☐ Northrop HL-10 (FSM)				PV
☐ Piper J-3C-65 Cub	N6003H	19138	NC6003H	PV
☐ Pitts S-1S Special				PV
☐ Republic F-84F Thunderstreak	51-1786			PV
☐ Rutan 33 Vari-Eze				PV
☐ Schleicher ASW-12	N491V	12013	On loan from National Soaring Museum, NY.	PV
☐ Wright Flyer (R)				PV

VIRGINIA AVIATION MUSEUM (VA36)

Address:	5701 Huntsman Road, Richmond, Virginia 23250-2416.
Tel:	804-236-3622 Email: mboehme@smv.org
Admission:	Tuesday-Saturday 0900-1700; Sunday 1200-1700.
Location:	At Richmond International Airport which is about 5 miles east of the city off Route 60.

Sidney Shannon opened a museum at his airport in Fredericksburg in Virginia in 1976 to house his vintage aircraft, engines, models, photographs, documents and memorabilia. He died in 1981 and the collection closed for a time.

The aircraft were left to the Virginia Aeronautical Historical Society which decided to raise funds for a new museum. A site was obtained at Byrd Airport and the first phase was completed by early 1987. This building was named the Freedlander Wing after a local resident, Eric Freedlander, who made a large donation towards its construction. The society transferred the museum to the Science Museum of Virginia in July 1990. The building has since been enlarged and further development is planned.

The Shannon aircraft were moved to their new home early in 1987 and although most were in airworthy condition only the Curtiss Robin flew to Richmond. This collection contained several rarities including the only surviving Vultee V-1. Just 27 V-1s were built with the Richmond example being the only V-1AD Special. Originally delivered to the newspaper magnate Randolph Hearst, the aircraft spent many years in Latin America before returning to the USA to undergo restoration between 1965 and 1971.

Only two complete examples of the Bellanca CH-400 dating from the early 1930s are thought to remain. These rugged high wing monoplanes were in demand for freight duties in remote areas. The example on show was converted from a Pacemaker at some time during its life. Just two Standard E-1s are known to exist. Designed as a fighter, two prototypes were built but the biplane was used as an advanced trainer. Just over 90 were delivered to the military.

The Fairchild FC-2W2 was used by Admiral Richard Byrd on his Antarctic exploration journeys. On 15th January 1929 it became the first American aircraft to fly in the region. From 1930 until 1934 it was stored in a hangar made of snow blocks. The monoplane was then returned to use for his second expedition.

To commemorate the centenary of powered flight a collection of replicas of Wright designs were built. The development of their gliders over the three years up to their Flyer can be seen. There are many excellent associated displays to be seen.

TYPE	REG/SER	CON. NO.	PI/NOTES	STATUS
☐ Aeronca C-2N	N11417	A-151	NC11417	PV
☐ Aeronca C-3	NC14640	A-526	NC14640, N14640	PV
☐ Bell 205 Iroquois (UH-1H) (UH-1V)	68-16623	11282		PV
☐ Bellanca CH-400 Skyrocket (CH-300 Pacemaker)	NX237	187		PV
☐ Brunner-Winkle Bird A	N831W	2025-96	NC831W	PV
☐ Bücker Bü 133C Jungmeister	N133BU	251	EC-AKA, PI-X-388, N859K	PV
☐ Curtiss 1C Jenny (JN-4D)	N2975	450		PV
☐ Curtiss 50H Robin J-1	N532N	733	NC532N	PV
☐ Curtiss-Wright A-14D Sportsman	NC12329	14-2009	NC12329, N12329	PV
☐ Douglas A-4C Skyhawk (A4D-2N)	Bu148543	12736		PV
☐ Ercoupe 415C	N99143	1766		PV
☐ Fairchild FC-2W2	NX8006	140	On loan from NASM, DC.	PV
☐ Fairchild 24G	N19123	2983	NC19123	PV
☐ Fleet 1	NC766V	347	NC766V, N766V	PV
☐ Grumman G-303 Tomcat (F-14D)	Bu164346	621/D26		PV
☐ Heath Super Parasol	N1926	31919		PV
☐ Lockheed SR-71A Blackbird	61-7968	2019		PV
☐ Pietenpol B4-A Aircamper	N9040N	410		PV
☐ Piper J-3C-65 Cub	N42535	14812	NC42535	PV
☐ Pitcairn PA-5 Mailwing	NC3835	9	NC3835, N3835	PV
☐ Quickie Aircraft Quickie 200 (Rutan 54)	N200XQ	2725		PV
☐ SPAD VII (R)	B9913		N1916S	PV
☐ Standard E-1				PV
☐ Stinson SR-10G Reliant	NC21135	5903	NC21135, N21135	PV
☐ Taylor E-2 Cub	NC12628	33	NC12628, N12628	PV
☐ Travel Air 2000	NC6282	721	NC6282, N6282	PV
☐ Vought A-7D Corsair II	70-0966	D112		RA
☐ Vultee V-1AD Special	NC16099	25	NC16099, RX-19, AN-ABI, RX-158, HP-158	PV
☐ Waco YOC	NC17740	4279	NC17740, N540Y	PV
☐ Wright 1899 Kite (R)				PV
☐ Wright 1900 Glider (R)				PV
☐ Wright 1901 Glider (R)				PV
☐ Wright 1902 Glider (R)				PV
☐ Wright Flyer (R)				PV

VIRGINIA MUSEUM OF TRANSPORTATION (VA37)

Address:	303 Norfolk Avenue South West, Roanoke, Virginia 24016.
Tel:	540-342-5670 Email: info@vmt.org
Admission:	Monday-Saturday 1000-1700; Sunday 1300-1700.
Location:	In the centre of the city.

Located in a restored railway freight station the museum has an excellent collection of locomotives and carriages on show. Also displayed are early cars, lorries, fire engines and horse drawn carriages.

The small aeronautical section has a collection of photographs showing the pioneer aviators of the Roanoke Valley. The history of Piedmont Airlines is also featured. The sole aircraft on display is a low wing monoplane built in Greenville, Tennessee. The machine flew from 1964 to 1980 and was then stored for eight years. The designer reassembled it and flew it to Roanoke for display in the museum in 1988.

TYPE	REG/SER	CON. NO.	PI/NOTES	STATUS
☐ Tucker LGT.1	N1295V	LGT.5		PV

WASHINGTON

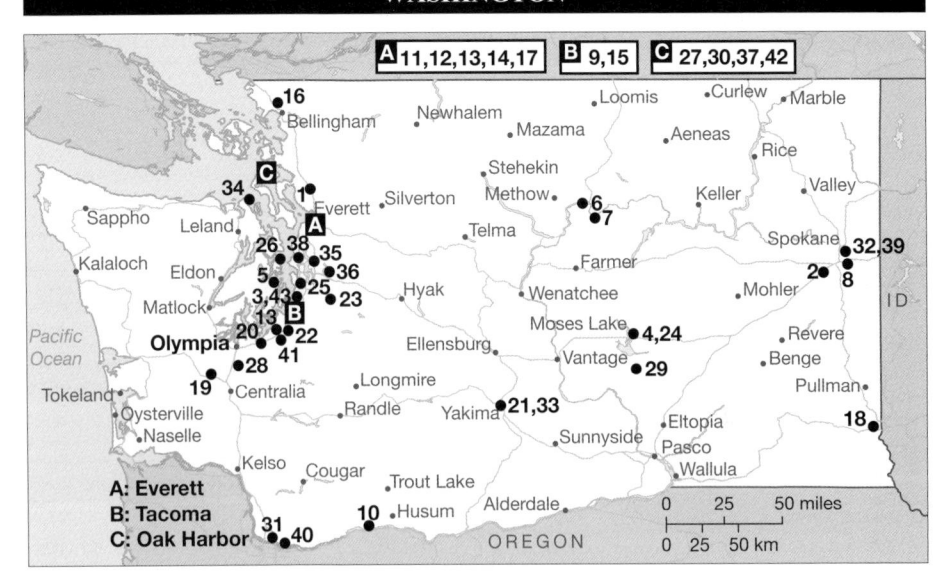

ARLINGTON NAVAL MUSEUM (WA1)

Address:	Arlington Airport, Arlington, Washington 98223.
Tel:	360-403-4321 (Airport)
Admission:	By prior permission only.
Location:	About 2 miles south west of the town which is about 20 miles north of Everett.

The Tracker was ferried to Arlington in 2005 for operation by a group who had plans to maintain it in airworthy condition. The now defunct Air Station Museum acquired the aircraft in 2008 and after their demise this new museum was set up to keep the aircraft at Arlington. There are plans to acquire other types.

TYPE	REG/SER	CON. NO.	PI/NOTES	STATUS
☐ Grumman G-89 Tracker (S2F-1) (S-2A) (US-2B)	N8112A	336	Bu136427	RA

ARMED FORCES AND AEROSPACE MUSEUM (WA2)

Address:	5813 East 4th Avenue, Spokane Valley, Washington 99212-0308
Tel:	509-244-0244 Email: mail@armedforces-aerospacemus.org
Admission:	Not yet open.
Location:	To be constructed at Spokane IAP which is about 4 miles south west of the city off Route 2. The US military aircraft are still at Fairchild AFB which is about 12 miles west of Spokane on Route 2.

The museum is raising funds for a new facility which will be constructed on land adjacent to Spokane International Airport.

The Fairchild Heritage Museum has closed and the artefacts are in store. The aircraft preserved on the Air Force Base are still there and can be viewed with special permission. When the first phase of the building is ready these military aircraft will be moved the short distance to the airport. The personal collection of vintage aircraft owned by Ed Carlson will eventually be displayed in the museum. At the current time he has loaned one of his Stearmans to the museum and this is under rebuild in a hangar on the field. The Polish-built MiG-17 is parked at the airport. There is the potential for an excellent display and hopefully the initial plans will be realised in the not too distant future.

The Fairchild Heritage Museum was established on 18th April 1980 and the initial exhibition was staged in the Base Recreation Center. In 1982 the display moved to a World War II barrack block. The following year artefacts from the nearby Fort George Wright were moved to Fairchild. On show were items from the Civil War and the Spanish-American conflicts. The history of the base, Fort George Wright and the local Air National Guard units were also portrayed.

The B-52D was delivered to the base in August 1957 and during service in Vietnam it became the first of its type to shoot down a MiG fighter. The Canadair Sabre was flown at Mojave in California by Flight Systems in the mid-1980s. The jet fighter joined the museum collection in 1988.

The C-47 was operated by NASA at Langley in Virginia, in the early 1950s. The aircraft them moved to Cleveland in Ohio before flying across the country to join the Dryden Flight Center at Edwards Air Force Base in California. After retirement in late 1984 it moved north to Fairchild and is now painted in military markings. When the exhibition hall is completed several privately owned types will be put on show.

TYPE	REG/SER	CON. NO.	PI/NOTES	STATUS
☐ Boeing 464-201-7 Stratofortress (B-52D)	56-0676	464047		RA
☐ Boeing 464-253 Stratofortress (B-52G)	58-0158	464226	Front fuselage only.	RA

☐ Boeing 717-148 Stratotanker (KC-135A) (KC-135E)	58-0082	17827		RA
☐ Canadair CL-13A Sabre 5 [North American F-86E]	'91086'	1134	23344 (Canada), N86EC	RAX
☐ Cessna 318B Tweety Bird (318A) (T-37A) (T-37B)	57-2352	40285		RA
☐ Convair 8-10 Delta Dagger (F-102A)	56-1115	8-10-332		RA
☐ Douglas DC-3A-467 Skytrain (C-47B)	43-49526	15342/26787	43-49526, NASA501, N501NA, N636NA, N817NA, N827NA	RA
☐ Douglas A-26B Invader	44-34423	27702	44-34423, N9594Z, C-GHLI	RA
☐ Lockheed 580 (T-33A)	58-0532	580-1501		PV
☐ McDonnell M.36BA Voodoo (F-101B)	'57-0439'	707	58-0335	RAX
☐ Republic F-105B Thunderchief	57-5823	B-60		RA
☐ Stearman C3B (C2C) (C3D)	NC1598	173	NC6433 – on loan from Carlson Collection, WA.	RAC
☐ WSK Lim-5R (Lim-5) [MiG-17F]	726	1C 17-26	1726 (Poland)	RA

AUBURN MONUMENT (WA3)

Location:	On permanent view in the Super Mall in the town.

TYPE	REG/SER	CON. NO.	PI/NOTES	STATUS
☐ Pietenpol B4-A Aircamper				PV

BIG BEND COMMUNITY COLLEGE (WA4)

Address:	7662 Chanute Street, Moses Lake, Washington 98837-3299.
Tel:	509-793-2241 Email: aviation@bigbend.edu
Admission:	By prior permission only.
Location:	At the airport which is about 3 miles north of the town off Route 17.

The college was established in 1961 and offers a wide range of courses. Five years later it moved to a site on the former Larson Air Force Base. The aviation section housed at the airport trains pilots, air traffic controllers and mechanics. Ten aircraft are used for technical work and 27 for flight training.

TYPE	REG/SER	CON. NO.	PI/NOTES	STATUS
☐ Beech 58TC Baron				RA
☐ Beech 95-B55 Baron				RA
☐ Bell 205 Iroquois (UH-1H)	74-22374	13698		RA
☐ Bell 47G-3B-1	N8500L	3817		RA
☐ Boeing 727-22F	N151FE	19147	N7083U	RA
☐ Cessna 170	N3823V	18681		RA
☐ Cessna 172F Mescalero (T-41A)				RA
☐ Emair MA-1	N9928M	028		RA
☐ North American NA-265 Sabreliner (T-39A) (CT-39A)	60-3493	265-21		RA
☐ Piper PA-32R-300 Cherokee Lance	N1212E	32R-7680249		RA

BREMERTON MONUMENT (WA5)

Location:	On permanent view in a park on Kitsap Way in the western part of the town.

TYPE	REG/SER	CON. NO.	PI/NOTES	STATUS
☐ Vought F-8H Crusader (F8U-2N) (F-8D)	Bu147909			PV

BREWSTER MONUMENT (WA6)

Location:	On permanent view at ALP 97 on East Main Avenue in the northern part of the town.

TYPE	REG/SER	CON. NO.	PI/NOTES	STATUS
☐ Lockheed 580 (T-33A)	'5-29667'	580-5554	51-4259	PVX

BRIDGEPORT WAR MEMORIAL (WA7)

Address:	Berryman Memorial Park, Bridgeport, Washington 98813.
Admission:	On permanent view.
Location:	In the south western part of the town.

Currently there are two aircraft on show at this memorial. The Sabre has been at the park for more than four decades. The Workhorse was at Paine Field near Everett in the 1990s. This helicopter replaced the Vought Cutlass now under rebuild at the Museum of Flight Restoration Center at Paine Field. The navy fighter was displayed in the park from 1958 until 1992.

TYPE	REG/SER	CON. NO.	PI/NOTES	STATUS
☐ North American NA-173 Sabre (F-86D) (F-86L)	51-6069	173-213		PV
☐ Piasecki PD-22 Work Horse (H-21B) (CH-21B)	53-4323	B.73	53-4323, N6793	PV

CARLSON COLLECTION (WA8)

Address:	South 7824 Cedar Road, Spokane, Washington 99224-9614.
Email:	oxmeadows@att.net
Admission:	By prior permission only.
Location:	At a private airfield south east of the town.

Washington

This interesting private collection contains a number of rarities. Designed as a pursuit aircraft in 1916, the Thomas Morse S-4C was ordered as an advanced trainer. Just over 600 examples of this biplane were built and gave excellent service for several years.

Lloyd Stearman was chief engineer of the Swallow Company in 1923. The following year he designed the original Travel Air before setting up his own company in California in 1926. He moved back to Wichita and the C2C appeared in 1928. The example in the collection was modified to C3 configuration in the 1960s. The Canuck is a Canadian-built Curtiss Jenny and the Puss Moth is one of 25 built by de Havilland Canada.

Only small numbers of Student Prince biplanes were constructed in Portland, Oregon in the early 1930s. Powered by a 95 hp Cirrus engine the type was intended to serve with the Rankin Flying School chain but these plans failed to materialise.

The Aeronca C-2 was based on the Roche-Dohse Monoplane of 1926. The type, powered by a 26 h.p. Aeronca twin cylinder motor, appeared in 1929 and 112 left the Cincinnati, Ohio factory. Ed Heath built his first Parasol in 1926. The wings were from a Thomas-Morse S-4 and a 20 h.p. Henderson motor cycle engine was fitted. Only about 50 were produced by the factory but over 1,000 kits were sold after plans appeared in 'Modern Mechanix' magazine.

Two early Cubs are in the collection along with a post-war Cub Special. The PA-11 was developed from the popular J-3 and made its maiden flight in March 1946 and over 1,000 were completed over the next few years. Eventually this collection will go on display at the Armed Forces and Aerospace Museum at Spokane International Airport.

TYPE	REG/SER	CON. NO.	PI/NOTES	STATUS
☐ Aeronca C-2	N1020	A-71	NC1020	RA
☐ Aircraft Builders Corporation Student Prince X	N893K	102	NC893K	RAA
☐ Bellanca 14-13-2 Crusair Senior	N74450	1563	NC74450	RAA
☐ Cessna 172	N5116A	28116		RAA
☐ Curtiss JN-4 Canuck	NC11917	C-1122		RAA
☐ De Havilland DH.80A Puss Moth	N223EC	DHC.223	CF-AVA	RAA
☐ De Havilland DH.82A Tiger Moth	N7966	83462	T5753, NZ660, ZK-AIW	RAA
☐ Fleet 2	N620R	196		RA
☐ Heath Parasol	N2768P	102		RAA
☐ Mono Aircraft Monocoupe 90A	N8057E	A-769	NC8057E	RAA
☐ Piper J-3C-65 Cub	N92096	16531	NC92096	RAA
☐ Piper J-3C-65 Cub	NC22842	2765	NC22842, N22842	RAA
☐ Piper PA-11 Cub Special	N4938M	11-1610		RAA
☐ Piper PA-22-135 Tripacer	N1392C	22-1146		RAA
☐ Piper PA-22-150 Tripacer	N7008D	22-4901		RAA
☐ Rearwin 185 Skyranger	N90695	1790		RAA
☐ Stinson V-76 Sentinel (L-5)	N49324	76-530	42-98289 (?)	RAA
☐ Stits SA-11A Playmate	N6404B	EDC-1		RAA
☐ Taylor E-2 Cub	NC15083	222	NC15083, N15083	RAA
☐ Taylor J-2 Cub	NC16316	549	NC16316, N16316	RAA
☐ Thomas-Morse S-4C	N3307T		SC38898	RAA
☐ Waco 10 (GXE)	NC6777	1579	NC6777, N6777	RAA

CLOVER PARK TECHNICAL COLLEGE (WA9)

Address: 17214 110th Avenue East, South Hill, Washington 98374.
Tel: 253-583-8904   **Email:** andy.bird@cptc.edu
Admission: By prior permission only.
Location: At Thun Field, Puyallup which is south of the townn off Route 161.

The college has its main campus at Lakewood and the aviation centre is at Thun Field. The institution was created in 1942 as a vocational school to train auto mechanics for Fort Lewis and McChord Field along with tradesman for the Tacoma shipyards. The fleet of instructional airframes includes a number of former military helicopters as well as familiar civilian types. The Cessna 402 was once used on a variety of tasks by NASA at Langley in Virginia. The Ecureuil helicopter is a recent addition to the fleet.

TYPE	REG/SER	CON. NO.	PI/NOTES	STATUS
☐ Aérospatiale AS.350 Ecureuil				RA
☐ Bell 205 Iroquois (UH-1D) (UH-1H)	N45AD	9003	66-16899	RA
☐ Bell 205 Iroquois (UH-1D) (UH-1V)	N772CP	5255	66-0772	RA
☐ Bell 206A Kiowa (OH-58A)	70-15088	40639		RA
☐ Bell 206A Kiowa (OH-58A)	71-20723	41584		RA
☐ Bell 206A Kiowa (OH-58A) (OH-58C)	71-20574	41435		RA
☐ Bell 206A Kiowa (OH-58A) (OH-58C)	70-15497	41048		RA
☐ Bell 209 Huey Cobra (AH-1S) (AH-1P)	76-22700	24053		RA
☐ Bell 209 Huey Cobra (AH-1S) (AH-1P)	77-22751	24089		RA
☐ Cessna 172N	N739MF	17270645		RA
☐ Cessna 172N	N5955E	17271975		RA
☐ Cessna 172N	N4725D	17272340		RA
☐ Cessna 402B	N503NA	402B0313		RA
☐ Cessna R182 Skylane RG	N7592Y	R18200141		RA
☐ Hughes 269A Osage (TH-55A)	67-16848	0955		RA
☐ Hughes 269A Osage (TH-55A)	67-16924	1031		RA
☐ North American NA-276 Sabreliner (T-39A) (CT-39A)	62-4459	276-12		RA
☐ Piper PA-23 Apache	N1248P	23-274		RA
☐ Piper PA-23 Apache	N2269P	24-879		RA

COLUMBIA GORGE INTERPRETIVE CENTER (WA10)

Address: PO Box 396, 990 South West Rock Creek Drive, Stevenson, Washington 98648.
Tel: 509-427-2811   **Fax:** 509-427-7429   **Email:** info@columbiagorge.org
Admission: Daily 1000-1700.
Location: About 35 miles east of Vancouver, WA off Route 14.

This museum opened in 2001 close to the Columbia River Gorge National Scenic Area. The displays trace the cultural and natural history of the region.
There are galleries on three floors with many innovative exhibits. The only aircraft is a 1917 Curtiss Jenny.

Wally Olsen, owner of Evergreen Airport, found the biplane in pieces in Spokane in the early 1980s. He restored and flew it but it crashed and the rebuild started again. The aircraft spent some time on show at the Pearson Air Museum before moving to its new home.

TYPE	REG/SER	CON. NO.	PI/NOTES	STATUS
☐ Curtiss 1C Jenny (JN-4D)	'C300'	5111	, ????, N511JN	PVX

EVERETT COMMUNITY COLLEGE (WA11)

Address:	2000 Tower Street, Everett, Washington 98201.
Tel:	425-388-9100 Email: kbrame@everettcc.edu
Admission:	By prior permission only.
Location:	At Paine Field, which is about 5 miles south of Everett off Route 526.

The college was founded in 1941 and has its main campus in the town. The aviation section is housed in hangars at Paine Field which is also home to a number of collections of historic aircraft.

TYPE	REG/SER	CON. NO.	PI/NOTES	STATUS
☐ Beech 65 Queen Air	N831Q	LC-56		RA
☐ Bell 47D-1 Sioux (HTL-4) (TH-13L)	N311WN	223	Bu128887	RA
☐ Bell 205 Iroquois (UH-1H)	66-16493	89687		RA
☐ Bell 206A Kiowa (OH-58A)	69-16344	40565		RA
☐ Boeing 727-25F	N511FE	18283	N8132N	RA
☐ Cessna 205	N8471Z	2050471		RA
☐ Cessna 310A Blue Canoe (L-27A) (U-3A)	N167Z	38094	58-2120	RA
☐ Hughes 269A Osage (TH-55A)	67-16968	1075		RA
☐ North American NA-265 Sabreliner (T-39A) (CT-39A)	61-0650	265-53		RA
☐ Piper PA-23-160 Apache	N3266P	23-1211		RA

FLYING HERITAGE COLLECTION (WA12)

Address:	3407 109th Street South West, Everett, Washington 98204.
Tel:	206-342-4242 Email: press@flyingheritage.com
Admission:	May–August daily 100-1600; September–April Tuesday-Sunday 1000-1600.
Location:	At Paine Field, which is about 5 miles south of Everett off Route 526.

Paul Allen of Microsoft started collecting aircraft in the late 1990s. He has obtained warbirds from many sources and a number of these are being rebuilt around the country.
A small display was opened at Arlington but the collection moved to Paine Field in 2007. Classic types from several countries have been obtained. Rarities include the Hayabusha and Polikarpov I-16 obtained from New Zealand. Both these were on show in the Alpine Fighter Collections premises in Wanaka.
The Focke-Wulf Fw 190A-5/U-3 crashed near Leningrad in 1943. The airframe was recovered by helicopter in 1990 and the fighter was taken to England. Restoration to flying condition started before the move to the USA One of many long-term projects will be the rebuild of the Mosquito. The aircraft flew in the 1960s film '633 Squadron' and then joined the collection of the Imperial War Museum. Unfortunately the outer starboard wing was cut off during this period.
The Messerschmitt Bf 109 crashed on a beach in France during World War II. The major components were recovered and an extensive rebuild took place in England. The fighter, painted in JG 51 markings, underwent taxiing trials at Wattisham airfield before being crated for transport across the Atlantic. The larger premises will enable more of the collection to be viewed.

TYPE	REG/SER	CON. NO.	PI/NOTES	STATUS
☐ Avro 683 Lancaster B.I	TW911		Front fuselage only.	PV
☐ Boeing 299-O Fortress (B-17E)	N12355	2682	41-9210, N5842N, CF-ICB, N9720F, CP-753, N8WJ	RAC
☐ CASA 2.111B [Heinkel He 111H-16]	G-AWHB	049	BR.2I-37, G-AWHB	RA
☐ CASA 2.111B [Heinkel He 111H-16]	N11105	169	B2I-39	RA
☐ Curtiss 1C Jenny (JN-4D)	N3712	3712		PVA
☐ Curtiss H81-A2 Warhawk (P-40C)	NX2689	16194	41-13390, 53 (Soviet), NX80FR, G-TOMA	PVA
☐ De Havilland DH.98 Mosquito T.III	TV959		TV959, 'MM398'	RA
☐ Dornier-Breguet Alpha Jet A	N512AF	0115	41+15	RAA
☐ Fieseler Fi 103A-1		2255		RA
☐ Fieseler Fi 103R		44329		PV
☐ Fieseler Fi 156C-2 Storch	NX436FS/ '2E+RA'	4362	(Luftwaffe)	PVA
☐ Focke-Wulf Fw 189A-2	N189FW	112100	V7+1H, G-BZKY	RAC
☐ Focke-Wulf Fw 190A-5/U-3	N19027	0151227	DG+HO,G-FOKW	PVA
☐ Focke-Wulf Fw 190D-13/R11	NX190D	836017	836017, FE-118 – registered with c/n 174103.	PV
☐ Grumman G-40 Avenger (TBM-3)	N7835C	4169	Bu91264	RA
☐ Grumman G-50 Hellcat (F6F-5) (F6F-5K)	N79863	A-11008	Bu79863	PV
☐ Hawker Hurricane IIC	'5429'	CCF/R32007	BW881, G-KAMM, NX54FH	PVAX
☐ Hawker-Siddeley P.1127 Harrier GR.3 (GR.1) (GR.1A)	N4320W	41H/712001	XV738, 9074M,XV738	RA
☐ Hawker-Siddeley P.1127 Harrier GR.3	XZ967	41H/712603	XZ967, 9077M	RA
☐ Ilyushin Il-2m3				RAC
☐ Lockheed 222-60-15 Lightning (P-38F)			Composite obtained from several crash sites.	RAC
☐ Lockheed 422-81-14 Lightning (P-38J)	N38LL	422-2922	42-104088, N5260N	RAC
☐ Messerschmitt Bf 109E-3	NX342FH	1342	G-BYDS	PVA

Washington

☐ Messerschmitt Me 163B-1a Komet	191660	191660	C/n 191400 on port wing – may contain parts of c/n 191060 VF241	PV
☐ Messerschmitt Me 262A-1a/U3	N94503	500453	500453, FE-4012, T2-4012	RAC
☐ Mikoyan-Gurevich MiG-21R	N7803Z	94R01904	1904 (Czechoslovakia)	RA
☐ Mikoyan-Gurevich MiG-21UM	N7803S	04695168	0468 (Czechoslovakia)	RA
☐ Mitsubishi A6M3 Zero Sen Model 32	N3852	3852	N385HF	PV
☐ Mitsubishi A6M5 Zero Sen Model 52	N1303	1303		RA
☐ Mitsubishi A6M5 Zero Sen Model 52	N652Z/'HK-102'	4400	82020	RA
☐ Nakajima Ki-43-Ic Hayabusa	N750N	4950	750, ZK-OSC	PV
☐ Noorduyn Norseman VI (C-64A) (UC-64A)	N4474	778	44-70513	RA
☐ North American NA-108 Mitchell (B-25J) (TB-25K) (Mitchell III)	N41123	108-33529	44-30254, 5211 (Canada), CF-MWC	RAA
☐ North American NA-122 Mustang (P-51D) (J 26)	NL723FH	122-38823	44-72364, Fv72061, 1916 (Dominica)	PVA
☐ North American NA-161 Sabre (P-86A) (F-86A)	N4912	161-211	49-1217, G-BZNL	RAC
☐ North American NA-172 Sabre (F-86F)	N186SE	172-358	51-13067 – possible identity.	RAA
☐ Polikarpov I-16 tip 24 (tip 29)	NX7459	2421014	45, ZK-JIP	PVA
☐ Polikarpov Po-2	NX46GU	641543		PVA
☐ Republic P-47D Thunderbolt	NX7159Z	399.55945	45-49406, 4192 (Brazil)	PVA
☐ Republic F-84G Thunderjet	N6599V		51-10586, 586 (Turkey)	RAC
☐ Republic F-84G Thunderjet	52-8365			RAC
☐ Republic F-105G Thunderchief (F-105F)	'63-8332'	F-113	63-8336	RAX
☐ Scaled Composites 316 SpaceShipOne (R)	'N328KF'			PVX
☐ Supermarine 349 Spitfire LF.Vc	NX614VC	WASP/20/288	AR614, 5378M, 7555M, C-FDUY, G-BUWA	PVA
☐ Vought FG-1D Corsair	NX700G	3117	Bu88303, N6594D	RAC
☐ Vought F-8K Crusader (F8U-2) (F-8C)	N19TB	A35-17	Bu145592	RA
☐ Vought F-8L Crusader (F8U-1E) (F-8B)	N37TB	A35-30	Bu145527	RA
☐ Yakovlev Yak-3U				RA

FORT LEWIS MILITARY MUSEUM (WA13)

Address: AFZH-PTM-ON, PO Box 331001, Fort Lewis, Washington 98433-1001.
Tel: 253-967-7207 **Email:** lewisdptmmuseum@conus.army.mil
Admission: Wednesday-Sunday 1200-1600.
Location: About 12 miles south west of Tacoma off Interstate 5.

Displays tracing the history of the fort and the story of the US Army in the Pacific Northwest can be seen in this museum. The exhibition is housed in the old Fort Lewis Inn constructed in 1918 by the Salvation Army. In 1973 the museum took over the building and the exhibition has steadily been developed. Four helicopters, representing types which have flown from Gray Army Airfield, are preserved around the site with one outside the museum. The other three are with base units. The site is now part of a joint base along with McChord AFB.

TYPE	REG/SER	CON. NO.	PI/NOTES	STATUS
☐ Bell 204 Iroquois (UH-1C) (UH-1M)	66-0722	1704		RA
☐ Bell 205 Iroquois (UH-1H)	67-17455	9853	With boom from c/n 13698 74-22374.	RA
☐ Bell 205 Iroquois (UH-1H)	69-15425	11713		RA
☐ Bell 209 Huey Cobra (AH-1S) (AH-1P)	76-22583	24017		RA

FUTURE OF FLIGHT CENTER AND BOEING TOUR (WA14)

Address: 8415 Paine Field Boulevard, Mukilteo, Washington 98275.
Tel: 425-438-8100 **Fax:** 425-265-9808 **Email:** info@futureofflight.org
Admission: Daily 0830-1730. Factory tours on the hour from 0900-1500.
Location: About 5 miles south west of Everett off Route 526.

This interpretative display opened in December 2005. The history of the Boeing company is portrayed with models of all their designs. There is a flight simulator and the visitor can use computer programmes to design an aircraft.
The latest advances in engineering can be viewed. Fuselage sections of a Boeing 707 and a 787 can be compared to see the advances in construction techniques over the last half century. Tours of the giant Boeing factory to see the airliner production occur regularly.
Aircraft from the Museum of Flight have been loaned to enhance the display. All are modern types using composite materials.

TYPE	REG/SER	CON. NO.	PI/NOTES	STATUS
☐ Beech 2000A Starship I	N8158X	NC-42	Museum of Flight aircraft.	PV
☐ Boeing 707			Fuselage section only.	PV
☐ Boeing 727-25QC	N124FE	19360	N8160G – front fuselage only – Museum of Flight aircraft.	PV
☐ Boeing 787			Fuselage section only.	PV
☐ Quickie Aircraft Quickie 51 (Rutan 54)	N77Q	001	Museum of Flight aircraft.	PV
☐ Stoddard-Hamilton SH-2 Glasair TG-1	N83JR	364	Museum of Flight aircraft.	PV
☐ Stoddard-Hamilton SH-2 Glasair III	N12JR	3006	Museum of Flight aircraft.	PV

GLEN SPIETH MUSEUM ANTIQUES (WA15)

Address: 5928 Steilacoom Boulevard, Tacoma, Washington 98499.
Tel: 206-584-3930
Admission: Saturday 1100-1700.
Location: In the centre of the town.

This private collection includes many aircraft components, instruments, engines and items of memorabilia. Two complete T-33s and the fuselage of another can be seen.

TYPE	REG/SER	CON. NO.	PI/NOTES	STATUS
☐ Lockheed 580 (T-33A)	51-4298	580-5593		PV
☐ Lockheed 580 (T-33A)	52-9395	580-7505		PV
☐ Lockheed 580 (T-33A)	52-9646	580-7831	Fuselage only.	PV

HERITAGE FLIGHT MUSEUM (WA16)

Address: 4165 Mitchell Way, Bellingham, Washington 98226.
Tel: 360-733-4422 **Fax:** 360-733-4423 **Email:** kate@heritageflight.org
Admission: Thursday-Saturday 1200-1600.
Location: About 4 miles north west of the town off Interstate 5.

Former astronaut Bill Anders has set up this museum of flying aircraft with the aim of showing the contribution military aircraft have made to the heritage, security and freedom of America. The Skyraider is one of a large batch supplied to France. Several of these made their way south to Africa and the one in the collection served in Chad. Later it flew with the Vormezeele Collection in Belgium.

TYPE	REG/SER	CON. NO.	PI/NOTES	STATUS
☐ Bell 47G	N2199	604		PV
☐ Boeing-Stearman E75 Kaydet (PT-13D) (N2S-5)	N65695	75-8584	42-109551, Bu43490	PV
☐ Cessna 305A Bird Dog	'12247'	2	N22SU	PVX
☐ Cessna 337M Super Skymaster (O-2A)	N3219K	337M0181	68-6892	PV
☐ Convair 105 (L-13B)	N7412H	292	47-412, N4898V	PV
☐ De Havilland DHC.2 Beaver	N682AF	1743	On loan.	PV
☐ Douglas AD-4NA Skyraider (AD-4N)	NX965AD	7765	Bu126965, 54 (France), (Chad), F-ZVMM, (OO-SKY), OO-FOR	PV
☐ Fairchild M-62A Cornell (PT-19A)	N977ED	T42-1811	42-2723, N46395	PV
☐ Max Holste MH.1521M Broussard	N4022	22	019 (France)	PV
☐ North American NA-88 Texan (SNJ-4)	N6413D	88-11850	Bu26991	PV
☐ North American NA-88 Texan (AT-6D)	N190FS	88-15143	42-44709, C.6-45, N4996P, N4292C	PV
☐ North American NA-121 Texan (AT-6F)	N706F	121-42615	44-81893, N7363C, N7463C	PV
☐ North American NA-124 Mustang (P-51D)	N151AF	124-48278	45-11525, (Indonesia), N91JB	PV
☐ Northrop N-160 Scorpion (N-68) (F-89D) (F-89J)	53-2453	N.4584	53-2453, N16565	PV

HISTORIC FLIGHT FOUNDATION (WA17)

Address: 10719 Bernie Webber Drive, Everett, Washington 98204.
Tel: 206-587-4040 **Email:** airborne@historicflight.org
Admission: Friday-Sunday 1000-1800.
Location: At Paine Field, which is about 5 miles south of Everett off Route 526.

This private collection is steadily acquiring an impressive fleet. The Tigercat flew from Duxford in England between 1988 and 1993 and was a popular performer at many airshows held at the Imperial War Museum airfield. The rare P-51B was built up from several aircraft and flew again in 2008.

TYPE	REG/SER	CON. NO.	PI/NOTES	STATUS
☐ Beech D17S (UC-43) (GB-2)	NC35JM	6914	(44-76069), Bu23734, N67737, CF-GLL	PVA
☐ Canadair CL-30 Silver Star 3 (CT-133) [Lockheed 580 (T-33AN)]	N303FS	T33-342	21342 (Canada), N144M	PVA
☐ De Havilland DHC.2 Beaver AL.1	N779XP/'52-6132'	1450	XP779. G-BTDL, G-DHCB, C-FLOR	PVAX
☐ Douglas DC-3A-467 Skytrain (C-47B)	N877MG	20806	43-16340, 100(?) (China), XT-20(?), N8350C, N37800, N800J, N8009	RAC
☐ Grumman G-51 Tigercat (F7F-3)	NX6178C	C.225	Bu80483	PVA
☐ Mikoyan-Gurevich MiG-29UB	N29UB	50903014896	64 (Soviet), 64 (Ukraine)	PVA
☐ North American NA-77 Texan (AT-6F)				PVA
☐ North American NA-100 Mitchell (B-25D) (Mitchell II)	N88972	100-23644	43-3318, KL161, CF-OGQ, N88972, G-BYDR	PVA
☐ North American NA-104 Mustang (P-51B)	NX5087F	104-23025	42-106638 – composite.	PVA
☐ Supermarine 361 Spitfire LF.IXe	N633VS/SL633	CBAF-IX-571	SL633 (Czech), 204 (Israel), UB-245 (Myanmar), 'UB424', G-CZAF	PVA
☐ Waco UPF-7	NC32018	5650	NC32018, N32018	PVA

INLAND NORTHWEST MUSEUM OF TRANSPORTATION AND HISTORY (WA18)

Address: PO Box 97, 1342 Bridge Street, Clarkston, Washington 99403-0097.
Admission: Unknown.
Location: Unknown.

The Beech 17 which was built in 1936 was registered to the museum in 2008. The address stated is home to a weekly Flea Market. I have not been able to find out any more information on the organisation.

TYPE	REG/SER	CON. NO.	PI/NOTES	STATUS
☐ Beech C17R	N15835	74	NC15833, N996	PV

KIMBREL COLLECTION (WA19)

Address:	1333 Garrard Creek Road, Oakville, Washington 98568-9703.
Tel:	
Admission:	By prior permission only.
Location:	At a private airfield outside the town which is about 20 miles south west of Olympia on Route 12.

Many interesting types are operated by this family collection.
The star is the de Havilland Dragon. This classic biplane was built in 1935 and flew on Railway Air Services routes. The airliner was damaged when it ran into a hedge at Land's End Airport in September 1938. During the war it flew services around Britain. In the 1950s it was one of a pair operated by Air Navigation and Trading Company. Flights around Blackpool Tower from Squires Gate Airport were operated on most days. In the 1960s the Dragon was familiar at many airshows when in the colours of Chrisair it carried out joyriding. In 1971 it joined this collection and is still in Chrisair colours carrying the name 'Sir Geoffrey de Havilland'.

A Dragon Rapide was flown for many years but this is now in Missouri with the Historic Aircraft Restoration Museum. The DC-3 is an early example delivered to United Airlines in April 1941. The Antonov An-2 was operated by Aeroflot in the early 1980s and served with them for a dozen years. These three transports can be compared with a range of light types.

TYPE	REG/SER	CON. NO.	PI/NOTES	STATUS
☐ Aeronca 7AC Champion	N1023E	7AC-4574	NC1023E	RAA
☐ Antonov An-2R	N737SL	1G 193-43	CCCP-68073, RA-68073, FLARF-01492	RAA
☐ Bellanca 14-13 Crusair Senior	N86857	1219	NC86857	RAA
☐ Bellanca 14-19-2 Cruisemaster	N13235	4050	NC13235	RAA
☐ Cessna 150H	N23350	15068892		RAA
☐ Cessna 310G	N8979Z	310G0079		RAA
☐ De Havilland DH.84 Dragon	N34DH	6096	G-ADDI	RAA
☐ Dormoy Flying Bathtub (R)	N50645	1		RAA
☐ Douglas DC-3A-197E	NC33644	4123	NC33644, (G-APKO), N33644	RAA
☐ Grega GN-1 Aircamper	N48302	195		RAA
☐ Piper J-3C-65 Cub	N35634	6502	NC35634	RAA
☐ Sorrell SNS	N2976G	1		RAA
☐ Sorrell SNS	N2180	2		RAA
☐ Stits SA-6B Flut-R-Bug	N8518	WW-100		RAA

LACEY MONUMENT (WA20)

Location:	On view during opening hours in Cabela's store at 1600 Gateway Boulevard North East.

TYPE	REG/SER	CON. NO.	PI/NOTES	STATUS
☐ Piper J-3C-65 Cub	N70182	17167	NC70182	PV

McALLISTER MUSEUM OF AVIATION (WA21)

Address:	2008 South 16th. Avenue, Yakima, Washington 98903.
Tel:	509-457-4993 Email: McAllister@nwinfo.net
Admission:	Tuesday-Friday 1000-1600; Saturday 0900-1600. Winter Friday-Saturday 1000-1600.
Location:	The airfield is about 5 miles west of the town.

In 1926 brothers Charlie and Alister McAllister opened a flying school in a field which is now Yakima Airport. Their first aircraft was a Standard J-1 biplane. The company remained in business for 73 years until Charlie's death in 1999, five years short of his century.
The hangar, offices and workshops became a museum. The history of flying in the Yakima region and the brothers' careers are portrayed. There are many interesting photographs, models and items of memorabilia on view.

Charlie built his first glider in 1918 and several more followed over the next decade. The Yakima Clipper, glider which can now be seen in the Museum of Flight at Seattle, was built in 1931/2. The design was based on pictures of German types seen in books.
In 1933 Charlie attempted to set a world endurance record but was forced to land after eight hours and 52 minutes when the wind dropped. The Tri-Traveler is being rebuilt to flying condition by volunteers.

TYPE	REG/SER	CON. NO.	PI/NOTES	STATUS
☐ Champion 7FC Tri-Traveler	N50778	432		PVC

McCHORD AIR MUSEUM (WA22)

Address:	PO Box 4205, 100 Main Street, McChord Air Force Base, Washington 98438-1109.
Tel:	253-982-2485/2419 Email: mamfound@mcchordairmuseum.org
Admission:	Wednesday-Saturday 1200-1600 (Subject to security clearance)
Location:	About 8 miles south of Tacoma off Interstate 5.

The airfield opened as the airport for Tacoma in the 1920s and was donated to the military in May 1938. Harold Bromley attempted a trans-Pacific flight from the site in 1929. The base is named after Colonel William S. McChord who was killed in a forced landing in Virginia in 1937.
Over the years many units have been resident at the field which is now home to an Airlift Wing. In 1942 personnel for the famous Doolittle raid on Tokyo were selected from squadrons based at McChord. Crews for the first batch of B-17s supplied to the Royal Air Force were trained here. The museum was set up in the early 1980s in a building in the camp. The indoor display traces the history of the base and its units. There is an excellent collection of models, photographs, uniforms, badges, components and memorabilia to be seen.
The rare B-18 has been under restoration for a long time and another Douglas bomber, the B-23, is parked outside the building. The C-124 was used for many years by a training school at Willow Run in Michigan. On 9th October 1986 it made what will probably be the last flight by the type when it was delivered to the museum. A new air park has

been constructed to house the larger aircraft and the C-124 and C-141 are now parked here. The museum has a hangar/workshop on the base and the CF-101F and F-102A have been restored to the colours they wore when operational. The top of the old McChord control tower, which was in use from 1952 to 1995 was moved to the museum in 1997. The Phantom is mounted on a pole outside the North West Headquarters of NORAD. A Hercules had been allocated to the collection but a change in policy has resulted in the aircraft being stored for future operational use.

TYPE	REG/SER	CON. NO.	PI/NOTES	STATUS
☐ Beech D18S Expeditor (C18S) (JRB-3) (SNB-5) (UC-45J)	'210613'		Bu89484, N40093	RAX
☐ Consolidated 28-5A Catalina (PBY-5A) (OA-10A)	'44-34033'	1547	(Bu33993), 43-43847, N4760C	PVX
☐ Convair 8-10 Delta Dagger (F-102A)	56-1515	8-10-732		PV
☐ Convair 8-24 Delta Dart (F-106A)	56-0459	8-24-09		PV
☐ Douglas B-18A Bolo	37-505	2505	37-505, N67947, XB-LAJ, N18AC	RAC
☐ Douglas DC-3A-467 Skytrain (TC-47B) (C-47D)	44-76502	16086/32834	44-76502, 476502 (France), 476502 (South Vietnam)	PV
☐ Douglas UC-67 Dragon (B-23)	'39-010'	2722	39-036, NR52327, N52327	PVX
☐ Douglas 1317 Globemaster II (C-124C)	52-0994	43903	52-0994, N86599	RA
☐ Fairchild 78 Packet (C-82A)	48-0574	10209	48-0574, N4753C	PV
☐ Fairchild-Republic A-10A Thunderbolt II	75-0270	A10-19		PV
☐ General Dynamics 401 Fighting Falcon (F-16A)	82-0929	61-522		RA
☐ Lockheed 300 Starlifter (C-141A) (C-141B)	65-0277	300-6129		RA
☐ Lockheed 382-4B Hercules (C-130E)	62-1789	382-3736	May join museum.	RA
☐ Lockheed 580 (T-33A)	58-2106	580-1692		PV
☐ McDonnell M.199-1A Eagle (F-15A)	'76-0008'	231/A200	76-0048	PVX
☐ McDonnell M.36BA Voodoo (TF-101B) (CF-101F)	101022	500	57-0322 – in Canadian markings	PV
☐ McDonnell M.98DE Phantom II (F-4C)	63-7584	636		PV
☐ North American NA-190 Sabre (F-86D)	'15976'	190-72	52-3669	PVX

MILITARY BEECH 18 HERITAGE FOUNDATION (WA23)

Address:	PO Box 200, Maple Valley, Washington 98038-2000.
Tel:	425-413-3830 Email: m2kopp@msn.com
Admission:	By prior permission only.
Location:	At Auburn Municipal Airport which is about 2 miles north of the town.

The foundation has been set up to educate the public on the role that the type played in military service both in the USA and around the world. Their aircraft was delivered to the US Navy in 1944 and initially served at Corpus Christi in Texas. Withdrawn in 1972, the Beech 18 spent time at Davis-Monthan AFB and at the Pima Air and Space Museum. The aircraft was restored at Stockton in California and won the 'Most Original Warbird' award at Oshkosh in 2006. The group acquired it a few months later and it regularly appears at shows in the north west.

TYPE	REG/SER	CON. NO.	PI/NOTES	STATUS
☐ Beech D18S Expeditor (C18S) (SNB-2C) (SNB-3) (SNB-5P) (RC-45J)	N585PB	7121	Bu29585, N75018	RAA

MOSES LAKE MONUMENT (WA24)

Location:	By prior permission only at a house in Harris Road North East.

TYPE	REG/SER	CON. NO.	PI/NOTES	STATUS
☐ Boeing 367-76-66 Stratofreighter (KC-97G)	N31338	16725	52-2694	RA

MUSEUM OF FLIGHT (WA25)

Address:	9404 East Marginal Way South, Seattle, Washington 98108-4046.
Tel:	206-764-5720 Fax: 206-764-5707 Email: curator@museumofflight.org
Admission:	Main museum daily 1000-1700.
	Paine Field Tuesday-Thursday 0800-1600; Saturday 0900-1700.
Location:	On the west side of Boeing Field which is about 8 miles south of Seattle off Interstate 5.
	Paine Field is about 5 miles south west of Everett off Route 526.

In 1915 local timber merchant William Boeing went into partnership with Seattle-based naval officer Conrad Westervelt. Their first aircraft was the B & W floatplane constructed on the shores of Lake Union. This biplane flew in June 1916 after Westervelt had been posted away from the area.

Boeing then set up his own company and today airliners bearing his name are still being produced in several factories in the Seattle region. Over the last 80 years the Boeing company has designed a wide range of both civil and military aircraft including bombers such as the B-17, B-29, B-47 and B-52 which served in large numbers with the Air Force.

In 1964 a local group of enthusiasts set up the Pacific Northwest Aviation Historical Foundation with the aim of saving aircraft and artefacts. Four years later a small display was staged at the Seattle Center and this remained open until 1979. In 1917 the Boeing Airplane Company moved into a wooden building at Lake Union. In the early 1970s this shed, known as 'The Red Barn', was derelict and in danger of being demolished. The Foundation acquired the building in 1975 and moved it to Boeing Field where it was restored.

The Museum of Flight opened in the Red Barn. Funds were raised for a large hall which was completed in 1987. This structure, known as the Great Gallery, features a large glass walled exhibition area along with offices and an excellent library and archive section. Two hangars are used at Paine Field, north of Seattle, where a restoration facility is located. This is staffed by a team of volunteers, which includes many past and present employees of the Boeing company.

In 1965 a Boeing 80A which had been flown in Alaska was found on a dump in Anchorage. The giant biplane was moved to Seattle and restored to its former glory. Soon after a B-47 Stratojet flew into Boeing Field. The displays in the Great Gallery have recently been improved and a range of aircraft from a replica Wright Flyer to a SR-71 Blackbird can be seen.

There are many rare types on show covering all aspects of flying and Boeing aircraft feature prominently. Examples of their famous bombers along with their jet airliners are in the collection. The B-29 arrived from Lowry Air Force Base in Colorado in the mid-1990s. Parked outside the main building is a VC-137B which was used by Presidents Eisenhower, Kennedy and Nixon with the famous callsign 'Air Force One'.

The range of airliners covers many of the types which have been in service around the world. Later models will join the collection in due course. A highlight is an example of the supersonic Concorde. The former British Airways aircraft joined the exhibition when the type was withdrawn. The museum purchased the famous Champlin Fighter Collection and the majority of these aircraft are on show in the 'Personal Courage Wing' which opened on 6th June 2004 – the 60th anniversary of D-Day.

These aircraft consist mainly of World War I replicas and classic fighters of World War II. A rare original machine is the Austrian Aviatik D I designed by Julius Berg. Over 700 were built and the example on show survived because the designer modified it as a two-seat tourer. He hid it in a barn where it remained until 1976.

The Caproni Ca 20 dates from 1914 and is the first type specifically designed as a fighter. The aircraft was stored at the Caproni villa in northern Italy for over 85 years. The monoplane was transported to the museum and restored. The Spanish-built Messerschmitt Bf 109 was one of those that flew in the 'Battle of Britain' film. The museum has a display at Seattle-Tacoma Airport to publicise its work. Currently on view there is an Alexander Eaglerock biplane. There are plans to acquire additional land and erect more display halls.

Location Codes: 1 Main Museum; 2 Paine Field.

TYPE	REG/SER	CON. NO.	PI/NOTES	STATUS
☐ Aeronca C-2	N30RC	301-23	Not an original c/n	PV.1
☐ Aeronca 65TC Grasshopper (O-58B) (L-3B)	43-26785	9223	43-26785, N47427	PV.1
☐ Aérospatiale / British Aircraft Corporation Concorde 102	G-BOAG	100-014	G-BFKW	PV.1
☐ Aerosport Scamp	N23JF	12		PV.1
☐ Albatros D Va (R)	'5636/17'	0036	NX36DV	PVX.1
☐ Alexander Eaglerock 3-POLB	N4648	469	NC4648 – at Seattle-Tacoma Airport.	PV
☐ Antonov An-2R	N61SL	1G 175-27	CCCP-62504, FLA-01270	RA.2
☐ Aviatik D I	101.40		In Austro-Hungarian markings	PV.1
☐ Bede BD-5B	N2441Y	3820	Composite.	RA.2
☐ Beech D18S Expeditor (C-45G)	'N115MF'	AF-253	51-11696, (N1354N), N115ME	PVX.1
☐ Bell 47D-1 Sioux (H-13E) (OH-13E)	'N795'	795	51-14030	RAX.2
☐ Bell 205 Iroquois (UH-1H)	69-15140	11428		PV.2
☐ Bensen B-8M Gyrocopter	N8533E	1		PV.2
☐ Boeing B & W (R)	N1916L	1A	On loan.	PV.1
			Fuselage only.	PV.1
☐ Boeing 40A (R)				
☐ Boeing 40B (R)	'C290'			PVX.1
☐ Boeing 80A	NC224M	1082	NC224M, N224M	PV.1
☐ Boeing 100	'29-354'	1143	NX872R, NC872H, N872R	PVX.1
☐ Boeing 247D (247)	NC13347	1729	NC13347, CF-BTD, 7389 (Canada), CF-BTB, NC13347, TI-1012, N3977C	RAA.2
☐ Boeing 299-O Fortress (B-17F) (RB-17F) (TB-17F)	N17W	4896	42-29782, N6015V	RAA.1
☐ Boeing 345 Superfortress (B-29)	44-69729	10561		RAC
☐ Boeing 450-157-35 Stratojet (B-47E) (WB-47E)	51-7066	450609		PV.1
☐ Boeing 464-253 Stratofortress (B-52G)	59-2584	464347		RA.2
☐ Boeing 707-153 (VC-137A) (VC-137B)	58-6970	17925		PV.1
☐ Boeing 727-22	N7001U	18293		PV.2
☐ Boeing 727-223	N874AA	21386		PV.1
☐ Boeing 737-130	N515NA	19437	N73700, (N715NA),	PV.1
☐ Boeing 737-201	N213US	20213	N744N – forward fuselage on show.	PV.1
☐ Boeing 747-121	N7470	20235	N7470, N1352B	PV.1
☐ Boeing-Stearman A75 Kaydet (PT-13A)	N8FL	75-0055	37-99	PV.1
☐ Bowers Fly Baby 1A	N500F	1-1		PV.2
☐ Bowers Fly Baby 1A	N4339	68-15		PV.2
☐ Bowlus BA-100 Baby Albatross	N25605	114		PV.2
☐ Canadair CL-13B Sabre 6 (CL-13A Sabre 5) [North American F-86E]	23363	1153	23363 (Canada), N74180, N8686F	PV.1
☐ Caproni Ca.20		1		PV.1
☐ Cascade Kasperwing 180B				RA.2
☐ Cessna CG-2	N178V	50	NC178V	PV.1
☐ Chanute-Herring Glider (R)				PV.1
☐ Curtiss 1C Jenny (JN-4D)			Parts from 5362 – uncovered airframe.	PV.1
☐ Curtiss 50C Robin C-1	NX979K	628	Modified to J-1 'Newsboy'	PV.1
☐ Curtiss 87V Warhawk (P-40N)	NL10626	32932	44-7192, N4161K, N10626	PVX.1
☐ De Havilland DH.106 Comet 4C	N888WA	6424	G-AOVU, XA-NAR	PV.2
☐ Douglas A-4F Skyhawk	Bu154180	13637		PV.1
☐ Douglas DC-2-118A	N1934D	1368	NC14296, XA-BJL, LG-ACA, TG-ACA, N4867V, 'NC13717'	RAA
☐ Douglas DC-3-277C	'NC91008'	2245	NC15591, N138D	PV.1
☐ Durand V	N444JF	5		PV.2
☐ Eipper Cumulus VB Hang Glider				RA.1
☐ Ercoupe 415C	N2944H	3569		PV.2
☐ Fairchild 24W41	N37161	W41-206	NC37161	PV.1
☐ Fiat G.91PAN (G.91)	MM6244	10		PV.1
☐ Fieseler Fi 103A-1			Composite.	PV.1
☐ Fokker D VII (R)	'4539'	CFM002	NX38038	PVX.1
☐ Fokker D VIII (R)				RAD
☐ Fokker D VIII (R)	'545/18'	545/18	NX7557U	PVX.1
☐ Fokker Dr I (R)	'535/17'	535/17	NX2203	PVX.1
☐ Fokker E III (R)	'226/15'	AA-107	NX3363G	PVX.1
☐ Gates Learjet 23	'N407V'	23-034	N242WT, N241BN, N24FF, N154AG	PV.1

☐ Gates Learfan 2100	N626BL	E-001		PV.1
☐ Granville Gee Bee Z (R)	NR77V'	T-4		PVX.1
☐ Grumman G-36 Wildcat (FM-2)	Bu74512	4704		PV.2
☐ Grumman G-99 Cougar (F9F-8) (F-9J)	Bu131232	170C		PV.1
☐ Grumman G-128 Intruder (A-6E)	Bu158794	I-530		PV.1
☐ Grumman G-303 Tomcat (F-14A)	Bu160382	238		PV.1
☐ Hawker-Siddeley P.1127 Harrier 50 (AV-8A) (AV-8C)	Bu158977	P138		PV.1
☐ Hiller HJ.1 Hornet (YH-32)	55-4969	12		PV.1
☐ Hispano HA-1112M1L [Messerschmitt Bf 109G]	NX109J	186	C.4K-122, G-AWHL	PV.1
☐ Howard DGA-15P	NC52947	559	NC52947, N52947	PV.2
☐ Huber 101-1 Aero				RA.2
☐ Insitu Aerosonde				PV.1
☐ Lamson L.106 Alcor	N924LR	18		PV.1
☐ Letov LF-107 Lunak	N2170D	36		PV.2
☐ Lilienthal Normal-Segelapparat (R)				PV.1
☐ Lockheed 080 Shooting Star (P-80C) (F-80C) (TO-1) (TV-1)	Bu33841	080-2074	47-1388 -	RA.2
☐ Lockheed 383-04-05 Starfighter (F-104C)	'N820NA'	183-1222	56-0934	PVX.1
☐ Lockheed 422-87-23 Lightning (P-38L) (P-38M)	NL3JB	422-8352	44-53097, NX67861, (Cuba), 503 (Honduras), N9011R, N7TF	PV.1
☐ Lockheed 1049G-02-82 Super Constellation (L-1049C-55-94) (L-1049E-55-01)	CF-TGE	1049C-4544	CF-TGE, N8742R, CF-RNR	PV.1
☐ Lockheed 1329 JetStar	N329J	1329-1001		RA.2
☐ Lockheed A-12MD	60-6940	134		PV.1
☐ Lockheed SR-71A Blackbird	61-7977	2028	Front fuselage only.	PV.1
☐ MacCready Gossamer Albatross II				PV.1
☐ McAllister Yakima Clipper	NC10655			PV.1
☐ McDonnell M.98DJ Phantom II (F-4C)	64-0776	1079	On loan from Oregon Mil. Mus, OR.	PV.1
☐ Mikoyan-Gurevich MiG-15bis	079	124079	In Chinese markings.	PV.1
☐ Mikoyan-Gurevich MiG-17	'7469'	1406016	1FJ-10 (Morocco) – in false North Vietnamese markings.	PVX.1
☐ Mikoyan-Gurevich MiG-21PFM	5411	94A5411	In Czech markings.	PV.1
☐ Nakajima Ki-43-IIB Hayabusa				PV.1
☐ Nieuport 24 (R)	'127'		N24RL	PVX.1
☐ Nieuport 27 (R)	N5597M	S-8		PVX.1
☐ Nieuport 28C.1	N6493U	6493		PV.1
☐ North American NA-122 Mustang (P-51D)	'463607'		(USAAF), (Sweden), 146 (Israel)	PVX.1
☐ Northrop N-156F Freedom Fighter (YF-5A)	59-4987	N.6001	59-4987, N156F	PV.1
☐ Pfalz D XII (R)	'7511/18'	1	NX43C	PVX.1
☐ Piasecki PD-22 Work Horse (H-21B) (CH-21B)	53-4329	B.79	53-4329, N6794	PV.2
☐ Piper J-3C-65 Cub	NC88023	15641	NC88023, N88023	PV.1
☐ Pratt-Read PR-G1 (LNE-1)	N60353	PRG-01-13		PV.2
☐ Pterodactyl Ascender				PV.2
☐ Pterodactyl Ascender II				PV.2
☐ Quickie Aircraft Quickie 2 (Rutan 54)	N82SC	2062		PV.1
☐ Republic TP-47G Thunderbolt (P-47G)	NX14519		42-8205, NC75640, '007' (Bolivia)	PV.1
☐ Rotec Rally 3B				PV.2
☐ Rotorway Scorpion Too	N65229	75RJM		PV.1
☐ Royal Aircraft Factory S.E.5A (R)	'C6457'	0010	NX910AV	PVX.1
☐ Rumpler Taube (R)	'0039'	0039	NX1914R	PVX
☐ Rutan 27 Vari-Viggen	N27MS	115		PV.2
☐ Ryan M-1	N46853	HN-1		PV.1
☐ Sikorsky S-62A Seaguard (HH-52A)	1415	62099		PV.2
☐ SPAD XIII (R)	'S15155'	CFM003	NX3883F	PVX.1
☐ Sopwith F.1 Camel (R)	'N6330'	AA-105	NX6330	PVX.1
☐ Sopwith 7F.1 Snipe (R)	'E6837'	E6837	NX6765D	PVX.1
☐ Sopwith Pup (R)	'B1843'	A-635	NX6018	PVX.1
☐ Sopwith Triplane (R)	'N5487'	CFM001	NX3805Z	PVX.1
☐ Sorrell Parasol	N5087K	1		PV.2
☐ Stearman C3B	NC7550	166	NS7550, NC7550, NS8Y	PV.1
☐ Stephens Akro	N78JN	434		PV.1
☐ Stinson Junior SR	NC13477	8732	NC13477, N13477	PV.1
☐ Supermarine 361 Spitfire LF.IXc	NX521R	CBAF-IX-1886	MK923, H-104 (Netherlands), H-61 (Netherlands), SM-37 (Belgium), OO-ARF, N93081, N521R	PV.1
☐ Swallow J-5	NC6070	968	NC6070, N6070	PV.1
☐ Task Silhouette	N84TR	TR601		RA.2
☐ Taylor Aerocar III	N100D	1		PV.1
☐ Taylorcraft A	NC19893	398	NC19893, N19893	PV.2
☐ Taylorcraft BC-12D	N95871	8171	NC95871	PV.2
☐ Thorp T-18	N1093	1093		PV.1
☐ Vought FG-1D Corsair	Bu88382	3196		PV.1
☐ Vought F2G-1 Corsair	NX4324	6163	Bu88454	PV.1
☐ Vought V-366 Cutlass (F7U-3)	Bu129554		Bu129554, N7FU	PVC.2
☐ Vought V-383 Crusader (XF8U-1)	Bu138899	1	On loan from NASM, DC.	PV.2
☐ War Aircraft P-47D Thunderbolt				RA.2
☐ Wizard J-2				PV.2
☐ Wright 1902 Glider (R)			On loan from Seattle Museum of Science and Industry, WA.	PV.1
☐ Wright Flyer (R)				PV.1
☐ Yakovlev Yak-9U	36	0815346		PV.1

NAVAL UNDERSEA MUSEUM (WA26)

Address:	1 Garnett Way, Keyport, Washington 98345.
Tel:	360-396-4148 Email:museumcurator@navalundersemuseum.org
Admission:	June–September daily 1000-1600; October–May Wednesday-Monday 1000-1600.
Location:	In the northern part of the town.

The museum has a range of exhibits informing the visitor of the nature of the sea and the creatures that live there. On show are many torpedoes and mines. The history of submarines in World War II is portrayed and there is a simulation of the control room of the nuclear powered USS *Greenling*. The development of diving is shown. Outside are submersible vehicles and submarine parts. The Gyrodyne unmanned helicopter, is in store.

TYPE	REG/SER	CON. NO.	PI/NOTES	STATUS
☐ Gyrodyne QH-50C (DSN-3)				RA

OAK HARBOR MONUMENT (WA27)

Location:	On permanent view on Highway 20 in the northern part of the city.

TYPE	REG/SER	CON. NO.	PI/NOTES	STATUS
☐ Grumman G-128 Intruder (A-6A) (A-6E)	Bu152907	I-211		PV
☐ Grumman G-128 Prowler (EA-6B)	Bu158036	P13		PV

OLYMPIC FLIGHT MUSEUM (WA28)

Address:	7637-A Old Highway 99 South East, Olympia, Washington 98501-5737.
Tel:	360-705-3925 Fax: 360-236-9839 Email: info@olympicflightmuseum.com
Admission:	Wednesday-Sunday 110-1700.
Location:	At Olympia Airport which is about 3 miles south of the town off Route 121.

This impressive collection of warbirds opened to the public on 19th June 1999. The idea of a museum had been in the minds of owners of former military types based at the field for some time. The number of aircraft has grown steadily and there are many interesting machines on show. The Sabre served with the South African Air Force for a period before returning to North America. The early Starfighter is from the batch of just over 20 flown by the Jordanian Air Force up to the late 1970s. The Canadian-built Harvard has been mocked up to represent a Japanese Zero fighter The company which owns the museum has a helicopter business at the airport and some of their fleet of classic and modern types can often be seen on the ramp.

TYPE	REG/SER	CON. NO.	PI/NOTES	STATUS
☐ Aero L-39ZO Albatros	N39VC	232314	2314 (Libya), N4313Y, N162JC, (N4313Y)	PVA
☐ Bede BD-5G				PV
☐ Bell 204 Iroquois (HH-1K)				PVA
☐ Bell 205 Iroquois (UH-1H)	69-15931	12219		PV
☐ Bell 205 Iroquois (UH-1H)	N348DM	12219	69-15931	PVA
☐ Bell 205 Iroquois (UH-1H)	N348FB	13684	74-22360	PVA
☐ Bell 205 Iroquois (UH-1H) (UH-1V)	N347AM	13655	74-22331	PVA
☐ Bell 209 Huey Cobra (AH-1S) (AH-1E)	77-22791	22129		PV
☐ Bell 209 Huey Cobra (AH-1S) (AH-1P) (TAH-1P)	NX7239L	24035	76-22601	PV
☐ Bell 209 Huey Cobra (AH-1S) (AH-1P) (TAH-1P)	NX7239T	24079	77-22741	RAC
☐ British Aircraft Corporation 167 Strikemaster 84	'XR366'	EEP/JP/1934	G-27-143, G-AYHS, 314 (Singapore), N21463, N72445	PVAX
☐ Canadair CL-13B Sabre 6 [North American F-86E]	N3844E	1522	23692 (Canada), 373 (South Africa)	PVA
☐ Canadian Car & Foundry Harvard 4 [North American NA-186]	NX15796	CCF4-16	20225, N15796 – mocked up as a Zero.	PVA
☐ Cessna 318B Tweety Bird (318A) (T-37A) (T-37B)	57-2305	40238		PV
☐ Cessna 318E Dragonfly (A-37B)	N396WM	43122	68-7975, 715 (Vietnam)	PVA
☐ Fieseler Fi 103A-1 (FSM)				PV
☐ Fieseler Fi 103A-1/Re4 (FSM)				PV
☐ Grumman G-36 Wildcat (FM-2)	N49JC	5744	Bu86690, N20HA, N70637	RAA
☐ Hughes 369M Cayuse (HO-6) (OH-6A)	N41776	0860	67-16475	RAA
☐ Kaman K-600-3 Huskie (H-43B) (HH-43B)	N286M	110	60-0286	PVA
☐ Kaman K-600-3 Huskie (HH-43F)	N4069R		64-17558	
☐ Lockheed 183-93-02 Starfighter (F-104A)	N66228	183-1074	56-0786, 909 (Jordan)	PV
☐ North American NA-121 Texan (AT-6F)	N2834D	121-42475	44-81753	PVA
☐ North American NA-122 Mustang (P-51D) (Mustang IV)	'413926'	122-39895	44-73436, 9300 (Canada), N6313T, N51TK, N51KD, NL51KD	PVAX
☐ North American NA-168 Texan (T-6G)	N6253C	168-47	49-2943	PVA
☐ North American NA-174 Trojan (T-28A) (AT-28D)	51-7500	174-353	51-7500, 17500 (Philippines)	RA
☐ Vought FG-1D Corsair	'KD658'	3697	Bu92436, N3470G, CF-JJW, C-GCWX, N72NW	PVAX

OTHELLO MONUMENT (WA29)

Location:	On permanent view on Main Street in the town centre.

TYPE	REG/SER	CON. NO.	PI/NOTES	STATUS
☐ Lockheed 580 (T-33A)	52-9568	580-7728		PV

PBY MEMORIAL FOUNDATION (WA30)

Address:	315 West Pioneer Way, Oak Harbor, Washington 98277-0941.
Tel:	360-240-9500 Email: winvp91@whidbey.net
Admission:	Thursday-Saturday 1100-1700.
Location:	In the town.

Oak Harbor was an important Catalina base constructed in 1942. As many as 30 PBYs were often in residence.

The group has been formed to preserve the seaplane base and trace the history of operations from the site. Funds are being raised to construct a hangar to house an example of the famous amphibian. A theatre showing films of Catalina operations will be included. A number of artefacts and components have been donated and these are in store in the area.

After many disappointments the foundation has at last managed to acquire an example of the type. The aircraft was moved to its new home under a Chinook helicopter on 25th June 2010. The Catalina was badly damaged on a delivery flight to the Israeli Air Force museum when it ran off the runway at Lewistown in Montana in 1985. A prolonged rebuild commenced but in 1999 a windstorm caused further problems. The amphibian was transported by road to Skagit in Washington State where the work was completed.

TYPE	REG/SER	CON. NO.	PI/NOTES	STATUS
☐ Consolidated 28-5A Catalina (PBY-5A)	N84857	1522	Bu33968, N5582V, C-GVTF	PV

PEARSON AIR MUSEUM (WA31)

Address:	1115 East Fifth Street, Vancouver, Washington 98661-3802.
Tel:	360-694-7026 Fax: 360-694-0824 Email: kyle.kihs@vnhrt.org
Admission:	Wednesday-Saturday 1000-1700; In summer open on Tuesday 1000-1700.
Location:	Pearson Airpark is in the south eastern suburbs of Vancouver just east of Interstate 5.

Pearson Airpark is the oldest operating airfield in the country. In 1905 an airship, piloted by Lincoln Beachey, used the site. Six years later an aircraft took off from the polo fields of Vancouver Barracks. The Army Air Service set up a base in 1921 and an adjoining civil field was constructed. Lieutenant Alexander Pearson, a local resident, won the 1919 speed contest from New York to San Francisco and back. He also undertook the first aerial survey of the Grand Canyon and was killed in 1924 whilst practising for the Pulitzer Races.

The airfield was visited by the Douglas DWCs on their 1924 round-the-world flight and was also a stop on the original West Coast air mail route. On 20th July 1937 the Tupolev ANT-25 piloted by Valery Chkalov landed at Pearson after a 63-hour journey from Moscow. This was the first non-stop trans polar flight and a memorial can be seen on the south side of the field.

The museum was set up in the early 1990s to preserve this rich heritage. A hangar was obtained and several local men loaned their aircraft to the display. A move has now been made to an early hangar which has been superbly restored and enlarged. The informative displays trace the history of the field and local aviators. There are many photographs, documents, engines, models and components to be seen. The diminutive Trotter WSA.1 is one of the claimants to be the smallest aircraft in the world.

A rarity in the USA is the Yves Gardan designed Minicab. The prototype of this low wing monoplane flew in France in 1949 and both factory and amateur-built examples were constructed, Two post-war racers are the Owl and the Polen Special. The visitor can always see a number of aircraft under restoration in the workshop area.

TYPE	REG/SER	CON. NO.	PI/NOTES	STATUS
☐ Boeing-Stearman D75N1 Kaydet (PT-27)	N58617	75-3937	42-15748, FJ887	PV
☐ Cessna 170B	N3241A	25885		PVA
☐ De Havilland DH.82C Tiger Moth	N4030E	DHC.903	5103 (Canada)	PVA
☐ De Havilland DH.82C Tiger Moth	N4030E	DHC.903	5103 (Canada)	PVA
☐ Fleet 7	NC794V	375	NC794V, N794V	PV
☐ Fokker Dr I (R)	N43SB	29590ABV		PV
☐ Gardan GY-20 Minicab	N1615U	AJ-1		PV
☐ North American NA-88 Texan (AT-6D) (SNJ-5)	N7979C	88-16498	42-84717, Bu84827	PV
☐ Oldfield Baby Great Lakes	N22872	7411-M-542B		PV
☐ Owl OR.7B	N26RW	OR-71-B-RW1		PV
☐ Piper J-3C-65 Cub	N5066E	16582		PVA
☐ Polen Special	N106P	101		PV
☐ Ryan ST-3KR Recruit (PT-21)	N48778	1057	41-1936	PV
☐ Trotter WSA.1	N34517	001		PV
☐ Voisin LA-III (R)	N176V	27533SFB		PV
☐ Waco ASO	N4W	X3101		PV

PEMBERTON COLLECTION (WA32)

Address:	5302 North Vista Court, Spokane, Washington 99212-1639.
Tel:	biplane@pembertonandsons.com
Admission:	By prior permission only.
Location:	At Felts Field which is about 5 miles north east of the city off Rutter Road.

The family business restores vintage aircraft but it also has its own collection of them. Two examples of the Boeing 40 mailplane were recovered from crash sites and many components were taken back to the workshops.

Boeing Air Transport Corporation made a successful bid for the San Francisco–Chicago section of the transcontinental air mail route. The 40C was a four-passenger version and 10 were sold. The 40C in the collection crashed on Canyon Mountain in October 1928. The remains were taken to the hangar in 2000 and the rebuild was soon underway. This aircraft flew again on 17th February 2008 and is now on show at the Western Antique Aeroplane and Automobile Museum in Oregon.

The Stearman 4 is one of the few left in flying condition and was restored by the company in 1991. The Kaydet has been modified with the fitting of a 450 h.p. engine, a T-6 canopy over the cockpit area and wheel spats. This biplane is painted in the colours of a US Navy fighter of the 1930s. The Super Cub is used for training pilots to fly the higher powered vintage types. A cabin Waco biplane is under rebuild.

Washington

TYPE	REG/SER	CON. NO.	PI/NOTES	STATUS
☐ Boeing 40B-4	N29708	1423	NC10342	RAC
☐ Boeing-Stearman E75 Kaydet (PT-13D)	N4760V	75-5821	42-17658	RAA
☐ Cessna 185 Skywagon	N4031Y	1850231		RAA
☐ Piper PA-18-135 Super Cub	N9948Q	18-3557		RAA
☐ Stearman 4DM (4CM-1)	NC485W	4033		RAA
☐ Waco EQC-6	NC16591	4490	NC16591, N16591	RAC

PINGREY COLLECTION (WA33)

Address:	PO Box 130, Selah, Yakima, Washington 98942.
Admission:	By prior permission only.
Location:	At Yakima airfield which is about 5 miles west of the town and on private premises.

This collection contains three examples of the Swallow biplane. Matty Laird designed the original version which was successfully improved by Lloyd Stearman, Charles Laird and Waverly Stearman. Over 250 of all variants were produced at Wichita between 1920 and 1929. The TP, powered by either a Kinner or a Warner engine, appeared in 1928 and just over 100 were sold before the onset of the Great Depression.

TYPE	REG/SER	CON. NO.	PI/NOTES	STATUS
☐ Aerochair Ax.3-21 Hot Air Balloon	N1186M	002		RAA
☐ Balloon Works Firefly 7 Hot Air Balloon	N40688	10042		RAA
☐ Cessna 182B	N2617G	51917		RAA
☐ Piper J-3C-65 Cub (O-59A) (L-4A)	N48694	10377	43-29086	RAA
☐ Swallow	N6079	974	NC6097	RA
☐ Swallow	N7797	1012	NC7797	RA
☐ Swallow TP	N8755T	155	NC8755	RA

PORT TOWNSEND AERO MUSEUM (WA34)

Address:	PO Box 101, Chimacum, Washington 98325.
Tel:	360-379-5244 **Email:** ptam@olypen.com
Admission:	Wednesday-Sunday 0900-1600.
Location:	At Port Townsend Airport which is about 5 miles south of the town off Route 20.

The museum was formed in 2001 by Jerry and Peggy Thuotte who donated six of their vintage aircraft to the organisation. Over the last few years they have transferred more types to the group and the remainder will eventually follow.

Ground was broken for a new museum building on 14th April 2005. This impressive structure was completed in 2007 and the aircraft then moved into their new home. There is access to the nearby airport for the fleet, the majority of which will be maintained in flying condition. The de Havilland Queen Bee is one of three known to survive. The type was designed as radio-controlled pilotless target and incorporated the wooden fuselage of a Moth Major fitted with Tiger Moth wings and tail surfaces. The example owned by the museum was sent to the USA for testing. In 1955 it was obtained by Pathé News. The Queen Bee was flown from the front seat and a camera operator used the rear cockpit. The aircraft was found in store at Issaquah in Washington in 2002.

The diminutive Irwin Meteorplane is another rarity. The uncovered dismantled airframe was donated to the museum. A decision whether to rebuild it or display it 'as acquired' has not yet been made. The prototype first flew in 1919 and only 27 were manufactured over the next dozen years by the Sacramento based firm. The aircraft was powered by a 25 hp Irwin engine. Several kits were sold in this period and the museum example may be one of these. The replica Howard racer has been rebuilt after a crash but will not be flown.

The Fairchild 71 high wing transport first appeared in 1929 and well over 100 were built. The type was basically an enlarged FC-2W2. The rugged construction made the type popular with operators in remote parts of Canada. The museum acquired their example a few years ago.

A long-term project is the rebuild of the Fairchild Pilgrim. The aircraft was flying on a Pan Am mailplane service when it crashed in Alaska in the mid-1940s. The wreck was recovered in the early 1990s. Three examples of the type are known to exist with one on show in Alaska.

The single seat Turner T-40 is a low wing all wooden construction monoplane with folding wings. The prototype made its maiden flight in 1961 and plans were made available. The two seat T-40A appeared a few years later.

Hawley Bowlus was a well known glider designer in the inter-war period and his SP-1 flew in 1929. The Baby Albatross appeared in 1937 and 156 kits were sold.

TYPE	REG/SER	CON. NO.	PI/NOTES	STATUS
☐ Aeronca C-3	NC16529	A-673	NC16529, N16529	PVC
☐ Aeronca K	NC19349	K-207	NC19349, N19349	PVA
☐ Aeronca 65TC Grasshopper (O-58B) (L-3B)	N48145	7742	(USAAF)	PVA
☐ Aeronca 7AC Champion	N3011E	7AC-6597	NC3011E	PVA
☐ Aeronca 7BCM Champion (7AC)	N82106	7AC-732	NC82106	PVA
☐ Aeronca 11CC Super Chief	N4524	11CC-237A		PVA
☐ Blériot XI (R)				PV
☐ Bowlus BA-100 Baby Albatross	NC17641	174	NC17641, N17641	PV
☐ Cessna 140	NC89293	8319	NC89293, N89293	PVA
☐ Cessna 145 Airmaster	NC19489	459	NC19489, N19489	PV
☐ Cessna 180H Skywagon 180	N75KB	18051869		PVA
☐ Champion 7ECA Citabria	N11695	856-72		PVA
☐ Corben D Baby Ace	N49A	1		PVA
☐ Curtiss 50C Robin C-1	NC917K	574	NC917K, N917K	PVA
☐ Curtiss-Wright CW-1 Junior	NC11809	1184	NC11809, N11809	PVA
☐ Curtiss-Wright CW-1 Junior (R)	N7201C	CW-1-001-71		PVA
☐ De Havilland DH.82B Queen Bee	N2726A	5447	V4760, N726A (?)	RAC
☐ Fairchild 71	NC9135	631	C-9135, N9135	PV
☐ Fairchild Pilgrim 100-A	N73706	6701		RA
☐ Funk B-75L	N24170	196	NC24170	PVA
☐ Howard DGA-4 (R)	'NR3777'	1	N30154	PVX
☐ Irwin F-A-1 Meteorplane				PVC

635

☐ Laister-Kauffman LK.10A	N5362S	61		PV
☐ Luscombe 8A Silvaire	N77948	3675	NC77948	PVA
☐ Pietenpol P-9 Sky Scout (R)	NX899EM	002		PVA
☐ Piper J-2 Cub	NC19213	1613	NC19213, N19213	PVA
☐ Piper J-3C-65 Cub	NC70109	17083	NC70109, N70109	PVA
☐ Piper J-5A Cub Cruiser	NC38030	5-838	NC38030, N38030	PVA
☐ Ryan ST-3KR Recruit (PT-22)	N62130	1812	41-20603	PVA
☐ Schleicher Ka-6E Rhönsegler	N4784S	4010		PV
☐ Stinson SM-8A Junior	NC418M	4009	NC418M, N418M	PV
☐ Stinson SM-8A Junior	NC930W	M4098	NC930W, N930W	PVA
☐ Stinson SR-10E Reliant	N27782	5949	NC27782	PV
☐ Travel Air 2000	NC6147	645	NC6147, N6147	PV
☐ Travel Air 4000	NC2928	157	NC2928, N2928	PVA
☐ Travel Air 4000 (W-4000)	NC9049	850		PVA
☐ Turner T-40A	N1525	54		PVA
☐ Waco YKS-6	NC16211	4416	NC16211, N16211	PVA

SEATTLE MUSEUM OF HISTORY AND INDUSTRY (WA35)

Address:	2700 24th Avenue East, Seattle, Washington 98112-2099.
Tel:	206-324-1126 **Fax:** 206-324-1346 **Email:** information@seattlehistory.com
Admission:	Tuesday-Friday 1100-1700; Saturday-Sunday 1000-1700.
Location:	In McCurdy Park near the University of Washington Stadium.

This museum was opened by the Seattle Historical Society in February 1952. There are many interesting items, including vehicles and machinery, to be seen.

There is a small aviation section devoted to the history of flying in the area. The sole B-1 flying boat was built in 1919 and used by Eddie Hubbard to fly the first international air mail contract from Seattle to Vancouver in British Columbia. He operated the B-1 for eight years.

The Society acquired the aircraft in 1934 and put it on outside display at Boeing Field. The boat was then put into store at the Boeing factory until rebuilt and moved to this museum in 1954.

TYPE	REG/SER	CON. NO.	PI/NOTES	STATUS
☐ Boeing 6 B-1	N-ABNA	86	N-CADS, N-ABNA, 4985, NC1974	PV

SEATTLE WORLD CRUISER ASSOCIATION (WA36)

Address:	550 Airport Way, Renton, Washington 98057.
Tel:	206-772-1623 **Email:** r.dempster@clearwire.net
Admission:	By prior permission only.
Location:	In the north western suburbs of the town.

Four Douglas DWCs left Sand Point Flying Field on Lake Washington on 6th April 1924 at the start of the first round-the-world flight. The 'Seattle' crashed in Alaska a few days into the flight and the group is building a replica of this aircraft. The aircraft will be constructed using modern materials and equipment for safety and reliability. The external appearance will be authentic. The ambitious plan is to re-enact the original flight. A five-man team led by Bob Dempster, a retired Boeing research and development engineer, are working on the DWC in a hangar at Renton. The project is making steady progress but it will be some time before it is completed.

TYPE	REG/SER	CON. NO.	PI/NOTES	STATUS
☐ Douglas DWC (R)				RAC

SKAGIT AERO EDUCATION MUSEUM (WA37)

Address:	7879 Superior Avenue, Concrete, Washington 98237.
Tel:	360-770-4848 **Email:** info@skagitaero.com
Admission:	By appointment only.
Location:	At Concrete Airport which is just southwest of the town on Highway 20.

The museum was founded by the late Harold Hanson and currently occupies five hangars at the airfield. These are well laid out and the exhibits can be seen easily. In addition to the aircraft there are paintings, models, motor cycles and vintage cars.

A major project is the construction of a replica of the Hall Springfield Bulldog. In 1931 Bob Hall resigned from the Granville Brothers Aircraft Company. He was their chief designer and his aircraft had achieved many racing successes. The following year Russell Thaw ordered a racing aircraft from Hall. He was not happy with the Bulldog but Hall flew it in the 1931 Thompson Trophy. He finished sixth and soon after the aircraft was dismantled and never took to the skies again. Jim Jenkins built a Granville E replica in the 1980s and became interested in the Bulldog. Construction started in 1990 but he stopped in 1994. The aircraft is now at the museum and work is proceeding. The Rose Parakeet biplane first flew in 1931 and eight were built by the company. An unusual feature was the use of a single bracing strut instead of flying wires. The design was revived after World War II and kits were made available. In the late 1960s Doug Rhinehart built five new examples.

Jim Moss of Buckley has built a number of aircraft including a replica of the Granville Brothers QED racer. One of his original designs is on show. The Ryan STA low wing monoplane entered production in 1935 and 71 were completed. The Special version with a supercharged Menasco engine featured in 1936 and 11 were sold. Tex Rankin won the 1937 US aerobatic Championships in one of these. There are many interesting types in the collection and other restoration projects will be acquired.

TYPE	REG/SER	CON. NO.	PI/NOTES	STATUS
☐ Aeronca 7AC Champion	N85337	7AC-4076	NC85337	PVA
☐ Aeronca 11AC Chief	N9460E	11AC-1098	NC9460E	RAA
☐ Beech K35 Bonanza	N6010E	D-5942		PVA

Washington

☐ Callair A-2	N2907V	123		RAA
☐ Cessna 120	NC77016	11462	NC77016, N77016	PVA
☐ Cessna 150J	N61145	15070836		RAA
☐ Cessna A185E Skywagon 185	N70112	18501995		PVA
☐ Champion 7ECA Citabria	N1634G	629		PVA
☐ Corben C-1 Baby Ace	N853BS	135		RAA
☐ Culver LCA Cadet	NC29279	148	NC29279, N29279	PVA
☐ Fairchild 24G	N23E	2926		PVA
☐ Fairchild M-62A Cornell (PT-19B)	N54977	T43-5770	42-83183	PVA
☐ Grumman G-44A Widgeon (J4F-2)	N62096	1393	Bu37763	PVC
☐ Hall Springfield Bulldog (R)				RAC
☐ Luscombe 8A Silvaire	N71381	2808	NC71381	RAA
☐ Mooney M-18C Mite	N4149E	315		PVA
☐ Mooney M-18L Mite	N4103	137		RAA
☐ Moss MT1	N6115	1		RAA
☐ Oldfield Baby Great Lakes	N25RG	7925-A-736-B		PVA
☐ Pietenpol P-9 Sky Scout				RAC
☐ Piper J-3C-65 Cub	NC70129	17107	NC70129, N70129	RAA
☐ Piper J-5A Cub Cruiser	N38874	5-1097	NC38874	PVA
☐ Piper PA-15 Vagabond	N4559H	15-333	NC4559H	PVA
☐ Piper PA-16 Clipper	N5732H	16-346		PVA
☐ Piper PA-20-135 Pacer	N2675A	20-952		PVA
☐ Piper PA-22-108 Colt	N5191Z	22-8859		PVA
☐ Piper PA-22-135 Tripacer	N3328A	22-1603		PVA
☐ Rose Parakeet A-1 (R)	NX858Y			RAA
☐ Ryan STA Special	NC17368	173	NC17368, N17368	PVA
☐ Stinson SR-9C Reliant	N18406	5312	NC18406	PVA
☐ Stolp SA.100 Starduster	N112P	HD101		PVA
☐ Stolp SA.300 Starduster Too	N51144	233		RAA
☐ Taylorcraft BC-12D	N5037M	10337	NC5037M	PVA
☐ Temco GC-1B Swift	N78045	2045		RAA
☐ Waco INF	N619Y	3364	NC619Y	PVA
☐ Waco QCF	N1149J	3535	NC11451, N11451	PVA
☐ Wag Aero L-4 Cuby Flitfire	N1775	1993		RAA

SOUTH SEATTLE COMMUNITY COLLEGE (WA38)

Address: 6000 16th Avenue South West, Seattle, Washington 98106-1499.
Tel: 206-764-5273   **Email:** btaves@sccd.ctc.edu
Admission: By prior permission only.
Location: In the western part of the town.

The college was established in 1970 and offers a range of courses. The aviation maintenance section is housed in a purpose-built structure with well equipped workshops for engines and systems. The fleet of instructional airframes includes a number of business jets and turboprops as well as some former military machines.

TYPE	REG/SER	CON. NO.	PI/NOTES	STATUS
☐ Aero Commander 680F	N72W	1104-70	N6262X	RA
☐ Beech 65-90 King Air	N735K	LJ-35		RA
☐ Beech C50 Seminole (L-23D) (U-8D)	N22757	RLH-44	57-6072	RA
☐ Beech C50 Seminole (L-23D) (U-8G)	N9182F	RLH-58	58-3057	RA
☐ Beech C50 Seminole (RL-23D) (RU-8D) (RU-8G)	N9183F	LH-196	59-4990	RA
☐ Bell 47G				RA
☐ Cessna 150E	N3024J	15061124		RA
☐ Cessna 150F	N8711S	15062011		RA
☐ Cessna 172G	N5951R	17253620		RA
☐ Lockheed 1329 JetStar 6	N66MP	1329-5015	NASA4, N172L, N103KC, N505T, N9046F	RA
☐ Lockheed 1329 JetStar 6	N96BB	1329-5049	N9216R, N1230R, N96B	RA
☐ North American NA-265 Sabreliner (T-39A) (CT-39A)	N8052V	265-18	60-3490	RA

SPOKANE COMMUNITY COLLEGE (WA39)

Address: 1810 North Green Street, MS 1010, Spokane, Washington 99217-5399.
Tel: 509-533-7250   **Email:** BMartinson@scc.spokane.edu
Admission: By prior permission only.
Location: At Felts Field which is the north eastern suburbs of the city.

The aviation section of the college is located at Felts Field which served as the airport for the city for many years. A number of historic buildings including the terminal are on the National Register of Historic Places. The college has its workshops in a hangar where the instructional airframes reside.

TYPE	REG/SER	CON. NO.	PI/NOTES	STATUS
☐ Beech 95-55 Baron	N371Z	TC-131		RA
☐ Cessna 150J	N50949	15069669		RA
☐ Cessna 150M	N66043	15075796		RA
☐ Cessna 150M	N704QA	15078779		RA
☐ Cessna 310C	N1722R	35822		RA
☐ Cessna 421B Golden Eagle	N31KC	421B0344		RA
☐ North American NA-265 Sabreliner (T-39A) (CT-39A)	N6581E	265-82	61-0679	RA
☐ Vans RV-8				RA

VANCOUVER VETERANS AFFAIRS MONUMENT (WA40)

Location: On permanent view at 1601 East Fourth Plain Boulevard in the town.

TYPE	REG/SER	CON. NO.	PI/NOTES	STATUS
☐ Bell 204 Iroquois (HU-1B) (UH-1B)	62-1984	504	62-1984,N332WN – possible identity.	PV

WASHINGTON NATIONAL GUARD STATE HISTORICAL SOCIETY MUSEUM (WA41)

Address: The Arsenal, Camp Murray, Tacoma, Washington 98430-5000.
Tel: 206-581-8464
Admission: By appointment only.
Location: About 10 miles south west of the city off Interstate 5.

Housed in a renovated 1915 Arsenal at Camp Murray, the displays trace the military history of the state. The exhibition is not yet open on a regular basis. The exhibition has a large collection of uniforms, documents, weapons and models on show. The Voodoo, used by the Washington Air National Guard in the 1970s, is mounted near the entrance to the base. The 116th Fighter Squadron operated the F-101 from Geiger Field, now Spokane International Airport, and Fairchild Air Force Base. The Cobra, a type flown by several Army National Guard squadrons, is on display near the Headquarters Building.

TYPE	REG/SER	CON. NO.	PI/NOTES	STATUS
☐ Bell 209 Huey Cobra (AH-1G) (AH-1F)	66-15285	20041		RA`
☐ McDonnell M.36BA Voodoo (F-101B)	57-0294	472		PV

WHIDBEY ISLAND NAVAL AIR STATION (WA42)

Address: 3730 North Charles Porter Avenue, Oak Harbor, Washington 98278-5000.
Tel: 360-257-2211   **Email:** whdb_webmaster@navy.mil
Admission: By prior permission only.
Location: About 3 miles west of Oak Harbor.

This station opened in 1942 and originally had a seaplane base on the eastern shore and an airfield on the opposite side of the island. The field is named after Commander William B Ault who was listed as 'missing in action' during the Battle of the Coral Sea. The first aircraft to arrive were Grumman Wildcats and Hellcats. Lockheed Venturas and Douglas Dauntless dive-bombers soon followed. The seaplane base was home to Consolidated Catalinas and Martin Mariners. The base was closed for a period at the end of World War II but the onset of the conflict in Korea saw in reopen and major construction work took place. The A-6 Intruder and its electronic countermeasures development the EA-6 Prowler arrived at the field in 1967 and served for almost 30 years. Orion squadrons have been based here since 1993. Helicopter squadrons are also in residence along with Boeing EA-18G Growler electronic versions of the McDonnell Super Hornet and a few Douglas DC-9s.

TYPE	REG/SER	CON. NO.	PI/NOTES	STATUS
☐ Douglas NRA-3B Skywarrior (A3D-2P) (RA-3B)	N878RS	12071	Bu144825, N578HA	RA
☐ Grumman G-128 Intruder (A2F-1) (A-6A) (KA-6D)	Bu149482	I-11		RA
☐ Grumman G-128 Prowler (EA-6B) (NEA-6B)	Bu156478	P1		RA
☐ Lockheed 185 Orion (P-3B)	Bu152764	185-5209		RA

WILLIAMS AERONAUTICAL COLLECTION (WA43)

Address: 11023 South East 24 Place, Bellevue, Washington 98004-7320
Admission: By prior permission only.
Location: At Auburn Municipal Airport which is about 2 miles north of the town.

This private collection includes a number of now rare types. The St. Louis Cardinal was designed by Harry MacKay and first flew in 1929. The high-wing cabin two-seater was powered by a variety of engines. Only 20 were completed.

The all metal Harlow PJC-1 was built by students at Pasedena College in California but crashed during its certification programme in 1938. A dozen improved PJC-2s were completed at Alhambra, California by the new Harlow Company. A number of kits of a tandem version, the PC-5A, were supplied to India for assembly by the Hindustan company. Max Harlow had previously worked for the Kinner company and had been part of the team who produced the Sportster. This low wing side-by-side two seater first flew in 1932 and the K version was fitted with a 100hp Kinner radial engine. The design featured folding wings.

Al Mooney was the designer of the low wing cabin Dart G. The Monocoupe company sold the type to the K.K. Culver firm in Columbus, Ohio who put the aircraft into production. Only 50, with a variety of engines, were completed before Culver moved to Wichita to produce the Cadet series. From a slightly earlier period is the parasol wing open cockpit Fairchild 22 of which well over 100 were sold in the early 1930s.

TYPE	REG/SER	CON. NO.	PI/NOTES	STATUS
☐ Bellanca 14-19-2 Cruisemaster	N7677B	4028		RAA
☐ Cessna 165 Airmaster	NC25485	580	NC25485, N25485	RA
☐ Dart G	NC18443	G-6	NC18443, N18443	RA
☐ Fairchild 22 C7F (C7E)	NC9484	1607	NC9484, N9484	RA
☐ Harlow PJC-2	N1998J	9	NC19983	RA
☐ Kinner Sportster K	NC13700	40	NC13700, N13700	RA
☐ Porterfield 35-70	NC17029	229	NC17029, N17029	RA
☐ Rearwin 9000L Sportster	NC20746	637D	NC20746, N20746	RA
☐ Ryan SCW-145	NC18914	208	NC18914, N18914	RAA
☐ St. Louis C-2-110 Super Cardinal	NC561N	117	NC561N, N561N	RA
☐ Waco YQC-6	NC46290	4387	NC15709, N15709	RA

WEST VIRGINIA

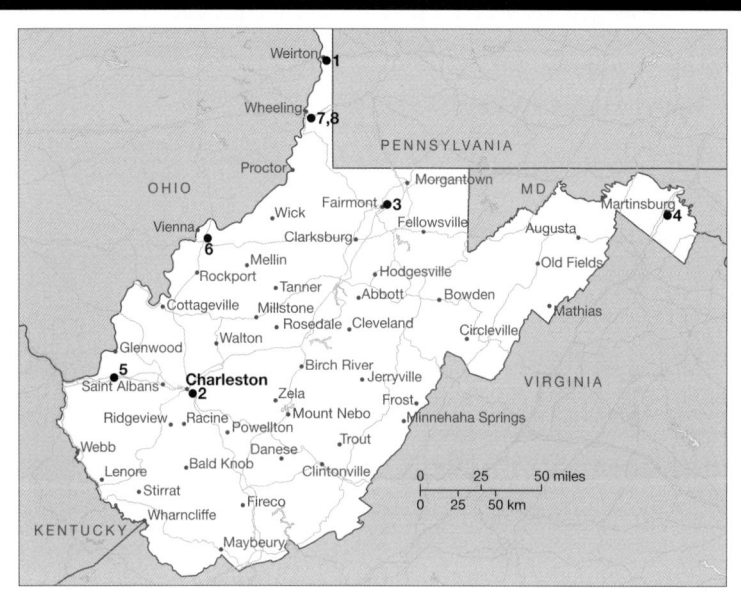

BROOKE-HANCOCK COUNTY VETERANS MEMORIAL BRIDGE AND PARK (WV1)

Address:	Freedom Way, Weirton, West Virginia 26062.
Admission:	On permanent view.
Location:	In the centre of the town near the Ohio River.

The spectacular bridge over the Ohio River was constructed during the 1980s. Close by is the park which is dedicated to the local people who have fought for America. Two aircraft, tanks and weapons can be seen. There are a number of memorials dedicated to local people who have lost their lives in military service.

TYPE	REG/SER	CON. NO.	PI/NOTES	STATUS
☐ Bell 209 Huey Cobra (AH-1G) (AH-1F)	66-15307	20063		PV
☐ Vought A-7D Corsair II	69-6241	D71		PV

CHARLESTON AIR NATIONAL GUARD BASE (WV2)

Location:	By prior permission only at Yeager Airport which is about 4 miles north of the city off Route 114.

TYPE	REG/SER	CON. NO.	PI/NOTES	STATUS
☐ North American NA-122 Mustang (P-51D)	44-72948	122-39407	At Charleston	RA

MARION COUNTY VIETNAM VETERANS MEMORIAL (WV3)

Address:	East Marion Park Entrance, Fairmont, West Virginia 26554.
Tel:	304-367-5398
Admission:	On permanent view.
Location:	In the eastern part of the town.

This display is dedicated to local people who lost their lives in the war. Surrounded by flags is a large monument bearing their names. There are bronze statues depicting soldiers from World War I, World war II, the Korean and Vietnam wars. The Iroquois on show operated in Vietnam during the conflict.

TYPE	REG/SER	CON. NO.	PI/NOTES	STATUS
☐ Bell 205 Iroquois (UH-1D) (UH-1H)	66-16109	5803		PV

MARTINSBURG AIR NATIONAL GUARD BASE (WV4)

Location:	By prior permission only at Shepherd Field which is about 5 miles south of the town.

TYPE	REG/SER	CON. NO.	PI/NOTES	STATUS
☐ North American NA-187 Sabre (F-86H)	52-2058	187-84	52-2058, N205P	RA

MILTON MONUMENT (WV5)

Location:	On permanent view in a park on Route 60 in the western part of the town.

TYPE	REG/SER	CON. NO.	PI/NOTES	STATUS
☐ North American NA-173 Sabre (F-86D) (F-86L)	51-6078	173-222		PV

VIENNA MONUMENT (WV6)

Location:	On permanent view in Jackson Memorial Park on 34th Street in the eastern part of the town.

TYPE	REG/SER	CON. NO.	PI/NOTES	STATUS
☐ Republic F-84F Thunderstreak	52-7066			PV

WHEELING AIRPORT MUSEUM (WV7)

Address:	Route 5, Box 5, Wheeling, West Virginia 26003.
Tel:	304-234-3865 Fax: 304-234-3864
Admission:	When the terminal is open.
Location:	About 7 miles north of the town on Route 5.

The airport opened in 1946 and the first commercial flight was made by a Pennsylvania Central Airlines DC-3. The display in the lobby of the terminal building traces the history of the field. On show are components, including a propeller from a Constellation, and airfield equipment. The America Fokker factory was in nearby Glendale and there is an original sign and other items from here. Displays highlighting the airlines which have used the airport can be seen.

WHEELING MONUMENT (WV8)

Location:	On view during opening hours in Cabela's store at One Cabela Drive in the eastern part of the town.

TYPE	REG/SER	CON. NO.	PI/NOTES	STATUS
☐ Piper PA-18-150 Super Cub				PV

WISCONSIN

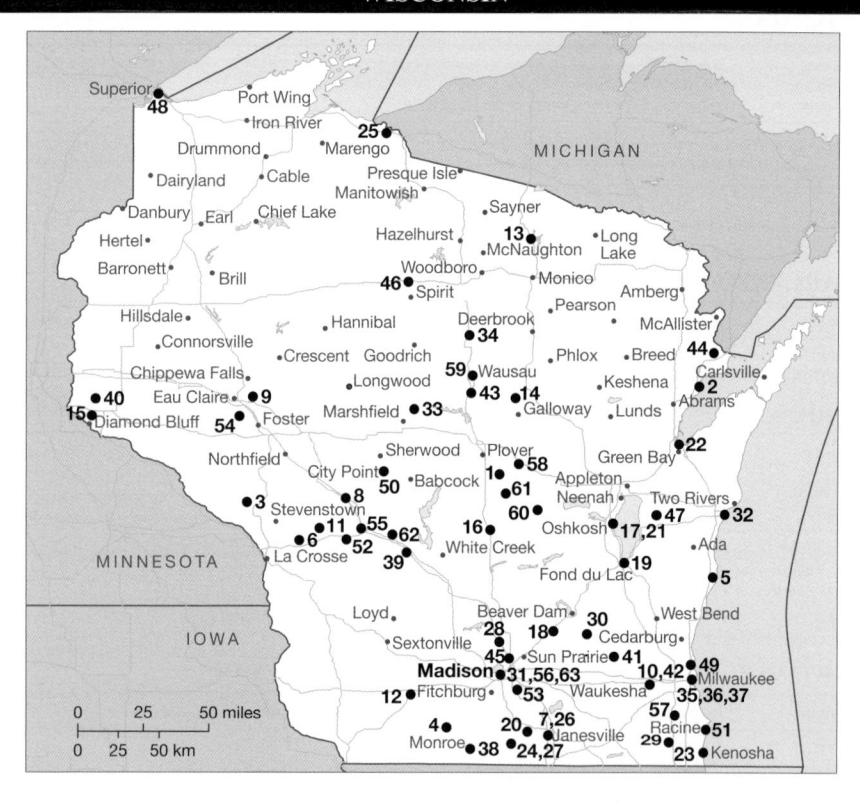

ALMOND MONUMENT (WI1)

Location:	On permanent view in a park on Route D just west of the town centre.

TYPE	REG/SER	CON. NO.	PI/NOTES	STATUS
☐ Bell 209 Huey Cobra (AH-1G) (AH-1S)	68-15169	20703		PV

APPLETON MONUMENT (WI2)

Location:	On permanent view at ALP 38 at 3228 West College Avenue west of the town centre.

TYPE	REG/SER	CON. NO.	PI/NOTES	STATUS
☐ North American NA-173 Sabre (F-86D) (F-86L)	51-5938	173-82		PV

ARCADIA MONUMENT (WI3)

Location:	On permanent view in the Memorial Park just south of the town centre.

TYPE	REG/SER	CON. NO.	PI/NOTES	STATUS
☐ General Dynamics 401 Fighting Falcon (F-16A)	78-0058	61-54		PV

ARGYLE MONUMENT (WI4)

Location:	On permanent view in the Legion Community Park on Route 78 just north of the town centre.

TYPE	REG/SER	CON. NO.	PI/NOTES	STATUS
☐ North American NA-203 Sabre (F-86H)	53-1359	203-131		PV

AVIATION HERITAGE CENTER (WI5)

Address:	N6191 Resource Drive, Sheybogan Falls, Wisconsin 53085-2348.
Tel:	920-467-2043
Admission:	April–October Monday-Friday 1000-1700, Saturday 0900-1300; November–March Thursday-Friday 1000-1700, Saturday 0900-1300.
Location:	At the airport which is about 5 miles west of the town.

The idea of the exhibition was put forward by members of the local EAA Chapter 766. Work on the building started in 2004 and it opened the following June. Inside is a library and laboratory along with a museum tracing the history of aviation with particular reference to the local area. The T-33 is being restored for the display.

TYPE	REG/SER	CON. NO.	PI/NOTES	STATUS
☐ Lockheed 580 (T-33A)				PVC

BANGOR MONUMENT (WI6)

Location:	On permanent view in the town.

TYPE	REG/SER	CON. NO.	PI/NOTES	STATUS
☐ Bell 209 Huey Cobra (AH-1G) (AH-1F)	67-15824	20488		PV

BLACKHAWK TECHNICAL COLLEGE (WI7)

Address:	4618 South Columbia Drive, Janesville, Wisconsin 53546.
Tel:	608-757-7743 Email: Lbrown@blackhawk.edu
Admission:	By prior permission only.
Location:	At South Wisconsin Regional Airport on Highway 51 about 2 miles south of the town.

The first vocational schools in the area were set up in 1911 and over 50 years later they were merged to form Blackhawk Technical Institution. The main college campus is located between Beloit and Janesville. An aviation centre has been set up at the airport where there is a large fleet of instructional airframes.

TYPE	REG/SER	CON. NO.	PI/NOTES	STATUS
☐ Beech 18D (D18S Expeditor (SNB-5)	N61912		Bu134705, 134705 (France)	RA
☐ Beech 95-B55B Cochise (T-42A)	N242BT	TF.24	65-12702	RA
☐ Beech C90 King Air	N90WJ	LJ-525	N1857W, N1857A, ZK-UPA, N70MT	RA
☐ Bell 47G Sioux (H-13G) (OH-13G)	52-7893	1120		RA
☐ Bell 205 Iroquois (UH-1H)	70-16283	12588		RA
☐ Cessna 150E	N232BT	15061302	N3902U	RA
☐ Cessna 172	N233BT	29977	N8177B	RA
☐ Cessna TU.206G Stationair	N235BT	U2060958		RA
☐ Cessna U206B Super Skywagon	N3967G	U2060967		RA
☐ Cessna 210	N9442T	57242		RA
☐ Lockheed 580 (T-33A)	58-2100	580-1686		RA
☐ North American NA-265 Sabreliner (T-39A) (CT-39A)	N21092	265-42	61-0637	RA
☐ Sikorsky S-61R Pelican (HH-3F)	1467	61629		RA
☐ Sikorsky S-61R Pelican (HH-3F)	1479	61656		RA

BLACK RIVER FALLS MONUMENT (WI8)

Location:	On permanent view in the town.

TYPE	REG/SER	CON. NO.	PI/NOTES	STATUS
☐ Bell 209 Huey Cobra (AH-1G) (AH-1F)	66-15316	20072		PV

CADOTT MONUMENT (WI9)

Location:	On permanent view at a Veterans Memorial on Route 29 in the south western part of the town.

TYPE	REG/SER	CON. NO.	PI/NOTES	STATUS
☐ Bell 209 Huey Cobra (AH-1G) (AH-1S)	70-15948	20892		PV

COMMEMORATIVE AIR FORCE (WISCONSIN WING) (WI10)

Address:	PO Box 1998, Waukesha, Wisconsin 53187-1998.
Tel:	262-547-1775 Email: stangoran610@hotmail.com
Admission:	Saturday 0800-1600 and by appointment.
Location:	At Crites Field which is about 15 miles west of Milwaukee off Route J.

Formed in 1982 the wing was restoring a Lockheed PV-2D Harpoon to original condition. This aircraft has moved to the Cavanaugh Flight Museum in Texas. The group now operates a Cornell painted in an all yellow World War II Royal Canadian Air Force colours. The aircraft regularly visits shows in the area.

TYPE	REG/SER	CON. NO.	PI/NOTES	STATUS
☐ Fairchild M-62A-4 Cornell II	N103JC	FC.119	10618 (Canada), C-GVEH	PVA

DEKE SLAYTON MEMORIAL SPACE AND BIKE MUSEUM (WI11)

Address:	200 West Main Street, Sparta, Wisconsin 54656-2141.
Tel:	608-269-0033 Fax: 608-269-4423 Email: Info@DekeSlayton.com
Admission:	Summer Monday-Saturday 1000-1630, Sunday 1300-1600; Winter Monday-Friday 1000-1600.
Location:	In the centre of the town.

This museum has an excellent collection of bicycles, a display relating to aviation in Monroe County and also traces the life of local astronaut Donald Slayton. The only aircraft on show is the Pietenpol donated by Donald Campbell of Chicago. The aircraft arrived from Brodhead Airfield in Wisconsin in November 2004.

TYPE	REG/SER	CON. NO.	PI/NOTES	STATUS
☐ Pietenpol B4-A Aircamper				PV

DODGEVILLE MONUMENT (WI12)

Location:	On permanent view by an inn near the airport which is about 3 miles north of the town on Route 23.

TYPE	REG/SER	CON. NO.	PI/NOTES	STATUS
☐ Boeing 367-76-66 Stratofreighter (KC-97G)	N227AR	16795	52-2764	PV

EAGLE RIVER MONUMENT (WI13)

Location:	On permanent view on Route 32 in the south eastern part of the town.

TYPE	REG/SER	CON. NO.	PI/NOTES	STATUS
☐ Bell 209 Huey Cobra (AH-1G) (AH-1S)	68-15151	20685		PV

ELDERON MONUMENT (WI14)

Location:	On permanent view at VFW 8068 on Highway 153 in the western part of the town.

TYPE	REG/SER	CON. NO.	PI/NOTES	STATUS
☐ Bell 209 Huey Cobra (AH-1G) (AH-1S)	70-16047	20991		PV

ELLSWORTH MONUMENT (WI15)

Location:	On permanent view at VVA 331 which is about 5 miles west of the town on Route 10.

TYPE	REG/SER	CON. NO.	PI/NOTES	STATUS
☐ Bell 205 Iroquois (UH-1H)	74-22438	13762	With boom from c/n 11867 69-15579	PV

ENDEAVOR MONUMENT (WI16)

Location:	On permanent view in a park on County Road CX about 2 miles south of the town.

TYPE	REG/SER	CON. NO.	PI/NOTES	STATUS
☐ Bell 205 Iroquois (UH-1H) (UH-1V)	66-17059	9253		PV

EXPERIMENTAL AIRCRAFT ASSOCIATION AIRVENTURE MUSEUM (WI17)

Address:	3000 Poberezny Road, Wittman Field, Oshkosh, Wisconsin 54903-3086.
Tel:	920-426-4818 Email: museum@eaa.org
Admission:	Monday-Saturday 0830-1700; Sunday 1000-1700.
Location:	In the southern suburbs of the town off Route 41.

The EAA was founded in 1953 by Paul H. Poberezny to cater for the growing interest in homebuilt aircraft which re-emerged after World War II. The organisation has grown to a world wide force with divisions also covering antique, classic, warbird and aerobatic aircraft.

The EAA held its first convention at Timmerman Field at Milwaukee in 1953 and, after a spell at Rockford in Illinois, moved to Oshkosh in 1970. Now the annual nine-day event usually attracts in excess of 1,500 show aircraft to the field along with around 1,000,000 people.

A museum foundation was set up in 1964 and aircraft began to be collected. An exhibition area was constructed at the headquarters in Hales Corner in the suburbs of Milwaukee. By the early 1980s well over 100 aircraft were on show in the now enlarged museum. A fund was started to improve the facilities and a decision was made to move both the headquarters and the museum to Oshkosh.

Ground was broken at Wittman Field in 1981 and the magnificent complex was dedicated at the 31st Convention in July 1983. The museum at Hales Corner remained open until the end of that year. The EAA Flight Test Center at Burlington also closed about this time and the flyable aircraft moved to Oshkosh. The Kermit Weeks Flight Research Center at Wittman Field now carries out this work.

The main museum has aircraft on show from all periods in the history of flight. There are many associated displays tracing the development of aviation with special emphasis on the history of the EAA and the homebuilding movement.

The first machine viewed is a faithful replica of the Wright Flyer and close by is a 1911 Curtiss Pusher. Sections are devoted to the Great War, the Golden Years, the Racers,

Aerobatics, Homebuilts and the Air Challengers. In all areas there are ranges of aircraft imaginatively displayed.

An addition to the original main building is the 'Eagle Hangar', which is dedicated to the memory of those who served in World War II. A superb collection of warbirds can be seen along with many associated displays. The story of the conflict is portrayed with engines, components and memorabilia on view.

Steve Wittman was born in 1904 and died in a crash in 1995. He designed 13 types and was a successful racing pilot. His first aircraft was the Hardy Abelson which he built when he was 19 years old. In the 1930s in his Chief Oshkosh he won many races and also set a number of World records. He continued racing until the 1970s and the WV was specially designed for the Formula V class. The Tailwind first flew in 1953 and plans were made available. Large numbers have been constructed in many countries. The work of this local aviator is told in a special display. The 'Racers' section of the display features a number of types mounted spectacularly. They are shown as though they were turning around pylons on a circuit.

In 1984 construction of the Pioneer Airport started on land adjacent to the museum. This facility is only open in the summer months. The aim was to recreate a 1930s style aerodrome. The second hangar to be placed on the site was Bernard Pietenpol's building brought from his private airfield. Now around 50 aircraft are located at this field with many in flying condition. Regular open days are held when some of the aircraft are flown. There are many highlights in this outstanding exhibition. Some of the aircraft are housed for most of the year in buildings on the convention site and these are often seen outside during the event.

TYPE	REG/SER	CON. NO.	PI/NOTES	STATUS
☐ Aero Gare Sea Hawk	N83SH	001		PV
☐ Aerodyne Vector 627		1730		RA
☐ Aerojet-General V-260/USD		1		RA
☐ Aeronca C-2N	NC13089	A-253	NC13089, N13089	PV
☐ Aeronca C-3	N16291	A-668	NC16291	PVA
☐ Aeronca K	NC19723	K-244	NC19723, N19723	PV
☐ Aeronca LC	NC17484	2060		PV
☐ Anderson Double Eagle V		1	Gondola only.	PV
☐ Antares MA-30				PV
☐ Bates Tractor				PV
☐ Bede BD-2	N1982A	1		PV
☐ Bede BD-5A	N500BD	5-001		RA
☐ Bell 47G-2	N2490B	1516		PVA
☐ Bensen B-11M Kopter-Kart	N63U	1		PV
☐ Boeing 299-O Fortress (B-17G)	N5017N	8649	44-85740, NL5017N	RAA
☐ Boeing-Stearman E75 Kaydet (PT-13D) (N2S-5)	N5051V	75-8798	42-109765, Bu52616	PV
☐ Brock KB-2G	N2303	1006		PV
☐ Bücker Bü 133 Jungmeister (R)	N258H	1		PV
☐ Bücker Bü 133L Jungmeister (Bü 133C)	N515	31	U-84 (Swiss), HB-MKE	PV
☐ Buckeye 582 Dream Machine		4070	On loan to FAA Oklahoma City, OK.	-
☐ Bugatti 100				PV
☐ Canadair CL-13A Sabre 5 [North American F-86E]	N86JR	1120	23330 (RCAF), N86FN	RA
☐ Cessna CG-2	N186V	58	NC186V	PV
☐ Cessna 150H	N23107	15068729		RA
☐ Cessna 210J Centurion	N3311S	21059111		RAA
☐ Chambliss Kirby Z-Edge 540	N540KC	010		PV
☐ Chandelle Standard				PV
☐ Chanute Glider (R)				PV
☐ Chase Church JC-1 Midwing	NX9167	3		PV
☐ Chengdu J-7 I [Mikoyan-Gurevich MiG-21F-13]	'4326'		1603 (China), N610DM, N21MG – in false North Vietnamese markings.	RAX
☐ Chester Special Jeep	NR12930	1		PV
☐ Christen Eagle 1F	N41ET	0002		PV
☐ Christen Eagle 1F	N42ET	0003		PV
☐ Christen Eagle 1F	N43ET	0004		PV
☐ Christen Eagle II	N160ER	0431		RA

☐ Cirrus VK30	N33VK	005		PV
☐ Colomban MC-12 Cri-Cri	N1377L	1		PV
☐ Consolidated 2 Trusty (PT-3)	N31PT	1	Part replica incorporating containing some Consolidated 1 (PT-1) parts.	PVA
☐ Corben C-1 Baby Ace	N9050C	101C		PV
☐ Corben D Baby Ace Seaplane	N9017C	3		PV
☐ Crosby CR-4	NX92Y	101		PV
☐ Culver NR-D Cadet (PQ-14B)	N999ML		44-68334, N10146	PV
☐ Curtiss E A-1	N24034	12		PV
☐ Curtiss 1C Jenny (JN-4D)	N5357	4904		PV
☐ Curtiss 35 Hawk (P-6E)	NX606PE		32-260 – partial replica.	PV
☐ Curtiss 50B Robin B-2	NC50H	403	NC50H, N50H	PVA
☐ Davis D-1W	NC13546	304	NC13546, N13546	RA
☐ De Havilland DH.82C Tiger Moth	N667EA	DHC.1667	8865 (RCAF), CF-IVO	PV
☐ De Havilland DH.98 Mosquito TT.35 (B.35)	NX35MK		RS712, G-ASKB, 'RF580' – on loan from Fantasy of Flight, FL.	PV
☐ De Havilland DHC.1 Chipmunk 1B-2-S3 (mod)	N1114V	116-154	CF-CXL	PV
☐ Douglas DC-3-455 (C-49K)	'223835'	6338	NC30036, 43-2014, NC12945, N77D, N7222, N7772	PVX
☐ Driggers L-A Sunshine Girl	N891H	1-A		PV
☐ Eipper MX Quicksilver				RA
☐ Eipper MX-1 Quicksilver		3746		PV
☐ Ercoupe 415C	NC28961	57	NC28961, N28961	PV
☐ Estupian-Hovey WD-II Whing-Ding	N6272	1		RA
☐ Evans VP-1 Volksplane	N6414	WE-1		PV
☐ Experimental Aircraft Association A-1 Biplane	N6077V	A1		PV
☐ Experimental Aircraft Association P-8 Acrosport	N1AC	108		RA
☐ Experimental Aircraft Association P-8A Super Acrosport	N76BM	280		PV
☐ Experimental Aircraft Association P-9 Pober Pixie	N9PH	109		PV
☐ Explorer PG-1 Aqua Glider	N6498D	1001		RA
☐ Fairchild FC-2W2	NC3569	35	NC3569, N3569	PV
☐ Fairchild 24 C8	NC13191	2009	NC13191, N13191	PV
☐ Fairchild 24H	NC16902	3211	NC16902, N16902	PVA
☐ Fairchild M-62A Cornell (PT-19A)	N61013	T43-7240	42-83653	RA
☐ Falck Racer			Fuselage only.	RA
☐ Fike C	N13390	4	Fuselage only.	PV
☐ Flightstar FS-II SL	N97UL	182		RA
☐ Fokker Dr 1 (R)	'152/17'	105	N105RF	PVX
☐ Folkerts Gullwing				PV
☐ Folkerts-Henderson Highwing	8902			PV
☐ Ford 1 Flivver (R)	'268'			PVX
☐ Ford 4-AT-E	NC8407	4-AT-69	NC8407, (Cuba), (Dominica)	PVA
☐ Fouga CM.170R Magister	N300FM	494	494 (France)	RA
☐ Funk B	NC24116	45	NC24119, N2974L	PV
☐ Goodyear GA-22A Drake	N5516M	4040		RAD
☐ Great Lakes 2T-1A	N77RF	260		PV
☐ Grumman G-15 Duck (J2F-6)	N1196N		Bu36976	PV
☐ Gunderson Burke Penguin	N41047	1		RA
☐ Harlow PJC-2	N3947B	6	NC15	PV
☐ Haufe Dale Hawk 2	N18278	100		PV
☐ Heath Feather		1		PV
☐ Heath LNA-40 Parasol	N16GR	161	N12814	RA
☐ Heath LNB-4 Super Parasol	N953M	1		PV
☐ Heath Parasol				PV
☐ Heath Super Parasol				PV
☐ Hegy R.C.H.A. El Chuparosa	N9360	1		PV
☐ Helisoar HP-10	N319Y	101		PV
☐ Henderschott Monoplane			Fuselage only.	RA
☐ Hill Hummer	N90381	01		PV
☐ Hispano HA-1112M1L [Messerschmitt Bf 109G]	N109BF	199	C.4K-127, G-AWHO, N90601	PVX
☐ Howard Pete III	'N27B'	1	N111PL	PVX
☐ Jurca MJ.5J2 Scirocco	N8038E	222		RA
☐ Keech LW-5	N100MK	1		PV
☐ Keith Rider R-5	NX264Y	A-1		PV
☐ Kiceniuk Icarus V				RA
☐ Kreider-Reisner KR-21B	NC954V	1502		PV
☐ Laird LC-DW-500 Super Solution (R)	NR12048	200		PVX
☐ Langley Aerodrome (Scale R)				PV
☐ Leak Avid Flyer	N4636J	42	On loan to Supple Restaurant, Green Bay, WI.	-
☐ Lesher Teal	N4291C	2		PV
☐ Lincoln PT-K	NC275N	602		PV
☐ Lobet Ganagobie	N60G	60		PV
☐ Lockheed 080 Shooting Star (P-80C) (F-80C)	N80PP	080-2125	48-0868, '45-8398'	PV
☐ Lockheed 422-87-23 Lightning (P-38L) (P-38M)	'42-103993'	422-8342	44-53087, NX62887, N62887, CF-GDS, N1107V, YV-C-BAR, N1107V, N3800L	PVX
☐ Lockheed 580 (T-33A)	51-8627	580-6411		PV
☐ Lockheed 580 (T-33A)	53-5250	580-8589		RA
☐ Lockwood Air Cam	N5084T	001		PV
☐ Loudenschlager Shark	N810LL	1		RA
☐ Loving-Wayne WR-1 Love	N351C	1		PV
☐ Marinac Flying Mercury	N6V			RA
☐ Meyers OTW-145	N34357	102	NC34357	PV
☐ Mignet HM-20-ME-2-Y Pou-du-Ciel	N43993	2		PV

Wisconsin

☐ Mikoyan-Gurevich MiG-15bis	N15MG/'4115'		1411 (China)	RAX
☐ Miller-Bohannon JM2 Special	N189BB	M-105		PV
☐ Mitchell Wing A-10		A101		RA
☐ Monnett Monex	N82MX	001		PV
☐ Monnett Moni	N107MX	001		PV
☐ Monnett Sonerai II				RA
☐ Monnett Sonerai II	N11ME	1		PV
☐ Mono Aircraft Monocoupe 90AW	N38904	A-827	NC38904	PVC
☐ Mono Aircraft Monocoupe 110 Special	N15E	7W97	NC15E	PV
☐ Mono Aircraft Monocoupe 113	NC7808	247	NC7808, N7808	PV
☐ Myers PM-1 Special	N42963	1		PV
☐ Neibauer Lancair 200	N384L	LN1984		PV
☐ Nicholas-Beazley Special (R)	N6119G	T-9		PV
☐ Nieuport 11 (R)	N2001			PV
☐ North American NA-68 (P-64) (RP-64)	N840	68-3061	41-19085, NX37498, XB-KUU, N68822	PVA
☐ North American NA-73 Mustang (XP-51)	NX51NA/41-038	73-3101	(AG348), 41-038	PV
☐ North American NA-98 Mitchell (B-25H)	N10V/43-4432	98-21433	43-4432, N90399, N10V, N410V	PVA
☐ North American NA-122 Mustang (P-51D)	N3451D	122-41547	44-75007, N5462V	PV
☐ North American NA-187 Sabre (F-86H)	52-1993	187-19		PV
☐ Northrop N-160 Scorpion (N-68) (F-89J) (F-89J)	N32536	N.4661	53-2530	PV
☐ Option Air Reno Acapella 100L	N455CB	0002		RA
☐ Payne M-6 Knight Twister Imperial	N28VP	1		RA
☐ Pedal Plane				RA
☐ Peel Z-1 Glider Boat		20		RA
☐ Pereira GP.3 Osprey II	N346JS	JS-3		RA
☐ Pheasant H-10	NC151N	136		PV
☐ Pietenpol B4-A Aircamper	N12937	1		PV
☐ Pietenpol B4-A Aircamper	N7533U	20		PV
☐ Pietenpol B4-A Aircamper			Fuselage only.	PV
☐ Pietenpol P-9 Sky Scout	N12941	109	Fuselage only.	PV
☐ Piper J-3C-65 Cub	NC3403K	22094	NC3403K, N3403K	PV
☐ Piper PA-23-250 Aztec E	N7CB	27-4802	N14247	RAA
☐ Pitcairn PA-6 Super Mailwing			Fuselage only.	PV
☐ Pitcairn PA-7S Sport Mailwing	NC95W	147	NC95W, N95W	PVA
☐ Pitcairn PCA-2	NC11609	B-27 (4123)		PV
☐ Pitcairn-Larsen PA-39	N3908	M-98	BW830	PV
☐ Pitts 1 (R)	'NX528'	001		RAX
☐ Pitts S-1S Special	N58J	107		PV
☐ Pitts S-1S Special	N442X	117H		PV
☐ Pitts S-1S Special	N9J	LPS-1		PV
☐ Pitts S-2 Special	N22Q	1001		PV
☐ Player Sportplane	N21778	1		PV
☐ Pober P-5 Pober Sport	N51G	105		PV
☐ Prescott Pusher	N35PP	35		RA
☐ Puffer CO-Z Cozy	N22CZ	1		PV
☐ Questair 200 Venture	N62V	0001		RA
☐ Quickie Aircraft Quickie 1 (Rutan 54)	N2WX	0004		RA
☐ Rand Robinson KR-1	N1436	1		RA
☐ Rasor 21 Balloon			Basket only.	PV
☐ Rearwin 6000M Speedster	N20741	311	NC20741	PV
☐ Republic F-84C Thunderjet (P-84C)	47-1498			RA
☐ Roloff RLU-1 Breezy	N59Y	5537		PV
☐ Rotorway Executive	N3WN	E-3076		PV
☐ Rotorway Scorpion 1	N6165	1289		PV
☐ Rotorway Scorpion Too	N40WM	194053		RA
☐ Rutan 27 Vari-Viggen	N27VV	001		PV
☐ Rutan 31 Vari-Eze	N7EZ	001		PV
☐ Rutan 68 Amsoil Racer	N301LS			PV
☐ Rutan 72 Grizzly	N80RA	001		RA
☐ Rutan 77-6 Solitaire	N142SD	6		RA
☐ Ryan NYP (R)	'NX-211'	1		PV
☐ Ryan NYP (R)	N211	2		PVA
☐ Ryan SCW-145	NC17372	201	NC17372, XC-CUT, N17372	PV
☐ Ryan STA Special	N17349	195	(Guatemala), NC17372	PVA
☐ Scaled Composites 271 V-Jet II	N222FJ	001		RA
☐ Schreder HP-18-LK-G	N96326	56		PV
☐ Smith DSA-1 Miniplane	N358L	CG-1	On show at Hilton Garden Inn, Oshkosh, WI.	PV
☐ Smith DSA-1 Miniplane	N90P	FWS-1		RA
☐ Snyder Baby Bomber	N1034	1		PV
☐ Spartan C-3-225	NC718N	A-12	NC718N, N718N	PVA
☐ Spartan 7W Executive	NC13993	7W-2	NC13993, N13993	PV
☐ Standard J-1	N6948	1956		PV
☐ Stier Penguin Trainer				RA
☐ Stinson SM-8A Junior	NC408Y	M4243	NC408Y, N408Y	PV
☐ Stinson V-76 Sentinel (L-5E)	N9658H	76-4297	(USAAF)	PV
☐ Stits DS-1 Baby Bird	N4453H	001		PV
☐ Stits SA-2A Skybaby	N5K	2	N8476H – on loan from NASM, DC.	PV
☐ Stits SA-3A Playboy	N8KK	3		RA
☐ Stits SA-8 Skeeto	N6048C	301	Fuselage only.	RA
☐ Stits SA-11A Playmate	N9681Z	64-1	N5K	RA
☐ Stoddard-Hamilton SH-2 Glasair HAM-2	N88TH	101		PV
☐ Stoddard-Hamilton SH-4 GlaStar	N824G	01-P		RA
☐ Stoddard-Hamilton SH-4 GlaStar	N232YE	5265		PVA
☐ Stoddard-Hamilton SH-4 GlaStar III	N231YE	5192		PVA

☐ Stolp SA.300 Starduster Too					RA
☐ Stolp SA.300 Starduster Too					RA
☐ Stolp SA.300 Starduster Too	N32CH	1961			RA
☐ Supermarine 509 Spitfire T.9	N8R	CBAF-7269	MJ772, 159 (Ireland), G-AVAV – on loan from Museum of Flight, WA.		PV
☐ Swallow OX-5	N4028	899	NC4028		PVA
☐ Taylor Aerocar	N4994P	1	N4994P, N31214		PV
☐ Taylor E-2 Cub	N15045	196	NC15045		PV
☐ Taylor JT.1 Monoplane	N5406E	PAT			RA
☐ Taylorcraft BF-50 (BC-50)	N21292	1086	NC21292		PV
☐ Tessier Biplane			On loan to Fratello's, Oshkosh, WI.		-
☐ Thorp T-18	N455DT	455			PV
☐ Travel Air E-4000	NC648H	1224			PVA
☐ Ultralight Flying Machines Easy Riser					RA
☐ Ultralight Flying Machines Easy Riser					RA
☐ Ultralight Flying Machines Solar Riser					PV
☐ Vans RV-3	N17RV	173			PVA
☐ Vans RV-4	N14RV	1			RA
☐ Vans RV-6A	N6YE	2557			RA
☐ Vitanza LV56	N56LV	0693			RA
☐ Volmer Jensen VJ-23E		B-47			RA
☐ Vought F4U-4 Corsair	NX6667	9413	Bu97259, N3728A, N6667		PVA
☐ Voyager Aircraft Voyager (Rutan 76) (R)			Cockpit section only.		PV
☐ Waco ARE	NC20953	5080	NC20953, N20953		PV
☐ Waco ATO	NC5814	A-4	NC5814, N83J		PV
☐ Waco CTO	NC7527	A-33	NC7527, N7527		PV
☐ Waco NAZ Primary Glider					PVA
☐ Waco RNF	NC140Y	3317			PV
☐ Waco UEC	NC12472	3638	NC12472, N12472		PV
☐ Wag Aero Cuby	N1933J	303			PVA
☐ Warwick W-4 Hot Canary	N477W	1			RA
☐ Warwick W-5 Cosmic Wind	N99CW	4			RA
☐ Waspair HM-81 Tomcat Tourer					RA
☐ Weedhopper JC-24B		137			RA
☐ Wittman DFA	N1292	7			PV
☐ Wittman Hardly Ableson (R)	'NR13688'	3			PVX
☐ Wittman Midwing	N4486E	3	NX13688		PV
☐ Wittman W.8C Tailwind	N37SW	12	In Oshkosh Airport Terminal, WI.		PV
☐ Wittman W.8C Tailwind	N5747N	8			PV
☐ Wittman WV	N3259	11			PV
☐ Wittman WX Buttercup	N18268	5			PV
☐ Worthington		4			RA
☐ Wright Flyer (R)					PV

FALL RIVER MONUMENT (WI18)

Location: On permanent view at VFW 2219 in Bradley Avenue in the northern part of the town.

TYPE	REG/SER	CON. NO.	PI/NOTES	STATUS
☐ Lockheed 580 (T-33A)	53-4897	580-8236		PV

FOND DU LAC MONUMENT (WI19)

Location: On permanent view at ALP 75 at 500 Fond du Lac Avenue in the south eastern part of the town.

TYPE	REG/SER	CON. NO.	PI/NOTES	STATUS
☐ Bell 209 Huey Cobra (AH-1G) (AH-1S)	68-17026	20754		RA

FOOTVILLE MONUMENT (WI20)

Location: On permanent view at ALP 237 at 406 Old Highway 11 in the south western part of the town.

TYPE	REG/SER	CON. NO.	PI/NOTES	STATUS
☐ Bell 209 Huey Cobra (AH-1G) (AH-1F)	68-15133	20667	Tail boom from c/n 20829 68-17101.	PV

FOX VALLEY TECHNICAL COLLEGE (WI21)

Address: 1825 North Bluemond Drive, Appleton, Wisconsin 54912-2277.
Tel: 920-735-5600   **Email:** info@fvtc.edu
Admission: By prior permission only.
Location: At 3601 Oregon Street, Oshkosh on the east side of the airport.

The college was established in 1967 although vocational schools had been operating in the area since 1912. The state decided to merge many at this time. An aviation centre has been set up at the airport where a fleet of instructional aircraft are in use. Courses leading to qualifications in airframe maintenance, engines and aircraft electronics are run. The well equipped workshops also contain engines and several test rigs.

Wisconsin

TYPE	REG/SER	CON. NO.	PI/NOTES	STATUS
☐ Beech 58 Baron	N38CL	TH-829		RA
☐ Beech 65-A90 King Air	N90FA	LJ-133	N1905L, N90SA	RA
☐ Beech 76 Duchess	N66272	ME-216		RA
☐ Beech 76 Duchess	N969RA	ME-317		RA
☐ Cessna A150L Aerobat	N4668F	A1500416		RA
☐ Cessna 337M Super Skymaster (O-2A)				RA
☐ Cessna 411	N4977T	4110177		RA

FULWILER COLLECTION (WI22)

Address: 1931 Airport Drive, Green Bay, Wisconsin 54313-5537.
Tel: 920-494-3733.
Admission: By prior permission only.
Location: In the western suburbs of the town.

The company which runs a maintenance business at the airport has a number of interesting types in its hangars. The Nardi FN.333 amphibian made its maiden flight in December 1952. The two examples in the collection were acquired in 2002 and one needs repairs before it can fly again.
Two original homebuilts are in the hangars. The Air Shark was registered in 1986 and the Thunder Mustang a dozen years later The prototype White der Jager was designed and built in California and made its maiden flight in September 1969. The biplane is reminiscent of a German World War I fighter, hence its name. The wings are based on those of an Albatros D V and the tail on that of a Fokker D VII. Plans were sold and well over 30 have been completed.

TYPE	REG/SER	CON. NO.	PI/NOTES	STATUS
☐ Beech 65-A90 King Air	N198KA	LJ-162	N235HM, N13ST, N198T	RAA
☐ Beech D50C Twin Bonanza	N9664R	DH-246		RAA
☐ Bellanca 7GCBC Citabria	N154RA	1391-2005		RAA
☐ Denney Kitfox IV	N127RF	1467		RAA
☐ Fulwiler Air Shark I	N303FM	003		RAA
☐ Fulwiler Thunder Mustang	N7007A	007		RAA
☐ Luscombe T-8F	N1824B	6251	NC1824B	RAA
☐ Nardi FN.333 Riviera	N993DM	0106	N916NS, C-GKMD	RAA
☐ Nardi FN.333 Riviera	N913NS	0107		RAA
☐ White D-IX Der Jager	N1007	007		RAA

GATEWAY TECHNICAL COLLEGE (WI23)

Address: 3520 30th Avenue, Kenosha, Wisconsin 53144-1619.
Tel: 262-564-2200
Admission: By prior permission only.
Location: At the airport which is about 5 miles west of the town.

The college trains pilots but also has a small maintenance section where at least two airframes are in use. A Thunderstreak was mounted outside the hangar but this disappeared a few years ago.

TYPE	REG/SER	CON. NO.	PI/NOTES	STATUS
☐ Champion 7ECA Citabria	N278GT	137-098		RA
☐ Piper PA-23-250 Aztec	N4648P	27-169		RA

HMS HISTORICAL TRANSPORTATION FOUNDATION (WI24)

Address: Brodhead Airport, Wisconsin 53520.
Email: info@flyingflea.org
Admission: By prior permission only.
Location: About 3 miles south west of the town.

The foundation was set up to honour the work of Henri Mignet and to collect his designs and other ultralight aircraft. The majority of the fleet is housed in a hangar at the grass airfield at Brodhead. Members of the association around the world own many other Mignet types. For example there is an HM-8 in Canada, an HM-14 in England and many in France.
The HM-8 and HM-14 really started the homebuilding movement in Europe. The prototype of this parasol wing design flew in the mid-1920s. Mignet had used some parts from his earlier designs and combined these with new components. The first amateur-built example flew in May 1929 and about 200 are believed to have been constructed. Some modern examples are flying in France and North America.
At Brodhead there are three amateur-built HM-293s. This single-seater first flew in the late 1940s and proved to be quite popular. Bernard Domont built the HM-381 at Villeneuve-sur-Lot in France in the early 1980s. This Flea joined the foundation in 2000. The HM-1000 Balerit microlight was designed by Pierre, the son of Henri. The type first took to the air in April 1984 and several examples have been produced. The HM-1100 has an epoxy resin fuselage and fabric covered metal wings. The Curtiss Racer was built in Texas by Julius Junge as were the Blériot XI, the Farman Moustique, the HM-160 and the HM-290E.
Glenn Curtiss was urged by the Aeronautical Society of New York to represent them at the 1909 Gordon Bennett Cup race to be held at Reims in France. He built a larger version of his Golden Flyer pusher and fitted it with a 60 hp V-8 engine.
Flying against the clock he set a world record speed of 43.35 mph over the 20 km closed course. The aircraft was taken back to the USA and flown by him and his pilots on exhibition flights.
The collection also includes some modern ultralights. The Diehl XTC is an amphibian first flown in the early 1980s and was one of the first to be constructed mainly of composite materials. A pusher propeller was mounted to the engine fitted above the wing.

TYPE	REG/SER	CON. NO.	PI/NOTES	STATUS
☐ Avid Catalina	N429A	001		RAA
☐ American Aerolights Eagle Seaplane				RAA
☐ Blériot XI (R)	N6202F	1		RAA
☐ Curtiss Gordon Bennett Racer (R)				RAA
☐ Diehl XTC				RAA
☐ Farman Moustique (R)				RAA
☐ Mignet HM-8 (R)				RAA
☐ Mignet HM-160				RAA
☐ Mignet HM-290E Pou-du-Ciel				RAA
☐ Mignet HM-293 Pou-du-Ciel	N114HM	1		RAA
☐ Mignet HM-293 Pou-du-Ciel	N122HM	1		RAA
☐ Mignet HM-293 Pou-du-Ciel	N124HM	1		RAA
☐ Mignet HM-360 Pou-du-Ciel	N360HM	001		RAA
☐ Mignet HM-381 Pou-du-Ciel	F-PZTJ	85	F-WZTJ	RAA
☐ Mignet HM-1000 Balerit	N109HM	65		RAA
☐ Mignet HM-1000 Balerit	N120HM	96		RAA
☐ Mignet HM-1000 Balerit	N121HM	105		RAA
☐ Mignet HM-1000 Balerit	N107HM	107		RAA
☐ Mignet HM-1000 Balerit	N129HM	113		RAA
☐ Mignet HM-1000 Balerit	N128HM	128		RAA
☐ Mignet HM-1100 Cordouan	N130HM	7		RAA
☐ Pietenpol B4-A Aircamper				RAA
☐ SkyRaider Seaplane				RAA
☐ Ultraflight Lazair 1 Seaplane				RAA
☐ Weedhopper Seaplane	N125HM	1		RAA

HURLEY MONUMENT (WI25)

Location: On permanent view by the Iron County Courthouse in Taconite Street in the southern part of the town.

TYPE	REG/SER	CON. NO.	PI/NOTES	STATUS
☐ Bell 209 Huey Cobra (AH-1G) (AH-1S)	70-15975	20919		PV

JANESVILLE MONUMENT (WI26)

Location: On permanent view at VFW 1621 at 1015 Center Avenue in the southern part of the town.

TYPE	REG/SER	CON. NO.	PI/NOTES	STATUS
☐ Bell 209 Huey Cobra (AH-1G) (AH-1F)	67-15491	20155		PV
☐ Grumman G-79 Panther (F9F-2)	Bu123557			PV

KELCH COLLECTION (WI27)

Address: 7018 West Boniwell Road, Mequon, Wisconsin 53097-2136.
Admission: By prior permission only.
Location: At Brodhead Airfield which is 3 miles south west of the town.

Alfred Kelch was born in 1918 and became interested in aviation at an early age when his uncle bought a Curtiss Jenny. Over the years he acquired and restored many aircraft. He was an early member of the EAA and a Director of their Vintage Division for many years. He died in 2004 and this interesting collection is now maintained by his widow Lois and their family. He also obtained a large amount of memorabilia including some items once owned by Charles Lindbergh.

The Franklin 90 biplane made its maiden flight in 1931. The two seater was powered by a 90 h.p. Lambert radial. Orders were slow and only a handful were produced over the next few years. Ohio native Orin Welch made his first solo flight in 1923 at the age of 17. He soon went barnstorming in a Standard J-1 He moved into aircraft manufacture and his first design a two seat open cockpit biplane flew in 1927. Other types soon followed and in 1929 the first of a series of light high wing monoplanes appeared. The OW-8M in the collection was built in 1938 as an OW-5M powered by a 40 h.p. Continental A-40 motor. The aircraft was active until about 1950. The airframe was found and rebuilt with a Franklin engine. The type suffered with the onset of the depression and sales were slow.

The unique Mathieu-Russell was built in 1929 and powered by the unreliable 40 h.p. Szekely engine. The high-wing parasol monoplane was withdrawn in the 1930s. After a long time in store it was restored and flew again in 2000. Kelch's own design, the TA-12, is powered by a Warner Scarab radial and first flew in the early 1990s.

The American Eaglet parasol wing monoplane designed by Douglas Webber and Noel Hockaday flew in June 1930. Powered by a 25 hp Cleone two stoke twin it crashed and was re-engined with the 30 hp Szekely motor and became the 230. The B-31 had the higher powered 45 hp Szekely and the 231 a 40 hp Salmson radial. About 90 were built and designs developed from the Eaglet included the Rearwin Junior and the Porterfield Flyabout.

TYPE	REG/SER	CON. NO.	PI/NOTES	STATUS
☐ American Eagle Eaglet 230K	N475V	SR3-210-1034	NC475V	RAA
☐ American Eagle Eaglet 231	N487V	1044	NC487V	RAA
☐ Franklin Sport 90	N13139	105	NC13139	RAA
☐ Kelch TA-12	N412W	2013-1990		RAA
☐ Piper J-3L-65 Cub	N32920	5702	NC32920	RAA
☐ Scott Mathieu-Russell	N996N	A1		RAA
☐ Stearman C3B	NC8811	221	NC8811, N8811	RAA
☐ Taylor E-2 Cub	NC10547	283	NC15393, N15393	RAA
☐ Travel Air 12Q	N439W	2005	NC439W	RAA
☐ Travel Air 4000 (BW)	N2709Y	168	NC2709, N2709	RAA
☐ Travel Air 4000	N2709	475	NC5235, N5235G	RAA
☐ Welch OW-8M (OW-5M)	NX204KW	136	NC20404, N20404	RAA

Wisconsin

KENDALL MONUMENT (WI28)

Location:	On permanent view at ALP 309 on Route 71 just south east of the village.

TYPE	REG/SER	CON. NO.	PI/NOTES	STATUS
☐ Bell 209 Huey Cobra (AH-1G) (AH-1S)	68-17099	20827		PV

LAKE GENEVA MONUMENT (WI29)

Location:	On permanent view at ALP 75 at Henry Street in the town.

TYPE	REG/SER	CON. NO.	PI/NOTES	STATUS
☐ Bell 209 Huey Cobra (AH-1G) (AH-1F)	71-21044	21115		PV

LOWELL MONUMENT (WI30)

Location:	On permanent view at VFW 9392 at 230 South Street just south of the town centre.

TYPE	REG/SER	CON. NO.	PI/NOTES	STATUS
☐ Bell 209 Huey Cobra (AH-1G) (AH-1S)	68-15123	20657		PV
☐ Lockheed 580 (T-33A)	'979392'	580-8030	52-9770	PV

MADISON MONUMENT (WI31)

Location:	On permanent view at VFW 8483 at 5737 County Road CV just north of the airport.

TYPE	REG/SER	CON. NO.	PI/NOTES	STATUS
☐ Lockheed 580 (T-33A)	53-4903	580-8242		PV

MANITOWOC MONUMENT (WI32)

Location:	On permanent view at the airport which is in the northern suburbs of the town.

TYPE	REG/SER	CON. NO.	PI/NOTES	STATUS
☐ Republic RC-3 Seabee	N6525K	791	NC6525K	PV

MARSHFIELD MONUMENT (WI33)

Location:	On permanent view in Park Street in the centre of the town.

TYPE	REG/SER	CON. NO.	PI/NOTES	STATUS
☐ Bell 209 Huey Cobra (AH-1G) (AH-1S)	68-15022	20556		PV

MERRILL MONUMENT (WI34)

Location:	At the airport which is about 2 miles north west of the town.

TYPE	REG/SER	CON. NO.	PI/NOTES	STATUS
☐ Republic F-84F Thunderstreak	51-9381			PV

MILWAUKEE AREA TECHNICAL COLLEGE (WI35)

Address:	700 West State Street, Milwaukee, Wisconsin 53233.
Tel:	414-297-6282 **Email:** info@matc.edu
Admission:	By prior permission only.
Location:	At the airport which is about 4 miles south of the city off Route 38.

Formed in 1912 the college took up its present name in 1923 when large new premises were constructed in the city. The aviation section occupies hangars and workshops at the airport where a number of instructional airframes are in use. Also in the complex are engines, components and test rigs.

TYPE	REG/SER	CON. NO.	PI/NOTES	STATUS
☐ Beech D45 Mentor (T-34B)	N18FC	BG-226	Bu140892 – fuselage only.	RA
☐ Beech 60 Duke	N164MC	P-12	N88D	RA
☐ Beech 65-A90 King Air	N123V	LJ-258	N915BD	RA
☐ Cessna 310A Blue Canoe (L-27A) (U-3A)	N88928	38040	57-5885	RA
☐ Hughes 269A Osage (TH-55A)	64-18208	56-0520		RA
☐ Mitsubishi MU-2B	N155MA	014	N3546X, N4WD	RA
☐ North American NA-276 Sabreliner (T-39A) (CT-39A)	62-4475	276-28		RA
☐ North American NA-276 Sabreliner (T-39A) (CT-39A)	'N269Y'	276-30	62-4477	RAX
☐ North American NA-276 Sabreliner (T-39A) (CT-39A)	62-4500	276-53		RA
☐ North American NA-285 Sabreliner (T3J-1) (T-39D)	Bu151422	285-31		RA
☐ Piper PA-23-250 Aztec D	N151ZL	27-3990	N6672Y	RA

MILWAUKEE MONUMENTS (WI36)

Location:	On permanent view at two locations in the city.

TYPE	REG/SER	CON. NO.	PI/NOTES	STATUS
☐ Cassutt IIIM			At Amelia's Restaurant at 724 East Layton Avenue.	PV
☐ Cessna 150F	N8617G	15062717	At the Final Approach Restaurant near the airport.	PV

MITCHELL GALLERY OF FLIGHT (WI37)

Address: 5300 South Howell Avenue, General Mitchell Airport, Milwaukee, Wisconsin 53207-6156.
Tel: 414-747-5703   **Email:** FlyMitchell@MitchellGallery.org
Admission: Daily 0700-2300.
Location: About 4 miles south of the city off Route 38.

The Friends of the Mitchell Gallery of Flight came into existence in May 1985 and over the last few years have managed to stage a most interesting exhibition in the airport terminal.
 Highlighted in the displays are the aviation pioneers of the region and the history of the airport. The life of General Billy Mitchell, who in the 1920s advocated the use of heavy bombers in aerial warfare, is portrayed. Many aviators with connections to the area are honoured. There is a display tracing the career of World War II pilot Richard Bong.
 Hanging from the roof of the main concourse is a Curtiss Pusher replica built and flown by Dale Crites. The veteran aviator rebuilt and flew the Pusher now on show in the EAA Museum at nearby Oshkosh. He enjoyed the experience so much that he decided to construct the replica, which performed at many Oshkosh conventions.

TYPE	REG/SER	CON. NO.	PI/NOTES	STATUS
☐ Curtiss D Pusher (R)				PV
☐ McDonnell M.98DE Phantom II (F-4C)	'64-0751'	848	63-7704	RAX
☐ North American NA-108 Mitchell (B-25J) (TB-25M)	44-30444	108-33719	44-30444, (Canada)	PV

MONROE MONUMENT (WI38)

Location:	On permanent view in Twining Park in the northern part of the town.

TYPE	REG/SER	CON. NO.	PI/NOTES	STATUS
☐ North American NA-173 Sabre (F-86D)	51-8455	173-588		PV

NEW LISBON MONUMENT (WI39)

Location:	On permanent view at ALP 110 at 110 Welch Prairie Road just east of the town centre.

TYPE	REG/SER	CON. NO.	PI/NOTES	STATUS
☐ Bell 209 Huey Cobra (AH-1G) (AH-1S)	70-16044	20988		PV

NEW RICHMOND MONUMENT (WI40)

Location:	On permanent view at ALP 80 at County Highway CC – north of Route 64..

TYPE	REG/SER	CON. NO.	PI/NOTES	STATUS
☐ Lockheed 580 (T-33A)	53-6026	580-9558		PV

NORTH LAKE MONUMENT (WI41)

Location:	On permanent view in a park near the Town Hall.

TYPE	REG/SER	CON. NO.	PI/NOTES	STATUS
☐ Bell 209 Huey Cobra (AH-1G) (AH-1F)	68-15106	20640		PV

O'BRIEN – CRITES FIELD AVIATION MUSEUM (WI42)

Address: 2525 Aviation Drive, Waukesha, Wisconsin 53186.
Tel: 262-547-7300
Admission: Daily 0700-2000.
Location: At Crites Field which is about 15 miles west of Milwaukee off Route J.

The Crites twins Dale and Dean were born in the area in 1907. At the age of 12 they helped Robert Huggins construct a glider in their hometown of Honey Creek. They built their first aircraft using parts from scrap machines in 1934 and discovered a Curtiss Pusher in the early 1940s. This aircraft had been stored in a Wisconsin barn since 1915.
 The biplane took to the air again in 1966 and was donated to the EAA Museum at Hales Corners in 1969. At the time it was the oldest licensed aircraft in the USA. They had a long career in aviation and are regarded as one of the major contributors to aviation in Wisconsin. The pair carried out aeronautical research and Dean became noted as a precision flyer often picking up a handkerchief with a spike on his wing tip.
 Dale died in 1991 and Dean in 2005. They were active members of the Waukesha Aviation Club which has set up this museum in the terminal building. On show are items of memorabilia tracing their eventful careers. One of the original hangars has been moved to the Vintage Wings and Wheels Museum at Poplar Grove in Illinois. The structure has now been named the 'Crites Hangar'.

PEPLIN MONUMENT (WI43)

Location:	On permanent view at VFW 8280 at 3332 Highway 153 about 2 miles east of the town.

TYPE	REG/SER	CON. NO.	PI/NOTES	STATUS
☐ Bell 209 Huey Cobra (AH-1G) (AH-1F)	68-15152	20686		PVG

POUND MONUMENT (WI44)

Location:	On permanent view in the town.

TYPE	REG/SER	CON. NO.	PI/NOTES	STATUS
☐ Bell 209 Huey Cobra (AH-1G) (AH-1F)	71-21003	21074		PV

PRAIRIE DU SAC MONUMENT (WI45)

Location:	On permanent view at VFW 7694 on Route 78 in the town.

TYPE	REG/SER	CON. NO.	PI/NOTES	STATUS
☐ Bell 209 Huey Cobra (AH-1G) (AH-1S)	70-15998	20942		PV

PRENTICE MONUMENT (WI46)

Location:	On permanent view in South Street in the town.

TYPE	REG/SER	CON. NO.	PI/NOTES	STATUS
☐ Lockheed 580 (T-33A)	51-8814	580-6598		PV

REEDSVILLE MONUMENT (WI47)

Location:	On permanent view in a park off 3rd Street.

TYPE	REG/SER	CON. NO.	PI/NOTES	STATUS
☐ Lockheed 580 (T-33A)	53-5986	580-9468		PV

RICHARD IRA BONG VETERANS HISTORICAL CENTER (WI48)

Address:	305 Harbor View Parkway, Superior, Wisconsin 54880.
Tel:	715-392-7151 Fax: 715-395-5526 Email: info@bongheritagecenter.org
Admission:	May–mid October Monday-Saturday 0900-1700, Sunday 1200-1700; Mid October–April Tuesday-Saturday 0900-1700.
Location:	In the centre of Poplar on Route 2.

Major Richard Bong was one of the top US fighter pilots of World War II. Between September 1942 and December 1944 he flew 146 missions in the Pacific area and downed 40 enemy aircraft. He was then sent home and lost his life testing a Lockheed P-80 on 6th August 1945, the day the atomic bomb was dropped on Hiroshima.

A P-38 Lightning, painted in the colours of his aircraft, was displayed on a pedestal in Poplar. This memorial was erected in 1955 and taken down in 1993. The Bong family has been instrumental in raising funds for the new centre which opened in September 2002. A hangar typical of the World War II period has been constructed to house the aircraft and the Lightning was restored over a three-year period by members of the Wisconsin ANG. The Center has taped many interviews with pilots and aircrew who flew in World War II.

TYPE	REG/SER	CON. NO.	PI/NOTES	STATUS
☐ Lockheed 422-87-23 Lightning (P-38L)	'423964'	422-8491	44-53236	PVX

RICHFIELD MONUMENT (WI49)

Location:	On view during opening hours in Cabela's store at One Cabela Way in the town.

TYPE	REG/SER	CON. NO.	PI/NOTES	STATUS
☐ Aeronca 7AC Champion				PV

SHERWOOD MONUMENT (WI50)

Location:	On permanent view by the Community Center in the centre of the town.

TYPE	REG/SER	CON. NO.	PI/NOTES	STATUS
☐ Lockheed 580 (T-33A)	53-5849	580-9250		PV

SOUTHEAST WISCONSIN AVIATION MUSEUM (WI51)

Address:	Experimental Aircraft Association Chapter 838, 333 North Green Bay Road, Racine, Wisconsin 53404.
Tel:	262-634-7575 Email: webmaster@eaa838.org
Admission:	Wednesday 1130-1500; Saturday 0900-1500; Sunday 1000-1600.
Location:	At the airport which is just north of the town.

The Racine chapter has set up a museum in their hangar at the airport. On show is the first aircraft owned by Johnson Wax Company, a Waco ATO biplane delivered in 1929. The company was formed in the town and was one of the first in the country to purchase an aircraft for business use. This aircraft, resplendent in its original colours, is surrounded by memorabilia. In the early 1930s the biplane made a 12,000 mile tour around the country to promote the products of the company.

In 1935 a flight to the Amazon Basin was undertaken in a Sikorsky S-38 amphibian to search for sources of the Carnauba palm which was used in their products. Born Again Restorations at Owatonna, Minnesota built a replica of the design and Sam Johnson and his two sons followed the original route. This aircraft is displayed along with maps and photos showing the eventful journey. The Tripacer is under conversion to the earlier model.

John Moody was a keen hang gliding pilot but the lack of hills in the area saw him fit a 12.5 h.p. engine to his Icarus Hang Glider. This was one of the first ultralight aircraft to fly when he took to the skies on 25th March 1975. He later fitted wheels so that it could take off under its own power.

A section is devoted to Green Bay resident Alfred Lawson who built the first airliner in the country, the 18 seat L-2, in 1919 and also constructed the larger L-4. The Kitfox was donated to the museum by a local aviator. The aircraft is used as a 'hands-on' educational exhibit to explain aircraft construction and design. The Hercules was operated by NASA from their Wallops Island site in Virginia.

Also on show are many items tracing the history of flying in the area. There is an excellent display of postage stamps and first day covers on show. The South East Wisconsin Aviation Hall of Fame is located in the nearby chapter buildings.

TYPE	REG/SER	CON. NO.	PI/NOTES	STATUS
☐ Denney Kitfox II				PV
☐ Fairchild 24R46	N81306	R46-206	NC81306	PV
☐ Lockheed 382C-85D Hercules (EC-130J)	N427NA	382-4901	Bu161495	PV
☐ Monnett Moni Tri-Gear	N192BB	192		PV
☐ Moody Ultralight	N427NA	382-4901	Bu161495	PV
☐ Piper PA-20 Pacer 125 (PA-22 Tripacer 125)				PVC
☐ Sikorsky S-38B (R)	NC6V	B314-12		PV
☐ Waco CTO (ATO)	NC8584	A-98	NC8584, N8584	PV

SPARTA MONUMENT (WI52)

Location: On permanent view at ALP 100 at 9929 Angelo Road just north east of the town on Route 21.

TYPE	REG/SER	CON. NO.	PI/NOTES	STATUS
☐ Bell 209 Huey Cobra (AH-1G) (AH-1S)	67-15661	20325		PV

STOUGHTON MONUMENT (WI53)

Location: On permanent view at VFW 328 on Country Route A in the town.

TYPE	REG/SER	CON. NO.	PI/NOTES	STATUS
☐ Lockheed 580 (T-33A)	'53-0905'	580-9381	53-5905	PV

STRUM MONUMENT (WI54)

Location: On permanent view at VFW 6550 in the southern part of the town.

TYPE	REG/SER	CON. NO.	PI/NOTES	STATUS
☐ Bell 209 Huey Cobra (AH-1G) (AH-1F)	67-15659	20323		PV

TOMAH MONUMENT (WI55)

Location: On permanent view at the Veterans Hospital in the north eastern part of the town.

TYPE	REG/SER	CON. NO.	PI/NOTES	STATUS
☐ Vought A-7D Corsair II	68-8220	D6		PV

TRUAX FIELD COLLECTION (WI56)

Address: Dane County Regional Airport, Madison, Wisconsin 53704.
Tel: 608-266-5000
Admission: Some on permanent view.
Location: In the north eastern suburbs of the city off Route 51.

The site opened in June 1942 as Madison Army Airfield. During World War II it was the Eastern Technical Training Center where large numbers of radio operators and airfield controllers learned their trades. In 1943 a special unit was set up to train personnel on the Boeing B-29 Superfortress. The airfield closed as an active AAF base on 30th November 1945.

After a period as a civil airport and home to ANG units the base was reactivated in February 1952. The facilities were improved and fighter squadrons were in residence until the mid-1960s. The airfield serves as the civil airport for the state capital and is also home to units of the Air and Army National Guard. The civil terminal main hall has a display of modern art and a restored mural dating from the opening of the art-deco terminal in 1936. The Corben Super Ace hangs in this area. O.G. Corben designed the Baby Ace in 1929. Six were built at the factory in Topeka, Kansas and many kits were sold. The Super Ace appeared in 1940 and about half a dozen were built before World War II. The example on show was constructed locally in the mid-1930s and flew for a period before being placed in store during World War II.

TYPE	REG/SER	CON. NO.	PI/NOTES	STATUS
☐ Bell 205 Iroquois (UH-1H)				RA
☐ Bell 209 Huey Cobra (AH-1G) (AH-1S)	66-15303	20059		PV
☐ Corben Super Ace	NC13697	341	In civil terminal.	PVX
☐ General Dynamics 401 Fighting Falcon (F-16A)	79-0368	61-153		RA

WATERFORD MONUMENTS (WI57)

Location:	On permanent view at VFW 8343 at 29224 Evergreen Drive on Route 20 just south of the town.

TYPE	REG/SER	CON. NO.	PI/NOTES	STATUS
☐ Bell 209 Huey Cobra (AH-1G) (AH-1F)	67-15813	20477		PV
☐ Lockheed 580 (T-33A)	53-5476	580-8815		RA
☐ Vought A-7A Corsair II	Bu153266	A175		PV

WAUPACA MONUMENT (WI58)

Location:	On permanent view at VFW 1037 on 244 North Industrial Drive in the eastern part of the town.

TYPE	REG/SER	CON. NO.	PI/NOTES	STATUS
☐ Bell 205 Iroquois (UH-1D) (UH-1H)	65-9803	4847		PV

WAUSAU MONUMENT (WI59)

Location:	On permanent view at VFW 388 at 388 River Drive in the town centre

TYPE	REG/SER	CON. NO.	PI/NOTES	STATUS
☐ Vought A-7D Corsair II	'70-0970'	D22	69-6192	PVX

WAUTOMA MONUMENT (WI60)

Location:	On permanent view at a Shell filling station in the town.

TYPE	REG/SER	CON. NO.	PI/NOTES	STATUS
☐ Ercoupe 415C				PVX

WILD ROSE MONUMENT (WI61)

Location:	Stored in the town with a member of ALP 370.

TYPE	REG/SER	CON. NO.	PI/NOTES	STATUS
☐ Bell 209 Huey Cobra (AH-1G) (AH-1S)	66-15302	20058		PV

WISCONSIN NATIONAL GUARD MEMORIAL LIBRARY AND MUSEUM (WI62)

Address:	Camp Williams – Volk Field, Camp Douglas, Wisconsin 54618-5001.
Tel:	608-427-1280 Email: eric.lent@dva.state.wi.us
Admission:	Wednesday-Saturday 0900-1600; Sunday 1000-1400.
Location:	About 10 miles south east of Tomah off Interstate 90.

In 1888 General Chandler Chapman purchased a site for a rifle range and offered it to the state for use as a camp. More land was acquired and by 1903 it covered more than 800 acres. The site was renamed in 1927 after Lieutenant Colonel Charles Williams. An airstrip was soon added and the first hard runways were laid in the mid-1930s. The airfield was named in honour of Lieutenant Charles Volk, who was the first Wisconsin Air National Guard pilot killed in combat in the Korean War.

An 1896 log building, which once served as the officers' club at Camp Williams, is home to the museum. The interior was remodelled and the display opened in 1989. The exhibits trace the story of the Wisconsin National Guard from its early times. The eastern room has been dedicated as the 'Gallery of the World Wars' where the exploits of the 32nd Infantry Division from its Mexican Border service in 1916 is honoured. Other rooms show the development of Camp Williams and Volk Field and history of the Wisconsin Air National Guard. There are many weapons, unit badges and flags on show along with regimental trophies.

Displayed around the camp are aircraft which have flown with squadrons around the state. The P-51D Mustang entered service in the state in 1947 and flew with units at Milwaukee and Truax Field until the introduction of jet fighters. The Boeing KC-97 arrived at the Milwaukee squadron in 1962 when the unit converted to the tanker role and was in use until 1977.

TYPE	REG/SER	CON. NO.	PI/NOTES	STATUS
☐ Bell 205 Iroquois (UH-1D)	66-0759	5242	At Hardwood Ranges.	PV
☐ Bell 205 Iroquois (UH-1D) (UH-1H)	66-16171	5865		RA
☐ Bell 206A Kiowa (OH-58A) (OH-58C)	69-16249	40470	At Hardwood Ranges.	PV
☐ Bell 209 Huey Cobra (AH-1G) (AH-1S)	70-16000	20944		PV
☐ Boeing 367-76-66 Stratofreighter (KC-97G) (KC-97L)	52-0905	16599		RA
☐ Convair 8-10 Delta Dagger (F-102A)	56-1273	8-10-490		PV
☐ Convair 8-12 Delta Dagger (TF-102A)	56-2353	8-12-85		PV
☐ Fairchild-Republic A-10A Thunderbolt II	77-0244	A10-169		RA
☐ McDonnell M.98DE Phantom II (F-4C)	63-7594	653	At Hardwood Ranges.	PV
☐ McDonnell M.98DJ Phantom II (F-4C)	64-0891	1307		PV
☐ North American NA-122 Mustang (P-51D)	44-72989	122-39448		PV
☐ North American NA-203 Sabre (F-86H)	53-1358	203-130		PV
☐ North American NA-217 Super Sabre (F-100C)	54-2106	217-367		PV
☐ Republic F-84F Thunderstreak	51-9365			PV
☐ Republic F-105B Thunderchief	57-5838	B-75		PV
☐ Vought A-7D Corsair II	70-0982	D128		RA

WISCONSIN VETERANS MUSEUM (WI63)

Address:	30 West Mifflin Street, Madison, Wisconsin 53703.
Tel:	608-267-1799 Email: veterans.museum@dva.state.wi.us
Admission:	All year Tuesday-Saturday 0930-1630 and April-September Sunday 1200-1600.
Location:	In the centre of the city near the state capitol.

The museum was first located in the grounds of the Veterans Home near Waupaca and it moved to its present building in 1993. The 19th century gallery highlights the role of Wisconsin citizen-soldiers in the Civil War and the Spanish-American conflict. The 20th century area covers the Mexican border campaign, the two World Wars, the Korean and Vietnam conflicts and the Gulf campaign.

The exhibition is regularly updated as new tasks are carried out by the state forces. There are many weapons, uniforms, badges, flags to be seen along with a wide range of weapons. During World War I Lieutenant Rodney Williams became Wisconsin's only ace flying a Sopwith Camel. He joined the Royal Canadian Air Force in April 1917 and was soon sent to France. He shot down four enemy aircraft and one balloon to gain this accolade. He was badly wounded on his last mission and spent a long period in hospital.

The Iroquois is displayed in a typical 'Vietnam' situation. The two replicas represent the two World Wars. Units of the Wisconsin Air National Guard operated Mustangs from their bases at Mitchell and Truax Fields in the late 1940s and early 1950s.

TYPE	REG/SER	CON. NO.	PI/NOTES	STATUS
☐ Bell 204 Iroquois (UH-1C) (UH-1M)	64-14157	1281		PV
☐ North American NA-122 Mustang (P-51D) (FSM)	'412067'			PVX
☐ Sopwith F.1 Camel (R)	'D659'			PVX

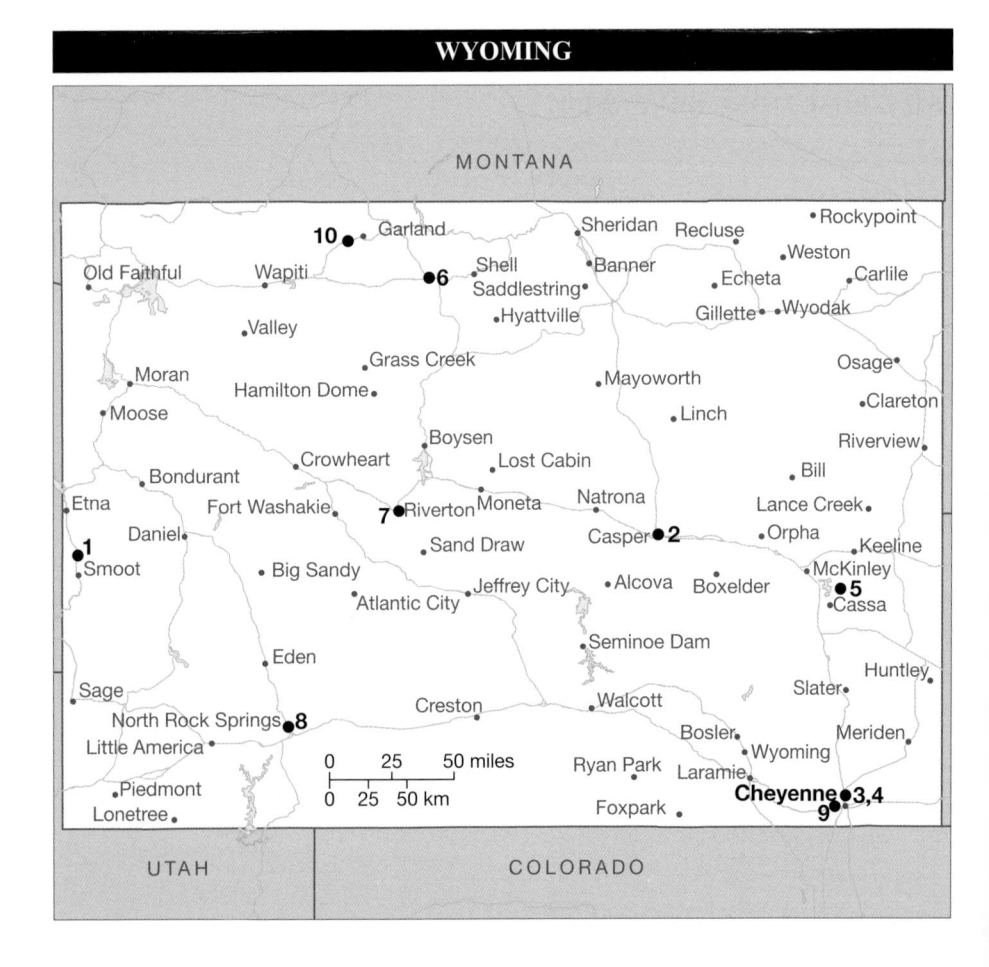

WYOMING

CALLAIR MUSEUM (WY1)

Address:	150 South Washington, Afton, Wyoming 83110.
Tel:	307-885-2001
Admission:	Monday-Friday 0800-1700.
Location:	In the centre of the town.

The Call brothers designed their first aircraft the Model A in the late 1930s and it took to the air in 1940. The side by side two-seat low-wing monoplane was underpowered. In 1944 it was re-engined with a 100 hp Lycoming engine which was more suitable for operations from the high altitude of Afton. Four A-1s were built and A-2 and A-3 models followed. The three-seat A-4 flew in 1954. The company introduced the A-5 which was specifically intended for agricultural work. The A-6 and A-7 were similar but featured different engines and design improvements. In 1962 the assets of the company were purchased by the Intermountain Manufacturing Company who developed the A-7 into the A-9. In 1966 the B-1 appeared and 35 examples of this version were completed. The first museum was located in a hangar at the airfield but this closed in 2002.

The new exhibition located in the Afton Civic Center opened to the public on 8th September 2008. On show are three aircraft displayed in imaginative scenes. The B-1 hangs in front of a large photographs of typical Wyoming scenery. Behind the A-6 is a view of a line of aircraft as they emerged from the factory. The A-3 is spectacularly mounted in front of a picture of snow covered mountains.

TYPE	REG/SER	CON. NO.	PI/NOTES	STATUS
☐ Callair A-3	NC2905V	121		PV
☐ Callair A-6	N2939G	294		PV
☐ Callair B-1A				PV

CASPER MONUMENT (WY2)

Location:	On permanent view at VFW 9439 at 1800 Brian Stock Trail in the north eastern part of the town.

TYPE	REG/SER	CON. NO.	PI/NOTES	STATUS
☐ Bell 205 Iroquois (UH-1H)	69-15660	11948		PV

CHEYENNE AIR NATIONAL GUARD BASE (WY3)

Address:	153AW/PA, PO Box 2268, Cheyenne Municipal Airport, Wyoming 82003-2268.
Tel:	307-772-2601
Admission:	By prior permission only.
Location:	In the northern suburbs of the town.

Cheyenne Airport opened in the 1920s when an airmail service for Salt Lake City left in a de Havilland DH-4. Commercial passenger services followed a few years later. The terminal building, hangar and fountain built in the late 1920s are on the National Register of Historic Places. During World War II modification work on Boeing B-17s was carried out.

At over 6,000 feet above sea level the field is often used by manufacturers to test airliners at high altitude. The 187th Squadron was allocated to the Wyoming Air National Guard in 1946 and equipped with P-51 Mustangs. In December 1951 the unit was called up for active duty and moved to Clovis Air Force base in New Mexico where it remained until returned to state control in January 1953. Fighters and fighter bombers were flown until 1961 when it became an aeromedical squadron. Since 1964 it has operated mainly in the transport role.

The preserved aircraft are mainly parked near the main gate to the base.

TYPE	REG/SER	CON. NO.	PI/NOTES	STATUS
☐ Bell 205 Iroquois (UH-1D) (UH-1H)	66-1135	5618		RA
☐ Lockheed 382-8B Hercules (C-130E)	63-7861	382-3931		PV
☐ Lockheed 580 (T-33A)	'36661'	580-1145	56-3661, N83615	RAX
☐ North American NA-201 Sabre (F-86D) (F-86L)	53-0806	201-250		RA
☐ Republic F-84F Thunderstreak	52-7019		52-7019, N5894	RA
☐ Vought A-7D Corsair II	70-1046	D192		RA

CHEYENNE MONUMENT (WY4)

Location:	On permanent view at the ANG Headquarters in the town near Exit 12 of Interstate 25.

TYPE	REG/SER	CON. NO.	PI/NOTES	STATUS
☐ North American NA-201 Sabre (F-86D) (F-86L)	'52-3153'		At ANG Headquarters.	PVX

GUERNSEY MONUMENT (WY5)

Location:	On permanent view at the National Guard Camp in the south eastern part of the town.

TYPE	REG/SER	CON. NO.	PI/NOTES	STATUS
☐ Bell 205 Iroquois (UH-1H)				PV

MUSEUM OF AVIATION AND AERIAL FIREFIGHTING (WY6)

Address:	2441 Highway 20 West, PO Box 391 Greybull, Wyoming 82426-0391
Tel:	307-765-4322 Fax: 307-765-2535 Email: flight@tctwest.net
Admission:	Monday-Friday 0800-1900; Saturday-Sunday 1000-1900. (provisional)
Location:	About 3 miles west of the town on Route 20.

Dan Hawkins and Gene Powers founded Hawkins and Powers Aviation in 1969. The initial fleet consisted of one PB4Y Privateer, two Cessna 180s, two Beech 18s, two Hiller 360s and a number of B-25 Mitchells.

The company grew into one of the largest fire-fighting organisations in the country. Unfortunately the firm went into receivership in 2006 and some of the aircraft were sold and others scrapped. The company was the last to use the Privateer but one crashed in Colorado in July 2002 due to structural failure. The three survivors owned by Hawkins and Powers were grounded.

The museum was set up in 1992 to preserve aircraft and equipment used in combating forest fires. Displays in the building trace the development of aerial fire-fighting. There are photographs of the types used and details of equipment carried. The history of Hawkins and Powers and their varied fleet is portrayed. The aircraft listed below are those which the museum says will remain at Greybull.

TYPE	REG/SER	CON. NO.	PI/NOTES	STATUS
☐ Beech C18S Expeditor (C-45F) (UC-45F)	N7391C	8460	44-87201	PV
☐ Boeing 367-76-66 Stratofreighter (KC-97G) (KC-97L)	N29866	16726	52-2695 – with tail from 52-2680	PV
☐ Consolidated 40 Privateer (PB4Y-2) (P4Y-2) (Convair 100)	N6884C		Bu59701, N3432G	PV
☐ Fairchild 110 Flying Boxcar (C-119F)	N5215R	10773	22108 (Canada)	PV
☐ Fairchild 110 Flying Boxcar (C-119F)	'N5216R'	10824	22113 (Canada), N3835	PVX

RIVERTON MONUMENT (WY7)

Location:	On permanent view at the airport about 3 miles north west of the town off Route 26.

TYPE	REG/SER	CON. NO.	PI/NOTES	STATUS
☐ Lockheed 580 (T-33A)	51-4489	580-5784		PV

ROCK SPRINGS MONUMENT (WY8)

Location:	On permanent view in the City Park in the town.

TYPE	REG/SER	CON. NO.	PI/NOTES	STATUS
☐ McDonnell M.36BA Voodoo (F-101B)	58-0317	689	May be c/n 684 58-0312.	PV

WARREN ICBM AND HERITAGE MUSEUM (WY9)

Address:	90 SW/MU, 7405 Maine Loop, Building 210, F.E. Warren Air Force Base, Wyoming 82005-5000.
Tel:	307-773-2980
Admission:	Monday-Friday 0800-1600.
Location:	In the western suburbs of Cheyenne off Interstate 25.

The Army first occupied this site, called Fort D.A. Russell, in 1867 and 80 years later control passed to the Air Force. The base was renamed in 1930 after a former territorial governor. The vast area houses intercontinental ballistic missiles. A small museum tracing the history of the base has been set up in a building near the main gate. The UH-1 was used at Warren to assist in the missile operations.

TYPE	REG/SER	CON. NO.	PI/NOTES	STATUS
☐ Bell 204 Iroquois (UH-1F)	65-7953	7094		PV

WENGAIR COLLECTION (WY10)

Address:	PO Box 813, Powell, Wyoming 82435-0813.
Admission:	By prior permission only.
Location:	The airport is 3 miles north of the town on Route 295.

This collection of powered aircraft and gliders contains a number of interesting types. The classic Rhönbussard glider dates from 1935 and is believed to be only one in the USA. The sailplane is currently in flying condition. Six examples of the Waco series of open cockpit biplanes are owned. Two, the ASO and ATO, are examples of the well known 'Taperwing'.

The Schweizer company manufactured over 2,000 training and high performance sailplanes at its Elmira factory in New York State between 1930 and 1980. Examples were used by the military and many civilian gliding clubs. A large number are still in everyday use.

TYPE	REG/SER	CON. NO.	PI/NOTES	STATUS
☐ AMS-Flight Carat A	N118VS	CA023		RAA
☐ Bellanca 7GCBC Citabria	N233RA	1381-2005		RAA
☐ Grob G.103C Twin III Acro SL	N103LD	35019		RAA
☐ Jacobs Rhönbussard (DFS 108-50)	N158RB	50		RAA
☐ Müller Moswey III	N379HB	379		RAA
☐ Piper PA-25-235 Pawnee C	N4707Y	25-4639		RAA
☐ Schleicher K.7	N4280C	7155		RAA
☐ Schneider Grunau Baby IIB	N58GB	2		RAA
☐ Schweizer SGS.2-33	N5709S	56		RAA
☐ Schweizer SGS.2-33A	N7773S	143		RAA
☐ Schweizer SGS.1-36	N3616F	7		RAA
☐ Spalinger S-18-III	N458HB	458		RAA
☐ Waco ASO	NC612N	A-116	NC751E, N751E	RAA
☐ Waco ATO	N6714	A-20	NC6711, N6711	RAA
☐ Waco DSO	NC762K	A-137	NC762K, N762K	RAA
☐ Waco UBF	NC13027	3660	NC13027, N13027	RAA
☐ Waco UPF-7	NC32080	5712	NC32080, N32080	RAA
☐ Waco YPF	NC15700	4375	NC15700, N15700	RAA

INDEX

All aircraft are listed alphabetically by manufacturer or designer (in the case of some gliders and homebuilt aircraft) followed by the type. Each state is denoted by the standard two letter code and each museum/collection a number e.g. NY23 is the twenty-third museum/collection in alphabetical order in New York State.

State codes are as follows:
AL Alabama; **AK** Alaska; **AZ** Arizona; **AR** Arkansas; **CA** California; **CO** Colorado; **CT** Connecticut; **DE** Delaware; **DC** District of Columbia; **FL** Florida; **GA** Georgia; **HI** Hawaii; **ID** Idaho; **IL** Illinois; **IN** Indiana; **IA** Iowa; **KS** Kansas; **KY** Kentucky; **LA** Louisiana; **ME** Maine; **MD** Maryland; **MA** Massachusetts; **MI** Michigan; **MN** Minnesota; **MS** Mississippi; **MO** Missouri; **MT** Montana; **NE** Nebraska; **NV** Nevada; **NH** New Hampshire; **NJ** New Jersey; **NM** New Mexico; **NY** New York; **NC** North Carolina; **ND** North Dakota; **OH** Ohio; **OK** Oklahoma; **OR** Oregon; **PA** Pennsylvania; **RI** Rhode Island; **SC** South Carolina; **SD** South Dakota; **TN** Tennessee; **TX** Texas; **UT** Utah; **VT** Vermont; **VA** Virginia; **WA** Washington; **WV** West Virginia; **WI** Wisconsin; **WY** Wyoming.

Aaaro Aeroncopy C3L-65	NY16	Aero L-29 Delfin	AZ33, 46, CA35, 53, 111, 114, IN28, NH2, NY23, 62, OR21, TX19, 80
AAI RQ-2A Pioneer	DC3		
AAI RQ-2B Pioneer	NC17, VA22		
AAI RQ-7A Shadow	DC3	Aero L-29C Delfin	CA150
AB Sportline Aviacija Genesis 2	NM20	Aero L-29L Delfin	IL20, TX57
Abernathy Streaker	FL22	Aero L-29R Delfin	DE12, TX92
Ableiter Green Hornet	CA155	Aero L-39C Albatros	AL32, CA65, DE12, FL86, ID24, IL20, 72, 73, 81, NM8, NY4, 62, OK27, OR 11, TX19, VA8
Abrams Explorer	MD15		
Abruzzo Grom 1 Peak Express	NM2		
Adam Aircraft M309 CarbonAero	CO32		
Adams A.55 Hot Air Balloon	IA29		
Adams-Wilson 101 Hobbycopter	CA37, OR7, 13	Aero L-39MS Albatros	DE12, IL81
Advanced Aviation Buccaneer II	MD14	Aero L-39TC Albatros	FL5
Aerial Experiment Association Glider (R)	NY24	Aero L-39V Albatros	KS10
		Aero L-39ZA Albatros	NY4, TX19
Aerial Experiment Association June Bug II (R)	NY24	Aero L-39ZO Albatros	WA28
		Aero Spacelines 377-MG Mini-Guppy (Boeing 377-10-26 Stratocruiser)	OR21
Aerial Experiment Association Silver Dart (R)	NY24		
Aermacchi MB.339A	NY34	Aero Spacelines 377-SG Super Guppy (Boeing 377-10-26 Stratocruiser)	AZ30
Aero Adventure Aventura	AR2		
Aero Commander L.3805	OK23		
Aero Commander 100	NY74, SD4	Aerochair Ax.3-21 Hot Air Balloon	WA33
Aero Commander 100-180	CA126	Aerocycle Penguin	CA105
Aero Commander 1121B	PA49	Aerodyne Vector 627	WI17
Aero Commander 200D	CA151	Aerojet-General V-260/USD	WI17
Aero Commander 500A	CA63	Aeromarine 39B	NY63
Aero Commander 500S	VA19	Aeromarine-Klemm AKL-26A	NY63
Aero Commander 500U	IL3	Aeromet Aura	OK43
Aero Commander 520	FL54, IL60, KS26, TX59, 132	Aeronca C-2	CA160, OH53, 59, VA19, WA8, 25
Aero Commander 520 (YL-26) (YU-9A)	AL36, CA85, OH22	Aeronca C-2N	VA36, WI17
		Aeronca C-3	CA122, 149, 158, FL23, IA1, IL18, 46, MN18, NC40, NY63, OH16, 37, 63, OR24, PA23, 35, 56, VA36, WA34, WI17
Aero Commander 560A	CA50		
Aero Commander 560A (L-26B) (U-4A)	NC38		
Aero Commander 560F	CA13		
Aero Commander 680	AL32, IA27, NC15, RI1		
Aero Commander 680 (L-26C) (U-4B)	LA19, OH55	Aeronca PC-3 (C-3)	PA17
		Aeronca K	AL32, CA64, 130, IA1, KS26, KY2, MO15, NH5, OR20, 24, PA35, VA13, WA34, WI17
Aero Commander 680 (L-26C) (U-9C)	IL62		
Aero Commander 680F	GA45, IL38, WA38		
Aero Commander 680T	OR19	Aeronca KC	AZ45, NH7
Aero Commander 680V	AZ9, MA10, NY37, OH18	Aeronca KCA	OR24
Aero Commander 680V (680T)	GA9, TX140	Aeronca LB	FL23, IN40
Aero Commander 680W	CA107, DC7, OK46, PA44, TN34	Aeronca LC	OR24, WI17
		Aeronca 50C Chief	CT9
Aero Commander 681	FL7	Aeronca 50F Chief	OR20
Aero Commander 690B	IL18	Aeronca 65-TAL Defender	OR24, TX32
Aero Jet Commander 1121	NY76	Aeronca 65C Chief	AK3, IL65, KS26, NH5
Aero Designs Pulsar	KY2	Aeronca 65CA Chief	IA1
Aero Designs Pulsar 912XP	IL66	Aeronca 65CA Super Chief	IL70, MI2, NH5, PA56, TX28
Aero Falcon Knight Falcon	TX151		
Aero Gare Sea Hawk	WI17	Aeronca 65LA	AR23, CA36
		Aeronca 65LB Chief	IL50, NY21
		Aeronca 65TAC	GA35

657

Aeronca 65TAC	MO10	Alliance Argo	MN18, OH59
Aeronca 65TC	HI6, OK12	Allison Sport Plane	PA23
Aeronca 65TC Grasshopper (O-58B) (L-3B)	AR19, AZ30, CA53, 91, IA1, 8, ID1, KS26, MI2, MO1, MT9, NY82, OH55, OR24, TX2, 16, 34, 40, VA20, WA25, 34	Alon A-2	CA151, ID2, OR24
		American Aerolights Double Eagle	PA35, VA19
		American Aerolights Eagle	IL50, PA35, VA29
		American Aerolights Eagle II	OR7
		American Aerolights Eagle Seaplane	WI24
		American Aerolights Eaglet	FL23
Aeronca 65TC Grasshopper (L-3C)	TX45	American Aviation AA-1A Trainer	NC10, VA35
Aeronca 65TF Defender	NY82, OH37, TX151	American Aviation AA-1B Trainer	OK19
Aeronca 65TL Defender	AL36, OH37	American Aviation AA-5A Cheetah	AZ42, OH12
Aeronca 7AC Champion	AZ45, CA53, 61, 121, 130, CT4, FL46, GA45, IA1, IN21, 25, 40, KS26, LA10, MO15, 36, NC40, NY7, 74, OH56, 64, OR24, PA17, UT8, VA13, WA19, 34, 37, WI49	American Eagle A-101	CA19, 158, 160, FL73, 77, OK28
		American Eagle A-101 (A-1)	CA158, OR20, 24
		American Eagle A-129	AZ30, KS18, NY63, 82
		American Eagle Eaglet 230K	WI27
		American Eagle Eaglet 231	CA130, NY74, PA35, WI27
		American Eagle Eaglet A31-1B	OH53
Aeronca 7BCM Champion (7AC)	WA34	American Eagle Eaglet B-31	IA1, OR24, RI1
Aeronca 7BCM Champion (L-16A)	AL36, AR2, CA61, 88, GA21, KS26	American Eagle RF-1 Frigate	OH59
		American Flea Triplane	SD8, TX151
Aeronca 7CCM Champion (7BCM)	MD14	American Helicopter XA-6	CA37
Aeronca 7CCM Champion (L-16B)	GA35, ID1, ND23	American Helicopter XA-8 Jet Jeep (XH-26)	AL36, OH55
Aeronca 7DC Champion (7AC)	AK19, TX92		
Aeronca 11AC Chief	AL32, IA1, IN40, MD7, MT9, NH5, NY7, OH18, TX32, 151, WA37	Ames-Dryden AD-1 (Rutan 35)	CA65
		AMS-Flight Carat A	WY10
		Anderson Double Eagle V	WI17
		Anderson Kingfisher	FL23
Aeronca 11BC Chief (11AC)	OH53	Anderson Phoenix X-1A	CA130
Aeronca 11CC Chief	NV5	Anderson Z	IA1
Aeronca 11CC Super Chief	WA34	Angel 44	IA27
Aeronca 15AC Sedan	AL32, CA9	Anglin Spacewalker 2	FL23
Aérospatiale / British Aircraft Corporation Concorde 101	VA19	Ansaldo A-1 Balilla (R)	NY63
		Antares MA-30	WI17
Aérospatiale / British Aircraft Corporation Concorde 102	NY34, WA25	Antonov An-2	ID1, TX19
		Antonov An-2M	MD15
Aérospatiale AS.350 Ecureuil	WA9	Antonov An-2P	MO15
Aérospatiale AS.366G Dauphin (HH-65A)	NC12	Antonov An-2R	CA35, 41, 63, 85, NY74, TX40, WA19, 25
Aerosport Quail	AZ30, NC24	Antonov An-2T	CA111
Aerosport Scamp	WA25	Antonov An-2TP	IN48, MO15
Aerostar S-60A Hot Air Balloon	FL22, 55	Antonov An-24RV	FL40
AeroVironment MQ-11 Raven	DC3	Applebay Zia	NM20
Agusta-Bell 206B1 Jet Ranger	IL66	Applebay Zuni II	MD15, OH55
Aichi B7A1 Ryusei	MD15	Arado Ar 196A-5	FL55, MD15
Aichi D3A2-22	CA111, TX103	Arado Ar 234B-2	VA19
Aichi M6A1 Seiran	VA19	Arctic Sparrow	AK4
Air and Space 18A	IN3, NJ21	Arlington Sisu 1-A	KY2, NY50, VA19
Air Command 447 Commander Sport	PA4	Armstrong Aeronaut	KS26
Air Command Autogyro	NY74	Armstrong Whitworth AW.650 Argosy 100	MI58
Aircraft Builders Corporation Student Prince X	OR20, WA8		
		Armstrong Whitworth AW.660 Argosy C.1	IA27
Aircraft Dynamics Nuwaco T-10	MO15		
Aircraft Engineering Company Ace	NY14	Armstrong Whitworth AW.660 Argosy T.2 (C.1)	CA88
Aircraft Manufacturing and Design Alarus CH2000	PA12		
		Arnold AR-5	CA65
Aircraft Manufacturing Company Texas Bullet 205	MN21, TN32	Arrow Sport A2-60	ND5, VA19
		Arrow Sport F	CA83, 105, IA1, ND5, OR24, PA35
Airspeed AS.58 Horsa II (FSM)	TX124		
Akerman 1-1936 Tailless	MD15	Arrow Sport M (F)	MN18
Alarus CH2000	UT10	Arrow Sport Pursuit	OR24
Albatros D Va	DC3	Atlas-Aermacchi MB.326M Impala I	CA91
Albatros D Va (R)	AZ30, CA122, NY63, OH55, VA17, WA25	Auster B.5 AOP.9	AL36, FL23
		Auster J/1 Autocrat	PA35
Albree Pigeon Fraser	NY63	Auster K AOP.6	NY7, OR7
Alenia G.222 Spartan (C-27A)	AZ1	Avian Falcon II Hot Air Balloon	AZ30, NM2
Alexander Eaglerock 3-POLB	IA39, OR24, WA25	Avian Hot Air Balloon	IA29
Alexander Eaglerock A-1	IA39, TX114	Aviat A-1 Husky	FL5, MN18
Alexander Eaglerock A-3	IA39	Aviat A-1B Husky	MN18
Alexander Eaglerock A-4	IL82, PA17	Aviatik D I	WA25
Alexander Eaglerock A-12	IL82	Aviation Restoration and Testing ART-38	TX3
Alexander Eaglerock A-14	CO11, IL82		
Alexander Eaglerock Long Wing	AL32, CO32	Avid Catalina	WI24
Alexander Flyabout D-2	OR24	Avid Magnum	MS20
Alexander Primary Glider	CA158		

Index

Avro 504J	FL22	Beech D17S (UC-43)	CA75, 160, ND23
Avro 504K (R)	KS26, NY63, OH55, VA17	Beech D17S (UC-43) (GB-2)	CA66, FL22, 55, IL63, NY74, OH55, PA29, TX12, WA17
Avro 594 Avian II	MN18		
Avro 616 Avian IVM	CA158	Beech E17B (UC-43D)	TX69
Avro 643 Cadet II	FL22	Beech E17L (E17B) (UC-43D)	TN4
Avro 683 Lancaster B.I	WA12	Beech F17D	KS26
Avro 683 Lancaster B.X	FL22	Beech F17D (UC-43C)	ID2, TN4
Avro 683 Lancaster 10(AR) (B.X)	FL22	Beech F17D (E17B) (UC-43D)	TN4
Avro 696 Shackleton AEW.2 (MR.2)	AZ30	Beech G17S	CA17, MO15, TN4
Avro 698 Vulcan B.2	CA32, LA7, NE23	Beech C18S	AK16
Avro Canada C.100 Canuck 4D (4) (CF-100)	OH55	Beech C18S Expeditor (C-45B)	OH40
		Beech C18S Expeditor (C-45F) (Expeditor 3T)	CA15
Avro Canada C.100 Canuck 5 (CF-100)	CA32, CO24, OH71	Beech C18S Expeditor (C-45F) (UC-45F)	AK3, 8, CA115, IL26, MD22, MT9, WY6
Avro Canada Model 1 Avrocar (VZ-9V)	OH55, VA34	Beech C18S Expeditor (C-45F) (UC-45F) (JRB-4)	AR19, IN29
Bachem Ba 349B-1 Natter (BP-20)	VA19	Beech C18S Expeditor (SNB-1)	TX119
Bachem Ba 349A-1 Natter (BP 20) (FSM)	CA111, FL22	Beech C18S Navigator (AT-7)	AZ30, CO14, DE11, MI53
Backstrom EPB-1A Flying Plank	NY50	Beech C18S Navigator (AT-7C)	CA128, KS26
Backstrom EPB-1C Flying Plank	NY50	Beech C18S Kansan (AT-11)	AZ30, 47, CA53, 139, CO32, FL22, 24, GA45, IL3, 39, IN25, LA7, 12, MI53, 58, NM5, OH55, TX40, 76, VT1
Backstrom Flying Plank II	IA1		
Bailey-Moyes Dragonfly	MD14		
Bailey-Moyes Tempest	MD14		
Bakeng Double Duce	PA49		
Bakeng Duce F.M.1	AK5		
Baker-McMillen Cadet	NY50, PA56	Beech C18S Kansan (AT-11C)	OH71
Baldwin Red Devil	VA19	Beech D18S	AL13, AZ10, 11, CA104, GA21, ID8, MD18, NC38, NM6, NY4, OK49, PA61, TN4, TX32, 38, 40, 59,151, VA19
Balkema 2/3 Jenny	MI2		
Ball-Bartoe JW-1 Jetwing	CO32		
Balloon Works Firefly 7 Hot Air Balloon	AZ30, CA105, NM2, TX69, WA33		
Balloon Works Firefly 7-B Hot Air Balloon	IL50		
		Beech D18S Expeditor (C-18S) (SNB-2) (SNB-5P) (RC-45J)	GA58
Balloon Works Firefly F7 Hot Air Balloon	NM2	Beech D18S Expeditor (C18S) (SNB-1) (SNB-5) (TC-45J) (UC-45J)	AZ9
Balloon Works Firefly 8-B Hot Air Balloon	NM2		
Bamber Glider (R)	PA56	Beech D18S Expeditor (C18S) (AT-7) (SNB-5) (TC-45J) (UC-45J)	GA52
Banks Lonestar Spirit Helico	OK28		
Barber Valkyrie	FL22	Beech D18S Expeditor (C18S) (AT-7C) (SNB-2C) (JRB-4) (TC-45J) (UC-45J)	CA111
Barnes AX-7 Hot Air Balloon	IA29		
Baslee Pfalz E-1 (Scale R)	KS9		
Bates Tractor	WI17	Beech D18S Expeditor (C18S) (AT-7C) (SNB-2C) (SNB-3P) (SNB-5) (RC-45J)	AZ30
Bauer Scale Corsair	AZ22		
Baum Balloon	IA29		
Baumann RB-1 Racer	MI25	Beech D18S Expeditor (C18S) (C-45F) (UC-45F) (JRB-4) (JRB-6)	CA85
Beachey Little Looper (R)	CA65		
Beagle B.206 Series 1	AL32		
Beagle B.206 Series 2	AL32, OK19	Beech D18S Expeditor (C18S) (C-45F) (UC-45F) (JRB-4) (SNB-5)	NY32, OK3
Beatty-Oram Hang Glider	CA111		
Bede BD-2	WI17		
Bede BD-4	AL32, AZ30, FL23	Beech D18S Expeditor (C18S) (JRB-2) (SNB-5)	TX151
Bede BD-5	AK3, AZ22, KY9		
Bede BD-5A	WI17	Beech D18S Expeditor (C18S) (JRB-2) (SNB-5P) (RC-45J)	FL55
Bede BD-5A/B	VA19		
Bede BD-5B	AL32, CA65, 105, 155, FL23, IA1, IL24, KS18, ND5, OK28, OR7, PA35, 56, TX8, WA25	Beech D18S Expeditor (C18S) (JRB-3) (SNB-5) (TC-45J)	CA111
		Beech D18S Expeditor (C18S) (JRB-3) (SNB-5) (UC-45J)	WA22
Bede BD-5G	WA28	Beech D18S Expeditor (C18S) (JRB-4) (SNB-5) (TC-45J)	HI1, 6, OR19
Bede BD-5J	AZ30, CA53, 96, 109, 114		
Bee Aviation Honey Bee	CA122	Beech D18S Expeditor (C18S) (UC-45J)	
Bee Aviation Wee Bee (R)	CA122	Beech D18S Expeditor (C18S) (SNB-1) (SNB-4) (SNB-5) (TC-45J) (UC-45J)	NV13
Beech 17R	TN4		
Beech B17L	KS36, TN4		
Beech C17B	OH53	Beech D18S Expeditor (C18S) (SNB-1) (SNB-5)	AR24
Beech C17L	TN4		
Beech C17L (C-17B)	DC3	Beech D18S Expeditor (C18S) (SNB-1) (SNB-5) (TC-45J) (UC-45J)	AZ9, FL29
Beech C17R	WA18		
Beech D17A (UC-43F)	OR7		
Beech D17S	AZ45	Beech D18S Expeditor (C18S) (SNB-2) (SNB-2P) (SNB-5) (TC-45J) (UC-45J)	GA40, 58, LA7, TN28, TX134
Beech D17S	ID8, LA27, TN4		
Beech D17S (GB-2)	ID15, MT13, OR24		

Beech D18S Expeditor (C18S) (SNB-2) (SNB-2P) (SNB-5P) (RC-45J)	AZ30, TN33	Beech 35-33 Debonair Beech A36 Bonanza 36 Beech 45 Mentor (YT-34)	PA49 IN58, MT13, TN4 CA32
Beech D18S Expeditor (C18S) (SNB-2) (SNB-3) (SNB-5) (TC-45J) (UC-45J)	CA4, GA52, IL60	Beech A45 Mentor (T-34A)	CA95, 150, FL5, IL3, 18, IN44, MI2, MT13, NC15, 24, NM8, NV18, NY34, OH19, 55, TN1, TX23, 28, 147, VA17
Beech D18S Expeditor (C18S) (SNB-2) (SNB-5)	AK3, IL38		
Beech D18S Expeditor (C18S) (SNB-2) (SNB-5) (TC-45J) (UC-45J)	CA3, CO6, FL13, 16, GA9, IA21, KS9, OH48, 71 TX40	Beech D45 Mentor (T-34B)	AL32, AR20, CA45, 53, 58, 95, 122, CO25, FL45, 55, 58, GA52, ID24, IN48, MD11, 19, MI2, NC6, OR7, 13, PA1, TN1, TX51, 88, 119, 149, WI35
Beech D18S Expeditor (C18S) (SNB-2) (SNB-5P) (RC-45J)	TX40, UT2		
Beech D18S Expeditor (C18S) (SNB-2C) (SNB-3) (SNB-5) (TC-45J) (UC-45J)	FL22, 29, GA58, IL60		
		Beech D45 Mentor (T-34B) (YT-34C)	FL83
Beech D18S Expeditor (C18S) (SNB-2C) (SNB-3) (SNB-5P) (RC-45J)	IA20, WA23	Beech D45 Mentor (T-34C) Beech B50 Twin Bonanza Beech C50 Twin Bonanza	AL5, VA16 AK3, CA121 CA9, PA49
Beech D18S Expeditor (C18S) (SNB-2C) (SNB-3E) (SNB-5) (TC-45J) (UC-45J)	LA6	Beech C50 Seminole (L-23D) (RL-23D) (RU-8D)	AZ47, MI36
Beech D18S Expeditor (C18S) (SNB-2C) (SNB-3Q) (SNB-5)	AL32	Beech C50 Seminole (L-23D) (RL-23D) (RU-8D) (RU-8G)	AZ9
Beech D18S Expeditor (C18S) (SNB-2C) (SNB-3Q) (SNB-5) (TC-45J)	MN30	Beech C50 Seminole (L-23D) (U-8D)	AL11, 36, AR20, AZ30, CA36, 107, CO4, IL60, NM7, PA44, 49, SD7, VA34, WA38
Beech D18S Expeditor (C18S) (SNB-2C) (SNB-5) (TC-45J) (UC-45J)	TX88, 147	Beech C50 Seminole (L-23D) (U-8D) (U-8G)	WA38
Beech D18S Expeditor (C18S) (UC-45F) (JRB-4) (SNB-5) (TC-45J)	TN4	Beech C50 Seminole (L-23E) (U-8E) (U-8G)	AZ9
		Beech C50 Seminole (RL-23D) (RU-8D)	KS9, MD16
Beech D18S Expeditor (C-45G)	AK8, CA32, 150, DE1, GA45, IL70, KS40, LA6, NV4, NY61, 74, OH36, 71, TX34, WA25	Beech C50 Seminole (RL-23D) (RU-8D) (RU-8G)	AL36, SC13, WA38
		Beech C50 Seminole (RL-23D) (RU-8D) (U-8G)	MS20
Beech D18S Expeditor (C-45H)	AK5, AZ24, CA139, FL33, IA21, ID1, IL48, 64, MN27, NC24, OH22, 36, 55, OK9, SD7, TN4, TX40, UT5, VT6	Beech D50 Twin Bonanza Beech D50C Twin Bonanza Beech D50E Twin Bonanza Beech E55 Baron Beech 58 Baron Beech 58P Baron	IL18, KS26 PA49, WI22 TN4 IL38 IN28, NJ8, WI21 ID14, KS41, NH8, PA44, SD4, UT11
Beech D18S Expeditor (TC-45G)	OH22		
Beech D18S Expeditor 3N	CA114	Beech 58TC Baron	FL22, MO19, MS12, WA4
Beech D18S Expeditor 3NM	AR19, ND2, 5, TX32		
Beech D18S Expeditor 3TM	OH71	Beech 60 Duke	IN53, WI35
Beech E18S	AZ45, CA89, MI29, OR24, TN4	Beech B60 Duke Beech 65 Queen Air	CA123 WA11
Beech G18S	AR23, PA35	Beech 65-80 Queen Air	CT11, GA9, IA27
Beech H18S	TX54, 92	Beech 65-80 Seminole (L-23F) (U-8F)	IL66, IN53, KS18, MN32
Beech S18D	AZ30, TN4		
Beech 18D (D18S Expeditor (SNB-5)	WI8	Beech 65-A80 Queen Air	OR19
Beech B19 Musketeer Sport	KS26	Beech 65-90 King Air	IL60, IN53, NY76, OH24, 34, OK23, VA19, WA38
Beech 23 Musketeer	CA158, MN32, NC15		
Beech A23 Musketeer II	IN46		
Beech C23 Sundowner 180	FL54, SD4, VA18	Beech 65-A90 King Air	LA22, OK29, TX141, VA4, WI21, 22, 35
Beech B24R Sierra	GA52		
Beech B24R Sierra 200	CA94	Beech 65-A90 King Air (VC-6A)	NM26
Beech 26 (AT-10)	OH55	Beech 65-A90-1 Ute (RU-21E) (JU-21H)	AL36
Beech 35 Bonanza	CA66, FL25, KS26, OR7, TN4, TX3, VA19		
		Beech 65-A90-1 Ute (U-21A)	GA34, SD4, TX89
Beech A35 Bonanza	AZ42	Beech 73 Jet Mentor	KS18
Beech B35 Bonanza	CA130, KS18	Beech 76 Duchess	WI21
Beech C35 Bonanza	AZ7, CO26	Beech B90 King Air	GA42
Beech E35 Bonanza	IL46	Beech B90 King Air (VC-6A)	OH55
Beech F33A Bonanza	TX98	Beech C 90 King Air	MS12, WI8
Beech H35 Bonanza	TN4	Beech C90A King Air	FL73
Beech J35 Bonanza	OK2	Beech 95-55 Baron	OK29, TN4, WA39
Beech K35 Bonanza	WA37	Beech 95-A55 Baron	DE7, NC10
Beech M35 Bonanza	CA105, ID14	Beech 95-B55 Baron	MI2, MT13, TX54, WA4
Beech N35 Bonanza	AZ30	Beech 95-B55B Cochise (T-42A)	AL36, CA126, IA25, NY52, 76, WI8
Beech S35 Bonanza	MO15		
Beech V35 Bonanza	TN4	Beech B95 Travel Air	CO4, NY4, 76
Beech V35B Bonanza	IL18	Beech B100 King Air	ID14

Index

Beech 200 Super King Air	CA107, FL22	Bell 47G-3B-1	AZ21, IL66, WA4
Beech A200 Huron (C-12A) (C-12C)	AL36, MS12	Bell 47G-3B-1 Sioux (TH-13T)	AL36, AZ21, CA104, 110, 123, 153, CO25, IL26, 66, NJ29, TX16, 69, UT5
Beech A200 Huron (C-12D) (RC-12D) (RC-12G)	AZ18		
Beech A200C Huron (UC-12B)	AZ1, TX43		
Beech A200CT Huron (C-12D) (RC-12D)	AL36, TX58	Bell 47G-3B-2	ID2, 24
		Bell 47G-4	AZ10, NY13
Beech A200CT Huron (C-12D) (RC-12G)	TX61	Bell 47G-4A	AL32
		Bell 47G-5	CA29
Beech 1079 (QU-22B)	NY47, OH55	Bell 47H-1	IN33, NY35, PA4
Beech 2000 Starship I	AL32, KS26, 41, UT10, WA14	Bell 47J	OK36
		Bell 47J (HUL-1) (UH-13P)	MO37
Beech 2000A Starship I	AZ30, KS18, OR7, TN4, WA25	Bell 47J-1 Sioux (H-13J) (UH-13J)	OH55, VA19
		Bell 47K (HTL-7)	CA61
Beech PD-373 Texan II	MD19	Bell 47K Sioux (HTL-7) (TH-13N)	AZ30, OK43
Bell 14 Airacobra (P-400)	VA17	Bell 52 (XS-2) (X-2) (FSM)	CA111
Bell 26C Airacobra (P-39N)	CA89, 111, FL27, OH71, OR21, PA1	Bell 58 (X-1B)	OH55
		Bell 60 (X-5)	OH55
Bell 26E Airacobra (P-39Q)	AZ30, CA85, 89, NY9, 35, TX23, 40, 91, VA17, 19, 35	Bell 65 ATV	VA19
		Bell 68 (X-14) (X-14A) (X-14B)	IN48
		Bell 200 (XH-33) (XV-3A)	OH55
Bell 26E Airacobra (P-39Q) (RP-39Q) (TP-39Q)	MI2, OH55	Bell 204	SC23
		Bell 204 (XH-40) (XHU-1)	AL36
Bell 26F Airacobra (P-39N)	CA89, 160	Bell 204 (YH-40) (YUH-1B)	VA32
Bell 27 Airacomet (XP-59A)	DC3	Bell 204 Iroquois (HU-1A) (UH-1A)	AL36, HI9, IL33, KY5, MN29, NC1, NY34, PA6, TX58, 144, VA34
Bell 27 Airacomet (YP-59A)	CA111		
Bell 27 Airacomet (P-59A)	CA85		
Bell 27 Airacomet (P-59B)	CA4, NE12, OH55	Bell 204 Iroquois (HU-1B) (UH-1B)	AL1, 36, CA62, 63, 137, 145, 157, CO4, FL79, GA15, 52, IA20, IL50, KY5, LA9, MI8, NV11, PA64, TX19, 62, 144, 147, VA34, WA40
Bell 30	NY8, VA19		
Bell 33 Kingcobra (P-63A)	CA160, GA21, ID15, OH71, TX40, VA17, 19		
Bell 33 Kingcobra (P-63A) (RP-63A)	CA110		
Bell 33 Kingcobra (P-63C)	FL23, OR4	Bell 204 Iroquois (UH-1B)	AL11, 17, 38, CA136, CT8, 9, GA6, 52, IN48, KY14, LA22, MD3, MI47, MN35, MO17, MT8, NC16, NM7, 11, NY13, OH57, OK1, 6, 17, OR3, PA44, SC10, 17, TX6, 16, 77, 128
Bell 33 Kingcobra (P-63E)	AZ30, OH55, TX23, VA17		
Bell 33 Kingcobra (P-63F)	TX40		
Bell 33 Kingcobra (RP-63G) (QF-63G)	TX147		
Bell 44 (XS-1) (X-1)	DC3		
Bell 44 (XS-1) (X-1) (FSM)	CA4, 29, 111, 115, KS20, NY55	Bell 204 Iroquois (HU-1E) (UH-1E) (NUH-1E)	FL55
Bell 44 (XS-1) (X-1) (X-1E)	CA99	Bell 204 Iroquois (TH-1F)	TX101
Bell 47	NY13, 35	Bell 204 Iroquois (TH-1L)	CA58, FL72, 83, GA6, MD19, PA4, TX69
Bell 47A Sioux (YR-13) (YH-13)	SD9		
Bell 47B	AK7, PA4, VA19		
Bell 47B-3	CA37, NY35	Bell 204 Iroquois (HU-1C) (UH-1C) (UH-1M)	CA10
Bell 47D (HTL-2)	AZ30, CA116		
Bell 47D Sioux (H-13B)	AL36	Bell 204 Iroquois (UH-1C)	AR15, CA97, GA2, 34, IL37, IN22, MI47, NY41
Bell 47D Sioux (H-13B) (H-13C)	AL36		
Bell 47D-1	NY49		
Bell 47D-1 (B-3)	AZ22	Bell 204 Iroquois (UH-1C) (UH-1M)	AL28, 36, AR7, 16, 19, AZ4, 30, CA16, 33, 78, 100, 115, 128, CO2, 9, CT7, FL45, 76, GA2, 6, HI11, IA3, 27, 38, ID7, IL16, 42, 62, KS9, MA3, 15, MD5, MI38, MT6, NC1, 29, 31, NE14, NJ21, NM26, NY16, 21, PA3, 34, 41, 57, 62, RI1, SC1, 18, TX138, UT1, 9, VA35, WA13, WI63
Bell 47D-1 (HTL-5)	IL66		
Bell 47D-1 Sioux (H-13D) (OH-13D)	CA122, PA4, TX148		
Bell 47D-1 Sioux (H-13E) (OH-13E)	AL36, AZ46, CA26, 160, CT9, GA2, MT14, NJ3, NM12, OK1, OR7, TX58, 104, 127, 144, VA34, VT7, WA25		
Bell 47D-1 Sioux (HTL-4) (TH-13L)	CA50, FL55, VA22, WA11		
Bell 47E (HTL-3)	OR7		
Bell 47G	MD14, MN32, OH18, 24, 71, TX40, 65, WA16, 38	Bell 204 Iroquois (UH-1E)	MA4, VA22
		Bell 204 Iroquois (XH-48A) (UH-1F)	AZ30
Bell 47G Sioux (H-13G) (OH-13G)	CA38, 58, FL61, MN29, NJ20, 21, OH34, PA26, WI8	Bell 204 Iroquois (UH-1F)	CA85, GA45, MO48, MT7, NC42, ND11, 20, NM12, OH55, SD7, WY9
Bell 47G Sioux (HTL-6) (TH-13M)	FL22, 55, GA45		
Bell 47G-2	AZ21,CA32, 37, FL16, NY13, WI17	Bell 204 Iroquois (UH-1F) (UH-1P)	FL36, GA45, OH55
		Bell 204 Iroquois (HH-1K)	CA143, FL55, IN20, MI18, WA28
Bell 47G-2 Sioux (H-13H) (OH-13H)	AL39, CT2, IN33, KS26, MT8, 14, NM7, OR19, SD7	Bell 205 Iroquois (YHU-1D) (YUH-1D) (UH-1D)	AL36, TX148
Bell 47G-2A	CA37	Bell 205 Iroquois (HU-1D) (UH-1D) (UH-1H)	MO24, NY44
Bell 47G-3B Sioux (OH-13S)	CA58, TX3		

Bell 205 Iroquois (UH-1D) AR19, CA33, FL24, GA29, KS26, SC18, TX58, WI62
Bell 205 Iroquois (UH-1D) (UH-1H) AK3, 5, AL4, 8, 10, 31, 36, 39, AR19, AZ30, CA53, 63, 70, 81, 137, CO2, 15, 19, 21, CT5, 11, DC4, FL9, 30, 56, GA6, 11, 48, IA10, 16, 24, 28, ID14, IL7, 13, 26, 62, 74, IN1, 29, 33, 48, KS6, 9, 14, 15, 22, 25, 28, LA5, 12, 14, 16, 22, 26, ME1, 3, 5, 6, MI17, 31, 42, 43, 48, 57, 58, MN27, MO7, 18, MS2, MT12, NC6, 23, 29, 32, ND2, NE14, NJ5, NM23, NY9, 21, 35, 38, 47, 64, 80, 82, OH7, 22, 32, 33, 38, 77, OK18, 31, OR7, PA22, 24, 31, 51, 59, RI1, SC7, 13, 23, TN15, 30, TX63, 72, 99, 104, 131, 138, 142, 147, 148, 150, VA19, 30, 32, VT7, WA9, WI58, 62, WV3, WY3
Bell 205 Iroquois (UH-1D) (UH-1S) MI22
Bell 205 Iroquois (UH-1D) (UH-1V) AL9, FL56, 80, NY5, 43, PA7, WA9
Bell 205 Iroquois (HH-1H) AR15, AZ1, TX83, UT5
Bell 205 Iroquois (UH-1H) AK2, 6, 9, 16, AL3, 6, 7, 11, 21, 26, 27, 32, 34, 36, 37, 38, AR2, 13, 22, AZ6, 19, CA3, 16, 46, 63, 100, 107, 109, 113, 119, 121, 125, 135, 143, CO25, 31, DE1, 3, 4, 10, FL6, 9, 29, 32, 60, GA5, 6, 10, 14, 15, 18, 22, 57, HI1, 6, 10, IA18, ID3, 5, 7, IL2, 33, 35, 38, 39, 51, 53, 57, 58, 62, 66, 71, IN1, 6, 13, 20, 22, 27, 39, 45, 51, KS1, 30, 38, KY5, 7, 10, LA2, 9, 21, MA10, MD16, ME4, MI1, 3, 4, 5, 10, 19, 30, 34, 51, 53, 54, MN5, 16, 22, 23, 29, 32, 41, MO27, 39, 43, MS2, 6, 13, 15, 18, 25, 29, MT14, NC3, 5, 25, 29, 39, ND8, 17, 19, 21, NE9, NE 14, 15, 19, 20, NH3, NJ11, 20, NV1, 19, 22, NY17, 18, 25, 37, 42, 79, 82, OH5, 6, 29, 41, 52, 54, 63, 75, 80, OR5, 18, 19, 23, PA15, 45, 55, 57, 58, RI2, SC1, 3, 13, TX6, 40, 41, 42, 46, 52, 58, 68, 96, 98, 104, 112, 121, 139, 141, 144, UT3, VA10, 23, 32, 34, VT6, WA4, 11, 13, 25, 28, WI8, 15, 56, WY2, 5
Bell 205 Iroquois (UH-1H) (EH-1X) NJ21
Bell 205 Iroquois (UH-1H) (JUH-1H) AZ23, CA100
Bell 205 Iroquois (UH-1H) (UH-1V) AK12, AL12, FL20, GA6, 36, 53, IA3, IN36, KY8, MI41, MO24, ND1, NY1, 15, 59,

Bell 205 Iroquois (UH-1H) (UH-1V) (continued) OK13, 23, PA2, 26, 37, 39, 60, TX58, 92, 140, VA36, WA28, WI16
Bell 206 Jet Ranger IN53, TX98
Bell 206 Kiowa (YHO-4A) (YOH-4A) AL36
Bell 206A Jet Ranger IL66, PA4, TX107
Bell 206A Kiowa (OH-58A) AL4, 36, AZ30, 38, CA157, CO2, CT5, DE6, FL9, 32, HI11, IA25, ID6, IL62, KS22, 28, KY2, 3, 6, LA5, MN29, MS10, 26, NC6, OH34, 48, OK1, 3, OR16, 21, RI1, SC1, SD4, TN25, TX66, 127, 138, 142, VA32, WA9, 11
Bell 206A Kiowa (OH-58A) (OH-58C) AR23, CA104, 110, 157, CO21, FL83, KS23, KY5, LA9, MI29, MS12, NY1, PA49, TX58, 63, UT10, WA9, WI62
Bell 206A Kiowa (OH-58A) (OH-58D) AL36
Bell 206A Kiowa (OH-58D) VA32
Bell 206A Sea Ranger (TH-57A) FL55, 83, OR21
Bell 206A Sea Ranger (TH-57C) FL55, HI3
Bell 206B Jet Ranger AK6, CA63, ID2, MT13, OR7
Bell 206L-1 Long Ranger DC3
Bell 207 Sioux Scout AL36
Bell 209 Huey Cobra (AH-1G) AL36, 38, GA2, 45, TX58
Bell 209 Huey Cobra (AH-1G) (AH-1F) AL8, 16, 20, 28, 33, 36, AR4, 6, 8, 24, AZ23, 38, 39, 48, CA16, 85, 91, 100, 135, CO18, 19, 30, CT3, 5, 10, 12, FL6, 17, 32, 59, 66, GA1, 4, 6, 25, HI9, IA32, ID7, IL13, 34, 40, 62, 75, IN25, KS4, 34, KY2, 4, 16, MI9, 11, 13, 53, MN17, 20, 29, 31, 38, MO46, NC10, 25, 35, ND16, NE10, 25, NJ6, 11, 18, 21, 27, 28, NY10, 11, 20, 28, 30, 35, 40, 43, 51, 64, 69, OH30, 44, 50, 54, 63, 66, 69, 85, OR7, PA4, 5, 9, 10, 11, 16, 40, 45, 50, RI2, SC6, 8, 14, TN9, 13, 23, 29, 31, TX16, 61, 78, 117, 137, 142, VA3, 5, 32, WA41, WI6, 7, 20, 26, 29, 41, 43, 44, 54, 57, WV1
Bell 209 Huey Cobra (AH-1G) (AH-1Q) (AH-1S) AL36, AZ1, 4, 30, CO21, CT9, MI38, MS2, TX144, UT3
Bell 209 Huey Cobra (AH-1G) (AH-1S) AL32, 36, 39, AR2, 7, 19, AZ38, CA2, 60, 110, 134, CO3, 21, FL55, 78, GA6, 34, HI6, 11, IA6, 19, 22, 24, 31, IL27, 28, 33, KS26, 28, KY5, 15, LA9, 28, MA1, 3, MD20, MI22, 30, 45, MN4, 16, MO1, 8, 11, 24, 29, 30, 39, MT6, NC29, NJ3, 20, NY1, 6, 34, 66, OH3, 32, 48, 62, 65, OK3, PA14, 32, 36, 57, 59, RI1, TX19, 40, 58, 82,

Index

Bell 209 Huey Cobra (AH-1G) (AH-1S)	138, 150, VA10, 32, WI1, 9, 13, 14, 19, 25, 28, 30, 33, 39, 45, 52, 56, 61, 62	Benoist 14 (R)	FL22, 68
		Benoist Biplane	IA36
		Benoist-Korn	VA19
		Bensen B-2 Gyroglider	NC40
Bell 209 Huey Cobra (AH-1G) (TAH-1F)	FL55	Bensen B-6 Gyroglider	NE12, NY16, VA19
		Bensen B-7 Gyroglider	IN3
Bell 209 Huey Cobra (AH-1S)	VA23	Bensen B-7M Gyrocopter	IN3, NE12
Bell 209 Huey Cobra (AH-1S) (AH-1E)	AZ26, CA122, MO47, NC1, NY58, TX84, 149, WA28	Bensen B-8 Gyroglider	CA111, IN3, KY2, PA56, RI1
		Bensen B-8 Gyroglider (X-25B)	CA4
Bell 209 Huey Cobra (AH-1S) (AH-1F)	AL28, 36, CO2, 21, GA6, IL10, MA5, MO48, NE15, NJ14, NY1, 3, 22,	Bensen B-8M Gyrocopter	AK3, AL32, AR2, CA37, 39, 85, 158, CT9, FL23, GA45, ID26, IN3, MO25, NC27, NJ3, NM20, NY16, OH53, 59, OR7, 21, PA4, 35, 56, VA19, WA25
Bell 209 Huey Cobra (AH-1S) (AH-1P)	LA9, NY1, SC2, 6, WA9, 13		
Bell 209 Huey Cobra (AH-1S) (AH-1P) (TAH-1P)	WA28		
Bell 209 Sea Cobra (AH-1J)	AZ1, CA30, 58, FL55, 58, 63, IL57, LA18, MD19, MI2, NC6, NY34, SC18, VA22	Bensen B-8M Gyrocopter (X-25A)	OH55
		Bensen B-9 Little Zipster	IN3
		Bensen B-11M Kopter-Kart	WI17
		Berkshire Concept 70	NY50
Bell 209 Sea Cobra (AH-1T) (AH-1W)	KS26, VA22	Berliner 5 Helicopter	MD7
		Bertelson Aeromobile	MD15
Bell 212	ID2	Bierman 1600R Eros	CA105
Bell 212 Iroquois (UH-1N)	CA30, FL58	Bilstrom and Jucewick BJ-1 Glider	OK43
Bell 212 Iroquois (UH-1N) (HH-1N)	AL37, AZ48, NV11	BJ Sportster (Piper J-3C-65 Cub modified)	MT9
Bell 214J	IL66		
Bell 214ST	CA58	Blanchard Balloon (FSM)	CT9
Bell 222	IL66	Blériot XI	CA15, CT9, DC3, FL55, IA36, MI25, NY14, 63, OH55
Bell 222 (FSM)	TN33		
Bell 301 (XV-15)	VA19		
Bell 309 King Cobra	AL36	Blériot XI (R)	AL36, CA122, 130, CO25, IA13, MA4, MD7, ME7, NV23, NY7, OK40, OR7, TX92, 114, 135, VA17, WA34, WI24
Bell 409 (YAH-63A)	AL36		
Bell D2127 (X-22A)	NY35		
Bell Jet Flying Belt	MD15, VA34		
Bell Rocket Belt	CA65		
Bell-Boeing V-22A Osprey	NC21, NY82, PA4		
Bellanca Monoplane (R)	NY14	Blériot XI (Scale R)	OH59
Bellanca CF	VA19	Blohm und Voss Bv 155B	MD15
Bellanca CH-300 Pacemaker	AK3	Bloomquist Staggerwing	TN5
Bellanca CH-400 Skyrocket	PA17	Bobcat Ultralight	PA56
Bellanca CH-400 Skyrocket (CH-300 Pacemaker)	VA36	Boeing B & W (R)	WA25
		Boeing 6 B-1	WA35
Bellanca 14-9L Crusair	NC6	Boeing 40A (R)	WA25
Bellanca 14-13 Crusair Senior	IL18, WA19	Boeing 40B (R)	WA25
Bellanca 14-13-2 Crusair Senior	AZ30, KS26, MD15, VA13, WA8	Boeing 40B-4	IL45, MI25, WA32
		Boeing 40C	OR24
Bellanca 14-13-3 Crusair Senior	PA12	Boeing 67 Hawk (FB-5)	CA111, 122, VA19
Bellanca 14-19 Cruisemaster	GA12	Boeing 80A	WA25
Bellanca 14-19-2 Cruisemaster	ID1, MI14, WA19, 43	Boeing 99 (F4B-1) (R)	CA7, TN5
Bellanca 14-19-3 260	KS26	Boeing 100	FL22, WA25
Bellanca 14-19-3A Cruisemaster	IA39	Boeing 100 (R)	FL22
Bellanca 14-19-3M Cruisemaster	IN57	Boeing 102 (P-12B) (R)	FL22
Bellanca 17-30A Super Viking	AZ7, NJ25, OR11	Boeing 222 (P-12C) (R)	FL22
Bellanca 17-31ATC Super Viking	CA160	Boeing 234 (P-12E)	CA111, OH55
Bellanca 31-42 Pacemaker	MN18	Boeing 234 (P-12E) (R)	CA85
Bellanca 31-42 Senior Pacemaker	AK3	Boeing 235 (F4B-2) (R)	FL22
Bellanca 66-75 Aircruiser	OR21	Boeing 235 (F4B-3) (R)	NC17
Bellanca 7GCBC Citabria	IL63, ND24, VA13, WI22, WY10	Boeing 235 (F4B-4)	DC3
		Boeing 235 (F4B-4) (FSM)	FL55
Bellanca 7KCAB Citabria	CA95, NC40	Boeing 235 (F4B-4) (R)	CA122
Bellanca 8GCBC Scout	IL18, TN5	Boeing 235 (F4B-4) (Scale R)	FL55
Bellanca 8KCAB Decathlon	AL32, CA130, FL86, ID2, IL20	Boeing 247D	DC3
		Boeing 247D (247)	WA25
Bennett Delta Wing 162 Hang Glider	VA19	Boeing 251 (P-12F)	FL55
Bennett Delta Wing Mariah M-9 Hang Glider	VA19	Boeing 266 Pea Shooter (P-26A)	CA111, VA19
		Boeing 266 Pea Shooter (P-26A) (R)	CA122, OH55
Bennett Delta Wing Phoenix 6 Hang Glider	VA19	Boeing 266 Pea Shooter (P-26D) (R)	VA17
		Boeing 299H Fortress (B-17D) (RB-17D)	OH55
Bennett Delta Wing Phoenix 6B Hang Glider	VA19		
		Boeing 299-O Fortress (B-17E) (XC-108A)	IL36
Bennett Delta Wing Phoenix Streak 130 Hang Glider	VA19		
		Boeing 299-O Fortress (B-17E)	AZ30, OH9, WA12
Bennett Delta Wing Phoenix Viper 175 Hang Glider	VA19	Boeing 299-O Fortress (B-17F)	GA43

Index

Boeing 299-O Fortress (B-17F) (RB-17F) — NE18
Boeing 299-O Fortress (B-17F) (RB-17F) (TB-17F) — WA25
Boeing 299-O Fortress (B-17F) (TB-17F) — OH55
Boeing 299-O Fortress (B-17G) — GA37, 43, LA17, OH55, OR2, TX92, VA19, WI17
Boeing 299-O Fortress (B-17G) (B-17H) (TB-17H) (SB-17G) — FL22
Boeing 299-O Fortress (B-17G) (CB-17G) (VB-17G) — CA84, NY74
Boeing 299-O Fortress (B-17G) (CB-17G) (VB-17G) (CB-17G) (VB-17G) — CA85, OR7
Boeing 299-O Fortress (B-17G) (DB-17G) — FL22
Boeing 299-O Fortress (B-17G) (DB-17G) (DB-17P) — CA111, FL22, IN20, NE23
Boeing 299-O Fortress (B-17G) (DB-17G) (EDB-17G) (DB-17G) — CA11
Boeing 299-O Fortress (B-17G) (EDB-17G) (DB-17G) (DB-17P) — TX51
Boeing 299-O Fortress (B-17G) (MB-17G) (TB-17G) (DB-17G) (DB-17P) — DE1
Boeing 299-O Fortress (B-17G) (PB-1G) — AZ2, MI58
Boeing 299-O Fortress (B-17G) (PB-1W) — FL76, LA7, TX29, 40
Boeing 299-O Fortress (B-17G) (RB-17G) (DB-17G) (DB-17P) — AZ11, TX40
Boeing 299-O Fortress (B-17G) (TB-17G) — TX147, UT5
Boeing 299-O Fortress (B-17G) (TB-17G) (EB-17G) (ETB-17G) (TB-17G) — CA32
Boeing 299-O Fortress (B-17G) (TB-17G) (ETB-17G) (JTB-17G) — VA17
Boeing 299-O Fortress (B-17G) (TB-17G) (VB-17G) — CA110
Boeing 299-O Fortress (B-17G) (TB-17H) (SB-17G) — MA4
Boeing 299-O Fortress (B-17G) (VB-17G) — FL22
Boeing 299-O Fortress (299-O) (299-Z) (B-17G) — GA37
Boeing 299Z Fortress (299-O) (B-17G) (EB-17G) (JB-17G) — OH15
Boeing S-307 Stratoliner — VA19
Boeing 345 Superfortress (B-29) — CA32, 133, FL22, NM5, 14, OH55, OK41, VA19, WA25
Boeing 345 Superfortress (B-29) (P2B-1S) — FL22
Boeing 345 Superfortress (B-29) (SB-29) — CA139, FL22
Boeing 345 Superfortress (B-29) (TB-29) — AZ30, GA24, KS18, LA7, NE23
Boeing 345 Superfortress (B-29) (TB-29) (B-29M) (KB-29B) — SD7
Boeing 345 Superfortress (B-29A) — CO25, OH55, TX40, 147, UT5
Boeing 345 Superfortress (B-29A) (F-13A) (FB-29A) (RB-29A) — GA29
Boeing 345 Superfortress (B-29A) (SB-29) — CA85, MO48
Boeing 345 Superfortress (B-29A) (TB-29A) — CT9, GA45
Boeing 345 Superfortress (B-29B) (KB-29P) — AK11
Boeing 345 Superfortress (B-29B) (TB-29B) — GA45
Boeing 345-2-1 Superfortress (B-29D) (B-50A) — CA111
Boeing 345-9-6 Superfortress (B-50D) (JB-50D) (WB-50D) — OH55
Boeing 345-9-6 Superfortress (B-50D) (KB-50J) — AZ30, DE1, FL48
Boeing 345-9-6 Superfortress (B-50D) (WB-50D) — CA32
Boeing 367-76-29 Stratofreighter (KC-97F) — OH71
Boeing 367-76-66 Stratofreighter (KC-97G) — AZ30, CA109, NC6, NE23, NJ4, WA24, WI12
Boeing 367-76-66 Stratofreighter (KC-97G) (C-97G) — AZ30, CA88, IL50
Boeing 367-76-66 Stratofreighter (KC-97G) (C-97K) — CA143
Boeing 367-76-66 Stratofreighter (KC-97G) (KC-97L) — CA32, 42, 71, 82, 85, CO5, DE1, GA45, IN20, LA7, MD15, MN27, MO48, MT7, OH55, OR12, TX51, WI62, WY6
Boeing 367-80 — VA19
Boeing 450-3-3 Stratojet (XB-47) — IL50
Boeing 450-10-9 Stratojet (B-47A) — AZ30
Boeing 450-11-10 Stratojet (B-47B) (TB-47B) — GA43
Boeing 450-67-27 Stratojet (B-47B) — CA4, IN20, MO48
Boeing 450-157-35 Stratojet (B-47E) — AR15, CA32, 85, KS37, LA7, NE23, NY60, OH55, OK3
Boeing 450-157-35 Stratojet (B-47E) (EB-47E) — AZ30, OH55, TX51
Boeing 450-157-35 Stratojet (B-47E) (FSM) — CA85
Boeing 450-157-35 Stratojet (B-47E) (JB-47E) — OH55
Boeing 450-157-35 Stratojet (B-47E) (NB-47E) — CO25
Boeing 450-157-35 Stratojet (B-47E) (WB-47E) — KS18, UT5, WA25
Boeing 450-158-36 Stratojet (RB-47E) — OK41
Boeing 450-171-51 Stratojet (RB-47H) — FL76, OH55
Boeing 464-201-0 Stratofortress (B-52A) (NB-52A) — AZ30
Boeing 464-201-3 Stratofortress (B-52B) — OH71
Boeing 464-201-3 Stratofortress (RB-52B) — CO32, NE23, NM14
Boeing 464-201-3 Stratofortress (RB-52B) (NB-52B) — CA4, 99
Boeing 464-201-7 Stratofortress (B-52D) — AL24, 35, 37, AZ13, 30, CA4, 32, 85, 139, CO28, FL50, GA45, IL50, KS18, LA7, MI28, 58, MO48, OH55, OK41, SD7, TX51, 76, 123, 147, WA2
Boeing 464-253 Stratofortress (B-52G) — AZ1, 30, FL76, LA7, ND11, 20, NE18, NY26, TX123, UT5, VA31, WA2, 25
Boeing 464-259 Stratofortress (B-52E) — CA85, HI6
Boeing 464-260 Stratofortress (B-52F) — CA68, 160
Boeing 464-261 Stratofortress (B-52H) — TX123
Boeing 541 Scout (YL-15) — AL36
Boeing 707 — WA14
Boeing 707-153 (VC-137A) (VC-137B) — AZ30, WA25
Boeing 707-353B (VC-137C) — CA118
Boeing 707-353B (VC-137C) (C-137C) — OH55

Index

Boeing 707-355C (EC-137D)	AZ1	Boeing 747-136	CA65
Boeing 707-458	NY14	Boeing 747-151	DC3
Boeing 717-100A Stratotanker (KC-135A)	CA32, 85	Boeing 767-232	GA23
Boeing 717-100A Stratotanker (KC-135A) (EC-135K)	KS37	Boeing 787	WA14
		Boeing 953 (YC-14A)	AZ1, 30
Boeing 717-100A Stratotanker (KC-135A) (JKC-135A) (NKC-135A)	OH55	Boeing 2707-300 SST (Mock Up)	CA65
		Boeing Bird of Prey	OH55
		Boeing Condor	CA65
Boeing 717-146 Stratotanker (KC-135A)	AZ30, CA4, IL64, LA7, ND11, TX51	Boeing X-32A	OH55
		Boeing X-32B	MD19
Boeing 717-146 Stratotanker (KC-135A) (EC-135A)	NE18, SD7	Boeing X-40A	OH55
		Boeing X-45A	DC3, OH55
Boeing 717-146 Stratotanker (KC-135A) (KC-135E)	AR15, IL64, KS18, TX123	Boeing X-46A	OH55
		Boeing-Sikorsky RAH-66 Comanche	AL36
Boeing 717-146 Stratotanker (KC-135A) (EC-135K)	AZ1	Boeing-Stearman 75 Kaydet (PT-13)	CA149, GA17
		Boeing-Stearman A75 Kaydet (PT-13A)	OH12, WA25
Boeing 717-146 Stratotanker (KC-135A) (EC-135L)	IN20	Boeing-Stearman A75 Kaydet (PT-13B)	CA66, 90, KS10, MO15, OR24, TX16
Boeing 717-148 Stratotanker (KC-135A)	OK3	Boeing-Stearman A75L3 Kaydet (B75N1) (N2S-3)	NH5
Boeing 717-148 Stratotanker (KC-135A)	TX56	Boeing-Stearman A75N1 Kaydet (N2S-1)	FL34, NH5, TX36
Boeing 717-148 Stratotanker (KC-135A) (KC-135E)	AK11, DE1, IL64, KS28, NE15, NH10, NJ17, TX123, 147, UT5, WA2	Boeing-Stearman A75N1 Kaydet (N2S-4)	CA130, FL38, IL72, NM6, TX16
		Boeing-Stearman A75N1 Kaydet (PT-17)	AL32, AR2, AZ24, 30, CA17, 32, 85, 91, 96, 130, CT9, DE1, FL22, 53, GA12, 45, 58, IL18, 63, IN25, 28, 48, KY2, LA22, 27, MA4, MD7, ME7, MO1, 36, MT9, NC6, 24, NH5, NJ7, 21, NM24, NY52, OH55, OR21, 24, PA35, TX8, 25, 32, 40, 65, UT5, VA13, 17
Boeing 717-157 Stratolifter (C-135A)	CA4		
Boeing 717-157 Stratolifter (C-135A) (EC-135N)	GA45		
Boeing 717-157 Stratolifter (C-135A) (EC-135N) (EC-135E)	OH55		
Boeing 717-158 Stratolifter (C-135B) (C-135C)	CA4		
Boeing 717-158B Stratolifter (C-135B) (WB-135B) (C-135B) (C-135C)	OK41		
Boeing 717-166 Stratotanker (KC-135B) (EC-135C)	AZ1, NE23	Boeing-Stearman A75N1 Kaydet (PT-17) (N2S-4)	AZ11, VA13
Boeing 717-166 Stratotanker (KC-135B) (EC-135C) (EC-135J)	AZ30	Boeing-Stearman B75 Kaydet (N2S-2)	CA111, FL42, NY7
Boeing 720-023B	CA82	Boeing-Stearman B75N1 Kaydet (N2S-3)	AL36, CA7, 17, 67, 110, 122, 130, FL55, GA43, 59, HI6, ID2, 8, 15, MD14, MO15, ND24, NJ21, NY7, 82, OH74, SC18, TX26, 40, 92, UT4, VA9, 13, 35
Boeing 727	AK3, CA96, IL69, NY72, TX65		
Boeing 727-14	MN32		
Boeing 727-22	AZ1, CA126, DC3, TN8, WA25		
Boeing 727-22F	AR23, CA147, FL7, GA27, IN46, LA22, NC15, NM7, OH61, TX74, WA4	Boeing-Stearman Custom 450 (B75N1) Kaydet (N2S-3))	CA7
		Boeing-Stearman D75N1 Kaydet (PT-27)	CA130, MT13, NY78, PA29, TX151, WA31
Boeing 727-22QC	AL25, OH24	Boeing-Stearman E75 Kaydet (PT-13B)	CA91
Boeing 727-24C	NY52		
Boeing 727-25F	FL25, TN34, WA11		
Boeing 727-25QC	AR18, MI2, NY45, TN25, WA14	Boeing-Stearman E75 Kaydet (PT-13D)	AZ11, 33, CA3, 67, 90, 110, 111, CO25, FL42, MI2, MN18, MS19, OH55, TX8, 37, 87, WA32
Boeing 727-81	OK23		
Boeing 727-100	IL45		
Boeing 727-116C	AZ31		
Boeing 727-173C	KS18	Boeing-Stearman E75 Kaydet (PT-13D) (N2S-5)	CA15, FL73, 83, GA52, IL43, ND8, NJ21, NM6, NY32, OR7, PA17, TX28, 34, 40, 92, UT2, VA13, 19, WA16, WI17
Boeing 727-200	GA47, IA27, MN32		
Boeing 727-214	OK46		
Boeing 727-223	WA25		
Boeing 727-277F	IA27		
Boeing 727-284	OR8		
Boeing 727-287A	AZ31	Boeing-Vertol 237 (YUH-61A)	AL36
Boeing 737-130	WA25	Boeing-Vertol 347 (Vertol V.114 (CH-47A))	AL36
Boeing 737-200-2H4	KS18, TX69		
Boeing 737-201	WA25	Boeing-Vertol BV.360	PA4
Boeing 737-222	CA65, IL38, 66, IN53	Bogardus Little Gee Bee	VA19
Boeing 737-253 (T-43)	AZ1, TX119	Boland Albatross Hot Air Balloon	VT3
Boeing 737-290C	AK3	Boland Ax.1-5 Hot Air Balloon	VT3
Boeing 737-293	MD4	Boland Ax.8 Hot Air Balloon	VT3
Boeing 737-2H4	AR25	Boland Baggage Hot Air Balloon	VT3
Boeing 747-121	WA25	Boland Fred Hot Air Balloon	VT3
Boeing 747-132C	OR7	Boland Hot Air Balloon	VA15
		Boland Mong Biplane	CA111

Boland Overseas Hot Air Balloon	VT3	Bücker Bü 133L Jungmeister (Bü 133C)	WI17
Boland Phoenix Hot Air Balloon	VT3		
Boland Rover Hot Air Balloon	VT3	Bücker Bü 133S Jungmeister	TX69
Boland/Raven RX.6 Hot Air Balloon	VT3	Bücker Bü 181B-1 Bestmann	VA19
Bölkow BO 102B Helitrainer	CA37	Bücker Bü 181B-1 Bestmann (Sk 25)	GA17
Bölkow BO 105 (FSM)	PA21	Buckeye 582 Dream Machine	WI17
Bölkow BO 105C	PA4, 44	Bud Light Spirit of Freedom	DC3
Bölkow BO 208A-1 Junior	IA1	Budd BB-1	PA21
Bölkow Phoebus C	NY50	Budd RB-1 Conestoga	AZ30
Bölkow Phoebus C-1	CA158	Bugatti 100	WI17
Bounsall Prospector	IA1	Buhl Autogyro	CA65
Bowers Fly Baby 1A	AK16, AZ30, CA128, 158, KS26, ND2, OH18, 59, 64, WA25	Buhl CA-3D/E Airsedan	MN18
		Buhl LA-1 Flying Bull Pup	CA17, 64, OH53, OR24
		Bureau of Standards Bat	CA111
Bowers Fly Baby 1A Biplane	NY16	Burgess H (R)	TX92, 136
Bowlus Albatross SP-1 (R)	CA122	Burgess Scale P-51D	OH40
Bowlus BA-100 Baby Albatross	CA154, 158, IL80, NY50, PA56, VA19, WA25, 34	Burgess-Curtiss Shoemaker Biplane	MD15
		Burgess-Wright F	UT5
		Burnelli CBY-3 Loadmaster (Cancargo)	CT9
Bowlus BA-102-2 Senior Albatross	NY50		
Bowlus BS-100 Super Albatross	CA158, NM20, NY50	Bushby-Long M-1 Midget Mustang	IL18, NC6, PA35
Bowlus S-1,000	CA158	Bushby M.II Mustang II	AL32, AZ30, KS26
Bowlus-Dupont 1-S-2100 Falcon	VA19	Bushmaster 2000	MN18
Boyce-Maynard MB-2	VA15	Butler Blackhawk	MO35
Boyd C2	MD7	Byfield HTH-1	PA61
Brantly B.2	AZ42	Callair A-2	MN18, WA37
Brantly B.2 (YHO-3)	AL36	Callair A-3	ND5, WY1
Brantly B.2B	CA107, PA4	Callair A-4	CA111
Brantly 305	AZ42, CA37	Callair A-6	WY1
Breese Penguin	NY14	Callair A-9B	ND23
Breese Penguin (R)	CA7, 158, KS22, NV23	Callair B-1	IA1
Breeze Bee	OR13	Callair B-1A	WY1
Breguet Biplane	NY63	Cameron A-105 Hot Air Balloon	FL22
Breitling Orbiter 3	DC3	Cameron AT-165 Hot Air Balloon	NM2
Brewster B.239 Buffalo	FL55	Cameron Hot Air Balloon	FL55
Brewster B.239 Buffalo (F2A-2) (R)	NY14	Cameron O-65 Hot Air Balloon	IA29
Brewster B.340 Buccaneer (SB2A-2)	FL55	Cameron O-105 Hot Air Balloon	VT3
Brewster B.340 Buccaneer (SB2A-4)	FL55	Cameron R-36 Gas Balloon	NM2
Brewster B.340E Bermuda	AZ30	Cameron V-65 Hot Air Balloon	NM2
Brewster Fleet B-1 (Fleet 16F)	IA1	Cameron V-77 Hot Air Balloon	VT3
Briegleb BG-7	NY16	Cameron Z-105 Hot Air Airship	IA29
Briegleb BG-12A	ND2	Campbell CSG-1	NM20
Briegleb BG-12ABD	NY50	Canadair CL-13 Sabre 2 [North American F-86E]	IL67
Briegleb BG-12B	CA88, NM20		
Briegleb BG-12BD	FL23	Canadair CL-13A Sabre 5 [North American F-86E]	AZ30, CA68, 112, 160, ID24, LA8, TX16, WA2, WI17
Briegleb BG-12B-GT	PA35		
Bristol Boxkite (R)	TN6		
Bristol 14 F.2B Fighter	TX114	Canadair CL-13B Sabre 6 (CL-13A Sabre 5) [North American F-86E]	WA25
Bristol 14 F.2B Fighter (R)	AZ33, CA111, TX114		
Bristol 20 M.1C (R)	NY63	Canadair CL-13B Sabre 6 [North American F-86E]	CA63, 160, ID24, MI37, MT2, NC33, NM24, OK40, OR4, TX33, TX20, WA28
Bristol 149 Bolingbroke IVT	AZ30, CA89, FL22, TN6		
Bristol 156 Beaufighter IC	OH55		
British Aircraft Corporation 167 Strikemaster 80	TX34		
		Canadair CL-30 Silver Star 3 (CT-133) [Lockheed 580 (T-33AN)]	AZ11, CA63, 89, 111, FL73, MT2, NM8, 24, NV6, NY74, OH71, OK40, TN1, 33, TX151, WA17
British Aircraft Corporation 167 Strikemaster 84	NY23, WA28		
Brock KB-2	KS8		
Brock KB-2G	WI17	Canadair CL-41G-5 Tebuan	FL21, NC38
Brokaw BJ.520 Bullet	FL23	Canadair CL-90 Starfighter (CF-104) [Lockheed 683-04-12]	FL70
Brooks Balloon	CT9		
Brown B-1	FL86	Canadair CL-219-1A17 Freedom Fighter (CF-116) (CF-116D) (CF-5D) [Northrop N-156B]	TX91
Brown B-2 (R)	FL22		
Brown Miles and Atwood Special (R)	CA111, OH64		
Brown Star-Lite	NY21	Canadair CL-226 Freedom Fighter (NF-5B) [Northrop N-156B]	OK47
Brunner-Winkle Bird A	IL29, IN25, MO15, NY14, OR24, VA36		
		Canadair RJ-200	MO32
Brunner-Winkle Bird A-T (A)	PA35	Canadian Car & Foundry Harvard 4 [North American NA-186]	AK10, GA21, KS9, MN10, MT13, ND8, TX16, 23, 25, 29, 40, WA28
Brunner-Winkle Bird BK	CA160, IL29, 70, NY7		
Brunner-Winkle Bird CK	IL46, NY63, PA17, 23		
Brunner-Winkle Bird CK (BK)	OR24		
Bücker Bü 131B Jungmann	FL22	Canadian Car & Foundry Harvard 4 [North American NA-186 (T-6J)]	NV5
Bücker Bü 133 Jungmeister (R)	CA105, OK28, WI17		
Bücker Bü 133C Jungmeister	CA130, FL22, IN57, VA17, 19, 36	Cangie WC.1	CA122
		Caproni Ca.20	WA25
Bücker Bü 133D Jungmeister (Bü 133D)	CA17	Caproni Ca.36M (Ca.3 mod)	OH55

Index

Caquot Balloon	OH55	Cessna 150M Commuter	CA63, PA35
CASA 1.131E [Bücker Bü 131 Jungmann]	CA17, 130, MD14, TX59	Cessna 152	AR18, 20, 23, CA77, 94, 116, 137, FL45, GA45,
CASA 2.111B [Heinkel He 111H-16]	OH55, TX16, WA12		IL18, 26, 50, IN46,
CASA 352L [Junkers Ju 52/3m]	FL22, OH55, VA17, 19		KS12, KY9, MI36, 42,
Cascade Kasperwing 180B	MD15, NM20, WA25		MO19, 32, NC10,
Cassutt B Special	NY14		OK23, PA49, SC23,
Cassutt IIIM	AZ30, CA65, KY9, WI36		TX132, UT11
Caudron G.3 (R)	NY63	Cessna A152 Aerobat	VA19
Caudron G.4	VA19	Cessna 165 Airmaster	AZ33, KS26, TX21, 40,
Caudron C.460 (R)	CA151		WA43
Cavalier Mustang II (F-51D) (North American NA-109)	FL76	Cessna 170	ID14, IL70, MD14, PA12, WA4
Cavalier Mustang II (F-51D) (North American NA-122)	AZ10, CA111, ID15, MN27	Cessna 170A	IL82
		Cessna 170B	AZ9, CO4, IL18, NC40, NJ8, NY7, WA31
Cavalier Mustang II (F-51D) (North American NA-122) (Mustang IV)	TX92	Cessna 172	FL22, 45, IL39, IN53, MN32, MO15, NV14,
Cayley Glider (R)	CA122, ME7, TX92		NY14, OK35, UT10,
Centrair 101 (Convair 105 (L-13A))	AK3		WA8, WI8
Cessna CG-2	WA25, WI17	Cessna 172A	CA38, 160, NE26
Cessna AW	CA160, NE12, PA23	Cessna 172B	CA125
Cessna AW (BW)	IL70, 80	Cessna 172C	PA49
Cessna C-34 Airmaster	AK16, CA128, OR20	Cessna P172D	TN33
Cessna T-50 Bobcat (AT-17)	CA91	Cessna 172E	CA23, OK23
Cessna T-50 Bobcat (AT-17B) (UC-78B)	AK3, AZ11, 30, DE5, FL55, GA45, IA1, KS11, LA3, OH55, OR24, TX40, 92, 105	Cessna 172E Skyhawk	IL26
		Cessna R172E Mescalero (T-41B)	AL11, 36, CA63, FL24, GA6, NC24, OK17, PA44
Cessna T-50 Bobcat (AT-17D) (UC-78C)	AZ30	Cessna R172E Mescalero (T-41C)	SD4
Cessna T-50 Bobcat (C-78) (UC-78)	AK16, CA3, 32, 139, 160, IL29, IN25, KS26, MA4, OH71, PA35	Cessna 172F	AR23, IL60, OK23, VA17
		Cessna 172F Mescalero (T-41A)	CO28, IL62, IN20, MI29, OH55, OK7, 35, 48, SC22, TX119, WA4
Cessna T-50 Crane 1	TX36, 40	Cessna 172G	MA10, OK23, WA38
Cessna 120	AZ30, CA121, IL63, IN40, KS26, WA37	Cessna 172K	AR5, CA75, 89, HI10, KY9, MS12
Cessna 140	CA66, CO22, 29, ID1, 14, IL70, IN53, KS26, MD14, MN21, NY7, PA28, RI1, TX75, WA34	Cessna 172L	CA81
		Cessna 172L Skyhawk	PA35
		Cessna 172M	CA95, FL29, GA42, MI12, NV5, VA4
Cessna 140A	MN21, NM24, PA12	Cessna 172N	CA62, 107, 137, CO26, FL29, HI10, NC10, OK29, SC23, TX34, WA9
Cessna 145 Airmaster	KS26, WA34		
Cessna 150	CA123, 126, DC3, FL29, IL66, IN31, MD9, NJ7, OK35, OR19, PA33		
		Cessna 172P	AR21, FL29
Cessna 150A	FL29	Cessna 172R	MI12, 29, MS12
Cessna 150B	AZ21, OK36	Cessna 172RG	AZ7, CA137, TX141
Cessna 150C	MN21, TX153	Cessna 172S	CA137, TX98, 141
Cessna 150D	CA34, OH18	Cessna 175	KS26
Cessna 150E	WA38, WI8	Cessna 175B	CA64
Cessna 150F	AR20, 23, GA42, LA22, NC10, OH34, OK36, 45, WA38, WI36	Cessna 177B Cardinal	CA65, KS18
		Cessna 177RG Cardinal RG	OK29
		Cessna 180	CA67, 149, ID1, 8, IL63, OH37, TX18, VA19
Cessna 150G	AR20, 23, CA36, 62, 107, 149, DE7, FL7, 25, MA10, NC10, UT10		
		Cessna 180A	AK6
		Cessna 180B	MO32
Cessna 150H	CA38, 104, ID1, IN53, KS23, MD14, MI29, MN30, NC10, NY52, 76, WA19, WI17	Cessna 180F	OR21
		Cessna 180H Skywagon 180	WA34
		Cessna 180K Skywagon 180	OH58
		Cessna 182	ID14, OH53, UT10
Cessna 150J	AR20, CA34, 81, 125, 153, KS23, MI12, NJ29, NY52, OH21, TX141, 153, WA37, 39	Cessna R182 Skylane RG	WA9
		Cessna 182A	IA25, PA12
		Cessna 182B Skylane	WA33
		Cessna 182D	LA22
Cessna 150K	AL11	Cessna 182F	OR10
Cessna 150L	CA104, CT2, DE7, GA9, IL66, KS23, MI12, MS12, NC38, OK36, PA12	Cessna 182J	DC7
		Cessna 182J Skylane	CA95
		Cessna 182Q	GA28, 52
		Cessna 182Q Skylane II	ID8, MN18
Cessna 150L Commuter	AZ30, ND23, VA19	Cessna 185 Skywagon	ID1, WA32
Cessna A150L Aerobat	WI21	Cessna A185E Skywagon 185	WA37
Cessna 150M	AR5, 20, CA94, 123, 126, FL29, IA20, IL60, NC10, NJ29, NY74, OK36, OR19, WA39	Cessna A185F Skywagon 185	FL73
		Cessna A188B Agwagon 300	ID1
		Cessna 190	ID1, MI12, NY7
		Cessna 195	CA130, PA23

Cessna 195 (LC-126A)	OH55	Cessna 318B Tweety Bird (318A)	TX51, 66, 88, 119, 123,
Cessna 195 (LC-126B) (U-20B)	ND23	(T-37A) (T-37B) (*continued*)	UT5, WA2, 28
Cessna 195 (LC-126C) (U-20A)	AL36, TX75	Cessna 318B Tweety Bird (T-37B)	AZ1, 33, CA4, 137, 160,
Cessna 195A	AZ46, CA17, 114, ID1,		CO25, GA45, IA20,
	KS26, ND5, NY74, 78,		MI28, NM24, OK48,
	OK23		TX31, 61, 80, 113, 123,
Cessna 195B	AZ10, CA130, 139, KS26		127, UT5
Cessna 195B (190)	TX75	Cessna 318D Dragonfly (318A)	GA45, TX76
Cessna 205	CA123, WA11	(T-37A) (T-37B) (A-37A)	
Cessna 206 Super Skywagon	KS18	Cessna 318D Dragonfly (318C)	OH55, TX123
Cessna P206A Super Skylane	NE26	(T-37C) (YAT-37D) (YA-37A)	
Cessna U206B Super Skywagon	WI8	Cessna 318D Dragonfly (A-37A)	IN28
Cessna U206F Stationair	MN21	Cessna 318E Dragonfly (318A)	TX92
Cessna U206G Stationair 6	CA66	(T-37A) (T-37B) (A-37A)	
Cessna TU.206G Stationair	ID2, WI8	Cessna 318E Dragonfly (A-37B)	CA85, FL24, MT13,
Cessna 210	CA132, ID14, MO19,		NY82, WA28
	NY45, TX3, WI8	Cessna 318E Dragonfly (A-37B)	CA4, TX147
Cessna 210A	CA61	(NOA-37B)	
Cessna 210C	OK29	Cessna 318E Dragonfly (A-37B)	CA159, FL36, IL54,
Cessna 210E Centurion	NM7, OH24	(OA-37B)	PA64, TX83
Cessna T210G Turbo Centurion	TX132	Cessna 320C Skyknight	KY9, OH18
Cessna 210J Centurion	WI17	Cessna 321 Bird Dog (OE-2) (O-1C)	NJ21
Cessna 210N Centurion	OK19	Cessna 337 Super Skymaster	IN48, 53, VA17
Cessna 305 Bird Dog	CO27	Cessna 337A Super Skymaster	KS26, MS5, NY47
Cessna 305A Bird Dog	WA16	Cessna 337A Super Skymaster	CA85, KS18, TX147
Cessna 305A Bird Dog (L-19A)	FL42	(O-2B)	
Cessna 305A Bird Dog (L-19A)	AL24, 29, 36, AZ13, 24,	Cessna 337B Super Skymaster	AL32, MI36, RI1
(O-1A)	CA26, 43, 111, 145,	Cessna 337E Super Skymaster	IA12
	CT2, FL55, GA45, 58,	Cessna T337G Super Skymaster	OR19
	IL72, MI2, 57, MN3,	Cessna T337H Super Skymaster	ID2
	29, 32, NC6, 24, ND8,	Cessna 337M Super Skymaster	AK11, AL32, AZ1, 30,
	NH6, OK1, 17, OR16,	(O-2A)	CA32, 53, 81, 114, 126,
	19, TN1, VA19, 34		139, CO4, CT2, FL36,
			76, 80, GA45, 52, HI6,
Cessna 305A Bird Dog (L-19A)	CA17		IL50, 54, 62, IN20, 48,
(O-1A) (CO-119)			MA10, MI53, MN3,
Cessna 305B Bird Dog (TL-19D)	GA6		32, MS5, OH48, 55, 70,
(TO-1D)			OK46, RI1, SC13, 19,
Cessna 305C Bird Dog (L-19E)	CA84, 111, 114, FL36,		SD4, 7, TX51, 66, 139,
(O-1E)	ID5		UT5, 11, VA19, WA16,
Cessna 305D Bird Dog (305A)	OH55		WI21
(L-19A) (O-1A) (O-1G)		Cessna 401	OK29
Cessna 310	AL32, AR5, 23, AZ7,	Cessna 402	MI42, MN32
	CA107, 130, IA20,	Cessna 402B	WA9
	MI29, 42, NC15,	Cessna 402C	GA28, KS41
	NY45, OH46, OK36,	Cessna 404 Titan	CA116
	OR7	Cessna 411	NY52, OK29, WI21
Cessna 310A	MO32, PA49, SC23	Cessna 414	AR20, NE26
Cessna 310A Blue Canoe (L-27A)	AL36, AZ30, CA32, 36,	Cessna 421	FL29, ID14, NM7, SC23
(U-3A)	126, 139, CO32, DE1,	Cessna 421B Golden Eagle	CA62, KS23, WA39
	ID14, IN20, MI53,	Cessna 552 Citation II (T-47A)	OH24
	NM7, NY4, 37, 52, 76,	Cessna CH-1B Seneca (YH-41)	AL36
	OH55, OK1, SD7,	Chadwick C122S Helicopter	OR7
	TX3, 132, 141, 151,	Chalais-Meudon Airship	CT9
	UT5, WA11, WI35	Chambliss Kirby Z-Edge 540	WI7
Cessna 310B	CA38, IL57, MS20, PA49,	Chamberlin Monoplane	NY63
	TX23, 40, 132	Champion 7EC Traveler	AZ11, CA130, FL55,
Cessna 310C	AZ30, CA132, WA39		MD14, TX40
Cessna 310D	GA58, HI10, IA13, MS21	Champion 7ECA Citabria	CA130, NY16, WA34, 37,
Cessna 310E	AK6		WI23
Cessna 310F	KS18, UT10	Champion 7FC Traveler (7FC	IL30
Cessna 310G	WA19	Tri-Traveler)	
Cessna 310H	CA38, FL54	Champion 7FC Tri-Traveler	CA61, DE5, WA21
Cessna 310J	AR23, IL66	Champion 7GCAA	CA130, IN40
Cessna 310M Blue Canoe (310E)	GA45, IA18	Chandelle Standard	WI17
(L-27B) (U-3B)		Chanute Glider	NY21
Cessna 310Q	CA126, 137, OH24, OR19	Chanute Glider (R)	CA111, 122, CT9, GA45,
Cessna 310R	CA95, IN46		IL50, IN17, 30, KS5,
Cessna T310R	CO4, GA20		ME7, MT5, NY63,
Cessna 318 Tweety Bird (XT-37)	KS26		OH55, WI17
Cessna 318B Tweety Bird (318A)	AL32, 36, AR7, AZ30,	Chanute Triplane (R)	MT5
(T-37A) (T-37B)	CA53, 85, 109, 139,	Chanute-Herring Glider	NY50
	160, CO2, FL4, IN20,	Chanute-Herring Glider (R)	WA25
	KS18, MS4, NY73,	Chase Church JC-1 Midwing	WI17
	OH48, 55, OK16, 21,	Chengdu J-7 [Mikoyan-Gurevich	WI17
	33, 48, RI3, SC7,	MiG-21F-13]	

Index

Chester Goon	OH27	Consolidated 32 Liberator (B-24L)	MI35
Chester Special Jeep	WI17	Consolidated 32 Liberator (B-24M)	TX147
Chris-Tena Mini Coupe	IL18, OR21	(FSM)	
Christen Eagle I	TX69	Consolidated 32 Liberator (B-24M)	CA32
Christen Eagle 1F	WI17	(PB4Y-1)	
Christen Eagle II	CA65, 130, CO32, CT2, IL38, MI2, OR7, TX16, WI17	Consolidated 36 Peacemaker (YB-36) (YB-36A) (RB-36E)	OH71
		Consolidated 37 (XC-99)	OH55
Christofferson Biplane (R)	TX135	Consolidated 40 Privateer (PB4Y-2)	MI58, TX92, WY6
Cianchette Lionheart	TN4	(P4Y-2) (Convair 100)	
Cierva C.30A (Avro 671)	FL22	Consolidated 40 Privateer (PB4Y-2)	CA160, FL55, MI58
Cirigliano SC-1 Baby Hawk	CA130	(P4Y-2) (P4Y-2G) (Convair 100)	
Cirrus 2 Hang Glider	VA29	Consolidated TBY-2 Sea Wolf (R)	PA52
Cirrus 3 Hang Glider	OK28	Convair 2 Seadart (YF2Y-1) (YF-7A)	CA122, FL23, MD15, PA26
Cirrus VK30	WI17		
Clark Ornithopter	ME7	Convair 4 Hustler (YB-58A)	CA4, IN20, TX92
Clark Special 3	MT9	(TB-58A)	
Classic Aircraft Waco F-5	IL31, VA17	Convair 4 Hustler (YB-58A)	IL50
Clemson AM A-100	SC20	(YRB-58A)	
Cloud Dancer Jenny	OH60	Convair 4 Hustler (B-58A)	AZ30, NE23, OH55, TX83
Cocke Nighthawk	CA79		
Coffee Mitsubishi A6M2-21 (R)	OR13	Convair 5 (XFY-1)	MD15
Coffman Glider	TX124	Convair 7-002 (XF-92A)	OH55
Coffman Monoplane	OK28	Convair 8-10 Delta Dagger (F-102A)	AK12, 16, AR7, AZ30, 41, CA2, 3, 32, 85, 122, 139, 160, CO24, 32, CT1, 9, FL37, GA45, HI2, 6, ID7, MI2, MN27, MT1, 14, ND20, 22, NE23, NY21, 71, OH48, 55, OR7, PA48, SC1, SD6, 7, TX56, 123, UT5, VT6, WA2, 22, WI62
Colomban MC-10 Cri-Cri	FL23		
Colomban MC-12 Cri-Cri	OK28, WI17		
Colomban MC-15 Cri-Cri	CA111		
Columbia XJL-1	AZ30		
Command-Aire 3C3	CA160		
Command-Aire 5C3	AR1, CA19, FL46		
Command-Aire Little Rocket (R)	FL23		
Commonwealth CA-13 Boomerang II	FL22		
Commonwealth CA-16 Wirraway III [North American NA-33]	FL22		
Commonwealth CA-17 Mustang 20 [North American P-51D]	AL29, OR21	Convair 8-12 Delta Dagger (TF-102A)	AL32, AZ30, CA4, 32, IN20, MI53, PA45, TX66, WI62
Commonwealth CA-18 Mustang 22 [North American P-51D]	TX91	Convair 8-24 Delta Dart (F-106A)	AZ1, 30, CA3, 32, 109, FL9, 37, 80, MI28, 53, MT1, ND20, OH55, UT5, WA22
Commonwealth CA-27 Sabre 30 [North American F-86F]	IN54		
Commonwealth CA-27 Sabre 31 [North American F-86F]	VA17	Convair 8-24 Delta Dart (F-106A) (QF-106A)	DE1, NM11, TX17
Condor Hang Glider	CA29	Convair 8-27 Delta Dart (F-106B)	CA160, NJ2, TX83, VA35
Consolidated 1 Trusty (PT-1)	CA122, OH55	Convair 8-27 Delta Dart (F-106B)	TX17
Consolidated 2 Trusty (PT-3)	OH37, WI17	(QF-106B)	
Consolidated 28-5 Catalina (PBY-5)	CA160, FL55	Convair 8-31 Delta Dart (F-106A)	AL32, CA2, CO24, FL74, GA45, OR7
Consolidated 28-5A Canso A	AK3, AZ24, TX54, 80, 92		
Consolidated 28-5A Catalina (PBV-1A) (OA-10A)	AK3, AZ30	Convair 8-32 Delta Dart (F-106B)	CA4
Consolidated 28-5A Catalina (PBY-5A)	AZ30, CA110, 122, FL22, 38, 55, 86, NM12, NY32, OH55, OR21, VA17, WA30	Convair 8-90 Delta Dagger (YF-102A)	LA12, NC6
		Convair 36 Peacemaker (B-36J)	AZ30, NE23, OH55
		Convair 36 Peacemaker (RB-36H)	CA32
		Convair 102 (XP-81) (XF-81)	OH55
Consolidated 28-5A Catalina (PBY-5A) (OA-10A)	WA22	Convair 105 (L-13A)	AL36, AR19, AZ33, CA32, 111, FL80, GA58, NJ31, NM24
Consolidated 28-5A Catalina (PBY-5B)	FL55		
		Convair 105 (L-13B)	WA16
Consolidated 28-5ACF Catalina (28-6A) (PBY-6A)	MN9, TX40	Convair 240	CA96
		Convair 240-0	FL77, MD15, OH67
Consolidated 28-6A Catalina (PBY-6A)	MN9, NY4, TX40, 54	Convair 240-1	AZ33
		Convair 240-5	CA9
Consolidated 29 Coronado (PB2Y-3) (PB2Y-5R)	FL55	Convair 240-11	CA32
		Convair 240-17 (T-29A)	AR3, CA141, GA45, NE23, TX123
Consolidated LB-30 Liberator	AK3		
Consolidated RLB-30 Liberator (LB-30A)	TX40	Convair 240-27 (T-29B)	AZ30, GA16
		Convair 240-27 (T-29B) (VT-29B)	TX147
Consolidated 32 Liberator (B-24A) (RB-24A)	MI58	Convair 240-27 (T-29C)	TX51, 119, UT5
		Convair 240-53 Samaritan (C-131A) (HC-131A)	CA27, CO25
Consolidated 32 Liberator (B-24D)	FL22, LA17, OH55, UT5		
Consolidated 32 Liberator (B-24D) (B.III)	CA89, VA35	Convair 30A-5 Coronado 990	CA93
		Convair 340	NY14
Consolidated 32 Liberator (B-24J)	GA43, LA7	Convair 340-31	OH45
Consolidated 32 Liberator (B-24J) (B.VII)	AZ30, FL22	Convair 340-67 Samaritan (VC-131D)	AZ24, CA3, 85
Consolidated 32 Liberator (B-24J) (B.VII) (GR.VI)	MA4	Convair 340-70 Samaritan (C-131B)	FL76

Convair 340-70 Samaritan (C-131B) (EC-131B) (C-131H) (NC-131H)	OH55	Curtiss E Hydro	OH27
		Curtiss H-1 (R)	NY24
Convair 340-71 Samaritan (R4Y-1) (C-131F)	AZ1, 30, CA160, FL55	Curtiss 1A Jenny (JN-4A)	NY14
		Curtiss 1A Jenny (JN-4A) (R)	OR7
Convair 340-79 Samaritan (C-131D)	CA139, DE1, VT6	Curtiss 1C Jenny (JN-3) (R)	NM16
Convair 340-79 Samaritan (C-131D) (VC-131D)	UT5	Curtiss 1C Jenny (JN-4D)	AK3, 18, AL36, AR1, CA53, 65, 122, 160, CO11, FL55, GA17, ID9, IL45, MD7, ME7, MT13, NE12, NY14, 24, 35, OH55, OR24, PA23, TX53, 100, 114, 147, UT5, VA19, 36, WA10, 12, 25, WI17
Convair 440 (340-41)	CA111		
Convair 440 (340-51)	FL22		
Convair 440-61 Samaritan (TC-131E)	MN27		
Convair 440-71 (C-131E) (R4Y-2) (C-131G)	OK46		
Convair 440-79 Samaritan (C-131D)	MI53, OH55, SD7		
Convair 580 (440) (340-38)	TX141		
Convair 640 (340-32)	TX151	Curtiss 1C Jenny (JN-4D) (R)	CA160, FL22, GA45, IL50, MN28
Convair 640 (340-33)	TX151		
Convair 880-22-1	CA82, GA8, NJ3, TN18	Curtiss 1C Jenny (JN-4D2) (R)	KS9
Convertawings A Quadrotor	NY14	Curtiss 1E Jenny (JN-4H)	CA130, NY63
Cook and Frazee Primary Training Glider	IA36	Curtiss 1E Jenny (JN-4HG)	VA22
		Curtiss JN-4 Canuck	MI25, MO15, OH53, TX114, WA8
Corben B-1 Baby Ace	IL70		
Corben C-1 Baby Ace	IL65, NC15, OH64, WA37, WI17	Curtiss 12 (NC-4)	FL55
		Curtiss 12 (NC-4) (R)	NY24
Corben C-1 Baby Ace (R)	WI56	Curtiss 17 Oriole	FL22, NY24, OH27
Corben D Baby Ace	IL82, PA56, WA34	Curtiss 17 Oriole (R)	MN27
Corben D Baby Ace Seaplane	WI37	Curtiss 18 Seagull (MF)	FL55
Corben D Junior Ace	NY16	Curtiss 25 Seagull (MF)	NY24
Corben E Junior Ace	CT9, IL70, NC40, NY16	Curtiss 34C Hawk (F6C-1) (R)	FL55
Corben MJA Sport	VA13	Curtiss 34H Hawk (F6C-4)	VA22
Corben Super Ace	OH55	Curtiss 35 Gulfhawk 1	VA19
Corben T.1 Baby Ace	OR20	Curtiss 35 Hawk (P-6E)	OH55, WI17
Cosmos Phase II	VA19	Curtiss 35 Hawk (P-6E) (Scale R)	CA85
Croff Batwing Hang Glider	NY50	Curtiss 42A (R3C-2)	DC3
Crosby CR-4	WI17	Curtiss 42A (R3C-2) (R)	CA111
Crosley Moonbeam	KY2	Curtiss 43 Seahawk (F7C-1)	FL55
Crosley-Mignet Pou-du-Ciel	VA19	Curtiss 48A Fledgling (N2C-2)	FL55
Crowley Hydro Air Vehicle	MD15	Curtiss 5 (N-9H)	VA19
Crown City CC-4	CA154	Curtiss 50 Robin	AZ37, GA17, IA22, NV23, PA17
Cub Crafters PA-18-150	AZ24		
CSS 13 [Polikarpov Po-2]	FL22	Curtiss 50B Robin B	CA160, FL22, GA12, MO15, NH5, NY24, OR20
Culver LCA Cadet	AL32, CA17, 111, IL70, MN40, MO15, NY74, OH59, OR24, PA35, WA37		
		Curtiss 50B Robin B-1	CA122
		Curtiss 50B Robin B-2	WI17
		Curtiss 50C Robin 4C-1	NC40
Culver LCA Cadet (LFA)	IA1	Curtiss 50C Robin C-1	AK3, AZ33, CA105, 160, GA17, NY7, 14, OR7, WA25, 34
Culver LFA Cadet	CA95, 158, OK19, PA23, TX21, 31		
Culver NR-D Cadet (PQ-14A) (TD2C-1)	CA111, FL58, MD15		
		Curtiss 50C Robin C-2	ID9, NH5
Culver NR-D Cadet (PQ-14B)	AZ30, IA1, OH55, WI17	Curtiss 50H Robin J-1	CA160, DC3, NY63, OR24, VA36
Culver Rigid Midget	NY50		
Culver V Satellite	CA23, FL23, KS18, 26	Curtiss 51 Fledgling	MN18, NY24, 63, OR7, PA23, 29
Cumulus 2F	AL32		
Cunningham Hall PT-6	AK16	Curtiss 58A Sparrowhawk (F9C-2)	FL55
Cunningham Hall PT-6F	MN18	Curtiss 58A Sparrowhawk (XF9C-2)	FL55, VA19
Cunningham-Hall GA-36	NY35	Curtiss 67A Hawk (F11C-2) (BFC-2)	FL55
Curtiss A Pusher (R)	NY35	Curtiss 75L Hawk (P-36A)	OH55
Curtiss A-1 (R)	NY24, TX92	Curtiss H81-A2 Warhawk (P-40C)	WA12
Curtiss-Thompson A-1	CA65	Curtiss H81-A2 Warhawk (P-40C) (Tomahawk IIB)	FL55
Curtiss A-2 (R)	VA22		
Curtiss Albany Flyer (R)	NY24	Curtiss H81-A2 Warhawk (P-40C) (Tomahawk IIB) (FSM)	CA115, IL2, NY2
Curtiss Little Looper	CA122		
Curtiss D Pusher	CA65, CT9, DC3, IA13, 36, ND2, NE12, NM1, OH59, OK40	Curtiss 84B Shrike (S84) (A-25A) (SB2C-1A)	OH55
		Curtiss 84E Helldiver (SB2C-3)	CA160
Curtiss D Pusher (R)	AL32, CA65, 88, 111, FL22, ID11, IL45, MD7, ME7, NY24, 63, OH55, OK28, OR7, 24, TX135, WI37	Curtiss 84F Helldiver (SB2C-4)	FL55
		Curtiss 84G Helldiver (SB2C-5)	MN14, TX38, 40, VA19
		Curtiss 85 Owl (O-52)	AZ30, CA160, OH55
		Curtiss A87-A2 Kittyhawk I	CA18, 160, FL22, HI6, ID26, IL18, MN14, MT13, NM24, NY78, OH55, VA19
Curtiss D Pusher Racer	WI37		
Curtiss E	VA19		
Curtiss E (R)	NY24	Curtiss A87-A2 Kittyhawk IA	ND5
Curtiss E A-1	WI17	Curtiss 87-A3 Warhawk (P-40M) (Kittyhawk III)	NY4
Curtiss E A-1 (R)	CA122, FL55		

Index

Curtiss 87-A4 Warhawk (P-40E) (Kittyhawk IA)	GA59, VA17	Dassault Falcon 200	TX16
Curtiss 87-A4 Warhawk (P-40E) (Scale R)	NY24	Dassault Mystère IVA	OH55
		Davis D-1 (V-3)	IN55
		Davis D-1K	OR24
Curtiss 87-A4 Warhawk (P-40M) (Kittyhawk III)	OH74	Davis D-1W	NY63, WI17
		Davis DA-2	AL32
Curtiss 87-B2 Warhawk (P-40E) (FSM)	HI6	Dawydoff UT-1 Cadet	NY50
		De Havilland DH.2 (R)	CA54, MO26
Curtiss 87-B3 Warhawk (P-40K)	AK3, AZ30, FL5, MN14, OR7	De Havilland DH-4	DC3, FL22
		De Havilland DH-4 (R)	CA51, DC5
Curtiss 87V Warhawk (P-40N)	CA130, GA44, IA27, MI2, TX16, WA25	De Havilland DH-4A (R)	VA22
		De Havilland DH-4B	FL22, OH55
Curtiss 87V Warhawk (P-40N) (Kittyhawk IV)	AZ30, CA111, ID26, TX23, 40	De Havilland DH-4BM	FL22
		De Havilland DH-4M	OR7
Curtiss 87V Warhawk (P-40N) (TP-40N)	CA110, FL22, GA45	De Havilland DH-4M2A	MO15
		De Havilland DH.60 Moth	CA17
Curtiss 87V Warhawk (P-40N) (FSM)	CA33, 85, 146, CO24, LA6, 24, MA6, MD1, TX51	De Havilland DH.60GM Moth	NE12
		De Havilland DH.60GMW Moth	MT9
		De Havilland DH.60M Moth	CA160
Curtiss 87V Warhawk (P-40N) (R)	UT5	De Havilland DH.60X Moth	CA17
Curtiss 99 (XF15C-1)	RI1	De Havilland DH.80A Puss Moth	NY63, WA8
Curtiss-Wright 200 (X-19A)	OH55	De Havilland DH.82A Tiger Moth	CA17, 130, FL5, 80, MT13, NM24, NY7, 63, OH55, PA12, 17, TX69, 92, VA17, WA8
Curtiss-Wright A-14D Sportsman	VA36		
Curtiss-Wright CW-1 Junior	FL22, KS26, MN13, NV23, NY16, 24, 63, OH53, 59, OR20, 24, PA23, VA19, WA34		
		De Havilland DH.82A Tiger Moth (R)	IN57
Curtiss-Wright CW-1 Junior (R)	AR2, CA130, WA34	De Havilland DH.82B Queen Bee	WA34
Curtiss-Wright CW-12W Sport Trainer	MT13, OR24	De Havilland DH.82C Tiger Moth	CA155, FL22, IA22, WA31, WI17
Curtiss-Wright CW-15C Sedan	MO15	De Havilland DH.82C Tiger Moth (PT-24)	TX26
Curtiss-Wright CW-15D Sedan	OR7		
Curtiss-Wright CW-16E Light Sport	MO15	De Havilland DH.84 Dragon	WA19
Curtiss-Wright CW-19R	CA130	De Havilland DH.88 Comet (R)	CA151
Curtiss-Wright CW-20B Commando (C-46A)	CA160, FL55, OH22	De Havilland DH.89A Dragon Rapide (DH.89B Dominie I)	MO15, OH55, VA17
Curtiss-Wright CW-20B-2 Commando (C-46D)	AZ30, CA32, 68, 111, FL36, GA45, OH55, 71	De Havilland DH.94 Moth Minor	TX34, 40
		De Havilland DH.98 Mosquito T.III	WA12
Curtiss-Wright CW-20B-4 Commando (C-46F)	CA45, NC1, NY24, TX40	De Havilland DH.98 Mosquito FB.26	VA17
		De Havilland DH.98 Mosquito B.35 (TT.35) (B.35)	VA19
Curtiss-Wright CW-A22 Falcon	OR7		
Curtiss-Wright CW-22N Falcon (SNC-1)	FL22, 55	De Havilland DH.98 Mosquito TT.35 (B.35)	OH55, WI17
Curtiss-Wright CW-24 Ascender (XP-55)	MI2	De Havilland DH.100 Vampire F.3	AZ33, NY23
		De Havilland DH.100 Vampire FB.6	CA111, FL22, NY62
Curtiss-Wright CW-25 Jeep (AT-9)	OH55	De Havilland DH.100 Vampire FB.52	OR7
Curtiss-Wright CW-25 Jeep (AT-9A)	AZ30	De Havilland DH.104 Dove 2A	TX134
Curtiss-Wright Gem	VA34	De Havilland DH.104 Dove 5A	PA35
Curtiss-Wright VZ-7AP Aerial Jeep	AL36	De Havilland DH.104 Dove 6A (2A)	PA35
Curtiss-Wright X-100	VA19	De Havilland DH.106 Comet 4C	WA25
Custer CCW-1	MD15	De Havilland DH.112 Sea Venom FAW.53	OR11
Custer CCW-5	PA35		
Cutter Hot Air Balloon	IA29	De Havilland DH.112 Venom FB.1	CO27, DE2
Cvjetkovic CA-61 Mini-Ace	IA27	De Havilland DH.115 Vampire T.11	CA53, NC18, SD11
D'Apuzzo D-260	IA39	De Havilland DH.115 Vampire T.35	IN48, OR11
Da Vinci Glider (R)	CA110	De Havilland DH.115 Vampire T.55	NY23
Da Vinci Flying Machine (FSM)	IA27	De Havilland DH.125 Series 400A	GA28
Da Vinci Ornithopter (R)	CA122, 158, NC40	De Havilland DHC.1 Chipmunk 1A-1 (mod)	VA19
Dake Mullicoupe	MN21		
Dale Fisher Classic	FL80	De Havilland DHC.1 Chipmunk 1B-2-S3 (mod)	WI17
Daphne SD-1A	TX151		
Dart BAC-2 [Bensen B-8M Gyrocopter]	NY16	De Havilland DHC.1 Chipmunk 1B-2-S5	ID2
Dart CW-3	NY16	De Havilland DHC.1 Chipmunk 1B-2-S5 (CT-120)	CA17
Dart G	OH59, OR24, WA43		
Dart GC	MO15, TX69	De Havilland DHC.1 Chipmunk T.10	VA17
Dart JN-4D	NY16	De Havilland DHC.1 Chipmunk T.20	CO7, VA8
Dart Special	NY16	De Havilland DHC.1 Chipmunk 22 (T.10)	IL18, IN28, PA12
Dart ULA-1 Skycycle	NY16		
Dassault Etendard IVM	NY34	De Havilland DHC.2 Beaver	AK3, WA16
Dassault Falcon 10	CA3	De Havilland DHC.2 Beaver (L-20A) (U-6A)	CA26, 32, CT9, FL24, 55, GA45, OH55, OK1, TN25, VA34
Dassault Falcon 20C	TN24		
Dassault Falcon 20DC	VA19		
Dassault Falcon 20G (HU-25A)	AZ1	De Havilland DHC.2 Beaver (YL-20A) (YU-6A)	AL36
Dassault Falcon 20G (HU-25B)	NC12		

671

De Havilland DHC.2 Beaver AL.1	WA17	Douglas DC-3-262	MO2
De Havilland DHC.3 Otter (U-1A)	AL36, VA34	Douglas DC-3-277	OK43
De Havilland DHC.3 Otter (UC-1) (U-1B) (NU-1B)	FL55	Douglas DC-3-277B	TX5, 92
		Douglas DC-3-277C	WA25
De Havilland DHC.4 Caribou	MI58	Douglas DC-3-313B (C-49E)	NM9
De Havilland DHC.4 Caribou (YAC-1) (YCV-2A) (YC-7A)	AL36, NC1, TX51, VA34	Douglas DC-3-357	GA23
		Douglas DC-3-362	CA57
De Havilland DHC.4A Caribou (AC-1) (CV-2A) (C-7A)	FL1	Douglas DC-3-454 (C-49J)	CT9
		Douglas DC-3-455 (C-49K)	WI17
De Havilland DHC.4 Caribou (AC-1) (CV-2A) (C-7A)	CA139	Douglas DC-3A (DC-3-201E)	CA82
		Douglas DC-3A-197	MD14, OR7
De Havilland DHC.4 Caribou (CV-2A) (C-7A)	TX16	Douglas DC-3A-197E	WA19
		Douglas DC-3A-228C	FL22
De Havilland DHC.4A Caribou (CV-2B) (C-7B)	CA4, CT9, DE1, GA45, OH55, UT5	Douglas DC-3A-228D	GA33
		Douglas DC-3A-269C	LA6
De Havilland DHC.5 Buffalo QSRA (C-8A)	CA98	Douglas DC-3A-314A	GA17
		Douglas DC-3A-360 Skytrain (C-47)	AK16, AZ30, MO31, NC6, ND8
De Havilland DHC.8-100	AZ31		
De Lackner Aerocycle	VA34	Douglas DC-3A-360 Skytrain (C-47) (R4D-1)	OR21
De Pischoff Biplane (R)	NY21		
Del Mar DH.1A Whirlymite	AL36	Douglas DC-3A-405 Skytrooper (C-53)	CA89, FL24, NC28
Denney Kitfox I	CA122, CO32, FL23		
Denney Kitfox II	WI51	Douglas DC-3A-405 Skytrooper (C-53) (R4D-3)	CA4, 96
Denney Kitfox IV	WI22		
Denney Kitfox IV Speedster	VA35	Douglas DC-3A-456 Skytrain (C-47A)	AK1, 14, 16, AZ30, 34, 45, 46, CA32, 84, 122, 139, 160, DE1, FL35, 80, 86, GA45, 46, IN29, KY5, LA7, 17, MD22, MI2, MO25, MS22, MT9, NC3, ND5, NE23, NH4, NM24, NY74, OH15, OK23, OR7, TX16, 151
Department of Aircraft Production Beaufort VIII [Bristol 152]	CA89, TN6		
Deperdussin 1913 (R)	CA111		
Deperdussin C	CA122		
Deperdussin Monocoque (R)	ME7		
Deperdussin Monoplane (R)	NV23, NY63		
Detroit Gull	KS18		
Deutsch Aerospace / Rockwell Ranger 2000	OK43		
Dewoitine D.26	FL22	Douglas DC-3A-456 Skytrain (C-47A) (C-117C) (VC-117A)	TX73
Dickenson-Howard DGA-21	CA17		
Dickson Primary (R)	NY63	Douglas DC-3A-456 Skytrain (C-47A) (C-47D) (NC-47B)	IN27
Diehl Aeronautical XTC	OK43		
Diehl XTC	WI24	Douglas DC-3A-456 Skytrain (C-47A) (Dakota III)	CA111, GA59, OK52, OR4, TX143
Doak 16 (VZ-4)	VA34		
Dobbins Simcopter	CA158	Douglas DC-3A-456 Skytrain (C-47A) (R4D-5)	NJ16, NY82, SD7
Doman LZ-5	CA37		
Doman LZ-5 (XH-31)	CT9	Douglas DC-3A-456 Skytrain (C-47A) (R4D-5) (C-47H)	FL9, IL47
Domenjoz Sailing Glider	ME7		
Dominator 1	AK5	Douglas DC-3A-456 Skytrain (C-47A) (R4D-5) (EC-47H)	ID4
Dormoy Flying Bathtub (R)	MT5, PA23, TX114, WA19		
		Douglas DC-3A-456 Skytrain (C-47A) (R4D-5) (R4D-6S)	TX51
Dornier Do 27B-1	AL36		
Dornier Do 335A-1	VA19	Douglas DC-3A-456 Skytrain (C-47A) (R4D-5) (SC-47H)	CO25
Dornier-Breguet Alpha Jet A	AZ30, ID19, WA12		
Double Eagle II	VA19	Douglas DC-3A-456 Skytrain (C-47A) (R4D-5L) (C-47H)	FL55
Douglas DWC	AK3, CA96, DC3		
Douglas DWC (R)	WA36	Douglas DC-3A-456 Skytrain (C-47A) (SC-47A)	NM12
Douglas M-2	VA19		
Douglas Dolphin 8	FL55	Douglas DC-3A-456 Skytrain (C-47A) (VC-47A)	CA85, ND2
Douglas O-38F	OH55		
Douglas O-46A	OH55	Douglas DC-3A-457 Skytrooper (C-53D)	CA3, 44, TX40
Douglas B-18A Bolo	AZ30, CO32, OH55, WA22		
		Douglas DC-3A-467 Skytrain (C-47B)	AZ30, CA9, 53, 71, 84, FL22, 80, MS2, NY4, 14, 32, 74, OH48, OK3, TX147, VT6, WA2, 17
Douglas B-18B Bolo (B-18)	CA32		
Douglas B-23 Dragon	FL22, OH55		
Douglas UC-67 Dragon (B-23)	AZ30, CA32, NY74, WA22		
		Douglas DC-3A-467 Skytrain (C-47B) (C-47D)	IN20, KS2, OH55
Douglas XB-42A Mixmaster (XB-42)	OH55		
Douglas YB-43 Jetmaster	OH55	Douglas DC-3A-467 Skytrain (C-47B) (Dakota IV)	CA110, NC6, NY4, OR21, TX31, 40
Douglas RB-66B Destroyer	IL50, OH55, TX51		
Douglas EB-66C Destroyer (RB-66C)	SC19	Douglas DC-3A-467 Skytrain (C-47B) (R4D-6)	OK20
Douglas WB-66D Destroyer	AZ30, GA45, TX147		
Douglas DC-2-118B	WA25	Douglas DC-3A-467 Skytrain (C-47B) (R4D-6) (C-47J)	AL35, CA111, GA45, NJ19, NY54
Douglas DC-2-243 (C-39)	OH55		
Douglas DST-217A (C-49E)	CA130, IL63	Douglas DC-3A-467 Skytrain (C-47B) (R4D-6) (EC-47J)	AL32, OK41
Douglas DST-406 (C-49F)	CA115		
Douglas DC-3-178	IL17, MO13	Douglas DC-3A-467 Skytrain (C-47B) (R4D-6) (R4D-6E) (R4D-6S)	ND5
Douglas DC-3-201	DC3		
Douglas DC-3-201B	MI25	Douglas DC-3A-467 Skytrain (C-47B) (R4D-6) (R4D-6R)	MN27
Douglas DC-3-201F	OK52		

Index

Douglas DC-3A-467 Skytrain (C-47B) (R4D-6) (R4D-6S) (SC-47J)	PA35
Douglas DC-3A-467 Skytrain (C-47B) (R4D-6) (SC-47J)	TX25, 40, 124
Douglas DC-3A-467 Skytrain (C-47B) (R4D-7) (TC-47B) (NC-47K) (NEC-47H)	FL76
Douglas DC-3A-467 Skytrain (C-47B) (VC-47D)	AL37, IL50, NC1, SC22, TX147, UT5
Douglas DC-3A-467 Skytrain (TC-47B) (C-47D)	WA32
Douglas DC-3A-467 Skytrain (TC-47B) (R4D-6) (R4D-6R) (R4D-6S) (SC-47J) (TC-47J)	NC30
Douglas DC-3A-467 Skytrain (TC-47B) (R4D-7) (R4D-6R)	IL11, TX40
Douglas DC-3A-467 Skytrain (TC-47B) (R4D-7) (R4D-6R) (R4D-6V)	OK28
Douglas DC-3A-467 Skytrain (TC-47B) (R4D-7) (R4D-6R) (TC-47J)	IN27
Douglas DC-3A-467 Skytrain (TC-47B) (TC-47D)	MI58
Douglas DC-3A-467 Skytrain (TC-47B) (VC-47D)	KS9
Douglas Super DC-3 (R4D-8) (C-117D)	AZ30, CA58, 143, FL55
Douglas DC-4 Skymaster (C-54A)	CA58
Douglas DC-4 Skymaster (C-54A) (VC-54C)	OH55
Douglas DC-4 Skymaster (C-54B) (R5D-3) (C-54P)	CA139
Douglas DC-4 Skymaster (C-54D)	AZ30, NE23, TX40
Douglas DC-4 Skymaster (C-54D) (R5D-3) (C-54Q)	CA3, 85
Douglas DC-4 Skymaster (C-54D) (R5D-3) (C-54S)	SD7
Douglas DC-4 Skymaster (C-54E) (C-54M)	DE1
Douglas DC-4 Skymaster (C-54E) (R5D-4R) (C-54R)	CA32, NJ4
Douglas DC-4 Skymaster (C-54G)	GA45, UT5
Douglas DC-6	AK17
Douglas DC-6 Liftmaster (VC-118)	OH55
Douglas DC-6A Liftmaster (C-118A)	AK3, HI6
Douglas DC-6A Liftmaster (C-118A) (C-118B) (VC-118A)	NJ17
Douglas DC-6A Liftmaster (C-118A) (VC-118A)	AZ30
Douglas DC-6A Liftmaster (R6D-1) (C-118A)	CA139, TX147
Douglas DC-6A Liftmaster (R6D-1) (C-118A) (R6D-1) (C-118B)	CA109
Douglas DC-6A Liftmaster (R6D-1) (C-118B)	FL33, 55, OK8
Douglas DC-6B	AK13, CA105, 109, MI58, TX143
Douglas DC-7	CO12, DC3
Douglas DC-7B	AZ30, FL33, 77, OH71
Douglas DC-7BF (DC-7B)	FL33
Douglas DC-7C	AZ11, FL77
Douglas DC-8-52	CA29
Douglas DC-8-54F (EC-24A)	AZ1
Douglas DC-9-14	MN32
Douglas DC-9-15	CA107
Douglas DC-9-32	GA28, OR7, VA35
Douglas DC-9-32CF Nightingale (C-9A)	AZ1, DE1, IL64, MD3, TX147
Douglas DC-9-32RC Skytrain II (C-9B)	AZ1, FL55, TX149
Douglas DC-9-33RC Skytrain II (C-9B)	AZ30
Douglas DC-9-41	FL71
Douglas DC-9-51	HI10
Douglas 1129A Globemaster II (C-124A)	DE1, OH71
Douglas 1129A Globemaster II (C-124A) (C-124C)	GA45
Douglas 1317 Globemaster II (C-124C)	AZ30, CA139, OH55, SC22, UT5, WA22
Douglas 1333 Cargomaster (C-133A)	CA139, IL50, OH55
Douglas 1430 Cargomaster (C-133B)	AZ30, DE1
Douglas A-20G Havoc	AZ30, FL22, OH55, VA17
Douglas A-20H Havoc	NY74
Douglas A-20J Havoc	TX91
Douglas A-24A Dauntless	OR21
Douglas A-24B Dauntless	AZ30, FL22, GA21, OH55, TX40, 92
Douglas A-26A Invader (A-26B) (B-26K)	OH55, TX151
Douglas A-26A Invader (A-26B) (TB-26B) (B-26K)	AZ30
Douglas A-26A Invader (A-26C) (B-26K)	FL36, SD7
Douglas A-26B Invader	AZ24, 28, 33, CA32, 84, 89, 109, 122, DE9, FL22, 55, MA4, MS13, NV9, 18, NY82, OH40, 71, OK14, TX8, 33, 40, VA17, WA2
Douglas TB-26B Invader (A-26B)	CA4, OK48, OR21
Douglas VB-26B Invader (A-26B)	VA19
Douglas VB-26B Invader (A-26B) (TB-26B)	NE23
Douglas A-26C Invader	AL32, AZ11, 30, CA85, 89, 110, 133, 139, CO25, CT9, DE1, FL22, 44, GA45, IL36, KS13, LA12, MI53, NC6, ND11, OH15, 55, OK11, OR4, 7, TX16, 51, 88, 147
Douglas RB-26C Invader (A-26C)	HI2, NM24, UT5
Douglas SBD-1 Dauntless	CA145
Douglas SBD-2 Dauntless	FL22, 55, HI6
Douglas SBD-3 Dauntless	FL55, LA17, MI2, TX149, VA22
Douglas SBD-3 Dauntless (FSM)	CA115
Douglas SBD-4 Dauntless	CA122, 144, 160, FL55, IL9, OH55
Douglas SBD-5 Dauntless	CA110, 111, FL55, HI6, SC18
Douglas SBD-5 Dauntless (FSM'	HI6
Douglas SBD-6 Dauntless	CA145, DC3
Douglas XAD-1 Destroyer II (XBT2D-1)	OH71, VA27
Douglas BTD-1 Destroyer	NY82
Douglas TBD-1 Devastator	FL55
Douglas AD-1 Skyraider (BT2D-1)	IL72
Douglas AD-3 Skyraider	PA38
Douglas AD-4 Skyraider	VA17
Douglas AD-4B Skyraider	NV11
Douglas AD-4N Skyraider	CA143
Douglas AD-4NA Skyraider (AD-4N)	AZ33, CA160, ID15, OR21, WA16
Douglas AD-4W Skyraider (AEW.1)	CA145, OR21
Douglas A-1D Skyraider (AD-4N) (AD-4NA)	MI2, SC18, TX92
Douglas A-1E Skyraider (AD-5)	CA3, ID15, OH55, UT5
Douglas EA-1E Skyraider (AD-5W)	CA85, OK27, TX16
Douglas NA-1E Skyraider (AD-5) (A-1E)	TX80
Douglas EA-1F Skyraider (AD-5N) (AD-5Q)	AZ30, FL55, OR7
Douglas A-1G Skyraider (AD-5N)	FL36
Douglas A-1H Skyraider (AD-6)	CA74, FL55, OH55, 71, VA19
Douglas XA-3 Skywarrior (XA3D-1)	NY36
Douglas YEA-3A Skywarrior (YA3D-1)	AZ30

Index

Douglas A-3A Skywarrior (A3D-1)	CA4, FL55, OR21	Douglas F-6A Skyray (F4D-1)	AZ30, CA58, CO25, CT9, FL55, MD19, VA27
Douglas A-3B Skywarrior (A3D-2)	CT9		
Douglas EA-3B Skywarrior (A3D-2Q)	AL37, MD16, SC18	Douglas EF-10B Skynight (F3D-2) (F3D-2Q)	CA4, 58, RI1, VA22
Douglas EKA-3B Skywarrior (A3D-2) (A-3B)	CA145	Douglas F-10B Skynight (F3D-2)	CA72, FL55, KS9
Douglas KA-3B Skywarrior (A3D-2) (A-3B)	CA105, 160, TX149	Douglas TF-10B Skynight (F3D-2) (F3D-2T)	AZ30, NY34
Douglas KA-3B Skywarrior (A3D-2) (A-3B) (NA-3B)	AZ1	Douglas F5D-1 Skylancer	OH56, OR11
		Douglas X-3 Stiletto	OH55
Douglas RA-3B Skywarrior (A3D-2P)	CA32	Driggers L-A Sunshine Girl	WI17
		Driggs Dart II	MO15
Douglas NRA-3B Skywarrior (A3D-2P) (RA-3B)	WA42	Driggs Skylark III	MI49, 50
		DSK Aircraft Corporation BJ.1B Duster	OK28
Douglas TA-3B Skywarrior (A3D-2T)	FL55	Duede Biplane	IA36
		Durand V	WA25
Douglas XA-4A Skyhawk (XA4D-1)	FL55	Dyndiuk Sport	CT9
Douglas YA-4A Skyhawk (YA4D-1)	CA143	Eagle AX-7 Hot Air Balloon	IA29
Douglas A-4A Skyhawk (A4D-1)	CA74, 155, 160, CT9, FL61, GA10, IL50, IN42, KS9, MD24, NC6, NJ21	Eaglet 1A	TX118
		Early Bird Jenny	IA1
		Ecker Flying Boat	DC3
		Egglestone Airvane	CA155
Douglas A-4A Skyhawk (YA4D-1) (YA-4A)	CA53	Eichmann Aerobat III	TX135
		Eipper Cumulus VB Hang Glider	WA25
Douglas A-4B Skyhawk (A4D-2)	CA58, 74, 115, 122, 143, 160, FL29, 56, GA32, IL72, IN48, MA13, MI2, 53, MO33, NH9, NJ9, 15, NV11, NY32, 34, OR21, TX11, 149	Eipper MX Quicksilver	AK5, CA29, 55, FL22, MD14, VA29, WI17
		Eipper MX-1 Quicksilver	WI17
		Eipper-Formance Cumulus 10 Hang Glider	VA19
		EKW C-3605 (C-3603-1)	CA111, FL22
Douglas TA-4B Skyhawk (A4D-2)	AZ30	Elias EC-1 Aircoupe	PA35
Douglas YA-4C Skyhawk (A4D-2N) (YA4D-2N)	CA68	Elliott AP.5 EoN Olympia 2	NM20
		Elliott GE-2	NY16
Douglas A-4C Skyhawk (A4D-2N)	AL32, AR2, AZ30, CA3, 6, 58, 102, 113, 122, 160, CO10, 25, DC3, FL24, 38, 55, IL23, LA13, 14, MN32, NE9, NJ1, OK5, OR13, 21, RI1, TN12, 33, TX66, 85, VA36	Elmira Dagling	NY50
		Emair MA-1	WA4
		Emair MA-1B	HI10
		Emeott 40 Hot Air Balloon	IA29
		Emigh Trojan A-2	AZ5, OR24
		English Electric EA.1 Canberra TT.18 (B.2)	AZ11, OK26
Douglas YA-4E Skyhawk (YA4D-5)	NY57	English Electric P.26 Lightning F.53	GA45
Douglas A-4E Skyhawk (A4D-5)	CA109, 111, 160, FL41, 55, HI1, 4, NY28, VA24, 27	English Electric P.27 Lightning T.5	MS1
		Enstrom F-28A	IL66, NH5, PA4
		Enstrom F-28F	NH5
Douglas A-4E Skyhawk	HI1, OR7, VA22	Epps Monoplane (R)	FL80, GA45
Douglas A-4F Skyhawk	CA58, 144, 145, FL55, NJ19, NV11, NY21, RI1, VA1, WA25	Ercoupe 415	VA19
		Ercoupe 415C	AR2, AZ30, CA33, 96, 110, 130, KS26, KY9, MD7, MN30, NC6, 40, ND5, NE12, NJ7, 23, NY7, 16, 74, OH19, 55, OR21, PA23, 61, TX19, 34, VA36, WA25, WI17, 60
Douglas TA-4F Skyhawk	FL38, NY52		
Douglas NTA-4F Skyhawk (TA-4E) (TA-4F)	CA143		
Douglas TA-4J Skyhawk (TA-4F)	AZ1, CA53, 85, 110, FL55, 80, IL2, IN20, MA4, MD12, MO6, TX85		
		Ercoupe 415C (XPQ-13)	TX69
		Ercoupe 415CD	PA12
Douglas TA-4J Skyhawk	AZ1, CA52, 58, 144, FL55, 58, ID24, KS9, MD20, MI20, MS17, NJ21, TX43, 66, 80, 85, 149, VT5	Ercoupe 415D	CA151, 160, FL23, MD7, OK27, SC23, UT2
		Ercoupe 415G	KS26, PA35
		Estupian-Hovey WD-II Whing-Ding	WI17
Douglas NTA-4J Skyhawk (TA-4F) (TA-4J)	CA105	Etrich Taube (R)	ME7
Douglas A-4L Skyhawk (A4D-2N) (A-4C)	AL37, AZ48, CA32, 86, 111, 128, CO10, GA51, ID1, KS26, 29, KY2, LA18, NC18, OR11, SC4, 18, TN11	Evans VP-1 Volksplane	AZ7, 30, CO10, FL23, ND5, TX92, WI17
		Exline PX-1	PA56
		Experimental Aircraft Association A-1 Biplane	WI17
		Experimental Aircraft Association P-1 Biplane	CA158, NY7, 52, PA23
Douglas A-4M Skyhawk	CA58, 65, 105, 127, IL57, MS9, NC17, PA26, RI1, TX63	Experimental Aircraft Association P-8 Acrosport	WI17
Douglas NA-4M Skyhawk (A-4F)	MD19	Experimental Aircraft Association P-8A Super Acrosport	WI17
Douglas OA-4M Skyhawk (TA-4F)	VA22		
Douglas D-558-1 Skystreak	FL55, NC6	Experimental Aircraft Association P-9 Pober Pixie	KS26, VT3, WI17
Douglas D-558-2 Skyrocket	CA13, 111, DC3	Explorer PG-1 Aqua Glider	WI17
Douglas XF4D-1 Skyray	CA143	Fairchild FC-2	DC3

Index

Fairchild FC-2W2	AK3, MN18, VA36, WI17	Fairchild 110 Flying Boxcar (R4Q-1)	KY5
Fairchild 22 C7	CA130	Fairchild 110 Flying Boxcar (R4Q-2)	CA58, CO25, PA35
Fairchild 22 C7A	OR24	Fairchild 205 Provider (C-123B)	AK16, AZ30
Fairchild 22 C7B	CA130, OR24	Fairchild 473 Provider (205)	AK1, 3
Fairchild 22 C7D	CA65, TX114	(C-123B) (C-123J)	
Fairchild 22 C7F	NC24	Fairchild 473 Provider (205)	AR15, AZ30, CA4, 32,
Fairchild 22 C7F (C7E)	WA43	(C-123B) (C-123K)	85, 89, 139, FL1, 36,
Fairchild 24 C8	IA13, WI17		IA27, NC1, 30, OH55,
Fairchild 24 C8A	CA149, IL18, MO15		PA1, TX147, UT5
Fairchild 24 C8C	CA65, ND5, OR20, PA1	Fairchild 473 Provider (205)	DE1, GA45, TX51
Fairchild 24 C8F	KS26, OH55	(C-123B) (C-123K) (UC-123K)	
Fairchild 24 C8F (24H)	NY63	Fairchild Black Fly	MD13
Fairchild 24G	AK3, IA13, NY7, PA12,	Fairchild F-27 Friendship	MT9
	35, VA36, WA37	Fairchild F-27A Friendship (F-27)	CA82
Fairchild 24H	WI17	Fairchild F-27F Friendship	ID14
Fairchild 24J	AK5	Fairchild F-27F Friendship (F-27A)	OK34
Fairchild 24R9 Forwarder (UC-61C)	MD13	Fairchild Pilgrim 100-A	AK3, WA34
Fairchild 24R40 (UC-86)	OR24	Fairchild-Hiller FH-1100	CA65, NY13
Fairchild 24R40A (XUC-86A)	OH55	Fairchild-Hiller FH-1100 (OH-5A)	AL36
Fairchild 24R46	CA45, 130, MO15, NC40,	Fairchild-Hiller FH-227B (FH-227)	MI29
	TX30, 40, WI51	Fairchild-Republic YA-10A	LA8, TX123
Fairchild 24W40	AK3	Thunderbolt II	
Fairchild 24W40 (GK-1)	OR21	Fairchild-Republic A-10A	AK11, AZ1, 13, 30, CA3,
Fairchild 24W41	WA25	Thunderbolt II	CO28, CT1, 9, FL76,
Fairchild 24W46	CA130, IL3, KS9		78, GA44, 45, ID7,
Fairchild 42	AK16		IN20, KY5, LA7, MA2,
Fairchild 45A	MN18		MI53, MO17, 48,
Fairchild M-62A Cornell (PT-19)	CA45, MN14, NY82,		NV17, NY4, 14, 21, 73,
	OH22, 71, PA35,		82, OH55, PA14, 64,
	TX29, 32, 40		SC16, 19, TX58, 76,
Fairchild M-62A Cornell (PT-19A)	AZ30, CA28, 89, 139,		123, 147, UT5, VA10,
	CO27, GA21, 45, IA21,		WA22, WI62
	KS26, MD13, 15,	Fairchild-Republic A-10B	CA4
	MN18, ND8, NM6,	Thunderbolt II (A-10A)	
	NY77, 82, OH37, 48,	Fairchild-Republic NGT (T-46A)	AZ1, CA4, OH55
	55, OK8, 10, 12, PA12,	Fairey Swordfish II	FL22
	TX8, 24, 26, 30, 34, 40	Fairey Swordfish III	TN6
	71, 105, WA16, WI17	Fairey Swordfish IV	TX40
Fairchild M-62A Cornell (PT-19B)	AL32, CA3, 85, FL23,	Fairey Gannet AEW.3	AZ30
	KS10, NY82, OK8,	Falck Racer	WI17
	OR7, 24, PA12, 35,	Farman HF-3 (R)	ME7
	TX16, WA37	Farman HF.206 Moustique (R)	WI24
Fairchild M-62A-3 (Fairchild M-62A	OH12	Farman F.65 Sport	VA19
Cornell (PT-19A))		Fauvel AV.361	MN3
Fairchild M-62A-4 Cornell (PT-26)	AL32, CA3, 160, TX8	Felixstowe F.5L	VA19
Fairchild M-62A-4 Cornell (PT-26)	AK3, CA111, MN14, 18,	Fellers Sierra Sr.1	CA155
(Cornell I)	TX28	Ferguson Monoplane	NY16
Fairchild M-62A-4 Cornell (PT-26A)	IN10, OK8, TX31, 40	Fiat G.55 (R)	IL18
Fairchild M-62A-4 Cornell (PT-26A)	FL73, KS26, MD22, NM6	Fiat G.59-4B	VA17
(Cornell II)		Fiat G.91PAN (G.91)	WA25
Fairchild M-62A-4 Cornell (PT-26B)	NY32, TX34, 40	Fiat G.91T/3 (T/1)	FL47
(Cornell II)		Fibera KK-1e Utu	NM20
Fairchild M-62A-4 Cornell II	AZ30, MN18, NM5,	Fieseler Fi 103A-1	AZ30, CA111, 160, DC3,
	OH55, TX28, 40, WI10		KS20, MD23, VA17,
Fairchild M-62C Cornell (PT-23)	CT9, ID12, IL18, KS11,		WA12, 25
	26, MA11, MI2, OH22,	Fieseler Fi 103A-1 (FSM)	FL22, WA28
	TX40	Fieseler Fi 103A-1/Re4 (FSM)	WA28
Fairchild M-62C Cornell (PT-23A)	CA32, MN18	Fieseler Fi 103R	WA12
Fairchild 71	AK16, MO15, WA34	Fieseler Fi 156C-1 Storch	MA4
Fairchild 78 Packet (C-82A)	AZ30, MD13, OH55, 71,	Fieseler Fi 156C-2 Storch	FL22, OH55, WA12
	WA22	Fike C	WI17
Fairchild 110 Flying Boxcar	CA4, 88	Fike F	AK16
(C-119B)		Firestone 45C (XR-9)	AL36
Fairchild 110 Flying Boxcar	AZ30, CA32, GA45,	Fischer Mini-Mustang	FL80
(C-119C)	NC30, TX147	Fisher FP-202 Koala II	KS26
Fairchild 110 Flying Boxcar (C-119F)	AZ24, CA3, 85, 139, DE1,	Fisher FP-303	FL23, NY21
	GA46, KY5, MD13,	Fisher FP-404	CO32, ND8, NJ1, OR7
	NV3, NY54, 74, UT5,	Fisher Mk1 912 Floatplane	PA56
	WY6	Fisher P-75A Eagle	OH55
Fairchild 110 Flying Boxcar (C-119F)	NE23	Fisher Q-Lite	OR7
(C-119G)		Flagg F-13	MO15
Fairchild 110 Flying Boxcar (C-119F)	OH55	Flaglor Sky Scooter	AZ30, NY21, VA29
(C-119J)		Fleet 1	CA130, IL65, IN48,
Fairchild 110 Flying Boxcar	IN20		NY56, VA17, 36
(C-119G)			
Fairchild 110 Flying Boxcar	AR15, AZ17, FL36, NC1		
(C-119G) (C-119L)			

Fleet 2	AZ30, 37, CA122, 128, IL65, IN40, 44, NY14, OH64, WA8, 31	Ford 1 Flivver	MI25
		Ford 1 Flivver (FSM)	FL23, 68
		Ford 1 Flivver (R)	WI17
Fleet 2 (N2Y-1)	FL55	Ford 4-AT-A	MN18
Fleet 7	CA85, IL70, MO15, PA35, VA13	Ford 4-AT-B	FL22, MI25
		Ford 4-AT-B (4-AT-A)	MN18
Fleet 7 (2)	IA1, OR24	Ford 4-AT-E	AZ10, MN18, WI17
Fleet 8	NY53	Ford 4-AT-E (4-AT-B)	FL55
Fleet 9	IL3	Ford 5-AT-B	CA122, DC3, FL22, OH31, OR7
Fleet 16B Finch II	IL65, NY7, 16, 63, TX34, 40		
		Ford 5-AT-C	AZ37, MI2
Fleet Super V (Beech 35 Bonanza)	TN4	Ford 5-AT-D	MT9
Fleetwings F5 Seabird	CA19	Ford JB-2 [Fieseler Fi 103A-1]	AK16, AL38, CA112, CT9, IL44, IN19, MI2, MS14, OH55, OR7, TX147
Fleetwings F401 Seabird	MN18		
Fleetwings XBT-12	OH71		
Flightstar FS-II SL	OH18, WI17		
Floyd BF-5	PA49	Forney F.1A	AL32, AZ24, CO14
Floyd BF-6	NY74	Foss Special	CA17
Flug Werk FW 190A-8/N	OH74, VA17	Foster AA-1 Hot Air Balloon	NM2
Flug Werk FW 190A-9/N	IL18	Foster AS-2 Hot Air Balloon	NM2
Focke-Achgelis Fa 330A-1 Bachstelze	OH55, VA19	Foster AX-1 Hot Air Balloon	NM2
		Foster AX-2 Hot Air Balloon	NM2
Focke-Wulf Fw 44J Stieglitz	AZ30, FL22, TX34, 40, VA17	Foster Dragonfly III	AZ22
		Fouga CM.170-2 Magister (CM.170A)	FL42, NY23, OR4, TX19
Focke-Wulf Ta 152H-0	VA19		
Focke-Wulf Fw 189A-2	WA12	Fouga CM.170R Magister	CA28, 53, 63, NM8, NY4 62, WI17
Focke-Wulf Fw 190A-5/U-3	WA12		
Focke-Wulf Fw 190A-7	FL82	Fournier RF-4D	CA17
Focke-Wulf Fw 190A-8	TX135, VA17	Fowler Gage Tractor	VA19
Focke-Wulf Fw 190D-13/R11	WA12	Francis-Angell A-15 Special	MI2
Focke-Wulf Fw 190D-9	OH55	Frankfort Cinema B (TG-1A)	MN18, NM20, VA19
Focke-Wulf Fw 190F-8	FL82	Franklin A	PA43
Focke-Wulf Fw 190F-8/R1 (A-7)	VA19	Franklin PS-2 Eagle	FL55, MD15, NM20, NY50, OH53
Focke-Wulf Weihe 50	NM20		
Fogle Skycat V-333	NC6	Franklin Sport 90	OR24, WI27
Fokker C IVA	ME7	Fronius DF-7	CA154
Fokker D VI (R)	CA15, PA29	Fuji LM-1	DE5
Fokker D VII	DC3	Fulton FA-3 Aerocar	VA19
Fokker D VII (FSM)	CA115, FL10, 55, MO24	Fulwiler Air Shark I	WI22
Fokker D VII (R)	AL32, CA15, 33, 111, CO29, IN25, MO26, NY63, OH55, TX16, 114, VA17, WA25	Fulwiler Thunder Mustang	WI22
		Funk B	CA105, KS8, OH53, WI17
		Funk B-75L	CA130, KS8, 26, OH53, PA61, WA34
Fokker D VIII (R)	AZ11, 37, CA15, CO29, FL22, WA25		
		Funk B-85C	KS18, TX135
Fokker D VIII (Scale R)	PA26	Funk B-85C (B)	IA1
Fokker D XII	OH55	Funk F-23	TX134
Fokker Dr I (FSM)	CA1, 96, 122, CT9, FL10, 61, IL79, OK28	Funk F-23B (F-23)	TX134
		Galaxy 7 Hot Air Balloon	VT3
Fokker Dr I (R)	AZ22, CA15, 91, 111, 114, CO29, FL22, IA13, 27, ID26, MA4, ME7, MI2, MT13, NY63, OH55, 64, OK43, OR7, 13, PA23, TN5, TX16, 30, 40, 114, VA17, WA25, 31, WI17	Gallaudet Hydro Kite	DC3
		Gannett Peak Aviation 2PCLM-T LFO-14-1	ID1
		Gardan GY-20 Minicab	WA31
		Gas Balloon	IA29, NM2
		Gates Learjet 23	AR2, AZ7, 30, CA160, KS18, MI2, MO3, OH34, OR7, VA19, WA25
Fokker E III (FSM)	CA122		
Fokker E III (R)	CA15, IL32, NY63, OK27, WA25	Gates Learjet 24	AR20, CO32, FL54, IL38, NC10
Fokker E V (FSM)	AL36	Gates Learjet 24A (23)	AR23
Fokker F.IV (T-2)	DC3	Gates Learjet 24D	CO27, OK43, TX69, VA16
Fokker F.VIIa	ND3		
Fokker F.VIIa/3m	MI25	Gates Learjet 24XR	CO26
Fokker Super Universal	AK5	Gates Learjet 25	AL11, MS24, VA16
Fokker F.27 Friendship 500	NC18	Gates Learjet 25D	OH24
Fokker 100 (FSM)	TX5	Gates Learjet 35	CO11, KS40
Folkerts Gullwing	WI17	Gates Learjet 45	AZ31
Folkerts-Henderson Highwing	WI17	Gates Learfan 2100	TX69, WA25
Folland Fo.141 Gnat F.1	CA85, 89, 142, NY21, OH40, TN6	Gazda 100 Helicospeeder	ME7
		Gehrlein GP-1	PA56
Folland Fo.144 Gnat T.1	AZ30, CA28, 111, 128, CO10, 27, DE9, FL86, KS26	Gehrlein Precursor	PA56
		General Aircraft Company Thunderbird W-14	PA17
Foose Tigercat	IL50	General Aircraft Corporation Aristocrat 102-A	CA149
Forbes Cobra	AR1		

Index

General Aircraft Genairco Cabin	FL22
General Atomics MQ-9 Reaper	OH55
General Atomics RQ-1A Predator	OH55
General Atomics RQ-1K Predator	CA122
General Balloon Ax-6	PA56
General Dynamics F-111A	AL32, 38, CA3, 4, ID18, IL3, 50, NM4, NV3, 17, NY4, OH55, OR11, TX14, 51, 80, 123
General Dynamics FB-111A	CA32, 85, CO32, LA7, MI28, NE23, NY60, OK28, SD7, TX147
General Dynamics EF-111A (F-111A)	AZ1, ID18, NM4, NV20, OH55
General Dynamics RF-111A (F-111A)	ID18
General Dynamics F-111 AFTI (F-111A)	CA4
General Dynamics F-111B	CA143
General Dynamics F-111D	CA109, 160, NM4, TX16
General Dynamics F-111E	AZ1, 30, FL76, GA45, LA7, TX40, 66, UT5
General Dynamics F-111F	NM17, 18, OH55, TX69
General Dynamics F-111G (FB-111A)	AZ1, CA3, MO48
General Dynamics 401 Fighting Falcon (YF-16A)	VA35
General Dynamics 401 Fighting Falcon (F-16A)	AK11, AL7, 19, 37, AR10, AZ1, 14, 25, 41, CA76, CO2, 28, FL19, 35, 37, 48, 58, 64, 76, 78, GA44, 45, 49, IA35, ID18, IN52, KS37, 41, LA11, MI3, 53, MN27, MT1, ND22, NM4, 18, NV17, 21, NY34, 73, OH55, 84, OK44, OR9, 12, SC1, 19, SD6, TN2, TX56, 83, 123, 147, UT5, 6, VA31, 35, VT6, WA22, WI3, 56
General Dynamics 401 Fighting Falcon (F-16A) (NF-16A) (AFTI/F-16)	OH55
General Dynamics 401 Fighting Falcon (F-16B)	AL38, CA4, IL54, NJ2, OK40, TX69, 123, 147
General Dynamics 401 Fighting Falcon (F-16C)	IN14, SD6, TX123, VT6
General Dynamics 401 Fighting Falcon (F-16D)	TX123
General Dynamics 401 Fighting Falcon (F-16N)	CA109, 110, 122, FL55, 78, NV11, TX63
General G-1-80 Skyfarer	OR20
Gerath Hang Glider	CT9
Gilbert DG-1	CA122
Gilbert Robert DGA-1A	NC40
Gittens Ikenga 530Z	VA19
Glasflügel BS-1	NY50, TX69
Glasflügel H201B Standard Libelle	NY82
Glasflügel H301 Libelle	NY50
Glasflügel H301B Libelle	NY50
Glasflügel H303 Mosquito	NM20
Glasflügel H401 Kestrel	NM20
Glatfelter Galaxie XRG-65 Glaticopter	PA4
Glider	IN7
Globe GC-1A Swift	CA88, MN21, TN32, VA19
Globe GC-1B Swift	AR2, CA66, 130, NJ25, NM24, NY7, OK19, TN32, TX75
Globe GC-1B Super Swift (GC-1B Swift)	TN32
Gloster Meteor F.4	CA111, FL22
Gloster Meteor NF.11	CA4
Goldwing ST	IL18

Gonzales Biplane	CA65, 139
Goodyear GA-22A Drake	WI17
Goodyear GA-33 Inflatoplane	OH59
Goodyear GA-400R-3 Gizmo (GA-400R-2J)	CA37
Goodyear GA-466 Inflatoplane	MT13
Goodyear GA-468 Inflatoplane (XAO-3)	AL36, FL55, MD19
Goodyear K-28 Puritan (ZNPK)	CT9
Goodyear K-47	FL55, VA19
Goodyear Pilgrim	FL55
Goodyear S-94 Hot Air Balloon	NM2
Goodyear ZPG-2 (ZP2N-1)	FL55
Goodyear ZPG-3W	DC3
Göppingen Gö 1 Wolf (DFS 108-58)	NY50
Göppingen Gö 3 Minimoa	NY50
Gotha G IV (R)	TN5
Gotha Go 229 (Horten Ho IX V3)	MD15
Gotha Go 229 (Horten Ho IX V3) (FSM)	CA122
Government Aircraft Factory Jindivik 203B (IIIB)	IN48
Government Aircraft Factory N.22SL Nomad	AZ30
Government Aircraft Factory N.24A Nomad	CA110
Granville A Gee Bee Sportster	CT9
Granville Gee Bee R (R)	FL22, MD15
Granville Gee Bee R-1	MO15
Granville Gee Bee R-1 (FSM)	MA17
Granville Gee Bee R-1 (R)	CA111, 122, CT9, OH27
Granville Gee Bee Sports E (R)	OR7
Granville Gee Bee Y (R)	FL22
Granville Gee Bee Z (R)	FL22, WA25
Great Lakes 2T-1	OH27, OR20
Great Lakes 2T-1A	CA88, 130, CO29, CT9, IA1, MN21, OH53, OR15, PA23, 33, WI17
Great Lakes 2T-1A (mod)	CA128
Great Lakes 2T-1A-2	AL32, MT13, NY63, TX59
Great Lakes 2T-1A-E (R)	IL18
Great Lakes 2T-1L	PA23
Great Lakes 2T-1MS	NY63
Great Lakes 2T-1R	NY63
Great Lakes Special	KS32
Grega GN-1 Aircamper	NH5, WA19
Griswold Slotted Wing	PA56
Grob G.102 Standard Astir III	VA19
Grob G.103C Twin III Acro SL	WY10
Grob G.109B	ID2
Gross Pioneer II	CA158
Gross Sky Ghost	NY50
Grumman G-15 Duck (J2F-6)	CA111, FL22, 55, OH55, OR21, WI17
Grumman G-21A Goose	NY14, VA19
Grumman G-21A Goose (G-39) (JRF-5)	AK3, CA160, NY32, TX54
Grumman G-21A Goose (G-39) (JRF-6B) (Goose IA)	TX54
Grumman G-22 Gulfhawk II	VA19
Grumman G-23	FL55
Grumman G-32A (UC-107)	AZ33
Grumman G-36 Wildcat (F4F-3)	CA145, FL55, IL49, NY14, TX91
Grumman G-36 Wildcat (F4F-3A)	FL55, HI6, SC18
Grumman G-36 Wildcat (F4F-4)	CA122, VA22
Grumman G-36 Wildcat (F4F-4) (FSM)	CA115
Grumman G-36 Wildcat (F4F-4) (Scale R)	VA21
Grumman G-36 Wildcat (FM-1)	DC3, FL80

Grumman G-36 Wildcat (FM-2)	AZ30, CA58, 110, 111, 144, 160, CT9, FL22, 55, ID26, IL18, MI2, OR21, PA12, TX16, 40, 103, VA17, WA25, 28	Grumman G-79 Panther (F9F-2)	CA58, 160, CT9, FL22, 55, PA26, VA22, 27, WI26
		Grumman G-79 Panther (F9F-2) (F9F-2B)	TX16
		Grumman G-79 Panther (F9F-4)	AZ30, CA49
Grumman G-36 Wildcat (FM-2) (FM-2P)	TX12	Grumman G-79 Panther (F9F-5)	CA145, 160, FL80, KS9, KY1
Grumman G-37 (F3F-2)	CA111, 130, FL22, 55	Grumman G-79 Panther (F9F-5P)	AL37, CA111
Grumman G-37 (F3F-2) (R)	NY14	Grumman G-79 Panther (F9F-5P) (F9F-5KD) (DF-9E)	AZ47
Grumman G-39 Goose (JRF-3)	FL55		
Grumman G-39 Goose (JRF-6B) (Goose 1A)	CA110	Grumman G-82 Guardian (AF-2S)	AZ11, 30, CA35, FL55, TX40
Grumman G-40 Avenger (TBF-1)	FL16, VA19	Grumman G-89 Tracker (S2F-1)	CA105, 119, 131, FL22, 55, KS26, MA4, OR11
Grumman G-40 Avenger (TBF-1C)	CA160, IN48	(S-2A)	
Grumman G-40 Avenger (TBM-1)	NY34	Grumman G-89 Tracker (S2F-1) (S-2A) (S-2F)	AZ1
Grumman G-40 Avenger (TBM-3)	AR19, AZ30, CT9, FL38, KS26, MO10, 44, NY4, 82, PA35, TX40, 70, WA12	Grumman G-89 Tracker (S2F-1) (S-2A) (TS-2A)	AL32, CA3, 109, FL83
		Grumman G-89 Tracker (S2F-1) (S-2A) (US-2A)	KS9, OH48, 71
Grumman G-40 Avenger (TBM-3) (FSM)	CA115, LA17	Grumman G-89 Tracker (S2F-1) (S-2A) (US-2B)	FL42, MI53, TX16, WA1
Grumman G-40 Avenger (TBM-3) (TBM-3E)	AZ24, CA58, 110, 111, 145, CO7, FL22, 55, ID15, MA4, MI58, MO44, ND24, NJ8, NM24, NY14, OK20, OR7, 21, RI1, SC18, TX16, 40, 103, 149, VA17, 22	Grumman G-89 Tracker (S2F-1) (S2F-1S) (S-2F)	FL80
		Grumman G-89 Tracker (S2F-1) (S2F-1S) (US-2B)	CA144
		Grumman G-89 Tracker (S2F-1) (S2F-1S1) (S-2F)	AZ30
		Grumman G-89 Tracker (S2F-1) (S2F-1T) (TS-2A)	NY21
Grumman G-40 Avenger (TBM-3) (TBM-3E) (AS.3)	MO44	Grumman G-89 Tracker (S2F-1) (S2F-2U) (US-2C)	MN3
Grumman G-40 Avenger (TBM-3) (TBM-3E) (AS.3M)	TX54, VA8	Grumman G-89 Tracker (S2F-1) (US-2B)	MO44
Grumman G-40 Avenger (TBM-3) (TBM-3N)	OH71	Grumman G-89 Tracker (S2F-1T) (TS-2A)	CA53
Grumman G-40 Avenger (TBM-3) (TBM-3R)	CA144	Grumman G-89 Tracker (S2F-2) (S2F-2U) (US-2C)	OR11
Grumman G-40 Avenger (TBM-3) (TBM-3S)	TX40	Grumman G-93 Cougar (XF9F-6)	VA19
Grumman G-40 Avenger (TBM-3) (TBM-3S) (AS.3)	CA15, FL12, NJ21, TX40	Grumman G-93 Cougar (F9F-6) (F-9F)	FL55, MN6
Grumman G-40 Avenger (TBM-3) (TBM-3S) (AS.3M)	OH74	Grumman G-93 Cougar (F9F-6P) (RF-9F)	CA12, FL55, NC17, NY75, OH22, VA22
Grumman G-40 Avenger (TBM-3) (TBM-3U)	FL80, TX92	Grumman G-93 Cougar (F9F-7) (F-9H)	NY14, 82
Grumman G-44 Widgeon	NJ8	Grumman G-96 Trader (TF-1) (C-1A)	AZ1, 24, CA110, 145, FL42, 55, IN20, KS2, PA26, RI1, TX92
Grumman G-44 Widgeon (J4F-1)	FL55		
Grumman G-44A Widgeon (J4F-2)	AK3, AZ30, CA160, WA37		
Grumman G-50 Hellcat (F6F-3)	CA111, 122, 160, FL22, 55, OR7, VA19	Grumman G-98 Tiger (F11F-1) (F-11A)	AZ30, 33, CA52, 143, 144, 160, CO1, 25, FL55, 67, 80, IN20, KS9, LA23, MI2, NC20, 41, NJ15, NY14, 34, OH48, 71, OK42, TN1, 26, VA27
Grumman G-50 Hellcat (F6F-5)	CA45, 95, 160, FL55, MD3, MI2, RI1, TX40		
Grumman G-50 Hellcat (F6F-5) (F6F-5K)	CT9, FL55, NY14, SC18, WA12		
Grumman G-50 Hellcat (F6F-5) (F6F-5N)	HI6, TX92	Grumman G-98 Tiger (F11F-1F) (F-11B)	CA143
Grumman G-50 Hellcat (F6F-5) (F6F-5N) (F6F-5K)	CA110	Grumman G-99 Cougar (F9F-8) (F-9J)	AZ30, CO25, FL55, MD19, NY34, OH22, TX80, 134, WA25
Grumman G-50 Hellcat (F6F-5) (FSM)	NY74	Grumman G-99 Cougar (F9F-8P) (RF-9J)	AZ30, CA58, 145, 160, IL36
Grumman G-51 Tigercat (F7F-3)	AZ30, CA110, FL22, 55, OR11, TX91, WA17	Grumman G-99 Cougar (F9F-8P) (RF-9J) (TAF-9J)	NY82
Grumman G-51 Tigercat (F7F-3N)	CA111		
Grumman G-51 Tigercat (F7F-3P)	TX91	Grumman G-105 Cougar (F9F-8T) (TF-9J)	AL18, 39, AZ30, CA143, MD12, MI2, MS27, NY84, OR7, SC18, TX149
Grumman G-58 Bearcat (F8F-1)	TX91		
Grumman G-58 Bearcat (F8F-1) (F8F-1D)	TX12		
Grumman G-58 Bearcat (F8F-1B)	IN58	Grumman G-111 Albatross (G-64) (SA-16A) (SA-16B) (HU-16B)	AZ30, CA32, 160, FL11, GA45, IL50, MD12, NE23, OH55, TX51
Grumman G-58 Bearcat (F8F-2)	CA45, 95, 111, TX40, 91, 92, VA19		
Grumman G-58 Bearcat (F8F-2) (F8F-2P)	FL55	Grumman G-111 Albatross (G-64) (SA-16A) (UF-1L) (LU-16C)	AK6
Grumman G-58A Bearcat	CA110	Grumman G-111 Albatross (G-64) (UF-1) (HU-16C)	AZ24, FL61, ID24, TX16
Grumman G-63 Kitten I	NY14		
Grumman G-73 Mallard	ID24, MI2, TX54		

Index

Grumman G-111 Albatross (G-64) (UF-1) (UF-2S) (HU-16B)	NM12	Grumman G-134 Mohawk (OV-1C) (OV-1D) (RV-1D)	GA21
Grumman G-111 Albatross (G-64) (UF-1G) (UF-2G) (HU-16E)	CA85, 109	Grumman G-134 Mohawk (OV-1D)	FL80, IL62, MI2, MN3, TX58
Grumman G-111 Albatross (SA-16B) (HU-16B) (HU-16E)	TN33	Grumman G-159 Gulfstream I	AZ30, FL61, IA12, KS33, MO8
Grumman G-111 Albatross (SA-16B) (UF-2G) (HU-16E)	TX54	Grumman G-159C Academe (TC-4C)	AZ1, FL55
Grumman G-111 Albatross (UF-2S) (HU-16D)	FL61	Grumman G-164 Ag-Cat	MS19, NY14, TX141, VA19
Grumman G-117 Tracer (WF-2) (E-1B)	AZ30, CT9, FL55, NY34, SC18	Grumman G-164A Super Ag-Cat	FL22
Grumman G-121 Tracker (S-2E)	FL55, NY32, SC18	Grumman G-234 Albatross (G-64) (SA-16A) (UF-1G) (UF-2G) (HU-16E)	AL37, CA3, 139, CT9, FL55, MA8, NC12, NY32, TX54
Grumman G-121 Tracker (S2F-3) (S-2D)	FL38, HI3, MD19	Grumman G-303 Tomcat (YF-14A)	FL55, NY14
Grumman G-123 Greyhound (C-2A)	CA102	Grumman G-303 Tomcat (YF-14A) (YF-14B) (YF-14D)	NY34
Grumman G-123 Hawkeye (E-2A) (E-2B)	MD19, NJ1	Grumman G-303 Tomcat (F-14A)	AL32, 37, 38, AZ1, 30, CA52, 85, 109, 110, 111, 112, 118, 122, 128, 144, 145, 155, 160, CO32, FL38, 55, 78, 80, GA10, KS9, 26, 39, MI2, 53, MN43, NJ1, 15, NV11, NY14, 21, 27, 82, OK43, OR21, PA19, 26, 38, 57, 63, RI1, SC18, TX40, 63, 134, 149, VA10, 26, 27, WA25
Grumman G-123 Hawkeye (E-2C)	AZ1, CA112, 145, 160, FL58, LA18, NV11, NY14, VA12, 27		
Grumman G-123 Hawkeye (W2F-1) (E-2A) (E-2B)	FL55, VA26		
Grumman G-128 Intruder (YA2F-1) (YA-6A) (EA-6A)	FL41, NC8		
Grumman G-128 Intruder (YA2F-1) (YA-6A) (NA-6A)	PA2		
Grumman G-128 Intruder (A2F-1) (A-6A) (KA-6D)	VA27, WA42		
Grumman G-128 Intruder (A-6A)	IN47	Grumman G-303 Tomcat (F-14A) (NF-14A)	CA105, MD20
Grumman G-128 Intruder (A-6A) (A-6E)	AZ30, CA53, 58, 109, 110, 143, 145, 160, CO1, FL9, 55, GA10, MI58, NV11, NY21, PA38, RI1, SC18, VA10, 19, 26, 35, WA27	Grumman G-303 Tomcat (F-14A) (F-14B)	FL16, KY2, NJ21, OH48
		Grumman G-303 Tomcat (F-14B)	CA53, CT9, FL41, IN20, PA18
		Grumman G-303 Tomcat (F-14D)	AZ1, CA3, 32, 68, FL86, HI6, NC18, NY4, OR7, TN2, VA27, 36
Grumman G-128 Intruder (EA-6A)	IA27		
Grumman G-128 Intruder (A-6A) (A-6E) (NA-6E)	MD19	Grumman G-712 (X-29A)	CA99, OH55
		Grumman G-712 (X-29A) (R)	DC3
Grumman G-128 Intruder (A-6A) (KA-6D)	AL37, CA105, FL78	Grumman G-1159 Gulfstream II	AZ30
		Grumman G-1159 Gulfstream IISP	MD13
Grumman G-128 Intruder (A-6E)	AZ1, CA52, 122, 143, 160, FL16, 80, MD20, NC17, NY14, 27, OR13, PA44, TX149, WA25	Gulfstream 550 Peregrine	OK28
		Gunderson Burke Penguin	WI17
		Gyrodyne QH-50C (DSN-3)	WA26
		Gyrodyne GCA.2C	NY14
		Gyrodyne QH-50C (DSN-3)	AZ30, CT9, GA45, IL62, LA25, MA3, NC6, NY14, OH76, OR13, PA4, SC18, 19
Grumman G-128 Intruder (A-6F)	NY14		
Grumman G-128 Intruder (A-6F) (A-6DSD)	NY34		
Grumman G-128 Prowler (EA-6B)	FL55, 58, MD19, WA27	Gyrodyne QH-50D	MD19, NV12
Grumman G-128 Prowler (EA-6B) (NEA-6B)	WA42	Gyrodyne XRON-1 (XHOG-1)	CT9, FL55, MO25, NY9, 14, SC18, VA22
Grumman G-134 Mohawk (YAO-1A) (YOV-1A)	AL36	Haigh SuperStar	MI2
		Halberstadt CL II (R)	NV23
Grumman G-134 Mohawk (AO-1A) (OV-1A)	CA111, IN48, MN39, NJ3	Halberstadt CL IV	VA19
		Halberstadt CL IV (C-5)	OH55
Grumman G-134 Mohawk (AO-1A) (OV-1A) (JOV-1A)	MN3	Halberstadt CL IV (R)	VA17
		Halberstadt CLS I	OH55
Grumman G-134 Mohawk (OV-1A)	MN3, TX134	Hall Cherokee II	IA22, NM20
Grumman G-134 Mohawk (AO-1B) (OV-1B)	CA110, MN3, NY14, TX16	Hall Cherokee IIRM	NY50
		Hall Cherokee RM	NM20
Grumman G-134 Mohawk (AO-1B) (OV-1B) (OV-1D)	GA6	Hall SAH-8 Ibex	NY50
		Hall Springfield Bulldog (R)	WA37
Grumman G-134 Mohawk (OV-1B)	AL36, FL80, GA38, IL59, TX4, VA23	Hallock Road Wing HT-1	TX69
		Hamilton H-45	AK5
Grumman G-134 Mohawk (OV-1B) (OV-1D)	GA39, NC6	Hamilton H-47	AK3
		Hammond Bill 01	FL23
Grumman G-134 Mohawk (OV-1B) (RV-1D)	MN3, MS2, PA57	Handley Page HP.80 Victor K.2 (B.2)	OH71
		Handley Raven 2300	OR7
Grumman G-134 Mohawk (AO-1C) (OV-1C)	AZ30, FL24, GA24, IN48, MN3, 24, RI1, TX58	Hang Glider	CA55, CO32, NV23
		Hanriot HD-1	CA111, FL55
Grumman G-134 Mohawk (OV-1C)	AZ1, 18, GA34, IL62, MN3, NY82	Hanriot Monoplane (R)	NY63
		Hargrave Ornithopter	DC3
Grumman G-134 Mohawk (OV-1C) (OV-1D)	GA6, IN22, 48, MN3, OR7, 16, PA1, TX61	Harlow PJC-2	WA43, WI17
		Harrison Mini Mac	AL32

Hartman Monoplane	NE12	Hill Hummer	WI17
Hatz CB-1	CA130, NY16, OH37	Hiller XH44	VA19
Haufe Dale Hawk 2	WI17	Hiller XH44 (R)	CA65
Hawker Fury (R)	VA17	Hiller UH4 Commuter	CA65
Hawker Hurricane I	CO27	Hiller UH5B	CA65
Hawker Sea Hurricane I	CA111	Hiller UH12A	NY13
Hawker Hurricane II	VA17	Hiller UH12A (HTE-1)	FL55
Hawker Hurricane IIB	FL22, TX92	Hiller UH12A Model 360	CA65
Hawker Hurricane IIC	AZ30, VA19, WA12	Hiller UH12A Raven (H-23A)	AL36, CA65, KS9, MI2, OK22
Hawker Hurricane XII	FL22, OH55, VA17		
Hawker Tempest V	FL22	Hiller UH12B	MI12
Hawker Fury FB.10	CA89, NM24, TX12	Hiller UH12B Raven (H-23B)	AL36, CA37, 65, 116,
Hawker Sea Fury FB.11	FL22, ID26, TN10, TX40, 91, VA17	(OH-23B)	GA6, 9, 45, 52, IL62, LA9, 12, MI2, 22,
Hawker Sea Fury T.20	TX16		OH34, 40, OR7, 16,
Hawker Sea Fury T.20S (T.20)	TX91		PA44, TX138, VA34
Hawker P.1067 Hunter F.51	CA88, ND2, OR4	Hiller UH12C	AZ30
Hawker P.1099 Hunter F.58	AZ30	Hiller UH12C Raven (H-23C)	CA26, 65, IA25, MN29,
Hawker P.1101 Hunter T.7	CA160	(OH-23C)	30, OK1, OR19
Hawker P.1127 Kestrel (XV-6A)	AL36, OH55, VA2, 35	Hiller UH12C Raven (H-23G)	AZ42, CA97, 100, CT9,
Hawker-Siddeley P.1127 Harrier 50 (AV-8A)	AZ48, CA122, 143, FL55, 78, NC17, 20, PA38	(OH-23G)	HI10, 11, IL38, MI29, OK17, PA4, TX132
Hawker-Siddeley P.1127 Harrier 50 (AV-8A) (AV-8C)	AZ30, CA58, 109, 143, FL55, 58, NY34, RI3, TX76, WA25	Hiller UH12D Raven (H-23D) (OH-23D)	CA65, 123, FL42, NJ21, NY13, OH22, TX104, 140
Hawker-Siddeley P.1127 Harrier GR.3 (GR.1) (GR.1A)	WA12	Hiller UH12E	CA65, 111, OR7
Hawker-Siddeley P.1127 Harrier GR.3	CA160, WA12	Hiller UH12E Raven (H-23F) (OH-23F)	AL36, CA65, OK17
Hawker-Siddeley P.1127 Harrier T.54 (TAV-8A)	CA105	Hiller UH12E4 (Mock up)	CA65
		Hiller UH12E5	CA65
Hawker-Siddeley P.1184 Sea Harrier FA.2 (FRS.1)	VA8	Hiller UH12L-4	CA65
		Hiller YHJ.1 Hornet	CA65
Hawker-Siddeley Harrier II (YAV-8B)	AL38	Hiller HJ.1 Hornet	CA65
		Hiller HJ.1 Hornet (XHOE-1)	VA19
Hawker-Siddeley Harrier II (AV-8B)	FL58, MD17, NC6, 8, VA22	Hiller HJ.1 Hornet (YH-32)	AL36, CA37, 65, FL22, WA25
HD-2M Sportster	CA65	Hiller HJ.1 Hornet (YH-32) (XHOE-1)	CA65
Heath Baby Bullet (R)	PA56		
Heath Feather	WI17	Hiller ULV (HJ.1 Hornet) (YH-32)	CA65
Heath CNA-40	KY2, PA35	Hiller 1031 Flying Platform (VZ-1)	VA19
Heath Parasol	MI2, NE12, OR20, PA23, 56, WA8, WI17	Hiller 1033 Rotor Cycle (XROE-1)	CA65
		Hiller 1033 Rotor Cycle (YROE-1)	AL36, CA65, OR7, VA19
Heath Super Parasol	AL32, NY16, OR24, VA36, WI17	Hiller 1099	CA65
		Hiller Camel (Mock up)	CA65
Heath LNA-40 Parasol	NY63, WA25, WI17	Hiller J10 (R)	CA65
Heath LNB-4 Parasol	CT9, NC40, PA35	Hiller VXT-8 (R)	CA65
Heath LNB-4 Super Parasol	WI17	Hipp's Reliant	OH18
Heath Super Parasol IV	FL23	Hispano HA-1112M1L	CA111, MI2, NY74,
Hegy R.C.H.A. El Chuparosa	WI17	[Messerschmitt Bf 109G]	OH55, OR21, TX16, 54, VA17, WA25,
Heinkel He 100D-1 (FSM)	CA111		WI17
Heinkel He 162A-1 (R)	NY82	Hispano HA-1112M4L [Messerschmitt Bf 109G] (two seater)	TX54
Heinkel He 162A-2	CA111, VA19		
Heinkel He 219A	VA19		
Helicraft Tip-Jet	IN3	Hispano HA.200A Saeta (HA.200R1)	CA38, NY23, 62
Helio No.1	VA19	Hispano HA.200B Saeta	MD15, NY23
Helio H-295 Super Courier	CA130	Hispano HA.200D Saeta	CA38, NC18, NY23
Helio H-295 Super Courier (H-395) (U-10B) (U-10D)	GA45	Homebuilt Aircraft	OR13
		Homebuilt Biplane	CA124, OH23
Helio H-295 Super Courier (U-10D)	OH55	Homebuilt Helicopter	NY16
Helio H-391 Courier (YL-24)	AL36	Homebuilt Hot Air Balloon	NM2
Helio H-395 Super Courier (U-10A)	FL36	Homebuilt Monoplane	IN48, NY16
Helio H-395 Super Courier (U-10B)	NC19	Horten Ho IIIf (DFS 108-250)	VA19
Helisoar HP-10	PA12, WI17	Horten Ho IIIh (DFS 108-250)	VA19
Helmerichs 32	MT9	Horten Ho IIIL	DC3
Helton Lark 95	AZ30, IA1, TX141	Horten Ho IVa (DFS 108-251)	CA111
Henderschott Monoplane	WI17	Horten Ho VI V2 (DFS 108-253)	VA19
Henderson Power	NY16	Horten Ho IX V3 (See Gotha Go 229)	MD15
Henschel Hs 293A-1	MD23		
Herbert Trautman Road Air	FL22	Hot Air Balloon	NM2, TN8
Herrick HV2A Convertoplane	VA19	Howard 250 (Lockheed 18-50-23 Lodestar (R5O-5))	CA111
Herring Sport Fan	KS18		
Herring-Arnot Hang Glider (R)	NY50	Howard DGA-3 Pete	NV23, OH27
Herring-Curtiss 1 (R)	NY14	Howard DGA-4	OH58
Hickman Jungmeister DH-1	OK28	Howard DGA-4 (R)	WA34
Hild-Marshonet 17 (R)	PA35	Howard DGA-5 (R)	CA111

Index

Howard DGA-6 (R)	AR2
Howard DGA-11	CA17
Howard DGA-11 (DGA-9)	AR2
Howard DGA-15P	CA17, ID15, MI2, ND24, OH71, WA25
Howard DGA-15P (GH-2)	CA133
Howard DGA-15P (GH-3)	TX149
Howard DGA-15P (NH-2)	TX75
Howard DGA-18K	AR2
Howard Pete III	WI17
Howard S-51-D Mustang	IN25
Howard Super Ventura (Lockheed 237-27-01 Ventura (PV-1))	CA35, 108
Huber 101-1 Aero	WA25
Huff-Daland Duster	AL32, VA19
Hughes H-1	DC3
Hughes H-1 (R)	CA111, 128
Hughes H-4 Hercules (HK-1)	OR7
Hughes 269A	MO19, NC10, NJ22, OR7, TX19
Hughes 269A Osage (TH-55A)	AL36, 38, AZ30, CA36, 50, 61, 77, 104, 126, 157, GA6, IA25, IL24, 33, 60, 62, IN22, 46, KS23, LA22, MA10, MN32, MO8, NJ10, 21, NY38, OH48, OK29, PA4, TX104, 132, 139, 142, VA34, WA9, 11, WI35
Hughes 269A-1	CO10
Hughes 269C	CA107
Hughes 269C-1	TX19
Hughes 369	GA52, NJ24, TX102
Hughes 369D	OR7
Hughes 369HS	CA107, NY13
Hughes 369M Cayuse (YHO-6) (YOH-6A)	MS10
Hughes 369M Cayuse (HO-6) (OH-6A)	AL31, 32, 36, AZ30, 42, CA85, 137, CO2, CT9, FL32, GA6, 38, IL62, KS26, 28, KY3, 5, LA6, MA16, MS2, 13, 26, NC29, NJ20, 21, NY16, 21, 82, OR19, PA4, 32, 45, 57, RI1, 2, SD9, TX58, 104, UT3, 9, VT4, 6, 7, WA28
Hughes 369M Cayuse (HO-6) (OH-6A) (AH-6C)	KY5
Hughes 369M Cayuse (HO-6) (OH-6A) (TH-6B)	MD20
Hughes 369M Cayuse (HO-6) (OH-6A) (MH-6B)	OK1
Hughes 369M Cayuse (HO-6) (OH-6A) (MH-6C)	NC3
Hughes 369M Cayuse (MH-6E)	PA4
Hughes 77 Apache (YAH-64A)	AL36
Hughes 77 Apache (AH-64A)	AL28, TX134, VA32
Hugo Hu-Go Craft VPS	OK43
Hunting-Percival P.84 Jet Provost T.3	UT10
Hunting-Percival P.84 Jet Provost T.3A (T.3)	AZ30, OR4, UT2, 4, 13
Hunting-Percival P.84 Jet Provost T.5	CO27, FL86
Hunting-Percival P.84 Jet Provost T.5A (T.5)	GA42
Hütter H 17	NY50
Icarus I Hang Glider	CA154, MD15, OR13
Ikarus Aero 3A	CA105, FL22
Ilyushin Il-2m3	AZ30, VA19, WA12
Ilyushin Il-14P	CA109
Inland Sport W-500	PA29
Insitu A-20 Scan Eagle	OR7
Insitu Aerosonde	WA25
Interavia E-3	ID15
Interstate S-1A Cadet	IA1, KS26, MN18, ND23, OR20, TX23
Interstate S1B1 Cadet (O-63) (L-6)	AL36, AZ30, ND8, 24, NJ7, OH55, 64, TX2, 36, 40
Interstate TDR-1	FL55
Irvin Aero Cycloid (R)	CA65
Irwin F-A-1 Meteorplane	CA106, WA34
Isaacs Fury	AL32
Israeli Aircraft Industries Kfir C.1 (F-21A)	NY34
Israeli Aircraft Industries-Mazlat Mastiff III	OR7
Jacobs Rhönadler 35 (DFS 108-47)	PA56
Jacobs Rhönbussard (DFS 108-50)	WY10
Jansson BJ-1B Duster	NM20
Jayhawk	KS18
Jeffair Barracuda	FL23, MI57
Jensen Slipknot	FL42
Johnston ONR Flying Platform	CA65
Junkers W 33 b	MI25
Junkers Ju 87R-2/trop	IL45
Junkers Ju 88D-1/trop	OH55
Junkers Ju 388L-1	VA19
Jurca MJ.5J2 Scirocco	WI17
Jurca MJ.77 Mustang	CA105
Kaman K-16B (Grumman G-39 Goose (JRF-5))	CT9
Kaman K-20 Seasprite (HU2K-1) (UH-2A) (HH-2D)	PA4
Kaman K-20 Seasprite (HU2K-1) (UH-2A) (SH-2F)	CA102, 144, FL55, VA26
Kaman K-20 Seasprite (HU2K-1U) (UH-2B) (HH-2C) (SH-2F)	AL37
Kaman K-20 Seasprite (HU2K-1U) (UH-2B) (SH-2F)	AK16, AZ1, 30, CA145, FL55, NJ30, OR7
Kaman K-20 Seasprite (UH-2B) (SH-2F)	LA14
Kaman K-20 Seasprite (SH-2F)	AL38, MD19, PA26
Kaman K-225	CT9
Kaman K-225 Huskie (XHOK-1)	VA19
Kaman K-240 Huskie (HTK-1) (TH-43E)	CT9, OR21
Kaman K-600 Huskie (HOK-1) (OH-43D)	AL36, AZ30, CA58, CT9, NC6
Kaman K-600 Huskie (HUK-1) (UH-43C)	CA37
Kaman K-600-1 Huskie (H-43A) (HH-43A)	CA37, CT9, GA45
Kaman K-600-3 Huskie (H-43B) (HH-43B)	CT9, GA45, NM12, OH55, TX73, UT5, WA28
Kaman K-600-3 Huskie (H-43B) (HH-43B) (HH-43F)	AZ30, CA32, DE1
Kaman K-600-3 Huskie (HH-43F)	WA28
Kaminskas RK-3 Jungster II	MT9
Kaminskas RK-3 Jungster III	CA128
Kamov Ka-26	CA37, VT2
Kantor Strat M-21	NY21
Karp Pusher 107	MI2
Kawanishi N1K1 Kyofu	FL55, MD15, TX103
Kawanishi N1K2-J Shiden Kai	FL55, OH55, VA19
Kawasaki Ki-45 Toryu	VA19
Kawasaki Ki-61-I Hien	FL22, VA17
Keech LW-5	WI17
Keith Rider R-4	CA111
Keith Rider R-5	WI17
Keith Rider R-6	CA111
Kelch TA-12	WI27
Kellett K-3	OH55
Kellett KD.1 (XO-60)	VA19
Kellett KD.1 (YG-1B)	CA160
Kellett KD.1A (KD.1)	PA35
Kellett XR-8	VA19
Kellner KR-1 Seagull	AK16
Kensrue MSK-10	NM20

Kersten Merope Hot Air Balloon	IA29	Lincoln Page LP-3	CA160, KS7, NE12, OR24
Keystone B-6A	LA7		
Keystone Loening K84 Commuter	AK3, MN18	Lincoln Page LP-3A	IL25
Kiceniuk Icarus V	WI17	Lincoln PT-K	WI17
Kinner Playboy R-5	PA29	Lincoln PT-W	MT13
Kinner Sportster B	PA17	Lincoln Sport	PA17
Kinner Sportster B-1	PA35	Lincoln Sport LS-2	PA17
Kinner Sportster K	WA43	Ling-Temco-Vought L450F	TX151
Knabenshue Toledo 2 Airship	OH56	Ling-Temco-Vought L450F (XQM-93A)	TX69
Knepper KA-1 Crusader	PA54		
Kolb III Classic	NY74	Ling-Temco-Vought XC-142A	OH55
Kolb Twinstar IIIX	MD14	Lippisch DM 1	MD15
Kotula-Lundy Graflite	IA27	Lippisch X-114	IA1
Kreider-Reisner KR-21A	MO15	Lithuanian Hot Air Balloon	NM2
Kreider-Reisner KR-21B	WI17	Lobet Ganagobie	WI17
Kreider-Reisner KR-31 Challenger (C-2)	CA130, MD13, MO15, PA17, TX114	Lockheed 1 Vega	MI25, PA29
		Lockheed 5 Vega	PA29
Kreider-Reisner KR-34C Challenger	GA12, MN18, VA19	Lockheed 5B Vega (5)	DC3
Kreutzer K-5 (K-2) (K-3)	MN18	Lockheed 5B Vega (FSM)	CA122
Krieg Ax.6 Smoke Balloon	NM2	Lockheed 5B Vega (R)	CA96, FL22
Krier-Kraft Aero-Master	KS32	Lockheed 5C Vega	PA29
Krist Cloud Cutter	OK28	Lockheed 5C Vega (5B)	VA19
Kyushu J7W1 Shinden	MD15	Lockheed 8 Sirius	DC3
Laird Biplane	MI25	Lockheed 10-A Electra	CA105, FL55
Laird Biplane (R)	FL23	Lockheed 10-A Electra (UC-36A)	AZ30
Laird Swallow	KS18	Lockheed 10-A Electra (XR2O-1)	CT9
Laird LC-1B-300	OH53	Lockheed 10-E Electra (XC-35)	MD15
Laird LC-B-200	IL31, OH53	Lockheed 10-E Electra (FSM)	NY21
Laird LC-R-200 (LC-B)	OH53	Lockheed 12-A Electra Junior (C-40D) (UC-40D)	CA160
Laird LC-RW300	OH53		
Laird LC-RW300 (LC-R200)	OH53	Lockheed 14-H2 Super Electra	FL22
Laird LCR-300	OH53	Lockheed 15-27-01 Harpoon (PV-2)	AZ30, 46, CA33, 90, 110, 142, FL22, 55, IN2, MO5, OH55, SC17, UT2
Laird LC-DW-300 Solution	CT9		
Laird LC-DW-500 Super Solution (R)	FL22, WI17		
Laird-Turner LTR-14 Meteor	VA19		
Laird-Turner LTR-14 Meteor (R)	CA111	Lockheed 15-27-01 Harpoon (PV-2D)	AZ46, OR21, TX16, 40, 92
Laister LP-46	NM20		
Laister Nugget JP-15	NY50	Lockheed 18-08-01 Lodestar	CA32
Laister-Kauffman LK.10A	AL32, CA154, MO15, NM20, NY16, 50, PA56, VA17, WA34	Lockheed 18-40-03 Lodestar (C-56)	CA139
		Lockheed 18-56-23 Lodestar (C-60A)	AL29, CA90, 96, 111, FL61, GA45, OH55, TX37, 40, 143, VA9
Laister-Kauffman LK.10B (TG-4A)	CA111, DE1, GA45, MI2, OH55, TX124		
		Lockheed 18-56-23 Lodestar (R5O-6)	TX92
Lake LA-250 Renegade	MT13	Lockheed 18-56-24 Lodestar (R5O-5)	AZ30, CA85
Lake LA-4-200 Buccaneer	CA63, IN28	Lockheed 026-49-01 Neptune (P2V-1)	FL55
Lamson L.106 Alcor	WA25		
Lancair Legacy 2000	TX75	Lockheed 049-46-25 Constellation (049-46-10) (C-69)	AZ30
Langley Aerodrome (Scale R)	WI17		
Langley Aerodrome 4 (R)	CO32	Lockheed 049-51-26 Constellation	NJ12
Langley Aerodrome 5	DC3	Lockheed 080 Shooting Star (XP-80A)	CA76
Langley Aerodrome 5 (R)	NY14		
Langley Aerodrome 6	MD15	Lockheed 080 Shooting Star (P-80A) (F-80A)	CA111, FL55, GA45, MI2, NJ1, UT5
Langley Aerodrome A	VA19		
Lark Termite H-1	IA1	Lockheed 080 Shooting Star (P-80A) (F-80A) (EF-80A)	CA4
Lavochkin La-9	VA17		
Lavochkin La-11	FL22	Lockheed 080 Shooting Star (P-80B) (F-80B)	AZ30, CA3, 32, NM12
Lazor-Rautenstrauch LR-1A	CT9		
Le Bel Jet	CA111	Lockheed 080 Shooting Star (P-80B) (P-80R)	OH55
Le Vier Cosmic Wind	CA111		
Leak Avid Flyer	AK3, FL22, KS26, MI2, WI17	Lockheed 080 Shooting Star (P-80C) (F-80C)	AK1, CA160, CO25, FL76, KS26, 37, NM11, OH55, TX51, WI17
Lesher SN-1 Nomad	MI55		
Lesher Teal	WI17		
Let C-11 [Yakovlev Yak-11]	CA110, 111, FL22, ID1	Lockheed 080 Shooting Star (P-80C) (F-80C) (TO-1) (TV-1)	CA58, 87, NC6, PA26, TX63, WA25
Let L-13 Blanik	ND23		
Let L-200A Morava	AL11	Lockheed 080 Shooting Star (P-80C) (F-80C) (FSM)	CA115
Letov LF-107 Lunak	WA25		
Levasseur Antoinette (R)	ME7	Lockheed 081-40-01 Salmon (XFV-1)	FL23
Lewann Biplane DD-1	AZ33		
Light Helicopter	CA37	Lockheed 090-32-01 (XP-90) (XF-90)	OH55
Lilienthal Normal-Segelapparat	DC3		
Lilienthal Normal-Segelapparat (R)	CA29, 111, 122, ME7, NY14, TX92, WA25	Lockheed 137-27-01 Ventura II	CO25
		Lockheed 137-27-02 Ventura IIA (B-34) (RB-34)	FL57
Limbach Gusty	MN13	Lockheed 140 Shooting Star (XP-80)	DC3

Index

Lockheed 182-1A Hercules (182-44-03) (C-130A)	AR15, AZ30, CA89, GA45, IL50, MD15, 16, TX51, 123, VA19	Lockheed 382-4B Hercules (C-130E)	AR15, CA105, MI3, 53, NC7, TX123, UT5, VA33, WA22
Lockheed 182-1A Hercules (182-44-03) (C-130A) (AC-130A)	FL36, 76, GA45, OH55	Lockheed 382-4B Hercules (EC-130E) (HC-130E)	NY21
Lockheed 182-1A Hercules (182-44-03) (C-130A) (AC-130A) (C-130A) (JC-130A) (AC-130A)	GA24	Lockheed 382-4B Hercules (C-130G) (EC-130G) (TC-130G)	FL55
Lockheed 182-1A Hercules (182-44-03) (C-130A) (C-130D)	AZ30, MN27, NY70, TX123	Lockheed 382-8B Hercules (C-130E)	AK1, 12, GA45, ID7, IL54, 64, NC1, TX83, 123, WY3
Lockheed 182-1A Hercules (182-44-03) (C-130A) (DC-130A)	CA143	Lockheed 382-8B Hercules (C-130E) (EC-130E)	PA5
Lockheed 182-1A Hercules (182-44-03) (C-130A) (DC-130A) (C-130A)	AZ1	Lockheed 382C-15D Hercules (C-130E)	DE1, NC30, TX51
Lockheed 182-1A Hercules (182-44-03) (C-130A) (JC-130A) (C-130A) (AC-130A)	OH55	Lockheed 382C-32D Hercules (EC-130Q) (TC-130Q)	OK41
Lockheed 182-1A Hercules (182-44-03) (C-130A) (JC-130A) (RC-130S)	AZ13	Lockheed 382C-41D Hercules (C-130H) (YMC-130H)	GA45
Lockheed 182-1A Hercules (182-44-03) (C-130A) (NC-130A)	FL19	Lockheed 382C-85D Hercules (EC-130Q)	IL62, WI51
Lockheed 182-2A Hercules (RC-130A) (C-130A)	MI53	Lockheed 383-04-05 Starfighter (F-104C)	AL32, AZ25, 27, CA4, 68, CO24, 32, CT9, GA13, KS26, MI2, MS14, ND25, NM11, OH55, OK40, SC1, TN20, TX123, VA35, WA25
Lockheed 183-93-02 Starfighter (F-104A)	CA4, 53, 63, 85, 139, 160, GA45, IL50, OH55, OR11, TX16, 51, 80, UT5, WA28		
		Lockheed 394 Viking (YS-3A) (NS-3A)	FL38
Lockheed 183-93-02 Starfighter (YF-104A) (F-104A)	CO25, DC3	Lockheed 394 Viking (S-3A)	CA102
Lockheed 183-93-02 Starfighter (F-104A) (NF-104A)	CA4, 101	Lockheed 394 Viking (S-3A) (ES-3A)	AZ1
Lockheed 185 Orion (P3V-1) (P-3A)	AL38, AZ1, CA92, FL38, 55	Lockheed 394 Viking (S-3A) (S-3B)	AZ1, 30, CA144, 145, FL55, 58, GA10, MD19, MI2, NV11, SC18
Lockheed 185 Orion (P3V-1) (P-3A) (NP-3D)	MD20		
Lockheed 185 Orion (P3V-1) (P-3A) (TP-3A)	HI3	Lockheed 402-2 Bushmaster	NJ3, 29
Lockheed 185 Orion (P3V-1) (P-3A) (VP-3A)	AZ30	Lockheed 422-81-14 Lightning (P-38J)	WA12
Lockheed 185 Orion (P-3A)	FL55, ME2, TX141	Lockheed 422-81-14 Lightning (P-38J) (FSM)	IL1
Lockheed 185 Orion (P-3A) (UP-3A)	HI1	Lockheed 422-81-22 Lightning (P-38J)	CA111, UT5, VA19
Lockheed 185 Orion (P-3B)	LA18, MI53, PA64, WA42	Lockheed 422-87-23 Lightning (P-38L)	AK3, CA160, NJ17, OR7, TX20, VA17, WI48
Lockheed 185 Orion (P-3C)	AZ1	Lockheed 422-87-23 Lightning (P-38L) (F-5G)	CA111, FL22, MN14, NM24, OH55, OR21
Lockheed 185 Orion [188 Electra] (YP3V-1) (YP-3A) (NP-3A)	FL55	Lockheed 422-87-23 Lightning (P-38L) (FSM)	CA115, 138, TX147
Lockheed 186 (XH-51A)	AL36		
Lockheed 187 Cheyenne (AH-56A)	AL36, KY5, LA9	Lockheed 422-87-23 Lightning (P-38L) (P-38M)	WA25, WI17
Lockheed 222-60-15 Lightning (P-38F)	TX91, WA12	Lockheed 426-42-13 Neptune (P2V-5) (P2V-5F) (P2V-5FS) (SP-2E)	CO25, ME2
Lockheed 222-68-12 Lightning (P-38G)	AK12	Lockheed 426-42-13 Neptune (P2V-5) (P2V-5FD) (DP-2E)	CA92
Lockheed 237-27-01 Ventura (PV-1)	CA89, VA22	Lockheed 426-42-15 Neptune (P2V-5) (P2V-5F) (P-2E)	FL38, OH8
Lockheed 282-1B Hercules (C-130B)	TX147		
Lockheed 282-1B Hercules (C-130B) (JC-130B) (C-130B) (NC-130B)	UT5	Lockheed 426-42-15 Neptune (P2V-5) (P2V-5F) (P2V-5FS) (SP-2E)	RI1
Lockheed 282-3B Hercules (GV-1) (KC-130F)	AZ1, FL55		
Lockheed 282-6B Hercules (UV-1L) (LC-130F)	AZ1	Lockheed 426-45-15 Neptune (P2V-5) (P2V-5F) (P-2E) (AP-2E)	AL36
Lockheed 283-93-03 Starfighter (F-104B)	CA3, FL70, KS20	Lockheed 426-45-15 Neptune (P2V-5) (P2V-5F) (P2V-5FS) (SP-2E)	NY32
Lockheed 300 Starlifter (C-141A) (NC-141A)	CA4, DE1		
Lockheed 300 Starlifter (C-141A) (C-141B)	AZ30, CA85, 139, DE1, GA10, 45, IL64, NJ17, OK3, 35, SC22, WA22	Lockheed 426-45-15 Neptune (P2V-5) (P2V-5S) (SP-2E)	OR7
		Lockheed 483-04-06 Starfighter (F-104D)	AZ30, CA25, 29, 32, FL76, IN26, MT4, NJ26, TX147
Lockheed 300 Starlifter (C-141A) (C-141B) (C-141C)	IL64		
Lockheed 300 Starlifter (C-141A) (C-141C)	OH55	Lockheed 580 (T-33A)	AK1, 11, 12, 15, AL15, 25, 26, 30, 32, 34, AR3, 11, 12, 19, 23, AZ3, 25, 27, 30, 33, 46, CA2, 3, 4, 9, 32, 33, 35, 36, 38, 50, 53, 68, 80, 85, 91,
Lockheed 300-50A-01 Starlifter	CA98		
Lockheed 326-59-04 Neptune (P2V-3W)	CA33		

683

Lockheed 580 (T-33A) *(continued)*	96, 104, 109, 111, 122, 123, 139, 155, 160, CO13, 24, 27, 32, DE1, FL2, 15, 16, 24, 37, 45, 55, 76, 80, GA16, 29, 31, 38, 41, 45, 54, 55, 56, 59, HI10, IA4, 7, 30, 33, 34, 35, ID3, 7, 16, 17, 25, IL8, 26, 28, 32, 50, 52, 55, 57, 62, 66, 78, IN9, 11, 20, 24, 26, 29, 36, KS9, 27, 37, LA4, 7, 11, 12, 20, MA2, 4, 8, MD8, 12, 21, MI7, 14, 23, 24, 27, 28, 52, 53, 57, 58, MN1, 2, 7, 11, 19, 24, 30, MO1, 7, 10, 23, 25, 34, MS3, 7, 8, 14, MT1, 7, 8, 13, 15, NC2, 18, 41, ND3, 5, 7, 10, 13, 15, 20, 26, NE2, 7, 8, 11, 15, 23, NJ21, NM4, 21, NY4, 67, 77, OH10, 11, 13, 22, 49, 55, 69, 71, 79, OK1, 15, 24, 28, 33, 46, 48, OR1, 7, 11, PA21, 41, 42, SC1, 9, 15, 21, SD3, 5, 7, TN12, 14, 19, 33, TX7, 23, 26, 48, 51, 52, 56, 57, 69, 76, 79, 80, 88, 93, 108, 115, 119, 121, 130, 131, 133, 134, 145, UT5, VA2, 11, 19, VT6, WA2, 6, 15, 22, 29, WI5, 8, 17, 18, 30, 31, 40, 46, 47, 50, 53, 57, WY3, 7
Lockheed 580 (T-33A) (NT-33A)	OH55
Lockheed 580 (T-33A) (RT-33A)	OR11
Lockheed 580 (T-33A) (TV-2) (T-33B)	AZ30, CA91, 110, 111, CO8, 25, CT2, 9, FL55, IN29, 36, KS18, MI2, 26, MO4, NC6, NM25, NY81, RI3, SD6, TN10, TX40, 123
Lockheed 583-04-15 Starfighter (CF-104D)	FL70
Lockheed 583-10-20 Starfighter (TF-104G)	CA53, 98, OR4
Lockheed 683-04-10 Starfighter (RF-104G)	CA99
Lockheed 683-10-19 Starfighter (F-104G)	CA111, FL42, LA1, NJ1, OK28, OR4, 7
Lockheed 683-10-19 Starfighter (F-104N)	AZ16, CA76
Lockheed 726-45-14 Neptune (P2V-7) (P-2H)	OH71
Lockheed 726-45-14 Neptune (P2V-7) (P-2H) (AP-2H)	AZ30
Lockheed 726-45-14 Neptune (P2V-7) (P2V-7S) (SP-2H)	FL55
Lockheed 726-45-17 Neptune (P2V-7) (P-2H)	GA45
Lockheed 726-45-17 Neptune (P2V-7) (P2V-7S) (SP-2H)	AZ1, CA35, GA52, HI3, OR21, PA35
Lockheed 749A-79-38 Constellation (C-121A) (VC-121A)	AZ30, 33
Lockheed 749A-79-43 Constellation (PO-1W) (WV-1)	KS26
Lockheed 780-76-12 Starfire (F-94A)	NY35, OH55, VT6
Lockheed 780-76-12 Starfire (F-94B) (YF-94A) (YF-94C)	NY73
Lockheed 780-76-12 Starfire (TF-80C) (YF-94A)	CA4
Lockheed 826-45-14 Neptune (P2V-7) (P-2H)	AZ30
Lockheed 880-75-13 Starfire (F-97A) (F-94C)	AZ30, CO24, CT9, MN22, 27, NC4, ND22, OH55, PA20
Lockheed 1049A-55-137 Super Constellation (1049A-55-86) (WV-2) (EC-121K)	CA3, IL50
Lockheed 1049A-55-137 Super Constellation (1049A-55-86) (WV-2) (EC-121K) (NC-121K)	GA45, NC34
Lockheed 1049A-55-137 Super Constellation (WV-2) (EC-121K)	FL55
Lockheed 1049A-55-86 Super Constellation (RC-121D) (EC-121D)	OH55
Lockheed 1049A-55-86 Super Constellation (RC-121D) (EC-121D) (EC-121T)	AZ30, CA160, CO24, KS9, OR7
Lockheed 1049A-55-86 Super Constellation (WV-2) (EC-121K)	OK41
Lockheed 1049B-55-97 Super Constellation (1049B-55-75) (R7V-1) (VC-121E)	OH55
Lockheed 1049E-55-115 Super Constellation (1049E-55-93)	DE1
Lockheed 1049F-55-96 Super Constellation (C-121C)	CA48, SC22, VA19
Lockheed 1049F-55-96 Super Constellation (C-121C) (EC-121S)	TX147
Lockheed 1049G-02-82 Super Constellation (L-1049C-55-94) (L-1049E-55-01)	WA25
Lockheed 1049H-03-152 Super Constellation (1049H-03-148)	MO2
Lockheed 1080-91-08 SeaStar (T2V-1) (T-1A)	AZ1, 30
Lockheed L-1011-1 TriStar	CA68, GA23, MO2
Lockheed L-1011-100 TriStar	AZ31
Lockheed 1329 JetStar	MD3, WA25
Lockheed 1329 JetStar 6	CA68, FL61, GA10, TN18, TX153, WA38
Lockheed 1329 JetStar 6 (C-140A)	CA4, 139, IL64
Lockheed 1329 JetStar 6 (VC-140B) (C-140B)	AZ30, GA45, OH55, TX94, UT5
Lockheed 1329 JetStar 8	IL24, KS35, SC13
Lockheed 1329 JetStar 731	MO41
Lockheed 1329-25 JetStar II	TX16
Lockheed 1649A-98-17 Starliner	FL22, 77
Lockheed A-10 (FSM)	TX7
Lockheed A-12	AL32, 37, 38, CA21, 29, 122, NY34, VA6
Lockheed A-12MD	WA25
Lockheed CL-475	AL36
Lockheed F-117A	CA21, 76, NM11
Lockheed Q-Star (YO-3A)	AL36, AZ30, CA41, 65
Lockheed SR-71A Blackbird	AZ30, CA4, 20, 21, 32, 85, 99, FL76, GA45, KS20, LA7, NE23, OH55, OR7, TX147, VA19, 36, WA25
Lockheed SR-71B Blackbird	MI2
Lockheed SR-71C Blackbird	UT5
Lockheed U-2A	OH55
Lockheed U-2C (U-2A)	AZ13, CA20, 98, DC3, NE23, TX88
Lockheed U-2C (U-2B)	GA45
Lockheed U-2D (U-2B)	CA21
Lockheed YF-12A	OH55
Lockheed YF-22A	CA4
Lockheed YF-117A	NV17, OH55
Lockheed-Boeing Dark Star	OH55
Lockheed-Boughton Air Rep P-38	CA128
Lockheed-Martin F-22A Raptor	OH55
Lockheed-Martin RQ-3A	DC3, OH55, WA25
Lockheed-Martin X-35	OH55

Index

Lockheed-Martin X-35B	VA19
Lockheed-Martin X-35C (X-35A)	MD19
Lockheed-Martin YF-22A Raptor	OH55
Lockheed/Schweizer SGS.2-32 (X-26A)	OH22
Lockheed/Schweizer SGS.2-32 (X-26B) (QT-2)	AL36
Lockwood Air Cam	WI17
Loening OA-1A	VA19
Long Henderson Longster (R)	MI2, NY16, OR13
Long Henderson Longster III (R)	OR24
Long Wimpy	OR15
Longren Pusher	KS21
Loudenschlager Shark	WI17
Loving-Wayne WR-1 Love	FL23, WI17
Loving-Wayne WR-3	IN25
Lunger Beta 1	CO32
Luscombe 1 Phantom	ND23, OH53, TX118
Luscombe 8A Silvaire	AZ46, CA17, 23, 111, 130, IA1, IL18, 38, 80, KS26, ME4, MN12, 21, 30, ND5, NJ25, OH55, 64, OK19, OR24, TX114, 118, WA34, 37
Luscombe 8C Silvaire	PA17, TX92
Luscombe 8E Silvaire	AK3, AR2, CA130, IN40, TX89
Luscombe 8F Silvaire	MN21, OK19, TX111
Luscombe T-8F	KS26, WI22
Luscombe 11A	CA130, TX118
Luton LA.4A Minor	FL51
Lutz Flying Dutchman	ID1
Macchi M.39 (FSM)	CA111
Macchi MC.200 Saetta	OH55
Macchi MC.202 Folgore	DC3
Macchi M.416 [Fokker S-11]	AZ33
MacCready Gossamer Albatross II	WA25
MacCready Gossamer Condor	DC3
MacCready Gossamer Penguin	CA154, TX69
MacCready Solar Challenger	VA29
Mackie 1	NY83
Mahoney Sorceress	VA19
Maneval Helicopter	KS21
Mann SB-26	PA12
Manta Pterodactyl	VA19
Marcoux-Bromberg R-3 (Keith Rider R-3)	CT9
Marinac Flying Mercury	WI17
Marketello Stahltaube	CA158
Marquart MA-3 Maverick	CA151
Marriott Avitor Hermes (R)	CA65
Marske Genesis I	NY50
Martin 139A (YB-10)	OH55
Martin 162 Mariner (PBM-5)	FL55
Martin 162A	MD6
Martin 162G Mariner (PBM-5A)	AZ30
Martin 179 Marauder (B-26)	CA89, FL22, OH48, UT5
Martin 179B Marauder (B-26B)	AZ30, DC3
Martin 179G Marauder (B-26G)	OH55
Martin 2-0-2A	NJ3
Martin 210A Mauler (AM-1)	CA111, FL55, MD12, OR21
Martin 237B Marlin (P5M-2S) (SP-5B)	FL55
Martin 272A Canberra (RB-57A)	CT9, GA45, IL57, KS28, MD12, MI53, 58, NY82, OH71, TX147, UT5
Martin 272B Canberra (B-57B)	MI2
Martin 272B Canberra (B-57B) (EB-57B)	AZ1, CA85, FL76, KS28, MD15, MT7, OH55, SD7, TX51, 88, VT6
Martin 272B Canberra (B-57B) (RB-57B)	CA4
Martin 272C Canberra (B-57C)	AR15
Martin 272E Canberra (B-57E)	AZ30, NE23
Martin 272E Canberra (B-57E) (EB-57E)	CA32, CO24, 32
Martin 275B Seamaster (P6M-2)	MD12
Martin 294 Canberra (RB-57D) (EB-57D)	OH55
Martin 4-0-4	AZ30, 33, CA160, FL22, GA47, MD12, MO2, PA35, TX109
Martin 744 Canberra (272) (B-57B) (RB-57F) (WB-57F)	AZ1, GA45
Martin 744 Canberra (294) (RB-57D) (RB-57F) (WB-57F)	AZ30
Martin J.V. K-III Kitten	VA19
Martin MB-2 (R)	OH55
Martin Sport Plane	NY16
Martin SV-5J	OH55
Martin SV-5J (X-24A)	CO28
Martin SV-5P (X-24A) (X-24B)	OH55
Martin SV-5P (X-24A) (FSM)	AL38
Martin X-23A (SV-5D)	OH55
Martin W.M. Glider	OH48
Massachusetts Institute of Technology Daedulus	MA9
Massachusetts Institute of Technology Monarch	MA9
Maule M-4-220C Strata Rocket	MN21
Maule M-4C	OR20
Maupin Lanteri Black Diamond	MD15
Maupin Woodstock 1	OK28
Max Holste MH.1521M Broussard	WA16
Maxair Drifter	NY16
Maxair Hummer	PA56
Maxair Super Drifter	MD14
McAllister Yakima Clipper	WA25
McCabe Aeroplane	NE6
McCulloch J-2	AZ30, CA37, FL22, KS26, NJ21
McCulloch MC-4A (XHUM-1) (HUM-1)	AZ30, CA160
McCulloch MC-4C	CA37, 65
McCulloch MC-4C (YH-30)	AL36
McDonald Primary Glider	CO32
McDonnell M.23 Phantom I (FD-1) (FH-1)	DC3, FL55, NY82
McDonnell M.24 Banshee (F2H-2)	CA58, LA4, TX149
McDonnell M.24 Banshee (F2H-2P)	FL55, NY82
McDonnell M.24 Banshee (F2H-3)	OH71, RI1
McDonnell M.24 Banshee (F2H-4) (F-2D)	FL55, VA27
McDonnell M.27D Goblin (XF-85)	NE23, OH55
McDonnell M.36BA Voodoo (F-101B)	AR22, AZ1, 30, CA3, 4, 32, 85, 139, CO24, 32, DE1, FL8, 62, 76, ID21, IN20, MD12, MI28, 39, MO42, ND11, 22, NE23, OH55, 81, OR14, PA46, SC19, SD7, TN7, TX10, 56, 125, 134, 135, 147, UT5, VA2, WA2, 41, WY8
McDonnell M.36BA Voodoo (F-101B) (CF-101B)	CO24, ME1, MN27
McDonnell M.36BA Voodoo (F-101B) (CF-101B) (RF-101B)	NV16
McDonnell M.36BA Voodoo (F-101B) (JF-101B)	KS9
McDonnell M.36BA Voodoo (F-101B) (JF-101B) (NF-101B)	MI58
McDonnell M.36BA Voodoo (F-101B) (NF-101B)	IL50
McDonnell M.36BA Voodoo (F-101B) (F-101F)	NC6
McDonnell M.36BA Voodoo (TF-101B) (CF-101F)	AZ32, WA22

685

McDonnell M.36BA Voodoo (TF-101B) (CF-101F) (TF-101F)	FL80	McDonnell M.98DH Phantom II (RF-4B)	CA52, 58, 143, FL55, NC8, 17
McDonnell M.36BA Voodoo (TF-101B) (TF-101F)	AL32, CA68, FL62, GA45, MN36, MO14, MT7, ND6, NY9, 21, OH48, TX51, 147	McDonnell M.98DJ Phantom II (F-4C)	AK11, AL18, 38, AZ13, 30, CA3, 11, 26, 93, 109, CO24, FL76, GA43, HI6, ID18, IL53, IN4, 7, 20, MD12, MI53, MT8, NC33, ND2, NV17, NY54, OH55, SC2, TX16, 66, 138, UT5, VA31, WA25, WI62
McDonnell M.36CA Voodoo (RF-101C)	AL24, AR7, 15, AZ19, 30, GA45, KY2, MD15, MI53, MS7, 14, NM4, NY54, OH55, SC19		
McDonnell M.36CM Voodoo (F-101C)	TX123	McDonnell M.98EN Phantom II (F-4D)	AL7, 17, 24, CA2, 68, 73, CO28, CT9, FL3, 19, 35, GA45, IL54, 67, KS1, 9, 26, 28, 37, KY1, 12, MA4, MD3, 23, MI18, MN11, ND8, 22, NE13, NJ20, NY21, OH55, OK41, OR11, TX9, 44, 51, 56, 63, 72, 80, 110, UT5, VT6, 7
McDonnell M.36CM Voodoo (F-101C) (RF-101H)	AR10, KY11		
McDonnell M.36W Voodoo (F-101A)	OR7		
McDonnell M.36Y Voodoo (RF-101A)	UT5		
McDonnell M.38 (XH-20)	OH55		
McDonnell M.58 Demon (F3H-2) (F-3B)	AZ30, FL24		
McDonnell M.58 Demon (F3H-2M) (MF-3B)	FL55	McDonnell M.98EN Phantom II (F-4D) (NF-4D)	CA39
McDonnell M.58 Demon (F3H-2N) (F-3C)	NY34	McDonnell M.98EV Phantom II (F-4J)	FL80, LA4, MD19, MO37, NC8, NJ15, OH51, SC18
McDonnell M.82 (XL-25) (XH-35) (XV-1)	AL36, VA19	McDonnell M.98EV Phantom II (F-4J) (F-4S)	AZ48, CA53, 58, 112, 122, 128, 144, 145, 160, FL55, HI3, IN6, KY2, NC6, OH48, TX134, 149, VA19
McDonnell M.98AM Phantom II (F4H-1F) (F-4A)	CA157, FL24, MD15, 24, NJ1, RI1, TX149, VA22, 27		
McDonnell M.98AM Phantom II (F4H-1) (F-4B)	AZ48, CA58, 144, FL55, IL2, 26, MN27, MO42, NC18, NY31,RI3, TX147	McDonnell M.98EV Phantom II (F-4J) (F-4S) (QF-4S)	CA110, TX66
		McDonnell M.98HO Phantom II (F-4E)	AZ1, 25, CA85, CO32, FL48, IN14, MI2, MO40, NC33, NJ17, OH51, TX14, 40, 63, 68, 150, UT5, VA35
McDonnell M.98AM Phantom II (F4H-1) (F-4B) (YF-4J)	AZ30, CA143		
McDonnell M.98AM Phantom II (F4H-1) (F-4B) (F-4N)	AZ13, CA143, IL57, LA23, NV11, NY34, OH55		
		McDonnell M.98HO Phantom II (F-4E) (NF-4E)	AZ12, 30, CA32, MO22, NJ14, TN3
McDonnell M.98AM Phantom II (F-4B)	NY82	McDonnell M.98HO Phantom II (F-4E) (F-4G)	ID7, OH55
McDonnell M.98AM Phantom II (F-4B) (EF-4B)	MD19	McDonnell M.98HO Phantom II (M.98EN) (F-4D) (YF-4EJ)	CA4
McDonnell M.98AM Phantom II (F-4B) (F-4N)	AL32, AR26, AZ11, 30, CA58, 109, FL41, 55, HI1, LA27, SC4	McDonnell M.98NQ Phantom II (F-4F)	NM26
McDonnell M.98AM Phantom II (F-4B) (F-4N) (QF-4N)	CA145	McDonnell M.199-1A Eagle (YF-15A) (F-15A)	TX147, VA31
McDonnell M.98DE Phantom II (F-4C)	AK12, AL37, AR7, 10, CA85, 139, 148, 160, CO19, GA30, 45, HI2, IA26, ID25, IL14, IN13, 52, KS34, LA7, 12, MI53, 58, MN27, MS10, ND4, NM11, OH57, OK16, OR7, 9, 14, PA61, SC5, TN2, TX53, 81, 83, 95, 123, 135, UT5, WA22, WI37, 62	McDonnell M.199-1A Eagle (F-15A)	AK3, 12, AL37, AZ1, 30, CA4, 32, 85, 109, CO24, 28, FL8, 14, 20, 37, 58, 60, 74, 76, 78, GA45, HI2, 6, ID18, IL50, LA5, 12, 18, MA2, 6, 8, MO38, 40, ND22, NM11, NY82, OH55, 84, OR7, 9, 14, PA1, TN2, TX83, 123, UT5, VA10, WA22
		McDonnell M.199-1A Eagle (F-15A) (FSM)	AK12
McDonnell M.98DE Phantom II (F-4C) (NF-4C)	CA4, FL74, TN17	McDonnell M.199-1B Eagle (TF-15A) (F-15B)	AZ25, CA4, GA45, IL62, NC33, TX123
McDonnell M.98DE Phantom II (RF-110A) (RF-4C)	IL50, 62	McDonnell M.199-1D Eagle (F-15D)	TX123
McDonnell M.98DF Phantom II (YRF-110A) (YRF-4C) (YF-4E)	OH55	McDonnell M.199-1E Eagle (F-15E)	TX123
		McDonnell M.267A Hornet (YF-18A)	VA12
McDonnell M.98DF Phantom II (RF-4C)	AL22, 31, AZ1, CA4, 85, 135, FL76, GA54, ID7, 12, KY11, MN27, NE15, 23, NV16, OH55, SC19, TX49, 50, 73, 87, 147, UT5, VA2	McDonnell M.267 Hornet (F/A-18A)	AL37, CA52, 58, 73, 74, 105, 110, 122, 143, 145, 160, FL25, 38, 55, 58, 61, 78, 83, LA18, MD19, 24, MI2, MO42, NV11, PA38, 64, SC4, 18, TN2, 33, TX43, 63, 85, 134, 149, UT5, VA10, 25, 27, 35
McDonnell M.98DF Phantom II (RF-4C) (NRF-4C)	AZ35		

Index

McDonnell M.267 Hornet (F/A-18A) (NF/A-18A)	MD20
McDonnell M.267 Hornet (TF-18A) (F/A-18B)	CA102, FL55
McDonnell M.267 Hornet (F/A-18C)	VA26
McDonnell M.267 Hornet (F/A-18D)	SC4
McDonnell M.267 Hornet (F/A-18E)	MD19, 20
McDonnell M.267 Hornet (F/A-18F)	FL58
McDonnell XHJH-1 Whirlaway (XHJD-1)	MD15
McDonnell YC-15A	AZ1, CA4
McDonnell-Douglas C-17A Globemaster III	VA33
McDonnell-Douglas MD-82	FL29
McDonnell-Douglas T-45A Goshawk (FSM)	MS17, TX43, 85
McDonnell-Douglas X-36	CA4, OH55
McEwan M-2-153	NM20
McKinnie 165	ND2
McLeod K & S 102.5 Cavalier	KS26
McManiman Springfield Cadet	OR15
McNeal Ranchaero HR	FL23
Mead Primary Glider	IA22
Mead Primary Glider (R)	CA122
Mead Rhön Ranger	CT9, NY16
Mead Rhön Ranger (R)	ME7
Medway Half Pint	CA139
Melfa VCA-1 XP-52	IA1
Mercury Air Shoestring	CA111, 122
Mercury Chic T-2	NY24
Mercury S-1 White Racer	NY24
Merlin Aircraft Merlin GT	ND8
Merlin Hang Glider	NY14
Messerschmitt Bf 108B-1 Taifun	FL22
Messerschmitt Bf 108B-2 Taifun	CA111
Messerschmitt Bf 108D-1 Taifun	NM6, TX40
Messerschmitt Bf 109 (Scale R)	OR13
Messerschmitt Bf 109E (FSM)	CA115, IL2
Messerschmitt Bf 109E-3	WA12
Messerschmitt Bf 109E-7	CA111, GA43, VA17
Messerschmitt Bf 109F (FSM)	KS9
Messerschmitt Bf 109F-4	CO27
Messerschmitt Bf 109F-4/trop	TX134
Messerschmitt Bf 109G	VA17
Messerschmitt Bf 109G (FSM)	GA43
Messerschmitt Bf 109G-14	LA17
Messerschmitt Bf 109G-2	TX134
Messerschmitt Bf 109G-4 (FSM)	CA122
Messerschmitt Bf 109G-6	OH55
Messerschmitt Bf 109G-6/R3	DC3
Messerschmitt Bf 109G-10/U4	AZ33, OR7
Messerschmitt Me 163B-1a Komet	OH55, VA19, WA12
Messerschmitt Me 163B-1a Komet (FSM)	CA111
Messerschmitt Me 262A-1	VA17
Messerschmitt Me 262A-1 (R)	OR7
Messerschmitt Me 262A-1a	DC3, OH55
Messerschmitt Me 262A-1a/U3	WA12
Messerschmitt Me 262B-1 (FSM)	NJ1
Messerschmitt Me 262B-1a	FL55
Messerschmitt Me 262B-1c	MA4
Messerschmitt Me 410A-2/U1	VA19
Meyers Little Toot	TX69
Meyers OTW-125	IL24, KS9, TX114
Meyers OTW-145	WI17
Meyers OTW-160	OH64
Meyers OTW-160 (OTW-125)	FL55, IL63
Meyers Racer	RI1
Microlight	IN7
Mignet HM-8	WI24
Mignet HM-14 Pou-du-Ciel	MO28, NY16
Mignet HM-20-ME-2-Y Pou-du-Ciel	WI17
Mignet HM-160 Pou-du-Ciel	WI24
Mignet HM-290 Pou-du-Ciel	ND24
Mignet HM-293 Pou-du-Ciel	WI24
Mignet HM-297 Pou-du-Ciel	FL23
Mignet HM-360 Pou-du-Ciel	WI24
Mignet HM-380 Pou-du-Ciel	TN22
Mignet HM-381 Pou-du-Ciel	WI24
Mignet HM-1000 Balerit	WI24
Mignet HM-1100 Cordouan	WI24
Mikoyan-Gurevich MiG-3	VA17
Mikoyan-Gurevich MiG-15	CA58, 111, CT9, DE5, FL22, IL3, NJ21, NY34, OH55
Mikoyan-Gurevich MiG-15bis	AZ11, CA105, 111, 122, FL55, VA19, WA25, WI17
Mikoyan-Gurevich UTI-MiG-15	DE5, ID13
Mikoyan-Gurevich MiG-17	AL37, CO27, DE5, OH55, OR7, 11, 13, WA25
Mikoyan-Gurevich MiG-17F	CA32, 122, GA43, 45, TX40
Mikoyan-Gurevich MiG-19S	CA85, OH55
Mikoyan-Gurevich MiG-21	FL55, 78
Mikoyan-Gurevich MiG-21bis	CA122, NV11
Mikoyan-Gurevich MiG-21F	LA7, NE23, NM12
Mikoyan-Gurevich MiG-21F-13	CA3, FL76, NV11, 17, OH55, OR4, 11, RI1, TX90, UT5, VA19
Mikoyan-Gurevich MiG-21FR (MiG-21F-13)	CA85
Mikoyan-Gurevich MiG-21MF	CA114, FL65, GA43, NJ3, TX57
Mikoyan-Gurevich MiG-21MF-75	OR7
Mikoyan-Gurevich MiG-21PF	AZ11, 30, CA122, 128, NY21, OH55
Mikoyan-Gurevich MiG-21PFM	DE5, KS9, MI2, NY34, 82, OR11, WA25
Mikoyan-Gurevich MiG-21R	CA111, OK40, WA12
Mikoyan-Gurevich MiG-21SMT	FL42
Mikoyan-Gurevich MiG-21SPS (MiG-21PFM)	NM24
Mikoyan-Gurevich MiG-21U-600	CA28, FL65, 80, NY62
Mikoyan-Gurevich MiG-21UM	AL32, DE12, IL81, NY4, OH55, OR4, TX19, WA12
Mikoyan-Gurevich MiG-21US	DE12, TN33, TX16
Mikoyan-Gurevich MiG-23BN	CA85
Mikoyan-Gurevich MiG-23MF	OR11
Mikoyan-Gurevich MiG-23K	OH55
Mikoyan-Gurevich MiG-23ML	FL3, 28, NV11, 17, TX73
Mikoyan-Gurevich MiG-23MLD	AZ30, OH55
Mikoyan-Gurevich MiG-23UB	DE12, TX19
Mikoyan-Gurevich MiG-25RB	OH55
Mikoyan-Gurevich MiG-29	NV17, OR7, TX73
Mikoyan-Gurevich MiG-29A	AZ30, NV11, OH55
Mikoyan-Gurevich MiG-29UB	FL78, IL81, OH84, WA17
Mil Mi-2	CA37, LA9, TX19
Mil Mi-8T	NV17
Mil Mi-24	IL62
Mil Mi-14PL	NV17
Mil Mi-24D	NV17, TX19, 25
Military Gas Balloon	NM2
Miller DK-1	CO32
Miller S-1 Fly Rod	KS26
Miller Special JM-1	CA156
Miller Tern	NY50
Miller Zeta	MA14
Miller-Bohannon JM2 Special	WI17
Milliken M-1 Special	ME7
Mirage Ultralight	MA14
Mitchell Nimbus 3L	NY50
Mitchell P-38	FL23, MI2
Mitchell Wing A-10	WI17
Mitchell Wing B-10	AK5, 16, AL32, AZ30, NM20, OK28, OR13, PA35
Mitchell Wing U-2	KS8, NY50, VA19
Mitsubishi A6M2 Zero Sen Model 21	FL55, HI6, ND8, OH55
Mitsubishi A6M3 Zero Sen Model 22	CA45, TX40

687

Mitsubishi A6M3 Zero Sen Model 32	OR7, WA12	Morane-Saulnier MS.505 Criquet (MS.500) [Fieseler Fi 156 Storch]	CA88
Mitsubishi A6M5 Zero Sen Model 52	CA111, DC3, FL22, WA12	Morrisey 2000C	TX151
Mitsubishi A6M7 Zero Sen Model 63	CA122	Morrisey OM-1-2 Bravo	IA1
Mitsubishi G4M1	CA111	Moss MT1	WA37
Mitsubishi G4M3	VA19	Müller Moswey III	WY10
Mitsubishi J2M3 Raiden	CA111	Murphy Renegade Spirit	MI2, TX92
Mitsubishi J8M1 Shusui	CA111	Murray A	CO32
Mitsubishi Marquise (MU-2B-60)	CO26	Murray JN-2D-1	NY21
Mitsubishi MU-2B	MN32, OK45, TX132, WI35	Murray T	CO32
		Mustang Golden Commuter	OR21
Mitsubishi MU-2D (MU-2B-10)	AK6, NM7	Mutual Aircraft Blackbird	CA160
Mitsubishi MU-2J (MU-2B-35)	TN34, TX139	Myers PM-1 Special	WI17
Monarch Hang Glider	OK28	Nagler-Rolz NR 54	VA19
Mong MS-1 Sport	GA3	Nakajima B6N2 Tenzan	MD15
Mong Special MS.3	OK28	Nakajima C6N1-S Saiun	MD15
Mong Sport	IL50	Nakajima J1N1-S Gekko	VA19
Monnett Monerai S	AL32, CT9, NM20, NY14, OR13	Nakajima J5N1 Tenrai	MD15
		Nakajima Ki-43 Hayabusa	OR21
Monnett Monex	WI17	Nakajima Ki-43-Ic Hayabusa	WA12
Monnett Moni	CA128, FL23, IA27, KS26, TX92, VA19, WI17	Nakajima Ki-43-IIb Hayabusa	AZ30, WA25
		Nakajima Ki-115 Tsurugi	MD15
		Nakajima Kikka	MD15
Monnett Moni Tri-Gear	CO32, WI51	NAMC YS-11-120	IN20
Monnett Sonerai II	CA110, 122, KS18, NY21, PA35, WI17	Nanchang CJ-6A	CA130, DE5, FL86, PA12, TX19, 23, UT2
Monnett Sonerai II-LT	AL32, CA128	Nanchang Y-5 [Antonov An-2]	FL22
Monnett Sonerai II-S2-MLI	IN32	Nardi FN.305D	FL22
Monnett Sonex	CA122	Nardi FN.333 Riviera	CA107, WI22
Mono Aircraft Monocoupe 70	CA29, 64, 65, PA23	NASA DS-1	MD15
Mono Aircraft Monocoupe 90	MO15, NY7, 63	NASA Parasev 1L-B	VA19
Mono Aircraft Monocoupe 90A	CA128, 130, IL31, MO15, 36, PA23, WA8	NASA Pathfinder Plus	VA19
		National Ballooning Ax-8 Hot Air Balloon	CT9, IA29
Mono Aircraft Monocoupe 90AF	CA23, MO15		
Mono Aircraft Monocoupe 90AL-115	MO15, OK19	Naval Aircraft Factory N3N-3	AZ30, 45, CA108, 111, 160, FL22, 55, IA21, ID24, MI2, MN3, MO15, NV8, NY7, 74, OH22, OR7, 24, PA35, TX37, 40, 92, 149, VA9, 17, 19
Mono Aircraft Monocoupe 90AW	WI17		
Mono Aircraft Monocoupe 110	CA105, MD7, ND5, 23		
Mono Aircraft Monocoupe 110 Special	MO21, ND23, VA19, WI17		
Mono Aircraft Monocoupe 113	NY63, WI17		
Mono Aircraft Monocoupe D-145	LA27, MO15, 21		
Mono Aircraft Monoprep 218	IA1	Naval Aircraft Factory TS-1 (Curtiss 28)	FL55
Mono Aircraft Monosport	MO15		
Montanair Scale Mustang	MT13	Navy Gas Training Balloon	CT9
Montanair Spirit 2180	MT13	Neibauer Lancair 200	WI17
Montecopter 12	CA65	Neibauer Lancair 235	AZ22, 33, NY74
Montecopter 15	CA37	Neibauer Lancair 320	OR7
Montgolfier Balloon (R)	MI2	Neibauer Lancair IVP	IN58
Montgomery 1893 Glider (R)	CA155	Nelson Dragonfly BB-1	CA158, NY50, VA19
Montgomery Evergreen	CA122	Nelson PG-185B Hummingbird	CA65, MD15, NM20, NY50
Montgomery Evergreen (R)	CA65		
Montgomery Gull (R)	CA65	Nesmith Cougar	NY16
Montgomery Santa Clara	MD15	New Standard D-25	CA67, FL46, NY63
Montgomery Santa Clara (R)	CA65	New Standard D-25 (1/4 scale)	MD15
Moody Ultralight	WI51	New Standard D-25A	FL46
Mooney M-18C Mite	IA1, KS18, 26, MO15, TX118, VA19, WA37	New Standard D-29 (NT-1)	FL55
		New Standard D-31	OH64
Mooney M-18L Mite	AL32, FL23, WA37	Nicholas-Beazley NB-3G	MO28
Mooney M-18LA Mite	NY21	Nicholas-Beazley NB-8	OR24
Mooney M.20A	MO15	Nicholas-Beazley NB-8G	MO15, 28, NY63
Mooney M.20C	IL18, ND23	Nicholas-Beazley Special (R)	WI17
Mooney M.20E	ND23, OK29, TX37	Nieuport 2N (R)	NY63
Mooney M.20F	ND23	Nieuport 10/83E	NY63
Mooney M.20K	AZ10	Nieuport 11 (R)	AZ22, CA15, 122, IA27, IL32, KS26, NC40, NY16, 63, OK28, PA56, WI17
Mooney M.22	ND23		
Mooney/Cox M-18C-X Mite	AZ33		
Moore SS-1	NM20		
Morane-Saulnier A1	FL22, NY63	Nieuport 11 (R)	CA22
Morane-Saulnier H	IL45	Nieuport 11 (Scale R)	CA85, IN25
Morane-Saulnier N (R)	NY63	Nieuport 12	MD15
Morane-Saulnier MS.130Et2	NY63	Nieuport 12 (R)	IL32, MO26
Morane-Saulnier MS.230	FL22	Nieuport 12 (Scale R)	GA21, TX40
Morane-Saulnier MS.500 Criquet [Fieseler Fi 156 Storch]	AZ30, CA89, MD15, VA17	Nieuport 17 (R)	AZ33, FL22, OR13
		Nieuport 24 (R)	NV23, WA25
Morane-Saulnier MS.502 Criquet [Fieseler Fi 156 Storch]	CA111, NJ7, NM24, TX40	Nieuport 24 (Scale R)	IN25
		Nieuport 24bis	CA15

Nieuport 24bis (R)	NY63	North American NA-88 Texan	MD22, NJ7, 8, NY4,
Nieuport 27 (R)	OH15, VA17, WA25	(AT-6D) (SNJ-5) (*continued*)	TX16, 18, 25, 29, 40,
Nieuport 28C.1	AL36, WA25		54, 92, VA8, 22, WA31
Nieuport 28C.1 (R)	CA15, 122, FL55, 80, IA13, ME7, OH55, VA19	North American NA-88 Texan (AT-6D) (SNJ-5) (SNJ-5B)	HI6, IN2
		North American NA-88 Texan	AR19, CA40, 47, FL55,
Nieuport 28C.1 (Scale R)	FL22	(SNJ-5)	86, IL18, IN54, MO15,
Nixon Special	CT9		NY52, TX40, 147, 149
Noorduyn Norseman IV (YC-64)	MD15	North American NA-88 Texan	ND23, TX151
Noorduyn Norseman V	LA7	(AT-6D) (Harvard III)	
Noorduyn Norseman VI (C-64A) (UC-64A)	AK3, 5, OH55, TX92, WA12	North American NA-88 Texan (AT-6D) (Harvard IIIA)	ND5
Nord N.1002 Pingouin II [Messerschmitt Bf 108B]	PA35, VA17	North American NA-88 Texan (AT-6D) (XAT-6E)	CA155
Nord N.1101 Noralpha (Ramier I) [Messerschmitt Me 208]	OR21, VA17	North American NA-97 Apache (A-36A)	CA111, MA4, OH55
Nord N.1101 Ramier I [Messerschmitt Me 208]	FL80, RI1	North American NA-98 Mitchell (B-25H)	CT9, FL34, WI17
Nord N.2000 [Jacobs Meise]	NY50	North American NA-98 Mitchell	MI2
Nord N.3202	CA89, CO32	(B-25H) (TB-25H) (RB-25H)	
North American NA-25 (O-47A)	CA111, VA19	North American NA-99 Mustang	CA111, 160, FL22
North American NA-50	TX91	(P-51A)	
North American NA-51 (O-47B)	KS9, OH55	North American NA-100 Mitchell	MI58
North American NA-59 Texan (AT-6)	MN27	(B-25D) North American NA-100 Mitchell	OH55
North American NA-62 Mitchell (B-25) (RB-25)	NY4	(B-25D) (F-10) (RB-25D) North American NA-100 Mitchell	TX68, WA17
North American NA-62 Mitchell (B-25B)	HI6	(B-25D) (Mitchell II) North American NA-103 Mustang	FL22, ID26, MA4, MN10,
North American NA-64 Yale	AZ30, CA88, OH55, TX35, 40	(P-51C) North American NA-104 Mustang	TX20, 40 WA17
North American NA-65 Texan (SNJ-2)	NY19, VA17	(P-51B) North American NA-108 Mitchell	IL69, TN33, UT5, VA22
North American NA-66 Harvard II	CA32, 95, NV5, OH19	(B-25J)	
North American NA-66 Harvard IIA (II)	NY74	North American NA-108 Mitchell (B-25J) (CB-25J) (TB-25J) (TB-25N)	OR18
North American NA-68 (P-64) (RP-64)	WI17	North American NA-108 Mitchell (B-25J) (EB-25) (JB-25J)	CA32
North American NA-73 Mustang (XP-51)	WI17	North American NA-108 Mitchell (B-25J) (JB-25J)	FL76
North American NA-75 Harvard II	CA47, ID2, TX40	North American NA-108 Mitchell	CA45, TX40
North American NA-77 Texan (AT-6A)	AZ45, NV5, WA17	(B-25J) (PBJ-1J) North American NA-108 Mitchell	AZ11, 24, CA160, FL36,
North American NA-78 Texan (AT-6A)	MN44, UT5	(B-25J) (TB-25J)	GA45, MO10, NE23, TX40, 103, VA17
North American NA-78 Texan (AT-6A) (SNJ-3)	ID15, NY19, 82	North American NA-108 Mitchell (B-25J) (TB-25J) (JB-25J)	CA111
North American NA-79 Texan (SNJ-2)	NY19	(TB-25J) North American NA-108 Mitchell	CA58, FL80, GA59
North American NA-81 Harvard II	CA41, TX40	(B-25J) (TB-25J) (Mitchell III)	
North American NA-81 Harvard IIA	OK47	North American NA-108 Mitchell	MN10, TX40
North American NA-82 Mitchell (B-25C)	AL32, CA88, SC6	(B-25J) (TB-25J) (TB-25K) North American NA-108 Mitchell	GA21
North American NA-84 Texan (AT-6B)	CA47, IL50, TX29, 40	(B-25J) (TB-25J) (TB-25L) North American NA-108 Mitchell	AL24, 37, AZ30, CA33,
North American NA-87 Mitchell (B-25D) (TB-25D)	SC18	(B-25J) (TB-25J) (TB-25N)	85, 89, 110, DE5, FL55, IN20, KS26,
North American NA-88 Texan (AT-6C)	AZ25, 45, FL34, OH55, OR7, TX38, 73, 88		LA17, MA4, MT7, NE23, NJ8, NV18,
North American NA-88 Texan (AT-6C) (Harvard II)	IN44		OH15, 74, PA35, TX16, 40, 73, UT5
North American NA-88 Texan (AT-6C) (Harvard IIA)	OH15, TX23	North American NA-108 Mitchell (B-25J) (TB-25J) (VB-25J)	TX147
North American NA-88 Texan (SNJ-4)	CA45, 47, 85, 111, 130, GA21, IN44, MS5, NM6, NV5, NY4, OH22, 25, PA35, TN33, TX30, 31, 40, VA17, 19, WA16	(TB-25J) (TB-25N) North American NA-108 Mitchell (B-25J) (TB-25J) (VB-25J) (VB-25N) North American NA-108 Mitchell (B-25J) (TB-25K)	CA9, OH71, TX151 AL29, TX27, 40
North American NA-88 Texan (AT-6D)	CA47, 47, 111, 128, FL86, NY37, 39, OH40, 48, 55, 74, OK48, TN1, TX16, WA16	North American NA-108 Mitchell (B-25J) (TB-25K) (Mitchell III) North American NA-108 Mitchell (B-25J) (TB-25M)	WA12 WI37
North American NA-88 Texan (AT-6D) (SNJ-5)	AZ11, 24, CA42, 45, 47, 58, 71, 96, 108, 111, 160, GA21, 59, IA21, ID15, 24, IL20, IN58,	North American NA-108 Mitchell (B-25J) (TB-25N)	CA84, FL22, IL50, ND11, TX39, 40, 91, 92, VA17, 19

689

Index

North American NA-108 Mitchell (B-25J) (VB-25J) — SD7
North American NA-109 Mustang (P-51D) — OR21, UT5
North American NA-111 Mustang (P-51C) — VA19
North American NA-111 Mustang (P-51K) — CA18, OH27, TX20
North American NA-111 Mustang (P-51K) (F-6K) — TX20
North American NA-111 Mustang (P-51K) (FSM) — SC1
North American NA-120 Twin Mustang (XP-82) — GA59
North American NA-121 Texan (AT-6D) — CA47, VA8
North American NA-121 Texan (AT-6D) (SNJ-5) — CA47, 130, 145, MI2, NC6, ND24, NV5, NY78, TX29, 37
North American NA-121 Texan (AT-6F) — FL86, GA59, MA4, MO10, NM24, NY52, TX45, 51, 119, WA16, 28
North American NA-121 Texan (AT-6F) (SNJ-6) — CA47, CO7, FL34, 42, 55, 83, 86, IL18, TX18, 28, 29, 40
North American NA-121 Texan (AT-6F) (SNJ-6) (SNJ-7) — OH71
North American NA-122 Mustang (P-51D) — AL36, 37, AZ30, CA2, 71, 95, 96, 111, 122, 155, 160, CO27, CT9, DC3, FL5, 23, FL69, GA45, 59, IA8, IL3, IN54, LA7, 17, MT13, NC33, ND8, 22, NJ8, NM24, NY78, OH55, OK27, OR7, TX16, 20, 40, 54, WI17, 62, WV2
North American NA-122 Mustang (P-51D) (J 26) — CA45, 130, ID19, MN14, WA12
North American NA-122 Mustang (P-51D) (Mustang IV) — AZ11, CA110, FL69, GA21, ID15, IN58, TX40, 91, VA17, WA28
North American NA-122 Mustang (P-51D) (TF-51D) — FL69
North American NA-122 Mustang (P-51D) (FSM) — CA1, 115, GA43, IA11, 37, IL1, 2, MD1, MO45, NM12, NY4, OH1, PA27, 48, TN33, 35, WI63
North American NA-123 Twin Mustang (P-82B) (F-82B) — OH55
North American NA-124 Mustang (P-51D) — AZ45, CA95, 111, CO27, FL22, IL63, IN28, 54, ND24, OH74, WA16, 25
North American NA-124 Mustang (P-51D) (F-6D) — IL43
North American NA-124 Mustang (P-51D) (TF-51D) — ID19, NM24
North American NA-126 Mustang (P-51H) — CA95, IL50, TX147
North American NA-141 Fury (FJ-1) — CA160, MD15
North American NA-144 Twin Mustang (P-82E) (F-82E) — TX147
North American NA-145 Navion — CA17, 45, 111, 150, KS36, OK1, TX34, 67, 75
North American NA-147 Tornado (B-45A) — AZ30, CA32
North American NA-151 Sabre (P-86A) (F-86A) — IL50, MT1, VA19
North American NA-151 Sabre (P-86A) (F-86A) (EF-86A) — TX147
North American NA-153 Tornado (B-45C) — OH55
North American NA-153 Tornado (RB-45C) — NE23
North American NA-154 Navion (L-17A) — NH7
North American NA-154 Navion (L-17A) — AL36, CA53, OH55
North American NA-159 Trojan (T-28A) — CA95, 109, 114, NV6, OK48, OR11, TX40, 73, 76, 88, 119, 147
North American NA-159 Trojan (T-28A) (AT-28D) — VA17
North American NA-159 Trojan (T-28A) (JT-28A) — OH55
North American NA-159 Trojan (T-28A) (T-28D) — FL36
North American NA-161 Sabre (P-86A) (F-86A) — AK1, AL24, AZ33, CA2, MI53, OH55, UT9, WA12
North American NA-165 Sabre (F-86D) — OH55
North American NA-165 Sabre (F-86D) (F-86L) — CA85
North American NA-168 Texan (T-6G) — AK1, AL29, 32, AZ30, 33, 45, CA45, 110, 114, CO2, FL22, 73, GA45, IL43, 72, 73, KS10, MD13, MI2, NC6, NM6, NV5, NY4, 52, OH71, OR21, TX25, 59, 91, 134, VA8, WA28
North American NA-170 Sabre (F-86E) — AZ30, HI2, IN31, 34, TX146
North American NA-171 Trojan (T-28A) — CA111, ND5
North American NA-172 Sabre (F-86E) — CA111, HI6, NM11, NV17, OH71, OR11
North American NA-172 Sabre (F-86F) — CO2, WA12
North American NA-173 Sabre (F-86D) — AZ8, 36, CA111, WI38
North American NA-173 Sabre (F-86D) (F-86L) — AZ13, GA51, OK44, TX113, UT5, WA7, WI2, WV5
North American NA-174 Trojan (T-28A) — CA89, 139, GA45, ID26, MS14, UT2, WA31
North American NA-174 Trojan (T-28A) (AT-28D) — WA28
North American NA-176 Sabre (F-86F) — CA3, CT9, PA35
North American NA-176 Sabre (F-86F) (QF-86F) — AZ41
North American NA-177 Sabre (F-86D) (F-86L) — AL37, CA3, VA2
North American NA-180 Super Sabre (YF-100A) — CA4
North American NA-181 Fury (FJ-2) — CA144, FL55, NM24
North American NA-182 Texan (T-6G) — CA3, 18, ID1, IN28, TX69, VA8, 9
North American NA-184 Savage (AJ-2) — FL55
North American NA-187 Sabre (F-86H) — CA5, 105, GA45, IL12, MD10, NJ5, SC12, VA15, 31, WI17, WV4
North American NA-190 Sabre (F-86D) — CA152, MO4, 42, NE4, OK1, TN20, VT1, WA22
North American NA-190 Sabre (F-86D) (F-86L) — AL32, AZ43, FL74, GA39, 54, HI6, KS37, LA12, NC6, 7, NY48, TX138
North American NA-191 Sabre (F-86F) — CA4, 53, 111, FL80, ID26, IL72, IN58, MI2, NV8, OH55, OR13, TX40, 151, UT5
North American NA-191 Sabre (F-86F) (FSM) — CA115

Index

North American NA-191 Sabre (F-86F) (RF-86F)	CA109, OH55
North American NA-192 Super Sabre (F-100A)	CA4, 139, CO2, CT9, MI21, NC33, NM12, 13, 22, OH72, SD7, TX40, 80, 147, UT5
North American NA-193 Sabre (F-86F)	AZ25, FL76, IN5, PA61
North American NA-193 Sabre (F-86F) (RF-86F)	IL2
North American NA-194 Fury (FJ-3) (F-1C)	AL14, CA58, 111, NY34, OR7
North American NA-194 Fury (FJ-3) (FJ-3M) (MF-1C)	VA27
North American NA-197 Texan (T-6G)	CO27, FL69
North American NA-200 Trojan (T-28B)	AK8, AL36, AZ33, CA3, 4, 53, 90, 144, DC1, FL55, 83, 86, IL38, 43, 72, KY2, MN27, NC6, NM24, NY62, OH19, 71, OR7, 21, PA1, TN33, TX16, 134, 149, UT5, VA8, 9
North American NA-200 Trojan (T-28B) (DT-28B)	CA90
North American NA-200 Trojan (T-28B) (AT-28D)	UT4
North American NA-201 Sabre (F-86D) (F-86L)	AL11, AZ30, CA2, 94, 139, CO24, IA23, ID10, IL6, MI58, MN42, MS11, MT3, NE15, NJ1, NV22, OH48, 71, OK25, OR11, 22, PA30, 48, SC1, TN27, TX51, 63, UT7, WY3, 4
North American NA-202 Sabre (F-86F)	CA122
North American NA-203 Sabre (F-86H)	AZ30, CA14, 32, 85, 109, 111, CO32, DC8, DE10, FL26, GA45, IN8, KS9, 26, KY13, MA2, 6, 8, MD12, MN25, NC14, ND12, 14, 28, NE16, 23, NM4, NY12, 68, 73, OH17, 55, PA1, SC1, SD7, WI4, 62
North American NA-209 Fury (FJ-4) (F-1E)	FL55, TX80
North American NA-209 Fury (FJ-4B) (AF-1E)	AZ30
North American NA-212 (YF-100B) (YF-107A)	AZ30, OH55
North American NA-214 Super Sabre (F-100C)	AZ25, CA32, IN20
North American NA-215 Fury (FJ-3M) (MF-1C)	NC18, SC4
North American NA-217 Super Sabre (F-100C)	AL32, AZ30, CA85, 160, FL76, GA45, IA35, ID18, IL50, 57, KS37, TX51, WI62
North American NA-219 Trojan (T-28B)	IN28, OH55, TX43, VA8
North American NA-223 Super Sabre (F-100D)	AL24, AR10, AZ20, CA3, 68, CO25, CT1, MD15, MO40, NV17, OH55, OK44, TX4, 123, VA2
North American NA-224 Super Sabre (F-100D)	OH65, 73, OK1
North American NA-226 Trojan (T-28C)	AL14, 32, AZ24, 30, 33, CO25, MA3, NJ21, OH19, OK27, TX54
North American NA-227 Sabre (F-86F)	AL32, AZ27, CA122, 143, 155
North American NA-231 Sabre (F-86F)	CA128, NV11
North American NA-235 Super Sabre (F-100D)	AZ41, CA3, 111, CO2, GA45, IN14, 52, LA5, 12, MA2, 8, MI53, NC6, ND9, NM4, 11, NY54, OH47, 48, SC16, SD6, TX83, 92
North American NA-240 (X-15) (X-15A)	DC3
North American NA-240 (X-15) (X-15A) (X-15A-2)	OH55
North American NA-240 (X-15) (X-15A) (FSM)	AZ30, CA4, 99, KS20, OR7
North American NA-243 Super Sabre (F-100F)	AL6, AR3, AZ13, 15, CO28, ID23, KS17, MD12, MI53, MT2, NE1, NJ2, NM15, OR7, TX17, 31, 76, 86, 136
North American NA-243 Super Sabre (F-100F) (QF-100F)	AZ1, OH55
North American NA-244 Fury (FJ-4B) (AF-1E)	GA29, ID24, NY9, PA26
North American NA-245 Super Sabre (F-100D)	AR7, CO32, IA11, VA19
North American NA-247 Vigilante (A3J-1) (A-5A)	MD20
North American NA-252 Trojan (T-28C)	CA150, CO4, ID24
North American NA-253 Buckeye (T2J-1) (T-2A)	CA111, MS16, 17, 23
North American NA-255 Super Sabre (F-100F)	TX53
North American NA-256 Sabre (F-86F)	CA8
North American NA-260 Nomad (NA-174 Trojan (T-28A))	MI2
North American NA-265 Sabreliner (T-39A)	CA32
North American NA-265 Sabreliner (T-39A) (CT-39A)	AL36, AZ7, CA3, 4, 36, 105, 107, 139, 153, IA12, 25, IL2, 59, 60, 64, LA15, MI36, MN24, 32, MO8, MT14, NM12, OK23, OR7, SC23, SD4, TN34, TX51, 89, UT5, WA4, 11, 38, 39, WI8
North American NA-266 Buckeye (T2J-1) (T-2A)	NC6
North American NA-276 Sabreliner (T-39A)	OH55
North American NA-276 Sabreliner (T-39A) (CT-39A)	AZ30, CA50, 85, 126, 139, CO4, GA45, IA20, IL50, MA10, MI12, MO42, NC15, NE23, OK23, PA44, SC23, TN25, UT10, 11, WA9, WI35
North American NA-278 Valkyrie (XB-70)	OH55
North American NA-282 Sabreliner 40	MO41, OK46, PA49, VA16
North American NA-282 Sabreliner 40 (CT-39E)	OK46
North American NA-283 Vigilante (RA-5C)	CO25, MD15
North American NA-285 Sabreliner (T3J-1) (T-39D)	AL32, FL55, IA18, MD19, WI35
North American NA-296 Vigilante (NA-269) (A3J-1) (A3J-3P) (RA-5C)	AZ30
North American NA-300 Bronco (YOV-10A)	KS26, TX66
North American NA-305 Bronco (OV-10A)	AZ13, CA53, FL36, GA45, IN48, TX66, UT5

691

North American NA-305 Bronco (OV-10A) (OV-10D)	AZ30, CA58, FL55, 80, IL62, TN33, TX104	Northrop N-160 Scorpion (N-68) (F-89D) (F-89J)	AZ30, 33, CA4, 32, 85, 111, 155, CO24, CT9, GA45, IN20, ME1, MN27, MT1, ND22, OH55, 70, OR7, SD2, 7, VA2, VT6, WA16, WI17
North American NA-306 Sabreliner 60	SC13		
North American NA-306 Sabreliner 60 (CT-39G)	CA4, FL55		
North American NA-310 Buckeye (T-2B)	ID24, IL72	Northrop N-311 Tiger II (F-5E)	AR3, AZ48, CA53, 58, 68, 109, 114, 160, FL80, MD12, MN3, NC18, NJ21, NV11, 17, NY21, OH55, OR7, TX66, UT5
North American NA-316 Vigilante (RA-5C)	CA143, 145, FL41, 55, 57, MD19, NV11, NY21, TN26		
North American NA-318 Buckeye (T-2C)	AZ1, CA145, FL80, NY21		
North American NA-321 Bronco (OV-10A)	OH55, TX66	Northrop N-311 Tiger II (F-5F)	TX83
		Northrop P.600 (YF-17A)	AL37, CA155
North American NA-332 Buckeye (T-2C)	AZ30, FL55, 83, PA14, TX80	Northrop HL-10	CA29, 99
		Northrop HL-10 (FSM)	VA35
North American NA-338 Bronco (OV-10B)	NV6	Northrop M2-F1	MD15
		Northrop M2-F3	DC3
North American NA-340 Buckeye (T-2C)	FL55, MD20, OR7	Northrop B-2 Spirit	OH55
		Northrop B-2 Spirit (Scale R)	SD7
North American NA-346 Buckeye (T-2C)	FL55, IN20, NY67, TX85, 134	Northrop F-20A Tigershark (F-5G)	CA29, 155
		Northrop F-20A Tigershark (F-5G) (Mock up)	CA4
North American NA-352 Buckeye (T-2C)	AR19, IL32, TX149		
		Northrop Tacit Blue	OH55
North American NA-367 Buckeye (T-2C)	AL32, MS17	Northrop X-21A (Douglas WB-66D Destroyer)	CA4
North American X-10	OH55	Northrop X-47A Pegasus (FSM)	MD19
North American Rotorworks Pitbull	OK43	Northrop YA-9A	CA4, 85
Northrop 4A Alpha	CA111, DC3	Northrop-Grumman RQ-4A Global Hawk	OH55
Northrop Gamma	DC3		
Northrop Gamma 2F (A-17A)	OH55	Northrop-Grumman RQ-4A Global Hawk (FSM)	OR7
Northrop N-1M	VA19		
Northrop N-2B (XP-56C)	MD15	Northrop-Grumman RQ-8A Fire Scout	CA122, NJ15, PA38
Northrop N-8D Black Widow (P-61B)	PA35		
		Northrop/McDonnell Douglas YF-23A	CA155, OH55
Northrop N-8E Black Widow (P-61C)	OH55, VA19		
Northrop N-9MB	CA111	Northrup Primary Glider	IA22, NM20
Northrop N-16 Bat (JB-1)	CA143, 155	Nussbaumer Baumer-Heath	PA17
Northrop N-23 Raider (YC-125A)	AZ30	Ohm & Stopplebein Special	NY65
Northrop N-23 Raider (YC-125B)	OH55	Oldershaw Jana Linn 02	NM20
Northrop N-26 (XS-4) (X-4)	CA4, OH55	Oldershaw O-3	NM20
Northrop N-35 Scorpion (P-89A) (F-89A) (F-89B) (EF-89A)	TX135	Oldfield Baby Great Lakes	KS18, 26, OR7, TX92, WA31, 37
		Oldfield Baby Great Lakes Special	NC40
Northrop N-35 Scorpion (P-89B) (F-89B)	ID20	Oldfield Baby Great Lakes WR-1	OH64
		Olmstead Amphibian	MD15
Northrop N-68 Scorpion (F-89D)	AK12, FL76	Omega 7 Hot Air Balloon	NM2
Northrop N-138 Scorpion (F-89H)	TX51, UT5	Option Air Reno Acapella 100L	WI17
Northrop N-156A Freedom Fighter (F-5A)	CA155, MT13	Orenco F	FL22
		Orlowski HO.1	CA111
Northrop N-156B Freedom Fighter (F-5B)	AZ30, IL50, TX147, UT5	Osterreichischer Aero Club Standard Austria	IL24
Northrop N-156F Freedom Fighter (YF-5A)	OH55, WA25	Owl OR.7B	WA31
		Pacific Airways 89	AZ30
Northrop N-156T Talon (YT-38) (YT-38A)	CA29, SD7	Packard C2	OH55
		Palmer Sunshine Clipper	FL23
Northrop N-156T Talon (T-38A)	AL24, 32, 38, AZ1, 30, 44, CA4, 20, 50, 68, 69, 85, 103, 109, 137, 155, 160, CO16, 28, CT2, FL39, 55, GA45, IL19, 57, IL62, IN12, KS20, 26, 34, MD15, 20, MI46, MO48, MS4, NE22, NM10, OH22, OK32, 40, 48, RI3, TN27, TX51, 55, 69, 76, 88, 104, 119, 122, 123, 126, 147, UT5	Panavia PA200 Tornado GR.1B (GR.1)	OH55
		Panavia PA200 Tornado IDS	AZ30, NM11
		Paramotor FX-5	NY14
		Paramount Cabinaire 165	MN18
		Park Brothers Primary Glider	KS18
		Parker Jeanie's Teenie	NY74
		Parker JP.001 American Special	NC40
		Parker Pusher	OK30, 45
		Parker RP.9	CA128
		Parker Teenie Too	IA27
		Parker-Thompson Tiny Mite	PA56
		Parks P-1	MO32
Northrop N-156T Talon (T-38A) (AT-38B)	CA14, FL58, IL62, KY2, MI33, MN34, ND20, NM11, 24, NY46, OH55, OK41, OR7, SD12, TX31, VA16	Parsons (Marvel) XV-11A	AL32
		Parsons Sport Autogyro	PA4
		Passett Ornithopter (R)	NY63
		Payne Knight Twister	AZ37, OH53
		Payne M-6 Knight Twister Imperial	WI17
		Pazmany PL-1	IL32

Index

Pazmany PL-4	MI14	Pioneer UAV	MD15
Pazmany PL-4A	AL32	Piper J-2 Cub	CA19, DC3, NY7, 16, PA47, WA34
Pedal Plane	WI17		
Peel Z-1 Glider Boat	CA158, NY14, WI17	Piper J-3C Cub (Scale R)	ND5
Penaud Planafore (R)	ME7	Piper J-3C-100 Cub (J-3C-65)	ID2
Pentecost E III Hoppicopter	AZ30	Piper J-3C-40 Cub	OR24
Percival P.40 Prentice T.1	CA9	Piper J-3C-65 Cub	AK6, AL36, AR1, 9, 19, CA9, 17, 32, 75, 90, 95, 111, 122, 130, CO7, 32, FL61, GA12, 38, IA22, ID22, IL18, 46, 65, 70, IN20, 28, 57, KS26, 32, LA27, MD14, ME9, MI2, MN14, 37, MO44, MS19, MT8, NC6, 24, NC40, ND5, NH7, NJ7, NM24, NV5, NY7, 16, 82, OH58, OK19, 20, OR24, PA12, 29, 47, 54, TX2, 15, 16, 31, 32, 34, 40, 64, 75, 114, 135, UT4, 5, VA8, 13, 19, 29, 35, 36, WA8, 19, 20, 25, 31, 34, 37, WI17
Percival P.56 Provost T.1	MA11		
Percival P.66 Pembroke C.51	AZ47, TN6		
Pereira GP.2 Osprey I	MI2		
Pereira GP.2 Osprey I (X-28A)	KS26		
Pereira GP.3 Osprey II	AK5, AZ30, FL23, WI17		
Perl PG-130 Penetrator	NY50		
Peryra Adventura	AR1		
Peterson J-4 Javelin	NY21		
Pfalz D III (R)	CA15, NV23		
Pfalz D XII	DC3		
Pfalz D XII (R)	WA25		
Pheasant H-10	NY7, WI17		
Phoenix 6C Hang Glider	KS26		
Piaggio FWP.149D	FL47, GA21		
Piaggio P.136L-1	TX54, 151		
Piaggio P.166AL-1	TX54		
Piasecki PV-2	VA19	Piper J-3C-65 Cub (J-3L)	CA110
Piasecki PV-3 Rescuer (XHRP-1)	MD15	Piper J-3C-65 Cub (O-59) (L-4)	TX87
Piasecki PV-3 Rescuer (HRP-1)	CA37	Piper J-3C-65 Cub (O-59A) (L-4A)	AL36, CA114, OH55, OR24, TX12, WA33
Piasecki PV-14 (XHJP-1)	PA4		
Piasecki PV-17 (HRP-2)	IN49, PA4	Piper J-3C-65 Cub (L-4B)	AL36, CA139, NJ8, OH53, OK1, PA17, TX23, 138
Piasecki PV-18 Retriever (HUP-1)	CA144, NV12		
Piasecki PV-18 Retriever (HUP-2) (UH-25B)	AZ30, 47, CA37, 58, 145, 160, CT9, IN20, NY34, OH22, PA4, 26, VA34	Piper J-3C-65 Cub (L-4H)	CA111, IA1, MI2, MN27, OR7, TX124
Piasecki PD-18 Retriever (H-25A)	AL36	Piper J-3C-65 Cub (L-4J)	FL22, 80, 84, KY2, MO36, ND24, OH58, OK17, OR24, TX8, 16, UT2, VA13
Piasecki PD-18 Retriever (H-25A) (HUP-3)	CA37		
Piasecki PD-18 Retriever (H-25A) (HUP-3) (UH-25C)	AZ30, CA160, FL55, KS26, MI2	Piper J-3C-65 Cub (mod)	PA56
		Piper J-3C-65 Cub (NE-1)	PA35
Piasecki PD-22 Work Horse (H-21A) (CH-21A)	PA35	Piper J-3C-85 Cub (J-3C-65)	IN25, ME7
		Piper J-3F-50 Cub	OR24
Piasecki PD-22 Work Horse (H-21B) (CH-21B)	AK3, 12, 16, AL36, 37, AR19, AZ46, CA37, 85, 139, CO25, GA45, NE23, NM12, OH22, 55, PA4, 35, WA7, 25	Piper J-3F-65 Cub	CA66, 149, ND2
		Piper J-3L-50 Cub	CT9, PA12
		Piper J-3L-65 Cub	IL82, MO15, MT13, OR7, 24, TX118, WI27
Piasecki 59K Aerial Jeep (VZ-8P)	PA4, VA34	Piper J-3P Cub	OR24
Piccard AX-3M Hot Air Balloon	NY63	Piper J-4A Cub Coupe	AZ30, CA64, NH7, NY16, OR24, TX114
Piccard AX-4 Hot Air Balloon	PA56		
Piccard AX-5 Hot Air Balloon	CT9	Piper J-4B Cub Coupe	NY82
Piccard AX-6 Body Glove Hot Air Balloon	NM2	Piper J-4E Cub Coupe	CA64
		Piper J-4F Cub Coupe	KS26
Piccard AX-6 Hot Air Balloon	IA29, OH59	Piper J-5 Cub Cruiser	NC40
Piccard AX-7 Hot Air Balloon	IA29	Piper J-5 Cub Cruiser (HE-1) (AE-1)	OR24
Piccard Balloon	IL3, 45	Piper J-5A Cub Cruiser	CA44, 130, OR24, TX40, WA34, 37
Piel CP.301 Emeraude	AL32		
Piel CP.301C Emeraude	NY16	Piper J-5C Cub Cruiser	CA149
Piel CP.305 Emeraude	CA158	Piper PA-11 Cub Special	IL63, MO15, ND23, WA8
Pierce-Sawyer JP-51	OK28	Piper PA-12 Super Cruiser	CA149, OH58, PA47, VA19
Pietenpol / St Croix Jenny Replica	IL24		
Pietenpol B4-A Aircamper	AR2, CA65, 88, 91, 122, 158, FL23, IA1, IL65, 68, 80, IN32, KS26, MN13, 15, MT5, 10, 11, ND2, 5, NY35, 63, OR7, PA23, 35, RI1, TX135, VA17, 36, WA3, WI11, 17, 24	Piper PA-15 Vagabond	IA20, MD14, MO15, NY7, PA1, WA37
		Piper PA-16 Clipper	CA130, OH74, WA37
		Piper PA-17 Vagabond	CA130
		Piper PA-18-95 Super Cub (L-18C)	AL36, CA32, NY76
		Piper PA-18-105 Super Cub	PA29
		Piper PA-18-105 Super Cub Special	NH7
		Piper PA-18-125 Super Cub	NM24, TX69
Pietenpol P-9 Sky Scout	MN15, TN5, WA37, WI17	Piper PA-18-125 Super Cub (L-21A)	CA32, TX138
		Piper PA-18-125 Super Cub (L-21A) (TL-21A) (U-7A)	AL36
Pietenpol P-9 Sky Scout (R)	IA1, OR24, TX114, WA34	Piper PA-18-135 Super Cub	VA19, WA32
		Piper PA-18-135 Super Cub (L-21B)	IN40, LA22, PA1, 35, TX132
Pietsch SD-TWO	ND5, 23		
Pietsch-Warren IT	ND23		
Pietsch-Warren Taylorcraft GJ	ND23	Piper PA-18-150 Super Cub	AK5, AZ20, CA130, ID2, KS19, ME7, OK19, PA12, 25, TX54, 102, WV8
Pilatus P.2-05	CA111, 130		
Pilatus P.3-05	NC24		
Pioneer Flightstar MC	CT9		

Index

Piper PA-20 Pacer 125	MN21, NY7, PA12, TX69
Piper PA-20 Pacer 125 (PA-22 Tripacer 125)	WI51
Piper PA-20-135 Pacer	WA37
Piper PA-20-135 Pacer (PA-22-135 Tripacer)	OR24
Piper PA-20-150 Pacer (PA-22-150 Tripacer)	MD14
Piper PA-20-160 Pacer (PA-22-160 Tripacer)	AZ22
Piper PA-22-108 Colt	CA130, MD14, MN30, NC40, WA37
Piper PA-22 Tripacer 125	CA88, IN32, NY42, PA35
Piper PA-22-135 Tripacer	IL29, 39, 50, 63, 66, KS26, WA8, 37
Piper PA-22-150 Tripacer	CA75, IA7, MI14, PA47, TX1, WA8
Piper PA-22-150 Caribbean	MA10, PA35
Piper PA-22-160 Tripacer	AR2, CA130, CO29, IA20
Piper PA-23 Apache	FL29, ID1, IL70, KS26, MA10, MO32, NE12, NH8, OH24, OK7, TX132, 141, VA19, WA9
Piper PA-23-160 Apache	AZ7, IL38, IN53, NJ13, NY76, OK36, PA12, TX132, WA11
Piper PA-23-160 Apache G	LA22
Piper PA-23-250 Aztec	AR5, CA137, 149, KS26, MN30, TX127, 140, WI23
Piper PA-23-250 Aztec (UO-1) (U-11A)	AZ9, 30, UT10
Piper PA-23-250 Aztec B	AR23, CA153,
Piper PA-23-250 Aztec C	CA126, FL29, IA25, MN32, NJ29, OH34,TX132
Piper PA-23-250 Aztec D	IL66, NC15, WI35
Piper PA-23-250 Aztec E	PA47, WI17
Piper PA-23-250 Aztec F	IL18
Piper PA-24 Comanche	CA75, OH24, PA47
Piper PA-24-250 Comanche	CA104, 132, KS26, TX141
Piper PA-24-260 Comanche	CA130
Piper PA-25 Pawnee	AR23, MN32, MS19, NC38
Piper PA-25 Pawnee C	WY10
Piper PA-25 Pawnee D	NY82
Piper PA-28-140 Cherokee	AL32, CT11, DE7, FL13, 54, HI10, MI42, MO15, 15, NY14, OR10, 19, TX3, 153
Piper PA-28-140 Cherokee C	CA121, KS23
Piper PA-28-140 Cherokee F	MA10, NC10
Piper PA-28-151 Cherokee Warrior	MN32, OH24
Piper PA-28-160 Cherokee	AR5, CA61, KY9
Piper PA-28-161 Warrior II	MO32, NJ13
Piper PA-28-180 Cherokee	NC38, TX140
Piper PA-28-180 Cherokee B	CA137
Piper PA-28-181 Cherokee Archer II	AZ42, IL18
Piper PA-28-235 Cherokee	DE7
Piper PA-28R-200 Cherokee Arrow II	MS12, OK29
Piper PA-29 Papoose	PA47
Piper PA-30 Twin Comanche	CA77, NY74, SC23
Piper PA-30 Twin Comanche B	CA116
Piper PA-31 Turbo Navajo	IN53, OK35, PA47
Piper PA-31-350 Navajo Chieftain	KS41, PA47
Piper PA-31-353 T-1020	PA47
Piper PA-31P-350 Mojave	PA47
Piper PA-31T Cheyenne	OR19, PA47
Piper PA-32-260 Cherokee Six	CA62
Piper PA-32R-300 Cherokee Lance	WA4
Piper PA-34-200 Seneca	CA50, PA35, TN34
Piper PA-34-200T Seneca II	IN53
Piper PA-36-285 Pawnee Brave	PA44
Piper PA-38-112 Tomahawk	AK6, CA36, 88, 123, 137, ID14, IN46, KS24, MO18, NC10, NJ21, OK 36, OR19, PA47
Piper PA-40 Arapaho	IN46
Piper PA-41P (pressurized Aztec)	PA47
Piper PA-42-720 Cheyenne IIIA	AR23
Piper PA-42-1000 Cheyenne 400LS	MT13
Piper PA-42-1000 Cheyenne 400 (R)	PA47
Piper PA-44-180 Seminole	IN53, TX141
Piper PA-48 Enforcer	CA4, OH55
Piper PT-1	PA47
Piper TG-8	OR24
Pitcairn PAA-1	NE12
Pitcairn PCA-1A	MD15, PA4
Pitcairn PCA-2	MI25, WI17
Pitcairn PA-5 Mailwing	DC3, IL31, VA36
Pitcairn PA-5S Sport Mailwing	NJ25
Pitcairn PA-6 Super Mailwing	NY63, PA17, 29, WI17
Pitcairn PA-7S Sport Mailwing	NJ25, PA29, WI17
Pitcairn PA-8 Mailwing	NJ25
Pitcairn PA-18	OH15
Pitcairn AC-35	VA19
Pitcairn-Cierva C.8	MD15
Pitcairn-Larsen PA-39	WI17
Pitts 'Lil' Monster	LA27
Pitts 1 (R)	WI17
Pitts S-1 Special	AZ30, ND2, 8, VA19
Pitts S-1C Special	AL32, AZ30, CA109, GA45, IA22, ID1, IL38, IN25, NY35
Pitts S-1D Special	IN57, PA56
Pitts S-1S Special	CA3, 65, 111, 122, 130, CO32, DC3, TX16, 75, UT4, VA35, WI17
Pitts S-1T Special	VA13
Pitts S-2 Special	WI17
Pitts S-2A Special	ND23, NY7
Pitts S-2B Special	OR7, TX69
Pitts SC-1 Special	GA3
Pitts P-6 Special	FL23
Pitts 12	IL18, MN14
Platt-Le Page XR-1	MD15
Player Sportplane	WI17
Pliska Biplane	TX116
Pober P-5 Pober Sport	WI17
Pober P.10 Cuby	IL18
Polen Special	WA31
Polikarpov Po-2	NY7, VA17, WA12
Polikarpov I-153	VA17
Polikarpov I-15bis	VA17
Polikarpov I-16	VA17
Polikarpov I-16 tip 24	CA45, TX40, VA17
Polikarpov I-16 tip 24 (tip 29)	WA12
Politechnika Warszawska PW-5 Smyk	NY50
Polliwagen	CA88, KY2
Polson Special	PA17
Porterfield 35-70	CA23, 130, WA43
Porterfield CP-40	IA1, OR20
Porterfield CP-50	IA1
Porterfield CP-65	CA33, 130, FL23, KS26
Porterfield LP-65	CA130, MO15
Posnansky-Fronius PF-1	CA154
Potez 25 (R)	TX143
Potez 842	CA89
Pratt-Read PR-G1 (XLNE-1)	IN25
Pratt-Read PR-G1 (LNE-1)	AL32, CA111, CT9, IN25, KY2, ND2, NY82, OH55, WA25
Pratt-Read PR-G1 (LNE-1) (TG-32)	MD22, TX124
Prescott Pusher	KS18, WI17
Prest Baby Pursuit	OR20
Princeton Air Scooter	MD15
PrincetonGem X-2 Air Scooter	PA4
Proctor-Varner-Austin Clip Wing Dart	OH53

Index

Progressive Aerodyne SeaRey	MD14
Prue 215	NY50
Prue IIA	NY50
Pterodactyl Ascender	WA25
Pterodactyl Ascender II	WA25
Puffer CO-Z Cozy	WI17
Purvis-Wilson Helicopter (R)	KS16
Putzer/Raab Doppleraab	NY24
PZL Koliber 150A	PA12
PZL TS-11 Iskra 100bisA	ND8
PZL TS-11 Iskra 100bisB	CA38, 111, DE5, OH19, 21, TX16, 57, 80
PZL TS-11 Iskra 200bisC	CA28
Questair 200 Venture	WI17
Quick Monoplane	AL38
Quickarus Hang Glider	CA154
Quickie Aircraft Quickie 1 (Rutan 54)	AZ30, CA158, CO14, CT9, FL23, KS26, MO25, PA21, VA19, WI17
Quickie Aircraft Quickie 2 (Rutan 54)	CA96, 111, IA36, IL18, OR7, 21, WA25
Quickie Aircraft Quickie 51 (Rutan 54)	WA14, 25
Quickie Aircraft Quickie 200 (Rutan 54)	FL23, VA36
Quicksilver Sprint II	FL22
Raab-Katzenstein RK 7 Schmetterling	NY63
RagWing Ultra-Piet	IA22
Ramsey Bathtub	TN5
Rand Robinson KR-1	AK5, AL32, CO10, 32, FL23, KS26, WI17
Rand Robinson KR-2	AZ31, CA128, IA27, NY21, PA35
Rans S-9	FL23
Rase R-1	IA39
Rasor 21 Balloon	WI17
Raven CA-50 Hot Air Balloon	IA29
Raven Hot Air Balloon	IA29
Raven Jules Verne Hot Air Balloon (Kittyhawk)	NM2
Raven NO5ST-15/15T Hot Air Balloon	NM2
Raven Orbitor Gas Balloon	IA29
Raven R Hot Air Balloon	NM2
Raven Rally RX-6 Hot Air Balloon	IA29, ND24
Raven RX.6-56 Hot Air Balloon	NM2
Raven S-40 Hot Air Balloon	CT9
Raven S-40A Hot Air Balloon	IA29, NM2
Raven S-50 Hot Air Balloon	AK5, NM2
Raven S-50A Hot Air Balloon	VA19
Raven S-55A Hot Air Balloon	IA29, NM2
Raven S-60 Hot Air Balloon	IA29
Raven S-60A Hot Air Balloon	NM2
Raven S-100 Hot Air Balloon	NM2
Rawdon R-1	KS18
Rawdon T-1	KS18, MO15
Raytheon T-6A Texan II [Pilatus PC-9]	OH55
Razor Balloon	OH56
Rearwin 6000M Speedster	OR20, 24, WI17
Rearwin 7000 Sportster	CA23, IA1, KS26, MO15, TX114
Rearwin 8135 Cloudster	CA122, CT9, IA1, OR20, PA35
Rearwin 8500 Sportster	OR24
Rearwin 9000L Sportster	OR24, WA43
Rearwin 175 Skyranger	KS26, NY14
Rearwin 185 Skyranger	NC28, OR24, PA35, WA8
Rearwin 190F	IA1
Rearwin Ken-Royce 2000R	TX114
Reid Flying Submarine	PA35
Reno P-5151	TX40
Rensselaer Polytechnic Institute RP-1	NY21
Rensselaer Polytechnic Institute RP-3	NY53
Replica Plans S.E.5A	AZ11, CO29
Republic P-47D Thunderbolt	AZ30, CA110, 160, CT9, FL22, MI2, NC6, NJ8, NY4, OH55, 71, OR21, TN33, TX91, 92, UT5, VA19, WA12
Republic P-47D Thunderbolt (FSM)	CA1, 115, IL1, 2, MD1, NY2, PA48, SC19
Republic P-47G Thunderbolt	CA111
Republic TP-47G Thunderbolt (P-47G)	WA25
Republic YP-47M Thunderbolt (P-47D)	CA160
Republic P-47N Thunderbolt	CO24, FL76, NY14, TX40, 147
Republic XF-84 Thunderjet (XP-84)	VA19
Republic YF-84A Thunderjet (YP-84A)	CA111, IL50
Republic F-84B Thunderjet (P-84B)	AZ33, CA3, NY14, 73, PA35
Republic F-84C Thunderjet (P-84C)	AZ27, 30, CA85, CO25, KS37, NM4, WI17
Republic F-84D Thunderjet	GA51
Republic F-84E Thunderjet	CA160, GA45, NY4, 35, OH55, 71
Republic YF-84F Thunderstreak (YF-96A)	OH55
Republic F-84F Thunderstreak	AL23, 32, AR7, AZ19, 25, 30, 41, CA3, 4, 32, 85, 109, 111, 139, 160, FL76, 80, 81, GA7, 16, 19, 29, 45, IA7, 9, 14, 15, 21, 24, 35, ID18, IL22, 33, 50, 54, 62, 67, 76, 77, IN14, 15, 20, 23, 37, 38, 50, 52, 56, KS8, 9, 18, LA7, 8, MA2, 8, MI2, 15, 53, 58, MN32, MO12, 39, MT7, ND18, NE3, 19, 23, NJ17, 20, NM3, 4, 11, 24, NV15, NY14, 18, 21, OH47, 48, 55, 65, 71, 72, 73, OR7, PA48, SD7, TX4, 16, 51, 56, 88, 147, UT5, VA10, 28, 35, WI34, 62, WV6, WY3
Republic RF-84F Thunderflash	AL7, 31, AR10, 15, AZ30, CA105, IA17, 35, MD12, MI53, 58, MS7, NC13, NE5, 15, 17, 24, 27, NY4, OH71, OK38, TN27, TX51, UT5
Republic RF-84K Thunderflash (RF-84F) (GRF-84F)	CA111, CO32, OH55
Republic F-84G Thunderjet	NC6, OH72, TX16, UT5, WA12
Republic XF-84H Thunderstreak (XF-106)	OH55
Republic XF-91 Thunderceptor (XP-91)	OH55
Republic YF-105B Thunderchief	AL37
Republic F-105B Thunderchief	AZ33, CA32, 85, CT9, IL50, MO9, NC18, NJ17, NY14, OH48, 85, SC19, SD7, TX125, WA2, WI62
Republic JF-105B Thunderchief	TX147
Republic F-105D Thunderchief	AL24, AZ13, 30, CA3, 4, 85, 139, 160, CO28, 32, DC2, FL76, 80, GA26, 44, IL2, 8, 13, IN20, KS9, 37, MD3, MO4, MS14, NC33, NE23, NM7, 11, 14, NY4, 16, OH20, 55, OK41, 48, OR11, TN2, TX40, 51, 63, 66, 80, 123, 134,

Republic F-105D Thunderchief (*continued*)	147, UT5, 6, VA2, 19, 28, 31	Rumpler C V (R)	PA23
		Rumpler Taube (R)	WA25
Republic F-105F Thunderchief	AL32, AR14, CA109, GA45, IL50, KS37, TX16	Rupert Special	OR15
		Russian Tilt Wing (FSM)	IL62
		Rutan 27 Vari-Viggen	AL32, CA96, FL23, TX8, WA25, WI17
Republic F-105G Thunderchief (F-105F)	AR3, AZ13, 30, CA68, 120, GA45, KS26, LA8, MD12, MI6, NV17, NY21, OH55, OR7, TX135, UT5, WA12	Rutan 31 Vari-Eze	WI17
		Rutan 33 Vari-Eze	AK5, AL32, 38, CA4, 53, 65, 105, 122, CT9, FL23, KS26, MT9, ND5, PA35, VA19, 35
		Rutan 40 Defiant	CA65
Republic RC-3 Seabee	AL32, CA66, 71, 95, 130, CT9, FL40, 61, IA1, ID2, 14, MA7, MO5, NY7, 14, OR7, PA35, SC11, 17, TX47, VA19, WI32	Rutan 61 Long Ez	AK3, AZ30, 33, CA28, FL23, IL32, MT13
		Rutan 68 Amsoil Racer	WI17
		Rutan 72 Grizzly	WI17
		Rutan 73	NY14
Republic JB-2 [Fieselar Fi 103A-1]	UT5, NY14, VA19	Rutan 77-6 Solitaire	RI1, WI17
Republic LTV-N-2 [Fieseler Fi 103A-1]	MD15, NC18, NM26, VA2	Ryan M-1	MO15, WA25
		Ryan M-1 (R)	CA122
Revolution Mini-500	AR2, FL22, IN25, PA49	Ryan B-1 Brougham	CA160
Richter Ric Jet 4	CA111	Ryan B-5 Brougham	CA122
Riley Turbine Eagle (Cessna 421C)	ID2	Ryan NYP	DC3
Ritz Standard A	IA1	Ryan NYP (FSM)	IL50, MN8
Robinson JR-5	CA154	Ryan NYP (R)	CA122, FL22, NY63, OK40, OR20, WI17
Robinson Mere-Merit	IA1		
Robinson R-22	CA107, MA10, PA4, VA19	Ryan NYP (R) (B-1)	MI25, MO21, NY14
		Ryan SCW-145	CA130, WA43, WI17
Robinson R-44 Astro	VA19	Ryan STA	CA17, 110, 122, 130, 149, IA1, OH55
Robinson R-44 Raven	CA122, FL42		
Rockwell B-1A Lancer	CA4, CO32, NE23	Ryan STA Special	WA37, WI17
Rockwell B-1B Lancer	AZ1, CA4, GA45, ID18, KS37, OH55, OK41, SD7, TX51, UT5	Ryan STA Special (ST-3KR Recruit (PT-22))	MO15
		Ryan STM-2	CA7
Rockwell B-1B Lancer (FSM)	TX123	Ryan ST-3KR Recruit (PT-21)	CA23, 33, 95, GA45, MN10, TX91, WA31
Rockwell HiMAT	DC3		
Rockwell OV-101 Space Shuttle	VA19	Ryan ST-3KR Recruit (PT-22)	AK5, AZ30, CA7, 17, 23, 32, 33, 44, 66, 91, 114, 122, CT9, FL42, 55, 73, 86, IA1, IL3, 25, KS11, 26, MI2, OH55, 64, OK28, OR7, 24, TX16, 34, 40, 69, 151, VA9, 17, WA34
Roe 1910 Triplane (Scale R)	TX135		
Rogallo Hang Glider	NY50		
Rogallo Standard Hang Glider	NC27		
Rolladen-Schneider LS-1F	PA56		
Roloff RLU-1 Breezy	IL18, KS8, 26, ND5, OR13, PA23, WI17		
Rose Parakeet A-1	IA1		
Rose Parakeet A-1 (R)	WA37	Ryan ST-3KR Recruit (PT-22A)	VA19
Rose Parakeet A4-C	CA130	Ryan 28 Fireball (FR-1)	CA111
Ross Johnson RHJ-6 Adastra	NY50	Ryan 69 Vertijet (X-13) (X-13A)	CA122, OH55
Ross Johnson RJ-6	NY50	Ryan 92 (VZ-3)	AL36
Ross Johnson RJK-5	NY50	Ryan 143 Vertifan (VZ-11) (XV-5A) (XV-5B)	AL36
Ross Seabird	AL32		
Rotary Rocket Company Roton ATV	CA93	Ryan Navion A	CA88, FL12, KS2, TX31, 40
Rotec Panther 2	AK16		
Rotec Rally 2B	AL32, ND5	Ryan Navion A (L-17B) (U-18B)	AL36, OH48
Rotec Rally 3	KS26	Ryan Navion B	AZ24, NY74
Rotec Rally 3B	WA25	Saab 29E (29B) (J 29B) (J 29E)	MD15
Rotorway Executive	AL32, IN3, ND5, WI17	Saab 32A Lansen (A 32A)	CA53, 142
Rotorway Executive 90	IN28, MI2	Saab 37 Viggen (Sk 37) (Sk 37E)	MA4
Rotorway Executive 162F	FL23	Santos-Dumont XX Demoiselle	IN32
Rotorway Scorpion 1	AL36, CA88, 158, FL29, ME4, NY4, WI17	Santos-Dumont XX Demoiselle (R)	FL22, MS28, NV23, NY63, OH15
		Sauser QC	CA85
Rotorway Scorpion 133	AK5, CA37, KS26, OR21, PA4	Savoia-Marchetti SM.56	NC24, NY14
		Scaled Composites 133-4.62	CA4
Rotorway Scorpion Too	IN3, 22, NJ3, PA4, VA19, WA25, WI17	Scaled Composites 143 Triumph	CA68
		Scaled Composites 271 V-Jet II	WI17
Royal Aircraft Factory B.E.2c (R)	AL36	Scaled Composites 311	VA19
Royal Aircraft Factory F.E.8 (R)	DC3, ME7, NY63	Scaled Composites 316 SpaceShipOne	DC3
Royal Aircraft Factory S.E.5A (FSM)	AL36, FL10		
Royal Aircraft Factory S.E.5A (R)	CA15, CO29, FL23, IL18, 82, ME7, MI44, NY7, 16, 63, OH64, PA29, TN5, TX114, WA25	Scaled Composites 316 SpaceShipOne (R)	CA69, 93, WA12
		Scheibe L-Spatz 55	NY50, PA56
Royal Aircraft Factory S.E.5A (Scale R)	AR2, NY24, VT7	Scheibe SF-24A Motor Spatz	PA12
		Scheibe SF-27 Zugvogel IIIB	AZ30
Royal Aircraft Factory S.E.5E	OH55	Schempp-Hirth HS-3 Nimbus 3L	KY2
Royal Aircraft Factory S.E.5E (R)	NC40	Schempp-Hirth SHK-1	AZ30
Rumpler C IV (R)	TN5	Schleicher Ka-3	NM20

Index

Schleicher Ka-4 Rhönlerche II	NM20, PA23
Schleicher Ka-6CR Rhönsegler	NM20
Schleicher Ka-6E Rhönsegler	NM20, NY50, OK43, WA34
Schleicher K.7	WY10
Schleicher ASW-12	VA35
Schleicher ASW-15	NM20
Schmidt Commuter	AZ33
Schneider ESG 29 Grunau 9 (DFS 108-10)	MD15
Schneider ESG 31 Grunau Baby II (DFS 108-49)	VA19
Schneider Grunau Baby IIB	WY10
Schneider-Hofmann-Rehberg SG-38 (DFS 108-14)	MD15
Schneider-Hofmann-Rehberg SG-38 (DFS 108-14) (R)	TX32
Schopal and Nylander Flying Wing	CA111
Schreder HP-8	NY50
Schreder HP-10	NY50
Schreder HP-11A	CA35, NM20, NY50
Schreder HP-16	NY50
Schreder HP-18	NM20, NY50
Schreder HP-18-LK-G	WI17
Schultz ABC	CA160
Schweizer SGP.1-1 (R)	NY50
Schweizer SGU.1-7	NY50
Schweizer SGS.2-8	CA85, 154, NY50
Schweizer SGS.2-8 (LNS-1)	FL55, MI2, NY82
Schweizer SGS.2-8 (TG-2)	IN4, TX124
Schweizer SGS.2-12 (TG-3A)	AZ11, 30, CA32, 160, MO1, NM20, NY16, 50, OH55, OK28, TX40, 124
Schweizer SGU.1-19	NY50, PA56
Schweizer SGU.1-20	IA22
Schweizer SGU.2-22	CA130, MD14, NM20, NY16, VA19
Schweizer SGS.1-23D	NY50
Schweizer SGS.1-23E	CA67
Schweizer SGS.1-23HM	NY35
Schweizer SGS.1-24	CO32
Schweizer SGS.2-25	OH55
Schweizer SGS.1-26	NY50
Schweizer SGS.1-26A	NM20, PA56
Schweizer SGS.1-26B	PA56
Schweizer SGS.1-26C	FL86
Schweizer SGS.1-26D	CA95, PA56
Schweizer SGS.1-26E	IL62, NY50, 82
Schweizer SGS.1-29	NY50
Schweizer SGS.2-33	WY10
Schweizer SGS.2-33A	ID2, IL18, NY82, WY10
Schweizer SGS.2-33A (TG-4A)	CO28, 32
Schweizer SGS.1-34	NM20, NY50
Schweizer SGS.1-35	NY50
Schweizer SGS.1-36	NY82, WY10
Schweizer SGS.2-32	NY50, 82, OR7
Schweizer SGM.2-37 (TG-7A)	OH34, OK46, SD4
Scott Mathieu-Russell	WI27
Seagull Hang Glider	NM20
Seahawk Industries Condor II	FL86
Seawind Seawind 3000	FL75
Security S-1-B Airster	CA158
Selcher Sport	IN44
Sellers Quadriplane (R)	KY2
Sellmer Sportsplane D-1	CA23
Semco Ax.5 Model T Hot Air Balloon	NM2
Semco Ax.5 Model T 65 K Hot Air Balloon	NM2
Semco Ax.6 Hot Air Balloon (Ax.5)	NM2
Semco TC-4 Hot Air Balloon	IA29
Sequoia F.8L Falco	SD4
Seversky 2PA Guardsman (AT-12)	CA111
Seversky AP-1 (P-35)	OH55
Seversky EP-106 (P-35A)	FL22
Sharp J-4 Nemesis	VA19
Shavrov Sh-2	MO15
Shenyang J-6 I [Mikoyan-Gurevich MiG-19SF]	AZ30
Shenyang J-8II	KS9
Shenyang J-5	CO27
Shober Willie II	KS26
Shoemaker Cannonhouse	MD15
Short S.25 Sunderland MR.V	FL22
Short S.29 (R)	NY63
Short S.45 Solent 3 (Seaford 1)	CA105
Short SD.3-30 Sherpa (C-23A)	AL11, NJ19
Siemens-Schuckert D IV (R)	AZ33, NY63
Sikorsky S-16 (FSM)	CT9
Sikorsky S-38B (R)	WI51
Sikorsky S-39-B (S-39-A)	CT9
Sikorsky S-39-C (S-39-A)	MN18
Sikorsky S-39-C (S-39-B)	NH7
Sikorsky S-43	AK3, AZ30
Sikorsky S-43 (JRS-1)	MD15
Sikorsky S-43 (OA-11)	TX143
Sikorsky VS-44A (XJRS-1)	CT9
Sikorsky VS-300	MI25
Sikorsky VS-300 (R)	PA4
Sikorsky VS-316A Hoverfly (R-4B)	AL36, CA160, CT9, OH55
Sikorsky VS-316A Hoverfly (R-4B) (HNS-1)	FL55
Sikorsky VS-316A Hoverfly (XR-4)	VA19
Sikorsky VS-316A Hoverfly (YR-4B) (HNS-1)	NE12
Sikorsky VS-316B Hoverfly II (R-6A)	AL36, OH55, PA4
Sikorsky VS-316B Hoverfly II (R-6A) (Doman mod)	CT9
Sikorsky VS-372 Dragonfly (XR-5)	VA19
Sikorsky VS-372 Dragonfly (YR-5A) (YH-5A)	OH55
Sikorsky S-51 Dragonfly	AL36, NM12, OR7, PA4
Sikorsky S-51 Dragonfly (R-5A) (R-5D) (H-5D)	AL36
Sikorsky S-51 Dragonfly (H-5G)	AK3, AL36, AZ30, PA4
Sikorsky S-51 Dragonfly (H-5H)	AK16, CT9
Sikorsky S-51 Dragonfly (HO3S-1)	AL36, AZ30, NC6, VA22
Sikorsky S-51 Dragonfly (HO3S-1G)	FL55, OR7
Sikorsky S-52-2 (YH-18A)	AL36, CA37
Sikorsky S-52-3 (HO5S-1)	CT2, FL16, 55, PA4, VA19
Sikorsky S-55B (HO4S-1)	TX80
Sikorsky S-55B (HRS-1)	VA19, 22
Sikorsky S-55B Chickasaw (H-19C) (UH-19C)	AL36, OH22
Sikorsky S-55D (HO4S-3) (UH-19F)	AZ46, NM12
Sikorsky S-55D (HO4S-3G)	NY34
Sikorsky S-55D (HRS-3) (CH-19E)	CA58, FL55, GA9
Sikorsky S-55D Chickasaw (H-19B) (UH-19B)	AZ30, FL80, NE23, OH55
Sikorsky S-55D Chickasaw (H-19D) (UH-19D)	AL36, 37, AZ11, CA4, 26, 37, 88, CT2, 9, GA45, IA25, MT8, ND11, OH22, 71, OR7, TX40, VA34
Sikorsky S-56 Mojave (H-37A) (CH-37A) (CH-37B)	OR7
Sikorsky S-56 Mojave (H-37A) (H-37B) (CH-37B)	AL36, AZ30, CA37, VA34
Sikorsky S-56 Mojave (HR2S-1) (CH-37C)	FL55
Sikorsky S-58	NY13
Sikorsky S-58 Choctaw (H-34A) (CH-34A)	AL36, CT2, GA46, HI10, PA2
Sikorsky S-58 Choctaw (H-34A) (CH-34A) (CH-34C)	CA26, 109, 129, MO4, NC6
Sikorsky S-58 Choctaw (H-34A) (UH-34A)	IL62

Sikorsky S-58 Choctaw (H-34A) (VH-34A)	AL36, CO21	Sikorsky S-65A (CH-53C) (MH-53J) (MH-53M)	FL36
Sikorsky S-58 Choctaw (H-34A) (VH-34C)	AZ30, CA4, 139, VA34	Sikorsky S-65A (HH-53B) (MH-53H) (MH-53J)	NM12
Sikorsky S-58 Seabat (XHSS-1) (YHSS-1) (YSH-34G)	CA129	Sikorsky S-65A (HH-53C) (HH-53H) (MH-53M)	AZ30, GA45
Sikorsky S-58 Seabat (HSS-1) (SH-34G) (UH-34G)	TN33	Sikorsky S-65A (HH-53C) (MH-53J) (MH-53M)	AL24, FL76, OH55, TX123, 147, UT5
Sikorsky S-58 Seabat (HSS-1) (UH-34G)	CA4, 91, MO4, OH71	Sikorsky S-65A Sea Dragon (MH-53E)	AZ1
Sikorsky S-58 Seabat (HSS-1) (SH-34J)	OK53	Sikorsky S-65A Sea Stallion (CH-53A)	FL55, IL62, MI2, NC21, TX123, VA22
Sikorsky S-58 Seabat (HSS-1N) (SH-34J)	CA37, 145, CO25, GA45, NM12, PA26, 35, UT5	Sikorsky S-65A Sea Stallion (CH-53A) (NCH-53A)	KS9, MD19, VA32
Sikorsky S-58 Seahorse (HUS-1) (UH-34D)	AZ3, CA58, 110, 129, 144, FL55, MN3, NY33, OK53, OR7, SC18, TN21, TX16, 63, VA19	Sikorsky S-65A Sea Stallion (CH-53D)	CA58, HI1, 3
		Sikorsky S-65A Sea Stallion (RH-53D)	HI3, NJ1, PA64, VA26
		Sikorsky S-69 (XH-59A)	AL36
Sikorsky S-58 Seahorse (HUS-1A) (UH-34E)	TX135	Sikorsky S-70A Black Hawk (UH-60A)	VA32
Sikorsky S-58 Seahorse (HUS-1G) (HH-34F)	FL24	Sikorsky S-70A Black Hawk (YUH-60A)	AL36
Sikorsky S-58 Seahorse (HUS-1L) (LH-34D)	CT9	Sikorsky S-70B Sea Hawk (YSH-60B)	FL49
Sikorsky S-58 Seahorse (HUS-1N) (UH-34J)	CA88, 129, TX16	Sikorsky S-70B Sea Hawk (SH-60B)	AL37, CA102, FL55, 58, MD20, NC10, 12
Sikorsky S-58 Seahorse (HUS-1Z) (VH-34D)	NC21, VA22	Sikorsky S-70B Sea Hawk (SH-60F)	CA145, NC10
Sikorsky S-58B	CA160, TX143	Sikorsky S-72	AL36
Sikorsky S-59	CT9	Sikorsky S-76	CT8
Sikorsky S-59 (XH-39)	AL36	Simplex Red Arrow K2C	OH59
Sikorsky S-60 Skycrane	CT9	Sino-Swearingen SJ30-2	TX92
Sikorsky S-61B Sea King (HSS-2) (HH-3A)	FL55, PA4	Sioux Coupe 60	OR20
		Sioux Coupe 90-B	IA22
		Sisler SF-2M	MN13
Sikorsky S-61B Sea King (HSS-2) (HH-3A) (UH-3A)	HI7	Sisler SP.1 Pipit	RI1
		Skandinavisk Aero Industri (SAI) KZ III U-2	MO15
Sikorsky S-61B Sea King (HSS-2) (SH-3A) (SH-3G)	CA85, 102, FL38, SC18	Skyfly CA-65	CA155
Sikorsky S-61B Sea King (HSS-2) (SH-3A) (SH-3H)	CA144, 145, FL55, OR7, RI1	SkyRaider Ultralight Seaplane	WI24
		Slingsby T.15 Gull	NY50
Sikorsky S-61B Sea King (HSS-2) (SH-3A) (UH-3A) (SH-3H)	VA26	Slingsby T.21B Sedbergh TX.1	NM20
		Slingsby T.31B Cadet TX.3	NM20
Sikorsky S-61B Sea King (HSS-2A) (SH-3A) (SH-3H)	HI1	Slingsby T.38 Grasshopper TX.1	NY50
		Slingsby T.43 Skylark 3B	NY50
Sikorsky S-61B Sea King (HSS-2Z) (VH-3A)	CA117, 118, FL55	Slingsby T.50 Skylark 4	IA39
		Slingsby T.56 [Royal Aircraft Factory S.E.5A (R)]	NY16
Sikorsky S-61B Sea King (SH-3D) (SH-3H)	AZ1, FL38, 55	Slingsby T.67C Firefly	FL65
Sikorsky S-61B Sea King (SH-3D) (UH-3H)	FL41, HI1, 6, 7	Slipstream Genesis	MD14
		Slipstream Revalation	MD14
Sikorsky S-61R (CH-3C) (CH-3E)	AZ13, CA160, FL36, IL62, NC6, OH55, TX130, UT5	Smith Aeroplane	IN18
		Smith DK-1	KS26
Sikorsky S-61R (CH-3C) (CH-3E) (JCH-3E)	CA4	Smith DSA-1 Miniplane	CA124, IA1, MD14, NJ24, NY16, OH43, 64, WI17
Sikorsky S-61R (CH-3C) (HH-3E)	NM12, OH55		
Sikorsky S-61R (CH-3E) (HH-3E)	GA45	Smith DSA-2 Miniplane	IN25
Sikorsky S-61R (HH-3E)	NY71	Smith Termite	CO10, OH59, OR13
Sikorsky S-61R (S-61A) (CH-3C) (CH-3E)	CA3	Smyth Sidewinder	FL23
		Snow S-2A	MS19, MT9, OH64
Sikorsky S-61R Pelican (HH-3F)	AZ30, CT13, FL24, 55, IL62, 66, NY32, TX68, WI8	Snow S-2R	ID1, TX54
		Snyder Baby Bomber	WI17
		Snyder R-1	NJ3
Sikorsky S-62A Seaguard (HH-52A)	AL37, AR5, AZ30, CA53, 103, 107, 160, CO4, CT9, FL7, 55, HI3, IL21, MI42, 53, MN24, 30, NC12, NE9, NJ3, 21, NY34, PA4, 35, TX3, UT11, WA25	Soko 522	GA21
		Soko N-60 Galeb G-2A	IL3
		Solo System Hot Air Balloon	IA29
		Sopwith 1 1/2 Strutter (R)	CA15, FL22
		Sopwith F.1 Camel	AR1
		Sopwith F.1 Camel (R)	AL36, CA15, 111, FL22, 55, MI2, NY63, OH55, OR7, PA29, TX16, 114, WA25, WI63
Sikorsky S-64A Tarhe (YCH-54A)	VA34		
Sikorsky S-64A Tarhe (CH-54A)	AL36, AZ30, IL62, KS9, 28, MS2, NV19, TX58		
		Sopwith 5F.1 Dolphin (R)	NY63
Sikorsky S-64A Tarhe (CH-54B)	AK2, AL31, 32, CT9, IL62	Sopwith 7F.1 Snipe	DC3
		Sopwith 7F.1 Snipe (R)	CA15, WA25

Index

Sopwith Pup (R)	CA15, 122, 158, CO29, FL22, IA13, ME7, MO15, OK40, PA23, TN5, TX69, WA25
Sopwith Pup (Scale R)	VA17
Sopwith Tabloid (R)	CA15
Sopwith Triplane (R)	CA15, NY63, OH48, WA25
Sorrell Parasol	WA25
Sorrell SNS	WA19
Sorta Baby Lakes	AZ33
SPAD VII	CA122, FL22, 58, OH55
SPAD VII (R)	CA158, CO29, MI2, NY63, VA36
SPAD VIII (R)	IA13
SPAD XIII	AZ29, DC3, OR21
SPAD XIII (FSM)	CA115, MI53
SPAD XIII (R)	CA15, ME7, WA25
SPAD XIIIC.1	OH55
SPAD XVI	VA19
SPAD XII	NY63
Spalinger S-18-III	WY10
Spartan C-2-45	OH53
Spartan C-2-60	MN18, OK43, OR24
Spartan C-3-135	PA12
Spartan C-3-165	NY63
Spartan C-3-220 (NP-1)	OK43
Spartan C-3-225	MO15, OK36, WI17
Spartan 7W Executive	AK3, AZ10, WI17
Spartan 7W Executive (UC-71)	MO15
Spencer S-12E Aircar	AK3
Sperry Aerial Torpedo (R)	NY14
Sperry-Verville M-1 Messenger	OH55, OR24
Sperry-Verville M-1 Messenger (R)	NY14, PA23
Spezio Sport Tuholer	OH64
Spirit of Lawrence Tech	MI32
Sportline Aviacija Genesis 2	ID24
Sportswings Valkyrie Hang Glider	VA19
Spratt 108	PA35
Squadron Aviation SPAD XIII	AZ30
St. Louis C-2-110 Super Cardinal	MO15, WA43
Staib LB-5	KS26
Stamer-Lippisch Z-12 Zögling	NY50
Stamer-Lippisch Z-12 Zögling (R)	NM20
Stampe & Vertongen S.V.4B	NY63
Stampe & Vertongen S.V.4C	FL22, NC40
Standard A-3	NY8
Standard E-1	FL22, VA36
Standard H-3	NY8
Standard J-1	AZ33, CA65, 122, 160, FL22, ME7, MO15, ND8, NE12, NY24, OH37, 55, PA23, 29, TX114, VA19, WI17
Stanford Swift	CA65
Stanley Nomad	VA19
Star Cavalier (R)	OK43
Star Cavalier B	MO15, PA23
Star Cavalier E	MO15, PA23
Star Cavalier E (B)	OK28
Starks Taube (Scale R)	KS9
Starr Bumble Bee	AZ30
Stearman C2B (C2M)	AK3
Stearman C3B	GA17, KS18, OR20, 24, WA25, WI27
Stearman C3B (C2C) (C3D)	WA2
Stearman C3B (C3L)	MN18
Stearman C3MB	OR20
Stearman C3R	CA7, IA22
Stearman 4CM-1	CA149
Stearman 4D	KS18
Stearman 4DM (4CM-1)	WA32
Stearman 4E (4D)	CA160
Stearman 4E Junior Speedmail	NV23
Stearman 6C	FL46
Stearman 6L (6A)	CA160
Stearman 6L (6F)	MN18
Stearman 6L (XPT-912) (6A) (6P)	GA17
Stearman 70	OR24
Stearman 73 (NS-1)	KS18
Stearman B Ariel	KS18
Stearman-Hammond Y-1S	CA65, VA19
Steckler STS.1 Tern	IL57
Steen Skybolt	CA45, IL50, KS26, PA35, TX92
Steinhauser S-2	PA56
Stephens Akro	VA19, WA25
Stephens Super Akro	FL22
Stevens Jet	NY16
Stewart JD-HW.1.7Headwind	AR1
Stewart Mustang	FL80
Stier Penguin Trainer	WI17
Stinson A	MN18
Stinson SM-1 Detroiter	IL42, MI25
Stinson SM-1B Detroiter	AZ37
Stinson SM-1B Detroiter (SM-1DX)	MN18
Stinson SM-1F Detroiter	NV23
Stinson SM-6000B	FL22, MN18
Stinson SM-7A Junior	MN18
Stinson SM-7B Junior	NV23
Stinson SM-8A Junior	AK3, AZ37, CA122, MO15, NE12, OH53, WA34, WI17
Stinson Junior R	OR24
Stinson Junior S	AR2, CA71, 149, IA1, OH37
Stinson Junior SR	AK3, 5, NH7, WA25
Stinson SR-5 Reliant	AL32, CT9, NH5
Stinson SR-5A Reliant	MO15, ND5
Stinson SR-5B Reliant	MO15
Stinson SR-5E Reliant	OR15
Stinson SR-6 Reliant	AK3, MO15
Stinson SR-8B Reliant	AK16
Stinson SR-8D Reliant	GA23
Stinson SR-9 Reliant	AK16, AL32
Stinson SR-9C Reliant	AK3, IN25, WA37
Stinson SR-10E Reliant	WA34
Stinson SR-10F Reliant	DC5
Stinson SR-10G Reliant	VA36
Stinson V-74 Vigilant (O-49) (L-1)	AL36, FL22
Stinson V-74 Vigilant (O-49A) (L-1A)	FL22, OH55
Stinson V-74 Vigilant (O-49A) (L-1A) (L-1F)	AK3
Stinson HW.75	OR24, TX30, 40
Stinson V-76 Sentinel (O-62) (L-5)	CA42, 58, 85, 160, ND8, NM24, TX25, 31, 40, 45, VA9
Stinson V-76 Sentinel (L-5)	AL36, CA89, 160, GA45, MN10, NM6, NY82, OH40, 55, OR24, TX28, 40, 45, 92, UT2, VA19, WA8
Stinson V-76 Sentinel (L-5) (OY-1)	FL55, TX40, VA8
Stinson V-76 Sentinel (L-5B)	AZ30, IA8, KS26, TX45
Stinson V-76 Sentinel (L-5B) (OY-1)	CA139, TX40
Stinson V-76 Sentinel (L-5C)	TX2, 26
Stinson V-76 Sentinel (L-5E)	CA43, 53, 149, HI6, IN59, OK20, TX16, 34, 40, 151, VA17, WI17
Stinson V-76 Sentinel (L-5E) (OY-1)	OH26, TX40, VA22
Stinson V-76 Sentinel (L-5G)	AK3, AL36, AZ33, CA32, 91, 128, ID1, IN10, NY77, SD7
Stinson V-76 Sentinel (L-5G) (OY-1)	PA13
Stinson V-77 Reliant (AT-19)	AK3, 5, AZ33, 37, CA53, 82, 90, 128, IN25, 40, KS26, MD14, MI58, MN26, NC9, ND8, NM24, NV9, NY74, 77, OR21, PA33, TX40, 134, 151

699

Stinson 10A Voyager	AL32, CA130, 158, CT9, IA1, KS26, MI57, MS5, NY74, PA13, RI1, TX40, 134
Stinson 105	CA88
Stinson 108-1 Voyager	AK3, CA155, OR24, TX37, 40, 118
Stinson 108-2 Voyager	CA45, KY2, NY4, OK28
Stinson 108-3 Voyager	CA130, IN44, NY7
Stits DS-1 Baby Bird	WI17
Stits SA-2A Skybaby	WI17
Stits SA-3A Playboy	IL38, WI17
Stits SA-3B Playboy	ND2
Stits SA-5A Flut-R-Bug	CA158
Stits SA-6B Flut-R-Bug	NY16, WA19
Stits SA-7D Skycoupe	NY21
Stits SA-8 Skeeto	WI17
Stits SA-11A Playmate	FL23, SD8, WA8, WI17
Stockwell Chum (Huntington Chum)	NY21
Stoddard-Hamilton SH-2 Glasair	CA105
Stoddard-Hamilton SH-2 Glasair 1-RG	FL23
Stoddard-Hamilton SH-2 Glasair HAM-2	WI17
Stoddard-Hamilton SH-2 Glasair II	OR7
Stoddard-Hamilton SH-2 Glasair IIFT	AL32
Stoddard-Hamilton SH-2 Glasair III	FL65, WA14
Stoddard-Hamilton SH-2 Glasair IIR	IL38
Stoddard-Hamilton SH-2 Glasair TG-1	WA14
Stoddard-Hamilton SH-4 GlaStar	AZ7, WI17
Stoddard-Hamilton SH-4 GlaStar III	WI17
Stoddard-Hamilton SH-4 GlaStar IIRG	NY21
Stolp SA.100 Starduster	AL32
Stolp SA.100 Starduster	WA37
Stolp SA.300 Starduster Too	MA10, PA12, RI1, WA37, WI17
Stolp SA.500L Starlet	GA3
Stolp SA.900 V-Star	IA27
Stout Skycar	VA19
Strang Flyer (R)	KS31
Striplin Lone Ranger	OR13
Sud Fennec [North American NA-174 Trojan (T-28A)]	AL29, CA89, IL63, ND8, OH48
Sud Fennec [North American NA-189 Trojan (T-28A)]	KS26
Sud SA.341G Gazelle	CA37
Sud-Est SE.210 Caravelle VI-R	AZ30, 31, CT9
Sud-Est SE.3130 Alouette II	ID24
Sud-Ouest SO.1221S Djinn	CA37, PA4
Sugden Mini 500	ID24
Sukhoi Su-7BM	NV17
Sukhoi Su-22M4	OH55
Sukhoi Su-26M	VA19
Summers WH-1 (Hansen Special)	CA111
Sunbird Hang Glider	CA155
Supermarine S.6B (FSM)	CA111
Supermarine 300 Spitfire F.I (FSM)	CA33
Supermarine 300 Spitfire F.Ia	IL45
Supermarine 329 Spitfire F.IIa (FSM)	CA115
Supermarine 349 Spitfire F.Vc	OH55
Supermarine 349 Spitfire LF.V (Scale R)	MN27
Supermarine 349 Spitfire LF.Vb	LA17, TX91
Supermarine 349 Spitfire LF.Vb (FSM)	AZ33
Supermarine 349 Spitfire LF.Vc	CA111, TX20, WA12
Supermarine 359 Spitfire HF.VIIc	DC3
Supermarine 359 Spitfire LF.VIIIc	TX16
Supermarine 361 Spitfire LF.IXb	TX54
Supermarine 361 Spitfire LF.IXc	CA111, NJ8, WA25
Supermarine 361 Spitfire LF.IXc (FSM)	MD1
Supermarine 361 Spitfire LF.IXe	FL5, VA17, WA17
Supermarine 361 Spitfire LF.IXe (FSM)	FL5
Supermarine 361 Spitfire LF.XVIe	CA18, 122, FL5, 22, NY74, OR7, TX92
Supermarine 365 Spitfire PR.XI	OH55
Supermarine 379 Spitfire F.XIV	CA111
Supermarine 379 Spitfire FR.XIVc	CA110, FL5
Supermarine 379 Spitfire FR.XIVe	CA45, FL22, TX40
Supermarine 386 Seafire F.XV	MO44
Supermarine 388 Seafire FR.47	MT13
Supermarine 394 Spitfire FR.XVIIIe	IL18
Supermarine 509 Spitfire T.9	WI17
Supermarine 544 Scimitar F.1	NY34
Swallow	WA33
Swallow 3POLB	NE12
Swallow A Ultralight	AZ30
Swallow J-5	ND2, WA25
Swallow J-5 (F-165)	KS18
Swallow New Swallow	KS18
Swallow OX-5	KS18, OR20, WI17
Swallow TP	CA160, WA33
Swallow TP-W	KS18
Swanson SF-4	PA17
Swearingen SA.26T Merlin II	AR23
Swearingen SA.26T Merlin IIA	AL11
Swift 18	KS18
Symonds Supercat	ID1
Task Silhouette	WA25
Taylor Aerocar	FL 42, MN18, WI17
Taylor Aerocar III	WA25
Taylor Chummy (R)	NY65
Taylor Coot A	NC28
Taylor E-2 Cub	FL23, IL4, 29, 70, MO15, NC40, OH59, OR24, PA23, VA36, WA8, WI17, 27
Taylor J-2 Cub	AL32, CA64, 75, IA22, IL29, 63, MD7, MO36, NC40, ND5, NE12, NH7, NY63, OR20, 24, PA35, WA8
Taylor JT.1 Monoplane	PA35, WI17
Taylor JT.2 Titch	CA35, 158
Taylor-Berry 2100 Bullet	OR13
Taylor-Young A	PA23, 35
Taylorcraft A	OH53, OR20, WA25
Taylorcraft BC-12-65	NY56, OR24
Taylorcraft BC-12D	AK3, AR2, 5, AZ30, CO29, IA22, IN48, ND5, NY16, PA12, 23, TX1, 134, WA25, 37
Taylorcraft BC-65	OH21, OR24
Taylorcraft BF-50 (BC-50)	WI17
Taylorcraft BL-65	FL23, MD7, PA8
Taylorcraft DCO-65 Grasshopper (O-57A) (L-2A)	AL36, CA32, IL24, IN10, MI56, NJ31, TX40
Taylorcraft DCO-65 Grasshopper (L-2B)	AR19, IL3, PA12
Taylorcraft DCO-65 Grasshopper (L-2M)	AZ30, CA3, 43, 130, GA35, 58, ID14, 15, IL3, IN28, KS10, 26, MN3, MO15, ND8, NH6, OH48, 55, OR24, PA12, TX2, 32, 34, 134
Taylorcraft DCO-65 Grasshopper (L-2MK)	AK3
Taylorcraft DCO-65 Grasshopper (ST-100D) (TG-6) (L-2M)	TX2
Taylorcraft ST-100 (TG-6)	AZ30, MO28, OR24
Team Minimax	IL24
Team Minimax 110R	CO32
Team Minimax 1600	AZ33
Temco D.16 Twin Navion	AZ30, KS26
Temco D.16A Twin Navion	IA21
Temco GC-1B Swift	CA130, IL18, KS26, MN21, TN32, WA37

Index

Temco T.51 Pinto (TT-1)	CA95, TX92	United States Lighter Then Air Corporation 138-SC (Grace GAC-20)	OR21
Temco TE.1B Buckaroo (T-35A)	TN32		
Temple Sportsman	TX69		
Tessier Biplane	WI17	Universal Systems Hot Air Balloon	IA29
Thaden T-1 Argomaut	CA65	University of Liverpool Man Powered Aircraft	PA12
Thomas E Pusher	NY63		
Thomas Pigeon	CA160	Unknown Glider	ND5
Thomas-Morse S-4B	NY63	Unruh Pretty Prairie Special	KS18
Thomas-Morse S-4B/C	VA22	UP Hang Glider	NM20
Thomas-Morse S-4C	CA122, 160, FL22, 55, NY14, OH27, 55, TX114, WA8	Utva Fabrica Aviona 66	FL80
		Valentin Taifun 17E	MT13
		Van Dellen LH-2	IA1
Thomas-Morse S-4C (R)	TX114	Vanek Gyrocopter C	OR21
Thomas-Morse S-5	TX114	Vans RV-3	AZ7, WI17
Thompson 28	OR21	Vans RV-4	CA122, 151, IN28, ND24, OH18, WI17
Thorp T-18	CA122, IA27, KS26, OR7, 13, TX69, WA25, WI17		
		Vans RV-6	CA17
		Vans RV-6A	CA94, WI17
Thorp TB-3	CA65	Vans RV-7	MD14
Thunder & Colt Hot Air Balloon	OR7	Vans RV-8	CA130, KY2, NC24, ND8, WA39
Thunder AX-7-77A Hot Air Balloon	IA29		
Thunder Hot Air Balloon.	NM2	Velocity Aircraft Velocity	PA44
Tilbury Flash	IL41	Vertol V.43 Shawnee (H-21C) (CH-21C)	AL36, AZ30, CA3, 4, OR7, PA4, UT5, VA34
Timm (Aetna) 2-SA Aerocraft	IA22		
Timm Collegiate	MO15, OR20	Vertol V.76 (VZ-2)	MD15
Timm PT.175K Tutor (N2T-1)	FL55, MI2	Vertol V.107M Sea Knight (HRB-1) (CH-46A) (HH-46A) (HH-46D)	CA102, NC17
Titan T-51 Mustang	AZ11		
Tracy Kona Wind	CA111	Vertol V.107M Sea Knight (HRB-1) (CH-46A) (UH-46A) (HH-46D)	CA145, NC10
Travel Air D-4D Speedwing	CA65, NY24, VA19		
Travel Air 6-B	GA23	Vertol V.107M Sea Knight (CH-46A) (HH-46A) (HH-46D)	AZ1, FL83, NC8, SC4, VA26
Travel Air 10-D	PA17		
Travel Air 12Q	WI27	Vertol V.107M Sea Knight (CH-46A) (UH-46D) (CH-46D)	FL55
Travel Air B-14B	CA3		
Travel Air 1000	TN4	Vertol V.107M Sea Knight (CH-46D)	NC6, VA22
Travel Air 2000	GA50, IL63, MO15, OR20, 24, VA36, WA34	Vertol V.107M Sea Knight (CH-46D) (CH-46E)	CA30, 58, FL58, NC21
		Vertol V.114 Chinook (CH-47A)	AL36, KY5
Travel Air 2000 (B)	PA23	Vertol V.114 Chinook (CH-47A) (ACH-47A)	AL28
Travel Air 3000	MO15, OR24, PA17		
Travel Air 4000	CA67, FL46, MO15, OR24, TN4, WA34, WI27	Vertol V.114 Chinook (CH-47D)	IL62, VA32
		Vertol V.114 Chinook (YHC-1B) (YCH-47A) (YCH-47B)	VA34
Travel Air 4000 (BW)	WI27	Verville AT Sportsman	VA19
Travel Air 4000 (W-4000)	WA34	Vickers 724 Viscount	AZ30
Travel Air B-4000	FL22	Vickers 745D Viscount	CA158
Travel Air D-4000	AR2, CA75, OK28, 39	Vickers 757 Viscount	TX13
Travel Air E-4000	IL46, WI17	Vickers 798D Viscount (745D)	PA35
Travel Air 5000MA	OK51	Vickers 831 Viscount	AZ31
Travel Air 6000-B	AR1	Viking B-8 Kittyhawk	CT9
Travel Air A-6000A	AZ37, MN18	Viking Dragonfly	CA17, FL23, KS26
Travel Air R	IL45, TN4	Vitanza LV56	WI17
Travel Air R (R)	MI2	Voisin LA-III (R)	WA31
Trek Solotrek XFV	CA65	Voisin 8	DC3
Trotter WSA.1	WA31	Voisin 8 (R)	NY63
Troyer VX-1	PA35	Vollmann Eagle Heli	ID1
Truax Papoose	MD13	Volmer Jensen VJ-21	CA128, 158
Tucker LGT.1	VA37	Volmer Jensen VJ-22 Sportsman	CA158, KY2, NY16, VT3
Tupolev ANT-7 (R-6)	VA17	Volmer Jensen VJ-23	AK3, IA1, NY16, PA56
Tupolev Tu-2S	FL22, NM24	Volmer Jensen VJ-23E	CA158, WI17
Turner Monoplane	CA39	Volmer Jensen VJ-24	FL23
Turner Nieuport 27 (Scale R)	KS9	Volmer Jensen VJ-24E	CA158
Turner T-40	IA27	Volmer Jensen VJ-24W	CA158
Turner T-40A	TX92, WA34	Von Pomer Pusher	NY21
Ultraflight Lazair 1	FL23	Vought VE-7 (R)	TX152
Ultraflight Lazair 1 Seaplane	WI24	Vought V-56 Vindicator (SB2U-2)	FL55
Ultraflight Lazair SS EC	VA19	Vought V-173	MD15, TX152
Ultralight 166 Mosquito	CT9	Vought V-310 Kingfisher (OS2U-2)	NC37
Ultralight Flying Machines Easy Riser	AZ30, CA105, 111, 154, IA22, NM20, NY16, WI17	Vought V-310 Kingfisher (OS2U-3)	AL37, CA160, FL55, VA17, 19
		Vought O3U Corsair	FL55
Ultralight Flying Machines Solar Riser	WI17	Vought XF4U-4 Corsair	CT9
		Vought F4U-1 Corsair	FL55
Ultralite Products Dragonfly 1 Hang Glider	AK16	Vought F4U-1A Corsair	CA111
		Vought F4U-1D Corsair	VA19

701

Vought F4U-4 Corsair	AZ30, CA111, 145, 160, FL22, ND8, 24, NM24, TX12, 152, VA22, WI17	Vought A-7D Corsair II (*continued*)	9, 10, TX16, 31, 147, VA28, 36, WI55, 59, 62, WV1, WY3
Vought F4U-4 Corsair (FSM)	MD14, NY2	Vought A-7E Corsair II	AL32, 34, AR17, AZ30, CA105, FL9, 38, 43, 55, GA10, IL2, 15, 26, KS29, LA18, 24, NC6, NM24, NV10, NY21, OH48, OR21, SC18, SD4, TN16, VA2, 27
Vought F4U-5N Corsair (F4U-5)	CA58, IN28, KS26, TX92		
Vought F4U-5N Corsair (F4U-5P)	MT13		
Vought F4U-5NL Corsair	IL3, MA4		
Vought F4U-7 Corsair	CA122, OR21		
Vought FG-1A Corsair	OH71, VA22		
Vought FG-1D Corsair	CA15, 110, CO32, CT2, DC6, FL22, 55, IN54, MI2, 53, NJ8, NY4, 82, OH48, 71, 74, OR7, SC18, TX16, 25, 40, 91, VA17, WA12, 25, 28	Vought YA-7F Corsair II (A-7D)	CA4, UT5
		Vought A-7K Corsair II	AZ1, IA27
		Vought EA-7L Corsair II (A-7C) (TA-7C)	IL62
		Voyager Aircraft Voyager (Rutan 76)	DC3
		Voyager Aircraft Voyager (Rutan 76) (R)	WI17
Vought FG-1D Corsair (FSM)	CA115, TX149	Vultee V-1AD Special	VA36
Vought F2G-1 Corsair	ND8, OH27, WA25	Vultee V-54D Valiant (BT-13)	AR24, CA91, 111, ND8, TX7, 40
Vought V-352 Pirate (F6U-1)	TX152		
Vought V-366 Cutlass (F7U-3)	CA145, OH71, PA26, WA25	Vultee V-72 Vengeance I (A-35A)	VA17
		Vultee V-74 Valiant (BT-13A)	AZ30, CA31, 32, 33, 43, 53, 85, 105, 139, CO29, DE1, FL22, 73, IL43, IN2, 10, 29, KS9, 10, MN10, 14, MT2, ND2, NJ8, 21, NV23, OH40, 71, OK48, PA35, SD7, TX21, 28, 29, 37, 40, 45, 73, VA8, 19
Vought V-366 Cutlass (F7U-3) (F7U-3M)	FL55		
Vought V-383 Crusader (XF8U-1)	WA25		
Vought F-8A Crusader (F8U-1)	CA99, 111, CO25, FL55, NJ15, PA26		
Vought TF-8A Crusader (F8U-1) (F8U-1T)	FL38		
Vought YF-8C Crusader (F8U-1) (YF8U-2)	TX152		
		Vultee V-74 Valiant (BT-13A) (SNV-1)	FL55, MI2
Vought F-8C Crusader (F8U-2)	CA99	Vultee V-74 Valiant (SNV-1)	CA114
Vought F-8E Crusader (F8U-2NE)	VA27	Vultee V-74A Valiant (BT-15)	AL35, AZ33, 46, FL80, KS26, MN44, OH71, TX22, 25, 40
Vought DF-8F Crusader (F8U-1) (F-8A)	AZ30, CA144, FL55		
Vought RF-8G Crusader (F8U-1P) (RF-8A)	AL37, AZ1, CA32, 58, 109, FL55, TX66, 69, VA19	Vultee V-79 Valiant (BT-13B)	AL32, AZ46, CA160, GA45, OH55, UT5
Vought F-8H Crusader (F8U-2N) (F-8D)	CA111, FL55, KS26, WA5	Vultee V-79 Valiant (BT-13B) (SNV-2)	CA90, NM24, OH22, OK20, PA12, TX16, VA17
Vought F-8J Crusader (F8U-2NE) (F-8E)	CA58, 122, FL55, MI2, NY34, OR21	Waco 4 (R)	OH78
Vought F-8K Crusader (F8U-2) (F-8C)	CA109, 144, 145, FL80, HI3, SC4, 18, WA12	Waco 9	IL31, NY63, OH53, 78, PA53, VA19
		Waco 10 (GXE)	CA6, 95, 96, 158, 160, IA39, ID2, IL31, MO15, ND5, 24, NY63, OH39, 53, 78, OR24, PA17, 29, TX135, WA8
Vought F-8K Crusader (F8U-2) (F-8C) (RF-8G)	CA53		
Vought F-8L Crusader (F8U-1E) (F-8B)	WA12		
Vought DF-8L Crusader (F8U-1E) (F-8B) (F-8L)	CA143, NV11		
		Waco 125	OH39
Vought F-8P Crusader (F-8E(FN))	FL65	Waco ARE	WI17
Vought A-7A Corsair II	AL38, AR5, CA109, FL18, 31, 55, 80, IL45, 57, 61, LA8, MD19, NC18, OH4, WI57	Waco ASO	FL21, IL31, 70, ND23, OH53, PA23, 29, WA31, WY10
		Waco ASO (DSO)	PA29
Vought A-7B Corsair II	AR19, CA6, 68, 122, 145, 160, FL22, LA23, MS24, NJ1, 15, NV11, TX66, 69, 134, 149	Waco ATO	CA17, IL31, 70, MO15, ND23, OH39, 53, PA29, WI17, WY10
		Waco AVN-8	MO15
		Waco BSO	PA29
Vought A-7C Corsair II	CA53, 74, 143	Waco BSO (DSO)	ND23
Vought NA-7C Corsair II (A-7C)	NV11	Waco CJC	OH53
Vought TA-7C Corsair II (A-7B)	CA52, MN3, NM14	Waco Cootie (R)	OH78
Vought TA-7C Corsair II (A-7C)	KS29	Waco CPF-1	OH53
Vought YA-7D Corsair II	CA4	Waco CRG	OH53
Vought A-7D Corsair II	AL2, AZ4, 13, 30, 41, CA3, 4, 85, CO2, 16, 17, 20, 32, CT9, GA44, IA2, 5, 9, 11, 22, 24, 28, 35, IL5, 12, 50, 56, IN43, KS26, LA7, MD12, MI53, MT8, ND5, 27, NE9, 21, NM9, 12, 19, NY82, OH9, 54, 55, 65, 72, 73, OK1, 41, 44, 46, OR7, 11, PA48, RI1, SC1, 16, SD1, 3, 6, 7,	Waco CSO	IL31, MO15, OH53
		Waco CSO (10 (GXE))	OR24
		Waco CTO	MO15, OR24, PA17, WI17
		Waco CTO (ATO)	IL31, OH78, WI51
		Waco CUC-1	MN18
		Waco DSO	OR24, WY10
		Waco EGC-8	NM24
		Waco EQC-6	WA32
		Waco INF	CA17, IN40, MI2, WA37
		Waco JWM	MO15
		Waco JYM	MO15

Index

Waco KNF	OH53	Watkin Skylark SL	KS18
Waco KNF (RNF)	OH39	Watson Hybrid Dirigible Research Vehicle	CA65
Waco NAZ Primary Glider	MD15, OH78, OR24, WI17	Wedell-Williams 44	OH27
Waco NEU (CG-15A)	MD22, NC1, 6, OH78	Wedell-Williams 44 (R)	LA27
Waco NZR Hadrian (CG-4A)	AZ30, CA139, 160, DE1, GA45, 46, ID26, IN4, KY5, MD22, MI2, 16, 57, NC3, NY14, 50, OH55, 78, TX40, 124	Wedell-Williams 45 (R)	LA27
		Wedell-Williams Wee-Will Junior (R)	LA27
		Weedhopper JC-24	ND2, NE12
		Weedhopper JC-24 Seaplane	WI24
Waco PBA	MO15	Weedhopper JC-24B	WI17
Waco PBF	NH7	Weedhopper JC-24C	VA19
Waco PBF-2	IL31	Weeks Quicksilver Sprint II	FL22
Waco PCF	OH53	Weeks S-1W	FL22
Waco PLA	OH53	Weeks SW-1S Solution	FL22
Waco QCF	CA17, IL31, MO15, NY63, WA37	Welch OW-8M (OW-5M)	WI27
		Wemple Solitaire	CA122
Waco QCF-2	MO15, ND5, OH53	Westland Lysander IIIA	FL23, TN6, VA19
Waco QDC	CA23, OH53	Westland Wasp HAS.1	CA37
Waco RNF	AZ30, GA50, IL31, IN40, OH39, 53, OR24, WI17	Westland-Sikorsky WS-55 Whirlwind HAR.10 (HAR.2)	NY82
Waco S3HD	NH7	White D-IX Der Jager	FL22, WI22
Waco SRE (UC-72)	MO15	White D-XII Der Jager	PA23
Waco SRE (UC-72C)	IL70	White Monoplane (R)	TX97
Waco STO (R)	IN57	White P	PA23
Waco UBA	OH53	Whithead 21 (Scale R)	CT6
Waco UBF	WY10	Wilcox Great Lakes Replica	TX114
Waco UBF-2	ME7, MO15	Wiley Post A	OK28
Waco UEC	CA160, WI17	Wilkes BMW-1	IA1
Waco UIC	AK3, AZ24, VA19	Wille Excelsior	IA39
Waco UKC	MN18	Wille Vancraft	IA39
Waco ULA	OH53	Williams CW-2	IL80
Waco UMF (YMF-3)	NH7	Williams Rigid Midget	CA154
Waco UMF-3	OH39, 53	Williams Super 8	IN57
Waco UPF-7	AZ30, CA17, FL46, ND5, NY4, OH39, 53, 58, 78, VA13, WA17, WY10	Williams W.17	CA111
		Williams WAF-2C	OH59
		Wills Wing Hang Glider	NM20
Waco UPF-7 (PT-14)	VA13	Windecker A/C7 Eagle I	AL36, VA19
Waco VKS-7	CA111	Winstead Special	PA23
Waco VPF-7	MI2	Wise RW.500	CA88
Waco YKC-S	AK3, CT9, MO15, OH39	Wiseman Cooke	DC5
Waco YKS-6	CA130, PA29, WA34	Wittman Buster	DC3
Waco YKS-7	CA19, 122, MO15	Wittman DFA	WI17
Waco YMF-3	OH53	Wittman Hardly Ableson (R)	WI17
Waco YMF-5	GA17, OH53	Wittman Midwing	WI17
Waco YMF-5 (YMF-3)	OH39	Wittman WV	WI17
Waco YOC	VA36	Wittman WX Buttercup	WI17
Waco YPF	WY10	Wittman W.8 Tailwind	NC40, TX69
Waco YPF-6	OH53	Wittman W.8C Tailwind	WI17
Waco YQC-6	WA43	Wittman W.10 Tailwind	PA12
Waco ZGC-7	PA29	Wittman W.18 Tailwind	MS5
Waco ZKS-6	AZ30	Wizard Hang Glider	CO32
Waco ZKS-7	MO15	Wizard J-2	WA25
Waco ZKS-7 (UC-72M)	AZ45	Wolf W-II Boredom Fighter	MI2, ND5, TX40
Waco ZPF-6	FL73, IL31, MO15	Woods Woody Pusher	FL23, OR20
Waco ZQC-6	PA29	Woods Woody Pusher WAS-2	CO32
Wag Aero Cuby	WI17	Worthington	WI17
Wag Aero Cuby L-21B-135	NY74	Wozniak Double Eagle 1	CA160
Wag Aero L-4 Cuby Flitfire	WA37	Wright 1899 Glider (R)	OH83
Wagner Formula One Racer	ID1	Wright 1899 Kite (R)	VA36
Wallis WA.116/6-1	NY21	Wright 1900 Glider (R)	DC3, MT5, OH83, VA36
Walter Extra EA-260	DC3	Wright 1901 Glider (R)	CA122, OH83, VA36
Walter Extra EA-300	IL20, VA13	Wright 1902 Glider (R)	CA29, 122, 128, DC3, ID9, MA4, MD7, NC6, 43, NY50, OH27, 28, 40, 78, 83, TN33, VA29, 36, WA25, 35
Walter Extra EA-300L	ID24, IL3, MN14		
War Aircraft F4U Corsair	MI2, OR13		
War Aircraft FW 190	CA88, ND8		
War Aircraft P-40	NY24		
War Aircraft P-47D Thunderbolt	AK5, AZ2, 11, 30, WA25	Wright 1903 Glider (R)	NY63
War Aircraft P-51 Mustang	NJ1, TX32	Wright 1911 Glider (R)	NY50
Warwick W-4 Hot Canary	WI17	Wright Glider (R)	OK40
Warwick W-5 Cosmic Wind	WI17	Wright Flyer	DC3
Waspair HM-81 Tomcat Tourer	WI17	Wright Flyer (R)	AL32, AR1, AZ30, CA56, 65, 96, 111, 122, 158, 160, FL21, 22, IL50, IN56, MI2, 25, MO39,
Waterman Gull (R)	CA154		
Waterman W-5 Arrowbile	VA19		
Waterman Whatsit	MD15		

Wright Flyer (R) (*continued*)		NC27, 28, 43, ND5, NE12, NJ1, NY32, 63, OH28, 55, 83, OK40, OR7, SC18, TX69, UT5, VA35, 36, WA25, WI17	WSK Lim-6bis (LiM-5M) WSK Lim-6M (Lim-5P) [MiG-17PF] WSK Lim-6MR (Lim-5P) [MiG-17PF] WSK Lim-6R Xiamen AD-100T	OR21, RI1 AL38 AZ30 DE5, KS9, OH48 OR13
Wright Flyer (Scale R)		PA35, TX92	Yakovlev Yak-3	CA45, 96
Wright Flyer 3		OH14, 83	Yakovlev Yak-3M	VA17
Wright B		PA21	Yakovlev Yak-3U	CA111, WA12
Wright B (R)		AL36, CA65, MD7, OH15, 35, 42, 82, VA17	Yakovlev Yak-3UA Yakovlev Yak-9U Yakovlev Yak-12	VA8 WA25 NY7
Wright B Modified		OH55	Yakovlev Yak-18	CA23, 111, VA17, 19
Wright B-1 (R)		MD24	Yakovlev Yak-50	NY62, OR7
Wright EX Vin Fiz		CA122, DC3	Yakovlev Yak-52	AZ46, CA35, 114, DE12,
Wright EX Vin Fiz (R)		CA65, 105, MA4, NY14, 63, OH83		FL86, IN44, MO15, NY62
Wright G		DC3	Yakovlev Yak-55	VA17
Wright Military Flyer		DC3	Yakovlev Yak-55M	MN14, NY62
Wright Military Flyer (R)		OH55	Yokosuka D4Y1 Suisei	AZ33
Wright Type Glider		MO25	Yokosuka MXY-7 Ohka 11	AZ33, CA111, 160, VA22
WSK Lim-2 [MiG-15bis]		AL32, AZ30, 33, CA85, 111, HI6, KS9, MI2, NM24, NV11	Yokosuka MXY-7 Ohka 11 (R) Yokosuka MXY-7 Ohka 22 Yokosuka MXY-7-K1 Ohka 11	NY82 VA19 DC6, OH55
WSK SBLim-2 (Lim-1) (MiG-15)		AZ11, CA111, DE5, FL65, 80, 85, NM8, NY23, 62, PA33, RI1	Yokosuka MXY-7-K2 Ohka Yokosuka P1Y1-C Ginga Yost GBN-41-1000 Gas Balloon	MD15 MD15 NM2
WSK SBLim-2 [MiG-15]		ID24	Yost GBN-41-1000 Helium Balloon	NM2
WSK SBLim-2 [MiG-15bis]		OR7, TX16, UT4	Yost GBN-41-1000 Hot Air Balloon	NM2
WSK SBLim-2A (Lim-1) [MiG-15] [MiG-15UTI]		AZ30, NM24	Yost GB-47 Hot Air Balloon Yost GB-55 Hot Air Balloon	NM2 VA19
WSK SBLim-2M (Lim-1) [MiG-15]		TX20	Yost Helium Balloon	NM2
WSK SBLim-2M (SB-LiM-2A) [MiG-15bis]		MN27	Zenair CH-200 Zenith Zenair CH-250	CA122 MI2
WSK Lim-5 [MiG-17F]		CA85, 111, 155, DE5, FL42, ID24, KS10, NV11, 17, NY21, 34, OH21, OR4, TN33, TX16, 57, 60, 80, UT5, 13	Zenith Z6A Zephyr ZAL Zimmermann Flying Platform Zlin Z-381 [Bücker Bü 181D Bestmann]	MO15 CT9 MD15 FL22
WSK Lim-5P [MiG-17PF]		CA3, FL80, NY82	Zlin Z-526 Trenér Master	NY62
WSK Lim-5R (Lim-5) [MiG-17F]		AZ30, TN33, WA2	Zlin Z-526F Trenér Master	CA105

COMPANY NAME ABBREVIATIONS

These have been used in the tables of aircraft and in the index.

CASA - Construcciones Aeronáuticas
CSS – Centralne Studium Samolotow
CVT - Centro Volo a Vela del Politecnico di Torino
EKW – Eidgenossische Flugwerke Emmen
NAMC – Nihon Kokuki Seizo Kabushiki Kaisha
NASA – National Aeronautics and Space Administration
PZL – Panstwowe Zaklady Lotnicze
Saab - Svenska Aeroplan Aktiebolaget
SCAN- Société de Construction Aéro-navales
SPAD - Société Pour l'Aviation et ses Derives
WSK - Wytwornia Sprzetu Komunikacyjnego